PRESENTED BY

TIME

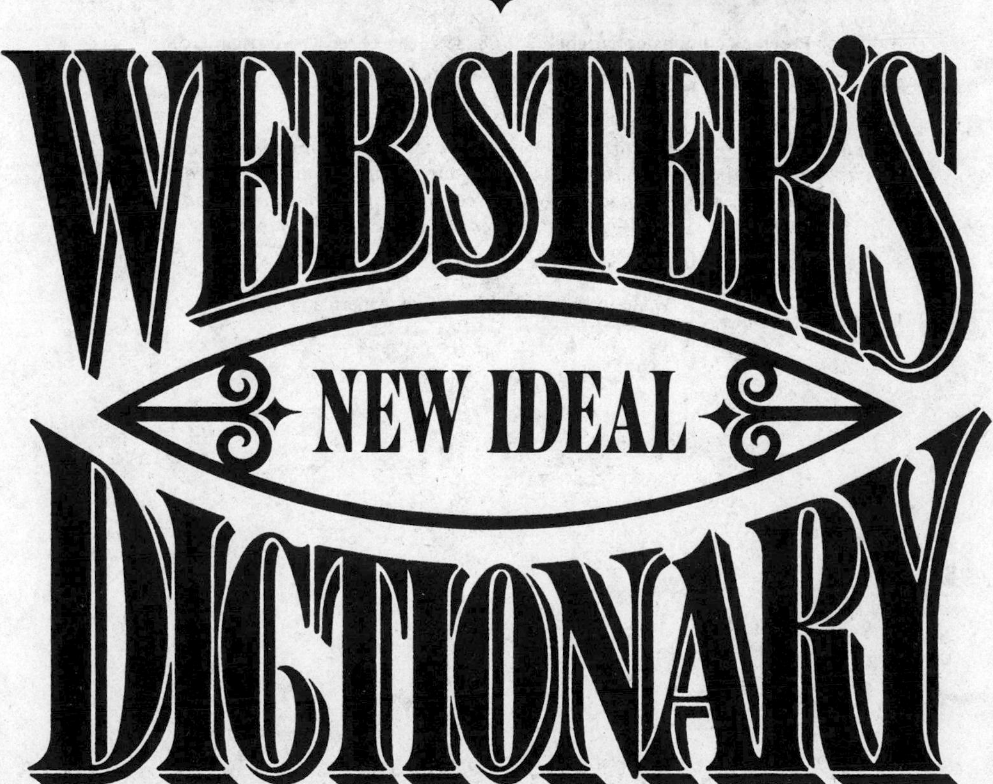

ISBN 0-87779-249-6

Made in the United States of America

CONTENTS

Preface 4a

Front Matter

Explanatory Notes 5a
Pronunciation Symbols 8a

A Dictionary of the English Language 1

Back Matter

Abbreviations 629
Pronouncing Vocabulary of Common English Given Names 634
Foreign Words and Phrases 640
Table of Chemical Elements 645
Measures and Weights 646
Metric Measures, Decimal and Fractional Equivalents 647
Standard Time Around the World, Jewish Years, Easter Dates . 648
Declaration of Independence 649
Constitution of the United States 650
Population of Urban Places in the United States 655

PREFACE

The publishers of the MERRIAM-WEBSTER series of dictionaries present herewith a concise dictionary. Including all boldface entries, the vocabulary contains over 54,000 words, pronounced, syllabified, and defined. The supplementary matter sets forth considerable additional information in handy arrangement. The subjects are listed in the table of contents on the preceding page. In the selection of the vocabulary for this abridged dictionary, obsolete, rare, and highly technical words and obsolete meanings of common words have been omitted. The vocabulary thus becomes a list of the words most likely to be looked up by any person searching for a meaning, a pronunciation, or a syllabication. Pronunciations are given in MERRIAM-WEBSTER symbols. A general key to these symbols is presented in the introductory material, and a key line for easy reference is placed at the bottom of the pages of the vocabulary.

This dictionary has been prepared to meet the needs of the user in his daily reading or writing. Within the limits adopted for its vocabulary, it presents a useful, accurate, and adequate selection. The fact that its definitions are based on WEBSTER'S THIRD NEW INTERNATIONAL DICTIONARY gives assurance of quality for this abridged work. A more elaborate treatment of word origins, derivatives, uncommon senses, and other lexicographic features may be found in WEBSTER'S SEVENTH NEW COLLEGIATE DICTIONARY and in other MERRIAM-WEBSTER dictionaries edited especially for secondary-school use.

To get satisfactory and pleasing rewards from looking into a dictionary one must learn how to use it, that is, how to interpret the information that is contained at each entry. This knowledge involves mainly an ability to recognize different typefaces, a small number of abbreviations that occur over and over, and a few traditional dictionary devices. Every user is, therefore, urged to find time to read the following pages carefully.

G. & C. MERRIAM COMPANY

EXPLANATORY NOTES

THE ENTRY

The entries in this dictionary begin on page 1 and continue in alphabetical order from A to Z. Each page contains, set off at the top, a pair of guide words to the entries contained alphabetically between them on the page. The entries are printed in heavy black letters (**boldface type**) set flush with the left-hand margin or run on after a dash. The left-hand words (like **abbot**) are MAIN ENTRIES and determine the alphabetical order. Those following dashes (like **absolutely** at **absolute**) are DERIVATIVE ENTRIES, derived from or formed on the main entry.

Most English words, especially nouns and verbs, change their forms to agree with their varying roles in context. Nouns have plural forms (as *boys* and *houses*). Verbs have past forms (as *walked* and *amplified*) and participial forms (as *walking, amplifying,* and *shown*). Adjectives and adverbs have comparative forms (like *cheaper* and *happier*) and superlative forms (like *cheapest* and *happiest*). When these forms are made regularly like thousands of other words, the forms are not shown in this dictionary because every native speaker of English is able to form them himself by repeated use of similar forms. If, however, these forms are irregular, they appear in boldface type and are called INFLECTIONAL ENTRIES. Examples: **mice** at **mouse, beeves** *or* **beefs** at **beef, beaux** *or* **beaus** at **beau, indexes** *or* **indices** at **index, saw** and **seen** at **see**, **abetted** and **abetting** at **abet**, **bivouacked** and **bivouacking** at **bivouac**, **worse** and **worst** at **bad**. Occasionally these inflectional forms are shown only as parts of words preceded by a hyphen (like **-plied** and **-plying** for *multiplied* and *multiplying* at **multiply**) which indicates that the user can supply the missing syllable or syllables from the main entry.

CENTERED PERIODS in boldface within entry words (as in **an·ti·bi·ot·ic**) indicate division points at which a hyphen may be put at the end of a line of handwriting, typewriting, or printing. In accordance with widespread practice among publishers in making syllabic divisions at the end of a line, this book does not show a division after a single initial letter of a word, before a single final letter of a word, or before a single final letter of an English prefix. Examples: **ane·mia**, **Pass·over, semi·fi·nal** rather than *a·ne·mi·a, Pass·o·ver, sem·i·fi·nal.* A single hyphen in a boldface word at the end of a line (as **con·tent-** in **contentedly** at **contented**) replaces a centered period.

The syllabic division of an entry is based on the pronunciation variant shown first in this book if another variant requires a different division.

A DOUBLE HYPHEN ⸗ at the end of a line in this dictionary (as at **pukka**) stands for a hyphen that belongs at that point in a hyphened word and should be retained when the word is written as a unit on one line of writing or type.

When one main entry has exactly the same written form as another that follows it, they are distinguished by SUPERIOR NUMBERS preceding each word (like **¹chase, ²chase, ³chase,** and **⁴chase**). Such words are called homographs. Some homographs are related to each other through being derived from the same base word. Others have no relationship beyond the accident of spelling.

PRONUNCIATION

A set of reversed virgules \ \ usually follows the boldface entries. The symbols within these slant lines indicate pronunciation. A tabular key to the Merriam-Webster pronunciation symbols appears on the page immediately following these notes. Also a simplified key for quick reference is shown in the lines at the bottom of the page.

A high-set mark ˈ indicates that the syllable following has primary (strongest) stress; a low⸗set mark ˌ indicates that the syllable following has secondary (next-strongest) stress (as \ˈded-ˌlīn\ at **deadline**). A syllable with neither a high-set mark nor a low-set mark is unstressed (as the middle syllable of \ˈab-di-ˌkāt\ at **abdicate**).

Parentheses mean that whatever is indicated within them is (1) present in the pronunciation of some speakers and absent from the pronunciation of other speakers, (2) present in some utterances and absent from other utterances of the same speaker, or (3) simply sometimes heard and sometimes not heard. The pronunciation \ˈfak-t(ə-)rē\ at **factory** shows that the pronunciation may be in three syllables \ˈfak-tə-rē\ or two syllables \ˈfak-trē\.

The placement of syllable divisions in the pronunciation transcriptions is based only on phonetic considerations. Thus *miner* and *minor* are identical in pronunciation and the two transcriptions are identically syllabified. (In syllabifying the boldface entry, however, other considerations may prevail, for the sole purpose of this division is to indicate desirable places to insert a hyphen at the end of a line of print or writing.

Thus the entry **miner**, which is composed of the verb *mine* and the suffix *-er,* is divided after the *n*, whereas the identically pronounced entry **mi-nor**, which does not contain two meaningful English elements, is divided before the *n*.)

An entry is usually not pronounced if it is identical in spelling, division, and pronunciation with a preceding entry (as **²meet** and **³meet** are like **¹meet** and **siphon** *verb* is like **siphon** *noun*). An entry is often not pronounced if it consists of a preceding entry and a suffix that is entered at its alphabetical place with pronunciation (as the pronunciation of **certainly** is that at **certain** plus that at **-ly**).

A syllable or syllable sequence at the beginning of a pronunciation at a derivative entry may be omitted if it is identical with the beginning of a pronunciation at the main entry (as the pronunciation of **macabrely** gets its first syllable from the pronunciation of **macabre**).

VARIANTS

Variant entries are joined by an italicized *or* (as **caddie** *or* **caddy, -celed** *or* **-celled** at **cancel,** and **legging** *or* **leggin**). The *or* joins equal variants. This means that neither is to be preferred to the other as a matter of correctness. The individual may use one or the other.

Variant pronunciations are separated within the pronunciation virgules by a comma. The presence of variant pronunciations simply indicates that not all educated speakers pronounce the word the same way. A second-place variant is not to be regarded as per se a less desirable variant than the one given first. In fact, it may be used by as many educated speakers as the first variant. Some variant pronunciations (as \\'ē-t͟hər, 'ī-\\ at **either,** \\'grē-sē, -zē\\ at **greasy**) are the kind that one speaker uses but another does not for the reason that their dialects are different and that the speech habits of one are different from those of the other.

ITALIC LABELS

An italic label following the pronunciation or, if no pronunciation is given, following the entry itself, indicates the part of speech. The eight traditional parts of speech are thus abbreviated:

ac·tive . . . *adj*	(adjective)
¹across . . . *adv*	(adverb)
al·though . . . *conj*	(conjunction)
ahoy . . . *interj*	(interjection)
¹act . . . *n*	(noun)
²across *prep*	(preposition)
¹he . . . *pron*	(pronoun)
²act *vb*	(verb)

These labels are sometimes combined [as at **awash** *adv* (*or adj*)] and especially at undefined derivatives (like **seventieth** *adj or n*).

Other italic labels sometimes occurring in the same position as the part-of-speech label are:

re- . . . *prefix*
may . . . *auxiliary verb*
⁴haw *imperative verb*
²a . . . *indefinite article*

avow . . . *vt*	(verb transitive)
²faint *vi*	(verb intransitive)

The label *pl* means PLURAL. This occurs after a comma to introduce the boldface plural form of a singular entry (as at **abacus** . . . *n, pl* **-ci** . . .) or without a comma to indicate that the preceding boldface is a plural (as **environs** *n pl*).

No italic labels are regularly used to indicate inflectional verb parts since their position after the infinitive of the entry form is regular. At **¹dive** the past, in second position, is **dived** or **dove**; the present participle, in third position, is **diving**. If the past participle differs from the past tense, it is shown in third position (as **swum** at **swim**).

CAPITALIZATION

Words nearly always capitalized are capitalized in the boldface entry (as **Fa·bi·an**) unless it is the second or third or fourth sense of a lowercase word. In the latter situation it is labeled *cap* (as at **dem·o·crat** . . . 2 *cap* . . .). Sometimes the letters to be capitalized are specified (as at **union jack** . . . 2 *cap U & J* . . .).

Words entered with an initial boldface lowercase letter sometimes bear a label to indicate that it is not always written lowercase:

al·ex·an·drine . . . *often cap*
¹word . . . 4 *often cap*

SYMBOLIC COLON

This dictionary uses a boldface character recognizably distinct from the usual roman colon as a linking symbol between the main entry and a definition. It stands for an unexpressed simple predicate that may be read "is being here defined as (or by)". It indicates that the supporting orientation immediately after the main entry is over and thus facilitates a visual jumping from word to definition:

¹beach . . . **:** a shore of an ocean, sea, or lake
de·bunk . . . **:** to expose the sham or falseness in

Words that have two or more definitions have two or more symbolic colons. The signal for another definition is another colon:

con·quer·or . . . **:** one that conquers **:** VICTOR

SENSE DIVISION

Boldface arabic numerals within an entry separate the senses of a word that has more than a single sense:

loop·hole . . . *n* **1 :** a small opening in a wall through which small firearms may be discharged **2 :** a means of escape

No one of the senses, as defined, is better or more important than another, but one may have more appropriate meaning in a specific context. Senses closely related, as two aspects of the same sense, are usually joined by a semicolon plus *also* or *esp:*

[1]ash . . . : any of a genus of trees of the olive family with thin furrowed bark and winged seeds; *also* : its tough elastic wood

all–Amer·i·can . . . : representative of the U.S. as a whole; *esp* : selected as the best in the U.S.

USAGE NOTES

A usage note is introduced by a lightface dash. A usage note provides information about the use of the word being defined and so always modifies the word that is the main entry. It may be in the form of a comment on idiom, syntax, semantic relationship, status, or various other matters:

[1]al·le·gro . . . — used as a direction in music

[1]gob·ble . . . — usu. used with *up*

jaw . . . — usu. used in pl.

sir . . . — used as a title before the given name of a knight or baronet

A usage note may stand in place of a definition and without the symbolic colon. Some function words have little or no semantic content, and most interjections express feelings but otherwise are untranslatable into a meaning that can be substituted. Many other words (as some oaths and imprecations, calls to animals, specialized signals, song refrains, and honorific titles), though genuinely a part of the language, have a usage note instead of a definition:

fie . . . *interj* — used to express disgust or shock

be·hold . . . *vb* . . . — used in the imperative esp. to call attention

and/or . . . *conj* — used as a function word to indicate that either *and* or *or* may apply

CROSS-REFERENCES

A sequence of lightface SMALL CAPITALS used in a definition is identical letter-by-letter with a boldface entry (or with one of its inflectional forms) at its own alphabetical place. This sequence is a cross-reference. It is not a definition but an indication that a definition at its boldface equivalent can be substituted at the place where the small capitals are used. It appears sometimes with a full definition, sometimes by itself:

ab·sorb . . . : to take in or swallow up : INCORPORATE

[2]gob . . . : SAILOR

same·ness . . . : MONOTONY, UNIFORMITY

Sometimes the small capitals simply direct the user to another place in the vocabulary:

ran *past of* RUN

mice *pl of* MOUSE

[1]bet·ter . . . *comparative of* GOOD

disc *var of* DISK

him . . . *objective case of* HE

ABBREVIATIONS

Abbreviations are not included as main entries in the vocabulary but they are classed as vocabulary entries. They are separately alphabetized in a section of back matter titled "Abbreviations".

Symbols for chemical elements are included alphabetically among the abbreviations in the back matter.

PRONUNCIATION SYMBOLS

ə . . . . banan**a**, hum**drum**

^{ə} . . . . immediately preceding \l\, \n\, \ŋ\, as in batt**le**, mitt**en**, and sometimes lock **and** key \-^{ə}ŋ-\; immediately following \l\, \m\, \r\, as often in French tab**le**, pris**me**, tit**re**

ər . . . . **oper**ation, **fur**

a . . . . **mat**

ā . . . . **day**

ä . . . . b**o**ther, c**o**t, and, with most American speakers, f**a**ther, c**a**rt

ȧ . . . . vowel between \a\ and \ä\, as in some pronunciations of **au**nt, f**a**ther, c**a**rt, and as in French p**a**tte

aů . . . . n**ow**, **ou**t

b . . . . **b**a**b**y, ri**b**

ch . . . . **ch**in, na**t**ure \'nā-chər\ (actually, this sound is \t\ + \sh\)

d . . . . **d**i**d**, a**dd**er

e . . . . b**e**t

ē . . . . b**ea**t, noseble**e**d, **ea**s**y**

f . . . . **f**i**f**ty, cu**ff**, **ph**one

g . . . . **g**o, bi**g**

h . . . . **h**at, a**h**ead

hw . . . **wh**ale

i . . . . t**i**p, ban**i**sh, act**i**ve

ī . . . . s**i**te, s**i**de, (actually, this sound is \ä\ + \i\, or \ȧ\ + \i\)

j . . . . **j**u**dg**e (actually, this sound is \d\ + \zh\)

k . . . . **k**in

k̲ . . . . German i**ch**, Bu**ch**

l . . . . **l**i**l**y

m . . . . **m**ur**m**ur

n . . . . **n**o, ow**n**

^{n} . . . . indicates that a preceding vowel or diphthong is pronounced with the nasal passages open, as in French *un bon vin blanc* \œ^{n}-bō^{n}-va^{n}-blä^{n}\

ŋ . . . . si**ng** \'siŋ\, si**ng**er \'siŋ-ər\, fi**ng**er \'fiŋ-gər\, i**n**k \'iŋk\

ō . . . . b**o**ne

ȯ . . . . s**aw**

œ . . . . French b**œu**f, German H**ö**lle (\e\ with rounded lips)

œ̄ . . . . French f**eu**, German H**öh**le (\ā\ with rounded lips)

ȯi . . . . c**oi**n, destr**oy**

p . . . . **p**e**pp**er, li**p**

r . . . . **r**a**r**ity

s . . . . **s**our**c**e, le**ss**

sh . . . **sh**y, mi**ss**ion

t . . . . **t**ie, a**tt**ack

th . . . **th**in, e**th**er

th̲ . . . **th**en, ei**th**er

ü . . . . r**u**le, y**ou**th

u̇ . . . . p**u**ll, w**oo**d, b**oo**k

ue . . . . German f**ü**llen, h**ü**bsch (\i\ with rounded lips)

ue̅ . . . . French r**ue**, German f**üh**len (\ē\ with rounded lips)

v . . . . **v**i**v**id

w . . . . **w**e, a**w**ay

y . . . . **y**ard

^{y} . . . . indicates that the sound preceding it is modified by the placing of the tongue tip against the lower front teeth, as in French di**gne** \dēn^{y}\, Italian **gli** \l^{y}ē\

yü . . . **you**th, **u**nion, c**ue**, f**ew**, m**u**te

yu̇ . . . c**u**rable, f**u**ry

z . . . . **z**one, rai**s**e

zh . . . vi**s**ion, a**z**ure \'azh-ər\

\ . . . . slant line used in pairs to mark the beginning and end of a transcription \'pen\

' . . . . mark preceding a syllable with primary (strongest) stress: \'pen-mən\

ˌ . . . . mark preceding a syllable with secondary (next-strongest) stress: \'pen-mən-ˌship\

\- . . . . mark of syllable division

() . . . . indicate that what is symbolized between is present in some utterances but not in others: at *factory*, \'fak-t(ə-)rē\ = \'fak-tə-rē, 'fak-trē\ or \'fak-trē, 'fak-tə-rē\

A DICTIONARY OF THE ENGLISH LANGUAGE

¹a \'ā\ *n, often cap* **1 :** the 1st letter of the English alphabet **2 :** the musical tone A **3 :** a grade rating a student's work as superior

²a \ə, (')ā\ *indefinite article* **1 :** some one unspecified **2 :** ONE **:** the same **3 :** ANY **4 :** in each **:** to each **:** for each — used in all senses before words beginning with a consonant sound

aard·vark \'ärd-ˌvärk\ *n* **:** a large African mammal that burrows in the ground and lives on ants which it catches with its long sticky tongue

aback \ə-'bak\ *adv* **:** by surprise **:** UNAWARES

ab·a·cus \'ab-ə-kəs\ *n, pl* **-ci** \-ˌsī, -ˌkē\ *or* **-cus·es** \-kə-səz\ **:** an instrument for making calculations by sliding counters along rods or in grooves

¹abaft \ə-'baft\ *adv* **:** toward the stern **:** at the stern **:** AFT

²abaft *prep* **:** to the rear of; *esp* **:** toward the stern from

ab·a·lo·ne \ˌab-ə-'lō-nē\ *n* **:** a mollusk with a flattened slightly spiral shell perforated along the edge and lined with mother-of-pearl

¹aban·don \ə-'ban-dən\ *vt* **1 :** to give up completely **2 :** to withdraw from often in the face of danger **3 :** to withdraw protection, support, or help from **:** DESERT **4 :** to give (oneself) over to a feeling or emotion without restraint — **aban·don·er** *n* — **aban·don·ment** *n*

²abandon *n* **1 :** a thorough yielding to natural impulses **2 :** ENTHUSIASM, EXUBERANCE

aban·doned \ə-'ban-dənd\ *adj* **1 :** DESERTED, FORSAKEN **2 :** wholly given up to wickedness or vice

abase \ə-'bās\ *vt* **:** to lower in rank or position **:** HUMBLE, DEGRADE — **abase·ment** *n*

abash \ə-'bash\ *vt* **:** to destroy the self-possession or self-confidence of **:** DISCONCERT — **abash·ment** *n*

abate \ə-'bāt\ *vb* **:** to reduce or decrease in degree, amount, or intensity **:** DIMINISH, LESSEN — **abat·er** *n*

abate·ment \ə-'bāt-mənt\ *n* **1 :** the act or process of abating **:** the state of being abated **2 :** an amount abated; *esp* **:** a deduction from the full amount of a tax

ab·a·tis \'ab-ə-ˌtē, 'ab-ət-əs\ *n, pl* **-a·tis** \-ə-ˌtēz\ *or* **-a·tis·es** \-ət-ə-səz\ **:** a defensive obstacle formed by cut-down trees with sharpened branches facing the enemy

ab·at·toir \'ab-ə-ˌtwär\ *n* **:** SLAUGHTERHOUSE

ab·ba·cy \'ab-ə-sē\ *n, pl* **-cies :** the office, term of office, position, or jurisdiction of an abbot

ab·bé \a-'bā, 'ab-ˌā\ *n* **:** a French cleric not in a religious order — used as a title

ab·bess \'ab-əs\ *n* **:** a woman who is the superior of a convent of nuns

ab·bey \'ab-ē\ *n, pl* **abbeys 1 a :** a monastery governed by an abbot **b :** a convent governed by an abbess **2 :** a church that once belonged to an abbey

ab·bot \'ab-ət\ *n* **:** the superior of an abbey for men

ab·bre·vi·ate \ə-'brē-vē-ˌāt\ *vt* **:** to make briefer **:** SHORTEN; *esp* **:** to reduce (as a word or phrase) to a shorter form intended to stand for the whole — **ab·bre·vi·a·tor** \-ˌāt-ər\ *n*

ab·bre·vi·a·tion \ə-ˌbrē-vē-'ā-shən\ *n* **1 :** the act or result of abbreviating **:** ABRIDGMENT **2 :** a shortened form of a word or phrase used for brevity esp. in writing in place of the whole

ABC \ˌā-(ˌ)bē-'sē\ *n* **1 :** ALPHABET — usu. used in pl. **2 a :** the rudiments of reading, writing, and spelling — usu. used in pl. **b :** the rudiments of any subject

ab·di·cate \'ab-di-ˌkāt\ *vb* **1 :** to relinquish (as sovereign power) formally **:** RENOUNCE **2 :** to renounce a throne, high office, dignity, or function — **ab·di·ca·tion** \ˌab-di-'kā-shən\ *n*

ab·do·men \'ab-də-mən, ab-'dō-mən\ *n* **:** the part of the body between the chest and the pelvis; *also* **:** the body cavity containing the chief digestive organs — **ab·dom·i·nal** \ab-'däm-ən-ᵊl\ *adj* — **ab·dom·i·nal·ly** \-ᵊl-ē\ *adv*

ab·duct \ab-'dəkt\ *vt* **:** to carry (a person) off by force — **ab·duc·tion** \-'dək-shən\ *n*

abeam \ə-'bēm\ *adv (or adj)* **:** on a line at right angles to a ship's keel

abed \ə-'bed\ *adv (or adj)* **:** in bed

ab·er·rance \a-'ber-ən(t)s\ *or* **ab·er·ran·cy** \-ən-sē\ *n, pl* **ab·er·ranc·es** *or* **aberrancies :** DEVIATION

ab·er·rant \a-'ber-ənt\ *adj* **1 :** straying from the right or normal way **2 :** deviating from the usual or natural type — **ab·er·rant·ly** *adv*

ab·er·ra·tion \ˌab-ə-'rā-shən\ *n* **1 :** the act of deviating esp. from a moral standard or normal state **2 :** failure of a mirror or lens to produce exact point-to-point correspondence between an object and its image **3 :** unsoundness or disorder of the mind — **ab·er·ra·tion·al** \-shnəl, -shən-ᵊl\ *adj*

abet \ə-'bet\ *vt* **abet·ted; abet·ting 1 :** to instigate, encourage, or aid in doing wrong **2 :** to assist in the achievement of a purpose — **abet·ment** *n* — **abet·tor** *or* **abet·ter** \-'bet-ər\ *n*

abey·ance \ə-'bā-ən(t)s\ *n* **:** a state of suspension or temporary inactivity — **abey·ant** \-ənt\ *adj*

ab·hor \ab-'hȯ(ə)r, əb-\ *vt* **ab·horred; ab·hor·ring 1 :** to feel extreme repugnance toward **:** LOATHE **2 :** to turn aside or shrink from in scorn or disgust **:** REJECT — **ab·hor·rence** \-'hȯr-ən(t)s, -'här-\ *n* — **ab·hor·rer** \-'hȯr-ər\ *n*

ab·hor·rent \-'hȯr-ənt, -'här-\ *adj* **1 :** feeling or showing abhorrence **2 :** not agreeable **3 :** DETESTABLE — **ab·hor·rent·ly** *adv*

abide \ə-'bīd\ *vb* **abode** \-'bōd\ *or* **abid·ed; abid·ing 1 a :** to endure without yielding **:** WITHSTAND **b :** to bear patiently

: TOLERATE 2 : to accept without objection 3 : to remain stable or fixed in a state 4 : to reside or continue in a place : DWELL — **abid·er** *n* — **abide by** : to accept the terms of : be obedient to

abid·ing \ə-ˈbīd-iŋ\ *adj* : ENDURING, LASTING, PERMANENT

abil·i·ty \ə-ˈbil-ət-ē\ *n, pl* **-ties** 1 a : the quality or state of being able; *esp* : physical, mental, or legal power to do something b : competence in doing : SKILL 2 : natural talent or acquired proficiency : APTITUDE

ab·ject \ˈab-ˌjekt, ab-ˈ\ *adj* 1 : sunk to a low condition 2 a : having no pride or spirit : SERVILE b : showing utter resignation : HOPELESS — **ab·ject·ly** *adv* — **ab·ject·ness** *n*

ab·jure \ab-ˈju̇(ə)r\ *vt* 1 a : to renounce upon oath b : to reject solemnly : REPUDIATE 2 : to abstain from : AVOID — **ab·ju·ra·tion** \ˌab-jə-ˈrā-shən\ *n* — **ab·jur·er** *n*

ab·late \a-ˈblāt\ *vb* : to remove or become removed by cutting, melting, evaporation, or vaporization — **ab·la·tion** \-ˈblā-shən\ *n*

ab·la·tive \ˈab-lət-iv\ *adj* : of, relating to, or constituting a grammatical case expressing typically the relations of separation and source and also frequently such relations as cause or instrument — **ablative** *n*

ablaze \ə-ˈblāz\ *adj* 1 : being on fire 2 : radiant with light or bright color

able \ˈā-bəl\ *adj* 1 a : having sufficient power, skill, or resources to do something b : free from restrictions preventing an action 2 : marked by intelligence, knowledge, skill, or competence

able–bod·ied \ˌā-bəl-ˈbäd-ēd\ *adj* : having a sound strong body : physically fit

able–bodied seaman *n* : an experienced deckhand qualified to perform routine duties at sea

abloom \ə-ˈblüm\ *adj* : BLOOMING

ab·lu·tion \a-ˈblü-shən, ə-ˈblü-\ *n* : the ceremonial washing of one's body or part of it — **ab·lu·tion·ary** \-shə-ˌner-ē\ *adj*

ably \ˈā-blē\ *adv* : in an able manner

ab·ne·gate \ˈab-ni-ˌgāt\ *vt* 1 : to give up or surrender (as a right or privilege) : RELINQUISH 2 : to deny to or reject for oneself : RENOUNCE — **ab·ne·ga·tion** \ˌab-ni-ˈgā-shən\ *n* — **ab·ne·ga·tor** \ˈab-ni-ˌgāt-ər\ *n*

ab·nor·mal \(ˈ)ab-ˈnȯr-məl\ *adj* : differing from the normal or average; *esp* : markedly irregular — **ab·nor·mal·ly** \-mə-lē\ *adv*

ab·nor·mal·i·ty \ˌab-nȯr-ˈmal-ət-ē\ *n, pl* **-ties** 1 : the quality or state of being abnormal 2 : something abnormal

¹**aboard** \ə-ˈbōrd\ *adv* 1 : on, onto, or within a ship, a railway car, or a passenger vehicle 2 : ALONGSIDE

²**aboard** *prep* : on or into esp. for passage

abode \ə-ˈbōd\ *n* : the place where one abides : dwelling place : RESIDENCE, HOME

abol·ish \ə-ˈbäl-ish\ *vt* : to do away with wholly : put an end to — **abol·ish·a·ble** *adj* — **abol·ish·er** *n* — **abol·ish·ment** *n*

ab·o·li·tion \ˌab-ə-ˈlish-ən\ *n* : the act of abolishing : the state of being abolished; *esp* : the abolishing of slavery

ab·o·li·tion·ist \-ˈlish-(ə-)nəst\ *n* : a person who is in favor of abolition; *esp* : one favoring the abolition of Negro slavery —**ab·o·li·tion·ism** \-ˈlish-ə-ˌniz-əm\ *n*

A–bomb \ˈā-ˌbäm\ *n* : ATOM BOMB — **A–bomb** *vb*

abom·i·na·ble \ə-ˈbäm-(ə-)nə-bəl\ *adj* 1 : deserving or causing loathing or hatred : DETESTABLE 2 : quite disagreeable or unpleasant — **abom·i·na·bly** \-blē\ *adv*

abom·i·nate \ə-ˈbäm-ə-ˌnāt\ *vt* : to hate or loathe intensely : ABHOR — **abom·i·na·tor** \-ˌnāt-ər\ *n*

abom·i·na·tion \ə-ˌbäm-ə-ˈnā-shən\ *n* 1 : something abominable 2 : extreme disgust and hatred : LOATHING

ab·o·rig·i·nal \ˌab-ə-ˈrij-nəl, -ən-ᵊl\ *adj* 1 : INDIGENOUS, ORIGINAL, PRIMITIVE 2 : of or relating to aborigines — **ab·o·rig·i·nal·ly** \-ē\ *adv*

ab·o·rig·i·ne \ˌab-ə-ˈrij-ə-(ˌ)nē\ *n* : an indigenous inhabitant esp. as contrasted with an invading or colonizing people

aborn·ing \ə-ˈbȯr-niŋ\ *adv* : while being born or produced

abort \ə-ˈbȯrt\ *vb* 1 : to bring forth premature or stillborn offspring 2 : to become checked in development 3 : to terminate prematurely

abor·tion \ə-ˈbȯr-shən\ *n* 1 : a premature birth occurring before the fetus can survive 2 : failure to reach full development; *also* : a result of such failure

abor·tive \ə-ˈbȯrt-iv\ *adj* 1 : failing to achieve the desired end : UNSUCCESSFUL 2 : imperfectly formed or developed : RUDIMENTARY — **abor·tive·ly** *adv* — **abor·tive·ness** *n*

abound \ə-ˈbau̇nd\ *vi* 1 : to be present in large numbers or in great quantity 2 : to become copiously supplied

¹**about** \ə-ˈbau̇t\ *adv* 1 : on all or various sides : AROUND 2 a : APPROXIMATELY b : ALMOST 3 : in succession : ALTERNATELY 4 a : in the opposite direction b : in reverse order

²**about** *prep* 1 : on every side of : AROUND 2 a : in the immediate neighborhood of : NEAR b : on or near the person of c : in the makeup of d : at the command of 3 a : engaged in b : on the verge of 4 : with regard to : CONCERNING 5 : over or in different parts of

about–face \ə-ˈbau̇t-ˈfās\ *n* 1 : a reversal of direction 2 : a reversal of attitude or point of view — **about–face** *vi*

¹**above** \ə-ˈbəv\ *adv* 1 : in or to a higher place : OVERHEAD 2 : higher on the same page or on a preceding page 3 : in or to a higher rank or number

²**above** *prep* 1 : in or to a higher place than : OVER 2 a : superior to (as in rank, quality, or degree) b : out of reach of c : too proud or honorable to stoop to 3 : exceeding in number, quantity, or size

³**above** *n* : something that is above

⁴**above** *adj* : written higher on the same page or on a preceding page

above·board \ə-ˈbəv-ˌbōrd\ *adv (or adj)* : in open sight : in a straightforward manner : without concealment or deceit

ab·ra·ca·dab·ra \ˌab-rə-kə-ˈdab-rə\ *n* 1 : a magical charm or incantation against calamity 2 : unintelligible language : JARGON

abrade \ə-ˈbrād\ *vb* 1 a : to rub or wear away esp. by friction : ERODE b : to irritate or roughen by rubbing 2 : to undergo abrasion — **abrad·er** *n*

abra·sion \ə-ˈbrā-zhən\ *n* 1 : a rubbing or wearing away 2 : a place where the surface has been rubbed or scraped off

¹**abra·sive** \ə-ˈbrā-siv\ *adj* : having the effect of abrading

²**abrasive** *n* : a substance (as emery, pumice, or fine sand) used for grinding, smoothing, or polishing

abreast \ə-ˈbrest\ *adv (or adj)* 1 : side by side with bodies in line 2 : up to a standard or level esp. of knowledge

abridge \ə-ˈbrij\ *vt* 1 : to make less : DIMINISH, CURTAIL 2 : to shorten in duration or extent 3 : to shorten by omission of words while retaining the substance : CONDENSE — **abridg·er** *n*

abridg·ment *or* **abridge·ment** \ə-ˈbrij-mənt\ *n* 1 a : the action of abridging b : the state of being abridged 2 : a shortened form of a work retaining the general sense and unity of the original

abroad \ə-ˈbrȯd\ *adv (or adj)* 1 : over a wide area : WIDELY 2 : outside of an implied place; *esp* : in the open 3 : in or to foreign countries 4 : in wide circulation : going about

ab·ro·gate \ˈab-rə-ˌgāt\ *vt* 1 : to annul or repeal by authoritative action 2 : to do away with — **ab·ro·ga·tion** \ˌab-rə-ˈgā-shən\ *n*

abrupt \ə-ˈbrəpt\ *adj* 1 : broken off; *also* : suddenly terminating as if cut or broken off 2 a : SUDDEN b : unceremoniously curt c : DISCONNECTED 3 : rising or dropping sharply : PRECIPITOUS, STEEP — **abrupt·ly** *adv* — **abrupt·ness** \ə-ˈbrəp(t)-nəs\ *n*

ab·scess \'ab-ˌses\ *n* : a localized collection of pus surrounded by inflamed tissue — **ab·scessed** \-ˌsest\ *adj*
ab·scond \ab-'skänd\ *vi* : to depart secretly and hide oneself — **ab·scond·er** *n*
ab·sence \'ab-sən(t)s\ *n* **1** : the state of being absent **2** : WANT, LACK **3** : inattention to things present
[1]**ab·sent** \'ab-sənt\ *adj* **1** : not present or attending : MISSING **2** : not existing : LACKING **3** : INATTENTIVE — **ab·sent·ly** *adv*
[2]**ab·sent** \ab-'sent\ *vt* : to keep (oneself) away
ab·sen·tee \ˌab-sən-'tē\ *n* **1** : a person who is absent or who absents himself **2** : a proprietor that lives away from his estate or business — **absentee** *adj*
ab·sen·tee·ism \ˌab-sən-'tē-ˌiz-əm\ *n* **1** : protracted absence of an owner from his property **2** : chronic absence from work or other duty
ab·sent·mind·ed \ˌab-sənt-'mīn-dəd\ *adj* : lost in thought and unaware of one's surroundings or action; *also* : given to absence of mind — **ab·sent·mind·ed·ly** *adv* — **ab·sent·mind·ed·ness** *n*
ab·sinthe *or* **ab·sinth** \'ab-ˌsin(t)th\ *n* : a green liqueur flavored with aromatics (as wormwood and anise)
ab·so·lute \'ab-sə-ˌlüt\ *adj* **1 a** : free from imperfection : PERFECT **b** : free or relatively free from mixture : PURE **2** : completely free from constitutional or other restraint or limitation **3 a** : lacking grammatical connection with any other word in a sentence **b** : standing alone without a modified substantive **c** : having no object in the particular construction under consideration though normally transitive **4** : having no restriction, exception, or qualification **5** : free from doubt : CERTAIN, UNQUESTIONABLE **6** : FUNDAMENTAL, ULTIMATE — **absolute** *n* — **ab·so·lute·ly** \'ab-sə-ˌlüt-lē, ˌab-sə-'\ *adv* — **ab·so·lute·ness** \-ˌlüt-nəs, -'lüt-\ *n*
ab·so·lu·tion \ˌab-sə-'lü-shən\ *n* : the act of absolving; *esp* : a forgiving of sins by a confessor in the sacrament of penance
ab·so·lut·ism \'ab-sə-ˌlüt-ˌiz-əm\ *n* **1 a** : a political theory that absolute power should be vested in one or more rulers **b** : government by an absolute ruler or authority **2** : advocacy of absolute standards or principles — **ab·so·lut·ist** \-ˌlüt-əst\ *n or adj*
ab·solve \əb-'sälv, -'zälv\ *vt* **1** : to set free from an obligation or from the consequences of guilt **2** : to forgive (a sin) by absolution — **ab·solv·er** *n*
ab·sorb \əb-'sȯrb, -'zȯrb\ *vt* **1** : to take in or swallow up : INCORPORATE **2** : to suck or take up or in **3** : to engage or engross wholly **4** : to receive without recoil or echo — **ab·sorb·a·bil·i·ty** \əb-ˌsȯr-bə-'bil-ət-ē, -ˌzȯr-\ *n* — **ab·sorb·a·ble** *adj* — **ab·sorb·er** *n*
ab·sorbed \-'sȯrbd, -'zȯrbd\ *adj* : wholly occupied or interested in a thought or activity : ENGROSSED
ab·sorb·en·cy \əb-'sȯr-bən-sē, -'zȯr-\ *n, pl* **-cies** : the quality or state of being absorbent
ab·sorb·ent \-bənt\ *adj* : able to absorb — **absorbent** *n*
ab·sorb·ing \-biŋ\ *adj* : fully taking attention : ENGROSSING — **ab·sorb·ing·ly** *adv*
ab·sorp·tion \əb-'sȯrp-shən, -'zȯrp-\ *n* **1** : the process of absorbing or being absorbed **2** : entire occupation of the mind — **ab·sorp·tive** \-tiv\ *adj*
ab·stain \əb-'stān\ *vi* : to refrain voluntarily esp. from an action — **ab·stain·er** *n*
ab·ste·mi·ous \ab-'stē-mē-əs\ *adj* **1** : sparing esp. in eating and drinking **2** : sparingly used or indulged in — **ab·ste·mi·ous·ly** *adv*
ab·sten·tion \əb-'sten-chən\ *n* : the act or practice of abstaining; *esp* : a usu. formal refusal to vote — **ab·sten·tious** \-chəs\ *adj*
ab·sti·nence \'ab-stə-nən(t)s\ *n* **1** : a restraining of oneself from indulgence of appetite or from eating certain foods **2** : an abstaining from drinking alcoholic liquors — **ab·sti·nent** \-nənt\ *adj* — **ab·sti·nent·ly** *adv*
[1]**ab·stract** \'ab-ˌstrakt, ab-'\ *adj* **1 a** : considered apart from application to any specific instance or particular object **b** : existing as a concept and not in any particular object or specific instance **c** : IDEAL **d** : existing in theory and not in practice : purely formal **2** : standing for an abstract quality or idea **3** : difficult to understand : ABSTRUSE **4** : dealing with a subject in purely abstract terms : THEORETICAL **5** : having only intrinsic form with little or no attempt at pictorial representation — **ab·stract·ly** *adv* — **ab·stract·ness** *n*
[2]**abstract** \'ab-ˌstrakt\ *n* **1** : a brief statement of the main points or facts : SUMMARY **2** : an abstract thing or state **3** : ABSTRACTION 4
[3]**ab·stract** \ab-'strakt, 'ab-ˌ\ *vt* **1** : REMOVE, SEPARATE **2** : to consider apart from application to a particular instance **3** : to make an abstract of : SUMMARIZE **4** : to draw away the attention of **5** : to take away secretly or dishonestly — **ab·strac·tor** *or* **ab·stract·er** *n*
ab·stract·ed \ab-'strak-təd, 'ab-ˌ\ *adj* : PREOCCUPIED, ABSENT-MINDED — **ab·stract·ed·ly** *adv* — **ab·stract·ed·ness** *n*
ab·strac·tion \ab-'strak-shən\ *n* **1 a** : the act or process of abstracting : the state of being abstracted **b** : an abstract idea or term **c** : a purely imaginary or visionary idea **2** : a state of not paying attention to nearby persons or things : ABSENT-MINDEDNESS **3** : abstract quality or character **4** : a composition or creation esp. in the art of painting or sculpture characterized by designs not recognizably representing objects in actual existence or by designs not precisely representing concrete objects or figures but with recognizable elements
ab·struse \ab-'strüs, əb-\ *adj* : hard to understand : RECONDITE — **ab·struse·ly** *adv* — **ab·struse·ness** *n*
ab·surd \əb-'sərd, -'zərd\ *adj* : ridiculously unreasonable, unsound, or incongruous — **ab·surd·ly** *adv* — **ab·surd·ness** *n*
ab·surd·i·ty \əb-'sərd-ət-ē, -'zərd-\ *n, pl* **-ties** **1** : the state of being absurd **2** : something that is absurd
abun·dance \ə-'bən-dən(t)s\ *n* **1** : an ample or overflowing quantity : PROFUSION **2** : AFFLUENCE, WEALTH **3** : relative degree of plentifulness
abun·dant \-dənt\ *adj* : existing in or possessing abundance : ABOUNDING — **abun·dant·ly** *adv*
[1]**abuse** \ə-'byüz\ *vt* **1** : to attack in words : REVILE **2** : to treat cruelly : MISTREAT **3** : to put to a wrong or improper use : MISUSE **4** : to use so as to injure or damage : MALTREAT — **abus·er** *n*
[2]**abuse** \ə-'byüs\ *n* **1** : a corrupt practice or custom **2** : improper use or treatment : MISUSE **3** : abusive language **4** : physical maltreatment
abu·sive \ə-'byü-siv, -ziv\ *adj* **1** : using or characterized by harsh insulting language : serving to abuse **2** : physically injurious — **abu·sive·ly** *adv* — **abu·sive·ness** *n*
abut \ə-'bət\ *vb* **abut·ted**; **abut·ting** **1** : to touch along a border or with a projecting part : BORDER **2 a** : to terminate at a point of contact **b** : to lean for support — **abut·ter** *n*
abut·ment \ə-'bət-mənt\ *n* **1** : the action or place of abutting **2** : something against which another thing rests its weight or pushes with force
abysm \ə-'biz-əm\ *n* : ABYSS
abys·mal \ə-'biz-məl\ *adj* : having the character of an abyss : immeasurably deep : BOTTOMLESS — **abys·mal·ly** \-mə-lē\ *adv*
abyss \ə-'bis\ *n* **1** : the bottomless gulf, pit, or chaos of the old descriptions of the origins of the universe **2** : an immeasurably deep gulf or great space
abys·sal \ə-'bis-əl\ *adj* **1** : UNFATHOMABLE **2** : of or relating to the bottom waters of the ocean depths
aca·cia \ə-'kā-shə\ *n* **1** : any of numerous woody plants of the

legume family with ball-shaped white or yellow flower clusters and often pinnate leaves **2** : GUM ARABIC

ac·a·dem·ic \ˌak-ə-ˈdem-ik\ *adj* **1** : of, relating to, or associated with an academy or school esp. of higher learning **2** : of or relating to liberal arts rather than technical or professional studies **3** : conforming to the traditions or rules of a school (as of literature or art) or an official academy : CONVENTIONAL **4** : having no immediate or practical significance : THEORETICAL — **ac·a·dem·i·cal·ly** \-ˈdem-i-k(ə-)lē\ *adv*

ac·a·de·mi·cian \ˌak-əd-ə-ˈmish-ən, ə-ˌkad-ə-\ *n* : a member of an academy for promoting science, art, or literature

acad·e·my \ə-ˈkad-ə-mē\ *n, pl* **-mies** **1** *cap* : the school of philosophy founded by Plato **2 a** : a private high school **b** : an institution for training in special subjects or skills **3** : a society of learned persons united to advance art, science, or literature

acan·thus \ə-ˈkan(t)-thəs\ *n* **1** : any of a genus of prickly herbs of the Mediterranean region **2** : an ornamentation representing the leaves of the acanthus

a cap·pel·la \ˌäk-ə-ˈpel-ə\ *adv (or adj)* : without instrumental accompaniment

ac·cede \ak-ˈsēd\ *vi* **1 a** : to adhere to an agreement **b** : to give consent : AGREE **2** : to enter upon an office or dignity

ac·ce·le·ran·do \(ˌ)ä-ˌchel-ə-ˈrän-dō\ *adv (or adj)* : gradually faster — used as a direction in music

ac·cel·er·ate \ik-ˈsel-ə-ˌrāt, ak-\ *vb* **1** : to bring about at an earlier point of time **2 a** : to hasten the ordinary progress or development of **b** : to speed up (a course of study) **3 a** : to add to the speed of **b** : to cause to undergo acceleration; *esp* : to increase the velocity of **4** : to move or progress faster — **ac·cel·er·a·tive** \-ˌrāt-iv\ *adj* — **ac·cel·er·a·tor** \-ˌrāt-ər\ *n*

ac·cel·er·a·tion \ik-ˌsel-ə-ˈrā-shən, (ˌ)ak-\ *n* : the act or process of accelerating : the state of being accelerated

¹ac·cent \ˈak-ˌsent\ *n* **1** : a peculiar or characteristic manner of speech **2** : special prominence given to one syllable of a word or group of words in speaking esp. by increase of stress or change of pitch **3** : rhythmically significant stress on the syllables of a verse usu. at regular intervals **4 a** : a mark (as ´, `, ^) used chiefly to indicate a specific sound value, stress, or pitch **b** : a mark (as ˈ or ˌ) identifying a syllable that is accented in speaking **5 a** : EMPHASIS **b** : a small detail in sharp contrast with its surroundings — **ac·cen·tu·al** \ak-ˈsench-(ə-)wəl\ *adj*

²ac·cent \ak-ˈsent, ˈak-ˌ\ *vt* **1 a** : to utter with accent : STRESS **b** : to mark with a written or printed accent **2** : to give prominence to or increase the prominence of

ac·cen·tu·ate \ak-ˈsen-chə-ˌwāt\ *vt* **1** : to pronounce or mark with an accent **2** : EMPHASIZE — **ac·cen·tu·a·tion** \(ˌ)ak-ˌsen-chə-ˈwā-shən\ *n*

ac·cept \ik-ˈsept, ak-\ *vb* **1** : to receive with consent or approval **2** : to agree or assent to: as **a** : to receive as true **b** : to regard as proper, normal, or inevitable **c** : to take without protest : TOLERATE **3 a** : to make an affirmative or favorable response to **b** : to undertake the responsibility of **4** : to assume an obligation to pay **5** : to receive officially — **ac·cept·er** *or* **ac·cep·tor** \-ˈsep-tər\ *n*

ac·cept·a·ble \ik-ˈsep-tə-bəl, ak-\ *adj* **1** : capable or worthy of being accepted : SATISFACTORY **2** : barely adequate — **ac·cept·a·bil·i·ty** \-ˌsep-tə-ˈbil-ət-ē\ *n* — **ac·cept·a·ble·ness** *n* — **ac·cept·a·bly** \-blē\ *adv*

ac·cept·ance \ik-ˈsep-tən(t)s, ak-\ *n* **1** : the act of accepting **2** : the quality or state of being accepted or acceptable

ac·cep·ta·tion \ˌak-ˌsep-ˈtā-shən\ *n* **1** : ACCEPTANCE **2** : the generally accepted meaning of a word or expression

ac·cess \ˈak-ˌses\ *n* **1** : a fit of intense feeling : OUTBURST **2 a** : permission, liberty, or ability to enter, approach, communicate with, pass to and from, or make use of **b** : a way or means of approach **3** : an increase by addition

ac·ces·si·ble \ak-ˈses-ə-bəl, ik-\ *adj* **1** : easy of access **2** : open to influence **3** : OBTAINABLE — **ac·ces·si·bil·i·ty** \(ˌ)ak-ˌses-ə-ˈbil-ət-ē, ik-\ *n* — **ac·ces·si·ble·ness** *n* — **ac·ces·si·bly** \-blē\ *adv*

ac·ces·sion \ak-ˈsesh-ən, ik-\ *n* **1** : something added : ACQUISITION **2** : ADHERENCE **3 a** : increase by something added **b** : acquisition of additional property by growth, increase, or other addition to existing property **4** : the act of assenting or agreeing **5** : the act of coming to high office or a position of honor or power **6** : ACCESS 1 — **ac·ces·sion·al** \-ˈsesh-nəl, -ən-ᵊl\ *adj*

¹ac·ces·so·ry \ak-ˈses-(ə-)rē, ik-\ *n, pl* **-ries** **1 a** : a thing of secondary or subordinate importance : ADJUNCT **b** : an object or device not essential in itself but adding to the beauty, convenience, or effectiveness of something else **2** : a person who aids or encourages another in the commission of a crime or who aids an offender in an attempt to escape justice

²accessory *adj* : aiding or contributing in a secondary way : SUPPLEMENTARY

ac·ci·dent \ˈak-səd-ənt\ *n* **1 a** : an event occurring by chance or from unknown causes **b** : lack of intention or necessity : CHANCE **2** : an unintended and usu. sudden and unexpected happening or change occurring through carelessness or ignorance or from unavoidable causes and resulting usu. in loss or injury **3 a** : a nonessential property : ATTRIBUTE **b** : a chance circumstance

¹ac·ci·den·tal \ˌak-sə-ˈdent-ᵊl\ *adj* **1** : arising from extrinsic causes : NONESSENTIAL **2 a** : occurring unexpectedly or by chance **b** : happening without intent or from carelessness often with unfortunate results — **ac·ci·den·tal·ly** \-ˈdent-lē, -ˈdent-ᵊl-ē\ *adv* — **ac·ci·den·tal·ness** *n*

²accidental *n* : a chromatically altered note (as a sharp or flat) foreign to a key indicated by a signature

¹ac·claim \ə-ˈklām\ *vb* **1** : to welcome with applause or great praise **2** : to declare or proclaim by or as if by acclamation — **ac·claim·er** *n*

²acclaim *n* **1** : the act of acclaiming **2** : APPLAUSE, PRAISE

ac·cla·ma·tion \ˌak-lə-ˈmā-shən\ *n* **1** : a loud eager expression of approval, praise, or assent **2** : an overwhelming affirmative vote by cheers, shouts, or applause rather than by ballot

ac·cli·mate \ə-ˈklī-mət, ˈak-lə-ˌmāt\ *vt* : ACCLIMATIZE — **ac·cli·ma·tion** \ˌak-ˌlī-ˈmā-shən, ˌak-lə-\ *n*

ac·cli·ma·tize \ə-ˈklī-mə-ˌtīz\ *vb* : to adapt to a new temperature, altitude, climate, environment, or situation — **ac·cli·ma·ti·za·tion** \ə-ˌklī-mət-ə-ˈzā-shən\ *n*

ac·cliv·i·ty \ə-ˈkliv-ət-ē\ *n, pl* **-ties** : a slope that ascends

ac·co·lade \ˈak-ə-ˌlād\ *n* **1** : a ceremonial embrace **2** : a formal salute (as a tap on the shoulder with the blade of a sword) that marks the conferring of knighthood **3 a** : a mark of recognition of merit : COMMENDATION **b** : AWARD

ac·com·mo·date \ə-ˈkäm-ə-ˌdāt\ *vb* **1 a** : to make fit or suitable : ADAPT **b** : to adapt oneself; *esp* : to undergo accommodation **2** : to furnish with something desired: as **a** : to provide with lodgings **b** : to make room for **c** : to hold without crowding — **ac·com·mo·da·tive** \-ˌdāt-iv\ *adj* — **ac·com·mo·da·tive·ness** *n*

ac·com·mo·dat·ing \-ˌdāt-iŋ\ *adj* : disposed to be helpful or obliging — **ac·com·mo·dat·ing·ly** *adv*

ac·com·mo·da·tion \ə-ˌkäm-ə-ˈdā-shən\ *n* **1 a** : something supplied for convenience or to satisfy a need **b** *pl* : lodging and meals or traveling space and related services **2** : the act of accommodating : the state of being accommodated

ac·com·pa·ni·ment \ə-ˈkəmp-(ə-)nē-mənt\ *n* **1** : a subordinate instrumental or vocal part designed to support or complement a principal voice or instrument **2** : an accompanying object, situation, or occurrence

ac·com·pa·ny \ə-ˈkəmp-(ə-)nē\ *vb* **-nied**; **-ny·ing** **1** : to go with or attend as an associate or companion **2** : to perform an accompaniment to or for **3 :** to occur at the same time as or along with — **ac·com·pa·nist** \-(ə-)nəst\ *n*

ac·com·plice \ə-'käm-pləs, -'kəm-\ *n* **:** one associated with another in wrongdoing

ac·com·plish \ə-'käm-plish, -'kəm-\ *vt* **1 :** to execute fully **:** PERFORM **2 a :** FULFILL **b :** TRAVERSE, COVER **3 :** PERFECT — **ac·com·plish·a·ble** *adj*

ac·com·plished \-plisht\ *adj* **1 :** COMPLETED, EFFECTED **2 a :** complete in skills or acquirements as the result of practice or training **:** EXPERT **b :** having many accomplishments

ac·com·plish·ment \-plish-mənt\ *n* **1 :** the act of accomplishing **:** COMPLETION **2 :** something accomplished **:** ACHIEVEMENT **3 :** an ability, a social quality, or a special skill acquired by training or practice

[1]**ac·cord** \ə'kȯ(ə)rd\ *vb* **1 :** to grant as suitable or proper **2 :** to be in harmony **:** AGREE

[2]**accord** *n* **1 a :** AGREEMENT, HARMONY **b :** an agreement between parties **2 :** voluntary or spontaneous impulse to act **:** WILLINGNESS

ac·cord·ance \ə-'kȯrd-ᵊn(t)s\ *n* **:** AGREEMENT, CONFORMITY

ac·cord·ant \-'kȯrd-ᵊnt\ *adj* **1 :** AGREEING **2 :** HARMONIOUS — **ac·cord·ant·ly** *adv*

ac·cord·ing as \-,kȯrd-iŋ-\ *conj* **1 :** in accord with the way in which **2 a :** depending on how **b :** depending on whether **:** IF

ac·cord·ing·ly \ə-'kȯrd-iŋ-lē\ *adv* **1 :** in accordance **:** CORRESPONDINGLY **2 :** CONSEQUENTLY, SO

according to *prep* **1 :** in agreement or conformity with **2 :** as stated by **3 :** depending on

[1]**ac·cor·di·on** \ə-'kȯrd-ē-ən\ *n* **:** a portable keyboard wind instrument in which the wind is forced past metallic reeds by means of a hand-operated bellows — **ac·cor·di·on·ist** \-ē-ə-nəst\ *n*

[2]**accordion** *adj* **:** folding or creased or hinged to fold like an accordion

ac·cost \ə-'kȯst\ *vt* **:** to approach and speak first to **:** ADDRESS

[1]**ac·count** \ə-'kau̇nt\ *n* **1 :** a chronological record of debits and credits covering transactions involving a particular item, person, or concern **2 :** a collection of items to be balanced **3 :** an explanation of one's conduct **4 a :** a periodically rendered reckoning listing charged purchases and credits **b :** the transactions between a business and an individual customer **5 a :** VALUE **b :** ESTEEM **6 :** PROFIT, ADVANTAGE **7 a :** a statement of reasons, causes, or motives **b :** a reason giving rise to an action or other result **c :** careful thought **:** CONSIDERATION **8 :** a statement of facts or events **:** RELATION **9 :** HEARSAY, REPORT **10 :** a sum of money deposited in a bank and subject to withdrawal by the depositor — **on account of** **:** for the sake of **:** by reason of **:** because of — **on no account** **:** under no circumstances

[2]**account** *vb* **1 :** to think of as **2 :** to furnish a detailed analysis or a justifying explanation **3 a :** to be the sole or primary factor **b :** to bring about the capture or destruction of something

ac·count·a·ble \ə-'kau̇nt-ə-bəl\ *adj* **1 :** responsible for giving an account (as of one's acts) **:** ANSWERABLE **2 :** capable of being accounted for **:** EXPLAINABLE — **ac·count·a·bil·i·ty** \-,kau̇nt-ə-'bil-ət-ē\ *n* — **ac·count·a·ble·ness** *n* — **ac·count·a·bly** \-'kau̇nt-ə-blē\ *adv*

ac·count·an·cy \ə-'kau̇nt-ᵊn-sē\ *n* **:** ACCOUNTING

ac·count·ant \ə-'kau̇nt-ᵊnt\ *n* **:** a person professionally trained in the practice of accounting

ac·count·ing \ə-'kau̇nt-iŋ\ *n* **1 :** the skill, system, or practice of recording and analyzing money transactions of a person or business **2 :** the action of giving an account

ac·cou·tre *or* **ac·cou·ter** \ə-'küt-ər\ *vt* **-cou·tred** *or* **-cou·tered; -cou·tring** *or* **-cou·ter·ing** \-'küt-ə-riŋ, -'kü-triŋ\ **:** to provide with equipment or furnishings **:** OUTFIT

ac·cou·tre·ment *or* **ac·cou·ter·ment** \ə-'kü-trə-mənt, -'küt-ər-mənt\ *n* **1 :** the act of accoutring **:** the state of being accoutred **2 :** EQUIPMENT; *esp* **:** a soldier's outfit usu. not including clothes and weapons.

ac·cred·it \ə-'kred-ət\ *vt* **1 :** to give official authorization or approval to: **a :** to send with credentials and authority to act as an official representative **b :** to vouch for as in conformity with a standard **c :** to recognize (an educational institution) as maintaining standards that qualify the graduates for admission to higher or more specialized institutions or for professional practice **2 :** CREDIT — **ac·cred·i·ta·tion** \ə-,kred-ə-'tā-shən\ *n*

ac·cre·tion \ə-'krē-shən\ *n* **1 :** the process of growth or enlargement; *esp* **:** increase by external addition or accumulation **2 :** a product or result of accretion — **ac·cre·tion·ary** \-shə-,ner-ē\ *adj* — **ac·cre·tive** \ə-'krēt-iv\ *adj*

ac·cru·al \ə-'krü-əl\ *n* **1 :** the action or process of accruing **2 :** something that accrues or has accrued

ac·crue \ə-'krü\ *vb* **1 :** to come by way of increase or addition **2 :** to accumulate over a period of time — **ac·crue·ment** *n*

ac·cu·mu·late \ə-'kyü-myə-,lāt\ *vb* **1 :** to pile up **:** AMASS **2 :** COLLECT, GATHER **3 :** to increase in quantity, number, or amount

ac·cu·mu·la·tion \ə-,kyü-myə-'lā-shən\ *n* **1 :** a collecting together **:** AMASSING **2 :** increase or growth by addition esp. when continuous or repeated **3 :** something that has accumulated or has been accumulated

ac·cu·mu·la·tive \ə-'kyü-myə-,lāt-iv, -lət-\ *adj* **:** CUMULATIVE — **ac·cu·mu·la·tive·ly** *adv*

ac·cu·ra·cy \'ak-yə-rə-sē\ *n, pl* **-cies** **1 :** freedom from mistake or error **:** CORRECTNESS **2 :** conformity to a standard **:** EXACTNESS

ac·cu·rate \'ak-yə-rət\ *adj* **1 :** free from mistakes esp. as the result of care **2 :** conforming exactly to truth or to a standard **:** EXACT — **ac·cu·rate·ly** *adv* — **ac·cu·rate·ness** *n*

ac·curs·ed \ə-'kər-səd, -'kərst\ *or* **ac·curst** \ə-'kərst\ *adj* **1 :** being under a curse **2 :** DAMNABLE, DETESTABLE — **ac·curs·ed·ly** \-'kər-səd-lē\ *adv*

ac·cu·sa·tion \,ak-yə-'zā-shən\ *n* **1 :** the act of accusing **:** the state or fact of being accused **2 :** a charge of wrongdoing

ac·cu·sa·tive \ə-'kyü-zət-iv\ *adj* **1 :** of, relating to, or constituting the grammatical case that marks the direct object of a verb or the object of any of several prepositions **2 :** ACCUSATORY — **accusative** *n* — **ac·cu·sa·tive·ly** *adv*

ac·cu·sa·to·ry \ə-'kyü-zə-,tōr-ē\ *adj* **:** expressing accusation

ac·cuse \ə-'kyüz\ *vb* **:** to charge with a fault or wrong or esp. with a criminal offense — **ac·cus·er** *n* — **ac·cus·ing·ly** \-'kyü-ziŋ-lē\ *adv*

ac·cused \ə-'kyüzd\ *n, pl* **accused** **:** one charged with an offense; *esp* **:** the defendant in a criminal case

ac·cus·tom \ə-'kəs-təm\ *vt* **:** to make familiar through use or experience **:** HABITUATE

ac·cus·tomed \-təmd\ *adj* **:** familiar through use or long experience: **a :** CUSTOMARY, USUAL **b :** USED, WONT

[1]**ace** \'ās\ *n* **1 :** a playing card bearing in its center one large pip **2 :** a very small amount or degree **3 :** a point scored on a stroke (as in tennis) that an opponent fails to touch **4 :** a golf hole made in one stroke **5 :** a combat pilot who has brought down at least five enemy airplanes **6 :** one that excels at something

[2]**ace** *vt* **:** to score an ace against (as a tennis opponent)

[3]**ace** *adj* **:** of first or high rank or quality

acer·bi·ty \ə-'sər-bət-ē\ *n, pl* **-ties** **:** acidity of temper, manner, or tone

ac·et·an·i·lide *or* **ac·et·an·i·lid** \,as-ə-'tan-ᵊl-,īd, -ᵊl-əd\ *n* **:** a white crystalline compound used esp. to check pain or fever

ac·e·tate \'as-ə-,tāt\ *n* **1 :** a salt or ester of acetic acid **2 :** a fast-drying fabric made of fiber derived from cellulose and acetic acid; *also* **:** a plastic of similar composition used for wrapping film and phonograph records

ace·tic \ə-'sēt-ik\ *adj* : of, relating to, or producing acetic acid or vinegar
acetic acid *n* : a colorless pungent liquid acid that is the chief acid of vinegar and that is used esp. in synthesis (as of plastics)
ac·e·tone \'as-ə-,tōn\ *n* : a volatile fragrant flammable liquid compound used chiefly as a solvent and in organic synthesis
acet·y·lene \ə-'set-ᵊl-ən, -ᵊl-,ēn\ *n* : a colorless flammable gas used chiefly in welding and soldering and in organic synthesis
¹ache \'āk\ *vi* **1** : to suffer a usu. dull persistent pain **2** : to become filled with painful yearning
²ache *n* : a usu. dull persistent pain — **achy** \'ā-kē\ *adj*
achieve \ə-'chēv\ *vb* **1** : to bring to a successful conclusion : ACCOMPLISH **2** : to get as the result of exertion : WIN — **achiev·a·ble** *adj*
achieve·ment \-mənt\ *n* **1** : the act of achieving **2** : something achieved; *esp* : something accomplished by great effort or persistence
ach·ro·mat·ic \,ak-rə-'mat-ik\ *adj* : giving an image practically free from colors not in the object
¹ac·id \'as-əd\ *adj* **1** : sour, sharp, or biting to the taste : resembling vinegar in taste **2** : sour in temper : CROSS **3** : of, relating to, or having the characteristics of an acid — **ac·id·ly** *adv* — **ac·id·ness** *n*
²acid *n* **1** : a sour substance **2** : any of various typically water-soluble and sour compounds that are capable of reacting with a base to form a salt, that redden litmus, that evolve hydrogen on reaction with various metals, that in water solution yield hydrogen ions, and that have hydrogen-containing molecules or ions able to give up a proton to a base or that are substances able to accept an unshared pair of electrons from a base **3** : LSD
acid·ic \ə-'sid-ik\ *adj* **1** : acid-forming **2** : ACID
acid·i·fy \ə-'sid-ə-,fī\ *vb* **-fied**; **-fy·ing** **1** : to make or become acid **2** : to change into an acid — **acid·i·fi·ca·tion** \ə-,sid-ə-fə-'kā-shən\ *n*
acid·i·ty \ə-'sid-ət-ē\ *n, pl* **-ties** **1** : the quality, state, or degree of being acid : TARTNESS **2** : HYPERACIDITY
ac·i·do·sis \,as-ə-'dō-səs\ *n* : an abnormal state of reduced alkalinity of the blood and of the body tissues — **ac·i·dot·ic** \-'dät-ik\ *adj*
acid test *n* : a severe or crucial test
acid·u·lous \ə-'sij-ə-ləs\ *adj* : acid in taste or manner : HARSH
ac·knowl·edge \ik-'näl-ij, ak-\ *vt* **1** : to own or admit the truth or existence of **2** : to recognize the rights, authority, or status of **3 a** : to take notice of **b** : to make known the receipt of — **ac·knowl·edge·a·ble** *adj*
ac·knowl·edged \-ijd\ *adj* : generally recognized or accepted — **ac·knowl·edged·ly** \-ij(-ə)d-lē\ *adv*
ac·knowl·edg·ment \ik-'näl-ij-mənt, ak-\ *n* **1 a** : the act of acknowledging **b** : recognition or favorable notice of an act or achievement **2** : a thing done or given in recognition of something received
ac·me \'ak-mē\ *n* : the highest point : PEAK
ac·ne \'ak-nē\ *n* : a disorder of the skin caused by inflammation of skin glands and hair follicles and marked by pimples esp. on the face
ac·o·lyte \'ak-ə-,līt\ *n* **1** : a man or boy who assists the clergyman in a liturgical service **2** : one who attends or assists : FOLLOWER
ac·o·nite \'ak-ə-,nīt\ *n* **1** : any of a genus of poisonous usu. blue-flowered or purple-flowered plants related to the buttercups **2** : a drug obtained from the common Old World monkshood
acorn \'ā-,kȯrn, -kərn\ *n* : the nut of the oak tree
acous·tic \ə-'kü-stik\ *adj* : of or relating to the sense or organs of hearing, to sound, or to the science of sounds: as **a** : deadening sound **b** : operated by or utilizing sound waves — **acous·ti·cal** \-sti-kəl\ *adj* — **acous·ti·cal·ly** \-sti-k(ə-)lē\ *adv*
acous·tics \ə-'kü-stiks\ *n sing or pl* **1** : the science dealing with sound **2** : the qualities in a room or hall that make it easy or hard for a person in it to hear distinctly
ac·quaint \ə-'kwānt\ *vt* **1** : to cause to know socially **2** : to cause to know firsthand : INFORM
ac·quaint·ance \ə-'kwānt-ᵊn(t)s\ *n* **1** : knowledge gained by personal observation, contact, or experience **2** : a person one knows but not familiarly or intimately — **ac·quaint·ance·ship** \-,ship\ *n*
ac·qui·esce \,ak-wē-'es\ *vi* : to accept, agree, or give implied consent by keeping silent or by not raising objections — **ac·qui·es·cence** \-'es-ᵊn(t)s\ *n*
ac·qui·es·cent \-'es-ᵊnt\ *adj* : acquiescing or disposed to acquiesce — **ac·qui·es·cent·ly** *adv*
ac·quire \ə-'kwī(ə)r\ *vt* **1** : to come into possession of esp. by one's own efforts : GAIN **2 a** : to come to have as a characteristic, trait, or ability often by sustained effort **b** : to develop after birth usu. as a result of environmental forces — **ac·quir·a·ble** *adj*
ac·quire·ment \-'kwī(ə)r-mənt\ *n* **1** : the act of acquiring **2** : an attainment of mind or body usu. resulting from continued endeavor
ac·qui·si·tion \,ak-wə-'zish-ən\ *n* **1** : the act of acquiring **2** : something acquired or gained
ac·quis·i·tive \ə-'kwiz-ət-iv\ *adj* : strongly desirous of acquiring : GRASPING — **ac·quis·i·tive·ly** *adv* — **ac·quis·i·tive·ness** *n*
ac·quit \ə-'kwit\ *vt* **-quit·ted**; **-quit·ting** **1** : to set free or discharge completely (as from an obligation or accusation) **2** : to conduct (oneself) usu. satisfactorily — **ac·quit·ter** *n*
ac·quit·tal \ə-'kwit-ᵊl\ *n* : the setting free of a person from the charge of an offense by verdict, sentence, or other legal process
acre \'ā-kər\ *n* **1** *pl* : LANDS, ESTATE **2** : a unit of area equal to 160 square rods **3** : a broad expanse or great quantity
acre·age \'ā-k(ə-)rij\ *n* : area in acres : ACRES
ac·rid \'ak-rəd\ *adj* **1** : sharp and harsh or unpleasantly pungent in taste or odor : IRRITATING, BITTER **2** : bitterly irritating to the feelings — **acrid·i·ty** \a-'krid-ət-ē, ə-\ *n* — **ac·rid·ly** \'ak-rəd-lē\ *adv* — **ac·rid·ness** *n*
ac·ri·mo·ni·ous \,ak-rə-'mō-nē-əs\ *adj* : marked by acrimony : BITTER, RANCOROUS — **ac·ri·mo·ni·ous·ly** *adv* — **ac·ri·mo·ni·ous·ness** *n*
ac·ri·mo·ny \'ak-rə-,mō-nē\ *n, pl* **-nies** : harsh or biting sharpness esp. of words, manner, or disposition
ac·ro·bat \'ak-rə-,bat\ *n* : one that performs gymnastic feats requiring skillful control of the body — **ac·ro·bat·ic** \,ak-rə-'bat-ik\ *adj* — **ac·ro·bat·i·cal·ly** \-'bat-i-k(ə-)lē\ *adv*
ac·ro·bat·ics \,ak-rə-'bat-iks\ *n sing or pl* **1** : the art or performance of an acrobat **2** : a striking performance involving great agility or maneuverability
ac·ro·nym \'ak-rə-,nim\ *n* : a word (as *radar*) formed from the initial letter or letters of each of the successive parts or major parts of a compound term
ac·ro·pho·bia \,ak-rə-'fō-bē-ə\ *n* : abnormal dread of being at a great height
acrop·o·lis \ə-'kräp-ə-ləs\ *n* : the upper fortified part of an ancient Greek city
¹across \ə-'krȯs\ *adv* **1** : so as to reach or pass from one side to the other **2** : to or on the opposite side
²across *prep* **1** : to or on the opposite side of **2** : so as to intersect or pass at an angle **3** : into an accidental or transitory meeting or contact with
across–the–board *adj* **1** : placed to pay off if a competitor wins, places, or shows **2** : including all classes or categories
acros·tic \ə-'krȯ-stik\ *n* : a composition usu. in verse in which sets of letters (as the initial or final letters of the lines) taken in

order form a word or phrase or a regular sequence of letters of the alphabet —**acros·ti·cal·ly** \-sti-k(ə-)lē\ *adv*

¹act \'akt\ *n* **1 :** something that is done : DEED **2 :** the doing of something **3 :** a law made by a governing body (as a legislature) **4 a :** one of the main divisions of a play or opera **b :** one of the successive parts of a variety show or circus

²act *vb* **1 :** to perform by action esp. on the stage **2 :** to play the part of **3 a :** to behave in a manner suitable to **b :** to conduct oneself **4 :** PRETEND **5 :** to take action : MOVE **6 a :** to perform a specified function : discharge the duties of a specified office : SERVE **b :** to produce an effect : WORK **7 :** to make a decision — **act·a·bil·i·ty** \,ak-tə-'bil-ət-ē\ *n* — **act·a·ble** *adj*

¹act·ing \'ak-tiŋ\ *adj* **:** serving temporarily or for another

²acting *n* **:** the art or practice of representing a character on a stage or before cameras

ac·ti·nism \'ak-tə-,niz-əm\ *n* **:** the property of radiant energy by which chemical changes are produced — **ac·tin·ic** \ak-'tin-ik\ *adj*

ac·tin·i·um \ak-'tin-ē-əm\ *n* **:** a radioactive metallic element found esp. in pitchblende

ac·tion \'ak-shən\ *n* **1 :** a proceeding in a court of justice by which one demands or enforces one's right or the redress or punishment of a wrong **2 :** the bringing about of an alteration by force or through a natural agency **3 :** the process or manner of acting or functioning : PERFORMANCE **4 a :** a thing done : DEED **b** *pl* **;** BEHAVIOR, CONDUCT **5 :** combat in war : BATTLE **6 :** the unfolding of the events of a drama or work of fiction : PLOT **7 :** an operating mechanism; *also* **:** the way it operates **8 :** the greatest activity or excitement in a particular field or group

ac·ti·vate \'ak-tə-,vāt\ *vt* **:** to make active or more active: as **a :** to make (as molecules) reactive **b :** to make (a substance) radioactive **c :** to aerate (sewage) so as to favor the growth of organisms that cause decomposition — **ac·ti·va·tion** \,ak-tə-'vā-shən\ *n* — **ac·ti·va·tor** \'ak-tə-,vāt-ər\ *n*

ac·tive \'ak-tiv\ *adj* **1 :** characterized by action rather than contemplation **2 :** productive of or involving action or movement **3 :** of, relating to, or constituting a verb form or voice indicating that the person or thing represented by the grammatical subject performs the action represented by the verb **4 :** quick in physical movement : LIVELY **5 a :** disposed to action : ENERGETIC **b :** engaged in an action or activity : PARTICIPATING **6 :** engaged in full-time service esp. in the armed forces **7 :** marked by present action, operation, movement, or use **8 a :** capable of acting or reacting **b :** tending to progress or increase — **ac·tive·ly** *adv* — **ac·tive·ness** *n*

ac·tiv·ism \'ak-ti-,viz-əm\ *n* **:** a doctrine or practice that emphasizes vigorous action and esp. the use of force for political ends — **ac·tiv·ist** \-vəst\ *n or adj*

ac·tiv·i·ty \ak-'tiv-ət-ē\ *n, pl* **-ties 1 :** the quality or state of being active **2 :** vigorous or energetic action : LIVELINESS **3 a :** natural or normal function **b** (1) **:** a process that an organism carries on or participates in by virtue of being alive (2) **:** a similar process actually or potentially involving mental function **4 :** an educational procedure designed to stimulate learning by firsthand experience **5 :** an active force **6 a :** PURSUIT 2 **b :** a form of organized, supervised, often extracurricular recreation **c :** the work or duties of a government unit or agency organized for a specific function

ac·tor \'ak-tər\ *n* **1 a :** one that acts : DOER **b :** one that acts a part; *esp* **:** a theatrical performer **2 :** PARTICIPANT — **ac·tress** \'ak-trəs\ *n*

ac·tu·al \'ak-ch(ə-w)əl\ *adj* **1 a :** existing in act and not merely potentially **b :** existing in fact or reality as distinguished from being ideal or nominal **c :** not false : REAL **2 :** present or active at the time : CURRENT

ac·tu·al·i·ty \,ak-chə-'wal-ət-ē\ *n, pl* **-ties 1 :** the quality or state of being actual **2 :** something that is actual

ac·tu·al·ly \'ak-ch(ə-w)ə-lē\ *adv* **:** in act or in fact : REALLY

ac·tu·ary \'ak-chə-,wer-ē\ *n, pl* **-ar·ies :** one who calculates insurance premiums and dividends — **ac·tu·ar·i·al** \,ak-chə-'wer-ē-əl\ *adj* — **ac·tu·ar·i·al·ly** \-ē-ə-lē\ *adv*

ac·tu·ate \'ak-chə-,wāt\ *vt* **1 :** to put into action **2 :** to move to action : arouse to activity — **ac·tu·a·tion** \,ak-chə-'wā-shən\ *n*

acu·i·ty \ə-'kyü-ət-ē\ *n* **:** keenness of perception : SHARPNESS

acu·men \ə-'kyü-mən\ *n* **:** keenness of insight esp. in practical matters : SHREWDNESS

acute \ə-'kyüt\ *adj* **1 a :** measuring less than a right angle **b :** composed of acute angles **2 a :** marked by keen discernment or intellectual perception esp. of subtle distinctions : PENETRATING **b :** responsive to slight impressions or stimuli **3 :** marked by sharpness or severity **4 :** HIGH, SHRILL **5 a :** having a sudden onset and short duration **b :** being at or near a turning point : URGENT, CRITICAL **6 :** of, marked by, or being an accent mark having the form ′ — **acute·ly** *adv* — **acute·ness** *n*

ad \'ad\ *n* **:** ADVERTISEMENT 2

ad·age \'ad-ij\ *n* **:** a saying embodying common observation often in metaphorical form

¹ada·gio \ə-'däj-ō, -'däj-ē-,ō, -'däzh-\ *adv* (*or adj*) **:** in an easy graceful manner : SLOWLY — used chiefly as a direction in music

²adagio *n* **1 :** a musical composition or movement in adagio tempo **2 :** a ballet duet or trio displaying difficult feats of balance, lifting, or spinning

¹ad·a·mant \'ad-ə-mənt\ *n* **:** a stone believed to be of impenetrable hardness

²adamant *adj* **:** unshakable or immovable esp. in opposition : UNYIELDING — **ad·a·mant·ly** *adv*

ad·a·man·tine \,ad-ə-'man-,tēn, -,tīn\ *adj* **1 :** made of or having the quality of adamant **2 :** rigidly firm : UNYIELDING **3 :** resembling the diamond in hardness or luster

Ad·am's apple \,ad-əmz-\ *n* **:** the projection in the front of the neck formed by the largest cartilage of the larynx

adapt \ə-'dapt\ *vb* **:** to make or become suitable; *esp* **:** to change so as to fit a new or specific use or situation — **adapt·a·bil·i·ty** \-,dap-tə-'bil-ət-ē\ *n* — **adapt·a·ble** *adj* — **adapt·er** *n*

ad·ap·ta·tion \,ad-,ap-'tā-shən\ *n* **1 a :** the act or process of adapting **b :** the state of being adapted **2 :** adjustment to environmental conditions **3 :** something that is adapted; *esp* **:** a composition rewritten into a new form — **ad·ap·ta·tion·al** \-shnəl, -shən-ᵊl\ *adj* — **ad·ap·ta·tion·al·ly** \-ē\ *adv*

adapt·ed \ə-'dap-təd\ *adj* **:** SUITABLE

adap·tive \ə-'dap-tiv\ *adj* **:** showing or having a capacity for or tendency toward adaptation — **adap·tive·ly** *adv*

add \'ad\ *vb* **1 a :** to join or unite to a thing so as to enlarge, increase, or enhance it **b :** to unite in a single whole **2 :** to put or say something more **3 :** to combine numbers into a single sum — **add·a·ble** *or* **add·i·ble** \'ad-ə-bəl\ *adj*

ad·dend \'ad-,end\ *n* **:** a number that is to be added to another number

ad·den·dum \ə-'den-dəm\ *n, pl* **-den·da** \-'den-də\ **1 :** a thing added : ADDITION **2 :** a supplement to a book : APPENDIX

¹ad·der \'ad-ər\ *n* **1 :** a poisonous European viper; *also* **:** any of several related snakes **2 :** any of several harmless No. American snakes

²add·er \'ad-ər\ *n* **:** one that adds

¹ad·dict \ə-'dikt\ *vt* **:** to devote or surrender (oneself) to something habitually or obsessively

²ad·dict \'ad-(,)ikt\ *n* **:** one who is addicted (as to a drug)

ad·dic·tion \ə-'dik-shən\ *n* **:** the quality or state of being addicted; *esp* **:** compulsive use of habit-forming drugs

ad·dic·tive \ə-ˈdik-tiv\ *adj* : causing or characterized by addiction

ad·di·tion \ə-ˈdish-ən\ *n* **1** : the result of adding : INCREASE **2** : the act or process of adding **3** : the operation of adding numbers to obtain their sum **4** : a part added (as to a building or residential section) — **in addition** : BESIDES — **in addition to** : over and above

ad·di·tion·al \-ˈdish-nəl, -ˈdish-ən-ᵊl\ *adj* : ADDED, EXTRA — **ad·di·tion·al·ly** \-ē\ *adv*

¹**ad·di·tive** \ˈad-ət-iv\ *adj* : relating to or produced by addition — **ad·di·tive·ly** *adv*

²**additive** *n* : a substance added to another in relatively small amounts to impart or improve desirable properties or suppress undesirable properties

ad·dle \ˈad-ᵊl\ *vb* **ad·dled**; **ad·dling** \ˈad-liŋ, -ᵊl-iŋ\ **1** : to make or become confused **2** : to become rotten

¹**ad·dress** \ə-ˈdres\ *vt* **1** : to direct the attention of (oneself) **2 a** : to communicate directly to a person or group **b** : to deliver a formal speech to **3** : to mark directions for delivery on **4** : to greet by a prescribed form — **ad·dress·er** *n*

²**ad·dress** \ə-ˈdres, ˈad-ˌres\ *n* **1 a** : a formal usu. prepared speech **b** : PETITION **2 a** : a place where a person or organization may be communicated with **b** : directions for delivery on the outside of an object (as a letter or package) **c** : the designation of place of delivery above the salutation on a business letter

ad·dress·ee \ˌad-ˌres-ˈē, ə-ˌdres-ˈē\ *n* : one to whom something is addressed

ad·duce \ə-ˈd(y)üs\ *vt* : to offer as example, reason, or proof in discussion or analysis — **ad·duc·er** *n*

ad·e·noid \ˈad-ᵊn-ˌȯid, ˈad-ˌnȯid\ *n* : an enlarged mass of tissue at the back of the pharynx characteristically obstructing breathing — usu. used in pl.

¹**ad·ept** \ˈad-ˌept\ *n* : a highly skilled or well-trained individual : EXPERT

²**adept** \ə-ˈdept\ *adj* : thoroughly proficient : EXPERT — **adept·ly** *adv* — **adept·ness** *n*

ad·e·qua·cy \ˈad-i-kwə-sē\ *n* : the quality or state of being adequate

ad·e·quate \ˈad-i-kwət\ *adj* **1** : suitable or fully sufficient for a specific requirement **2** : barely sufficient or satisfactory — **ad·e·quate·ly** *adv* — **ad·e·quate·ness** *n*

ad·here \ad-ˈhi(ə)r, əd-\ *vi* **1** : to give support or maintain loyalty (as to a cause or belief) **2** : to hold fast or stick by or as if by gluing : CLING **3** : to agree to accept as binding

ad·her·ence \-ˈhir-ən(t)s\ *n* **1** : the action or quality of adhering **2** : steady or faithful attachment : FIDELITY

¹**ad·her·ent** \-ˈhir-ənt\ *adj* : able or tending to adhere — **ad·her·ent·ly** *adv*

²**adherent** *n* : one that adheres: as **a** : a follower of a leader or party **b** : a believer in or advocate of something (as an idea, church, or doctrine)

ad·he·sion \ad-ˈhē-zhən, əd-\ *n* **1** : steady or firm attachment : ADHERENCE **2** : the action or state of adhering **3** : tissues abnormally united by fibrous tissue following inflammation (as after surgery) — **ad·he·sion·al** \-ˈhēzh-nəl, -ˈhē-zhən-ᵊl\ *adj*

¹**ad·he·sive** \ad-ˈhē-siv, əd-\ *adj* **1** : tending to remain in association or memory **2** : tending to adhere : prepared for adhering : STICKY — **ad·he·sive·ly** *adv* — **ad·he·sive·ness** *n*

²**adhesive** *n* : an adhesive substance (as glue or cement)

adieu \ə-ˈd(y)ü\ *n, pl* **adieus** *or* **adieux** \-ˈd(y)üz\ : FAREWELL — often used interjectionally

ad in·fi·ni·tum \ˌad-ˌin-fə-ˈnīt-əm\ *adv* (*or adj*) : without end or limit

¹**ad in·ter·im** \(ˈ)ad-ˈin-tə-rəm\ *adv* : for the intervening time : TEMPORARILY

²**ad interim** *adj* : made or serving ad interim

adi·os \ˌad-ē-ˈōs, ˌäd-\ *interj* — used to express farewell

ad·i·pose \ˈad-ə-ˌpōs\ *adj* : of or relating to animal fat : FATTY — **ad·i·pos·i·ty** \ˌad-ə-ˈpäs-ət-ē\ *n*

ad·ja·cent \ə-ˈjās-ᵊnt\ *adj* : lying next or near : having a common border — **ad·ja·cent·ly** *adv*

ad·jec·ti·val \ˌaj-ik-ˈtī-vəl\ *adj* : ADJECTIVE — **ad·jec·ti·val·ly** \-və-lē\ *adv*

¹**ad·jec·tive** \ˈaj-ik-tiv\ *adj* **1** : of, relating to, or functioning as an adjective **2** : not standing by itself : DEPENDENT — **ad·jec·tive·ly** *adv*

²**adjective** *n* : a word typically serving as a modifier of a noun

ad·join \ə-ˈjȯin\ *vt* : to lie next to or in contact with

ad·journ \ə-ˈjərn\ *vb* : to suspend further proceedings or business for an indefinite or stated period of time — **ad·journ·ment** *n*

ad·judge \ə-ˈjəj\ *vt* **1** : ADJUDICATE **2** : to hold or pronounce to be : DEEM

ad·ju·di·cate \ə-ˈjüd-i-ˌkāt\ *vt* : to decide, award, or sentence judicially — **ad·ju·di·ca·tive** \-ˌkāt-iv\ *adj* — **ad·ju·di·ca·tor** \-ˌkāt-ər\ *n*

ad·ju·di·ca·tion \-ˌjüd-i-ˈkā-shən\ *n* **1** : the act or process of adjudicating **2** : a judicial decision

¹**ad·junct** \ˈaj-ˌən(k)t\ *n* : something joined or added to another thing but not essentially a part of it

²**adjunct** *adj* **1** : added or joined as an accompanying object or circumstance **2** : attached in a subordinate or temporary capacity to a staff — **ad·junct·ly** *adv*

ad·jure \ə-ˈju̇(ə)r\ *vt* **1** : to charge or command solemnly under or as if under oath or penalty of a curse **2** : to entreat earnestly : CHARGE — **ad·ju·ra·tion** \ˌaj-ə-ˈrā-shən\ *n* — **ad·jur·a·to·ry** \ə-ˈju̇r-ə-ˌtōr-ē\ *adj*

ad·just \ə-ˈjəst\ *vb* **1** : to bring to a more satisfactory state: **a** : SETTLE, RESOLVE **b** : RECTIFY **2** : to move the parts of an instrument or a piece of machinery until they fit together in the best working order : REGULATE **3** : to determine the amount of an insurance claim **4** : to adapt or accommodate oneself to external conditions — **ad·just·a·ble** *adj* — **ad·just·er** *n*

ad·just·ment \ə-ˈjəs(t)-mənt\ *n* **1** : the act or process of adjusting **2** : a settlement of a claim or debt **3** : the state of being adjusted **4** : a means of adjusting one part (as in a machine) to another **5** : a correction or modification to reflect actual conditions — **ad·just·ment·al** \ə-ˌjəs(t)-ˈment-ᵊl\ *adj*

ad·ju·tan·cy \ˈaj-ət-ən-sē\ *n* : the office or rank of an adjutant

ad·ju·tant \ˈaj-ət-ənt\ *n* **1** : a staff officer (as in the army) assisting the commanding officer and responsible esp. for correspondence **2** : one who helps : ASSISTANT

adjutant general *n, pl* **adjutants general** : the chief administrative officer of an army or of one of its major units (as a division or corps)

ad·ju·vant \ˈaj-ə-vənt\ *n* : something that enhances the effectiveness of medical treatment

ad lib \(ˈ)ad-ˈlib\ *adv* : without restraint or limit

¹**ad–lib** \(ˈ)ad-ˈlib\ *adj* : spoken, composed, or performed without preparation

²**ad–lib** *vb* **ad–libbed**; **ad–lib·bing** **1** : to deliver spontaneously **2** : to improvise lines or a speech

ad li·bi·tum \(ˈ)ad-ˈlib-ət-əm\ *adv* : freely in accordance with one's wishes — used as a direction in music

ad·man \ˈad-ˌman\ *n* : one who writes, solicits, or places advertisements

ad·min·is·ter \əd-ˈmin-ə-stər\ *vb* **ad·min·is·tered**; **ad·min·is·ter·ing** \-st(ə-)riŋ\ **1 a** : to superintend the execution, use, or conduct of **b** : to manage or direct the affairs of **c** : SETTLE 7a **2 a** : to mete out : DISPENSE **b** : to give ritually **c** : to give remedially **3** : to furnish a benefit : MINISTER — **ad·min·is·tra·ble** \-strə-bəl\ *adj* — **ad·min·is·trant** \-strənt\ *n*

ad·min·is·tra·tion \əd-ˌmin-ə-ˈstrā-shən, (ˌ)ad-\ *n* **1** : the act or process of administering **2** : performance of executive duties

: MANAGEMENT **3** : the execution of public affairs as distinguished from policy making **4 a** : a body of persons who administer **b** *cap* : a group constituting the political executive in a presidential government **c** : a governmental agency or board **5** : the term of office of an administrative officer or body

ad·min·is·tra·tive \əd-ˈmin-ə-ˌstrāt-iv\ *adj* : of or relating to administration

ad·min·is·tra·tor \əd-ˈmin-ə-ˌstrāt-ər\ *n* : one that administers; *esp* : a person legally vested with the right of administration of an estate — **ad·min·is·tra·trix** \əd-ˌmin-ə-ˈstrā-triks\ *n*

ad·mi·ra·ble \ˈad-m(ə-)rə-bəl\ *adj* : deserving to be admired : EXCELLENT — **ad·mi·ra·bly** \-blē\ *adv*

ad·mi·ral \ˈad-m(ə-)rəl\ *n* : a commissioned officer in the navy ranking next below a fleet admiral

ad·mi·ral·ty \ˈad-m(ə-)rəl-tē\ *adj* : of, relating to, or having jurisdiction over maritime affairs

Admiralty *n* : the body of officials having jurisdiction over the British navy

ad·mi·ra·tion \ˌad-mə-ˈrā-shən\ *n* **1** : an object of admiring esteem **2** : delighted or astonished approval

ad·mire \əd-ˈmī(ə)r\ *vt* **1** : to regard with admiration **2** : to esteem highly — **ad·mir·er** *n*

ad·mis·si·ble \əd-ˈmis-ə-bəl\ *adj* : that can be or is worthy to be admitted or allowed : ALLOWABLE — **ad·mis·si·bil·i·ty** \-ˌmis-ə-ˈbil-ət-ē\ *n* — **ad·mis·si·bly** \-ˈmis-ə-blē\ *adv*

ad·mis·sion \əd-ˈmish-ən\ *n* **1** : the act of admitting **2** : the right or permission to enter **3** : the price of entrance to a place **4** : a granting of something that has not been fully proved

ad·mit \əd-ˈmit\ *vb* **ad·mit·ted**; **ad·mit·ting** **1** : to allow scope for : PERMIT **2** : to allow entry : let in **3** : to confess to : make acknowledgment — **ad·mit·ted·ly** \-ˈmit-əd-lē\ *adv*

ad·mit·tance \əd-ˈmit-ᵊn(t)s\ *n* : permission to enter a place : ENTRANCE

ad·mix \ad-ˈmiks\ *vt* : MINGLE, MIX

ad·mix·ture \ad-ˈmiks-chər\ *n* **1 a** : the act or process of mixing **b** : the fact of being mixed **2** : something formed by mixing : MIXTURE **3** : something added to another thing in mixing

ad·mon·ish \ad-ˈmän-ish\ *vt* **1 a** : to indicate duties or obligations to **b** : to reprove gently but seriously : warn of a fault **2** : to give friendly earnest advice or encouragement to — **ad·mon·ish·er** *n* — **ad·mon·ish·ing·ly** \-ˈmän-i-shiŋ-lē\ *adv* — **ad·mon·ish·ment** *n*

ad·mo·ni·tion \ˌad-mə-ˈnish-ən\ *n* **1** : gentle or friendly reproof **2** : counsel or warning against fault or oversight

ad·mon·i·to·ry \ad-ˈmän-ə-ˌtōr-ē\ *adj* : expressing admonition : WARNING

ad nau·se·am \ad-ˈnȯ-zē-əm\ *adv* : to a sickening degree

ado \ə-ˈdü\ *n* : FUSS, TROUBLE

ado·be \ə-ˈdō-bē\ *n* **1** : a brick made of clayey mud dried in the sun **2** : a building made of adobe bricks

ad·o·les·cence \ˌad-ᵊl-ˈes-ᵊn(t)s\ *n* : the state or process of growing up; *also* : the period of life from puberty to maturity

¹**ad·o·les·cent** \-ᵊnt\ *n* : one that is in the state of adolescence : a person not fully mature

²**adolescent** *adj* : of, relating to, or being in adolescence — **ad·o·les·cent·ly** *adv*

adopt \ə-ˈdäpt\ *vt* **1** : to take by choice into a relationship; *esp* : to take (a child of other parents) voluntarily and usu. by formal legal act as one's own child **2** : to take up and practice as one's own **3** : to accept formally and put into effect — **adopt·a·bil·i·ty** \ə-ˌdäp-tə-ˈbil-ət-ē\ *n* — **adopt·a·ble** *adj* — **adopt·er** *n*

adop·tion \ə-ˈdäp-shən\ *n* : the act of adopting : the state of being adopted

adop·tive \ə-ˈdäp-tiv\ *adj* : made or acquired by adoption — **adop·tive·ly** *adv*

ador·a·ble \ə-ˈdōr-ə-bəl\ *adj* **1** : deserving to be adored **2** : CHARMING, LOVELY — **ador·a·bil·i·ty** \ə-ˌdōr-ə-ˈbil-ət-ē\ *n* — **ador·a·ble·ness** *n* — **ador·a·bly** \ə-ˈdōr-ə-blē\ *adv*

ad·o·ra·tion \ˌad-ə-ˈrā-shən\ *n* : the act of adoring : the state of being adored

adore \ə-ˈdō(ə)r\ *vt* **1** : WORSHIP **2** : to be extremely fond of — **ador·er** *n*

adorn \ə-ˈdȯrn\ *vt* : to decorate with ornaments : BEAUTIFY

adorn·ment \-mənt\ *n* **1** : the action of adorning : the state of being adorned **2** : something that adorns

adre·nal \ə-ˈdrēn-ᵊl\ *adj* **1** : adjacent to the kidneys **2** : of, relating to, or derived from adrenal glands or secretion

adrenal gland *n* : either of a pair of complex endocrine organs occurring one near each kidney that produce several hormones

adren·a·line \ə-ˈdren-ᵊl-ən\ *n* : a hormone of the adrenal gland acting esp. on involuntary muscle, causing narrowing of blood vessels, and raising blood pressure

adrift \ə-ˈdrift\ *adv (or adj)* **1** : without motive power, anchor, or mooring **2** : without guidance or purpose

adroit \ə-ˈdrȯit\ *adj* **1** : dexterous in the use of the hands **2** : showing shrewdness, craft, or resourcefulness in coping with difficulty or danger — **adroit·ly** *adv* — **adroit·ness** *n*

ad·sorb \ad-ˈsȯrb, -ˈzȯrb\ *vt* : to take up and hold by adsorption — **ad·sorb·ent** \-ˈsȯr-bənt, -ˈzȯr-\ *adj or n*

ad·sorp·tion \-ˈsȯrp-shən, -ˈzȯrp-\ *n* : the adhesion in an extremely thin layer of molecules (as of gases, solutes, or liquids) to the surfaces of solid bodies or liquids with which they are in contact — **ad·sorp·tive** \-ˈsȯrp-tiv, -ˈzȯrp-\ *adj*

ad·u·late \ˈaj-ə-ˌlāt\ *vt* : to flatter or admire excessively or slavishly — **ad·u·la·tion** \ˌaj-ə-ˈlā-shən\ *n* — **ad·u·la·to·ry** \ˈaj-ə-lə-ˌtōr-ē\ *adj*

¹**adult** \ə-ˈdəlt, ˈad-ˌəlt\ *adj* **1** : fully developed and mature : GROWN-UP **2** : of, relating to, or characteristic of adults — **adult·hood** \ə-ˈdəlt-ˌhu̇d\ *n* — **adult·ness** *n*

²**adult** *n* **1** : a fully grown person, animal, or plant **2** : a person having attained legal majority

adul·ter·ant \ə-ˈdəl-tə-rənt\ *n* : something used to adulterate another thing

adul·ter·ate \ə-ˈdəl-tə-ˌrāt\ *vt* : to make impure or weaker by adding a foreign or inferior substance; *esp* : to prepare for sale by using in whole or in part a substance that reduces quality or strength — **adul·ter·a·tion** \ə-ˌdəl-tə-ˈrā-shən\ *n* — **adul·ter·a·tor** \ə-ˈdəl-tə-ˌrāt-ər\ *n*

adul·tery \ə-ˈdəl-t(ə-)rē\ *n, pl* **-ter·ies** : voluntary sexual intercourse between a married person and someone other than his or her spouse — **adul·ter·er** \-tər-ər\ *n* — **adul·ter·ess** \-t(ə-)rəs\ *n* — **adul·ter·ous** \-t(ə-)rəs\ *adj*

ad·um·brate \ˈad-əm-ˌbrāt\ *vt* **1** : to suggest or disclose partially **2** : SHADE, OBSCURE — **ad·um·bra·tion** \ˌad-(ˌ)əm-ˈbrā-shən\ *n* — **ad·um·bra·tive** \ə-ˈdəm-brət-iv\ *adj* — **ad·um·bra·tive·ly** *adv*

ad va·lo·rem \ˌad-və-ˈlōr-əm\ *adj* : based on a percentage of the monetary value of the goods imported

¹**ad·vance** \əd-ˈvan(t)s\ *vb* **1** : to move forward **2** : to further the progress of **3** : to raise to a higher rank or position : PROMOTE **4** : to supply or furnish in expectation of repayment **5** : to bring forward : PROPOSE **6** : to raise or rise in rate or price : INCREASE — **ad·vanc·er** *n*

²**advance** *n* **1** : a forward movement **2** : progress in development : IMPROVEMENT **3** : a rise in price, value, or amount **4** : a first step or approach made : OFFER **5 a** : a provision of something (as money or goods) before a return is received **b** : the money or goods supplied — **in advance** : BEFOREHAND

³**advance** *adj* **1** : made, sent, or furnished ahead of time **2** : going or situated before

ad·vanced \əd-ˈvan(t)st\ *adj* **1** : far on in time or course **2 a** : being beyond the elementary or introductory **b** : being beyond others in progress or development

ad•vance•ment \əd-'van(t)s-mənt\ *n* 1 : the action of advancing : the state of being advanced: a : promotion or elevation to a higher rank or position b : progression to a higher stage of development 2 : money or property given in advance
ad•van•tage \əd-'vant-ij\ *n* 1 : superiority of position or condition 2 : BENEFIT, GAIN; *esp* : benefit resulting from some course of action 3 : the 1st point won in tennis after deuce
ad•van•ta•geous \,ad-vən-'tā-jəs, -,van-\ *adj* : giving an advantage : HELPFUL, FAVORABLE — **ad•van•ta•geous•ly** *adv* — **ad•van•ta•geous•ness** *n*
Ad•vent \'ad-,vent\ *n* 1 : a penitential season beginning four Sundays before Christmas 2 : the coming of Christ at the incarnation or as judge on the last day 3 *not cap* : COMING, ARRIVAL
ad•ven•ti•tious \,ad-vən-'tish-əs\ *adj* 1 : added externally and not becoming an essential part : ACCIDENTAL 2 : appearing out of the usual or normal place — **ad•ven•ti•tious•ly** *adv* — **ad•ven•ti•tious•ness** *n*
[1]**ad•ven•ture** \əd-'ven-chər\ *n* 1 a : an undertaking involving unknown dangers and risks b : the encountering of risks 2 : an unusual experience
[2]**adventure** *vb* **-ven•tured**; **-ven•tur•ing** \-'vench-(ə-)riŋ\ 1 : RISK, VENTURE 2 : to proceed despite danger or risk
ad•ven•tur•er \-'ven-chər-ər\ *n* 1 : one that adventures: as a : SOLDIER OF FORTUNE b : one that engages in risky commercial enterprises for profit 2 : one that seeks position or wealth by sharp practice and dubious methods
ad•ven•ture•some \-'ven-chər-səm\ *adj* : inclined to take risks : DARING
ad•ven•tur•ess \-'vench-(ə-)rəs\ *n* : a female adventurer
ad•ven•tur•ous \əd-'vench-(ə-)rəs\ *adj* 1 : ready to seek adventure or to cope with the new and unknown 2 : characterized by unknown dangers and risks — **ad•ven•tur•ous•ly** *adv* — **ad•ven•tur•ous•ness** *n*
ad•verb \'ad-,vərb\ *n* : a word used to modify a verb, an adjective, or another adverb — **adverb** *adj*
ad•ver•bi•al \ad-'vər-bē-əl\ *adj* : of, relating to, or having the function of an adverb — **ad•ver•bi•al•ly** \-bē-ə-lē\ *adv*
ad•ver•sary \'ad-və(r)-,ser-ē\ *n, pl* **-sar•ies** : one that contends with, opposes, or resists
ad•verse \ad-'vərs, 'ad-,vərs\ *adj* 1 : acting in a contrary direction 2 : actively opposed : ANTAGONISTIC 3 : having a harmful or hindering effect : UNFAVORABLE — **ad•verse•ly** *adv* — **ad•verse•ness** *n*
ad•ver•si•ty \ad-'vər-sət-ē\ *n, pl* **-ties** : a condition or experience of serious or continued misfortune
ad•vert \ad-'vərt\ *vb* : to direct attention (as in speaking or writing) : REFER
ad•ver•tise \'ad-vər-,tīz\ *vb* 1 : to announce publicly esp. by a printed notice or a broadcast 2 : to call public attention to esp. by emphasizing desirable qualities so as to arouse a desire to buy or patronize 3 : to issue or sponsor advertising — **ad•ver•tis•er** *n*
ad•ver•tise•ment \,ad-vər-'tīz-mənt, ad-'vərt-əz-\ *n* 1 : the act or process of advertising 2 : a public notice; *esp* : one published or broadcast
ad•ver•tis•ing \'ad-vər-,tī-ziŋ\ *n* 1 : the action of calling something to the attention of the public esp. by paid announcements 2 : ADVERTISEMENTS 3 : the business of preparing advertisements for publication or broadcast
ad•vice \əd-'vīs\ *n* : recommendation regarding a decision or course of conduct : COUNSEL
ad•vis•a•ble \əd-'vī-zə-bəl\ *adj* : reasonable or proper under the circumstances : WISE, PRUDENT — **ad•vis•a•bil•i•ty** \əd-,vī-zə-'bil-ət-ē\ *n* — **ad•vis•a•bly** \əd-'vī-zə-blē\ *adv*
ad•vise \əd-'vīz\ *vb* 1 a : to give advice to : COUNSEL b : RECOMMEND 2 : to give information or notice to : INFORM 3 : to take counsel : CONSULT — **ad•vis•er** *or* **ad•vi•sor** \-'vī-zər\ *n*
ad•vised \-'vīzd\ *adj* : thought out : CONSIDERED — **ad•vis•ed•ly** \-'vī-zəd-lē\ *adv*
ad•vise•ment \əd-'vīz-mənt\ *n* : careful consideration
ad•vi•so•ry \əd-'vīz-(ə-)rē\ *adj* 1 : having the power or right to advise 2 : giving or containing advice
ad•vo•ca•cy \'ad-və-kə-sē\ *n* : the act of advocating : public support
[1]**ad•vo•cate** \'ad-və-kət, -,kāt\ *n* 1 : one that pleads the cause of another esp. before a judicial tribunal 2 : one that argues for, recommends, or supports a cause or policy
[2]**ad•vo•cate** \-,kāt\ *vt* : to speak in favor of : support or recommend openly
adz *or* **adze** \'adz\ *n* : a cutting tool with a thin arched blade at right angles to the handle that is used for shaping wood
ae•gis \'ē-jəs\ *n* 1 : PROTECTION, DEFENSE 2 : SPONSORSHIP
ae•o•li•an harp \ē-,ō-lē-ən-\ *n* : a box-shaped musical instrument having stretched strings on which the wind produces varying harmonics over the same fundamental tone
ae•on \'ē-ən, 'ē-,än\ *n* : an immeasurably or indefinitely long period of time : AGE
aer•ate \'a(-ə)r-,āt\ *vt* 1 : to supply (blood) with oxygen by respiration 2 : to supply or impregnate with air 3 : to combine or charge with gas — **aer•a•tion** \,a(-ə)r-'ā-shən\ *n* — **aer•a•tor** \'a(-ə)r-,āt-ər\ *n*
[1]**ae•ri•al** \'ar-ē-əl, ā-'ir-ē-əl\ *adj* 1 : inhabiting, produced by, or done in the air 2 a : lacking substance : THIN b : IMAGINARY, ETHEREAL 3 : of or relating to aircraft — **ae•ri•al•ly** \-ē-ə-lē\ *adv*
[2]**aer•i•al** \'ar-ē-əl\ *n* : ANTENNA 2
ae•ri•al•ist \'ar-ē-ə-ləst, ā-'ir-\ *n* : a performer of feats above the ground esp. on a flying trapeze
ae•rie \'a(ə)r-ē, 'i(ə)r-\ *n* 1 : the nest of a bird on a cliff or a mountaintop 2 : a dwelling on a height
aero \'a(-ə)r-ō\ *adj* 1 : of or relating to aircraft 2 : designed for aerial use
aer•o•bic \,a(-ə)-'rō-bik\ *adj* : living or active only in the presence of oxygen — **aer•obe** \'a(-ə)r-,ōb\ *n* — **aer•o•bi•cal•ly** \,a(-ə)-'rō-bi-k(ə-)lē\ *adv*
aer•o•bics \,a(-ə)-'rō-biks\ *n* : physical conditioning exercises (as running or swimming) intended to increase oxygen consumption and improve the functioning of the heart and lungs
aer•o•naut \'ar-ə-,nȯt\ *n* : one that operates or travels in an airship or balloon
aer•o•nau•tics \,ar-ə-'nȯt-iks\ *n* : a science dealing with aircraft operation or aircraft design and manufacture — **aer•o•nau•tic** \-'nȯt-ik\ *adj* — **aer•o•nau•ti•cal** \-'nȯt-i-kəl\ *adj*
aero•sol \'ar-ə-,sȯl, -,säl\ *n* : a suspension of fine solid or liquid particles (as of smoke, fog, or an insecticide) in gas
aero•space \'ar-ō-,spās\ *n* : the earth's atmosphere and the space beyond
aes•thete \'es-,thēt\ *n* : one having or affecting sensitivity to the beautiful esp. in art
aes•thet•ic \es-'thet-ik\ *adj* 1 : having to do with beauty or with what is beautiful esp. as distinguished from what is useful 2 : appreciative of or responsive to what is beautiful — **aes•thet•i•cal•ly** \-'thet-i-k(ə-)lē\ *adv*
aes•thet•ics \-iks\ *n* : a branch of philosophy that studies and explains the principles and forms of beauty esp. in art and literature
aes•ti•vate \'es-tə-,vāt\ *vi* : to pass the summer in a state of torpor
aes•ti•va•tion \,es-tə-'vā-shən\ *n* : the state of one that aestivates
afar \ə-'fär\ *adv* : to or at a great distance
af•fa•ble \'af-ə-bəl\ *adj* 1 : being pleasant and at ease in talking to others 2 : characterized by ease and friendliness — **af•fa•bil•i•ty** \,af-ə-'bil-ət-ē\ *n* — **af•fa•bly** \'af-ə-blē\ *adv*
af•fair \ə-'fa(ə)r\ *n* 1 a *pl* : commercial, professional, or public

business **b** : MATTER, CONCERN **2 a** : EVENT, ACTIVITY **b** : PRODUCT, THING **3 a** : a romantic or passionate attachment typically of limited duration **b** : a matter occasioning public anxiety, controversy, or scandal : CASE

¹af·fect \ə-ˈfekt, a-\ *vt* **1** : to be given to : FANCY **2** : to make a display of liking or using : CULTIVATE **3** : to put on a pretense of : FEIGN

²affect *vt* : to have an effect upon : INFLUENCE

af·fec·ta·tion \ˌaf-ˌek-ˈtā-shən\ *n* **1** : an assuming or displaying of an attitude or kind of behavior not natural or not genuine **2** : unnatural speech or conduct

af·fect·ed \ə-ˈfek-təd\ *adj* : not natural or genuine — **af·fect·ed·ly** *adv*

af·fect·ing \-tiŋ\ *adj* : arousing pity, sympathy, or sorrow — **af·fect·ing·ly** *adv*

¹af·fec·tion \ə-ˈfek-shən\ *n* **1** : a feeling of attachment : FONDNESS **2** : PROPENSITY, DISPOSITION

²af·fec·tion *n* : DISEASE, DISORDER

af·fec·tion·ate \ə-ˈfek-sh(ə-)nət\ *adj* : feeling or showing a great liking for a person or thing : TENDER — **af·fec·tion·ate·ly** *adv*

af·fer·ent \ˈaf-ə-rənt, -ˌer-ənt\ *adj* : bearing or conducting inward toward a more central part — **af·fer·ent·ly** *adv*

af·fi·ance \ə-ˈfī-ən(t)s\ *vt* : to solemnly promise (oneself or another) in marriage : BETROTH

af·fi·da·vit \ˌaf-ə-ˈdā-vət\ *n* : a sworn written statement; *esp* : one made under oath before an authorized official

¹af·fil·i·ate \ə-ˈfil-ē-ˌāt\ *vb* : to connect closely often as a member, branch, or associate — **af·fil·i·a·tion** \ə-ˌfil-ē-ˈā-shən\ *n*

²af·fil·i·ate \ə-ˈfil-ē-ət\ *n* : an affiliated person or organization

af·fin·i·ty \ə-ˈfin-ət-ē\ *n, pl* **-ties** **1** : relationship by marriage **2 a** : RELATIONSHIP, KINSHIP **b** : ATTRACTION

af·firm \ə-ˈfərm\ *vb* **1 a** : CONFIRM, RATIFY **b** : to state positively or with confidence : declare to be true **2** : to make a solemn and formal declaration or assertion in place of an oath — **af·fir·ma·tion** \ˌaf-ər-ˈmā-shən\ *n*

¹af·firm·a·tive \ə-ˈfər-mət-iv\ *adj* **1** : asserting a predicate of a subject **2** : asserting that the fact is so **3** : POSITIVE **4** : favoring or supporting a proposition or motion — **af·firm·a·tive·ly** *adv*

²affirmative *n* **1** : an expression (as the word *yes*) of affirmation or assent **2** : an affirmative proposition **3** : the affirmative side in a debate or vote

¹af·fix \ə-ˈfiks\ *vt* **1** : to attach physically : FASTEN **2** : to add as an associated part (as to a document) — **af·fix·a·tion** \ˌaf-ˌik-ˈsā-shən\ *n*

²af·fix \ˈaf-ˌiks\ *n* : one or more sounds or letters attached to the beginning or end of a word and serving to produce a derivative word or an inflectional form

af·flict \ə-ˈflikt\ *vt* **1** : to distress severely so as to cause continued suffering **2** : TROUBLE, INJURE

af·flic·tion \ə-ˈflik-shən\ *n* **1** : the state of being afflicted **2** : the cause of continued pain or distress

af·flu·ence \ˈaf-ˌlü-ən(t)s, a-ˈflü-, ə-\ *n* **1** : an abundant flow or supply **2** : abundance of wealth or property

af·flu·ent \-ənt\ *adj* **1** : flowing in abundance : COPIOUS **2** : having an abundance of material possessions : WEALTHY, RICH — **af·flu·ent·ly** *adv*

af·ford \ə-ˈfōrd\ *vt* **1** : to have resources enough to pay for **2** : to be able to do or to bear without serious harm **3** : PROVIDE, FURNISH

af·fray \ə-ˈfrā\ *n* : a noisy quarrel or fight : BRAWL

af·fright \ə-ˈfrīt\ *vt* : FRIGHTEN, ALARM

¹af·front \ə-ˈfrənt\ *vt* **1** : to insult esp. to the face : OFFEND **2** : to face in defiance : CONFRONT

²affront *n* **1** : a deliberately offensive act or utterance **2** : an offense to one's self-respect : INSULT

af·ghan \ˈaf-gən, -ˌgan\ *n* : a blanket or shawl of colored wool knitted or crocheted in strips or squares

afi·ci·o·na·do \ə-ˌfis-ē-ə-ˈnäd-ō\ *n, pl* **-dos** : DEVOTEE, FAN

afield \ə-ˈfēld\ *adv* **1** : to, in, or on the field **2** : away from home **3** : out of one's regular course : ASTRAY

afire \ə-ˈfī(ə)r\ *adj* : on fire : BURNING

aflame \ə-ˈflām\ *adj* : FLAMING, GLOWING

afloat \ə-ˈflōt\ *adv (or adj)* **1 a** : borne on or as if on the water **b** : at sea **2** : free of difficulties : SELF-SUFFICIENT **3 a** : circulating about : RUMORED **b** : ADRIFT **4** : flooded with or submerged under water : AWASH

aflut·ter \ə-ˈflət-ər\ *adj* **1** : FLUTTERING **2** : nervously excited

afoot \ə-ˈfu̇t\ *adv (or adj)* **1** : on foot **2 a** : on the move : ASTIR **b** : in progress

afore·men·tioned \ə-ˈfō(ə)r-ˌmen-chənd\ *adj* : mentioned previously

afore·said \-ˌsed\ *adj* : said or named previously

afore·thought \-ˌthȯt\ *adj* : thought of, deliberated, or planned beforehand : PREMEDITATED

a for·ti·o·ri \ˌä-ˌfȯrt-ē-ˈōr-ē\ *adv* : with greater reason or more convincing force

afoul of \ə-ˈfau̇l-əv\ *prep* **1** : in or into collision or entanglement with **2** : in or into conflict with

afraid \ə-ˈfrād\ *adj* **1** : filled with fear or apprehension **2** : filled with concern or regret over an unwanted contingency **3** : DISINCLINED, RELUCTANT

afresh \ə-ˈfresh\ *adv* : from a new start : AGAIN

Af·ro \ˈaf-rō\ *n, pl* **Afros** : a style of wearing the hair in which the hair forms a round bushy mass

aft \ˈaft\ *adv* : near, toward, or in the stern of a ship or the tail of an aircraft

¹af·ter \ˈaf-tər\ *adv* : following in time or place : AFTERWARD

²after *prep* **1 a** : behind in place **b** : later in time than **c** : following in rank or order **d** (1) : later than and in consequence of (2) : later than and in spite of **2** — used as a function word to introduce an object or goal **3 a** : in accordance with **b** : with the name of or a name derived from that of **c** : in imitation or resemblance of

³after *conj* : later than the time when

⁴after *adj* **1** : LATER **2** : located toward the rear

af·ter·birth \ˈaf-tər-ˌbərth\ *n* : the placenta and fetal membranes that are expelled after delivery

af·ter·care \-ˌke(ə)r\ *n* : the care, nursing, or treatment of a convalescent patient

af·ter·deck \-ˌdek\ *n* : the rear half of the deck of a ship

af·ter·ef·fect \-ə-ˌfekt\ *n* **1** : an effect that follows its cause after some time has passed **2** : a secondary effect coming on after the first or immediate effect has subsided

af·ter·glow \-ˌglō\ *n* **1** : a glow remaining (as in the sky after sunset) where a light has disappeared **2** : a reflection of past splendor, success, or emotion

af·ter·life \-ˌlīf\ *n* **1** : an existence after death **2** : a later period in one's life

af·ter·math \-ˌmath\ *n* **1** : a second-growth crop esp. of hay **2** : CONSEQUENCE, RESULT

af·ter·noon \ˌaf-tər-ˈnün\ *n* : the part of day between noon and sunset — **afternoon** *adj*

af·ter·taste \ˈaf-tər-ˌtāst\ *n* : a sensation (as of flavor) continuing after the stimulus causing it has ended

af·ter·thought \-ˌthȯt\ *n* : a later thought about something one has done or said

af·ter·ward \ˈaf-tə(r)-wərd\ *or* **af·ter·wards** \-wərdz\ *adv* : at a later time

af·ter·world \ˈaf-tər-ˌwərld\ *n* : a future world : a world after death

again \ə-ˈgen\ *adv* **1** : in return **2** : another time : ANEW **3** : in addition **4** : on the other hand **5** : FURTHER, MOREOVER

against \ə-ˈgen(t)st\ *prep* **1** : directly opposite : FACING **2 a** : in opposition or hostility to **b** : as a defense or protection from **3** : in preparation or provision for **4 a** : in the direction of and into contact with **b** : in contact with **5** : in a direction opposite to the motion or course of **6** : before the background of **7** : as a basis for disapproval of **8** : in exchange for

¹agape \ə-ˈgāp\ *adj* : having the mouth open in wonder or surprise : GAPING

²aga·pe \ä-ˈgäp-ˌā, ˈäg-ə-ˌpā\ *n* : LOVE 3a

ag·ate \ˈag-ət\ *n* **1** : a fine-grained variegated quartz having its colors arranged in stripes, blended in clouds, or showing mosslike forms **2** : a child's playing marble of agate or of glass resembling it

aga·ve \ə-ˈgäv-ē\ *n* : any of a genus of plants of the amaryllis family having spiny-edged leaves and flowers

¹age \ˈāj\ *n* **1 a** : the time from birth to a specified date **b** : the time of life when a person attains some right or capacity; *esp* : MAJORITY **c** : normal lifetime **d** : the later part of life **2** : a period of time in history or in the development of man or in the history of the earth; *esp* : one characterized by some distinguishing feature **3** : a long period of time

²age *vb* **aged**; **ag·ing** *or* **age·ing** **1** : to become old : show the effects or the characteristics of increasing age **2** : to become or cause to become mellow or mature : RIPEN **3** : to cause to seem or appear old esp. prematurely (as by strain or suffering)

aged \ˈā-jəd, *in senses 1b and 2b* ˈājd\ *adj* **1** : grown old: as **a** : of an advanced age **b** : having attained a specified age **2 a** : typical of old age **b** : having acquired a desired quality with age — **aged·ness** *n*

age·less \ˈāj-ləs\ *adj* **1** : not growing old or showing the effects of age **2** : TIMELESS, ETERNAL — **age·less·ly** *adv*

age·long \ˈāj-ˌlȯŋ\ *adj* : lasting for an age : EVERLASTING

agen·cy \ˈā-jən-sē\ *n, pl* **-cies** **1** : the capacity, condition, or state of acting or of exerting power : OPERATION **2** : a person or thing through which power is exerted or an end is achieved **3 a** : the office or function of an agent **b** : the relationship between a principal and his agent **4** : an establishment doing business under a franchise from another **5** : an administrative division (as of a government)

agen·da \ə-ˈjen-də\ *n* : a list of the items of business to be considered (as at a meeting)

agent \ˈā-jənt\ *n* **1** : something that produces an effect : an active or efficient cause **2** : one that acts or exerts power **3** : MEANS, INSTRUMENT **4** : one who acts for or in the place of another and by his authority

age–old \ˈāj-ˈōld\ *adj* : having existed for ages : ANCIENT

ag·glom·er·a·tion \ə-ˌgläm-ə-ˈrā-shən\ *n* **1** : the action or process of collecting in a mass **2** : a heap or cluster of dissimilar elements — **ag·glom·er·a·tive** \ə-ˈgläm-ə-ˌrāt-iv\ *adj*

ag·glu·ti·nate \ə-ˈglüt-ᵊn-ˌāt\ *vb* **1** : to cause to adhere : FASTEN **2** : to cause to clump or undergo agglutination **3** : to unite into a group or gather into a mass **4** : to form words by agglutination

ag·glu·ti·na·tion \ə-ˌglüt-ᵊn-ˈā-shən\ *n* **1** : the action or process of agglutinating **2** : a mass or group formed by the union of separate elements **3** : the formation of derivative or compound words by putting together constituents of which each expresses a single definite meaning — **ag·glu·ti·na·tive** \ə-ˈglüt-ᵊn-ˌāt-iv\ *adj*

ag·gran·dize \ə-ˈgran-ˌdīz, ˈag-rən-\ *vt* : to make great or greater (as in power, rank, size, or resources) — **ag·gran·dize·ment** \ə-ˈgran-dəz-mənt, -ˌdīz-; ˌag-rən-ˈdīz-mənt\ *n* — **ag·gran·diz·er** *n*

ag·gra·vate \ˈag-rə-ˌvāt\ *vt* **1** : to make worse, more serious, or more severe **2** : EXASPERATE, ANNOY

ag·gra·va·tion \ˌag-rə-ˈvā-shən\ *n* **1** : the act of making something worse or more severe : an increase in severity **2** : something that makes a thing worse or more severe **3** : IRRITATION, PROVOCATION

¹ag·gre·gate \ˈag-ri-gət\ *adj* **1** : formed by the collection of units or particles into a body, mass, or amount : COLLECTIVE **2** : clustered in a dense mass or head — **ag·gre·gate·ly** *adv* — **ag·gre·gate·ness** *n*

²ag·gre·gate \-ˌgāt\ *vt* **1** : to collect or gather into a mass or whole **2** : to amount in the aggregate to

³ag·gre·gate \-gət\ *n* **1** : a mass or body of units or parts somewhat loosely associated with one another **2** : the whole sum or amount

ag·gre·ga·tion \ˌag-ri-ˈgā-shən\ *n* **1** : the collecting of units or parts into a mass or whole **2** : a group, body, or mass composed of many distinct parts : ASSEMBLAGE

ag·gres·sion \ə-ˈgresh-ən\ *n* **1** : an offensive action or procedure; *esp* : an unprovoked attack **2** : the practice of making attacks or encroachments; *esp* : unprovoked violation by one country of the territorial integrity of another usu. by actual or threatened military action

ag·gres·sive \ə-ˈgres-iv\ *adj* **1 a** : showing a readiness to attack others **b** : practicing or marked by aggression **2 a** : ENERGETIC, FORCEFUL **b** : obtrusively self-assertive — **ag·gres·sive·ly** *adv* — **ag·gres·sive·ness** *n*

ag·gres·sor \ə-ˈgres-ər\ *n* : one that makes an unprovoked attack; *esp* : a country that commits aggression

ag·grieved \ə-ˈgrēvd\ *adj* **1** : troubled or distressed in spirit **2** : having a grievance; *esp* : suffering from injury or loss

aghast \ə-ˈgast\ *adj* : struck with terror, amazement, or horror : SHOCKED

ag·ile \ˈaj-əl\ *adj* **1** : able to move quickly and easily : readily active : NIMBLE **2** : mentally quick — **ag·ile·ly** \-ə(l)-lē\ *adv*

agil·i·ty \ə-ˈjil-ət-ē\ *n* : the quality or state of being agile

aging *pres part of* AGE

ag·i·tate \ˈaj-ə-ˌtāt\ *vb* **1** : to shake jerkily : set in violent irregular motion **2** : to stir up : EXCITE, DISTURB **3** : to attempt to arouse or influence public interest in something esp. by discussion or appeals — **ag·i·tat·ed·ly** \-ˌtāt-əd-lē\ *adv* — **ag·i·ta·tion** \ˌaj-ə-ˈtā-shən\ *n*

ag·i·ta·tor \ˈaj-ə-ˌtāt-ər\ *n* : one that agitates: as **a** : one who stirs up public feeling on a controversial issue **b** : a device for stirring or shaking

agleam \ə-ˈglēm\ *adj* : GLEAMING

aglit·ter \ə-ˈglit-ər\ *adj* : GLITTERING

aglow \ə-ˈglō\ *adj* : GLOWING

ag·nos·tic \ag-ˈnäs-tik\ *n* : a person who does not deny the possible existence of God but holds that this existence and the origin of the universe are not known and probably cannot be known — **agnostic** *adj* — **ag·nos·ti·cism** \-ˈnäs-tə-ˌsiz-əm\ *n*

ago \ə-ˈgō\ *adj (or adv)* : earlier than the present time

agog \ə-ˈgäg\ *adj* : full of intense interest or excitement : EAGER

ag·o·nize \ˈag-ə-ˌnīz\ *vb* **1** : to suffer or cause to suffer extreme pain or anguish of body or mind **2** : to strive desperately : STRUGGLE — **ag·o·niz·ing·ly** \-ˌnī-ziŋ-lē\ *adv*

ag·o·ny \ˈag-ə-nē\ *n, pl* **-nies** **1 a** : intense pain of mind or body : ANGUISH, TORTURE **b** : the throes of death **2** : a strong sudden display (as of joy or delight) : OUTBURST

ag·o·ra \ˈag-ə-rə\ *n, pl* **-ras** *or* **-rae** \-ˌrē, -ˌrī\ : the marketplace or place of assembly in an ancient Greek city

ag·o·ra·pho·bia \ˌag-ə-rə-ˈfō-bē-ə\ *n* : abnormal fear of crossing or of being in open spaces

¹agrar·i·an \ə-ˈgrer-ē-ən\ *adj* **1** : of or relating to the land or its ownership **2** : of, relating to, or concerned with farmers or peasants or farming interests **3** : AGRICULTURAL 2

²agrarian *n* : a member of an agrarian party or movement

agrar·i·an·ism \-ē-ə-ˌniz-əm\ *n* : a social or political movement designed chiefly to improve the economic status of the farmer or peasant

agree \ə-ˈgrē\ *vb* **agreed**; **agree·ing** **1** : to give one's approval : CONSENT 2 : ADMIT, CONCEDE 3 : to be alike : CORRESPOND 4 : to get on well together 5 : to come to a harmonious understanding 6 : to be fitting, pleasing, or healthful : SUIT 7 : to be alike or correspond grammatically in gender, number, case, or person

agree·a·ble \ə-'grē-ə-bəl\ *adj* 1 : pleasing to the mind or senses : PLEASANT 2 : ready or willing to agree 3 : being in harmony : CONSONANT — **agree·a·ble·ness** *n* — **agree·a·bly** \-blē\ *adv*

agreed \ə-'grēd\ *adj* : settled by agreement

agree·ment \ə-'grē-mənt\ *n* 1 a : the act of agreeing b : harmony of opinion, action, or character : CONCORD 2 a : a mutual arrangement or understanding (as a contract or treaty) between two or more parties about some course of action b : a written record of such an agreement 3 : the fact of agreeing grammatically

ag·ri·cul·tur·al \,ag-ri-'kəlch-(ə-)rəl\ *adj* 1 : of, relating to, or used in agriculture 2 : engaged in or concerned with agriculture — **ag·ri·cul·tur·al·ly** \-ē\ *adv*

ag·ri·cul·ture \'ag-ri-,kəl-chər\ *n* : the science, art, or occupation of cultivating the soil, producing crops, and raising livestock : FARMING — **ag·ri·cul·tur·ist** \,ag-ri-'kəlch-(ə-)rəst\ *or* **ag·ri·cul·tur·al·ist** \-(ə-)rə-ləst\ *n*

aground \ə-'grau̇nd\ *adv* (*or adj*) 1 : with the bottom lodged on the ground or on the shore : STRANDED 2 : on the ground

ague \'ā-gyü\ *n* 1 : a fever (as malaria) marked by outbreaks of chills, fever, and sweating that recur at regular intervals 2 : a fit of shivering : CHILL

ah \'ä\ *interj* — used to express delight, relief, regret, or contempt

aha \ä-'hä\ *interj* — used to express surprise, triumph, or derision

ahead \ə-'hed\ *adv* 1 a : in a forward direction or position : FORWARD b : in front 2 : in, into, or for the future 3 : in or toward a more advantageous position 4 : in advance — **ahead** *adj*

ahead of *prep* 1 : in front or advance of 2 : in excess of : ABOVE

ahoy \ə-'hȯi\ *interj* — used in hailing

[1]**aid** \'ād\ *vb* 1 : to provide with what is useful or necessary in achieving an end : ASSIST 2 : to give assistance — **aid·er** *n*

[2]**aid** *n* 1 : the act of helping or the help given : ASSISTANCE 2 a : an assisting person or group b : an auxiliary device

aide \'ād\ *n* 1 : a military or naval officer acting as assistant to a superior 2 : a person who acts as an assistant or helper

aide–de–camp \,ād-di-'kamp, -'kän\ *n, pl* **aides–de–camp** \,ādz-di-\ : AIDE 1

ai·grette \ā-'gret, 'ā-,\ *n* : a plume or decorative tuft for the head

ail \'āl\ *vb* 1 : to be the matter with : TROUBLE 2 : to have something the matter; *esp* : to suffer ill health

ai·le·ron \'ā-lə-,rän\ *n* : a movable portion of an airplane wing; *also* : a movable airfoil external to the wing

ail·ment \'āl-mənt\ *n* : a bodily disorder : SICKNESS

[1]**aim** \'ām\ *vb* 1 a : to direct a course b : to point a weapon 2 : ASPIRE, INTEND 3 a : POINT b : to direct to or toward a specified object or goal

[2]**aim** *n* 1 : the directing of a weapon or a missile at a mark 2 : GOAL, PURPOSE

aim·less \'ām-ləs\ *adj* : lacking aim or purpose — **aim·less·ly** *adv* — **aim·less·ness** *n*

ain't \(')ānt\ 1 a : are not b : is not c : am not — though disapproved by many and more common in less educated speech, used orally in most parts of the U.S. by many educated speakers esp. in the phrase *ain't I* 2 *substand* a : have not b : has not

[1]**air** \'a(ə)r\ *n* 1 : the invisible mixture of odorless tasteless gases (as nitrogen and oxygen) that surrounds the earth 2 : a light breeze 3 : compressed air 4 : AIRCRAFT 5 : AVIATION 6 : the medium of transmission of radio waves; *also* : RADIO, TELEVISION 7 a : outward appearance : apparent nature b *pl* : an artificial or affected manner : HAUGHTINESS c : a surrounding or pervading influence : ATMOSPHERE 8 : TUNE, MELODY

[2]**air** *vt* 1 : to place in the air for cooling, refreshing, or cleansing 2 : to make known in public

air bag *n* : an automobile safety device consisting of a bag that automatically inflates in front of riders in the event of an accident

air·borne \-,bōrn\ *adj* : supported or transported by air

air·brush \-,brəsh\ *n* : an atomizer for applying by compressed air a fine spray (as of paint or a protective coating) — **airbrush** *vt*

air–con·di·tion \,a(ə)r-kən-'dish-ən\ *vt* : to equip with an apparatus for washing air and controlling its humidity and temperature; *also* : to subject (air) to these processes — **air–con·di·tion·er** *n*

air·craft \'a(ə)r-,kraft\ *n, pl* **aircraft** : a weight-carrying machine for navigation of the air that is supported either by its own buoyancy or by the action of the air against its surfaces

air·drome \-,drōm\ *n* : AIRPORT

air·drop \-,dräp\ *n* : delivery of cargo or personnel by parachute from an airplane in flight — **air–drop** \-,dräp\ *vt*

air·field \-,fēld\ *n* 1 : the landing field of an airport 2 : AIRPORT

air·foil \-,fȯil\ *n* : an airplane surface (as a wing or rudder) designed to produce reaction from the air through which it moves

air force *n* : the military organization of a nation for air warfare

air·lift \'a(ə)r-,lift\ *n* : a supply line operated by aircraft — **airlift** *vt*

air·line \-,līn\ *n* 1 : an established system of transportation by airplanes, its equipment, or the organization owning or operating it 2 : a regular route followed in transportation by air

air·lin·er \-,lī-nər\ *n* : a large passenger airplane operating over an airline

air·mail \-'māl\ *n* : the system of transporting mail by airplanes; *also* : the mail transported — **airmail** *vt*

air·man \-mən\ *n* 1 : an enlisted man in the air force; *esp* : one of any of four ranks below a staff sergeant 2 : a civilian or military pilot or aviator

air–mind·ed \-'mīn-dəd\ *adj* : interested in aviation or in air travel — **air–mind·ed·ness** *n*

air·plane \-,plān\ *n* : a fixed-wing aircraft heavier than air that is driven by a propeller or by a rearward jet and supported by the reaction of the air against its wings

air·port \'a(ə)r-,pōrt\ *n* : a tract of land or water that is maintained for the landing and takeoff of airplanes and for receiving and discharging passengers and cargo and that usu. has facilities for the shelter, supply, and repair of planes

air·post \-'pōst\ *n* : AIRMAIL

air·ship \-,ship\ *n* : an aircraft lighter than air that is borne in the air by a gas-filled container and has an engine, propeller, and rudder

air·sick \-,sik\ *adj* : affected with motion sickness associated with flying — **air·sick·ness** *n*

air·space \-,spās\ *n* : the space lying above a nation and coming under its jurisdiction

air·speed \-,spēd\ *n* : the speed of an airplane with relation to the air as distinguished from its speed relative to the earth

air·strip \-,strip\ *n* : a runway without normal air base or airport facilities

air·tight \-'tīt\ *adj* 1 : so tightly sealed that no air can get in or out 2 : leaving no opening for attack

air·wave \-,wāv\ *n* : the medium of radio and television transmission — usu. used in pl.

air·way \-ˌwā\ *n* **1 :** a regular route for airplanes from airport to airport; *esp* **:** such a route equipped with navigational aids **2 :** AIRLINE 1
air·wor·thy \-ˌwər-t͟hē\ *adj* **:** fit or safe for operation in the air — **air·wor·thi·ness** *n*
airy \ˈa(ə)r-ē\ *adj* **1 :** of, relating to, or living in the air **:** AERIAL **2 :** open to the air **:** BREEZY **3 :** resembling air in lightness **:** DELICATE, GRACEFUL, ETHEREAL **4 :** lacking a sound or solid basis — **air·i·ly** \ˈar-ə-lē\ *adv* — **air·i·ness** \ˈar-ē-nəs\ *n*
aisle \ˈīl\ *n* **1 :** the side of a church separated by piers from the nave **2 :** a passage between sections of seats
¹ajar \ə-ˈjär\ *adv (or adj)* **:** slightly open
²ajar *adj* **:** DISCORDANT
akim·bo \ə-ˈkim-bō\ *adv (or adj)* **:** with the hand on the hip and the elbow turned outward
akin \ə-ˈkin\ *adj* **1 :** related by blood **:** descended from a common ancestor or prototype **2 :** essentially similar or related **:** ALIKE
a la *or* **à la** \ˌal-ə, ˌäl-ə\ **:** in the manner of
al·a·bas·ter \ˈal-ə-ˌbas-tər\ *n* **:** a compact fine-textured usu. white and translucent gypsum that is carved into objects (as vases)
a la carte \ˌal-ə-ˈkärt, ˌäl-\ *adv (or adj)* **:** with a separate price for each item on the menu
alac·ri·ty \ə-ˈlak-rət-ē\ *n* **:** a cheerful readiness to do something **:** BRISKNESS, LIVELINESS — **alac·ri·tous** \-rət-əs\ *adj*
a la mode \ˌal-ə-ˈmōd, ˌäl-\ *adj* **1 :** FASHIONABLE, STYLISH **2 :** topped with ice cream
¹alarm \ə-ˈlärm\ *n* **1 a :** a sound or signal giving notice of danger or calling attention to some event or condition **b :** a device that warns or signals (as by a bell) **2 :** the fear caused by a sudden sense of danger
²alarm *vt* **1 :** to notify of danger **2 :** to arouse to a sense of danger **:** FRIGHTEN, DISTURB — **alarm·ing·ly** \-ˈlär-miŋ-lē\ *adv*
alarm·ist \ə-ˈlär-məst\ *n* **:** a person who is given to alarming others esp. needlessly — **alarm·ism** \-ˌmiz-əm\ *n*
alas \ə-ˈlas\ *interj* — used to express unhappiness, pity, or concern
alb \ˈalb\ *n* **:** a basic full-length white linen vestment with close sleeves worn at the Eucharist
al·ba·core \ˈal-bə-ˌkō(ə)r\ *n, pl* **-core** *or* **-cores :** any of several tunas
al·ba·tross \ˈal-bə-ˌtrȯs, -ˌträs\ *n, pl* **-tross** *or* **-tross·es :** any of various large web-footed seabirds that are related to the petrels and include the largest birds of the sea
al·be·it \ȯl-ˈbē-ət, al-\ *conj* **:** even though **:** ALTHOUGH
al·bi·no \al-ˈbī-nō\ *n, pl* **-nos :** a human being or lower animal that is congenitally deficient in pigment and usu. has a milky or translucent skin, white or colorless hair, and eyes with pink or blue iris and deep red pupil — **al·bin·ic** \al-ˈbin-ik\ *adj* — **al·bi·nism** \ˈal-bə-ˌniz-əm, al-ˈbī-\ *n* — **al·bi·nis·tic** \ˌal-bə-ˈnis-tik\ *adj* — **albino** *adj* — **al·bi·not·ic** \ˌal-bə-ˈnät-ik, -ˌbī-\ *adj*
al·bum \ˈal-bəm\ *n* **1 a :** a book with blank pages for autographs, stamps, or photographs **b :** a container with envelopes for phonograph records **c :** one or more phonograph records or tape recordings carrying a major musical work or a group of related selections **2 :** a collection usu. in book form of literary selections, musical compositions, or pictures **:** ANTHOLOGY
al·bu·men \al-ˈbyü-mən\ *n* **1 :** the white of an egg **2 :** ALBUMIN
al·bu·min \al-ˈbyü-mən\ *n* **:** any of numerous water-soluble proteins found esp. in blood, the whites of eggs, and various animal and plant tissues
al·bu·min·ous \al-ˈbyü-mə-nəs\ *adj* **:** relating to, containing, or having the properties of albumen or albumin
al·che·mist \ˈal-kə-məst\ *n* **:** one who studies or practices alchemy
al·che·my \ˈal-kə-mē\ *n* **1 :** a medieval chemical science and philosophy aiming to achieve the conversion of the base metals into gold, the discovery of a universal cure for disease, and the discovery of a means of indefinitely prolonging life **2 :** a power or process of transforming something common into something precious — **al·chem·i·cal** \al-ˈkem-i-kəl\ *adj* — **al·chem·i·cal·ly** \-k(ə-)lē\ *adv*
al·co·hol \ˈal-kə-ˌhȯl\ *n* **1 a :** a colorless volatile flammable liquid that is the intoxicating agent in fermented and distilled liquors (as beer, wine, whiskey) **b :** any of various carbon compounds that are similar to alcohol **2 :** a liquor (as beer, wine, or whiskey) containing alcohol; *also* **:** LIQUORS
¹al·co·hol·ic \ˌal-kə-ˈhȯl-ik, -ˈhäl-\ *adj* **1 :** of, relating to, caused by, or containing alcohol **2 :** affected with alcoholism — **al·co·hol·i·cal·ly** \-i-k(ə-)lē\ *adv*
²alcoholic *n* **:** one affected with alcoholism
al·co·hol·ism \ˈal-kə-ˌhȯl-ˌiz-əm\ *n* **:** continued excessive and usu. uncontrollable use of alcoholic drinks; *also* **:** the abnormal state associated with such use
al·cove \ˈal-ˌkōv\ *n* **1 a :** a nook or small recess opening off a larger room **b :** a niche or arched opening (as in a wall) **2 :** SUMMERHOUSE
al·der \ˈȯl-dər\ *n* **:** any of a genus of toothed-leaved trees or shrubs related to the birches and found esp. in moist ground
al·der·man \ˈȯl-dər-mən\ *n* **1 :** a specially chosen member of a British county or borough council **2 :** a member of a municipal legislative body in a U.S. city — **al·der·man·ic** \ˌȯl-dər-ˈman-ik\ *adj*
ale \ˈāl\ *n* **:** an alcoholic drink made from malt and flavored with hops; *esp* **:** one that is brewed by rapid fermentation and is heavier bodied and more bitter than beer
alee \ə-ˈlē\ *adv (or adj)* **:** on or toward the lee
ale·house \ˈāl-ˌhau̇s\ *n* **:** a place where ale is sold to be drunk on the premises
alem·bic \ə-ˈlem-bik\ *n* **:** an apparatus formerly used in distillation
¹alert \ə-ˈlərt\ *adj* **1 a :** being watchful and prompt to meet danger **b :** quick to perceive and act **2 :** ACTIVE, BRISK — **alert·ly** *adv* — **alert·ness** *n*
²alert *n* **1 :** a signal (as an alarm) of danger **2 :** the period during which an alert is in effect — **on the alert :** on the lookout for danger
³alert *vt* **:** to call to a state of readiness **:** WARN
ale·wife \ˈāl-ˌwīf\ *n* **:** a woman who keeps an alehouse
al·ex·an·drine \ˌal-ig-ˈzan-drən\ *n, often cap* **:** a line consisting of six iambic feet
al·fal·fa \al-ˈfal-fə\ *n* **:** a deep-rooted European leguminous plant with purple flowers and leaves like clover that is widely grown for hay and forage
al·fres·co \al-ˈfres-kō\ *adv (or adj)* **:** in the open air
al·ga \ˈal-gə\ *n, pl* **al·gae** \ˈal-(ˌ)jē\ **:** any plant of a group that forms the lowest division of the plant kingdom and includes seaweeds and related forms mostly growing in water, lacking a vascular system, and having chlorophyll often masked by brown or red coloring matter — **al·gal** \ˈal-gəl\ *adj*
al·ge·bra \ˈal-jə-brə\ *n* **:** a branch of mathematics in which symbols (as letters and numbers) representing various entities are combined according to special rules of operation
al·ge·bra·ic \ˌal-jə-ˈbrā-ik\ *adj* **:** of or relating to algebra — **al·ge·bra·i·cal·ly** \-ˈbrā-ə-k(ə-)lē\ *adv*
¹ali·as \ˈā-lē-əs\ *adv* **:** otherwise called **:** otherwise known as
²alias *n* **:** an assumed name
¹al·i·bi \ˈal-ə-ˌbī\ *n, pl* **-bis** \-ˌbīz\ **1 :** the plea made by a person accused of a crime that he was at another place when the crime occurred **2 :** a plausible excuse
²alibi *vb* **-bied**; **-bi·ing 1 :** to offer an excuse **2 :** to make an excuse for

[1]**alien** \ˈā-lē-ən, ˈāl-yən\ *adj* **1 a :** relating or belonging to another country **b :** owing allegiance to a foreign country **2 :** wholly different in nature or character

[2]**alien** *n* **1 :** a person of another family, race, or nation **2 :** a foreign-born resident who has not been naturalized and is still a subject or citizen of a foreign country

alien·a·ble \ˈā-lē-ə-nə-bəl, ˈāl-yə-nə-\ *adj* **:** transferable to the ownership of another — **alien·a·bil·i·ty** \ˌā-lē-ə-nə-ˈbil-ət-ē, ˌāl-yə-nə-\ *n*

alien·ate \ˈā-lē-ə-ˌnāt, ˈāl-yə-ˌnāt\ *vt* **1 :** to convey or transfer (as a title, property, or right) to another **2 :** to cause to lose former feelings of love, loyalty, attachment, or a sense of filling a useful and respected position in a society **:** ESTRANGE **3 :** to cause to be withdrawn or diverted — **alien·a·tion** \ˌā-lē-ə-ˈnā-shən, ˌāl-yə-ˈnā-\ *n* — **alien·a·tor** \ˈā-lē-ə-ˌnāt-ər, ˈāl-yə-ˌnāt-\ *n*

alien·ist \ˈā-lē-ə-nəst, ˈāl-yə-nəst\ *n* **:** PSYCHIATRIST; *esp* **:** one who testifies in a legal proceeding

[1]**alight** \ə-ˈlīt\ *vi* **alight·ed** \-ˈlīt-əd\; **alight·ing** **1 :** to get down **:** DISMOUNT **2 :** to descend from the air and settle **:** LAND

[2]**alight** *adj* **:** LIGHTED, AFLAME

align \ə-ˈlīn\ *vb* **1 :** to bring into line or alignment **2 :** to array on the side of or against a party or cause **3 :** to be in or come into alignment — **align·er** *n*

align·ment \ə-ˈlīn-mənt\ *n* **1 a :** the act of aligning **:** the state of being aligned **b :** the proper positioning of parts in relation to each other **2 :** an arrangement of groups or forces in relation to one another

[1]**alike** \ə-ˈlīk\ *adj* **:** LIKE — **alike·ness** *n*

[2]**alike** *adv* **:** in the same manner, form, or degree **:** EQUALLY

al·i·men·ta·ry \ˌal-ə-ˈment-ə-rē, -ˈmen-trē\ *adj* **:** of or relating to nourishment or nutrition

alimentary canal *n* **:** the tube that extends from mouth to anus and functions in direction and absorption of food and in elimination of residual waste

al·i·mo·ny \ˈal-ə-ˌmō-nē\ *n* **:** an allowance of money made by a man to a woman for her support during or after her divorce or legal separation from him

alive \ə-ˈlīv\ *adj* **1 a :** having life **:** not dead or inanimate **b :** LIVING **2 :** still in existence, force, or operation **:** ACTIVE **3 :** knowingly aware or conscious **:** SENSITIVE **4 :** marked by much life, animation, or activity **:** SWARMING — **alive·ness** *n*

al·ka·li \ˈal-kə-ˌlī\ *n, pl* **-lies** *or* **-lis** **1 :** a substance (as hydroxide of sodium) that has marked basic properties (as an acrid taste and the power to neutralize acids, form salts, and turn red litmus blue) **2 :** a soluble salt or a mixture of soluble salts present in some soils of arid regions

al·ka·line \ˈal-kə-ˌlīn, -lən\ *adj* **:** of, relating to, or having the properties of an alkali — **al·ka·lin·i·ty** \ˌal-kə-ˈlin-ət-ē\ *n*

al·ka·lin·ize \ˈal-kə-lə-ˌnīz\ *vt* **:** to make alkaline — **al·ka·lin·i·za·tion** \ˌal-kə-ˌlin-ə-ˈzā-shən\ *n*

al·ka·loid \ˈal-kə-ˌlȯid\ *n* **:** any of numerous usu. colorless, complex, and bitter organic basic compounds containing nitrogen and usu. oxygen that occur esp. in seed plants — **al·ka·loi·dal** \ˌal-kə-ˈlȯid-ᵊl\ *adj*

[1]**all** \ˈȯl\ *adj* **1 a :** the whole of **b :** as much as possible **2 :** every member or individual component of **3 :** the whole number or sum of **4 :** EVERY **5 :** any whatever **6 :** nothing but **:** ONLY **7 :** being more than one person or thing

[2]**all** *adv* **1 :** WHOLLY, ALTOGETHER — often used as an intensive **2 :** so much **3 :** for each side **:** APIECE

[3]**all** *pron* **1 :** the whole number, quantity, or amount **2 :** EVERYBODY, EVERYTHING

Al·lah \ˈal-ə\ *n* **:** the Supreme Being of the Muslims

all–Amer·i·can \ˌȯl-ə-ˈmer-ə-kən\ *adj* **1 :** composed wholly of American elements **2 :** representative of the U.S. as a whole; *esp* **:** selected as the best in the U.S.

all–around \ˌȯl-ə-ˈrau̇nd\ *adj* **1 :** competent in many fields **2 :** having general utility

al·lay \ə-ˈlā\ *vt* **1 :** to make less severe **:** RELIEVE **2 :** to make quiet **:** CALM

all clear *n* **:** a signal that a danger has passed

al·le·ga·tion \ˌal-i-ˈgā-shən\ *n* **1 :** the act of alleging **2 :** something alleged: **a :** a positive assertion **b :** a statement by a party to a legal action of what he undertakes to prove **c :** an assertion unsupported by proof or evidence

al·lege \ə-ˈlej\ *vt* **1 :** to state positively but without proof or before attempting to prove **:** DECLARE **2 :** to offer as a reason or an excuse — **al·leg·ed·ly** \ə-ˈlej-əd-lē\ *adv*

al·le·giance \ə-ˈlē-jən(t)s\ *n* **1 :** the obligation of fidelity and obedience owed by a subject or citizen to his sovereign or government **2 :** devotion or loyalty to a person, group, or cause

al·le·gor·i·cal \ˌal-ə-ˈgȯr-i-kəl\ *adj* **:** consisting of or containing allegory **:** having the characteristics of allegory — **al·le·gor·i·cal·ly** \-i-k(ə-)lē\ *adv*

al·le·go·rize \ˈal-ə-ˌgōr-ˌīz, -gə-ˌrīz\ *vt* **1 :** to make into allegory **2 :** to treat or explain as allegory

al·le·go·ry \ˈal-ə-ˌgōr-ē\ *n, pl* **-ries** **:** a story in which the characters and events are symbols expressing truths about human life

[1]**al·le·gro** \ə-ˈleg-rō, -ˈlā-grō\ *adv* (*or adj*) **:** in a brisk lively manner — used as a direction in music

[2]**allegro** *n, pl* **-gros** **:** a piece or movement in allegro tempo

al·le·lu·ia \ˌal-ə-ˈlü-yə\ *interj* **:** HALLELUJAH

al·ler·gen \ˈal-ər-jən\ *n* **:** a substance that induces allergy — **al·ler·gen·ic** \ˌal-ər-ˈjen-ik\ *adj*

al·ler·gic \ə-ˈlər-jik\ *adj* **1 :** of, relating to, or inducing allergy **2 :** disagreeably sensitive

al·ler·gist \ˈal-ər-jəst\ *n* **:** a specialist in allergy

al·ler·gy \ˈal-ər-jē\ *n, pl* **-gies** **1 a :** altered bodily reactivity **b :** exaggerated or abnormal reaction (as by sneezing, itching, or rashes) to substances, situations, or physical states that are harmless to most people **2 :** a feeling of dislike

al·le·vi·ate \ə-ˈlē-vē-ˌāt\ *vt* **1 :** to make easier to be endured **:** RELIEVE **2 :** to remove or correct in part **:** lessen the presence of — **al·le·vi·a·tion** \ə-ˌlē-vē-ˈā-shən\ *n*

al·ley \ˈal-ē\ *n, pl* **al·leys** **1 :** a garden or park walk bordered by trees or bushes **2 :** a place for bowling; *esp* **:** a hardwood lane **3 :** a narrow street or passageway between buildings; *esp* **:** one giving access to the rear of buildings

al·ley·way \-ˌwā\ *n* **1 :** a narrow passageway **2 :** ALLEY 3

All·hal·lows \ȯl-ˈhal-ōz\ *n* **:** ALL SAINTS' DAY

al·li·ance \ə-ˈlī-ən(t)s\ *n* **1 a :** the state of being allied **:** the action of allying **b :** a union or connection between families, parties, or individuals **2 a :** an association to further the common interests of the members; *esp* **:** one formed by two or more nations usu. by treaty and often for their mutual assistance and protection **b :** a treaty of alliance **3 :** union by relationship in qualities **:** AFFINITY

al·lied \ə-ˈlīd, ˈal-ˌīd\ *adj* **1 :** JOINED, CONNECTED **2 :** joined in alliance esp. by treaty **3 :** related esp. by common properties, characteristics, or ancestry

al·li·ga·tor \ˈal-ə-ˌgāt-ər\ *n* **:** either of two large short-legged reptiles resembling crocodiles but having a shorter and broader snout

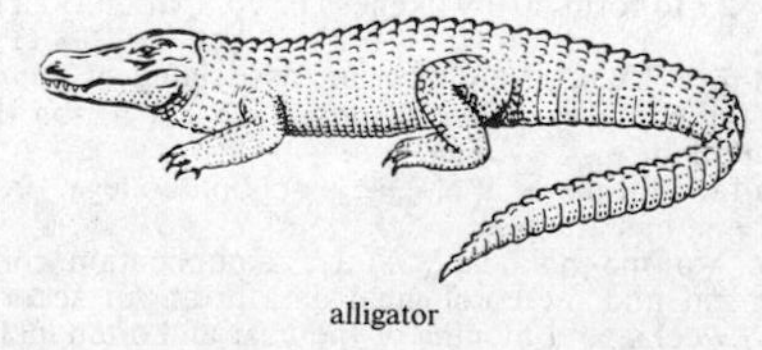

alligator

al·lit·er·a·tion \ə-ˌlit-ə-ˈrā-shən\ *n* : the repetition of a sound at the beginning of two or more neighboring words — **al·lit·er·a·tive** \ə-ˈlit-ə-ˌrāt-iv\ *adj* — **al·lit·er·a·tive·ly** *adv*

al·lo·cate \ˈal-ə-ˌkāt\ *vt* **1** : to apportion for a specific purpose or among particular persons or things : DISTRIBUTE **2** : to set apart and designate : ASSIGN — **al·lo·ca·tion** \ˌal-ə-ˈkā-shən\ *n*

al·lo·phone \ˈal-ə-ˌfōn\ *n* : one of two or more variants of the same phoneme — **al·lo·phon·ic** \ˌal-ə-ˈfän-ik\ *adj*

al·lot \ə-ˈlät\ *vt* **al·lot·ted**; **al·lot·ting** **1** : to assign as a share or portion : ALLOCATE **2** : to distribute by or as if by lot

al·lot·ment \ə-ˈlät-mənt\ *n* **1** : the act of allotting **2** : something that is allotted

all–out \ˈȯl-ˈau̇t\ *adj* : made with maximum effort : EXTREME

all over *adv* : EVERYWHERE

all·over \ˈȯl-ˌō-vər\ *adj* : covering the whole extent or surface

al·low \ə-ˈlau̇\ *vb* **1 a** : to assign as a share or suitable amount (as of time or money) **b** : to allot as a deduction or an addition **2** : ADMIT, CONCEDE **3 a** : PERMIT **b** : to neglect to restrain or prevent **4** : to make allowance

al·low·a·ble \-ə-bəl\ *adj* : not forbidden : not unlawful or improper : PERMISSIBLE — **al·low·a·bly** \-blē\ *adv*

al·low·ance \ə-ˈlau̇-ən(t)s\ *n* **1 a** : a share or portion allotted or granted **b** : a sum granted as a reimbursement or bounty or for expenses **2** : the act of allowing : PERMISSION **3** : the taking into account of things that may partly excuse an offense or mistake

¹al·loy \ˈal-ˌȯi, ə-ˈlȯi\ *n* : a substance composed of two or more metals or of a metal and a nonmetal united usu. by being melted together

²al·loy \ə-ˈlȯi, ˈal-ˌȯi\ *vt* **1** : to reduce the purity of by mixing with a less valuable metal **2** : to mix so as to form an alloy **3** : to debase by admixture

¹all right *adv* **1** : SATISFACTORILY **2** : very well : YES **3** : beyond doubt : CERTAINLY

²all right *adj* **1** : SATISFACTORY, CORRECT **2** : SAFE, WELL

All Saints' Day *n* : November 1 observed as a church festival in honor of the saints

All Souls' Day *n* : November 2 observed in some churches as a day of prayer for the souls in purgatory

all·spice \ˈȯl-ˌspīs\ *n* : the berry of a West Indian tree of the myrtle family or a mildly pungent and aromatic spice prepared from it

all told *adv* : with everything counted : in all

al·lude \ə-ˈlüd\ *vi* : to make indirect reference

¹al·lure \ə-ˈlu̇(ə)r\ *vt* : to entice by charm or attraction

²allure *n* : ATTRACTION, CHARM

al·lure·ment \-mənt\ *n* **1** : the action of alluring : FASCINATION **2** : something that allures : ATTRACTION

al·lu·sion \ə-ˈlü-zhən\ *n* **1** : the act of alluding or hinting **2** : an implied or indirect reference — **al·lu·sive** \ə-ˈlü-siv\ *adj* — **al·lu·sive·ly** *adv* — **al·lu·sive·ness** *n*

al·lu·vi·al \ə-ˈlü-vē-əl\ *adj* : relating to, composed of, or found in alluvium

al·lu·vi·um \-vē-əm\ *n, pl* **-vi·ums** *or* **-via** \-vē-ə\ : soil material (as clay, silt, sand, or gravel) deposited by running water

¹al·ly \ə-ˈlī, ˈal-ˌī\ *vb* **al·lied**; **al·ly·ing** **1** : to form (as by marriage or treaty) a connection between : join in an alliance : UNITE **2** : to form (as by likeness or compatibility) a relation between

²al·ly \ˈal-ˌī, ə-ˈlī\ *n, pl* **al·lies** : one associated or united with another for some common purpose; *esp* : a nation that has joined an alliance

al·ma ma·ter \ˌal-mə-ˈmät-ər\ *n* : a school, college, or university that one has attended

al·ma·nac \ˈȯl-mə-ˌnak, ˈal-\ *n* **1** : a publication containing astronomical and meteorological data arranged according to the days, weeks, and months of the year and often including a miscellany of other information **2** : a publication containing statistical, tabular, and general information

al·mighty \ȯl-ˈmīt-ē\ *adj* **1** *often cap* : having absolute power over all **2** : relatively unlimited in power

Almighty *n* : ²GOD — used with *the*

al·mond \ˈäm-ənd, ˈam-; ˈal-mənd\ *n* : a small tree of the rose family having flowers like those of a peach tree; *also* : the edible kernel of its fruit used as a nut

al·mo·ner \ˈal-mə-nər, ˈäm-ə-\ *n* : a person who distributes alms for someone else

al·most \ˈȯl-ˌmōst, ȯl-ˈ\ *adv* : only a little less than : NEARLY

alms \ˈämz\ *n, pl* **alms** : something and esp. money given freely to help the poor : CHARITY — **alms·giv·er** \-ˌgiv-ər\ *n* — **alms·giv·ing** \-ˌgiv-iŋ\ *n*

alms·house \-ˌhau̇s\ *n* : POORHOUSE

al·oe \ˈal-ō\ *n* **1** : any of a large genus of succulent chiefly southern African plants of the lily family with spikes of often showy flowers **2** *pl* : the dried bitter juice of the leaves of an aloe used as a purgative and tonic

aloft \ə-ˈlȯft\ *adv (or adj)* **1** : at or to a great height **2** : in the air; *esp* : in flight **3** : at, on, or to the masthead or the higher rigging

alo·ha \ə-ˈlō-ə, ä-ˈlō-ˌhä\ *interj* — used to express greeting or farewell

¹alone \ə-ˈlōn\ *adj* **1** : separated from others : ISOLATED **2** : exclusive of anyone or anything else

²alone *adv* **1** : SOLELY, EXCLUSIVELY **2** : without company, aid, or support

¹along \ə-ˈlȯŋ\ *prep* **1** : lengthwise of : parallel with the length or direction of **2** : in accordance with : IN

²along *adv* **1** : FORWARD, ON **2** : as a companion or associate **3** : at or on hand

along·shore \-ˈshō(ə)r\ *adv (or adj)* : along the shore or coast

¹along·side \-ˈsīd\ *adv* : along or close at the side : in parallel position

²alongside *prep* : side by side with; *esp* : parallel to

¹aloof \ə-ˈlüf\ *adv* : at a distance : out of involvement

²aloof *adj* : removed or distant in interest or feeling : RESERVED — **aloof·ly** *adv* — **aloof·ness** *n*

aloud \ə-ˈlau̇d\ *adv* : with the speaking voice

alp \ˈalp\ *n* : a high rugged mountain

al·paca \al-ˈpak-ə\ *n* **1** : a mammal with fine long woolly hair domesticated in Peru and related to the llama **2** : wool of the alpaca or a thin cloth made of or containing it; *also* : a rayon or cotton imitation of this cloth

al·pen·stock \ˈal-pən-ˌstäk\ *n* : a long iron-pointed staff used in mountain climbing

al·pha·bet \ˈal-fə-ˌbet, -bət\ *n* **1** : the characters (as letters) of a written language arranged in their customary order **2** : a system of signs or signals that serve as equivalents for letters

al·pha·bet·ic \ˌal-fə-ˈbet-ik\ *adj* : arranged in the order of the letters of the alphabet — **al·pha·bet·i·cal** \-ˈbet-i-kəl\ *adj* — **al·pha·bet·i·cal·ly** \-i-k(ə-)lē\ *adv*

al·pha·bet·ize \ˈal-fə-bə-ˌtīz\ *vt* : to arrange in alphabetic order — **al·pha·bet·i·za·tion** \ˌal-fə-ˌbet-ə-ˈzā-shən\ *n* — **al·pha·bet·iz·er** \ˈal-fə-bə-ˌtī-zər\ *n*

alpha particle *n* : a positively charged particle that is identical with the nucleus of a helium atom, consists of 2 protons and 2 neutrons, and is ejected at high speed in various radioactive transformations

alpha ray *n* : a stream of alpha particles

al·pine \ˈal-ˌpīn\ *n* : a plant native to alpine or boreal regions

Alpine *adj, often not cap* **1** : relating to or resembling the Alps or any mountains **2** : of, relating to, or growing on upland slopes above timberline

al·ready \ȯl-ˈred-ē\ *adv* **1** : before a stated or implied time : PREVIOUSLY **2** : so soon

al·right \ȯl-ˈrīt\ *adv (or adj)* : all right

al·so \'ȯl-sō\ *adv* **1 :** LIKEWISE **2 :** in addition **:** TOO
al·so–ran \-ˌran\ *n* **1 :** a horse or dog that finishes out of the money in a race **2 :** a contestant that does not win
al·tar \'ȯl-tər\ *n* **1 :** a usu. raised structure or place on which sacrifices are offered or incense is burned in worship **2 :** a usu. enclosed table used in consecrating the eucharistic elements or as a center of worship or ritual
altar boy *n* **:** ACOLYTE 1
altar rail *n* **:** a railing in front of an altar separating the chancel from the body of the church
al·ter \'ȯl-tər\ *vb* **1 :** to change partly but not completely **:** make or become different in some details **2 :** CASTRATE, SPAY — **al·ter·a·bil·i·ty** \ˌȯl-tə-rə-'bil-ət-ē\ *n* — **al·ter·a·ble** \'ȯl-tə-rə-bəl\ *adj* — **al·ter·a·bly** \-blē\ *adv*
al·ter·ation \ˌȯl-tə-'rā-shən\ *n* **1 a :** the act or process of altering **b :** the state of being altered **2 :** the result of altering **:** MODIFICATION
al·ter·ca·tion \ˌȯl-tər-'kā-shən\ *n* **:** a noisy or angry dispute **:** WRANGLE
al·ter ego \ˌȯl-tər-'ē-gō\ *n* **:** a second self; *esp* **:** a trusted friend
¹al·ter·nate \'ȯl-tər-nət, 'al-\ *adj* **1 :** occurring or succeeding by turns **2 :** every other **:** every second **3 :** ALTERNATIVE, SUBSTITUTE — **al·ter·nate·ly** *adv*
²al·ter·nate \-ˌnāt\ *vb* **1 :** to do, occur, or act by turns **2 :** to cause to alternate
³al·ter·nate \-nət\ *n* **1 :** ALTERNATIVE **2 :** one that alternates with another; *esp* **:** a person named to take the place of another whenever necessary
alternating current *n* **:** an electric current that reverses its direction at regular intervals
al·ter·na·tion \ˌȯl-tər-'nā-shən, ˌal-\ *n* **1 :** the act or process of alternating **2 :** alternate position or occurrence **:** SUCCESSION
¹al·ter·na·tive \ȯl-'tər-nət-iv, al-\ *adj* **1 :** offering or expressing a choice **2 :** ALTERNATE — **al·ter·na·tive·ly** *adv* — **al·ter·na·tive·ness** *n*
²alternative *n* **1 :** a chance to choose between two things **2 :** one of the two or sometimes more things between which a choice is to be made
al·though \ȯl-'t͟hō\ *conj* **:** in spite of the fact that **:** THOUGH
al·tim·e·ter \al-'tim-ət-ər, 'al-tə-ˌmēt-ər\ *n* **:** an instrument for measuring altitude
al·ti·tude \'al-tə-ˌt(y)üd\ *n* **1 a :** the angular height of a celestial object above the horizon **b :** the vertical distance of an object above sea level **2 a :** vertical distance or extent **b :** position at a height **c :** an elevated region **:** EMINENCE — usu. used in pl. — **al·ti·tu·di·nal** \ˌal-tə-'t(y)üd-nəl, -ᵊn-əl\ *adj*
al·to \'al-tō\ *n, pl* **altos** **1 a :** CONTRALTO **b :** the voice part next to the highest in 4-part harmony **2 :** the second highest member of a family of musical instruments — **alto** *adj*
al·to·geth·er \ˌȯl-tə-'get͟h-ər\ *adv* **1 :** WHOLLY, THOROUGHLY **2 :** on the whole
al·tru·ism \'al-trü-ˌiz-əm\ *n* **:** unselfish interest in or care for the welfare of others — **al·tru·ist** \-trü-əst\ *n* — **al·tru·is·tic** \ˌal-trü-'is-tik\ *adj* — **al·tru·is·ti·cal·ly** \-'is-ti-k(ə-)lē\ *adv*
al·um \'al-əm\ *n* **1 :** either of two colorless crystalline compounds containing aluminum that have a sweetish-sourish taste and a puckering effect on the mouth and are used in medicine (as to check local sweating or to stop bleeding) **2 :** an aluminum compound made from bauxite and used in paper manufacture, dyeing, and sewage treatment
alu·mi·na \ə-'lü-mə-nə\ *n* **:** the oxide of aluminum that occurs native as corundum and in bauxite and is used as a source of aluminum, as an abrasive, and as an absorbent
alu·mi·num \ə-'lü-mə-nəm\ *n* **:** a silver-white malleable ductile light metallic element with good electrical and thermal conductivity and resistance to oxidation that is the most abundant metal in the earth's crust
alum·na \ə-'ləm-nə\ *n, pl* **-nae** \-(ˌ)nē\ **:** a girl or woman who has attended or has graduated from a particular school, college, or university
alum·nus \ə-'ləm-nəs\ *n, pl* **-ni** \-ˌnī\ **:** one that has attended or graduated from a particular school, college, or university
al·ways \'ȯl-wēz, -wəz, -ˌwāz\ *adv* **1 :** at all times **:** INVARIABLY **2 :** FOREVER, PERPETUALLY
am *pres 1st sing of* BE
amah \'äm-ə, 'äm-ˌä\ *n* **:** a female servant typically Chinese; *esp* **:** NURSE
amain \ə-'mān\ *adv* **1 :** with all one's might **2 a :** at full speed **b :** in great haste
amal·gam \ə-'mal-gəm\ *n* **1 :** an alloy of mercury with some other metal or metals that is used in filling teeth **2 :** a combination or mixture of different elements
amal·ga·mate \ə-'mal-gə-ˌmāt\ *vb* **:** to unite in or as if in an amalgam; *esp* **:** to combine into a single body
amal·ga·ma·tion \ə-ˌmal-gə-'mā-shən\ *n* **1 a :** the act or process of amalgamating **b :** the state of being amalgamated **2 :** the result of amalgamating; *esp* **:** a combination of different elements (as races or business corporations) into a single body — **amal·ga·ma·tive** \-'mal-gə-ˌmāt-iv\ *adj*
aman·u·en·sis \ə-ˌman-yə-'wen(t)-səs\ *n, pl* **aman·u·en·ses** \-'wen(t)-sēz\ **:** a person employed to write from dictation or to copy manuscript **:** SECRETARY
am·a·ranth \'am-ə-ˌran(t)th\ *n* **1 :** an imaginary flower that never fades **2 :** any of a large genus of coarse herbs sometimes cultivated for their showy flowers
am·a·ran·thine \ˌam-ə-'ran(t)-thən, -'ran-ˌthīn\ *adj* **:** relating to or resembling amaranth **:** UNFADING, UNDYING
am·a·ryl·lis \ˌam-ə-'ril-əs\ *n* **:** any of various plants of a family related to the lily family; *esp* **:** any of several African bulbous herbs grown for their umbels of large showy flowers
amass \ə-'mas\ *vt* **1 :** to collect for oneself **:** ACCUMULATE **2 :** to pile up into a mass **:** GATHER — **amass·er** *n*
am·a·teur \'am-ə-ˌtər, -ət-ər, -ə-ˌt(y)ů(ə)r\ *n* **1 :** a person who takes part in sports or occupations for pleasure and not for pay **2 :** a person who engages in something without experience or competence — **amateur** *adj* — **am·a·teur·ish** \ˌam-ə-'tər-ish, -'t(y)ů(ə)r-ish\ *adj* — **am·a·teur·ish·ly** *adv* — **am·a·teur·ish·ness** *n* — **am·a·teur·ism** \'am-ə-ˌtər-ˌiz-əm, -ət-ər-, -ə-ˌt(y)ů(ə)r-\ *n*
am·a·to·ry \'am-ə-ˌtōr-ē\ *adj* **:** of, relating to, or expressing sexual love
amaze \ə-'māz\ *vt* **:** to surprise or astonish greatly **:** fill with wonder **:** ASTOUND
amaze·ment \ə-'māz-mənt\ *n* **:** great surprise or astonishment
am·a·zon \'am-ə-ˌzän, -ə-zən\ *n* **1** *cap* **:** a member of a race of female warriors repeatedly warring with the ancient Greeks of mythology **2 :** a tall strong masculine woman
Am·a·zo·ni·an \ˌam-ə-'zō-nē-ən\ *adj* **1 a :** of, relating to, or resembling an Amazon **b** *not cap* **:** MASCULINE, WARLIKE **2 :** of or relating to the Amazon river or its valley
am·bas·sa·dor \am-'bas-əd-ər\ *n* **1 :** an official envoy; *esp* **:** a diplomatic agent of the highest rank accredited to a foreign sovereign or government as the resident representative of his own sovereign or government or appointed for a special and often temporary diplomatic assignment **2 :** an authorized representative or messenger — **am·bas·sa·do·ri·al** \(ˌ)am-ˌbas-ə-'dōr-ē-əl\ *adj* — **am·bas·sa·dor·ship** \am-'bas-əd-ər-ˌship\ *n*
am·bas·sa·dress \-'bas-ə-drəs\ *n* **:** a female ambassador
am·ber \'am-bər\ *n* **1 :** a hard yellowish to brownish translucent resin from trees long dead that takes a fine polish and is used in making ornamental objects (as beads) **2 :** a variable color averaging a dark orange yellow
am·ber·gris \'am-bər-ˌgris, -ˌgrēs\ *n* **:** a waxy substance from the sperm whale used in the manufacture of perfumes
am·bi·dex·trous \ˌam-bi-'dek-strəs\ *adj* **1 :** using both hands

with equal ease **2 :** unusually skillful **:** VERSATILE **3 :** characterized by duplicity **:** DOUBLE-DEALING — **am·bi·dex·trous·ly** *adv*

am·bi·ence *or* **am·bi·ance** \äⁿ-byäⁿs, 'am-bē-ən(t)s\ *n* **:** a surrounding or pervading atmosphere **:** ENVIRONMENT

am·bi·ent \'am-bē-ənt\ *adj* **:** surrounding on all sides **:** ENCOMPASSING

am·bi·gu·i·ty \ˌam-bə-'gyü-ət-ē\ *n, pl* **-ties 1 :** uncertainty or confusion of meaning (as of a word or phrase) **2 :** an ambiguous word or passage

am·big·u·ous \am-'big-yə-wəs\ *adj* **:** not clear in meaning because able to be understood in more than one way **:** EQUIVOCAL — **am·big·u·ous·ly** *adv* — **am·big·u·ous·ness** *n*

am·bi·tion \am-'bish-ən\ *n* **1 a :** an ardent desire for rank, fame, or power **b :** desire to achieve a particular end **:** ASPIRATION **2 :** the object of ambition

am·bi·tious \am-'bish-əs\ *adj* **1 :** stirred by or possessing ambition **2 :** showing ambition — **am·bi·tious·ly** *adv*

am·biv·a·lence \am-'biv-ə-lən(t)s\ *n* **:** simultaneous attraction toward and repulsion from something or someone — **am·biv·a·lent** \-lənt\ *adj*

¹am·ble \'am-bəl\ *vi* **am·bled; am·bling** \-b(ə-)liŋ\ **:** to go at an amble **:** SAUNTER — **am·bler** \-b(ə-)lər\ *n*

²amble *n* **1 :** an easy gait of a horse in which the legs on the same side of the body move together **2 :** a gentle easy gait

am·bro·sia \am-'brō-zh(ē-)ə\ *n* **:** the food of the Greek and Roman gods — **am·bro·sial** \-zh(ē-)əl\ *adj*

am·bu·lance \'am-byə-lən(t)s\ *n* **:** a vehicle equipped for transporting the injured or the sick

¹am·bu·la·to·ry \'am-byə-lə-ˌtōr-ē, -ˌtȯr-\ *adj* **1 :** of, relating to, or adapted to walking **2 :** able to walk about

²ambulatory *n, pl* **-ries :** a sheltered place (as a cloister) for walking

am·bus·cade \'am-bə-ˌskād\ *n* **:** AMBUSH — **ambuscade** *vb* — **am·bus·cad·er** *n*

¹am·bush \'am-ˌbu̇sh\ *vt* **1 :** to station in ambush **2 :** to attack from an ambush **:** WAYLAY

²ambush *n* **:** a trap in which concealed persons lie in wait to attack by surprise; *also* **:** the persons so concealed or their position

ame·lio·rate \ə-'mēl-yə-ˌrāt\ *vb* **:** to make or grow better or more tolerable — **ame·lio·ra·tion** \-ˌmēl-yə-'rā-shən\ *n* — **ame·lio·ra·tive** \-'mēl-yə-ˌrāt-iv\ *adj*

amen \(')ā-'men, (')ä-\ *interj* — used to express solemn agreement or hearty approval

ame·na·ble \ə-'mē-nə-bəl, -'men-ə-\ *adj* **1 :** subject to some authority and therefore liable to be called to account by it **2 :** easily influenced or managed **:** RESPONSIVE — **ame·na·bil·i·ty** \-ˌmē-nə-'bil-ət-ē, -ˌmen-ə-\ *n* — **ame·na·bly** \-'mē-nə-blē, -'men-ə-\ *adv*

amend \ə-'mend\ *vb* **1 :** to put right; *esp* **:** to make emendations in **2 a :** to change for the better **:** IMPROVE **b :** to alter esp. in phraseology; *esp* **:** to alter formally by modification, deletion, or addition — **amend·a·ble** *adj* — **amen·da·to·ry** \-'men-də-ˌtōr-ē\ *adj* — **amend·er** *n*

amend·ment \ə-'men(d)-mənt\ *n* **1 :** the act or process of amending esp. for the better **2 :** a modification, addition, or deletion (as to a law, bill, or motion) made or proposed

amends \ə-'men(d)z\ *n sing or pl* **:** something done or given by a person to make up for a loss or injury he has caused

amen·i·ty \ə-'men-ət-ē, -'mē-nət-\ *n, pl* **-ties 1 :** the quality of being pleasant or agreeable **2 :** something (as a conventional social gesture) that adds to material comfort or convenience or to smoothness of social intercourse — usu. used in pl.

amerce \ə-'mərs\ *vt* **:** to punish by a fine fixed in amount by the court — **amerce·ment** *n* — **amer·cia·ble** \-'mər-sē-ə-bəl, -'mər-shə-bəl\ *adj*

Amer·i·can·ism \ə-'mer-ə-kə-ˌniz-əm\ *n* **1 :** a characteristic feature of English as used in the U.S. **2 :** attachment or loyalty to the traditions, interests, or ideals of the U.S. **3 :** a custom or trait peculiar to the U.S. or to Americans

amer·i·can·ize \-kə-ˌnīz\ *vb, often cap* **:** to make or become American (as in customs, habits, dress, or speech) — **amer·i·can·i·za·tion** \ə-ˌmer-ə-kə-nə-'zā-shən\ *n, often cap*

am·er·i·ci·um \ˌam-ə-'ris(h)-ē-əm\ *n* **:** a radioactive metallic chemical element produced by bombardment of uranium with high-energy helium nuclei

am·e·thyst \'am-ə-thəst\ *n* **:** a clear purple or bluish violet variety of crystallized quartz used as a jeweler's stone

ami·a·ble \'ā-mē-ə-bəl\ *adj* **:** generally agreeable **:** having a friendly, sociable, and congenial disposition — **ami·a·bil·i·ty** \ˌā-mē-ə-'bil-ət-ē\ *n* — **ami·a·ble·ness** *n* — **ami·a·bly** \-blē\ *adv*

am·i·ca·ble \'am-i-kə-bəl\ *adj* **:** characterized by friendship and goodwill **:** PEACEABLE — **am·i·ca·bil·i·ty** \ˌam-i-kə-'bil-ət-ē\ *n* — **am·i·ca·ble·ness** *n* — **am·i·ca·bly** \-blē\ *adv*

am·ice \'am-əs\ *n* **:** a white linen cloth worn about the neck and shoulders under other vestments

amid \ə-'mid\ *or* **amidst** \-'midst\ *prep* **:** in or into the middle of **:** AMONG

amid·ships \ə-'mid-ˌships\ *adv* **:** in or near the middle of a ship

ami·no acid \ə-ˌmē-nō-, ˌam-ə-ˌnō-\ *n* **:** any of numerous nitrogen-containing acids that include some which are the building blocks of proteins and are synthesized by living cells or are obtained as essential components of the diet

¹amiss \ə-'mis\ *adv* **1 :** WRONGLY, FAULTILY **2 :** ASTRAY

²amiss *adj* **:** WRONG, FAULTY, IMPROPER

am·i·ty \'am-ət-ē\ *n, pl* **-ties :** FRIENDSHIP; *esp* **:** friendly relations between nations

am·me·ter \'am-ˌēt-ər\ *n* **:** an instrument for measuring electric current in amperes

am·mo \'am-ō\ *n, pl* **ammos :** AMMUNITION

am·mo·nia \ə-'mō-nyə\ *n* **1 :** a colorless gas that is a compound of nitrogen and hydrogen, has a sharp smell and taste, is very soluble in water, can be easily liquefied by cold and pressure, and is used in the manufacture of ice, fertilizers, and explosives **2 :** a solution of ammonia in water — **am·mo·ni·a·cal** \ˌam-ə-'nī-ə-kəl\ *adj*

am·mo·nite \'am-ə-ˌnīt\ *n* **:** any of numerous flat spiral fossil shells of mollusks — **am·mo·nit·ic** \ˌam-ə-'nit-ik\ *adj*

am·mu·ni·tion \ˌam-yə-'nish-ən\ *n* **1 :** something that can be hurled at a target; *esp* **:** something (as a bullet, shell, grenade, or bomb) propelled by or containing explosives **2 :** a material that may be used (as in a controversy) in attack or defense

am·ne·sia \am-'nē-zhə\ *n* **:** loss of memory due usu. to brain injury, shock, fatigue, repression, or illness— **am·ne·si·ac** \-z(h)ē-ˌak\ *or* **am·ne·sic** \-zik, -sik\ *adj or n*

am·nes·ty \'am-nə-stē\ *n, pl* **-ties :** a general pardon granted by a ruler or government to a large group of persons guilty of a political offense (as treason or rebellion)

amoe·ba \ə-'mē-bə\ *n, pl* **amoebas** *or* **amoe·bae** \-(ˌ)bē\ **:** any of numerous protozoans that have no permanent cell organs or supporting structures and are widespread in fresh and salt water and in moist soils — **amoe·bic** \-bik\ *adj*

amok \ə-'mək, -'mäk\ *adv* **:** in a murderously frenzied state or violently raging manner — **amok** *adj*

among \ə-'məŋ\ *prep* **1 :** in or through the midst of **2 :** in company or association with **3 :** by or through the whole or a large part of **4 :** in the number or class of **5 :** in shares to each of **6 :** through the reciprocal or joint action of

amor·al \(')ā-'mȯr-əl\ *adj* **:** neither moral nor immoral; *esp* **:** outside the sphere to which moral judgments apply — **amor·al·ly** \-ə-lē\ *adv*

am·o·rous \'am-(ə-)rəs\ *adj* **1 a :** inclined to love **:** easily falling in love **b :** being in love **:** ENAMORED **2 :** of, relating to, or caused by love — **am·o·rous·ly** *adv* — **am·o·rous·ness** *n*

amor·phous \ə-'mȯr-fəs\ *adj* **:** having no determinate form

: SHAPELESS: as **a** : lacking complex bodily organization **b** : UNCRYSTALLIZED — **amor·phous·ly** *adv* — **amor·phous·ness** *n*

am·or·tize \'am-ər-ˌtīz, ə-'mȯr-ˌtīz\ *vt* : to extinguish (as a mortgage) usu. by payment on the principle at the time of each periodic interest payment — **am·or·ti·za·tion** \ˌam-ərt-ə-'zā-shən, ə-ˌmȯrt-ə-\ *n*

¹amount \ə-'maůnt\ *vi* **1** : to add up **2** : to be equivalent

²amount *n* **1** : the total number or quantity : AGGREGATE **2** : the whole effect, significance, or import **3** : a principal sum and the interest on it

amour \ə-'mů(ə)r, a-, ä-\ *n* : a love affair; *esp* : a secret love affair

amour pro·pre \ˌam-ˌůr-'prōprᵊ\ *n* : SELF-ESTEEM

am·per·age \'am-pə-rij\ *n* : the strength of a current of electricity expressed in amperes

am·pere \'am-ˌpi(ə)r\ *n* : a unit of electric current that is equivalent to a steady current produced by one volt applied across a resistance of one ohm

am·per·sand \'am-pər-ˌsand\ *n* : a character & standing for the word *and*

am·phib·i·an \am-'fib-ē-ən\ *n* **1** : an amphibious organism; *esp* : any of a class of cold-blooded vertebrate animals (as frogs and newts) intermediate between fishes and reptiles **2** : an airplane designed to take off from and land on either land or water — **amphibian** *adj*

am·phib·i·ous \-ē-əs\ *adj* **1** : able to live both on land and in water **2 a** : relating to or adapted for both land and water **b** : executed by coordinated action of land, sea, and air forces organized for invasion from the sea; *also* : trained or organized for such action — **am·phib·i·ous·ly** *adv* — **am·phib·i·ous·ness** *n*

am·phi·the·a·ter \'am(p)-fə-ˌthē-ət-ər\ *n* **1** : a round or oval building with seats rising in curved rows around an open space on which games and plays take place **2** : something resembling an amphitheater (as a piece of level ground surrounded by hills)

am·ple \'am-pəl\ *adj* **1** : generous or more than adequate in size, scope, or capacity : COPIOUS **2** : enough to satisfy : ABUNDANT — **am·ple·ness** *n* — **am·ply** \-plē\ *adv*

am·pli·fi·ca·tion \ˌam-plə-fə-'kā-shən\ *n* **1** : an act, example, or product of amplifying **2 a** : matter by which a statement is expanded **b** : an expanded statement

am·pli·fi·er \'am-plə-ˌfī(-ə)r\ *n* : one that amplifies

am·pli·fy \'am-plə-ˌfī\ *vt* **-fied; -fy·ing** **1** : ENLARGE; *esp* : to expand by addition of detail or illustration **2** : to increase (voltage, current, or power) in magnitude or strength (as by use of a vacuum tube) **3** : to make louder

am·pli·tude \'am-plə-ˌt(y)üd\ *n* **1** : the quality or state of being ample : FULLNESS **2** : the extent or range of a quality, property, process, or phenomenon; *esp* : the extent of a vibratory movement (as of a pendulum) or of an oscillation (as of an alternating current or a radio wave)

amplitude modulation *n* : modulation of the amplitude of a radio carrier wave in accordance with the strength of the audio or other signal; *also* : a broadcasting system using such modulation

am·pul *or* **am·poule** \'am-ˌp(y)ül\ *n* : a small sealed bulbous glass vessel used to hold a solution for hypodermic injection

am·pu·tate \'am-pyə-ˌtāt\ *vt* : to cut or lop off : PRUNE; *esp* : to cut (as a limb) from the body — **am·pu·ta·tion** \ˌam-pyə-'tā-shən\ *n* — **am·pu·ta·tor** \'am-pyə-ˌtāt-ər\ *n*

am·pu·tee \ˌam-pyə-'tē\ *n* : one that has had a limb amputated

am·u·let \'am-yə-lət\ *n* : a small object worn as a charm against evil

amuse \ə-'myüz\ *vt* **1** : to occupy with something pleasant : DIVERT **2** : to please or delight the sense of humor of — **amus·ing·ly** *adv*

amuse·ment \ə-'myüz-mənt\ *n* **1** : the condition of being amused **2** : pleasant diversion **3** : something that amuses or entertains

an \ən, (')an\ *indefinite article* : ²A — in standard speech and writing used (1) invariably before words beginning with a vowel letter and sound; (2) invariably before *h*-initial words in which the *h* is silent; (3) frequently before *h*-initial words which have in an initial unstressed syllable an \h\ sound often lost after the *an*; (4) sometimes esp. in England before words like *union* and *European* whose initial letter is a vowel and whose initial sounds are \yü\ or \yů\

anach·ro·nism \ə-'nak-rə-ˌniz-əm\ *n* **1** : an error in chronology; *esp* : a chronological misplacing of persons, events, objects, or customs in regard to each other **2** : a person or a thing that is chronologically out of place; *esp* : something from a former age incongruous in the present — **anach·ro·nis·tic** \ə-ˌnak-rə-'nis-tik\ *adj* — **anach·ro·nis·ti·cal·ly** \-ti-k(ə-)lē\ *adv*

an·a·con·da \ˌan-ə-'kän-də\ *n* : a large So. American snake of the boa family that crushes its prey in its coils

an·aer·o·bic \ˌan-ə-'rō-bik\ *adj* : living, active, or occurring in the absence of free oxygen — **an·aer·obe** \(')an-'a(-ə)r-ˌōb\ *n* — **an·aer·o·bi·cal·ly** *adv*

ana·gram \'an-ə-ˌgram\ *n* : a word or phrase made out of another by changing the order of the letters

anal \'ān-ᵊl\ *adj* : of, relating to, or situated near the anus — **anal·ly** \-ᵊl-ē\ *adv*

an·al·ge·sia \ˌan-ᵊl-'jē-zhə\ *n* ; insensibility to pain without loss of consciousness — **an·al·ge·sic** \-'jē-zik, -sik\ *adj or n* — **an·al·get·ic** \-'jet-ik\ *adj or n*

an·a·log·i·cal \ˌan-ᵊl-'äj-i-kəl\ *adj* **1** : of, relating to, or based on analogy **2** : expressing or implying analogy — **an·a·log·i·cal·ly** \-k(ə-)lē\ *adv*

anal·o·gous \ə-'nal-ə-gəs\ *adj* **1** : showing an analogy or a likeness permitting one to draw an analogy **2** : being or related to as an analogue — **anal·o·gous·ly** *adv* — **anal·o·gous·ness** *n*

an·a·logue *or* **an·a·log** \'an-ᵊl-ˌȯg\ *n* : something that is analogous or similar to something else

anal·o·gy \ə-'nal-ə-jē\ *n, pl* **-gies** **1** : an inference that if two or more things agree with one another in some respects they will prob. agree in others **2** : resemblance in some particulars between things otherwise unlike : SIMILARITY

anal·y·sis \ə-'nal-ə-səs\ *n, pl* **anal·y·ses** \-'nal-ə-ˌsēz\ **1** : separation of a whole into its component parts **2 a** : an examination of a whole to discover its elements and their relations **b** : a statement of such an analysis **c** : an examination and interpretation of the nature and significance of something (as news events or business conditions) **3** : PSYCHOANALYSIS

an·a·lyst \'an-ᵊl-əst\ *n* **1** : a person who analyzes or who is skilled in analysis **2** : PSYCHOANALYST

an·a·lyt·ic \ˌan-ᵊl-'it-ik\ *adj* **1** : of or relating to analysis; *esp* : separating something into component parts or constituent elements **2** : skilled in or using analysis — **an·a·lyt·i·cal** \-i-kəl\ *adj* — **an·a·lyt·i·cal·ly** \-k(ə-)lē\ *adv*

an·a·lyze \'an-ᵊl-ˌīz\ *vt* : to make an analysis of; *esp* : to study or determine the nature and relationship of the parts of by analysis — **an·a·lyz·a·ble** *adj* — **an·a·lyz·er** *n*

an·a·pest \'an-ə-ˌpest\ *n* : a metrical foot consisting of two unaccented syllables followed by one accented syllable (as in *the accused*) — **an·a·pes·tic** \ˌan-ə-'pes-tik\ *adj*

an·ar·chic \a-'när-kik\ *adj* : of, relating to, or tending toward anarchy : LAWLESS — **an·ar·chi·cal** \-ki-kəl\ *adj*

an·ar·chism \'an-ər-ˌkiz-əm\ *n* **1** : a political theory holding all governmental authority to be unnecessary and undesirable and advocating a society based on the voluntary cooperation of individuals and groups **2** : the advocacy or practice of anarchistic principles

an·ar·chist \'an-ər-kəst\ *n* **1 :** one who rebels against any authority, established order, or ruling power **2 :** one who believes in, advocates, or promotes anarchism; *esp* **:** one who uses violent means to overthrow the established order — **anarchist** *or* **an·ar·chis·tic** \ˌan-ər-'kis-tik\ *adj*

an·ar·chy \'an-ər-kē\ *n* **1 :** the condition of a society without a government **2 :** a state of lawlessness, confusion, or disorder **3 :** an ideal society having no government and made up of individuals who enjoy complete freedom

anath·e·ma \ə-'nath-ə-mə\ *n* **1 a :** a curse solemnly pronounced by ecclesiastical authority and accompanied by excommunication **b :** a vigorous denunciation **:** CURSE **2 :** a person or thing that is cursed or intensely disliked or loathed

anat·o·mize \ə-'nat-ə-ˌmīz\ *vt* **1 :** to dissect so as to show or examine the structure and use of the parts **2 :** ANALYZE

anat·o·my \ə-'nat-ə-mē\ *n, pl* **-mies 1 :** a branch of knowledge that deals with the structure of organisms **2 :** structural makeup esp. of an organism or any of its parts **3 :** a separating into parts for examination **:** ANALYSIS — **an·a·tom·ic** \ˌan-ə-'täm-ik\ *or* **an·a·tom·i·cal** \-'täm-i-kəl\ *adj* — **an·a·tom·i·cal·ly** \-k(ə-)lē\ *adv* — **anat·o·mist** \ə-'nat-ə-məst\ *n*

an·ces·tor \'an-ˌses-tər\ *n* **1 :** one from whom an individual or kind of individual is descended and who is usu. more remote in the line of descent than a grandparent **2 :** FORERUNNER, PROTOTYPE — **an·ces·tress** \-trəs\ *n*

an·ces·tral \an-'ses-trəl\ *adj* **:** of, relating to, or derived from an ancestor — **an·ces·tral·ly** \-trə-lē\ *adv*

an·ces·try \'an-ˌses-trē\ *n, pl* **-tries 1 :** line of descent **:** LINEAGE **2 :** a series of ancestors

[1]**an·chor** \'aŋ-kər\ *n* **1 :** a heavy iron or steel device attached to a boat or ship by a cable or chain and so made that when thrown overboard it digs into the earth and holds the boat or ship in place **2 :** something that secures or steadies or that gives a feeling of stability

[2]**anchor** *vb* **an·chored; an·chor·ing** \-k(ə-)riŋ\ **1 :** to hold in place by means of an anchor **2 :** to fasten securely to a firm foundation **3 :** to drop anchor **:** become anchored

an·chor·age \'aŋ-k(ə-)rij\ *n* **1 :** a place where boats may be anchored **2 :** a secure hold to resist a strong pull **3 :** a means of security **:** REFUGE

an·cho·rite \'aŋ-kə-ˌrīt\ *n* **:** a person who gives up worldly things and lives in solitude usu. for religious reasons

an·chor·man \'aŋ-ker-ˌman\ *n* **:** a news broadcaster who is the principal reporter and who coordinates news stories from other reporters into a unified program

an·cho·vy \'an-ˌchō-vē, an-'\ *n, pl* **-vies** *or* **-vy :** any of numerous small fishes resembling herrings; *esp* **:** a common Mediterranean fish used esp. for sauces and relishes

an·cien ré·gime \ä^{n}s-ya^{n}-rā-zhēm\ *n* **1 :** the political and social system of France before the Revolution of 1789 **2 :** a system or mode no longer prevailing

[1]**an·cient** \'ān-shənt, -chənt; 'āŋ(k)-shənt\ *adj* **1 :** having existed for many years **:** very old **2 :** of or relating to a period of time long past or to those living in such a period; *esp* **:** of or relating to the historical period from the earliest civilizations to the fall of the western Roman Empire A.D. 476 **3 :** having the qualities of age or long existence: **a :** VENERABLE **b :** OLD-FASHIONED, ANTIQUE — **an·cient·ness** *n*

[2]**ancient** *n* **1 :** an aged person **2** *pl* **:** the civilized peoples of ancient times and esp. of Greece and Rome

an·cient·ly \-lē\ *adv* **:** in ancient times

and \ənd(d), (')an(d), *usu* ᵊn(d) *after* t, d, s, *or* z, *often* ᵊm *after* p *or* b, *sometimes* ᵊŋ *after* k *or* g\ *conj* — used as a function word to join words or word groups of the same grammatical rank or function (as two nouns that are subjects of the same verb, two relative clauses modifying the same noun, or an adverb and a prepositional phrase modifying the same verb) and to express connection or addition

an·dan·te \än-'dän-ˌtā, an-'dant-ē\ *adv (or adj)* **:** moderately slow — used as a direction in music

and·iron \'an-ˌdī(-ə)rn\ *n* **:** one of a pair of metal supports for wood in a fireplace

and/or \'and-'ō(ə)r\ *conj* — used as a function word to indicate that either *and* or *or* may apply

an·dro·gen \'an-drə-jən\ *n* **:** a male sex hormone — **an·dro·gen·ic** \ˌan-drə-'jen-ik\ *adj*

an·ec·dote \'an-ik-ˌdōt\ *n* **:** a short narrative of an interesting, amusing, or biographical incident — **an·ec·dot·al** \ˌan-ik-'dōt-ᵊl\ *adj* — **an·ec·dot·al·ly** \-ᵊl-ē\ *adv*

ane·mia \ə-'nē-mē-ə\ *n* **1 :** a condition in which the blood is deficient in red blood cells, in hemoglobin, or in total volume and which is usu. marked by pale skin, shortness of breath, and irregular heart action **2 :** lack of vitality — **ane·mic** \-mik\ *adj* — **ane·mi·cal·ly** \-mi-k(ə-)lē\ *adv*

an·e·mom·e·ter \ˌan-ə-'mäm-ət-ər\ *n* **:** an instrument for measuring the force or speed of the wind

anem·o·ne \ə-'nem-ə-nē\ *n* **:** any of a large genus of herbs related to the buttercups that have showy flowers without petals but with conspicuous often colored sepals

an·es·the·sia \ˌan-əs-'thē-zhə\ *n* **:** loss of bodily sensation with or without loss of consciousness

[1]**an·es·thet·ic** \ˌan-əs-'thet-ik\ *adj* **:** of, relating to, or capable of producing anesthesia — **an·es·thet·i·cal·ly** \-'thet-i-k(ə-)lē\ *adv*

[2]**anesthetic** *n* **:** a substance that produces either local or general anesthesia

anes·the·tist \ə-'nes-thət-əst\ *n* **:** one who administers anesthetics

anes·the·tize \ə-'nes-thə-ˌtīz\ *vt* **:** to make insensible to pain esp. by the use of an anesthetic

anew \ə-'n(y)ü\ *adv* **1 :** over again **:** for an additional time **:** AFRESH **2 :** in a new or different form

an·gel \'ān-jəl\ *n* **1 a :** a spiritual being serving God esp. as a messenger or as a guardian of men; *esp* **:** one in the lowest rank **b :** a white-robed winged figure of human form in fine art representing an angel **2 :** an attendant spirit or guardian **3 :** MESSENGER, HARBINGER **4 :** a person felt to resemble (as in virtue, innocence, or beauty) an angel **5 :** a financial backer of a theatrical venture or other enterprise — **an·gel·ic** \an-'jel-ik\ *or* **an·gel·i·cal** \-i-kəl\ *adj* — **an·gel·i·cal·ly** \-i-k(ə-)lē\ *adv*

[1]**an·ger** \'aŋ-gər\ *n* **:** a strong feeling of displeasure and usu. of antagonism

[2]**anger** *vt* **an·gered; an·ger·ing** \-g(ə-)riŋ\ **:** to make angry

an·gi·na \an-'jī-nə\ *n* **:** a disorder (as of the heart) marked by spasmodic attacks of intense pain — **an·gi·nal** \-'jīn-ᵊl\ *adj*

[1]**an·gle** \'aŋ-gəl\ *n* **1 :** the figure formed by two lines extending from the same point or by two surfaces diverging from the same line **2 :** a sharp projecting corner **3 a :** ASPECT **b :** a special approach or technique for accomplishing an objective **4 :** a course or direction abruptly diverging from the one orig. pursued — **an·gled** \-gəld\ *adj*

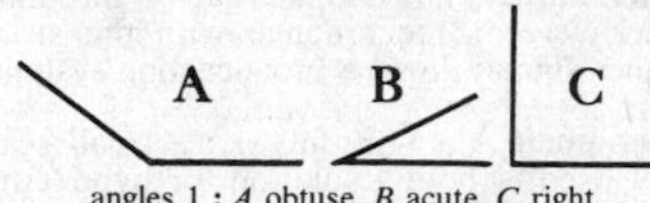

angles 1 : *A* obtuse, *B* acute, *C* right

[2]**angle** *vb* **an·gled; an·gling** \-g(ə-)liŋ\ **1 :** to turn, move, or direct at an angle **2 :** to present (as a news story or speech) from a particular often biased point of view **:** SLANT

[3]**angle** *vi* **an·gled; an·gling** \-g(ə-)liŋ\ **1 :** to fish with hook and line **2 :** to use artful means to attain an objective

an·gler \'aŋ-glər\ *n* **:** one who fishes especially for sport

an·gle·worm \'aŋ-gəl-ˌwərm\ *n* **:** EARTHWORM

An·gli·can \'aŋ-gli-kən\ *n* **:** a member of the Church of England or of one of the related churches in communion with it — **Anglican** *adj*

an·gli·cize \'aŋ-glə-ˌsīz\ *vt, often cap* **1** : to make English (as in habits, speech, character, or outlook) **2** : to borrow (a foreign word or phrase) into English without changing form or spelling and sometimes without changing pronunciation — **an·gli·ci·za·tion** \ˌaŋ-glə-sə-'zā-shən\ *n, often cap*

an·gling \'aŋ-gliŋ\ *n* : the act of fishing with hook and line usu. for sport

an·glo·phile \'aŋ-glə-ˌfīl\ *n, often cap* : one who greatly admires England and things English

an·glo·phobe \-ˌfōb\ *n, often cap* : one who is averse to England and things English

an·go·ra \aŋ-'gōr-ə, an-\ *n* **1** *cap* : a cat, goat, or rabbit with a long silky coat **2** : yarn or cloth made from the hair of the Angora goat or the Angora rabbit

an·gry \'aŋ-grē\ *adj* **1 a** : stirred by anger : ENRAGED, WRATHFUL **b** : showing or arising from anger **c** : threatening as if in anger **2** : painfully inflamed — **an·gri·ly** \-grə-lē\ *adv* — **an·gri·ness** \-grē-nəs\ *n*

an·guish \'aŋ-gwish\ *n* : extreme pain or distress of body or mind

an·guished \'aŋ-gwisht\ *adj* : full of anguish : TORMENTED

an·gu·lar \'aŋ-gyə-lər\ *adj* **1 a** : having one or more angles **b** : forming an angle : sharp-cornered : POINTED **2** : measured by an angle **3** : being lean and bony — **an·gu·lar·i·ty** \ˌaŋ-gyə-'lar-ət-ē\ *n* — **an·gu·lar·ly** *adv*

an·hy·drous \(ˈ)an-'hī-drəs\ *adj* : free from water

an·i·line \'an-ᵊl-ən\ *n* : an oily poisonous liquid used chiefly in organic synthesis (as of dyes)

an·i·mad·ver·sion \ˌan-ə-ˌmad-'vər-zhən\ *n* **1** : a critical remark or comment **2** : hostile criticism

an·i·mad·vert \-'vərt\ *vi* : to make a critical remark : comment unfavorably

[1]**an·i·mal** \'an-ə-məl\ *n* **1** : any of a kingdom of living beings typically differing from plants in capacity for active movement, in rapid response to stimulation, and in lack of cellulose cell walls **2 a** : one of the lower animals as distinguished from man **b** : MAMMAL

[2]**animal** *adj* **1** : of, relating to, or derived from animals **2** : of or relating to the physical nature of a person as contrasted with the intellectual; *esp* : SENSUOUS

an·i·mal·cule \ˌan-ə-'mal-ˌkyül\ *n* : a very small animal that is invisible or nearly invisible to the naked eye — **an·i·mal·cu·lar** \-'mal-kyə-lər\ *adj*

an·i·mal·ism \'an-ə-mə-ˌliz-əm\ *n* **1** : qualities typical of animals **2** : preoccupation with the satisfaction of physical drives or wants — **an·i·mal·ist** \-mə-ləst\ *n* — **an·i·mal·is·tic** \ˌan-ə-mə-'lis-tik\ *adj*

[1]**an·i·mate** \'an-ə-mət\ *adj* **1** : having life : ALIVE **2** : ANIMATED, LIVELY — **an·i·mate·ness** *n*

[2]**an·i·mate** \'an-ə-ˌmāt\ *vt* **1** : to give life to : make alive **2** : to give spirit and vigor to : ENLIVEN **3** : to give the appearance of life to; *esp* : to make appear to move

an·i·mat·ed \-ˌmāt-əd\ *adj* **1 a** : ALIVE, LIVING **b** : full of movement and activity **c** : full of vigor and spirit : VIVACIOUS **2** : having the appearance or movement of something alive — **an·i·mat·ed·ly** *adv*

an·i·ma·tion \ˌan-ə-'mā-shən\ *n* **1** : SPIRIT, LIVELINESS **2** : an animated cartoon

an·i·ma·to \ˌan-ə-'mät-ō\ *adv (or adj)* : with animation — used as a direction in music

an·i·mism \'an-ə-ˌmiz-əm\ *n* : attribution of conscious life to nature as a whole or to inanimate objects — **an·i·mist** \-məst\ *n* — **an·i·mis·tic** \ˌan-ə-'mis-tik\ *adj*

an·i·mos·i·ty \ˌan-ə-'mäs-ət-ē\ *n, pl* **-ties** : ill will or resentment tending toward active hostility

an·i·mus \'an-ə-məs\ *n* **1** : basic attitude : DISPOSITION, INTENTION **2** : deep-seated hostility : ANTAGONISM

an·ise \'an-əs\ *n* : an herb of the carrot family with aromatic seeds; *also* : ANISEED

ani·seed \'an-ə(s)-ˌsēd\ *n* : the seed of anise often used as a flavoring in cordials and in cooking

an·kle \'aŋ-kəl\ *n* : the joint between the foot and the leg; *also* : the region of this joint

an·klet \'aŋ-klət\ *n* **1** : something (as an ornament) worn around the ankle **2** : a short sock reaching slightly above the ankle

an·nal·ist \'an-ᵊl-əst\ *n* : a writer of annals : HISTORIAN

an·nals \'an-ᵊlz\ *n pl* **1** : a record of events arranged in yearly sequence **2** : historical records : CHRONICLES **3** : records of the activities of an organization

an·neal \ə-'nēl\ *vt* : to heat and then cool (as steel or glass) for softening and making less brittle

[1]**an·nex** \ə-'neks, 'an-ˌeks\ *vt* **1** : to add as a subsidiary part : APPEND **2** : to incorporate (a country or other territory) within one's own domain — **an·nex·a·tion** \ˌan-ˌek-'sā-shən\ *n* — **an·nex·a·tion·al** \-shnəl, -shən-ᵊl\ *adj* — **an·nex·a·tion·ist** \-sh(ə-)nəst\ *n*

[2]**an·nex** \'an-ˌeks, 'an-iks\ *n* : something annexed or appended; *esp* : an added part of a building

an·ni·hi·late \ə-'nī-ə-ˌlāt\ *vt* : to destroy entirely : put completely out of existence : SHATTER — **an·ni·hi·la·tion** \-ˌnī-ə-'lā-shən\ *n* — **an·ni·hi·la·tor** \-'nī-ə-ˌlāt-ər\ *n*

an·ni·ver·sa·ry \ˌan-ə-'vərs-(ə-)rē\ *n, pl* **-ries** **1** : the annual recurrence of a date marking a notable event **2** : the celebration of an anniversary

an·no Do·mi·ni \ˌan-ō-'däm-ə-nē\ *adv, often cap A* — used to indicate that a time division falls within the Christian era

an·no·tate \'an-ə-ˌtāt\ *vb* : to make or furnish critical or explanatory notes or comment — **an·no·ta·tor** \-ˌtāt-ər\ *n*

an·no·ta·tion \ˌan-ə-'tā-shən\ *n* **1** : the act of annotating **2** : a note added by way of comment or explanation

an·nounce \ə-'naủn(t)s\ *vb* **1** : to make known publicly : PROCLAIM **2 a** : to give notice of the arrival, presence, or readiness of **b** : to indicate beforehand : FORETELL **3** : to serve as an announcer

an·nounce·ment \ə-'naủn(t)s-mənt\ *n* **1** : the act of announcing **2** : a public notice announcing something

an·nounc·er \ə-'naủn(t)-sər\ *n* : one that announces; *esp* : one that introduces television or radio programs, makes announcements, and gives the news and station identification

an·noy \ə-'nȯi\ *vb* : to disturb or irritate esp. by repeated disagreeable acts : VEX — **an·noy·er** *n* — **an·noy·ing·ly** *adv*

an·noy·ance \ə-'nȯi-ən(t)s\ *n* **1 a** : the act of annoying or of being annoyed **b** : the state or feeling of being annoyed : VEXATION **2** : a source of vexation or irritation : NUISANCE

[1]**an·nu·al** \'an-y(ə-w)əl\ *adj* **1** : covering the period of a year **2** : occurring or performed once a year : YEARLY **3** : completing the life cycle in one growing season — **an·nu·al·ly** \-ē\ *adv*

[2]**annual** *n* **1** : a publication appearing yearly **2** : an event that occurs yearly **3** : an annual plant

an·nu·i·ty \ə-'n(y)ü-ət-ē\ *n, pl* **-ties** **1** : a sum of money paid at regular intervals (as every year) **2** : an insurance contract providing for the payment of an annuity

an·nul \ə-'nəl\ *vt* **an·nulled**; **an·nul·ling** **1** : to reduce to nothing : OBLITERATE **2** : to make ineffective or inoperative : NEUTRALIZE, CANCEL **3** : to declare or make legally void

an·nu·lar \'an-yə-lər\ *adj* : of, relating to, or forming a ring — **an·nu·lar·i·ty** \ˌan-yə-'lar-ət-ē\ *n*

an·nul·ment \ə-'nəl-mənt\ *n* : the act of annulling or of being annulled; *esp* : a legal declaration that a marriage is invalid

an·nun·ci·ate \ə-'nən(t)-sē-ˌāt\ *vt* : ANNOUNCE — **an·nun·ci·a·tor** \-ˌāt-ər\ *n*

an·nun·ci·a·tion \ə-ˌnən(t)-sē-'ā-shən\ *n* : the act of announcing : ANNOUNCEMENT

Annunciation *n* : March 25 observed as a church festival in commemoration of the announcement of the Incarnation

an·ode \ˈan-ˌōd\ *n* **1** : the positive electrode of an electrolytic cell to which the negative ions are attracted **2** : the negative terminal of a primary cell or of a storage battery that is delivering current **3** : the electron-collecting electrode of an electron tube — **an·od·ic** \a-ˈnäd-ik\ *adj*

an·o·dyne \ˈan-ə-ˌdīn\ *n* : something that relieves pain : a soothing agent — **an·o·dyn·ic** \ˌan-ə-ˈdin-ik\ *adj*

anoint \ə-ˈnȯint\ *vt* **1** : to rub over with oil esp. as a sacred rite **2** : to consecrate with or as if with oil — **anoint·er** *n* — **anoint·ment** *n*

anom·a·lous \ə-ˈnäm-ə-ləs\ *adj* **1** : deviating from a general rule, method, or analogy or from accepted notions of fitness or order : ABNORMAL **2** : being not what would naturally be expected — **anom·a·lous·ly** *adv* — **anom·a·lous·ness** *n*

anom·a·ly \ə-ˈnäm-ə-lē\ *n, pl* **-lies** **1** : deviation from the common rule : IRREGULARITY **2** : something anomalous

anon \ə-ˈnän\ *adv* : SOON, PRESENTLY; *also* : LATER

an·o·nym·i·ty \ˌan-ə-ˈnim-ət-ē\ *n, pl* **-ties** : the quality or state of being anonymous

anon·y·mous \ə-ˈnän-ə-məs\ *adj* **1** : having or giving no name **2** : of unknown or unnamed source or origin — **anon·y·mous·ly** *adv* — **anon·y·mous·ness** *n*

anoph·e·les \ə-ˈnäf-ə-ˌlēz\ *n* : any of a genus of mosquitoes that includes all mosquitoes which transmit malaria to man — **anoph·e·line** \-ˌlīn\ *adj or n*

[1]**an·oth·er** \ə-ˈnəth-ər\ *adj* **1** : different or distinct from the one considered **2** : some other : LATER **3** : being one more in addition : NEW

[2]**another** *pron* **1** : an additional one **2** : one that is different from the first or present one

[1]**an·swer** \ˈan(t)-sər\ *n* **1 a** : something spoken or written in reply esp. to a question **b** : a correct response **2** : a reply to a charge or accusation : DEFENSE **3** : an act done in response **4** : a solution of a problem

[2]**answer** *vb* **an·swered**; **an·swer·ing** \ˈan(t)s-(ə-)riŋ\ **1** : to speak or write in or by way of reply **2 a** : to be or make oneself responsible or accountable **b** : to make amends : ATONE **3** : CONFORM, CORRESPOND **4** : to act in response **5** : to be adequate : SERVE **6** : to offer a solution for; *esp* : SOLVE — **an·swer·er** \ˈan(t)-sər-ər\ *n*

an·swer·a·ble \ˈan(t)s-(ə-)rə-bəl\ *adj* **1** : liable to be called to account : RESPONSIBLE **2**: capable of being proved wrong

ant \ˈant\ *n* : any of a family of colonial insects that are related to the wasps and bees and have a complex social organization with various castes performing special duties

ant- — see ANTI-

ant·ac·id \(ˈ)ant-ˈas-əd\ *adj* : counteractive of acidity — **antacid** *n*

an·tag·o·nism \an-ˈtag-ə-ˌniz-əm\ *n* **1 a** : active opposition, hostility, or antipathy **b** : opposition between two conflicting forces, tendencies, or principles **2** : opposition in physiological action (as of two drugs or muscles)

an·tag·o·nist \-nəst\ *n* : one that opposes another esp. in combat : ADVERSARY

an·tag·o·nis·tic \(ˌ)an-ˌtag-ə-ˈnis-tik\ *adj* : characterized by or resulting from antagonism : OPPOSING — **an·tag·o·nis·ti·cal·ly** \-ti-k(ə-)lē\ *adv*

an·tag·o·nize \an-ˈtag-ə-ˌnīz\ *vt* **1** : to act in opposition to : COUNTERACT **2** : to incur or provoke the hostility of

ant·arc·tic \(ˈ)ant-ˈärk-tik, -ˈärt-ik\ *adj, often cap* : of or relating to the south pole or to the region near it

antarctic circle *n, often cap A & C* : a small circle of the earth parallel to its equator approximately 23° 27′ from the south pole

[1]**an·te** \ˈant-ē\ *n* : a poker stake usu. put up before the deal to build the pot

[2]**ante** *vt* **an·ted**; **an·te·ing** : to put up (an ante); *also* : PAY

an·te·bel·lum \ˌant-i-ˈbel-əm\ *adj* : existing before a war; *esp* : existing before the Civil War

[1]**an·te·ce·dent** \ˌant-ə-ˈsēd-ᵊnt\ *n* **1** : a noun, pronoun, phrase, or clause referred to by a personal or relative pronoun **2** : the first term of a mathematical ratio **3** : a preceding event, condition, or cause **4 a** : a predecessor in a series; *esp* : a model or stimulus for later developments **b** *pl* : ANCESTORS, PARENTS

[2]**antecedent** *adj* **1** : coming earlier in time or order : existing or occurring before **2** : causally or logically prior — **an·te·ce·dent·ly** *adv*

an·te·cham·ber \ˈant-i-ˌchām-bər\ *n* : an outer room leading to another usu. more important room

an·te·date \ˈant-i-ˌdāt\ *vt* **1** : to date with a date prior to that of execution or occurrence **2** : to precede in time

an·te·di·lu·vi·an \ˌant-i-də-ˈlü-vē-ən, -dī-\ *adj* **1** : of or relating to the period before the Flood described in the Bible **2** : OLD-FASHIONED, OUTMODED — **antediluvian** *n*

an·te·lope \ˈant-ᵊl-ˌōp\ *n, pl* **-lope** *or* **-lopes** : any of various Old World ruminant mammals that are related to the goats and oxen but differ from the true oxen esp. in lighter racier build and horns directed upward and backward

an·te me·ri·di·em \ˌant-i-mə-ˈrid-ē-əm, -ē-ˌem\ *adj* : being before noon

an·te·mor·tem \ˌant-i-ˈmȯrt-əm\ *adj* : preceding death

an·te·na·tal \ˌant-i-ˈnāt-ᵊl\ *adj* **1** : of or relating to an unborn child **2** : occurring during pregnancy

an·ten·na \an-ˈten-ə\ *n, pl* **-ten·nae** \-ˈten-(ˌ)ē\ *or* **-tennas** **1** : any of one or two pairs of long slender segmented sensory organs on the head of an arthropod (as an insect or a crab) **2** *pl usu antennas* : a usu. metallic device (as a rod or wire) for radiating or receiving radio waves

an·te·ri·or \an-ˈtir-ē-ər\ *adj* **1** : situated before or toward the front **2** : coming before in time : ANTECEDENT — **an·te·ri·or·ly** *adv*

an·te·room \ˈant-i-ˌrüm, -ˌru̇m\ *n* : a room used as an entrance to another : WAITING ROOM

an·them \ˈan(t)-thəm\ *n* **1** : a sacred vocal composition with words usu. from the Scriptures **2** : a song of praise or joy

an·ther \ˈan(t)-thər\ *n* : the part of a stamen that produces and contains pollen and is usu. borne on a stalk

ant·hill \ˈant-ˌhil\ *n* : a mound thrown up by ants or termites in digging their nest

an·thol·o·gy \an-ˈthäl-ə-jē\ *n, pl* **-gies** : a collection of selected literary pieces or passages — **an·thol·o·gist** \-jəst\ *n*

an·thra·cite \ˈan(t)-thrə-ˌsīt\ *n* : a hard glossy coal that burns without much smoke or flame

an·thrax \ˈan-ˌthraks\ *n* : an infectious and usu. fatal bacterial disease of warm-blooded animals (as cattle and sheep)

an·thro·po·cen·tric \ˌan(t)-thrə-pə-ˈsen-trik\ *adj* : interpreting or regarding the world in terms of human values and experiences

[1]**an·thro·poid** \ˈan(t)-thrə-ˌpȯid\ *adj* **1** : resembling man **2** : resembling an ape

[2]**anthropoid** *n* : any of several large higher apes (as a gorilla) — **an·thro·poi·dal** \ˌan(t)-thrə-ˈpȯid-ᵊl\ *adj*

an·thro·pol·o·gy \ˌan(t)-thrə-ˈpäl-ə-jē\ *n* : a science that collects and studies the facts about man and esp. about his physical characteristics, the origin and distribution of races, human environment and social relations, and culture — **an·thro·po·log·i·cal** \-pə-ˈläj-i-kəl\ *adj* — **an·thro·po·log·i·cal·ly** \-ˈläj-i-k(ə-)lē\ *adv* — **an·thro·pol·o·gist** \-ˈpäl-ə-jəst\ *n*

an·thro·po·mor·phic \ˌan(t)-thrə-pə-ˈmȯr-fik\ *adj* **1** : described or thought of as having a human form or human attributes **2** : ascribing human characteristics to nonhuman things — **an·thro·po·mor·phi·cal·ly** \-fi-k(ə-)lē\ *adv* — **an·thro·po·mor·phism** \-ˌfiz-əm\ *n*

[1]**an·ti** \ˈan-ˌtī, ˈant-ē\ *n* : one who is opposed

[2]**anti** *prep* : opposed to : AGAINST

anti- \ˌant-i, -ē; ˌan-ˌtī\ *or* **ant-** *prefix* 1 : opposite in kind, position, or action 2 : opposing : hostile toward 3 : counteractive 4 : preventive of : curative of

antiaircraft
antibacterial
anticapitalist
anticlerical
anticolonial
anti–Communism
anti–Communist
anticorrosion
antidemocratic
antidiabetic
antifascist
antigravity
anti–imperialism
anti–imperialist
antilabor
antimagnetic
antimalarial
antimicrobial
antislavery
antispasmodic
antisubmarine
antitank
antitrust

an·ti·bal·lis·tic missile \ˌant-i-bə-ˌlis-tik-\ *n* : a missile for intercepting and destroying an enemy missile in flight

an·ti·bi·ot·ic \ˌant-i-bī-ˈät-ik\ *n* : a substance produced by an organism and usu. by a fungus or bacterium that in dilute solution inhibits or kills a harmful microorganism — **antibiotic** *adj* — **an·ti·bi·ot·i·cal·ly** \-ˈät-i-k(ə-)lē\ *adv*

an·ti·body \ˈant-i-ˌbäd-ē\ *n* : an immune substance of the body that counteracts the effects of a disease-producing microorganism or its poisons

[1]**an·tic** \ˈant-ik\ *n* : a grotesquely ludicrous act or action : CAPER

[2]**antic** *adj* : whimsically gay : FROLICSOME

an·ti·christ \ˈant-i-ˌkrīst\ *n* 1 : one who denies or opposes Christ 2 : a false Christ

an·tic·i·pate \an-ˈtis-ə-ˌpāt\ *vb* 1 a : to do something before the appointed time b : to take up, use, or introduce ahead of time 2 : to be before in doing or acting : FORESTALL 3 : to see and perform beforehand 4 : to experience beforehand : look forward to : EXPECT — **an·tic·i·pa·tor** \-ˌpāt-ər\ *n*

an·tic·i·pa·tion \(ˌ)an-ˌtis-ə-ˈpā-shən\ *n* 1 a : a prior action that takes into account or forestalls a later action b : the act of looking forward : EXPECTATION; *esp* : pleasurable expectation 2 : a picturing beforehand of a future event or state — **an·tic·i·pa·to·ry** \an-ˈtis-ə-pə-ˌtōr-ē\ *adj*

an·ti·cli·max \ˌant-i-ˈklī-ˌmaks\ *n* 1 : the usu. sudden transition in writing or speaking from a significant idea to a trivial or ludicrous idea; *also* : an instance of such transition 2 : an event esp. closing a series that is strikingly less important than what has preceded it — **an·ti·cli·mac·tic** \-klī-ˈmak-tik\ *adj*

an·ti·clock·wise \ˌant-i-ˈkläk-ˌwīz\ *adj or adv* : COUNTERCLOCKWISE

an·ti·dote \ˈant-i-ˌdōt\ *n* 1 : a remedy to counteract the effects of poison 2 : something that relieves, prevents, or counteracts — **an·ti·dot·al** \ˌant-i-ˈdōt-ᵊl\ *adj* — **an·ti·dot·al·ly** \-ᵊl-ē\ *adv*

an·ti·freeze \ˈant-i-ˌfrēz\ *n* : a substance added to the liquid in an automobile radiator to prevent its freezing

an·ti·his·ta·mine \ˌant-i-ˈhis-tə-ˌmēn\ *n* : any of various drugs used for treating allergic reactions and cold symptoms presumably by inactivating histamine

an·ti–in·tel·lec·tu·al·ism \ˌant-i-ˌint-ᵊl-ˈek-ch(ə-w)ə-ˌliz-əm, ˌan-ˌtī-\ *n* : hostility toward or suspicion of intellectuals or intellectual traits and activities

an·ti·knock \ˌant-ē-ˈnäk\ *n* : a substance that when added to the fuel of an internal-combustion engine helps to prevent knocking

an·ti·log·a·rithm \ˌant-i-ˈlȯg-ə-ˌrith-əm, ˌan-ˌtī-, -ˈläg-\ *n* : the number corresponding to a given logarithm

an·ti·ma·cas·sar \ˌant-i-mə-ˈkas-ər\ *n* : a cover to protect the back or arms of furniture

an·ti·mo·ny \ˈant-ə-ˌmō-nē\ *n* : a metallic silvery white crystalline and brittle element that is used esp. as a constituent of alloys and in medicine — **an·ti·mo·ni·al** \ˌant-ə-ˈmō-nē-əl\ *adj*

an·ti·pas·to \ˌant-i-ˈpas-tō, -ˈpäs-\ *n* : HORS D'OEUVRE

an·tip·a·thy \an-ˈtip-ə-thē\ *n, pl* **-thies** 1 : strong feeling against someone or something : deep-seated dislike 2 : a person or thing that arouses strong feelings of dislike

an·ti·per·son·nel \ˌant-i-ˌpərs-ᵊn-ˈel, ˌan-ˌtī-\ *adj* : designed for use against military personnel

an·tiph·o·nal \an-ˈtif-ən-ᵊl\ *adj* : performed by two alternating groups : ANSWERING — **an·tiph·o·nal·ly** \-ᵊl-ē\ *adv*

an·tip·o·des \an-ˈtip-ə-ˌdēz\ *n pl* : the parts of the earth diametrically opposite — **an·tip·o·dal** \-ˈtip-əd-ᵊl\ *adj*

[1]**an·ti·quar·i·an** \ˌant-ə-ˈkwer-ē-ən\ *n* : ANTIQUARY

[2]**antiquarian** *adj* : of or relating to antiquaries or antiquities

an·ti·quary \ˈant-ə-ˌkwer-ē\ *n, pl* **-quar·ies** : a person who collects or studies antiquities

an·ti·quate \ˈant-ə-ˌkwāt\ *vt* : to make old or obsolete

an·ti·quat·ed \-əd\ *adj* 1 : OLD-FASHIONED, OUTMODED 2 : advanced in age

[1]**an·tique** \an-ˈtēk\ *adj* 1 a : belonging to antiquity b : being among the oldest of its class 2 : belonging to earlier periods : ANCIENT 3 : belonging to or resembling a former style or fashion : OLD-FASHIONED — **an·tique·ly** *adv* — **an·tique·ness** *n*

[2]**antique** *n* : an object of an earlier period; *esp* : a work of art, piece of furniture, or decorative object made at an earlier period

an·tiq·ui·ty \an-ˈtik-wət-ē\ *n, pl* **-ties** 1 : ancient times; *esp* : those before the Middle Ages 2 : the quality of being ancient : very great age 3 *pl* a : relics or monuments of ancient times b : matters relating to the life or culture of ancient times

an·ti–Sem·ite \ˌant-i-ˈsem-ˌīt, ˌan-ˌtī-\ *n* : one who is hostile to or discriminates against Jews — **an·ti–Se·mit·ic** \-sə-ˈmit-ik\ *adj* — **an·ti–Sem·i·tism** \-ˈsem-ə-ˌtiz-əm\ *n*

an·ti·sep·tic \ˌant-ə-ˈsep-tik\ *adj* 1 : preventing or arresting the growth of germs that cause disease or decay 2 : relating to or characterized by the use of antiseptics 3 a : protecting or protected from what is undesirable b : neat to the point of being bare or uninteresting c : COLD, IMPERSONAL — **antiseptic** *n* — **an·ti·sep·ti·cal·ly** \-ti-k(ə-)lē\ *adv*

an·ti·so·cial \ˌant-i-ˈsō-shəl, ˌan-ˌtī-\ *adj* 1 : contrary or hostile to the well-being of society 2 : disliking the society of others : MISANTHROPIC

an·tith·e·sis \an-ˈtith-ə-səs\ *n, pl* **-tith·e·ses** \-ˈtith-ə-ˌsēz\ 1 : the rhetorical contrast of ideas by means of parallel arrangements of words, clauses, or sentences 2 a : OPPOSITION, CONTRAST b : the second of two contrasted things 3 : the direct opposite : CONTRARY — **an·ti·thet·ic** \ˌant-ə-ˈthet-ik\ *adj* — **an·ti·thet·i·cal** \-ˈthet-i-kəl\ *adj*

an·ti·tox·in \ˌant-i-ˈtäk-sən\ *n* : an antibody capable of neutralizing a particular toxin that is formed when the toxin is introduced into the body and is produced commercially in lower animals for use in treating human diseases (as diphtheria) in which such a toxin is present — **an·ti·tox·ic** \-sik\ *adj*

ant·ler \ˈant-lər\ *n* : the solid deciduous horn of an animal of the deer family or a branch of such horn — **ant·lered** \-lərd\ *adj*

an·to·nym \ˈan-tə-ˌnim\ *n* : a word of opposite meaning — **an·ton·y·mous** \an-ˈtän-ə-məs\ *adj*

an·trum \ˈan-trəm\ *n, pl* **an·tra** \-trə\ : the cavity of a hollow organ or a sinus

anus \ˈā-nəs\ *n* : the posterior opening of the alimentary canal

an·vil \ˈan-vəl\ *n* : a heavy usu. steel-faced iron block on which metal is shaped

anx·i·e·ty \aŋ-ˈzī-ət-ē\ *n, pl* **-ties** 1 : painful or apprehensive uneasiness of mind usu. over an impending or anticipated ill 2 : solicitous concern or interest

anx·ious \ˈaŋ(k)-shəs\ *adj* 1 : fearful of what may happen : WORRIED 2 : desiring earnestly — **anx·ious·ly** *adv* — **anx·ious·ness** *n*

[1]**any** \ˈen-ē\ *adj* 1 a : one taken at random b : EVERY — used to indicate one selected without restriction 2 : one, some, or all indiscriminately of whatever quantity 3 : unmeasured or unlimited in amount, number, or extent

²any *pron* 1 : any person or persons 2 **a** : any thing or things **b** : any part, quantity, or number
³any *adv* : to any extent or degree : at all
any·body \'en-ē-ˌbäd-ē\ *pron* : ANYONE
any·how \-ˌhau̇\ *adv* 1 : in any way, manner, or order 2 : at any rate : in any case
any·more \ˌen-ē-'mō(ə)r\ *adv* : at the present time : NOWADAYS
any·one \'en-ē-(ˌ)wən\ *pron* : any person at all
any·place \-ˌplās\ *adv* : in any place : ANYWHERE
any·thing \-ˌthiŋ\ *pron* : any thing at all
any·way \-ˌwā\ *adv* : ANYHOW
any·where \-ˌhwe(ə)r\ *adv* : in, at, or to any place
any·wise \'en-ē-ˌwīz\ *adv* : in any way whatever : at all
A1 \'ā-'wən\ *adj* : of the finest quality : FIRST-RATE
aor·ta \ā-'ȯrt-ə\ *n, pl* **aortas** *or* **aor·tae** \-'ȯr-ˌtē\ : the main artery that carries blood from the heart to be distributed by branch arteries through the body — **aor·tal** \-'ȯrt-ᵊl\ *adj* — **aor·tic** \-'ȯrt-ik\ *adj*
apace \ə-'pās\ *adv* : at a quick pace : SWIFTLY
¹apart \ə-'pärt\ *adv* 1 : at a distance in space or time 2 : as a separate unit : INDEPENDENTLY 3 : ASIDE 4 : into two or more parts : to pieces
²apart *adj* 1 : SEPARATE, ISOLATED 2 : DIVIDED — **apart·ness** *n*
apart·heid \ə-'pär-ˌtāt, -ˌtīt\ *n* : a policy of racial segregation practiced in the Republic of So. Africa
apart·ment \ə-'pärt-mənt\ *n* 1 : a room or set of rooms used as a dwelling 2 : a building divided into individual dwelling units
ap·a·thet·ic \ˌap-ə-'thet-ik\ *adj* 1 : having or showing little or no feeling or emotion : SPIRITLESS 2 : having little or no interest or concern : INDIFFERENT — **ap·a·thet·i·cal·ly** \-'thet-i-k(ə-)lē\ *adv*
ap·a·thy \'ap-ə-thē\ *n, pl* **-thies** 1 : lack of feeling or emotion 2 : lack of interest or concern : INDIFFERENCE
¹ape \'āp\ *n* 1 : any of the larger tailless primates (as a baboon or gorilla); *also* : MONKEY 2 **a** : MIMIC **b** : a large uncouth person
²ape *vt* : COPY, MIMIC — **ap·er** *n*
ap·er·ture \'ap-ə-(r)-ˌchu̇(ə)r, -chər\ *n* : an opening or open space : HOLE
apex \'ā-ˌpeks\ *n, pl* **apex·es** *or* **api·ces** \'ā-pə-ˌsēz, 'ap-ə-\ 1 **a** : the uppermost point : VERTEX **b** : the narrowed or pointed end : TIP 2 : the highest or culminating point
apha·sia \ə-'fā-zh(ē-)ə\ *n* : loss or impairment of the power to use and understand words — **apha·si·ac** \-zē-ˌak\ *adj* — **apha·sic** \-zik\ *n or adj*
aphid \'ā-fəd, 'af-əd\ *n* : any of numerous small sluggish insects that suck the juices of plants
aphis \'ā-fəs, 'af-əs\ *n, pl* **aphi·des** \'ā-fə-ˌdēz, 'af-ə-\ : APHID
aph·o·rism \'af-ə-ˌriz-əm\ *n* : a short sentence stating a general truth or practical observation — **aph·o·ris·tic** \ˌaf-ə-'ris-tik\ *adj* — **aph·o·ris·ti·cal·ly** \-ti-k(ə-)lē\ *adv*
aph·ro·dis·i·ac \ˌaf-rə-'diz-ē-ˌak\ *adj* : exciting sexual desire — **aphrodisiac** *n* — **aph·ro·di·si·a·cal** \ˌaf-rəd-ə-'zī-ə-kəl, -'sī-\ *adj*
api·ary \'ā-pē-ˌer-ē\ *n, pl* **-ar·ies** : a place where bees are kept; *esp* : a collection of hives of bees — **api·ar·i·an** \ˌā-pē-'er-ē-ən\ *adj* — **api·a·rist** \'ā-pē-ə-rəst\ *n*
apiece \ə-'pēs\ *adv* : for each one : INDIVIDUALLY
ap·ish \'ā-pish\ *adj* 1 : given to slavish imitation 2 : extremely silly or affected — **ap·ish·ly** *adv* — **ap·ish·ness** *n*
aplomb \ə-'pläm, -'pləm\ *n* : complete composure or self-assurance : POISE
apoc·a·lypse \ə-'päk-ə-ˌlips\ *n* 1 : a writing envisaging a world cataclysm 2 : CATACLYSM — **apoc·a·lyp·tic** \ə-ˌpäk-ə-'lip-tik\ *adj* — **apoc·a·lyp·ti·cal·ly** \-'lip-ti-k(ə-)lē\ *adv*
apoc·ry·pha \ə-'päk-rə-fə\ *n sing or pl* 1 : writings or statements of dubious authenticity 2 *cap* **a** : books included in the Septuagint and Vulgate but excluded from the Jewish and Protestant canons of the Old Testament **b** : early Christian writings not included in the New Testament
apoc·ry·phal \-fəl\ *adj* 1 *often cap* : of or resembling the Apocrypha 2 : not canonical : SPURIOUS — **apoc·ry·phal·ly** \-ē\ *adv* — **apoc·ry·phal·ness** *n*
apo·gee \'ap-ə-(ˌ)jē\ *n* 1 : the point in the orbit of a satellite of the earth or of a vehicle orbiting the earth that is at the greatest distance from the center of the earth; *also* : the point farthest from a planet or a satellite (as the moon) reached by any object orbiting it 2 : the farthest or highest point : CULMINATION
apol·o·get·ic \ə-ˌpäl-ə-'jet-ik\ *adj* 1 : offered by way of excuse or apology 2 : expressing or seeming to express apology — **apol·o·get·i·cal·ly** \-'jet-i-k(ə-)lē\ *adv*
apol·o·gist \ə-'päl-ə-jəst\ *n* : one who speaks or writes in defense of a faith, a cause, or an institution
apol·o·gize \ə-'päl-ə-ˌjīz\ *vi* : to make an apology : express regret for something one has done — **apol·o·giz·er** *n*
apol·o·gy \-jē\ *n, pl* **-gies** 1 : a formal justification or defense 2 : an admission of error or discourtesy accompanied by an expression of regret 3 : a poor substitute
ap·o·plec·tic \ˌap-ə-'plek-tik\ *adj* 1 : of, relating to, or caused by apoplexy 2 : affected with or inclined to apoplexy — **ap·o·plec·ti·cal·ly** \-ti-k(ə-)lē\ *adv*
ap·o·plexy \'ap-ə-ˌplek-sē\ *n, pl* **-plex·ies** : sudden weakening or loss of consciousness, sensation, and voluntary motion caused by rupture or obstruction of an artery of the brain (as by a clot)
aport \ə-'pōrt\ *adv (or adj)* : on or toward the left side of a ship
apos·ta·sy \ə-'päs-tə-sē\ *n, pl* **-sies** 1 : renunciation of a religious faith 2 : abandonment of a previous loyalty : DEFECTION
apos·tate \ə-'päs-ˌtāt, -tət\ *n* : one who commits apostasy — **apostate** *adj*
a pos·te·ri·o·ri \ˌä-pō-ˌstir-ē-'ōr-ē\ *adj* : of or relating to reasoning from known or observed facts to a conclusion — **a posteriori** *adv*
apos·tle \ə-'päs-əl\ *n* 1 : one sent on a religious mission 2 : ADVOCATE, PROPAGANDIST; *esp* : one who first advocates a viewpoint — **apos·tle·ship** \-əl-ˌship\ *n*
apos·to·late \ə-'päs-tə-ˌlāt, -lət\ *n* : the office or mission of an apostle
ap·os·tol·ic \ˌap-ə-'stäl-ik\ *adj* 1 **a** : of or relating to an apostle **b** : of or relating to the New Testament apostles or their times 2 : of or forming a succession of spiritual authority from the apostles held in Catholic tradition to be perpetuated by successive ordinations of bishops and to be necessary for the validity of sacraments and orders — **apos·to·lic·i·ty** \ə-ˌpäs-tə-'lis-ət-ē\ *n*
¹apos·tro·phe \ə-'päs-trə-(ˌ)fē\ *n* : the rhetorical addressing of an absent person as if present or of an abstract idea or inanimate object as if capable of understanding (as in "O grave, where is thy victory?")
²apostrophe *n* : a mark ' or ˈ used to show the omission of letters or figures (as in *can't* for *cannot* or '*76* for *1776*), the possessive case (as in *James's*), or the plural of letters or figures (as in *cross your t's, six 7's*)
apos·tro·phize \ə-'päs-trə-ˌfīz\ *vb* 1 : to address by or in apostrophe 2 : to make use of apostrophe
apothecaries' measure *n* : a measure of capacity used by pharmacists
apothecaries' weight *n* : a measure of weight used by pharmacists
apoth·e·cary \ə-'päth-ə-ˌker-ē\ *n, pl* **-car·ies** : DRUGGIST
apo·thegm \'ap-ə-ˌthem\ *n* : a short, pithy, and instructive saying or formulation : APHORISM

apo·the·o·sis \ə-ˌpäth-ē-ˈō-səs, ˌap-ə-ˈthē-ə-səs\ *n, pl* **-o·ses** \-ˈō-ˌsēz, -ə-ˌsēz\ **1 :** elevation to divine status : DEIFICATION **2 :** a perfect example — **ap·o·the·o·size** \ˌap-ə-ˈthē-ə-ˌsīz, ə-ˈpäth-ē-ə-\ *vt*

ap·pall \ə-ˈpȯl\ *vt* **ap·palled; ap·pal·ling :** to overcome with fear or dread

ap·pall·ing \-iŋ\ *adj* **:** inspiring horror or dismay : SHOCKING — **ap·pall·ing·ly** *adv*

ap·pa·nage \ˈap-ə-nij\ *n* **1 a :** a grant (as of land or revenue) made by a sovereign or a legislative body to a member of the royal family or a nobleman **b :** a customary or rightful possession or privilege **2 :** a natural accompaniment or endowment

ap·pa·rat·us \ˌap-ə-ˈrat-əs, -ˈrāt-\ *n, pl* **-ratus** *or* **-rat·us·es** **1 a :** the equipment used to do a particular kind of work **b :** an instrument or appliance for a specific operation **2 :** the system of persons and agencies through which an organization functions

¹ap·par·el \ə-ˈpar-əl\ *vt* **-eled** *or* **-elled; -el·ing** *or* **-el·ling** **1 :** CLOTHE, DRESS **2 :** ADORN, EMBELLISH

²apparel *n* **:** personal attire : CLOTHING

ap·par·ent \ə-ˈpar-ənt\ *adj* **1 :** open to view : VISIBLE **2 :** clear to the understanding : EVIDENT **3 :** appearing as actual to the eye or mind **4 :** appearing to be reasonably true — **ap·par·ent·ly** *adv* — **ap·par·ent·ness** *n*

ap·pa·ri·tion \ˌap-ə-ˈrish-ən\ *n* **1 a :** an unusual or unexpected sight : PHENOMENON **b :** a ghostly figure : GHOST **2 :** APPEARANCE

¹ap·peal \ə-ˈpēl\ *n* **1 a :** a legal proceeding by which a case is brought from a lower to a higher court for a reexamination **b :** a request for a review of a decision by a higher authority **2 :** an earnest request : PLEA **3 :** the power of arousing a sympathetic response : ATTRACTION

²appeal *vb* **1 :** to charge with a crime : ACCUSE **2 :** to take action to have a case or decision reviewed by a higher court or authority **3 :** to call upon another for corroboration or vindication **4 :** to make an earnest request **5 :** to arouse a sympathetic response — **ap·peal·a·ble** *adj*

ap·peal·ing \-iŋ\ *adj* **:** arousing interest esp. by beauty or charm : ATTRACTIVE — **ap·peal·ing·ly** *adv*

ap·pear \ə-ˈpi(ə)r\ *vi* **1 :** to come into sight : become evident : SHOW **2 :** to present oneself formally (as to answer a charge, give testimony, or plead a cause) **3 :** to become clear to the mind **4 a :** to come out in printed form **b :** to come before the public on stage or screen **5 :** SEEM, LOOK

ap·pear·ance \ə-ˈpir-ən(t)s\ *n* **1 :** the act, action, or process of appearing **2 a :** outward aspect : LOOK **b :** external show : SEMBLANCE **c** *pl* **:** outward indications **3 a :** something that appears : PHENOMENON **b :** an instance of appearing

ap·pease \ə-ˈpēz\ *vt* **1 :** to make calm or quiet : ALLAY **2 :** to make concessions to (a potential aggressor) usu. at the sacrifice of principles in order to avoid war : CONCILIATE — **ap·pease·ment** *n* — **ap·peas·er** *n*

¹ap·pel·lant \ə-ˈpel-ənt\ *adj* **:** making an appeal

²appellant *n* **:** one that appeals; *esp* **:** one that appeals from a judicial decision or decree

ap·pel·late \ə-ˈpel-ət\ *adj* **:** of or relating to appeals; *esp* **:** having the power to review the decisions of a lower court

ap·pel·la·tion \ˌap-ə-ˈlā-shən\ *n* **:** identifying or descriptive name or title : DESIGNATION

ap·pend \ə-ˈpend\ *vt* **1 :** ATTACH, AFFIX **2 :** to add as a supplement or appendix

ap·pend·age \ə-ˈpen-dij\ *n* **:** something attached to a larger or more important thing

ap·pen·dec·to·my \ˌap-ən-ˈdek-tə-mē\ *n, pl* **-mies :** surgical removal of the human appendix

ap·pen·di·ci·tis \ə-ˌpen-də-ˈsīt-əs\ *n* **:** inflammation of the appendix

ap·pen·dix \ə-ˈpen-diks\ *n, pl* **-dix·es** *or* **-di·ces** \-də-ˌsēz\ **1 :** supplementary material usu. attached at the end of a piece of writing **2 :** a small tubular outgrowth from the cecum of the intestine

ap·per·tain \ˌap-ər-ˈtān\ *vi* **:** to belong or be connected as a possession, part, or right : PERTAIN

ap·pe·tite \ˈap-ə-ˌtīt\ *n* **1 :** one of the instinctive desires necessary to keep up organic life; *esp* **:** the desire to eat **2 a :** an inherent craving **b :** TASTE, PREFERENCE

ap·pe·tiz·er \-ˌtī-zər\ *n* **:** a food or drink that stimulates the appetite and is usu. served before a meal

ap·pe·tiz·ing \-ˌtī-ziŋ\ *adj* **:** appealing to the appetite

ap·plaud \ə-ˈplȯd\ *vb* **1 :** PRAISE, APPROVE **2 :** to show approval esp. by clapping the hands — **ap·plaud·a·ble** *adj* — **ap·plaud·er** *n*

ap·plause \ə-ˈplȯz\ *n* **:** approval publicly expressed (as by clapping the hands) : ACCLAIM

ap·ple \ˈap-əl\ *n* **:** a rounded fruit with a red, yellow, or green skin, firm white flesh, a seedy core, and usu. a tart taste; *also* **:** the tree of the rose family that bears this fruit

ap·ple·jack \ˈap-əl-ˌjak\ *n* **:** brandy distilled from cider

ap·pli·ance \ə-ˈplī-ən(t)s\ *n* **1 :** a piece of equipment for adapting a tool or machine to a special purpose : ATTACHMENT **2 :** an instrument or device designed for a particular use **3 :** a piece (as a stove, toaster, refrigerator, or vacuum cleaner) of household or office equipment that is operated by gas, electricity, or a small electric motor

ap·pli·ca·ble \ˈap-li-kə-bəl, ə-ˈplik-ə-\ *adj* **:** capable of being or suitable to be applied : APPROPRIATE — **ap·pli·ca·bil·i·ty** \ˌap-li-kə-ˈbil-ət-ē, ə-ˌplik-ə-\ *n*

ap·pli·cant \ˈap-li-kənt\ *n* **:** one who applies for something

ap·pli·ca·tion \ˌap-lə-ˈkā-shən\ *n* **1 :** the act or an instance of applying **2 :** something put or spread on a surface **3 :** ability to fix one's attention on a task **4 a :** PETITION **b :** a request made personally or in writing; *also* **:** a form used in making such a request **5 :** capacity for practical use

ap·pli·ca·tor \ˈap-lə-ˌkāt-ər\ *n* **:** one that applies; *esp* **:** a device for applying a substance (as medicine or polish)

ap·plied \ə-ˈplīd\ *adj* **:** put to practical use; *esp* **:** applying general principles to solve definite problems

¹ap·pli·qué \ˌap-lə-ˈkā\ *n* **:** a cutout decoration fastened to a larger piece of material

²appliqué *vt* **-quéd; -qué·ing :** to apply (as a decoration or ornament) to a larger surface

ap·ply \ə-ˈplī\ *vb* **ap·plied; ap·ply·ing** **1 a :** to put to use esp. for some practical or specific purpose **b :** to bring into action **c :** to lay or spread on **d :** to place in contact **e :** to put into operation or effect **2 :** to employ diligently or with close attention **3 :** to have relevance or a valid connection **4 :** to make an appeal or request esp. in the form of a written application — **ap·pli·er** *n*

ap·point \ə-ˈpȯint\ *vt* **1 :** to fix or set officially **2 :** to name officially esp. to an office or position

ap·point·ed \-əd\ *adj* **:** FURNISHED, EQUIPPED

ap·poin·tee \ə-ˌpȯin-ˈtē, ˌa-ˌpȯin-\ *n* **:** a person appointed to a position or an office

ap·point·ive \ə-ˈpȯint-iv\ *adj* **:** of, relating to, or filled by appointment

ap·point·ment \ə-ˈpȯint-mənt\ *n* **1 :** the act or an instance of appointing : DESIGNATION **2 :** a position or office to which a person is named but not elected **3 :** an agreement to meet at a fixed time **4 :** EQUIPMENT, FURNISHINGS — usu. used in pl.

ap·por·tion \ə-ˈpōr-shən\ *vt* **-tioned; -tion·ing** \-sh(ə-)niŋ\ **:** to divide and distribute proportionately

ap·por·tion·ment \-shən-mənt\ *n* **:** the act or result of apportioning; *esp* **:** the apportioning of representatives or taxes among states or districts according to population

ap·po·site \'ap-ə-zət\ *adj* : highly pertinent or appropriate : APT — **ap·po·site·ly** *adv* — **ap·po·site·ness** *n*

ap·po·si·tion \ˌap-ə-'zish-ən\ *n* : a grammatical construction in which a noun or noun equivalent is followed by another that explains it (as *the poet* and *Burns* in "a biography of the poet Burns"); *also* : the relation of one of such a pair of nouns or noun equivalents to the other — **ap·po·si·tion·al** \-'zish-nəl, -ən-ᵊl\ *adj* — **ap·po·si·tion·al·ly** \-ē\ *adv*

[1]**ap·pos·i·tive** \ə-'päz-ət-iv\ *adj* : of, relating to, or standing in grammatical apposition — **ap·pos·i·tive·ly** *adv*

[2]**appositive** *n* : the second of a pair of nouns or noun equivalents in apposition

ap·prais·al \ə-'prā-zəl\ *n* **1** : an act or instance of appraising **2** : a determination of the value of property by an appraiser; *also* : the value so determined

ap·praise \ə-'prāz\ *vt* : to set a value on; *esp* : to determine the money value of — **ap·praise·ment** *n*

ap·prais·er \ə-'prā-zər\ *n* : one that appraises; *esp* : an official who appraises real estate and personal property for purposes of taxation

ap·pre·cia·ble \ə-'prē-shə-bəl\ *adj* : large enough to be recognized and measured or to be felt — **ap·pre·cia·bly** \-blē\ *adv*

ap·pre·ci·ate \ə-'prē-shē-ˌāt\ *vb* **1 a** : to evaluate the worth, quality, or significance of **b** : to admire greatly **c** : to judge with heightened perception or understanding : be fully aware of **d** : to recognize with gratitude **2** : to increase in number or value — **ap·pre·ci·a·tor** \-ˌāt-ər\ *n* — **ap·pre·cia·to·ry** \-shə-ˌtōr-ē\ *adj*

ap·pre·ci·a·tion \ə-ˌprē-shē-'ā-shən\ *n* **1** : the act of appreciating **2** : awareness or understanding of worth or value **3** : a rise in value

ap·pre·cia·tive \ə-'prē-shət-iv, -shē-ˌāt-iv\ *adj* : having or showing appreciation — **ap·pre·cia·tive·ly** *adv*

ap·pre·hend \ˌap-ri-'hend\ *vb* **1** : ARREST, SEIZE **2 a** : to become aware of : PERCEIVE **b** : to anticipate esp. with anxiety, dread, or fear **3** : to grasp with the understanding : UNDERSTAND — **ap·pre·hen·si·ble** \-'hen(t)-sə-bəl\ *adj* — **ap·pre·hen·si·bly** \-blē\ *adv*

ap·pre·hen·sion \ˌap-ri-'hen-chən\ *n* **1** : CAPTURE, ARREST **2** : UNDERSTANDING, COMPREHENSION **3** : fear of what may be coming : dread of the future

ap·pre·hen·sive \ˌap-ri-'hen(t)-siv\ *adj* : feeling apprehension : fearful of what may be coming — **ap·pre·hen·sive·ly** *adv* — **ap·pre·hen·sive·ness** *n*

[1]**ap·pren·tice** \ə-'prent-əs\ *n* **1** : one legally bound to serve a master for a term in consideration of instruction in an art or trade and formerly usu. of maintenance **2** : one who is learning a trade, art, or calling by practical experience under skilled workers — **ap·pren·tice·ship** \-ˌship\ *n*

[2]**apprentice** *vt* : to bind or set at work as an apprentice

ap·prise \ə-'prīz\ *vt* : to give notice to : INFORM

[1]**ap·proach** \ə-'prōch\ *vb* **1 a** : to draw close : come near or nearer : NEAR **b** : APPROXIMATE **2** : to take preliminary steps toward

[2]**approach** *n* **1 a** : an act or instance of approaching **b** : APPROXIMATION **2 a** : a preliminary step **b** : manner of advance **3** : a means of access : AVENUE

ap·proach·a·ble \ə-'prō-chə-bəl\ *adj* : capable of being approached : ACCESSIBLE; *esp* : easy to meet or deal with

ap·pro·ba·tion \ˌap-rə-'bā-shən\ *n* : COMMENDATION, PRAISE

[1]**ap·pro·pri·ate** \ə-'prō-prē-ˌāt\ *vt* **1** : to take exclusive possession of : ANNEX **2** : to set apart for a particular purpose or use **3** : to take without permission — **ap·pro·pri·a·tor** \-ˌāt-ər\ *n*

[2]**ap·pro·pri·ate** \-prē-ət\ *adj* : especially suitable or fitting : PROPER — **ap·pro·pri·ate·ly** *adv* — **ap·pro·pri·ate·ness** *n*

ap·pro·pri·a·tion \ə-ˌprō-prē-'ā-shən\ *n* **1** : an act or instance of appropriating **2** : something that has been appropriated; *esp* : a sum of money formally set aside for a specific use

ap·prov·al \ə-'prü-vəl\ *n* : an act or instance of approving : APPROBATION — **on approval** : subject to a prospective buyer's acceptance or refusal

ap·prove \ə-'prüv\ *vb* **1** : to have or express a favorable judgment : take a favorable view **2 a** : to accept as satisfactory **b** : to give formal or official sanction to — **ap·prov·ing·ly** *adv*

[1]**ap·prox·i·mate** \ə-'präk-sə-mət\ *adj* : nearly correct or exact — **ap·prox·i·mate·ly** *adv*

[2]**ap·prox·i·mate** \-ˌmāt\ *vt* **1 a** : to bring near or close **b** : to bring together **2** : to come near : APPROACH

ap·prox·i·ma·tion \ə-ˌpräk-sə-'mā-shən\ *n* **1** : the act or process of approximating **2** : the quality or state of being close esp. in value **3** : something that is approximate; *esp* : a nearly exact estimate of a value — **ap·prox·i·ma·tive** \ə-'präk-sə-ˌmāt-iv\ *adj* — **ap·prox·i·ma·tive·ly** *adv*

ap·pur·te·nance \ə-'pərt-nən(t)s, -ᵊn-ən(t)s\ *n* : something (as a right or fixture) that belongs to or goes along with another usu. larger and more important thing — **ap·pur·te·nant** \-'pərt-nənt, -ᵊn-ənt\ *adj*

apri·cot \'ap-rə-ˌkät, 'ā-prə-\ *n* : an oval orange-colored fruit resembling the related peach and plum in flavor; *also* : a tree that bears apricots

April \'ā-prəl\ *n* : the 4th month of the year

a pri·o·ri \ˌä-prē-'ōr-ē\ *adj* **1** : of or relating to reasoning from self-evident propositions **2** : estimated from available facts without close examination : PRESUMPTIVE — **a priori** *adv*

apron \'ā-prən, -pərn\ *n* **1** : a garment worn on the front of the body to protect the clothing **2** : something resembling an apron in shape, position, or use: as **a** : the part of the stage in front of the proscenium arch **b** : the extensive paved part of an airport immediately adjacent to the terminal area or hangars

[1]**ap·ro·pos** \ˌap-rə-'pō, 'ap-rə-ˌ\ *adv* **1** : at the right time : SEASONABLY **2** : INCIDENTALLY

[2]**apropos** *adj* : being to the point : PERTINENT

apropos of *prep* : with regard to : CONCERNING

apse \'aps\ *n* : a vaulted semicircular or polygonal projection on the end of a church or other building

apt \'apt\ *adj* **1** : FITTING, SUITABLE **2** : having an habitual tendency or inclination : LIKELY **3** : quick to learn — **apt·ly** *adv* — **apt·ness** *n*

ap·ti·tude \'ap-tə-ˌt(y)üd\ *n* **1** : capacity for learning : APTNESS **2 a** : INCLINATION, TENDENCY **b** : a natural ability : TALENT **3** : general suitability : APPROPRIATENESS — **ap·ti·tu·di·nal** \ˌap-tə-'t(y)üd-ᵊn-əl\ *adj*

aq·ua·cade \'ak-wə-ˌkād, 'äk-\ *n* : an elaborate water spectacle consisting of exhibitions of swimming, diving, and acrobatics accompanied by music

aqua·lung·er \'ak-wə-ˌləŋ-ər, 'äk-\ : one who swims under water with the aid of scuba gear

aq·ua·ma·rine \ˌak-wə-mə-'rēn, ˌäk-\ *n* : a transparent semiprecious bluish or greenish stone that is a variety of beryl

aq·ua·plane \'ak-wə-ˌplān, 'äk-\ *n* : a board towed behind a speeding motorboat and ridden by a person standing on it — **aquaplane** *vi* — **aq·ua·plan·er** *n*

aquar·ist \ə-'kwer-əst\ *n* : a person who keeps an aquarium

aquar·i·um \ə-'kwer-ē-əm\ *n, pl* **-i·ums** *or* **-ia** \-ē-ə\ : a container (as a glass tank) in which living water animals or plants are kept; *also* : an establishment where such aquatic collections are kept and shown

[1]**aquat·ic** \ə-'kwät-ik, -'kwat-\ *adj* **1** : growing or living in or frequenting water **2** : performed in or on water

[2]**aquatic** *n* **1** : an aquatic animal or plant **2** *pl* : water sports

aq·ua·tint \'ak-wə-ˌtint, 'äk-\ *n* : an etching in which spaces are eaten in with nitric acid to produce an effect resembling a drawing (as in watercolors)

aq·ue·duct \'ak-wə-ˌdəkt\ *n* **1 :** an artificial channel for carrying flowing water from place to place; *esp* **:** a structure that carries the water of a canal across a river or hollow **2 :** a canal or passage in a body part or organ

aque·ous \'ā-kwē-əs, 'ak-wē-\ *adj* **1 :** of, relating to, or resembling water **2 :** made of, by, or with water

aq·ui·line \'ak-wə-ˌlīn, -lən\ *adj* **1 :** of, relating to, or resembling an eagle **2 :** curving like an eagle's beak — **aq·ui·lin·i·ty** \ˌak-wə-'lin-ət-ē\ *n*

ar·a·besque \ˌar-ə-'besk\ *n* **:** an ornament or a style of decoration consisting of interlacing lines and figures usu. of flowers, foliage, or fruit — **arabesque** *adj*

ar·a·bic numeral \ˌar-ə-bik-\ *n, often cap A* **:** one of the number symbols 1, 2, 3, 4, 5, 6, 7, 8, 9, and 0

ar·a·ble \'ar-ə-bəl\ *adj* **:** fit for or cultivated by plowing or tillage **:** suitable for producing crops — **ar·a·bil·i·ty** \ˌar-ə-'bil-ət-ē\ *n* — **arable** *n*

ar·ba·lest *or* **ar·ba·list** \'är-bə-ləst\ *n* **:** a medieval crossbow with a steel bow

ar·bi·ter \'är-bət-ər\ *n* **1 :** a person delegated to decide a dispute **:** ARBITRATOR, UMPIRE **2 :** a person having absolute authority to judge and decide what is right or proper

ar·bit·ra·ment \är-'bi-trə-mənt\ *n* **1 :** the settling of a dispute by an arbiter **2 :** a decision or award made by an arbiter

ar·bi·trary \'är-bə-ˌtrer-ē\ *adj* **1 :** depending on choice or discretion **2 :** arising from or guided by ungoverned will, impulse, caprice, or judgment **3 :** selected at random or without reason — **ar·bi·trar·i·ly** \ˌär-bə-'trer-ə-lē\ *adv* — **ar·bi·trar·i·ness** \'är-bə-ˌtrer-ē-nəs\ *n*

ar·bi·trate \'är-bə-ˌtrāt\ *vb* **1 :** to settle a dispute after hearing and considering the arguments of both sides **:** hear and decide as an arbiter **2 :** to refer a dispute to others for settlement **:** submit to arbitration — **ar·bi·tra·ble** \-bə-trə-bəl\ *adj* — **ar·bi·tra·tive** \-ˌtrāt-iv\ *adj*

ar·bi·tra·tion \ˌär-bə-'trā-shən\ *n* **:** the act of arbitrating; *esp* **:** the settling of a dispute in which both parties agree beforehand to abide by the decision of an arbitrator

ar·bi·tra·tor \'är-bə-ˌtrāt-ər\ *n* **:** a person chosen to settle differences between two parties in controversy **:** ARBITER

ar·bor \'är-bər\ *n* **:** a bower of vines or branches or of latticework covered with climbing shrubs or vines

ar·bo·re·al \är-'bōr-ē-əl\ *adj* **1 :** of, relating to, or resembling a tree **2 :** living in or frequenting trees — **ar·bo·re·al·ly** \-ē\ *adv*

ar·bo·re·tum \ˌär-bə-'rēt-əm\ *n, pl* **-retums** *or* **-re·ta** \-'rēt-ə\ **:** a place where trees and plants are grown for scientific and educational purposes

ar·bor·ist \'är-bə-rəst\ *n* **:** a specialist in the care and maintenance of trees

ar·bor·vi·tae \ˌär-bər-'vīt-ē\ *n* **:** any of various evergreen trees of the pine family with closely overlapping scale leaves that are often grown for ornament and hedges

ar·bu·tus \är-'byüt-əs\ *n* **:** any of a genus of shrubs and trees of the heath family with white or pink flowers and scarlet berries; *also* **:** a related trailing plant of eastern No. America with fragrant pinkish flowers borne in early spring

arc \'ärk\ *n* **1 :** something arched or curved; *esp* **:** a sustained luminous discharge of electricity across a gap in a circuit or between electrodes **2 :** a continuous portion of a circle or other curve

ar·cade \är-'kād\ *n* **1 :** a row of arches with the columns that support them **2 :** an arched or covered passageway; *esp* **:** one lined with shops — **ar·cad·ed** \-əd\ *adj*

ar·cane \är-'kān\ *adj* **:** SECRET, MYSTERIOUS

¹arch \'ärch\ *n* **1 :** a usu. curved structural member spanning an opening and serving as a support (as for the wall above the opening) **2 :** something resembling an arch in form or function **3 :** ARCHWAY

²arch *vb* **1 :** to cover or provide with an arch **2 :** to form or bend into an arch **3 :** to move in an arch

³arch \'ärch\ *adj* **1 :** PRINCIPAL, CHIEF **2 a :** cleverly sly and alert **b :** playfully saucy **:** ROGUISH

ar·chae·ol·o·gy *or* **ar·che·ol·o·gy** \ˌär-kē-'äl-ə-jē\ *n* **:** the science that deals with past human life and activities as shown by fossil relics and the monuments and artifacts left by ancient peoples — **ar·chae·o·log·i·cal** \-kē-ə-'läj-i-kəl\ *adj* — **ar·chae·ol·o·gist** \-kē-'äl-ə-jəst\ *n*

ar·cha·ic \är-'kā-ik\ *adj* **1 :** of, relating to, or characteristic of an earlier or more primitive time **:** ANTIQUATED **2 :** having the characteristics of the language of the past and surviving chiefly in specialized uses **3 :** surviving from an earlier period

ar·cha·ism \'är-kē-ˌiz-əm, -kā-\ *n* **1 :** the use of archaic words **2 :** an archaic word or expression

arch·an·gel \'ärk-ˌān-jəl\ *n* **:** an angel of high rank — **arch·an·gel·ic** \ˌärk-ˌan-'jel-ik\ *adj*

arch·bish·op \(')ärch-'bish-əp\ *n* **:** the bishop of highest rank in a group of dioceses — **arch·bish·op·ric** \-'bish-ə-(ˌ)prik\ *n*

arch·dea·con \(')ärch-'dē-kən\ *n* **:** an Anglican priest who supervises a part of a diocese or the missionary work of a diocese — **arch·dea·con·ate** \-kə-nət\ *n* — **arch·dea·con·ry** \-kən-rē\ *n*

arch·di·o·cese \(')ärch-'dī-ə-səs\ *n* **:** the diocese of an archbishop — **arch·di·oc·e·san** \ˌärch-dī-'äs-ə-sən\ *adj*

arch·du·cal \(')ärch-'d(y)ü-kəl\ *adj* **:** of or relating to an archduke or archduchy

arch·duch·ess \(')ärch-'dəch-əs\ *n* **1 :** the wife or widow of an archduke **2 :** a woman having in her own right the rank of archduke

arch·duchy \-'dəch-ē\ *n* **:** the territory of an archduke or archduchess

arch·duke \-'d(y)ük\ *n* **:** a sovereign prince; *esp* **:** a prince of the imperial family of Austria — **arch·duke·dom** \-dəm\ *n*

arch·en·e·my \(')ärch-'en-ə-mē\ *n* **:** a principal enemy

ar·cher \'är-chər\ *n* **:** one who uses a bow and arrow

ar·chery \'ärch-(ə-)rē\ *n* **1 :** the art, practice, or skill of shooting with bow and arrow **2 :** a body of archers

ar·che·type \'är-ki-ˌtīp\ *n* **:** the original pattern or model of a work or the model from which others are copied — **ar·che·typ·al** \ˌär-ki-'tī-pəl\ *or* **ar·che·typ·i·cal** \-'tip-i-kəl\ *adj*

arch·fiend \(')ärch-'fēnd\ *n* **:** a chief fiend; *esp* **:** SATAN

ar·chi·epis·co·pal \ˌär-kē-ə-'pis-kə-pəl\ *adj* **:** of or relating to an archbishop

ar·chi·pel·a·go \ˌär-kə-'pel-ə-ˌgō, ˌär-chə-\ *n, pl* **-goes** *or* **-gos** **:** a sea or other expanse of water with many scattered islands; *also* **:** a group of islands in such a body of water — **ar·chi·pe·lag·ic** \-pə-'laj-ik\ *adj*

ar·chi·tect \'är-kə-ˌtekt\ *n* **:** a person who designs buildings and oversees their construction

ar·chi·tec·ton·ic \ˌär-kə-ˌtek-'tän-ik\ *adj* **:** of, relating to, or according with the principles of architecture **:** ARCHITECTURAL — **ar·chi·tec·ton·i·cal·ly** \-'tän-i-k(ə-)lē\ *adv*

ar·chi·tec·ton·ics \-'tän-iks\ *n sing or pl* **:** structural design **:** STRUCTURE, ORDER, PLAN

ar·chi·tec·tur·al \ˌär-kə-'tek-chə-rəl\ *adj* **:** of, relating to, or conforming to the rules of architecture — **ar·chi·tec·tur·al·ly** \-ē\ *adv*

ar·chi·tec·ture \'är-kə-ˌtek-chər\ *n* **1 :** the art of making plans for buildings **2 :** the style of building that architects produce or imitate **3 :** architectural work **:** BUILDINGS

ar·chi·trave \'är-kə-ˌtrāv\ *n* **:** the supporting horizontal member just above the columns in a building in the classical style of architecture

ar·chive \'är-ˌkīv\ *n* **:** a place in which public records or historical documents are preserved; *also* : the material preserved — usu. used in pl. — **ar·chi·val** \är-'kī-vəl\ *adj*

ar·chi·vist \'är-kə-vəst, -ˌkī-\ *n* : a person in charge of archives

arch·ly \'ärch-lē\ *adv* : in an arch manner : ROGUISHLY, MISCHIEVOUSLY

ar·chon \'är-ˌkän, -kən\ *n* : one of the chief magistrates in ancient Athens

arch·way \'ärch-ˌwā\ *n* : a way or passage under an arch; *also* : an arch over a passage

¹arc·tic \'ärk-tik, 'ärt-ik\ *adj* **1** *often cap* : of or relating to the north pole or the region around it **2** : very cold : FRIGID

²arc·tic \'ärt-ik, 'ärk-tik\ *n* : a rubber overshoe reaching to the ankle or above

arctic circle *n, often cap A & C* : a circle of the earth parallel to its equator approximately 23° 27′ from the north pole

ar·dent \'ärd-ᵊnt\ *adj* **1 a** : characterized by warmth of feeling : PASSIONATE **b** : ZEALOUS, DEVOTED **2** : FIERY, HOT **3** : GLOWING, SHINING — **ar·den·cy** \-ᵊn-sē\ *n* — **ar·dent·ly** *adv*

ar·dor \'ärd-ər\ *n* **1 a** : a warmth of feeling or sentiment **b** : extreme vigor or energy : INTENSITY **2** : ZEAL, EAGERNESS

ar·du·ous \'ärj-(ə-)wəs\ *adj* : extremely difficult : LABORIOUS, STRENUOUS — **ar·du·ous·ly** *adv* — **ar·du·ous·ness** *n*

¹are *pres 2d sing or pres pl of* BE

²are \'a(ə)r, 'e(ə)r, 'är\ *n* : a unit of area equal to 100 square meters

ar·ea \'ar-ē-ə\ *n* **1** : a flat surface or space; *esp* : a level piece of ground **2** : the amount of surface included within a closed figure; *also* : the number of unit squares equal in measure to the surface **3 a** : REGION **b** : a field of activity — **ar·e·al** \-ē-əl\ *adj* — **ar·e·al·ly** \-ē-ə-lē\ *adv*

area·way \-ē-ə-ˌwā\ *n* : a sunken space affording access, air, and light to a basement

are·na \ə-'rē-nə\ *n* **1** : an area in a Roman amphitheater for gladiatorial combats **2 a** : an enclosed area used for public entertainment **b** : a building containing an arena **3** : a sphere of interest or activity

arête \ə-'rāt\ *n* : a sharp-crested ridge in rugged mountains

ar·gent \'är-jənt\ *adj* : of or resembling silver : SILVERY, WHITE, SHINING

ar·gon \'är-ˌgän\ *n* : a colorless odorless inert gaseous chemical element found in the air and in volcanic gases and used for filling electric light bulbs

ar·go·sy \'är-gə-sē\ *n, pl* **-sies** **1** : a large ship; *esp* : a large merchant ship **2** : a fleet of ships

ar·got \'ar-gət, -ˌgō\ *n* : the language of a particular group or class esp. of the underworld

ar·gu·a·ble \'är-gyə-wə-bəl\ *adj* : open to argument, dispute, or question — **ar·gu·a·bly** \-blē\ *adv*

ar·gue \'är-(ˌ)gyü\ *vb* **1** : to give reasons for or against **2** : to debate or discuss some matter : DISPUTE **3** : to persuade by giving reasons **4** : INDICATE — **ar·gu·er** *n*

ar·gu·ment \'är-gyə-mənt\ *n* **1 a** : a reason for or against something **b** : a discussion in which arguments are presented : DISPUTE, DEBATE **2** : a heated dispute : QUARREL **3** : the subject matter or topic (as of a book) or a summary of such subject matter

ar·gu·men·ta·tion \ˌär-gyə-mən-'tā-shən\ *n* **1** : the act or process of forming reasons and of drawing conclusions and applying them to a case under discussion **2** : DEBATE, DISCUSSION

ar·gu·men·ta·tive \ˌär-gyə-'ment-ət-iv\ *adj* : marked by or given to argument : DISPUTATIOUS — **ar·gu·men·ta·tive·ly** *adv*

ar·gyle \'är-ˌgīl\ *n* : a geometric knitting pattern of varicolored diamonds on a single background color; *also* : a sock knit in this pattern

aria \'är-ē-ə\ *n* : AIR, MELODY, TUNE; *esp* : an accompanied elaborate melody sung (as in an opera) by a single voice

ar·id \'ar-əd\ *adj* : excessively dry; *esp* : having insufficient rainfall to support agriculture — **arid·i·ty** \ə-'rid-ət-ē, a-\ *n*

aright \ə-'rīt\ *adv* : RIGHTLY, CORRECTLY

arise \ə-'rīz\ *vi* **arose** \-'rōz\; **aris·en** \-'riz-ᵊn\; **aris·ing** \-'rī-ziŋ\ **1** : to move upward : ASCEND **2** : to get up from sleep or after lying down **3** : to come into existence from or as if from a source : spring up : OCCUR

ar·is·toc·ra·cy \ˌar-ə-'stäk-rə-sē\ *n, pl* **-cies** **1** : government by the best individuals or by a small privileged class **2 a** : a government in which power is exercised by a minority esp. of those felt to be best qualified **b** : a state with such a government **3 a** : a governing body or upper class usu. made up of an hereditary nobility **b** : a group felt to be superior (as in wealth, culture, or intelligence)

aris·to·crat \ə-'ris-tə-ˌkrat\ *n* **1** : a member of an aristocracy; *esp* : NOBLE **2** : one who has habits and viewpoints (as snobbishness) that are typical of the aristocracy — **aris·to·crat·ic** \ə-ˌris-tə-'krat-ik\ *adj* — **aris·to·crat·i·cal·ly** \-'krat-i-k(ə-)lē\ *adv*

arith·me·tic \ə-'rith-mə-ˌtik\ *n* **1** : a branch of mathematics that deals with computations with numbers **2** : an act or method of computing : CALCULATION — **ar·ith·met·ic** \ˌar-ith-'met-ik\ *or* **ar·ith·met·i·cal** \-'met-i-kəl\ *adj* — **ar·ith·met·i·cal·ly** \-k(ə-)lē\ *adv* — **arith·me·ti·cian** \ə-ˌrith-mə-'tish-ən\ *n*

ark \'ärk\ *n* **1** : the ship in which Noah and his family were preserved from the Deluge **2** : a sacred chest in which the ancient Hebrews kept the two tablets of the Law

¹arm \'ärm\ *n* **1** : a human upper limb; *esp* : the part between the shoulder and wrist **2** : something resembling an arm **3** : POWER, MIGHT **4** : a support (as on a chair) for the elbow and forearm **5** : SLEEVE **6** : a division of an organization — **armed** \'ärmd\ *adj* — **arm·less** \'ärm-ləs\ *adj*

²arm *vb* **1** : to provide with weapons **2** : to provide with a means of defense **3** : to provide oneself with arms and armament **4** : to equip or ready for action or operation

³arm *n* **1 a** : a means of offense or defense : WEAPON; *esp* : FIREARM **b** : a branch of an army (as the infantry or artillery) that actually fights **c** : a branch of the military forces (as the navy) **2** *pl* : the heraldic devices of a family or a government **3 a** *pl* : active hostilities : WARFARE **b** *pl* : military service

ar·ma·da \är-'mäd-ə, -'mād-\ *n* : a large fleet of warships

ar·ma·dil·lo \ˌär-mə-'dil-ō\ *n, pl* **-los** : any of several small burrowing chiefly nocturnal mammals of warm parts of the Americas having body and head encased in an armor of small bony plates

Ar·ma·ged·don \ˌär-mə-'ged-ᵊn\ *n* **1 a** : a final and conclusive battle between the forces of good and evil **b** : the site or time of Armageddon **2** : a vast decisive conflict

ar·ma·ment \'är-mə-mənt\ *n* **1** : the whole military strength and equipment of a nation **2** : the total supply of weapons, ammunition, and related equipment of a ship, fort, military unit, or system of defense **3** : means of protection or defense : ARMOR **4** : the process of preparing for war

ar·ma·ture \'är-mə-chər, -ˌchu̇(ə)r\ *n* **1** : a protective or defensive mechanism or covering (as the spines of a cactus) **2** : the part of an electric generator that consists of coils of wire around an iron core and that induces an electric current when it is rotated in a magnetic field **3** : the part of an electric motor that consists of coils of wire around an iron core and that is caused to rotate in a magnetic field when an electric current is passed through the coils **4** : the movable part of an electromagnetic device (as an electric bell)

¹arm·chair \'ärm-ˌche(ə)r\ *n* : a chair with arms

²armchair *adj* **1** : remote from direct dealing with problems **2** : sharing vicariously in another's experiences

armed forces *n pl* : the combined military, naval, and air forces of a nation

ar·mful \'ärm-ˌfu̇l\ *n, pl* **ar·mfuls** \-ˌfu̇lz\ *or* **arms·ful** \'ärmz-ˌfu̇l\ : as much as a person's arm can hold
arm·hole \'ärm-ˌhōl\ *n* : an opening for the arm in a garment
ar·mi·stice \'är-mə-stəs\ *n* : temporary suspension of fighting brought about by agreement between the two sides : TRUCE
Armistice Day *n* : VETERANS DAY
arm·let \'ärm-lət\ *n* : a bracelet or band for the upper arm
ar·mor \'är-mər\ *n* 1 : defensive covering for the body; *esp* : covering (as of metal) used in combat 2 : something that affords protection 3 : a protective covering (as the steel plates of a battleship or a sheathing for wire) 4 : armored forces and vehicles (as tanks) — **ar·mored** *adj*
ar·mor·er \-mər-ər\ *n* 1 : one that makes armor or arms 2 : one that repairs, assembles, and tests firearms or that services and loads aircraft armament including bombs
ar·mo·ri·al \är-'mōr-ē-əl\ *adj* : of, relating to, or bearing heraldic arms
ar·mo·ry \'ärm-(ə-)rē\ *n, pl* **-ries** 1 : a supply of arms 2 : a place where arms are stored; *esp* : one used for training military reserve personnel 3 : a place where arms are manufactured
arm·pit \'ärm-ˌpit\ *n* : the hollow beneath the junction of the arm and shoulder
ar·my \'är-mē\ *n, pl* **ar·mies** 1 a : a large organized body of men armed and trained for land warfare b : a military unit capable of independent action and consisting usu. of a headquarters, two or more corps, and auxiliary troops c *often cap* : the complete military organization of a nation for land warfare 2 : a great multitude 3 : a body of persons organized to advance a cause
ar·ni·ca \'är-ni-kə\ *n* : dried flower heads of a mountain herb related to the daisies and used esp. in the form of a tincture as a liniment; *also* : this tincture
aro·ma \ə-'rō-mə\ *n* 1 : a distinctive, pleasing, and usu. penetrating odor 2 : a distinctive but faint quality : FLAVOR
ar·o·mat·ic \ˌar-ə-'mat-ik\ *adj* : of, relating to, or having aroma — **aromatic** *n*
arose *past of* ARISE
[1]**around** \ə-'rau̇nd\ *adv* 1 a : in circumference b : in, along, or through a curving or roundabout course 2 a : on all or various sides b : NEARBY 3 : here and there in various places 4 : in or to an opposite direction or position
[2]**around** *prep* 1 a : on all or various sides of b : so as to encircle or enclose c : on or to another side of 2 : here and there in or throughout 3 : not far from in number or amount
arouse \ə-'rau̇z\ *vb* 1 : to awaken from sleep 2 : to rouse to action : EXCITE
ar·peg·gio \är-'pej-ō, -'pej-ē-ˌō\ *n, pl* **-gios** 1 : production of the tones of a chord in succession and not simultaneously 2 : a chord played in arpeggio
ar·raign \ə-'rān\ *vt* 1 : to call before a court to answer to an indictment : CHARGE 2 : ACCUSE, DENOUNCE — **ar·raign·ment** *n*
ar·range \ə-'rānj\ *vb* 1 : to put in order; *esp* : to put in a particular order 2 : to make plans for : PREPARE 3 : ADJUST, SETTLE 4 a : to adapt a musical composition for voices or instruments other than those orig. intended b : ORCHESTRATE — **ar·rang·er** *n*
ar·range·ment \ə-'rānj-mənt\ *n* 1 : a putting in order : the order in which things are put 2 : PREPARATION, PLAN 3 : something made by arranging 4 a : ADAPTATION; *esp* : an adaptation of a piece of music to voices or instruments other than those orig. intended b : ORCHESTRATION
ar·rant \'ar-ənt\ *adj* : THOROUGHGOING, CONFIRMED — **ar·rant·ly** *adv*
ar·ras \'ar-əs\ *n, pl* **arras** 1 : a tapestry of Flemish origin used esp. for wall hangings and curtains 2 : a wall hanging or screen of tapestry
[1]**ar·ray** \ə-'rā\ *vt* 1 : to set in order : draw up : MARSHAL 2 : to clothe or dress esp. in splendid or impressive attire : ADORN — **ar·ray·er** *n*
[2]**array** *n* 1 : regular order or arrangement; *also* : persons (as troops) in array 2 a : CLOTHING, ATTIRE b : rich or beautiful apparel : FINERY 3 : an imposing group : large number
ar·rears \ə-'ri(ə)rz\ *n pl* 1 : the state of being behind in the discharge of debts owed 2 : an unpaid and overdue debt
[1]**ar·rest** \ə-'rest\ *vt* 1 : to stop the progress or movement of : CHECK, SLOW 2 : SEIZE, CAPTURE; *esp* : to take or keep in custody by authority of law 3 : to attract and hold the attention of
[2]**arrest** *n* 1 a : the act of stopping : CHECK b : the state of being stopped 2 : the act of taking or holding in custody by authority of law
ar·rest·ing \-iŋ\ *adj* : STRIKING, IMPRESSIVE
ar·riv·al \ə-'rī-vəl\ *n* 1 : the act of arriving 2 : a person or thing that has arrived
ar·rive \ə-'rīv\ *vi* 1 : to reach a place and esp. one's destination 2 : to gain an end or object 3 : COME
ar·ro·gance \'ar-ə-gən(t)s\ *n* : a sense of one's own superiority that shows itself in an offensively proud manner : HAUGHTINESS
ar·ro·gant \-gənt\ *adj* 1 : exaggerating one's own worth or importance in an overbearing manner 2 : marked by arrogance — **ar·ro·gant·ly** *adv*
ar·ro·gate \'ar-ə-ˌgāt\ *vt* 1 : to take or claim for one's own without right or in a haughty manner 2 : to ascribe to another esp. unduly or without right — **ar·ro·ga·tion** \ˌar-ə-'gā-shən\ *n*
ar·row \'ar-ō\ *n* 1 : a missile weapon shot from a bow and usu. having a slender shaft, a pointed head, and feathers at the butt 2 : a mark (as on a map or signboard) to indicate direction
ar·row·head \-ˌhed\ *n* 1 : the usu. separate wedge-shaped striking end of an arrow 2 : something (as a wedge-shaped mark) resembling an arrowhead
ar·row·root \-ˌrüt, -ˌru̇t\ *n* : any of several tropical American plants with starchy tuberous roots; *also* : an edible starch from these roots
ar·royo \ə-'rȯi-ō, -'rȯi-ə\ *n, pl* **-roy·os** 1 : a watercourse (as a creek or stream) in a dry region 2 : an often dry gully or channel carved by water
ar·se·nal \'ärs-nəl, -ᵊn-əl\ *n* 1 a : a place for the manufacture or storage of arms b : a collection of weapons 2 : STORE, STOREHOUSE, REPERTORY
ar·se·nic \'ärs-nik, -ᵊn-ik\ *n* 1 : a solid poisonous chemical element commonly metallic steel-gray, crystalline, and brittle 2 : a white or transparent extremely poisonous chemical compound used in making glass and insecticides
ar·sen·i·cal \är-'sen-i-kəl\ *adj* : of, relating to, or containing arsenic — **arsenical** *n*
ar·son \'ärs-ᵊn\ *n* : the malicious burning of a building or property (as a dwelling house) — **ar·son·ist** \'ärs-nəst, -ᵊn-əst\ *n*
art \'ärt\ *n* 1 : the power of doing something easily and skillfully : skill in performance : KNACK 2 : an occupation that requires a natural skill in addition to training and practice 3 : the rules or ideas that a person must know in order to follow a profession or craft 4 : a branch of learning; *esp* : one of the nonscientific branches of learning (as history, philosophy, or literature) — usu. used in pl. 5 : the study of drawing, painting, and sculpture 6 : the works produced by artists (as painters, sculptors, or writers) : a product of creative imagination
ar·te·ri·al \är-'tir-ē-əl\ *adj* 1 : of or relating to an artery 2 : being the bright red oxygen-rich blood present in most arteries — **ar·te·ri·al·ly** \-ē-ə-lē\ *adv*
ar·te·rio·scle·ro·sis \är-ˌtir-ē-ō-sklə-'rō-səs\ *n* : a chronic disease characterized by abnormal thickening and hardening of the arterial walls — **ar·te·rio·scle·rot·ic** \-'rät-ik\ *adj or n*

ar·tery \'ärt-ə-rē\ *n, pl* **-ter·ies** **1** : one of the tubular branching muscular-walled and elastic-walled vessels that carry blood from the heart through the body **2** : a channel (as a river or highway) of communication
ar·te·sian well \är-ˌtē-zhən-\ *n* **1** : a bored well from which water flows up like a fountain **2** : a deep-bored well
art·ful \'ärt-fəl\ *adj* **1** : performed with or showing art or skill **2** : ARTIFICIAL **3** : skillful or ingenious in gaining an end; *also* : CRAFTY, WILY — **art·ful·ly** \-fə-lē\ *adv* — **art·ful·ness** *n*
ar·thri·tis \är-'thrīt-əs\ *n* : inflammation of the joints — **ar·thrit·ic** \-'thrit-ik\ *adj or n* — **ar·thrit·i·cal·ly** \-'thrit-i-k(ə-)lē\ *adv*
ar·thro·pod \'är-thrə-ˌpäd\ *n* : any of a phylum of invertebrate animals (as insects, spiders, or crabs) with body and limbs segmented — **arthropod** *adj* — **ar·throp·o·dal** \är-'thräp-əd-ᵊl\ *or* **ar·throp·o·dan** \-əd-ən\ *or* **ar·throp·o·dous** \-əd-əs\ *adj*
ar·ti·choke \'ärt-ə-ˌchōk\ *n* : a tall composite herb like a thistle with coarse pinnately incised leaves; *also* : its edible flower head which is cooked as a vegetable
¹ar·ti·cle \'ärt-i-kəl\ *n* **1** : a distinct part of a document (as a constitution, contract, or treaty) dealing with a single subject **2** : a nonfictional prose composition forming an independent part of a publication and usu. dealing with a single topic **3** : any of a small set of words (as *a, an,* or *the*) used with nouns to limit or give definiteness to their application **4** : a member of a class of things; *esp* : COMMODITY
²article *vt* **-cled**; **-cling** \-k(ə-)liŋ\ : to bind by the articles of a contract
ar·tic·u·lar \är-'tik-yə-lər\ *adj* : of or relating to a joint
¹ar·tic·u·late \är-'tik-yə-lət\ *adj* **1 a** : divided clearly into words and syllables : INTELLIGIBLE **b** : able to speak; *esp* : able to express oneself effectively **2** : consisting of segments united by joints : JOINTED — **ar·tic·u·late·ly** *adv* — **ar·tic·u·late·ness** *n*
²ar·tic·u·late \-ˌlāt\ *vb* **1 a** : to make articulate sounds **b** : to speak in distinct syllables or words : express clearly and distinctly **2** : to unite or become united or connected by or as if by a joint — **ar·tic·u·la·tor** \-ˌlāt-ər\ *n*
ar·tic·u·la·tion \(ˌ)är-ˌtik-yə-'lā-shən\ *n* **1** : the making of articulate sounds (as in pronunciation) **2** : a joint between rigid parts of an animal; *esp* : one between bones or cartilages — **ar·tic·u·la·to·ry** \är-'tik-yə-lə-ˌtōr-ē\ *adj*
ar·ti·fact *or* **ar·te·fact** \'ärt-ə-ˌfakt\ *n* : a usu. simple object (as a tool or ornament) showing human workmanship or modification
ar·ti·fice \'ärt-ə-fəs\ *n* **1** : SKILL, INGENUITY **2 a** : a clever or esp. a crafty device : a cunning trick **b** : GUILE, TRICKERY
ar·tif·i·cer \är-'tif-ə-sər\ *n* : a skilled or artistic workman : CRAFTSMAN
ar·ti·fi·cial \ˌärt-ə-'fish-əl\ *adj* **1** : not natural : produced by a human agency **2** : made or changed to resemble something natural **3** : not genuine or sincere : FORCED — **ar·ti·fi·ci·al·i·ty** \-ˌfish-ē-'al-ət-ē\ *n* — **ar·ti·fi·cial·ly** \-'fish-(ə-)lē\ *adv* — **ar·ti·fi·cial·ness** *n*
ar·til·ler·ist \är-'til-ə-rəst\ *n* : ARTILLERYMAN
ar·til·lery \är-'til-(ə-)rē\ *n* **1** : large caliber crew-served mounted firearms (as guns, howitzers, rockets) : ORDNANCE **2** : a branch of an army armed with artillery — **ar·til·lery·man** \-mən\ *n*
ar·ti·san \'ärt-ə-zən\ *n* : a person (as a carpenter) trained to have manual dexterity or skill in a trade
art·ist \'ärt-əst\ *n* **1** : a person skilled in one of the arts (as painting, sculpture, music, or writing); *esp* : PAINTER **2** : a person showing unusual ability in an occupation requiring skill
ar·tis·tic \är-'tis-tik\ *adj* **1** : relating to or characteristic of art or artists **2** : showing taste in arrangement or execution — **ar·tis·ti·cal·ly** \-'tis-ti-k(ə-)lē\ *adv*
art·ist·ry \'ärt-ə-strē\ *n* **1** : artistic quality of effect or workmanship **2** : artistic ability
art·less \'ärt-ləs\ *adj* **1** : lacking art, knowledge, or skill : UNCULTURED **2 a** : made without skill : RUDE **b** : being simple and sincere : NATURAL **3** : free from deceit — **art·less·ly** *adv* — **art·less·ness** *n*
arty \'ärt-ē\ *adj* **1** : showily imitative of art **2** : aspiring to be artistic : DILETTANTE — **art·i·ly** \'ärt-ᵊl-ē\ *adv* — **art·i·ness** \'ärt-ē-nəs\ *n*
ar·um \'ar-əm\ *n* : any of a family of plants having heart-shaped or sword-shaped leaves and flowers in a fleshy spike enclosed in a leafy sheath
¹as \əz, (ˌ)az\ *adv* **1** : to the same degree or extent **2** : for instance
²as *conj* **1** : in or to the same degree that **2** : in the way or manner that **3** : WHILE, WHEN **4** : regardless of the degree to which : THOUGH **5** : for the reason that **6** : that the result is — used after *so* or *such*
³as *pron* **1** : THAT, WHO, WHICH — used in standard English after *same* or *such* **2** : a fact that
⁴as *prep* **1** : LIKE 2 **2** : in the character or position of
as·a·fet·i·da *or* **as·a·foe·ti·da** \ˌas-ə-'fit-əd-ē, -'fet-əd-ə\ *n* : a resin that has an unpleasant smell and taste and comes from several oriental plants of the carrot family formerly used in medicine
as·bes·tos \as-'bes-təs, az-\ *n* : a noncombustible and heat-resistant grayish mineral that readily separates into long flexible fibers and is used in making various fireproof, nonconducting, and chemically resistant materials
as·cend \ə-'send\ *vb* : to go up : slope upward : CLIMB, RISE — **as·cend·a·ble** *or* **as·cend·i·ble** \-'sen-də-bəl\ *adj*
as·cend·an·cy \ə-'sen-dən-sē\ *or* **as·cend·ance** \-dən(t)s\ *n* : governing or controlling influence : DOMINATION
¹as·cend·ant \ə-'sen-dənt\ *n* : a state or position of dominant power
²ascendant *adj* **1** : moving upward : RISING **2 a** : SUPERIOR **b** : DOMINANT
as·cen·sion \ə-'sen-chən\ *n* : the act or process of ascending
Ascension Day *n* : the Thursday 40 days after Easter observed in some churches in commemoration of Christ's ascension into heaven
as·cent \ə-'sent\ *n* **1** : the act of rising or mounting upward : CLIMB **2** : an upward slope : RISE
as·cer·tain \ˌas-ər-'tān\ *vt* : to learn with certainty : find out — **as·cer·tain·a·ble** *adj* — **as·cer·tain·ment** *n*
as·cet·ic \ə-'set-ik\ *adj* **1** : practicing strict self-denial esp. as a means of religious discipline **2** : AUSTERE — **ascetic** *n* — **as·cet·i·cism** \ə-'set-ə-ˌsiz-əm\ *n*
ascor·bic acid \ə-ˌskȯr-bik-\ *n* : VITAMIN C
as·cot \'as-kət, -ˌkät\ *n* : a broad neck scarf that is looped under the chin and sometimes pinned
as·cribe \ə-'skrīb\ *vt* : to refer to a supposed cause, source, or author : ATTRIBUTE — **as·crib·a·ble** *adj*
as·crip·tion \ə-'skrip-shən\ *n* : the act of ascribing : ATTRIBUTION
asep·tic \(')ā-'sep-tik\ *adj* **1** : free or freed from disease-causing microorganisms **2 a** : lacking life, emotion, or warmth **b** : DETACHED, OBJECTIVE — **asep·ti·cal·ly** \-ti-k(ə-)lē\ *adv*
asex·u·al \(')ā-'sek-sh(ə-w)əl\ *adj* **1** : lacking sex **2** : occurring or formed without sexual action — **asex·u·al·ly** \-ē\ *adv*
as for *prep* : with regard to : CONCERNING
as good as *adv* : in effect : for all practical purposes
¹ash \'ash\ *n* : any of a genus of trees of the olive family with thin furrowed bark and winged seeds; *also* : its tough elastic wood
²ash *n* **1 a** : the solid residue left when material is thoroughly burned or is oxidized by chemical means **b** : fine particles of mineral matter from a volcanic vent **2** *pl* **a** : a collection of ash

left after something has been burned **b** : the remains of the dead human body esp. after cremation **c** : ruins or last traces **3** *pl* : something that symbolizes grief, repentance, or humiliation **4** *pl* : deathly pallor

ashamed \ə-'shāmd\ *adj* **1** : feeling shame, guilt, or disgrace **2** : kept back by anticipation of shame — **asham•ed•ly** \-'shā-məd-lē\ *adv*

ash•en \'ash-ən\ *adj* **1** : of the color of ashes **2** : deadly pale : BLANCHED

ash•lar \'ash-lər\ *n* : hewn or squared stone; *also* : masonry of such stone

ashore \ə-'shō(ə)r\ *adv (or adj)* : on or to the shore

Ash Wednesday *n* : the first day of Lent

ashy \'ash-ē\ *adj* **1** : of, relating to, or resembling ashes **2** : deadly pale

¹aside \ə-'sīd\ *adv* **1** : to or toward the side **2** : out of the way : AWAY **3** : away from one's thought : APART

²aside *n* **1** : words meant to be inaudible to someone; *esp* : an actor's words supposedly not heard by others on the stage **2** : DIGRESSION

aside from *prep* **1** : in addition to : BESIDES **2** : except for

as if *conj* **1** : as it would be if **2** : as one would do if **3** : THAT

as•i•nine \'as-ᵊn-,īn\ *adj* : of, relating to, or resembling an ass esp. in stupidity or obstinacy — **as•i•nine•ly** *adv* — **as•i•nin•i•ty** \,as-ᵊn-'in-ət-ē\ *n*

ask \'ask\ *vb* **1** : to seek information : put a question to someone or about something : INQUIRE **2** : to make a request **3** : to set as a price : DEMAND **4** : INVITE **5** : LOOK — **ask•er** *n*

askance \ə-'skan(t)s\ *adv* **1** : with a side glance : OBLIQUELY **2** : with distrust, suspicion, or disapproval

askew \ə-'skyü\ *adv (or adj)* : out of line : AWRY, AMISS

¹aslant \ə-'slant\ *adv* : in a slanting direction

²aslant *prep* : over or across in a slanting direction

¹asleep \ə-'slēp\ *adj* **1** : SLEEPING **2** : lacking sensation : NUMB **3** : INACTIVE, SLUGGISH

²asleep *adv* : into a state of sleep

as long as *conj* **1** : PROVIDED **2** : inasmuch as : SINCE

as of *prep* : ON, AT, DURING, FROM

asp \'asp\ *n* : a small venomous snake of Egypt

as•par•a•gus \ə-'spar-ə-gəs\ *n* : a tall branching perennial herb of the lily family widely grown for its thick edible young shoots

as•pect \'as-,pekt\ *n* **1** : a position facing a particular direction : EXPOSURE **2** : a particular status or phase in which something appears or may be regarded **3** : MIEN

as•pen \'as-pən\ *n* : any of several poplars with leaves that flutter in the lightest breeze

as•per•i•ty \a-'sper-ət-ē, ə-'sper-\ *n, pl* **-ties** **1** : RIGOR, SEVERITY **2** : roughness of surface : UNEVENNESS **3** : harshness of temper, manner, or tone

as•per•sion \ə-'spər-zhən\ *n* : an injurious or offensive charge or implication

as•phalt \'as-,fȯlt\ *or* **as•phal•tum** \as-'fȯl-təm\ *n* **1** : a brown to black substance that is found in natural beds or obtained as a residue in petroleum or coal-tar refining and that consists chiefly of hydrocarbons **2** : any of various compositions of asphalt having diverse uses (as for pavement or for waterproof cement or paint) — **as•phal•tic** \as-'fȯl-tik\ *adj*

as•pho•del \'as-fə-,del\ *n* : any of several herbs of the lily family with white or yellow flowers in long erect spikes

as•phyx•ia \as-'fik-sē-ə\ *n* : a lack of oxygen or an excess of carbon dioxide in the body usu. caused by interruption of breathing and resulting in unconsciousness

as•phyx•i•ate \as-'fik-sē-,āt\ *vt* : to cause asphyxia in; *also* : to kill or make unconscious by interference with the normal oxygen intake — **as•phyx•i•a•tion** \(,)as-,fik-sē-'ā-shən\ *n* — **as•phyx•i•a•tor** \as-'fik-sē-,āt-ər\ *n*

as•pic \'as-pik\ *n* : a savory jelly of fish or meat stock used cold esp. to make a mold of meat, fish, or vegetables

as•pi•rant \'as-p(ə-)rənt, ə-'spī-rənt\ *n* : one who aspires

¹as•pi•rate \'as-pə-,rāt\ *vt* **1** : to pronounce with an initial *h*-sound **2** : to draw or remove by suction

²as•pi•rate \'as-p(ə-)rət\ *n* : an independent sound \h\ or a character (as the letter *h*) representing it

as•pi•ra•tion \,as-pə-'rā-shən\ *n* **1 a** : pronunciation with an aspirate **b** : an independent sound \h\ or its symbol **2** : a drawing of something in, out, up, or through by or as if by suction **3 a** : a strong desire to achieve something high or great **b** : an object of such desire

as•pire \ə-'spī(ə)r\ *vb* : to seek to attain something high or great : desire eagerly — **as•pir•er** *n*

as•pi•rin \'as-p(ə-)rən\ *n* : a white crystalline drug used as a remedy for pain and fever

ass \'as\ *n* **1** : an animal resembling but smaller than the related horse and having a shorter mane, shorter hair on the tail, and longer ears : DONKEY **2** : a stupid, obstinate, or perverse person

as•sail \ə-'sāl\ *vt* : to attack violently with blows or words — **as•sail•a•ble** *adj* — **as•sail•ant** \-'sā-lənt\ *n*

as•sas•sin \ə-'sas-ᵊn\ *n* : a person who kills another by a surprise or secret attack; *esp* : a hired murderer of a prominent person

as•sas•si•nate \ə-'sas-ᵊn-,āt\ *vt* : to murder (a usu. prominent person) by a surprise or secret attack esp. for pay — **as•sas•si•na•tion** \ə-,sas-ᵊn-'ā-shən\ *n*

¹as•sault \ə-'sȯlt\ *n* **1** : a violent or sudden attack : ONSLAUGHT **2** : an apparent attempt or a threat to do harm to another

²assault *vt* : to make an assault upon

¹as•say \'as-,ā, a-'sā\ *n* : examination or analysis (as of an ore, a metal, or a drug) for the purpose of determining composition, measure, or quality or of determining the quantity of one or more components

²as•say \a-'sā, 'as-,ā\ *vb* **1** : TRY, ATTEMPT **2 a** : to analyze (as an ore) for one or more valuable components **b** : ESTIMATE **3** : to prove up in an assay — **as•say•er** *n*

as•sem•blage \ə-'sem-blij\ *n* **1** : a collection of persons or things : GATHERING **2** : the act of assembling : the state of being assembled

as•sem•ble \ə-'sem-bəl\ *vb* **-bled**; **-bling** \-b(ə-)liŋ\ **1** : to collect into one place or group **2** : to fit together the parts of **3** : to meet together : CONVENE — **as•sem•bler** *n*

as•sem•bly \ə-'sem-blē\ *n, pl* **-blies** **1** : a body of persons gathered together (as for deliberation, worship, or entertainment) **2** *cap* : a legislative body; *esp* : the lower house of a legislature **3** : ASSEMBLAGE **4** : a signal given (as by drum or bugle) for troops to assemble or fall in **5** : a collection of parts that go to make up a complete unit

as•sem•bly•man \-mən\ *n* : a member of a legislative assembly

¹as•sent \ə-'sent\ *vi* : AGREE, CONCUR

²assent *n* : an act of assenting : ACQUIESCENCE, AGREEMENT

as•sert \ə-'sərt\ *vt* **1** : to state clearly and strongly : declare positively **2** : MAINTAIN, DEFEND

as•ser•tion \ə-'sər-shən\ *n* : the act of asserting; *also* : something asserted : DECLARATION

as•sert•ive \ə-'sərt-iv\ *adj* : disposed to bold or confident assertion — **as•sert•ive•ly** *adv* — **as•sert•ive•ness** *n*

as•sess \ə-'ses\ *vt* **1** : to determine the rate or amount of **2** : to set a value on (as property) for purposes of taxation **3** : to lay a tax or charge on **4** : to determine the importance, size, or value of — **as•sess•a•ble** *adj*

as•sess•ment \ə-'ses-mənt\ *n* **1** : the act of assessing : APPRAISAL **2** : the amount or value assessed

as•ses•sor \ə-'ses-ər\ *n* : an official who assesses property for purposes of taxation

as·set \'as-ˌet\ *n* 1 *pl* : all the property (as cash, securities, real property, goods, accounts receivable) of a person, corporation, or estate that may be used in payment of debts 2 : ADVANTAGE, RESOURCE
as·sev·er·ate \ə-'sev-ə-ˌrāt\ *vt* : to declare positively or earnestly : AVER — **as·sev·er·a·tion** \ə-ˌsev-ə-'rā-shən\ *n*
as·si·du·ity \ˌas-ə-'d(y)ü-ət-ē\ *n* : the quality or state of being assiduous : DILIGENCE
as·sid·u·ous \ə-'sij-(ə-)wəs\ *adj* : steadily attentive : DILIGENT — **as·sid·u·ous·ly** *adv* — **as·sid·u·ous·ness** *n*
as·sign \ə-'sīn\ *vt* 1 : to transfer to another 2 a : to appoint to a post or duty b : PRESCRIBE 3 : to fix authoritatively : SPECIFY 4 : ASCRIBE, REFER 1 — **as·sign·a·ble** *adj* — **as·sign·er** \ə-'sī-nər\ *or* **as·sign·or** \ə-'sī-nər; ə-ˌsī-'nȯ(ə)r, ˌas-ˌī-; ˌas-ə-'nȯ(ə)r\ *n*
as·sig·na·tion \ˌas-ig-'nā-shən\ *n* 1 : ASSIGNMENT 2 : a usu. clandestine or illicit meeting esp. for lovemaking; *also* : an appointment for such a meeting
as·sign·ee \ə-ˌsī-'nē, ˌas-ˌī-\ *n* : a person to whom an assignment is made
as·sign·ment \ə-'sīn-mənt\ *n* 1 : the act of assigning 2 : something assigned : an assigned task
as·sim·i·late \ə-'sim-ə-ˌlāt\ *vb* 1 a : to take something in and make it part of and like the thing it has joined b : to comprehend thoroughly : ABSORB 2 a : to make similar b : to alter by assimilation — **as·sim·i·la·bil·i·ty** \-ˌsim-ə-lə-'bil-ət-ē\ *n* — **as·sim·i·la·ble** \-'sim-ə-lə-bəl\ *adj* — **as·sim·i·la·tor** \-'sim-ə-ˌlāt-ər\ *n*
as·sim·i·la·tion \ə-ˌsim-ə-'lā-shən\ *n* 1 : the act or process of assimilating; *esp* : the conversion of nutrients (as digested food) into protoplasm 2 : change of a sound so that it becomes identical with or similar to a neighboring sound — **as·sim·i·la·tive** \-'sim-ə-ˌlāt-iv\ *adj*
¹as·sist \ə-'sist\ *vb* : to give support or aid : HELP
²assist *n* : an act of assistance : AID
as·sist·ance \ə-'sis-tən(t)s\ *n* : the act of assisting or the aid supplied : SUPPORT
as·sist·ant \ə-'sis-tənt\ *n* : one who assists : HELPER; *also* : one who serves in a subordinate capacity — **assistant** *adj*
as·size \ə-'sīz\ *n* : a session of an English superior court held for the trial of civil and criminal cases three or four times a year in most counties by judges traveling on circuit — usu. used in pl.
¹as·so·ci·ate \ə-'sō-s(h)ē-ˌāt\ *vb* 1 : to join or come together as partners, friends, or companions 2 : to connect or bring (as ideas) together 3 : to combine or join with other parts : UNITE
²as·so·ci·ate \ə-'sō-s(h)ē-ət, -shət\ *n* 1 : a fellow worker : PARTNER, COLLEAGUE 2 : COMPANION — **associate** *adj*
as·so·ci·a·tion \ə-ˌsō-s(h)ē-'ā-shən\ *n* 1 : the act of associating : the state of being associated 2 : an organization of persons having a common interest : SOCIETY 3 : something linked mentally (as with a thing or person); *also* : the process of forming such links — **as·so·ci·a·tion·al** \-shnəl, -shən-ᵊl\ *adj*
as·so·ci·a·tive \ə-'sō-s(h)ē-ˌāt-iv, -shət-iv\ *adj* 1 : of, relating to, or involved in association and esp. mental association 2 : dependent on or acquired by association or learning — **as·so·ci·a·tive·ly** *adv* — **as·so·cia·tiv·i·ty** \ə-ˌsō-s(h)ē-ə-'tiv-ət-ē, -ˌsō-shə-'tiv-\ *n*
as·so·nance \'as-ə-nən(t)s\ *n* 1 : resemblance of sound in words or syllables 2 : repetition of vowels without repetition of consonants (as in *story* and *holy*) used as an alternative to rhyme in verse — **as·so·nant** \-nənt\ *adj or n*
as·sort \ə-'sȯrt\ *vb* 1 : to distribute into groups of a like kind : CLASSIFY 2 : to agree in kind : HARMONIZE — **as·sort·a·tive** \ə-'sȯrt-ət-iv\ *adj* — **as·sort·er** *n*
as·sort·ed \ə-'sȯrt-əd\ *adj* 1 : consisting of various kinds 2 : MATCHED, SUITED
as·sort·ment \ə-'sȯrt-mənt\ *n* 1 a : arrangement in classes b : VARIETY 2 : a collection containing a variety of sorts
as·suage \ə-'swāj\ *vt* 1 : to lessen the intensity of (as pain) : EASE, QUIET 2 : SATISFY, QUENCH — **as·suage·ment** *n*
as·sume \ə-'süm\ *vb* 1 a : to take to or upon oneself : UNDERTAKE b : to put on (clothing) : DON 2 : SEIZE, USURP 3 : to put on in appearance only : FEIGN 4 : to take for granted : SUPPOSE
as·sum·ing \-iŋ\ *adj* : PRETENTIOUS, PRESUMPTUOUS
as·sump·tion \ə-'səm(p)-shən\ *n* 1 *cap* : August 15 observed as a church festival in commemoration of the Assumption of Mary 2 : a taking to or upon oneself 3 : the act of laying claim to or taking possession of 4 a : the supposition that something is true b : a fact or statement taken for granted
as·sur·ance \ə-'shu̇r-ən(t)s\ *n* 1 : the act of assuring : PLEDGE 2 : the state of being sure or certain 3 : SECURITY, SAFETY 4 : SELF-CONFIDENCE, SELF-RELIANCE 5 : AUDACITY, PRESUMPTION
as·sure \ə-'shu̇(ə)r\ *vt* 1 : INSURE 2 : REASSURE 3 : to make sure or certain 4 : to inform positively
¹as·sured \ə-'shu̇(ə)rd\ *adj* 1 : made sure or certain: as a : SAFE b : UNQUESTIONABLE c : GUARANTEED 2 a : CONFIDENT b : COMPLACENT — **as·sur·ed·ly** \-'shu̇r-əd-lē\ *adv* — **as·sur·ed·ness** \-əd-nəs\ *n*
²assured *n* : a person whose life or property is insured
astar·board \ə-'stär-bərd\ *adv* : toward or on the starboard side of a ship
as·ta·tine \'as-tə-ˌtēn\ *n* : a radioactive chemical element discovered by bombarding bismuth with helium nuclei
as·ter \'as-tər\ *n* : any of various mostly fall-blooming leafy-stemmed composite herbs usu. with showy white, pink, purple, or yellow flower heads
as·ter·isk \'as-tə-ˌrisk\ *n* : a character * used as a reference mark or to show the omission of letters or words — **asterisk** *vt*
astern \ə-'stərn\ *adv* 1 : behind a ship or airplane : in the rear 2 : at or toward the stern of a ship or aircraft 3 : BACKWARD
as·ter·oid \'as-tə-ˌrȯid\ *n* : one of thousands of small planets between Mars and Jupiter with diameters from a fraction of a mile to nearly 500 miles
asth·ma \'az-mə\ *n* : a condition often of allergic origin that is marked by labored breathing with wheezing, a feeling of tightness in the chest, and coughing — **asth·mat·ic** \az-'mat-ik\ *adj or n* — **asth·mat·i·cal·ly** \-'mat-i-k(ə-)lē\ *adv*
as though *conj* : as if
astig·ma·tism \ə-'stig-mə-ˌtiz-əm\ *n* : a defect of an optical system (as of the eye) that prevents light from focusing accurately and results in a blurred image or indistinct vision — **as·tig·mat·ic** \ˌas-tig-'mat-ik\ *adj* — **as·tig·mat·i·cal·ly** \-'mat-i-k(ə-)lē\ *adv*
astir \ə-'stər\ *adj* 1 : being in a state of activity : STIRRING 2 : out of bed : UP
as to *prep* 1 : with regard or reference to : as for : ABOUT 2 : according to : BY
as·ton·ish \ə-'stän-ish\ *vt* : to strike with sudden wonder : surprise greatly : AMAZE
as·ton·ish·ing \-iŋ\ *adj* : causing astonishment : SURPRISING — **as·ton·ish·ing·ly** *adv*
as·ton·ish·ment \ə-'stän-ish-mənt\ *n* 1 : the state of being astonished; *also* : CONSTERNATION 2 : a cause of amazement or wonder
as·tound \ə-'stau̇nd\ *vb* : to fill with bewildered wonder
¹astrad·dle \ə-'strad-ᵊl\ *adv* : on or above and extending onto both sides : ASTRIDE
²astraddle *prep* : with one leg on each side of : ASTRIDE
as·tra·khan *or* **as·tra·chan** \'as-trə-kən, -ˌkan\ *n, often cap* 1 : karakul of Russian origin 2 : a cloth with a usu. wool, curled, and looped pile resembling karakul

as·tral \'as-trəl\ *adj* : of or relating to the stars : STARRY — **as·tral·ly** \-trə-lē\ *adv*
astray \ə-'strā\ *adv* (*or adj*) **1** : off the right path or route : STRAYING **2** : into error : MISTAKEN
¹astride \ə-'strīd\ *adv* : with one leg on each side
²astride *prep* : on or above and with one leg on each side of
¹as·trin·gent \ə-'strin-jənt\ *adj* **1** : able or tending to shrink body tissues : CONTRACTING, PUCKERY **2** : STERN, AUSTERE — **as·trin·gen·cy** \-jən-sē\ *n* — **as·trin·gent·ly** *adv*
²astringent *n* : an astringent agent or substance
as·tro·labe \'as-trə-,lāb\ *n* : a compact instrument for observing the positions of celestial bodies that is superseded by the sextant
as·trol·o·ger \ə-'sträl-ə-jər\ *n* : one who practices astrology
as·trol·o·gy \-jē\ *n* : divination based on the supposed influence of the stars upon human events — **as·tro·log·i·cal** \,as-trə-'läj-i-kəl\ *adj* — **as·tro·log·i·cal·ly** \-i-k(ə-)lē\ *adv*
as·tro·naut \'as-trə-,nȯt\ *n* : a traveler in a spaceship — **as·tro·nau·ti·cal** \,as-trə-'nȯt-i-kəl\ *adj* — **as·tro·nau·ti·cal·ly** \-i-k(ə-)lē\ *adv*
as·tro·nau·tics \,as-trə-'nȯt-iks\ *n* : the science of the construction and operation of spaceships
as·tron·o·mer \ə-'strän-ə-mər\ *n* : one who is skilled in astronomy or who makes observations of celestial phenomena
as·tro·nom·i·cal \,as-trə-'näm-i-kəl\ *or* **as·tro·nom·ic** \-'näm-ik\ *adj* **1** : of or relating to astronomy **2** : extremely or unimaginably large — **as·tro·nom·i·cal·ly** \-'näm-i-k(ə-)lē\ *adv*
as·tron·o·my \ə-'strän-ə-mē\ *n* : the science of the celestial bodies and of their magnitudes, motions, and constitution
as·tro·phys·ics \,as-trə-'fiz-iks\ *n* : a branch of astronomy dealing with the physical and chemical constitution of the celestial bodies — **as·tro·phys·i·cal** \-'fiz-i-kəl\ *adj* — **as·tro·phys·i·cist** \-'fiz-ə-səst\ *n*
as·tute \ə-'st(y)üt, a-\ *adj* : CLEVER, SAGACIOUS; *also* : WILY — **as·tute·ly** *adv* — **as·tute·ness** *n*
asun·der \ə-'sən-dər\ *adv* (*or adj*) **1** : into parts **2** : APART
as well as *prep* : in addition to : BESIDES
as yet *adv* : up to the present time : YET
asy·lum \ə-'sī-ləm\ *n* **1** : an inviolable place of refuge and protection giving shelter to criminals and debtors : SANCTUARY **2** : a place of retreat and security : SHELTER **3** : protection or inviolability afforded by or as if by an asylum : REFUGE **4** : an institution for the relief or care of the destitute or afflicted and esp. the insane
asym·met·ric \,ā-sə-'me-trik\ *adj* : not symmetrical — **asym·met·ri·cal** \-tri-kəl\ *adj* — **asym·met·ri·cal·ly** \-tri-k(ə-)lē\ *adv* — **asym·me·try** \(')ā-'sim-ə-trē\ *n*
at \ət, (')at\ *prep* — used as a function word to introduce an expression indicating (1) a place or location, (2) a goal of action or motion, (3) that with which one is occupied or employed, (4) a condition, (5) a means, cause, or manner, or (6) a rate, degree, or position in a scale or series
at all *adv* **1** : in all ways : INDISCRIMINATELY **2** : in any way or respect : to the least extent or degree : under any circumstances
at·a·vism \'at-ə-,viz-əm\ *n* : appearance in an individual of a remotely ancestral character; *also* : such an individual or character — **at·a·vis·tic** \,at-ə-'vis-tik\ *adj* — **at·a·vis·ti·cal·ly** \-'vis-ti-k(ə-)lē\ *adv*
ate *past of* EAT
ate·lier \,at-ᵊl-'yā\ *n* **1** : an artist's studio **2** : WORKSHOP
athe·ism \'ā-thē-,iz-əm\ *n* : the belief that there is no God : denial of the existence of a supreme being
athe·ist \-thē-əst\ *n* : a person who believes there is no God — **athe·is·tic** \,ā-thē-'is-tik\ *adj* — **athe·is·ti·cal·ly** \-'is-ti-k(ə-)lē\ *adv*
ath·e·nae·um *or* **ath·e·ne·um** \,ath-ə-'nē-əm\ *n* **1** : a literary or scientific association **2** : a building or room in which books, periodicals, and newspapers are kept for use
athirst \ə-'thərst\ *adj* **1** : THIRSTY **2** : EAGER, LONGING
ath·lete \'ath-,lēt\ *n* : a person who is trained in or good at games and exercises that require physical skill, endurance and strength
ath·let·ic \ath-'let-ik\ *adj* **1** : of, relating to, or characteristic of athletes or athletics **2** : VIGOROUS, ACTIVE — **ath·let·i·cal·ly** \-'let-i-k(ə-)lē\ *adv*
ath·let·ics \ath-'let-iks\ *n sing or pl* : games, sports, and exercises requiring strength and skill
¹athwart \ə-'thwȯrt\ *adv* : ACROSS : obliquely across
²athwart *prep* **1** : ACROSS **2** : in opposition to
at·las \'at-ləs\ *n* : a book of maps often including descriptive text
at·mo·sphere \'at-mə-,sfi(ə)r\ *n* **1** : the whole mass of air surrounding the earth **2** : the air in a particular place **3** : a surrounding influence or set of conditions : ENVIRONMENT **4** : a unit of pressure equal to the pressure of the air at sea level or approximately 14.7 pounds to the square inch
at·mo·spher·ic \,at-mə-'sfi(ə)r-ik, -'sfer-\ *adj* : of or relating to the atmosphere — **at·mo·spher·i·cal·ly** \-i-k(ə-)lē\ *adv*
atoll \'a-,tȯl\ *n* : a ring-shaped coral island or string of islands consisting of a coral reef surrounding a lagoon

atoll

at·om \'at-əm\ *n* **1** : a tiny particle : BIT **2** : the smallest particle of an element that can exist either alone or in combination
atom bomb *n* : a bomb whose violent explosive power is due to the sudden release of atomic energy resulting from the splitting of nuclei of a heavy chemical element (as plutonium or uranium) by neutrons in a very rapid chain reaction — **at·om–bomb** \,at-əm-'bäm\ *vt*
atom·ic \ə-'täm-ik\ *adj* **1** : of, relating to, or concerned with atoms, atomic energy, or atomic bombs **2** : extremely small : MINUTE — **atom·i·cal·ly** \-i-k(ə-)lē\ *adv*
atomic bomb *n* : ATOM BOMB
atomic energy *n* : energy that can be liberated by changes (as by fission or fusion) in the nucleus of an atom
atom·ics \ə-'täm-iks\ *n* : the science of atoms esp. when involving atomic energy
at·om·ize \'at-ə-,mīz\ *vt* **1** : to reduce to minute particles or to a fine spray **2** : to treat as made up of many discrete units **3** : to subject to atomic bombing — **at·om·i·za·tion** \,at-ə-mə-'zā-shən\ *n*
at·om·iz·er \'at-ə-,mī-zər\ *n* : a device for spraying a liquid (as a perfume or disinfectant)
aton·al \(')ā-'tōn-ᵊl\ *adj* : characterized by avoidance of traditional musical tonality — **ato·nal·i·ty** \,ā-tō-'nal-ət-ē\ *n* — **aton·al·ly** *adv*
atone \ə-'tōn\ *vb* : to do something to make up for a wrong done : make amends : EXPIATE
atone·ment \-mənt\ *n* **1** : the reconciliation of God and man through the death of Jesus Christ **2** : reparation for an offense or injury : SATISFACTION
atop \ə-'täp\ *prep* : on top of
atri·um \'ā-trē-əm\ *n, pl* **atria** \-trē-ə\ **1** : the central hall of a Roman house **2** : an anatomical cavity or passage; *esp* : the main chamber of an auricle of the heart or the entire auricle
atro·cious \ə-'trō-shəs\ *adj* **1** : extremely wicked, brutal, or

cruel 2 : savagely fierce : MURDEROUS 3 : APPALLING, TERRIBLE 4 : very bad : ABOMINABLE — **atro·cious·ly** *adv* — **atro·cious·ness** *n*

atroc·i·ty \ə-'träs-ət-ē\ *n, pl* **-ties** 1 : the quality or state of being atrocious 2 : an atrocious act, object, or situation

¹at·ro·phy \'a-trə-fē\ *n, pl* **-phies** : decrease in size or wasting away of a body part or tissue — **atroph·ic** \ə-'träf-ik\ *adj*

²atrophy *vi* **-phied**; **-phy·ing** : to undergo atrophy

at·ro·pine \'a-trə-,pēn, -pən\ *n* : a poisonous white crystalline compound from belladonna and related plants used esp. to relieve spasms and to dilate the pupil of the eye

at·tach \ə-'tach\ *vb* 1 : to take money or property by legal authority esp. to secure payment of a debt 2 : to fasten or join one thing to another : TIE 3 : to tie or bind by feelings of affection 4 : to assign by authority : APPOINT 5 : to think of as belonging to something : ATTRIBUTE 6 : to be associated or connected — **at·tach·a·ble** *adj*

at·ta·ché \,at-ə-'shā, ,a-,ta-\ *n* : a technical expert on the diplomatic staff of his country at a foreign capital

at·tach·ment \ə-'tach-mənt\ *n* 1 : a seizure by legal process or the writ commanding such seizure 2 : the state of being personally attached : FIDELITY, FONDNESS 3 : a device attached to a machine or implement 4 : the physical connection by which one thing is attached to another

¹at·tack \ə-'tak\ *vb* 1 : to set upon forcefully 2 : to use unfriendly or bitter words against 3 : to begin to affect or to act upon injuriously 4 : to set to work upon — **at·tack·er** *n*

²attack *n* 1 : the act of attacking : ASSAULT 2 : a setting to work : START 3 : a fit of sickness; *esp* : an active episode of a chronic or recurrent disease

at·tain \ə-'tān\ *vb* 1 : ACHIEVE, ACCOMPLISH 2 : to come into possession of : OBTAIN 3 : to arrive at : ARRIVE, REACH — **at·tain·a·bil·i·ty** \ə-,tā-nə-'bil-ət-ē\ *n* — **at·tain·a·ble** *adj* — **at·tain·a·ble·ness** *n*

at·tain·der \ə-'tān-dər\ *n* : the taking away of a person's civil rights when he has been declared an outlaw or sentenced to death

at·tain·ment \ə-'tān-mənt\ *n* 1 : the act of attaining : the state of being attained 2 : something attained : ACCOMPLISHMENT

at·tar \'at-ər, 'a-,tär\ *n* : a fragrant essential oil (as from rose petals)

¹at·tempt \ə-'tem(p)t\ *vt* 1 : to make an effort to accomplish 2 : to try to take by force : ATTACK 3 : ENDEAVOR

²attempt *n* : the act or an instance of attempting; *esp* : an unsuccessful effort

at·tend \ə-'tend\ *vb* 1 : to care for : look after : take charge of 2 : to wait on : SERVE 3 : to go or stay with as a servant or companion 4 : to be present at 5 : to be present with : ACCOMPANY 6 : to pay attention

at·tend·ance \ə-'ten-dən(t)s\ *n* 1 : the act of attending 2 **a** : the persons or number of persons attending **b** : the number of times a person attends

¹at·tend·ant \ə-'ten-dənt\ *adj* : accompanying or following as a consequence

²attendant *n* : one who attends another to perform a service; *esp* : an employee who waits on customers

at·ten·tion \ə-'ten-chən\ *n* 1 : the act or the power of fixing one's mind upon something : careful listening or watching 2 : careful consideration of something with a view to taking action on it 3 : an act of kindness, care, or courtesy 4 : a military position of readiness to act on the next command

at·ten·tive \ə-'tent-iv\ *adj* 1 : paying attention : HEEDFUL, OBSERVANT 2 : heedful of the comfort of others : COURTEOUS — **at·ten·tive·ly** *adv* — **at·ten·tive·ness** *n*

at·ten·u·ate \ə-'ten-yə-,wāt\ *vb* 1 : to make thin or slender 2 : to make less in amount, force, value, virulence, vitality, or density : WEAKEN, RAREFY 3 : to become thin, fine, or less — **at·ten·u·a·tion** \ə-,ten-yə-'wā-shən\ *n*

at·test \ə-'test\ *vb* : to give proof of : testify to : CERTIFY — **at·tes·ta·tion** \,a-,tes-'tā-shən\ *n* — **at·test·er** *n*

at·tic \'at-ik\ *n* : a room or a space immediately below the roof of a building

¹at·tire \ə-'tī(ə)r\ *vt* 1 : DRESS, ARRAY 2 : to clothe in rich garments

²attire *n* : DRESS, CLOTHES; *esp* : fine clothing

at·ti·tude \'at-ə-,t(y)üd\ *n* 1 : the arrangement of the body or figure : POSTURE 2 : a mental position or feeling regarding a fact or state 3 : the position of something in relation to something else (as a line or plane) that serves as a reference

at·tor·ney \ə-'tər-nē\ *n, pl* **-neys** : one who is legally appointed by another to transact business for him; *esp* : a legal agent qualified to act for suitors and defendants in legal proceedings

attorney general *n, pl* **attorneys general** *or* **attorney generals** : the chief law officer of a nation or state who represents the government in legal matters and serves as its principal legal advisor

at·tract \ə-'trakt\ *vb* 1 : to draw to or toward oneself or itself : cause to approach or adhere 2 : to draw by appealing to interest or feeling

at·trac·tion \ə-'trak-shən\ *n* 1 : the act, process, or power of attracting; *esp* : personal charm or beauty 2 : an attractive quality, object, or feature 3 : a force tending to draw particles together

at·trac·tive \ə-'trak-tiv\ *adj* : having the power or quality of attracting; *esp* : CHARMING, PLEASING — **at·trac·tive·ly** *adv* — **at·trac·tive·ness** *n*

¹at·tri·bute \'a-trə-,byüt\ *n* 1 : an inherent characteristic : a quality belonging to a particular person or thing 2 : an object closely associated with a specific person, thing, or office

²at·trib·ute \ə-'trib-yət\ *vt* 1 : to explain by way of cause 2 **a** : to regard as a characteristic of a person or thing **b** : to reckon as made or originated in an indicated fashion — **at·trib·ut·a·ble** *adj* — **at·trib·ut·er** *n*

at·tri·bu·tion \,a-trə-'byü-shən\ *n* : the act of attributing; *also* : an ascribed quality, character, or right

at·trib·u·tive \ə-'trib-yət-iv\ *adj* : relating to or of the nature of an attribute; *esp* : joined directly to a modified noun without a copulative verb — **attributive** *n* — **at·trib·u·tive·ly** *adv*

at·tri·tion \ə-'trish-ən\ *n* 1 : the act of wearing or grinding down by friction 2 : the act of weakening or exhausting by constant harassment or abuse

at·tune \ə-'t(y)ün\ *vt* : to bring into harmony : TUNE

atyp·i·cal \(')ā-'tip-i-kəl\ *adj* : not typical : IRREGULAR — **atyp·i·cal·ly** \-k(ə-)lē\ *adv*

au·burn \'ȯ-bərn\ *n* : a moderate brown

¹auc·tion \'ȯk-shən\ *n* : a public sale in which persons bid on property to be sold and the property is sold to the highest bidder

²auction *vt* **auc·tioned**; **auc·tion·ing** \-sh(ə-)niŋ\ : to sell at auction

auc·tion·eer \,ȯk-shə-'ni(ə)r\ *n* : an agent who sells goods for another at auction — **auctioneer** *vt*

au·da·cious \ȯ-'dā-shəs\ *adj* 1 **a** : intrepidly daring : ADVENTUROUS **b** : recklessly bold : RASH 2 : INSOLENT, IMPUDENT — **au·da·cious·ly** *adv* — **au·da·cious·ness** *n*

au·dac·i·ty \ȯ-'das-ət-ē\ *n, pl* **-ties** 1 : BOLDNESS, DARING 2 : IMPUDENCE

au·di·ble \'ȯd-ə-bəl\ *adj* : loud enough to be heard — **au·di·bil·i·ty** \,ȯd-ə-'bil-ət-ē\ *n* — **au·di·bly** \'ȯd-ə-blē\ *adv*

au·di·ence \'ȯd-ē-ən(t)s\ *n* 1 : the act or state of hearing 2 : an assembled group that listens or watches (as at a play, concert, or sports event) 3 : an opportunity of being heard; *esp* : a formal interview with a person of very high rank 4 : those of the general public who give attention to something said, done, or written

au·dio \'ȯd-ē-,ō\ *adj* 1 : of or relating to electrical or other vibrational frequencies corresponding to normally audible sound waves **2 a :** of or relating to sound or its reproduction and esp. high-fidelity reproduction **b :** relating to or used in the transmission or reception of sound — **audio** *n*

au·dio·phile \'ȯd-ē-ə-ˌfīl\ *n* **:** one who is enthusiastic about high-fidelity sound reproduction

au·dio·vi·su·al \ˌȯd-ē-ō-'vizh-(ə-)wəl, -'vizh-əl\ *adj* **:** of, relating to, or making use of both hearing and sight

¹au·dit \'ȯd-ət\ *n* **:** a searching examination and verification of accounts and account books esp. of a business or society; *also* **:** the final report of such an examination

²audit *vt* **:** to make an audit of

¹au·di·tion \ȯ-'dish-ən\ *n* **1 :** the power or sense of hearing **2 :** a critical hearing; *esp* **:** a trial performance to appraise an entertainer's merits

²audition *vb* **-di·tioned**; **-di·tion·ing** \-'dish-(ə-)niŋ\ **1 :** to test in an audition **2 :** to give a trial performance

au·di·tor \'ȯd-ət-ər\ *n* **1 :** one that hears or listens **2 :** a person authorized to examine and verify accounts

au·di·to·ri·um \ˌȯd-ə-'tōr-ē-əm\ *n* **1 :** the part of a public building where an audience sits **2 :** a room, hall, or building used for public gatherings

au·di·to·ry \'ȯd-ə-ˌtōr-ē\ *adj* **:** of or relating to hearing or to the sense or organs of hearing

auf Wie·der·seh·en \au̇f-'vēd-ər-ˌzā(-ə)n\ *interj* — used to express farewell

au·ger \'ȯ-gər\ *n* **:** a boring tool

¹aught \'ȯt, 'ät\ *pron* **:** ALL

²aught *n* **:** ZERO, CIPHER

aug·ment \ȯg-'ment\ *vb* **1 :** to enlarge or increase esp. in size, amount, or degree **2 :** to become augmented **:** INCREASE — **aug·ment·a·ble** *adj* — **aug·ment·er** *n*

aug·men·ta·tion \ˌȯg-mən-'tā-shən, -ˌmen-\ *n* **1 :** the act of augmenting **2 :** something that augments **:** INCREASE, ENLARGEMENT

aug·men·ta·tive \ȯg-'ment-ət-iv\ *adj* **:** capable of augmenting or serving to augment

au gra·tin \ō-'grät-ᵊn, ȯ-, -'grat-\ *adj* **:** covered with bread crumbs, butter, and cheese and browned

¹au·gur \'ȯ-gər\ *n* **1 :** an official diviner of ancient Rome **2 :** SOOTHSAYER, DIVINER

²augur *vb* **1 :** to predict or foretell esp. from signs or omens **2 :** to serve as a sign **:** INDICATE

au·gu·ry \'ȯ-g(y)ə-rē\ *n, pl* **-ries 1 :** divination from omens or portents or from chance events (as the fall of lots) **2 :** an indication of the future **:** OMEN

au·gust \ȯ-'gəst\ *adj* **:** marked by majestic dignity or grandeur — **au·gust·ly** *adv* — **au·gust·ness** *n*

Au·gust \'ȯ-gəst\ *n* **:** the 8th month of the year

auk \'ȯk\ *n* **:** any of several thickset black-and-white short-necked diving seabirds that breed in colder parts of the northern hemisphere

auld lang syne \ˌōl-ˌ(d)laŋ-'zīn, ˌȯl-\ *n* **:** the good old times

aunt \'ant, 'ȧnt\ *n* **1 :** the sister of one's father or mother **2 :** the wife of one's uncle

au·ra \'ȯr-ə\ *n* **1 a :** a subtle sensory stimulus (as an aroma) **b :** a distinctive atmosphere or impression surrounding a person or thing **2 :** a luminous radiation **:** NIMBUS

au·ral \'ȯr-əl\ *adj* **:** of or relating to the ear or sense of hearing — **au·ral·ly** \-ē\ *adv*

au·re·ate \'ȯr-ē-ət\ *adj* **1 :** of a golden color or brilliance **2 :** RESPLENDENT, ORNATE, GRANDILOQUENT

au·re·ole \'ȯr-ē-ˌōl\ *or* **au·re·o·la** \ȯ-'rē-ə-lə\ *n* **:** HALO, NIMBUS

au re·voir \ˌōr-əv-'wär\ *n* **:** GOOD-BYE

au·ri·cle \'ȯr-i-kəl\ *n* **1 :** the external ear **2 :** the chamber or either of the chambers of the heart that receives blood from the veins

au·ric·u·lar \ȯ-'rik-yə-lər\ *adj* **1 :** of or relating to the ear or the sense of hearing **2 :** told privately **3 :** known by the sense of hearing **4 :** of or relating to an auricle

au·ro·ra \ə-'rōr-ə\ *n, pl* **-ras** *or* **-rae** \-'rōr-(ˌ)ē\ **1 :** AURORA BOREALIS **2 :** AURORA AUSTRALIS — **au·ro·ral** \-əl\ *adj*

aurora aus·tra·lis \-ȯ-'strā-ləs, -ä-\ *n* **:** a display of light in the southern hemisphere corresponding to the aurora borealis

aurora bo·re·al·is \-ˌbōr-ē-'al-əs\ *n* **:** streamers or arches of light in the sky at night that are held to be of electrical origin and appear to best advantage in the arctic regions

aus·pice \'ȯ-spəs\ *n* **1 :** observation in augury esp. of the flight and feeding of birds **2 :** a prophetic sign **:** AUGURY; *esp* **:** a favorable sign **3** *pl* **:** kindly patronage and guidance **:** PROTECTION

aus·pi·cious \ȯ-'spish-əs\ *adj* **1 :** promising success **:** FAVORABLE **2 :** PROSPEROUS, FORTUNATE — **aus·pi·cious·ly** *adv* — **aus·pi·cious·ness** *n*

aus·tere \ȯ-'sti(ə)r\ *adj* **1 a :** stern and forbidding in appearance and manner **b :** SOMBER, GRAVE **2 :** rigidly abstemious **:** ASCETIC **3 :** UNADORNED, SIMPLE — **aus·tere·ly** *adv* — **aus·tere·ness** *n*

aus·ter·i·ty \ȯ-'ster-ət-ē\ *n, pl* **-ties 1 :** the quality or state of being austere **2 a :** an austere act, manner, or attitude **b :** an ascetic practice **3 :** enforced or extreme economy

aus·tral \'ȯs-trəl, 'äs-\ *adj* **:** SOUTHERN

au·then·tic \ȯ-'thent-ik, ə-\ *adj* **1 :** being really what it seems to be **:** GENUINE **2 :** TRUE, CORRECT — **au·then·ti·cal·ly** \-'thent-i-k(ə-)lē\ *adv* — **au·then·tic·i·ty** \ˌȯ-ˌthen-'tis-ət-ē\ *n*

au·then·ti·cate \ȯ-'thent-i-ˌkāt, ə-\ *vt* **:** to prove, establish, or attest the authenticity of — **au·then·ti·ca·tion** \-ˌthent-i-'kā-shən\ *n* — **au·then·ti·ca·tor** \-'thent-i-ˌkāt-ər\ *n*

au·thor \'ȯ-thər\ *n* **1 :** one that writes or composes a literary work (as a book) **2 :** one that originates or makes; *esp* **:** GOD — **author** *vt* — **au·thor·ess** \'ȯ-th(ə-)rəs\ *n* — **au·tho·ri·al** \ȯ-'thōr-ē-əl\ *adj*

au·thor·i·tar·i·an \ə-ˌthȯr-ə-'ter-ē-ən, ȯ-\ *adj* **:** relating to, advocating, or demanding total submission to authority as concentrated in a leader or an elite not constitutionally responsible to the people — **authoritarian** *n* — **au·thor·i·tar·i·an·ism** \-ē-ə-ˌniz-əm\ *n*

au·thor·i·ta·tive \ə-'thȯr-ə-ˌtāt-iv, ȯ-\ *adj* **1 :** having authority **:** coming from or based on authority **2 :** entitled to obedience or acceptance **3 :** having an air of authority **:** POSITIVE — **au·thor·i·ta·tive·ly** *adv* — **au·thor·i·ta·tive·ness** *n*

au·thor·i·ty \ə-'thȯr-ət-ē, ȯ-\ *n, pl* **-ties 1 a :** a fact or statement used to support a position; *also* **:** a person, text, or prior decision that is the source of such a fact or statement **b :** a person appealed to as an expert **2 a :** the right to give commands and the power to enforce obedience **b :** delegated power **3 a :** a person or persons having powers of government **b :** a government agency or corporation that administers a revenue-producing public enterprise

au·tho·rize \'ȯ-thə-ˌrīz\ *vt* **1 :** to give authority to **:** EMPOWER **2 :** to give legal or official approval or permission to **3 :** to establish by or as if by authority **:** SANCTION, APPROVE — **au·tho·ri·za·tion** \ˌȯ-th(ə-)rə-'zā-shən\ *n* — **au·tho·riz·er** *n*

au·thor·ship \'ȯ-thər-ˌship\ *n* **1 :** the profession of writing **2 a :** the origin of a literary production **b :** the state or act of creating or causing

au·to \'ȯt-ō\ *n* **:** AUTOMOBILE

au·to·bi·og·ra·phy \ˌȯt-ə-bī-'äg-rə-fē\ *n* **:** the biography of a person narrated by himself — **au·to·bi·og·ra·pher** \-rə-fər\ *n* — **au·to·bio·graph·ic** \-ˌbī-ə-'graf-ik\ *or* **au·to·bio·graph·i·cal** \-'graf-i-kəl\ *adj* — **au·to·bio·graph·i·cal·ly** \-i-k(ə-)lē\ *adv*

au·toc·ra·cy \ȯ-'täk-rə-sē\ *n, pl* **-cies 1 :** government in which one person possesses unlimited power **2 :** the authority or rule of an autocrat **3 :** a community or state governed by autocracy

au·to·crat \'ȯt-ə-ˌkrat\ *n* : a person (as a monarch) ruling with unlimited authority

au·to·crat·ic \ˌȯt-ə-'krat-ik\ *adj* : of, relating to, characteristic of, or resembling autocracy or an autocrat : DESPOTIC — **au·to·crat·i·cal·ly** \-'krat-i-k(ə-)lē\ *adv*

[1]**au·to·graph** \'ȯt-ə-ˌgraf\ *n* : something written with one's own hand; *esp* : a person's handwritten signature

[2]**autograph** *vt* : to write one's signature in or on

au·to·in·tox·i·ca·tion \ˌȯt-ō-in-ˌtäk-sə-'kā-shən\ *n* : a state of being poisoned by substances produced within the body

au·to·mate \'ȯt-ə-ˌmāt\ *vt* **1** : to operate by automation **2** : to convert to automatic operation

[1]**au·to·mat·ic** \ˌȯt-ə-'mat-ik\ *adj* **1 a** : largely or wholly involuntary **b** : acting or done spontaneously or unconsciously; *also* : resembling an automaton : MECHANICAL **2** : having a self-acting or self-regulating mechanism — **au·to·mat·i·cal·ly** \-'mat-i-k(ə-)lē\ *adv*

[2]**automatic** *n* : an automatic machine or apparatus; *esp* : an automatic firearm

au·to·ma·tion \ˌȯt-ə-'mā-shən\ *n* **1** : the method of making an apparatus, a process, or a system operate automatically **2** : the state of being operated automatically **3** : automatic operation of an apparatus, process, or system by mechanical or electronic devices that take the place of human operators

au·tom·a·tize \ȯ-'täm-ə-ˌtīz\ *vt* : to make automatic — **au·tom·a·ti·za·tion** \ȯ-ˌtäm-ət-ə-'zā-shən\ *n*

au·tom·a·ton \ȯ-'täm-ət-ən, -'täm-ə-ˌtän\ *n, pl* **-atons** *or* **-a·ta** \-ət-ə\ **1** : a machine that can move by itself; *esp* : one made to imitate the motions of a man or an animal **2** : a person who acts in a mechanical fashion

au·to·mo·bile \ˌȯt-ə-mō-'bēl, -'mō-ˌbēl\ *n* : a usu. four-wheeled automotive vehicle designed for passenger transportation on streets and roadways and commonly propelled by an internal-combustion engine — **automobile** *vi* — **au·to·mo·bil·ist** \-mō-'bē-ləst\ *n*

au·to·mo·tive \ˌȯt-ə-'mōt-iv\ *adj* **1** : SELF-PROPELLED **2** : of, relating to, or concerned with automotive vehicles and esp. automobiles and motorcycles

au·ton·o·mous \ȯ-'tän-ə-məs\ *adj* **1** : relating to, marked by, or possessing autonomy; *esp* : independent of outside control : SELF-GOVERNING **2** : existing, responding, reacting, or developing independently of the whole — **au·ton·o·mous·ly** *adv*

au·ton·o·my \-mē\ *n, pl* **-mies** : the quality or state of being self-governing; *also* : the power or right of self-government

au·top·sy \'ȯ-ˌtäp-sē, 'ȯt-əp-\ *n, pl* **-sies** : an examination of a dead body usu. to determine the cause of death — **autopsy** *vt*

au·tumn \'ȯt-əm\ *n* **1** : the season between summer and winter comprising in the northern hemisphere usu. the months of September, October, and November or as reckoned astronomically extending from the September equinox to the December solstice **2** : a time or season of maturity or decline — **au·tum·nal** \ȯ-'təm-nəl\ *adj*

[1]**aux·il·ia·ry** \ȯg-'zil-yə-rē\ *adj* **1 a** : offering or providing help **b** : functioning in a subsidiary capacity : SUPPLEMENTARY, RESERVE **2** : being a verb that accompanies another verb and typically expresses such things as person, number, mood, or tense

[2]**auxiliary** *n, pl* **-ries** **1** : an auxiliary person, group, or device; *esp* : a member of a foreign force serving a nation at war **2** : an auxiliary verb

aux·in \'ȯk-sən\ *n* : a plant hormone; *esp* : one that stimulates shoot elongation

[1]**avail** \ə-'vāl\ *vb* : to be of use or advantage : HELP, BENEFIT

[2]**avail** *n* : help or benefit toward attainment of a goal : USE

avail·a·bil·i·ty \ə-ˌvā-lə-'bil-ət-ē\ *n, pl* **-ties** **1** : the quality or state of being available **2** : an available person or thing

avail·a·ble \ə-'vā-lə-bəl\ *adj* **1** : such as may be availed of : USABLE **2** : ACCESSIBLE, OBTAINABLE — **avail·a·ble·ness** *n* — **avail·a·bly** \-blē\ *adv*

av·a·lanche \'av-ə-ˌlanch\ *n* : a large mass of snow and ice or of earth and rock sliding down a mountainside or over a steep cliff

avant–garde \ˌäv-ˌän(t)-'gärd, ˌäv-ˌäⁿ-\ *n* : those in the arts who create or apply new or highly experimental ideas — **avant–garde** *adj* — **avant–gard·ism** \-'gärd-ˌiz-əm\ *n* — **avant–gard·ist** \-'gärd-əst\ *n*

av·a·rice \'av-(ə-)rəs\ *n* : excessive or insatiable desire for wealth or gain : GREED

av·a·ri·cious \ˌav-ə-'rish-əs\ *adj* : greedy of gain : GRASPING — **av·a·ri·cious·ly** *adv* — **av·a·ri·cious·ness** *n*

avast \ə-'vast\ *imperative verb* — a nautical command to stop or cease

av·a·tar \'av-ə-ˌtär\ *n* : an embodiment (as of a concept, philosophy, or tradition) usu. in human form

Ave Ma·ria \ˌäv-ˌā-mə-'rē-ə\ *n* : a salutation and prayer to the Virgin Mary

avenge \ə-'venj\ *vt* **1** : to take vengeance for or on behalf of **2** : to exact satisfaction for (a wrong) by punishing the wrongdoer — **aveng·er** *n*

av·e·nue \'av-ə-ˌn(y)ü\ *n* **1** : an opening or passageway to a place **2** : a way or means to an end **3** : a street esp. when broad and attractive

aver \ə-'vər\ *vt* **averred**; **aver·ring** : to declare positively : ASSERT, ALLEGE

[1]**av·er·age** \'av-(ə-)rij\ *n* **1** : a value computed by dividing the sum of a set of terms by the number of terms **2** : something typical of a group, class, or series **3** : a ratio (as a rate per thousand) of successful tries to total tries

[2]**average** *adj* **1** : equaling or approximating an average **2 a** : being about midway between extremes **b** : being not out of the ordinary : COMMON — **av·er·age·ly** *adv* — **av·er·age·ness** *n*

[3]**average** *vb* **1** : to be at or come to an average **2** : to amount to on the average : be usually **3** : to find the average of **4** : to bring toward an average

averse \ə-'vərs\ *adj* : having an active feeling of repugnance or distaste — **averse·ly** *adv* — **averse·ness** *n*

aver·sion \ə-'vər-zhən\ *n* **1** : a feeling of repugnance toward something with a desire to avoid or turn from it **2** : a settled dislike : ANTIPATHY

avert \ə-'vərt\ *vt* **1** : to turn away **2** : to prevent from happening : ward off

avi·an \'ā-vē-ən\ *adj* : of, relating to, or derived from birds

avi·ary \'ā-vē-ˌer-ē\ *n, pl* **-ar·ies** : a place (as a large cage or a building) where many live birds are kept usu. for exhibition — **avi·a·rist** \-vē-ə-rəst\ *n*

avi·a·tion \ˌā-vē-'ā-shən, ˌav-ē-\ *n* **1** : the operation of heavier-than-air aircraft **2** : military airplanes — **aviation** *adj*

aviation cadet *n* : a student officer in the air force

avi·a·tor \'ā-vē-ˌāt-ər, 'av-ē-\ *n* : the pilot of a heavier-than-air aircraft

avi·a·trix \ˌā-vē-'ā-triks, ˌav-ē-\ *n* : a woman aviator

av·id \'av-əd\ *adj* **1** : craving eagerly : GREEDY **2** : marked by eagerness and enthusiasm — **avid·i·ty** \ə-'vid-ət-ē, a-\ *n* — **av·id·ly** *adv* — **av·id·ness** *n*

av·o·ca·do \ˌav-ə-'käd-ō\ *n, pl* **-dos** : the usu. green pulpy pear-shaped or egg-shaped oily edible fruit of a tropical American tree; *also* : the tree that bears this fruit

av·o·ca·tion \ˌav-ə-'kā-shən\ *n* : a subordinate occupation pursued in addition to one's vocation esp. for enjoyment : HOBBY — **av·o·ca·tion·al** \-shnəl, -shən-ᵊl\ *adj*

avoid \ə-'vȯid\ *vt* **1** : to make legally void : ANNUL **2 a** : to keep away from : SHUN **b** : to refrain from — **avoid·a·ble** *adj* — **avoid·a·bly** \-ə-blē\ *adv*

avoid·ance \ə-'vȯid-ᵊn(t)s\ *n* **1** : the act of annulling **2** : the act of keeping away from or clear of

av·oir·du·pois \ˌav-ərd-ə-'pȯiz\ *n* **1** : AVOIRDUPOIS WEIGHT **2** : WEIGHT, HEAVINESS

avoirdupois weight *n* : the series of units of weight based on the pound of 16 ounces and the ounce of 16 drams

avouch \ə-'vau̇ch\ *vt* 1 : to declare positively : AFFIRM 2 : to vouch for : GUARANTEE

avow \ə-'vau̇\ *vt* : to declare or acknowledge openly and frankly

avow·al \ə-'vau̇(-ə)l\ *n* : an open declaration or acknowledgment

avowed \ə-'vau̇d\ *adj* : openly acknowledged or declared : ADMITTED — **avowed·ly** \-'vau̇(-ə)d-lē\ *adv*

avun·cu·lar \ə-'vəŋ-kyə-lər\ *adj* : of, relating to, or characteristic of an uncle

await \ə-'wāt\ *vb* 1 : to wait for : stay for : EXPECT 2 : to be ready or waiting for

[1]**awake** \ə-'wāk\ *vb* **awoke** \-'wōk\ *or* **awaked** \-'wākt\; **awak·ing** 1 : to cease sleeping 2 : to become conscious or aware of something 3 : to arouse from sleep 4 : to make or become active : STIR

[2]**awake** *adj* : roused from sleep : ALERT

awak·en \ə-'wā-kən\ *vb* **awak·ened**; **awak·en·ing** \-'wāk-(ə-)niŋ\ : AWAKE — **awak·en·er** *n*

[1]**award** \ə-'wȯrd\ *vt* 1 : to give by judicial decision (as after a lawsuit) : ADJUDGE 2 : to give or grant as a reward — **award·a·ble** *adj* — **award·er** *n*

[2]**award** *n* 1 : JUDGMENT, DECISION; *esp* : the decision of arbitrators in a case submitted to them 2 : something that is conferred or bestowed : PRIZE

aware \ə-'wa(ə)r\ *adj* : having or showing realization, perception, or knowledge : CONSCIOUS — **aware·ness** *n*

awash \ə-'wȯsh, -'wäsh\ *adv (or adj)* 1 : washed by waves or tide 2 : washing about : AFLOAT 3 : overflowed by water

[1]**away** \ə-'wā\ *adv* 1 : on the way : ALONG 2 : from this or that place : HENCE, THENCE 3 **a** : in another place **b** : in another direction 4 : out of existence : to an end 5 : from one's possession 6 **a** : UNINTERRUPTEDLY, ON **b** : without hesitation or delay 7 : by a long distance or interval : FAR

[2]**away** *adj* 1 : absent from a place : GONE 2 : DISTANT

[1]**awe** \'ȯ\ *n* 1 : a profoundly humble and reverential attitude in the presence of deity 2 : abashed fear inspired by authority or power 3 : veneration inspired by something sacred, mysterious, or sublime

[2]**awe** *vt* 1 : to inspire with awe 2 : to control or check by inspiring with awe

aweigh \ə-'wā\ *adj* : just clear of the bottom and hanging perpendicularly

awe·some \'ȯ-səm\ *adj* 1 : expressive of awe 2 : inspiring awe — **awe·some·ly** *adv* — **awe·some·ness** *n*

awe·strick·en \'ȯ-ˌstrik-ən\ *or* **awe·struck** \-ˌstrək\ *adj* : filled with awe

[1]**aw·ful** \'ȯ-fəl\ *adj* 1 : inspiring awe 2 : extremely disagreeable or objectionable 3 : exceedingly great — used as an intensive — **aw·ful·ness** *n*

[2]**awful** *adv* : AWFULLY, VERY, EXTREMELY

aw·ful·ly *usu* 'ȯ-fə-lē *in sense* 1, 'ȯ-flē *in senses* 2 & 3\ *adv* 1 : in a manner to inspire awe 2 : in a disagreeable or objectionable manner 3 : EXCEEDINGLY, EXTREMELY

awhile \ə-'hwīl\ *adv* : for a while : for a short time

awhirl \ə-'hwərl\ *adv (or adj)* : in a whirl : WHIRLING

awk·ward \'ȯ-kwərd\ *adj* 1 : lacking dexterity or skill esp. in the use of the hands or of instruments : CLUMSY 2 **a** : lacking ease or grace of movement or expression **b** : appearing ill-proportioned, outsize, or poorly fitted together : UNGAINLY 3 : causing embarrassment 4 : poorly adapted for use or handling — **awk·ward·ly** *adv* — **awk·ward·ness** *n*

awl \'ȯl\ *n* : a pointed tool for making small holes (as in leather or wood)

awn \'ȯn\ *n* : one of the bristles on a spike of grass — **awned** \'ȯnd\ *adj* — **awn·less** \'ȯn-ləs\ *adj*

aw·ning \'ȯn-iŋ, 'än-\ *n* : a cover esp. of canvas resembling a roof and extended over or in front of something to provide shade or shelter

awoke *past of* AWAKE

AWOL \'ā-ˌwȯl, ˌā-ˌdəb-əl-yü-ˌō-'el\ *n* : a person who is absent without permission — **AWOL** *adv (or adj)*

awry \ə-'rī\ *adv (or adj)* 1 : turned or twisted toward one side : ASKEW 2 : out of the right course : AMISS

ax *or* **axe** \'aks\ *n* : a cutting tool that consists of a heavy edged head fixed to a handle and is used for chopping and splitting wood

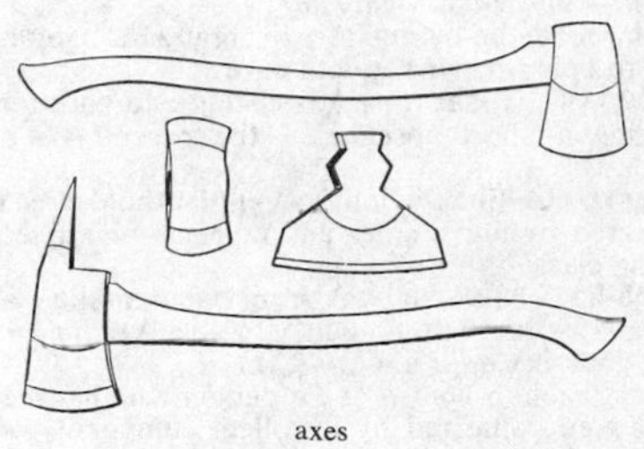

axes

ax·i·al \'ak-sē-əl\ *or* **ax·al** \-səl\ *adj* 1 : of, relating to, or functioning as an axis 2 : situated around, in the direction of, on, or along an axis — **ax·i·al·ly** \-sē-ə-lē\ *adv*

ax·i·om \'ak-sē-əm\ *n* 1 : a maxim widely accepted on its intrinsic merit 2 **a** : a proposition regarded as a self-evident truth **b** : POSTULATE

ax·i·om·at·ic \ˌak-sē-ə-'mat-ik\ *adj* : of, relating to, or having the nature of an axiom : SELF-EVIDENT — **ax·i·om·at·i·cal·ly** \-'mat-i-k(ə-)lē\ *adv*

ax·is \'ak-səs\ *n, pl* **ax·es** \'ak-ˌsēz\ 1 **a** : a straight line about which a body or a geometric figure rotates or may be supposed to rotate **b** : a straight line with respect to which a body or figure is symmetrical 2 : a main line of direction, motion, growth, or extension 3 : a central, crucial, or fundamental part : PIVOT 4 : PARTNERSHIP, ALLIANCE

ax·le \'ak-səl\ *n* 1 : a pin or shaft on or with which a wheel or pair of wheels revolves 2 : AXLETREE

axle·tree \-(ˌ)trē\ *n* : a fixed bar with bearings at its ends on which wheels (as of a cart) revolve

[1]**aye** \'ā\ *adv* : FOREVER, ALWAYS, CONTINUALLY

[2]**aye** \'ī\ *adv* : YES

[3]**aye** \'ī\ *n, pl* **ayes** : an affirmative vote or voter

aza·lea \ə-'zāl-yə\ *n* : any of numerous rhododendrons with funnel-shaped flowers and usu. deciduous leaves including many grown as ornamentals

az·i·muth \'az-(ə-)məth\ *n* : horizontal direction

azure \'azh-ər\ *n* : the blue color of the clear sky — **azure** *adj*

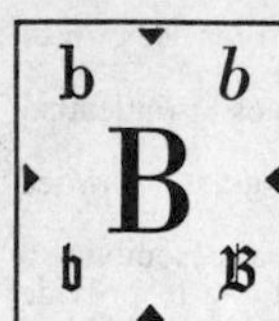

b \'bē\ *n, often cap* **1 :** the 2d letter of the English alphabet **2 :** the musical tone B **3 :** a grade rating a student's work as good
bab•ble \'bab-əl\ *vb* **bab•bled; bab•bling** \'bab-(ə-)liŋ\ **1 :** to utter meaningless sounds **2 :** to talk foolishly or excessively — **babble** *n* — **bab•bler** \'bab-(ə-)lər\ *n*
babe \'bāb\ *n* **:** INFANT, BABY
ba•bel \'bā-bəl, 'bab-əl\ *n, often cap* **1 :** a confusion of sounds or voices **2 :** a scene of noise or confusion
ba•boon \ba-'bün\ *n* **:** any of several large African and Asiatic apes having doglike muzzles and short tails
ba•bush•ka \bə-'bu̇sh-kə\ *n* **:** a kerchief for the head usu. folded triangularly
¹ba•by \'bā-bē\ *n, pl* **ba•bies** **1 a :** an extremely young child **b :** the youngest of a group **2 :** a childish person — **ba•by•hood** \-,hu̇d\ *n* — **ba•by•ish** \-ish\ *adj*
²baby *vt* **ba•bied; ba•by•ing** **1 :** to treat as a baby **:** FONDLE, PET **2 :** to operate or treat with care
ba•by–sit \-,sit\ *vi* **-sat** \-,sat\; **-sit•ting :** to care for children usu. during a short absence of the parents — **ba•by–sit•ter** *n*
bac•ca•lau•re•ate \,bak-ə-'lȯr-ē-ət\ *n* **1 :** the degree of bachelor conferred by universities and colleges **2 :** a sermon to a graduating class
bac•cha•na•lia \,bak-ə-'nāl-yə\ *n, pl* **bacchanalia :** a drunken feast **:** ORGY — **bac•cha•na•lian** \-'nāl-yən\ *adj or n*
bac•chic \'bak-ik\ *adj* **:** BACCHANALIAN
bach•e•lor \'bach-(ə-)lər\ *n* **1 :** a person who has received the lowest degree conferred by a college, university, or professional school **2 :** an unmarried man — **bach•e•lor•hood** \-,hu̇d\ *n*
bac•il•lary \'bas-ə-,ler-ē\ *or* **ba•cil•lar** \bə-'sil-ər\ *adj* **:** of, relating to, or produced by bacilli
ba•cil•lus \bə-'sil-əs\ *n, pl* **-cil•li** \-'sil-,ī, -'sil-ē\ **:** any of numerous straight aerobic rod-shaped bacteria; *also* **:** a disease-producing bacterium
¹back \'bak\ *n* **1 a :** the rear part of the human body esp. from the neck to the end of the spine **b :** the corresponding part of a lower animal **2 :** the hinder part **:** REAR; *also* **:** the farther or reverse side **3 :** a player in the backfield in football — **backed** \'bakt\ *adj* — **back•less** \'bak-ləs\ *adj*
²back *adv* **1 a :** to, toward, or at the rear **b :** in or into the past **:** AGO **c :** in or into a reclining position **d :** under restraint **2 a :** to, toward, or in a place or state from which a person or thing came **b :** in return or reply
³back *adj* **1 :** being at or in the back **2 :** being in arrears **:** OVERDUE **3 :** not current
⁴back *vb* **1 :** to give aid or support to **:** ASSIST **2 :** to move or cause to move back, backward, or in reverse **3 a :** to furnish with a back **b :** to be or be at the back of — **back•er** *n*
back•bite \-,bīt\ *vb* **:** to say mean or spiteful things about someone who is absent **:** SLANDER — **back•bit•er** *n*
back•board \-,bōrd\ *n* **:** a board or construction placed at the back or serving as a back
back•bone \-'bōn, -,bōn\ *n* **1 :** SPINAL COLUMN **2 :** the foundation or sturdiest part of something **3 :** firm and resolute character — **back•boned** \-'bōnd, -,bōnd\ *adj*
back•drop \-,dräp\ *n* **:** a painted cloth hung across the rear of a stage
back•field \-,fēld\ *n* **:** the football players who line up behind the line of scrimmage
¹back•fire \-,fī(ə)r\ *n* **:** an improperly timed explosion of fuel mixture in the cylinder of an internal-combustion engine
²backfire *vi* **1 :** to make a backfire **2 :** to have an effect that is the reverse of the one desired or expected
back•gam•mon \'bak-,gam-ən\ *n* **:** a game played by two persons on a double board with pieces whose movements are determined by throwing dice
back•ground \-,grau̇nd\ *n* **1 :** the scenery, ground, or surface behind an object seen or represented (as in a painting) **2 a :** the setting within which something takes place **b :** information essential to understanding a problem or situation **c :** the total of a person's experience, knowledge, and education
back•hand \'bak-,hand\ *n* **:** a stroke made with the back of the hand turned in the direction of movement — **backhand** *adj*
back•hand•ed \-,han-dəd\ *adj* **:** DEVIOUS; *esp* **:** SARCASTIC
back•ing \'bak-iŋ\ *n* **1 :** something forming a back **2 a :** SUPPORT, AID **b :** ENDORSEMENT, APPROVAL **3 :** those who support a person or enterprise
back•lash \'bak-,lash\ *n* **:** a sudden violent backward movement or reaction
back•log \-,lȯg, -,läg\ *n* **1 :** a large log at the back of a hearth fire **2 :** a reserve esp. of unfilled orders **3 :** an accumulation of unperformed tasks
back of *prep* **:** BEHIND
back•side \'bak-'sīd\ *n* **:** BUTTOCKS
back•slide \-,slīd\ *vi* **-slid** \-,slid\; **-slid** *or* **-slid•den** \-,slid-ᵊn\; **-slid•ing** \-,slīd-iŋ\ **:** to lapse morally or in the practice of religion — **back•slid•er** \-,slīd-ər\ *n*
back•spin \-,spin\ *n* **:** a backward rotary motion of a ball
back•stop \-,stäp\ *n* **:** something serving as a stop behind something else; *esp* **:** a screen or fence used in a game (as baseball) to keep a ball from leaving the field of play
back•stretch \-,strech, -'strech\ *n* **:** the side opposite the homestretch on a racecourse
back•stroke \-,strōk\ *n* **:** a swimming stroke executed by a swimmer lying on his back
back•track \-,trak\ *vi* **:** to retrace one's course
¹back•ward \-wərd\ *or* **back•wards** \-wərdz\ *adv* **1 a :** toward the back **b :** with the back foremost **2 a :** in a reverse or contrary direction or way **b :** toward the past **c :** toward a worse state
²backward *adj* **1 :** directed or turned backward **2 :** DIFFIDENT, SHY **3 :** retarded in development — **back•ward•ly** *adv* — **back•ward•ness** *n*
back•wash \-,wȯsh, -,wäsh\ *n* **:** backward movement (as of water or air) produced by motion of oars or other propelling force
back•woods \-'wu̇dz, -,wu̇dz\ *n pl* **1 :** wooded or partly cleared areas on the frontier **2 :** a remote culturally backward area — **back•woods•man** \-mən\ *n*
ba•con \'bā-kən\ *n* **:** salted and smoked meat from the sides and sometimes the back of a pig
bac•te•ri•ol•o•gy \bak-,tir-ē-'äl-ə-jē\ *n* **1 :** a science that deals with bacteria **2 :** bacterial life and phenomena — **bac•te•ri•o•log•ic** \-ē-ə-'läj-ik\ *or* **bac•te•ri•o•log•i•cal** \-'läj-i-kəl\ *adj* — **bac•te•ri•o•log•i•cal•ly** \-'läj-i-k(ə-)lē\ *adv* — **bac•te•ri•ol•o•gist** \-ē-'äl-ə-jəst\ *n*
bac•te•ri•um \bak-'tir-ē-əm\ *n, pl* **-ria** \-ē-ə\ **:** any of a class of microscopic plants living in soil, water, organic matter, or the bodies of plants and animals and being important to man because of their chemical effects and as causers of disease — **bac•te•ri•al** \-ē-əl\ *adj*
¹bad \'bad\ *adj* **worse** \'wərs\; **worst** \'wərst\ **1 a :** below standard **:** POOR **b :** UNFAVORABLE **c :** DECAYED, SPOILED **2 a :** morally evil **b :** MISCHIEVOUS, DISOBEDIENT **3 :** INADEQUATE **4 :** DISAGREEABLE, UNPLEASANT **5 a :** INJURIOUS, HARMFUL **b :** SEVERE **6 :** INCORRECT, FAULTY **7 :** ILL, SICK **8 :** SORROWFUL, SORRY **9 :** INVALID, VOID — **bad** *adv* — **bad•ly** *adv* — **bad•ness** *n*
²bad *n* **:** an evil or unhappy state
bade *past of* BID
badge \'baj\ *n* **:** a mark or sign worn to show that a person belongs to a certain group, class, or rank

¹badg·er \ˈbaj-ər\ *n* : any of several sturdy burrowing mammals widely distributed in the northern hemisphere
²badger *vt* **badg·ered**; **badg·er·ing** \ˈbaj-(ə-)riŋ\ : to harass or annoy persistently
bad·i·nage \ˌbad-ᵊn-ˈäzh\ *n* : playful talk back and forth
bad·min·ton \ˈbad-ˌmint-ᵊn\ *n* : a court game played with a light racket and a shuttlecock volleyed over a net
¹baf·fle \ˈbaf-əl\ *vt* **baf·fled**; **baf·fling** \ˈbaf-(ə-)liŋ\ : to defeat or check by confusing : PERPLEX — **baf·fle·ment** *n* — **baf·fler** \-(ə-)lər\ *n*
²baffle *n* : a plate, wall, screen, or other device to deflect, check, or regulate flow
¹bag \ˈbag\ *n* **1** : a flexible usu. closed container for holding, storing, or carrying something **2** : something resembling a bag — **in the bag** : SURE, CERTAIN
²bag *vb* **bagged**; **bag·ging** **1** : to swell out : BULGE **2** : to put into a bag **3 a** : to take (animals) as game **b** : CAPTURE, SEIZE; *also* : to shoot down : DESTROY
bag·a·telle \ˌbag-ə-ˈtel\ *n* : TRIFLE
ba·gel \ˈbā-gəl\ *n* : a hard glazed doughnut-shaped roll
bag·gage \ˈbag-ij\ *n* **1** : the traveling bags and belongings of a traveler **2** : a worthless saucy woman or girl
bag·gy \ˈbag-ē\ *adj* : loose, puffed out, or hanging like a bag
ba·gnio \ˈban-yō\ *n, pl* **bagnios** : BROTHEL
bag·pipe \ˈbag-ˌpīp\ *n* : a wind instrument consisting of a leather bag, a valve-stopped tube, and three or four sounding pipes — often used in pl. — **bag·pip·er** *n*
¹bail \ˈbāl\ *n* **1** : security given to guarantee the appearance of a prisoner when legally required **2** : the temporary release of a prisoner upon security **3** : one who provides bail
²bail *vt* **1 a** : to release under bail **b** : to gain the release of by giving bail **2** : to help from a predicament usu. by financial aid
³bail *vt* : to clear (water) from a boat by dipping and throwing over the side
⁴bail *n* : the arched handle of a kettle or pail
bai·liff \ˈbā-ləf\ *n* **1** : an official employed by a British sheriff to serve writs and make arrests and executions **2** : a minor officer of some U.S. courts usu. serving as a messenger or doorkeeper — **bai·liff·ship** \-ˌship\ *n*
bai·li·wick \ˈbā-li-ˌwik\ *n* **1** : the office or jurisdiction of a bailiff or a sheriff **2** : one's special province or domain
¹bait \ˈbāt\ *vt* **1** : to persecute or exasperate by repeated attacks **2** : to harass with dogs usu. for sport **3 a** : to furnish (as a hook) with bait **b** : ENTICE, LURE **4** : to give food and drink to (an animal) — **bait·er** *n*
²bait *n* **1** : something used in luring esp. to a hook or trap **2** : LURE, TEMPTATION
baize \ˈbāz\ *n* : a coarse fabric napped to imitate felt
¹bake \ˈbāk\ *vb* **1** : to cook or become cooked in a dry heat esp. in an oven **2** : to dry or harden by heat — **bak·er** *n*
²bake *n* **1** : the act or process of baking **2** : a social gathering at which a baked food is served
bak·ery \ˈbā-k(ə-)rē\ *n, pl* **-er·ies** : a place where bread, cakes, and pastry are made or sold
bake·shop \ˈbāk-ˌshäp\ *n* : BAKERY
bak·sheesh \ˈbak-ˌshēsh, bak-ˈ\ *n, pl* **baksheesh** : a gift of money esp. in the Near East : GRATUITY
¹bal·ance \ˈbal-ən(t)s\ *n* **1** : an instrument for weighing **2** : a means of judging or deciding **3** : a counterbalancing weight, force, or influence **4** : a vibrating wheel used to regulate the movement of a timepiece **5 a** : equipoise between contrasting or interacting elements **b** : equality between the totals of the two sides of an account **6** : something left over : REMAINDER; *esp* : the amount by which one side of an account is greater than the other **7** : mental and emotional steadiness
²balance *vb* **1 a** : to compute the difference between the debits and credits of an account **b** : to make two parts exactly equal **2 a** : COUNTERBALANCE, OFFSET **b** : to equal or equalize in weight, number, or proportion **3** : WEIGH **4 a** : to bring or come to a state or position of equipoise **b** : to poise in or as if in balance **c** : to bring into harmony or proportion — **bal·anc·er** *n*
bal·co·ny \ˈbal-kə-nē\ *n, pl* **-nies** **1** : a platform enclosed by a low wall or a railing and built out from the side of a building **2** : a gallery inside a building (as a theater)
bald \ˈbȯld\ *adj* **1** : lacking a natural or usual covering (as of hair) **2** : UNADORNED, PLAIN, SIMPLE — **bald·ly** *adv* — **bald·ness** *n*
bal·der·dash \ˈbȯl-dər-ˌdash\ *n* : NONSENSE
bal·dric \ˈbȯl-drik\ *n* : an often ornamented belt worn over one shoulder to support a sword or bugle
¹bale \ˈbāl\ *n* **1** : great evil **2** : WOE, SORROW
²bale *n* : a large bundle of goods; *esp* : a large closely pressed package of merchandise bound and usu. wrapped
³bale *vt* : to make up into a bale — **bal·er** *n*
ba·leen \bə-ˈlēn\ *n* : WHALEBONE
bale·ful \ˈbāl-fəl\ *adj* **1** : deadly or harmful in influence **2** : foreboding evil : OMINOUS — **bale·ful·ly** \-fə-lē\ *adv* — **bale·ful·ness** *n*
¹balk \ˈbȯk\ *n* : HINDRANCE, CHECK
²balk *vb* **1** : to check or stop by or as if by an obstacle : BLOCK **2** : to stop short and refuse to go : refuse abruptly — **balk·er** *n*
balky \ˈbȯ-kē\ *adj* : likely to balk : BALKING
¹ball \ˈbȯl\ *n* **1** : a round or roundish body or mass: as **a** : a spherical or ovoid body used in a game or sport **b** : EARTH, GLOBE **c** : a usu. round solid shot for a firearm **d** : the rounded bulge at the base of the thumb or great toe **2** : a game played with a ball **3** : a pitched baseball not struck at by the batter that fails to pass through the strike zone
²ball *vb* : to form or gather into a ball
³ball *n* : a large formal gathering for social dancing
bal·lad \ˈbal-əd\ *n* **1** : a simple song : AIR **2** : a narrative poem usu. in stanzas of two or four lines and suitable for singing **3** : a slow romantic dance song — **bal·lad·ry** \-ə-drē\ *n*
bal·last \ˈbal-əst\ *n* **1** : something heavy carried in a ship to steady it **2** : something heavy put into the car of a balloon to steady it or to control its ascent **3** : gravel, cinders, or crushed stone used in making a roadbed
ball·car·ri·er \ˈbȯl-ˌkar-ē-ər\ *n* : the football player carrying the ball in an offensive play
bal·le·ri·na \ˌbal-ə-ˈrē-nə\ *n* : a female ballet dancer
bal·let \ˈba-ˌlā, ba-ˈ\ *n* **1 a** : dancing in which conventional poses and steps are combined with light flowing figures and movements **b** : a theatrical art form using ballet dancing to convey a story, theme, or atmosphere **2** : music for a ballet **3** : a group that performs ballets
bal·lis·tic \bə-ˈlis-tik\ *adj* : of or relating to ballistics or to a body in motion according to the laws of ballistics
bal·lis·tics \-tiks\ *n sing or pl* **1** : the science that deals with the motion of projectiles (as bullets) **2** : the flight characteristics of a projectile
¹bal·loon \bə-ˈlün\ *n* **1** : an airtight bag filled with heated air or with a gas lighter than air so as to rise and float above the ground **2** : a toy consisting of a rubber bag that can be inflated with air or gas — **bal·loon·ist** \-ˈlü-nəst\ *n*
²balloon *vb* **1** : to ascend or travel in a balloon **2** : to swell or puff out **3** : to increase rapidly
¹bal·lot \ˈbal-ət\ *n* **1** : a sheet of paper used to cast a vote **2 a** : the action or system of voting **b** : the right to vote **3** : the number of votes cast
²ballot *vi* : to vote or decide by ballot — **bal·lot·er** *n*
ball·room \ˈbȯl-ˌrüm, -ˌru̇m\ *n* : a large room for dances
bal·ly·hoo \ˈbal-ē-ˌhü\ *n, pl* **-hoos** **1** : a noisy attention-getting demonstration or talk **2** : grossly exaggerated or sensational advertising or propaganda — **ballyhoo** *vt*

balm \'bäm, 'bälm\ *n* **1 :** a fragrant healing or soothing preparation (as an ointment) **2 :** something that comforts or refreshes **3 :** any of several spicy fragrant herbs

balmy \'bäm-ē, 'bäl-mē\ *adj* **1 a :** having the qualities of balm : SOOTHING **b :** MILD **2 :** FOOLISH, INSANE

bal·sa \'bȯl-sə\ *n* **:** a tropical American tree with extremely light strong wood used esp. for floats; *also* **:** its wood

bal·sam \'bȯl-səm\ *n* **1 a :** an aromatic and usu. oily and resinous substance flowing from various plants **b :** a preparation containing or smelling like balsam **2 a :** a balsam-yielding tree **b :** any of several showy garden plants — **bal·sam·ic** \bȯl-'sam-ik\ *adj*

bal·us·ter \'bal-ə-stər\ *n* **:** an upright support of a rail (as in the railing of a staircase or balcony)

bal·us·trade \'bal-ə-ˌstrād\ *n* **:** a row of balusters topped by a rail to serve as an open barrier

bam·boo \bam-'bü\ *n, pl* **bamboos :** any of various chiefly tropical tall woody grasses including some with strong hollow stems used for building, furniture, or utensils — **bamboo** *adj*

bam·boo·zle \bam-'bü-zəl\ *vt* **-boo·zled; -boo·zling** \-'büz-(ə-)liŋ\ **:** to deceive by trickery : HOODWINK — **bam·boo·zle·ment** n

[1]**ban** \'ban\ *vb* **banned; ban·ning :** to prohibit esp. by legal means or social pressure

[2]**ban** *n* **1 :** ANATHEMA, EXCOMMUNICATION **2 :** MALEDICTION, CURSE **3 :** an official prohibition

ba·nal \bə-'näl, -'nal; 'bān-ᵊl\ *adj* **:** TRITE, COMMONPLACE, ORDINARY — **ba·nal·i·ty** \bā-'nal-ət-ē, bə-\ *n* — **ba·nal·ly** \bə-'näl-lē, -'nal-; 'bān-ᵊl-(l)ē\ *adv*

ba·nana \bə-'nan-ə\ *n* **:** a treelike tropical plant with large leaves and flower clusters that develop into a bunch of finger-shaped fruit which are yellow or red when ripe; *also* **:** its fruit

[1]**band** \'band\ *n* **1 :** something (as a fetter or shackle) that confines or constricts **2 :** something that binds or restrains legally, morally, or spiritually **3 :** a strip serving to join or hold things together **4 :** a thin encircling strip that confines, supports, or protects **5 :** a range of wavelengths or frequencies between two specified limits — **band·ed** \'ban-dəd\ *adj*

[2]**band** *vb* **1 :** to put a band on or tie up with a band **2 :** to finish with a band **3 :** to gather together or unite in a company or for a common purpose — **band·er** *n*

[3]**band** *n* **:** a group of persons, animals, or things; *esp* **:** a group of musicians organized for playing together

[1]**ban·dage** \'ban-dij\ *n* **:** a strip of fabric used esp. to dress and bind up wounds

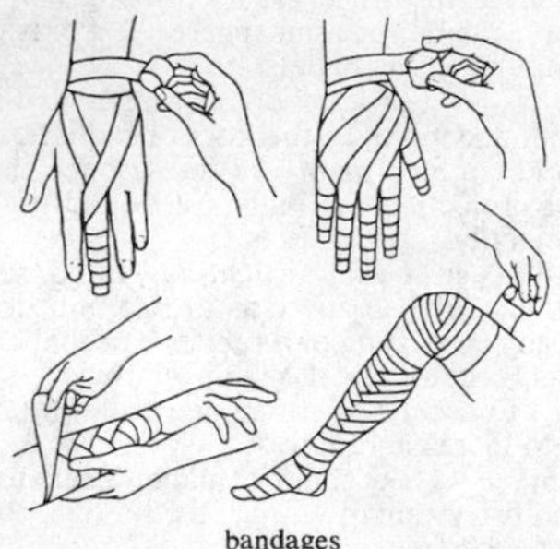

bandages

[2]**bandage** *vt* **:** to bind, dress, or cover with a bandage — **ban·dag·er** *n*

ban·dan·na *or* **ban·dana** \ban-'dan-ə\ *n* **:** a large figured handkerchief with usu. a red or blue background

band·box \'ban(d)-ˌbäks\ *n* **:** a usu. cylindrical box of pasteboard or thin wood for holding light articles of attire

ban·deau \ban-'dō\ *n, pl* **ban·deaux** \-'dōz\ **1 :** a fillet or band esp. for the hair **2 :** BRASSIERE

ban·dit \'ban-dət\ *n* **1 :** OUTLAW, BRIGAND **2 :** one who steals, profiteers, or kills : GANGSTER, CRIMINAL — **ban·dit·ry** \'ban-də-trē\ *n*

ban·do·lier *or* **ban·do·leer** \ˌban-də-'li(ə)r\ *n* **:** a belt worn over the shoulder esp. to carry ammunition

band·stand \'ban(d)-ˌstand\ *n* **:** a usu. roofed outdoor stand or platform on which a band or orchestra performs

band·wag·on \'ban(d)-ˌwag-ən\ *n* **1 :** a wagon carrying musicians in a parade **2 :** a candidate, side, or movement that attracts open support or approval because it seems to be winning or gaining popularity — used in phrases like *climb on the bandwagon*

[1]**ban·dy** \'ban-dē\ *vb* **ban·died; ban·dy·ing 1 :** to toss from side to side or from one to another **2 :** EXCHANGE; *esp* **:** to exchange (words) argumentatively **3 :** to discuss banteringly or as a subject of gossip

[2]**bandy** *adj* **:** curved esp. outward : BOWED

ban·dy–legged \ˌban-dē-'leg(-ə)d\ *adj* **:** BOWLEGGED

bane \'bān\ *n* **1 :** deadly poison **2 :** a source of injury, harm, ruin, or woe : a destructive influence

bane·ful \'bān-fəl\ *adj* **:** creating destruction or woe : RUINOUS — **bane·ful·ly** \-fə-lē\ *adv*

[1]**bang** \'baŋ\ *vb* **1 :** to strike against : BUMP **2 :** to strike with a sharp noise

[2]**bang** *n* **1 :** a resounding blow **2 :** a sudden loud noise

[3]**bang** *adv* **:** RIGHT, DIRECTLY

[4]**bang** *n* **:** a fringe of banged hair

[5]**bang** *vt* **:** to cut (as front hair) short and squarely across

ban·gle \'baŋ-gəl\ *n* **1 :** a stiff usu. ornamental bracelet or anklet slipped or clasped on **2 :** a small ornament hanging (as from a bracelet) loosely

bang–up \'baŋ-ˌəp\ *adj* **:** FIRST-RATE, EXCELLENT

ban·ish \'ban-ish\ *vt* **1 :** to compel by authority to leave a country **2 :** to drive out from or as if from a home : EXPEL — **ban·ish·er** *n* — **ban·ish·ment** *n*

ban·is·ter \'ban-ə-stər\ *n* **1 :** one of the slender posts used to support the handrail of a staircase **2 :** the handrail of a staircase

ban·jo \'ban-ˌjō\ *n, pl* **banjos :** a musical instrument of the guitar class with a long narrow fretted neck and small drum-shaped body — **ban·jo·ist** \-ˌjō-əst\ *n*

[1]**bank** \'baŋk\ *n* **1 :** a mound, pile, or ridge esp. of earth **2 :** a piled up mass of cloud or fog **3 :** an undersea elevation : SHOAL **4 :** the rising ground bordering a lake, river, or sea **5 :** a steep slope (as of a hill) **6 :** the inward tilt of a surface along a curve or of a vehicle (as an airplane) when taking a curve

[2]**bank** *vb* **1 :** to raise a bank about **2 :** to heap or pile in a bank **3 :** to build (a curve) with the roadbed or track inclined laterally upward from the inside edge **4 :** to incline an airplane laterally **5 :** to form or group in a tier

[3]**bank** *n* **1 :** a bench for the rowers of a galley **2 :** a group or series of objects arranged near together in a row or a tier

[4]**bank** *n* **1 :** a place of business that receives, lends, issues, exchanges, and takes care of money, extends credit, and provides ways of sending money and credit quickly from place to place **2 :** a small container in which coins or bills are saved **3 :** a supply of something held in reserve **4 :** a storage place for a reserve supply

[5]**bank** *vb* **1 :** to keep a bank : act as a banker **2 :** to have an account in a bank **3 :** to deposit in a bank — **bank·er** *n* — **bank on** *or* **bank upon :** to depend upon

bank·book \'baŋk-ˌbu̇k\ *n* **:** the depositor's book in which a bank enters his deposits and withdrawals

bank·ing \'baŋ-kiŋ\ *n* : the business of a bank or a banker

[1]**bank·rupt** \'baŋ-(,)krəpt\ *n* : a person who becomes unable to pay his debts; *esp* : one whose property by court order is turned over to a trustee to be administered for the benefit of his creditors

[2]**bankrupt** *vt* : to reduce to bankruptcy

[3]**bankrupt** *adj* **1 a** : fallen into a state of financial ruin : IMPOVERISHED **b** : legally declared a bankrupt **2 a** : BROKEN, RUINED **b** : DEPLETED, STERILE **c** : DESTITUTE

bank·rupt·cy \'baŋ-(,)krəp-(t)sē\ *n, pl* **-cies** : the condition of being bankrupt

[1]**ban·ner** \'ban-ər\ *n* **1 a** : a piece of cloth attached by one edge to a staff and used as a standard **b** : [3]FLAG **2** : a strip of cloth on which a sign is painted

[2]**banner** *adj* : distinguished from all others esp. in excellence

ban·nock \'ban-ək\ *n* : an often unleavened bread of oat or barley flour baked in flat loaves

banns \'banz\ *n pl* : public announcement esp. in church of a proposed marriage

[1]**ban·quet** \'baŋ-kwət, 'ban-, -,kwet\ *n* : an elaborate often ceremonious meal for numerous people

[2]**banquet** *vb* **1** : to treat with a banquet : FEAST **2** : to partake of a banquet — **ban·quet·er** *n*

ban·quette \baŋ-'ket, ban-\ *n* **1** : a raised way along the inside of a parapet or trench for gunners or guns **2** : a long upholstered seat esp. along a wall

ban·shee \'ban-(,)shē\ *n* : a female spirit in Gaelic folklore whose wailing warns a family of the approaching death of a member

[1]**ban·tam** \'bant-əm\ *n* **1** : any of numerous small domestic fowls that are often miniatures of members of the standard breeds **2** : a person of diminutive stature and often combative disposition

[2]**bantam** *adj* : SMALL, DIMINUTIVE

[1]**ban·ter** \'bant-ər\ *vb* **1** : to speak to in a witty and teasing manner : RALLY **2** : to talk or act in a humorous way — **ban·ter·er** *n* — **ban·ter·ing·ly** *adv*

[2]**banter** *n* : good-natured and usu. witty teasing

bant·ling \'bant-liŋ\ *n* : a very young child

ban·yan \'ban-yən\ *n* : a large East Indian tree from whose branches aerial roots grow downward into the ground and form new supporting trunks

banyan

bao·bab \'baù-,bab, 'bā-ə-,bab\ *n* : an Old World tropical tree with a broad trunk and an edible acid fruit resembling a gourd

bap·tism \'bap-,tiz-əm\ *n* **1** : a Christian sacrament signifying spiritual rebirth and symbolized by the ritual use of water **2** : an act of baptizing — **bap·tis·mal** \bap-'tiz-məl\ *adj* — **bap·tis·mal·ly** \-mə-lē\ *adv*

Bap·tist \'bap-təst\ *n* : a Protestant of an evangelical denomination practicing congregational government and baptism by immersion for believers — **Baptist** *adj*

bap·tis·tery *or* **bap·tis·try** \'bap-tə-strē\ *n, pl* **-ter·ies** *or* **-tries** : a place esp. in a church used for baptism

bap·tize \bap-'tīz, 'bap-,\ *vt* **1** : to administer baptism to **2** : to purify esp. by an ordeal **3** : to give a name to (as at baptism) : CHRISTEN — **bap·tiz·er** *n*

[1]**bar** \'bär\ *n* **1** : a rigid piece (as of wood or metal) that is longer than it is wide and has various uses (as for a lever, barrier, or fastening) **2** : something that obstructs or prevents passage, progress, or action : IMPEDIMENT **3 a** : the railing in a courtroom that encloses the place where the business of the court is transacted **b** : the body of lawyers qualified to practice in a jurisdiction; *also* : the profession of lawyer **4** : a straight stripe, band, or line much longer than it is wide **5 a** : a counter for serving food or esp. alcoholic beverages **b** : BARROOM **6** : a vertical line across the musical staff

[2]**bar** *vt* **barred**; **bar·ring** **1 a** : to fasten with a bar **b** : to place bars across to prevent passage **2** : to mark with bars : STRIPE **3** : OBSTRUCT **4 a** : to set aside : rule out **b** : to keep out : EXCLUDE **c** : PREVENT, FORBID

[3]**bar** *prep* : with the exception of

[1]**barb** \'bärb\ *n* : a sharp projection extending backward (as from the point of an arrow or fishhook) and preventing easy extraction — **barbed** \'bärbd\ *adj*

[2]**barb** *vt* : to furnish with a barb

bar·bar·i·an \bär-'ber-ē-ən\ *adj* : of, relating to, or being a land, culture, or people alien to and usu. believed to be inferior to one's own — **barbarian** *n* — **bar·bar·i·an·ism** \-ē-ə-,niz-əm\ *n*

bar·bar·ic \bär-'bar-ik\ *adj* **1** : of, relating to, or characteristic of barbarians **2 a** : WILD **b** : having a bizarre, primitive, or unsophisticated quality

bar·ba·rism \'bär-bə-,riz-əm\ *n* **1** : a word or expression not accepted as belonging to the standard language **2 a** : a barbarian state of social or intellectual development **b** : the practice or display of barbarian acts, attitudes, or ideas

bar·bar·i·ty \bär-'bar-ət-ē\ *n, pl* **-ties** **1** : BARBARISM **2** : barbarous cruelty : INHUMANITY

bar·ba·rous \'bär-b(ə-)rəs\ *adj* **1** : characterized by the use of barbarisms in speech or writing **2 a** : UNCIVILIZED **b** : lacking culture or refinement **3** : mercilessly harsh or cruel — **bar·ba·rous·ly** *adv* — **bar·ba·rous·ness** *n*

[1]**bar·be·cue** \'bär-bi-,kyü\ *n* **1** : a large animal (as a hog or steer) roasted or broiled whole or split over an open fire or bed of hot coals **2** : a social gathering at which barbecued food is eaten

[2]**barbecue** *vt* **1** : to cook over hot coals or on a revolving spit **2** : to cook in a highly seasoned vinegar sauce

bar·bell \'bär-,bel\ *n* : a bar with adjustable weights attached to each end used for exercise and in weight-lifting competition

[1]**bar·ber** \'bär-bər\ *n* : one whose business is cutting and dressing hair or shaving and trimming beards

[2]**barber** *vb* **bar·bered**; **bar·ber·ing** \-b(ə-)riŋ\ : to perform the services of a barber

bar·ber·ry \'bär-,ber-ē\ *n* : any of a genus of spiny yellow-flowered shrubs often grown for hedges

bar·bi·can \'bär-bi-kən\ *n* : an outer defensive work

bar·bi·tu·rate \bär-'bich-ə-rət\ *n* : a salt or ester of an organic acid; *esp* : one used esp. as a sedative or hypnotic

bar·ca·role *or* **bar·ca·rolle** \'bär-kə-,rōl\ *n* **1** : a Venetian boat song characterized by a beat suggesting a rowing rhythm **2** : a piece of music imitating a barcarole

bard \'bärd\ *n* : POET — **bard·ic** \'bärd-ik\ *adj*

[1]**bare** \'ba(ə)r\ *adj* **1** : NAKED **2** : open to view : EXPOSED **3 a** : EMPTY **b** : DESTITUTE **4 a** : having nothing left over or added : MERE **b** : not adorned or expanded : PLAIN — **bare·ly** *adv* — **bare·ness** *n*

[2]**bare** *vt* : to make or lay bare : UNCOVER, REVEAL

bare·back \-,bak\ *or* **bare·backed** \-'bakt\ *adv* (*or adj*) : on the bare back of a horse : without a saddle

bare·faced \-'fāst\ *adj* : SHAMELESS, BOLD

bare·foot \-ˌfu̇t\ *or* **bare·foot·ed** \-'fu̇t-əd\ *adv* (*or adj*) : with the feet bare : UNSHOD
bare·hand·ed \-'han-dəd\ *adv* (*or adj*) 1 : without gloves or mittens 2 : without tools or weapons
bare·head·ed \-'hed-əd\ *adv* (*or adj*) : without a hat
[1]**bar·gain** \'bär-gən\ *n* 1 : AGREEMENT 2 : an advantageous purchase 3 : a situation or event with important good or bad results
[2]**bargain** *vb* 1 : to talk over the terms of a purchase, agreement, or contract 2 : to come to terms : AGREE 3 : BARTER — **bar·gain·er** *n*
[1]**barge** \'bärj\ *n* 1 : a broad flat-bottomed boat used chiefly on rivers and canals 2 : a ship's boat for the use of a naval officer ranking above a captain
[2]**barge** *vb* 1 : to carry by barge 2 : to move or thrust oneself clumsily or rudely
bar·i·tone \'bar-ə-ˌtōn\ *n* : a male singing voice between bass and tenor; *also* : a man having such a voice
bar·i·um \'bar-ē-əm\ *n* : a silver-white malleable toxic metallic chemical element that occurs only in combination
[1]**bark** \'bärk\ *vb* 1 : to make the characteristic short loud cry of a dog or a similar noise 2 : to speak or utter in a curt loud usu. angry tone
[2]**bark** *n* : the sound made by a barking dog
[3]**bark** *n* : the tough largely corky exterior covering of a woody root or stem
[4]**bark** *vt* 1 : to strip the bark from 2 : to rub off or abrade the skin of
[5]**bark** *or* **barque** *n* 1 : a small sailing ship 2 : a 3-masted ship with foremast and mainmast square-rigged
bar·keep·er \'bär-ˌkē-pər\ *or* **bar·keep** \-ˌkēp\ *n* : one that keeps or tends a bar for the sale of liquors
bark·er \'bär-kər\ *n* : a person who stands at the entrance to a show or a store and tries to attract customers to it
bar·ley \'bär-lē\ *n* : a cereal grass with seeds used as food and in making malt liquors; *also* : its seed
bar·ley·corn \-ˌko̍rn\ *n* : a grain of barley
bar mitz·vah \bär-'mits-və\ *n, often cap B & M* 1 : a Jewish boy who reaches his 13th birthday and attains the age of religious duty and responsibility 2 : the initiatory ceremony recognizing a boy as a bar mitzvah
barn \'bärn\ *n* : a building used chiefly for storing grain and hay and for housing farm animals (as cows and horses)
bar·na·cle \'bär-ni-kəl\ *n* : any of numerous marine crustaceans that are free-swimming as larvae but fixed (as to rocks or pilings) as adults — **bar·na·cled** \-kəld\ *adj*
barn·storm \'bärn-ˌsto̍rm\ *vi* 1 : to tour through rural districts staging theatrical performances usu. in one-night stands 2 : to travel from place to place making brief stops (as in political campaigning) — **barn·storm·er** *n*
barn·yard \-ˌyärd\ *n* : a usu. fenced area adjoining a barn
ba·rom·e·ter \bə-'räm-ət-ər\ *n* : an instrument for determining the pressure of the atmosphere and hence for assisting in judgment as to probable weather changes — **bar·o·met·ric** \ˌbar-ə-'me-trik\ *adj*
bar·on \'bar-ən\ *n* 1 : a member of the lowest grade of the British peerage 2 : a man of great or excessive power or influence in some field
bar·on·age \-ə-nij\ *n* : the whole body of barons or peers
bar·on·ess \-ə-nəs\ *n* 1 : the wife or widow of a baron 2 : a woman who holds a baronial title in her own right
bar·on·et \'bar-ə-nət\ *n* : a man holding a rank of honor below a baron but above a knight
ba·ro·ni·al \bə-'rō-nē-əl\ *adj* : of, relating to, or suitable for a baron or the baronage
bar·ony \'bar-ə-nē\ *n, pl* **bar·on·ies** : the domain, rank, or dignity of a baron
ba·roque \bə-'rōk, ba-, -'räk\ *adj* : marked by elaborate and sometimes grotesque ornamentation and esp. by curved and plastic figures
ba·rouche \bə-'rüsh\ *n* : a four-wheeled carriage with a driver's seat high in front and a folding top
bar·racks \'bar-əks, -iks\ *n sing or pl* : a building or group of buildings in which soldiers are quartered
bar·ra·cu·da \ˌbar-ə-'küd-ə\ *n, pl* **-da** *or* **-das** : any of several large gluttonous and fierce marine fishes of warm seas related to the gray mullets

barracuda

bar·rage \bə-'räzh, -'räj\ *n* : a barrier formed by continuous artillery or machine-gun fire directed upon a narrow strip of ground
bar·ra·try \'bar-ə-trē\ *n, pl* **-tries** 1 : the purchase or sale of office or preferment in church or state 2 : a fraudulent breach of duty by the master or crew of a ship intended to harm the owner or cargo
barred \'bärd\ *adj* : having bands of different color
[1]**bar·rel** \'bar-əl\ *n* 1 : a round bulging container that has flat ends 2 : the amount held by a barrel 3 : a cylindrical or tubular part — **bar·reled** \-əld\ *adj*
[2]**barrel** *vb* **-reled** *or* **-relled**; **-rel·ing** *or* **-rel·ling** 1 : to put or pack in a barrel 2 : to travel at a high speed
[1]**bar·ren** \'bar-ən\ *adj* 1 : not reproducing 2 a : producing inferior or scanty vegetation b : unproductive of results or gain : FRUITLESS 3 : lacking interest, information, or charm — **bar·ren·ly** *adv* — **bar·ren·ness** *n*
[2]**barren** *n* : a tract of barren land
bar·rette \bä-'ret, bə-\ *n* : a clip or bar for holding a woman's hair in place
[1]**bar·ri·cade** \'bar-ə-ˌkād, ˌbar-ə-'\ *vt* 1 : to block off or stop up with a barricade 2 : to prevent access to by means of a barricade
[2]**barricade** *n* : an obstruction or rampart thrown up across a way or passage to check an advance or block passage
bar·ri·er \'bar-ē-ər\ *n* 1 : a material object or set of objects that separates or marks off or serves as a barricade 2 : something immaterial that separates
bar·ring \'bär-iŋ\ *prep* 1 : with the exception of 2 : apart from the possibility of
bar·ris·ter \'bar-ə-stər\ *n* : a lawyer who is permitted to plead cases in any English court
bar·room \'bär-ˌrüm, -ˌru̇m\ *n* : a room or establishment whose main feature is a bar for the sale of liquor
[1]**bar·row** \'bar-ō\ *n* : a large burial mound of earth or stones
[2]**barrow** *n* : a male hog castrated before sexual maturity
[3]**barrow** *n* 1 : a framework that has handles and sometimes a wheel and is used for carrying things 2 : a cart with a shallow box body and shafts for pushing it
bar·tend·er \'bär-ˌten-dər\ *n* : one that serves liquor at a bar
[1]**bar·ter** \'bärt-ər\ *vb* : to trade one commodity directly for another without the use of money — **bar·ter·er** *n*
[2]**barter** *n* : the exchange of goods without the use of money
bas·al \'bā-səl\ *adj* 1 : relating to, situated at, or forming the base 2 : FUNDAMENTAL — **bas·al·ly** \-ə-lē\ *adv*
ba·salt \bə-'so̍lt, 'bā-ˌ\ *n* : a dark fine-grained igneous rock — **ba·sal·tic** \bə-'so̍l-tik\ *adj*
[1]**base** \'bās\ *n, pl* **bas·es** \'bā-səz\ 1 : the bottom of something considered as its support : FOUNDATION 2 a : a main ingredient b : a supporting or carrying ingredient (as of a

medicine) **3 :** the fundamental part of something : GROUNDWORK **4 a :** the point or line from which a start is made in an action or undertaking **b :** the locality or installations from which a military force operates **5 a :** the starting place or goal in various games **b :** any one of the four stations at the corners of a baseball infield **6 :** any of various compounds (as lime) that are capable of reacting with an acid to form a salt, that when dissolved in water have a strong somewhat salty taste, and that turn litmus blue — **based** \'bāst\ *adj*

²base *vt* **1 :** to make, form, or serve as a base for **2 :** to use as a base or basis for : ESTABLISH

³base *adj* : constituting or serving as a base

⁴base *adj* **1 a :** of inferior quality; *esp* : alloyed with or made of inferior metal **b :** of comparatively little value **2 :** morally low : MEAN, CONTEMPTIBLE — **base•ly** *adv* — **base•ness** *n*

base•ball \'bās-ˌbȯl\ *n* : a game played with a bat and ball between two teams of nine players each on a field with four bases that mark the course a runner must take to score; *also* : the ball used in this game

base•board \-ˌbōrd\ *n* : a line of boards or molding covering the joint of a wall and the adjoining floor

base•born \-'bȯrn\ *adj* **1 :** of humble birth : LOWLY **2 :** of illegitimate birth : BASTARD

base•less \'bās-ləs\ *adj* : having no basis or reason

base•ment \'bās-mənt\ *n* **1 :** the part of a building that is wholly or partly below ground level **2 :** the lowest or fundamental part of something

base on balls : an advance to first base given to a baseball player who receives four balls

base runner *n* : a baseball player of the team at bat who is on base or is attempting to reach base

bash \'bash\ *vb* **1 :** to strike violently : BEAT **2 :** to smash by a blow **3 :** CRASH

bash•ful \'bash-fəl\ *adj* : inclined to shrink from public attention : SHY — **bash•fully•ly** \-fə-lē\ *adv* — **bash•ful•ness** *n*

¹ba•sic \'bā-sik\ *adj* **1 :** of, relating to, or forming the base or foundation : FUNDAMENTAL **2 :** constituting or serving as a basis or starting point **3 :** of, relating to, containing, or having the character of a base; *also* : having an alkaline reaction — **ba•si•cal•ly** \-si-k(ə-)lē\ *adv*

²basic *n* : something that is basic : FUNDAMENTAL

bas•il \'baz-əl, 'bās-, 'bas-, 'bāz-\ *n* : an aromatic mint used in cookery

ba•sil•i•ca \bə-'sil-i-kə, -'zil-\ *n* **1 :** an early Christian church building consisting of nave and aisles with clerestory and apse **2 :** a Roman Catholic church with ceremonial privileges — **ba•sil•i•can** \-kən\ *adj*

bas•i•lisk \'bas-ə-ˌlisk, 'baz-\ *n* : a legendary reptile with fatal breath and glance

ba•sin \'bās-ᵊn\ *n* **1 :** a wide shallow usu. round dish or bowl with sloping or curving sides for holding liquid (as water) **2 :** a natural or artificial hollow, depression, or enclosure containing water **3 :** the land drained by a river and its branches

ba•sis \'bā-səs\ *n, pl* **ba•ses** \'bā-ˌsēz\ **1 :** the base, foundation, or chief supporting part **2 :** a fundamental principal

bask \'bask\ *vi* : to lie in or expose oneself to a pleasant warmth or atmosphere

bas•ket \'bas-kət\ *n* **1 :** a container made by weaving together the constituent material (as twigs, straw, cane, or strips of wood) **2 :** something that resembles a basket in shape or use — **bas•ket•work** \-ˌwərk\ *n*

bas•ket•ball \-ˌbȯl\ *n* : a usu. indoor court game in which each of two teams tries to toss an inflated ball through a raised goal; *also* : the ball used in this game

bas–re•lief \ˌbä-ri-'lēf\ *n* : a sculpture in relief in which the design is raised very slightly from the background

¹bass \'bas\ *n, pl* **bass** *or* **bass•es** : any of several spiny-finned freshwater sport and food fishes of eastern No. America

²bass \'bās\ *n* **1 :** a deep sound or tone **2 :** the lowest part in polyphonic or harmonic music **3 :** the lowest male singing voice **4 :** a singer having a bass voice **5 :** the lowest member in range of a family of instruments — **bass** *adj*

bas•si•net \ˌbas-ə-'net\ *n* : a basket often with a hood over one end used as an infant's bed

bas•so \'bas-ō, 'bäs-\ *n, pl* **bassos** : a bass singer

bas•soon \ba-'sün, bə-\ *n* : a tenor or bass double-reed woodwind instrument having a long doubled conical wooden body connected to the mouthpiece by a thin metal tube — **bas•soon•ist** \-'sü-nəst\ *n*

bass•wood \'bas-ˌwu̇d\ *n* **1 :** any of several trees of the linden family; *also* : TULIP TREE **2 :** the pale straight-grained wood of a basswood

bast \'bast\ *n* : a strong woody fiber obtained chiefly from the phloem of plants and used esp. in cordage and matting

¹bas•tard \'bas-tərd\ *n* **1 :** an illegitimate child **2 :** something spurious or irregular — **bas•tard•ly** *adj*

²bastard *adj* **1 :** ILLEGITIMATE **2 :** of an inferior or atypical kind, stock, or form **3 :** SPURIOUS — **bastardy** *n*

¹baste \'bāst\ *vt* : to sew with long loose stitches in order to hold the work temporarily in place — **bast•er** *n*

²baste \'bāst\ *vt* : to moisten (as roasting meat) with melted butter or fat — **bast•er** *n*

bas•ti•na•do \ˌbas-tə-'nād-ō, -'näd-\ *n, pl* **-does** **1 :** a blow with a stick or cudgel **2 :** a punishment consisting of beating the soles of the feet with a stick — **bastinado** *vt*

bas•tion \'bas-chən\ *n* **1 :** a projecting part of a fortification **2 :** a fortified area or position **3 :** STRONGHOLD, BULWARK

¹bat \'bat\ *n* **1 :** a stout solid stick : CLUB **2 :** a sharp blow **3 :** a wooden implement used for hitting the ball (as in baseball) **4 :** a turn at batting

²bat *vb* **bat•ted; bat•ting :** to strike or hit with or as if with a bat

³bat *n* : any of a large group of nocturnal flying mammals with the forelimbs modified to form wings

⁴bat *vt* **bat•ted; bat•ting :** to wink esp. in surprise

batch \'bach\ *n* **1 :** a quantity baked at one time **2 :** a quantity of any material for use at one time or produced at one operation **3 :** a group of persons or things : LOT

bate \'bāt\ *vt* **1 :** to reduce the force or intensity of **2 :** to take away : DEDUCT

bath \'bath, 'bȧth\ *n, pl* **baths** \'ba<u>th</u>z, 'baths, 'bȧ<u>th</u>z, 'bȧths\ **1 :** a washing or soaking (as in water or steam) of all or part of the body **2 a :** water used for bathing **b :** a liquid in which objects are placed so that it can act upon them **3 :** BATHROOM

bathe \'bā<u>th</u>\ *vb* **1 :** to take a bath **2 :** to go swimming **3 a :** to wash in a liquid (as water) **b :** MOISTEN, WET **4 :** to apply water or a liquid medicament to **5 :** to flow along the edge of : LAVE **6 :** SUFFUSE, OVERSPREAD — **bath•er** *n* — **bath•ing** *n*

ba•thet•ic \bə-'thet-ik\ *adj* : characterized by bathos — **ba•thet•i•cal•ly** \-i-k(ə-)lē\ *adv*

bath•house \'bath-ˌhau̇s, 'bȧth-\ *n* **1 :** a building equipped for bathing **2 :** a building containing dressing rooms for bathers

ba•thos \'bā-ˌthäs\ *n* **1 :** the sudden appearance of the commonplace in otherwise elevated matter or style **2 :** insincere or overdone pathos

bath•robe \'bath-ˌrōb, 'bȧth-\ *n* : a loose usu. absorbent robe worn before and after bathing or as a dressing gown

bath•room \-ˌrüm, -ˌru̇m\ *n* : a room containing a bathtub or shower and usu. a washbowl and toilet

bath•tub \-ˌtəb\ *n* : a usu. fixed tub for bathing

ba•tiste \bə-'tēst, ba-\ *n* : a fine soft sheer fabric of plain weave made of various fibers

ba•ton \bə-'tän, bə-\ *n* : STAFF, ROD; *esp* : a stick or wand with which a leader directs a band or orchestra

ba•tra•chi•an \bə-'trā-kē-ən\ *n* : FROG, TOAD — **batrachian** *adj*

bats•man \'bats-mən\ *n* : ³BATTER

bat•tal•ion \bə-'tal-yən\ *n* **1 :** a large organized body of troops

2 : a military unit composed of a headquarters and two or more companies, batteries, or subunits

[1]**bat·ten** \'bat-ᵊn\ *vb* **bat·tened**; **bat·ten·ing** \'bat-niŋ, -ᵊn-iŋ\ 1 : to grow or make fat 2 : THRIVE

[2]**batten** *n* : a thin narrow strip of lumber used esp. to seal or reinforce a joint

[3]**batten** *vt* : to furnish or fasten with battens

[1]**bat·ter** \'bat-ər\ *vb* 1 : to beat with successive violent, heavy, or shattering blows 2 : to wear or damage by blows or hard usage

[2]**batter** *n* : a mixture that consists chiefly of flour and liquid and is thin enough to pour or drop from a spoon

[3]**batter** *n* : one that bats; *esp* : the baseball player at bat

bat·ter·ing ram \'bat-ər-iŋ-\ *n* : a military siege engine used in ancient times to beat down the walls of a besieged place

bat·tery \'bat-ə-rē, 'ba-trē\ *n, pl* **-ter·ies** 1 **a** : the act of battering or beating **b** : the unlawful beating of or use of force on a person 2 **a** : a tactical grouping of artillery pieces **b** : the guns of a warship 3 : a group of two or more electric cells for furnishing electric current; *also* : a single electric cell 4 : a number of similar items grouped or used as a unit 5 : the pitcher and catcher of a baseball team

bat·ting \'bat-iŋ\ *n* : layers or sheets of raw cotton or wool used for lining quilts or for stuffing or packaging

[1]**bat·tle** \'bat-ᵊl\ *n* 1 : a general encounter between armies, ships of war, or airplanes 2 : an extended contest, struggle, or controversy

[2]**battle** *vb* **bat·tled**; **bat·tling** \'bat-liŋ, -ᵊl-iŋ\ 1 : to engage in battle : FIGHT 2 : to contend with full strength, craft, or resources : STRUGGLE 3 : to fight against

bat·tle–ax *or* **bat·tle–axe** \'bat-ᵊl-ˌaks\ *n* : a long-handled ax formerly used as a weapon of war

bat·tle·dore \'bat-ᵊl-ˌdō(ə)r\ *n* : a light flat bat or racket used in striking a shuttlecock

bat·tle·field \-ˌfēld\ *n* : a place where a battle is fought

bat·tle·ment \'bat-ᵊl-mənt\ *n* : a parapet with open spaces that surmounts a wall and is used for defense or decoration — **bat·tle·ment·ed** \-ˌment-əd\ *adj*

bat·tle·ship \'bat-ᵊl-ˌship\ *n* : a warship of the largest and most heavily armed and armored class

bau·ble \'bȯ-bəl\ *n* 1 : TRINKET 2 : TRIFLE

baux·ite \'bȯk-ˌsīt\ *n* : a mineral that is the principal ore of aluminum

bawd \'bȯd\ *n* 1 : one who keeps a house of prostitution 2 : PROSTITUTE

bawdy \'bȯd-ē\ *adj* : OBSCENE, LEWD — **bawd·i·ly** \'bȯd-ᵊl-ē\ *adv* — **bawd·i·ness** *n*

[1]**bawl** \'bȯl\ *vb* 1 : to cry out loudly 2 : WAIL 3 : to scold severely — used with *out* — **bawl·er** *n*

[2]**bawl** *n* : a loud prolonged cry : OUTCRY

[1]**bay** \'bā\ *n* 1 : a horse with a reddish brown body and black mane, tail, and points 2 : a reddish brown

[2]**bay** *n* 1 : LAUREL 1 2 : any of several shrubs or trees resembling the laurel

[3]**bay** *n* 1 : a section of a building set off from other parts (as by pillars or beams) 2 : a compartment projecting outward from the wall of a building and containing a window

[4]**bay** *vb* : to bark with long deep tones

[5]**bay** *n* 1 : the position of one unable to retreat and forced to face danger 2 : the baying of a dog : a deep bark

[6]**bay** *n* : an inlet or indentation of a body of water (as the sea)

bay·ber·ry \'bā-ˌber-ē\ *n* 1 : a West Indian tree of the myrtle family yielding a yellow aromatic oil 2 : WAX MYRTLE; *also* : its fruit used esp. in making candles

[1]**bay·o·net** \'bā-ə-nət, ˌbā-ə-'net\ *n* : a steel blade made to be attached at the muzzle end of a rifle

[2]**bayonet** *vb* **-net·ed**; **-net·ing** : to stab with a bayonet

bay·ou \'bī-ō, 'bī-ü\ *n* : a usu. marshy or sluggish body of water (as a stream on a delta or an offshoot of a river)

ba·zaar \bə-'zär\ *n* 1 : an Oriental market consisting of rows of shops or stalls selling miscellaneous goods 2 : a place for the sale of goods 3 : a fair for the sale of articles esp. for charitable purposes

ba·zoo·ka \bə-'zü-kə\ *n* : a light portable shoulder weapon that consists of a tube open at both ends and shoots an explosive rocket able to pierce armor

be \(')bē\ *vb, past 1st & 3d sing* **was** \(')wəz, 'wäz\; *2d sing* **were** \(')wər\; *pl* **were**; *past subjunctive* **were**; *past part* **been** \(')bin, *chiefly Brit* (')bēn\; *pres part* **be·ing** \'bē-iŋ\; *pres 1st sing* **am** \(ə)m, (')am\; *2d sing* **are** \ər, (')är\; *3d sing* **is** \(')iz, (ə)z\; *pl* **are**; *pres subjunctive* **be** 1 **a** : to have the same meaning as : serve as a sign for **b** : to have identity with **c** : to constitute the same class as **d** : to have a specified qualification or characterization **e** : to belong to the class of — used regularly in senses 1a through 1e as the copula of simple predication 2 **a** : to have reality : EXIST, LIVE **b** : to have, keep, or occupy a place, situation, or position **c** : to remain unmolested, undisturbed, or uninterrupted — used only in infinitive form **d** : OCCUR : take place 3 — used with the past participle of transitive verbs as a passive-voice auxiliary 4 — used as the auxiliary of the present participle in expressing continuous action 5 — used with the infinitive with *to* to express futurity, arrangement in advance, or obligation

[1]**beach** \'bēch\ *n* : a shore of an ocean, sea, or lake

[2]**beach** *vt* : to run or drive ashore

beach·comb·er \'bēch-ˌkō-mər\ *n* 1 : a drifter, loafer, or casual worker along the seacoast 2 : one who searches along a shore for useful or salable flotsam and refuse

beach flea *n* : any of numerous small leaping crustaceans common on sea beaches

beach·head \'bēch-ˌhed\ *n* 1 : an area on an enemy-held shore occupied by an advance attacking force to protect the later landing of troops or supplies 2 : FOOTHOLD

bea·con \'bē-kən\ *n* 1 : a signal fire 2 **a** : a signal (as a lighthouse) for guidance **b** : a radio transmitter emitting signals for guidance of airplanes

[1]**bead** \'bēd\ *n* 1 *pl* : a series of prayers and meditations made with a rosary 2 : a small piece of material pierced for threading on a string or wire 3 : a small ball-shaped body 4 : a projecting rim, band, or molding

[2]**bead** *vb* 1 : to adorn or cover with beads or beading 2 : to string together like beads

bead·ing \'bēd-iŋ\ *n* 1 : material or a part or a piece consisting of a bead 2 : a beaded molding

bea·dle \'bēd-ᵊl\ *n* : a minor parish official whose duties include ushering and keeping order in church

bead·work \'bēd-ˌwərk\ *n* : ornamental work in beads

beady \'bēd-ē\ *adj* 1 : resembling beads 2 : marked by beads

bea·gle \'bē-gəl\ *n* : a small short-legged smooth-coated hound

beak \'bēk\ *n* 1 : the bill of a bird; *esp* : the bill of a bird of prey adapted for striking and tearing 2 : a pointed structure or formation — **beaked** \'bēkt\ *adj*

bea·ker \'bē-kər\ *n* 1 : a large drinking cup with a wide mouth 2 : a deep thin laboratory vessel having a wide mouth and often a projecting lip

[1]**beam** \'bēm\ *n* 1 : a long heavy piece of timber used esp. as a main horizontal support of a building or a ship 2 : the bar of a balance from which the scales hang 3 : the width of a ship at its widest part 4 **a** : a ray or shaft of light **b** : a collection of nearly parallel rays (as X rays) or particles (as electrons) 5 : a directed flow of radio signals for the guidance of pilots; *also* : the course indicated by this flow

[2]**beam** *vb* 1 : to emit in beams or as a beam 2 : to aim (a broadcast) by directional antennas 3 : to send out beams of light 4 : to smile with joy

bean \'bēn\ *n* 1 **a** : the seed or pod of any of various erect or climbing leguminous plants **b :** a plant bearing beans **2 :** a seed or fruit like a bean

[1]bear \'ba(ə)r\ *n, pl* **bear** *or* **bears** **1 :** any of a family of large heavy mammals having long shaggy hair and rudimentary tail **2 :** a surly, uncouth, or shambling person **3 :** one that sells securities or commodities in expectation of a price decline

[2]bear *vb* **bore** \'bō(ə)r\; **borne** \'bōrn\; **bear·ing** **1 a :** to move while holding up : CARRY **b :** to be furnished with **c :** to have as a feature or characteristic **d :** to hold in the mind : HARBOR **e :** DISSEMINATE **f :** to bring forward in testifying **g :** BEHAVE, CONDUCT **2 a :** to give birth to **b :** PRODUCE, YIELD **3 a :** to support the weight of : hold up : SUSTAIN **b :** to support a burden or strain **c :** ENDURE **4 :** THRUST, PRESS **5 :** to move, extend, or incline in an indicated direction — **bear·er** *n*

bear·a·ble \'bar-ə-bəl\ *adj* **:** capable of being borne

[1]beard \'bi(ə)rd\ *n* **1 :** the hair that grows on a man's face often excluding the moustache **2 :** a hairy or bristly growth or tuft (as on the chin of a goat or on a head of rye) — **beard·ed** \-əd\ *adj* — **beard·less** \-ləs\ *adj*

[2]beard *vt* **:** to confront and oppose daringly : DEFY

bear·ing \'ba(ə)r-iŋ\ *n* **1 :** the manner in which one bears or comports oneself : CARRIAGE, BEHAVIOR **2 a :** an object, surface, or point that supports something **b :** a machine part in which one part (as a journal or pin) turns **3 :** a charge in a coat of arms **4 a :** the position or direction of one point with respect to another or to the compass **b :** a determination of position **c** *pl* **:** comprehension of one's position, environment, or situation **d :** RELATION, CONNECTION; *also* **:** PURPORT

bear·ish \-ish\ *adj* **1 :** resembling a bear **2 :** marked by, tending to, or expecting a decline in stock prices — **bear·ish·ly** *adv* — **bear·ish·ness** *n*

bear·skin \'ba(ə)r-ˌskin\ *n* **:** an article made of the skin of a bear; *esp* **:** a military hat made of the skin of a bear

beast \'bēst\ *n* **1 :** ANIMAL 1; *esp* **:** a lower mammal **2 :** a contemptible person

beast·ly \'bēst-lē\ *adj* **1 :** of, relating to, or resembling a beast **2 :** BESTIAL **3 :** ABOMINABLE, DISGUSTING — **beast·li·ness** *n*

[1]beat \'bēt\ *vb* **beat**; **beat·en** \'bēt-[ə]n\ *or* **beat**; **beat·ing** **1 :** to strike repeatedly: **a :** to dash against **b :** to mix by stirring : WHIP **2 a :** to drive or force by blows **b :** to make by repeated treading or driving over **c :** to shape by repeated blows **3 :** to cause to strike or flap repeatedly **4 a :** OVERCOME, DEFEAT; *also* **:** SURPASS **b :** BEWILDER, BAFFLE **c :** EXHAUST, DISPIRIT **5 a :** to act ahead of usu. so as to forestall **b :** to come or arrive before **6 :** to indicate by beats **7 a :** DASH **b :** to glare or strike with oppressive intensity **8 :** PULSATE — **beat·er** *n*

[2]beat *n* **1 :** a single stroke or blow esp. in a series; *also* **:** PULSATION **2 :** a metrical or rhythmic stress in poetry or music or the rhythmic effect of these stresses **3 :** a regularly traversed round **4 :** the reporting of a news story ahead of competitors

[3]beat *adj* **1 :** EXHAUSTED **2 :** sapped of resolution or morale **3 :** of or relating to beatniks

be·a·tif·ic \ˌbē-ə-'tif-ik\ *adj* **:** giving or expressing great joy or blessedness : BLISSFUL — **be·a·tif·i·cal·ly** \-'tif-i-k(ə-)lē\ *adv*

be·at·i·fy \bē-'at-ə-ˌfī\ *vt* **-fied**; **-fy·ing** **1 :** to make supremely happy **2 :** to declare to have attained the blessedness of heaven and authorize the title "Blessed" and limited public religious honor for — **be·at·i·fi·ca·tion** \-ˌat-ə-fə-'kā-shən\ *n*

be·at·i·tude \bē-'at-ə-ˌt(y)üd\ *n* **1 :** supreme bliss **2 :** a declaration made in the Sermon on the Mount (Matthew 5:3–12) beginning "Blessed are"

beat·nik \'bēt-nik\ *n* **:** a person who behaves and dresses unconventionally and is inclined to exotic philosophizing and extreme self-expression

beau \'bō\ *n, pl* **beaux** \'bōz\ *or* **beaus** \'bōz\ **1 :** a man who dresses very carefully in the latest fashion : DANDY **2 a :** a man who is courting : LOVER, ADMIRER **b :** ESCORT

beau monde \bō-'mänd\ *n, pl* **beau mondes** *or* **beaux mondes** \bō-'män(d)z\ **:** the world of high society and fashion

beau·te·ous \'byüt-ē-əs\ *adj* **:** BEAUTIFUL — **beau·te·ous·ly** *adv* — **beau·te·ous·ness** *n*

beau·ti·cian \byü-'tish-ən\ *n* **:** COSMETOLOGIST

beau·ti·ful \'byüt-i-fəl\ *adj* **:** having qualities of beauty : exciting aesthetic pleasure — **beau·ti·ful·ly** \-f(ə-)lē\ *adv* — **beau·ti·ful·ness** *n*

beau·ti·fy \'byüt-ə-ˌfī\ *vt* **-fied**; **-fy·ing** **:** to make beautiful or add beauty to : EMBELLISH — **beau·ti·fi·ca·tion** \ˌbyüt-ə-fə-'kā-shən\ *n* — **beau·ti·fi·er** *n*

beau·ty \'byüt-ē\ *n, pl* **beauties** **1 :** the qualities of a person or a thing that give pleasure to the senses : LOVELINESS **2 :** a lovely person or thing; *esp* **:** a lovely woman

bea·ver \'bē-vər\ *n, pl* **beaver** *or* **beavers** **:** a large fur-bearing mammal with webbed hind feet and a broad flat tail that builds dams and underwater houses of mud and branches; *also* **:** its fur

be·calm \bi-'käm\ *vt* **1 :** to bring to a stop or keep motionless by lack of wind **2 :** to make calm

be·cause \bi-'kȯz\ *conj* **:** for the reason that

because of *prep* **:** by reason of

beck \'bek\ *n* **1 :** a beckoning gesture **2 :** BIDDING, SUMMONS

beck·on \'bek-ən\ *vb* **beck·oned**; **beck·on·ing** \'bek-(ə-)niŋ\ **1 :** to summon or signal to a person by gesture (as a wave or nod) **2 :** to appear inviting : ATTRACT

be·cloud \bi-'klau̇d\ *vt* **:** OBSCURE

be·come \bi-'kəm\ *vb* **-came** \-'kām\; **-come**; **-com·ing** **1 :** to come or grow to be **2 :** to suit or be suitable

be·com·ing \bi-'kəm-iŋ\ *adj* **:** SUITABLE, FITTING; *esp* **:** attractively suitable — **be·com·ing·ly** *adv*

[1]bed \'bed\ *n* **1 a :** a piece of furniture on or in which one may lie and sleep **b :** a place or time for sleeping **2 a :** a plot of ground prepared for plants **b :** the bottom of a body of water **3 :** FOUNDATION **4 :** LAYER

[2]bed *vb* **bed·ded**; **bed·ding** **1 a :** to furnish with a bed or bedding **b :** to put or go to bed **2 a :** to fix in a foundation : EMBED **b :** to plant or arrange in beds **3 :** to lay flat or in a layer **4 :** to form a layer

be·daub \bi-'dȯb\ *vt* **:** to daub over : SMEAR

be·daz·zle \bi-'daz-əl\ *vt* **:** to confuse by or as if by a strong light : DAZZLE — **be·daz·zle·ment** *n*

bed·bug \'bed-ˌbəg\ *n* **:** a wingless bloodsucking bug sometimes infesting houses and esp. beds

bed·clothes \'bed-ˌklō(th)z\ *n pl* **:** the covering (as sheets and blankets) used on a bed

bed·ding \'bed-iŋ\ *n* **1 :** BEDCLOTHES **2 :** a bottom layer : FOUNDATION **3 :** material to provide a bed for livestock

be·deck \bi-'dek\ *vt* **:** to deck out : ADORN

be·dev·il \bi-'dev-əl\ *vt* **:** to drive frantic : confuse utterly : HARASS — **be·dev·il·ment** *n*

be·dew \bi-'d(y)ü\ *vt* **:** to wet with or as if with dew

bed·fast \'bed-ˌfast\ *adj* **:** BEDRIDDEN

bed·fel·low \'bed-ˌfel-ō\ *n* **:** one who shares a bed with another

be·dim \bi-'dim\ *vt* **:** to make dim or obscure

be·di·zen \bi-'dīz-[ə]n, -'diz-\ *vt* **:** to dress or adorn in a showy way esp. with gaudy finery

bed·lam \'bed-ləm\ *n* **:** a place or scene of uproar and confusion

bed·ou·in \'bed-ə-wən\ *n, pl* **bedouin** *or* **bedouins** *often cap* **:** a nomadic Arab of the Arabian, Syrian, or No. African deserts

be·drag·gle \bi-'drag-əl\ *vt* **:** to wet and usu. soil thoroughly (as by rain or mud)

bed·rid·den \'bed-ˌrid-[ə]n\ *adj* **:** confined to bed by illness or weakness

bed·rock \'bed-'räk, -ˌräk\ *n* **1 :** the solid rock underlying surface materials (as soil) **2 :** a solid foundation

bed·roll \-ˌrōl\ *n* **:** bedding rolled up for carrying

bed•room \-ˌrüm, -ˌru̇m\ *n* : a room furnished with a bed and used for sleeping
bed•side \-ˌsīd\ *n* : the side of a bed or the place beside a bed esp. of a sick or dying person
bed•spread \-ˌspred\ *n* : a usu. decorative cloth cover for a bed
bed•stead \-ˌsted\ *n* : the framework of a bed usu. including head, foot, and side rails
bed•time \-ˌtīm\ *n* : time to go to bed
bee \ˈbē\ *n* **1** : a social colonial 4-winged insect often kept in hives for the honey that it produces; *also* : any of numerous related insects **2** : an eccentric notion : FANCY **3** : a gathering of people for a specific purpose
beech \ˈbēch\ *n, pl* **beech•es** *or* **beech** : any of a genus of hardwood trees with smooth gray bark and small edible nuts; *also* : its wood — **beech•en** \ˈbē-chən\ *adj* — **beech•wood** \ˈbēch-ˌwu̇d\ *n*
beef \ˈbēf\ *n, pl* **beeves** \ˈbēvz\ *or* **beefs** **1** : the flesh of a steer, cow, or bull; *also* : the dressed carcass of a beef animal **2** : a steer, cow, or bull esp. when fattened for food **3** : muscular flesh : BRAWN
beef•steak \-ˌstāk\ *n* : a slice of beef suitable for broiling or frying
beefy \ˈbē-fē\ *adj* : BRAWNY, THICKSET
bee•hive \ˈbē-ˌhīv\ *n* **1** : a hive for bees **2** : a scene of crowded activity
bee•keep•er \-ˌkē-pər\ *n* : one that raises bees — **bee•keep•ing** *n*
bee•line \ˈbē-ˌlīn\ *n* : a straight direct course
been *past part of* BE
beer \ˈbi(ə)r\ *n* : an alcoholic drink made from malt and flavored with hops — **beery** \ˈbi(ə)r-ē\ *adj*
bees•wax \ˈbēz-ˌwaks\ *n* : WAX 1
beet \ˈbēt\ *n* : a biennial garden plant with thick long-stalked edible leaves and a swollen root used as a vegetable, as a source of sugar, or for forage; *also* : this root
[1]**bee•tle** \ˈbēt-ᵊl\ *n* : any of an order of insects having four wings of which the outer pair are modified into stiff cases that protect the inner pair when at rest
[2]**beetle** *adj* : being prominent and overhanging
[3]**beetle** *vi* **bee•tled**; **bee•tling** \ˈbēt-liŋ, -ᵊl-iŋ\ : PROJECT, JUT
be•fall \bi-ˈfȯl\ *vb* **-fell** \-ˈfel\; **-fall•en** \-ˈfȯ-lən\; **-fall•ing** **1** : to come to pass : HAPPEN **2** : to happen to
be•fit \bi-ˈfit\ *vt* : to be suitable to or proper for
be•fog \bi-ˈfȯg, -ˈfäg\ *vt* **1** : OBSCURE **2** : CONFUSE
be•fool \bi-ˈfül\ *vt* : DECEIVE
[1]**be•fore** \bi-ˈfō(ə)r\ *adv* **1** : in advance : AHEAD **2** : EARLIER, PREVIOUSLY
[2]**before** *prep* **1 a** (1) : in front of (2) : in the presence of **b** : under the consideration of **c** : in store for **2** : earlier than : previously to **3** : in a higher or more important position than
[3]**before** *conj* **1** : earlier than the time when **2** : more willingly than
be•fore•hand \-ˌhand\ *adv* : in advance : ahead of time
be•foul \bi-ˈfau̇l\ *vt* : to make dirty : SOIL
be•friend \bi-ˈfrend\ *vt* : to act as a friend to
be•fud•dle \bi-ˈfəd-ᵊl\ *vt* **1** : to muddle the senses of **2** : CONFUSE, PERPLEX — **be•fud•dle•ment** *n*
beg \ˈbeg\ *vb* **begged**; **beg•ging** **1** : to ask for money, food, or help as a charity **2** : to ask earnestly or politely — **beg the question** : to assume as true or take for granted the thing that is the subject of the argument
be•get \bi-ˈget\ *vt* **-got** \-ˈgät\; **-got•ten** \-ˈgät-ᵊn\ *or* **-got**; **-get•ting** **1** : to become the father of : SIRE **2** : CAUSE — **be•get•ter** *n*
[1]**beg•gar** \ˈbeg-ər\ *n* **1** : one that begs; *esp* : one that lives by asking for gifts **2** : PAUPER **3** : FELLOW
[2]**beggar** *vt* : to reduce to beggary
beg•gar•ly \ˈbeg-ər-lē\ *adj* **1** : marked by extreme poverty **2** : MEAN — **beg•gar•li•ness** *n*
beg•gary \ˈbeg-ə-rē\ *n* : extreme poverty or want
be•gin \bi-ˈgin\ *vb* **be•gan** \-ˈgan\; **be•gun** \-ˈgən\; **be•gin•ning** **1 a** : to do the first part of an action **b** : to undertake or undergo initial steps : COMMENCE **2 a** : to come into existence : ARISE **b** : to have a starting point **3** : to do or succeed in the least degree **4** : FOUND, ORIGINATE, INVENT **5** : to come first in
be•gin•ner \bi-ˈgin-ər\ *n* : one that is beginning something or doing something for the first time
be•gin•ning \bi-ˈgin-iŋ\ *n* **1** : the point at which something begins **2** : the first part **3** : ORIGIN, SOURCE **4** : a first stage or early period
be•gone \bi-ˈgȯn\ *vi* : to go away : DEPART — used esp. in the imperative
be•go•nia \bi-ˈgō-nyə\ *n* : any of a large genus of tropical herbs often grown for their shining leaves and bright waxy flowers
be•grime \bi-ˈgrīm\ *vt* : to make dirty with grime
be•grudge \bi-ˈgrəj\ *vt* **1** : to give, do, or concede reluctantly **2** : to grumble at or be annoyed by **3** : to envy a person's possession or enjoyment of something — **be•grudg•ing•ly** *adv*
be•guile \bi-ˈgīl\ *vt* **1** : to deceive by means of flattery or by a trick or lie **2** : to draw notice or interest by wiles or charm **3** : to cause time to pass pleasantly : while away — **be•guile•ment** *n* — **be•guil•er** *n*
be•gum \ˈbē-gəm\ *n* : a Muslim woman of high rank
be•half \bi-ˈhaf, -ˈhȧf\ *n* : INTEREST, BENEFIT; *also* : SUPPORT, DEFENSE
be•have \bi-ˈhāv\ *vb* **1** : to bear or comport oneself in a particular way **2** : to conduct oneself in a proper manner **3** : to act, function, or react in a particular way : exhibit reaction (as to an environment)
be•hav•ior \bi-ˈhāv-yər\ *n* : way of behaving; *esp* : personal conduct — **be•hav•ior•al** \-yə-rəl\ *adj* — **be•hav•ior•al•ly** \-rə-lē\ *adv*
be•head \bi-ˈhed\ *vt* : to cut off the head of
be•he•moth \bi-ˈhē-məth, ˈbē-ə-ˌmȯth\ *n* : something of oppressive or monstrous size or power
be•hest \bi-ˈhest\ *n* : COMMAND, ORDER
[1]**be•hind** \bi-ˈhīnd\ *adv* **1 a** : in a place, situation, or time that is being or has been departed from **b** : at, to, or toward the back **2 a** : in a secondary or inferior position **b** : in a state of failing to keep up to schedule
[2]**behind** *prep* **1 a** : in a place, situation, or time left by **b** : at, to, or toward the back of **2** : inferior to **3** : retarded in relation to **4 a** : MOTIVATING **b** : SUPPORTING
[3]**behind** *n* : BUTTOCKS
be•hind•hand \bi-ˈhīnd-ˌhand\ *adv* (*or adj*) : not keeping up : LATE, BACKWARD, BEHIND
be•hold \bi-ˈhōld\ *vb* **1** : SEE **2** : to gaze upon : OBSERVE **3** — used in the imperative esp. to call attention — **be•hold•er** *n*
be•hold•en \bi-ˈhōl-dən\ *adj* : OBLIGATED, INDEBTED
be•hoof \bi-ˈhüf\ *n* : PROFIT, ADVANTAGE, BENEFIT
be•hoove \bi-ˈhüv\ *or* **be•hove** \-ˈhōv\ *vt* : to be necessary for as a matter of duty or obligation
beige \ˈbāzh\ *n* : a pale dull yellowish brown — **beige** *adj*
be•ing \ˈbē-iŋ\ *n* **1 a** : EXISTENCE **b** : LIFE **2** : the totality of existing things **3** : a living thing; *esp* : PERSON
be•la•bor \bi-ˈlā-bər\ *vt* **1** : to work on or at to absurd lengths **2** : ASSAIL, ATTACK
be•lat•ed \bi-ˈlāt-əd\ *adj* : delayed beyond the usual time : LATE — **be•lat•ed•ly** *adv* — **be•lat•ed•ness** *n*
be•lay \bi-ˈlā\ *vb* **1 a** : to secure (as a rope) by turns around a cleat or pin **b** : to make fast **2** : STOP
belch \ˈbelch\ *vb* **1** : to expel gas suddenly from the stomach through the mouth **2** : to eject, emit, or issue forth violently — **belch** *n*

bel·dam *or* **bel·dame** \'bel-dəm\ *n* : an old woman; *esp* : HAG
be·lea·guer \bi-'lē-gər\ *vt* **-guered**; **-guer·ing** \-g(ə-)riŋ\ **1** : to surround with an army so as to prevent escape : BESIEGE **2** : BESET, HARASS
bel·fry \'bel-frē\ *n, pl* **belfries** : a tower or a room in a tower for a bell or set of bells
be·lie \bi-'lī\ *vt* **-lied**; **-ly·ing** **1** : MISREPRESENT **2** : to be false or unfaithful to **3** : to show to be false — **be·li·er** *n*
be·lief \bə-'lēf\ *n* **1** : CONFIDENCE, FAITH, TRUST **2** : religious faith; *esp* : CREED **3** : the thing that is believed : CONVICTION, OPINION
be·lieve \bə-'lēv\ *vb* **1** : to have a firm religious faith **2** : to have a firm conviction as to the reality or goodness of something **3** : to take as true or honest **4** : to hold as an opinion : THINK, SUPPOSE — **be·liev·a·ble** *adj* — **be·liev·a·bly** \-'lē-və-blē\ *adv* — **be·liev·er** *n*
be·lit·tle \bi-'lit-ᵊl\ *vt* **-lit·tled**; **-lit·tling** \-'lit-liŋ, -'lit-ᵊl-iŋ\ : to make (a person or a thing) seem little or unimportant : speak of in a slighting way — **be·lit·tle·ment** *n*
¹**bell** \'bel\ *n* **1** : a hollow usu. cup-shaped metallic device that makes a ringing sound when struck **2** : the stroke or sound of a bell that tells the hour esp. on shipboard **3** : the time indicated by the stroke of a bell **4** : something shaped like a bell
²**bell** *vb* : to provide with a bell
bel·la·don·na \ˌbel-ə-'dän-ə\ *n* : a European poisonous herb of the nightshade family with reddish bell-shaped flowers and shining black berries; *also* : a drug or extract from this plant used esp. to relieve spasms and to dilate the eye
bell·boy \'bel-ˌbȯi\ *n* : a hotel or club employee who escorts guests to rooms, assists them with luggage, and runs errands
belle \'bel\ *n* : a popular attractive girl or woman
belles let·tres \bel-letrᵊ\ *n pl* : literature that is an end in itself and not practical or purely informative — **bel·le·tris·tic** \ˌbel-ə-'tris-tik\ *adj*
bell·hop \'bel-ˌhäp\ *n* : BELLBOY
bel·li·cose \'bel-ə-ˌkōs\ *adj* : inclined to quarrel or fight : WARLIKE — **bel·li·cos·i·ty** \ˌbel-ə-'käs-ət-ē\ *n*
bel·lig·er·ence \bə-'lij-(ə-)rən(t)s\ *n* : an aggressive or truculent attitude, atmosphere, or disposition
bel·lig·er·en·cy \-(ə-)rən-sē\ *n* **1** : the status of a nation that is at war **2** : WARFARE
bel·lig·er·ent \bə-'lij-(ə-)rənt\ *adj* **1** : waging war **2** : inclined to or exhibiting assertiveness or combativeness — **belligerent** *n* — **bel·lig·er·ent·ly** *adv*
bel·low \'bel-ō\ *vb* **1** : to make the loud deep hollow sound characteristic of a bull **2** : to shout in a deep voice : BAWL — **bellow** *n*
bel·lows \'bel-ōz, -əz\ *n sing or pl* : a device (as for blowing fires or operating an organ) that by alternate expansion and contraction of a closed box draws in air through a valve and expels it forcibly through a tube
bell·weth·er \'bel-'weth-ər\ *n* : one that takes the lead or initiative : LEADER
¹**bel·ly** \'bel-ē\ *n, pl* **bellies** **1 a** : ABDOMEN **b** : the undersurface of an animal's body **c** : STOMACH 1a **2** : a surface or object curved or rounded like a human belly
²**belly** *vb* **bel·lied**; **bel·ly·ing** : to swell or bulge out
bel·ly–land \'bel-ē-ˌland\ *vb* : to land an airplane without use of landing gear — **belly landing** *n*
be·long \bə-'lȯŋ\ *vi* **1 a** : to be suitable, appropriate, or advantageous **b** : to be in a proper situation **2 a** : to be the property of a person or thing — used with *to* **b** : to become attached or bound by birth, allegiance, or dependency **3** : to be an attribute, part, adjunct, or function of a person or thing **4** : to be properly classified
be·long·ings \bə-'lȯŋ-iŋz\ *n pl* : EFFECTS, POSSESSIONS
be·lov·ed \bi-'ləv(-ə)d\ *adj* : dearly loved — **beloved** *n*
¹**be·low** \bə-'lō\ *adv* **1** : in or to a lower place **2 a** : on earth **b** : in or to Hades or hell **3** : on or to a lower floor or deck **4** : lower on the same page or on a following page
²**below** *prep* : lower than in place, rank, or value
¹**belt** \'belt\ *n* **1** : a strip of flexible material (as leather or cloth) worn around the waist **2** : a flexible endless band running around wheels or pulleys and used for moving or carrying something **3** : a natural area characterized by some distinctive feature; *esp* : one suited to a particular crop — **belt·ed** \'bel-təd\ *adj*
²**belt** *vt* **1** : to put a belt on or around **2** : to beat with or as if with a belt : THRASH, STRIKE **3** : to mark with a band
³**belt** *n* : a jarring blow
be·mire \bi-'mī(ə)r\ *vt* : to cover or soil with or sink in mire
be·moan \bi-'mōn\ *vt* : LAMENT, DEPLORE
be·muse \bi-'myüz\ *vt* : to make confused : BEWILDER
bench \'bench\ *n* **1** : a long seat for two or more persons **2** : a long table for holding work and tools **3 a** : the seat where a judge sits in a court of law **b** : the position or rank of a judge **c** : a person sitting as a judge or the persons who sit as judges taken together
¹**bend** \'bend\ *n* : a knot by which one rope is fastened to another or to some object
²**bend** *vb* **bent** \'bent\; **bend·ing** **1** : to pull taut or tense **2** : to curve or cause a change of shape **3** : to turn in a certain direction : DIRECT **4** : to force to yield **5 a** : to apply closely **b** : to apply oneself closely or vigorously **6** : to curve out of line **7** : to curve downward : STOOP **8** : YIELD, SUBMIT
³**bend** *n* **1** : the act or process of bending : the state of being bent **2** : something that is bent; *esp* : a curved part of a stream **3** *pl* : a painful and dangerous disorder resulting from too sudden removal (as of a diver) from a compressed atmosphere
¹**be·neath** \bi-'nēth\ *adv* **1** : in or to a lower position **2** : directly under
²**beneath** *prep* **1 a** : in or to a lower position than **b** : directly under **2** : unworthy of
ben·e·dict \'ben-ə-ˌdikt\ *n* : a newly married man who has long been a bachelor
ben·e·dic·tion \ˌben-ə-'dik-shən\ *n* : the invocation of a blessing; *esp* : the short blessing with which public worship is concluded — **ben·e·dic·to·ry** \-'dik-t(ə-)rē\ *adj*
ben·e·fac·tion \'ben-ə-ˌfak-shən, ˌben-ə-'\ *n* **1** : the action of benefiting **2** : a benefit conferred; *esp* : a charitable donation
ben·e·fac·tor \'ben-ə-ˌfak-tər\ *n* : one that confers a benefit; *esp* : one that makes a gift or bequest
ben·e·fice \'ben-ə-fəs\ *n* : an ecclesiastical post to which the revenue from an endowment is attached — **benefice** *vt*
be·nef·i·cence \bə-'nef-ə-sən(t)s\ *n* **1** : the quality or state of being beneficent **2** : BENEFACTION
be·nef·i·cent \-sənt\ *adj* **1** : doing or producing good; *esp* : performing acts of kindness and charity **2** : productive of benefit — **be·nef·i·cent·ly** *adv*
ben·e·fi·cial \ˌben-ə-'fish-əl\ *adj* : conferring benefits : ADVANTAGEOUS — **ben·e·fi·cial·ly** \-'fish-ə-lē\ *adv* — **ben·e·fi·cial·ness** *n*
ben·e·fi·ci·ary \-'fish-ē-ˌer-ē, -'fish-(ə-)rē\ *n, pl* **-ar·ies** : a person who benefits or is expected to benefit from something (as a life insurance policy)
¹**ben·e·fit** \'ben-ə-ˌfit\ *n* **1 a** : something that promotes well-being : ADVANTAGE **b** : useful aid : HELP **2** : assistance (as money) provided for under an annuity, pension plan, or insurance policy **3** : an entertainment or social event to raise funds for a person or cause
²**benefit** *vb* **-fit·ed** *or* **-fit·ted**; **-fit·ing** *or* **-fit·ting** **1** : to be useful or profitable to **2** : to receive benefit
be·nev·o·lence \bə-'nev-(ə-)lən(t)s\ *n* **1** : disposition to do good **2 a** : an act of kindness **b** : a generous gift
be·nev·o·lent \-(ə-)lənt\ *adj* **1** : having or showing goodwill

to others : KINDLY 2 : freely or generously giving to charity — **be·nev·o·lent·ly** *adv* — **be·nev·o·lent·ness** *n*
be·night·ed \bi-ˈnīt-əd\ *adj* 1 : overtaken by night or darkness 2 : IGNORANT
be·nign \bi-ˈnīn\ *adj* 1 : of a gentle disposition : GRACIOUS 2 a : manifesting kindness and gentleness b : FAVORABLE 3 : of a mild character; *esp* : not malignant — **be·nig·ni·ty** \-ˈnig-nət-ē\ *n* — **be·nign·ly** *adv*
be·nig·nant \bi-ˈnig-nənt\ *adj* 1 : KINDLY, GENTLE 2 : FAVORABLE, BENEFICIAL — **be·nig·nant·ly** *adv*
ben·i·son \ˈben-ə-sən, -zən\ *n* : BLESSING, BENEDICTION
bent \ˈbent\ *n* 1 a : strong inclination or interest b : a natural capacity 2 : capacity of endurance
be·numb \bi-ˈnəm\ *vt* : to make numb esp. by cold
ben·zene \ˈben-ˌzēn, ben-ˈ\ *n* : a colorless volatile flammable liquid obtained chiefly in the distillation of coal and used as a solvent and in making dyes and drugs
ben·zine \ˈben-ˌzēn, ben-ˈ\ *n* 1 : BENZENE 2 : any of various volatile flammable petroleum distillates used esp. as solvents for fatty substances or as motor fuels
ben·zo·ic acid \(ˌ)ben-ˌzō-ik-\ *n* : a white crystalline acid found naturally (as in cranberries) or made synthetically and used esp. as a preservative and as an antiseptic
ben·zol \ˈben-ˌzȯl\ *n* : BENZENE
be·queath \bi-ˈkwēth, -ˈkwēt͟h\ *vt* 1 : to give or leave esp. personal property by will 2 : to hand down — **be·queath·al** \-əl\ *n*
be·quest \bi-ˈkwest\ *n* 1 : the action of bequeathing 2 : something bequeathed : LEGACY
be·rate \bi-ˈrāt\ *vt* : to scold violently
ber·ceuse \ber-ˈsə(r)z\ *n, pl* **ber·ceuses** \-ˈsə(r)z(-əz)\ 1 : LULLABY 2 : a musical composition of a tranquil nature
be·reave \bi-ˈrēv\ *vt* **be·reaved** \-ˈrēvd\ *or* **be·reft** \-ˈreft\; **be·reav·ing** : to deprive of something cherished esp. by death : STRIP, DISPOSSESS — **be·reave·ment** *n*
be·ret \bə-ˈrā\ *n* : a soft flat visorless wool cap
berg \ˈbərg\ *n* : ICEBERG
ber·i·beri \ˌber-ē-ˈber-ē\ *n* : a deficiency disease marked by weakness, wasting, and damage to nerves and caused by a dietary lack of or inability to assimilate thiamine
berke·li·um \ˈbər-klē-əm, (ˌ)bər-ˈkē-lē-əm\ *n* : an artificially prepared radioactive chemical element
[1]**ber·ry** \ˈber-ē\ *n, pl* **berries** 1 a : a small pulpy and usu. edible fruit b : a simple fruit (as a currant, grape, tomato, or banana) with the wall of the ripened ovary pulpy or fleshy 2 : the dry seed of some plants (as coffee)
[2]**berry** *vi* **ber·ried**; **ber·ry·ing** 1 : to bear or produce berries 2 : to gather or seek berries
ber·serk \bə(r)-ˈsərk, -ˈzərk, ˈbər-ˌ\ *adj* : FRENZIED, CRAZED — **berserk** *adv*
[1]**berth** \ˈbərth\ *n* 1 : distance sufficient to maneuver a ship 2 : a place where a ship lies at anchor 3 : a place to sit or sleep on a ship or vehicle 4 : JOB, POSITION
[2]**berth** *vb* 1 : to bring or come into a berth 2 : to allot a berth to
ber·yl \ˈber-əl\ *n* : a hard silicate mineral occurring in green, yellow, pink, or white crystals
be·ryl·li·um \bə-ˈril-ē-əm\ *n* : a steel-gray light strong brittle metallic element
be·seech \bi-ˈsēch\ *vb* **be·sought** \-ˈsȯt\ *or* **be·seeched**; **be·seech·ing** : to ask earnestly for : IMPLORE
be·set \bi-ˈset\ *vt* **-set**; **-set·ting** 1 : TROUBLE, HARASS 2 a : to set upon : ASSAIL b : to hem in : SURROUND
be·set·ting \bi-ˈset-iŋ\ *adj* : constantly present or attacking
be·side \bi-ˈsīd\ *prep* 1 a : by the side of b : in comparison with 2 : BESIDES 3 : not relevant to — **beside oneself** : out of one's wits
[1]**be·sides** \bi-ˈsīdz\ *adv* : in addition : ALSO
[2]**besides** *prep* 1 : in addition to 2 : other than
be·siege \bi-ˈsēj\ *vt* 1 : to surround with armed forces : lay siege to 2 : to crowd around : BESET — **be·sieg·er** *n*
be·smear \bi-ˈsmi(ə)r\ *vt* : SMEAR
be·smirch \bi-ˈsmərch\ *vt* : SULLY, SOIL
be·som \ˈbē-zəm\ *n* : a broom made of twigs
be·sot \bi-ˈsät\ *vt* **be·sot·ted**; **be·sot·ting** : to make dull or stupid : STUPEFY; *esp* : to muddle with drink
be·spat·ter \bi-ˈspat-ər\ *vt* : SPATTER
be·speak \bi-ˈspēk\ *vt* **-spoke** \-ˈspōk\; **-spo·ken** \-ˈspō-kən\; **-speak·ing** 1 a : to ask or arrange for beforehand b : REQUEST 2 a : INDICATE, SIGNIFY b : FORETELL
[1]**best** \ˈbest\ *adj, superlative of* GOOD 1 : good or useful in the highest degree : most excellent 2 : MOST, LARGEST
[2]**best** *adv, superlative of* WELL 1 : in the best way 2 : to the highest degree : MOST
[3]**best** *n* 1 : the best state or part 2 : one that is best 3 : one's maximum effort 4 : best clothes
[4]**best** *vt* : to get the better of : OUTDO
bes·tial \ˈbes-chəl\ *adj* 1 : of or relating to beasts 2 a : lacking intelligence or reason b : VICIOUS, BRUTAL — **bes·tial·ly** \-chə-lē\ *adv*
bes·ti·al·i·ty \ˌbes-chē-ˈal-ət-ē\ *n* : display or gratification of bestial traits or impulses
be·stir \bi-ˈstər\ *vt* : to stir up : rouse to action
be·stow \bi-ˈstō\ *vt* 1 : USE, APPLY 2 : to present as a gift : CONFER — **be·stow·al** \-ˈstō-əl\ *n*
be·stride \bi-ˈstrīd\ *vt* **-strode** \-ˈstrōd\; **-strid·den** \-ˈstrid-ᵊn\; **-strid·ing** 1 : to ride, sit, or stand astride : STRADDLE 2 : to tower over : DOMINATE
[1]**bet** \ˈbet\ *n* 1 a : an agreement requiring the person whose guess about the result of a contest or the outcome of an event proves wrong to give something to a person whose guess proves right b : the making of such an agreement : WAGER 2 : the money or thing risked
[2]**bet** *vb* **bet** *or* **bet·ted**; **bet·ting** 1 : to stake on the outcome of an issue 2 : to make a bet with 3 : to lay a bet
be·take \bi-ˈtāk\ *vt* : to cause (oneself) to go
be·ta particle \ˈbāt-ə-\ *n* : an electron or positron ejected from the nucleus of an atom during radioactive transformation
beta ray *n* 1 : BETA PARTICLE 2 : a stream of beta particles
be·tel \ˈbēt-ᵊl\ *n* : a climbing pepper whose dried leaves are chewed together with betel nut and lime as a stimulant esp. by southeastern Asians
betel nut *n* : the astringent seed of an Asiatic palm
bête noire \ˌbāt-nə-ˈwär, bāt-ˈnwär\ *n, pl* **bêtes noires** \-ˈwär(z), -ˈnwär(z)\ : a person or thing strongly detested or avoided : BUGBEAR
beth·el \ˈbeth-əl\ *n* : a place of worship esp. for seamen
be·think \bi-ˈthiŋk\ *vt* **-thought** \-ˈthȯt\; **-think·ing** 1 a : REMEMBER, RECALL b : to cause (oneself) to be reminded 2 : to cause (oneself) to consider
be·tide \bi-ˈtīd\ *vb* : to happen or happen to : BEFALL
be·times \bi-ˈtīmz\ *adv* : in time : EARLY
be·to·ken \bi-ˈtō-kən\ *vt* : to be a sign of : INDICATE
be·tray \bi-ˈtrā\ *vt* 1 : to give over to an enemy by treachery or fraud 2 : to be unfaithful or treacherous to : FAIL 3 : to lead into error, sin, or danger : DECEIVE, SEDUCE 4 : to reveal unintentionally 5 : to tell in violation of a trust — **be·tray·al** \-ˈtrā(-ə)l\ *n* — **be·tray·er** *n*
be·troth \bi-ˈtrȯth, -ˈtrōt͟h\ *vt* : to promise to marry or give in marriage — **be·troth·al** \-əl\ *n*
be·trothed \bi-ˈtrȯtht, -ˈtrōt͟hd\ *n* : the person to whom one is betrothed
[1]**bet·ter** \ˈbet-ər\ *adj, comparative of* GOOD 1 : more than half 2 : improved in health 3 : of higher quality
[2]**better** *adv, comparative of* WELL 1 : in a more excellent manner 2 a : to a higher or greater degree b : MORE

[3]**better** *n* **1 a :** something better **b :** a superior esp. in merit or rank **2 :** ADVANTAGE, VICTORY

[4]**better** *vt* **1 :** to make better **2 :** to surpass in excellence

bet·ter·ment \'bet-ər-mənt\ *n* **:** IMPROVEMENT

bet·tor *or* **bet·ter** \'bet-ər\ *n* **:** one that bets

[1]**be·tween** \bi-'twēn\ *prep* **1 :** by the common action of **:** in common to **2 :** in the time, space, or interval that separates **3 :** DISTINGUISHING **4 :** by comparison of **5 :** from one to the other or another of

[2]**between** *adv* **:** in an intermediate space or interval — **be·tween·ness** *n*

[1]**bev·el** \'bev-əl\ *adj* **:** OBLIQUE, BEVELED

[2]**bevel** *n* **1 :** the angle or slant that one surface or line makes with another when they are not at right angles **2 :** an instrument for drawing angles or adjusting surfaces to be given a bevel

[3]**bevel** *vb* **bev·eled** *or* **bev·elled**; **bev·el·ing** *or* **bev·el·ling** \'bev-(ə-)liŋ\ **1 :** to cut or shape (as an edge or surface) to a bevel **2 :** INCLINE, SLANT

bev·er·age \'bev-(ə-)rij\ *n* **:** liquid for drinking; *esp* **:** such liquid other than water

bevy \'bev-ē\ *n, pl* **bev·ies :** GROUP, CLUSTER

be·wail \bi-'wāl\ *vt* **1 :** to wail over **2 :** to express deep regret for

be·ware \bi-'wa(ə)r\ *vb* **1 :** to be on one's guard **2 :** to be wary of

be·wil·der \bi-'wil-dər\ *vt* **-dered**; **-der·ing** \-d(ə-)riŋ\ **:** PERPLEX, CONFUSE — **be·wil·der·ment** *n*

be·witch \bi-'wich\ *vt* **1 :** to affect by witchcraft **2 :** CHARM, FASCINATE — **be·witch·ery** \-ə-rē\ *n*

bey \'bā\ *n* **1 :** a provincial governor in the Ottoman Empire **2 :** the former native ruler of Tunis

[1]**be·yond** \bē-'änd\ *adv* **:** on or to the farther side

[2]**beyond** *prep* **1 :** on or to the farther side of **2 :** out of the reach or sphere of

[3]**beyond** *n* **:** HEREAFTER

bez·el \'bez-əl\ *n* **1 :** a sloping edge on a cutting tool **2 a :** the top part of a ring setting **b :** the upper faceted portion of a cut gem projecting from the setting **3 :** the grooved rim that holds the crystal on a watch

bhang \'baŋ\ *n* **:** a narcotic product of hemp

bi·an·nu·al \(')bī-'an-yə(-wə)l\ *adj* **:** occurring twice a year — **bi·an·nu·al·ly** \-ē\ *adv*

[1]**bi·as** \'bī-əs\ *n* **1 :** a line diagonal to the grain of a fabric **2 :** PREJUDICE, BENT

[2]**bias** *adj* **:** DIAGONAL, SLANTING

[3]**bias** *vt* **bi·ased** *or* **bi·assed**; **bi·as·ing** *or* **bi·as·sing :** to give a bias to **:** PREJUDICE

bib \'bib\ *n* **:** a cloth or plastic shield tied under a child's chin to protect the clothes

bib·ber \'bib-ər\ *n* **:** TIPPLER — **bib·bery** \-ə-rē\ *n*

Bi·ble \'bī-bəl\ *n* **1 :** the sacred scriptures of Christians comprising the Old Testament and the New Testament **2 :** the sacred scriptures of Judaism or of some other religion **3** *not cap* **:** a publication that is preeminent esp. in authoritativeness

bib·li·cal \'bib-li-kəl\ *adj* **1 :** of, relating to, or being in accord with the Bible **2 :** suggestive of the Bible or Bible times — **bib·li·cal·ly** \-k(ə-)lē\ *adv*

bib·li·og·ra·pher \ˌbib-lē-'äg-rə-fər\ *n* **1 :** an expert in bibliography **2 :** a compiler of bibliography

bib·li·og·ra·phy \ˌbib-lē-'äg-rə-fē\ *n, pl* **-phies 1 :** the history, identification, or description of writings or publications **2 :** a list of writings relating to a particular subject, period, or author — **bib·li·o·graph·ic** \ˌbib-lē-ə-'graf-ik\ *or* **bib·li·o·graph·i·cal** \-'graf-i-kəl\ *adj* — **bib·li·o·graph·i·cal·ly** \-'graf-i-k(ə-)lē\ *adv*

bib·lio·phile \'bib-lē-ə-ˌfīl\ *n* **:** a lover of books

THE BOOKS OF THE OLD TESTAMENT

DOUAY VERSION	AUTHORIZED VERSION
Genesis	Genesis
Exodus	Exodus
Leviticus	Leviticus
Numbers	Numbers
Deuteronomy	Deuteronomy
Josue	Joshua
Judges	Judges
Ruth	Ruth
1 & 2 Kings	1 & 2 Samuel
3 & 4 Kings	1 & 2 Kings
1 & 2 Paralipomenon	1 & 2 Chronicles
1 Esdras	Ezra
2 Esdras	Nehemiah
Tobias	
Judith	
Esther	Esther
Wisdom	
Ecclesiasticus	
Isaias	Isaiah
Jeremias	Jeremiah
Lamentations	Lamentations
Baruch	
Ezechiel	Ezekiel
Daniel	Daniel
Osee	Hosea
Joel	Joel
Amos	Amos
Abdias	Obadiah
Jonas	Jonah
Micheas	Micah
Nahum	Nahum
Habacuc	Habakkuk
Sophonias	Zephaniah
Job	Job
Psalms	Psalms
Proverbs	Proverbs
Ecclesiastes	Ecclesiastes
Canticle of Canticles	Song of Solomon
Aggeus	Haggai
Zacharias	Zechariah
Malachias	Malachi
1 & 2 Machabees	

THE BOOKS OF THE NEW TESTAMENT (*DV* and *AV* names the same)

Matthew
Mark
Luke
John
Acts of the Apostles
Romans
1 & 2 Corinthians
Galatians
Ephesians
Philippians
Colossians
1 & 2 Thessalonians
1 & 2 Timothy
Titus
Philemon
Hebrews
James
1 & 2 Peter
1, 2, 3 John
Jude
Revelation (*DV*: Apocalypse)

PROTESTANT APOCRYPHA

1 & 2 Esdras[1]
Tobit
Judith
part of Esther[2]
Wisdom of Solomon
Ecclesiasticus or the Wisdom of Jesus Son of Sirach
Baruch
Prayer of Azariah and the Song of the Three Holy Children[3]
Susanna[4]
Bel and the Dragon[5]
The Prayer of Manasses[6]
1 & 2 Maccabees

[1]not the same as 1 & 2 Esdras in *DV*
[2]ch. 11–16 in *DV*
[3]from ch. 3 of *DV* Daniel
[4]ch. 13 of *DV* Daniel
[5]ch. 14 of *DV* Daniel
[6]not in *DV*

bib·u·lous \'bib-yə-ləs\ *adj* **1 :** highly absorbent **2 :** inclined to drink — **bib·u·lous·ly** *adv* — **bib·u·lous·ness** *n*

bi·cam·er·al \(')bī-'kam(-ə)-rəl\ *adj* **:** having, consisting of, or based upon two legislative chambers — **bi·cam·er·al·ism** \-rə-ˌliz-əm\ *n*

bi·car·bon·ate of soda \bī-ˌkär-bə-nət-, -ˌnāt-\ **:** SODIUM BICARBONATE

bi·cen·te·na·ry \ˌbī-sen-'ten-ə-rē, (')bī-'sent-ᵊn-ˌer-ē\ *adj* **:** BICENTENNIAL — **bicentenary** *n*

bi·cen·ten·ni·al \ˌbī-sen-'ten-ē-əl\ *adj* **:** relating to a 200th anniversary — **bicentennial** *n*

bi·ceps \'bī-ˌseps\ *n* **:** a muscle having two heads; *esp* **:** a large muscle of the front of the upper arm

bi·chlo·ride \(')bī-'klōr-ˌīd\ *n* **:** any of several chlorides; *esp*

: one that is a poisonous compound of mercury and chlorine used as an antiseptic and fungicide

bick•er \'bik-ər\ *vi* **bick•ered**; **bick•er•ing** \'bik-(ə-)riŋ\ : to quarrel petulantly or pettily : WRANGLE — **bicker** *n*

bi•cus•pid \(')bī-'kəs-pəd\ *n* : either of two double-pointed teeth next to the canine on each side of each jaw in man

[1]**bi•cy•cle** \'bī-ˌsik-əl\ *n* : a vehicle with two wheels tandem, a steering handle, a saddle seat, and pedals by which it is propelled — **bi•cy•clist** \-ˌsik-(ə-)ləst\ *n*

[2]**bicycle** *vi* **bi•cy•cled**; **bi•cy•cling** \-ˌsik-(ə-)liŋ\ : to ride a bicycle — **bi•cy•cler** \-ˌsik-(ə-)lər\ *n*

[1]**bid** \'bid\ *vb* **bade** \'bad, 'bād\ *or* **bid**; **bid•den** \'bid-ᵊn\ *or* **bid**; **bid•ding** **1 a** : to issue an order to : TELL **b** : to request to come : INVITE **2** : to give expression to **3** *past* **bid** : to make a bid : OFFER — **bid•der** *n*

[2]**bid** *n* **1** : an offer to pay a certain sum for something or to perform certain work at a stated fee; *also* : the price or fee offered **2** : an opportunity or turn to bid **3** : INVITATION **4** : an announcement of what a card player proposes to undertake **5** : an attempt to win or gain

bid•da•ble \'bid-ə-bəl\ *adj* **1** : OBEDIENT, DOCILE **2** : capable of being bid — **bid•da•bly** \-blē\ *adv*

bide \'bīd\ *vb* **bode** \'bōd\ *or* **bid•ed**; **bided**; **bid•ing** **1** : to continue in a state or condition : WAIT **2** : to wait for — **bid•er** *n*

bi•en•ni•al \(')bī-'en-ē-əl\ *adj* **1** : occurring every two years **2 a** : continuing or lasting for two years **b** : producing leaves the first year and fruiting and dying the second — **biennial** *n* — **bi•en•ni•al•ly** \-ē-ə-lē\ *adv*

bi•en•ni•um \bī-'en-ē-əm\ *n* : a period of two years

bier \'bi(ə)r\ *n* : a stand bearing a corpse or coffin

[1]**bi•fo•cal** \(')bī-'fō-kəl\ *adj* : having two focal lengths

[2]**bifocal** *n* **1** : a bifocal glass or lens **2** *pl* : eyeglasses with bifocal lenses

bi•fur•cate \'bī-fər-ˌkāt, bī-'fər-\ *vb* : to divide into two branches or parts — **bi•fur•cate** \(')bī-'fər-kət, -ˌkāt; 'bī-fər-ˌkāt\ *adj* — **bi•fur•cate•ly** *adv* — **bi•fur•ca•tion** \ˌbī-(ˌ)fər-'kā-shən\ *n*

big \'big\ *adj* **1** : of great force **2** : large in size, amount, or scale **3 a** : PREGNANT **b** : full to bursting : SWELLING **4 a** : CHIEF, PREEMINENT **b** : of great importance or significance **c** : IMPOSING, PRETENTIOUS; *also* : BOASTFUL **d** : MAGNANIMOUS, GENEROUS — **big** *adv* — **big•ness** *n*

big•a•mist \'big-ə-məst\ *n* : one who practices bigamy

big•a•my \'big-ə-mē\ *n* : the act of marrying one person while still legally married to another — **big•a•mous** \-məs\ *adj* — **big•a•mous•ly** *adv*

big•horn \'big-ˌhȯrn\ *n, pl* **bighorn** *or* **bighorns** : a wild sheep of mountainous western No. America

bight \'bīt\ *n* **1** : the slack middle part of a rope fastened at both ends : a loop or double part of a bent rope **2** : a bend in a coast or the bay it forms

big•ot \'big-ət\ *n* : a person obstinately or intolerantly devoted to his own group, beliefs, or opinions — **big•ot•ed** *adj*

big•ot•ry \'big-ə-trē\ *n, pl* **-ries** : the state of mind of a bigot; *also* : behavior or beliefs arising from it

big•wig \'big-ˌwig\ *n* : an important person

bike \'bīk\ *n or vi* : BICYCLE — **bik•er** *n*

bike•way \'bī-ˌkwā\ *n* : a thoroughfare for bicycles

bi•ki•ni \bə-'kē-nē\ *n* : a woman's abbreviated two-piece bathing suit

bi•lat•er•al \(')bī-'lat-ə-rəl, -'la-trəl\ *adj* : having or involving two sides; *esp* : affecting reciprocally two sides or parties — **bi•lat•er•al•ism** \-ˌiz-əm\ *n* — **bi•lat•er•al•ly** \-ē\ *adv* — **bi•lat•er•al•ness** *n*

bile \'bīl\ *n* **1** : a thick bitter yellow or greenish fluid secreted by the liver that aids in the digestion of fats **2** : proneness to anger : SPLEEN

bilge \'bilj\ *n* **1** : the part of a ship's hull between the flat of the bottom and the vertical topsides **2** : foul water that collects in the bottom of a ship

bi•lin•gual \(')bī-'liŋ-gwəl\ *adj* **1** : of, containing, or expressed in two languages **2** : using or able to use two languages

bil•ious \'bil-yəs\ *adj* **1** : marked by or suffering from disordered liver function **2** : of a peevish ill-natured disposition — **bil•ious•ly** *adv* — **bil•ious•ness** *n*

bilk \'bilk\ *vt* : to cheat out of what is due : SWINDLE

[1]**bill** \'bil\ *n* **1** : the jaws of a bird together with their horny covering **2** : a beak (as of a turtle) or mouth structure resembling a bird's bill **3** : the visor of a cap — **billed** \'bild\ *adj*

bills of birds

[2]**bill** *vi* **1** : to touch bill to bill **2** : to caress affectionately

[3]**bill** *n* **1** : a draft of a law presented to a legislature for enactment **2** : a written declaration of a wrong suffered or of a breach of law **3** : a written list or statement of particulars **4** : an itemized account (as of the cost of goods sold or work done) : INVOICE **5** : an advertisement posted or distributed to announce an event (as a theatrical entertainment) of interest to the public **6** : a piece of paper money

[4]**bill** *vt* **1 a** : to enter in a book of accounts : make a bill of (charges) **b** : to submit a bill of charges to **2 a** : to advertise esp. by posters or placards **b** : to arrange for the presentation of — **bill•er** *n*

bill•board \'bil-ˌbōrd\ *n* : a flat surface on which advertising bills are posted

[1]**bil•let** \'bil-ət\ *n* **1** : an official order directing that a soldier be lodged (as in a private home) **2** : quarters assigned by or as if by a billet **3** : BERTH, POSITION

[2]**billet** *vb* : to assign lodging to by a billet : QUARTER

bil•let–doux \ˌbil-(ˌ)ā-'dü\ *n, pl* **bil•lets–doux** \-(ˌ)ā-'dü(z)\ : a love letter

bill•fold \'bil-ˌfōld\ *n* : WALLET 2

bill•head \-ˌhed\ *n* : a printed form usu. headed with a business address and used for billing charges

bil•liards \'bil-yərdz\ *n* : any of several games played on an oblong table by driving small balls against one another or into pockets with a cue

bil•lings•gate \'bil-iŋz-ˌgāt\ *n* : coarsely abusive language

bil•lion•aire \ˌbil-yə-'na(ə)r, 'bil-yə-ˌ\ *n* : one whose wealth is a billion or more

bill of exchange : a written order from one person to another to pay a specified sum of money to a designated person

[1]**bil•low** \'bil-ō\ *n* **1** : WAVE; *esp* : a great wave **2** : a rolling mass (as of flame or smoke) like a high wave

[2]**billow** *vb* **1** : to rise or roll in waves or surges **2** : to bulge or swell out

bil•lowy \'bil-ə-wē\ *adj* : characterized by billows

bil•ly \'bil-ē\ *n, pl* **billies** : a heavy usu. wooden club; *esp* : a policeman's club

bi•met•al•lism \(')bī-'met-ᵊl-ˌiz-əm\ *n* : the use of two metals (as gold and silver) jointly as a monetary standard with both

constituting legal tender at a legally fixed ratio — **bi·met·al·list** \-ᵊl-əst\ *n*
bin \'bin\ *n* : a box, crib, or enclosed place for storage
¹bi·na·ry \'bī-nə-rē\ *adj* : compounded or consisting of or characterized by two often similar things or parts
²binary *n, pl* **-ries** : something constituted of two things or parts
bin·au·ral \(')bī-'nȯr-əl\ *adj* : of, relating to, or characterized by the placement of sound sources (as in sound transmission and recording) to achieve in sound reproduction an effect of hearing the sound sources in their original positions — **bin·au·ral·ly** \-ə-lē\ *adv*
¹bind \'bīnd\ *vb* **bound** \'bau̇nd\; **bind·ing** **1 a** : to make secure by tying **b** : to confine, restrain, or restrict as if with bonds **c** : to put under an obligation **2 a** : to wrap around with something so as to enclose, encircle, or cover **b** : BANDAGE **3** : to tie or fasten together **4 a** : to stick together **b** : to form a cohesive mass **5** : CONSTIPATE **6** : to make firm or sure **7 a** : to protect, strengthen, or decorate by a band or binding **b** : to apply the parts of the cover to (a book) **8** : APPRENTICE **9** : to cause to be attached (as by gratitude) — **bind·er** *n*
²bind *n* : something that binds
bind·ing \'bīn-diŋ\ *n* : a material or device used to bind
binge \'binj\ *n* : CAROUSAL, SPREE
bin·na·cle \'bin-i-kəl\ *n* : a case, box, or stand containing a ship's compass and a lamp
¹bin·oc·u·lar \bī-'näk-yə-lər, bə-\ *adj* : of, relating to, using, or adapted to the use of both eyes — **bin·oc·u·lar·ly** *adv*
²bin·oc·u·lar \bə-'näk-yə-lər, bī-\ *n* **1** : a binocular optical instrument **2** : FIELD GLASS — usu. used in pl.
bi·no·mi·al \bī-'nō-mē-əl\ *n* **1** : a mathematical expression consisting of two terms connected by a plus sign or minus sign **2** : a biological species name consisting of two terms — **binomial** *adj* — **bi·no·mi·al·ly** \-mē-ə-lē\ *adv*
bio·chem·i·cal \ˌbī-ō-'kem-i-kəl\ *adj* : of or relating to biochemistry — **bio·chem·i·cal·ly** \-k(ə-)lē\ *adv*
bio·chem·is·try \-'kem-ə-strē\ *n* : chemistry that deals with the chemical compounds and processes occurring in organisms — **bio·chem·ist** \-'kem-əst\ *n*
bio·de·grad·a·ble \-di-'grād-ə-bəl\ *adj* : capable of being broken down esp. into innocuous products by the action of living beings (as microorganisms)
bio·ge·og·ra·phy \-jē-'äg-rə-fē\ *n* : a branch of biology that deals with the geographical distribution of animals and plants — **bio·ge·og·ra·pher** \-jē-'äg-rə-fər\ *n* — **bio·geo·graph·ic** \-ˌjē-ə-'graf-ik\ *or* **bio·geo·graph·i·cal** \-'graf-i-kəl\ *adj*
bi·og·ra·pher \bī-'äg-rə-fər, bē-\ *n* : a writer of a biography
bio·graph·i·cal \ˌbī-ə-'graf-i-kəl\ *or* **bio·graph·ic** \-'graf-ik\ *adj* **1** : of, relating to, or constituting biography **2** : consisting of biographies — **bio·graph·i·cal·ly** \-'graf-i-k(ə-)lē\ *adv*
bi·og·ra·phy \bī-'äg-rə-fē, bē-\ *n, pl* **-phies** **1** : a usu. written history of a person's life **2** : biographical writings in general
bi·o·log·i·cal \ˌbī-ə-'läj-i-kəl\ *or* **bi·o·log·ic** \-'läj-ik\ *adj* : of or relating to biology or to life and living processes — **bi·o·log·i·cal·ly** \-'läj-i-k(ə-)lē\ *adv*
biological warfare *n* : warfare in which living organisms (as disease germs) are used to harm the enemy
bi·ol·o·gy \bī-'äl-ə-jē\ *n* **1 a** : a branch of knowledge that deals with living organisms and life processes **b** : ECOLOGY **2** : the laws and phenomena relating to an organism or group — **bi·ol·o·gist** \-jəst\ *n*
bi·op·sy \'bī-ˌäp-sē\ *n, pl* **-sies** : the removal and examination of tissue, cells, or fluids from the living body
bi·o·tin \'bī-ə-tən\ *n* : a colorless crystalline growth vitamin of the vitamin B complex found esp. in yeast, liver, and egg yolk
bi·pa·ren·tal \ˌbī-pə-'rent-ᵊl\ *adj* : involving or derived from two parents
bi·par·ti·san \(')bī-'pärt-ə-zən\ *adj* : representing, composed of, or formulated by members of two parties — **bi·par·ti·san·ship** \-ˌship\ *n*
bi·par·tite \(')bī-'pär-ˌtīt\ *adj* **1** : being in two parts **2** : shared by two — **bi·par·tite·ly** *adv* — **bi·par·ti·tion** \ˌbī-ˌpär-'tish-ən\ *n*
bi·ped \'bī-ˌped\ *n* : a 2-footed animal — **biped** *or* **bi·ped·al** \(')bī-'ped-ᵊl\ *adj*
bi·plane \'bī-ˌplān\ *n* : an airplane with two main supporting surfaces usu. placed one above the other
bi·ra·cial \(')bī-'rā-shəl\ *adj* : of, relating to, or involving members of two races — **bi·ra·cial·ism** \-shə-ˌliz-əm\ *n*
¹birch \'bərch\ *n* **1** : any of a genus of deciduous usu. short-lived trees or shrubs with typically a layered membranous outer bark that peels readily; *also* : its hard pale close-grained wood **2** : a birch rod or bundle of twigs for flogging — **birch** *or* **birch·en** \'bər-chən\ *adj*
²birch *vt* : to beat with or as if with a birch : WHIP
bird \'bərd\ *n* : any of a class of warm-blooded egg-laying vertebrate animals with the body covered with feathers and the forelimbs modified as wings
bird·bath \-ˌbath, -ˌbȧth\ *n* : a usu. ornamental basin set up for birds to bathe in
bird·house \-ˌhau̇s\ *n* : an artificial nesting place for birds; *also* : AVIARY
bird·ie \'bərd-ē\ *n* : a golf score of one stroke less than par on a hole
bird·lime \'bərd-ˌlīm\ *n* : a sticky substance smeared on twigs to catch and hold small birds
bird·seed \-ˌsēd\ *n* : a mixture of small seeds (as of hemp or millet) used chiefly for feeding cage birds
bird's–eye \'bərd-ˌzī\ *adj* **1 a** : seen from above as if by a flying bird **b** : CURSORY **2** : marked with spots resembling birds' eyes; *also* : made of bird's-eye wood
bi·reme \'bī-ˌrēm\ *n* : a galley with two banks of oars
bi·ret·ta \bə-'ret-ə\ *n* : a square cap with three upright projecting pieces on top worn ceremonially by clergymen esp. of the Roman Catholic Church
birth \'bərth\ *n* **1 a** : the emergence of a new individual from the body of its parent **b** : the act or process of bringing forth young from the womb **2** : LINEAGE, EXTRACTION **3** : BEGINNING, ORIGIN
birth·day \-ˌdā\ *n* **1** : the day or anniversary of one's birth **2** : the day or anniversary of a beginning
birth·mark \-ˌmärk\ *n* : an unusual mark or blemish on the skin at birth — **birthmark** *vt*
birth·place \-ˌplās\ *n* : place of birth or origin
birth·rate \-ˌrāt\ *n* : the number of births for every hundred or every thousand persons in a given area or group during a given time
birth·right \-ˌrīt\ *n* : a right, privilege, or possession to which a person is entitled by birth
birth·stone \-ˌstōn\ *n* : a precious stone associated symbolically with the month of one's birth
bis·cuit \'bis-kət\ *n* **1** : a crisp flat cake **2** : a small quick bread made from dough that has been rolled and cut or dropped from a spoon
bi·sect \'bī-ˌsekt, bī-'\ *vb* : to divide into two usu. equal parts : SEPARATE; *also* : CROSS, INTERSECT — **bi·sec·tion** \'bī-ˌsek-shən, bī-'\ *n* — **bi·sec·tion·al** \-shnəl, -shən-ᵊl\ *adj* — **bi·sec·tion·al·ly** \-ē\ *adv*
bi·sex·u·al \(')bī-'sek-sh(ə-w)əl\ *adj* **1** : possessing characters of or sexually oriented toward both sexes **2** : of, relating to, or involving two sexes — **bisexual** *n* — **bi·sex·u·al·i·ty** \ˌbī-ˌsek-shə-'wal-ət-ē\ *n* — **bi·sex·u·al·ly** \(')bī-'sek-sh(ə-w)ə-lē\ *adv*
bish·op \'bish-əp\ *n* **1 a** : a clergyman ranking above a priest, having authority to ordain and confirm, and typically governing a diocese **b** : a clergyman who oversees a church district **2** : a chess piece that can move diagonally across any number of unoccupied squares

bish·op·ric \'bish-ə-(ˌ)prik\ *n* **1 :** DIOCESE **2 :** the office of bishop **3 :** a bishop's seat or residence

bis·muth \'biz-məth\ *n* **:** a heavy brittle grayish white metallic element used in alloys and medicine

bi·son \'bīs-ᵊn, 'bīz-\ *n, pl* **bison :** a large shaggy-maned hump-shouldered wild ox formerly abundant on the plains of the central U.S.

bisque \'bisk\ *n* **1 :** a thick cream soup **2 :** ice cream containing powdered nuts or macaroons

¹bit \'bit\ *n* **1 :** the part of a bridle inserted in the mouth of a horse **2 :** a drilling or boring tool used in a brace **3 :** something that curbs or restrains

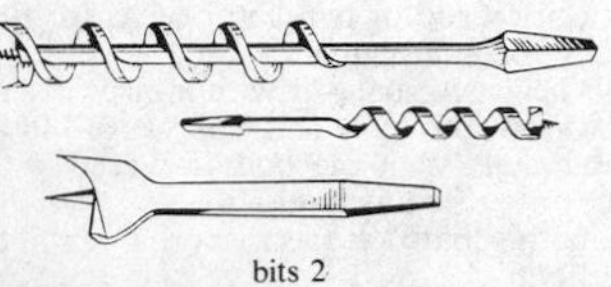

bits 2

²bit *n* **1 a :** a small piece **b :** AMOUNT, QUANTITY; *esp* **:** a small amount or quantity **2 :** a short time **:** WHILE **3 :** SOMEWHAT

bitch \'bich\ *n* **:** the female of the dog

¹bite \'bīt\ *vb* **bit** \'bit\; **bit·ten** \'bit-ᵊn\; **bit·ing** \'bīt-iŋ\ **1 :** to seize, grip, or cut into with or as if with teeth **2 :** to wound or pierce with or as if with fangs **3 :** to make a gash or cut **4 :** to cause to smart **:** STING **5 :** to eat into **:** CORRODE **6 :** to respond to a lure **:** take a bait — **bit·er** *n*

²bite *n* **1 :** a seizing of something by biting; *also* **:** the grip taken in biting **2 a :** the amount of food taken at a bite **b :** SNACK **3 :** a wound made by biting **4 :** a keen incisive quality or sharp penetrating effect

bit·ing \'bīt-iŋ\ *adj* **:** SHARP, CUTTING

bit·ter \'bit-ər\ *adj* **1 :** having or being a disagreeable acrid taste that is one of the four basic taste sensations **2 :** marked by intensity or severity: **a :** hard to bear **:** PAINFUL **b :** VEHEMENT, RELENTLESS **c :** sharp and resentful **d :** intensely unpleasant esp. in coldness or rawness **3 :** expressive of severe pain, grief, or regret — **bit·ter·ish** \'bit-ə-rish\ *adj* — **bit·ter·ly** *adv* — **bit·ter·ness** *n*

bit·tern \'bit-ərn\ *n* **:** any of various small or medium-sized nocturnal herons with a characteristic booming cry

bit·ters \'bit-ərz\ *n sing or pl* **:** a usu. alcoholic solution of bitter and often aromatic plant products used in mixing drinks and as a mild tonic

¹bit·ter·sweet \'bit-ər-ˌswēt\ *n* **1 :** a sprawling poisonous weedy nightshade with purple flowers and oval reddish orange berries **2 :** a No. American woody climbing plant with yellow capsules that open when ripe and disclose the scarlet seed covers

²bittersweet *adj* **:** being both bitter and sweet

bi·tu·men \bə-'t(y)ü-mən, bī-\ *n* **:** any of various mixtures of hydrocarbons (as asphalt, crude petroleum, or tar)

bi·tu·mi·nous \-mə-nəs\ *adj* **1 :** resembling, containing, or impregnated with bitumen **2 :** of or relating to coal that when heated yields considerable volatile bituminous matter

¹bi·valve \'bī-ˌvalv\ *adj* **:** having a shell composed of two movable valves

²bivalve *n* **:** an animal (as a clam) with a bivalve shell

¹biv·ouac \'biv-ˌwak, -ə-ˌwak\ *n* **1 :** an encampment under little or no shelter usu. for a short time **2 :** a camping out for a night; *also* **:** a temporary shelter or settlement

²bivouac *vi* **biv·ouacked**; **biv·ouack·ing :** to encamp with little or no shelter

bi·zarre \bə-'zär\ *adj* **:** strikingly unusual or odd in appearance (as in fashion, design, or color) — **bi·zarre·ly** *adv* — **bi·zarre·ness** *n*

blab \'blab\ *vb* **blabbed**; **blab·bing :** to reveal esp. by talking without reserve or discretion **:** TATTLE

blab·ber \'blab-ər\ *vb* **blab·bered**; **blab·ber·ing** \'blab-(ə-)riŋ\ **:** BABBLE, CHATTER

¹black \'blak\ *adj* **1 a :** of the color black **b :** very dark **2 :** having dark skin, hair, and eyes **:** SWARTHY; *esp* **:** NEGROID **3 a :** EVIL, WICKED **b :** invoking evil supernatural powers **4 a :** GLOOMY, CALAMITOUS; *esp* **:** DISASTROUS **b :** SULLEN, HOSTILE — **black·ish** \-ish\ *adj* — **black·ly** *adv* — **black·ness** *n*

²black *n* **1 :** a black pigment or dye **2 :** the characteristic color of soot or coal **3 :** something that is black; *esp* **:** black clothing **4 :** a person belonging to a dark-skinned race **5 :** the condition of making a profit

³black *vb* **:** BLACKEN

black·a·moor \'blak-ə-ˌmu̇(ə)r\ *n* **:** NEGRO

black–and–blue \ˌblak-ən-'blü\ *adj* **:** darkly discolored (as from a bruise)

black·ball \'blak-ˌbȯl\ *n* **1 :** a small black ball used to cast a negative vote **2 :** an adverse vote — **blackball** *vt*

black·ber·ry \'blak-ˌber-ē\ *n* **1 :** the usu. black or dark purple juicy but seedy edible fruit of various brambles **2 :** a plant that bears blackberries

black·bird \-ˌbərd\ *n* **:** any of various birds of which the males are largely or entirely black

black·board \-ˌbōrd\ *n* **:** a hard smooth dark surface used for writing or drawing on usu. with chalk

black·en \'blak-ən\ *vb* **black·ened**; **black·en·ing** \'blak-(ə-)niŋ\ **1 :** to make or become black **2 :** SOIL, DIRTY **3 :** to injure the reputation of **:** DEFAME

black·face \'blak-ˌfās\ *n* **:** makeup for a Negro role esp. in a minstrel show

black·guard \'blag-ərd, -ˌärd; 'blak-ˌgärd\ *n* **:** a rude or unscrupulous person — **black·guard·ly** *adj or adv*

black·head \'blak-ˌhed\ *n* **:** a small oily plug blocking the outlet of a skin gland

black·ing \'blak-iŋ\ *n* **:** a substance that is applied to an object to make it black

black·jack \'blak-ˌjak\ *n* **1 :** a small leather-covered club with a flexible handle **2 :** a card game in which the object is to be dealt cards having a higher count than the dealer but not exceeding 21

black·list \-ˌlist\ *n* **:** a list of persons who are disapproved of and are to be punished (as by refusal of jobs or a boycott) — **blacklist** *vt*

black·mail \-ˌmāl\ *n* **:** extortion of money from a person by a threat esp. of public exposure; *also* **:** the money extorted — **blackmail** *vt* — **black·mail·er** *n*

black out \(')blak-'au̇t\ *vb* **:** to undergo a temporary loss of vision, consciousness, or memory

black·out \'blak-ˌau̇t\ *n* **:** a transient dulling or loss of vision or consciousness

black sheep *n* **:** a discreditable member of an otherwise respectable group

black·smith \'blak-ˌsmith\ *n* **:** a workman who shapes iron by heating it and then hammering it on an iron block — **black·smith·ing** *n*

black·thorn \-ˌthȯrn\ *n* **1 :** a European spiny plum **2 :** any of several American hawthorns

blad·der \'blad-ər\ *n* **1 :** a membranous sac in an animal in which a liquid or gas is stored; *esp* **:** one in a vertebrate into which urine passes from the kidneys **2 :** something resembling a bladder — **blad·der·like** *adj*

blade \'blād\ *n* **1 a :** a leaf of a plant and esp. of a grass **b :** the broad flat part of a leaf as distinguished from its stalk **2 :** something (as the flat part of an oar or an arm of a propeller) resembling the blade of a leaf **3 a :** the cutting part of an implement **b** (1) : SWORD (2) : SWORDSMAN (3) : a dashing fellow — **blad·ed** \'blād-əd\ *adj*

[1]**blame** \'blām\ *vt* **1** : to find fault with : CENSURE **2 a** : to hold responsible **b** : to place responsibility for — **blam·a·ble** *adj* — **blam·a·bly** \'blā-mə-blē\ *adv* — **blam·er** *n*

[2]**blame** *n* **1** : expression of disapproval **2** : responsibility for something that fails : FAULT

blame·less \'blām-ləs\ *adj* : free from blame or fault — **blame·less·ly** *adv* — **blame·less·ness** *n*

blame·wor·thy \'blām-ˌwər-th̲ē\ *adj* : deserving blame — **blame·wor·thi·ness** *n*

blanch \'blanch\ *vb* **1** : to take the color out of **2** : to become white or pale — **blanch·er** *n*

blanc·mange \blə-'mänj\ *n* : a dessert made from gelatin or a starchy substance and milk usu. sweetened and flavored

bland \'bland\ *adj* **1** : smooth and soothing in manner : GENTLE **2** : having soft and soothing qualities : not irritating — **bland·ly** *adv* — **bland·ness** *n*

blan·dish \'blan-dish\ *vt* : to coax with flattery : CAJOLE — **blan·dish·er** *n* — **blan·dish·ment** *n*

[1]**blank** \'blaŋk\ *adj* **1** : being without writing, printing, or marks **2** : appearing dazed or confused : EXPRESSIONLESS **3** : DULL, EMPTY **4** : ABSOLUTE, UNQUALIFIED **5** : not shaped into finished form — **blank·ly** *adv* — **blank·ness** *n*

[2]**blank** *n* **1 a** : an empty space (as on a paper) **b** : a paper with spaces for the entry of data **2** : an empty space or period **3** : the bull's-eye of a target **4** : a cartridge loaded with powder but no bullet

[3]**blank** *vt* **1 a** : OBSCURE, OBLITERATE **b** : to stop up : SEAL **2** : to keep from scoring

[1]**blan·ket** \'blaŋ-kət\ *n* **1** : a heavy woven often woolen covering used for beds **2** : a covering of any kind

[2]**blanket** *vt* : to cover with or as if with a blanket

[3]**blanket** *adj* : covering all instances or members of a group or class

blank verse *n* : unrhymed iambic pentameter verse

[1]**blare** \'bla(ə)r\ *vb* **1** : to sound loud and harsh **2** : to utter or proclaim in a harsh noisy manner

[2]**blare** *n* : a loud strident noise

blar·ney \'blär-nē\ *n* : skillful flattery — **blarney** *vb*

bla·sé \blä-'zā\ *adj* : not responsive to pleasure or excitement as a result of excessive indulgence; *also* : SOPHISTICATED

blas·pheme \blas-'fēm, 'blas-ˌ\ *vb* **1 a** : to speak of or address with irreverence **b** : to utter blasphemy **2** : REVILE, ABUSE — **blas·phem·er** *n*

blas·phe·my \'blas-fə-mē\ *n, pl* **-mies** : great disrespect shown to God or to sacred persons or things — **blas·phe·mous** \-məs\ *adj* — **blas·phe·mous·ly** *adv* — **blas·phe·mous·ness** *n*

[1]**blast** \'blast\ *n* **1** : a strong gust of wind **2** : a current of air or gas forced through an opening (as in an organ or furnace) **3** : the sound made by a wind instrument or by a whistle **4 a** : EXPLOSION **b** : the sudden air pressure produced in the vicinity of an explosion that has the effect of a violent wind

[2]**blast** *vb* **1** : to produce a strident sound **2 a** : to use an explosive **b** : SHOOT **3** : to injure by or as if by the action of wind : BLIGHT **4** : to shatter by or as if by an explosive : DEMOLISH — **blast·er** *n*

blast off \(')blas-'tȯf\ *vi* : to take off — used of rocket-propelled missiles and vehicles — **blast–off** \'blas-ˌtȯf\ *n*

blat \'blat\ *vi* **blat·ted**; **blat·ting** : to cry like a calf or sheep — **blat** *n*

bla·tant \'blāt-ᵊnt\ *adj* **1** : noisy esp. in a vulgar or offensive manner : CLAMOROUS **2** : OBTRUSIVE, BRAZEN — **bla·tan·cy** \-ᵊn-sē\ *n* — **bla·tant·ly** *adv*

blath·er \'blat̲h̲-ər\ *vi* **blath·ered**; **blath·er·ing** \-(ə-)riŋ\ : to talk foolishly — **blather** *n* — **blath·er·er** *n*

blath·er·skite \'blat̲h̲-ər-ˌskīt\ *n* : a blustering talkative person

[1]**blaze** \'blāz\ *n* **1 a** : an intensely burning fire **b** : intense direct light often accompanied by heat **2 a** : a dazzling display **b** : a sudden outburst

[2]**blaze** *vi* **1 a** : to burn brightly **b** : to flare up : FLAME **2** : to be conspicuously brilliant

[3]**blaze** *vt* : to make public : PROCLAIM

[4]**blaze** *n* **1** : a white mark on the face of an animal **2** : a mark made on a tree by chipping off a piece of bark

[5]**blaze** *vt* : to mark (as a trail) with blazes

blaz·er \'blā-zər\ *n* : a sports jacket often with notched collar and pockets that are stitched on

[1]**bla·zon** \'blāz-ᵊn\ *n* **1** : COAT OF ARMS **2** : ostentatious display : SHOW

[2]**blazon** *vt* **bla·zoned**; **bla·zon·ing** \'blāz-niŋ, -ᵊn-iŋ\ **1** : to publish abroad **2** : DECK, ADORN

[1]**bleach** \'blēch\ *vb* **1** : to make whiter or lighter **2** : to grow white : lose color

[2]**bleach** *n* : a preparation used in bleaching

bleach·ers \'blē-chərz\ *n pl* : a usu. uncovered stand of tiered planks providing seats for spectators

bleak \'blēk\ *adj* **1** : exposed to wind or weather **2** : DREARY, CHEERLESS **3** : COLD, RAW **4** : severely simple — **bleak·ly** *adv* — **bleak·ness** *n*

[1]**blear** \'bli(ə)r\ *vt* **1** : to make (the eyes) sore or watery **2** : DIM, BLUR

[2]**blear** *adj* **1** : dim with water or tears **2** : DULL, DIM — **blear–eyed** \-'īd\ *adj*

bleary \'bli(ə)r-ē\ *adj* **1** : dull or dimmed esp. from fatigue or sleep **2** : poorly outlined or defined : DIM

bleat \'blēt\ *vb* : to utter the natural cry of a sheep or goat — **bleat** *n*

bleed \'blēd\ *vb* **bled** \'bled\; **bleed·ing** **1** : to lose or shed blood **2** : to be wounded **3** : to feel pain or deep sympathy **4** : to run out from a wounded surface **5** : to draw liquid (as blood or sap) from **6** : to extort money from

bleed·er \'blēd-ər\ *n* : one that bleeds; *esp* : HEMOPHILIAC

[1]**blem·ish** \'blem-ish\ *vt* : to spoil by a flaw : MAR

[2]**blemish** *n* : a noticeable imperfection

[1]**blench** \'blench\ *vi* : to shrink back out of fear : FLINCH

[2]**blench** *vb* : to grow or make pale : BLANCH

[1]**blend** \'blend\ *vb* **1** : to mix thoroughly so that the separate things mixed cannot be distinguished **2** : to shade into each other : MERGE, HARMONIZE — **blend·er** *n*

[2]**blend** *n* **1** : thorough mixture **2** : a product (as coffee) prepared by blending

bless \'bles\ *vt* **blessed** \'blest\; **bless·ing** **1** : to hallow or consecrate by religious rite or word **2** : to make the sign of the cross upon or over **3** : to invoke divine care or protection for **4** : PRAISE, GLORIFY **5** : to confer prosperity or happiness upon

bless·ed \'bles-əd\ *or* **blest** \'blest\ *adj* **1** : HOLY **2** : of or enjoying happiness; *esp* : enjoying the bliss of heaven — **bless·ed·ly** *adv* — **bless·ed·ness** *n*

bless·ing \'bles-iŋ\ *n* **1** : the act of one that blesses **2** : a thing conducive to happiness **3** : grace said at a meal

blew *past of* BLOW

[1]**blight** \'blīt\ *n* **1 a** : a disease or disorder of plants resulting in withering and death without rotting **b** : an organism that causes blight **2 a** : something that impairs or destroys **b** : an impaired or deteriorated condition

[2]**blight** *vb* **1** : to affect with blight **2** : to cause to deteriorate **3** : to suffer from or become affected with blight

blimp \'blimp\ *n* : a small balloon-shaped airship

[1]**blind** \'blīnd\ *adj* **1** : sightless or grossly defective in power to see **2** : lacking in judgment or understanding **3** : closed at one end **4** : made or done without the aid of sight; *esp* : performed solely by the aid of instruments within an airplane — **blind·ly** *adv* — **blind·ness** *n*

²blind *vt* 1 : to make blind 2 : to make temporarily blind : DAZZLE 3 : to deprive of judgment or understanding

³blind *n* 1 : a device (as a window shade) to hinder sight or keep out light 2 : a place of concealment esp. for hunters

¹blind·fold \ˈblīn(d)-ˌfōld\ *vt* : to cover the eyes of with or as if with a bandage — **blindfold** *adj*

²blindfold *n* : a bandage for covering the eyes

¹blink \ˈbliŋk\ *vb* 1 : to look with half-shut winking eyes 2 : to wink quickly 3 : TWINKLE 4 : to shine with a light that goes or seems to go on and off

²blink *n* 1 : GLIMMER, SPARKLE 2 : a usu. involuntary shutting and opening of the eye

blink·er \ˈbliŋ-kər\ *n* : a blinking light for signaling

bliss \ˈblis\ *n* : great happiness : JOY — **bliss·ful** \-fəl\ *adj* — **bliss·ful·ly** \-fə-lē\ *adv* — **bliss·ful·ness** *n*

¹blis·ter \ˈblis-tər\ *n* 1 : a raised area of the outer skin containing watery liquid 2 : a raised spot (as in paint) resembling a blister — **blis·tery** \-t(ə-)rē\ *adj*

²blister *vb* **blis·tered**; **blis·ter·ing** \-t(ə-)riŋ\ 1 : to develop a blister : rise in blisters 2 : to raise a blister on

blithe \ˈblīth, ˈblīth\ *adj* 1 : of a happy lighthearted character or disposition 2 : HEEDLESS — **blithe·ly** *adv*

blithe·some \ˈblīth-səm, ˈblīth-\ *adj* : GAY, MERRY

blitz \ˈblits\ *n* 1 : an intensive series of air raids; *also* : AIR RAID 2 : a fast intensive campaign — **blitz** *vt*

blitz·krieg \ˈblits-ˌkrēg\ *n* : a violent swift surprise offensive by coordinated air and ground forces — **blitzkrieg** *vt*

bliz·zard \ˈbliz-ərd\ *n* 1 : a long severe snowstorm 2 : an intensely strong cold wind filled with fine snow

bloat \ˈblōt\ *vb* : to swell by filling with or as if with water or air : puff up

bloat·er \ˈblōt-ər\ *n* : a large fat herring or mackerel lightly salted and briefly smoked

blob \ˈbläb\ *n* : a small lump or drop of something (as paste or paint) of a thick consistency

bloc \ˈbläk\ *n* : a combination of persons, groups, or nations united by treaty, agreement, or common interest

¹block \ˈbläk\ *n* 1 : a solid piece of material (as stone or wood) usu. with one or more flat sides; *also* : a hollow rectangular building unit (as of glass) 2 a : OBSTACLE b : interruption of normal function of body or mind 3 : a wooden or metal case enclosing one or more pulleys 4 : a number of things thought of as forming a group or unit 5 a : a large building divided into separate houses or shops b : a space enclosed by streets c : the length of one of the sides of such a block 6 : a piece of material having on its surface a hand-cut design from which impressions are to be printed

²block *vt* 1 a : to stop up or close off : OBSTRUCT b : to hinder the progress or advance of c : to prevent normal functioning of 2 : to mark the chief lines of 3 : to shape on, with, or as if with a block 4 : to secure, support, or provide with a block — **block·er** *n*

block·ade \blä-ˈkād\ *n* : the shutting off of a place usu. by troops or ships to prevent passage in or out — **blockade** *vt* — **block·ad·er** *n*

block·bust·er \ˈbläk-ˌbəs-tər\ *n* : a very large high-explosive demolition bomb

block·head \ˈbläk-ˌhed\ *n* : a stupid person

block·house \-ˌhau̇s\ *n* : a small strong building used as a shelter (as from enemy fire) or observation post (as of operations producing blast or radiation)

blocky \ˈbläk-ē\ *adj* : resembling a block; *esp* : solidly built

¹blond \ˈbländ\ *adj* 1 : fair in complexion 2 : of a light color — **blond·ness** *n*

²blond *or* **blonde** \ˈbländ\ *n* : a blond person

blood \ˈbləd\ *n* 1 : the red fluid that circulates in the heart, arteries, capillaries, and veins of a vertebrate animal 2 a : LINEAGE, DESCENT; *esp* : royal lineage b : relationship by descent from a common ancestor : KINSHIP; *also* : KINDRED 3 a : EMOTIONS, TEMPER b : ANGER

blood·bath \-ˌbath, -ˌbȧth\ *n* : a great slaughter : MASSACRE

blood·cur·dling \ˈbləd-ˌkərd-liŋ\ *adj* : seeming to have the effect of congealing the blood through fear or horror

blood·ed \ˈbləd-əd\ *adj* 1 : entirely or largely of pure blood or stock 2 : having blood of a specified kind

blood·hound \ˈbləd-ˌhau̇nd\ *n* : a large powerful hound remarkable for keenness of smell

blood·less \ˈbləd-ləs\ *adj* 1 : deficient in blood 2 : not accompanied by loss of blood or by bloodshed or slaughter — **blood·less·ly** *adv* — **blood·less·ness** *n*

blood·mo·bile \ˈbləd-mō-ˌbēl\ *n* : an automobile staffed and equipped for collecting blood from donors

blood pressure *n* : pressure of the blood on the walls of blood vessels and esp. arteries

blood·red \ˈbləd-ˈred\ *adj* : having the color of blood

blood·shed \ˈbləd-ˌshed\ *n* 1 : the shedding of blood 2 : the taking of life : SLAUGHTER

blood·shot \-ˌshät\ *adj* : inflamed to redness

blood·stone \-ˌstōn\ *n* : a green quartz with red spots

blood·stream \-ˌstrēm\ *n* : the flowing blood in a circulatory system

blood·suck·er \-ˌsək-ər\ *n* : an animal that sucks blood; *esp* : LEECH — **blood·suck·ing** *adj*

blood·thirsty \ˈbləd-ˌthər-stē\ *adj* : eager to shed blood : CRUEL — **blood·thirst·i·ly** \-stə-lē\ *adv* — **blood·thirst·i·ness** \-stē-nəs\ *n*

bloody \ˈbləd-ē\ *adj* 1 : smeared or stained with blood; *also* : BLEEDING 2 : causing or accompanied by bloodshed 3 : BLOODTHIRSTY, MURDEROUS — **blood·i·ly** \ˈbləd-ᵊl-ē\ *adv* — **blood·i·ness** \ˈbləd-ē-nəs\ *n* — **bloody** *vt*

¹bloom \ˈblüm\ *n* 1 a : FLOWER b : flowers or amount of flowers (as of a plant) c : the period or state of flowering 2 : a state or time of beauty, freshness, and vigor 3 a : a delicate powdery coating on some fruits and leaves b : a rosy appearance of the cheeks; *also* : an outward evidence of freshness or healthy vigor 4 : the bouquet of a wine — **bloomy** \ˈblü-mē\ *adj*

²bloom *vi* 1 : to produce or yield flowers 2 : to be in a state of youthful beauty or freshness : FLOURISH — **bloom·er** *n*

bloo·mers \ˈblü-mərz\ *n pl* : full loose trousers gathered at the knee formerly worn by women

bloop·er \ˈblü-pər\ *n* : an embarrassing blunder made in public

¹blos·som \ˈbläs-əm\ *n* 1 a : the flower of a seed plant b : the period or state of flowering 2 : a period or stage of development suggesting the unfolding of a flower — **blos·somy** \-ə-mē\ *adj*

²blossom *vi* 1 : BLOOM 2 : to unfold like a blossom

¹blot \ˈblät\ *n* 1 : SPOT, STAIN 2 : DISGRACE, BLEMISH

²blot *vb* **blot·ted**; **blot·ting** 1 a : SPOT, STAIN b : SPATTER 2 : OBSCURE, DIM 3 : DISGRACE 4 a : to dry with blotting paper or other absorbing agent b : to remove by blotting the surface 5 : to become marked with a blot

blotch \ˈbläch\ *n* 1 : IMPERFECTION, BLEMISH 2 : a spot or mark (as of color or ink) esp. when large or irregular — **blotch** *vt* — **blotched** \ˈblächt\ *adj* — **blotchy** \ˈbläch-ē\ *adj*

blot·ter \ˈblät-ər\ *n* 1 : a piece of blotting paper 2 : a book in which entries are made temporarily pending their transfer to permanent record books

blot·ting paper \ˈblät-iŋ-\ *n* : a soft spongy paper used to absorb wet ink

blouse \ˈblau̇s, ˈblau̇z\ *n* 1 : a loose outer garment like a shirt or smock 2 : the upper outer garment of a uniform 3 : a usu. loose-fitting garment covering the body from the neck to the waist

¹blow \ˈblō\ *vb* **blew** \ˈblü\; **blown** \ˈblōn\; **blow·ing** 1 : to move esp. rapidly or with power 2 : to send forth a strong current of air **3 :** to sound or cause to sound by blowing **4 :** PANT, GASP **5 a :** to melt when overloaded **b :** to cause (a fuse) to blow **6 :** to have or cause to have a blowout **7 :** to produce or shape by the action of blown or injected air **8 :** to shatter or destroy by explosion **9 :** to put out of breath with exertion **10 a :** to spend (money) recklessly **b :** TREAT — **blow·er** *n*

²blow *n* **1 :** a blowing of wind esp. when violent **:** GALE **2 :** a forcing of air from the mouth or nose or through some instrument

³blow *vi* **blew** \'blü\; **blown** \'blōn\; **blow·ing :** FLOWER, BLOOM

⁴blow *n* **:** BLOOM 1c

⁵blow *n* **1 :** a forcible stroke delivered with a part of the body or with an instrument **2 :** a hostile act **:** COMBAT **3 :** a forcible or sudden act or effort **:** ASSAULT **4 :** a severe and sudden calamity

blow·gun \'blō-ˌgən\ *n* **:** a tube from which an arrow or a dart may be shot by the force of the breath

blow·out \-ˌau̇t\ *n* **:** a bursting of a container (as a tire) by pressure of the contents on a weak spot

blow·pipe \-ˌpīp\ *n* **1 :** a small round tube for blowing a jet of gas (as air) into a flame so as to concentrate and increase the heat **2 :** BLOWGUN

blow·sy \'blau̇-zē\ *adj* **:** DISHEVELED, SLOVENLY; *also* **:** COARSE

blow·torch \'blō-ˌtȯrch\ *n* **:** a small portable burner that intensifies combustion by means of a blast of air or oxygen

blow·up \'blō-ˌəp\ *n* **1 :** EXPLOSION **2 :** an outburst of temper **3 :** a photographic enlargement

blowy \'blō-ē\ *adj* **:** WINDY

¹blub·ber \'bləb-ər\ *n* **1 :** the fat of large sea mammals (as whales) **2 :** the action of blubbering

²blubber *vb* **blub·bered; blub·ber·ing** \-(ə-)riŋ\ **:** to weep noisily and childishly

blu·cher \'blü-chər, -kər\ *n* **:** a shoe having the tongue and vamp cut in one piece

bludg·eon \'bləj-ən\ *n* **:** a short club with one end thicker and heavier than the other — **bludgeon** *vt*

¹blue \'blü\ *adj* **1 :** of the color blue **2 a :** BLUISH **b :** LIVID **3 a :** low in spirits **:** MELANCHOLY **b :** DEPRESSING **4 :** PURITANICAL — **blu·ish** *or* **blue·ish** \-ish\ *adj* — **blue·ly** *adv* — **blue·ness** *n*

²blue *n* **1 :** a color whose hue is that of the clear daytime sky or that of the portion of the color spectrum lying between green and violet **2 :** blue clothing or cloth **3 a :** SKY **b :** the far distance

blue·beard \'blü-ˌbi(ə)rd\ *n* **:** a man who marries and kills one woman after another

blue·bell \-ˌbel\ *n* **:** any of various plants with blue bell-shaped flowers; *esp* **:** HAREBELL

blue·ber·ry \'blü-ˌber-ē, -b(ə-)rē\ *n* **:** the edible blue or blackish small-seeded berry of any of several plants of the heath family; *also* **:** a shrub producing these berries

blue·bird \-ˌbərd\ *n* **:** any of several small No. American songbirds related to the robin but more or less blue above

blue blood *n* **:** a member of a noble or socially prominent family

blue·bon·net \'blü-ˌbän-ət\ *n* **:** a low-growing annual lupine of Texas with silky foliage and blue flowers

blue·fish \-ˌfish\ *n* **:** an active greedy saltwater food and sport fish that is bluish above and silvery below

blue·grass \-ˌgras\ *n* **:** a valuable pasture and lawn grass with bluish green stems

blue·jack·et \-ˌjak-ət\ *n* **:** an enlisted man in the navy

blue jay *n* **:** any of several crested and largely blue American jays

blue jeans *n pl* **:** work pants or overalls usu. of blue denim

blue·print \'blü-ˌprint\ *n* **1 :** a photographic print in white on a bright blue ground used esp. for copying mechanical drawings and architects' plans **2 :** a detailed plan or program of action — **blueprint** *vt*

blues \'blüz\ *n pl* **1 :** low spirits **:** MELANCHOLY **2 :** music in a style of American Negro origin marked by recurrent minor intervals and melancholy lyrics

blue·stock·ing \'blü-ˌstäk-iŋ\ *n* **:** a woman having intellectual or literary interests

blu·et \'blü-ət\ *n* **:** a low American herb with dainty solitary bluish flowers

¹bluff \'bləf\ *adj* **1 :** rising steeply with a broad front (as from a plain or shore) **2 :** frank and outspoken in a rough but good-natured manner — **bluff·ly** *adv* — **bluff·ness** *n*

²bluff *n* **:** a high steep bank **:** CLIFF

³bluff *vb* **:** to deceive or frighten by pretending to have strength or confidence that one does not really have — **bluff·er** *n*

⁴bluff *n* **1 a :** an act or instance of bluffing **b :** the practice of bluffing **2 :** one who bluffs

blu·ing *or* **blue·ing** \'blü-iŋ\ *n* **:** a preparation of blue or violet dyes used in laundering to counteract yellowing of white fabrics

¹blun·der \'blən-dər\ *vb* **blun·dered; blun·der·ing** \-d(ə-)riŋ\ **1 :** to move unsteadily or confusedly **2 :** to make a mistake through stupidity, ignorance, confusion, or carelessness — **blun·der·er** *n*

²blunder *n* **:** a gross error or mistake resulting from stupidity, ignorance, confusion, or carelessness

blun·der·buss \'blən-dər-ˌbəs\ *n* **1 :** an obsolete short firearm having a large bore and usu. a flaring muzzle **2 :** a blundering person

¹blunt \'blənt\ *adj* **1 :** slow or deficient in feeling **:** INSENSITIVE **2 :** not sharp **3 :** lacking refinement or tact **:** ABRUPT — **blunt·ly** *adv* — **blunt·ness** *n*

²blunt *vb* **:** to make or become blunt

¹blur \'blər\ *n* **1 :** a smear or stain that obscures but does not efface **2 :** something vague or lacking definite outline — **blur·ry** \-ē\ *adj*

²blur *vb* **blurred; blur·ring 1 :** to obscure or blemish by smearing **2 :** to make indistinct or confused **3 :** to become vague, indistinct, or indefinite

blurb \'blərb\ *n* **:** a brief notice esp. in advertising praising a product extravagantly

blurt \'blərt\ *vt* **:** to utter suddenly and without thinking

¹blush \'bləsh\ *vi* **:** to become red in the face esp. from shame, modesty, or confusion — **blush·er** *n*

²blush *n* **:** a reddening of the face esp. from shame or modesty — **blush·ful** \-fəl\ *adj*

blus·ter \'bləs-tər\ *vb* **blus·tered; blus·ter·ing** \-t(ə-)riŋ\ **1 :** to blow violently and noisily **2 :** to talk or act in a noisy boastful way **:** SWAGGER, RAGE — **bluster** *n* — **blus·tery** \-t(ə-)rē\ *adj*

boa \'bō-ə\ *n* **1 :** a large snake (as the anaconda or python) that crushes its prey **2 :** a long fluffy scarf of fur, feathers, or delicate fabric

boar \'bō(ə)r\ *n* **1 :** a male swine **2 :** the Old World wild hog from which most domestic swine derive — **boar·ish** \-ish\ *adj*

¹board \'bōrd\ *n* **1 :** the side of a ship — often used in combination **2 a :** a thin flat relatively long piece of sawed lumber **b** *pl* **:** STAGE 2 **3 a :** a dining table **b :** daily meals esp. when furnished for pay **c :** a group of persons having managerial, supervisory, or investigatory powers and functions **4 :** a flat usu. rectangular piece of material designed for a special purpose **5 :** any of various wood pulps or composition materials formed into flat rectangular sheets — **by the board 1 :** over the side of a ship **2 :** into a state of discard, neglect, or ruin — **on board :** ABOARD

²board *vb* **1 :** to go aboard **:** get on **2 :** to cover with boards **3 :** to provide or be provided with regular meals and often lodging usu. for pay — **board·er** *n*

board·ing·house \ˈbōrd-iŋ-ˌhau̇s\ *n* : a house at which persons are boarded

board·walk \ˈbōrd-ˌwȯk\ *n* : a promenade orig. of planking along a beach

[1]**boast** \ˈbōst\ *n* **1** : the act of boasting : BRAG **2** : a cause for pride — **boast·ful** \ˈbōst-fəl\ *adj* — **boast·ful·ly** \-fə-lē\ *adv* — **boast·ful·ness** *n*

[2]**boast** *vb* **1** : to praise oneself **2** : to tell with extreme pride : BRAG **3** : to possess or display proudly — **boast·er** *n*

[1]**boat** \ˈbōt\ *n* **1** : a small vessel propelled by oars or paddles or by sail or power **2** : SHIP

[2]**boat** *vb* **1** : to place in or bring into a boat **2** : to travel by boat — **boat·er** *n*

boat hook *n* : a pole-handled hook used esp. to pull or push a boat, log, or raft into place

boat·house \ˈbōt-ˌhau̇s\ *n* : a house or shelter for boats

boat·man \ˈbōt-mən\ *n* : a man who manages, works on, or deals in boats — **boat·man·ship** \-ˌship\ *n*

boat·swain \ˈbōs-ᵊn\ *n* : a subordinate officer on a ship in charge of the hull and all related equipment

[1]**bob** \ˈbäb\ *vb* **bobbed**; **bob·bing** **1** : to move or cause to move up and down in a short quick movement **2** : to emerge, arise, or appear suddenly or unexpectedly

[2]**bob** *n* : a short jerky motion

[3]**bob** *n* **1** : a woman's or child's short haircut **2** : a ball or weight hanging from a rod or line **3** : a device (as a cork) for buoying up the baited end of a fishing line

[4]**bob** *vt* **bobbed**; **bob·bing** : to cut (hair) in a bob

bob·bin \ˈbäb-ən\ *n* : a cylinder or spindle on which yarn or thread is wound (as in a sewing machine)

bob·ble \ˈbäb-əl\ *vb* **bob·bled**; **bob·bling** \ˈbäb-(ə-)liŋ\ **1** : [1]BOB **2** : FUMBLE — **bobble** *n*

bob·by–sox·er \ˈbäb-ē-ˌsäk-sər\ *or* **bob·by–sock·er** \-ˌsäk-ər\ *n* : an adolescent girl

bob·cat \ˈbäb-ˌkat\ *n* : a common usu. rusty-colored No. American lynx

bob·o·link \ˈbäb-ə-ˌliŋk\ *n* : an American migratory songbird related to the blackbirds

bob·sled \ˈbäb-ˌsled\ *n* **1** : a short sled usu. used as one of a joined pair **2** : a racing sled that has two sets of runners in tandem, a steering device, and a brake — **bobsled** *vi*

bob·tail \-ˌtāl\ *n* **1** : a bobbed tail **2** : a horse or dog with a bobbed tail — **bobtail** *or* **bob·tailed** \-ˌtāld\ *adj*

bob·white \(ˈ)bäb-ˈhwīt\ *n* : any of several American quails

boc·cie *or* **boc·ci** *or* **boc·ce** \ˈbäch-ē\ *n* : an Italian bowling game played on a long narrow dirt court

bock \ˈbäk\ *n* : a heavy dark rich beer usu. sold in the early spring

[1]**bode** \ˈbōd\ *vt* : to indicate (as a future event) by signs : PRESAGE — **bode·ment** *n*

[2]**bode** *past of* BIDE

bod·ice \ˈbäd-əs\ *n* : the upper part of a woman's dress

bod·ied \ˈbäd-ēd\ *adj* : having a body or such a body

bod·i·less \ˈbäd-ē-ləs, -ᵊl-əs\ *adj* : having no body : INCORPOREAL

[1]**bod·i·ly** \ˈbäd-ᵊl-ē\ *adj* : of or relating to the body

[2]**bodily** *adv* **1** : in the flesh **2** : as a whole : ENTIRELY

bod·ing \ˈbōd-iŋ\ *n* : FOREBODING

bod·kin \ˈbäd-kən\ *n* **1 a** : DAGGER, STILETTO **b** : a sharp thin tool for making holes in cloth **2** : a blunt needle with a large eye for drawing tape or ribbon through a loop or hem

body \ˈbäd-ē\ *n, pl* **bod·ies** **1 a** : the physical whole of a living or dead organism **b** : the trunk or main part of an organism as distinguished from the head or appendages **c** : a human being : PERSON **2** : the main or central part (as the box of a vehicle carrying the load) **3** : a mass or portion of matter distinct from other masses **4 a** : a group of individuals united for some purpose **b** : a unit formed of a number of persons or things : a collective whole **5 a** : VISCOSITY **b** : richness of flavor (as of wine)

body·guard \ˈbäd-ē-ˌgärd\ *n* : a man or group of men whose duty it is to protect a person

body·surf \-ˌsərf\ *vi* : to ride waves without a surfboard

[1]**bog** \ˈbäg, ˈbȯg\ *n* : wet spongy and usu. acid ground — **bog·gy** \-ē\ *adj*

[2]**bog** *vb* **bogged**; **bog·ging** : to sink into or as if into a bog

bo·gey *or* **bo·gy** *or* **bo·gie** *n, pl* **bogeys** *or* **bogies** **1** \ˈbu̇g-ē, ˈbō-gē, ˈbü-gē, ˈbu̇g-ər\ : SPECTER, PHANTOM **2** \ˈbō-gē *also* ˈbu̇g-ē *or* ˈbü-gē\ : a source of annoyance, perplexity, or harassment **3** \ˈbō-gē\ : one golf stroke over par on a hole

bo·gey·man \ˈbu̇g-ē-ˌman, ˈbō-gē-, ˈbü-gē-, ˈbu̇g-ər-\ *n* : a terrifying person or thing; *esp* : a monstrous imaginary figure used in threatening children

bog·gle \ˈbäg-əl\ *vb* **bog·gled**; **bog·gling** \ˈbäg-(ə-)liŋ\ **1** : to start with fright or amazement **2** : to hesitate because of doubt, fear, or scruples **3** : BUNGLE — **boggle** *n*

bo·gus \ˈbō-gəs\ *adj* : not genuine : SPURIOUS, SHAM

bo·he·mi·an \bō-ˈhē-mē-ən\ *n, often cap* **1** : VAGABOND, WANDERER; *esp* : GYPSY **2** : a writer or artist living an unconventional life — **bohemian** *adj, often cap* — **bo·he·mi·an·ism** \-mē-ə-ˌniz-əm\ *n, often cap*

[1]**boil** \ˈbȯil\ *n* : a painful swollen inflamed area in the skin containing pus

[2]**boil** *vb* **1 a** : to generate bubbles of vapor when heated **b** : to come or bring to the boiling point **2** : to become agitated like boiling water : SEETHE **3** : to act or be acted on by a boiling liquid

[3]**boil** *n* : the act or state of boiling

boil·er \ˈbȯi-lər\ *n* **1** : a container in which something is boiled **2** : a tank holding hot water **3** : a strong metal container used in making steam for heating buildings or for driving engines

bois·ter·ous \ˈbȯi-st(ə-)rəs\ *adj* **1 a** : noisily turbulent : ROWDY **b** : marked by exuberance and high spirits **2** : STORMY, TUMULTUOUS — **bois·ter·ous·ly** *adv* — **bois·ter·ous·ness** *n*

bold \ˈbōld\ *adj* **1** : fearless before danger : INTREPID **2** : IMPUDENT, PRESUMPTUOUS **3** : SHEER, STEEP **4** : ADVENTUROUS, DARING **5** : standing out prominently : CONSPICUOUS — **bold·ly** *adv* — **bold·ness** *n*

bold·face \ˈbōl(d)-ˌfās\ *n* : a heavy-faced type

bold–faced \-ˈfāst\ *adj* **1** : bold in manner or conduct : IMPUDENT **2** : set in boldface

bole \ˈbōl\ *n* : the trunk of a tree

bo·le·ro \bə-ˈle(ə)r-ō\ *n, pl* **-ros** **1** : a Spanish dance in ¾ time; *also* : the music for it **2** : a loose waist-length jacket open at the front

boll \ˈbōl\ *n* : a seedpod of a plant (as cotton)

bo·lo \ˈbō-lō\ *n, pl* **bolos** : a long heavy single-edged knife used in the Philippines

bo·lo·gna \bə-ˈlō-nē *also* -n(y)ə\ *n* : a large smoked sausage of beef, veal, and pork

Bol·she·vik \ˈbōl-shə-ˌvik\ *n, pl* **Bolsheviks** *or* **Bol·she·vi·ki** \ˌbōl-shə-ˈvik-ē\ **1** : a member of the party that seized power in Russia during the revolution of 1917–20 **2** : COMMUNIST — **Bolshevik** *adj*

Bol·she·vism \ˈbōl-shə-ˌviz-əm\ *n* : the theories and practices of Bolsheviks — **Bol·she·vist** \-vəst\ *n or adj* — **Bol·she·vis·tic** \ˌbōl-shə-ˈvis-tik\ *adj*

[1]**bol·ster** \ˈbōl-stər\ *n* : a long pillow or cushion extending the full width of a bed

[2]**bolster** *vt* **bol·stered**; **bol·ster·ing** \-st(ə-)riŋ\ : to support with or as if with a bolster; *also* : REINFORCE — **bol·ster·er** *n*

[1]**bolt** \ˈbōlt\ *n* **1 a** : a shaft or missile for a crossbow or catapult **b** : a lightning stroke : THUNDERBOLT **2** : a sliding bar used to fasten a door **3** : a metal pin or rod usu. with a head at one end and a screw thread at the other that is used to hold

something in place 4 : a roll of cloth or wallpaper of a specified length

[2]**bolt** *vb* 1 : to move suddenly or nervously 2 : to move rapidly : DASH 3 : to run away 4 : to break away from or oppose one's political party 5 : to fasten with a bolt 6 : to swallow hastily or without chewing — **bolt•er** *n*

[3]**bolt** *n* : an act of bolting

[4]**bolt** *vt* : to sift (as flour) usu. through fine-meshed cloth

bo•lus \'bō-ləs\ *n* : a rounded mass: as **a** : a large pill **b** : a soft mass of chewed food

[1]**bomb** \'bäm\ *n* 1 : a hollow case or shell containing explosive material and variously made to be dropped from an airplane, thrown by hand, or set off by a fuse 2 : a container in which a substance (as an insecticide) is stored under pressure and from which it is released in the form of a fine spray

[2]**bomb** *vb* : to attack with bombs

bom•bard \bäm-'bärd, bəm-\ *vt* 1 : to attack with artillery 2 : to assail vigorously or persistently (as with questions) 3 : to subject to the impact of rapidly moving particles (as electrons) — **bom•bard•ment** *n*

bom•bar•dier \ˌbäm-bə(r)-'di(ə)r\ *n* : a bomber-crew member who releases the bombs

bom•bast \'bäm-ˌbast\ *n* : pretentious inflated speech or writing — **bom•bas•tic** \bäm-'bas-tik\ *adj* — **bom•bas•ti•cal•ly** \-ti-k(ə-)lē\ *adv*

bomb•er \'bäm-ər\ *n* : one that bombs; *esp* : an airplane designed for dropping bombs

bomb•shell \'bäm-ˌshel\ *n* 1 : BOMB 1 2 : a devastating surprise

bo•na fide \'bō-nə-ˌfīd, ˌbō-nə-'fīd-ē\ *adj* 1 **a** : made or carried out in good faith without fraud or deceit **b** : acting in good faith without fraud or deceit 2 : GENUINE

bo•nan•za \bə-'nan-zə\ *n* 1 : a rich mass of ore in a mine 2 : something that brings a rich return

bon•bon \'bän-ˌbän\ *n* : a candy with chocolate or fondant coating and fondant center with fruits and nuts sometimes added

[1]**bond** \'bänd\ *n* 1 : something that restrains : FETTER 2 : a binding agreement : COVENANT 3 : a material or device for binding 4 : a tie of loyalty, sentiment, or friendship 5 **a** : one who gives bail or acts as surety **b** : a certificate bearing interest issued by a government or corporation as an evidence of indebtedness 6 : the state of goods manufactured, stored, or transported under the care of bonded agencies until taxes on them are paid

[2]**bond** *vb* 1 : to protect or secure by or operate under a bond; *esp* : to secure payment of taxes on (goods) by giving a bond 2 : to hold together or solidify by or as if by means of a bond or binder : COHERE — **bond•a•ble** *adj* — **bond•er** *n*

bond•age \'bän-dij\ *n* : SERVITUDE, SLAVERY

bond•hold•er \'bänd-ˌhōl-dər\ *n* : one that owns a government or corporation bond

bond•man \'bän(d)-mən\ *n* : SLAVE, SERF — **bond•wom•an** \'bänd-ˌwu̇m-ən\ *n*

[1]**bonds•man** \'bän(d)z-mən\ *n* : BONDMAN

[2]**bondsman** *n* : SURETY

[1]**bone** \'bōn\ *n* 1 **a** : the hard largely calcareous tissue of which the skeleton of most vertebrate animals is formed; *also* : one of the hard pieces in which this tissue occurs **b** : a similar hard animal substance (as whalebone or ivory) 2 *pl* : something (as dice) usu. or orig. made from bone — **bone•less** \-ləs\ *adj*

[2]**bone** *vb* 1 : to remove the bones from 2 : to study hard

bone•head \-ˌhed\ *n* : a stupid person : NUMSKULL

bon•er \'bō-nər\ *n* : BLUNDER, HOWLER

bon•fire \'bän-ˌfī(ə)r\ *n* : a large fire built in the open air

bon•go \'bäŋ-gō\ *n* : one of a pair of small tuned drums played with the hands

bon•ho•mie \ˌbän-ə-'mē, ˌbō-nə-\ *n* : good-natured easy friendliness : GENIALITY

bo•ni•to \bə-'nēt-ō\ *n, pl* **bonitos** *or* **bonito** : any of various medium-sized tunas

bon mot \bōn-'mō\ *n, pl* **bons mots** \bōn-'mō(z)\ *or* **bon mots** \-'mō(z)\ : a clever remark : WITTICISM

bon•net \'bän-ət\ *n* : a head covering often tied under the chin by ribbons or strings and worn by women and small children

bo•nus \'bō-nəs\ *n* : something and esp. money given in addition to what is usual or due

bon vi•vant \ˌbän-vē-'vänt, ˌbōn-vē-'vän\ *n, pl* **bons vivants** \ˌbän-vē-'vänts, ˌbōn-vē-'vän(z)\ *or* **bon vivants** *same*\ : a person having cultivated or refined tastes esp. in food and drink

bon voy•age \ˌbōnv-ˌwī-'äzh, -ˌwä-'yäzh\ *n* : a good trip : FAREWELL — often used interjectionally

bony \'bō-nē\ *adj* 1 : of or relating to bone 2 : full of bones 3 : resembling bone esp. in hardness 4 : having large or prominent bones; *also* : SKINNY, SCRAWNY

boo \'bü\ *n* : a shout of disapproval or contempt — **boo** *vb*

boob \'büb\ *n* : SIMPLETON; *also* : BOOR

boo•by \'bü-bē\ *n, pl* **boobies** : a foolish person : DOPE

[1]**book** \'bu̇k\ *n* 1 **a** : a set of written, printed, or blank sheets of paper bound together into a volume **b** : a long written or printed literary composition **c** : a major division of a literary work 2 *cap* : BIBLE

[2]**book** *vb* 1 : to engage transportation or reserve lodgings 2 : to enter charges against in a police register

book•end \'bu̇k-ˌend\ *n* : a support placed at the end of a row of books to hold them up

book•ie \'bu̇k-ē\ *n* : BOOKMAKER

book•ish \'bu̇k-ish\ *adj* 1 : fond of books and reading 2 : inclined to rely unduly on knowledge from books — **book•ish•ly** *adv* — **book•ish•ness** *n*

book•keep•er \'bu̇k-ˌkē-pər\ *n* : a person who keeps accounts (as of a business) — **book•keep•ing** \-piŋ\ *n*

book•let \'bu̇k-lət\ *n* : a little book; *esp* : PAMPHLET

book•mak•er \'bu̇k-ˌmā-kər\ *n* : one who determines odds and receives and pays off bets — **book•mak•ing** *n*

book•mark \-ˌmärk\ *n* : a marker for finding a place in a book

book•mo•bile \'bu̇k-mō-ˌbēl\ *n* : a truck that serves as a traveling library

book•plate \'bu̇k-ˌplāt\ *n* : a label placed in a book showing who owns it

book•sell•er \-ˌsel-ər\ *n* : the proprietor of a bookstore

book•worm \-ˌwərm\ *n* : a person unusually devoted to reading or study

[1]**boom** \'büm\ *n* 1 : a long pole; *esp* : one for stretching the bottom of a sail 2 : a long beam projecting from the mast of a derrick to support or guide the thing that is being lifted 3 : a line of connected floating timbers to hold logs together in a river

[2]**boom** *vi* 1 : to make a deep hollow sound 2 **a** : to increase in esteem or importance **b** : to experience a sudden rapid growth and expansion **c** : to develop rapidly in population and importance

[3]**boom** *n* 1 : a booming sound or cry 2 : a rapid expansion or increase

[1]**boo•mer•ang** \'bü-mə-ˌraŋ\ *n* : a curved club or stick usu. somewhat flat that can be thrown so as to return to the thrower

[2]**boomerang** *vi* : to return in the manner of a boomerang; *esp* : to injure the originator instead of an intended target

[1]**boon** \'bün\ *n* : BENEFIT, FAVOR, BLESSING

[2]**boon** *adj* : MERRY, JOVIAL; *also* : INTIMATE

boon•dog•gling \'bün-ˌdȯg-(ə-)liŋ\ *n* : a trivial, useless, or wasteful activity

boor \ˈbu̇(ə)r\ *n* **1 :** PEASANT; *esp* **:** a rough clownish rustic **:** YOKEL **2 :** a rude or insensitive person

boor·ish \ˈbu̇(ə)r-ish\ *adj* **:** resembling a boor **:** RUDE — **boor·ish·ly** *adv* — **boor·ish·ness** *n*

boost \ˈbüst\ *vt* **1 :** to push or shove up from below **2 :** to increase in force, power, or amount; *also* **:** RAISE, PROMOTE — **boost** *n* — **boost·er** *n*

[1]boot \ˈbüt\ *n* **1 :** a covering (as of leather or rubber) for the foot and leg **2 :** a protective sheath or casing **3 :** a patch for the inside of a tire casing **4 :** a blow delivered by the foot **:** KICK; *also* **:** a rude discharge or dismissal

[2]boot *vt* **1 :** KICK **2 :** to discharge rudely

boot·black \ˈbüt-ˌblak\ *n* **:** a person who shines shoes

boot·ee *or* **boot·ie** \ˈbüt-ē\ *n* **:** an infant's knitted or crocheted sock

booth \ˈbüth\ *n, pl* **booths** \ˈbüt͟hz, ˈbüths\ **1 :** a temporary shelter **2 a :** a stall or stand for the sale or exhibition of goods (as at a fair, market, or exhibition) **b :** a small enclosure affording privacy for one person at a time **c :** a restaurant accommodation consisting of a table between two backed benches

[1]boot·leg \ˈbüt-ˌleg\ *vb* **1 :** to make or transport for sale alcoholic liquor contrary to law **2 a :** to produce or sell illicitly **b :** SMUGGLE — **boot·leg·ger** *n*

[2]bootleg *n* **:** something bootlegged — **bootleg** *adj*

boot·less \ˈbüt-ləs\ *adj* **:** USELESS, UNPROFITABLE — **boot·less·ly** *adv* — **boot·less·ness** *n*

boo·ty \ˈbüt-ē\ *n* **:** SPOILS, PLUNDER

[1]booze \ˈbüz\ *vi* **:** to drink intoxicating liquor to excess — **booz·er** *n* — **boozy** \ˈbü-zē\ *adj*

[2]booze *n* **:** intoxicating liquor

bo·rac·ic acid \bə-ˌras-ik-\ *n* **:** BORIC ACID

bo·rax \ˈbō(ə)r-ˌaks\ *n* **:** a crystalline slightly alkaline compound that occurs as a mineral and is used as a flux, cleansing agent, and antiseptic

[1]bor·der \ˈbȯrd-ər\ *n* **1 :** an outer part or edge **2 :** BOUNDARY, FRONTIER — **bor·dered** \-ərd\ *adj*

[2]border *vb* **bor·dered; bor·der·ing** \ˈbȯrd-(ə-)riŋ\ **1 :** to put a border on **2 :** to touch at the edge or boundary **:** BOUND **3 :** VERGE — **bor·der·er** *n*

bor·der·land \ˈbȯrd-ər-ˌland\ *n* **1 :** territory at or near a border **:** FRONTIER **2 :** an outlying or intermediate region often not clearly defined

bor·der·line \-ˌlīn\ *adj* **1 :** situated at or near a border or boundary **2 :** UNCERTAIN **3 :** INTERMEDIATE

[1]bore \ˈbō(ə)r\ *vb* **1 :** to make a hole in esp. with a tool that turns round **:** PIERCE **2 :** to make by piercing or drilling **3 :** to make a hole by boring — **bor·er** *n*

[2]bore *n* **1 :** a hole made by or as if by boring **2 :** an interior lengthwise cylindrical cavity **3 a :** the diameter of a hole or tube; *esp* **:** the interior diameter of a gun barrel **b :** the diameter of an engine cylinder

[3]bore *past of* BEAR

[4]bore *n* **:** one that causes boredom

[5]bore *vt* **:** to weary by being dull or monotonous

bo·re·al \ˈbōr-ē-əl\ *adj* **:** of, relating to, or located or growing in northern or mountainous regions

bore·dom \ˈbōrd-əm\ *n* **:** the state of being bored

bo·ric acid \ˌbōr-ik-\ *n* **:** a white crystalline weak acid that contains boron, occurs naturally in solution, and is used as a mild antiseptic

born \ˈbȯrn\ *adj* **1 a :** brought into life by birth **b :** NATIVE **2 :** having special natural abilities or character from birth

borne *past part of* BEAR

bo·ron \ˈbō(ə)r-ˌän\ *n* **:** a chemical element that occurs in nature only in combination (as in borax) and is used esp. in metallurgy

bor·ough \ˈbər-ō\ *n* **1 :** a British town that sends one or more members to parliament; *also* **:** an incorporated British urban area **2 :** an incorporated town or village in some U.S. states; *also* **:** any of the 5 political divisions of New York City

bor·row \ˈbär-ō\ *vb* **1 :** to take or receive something with the promise or intention of returning it **2 a :** to take for one's own use **b :** COPY, IMITATE **c :** ADOPT — **bor·row·er** *n*

bosh \ˈbäsh\ *n* **:** foolish talk **:** NONSENSE

bosky \ˈbäs-kē\ *adj* **:** covered with trees or shrubs

[1]bos·om \ˈbu̇z-əm\ *n* **1 :** the front of the human chest; *esp* **:** the female breasts **2 :** the center of secret thoughts and feelings **3 :** the part of a garment covering the breast — **bos·omed** \-əmd\ *adj*

[2]bosom *adj* **:** CLOSE, INTIMATE

[1]boss \ˈbȯs, ˈbäs\ *n* **:** an ornament resembling a knob

[2]boss *vt* **:** to ornament with bosses **:** EMBOSS

[3]boss \ˈbȯs\ *n* **1 :** one who exercises control or authority; *esp* **:** one who directs or supervises workers **2 :** a politician who controls votes or dictates policies — **boss** *adj* — **boss·ism** \-ˌiz-əm\ *n*

[4]boss \ˈbȯs\ *vt* **1 :** DIRECT, SUPERVISE **2 :** ORDER

[1]bossy \ˈbȯs-ē, ˈbä-sē\ *adj* **:** ornamented with bosses

[2]bossy \ˈbȯ-sē\ *n, pl* **boss·ies :** COW, CALF

[3]bossy \ˈbȯ-sē\ *adj* **:** DICTATORIAL — **boss·i·ness** *n*

bo·tan·i·cal \bə-ˈtan-i-kəl\ *or* **bo·tan·ic** \-ik\ *adj* **1 :** of or relating to plants or botany **2 :** derived from plants — **bo·tan·i·cal·ly** \-i-k(ə-)lē\ *adv*

bot·a·nize \ˈbät-ᵊn-ˌīz\ *vi* **:** to collect and study plants

bot·a·ny \ˈbät-ᵊn-ē, ˈbät-nē\ *n* **:** a branch of biology dealing with plants and plant life — **bot·a·nist** \ˈbät-ᵊn-əst, ˈbät-nəst\ *n*

[1]botch \ˈbäch\ *vt* **1 :** to patch clumsily **2 :** BUNGLE

[2]botch *n* **:** a botched job **:** BUNGLE, MESS — **botchy** \-ē\ *adj*

[1]both \ˈbōth\ *adj* **:** being the two **:** affecting or involving the one and the other

[2]both *pron* **:** the one as well as the other

[3]both *conj* — used as a function word to indicate and stress the inclusion of each of two or more things specified by coordinated words, phrases, or clauses

[1]both·er \ˈbät͟h-ər\ *vb* **both·ered; both·er·ing** \-(ə-)riŋ\ **1 a :** ANNOY, IRK **b :** PESTER **2 :** to cause to be anxious or concerned **:** TROUBLE **3 :** to take pains

[2]bother *n* **1 a :** a state of petty annoyance **b :** something that causes petty annoyance **2 :** FUSS, DISTURBANCE

both·er·some \ˈbät͟h-ər-səm\ *adj* **:** causing bother

[1]bot·tle \ˈbät-ᵊl\ *n* **1 :** a container typically of glass or plastic with a narrow neck and mouth and no handle **2 :** the quantity held by a bottle — **bot·tle·ful** \-ˌfu̇l\ *n*

[2]bottle *vt* **bot·tled; bot·tling** \ˈbät-liŋ, -ᵊl-iŋ\ **:** to put into a bottle — **bot·tler** \ˈbät-lər, -ᵊl-ər\ *n*

bot·tle·neck \ˈbät-ᵊl-ˌnek\ *n* **1 :** a narrow passageway **2 :** a place, condition, or point where progress is held up

[1]bot·tom \ˈbät-əm\ *n* **1 a :** the under surface of something **b :** a supporting surface or part **:** BASE **c :** BUTTOCKS, RUMP **2 :** the bed of a body of water **3 :** BOAT, SHIP **4 :** the lowest part, place, or point — **bot·tomed** \-əmd\ *adj* — **at bottom :** BASICALLY, REALLY

[2]bottom *vb* **:** to rest on, bring to, or reach the bottom

bot·tom·less \ˈbät-əm-ləs\ *adj* **1 :** having no bottom **2 :** very deep — **bot·tom·less·ly** *adv*

bou·doir \ˈbüd-ˌwär, ˈbu̇d-\ *n* **:** a woman's dressing room, bedroom, or private sitting room

bough \ˈbau̇\ *n* **:** a branch of a tree; *esp* **:** a main branch — **boughed** \ˈbau̇d\ *adj*

bought *past of* BUY

bouil·lon \ˈbü-ˌyän; ˈbu̇l-ˌyän, -yən\ *n* **:** a clear seasoned soup made usu. from lean beef

boul·der \ˈbōl-dər\ *n* **:** a detached and rounded or much-worn mass of rock — **boul·dery** \-d(ə-)rē\ *adj*

bou•le•vard \'bu̇l-ə-ˌvärd, 'bül-\ *n* : a broad often landscaped thoroughfare
bounce \'bau̇n(t)s\ *vb* 1 a : to cause to rebound b : to spring backward after striking 2 : to recover quickly — usu. used with *back* 3 : to be returned by a bank as no good — **bounce** *n*
bounc•er \'bau̇n(t)-sər\ *n* : a man employed in a public place to remove disorderly persons
bounc•ing \-siŋ\ *adj* : HEALTHY, ROBUST
[1]**bound** \'bau̇nd\ *adj* : going or intending to go
[2]**bound** *n* 1 : a boundary line (as of a piece of property) 2 : a point or a line beyond which one cannot go : LIMIT
[3]**bound** *vt* 1 : to set limits to : CONFINE 2 : to form the boundary of 3 : to name the boundaries of
[4]**bound** *adj* 1 a : fastened by or as if by a band : CONFINED b : CERTAIN, SURE 2 a : OBLIGED b : RESOLVED, DETERMINED
[5]**bound** *n* 1 : LEAP, JUMP 2 : BOUNCE, REBOUND
[6]**bound** *vi* 1 : to move by leaping 2 : REBOUND, BOUNCE
bound•a•ry \'bau̇n-d(ə-)rē\ *n, pl* **-ries** : something that marks or shows a limit or end (as of territory)
bound•en \'bau̇n-dən\ *adj* : OBLIGATORY, BINDING
bound•less \'bau̇nd-ləs\ *adj* : having no boundaries; *also* : VAST — **bound•less•ly** *adv* — **bound•less•ness** *n*
boun•te•ous \'bau̇nt-ē-əs\ *adj* 1 : GENEROUS 2 : given plentifully — **boun•te•ous•ly** *adv* — **boun•te•ous•ness** *n*
boun•ti•ful \'bau̇nt-i-fəl\ *adj* 1 : giving in abundance : GENEROUS 2 : PLENTIFUL, ABUNDANT — **boun•ti•ful•ly** \-f(ə-)lē\ *adv* — **boun•ti•ful•ness** *n*
boun•ty \'bau̇nt-ē\ *n, pl* **bounties** 1 a : GENEROSITY b : something given generously 2 : money given as a reward or inducement (as for the killing of vermin)
bou•quet \bō-'kā, bü-\ *n* 1 : a bunch of flowers 2 : FRAGRANCE, AROMA
bour•bon \'bər-bən\ *n* : a whiskey distilled from corn mash
[1]**bour•geois** \'bu̇(ə)rzh-ˌwä, bu̇rzh-'\ *n, pl* **bour•geois** \-ˌwä(z), -'wä(z)\ : a person whose social behavior and political views are held to be influenced by his interest in private property; *esp* : CAPITALIST
[2]**bourgeois** *adj* 1 : of, relating to, or characteristic of the middle class 2 : marked by a concern for material interests and respectability and a tendency toward mediocrity 3 : CAPITALISTIC
bour•geoi•sie \ˌbu̇rzh-ˌwä-'zē\ *n, pl* **bourgeoisie** : a social order dominated by bourgeois
bourn *or* **bourne** \'bōrn, 'bu̇(ə)rn\ *n* : STREAM, BROOK
bourse \'bu̇(ə)rs\ *n* : a European stock exchange
bout \'bau̇t\ *n* : a spell of activity: as a : an athletic match (as of boxing) b : OUTBREAK, ATTACK c : SESSION
bou•tique \bü-'tēk\ *n* : a small retail store; *esp* : a fashionable specialty shop for women
bou•ton•niere \ˌbüt-ᵊn-'i(ə)r, ˌbü-tən-'ye(ə)r\ *n* : a flower or bouquet worn in a buttonhole
bo•vine \'bō-ˌvīn, -ˌvēn\ *adj* 1 : of, relating to, or resembling the ox or cow 2 : sluggish or patient like an ox or cow — **bovine** *n*
[1]**bow** \'bau̇\ *vb* 1 : to bend the head, body, or knee in greeting, reverence, respect, or submission 2 : SUBMIT, YIELD 3 : BEND
[2]**bow** *n* : a bending of the head or body in respect, submission, assent, or greeting
[3]**bow** \'bō\ *n* 1 : RAINBOW 2 : a weapon for shooting arrows 3 : something shaped in a curve : BEND 4 : a wooden rod strung with horsehairs used for playing a violin or similar instrument 5 : a knot formed by doubling a ribbon or string into one or two loops
[4]**bow** \'bō\ *vb* 1 : to bend into a curve 2 : to play a stringed musical instrument with a bow
[5]**bow** \'bau̇\ *n* : the forward part of a ship
bowd•ler•ize \'bōd-lə-ˌrīz, 'bau̇d-\ *vt* : to expurgate (as a book) by omitting or modifying parts considered indelicate — **bowd•ler•i•za•tion** \ˌbōd-lə-rə-'zā-shən, ˌbau̇d-\ *n*
bow•el \'bau̇(-ə)l\ *n* 1 a : INTESTINE, GUT — usu. used in pl. b : a division of the intestine 2 *pl* : the interior parts
bow•er \'bau̇(-ə)r\ *n* : a shelter made with tree boughs or vines : ARBOR — **bow•ery** \-ē\ *adj*
bow•ie knife \'bü-ē-, 'bō-ē-\ *n* : a stout straight single-edged hunting knife
[1]**bowl** \'bōl\ *n* 1 : a rounded hollow dish generally deeper than a basin and larger than a cup 2 : the contents of a bowl 3 : a bowl-shaped part or structure
[2]**bowl** *n* 1 : a ball for rolling on a level surface in bowling 2 : a cast of the ball in bowling
[3]**bowl** *vb* 1 : to participate or roll a ball in bowling 2 : to travel smoothly and rapidly 3 a : to strike with a swiftly moving object b : to overwhelm with surprise
bow•leg \'bō-ˌleg, -'leg\ *n* : a leg bowed outward at or below the knee — **bow•legged** \'bō-'leg(-ə)d\ *adj*
[1]**bowl•er** \'bō-lər\ *n* : one that bowls
[2]**bow•ler** \'bō-lər\ *n* : DERBY 3
bowl•ing \'bō-liŋ\ *n* : a game played by rolling balls so as to knock down wooden pins set up at the far end of an alley; *esp* : TENPINS
bow•man \'bō-mən\ *n* : ARCHER
bow•sprit \'bau̇-ˌsprit, 'bō-\ *n* : a large spar projecting forward from the bow of a ship
bow•string \'bō-ˌstriŋ\ *n* : the cord connecting the two ends of a bow
[1]**box** \'bäks\ *n, pl* **box** *or* **box•es** : an evergreen shrub or small tree used esp. for hedges
[2]**box** *n* 1 a : a receptacle usu. having four sides, a bottom, and a cover b : the amount held by a box 2 : a small compartment for a group of spectators in a theater 3 : the driver's seat on a carriage 4 : a shed that protects 5 : a receptacle (as for a bearing) resembling a box 6 : printed matter enclosed by rules or white space 7 : a space on a baseball diamond where a batter, coach, pitcher, or catcher stands
[3]**box** *vt* : to enclose in or as if in a box
[4]**box** *n* : a punch or slap esp. on the ear
[5]**box** *vb* 1 : to strike with the hand 2 : to engage in boxing : fight with the fists
box•car \'bäks-ˌkär\ *n* : a roofed freight car usu. with sliding doors in the sides
[1]**box•er** \'bäk-sər\ *n* : one that engages in the sport of boxing
[2]**boxer** *n* : a compact medium-sized short-haired usu. fawn or brindle dog of a breed originating in Germany
box•ing \'bäk-siŋ\ *n* : the art of attack and defense with the fists practiced as a sport
box•like \'bäks-ˌlīk\ *adj* : resembling a box esp. in shape
boy \'bȯi\ *n* 1 : a male child : YOUTH 2 : SON 3 : a male servant — **boy•hood** \-ˌhu̇d\ *n* — **boy•ish** \-ish\ *adj* — **boy•ish•ly** *adv* — **boy•ish•ness** *n*
boy•cott \'bȯi-ˌkät\ *vt* : to engage in a joint refusal to have dealings with as an expression of disapproval or to force acceptance of terms — **boycott** *n*
boy•friend \'bȯi-ˌfrend\ *n* : a regular male companion of a girl or woman
bra \'brä\ *n* : BRASSIERE
[1]**brace** \'brās\ *n, pl* **brac•es** *or* **brace** 1 : two of a kind 2 : a crank-shaped instrument for turning a wood-boring bit 3 a : something that transmits, directs, resists, or supports weight or pressure b *pl* : SUSPENDERS c : a device for supporting a body part d : a dental appliance worn on the teeth to correct irregularities of growth and position 4 : a mark { or } or ⏝ used to connect words or items to be considered together
[2]**brace** *vb* 1 a : to make firm or taut b : to get ready or set : STEEL 2 a : to furnish or support with a brace : prop up

: REINFORCE **b** : INVIGORATE, FRESHEN **3 a** : to make rigid : STIFFEN **b** : to plant firmly **4** : to take heart

brace·let \'brā-slət\ *n* : an ornamental band or chain worn around the wrist

brack·en \'brak-ən\ *n* : a large coarse branching fern; *also* : a growth of such ferns

[1]**brack·et** \'brak-ət\ *n* **1** : a projecting member or fixture designed to support a vertical load **2** : a short wall shelf **3** : one of a pair of marks [ ] used to enclose interpolated matter **4** : a section of a continuously numbered or graded series; *esp* : one of a series of groups graded by income

[2]**bracket** *vt* **1** : to place within or as if within brackets **2** : to put into the same class : ASSOCIATE

brack·ish \'brak-ish\ *adj* : somewhat salty

bract \'brakt\ *n* : an often modified leaf on or at the base of a flower stalk — **bract·ed** \'brak-təd\ *adj*

brad \'brad\ *n* : a slender wire nail with a small deep round head

[1]**brag** \'brag\ *n* **1** : a pompous or boastful statement **2** : arrogant talk or manner : COCKINESS **3** : BRAGGART

[2]**brag** *vb* **bragged**; **brag·ging** : to talk or assert boastfully — **brag·ger** *n*

brag·ga·do·cio \ˌbrag-ə-'dō-s(h)ē-ˌō, -shō\ *n, pl* **-cios 1** : BRAGGART, BOASTER **2 a** : empty boasting **b** : COCKINESS

brag·gart \'brag-ərt\ *n* : a loud arrogant boaster — **braggart** *adj*

Brah·min \'bräm-ən\ *n* : an aloof intellectually and socially cultivated person

[1]**braid** \'brād\ *vt* **1** : to form (three or more strands) into a braid **2** : to ornament esp. with ribbon or braid — **braid·er** *n*

[2]**braid** *n* **1** : a cord or ribbon having usu. three or more component strands; *esp* : a narrow fabric of intertwined threads used esp. for trimming **2** : a length of braided hair

braille \'brāl\ *n, often cap* : a system of writing for the blind that uses characters made up of raised dots

a b c d e f g h i j
1 2 3 4 5 6 7 8 9 0

k l m n o p q r s t

u v x y z w Capital Sign Numeral Sign

braille alphabet and numerals

[1]**brain** \'brān\ *n* **1 a** : the portion of the vertebrate central nervous system that is the organ of thought and nervous coordination, is made up of neurons and supporting and nutritive structures, is enclosed within the skull, and is continuous with the spinal cord **b** : a major nervous center in an invertebrate animal **2** : INTELLECT, INTELLIGENCE — often used in pl.

[2]**brain** *vt* **1** : to kill by smashing the skull **2** : to hit on the head

brain·less \'brān-ləs\ *adj* : UNINTELLIGENT, SILLY — **brain·less·ly** *adv* — **brain·less·ness** *n*

brain·storm \'brān-ˌstȯrm\ *n* : a sudden burst of inspiration : a startling idea

brain·wash·ing \'brān-ˌwȯsh-iŋ, -ˌwäsh-\ *n* : a forcible attempt by indoctrination to induce someone to give up his basic political, social, or religious beliefs and attitudes and to accept contrasting regimented ideas

brainy \'brā-nē\ *adj* : INTELLIGENT, INTELLECTUAL — **brain·i·ness** *n*

braise \'brāz\ *vt* : to cook slowly in fat and little moisture in a closed pot

[1]**brake** \'brāk\ *n* : a large coarse fern : BRACKEN

[2]**brake** *n* : a device for slowing up or stopping motion (as of a wheel, vehicle, or engine) esp. by friction

[3]**brake** *vb* **1** : to retard or stop by or as if by a brake **2** : to operate a brake esp. on a vehicle

[4]**brake** *n* : rough or marshy land thickly overgrown usu. with one kind of plant — **braky** \'brā-kē\ *adj*

brake·man \'brāk-mən\ *n* : a freight or passenger train crew member whose duties include inspecting the train and assisting the conductor

bram·ble \'bram-bəl\ *n* : any of a large genus of usu. prickly shrubs of the rose family including the raspberries and blackberries — **bram·bly** \-b(ə-)lē\ *adj*

bran \'bran\ *n* : the broken coat of the seed of cereal grain separated from the flour or meal by sifting or bolting

[1]**branch** \'branch\ *n* **1** : a natural subdivision (as a bough or twig) of a plant stem **2** : something related to a larger whole like a branch to a tree: as **a** : a division of a family descending from a particular ancestor **b** : a division of an organization **c** : a subordinate office or part of a central system — **branched** \'brancht\ *adj* — **branch·less** \'branch-ləs\ *adj* — **branchy** \'bran-chē\ *adj*

[2]**branch** *vi* **1** : to put forth branches : spread or separate into branches **2** : to spring out (as from a main stem) : DIVERGE **3** : to extend activities

[1]**brand** \'brand\ *n* **1** : a charred or burning piece of wood **2** : SWORD **3 a** : a mark made (as by burning) usu. to identify **b** : a mark of disgrace : STIGMA **4 a** : a class of goods identified as the product of a single firm or manufacturer : MAKE **b** : a characteristic or distinctive kind : VARIETY

[2]**brand** *vt* **1** : to mark with or as if with a brand **2** : STIGMATIZE — **brand·er** *n*

bran·dish \'bran-dish\ *vt* **1** : to shake or wave (as a weapon) threateningly **2** : to display in a showy or aggressive manner — **brandish** *n*

brand–new \'bran-'n(y)ü\ *adj* : conspicuously new and unused

[1]**bran·dy** \'bran-dē\ *n, pl* **-dies** : an alcoholic liquor distilled from wine or fermented fruit juice

[2]**brandy** *vt* **bran·died**; **bran·dy·ing** : to flavor, blend, or preserve with brandy

brash \'brash\ *adj* **1** : IMPETUOUS, RASH **2 a** : aggressively self-assertive : IMPUDENT **b** : HARSH, BLATANT — **brash·ly** *adv* — **brash·ness** *n*

brass \'bras\ *n* **1** : an alloy consisting essentially of copper and zinc **2** : an object of brass **3** : brazen self-assurance : GALL — **brass** *adj*

bras·siere \brə-'zi(ə)r\ *n* : a woman's close-fitting undergarment having cups for bust support

brassy \'bras-ē\ *adj* **1** : BRAZEN, OBSTREPEROUS **2** : resembling brass esp. in color **3** : resembling the sound of a brass instrument — **brass·i·ly** \'bras-ə-lē\ *adv* — **brass·i·ness** *n*

brat \'brat\ *n* : CHILD; *esp* : an ill-mannered annoying child — **brat·tish** \'brat-ish\ *adj* — **brat·ty** \'brat-ē\ *adj*

bra·va·do \brə-'väd-ō\ *n, pl* **-does** *or* **-dos 1** : blustering swaggering conduct **2** : show of bravery

[1]**brave** \'brāv\ *adj* **1** : COURAGEOUS **2** : making a fine show : SPLENDID — **brave·ly** *adv*

[2]**brave** *vt* : to face or endure with courage

[3]**brave** *n* : a No. American Indian warrior

brav·ery \'brāv-(ə-)rē\ *n, pl* **-er·ies 1 a** : fine clothes **b** : showy display **2** : the quality or state of being brave : FEARLESSNESS

bra·vo \'bräv-ō, brä-'vō\ *n, pl* **bravos** : a shout of approval — often used interjectionally in applauding

bra•vu•ra \brə-ˈv(y)u̇r-ə\ *n* **1 :** a florid brilliant musical style **2 :** self-assured brilliant performance

[1]**brawl** \ˈbrȯl\ *vi* **:** to quarrel noisily **:** WRANGLE — **brawl•er** *n*

[2]**brawl** *n* **:** a noisy quarrel or fight

brawn \ˈbrȯn\ *n* **1 :** full strong muscles esp. of the arm or leg **2 :** muscular strength

brawny \ˈbrȯ-nē\ *adj* **:** MUSCULAR, STRONG — **brawn•i•ness** *n*

bray \ˈbrā\ *vb* **:** to utter the characteristic loud harsh cry of a donkey — **bray** *n*

braze \ˈbrāz\ *vb* **:** to solder with a relatively infusible alloy (as brass)

[1]**bra•zen** \ˈbrāz-ᵊn\ *adj* **1 :** made of brass **2 :** sounding harsh and loud like struck brass **3 :** IMPUDENT, SHAMELESS — **bra•zen–faced** \ˌbrāz-ᵊn-ˈfāst\ *adj* — **bra•zen•ly** *adv* — **bra•zen•ness** *n*

[2]**brazen** *vt* **bra•zened**; **bra•zen•ing** \ˈbrāz-niŋ, -ᵊn-iŋ\ **:** to face with defiance or impudence

[1]**bra•zier** \ˈbrā-zhər\ *n* **:** one that works in brass

[2]**brazier** *n* **1 :** a pan for holding burning coals **2 :** a utensil on which food is exposed to heat (as from burning charcoal) through a wire grill

[1]**breach** \ˈbrēch\ *n* **1 :** violation of a law, duty, or tie **2 a :** a broken, ruptured, or torn condition or area **b :** a gap (as in a wall) made by battering **3 a :** a break in accustomed friendly relations **b :** HIATUS

[2]**breach** *vb* **1 :** to make a breach in **2 :** BREAK, VIOLATE

[1]**bread** \ˈbred\ *n* **1 :** a baked food made of a mixture whose basic constituent is flour or meal **2 :** FOOD

[2]**bread** *vt* **:** to cover with bread crumbs

bread•bas•ket \ˈbred-ˌbas-kət\ *n* **:** a major cereal-producing region

bread•stuff \-ˌstəf\ *n* **1 :** GRAIN, FLOUR **2 :** BREAD

breadth \ˈbredth\ *n* **1 :** distance from side to side **:** WIDTH **2 a :** something of full width **b :** a wide expanse **3 :** COMPREHENSIVENESS, SCOPE

[1]**break** \ˈbrāk\ *vb* **broke** \ˈbrōk\; **bro•ken** \ˈbrō-kən\; **break•ing 1 a :** to separate into parts with suddenness or violence **:** SHATTER **b :** to curl over and fall apart in surf or foam **2 :** VIOLATE, TRANSGRESS **3 a :** to force a way into, out of, or through **b :** to escape with sudden forceful effort **c :** to develop, appear, or burst forth with suddenness or force **d :** to become fair **e :** to make a sudden dash **f :** to make or effect by cutting, forcing, or pressing **4 :** LOOSEN, SUNDER **5 :** to cut into and turn over the surface of **:** PLOW **6 a :** to disrupt the order, compactness, or uniformity of **b :** to decline suddenly and sharply in price or value **c :** to end a relationship or accord **7 a :** to subdue completely **:** CRUSH **b :** to lose or cause to lose health, strength, or spirit **c :** to become inoperative because of damage, wear, or strain **d :** to ruin financially **e :** to reduce in rank **8 :** to stop or bring to an end suddenly **9 a :** to make (an animal) fit for use (as by training) **b :** to accustom to an activity or occurrence **10 :** to make known **11 :** to turn aside or lessen the force or intensity of **12 :** EXCEED, SURPASS **13 :** SOLVE **14 :** to alter course sharply **15 :** HAPPEN, DEVELOP — **break•a•ble** *adj*

[2]**break** *n* **1 :** an act or action of breaking **2 :** a condition produced by breaking **3 :** an interruption in continuity **4 :** a rupture in previously friendly relations **5 :** a place or situation at which a break occurs **6 :** an awkward social blunder **7 :** a stroke of good luck

break•age \ˈbrā-kij\ *n* **1 a :** the action of breaking **b :** a quantity broken **2 :** an allowance for things broken

break•down \ˈbrāk-ˌdau̇n\ *n* **1 :** a failure to function properly; *esp* **:** a physical, mental, or nervous collapse **2 :** DISINTEGRATION **3 :** DECOMPOSITION **4 :** division into categories **:** CLASSIFICATION

break•er \ˈbrā-kər\ *n* **1 :** one that breaks **2 :** a wave breaking into foam against the shore

break•fast \ˈbrek-fəst\ *n* **:** the first meal of the day — **breakfast** *vb*

break•neck \ˈbrāk-ˌnek\ *adj* **:** extremely dangerous

break•through \-ˌthrü\ *n* **1 :** an act or point of breaking through an obstruction or defensive line **2 :** a sudden advance in knowledge or technique

break•wa•ter \-ˌwȯt-ər, -ˌwät-\ *n* **:** a structure to protect a harbor or beach from the force of waves

bream \ˈbrim\ *n, pl* **bream** *or* **breams :** any of various mostly freshwater spiny-finned fishes

[1]**breast** \ˈbrest\ *n* **1 :** either of two protuberant milk-producing glandular organs situated on the front of the chest in the human female and some other mammals **2 :** the fore or ventral part of the body between the neck and the abdomen **3 :** something resembling a breast — **breast•ed** \ˈbres-təd\ *adj*

[2]**breast** *vt* **1 :** FACE, CONFRONT **2 :** to struggle against courageously

breast•bone \ˈbres(t)-ˈbōn, -ˌbōn\ *n* **:** STERNUM

breast•plate \-ˌplāt\ *n* **:** a metal plate worn as defensive armor for the breast

breast•stroke \-ˌstrōk\ *n* **:** a swimming stroke executed by extending the arms in front of the head while drawing the knees forward and outward and then sweeping the arms back with palms out while kicking backward and outward

breast•work \ˈbrest-ˌwərk\ *n* **:** an improvised or temporary fortification

breath \ˈbreth\ *n* **1 a :** air charged with a fragrance or odor **b :** a slight indication **:** SUGGESTION **2 a :** the faculty of breathing **b :** RESPITE **3 :** a slight breeze **4 a :** air inhaled and exhaled in breathing **b :** something (as moisture on a cold surface) produced by breathing **5 :** a spoken sound **:** UTTERANCE — **out of breath :** breathing very rapidly (as from strenuous exercise)

breathe \ˈbrē<u>th</u>\ *vb* **1 :** to draw air into and expel it from the lungs **:** RESPIRE **2 :** LIVE **3 :** to pause and rest before continuing **4 :** to blow softly **5 a :** to send out by exhaling **b :** to instill by or as if by breathing **6 :** UTTER, EXPRESS — **breath•a•ble** *adj*

breath•er \ˈbrē-<u>th</u>ər\ *n* **:** a break in activity for rest

breath•less \ˈbreth-ləs\ *adj* **1 :** not breathing **2 :** panting or gasping for breath — **breath•less•ly** *adv* — **breath•less•ness** *n*

breath•tak•ing \ˈbreth-ˌtā-kiŋ\ *adj* **1 :** making one out of breath **2 :** EXCITING, THRILLING

breech \ˈbrēch; *"breeches" (garment) is usu* ˈbrich-əz\ *n* **1** *pl* **a :** short trousers fitting snugly at the lower edges at or just below the knee **b :** PANTS **2 :** BUTTOCKS **3 :** the back part of a cannon or gun behind the bore

[1]**breed** \ˈbrēd\ *vb* **bred** \ˈbred\; **breed•ing 1 a :** BEGET **1 b :** ORIGINATE **2 :** to propagate (plants or animals) sexually and usu. under controlled conditions **3 :** to bring up **:** NURTURE **4 :** to mate with **:** MATE — **breed•er** *n*

[2]**breed** *n* **1 :** a group of presumably related animals or plants visibly similar in most characters; *esp* **:** one differentiated from the wild type under the influence of man **2 :** a number of persons of the same stock **3 :** CLASS, KIND

breed•ing \ˈbrēd-iŋ\ *n* **1 :** ANCESTRY **2 :** training or education esp. in manners **3 :** the sexual propagation of plants or animals

[1]**breeze** \ˈbrēz\ *n* **1 :** a gentle wind **2 :** CINCH

[2]**breeze** *vi* **:** to proceed quickly and easily

breeze•way \ˈbrēz-ˌwā\ *n* **:** a roofed open passage usu. connecting two buildings (as a house and garage)

breezy \ˈbrē-zē\ *adj* **1 :** swept by breezes **2 :** BRISK, LIVELY — **breez•i•ly** \-zə-lē\ *adv* — **breez•i•ness** \-zē-nəs\ *n*

brethren *pl of* BROTHER — used chiefly in formal or solemn address

breve \ˈbrēv, ˈbrev\ *n* **:** a mark ˘ placed over a vowel to show that the vowel is short

[1]**bre·vet** \brə-'vet\ *n* : a commission giving a military officer higher nominal rank than that for which he receives pay

[2]**brevet** *vt* **bre·vet·ted** *or* **bre·vet·ed**; **bre·vet·ting** *or* **bre·vet·ing** : to confer rank upon by brevet

bre·via·ry \'brē-v(y)ə-rē, -vē-,er-ē\ *n, pl* **-ries** 1 : MANUAL, HANDBOOK 2 : a book containing the prayers, hymns, and readings prescribed esp. for priests for each day of the year

brev·i·ty \'brev-ət-ē\ *n* 1 : shortness of duration 2 : expression in few words : CONCISENESS

[1]**brew** \'brü\ *vb* 1 : to prepare (as beer or ale) by steeping, boiling, and fermentation or by infusion and fermentation 2 : CONTRIVE, PLOT 3 : to prepare (as tea) by infusion in hot water 4 : to be forming — **brew·er** *n*

[2]**brew** *n* 1 : a brewed beverage 2 : a product of brewing

brew·ery \'brü-ə-rē, 'brů(-ə)r-ē\ *n, pl* **-er·ies** : a plant where malt liquors are manufactured

[1]**bribe** \'brīb\ *n* : money or favor given or promised to a person in a position of trust to influence dishonestly his judgment or conduct

[2]**bribe** *vb* : to induce or influence by or as if by giving bribes — **brib·a·ble** *adj* — **brib·er** *n*

brib·ery \'brī-b(ə-)rē\ *n, pl* **-er·ies** : the act or practice of bribing

bric–a–brac \'brik-ə-,brak\ *n* : small ornamental articles : KNICKKNACKS, CURIOS

[1]**brick** \'brik\ *n* 1 **a** : a building or paving material made from clay molded into blocks and hardened in the sun or baked **b** : a rectangular block made of brick 2 : a brick-shaped mass

[2]**brick** *vt* : to close, face, or pave with bricks

brick·bat \-,bat\ *n* 1 : a piece of a broken brick; *esp* : one thrown as a missile 2 : an uncomplimentary remark

brick·lay·er \-,lā-ər\ *n* : a person who builds or paves with bricks — **brick·lay·ing** *n*

[1]**brid·al** \'brīd-ᵊl\ *n* : a wedding festival or ceremony : MARRIAGE

[2]**bridal** *adj* : of or relating to a bride or a wedding : NUPTIAL

bride \'brīd\ *n* : a woman newly married or about to be married

bride·groom \-,grüm, -,grům\ *n* : a man just married or about to be married

brides·maid \'brīdz-,mād\ *n* : a woman who attends a bride at her wedding

[1]**bridge** \'brij\ *n* 1 : a structure built over a depression or an obstacle (as a river or a railroad) for use as a passageway 2 : a platform above and across the deck of a ship for the captain or officer in charge 3 : something resembling a bridge in form or function 4 : something (as a partial denture anchored to adjacent teeth) that fills a gap

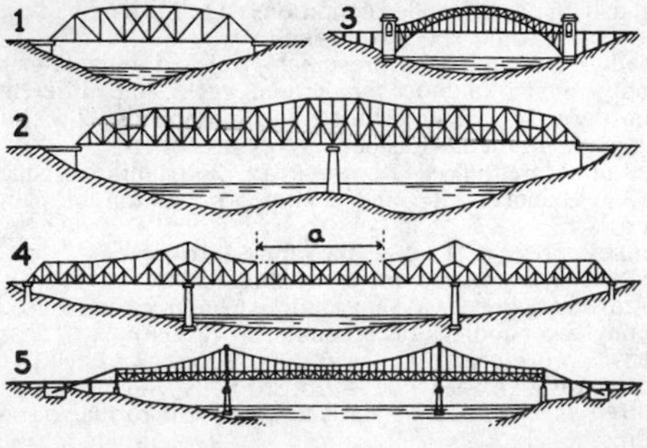

bridges: *1* simple truss, *2* continuous truss, *3* steel arch, *4* cantilever (*a* suspended span), *5* suspension

[2]**bridge** *vt* : to make a bridge over or across — **bridge·a·ble** *adj*

[3]**bridge** *n* : any of various card games for four players developed from whist

bridge·head \-,hed\ *n* : an advanced position seized in enemy territory as a foothold for further advance

[1]**bri·dle** \'brīd-ᵊl\ *n* 1 : the headgear with which a horse is controlled 2 : CURB, RESTRAINT

[2]**bridle** *vb* **bri·dled**; **bri·dling** \'brīd-liŋ, -ᵊl-iŋ\ 1 : to put a bridle upon 2 : to restrain with or as if with a bridle 3 : to show hostility or resentment

[1]**brief** \'brēf\ *adj* 1 : short in duration or extent 2 **a** : CONCISE **b** : CURT, ABRUPT — **brief·ly** *adv* — **brief·ness** *n*

[2]**brief** *n* 1 : a concise statement or document; *esp* : one summarizing a law client's case or a legal argument 2 *pl* : short snug underpants

[3]**brief** *vt* 1 : to give final precise instructions to 2 : to give essential information to

brief·case \-,kās\ *n* : a flat flexible case usu. of leather for carrying papers

[1]**bri·er** \'brī(-ə)r\ *n* : a plant (as the blackberry or the wild rose) with a thorny or prickly woody stem — **bri·ery** \'brī(-ə)r-ē\ *adj*

[2]**brier** *n* : a heath of southern Europe whose root is used for making tobacco pipes

[1]**brig** \'brig\ *n* : a 2-masted square-rigged ship

[2]**brig** *n* : a place (as on a ship) for temporary confinement of offenders in the U.S. Navy

bri·gade \brig-'ād\ *n* 1 : a military unit composed of a headquarters, one or more units of infantry or armor, and supporting units 2 : a group of people organized for special activity

brig·a·dier general \,brig-ə-,di(ə)r-\ *n* : a commissioned officer (as in the army) ranking next below a major general

brig·and \'brig-ənd\ *n* : BANDIT — **brig·and·age** \-ən-dij\ *n* — **brig·and·ism** \-,diz-əm\ *n*

brig·an·tine \'brig-ən-,tēn\ *n* : a 2-masted square-rigged ship not carrying a square mainsail

bright \'brīt\ *adj* 1 : shedding much light : SHINING, GLOWING 2 : very clear or vivid in color : of high saturation or brilliance 3 : CLEVER, INTELLIGENT 4 : LIVELY, CHEERFUL 5 : PROMISING — **bright** *adv* — **bright·ly** *adv* — **bright·ness** *n*

bright·en \'brīt-ᵊn\ *vb* **bright·ened**; **bright·en·ing** \'brīt-niŋ, -ᵊn-iŋ\ : to make or become bright or brighter

bril·liant \'bril-yənt\ *adj* 1 : very bright : GLITTERING 2 **a** : STRIKING, DISTINGUISHED **b** : unusually keen or alert in mind — **bril·liance** \-yən(t)s\ *or* **bril·lian·cy** \-yən-sē\ *n* — **bril·liant·ly** *adv* — **bril·liant·ness** *n*

bril·lian·tine \'bril-yən-,tēn\ *n* : a preparation for making hair glossy

[1]**brim** \'brim\ *n* 1 **a** : the rim esp. of a cup, bowl, or depression **b** : BRINK, VERGE 2 : the projecting rim of a hat — **brim·ful** \-'fůl\ *adj*

[2]**brim** *vb* **brimmed**; **brim·ming** 1 : to fill or become full to the brim 2 : to reach or overflow a brim

brim·stone \'brim-,stōn\ *n* : SULFUR

brin·dled \'brin-dᵊld\ *or* **brin·dle** \-dᵊl\ *adj* : having faint dark streaks or flecks on a gray or tawny ground

brine \'brīn\ *n* 1 : water containing a great deal of common salt 2 : OCEAN

bring \'briŋ\ *vt* **brought** \'brȯt\; **bring·ing** \'briŋ-iŋ\ 1 **a** : to convey, lead, carry, or cause to come along with one **b** : to cause to be, act, or move in a special way 2 : to cause to exist or occur 3 : to procure in exchange : sell for

bring about *vt* : to cause to take place : EFFECT

bring out *vb* : to present to the public

bring to *vt* : to restore to consciousness

bring up *vb* 1 : REAR, EDUCATE 2 : to stop suddenly 3 : to bring to attention : INTRODUCE 4 : VOMIT

brink \'briŋk\ *n* **1** : EDGE; *esp* : the edge at the top of a steep place **2** : the point of onset : VERGE

briny \'brī-nē\ *adj* : of or resembling brine : SALTY — **brin·i·ness** *n*

bri·quette *or* **bri·quet** \brik-'et\ *n* : a compacted often brick-shaped mass of usu. fine material

[1]**brisk** \'brisk\ *adj* **1** : very active or alert : LIVELY **2** : INVIGORATING, REFRESHING **3** : ENERGETIC, QUICK — **brisk·ly** *adv* — **brisk·ness** *n*

[2]**brisk** *vb* : to make or become brisk

bris·ket \'bris-kət\ *n* : the breast or lower chest of a quadruped animal

bris·ling *or* **bris·tling** \'briz-liŋ, 'bris-\ *n* : a small herring that resembles and is processed like a sardine

[1]**bris·tle** \'bris-əl\ *n* : a short stiff coarse hair or filament — **bris·tled** \-əld\ *adj* — **bris·tly** \'bris-(ə-)lē\ *adj*

[2]**bristle** *vi* **bris·tled**; **bris·tling** \'bris-(ə-)liŋ\ **1** : to rise up and stand stiffly erect **2** : to show signs of anger or defiance **3** : to appear as if covered with bristles — **bris·tly** \'bris-(ə-)lē\ *adj*

britch·es \'brich-əz\ *n pl* : BREECHES

brit·tle \'brit-ᵊl\ *adj* : being hard but not tough : easily broken, cracked, or snapped — **brit·tle·ness** *n*

[1]**broach** \'brōch\ *n* **1** : any of various pointed or tapered tools, implements, or parts **2** : BROOCH

[2]**broach** *vb* **1** : to pierce (as a cask) in order to draw the contents : TAP **2** : to shape or enlarge (a hole) with a broach **3** : to introduce as a topic of conversation — **broach·er** *n*

broad \'brȯd\ *adj* **1** : not narrow : WIDE **2** : extending far and wide : SPACIOUS **3** : CLEAR, FULL **4** : PLAIN, OBVIOUS **5** : COARSE, INDELICATE **6** : liberal in thought **7** : not limited : extended in range or amount **8** : being main and essential **9** : [3]LOW 12 — used specif. of *a* pronounced as in *father* — **broad·ly** *adv* — **broad·ness** *n*

broad·ax *or* **broad·axe** \'brȯd-,aks\ *n* : a broad-bladed ax

[1]**broad·cast** \'brȯd-,kast\ *adj* **1** : cast or scattered in all directions **2** : made public by means of radio or television — **broadcast** *adv*

[2]**broadcast** *n* **1** : the transmitting of sound or images by radio waves **2** : a single radio or television program

[3]**broadcast** *vb* **broadcast**; **broad·cast·ing** **1** : to scatter or sow (seed) broadcast **2** : to make widely known **3 a** : to send out a broadcast from a radio or television transmitting station **b** : to speak or perform on a broadcast program — **broad·cast·er** *n*

broad·cloth \'brȯd-,klȯth\ *n* **1** : a fine woolen or worsted fabric made compact and glossy in finishing **2** : a fine cloth usu. of cotton, silk, or rayon made in plain and ribbed weaves

broad·en \'brȯd-ᵊn\ *vb* **broad·ened**; **broad·en·ing** \'brȯd-niŋ, -ᵊn-iŋ\ : to make or become broad or broader

broad–mind·ed \'brȯd-'mīn-dəd\ *adj* : tolerant of varied views — **broad–mind·ed·ness** *n*

[1]**broad·side** \'brȯd-,sīd\ *n* **1** : the part of a ship's side above the waterline **2 a** : all the guns that can be fired from the same side of a ship **b** : a discharge of all these guns together **3** : a storm of abuse

[2]**broadside** *adv* **1** : with the broadside toward a given object or point **2** : in one volley — **broadside** *adj*

broad–spectrum *adj* : effective against various microorganisms

broad·sword \'brȯd-,sōrd\ *n* : a broad-bladed sword for cutting rather than thrusting

bro·cade \brō-'kād\ *n* : a rich fabric with raised patterns often in gold or silver thread — **bro·cad·ed** \-'kād-əd\ *adj*

broc·co·li \'bräk-(ə-)lē\ *n* : an open branching form of cauliflower whose young flowering shoots are used as a vegetable

bro·chure \brō-'shu̇(ə)r\ *n* : PAMPHLET

bro·gan \'brō-gən, brō-'gan\ *n* : a heavy shoe; *esp* : a coarse work shoe reaching to the ankle

brogue \'brōg\ *n* : a marked dialect or regional pronunciation; *esp* : an Irish accent

broi·der \'brȯid-ər\ *vt* : EMBROIDER — **broi·dery** \'brȯid-(ə-)rē\ *n*

[1]**broil** \brȯil\ *vb* **1** : to cook or become cooked by direct exposure to fire or flame **2** : to make or become extremely hot

[2]**broil** *n* : a confused or noisy disturbance

broil·er \'brȯi-lər\ *n* **1** : a rack and pan or an oven equipped with a rack and pan for broiling meats **2** : a young chicken suitable for broiling

[1]**broke** \'brōk\ *past of* BREAK

[2]**broke** *adj* : having no money : PENNILESS

bro·ken \'brō-kən\ *adj* **1** : shattered into pieces **2 a** : ROUGH, UNEVEN **b** : having gaps or breaks **3** : not kept **4** : SUBDUED, CRUSHED **5** : imperfectly spoken **6 a** : FRACTURED **b** : cut off : DISCONNECTED — **bro·ken·ly** *adv* — **bro·ken·ness** *n*

bro·ken·heart·ed \,brō-kən-'härt-əd\ *adj* : crushed by grief or despair

bro·ker \'brō-kər\ *n* : a person who acts as an agent for others in the purchase and sale of property

bro·ker·age \'brō-k(ə-)rij\ *n* **1** : the business of a broker **2** : the fee or commission charged by a broker

bro·mide \'brō-,mīd\ *n* **1** : any of various compounds of bromine with another element or a radical including some used as sedatives **2** : a commonplace or hackneyed statement or notion

bro·mine \'brō-,mēn\ *n* : a chemical element that is normally a deep red corrosive liquid giving off an irritating reddish brown vapor of disagreeable odor

bronc \'bräŋk\ *n* : BRONCO

bron·chi·al \'bräŋ-kē-əl\ *adj* : of, relating to, or involving the bronchi or their branches — **bron·chi·al·ly** \-ə-lē\ *adv*

bron·chi·tis \brän-'kīt-əs, bräŋ-\ *n* : inflammation of the bronchial tubes — **bron·chit·ic** \-'kit-ik\ *adj*

bron·chus \'bräŋ-kəs\ *n, pl* **bron·chi** \'brän-,kī, 'bräŋ-, -,kē\ : either of the main divisions of the trachea each leading to a lung

bron·co \'bräŋ-kō, 'brän-\ *n, pl* **broncos** : an unbroken or partly broken range horse of western No. America; *also* : MUSTANG

[1]**bronze** \'bränz\ *vt* : to give the appearance of bronze

[2]**bronze** *n* **1** : an alloy basically of copper and tin **2** : a work of art made of bronze **3** : a moderate yellowish brown — **bronzy** \'brän-zē\ *adj*

brooch \'brōch, 'brüch\ *n* : an ornament to be worn at or near the neck of a dress and held by a pin or clasp

[1]**brood** \'brüd\ *n* : a family of young animals or children; *esp* : the young (as of a bird) hatched or cared for at one time

[2]**brood** *vb* **1** : to sit on eggs in order to hatch them **2** : to cover young with the wings **3** : to think anxiously or moodily upon a subject — **brood·ing·ly** *adv*

[3]**brood** *adj* : kept for breeding

brood·er \'brüd-ər\ *n* **1** : a person or animal that broods **2** : a heated structure used for raising young fowl

broody \'brüd-ē\ *adj* **1** : physiologically ready to brood **2** : CONTEMPLATIVE, MOODY — **brood·i·ness** *n*

[1]**brook** \'bru̇k\ *vt* : to put up with : BEAR, TOLERATE

[2]**brook** *n* : CREEK

brook·let \'bru̇k-lət\ *n* : a small brook

broom \'brüm, 'bru̇m\ *n* **1** : a plant of the pea family with long slender branches along which grow many drooping yellow flowers **2** : a long-handled brush used for sweeping and orig. made from twigs of broom

broom·stick \-,stik\ *n* : the handle of a broom

broth \'brȯth\ *n, pl* **broths** \'brȯths, 'brȯt͟hz\ : liquid in which meat, fish, cereal grains, or vegetables have been cooked

broth·el \'bräth-əl, 'brȯth-\ *n* : an establishment in which prostitutes are available

broth•er \'brəth-ər\ *n, pl* **brothers** *or* **breth•ren** \'breth-(ə-)rən, 'breth-ərn\ **1** : a male who has one or both parents in common with another **2** : KINSMAN **3** : a fellow member **4** : one related to another by common ties or interests **5** *often cap* : a man who is a religious but not a priest
broth•er•hood \'brəth-ər-,hu̇d\ *n* **1** : the state of being brothers or a brother **2** : an association (as a labor union) for a particular purpose **3** : the whole body of persons engaged in a business or profession
broth•er–in–law \'brəth-(ə-)rən-,lȯ, 'brəth-ərn-,lȯ\ *n, pl* **brothers–in–law** \'brəth-ər-zən-\ **1** : the brother of one's spouse **2** : the husband of one's sister
broth•er•ly \'brəth-ər-lē\ *adj* **1** : of or relating to brothers **2** : natural or becoming to brothers : AFFECTIONATE — **broth•er•li•ness** *n*
brougham \'brü(-ə)m, 'brō-əm\ *n* **1** : a light closed carriage with seats inside for two or four **2** : a 2-door sedan; *esp* : one electrically driven
brought *past of* BRING
brow \'brau̇\ *n* **1 a** : EYEBROW **b** : the ridge on which the eyebrow grows **c** : FOREHEAD **2** : the edge or projecting upper part of a steep slope
brow•beat \'brau̇-,bēt\ *vt* : to frighten by a stern manner or threatening speech : BULLY, ABUSE
¹**brown** \'brau̇n\ *adj* : of the color brown; *esp* : of dark or tanned complexion
²**brown** *n* : a color like that of coffee or chocolate that is a blend of red and yellow darkened by black — **brown•ish** \'brau̇-nish\ *adj*
³**brown** *vb* : to make or become brown
brown•ie \'brau̇-nē\ *n* **1** : a good-natured goblin who performs helpful services at night **2** : a small square or rectangle of rich usu. chocolate cake containing nuts
¹**browse** \'brau̇z\ *n* : tender shoots, twigs, and leaves of trees and shrubs fit for food for cattle
²**browse** *vb* **1** : to nibble or feed on browse : GRAZE **2 a** : to skim a book reading random passages **b** : to look over books esp. in order to select one — **brows•er** *n*
¹**bruise** \'brüz\ *vb* **1** : to inflict a bruise on **2** : to break down (as leaves or berries) by pounding : CRUSH **3** : to wound or hurt the feelings of **4** : to become bruised
²**bruise** *n* : an injury (as from a blow) in which the skin is not broken but is discolored : CONTUSION
bruis•er \'brü-zər\ *n* : a big husky man
bruit \'brüt\ *vt* : to noise abroad : REPORT
brum•ma•gem \'brəm-i-jəm\ *adj* : being showy and cheap
brunch \'brənch\ *n* : a late breakfast, an early lunch, or a combination of the two
bru•net *or* **bru•nette** \brü-'net\ *adj* : of dark or relatively dark pigmentation; *esp* : having brown or black hair and eyes — **brunet** *n*
brunt \'brənt\ *n* : the main force of a blow or an attack : the heaviest shock, stress, or strain
¹**brush** \'brəsh\ *n* **1** : BRUSHWOOD **2 a** : scrub vegetation **b** : land covered with scrub vegetation
²**brush** *n* **1** : a device composed of bristles set into a handle and used esp. for sweeping, scrubbing, or painting **2** : a bushy tail (as of a fox or squirrel) **3 a** : an act of brushing **b** : a quick light touch or momentary contact
³**brush** *vb* **1 a** : to apply a brush to **b** : to apply with a brush **2 a** : to remove with or as if with a brush **b** : to dispose of in an offhand way : DISMISS **3** : to touch gently in passing — **brush•er** *n*
⁴**brush** *n* : a brief encounter or skirmish
brush–off \'brəsh-,ȯf\ *n* : an abrupt or offhand dismissal
brush•wood \-,wu̇d\ *n* **1** : small branches cut from trees or shrubs **2** : a thicket of shrubs and small trees
¹**brushy** \'brəsh-ē\ *adj* : SHAGGY, ROUGH
²**brushy** *adj* : covered with or abounding in brush or brushwood
brusque \'brəsk\ *adj* : markedly abrupt in manner or speech : being sharp and often harsh — **brusque•ly** *adv* — **brusque•ness** *n*
brus•sels sprout \,brəs-əlz-\ *n, often cap B* : one of the edible small green heads borne on the stem of a plant related to the cabbage; *also* : this plant
bru•tal \'brüt-ᵊl\ *adj* : ruthlessly violent : CRUEL, INHUMAN, SAVAGE — **bru•tal•ly** *adv*
bru•tal•i•ty \brü-'tal-ət-ē\ *n, pl* **-ties** **1** : the quality or state of being brutal **2** : a brutal act or course of action
¹**brute** \'brüt\ *adj* **1** : of, relating to, or typical of beasts **2** : having neither mind nor soul **3** : resembling an animal in quality, action, or instinct
²**brute** *n* **1** : BEAST **2** : a brutal person
brut•ish \'brüt-ish\ *adj* **1** : of or resembling a beast **2 a** : grossly sensual : INSENSITIVE **b** : UNREASONING, IRRATIONAL — **brut•ish•ly** *adv* — **brut•ish•ness** *n*
¹**bub•ble** \'bəb-əl\ *vb* **bub•bled**; **bub•bling** \'bəb-(ə-)liŋ\ **1** : to form or produce bubbles **2** : to flow out with a gurgling sound **3** : to seem to give off bubbles : EFFERVESCE **4 a** : to cause to bubble **b** : BURP
²**bubble** *n* **1 a** : a small body of gas within a liquid **b** : a thin film of liquid inflated with air or gas **2** : something that lacks firmness, solidity, or reality
bub•bler \'bəb-(ə-)lər\ *n* : a drinking fountain
bub•bly \'bəb-(ə-)lē\ *adj* **1** : full of bubbles : EFFERVESCENT **2** : resembling a bubble
bu•bon•ic plague \b(y)ü-,bän-ik-\ *n* : plague marked esp. by chills and fever and by inflammatory swellings
buc•ca•neer \,bək-ə-'ni(ə)r\ *n* : PIRATE — **buccaneer** *vi*
¹**buck** \'bək\ *n, pl* **buck** *or* **bucks** **1** : a male animal; *esp* : a male deer or antelope **2 a** : a male human being : MAN **b** : DANDY **3** : BUCKSKIN
²**buck** *vb* **1** : to spring with a quick plunging leap **2 a** : to charge against something as if butting **b** : to charge into (the opposing line) in football **c** : OPPOSE, RESIST **3** : to start, move, or react jerkily **4** : to strive for advancement or promotion — **buck•er** *n*
³**buck** *n* : an act or instance of bucking
buck•a•roo *or* **buck•er•oo** \,bək-ə-'rü\ *n, pl* **-aroos** *or* **-eroos** : COWBOY
buck•board \'bək-,bōrd\ *n* : a four-wheeled vehicle with a springy platform carrying the seat
¹**buck•et** \'bək-ət\ *n* **1** : a cylindrical vessel for holding liquids or solids **2** : an object resembling a bucket in collecting, scooping, or carrying something **3** : BUCKETFUL
²**bucket** *vb* : to draw or lift in or as if in buckets
buck•et•ful \'bək-ət-,fu̇l\ *n, pl* **buck•et•fuls** \-ət-,fu̇lz\ *or* **buck•ets•ful** \-əts-,fu̇l\ : the amount held by a bucket
¹**buck•le** \'bək-əl\ *n* : a fastening for two loose ends that is attached to one and holds the other by a catch
²**buckle** *vb* **buck•led**; **buck•ling** \'bək-(ə-)liŋ\ **1** : to fasten with a buckle **2** : to apply oneself with vigor **3** : to crumple up : BEND, COLLAPSE
³**buckle** *n* : a product of buckling : BEND
buck•ler \'bək-lər\ *n* : SHIELD
buck•ram \'bək-rəm\ *n* : a stiff-finished heavily sized fabric of cotton or linen used in garments, millinery, and bookbindings — **buckram** *adj*
buck•saw \'bək-,sȯ\ *n* : a saw set in a usu. H-shaped frame that is used for sawing wood on a sawbuck
buck•shot \-,shät\ *n* : a coarse lead shot used in shotgun shells
buck•skin \-,skin\ *n* **1 a** : the skin of a buck **b** : a soft usu. suede-finished leather **2** *pl* : buckskin breeches
buck•wheat \'bək-,hwēt\ *n* : any of several herbs with pinkish white flowers and triangular seeds; *also* : the seeds used as a cereal grain

bu·col·ic \byü-ˈkäl-ik\ *adj* **1 :** PASTORAL **2 :** RUSTIC — **bu·col·i·cal·ly** \-i-k(ə-)lē\ *adv*

[1]**bud** \ˈbəd\ *n* **1 :** a small growth at the tip or on the side of a plant stem that develops into a flower, leaf, or new shoot **2 :** a flower that has not fully opened **3 :** an asexual reproductive structure **4 :** an early stage or condition

[2]**bud** *vb* **bud·ded; bud·ding** **1 a :** to form or put forth buds **b :** to reproduce by asexual buds **2 :** to be or develop like a bud **3 :** to insert a bud from one plant into an opening cut in the bark of (another plant) in order to propagate a desired variety — **bud·der** *n*

Bud·dhism \ˈbü-ˌdiz-əm, ˈbu̇d-ˌiz-\ *n* **:** a religion of eastern and central Asia growing out of the teachings of Gautama Buddha — **Bud·dhist** \ˈbüd-əst, ˈbu̇d-\ *n or adj*

bud·dy \ˈbəd-ē\ *n, pl* **buddies :** COMPANION, PARTNER, PAL

budge \ˈbəj\ *vb* **:** MOVE, SHIFT; *esp* **:** YIELD

bud·ger·i·gar \ˈbəj-(ə-)rē-ˌgär\ *n* **:** a small Australian parrot bred under domestication in many colors

[1]**bud·get** \ˈbəj-ət\ *n* **1 :** STOCK, SUPPLY **2 a :** a statement of the estimated expenditures (as of a nation) during a period and of proposals to finance them **b :** a plan for using resources to finance expenditures

[2]**budget** *vb* **1 :** to include or assign in or as if in a budget **2 :** to provide a budget or detailed plan for **3 :** to draw up and operate under a budget

bud·get·ary \ˈbəj-ə-ˌter-ē\ *adj* **:** of or relating to a budget

[1]**buff** \ˈbəf\ *n* **1 :** a fuzzy-surfaced usu. oil-tanned leather; *also* **:** a garment of this **2 :** the bare skin **3 a :** a moderate orange yellow **b :** a light to moderate yellow **4 :** FAN, ENTHUSIAST

[2]**buff** *adj* **:** of the color buff

[3]**buff** *vt* **:** POLISH, SHINE

[1]**buf·fa·lo** \ˈbəf-ə-ˌlō\ *n, pl* **-lo** *or* **-loes :** any of several wild oxen; *esp* **:** a large shaggy-maned No. American wild ox with short horns and heavy forequarters bearing a large muscular hump

[2]**buffalo** *vt* **1 :** BEWILDER, BAFFLE **2 :** OVERAWE

[1]**buff·er** \ˈbəf-ər\ *n* **:** one that buffs

[2]**buf·fer** \ˈbəf-ər\ *n* **1 :** a device or material for reducing shock due to contact **2 :** a person who shields another esp. from annoying routine matters

[1]**buf·fet** \ˈbəf-ət\ *n* **:** BLOW, SLAP

[2]**buffet** *vb* **1 :** STRIKE, SLAP **2 :** to pound repeatedly **:** BATTER **3 :** CONTEND, STRUGGLE

[3]**buf·fet** \(ˌ)bə-ˈfā, bü-\ *n* **1 :** SIDEBOARD **2 a :** a counter for refreshments **b :** a meal set out on a buffet or table to be eaten without formal service

buf·foon \(ˌ)bə-ˈfün\ *n* **:** CLOWN — **buf·foon·ish** \-ˈfü-nish\ *adj* — **buf·foon·ery** \-ˈfün-(ə-)rē\ *n*

bug \ˈbəg\ *n* **1 a :** an insect or other creeping or crawling invertebrate; *esp* **:** an obnoxious insect (as a bedbug or head louse) **b :** any of a group of insects with sucking mouthparts that includes many destructive plant pests **2 :** an unexpected defect, fault, flaw, or imperfection **3 :** a disease-producing germ

bug·a·boo \ˈbəg-ə-ˌbü\ *n, pl* **-boos :** BUGBEAR, BOGEY

bug·bear \ˈbəg-ˌba(ə)r\ *n* **1 :** BOGEY **2 :** an object or source of dread

[1]**bug·gy** \ˈbəg-ē\ *adj* **:** infested with bugs

[2]**buggy** *n, pl* **buggies :** a light single-seated carriage usu. drawn by one horse

[1]**bu·gle** \ˈbyü-gəl\ *n* **:** a brass instrument with a cupped mouthpiece like the trumpet but having a shorter and more conical tube

[2]**bugle** *vb* **bu·gled; bu·gling** \-g(ə-)liŋ\ **1 :** to sound or summon by or as if by a bugle call **2 :** to sound a bugle — **bu·gler** \-glər\ *n*

[1]**build** \ˈbild\ *vb* **built** \ˈbilt\; **build·ing** **1 :** to make by putting together parts or materials **:** CONSTRUCT **2 :** to produce or create gradually esp. by effort **3 :** to cause to be constructed **4 :** to engage in building **5 :** INCREASE, ENLARGE **6 :** to progress toward a peak

[2]**build** *n* **:** form or mode of structure; *esp* **:** PHYSIQUE

build·er \ˈbil-dər\ *n* **:** one that builds

build·ing \ˈbil-diŋ\ *n* **1 :** a usu. roofed and walled structure built for permanent use (as for a dwelling) **2 :** the art, work, or business of assembling materials into a structure

built–in \ˈbilt-ˈin\ *adj* **1 :** forming an integral part of a structure **2 :** INHERENT

bulb \ˈbəlb\ *n* **1 a :** a plant underground resting stage consisting of a short stem base bearing one or more buds enclosed in thickened storage leaves **b :** a fleshy structure (as a tuber or corm) resembling a bulb in appearance or function **c :** a plant having or developing from a bulb **2 :** a bulb-shaped object or part — **bul·ba·ceous** \ˌbəl-ˈbā-shəs\ *adj* — **bulbed** \ˈbəlbd\ *adj*

bulb·ous \ˈbəl-bəs\ *adj* **1 :** having a bulb **:** growing from or bearing bulbs **2 :** resembling a bulb **:** ROUNDED, SWOLLEN — **bulb·ous·ly** *adv*

bul·bul \ˈbu̇l-ˌbu̇l\ *n* **:** a Persian songbird that is prob. a nightingale

[1]**bulge** \ˈbəlj\ *n* **:** a swelling or protuberant part **:** a part that has an outward bend

[2]**bulge** *vb* **:** to swell or bend outward

[1]**bulk** \ˈbəlk\ *n* **1 :** greatness of size or extent **2 :** a large body or mass **3 :** the main or greater part

[2]**bulk** *vb* **1 :** to have a bulky appearance **:** LOOM **2 :** to be weighty or impressive

bulk·head \ˈbəlk-ˌhed\ *n* **1 :** an upright partition separating compartments on a ship **2 :** a structure or partition to resist pressure or to shut off water, fire, or gas **3 :** a projecting framework with a sloping door giving access to a cellar stairway

bulky \ˈbəl-kē\ *adj* **:** having bulk: as **a :** being large and unwieldy **b :** having great volume in proportion to weight — **bulk·i·ly** \-kə-lē\ *adv* — **bulk·i·ness** *n*

[1]**bull** \ˈbu̇l\ *n* **1 :** an adult male bovine animal; *also* **:** a usu. adult male of various large animals **2 :** a person who buys something (as stocks) in expectation of a price rise or who acts to bring about such a rise

[2]**bull** *adj* **1 a :** MALE **b :** of, relating to, or resembling a bull **2 :** large of its kind **3 :** RISING

[3]**bull** *n* **:** a papal pronouncement of the most formal and important kind

[4]**bull** *n* **:** a grotesque blunder in language

[1]**bull·dog** \ˈbu̇l-ˌdȯg\ *n* **:** a compact muscular short-haired dog of English origin

[2]**bulldog** *adj* **:** resembling a bulldog **:** STUBBORN

bull·doze \ˈbu̇l-ˌdōz\ *vt* **1 :** BULLY **2 :** to move, clear, gouge out, or level off with a bulldozer **3 :** to force as if by using a bulldozer

bull·doz·er \-ˌdō-zər\ *n* **:** a tractor-driven machine having a broad horizontal blade for pushing

bul·let \ˈbu̇l-ət\ *n* **:** a shaped piece of metal made to be shot from a firearm

bul·le·tin \ˈbu̇l-ət-ᵊn\ *n* **1 :** a brief public notice issuing usu. from an authoritative source **2 :** a periodical publication; *esp* **:** the organ of an institution or association

bul·let·proof \ˌbu̇l-ət-ˈprüf\ *adj* **:** so made as to prevent the passing through of bullets

bull fiddle *n* **:** DOUBLE BASS — **bull fiddler** *n*

bull·fight \ˈbu̇l-ˌfīt\ *n* **:** a spectacle in which men ceremonially excite, fight with, and usu. kill bulls in an arena for public amusement — **bull·fight·er** *n*

bull·finch \-ˌfinch\ *n* **:** a thick-billed red-breasted European songbird often kept as a cage bird

bull·frog \-ˌfrȯg, -ˌfräg\ *n* : FROG; *esp* : a large heavy frog that makes a booming or bellowing sound
bull·head \-ˌhed\ *n* : any of various large-headed fishes
bull·head·ed \ˈbu̇l-ˈhed-əd\ *adj* : stupidly stubborn : HEADSTRONG — **bull·head·ed·ly** *adv* — **bull·head·ed·ness** *n*
bul·lion \ˈbu̇l-yən\ *n* : gold or silver metal; *esp* : gold or silver in bars or ingots
bull·ish \ˈbu̇l-ish\ *adj* 1 : marked by, tending to cause, or hopeful of rising prices (as in a stock market) 2 : OPTIMISTIC — **bull·ish·ly** *adv*
bull·ock \ˈbu̇l-ək\ *n* 1 : a young bull 2 : a castrated bull : STEER — **bull·ocky** \-ə-kē\ *adj*
bull·ring \ˈbu̇l-ˌriŋ\ *n* : an arena for bullfights
bull's–eye \ˈbu̇l-ˌzī\ *n* 1 : a small thick disk of glass inserted (as in a deck) to let in light 2 **a** : the center of a target **b** : a shot that hits a bull's-eye
¹**bul·ly** \ˈbu̇l-ē\ *n, pl* **bullies** : a blustering fellow; *esp* : one habitually cruel to others weaker than himself
²**bully** *adj* : EXCELLENT, FIRST-RATE — often used interjectionally
³**bully** *vb* **bul·lied**; **bul·ly·ing** 1 : BROWBEAT, INTIMIDATE, DOMINEER 2 : to act like a bully : BLUSTER
bul·rush \ˈbu̇l-ˌrəsh\ *n* : any of several large sedges growing in wet land or water
bul·wark \ˈbu̇l-(ˌ)wərk, -ˌwȯrk; ˈbəl-(ˌ)wərk\ *n* 1 : a solid wall-like structure raised for defense : RAMPART 2 : a strong support or protection in danger
¹**bum** \ˈbəm\ *vb* **bummed**; **bum·ming** 1 **a** : LOAF **b** : to wander like a tramp 2 : to obtain by begging
²**bum** *n* 1 : a person who avoids work and tries to live off others 2 : TRAMP, HOBO
³**bum** *adj* 1 : INFERIOR, WORTHLESS 2 : DISABLED
bum·ble·bee \ˈbəm-bəl-ˌbē\ *n* : any of numerous large robust hairy social bees
¹**bump** \ˈbəmp\ *vb* 1 : to strike or knock against something with force or violence 2 : to collide with 3 : to proceed in a series of bumps : JOLT
²**bump** *n* 1 : a sudden forceful blow, impact, or jolt 2 : a rounded projection or protuberance; *esp* : a swelling (as from a blow or sting) of tissue
¹**bump·er** \ˈbəm-pər\ *n* : a cup or glass filled to the brim
²**bumper** *adj* : unusually large or fine
³**bumper** *n* : a device for absorbing shock or preventing damage (as in collision); *esp* : a metal bar at the end of an automobile
bump·kin \ˈbəm(p)-kən\ *n* : an awkward and unsophisticated rustic
bump·tious \ˈbəm(p)-shəs\ *adj* : obtusely and often noisily self-assertive : PRESUMPTUOUS — **bump·tious·ly** *adv* — **bump·tious·ness** *n*
bumpy \ˈbəm-pē\ *adj* 1 : having or covered with bumps 2 : causing or marked by bumps or jolts — **bump·i·ly** \-pə-lē\ *adv* — **bump·i·ness** *n*
bun \ˈbən\ *n* 1 : a sweet or plain small bread; *esp* : a round roll 2 : a knot of hair shaped like a bun
¹**bunch** \ˈbənch\ *n* 1 : a number of things of the same kind : CLUSTER 2 : GROUP, COLLECTION — **bunch·i·ly** \ˈbən-chə-lē\ *adv* — **bunchy** \-chē\ *adj*
²**bunch** *vb* : to form in or gather into a group or cluster
bun·co *or* **bun·ko** \ˈbəŋ-kō\ *n, pl* **buncos** *or* **bunkos** : a swindling game or scheme — **bunco** *vt*
¹**bun·dle** \ˈbən-dᵊl\ *n* 1 : a group of things tied together 2 : PACKAGE, PARCEL
²**bundle** *vb* **bun·dled**; **bun·dling** \ˈbən-dliŋ, -dᵊl-iŋ\ 1 : to make into a bundle : WRAP 2 : to hurry off unceremoniously : HUSTLE — **bun·dler** \-dlər, -dᵊl-ər\ *n*
¹**bung** \ˈbəŋ\ *n* : the stopper in the bunghole of a cask; *also* : BUNGHOLE
²**bung** *vt* 1 : to plug with or as if with a bung 2 : BATTER
bun·ga·low \ˈbəŋ-gə-ˌlō\ *n* : a usu. one-storied house characterized by low sweeping lines and a wide veranda
bung·hole \ˈbəŋ-ˌhōl\ *n* : a hole for emptying or filling a cask
bun·gle \ˈbəŋ-gəl\ *vb* **bun·gled**; **bun·gling** \-g(ə-)liŋ\ : to act, do, make, or work in a clumsy manner — **bungle** *n* — **bun·gler** \-g(ə-)lər\ *n*
bun·ion \ˈbən-yən\ *n* : an inflamed swelling on the first joint of the big toe
¹**bunk** \ˈbəŋk\ *n* 1 : a built-in bed (as on a ship) that is often one of a tier 2 : a sleeping place
²**bunk** *vb* 1 : to occupy a bunk 2 : to provide with a bunk
³**bunk** *n* : NONSENSE
bun·ker \ˈbəŋ-kər\ *n* 1 : a bin or compartment for storage (as for coal or oil on a ship) 2 **a** : a protective embankment or dugout; *esp* : a fortified chamber mostly below ground **b** : an embankment constituting a hazard on a golf course
bunk·house \ˈbəŋk-ˌhau̇s\ *n* : a rough simple building providing sleeping quarters (as for construction workers)
bun·kum *or* **bun·combe** \ˈbəŋ-kəm\ *n* : insincere or foolish talk : NONSENSE
bun·ny \ˈbən-ē\ *n, pl* **bunnies** : RABBIT
¹**bunt** \ˈbənt\ *vb* 1 : to strike or push with or as if with the head : BUTT 2 : to push or tap a baseball lightly without swinging the bat — **bunt·er** *n*
²**bunt** *n* : a bunted ball
¹**bun·ting** \ˈbənt-iŋ\ *n* : any of various stout-billed finches of the size and habits of a sparrow
²**bunting** *n* 1 : a thin fabric used chiefly for making flags 2 : flags or decorations made of bunting
¹**buoy** \ˈbü-ē, ˈbȯi\ *n* : a floating object anchored in a body of water to mark a channel or warn of danger
²**buoy** *vt* 1 : to mark by or as if by a buoy 2 **a** : to keep afloat **b** : to raise the spirits of : SUSTAIN
buoy·an·cy \ˈbȯi-ən-sē, ˈbü-yən-\ *n* 1 **a** : the tendency of a body to float or to rise when submerged in a fluid **b** : the power of a fluid to exert an upward force on a body placed in it 2 : natural lightness of spirit : LIGHTHEARTEDNESS
buoy·ant \ˈbȯi-ənt, ˈbü-yənt\ *adj* 1 : able to rise and float in the air or on the surface of a liquid 2 : able to keep a body afloat 3 : LIGHTHEARTED, CHEERFUL — **buoy·ant·ly** *adv*
bur *var of* BURR
¹**bur·den** \ˈbərd-ᵊn\ *n* 1 : something that is carried : LOAD 2 : something hard to bear : ENCUMBRANCE 3 **a** : CARGO, LADING **b** : capacity for carrying cargo
²**burden** *vt* **bur·dened**; **bur·den·ing** \ˈbərd-niŋ, -ᵊn-iŋ\ : LOAD, OPPRESS
³**burden** *n* 1 : the refrain or chorus of a song 2 : a main or recurring theme : central idea : GIST
bur·den·some \ˈbərd-ᵊn-səm\ *adj* : difficult or distressing to bear : OPPRESSIVE — **bur·den·some·ly** *adv*
bur·dock \ˈbər-ˌdäk\ *n* : any of a genus of coarse herbs related to the daisy that have globular flower heads with prickly bracts
bu·reau \ˈbyu̇(ə)r-ō\ *n* 1 : a low chest of drawers with a mirror for use in a bedroom 2 **a** : a specialized administrative unit; *esp* : a subdivision of a governmental department **b** : a commercial agency providing services for the public or for other businesses
bu·reau·cra·cy \byu̇-ˈräk-rə-sē\ *n, pl* **-cies** 1 : a body of appointed government officials 2 **a** : a system of administration characterized by specialization of functions, adherence to fixed rules, and a hierarchy of authority **b** : a system of administration marked by lack of initiative and flexibility
bu·reau·crat \ˈbyu̇r-ə-ˌkrat\ *n* : a member of a bureaucracy
bu·reau·crat·ic \ˌbyu̇r-ə-ˈkrat-ik\ *adj* : of, relating to, or having the characteristics of a bureaucracy or a bureaucrat — **bu·reau·crat·i·cal·ly** \-ˈkrat-i-k(ə-)lē\ *adv*
burg \ˈbərg\ *n* : a medieval fortress or walled town

bur·geon \'bər-jən\ *vi* **1 a :** to put forth new growth (as buds) **b :** BLOSSOM, BLOOM **2 :** EXPAND, FLOURISH
bur·gess \'bər-jəs\ *n* **:** a citizen of a British borough
burgh \'bər-ō\ *n* **:** a Scottish town
bur·gher \'bər-gər\ *n* **:** an inhabitant of a borough or a town; *esp* **:** a prosperous solid citizen
bur·glar \'bər-glər\ *n* **:** one who commits burglary **:** THIEF
bur·glary \'bər-glə-rē\ *n, pl* **-glar·ies :** the act of breaking into a building (as a house) esp. at night and with the intent of committing a crime (as stealing)
bur·go·mas·ter \'bər-gə-ˌmas-tər\ *n* **:** the chief magistrate of a town in some European countries
Bur·gun·dy \'bər-gən-dē\ *n* **:** a dry usu. red table wine
bur·i·al \'ber-ē-əl\ *n* **:** the act of burying
bur·lap \'bər-ˌlap\ *n* **:** a coarse fabric made usu. from jute or hemp and used esp. for bags
¹bur·lesque \(ˌ)bər-'lesk\ *n* **1 :** a witty or derisive literary or dramatic imitation **2 :** theatrical entertainment consisting of low comedy skits and dance routines — **burlesque** *adj*
²burlesque *vt* **:** to mock or ridicule through burlesque
bur·ly \'bər-lē\ *adj* **:** strongly and heavily built **:** HUSKY — **bur·li·ness** *n*
¹burn \'bərn\ *vb* **burned** \'bərnd\ *or* **burnt** \'bərnt\; **burn·ing** **1 a :** BLAZE **b :** to undergo combustion **2 a :** to feel hot **b :** to become altered by or as if by the action of fire or heat; *esp* **:** SCORCH **c :** to appear as if on fire **:** GLOW **d :** to cause to undergo combustion; *esp* **:** to destroy by fire **e :** to use as fuel **3 :** to produce by the action of fire or heat **4 :** to injure or alter by or as if by fire or heat — **burn·a·ble** *adj* — **burn·er** *n* — **burn·ing·ly** *adv*
²burn *n* **:** injury, damage, or effect produced by or as if by burning
bur·nish \'bər-nish\ *vt* **:** to make shiny or lustrous esp. by rubbing with a hard smooth tool — **bur·nish·er** *n*
bur·noose *or* **bur·nous** \(ˌ)bər-'nüs\ *n* **:** a hooded cloak worn by Arabs and Moors
¹burp \'bərp\ *n* **:** BELCH
²burp *vb* **1 :** BELCH **2 :** to help (a baby) expel gas from the stomach esp. by patting or rubbing the back
¹burr \'bər\ *n* **1** *usu* **bur a :** a rough or prickly envelope of a fruit **b :** a plant that bears burs **2 :** a roughness left (as in drilling or engraving) by a tool in cutting or shaping metal **3 :** a rough humming sound **:** WHIR — **burred** \'bərd\ *adj*
²burr *vb* **1 :** to make a whirring sound **2 a :** to form into a rough edge **b :** to remove burrs from — **burr·er** *n*
bur·ro \'bər-ō, 'bu̇r-\ *n, pl* **burros :** a usu. small donkey
¹bur·row \'bər-ō\ *n* **:** a hole in the ground made by an animal (as a rabbit) for shelter
²burrow *vb* **1 :** to construct by tunneling **2 a :** to make a burrow **b :** to progress by or as if by digging **3 :** to make a thorough search **:** DELVE **4 :** to enter by stealth — **bur·row·er** *n*
bur·ry \'bər-ē\ *adj* **1 :** containing burs **2 :** PRICKLY
bur·sar \'bər-sər, -ˌsär\ *n* **:** a treasurer esp. of a college or monastery
bur·sa·ry \'bərs-(ə-)rē\ *n, pl* **-ries :** the treasury of a college or monastery
bur·si·tis \(ˌ)bər-'sīt-əs\ *n* **:** inflammation of the serous sac of a joint (as the shoulder or elbow)
¹burst \'bərst\ *vb* **burst**; **burst·ing** **1 a :** to break open, apart, or into pieces from or as if from impact or from or as if from pressure within **b :** to cause to burst **2 :** to give vent suddenly to an emotion **3 a :** to emerge or spring suddenly **b :** LAUNCH, PLUNGE **4 :** to be filled to the breaking point
²burst *n* **1 a :** a sudden outbreak or outburst **b :** a sudden intense effort or exertion **2 :** an act of bursting **3 :** a result of bursting
bury \'ber-ē\ *vt* **bur·ied**; **bur·y·ing** **1 :** to deposit (a dead body) in or as if in the earth; *esp* **:** to inter with funeral ceremonies **2 :** to place in the ground and cover over **3 :** CONCEAL, HIDE **4 :** to remove from the world of action — **bur·i·er** *n*
¹bus \'bəs\ *n, pl* **bus·es** *or* **bus·ses :** a large motor-driven passenger vehicle
²bus *vb* **bussed**; **bus·sing :** to travel by bus
bus·boy \'bəs-ˌbȯi\ *n* **:** a man or boy employed in a restaurant to help (as by removing soiled dishes and cleaning and resetting tables after use)
bus·by \'bəz-bē\ *n, pl* **busbies :** a military full-dress fur hat with a bag hanging down on one side
bush \'bu̇sh\ *n* **1 :** SHRUB; *esp* **:** a low densely branched shrub **2 :** a large uncleared or sparsely settled area (as in Australia) **3 :** a bushy tuft or mass
bush·el \'bu̇sh-əl\ *n* **:** any of various units of dry capacity
bush·ing \'bu̇sh-iŋ\ *n* **:** a usu. removable cylindrical lining in an opening of a mechanical part to limit the size of the opening, resist wear (as in a bearing for an axle), or serve as a guide
bush·whack \'bu̇sh-ˌhwak\ *vb* **1 :** to live or hide out in the woods **2 :** AMBUSH — **bush·whack·er** *n* — **bush·whack·ing** *n*
bushy \'bu̇sh-ē\ *adj* **1 :** full of or overgrown with bushes **2 :** resembling a bush esp. in thick spreading form or growth — **bush·i·ness** *n*
busi·ness \'biz-nəs, -nəz\ *n* **1 a :** an activity that takes a major part of the time, attention, or effort of a person or group; *esp* **:** OCCUPATION **b :** a commercial or mercantile activity engaged in as a means of livelihood **2 :** an immediate task or objective **:** MISSION **3 a :** a commercial or industrial enterprise **b :** the area of economic activity that usu. includes trade, commerce, finance, and industry **4 :** AFFAIR, MATTER
busi·ness·like \'biz-nəs-ˌlīk, -nəz-\ *adj* **1 :** EFFICIENT, PRACTICAL **2 :** SERIOUS, PURPOSEFUL
busi·ness·man \-ˌman\ *n* **:** a man engaged in a commercial or industrial enterprise esp. on an executive level
bus·kin \'bəs-kən\ *n* **1 :** a boot reaching halfway to the knee **2 :** tragic drama
buss \'bəs\ *n* **:** KISS — **buss** *vt*
¹bust \'bəst\ *n* **1 :** a piece of sculpture representing the upper part of the human figure including the head and neck **2 :** the upper portion of the human torso between neck and waist; *esp* **:** the breasts of a woman
²bust *vb* **1 :** HIT, PUNCH **2 :** BREAK; *esp* **:** to break up or apart **3 :** to demote esp. in military rank — **bust·er** *n*
³bust *n* **1 a :** a complete failure **b :** a severe business depression or recession **2 :** SPREE
¹bus·tle \'bəs-əl\ *vi* **bus·tled**; **bus·tling** \'bəs-(ə-)liŋ\ **1 :** to move about with fussy or noisy activity **2 :** to be busily astir
²bustle *n* **:** noisy or energetic activity
³bustle *n* **:** a pad or a light frame formerly worn by women just below the back waistline to give fullness to the skirt
¹busy \'biz-ē\ *adj* **1 a :** engaged in action **:** OCCUPIED **b :** being in use **2 :** full of activity **:** BUSTLING — **bus·i·ly** \'biz-ə-lē\ *adv*
²busy *vb* **bus·ied**; **bus·y·ing** **1 :** to make or keep busy **:** OCCUPY **2 :** to be busy
busy·body \'biz-ē-ˌbäd-ē\ *n* **:** a person who meddles in the affairs of others
busy·ness \'biz-ē-nəs\ *n* **:** the quality or state of being busy
¹but \(ˌ)bət\ *conj* **1 a :** without the consequence or accompanying circumstance that **b :** that not **c :** THAT — used after a negative **2 a** (1) **:** on the contrary (2) **:** despite that fact **b :** with this exception, namely
²but *prep* **1 :** with the exception of **2 :** other than
³but *adv* **1 :** ONLY, MERELY **2 :** to the contrary
¹butch·er \'bu̇ch-ər\ *n* **1 a :** one who slaughters animals or dresses their flesh **b :** a dealer in meat **2 :** one that kills ruthlessly or brutally
²butcher *vt* **butch·ered**; **butch·er·ing** \-(ə-)riŋ\ **1 :** to slaughter and dress for meat **2 :** to kill in a barbarous manner — **butch·er·er** *n*

butch·ery \'bu̇ch-(ə-)rē\ *n, pl* **-er·ies** **1 :** the business of a butcher **2 :** brutal murder : great slaughter
but·ler \'bət-lər\ *n* **:** the chief male servant of a household
[1]**butt** \'bət\ *vb* **:** to strike with the head or horns
[2]**butt** *n* **:** a blow or thrust usu. with the head or horns
[3]**butt** *n* **1 a :** a mound, bank, or structure for stopping missiles shot at a target **b :** TARGET **2 :** a target of abuse or ridicule
[4]**butt** *vb* **1 :** ABUT **2 :** to place end to end without overlapping
[5]**butt** *n* **:** the large or thicker end (as of a weapon)
[6]**butt** *n* **1 :** a large cask esp. for wine, beer, or water **2 :** any of various units of liquid capacity
butte \'byüt\ *n* **:** an isolated hill with steep sides
[1]**but·ter** \'bət-ər\ *n* **1 :** a solid yellow emulsion of fat, air, and water made by churning milk or cream and used as food **2 :** a substance resembling butter in appearance, texture, or use
[2]**butter** *vt* **:** to spread with or as if with butter
but·ter·cup \'bət-ər-,kəp\ *n* **:** any of a genus of yellow-flowered herbs with usu. five petals and sepals
but·ter·fat \-,fat\ *n* **:** the natural fat of milk and chief constituent of butter
but·ter·fly \-,flī\ *n* **:** any of numerous slender-bodied day-flying insects with large broad usu. brightly colored wings
but·ter·milk \-,milk\ *n* **1 :** the liquid left after the butterfat has been churned from milk or cream **2 :** cultured milk made by the addition of certain organisms to sweet milk
but·ter·nut \-,nət\ *n* **:** the edible oily nut of an American tree of the walnut family; *also* **:** this tree
but·ter·scotch \-,skäch\ *n* **:** a candy made from sugar, corn syrup, and water; *also* **:** the flavor of such candy — **butterscotch** *adj*
but·tery \'bət-ə-rē\ *adj* **1 :** having the qualities, consistency, or appearance of butter **2 :** spread with butter
but·tocks \'bət-əks\ *n pl* **:** the seat of the body; *also* **:** RUMP
[1]**but·ton** \'bət-ᵊn\ *n* **1 :** a small knob or disk (as of shell, leather, or plastic) used for holding parts of a garment together or as an ornament **2 :** something that resembles a button
[2]**button** *vb* **but·toned**; **but·ton·ing** \'bət-niŋ, -ᵊn-iŋ\ **:** to close or fasten with buttons
[1]**but·ton·hole** \'bət-ᵊn-,hōl\ *n* **:** a slit or loop for fastening a button
[2]**buttonhole** *vt* **:** to detain in conversation by or as if by holding on to the outer garments of — **but·ton·hol·er** *n*
but·ton·hook \-,hu̇k\ *n* **:** a hook for drawing small buttons through buttonholes
[1]**but·tress** \'bə-trəs\ *n* **1 :** a projecting structure of masonry or wood for supporting or giving stability to a wall or building **2 :** something that supports, props, or strengthens
[2]**buttress** *vt* **:** to support with or as if with a buttress
bux·om \'bək-səm\ *adj* **:** vigorously or healthily plump; *esp* **:** full-bosomed — **bux·om·ly** *adv* — **bux·om·ness** *n*
[1]**buy** \'bī\ *vt* **bought** \'bȯt\; **buy·ing** **1 :** to get possession or ownership of by giving or agreeing to give money in exchange **:** PURCHASE **2 :** to secure decisive control over by bribery — **buy·er** *n*
[2]**buy** *n* **:** something sold or for sale at a price favorable to the purchaser **:** BARGAIN
[1]**buzz** \'bəz\ *vb* **1 :** to make a low continuous humming sound like that of a bee **2 :** to be filled with a confused murmur **3 :** to fly low and fast over
[2]**buzz** *n* **1 :** a persistent sound produced by or as if by fast pulsations (as of the wings of a bee) **2 :** a confused murmur or flurry of activity **3 :** a signal conveyed by buzzer
buz·zard \'bəz-ərd\ *n* **:** any of various usu. large slow-flying birds of prey
buzz·er \'bəz-ər\ *n* **:** an electric signaling device that makes a buzzing sound
[1]**by** \(')bī, *esp before consonants* bə\ *prep* **1 :** close to **:** NEAR **2 a :** ALONG, THROUGH **b :** PAST **3 a :** during the course of **b :** not later than **4 :** through the agency or instrumentality of **5 :** with the witness or sanction of **6 a :** in conformity with **b :** according to **7 :** with respect to **8 :** in or to the amount or extent of **9 :** in successive units of **10** — used as a function word in multiplication and in measurements
[2]**by** \'bī\ *adv* **1 a :** close at hand **:** NEAR **b :** at or to another's home **2 :** PAST **3 :** ASIDE, AWAY
by and large \,bī-ən-'lärj\ *adv* **:** on the whole **:** in general
by–elec·tion \'bī-ə-,lek-shən\ *n* **:** a special election held between regular elections in order to fill a vacancy
by·gone \'bī-,gȯn\ *adj* **:** gone by **:** PAST — **bygone** *n*
by·law \'bī-,lȯ\ *n* **:** a rule adopted by an organization (as a club or municipality) chiefly for the government of its members and the regulation of its affairs
by–line \-,līn\ *n* **:** a line at the head of a newspaper or magazine article giving the writer's name
[1]**by·pass** \-,pas\ *n* **:** a passage to one side; *esp* **:** an alternate route around a congested area
[2]**bypass** *vt* **:** to make a detour or circuit around **:** avoid by means of a bypass
by–prod·uct \'bī-,präd-(,)əkt\ *n* **1 :** something produced (as in manufacturing) in addition to the principal product **2 :** a secondary and often unexpected or unintended result
by·road \-,rōd\ *n* **:** BYWAY
by·stand·er \-,stan-dər\ *n* **:** a person present or standing near but taking no part in something going on
by·way \-,wā\ *n* **1 :** a side road; *esp* **:** one that is little traveled **2 :** a secondary aspect or field
by·word \-,wərd\ *n* **1 :** a proverbial saying **2 :** an object of scorn or contempt

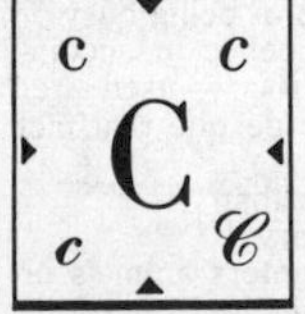

c \'sē\ *n, often cap* **1 :** the 3d letter of the English alphabet **2 :** the roman numeral 100 **3 :** the musical tone C **4 :** a grade rating a student's work as fair or mediocre
cab \'kab\ *n* **1 a :** CABRIOLET **b :** a light closed carriage (as a hansom) **2 :** TAXICAB **3 a :** the part of a locomotive that houses the engineer and operating controls **b :** a comparable shelter on a truck, tractor, or crane
ca·bal \kə-'bal\ *n* **:** a group of persons working together to promote their own interests esp. by intrigue
ca·bana \kə-'ban-(y)ə\ *n* **:** a beach shelter resembling a cabin usu. with an open side facing the sea
cab·a·ret \,kab-ə-'rā\ *n* **:** a restaurant serving liquor and providing entertainment (as by singers or dancers)
cab·bage \'kab-ij\ *n* **:** a garden plant related to the turnip and having a dense globular head of leaves used as a vegetable
cab·by *or* **cab·bie** \'kab-ē\ *n, pl* **cabbies :** a driver of a cab
cab·in \'kab-ən\ *n* **1 a :** a private room on a ship for one or a few persons **b :** a compartment below deck on a small boat for passengers or crew **c :** an airplane or airship compartment for cargo, crew, or passengers **2 :** a small one-story dwelling usu. of simple construction
cab·i·net \'kab-(ə-)nət\ *n* **1 a :** a case or cupboard usu. having doors and shelves **b :** an upright case housing a radio or

television : CONSOLE **2 a** : a group of ministers acting as advisers to a monarch or chief of state but constituting the real political executive **b** : a body of advisers to the president of the U.S. consisting chiefly of the heads of the executive departments

cab·i·net·mak·er \-ˌmā-kər\ *n* : a skilled woodworker who makes fine furniture — **cab·i·net·mak·ing** \-kiŋ\ *n*

cab·i·net·work \-ˌwərk\ *n* : the finished work of a cabinetmaker

[1]**ca·ble** \'kā-bəl\ *n* **1** : a very strong rope, wire, or chain **2 a** : a bundle of electrical conductors insulated from each other but held together usu. by being twisted around a central core **b** : CABLEGRAM

[2]**cable** *vb* **ca·bled**; **ca·bling** \'kā-b(ə-)liŋ\ : to telegraph by submarine cable

cable car *n* : a car moved on a railway by an endless cable or along an overhead cable

ca·ble·gram \'kā-bəl-ˌgram\ *n* : a message sent by submarine cable

cable TV *n* : COMMUNITY ANTENNA TELEVISION

ca·boose \kə-'büs\ *n* : a freight-train car attached usu. to the rear mainly for the use of the train crew and railroad workmen

cab·ri·o·let \ˌkab-rē-ə-'lā\ *n* **1** : a light 2-wheeled one-horse carriage with a folding leather hood and upward-curving shafts **2** : a convertible coupe

ca·cao \kə-'kaů, kə-'kā-ˌō\ *n, pl* **ca·caos** : a So. American tree with small yellowish flowers followed by fleshy yellow pods with many seeds; *also* : its dried partly fermented fatty seeds from which cocoa and chocolate are made

[1]**cache** \'kash\ *n* **1** : a place for hiding, storing, or safeguarding treasure, food, or other supplies **2** : the material hidden or stored in a cache

[2]**cache** *vt* : to place, hide, or store in a cache

ca·chet \ka-'shā\ *n* **1** : a seal esp. of official approval **2** : a characteristic feature or quality conferring prestige **3** : a commemorative device

cack·le \'kak-əl\ *vi* **cack·led**; **cack·ling** \-(ə-)liŋ\ **1** : to make the sharp broken noise or cry characteristic of a hen esp. after laying **2** : to laugh or chatter noisily — **cackle** *n* — **cack·ler** *n*

ca·coph·o·ny \ka-'käf-ə-nē\ *n, pl* **-nies** : harsh or discordant sound : DISSONANCE — **ca·coph·o·nous** \-nəs\ *adj*

cac·tus \'kak-təs\ *n, pl* **cac·tus·es** *or* **cac·ti** \-ˌtī, -(ˌ)tē\ : any of a large family of flowering plants able to live in dry regions and having fleshy stems and branches that bear scales or prickles instead of leaves

cad \'kad\ *n* : a person who behaves esp. deliberately in an ungentlemanly way

ca·dav·er \kə-'dav-ər\ *n* : a dead body esp. of a human being : CORPSE — **ca·dav·er·ic** \-'dav-ə-rik\ *adj*

ca·dav·er·ous \kə-'dav-(ə-)rəs\ *adj* : of, relating to, or having the look of a cadaver: as **a** : PALE, GHASTLY **b** : THIN, HAGGARD — **ca·dav·er·ous·ly** *adv*

[1]**cad·die** *or* **cad·dy** \'kad-ē\ *n, pl* **caddies** : a person who carries a golfer's clubs

[2]**caddie** *or* **caddy** *vi* **-died**; **-dy·ing** : to work as a caddie

cad·dish \'kad-ish\ *adj* : resembling a cad or the behavior of a cad — **cad·dish·ly** *adv* — **cad·dish·ness** *n*

cad·dy \'kad-ē\ *n, pl* **caddies** : a small box, can, or chest; *esp* : one to keep tea in

ca·dence \'kād-ᵊn(t)s\ *n* **1** : rhythmic flow of sounds in language **2** : the beat, time, or measure of rhythmical motion or activity — **ca·denced** \-ᵊn(t)st\ *adj*

ca·den·za \kə-'den-zə\ *n* : a technically brilliant sometimes improvised passage toward the close of a musical composition

ca·det \kə-'det\ *n* **1** : a younger brother or son **2** : one in training for a military commission; *esp* : a student in a service academy **3** : a student at a military school — **ca·det·ship** \-ˌship\ *n*

cadge \'kaj\ *vb* : BEG, SPONGE — **cadg·er** *n*

cad·mi·um \'kad-mē-əm\ *n* : a grayish white malleable ductile metallic element used esp. in protective platings and in bearing metals

cad·re \'kad-rē\ *n* : a nucleus of trained personnel capable of assuming leadership and of training others

ca·du·ce·us \kə-'d(y)ü-sē-əs\ *n, pl* **-cei** \-sē-ˌī\ : the staff of a herald; *esp* : a representation of a staff with two entwined snakes and two wings at the top

cae·su·ra \si-'z(h)ůr-ə\ *n, pl* **-su·ras** *or* **-su·rae** \-'z(h)ů(ə)r-(ˌ)ē\ : a break in the flow of sound usu. in the middle of a line of verse — **cae·su·ral** \-'z(h)ůr-əl\ *adj*

ca·fé \ka-'fā\ *n* **1** : COFFEEHOUSE **2** : BARROOM, SALOON **3** : RESTAURANT; *also* : NIGHTCLUB

ca·fé au lait \(ˌ)ka-ˌfā-ō-'lā\ *n* : coffee with usu. hot milk in about equal parts

caf·e·te·ria \ˌkaf-ə-'tir-ē-ə\ *n* : a restaurant in which the customers serve themselves or are served at a counter but take the food to tables to eat

caf·feine \ka-'fēn\ *n* : a bitter stimulating compound found esp. in coffee and tea

[1]**cage** \'kāj\ *n* **1** : a largely openwork enclosure for confining an animal **2** : an enclosure like a cage in form or purpose

[2]**cage** *vt* : to confine or keep in or as if in a cage

ca·gey \'kā-jē\ *adj* : wary of being trapped or deceived : SHREWD, CAUTIOUS — **ca·gi·ly** \-jə-lē\ *adv* — **ca·gi·ness** \-jē-nəs\ *n*

ca·hoot \kə-'hüt\ *n* : PARTNERSHIP, LEAGUE — usu. used in pl.

cairn \'ka(ə)rn\ *n* : a heap of stones piled up as a landmark or as a memorial

cais·son \'kā-ˌsän, 'kās-ᵊn\ *n* **1 a** : a chest for ammunition **b** : a 2-wheeled vehicle for artillery ammunition **2** : a watertight chamber used in construction work under water or as a foundation

cai·tiff \'kāt-əf\ *adj* : being base, cowardly, or despicable — **caitiff** *n*

ca·jole \kə-'jōl\ *vt* : to coax or persuade esp. by flattery or false promises : WHEEDLE — **ca·jol·ery** \-'jōl-(ə-)rē\ *n*

Ca·jun \'kā-jən\ *n* : a Louisianian descended from French-speaking immigrants from Acadia

[1]**cake** \'kāk\ *n* **1** : a small mass of food (as dough or batter, meat, or fish) baked or fried **2** : a baked food made from a mixture of flour, sugar, eggs, and flavoring **3** : a substance hardened or molded into a solid mass

[2]**cake** *vb* **1** : ENCRUST **2** : to form or harden into a mass

cal·a·bash \'kal-ə-ˌbash\ *n* : GOURD; *esp* : one whose hard shell is used for a utensil (as a bottle)

cal·a·mine \'kal-ə-ˌmīn\ *n* : a mixture of zinc oxide and ferric oxide used in lotions, liniments, and ointments

ca·lam·i·tous \kə-'lam-ət-əs\ *adj* : causing or accompanied by calamity : DISASTROUS — **ca·lam·i·tous·ly** *adv*

ca·lam·i·ty \kə-'lam-ət-ē\ *n, pl* **-ties** **1** : a state of deep distress or misfortune **2** : an event marked by great loss and lasting distress and affliction

cal·car·e·ous \kal-'kar-ē-əs\ *adj* **1** : resembling calcium carbonate esp. in hardness **2** : consisting of or containing calcium carbonate; *also* : containing calcium — **cal·car·e·ous·ly** *adv* — **cal·car·e·ous·ness** *n*

cal·ci·fi·ca·tion \ˌkal-sə-fə-'kā-shən\ *n* **1** : the process of calcifying **2** : a calcified structure

cal·ci·fy \'kal-sə-ˌfī\ *vb* **-fied**; **-fy·ing** **1** : to make calcareous by deposit of calcium salts **2** : to become calcareous

cal·ci·mine \'kal-sə-ˌmīn\ *n* : a thin water paint used esp. on plastered surfaces — **calcimine** *vt*

cal·cine \kal-'sīn\ *vt* : to heat to a high temperature but without fusing in order to drive off volatile matter and thus to disintegrate (as bone) or in order to produce an oxide of a metal — **cal·ci·na·tion** \ˌkal-sə-'nā-shən\ *n*

cal•ci•um \'kal-sē-əm\ *n* : a silver-white soft metallic chemical element that is found only in combination with other chemical elements (as in limestone) and that is one of the essential parts of the bodies of most plants and animals

calcium carbonate *n* : a solid substance found in nature as limestone and marble and in plant ashes, bones, and shells

cal•cu•late \'kal-kyə-ˌlāt\ *vb* **1 a** : to determine by mathematical processes **b** : to reckon by an informed guess : ESTIMATE **2** : to make a calculation **3** : to plan by careful thought **4** : RELY, DEPEND — **cal•cu•la•ble** \-kyə-lə-bəl\ *adj* — **cal•cu•la•bly** \-blē\ *adv*

cal•cu•lat•ed \-ˌlāt-əd\ *adj* : undertaken after estimating the probability of success or failure

cal•cu•lat•ing \-ˌlāt-iŋ\ *adj* **1** : designed to make calculations **2** : marked by shrewd analysis of one's own self-interest : SCHEMING

cal•cu•la•tion \ˌkal-kyə-'lā-shən\ *n* **1 a** : the process or an act of calculating **b** : the result of an act of calculating **2** : studied care in analyzing or planning : CAUTION

cal•cu•la•tor \'kal-kyə-ˌlāt-ər\ *n* **1** : one that calculates **2** : a machine for performing mathematical operations mechanically

cal•cu•lus \'kal-kyə-ləs\ *n, pl* **-li** \-ˌlī, -ˌlē\ : a method of computation or calculation in a special symbolic notation

cal•dron \'kȯl-drən\ *n* : a large kettle or boiler

[1]**cal•en•dar** \'kal-ən-dər\ *n* **1 a** : an arrangement of time into days, weeks, months, and years **b** : a sheet, folder, or book containing a record of such an arrangement for a certain period usu. a year **2** : an orderly list

[2]**calendar** *vt* : to enter in a calendar

[1]**cal•en•der** \'kal-ən-dər\ *vt* : to press (as cloth or paper) between rollers or plates in order to smooth and glaze or thin into sheets — **cal•en•der•er** *n*

[2]**calender** *n* : a machine for calendering cloth or paper

cal•ends \'kal-ən(d)z\ *n pl* : the first day of the ancient Roman month

[1]**calf** \'kaf, 'kȧf\ *n, pl* **calves** \'kavz, 'kȧvz\ **1 a** : the young of the domestic cow **b** : the young of various large animals (as the elephant or whale) **2** *pl* **calfs** : CALFSKIN **3** : an awkward or silly boy or youth

[2]**calf** *n, pl* **calves** : the fleshy back part of the leg below the knee

calf•skin \'kaf-ˌskin, 'kȧf-\ *n* : leather made of the skin of a calf

cal•i•ber *or* **cal•i•bre** \'kal-ə-bər\ *n* **1** : the diameter of a projectile **2** : the diameter of the bore of a gun **3 a** : mental ability or moral quality **b** : degree of excellence : QUALITY

cal•i•brate \'kal-ə-ˌbrāt\ *vt* **1** : to measure the caliber of **2** : to determine, correct, or put the measuring marks on (as a thermometer tube) — **cal•i•bra•tion** \ˌkal-ə-'brā-shən\ *n* — **cal•i•bra•tor** \'kal-ə-ˌbrāt-ər\ *n*

cal•i•co \'kal-i-ˌkō\ *n, pl* **-coes** *or* **-cos** : cotton cloth; *esp* : cotton cloth with a colored pattern printed on one side — **calico** *adj*

cal•i•for•ni•um \ˌkal-ə-'fȯr-nē-əm\ *n* : an artificially prepared radioactive chemical element

cal•i•per *or* **cal•li•per** \'kal-ə-pər\ *n* : a measuring instrument with two legs or jaws that can be adjusted to determine thickness, diameter, and distance between surfaces — usu. used in pl.

ca•liph *or* **ca•lif** \'kā-ləf, 'kal-əf\ *n* : a successor of Muhammad as temporal and spiritual head of Islam — used as a title — **ca•liph•ate** \-ˌāt\ *n*

cal•is•then•ics \ˌkal-əs-'then-iks\ *n sing or pl* : systematic bodily exercises without apparatus or with light hand apparatus — **cal•is•then•ic** \-ik\ *adj*

[1]**calk** \'kȯk\ *n* : a tapered piece projecting downward from a shoe (as of a horse) to prevent slipping

[2]**calk** *vt* **1** : to furnish with calks **2** : to wound with a calk

[1]**call** \'kȯl\ *vb* **1** : to speak in a loud distinct voice so as to be heard at a distance : CRY, SHOUT **2** : to utter in a loud clear voice **3** : to announce with authority : PROCLAIM **4** : to summon with a shout **5** : to bring into action or discussion **6** : to make an appeal, request, or demand **7** : to get in touch with by telephone **8** : SUMMON, CONVOKE **9** : to make a brief visit **10** : to give a name to : address by name **11** : to regard as being of a certain kind **12** : to estimate as being **13** *of an animal* : to utter a characteristic note or cry **14** : to make a demand in card games (as for a particular card or for a show of hands) **15** : SUSPEND — **call•er** *n*

[2]**call** *n* **1 a** : an act of calling with the voice : SHOUT **b** : a cry of an animal (as a bird) **2 a** : a request or command to assemble **b** : an invitation to become the minister of a church or to accept a professional appointment **3 a** : DEMAND, CLAIM **b** : NEED, JUSTIFICATION **c** : REQUEST **4** : a short visit **5** : a name or thing called **6** : the act of calling in a card game **7** : the act of calling on the telephone

cal•la \'kal-ə\ *n* : a plant of the arum family often grown for its white showy spathe surrounding a fleshy spike of yellow florets

cal•lig•ra•phy \kə-'lig-rə-fē\ *n* **1** : beautiful or elegant handwriting; *also* : the art of producing such writing **2** : PENMANSHIP — **cal•lig•ra•pher** \-fər\ *n* — **cal•li•graph•ic** \ˌkal-ə-'graf-ik\ *adj*

call•ing \'kȯ-liŋ\ *n* **1** : a strong inner impulse; *esp* : one accompanied by conviction of divine influence **2** : one's customary vocation or profession

cal•li•o•pe \kə-'lī-ə-(ˌ)pē, 'kal-ē-ˌōp\ *n* : a musical instrument consisting of a series of whistles played by keys arranged as in an organ

call off *vt* **1** : to draw away : DIVERT **2** : CANCEL

cal•los•i•ty \ka-'läs-ət-ē\ *n, pl* **-ties** **1** : the quality or state of being callous **2** : CALLUS 1

[1]**cal•lous** \'kal-əs\ *adj* **1** : so thickened and usu. hardened as to form a callus **2** : deficient in emotional response : UNFEELING — **cal•lous•ly** *adv* — **cal•lous•ness** *n*

[2]**callous** *vt* : to make callous

cal•low \'kal-ō\ *adj* : lacking adult sophistication : IMMATURE — **cal•low•ness** *n*

[1]**cal•lus** \'kal-əs\ *n* **1** : a thickening of or a hard thickened area on skin or bark **2** : a mass of tissue that is converted into bone in the healing of a bone fracture

[2]**callus** *vi* : to form callus

[1]**calm** \'käm\ *n* **1** : a period or condition of freedom from storm, wind, or rough activity of water **2** : a state of repose and freedom from turmoil or agitation

[2]**calm** *adj* **1** : marked by calm : STILL **2** : free from agitation, excitement, or disturbance — **calm•ly** *adv* — **calm•ness** *n*

[3]**calm** *vb* **1** : to become calm **2** : to make calm

cal•o•mel \'kal-ə-məl, -ˌmel\ *n* : a white tasteless substance that occurs as a mineral or is made chemically and that is used as a cathartic, fungicide, and insecticide

ca•lor•ic \kə-'lȯr-ik\ *adj* **1** : of or relating to heat **2** : of or relating to calories — **ca•lor•i•cal•ly** \-i-k(ə-)lē\ *adv*

cal•o•rie *or* **cal•o•ry** \'kal-(ə-)rē\ *n, pl* **-ries** : a unit of heat: **a** : the heat required to raise the temperature of one gram of water one degree centigrade **b** : 1000 small calories — used esp. to indicate the value of foods in producing heat and energy

cal•o•rif•ic \ˌkal-ə-'rif-ik\ *adj* : CALORIC

cal•o•rim•e•ter \ˌkal-ə-'rim-ət-ər\ *n* : an apparatus for measuring quantities of heat — **cal•o•ri•met•ric** \ˌkal-ə-rə-'me-trik\ *adj* — **cal•o•ri•met•ri•cal•ly** \-'me-tri-k(ə-)lē\ *adv* — **cal•o•rim•e•try** \-'rim-ə-trē\ *n*

cal•u•met \'kal-yə-ˌmet\ *n* : an ornamented ceremonial pipe of the American Indians

ca•lum•ni•ate \kə-'ləm-nē-ˌāt\ *vt* : to accuse falsely and maliciously : SLANDER — **ca·lum·ni·a·tion** \-ˌləm-nē-ˈā-shən\ *n* — **ca·lum·ni·a·tor** \-ˈləm-nē-ˌāt-ər\ *n*

cal·um·ny \ˈkal-əm-nē\ *n, pl* **-nies** : a false accusation made to injure another person's character — **ca·lum·ni·ous** \kə-ˈləm-nē-əs\ *adj* — **ca·lum·ni·ous·ly** *adv*

calve \ˈkav, ˈkȧv\ *vi* : to give birth to a calf

calves *pl of* CALF

Cal·vin·ism \ˈkal-və-ˌniz-əm\ *n* : the system of theological teachings and practices of John Calvin and his followers emphasizing the absolute power of God, the total depravity of man, and election — **Cal·vin·ist** \-və-nəst\ *n or adj* — **Cal·vin·is·tic** \ˌkal-və-ˈnis-tik\ *adj*

ca·lyp·so \kə-ˈlip-sō\ *n, pl* **-sos** : an improvised ballad usu. satirizing current events in a rhythmic style originating in the British West Indies

ca·lyx \ˈkā-liks, ˈkal-iks\ *n, pl* **ca·lyx·es** *or* **ca·ly·ces** \ˈkā-lə-ˌsēz, ˈkal-ə-\ : the external usu. green or leafy part of a flower consisting of sepals

cam \ˈkam\ *n* : a device that consists of a plate or cylinder on a revolving shaft and that transmits motion by means of its edge or a groove to another mechanical part (as a rod or lever) so that circular motion may be transformed into intermittent or back-and-forth motion

ca·ma·ra·de·rie \ˌkam-(ə-)ˈrad-ə-rē, ˌkäm-(ə-)ˈräd-\ *n* : good feeling existing between comrades

cam·ber \ˈkam-bər\ *n* : a slight convexity, arching, or curvature (as of a beam, deck, or road)

cam·bi·um \ˈkam-bē-əm\ *n, pl* **-bi·ums** *or* **-bia** \-bē-ə\ : a thin cell layer between the xylem and phloem of most vascular plants from which new cells (as of wood and bark) develop — **cam·bi·al** \-bē-əl\ *adj*

cam·bric \ˈkām-brik\ *n* : a fine thin white linen fabric; *also* : a similar cotton fabric

came *past of* COME

cam·el \ˈkam-əl\ *n* : either of two large cud-chewing mammals used as draft and saddle animals in desert regions esp. of Africa and Asia: **a** : a single-humped camel of southwestern Asia and Africa **b** : a two-humped camel of central Asian origin

cam·el·back \-ˌbak\ *n* : an uncured compound chiefly of reclaimed or synthetic rubber used for retreading or recapping pneumatic tires

ca·mel·lia \kə-ˈmēl-yə\ *n* : any of several shrubs or trees of the tea family grown in warm regions for their showy roselike flowers

ca·mel·o·pard \kə-ˈmel-ə-ˌpärd\ *n* : GIRAFFE

camel's hair *n* : a fabric made of the hair of camels or of a mixture of this hair with wool

cam·eo \ˈkam-ē-ˌō\ *n, pl* **-e·os** : a gem carved in such a way that the design is higher than its background

cam·era \ˈkam-(ə-)rə\ *n* **1** : a judge's private office **2** : a lighttight box fitted with a lens through the opening of which the image of an object is recorded on a material that is sensitive to light **3** : the part of a television transmitting apparatus in which the image to be televised is formed for change into electrical impulses

cam·era·man \-ˌman, -mən\ *n* : one that operates a camera

cam·i·sole \ˈkam-ə-ˌsōl\ *n* : a short sleeveless undergarment for women

cam·ou·flage \ˈkam-ə-ˌfläzh\ *n* **1 a** : the disguising of military equipment or installations with paint, nets, or foliage **b** : the disguise so applied **2** : behavior or a trick intended to deceive or hide — **camouflage** *vt*

¹camp \ˈkamp\ *n* **1 a** : ground on which temporary shelters are erected **b** : a group of tents or buildings erected on the ground **2** : a body of persons holding a theory or doctrine **3** : military service or life

²camp *vb* **1** : to make or occupy a camp **2** : to live in a camp or outdoors — **camp·er** *n*

cam·paign \kam-ˈpān\ *n* **1** : a series of military operations forming a distinct phase of a war **2** : a connected series of operations designed to bring about a particular result — **campaign** *vi* — **cam·paign·er** *n*

cam·pa·ni·le \ˌkam-pə-ˈnē-lē\ *n* : a bell tower; *esp* : one built separate from another building

cam·phor \ˈkam(p)-fər\ *n* : a tough gummy volatile fragrant crystalline compound obtained esp. from the wood and bark of the camphor tree and used esp. in medicine and the chemical industry

camphor tree *n* : a large evergreen Asiatic tree of the laurel family

camp meeting *n* : a series of evangelistic meetings held outdoors or in a tent

camp·o·ree \ˌkam-pə-ˈrē\ *n* : a gathering of boy or girl scouts from a given geographic area

camp·stool \ˈkamp-ˌstül\ *n* : a folding stool

cam·pus \ˈkam-pəs\ *n* : the grounds of a college or a school

¹can \kən, (ˈ)kan\ *auxiliary verb, past* **could** \kəd, (ˈ)kůd\; *pres sing & pl* **can** **1 a** : know how to **b** : be able to **c** : be permitted by conscience or feeling **d** : be inherently able or designed to **e** : be enabled by law, agreement, or custom to **2** : have permission to

²can \ˈkan\ *n* **1** : a usu. cylindrical metal receptacle **2** : the contents of a can

³can \ˈkan\ *vt* **canned**; **can·ning** : to put in a can; *esp* : to preserve by sealing in an airtight can or jar

ca·naille \kə-ˈnāl, -ˈnī\ *n* : RABBLE, RIFFRAFF

ca·nal \kə-ˈnal\ *n* **1** : a tubular anatomical passage or channel : DUCT **2** : an artificial waterway for navigation or for draining or irrigating land

ca·nard \kə-ˈnärd\ *n* : a false or unfounded report or story; *esp* : one deliberately made up

ca·nary \kə-ˈne(ə)r-ē\ *n, pl* **-nar·ies** **1** : a sweet wine made in the Canary islands **2** : a small usu. yellow or greenish finch often kept as a cage bird

ca·nas·ta \kə-ˈnas-tə\ *n* : rummy using two decks plus four jokers

can·can \ˈkan-ˌkan\ *n* : a woman's dance of French origin characterized by high kicking

¹can·cel \ˈkan(t)-səl\ *vb* **-celed** *or* **-celled**; **-cel·ing** *or* **-cel·ling** \-s(ə-)liŋ\ **1 a** : to mark or strike out for deletion **b** : OMIT, DELETE **2 a** : to destroy the force, effectiveness, or validity of : ANNUL **b** : to match in force or effect : OFFSET **3 a** : to remove (a common divisor) from numerator and denominator **b** : to remove (equivalents) on opposite sides of an equation or account **4** : to deface (a postage or revenue stamp) esp. with a set of parallel lines so as to invalidate for reuse — **can·cel·er** *or* **can·cel·ler** *n*

²cancel *n* : CANCELLATION

can·cel·la·tion \ˌkan(t)-sə-ˈlā-shən\ *n* **1** : an act of canceling **2** : a mark made to cancel something

can·cer \ˈkan(t)-sər\ *n* **1** : a malignant tumor that tends to spread locally and to other parts of the body **2** : a dangerous evil that eats away slowly but fatally — **can·cer·ous** \ˈkan(t)s-(ə-)rəs\ *adj*

can·de·la·bra \ˌkan-də-ˈläb-rə, -ˈlab-\ *n* : CANDELABRUM

can·de·la·brum \-rəm\ *n, pl* **-bra** \-rə\ *or* **-brums** : a candlestick that has several branches for holding more than one candle

can·did \ˈkan-dəd\ *adj* **1** : free from bias, prejudice, or malice : FAIR **2** : marked by honest sincere expression **3** : relating to photography of subjects acting naturally or spontaneously without being posed — **can·did·ly** *adv* — **can·did·ness** *n*

can·di·da·cy \ˈkan-dəd-ə-sē\ *n, pl* **-cies** : the state of being a candidate

can·di·date \ˈkan-də-ˌdāt\ *n* : one who offers himself or is proposed by others for an office, membership, right, or honor

can·died \'kan-dēd\ *adj* **1 :** encrusted or coated with sugar **2 :** baked with sugar or syrup until translucent

¹can·dle \'kan-dᵊl\ *n* **:** a long slender cylindrical mass of tallow or wax containing a loosely twisted linen or cotton wick that is burned to give light

²candle *vt* **can·dled**; **can·dling** \'kan-dliŋ, -dᵊl-iŋ\ **:** to examine (an egg) by holding between the eye and a light — **can·dler** \-dlər, -dᵊl-ər\ *n*

can·dle·light \'kan-dᵊl-ˌ(l)īt\ *n* **1 a :** the light of a candle **b :** a soft artificial light **2 :** the time when candles are lit **:** TWILIGHT

can·dle·lit \-dᵊl-ˌ(l)it\ *adj* **:** illuminated by candlelight

Can·dle·mas \'kan-dᵊl-məs\ *n* **:** February 2 observed as a church festival in commemoration of the presentation of Christ in the temple

can·dle·pin \'kan-dᵊl-ˌpin\ *n* **1 :** a slender bowling pin tapering toward top and bottom **2** *pl* **:** a bowling game using candlepins and a smaller ball than in tenpins

can·dle·stick \-ˌstik\ *n* **:** a holder with a socket for a candle

can·dor \'kan-dər\ *n* **1 :** freedom from prejudice **:** IMPARTIALITY **2 :** FRANKNESS, OUTSPOKENNESS

¹can·dy \'kan-dē\ *n, pl* **-dies :** a confection made of sugar often with flavoring and filling

²candy *vb* **can·died**; **can·dy·ing 1 :** to coat or become coated with sugar often by cooking **2 :** to make seem attractive **:** SWEETEN **3 :** to crystallize into sugar

¹cane \'kān\ *n* **1 a :** a hollow or pithy and usu. slender, flexible, and jointed stem (as of a reed or bramble) **b :** any of various tall woody grasses or reeds; *esp* **:** SUGARCANE **2 a :** a walking stick **b :** a rod for flogging

²cane *vt* **1 :** to beat with a cane **2 :** to make or repair with cane

cane·brake \-ˌbrāk\ *n* **:** a thicket of cane

¹ca·nine \'kā-ˌnīn\ *adj* **1 :** of or relating to dogs or to the family that includes the dogs, wolves, jackals, and foxes **2 :** of, relating to, or resembling a dog

²canine *n* **1 :** a conical pointed tooth next to the incisors **2 :** DOG

can·is·ter \'kan-əs-tər\ *n* **1 :** a small box or can for holding a dry product (as tea, coffee, flour, or sugar) **2 :** a shell for close-range artillery fire **3 :** a perforated box that contains material to absorb, filter, or make harmless a poisonous or irritating substance in the air

can·ker \'kaŋ-kər\ *n* **1 :** a spreading sore that eats into the tissue **2 :** a source of corruption or destruction — **can·ker·ous** \'kaŋ-k(ə-)rəs\ *adj*

can·ker·worm \'kaŋ-kər-ˌwərm\ *n* **:** an insect larva (as a caterpillar) that injures plants

canned \'kand\ *adj* **1 :** preserved in a sealed can or jar **2 :** transcribed for radio or television reproduction

can·nel coal \ˌkan-ᵊl-\ *n* **:** a bituminous coal containing much volatile matter that burns brightly

can·ner \'kan-ər\ *n* **:** a person whose business or occupation is canning food

can·nery \'kan-(ə-)rē\ *n, pl* **-ner·ies :** a factory for the canning of food

can·ni·bal \'kan-ə-bəl\ *n* **1 :** a human being who eats human flesh **2 :** an animal that eats its own kind — **cannibal** *adj* — **can·ni·bal·ism** \-bə-ˌliz-əm\ *n* — **can·ni·bal·is·tic** \ˌkan-ə-bə-'lis-tik\ *adj*

can·ni·bal·ize \'kan-ə-bə-ˌlīz\ *vb* **:** to dismantle a machine for parts to be used as replacements in other machines

can·non \'kan-ən\ *n, pl* **cannons** *or* **cannon :** a heavy gun mounted on a carriage and fired from that position

¹can·non·ade \ˌkan-ə-'nād\ *n* **:** a heavy firing of artillery

²cannonade *vb* **:** to attack with artillery

can·non·ball \'kan-ən-ˌbȯl\ *n* **:** a round solid missile made for firing from a cannon

can·non·eer \ˌkan-ə-'ni(ə)r\ *n* **:** an artilleryman who tends and fires cannon **:** GUNNER

can·not \'kan-(ˌ)ät; kə-'nät\ **:** can not — **cannot but :** to be bound to **:** MUST

can·ny \'kan-ē\ *adj* **:** being cautious and shrewd **:** watchful of one's own interests — **can·ni·ly** \'kan-ᵊl-ē\ *adv* — **can·ni·ness** \'kan-ē-nəs\ *n*

¹ca·noe \kə-'nü\ *n* **:** a long light narrow boat with sharp ends and curved sides that is usu. paddled by hand

²canoe *vb* **ca·noed**; **ca·noe·ing :** to travel or transport in a canoe — **ca·noe·ist** *n*

¹can·on \'kan-ən\ *n* **1 :** a church law or doctrinal decree **2 :** an official or authoritative list (as of the saints or of the books of the Bible) **3 :** an accepted principle or rule

²canon *n* **:** a clergyman on the staff of a cathedral

ca·non·i·cal \kə-'nän-i-kəl\ *adj* **1 :** of, relating to, or complying with church law **2 :** accepted as authoritative or genuine — **ca·non·i·cal·ly** \-k(ə-)lē\ *adv*

can·on·ize \'kan-ə-ˌnīz\ *vt* **1 :** to declare (a beatified person) to be a saint and worthy of public veneration throughout the church **2 :** GLORIFY, EXALT — **can·on·i·za·tion** \ˌkan-ə-nə-'zā-shən\ *n*

¹can·o·py \'kan-ə-pē\ *n, pl* **-pies 1 :** a covering suspended over a bed, throne, or shrine or carried on poles over a person of high rank or over some sacred object **2 :** an overhanging shade or shelter — **can·o·py·like** \-ˌlīk\ *adj*

²canopy *vt* **-pied**; **-py·ing :** to cover with a canopy

¹cant \'kant\ *n* **1 :** a slanting surface (as of a buttress or bank of earth) **2 :** TILT, SLOPE, INCLINE

²cant *vt* **1 :** to give a cant or oblique edge to **2 :** to set at an angle **:** TIP

³cant *vi* **1 :** BEG **2 :** to talk hypocritically

⁴cant *n* **1 a :** ARGOT **b :** JARGON **2 :** insincere speech; *esp* **:** pious words or statements

can·ta·bi·le \kän-'täb-ə-ˌlā\ *adv (or adj)* **:** in a singing manner — used as a direction in music

can·ta·loupe \'kant-ᵊl-ˌōp\ *n* **:** MUSKMELON; *esp* **:** a muskmelon with a hard ridged or warty rind and reddish orange flesh

can·tan·ker·ous \kan-'taŋ-k(ə-)rəs\ *adj* **:** ILL-NATURED, QUARRELSOME — **can·tan·ker·ous·ly** *adv* — **can·tan·ker·ous·ness** *n*

can·ta·ta \kən-'tät-ə\ *n* **:** a poem or narrative set to music to be sung by a chorus and soloists

can·teen \kan-'tēn\ *n* **1 :** a store (as in a camp or a factory) in which food, drinks, and small supplies are sold **2 :** a place of recreation and entertainment for servicemen **3 :** a small container used for carrying liquid (as drinking water)

¹can·ter \'kant-ər\ *vb* **:** to move or cause to move at or as if at a canter **:** LOPE

²canter *n* **:** a 3-beat gait (as of a horse) resembling but smoother and slower than the gallop

can·ti·cle \'kant-i-kəl\ *n* **1 :** SONG **2 :** one of several liturgical songs taken from the Bible

can·ti·le·ver \'kant-ᵊl-ˌē-vər, -ˌev-ər\ *n* **1 :** a projecting beam or structure fastened only at one end **2 :** either of two beams or structures that project from piers toward each other and when joined form a span in a bridge

can·tle \'kant-ᵊl\ *n* **:** the upwardly projecting rear part of a saddle

can·to \'kan-ˌtō\ *n, pl* **cantos :** one of the major divisions of a long poem

¹can·ton \'kant-ᵊn, 'kan-ˌtän\ *n* **:** a small territorial division of a country; *esp* **:** one of the states of the Swiss confederation — **can·ton·al** \'kant-ᵊn-əl, kan-'tän-ᵊl\ *adj*

²can·ton \'kant-ᵊn, 'kan-ˌtän, *in sense 2 usu* kan-'tōn *or* -'tän\ *vt* **1 :** to divide into cantons **2 :** to allot quarters to (troops)

can·ton·ment \kan-'tōn-mənt, -'tän-\ *n* **:** a group of temporary structures for housing troops

can·tor \'kant-ər\ *n* **:** a synagogue official who sings or chants the liturgy and leads the congregation in prayer

can·vas \'kan-vəs\ *n* **1 :** a strong cloth of hemp, flax, or cotton that is used esp. for making tents and sails **2 :** something made of canvas or on canvas; *esp* **:** an oil painting **3 :** the floor of a boxing or wrestling ring

can·vas·back \-ˌbak\ *n* **:** a No. American wild duck with reddish head and grayish back

can·vass \ˈkan-vəs\ *vb* **1 :** to examine in detail **2 a :** to go through (an area) soliciting something (as information, contributions, or votes) **b :** to ask for information, money, or votes — **canvass** *n* — **can·vass·er** *n*

can·yon \ˈkan-yən\ *n* **:** a deep valley with high steep slopes and often with a stream flowing through it

caou·tchouc \kau̇-ˈchük\ *n* **:** RUBBER 2

¹cap \ˈkap\ *n* **1 :** a head covering; *esp* **:** one for men and boys that has a visor and no brim **2 :** something like a cap in appearance, position, or function **3 :** a paper or metal container holding an explosive charge (as for a toy pistol)

²cap *vt* **capped; cap·ping** **1 :** to provide with a cap **2 :** to match with something equal or better

ca·pa·bil·i·ty \ˌkā-pə-ˈbil-ət-ē\ *n, pl* **-ties** **1 :** the quality or state of being capable **2 :** a feature or faculty capable of development **:** POTENTIALITY

ca·pa·ble \ˈkā-pə-bəl\ *adj* **1 :** having the ability, capacity, or power to do something **2 :** of such a nature as to permit **:** SUSCEPTIBLE **3 :** EFFICIENT, COMPETENT — **ca·pa·bly** \-blē\ *adv*

ca·pa·cious \kə-ˈpā-shəs\ *adj* **:** able to contain a great deal **:** not narrow — **ca·pa·cious·ly** *adv* — **ca·pa·cious·ness** *n*

ca·pac·i·ty \kə-ˈpas-ət-ē\ *n, pl* **-ties** **1 a :** the ability to hold or accommodate **b :** a measure of content **:** VOLUME **c :** productive ability or potential **2 :** legal competence **3 :** ABILITY, CALIBER **4 :** a position or character assigned or assumed

cap–a–pie *or* **cap–à–pie** \ˌkap-ə-ˈpē\ *adv* **:** from head to foot **:** at all points

ca·par·i·son \kə-ˈpar-ə-sən\ *n* **1 :** an ornamental covering for a horse **2 :** rich clothing **:** ADORNMENT — **caparison** *vt*

¹cape \ˈkāp\ *n* **:** a point or extension of land jutting out into water either as a peninsula or as a projecting point

²cape *n* **:** a sleeveless garment that fits closely at the neck and hangs loosely from the shoulders

¹ca·per \ˈkā-pər\ *n* **1 :** any of a genus of low prickly shrubs of the Mediterranean region **2 :** one of the flower buds of the caper pickled for use as a relish

²caper *vi* **ca·pered; ca·per·ing** \-p(ə-)riŋ\ **:** to leap about in a gay frolicsome way

³caper *n* **1 :** a gay bounding leap **2 :** PRANK, TRICK

cape·skin \ˈkāp-ˌskin\ *n* **:** a light flexible leather made from sheepskins with the natural grain retained

cap·il·lar·i·ty \ˌkap-ə-ˈlar-ət-ē\ *n* **:** the action by which the surface of a liquid where (as in a slender tube) it is in contact with a solid is raised or lowered depending upon the relative attraction of the molecules of the liquid for each other and for those of the solid

¹cap·il·lary \ˈkap-ə-ˌler-ē\ *adj* **1 :** resembling a hair; *esp* **:** having a very small bore **2 :** of or relating to capillaries or capillarity

²capillary *n, pl* **-lar·ies** **:** any of the tiny thin-walled tubes that carry blood between the smallest arteries and their corresponding veins

¹cap·i·tal \ˈkap-ət-ᵊl\ *adj* **1 a :** punishable by death **b :** resulting in death **2 :** being a letter that belongs to or conforms to the series A, B, C, etc. rather than a, b, c, etc. **3 a :** first in importance or influence **:** CHIEF **b :** being the seat of government **4 :** EXCELLENT

²capital *n* **1 a :** accumulated goods on hand at a specified time in contrast to income received over a specified period **b :** the excess of assets over liabilities **2 a :** capital goods and invested savings used in the process of production **b :** possessions (as money) used to bring in income **c :** persons owning or investing capital **:** CAPITALISTS **d :** the total face value of shares of stock issued by a company **3 :** ADVANTAGE, GAIN **4 :** a capital letter **5 :** a capital city

³capital *n* **:** the top part or piece of an architectural column

capital goods *n pl* **:** machinery, tools, factories, and commodities used in the production of goods

cap·i·tal·ism \ˈkap-ət-ᵊl-ˌiz-əm\ *n* **:** an economic system in which natural resources and means of production are privately owned and prices, production, and the distribution of goods are determined mainly by competition in a free market — **cap·i·tal·ist** \-ᵊl-əst\ *or* **cap·i·tal·is·tic** \ˌkap-ət-ᵊl-ˈis-tik\ *adj*

cap·i·tal·ist \ˈkap-ət-ᵊl-əst\ *n* **1 :** a person who has or controls a great amount of business capital **2 :** a person who favors capitalism

cap·i·tal·i·za·tion \ˌkap-ət-ᵊl-ə-ˈzā-shən\ *n* **1 :** the act or process of capitalizing **2 :** the amount of money used as capital in a business

cap·i·tal·ize \ˈkap-ət-ᵊl-ˌīz\ *vb* **1 :** to write or print with an initial capital or in capitals **2 a :** to charge (an expenditure) to a capital account **b** (1) **:** to supply capital for (2) **:** to use as capital **3 :** to act profitably

cap·i·tal·ly \ˈkap-ət-ᵊl-ē\ *adv* **:** in a capital manner

cap·i·ta·tion \ˌkap-ə-ˈtā-shən\ *n* **:** a direct uniform tax imposed upon each head or person

cap·i·tol \ˈkap-ət-ᵊl\ *n* **:** a building in which a legislative body meets

ca·pit·u·late \kə-ˈpich-ə-ˌlāt\ *vi* **:** to surrender usu. on terms agreed upon in advance

ca·pit·u·la·tion \kə-ˌpich-ə-ˈlā-shən\ *n* **1 :** a set of terms or articles constituting an agreement between governments **2 :** an act of capitulating

ca·pon \ˈkā-ˌpän\ *n* **:** a castrated male chicken — **ca·pon·ize** \ˈkā-pə-ˌnīz\ *vt*

ca·pric·cio \kə-ˈprē-chō, -chē-ˌō\ *n, pl* **-cios** **:** an instrumental piece in free form usu. lively in tempo and brilliant in style

ca·price \kə-ˈprēs\ *n* **1 :** a sudden unpredictable turn or change **2 :** a disposition to change one's mind impulsively **3 :** CAPRICCIO

ca·pri·cious \kə-ˈprish-əs\ *adj* **:** moved or controlled by caprice — **ca·pri·cious·ly** *adv* — **ca·pri·cious·ness** *n*

cap·size \ˈkap-ˌsīz, kap-ˈ\ *vb* **:** to turn over **:** UPSET

cap·stan \ˈkap-stən\ *n* **:** a mechanical device that consists of an upright revolving drum to which a rope is fastened and that is used on ships for moving or raising weights and for exerting pulling force

cap·su·lar \ˈkap-sə-lər\ *adj* **:** of, relating to, or resembling a capsule

cap·su·late \-ˌlāt, -lət\ *or* **cap·su·lat·ed** \-ˌlāt-əd\ *adj* **:** enclosed in a capsule

¹cap·sule \ˈkap-səl, -ˌsül\ *n* **1 :** an enveloping cover: as **a :** a dry dehiscent fruit made up of two or more united carpels **b :** an edible shell (as of gelatin) enclosing medicine **2 :** a small pressurized compartment for an aviator or astronaut for flight or emergency escape

²capsule *adj* **1 :** extremely brief **2 :** being small and very compact

¹cap·tain \ˈkap-tən\ *n* **1 :** a leader of a group **2 a :** a commissioned officer in the navy ranking next below a rear admiral or a commodore **b :** a commissioned officer (as in the army) ranking next below a major **3 :** the commanding officer of a ship — **cap·tain·ship** \-ˌship\ *n*

²captain *vt* **:** to be captain of **:** LEAD

cap·tain·cy \ˈkap-tən-sē\ *n, pl* **-cies** **:** a captain's rank or position

¹cap·tion \ˈkap-shən\ *n* **1 :** the heading esp. of an article or document **2 :** the explanatory comment or designation accompanying a pictorial illustration

²caption *vt* **:** to furnish with a caption **:** ENTITLE

cap·tious \'kap-shəs\ *adj* : quick to find fault esp. over trifles — **cap·tious·ly** *adv* — **cap·tious·ness** *n*
cap·ti·vate \'kap-tə-ˌvāt\ *vb* : to attract with appeal and win over : CHARM, FASCINATE — **cap·ti·va·tion** \ˌkap-tə-'vā-shən\ *n* — **cap·ti·va·tor** \'kap-tə-ˌvāt-ər\ *n*
[1]**cap·tive** \'kap-tiv\ *adj* **1 a** : taken and held prisoner esp. in war **b** : held or confined so as to prevent escape **2** : of or relating to captivity
[2]**captive** *n* : one that is captive : PRISONER
cap·tiv·i·ty \kap-'tiv-ət-ē\ *n, pl* **-ties** : the state of being captive
cap·tor \'kap-tər\ *n* : one that captures
[1]**cap·ture** \'kap-chər\ *n* **1** : the act of catching or gaining control by force, stratagem, or guile **2** : one that has been taken captive
[2]**capture** *vt* **cap·tured**; **cap·tur·ing** \'kap-chə-riŋ, 'kap-shriŋ\ **1** : to take captive : WIN, GAIN **2** : to preserve in a relatively permanent form
Cap·u·chin \'kap-yə-shən, kə-'p(y)ü-\ *n* : a member of an austere branch of the first order of St. Francis of Assisi engaged in missionary work and preaching
car \'kär\ *n* **1** : a vehicle moved on wheels **2** : the cage of an elevator **3** : the part of a balloon or an airship in which passengers or equipment are carried
ca·ra·bao \ˌkar-ə-'baů\ *n, pl* **-baos** : WATER BUFFALO
car·a·cole \'kar-ə-ˌkōl\ *n* : a half turn to right or left executed by a mounted horse — **caracole** *vb*
ca·rafe \kə-'raf\ *n* : a bottle with a wide base and flaring lip used to hold water or beverages
car·a·mel \'kar-ə-məl, 'kär-məl\ *n* **1** : a brittle brown and somewhat bitter substance obtained by heating sugar and used as a coloring and flavoring agent **2** : a firm chewy candy usu. in small blocks
car·a·mel·ize \-mə-ˌlīz\ *vb* : to turn into caramel — **car·a·mel·i·za·tion** \ˌkar-ə-mə-lə-'zā-shən, ˌkär-mə-\ *n*
car·a·pace \'kar-ə-ˌpās\ *n* : a protective case or shield covering the back of an animal (as a turtle)
car·at \'kar-ət\ *n* : a unit of weight for precious stones (as diamonds) equal to 200 milligrams
car·a·van \'kar-ə-ˌvan\ *n* **1 a** : a company of travelers on a journey through desert or hostile regions **b** : a group of vehicles traveling together in a file **2** : a covered vehicle; *esp* : one equipped as traveling living quarters
car·a·van·sa·ry \ˌkar-ə-'van(t)-sə-rē\ *n, pl* **-ries** **1** : an inn in eastern countries where caravans rest at night **2** : HOTEL, INN
car·a·vel \'kar-ə-ˌvel\ *n* : a small 15th and 16th century ship with broad bows, high narrow poop, and lateen sails
car·a·way \'kar-ə-ˌwā\ *n* : a usu. white-flowered aromatic herb of the carrot family with pungent fruits used in seasoning and medicine
car·bine \'kär-ˌbēn, -ˌbīn\ *n* : a short light rifle
car·bo·hy·drate \ˌkär-bō-'hī-ˌdrāt\ *n* : any of various neutral compounds of carbon, hydrogen, and oxygen (as sugars, starches, or celluloses)
car·bo·lat·ed \'kär-bə-ˌlāt-əd\ *adj* : impregnated with carbolic acid
car·bol·ic acid \ˌkär-ˌbäl-ik-\ *n* : PHENOL
car·bon \'kär-bən\ *n* **1** : a chemical element found native (as in the diamond and graphite) or as a constituent of coal, petroleum, and asphalt, of limestone and other carbonates, and of organic compounds **2 a** : a sheet of carbon paper **b** : a copy made with carbon paper
[1]**car·bon·ate** \'kär-bə-ˌnāt, -nət\ *n* : a salt or ester of carbonic acid
[2]**car·bon·ate** \-ˌnāt\ *vt* : to impregnate with carbon dioxide — **car·bon·a·tion** \ˌkär-bə-'nā-shən\ *n*
carbon copy *n* **1** : a copy made by carbon paper **2** : DUPLICATE
carbon dioxide *n* : a heavy colorless gas that does not support combustion, is formed esp. by the combustion and decomposition of organic substances, is absorbed from the air by plants in photosynthesis, and is used in the carbonation of beverages
carbon 14 *n* : a heavy radioactive form of carbon used for determining the age of very old specimens of formerly living materials
car·bon·ic acid \ˌkär-ˌbän-ik-\ *n* : a weak acid that decomposes readily into water and carbon dioxide
car·bon·if·er·ous \ˌkär-bə-'nif-(ə-)rəs\ *adj* : producing or containing carbon or coal
carbon monoxide *n* : a colorless odorless very poisonous gas formed by the incomplete burning of carbon
carbon paper *n* : a thin paper coated with a waxy substance containing pigment and used in making copies of written or printed matter
car·bun·cle \'kär-ˌbəŋ-kəl\ *n* : a painful inflammation of the skin and deeper tissues that discharges pus from several openings — **car·bun·cled** \-kəld\ *adj* — **car·bun·cu·lar** \kär-'bəŋ-kyə-lər\ *adj*
car·bu·re·tor \'kär-b(y)ə-ˌrāt-ər\ *n* : an apparatus for supplying an internal-combustion engine with vaporized fuel mixed with air in an explosive mixture
car·cass \'kär-kəs\ *n* : a dead body; *esp* : the dressed body of a meat animal
car·cin·o·gen \kär-'sin-ə-jən\ *n* : a substance or agent producing or inciting cancer — **car·ci·no·gen·ic** \ˌkärs-ᵊn-ō-'jen-ik\ *adj* — **car·ci·no·ge·nic·i·ty** \-jə-'nis-ət-ē\ *n*
[1]**card** \'kärd\ *vt* : to cleanse and untangle (fibers) by combing with a card before spinning — **card·er** *n*
[2]**card** *n* : an instrument usu. having bent wire teeth for combing fibers (as wool or cotton)
[3]**card** *n* **1** : PLAYING CARD **2** *pl* **a** : a game played with cards **b** : card playing **3** : a clownishly amusing person **4 a** : a stiff usu. small rectangular piece of paper or thin paperboard **b** : a sports program
card·board \'kärd-ˌbōrd\ *n* : a stiff moderately thick board made of paper
car·di·ac \'kärd-ē-ˌak\ *adj* **1** : of, relating to, situated near, or acting on the heart **2** : of, relating to, or being the part of the stomach into which the esophagus opens
car·di·gan \'kärd-i-gən\ *n* : a sweater usu. without a collar and opening the full length of the front
[1]**car·di·nal** \'kärd-nəl, -ᵊn-əl\ *adj* : of basic importance : MAIN, CHIEF, PRIMARY — **car·di·nal·ly** \-ē\ *adv*
[2]**cardinal** *n* **1** : one of the dignitaries of the Roman Catholic Church who rank next below the pope and elect his successor **2** : CARDINAL NUMBER **3** : any of several American finches of which the male is bright red with a black face and pointed crest
cardinal number *n* : a number (as 1, 5, 15) that is used in simple counting and that indicates how many elements there are in a collection — see NUMBER table
car·dio·vas·cu·lar \ˌkärd-ē-ō-'vas-kyə-lər\ *adj* : of, relating to, or involving the heart and blood vessels
card·play·er \'kärd-ˌplā-ər\ *n* : one that plays cards
[1]**care** \'ke(ə)r\ *n* **1** : a heavy sense of responsibility : WORRY, ANXIETY **2** : serious attention : HEED **3** : PROTECTION, SUPERVISION **4** : a person or thing that is an object of one's watchful attention
[2]**care** *vb* **1 a** : to feel trouble or anxiety **b** : to feel interest or concern **2** : to give care **3 a** : to have a liking, fondness, or taste **b** : to have an inclination
ca·reen \kə-'rēn\ *vb* **1** : to cause a boat to lean or tilt over on one side for cleaning, caulking, or repairing **2** : to sway from side to side : LURCH
[1]**ca·reer** \kə-'ri(ə)r\ *n* **1 a** : COURSE, PROGRESS **b** : full speed or exercise of activity **2** : a course of continued progress or activity **3** : a profession for which one trains and which is undertaken as a permanent calling

²career *vi* : to go at top speed esp. in a headlong manner
care·free \'ke(ə)r-ˌfrē\ *adj* : free from care or worry
care·ful \-fəl\ *adj* 1 : using care : taking care : WATCHFUL, CAUTIOUS 2 : made, done, or said with care — **care·ful·ly** \-f(ə-)lē\ *adv* — **care·ful·ness** \-fəl-nəs\ *n*
care·less \'ke(ə)r-ləs\ *adj* 1 : CAREFREE 2 : not taking proper care : HEEDLESS 3 : done, made, or said without due care — **care·less·ly** *adv* — **care·less·ness** *n*
¹ca·ress \kə-'res\ *n* : a tender or loving touch or embrace
²caress *vt* : to touch or stroke lightly in a loving or endearing manner — **ca·ress·er** *n*
car·et \'kar-ət\ *n* : a mark ∧ used to show where something is to be inserted
care·tak·er \'ke(ə)r-ˌtā-kər\ *n* : one that takes care of buildings or land often for an absent owner
care·worn \-ˌwōrn\ *adj* : showing the effect of grief or anxiety
car·fare \'kär-ˌfa(ə)r\ *n* : the fare charged for carrying a passenger on a car (as a streetcar)
car·go \'kär-ˌgō\ *n, pl* **cargoes** *or* **cargos** : the goods or merchandise conveyed in a ship, airplane, or vehicle : FREIGHT
car·i·bou \'kar-ə-ˌbü\ *n, pl* **-bou** *or* **-bous** : any of several large deer of northern No. America closely related to the reindeer
car·i·ca·ture \'kar-i-kə-ˌchů(ə)r\ *n* 1 : exaggeration by means of ludicrous distortion of parts or characteristics 2 : a representation esp. in literature or art that has the qualities of caricature — **caricature** *vt* — **car·i·ca·tur·ist** \-əst\ *n*
car·ies \'kar-ēz\ *n, pl* **caries** : tooth decay
car·il·lon \'kar-ə-ˌlän, -lən\ *n* : a set of fixed bells sounded by hammers controlled by a keyboard
car·load \'kär-'lōd\ *n* : a load that fills a car
car·min·a·tive \kär-'min-ət-iv\ *adj* : expelling gas from the alimentary canal — **carminative** *n*
car·mine \'kär-mən, -ˌmīn\ *n* : a vivid red
car·nage \'kär-nij\ *n* : great destruction of life (as in battle) : SLAUGHTER
car·nal \'kärn-ᵊl\ *adj* 1 : of or relating to the body 2 : SENSUAL — **car·nal·i·ty** \kär-'nal-ət-ē\ *n* — **car·nal·ly** \'kärn-ᵊl-ē\ *adv*
car·na·tion \kär-'nā-shən\ *n* : any of numerous cultivated usu. double-flowered pinks
car·nau·ba \kär-'nȯ-bə, ˌkär-nə-'ü-bə\ *n* : a Brazilian palm that yields a brittle yellowish wax used esp. in polishes; *also* : this wax
car·ne·lian \kär-'nēl-yən\ *n* : a hard tough reddish quartz used as a gem
car·ni·val \'kär-nə-vəl\ *n* 1 : a season of merrymaking before Lent 2 : a merrymaking, feasting, or masquerading 3 **a** : a traveling enterprise offering amusements **b** : an organized program of entertainment or exhibition
car·ni·vore \'kär-nə-ˌvō(ə)r\ *n* : a flesh-eating animal; *esp* : any of an order of flesh-eating mammals
car·niv·o·rous \kär-'niv-(ə-)rəs\ *adj* 1 : subsisting or feeding on animal tissues 2 : of or relating to the carnivores — **car·niv·o·rous·ly** *adv* — **car·niv·o·rous·ness** *n*
¹car·ol \'kar-əl\ *n* 1 : a song of joy or mirth 2 : a popular song of religious joy
²carol *vb* **-oled** *or* **-olled**; **-ol·ing** *or* **-ol·ling** 1 : to sing esp. in a joyful manner 2 : to sing carols — **car·ol·er** *or* **car·ol·ler** *n*
¹car·om \'kar-əm\ *n* 1 : a shot in billiards in which the cue ball strikes each of two object balls 2 : a rebounding esp. at an angle
²carom *vi* 1 : to make a carom 2 : to strike and rebound at an angle : GLANCE
car·o·tene \'kar-ə-ˌtēn\ *or* **car·o·tin** \'kar-ət-ᵊn\ *n* : any of several orange or red hydrocarbon pigments that occur in plants and in the fatty tissues of plant-eating animals and are convertible to vitamin A
ca·rous·al \kə-'raů-zəl\ *n* : CAROUSE
¹ca·rouse \kə-'raůz\ *n* : a drunken revel
²carouse *vi* 1 : to drink liquor freely 2 : to take part in a carouse — **ca·rous·er** *n*
¹carp \'kärp\ *vi* : to find fault — **carp·er** *n*
²carp *n, pl* **carp** *or* **carps** : a large soft-finned freshwater fish noted for its longevity and often raised for food
car·pel \'kär-pəl\ *n* : one of the highly modified leaves that together form the ovary of a flower — **car·pel·lary** \-pə-ˌler-ē\ *adj* — **car·pel·late** \-ˌlāt\ *adj*
car·pen·ter \'kär-pən-tər\ *n* : a workman who builds or repairs wooden structures — **carpenter** *vb* — **car·pen·try** \-trē\ *n*
car·pet \'kär-pət\ *n* : a heavy fabric used as a floor covering — **carpet** *vt*
car·pet·bag \-ˌbag\ *n* : a traveling bag made of carpeting common in the 19th century
car·pet·bag·ger \-ˌbag-ər\ *n* : a Northerner in the South during the reconstruction period seeking private gain by taking advantage of unsettled conditions and political corruption — **car·pet·bag·gery** \-ˌbag-ə-rē\ *n*
car·pet·ing \'kär-pət-iŋ\ *n* : material for carpets; *also* : CARPETS
car·port \'kär-ˌpōrt\ *n* : an open-sided automobile shelter
car·rel \'kar-əl\ *n* : a table with bookshelves often partitioned or enclosed for individual study in a library
car·riage \'kar-ij\ *n* 1 **a** : the act of carrying **b** : manner of bearing the body : POSTURE 2 : a wheeled vehicle; *esp* : a horse-drawn vehicle designed for private use and comfort 3 : a movable part of a machine for supporting or carrying some other movable object or part
carriage trade *n* : trade from well-to-do or upper-class people
car·ri·er \'kar-ē-ər\ *n* 1 : one that carries 2 **a** : a person or firm engaged in transporting passengers or goods **b** : a postal employee who delivers or collects mail **c** : one that delivers newspapers 3 : a bearer and transmitter of disease germs 4 : an electric wave or alternating current whose modulations are used as signals in radio, telephonic, or telegraphic transmission
car·ri·on \'kar-ē-ən\ *n* : dead and decaying flesh
car·rot \'kar-ət\ *n* : a biennial herb with a usu. orange spindle-shaped edible root; *also* : its root
car·rou·sel *or* **car·ou·sel** \ˌkar-ə-'sel\ *n* : MERRY-GO-ROUND
¹car·ry \'kar-ē\ *vb* **car·ried**; **car·ry·ing** 1 : to support and take from one place to another : TRANSPORT, CONVEY 2 : to influence by mental or emotional appeal 3 : to get possession or control of : CAPTURE 4 : to transfer from one place to another 5 : to contain and direct the course of : CONDUCT 6 : IMPLY, INVOLVE 7 : to conduct oneself 8 : to sustain the weight of 9 : to sing in correct pitch 10 : to keep in stock for sale 11 : to provide sustenance for 12 : to maintain on a list or record 13 : MAINTAIN, SUPPORT 14 : to prolong in space, time, or degree 15 **a** (1) : to gain victory for; *esp* : to secure the adoption or passage of (2) : to win adoption **b** : to succeed in (an election) 16 **a** : to bear the charges of holding (as merchandise) **b** : to keep on one's books as a debtor 17 : to penetrate to a distance
²carry *n, pl* **carries** 1 : the range of a gun or projectile or of a struck or thrown ball 2 **a** : the act or method of carrying **b** : PORTAGE
car·ry·all \'kar-ē-ˌȯl\ *n* : a passenger automobile similar to a station wagon but with a higher body often on a truck chassis
carry away *vt* : to arouse to a high and often excessive degree of emotion or enthusiasm
carry on *vb* 1 : CONDUCT, MANAGE 2 : to behave in a foolish, excited, or improper manner 3 : to continue in spite of hindrance or discouragement
carry out *vt* 1 : to put into execution 2 : to bring to a successful conclusion
¹cart \'kärt\ *n* 1 : a heavy usu. horse-drawn 2-wheeled vehicle used for haulage 2 : a light usu. 2-wheeled vehicle

[2]**cart** *vt* : to convey in or as if in a cart — **cart·er** *n*

cart·age \'kärt-ij\ *n* : the act of or rate charged for carting

carte blanche \'kärt-'blä^{n}sh, -'blänch\ *n, pl* **cartes blanches** *same*\ : full discretionary power

car·tel \kär-'tel\ *n* : a combination of independent commercial enterprises often international in scope designed to limit competition

car·ti·lage \'kärt-^{ə}l-ij\ *n* : a translucent elastic tissue that composes most of the skeleton of the embryonic and very young vertebrates and becomes for the most part converted into bone in the higher vertebrates

car·ti·lag·i·nous \ˌkärt-^{ə}l-'aj-ə-nəs\ *adj* : of, relating to, or resembling cartilage

car·tog·ra·phy \kär-'täg-rə-fē\ *n* : the making of maps — **car·tog·ra·pher** \-fər\ *n* — **car·to·graph·ic** \ˌkärt-ə-'graf-ik\ *adj*

car·ton \'kärt-^{ə}n\ *n* : a cardboard box or container

car·toon \kär-'tün\ *n* **1** : a preparatory design, drawing, or painting **2 a** : a satirical drawing commenting on public and usu. political matters **b** : COMIC STRIP — **cartoon** *vb* — **car·toon·ist** \-'tü-nəst\ *n*

car·tridge \'kär-trij\ *n* **1** : a tube of metal or paper containing a complete charge for a firearm **2** : an often cylindrical container of material for insertion into a larger mechanism or apparatus **3** : a phonograph part that translates stylus motion into electrical voltage

cart·wheel \'kärt-ˌhwēl\ *n* **1** : a large coin (as a silver dollar) **2** : a lateral handspring with arms and legs extended

carve \'kärv\ *vb* **1** : to cut with care or precision esp. artistically **2** : to cut into pieces or slices **3** : to cut up and serve meat — **carv·er** *n*

carv·ing \'kär-viŋ\ *n* **1** : the act or art of one who carves **2** : a carved object, design, or figure

car·y·at·id \ˌkar-ē-'at-əd\ *n, pl* **-at·ids** *or* **-at·i·des** \-'at-ə-ˌdēz\ : a sculptured figure of a woman in flowing robes used as an architectural column

ca·sa·ba \kə-'säb-ə\ *n* : any of several winter melons with yellow rind and sweet flesh

[1]**cas·cade** \kas-'kād\ *n* **1** : a steep usu. small fall of water; *esp* : one of a series **2** : something arranged in a series or in a succession of stages so that each stage derives from or acts upon the product of the preceding

[2]**cascade** *vi* : to fall in a cascade

cas·cara \kas-'kar-ə\ *n* : the dried laxative bark of a small Pacific coastal tree

[1]**case** \'kās\ *n* **1** : a special set of circumstances or conditions **2 a** : a situation requiring investigation or action (as by the police) **b** : an object of investigation or consideration **3 a** : an inflectional form of a noun, pronoun, or adjective indicating its grammatical relation to other words **b** : such a relation whether indicated by inflection or not **4** : what actually exists or happens : FACT **5 a** : a suit or action in law or equity **b** (1) : the evidence supporting a conclusion or judgment (2) : ARGUMENT; *esp* : a convincing argument **6 a** : an instance of disease or injury; *also* : PATIENT **b** : INSTANCE, EXAMPLE — **in case 1** : IF **2** : as a precaution **3** : as a precaution against the event that

[2]**case** *n* **1 a** : a box or receptacle to contain something **b** : SET; *esp* : PAIR **2** : an outer covering **3** : a shallow divided tray for holding printing type **4** : the frame of a door or window : CASING

[3]**case** *vt* : to enclose in or cover with a case : ENCASE

ca·sein \kā-'sēn, 'kā-sē-ən\ *n* : a whitish phosphorus-containing protein occurring in milk

case·ment \'kās-mənt\ *n* : a window sash opening on hinges like a door; *also* : a window with such a sash

[1]**cash** \'kash\ *n* **1** : ready money **2** : money or its equivalent paid promptly after purchasing

[2]**cash** *vt* : to pay or obtain cash for

cash·ew \'kash-ü, kə-'shü\ *n* : a tropical American tree of the sumac family; *also* : its edible nut

[1]**ca·shier** \ka-'shi(ə)r\ *vt* : DISCHARGE; *esp* : to discharge in disgrace from a position of responsibility or trust

[2]**cash·ier** *n* **1** : a high officer of a bank who is responsible for all money received and paid out **2** : an employee of a store or restaurant who receives and records payments made by customers

cashier's check *n* : a check drawn by a bank upon its own funds and signed by its cashier

cash·mere \'kazh-ˌmi(ə)r, 'kash-\ *n* : fine wool from the undercoat of an Indian goat or a yarn of this wool; *also* : a soft twilled fabric orig. from this wool

cash register *n* : a business machine usu. with a money drawer that records the amount of money received and exhibits the amount of each sale

cas·ing \'kā-siŋ\ *n* : something that encases

ca·si·no \kə-'sē-nō\ *n, pl* **-nos 1** : a building or room used for social amusements; *esp* : a building or room for gambling **2** *or* **cas·si·no** : a card game

cask \'kask\ *n* **1** : a barrel-shaped container usu. for liquids **2** : the quantity contained in a cask

cas·ket \'kas-kət\ *n* **1** : a small chest or box (as for jewels) **2** : a usu. ornamented and lined coffin

casque \'kask\ *n* : HELMET

cas·sa·va \kə-'säv-ə\ *n* : any of several plants of the spurge family grown in the tropics for their fleshy rootstocks which yield a nutritious starch

cas·se·role \'kas-ə-ˌrōl\ *n* **1** : a covered dish in which food can be baked and served **2** : the food cooked and served in a casserole

cas·sia \'kash-ə\ *n* **1** : a coarse cinnamon bark **2** : any of a genus of leguminous herbs, shrubs, and trees of warm regions some of which yield senna

cas·sock \'kas-ək\ *n* : a close-fitting ankle-length gown worn esp. by Roman Catholic and Anglican clergy

[1]**cast** \'kast\ *vb* **cast**; **cast·ing 1 a** (1) : THROW, FLING, TOSS (2) : to throw out a lure with a fishing rod **b** : DIRECT **c** : to deposit (a ballot) formally **d** : to throw off, out, or away: as (1) : EMIT (2) : DISCARD (3) : SHED, MOLT **2** : ADD, COMPUTE **3 a** : to assign the parts of to actors **b** : to assign (an actor) to a part **4 a** : to give shape to (a substance) by pouring in liquid or plastic form into a mold and letting harden without pressure **b** : to form by this process — **cast about** : to search here and there — **cast lots** : to draw lots to determine a matter by chance

[2]**cast** *n* **1 a** : an act of casting **b** : something that happens as a result of chance **2 a** : the form in which a thing is constructed **b** : the characters or the actors in a play or narrative **3** : a turning of the eye; *also* : EXPRESSION **4** : something thrown or the quantity thrown **5 a** : something formed by casting in a mold or form : CASTING **b** : a rigid dressing of gauze impregnated with plaster of paris for immobilizing a diseased or broken part **6** : an overspread of a color : SHADE **7 a** : SHAPE, APPEARANCE **b** : characteristic quality

cas·ta·net \ˌkas-tə-'net\ *n* : a rhythm instrument used esp. by dancers that consists of two small ivory, wood, or plastic shells fastened to the thumb and clicked together by the fingers — usu. used in pl.

cast·away \'kas-tə-ˌwā\ *adj* **1** : thrown away : REJECTED **2** : cast adrift or ashore as a survivor of a shipwreck — **castaway** *n*

caste \'kast\ *n* **1** : one of the hereditary classes formerly dividing Hindu society **2 a** : a division of society based upon differences of wealth, inherited rank, or occupation **b** : the position conferred by caste standing : PRESTIGE

cas·tel·lat·ed \'kas-tə-ˌlāt-əd\ *adj* : having battlements like a castle

cast·er \'kas-tər\ *n* 1 : one that casts 2 : a small container (as for salt) with a perforated top 3 : a wheel or set of wheels mounted in a swivel frame used for supporting furniture, trucks, and portable machines

cas·ti·gate \'kas-tə-,gāt\ *vt* : to punish, reprove, or criticize severely — **cas·ti·ga·tion** \,kas-tə-'gā-shən\ *n* — **cas·ti·ga·tor** \'kas-tə-,gāt-ər\ *n*

cast·ing \'kas-tiŋ\ *n* 1 : the act of one that casts 2 : something cast in a mold 3 : something that is cast out or off

cast iron *n* : a hard brittle alloy of iron, carbon, and silicon shaped by being poured into a mold while it is molten

cas·tle \'kas-əl\ *n* 1 a : a large fortified building or set of buildings b : a massive or imposing house 2 : ³ROOK

cast–off \'kas-,tȯf\ *adj* : thrown away as no longer wanted : DISCARDED — **castoff** *n*

cas·tor oil \,kas-tər-\ *n* : a thick yellowish oil extracted from the poisonous seeds of an herb and used as a lubricant, in soap, and as a cathartic

cas·trate \'kas-,trāt\ *vt* : to deprive of the sex glands and esp. the testes — **cas·tra·tion** \ka-'strā-shən\ *n*

ca·su·al \'kazh-(ə-)wəl, 'kazh-əl\ *adj* 1 : subject to or occurring by chance 2 : occurring without regularity : OCCASIONAL 3 a : feeling or showing little concern : NONCHALANT b : INFORMAL, NATURAL — **ca·su·al·ly** \-ē\ *adv* — **ca·su·al·ness** *n*

ca·su·al·ty \'kazh-əl-tē, 'kazh-(ə-)wəl-\ *n, pl* **-ties** 1 : serious or fatal accident : DISASTER 2 a : a military person lost (as by death or capture) during warfare b : a person or thing injured, lost, or destroyed

ca·su·ist·ry \'kazh-(ə-)wə-strē\ *n, pl* **-ries** : false reasoning or application of principles esp. with regard to morals — **ca·su·ist** \'kazh-(ə-)wəst\ *n* — **ca·su·is·tic** \,kazh-ə-'wis-tik\ *adj*

cat \'kat\ *n* 1 a : a small carnivorous mammal long domesticated and kept by man as a pet or for catching rats and mice b : an animal of the cat family including the lion, tiger, leopard, jaguar, cougar, wildcat, lynx, and cheetah 2 : CAT-O'-NINE-TAILS

cat·a·clysm \'kat-ə-,kliz-əm\ *n* 1 : a violent and destructive upheaval (as an earthquake) of nature 2 : a violent social or political upheaval — **cat·a·clys·mal** \,kat-ə-'kliz-məl\ *adj* — **cat·a·clys·mic** \-'kliz-mik\ *adj*

cat·a·comb \'kat-ə-,kōm\ *n* : an underground place of burial with galleries and recesses for tombs

cat·a·falque \'kat-ə-,falk, -,fȯ(l)k\ *n* : an ornamental structure sometimes used in solemn funerals to hold the body

cat·a·lep·sy \'kat-ᵊl-,ep-sē\ *n* : a condition of suspended animation and loss of voluntary motion — **cat·a·lep·tic** \,kat-ᵊl-'ep-tik\ *adj or n*

¹cat·a·log *or* **cat·a·logue** \'kat-ᵊl-,ȯg\ *n* : a list of names, titles, or articles arranged according to a system; *also* : a book or a file containing such a list or the items listed

²catalog *or* **catalogue** *vt* 1 : to make a catalog of 2 : to enter in a catalog — **cat·a·log·er** *or* **cat·a·logu·er** *n*

ca·tal·pa \kə-'tal-pə\ *n* : a small tree of America and Asia with broad oval leaves, flowers brightly striped inside and spotted outside, and long narrow pods

ca·tal·y·sis \kə-'tal-ə-səs\ *n* : the change and esp. increase in the rate of a chemical reaction brought about by a catalyst — **cat·a·lyt·ic** \,kat-ᵊl-'it-ik\ *adj* — **cat·a·lyt·i·cal·ly** \-'it-i-k(ə-)lē\ *adv*

cat·a·lyst \'kat-ᵊl-əst\ *n* : a substance that changes the rate of a chemical reaction but is itself unchanged at the end of the process

cat·a·ma·ran \,kat-ə-mə-'ran\ *n* 1 : a raft propelled by paddles or sails 2 : a boat with twin hulls

cat·a·mount \'kat-ə-,maůnt\ *n* : any of various wild cats: as a : COUGAR b : LYNX

¹cat·a·pult \'kat-ə-,pəlt, -,půlt\ *n* 1 : an ancient military device for hurling missiles 2 : a device for launching an airplane (as from the deck of a ship)

²catapult *vb* 1 : to throw or launch by or as if by a catapult 2 : to become catapulted

cat·a·ract \'kat-ə-,rakt\ *n* 1 : a clouding of the lens of the eye or of its capsule obstructing the passage of light 2 a : WATERFALL; *esp* : a large one over a precipice b : steep rapids in a river

ca·tarrh \kə-'tär\ *n* : inflammation of a mucous membrane esp. of the nose and throat — **ca·tarrh·al** \-'tär-əl\ *adj* — **ca·tarrh·al·ly** \-ə-lē\ *adv*

ca·tas·tro·phe \kə-'tas-trə-(,)fē\ *n* 1 : a momentous tragic event 2 : utter failure or ruin : FIASCO — **cat·a·stroph·ic** \,kat-ə-'sträf-ik\ *adj*

cat·bird \'kat-,bərd\ *n* : a dark gray American songbird with black cap and reddish under tail coverts

cat·boat \-,bōt\ *n* : a sailboat with a single mast set far forward and a single large sail extended by a long boom

cat·call \-,kȯl\ *n* : a sound like the cry of a cat or a noise made to express disapproval (as at a sports event)

¹catch \'kach, 'kech\ *vb* **caught** \'kȯt\; **catch·ing** 1 a : to capture or seize something in flight or motion b : TRAP, ENSNARE 2 a : to discover unexpectedly : come upon suddenly b : to check suddenly or momentarily 3 : to take hold of : SNATCH 4 a : to get entangled b : to engage firmly c : FASTEN 5 : to become affected by 6 : to take or get momentarily or quickly 7 a : OVERTAKE b : to get aboard in time 8 : to grasp by the senses or the mind : APPREHEND — **catch one's breath** : to pause or rest long enough to regain normal breathing

²catch *n* 1 : something caught 2 a : the act of catching b : a game in which a ball is thrown and caught 3 : something that checks or holds immovable 4 : one worth catching esp. as a spouse 5 : FRAGMENT, SNATCH 6 : a concealed difficulty

catch·all \'kach-,ȯl, 'kech-\ *n* : something to hold a variety of odds and ends

catch·er \'kach-ər, 'kech-\ *n* : one that catches; *esp* : a baseball player stationed behind home plate

catch·ing \-iŋ\ *adj* 1 : INFECTIOUS, CONTAGIOUS 2 : ALLURING, CATCHY

catch·word \-,wərd\ *n* 1 : either of the terms to right and left of the head of a page of an alphabetical reference work (as a dictionary) indicating the first and last entries on the page 2 : SLOGAN

catchy \'kach-ē, 'kech-ē\ *adj* 1 : likely to attract 2 : apt to entangle one : TRICKY

cat·e·chet·i·cal \,kat-ə-'ket-i-kəl\ *adj* : of or relating to instruction in religious doctrine

cat·e·chism \'kat-ə-,kiz-əm\ *n* : a summary of religious doctrine often in the form of questions and answers

cat·e·chist \'kat-i-kəst\ *n* : one that catechizes

cat·e·chize \'kat-ə-,kīz\ *vt* 1 : to instruct systematically esp. by questions, answers, and explanations and corrections 2 : to question systematically or searchingly — **cat·e·chiz·er** *n*

cat·e·gor·i·cal \,kat-ə-'gȯr-i-kəl\ *adj* 1 : being without qualification or reservation : ABSOLUTE 2 : of, relating to, or constituting a category — **cat·e·gor·i·cal·ly** \-i-k(ə-)lē\ *adv*

cat·e·go·rize \'kat-i-gə-,rīz\ *vt* : to put into a category : CLASSIFY — **cat·e·go·ri·za·tion** \,kat-i-gə-rə-'zā-shən\ *n*

cat·e·go·ry \'kat-ə-,gōr-ē\ *n, pl* **-ries** 1 : one of the divisions or groupings used in a system of classification 2 : CLASS, VARIETY, KIND

ca·ter \'kāt-ər\ *vi* 1 : to provide a supply of food 2 : to supply what is required or desired esp. by a special group — **ca·ter·er** *n*

cat·er·cor·ner \,kat-ē-'kȯr-nər, ,kat-ə-, ,kit-ē-\ *or* **cat·er–cor·nered** \-nərd\ *adv (or adj)* : in a diagonal or oblique position : on a diagonal or oblique line

cat·er·pil·lar \ˈkat-ə(r)-ˌpil-ər\ *n* : the long wormlike larva esp. of a butterfly or moth

cat·er·waul \ˈkat-ər-ˌwȯl\ *vi* : to make the characteristic harsh cry of a rutting cat — **caterwaul** *n*

cat·fish \ˈkat-ˌfish\ *n* : any of numerous large-headed gluttonous fishes with long sensory barbels

cat·gut \-ˌgət\ *n* : a tough cord made usu. from sheep intestines

ca·thar·sis \kə-ˈthär-səs\ *n, pl* **-thar·ses** \-ˈthär-ˌsēz\ **1** : PURGATION **2** : a purification that brings about spiritual renewal or release from tension

[1]**ca·thar·tic** \-ˈthärt-ik\ *adj* : of or relating to catharsis or to a cathartic

[2]**cathartic** *n* : PURGATIVE

ca·the·dral \kə-ˈthē-drəl\ *n* : a church that contains a bishop's throne and is the principal church of a diocese

cath·e·ter \ˈkath-ət-ər\ *n* : a slender tube for insertion (as for medication or removal of contents) into a bodily passage or cavity

cath·ode \ˈkath-ˌōd\ *n* **1** : the negative electrode of an electrolytic cell **2** : the positive terminal of a battery **3** : the electron-emitting electrode of an electron tube — **ca·thod·ic** \ka-ˈthäd-ik\ *adj*

cath·o·lic \ˈkath-(ə-)lik\ *adj* **1** : COMPREHENSIVE, UNIVERSAL **2** *cap* **a** : emphasizing historical continuity from apostolic times of doctrinal and liturgical traditions and of the succession of bishops **b** : of or relating to the church of which the pope is head : Roman Catholic

Catholic *n* : a member of a Catholic church; *esp* : ROMAN CATHOLIC

cath·o·lic·i·ty \ˌkath-ə-ˈlis-ət-ē\ *n* **1** *cap* : the character of being in conformity with a Catholic church **2 a** : liberality of sentiments or views **b** : comprehensive range

cat·kin \ˈkat-kən\ *n* : a flower cluster bearing crowded flowers and prominent bracts

cat·nap \ˈkat-ˌnap\ *n* : a very short light nap — **catnap** *vi*

cat·nip \-ˌnip\ *n* : a common strong-scented mint of which cats are especially fond

cat–o'–nine–tails \ˌkat-ə-ˈnīn-ˌtālz\ *n, pl* **cat–o'–nine–tails** : a whip made of nine knotted cords fastened to a handle

cat's cradle *n* : a game played with a string looped on the fingers in such a way as to resemble a small cradle

cat's–paw \ˈkats-ˌpȯ\ *n* : a person used by another for his own ends

cat·sup \ˈkech-əp, ˈkach-; ˈkat-səp\ *n* : a seasoned sauce of puree consistency usu. of tomatoes

cat·tail \ˈkat-ˌtāl\ *n* : a tall reedy marsh plant with brown furry spikes of very tiny flowers

cat·tle \ˈkat-ᵊl\ *n, pl* **cattle** : domesticated quadrupeds held as property or raised for use; *esp* : bovine animals kept on a farm or ranch

cat·tle·man \-mən, -ˌman\ *n* : a man who tends or raises cattle

cat·ty \ˈkat-ē\ *adj* **1** : resembling a cat **2** : slyly spiteful — **cat·ti·ly** \ˈkat-ᵊl-ē\ *adv* — **cat·ti·ness** \ˈkat-ē-nəs\ *n*

cat·walk \ˈkat-ˌwȯk\ *n* : a narrow walk or way (as along a bridge or over or around a large machine or tank)

Cau·ca·sian \kȯ-ˈkā-zhən, -ˈkazh-ən\ *adj* : of or relating to the white race of mankind — **Caucasian** *n* — **Cau·ca·soid** \ˈkȯ-kə-ˌsȯid\ *adj or n*

[1]**cau·cus** \ˈkȯ-kəs\ *n* : a meeting of members of a party or faction usu. to select candidates or decide policy

[2]**caucus** *vi* : to meet in caucus

cau·dal \ˈkȯd-ᵊl\ *adj* **1** : of, relating to, or being a tail **2** : situated in or directed toward the hind part of the body — **cau·dal·ly** \-ᵊl-ē\ *adv*

caught *past of* CATCH

cau·li·flow·er \ˈkȯ-li-ˌflau̇(-ə)r\ *n* : a garden plant closely related to the cabbage and grown for its compact edible head of usu. white undeveloped flowers

cauliflower ear *n* : an ear deformed from injury and excessive growth of scar tissue

caulk \ˈkȯk\ *vt* **1** : to stop up and make watertight the seams of by filling with waterproofing material **2** : to stop up and make tight against leakage — **caulk·er** *n*

caus·al \ˈkȯ-zəl\ *adj* **1** : expressing or indicating cause : CAUSATIVE **2** : of, relating to, or constituting a cause **3** : involving causation or a cause **4** : arising from a cause — **caus·al·ly** \-zə-lē\ *adv*

cau·sal·i·ty \kȯ-ˈzal-ət-ē\ *n, pl* **-ties** **1** : a causal quality or agency **2** : the relation between a cause and its effect or between regularly correlated events or phenomena

cau·sa·tion \kȯ-ˈzā-shən\ *n* **1 a** : the act or process of causing **b** : the act or agency by which an effect is produced **2** : CAUSALITY

[1]**cause** \ˈkȯz\ *n* **1** : something or someone that brings about a result : a person or thing that is the occasion of an action or state **2** : a good or adequate reason **3 a** : a ground of legal action **b** : CASE 5a **c** : a matter or question to be decided **4** : a principle or movement militantly supported — **cause·less** \-ləs\ *adj*

[2]**cause** *vt* **1** : to serve as cause or occasion of **2** : to effect by command, authority, or force — **caus·er** *n*

cause·way \ˈkȯz-ˌwā\ *n* : a raised way esp. across wet ground or water

[1]**caus·tic** \ˈkȯ-stik\ *adj* **1** : capable of destroying or eating away by chemical action : CORROSIVE **2** : INCISIVE, BITING — **caus·ti·cal·ly** \-sti-k(ə-)lē\ *adv*

[2]**caustic** *n* : a caustic substance

cau·ter·ize \ˈkȯt-ə-ˌrīz\ *vb* : to burn usu. to destroy infected tissue — **cau·ter·i·za·tion** \ˌkȯt-ə-rə-ˈzā-shən\ *n*

[1]**cau·tion** \ˈkȯ-shən\ *n* **1** : WARNING **2** : prudent forethought to minimize risk

[2]**caution** *vt* **cau·tioned**; **cau·tion·ing** \ˈkȯ-sh(ə-)niŋ\ : to advise caution to

cau·tion·ary \ˈkȯ-shə-ˌner-ē\ *adj* : serving as or offering a warning

cau·tious \ˈkȯ-shəs\ *adj* : marked by or given to caution — **cau·tious·ly** *adv* — **cau·tious·ness** *n*

cav·al·cade \ˌkav-əl-ˈkād, ˈkav-əl-ˌ\ *n* **1 a** : a procession of riders or carriages **b** : a procession of vehicles or ships **2** : a sequence of dramatic scenes : PAGEANT

[1]**cav·a·lier** \ˌkav-ə-ˈli(ə)r\ *n* **1** : a mounted soldier : KNIGHT **2** : GALLANT

[2]**cavalier** *adj* **1** : DEBONAIR **2** : marked by lofty disregard of others' interests or offhand dismissal of important matters : DISDAINFUL — **cav·a·lier·ly** *adv*

cav·al·ry \ˈkav-əl-rē\ *n, pl* **-ries** : a highly mobile army component mounted on horseback or moving in motor vehicles — **cav·al·ry·man** \-rē-mən, -ˌman\ *n*

[1]**cave** \ˈkāv\ *n* : a large natural underground cavity with an opening to the surface : CAVERN

[2]**cave** *vb* : to fall or cause to fall in or down esp. from being undermined : COLLAPSE

ca·ve·at emp·tor \ˌkā-vē-ˌat-ˈem(p)-tər, -ˌtȯ(ə)r\ *n* : a warning that without a warranty the buyer of goods takes the risk of their quality upon himself

cave–in \ˈkāv-ˌin\ *n* **1** : the action of caving in **2** : a place where earth has caved in

cave·man \ˈkāv-ˌman\ *n* **1** : one who lives in a cave; *esp* : a man of the Stone Age **2** : a man who acts with rough or violent directness esp. toward women

cav·ern \ˈkav-ərn\ *n* : an underground chamber often of large or indefinite extent : CAVE

cav·ern·ous \-ər-nəs\ *adj* **1** : having caverns or cavities **2** : constituting or suggesting a cavern — **cav·ern·ous·ly** *adv*

cav·i·ar *or* **cav·i·are** \ˈkav-ē-ˌär\ *n* : processed salted roe of a large fish (as the sturgeon) prepared as an appetizer

cav·il \'kav-əl\ *vb* **-iled** *or* **-illed**; **-il·ing** *or* **-il·ling** \-(ə-)liŋ\ : to raise trivial and frivolous objections : QUIBBLE — **cavil** *n* — **cav·il·er** *or* **cav·il·ler** \-(ə-)lər\ *n*

cav·i·ty \'kav-ət-ē\ *n, pl* **-ties** : an unfilled space within a mass : a hollow place : HOLE

ca·vort \kə-'vȯrt\ *vi* : to bound or frisk about : CAPER

ca·vy \'kā-vē\ *n, pl* **cavies** : any of several short-tailed rough-haired So. American rodents; *esp* : GUINEA PIG

caw \'kȯ\ *vi* : to utter the harsh raucous natural call of the crow or a similar cry — **caw** *n*

cay \'kē, 'kā\ *n* : a small low island or emergent reef of sand or coral : ISLET, KEY

cay·enne pepper \ˌkī-ˌen-, ˌkā-\ *n* : a pungent condiment consisting of the ground dried fruits or seeds of hot peppers; *also* : a plant bearing such fruits

cay·use \'kī-ˌ(y)üs, kī-'\ *n* : a native range horse of the western U.S.

1cease \'sēs\ *vb* : to come or bring to an end : leave off : DISCONTINUE

2cease *n* : CESSATION — usu. used with *without*

cease–fire \'sēs-'fī(ə)r\ *n* **1** : a military order to cease firing **2** : a suspension of active hostilities

cease·less \'sēs-ləs\ *adj* : CONSTANT, CONTINUAL — **cease·less·ly** *adv* — **cease·less·ness** *n*

ce·cum \'sē-kəm\ *n, pl* **ce·ca** \-kə\ : the blind pouch in which the large intestine begins and into which the small intestine opens from one side — **ce·cal** \-kəl\ *adj* — **ce·cal·ly** \-kə-lē\ *adv*

ce·dar \'sēd-ər\ *n* **1** : any of various cone-bearing trees noted for their fragrant durable wood **2** : the wood of a cedar

cede \'sēd\ *vt* **1** : to yield or grant typically by treaty **2** : ASSIGN, TRANSFER

ce·dil·la \si-'dil-ə\ *n* : a mark placed under the letter *c* (as ç) to show that the *c* is to be pronounced like *s*

ceil·ing \'sē-liŋ\ *n* **1** : the overhead inside lining of a room **2** : something that overhangs like a shelter **3 a** : the greatest height at which an airplane can maintain level flight or operate efficiently **b** : the height above the ground of the base of the lowest layer of clouds **4** : an upper usu. prescribed limit

cel·an·dine \'sel-ən-ˌdīn, -ˌdēn\ *n* : a yellow-flowered biennial herb related to the poppy

cel·e·brant \'sel-ə-brənt\ *n* : one who celebrates; *esp* : the priest officiating at the Eucharist

cel·e·brate \'sel-ə-ˌbrāt\ *vb* **1** : to perform publicly and according to rule or form **2** : to observe in some special way (as by merrymaking) **3** : to praise or make known publicly **4** : to observe a special day or event (as a holiday or anniversary) with festivities — **cel·e·bra·tion** \ˌsel-ə-'brā-shən\ *n* — **cel·e·bra·tor** \'sel-ə-ˌbrāt-ər\ *n*

cel·e·brat·ed \'sel-ə-ˌbrāt-əd\ *adj* : widely known and often referred to : RENOWNED — **cel·e·brat·ed·ness** *n*

ce·leb·ri·ty \sə-'leb-rət-ē\ *n, pl* **-ties** **1** : the state of being celebrated : FAME **2** : a celebrated person

ce·ler·i·ty \sə-'ler-ət-ē\ *n, pl* **-ties** : rapidity of motion : SWIFTNESS

cel·ery \'sel-(ə-)rē\ *n* : a European herb of the carrot family widely grown for its thick edible petioles

ce·les·tial \sə-'les-chəl\ *adj* **1** : of, relating to, or suggesting the spiritual heaven : HEAVENLY **2** : of or relating to the sky or heavens — **ce·les·tial·ly** \-chə-lē\ *adv*

cel·i·ba·cy \'sel-ə-bə-sē\ *n* **1** : the state of not being married **2** : the single life esp. of one bound by vow not to marry

cel·i·bate \'sel-ə-bət\ *n* : one who lives in celibacy — **celibate** *adj*

cell \'sel\ *n* **1 a** : a one-room dwelling occupied by a solitary person (as a hermit) **b** : a single room (as in a convent or prison) usu. for one person **2** : a small compartment, receptacle, cavity, or bounded space **3** : a tiny mass of protoplasm that includes a nucleus and is enclosed by a membrane and that is the fundamental unit of living matter **4** : a receptacle (as a jar) containing electrodes and an electrolyte either for generating electricity by chemical action or for use in electrolysis **5** : the basic and usu. smallest unit of an organization or movement — **celled** \'seld\ *adj*

cel·lar \'sel-ər\ *n* **1** : BASEMENT **2** : a stock of wines

cel·lar·age \'sel-ə-rij\ *n* : a cellar esp. for storage

cel·list \'chel-əst\ *n* : one that plays the cello

cel·lo \'chel-ō\ *n, pl* **cellos** : the bass member of the violin family tuned an octave below the viola

cel·lo·phane \'sel-ə-ˌfān\ *n* : a thin transparent material made from cellulose and used as a wrapping

cel·lu·lar \'sel-yə-lər\ *adj* **1** : of, relating to, or consisting of cells **2** : having a porous texture — **cel·lu·lar·i·ty** \ˌsel-yə-'lar-ət-ē\ *n* — **cel·lu·lar·ly** \'sel-yə-lər-lē\ *adv*

cel·lu·lose \'sel-yə-ˌlōs\ *n* : a complex carbohydrate of the cell walls of plants used in making various products (as rayon and cellophane)

cel·lu·los·ic \ˌsel-yə-'lō-sik\ *adj* : of, relating to, or made from cellulose — **cellulosic** *n*

Cel·si·us \'sel-sē-əs, 'sel-shəs\ *adj* : CENTIGRADE

cem·ba·lo \'chem-bə-ˌlō\ *n, pl* **-los** *or* **-li** \-ˌlē\ : HARPSICHORD

1ce·ment \si-'ment\ *n* **1** : a powder that is produced from a burned mixture chiefly of clay and limestone, that with water forms a paste that hardens into a stonelike mass, and that is used in mortars and concretes; *also* : CONCRETE, MORTAR **2** : a binding element or agency

2cement *vb* **1** : to unite by or as if by cement **2** : to overlay with concrete — **ce·ment·er** *n*

cem·e·tery \'sem-ə-ˌter-ē\ *n, pl* **-ter·ies** : a burial ground

cen·o·taph \'sen-ə-ˌtaf\ *n* : a tomb or a monument erected in honor of a person whose body is elsewhere

cen·ser \'sen(t)-sər\ *n* : a vessel for burning incense

1cen·sor \'sen(t)-sər\ *n* : an official who examines publications or communications for objectionable matter — **cen·so·ri·al** \sen-'sōr-ē-əl\ *adj*

2censor *vt* **cen·sored**; **cen·sor·ing** \'sen(t)s-(ə-)riŋ\ : to examine in order to suppress or delete anything thought to be harmful or dangerous

cen·so·ri·ous \sen-'sōr-ē-əs\ *adj* : sternly critical — **cen·so·ri·ous·ly** *adv* — **cen·so·ri·ous·ness** *n*

cen·sor·ship \'sen(t)-sər-ˌship\ *n* : the institution, system, or practice of censoring or censors

1cen·sure \'sen-chər\ *n* **1** : the act of blaming or condemning sternly **2** : an official reprimand

2censure *vt* **cen·sured**; **cen·sur·ing** \'sench-(ə-)riŋ\ : to find fault with : criticize as blameworthy

cen·sus \'sen(t)-səs\ *n* **1** : a periodic governmental counting of population **2** : COUNT, TALLY

cent \'sent\ *n* **1** : a unit of value equal to 1/100 part of a basic monetary unit (as in the U.S. and Canada 1/100 dollar) **2** : a coin, token, or note representing one cent

cent·are \'sen-ˌta(ə)r\ *or* **cen·ti·are** \'sent-ē-ˌa(ə)r\ *n* : a unit of area equal to one square meter

cen·taur \'sen-ˌtȯr\ *n* : one of a race in Greek mythology fabled to be half man and half horse

cen·te·nar·i·an \ˌsent-ᵊn-'er-ē-ən\ *n* : one that is 100 years old or older — **centenarian** *adj*

cen·ten·a·ry \sen-'ten-ə-rē, 'sent-ᵊn-ˌer-ē\ *adj or n* : CENTENNIAL

cen·ten·ni·al \sen-'ten-ē-əl\ *n* : a 100th anniversary or its celebration — **centennial** *adj* — **cen·ten·ni·al·ly** \-ē-ə-lē\ *adv*

1cen·ter \'sent-ər\ *n* **1** : the point at an equal distance or at the average distance from the exterior points of a geometric figure (as a circle or sphere) **2** : a place in or around which an activity concentrates or from which something originates **3 a** : a middle part (as of an army or stage) **b** *often cap* : individuals holding moderate political views esp. between those of conservatives and liberals **4 :** a player occupying a middle position on a team

²**center** *vb* **cen·tered**; **cen·ter·ing** \'sent-ə-riŋ, 'sen-triŋ\ **1 :** to place or fix at or around a center or central area or position **2 :** to gather to a center : CONCENTRATE **3 :** to have a center

cen·ter·board \'sent-ər-ˌbōrd\ *n* **:** a retractable keel used esp. in sailboats

cen·ter·piece \'sent-ər-ˌpēs\ *n* **:** an object occupying a central position; *esp* **:** an adornment in the center of a table

cen·ti·grade \'sent-ə-ˌgrād, 'sänt-\ *adj* **:** relating to, conforming to, or having a thermometer scale on which the interval between the freezing point and the boiling point of water is divided into 100 degrees with 0° representing the freezing point and 100° the boiling point — abbr. *C*

cen·ti·gram \-ˌgram\ *n* **:** a unit of weight equal to 1/100 gram

cen·ti·li·ter \-ˌlēt-ər\ *n* **:** a unit of capacity equal to 1/100 liter

cen·ti·me·ter \'sent-ə-ˌmēt-ər, 'sänt-\ *n* **:** a unit of length equal to 1/100 meter

cen·ti·pede \'sent-ə-ˌpēd\ *n* **:** any of a class of long flat many-legged arthropods

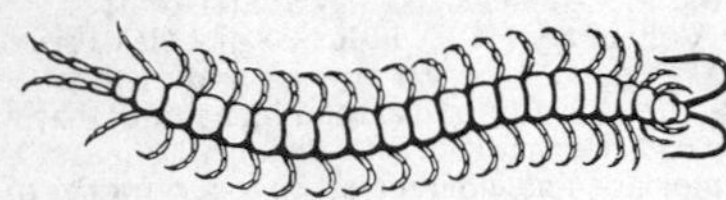

centipede

¹**cen·tral** \'sen-trəl\ *adj* **1 :** containing or constituting a center **2 :** ESSENTIAL, PRINCIPAL **3 :** situated at, in, or near the center **4 :** controlling or directing local or branch activities — **cen·tral·i·ty** \sen-'tral-ət-ē\ *n* — **cen·tral·ly** \'sen-trə-lē\ *adv*

²**central** *n* **:** a telephone exchange or operator

cen·tral·ize \'sen-trə-ˌlīz\ *vt* **:** to concentrate (as authority) in a center or central organization — **cen·tral·i·za·tion** \ˌsen-trə-lə-'zā-shən\ *n* — **cen·tral·iz·er** \'sen-trə-ˌlī-zər\ *n*

cen·trif·u·gal \sen-'trif-yə-gəl, -'trif-i-gəl\ *adj* **1 :** proceeding or acting in a direction away from a center or axis **2 :** using or acting by centrifugal force — **cen·trif·u·gal·ly** \-gə-lē\ *adv*

centrifugal force *n* **:** the force that tends to impel a thing or parts of a thing outward from a center of rotation

cen·tri·fuge \'sen-trə-ˌfyüj, 'sän-\ *n* **:** a machine using centrifugal force for separating substances of different densities, for removing moisture, or for simulating gravitational effects

cen·trip·e·tal \sen-'trip-ət-ᵊl\ *adj* **:** proceeding or acting in a direction toward a center or axis — **cen·trip·e·tal·ly** \-ᵊl-ē\ *adv*

cen·tu·ri·on \sen-'t(y)u̇r-ē-ən\ *n* **:** an officer commanding a Roman century

cen·tu·ry \'sench-(ə-)rē\ *n, pl* **-ries** **1 :** a subdivision of the Roman legion **2 :** a group, sequence, or series of 100 like things **3 :** a period of 100 years; *esp* **:** one of the 100-year divisions of the Christian era or of the preceding period

ce·phal·ic \sə-'fal-ik\ *adj* **1 :** of or relating to the head **2 :** directed toward or situated on or in or near the head — **ce·phal·i·cal·ly** \-i-k(ə-)lē\ *adv*

cephalic index *n* **:** the ratio multiplied by 100 of the maximum breadth of the head to its maximum length

¹**ce·ram·ic** \sə-'ram-ik\ *adj* **:** of or relating to a product (as earthenware, porcelain, or brick) made essentially from a nonmetallic mineral by firing at high temperatures

²**ceramic** *n* **1** *pl* **:** the art of making ceramic articles **2 :** a product of ceramic manufacture

ce·ram·ist \sə-'ram-əst\ *or* **ce·ram·i·cist** \-'ram-ə-səst\ *n* **:** one who engages in ceramics

ce·re·al \'sir-ē-əl\ *n* **1 :** a grass yielding grain suitable for food; *also* **:** its grain **2 :** a prepared foodstuff of grain

cer·e·bel·lum \ˌser-ə-'bel-əm\ *n, pl* **-bel·lums** *or* **-bel·la** \-'bel-ə\ **:** a large part of the brain esp. concerned with the coordination of muscles and the maintenance of bodily equilibrium and situated in front of and above the medulla which it partly overlaps — **cer·e·bel·lar** \-'bel-ər\ *adj*

ce·re·bral \sə-'rē-brəl, 'ser-ə-\ *adj* **1 a :** of or relating to the brain or the intellect **b :** of, relating to, or being the cerebrum **2 :** appealing to the intellect — **ce·re·bral·ly** \-brə-lē\ *adv*

cerebral palsy *n* **:** a disability caused by damage to the brain usu. before or during birth and marked by muscular incoordination and speech disturbances

cer·e·brate \'ser-ə-ˌbrāt\ *vi* **:** THINK — **cer·e·bra·tion** \ˌser-ə-'brā-shən\ *n*

ce·re·brum \sə-'rē-brəm, 'ser-ə-brəm\ *n, pl* **-brums** *or* **-bra** \-brə\ **:** the enlarged front and upper part of the brain that contains the higher nervous centers

cere·cloth \'si(ə)r-ˌklȯth\ *n* **:** cloth treated with melted wax or gummy matter and formerly used esp. for wrapping a dead body

cer·e·ment \'ser-ə-mənt, 'si(ə)r-mənt\ *n* **:** a shroud for the dead; *esp* **:** CERECLOTH — usu. used in pl.

¹**cer·e·mo·ni·al** \ˌser-ə-'mō-nē-əl\ *adj* **:** of, relating to, or forming a ceremony — **cer·e·mo·ni·al·ism** \-nē-ə-ˌliz-əm\ *n* — **cer·e·mo·ni·al·ly** \-nē-ə-lē\ *adv*

²**ceremonial** *n* **:** a ceremonial act, action, or system

cer·e·mo·ni·ous \ˌser-ə-'mō-nē-əs\ *adj* **1 :** of, relating to, or constituting a ceremony **2 :** devoted to forms and ceremony **:** PUNCTILIOUS **3 :** according to formal usage or prescribed procedures — **cer·e·mo·ni·ous·ly** *adv* — **cer·e·mo·ni·ous·ness** *n*

cer·e·mo·ny \'ser-ə-ˌmō-nē\ *n, pl* **-nies** **1 :** a formal act or series of acts prescribed by ritual or custom **2 :** a conventional act of politeness **3 :** the social behavior required by strict etiquette **:** FORMALITY

ce·rise \sə-'rēs\ *n* **:** a moderate red

ce·ri·um \'sir-ē-əm\ *n* **:** a malleable metallic element

cer·tain \'sərt-ᵊn\ *adj* **1 a :** FIXED, SETTLED **b :** proved to be true **2 :** implied as being specific but not named **:** PARTICULAR **3 a :** DEPENDABLE, RELIABLE **b :** INDISPUTABLE **4 a :** INEVITABLE **b :** incapable of failing **:** DESTINED **5 :** assured in mind or action — **cer·tain·ly** *adv*

cer·tain·ty \-tē\ *n, pl* **-ties** **1 :** something that is certain **2 :** the quality or state of being certain

cer·tif·i·cate \(ˌ)sər-'tif-i-kət\ *n* **1 :** a document containing a certified statement esp. as to the truth of something; *esp* **:** one certifying that a person has fulfilled the requirements of a school or profession **2 :** a document evidencing ownership or debt

cer·ti·fi·ca·tion \ˌsərt-ə-fə-'kā-shən\ *n* **1 :** the act of certifying **:** the state of being certified **2 :** a certified statement

certified check *n* **:** a check certified to be good by the bank upon which it is drawn

cer·ti·fy \'sərt-ə-ˌfī\ *vt* **-fied**; **-fy·ing** **1 :** to attest authoritatively; *esp* **:** to guarantee to be true or valid or as represented or meeting a standard **2 :** to inform with certainty **3 :** LICENSE — **cer·ti·fi·a·ble** \-ˌfī-ə-bəl\ *adj* — **cer·ti·fi·er** \-ˌfī(-ə)r\ *n*

cer·ti·tude \'sərt-ə-ˌt(y)üd\ *n* **1 :** the state of being or feeling certain **2 :** unfailingness of act or event

ce·ru·le·an \sə-'rü-lē-ən\ *adj* **:** somewhat resembling the blue of the sky

ce·si·um \'sē-zē-əm\ *n* **:** a silver-white soft ductile element

ces·sa·tion \se-'sā-shən\ *n* **:** a temporary or final ceasing (as of action) **:** STOP

ces·sion \'sesh-ən\ *n* **:** a yielding (as of territory) to another

cess·pool \'ses-ˌpül\ *n* **:** an underground pit or tank for liquid waste (as household sewage)

chafe \'chāf\ *vb* **1 a :** IRRITATE, VEX **b :** to feel discontent

: FRET **2 :** to warm by rubbing **3 a :** to rub so as to wear away : ABRADE **b :** to make sore by rubbing
cha·fer \'chā-fər\ *n* **:** any of various large beetles
[1]**chaff** \'chaf\ *n* **1 :** the debris (as seed coverings) separated from the seed in threshing grain **2 :** something light and worthless — **chaffy** \-ē\ *adj*
[2]**chaff** *n* **:** light jesting talk : BANTER
[3]**chaff** *vb* **:** to tease good-naturedly : BANTER
chaf·fer \'chaf-ər\ *vb* **:** to dispute about a price : BARGAIN
chaf·finch \'chaf-(,)inch\ *n* **:** a European finch of which the male has a reddish breast plumage and a cheerful song
chaf·ing dish \'chā-fing-\ *n* **:** a utensil for cooking or warming food at the table
[1]**cha·grin** \shə-'grin\ *n* **:** a feeling of annoyance caused by failure or disappointment
[2]**chagrin** *vt* **cha·grined** \-'grind\; **cha·grin·ing** \-'grin-iŋ\ **:** to cause to feel chagrin
[1]**chain** \'chān\ *n* **1 a :** a series of connected usu. metal links or rings **b** (1) **:** a measuring instrument of 100 links used in surveying (2) **:** a unit of length equal to 66 feet **2 :** something that confines or restrains **3 a :** a series of things linked, connected, or associated together **b :** a number of atoms united like links in a chain
[2]**chain** *vt* **:** to fasten, bind, or connect with a chain
chain gang *n* **:** a gang of convicts chained together
chain mail *n* **:** flexible armor of interlinked metal rings
chain reaction *n* **1 :** a series of events so related to each other that each one initiates the succeeding one **2 :** a chemical or nuclear reaction yielding energy or products that cause further reactions of the same kind and so becoming self-sustaining
chain store *n* **:** one of numerous usu. retail stores under the same ownership and selling the same lines of goods
chair \'che(ə)r\ *n* **1 :** a seat with legs and a back for use by one person **2 a :** an official seat or a seat of authority or dignity **b :** an office or position of authority or dignity **c :** CHAIRMAN **3 :** any of various supporting devices
chair·man \-mən\ *n* **:** the presiding officer of a meeting or an organization or committee — **chair·man·ship** \-,ship\ *n*
chair·per·son \-,pərs-ᵊn\ *n* **:** CHAIRMAN
chaise \'shāz\ *n* **1 :** a 2-wheeled carriage with a folding top **2 :** a light carriage or pleasure cart
chaise longue \'shāz-'lȯŋ\ *n, pl* **chaise longues :** a long reclining chair
chal·ced·o·ny \kal-'sed-ᵊn-ē\ *n, pl* **-nies :** a translucent pale blue or gray quartz with nearly waxy luster
cha·let \sha-'lā\ *n* **1 :** a remote herdsman's hut in the Alps **2 a :** a Swiss dwelling with a wide roof overhang **b :** a cottage in chalet style
chal·ice \'chal-əs\ *n* **:** a drinking cup; *esp* **:** the eucharistic cup
[1]**chalk** \'chȯk\ *n* **1 :** a soft limestone **2 :** chalk or chalky material used as a crayon — **chalky** \'chȯ-kē\ *adj*
[2]**chalk** *vt* **1 :** to rub or mark with chalk **2 :** to record or add up with or as if with chalk
chalk·board \-,bōrd\ *n* **:** BLACKBOARD
chalk up *vt* **1 :** ASCRIBE, CREDIT **2 :** ATTAIN, ACHIEVE
[1]**chal·lenge** \'chal-ənj\ *vb* **1 :** to claim as due or deserved **2 :** to question and demand the countersign from **3 a :** to take exceptions to : DISPUTE **b :** to question the legality or legal qualifications of **4 :** to issue an invitation to compete against one esp. in single combat : DARE, DEFY — **chal·leng·er** *n*
[2]**challenge** *n* **1 :** an exception taken to something as not being true, genuine, accurate, valid, or justified or to a person as not being qualified or acceptable **2 :** a sentry's command to halt and prove identity **3 :** a summons or invitation to compete; *esp* **:** a summons to single combat
chal·lis \'shal-ē\ *n, pl* **chal·lises** \-ēz\ **:** a lightweight soft clothing fabric esp. of cotton or wool
[1]**cham·ber** \'chām-bər\ *n* **1 :** ROOM; *esp* **:** BEDROOM **2 :** an enclosed space or compartment **3 a :** a meeting hall of a deliberative, legislative, or judicial body **b :** a room where a judge transacts business out of court **4 a :** a legislative or judicial body; *esp* **:** either of the houses of a bicameral legislature **b :** a voluntary board or council (as of businessmen) **5 :** a compartment in the cartridge cylinder of a revolver — **cham·bered** \-bərd\ *adj*
[2]**chamber** *adj* **:** intended for performance by a few musicians for a small audience
cham·ber·lain \'chām-bər-lən\ *n* **1 :** a chief officer in the household of a king or nobleman **2 :** TREASURER
cham·ber·maid \'chām-bər-,mād\ *n* **:** a maid who makes beds and does general cleaning of bedrooms (as in a hotel)
cham·bray \'sham-,brā, -brē\ *n* **:** a lightweight clothing fabric with colored and white yarns
cha·me·leon \kə-'mēl-yən\ *n* **:** a lizard that has the ability to vary the color of its skin
cham·ois \'sham-ē\ *n, pl* **cham·ois** \'sham-ēz\ **1 :** a small goatlike mountain antelope of Europe and the Caucasus **2 :** a soft pliant leather prepared from the skin of the chamois or from sheepskin
cham·o·mile \'kam-ə-,mīl\ *n* **:** any of a genus of strong-scented herbs related to the daisies with flower heads that contain a bitter medicinal principle
[1]**champ** \'champ\ *vb* **1 :** to bite and chew noisily **2 :** to show restive impatience
[2]**champ** *n* **:** CHAMPION
cham·pagne \sham-'pān\ *n* **:** a white sparkling wine
cham·paign \sham-'pān\ *n* **:** an expanse of level open country : PLAIN
[1]**cham·pi·on** \'cham-pē-ən\ *n* **1 :** a militant advocate or defender **2 a :** a person formally acknowledged as better than all others in a sport or in a game of skill **b :** the winner of first place in a competition
[2]**champion** *vt* **:** to protect or fight for as a champion
cham·pi·on·ship \-,ship\ *n* **1 :** the act of defending as a champion **2 a :** the position or title of champion **b :** a contest held to determine a champion
[1]**chance** \'chan(t)s\ *n* **1 :** the way in which things take place : FORTUNE **2 :** OPPORTUNITY **3 :** RISK, GAMBLE **4 :** the possibility of an indicated or a favorable outcome in an uncertain situation — **chance** *adj*
[2]**chance** *vb* **1 a :** to take place or come about by chance : HAPPEN **b :** to be found by chance **c :** to have the good or bad luck **2 :** to come casually and unexpectedly — used with *upon* **3 :** to accept the hazard of : RISK
chan·cel \'chan(t)-səl\ *n* **:** the part of a church containing the altar and seats for the clergy and choir
chan·cel·lery *or* **chan·cel·lory** \'chan(t)-s(ə-)lə-rē\ *n, pl* **-ler·ies** *or* **-lor·ies 1 a :** the position or department of a chancellor **b :** the building or room where a chancellor has his office **2 :** the office or staff of an embassy or consulate
chan·cel·lor \'chan(t)-s(ə-)lər\ *n* **1 :** the head of a university **2 :** a judge in a court of chancery or equity **3 :** the chief minister of state in some European countries; *also* **:** a high state official in various countries — **chan·cel·lor·ship** \-,ship\ *n*
chan·cery \'chan(t)s-(ə-)rē\ *n, pl* **-cer·ies 1 :** a court having jurisdiction in equity; *also* **:** the principles and practices of judicial equity **2 :** a record office for public or for ecclesiastical, legal, or diplomatic archives **3 :** CHANCELLERY
chan·cre \'shaŋ-kər\ *n* **:** a primary sore or ulcer at the site of entry of an infective agent (as of syphilis) — **chan·crous** \-k(ə-)rəs\ *adj*
chan·de·lier \,shan-də-'li(ə)r\ *n* **:** a branched often ornate lighting fixture usu. suspended from a ceiling
chan·dler \'chan-dlər\ *n* **:** a dealer in provisions and supplies esp. for ships — **chan·dlery** \-dlə-rē\ *n*
[1]**change** \'chānj\ *vb* **1 :** to make or become different : MOD-

IFY, TRANSFORM **2 a :** to give a different position, course, or direction to **b :** REVERSE **3 :** to replace with another; *also* **:** SWITCH **4 :** to put fresh clothes or covering on **5 :** to shift one's means of conveyance **:** TRANSFER **6 :** to undergo transformation, transition, or substitution **7 :** to put on different clothes **8 :** to give up one thing for something else in return **:** EXCHANGE — **chang·er** *n*

²change *n* **1 :** the act, process, or result of changing: as **a :** ALTERATION **b :** TRANSFORMATION **c :** SUBSTITUTION **2 :** a fresh set of clothes **3 a :** money in small denominations received in exchange for an equivalent sum in larger denominations **b :** money returned when a payment exceeds the amount due **c :** COINS

change·a·ble \ˈchān-jə-bəl\ *adj* **1 :** capable of or given to change **:** VARIABLE, ALTERABLE **2 :** appearing different (as in color) from different points of view — **change·a·bil·i·ty** \ˌchān-jə-ˈbil-ət-ē\ *n* — **change·a·ble·ness** *n* — **change·a·bly** \ˈchān-jə-blē\ *adv*

change·ful \ˈchānj-fəl\ *adj* **:** full of or given to change **:** UNCERTAIN — **change·ful·ly** \-fə-lē\ *adv*

change·less \ˈchānj-ləs\ *adj* **:** UNCHANGING, CONSTANT — **change·less·ly** *adv* — **change·less·ness** *n*

change·ling \ˈchānj-liŋ\ *n* **:** a child secretly exchanged for another in infancy by fairies or elves

change of life : MENOPAUSE

change ringing *n* **:** the art or practice of ringing a set of tuned bells in continually varying order

¹chan·nel \ˈchan-ᵊl\ *n* **1 :** the bed of a stream **2 :** the deeper part of a river, harbor, or strait **3 :** a strait or a narrow sea between two close land masses **4 :** a closed course (as a tube) through which something flows **:** PASSAGEWAY **5 :** a long gutter, groove, or furrow **6 :** a means of passage or transmission **7 :** a range of frequencies of sufficient width for a single radio or television transmission

²channel *vt* **-neled** *or* **-nelled**; **-nel·ing** *or* **-nel·ling 1 a :** to form, cut, or wear a channel in **b :** GROOVE **2 :** to direct into or through a channel

chan·nel·ize \ˈchan-ᵊl-ˌīz\ *vt* **:** CHANNEL — **chan·nel·i·za·tion** \ˌchan-ᵊl-ə-ˈzā-shən\ *n*

chan·son \shäⁿ-sōⁿ\ *n, pl* **chan·sons** \-sōⁿ(z)\ **:** SONG; *esp* **:** a French song

¹chant \ˈchant\ *vb* **1 :** SING; *esp* **:** to sing a chant **2 :** to recite in a monotonous repetitive tone

²chant *n* **1 :** a melody in which several words are sung on one tone **2 :** SONG **3 :** a rhythmic monotonous utterance

chan·tey *or* **chan·ty** \ˈshant-ē, ˈchant-\ *n, pl* **chanteys** *or* **chanties :** a song sung by sailors in rhythm with their work

chan·ti·cleer \ˌchant-ə-ˈkli(ə)r\ *n* **:** ¹COCK 1

cha·os \ˈkā-ˌäs\ *n* **:** complete confusion and disorder — **cha·ot·ic** \kā-ˈät-ik\ *adj* — **cha·ot·i·cal·ly** \-i-k(ə-)lē\ *adv*

¹chap \ˈchap\ *n* **:** FELLOW

²chap *vb* **chapped**; **chap·ping :** to open in slits **:** CRACK

³chap \ˈchäp, ˈchap\ *n* **:** JAW **:** the fleshy covering of a jaw; *also* **:** the forepart of the face — usu. used in pl.

chap·ar·ral \ˌshap-ə-ˈral\ *n* **:** a thicket of dwarf evergreen oaks; *also* **:** a dense impenetrable thicket

chap·el \ˈchap-əl\ *n* **1 :** a place of worship in a residence or institution **2 :** a building or a room or recess esp. in a church for prayer or special religious services **3 :** a service of worship or an assembly in a school or college

¹chap·er·on *or* **chap·er·one** \ˈshap-ə-ˌrōn\ *n* **:** a person and esp. a married woman who accompanies and is responsible for (as at a dance) a young woman or a group of young people

²chaperon *or* **chaperone** *vb* **:** to act as a chaperon **:** ESCORT — **chap·er·on·age** \-ˌrō-nij\ *n*

chap·fall·en \ˈchap-ˌfȯ-lən, ˈchäp-\ *adj* **1 :** having the lower jaw hanging loosely **2 :** DEJECTED, DEPRESSED

chap·lain \ˈchap-lən\ *n* **1 :** a clergyman appointed to serve a dignitary, institution, or military force **2 :** a person chosen to conduct religious exercises for an organization — **chap·lain·cy** \-sē\ *n* — **chap·lain·ship** \-ˌship\ *n*

chap·let \ˈchap-lət\ *n* **1 :** a wreath worn on the head **2 :** a string of beads

chaps \ˈshaps\ *n pl* **:** leather leggings resembling trousers without a seat that are worn esp. by western ranch hands

chap·ter \ˈchap-tər\ *n* **1 :** a main division of a book or of a law code **2 :** the body of canons of a cathedral or collegiate church **3 :** a local branch of a society or fraternity

char \ˈchär\ *vb* **charred**; **char·ring 1 :** to change to charcoal by burning **2 :** to burn slightly **:** SCORCH **3 :** to burn to a cinder

char·ac·ter \ˈkar-ik-tər\ *n* **1 :** a mark or symbol (as a letter of an alphabet) used in writing or printing **2 a :** a distinguishing feature **:** CHARACTERISTIC **b :** the total sum of the distinguishing qualities of a person, group, or thing **:** NATURE **3 :** a person having notable traits or characteristics; *esp* **:** an odd or peculiar person **4 :** a person in a story, novel, or play **5 :** REPUTATION **6 :** moral excellence and strength — **char·ac·ter·less** \-ləs\ *adj*

¹char·ac·ter·is·tic \ˌkar-ik-tə-ˈris-tik\ *adj* **:** serving to mark the distinctive character of an individual, group, or class — **char·ac·ter·is·ti·cal·ly** \-ti-k(ə-)lē\ *adv*

²characteristic *n* **:** a distinguishing trait, quality, or property

char·ac·ter·i·za·tion \ˌkar-ik-tə-rə-ˈzā-shən\ *n* **1 :** the act of characterizing **2 :** the creation of characters in fiction or drama

char·ac·ter·ize \ˈkar-ik-tə-ˌrīz\ *vt* **1 :** to indicate the character or quality of **2 :** to be characteristic of

cha·rades \shə-ˈrādz\ *n pl* **:** a game in which each syllable of a word to be guessed is acted out by some of the contestants while the others try to guess the word

char·coal \ˈchär-ˌkōl\ *n* **1 :** a dark or black porous carbon prepared from vegetable or animal substances (as from wood by charring in a kiln from which air is excluded) **2 a :** a piece or pencil of fine charcoal used in drawing **b :** a charcoal drawing

chard \ˈchärd\ *n* **:** a beet that lacks a swollen root and forms large leaves and succulent stalks often cooked as a vegetable

¹charge \ˈchärj\ *vb* **1 a :** to place a charge (as of powder) in **b :** to load or fill to capacity **c (1) :** to impart an electric charge to **(2) :** to restore the active materials in (a storage battery) by the passage of a direct current through in the opposite direction to that of discharge **2 a :** to impose a task or responsibility on **b :** to command, instruct, or exhort with right or authority **3 :** ACCUSE, BLAME **4 :** to rush against or bear down upon a place **:** ASSAULT, ATTACK **5 a :** to impose a monetary charge upon a person **b :** to fix or ask as fee or payment **c :** to ask or set a price — **charge·a·ble** *adj*

²charge *n* **1 a :** the quantity (as of powder) that an apparatus (as a gun) is intended to receive and fitted to hold **b :** a store or accumulation of force **c :** a definite quantity of electricity **2 a :** OBLIGATION, REQUIREMENT **b :** MANAGEMENT, SUPERVISION; *also* **:** CARE, CUSTODY **c :** a person or thing committed to the care of another **3 a :** INSTRUCTION, COMMAND **b :** an instruction in points of law given by a court to a jury **4 a :** EXPENSE, COST **b :** PRICE **c :** a debit to an account **5 a :** ACCUSATION, INDICTMENT **b :** a complaint of error, failure, or wrong **6 :** a rush to attack an enemy

char·gé d'af·faires \ˈshär-ˌzhād-ə-ˈfa(ə)r\ *n, pl* **char·gés d'af·faires** \-ˌzhād-ə-, -ˌzhāz-də-\ **:** a diplomat who substitutes for an absent ambassador or minister

charg·er \ˈchär-jər\ *n* **1 :** a cavalry horse **2 :** a device for charging storage batteries

char·i·ot \ˈchar-ē-ət\ *n* **:** a 2-wheeled horse-drawn battle car of ancient times used also in processions and races

char·i·o·teer \ˌchar-ē-ə-ˈti(ə)r\ *n* **:** a driver of a chariot

char·is·mat·ic \ˌkar-əz-ˈmat-ik\ *adj* **:** having or showing a personal quality of leadership that arouses special popular loyalty or enthusiasm

char•i•ta•ble \'char-ət-ə-bəl\ *adj* **1** : liberal with money or help for poor and needy persons : GENEROUS **2** : given for the needy **3** : generous and kindly in judging other people : FORGIVING, LENIENT — **char•i•ta•bly** \-blē\ *adv*

char•i•ty \'char-ət-ē\ *n, pl* **-ties** **1** : love for one's fellowmen **2** : kindliness in judging others **3 a** : the giving of aid to the poor and suffering **b** : public aid for the poor **c** : an institution or fund for aiding the needy

char•la•tan \'shär-lə-tən\ *n* : a person who pretends to have knowledge or ability he does not have : QUACK

char•ley horse \'chär-lē-ˌhȯrs\ *n* : pain and stiffness from muscular strain esp. in a leg

[1]**charm** \'chärm\ *n* **1** : a word, action, or thing believed to have magic powers **2** : something worn or carried to keep away evil and bring good luck **3** : a small decorative object worn on a chain or bracelet **4** : a quality that attracts and pleases; *also* : physical grace or attractiveness

[2]**charm** *vt* **1** : to affect or influence by or as if by magic : COMPEL; *also* : DELIGHT **2** : to protect by or as if by a charm **3** : to attract by grace or beauty — **charm•er** *n*

char•nel \'chärn-ᵊl\ *n* : a building or chamber in which dead bodies or bones are deposited — **charnel** *adj*

[1]**chart** \'chärt\ *n* **1** : MAP **2** : a sheet giving information in the form of a table or of lists or by means of diagrams or graphs; *also* : GRAPH **3** : a sheet of paper ruled and graduated for use in a recording instrument

[2]**chart** *vt* **1** : to make a map or chart of **2** : to lay out a plan for

[1]**char•ter** \'chärt-ər\ *n* **1 a** : an instrument in writing issued by the sovereign power of a state, country, or authority granting, guaranteeing, or defining the rights and duties of the body (as a municipality, corporation, or a local society) to which it is issued **b** : CONSTITUTION **2** : a special privilege or immunity **3** : a contract by which the owners of a ship lease it to others

[2]**charter** *vt* **1** : to grant a charter to **2** : to hire (as a ship or a bus) for one's own use — **char•ter•er** *n*

char•treuse \shär-'trüz, -'trüs\ *n* **1** : a usu. green or yellow liqueur **2** : a variable color averaging a brilliant yellow green

char•wom•an \'chär-ˌwu̇m-ən\ *n* : a cleaning woman usu. in a large building

chary \'cha(ə)r-ē\ *adj* **1** : cautiously sparing or frugal **2** : cautiously watchful esp. in preserving something — **char•i•ly** \'char-ə-lē\ *adv* — **char•i•ness** \'char-ē-nəs\ *n*

[1]**chase** \'chās\ *vb* **1 a** : to follow rapidly : PURSUE **b** : HUNT **2** : to seek out **3** : to drive away or out

[2]**chase** *n* **1 a** : the act of chasing : PURSUIT **b** : HUNTING — used with *the* **2** : something pursued **3** : a tract of unenclosed land used as a game preserve

[3]**chase** *vt* : to ornament (metal) by embossing or engraving

[4]**chase** *n* **1** : GROOVE **2** : TRENCH

chas•er \'chā-sər\ *n* **1** : one that chases **2** : a mild drink (as water or beer) taken after hard liquor

chasm \'kaz-əm\ *n* : a deep cleft in the earth : GORGE

chas•seur \sha-'sər\ *n* : one of a body of light cavalry or infantry trained for rapid maneuvering

chas•sis \'shas-ē, 'chas-ē\ *n, pl* **chas•sis** \-ēz\ : a supporting framework (as for the body of an automobile or the parts of a radio set)

chaste \'chāst\ *adj* **1** : innocent of unlawful sexual intercourse **2** : CELIBATE **3** : pure in thought : MODEST **4** : severe in design and expression — **chaste•ly** *adv* — **chaste•ness** *n*

chas•ten \'chās-ᵊn\ *vt* **chas•tened**; **chas•ten•ing** \'chās-niŋ, -ᵊn-iŋ\ : to correct by punishment or suffering : DISCIPLINE; *also* : PURIFY — **chas•ten•er** \'chās-nər, -ᵊn-ər\ *n*

chas•tise \chas-'tīz\ *vt* **1** : to inflict punishment on (as by whipping) **2** : to censure severely : CASTIGATE — **chas•tise•ment** \chas-'tīz-mənt, 'chas-təz-\ *n* — **chas•tis•er** \chas-'tī-zər\ *n*

chas•ti•ty \'chas-tət-ē\ *n, pl* **-ties** : the quality or state of being chaste; *esp* : personal purity and modesty

cha•su•ble \'chaz(h)-ə-bəl, 'chas-ə-\ *n* : a sleeveless outer vestment worn by the officiating priest at mass

[1]**chat** \'chat\ *vi* **chat•ted**; **chat•ting** **1** : CHATTER, PRATTLE **2** : to talk in a light, informal, or familiar manner

[2]**chat** *n* : light familiar talk; *also* : an informal conversation

châ•teau \sha-'tō\ *n, pl* **châ•teaus** \-'tōz\ *or* **châ•teaux** \-'tō(z)\ **1** : a feudal castle in France **2** : a large country house

chat•e•laine \'shat-ᵊl-ˌān\ *n* **1** : the mistress of a château or a household **2** : an ornamental clasp or hook for a watch, purse, or bunch of keys

chat•tel \'chat-ᵊl\ *n* **1** : SLAVE, BONDMAN **2** : an item of property (as animals, furniture, money, or goods) other than real estate

chat•ter \'chat-ər\ *vb* **1** : to utter rapidly succeeding sounds suggesting speech but lacking meaning **2** : to speak idly, incessantly, or rapidly : JABBER **3** : to click repeatedly or uncontrollably — **chatter** *n* — **chat•ter•er** *n*

chat•ter•box \-ˌbäks\ *n* : a constant chatterer

chat•ty \'chat-ē\ *adj* **1** : TALKATIVE **2** : having the style and manner of light familiar conversation — **chat•ti•ly** \'chat-ᵊl-ē\ *adv* — **chat•ti•ness** \'chat-ē-nəs\ *n*

[1]**chauf•feur** \'shō-fər, shō-'\ *n* : a person employed to drive an automobile

[2]**chauffeur** *vb* : to work or operate as chauffeur

chau•vin•ism \'shō-və-ˌniz-əm\ *n* **1** : excessive or blind patriotism **2** : an attitude of superiority toward members of the opposite sex — **chau•vin•ist** \-və-nəst\ *n*

cheap \'chēp\ *adj* **1** : of low cost or price **2** : worth little : of inferior quality **3** : gained with little effort **4** : worthy of scorn or contempt **5 a** : charging low prices **b** : dealing in inferior goods **6 a** : depreciated in value or purchasing power (as by inflation) **b** : obtainable at a low rate of interest — **cheap** *adv* — **cheap•ly** *adv* — **cheap•ness** *n*

cheap•en \'chē-pən\ *vb* **cheap•ened**; **cheap•en•ing** \'chēp-(ə-)niŋ\ : to make or become cheap or cheaper

cheap•skate \'chēp-ˌskāt\ *n* : a shabby or miserly person

[1]**cheat** \'chēt\ *n* **1** : an act of cheating : DECEPTION, FRAUD **2** : one that cheats : DECEIVER

[2]**cheat** *vb* **1** : to rob by deceit or fraud **2** : to influence or lead astray by deceit, trick, or artifice **3** : to defeat in an expectation or purpose by deceit and trickery **4 a** : to practice fraud or trickery **b** : to violate rules dishonestly (as at cards)

[1]**check** \'chek\ *n* **1** : a stoppage of progress : ARREST, PAUSE **2** : something that arrests, limits, or restrains : RESTRAINT **3 a** : a standard for testing and evaluation : CRITERION **b** : EXAMINATION, INVESTIGATION, VERIFICATION **4** : an order directing a bank to pay out money in accordance with instructions written thereon **5 a** : a ticket or token that shows that the bearer has a claim to property or has made payment for a previous performance that did not take place **b** : a slip indicating the amount due : BILL **6 a** : a pattern in squares that resembles a checkerboard **b** : a fabric with such a design **7** : a mark √ placed beside an item to show it has been noted **8** : CRACK, BREAK

[2]**check** *vb* **1 a** : to bring to a sudden pause : STOP **b** : to halt through caution, uncertainty, or fear **2** : RESTRAIN, CURB **3 a** : to make sure of the correctness or satisfactoriness of **b** : to mark printing or writing with a check to show that something has been specially noted **4** : to mark with squares or checks **5** : to leave or accept for safekeeping in a checkroom or for shipment as baggage **6** : to investigate conditions **7** : to correspond point for point : TALLY **8** : to develop small cracks

check•book \-ˌbu̇k\ *n* : a book containing blank checks to be drawn on a bank

[1]**check•er** \'chek-ər\ *n* : a piece in the game of checkers

²check·er *vt* **check·ered; check·er·ing** \'chek-(ə-)riŋ\ **1 :** to mark with squares or spots of different colors **2 :** to subject to frequent changes (as of fortune)

³checker *n* **:** one that checks; *esp* **:** an employee who checks out purchases in a supermarket

check·ers \'chek-ərz\ *n* **:** a game played on a board by two persons with each having 12 men

check·list \'chek-ˌlist\ *n* **:** a list of items that may easily be referred to

check·mate \-ˌmāt\ *vt* **1 :** to arrest or frustrate completely **2 :** to check (a chess opponent's king) so that escape is impossible — **checkmate** *n*

check·point \'chek-ˌpȯint\ *n* **:** a point at which vehicular traffic is halted for inspection or clearance

check·room \-ˌrüm, -ˌru̇m\ *n* **:** a room at which baggage, parcels, or clothing is checked

check·up \-ˌəp\ *n* **:** EXAMINATION; *esp* **:** a general physical examination

ched·dar \'ched-ər\ *n, often cap* **:** a hard pressed cheese of smooth texture

cheek \'chēk\ *n* **1 :** the fleshy side of the face below the eye and above and to the side of the mouth **2 :** saucy speech or behavior **:** IMPUDENCE — **cheek by jowl :** in close proximity

cheek·bone \-'bōn, -ˌbōn\ *n* **:** the bone or the bony prominence below the eye

cheeky \'chē-kē\ *adj* **:** SAUCY, IMPUDENT — **cheek·i·ness** *n*

cheep \'chēp\ *vb* **:** to utter faint shrill sounds **:** PEEP, CHIRP — **cheep** *n*

¹cheer \'chi(ə)r\ *n* **1 :** state of mind or heart **:** SPIRIT **2 :** ANIMATION, GAIETY **3 :** food and drink for a feast **:** FARE **4 :** something that gladdens **5 :** a shout of applause or encouragement

²cheer *vb* **1 :** to give hope to or make happier **:** COMFORT **2 :** to urge on esp. with shouts or cheers **3 :** to shout with joy, approval, or enthusiasm **4 :** to grow or be cheerful **:** REJOICE — usu. used with *up*

cheer·ful \'chir-fəl\ *adj* **1 :** full of good spirits **:** GAY **2 :** pleasantly bright — **cheer·ful·ly** \-f(ə-)lē\ *adv* — **cheer·ful·ness** \-fəl-nəs\ *n*

cheer·lead·er \'chi(ə)r-ˌlēd-ər\ *n* **:** a person who directs organized cheering esp. at a sports event

cheer·less \'chi(ə)r-ləs\ *adj* **:** lacking in warmth or kindliness **:** DEPRESSING, GLOOMY

cheery \'chi(ə)r-ē\ *adj* **:** causing or suggesting cheerfulness — **cheer·i·ly** \'chir-ə-lē\ *adv* — **cheer·i·ness** \'chir-ē-nəs\ *n*

cheese \'chēz\ *n* **:** the curd of milk pressed and used as food

cheese·cloth \-ˌklȯth\ *n* **:** a thin loose-woven cotton cloth

cheesy \'chē-zē\ *adj* **:** resembling or suggesting cheese (as in texture or odor)

chef \'shef\ *n* **:** COOK; *esp* **:** a head cook

chef d'oeu·vre \shā-dœvrᵊ\ *n, pl* **chefs d'oeuvre** *same*\ **:** a masterpiece esp. in art or literature

che·la \'kē-lə\ *n, pl* **che·lae** \-(ˌ)lē\ **:** a pincerlike organ or claw on a limb of a crustacean

che·late \'kē-ˌlāt\ *adj* **:** resembling or having chelae

¹chem·i·cal \'kem-i-kəl\ *adj* **1 :** of, relating to, used in, or produced by chemistry **2 :** acting or operated or produced by chemicals — **chem·i·cal·ly** \-i-k(ə-)lē\ *adv*

²chemical *n* **1 :** a substance formed when two or more other substances act upon one another to cause a permanent change **2 a :** a substance that is prepared for use in the manufacture of another substance **b :** a substance that acts upon something else to cause a permanent change

che·mise \shə-'mēz\ *n* **1 :** a woman's one-piece undergarment **2 :** a loose straight-hanging dress

chem·ist \'kem-əst\ *n* **:** one trained or engaged in chemistry

chem·is·try \'kem-ə-strē\ *n* **1 :** a science that deals with the composition, structure, and properties of substances and of the changes that they undergo **2 :** chemical composition, properties, or processes

che·nille \shə-'nēl\ *n* **:** a fabric with a deep fuzzy pile used for bedspreads and rugs

cher·ish \'cher-ish\ *vt* **1 a :** to hold dear **:** feel or show affection for **b :** to keep with care and affection **:** NURTURE **2 :** to harbor in the mind

che·root \shə-'rüt\ *n* **:** a cigar cut square at both ends

cher·ry \'cher-ē\ *n, pl* **cherries** **1 a :** any of numerous trees and shrubs of the rose family with rather small pale yellow to deep blackish red smooth-skinned fruits **b :** the fruit or wood of a cherry **2 :** a variable color averaging a moderate red — **cherry** *adj*

chert \'chərt, 'chat\ *n* **:** a rock resembling flint and consisting essentially of fine crystalline quartz or fibrous chalcedony

cher·ub \'cher-əb\ *n* **1** *pl* **cher·u·bim** \'cher-(y)ə-ˌbim\ **:** an angel of high rank **2** *pl* **cher·ubs** \'cher-əbz\ **:** a chubby rosy child — **che·ru·bic** \chə-'rü-bik\ *adj*

chess \'ches\ *n* **:** a game played on a board by two persons with each having 16 men — **chess·board** \-ˌbōrd\ *n* — **chess·man** \-ˌman, -mən\ *n*

chest \'chest\ *n* **1 :** a container for storage or shipping; *esp* **:** a box with a lid esp. for safekeeping of belongings **2 :** the part of the body enclosed by the ribs and breastbone — **chest·ed** \'ches-təd\ *adj*

ches·ter·field \'ches-tər-ˌfēld\ *n* **:** an overcoat with a velvet collar

¹chest·nut \'ches-(ˌ)nət\ *n* **1 :** an edible nut from several trees or shrubs of the beech family; *also* **:** a plant bearing chestnuts or its wood **2 :** a horse with the body colored pure or reddish brown and the mane, tail, and points of the same or a lighter shade **3 :** an often repeated old joke or story

²chestnut *adj* **:** of a grayish to reddish brown color

chev·a·lier \ˌshev-ə-'li(ə)r\ *n* **:** a member of any of various orders of knighthood or of merit

chev·i·ot \'shev-ē-ət\ *n* **1 :** a heavy rough napped woolen or worsted fabric **2 :** a sturdy cotton shirting

chev·ron \'shev-rən\ *n* **1 :** a figure resembling an upside down V **2 :** a sleeve badge usu. indicating military rank

¹chew \'chü\ *vb* **:** to crush or grind (as food) with the teeth — **chew·a·ble** *adj* — **chew·er** *n* — **chewy** \'chü-ē\ *adj*

²chew *n* **1 :** the act of chewing **2 :** something for chewing

chiar·oscu·ro \kē-ˌär-ə-'sk(y)u̇(ə)r-ō\ *n* **1 :** pictorial representation in terms of light and shade without regard to color **2 :** the arrangement or treatment of light and dark parts in a pictorial work of art — **chiar·oscu·rist** \-'sk(y)u̇r-əst\ *n*

¹chic \'shēk\ *n* **:** STYLISHNESS

²chic *adj* **:** cleverly stylish **:** SMART

chi·ca·nery \shik-'ān-(ə-)rē\ *n, pl* **-ner·ies :** TRICKERY, DECEIT

Chi·ca·no \chi-'kän-ō\ *n, pl* **-nos :** an American of Mexican descent — **Chicano** *adj*

chick \'chik\ *n* **1 :** CHICKEN; *esp* **:** one newly hatched **2 :** the young of any bird

chick·a·dee \'chik-əd-(ˌ)ē\ *n* **:** any of several crestless American titmice usu. with the crown of the head darker than the body

chick·en \'chik-ən\ *n* **:** the common domestic fowl esp. when young; *also* **:** its flesh used as food

chick·en·heart·ed \ˌchik-ən-'härt-əd\ *adj* **:** TIMID, COWARDLY

chick·weed \'chik-ˌwēd\ *n* **:** any of several low-growing small-leaved weedy plants of the pink family

chic·o·ry \'chik-(ə-)rē\ *n, pl* **-ries :** a thick-rooted usu. blue-flowered perennial herb related to the daisies and grown for its roots and as a salad plant; *also* **:** its dried ground roasted root used to flavor or adulterate coffee

chide \'chīd\ *vb* **chid** \'chid\ *or* **chid·ed** \'chīd-əd\; **chid** *or* **chid·den** \'chid-ᵊn\ *or* **chided; chid·ing** \'chīd-iŋ\ **:** to voice disapproval to **:** SCOLD, REBUKE

¹chief \'chēf\ *n* : the head of a body or organization : LEADER
²chief *adj* **1** : highest in rank, office, or authority **2** : of greatest importance, significance, or influence
chief·ly \'chē-flē\ *adv* **1** : most importantly : PRINCIPALLY, ESPECIALLY **2** : for the most part : MOSTLY
chief master sergeant *n* : a noncommissioned officer in the air force of the highest enlisted rank
chief petty officer *n* : a noncommissioned officer in the navy ranking next below a senior chief petty officer
chief·tain \'chēf-tən\ *n* : a chief esp. of a band, tribe, or clan — **chief·tain·cy** \-sē\ *n* — **chief·tain·ship** \-ˌship\ *n*
chief warrant officer *n* : a warrant officer of senior rank
chif·fon \shif-'än\ *n* : a sheer silk fabric
chif·fo·nier \ˌshif-ə-'ni(ə)r\ *n* : a high narrow chest of drawers often with a mirror
chig·ger \'chig-ər\ *n* : a 6-legged larval mite that sucks the blood of vertebrates and causes intense irritation
chi·gnon \'shēn-ˌyän\ *n* : a knot of hair worn at the back of the head
chil·blain \'chil-ˌblān\ *n* : an inflammatory swelling or sore caused by exposure (as of the feet or hands) to cold
child \'chīld\ *n, pl* **chil·dren** \'chil-drən\ **1** : an unborn or recently born person **2** : a young person of either sex esp. between infancy and youth **3** : a son or daughter of human parents **4** : one strongly influenced by another or by a place or state of affairs — **child·less** \-ləs\ *adj* — **with child** : PREGNANT
child·birth \-ˌbərth\ *n* : PARTURITION
child·hood \-ˌhu̇d\ *n* : the state or time of being a child
child·ish \'chīl-dish\ *adj* **1** : of, resembling, or suitable to a child **2** : FOOLISH, SILLY — **child·ish·ly** *adv* — **child·ish·ness** *n*
child·like \'chīld-ˌlīk\ *adj* : of, relating to, or resembling a child or childhood; *esp* : marked by simplicity, innocence, and trust — **child·like·ness** *n*
chili *or* **chile** *or* **chil·li** \'chil-ē\ *n, pl* **chil·ies** *or* **chil·es** *or* **chil·lies** : CHILI CON CARNE
chili con car·ne \ˌchil-ē-ˌkän-'kär-nē\ *n* : a stew of ground beef, hot pepper, and usu. beans
¹chill \'chil\ *vb* **1** : to become cold **2** : to make cold or chilly **3** : to harden the surface of (metal) by sudden cooling — **chill·er** *n* — **chill·ing·ly** *adv*
²chill *adj* **1 a** : moderately cold **b** : COLD, RAW **2** : not cordial : DISTANT, FORMAL
³chill *n* **1** : a sensation of cold accompanied by shivering **2** : a moderate but disagreeable degree of cold **3** : a check to enthusiasm or warmth of feeling
chilly \'chil-ē\ *adj* **1** : noticeably cold : CHILLING **2** : unpleasantly affected by cold **3** : lacking warmth of feeling — **chill·i·ness** *n*
¹chime \'chīm\ *n* **1** : a musically tuned set of bells **2 a** : the sound of a set of bells — usu. used in pl. **b** : a musical sound suggesting that of bells
²chime *vb* **1 a** : to make a musical esp. harmonious sound **b** : to make the sounds of a chime **2** : to be or act in accord **3** : to call or indicate by chiming
chime in *vb* : to break into or join in a conversation
chi·me·ra *or* **chi·mae·ra** \kī-'mir-ə, kə-\ *n* : an often grotesque creation of the imagination
chi·mer·i·cal \-'mer-i-kəl\ *or* **chi·mer·ic** \-ik\ *adj* **1** : existing only in the imagination : FANCIFUL, FANTASTIC **2** : inclined to favor fantastic ideas or schemes
chim·ney \'chim-nē\ *n, pl* **chimneys** **1** : a passage for smoke; *esp* : an upright structure of brick or stone extending above the roof of a building **2** : a glass tube around a lamp flame
chimp \'chimp, 'shimp\ *n* : CHIMPANZEE
chim·pan·zee \ˌchim-ˌpan-'zē, ˌshim-; chim-'pan-zē, shim-\ *n* : an African anthropoid ape that is smaller, more arboreal, and less fierce than the gorilla
¹chin \'chin\ *n* : the part of the face below the lower lip and including the prominence of the lower jaw
²chin *vb* **chinned**; **chin·ning** : to raise (oneself) while hanging by the hands until the chin is level with the support
chi·na \'chī-nə\ *n* : vitreous porcelain ware orig. from the Orient; *also* : pottery (as dishes) for domestic use
chi·na·ware \-ˌwa(ə)r\ *n* : CHINA
chinch bug \'chinch-\ *n* : a small black-and-white bug very destructive to cereal grasses
chin·chil·la \chin-'chil-ə\ *n* **1** : a So. American rodent the size of a large squirrel widely bred in captivity for its very soft fur of a pearly gray color; *also* : its fur **2** : a heavy twilled woolen coating
chine \'chīn\ *n* : BACKBONE, SPINE
¹chink \'chiŋk\ *n* : a narrow slit or crack (as in a wall)
²chink *vt* : to fill the chinks of (as by caulking) : stop up
³chink *n* : a short sharp sound
⁴chink *vb* : to make or cause to make a chink
chintz \'chin(t)s\ *n* **1** : a printed calico from India **2** : a usu. glazed printed cotton fabric
¹chip \'chip\ *n* **1 a** : a small piece (as of wood, stone, or glass) broken off by a sharp blow : FLAKE **b (1)** : a thin crisp slice of potato **(2)** : FRENCH FRY **2** : a counter used in poker **3** : a flaw left after a small piece has been broken off
²chip *vb* **chipped**; **chip·ping** **1 a** : to cut or hew with an edged tool **b (1)** : to cut or break (a small piece) from something **(2)** : to cut or break a chip from **2** : to break off in small pieces
chip·munk \'chip-ˌməŋk\ *n* : any of numerous small striped largely terrestrial American squirrels
chipped beef \'chipt-\ *n* : smoked dried beef sliced thin
chip·per \'chip-ər\ *adj* : GAY, SPRIGHTLY
chi·rog·ra·phy \kī-'räg-rə-fē\ *n* **1** : HANDWRITING, PENMANSHIP **2** : CALLIGRAPHY 1 — **chi·rog·ra·pher** \-fər\ *n* — **chi·ro·graph·ic** \ˌkī-rə-'graf-ik\ *adj*
chi·rop·o·dy \kə-'räp-əd-ē\ *n* : professional care and treatment of the human foot — **chi·rop·o·dist** \-əd-əst\ *n*
chi·ro·prac·tic \'kī-rə-ˌprak-tik\ *n* : a system of healing based on manipulation and specific adjustment of body structures — **chi·ro·prac·tor** \-tər\ *n*
chirp \'chərp\ *n* : a short sharp sound characteristic of a small bird or cricket — **chirp** *vb*
chir·rup \'chər-əp, 'chir-\ *n* : CHIRP — **chirrup** *vb*
¹chis·el \'chiz-əl\ *n* : a metal tool with a cutting edge at the end of a blade used to shape or chip away stone, wood, or metal

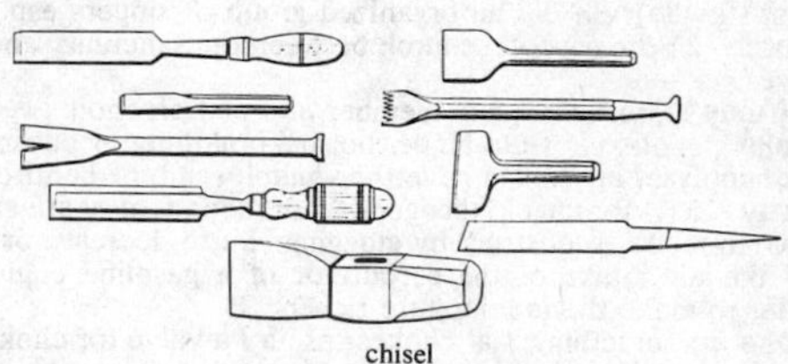
chisel

²chisel *vb* **-eled** *or* **-elled**; **-el·ing** *or* **-el·ling** \'chiz-(ə-)liŋ\ **1** : to cut or work with or as if with a chisel **2 a** : to use shrewd sometimes unfair practices **b** : CHEAT — **chis·el·er** \'chiz-(ə-)lər\ *n*
chis·eled *or* **chis·elled** \'chiz-əld\ *adj* **1** : cut or shaped with a chisel **2** : finely cut
¹chit \'chit\ *n* **1** : CHILD **2** : a pert young woman
²chit *n* : a short letter or note
chi·val·ric \shə-'val-rik\ *adj* : of or relating to chivalry

chiv·al·rous \'shiv-əl-rəs\ *adj* **1** : VALIANT **2** : of or relating to chivalry **3 a** : marked by honor, generosity, and courtesy **b** : marked by especial courtesy and consideration to women — **chiv·al·rous·ly** *adv* — **chiv·al·rous·ness** *n*

chiv·al·ry \-rē\ *n* **1** : a body of knights **2** : the system, spirit, ways, or customs of medieval knighthood **3** : the qualities held to characterize an ideal knight

chive \'chīv\ *n* : a perennial herb related to the onion and used for flavoring

chlo·ral \'klōr-əl\ *n* : a bitter white crystalline drug used to bring sleep

chlor·dane \'klōr-ˌdān\ *or* **chlor·dan** \-ˌdan\ *n* : a viscous volatile liquid insecticide

chlo·ride \'klōr-ˌīd\ *n* : a chemical compound of chlorine with another element or radical

chlo·ri·nate \'klōr-ə-ˌnāt\ *vt* : to treat or cause to combine with chlorine esp. for purifying — **chlo·ri·na·tion** \ˌklōr-ə-'nā-shən\ *n* — **chlo·ri·na·tor** \'klōr-ə-ˌnāt-ər\ *n*

chlo·rine \'klōr-ˌēn\ *n* : a chemical element that is a heavy greenish yellow irritating gas of pungent odor used esp. as a bleach, oxidizing agent, and disinfectant

[1]**chlo·ro·form** \'klōr-ə-ˌfórm\ *n* : a colorless volatile heavy poisonous liquid that smells like ether and is used esp. as a solvent or as a general anesthetic

[2]**chloroform** *vt* : to treat with chloroform esp. so as to produce anesthesia or death

chlo·ro·phyll \'klōr-ə-ˌfil\ *n* : the green magnesium-containing photosynthetic coloring matter of plants — **chlo·ro·phyl·lose** \ˌklōr-ə-'fil-ˌōs\ *adj* — **chlo·ro·phyl·lous** \-'fil-əs\ *adj*

[1]**chock** \'chäk\ *n* : a wedge or block for steadying a body (as a cask) and holding it motionless or for blocking the movement of a wheel

[2]**chock** *vt* : to stop or make fast with or as if with chocks

chock·a·block \'chäk-ə-ˌbläk\ *adj* : very full : CROWDED

chock–full \'chäk-'fu̇l\ *adj* : full to the limit

choc·o·late \'chäk-(ə-)lət, 'chök-\ *n* **1** : a food prepared from ground roasted cacao beans **2** : a beverage of chocolate in water or milk **3** : a candy with a chocolate coating **4** : a variable color averaging a brownish gray — **chocolate** *adj*

[1]**choice** \'chȯis\ *n* **1** : the act of choosing : SELECTION **2** : power of choosing : OPTION **3 a** : a person or thing chosen **b** : the best part : CREAM **4** : a sufficient number and variety for wide or free selection

[2]**choice** *adj* **1** : very fine : better than most **2** : of a grade between prime and good — **choice·ly** *adv* — **choice·ness** *n*

choir \'kwī(ə)r\ *n* **1** : an organized group of singers esp. in a church **2** : the part of a church between the sanctuary and the nave

choir·boy \-ˌbȯi\ *n* : a boy member of a church choir

[1]**choke** \'chōk\ *vb* **1** : to hinder normal breathing by cutting off the supply of air **2** : to have the windpipe stopped entirely or partly **3** : to check the growth or action of : SUPPRESS, SMOTHER **4** : to obstruct by clogging **5** : to decrease or shut off the air intake of the carburetor of a gasoline engine in order to make the fuel mixture richer

[2]**choke** *n* : something that chokes: as **a** : a valve for choking a gasoline engine **b** : a narrowing toward the muzzle in the bore of a gun

chol·er \'käl-ər, 'kō-lər\ *n* : IRASCIBILITY, TEMPER

chol·era \'käl-ə-rə\ *n* : any of several diseases usu. marked by severe vomiting and dysentery

chol·er·ic \'käl-ə-rik, kə-'ler-ik\ *adj* **1** : easily moved to anger **2** : ANGRY, IRATE

cho·les·ter·ol \kə-'les-tə-ˌrōl\ *n* : a physiologically important waxy substance present in animal cells and tissues

choose \'chüz\ *vb* **chose** \'chōz\; **cho·sen** \'chōz-ᵊn\; **choos·ing** \'chü-ziŋ\ **1** : to select esp. freely and after consideration **2 a** : DECIDE **b** : PREFER **3** : to see fit : INCLINE — **choos·er** *n*

[1]**chop** \'chäp\ *vb* **chopped**; **chop·ping** **1** : to cut by striking esp. repeatedly with something sharp **2** : to cut into small pieces : MINCE **3** : to strike quickly or repeatedly (as with an ax) — **chop·per** *n*

[2]**chop** *n* **1** : a sharp downward blow or stroke **2** : a small cut of meat often including a part of a rib **3** : a short quick motion (as of a wave)

chop·pi·ness \'chäp-ē-nəs\ *n* : the quality or state of being choppy

[1]**choppy** \'chäp-ē\ *adj* : CHANGEABLE, VARIABLE

[2]**choppy** *adj* **1** : rough with small waves **2** : JERKY, DISCONNECTED

chops \'chäps\ *n pl* : the fleshy covering of the jaws

chop·stick \'chäp-ˌstik\ *n* : one of a pair of slender sticks used chiefly in oriental countries to lift food to the mouth

chop su·ey \chäp-'sü-ē\ *n* : a dish prepared chiefly from bean sprouts, bamboo shoots, celery, onions, mushrooms, and meat or fish

cho·ral \'kōr-əl\ *adj* : of, relating to, or performed by a chorus or choir or in chorus — **cho·ral·ly** \-ə-lē\ *adv*

cho·rale \kə-'ral\ *n* **1** : a hymn or psalm sung in church; *also* : a hymn tune or a harmonization of a traditional melody **2** : CHORUS, CHOIR

[1]**chord** \'kȯrd\ *n* : a combination of tones that blend harmoniously when sounded together

[2]**chord** *n* **1** : CORD 3 **2** : a straight line joining two points on a curve **3** : an individual emotion or disposition

chore \'chō(ə)r\ *n* **1** *pl* : the regular light work of a household or farm **2** : a routine task or job **3** : a difficult or disagreeable task

cho·rea \kə-'rē-ə\ *n* : a nervous disorder marked by spasmodic uncontrolled movements

cho·re·og·ra·phy \ˌkōr-ē-'äg-rə-fē\ *n* : the art of dancing or of arranging dances and esp. ballets — **cho·re·og·ra·pher** \-fər\ *n* — **cho·re·o·graph·ic** \-ē-ə-'graf-ik\ *adj*

cho·ris·ter \'kōr-ə-stər\ *n* : a singer in a choir

chor·tle \'chȯrt-ᵊl\ *vi* **chor·tled**; **chor·tling** \'chȯrt-liŋ, -ᵊl-iŋ\ : to laugh or chuckle esp. in satisfaction or exultation — **chortle** *n* — **chor·tler** \'chȯrt-lər, -ᵊl-ər\ *n*

[1]**cho·rus** \'kōr-əs\ *n* **1 a** : an organized group of singers : CHOIR **b** : a group of supporting dancers and singers in a musical comedy or revue **2 a** : a recurring part of a song or hymn **b** : a composition to be sung by a number of voices in concert **3** : something uttered simultaneously by a number of persons

[2]**chorus** *vb* : to sing or utter in chorus

chose *past of* CHOOSE

cho·sen \'chōz-ᵊn\ *adj* : selected or marked for favor or special privilege

chow \'chau̇\ *n* : a thick-coated straight-legged muscular dog with a blue-black tongue and a short tail curled close to the back

chow·der \'chau̇d-ər\ *n* : a soup or stew made of fish, clams, or a vegetable usu. stewed in milk

chow mein \'chau̇-'mān\ *n* **1** : fried noodles **2** : a thick stew of shredded meat, mushrooms, and vegetables served with fried noodles

chrism \'kriz-əm\ *n* : consecrated oil used esp. in baptism, confirmation, and ordination

Christ \'krīst\ *n* : Jesus esp. in his character as the Messiah

chris·ten \'kris-ᵊn\ *vt* **chris·tened**; **chris·ten·ing** \'kris-niŋ, -ᵊn-iŋ\ **1 a** : BAPTIZE **b** : to name at baptism **2** : to name or dedicate (as a ship) by a ceremony suggestive of baptism

Chris·ten·dom \'kris-ᵊn-dəm\ *n* **1** : the entire body of Christians **2** : all the countries or peoples that are predominantly Christian

[1]**Chris·tian** \'kris-chən\ *n* **1 :** an adherent of Christianity **2 :** a member of one of several Protestant religious bodies dedicated to the restoration of a united New Testament Christianity
[2]**Christian** *adj* **1 :** of or relating to Jesus Christ or the religion deriving from him **2 :** of or relating to Christians **3 :** befitting a Christian **:** KIND, DECENT
Chris·ti·an·i·ty \ˌkris-chē-'an-ət-ē\ *n* **1 :** the religion deriving from Jesus Christ **2 :** Christian belief or practice
Chris·tian·ize \'kris-chə-ˌnīz\ *vt* **:** to make Christian — **Chris·tian·i·za·tion** \ˌkris-chə-nə-'zā-shən\ *n* — **Chris·tian·iz·er** *n*
Christian Science *n* **:** a religion and system of healing founded by Mary Baker Eddy and taught by the Church of Christ, Scientist — **Christian Scientist** *n*
Christ·like \'krīst-ˌlīk\ *adj* **:** resembling Christ in character or spirit
Christ·mas \'kris-məs\ *n* **1 :** December 25 celebrated as a church festival in commemoration of the birth of Christ and observed as a legal holiday **2 :** CHRISTMASTIDE
Christ·mas·tide \'kris-məs-ˌtīd\ *n* **:** the season of Christmas
chro·mat·ic \krō-'mat-ik\ *adj* **1 :** of or relating to color or color phenomena; *esp* **:** being a shade other than black, gray, or white **2 :** proceeding by half steps of the musical scale — **chro·mat·i·cal·ly** \-'mat-i-k(ə-)lē\ *adv*
chrome \'krōm\ *n* **1 a :** CHROMIUM **b :** a chromium pigment **2 :** something plated with an alloy of chromium
chro·mi·um \'krō-mē-əm\ *n* **:** a blue-white metallic element used esp. in alloys, as a lustrous rust-resisting plating, and in its compounds in paints and in electroplating
chro·mo·some \'krō-mə-ˌsōm\ *n* **:** one of the usu. elongated bodies of a cell nucleus that contains the genes — **chro·mo·som·al** \ˌkrō-mə-'sō-məl\ *or* **chro·mo·so·mic** \-'sō-mik\ *adj*
chron·ic \'krän-ik\ *adj* **1 a :** marked by long duration or frequent recurrence **b :** suffering from a chronic disease **2 a :** constantly present or frequently recurring **b :** HABITUAL, ACCUSTOMED — **chron·i·cal·ly** \-i-k(ə-)lē\ *adv* — **chro·nic·i·ty** \krä-'nis-ət-ē\ *n*
[1]**chron·i·cle** \'krän-i-kəl\ *n* **:** HISTORY, NARRATIVE
[2]**chronicle** *vt* **chron·i·cled**; **chron·i·cling** \-k(ə-)liŋ\ **:** to record in or as if in a chronicle **:** tell the story of — **chron·i·cler** \-k(ə-)lər\ *n*
chron·o·graph \'krän-ə-ˌgraf\ *n* **:** an instrument for measuring and recording time intervals with accuracy — **chron·o·graph·ic** \ˌkrän-ə-'graf-ik\ *adj* — **chro·nog·ra·phy** \krə-'näg-rə-fē\ *n*
chron·o·log·i·cal \ˌkrän-ᵊl-'äj-i-kəl\ *adj* **:** arranged in or according to the order of time — **chron·o·log·i·cal·ly** \-'äj-i-k(ə-)lē\ *adv*
chro·nol·o·gy \krə-'näl-ə-jē\ *n, pl* **-gies 1 :** the science that deals with measuring time by regular divisions and that assigns to events their proper dates **2 :** a chronological table or list **3 :** an arrangement (as of events) in order of occurrence — **chro·nol·o·gist** \-jəst\ *n*
chro·nom·e·ter \krə-'näm-ət-ər\ *n* **:** an instrument for measuring time; *esp* **:** one intended to keep time with great accuracy — **chron·o·met·ric** \ˌkrän-ə-'me-trik\ *adj*
chrys·a·lis \'kris-ə-ləs\ *n, pl* **chry·sal·i·des** \krə-'sal-ə-ˌdēz\ *or* **chrys·a·lis·es** \'kris-ə-lə-səz\ **:** the pupa of insects (as butterflies) that pass the pupal stage in a quiescent condition enclosed in a firm case
chry·san·the·mum \kris-'an(t)-thə-məm\ *n* **1 :** any of a genus of plants related to the daisies that include ornamentals grown for their brightly colored flower heads and important sources of medicinals and insecticides **2 :** a flower head of an ornamental chrysanthemum
chub \'chəb\ *n, pl* **chub** *or* **chubs :** any of several small freshwater fishes related to the carp
chub·by \'chəb-ē\ *adj* **:** PLUMP — **chub·bi·ness** *n*
[1]**chuck** \'chək\ *vt* **1 :** to give a pat or tap **2 :** TOSS
[2]**chuck** *n* **1 :** a pat or nudge under the chin **2 :** TOSS, JERK
[3]**chuck** *n* **1 :** a portion of a side of dressed beef **2 :** a device for holding work or a tool in a machine and esp. in a lathe
chuck·hole \-ˌhōl\ *n* **:** a hole or rut in a road
chuck·le \'chək-əl\ *vi* **chuck·led**; **chuck·ling** \'chək-(ə-)liŋ\ **:** to laugh inwardly or quietly — **chuckle** *n*
chuck wagon \'chək-\ *n* **:** a wagon carrying a stove and provisions for cooking (as on a ranch)
[1]**chug** \'chəg\ *n* **:** a dull explosive sound made by or as if by a laboring engine
[2]**chug** *vi* **chugged**; **chug·ging :** to move or go with chugs
[1]**chum** \'chəm\ *n* **:** a steady companion **:** a close friend
[2]**chum** *vi* **chummed**; **chum·ming :** to go about with a person **:** be on terms of close friendship
chum·my \'chəm-ē\ *adj* **:** INTIMATE, SOCIABLE
chump \'chəmp\ *n* **:** FOOL, DUPE
chunk \'chəŋk\ *n* **:** a short thick piece or lump (as of coal)
chunky \'chəŋ-kē\ *adj* **:** STOCKY
church \'chərch\ *n* **1 :** a building for public worship esp. by a Christian parish or congregation **2 :** a body or organization of religious believers **3 :** public worship esp. in a church — **church·ly** \-lē\ *adj*
church·man \-mən\ *n* **1 :** CLERGYMAN **2 :** a church member
church·yard \'chərch-ˌyärd\ *n* **:** a yard that belongs to a church and is often used as a burial ground
churl \'chərl\ *n* **1 :** a medieval peasant **2 :** RUSTIC, COUNTRYMAN **3 a :** a rude ill-bred person **b :** a surly person
churl·ish \'chər-lish\ *adj* **:** SURLY, RUDE, ILL-MANNERED — **churl·ish·ly** *adv* — **churl·ish·ness** *n*
[1]**churn** \'chərn\ *n* **:** a vessel in which cream is agitated to separate the butterfat from the other constituents
[2]**churn** *vb* **1 :** to agitate cream in a churn in making butter **2 a :** to stir or agitate violently **b :** to make (as foam) by stirring **3 :** to be in violent agitation
chute \'shüt\ *n* **1 :** an inclined plane, trough, or passage down or through which things may pass **2 :** PARACHUTE
chut·ney \'chət-nē\ *n, pl* **chutneys :** a condiment of acid fruits with raisins, dates, and onions
chutz·pah *or* **chutz·pa** \'hůt-spə, 'ku̇t-, -spä\ *n* **:** supreme self-confidence **:** NERVE, GALL
ci·ca·da \sə-'kād-ə\ *n* **:** any of a family of stout-bodied insects that are related to the bugs and have a wide blunt head and large transparent wings
cic·a·trix \'sik-ə-(ˌ)triks\ *n, pl* **cic·a·tri·ces** \ˌsik-ə-'trī-(ˌ)sēz\ **:** a scar resulting from formation and contraction of fibrous tissue in a flesh wound — **cic·a·tri·cial** \ˌsik-ə-'trish-əl\ *adj*
ci·der \'sīd-ər\ *n* **:** the expressed juice of fruit (as apples) used as a beverage or for making other products (as vinegar)
ci·gar \sig-'är\ *n* **:** a roll of tobacco for smoking
cig·a·rette \ˌsig-ə-'ret, 'sig-ə-ˌ\ *n* **:** a small roll of cut tobacco wrapped in paper for smoking
[1]**cinch** \'sinch\ *n* **1 :** a strong girth for a pack or saddle **2 :** a tight grip **3 a :** a thing done with ease **b :** CERTAINTY
[2]**cinch** *vt* **1 :** to put a cinch on **2 :** to make certain
cin·cho·na \siŋ-'kō-nə\ *n* **1 :** any of a genus of So. American trees and shrubs **2 :** the dried bark of a cinchona containing alkaloids (as quinine) and having use as a specific in malaria
cinc·ture \'siŋ(k)-chər\ *n* **:** GIRDLE, BELT
cin·der \'sin-dər\ *n* **1 :** waste matter from the smelting of metal ores **:** SLAG **2 a :** a piece of partly burned coal or wood in which fire is extinct **b :** a hot coal without flame **3** *pl* **:** ASHES — **cin·dery** \-d(ə-)rē\ *adj*
cin·e·ma \'sin-ə-mə\ *n* **:** MOVIES — **cin·e·mat·ic** \ˌsin-ə-'mat-ik\ *adj* — **cin·e·mat·i·cal·ly** \-'mat-i-k(ə-)lē\ *adv*
cin·e·ma·tog·ra·phy \ˌsin-ə-mə-'täg-rə-fē\ *n* **:** the art or science of motion-picture photography — **cin·e·mat·o·graph·ic** \-ˌmat-ə-'graf-ik\ *adj*

cin·na·bar \'sin-ə-ˌbär\ *n* : a red mineral that is the only important ore of mercury
cin·na·mon \'sin-ə-mən\ *n* : the highly aromatic bark of any of several trees of the laurel family used as a spice — **cin·na·mon·ic** \ˌsin-ə-'män-ik\ *adj*
cinque·foil \'siŋk-ˌfȯil, 'saŋk-\ *n* : a design enclosed by five joined foils
[1]**ci·pher** \'sī-fər\ *n* **1 a** : ZERO **b** : an insignificant individual : NONENTITY **2** : a method of transforming a text in order to conceal its meaning **3** : a combination of symbolic letters; *esp* : the interwoven initials of a name
[2]**cipher** *vb* **ci·phered**; **ci·pher·ing** \-f(ə-)riŋ\ : to compute arithmetically
cir·ca \'sər-kə\ *prep* : at, in, or of approximately — used with numerals and esp. with dates
[1]**cir·cle** \'sər-kəl\ *n* **1 a** : RING, HALO **b** : a closed plane curve every point of which is equidistant from a fixed point within the curve **2** : something in the form of a circle or section of a circle **3** : an area of action or influence : REALM **4** : CYCLE, ROUND **5** : a group bound by a common tie; *esp* : COTERIE
[2]**circle** *vb* **cir·cled**; **cir·cling** \-k(ə-)liŋ\ **1** : to enclose in a circle **2** : to move or revolve around **3** : to move in a circle — **cir·cler** \-k(ə-)lər\ *n*
cir·clet \'sər-klət\ *n* : a little circle; *esp* : an ornament for the person in the form of a circle
[1]**cir·cuit** \'sər-kət\ *n* **1** : a boundary around an enclosed space **2** : a moving or revolving around (as in a circle or orbit) : CIRCLING **3** : a regular tour (as by a judge) around an assigned territory **4 a** : an association of similar groups : LEAGUE **b** : a chain of theaters at which productions are successively presented **5** : the complete path of an electric current or any part of this path — **cir·cuit·al** \-kət-ᵊl\ *adj*
[2]**circuit** *vb* : to make a circuit about something
cir·cu·i·tous \(ˌ)sər-'kyü-ət-əs\ *adj* **1** : marked by a circular or winding course **2** : marked by roundabout or indirect procedure — **cir·cu·i·tous·ly** *adv* — **cir·cu·i·tous·ness** *n*
cir·cuit·ry \'sər-kə-trē\ *n* : the plan or the components of an electric circuit
[1]**cir·cu·lar** \'sər-kyə-lər\ *adj* **1** : having the form of a circle : ROUND **2** : moving in or describing a circle **3** : CIRCUITOUS, ROUNDABOUT **4** : sent around to a number of persons — **cir·cu·lar·i·ty** \ˌsər-kyə-'lar-ət-ē\ *n* — **cir·cu·lar·ly** *adv* — **cir·cu·lar·ness** *n*
[2]**circular** *n* : a paper (as a leaflet containing an advertisement) intended for wide distribution
cir·cu·lar·ize \'sər-kyə-lə-ˌrīz\ *vt* **1** : to send circulars to **2** : to poll by questionnaire — **cir·cu·lar·i·za·tion** \ˌsər-kyə-lə-rə-'zā-shən\ *n*
cir·cu·late \'sər-kyə-ˌlāt\ *vb* **1** : to move or cause to move in a circle, circuit, or orbit **2** : to pass from person to person or place to place — **cir·cu·la·tor** \-ˌlāt-ər\ *n*
cir·cu·la·tion \ˌsər-kyə-'lā-shən\ *n* **1** : FLOW **2** : orderly movement through a circuit **3** : passage or transmission from person to person or place to place
cir·cu·la·to·ry \'sər-kyə-lə-ˌtōr-ē\ *adj* : of or relating to circulation (as of the blood)
cir·cum·am·bi·ent \ˌsər-kəm'am-bē-ənt\ *adj* : SURROUNDING
cir·cum·cise \'sər-kəm-ˌsīz\ *vt* : to cut off the foreskin of
cir·cum·ci·sion \ˌsər-kəm-'sizh-ən\ *n* : the act of circumcising or being circumcised
cir·cum·fer·ence \sə(r)-'kəm(p)-f(ə-)rən(t)s\ *n* **1** : the perimeter of a circle **2** : the external boundary or surface of a figure or object : PERIPHERY — **cir·cum·fer·en·tial** \-ˌkəm(p)-fə-'ren-chəl\ *adj*
cir·cum·flex \'sər-kəm-ˌfleks\ *n* : a mark ˆ, ˜, or ˜ used chiefly to indicate length, contraction, or a specific vowel quality
cir·cum·lo·cu·tion \ˌsər-kəm-lō-'kyü-shən\ *n* **1** : the use of an unnecessarily large number of words to express an idea **2** : evasion in speech — **cir·cum·loc·u·to·ry** \-'läk-yə-ˌtōr-ē\ *adj*
cir·cum·nav·i·gate \-'nav-ə-ˌgāt\ *vt* : to go completely around (as the earth) esp. by water — **cir·cum·nav·i·ga·tion** \-ˌnav-ə-'gā-shən\ *n* — **cir·cum·nav·i·ga·tor** \-'nav-ə-ˌgāt-ər\ *n*
cir·cum·scribe \'sər-kəm-ˌskrīb\ *vt* **1** : to draw a line around **2** : to limit narrowly the range or activity of
cir·cum·scrip·tion \ˌsər-kəm-'skrip-shən\ *n* **1** : something that circumscribes **2** : the act of circumscribing : the state of being circumscribed
cir·cum·spect \'sər-kəm-ˌspekt\ *adj* : careful to consider all circumstances and possible consequences : PRUDENT — **cir·cum·spect·ly** *adv*
cir·cum·spec·tion \ˌsər-kəm-'spek-shən\ *n* : circumspect action or behavior : CAUTION, PRUDENCE
cir·cum·stance \'sər-kəm-ˌstan(t)s\ *n* **1** : a fact or event that must be considered along with another fact or event **2** *pl* : surrounding conditions **3** *pl* : condition or situation with respect to wealth **4** : formality accompanying an event : CEREMONY **5** : CHANCE, FATE
cir·cum·stanced \-ˌstan(t)st\ *adj* : placed in particular circumstances esp. in regard to property or income
cir·cum·stan·tial \ˌsər-kəm-'stan-chəl\ *adj* **1** : consisting of or dependent on circumstances **2** : relating to a matter but not essential to it : INCIDENTAL **3** : containing full details — **cir·cum·stan·tial·ly** \-'stanch-(ə-)lē\ *adv*
cir·cum·vent \ˌsər-kəm-'vent\ *vt* : to check or defeat esp. by ingenuity or stratagem — **cir·cum·ven·tion** \-'ven-chən\ *n*
cir·cus \'sər-kəs\ *n* **1 a** : an arena often covered by a tent and used for variety shows usu. including feats of physical skill and daring, wild animal acts, and performances by jugglers and clowns **b** : a circus performance **2** : the physical plant, livestock, and personnel of a circus
cir·rus \'sir-əs\ *n*, *pl* **cir·ri** \'sir-ˌī\ : a wispy white cloud usu. of minute ice crystals formed at altitudes of 20,000 to 40,000 feet
cis·tern \'sis-tərn\ *n* : an often underground artificial reservoir or tank for storing water
cit·a·del \'sit-əd-ᵊl, -ə-ˌdel\ *n* **1** : a fortress that commands a city **2** : STRONGHOLD
ci·ta·tion \sī-'tā-shən\ *n* **1** : an official summons to appear (as before a court) **2 a** : an act or instance of quoting **b** : a word or passage quoted : EXCERPT **3 a** : a formal statement of the achievements of a person receiving an award **b** : specific reference in a military dispatch to meritorious performance of duty
cite \'sīt\ *vt* **1** : to summon to appear before a court **2** : to quote as an example, authority, or proof **3** : to refer to esp. in commendation or praise
cit·i·fy \'sit-i-ˌfī\ *vt* **-fied**; **-fy·ing** : to accustom to urban ways
cit·i·zen \'sit-ə-zən\ *n* **1** : an inhabitant of a city or town **2** : a person who owes allegiance to a government and is entitled to protection from it — **cit·i·zen·ly** \-lē\ *adj*
cit·i·zen·ess \-zə-nəs\ *n* : a female citizen
cit·i·zen·ry \-zən-rē\ *n* : the whole body of citizens
citizens band *n* : one of the radio communications bands allocated in the U. S. for private use
cit·i·zen·ship \-zən-ˌship\ *n* **1** : the status of being a citizen **2** : the quality of an individual's response to membership in a community
cit·ric acid \ˌsi-trik-\ *n* : a pleasantly sour-tasting acid obtained esp. from lemon and lime juices or by fermentation of sugars and used as a flavoring
cit·ron \'si-trən\ *n* **1** : a fruit like the lemon in appearance and structure but larger; *also* : the citrus tree producing this fruit **2** : a small hard-fleshed watermelon used esp. in pickles and preserves
cit·ro·nel·la \ˌsi-trə-'nel-ə\ *n* : a fragrant grass of southern Asia that yields an oil used esp. as an insect repellent

cit·rus \'si-trəs\ *n, pl* **citrus** *or* **cit·rus·es** : any of a genus of often thorny trees and shrubs grown in warm regions for their fruits (as orange, grapefruit, or lemon)
city \'sit-ē\ *n, pl* **cit·ies** **1 a** : an inhabited place of greater size or importance than a town **b** : a usu. large or important municipality in the U.S. governed under a charter granted by the state **2** : the people of a city
civ·et \'siv-ət\ *n* : a thick yellowish musky-odored substance obtained from the civet cat and used in perfume
civet cat *n* : a long-bodied short-legged African mammal that produces most of the civet of commerce
civ·ic \'siv-ik\ *adj* : of or relating to a citizen, a city, citizenship, or civil affairs — **civ·i·cal·ly** \'siv-i-k(ə-)lē\ *adv*
civ·ics \'siv-iks\ *n* : a social science dealing with the rights and duties of citizens
civ·il \'siv-əl\ *adj* **1** : of or relating to citizens **2** : of or relating to the state as a political body **3** : of or relating to the general population as distinguished from military or religious personnel **4** : marked by courtesy or politeness **5** : relating to legal proceedings in connection with private rights and obligations
civil engineering *n* : engineering that deals with the designing and construction of public works (as roads or harbors) and of various private works — **civil engineer** *n*
ci·vil·ian \sə-'vil-yən\ *n* : one not on active duty in a military, police, or fire-fighting force — **civilian** *adj*
ci·vil·i·ty \sə-'vil-ət-ē\ *n, pl* **-ties** **1** : POLITENESS, COURTESY **2** : a polite act or expression
civ·i·li·za·tion \ˌsiv-ə-lə-'zā-shən\ *n* **1 a** : a relatively high level of cultural and technological development **b** : the special culture of a people or a period **2** : refinement of thought, manners, or taste
civ·i·lize \'siv-ə-ˌlīz\ *vt* **1** : to raise out of a savage state to an advanced and ordered stage of cultural development **2** : REFINE — **civ·i·lized** *adj*
civ·il·ly \'siv-ə(l)-lē\ *adv* : in a civil manner : POLITELY
[1]**clack** \'klak\ *vb* **1** : CHATTER, PRATTLE **2** : to make or cause to make a clatter — **clack·er** *n*
[2]**clack** *n* **1** : rapid continuous talk : CHATTER **2** : a sound of clacking
clad \'klad\ *adj* : CLOTHED, COVERED
[1]**claim** \'klām\ *vt* **1 a** : to ask for as rightfully belonging to oneself **b** : to take as the rightful owner **c** : to call for : REQUIRE **2** : to state as a fact : MAINTAIN — **claim·a·ble** *adj* — **claim·er** *n*
[2]**claim** *n* **1** : a demand for something due or believed to be due **2 a** : a right to something usu. in the possession of another **b** : an assertion open to challenge **3** : something claimed
claim·ant \'klā-mənt\ *n* : a person who claims or asserts his right to something
clair·voy·ance \kla(ə)r-'vȯi-ən(t)s\ *n* **1** : the professed power of seeing or knowing about things that are not present to the senses **2** : keenness of perception
[1]**clair·voy·ant** \-ənt\ *adj* **1** : unusually perceptive : DISCERNING **2** : of or relating to clairvoyance — **clair·voy·ant·ly** *adv*
[2]**clairvoyant** *n* : a person held to have the power of clairvoyance
[1]**clam** \'klam\ *n* : any of numerous edible bivalve mollusks
[2]**clam** *vi* **clammed**; **clam·ming** : to gather clams esp. by digging
clam·bake \-ˌbāk\ *n* : a party or gathering (as at the seashore) at which food (as clams, potatoes) is cooked usu. on heated rocks covered by seaweed
clam·ber \'klam-bər\ *vb* **clam·bered**; **clam·ber·ing** \-b(ə-)riŋ\ : to climb awkwardly (as by scrambling) — **clam·ber·er** *n*
clam·my \'klam-ē\ *adj* : being damp, soft, sticky, and usu. cool — **clam·mi·ness** *n*
[1]**clam·or** \'klam-ər\ *n* **1 a** : noisy shouting **b** : a loud continuous noise **2** : vigorous and insistent protest or demand
[2]**clamor** *vb* **clam·ored**; **clam·or·ing** \'klam-(ə-)riŋ\ : to make a clamor
clam·or·ous \'klam-(ə-)rəs\ *adj* : full of clamor : NOISY — **clam·or·ous·ly** *adv*
[1]**clamp** \'klamp\ *n* : a device that holds or presses two or more parts together firmly
[2]**clamp** *vb* : to fasten with or as if with a clamp
clamp down *vt* : to impose harsh penalties and restrictions
clan \'klan\ *n* : a group (as in the Scottish Highlands) made up of households whose heads claim descent from a common ancestor
clan·des·tine \klan-'des-tən\ *adj* : managed with planned secrecy : UNDERHAND — **clan·des·tine·ly** *adv*
[1]**clang** \'klaŋ\ *vb* : to make or cause to make a clang
[2]**clang** *n* : a loud ringing sound like that made by pieces of metal striking each other
clan·gor \'klaŋ-(g)ər\ *n* : a resounding clang or medley of clangs — **clangor** *vi* — **clan·gor·ous** \-(g)ə-rəs\ *adj* — **clan·gor·ous·ly** *adv*
[1]**clank** \'klaŋk\ *vb* **1** : to make or cause to make a clank or series of clanks **2** : to move with a clank
[2]**clank** *n* : a sharp brief metallic ringing sound
clan·nish \'klan-ish\ *adj* **1** : of or relating to a clan **2** : tending to associate only with a group of similar background or status — **clan·nish·ness** *n*
[1]**clap** \'klap\ *vb* **clapped**; **clap·ping** **1** : to strike noisily : SLAM, BANG **2** : to strike the hands together repeatedly in applause : APPLAUD **3** : to strike with the open hand **4** : to put hastily
[2]**clap** *n* **1** : a loud noisy crash **2** : a hard slap **3** : the sound made by clapping the hands together : APPLAUSE
clap·board \'klab-ərd; 'kla(p)-ˌbōrd\ *n* : a narrow board thicker at one edge than at the other used horizontally for covering wooden buildings — **clapboard** *vt*
clap·per \'klap-ər\ *n* : one that makes a clapping sound; *esp* : the tongue of a bell
clap·trap \'klap-ˌtrap\ *n* : pretentious nonsense
claque \'klak\ *n* **1** : a group hired to applaud at a performance **2** : a group of toadies
clar·et \'klar-ət\ *n* : a dry red table wine
clar·i·fi·ca·tion \ˌklar-ə-fə-'kā-shən\ *n* : the act or process of clarifying
clar·i·fy \'klar-ə-ˌfī\ *vb* **-fied**; **-fy·ing** **1** : to make or become pure or clear **2** : to make or become more readily understandable — **clar·i·fi·er** \-ˌfī(-ə)r\ *n*
clar·i·net \ˌklar-ə-'net\ *n* : a single-reed woodwind instrument in the form of a cylindrical tube with moderately flaring end

clarinet

clar·i·net·ist *or* **clar·i·net·tist** \-'net-əst\ *n* : a person who plays a clarinet
clar·i·on \'klar-ē-ən\ *adj* : brilliantly clear
clar·i·ty \'klar-ət-ē\ *n* : CLEARNESS
[1]**clash** \'klash\ *vb* **1** : to make a clash **2 a** : to come into conflict **b** : to be sharply out of harmony **3** : to cause to clash — **clash·er** *n*
[2]**clash** *n* **1** : a noisy usu. metallic sound of collision **2 a** : a hostile encounter **b** : a sharp conflict
[1]**clasp** \'klasp\ *n* **1** : a device for holding together two objects or two parts of something **2** : EMBRACE, GRASP
[2]**clasp** *vt* **1** : to fasten with a clasp **2** : EMBRACE **3** : to seize with or as if with the hand : GRASP — **clasp·er** *n*
[1]**class** \'klas\ *n* **1 a** : a group of the same general status or level **b** : social rank or level **c** : high quality **2 a** : a course of instruction **b** : the group of pupils meeting regularly in a

course **c** : the period during which a study group meets **d** : a group of students or alumni whose graduation date is the same **3** : a division or rating based on grade or quality — **class·less** \-ləs\ *adj*

²class *vt* : CLASSIFY

¹clas·sic \'klas-ik\ *adj* **1 a** : serving as a standard of excellence **b** : TRADITIONAL, ENDURING **2** : of or relating to the ancient Greeks and Romans or their culture : CLASSICAL **3 a** : notable as the best or most typical instance **b** : AUTHENTIC

²classic *n* **1** : a literary work of ancient Greece or Rome **2** : a work of enduring excellence; *also* : its author **3** : a traditional event

clas·si·cal \'klas-i-kəl\ *adj* **1** : CLASSIC **2** : of or relating to the ancient Greek and Roman classics **3** : of or relating to the first developed form or system of a science, art, or discipline **4** : concerned with a general study of the arts and sciences

clas·si·cal·ly \'klas-i-k(ə-)lē\ *adv* : in a classic or classical manner

clas·si·cism \'klas-ə-ˌsiz-əm\ *n* **1** : the principles or style embodied in the literature, art, or architecture of ancient Greece and Rome **2** : adherence to traditional standards universally and lastingly valid

clas·si·cist \-səst\ *n* **1** : an advocate or follower of classicism **2** : a classical scholar — **clas·si·cis·tic** \ˌklas-ə-'sis-tik\ *adj*

clas·si·fi·ca·tion \ˌklas-ə-fə-'kā-shən\ *n* **1** : the act or process of classifying **2** : CLASS, CATEGORY — **clas·si·fi·ca·to·ry** \'klas-(ə-)fə-kə-ˌtōr-ē\ *adj*

clas·si·fied \'klas-ə-ˌfīd\ *adj* : withheld from general circulation for reasons of national security

clas·si·fy \'klas-ə-ˌfī\ *vt* **-fied**; **-fy·ing** : to arrange in or assign to classes — **clas·si·fi·a·ble** *adj* — **clas·si·fi·er** *n*

class·mate \'klas-ˌmāt\ *n* : a member of the same class in a school or college

class·room \-ˌrüm, -ˌru̇m\ *n* : a room in a school or college in which classes meet

¹clat·ter \'klat-ər\ *vb* : to make or cause to make a rattling sound — **clat·ter·er** *n* — **clat·ter·ing·ly** *adv*

²clatter *n* : a rattling sound (as of hard bodies striking together) — **clat·tery** \'klat-ə-rē\ *adj*

clause \'klȯz\ *n* **1** : a separate distinct part of an article or document **2** : a group of words having its own subject and predicate but forming only part of a compound or complex sentence

claus·tro·pho·bia \ˌklȯ-strə-'fō-bē-ə\ *n* : abnormal dread of being in closed or narrow spaces — **claus·tro·pho·bic** \-bik\ *adj*

clav·i·chord \'klav-ə-ˌkȯrd\ *n* : an early keyboard instrument in use before the piano

clav·i·cle \'klav-i-kəl\ *n* : a bone of the shoulder that joins the breastbone and the shoulder blade — **cla·vic·u·lar** \kla-'vik-yə-lər\ *adj*

cla·vier \klə-'vi(ə)r, 'klāv-ē-ər\ *n* **1** : the keyboard of a musical instrument **2** : an early keyboard instrument

¹claw \'klȯ\ *n* **1 a** : a sharp usu. curved nail on the toe of an animal **b** : a sharp curved process esp. if at the end of a limb (as of an insect); *also* : one of the pincerlike organs terminating some limbs of arthropods (as a lobster) **2** : something that resembles a claw in shape or use — **clawed** \'klȯd\ *adj*

²claw *vb* : to rake, seize, or dig with or as if with claws

clay \'klā\ *n* **1 a** : an earthy material that is plastic when moist but hard when fired, is composed chiefly of silicates of aluminum and water, and is used for brick, tile, and earthenware; *also* : soil composed chiefly of this material **b** : EARTH, MUD **2** : the mortal human body — **clay·ish** \'klā-ish\ *adj*

clay·ey \'klā-ē\ *adj* : resembling or containing clay

clay·more \'klā-ˌmō(ə)r\ *n* : a large 2-edged sword formerly used by Scottish Highlanders

clay pigeon *n* : a saucer-shaped target thrown from a trap in trapshooting

¹clean \'klēn\ *adj* **1 a** : free from dirt, foreign matter, or leavings **b** : free from contamination or disease **2** : free from admixture : PURE **3** : characterized by moral integrity : HONORABLE **4** : THOROUGH, COMPLETE **5 a** : being trim and well-formed **b** : EVEN, SMOOTH **6** : habitually neat — **cleanness** *n*

²clean *adv* **1 a** : so as to clean **b** : in a clean manner **2** : all the way : COMPLETELY

³clean *vb* **1** : to make or become clean **2** : to remove or exhaust the contents or resources of **3** : SETTLE — **clean·er** *n*

clean–cut \'klēn-'kət\ *adj* **1** : cut so that the surface or edge is smooth and even **2** : sharply defined or outlined **3** : giving an effect of wholesomeness

clean–limbed \-'limd\ *adj* : well proportioned : TRIM

¹clean·ly \'klen-lē\ *adj* **1** : careful to keep clean **2** : habitually kept clean — **clean·li·ness** *n*

²clean·ly \'klēn-lē\ *adv* : in a clean manner

cleanse \'klenz\ *vt* : to make clean

cleans·er \'klen-zər\ *n* : a preparation (as a scouring powder) used for cleaning

¹clear \'kli(ə)r\ *adj* **1 a** : BRIGHT, LUMINOUS **b** : free from clouds, haze, or mist **c** : UNTROUBLED, SERENE **2** : CLEAN, PURE; *also* : TRANSPARENT **3** : easily heard, seen, or understood **4** : free from doubt : SURE **5** : free from guile or guilt : INNOCENT **6** : unhampered by restriction or limitation — **clear·ly** *adv* — **clear·ness** *n*

²clear *adv* **1** : in a clear manner **2** : all the way : COMPLETELY

³clear *vb* **1 a** : to make or become clear or translucent **b** : to go away : DISPERSE **2 a** : to free from accusation or blame **b** : to certify as trustworthy **3** : EXPLAIN **4** : to get free from obstruction **5** : SETTLE **6** : to go through (customs) **7** : NET **8** : to get rid of : REMOVE **9 a** : to jump or go by without touching **b** : PASS

⁴clear *n* : a clear space or part

clear·ance \'klir-ən(t)s\ *n* **1** : an act or process of clearing **2** : the distance by which one object clears another or the clear space between them

clear–cut \'kli(ə)r-'kət\ *adj* **1** : sharply outlined : DISTINCT **2** : DEFINITE, UNEQUIVOCAL

clear·head·ed \-'hed-əd\ *adj* : having a clear understanding : PERCEPTIVE — **clear·head·ed·ly** *adv* — **clear·head·ed·ness** *n*

clear·ing \'kli(ə)r-iŋ\ *n* **1** : a tract of land cleared of wood and brush **2** : the passage of checks and claims through a clearinghouse

clear·ing·house \-ˌhau̇s\ *n* : an institution established and maintained by banks for making an exchange of checks and claims held by each bank against other banks

clear–sight·ed \'kli(ə)r-'sīt-əd\ *adj* **1** : having clear vision **2** : DISCERNING — **clear–sight·ed·ly** *adv* — **clear–sight·ed·ness** *n*

cleat \'klēt\ *n* : a strip or projecting piece fastened on or across something to give strength, to provide a grip, or to prevent slipping

cleav·a·ble \'klē-və-bəl\ *adj* : capable of being split

cleav·age \'klē-vij\ *n* : the action of cleaving : the state of being cleft

¹cleave \'klēv\ *vi* **cleaved** \'klēvd\ *or* **clove** \'klōv\; **cleav·ing** : ADHERE, CLING

²cleave *vb* **cleaved** \'klēvd\; **cleav·ing** **1 a** : to split by or as if by a cutting blow **b** : DIVIDE, SEPARATE **2** : PENETRATE

cleav·er \'klē-vər\ *n* : one that cleaves; *esp* : a heavy butcher's knife for cutting up meat

clef \'klef\ *n* : a sign placed on the staff in music to show what pitch is represented by each line and space

cleft \'kleft\ *n* : a space or opening made by splitting : FISSURE

clem·a·tis \'klem-ət-əs, kli-'mat-əs\ *n* : a vine or herb related to the buttercups that is widely grown for its showy usu. white or purple flowers

clem·en·cy \'klem-ən-sē\ *n, pl* **-cies** 1 : disposition to be merciful 2 : mildness of weather

clem·ent \'klem-ənt\ *adj* 1 : inclined to be merciful : LENIENT 2 : TEMPERATE, MILD — **clem·ent·ly** *adv*

clench \'klench\ *vb* 1 : CLINCH 1 2 : to hold fast : CLUTCH 3 : to set or close tightly

clere·sto·ry *or* **clear·sto·ry** \'kli(ə)r-ˌstōr-ē\ *n, pl* **-ries** : an outside wall of a room or building that rises above an adjoining roof and contains windows

cler·gy \'klər-jē\ *n, pl* **clergies** : the body of men ordained for service in the Christian church

cler·gy·man \-ji-mən\ *n* : a member of the clergy

cler·ic \'kler-ik\ *n* : CLERGYMAN

cler·i·cal \'kler-i-kəl\ *adj* 1 : of, relating to, or characteristic of the clergy or a clergyman 2 : of or relating to a clerk or office worker — **cler·i·cal·ly** \'kler-i-k(ə-)lē\ *adv*

cler·i·cal·ism \'kler-i-kə-ˌliz-əm\ *n* : a policy of maintaining or increasing the power of a religious hierarchy

[1]**clerk** \'klərk\ *n* 1 : CLERIC 2 a : an official responsible for correspondence, records, and accounts b : one employed to keep records or accounts or to perform general office work c : a salesman in a store

[2]**clerk** *vi* : to act or work as a clerk

clerk·ly \'klər-klē\ *adj* : of or relating to a clerk

clerk·ship \'klərk-ˌship\ *n* : the office or business of a clerk

clev·er \'klev-ər\ *adj* 1 a : showing skill or resourcefulness b : quick in learning 2 : marked by wit or ingenuity — **clev·er·ish** \'klev-(ə-)rish\ *adj* — **clev·er·ly** *adv* — **clev·er·ness** *n*

[1]**clew** *or* **clue** \'klü\ *n* 1 : a ball of thread, yarn, or cord 2 *usu clue* : something that guides through an intricate procedure or maze of difficulties; *esp* : a piece of evidence guiding one to the solution of a problem 3 : a metal loop attached to the lower corner of a sail

[2]**clew** *or* **clue** *vt* **clewed** *or* **clued**; **clew·ing** *or* **clue·ing** *or* **clu·ing** 1 : to roll into a ball 2 *usu clue* : to provide with a clue 3 : to haul (a sail) up or down by ropes through the clews

cli·ché \klē-'shā\ *n* : a trite phrase or expression; *also* : the idea expressed by it — **cliché** *adj*

[1]**click** \'klik\ *n* : a slight sharp noise

[2]**click** *vb* 1 : to make or cause to make a click 2 : to fit or work together smoothly

cli·ent \'klī-ənt\ *n* 1 : a person under the protection of another : DEPENDENT 2 a : a person who engages the professional services of another b : PATRON, CUSTOMER

cli·en·tele \ˌklī-ən-'tel\ *n* : a body of clients and esp. of customers

cliff \'klif\ *n* : a high steep face of rock

cliff–hang·er \'klif-ˌhaŋ-ər\ *n* 1 : an adventure serial or melodrama; *esp* : one presented in installments each ending in suspense 2 : a contest whose outcome is in doubt up to the very end

cli·mac·tic \klī-'mak-tik\ *adj* : of, relating to, or constituting a climax — **cli·mac·ti·cal·ly** \-ti-k(ə-)lē\ *adv*

cli·mate \'klī-mət\ *n* 1 : the average weather conditions of a place or region over a period of years 2 : the prevailing temper or environment — **cli·mat·ic** \klī-'mat-ik\ *adj* — **cli·mat·i·cal·ly** \-'mat-i-k(ə-)lē\ *adv*

[1]**cli·max** \'klī-ˌmaks\ *n* 1 a : a series of ideas or statements so arranged that they increase in force and power from the first to the last b : the highest or most forceful in a series 2 : the highest point : CULMINATION

[2]**climax** *vb* : to come or bring to a climax

[1]**climb** \'klīm\ *vb* 1 a : to go up or down by grasping or clinging with hands and feet b : to ascend in growth (as by twining) 2 : to rise gradually to a higher point — **climb·a·ble** \'klī-mə-bəl\ *adj* — **climb·er** \'klī-mər\ *n*

[2]**climb** *n* 1 : a place where climbing is necessary 2 : the act of climbing : ascent by climbing

clime \'klīm\ *n* : CLIMATE

[1]**clinch** \'klinch\ *vb* 1 a : to turn over or flatten the protruding end of (as a driven nail) b : to fasten by clinching 2 : CLENCH 2 3 : to make final or irrefutable : SETTLE 4 : to seize or grasp one another : GRAPPLE

[2]**clinch** *n* 1 : a fastening by means of a clinched nail, rivet, or bolt 2 : an act or instance of clinching in boxing

clinch·er \'klin-chər\ *n* : one that clinches; *esp* : a decisive fact, argument, act, or remark

cling \'kliŋ\ *vi* **clung** \'kləŋ\; **cling·ing** \'kliŋ-iŋ\ 1 a : to adhere as if glued cohesively and firmly : STICK b : to hold or hold on tightly or tenaciously 2 : to have a strong emotional attachment or dependence

clin·ic \'klin-ik\ *n* 1 : a class of medical instruction in which patients are examined and discussed 2 : a medical facility in which persons not bedridden are diagnosed or treated

clin·i·cal \'klin-i-kəl\ *adj* 1 a : of, relating to, or conducted in or as if in a clinic b : involving direct observation of the patient 2 : being analytical, detached, or coolly dispassionate — **clin·i·cal·ly** \-i-k(ə-)lē\ *adv*

[1]**clink** \'kliŋk\ *vb* : to make or cause to make a slight sharp short metallic sound

[2]**clink** *n* : a clinking sound

clin·ker \'kliŋ-kər\ *n* : a mass of stony matter fused together by fire (as in a furnace from impurities in the coal)

[1]**clip** \'klip\ *vb* **clipped**; **clip·ping** 1 : to clasp or fasten with a clip 2 : to block (a football opponent) illegally from behind

[2]**clip** *n* 1 : a device that grips, clasps, or hooks 2 : a device to hold cartridges for a rifle or automatic handgun

[3]**clip** *vb* **clipped**; **clip·ping** 1 : to cut or cut off with shears 2 : CURTAIL, DIMINISH 3 : HIT, PUNCH

[4]**clip** *n* 1 : a 2-bladed instrument for cutting esp. the nails 2 : something that is clipped 3 : a sharp blow 4 : a rapid pace

clip·board \'klip-ˌbōrd\ *n* : a small writing board with a spring clip at the top for holding papers

clip·per \'klip-ər\ *n* 1 : one that clips 2 *pl* : an implement for clipping esp. hair, fingernails, or toenails 3 : a fast sailing ship

clip·ping \'klip-iŋ\ *n* : a piece clipped from something

clique \'klēk, 'klik\ *n* : a small exclusive group or set of people : COTERIE — **cliqu·ey** *or* **cliquy** \-ē\ *adj* — **cliqu·ish** \-ish\ *adj*

cli·to·ris \'klit-ə-rəs, kli-'tōr-əs\ *n, pl* **cli·to·ri·des** \kli-'tōr-ə-ˌdēz\ *or* **cli·to·ris·es** : a small organ at the anterior or ventral part of the vulva homologous to the penis — **clit·o·ral** \'klit-ə-rəl\ *adj*

[1]**cloak** \'klōk\ *n* 1 : a loose outer garment usu. longer than a cape 2 : something that conceals or covers

[2]**cloak** *vt* : to cover or hide with a cloak

cloche \'klōsh\ *n* : a woman's small helmetlike hat

[1]**clock** \'kläk\ *n* : a timepiece not meant to be worn on the person

[2]**clock** *vt* 1 : to time with a timing device 2 : to register on a mechanical recording device

clock·wise \-ˌwīz\ *adv* : in the direction in which the hands of a clock rotate — **clockwise** *adj*

clock·work \-ˌwərk\ *n* : machinery (as in a mechanical toy) containing a train of wheels of small size

clod \'kläd\ *n* 1 : a lump or mass esp. of earth or clay 2 : a dull or insensitive person : OAF — **clod·dy** \'kläd-ē\ *adj*

clod·hop·per \'kläd-ˌhäp-ər\ *n* 1 : a clumsy and uncouth rustic 2 : a large heavy shoe

[1]**clog** \'kläg\ *n* 1 : a weight attached to a man or an animal to hinder motion 2 : a shoe having a thick typically wooden sole

[2]**clog** *vb* **clogged**; **clog·ging** 1 : to impede with a clog : HINDER 2 : to obstruct passage through : OVERLOAD 3 : to become filled with extraneous matter

[1]**clois·ter** \'klòi-stər\ *n* 1 a : a monastic establishment b : mo-

nastic life 2 : a covered passage on the side of or around a court — **clois·tral** \-strəl\ *adj*

[2]**cloister** *vt* : to shut away from the world in or as if in a cloister

[1]**close** \'klōz\ *vb* 1 : to bar passage through 2 : to suspend or stop the operations of 3 : to bring or come to an end or period : TERMINATE 4 a : to bring or bind together the parts or edges of b : to fill or stop up 5 : to engage in a struggle at close quarters : GRAPPLE 6 : to enter into or complete an agreement — **clos·a·ble** *or* **close·a·ble** *adj* — **clos·er** *n*

[2]**close** \'klōz\ *n* : CONCLUSION, END

[3]**close** \'klōs\ *n* : an enclosed area

[4]**close** \'klōs\ *adj* 1 : having no openings : CLOSED 2 : confined or confining strictly 3 : restricted to a privileged class 4 a : SECLUDED, SECRET b : SECRETIVE 5 : STRICT, RIGOROUS 6 : SULTRY, STUFFY 7 : STINGY, TIGHTFISTED 8 : having little space between items or units 9 a : fitting tightly or exactly b : very short 10 : being near in time, space, effect, or degree 11 : INTIMATE, FAMILIAR 12 : ACCURATE, PRECISE 13 : decided by a narrow margin — **close·ly** *adv* — **close·ness** *n*

[5]**close** \'klōs\ *adv* : in a close position or manner : NEAR

closed circuit *n* : a television installation in which the signal is transmitted by wire

close·fist·ed \'klōs-'fis-təd\ *adj* : STINGY, TIGHTFISTED

[1]**clos·et** \'kläz-ət\ *n* 1 : a small room for privacy 2 : a cabinet or recess for china, household utensils, or clothing 3 : WATER CLOSET

[2]**closet** *vt* : to take into a private room for an interview

close–up \'klōs-,əp\ *n* 1 : a photograph or movie shot taken at close range 2 : an intimate view or examination of something

clo·sure \'klō-zhər\ *n* 1 : an act of closing : the condition of being closed 2 : something that closes 3 : CLOTURE

[1]**clot** \'klät\ *n* : a mass or lump made by a portion of a liquid substance thickening and sticking together

[2]**clot** *vb* **clot·ted**; **clot·ting** : to become or cause to become a clot : form clots

cloth \'klȯth\ *n, pl* **cloths** \'klȯt͟hz, 'klȯths\ 1 : a pliable fabric made usu. by weaving or knitting natural or synthetic fibers and filaments 2 : TABLECLOTH 3 : distinctive dress of a profession or calling and esp. of the clergy; *also* : CLERGY

clothe \'klōt͟h\ *vt* **clothed** *or* **clad** \'klad\; **cloth·ing** 1 : DRESS 2 : to express or enhance by suitably significant language : COUCH

clothes \'klō(t͟h)z\ *n pl* 1 : CLOTHING 2 : BEDCLOTHES

clothes·horse \-,hȯrs\ *n* 1 : a frame on which to hang clothes 2 : a conspicuously dressy person

clothes·pin \-,pin\ *n* : a forked piece of wood or plastic or a small spring clamp used for fastening clothes on a line

clothes·press \-,pres\ *n* : a receptacle for clothes

cloth·ier \'klōt͟h-yər, 'klō-t͟hē-ər\ *n* : one who makes or sells cloth or clothing

cloth·ing \'klō-t͟hiŋ\ *n* : garments in general

clo·ture \'klō-chər\ *n* : the closing or limitation (as by calling for a vote) of debate in a legislative body

[1]**cloud** \'klau̇d\ *n* 1 : a visible mass of particles of water or ice suspended usu. at a considerable height in the air 2 : a visible mass of minute particles in the air 3 : a great crowd or multitude massed together : SWARM 4 : something that has a dark, lowering, or threatening aspect

[2]**cloud** *vb* 1 : to grow cloudy 2 : to darken, envelop, or hide with a cloud 3 : to make unclear : OBSCURE 4 : TAINT, SULLY

cloud·burst \-,bərst\ *n* : a sudden heavy rainfall

cloud·less \-ləs\ *adj* : free from any cloud : CLEAR

cloud·let \-lət\ *n* : a small cloud

cloudy \'klau̇d-ē\ *adj* 1 : of, relating to, or resembling cloud 2 : darkened by gloom or anxiety 3 : overcast with clouds 4 : obscure in meaning 5 : not clear : MURKY — **cloud·i·ly** \'klau̇d-ᵊl-ē\ *adv* — **cloud·i·ness** \'klau̇d-ē-nəs\ *n*

[1]**clout** \'klau̇t\ *n* : a blow esp. with the hand; *also* : a hard hit

[2]**clout** *vt* : to hit forcefully

[1]**clove** \'klōv\ *past of* CLEAVE

[2]**clove** *n* : the dried flower bud of a tropical tree of the myrtle family used esp. as a spice

clo·ver \'klō-vər\ *n* : any of a genus of leguminous herbs having leaves with three leaflets and flowers in dense heads

clo·ver·leaf \-,lēf\ *n* : a road plan that in shape resembles a four-leaf clover and that is used for passing one highway over another and for routing traffic so that all turns are from the right

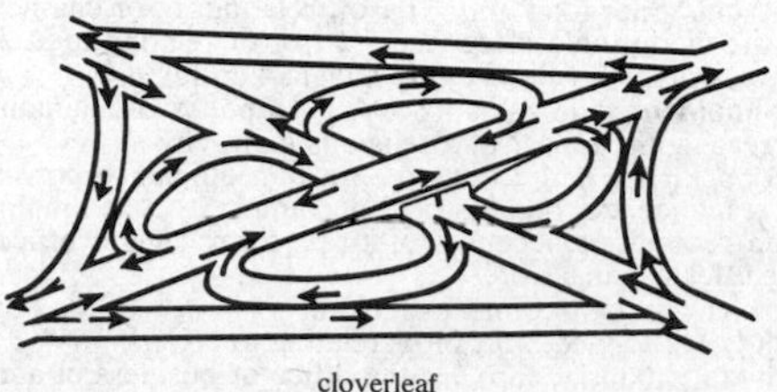

cloverleaf

[1]**clown** \'klau̇n\ *n* 1 : BOOR 2 : a fool, jester, or comedian in an entertainment (as a play)

[2]**clown** *vi* : to act as or like a clown

clown·ish \'klau̇-nish\ *adj* : of or resembling a clown : RUDE — **clown·ish·ly** *adv* — **clown·ish·ness** *n*

cloy \'klȯi\ *vb* : to disgust or nauseate with an excess usu. of something orig. pleasing : SURFEIT — **cloy·ing·ly** *adv*

[1]**club** \'kləb\ *n* 1 a : a heavy usu. tapering staff esp. of wood wielded as a weapon b : a stick or bat used for hitting a ball in a game c : any of a suit of playing cards marked with a black figure resembling a clover leaf 2 a : an association of persons for some common object b : the meeting place of a club

[2]**club** *vb* **clubbed**; **club·bing** 1 : to beat or strike with a club 2 : to unite or combine for a common cause — often used with *together*

club·foot \'kləb-'fu̇t\ *n* : a misshapen foot twisted out of position from birth — **club·foot·ed** \-əd\ *adj*

[1]**cluck** \'klək\ *vb* : to make or call with a cluck

[2]**cluck** *n* : the characteristic sound made by a hen esp. in calling her chicks

clue *var of* CLEW

[1]**clump** \'kləmp\ *n* 1 : a group of things clustered together 2 : a heavy tramping sound — **clumpy** \'kləm-pē\ *adj*

[2]**clump** *vb* 1 : to tread clumsily and noisily 2 : to form or cause to form clumps

clum·sy \'kləm-zē\ *adj* 1 a : lacking dexterity, nimbleness, or grace b : lacking tact or subtlety 2 : UNWIELDY — **clum·si·ly** \-zə-lē\ *adv* — **clum·si·ness** \-zē-nəs\ *n*

clung *past of* CLING

[1]**clus·ter** \'kləs-tər\ *n* : BUNCH

[2]**cluster** *vb* **clus·tered**; **clus·ter·ing** \-t(ə-)riŋ\ : to grow, collect, or assemble in a cluster

[1]**clutch** \'kləch\ *vb* : to grasp or hold with or as if with the hand or claws usu. strongly, tightly, or suddenly

[2]**clutch** *n* 1 a : the claws or a hand in the act of grasping b : CONTROL, POWER 2 : a device for gripping an object 3 : a coupling used to connect and disconnect a driving and a driven part of a mechanism 4 : a critical situation

[1]**clut·ter** \'klət-ər\ *vt* : to fill or cover with scattered things that impede movement or reduce effectiveness
[2]**clutter** *n* : a crowded or confused mass or collection
[1]**coach** \'kōch\ *n* **1 a** : a large usu. closed four-wheeled carriage having doors in the sides and an elevated seat in front for the driver **b** : a railroad passenger car intended primarily for day travel **c** : BUS **d** : an automobile body esp. of a closed model; *also* : a closed 2-door automobile for 4 or 5 passengers **2 a** : a private tutor **b** : one who instructs players in the fundamentals of a sport and directs team strategy
[2]**coach** *vb* **1** : to instruct, direct, or prompt as a coach **2** : to go in a horse-drawn coach — **coach·er** *n*
coach·man \-mən\ *n* : a man whose business is driving a coach or carriage
co·ad·ju·tor \ˌkō-ə-'jüt-ər, kō-'aj-ət-ər\ *n* : ASSISTANT; *esp* : a bishop assisting a diocesan bishop and having the right of succession — **coadjutor** *adj*
co·ag·u·late \kō-'ag-yə-ˌlāt\ *vb* : CLOT — **co·ag·u·la·tion** \(ˌ)kō-ˌag-yə-'lā-shən\ *n*
[1]**coal** \'kōl\ *n* **1** : EMBER **2** : a black solid mineral mined for use as a fuel
[2]**coal** *vb* **1** : to supply with coal **2** : to take in coal
co·a·lesce \ˌkō-ə-'les\ *vi* **1** : to grow together **2** : to unite into a whole : FUSE — **co·a·les·cence** \-'les-ᵊn(t)s\ *n* — **co·a·les·cent** \-ᵊnt\ *adj*
co·a·li·tion \ˌkō-ə-'lish-ən\ *n* : UNION, COMBINATION; *esp* : a temporary union of persons, parties, or countries for a common purpose — **co·a·li·tion·ist** \-'lish-(ə-)nəst\ *n*
coal oil *n* : KEROSENE
coal tar *n* : tar obtained by distilling bituminous coal and used in making drugs, dyes, and explosives
coarse \'kōrs\ *adj* **1** : of ordinary or inferior quality or appearance : COMMON **2 a** : composed of relatively large parts or particles **b** : loose or rough in texture **3** : crude in taste, manners, or language **4** : harsh or rough in tone — **coarse·ly** *adv* — **coarse·ness** *n*
coars·en \'kōrs-ᵊn\ *vb* **coars·ened**; **coars·en·ing** \'kōrs-niŋ, -ᵊn-iŋ\ : to make or become coarse
[1]**coast** \'kōst\ *n* **1** : the land near a shore : SEASHORE **2** : a slide down a slope
[2]**coast** *vb* **1** : to sail along the shore **2 a** : to slide, run, or glide downhill by the force of gravity **b** : to move along without application of power
coast·al \'kōst-ᵊl\ *adj* : located on, near, or along a coast
coast·er \'kō-stər\ *n* **1** : one that coasts **2** : a shallow container or a plate or mat to protect a surface
coast guard *n* : a military force employed in guarding or patrolling a coast
coast·line \'kōst-ˌlīn\ *n* : the outline or shape of a coast
coast·ward \'kōs-twərd\ *or* **coast·wards** \-twərdz\ *adv* : toward the coast — **coastward** *adj*
[1]**coat** \'kōt\ *n* **1** : an outer garment for the upper part of the body **2** : the external growth (as of fur) on an animal **3** : a layer of one substance covering another — **coat·ed** *adj*
[2]**coat** *vt* : to cover usu. with a finishing or protecting coat
coat·ing \'kōt-iŋ\ *n* : COAT, COVERING
coat of arms : the particular heraldic bearings (as of a person) usu. depicted on an escutcheon
coat of mail : a garment of metal scales or rings worn as armor
co·au·thor \(')kō-'ȯ-thər\ *n* : a joint or associate author
coax \'kōks\ *vb* **1** : WHEEDLE **2** : to draw or gain by gentle urging or flattery — **coax·er** *n*
co·ax·i·al \(')kō-'ak-sē-əl\ *adj* **1** : having coincident axes **2** : being an electrical cable that consists of a tube of conducting material surrounding a central conductor — **co·ax·i·al·ly** \-sē-ə-lē\ *adv*
cob \'käb\ *n* **1** : a male swan **2** : CORNCOB **3** : a short-legged stocky horse
co·balt \'kō-ˌbȯlt\ *n* : a tough shiny silver-white magnetic metallic element that occurs with iron and nickel — **co·bal·tic** \kō-'bȯl-tik\ *adj* — **co·bal·tous** \-təs\ *adj*
cob·ble \'käb-əl\ *vt* **cob·bled**; **cob·bling** \-(ə-)liŋ\ : to make or put together roughly or hastily
cob·bler \'käb-lər\ *n* **1** : a mender or maker of shoes **2** : a deep-dish fruit pie with a thick top crust
cob·ble·stone \'käb-əl-ˌstōn\ *n* : a naturally rounded stone larger than a pebble and smaller than a boulder
co·bra \'kō-brə\ *n* : any of several venomous Asiatic and African snakes that when excited expand the skin of the neck into a hood
cob·web \'käb-ˌweb\ *n* **1** : the network spread by a spider; *also* : a single thread spun by a spider or insect larva **2** : something resembling a spider web — **cob·webbed** \-ˌwebd\ *adj* — **cob·web·by** \-ˌweb-ē\ *adj*
co·caine \kō-'kān\ *n* : a bitter addictive drug obtained from the leaves of a South American plant and sometimes used as a local anesthetic
coch·i·neal \'käch-ə-ˌnēl\ *n* : a red dyestuff consisting of the dried bodies of a tropical American insect
co·chlea \'kō-klē-ə, 'käk-lē-\ *n, pl* **co·chle·as** *or* **co·chle·ae** \-(k)lē-ˌē, -ˌī\ : a part of the inner ear that is usu. coiled like a snail shell and is the seat of the hearing organ — **coch·le·ar** \-lē-ər\ *adj*
[1]**cock** \'käk\ *n* **1** : the adult male of a bird and esp. the domestic fowl **2** : a device for regulating the flow of a liquid **3** : the cocked position of the hammer of a firearm
[2]**cock** *vt* **1** : to draw the hammer of (a firearm) back **2** : to set erect **3** : to turn up (as a hat brim)
[3]**cock** *n* : a small pile (as of hay)
cock·ade \kä-'kād\ *n* : a rosette or a similar ornament worn on the hat as a badge
cock·a·too \'käk-ə-ˌtü\ *n, pl* **-toos** : any of numerous large noisy usu. showy and crested chiefly Australasian parrots
cock·crow \'käk-ˌkrō\ *n* : early morning
cock·er·el \'käk-(ə-)rəl\ *n* : a young male domestic fowl
cock·eye \'käk-'ī, -ˌī\ *n* : a squinting eye
cock–eyed \-'īd\ *adj* : having a cockeye
cock·fight \-ˌfīt\ *n* : a contest of gamecocks usu. fitted with metal spurs — **cock·fight·ing** *adj or n*
[1]**cock·le** \'käk-əl\ *n* : any of several grainfield weeds
[2]**cockle** *n* : an edible shellfish with a heart-shaped 2-valved shell
cock·le·shell \'käk-əl-ˌshel\ *n* **1** : a shell or shell valve of a cockle **2** : a light flimsy boat
cock·ney \'käk-nē\ *n, pl* **cockneys** *often cap* **1** : a native of London and esp. of the East End of London **2** : the dialect of a cockney — **cockney** *adj*
cock·pit \'käk-ˌpit\ *n* **1** : a pit for cockfights **2 a** : an open space aft of a decked area from which a small boat is steered **b** : a space in the fuselage of an airplane for the pilot or the pilot and passengers or the pilot and crew
cock·roach \'käk-ˌrōch\ *n* : any of an order of mostly nocturnal insects some of which are domestic pests
cock·sure \'käk-'shu̇(ə)r\ *adj* **1** : CERTAIN **2** : COCKY
cock·tail \-ˌtāl\ *n* **1** : an iced drink of distilled liquor mixed with flavoring ingredients **2** : an appetizer (as tomato juice) served as a first course at a meal
cocky \'käk-ē\ *adj* : PERT, CONCEITED — **cock·i·ness** \'käk-ē-nəs\ *n*
co·co \'kō-kō\ *n, pl* **cocos** : the coconut palm or its fruit
co·coa \'kō-kō\ *n* **1** : a cacao tree **2 a** : chocolate freed of some of its fat and ground **b** : a beverage prepared by cooking cocoa powder with water or milk
co·co·nut \'kō-kə-(ˌ)nət\ *n* : the fruit of a tall tropical palm with an outer fibrous husk and a nut containing thick edible meat and coconut milk

co·coon \kə-'kün\ *n* : a usu. largely silken envelope which an insect larva (as a caterpillar) forms about itself and in which it passes the pupa stage

cod \'käd\ *n, pl* **cod** : a soft-finned fish of the colder parts of the No. Atlantic that is a major food fish

co·da \'kōd-ə\ *n* : a closing section in a musical composition that is formally distinct from the main structure

cod·dle \'käd-ᵊl\ *vt* **cod·dled**; **cod·dling** \'käd-liŋ, -ᵊl-iŋ\ **1** : to cook slowly in water below the boiling point **2** : to treat as a little child or a pet : PAMPER

¹code \'kōd\ *n* **1** : a systematic statement of a body of law **2** : a system of principles or rules **3** : a system of signals **4** : a system of letters or symbols used (as in a computing machine) with special meanings

²code *vt* : to put in or into the form or symbols of a code — **cod·er** *n*

co·deine *or* **co·dein** \'kō-ˌdēn, 'kōd-ē-ən\ *n* : a drug obtained from opium and used in cough remedies

co·dex \'kō-ˌdeks\ *n, pl* **co·di·ces** \'kōd-ə-ˌsēz, 'käd-\ : a manuscript book (as of the Scriptures)

cod·fish \'käd-ˌfish\ *n* : COD; *also* : its flesh used as food

codg·er \'käj-ər\ *n* : an odd or cranky fellow

cod·i·cil \'käd-ə-səl\ *n* : a legal instrument modifying an earlier will

cod·i·fy \'käd-ə-ˌfī, 'kōd-\ *vt* **-fied**; **-fy·ing** : to arrange (as a collection of laws) in a systematic form — **cod·i·fi·ca·tion** \ˌkäd-ə-fə-'kā-shən, ˌkōd-\ *n*

cod·ling \'käd-liŋ\ *n* **1** : a young cod **2** : HAKE

¹co·ed \'kō-ˌed\ *n* : a female student in a coeducational institution

²coed *adj* **1** : COEDUCATIONAL **2** : of or relating to a coed

co·ed·u·ca·tion \(ˌ)kō-ˌej-ə-'kā-shən\ *n* : the education of male and female students at the same school or college — **co·ed·u·ca·tion·al** \-shnəl, -shən-ᵊl\ *adj*

co·ef·fi·cient \ˌkō-ə-'fish-ənt\ *n* **1** : any of the factors of a product considered in relation to a specific factor **2** : a number that serves as a measure of some property or characteristic (as of a substance or device)

co·equal \(')kō-'ē-kwəl\ *adj* : equal esp. in rank or status

co·erce \kō-'ərs\ *vt* **1** : to restrain or dominate by nullifying individual will **2** : to compel to an act or a choice **3** : to enforce by force or threat — **co·erc·i·ble** \-'ər-sə-bəl\ *adj*

co·er·cion \kō-'ər-zhən, -shən\ *n* : the act, process, or power of coercing

co·er·cive \-'ər-siv\ *adj* : serving or intended to coerce

co·eval \kō-'ē-vəl\ *adj* : of the same age — **coeval** *n*

co·ex·ist \ˌkō-ig-'zist\ *vi* **1** : to exist together or at the same time **2** : to live in peace with each other — **co·ex·ist·ence** \-'zis-tən(t)s\ *n* — **co·ex·ist·ent** \-tənt\ *adj*

co·ex·ten·sive \ˌkō-ik-'sten(t)-siv\ *adj* : having the same scope or extent in space or time — **co·ex·ten·sive·ly** *adv*

cof·fee \'kȯ-fē\ *n* **1** : a drink made from the roasted and ground seeds of a tropical tree or shrub; *also* : these seeds or a plant producing them **2** : a cup of coffee

cof·fee·house \-ˌhau̇s\ *n* : a place where refreshments (as coffee) are sold

cof·fee·pot \-ˌpät\ *n* : a covered utensil for preparing or serving coffee

cof·fer \'kȯ-fər\ *n* : CHEST, BOX; *esp* : a strongbox for valuables

cof·fer·dam \-ˌdam\ *n* : a watertight enclosure from which water is pumped to expose the bottom of a body of water and permit construction

cof·fin \'kȯ-fən\ *n* : a box or chest for a corpse to be buried in

cog \'käg\ *n* : a tooth on the rim of a wheel adjusted to fit the notches in a receiving wheel or bar and to give or receive motion

co·gent \'kō-jənt\ *adj* : having power to compel or constrain : CONVINCING — **co·gen·cy** \-jən-sē\ *n* — **co·gent·ly** *adv*

cog·i·tate \'käj-ə-ˌtāt\ *vb* : to think over intently or deeply : PONDER — **cog·i·ta·tion** \ˌkäj-ə-'tā-shən\ *n*

co·gnac \'kōn-ˌyak\ *n* : a French brandy

cog·nate \'käg-ˌnāt\ *adj* **1** : related by descent from the same ancestral language **2** : related by adoption from one source language into two or more other languages **3** : of the same or similar nature — **cognate** *n*

cog·ni·tion \käg-'nish-ən\ *n* : the act or process of knowing — **cog·ni·tive** \'käg-nət-iv\ *adj*

cog·ni·zance \'käg-nə-zən(t)s\ *n* **1** : KNOWLEDGE **2** : NOTICE, HEED **3** : AWARENESS

cog·ni·zant \-zənt\ *adj* : having cognizance

cog·no·men \käg-'nō-mən, 'käg-nə-\ *n, pl* **-nomens** *or* **-no·mi·na** \-'näm-ə-nə, -'nō-mə-\ : NAME; *esp* : NICKNAME

cog·wheel \'käg-ˌhwēl\ *n* : a wheel with cogs on the rim

co·hab·it \kō-'hab-ət\ *vi* : to live together as husband and wife — **co·hab·i·ta·tion** \(ˌ)kō-ˌhab-ə-'tā-shən\ *n*

co·here \kō-'hi(ə)r\ *vi* **1 a** : to hold together firmly as parts of the same mass **b** : ADHERE **2** : to consist of parts that cohere — **co·her·ence** \-'hir-ən(t)s\ *or* **co·her·en·cy** \-ən-sē\ *n*

co·her·ent \kō-'hir-ənt\ *adj* **1** : having the quality of cohering **2** : logically consistent — **co·her·ent·ly** *adv*

co·he·sion \kō-'hē-zhən\ *n* **1** : the action of sticking together tightly **2** : molecular attraction by which the particles of a body are united throughout the mass

co·he·sive \kō-'hē-siv\ *adj* : exhibiting or producing cohesion — **co·he·sive·ly** *adv* — **co·he·sive·ness** *n*

co·hort \'kō-ˌhȯrt\ *n* **1** : a group of warriors or followers **2** : COMPANION, ACCOMPLICE

coif \'kȯif, *in sense 2 usu* 'kwäf\ *n* **1** : a close-fitting cap **2** : COIFFURE

coif·fure \kwä-'fyu̇(ə)r\ *n* : a manner of arranging the hair

¹coil \'kȯil\ *vb* **1** : to wind into rings or spirals **2** : to move in a circular, spiral, or winding course

²coil *n* **1** : a series of loops : SPIRAL **2** : a single loop of a coil

¹coin \'kȯin\ *n* **1** : a piece of metal issued by governmental authority as money **2** : metal money

²coin *vt* **1** : to make (a coin) esp. by stamping : MINT **2** : CREATE, INVENT — **coin·er** *n*

coin·age \'kȯi-nij\ *n* **1** : the act or process of coining **2 a** : COINS **b** : something (as a word) made up or invented

co·in·cide \ˌkō-ən-'sīd\ *vi* **1** : to occupy the same place in space or time **2** : to correspond or agree exactly

co·in·ci·dence \kō-'in(t)-səd-ən(t)s\ *n* **1** : the act or condition of coinciding **2** : two things that happen at the same time by accident but seem to have some connection

co·in·ci·dent \-səd-ənt\ *adj* **1** : occupying the same space or time **2** : of similar nature : HARMONIOUS — **co·in·ci·dent·ly** *adv*

co·in·ci·den·tal \(ˌ)kō-ˌin(t)-sə-'dent-ᵊl\ *adj* **1** : resulting from a coincidence **2** : occurring or existing at the same time — **co·in·ci·den·tal·ly** \-'dent-ᵊl-ē, -'dent-lē\ *adv*

co·i·tus \'kō-ət-əs\ *n* : sexual intercourse

coke \'kōk\ *n* : gray porous lumps of fuel made by heating soft coal until some of its gases have passed off

co·la \'kō-lə\ *n* : a carbonated soft drink containing sugar, caffeine, phosphoric acid or citric acid, caramel, and a characteristic flavoring

col·an·der \'kəl-ən-dər, 'käl-\ *n* : a perforated utensil for draining food

¹cold \'kōld\ *adj* **1** : having a low temperature or one decidedly below normal **2** : lacking warmth of feeling : UNFRIENDLY **3** : uncomfortable from lack of warmth — **cold·ly** *adv* — **cold·ness** *n* — **in cold blood** : with premeditation

²cold *n* **1 a** : a condition of low temperature **b** : cold weather **2** : bodily sensation produced by loss or lack of heat : CHILL **3** : a bodily disorder (as a respiratory inflammation) popularly associated with chilling

cold–blood·ed \'kōl(d)-'bləd-əd\ *adj* **1 :** lacking or showing a lack of natural human feelings **2 :** sensitive to cold — **cold–blood·ed·ly** *adv* — **cold–blood·ed·ness** *n*

cole·slaw \'kōl-ˌslȯ\ *n* **:** a salad made of sliced or chopped raw cabbage

col·ic \'käl-ik\ *n* **:** sharp sudden pain in the abdomen — **col·icky** \'käl-i-kē\ *adj*

col·i·se·um \ˌkäl-ə-'sē-əm\ *n* **:** a large building, amphitheater, or stadium for athletic contests or public entertainments

col·lab·o·rate \kə-'lab-ə-ˌrāt\ *vi* **1 :** to work jointly with others (as in writing a book) **2 :** to cooperate with or assist an enemy force occupying one's country — **col·lab·o·ra·tion** \-ˌlab-ə-'rā-shən\ *n* — **col·lab·o·ra·tion·ist** \-sh(ə-)nəst\ *n* — **col·lab·o·ra·tor** \-'lab-ə-ˌrāt-ər\ *n*

[1]**col·lapse** \kə-'laps\ *vb* **1 :** to break down completely **:** DISINTEGRATE **2 :** to fall or shrink together abruptly and completely **3 :** to fall in **:** give way **4 :** to break down physically or mentally through exhaustion or disease; *esp* **:** to fall helpless or unconscious — **col·laps·i·ble** \-'lap-sə-bəl\ *adj*

[2]**collapse** *n* **:** the act or an instance of collapsing

[1]**col·lar** \'käl-ər\ *n* **1 :** a band, strip, or chain worn around the neck or the neckline of a garment **2 :** something resembling a collar — **col·lar·less** \-ər-ləs\ *adj*

[2]**collar** *vt* **:** to seize by the collar; *also* **:** CAPTURE, GRAB

col·lar·bone \-ˌbōn\ *n* **:** CLAVICLE

col·late \kə-'lāt, 'käl-ˌāt\ *vt* **:** to compare carefully — **col·la·tor** \kə-'lāt-ər, 'käl-ˌāt-\ *n*

[1]**col·lat·er·al** \kə-'lat-ə-rəl, -'la-trəl\ *adj* **1 :** associated but of secondary importance **2 :** descended from the same ancestors but not in the same line **3 a :** of, relating to, or being collateral used as security **b :** secured by collateral — **col·lat·er·al·ly** \-ē\ *adv*

[2]**collateral** *n* **:** property (as stocks) handed over or pledged as security for the repayment of a loan

col·la·tion \kə-'lā-shən, kä-\ *n* **1 :** a light meal **2 :** the act, process, or result of collating

col·league \'käl-ˌēg\ *n* **:** an associate in a profession or office; *also* **:** a fellow worker

[1]**col·lect** \'käl-ikt\ *n* **:** a short prayer comprising an invocation, petition, and conclusion

[2]**col·lect** \kə-'lekt\ *vb* **1 a :** to bring together into one body or place **b :** to gather from a number of sources **2 :** to gain control of **3 :** to receive payment for — **col·lect·i·ble** *or* **col·lect·a·ble** \-'lek-tə-bəl\ *adj* — **col·lec·tor** \-'lek-tər\ *n*

[3]**col·lect** \kə-'lekt\ *adv* (*or adj*) **:** to be paid for by the receiver

col·lect·ed \kə-'lek-təd\ *adj* **:** SELF-POSSESSED, CALM — **col·lect·ed·ly** *adv* — **col·lect·ed·ness** *n*

col·lec·tion \kə-'lek-shən\ *n* **1 :** the act or process of collecting **2 :** something collected **3 :** a gathering of money (as for charitable purposes)

[1]**col·lec·tive** \kə-'lek-tiv\ *adj* **1 :** of, relating to, or denoting a number of persons or things considered as a whole **2 :** formed by collecting **3 :** shared or assumed by all members of the group — **col·lec·tive·ly** *adv*

[2]**collective** *n* **1 :** a collective body **:** GROUP **2 :** a cooperative unit or organization

col·lec·tiv·ism \kə-'lek-ti-ˌviz-əm\ *n* **:** a political or economic theory advocating collective control esp. over production and distribution — **col·lec·tiv·ist** \-vəst\ *adj or n*

col·lec·tiv·i·ty \ˌkäl-ˌek-'tiv-ət-ē, kə-ˌlek-\ *n, pl* **-ties :** a collective whole

col·lec·tiv·ize \kə-'lek-ti-ˌvīz\ *vt* **:** to organize under collective control — **col·lec·tiv·i·za·tion** \-ˌlek-ti-və-'zā-shən\ *n*

col·leen \kä-'lēn, 'käl-ˌēn\ *n* **:** an Irish girl

col·lege \'käl-ij\ *n* **1 :** a building used for an educational or religious purpose **2 a :** an institution of higher learning offering courses leading to a bachelor's degree **b :** an institution offering instruction usu. in a professional, vocational, or technical field **3 :** an organized body of persons having common interests or duties

col·le·gian \kə-'lē-j(ē-)ən\ *n* **:** a college student

col·le·giate \kə-'lē-j(ē-)ət\ *adj* **:** of or relating to a college or college students

col·le·gi·um \kə-'leg-ē-əm, -'lāg-\ *n* **:** a governing group in which each member has equal power and authority

col·lide \kə-'līd\ *vi* **1 :** to come together with solid impact **2 :** CLASH

col·lie \'käl-ē\ *n* **:** a large usu. long-coated dog of a Scottish breed used in herding sheep

col·lier \'käl-yər\ *n* **1 :** a coal miner **2 :** a ship for carrying coal

col·liery \'käl-yə-rē\ *n, pl* **-lier·ies :** a coal mine

col·li·sion \kə-'lizh-ən\ *n* **:** an act or instance of colliding

col·lo·ca·tion \ˌkäl-ə-'kā-shən\ *n* **:** a placing together or side by side; *also* **:** the result of such placing

col·lo·di·on \kə-'lōd-ē-ən\ *n* **:** a sticky substance that hardens in the air and is used esp. as a coating for wounds or for photographic films

col·loid \'käl-ˌȯid\ *n* **:** a substance in a fine state of division with particles that are not visible in an ordinary microscope but that when in suspension in a liquid or gas are made visible by a beam of light and do not settle out; *also* **:** such a substance together with the gaseous, liquid, or solid substance in which it is dispersed — **col·loi·dal** \kə-'lȯid-ᵊl, kä-\ *adj* — **col·loi·dal·ly** \-ᵊl-ē\ *adv*

col·lo·qui·al \kə-'lō-kwē-əl\ *adj* **1 :** CONVERSATIONAL **2 :** used in or characteristic of familiar and informal conversation — **col·lo·qui·al·ly** \-kwē-ə-lē\ *adv*

col·lo·qui·al·ism \-kwē-ə-ˌliz-əm\ *n* **1 :** a colloquial expression **2 :** colloquial style

col·lo·quy \'käl-ə-kwē\ *n, pl* **-quies :** CONVERSATION; *esp* **:** a formal conversation or conference

col·lu·sion \kə-'lü-zhən\ *n* **:** secret agreement or cooperation for a fraudulent or deceitful purpose — **col·lu·sive** \-'lü-siv\ *adj* — **col·lu·sive·ly** *adv*

co·logne \kə-'lōn\ *n* **:** a perfumed liquid composed of alcohol and certain aromatic oils

[1]**co·lon** \'kō-lən\ *n* **:** the part of the large intestine that extends from the cecum to the rectum — **co·lon·ic** \kō-'län-ik\ *adj*

[2]**colon** *n* **:** a punctuation mark **:** used chiefly to direct attention to what follows (as a list, explanation, or quotation)

col·o·nel \'kərn-ᵊl\ *n* **:** a commissioned officer (as in the army) ranking next below a brigadier general — **col·o·nel·cy** \-ᵊl-sē\ *n*

[1]**co·lo·nial** \kə-'lō-nyəl, -nē-əl\ *adj* **1 :** of, relating to, or characteristic of a colony **2** *often cap* **:** of or relating to the original 13 colonies forming the United States **3 :** possessing, forming, or composed of colonies

[2]**colonial** *n* **:** a member or inhabitant of a colony

co·lo·nial·ism \-nyə-ˌliz-əm, -nē-ə-ˌliz-\ *n* **:** control by one power over a dependent area or people; *also* **:** a policy advocating or based on such control — **co·lo·nial·ist** \-ləst\ *n or adj*

col·o·nist \'käl-ə-nəst\ *n* **1 :** an inhabitant or member of a colony **2 :** a person who takes part in founding a colony

col·o·nize \'käl-ə-ˌnīz\ *vb* **1 :** to establish a colony in or on **2 :** to establish in a colony — **col·o·ni·za·tion** \ˌkäl-ə-nə-'zā-shən\ *n* — **col·o·niz·er** *n*

col·on·nade \ˌkäl-ə-'nād\ *n* **:** a row of columns usu. supporting the base of the roof structure

col·o·ny \'käl-ə-nē\ *n, pl* **-nies 1 a :** a body of people sent out by a state to a new territory **b :** the territory inhabited by people sent to new territory **2 :** a distinguishable localized population of organisms **3 :** a group of individuals with common interests; *also* **:** the section occupied by such a group

[1]**col·or** \'kəl-ər\ *n* **1 a :** a phenomenon of light (as red, brown, pink, gray) or visual perception that enables one to differenti-

ate otherwise identical objects **b :** a hue as contrasted with black, white, or gray **2 :** an outward often deceptive show : APPEARANCE **3 :** complexion tint **4** *pl* **a :** an identifying flag, ensign, or pennant **b :** service in the armed forces **5 :** VITALITY, INTEREST

²color *vb* **1 a :** to give color to **b :** to change the color of : PAINT **2 :** MISREPRESENT, DISTORT **3 :** BLUSH — **col·or·er** *n*

col·or·a·tion \ˌkəl-ə-ˈrā-shən\ *n* : use or arrangement of colors or shades

col·or·a·tu·ra \ˌkəl-ə-rə-ˈt(y)u̇r-ə\ *n* **1 :** florid ornamentation in vocal music **2 :** a soprano specializing in coloratura

col·ored \ˈkəl-ərd\ *adj* **1 :** having color **2 :** SLANTED, BIASED **3 :** of a race other than the white; *esp* : NEGRO

col·or·fast \ˈkəl-ər-ˌfast\ *adj* : having color that does not fade or run — **col·or·fast·ness** *n*

col·or·ful \ˈkəl-ər-fəl\ *adj* **1 :** having striking colors **2 :** full of variety or interest — **col·or·ful·ly** \-f(ə-)lē\ *adv*

col·or·ing \ˈkəl-ə-riŋ\ *n* **1 :** the act of applying colors **2 :** something that produces color **3 a :** the effect produced by applying or combining colors **b :** natural color **c :** COMPLEXION, COLORATION

col·or·less \ˈkəl-ər-ləs\ *adj* **1 :** lacking color **2 :** PALLID, BLANCHED **3 :** DULL, UNINTERESTING — **col·or·less·ly** *adv* — **col·or·less·ness** *n*

co·los·sal \kə-ˈläs-əl\ *adj* **1 :** of very great size **2 :** EXCEPTIONAL, ASTONISHING

co·los·sus \kə-ˈläs-əs\ *n, pl* **-los·sus·es** *or* **-los·si** \-ˈläs-ˌī, -(ˌ)ē\ **1 :** a statue of gigantic size and proportions **2 :** one resembling a colossus esp. in size

colt \ˈkōlt\ *n* **1 :** FOAL **2 :** a young male horse

colt·ish \ˈkōl-tish\ *adj* **1 :** FRISKY, PLAYFUL **2 :** of, relating to, or resembling a colt — **colt·ish·ly** *adv*

col·um·bine \ˈkäl-əm-ˌbīn\ *n* : any of a genus of plants related to the buttercups that have showy flowers with usu. five spurred petals

col·umn \ˈkäl-əm\ *n* **1 a :** one of two or more vertical sections of a printed page **b :** a special department in a newspaper or periodical **2 :** a supporting pillar; *esp* : one consisting of a usu. round shaft, a capital, and a base **3 :** something resembling a column **4 :** a long row (as of soldiers) — **co·lum·nar** \kə-ˈləm-nər\ *adj*

col·um·nist \ˈkäl-əm-(n)əst\ *n* : a person who writes a newspaper column

co·ma \ˈkō-mə\ *n* : a state of profound unconsciousness caused by disease, injury, or poison — **co·ma·tose** \-ˌtōs\ *adj*

¹comb \ˈkōm\ *n* **1 a :** a toothed implement to smooth and arrange the hair or worn in the hair to hold it in place **b :** a toothed instrument for separating fibers (as of wool or flax) **2 :** a fleshy crest on the head of a fowl **3 :** HONEYCOMB — **combed** \ˈkōmd\ *adj*

combs of various roosters

²comb *vb* **1 :** to smooth, arrange, or untangle with a comb **2 :** to go over or through carefully in search of something

¹com·bat \kəm-ˈbat, ˈkäm-ˌ\ *vb* **-bat·ed** *or* **-bat·ted**; **-bat·ing** *or* **-bat·ting** **1 :** to fight with **2 :** to struggle against

²com·bat \ˈkäm-ˌbat\ *n* **1 :** a fight or contest between individuals or groups **2 :** CONFLICT, CONTROVERSY **3 :** active fighting in a war

com·bat·ant \kəm-ˈbat-ᵊnt, ˈkäm-bət-ənt\ *adj* : engaging in or ready to engage in combat — **combatant** *n*

com·bat·ive \kəm-ˈbat-iv\ *adj* : eager to fight : PUGNACIOUS — **com·bat·ive·ly** *adv* — **com·bat·ive·ness** *n*

comb·er \ˈkō-mər\ *n* **1 :** one that combs fibers (as of wool) **2 :** a long curling wave rolling in from the ocean

com·bi·na·tion \ˌkäm-bə-ˈnā-shən\ *n* **1 :** a result or product of combining **2 :** a sequence of letters or numbers chosen in setting a lock **3 a :** the act or process of combining **b :** the quality or state of being combined

¹com·bine \kəm-ˈbīn\ *vb* **1 :** to bring into close relationship : UNIFY **2 :** INTERMIX, BLEND **3 :** to become one — **com·bin·a·ble** *adj* — **com·bin·er** *n*

²com·bine \ˈkäm-ˌbīn\ *n* **1 :** a combination to gain an often illicit end **2 :** a harvesting machine that harvests, threshes, and cleans grain while moving over a field

comb·ings \ˈkō-miŋz\ *n pl* : loose hairs or fibers removed by a comb

com·bin·ing form \kəm-ˌbī-niŋ-\ *n* : a linguistic form that occurs only in compounds or derivatives

com·bo \ˈkäm-ˌbō\ *n, pl* **combos** : a small jazz or dance band

com·bus·ti·ble \kəm-ˈbəs-tə-bəl\ *adj* **1 :** capable of being burned **2 :** catching fire or burning easily — **com·bus·ti·bil·i·ty** \-ˌbəs-tə-ˈbil-ət-ē\ *n* — **combustible** *n*

com·bus·tion \kəm-ˈbəs-chən\ *n* **1 :** the process of burning **2 :** a chemical process in which substances combine with oxygen

come \(ˈ)kəm\ *vi* **came** \ˈkām\; **come**; **com·ing** \ˈkəm-iŋ\ **1 :** to move toward something : APPROACH **2 :** to move toward or enter a scene of action or into a field of interest **3 a :** to reach the point of being or becoming **b :** AMOUNT **4 a :** to have a place (as in a series) **b :** to proceed as a consequence, effect, or conclusion **5 :** ORIGINATE, ARISE **6 :** to be obtainable **7 :** EXTEND, REACH **8 a :** to arrive at a particular place, end, result, or conclusion **b :** HAPPEN, OCCUR **9 :** to fall within a scope — **come across :** to meet or find by chance — **come at** : to reach a mastery of : ATTAIN — **come by** : ACQUIRE — **come into :** to acquire as an inheritance

come about *vi* **1 :** to come to pass **2 :** to change direction

come around *vi* : to come round

come·back \ˈkəm-ˌbak\ *n* **1 :** RETORT **2 :** a return to a former position or condition (as of health, power, popularity, or prosperity) : RECOVERY

co·me·di·an \kə-ˈmēd-ē-ən\ *n* **1 :** an actor who plays in comedy **2 :** a comical individual

co·me·di·enne \kə-ˌmēd-ē-ˈen\ *n* : a female comedian

come down *vi* : to fall sick

come·down \ˈkəm-ˌdau̇n\ *n* : a descent in rank or dignity

com·e·dy \ˈkäm-əd-ē\ *n, pl* **-dies** **1 :** a drama of light and amusing character typically with a happy ending **2 :** a literary work written in a comic style or treating a comic theme

come in *vi* **1 :** to be the recipient **2 :** to attain maturity, fruitfulness, or production

come·ly \ˈkəm-lē\ *adj* : pleasing to the sight : good-looking — **come·li·ness** *n*

come out *vi* **1 a :** to come into view : EMERGE **b :** to make one's debut **2 :** to turn out **3 :** to declare oneself

com·er \ˈkəm-ər\ *n* **1 :** one that comes **2 :** a promising newcomer

come round *vi* **1 :** to come to **2 :** to change direction or opinion

¹co·mes·ti·ble \kə-ˈmes-tə-bəl\ *adj* : EDIBLE

²comestible *n* : FOOD — usu. used in pl.
com·et \'käm-ət\ *n* : a celestial body that consists of a fuzzy head usu. surrounding a bright nucleus, that often when in the part of its orbit near the sun develops a long tail which points away from the sun, and that has a nearly round or an elongated orbit
come to *vi* : to recover consciousness
come·up·pance \(,)kə-'məp-ən(t)s\ *n* : a deserved rebuke or penalty : DESERTS
com·fit \'kəm(p)-fət\ *n* : a confection consisting of a piece of fruit, a root, or a seed coated and preserved with sugar
¹com·fort \'kəm(p)-fərt\ *n* **1** : acts or words that comfort **2** : the feeling of the one that is comforted **3** : something that makes a person comfortable — **com·fort·less** \-ləs\ *adj*
²comfort *vt* **1** : to give strength and hope to : CHEER **2** : to ease the grief or trouble of : CONSOLE
com·fort·a·ble \'kəm(p)(f)-tə-bəl, 'kəm(p)-fərt-ə-bəl\ *adj* **1** : giving comfort **2** : more than adequate **3** : physically at ease — **com·fort·a·ble·ness** *n* — **com·fort·a·bly** \-blē\ *adv*
com·fort·er \'kəm(p)-fə(r)t-ər\ *n* **1** : one that gives comfort **2** : QUILT
¹com·ic \'käm-ik\ *adj* **1** : of, relating to, or marked by comedy **2** : causing laughter or amusement : FUNNY
²comic *n* **1** : COMEDIAN **2 a** : COMIC STRIP **b** *pl* : the part of a newspaper devoted to comic strips
com·i·cal \'käm-i-kəl\ *adj* : amusingly whimsical : DROLL, LAUGHABLE — **com·i·cal·i·ty** \,käm-i-'kal-ət-ē\ *n* — **com·i·cal·ly** \'käm-i-k(ə-)lē\ *adv*
comic strip *n* : a sequence of cartoons that tell a story
com·ing \'kəm-iŋ\ *adj* **1** : APPROACHING, NEXT **2** : gaining importance
co·mi·ty \'käm-ət-ē, 'kō-mət-\ *n, pl* **-ties** : courteous behavior
com·ma \'käm-ə\ *n* : a punctuation mark , used chiefly to show separation of words or word groups within a sentence
¹com·mand \kə-'mand\ *vb* **1 a** : to direct authoritatively : ORDER, GOVERN **b** : to have authority and control of a military force or post : be commander of **2 a** : to have at one's disposal **b** : to overlook from a strategic position
²command *n* **1** : the act of commanding **2** : an order given **3 a** : the ability to control : MASTERY **b** : the authority or right to command **c** : facility in using **4** : the personnel, area, or unit under a commander **5** : a position from which military operations are directed
³command *adj* : done on command or request
com·man·dant \'käm-ən-,dant, -,dänt\ *n* : COMMANDING OFFICER
com·man·deer \,käm-ən-'di(ə)r\ *vt* : to take arbitrary or forcible possession of esp. for military purposes
com·mand·er \kə-'man-dər\ *n* **1** : one in official command; *esp* : COMMANDING OFFICER **2** : a commissioned officer in the navy ranking next below a captain — **com·mand·er·ship** \-,ship\ *n*
commander in chief : one who holds the supreme command of an armed force
commanding officer *n* : a military or naval officer in command of a unit or post
com·mand·ment \kə-'man(d)-mənt\ *n* : something commanded; *esp* : one of the biblical Ten Commandments
com·man·do \kə-'man-dō\ *n, pl* **-dos** *or* **-does** : a member of a military unit trained and organized for surprise raids into enemy territory
com·mem·o·rate \kə-'mem-ə-,rāt\ *vt* **1** : to call to remembrance **2** : to mark by a ceremony : OBSERVE **3** : to be a memorial of — **com·mem·o·ra·tor** \-,rāt-ər\ *n*
com·mem·o·ra·tion \kə-,mem-ə-'rā-shən\ *n* **1** : the act of commemorating **2** : something that commemorates
com·mem·o·ra·tive \kə-'mem-ə-,rāt-iv\ *adj* : intended to commemorate an event — **commemorative** *n*
com·mence \kə-'men(t)s\ *vb* : BEGIN, START
com·mence·ment \-'men(t)s-mənt\ *n* **1** : an act, instance, or time of commencing **2** : the graduation ceremonies of a school or college
com·mend \kə-'mend\ *vb* **1** : to give into another's care : ENTRUST **2** : PRAISE — **com·mend·a·ble** *adj* — **com·mend·a·bly** \-'men-də-blē\ *adv*
com·men·da·tion \,käm-ən-'dā-shən\ *n* **1** : an act of commending **2** : something that commends — **com·men·da·to·ry** \kə-'men-də-,tōr-ē\ *adj*
com·men·su·rate \kə-'men(t)s-(ə-)rət, -'mench-(ə-)rət\ *adj* **1** : equal in measure or extent **2** : CORRESPONDING, PROPORTIONATE — **com·men·su·rate·ly** *adv*
¹com·ment \'käm-,ent\ *n* **1** : an expression of opinion **2 a** : REMARK **b** : a critical remark
²comment *vi* : to make a comment : REMARK
com·men·tary \'käm-ən-,ter-ē\ *n, pl* **-tar·ies** **1** : an explanatory or narrative treatise — often used in pl. **2** : a series of oral comments or written notes
com·men·ta·tor \-,tāt-ər\ *n* : one who gives a commentary; *esp* : one who reports and discusses news on radio or television
com·merce \'käm-(,)ərs\ *n* **1** : social intercourse **2** : the exchange or buying and selling of commodities on a large scale
¹com·mer·cial \kə-'mər-shəl\ *adj* **1** : of, relating to, or suitable for commerce **2** : viewed with regard to profit or mass appeal **3** : emphasizing skills and subjects useful in business — **com·mer·cial·ly** \-'mərsh-(ə-)lē\ *adv*
²commercial *n* : an advertisement broadcast on radio or television
com·mer·cial·ism \kə-'mər-shə-,liz-əm\ *n* : a spirit, method, or practice characteristic of business
com·mer·cial·ize \kə-'mər-shə-,līz\ *vt* **1** : to manage on a business basis for profit **2** : to exploit for profit — **com·mer·cial·i·za·tion** \-,mər-shə-lə-'zā-shən\ *n*
com·mie \'käm-ē\ *n, often cap* : COMMUNIST
com·min·gle \kə-'miŋ-gəl\ *vb* : MIX, MINGLE
com·mi·nute \'käm-ə-,n(y)üt\ *vt* : to reduce to minute particles — **com·mi·nu·tion** \,käm-ə-'n(y)ü-shən\ *n*
com·mis·er·ate \kə-'miz-ə-,rāt\ *vb* **1** : to feel or express sorrow or compassion for **2** : CONDOLE, SYMPATHIZE — **com·mis·er·a·tion** \-,miz-ə-'rā-shən\ *n*
com·mis·sar \'käm-ə-,sär\ *n* : a Communist party official assigned to a military unit to teach party principles and policies and to ensure party loyalty
com·mis·sar·i·at \,käm-ə-'ser-ē-ət\ *n* : a system for supplying an army with food
com·mis·sary \'käm-ə-,ser-ē\ *n, pl* **-sar·ies** : a store supplying provisions esp. to military personnel and dependents
¹com·mis·sion \kə-'mish-ən\ *n* **1 a** : a formal order granting the power to perform various acts or duties **b** : a certificate conferring military rank and authority **2** : an authorization or command to perform prescribed acts : CHARGE **3 a** : authority to act as agent for another **b** : a task or matter entrusted to an agent **4 a** : a group of persons directed to perform some duty **b** : a government agency having administrative, legislative, or judicial powers **5** : an act of committing (as a crime) **6** : a fee (as a percentage of money received) paid to an agent or employee
²commission *vt* **-mis·sioned**; **-mis·sion·ing** \-'mish-(ə-)niŋ\ **1** : to confer a commission on **2** : to order to be made **3** : to put (a ship) into a state of readiness for service
commissioned officer *n* : a military or naval officer holding by a commission a rank of second lieutenant or ensign or a higher rank
com·mis·sion·er \kə-'mish-(ə-)nər\ *n* **1** : a member of a commission **2** : an official in charge of a government department
com·mit \kə-'mit\ *vt* **com·mit·ted**; **com·mit·ting** **1 a** : to put

into charge or trust : ENTRUST **b** : to place in a prison or mental institution **c** : to consign for preservation, disposal, or safekeeping **2** : to bring about : PERFORM **3** : to pledge or assign to some particular course or use
com·mit·ment \kə-ˈmit-mənt\ *n* **1** : an act of committing to a charge or trust **2** : an agreement or pledge to do something
com·mit·tee \kə-ˈmit-ē\ *n* : a body of persons delegated to consider or take action on some matter
com·mit·tee·man \-mən, -ˌman\ *n* **1** : a member of a committee **2** : a party leader of a ward or precinct — **com·mit·tee·wom·an** \-ˌwu̇m-ən\ *n*
com·mode \kə-ˈmōd\ *n* : a movable washstand with a cupboard underneath
com·mo·di·ous \kə-ˈmōd-ē-əs\ *adj* : comfortably or conveniently spacious : ROOMY — **com·mo·di·ous·ly** *adv* — **com·mo·di·ous·ness** *n*
com·mod·i·ty \kə-ˈmäd-ət-ē\ *n, pl* **-ties** **1** : a product of agriculture or mining **2** : an article exchanged in commerce
com·mo·dore \ˈkäm-ə-ˌdō(ə)r\ *n* **1** : a commissioned officer in the navy ranking next below a rear admiral **2** : the chief officer of a yacht club
[1]**com·mon** \ˈkäm-ən\ *adj* **1** : having to do with, belonging to, or used by everybody : PUBLIC **2** : belonging to or shared by a number in a group **3** : widely or generally known, met, or seen **4** : FREQUENT, FAMILIAR **5** : not above the average in rank, merit, or social position **6** : PLAIN, PRACTICAL **7 a** : falling below ordinary standards **b** : lacking refinement — **com·mon·ly** *adv* — **com·mon·ness** \-ən-nəs\ *n*
[2]**common** *n* **1** *pl* : the common people **2** *pl* : a dining hall **3** *pl, cap* : the lower house of the British and Canadian parliaments **4** : a piece of land subject to common use — often used in pl. — **in common** : shared together
com·mon·al·i·ty \ˌkäm-ə-ˈnal-ət-ē\ *or* **com·mon·al·ty** \ˈkäm-ə-nəl-tē\ *n, pl* **-ties** : the common people
com·mon·er \ˈkäm-ə-nər\ *n* : one of the common people : one who is not of noble rank
[1]**com·mon·place** \ˈkäm-ən-ˌplās\ *n* : an obvious or trite remark
[2]**commonplace** *adj* : ORDINARY, UNREMARKABLE
com·mon·weal \ˈkäm-ən-ˌwēl\ *n* : the general welfare
com·mon·wealth \-ˌwelth\ *n* **1** : a political unit whose aim is the common good of all the people **2** : a state of the U.S. — used officially of Kentucky, Massachusetts, Pennsylvania, and Virginia **3** *often cap* : an association of self-governing states
com·mo·tion \kə-ˈmō-shən\ *n* **1** : disturbed or violent motion **2 a** : noisy excitement and confusion **b** : TUMULT
com·mu·nal \kə-ˈmyün-ᵊl\ *adj* **1** : of or relating to a commune or community **2** : characterized by collective ownership and use of property
[1]**com·mune** \kə-ˈmyün\ *vi* **1** : to receive Communion **2** : to communicate intimately
[2]**com·mune** \ˈkäm-ˌyün\ *n* : the smallest administrative district of many countries esp. in Europe
com·mu·ni·ca·ble \kə-ˈmyü-ni-kə-bəl\ *adj* : capable of being communicated : TRANSMITTABLE
com·mu·ni·cant \kə-ˈmyü-ni-kənt\ *n* **1** : a person who partakes of Communion : a church member **2** : a person who communicates — **communicant** *adj*
com·mu·ni·cate \kə-ˈmyü-nə-ˌkāt\ *vb* **1 a** : to make known **b** : TRANSFER, TRANSMIT **2** : to receive Communion **3** : to be in communication **4** : JOIN, CONNECT — **com·mu·ni·ca·tor** \-ˌkāt-ər\ *n*
com·mu·ni·ca·tion \kə-ˌmyü-nə-ˈkā-shən\ *n* **1** : an act or instance of transmitting **2** : MESSAGE **3** : an exchange of information **4** *pl* : a system (as of telephones) for communicating **5** *pl* : the business or technology of the transmission of information
com·mu·ni·ca·tive \kə-ˈmyü-nə-ˌkāt-iv, -ni-kət-\ *adj* **1** : TALKATIVE **2** : of or relating to communication
com·mu·nion \kə-ˈmyü-nyən\ *n* **1** : an act or instance of sharing **2 a** *cap* : a Christian sacrament in which bread and wine are partaken of as a commemoration of the death of Christ **b** : the act of receiving the sacrament **3** : COMMUNICATION **4** : a body of Christians having a common faith and discipline
com·mu·ni·qué \kə-ˈmyü-nə-ˌkā\ *n* : an official communication
com·mu·nism \ˈkäm-yə-ˌniz-əm\ *n* **1** : a social system in which property and goods are owned in common; *also* : a theory advocating such a system **2** *cap* : a doctrine based upon revolutionary Marxian socialism that is the official ideology of the U.S.S.R., the Chinese People's Republic, and several satellite nations
com·mu·nist \ˈkäm-yə-nəst\ *n* **1** : an adherent or advocate of communism **2** *cap* : a member or adherent of a Communist party or movement — **communist** *adj, often cap* — **com·mu·nis·tic** \ˌkäm-yə-ˈnis-tik\ *adj, often cap* — **com·mu·nis·ti·cal·ly** \-ti-k(ə-)lē\ *adv*
com·mu·ni·ty \kə-ˈmyü-nət-ē\ *n, pl* **-ties** **1 a** : the people living in an area **b** : a natural population of plants and animals occupying a common area **c** : a group of people with common interests living together within a larger society **2 a** : joint ownership **b** : LIKENESS **c** : FELLOWSHIP
com·mu·ta·tion \ˌkäm-yə-ˈtā-shən\ *n* **1** : a substitution of one form of payment for another **2** : a reduction of a legal penalty
community antenna television *n* : a system of television reception in which signals from distant stations are picked up by a tall or elevated antenna and sent by cable to the individual receivers of paying subscribers
commutation ticket *n* : a transportation ticket sold at a reduced rate for a fixed number of trips over the same route
com·mu·ta·tor \ˈkäm-yə-ˌtāt-ər\ *n* : a device (as on a generator or motor) for reversing the direction of electric current
com·mute \kə-ˈmyüt\ *vb* **1** : EXCHANGE **2** : to substitute a less severe penalty for a greater one **3** : to travel back and forth regularly — **com·mut·er** *n*
[1]**com·pact** \kəm-ˈpakt, ˈkäm-ˌ\ *adj* **1** : closely united, collected, or packed : SOLID **2** : arranged so as to save space **3** : not wordy : BRIEF **4** : not gangling or lanky in appearance — **com·pact·ly** *adv* — **com·pact·ness** *n*
[2]**compact** *vb* **1** : COMBINE, CONSOLIDATE **2** : COMPRESS — **com·pac·tor** *or* **com·pact·er** *n*
[3]**com·pact** \ˈkäm-ˌpakt\ *n* **1** : a small cosmetic case **2** : a relatively small automobile
[4]**com·pact** \ˈkäm-ˌpakt\ *n* : an agreement or covenant between two or more parties
[1]**com·pan·ion** \kəm-ˈpan-yən\ *n* **1** : one much in the company of another : COMRADE **2** : one of a pair of matching things
[2]**companion** *n* : COMPANIONWAY
com·pan·ion·a·ble \kəm-ˈpan-yə-nə-bəl\ *adj* : fitted to be a companion : SOCIABLE — **com·pan·ion·a·bly** \-blē\ *adv*
com·pan·ion·ship \kəm-ˈpan-yən-ˌship\ *n* : FELLOWSHIP
com·pan·ion·way \-ˌwā\ *n* : a ship's stairway from one deck to another
com·pa·ny \ˈkəmp-(ə-)nē\ *n, pl* **-nies** **1 a** : association with another : FELLOWSHIP **b** : COMPANIONS, ASSOCIATES **c** : VISITORS, GUESTS **2 a** : a group of persons or things **b** : a body of soldiers; *esp* : an infantry unit **c** : an organization of musical or dramatic performers **d** : the officers and men of a ship **e** : a fire-fighting unit **3** : an association of persons carrying on a commercial or industrial enterprise
com·pa·ra·ble \ˈkäm-p(ə-)rə-bəl\ *adj* **1** : capable of being compared **2** : worthy of being compared — **com·pa·ra·bly** \-blē\ *adv*
[1]**com·par·a·tive** \kəm-ˈpar-ət-iv\ *adj* **1** : of, relating to, or constituting the degree of grammatical comparison that denotes increase in the quality, quantity, or relation **2** : measured by comparison : RELATIVE — **com·par·a·tive·ly** *adv*

[2]**comparative** *n* : the comparative degree or a comparative form in a language

[1]**com·pare** \kəm-ˈpa(ə)r\ *vb* **1** : to represent as similar : LIKEN **2** : to examine in order to discover likenesses or differences **3** : to inflect or modify (an adjective or adverb) according to the degrees of comparison

[2]**compare** *n* : COMPARISON

com·par·i·son \kəm-ˈpar-ə-sən\ *n* **1** : the act of comparing : the state of being compared **2** : change in the form of an adjective or an adverb to show different levels of quality, quantity, or relation

com·part·ment \kəm-ˈpärt-mənt\ *n* **1** : one of the parts into which an enclosed space is divided **2** : a separate division or section — **com·part·ment·ed** \-ˌment-əd\ *adj*

com·part·men·tal·ize \kəm-ˌpärt-ˈment-ᵊl-ˌīz\ *vt* : to separate into compartments

[1]**com·pass** \ˈkəm-pəs, ˈkäm-\ *vt* **1** : CONTRIVE, PLOT **2 a** : ENCOMPASS **b** : to travel entirely around **3** : ACHIEVE, ACCOMPLISH

[2]**compass** *n* **1 a** : BOUNDARY, CIRCUMFERENCE **b** : an enclosed space **c** : RANGE, SCOPE **2 a** : a device for determining directions by means of a magnetic needle turning freely on a pivot and pointing to the magnetic north **b** : any of various nonmagnetic devices that indicate direction **c** : an instrument for describing circles or transferring measurements that consists of two pointed branches joined at the top by a pivot — usu. used in pl.

compass card *n* : the circular card attached to the needles of a mariner's compass on which are marked 32 points of the compass and the 360° of the circle

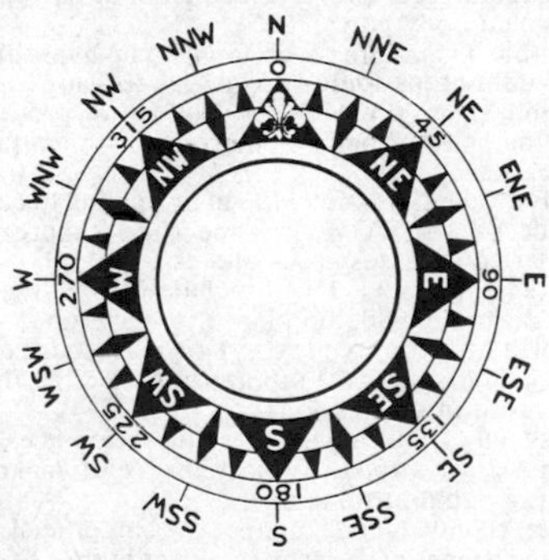

compass card

com·pas·sion \kəm-ˈpash-ən\ *n* : sorrow or pity aroused by the suffering or misfortune of another : SYMPATHY, MERCY

com·pas·sion·ate \kəm-ˈpash-(ə-)nət\ *adj* : having or showing compassion : SYMPATHETIC — **com·pas·sion·ate·ly** *adv*

com·pat·i·ble \kəm-ˈpat-ə-bəl\ *adj* : capable of existing together in harmony — **com·pat·i·bil·i·ty** \-ˌpat-ə-ˈbil-ət-ē\ *n* — **com·pat·i·bly** \-ˈpat-ə-blē\ *adv*

com·pa·tri·ot \kəm-ˈpā-trē-ət, -ˌät\ *n* **1** : a fellow countryman **2** : COLLEAGUE, COMPANION

com·peer \ˈkäm-ˌpi(ə)r, kəm-ˈ\ *n* : EQUAL, PEER

com·pel \kəm-ˈpel\ *vt* **com·pelled**; **com·pel·ling** **1** : to drive or urge with force : CONSTRAIN **2** : EXACT, EXTORT — **com·pel·ler** *n*

com·pen·di·ous \kəm-ˈpen-dē-əs\ *adj* : marked by brief expression of a comprehensive matter : CONCISE — **com·pen·di·ous·ly** *adv* — **com·pen·di·ous·ness** *n*

com·pen·di·um \-dē-əm\ *n, pl* **-di·ums** *or* **-dia** \-dē-ə\ : a brief summary of a larger work or of a field of knowledge : ABSTRACT

com·pen·sate \ˈkäm-pən-ˌsāt\ *vb* **1** : to be equivalent to in value or effect : COUNTERBALANCE **2** : to make equal return to : REMUNERATE, PAY — **com·pen·sa·tive** \ˈkäm-pən-ˌsāt-iv, kəm-ˈpen(t)-sət-\ *adj* — **com·pen·sa·tor** \ˈkäm-pən-ˌsāt-ər\ *n* — **com·pen·sa·to·ry** \kəm-ˈpen(t)-sə-ˌtōr-ē\ *adj*

com·pen·sa·tion \ˌkäm-pən-ˈsā-shən\ *n* **1** : the act of compensating : the state of being compensated **2** : payment to an unemployed or injured worker or his dependents

com·pete \kəm-ˈpēt\ *vi* : to vie with another for or as if for a prize : contend in rivalry : CONTEST

com·pe·tence \ˈkäm-pət-ən(t)s\ *n* **1** : means sufficient for the necessities of life **2** : the quality or state of being competent

com·pe·ten·cy \-ən-sē\ *n* : COMPETENCE

com·pe·tent \ˈkäm-pət-ənt\ *adj* **1** : having requisite ability or qualities : FIT **2** : rightfully belonging : PROPER **3** : legally qualified — **com·pe·tent·ly** *adv*

com·pe·ti·tion \ˌkäm-pə-ˈtish-ən\ *n* **1** : the act or process of competing **2** : a contest between rivals

com·pet·i·tive \kəm-ˈpet-ət-iv\ *adj* : relating to, characterized by, or based on competition — **com·pet·i·tive·ly** *adv* — **com·pet·i·tive·ness** *n*

com·pet·i·tor \kəm-ˈpet-ət-ər\ *n* : one that competes esp. in the selling of goods or services : RIVAL

com·pi·la·tion \ˌkäm-pə-ˈlā-shən\ *n* **1** : the act or process of compiling **2** : something compiled

com·pile \kəm-ˈpīl\ *vt* **1** : to collect into a volume **2** : to compose out of materials from other documents — **com·pil·er** *n*

com·pla·cence \kəm-ˈplās-ᵊn(t)s\ *n* : calm or secure satisfaction with one's self or lot : SELF-SATISFACTION

com·pla·cen·cy \-ᵊn-sē\ *n* : COMPLACENCE

com·pla·cent \kəm-ˈplās-ᵊnt\ *adj* : SATISFIED; *esp* : SELF-SATISFIED — **com·pla·cent·ly** *adv*

com·plain \kəm-ˈplān\ *vi* **1** : to express grief, pain, or discontent **2** : to make a formal accusation or charge — **com·plain·er** *n* — **com·plain·ing·ly** *adv*

com·plaint \kəm-ˈplānt\ *n* **1** : expression of grief, pain, or resentment **2** : a bodily ailment or disease **3** : a formal charge against a person

com·plai·sance \kəm-ˈplās-ᵊn(t)s, ˈkäm-plā-ˌzan(t)s\ *n* : disposition to please or oblige

com·plai·sant \kəm-ˈplās-ᵊnt, ˈkäm-plā-ˌzant\ *adj* **1** : marked by an inclination to please or oblige **2** : tending to consent to others' wishes — **com·plai·sant·ly** *adv*

com·plect·ed \kəm-ˈplek-təd\ *adj* : COMPLEXIONED

[1]**com·ple·ment** \ˈkäm-plə-mənt\ *n* **1** : a quantity necessary to make a thing complete **2** : full quantity, number, or amount **3** : an added word or group of words by which the predicate of a sentence is made complete

[2]**com·ple·ment** \-ˌment\ *vt* : to be complementary to

com·ple·men·tal \ˌkäm-plə-ˈment-ᵊl\ *adj* : relating to or being a complement

com·ple·men·ta·ry \ˌkäm-plə-ˈment-ə-rē, -ˈmen-trē\ *adj* : forming or serving as a complement : COMPLEMENTAL — **complementary** *n*

[1]**com·plete** \kəm-ˈplēt\ *adj* **1** : possessing all necessary parts : ENTIRE **2** : brought to an end : CONCLUDED **3** : fully carried out : THOROUGH — **com·plete·ly** *adv* — **com·plete·ness** *n*

[2]**complete** *vt* **1** : to bring to an end : accomplish or achieve fully **2** : to make whole or perfect

com·ple·tion \kəm-ˈplē-shən\ *n* : the act or process of completing : the state of being complete

[1]**com·plex** \käm-ˈpleks, kəm-\ *adj* **1** : composed of two or more parts **2** : consisting of a main clause and one or more subordinate clauses **3** : hard to separate, analyze, or solve — **com·plex·ly** *adv* — **com·plex·ness** *n*

[2]**com·plex** \ˈkäm-ˌpleks\ *n* **1** : a whole made up of complicated

or interrelated parts **2** : a system of repressed desires and memories that exerts a dominating influence upon the personality

com·plex·ion \kəm-ˈplek-shən\ *n* **1** : the hue or appearance of the skin and esp. of the face **2** : general appearance or impression — **com·plex·ioned** \-shənd\ *adj*

com·plex·i·ty \kəm-ˈplek-sət-ē, käm-\ *n, pl* **-ties** **1** : the quality or state of being complex **2** : something complex

com·pli·ance \kəm-ˈplī-ən(t)s\ *n* **1** : the act or process of complying to a desire, demand, or proposal **2** : a disposition to yield — **in compliance with** : in accordance with

com·pli·an·cy \-ən-sē\ *n* : COMPLIANCE

com·pli·ant \-ənt\ *adj* : ready or disposed to comply : SUBMISSIVE — **com·pli·ant·ly** *adv*

com·pli·cate \ˈkäm-plə-ˌkāt\ *vb* : to make or become complex, intricate, or difficult

com·pli·cat·ed \-əd\ *adj* **1** : consisting of parts intricately combined **2** : difficult to analyze, understand, or explain — **com·pli·cat·ed·ly** *adv*

com·pli·ca·tion \ˌkäm-plə-ˈkā-shən\ *n* **1** : a situation or a detail of character complicating the main thread of a plot **2** : a making difficult, involved, or intricate **3** : something that makes a situation more complicated or difficult

com·plic·i·ty \kəm-ˈplis-ət-ē\ *n, pl* **-ties** : association or participation in a wrongful act

¹com·pli·ment \ˈkäm-plə-mənt\ *n* **1** : a formal expression of esteem, respect, affection, or admiration; *esp* : a flattering remark **2** *pl* : best wishes : REGARDS

²com·pli·ment \-ˌment\ *vt* : to pay a compliment to

com·pli·men·ta·ry \ˌkäm-plə-ˈment-ə-rē, -ˈmen-trē\ *adj* **1** : expressing a compliment **2** : given free as a courtesy

com·ply \kəm-ˈplī\ *vi* **com·plied**; **com·ply·ing** : to conform or adapt one's actions to another's wishes, to a rule, or to necessity — **com·pli·er** *n*

¹com·po·nent \kəm-ˈpō-nənt, ˈkäm-ˌ\ *n* : a constituent part : INGREDIENT

²component *adj* : being or forming a part : CONSTITUENT

com·port \kəm-ˈpōrt\ *vb* **1** : ACCORD, SUIT **2** : CONDUCT

com·port·ment \-mənt\ *n* : BEHAVIOR, BEARING

com·pose \kəm-ˈpōz\ *vb* **1 a** : to form by putting together : FASHION **b** : to arrange (type) in order for printing : SET **2** : to create by mental or artistic labor **3** : to reduce to a minimum **4** : to arrange in proper form **5** : to free from agitation

com·posed \-ˈpōzd\ *adj* : free from agitation : CALM; *esp* : SELF-POSSESSED — **com·pos·ed·ly** \-ˈpō-zəd-lē\ *adv* — **com·pos·ed·ness** \-ˈpō-zəd-nəs\ *n*

com·pos·er \kəm-ˈpō-zər\ *n* : one that composes; *esp* : a person who writes music

¹com·pos·ite \käm-ˈpäz-ət, kəm-\ *adj* **1** : made up of distinct parts or elements **2** : of or relating to a very large group of flowering plants (as the daisy) that bear many small flowers arranged in dense heads resembling single flowers — **com·pos·ite·ly** *adv*

²composite *n* **1** : something that is made up of different parts **2** : a composite plant

com·po·si·tion \ˌkäm-pə-ˈzish-ən\ *n* **1** : a composing: as **a** : the art or practice of writing **b** : the work of a compositor **2** : the manner in which the parts of a thing are put together **3** : the makeup of a compound or mixture **4** : mutual settlement or agreement **5** : a product of combining various ingredients **6** : a literary, musical, or artistic production; *esp* : a short piece of writing done as an educational exercise — **com·po·si·tion·al** \-ˈzish-nəl, -ən-ᵊl\ *adj*

com·pos·i·tor \kəm-ˈpäz-ət-ər\ *n* : one who sets type

com·post \ˈkäm-ˌpōst\ *n* : a mixture of decayed organic matter used for fertilizing and conditioning land

com·po·sure \kəm-ˈpō-zhər\ *n* : SELF-POSSESSION

com·pote \ˈkäm-ˌpōt\ *n* **1** : fruits cooked in syrup **2** : a bowl (as of glass) usu. with a base and stem from which compotes, fruits, nuts, or sweets are served

¹com·pound \käm-ˈpau̇nd, kəm-\ *vb* **1** : to put together or be joined to form a whole **2** : to form by combining parts **3** : to settle peaceably **4 a** : to increase (as interest) by an amount that itself increases **b** : to add to **5** : to agree for a consideration not to prosecute (an offense) — **com·pound·a·ble** *adj*

²com·pound \ˈkäm-ˌpau̇nd\ *adj* **1** : composed of separate elements, ingredients, or parts **2** : consisting of two or more main clauses

³com·pound \ˈkäm-ˌpau̇nd\ *n* **1** : a word consisting of components that are words or word elements **2** : something formed by a union of elements, ingredients, or parts

⁴com·pound \ˈkäm-ˌpau̇nd\ *n* : an enclosure of European residences and commercial buildings esp. in the Orient

com·pre·hend \ˌkäm-pri-ˈhend\ *vt* **1** : to grasp the meaning of mentally **2** : to take in : EMBRACE — **com·pre·hend·i·ble** \-ˈhen-də-bəl\ *adj*

com·pre·hen·si·ble \-ˈhen(t)-sə-bəl\ *adj* : capable of being comprehended — **com·pre·hen·si·bil·i·ty** \-ˌhen(t)-sə-ˈbil-ət-ē\ *n* — **com·pre·hen·si·bly** \-ˈhen(t)-sə-blē\ *adv*

com·pre·hen·sion \ˌkäm-pri-ˈhen-chən\ *n* **1** : the act or process of including or comprising **2 a** : the act or action of grasping with the intellect **b** : the capacity for understanding

com·pre·hen·sive \-ˈhen(t)-siv\ *adj* **1** : INCLUSIVE **2** : having wide mental comprehension — **com·pre·hen·sive·ly** *adv* — **com·pre·hen·sive·ness** *n*

¹com·press \kəm-ˈpres\ *vb* : to press or become pressed together : reduce the volume of by pressure

²com·press \ˈkäm-ˌpres\ *n* : a folded cloth or pad applied so as to press upon a body part

com·press·i·ble \kəm-ˈpres-ə-bəl\ *adj* : capable of being compressed — **com·press·i·bil·i·ty** \-ˌpres-ə-ˈbil-ət-ē\ *n*

com·pres·sion \kəm-ˈpresh-ən\ *n* : the act or process of compressing : the state of being compressed — **com·pres·sion·al** \-ˈpresh-nəl, -ən-ᵊl\ *adj*

com·pres·sive \kəm-ˈpres-iv\ *adj* : of or relating to compression

com·pres·sor \-ˈpres-ər\ *n* **1** : one that compresses **2** : a machine that compresses gases and esp. air

com·prise \kəm-ˈprīz\ *vt* **1** : to include esp. within a particular scope **2** : to be made up of **3** : to make up

¹com·pro·mise \ˈkäm-prə-ˌmīz\ *n* **1** : a settlement of a dispute by mutual concessions **2** : SURRENDER **3** : the thing agreed upon as a result of concessions

²compromise *vb* **1** : to adjust or settle differences by mutual concessions **2** : to expose to discredit **3** : to make unworthy concessions — **com·pro·mis·er** *n*

comp·trol·ler \kən-ˈtrō-lər, ˈkäm(p)-ˌ\ *n* : an official who audits accounts and sometimes certifies expenditures — **comp·trol·ler·ship** \-ˌship\ *n*

com·pul·sion \kəm-ˈpəl-shən\ *n* **1** : an act of compelling : the state of being compelled **2** : an irresistible impulse

com·pul·sive \-ˈpəl-siv\ *adj* **1** : having power to compel **2** : of, relating to, or caused by psychological compulsion — **com·pul·sive·ly** *adv* — **com·pul·sive·ness** *n*

com·pul·so·ry \-ˈpəls-(ə-)rē\ *adj* **1** : ENFORCED, REQUIRED **2** : having the power of compelling

com·punc·tion \kəm-ˈpəŋ(k)-shən\ *n* **1** : sharp uneasiness caused by a sense of guilt : REMORSE **2** : a passing feeling of regret for some slight wrong

com·pu·ta·tion \ˌkäm-pyu̇-ˈtā-shən\ *n* **1** : the act or action of computing : CALCULATION **2** : a system of reckoning — **com·pu·ta·tion·al** \-shnəl, -shən-ᵊl\ *adj*

com·pute \kəm-ˈpyüt\ *vb* : to determine or calculate esp. by mathematical means : RECKON — **com·put·a·ble** *adj*

com·put·er \-ˈpyüt-ər\ *n* : one that computes; *esp* : an automatic electronic machine for performing calculations

com·rade \'käm-ˌrad, -rəd\ *n* : an intimate friend or associate : COMPANION
com·rade·ship \-ˌship\ *n* : association as comrades
[1]**con** \'kän\ *vt* **conned**; **con·ning** 1 : to study or examine closely : PERUSE 2 : to commit to memory
[2]**con** *adv* : in opposition
[3]**con** *n* : an argument or evidence in opposition
con·cave \kän-'kāv\ *adj* : hollowed or rounded inward like the inside of a bowl — **con·cave·ly** *adv*
con·cav·i·ty \kän-'kav-ət-ē\ *n, pl* **-ties** 1 : a concave surface or space 2 : the quality or state of being concave
con·ceal \kən-'sēl\ *vt* : to hide from sight
con·ceal·ment \-mənt\ *n* : the act of hiding : the state of being hidden
con·cede \kən-'sēd\ *vb* 1 : to grant as a right or privilege 2 : YIELD
con·ceit \kən-'sēt\ *n* 1 : excessive appreciation of one's own worth or virtue 2 **a** : a fanciful idea **b** : an elaborate metaphor
con·ceit·ed \-'sēt-əd\ *adj* : having an excessively high opinion of oneself — **con·ceit·ed·ly** *adv*
con·ceiv·a·ble \kən-'sē-və-bəl\ *adj* : capable of being conceived : IMAGINABLE — **con·ceiv·a·bly** \-blē\ *adv*
con·ceive \kən-'sēv\ *vb* 1 : to become pregnant 2 : to form an idea of : IMAGINE 3 : THINK
[1]**con·cen·trate** \'kän(t)-sən-ˌtrāt\ *vb* 1 : to gather into one body, mass, or force 2 : to make stronger by removing the diluting or admixing material 3 : to fix one's powers, efforts, or attentions on one thing — **con·cen·tra·tor** \-ˌtrāt-ər\ *n*
[2]**concentrate** *n* : something concentrated
con·cen·tra·tion \ˌkän(t)-sən-'trā-shən\ *n* 1 : the act or process of concentrating : the state of being concentrated; *esp* : direction of attention on a single object 2 : a concentrated mass 3 : the relative content of a component
con·cen·tric \kən-'sen-trik, (ˈ)kän-\ *adj* : having a common center — **con·cen·tri·cal·ly** \-tri-k(ə-)lē\ *adv*
con·cept \'kän-ˌsept\ *n* : THOUGHT, NOTION
con·cep·tion \kən-'sep-shən\ *n* 1 **a** : the act of conceiving or being conceived **b** : BEGINNING 2 : a general idea : CONCEPT 3 : the originating of something in the mind — **con·cep·tion·al** \-shnəl, -shən-ᵊl\ *adj* — **con·cep·tive** \-'sep-tiv\ *adj*
con·cep·tu·al \kən-'sep-chə(-wə)l\ *adj* : of, relating to, or consisting of concepts — **con·cep·tu·al·ly** \-ē\ *adv*
[1]**con·cern** \kən-'sərn\ *vt* 1 : to relate to 2 : to be the business of : AFFECT 3 : ENGAGE, OCCUPY
[2]**concern** *n* 1 : something that relates to or involves one : AFFAIR 2 **a** : marked regard or care usu. arising through a personal tie or relationship **b** : a state of uncertainty and apprehension 3 : a business or manufacturing establishment
con·cerned \-'sərnd\ *adj* : DISTURBED, ANXIOUS
con·cern·ing \-'sər-niŋ\ *prep* : relating to
con·cern·ment \-'sərn-mənt\ *n* 1 : something in which one is concerned 2 : IMPORTANCE, CONSEQUENCE
[1]**con·cert** \kən-'sərt\ *vb* : to plan or arrange together
[2]**con·cert** \'kän-(ˌ)sərt\ *n* 1 : agreement in design or plan 2 : a musical performance by several voices or instruments or both
con·cert·ed \kən-'sərt-əd\ *adj* : mutually contrived or agreed
con·cer·ti·na \ˌkän(t)-sər-'tē-nə\ *n* : a musical instrument of the accordion family
con·cert·mas·ter \'kän(t)-sərt-ˌmas-tər\ *n* : the leader of the first violins and assistant conductor
con·cer·to \kən-'chert-ō\ *n, pl* **-tos** *or* **-ti** \-(ˌ)ē\ : a symphonic piece for one or more soloists and orchestra
con·ces·sion \kən-'sesh-ən\ *n* 1 : the act or an instance of conceding 2 : something conceded 3 : a grant of property or of a right by a government 4 : a lease of a part of premises for some purpose
con·ces·sion·aire \kən-ˌsesh-ə-'na(ə)r\ *n* : the recipient or operator of a concession
con·ces·sive \kən-'ses-iv\ *adj* : tending toward, expressing, or being a concession — **con·ces·sive·ly** *adv*
conch \'käŋk, 'känch\ *n, pl* **conchs** \'käŋks\ *or* **conch·es** \'kän-chəz\ : a large spiral-shelled marine mollusk
con·cierge \kōⁿ-'syerzh\ *n* : an attendant at the entrance of a building esp. in France who oversees ingress and egress, handles mail, and acts as a janitor or porter
con·cil·i·ate \kən-'sil-ē-ˌāt\ *vt* 1 : to bring into agreement : RECONCILE 2 : to gain the goodwill or favor of — **con·cil·i·a·tion** \-ˌsil-ē-'ā-shən\ *n* — **con·cil·i·a·tor** \-'sil-ē-ˌāt-ər\ *n* — **con·cil·ia·to·ry** \-'sil-yə-ˌtōr-ē, -'sil-ē-ə-\ *adj*
con·cise \kən-'sīs\ *adj* : marked by brevity and compactness of expression or statement — **con·cise·ly** *adv* — **con·cise·ness** *n*
con·clave \'kän-ˌklāv\ *n* 1 : a private meeting or secret assembly 2 : ASSEMBLY, CONVENTION
con·clude \kən-'klüd\ *vb* 1 : to bring or come to an end : FINISH 2 : to form an opinion 3 : to bring about as a result
con·clu·sion \kən-'klü-zhən\ *n* 1 : a reasoned judgment : INFERENCE 2 : TERMINATION, END 3 : RESULT, OUTCOME
con·clu·sive \kən-'klü-siv\ *adj* : DECISIVE, CONVINCING, FINAL — **con·clu·sive·ly** *adv*
con·coct \kən-'käkt, kän-\ *vt* 1 : to prepare by combining various ingredients 2 : DEVISE, FABRICATE — **con·coct·er** *n* — **con·coc·tion** \-'käk-shən\ *n*
con·com·i·tant \kən-'käm-ət-ənt, kän-\ *adj* : accompanying esp. in a subordinate or incidental way — **concomitant** *n* — **con·com·i·tant·ly** *adv*
con·cord \'kän-ˌkȯrd, 'käŋ-\ *n* : a state of agreement : HARMONY
con·cord·ance \kən-'kȯrd-ᵊn(t)s\ *n* 1 : an alphabetical index of words in a book or in the works of an author with their immediate contexts 2 : CONCORD, AGREEMENT
con·cord·ant \-ᵊnt\ *adj* : AGREEING, CONSONANT — **con·cord·ant·ly** *adv*
con·cor·dat \kən-'kȯr-ˌdat\ *n* : COMPACT, COVENANT
con·course \'kän-ˌkōrs\ *n* 1 : a flocking together : GATHERING 2 : a place (as a boulevard) where many people pass or congregate
con·cres·cence \kən-'kres-ᵊn(t)s\ *n* : a growing together : COALESCENCE — **con·cres·cent** \-ᵊnt\ *adj*
[1]**con·crete** \kän-'krēt, 'kän-ˌ\ *adj* 1 : naming a real thing or class of things : not abstract 2 **a** : belonging to or derived from actual experience **b** : REAL, TANGIBLE — **con·crete·ly** *adv* — **con·crete·ness** *n*
[2]**con·crete** \'kän-ˌkrēt, kän-'\ *n* : a hard building material made by mixing cement, sand, and gravel or broken rock with water
[3]**con·crete** \'kän-ˌkrēt, kän-'\ *vb* 1 : SOLIDIFY 2 : to cover with, form of, or set in concrete
con·cre·tion \kän-'krē-shən\ *n* : a hard usu. inorganic mass formed in a living body
con·cu·bine \'käŋ-kyə-ˌbīn\ *n* 1 : a woman who lives with a man and among some peoples has a legally recognized position in his household less than that of a wife 2 : MISTRESS 3 — **con·cu·bi·nage** \kän-'kyü-bə-nij\ *n*
con·cu·pis·cence \kän-'kyü-pə-sən(t)s\ *n* : ardent sexual desire : LUST — **con·cu·pis·cent** \-sənt\ *adj*
con·cur \kən-'kər\ *vi* **con·curred**; **con·cur·ring** 1 : to happen together : COINCIDE 2 : to act together to a common end or single effect 3 : to be in agreement : ACCORD
con·cur·rence \kən-'kər-ən(t)s\ *n* 1 **a** : agreement in action, opinion, or intent **b** : CONSENT 2 : a coming together : CONJUNCTION
con·cur·rent \-'kər-ənt\ *adj* 1 : happening or operating at the same time 2 : joint and equal in authority — **concurrent** *n* — **con·cur·rent·ly** *adv*
con·cus·sion \kən-'kəsh-ən\ *n* 1 : SHAKING, AGITATION 2 : a smart or hard blow or collision 3 : bodily injury esp. of the

brain resulting from a sudden jar — **con·cus·sive** \-'kəs-iv\ *adj*

con·demn \kən-'dem\ *vt* **1 :** to declare to be wrong : CENSURE **2 a :** to pronounce guilty : CONVICT **b :** SENTENCE **3 :** to adjudge unfit for use **4 :** to take for public use — **con·dem·na·ble** \-'dem-(n)ə-bəl\ *adj*

con·dem·na·tion \ˌkän-ˌdem-'nā-shən, -dəm-\ *n* **1 :** CENSURE, BLAME **2 :** the act of judicially condemning **3 :** the state of being condemned — **con·dem·na·to·ry** \kən-'dem-nə-ˌtōr-ē\ *adj*

con·den·sa·tion \ˌkän-ˌden-'sā-shən, -dən-\ *n* **1 :** the act or process of condensing **2 :** the quality or state of being condensed **3 :** a product of condensing; *esp* **:** an abridgment of a literary work

con·dense \kən-'den(t)s\ *vb* **1 :** to make or become more close, compact, concise, or dense : CONCENTRATE, COMPRESS **2 :** to change from a less dense to a denser form — **con·dens·er** *n*

con·de·scend \ˌkän-di-'send\ *vi* **1 :** to descend in manner or behavior to a level considered less dignified or humbler than one's own **2 :** to grant favors with a superior air

con·de·scend·ing \-'sen-diŋ\ *adj* **:** showing or characterized by condescension : PATRONIZING — **con·de·scend·ing·ly** *adv*

con·de·scen·sion \ˌkän-di-'sen-chən\ *n* **:** a patronizing attitude

con·dign \kən-'dīn, 'kän-ˌ\ *adj* **:** DESERVED, APPROPRIATE

con·di·ment \'kän-də-mənt\ *n* **:** something used to give an appetizing taste to food; *esp* **:** a pungent seasoning

[1]**con·di·tion** \kən-'dish-ən\ *n* **1 :** a provision upon which the fulfillment of an agreement depends : STIPULATION **2 :** something essential to another : PREREQUISITE **3 a :** a restricting factor : QUALIFICATION **b :** an unsatisfactory academic grade that may be raised by doing additional work **4 a :** a state of being **b :** social status : RANK **c** *pl* **:** attendant circumstances **5 :** state of health

[2]**condition** *vt* **-di·tioned; -di·tion·ing** \-'dish-(ə-)niŋ\ **1 :** to put into a proper or desired condition **2 :** to adapt, modify, or mold to respond in a particular way — **con·di·tion·er** *n*

con·di·tion·al \kən-'dish-nəl, -ən-ᵊl\ *adj* **:** subject to, implying, or dependent upon a condition — **con·di·tion·al·ly** \-ē\ *adv*

con·di·tioned \-'dish-ənd\ *adj* **1 :** CONDITIONAL **2 :** brought or put into a specified state **3 :** determined or established by conditioning

con·dole \kən-'dōl\ *vi* **:** to express sympathetic sorrow

con·do·lence \kən-'dō-lən(t)s, 'kän-də-\ *n* **:** expression of sympathy with another in sorrow or grief

con·do·min·i·um \ˌkän-də-'min-ē-əm\ *n* **1 :** joint sovereignty by two or more nations **2 :** a politically dependent territory under condominium **3 :** individual ownership of a unit in a multi-unit structure (as an apartment building); *also* **:** a unit so owned

con·done \kən-'dōn\ *vt* **:** to pardon or overlook voluntarily — **con·do·na·tion** \ˌkän-dō-'nā-shən\ *n* — **con·don·er** *n*

con·dor \'kän-dər, -ˌdȯr\ *n* **:** a very large American vulture

con·duce \kən-'d(y)üs\ *vi* **:** to lead or tend to a usu. desirable result : CONTRIBUTE

con·du·cive \kən-'d(y)ü-siv\ *adj* **:** tending to promote or aid : CONTRIBUTING

[1]**con·duct** \'kän-(ˌ)dəkt\ *n* **1 :** the act, manner, or process of carrying on : MANAGEMENT **2 :** personal behavior

[2]**con·duct** \kən-'dəkt\ *vb* **1 :** GUIDE, ESCORT **2 :** LEAD, DIRECT **3 a :** to convey in a channel **b :** to act as a medium for conveying **4 :** BEHAVE **5 :** to act as leader or director — **con·duct·ance** \-'dək-tən(t)s\ *n* — **con·duct·i·bil·i·ty** \-ˌdək-tə-'bil-ət-ē\ *n* — **con·duct·i·ble** \-'dək-tə-bəl\ *adj* — **con·duc·tion** \-'dək-shən\ *n*

con·duc·tive \kən-'dək-tiv\ *adj* **:** having conductivity

con·duc·tiv·i·ty \ˌkän-ˌdək-'tiv-ət-ē\ *n, pl* **-ties :** the quality or power of conducting or transmitting

con·duc·tor \kən-'dək-tər\ *n* **:** one that conducts: as **a :** a person in charge of a public conveyance (as a bus or railroad train) **b :** the leader of a musical ensemble — **con·duc·to·ri·al** \ˌkän-ˌdək-'tōr-ē-əl\ *adj* — **con·duc·tress** \kən-'dək-trəs\ *n*

con·duit \'kän-ˌd(y)ü-ət, -dət\ *n* **1 :** a channel through which water or other fluid is conveyed **2 :** a pipe, tube, or tile for protecting electric wires or cables

cone \'kōn\ *n* **1 :** a mass of overlapping woody scales that esp. in trees of the pine family are arranged on an axis and bear seeds between them **2 :** a solid figure tapering evenly to a point from a circular base; *also* **:** something having a similar shape

Con·es·to·ga \ˌkän-ə-'stō-gə\ *n* **:** a broad-wheeled covered wagon usu. drawn by six horses and formerly used esp. for transporting freight across the prairies

co·ney \'kō-nē\ *n* **1 :** RABBIT **2 :** rabbit fur

con·fab·u·late \kən-'fab-yə-ˌlāt\ *vi* **1 :** CHAT **2 :** POWWOW — **con·fab·u·la·tor** \-'fab-yə-ˌlāt-ər\ *n*

con·fect \kən-'fekt\ *vt* **:** CONCOCT, COMPOUND

con·fec·tion \kən-'fek-shən\ *n* **:** something confected; *esp* **:** a fancy dish or sweet

con·fec·tion·er \-sh(ə-)nər\ *n* **:** a manufacturer of or dealer in confections

con·fec·tion·ery \-shə-ˌner-ē\ *n, pl* **-er·ies 1 :** sweet edibles (as candy) **2 :** a confectioner's shop

con·fed·er·a·cy \kən-'fed-(ə-)rə-sē\ *n, pl* **-cies 1 :** a loose league of persons, parties, or states : ALLIANCE, CONFEDERATION **2** *cap* **:** the 11 southern states that seceded from the U.S. in 1860 and 1861 — **con·fed·er·al** \-'fed-(ə-)rəl\ *adj*

[1]**con·fed·er·ate** \kən-'fed-(ə-)rət\ *adj* **1 :** united in a league : ALLIED **2** *cap* **:** of or relating to the Confederacy

[2]**confederate** *n* **1 :** ALLY, ACCOMPLICE **2** *cap* **:** a soldier, citizen, or adherent of the Confederacy

[3]**con·fed·er·ate** \-'fed-ə-ˌrāt\ *vb* **:** to unite in a confederacy

con·fed·er·a·tion \kən-ˌfed-ə-'rā-shən\ *n* **1 :** an act of confederating : a state of being confederated **2 :** LEAGUE

con·fer \kən-'fər\ *vb* **con·ferred; con·fer·ring 1 :** to give or grant publicly **2 :** to compare views : CONSULT — **con·fer·ral** \-'fər-əl\ *n* — **con·fer·rer** *n*

con·fer·ee *or* **con·fer·ree** \ˌkän-fə-'rē\ *n* **1 :** one conferred with **2 :** one on whom something is conferred

con·fer·ence \'kän-f(ə-)rən(t)s\ *n* **1 :** a meeting for formal discussion or exchange of opinions **2 :** an association of athletic teams representing educational institutions

con·fess \kən-'fes\ *vb* **1 :** to make acknowledgment of : ADMIT **2 a :** to acknowledge one's sins to God or to a priest **b :** to act as confessor for

con·fess·ed·ly \-'fes-əd-lē, -'fest-lē\ *adv* **:** ADMITTEDLY

con·fes·sion \kən-'fesh-ən\ *n* **1 :** an act of confessing (as in the sacrament of penance) **2 a :** an acknowledgment of guilt **b :** a formal statement of religious beliefs **3 :** a religious body having a common creed

con·fes·sion·al \-'fesh-nəl, -ən-ᵊl\ *n* **:** the enclosed place in which a priest sits and hears confessions

con·fes·sor \kən-'fes-ər\ *n* **1 :** one that confesses **2 :** a priest who hears confessions

con·fet·ti \kən-'fet-ē\ *n* **:** small bits of brightly colored paper made for throwing (as at weddings)

con·fi·dant \'kän-fə-ˌdant, -ˌdänt\ *n* **:** one to whom secrets are entrusted

con·fi·dante \'kän-fə-ˌdant, -ˌdänt\ *n* **:** a female confidant

con·fide \kən-'fīd\ *vb* **1 :** to have confidence : TRUST **2 :** to show confidence by imparting secrets **3 :** to tell confidentially **4 :** ENTRUST

con·fi·dence \'kän-fəd-ən(t)s, -fə-ˌden(t)s\ *n* **1 :** FAITH, TRUST **2 :** consciousness of feeling sure : ASSURANCE **3 a :** reliance on another's discretion **b :** legislative support **4 :** a communication made in confidence : SECRET

con·fi·dent \'kän-fəd-ənt, -fə-ˌdent\ *adj* : having or showing confidence : SURE, SELF-ASSURED — **con·fi·dent·ly** *adv*
con·fi·den·tial \ˌkän-fə-'den-chəl\ *adj* **1** : SECRET, PRIVATE **2** : INTIMATE, FAMILIAR **3** : trusted with secret matters — **con·fi·den·tial·ly** \-'dench-(ə-)lē\ *adv*
con·fid·ing \kən-'fīd-iŋ\ *adj* : tending to confide : TRUSTFUL — **con·fid·ing·ly** *adv*
con·fig·u·ra·tion \kən-ˌfig-(y)ə-'rā-shən\ *n* : relative arrangement of parts
¹con·fine \'kän-ˌfīn\ *n* : BOUNDARY, LIMIT
²con·fine \kən-'fīn\ *vt* **1** : to keep within limits : RESTRICT **2 a** : to shut up : IMPRISON **b** : to keep indoors
con·fine·ment \kən-'fīn-mənt\ *n* : an act of confining : the state of being confined
con·firm \kən-'fərm\ *vt* **1** : to make firm or firmer : STRENGTHEN **2** : to make sure of the truth of : VERIFY **3** : APPROVE, RATIFY **4** : to administer the rite of confirmation to
con·fir·ma·tion \ˌkän-fər-'mā-shən\ *n* **1** : an act or process of confirming; *esp* : a Christian rite or sacrament admitting a baptized person to full church privileges **2** : something that confirms : CORROBORATION — **con·fir·ma·to·ry** \kən-'fər-mə-ˌtōr-ē\ *adj*
con·firmed \kən-'fərmd\ *adj* **1** : made firm : STRENGTHENED **2** : deeply ingrained **3** : HABITUAL, CHRONIC
con·fis·cate \'kän-fə-ˌskāt\ *vt* : to seize by or as if by public authority — **con·fis·ca·tion** \ˌkän-fə-'skā-shən\ *n* — **con·fis·ca·tor** \'kän-fə-ˌskāt-ər\ *n* — **con·fis·ca·to·ry** \kən-'fis-kə-ˌtōr-ē\ *adj*
con·fla·gra·tion \ˌkän-flə-'grā-shən\ *n* : FIRE; *esp* : a large disastrous fire
¹con·flict \'kän-ˌflikt\ *n* **1** : FIGHT; *esp* : a prolonged struggle **2** : a clashing or sharp disagreement (as between ideas)
²con·flict \kən-'flikt\ *vi* : to be in opposition
con·flu·ence \'kän-ˌflü-ən(t)s\ *n* **1 a** : a flocking together to one place **b** : CROWD **2** : a flowing together or place of meeting esp. of two or more streams
con·flu·ent \-ˌflü-ənt\ *adj* : flowing or coming together
con·form \kən-'fórm\ *vb* **1** : to bring into harmony **2** : to be similar or identical **3** : to adapt oneself to prevailing standards or customs — **con·form·er** *n* — **con·form·ism** \-'fór-ˌmiz-əm\ *n* — **con·form·ist** \-məst\ *n*
con·form·a·ble \kən-'fór-mə-bəl\ *adj* **1** : corresponding in form or character **2** : SUBMISSIVE, COMPLIANT — **con·form·a·bly** \-blē\ *adv*
con·form·ance \kən-'fór-mən(t)s\ *n* : CONFORMITY
con·for·ma·tion \ˌkän-(ˌ)fór-'mā-shən\ *n* : arrangement and congruity of parts : FORM
con·for·mi·ty \kən-'fór-mət-ē\ *n, pl* **-ties** **1** : correspondence in form, manner, or character : AGREEMENT **2** : OBEDIENCE
con·found \kən-'fau̇nd, kän-\ *vt* **1** : to put to shame : DISCOMFIT **2** : DAMN **3** : to throw into disorder : CONFUSE
con·fra·ter·ni·ty \ˌkän-frə-'tər-nət-ē\ *n, pl* **-ties** : a society devoted to a religious or charitable cause
con·frere \'kōⁿ-ˌfre(ə)r, 'kän-\ *n* : COLLEAGUE, COMRADE
con·front \kən-'frənt\ *vt* **1** : to face esp. in challenge : OPPOSE **2** : to bring face-to-face : cause to meet — **con·fron·ta·tion** \ˌkän-(ˌ)frən-'tā-shən\ *n*
con·fuse \kən-'fyüz\ *vt* **1 a** : to make mentally unclear or uncertain : PERPLEX **b** : DISCONCERT **2** : to make indistinct : BLUR **3** : to mix up : JUMBLE — **con·fused·ly** \-'fyüz(-ə)d-lē\ *adv* — **con·fus·ing·ly** *adv*
con·fu·sion \-'fyü-zhən\ *n* **1** : an act or instance of confusing **2** : the quality or state of being confused
con·fute \kən-'fyüt\ *vt* : to overwhelm by argument — **con·fu·ta·tion** \ˌkän-fyu̇-'tā-shən\ *n*
con·ga \'käŋ-gə\ *n* : a Cuban dance of African origin performed by a group usu. in single file
con·geal \kən-'jēl\ *vb* **1** : FREEZE **2** : to make or become hard or thick : COAGULATE — **con·geal·ment** *n*
con·ge·ner \'kän-jə-nər\ *n* : one related to another — **con·ge·ner·ic** \ˌkän-jə-'ner-ik\ *adj* — **con·ge·ner·ous** \kən-'jē-nə-rəs, -'jen-ə-\ *adj*
con·ge·nial \kən-'jē-nyəl\ *adj* **1** : having the same nature, disposition, or tastes **2 a** : agreeably suited to one's nature, tastes, or outlook **b** : SOCIABLE, GENIAL — **con·ge·nial·ly** \-nyə-lē\ *adv*
con·ge·ni·al·i·ty \-ˌjē-nē-'al-ət-ē, -ˌjēn-'yal-\ *n* : the quality or state of being congenial
con·gen·i·tal \kən-'jen-ə-tᵊl\ *adj* : existing at or dating from birth but usu. not hereditary — **con·gen·i·tal·ly** \-tᵊl-ē\ *adv*
con·ger eel \ˌkäŋ-gər-\ *n* : a large edible saltwater eel
con·ge·ries \'kän-jə-(ˌ)rēz\ *n, pl* **congeries** *same*\ : AGGREGATION, COLLECTION
con·gest \kən-'jest\ *vb* **1** : to cause an excessive fullness of the blood vessels of (as an organ) **2** : CLOG, OVERCROWD — **con·ges·tion** \-'jes-chən\ *n* — **con·ges·tive** \-'jes-tiv\ *adj*
¹con·glom·er·ate \kən-'gläm-(ə-)rət\ *adj* **1** : made up of parts from various sources **2** : densely clustered
²con·glom·er·ate \-'gläm-ə-ˌrāt\ *vb* : to collect or form into a mass
³con·glom·er·ate \-(ə-)rət\ *n* : a composite mass or mixture; *esp* : rock composed of rounded fragments varying from small pebbles to large boulders in a cement (as of hardened clay)
con·glom·er·a·tion \kən-ˌgläm-ə-'rā-shən, ˌkän-\ *n* **1** : a conglomerating or the state of being conglomerated **2** : a conglomerate mass
con·grat·u·late \kən-'grach-ə-ˌlāt\ *vt* : to express sympathetic pleasure to on account of success or good fortune
con·grat·u·la·tion \-ˌgrach-ə-'lā-shən\ *n* **1** : the act of congratulating **2** : an expression of pleasure at another's success, happiness, or good fortune — usu. used in pl.
con·grat·u·la·to·ry \-'grach-ə-lə-ˌtōr-ē\ *adj* : expressing congratulations
con·gre·gate \'käŋ-gri-ˌgāt\ *vb* : to collect into a group or crowd : ASSEMBLE
con·gre·ga·tion \ˌkäŋ-gri-'gā-shən\ *n* **1** : the action of congregating : the state of being congregated **2** : an assembly of persons met esp. for religious worship **3** : the membership of a church or synagogue **4** : a company or order of religious persons under a common rule
con·gre·ga·tion·al \-'gā-shnəl, -shən-ᵊl\ *adj* **1** : of or relating to a congregation **2** *cap* : of or relating to a body of Protestant churches affirming the essential importance and the autonomy of the local congregation — **con·gre·ga·tion·al·ism** \-ˌiz-əm\ *n, often cap* — **con·gre·ga·tion·al·ist** \-əst\ *n or adj, often cap*
con·gress \'käŋ-grəs\ *n* **1** : a formal meeting of delegates for discussion and action **2** : the legislative body of a nation and esp. of a republic — **con·gres·sion·al** \kən-'gresh-nəl, -ən-ᵊl\ *adj*
con·gress·man \'käŋ-grəs-mən\ *n* : a member of a congress and esp. of the U.S. House of Representatives
con·gress·wom·an \-ˌwu̇m-ən\ *n* : a female member of a congress and esp. of the U.S. House of Representatives
con·gru·ence \kən-'grü-ən(t)s, 'käŋ-grə-wən(t)s\ *n* : the quality or state of according or coinciding
con·gru·ent \kən-'grü-ənt, 'käŋ-grə-wənt\ *adj* **1** : AGREEING, CORRESPONDING **2** : having the same size and shape — **con·gru·ent·ly** *adv*
con·gru·i·ty \kən-'grü-ət-ē, kän-\ *n* : AGREEMENT, HARMONY
con·gru·ous \'käŋ-grə-wəs\ *adj* **1** : being in agreement, harmony, or correspondence **2** : SUITABLE, APPROPRIATE — **con·gru·ous·ly** *adv* — **con·gru·ous·ness** *n*
con·ic \'kän-ik\ *adj* **1** : CONICAL **2** : of or relating to a cone
con·i·cal \'kän-i-kəl\ *adj* : resembling a cone — **con·i·cal·ly** \-i-k(ə-)lē\ *adv* — **con·i·cal·ness** *n*
con·i·fer \'kän-ə-fər, 'kō-nə-\ *n* : any of an order of mostly

evergreen cone-bearing trees and shrubs — **co·nif·er·ous** \kō-ˈnif-(ə-)rəs, kə-\ *adj*

con·jec·tur·al \kən-ˈjek-chə-rəl\ *adj* : of the nature of, involving, or based on conjecture — **con·jec·tur·al·ly** \-ē\ *adv*

¹con·jec·ture \kən-ˈjek-chər\ *n* : inference from inadequate evidence

²conjecture *vb* **-jec·tured**; **-jec·tur·ing** \-ˈjek-chə-riŋ, -ˈjek-shriŋ\ : to make conjectures as to : SURMISE — **con·jec·tur·er** *n*

con·join \kən-ˈjȯin, kän-\ *vb* : to join together

con·joint \-ˈjȯint\ *adj* **1** : UNITED, CONJOINED **2** : JOINT — **con·joint·ly** *adv*

con·ju·gal \ˈkän-ji-gəl, kən-ˈjü-\ *adj* : of or relating to marriage, the married state, or matrimonial relations — **con·ju·gal·ly** *adv*

¹con·ju·gate \ˈkän-ji-gət, -jə-ˌgāt\ *adj* **1** : joined together esp. in pairs : COUPLED **2** : acting or operating as if joined — **con·ju·gate·ly** *adv* — **con·ju·gate·ness** *n*

²con·ju·gate \ˈkän-jə-ˌgāt\ *vb* **1** : to give the various inflectional forms of (a verb) in a prescribed order **2** : to join together : COUPLE

³conjugate *like* ¹CONJUGATE\ *n* : something conjugate

con·ju·ga·tion \ˌkän-jə-ˈgā-shən\ *n* **1** : the act of conjugating : the state of being conjugated **2** : an orderly arrangement of the inflectional forms of a verb — **con·ju·ga·tion·al** \-shnəl, -shən-ᵊl\ *adj* — **con·ju·ga·tive** \ˈkän-jə-ˌgāt-iv\ *adj*

con·junct \kən-ˈjəŋ(k)t, kän-\ *adj* : JOINED, UNITED

con·junc·tion \kən-ˈjəŋ(k)-shən\ *n* **1** : the act or instance of conjoining : the state of being conjoined **2** : occurrence together in time or space **3** : an uninflected word or expression that joins together words or word groups — **con·junc·tion·al** \-shnəl, -shən-ᵊl\ *adj* — **con·junc·tion·al·ly** \-ē\ *adv*

con·junc·tive \kən-ˈjəŋ(k)-tiv\ *adj* **1** : CONNECTIVE **2** : done or existing in conjunction : CONJUNCT **3** : being or functioning like a conjunction — **conjunctive** *n*

con·junc·ture \kən-ˈjəŋ(k)-chər\ *n* **1** : CONJUNCTION, UNION **2** : a combination of circumstances or events esp. producing a crisis : JUNCTURE

con·ju·ra·tion \ˌkän-jə-ˈrā-shən, ˌkən-\ *n* **1** : the act of conjuring **2** : an expression or trick used in conjuring

con·jure \ˈkän-jər, ˈkən-; *in sense 1* kən-ˈju̇(ə)r\ *vb* **1** : to entreat earnestly or solemnly **2 a** : to summon by invocation or incantation **b** : to affect or effect by magic **3** : to practice magical arts

con·jur·er *or* **con·ju·ror** \ˈkän-jər-ər, ˈkən-\ *n* **1** : one that practices magic arts **2** : MAGICIAN, JUGGLER

conk \ˈkäŋk\ *vi* : to break down; *esp* : STALL

con·nect \kə-ˈnekt\ *vb* **1** : to join or link together **2** : to attach by personal relationship or association **3** : to associate in the mind **4** : to be related causally, logically, or spatially — **con·nec·tor** *or* **con·nect·er** \-ˈnek-tər\ *n*

con·nect·ed·ly \-ˈnek-təd-lē\ *adv* : in a connected manner : COHERENTLY

con·nec·tion \-ˈnek-shən\ *n* **1** : the act of connecting **2** : the fact or condition of being connected : RELATIONSHIP **3** : a means by which two things are connected : BOND, LINK **4** : a person connected with others esp. by marriage or kinship **5** : a set of persons associated together: as **a** : DENOMINATION **b** : CLAN

¹con·nec·tive \kə-ˈnek-tiv\ *adj* : connecting or tending to connect — **con·nec·tive·ly** *adv*

²connective *n* : something that connects; *esp* : a word (as a conjunction) that connects words or word groups

con·niv·ance \kə-ˈnī-vən(t)s\ *n* : the act of conniving

con·nive \kə-ˈnīv\ *vi* **1** : to pretend ignorance of something that one ought to oppose or stop **2** : to cooperate secretly or have a secret understanding — **con·niv·er** *n*

con·nois·seur \ˌkän-ə-ˈsər\ *n* : a person competent to act as a judge in matters involving taste and appreciation : EXPERT

con·no·ta·tion \ˌkän-ə-ˈtā-shən\ *n* : a meaning suggested by a word or an expression apart from and in addition to its denotation — **con·no·ta·tion·al** \-shnəl, -shən-ᵊl\ *adj*

con·no·ta·tive \ˈkän-ə-ˌtāt-iv, kə-ˈnōt-ət-iv\ *adj* **1** : connoting or tending to connote **2** : relating to connotation — **con·no·ta·tive·ly** *adv*

con·note \kə-ˈnōt\ *vt* **1** : to suggest or mean along with or in addition to the exact explicit meaning **2** : to be associated with as a consequence or concomitant

con·nu·bi·al \kə-ˈn(y)ü-bē-əl\ *adj* : of or relating to marriage : CONJUGAL — **con·nu·bi·al·ly** \-bē-ə-lē\ *adv*

con·quer \ˈkäŋ-kər\ *vb* **con·quered**; **con·quer·ing** \-k(ə-)riŋ\ **1** : to gain by force of arms : SUBJUGATE **2** : to overcome by force of arms **3** : to gain or win by overcoming obstacles or opposition

con·quer·or \ˈkäŋ-kər-ər\ *n* : one that conquers : VICTOR

con·quest \ˈkän-ˌkwest, ˈkäŋ-\ *n* **1** : the act or process of conquering **2 a** : something conquered **b** : a person whose affections have been won

con·quis·ta·dor \kōŋ-ˈkēs-tə-ˌdȯr, kän-ˈk(w)is-\ *n, pl* **con·quis·ta·do·res** \kōŋ-ˌkēs-tə-ˈdȯr-ēz, -ˈdōr-, kän-ˌk(w)is-\ *or* **con·quis·ta·dors** : CONQUEROR; *esp* : a leader in the Spanish conquest of America and esp. of Mexico and Peru in the 16th century

con·san·guin·e·ous \ˌkän-ˌsan-ˈgwin-ē-əs, -ˌsaŋ-\ *adj* : of the same blood or origin; *esp* : descended from the same ancestor — **con·san·guin·e·ous·ly** *adv* — **con·san·guin·i·ty** \-ˈgwin-ət-ē\ *n*

con·science \ˈkän-chən(t)s\ *n* : the sense or consciousness of the moral goodness or blameworthiness of one's own conduct, intentions, or character together with a feeling of obligation to do right or be good

con·sci·en·tious \ˌkän-chē-ˈen-chəs\ *adj* **1** : governed by or in accordance with one's conscience : SCRUPULOUS **2** : METICULOUS, CAREFUL — **con·sci·en·tious·ly** *adv* — **con·sci·en·tious·ness** *n*

con·scious \ˈkän-chəs\ *adj* **1** : perceiving or noticing with a degree of controlled thought or observation **2** : known or felt by one's inner self **3** : capable of or marked by thought, will, design, or perception **4** : having mental faculties undulled by sleep, faint, or stupor : AWAKE **5** : done or acting with critical awareness — **con·scious·ly** *adv*

con·scious·ness \ˈkän-chəs-nəs\ *n* **1** : awareness of something **2** : MIND **3** : the normal state of conscious life as distinguished from sleep or insensibility **4** : the upper level of mental life as contrasted with unconscious processes

¹con·script \ˈkän-ˌskript\ *n* : a conscripted person (as a military recruit)

²con·script \kən-ˈskript\ *vt* : to enroll into military service by compulsion : DRAFT

con·scrip·tion \kən-ˈskrip-shən\ *n* : compulsory enrollment of persons esp. for military service : DRAFT

con·se·crate \ˈkän(t)-sə-ˌkrāt\ *vb* **1** : to set apart to the service of God; *esp* : to ordain to the office of bishop **2** : to devote to a purpose with deep solemnity or dedication **3** : to make inviolate or venerable — **con·se·cra·tor** \-ˌkrāt-ər\ *n*

con·se·cra·tion \ˌkän(t)-sə-ˈkrā-shən\ *n* **1** : the act or ceremony of consecrating **2** : the state of being consecrated

con·sec·u·tive \kən-ˈsek-(y)ət-iv\ *adj* : following one after the other in order without gaps : CONTINUOUS — **con·sec·u·tive·ly** *adv* — **con·sec·u·tive·ness** *n*

con·sen·sus \kən-ˈsen(t)-səs\ *n* **1** : general agreement (as in opinion or testimony) : ACCORD **2** : the trend of opinion

¹con·sent \kən-ˈsent\ *vi* : to give assent or approval : AGREE — **con·sent·er** *n*

²consent *n* **1** : compliance in or approval of what is asked or proposed **2** : agreement as to action or opinion

con·se·quence \ˈkän(t)-sə-ˌkwen(t)s, -si-kwən(t)s\ *n* **1** : something produced by a cause or necessarily following from a set of conditions 2 : a conclusion that results from reason or argument 3 a : importance with respect to power to produce an effect b : social importance

con•se•quent \-si-kwənt, -sə-ˌkwent\ *adj* 1 : following as a result or effect 2 : observing logical sequence : RATIONAL

con•se•quen•tial \ˌkän(t)-sə-'kwen-chəl\ *adj* 1 : following as a consequence 2 : having significant consequences 3 : SELF-IMPORTANT — **con•se•quen•tial•ly** \-'kwench-(ə-)lē\ *adv* — **con•se•quen•tial•ness** *n*

con•se•quent•ly \'kän(t)-sə-ˌkwent-lē, -si-kwənt-\ *adv* : as a result : ACCORDINGLY

con•ser•va•tion \ˌkän(t)-sər-'vā-shən\ *n* : a careful preservation and protection; *esp* : planned management of a natural resource to prevent exploitation, destruction, or neglect — **con•ser•va•tion•al** \-shnəl, -shən-ᵊl\ *adj*

con•ser•va•tion•ist \-'vā-sh(ə-)nəst\ *n* : one who advocates conservation esp. of natural resources

con•serv•a•tism \kən-'sər-və-ˌtiz-əm\ *n* 1 : disposition in politics to preserve what is established 2 : tendency to prefer an existing situation and to be suspicious of change

[1]**con•serv•a•tive** \kən-'sər-vət-iv\ *adj* 1 : tending to conserve or preserve 2 : of or relating to conservatism 3 a : tending or disposed to maintain existing views, conditions, or institutions b : MODERATE, CAUTIOUS — **con•serv•a•tive•ly** *adv* — **con•serv•a•tive•ness** *n*

[2]**conservative** *n* : an adherent or advocate of conservatism

con•ser•va•toire \kən-'sər-və-ˌtwär\ *n* : CONSERVATORY

con•ser•va•tor \kən-'sər-vət-ər, 'kän(t)-sər-ˌvāt-ər\ *n* 1 : PROTECTOR 2 : one designated to take over and protect the interests of an incompetent

con•serv•a•to•ry \kən-'sər-və-ˌtōr-ē\ *n, pl* **-ries** 1 : a greenhouse for growing or displaying plants 2 : a school specializing in one of the fine arts

[1]**con•serve** \kən-'sərv\ *vt* 1 : to keep in a safe or sound state : PRESERVE 2 : to preserve with sugar — **con•serv•er** *n*

[2]**con•serve** \'kän-ˌsərv\ *n* 1 : CONFECTION; *esp* : a candied fruit 2 : PRESERVE; *esp* : one prepared from a mixture of fruits

con•sid•er \kən-'sid-ər\ *vb* **-sid•ered; -sid•er•ing** \-'sid-(ə-)riŋ\ 1 : to think over carefully : PONDER, REFLECT 2 : to regard highly : ESTEEM 3 : to think of in a certain way : regard as being

con•sid•er•a•ble \kən-'sid-ər-(ə-)bəl, -'sid-rə-bəl\ *adj* 1 : deserving consideration : IMPORTANT 2 : large in extent, amount, or quantity — **con•sid•er•a•bly** \-blē\ *adv*

con•sid•er•ate \kən-'sid-(ə-)rət\ *adj* : thoughtful of the rights and feelings of others — **con•sid•er•ate•ly** *adv* — **con•sid•er•ate•ness** *n*

con•sid•er•a•tion \kən-ˌsid-ə-'rā-shən\ *n* 1 : careful thought : DELIBERATION 2 : thoughtfulness for other people 3 : MOTIVE, REASON 4 : RESPECT, REGARD 5 : a payment made in return for something : COMPENSATION

con•sid•er•ing *prep* : in view of : taking into account

con•sign \kən-'sīn\ *vt* 1 : to give over to another's care : ENTRUST 2 : to give, transfer, or deliver formally 3 : to send or address to an agent to be cared for or sold — **con•sign•a•ble** *adj* — **con•sign•ee** \ˌkän-ˌsī-'nē, kən-\ *n* — **con•sign•or** \kən-'sī-nər, ˌkän-ˌsī-'nȯ(ə)r\ *n*

con•sign•ment \kən-'sīn-mənt\ *n* 1 : the act or process of consigning 2 : something consigned; *esp* : a single shipment of goods delivered to an agent for sale

con•sist \kən-'sist\ *vi* 1 : to be contained : LIE, RESIDE — used with *in* 2 : to be made up or composed — used with *of*

con•sist•ence \kən-'sis-tən(t)s\ *n* : CONSISTENCY

con•sist•en•cy \kən-'sis-tən-sē\ *n, pl* **-cies** 1 : the condition of adhering together : FIRMNESS 2 a : agreement or harmony of parts or features to one another or a whole b : harmony with past performance or with stated aims

con•sist•ent \kən-'sis-tənt\ *adj* 1 : possessing firmness or coherence 2 a : HARMONIOUS, COMPATIBLE b : uniform throughout 3 : living or acting conformably to one's own belief, professions, or character — **con•sist•ent•ly** *adv*

con•sis•to•ry \kən-'sis-t(ə-)rē\ *n, pl* **-ries** : a solemn meeting of Roman Catholic cardinals presided over by the pope — **con•sis•to•ri•al** \ˌkän-ˌsis-'tōr-ē-əl\ *adj*

con•so•la•tion \ˌkän(t)-sə-'lā-shən\ *n* : the act or an instance of consoling : the state of being consoled — **con•sol•a•to•ry** \kən-'säl-ə-ˌtōr-ē, -'sō-lə-\ *adj*

[1]**con•sole** \kən-'sōl\ *vt* : to comfort in times of grief or distress — **con•sol•a•ble** *adj*

[2]**con•sole** \'kän-ˌsōl\ *n* 1 : an architectural bracket used for ornament or support 2 a : the desk from which an organ is played b : a panel or cabinet on which are mounted dials and switches used in controlling electrical or mechanical devices 3 : a cabinet (as for a radio or television set) designed to rest directly on the floor

con•sol•i•date \kən-'säl-ə-ˌdāt\ *vb* 1 : to join together into one whole : UNITE 2 : to make firm or secure : STRENGTHEN 3 : to form into a compact mass

con•sol•i•da•tion \kən-ˌsäl-ə-'dā-shən\ *n* 1 : the act or process of consolidating : the state of being consolidated 2 : the merger of two or more corporations into one

con•som•mé \ˌkän(t)-sə-'mā\ *n* : a clear soup chiefly of meat stock

con•so•nance \'kän(t)-s(ə-)nən(t)s\ *n* 1 : harmony or agreement among components 2 : an agreeable combination or correspondence of musical tones or speech sounds

[1]**con•so•nant** \'kän(t)-s(ə-)nənt\ *n* 1 : a speech sound (as \p\, \n\, or \s\) characterized by narrowing or stoppage at one or more points in the breath channel 2 : a letter representing a consonant

[2]**consonant** *adj* : being in agreement or harmony — **con•so•nant•ly** *adv*

con•so•nan•tal \ˌkän(t)-sə-'nant-ᵊl\ *adj* : relating to, being, or marked by a consonant or group of consonants

[1]**con•sort** \'kän-ˌsȯrt\ *n* 1 : a wife or husband : SPOUSE 2 : a ship sailing in company with another ship

[2]**con•sort** \kən-'sȯrt\ *vb* 1 : to keep company : ASSOCIATE 2 : ACCORD, HARMONIZE

con•sor•tium \kən-'sȯr-sh(ē-)əm\ *n, pl* **-tia** \-sh(ē-)ə\ : an international business or banking agreement or combination

con•spec•tus \kən-'spek-təs\ *n* 1 : a brief survey or summary 2 : OUTLINE, SYNOPSIS

con•spic•u•ous \kən-'spik-yə-wəs\ *adj* : attracting attention : STRIKING — **con•spic•u•ous•ly** *adv* — **con•spic•u•ous•ness** *n*

con•spir•a•cy \kən-'spir-ə-sē\ *n, pl* **-cies** : an agreement among conspirators

con•spir•a•tor \kən-'spir-ət-ər\ *n* : one that conspires

con•spir•a•to•ri•al \kən-ˌspir-ə-'tōr-ē-əl\ *adj* : of, relating to, or characteristic of a conspiracy — **con•spir•a•to•ri•al•ly** \-ē\ *adv*

con•spire \kən-'spī(ə)r\ *vb* 1 : PLOT, CONTRIVE 2 : to agree secretly to do an unlawful or wrongful act

con•sta•ble \'kän(t)-stə-bəl, 'kən(t)-\ *n* : a public officer responsible for keeping the peace

con•stab•u•lary \kən-'stab-yə-ˌler-ē\ *n, pl* **-lar•ies** 1 : the organized body of constables of a particular district or country 2 : an armed police force organized on military lines but distinct from the regular army

con•stan•cy \'kän(t)-stən-sē\ *n* 1 : firmness in one's beliefs : STEADFASTNESS 2 : freedom from change

[1]**con•stant** \'kän(t)-stənt\ *adj* 1 : STEADFAST, RESOLUTE 2 : INVARIABLE, UNIFORM 3 : continually recurring : REGULAR — **con•stant•ly** *adv*

[2]**constant** *n* : something invariable or unchanging

con·stel·la·tion \ˌkän(t)-stə-ˈlā-shən\ *n* : any of 88 groups of stars forming patterns
con·ster·na·tion \ˌkän(t)-stər-ˈnā-shən\ *n* : amazement or dismay that hinders or throws into confusion
con·sti·pate \ˈkän(t)-stə-ˌpāt\ *vt* : to cause constipation in
con·sti·pa·tion \ˌkän(t)-stə-ˈpā-shən\ *n* : abnormally delayed or infrequent passage of dry hardened feces
con·stit·u·en·cy \kən-ˈstich-(ə-)wən-sē\ *n*, *pl* **-cies** **1** : the residents in an electoral district **2** : an electoral district
[1]**con·stit·u·ent** \kən-ˈstich-(ə-)wənt\ *n* **1** : one of the parts of which a thing is made up : COMPONENT **2** : one of a group who elects another to represent him in a public office
[2]**constituent** *adj* **1** : COMPONENT **2** : having the power to create a government or frame or amend a constitution — **con·stit·u·ent·ly** *adv*
con·sti·tute \ˈkän(t)-stə-ˌt(y)üt\ *vt* **1** : to appoint to an office or duty **2** : to set up : ESTABLISH, FIX **3** : to make up : FORM
con·sti·tu·tion \ˌkän(t)-stə-ˈt(y)ü-shən\ *n* **1** : the act of establishing, making, or setting up **2 a** : the physical makeup of the individual : PHYSIQUE **b** : the structure, composition, or nature of something **3 a** : the basic principles and laws of a nation, state, or social group **b** : a written instrument embodying the rules of a political or social organization — **con·sti·tu·tion·al** \-shnəl, -shən-ᵊl\ *adj* — **con·sti·tu·tion·al·ly** \-ē\ *adv*
constitutional *n* : a walk or other exercise taken for one's health
con·sti·tu·tion·al·ism \-ˌiz-əm\ *n* : adherence to or government according to constitutional principles — **con·sti·tu·tion·al·ist** \-əst\ *n*
con·sti·tu·tion·al·i·ty \ˌkän(t)-stə-ˌt(y)ü-shə-ˈnal-ət-ē\ *n* : accordance with the provisions of a constitution
con·sti·tu·tive \ˈkän(t)-stə-ˌt(y)üt-iv, kən-ˈstich-ət-iv\ *adj* : forming part of the structure of a thing : CONSTITUENT, ESSENTIAL — **con·sti·tu·tive·ly** *adv*
con·strain \kən-ˈstrān\ *vt* **1** : COMPEL **2** : to secure by or as if by bond : CONFINE **3** : to hold back by force : RESTRAIN
con·straint \kən-ˈstrānt\ *n* **1 a** : COMPULSION; *also* : RESTRAINT **b** : a constraining agency or force : CHECK **2** : repression of one's feelings, behavior, or actions
con·strict \kən-ˈstrikt\ *vb* **1 a** : to draw together **b** : COMPRESS, SQUEEZE **2** : to become narrower or smaller — **con·stric·tive** \-ˈstrik-tiv\ *adj*
con·stric·tion \kən-ˈstrik-shən\ *n* **1** : an act of constricting : the state of being constricted : TIGHTENING **2** : something that constricts : a part that is constricted
con·struct \kən-ˈstrəkt\ *vt* : to make or form by combining parts — **con·struct·i·ble** \-ˈstrək-tə-bəl\ *adj* — **con·struc·tor** \-ˈstrək-tər\ *n*
con·struc·tion \kən-ˈstrək-shən\ *n* **1** : the arrangement and connection of words or groups of words in a sentence **2** : the process, art, or manner of constructing; *also* : a thing constructed : STRUCTURE **3** : an interpretation or explanation of a statement or a fact — **con·struc·tion·al** \-shnəl, -shən-ᵊl\ *adj*
con·struc·tion·ist \kən-ˈstrək-sh(ə-)nəst\ *n* : one who construes an instrument (as the U.S. Constitution) in a specific way
con·struc·tive \kən-ˈstrək-tiv\ *adj* **1** : fitted for or given to constructing **2** : helping to develop or improve something — **con·struc·tive·ly** *adv*
con·strue \kən-ˈstrü\ *vb* **1** : to explain the grammatical relationships of the words in a sentence, clause, or phrase **2** : to understand or explain the sense or intention of : INTERPRET — **con·stru·a·ble** *adj*
con·sul \ˈkän(t)-səl\ *n* **1** : either of two joint annually elected chief magistrates of the Roman republic **2** : an official appointed by a government to reside in a foreign country to represent the commercial interests of citizens of the appointing country — **con·sul·ar** \-s(ə-)lər\ *adj* — **con·sul·ship** \-səl-ˌship\ *n*
con·sul·ate \ˈkän(t)-s(ə-)lət\ *n* **1** : a government by consuls **2** : the office, term of office, or jurisdiction of a consul **3** : the residence or official premises of a consul
con·sult \kən-ˈsəlt\ *vb* **1** : to seek the opinion or advice of **2** : to seek information from **3** : CONFER — **con·sult·er** *n*
con·sult·ant \kən-ˈsəlt-ᵊnt\ *n* **1** : one who consults another **2** : one who gives professional advice or services
con·sul·ta·tion \ˌkän(t)-səl-ˈtā-shən\ *n* **1** : COUNCIL, CONFERENCE; *esp* : a deliberation between physicians on a case or its treatment **2** : the act of consulting or conferring
con·sul·ta·tive \kən-ˈsəl-tət-iv\ *adj* : ADVISORY
con·sume \kən-ˈsüm\ *vb* **1** : to destroy or become destroyed by or as if by fire **2** : to use up : EXPEND **3** : to eat or drink up **4** : to take up one's attention — **con·sum·a·ble** *adj*
con·sum·er \kən-ˈsü-mər\ *n* : one that consumes; *esp* : one that utilizes economic goods
[1]**con·sum·mate** \kən-ˈsəm-ət, ˈkän(t)-sə-mət\ *adj* : of the highest degree or quality — **con·sum·mate·ly** *adv*
[2]**con·sum·mate** \ˈkän(t)-sə-ˌmāt\ *vt* : to make perfect : FINISH, COMPLETE — **con·sum·ma·tion** \ˌkän(t)-sə-ˈmā-shən\ *n*
con·sump·tion \kən-ˈsəm(p)-shən\ *n* **1** : the act or process of consuming; *esp* : the use of economic goods **2 a** : a progressive wasting away of the body **b** : TUBERCULOSIS
[1]**con·sump·tive** \kən-ˈsəm(p)-tiv\ *adj* **1** : tending to consume : DESTRUCTIVE **2** : of, relating to, or affected with consumption — **con·sump·tive·ly** *adv*
[2]**consumptive** *n* : a person affected with consumption
[1]**con·tact** \ˈkän-ˌtakt\ *n* **1** : union or junction of surfaces **2 a** : ASSOCIATION, RELATIONSHIP **b** : CONNECTION, COMMUNICATION
[2]**contact** *vb* **1** : to bring into contact **2 a** : to enter into or be in contact with **b** : to make contact
contact lens *n* : a thin lens designed to fit over the cornea
con·ta·gion \kən-ˈtā-jən\ *n* **1** : the passing of a disease from one individual to another by contact **2** : a contagious disease or its causative agent (as a virus) **3** : transmission of an influence to the mind of others
con·ta·gious \kən-ˈtā-jəs\ *adj* : communicable by contact : CATCHING; *also* : relating to contagion or contagious diseases — **con·ta·gious·ly** *adv* — **con·ta·gious·ness** *n*
con·tain \kən-ˈtān\ *vt* **1** : to keep within limits : RESTRAIN **2** : to have within : HOLD **3** : ENCLOSE, BOUND — **con·tain·a·ble** *adj*
con·tain·er \kən-ˈtā-nər\ *n* : RECEPTACLE
con·tam·i·nant \kən-ˈtam-ə-nənt\ *n* : something that contaminates
con·tam·i·nate \kən-ˈtam-ə-ˌnāt\ *vt* : to soil, stain, or infect by contact or association — **con·tam·i·na·tion** \-ˌtam-ə-ˈnā-shən\ *n* — **con·tam·i·na·tive** \-ˈtam-ə-ˌnāt-iv\ *adj* — **con·tam·i·na·tor** \-ˌnāt-ər\ *n*
con·temn \kən-ˈtem\ *vt* : to view or treat with contempt : DISDAIN — **con·tem·ner** \-ˈtem-ər, -ˈtem-nər\ *n*
con·tem·plate \ˈkänt-əm-ˌplāt\ *vb* **1** : to consider carefully and for a long time : MEDITATE **2** : to have in mind : INTEND
con·tem·pla·tion \ˌkänt-əm-ˈplā-shən\ *n* **1** : concentration on spiritual things as a form of private devotion **2** : STUDY **3** : the act of regarding steadily **4** : INTENTION
con·tem·pla·tive \kən-ˈtem-plət-iv, ˈkänt-əm-ˌplāt-\ *adj* : marked by or given to contemplation — **con·tem·pla·tive·ly** *adv* — **con·tem·pla·tive·ness** *n*
con·tem·po·ra·ne·ous \kən-ˌtem-pə-ˈrā-nē-əs\ *adj* : existing, occurring, or originating during the same time — **con·tem·po·ra·ne·ous·ly** *adv*
[1]**con·tem·po·rary** \kən-ˈtem-pə-ˌrer-ē\ *adj* **1** : living or occurring at the same period of time **2** : of the same age **3** : of the present time : MODERN
[2]**contemporary** *n*, *pl* **-rar·ies** **1** : one that is contemporary with another **2** : one of about the same age as another

con·tempt \kən-'tem(p)t\ *n* **1 :** the act of despising : the state of mind of one who despises **2 :** DISGRACE **3 :** disobedience or disrespect to a court, judge, or legislative body
con·tempt·i·ble \kən-'tem(p)-tə-bəl\ *adj* : deserving contempt — **con·tempt·i·bly** \-blē\ *adv*
con·temp·tu·ous \kən-'tem(p)-chə-wəs\ *adj* : feeling or showing contempt : SCORNFUL — **con·temp·tu·ous·ly** *adv* — **con·temp·tu·ous·ness** *n*
con·tend \kən-'tend\ *vb* **1 :** to compete with another in opposition or in rivalry **2 :** STRIVE, STRUGGLE **3 :** ARGUE, MAINTAIN — **con·tend·er** *n*
¹con·tent \kən-'tent\ *adj* : SATISFIED, CONTENTED
²content *vt* : to appease the desires of : SATISFY
³content *n* : CONTENTMENT
⁴con·tent \'kän-ˌtent\ *n* **1 :** something contained — usu. used in pl. **2 :** the subject matter or topics treated (as in a book) **3 :** the significant part (as of a book) **4 a :** CAPACITY **b :** the amount contained
con·tent·ed \kən-'tent-əd\ *adj* : satisfied or showing satisfaction with one's possessions, status, or situation — **con·tent·ed·ly** *adv*
con·ten·tion \kən-'ten-chən\ *n* **1 :** an act or instance of contending : STRIFE, DISPUTE **2 :** a point advanced or maintained in a debate or argument
con·ten·tious \kən-'ten-chəs\ *adj* : inclined to find or seek reasons for contention often over unimportant matters — **con·ten·tious·ly** *adv* — **con·ten·tious·ness** *n*
con·tent·ment \kən-'tent-mənt\ *n* : the state of being contented : peaceful satisfaction
con·ter·mi·nous \kən-'tər-mə-nəs, kän-\ *adj* : having the same or a common boundary
¹con·test \kən-'test\ *vb* **1 :** DISPUTE, CHALLENGE **2 :** to struggle over or for **3 :** STRIVE, VIE — **con·test·a·ble** *adj* — **con·test·er** *n*
²con·test \'kän-ˌtest\ *n* **1 :** a struggle for victory or superiority (as in strength, skill, or knowledge) : COMPETITION **2 :** OPPOSITION, RIVALRY
con·test·ant \kən-'tes-tənt\ *n* : one who takes part in a contest
con·text \'kän-ˌtekst\ *n* : the parts of a written or spoken passage that are near a certain word or group of words and that help to explain its meaning — **con·tex·tu·al** \kän-'teks-chə(-wə)l\ *adj* — **con·tex·tu·al·ly** \-ē\ *adv*
con·ti·gu·i·ty \ˌkänt-ə-'gyü-ət-ē\ *n* : the state of being contiguous
con·tig·u·ous \kən-'tig-yə-wəs\ *adj* **1 :** being in contact : TOUCHING **2 :** very near though not in actual contact — **con·tig·u·ous·ly** *adv* — **con·tig·u·ous·ness** *n*
con·ti·nence \'känt-ᵊn-ən(t)s\ *n* **1 :** SELF-RESTRAINT **2 :** ability to refrain from a bodily activity
¹con·ti·nent \'känt-ᵊn-ənt\ *adj* : exercising continence — **con·ti·nent·ly** *adv*
²con·ti·nent \'känt-ᵊn-ənt, 'känt-nənt\ *n* **1 :** MAINLAND **2 a :** one of the great divisions of land (as North America, South America, Europe, Asia, Africa, Australia, or Antarctica) on the globe **b** *cap* : the continent of Europe
¹con·ti·nen·tal \ˌkänt-ᵊn-'ent-ᵊl\ *adj* **1 :** of relating to, or characteristic of a continent; *esp* : of or relating to the continent of Europe as distinguished from the British Isles **2** *often cap* : of or relating to the colonies later forming the U.S. — **con·ti·nen·tal·ly** \-ᵊl-ē\ *adv*
²continental *n* **1** *often cap* : an American soldier of the Revolution in the Continental army **2 :** the least bit
con·tin·gen·cy \kən-'tin-jən-sē\ *n, pl* **-cies 1 :** the state of being contingent **2 :** a chance happening or event
¹con·tin·gent \-jənt\ *adj* **1 :** likely but not certain to happen : POSSIBLE **2 a :** happening by chance or unforeseen causes **b :** intended for use in circumstances not completely foreseen **3 :** dependent on or conditioned by something else — **con·tin·gent·ly** *adv*
²contingent *n* : a number of persons representing or drawn from an area or group
con·tin·u·al \kən-'tin-yə(-wə)l\ *adj* **1 :** continuing indefinitely in time without interruption **2 :** recurring in rapid succession — **con·tin·u·al·ly** \-ē\ *adv*
con·tin·u·ance \kən-'tin-yə-wən(t)s\ *n* **1 :** the act of continuing in a state, condition, or course of action **2 :** unbroken succession : CONTINUATION **3 :** postponement of proceedings in a court of law to a specified day
con·tin·u·a·tion \kən-ˌtin-yə-'wā-shən\ *n* **1 :** continuance in or prolongation of a state or activity **2 :** resumption after an interruption **3 :** something that continues, increases, or adds
con·tin·ue \kən-'tin-yü\ *vb* **1 :** to remain in a place or a condition : STAY **2 :** ENDURE, LAST **3 :** to go on or carry forward in a course **4 :** to go on or carry on after an interruption : RESUME **5 :** to postpone a legal proceeding to a later date **6 :** to allow to remain — **con·tin·u·er** *n*
con·ti·nu·i·ty \ˌkänt-ᵊn-'(y)ü-ət-ē\ *n, pl* **-ties 1 :** uninterrupted connection, succession, or union **2 a :** a script or scenario in the performing arts **b :** transitional spoken or musical matter for a radio or television program
con·tin·u·ous \kən-'tin-yə-wəs\ *adj* : being without break or interruption : CONTINUED, UNBROKEN — **con·tin·u·ous·ly** *adv* — **con·tin·u·ous·ness** *n*
con·tin·u·um \-yə-wəm\ *n, pl* **-ua** \-wə\ **1 :** something that is the same throughout **2 :** something that consists of a series of variations or of a sequence of things in regular order
con·tort \kən-'tȯrt\ *vb* : to twist into an unusual appearance or unnatural shape : DEFORM, DISTORT
con·tor·tion \kən-'tȯr-shən\ *n* **1 :** a contorting or a being contorted **2 :** a contorted shape or thing
con·tor·tion·ist \-sh(ə-)nəst\ *n* : a person who contorts; *esp* : an acrobat who puts himself into unusual postures
con·tour \'kän-ˌtu̇(ə)r\ *n* **1 :** the outline of a figure or body **2 :** SHAPE, FORM
con·tra·band \'kän-trə-ˌband\ *n* : goods or merchandise whose importation, exportation, or possession is forbidden; *also* : smuggled goods — **contraband** *adj*
con·tra·cep·tion \ˌkän-trə-'sep-shən\ *n* : voluntary prevention of conception
¹con·tra·cep·tive \-'sep-tiv\ *adj* : relating to or used for contraception
²contraceptive *n* : a contraceptive agent or device
¹con·tract \'kän-ˌtrakt\ *n* **1 :** a legally binding agreement : COVENANT **2 :** an undertaking to win a specified number of tricks or points in bridge
²con·tract \kən-'trakt, *oftenest for 2* 'kän-ˌ\ *vb* **1 :** to enter into by contract **2 :** to undertake by contract **3 :** to draw together or draw up so as to make or to become shorter and broader **4 a :** to diminish in size : SHORTEN, SHRINK **b :** to shorten (as a word) by omitting one or more sounds or letters **5 a :** GET, CATCH **b :** FORM — **con·tract·i·bil·i·ty** \kən-ˌtrak-tə-'bil-ət-ē, ˌkän-\ *n* — **con·tract·i·ble** \kən-'trak-tə-bəl, 'kän-ˌ\ *adj*
con·trac·tile \kən-'trak-tᵊl\ *adj* : capable of contracting — **con·trac·til·i·ty** \ˌkän-ˌtrak-'til-ət-ē\ *n*
con·trac·tion \kən-'trak-shən\ *n* **1 :** the act or process of contracting : the state of being contracted **2 :** a shortening of a word, syllable, or word group by omission of a sound or letter; *also* : a form produced by such shortening — **con·trac·tion·al** \-'trak-shnəl, -shən-ᵊl\ *adj* — **con·trac·tive** \-'trak-tiv\ *adj*
con·trac·tor \'kän-ˌtrak-tər\ *n* : one that contracts or is party to a contract
con·trac·tu·al \kən-'trak-chə(-wə)l, kän-\ *adj* : of, relating to, or constituting a contract

con·tra·dict \ˌkän-trə-ˈdikt\ *vt* **1** : to deny the truth of (as a statement) : state the contrary of **2** : to be contrary or opposed to
con·tra·dic·tion \-ˈdik-shən\ *n* **1** : a statement that contradicts another **2** : opposition existing between things
con·tra·dic·to·ry \ˌkän-trə-ˈdik-t(ə-)rē\ *adj* **1** : tending to contradict **2** : involving contradiction : OPPOSED
con·tra·dis·tinc·tion \ˌkän-trə-dis-ˈtiŋ(k)-shən\ *n* : distinction by contrast
con·tra·dis·tin·guish \-ˈtiŋ-gwish\ *vt* : to distinguish by contrast of qualities
con·trail \ˈkän-ˌtrāl\ *n* : streaks of condensed water vapor created in the air by an airplane or rocket at high altitudes
con·tral·to \kən-ˈtral-tō\ *n, pl* **-tos** : the lowest female singing voice; *also* : a singer with such a voice
con·trap·tion \kən-ˈtrap-shən\ *n* : CONTRIVANCE, DEVICE
con·tra·pun·tal \ˌkän-trə-ˈpənt-ᵊl\ *adj* : of or relating to counterpoint — **con·tra·pun·tal·ly** \-ᵊl-ē\ *adv*
con·tra·ri·ety \ˌkän-trə-ˈrī-ət-ē\ *n, pl* **-eties** **1** : the quality or state of being contrary **2** : something contrary
con·trari·wise \ˈkän-ˌtrer-ē-ˌwīz\ *adv* **1** : on the contrary **2** : vice versa : CONVERSELY **3** : PERVERSELY
¹**con·trary** \ˈkän-ˌtrer-ē\ *n, pl* **-trar·ies** **1** : a fact or condition incompatible with another : OPPOSITE **2** : one of a pair of opposites — **by contraries** : in a manner opposite to what is logical or expected — **on the contrary** : just the opposite — **to the contrary** : NOTWITHSTANDING
²**con·trary** \ˈkän-ˌtrer-ē, *4 is often* kən-ˈtre(ə)r-ē\ *adj* **1** : exactly opposite **2** : OPPOSED **3** : UNFAVORABLE **4** : inclined to oppose or resist — **con·trar·i·ly** \-ˌtrer-ə-lē, -ˈtrer-\ *adv* — **con·trar·i·ness** \-ˌtrer-ē-nəs, -ˈtrer-\ *n*
³**con·trary** *like* ²CONTRARY\ *adv* : CONTRARIWISE
¹**con·trast** \ˈkän-ˌtrast\ *n* **1** : the act or process of contrasting : the state of being contrasted **2** : a person or thing that exhibits differences when contrasted **3** : difference between associated things; *esp* : diversity of adjacent parts in color, emotion, tone, or brightness
²**con·trast** \kən-ˈtrast, ˈkän-ˌ\ *vb* **1** : to show noticeable differences **2** : to compare two persons or things so as to show the differences between them — **con·trast·a·ble** *adj*
con·tra·vene \ˌkän-trə-ˈvēn\ *vt* **1** : to go or act contrary to **2** : to oppose in argument
con·tra·ven·tion \ˌkän-trə-ˈven-chən\ *n* : the act of contravening : VIOLATION
con·tre·temps \ˈkän-trə-ˌtäⁿ\ *n, pl* **con·tre·temps** \-ˌtäⁿ(z)\ : an inopportune embarrassing occurrence : MISHAP
con·trib·ute \kən-ˈtrib-yət\ *vb* **1** : to give along with others **2** : to have a share in something **3** : to supply (as an article) for publication
con·tri·bu·tion \ˌkän-trə-ˈbyü-shən\ *n* **1** : LEVY, TAX **2** : the act of contributing; *also* : the sum or thing contributed **3** : a writing for publication esp. in a periodical
con·trib·u·tive \kən-ˈtrib-yət-iv\ *adj* : contributing or tending to contribute — **con·trib·u·tive·ly** *adv*
con·trib·u·tor \-yət-ər\ *n* : one that contributes (as for publication esp. in a periodical)
con·trib·u·to·ry \kən-ˈtrib-yə-ˌtōr-ē\ *adj* **1** : helping to accomplish a result **2 a** : of, relating to, or forming a contribution **b** : supported by contributions
con·trite \ˈkän-ˌtrīt, kən-ˈ\ *adj* : sorrowful for some wrong that one has done : deeply repentant — **con·trite·ly** *adv* — **con·trite·ness** *n*
con·tri·tion \kən-ˈtrish-ən\ *n* : the state of being contrite
con·triv·ance \kən-ˈtrī-vən(t)s\ *n* **1** : the act or faculty of contriving : the state of being contrived **2** : a thing contrived; *esp* : a mechanical device
con·trive \kən-ˈtrīv\ *vb* **1** : PLAN, PLOT, SCHEME **2** : to form or make in some skillful or ingenious way : INVENT, DESIGN **3** : to bring about : MANAGE — **con·triv·er** *n*
con·trived *adj* : ARTIFICIAL, UNNATURAL
¹**con·trol** \kən-ˈtrōl\ *vt* **con·trolled**; **con·trol·ling** **1** : to exercise restraining or directing influence over : REGULATE **2** : to have power over : RULE — **con·trol·la·ble** \-ˈtrō-lə-bəl\ *adj*
²**control** *n* **1** : the power or authority to control or command **2 a** : ability to control **b** : RESTRAINT, RESERVE **3** : a means or method of controlling; *esp* : a mechanism used to regulate or guide the operation of a machine, apparatus, or system
con·trol·ler \kən-ˈtrō-lər, ˈkän-ˌ\ *n* **1** : COMPTROLLER **2** : one that controls — **con·trol·ler·ship** \-ˌship\ *n*
con·tro·ver·sial \ˌkän-trə-ˈvər-shəl, -ˈvər-sē-əl\ *adj* **1** : of or relating to controversy **2** : open to or likely to cause controversy **3** : fond of controversy : ARGUMENTATIVE — **con·tro·ver·sial·ist** \-əst\ *n* — **con·tro·ver·sial·ly** \-ē\ *adv*
con·tro·ver·sy \ˈkän-trə-ˌvər-sē\ *n, pl* **-sies** **1** : a discussion marked esp. by expression of opposing views : DISPUTE **2** : QUARREL, STRIFE
con·tro·vert \ˈkän-trə-ˌvərt, ˌkän-trə-ˈ\ *vt* : to oppose by argument : DENY, CONTRADICT — **con·tro·vert·er** *n* — **con·tro·vert·i·ble** \-ə-bəl\ *adj*
con·tu·ma·cious \ˌkän-t(y)ə-ˈmā-shəs, ˌkän-chə-\ *adj* : stubbornly disobedient — **con·tu·ma·cious·ly** *adv*
con·tu·ma·cy \kən-ˈt(y)ü-mə-sē; ˈkän-t(y)ə-, ˈkän-chə-\ *n, pl* **-cies** : stubborn opposition to authority : DEFIANCE
con·tu·me·li·ous \ˌkän-t(y)ə-ˈmē-lē-əs, ˌkän-chə-\ *adj* : insolently abusive and humiliating — **con·tu·me·li·ous·ly** *adv*
con·tu·me·ly \kən-ˈt(y)ü-mə-lē; ˈkän-t(y)ə-ˌmē-lē, ˈkän-chə-\ *n, pl* **-lies** : rude language or treatment arising from haughtiness and contempt
con·tuse \kən-ˈt(y)üz\ *vt* : to injure (tissue) usu. without breaking the skin — **con·tu·sion** \-ˈt(y)ü-zhən\ *n*
co·nun·drum \kə-ˈnən-drəm\ *n* **1** : a riddle whose answer is or involves a pun **2** : an intricate problem
con·va·lesce \ˌkän-və-ˈles\ *vi* : to recover health and strength gradually after illness or weakness
con·va·les·cence \-ˈles-ᵊn(t)s\ *n* : the process or period of convalescing — **con·va·les·cent** \-ᵊnt\ *adj or n*
con·vec·tion \kən-ˈvek-shən\ *n* : the circulatory motion that occurs in a gas or liquid owing to the warmer portions rising and the colder denser portions sinking; *also* : the transfer of heat by this circulation — **con·vec·tion·al** \-shnəl, -shən-ᵊl\ *adj* — **con·vec·tive** \-ˈvek-tiv\ *adj*
con·vene \kən-ˈvēn\ *vb* **1** : to come together in a group or body : MEET **2** : to call together — **con·ven·er** *n*
con·ve·nience \kən-ˈvē-nyən(t)s\ *n* **1** : fitness or suitability for meeting a requirement **2** : personal comfort **3** : a suitable time : OPPORTUNITY **4** : something (as a device or a service) that gives comfort or advantage
con·ve·nient \kən-ˈvē-nyənt\ *adj* **1** : suited to personal comfort or to easy use **2** : near at hand — **con·ve·nient·ly** *adv*
con·vent \ˈkän-vənt, -ˌvent\ *n* : a local community or house of a religious order esp. of nuns — **con·ven·tu·al** \kən-ˈvench-(ə-)wəl, kän-\ *adj*
con·ven·tion \kən-ˈven-chən\ *n* **1** : AGREEMENT, COVENANT **2** : generally accepted custom, practice, or belief **3** : an assembly of persons met for a common purpose
con·ven·tion·al \kən-ˈvench-nəl, -ˈven-chən-ᵊl\ *adj* **1** : settled or prescribed by convention : CUSTOMARY **2** : COMMONPLACE, ORDINARY — **con·ven·tion·al·ly** \-ē\ *adv*
con·ven·tion·al·i·ty \kən-ˌven-chə-ˈnal-ət-ē\ *n, pl* **-ties** **1** : formality in social customs and practices **2** : CONVENTION
con·ven·tion·al·ize \kən-ˈvench-nə-ˌlīz, -ˈven-chən-ᵊl-ˌīz\ *vt* : to make conventional — **con·ven·tion·al·i·za·tion** \-ˌvench-nə-lə-ˈzā-shən, -ˌven-chə-nə-\ *n*
con·verge \kən-ˈvərj\ *vb* : to tend or move toward one point or one another : MEET
con·ver·gence \kən-ˈvər-jən(t)s\ *n* : the act or condition of

converging esp. toward union or uniformity — **con·ver·gent** \-jənt\ *adj*
con·ver·sant \kən-'vərs-ᵊnt\ *adj* : having knowledge or experience : FAMILIAR — **con·ver·sant·ly** *adv*
con·ver·sa·tion \ˌkän-vər-'sā-shən\ *n* : oral exchange of sentiments, observations, opinions, or ideas; *also* : TALK
con·ver·sa·tion·al \ˌkän-vər-'sā-shnəl, -shən-ᵊl\ *adj* : of, relating to, or suitable for informal friendly talk — **con·ver·sa·tion·al·ly** \-ē\ *adv*
¹con·verse \kən-'vərs\ *vi* : to exchange thoughts and opinions in speech : TALK
²con·verse \'kän-ˌvərs\ *n* : CONVERSATION
³con·verse \kən-'vərs, 'kän-ˌ\ *adj* : reversed in order, relation, or action — **con·verse·ly** *adv*
⁴con·verse \'kän-ˌvərs\ *n* : something that is the opposite of something else
con·ver·sion \kən-'vər-zhən\ *n* **1** : the act of converting : the state of being converted **2** : a change in the nature or form of a thing **3** : a spiritual change in a person associated with a decisive adoption of religion **4** : the taking and using of another's property without right as one's own — **con·ver·sion·al** \-'vərzh-nəl, -ən-ᵊl\ *adj*
¹con·vert \kən-'vərt\ *vb* **1 a** : to bring over from one belief, view, or party to another **b** : to bring about a religious conversion in **2 a** : to alter the physical or chemical nature of **b** : to exchange for an equivalent **3** : to appropriate without right — **con·vert·er** *or* **con·ver·tor** \-ər\ *n*
²con·vert \'kän-ˌvərt\ *n* : one that is converted; *esp* : one who has experienced religious conversion
¹con·vert·i·ble \kən-'vərt-ə-bəl\ *adj* **1** : capable of being converted **2** : having a top that may be lowered or removed — **con·vert·i·bil·i·ty** \-ˌvərt-ə-'bil-ət-ē\ *n* — **con·vert·i·bly** \-'vərt-ə-blē\ *adv*
²convertible *n* : a convertible automobile
con·vex \kän-'veks\ *adj* : curved or rounded like the exterior of a sphere or circle — **con·vex·ly** *adv* — **con·vex·ness** *n*
con·vex·i·ty \kən-'vek-sət-ē, kän-\ *n, pl* **-ties** **1** : the quality or state of being convex **2** : a convex surface or part
con·vey \kən-'vā\ *vt* **con·veyed**; **con·vey·ing** **1** : to carry from one place to another : TRANSPORT **2** : to serve as a means of transferring or transmitting **3** : to impart or communicate or serve as a means of imparting or communicating **4** : to transfer real estate or title to real estate by a sealed instrument — **con·vey·er** *or* **con·vey·or** \-'vā-ər\ *n*
con·vey·ance \kən-'vā-ən(t)s\ *n* **1** : the act of conveying **2 a** : an instrument by which title to property is conveyed **b** : VEHICLE
¹con·vict \kən-'vikt\ *vt* : to find or prove to be guilty
²con·vict \'kän-ˌvikt\ *n* **1** : a person convicted of a crime **2** : a person serving a prison sentence usu. for a long term
con·vic·tion \kən-'vik-shən\ *n* **1** : the act of convicting : the state of being convicted **2** : the state of mind of a person who is convinced that what he believes or says is true **3** : a strong belief or opinion
con·vince \kən-'vin(t)s\ *vt* : to bring by argument or evidence to assent or belief
con·vinc·ing \-'vin(t)-siŋ\ *adj* : strongly persuasive — **con·vinc·ing·ly** *adv* — **con·vinc·ing·ness** *n*
con·viv·i·al \kən-'viv-ē-əl, -'viv-yəl\ *adj* : relating to, occupied with, or fond of feasting, drinking, and good company — **con·viv·i·al·ly** \-ē\ *adv*
con·viv·i·al·i·ty \-ˌviv-ē-'al-ət-ē\ *n, pl* **-ties** : convivial spirit : FESTIVITY
con·vo·ca·tion \ˌkän-və-'kā-shən\ *n* **1** : the act of convoking **2** : ASSEMBLY, MEETING
con·voke \kən-'vōk\ *vt* : to call together to a meeting
con·vo·lut·ed \'kän-və-ˌlüt-əd\ *adj* **1** : folded in curved or tortuous windings **2** : INVOLVED, INTRICATE
con·vo·lu·tion \ˌkän-və-'lü-shən\ *n* **1** : one of the irregular ridges on the surface of the brain **2** : a convoluted form or structure — **con·vo·lu·tion·al** \-shnəl, -shən-ᵊl\ *adj*
¹con·voy \'kän-ˌvȯi, kən-'\ *vt* : to accompany for protection either by land or by sea : ESCORT
²con·voy \'kän-ˌvȯi\ *n* **1** : one that convoys; *esp* : a protective escort for ships, persons, or goods **2** : a group convoyed or organized for convenience or protection in moving
con·vulse \kən-'vəls\ *vt* : to shake or agitate violently
con·vul·sion \-'vəl-shən\ *n* **1** : an abnormal violent and involuntary contraction or series of contractions of the muscles **2** : a violent disturbance
con·vul·sive \-'vəl-siv\ *adj* : constituting or producing a convulsion — **con·vul·sive·ly** *adv*
coo \'kü\ *vi* **1** : to make the low soft cry of a dove or pigeon **2** : to talk fondly or amorously — **coo** *n*
¹cook \'ku̇k\ *n* : one who prepares food for eating
²cook *vb* **1** : to prepare food for eating by a heating process **2 a** : OCCUR, HAPPEN **b** : CONCOCT, IMPROVISE **3** : to subject to heat or fire — **cook·er** *n* — **cook one's goose** : to ruin (one) irretrievably
cook·book \-ˌbu̇k\ *n* : a book of cooking directions and recipes
cook·ery \'ku̇k-(ə-)rē\ *n* : the art or practice of cooking
cook·ie *or* **cooky** \'ku̇k-ē\ *n, pl* **cook·ies** : any of various small sweet flat or slightly raised cakes
cook·out \'ku̇k-ˌau̇t\ *n* : an outing at which a meal is cooked and served in the open; *also* : the meal cooked
¹cool \'kül\ *adj* **1** : moderately cold **2 a** : marked by steady calmness and self-control **b** : lacking ardor, excitement, or friendliness **3** : WHOLE, FULL — **cool·ish** \'kü-lish\ *adj* — **cool·ly** \'kül-(l)ē\ *adv* — **cool·ness** \'kül-nəs\ *n*
²cool *vb* : to make or become cool
³cool *n* : a cool time or place
cool·ant \'kü-lənt\ *n* : a usu. fluid cooling agent
cool·er \'kü-lər\ *n* **1** : one that cools: as **a** : a container for cooling liquids **b** : REFRIGERATOR **2** : LOCKUP, JAIL
coo·lie \'kü-lē\ *n* : an unskilled laborer or porter usu. in or from the Far East
coon \'kün\ *n* : RACCOON
coon·skin \-ˌskin\ *n* : the fur or pelt of the raccoon
¹coop \'küp, 'ku̇p\ *n* **1** : a small enclosure or building usu. for housing poultry **2** : a confined place
²coop *vt* : to place or keep in a coop : PEN
co–op \'kō-ˌäp\ *n* : COOPERATIVE
¹coo·per \'kü-pər, 'ku̇p-ər\ *n* : one that makes or repairs wooden casks or tubs
²cooper *vb* : to work or work on as a cooper
coo·per·age \'kü-p(ə-)rij, 'ku̇p-(ə-)rij\ *n* **1** : a cooper's place of business **2** : a cooper's work or products
co·op·er·ate \kō-'äp-(ə-)ˌrāt\ *vi* : to act, work, or associate with others esp. for mutual benefit
co·op·er·a·tion \kō-ˌäp-ə-'rā-shən\ *n* **1** : the act or process of cooperating **2** : association of individuals or groups for the purpose of mutual benefit
¹co·op·er·a·tive \kō-'äp-(ə-)rət-iv, -'äp-ə-ˌrāt-\ *adj* **1** : marked by cooperation or a willingness to cooperate **2** : of, relating to, or organized as a cooperative — **co·op·er·a·tive·ly** *adv* — **co·op·er·a·tive·ness** *n*
²cooperative *n* : an association formed to enable its members to buy or sell to better advantage
co–opt \kō-'äpt\ *vt* : to choose or elect as a fellow member or colleague — **co–op·tion** \-'äp-shən\ *n*
¹co·or·di·nate \kō-'ȯrd-nət, -ᵊn-ət\ *adj* **1** : equal in rank or order **2 a** : being of equal rank in a compound sentence **b** : joining words or word groups of the same grammatical rank — **co·or·di·nate·ly** *adv*
²coordinate *n* **1** : one who is of equal rank, authority, or importance **2** : any of a set of numbers used in specifying the

location of a point on a surface or in space

3**co·or·di·nate** \kō-'ȯrd-ᵊn-ˌāt\ *vb* **1** : to make or become coordinate **2** : to bring into a common action, movement, or condition — **co·or·di·na·tor** \-ˌāt-ər\ *n*

co·or·di·nat·ing \-ˌāt-iŋ\ *adj* : 1COORDINATE 2b

co·or·di·na·tion \kō-ˌȯrd-ᵊn-'ā-shən\ *n* **1** : the act of coordinating **2** : the state of being coordinate

coot \'küt\ *n* **1** : any of various sluggish slow-flying slaty-black birds of the rail family **2** : a harmless simple person

coo·tie \'küt-ē\ *n* : a body louse

cop \'käp\ *n* : POLICEMAN

co·part·ner \(')kō-'pärt-nər\ *n* : PARTNER — **co·part·ner·ship** \-ˌship\ *n*

1**cope** \'kōp\ *n* : a long enveloping ecclesiastical vestment

2**cope** *vi* : to struggle or contend esp. with some success

cop·i·er \'käp-ē-ər\ *n* : one that copies

co·pi·lot \'kō-ˌpī-lət\ *n* : an assistant airplane pilot

cop·ing \'kō-piŋ\ *n* : the top layer of a wall

co·pi·ous \'kō-pē-əs\ *adj* : very plentiful : LAVISH, ABUNDANT — **co·pi·ous·ly** *adv* — **co·pi·ous·ness** *n*

cop·per \'käp-ər\ *n* **1** : a reddish metallic element that is ductile and malleable and one of the best conductors of heat and electricity **2** : a copper or bronze coin — **cop·pery** \'käp-(ə-)rē\ *adj*

cop·per·as \'käp-(ə-)rəs\ *n* : a green sulfate of iron used in making inks and in dyeing

cop·per·head \'käp-ər-ˌhed\ *n* : a common largely coppery brown pit viper of upland eastern U.S.

cop·pice \'käp-əs\ *n* : a thicket, grove, or growth of small trees

co·pra \'kō-prə\ *n* : dried coconut meat yielding coconut oil

copse \'käps\ *n* : COPPICE

cop·u·la \'käp-yə-lə\ *n* : a word or expression (as a form of the verb *to be*) that links a subject with its predicate

cop·u·late \'käp-yə-ˌlāt\ *vi* : to engage in sexual intercourse — **cop·u·la·tion** \ˌkäp-yə-'lā-shən\ *n* — **cop·u·la·to·ry** \'käp-yə-lə-ˌtōr-ē\ *adj*

cop·u·la·tive \'käp-yə-ˌlāt-iv\ *adj* : being a copula — **cop·u·la·tive·ly** *adv*

1**copy** \'käp-ē\ *n, pl* **cop·ies** **1** : an imitation or reproduction of an original work **2** : one of the printed reproductions of an original text, engraving, or photograph **3** : matter to be set up for printing or photoengraving

2**copy** *vb* **cop·ied**; **cop·y·ing** **1** : to make a copy : DUPLICATE **2** : to model oneself on : IMITATE

copy·book \-ˌbu̇k\ *n* : a book containing copies esp. of penmanship for learners to imitate

copy·boy \-ˌbȯi\ *n* : one that carries copy and runs errands (as in a newspaper office)

copy·cat \-ˌkat\ *n* : a sedulous imitator

copy·desk \-ˌdesk\ *n* : the desk at which newspaper copy is edited

copy·ist \'käp-ē-əst\ *n* **1** : one who makes copies **2** : IMITATOR

copy·read·er \'käp-ē-ˌrēd-ər\ *n* : one who edits and writes headlines for newspaper copy; *also* : one who reads and corrects manuscript copy in a publishing house

1**copy·right** \-ˌrīt\ *n* : the sole right to reproduce, publish, and sell a literary or artistic work — **copyright** *adj*

2**copyright** *vt* : to secure a copyright on

co·quet *or* **co·quette** \kō-'ket\ *vi* **co·quet·ted**; **co·quet·ting** : FLIRT

co·que·try \'kō-kə-trē, kō-'ke-trē\ *n, pl* **-tries** : the conduct or art of a coquette : FLIRTATION

co·quette \kō-'ket\ *n* : FLIRT — **co·quett·ish** \-'ket-ish\ *adj* — **co·quett·ish·ly** *adv* — **co·quett·ish·ness** *n*

cor·a·cle \'kȯr-ə-kəl\ *n* : a boat made of hoops covered with horsehide or tarpaulin

cor·al \'kȯr-əl\ *n* **1 a** : the stony or horny skeletal deposit produced by various polyps; *esp* : a richly red material used in jewelry **b** : a polyp or polyp colony together with its membranes and skeleton **2** : a variable color averaging a deep pink — **coral** *adj*

1**cor·bel** \'kȯr-bəl\ *n* : a bracket-shaped architectural member that projects from a wall and supports a weight

2**corbel** *vt* **-beled** *or* **-belled**; **-bel·ing** *or* **-bel·ling** : to furnish with or make into a corbel

1**cord** \'kȯrd\ *n* **1** : a string or small rope consisting of several strands woven or twisted together **2** : a moral, spiritual, or emotional bond **3** : an anatomical structure (as a tendon or nerve) resembling a cord **4** : a unit of wood cut for fuel equal to a stack 4x4x8 feet **5** : a rib like a cord on a textile

2**cord** *vt* **1** : to furnish, bind, or connect with a cord **2** : to pile up (wood) in cords — **cord·er** *n*

cord·age \'kȯrd-ij\ *n* : ropes or cords; *esp* : the ropes in the rigging of a ship

1**cor·dial** \'kȯr-jəl\ *adj* : HEARTFELT, HEARTY — **cor·di·al·i·ty** \ˌkȯr-jē-'al-ət-ē\ *n* — **cor·dial·ly** \'kȯrj-(ə-)lē\ *adv* — **cor·dial·ness** \'kȯr-jəl-nəs\ *n*

2**cordial** *n* **1** : a stimulating medicine or drink **2** : LIQUEUR

cor·dil·le·ra \ˌkȯrd-ᵊl-'(y)er-ə, kȯr-'dil-ə-rə\ *n* : a group of mountain ranges — **cor·dil·le·ran** \-'(y)er-ən, -ə-rən\ *adj*

cor·don \'kȯrd-ᵊn, 'kȯr-ˌdän\ *n* **1** : an ornamental cord **2** : a line of persons or things around a person or place

cor·do·van \'kȯrd-ə-vən\ *n* : a soft fine-grained colored leather — **cordovan** *adj*

cor·du·roy \'kȯrd-ə-ˌrȯi\ *n* **1 a** : a durable ribbed usu. cotton fabric **b** *pl* : trousers of corduroy **2** : a road built of logs laid side by side transversely — **corduroy** *adj*

cord·wain·er \'kȯrd-ˌwā-nər\ *n* : SHOEMAKER

cord·wood \-ˌwu̇d\ *n* : wood cut for fuel and sold by the cord

1**core** \'kō(ə)r\ *n* **1** : a central or inmost part **2** : the usu. inedible central part of some fruits (as a pineapple or apple) **3** : a basic, essential, or enduring part

2**core** *vt* : to remove the core from — **cor·er** *n*

1**cork** \'kȯrk\ *n* **1 a** : the elastic tough outer tissue of a European oak used esp. for stoppers and insulation **b** : the tissue of a woody plant making up most of the bark **2** : a usu. cork stopper for a bottle or jug

2**cork** *vt* : to furnish, fit, or seal with a cork

cork·er \'kȯr-kər\ *n* : one that corks containers

1**cork·screw** \'kȯrk-ˌskrü\ *n* : a pointed spiral piece of metal with a handle used to draw corks from bottles

2**corkscrew** *adj* : resembling a corkscrew : SPIRAL

corky \'kȯr-kē\ *adj* : resembling cork esp. in dry porous quality

cor·mo·rant \'kȯrm-(ə-)rənt\ *n* : any of various dark-colored web-footed seabirds with a long neck, a wedge-shaped tail, a hooked bill, and a patch of bare often brightly colored skin under the mouth

1**corn** \'kȯrn\ *n* **1 a** : the seeds of a cereal grass and esp. of the important cereal crop of a region **b** : sweet corn served as a vegetable **2** : a plant that produces corn

2**corn** *vb* : to preserve by packing with salt or by soaking in brine

3**corn** *n* : a local hardening and thickening of skin (as on a toe)

corn bread *n* : bread made with cornmeal

corn·cob \'kȯrn-ˌkäb\ *n* : the woody axis on which the kernels of Indian corn are arranged

corn·crib \-ˌkrib\ *n* : a crib for storing ears of Indian corn

cor·nea \'kȯr-nē-ə\ *n* : the transparent part of the coat of the eyeball that covers the iris and pupil and admits light to the interior — **cor·ne·al** \-nē-əl\ *adj*

1**cor·ner** \'kȯr-nər\ *n* **1 a** : the point or place where converging lines, edges, or sides meet : ANGLE **b** : the place of intersection of two streets or roads **c** : a piece designed to form, mark, or protect a corner **2** : a position from which escape or retreat is difficult or impossible **3** : control or ownership of enough of the available supply of a commodity or security to permit manipulation of the price — **cor·nered** \-nərd\ *adj*

[2]**corner** *vb* **1** : to drive into a corner **2** : to get a corner on

cor·ner·stone \-ˌstōn\ *n* **1** : a stone forming part of a corner in a wall; *esp* : such a stone laid at the formal beginning of the erection of a building **2** : something of basic importance

cor·net \kȯr-ˈnet\ *n* : a brass instrument resembling the trumpet but having greater agility and a less brilliant tone

cor·nice \ˈkȯr-nəs\ *n* : the ornamental projecting piece that forms the top edge of the front of a building or of a pillar

corn·meal \ˈkȯrn-ˈmēl\ *n* : meal ground from corn

corn·stalk \ˈkȯrn-ˌstȯk\ *n* : a stalk of Indian corn

corn·starch \-ˌstärch\ *n* : a starch made from corn and used in cooking as a thickening agent

corn syrup *n* : a syrup obtained by partial hydrolysis of cornstarch and used in baked goods and candy

cor·nu·co·pia \ˌkȯr-n(y)ə-ˈkō-pē-ə\ *n* : a horn-shaped container overflowing with fruits and flowers used as a symbol of abundance

corny \ˈkȯr-nē\ *adj* : mawkishly old-fashioned or countrified : tiresomely simple or sentimental : OUTWORN

co·rol·la \kə-ˈräl-ə\ *n* : the petals of a flower

cor·ol·lary \ˈkȯr-ə-ˌler-ē\ *n, pl* **-lar·ies** **1** : an immediate inference from a proved proposition **2** : something that naturally follows : RESULT — **corollary** *adj*

co·ro·na \kə-ˈrō-nə\ *n* **1** : a usu. colored circle often seen around and close to a luminous body (as the sun or moon) **2** : the outermost part of the atmosphere of the sun appearing as a gray halo around the moon's black disk during a total eclipse of the sun

cor·o·nal \ˈkȯr-ən-ᵊl\ *n* : a circlet for the head

[1]**cor·o·nary** \ˈkȯr-ə-ˌner-ē\ *adj* : of or relating to the heart or its blood vessels

[2]**coronary** *n, pl* **-nar·ies** : coronary disease

cor·o·na·tion \ˌkȯr-ə-ˈnā-shən\ *n* : the ceremony of investing a sovereign or his consort with the royal crown

cor·o·ner \ˈkȯr-ə-nər\ *n* : a public officer whose chief duty is to discover the causes of any death possibly not due to natural causes

cor·o·net \ˌkȯr-ə-ˈnet\ *n* **1** : a small crown worn by a person of noble but not of royal rank **2** : an ornamental wreath or band worn around the head

[1]**cor·po·ral** \ˈkȯr-p(ə-)rəl\ *adj* : of or relating to the body

[2]**corporal** *n* : an enlisted man (as in the army) of the lowest noncommissioned rank

cor·po·rate \ˈkȯr-p(ə-)rət\ *adj* **1** : formed into an association and endowed by law with the rights and liabilities of an individual : INCORPORATED **2** : of or relating to a whole composed of individuals

cor·po·ra·tion \ˌkȯr-pə-ˈrā-shən\ *n* **1** : the municipal authorities of a town or city **2** : a body authorized by law to carry on an activity (as a business enterprise) with the rights and duties of a single person

cor·po·re·al \kȯr-ˈpōr-ē-əl\ *adj* **1** : PHYSICAL, MATERIAL **2** : BODILY

corps \ˈkō(ə)r\ *n, pl* **corps** \ˈkōrz\ **1** : an organized branch of a military establishment **2** : a group of persons associated together or acting under common direction

corpse \ˈkȯrps\ *n* : a dead body

cor·pu·lent \ˈkȯr-pyə-lənt\ *adj* : having a large bulky body : OBESE — **cor·pu·lence** \-lən(t)s\ *or* **cor·pu·len·cy** \-lən-sē\ *n* — **cor·pu·lent·ly** *adv*

cor·pus \ˈkȯr-pəs\ *n, pl* **cor·po·ra** \-p(ə-)rə\ **1** : the main or central part of a bodily structure **2** : the main body or principal substance (as of a field of study)

cor·pus·cle \ˈkȯr-(ˌ)pəs-əl\ *n* **1** : a minute particle **2** : a living cell; *esp* : one (as a blood or cartilage cell) not aggregated into continuous tissues — **cor·pus·cu·lar** \kȯr-ˈpəs-kyə-lər\ *adj*

cor·pus de·lic·ti \ˌkȯr-pəs-di-ˈlik-ˌtī, -(ˌ)tē\ *n, pl* **cor·po·ra delicti** \ˌkȯr-p(ə-)rə-\ **1** : the substantial fact necessary to prove the commission of a crime **2** : the body of a murder victim

[1]**cor·ral** \kə-ˈral\ *n* **1** : an enclosure for confining or capturing livestock **2** : an enclosure made with wagons for defense of an encampment

[2]**corral** *vt* **cor·ralled**; **cor·ral·ling** **1** : to confine in or as if in a corral **2** : SURROUND, CAPTURE

[1]**cor·rect** \kə-ˈrekt\ *vt* **1** : to make or set right : AMEND **2** : REBUKE, PUNISH — **cor·rect·a·ble** *adj* — **cor·rec·tor** \-ˈrek-tər\ *n*

[2]**correct** *adj* **1** : conforming to an approved or conventional standard **2** : agreeing with fact, logic, or known truth : ACCURATE — **cor·rect·ly** *adv* — **cor·rect·ness** *n*

cor·rec·tion \kə-ˈrek-shən\ *n* **1** : the action or an instance of correcting **2** : something substituted in place of what is wrong **3** : punishment intended to correct faults of character or behavior — **cor·rec·tion·al** \-shnəl, -shən-ᵊl\ *adj*

cor·rec·tive \kə-ˈrek-tiv\ *adj* : having the power of making right, normal, or regular — **corrective** *n*

cor·re·late \ˈkȯr-ə-ˌlāt\ *vb* **1** : to have reciprocal or mutual relations **2** : to establish a mutual or reciprocal relation of

cor·re·la·tion \ˌkȯr-ə-ˈlā-shən\ *n* **1** : the act or process of correlating **2** : the state of being correlated; *esp* : a mutual relation discovered to exist between things

[1]**cor·rel·a·tive** \kə-ˈrel-ət-iv\ *adj* **1** : mutually related **2** : regularly used together — **cor·rel·a·tive·ly** *adv*

[2]**correlative** *n* : either of two correlative things

cor·re·spond \ˌkȯr-ə-ˈspänd\ *vi* **1 a** : to be in agreement : SUIT **b** : MATCH **2** : to communicate by letter

cor·re·spond·ence \-ˈspän-dən(t)s\ *n* **1** : the agreement of things with one another **2** : communication by letters; *also* : the letters exchanged

[1]**cor·re·spond·ent** \ˌkȯr-ə-ˈspän-dənt\ *adj* **1** : SIMILAR **2** : CONFORMING, FITTING

[2]**correspondent** *n* **1** : something that corresponds to something else **2 a** : one who communicates with another by letter **b** : one who contributes news or comment to a newspaper often from a distant place

cor·re·spond·ing·ly \-ˈspän-diŋ-lē\ *adv* : in a corresponding manner : in such a way as to correspond

cor·ri·dor \ˈkȯr-əd-ər\ *n* **1** : a passageway into which compartments or rooms open (as in a hotel or school) **2** : a narrow strip of land esp. through foreign-held territory

cor·ri·gen·dum \ˌkȯr-ə-ˈjen-dəm\ *n, pl* **-da** \-də\ : an error in a printed work discovered after printing and shown with its correction on a separate sheet

cor·rob·o·rate \kə-ˈräb-ə-ˌrāt\ *vt* : to support with evidence or authority — **cor·rob·o·ra·tor** \-ˌrāt-ər\ *n*

cor·rob·o·ra·tion \kə-ˌräb-ə-ˈrā-shən\ *n* **1** : the act of corroborating **2** : something that corroborates

cor·rob·o·ra·tive \kə-ˈräb-ə-ˌrāt-iv, -ˈräb-(ə-)rət-\ *adj* : serving to corroborate — **cor·rob·o·ra·tive·ly** *adv*

cor·rob·o·ra·to·ry \kə-ˈräb-(ə-)rə-ˌtōr-ē\ *adj* : CORROBORATIVE

cor·rode \kə-ˈrōd\ *vb* : to eat or be eaten away by degrees as if by gnawing; *esp* : to wear away gradually usu. by chemical action — **cor·rod·i·ble** \-ˈrōd-ə-bəl\ *adj*

cor·ro·sion \kə-ˈrō-zhən\ *n* : the action, process, or effect of corroding

[1]**cor·ro·sive** \-ˈrō-siv\ *adj* : tending or having the power to corrode — **cor·ro·sive·ly** *adv* — **cor·ro·sive·ness** *n*

[2]**corrosive** *n* : something corrosive

cor·ru·gate \ˈkȯr-ə-ˌgāt\ *vb* : to form or shape into wrinkles or folds or ridges and grooves

cor·ru·ga·tion \ˌkȯr-ə-ˈgā-shən\ *n* **1** : the act of corrugating : the state of being corrugated **2** : a ridge or groove of a corrugated surface

[1]**cor·rupt** \kə-ˈrəpt\ *vb* **1** : to change from good to bad in

morals, manners, or actions; *esp* : to influence a public official improperly 2 : TAINT, ROT — **cor·rupt·er** *or* **cor·rup·tor** \-'rəp-tər\ *n*

[2]**corrupt** *adj* : morally perverted : DEPRAVED — **cor·rupt·ly** *adv* — **cor·rupt·ness** *n*

cor·rupt·i·ble \kə-'rəp-tə-bəl\ *adj* : capable of being corrupted — **cor·rupt·i·bil·i·ty** \-ˌrəp-tə-'bil-ət-ē\ *n*

cor·rup·tion \kə-'rəp-shən\ *n* 1 : physical decay or rotting 2 : impairment of integrity, virtue, or moral principle : DEPRAVITY 3 : inducement to do wrong by unlawful or improper means (as bribery)

cor·sage \kȯr-'säzh, -'säj\ *n* 1 : the waist of a woman's dress 2 : an arrangement of flowers to be worn by a woman

cor·sair \'kȯr-ˌsa(ə)r\ *n* : PIRATE; *esp* : a privateer of the Barbary coast

corse·let *or* **cors·let** \'kȯr-slət\ *n* : the body armor worn by a knight esp. on the upper part of the body

[1]**cor·set** \'kȯr-sət\ *n* : a tight-fitting stiffened undergarment worn by women to give shape to waist and hips

[2]**corset** *vt* : to dress in or fit with a corset

cor·tege \'kȯr-ˌtezh, kȯr-'\ *n* : PROCESSION; *esp* : a funeral procession

cor·tex \'kȯr-ˌteks\ *n, pl* **cor·ti·ces** \'kȯrt-ə-ˌsēz\ *or* **cor·tex·es** : an outer or covering layer of an organism or one of its parts; *esp* : the outer layer of gray matter of the brain — **cor·ti·cal** \'kȯrt-i-kəl\ *adj* — **cor·ti·cal·ly** \-i-k(ə-)lē\ *adv*

cor·ti·sone \'kȯrt-ə-ˌsōn, -ˌzōn\ *n* : a hormone of the adrenal cortex used esp. in treating arthritis

co·run·dum \kə-'rən-dəm\ *n* : a very hard aluminum-containing mineral used as an abrasive or in some crystalline forms as a gem

cor·us·cate \'kȯr-ə-ˌskāt\ *vi* : FLASH, SPARKLE — **cor·us·ca·tion** \ˌkȯr-ə-'skā-shən\ *n*

cor·vette \kȯr-'vet\ *n* : a highly maneuverable armed escort ship smaller than a destroyer

co·ry·za \kə-'rī-zə\ *n* : an acute inflammatory contagious disease involving the upper respiratory tract : the common cold — **co·ry·zal** \-zəl\ *adj*

co·sig·na·to·ry \(')kō-'sig-nə-ˌtōr-ē\ *n, pl* **-ries** : a joint signer

[1]**cos·met·ic** \käz-'met-ik\ *n* : a cosmetic preparation for external use

[2]**cosmetic** *adj* : relating to or making for beauty esp. of the complexion : BEAUTIFYING

cos·me·tol·o·gist \ˌkäz-mə-'täl-ə-jəst\ *n* : one who gives beauty treatments (as to skin) — **cos·me·tol·o·gy** \-jē\ *n*

cos·mic \'käz-mik\ *adj* 1 : of or relating to the cosmos 2 : extremely vast : GRAND — **cos·mi·cal·ly** \-mi-k(ə-)lē\ *adv*

cosmic ray *n* : a stream of atomic nuclei of extremely penetrating character that enter the earth's atmosphere from outer space at speeds approaching that of light

cos·mog·o·ny \käz-'mäg-ə-nē\ *n, pl* **-nies** : the creation or origination of the world or universe — **cos·mog·o·nist** \-nəst\ *n*

cos·mol·o·gy \käz-'mäl-ə-jē\ *n, pl* **-gies** : a study that deals with the origin and structure of the universe — **cos·mo·log·i·cal** \ˌkäz-mə-'läj-i-kəl\ *adj* — **cos·mol·o·gist** \käz-'mäl-ə-jəst\ *n*

cos·mo·naut \'käz-mə-ˌnȯt\ *n* : a traveler beyond the earth's atmosphere : ASTRONAUT

cos·mo·pol·i·tan \ˌkäz-mə-'päl-ət-ᵊn\ *adj* 1 : having worldwide scope or bearing 2 : having a broadly sophisticated and international outlook 3 : composed of persons, constituents, or elements from many parts of the world — **cosmopolitan** *n* — **cos·mo·pol·i·tan·ism** \-ᵊn-ˌiz-əm\ *n*

cos·mop·o·lite \käz-'mäp-ə-ˌlīt\ *n* : a cosmopolitan person or organism

cos·mos \'käz-məs\ *n* 1 : the orderly systematic universe 2 : a tall garden plant related to the daisies

cos·sack \'käs-ˌak, -ək\ *n* : a member of a group of frontiersmen of southern Russia organized as cavalry in the czarist army

[1]**cost** \'kȯst\ *n* 1 a : the amount paid or charged for something : PRICE b : the outlay or expenditure made to achieve an object 2 : loss or penalty incurred in gaining something

[2]**cost** *vb* **cost**; **cost·ing** 1 : to have a price of 2 : to cause one to pay, spend, or lose

cost·ly \'kȯst-lē\ *adj* 1 : of great cost or value 2 : made at heavy expense or sacrifice — **cost·li·ness** *n*

[1]**cos·tume** \'käs-ˌt(y)üm\ *n* 1 : a suit or dress characteristic of a period, country, class, or occupation esp. as worn on the stage or at a masquerade party 2 : a person's ensemble of outer garments; *esp* : a woman's ensemble of dress with coat or jacket — **costume** *adj*

[2]**costume** *vt* : to provide with a costume

cos·tum·er \'käs-ˌt(y)ü-mər\ *n* : one that makes, sells, or rents costumes

[1]**cot** \'kät\ *n* : a small house : COTTAGE

[2]**cot** *n* : a small often collapsible bed usu. of fabric stretched on a frame

cote \'kōt, 'kät\ *n* : a shed or coop (as for sheep or pigeons)

co·te·rie \'kōt-ə-(ˌ)rē\ *n* : an intimate often exclusive group of persons with a common interest or purpose

co·ter·mi·nal \(')kō-'tər-mən-ᵊl\ *adj* : having the same or coincident boundaries

co·ter·mi·nous \(')kō-'tər-mə-nəs\ *adj* : coextensive in scope or duration — **co·ter·mi·nous·ly** *adv*

co·til·lion \kō-'til-yən\ *n* 1 : an elaborate dance with frequent changing of partners executed under the leadership of one couple at formal balls 2 : a formal ball

cot·tage \'kät-ij\ *n* 1 : a small usu. frame one-family house 2 : a small house for vacation use

cottage cheese *n* : a soft uncured cheese made from soured milk

cot·tag·er \'kät-ij-ər\ *n* : one who lives in a cottage

cot·ter *or* **cot·tar** \'kät-ər\ *n* : a rural laborer occupying a small holding usu. in return for services

cotter pin *n* : a half-round metal strip bent into a pin whose ends can be flared after insertion through a slot or hole

[1]**cot·ton** \'kät-ᵊn\ *n* 1 a : a soft usu. white fibrous substance composed of the hairs surrounding the seeds of various erect freely branching tropical plants of the mallow family b : a crop of cotton 2 a : fabric made of cotton b : yarn spun from cotton — **cotton** *adj*

[2]**cotton** *vi* **cot·toned**; **cot·ton·ing** \'kät-niŋ, -ᵊn-iŋ\ : to take a liking

cot·ton·seed \-ˌsēd\ *n* : the seed of the cotton plant yielding a protein-rich meal and a fixed oil used esp. in cooking

cot·ton·tail \-ˌtāl\ *n* : any of several small brownish gray rabbits with white-tufted tail

cot·ton·wood \-ˌwu̇d\ *n* : a poplar with a tuft of cottony hairs on the seed

cot·tony \'kät-nē, -ᵊn-ē\ *adj* : resembling cotton in appearance or character

cot·y·le·don \ˌkät-ᵊl-'ēd-ᵊn\ *n* : the first leaf or one of the first pair or whorl of leaves developed by the embryo of a seed plant

[1]**couch** \'kau̇ch\ *vb* 1 : to recline for rest or sleep 2 : to phrase in a specified manner

[2]**couch** *n* : an article of furniture for sitting or reclining

couch·ant \'kau̇-chənt\ *adj* : lying down esp. with the head up

cou·gar \'kü-gər, -ˌgär\ *n* : a large powerful tawny brown cat formerly widespread in the Americas

[1]**cough** \'kȯf\ *vb* 1 : to force air from the lungs with sharp short noises 2 : to get rid of by coughing

[2]**cough** *n* 1 : a condition marked by repeated or frequent coughing 2 : an act or sound of coughing

could \kəd, (')ku̇d\ *past of* CAN — used as an auxiliary verb in

the past and as a polite or less forceful alternative to *can* in the present
coun·cil \'kau̇n(t)-səl\ *n* **1** : a meeting for consultation, advice, or discussion **2** : an elected or appointed advisory or legislative body
coun·cil·lor *or* **coun·cil·or** \'kau̇n(t)-s(ə-)lər\ *n* : a member of a council — **coun·cil·lor·ship** \-ˌship\ *n*
coun·cil·man \'kau̇n(t)-səl-mən\ *n* : a member of a council esp. in a city government
[1]**coun·sel** \'kau̇n(t)-səl\ *n* **1** : advice given esp. as a result of consultation **2** : DELIBERATION, CONSULTATION **3** *pl* **counsel** : LAWYER
[2]**counsel** *vb* **-seled** *or* **-selled**; **-sel·ing** *or* **-sel·ling** \-s(ə-)liŋ\ **1** : to give counsel : ADVISE **2** : to seek counsel : CONSULT
coun·sel·or *or* **coun·sel·lor** \'kau̇n(t)-s(ə-)lər\ *n* **1** : ADVISER **2** : LAWYER — **coun·sel·or·ship** \-ˌship\ *n*
[1]**count** \'kau̇nt\ *vb* **1 a** : to name by units or groups so as to find the total number **b** : to recite the numbers in order **c** : to include in a tally **2** : CONSIDER **3 a** : RELY, DEPEND **b** : RECKON, PLAN **4** : to have value, significance, or importance — **count·a·ble** *adj*
[2]**count** *n* **1** : the act of counting; *also* : a total obtained by counting **2** : ALLEGATION, CHARGE; *esp* : one stating a separate cause of action in a legal declaration or indictment
[3]**count** *n* : a European nobleman whose rank corresponds to that of a British earl
count·down \'kau̇nt-ˌdau̇n\ *n* : an audible backward counting off (as in seconds) to mark the time remaining before an event (as the launching of a rocket)
[1]**coun·te·nance** \'kau̇nt-ᵊn-ən(t)s, 'kau̇nt-nən(t)s\ *n* **1** : FACE, VISAGE; *esp* : facial indication of mood, emotion, or character **2** : appearance or expression seeming to approve or encourage
[2]**countenance** *vt* : to extend approval or toleration to : SANCTION — **coun·te·nanc·er** *n*
[1]**count·er** \'kau̇nt-ər\ *n* **1** : a piece (as of metal or ivory) used in counting or in games **2** : a level surface (as a table) over which food is served or on which goods are displayed or work is conducted
[2]**coun·ter** \'kau̇nt-ər\ *vb* **coun·tered**; **coun·ter·ing** \'kau̇nt-ə-riŋ, 'kau̇n-triŋ\ **1** : to act in opposition to : OPPOSE **2** : RETALIATE
[3]**coun·ter** *adv* : in a contrary manner or direction
[4]**coun·ter** *adj* **1** : moving in an opposite direction **2** : designed to oppose
coun·ter·act \ˌkau̇nt-ər-'akt\ *vt* : to lessen the force of : OFFSET — **coun·ter·ac·tion** \-'ak-shən\ *n* — **coun·ter·ac·tive** \-'ak-tiv\ *adj*
coun·ter·at·tack \'kau̇nt-ər-ə-ˌtak\ *n* : an attack made to counter an enemy's attack — **counterattack** *vb*
[1]**coun·ter·bal·ance** \'kau̇nt-ər-ˌbal-ən(t)s\ *n* **1** : a weight that balances another **2** : a force or influence that offsets or checks an opposing force
[2]**coun·ter·bal·ance** \ˌkau̇nt-ər-'\ *vt* : to oppose with an equal weight or force
coun·ter·claim \'kau̇nt-ər-ˌklām\ *n* : an opposing claim esp. in law — **counterclaim** *vb* — **coun·ter·claim·ant** \-ˌklā-mənt\ *n*
coun·ter·clock·wise \ˌkau̇nt-ər-'kläk-ˌwīz\ *adv* : in a direction opposite to that in which the hands of a clock rotate — **counterclockwise** *adj*
coun·ter·es·pi·o·nage \ˌkau̇nt-ər-'es-pē-ə-ˌnäzh, -nij\ *n* : the attempt to discover and defeat enemy espionage
[1]**coun·ter·feit** \'kau̇nt-ər-ˌfit\ *vb* **1** : to imitate or copy esp. with intent to deceive **2** : PRETEND, FEIGN — **coun·ter·feit·er** *n*
[2]**counterfeit** *adj* **1** : made in imitation of something else with intent to deceive : FORGED **2** : FEIGNED, SHAM
[3]**counterfeit** *n* : something counterfeit : FORGERY
coun·ter·in·tel·li·gence \ˌkau̇nt-ər-ən-'tel-ə-jən(t)s\ *n* : organized activities of an intelligence service designed to counter the activities of an enemy's intelligence service
coun·ter·mand \'kau̇nt-ər-ˌmand\ *vt* : to revoke (a former command) by a contrary order — **countermand** *n*
coun·ter·of·fen·sive \-ə-ˌfen(t)-siv\ *n* : a large-scale military offensive undertaken by a force previously on the defensive
coun·ter·pane \-ˌpān\ *n* : BEDSPREAD
coun·ter·part \-ˌpärt\ *n* **1** : a part or thing corresponding to another (as in appearance, position, or use) **2** : something that serves to complete something else : COMPLEMENT
[1]**coun·ter·plot** \-ˌplät\ *vb* : INTRIGUE; *also* : to foil with a plot
[2]**counterplot** *n* : a plot opposed to another
coun·ter·point \'kau̇nt-ər-ˌpȯint\ *n* : music in which one melody is accompanied by one or more independent melodies
coun·ter·poise \-ˌpȯiz\ *n* : COUNTERBALANCE
coun·ter·rev·o·lu·tion \ˌkau̇nt-ə(r)-ˌrev-ə-'lü-shən\ *n* : a revolution in opposition to a current or earlier one — **coun·ter·rev·o·lu·tion·ary** \-shə-ˌner-ē\ *adj or n* — **coun·ter·rev·o·lu·tion·ist** \-sh(ə-)nəst\ *n*
[1]**coun·ter·sign** \'kau̇nt-ər-ˌsīn\ *n* **1** : a signature attesting the authenticity of a document already signed by another **2** : a secret signal that must be given by one wishing to pass a guard
[2]**countersign** *vt* : to add one's signature to after another's in order to attest authenticity — **coun·ter·sig·na·ture** \ˌkau̇nt-ər-'sig-nə-ˌchu̇(ə)r, -chər\ *n*
[1]**coun·ter·sink** \'kau̇nt-ər-ˌsiŋk\ *vt* **-sunk** \-ˌsəŋk\; **-sink·ing** **1** : to form a hollowed-out place around the top of (a hole in wood or metal) into which a screw or bolt is to be placed **2** : to sink the head of (as a screw, bolt, or nail) even with or below the surface
[2]**countersink** *n* **1** : a funnel-shaped enlargement at the outer end of a drilled hole **2** : a bit or drill for making a countersink
coun·ter·spy \-ˌspī\ *n* : a spy used against enemy espionage
coun·ter·ten·or \-ˌten-ər\ *n* : a tenor with an unusually high range
coun·ter·weight \-ˌwāt\ *n* : COUNTERBALANCE — **counterweight** *vt*
count·ess \'kau̇nt-əs\ *n* **1** : the wife or widow of a count or an earl **2** : a woman who holds the rank of a count or an earl in her own right
count·ing·house \'kau̇nt-iŋ-ˌhau̇s\ *n* : a building or office used for keeping books and transacting business
count·less \'kau̇nt-ləs\ *adj* : too numerous to be counted
coun·tri·fied *or* **coun·try·fied** \'kən-trē-ˌfīd\ *adj* : looking or acting like a person from the country : RUSTIC
coun·try \'kən-trē\ *n, pl* **countries** **1** : an indefinite usu. extended expanse of land : REGION **2 a** : the land of a person's birth, residence, or citizenship **b** : a political state or nation or its territory **3** : the people of a state or district : POPULACE **4** : rural as distinguished from urban areas
country and western *n* : music derived from or imitating the folk style of the southern U.S. or of the Western cowboy
coun·try–dance \'kən-trē-ˌdan(t)s\ *n* : an English dance in which partners face each other esp. in rows
coun·try·man \'kən-trē-mən, *3 is often* -ˌman\ *n* **1** : an inhabitant or native of a specified country **2** : COMPATRIOT **3** : RUSTIC — **coun·try·wom·an** \-ˌwu̇m-ən\ *n*
coun·try·seat \ˌkən-trē-'sēt\ *n* : a dwelling or estate in the country
coun·try·side \'kən-trē-ˌsīd\ *n* : a rural area or its people
coun·ty \'kau̇nt-ē\ *n, pl* **counties** **1** : the domain of a count **2** : a territorial division of a country or state for purposes of local government
coup \'kü\ *n, pl* **coups** \'küz\ : a brilliant, sudden, and usu. highly successful stroke
coup de grace \ˌküd-ə-'gräs\ *n, pl* **coups de grace** \ˌküd-ə-\ **1** : a death blow **2** : a decisive finishing blow or event
coup d'e·tat \ˌküd-ə-'tä, ˌküd-ā-\ *n, pl* **coups d'e·tat** \ˌküd-ə-

'tä(z), ˌküd-ā-\ : a sudden political move by a small group overthrowing an existing government
cou·pé *or* **coupe** \kü-'pā, *2 is often* 'küp\ *n* **1** : a four-wheeled closed horse-drawn carriage for two persons inside with an outside seat for the driver in front **2** *usu coupe* : a closed 2-door automobile with one seat compartment and a separate luggage compartment
[1]**cou·ple** \'kəp-əl\ *vb* **cou·pled**; **cou·pling** \'kəp-(ə-)liŋ\ : to join together : CONNECT — **cou·pler** \'kəp-(ə-)lər\ *n*
[2]**couple** *n* **1 a** : a man and woman married, engaged, or otherwise paired **b** : any two persons paired together **2** : PAIR, BRACE **3** : an indefinite small number
cou·plet \'kəp-lət\ *n* : two successive rhyming lines of verse
cou·pling \'kəp-liŋ (*usual for 2*), -ə-liŋ\ *n* **1** : the act of bringing or coming together : PAIRING **2** : something that joins or connects two parts or things
cou·pon \'k(y)ü-ˌpän\ *n* **1** : a statement of due interest to be cut from a bond and presented for payment on a stated date **2** : a certificate or similar evidence of a purchase redeemable in premiums
cour·age \'kər-ij\ *n* : mental or moral strength to venture, persevere, and withstand danger, fear, or difficulty
cou·ra·geous \kə-'rā-jəs\ *adj* : having or characterized by courage : BRAVE — **cou·ra·geous·ly** *adv* — **cou·ra·geous·ness** *n*
cou·ri·er \'ku̇r-ē-ər, 'kər-ē-\ *n* : MESSENGER; *esp* : a member of a diplomatic service entrusted with bearing messages
[1]**course** \'kōrs\ *n* **1** : the act or action of moving in a path from point to point **2** : the ground or path over which something moves **3 a** : accustomed procedure or action **b** : a manner of conducting oneself : BEHAVIOR **c** : progression through a series of acts or events or a development or period **4** : an ordered process or succession; *esp* : a series of lectures or discussions dealing with a subject or a series of such courses constituting a curriculum **5** : a part of a meal served at one time — **of course 1** : following the ordinary way or procedure **2** : NATURALLY
[2]**course** *vb* **1** : to hunt (game) with dogs **2** : to run or move rapidly : RACE
cours·er \'kōr-sər\ *n* : a swift or spirited horse
[1]**court** \'kōrt\ *n* **1 a** : the residence of a sovereign or similar dignitary **b** : a sovereign's formal assembly of his councillors and officers **c** : the sovereign and his officials who constitute the governing power **2 a** : an open space surrounded by buildings **b** : a space arranged for playing one of various games with a ball **3 a** : an assembly for the transaction of judicial business **b** : a building or room for the administration of justice **c** : a judge in session **4** : attention designed to win favor or dispel hostility
[2]**court** *vb* **1 a** : to try to gain **b** : to act so as to provoke **2 a** : to seek the affections of **b** : to try to get the support of **3** : to engage in the personal relationship and activities usu. leading to marriage
cour·te·ous \'kərt-ē-əs\ *adj* : marked by respect for and consideration of others — **cour·te·ous·ly** *adv* — **cour·te·ous·ness** *n*
cour·te·san \'kōrt-ə-zən, 'kərt-\ *n* : a prostitute with a courtly, wealthy, or upper-class clientele
cour·te·sy \'kərt-ə-sē\ *n, pl* **-sies 1** : courtly politeness **2** : a favor courteously performed
court·house \'kōrt-ˌhau̇s\ *n* **1** : a building in which courts of law are held **2** : a building in which county offices are housed
court·ier \'kōrt-ē-ər\ *n* : a person in attendance at a royal court
court·ly \'kōrt-lē\ *adj* : of a quality befitting a royal court : ELEGANT — **court·li·ness** *n*
[1]**court–mar·tial** \'kōrt-ˌmär-shəl\ *n, pl* **courts–martial 1** : a military court for the trial of members of the armed forces or others within its jurisdiction **2** : a trial by court-martial
[2]**court–martial** *vt* **-mar·tialed**; **-mar·tial·ing** \-ˌmärsh-(ə-)liŋ\ : to subject to trial by court-martial
court·room \'kōrt-ˌrüm, -ˌru̇m\ *n* : a room in which a court of law is held
court·ship \-ˌship\ *n* : the act or process of courting
court·yard \-ˌyärd\ *n* : a court or enclosure attached to a building (as a palace)
cous·in \'kəz-ᵊn\ *n* **1 a** : a child of one's uncle or aunt **b** : a relative descended from a common ancestor in a different line **2** : a person belonging to an ethnically or culturally related group
cove \'kōv\ *n* **1** : a trough for concealed lighting at the upper part of a wall **2** : a small sheltered inlet or bay
[1]**cov·e·nant** \'kəv-(ə-)nənt\ *n* : a solemn and binding agreement : COMPACT
[2]**cov·e·nant** \'kəv-(ə-)nənt, -ə-ˌnant\ *vb* **1** : PLEDGE **2** : CONTRACT — **cov·e·nant·er** *or* **cov·e·nan·tor** \-ə-ˌnant-ər\ *n*
[1]**cov·er** \'kəv-ər\ *vb* **cov·ered**; **cov·er·ing** \'kəv-(ə-)riŋ\ **1 a** : to guard from attack **b** : to have within gunshot range **c** : to provide protection to or compensation for **2** : to hide from sight or knowledge **3** : to overlay so as to protect or shelter **4** : to spread or lie over or on **5** : to put something protective or concealing over **6** : to sit on and incubate (eggs) **7** : to have width or scope enough to include, take in, or make provisions for **8** : to have as one's territory or field of activity **9** : to pass over or through **10** : to accept an offered bet **11** : to buy securities or commodities for delivery so as to fulfill (an earlier short sale)
[2]**cover** *n* **1** : something that protects, shelters, or conceals **2** : something that is placed over or about another thing: **a** : LID, TOP **b** : a binding or case for a book **c** : an overlay or outer layer esp. for protection **d** : a tablecloth and tableware for one person **e** : a cloth used on a bed **3** : an envelope or wrapper for mail
cov·er·age \'kəv-(ə-)rij\ *n* **1** : the act or fact of covering; *also* : something that covers **2** : the number or amount covered : SCOPE
cov·er·all \'kəv-ər-ˌȯl\ *n* : a one-piece outer garment worn to protect one's clothes — usu. used in pl.
covering *n* : something that covers or conceals
cov·er·let \'kəv-ər-lət\ *n* : BEDSPREAD
[1]**cov·ert** \'kəv-ərt, 'kō-(ˌ)vərt\ *adj* **1** : partly hidden **2** : covered over : SHELTERED — **cov·ert·ly** *adv* — **cov·ert·ness** *n*
[2]**cov·ert** \'kəv-ərt, 'kō-vərt\ *n* **1 a** : SHELTER **b** : a thicket affording cover for game **2** : a feather covering the bases of the quills of the wings and tail of a bird **3** : a firm durable twilled cloth usu. of mixed-color yarns
cov·et \'kəv-ət\ *vb* : to wish for enviously — **cov·et·a·ble** *adj* — **cov·et·er** *n* — **cov·et·ing·ly** *adv*
cov·et·ous \'kəv-ət-əs\ *adj* : marked by a too eager desire for wealth or possessions or for another's possessions — **cov·et·ous·ly** *adv* — **cov·et·ous·ness** *n*
cov·ey \'kəv-ē\ *n, pl* **coveys** : a mature bird or pair of birds with a brood of young; *also* : a small flock
[1]**cow** \'kau̇\ *n* **1** : the mature female of cattle or of an animal (as the moose) the male of which is called *bull* **2** : a domestic bovine animal regardless of sex or age
[2]**cow** *vt* : to subdue the spirits or courage of : make afraid
cow·ard \'kau̇(-ə)rd\ *n* : one who shows ignoble fear or timidity — **coward** *adj*
cow·ard·ice \'kau̇(-ə)rd-əs\ *n* : lack of courage to face danger : shameful fear
cow·ard·ly \'kau̇(-ə)rd-lē\ *adj* **1** : lacking courage : not brave **2** : characteristic of a coward — **cow·ard·li·ness** *n*
cow·boy \'kau̇-ˌbȯi\ *n* : one who tends or drives cattle; *esp* : a usu. mounted cattle ranch hand — **cow·girl** \-ˌgərl\ *n*
cow·er \'kau̇(-ə)r\ *vi* : to crouch down (as from fear or cold)
cow·hide \'kau̇-ˌhīd\ *n* **1** : the hide of a cow or leather made from it **2** : a coarse whip of rawhide or braided leather

cowl \'kau̇l\ *n* **1 :** a hood or long hooded cloak esp. of a monk **2 :** the top portion of the front part of an automobile body forward of the two front doors to which the windshield is attached — **cowled** \'kau̇ld\ *adj*
cow·lick \'kau̇-ˌlik\ *n* **:** a turned-up tuft of hair that cannot be controlled
cowl·ing \'kau̇-liŋ\ *n* **:** a removable metal covering for the engine and sometimes a portion of the fuselage or nacelle of an airplane
cow·man \'kau̇-mən, -ˌman\ *n* **1 :** COWBOY **2 :** a cattle owner or rancher
co–work·er \'kō-ˌwər-kər\ *n* **:** a fellow worker
cow·punch·er \'kau̇-ˌpən-chər\ *n* **:** COWBOY
cow·slip \'kau̇-ˌslip\ *n* **:** a common Old World primrose with fragrant yellow or purplish flowers
cox \'käks\ *n* **:** COXSWAIN — **cox** *vb*
cox·comb \'käks-ˌkōm\ *n* **:** a conceited foolish person
cox·swain \'käk-sən, -ˌswān\ *n* **1 :** a sailor who has charge of a ship's boat **2 :** a steersman of a racing shell
coy \'kȯi\ *adj* **1 :** sensitively diffident **:** BASHFUL **2 :** affecting shy or demure reserve — **coy·ly** *adv* — **coy·ness** *n*
coy·ote \'kī-ˌōt, kī-'ōt-ē\ *n, pl* **coyotes** *or* **coyote :** a small wolf native to western No. America
coy·pu \'kȯi-ˌpü\ *n* **1 :** a So. American aquatic rodent with webbed feet and dorsal mammary glands **2 :** NUTRIA 2
coz·en \'kəz-ᵊn\ *vb* **:** CHEAT, DEFRAUD, DECEIVE — **coz·en·age** \-ᵊn-ij\ *n*
[1]**co·zy** \'kō-zē\ *adj* **:** SNUG, COMFORTABLE — **co·zi·ly** \-zə-lē\ *adv* — **co·zi·ness** \-zē-nəs\ *n*
[2]**cozy** *adv* **:** in a cautious manner
[3]**cozy** *n, pl* **cozies :** a padded covering for a vessel (as a teapot) to keep the contents hot
[1]**crab** \'krab\ *n* **:** a crustacean with a short broad shell, a small abdomen, and a front pair of limbs with strong pincers
[2]**crab** *vi* **crabbed; crab·bing :** to fish for crabs — **crab·ber** *n*
[3]**crab** *vb* **crabbed; crab·bing :** to find fault **:** COMPLAIN
[4]**crab** *n* **1 :** CRAB APPLE **2 :** a sour ill-tempered person
crab apple *n* **:** a small sour apple
crab·bed \'krab-əd\ *adj* **1 :** MOROSE, PEEVISH **2 :** difficult to read or understand — **crab·bed·ly** *adv*
crab·by \'krab-ē\ *adj* **:** CROSS, ILL-NATURED
[1]**crack** \'krak\ *vb* **1 :** to break with a sudden sharp sound **2 :** to break without total separation of parts **3 :** to tell esp. in a clever or witty way **4 a :** to lose control **b :** to fail in tone **5 :** to puzzle out and solve or discover the secret of **6 :** to subject (as a petroleum oil) to heat for breaking down into lighter products (as gasoline)
[2]**crack** *n* **1 :** a sudden sharp noise **2 :** a sharp witty remark **3 :** a narrow break **:** FISSURE **4 a :** WEAKNESS, FLAW **b :** a broken tone of the voice **5 :** MOMENT, INSTANT **6 :** a sharp resounding blow **7 :** ATTEMPT, TRY
[3]**crack** *adj* **:** of superior excellence
crack down *vi* **:** to take positive disciplinary action
crack·down \'krak-ˌdau̇n\ *n* **:** an act or instance of cracking down
crack·er \'krak-ər\ *n* **1 :** something (as a firecracker) that makes a cracking noise **2 :** a dry thin crisp bakery product made of flour and water
crack·er·jack \-ˌjak\ *n* **:** something very excellent — **crackerjack** *adj*
[1]**crack·le** \'krak-əl\ *vi* **crack·led; crack·ling** \'krak-(ə-)liŋ\ **1 :** to make small sharp sudden repeated noises **2 :** to develop a surface network of fine cracks
[2]**crackle** *n* **1 :** the noise of repeated small cracks **2 :** a network of fine cracks on a smooth surface
crack·pot \'krak-ˌpät\ *n* **:** an eccentric person — **crackpot** *adj*
crack–up \'krak-ˌəp\ *n* **:** CRASH, WRECK
[1]**cra·dle** \'krād-ᵊl\ *n* **1 a :** a bed or cot for a baby usu. on rockers **b :** place of origin **2 :** something serving as a framework or support **3 :** an implement with rods like fingers attached to a scythe and used formerly for harvesting grain
[2]**cradle** *vt* **cra·dled; cra·dling** \'krād-liŋ, -ᵊl-iŋ\ **1 :** to place or keep in or as if in a cradle **2 :** to shelter in childhood **:** REAR **3 :** to protect and cherish lovingly
cra·dle·land \'krād-ᵊl-ˌ(l)and\ *n* **:** region of origin
cra·dle·song \-ˌsȯŋ\ *n* **:** LULLABY
craft \'kraft\ *n* **1 :** DEXTERITY, SKILL **2 :** an occupation or trade requiring manual dexterity or artistic skill **3 :** CUNNING, GUILE **4** *pl usu* **craft a :** a boat esp. of small size **b :** AIRCRAFT
crafts·man \'kraf(t)s-mən\ *n* **:** a highly skilled artisan — **crafts·man·ship** \-ˌship\ *n*
crafty \'kraf-tē\ *adj* **:** skillful at deceiving others **:** CUNNING — **craft·i·ly** \-tə-lē\ *adv* — **craft·i·ness** \-tē-nəs\ *n*
crag \'krag\ *n* **:** a steep rugged rock or cliff — **crag·gy** \-ē\ *adj*
cram \'kram\ *vb* **crammed; cram·ming 1 :** to stuff or crowd in **2 :** to fill full **3 :** to study hastily in preparation for an examination **4 :** to eat greedily — **cram·mer** *n*
[1]**cramp** \'kramp\ *n* **1 :** a sudden painful involuntary contraction of muscle **2 :** sharp abdominal pain — usu. used in pl.
[2]**cramp** *vt* **1 :** to affect with cramp **2 :** CONFINE, RESTRAIN; *also* **:** HAMPER **3 :** to turn (the front wheels of a vehicle) to right or left
cran·ber·ry \'kran-ˌber-ē, -b(ə-)rē\ *n* **:** the bright red sour berry of several trailing plants of the heath family; *also* **:** a plant producing these
[1]**crane** \'krān\ *n* **1 :** any of a family of tall wading birds related to the rails **2 :** a machine for raising, shifting, and lowering heavy weights
[2]**crane** *vb* **:** to stretch one's neck forward to see better
cra·ni·al \'krā-nē-əl\ *adj* **1 :** of or relating to the skull or cranium **2 :** CEPHALIC — **cra·ni·al·ly** \-ə-lē\ *adv*
cra·ni·um \'krā-nē-əm\ *n, pl* **-ni·ums** *or* **-nia** \-nē-ə\ **:** SKULL; *esp* **:** the part that encloses the brain
[1]**crank** \'kraŋk\ *n* **1 :** a bent part of an axle or shaft or an arm at right angles to the end of a shaft by which circular motion is imparted to or received from it **2 a :** an eccentric person **b :** a bad-tempered person **:** GROUCH
[2]**crank** *vb* **:** to start or operate by turning a crank
crank·case \-ˌkās\ *n* **:** the housing of a crankshaft
crank·shaft \-ˌshaft\ *n* **:** a shaft turning or driven by a crank
cranky \'kraŋ-kē\ *adj* **1 :** being out of order **2 :** CROTCHETY, IRRITABLE — **crank·i·ness** *n*
cran·ny \'kran-ē\ *n, pl* **crannies :** a small break or slit
crape \'krāp\ *n* **1 :** CREPE **2 :** a band of crepe worn on a hat or sleeve as a sign of mourning
craps \'kraps\ *n pl* **:** a gambling game played with two dice
crap·shoot·er \'krap-ˌshüt-ər\ *n* **:** a person who plays craps — **crap·shoot·ing** \-ˌshüt-iŋ\ *n*
[1]**crash** \'krash\ *vb* **1 a :** to break violently and noisily **:** SMASH **b :** to damage an airplane in landing **2 :** to enter or attend without invitation or without paying **3 :** to decline or break suddenly — **crash·er** *n*
[2]**crash** *n* **1 :** a loud sound (as of things smashing) **2 :** a breaking to pieces by or as if by collision; *also* **:** an instance of crashing **3 :** a sudden failure (as of a business)
[3]**crash** *adj* **:** effected hastily on an emergency basis with all available means
[4]**crash** *n* **:** a coarse fabric used for draperies, toweling, and clothing
crash–land \'krash-'land\ *vb* **:** to land an airplane under emergency conditions usu. with damage to the craft
crass \'kras\ *adj* **:** GROSS, INSENSITIVE — **crass·ly** *adv* — **crass·ness** *n*
[1]**crate** \'krāt\ *n* **1 :** a box usu. ventilated and made of thin wooden slats for packing fruit or vegetables **2 :** an enclosing

framework for protecting something (as in shipment)
²crate *vt* : to pack in a crate
cra·ter \'krāt-ər\ *n* : the depression around the opening of a volcano; *also* : a bowl-shaped depression
cra·vat \krə-'vat\ *n* : NECKTIE
crave \'krāv\ *vb* **1** : to ask earnestly : BEG, ENTREAT **2** : to have a strong desire for : LONG
¹cra·ven \'krā-vən\ *adj* : COWARDLY — **cra·ven·ly** *adv*
²craven *n* : COWARD
crav·ing \'krā-viŋ\ *n* : an urgent or abnormal desire
craw·fish \'krȯ-ˌfish\ *n* **1** : CRAYFISH **2** : SPINY LOBSTER
¹crawl \'krȯl\ *vb* **1** : to move slowly with the body close to the ground : CREEP **2** : to drag along slowly or feebly **3** : to advance by guile or servility **4** : to be swarming with or have the sensation of swarming with creeping things — **crawl·er** *n*
²crawl *n* **1** : the act or motion of crawling **2** : a speed swimming stroke
cray·fish \'krā-ˌfish\ *n* : any of numerous freshwater crustaceans resembling but usu. much smaller than the lobster
cray·on \'krā-ˌän, -ən; 'kran\ *n* **1** : a stick of white or colored chalk or of colored wax used for writing or drawing **2** : a crayon drawing
¹craze \'krāz\ *vb* : to make or become insane
²craze \'krāz\ *n* : FAD, MANIA
cra·zy \'krā-zē\ *adj* **1 a** : mentally disordered : INSANE **b (1)** : wildly impractical **(2)** : ERRATIC **2** : distracted with desire or excitement — **cra·zi·ly** \-zə-lē\ *adv* — **cra·zi·ness** \-zē-nəs\ *n*
¹creak \'krēk\ *vi* : to make a prolonged grating or squeaking sound
²creak *n* : a rasping or grating noise — **creak·i·ly** \'krē-kə-lē\ *adv* — **creaky** \'krē-kē\ *adj*
¹cream \'krēm\ *n* **1** : the yellowish part of milk containing butterfat **2 a** : a food prepared with cream **b** : something having the consistency of cream (as a usu. emulsified medicinal or cosmetic preparation) **3** : the choicest part **4** : a pale yellow — **creamy** \'krē-mē\ *adj*
²cream *vb* **1** : to form cream **2** : to take the choicest part of something **3** : to furnish, prepare, or treat with cream **4** : to work or blend to the consistency of cream
cream cheese *n* : an unripened soft white cheese made from whole milk enriched with cream
cream·er \'krē-mər\ *n* : a small vessel for serving cream
cream·ery \'krēm-(ə-)rē\ *n, pl* **-er·ies** : an establishment where butter and cheese are made or where milk and cream are sold or prepared
¹crease \'krēs\ *n* : a line or mark made by or as if by folding a pliable substance
²crease *vb* **1** : to make a crease in or on : WRINKLE **2** : to wound slightly esp. by grazing **3** : to become creased
cre·ate \krē-'āt\ *vt* **1** : to bring into existence **2** : to invest with a new office or rank **3** : to bring about : CAUSE, MAKE, PRODUCE
cre·a·tion \krē-'ā-shən\ *n* **1** : the act of creating or fact of being created **2** : something created **3** : all created things : WORLD
cre·a·tive \krē-'āt-iv\ *adj* : having or showing the power to produce original work (as in literature) — **cre·a·tive·ly** *adv* — **cre·a·tive·ness** *n*
cre·a·tiv·i·ty \ˌkrē-ā-'tiv-ət-ē\ *n* : ability to create
cre·a·tor \krē-'āt-ər\ *n* : one that creates : MAKER
crea·ture \'krē-chər\ *n* **1** : a lower animal **2** : a human being : PERSON — **crea·tur·al** \'krēch-(ə-)rəl\ *adj*
crèche \'kresh\ *n* : a representation of the Nativity scene in the stable at Bethlehem
cre·dence \'krēd-ᵊn(t)s\ *n* : BELIEF
cre·den·tial \kri-'den-chəl\ *n* **1** : something that gives a title to credit or confidence **2** *pl* : documents showing that a person is entitled to confidence or has a right to exercise official power
cred·i·ble \'kred-ə-bəl\ *adj* : capable of being believed : deserving to be believed — **cred·i·bil·i·ty** \ˌkred-ə-'bil-ət-ē\ *n* — **cred·i·bly** \'kred-ə-blē\ *adv*
¹cred·it \'kred-ət\ *n* **1 a** : a favorable balance in a bank account **b** : an entry in an account representing an addition of revenue or net worth **c** : the right or privilege of taking present possession of money, goods, or services in exchange for a promise to pay for them at a future date **d** : reputation for fulfilling financial obligations **2 a** : reliance on the truth or reality of something : BELIEF **b** : reputation for honesty or integrity : ESTEEM **3** : a source of honor **4** : a unit of academic work
²credit *vt* **1** : BELIEVE **2** : to enter a sum upon the credit side of **3** : to give credit to
cred·it·a·ble \'kred-ət-ə-bəl\ *adj* : worthy of esteem or praise — **cred·it·a·bil·i·ty** \ˌkred-ət-ə-'bil-ət-ē\ *n* — **cred·it·a·bly** \'kred-ət-ə-blē\ *adv*
cred·i·tor \'kred-ət-ər\ *n* : a person to whom a debt is owed; *esp* : a person to whom money or goods are due
cre·do \'krēd-ō, 'krād-\ *n, pl* **credos** : CREED
cre·du·li·ty \kri-'d(y)ü-lət-ē\ *n* : a willingness to believe statements esp. on little or no evidence
cred·u·lous \'krej-ə-ləs\ *adj* : ready to believe esp. on slight or uncertain evidence — **cred·u·lous·ly** *adv* — **cred·u·lous·ness** *n*
creed \'krēd\ *n* **1** : a statement of the essential beliefs of a religious faith **2** : a set of guiding principles or beliefs — **creed·al** *or* **cre·dal** \'krēd-ᵊl\ *adj*
creek \'krēk, 'krik\ *n* : a natural stream of water usu. smaller than a river
creel \'krēl\ *n* : a wickerwork container (as for fish)
¹creep \'krēp\ *vi* **crept** \'krept\; **creep·ing 1** : to move along with the body prone and close to the ground; *also* : to move slowly on hands and knees **2** : to move or advance slowly, timidly, or stealthily **3** : to spread or grow over a surface like ivy **4** : to feel as though insects were crawling on the body — **creep·er** *n*
²creep *n* **1** : a creeping movement **2** : a feeling of horror — usu. used in pl.
creepy \'krē-pē\ *adj* : having or producing a nervous shivery fear — **creep·i·ness** *n*
cre·mate \'krē-ˌmāt, kri-'\ *vt* : to reduce (a dead body) to ashes by fire — **cre·ma·tion** \kri-'mā-shən\ *n*
cre·ma·to·ri·um \ˌkrē-mə-'tōr-ē-əm, ˌkrem-ə-\ *n, pl* **-ri·ums** *or* **-ria** \-ē-ə\ : CREMATORY
cre·ma·to·ry \'krē-mə-ˌtōr-ē, 'krem-ə-\ *n, pl* **-ries** : a furnace for cremating or a structure containing such a furnace
cren·el·late *or* **cren·el·ate** \'kren-ᵊl-ˌāt\ *vt* : to furnish with battlements — **cren·el·la·tion** \ˌkren-ᵊl-'ā-shən\ *n*
cre·o·sote \'krē-ə-ˌsōt\ *n* : a brownish oily liquid obtained by distillation of coal tar and used esp. as a wood preservative
crepe *or* **crêpe** \'krāp\ *n* : a thin crinkled fabric (as of silk, wool, or cotton) — **crepe** *adj*
crepe de chine \ˌkrāp-də-'shēn\ *n, often cap 2d C* : a soft fine clothing crepe
cre·pus·cu·lar \kri-'pəs-kyə-lər\ *adj* **1** : of, relating to, or resembling twilight : DIM **2** : active in the twilight
cre·scen·do \kri-'shen-dō\ *n, pl* **-dos** *or* **-does** : a swelling in volume of sound in music or a passage so performed — **crescendo** *adv (or adj)*
¹cres·cent \'kres-ᵊnt\ *n* **1** : the moon at any stage between new moon and first quarter and between last quarter and the succeeding new moon **2** : something shaped like a crescent — **cres·cen·tic** \kre-'sent-ik\ *adj*
²crescent *adj* : INCREASING
cress \'kres\ *n* : any of numerous plants of the mustard family whose leaves are used in salads

¹crest \'krest\ *n* **1 a :** a showy tuft or process on the head of an animal (as a bird) **b :** the plume worn on a knight's helmet **2 :** something suggesting a crest esp. in being an upper prominence, edge, or limit **3 :** a high point : CLIMAX, CULMINATION — **crest•ed** *adj* — **crest•less** \-ləs\ *adj*
²crest *vb* **1 :** to furnish with a crest : CROWN **2 :** to reach the crest of **3 :** to rise to a crest
crest•fall•en \'kres(t)-,fò-lən\ *adj* **:** DEJECTED; *also* **:** SHAMEFACED, HUMILIATED — **crest•fall•en•ness** *n*
cre•ta•ceous \kri-'tā-shəs\ *adj* **:** having the characteristics of or abounding in chalk
cre•tonne \'krē-,tän\ *n* **:** a strong printed cotton or linen cloth used esp. for furniture coverings and curtains
cre•vasse \kri-'vas\ *n* **1 :** a deep crevice or fissure (as in a glacier) **2 :** a breach in a levee
crev•ice \'krev-əs\ *n* **:** a narrow opening that results from a split or crack **:** FISSURE, CLEFT
crew \'krü\ *n* **1 :** a group or gathering of persons **2 :** a group of persons associated in joint work **3 :** the group of seamen who man a ship **4 :** the persons who man an airplane in flight — **crew•man** \-mən\ *n*
¹crib \'krib\ *n* **1 :** a manger for feeding animals **2 a :** a small child's bedstead with high enclosing usu. slatted sides **b :** a building for storage **:** BIN **3 a :** a literal translation; *esp* **:** PONY 3 **b :** a device used for cheating in an examination
²crib *vb* **cribbed; crib•bing 1 :** to copy (as an idea) and use as one's own **:** PLAGIARIZE **2 :** to make use of a translation or notes in a forbidden or dishonest way
crib•bage \'krib-ij\ *n* **:** a card game usu. played by two players and scored on a board
crick \'krik\ *n* **:** a painful spasm of muscles (as of the neck or back) — **crick** *vt*
¹crick•et \'krik-ət\ *n* **:** a small leaping insect noted for the chirping notes of the males
²cricket *n* **1 :** a game played with a ball and bat by two sides of usu. 11 players each on a large field centering upon two wickets **2 :** fair and honorable behavior — **crick•et•er** *n*
cri•er \'krī(-ə)r\ *n* **:** one that cries; *esp* **:** one who proclaims orders or announcements
crime \'krīm\ *n* **:** a serious offense against the law
¹crim•i•nal \'krim-ən-ᵊl\ *adj* **1 :** involving or being a crime **2 :** relating to crime or its punishment — **crim•i•nal•i•ty** \,krim-ə-'nal-ət-ē\ *n* — **crim•i•nal•ly** \'krim-ən-ᵊl-ē\ *adv*
²criminal *n* **:** one that has committed a crime **:** MALEFACTOR
crim•i•nol•o•gy \,krim-ə-'näl-ə-jē\ *n* **:** a scientific study of crime, of criminals, and of their punishment or correction — **crim•i•no•log•i•cal** \,krim-ən-ᵊl-'äj-i-kəl\ *adj* — **crim•i•nol•o•gist** \,krim-ə-'näl-ə-jəst\ *n*
¹crimp \'krimp\ *vt* **1 :** to cause to become wavy, bent, or warped **2 :** INHIBIT, HINDER — **crimp•er** *n*
²crimp *n* **1 :** something produced by or as if by crimping **2 :** something that cramps or inhibits
crimpy \'krim-pē\ *adj* **:** having a crimped appearance **:** FRIZZY
¹crim•son \'krim-zən\ *n* **:** any of several deep purplish reds — **crimson** *adj*
²crimson *vb* **:** to make or become crimson
cringe \'krinj\ *vi* **cringed; cring•ing 1 :** to draw in or contract one's muscles involuntarily **2 :** to shrink in fear or servility
¹crin•kle \'kriŋ-kəl\ *vb* **crin•kled; crin•kling** \-k(ə-)liŋ\ **1 :** to form little waves or wrinkles on the surface **:** WRINKLE, RIPPLE **2 :** RUSTLE
²crinkle *n* **:** WINDING, WRINKLE — **crin•kly** \-k(ə-)lē\ *adj*
crin•o•line \'krin-ᵊl-ən\ *n* **1 :** a cloth thread used for stiffening and lining **2 :** a very full stiff skirt — **crinoline** *adj*
¹crip•ple \'krip-əl\ *n* **:** a lame or disabled individual
²cripple *vt* **crip•pled; crip•pling** \'krip-(ə-)liŋ\ **1 :** to deprive of the use esp. of a leg **2 :** to deprive of strength, efficiency, or capability for service — **crip•pler** \-(ə-)lər\ *n*

cri•sis \'krī-səs\ *n, pl* **cri•ses** \'krī-,sēz\ **1 :** the turning point for better or worse in an acute disease or fever **2 :** a decisive moment or turning point **3 :** an unstable or crucial time or state of affairs
¹crisp \'krisp\ *adj* **1 :** CURLY, WAVY **2 :** easily crumbled **:** FLAKY **3 :** being firm and fresh **4 a :** being sharp, clean-cut, and clear **b :** noticeably neat **c :** SPRIGHTLY, LIVELY **d :** FROSTY, SNAPPY — **crisp•ly** *adv* — **crisp•ness** *n*
²crisp *vb* **:** to make or become crisp — **crisp•er** *n*
crispy \'kris-pē\ *adj* **:** CRISP — **crisp•i•ness** *n*
¹criss•cross \'kris-,kròs\ *n* **:** a pattern formed by crossed lines — **crisscross** *adj (or adv)*
²crisscross *vb* **1 :** to mark with intersecting lines **2 :** to go or pass back and forth
cri•te•ri•on \krī-'tir-ē-ən\ *n, pl* **-ria** \-ē-ə\ **:** a standard on which a judgment or decision may be based
crit•ic \'krit-ik\ *n* **1 :** a person who gives his judgment of the value, worth, beauty, or excellence of something **2 :** FAULTFINDER
crit•i•cal \'krit-i-kəl\ *adj* **1 a :** inclined to criticize **b :** using or involving careful judgment **2 a :** of, relating to, or being a turning point or specially important juncture **b :** CRUCIAL, DECISIVE **c :** indispensable for overcoming a crisis — **crit•i•cal•ly** \-i-k(ə-)lē\ *adv*
crit•i•cism \'krit-ə-,siz-əm\ *n* **1 :** the act of criticizing; *esp* **:** FAULTFINDING **2 :** a critical remark or observation **3 :** a careful judgment or review **4 :** the art of judging expertly works of art or literature
crit•i•cize \'krit-ə-,sīz\ *vb* **1 :** to examine and judge as a critic **:** EVALUATE **2 :** to find fault with
cri•tique \krə-'tēk\ *n* **:** a critical estimate or discussion
¹croak \'krōk\ *vb* **1 :** to make a deep harsh sound **2 :** GRUMBLE
²croak *n* **:** a hoarse harsh cry (as of a frog) — **croaky** \'krō-kē\ *adj*
¹cro•chet \krō-'shā\ *n* **:** needlework consisting of the interlocking of looped stitches formed with a single thread and a hooked needle
²crochet *vb* **:** to form a fabric by crochet
crock \'kräk\ *n* **:** a thick earthenware pot or jar
crock•ery \'kräk-(ə-)rē\ *n* **:** EARTHENWARE
croc•o•dile \'kräk-ə-,dīl\ *n* **:** any of several large greedy thick-skinned long-bodied aquatic reptiles of tropical and subtropical waters
cro•cus \'krō-kəs\ *n* **:** any of a large genus of small herbs of the iris family with showy solitary long-tubed flowers and slender linear leaves
crone \'krōn\ *n* **:** a withered old woman
cro•ny \'krō-nē\ *n, pl* **cronies :** an intimate companion
¹crook \'krùk\ *n* **1 :** an implement having a bent or hooked form **2 :** a shepherd's staff **3 :** a dishonest person; *esp* **:** CRIMINAL **4 :** BEND, CURVE **5 :** a hook-shaped, curved, or bent part
²crook *vb* **1 :** BEND **2 :** CURVE, WIND
crook•ed \'krùk-əd\ *adj* **1 :** having a crook or curve **:** BENT **2 :** DISHONEST; *esp* **:** CRIMINAL — **crook•ed•ly** *adv* — **crook•ed•ness** *n*
croon \'krün\ *vb* **1 :** to hum or sing in a low voice **2 :** to sing popular songs in an exaggerated sentimental style — **croon•er** *n*
¹crop \'kräp\ *n* **1 :** the stock or handle of a whip; *also* **:** a riding whip **2 :** a pouched enlargement of the gullet of a bird or insect that receives food **3 a :** a plant or animal or plant or animal product that can be grown and harvested **b :** the product or yield esp. of a harvested crop
²crop *vb* **cropped; crop•ping 1 a :** to remove the upper or outer parts of **b :** to cut off short **:** CLIP **2 :** to cause (land) to bear produce **3 :** to feed by cropping something **4 :** to appear unexpectedly or casually

crop·land \'kräp-ˌland\ *n* : land devoted to the production of plant crops

[1]**crop·per** \'kräp-ər\ *n* : one that raises crops; *esp* : SHARECROPPER

[2]**cropper** *n* **1** : a severe fall **2** : a sudden or violent failure

cro·quet \krō-'kā\ *n* : a game in which the players use mallets to drive wooden balls through a series of hoops set in the ground

cro·quette \krō-'ket\ *n* : a roll or ball of hashed meat, fish, or vegetables fried in deep fat

cro·sier \'krō-zhər\ *n* : a staff carried by bishops and abbots as a symbol of office

[1]**cross** \'krȯs\ *n* **1** : a structure consisting of an upright with a transverse beam **2** : a trying affliction **3** : a device or structure composed of an upright bar crossed by a horizontal one; *esp* : one used as a Christian emblem **4** : the intersection of two ways or lines : CROSSING **5 a** : an act of crossing unlike individuals **b** : a crossbred individual or kind **6** : a punch thrown over an opponent's lead in boxing

crosses 3

[2]**cross** *vb* **1 a** : to lie or be situated across **b** : INTERSECT **2** : to cancel by marking a cross on or drawing a line through **3** : to place or fold crosswise one over the other **4 a** : to run counter to : OPPOSE, THWART, OBSTRUCT **b** : BETRAY **5 a** : to extend across : TRAVERSE **b** : to go from one to the other side of **6** : to draw a line across **7** : INTERBREED, HYBRIDIZE **8** : to meet and pass on the way

[3]**cross** *adj* **1 a** : lying across **b** : moving across **2** : running counter : OPPOSED **3** : marked by bad temper **4** : CROSSBRED, HYBRID — **cross·ly** *adv* — **cross·ness** *n*

cross·bar \'krȯs-ˌbär\ *n* : a bar, piece, or stripe placed crosswise or across

cross·bones \-ˌbōnz\ *n pl* : two leg or arm bones placed or depicted crosswise

cross·bow \-ˌbō\ *n* : a short bow mounted crosswise near the end of a wooden stock that discharges stones and square-headed arrows — **cross·bow·man** \-mən\ *n*

[1]**cross·breed** \-ˌbrēd, -'brēd\ *vt* : HYBRIDIZE; *esp* : to interbreed two varieties or breeds of the same species

[2]**cross·breed** \-ˌbrēd\ *n* : HYBRID

cross–coun·try \-'kən-trē\ *adj* **1** : proceeding over the countryside (as fields) rather than by roads **2** : of or relating to cross-country sports — **cross–country** *adv*

cross·cur·rent \-'kər-ənt\ *n* **1** : a current running counter to another **2** : a conflicting tendency

[1]**cross·cut** \-ˌkət\ *vt* **-cut**; **-cut·ting** : to cut or saw crosswise esp. of the grain of wood

[2]**crosscut** *adj* **1** : made or used for cutting transversely **2** : cut across or transversely

[3]**crosscut** *n* : something that cuts across or through

cross–ex·am·i·na·tion \ˌkrȯs-ig-ˌzam-ə-'nā-shən\ *n* : the questioning of a witness in order to check, alter, expand, or discredit his testimony — **cross–ex·am·ine** \-'zam-ən\ *vt* — **cross–ex·am·in·er** *n*

cross–eye \'krȯs-ˌī\ *n* : an abnormality in which the eye turns inward toward the nose — **cross–eyed** \-'īd\ *adj*

cross–grained \'krȯs-'grānd\ *adj* : having the grain or fibers running diagonally, transversely, or irregularly

cross·ing \'krȯ-siŋ\ *n* **1 a** : the act or action of one that crosses **b** : a voyage across water **c** : INTERBREEDING, HYBRIDIZING **2** : a point of intersection **3** : a place where a street or stream is crossed

cross–legged \'krȯs-'leg(-ə)d\ *adv* : with the legs crossed and the knees spread wide

cross·over \'krȯs-ˌō-vər\ *n* : a crossing from one side, level, or track to another or a place or passage where such crossing is made

cross·piece \-ˌpēs\ *n* : a horizontal member (as of a figure or a structure)

cross–pol·li·nate \-'päl-ə-ˌnāt\ *or* **cross–pol·li·nize** \-'päl-ə-ˌnīz\ *vt* : to subject to cross-pollination

cross–pol·li·na·tion \ˌkrȯs-ˌpäl-ə-'nā-shən\ *n* : the transfer of pollen from one flower to the stigma of another

cross–re·fer \ˌkrȯs-ri-'fər\ *vb* : to refer by a notation or direction from one place to another (as in a book) — **cross–ref·er·ence** \'krȯs-'ref-ərn(t)s, -'ref-(ə-)rən(t)s\ *n*

cross·road \'krȯs-ˌrōd\ *n* **1** : a road that crosses a main road or runs between main roads **2** : the place of intersection of two or more roads — usu. used in pl.

cross section *n* **1 a** : a cutting made across something (as a log or apple) **b** : a representation of a cutting made across something **2** : a number of persons or things selected from a group to represent or show the general nature of the whole — **cross–sec·tion·al** \'krȯs-'sek-shnəl, -shən-ᵊl\ *adj*

cross·town \'krȯs-ˌtau̇n, -'tau̇n\ *adj* **1** : situated at opposite points of a town **2** : extending or running across a town — **crosstown** *adv*

cross·walk \'krȯs-ˌwȯk\ *n* : a specially paved or marked path for pedestrians crossing a street or road

cross·way \-ˌwā\ *n* : CROSSROAD — often used in pl.

[1]**cross·wise** \-ˌwīz\ *adv* : so as to cross something : ACROSS

[2]**crosswise** *adj* : extended or lying across

crotch \'kräch\ *n* : an angle formed by the parting of two legs, branches, or members

crotch·et \'kräch-ət\ *n* : a peculiar opinion or habit : WHIM

crotch·ety \'kräch-ət-ē\ *adj* : marked by or given to whims or ill temper

crouch \'krau̇ch\ *vb* **1** : to stoop with the limbs close to the body **2** : to bend or bow servilely — **crouch** *n*

croup \'krüp\ *n* : a laryngitis esp. of infants marked by difficult breathing and a hoarse metallic cough — **croup·ous** \'krü-pəs\ *adj* — **croupy** \-pē\ *adj*

crou·pi·er \'krü-pē-ər, -pē-ˌā\ *n* : an employee of a gambling casino who collects and pays bets at a gaming table

crou·ton \'krü-ˌtän, krü-'\ *n* : a small piece of toast

[1]**crow** \'krō\ *n* : any of various large usu. entirely glossy black birds related to the jays

[2]**crow** *vi* **1** : to make the loud shrill sound characteristic of a cock **2** : to utter a sound expressive of pleasure **3 a** : EXULT, GLOAT **b** : BRAG

[3]**crow** *n* **1** : the cry of the cock **2** : a triumphant cry

crow·bar \'krō-ˌbär\ *n* : an iron or steel bar usu. wedge-shaped at the end for use as a pry or lever

[1]**crowd** \'krau̇d\ *vb* **1** : to press forward **2** : to press close to something **3** : to collect in numbers : THRONG **4** : to fill or pack by pressing together

[2]**crowd** *n* **1** : a large number of persons collected into a body without order **2** : the great body of the people : POPULACE **3** : a large number of things close together

crow·foot \'krō-ˌfu̇t\ *n* : BUTTERCUP

[1]**crown** \'krau̇n\ *n* **1** : a wreath or band for the head; *esp* : one worn as a mark of victory or honor **2** : a royal headdress : DIADEM **3** : a top part (as of a tree or tooth) **4 a** *often cap* : imperial or regal power : SOVEREIGNTY **b** : SOVEREIGN **5** : the highest point of development : CULMINATION **6** : any of several coins; *esp* : an English silver coin worth five shillings — **crown** *adj, often cap* — **crowned** \'krau̇nd\ *adj*

[2]**crown** *vt* **1 a** : to place a crown on **b** : to recognize officially as **2** : BESTOW, ENDOW **3** : SURMOUNT, TOP **4** : to bring to a

successful conclusion : CLIMAX 5 : to put an artificial crown upon (a tooth)
crown prince *n* : the heir apparent to a crown or throne
crown princess *n* 1 : the wife of a crown prince 2 : a female heir apparent to a crown or throne
cru·cial \'krü-shəl\ *adj* 1 : marked by final determination of a doubtful issue : DECISIVE 2 : SEVERE, TRYING — **cru·cial·ly** \'krüsh-(ə-)lē\ *adv*
cru·ci·ble \'krü-sə-bəl\ *n* : a container used for holding a substance (as metal or ore) treated under great heat
cru·ci·fer \'krü-sə-fər\ *n* : one who carries a cross esp. at the head of an ecclesiastical procession — **cru·cif·er·ous** \krü-'sif-(ə-)rəs\ *adj*
cru·ci·fix \'krü-sə-ˌfiks\ *n* : a representation of Christ on the cross
cru·ci·fix·ion \ˌkrü-sə-'fik-shən\ *n* : an act of crucifying; *esp*, *cap* : the crucifying of Christ
cru·ci·form \'krü-sə-ˌfȯrm\ *adj* : forming or arranged in a cross — **cru·ci·form·ly** *adv*
cru·ci·fy \'krü-sə-ˌfī\ *vt* **-fied**; **-fy·ing** 1 : to put to death by nailing or binding the hands and feet to a cross 2 : to treat cruelly : TORTURE, PERSECUTE
crude \'krüd\ *adj* 1 : not refined : RAW 2 : lacking refinement, grace, or tact 3 : rough or inexpert in plan or execution — **crude·ly** *adv* — **crude·ness** *n* — **cru·di·ty** \'krüd-ət-ē\ *n*
cru·el \'krü(-ə)l\ *adj* **cru·el·er** *or* **cru·el·ler**; **cru·el·est** *or* **cru·el·lest** 1 : disposed to inflict pain 2 a : causing or helping to cause injury, grief, or pain b : devoid of kindness : MERCILESS — **cru·el·ly** \'krü-ə-lē, 'krü-lē\ *adv*
cru·el·ty \'krü(-ə)l-tē\ *n*, *pl* **-ties** 1 : the quality or state of being cruel 2 a : a cruel action b : inhuman treatment
cru·et \'krü-ət\ *n* : a small glass bottle for holding vinegar, oil, or sauce for table use
[1]**cruise** \'krüz\ *vb* 1 : to sail about touching at a series of ports 2 : to travel for enjoyment 3 : to go about the streets at random 4 : to travel at the most efficient operating speed
[2]**cruise** *n* : an act or an instance of cruising
cruis·er \'krü-zər\ *n* 1 : a boat or vehicle that cruises 2 : a large fast moderately armored and gunned warship 3 : a motorboat with arrangements necessary for living aboard
crul·ler \'krəl-ər\ *n* : a small sweet cake in the form of a twisted strip fried in deep fat
[1]**crumb** \'krəm\ *n* : a small fragment esp. of bread
[2]**crumb** *vt* 1 : to break into crumbs : CRUMBLE 2 : to cover or thicken with crumbs 3 : to remove crumbs from
crum·ble \'krəm-bəl\ *vb* **crum·bled**; **crum·bling** \-b(ə-)liŋ\ : to break into small pieces : DISINTEGRATE
crum·bly \-b(ə-)lē\ *adj* : easily crumbled
crum·pet \'krəm-pət\ *n* : a small round cake made of unsweetened batter cooked on a griddle
[1]**crum·ple** \'krəm-pəl\ *vb* **crum·pled**; **crum·pling** \-p(ə-)liŋ\ 1 : to press, bend, or crush out of shape : RUMPLE 2 : to become crumpled 3 : COLLAPSE
[2]**crumple** *n* : a wrinkle or crease made by crumpling
[1]**crunch** \'krənch\ *vb* : to chew, grind, or press with a crushing noise
[2]**crunch** *n* : an act or sound of crunching — **crunchy** \'krən-chē\ *adj*
[1]**cru·sade** \krü-'sād\ *n* 1 *cap* : any of the military expeditions undertaken by Christian countries in the 11th, 12th, and 13th centuries to recover the Holy Land from the Muslims 2 : a campaign to improve conditions that is undertaken with zeal
[2]**crusade** *vi* : to engage in a crusade — **cru·sad·er** *n*
cruse \'krüz, 'krüs\ *n* : a jar, pot, or cup for holding a liquid (as water or oil)
[1]**crush** \'krəsh\ *vb* 1 a : to squeeze or force by pressure so as to alter or destroy structure b : to squeeze together into a mass 2 : HUG, EMBRACE 3 : to reduce to particles by pounding or grinding 4 a : SUPPRESS, OVERWHELM b : SUBDUE, DEFEAT — **crush·er** *n*
[2]**crush** *n* 1 : an act of crushing 2 : a tightly packed crowd 3 : INFATUATION; *also* : the object of infatuation
crust \'krəst\ *n* 1 a : the hardened exterior surface of bread b : a piece of dry hard bread 2 : the pastry portion of a pie 3 : a hard external covering or surface layer — **crust** *vb*
crus·ta·cean \ˌkrəs-'tā-shən\ *n* : any of a large class of mostly aquatic arthropods (as lobsters or crabs) having a firm crust-like shell — **crustacean** *adj*
crust·al \'krəst-ᵊl\ *adj* : relating to a crust (as of the earth)
crusty \'krəs-tē\ *adj* 1 : having or being a crust 2 : SURLY, IRASCIBLE
crutch \'krəch\ *n* 1 : a support typically fitting under the armpit for use by the disabled in walking 2 : a usu. forked support or prop
crux \'krəks, 'krủks\ *n* 1 : a puzzling or difficult problem 2 : a crucial or critical point
[1]**cry** \'krī\ *vb* **cried**; **cry·ing** 1 : to call loudly : SHOUT 2 : WEEP, LAMENT 3 : to utter a characteristic sound or call 4 : BEG, BESEECH 5 : to proclaim publicly : call out
[2]**cry** *n*, *pl* **cries** 1 : a loud call or shout (as of pain, fear, or joy) 2 : APPEAL 3 : a fit of weeping 4 : the characteristic sound uttered by an animal (as a bird) 5 : SLOGAN, WATCHWORD
cry·ba·by \'krī-ˌbā-bē\ *n* : one who cries easily or often
cry·ing \'krī-iŋ\ *adj* 1 : calling for attention and correction 2 : NOTORIOUS
cry·on·ics \krī-'än-iks\ *n* : the practice of freezing a dead diseased human being in expectation of reviving him at a future time when a cure for his diease has been developed
crypt \'kript\ *n* : an underground vault or room; *esp* : one under the floor of a church used as a burial place
cryp·tic \'krip-tik\ *adj* 1 : HIDDEN, SECRET 2 : having or seeming to have a hidden meaning — **cryp·ti·cal·ly** \-ti-k(ə-)lē\ *adv*
cryp·to·gram \'krip-tə-ˌgram\ *n* : a writing in cipher or code
cryp·tog·ra·phy \krip-'täg-rə-fē\ *n* : the enciphering and deciphering of messages in code — **cryp·tog·ra·pher** \-fər\ *n*
crys·tal \'krist-ᵊl\ *n* 1 : transparent quartz 2 : something resembling crystal in transparency and colorlessness 3 : a body that is formed by the solidification of a substance or mixture and has a regularly repeating internal arrangement of its atoms and often external plane faces 4 : a clear colorless glass of superior quality 5 : the transparent cover over a watch dial
crys·tal·line \'kris-tə-lən\ *adj* 1 : made of crystal or composed of crystals 2 : TRANSPARENT 3 : of or relating to a crystal — **crys·tal·lin·i·ty** \ˌkris-tə-'lin-ət-ē\ *n*
crys·tal·lize \'kris-tə-ˌlīz\ *vb* 1 : to cause to form crystals or assume crystalline form 2 : to give a definite form to 3 : to become crystallized — **crys·tal·liz·a·ble** *adj* — **crys·tal·li·za·tion** \ˌkris-tə-lə-'zā-shən\ *n*
cub \'kəb\ *n* 1 : a young fox or other carnivorous mammal 2 : APPRENTICE; *esp* : an inexperienced newspaper reporter
cub·by·hole \'kəb-ē-ˌhōl\ *n* 1 : a snug or confined place (as for hiding) 2 : a small closet, cupboard, or compartment for storing things
[1]**cube** \'kyüb\ *n* 1 : a solid having six equal square sides 2 : the product obtained by taking a number three times as a factor
[2]**cube** *vt* 1 : to raise to the third power 2 a : to form into a cube b : to cut into cubes
cu·bic \'kyü-bik\ *adj* 1 : having the form of a cube : CUBICAL 2 : being the volume of a cube whose edge is a specified unit — **cu·bic·ly** *adv*
cu·bi·cal \'kyü-bi-kəl\ *adj* 1 : CUBIC; *esp* : shaped like a cube 2 : relating to volume — **cu·bi·cal·ly** \-k(ə-)lē\ *adv*
cu·bi·cle \'kyü-bi-kəl\ *n* 1 : a sleeping compartment partitioned off from a large room 2 : a small partitioned space

cu·bit \'kyü-bət\ *n* : an ancient unit of length equal to about 18 inches

cuck·old \'kək-əld, 'kuk-\ *n* : a man whose wife is unfaithful — **cuck·old·ry** \-əl-drē\ *n*

cuck·oo \'kük-ü, 'kuk-\ *n, pl* **cuckoos** : a largely grayish brown European bird that lays its eggs in the nests of other birds for them to hatch

cu·cum·ber \'kyü-(,)kəm-bər\ *n* : the long fleshy many-seeded fruit of a vine of the gourd family grown as a garden vegetable

cud \'kəd, 'kud\ *n* : food brought up into the mouth by a ruminating animal (as a cow) from the first stomach to be chewed again

[1]**cud·dle** \'kəd-ᵊl\ *vb* **cud·dled**; **cud·dling** \'kəd-liŋ, -ᵊl-iŋ\ : to lie close : NESTLE, SNUGGLE

[2]**cuddle** *n* : a close embrace : the act of nestling

[1]**cudg·el** \'kəj-əl\ *n* : a short heavy club

[2]**cudgel** *vt* **-eled** *or* **-elled**; **-el·ing** *or* **-el·ling** : to beat with or as if with a cudgel

[1]**cue** \'kyü\ *n* **1** : a word, phrase, or action in a play serving as a signal for the next actor to speak or act **2** : HINT

[2]**cue** *n* : a tapering rod for striking a ball in games (as billiards or pool)

[1]**cuff** \'kəf\ *n* **1** : a part of a sleeve or glove encircling the wrist **2** : the turned-back hem of a trouser leg

[2]**cuff** *vt* : to strike esp. with the palm of the hand

[3]**cuff** *n* : a blow with the hand esp. when open : SLAP

cui·rass \kwi-'ras\ *n* : a piece of armor covering the body from neck to girdle; *also* : the breastplate of such a piece

cui·sine \kwi-'zēn\ *n* : manner of preparing food

cul–de–sac \,kəl-di-'sak, ,kul-\ *n, pl* **culs–de–sac** \,kəl(z)-, ,kul(z)-\ : a street or passage closed at one end

cul·i·nary \'kəl-ə-,ner-ē, 'kyü-lə-\ *adj* : of or relating to the kitchen or cookery

[1]**cull** \'kəl\ *vt* **1** : to select from a group : CHOOSE **2** : to identify and remove the culls from — **cull·er** *n*

[2]**cull** *n* : something rejected as inferior or worthless

cul·mi·nate \'kəl-mə-,nāt\ *vi* : to reach the highest or a climactic or decisive point

cul·mi·na·tion \,kəl-mə-'nā-shən\ *n* **1** : the action of culminating **2** : the culminating position : SUMMIT

cul·pa·ble \'kəl-pə-bəl\ *adj* : deserving condemnation or blame — **cul·pa·bil·i·ty** \,kəl-pə-'bil-ət-ē\ *n* — **cul·pa·ble·ness** *n* — **cul·pa·bly** \'kəl-pə-blē\ *adv*

cul·prit \'kəl-prət, -,prit\ *n* : one accused of or charged with a crime

cult \'kəlt\ *n* **1** : formal religious veneration : WORSHIP **2** : a system of religious beliefs and ritual; *also* : its body of adherents **3 a** : enthusiastic and usu. temporary devotion to a person, idea, or thing **b** : a group of persons showing such devotion — **cult·ist** \'kəl-təst\ *n*

cul·ti·va·ble \'kəl-tə-və-bəl\ *adj* : capable of being cultivated — **cul·ti·va·bil·i·ty** \,kəl-tə-və-'bil-ət-ē\ *n*

cul·ti·vate \'kəl-tə-,vāt\ *vt* **1** : to prepare for the raising of crops : TILL; *also* : to loosen or break up the soil about (growing plants) **2 a** : to foster the growth of **b** : REFINE, IMPROVE **3** : FURTHER, ENCOURAGE **4** : to seek the society of — **cul·ti·va·tor** \-ər\ *n*

cul·ti·vat·ed \-əd\ *adj* **1** : subjected to or produced under cultivation **2** : REFINED, EDUCATED

cul·ti·va·tion \,kəl-tə-'vā-shən\ *n* **1** : the act or art of cultivating; *esp* : TILLAGE **2** : CULTURE, REFINEMENT

cul·tur·al \'kəlch-(ə-)rəl\ *adj* **1** : of or relating to culture **2** : concerned with the fostering of plant or animal growth — **cul·tur·al·ly** \-ē\ *adv*

cul·ture \'kəl-chər\ *n* **1** : CULTIVATION, TILLAGE **2 a** : the growing or development of a particular product, stock, or crop **b** : professional or expert care and training **3** : the improvement of the mind, tastes, and manners through careful training **4 a** : a particular stage of advancement in civilization **b** : the characteristic features of a civilization including its beliefs, its artistic and material products, and its social institutions

cul·tured \'kəl-chərd\ *adj* : CULTIVATED

cul·vert \'kəl-vərt\ *n* : a drain crossing under a road or railroad

cum·ber \'kəm-bər\ *vt* **cum·bered**; **cum·ber·ing** \-b(ə-)riŋ\ **1** : to hinder or hamper by being in the way **2** : to weigh down : BURDEN

cum·ber·some \'kəm-bər-səm\ *adj* **1** : CLUMSY, UNWIELDY **2** : slow-moving : LUMBERING — **cum·ber·some·ly** *adv* — **cum·ber·some·ness** *n*

cum·brous \'kəm-brəs\ *adj* : CUMBERSOME

cum·mer·bund \'kəm-ər-,bənd\ *n* : a broad sash worn as a waistband

cu·mu·la·tive \'kyü-myə-lət-iv, -,lāt-\ *adj* **1** : increasing (as in force, strength, or amount) by successive additions **2** : formed by addition of new material of the same kind — **cu·mu·la·tive·ly** *adv* — **cu·mu·la·tive·ness** *n*

cu·mu·lus \'kyü-myə-ləs\ *n, pl* **cu·mu·li** \-,lī, -,lē\ : a massy cloud form having a flat base and rounded outlines often piled up like a mountain

[1]**cu·ne·i·form** \kyu-'nē-ə-,fȯrm, 'kyü-n(ē-)ə-\ *adj* **1** : having the shape of a wedge **2** : composed of or written in wedge-shaped characters

[2]**cuneiform** *n* : cuneiform writing (as of ancient Assyria and Babylonia)

[1]**cun·ning** \'kən-iŋ\ *adj* **1** : exhibiting skill **2** : CRAFTY, ARTFUL **3** : prettily appealing : CUTE — **cun·ning·ly** *adv*

[2]**cunning** *n* **1** : SKILL, DEXTERITY **2** : SLYNESS, CRAFTINESS

[1]**cup** \'kəp\ *n* **1** : an open bowl-shaped drinking vessel usu. with a handle **2** : the contents of a cup **3** : a large ornamental cup offered as a prize **4** : something resembling a cup — **cup·like** *adj*

[2]**cup** *vt* **cupped**; **cup·ping** **1** : to curve into the shape of a cup **2** : to place in a cup — **cup·per** *n*

cup·bear·er \'kəp-,bar-ər\ *n* : one who has the duty of filling and handing cups of wine

cup·board \'kəb-ərd\ *n* : a closet with shelves for cups, dishes, or food; *also* : a small closet

cup·cake \'kəp-,kāk\ *n* : a small cake baked in a cuplike mold

cup·ful \'kəp-,ful\ *n, pl* **cup·fuls** \-,fulz\ *or* **cups·ful** \'kəps-,ful\ **1** : the amount held by a cup **2** : a half pint : eight ounces

cu·pid·i·ty \kyu-'pid-ət-ē\ *n* : excessive desire esp. for wealth : GREED

cu·po·la \'kyü-pə-lə, -,lō\ *n* **1** : a rounded roof or ceiling **2** : a small structure built on top of a roof

cur \'kər\ *n* : a mongrel or inferior dog

cur·a·ble \'kyur-ə-bəl\ *adj* : capable of being cured — **cur·a·bil·i·ty** \,kyur-ə-'bil-ət-ē\ *n* — **cur·a·ble·ness** *n* — **cur·a·bly** \'kyur-ə-blē\ *adv*

cu·ra·cy \'kyur-ə-sē\ *n, pl* **-cies** : the office or term of office of a curate

cu·rate \'kyur-ət\ *n* : a clergyman serving as assistant (as to a rector) in a parish

cu·ra·tive \'kyur-ət-iv\ *adj* : relating to or used in the cure of diseases — **cu·ra·tive·ly** *adv*

cu·ra·tor \kyu-'rāt-ər, 'kyur-,āt-\ *n* : one that has the care and superintendence of something; *esp* : one in charge of a museum or zoo

[1]**curb** \'kərb\ *n* **1** : a chain or strap on a bit used to restrain a horse **2** : CHECK, RESTRAINT **3** : an edging built along a street to form part of a gutter **4** : a market for trading in securities not listed on a stock exchange

[2]**curb** *vt* : to control by or furnish with a curb

curb·ing \'kər-biŋ\ *n* **1** : the material for a curb **2** : CURB

curb·stone \'kərb-,stōn\ *n* : a stone forming a curb

[1]**curd** \'kərd\ *n* : the thick casein-rich part of coagulated milk — **curdy** \-ē\ *adj*

[2]**curd** *vb* : COAGULATE, CURDLE
cur·dle \'kərd-ᵊl\ *vb* **cur·dled**; **cur·dling** \'kərd-liŋ, -ᵊl-iŋ\ 1 : to cause curds to form in 2 : to form curds : COAGULATE 3 : SPOIL, SOUR
[1]**cure** \'kyu̇(ə)r\ *n* 1 : spiritual charge : CARE 2 **a** : recovery or relief from a disease **b** : an agency that cures a disease **c** : a course or period of treatment 3 : a process or method of curing — **cure·less** \-ləs\ *adj*
[2]**cure** *vb* 1 **a** : to restore to health, soundness, or normality **b** : to bring about recovery from 2 : to prepare by processing for keeping or use 3 : to undergo a curing process — **cur·er** *n*
[3]**cu·ré** \kyu̇-'rā\ *n* : a parish priest
cure–all \'kyu̇(ə)r-ˌȯl\ *n* : a remedy for all ills : PANACEA
cur·few \'kər-ˌfyü\ *n* 1 : an order or regulation requiring persons of a usu. specified class to be off the streets at a stated time 2 : a signal (as the ringing of a bell) to announce the beginning of a curfew
cu·ria \'k(y)u̇r-ē-ə\ *n, pl* **cu·ri·ae** \'kyu̇r-ē-ˌē, 'ku̇r-ē-ˌī\ *often cap* : the body of congregations, tribunals, and offices through which the pope governs the Roman Catholic Church — **cu·ri·al** \'kyu̇r-ē-əl\ *adj*
cu·rio \'kyu̇r-ē-ˌō\ *n, pl* **-ri·os** : a rare or unusual article
cu·ri·os·i·ty \ˌkyu̇r-ē-'äs-ət-ē\ *n, pl* **-ties** 1 : an eager desire to learn and often to learn what does not concern one 2 : something strange or unusual; *esp* : CURIO
cu·ri·ous \'kyu̇r-ē-əs\ *adj* 1 : eager to learn 2 : marked by inquisitiveness about others' concerns 3 : STRANGE, RARE, UNUSUAL 4 : ODD, ECCENTRIC — **cu·ri·ous·ly** *adv* — **cu·ri·ous·ness** *n*
[1]**curl** \'kərl\ *vb* 1 : to form into coils or ringlets 2 : to form into a curved shape : TWIST 3 **a** : to grow in coils or spirals **b** : to move in curves or spirals
[2]**curl** *n* 1 : a lock of hair that coils : RINGLET 2 : something having a spiral or winding form : COIL
curl·er \'kər-lər\ *n* : one that curls; *esp* : a device for putting a curl into hair
cur·lew \'kərl-(y)ü\ *n, pl* **curlews** *or* **curlew** : any of various largely brownish mostly migratory birds related to the woodcocks and distinguished by long legs and a long slender down-curved bill
curli·cue \'kər-li-ˌkyü\ *n* : a fancifully curved or spiral figure
curl·ing \'kər-liŋ\ *n* : a game in which two teams of four men each slide special stones over ice toward a target circle
curly \'kər-lē\ *adj* : tending to curl; *also* : having curls — **curl·i·ness** *n*
cur·mudg·eon \(ˌ)kər-'məj-ən\ *n* : an irascible old man
cur·rant \'kər-ənt\ *n* 1 : a small seedless raisin 2 : the acid edible fruit of several shrubs related to the gooseberries; *also* : a plant bearing currants
cur·ren·cy \'kər-ən-sē\ *n, pl* **-cies** 1 : general use or acceptance 2 : coin, government notes, and bank notes circulating as a medium of exchange
[1]**cur·rent** \'kər-ənt\ *adj* 1 : occurring in or belonging to the present time 2 : used as a medium of exchange 3 : generally accepted, used, or practiced — **cur·rent·ly** *adv* — **cur·rent·ness** *n*
[2]**current** *n* 1 **a** : the part of a fluid body moving continuously in a certain direction **b** : the swiftest part of a stream 2 : general course or movement : TREND 3 : a movement of electricity analogous to the flow of a stream of water
cur·ric·u·lum \kə-'rik-yə-ləm\ *n, pl* **-la** \-lə\ *or* **-lums** : a course of study; *esp* : the body of courses offered in a school or college or in one of its departments — **cur·ric·u·lar** \-lər\ *adj*
[1]**cur·ry** \'kər-ē\ *vt* **cur·ried**; **cur·ry·ing** 1 : to dress the coat of with a currycomb 2 : to treat (tanned leather) esp. by incorporating oil or grease — **cur·ri·er** *n*
[2]**cur·ry** \'kər-ē\ *n, pl* **curries** 1 : CURRY POWDER 2 : a food seasoned with curry powder
cur·ry·comb \-ˌkōm\ *n* : a comb with rows of metallic teeth or serrated ridges used esp. to curry horses — **currycomb** *vt*
curry powder *n* : a condiment consisting of ground spices
[1]**curse** \'kərs\ *n* 1 : a prayer that harm or injury may come upon someone 2 : a word or an expression used in cursing or swearing 3 : evil or misfortune that comes as if in answer to a curse
[2]**curse** *vb* 1 **a** : to call upon divine or supernatural power to send injury upon **b** : EXECRATE 2 **a** : to use profanely insolent language against : BLASPHEME **b** : to utter imprecations : SWEAR 3 : to bring great evil upon : AFFLICT
cursed \'kər-səd, 'kərst\ *adj* : being under or deserving a curse — **cursed·ly** *adv* — **cursed·ness** *n*
[1]**cur·sive** \'kər-siv\ *adj* : written or formed with the strokes of the letters joined together and the angles rounded
[2]**cursive** *n* : a style of printed letter imitating handwriting
cur·so·ry \'kərs-(ə-)rē\ *adj* : rapidly and often superficially performed : HASTY — **cur·so·ri·ly** \-(ə-)rə-lē\ *adv* — **cur·so·ri·ness** \-(ə-)rē-nəs\ *n*
curt \'kərt\ *adj* : rudely abrupt or brief — **curt·ly** *adv* — **curt·ness** *n*
cur·tail \(ˌ)kər-'tāl\ *vt* : to shorten or reduce by cutting off the end or a part of — **cur·tail·er** *n* — **cur·tail·ment** *n*
[1]**cur·tain** \'kərt-ᵊn\ *n* 1 : a hanging screen that usu. can be drawn up or back (as at a window) 2 : the ascent or descent of a theater curtain 3 : something that covers, conceals, or separates like a curtain
[2]**curtain** *vt* **cur·tained**; **cur·tain·ing** \'kərt-niŋ, -ᵊn-iŋ\ 1 : to furnish with curtains 2 : to veil or shut off with a curtain
[1]**curt·sy** *or* **curt·sey** \'kərt-sē\ *n, pl* **curtsies** *or* **curtseys** : a courteous bow made esp. by women that consists of a slight lowering of the body and bending of the knees
[2]**curtsy** *or* **curtsey** *vi* **curt·sied** *or* **curt·seyed**; **curt·sy·ing** *or* **curt·sey·ing** : to make a curtsy
cur·va·ture \'kər-və-ˌchu̇(ə)r, -chər\ *n* 1 : the act of curving : the state of being curved 2 : a measure or amount of curving
[1]**curve** \'kərv\ *vb* : to turn, change, or deviate from a straight line without sharp breaks or angularity
[2]**curve** *n* 1 : a curving line or surface : BEND 2 : something curved 3 : a ball thrown so that it swerves from its normal course — **curved** \'kərvd\ *adj*
[1]**cur·vet** \(ˌ)kər-'vet\ *n* : a prancing leap of a horse
[2]**curvet** *vi* **cur·vet·ted** *or* **cur·vet·ed**; **cur·vet·ting** *or* **cur·vet·ing** : to make a curvet; *also* : CAPER, PRANCE
[1]**cush·ion** \'ku̇sh-ən\ *n* 1 : a soft pillow or pad to rest on or against 2 : something resembling a cushion in use, shape, or softness 3 : a pad of springy rubber along the inside of the rim of a billiard table
[2]**cushion** *vt* **cush·ioned**; **cush·ion·ing** \-(ə-)niŋ\ 1 : to seat or place on a cushion 2 : to furnish with a cushion 3 **a** : to mitigate the effects of **b** : to shield from harm or injury
cusp \'kəsp\ *n* 1 : POINT, APEX 2 : a point on the grinding surface of a tooth
cus·pid \'kəs-pəd\ *n* : a canine tooth
cus·pi·dor \'kəs-pə-ˌdȯr\ *n* : SPITTOON
[1]**cuss** \'kəs\ *n* 1 : CURSE 2 : FELLOW
[2]**cuss** *vb* : CURSE — **cuss·er** *n*
cuss·ed \'kəs-əd\ *adj* 1 : CURSED 2 : PERVERSE, OBSTINATE
cuss·ed·ness \-əd-nəs\ *n* : disposition to perversity
cus·tard \'kəs-tərd\ *n* : a sweetened mixture of milk and eggs baked, boiled, or frozen
cus·to·di·al \ˌkə-'stōd-ē-əl\ *adj* : of or relating to custodians
cus·to·di·an \ˌkə-'stōd-ē-ən\ *n* : one that guards and protects or maintains; *esp* : one entrusted with guarding and keeping property or records
cus·to·dy \'kəs-təd-ē\ *n* 1 : immediate charge and control

exercised by a person or an authority **2 :** legal confinement; *esp* **:** IMPRISONMENT

[1]**cus·tom** \ˈkəs-təm\ *n* **1 :** a usage or practice common to many or habitual with an individual **2** *pl* **:** duties, tolls, or imposts imposed by a country on imports or exports **3 a :** business patronage **b :** CUSTOMERS

[2]**custom** *adj* **1 :** made or performed according to personal order **2 :** specializing in custom work or operation

cus·tom·ary \ˈkəs-tə-ˌmer-ē\ *adj* **1 :** based on or established by custom **2 :** commonly practiced or observed **:** HABITUAL — **cus·tom·ar·i·ly** \ˌkəs-tə-ˈmer-ə-lē\ *adv*

cus·tom–built \ˌkəs-təm-ˈbilt\ *adj* **:** built to individual order

cus·tom·er \ˈkəs-tə-mər\ *n* **1 :** one that usu. buys from or patronizes the same firm **2 :** PERSON, FELLOW

cus·tom·house \ˈkəs-təm-ˌhau̇s\ *n* **:** a building where customs and duties are paid or collected and where ships are entered and cleared at a port

cus·tom–made \ˌkəs-təm-ˈmād\ *adj* **:** made to individual order

[1]**cut** \ˈkət\ *vb* **cut; cut·ting 1 a :** to penetrate with an edged instrument **:** GASH **b :** to function as or like an edged tool **c :** to experience the growth of (a tooth) through the gum **2 a :** to hurt emotionally **b :** to strike sharply **c :** to have validity or effect **d :** to cause constriction **:** CHAFE **3 a :** to make less in amount **b :** to shorten by omissions **4 a :** MOW, REAP **b :** to divide into parts with an edged tool **c :** FELL, HEW **5 :** to remove as if with an edged tool **6 a :** to turn sharply **b :** to move fast **c :** INTERSECT, CROSS **7 a :** STOP **b :** to refuse to recognize (an acquaintance) **c :** to fail to attend (as a meeting or class) **8 a :** to engage in **:** PERFORM **b :** to give the appearance of

[2]**cut** *n* **1 :** something cut or cut off: as **a :** a part of a meat carcass **b :** an allotted part **:** SHARE **2 :** an effect produced by cutting: as **a :** a wound made by something sharp **b :** a passage made by cutting **c :** a pictorial illustration **3 a :** a gesture or expression that wounds the feelings **b :** REDUCTION **4 :** a voluntary absence from a class **5 :** the shape and style in which a thing is cut, formed, or made

cut–and–dried \ˌkət-ᵊn-ˈdrīd\ *adj* **:** according to a plan, set procedure, or formula **:** ROUTINE

cut·away \ˈkət-ə-ˌwā\ *n* **1 :** a coat with skirts tapering from the front waistline to form tails at the back **2 :** a picture or representation having or showing parts cut away

cut back *vb* **1 :** PRUNE **2 :** REDUCE, DECREASE **3 :** to interrupt the sequence of a plot by introducing events prior to those last presented

cut·back \ˈkət-ˌbak\ *n* **1 :** something cut back **2 :** REDUCTION

cut down *vb* **1 :** to remake in a smaller size **2 :** to strike down by or as if by cutting **3 :** REDUCE

cute \ˈkyüt\ *adj* **1 :** CLEVER, SHREWD **2 :** attractive or pretty esp. by reason of daintiness or delicacy — **cute·ly** *adv* — **cute·ness** *n*

cu·ti·cle \ˈkyüt-i-kəl\ *n* **:** an outer layer (as of skin) — **cu·tic·u·lar** \kyu̇-ˈtik-yə-lər\ *adj*

cut in *vb* **1 :** to thrust oneself into a position between others or belonging to another **2 :** to join in something suddenly **3 :** to interrupt a dancing couple and take one of them as a partner **4 :** INCLUDE

cut·lass \ˈkət-ləs\ *n* **:** a short curved sword formerly used by sailors on warships

cut·ler \ˈkət-lər\ *n* **:** one who makes, deals in, or repairs cutlery

cut·lery \ˈkət-lə-rē\ *n, pl* **-ler·ies :** edged or cutting tools; *esp* **:** implements for cutting and eating food

cut·let \ˈkət-lət\ *n* **:** a small slice of meat broiled or fried

cut off *vt* **1 :** to strike off **:** SEVER **2 :** to kill usu. suddenly or prematurely **3 :** to stop the passage of **4 :** SEPARATE, ISOLATE **5 :** DISINHERIT **6 a :** to stop the operation of **b :** to stop or interrupt while in communication

cut·off \ˈkət-ˌȯf\ *n* **1 :** the action or act of cutting off **2 a :** the channel formed when a stream cuts through the neck of an oxbow **b :** SHORTCUT **3 :** a device for cutting off — **cutoff** *adj*

cut out *vb* **1 :** to form or shape by or as if by cutting **2 :** to determine or assign through necessity **3 :** to take the place of **:** SUPPLANT **4 :** to remove from a series or circuit **:** DISCONNECT **5 :** to cease operating **6 :** to swerve out of a traffic line

cut·out \ˈkət-ˌau̇t\ *n* **:** something cut out or prepared for cutting out from something else — **cutout** *adj*

cut·over \ˌkət-ˌō-vər\ *adj* **:** having most of its salable timber cut

cut–rate \ˈkət-ˈrāt\ *adj* **:** marked by, offering, or making use of a reduced rate or price

cut·ter \ˈkət-ər\ *n* **1 :** one that cuts **2 a :** a boat used by warships for carrying passengers and stores to and from the shore **b :** a small one-masted sailing boat **c :** a small armed boat in the coast guard

[1]**cut·throat** \ˈkət-ˌthrōt\ *n* **:** MURDERER

[2]**cutthroat** *adj* **1 :** MURDEROUS, CRUEL **2 :** MERCILESS, RUTHLESS

[1]**cut·ting** \ˈkət-iŋ\ *n* **1 :** something cut or cut off; *esp* **:** a section of a plant capable of developing into a new plant **2 :** something made by cutting; *esp* **:** RECORDING

[2]**cutting** *adj* **1 :** EDGED, SHARP **2 :** wounding the feelings of others **:** SARCASTIC **3 :** INTENSE — **cut·ting·ly** *adv*

cut·tle·fish \ˈkət-ᵊl-ˌfish\ *n* **:** a 10-armed marine mollusk differing from the related squid in having a calcified internal shell

cut up *vb* **1 :** to cut or be cut into parts or pieces **2 :** to damage by or as if by cutting **3 :** to clown or act boisterously

cut·up \ˈkət-ˌəp\ *n* **:** one who clowns or acts boisterously

cut·worm \-ˌwərm\ *n* **:** any of various smooth-bodied moth larvae that feed on plants at night

cy·a·nide \ˈsī-ə-ˌnīd, -nəd\ *n* **:** a very poisonous potassium-containing or sodium-containing substance used esp. in electroplating

cy·cla·men \ˈsī-klə-mən\ *n* **:** any of a genus of plants of the primrose family grown as pot plants for their showy nodding flowers

[1]**cy·cle** \ˈsī-kəl, *5 also* ˈsik-əl\ *n* **1 :** a period of time taken up by a series of events or actions that repeat themselves regularly and in the same order **2 a :** a course or series of events or operations that recur regularly **b :** one complete series of changes of value of an alternating electric current **3 :** a long period of time **:** AGE **4 :** a group of poems, plays, novels, or songs treating the same theme **5 a :** BICYCLE **b :** MOTORCYCLE — **cy·clic** \ˈsī-klik, ˈsik-lik\ *or* **cy·cli·cal** \ˈsī-kli-kəl, ˈsik-li-\ *adj* — **cy·cli·cal·ly** \-k(ə-)lē\ *adv*

[2]**cy·cle** \ˈsī-kəl, *also* ˈsik-əl\ *vb* **cy·cled; cy·cling** \ˈsī-k(ə-)liŋ, ˈsik(-ə)-\ **:** to ride a cycle — **cy·cler** \ˈsī-k(ə-)lər, ˈsik(-ə)-\ *n*

cy·clist \ˈsī-k(ə-)ləst, ˈsik(-ə)-\ *n* **:** one who rides a cycle and esp. a bicycle

cy·clom·e·ter \sī-ˈkläm-ət-ər\ *n* **:** a device designed to record revolutions of a wheel and often used to register distance traversed by a wheeled vehicle

cy·clone \ˈsī-ˌklōn\ *n* **1 :** a storm or system of winds that rotates about a center of low atmospheric pressure, advances at a speed of 20 to 30 miles an hour, and often brings abundant rain **2 :** TORNADO — **cy·clon·ic** \sī-ˈklän-ik\ *adj* — **cy·clon·i·cal·ly** \-ˈklän-i-k(ə-)lē\ *adv*

cy·clo·pe·dia *or* **cy·clo·pae·dia** \ˌsī-klə-ˈpēd-ē-ə\ *n* **:** ENCYCLOPEDIA — **cy·clo·pe·dic** \-ˈpēd-ik\ *adj*

cy·clo·tron \ˈsī-klə-ˌträn\ *n* **:** a device for giving high speeds to charged particles by magnetic and electrical means

cyg·net \ˈsig-nət\ *n* **:** a young swan

cyl·in·der \ˈsil-ən-dər\ *n* **1 :** the solid figure formed by turning a rectangle about one side as an axis; *also* **:** a body of this form **2 :** a long round solid or hollow body (as the piston chamber of an engine or the part of a revolver which turns and holds the cartridges) — **cyl•in•dered** \-dərd\ *adj*

cy•lin•dri•cal \sə-'lin-dri-kəl\ *or* **cy•lin•dric** \-drik\ *adj* : of, relating to, or having the form or properties of a cylinder — **cy•lin•dri•cal•ly** \-dri-k(ə-)lē\ *adv*

cym•bal \'sim-bəl\ *n* : a concave brass plate that produces a brilliant clashing tone and that is struck with a drumstick or is used in pairs struck glancingly together — **cym•bal•ist** \-bə-ləst\ *n*

cyn•ic \'sin-ik\ *n* : one who believes that human conduct is motivated wholly by self-interest — **cynic** *adj*

cyn•i•cal \'sin-i-kəl\ *adj* : having the attitude or temper of a cynic; *esp* : contemptuously distrustful of human nature and motives — **cyn•i•cal•ly** \-k(ə-)lē\ *adv*

cyn•i•cism \'sin-ə-ˌsiz-əm\ *n* : cynical character or quality; *also* : an expression of such quality

cy•no•sure \'sī-nə-ˌshu̇r, 'sin-ə-\ *n* : a center of attraction or attention

cy•press \'sī-prəs\ *n* **1 a** : any of a genus of symmetrical mostly evergreen trees of the pine family with overlapping scalelike leaves **b** : any of several related trees; *esp* : either of two large swamp trees of the southern U.S. with hard red wood used for shingles **2** : the wood of a cypress tree

cyst \'sist\ *n* : a closed sac developing abnormally in a cavity or structure of the body

cys•tic \'sis-tik\ *adj* : of, relating to, or containing cysts

czar \'zär\ *n* **1** : the ruler of Russia until the 1917 revolution **2** : one having great power or authority — **czar•dom** \'zärd-əm\ *n* — **czar•ism** \'zär-ˌiz-əm\ *n* — **czar•ist** \'zär-əst\ *adj or n*

cza•ri•na \zä-'rē-nə\ *n* **1** : the wife of a czar **2** : a woman who has the rank of czar in her own right

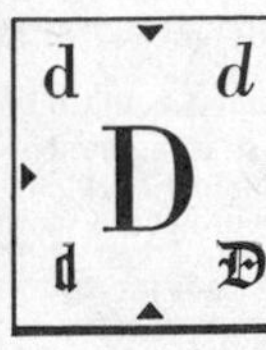

d \'dē\ *n, often cap* **1** : the 4th letter of the English alphabet **2** : the roman numeral 500 **3** : the musical tone D **4** : a grade rating a student's work as poor

[1]**dab** \'dab\ *n* **1** : a sudden blow or thrust : POKE **2** : a gentle touch or stroke : PAT

[2]**dab** *vb* **dabbed**; **dab•bing** **1** : to strike or touch lightly **2** : to apply lightly or irregularly : DAUB — **dab•ber** *n*

[3]**dab** *n* **1** : DAUB **2** : a small amount

dab•ble \'dab-əl\ *vb* **dab•bled**; **dab•bling** \'dab-(ə-)liŋ\ **1** : to wet by splashing : SPATTER **2** : to paddle or play in or as if in water **3** : to work or concern oneself lightly or superficially — **dab•bler** \-(ə-)lər\ *n*

dace \'dās\ *n, pl* **dace** : a small freshwater European fish related to the carp

dachs•hund \'däks-ˌhu̇nt\ *n, pl* **dachs•hunds** *or* **dachs•hun•de** \-ˌhu̇n-də\ : a small dog of a breed of German origin with a long body, short legs, and long drooping ears

dac•tyl \'dak-tᵊl\ *n* : a metrical foot consisting of one accented syllable followed by two unaccented syllables (as in *tenderly*) — **dac•tyl•ic** \dak-'til-ik\ *adj*

dad \'dad\ *n* : FATHER

dad•dy \'dad-ē\ *n, pl* **daddies** : FATHER

da•do \'dād-ō\ *n, pl* **dadoes** **1** : the part of a pedestal of a column between the base and the top moldings **2** : the lower part of an interior wall when specially decorated or faced

daemon *var of* DEMON

daf•fo•dil \'daf-ə-ˌdil\ *n* : a narcissus with usu. large flowers having a trumpetlike center

daft \'daft\ *adj* **1** : SILLY, FOOLISH **2** : MAD, INSANE — **daft•ly** *adv* — **daft•ness** *n*

dag•ger \'dag-ər\ *n* **1** : a short weapon for stabbing **2** : a character † used as a reference mark or to indicate a death date

da•guerre•o•type \də-'ger-(ē-)ə-ˌtīp\ *n* : an early photograph produced on a silver or a silver-covered copper plate

dahl•ia \'dal-yə, 'däl-\ *n* : any of a genus of American tuberous-rooted herbs related to the daisies that have opposite pinnate leaves and bright-petaled flower heads

[1]**dai•ly** \'dā-lē\ *adj* **1 a** : occurring, done, produced, or used every day or every weekday **b** : of or relating to every day **2** : computed in terms of one day — **daily** *adv*

[2]**daily** *n, pl* **dailies** : a newspaper published every weekday

[1]**dain•ty** \'dānt-ē\ *n, pl* **dainties** : DELICACY

[2]**dainty** *adj* **1** : pleasing to the taste : DELICIOUS **2** : delicately pretty **3 a** : having or showing delicate or finical taste **b** : FASTIDIOUS — **dain•ti•ly** \'dānt-ᵊl-ē\ *adv* — **dain•ti•ness** *n*

dai•qui•ri \'dī-kə-rē\ *n* : a cocktail made of rum, lime juice, and sugar

dairy \'de(ə)r-ē\ *n, pl* **dair•ies** **1** : CREAMERY **2** : a farm devoted to the production of milk

dair•y•ing \'der-ē-iŋ\ *n* : the business of operating a dairy

dair•y•maid \-ē-ˌmād\ *n* : a woman employed in a dairy

dair•y•man \-ē-mən, -ˌman\ *n* : one who operates a dairy farm or works in a dairy

da•is \'dā-əs\ *n* : a raised platform in a hall or large room giving prominence to those who occupy it

dai•sy \'dā-zē\ *n, pl* **daisies** : any of numerous plants of the composite family having flower heads in which the marginal flowers resemble petals

dale \'dāl\ *n* : VALLEY

dal•li•ance \'dal-ē-ən(t)s\ *n* **1** : PLAY; *esp* : amorous play (as flirting or caressing) **2** : frivolous action : TRIFLING

dal•ly \'dal-ē\ *vi* **dal•lied**; **dal•ly•ing** **1** : to act playfully; *esp* : to play amorously **2 a** : to waste time **b** : LINGER, DAWDLE — **dal•li•er** *n*

dal•ma•tian \dal-'mā-shən\ *n, often cap* : a large dog of a breed characterized by a white short-haired coat with black or brown spots

[1]**dam** \'dam\ *n* : a female parent — used esp. of a domestic animal

[2]**dam** *n* **1** : a barrier preventing the flow of a fluid (as water); *esp* : a barrier built across a watercourse **2** : a body of water confined by a dam

[3]**dam** *vt* **dammed**; **dam•ming** **1** : to provide or restrain with a dam **2** : to stop up : BLOCK

[1]**dam•age** \'dam-ij\ *n* **1** : a loss or harm resulting from injury to person, property, or reputation **2** *pl* : compensation in money imposed by law for loss or injury

[2]**damage** *vt* : to cause damage to

dam•ask \'dam-əsk\ *n* **1** : a firm lustrous reversible figured fabric used esp. for household linen **2** : a tough steel having decorative wavy lines — **damask** *adj*

dame \'dām\ *n* **1** : a woman of rank, station, or authority **2** : an elderly woman

[1]**damn** \'dam\ *vb* **1** : to condemn to a punishment or fate; *esp* : to condemn to hell **2** : to condemn as bad or as a failure **3** : to swear at : CURSE

[2]**damn** *n* **1** : the utterance of the word *damn* as a curse **2** : something of little value

dam•na•ble \'dam-nə-bəl\ *adj* **1** : liable to or deserving con-

demnation 2 : very bad : EXECRABLE — **dam·na·bly** \-blē\ *adv*
dam·na·tion \dam-ˈnā-shən\ *n* 1 : the act of damning 2 : the state of being damned
¹damp \ˈdamp\ *n* 1 : a noxious gas esp. in a coal mine 2 : MOISTURE, HUMIDITY 3 : DISCOURAGEMENT, CHECK
²damp *vt* 1 a : DEPRESS, DEJECT b : RESTRAIN, CHECK c : to check the vibration or oscillation of 2 : DAMPEN
³damp *adj* : MOIST — **damp·ly** *adv* — **damp·ness** *n*
damp·en \ˈdam-pən\ *vb* **damp·ened**; **damp·en·ing** \ˈdamp-(ə-)niŋ\ 1 : to check or diminish in activity or vigor : DEADEN 2 : to make or become damp — **damp·en·er** \ˈdamp-(ə-)nər\ *n*
damp·er \ˈdam-pər\ *n* : one that damps; *esp* : a valve or plate (as in the flue of a furnace) for regulating the draft
dam·sel \ˈdam-zəl\ *or* **dam·o·sel** *or* **dam·o·zel** \ˈdam-ə-ˌzel\ *n* : GIRL, MAIDEN
dam·son \ˈdam-zən\ *n* : an Asiatic plum grown for its small acid purple fruit; *also* : this fruit
¹dance \ˈdan(t)s\ *vb* 1 : to perform a rhythmic and patterned succession of bodily movements usu. to music 2 : to move quickly up and down or about 3 : to perform or take part in as a dancer — **danc·er** *n*
²dance *n* 1 : an act or instance of dancing 2 : a social gathering for dancing 3 : a piece of music by which dancing may be guided 4 : the art of dancing
dan·de·li·on \ˈdan-dᵊl-ˌī-ən\ *n* : any of a genus of yellow-flowered herbs related to chicory
dan·der \ˈdan-dər\ *n* : ANGER, TEMPER
dan·dle \ˈdan-dᵊl\ *vt* **dan·dled**; **dan·dling** \-dliŋ, -dᵊl-iŋ\ 1 : to move up and down in one's arms or on one's knee in affectionate play 2 : PAMPER, PET
dan·druff \ˈdan-drəf\ *n* : a scurf that forms on the scalp and comes off in small scales — **dan·druffy** \-ē\ *adj*
¹dan·dy \ˈdan-dē\ *n, pl* **dandies** 1 : a man unduly attentive to dress 2 : something excellent in its class — **dan·dy·ish** \-dē-ish\ *adj*
²dandy *adj* : very good : FIRST-RATE
dan·ger \ˈdān-jər\ *n* 1 : exposure or liability to injury, harm, or evil 2 : something that may cause injury or harm : a case of danger
dan·ger·ous \ˈdānj-(ə-)rəs\ *adj* 1 : exposing to or involving danger 2 : able or likely to injure — **dan·ger·ous·ly** *adv*
dan·gle \ˈdaŋ-gəl\ *vb* **dan·gled**; **dan·gling** \-g(ə-)liŋ\ 1 : to hang loosely esp. with a swinging motion 2 : to be a hanger-on or dependent 3 : to be left without proper grammatical connection in a sentence 4 : to cause to dangle : SWING 5 : to keep hanging uncertainly — **dan·gler** \-g(ə-)lər\ *n* — **dan·gling·ly** *adv*
dank \ˈdaŋk\ *adj* : unpleasantly moist or wet — **dank·ness** *n*
dan·seuse \däⁿ-ˈsə(r)z, -ˈsüz\ *n* : a female ballet dancer
dap·per \ˈdap-ər\ *adj* 1 : being neat and trim in dress or appearance : SPRUCE 2 : being alert and lively in movement and manners — **dap·per·ly** *adv* — **dap·per·ness** *n*
¹dap·ple \ˈdap-əl\ *n* 1 : any of numerous usu. cloudy and rounded spots of a color or shade different from their background 2 : a dappled state 3 : a dappled animal
²dapple *vb* **dap·pled**; **dap·pling** \ˈdap-(ə-)liŋ\ : to mark or become marked with dapples
¹dare \ˈda(ə)r\ *vb* 1 : to have sufficient courage : be bold enough to 2 : to challenge to perform an action esp. as a proof of courage 3 : to confront boldly
²dare *n* : an act or instance of daring : CHALLENGE
dare·dev·il \ˈda(ə)r-ˌdev-əl\ *n* : a recklessly bold person — **daredevil** *adj*
¹dar·ing \ˈda(ə)r-iŋ\ *adj* : venturesomely bold — **dar·ing·ly** *adv* — **dar·ing·ness** *n*
²daring *n* : venturesome boldness
¹dark \ˈdärk\ *adj* 1 a : being without light or without much light b : not giving off light 2 : not light in color; *esp* : of low lightness and medium saturation 3 : not bright and cheerful : GLOOMY 4 : being without knowledge and culture : IGNORANT 5 : SILENT, SECRETIVE 6 : not clear to the understanding — **dark·ish** \ˈdär-kish\ *adj* — **dark·ly** *adv* — **dark·ness** *n*
²dark *n* 1 a : absence of light : DARKNESS b : a place or time of little or no light : NIGHT, NIGHTFALL 2 : a dark or deep color
dark·en \ˈdär-kən\ *vb* **dark·ened**; **dark·en·ing** \ˈdärk-(ə-)niŋ\ 1 : to make or grow dark or darker 2 : to make less clear : DIM 3 : BESMIRCH, TARNISH 4 : to make or become gloomy or forbidding
¹dark·ling \ˈdär-kliŋ\ *adv* : in the dark
²darkling *adj* : DARK
dark·room \ˈdärk-ˌrüm, -ˌru̇m\ *n* : a room protected from rays of light harmful in the process of developing sensitive photographic plates and film
dark·some \ˈdärk-səm\ *adj* : gloomily somber : DARK
¹dar·ling \ˈdär-liŋ\ *n* 1 : a dearly loved person 2 : FAVORITE
²darling *adj* 1 : dearly loved : FAVORITE 2 : very pleasing : CHARMING — **dar·ling·ly** *adv*
¹darn \ˈdärn\ *vb* : to mend with interlacing stitches
²darn *n* : a place that has been darned
dar·nel \ˈdärn-ᵊl\ *n* : any of several usu. weedy grasses with bristly flower clusters
darning needle *n* 1 : a needle for darning 2 : DRAGONFLY
¹dart \ˈdärt\ *n* 1 a : a small missile usu. with a shaft pointed at one end and feathered on the other b *pl* : a game in which darts are thrown at a target 2 a : something projected with sudden speed; *esp* : a sharp glance b : something causing a sudden pain 3 : a stitched tapering fold in a garment 4 : a quick movement
²dart *vb* 1 : to throw with a sudden movement 2 : to thrust or move suddenly or rapidly
dart·er \ˈdärt-ər\ *n* : any of numerous small American freshwater fishes closely related to the perches
¹dash \ˈdash\ *vb* 1 : to knock, hurl, or thrust violently 2 : to break by striking or knocking 3 : SPLASH, SPATTER 4 a : DESTROY, RUIN b : DEPRESS, SADDEN 5 : to affect by mixing in something different 6 : to perform or finish hastily 7 : to move with sudden speed — **dash·er** *n*
²dash *n* 1 : a sudden burst or splash 2 a : a stroke of a pen b : a punctuation mark — used chiefly to indicate a break in the thought or structure of a sentence 3 : a small usu. distinctive addition 4 : conspicuous display 5 : animation in style and action 6 a : a sudden rush or attempt b : a short fast race 7 : DASHBOARD
dash·board \ˈdash-ˌbōrd\ *n* : an instrument panel below the windshield of an automobile or airplane
da·shi·ki \də-ˈshē-kē\ *n* : a usu. brightly colored loose-fitting pullover garment
dash·ing \-iŋ\ *adj* 1 : marked by vigorous action 2 : marked by smartness esp. in dress and manners — **dash·ing·ly** *adv*
das·tard \ˈdas-tərd\ *n* : COWARD; *esp* : one who sneakily commits malicious acts
das·tard·ly \-lē\ *adj* : treacherously cowardly — **das·tard·li·ness** *n*
da·ta \ˈdāt-ə, ˈdat-\ *n sing or pl* 1 : factual information (as measurements or statistics) used as a basis for reasoning, discussion, or calculation 2 : DATUM
¹date \ˈdāt\ *n* : the oblong edible fruit of a tall Old World palm; *also* : this palm
²date *n* 1 a : the time at which an event occurs b : a statement giving the time of execution or making (as of a coin or check) 2 : DURATION 3 : the period of time to which something belongs 4 a : APPOINTMENT; *esp* : a social engagement between two persons of opposite sex b : a person of the opposite sex with whom one has a social engagement — **to date** : up to the present moment

³**date** *vb* **1** : to determine the date of **2** : to record the date of or on **3** : to mark or reveal the date, age, or period of **4** : to make or have a date with **5 a** : ORIGINATE **b** : EXTEND **6** : to show qualities typical of a past period — **dat·a·ble** *or* **date·a·ble** *adj*
date·less \'dāt-ləs\ *adj* **1** : ENDLESS **2** : having no date **3** : too ancient to be dated **4** : TIMELESS
date·line \'dāt-ˌlīn\ *n* : a line in a publication giving the date and place of composition or issue
da·tive \'dāt-iv\ *adj* : of, relating to, or being the grammatical case that marks typically the indirect object of a verb — **dative** *n*
da·tum \'dāt-əm, 'dat-\ *n, pl* **da·ta** \-ə\ *or* **datums** : a single piece of data : FACT
¹**daub** \'dȯb\ *vb* **1** : to cover with soft adhesive matter : PLASTER **2** : SMEAR, SMUDGE **3** : to apply coloring material crudely to — **daub·er** *n*
²**daub** *n* **1** : something daubed on : SMEAR **2** : a crude picture
¹**daugh·ter** \'dȯt-ər\ *n* **1** : a female offspring esp. of human beings **2** : a human female having a specified ancestor or belonging to a group of common ancestry — **daugh·ter·ly** \-lē\ *adj*
²**daughter** *adj* : being offspring of the first generation
daugh·ter–in–law \'dȯt-ə-rən-ˌlȯ\ *n, pl* **daughters–in–law** : the wife of one's son
daunt \'dȯnt\ *vt* : to lessen the courage of : make afraid
daunt·less \-ləs\ *adj* : FEARLESS, UNDAUNTED — **daunt·less·ly** *adv* — **daunt·less·ness** *n*
dau·phin \'dȯ-fən\ *n, often cap* : the eldest son of a king of France
dav·en·port \'dav-ən-ˌpōrt\ *n* : a large upholstered sofa
da·vit \'dā-vət, 'dav-ət\ *n* : one of a pair of small cranes for raising and lowering small boats
daw·dle \'dȯd-ᵊl\ *vb* **daw·dled**; **daw·dling** \'dȯd-liŋ, -ᵊl-iŋ\ **1** : to spend time wastefully or idly : LINGER **2** : LOITER **3** : IDLE — **daw·dler** \'dȯd-lər, -ᵊl-ər\ *n*
¹**dawn** \'dȯn\ *vi* **1** : to begin to grow light as the sun rises **2** : to begin to appear or develop **3** : to begin to be perceived or understood
²**dawn** *n* **1** : the first appearance of light in the morning **2** : a first appearance : BEGINNING
day \'dā\ *n* **1 a** : the time of light between one night and the next **b** : DAYLIGHT **2** : the period of the earth's rotation on its axis **3** : a period of 24 hours beginning at midnight **4** : a specified day or date **5** : a specified time or period : AGE **6** : the conflict or contention of the day **7** : the time set apart by usage or law for work
day·book \'dā-ˌbu̇k\ *n* : DIARY, JOURNAL
day·break \-ˌbrāk\ *n* : DAWN
day coach *n* : COACH 1b
¹**day·dream** \'dā-ˌdrēm\ *n* : a dream experienced while awake; *esp* : a pleasant reverie usu. of wish fulfillment
²**daydream** *vi* : to have a daydream — **day·dream·er** *n*
day·light \'dā-ˌlīt\ *n* **1** : the light of day **2** : DAWN **3** : understanding of something that has been obscure
daylight saving time *n* : time usu. one hour ahead of standard time
Day of Atonement : YOM KIPPUR
day·star \'dā-ˌstär\ *n* : SUN 1a
day·time \'dā-ˌtīm\ *n* : the period of daylight
¹**daze** \'dāz\ *vt* **1** : to stupefy esp. by a blow : STUN **2** : to dazzle with light
²**daze** *n* : the state of being dazed
daz·zle \'daz-əl\ *vt* **daz·zled**; **daz·zling** \'daz-(ə-)liŋ\ **1** : to overpower with light **2** : to impress greatly or confound with brilliance — **dazzle** *n*
DDT \ˌdēd-(ˌ)ē-'tē\ *n* : a colorless odorless water-insoluble crystalline insecticide
dea·con \'dē-kən\ *n* : a subordinate officer in a Christian church — **dea·con·ess** \'dē-kə-nəs\ *n*
de·ac·ti·vate \(')dē-'ak-tə-ˌvāt\ *vt* : to make inactive or ineffective — **de·ac·ti·va·tion** \(ˌ)dē-ˌak-tə-'vā-shən\ *n*
¹**dead** \'ded\ *adj* **1** : deprived of life : having died : LIFELESS **2 a** : having the appearance of death : DEATHLY **b** : NUMB **c** : very tired **d** : UNRESPONSIVE **e** : EXTINGUISHED **3 a** : INANIMATE, INERT **b** : no longer producing or functioning : EXHAUSTED **4 a** : lacking power, significance, or effect **b** : no longer in use : OBSOLETE **c** : no longer active : EXTINCT **d** : lacking in gaiety or animation **e** : lacking in activity : QUIET **f** : IDLE, UNPRODUCTIVE **g** : lacking elasticity **h** : being out of action or out of use; *esp* : free from any connection to a source of voltage and free from electric charges **5 a** : not running or circulating : STAGNANT **b** : lacking warmth, vigor, or taste **6 a** : absolutely uniform **b** : UNERRING, EXACT **c** : ABRUPT **d** : COMPLETE, ABSOLUTE
²**dead** *n, pl* **dead** **1** : one that is dead — usu. used collectively **2** : the time of greatest quiet
³**dead** *adv* **1**: UTTERLY **2** : suddenly and completely **3** : DIRECTLY
dead·beat \'ded-ˌbēt\ *n* : one who persistently fails to pay his debts or his way
dead·en \'ded-ᵊn\ *vt* **dead·ened**; **dead·en·ing** \'ded-niŋ, -ᵊn-iŋ\ **1** : to impair in vigor or sensation : BLUNT **2 a** : to deprive of luster or spirit **b** : to make (as a wall) soundproof
dead end *n* : an end (as of a street) without an exit
dead–end \ˌded-ˌend\ *adj* : leading nowhere
dead·line \'ded-ˌlīn\ *n* : a date or time before which something must be done
dead·lock \-ˌläk\ *n* : a stoppage of action because neither of two equally powerful factions in a struggle will give in — **deadlock** *vt*
¹**dead·ly** \-lē\ *adj* **1** : likely to cause or capable of causing death **2 a** : aiming to kill or destroy : IMPLACABLE **b** : very accurate : UNERRING **3** : fatal to spiritual progress **4 a** : tending to deprive of force or vitality **b** : suggestive of death **5** : very great : EXTREME — **dead·li·ness** *n*
²**deadly** *adv* **1** : suggesting death **2** : EXTREMELY
dead·weight \'ded-'wāt\ *n* : the unrelieved weight of an inert mass
dead·wood \-ˌwu̇d\ *n* **1** : wood dead on the tree **2** : useless personnel or material
deaf \'def\ *adj* **1** : wholly or partly unable to hear **2** : unwilling to hear or listen — **deaf·ness** *n*
deaf·en \'def-ən\ *vb* **deaf·ened**; **deaf·en·ing** \'def-(ə-)niŋ\ **1** : to make deaf **2** : to cause deafness or stun with noise — **deaf·en·ing·ly** *adv*
deaf–mute \'def-'myüt\ *n* : a deaf person who cannot speak — **deaf–mute** *adj* — **deaf–mut·ism** \-'myüt-ˌiz-əm\ *n*
¹**deal** \'dēl\ *n* **1 a** : an indefinite quantity or degree **b** : a large quantity **2 a** : the act or right of distributing cards to players in a card game **b** : HAND 10b
²**deal** *vb* **dealt** \'delt\; **deal·ing** **1** : to give as one's portion : DISTRIBUTE **2** : ADMINISTER, BESTOW **3** : to have to do : TREAT **4** : to take action in regard to something **5 a** : to engage in bargaining : TRADE **b** : to sell or distribute something as a business — **deal·er** *n*
³**deal** *n* **1 a** : BARGAINING, NEGOTIATION **b** : the result of bargaining : a mutual agreement to do business (as to buy or sell) : TRANSACTION **2** : treatment received **3** : a secret or underhand agreement usu. to mutual advantage or to the disadvantage of other parties **4** : BARGAIN
⁴**deal** *n* : wood or a board of fir or pine — **deal** *adj*
deal·ing \-iŋ\ *n* **1** *pl* : INTERCOURSE, TRAFFIC; *esp* : business transactions **2** : a way of acting or of doing business
dean \'dēn\ *n* **1** : the head of the chapter of a collegiate or cathedral church **2 a** : the head of a division, faculty, college,

or school of a university **b** : a college or secondary school administrator in charge of counseling and disciplining students **3** : the senior member of a group — **dean·ship** \\-ˌship\\ *n*

dean·ery \\ˈdēn-(ə-)rē\\ *n, pl* **-er·ies** : the office, jurisdiction, or official residence of a clerical dean

¹dear \\ˈdi(ə)r\\ *adj* : SEVERE, SORE

²dear *adj* **1** : highly valued : PRECIOUS **2** : AFFECTIONATE, FOND **3** : high-priced : EXPENSIVE **4** : HEARTFELT — **dear** *adv* — **dear·ly** *adv* — **dear·ness** *n*

³dear *n* : a loved one : DARLING

dearth \\ˈdərth\\ *n* : SCARCITY, FAMINE

death \\ˈdeth\\ *n* **1** : a permanent cessation of all vital functions : the end of life **2** : the cause of loss of life **3** *cap* : the destroyer of life represented usu. as a skeleton with a scythe **4** : the state of being dead **5** : DESTRUCTION, EXTINCTION **6** : SLAUGHTER — **death·like** *adj*

death·bed \\ˈdeth-ˈbed\\ *n* **1** : the bed in which a person dies **2** : the last hours of life

death·blow \\-ˈblō\\ *n* : a destructive or killing stroke or event

death·less \\ˈdeth-ləs\\ *adj* : IMMORTAL, IMPERISHABLE

death·ly \\-lē\\ *adj* **1** : FATAL **2** : of, relating to, or suggestive of death — **deathly** *adv*

death's–head \\ˈdeths-ˌhed\\ *n* : a human skull emblematic of death

deb \\ˈdeb\\ *n* : DEBUTANTE

de·ba·cle \\di-ˈbäk-əl, -ˈbak-\\ *n* **1** : a violent disruption (as of an army) : ROUT **2** : BREAKDOWN, COLLAPSE

de·bar \\di-ˈbär\\ *vt* : to bar from having or doing something : PRECLUDE — **de·bar·ment** *n*

de·bark \\di-ˈbärk\\ *vb* : DISEMBARK — **de·bar·ka·tion** \\ˌdē-ˌbär-ˈkā-shən\\ *n*

de·base \\di-ˈbās\\ *vt* : to lower in character, dignity, quality, or value — **de·base·ment** *n* — **de·bas·er** *n*

de·bat·a·ble \\di-ˈbāt-ə-bəl\\ *adj* : able to be debated or disputed : open to question or dispute

¹de·bate \\di-ˈbāt\\ *n* **1** : the formal discussion of a motion before a deliberative body according to the rules of parliamentary procedure **2** : a regulated discussion of a proposition between two matched sides

²debate *vb* **1** : to discuss or examine a question by presenting and considering arguments on both sides **2** : to take part in a debate — **de·bat·er** *n*

de·bauch \\di-ˈbȯch\\ *vt* : to lead away from virtue or morality : SEDUCE, CORRUPT — **debauch** *n* — **de·bauch·ee** \\-ˌbȯch-ˈē\\ *n* — **de·bauch·er** *n*

de·bauch·ery \\-ˈbȯch-(ə-)rē\\ *n, pl* **-er·ies** : excessive indulgence of one's sensual desires

de·ben·ture \\di-ˈben-chər\\ *n* : a certificate of indebtedness; *esp* : a bond secured only by the general assets of the issuing government or corporation

de·bil·i·tate \\di-ˈbil-ə-ˌtāt\\ *vt* : to impair the strength of : WEAKEN — **de·bil·i·ta·tion** \\di-ˌbil-ə-ˈtā-shən\\ *n*

de·bil·i·ty \\di-ˈbil-ət-ē\\ *n, pl* **-ties** : an infirm or weakened state

¹deb·it \\ˈdeb-ət\\ *n* **1** : an entry in an account representing an amount paid out or owed **2** : a disadvantageous or unfavorable quality or character

²debit *vt* : to enter as a debit : charge with or as a debt

deb·o·nair \\ˌdeb-ə-ˈna(ə)r\\ *adj* : gaily and gracefully charming — **deb·o·nair·ly** *adv*

de·bouch \\di-ˈbüsh\\ *vi* : to march or issue out (as from a defile) into an open area — **de·bouch·ment** *n*

de·bris \\də-ˈbrē, ˈdā-ˌbrē\\ *n, pl* **de·bris** \\-ˈbrēz, -ˌbrēz\\ **1** : the remains of something broken down or destroyed : RUINS **2** : an accumulation of fragments of rock

debt \\ˈdet\\ *n* **1** : SIN, TRESPASS **2** : something owed to another : a thing or amount due : OBLIGATION **3** : a condition of owing; *esp* : the state of owing money in amounts greater than one can pay

debt·or \\ˈdet-ər\\ *n* **1** : SINNER **2** : one that owes a debt

de·bunk \\(ˈ)dē-ˈbəŋk\\ *vt* : to expose the sham or falseness in — **de·bunk·er** *n*

de·but \\ˈdā-ˌbyü, dā-ˈ\\ *n* **1** : a first public appearance **2** : a formal entrance into society

deb·u·tante \\ˈdeb-yu̇-ˌtänt\\ *n* : a young woman making her formal entrance into society

dec·ade \\ˈdek-ˌād, -əd\\ *n* : a period of 10 years

dec·a·dence \\ˈdek-əd-ən(t)s, di-ˈkād-ᵊn(t)s\\ *n* : DETERIORATION, DECLINE

dec·a·dent \\ˈdek-əd-ənt, di-ˈkād-ᵊnt\\ *adj* : marked by decay or decline — **decadent** *n* — **dec·a·dent·ly** *adv*

de·cal \\ˈdē-ˌkal\\ *n* : DECALCOMANIA

de·cal·ci·fy \\(ˈ)dē-ˈkal-sə-ˌfī\\ *vt* : to remove calcium or calcium compounds from — **de·cal·ci·fi·ca·tion** \\(ˌ)dē-ˌkal-sə-fə-ˈkā-shən\\ *n*

de·cal·co·ma·nia \\di-ˌkal-kə-ˈmā-nē-ə\\ *n* **1** : the art or process of transferring (as to glass) pictures and designs from specially prepared paper **2** : a picture or design prepared for transfer by decalcomania

dec·a·logue \\ˈdek-ə-ˌlȯg\\ *n* **1** *cap* : TEN COMMANDMENTS **2** : a basic set of rules carrying binding authority

de·camp \\di-ˈkamp\\ *vi* **1** : to break up a camp **2** : to depart suddenly : ABSCOND — **de·camp·ment** *n*

de·cant \\di-ˈkant\\ *vt* **1** : to pour from one vessel into another **2** : to draw off gently without disturbing any sediment — **de·can·ta·tion** \\ˌdē-ˌkan-ˈtā-shən\\ *n*

de·cant·er \\di-ˈkant-ər\\ *n* : an ornamental glass bottle used for serving wine

de·cap·i·tate \\di-ˈkap-ə-ˌtāt\\ *vt* : to cut off the head of : BEHEAD — **de·cap·i·ta·tion** \\di-ˌkap-ə-ˈtā-shən\\ *n*

deca·syl·lab·ic \\ˌdek-ə-sə-ˈlab-ik\\ *adj* : having or composed of verses having 10 syllables — **decasyllabic** *n*

de·cath·lon \\di-ˈkath-lən\\ *n* : an athletic contest in which each competitor participates in each of a series of 10 track-and-field events

de·cay \\di-ˈkā\\ *vb* **1** : to decline from a sound, prosperous, or healthy condition **2** : to undergo or cause to undergo decomposition — **decay** *n*

de·cease \\di-ˈsēs\\ *n* : passing from physical life : DEATH — **decease** *vi*

de·ceased \\-ˈsēst\\ *n, pl* **deceased** : a dead person

de·ceit \\di-ˈsēt\\ *n* **1** : the act or practice of deceiving : DECEPTION **2** : an attempt or device to deceive : TRICK **3** : DECEITFULNESS

de·ceit·ful \\-fəl\\ *adj* **1** : practicing or tending to practice deceit **2** : showing or containing deceit or fraud : MISLEADING, DECEPTIVE — **de·ceit·ful·ly** \\-fə-lē\\ *adv* — **de·ceit·ful·ness** *n*

de·ceive \\di-ˈsēv\\ *vb* **1** : to cause to believe what is untrue : MISLEAD **2** : to impose upon : deal with dishonestly : CHEAT **3** : to use or practice deceit — **de·ceiv·er** *n*

de·cel·er·ate \\(ˈ)dē-ˈsel-ə-ˌrāt\\ *vb* : to slow down — **de·cel·er·a·tion** \\(ˌ)dē-ˌsel-ə-ˈrā-shən\\ *n* — **de·cel·er·a·tor** \\(ˈ)dē-ˈsel-ə-ˌrāt-ər\\ *n*

De·cem·ber \\di-ˈsem-bər\\ *n* : the 12th month of the year

de·cen·cy \\ˈdēs-ᵊn-sē\\ *n, pl* **-cies** **1 a** : the quality or state of being decent : PROPRIETY **b** : conformity to standards of taste, propriety, or quality **2** : standard of propriety — usu. used in pl.

de·cen·ni·al \\di-ˈsen-ē-əl\\ *adj* **1** : consisting of 10 years **2** : happening every 10 years — **decennial** *n* — **de·cen·ni·al·ly** \\-ē-ə-lē\\ *adv*

de·cent \\ˈdēs-ᵊnt\\ *adj* **1 a** : conforming to standards of propriety, good taste, or morality **b** : modestly clothed **2** : free from immodesty or obscenity **3** : fairly good : ADEQUATE — **de·cent·ly** *adv*

de·cen·tral·ize \\(ˈ)dē-ˈsen-trə-ˌlīz\\ *vt* **1** : to disperse or distribute among various regional or local authorities **2** : to cause to withdraw from urban centers to outlying areas — **de·cen·tral·i·za·tion** \(,)dē-,sen-trə-lə-'zā-shən\ *n*

de·cep·tion \di-'sep-shən\ *n* **1 a :** the act of deceiving **b :** the fact or condition of being deceived **2 :** something that deceives : TRICK

de·cep·tive \di-'sep-tiv\ *adj* **:** tending or having power to deceive — **de·cep·tive·ly** *adv* — **de·cep·tive·ness** *n*

dec·i·bel \'des-ə-,bel\ *n* **1 :** a unit for expressing the ratio of two amounts of electric or acoustic signal power **2 :** a unit for measuring the relative loudness of sounds equal approximately to the smallest degree of difference of loudness ordinarily detectable by the human ear whose range includes about 130 decibels

de·cide \di-'sīd\ *vb* **1 :** to arrive at a solution that ends uncertainty or dispute about **2 :** to bring to a definitive end **3 :** to induce to come to a choice **4 :** to make a choice or judgment — **de·cid·a·ble** *adj* — **de·cid·er** *n*

de·cid·ed \-'sīd-əd\ *adj* **1 :** CLEAR, UNMISTAKABLE **2 :** FIRM, DETERMINED — **de·cid·ed·ly** *adv*

de·cid·u·ous \di-'sij-ə-wəs\ *adj* **1 :** falling off (as at the end of a growing period or stage of development) **2 :** having deciduous parts — **de·cid·u·ous·ly** *adv* — **de·cid·u·ous·ness** *n*

deci·gram \'des-ə-,gram\ *n* **:** a metric unit of mass and weight equal to 1/10 gram

deci·li·ter \'des-ə-,lēt-ər\ *n* **:** a metric unit of capacity equal to 1/10 liter

¹**dec·i·mal** \'des-ə-məl\ *adj* **1 :** numbered or proceeding by tens **2 :** based on the number 10 **3 :** expressed in a decimal fraction — **dec·i·mal·ly** \-mə-lē\ *adv*

²**decimal** *n* **:** a fraction in which the denominator is a power of 10 usu. not expressed but signified by a point placed at the left of the numerator (as .2 = 2/10, .25 = 25/100, .025 = 25/1000)

dec·i·mate \'des-ə-,māt\ *vt* **1 :** to take or destroy the tenth part of **2 :** to destroy a large part of — **dec·i·ma·tion** \,des-ə-'mā-shən\ *n*

deci·me·ter \'des-ə-,mēt-ər\ *n* **:** a metric unit of length equal to 1/10 meter

de·ci·pher \(')dē-'sī-fər\ *vt* **1 :** to convert into intelligible form; *esp* **:** to translate from secret writing (as code) **2 :** to make out the meaning of despite indistinctness or obscurity — **de·ci·pher·a·ble** *adj* — **de·ci·pher·ment** *n*

de·ci·sion \di-'sizh-ən\ *n* **1 :** the act or result of deciding esp. by giving judgment **2 :** promptness and firmness in deciding : DETERMINATION

de·ci·sive \di-'sī-siv\ *adj* **1 :** having the power to decide **2 :** of such nature as to settle a question or dispute **3 :** marked by or showing decision — **de·ci·sive·ly** *adv* — **de·ci·sive·ness** *n*

deci·stere \'des-ə-,sti(ə)r, -,ste(ə)r\ *n* **:** a metric unit of capacity equal to 1/10 cubic meter

¹**deck** \'dek\ *n* **1 :** a floorlike platform in a ship **2 :** something resembling the deck of a ship **3 :** a pack of playing cards

²**deck** *vt* **1 a :** to clothe elegantly : ARRAY **b :** DECORATE **2 :** to furnish with a deck

deck·hand \-,hand\ *n* **:** a seaman who performs manual duties

de·claim \di-'klām\ *vb* **:** to speak or deliver in the manner of a formal oration — **de·claim·er** *n* — **dec·la·ma·tion** \,dek-lə-'mā-shən\ *n*

de·clam·a·to·ry \di-'klam-ə-,tōr-ē\ *adj* **:** of, relating to, or marked by declamation or rhetorical display

dec·la·ra·tion \,dek-lə-'rā-shən\ *n* **1 :** the act of declaring : ANNOUNCEMENT **2 :** something declared or a document containing such a declaration

de·clar·a·tive \di-'klar-ət-iv\ *adj* **:** making a declaration or statement

de·clar·a·to·ry \di-'klar-ə-,tōr-ē\ *adj* **:** serving to declare

de·clare \di-'kla(ə)r\ *vb* **1 :** to make known formally or explicitly **2 :** to state emphatically : AFFIRM **3 :** to make a full statement of (taxable or dutiable property) — **de·clar·er** \-'klar-ər\ *n*

de·clen·sion \di-'klen-chən\ *n* **1 :** a schematic arrangement of the inflectional forms esp. of a noun or pronoun **2 :** DECLINE, DETERIORATION **3 :** DESCENT, SLOPE — **de·clen·sion·al** \-'klench-nəl, -ən-ᵊl\ *adj*

dec·li·na·tion \,dek-lə-'nā-shən\ *n* **1 :** a decline esp. from vigor **2 :** a bending downward : INCLINATION **3 :** a formal refusal — **dec·li·na·tion·al** \-'nā-shnəl, -shən-ᵊl\ *adj*

¹**de·cline** \di-'klīn\ *vb* **1 a :** to slope downward : DESCEND **b :** to bend down : DROOP **2 :** to reach or pass toward a lower level : RECEDE **3 :** to draw toward a close : WANE **4 a :** to withhold consent **b :** to refuse to undertake, engage in, or comply with **c :** to refuse to accept **5 :** to give in a prescribed order the inflectional forms of a noun, pronoun, or adjective — **de·clin·a·ble** *adj*

²**decline** *n* **1 :** the process of declining: **a :** a gradual sinking and wasting away **b :** a change to a lower state or level **2 :** the time when something is approaching its end **3 :** a downward slope : DECLIVITY **4 :** a wasting disease; *esp* **:** pulmonary tuberculosis

de·cliv·i·ty \di-'kliv-ət-ē\ *n, pl* **-ties** **1 :** downward inclination **2 :** a descending slope

de·coc·tion \di-'käk-shən\ *n* **:** an extracting (as of a flavor or active principle) by boiling in water; *also* **:** a product of this process

de·code \(')dē-'kōd\ *vt* **:** to convert (a coded message) into ordinary language — **de·cod·er** *n*

dé·col·le·té \(,)dā-,käl-ə-'tā\ *adj* **1 :** wearing a strapless or low-necked dress **2 :** having a low-cut neckline

de·col·or·ize \(')dē-'kəl-ə-,rīz\ *vt* **:** to remove color from — **de·col·or·iz·er** *n*

de·com·pose \,dē-kəm-'pōz\ *vb* **1 :** to separate a thing into its parts or into simpler compounds **2 :** to break down through chemical change : ROT — **de·com·pos·a·ble** *adj* — **de·com·po·si·tion** \(,)dē-,käm-pə-'zish-ən\ *n*

de·com·press \,dē-kəm-'pres\ *vt* **:** to release (as a diver) from pressure or compression — **de·com·pres·sion** \-'presh-ən\ *n*

de·con·tam·i·nate \,dē-kən-'tam-ə-,nāt\ *vt* **:** to rid of contamination — **de·con·tam·i·na·tion** \-,tam-ə-'nā-shən\ *n*

de·cor *or* **dé·cor** \dā-'kȯ(ə)r\ *n* **:** DECORATION; *esp* **:** the arrangement of accessories in interior decoration

dec·o·rate \'dek-ə-,rāt\ *vt* **1 :** to make more attractive by adding something beautiful or becoming **2 :** to award a decoration of honor to

dec·o·ra·tion \,dek-ə-'rā-shən\ *n* **1 :** the act or process of decorating **2 :** ORNAMENT **3 :** a badge of honor

dec·o·ra·tive \'dek-(ə-)rət-iv\ *adj* **:** serving to decorate : ORNAMENTAL

dec·o·ra·tor \'dek-ə-,rāt-ər\ *n* **:** one that decorates; *esp* **:** a person who designs or executes the interiors of buildings and their furnishings

dec·o·rous \'dek-ə-rəs, di-'kōr-əs\ *adj* **:** marked by propriety and good taste : CORRECT — **dec·o·rous·ly** *adv* — **dec·o·rous·ness** *n*

de·co·rum \di-'kōr-əm\ *n* **1 :** conformity to accepted standards of conduct : proper behavior **2 :** ORDERLINESS

¹**de·coy** \di-'kȯi, 'dē-,\ *n* **:** something intended to lure into a trap; *esp* **:** an artificial bird used to attract live birds within shot

²**decoy** *vt* **:** to lure by or as if by a decoy : ENTICE

¹**de·crease** \di-'krēs\ *vb* **:** to grow or cause to grow less

²**de·crease** \'dē-,krēs\ *n* **1 :** a process of decreasing : DIMINISHING, LESSENING **2 :** the amount by which a thing decreases : REDUCTION

¹**de·cree** \di-'krē\ *n* **1 :** an order usu. having the force of law : EDICT **2 :** a judicial decision

[2]**decree** *vb* **de·creed**; **de·cree·ing** 1 : to command or enjoin by decree 2 : to determine or order judicially
dec·re·ment \'dek-rə-mənt\ *n* 1 : gradual decrease 2 : the quantity lost by diminution or waste
de·crep·it \di-'krep-ət\ *adj* : broken down with age : worn out — **de·crep·it·ly** *adv* — **de·crep·it·ness** *n*
de·crep·i·tude \di-'krep-ə-ˌt(y)üd\ *n* : the quality or state of being decrepit : infirmity esp. from old age
de·cry \di-'krī\ *vt* 1 : to speak slightingly of : belittle publicly 2 : to find fault with : CONDEMN
de·cum·bent \di-'kəm-bənt\ *adj* : lying down — **de·cum·ben·cy** \-bən-sē\ *n*
ded·i·cate \'ded-i-ˌkāt\ *vt* 1 : to set apart for some purpose and esp. a sacred or serious purpose : DEVOTE 2 : to address or inscribe as a compliment — **ded·i·ca·tor** \-ˌkāt-ər\ *n*
ded·i·ca·tion \ˌded-i-'kā-shən\ *n* 1 a : an act or rite of dedicating to a divine being or to a sacred use b : a setting aside for a particular purpose 2 : a name and often a message prefixed to a literary work in tribute to a person or cause — **ded·i·ca·tive** \'ded-i-ˌkāt-iv\ *adj* — **ded·i·ca·to·ry** \'ded-i-kə-ˌtōr-ē\ *adj*
de·duce \di-'d(y)üs\ *vt* 1 : to trace the course or derivation of 2 a : to draw (a conclusion) necessarily from given premises b : to infer from a general principle — **de·duc·i·ble** \-'d(y)ü-sə-bəl\ *adj*
de·duct \di-'dəkt\ *vt* : SUBTRACT
de·duct·i·ble \di-'dək-tə-bəl\ *adj* : capable of being deducted : allowable as a deduction — **de·duct·i·bil·i·ty** \di-ˌdək-tə-'bil-ət-ē\ *n*
de·duc·tion \di-'dək-shən\ *n* 1 a : an act of taking away b : the deriving of a conclusion by reasoning 2 a : a conclusion reached by mental deduction b : something that is or may be subtracted : ABATEMENT — **de·duc·tive** \-'dək-tiv\ *adj* — **de·duc·tive·ly** *adv*
[1]**deed** \'dēd\ *n* 1 : something that is done : ACT 2 : a legal document by which one person transfers real property to another
[2]**deed** *vt* : to convey or transfer by deed
deem \'dēm\ *vb* : THINK, JUDGE, SUPPOSE
[1]**deep** \'dēp\ *adj* 1 a : extending far downward : having a great distance between the top and bottom surfaces : not shallow b : extending well inward from an outer surface c : extending well back from a front surface d : extending far outward from a center e : occurring or located near the outer limits 2 : having a specified extension downward or backward 3 a : difficult to understand b : MYSTERIOUS, OBSCURE c : WISE d : ENGROSSED, INVOLVED e : of great intensity : PROFOUND 4 a : high in saturation and low in lightness b : having a low musical pitch or range 5 a : coming from or situated well within b : covered, enclosed, or filled often to a specified degree — **deep·ly** *adv*
[2]**deep** *adv* 1 : to a great depth : DEEPLY 2 : far on : LATE
[3]**deep** *n* 1 : an extremely deep place or part; *esp* : OCEAN 2 : the middle or most intense part
deep·en \'dē-pən\ *vb* **deep·ened**; **deep·en·ing** \'dēp-(ə-)niŋ\ : to make or become deep or deeper
deep–root·ed \'dēp-'rüt-əd, -'rüt-\ *adj* : deeply implanted or established
deep–sea \'dēp-ˌsē\ *adj* : of, relating to, or occurring in the deeper parts of the sea
deep–seat·ed \'dēp-'sēt-əd\ *adj* 1 : situated far below the surface 2 : firmly established
deep–set \'dēp-'set\ *adj* : set far in
deer \'di(ə)r\ *n, pl* **deer** : any of a family of cloven-hoofed ruminant mammals with antlers borne by the males
deer·skin \-ˌskin\ *n* : leather made from the skin of a deer; *also* : a garment of such leather
de–es·ca·late \(')dē-'es-kə-ˌlāt\ *vb* : to decrease in extent, volume, or scope — **de–es·ca·la·tion** \(ˌ)dē-ˌes-kə-'lā-shən\ *n*
de·face \di-'fās\ *vt* : to destroy or mar the face or surface of — **de·face·ment** *n* — **de·fac·er** *n*
de fac·to \di-'fak-ˌtō\ *adj (or adv)* 1 : actually exercising power 2 : actually existing
de·fal·ca·tion \ˌdē-ˌfal-'kā-shən, -ˌfȯl-; ˌdef-əl-\ *n* : a misuse or theft of money by a person who holds it in trust for someone else
def·a·ma·tion \ˌdef-ə-'mā-shən\ *n* : the act of defaming : injury to the good name of another : SLANDER, LIBEL — **de·fam·a·to·ry** \di-'fam-ə-ˌtōr-ē\ *adj*
de·fame \di-'fām\ *vt* : to injure or destroy the good name of : speak evil of : LIBEL — **de·fam·er** *n*
[1]**de·fault** \di-'fȯlt\ *n* : failure to do something required by law or duty
[2]**default** *vb* : to fail to carry out a contract, obligation, or duty; *also* : to forfeit something by such failure — **de·fault·er** *n*
[1]**de·feat** \di-'fēt\ *vt* 1 : NULLIFY, FRUSTRATE 2 : to win victory over : BEAT
[2]**defeat** *n* 1 : frustration by prevention of success 2 a : an overthrow of an army in battle b : loss of a contest
de·feat·ism \-ˌiz-əm\ *n* : an attitude of expecting the defeat of one's own cause or of accepting such defeat — **de·feat·ist** \-əst\ *n or adj*
def·e·cate \'def-i-ˌkāt\ *vb* 1 : to free from impurity or corruption : REFINE 2 : to discharge feces from the bowels — **def·e·ca·tion** \ˌdef-i-'kā-shən\ *n*
[1]**de·fect** \'dē-ˌfekt, di-'\ *n* : a lack of something necessary for completeness or perfection : FAULT, IMPERFECTION
[2]**de·fect** \di-'fekt\ *vi* : to desert a cause or party often in order to espouse another — **de·fec·tion** \-'fek-shən\ *n* — **de·fec·tor** \-'fek-tər\ *n*
de·fec·tive \di-'fek-tiv\ *adj* : wanting in something essential : FAULTY — **de·fec·tive·ly** *adv* — **de·fec·tive·ness** *n*
de·fend \di-'fend\ *vb* 1 : to repel danger or attack 2 : to act as attorney for 3 : to oppose the claim of another in a lawsuit : CONTEST 4 : to maintain against opposition — **de·fend·er** *n*
de·fend·ant \di-'fen-dənt\ *n* : a person required to make answer in a legal action or suit
de·fense \di-'fen(t)s\ *n* 1 : the act of defending : resistance against attack 2 : capability of resisting attack 3 a : means or method of defending b : an argument in support or justification 4 : a defending party or group (as in a court of law or on a playing field) 5 : the answer made by the defendant in a legal action or suit — **de·fense·less** \-ləs\ *adj*
de·fen·si·ble \di-'fen(t)-sə-bəl\ *adj* : capable of being defended — **de·fen·si·bil·i·ty** \-ˌfen(t)-sə-'bil-ət-ē\ *n* — **de·fen·si·bly** \-'fen(t)-sə-blē\ *adv*
[1]**de·fen·sive** \di-'fen(t)-siv\ *adj* : of or relating to defense : serving or intended to defend or protect — **de·fen·sive·ly** *adv* — **de·fen·sive·ness** *n*
[2]**defensive** *n* : a defensive position
[1]**de·fer** \di-'fər\ *vt* **de·ferred**; **de·fer·ring** : to put off : DELAY — **de·fer·ra·ble** \-'fər-ə-bəl\ *adj*
[2]**defer** *vi* **de·ferred**; **de·fer·ring** : to submit or yield to another's wish or opinion
def·er·ence \'def-(ə-)rən(t)s\ *n* : courteous, respectful, or ingratiating regard for another's wishes
def·er·en·tial \ˌdef-ə-'ren-chəl\ *adj* : showing or expressing deference — **def·er·en·tial·ly** \-'rench-(ə-)lē\ *adv*
de·fer·ment \di-'fər-mənt\ *n* : the act of delaying; *esp* : official postponement of military service
de·fi·ance \di-'fī-ən(t)s\ *n* 1 : the act or an instance of defying 2 : disposition to resist : contempt of opposition
de·fi·ant \-ənt\ *adj* : full of defiance : BOLD, INSOLENT — **de·fi·ant·ly** *adv*
de·fi·cien·cy \di-'fish-ən-sē\ *n, pl* **-cies** 1 : the quality or state of being deficient 2 : INADEQUACY

de·fi·cient \di-ˈfish-ənt\ *adj* : lacking something necessary for completeness : DEFECTIVE — **de·fi·cient·ly** *adv*
def·i·cit \ˈdef-ə-sət\ *n* : a deficiency in amount; *esp* : an excess of expenditures over revenue
¹de·file \di-ˈfīl\ *vt* **1** : to make filthy : DIRTY **2** : to corrupt the purity or perfection of **3** : RAVISH, VIOLATE **4** : to make ceremonially unclean : DESECRATE **5** : SULLY, DISHONOR — **de·file·ment** *n* — **de·fil·er** *n*
²de·file \di-ˈfīl, ˈdē-ˌ\ *n* : a narrow passage or gorge
de·fine \di-ˈfīn\ *vb* **1 a** : to fix or mark the limits of **b** : to make distinct in outline **2 a** : to determine the essential qualities or precise meaning of **b** : to discover and set forth the meaning — **de·fin·a·ble** *adj* — **de·fin·er** *n*
def·i·nite \ˈdef-(ə-)nət\ *adj* **1** : having certain or distinct limits : FIXED **2** : clear in meaning : EXACT, EXPLICIT **3** : typically designating an identified or immediately identifiable person or thing — **def·i·nite·ly** *adv* — **def·i·nite·ness** *n*
def·i·ni·tion \ˌdef-ə-ˈnish-ən\ *n* **1** : an act of determining or settling the limits **2 a** : a statement of the meaning of a word or word group **b** : the action or process of stating such a meaning **3 a** : the action or the power of making definite and clear **b** : CLARITY, DISTINCTNESS — **def·i·ni·tion·al** \-ˈnish-nəl, -ˈnish-ən-ᵊl\ *adj*
de·fin·i·tive \di-ˈfin-ət-iv\ *adj* **1** : serving to provide a final solution : CONCLUSIVE **2** : being authoritative and apparently exhaustive **3** : serving to define or specify precisely **4** : fully differentiated or developed — **de·fin·i·tive·ly** *adv* — **de·fin·i·tive·ness** *n*
de·flate \di-ˈflāt\ *vb* **1** : to release air or gas from **2** : to cause to contract from an abnormally high level : reduce from a state of inflation **3** : to become deflated : COLLAPSE
de·fla·tion \-ˈflā-shən\ *n* **1** : an act or instance of deflating : the state of being deflated **2** : a contraction in the volume of available money or credit resulting in a decline of the general price level — **de·fla·tion·ary** \-shə-ˌner-ē\ *adj*
de·flect \di-ˈflekt\ *vb* : to turn or cause to turn aside (as from a course, direction, or position) — **de·flec·tion** \-ˈflek-shən\ *n*
de·form \di-ˈfȯrm\ *vb* **1** : to spoil the form or natural appearance of : DISFIGURE **2** : to become misshapen or changed in shape — **de·for·ma·tion** \ˌdē-ˌfȯr-ˈmā-shən, ˌdef-ər-\ *n*
de·formed \-ˈfȯrmd\ *adj* : distorted or unshapely in form
de·for·mi·ty \di-ˈfȯr-mət-ē\ *n, pl* **-ties** **1** : the state of being deformed **2** : a physical blemish or distortion : DISFIGUREMENT **3** : a moral or aesthetic flaw
de·fraud \di-ˈfrȯd\ *vt* : to deprive of something by trickery, deception, or fraud — **de·frau·da·tion** \ˌdē-ˌfrȯ-ˈdā-shən\ *n* — **de·fraud·er** *n*
de·fray \di-ˈfrā\ *vt* : to pay or provide for the payment of — **de·fray·a·ble** *adj* — **de·fray·al** \-ˈfrā(-ə)l\ *n*
de·frost \di-ˈfrȯst\ *vb* **1** : to release from a frozen state : thaw out **2** : to free from ice — **de·frost·er** *n*
deft \ˈdeft\ *adj* : quick and neat in action : SKILLFUL — **deft·ly** *adv* — **deft·ness** *n*
de·funct \di-ˈfəŋ(k)t\ *adj* : DEAD, EXTINCT
de·fy \di-ˈfī\ *vt* **de·fied**; **de·fy·ing** **1** : to challenge to do something considered impossible : DARE **2** : to refuse boldly to obey or to yield to : DISREGARD **3** : to resist attempts at : WITHSTAND, BAFFLE — **de·fi·er** *n*
de·gen·er·a·cy \di-ˈjen-(ə-)rə-sē\ *n, pl* **-cies** **1** : the state of being or process of becoming degenerate : DEGRADATION, DEBASEMENT **2** : sexual perversion
¹de·gen·er·ate \di-ˈjen-(ə-)rət\ *adj* : having sunk to a condition below that which is normal to a type : having declined (as in nature or character) from an ancestral or former state : DEBASED, DEGRADED — **de·gen·er·ate·ly** *adv* — **de·gen·er·ate·ness** *n*
²degenerate *n* : a degenerate person; *esp* : a sexual pervert
³de·gen·er·ate \-ə-ˌrāt\ *vi* : to pass from a higher to a lower type or condition : DETERIORATE
de·gen·er·a·tion \di-ˌjen-ə-ˈrā-shən\ *n* : a lowering of power, vitality, or essential quality to a feebler and poorer kind or state
de·gen·er·a·tive \di-ˈjen-ə-ˌrāt-iv\ *adj* : of, relating to, or tending to cause degeneration
deg·ra·da·tion \ˌdeg-rə-ˈdā-shən\ *n* **1 a** : a reduction in rank, dignity, or standing **b** : removal from office **2** : DISGRACE **3** : DETERIORATION, DEGENERATION
de·grade \di-ˈgrād\ *vb* **1** : to reduce from a higher to a lower rank or degree : deprive of an office or position **2** : to lower the character of : DEBASE **3** : to reduce the complexity of : DECOMPOSE — **de·grad·er** *n*
de·gree \di-ˈgrē\ *n* **1** : a step or stage in a process, course, or classificatory order **2 a** : the extent, intensity, or scope of something esp. as measured by a graded series **b** : one of the forms or sets of forms used in the comparison of an adjective or adverb **3 a** : a rank or grade of official, ecclesiastical, or social position **b** : the civil condition or status of a person **4** : a title conferred upon students by a college, university, or professional school upon completion of a unified program of study **5** : a 360th part of the circumference of a circle **6 a** : a line or space of the musical staff **b** : a step, note, or tone of a musical scale — **to a degree** **1** : to a remarkable extent **2** : in a small way
de·hu·man·ize \(ˈ)dē-ˈ(h)yü-mə-ˌnīz\ *vt* : to divest of human qualities or personality — **de·hu·man·i·za·tion** \(ˌ)dē-ˌ(h)yü-mə-nə-ˈzā-shən\ *n*
de·hy·drate \(ˈ)dē-ˈhī-ˌdrāt\ *vb* **1** : to remove water from (as foods) **2** : to lose water or body fluids — **de·hy·dra·tion** \ˌdē-ˌhī-ˈdrā-shən\ *n*
de·ice \(ˈ)dē-ˈīs\ *vt* : to keep free or rid of ice — **de·ic·er** *n*
de·i·fy \ˈdē-ə-ˌfī\ *vt* **-fied**; **-fy·ing** **1 a** : to make a god of **b** : to take as an object of worship **2** : to glorify as of supreme worth — **de·i·fi·ca·tion** \ˌdē-ə-fə-ˈkā-shən\ *n*
deign \ˈdān\ *vb* : CONDESCEND
de·ism \ˈdē-ˌiz-əm\ *n* : a movement or system of thought advocating natural religion based on human reason rather than revelation — **de·ist** \ˈdē-əst\ *n*
de·i·ty \ˈdē-ət-ē\ *n, pl* **-ties** **1 a** : DIVINITY 1 **b** *cap* : ²GOD **2 a** : GOD **b** : GODDESS
de·ject·ed \di-ˈjek-təd\ *adj* : cast down in spirits : LOW-SPIRITED, SAD, DEPRESSED — **de·ject·ed·ly** *adv*
de·jec·tion \di-ˈjek-shən\ *n* : lowness of spirits : SADNESS
de ju·re \(ˈ)dē-ˈju̇(ə)r-ē\ *adj (or adv)* : existing or exercising power by legal right
deka·gram \ˈdek-ə-ˌgram\ *n* : a metric unit of mass and weight equal to 10 grams
deka·li·ter \ˈdek-ə-ˌlēt-ər\ *n* : a metric unit of capacity equal to 10 liters
deka·me·ter \ˈdek-ə-ˌmēt-ər\ *n* : a metric unit of length equal to 10 meters
deka·stere \ˈdek-ə-ˌsti(ə)r, -ˌste(ə)r\ *n* : a metric unit of volume equal to 10 cubic meters
¹de·lay \di-ˈlā\ *n* **1** : the act of delaying : the state of being delayed **2** : the time during which something is delayed
²delay *vb* **1** : to put off : POSTPONE **2** : to stop, detain, or hinder for a time **3** : to move or act slowly
de·le \ˈdē-(ˌ)lē\ *vt* **de·led**; **de·le·ing** : to remove (as a word) from typeset matter : ERASE, DELETE
de·lec·ta·ble \di-ˈlek-tə-bəl\ *adj* **1** : highly pleasing : DELIGHTFUL **2** : DELICIOUS — **de·lec·ta·bly** \-blē\ *adv*
de·lec·ta·tion \ˌdē-ˌlek-ˈtā-shən\ *n* **1** : DELIGHT **2** : PLEASURE, ENJOYMENT, DIVERSION
¹del·e·gate \ˈdel-i-gət\ *n* : a person sent with power to act for another: as **a** : a representative to a convention, conference, or assembly **b** : a representative of a U.S. territory in the

House of Representatives **c :** a member of the lower house of the legislature of Maryland, Virginia, or West Virginia

²del·e·gate \-ˌgāt\ *vt* **1 :** to entrust to another **2 :** to appoint as one's delegate

del·e·ga·tion \ˌdel-i-ˈgā-shən\ *n* **1 :** the act of delegating power or authority to another **2 :** one or more persons chosen to represent others

de·lete \di-ˈlēt\ *vt* **:** to eliminate esp. by blotting out, cutting out, or erasing

del·e·te·ri·ous \ˌdel-ə-ˈtir-ē-əs\ *adj* **:** HARMFUL, NOXIOUS

de·le·tion \di-ˈlē-shən\ *n* **1 :** an act of deleting **2 :** something deleted

delft \ˈdelft\ *or* **delft·ware** \-ˌwa(ə)r\ *n* **1 :** a Dutch brown pottery covered with an opaque white glaze upon which the predominantly blue decoration is painted **2 :** glazed pottery esp. when blue and white

¹de·lib·er·ate \di-ˈlib-(ə-)rət\ *adj* **1 :** decided upon as a result of careful thought **:** carefully considered **2 :** weighing facts and arguments **:** careful and slow in deciding **3 :** slow in action **:** not hurried — **de·lib·er·ate·ly** *adv* — **de·lib·er·ate·ness** *n*

²de·lib·er·ate \di-ˈlib-ə-ˌrāt\ *vb* **:** to consider carefully

de·lib·er·a·tion \di-ˌlib-ə-ˈrā-shən\ *n* **1 :** the act of deliberating **2 :** a discussion and consideration of the reasons for and against a measure or question **3 :** the quality of being deliberate **:** DELIBERATENESS

de·lib·er·a·tive \di-ˈlib-ə-ˌrāt-iv, -ˈlib-(ə-)rət-\ *adj* **:** of or relating to deliberation **:** engaged in or devoted to deliberation — **de·lib·er·a·tive·ly** *adv*

del·i·ca·cy \ˈdel-i-kə-sē\ *n, pl* **-cies 1 :** something pleasing to eat because it is rare or luxurious **2 a :** FINENESS, DAINTINESS **b :** FRAILTY **3 :** nicety or subtle expressiveness of touch (as in painting or music) **4 a :** precise and refined perception and discrimination **b :** extreme sensitivity **:** PRECISION **5 a :** nice sensibility in feeling or conduct **b :** SQUEAMISHNESS **6 :** the quality or state of requiring delicate treatment

del·i·cate \ˈdel-i-kət\ *adj* **1 a :** pleasing to the sense of taste or smell esp. in a mild or subtle way **b :** marked by daintiness or charm of color, lines, or proportions **2 :** marked by keen sensitivity or fine discrimination **:** FASTIDIOUS **3 a :** marked by minute precision **b :** exhibiting extreme sensitivity **4 :** precariously balanced **5 a :** marked by meticulous technique or operation or by execution with adroit finesse **b :** marked by fineness of structure, workmanship, or texture **c :** easily torn or hurt; *also* **:** WEAK, SICKLY **d :** marked by fine subtlety **e :** marked by tact; *also* **:** requiring tact — **del·i·cate·ly** *adv*

del·i·ca·tes·sen \ˌdel-i-kə-ˈtes-ᵊn\ *n pl* **1 :** ready-to-eat food products (as cooked meats and prepared salads) **2** *sing, pl* **delicatessens :** a store selling delicatessen

de·li·cious \di-ˈlish-əs\ *adj* **:** affording great pleasure **:** DELIGHTFUL; *esp* **:** very pleasing to the taste or smell — **de·li·cious·ly** *adv* — **de·li·cious·ness** *n*

¹de·light \di-ˈlīt\ *n* **1 :** extreme pleasure or satisfaction **:** JOY **2 :** something that gives great pleasure

²delight *vb* **1 :** to take great pleasure **2 :** to give keen enjoyment **3 :** to give joy or satisfaction to **:** please greatly

de·light·ed \-əd\ *adj* **:** highly pleased **:** GRATIFIED, JOYOUS — **de·light·ed·ly** *adv* — **de·light·ed·ness** *n*

de·light·ful \di-ˈlīt-fəl\ *adj* **:** highly pleasing **:** giving delight — **de·light·ful·ly** \-fə-lē\ *adv* — **de·light·ful·ness** *n*

de·lim·it \di-ˈlim-ət\ *vt* **:** to fix the limits of **:** BOUND — **de·lim·i·ta·tion** \-ˌlim-ə-ˈtā-shən\ *n*

de·lin·e·ate \di-ˈlin-ē-ˌāt\ *vt* **1 a :** to indicate by lines drawn in the form or figure of **:** PORTRAY, SKETCH **b :** to represent accurately **2 :** to describe in usu. sharp or vivid detail — **de·lin·e·a·tor** \-ē-ˌāt-ər\ *n*

de·lin·e·a·tion \di-ˌlin-ē-ˈā-shən\ *n* **1 :** the act of representing, portraying, or describing graphically or verbally **2 :** something made by delineating

de·lin·quen·cy \di-ˈliŋ-kwən-sē\ *n, pl* **-cies :** the quality or state of being delinquent

¹de·lin·quent \-kwənt\ *n* **:** a delinquent person

²delinquent *adj* **1 :** offending by neglect or violation of duty or of law **2 :** being in arrears in payment

del·i·quesce \ˌdel-ə-ˈkwes\ *vi* **:** to melt away: **a :** to dissolve gradually by absorbing moisture from the air **b :** to become soft or liquid — **del·i·ques·cence** \-ˈkwes-ᵊn(t)s\ *n*

del·i·ques·cent \-ˈkwes-ᵊnt\ *adj* **:** marked by or undergoing deliquescence

de·lir·i·ous \di-ˈlir-ē-əs\ *adj* **1 :** of or relating to delirium **2 :** marked by delirium; *also* **:** wildly excited — **de·lir·i·ous·ly** *adv* — **de·lir·i·ous·ness** *n*

de·lir·i·um \-ˈlir-ē-əm\ *n* **1 :** a mental disturbance characterized by confusion, disordered speech, and hallucinations **2 :** frenzied excitement

de·liv·er \di-ˈliv-ər\ *vt* **de·liv·ered; de·liv·er·ing** \-ˈliv-(ə-)riŋ\ **1 :** to set free **:** SAVE **2 :** to hand over **:** CONVEY, SURRENDER **3 :** to assist in giving birth; *also* **:** to aid in the birth of **4 :** UTTER, RELATE, COMMUNICATE **5 :** to send to an intended target or destination — **de·liv·er·a·ble** *adj* — **de·liv·er·er** *n*

de·liv·er·ance \di-ˈliv-(ə-)rən(t)s\ *n* **1 :** a delivering or a being delivered **:** LIBERATION, RESCUE **2 :** something delivered or communicated; *esp* **:** a publicly expressed opinion

de·liv·ery \di-ˈliv-(ə-)rē\ *n, pl* **-er·ies 1 :** a delivering from restraint **2 a :** the act of handing over **b :** something delivered at one time or in one unit **3 :** the act of giving birth **4 :** a delivering esp. of a speech; *also* **:** manner or style of uttering in speech or song **5 :** the act or manner of sending forth or throwing

dell \ˈdel\ *n* **:** a secluded small valley

de·louse \(ˈ)dē-ˈlau̇s, -ˈlau̇z\ *vt* **:** to remove lice from

del·phin·i·um \del-ˈfin-ē-əm\ *n* **:** any of a large genus of chiefly perennial erect branching herbs related to the buttercups and widely grown for their irregular flowers in showy spikes

del·ta \ˈdel-tə\ *n* **:** the triangular or fan-shaped piece of land made by deposits of mud and sand at the mouth of a river — **del·ta·ic** \del-ˈtā-ik\ *adj*

de·lude \di-ˈlüd\ *vt* **:** to lead from truth or into error **:** mislead the mind or judgment of **:** DECEIVE, TRICK — **de·lud·er** *n* — **de·lud·ing·ly** *adv*

¹del·uge \ˈdel-(ˌ)yüj\ *n* **1 a :** an overflowing of the land by water **:** FLOOD **b :** a drenching rain **2 :** an irresistible rush

²deluge *vt* **1 :** to overflow with water **:** INUNDATE, FLOOD **2 :** to overwhelm as if with a deluge

de·lu·sion \di-ˈlü-zhən\ *n* **1 :** the act of deluding **:** the state of being deluded **2 a :** something that is falsely or delusively believed or propagated **b :** a persistent belief in something false typical of some mental disorders — **de·lu·sion·al** \-ˈlüzh-nəl, -ˈlü-zhən-ᵊl\ *adj*

de·lu·sive \-ˈlü-siv\ *adj* **:** deluding or apt to delude — **de·lu·sive·ly** *adv* — **de·lu·sive·ness** *n*

de·luxe \di-ˈlu̇ks, -ˈləks\ *adj* **:** notably luxurious or elegant

delve \ˈdelv\ *vi* **1 :** to dig or labor with a spade **2 :** to seek laboriously for information in written records (as books)

de·mag·ne·tize \(ˈ)dē-ˈmag-nə-ˌtīz\ *vt* **:** to deprive of magnetic properties — **de·mag·ne·ti·za·tion** \(ˌ)dē-ˌmag-nət-ə-ˈzā-shən\ *n* — **de·mag·ne·tiz·er** \(ˈ)dē-ˈmag-nə-ˌtī-zər\ *n*

dem·a·gogue *or* **dem·a·gog** \ˈdem-ə-ˌgäg\ *n* **:** a person who appeals to the emotions and prejudices of people in order to arouse discontent and advance his own political ends — **dem·a·gog·ic** \ˌdem-ə-ˈgäj-ik, -ˈgäg-\ *or* **dem·a·gog·i·cal** \-i-kəl\ *adj* — **dem·a·gogu·ery** \ˈdem-ə-ˌgäg-(ə-)rē\ *n* — **dem·a·gogy** \-ˌgäj-ē, -ˌgäg-ē\ *n*

¹de·mand \di-ˈmand\ *n* **1 a :** an act of demanding or asking esp. with authority **b :** something claimed as due **2 a :** an expressed desire to own or use something **b :** the ability and desire to purchase goods or services at a specified time and price **c** : the quantity of an article or service that is wanted at a stated price **3 a** : a seeking or state of being sought after **b** : urgent need **4** : a pressing need or requirement — **on demand** : upon request for payment

[2]**demand** *vb* **1** : to ask or call for with authority : claim as one's right **2** : to ask earnestly or in the manner of a command **3** : to call for : REQUIRE, NEED — **de•mand•a•ble** *adj* — **de•mand•er** *n*

de•mar•cate \di-ˈmär-ˌkāt, ˈdē-ˌmär-\ *vt* **1** : to mark the limits of **2** : to set apart : SEPARATE — **de•mar•ca•tion** \ˌdē-ˌmär-ˈkā-shən\ *n*

de•marche \dā-ˈmärsh\ *n* : a course of action : MANEUVER

[1]**de•mean** \di-ˈmēn\ *vt* : to conduct or behave (oneself) usu. in a proper manner

[2]**demean** *vt* : DEGRADE, DEBASE

de•mea•nor \di-ˈmē-nər\ *n* : CONDUCT, BEARING

de•ment•ed \di-ˈment-əd\ *adj* : MAD, INSANE — **de•ment•ed•ly** *adv* — **de•ment•ed•ness** *n*

de•men•tia \di-ˈmen-chə\ *n* : a condition of deteriorated mentality : INSANITY

de•mer•it \(ˈ)dē-ˈmer-ət\ *n* **1** : FAULT **2** : a mark placed against a person's record for some fault or offense

de•mesne \di-ˈmān, -ˈmēn\ *n* **1** : manorial land actually possessed by the lord and not held by free tenants **2 a** : ESTATE **b** : REGION, TERRITORY **3** : REALM, DOMAIN

demi•god \ˈdem-ē-ˌgäd\ *n* : a mythological being with more power than a mortal but less than a god

demi•john \-ˌjän\ *n* : a large glass or hard pottery bottle enclosed in wickerwork

de•mil•i•ta•rize \(ˈ)dē-ˈmil-ə-tə-ˌrīz\ *vt* : to strip of military forces, weapons, or fortification — **de•mil•i•ta•ri•za•tion** \(ˌ)dē-ˌmil-ə-tə-rə-ˈzā-shən\ *n*

demi•mon•daine \ˌdem-ē-ˌmän-ˈdān\ *n* : a woman of the demimonde

demi•monde \ˈdem-ē-ˌmänd\ *n* **1** : a class of women on the fringes of respectable society supported by wealthy lovers **2** : a group engaged in activity of doubtful legality or propriety

[1]**de•mise** \di-ˈmīz\ *vt* : LEASE

[2]**demise** *n* **1** : a letting of property : LEASE **2** : transfer of sovereignty to a successor **3 a** : DEATH **b** : a cessation of existence or activity

demi•tasse \ˈdem-ē-ˌtas, -ˌtäs\ *n* : a small cup of black coffee; *also* : the cup used to serve it

de•mo•bi•lize \di-ˈmō-bə-ˌlīz\ *vt* **1** : to dismiss from military service **2** : to change from a state of war to a state of peace — **de•mo•bi•li•za•tion** \-ˌmō-bə-lə-ˈzā-shən\ *n*

de•moc•ra•cy \di-ˈmäk-rə-sē\ *n, pl* **-cies** **1 a** : government by the people; *esp* : rule of the majority **b** : government in which the supreme power is vested in the people and exercised by them directly or indirectly through representation **2** : a political unit that has a democratic government **3 a** : the absence of hereditary or arbitrary class distinctions or privileges **b** : belief in or practice of social or economic equality for all people

dem•o•crat \ˈdem-ə-ˌkrat\ *n* **1 a** : an adherent of democracy **b** : one who practices social equality **2** *cap* : a member of the Democratic party of the U.S.

dem•o•crat•ic \ˌdem-ə-ˈkrat-ik\ *adj* **1** : of, relating to, or favoring political, social, or economic democracy **2** *often cap* : of or relating to one of the two major political parties in the U.S. associated in modern times with policies of broad social reform and internationalism **3** : of, relating to, or appealing to the broad masses of the people **4** : favoring social equality : not snobbish — **dem•o•crat•i•cal•ly** \-i-k(ə-)lē\ *adv*

de•mog•ra•phy \di-ˈmäg-rə-fē\ *n* : the statistical study of human populations and esp. their size and distribution and the number of births and deaths — **de•mog•ra•pher** \-fər\ *n* — **de•mo•graph•ic** \ˌdē-mə-ˈgraf-ik, ˌdem-ə-\ *adj* — **de•mo•graph•i•cal•ly** \-ˈgraf-i-k(ə-)lē\ *adv*

dem•oi•selle \ˌdem-(w)ə-ˈzel\ *n* : a young lady

de•mol•ish \di-ˈmäl-ish\ *vt* **1 a** : to tear down : RAZE **b** : to break to pieces : SMASH **2** : to do away with : put an end to — **de•mol•ish•er** *n* — **de•mol•ish•ment** *n*

dem•o•li•tion \ˌdem-ə-ˈlish-ən, ˌdē-mə-\ *n* : the act of demolishing; *esp* : destruction in war by means of explosives — **dem•o•li•tion•ist** \-ˈlish-(ə-)nəst\ *n*

de•mon *or* **dae•mon** \ˈdē-mən\ *n* **1** *usu daemon* : an attendant power or spirit : GENIUS **2 a** : an evil spirit **b** : an evil or undesirable emotion, trait, or state **3** : one that has unusual drive or effectiveness — **de•mon•ic** \di-ˈmän-ik\ *adj*

de•mon•e•tize \(ˈ)dē-ˈmän-ə-ˌtīz, -ˈmən-\ *vt* : to stop using as money or as a monetary standard — **de•mon•e•ti•za•tion** \(ˌ)dē-ˌmän-ət-ə-ˈzā-shən, -ˌmən-\ *n*

de•mo•ni•ac \di-ˈmō-nē-ˌak\ *adj* **1** : possessed or influenced by a demon **2** : of, relating to, or suggestive of a demon : DEVILISH, FIENDISH — **de•mo•ni•a•cal•ly** \ˌdē-mə-ˈnī-ə-k(ə-)lē\ *adv*

de•mon•stra•ble \di-ˈmän(t)-strə-bəl\ *adj* **1** : capable of being demonstrated or proved **2** : APPARENT, EVIDENT — **de•mon•stra•bil•i•ty** \di-ˌmän(t)-strə-ˈbil-ət-e\ *n* — **de•mon•stra•ble•ness** *n* — **de•mon•stra•bly** \di-ˈmän(t)-strə-blē\ *adv*

dem•on•strate \ˈdem-ən-ˌstrāt\ *vb* **1** : to show clearly **2 a** : to prove or make clear by reasoning or evidence **b** : to illustrate and explain esp. with many examples **3** : to show publicly the good qualities of a product **4** : to make a public display (as of feelings or military force)

dem•on•stra•tion \ˌdem-ən-ˈstrā-shən\ *n* **1** : an outward expression or display **2** : an act, process, or means of demonstrating

[1]**de•mon•stra•tive** \di-ˈmän(t)-strət-iv\ *adj* **1 a** : demonstrating as real or true **b** : characterized or established by demonstration **2** : pointing out the one referred to and distinguishing it from others of the same class **3** : marked by display of feeling — **de•mon•stra•tive•ly** *adv* — **de•mon•stra•tive•ness** *n*

[2]**demonstrative** *n* : a demonstrative word; *esp* : a demonstrative pronoun

dem•on•stra•tor \ˈdem-ən-ˌstrāt-ər\ *n* **1** : a person who makes or takes part in a demonstration **2** : a manufactured article (as an automobile) used for purposes of demonstration

de•mor•al•ize \di-ˈmȯr-ə-ˌlīz\ *vb* **1** : to corrupt in morals : make bad **2** : to destroy the morale of : weaken in discipline or spirit : DISORGANIZE — **de•mor•al•iza•tion** \di-ˌmȯr-ə-lə-ˈzā-shən\ *n* — **de•mor•al•iz•er** *n*

de•mote \di-ˈmōt\ *vt* : to reduce to a lower grade or rank — **de•mo•tion** \-ˈmō-shən\ *n*

de•mot•ic \di-ˈmät-ik\ *adj* : POPULAR, COMMON

[1]**de•mul•cent** \di-ˈməl-sənt\ *adj* : SOOTHING

[2]**demulcent** *n* : a usu. oily or somewhat thick and gelatinous preparation used to soothe or protect an abraded mucous membrane

[1]**de•mur** \di-ˈmər\ *vi* **de•murred**; **de•mur•ring** **1** : to enter a demurrer **2** : to take exception : OBJECT

[2]**demur** *n* **1** : HESITATION **2** : the act of objecting : PROTEST

de•mure \di-ˈmyu̇(ə)r\ *adj* **1** : SOBER, SERIOUS **2** : affectedly modest, reserved, or serious : PRIM — **de•mure•ly** *adv* — **de•mure•ness** *n*

de•mur•rage \di-ˈmər-ij\ *n* **1** : detention of a ship by the shipper or receiver beyond the time allowed for loading or unloading **2** : a charge on a shipper or receiver of goods for detaining a ship, freight car, or truck beyond the time necessary for loading or unloading

de•mur•rer \di-ˈmər-ər\ *n* **1** : a claim by the defendant in a legal action that the pleadings of the plaintiff are insufficient or otherwise defective **2** : OBJECTION

[1]**den** \ˈden\ *n* **1** : the shelter or resting place of a wild animal **2** : a hiding place (as for thieves) **3** : a dirty wretched place in

which people live or gather 4 : a quiet snug room; *esp* : one set apart for reading and relaxation

[2]**den** *vb* **denned**; **den·ning** : to live in or retire to a den

de·na·ture \(ˈ)dē-ˈnā-chər\ *vt* **de·na·tured**; **de·na·tur·ing** \-ˈnāch-(ə-)riŋ\ : to deprive of natural qualities; *esp* : to make (alcohol) unfit for drinking without impairing usefulness for other purposes — **de·na·tur·a·tion** \(ˌ)dē-ˌnā-chə-ˈrā-shən\ *n*

den·gue \ˈdeŋ-gē\ *n* : an acute infectious disease characterized by headache, severe joint pain, and rash

de·ni·al \di-ˈnī(-ə)l\ *n* 1 : a refusal to grant something asked for 2 : a refusal to admit the truth of a statement : CONTRADICTION 3 : a refusal to acknowledge something; *esp* : a statement of disbelief or rejection : DISAVOWAL 4 : a cutting down or limiting : RESTRICTION

[1]**de·ni·er** \di-ˈnī(-ə)r\ *n* : one that denies

[2]**den·ier** \ˈden-yər\ *n* : a unit of fineness for silk, rayon, or nylon yarn equal to the fineness of a yarn weighing one gram for each 9000 meters

den·im \ˈden-əm\ *n* 1 : a firm often coarse cotton cloth 2 : overalls or trousers of usu. blue denim

den·i·zen \ˈden-ə-zən\ *n* : INHABITANT; *esp* : a person, animal, or plant found or naturalized in a particular region or environment

de·nom·i·nate \di-ˈnäm-ə-ˌnāt\ *vt* : to give a name to

de·nom·i·na·tion \di-ˌnäm-ə-ˈnā-shən\ *n* 1 : an act of denominating 2 : NAME, DESIGNATION; *esp* : a general name for a class of things 3 : a religious organization uniting in a single body a number of congregations 4 : one of a series of related values each having a special name — **de·nom·i·na·tion·al** \-shnəl, -shən-ᵊl\ *adj* — **de·nom·i·na·tion·al·ly** \-ē\ *adv*

de·nom·i·na·tion·al·ism \-shnəl-ˌiz-əm, -shən-ᵊl-ˌiz-\ *n* 1 : devotion to denominational principles or interests 2 : SECTARIANISM

de·nom·i·na·tor \di-ˈnäm-ə-ˌnāt-ər\ *n* : the part of a fraction that is below the line : DIVISOR

de·no·ta·tion \ˌdē-nō-ˈtā-shən\ *n* 1 : an act or process of denoting 2 : MEANING; *esp* : a direct specific meaning as distinct from connotations 3 : NAME, SIGN

de·no·ta·tive \ˈdē-nō-ˌtāt-iv, di-ˈnōt-ət-iv\ *adj* 1 : denoting or tending to denote 2 : relating to denotation

de·note \di-ˈnōt\ *vt* 1 : to mark out plainly : point out : INDICATE 2 : to make known : SHOW 3 : to have the meaning of : MEAN, NAME

de·noue·ment \ˌdā-ˌnü-ˈmäⁿ\ *n* : the final solution or untangling of the conflicts or difficulties that make up the plot of a literary work

de·nounce \di-ˈnau̇n(t)s\ *vt* 1 : to point out as deserving blame or punishment 2 : to inform against : ACCUSE 3 : to announce formally the termination of (as a treaty) — **de·nounce·ment** *n* — **de·nounc·er** *n*

dense \ˈden(t)s\ *adj* 1 : marked by compactness or crowding together of parts 2 : mentally dull 3 : having high opacity — **dense·ly** *adv* — **dense·ness** *n*

den·si·ty \ˈden(t)-sət-ē\ *n, pl* **-ties** 1 : the quality or state of being dense 2 : the quantity of something per unit volume, unit area, or unit length 3 : STUPIDITY 4 : the degree of opacity of a translucent medium

[1]**dent** \ˈdent\ *n* 1 : a depression or hollow made by a blow or by pressure 2 a : an impression or effect made usu. against resistance b : initial progress

[2]**dent** *vb* 1 : to make a dent in or on 2 : to become marked by a dent

den·tal \ˈdent-ᵊl\ *adj* : of or relating to the teeth or dentistry — **den·tal·ly** \-ᵊl-ē\ *adv*

den·tate \ˈden-ˌtāt\ *or* **den·tat·ed** \-ˌtāt-əd\ *adj* : having pointed conical projections — **den·tate·ly** *adv* — **den·ta·tion** \den-ˈtā-shən\ *n*

den·ti·frice \ˈdent-ə-frəs\ *n* : a powder, paste, or liquid for cleaning the teeth

den·tist \ˈdent-əst\ *n* : one whose profession is the care, treatment, and repair of the teeth and the fitting of artificial teeth

den·tist·ry \ˈdent-ə-strē\ *n* : the profession or practice of a dentist

den·ti·tion \den-ˈtish-ən\ *n* 1 : the development and cutting of teeth 2 : the number, kind, and arrangement of teeth (as of a person)

den·ture \ˈden-chər\ *n* 1 : a set of teeth 2 : an artificial replacement for one or more teeth; *esp* : a set of false teeth

de·nude \di-ˈn(y)üd\ *vt* : to strip of covering : lay bare — **de·nu·da·tion** \ˌdē-(ˌ)n(y)ü-ˈdā-shən\ *n* — **de·nu·da·tion·al** \-shnəl, -shən-ᵊl\ *adj* — **de·nud·er** *n*

de·nun·ci·a·tion \di-ˌnən(t)-sē-ˈā-shən\ *n* : the act of denouncing; *esp* : a public accusation

de·ny \di-ˈnī\ *vt* **de·nied**; **de·ny·ing** 1 : to declare not to be true : CONTRADICT 2 : to refuse to grant 3 : to refuse to acknowledge : DISOWN 4 : to reject as false

de·odor·ant \dē-ˈōd-ə-rənt\ *n* : a preparation that destroys or masks unpleasant odors — **deodorant** *adj*

de·odor·ize \dē-ˈōd-ə-ˌrīz\ *vt* : to eliminate or prevent the offensive odor of — **de·odor·i·za·tion** \(ˌ)dē-ˌōd-ə-rə-ˈzā-shən\ *n* — **de·odor·iz·er** *n*

de·oxy·ri·bo·nu·cle·ic acid \(ˌ)dē-ˌäk-sē-ˈrī-bō-n(y)u̇-ˌklē-ik-\ *n* : any of various nucleic acids found esp. in cell nuclei and as a major constituent of chromatin

de·part \di-ˈpärt\ *vb* 1 a : to go away or go away from : LEAVE b : DIE 2 : to turn aside : DEVIATE

de·part·ment \di-ˈpärt-mənt\ *n* 1 : a distinct sphere : PROVINCE 2 a : a major administrative division of a government or business b : a division of a college or school giving instruction in a particular subject — **de·part·men·tal** \di-ˌpärt-ˈment-ᵊl\ *adj* — **de·part·men·tal·ly** \-ē\ *adv*

de·par·ture \di-ˈpär-chər\ *n* 1 : the act of going away 2 : a setting out (as on a new course) 3 : DIVERGENCE

de·pend \di-ˈpend\ *vi* 1 : to hang down 2 : to rely for support 3 : to be determined by or based on some action or condition 4 : TRUST, RELY

de·pend·a·ble \di-ˈpen-də-bəl\ *adj* : capable of being depended on : TRUSTWORTHY, RELIABLE — **de·pend·a·bil·i·ty** \-ˌpen-də-ˈbil-ət-ē\ *n* — **de·pend·a·bly** \-ˈpen-də-blē\ *adv*

de·pend·ence \di-ˈpen-dən(t)s\ *n* 1 : the quality or state of being dependent; *esp* : the quality or state of being influenced by or subject to another 2 : RELIANCE, TRUST 3 : something on which one relies

de·pend·en·cy \-dən-sē\ *n, pl* **-cies** 1 : DEPENDENCE 1 2 : a territory under the jurisdiction of a nation but not formally annexed by it

[1]**de·pend·ent** \di-ˈpen-dənt\ *adj* 1 : hanging down 2 a : determined or conditioned by another b : relying on another for support c : subject to another's jurisdiction 3 : SUBORDINATE 3a — **de·pend·ent·ly** *adv*

[2]**dependent** *n* : one that is dependent; *esp* : a person who relies on another for support

de·pict \di-ˈpikt\ *vt* 1 : to represent by a picture 2 : to describe in words — **de·pic·tion** \-ˈpik-shən\ *n*

de·pil·a·to·ry \di-ˈpil-ə-ˌtōr-ē\ *n, pl* **-ries** : an agent for removing hair, wool, or bristles — **depilatory** *adj*

de·plete \di-ˈplēt\ *vt* : to reduce in amount by using up : exhaust esp. of strength or resources — **de·ple·tion** \-ˈplē-shən\ *n*

de·plor·a·ble \di-ˈplōr-ə-bəl\ *adj* 1 : deserving to be deplored : LAMENTABLE 2 : very bad : WRETCHED — **de·plor·a·ble·ness** *n* — **de·plor·a·bly** \-blē\ *adv*

de·plore \di-ˈplō(ə)r\ *vt* 1 a : to feel or express grief for b : to regret strongly 2 : to consider unfortunate or deserving of disapproval — **de·plor·er** *n*

de·ploy \di-ˈplȯi\ *vb* 1 : to spread out (as troops or ships) in order for battle 2 : to undergo deployment

de·ploy·ment \-mənt\ *n* : an act of deploying
de·pop·u·late \(ˈ)dē-ˈpäp-yə-ˌlāt\ *vt* : to reduce greatly the population of (as a city or region) by destroying or driving away the inhabitants — **de·pop·u·la·tion** \(ˌ)dē-ˌpäp-yə-ˈlā-shən\ *n* — **de·pop·u·la·tor** \(ˈ)dē-ˈpäp-yə-ˌlāt-ər\ *n*
de·port \di-ˈpōrt\ *vt* **1** : CONDUCT, BEHAVE **2** : to force (an alien whose presence is unlawful or harmful) to leave a country — **de·por·ta·tion** \ˌdē-ˌpōr-ˈtā-shən\ *n*
de·port·ment \di-ˈpōrt-mənt\ *n* : manner of conducting oneself : BEHAVIOR
de·pose \di-ˈpōz\ *vb* **1** : to remove from a throne or other high position **2** : to testify under oath or by affidavit
[1]**de·pos·it** \di-ˈpäz-ət\ *vb* **1** : to place for safekeeping; *esp* : to put money in a bank **2** : to give as a pledge that a purchase will be made or a service used **3** : to lay down : PLACE, PUT **4** : to let fall or sink **5** : to become deposited : SETTLE — **de·pos·i·tor** \-ət-ər\ *n*
[2]**deposit** *n* **1** : the state of being deposited **2 a** : something placed for safekeeping; *esp* : money deposited in a bank **b** : money given as a pledge **3** : an act of depositing **4** : something laid or thrown down **5** : an accumulation of mineral matter (as iron ore, oil, or gas) in nature
dep·o·si·tion \ˌdep-ə-ˈzish-ən, ˌdē-pə-\ *n* **1** : the act of deposing a person from high office **2** : a statement esp. in writing made under oath **3** : the action or process of depositing **4** : something deposited : DEPOSIT — **dep·o·si·tion·al** \-ˈzish-nəl, -ˈzish-ən-ᵊl\ *adj*
de·pos·i·to·ry \di-ˈpäz-ə-ˌtōr-ē\ *n, pl* **-ries** : a place where something is deposited esp. for safekeeping
de·pot *1 & 3 are* ˈdep-ˌō *also* ˈdē-ˌpō, *2 is* ˈdē-ˌpō *also* ˈdep-ˌō\ *n* **1** : a place of deposit for goods : STOREHOUSE **2** : a building for railroad or bus passengers or freight : STATION **3** : a place where military supplies are kept or where troops are assembled and trained
de·prave \di-ˈprāv\ *vt* : CORRUPT, PERVERT
de·praved \-ˈprāvd\ *adj* : marked by corruption or evil; *esp* : PERVERTED
de·prav·i·ty \di-ˈprav-ət-ē\ *n, pl* **-ties** **1** : the quality or state of being depraved **2** : a corrupt act or practice
dep·re·cate \ˈdep-ri-ˌkāt\ *vt* **1** : to express disapproval of **2** : DEPRECIATE — **dep·re·cat·ing·ly** *adv* — **dep·re·ca·tion** \ˌdep-ri-ˈkā-shən\ *n*
dep·re·ca·to·ry \ˈdep-ri-kə-ˌtōr-ē\ *adj* **1** : serving to deprecate **2** : expressing deprecation : APOLOGETIC
de·pre·ci·ate \di-ˈprē-shē-ˌāt\ *vb* **1** : to lower the price or value of **2** : to represent as of little value : DISPARAGE **3** : to fall in value — **de·pre·cia·tive** \-shē-ˌāt-iv, -sh(ē-)ət-\ *adj* — **de·pre·cia·to·ry** \-sh(ē-)ə-ˌtōr-ē\ *adj*
de·pre·ci·a·tion \di-ˌprē-shē-ˈā-shən\ *n* **1** : a decline in the purchasing power or exchange value of money **2** : the act of belittling : DISPARAGEMENT **3** : a decline (as from age or wear and tear) in the value of something
dep·re·da·tion \ˌdep-rə-ˈdā-shən\ *n* : the action or an act of plundering or laying waste : RAVAGING, PILLAGING
de·press \di-ˈpres\ *vt* **1 a** : to press down **b** : to cause to sink to a lower position **2** : to lessen the activity or strength of **3** : SADDEN, DISCOURAGE **4** : to lessen in price or value : DEPRECIATE
de·pres·sant \di-ˈpres-ᵊnt\ *n* : one that depresses; *esp* : an agent that reduces bodily functional activity — **depressant** *adj*
de·pressed \-ˈprest\ *adj* **1** : low in spirits : SAD **2** : suffering from economic depression; *esp* : UNDERPRIVILEGED
de·pres·sion \di-ˈpresh-ən\ *n* **1** : an act of depressing : a state of being depressed: as **a** : a pressing down : LOWERING **b** : DEJECTION; *also* : a mental disorder marked by sadness, inactivity, and self-depreciation **c** (1) : a reduction in activity, amount, quality, or force (2) : a lowering of vitality or functional activity **2** : a depressed place or part : HOLLOW **3** : a period of low general economic activity with widespread unemployment
dep·ri·va·tion \ˌdep-rə-ˈvā-shən\ *n* **1** : an act or instance of depriving : LOSS **2** : the state of being deprived
de·prive \di-ˈprīv\ *vt* **1** : to take something away from **2** : to stop from having something
depth \ˈdepth\ *n, pl* **depths** \ˈdep(th)s\ **1 a** (1) : a deep place in a body of water (2) : a part that is far from the outside or surface (3) : ABYSS **b** (1) : the middle of a time (2) : an extreme state (as of misery) (3) : the worst part **2 a** : the perpendicular distance downward from a surface **b** : the distance from front to back **3** : the quality of being deep **4** : degree of intensity — **depth·less** \ˈdepth-ləs\ *adj*
dep·u·ta·tion \ˌdep-yə-ˈtā-shən\ *n* **1** : the act of appointing a deputy **2** : DELEGATION
de·pute \di-ˈpyüt\ *vt* : DELEGATE
dep·u·tize \ˈdep-yə-ˌtīz\ *vb* **1** : to appoint as deputy **2** : to act as deputy
dep·u·ty \ˈdep-yət-ē\ *n, pl* **-ties** **1** : a person appointed to act for or in place of another **2** : an assistant empowered to act as a substitute in the absence of his superior **3** : a member of a lower house of a legislative assembly — **deputy** *adj*
de·rail \di-ˈrāl\ *vt* : to cause to run off the rails — **de·rail·ment** *n*
de·range \di-ˈrānj\ *vt* **1** : to put out of order : DISARRANGE, UPSET **2** : to make insane — **de·range·ment** *n*
der·by \ˈdər-bē, *esp Brit* ˈdär-\ *n, pl* **derbies** **1** : a horse race usu. for three-year-olds held annually **2** : a race or contest open to all comers **3** : a man's stiff felt hat with dome-shaped crown and narrow brim
[1]**der·e·lict** \ˈder-ə-ˌlikt\ *adj* **1** : abandoned by the owner or occupant **2** : NEGLECTFUL, NEGLIGENT
[2]**derelict** *n* **1** : something voluntarily abandoned; *esp* : a ship abandoned on the high seas **2** : a person no longer able to support himself : BUM
der·e·lic·tion \ˌder-ə-ˈlik-shən\ *n* **1** : the act of abandoning : the state of being abandoned **2** : a failure in duty : DELINQUENCY
de·ride \di-ˈrīd\ *vt* : to laugh at scornfully : make fun of — **de·rid·er** *n*
de ri·gueur \də-(ˌ)rē-ˈgər\ *adj* : prescribed or required by fashion, etiquette, or custom : PROPER
de·ri·sion \di-ˈrizh-ən\ *n* **1** : scornful or contemptuous ridicule **2** : an object of ridicule
de·ri·sive \di-ˈrī-siv\ *adj* : expressing or causing derision — **de·ri·sive·ly** *adv* — **de·ri·sive·ness** *n*
de·riv·a·ble \di-ˈrī-və-bəl\ *adj* : capable of being derived
der·i·va·tion \ˌder-ə-ˈvā-shən\ *n* **1 a** : the formation (as by the addition of an affix) of a word from an earlier word or root **b** : an act of ascertaining or stating the derivation of a word **c** : ETYMOLOGY 1 **2 a** : SOURCE, ORIGIN **b** : ORIGINATION, DESCENT **c** : an act or process of deriving — **der·i·va·tion·al** \-shnəl, -shən-ᵊl\ *adj*
[1]**de·riv·a·tive** \di-ˈriv-ət-iv\ *adj* : derived from something else : not original or fundamental — **de·riv·a·tive·ly** *adv*
[2]**derivative** *n* **1** : a word formed by derivation **2** : something derived
de·rive \di-ˈrīv\ *vb* **de·rived**; **de·riv·ing** **1 a** : to receive or obtain from a source **b** : to obtain (as a chemical substance) from a parent substance **2** : to trace the origin, descent, or derivation of **3** : to come from a certain source **4** : INFER, DEDUCE
der·ma·ti·tis \ˌdər-mə-ˈtīt-əs\ *n* : inflammation of the skin
der·ma·tol·o·gy \ˌdər-mə-ˈtäl-ə-jē\ *n* : a branch of science dealing with the skin — **der·mat·o·log·ic** \(ˌ)dər-ˌmat-ᵊl-ˈäj-ik\ *or* **der·mat·o·log·i·cal** \-ˈäj-i-kəl\ *adj* — **der·ma·tol·o·gist** \ˌdər-mə-ˈtäl-ə-jəst\ *n*
der·o·gate \ˈder-ə-ˌgāt\ *vb* **1** : to cause to seem inferior : DISPARAGE **2** : to take away a part so as to impair : DETRACT —

der·o·ga·tion \ˌder-ə-'gā-shən\ *n* — **de·rog·a·tive** \di-'räg-ət-iv\ *adj*
de·rog·a·to·ry \di-'räg-ə-ˌtōr-ē\ *adj* : intended to lower the reputation of a person or thing : DISPARAGING — **de·rog·a·to·ri·ly** \-ˌräg-ə-'tōr-ə-lē\ *adv*
der·rick \'der-ik\ *n* **1** : any of various machines for moving or hoisting heavy weights by means of a long beam fitted with pulleys and ropes or cables **2** : a framework or tower built over an oil well for supporting machinery
der·ri·ere *or* **der·ri·ère** \ˌder-ē-'e(ə)r\ *n* : BUTTOCKS
der·ring–do \ˌder-iŋ-'dü\ *n* : daring action : DARING
der·rin·ger \'der-ən-jər\ *n* : a short-barreled pocket pistol
der·ris \'der-əs\ *n* : any of a large genus of leguminous tropical Old World shrubs and woody vines including commercial sources of rotenone; *also* : a derris insecticide
der·vish \'dər-vish\ *n* : a member of a Muslim religious order noted for devotional exercises (as bodily movements leading to a trance)
[1]**des·cant** \'des-ˌkant\ *n* **1** : a melody sung above a principal melody **2** : the art of composing or singing part music; *also* : a piece of music so composed
[2]**des·cant** \'des-ˌkant, des-'\ *vi* **1 a** : to sing or play a descant **b** : SING, WARBLE **2** : to talk or write at length
de·scend \di-'send\ *vb* **1 a** : to pass from a higher to a lower place or level **b** : to pass, move, or climb down or down along **2 a** : to come down from a stock or source : DERIVE **b** : to pass by inheritance **c** : to pass by transmission **3** : to incline, lead, or extend downward **4** : to swoop down in a sudden attack **5** : to sink in status, dignity, or condition
[1]**de·scend·ant** *or* **de·scend·ent** \di-'sen-dənt\ *adj* **1** : DESCENDING **2** : proceeding from an ancestor or source
[2]**descendant** *or* **descendent** *n* : one descended from another or from a common stock
de·scent \di-'sent\ *n* **1** : the act or process of descending **2** : a downward step (as in station or value) : DECLINE **3** : derivation from an ancestor : BIRTH **4 a** : an inclination downward : SLOPE **b** : a descending way (as a downgrade or stairway) **5** : a sudden hostile raid or assault
de·scribe \di-'skrīb\ *vt* **1** : to represent or give an account of in words **2** : to trace or traverse the outline of — **de·scrib·a·ble** *adj* — **de·scrib·er** *n*
de·scrip·tion \di-'skrip-shən\ *n* **1** : an account of something; *esp* : an account that presents a picture to a person who reads or hears it **2** : KIND, SORT
de·scrip·tive \-'skrip-tiv\ *adj* : serving to describe — **de·scrip·tive·ly** *adv* — **de·scrip·tive·ness** *n*
de·scry \di-'skrī\ *vt* **de·scried**; **de·scry·ing** **1** : to catch sight of : spy out or discover by the eye **2** : to discover or detect by observation or investigation
des·e·crate \'des-i-ˌkrāt\ *vt* : to violate the sanctity of : PROFANE — **des·e·crat·er** *or* **des·e·cra·tor** \-ˌkrāt-ər\ *n* — **des·e·cra·tion** \ˌdes-i-'krā-shən\ *n*
de·seg·re·gate \(')dē-'seg-ri-ˌgāt\ *vb* : to eliminate segregation in; *esp* : to end by law the isolation of members of a particular race in separate units — **de·seg·re·ga·tion** \(ˌ)dē-ˌseg-ri-'gā-shən\ *n*
[1]**des·ert** \'dez-ərt\ *n* : an arid barren tract incapable of supporting a considerable population without an artificial water supply
[2]**des·ert** \'dez-ərt\ *adj* : of, relating to, or resembling a desert; *esp* : being barren and without life
[3]**de·sert** \di-'zərt\ *n* **1** : worthiness of reward or punishment **2** : a just reward or punishment
[4]**de·sert** \di-'zərt\ *vb* **1** : to withdraw from : LEAVE **2** : to leave in the lurch : FORSAKE — **de·sert·er** *n*
de·ser·tion \di-'zər-shən\ *n* **1** : an act of deserting **2** : a state of being deserted or forsaken : DESOLATION
de·serve \di-'zərv\ *vb* : to be worthy of : MERIT — **de·serv·er** *n*
de·serv·ed·ly \di-'zər-vəd-lē\ *adv* : according to merit : JUSTLY
deserving *adj* : MERITORIOUS, WORTHY
des·ic·cant \'des-i-kənt\ *n* : a drying agent
des·ic·cate \-ˌkāt\ *vb* **1** : to dry up or become dried up **2** : to preserve (a food) by drying : DEHYDRATE — **des·ic·ca·tion** \ˌdes-i-'kā-shən\ *n* — **des·ic·ca·tor** \'des-i-ˌkāt-ər\ *n*
de·sid·er·a·tum \di-ˌsid-ə-'rät-əm\ *n, pl* **-ta** \-ə\ : something desired as essential or needed
[1]**de·sign** \di-'zīn\ *vt* **1 a** : to conceive and plan out in the mind **b** : DEVOTE, CONSIGN **c** : to have as a purpose : INTEND **d** : to devise for a specific function or end **2 a** : to make a pattern or sketch of **b** : to conceive and draw the plans for — **de·sign·er** *n*
[2]**design** *n* **1** : a project or scheme in which means to an end are laid down **2** : deliberate purposive planning **3 a** : a secret project or scheme : PLOT **b** *pl* : aggressive or evil intent — used with *on* or *against* **4** : a sketch or plan showing the main features of something to be executed **5** : the arrangement of elements that make up a structure or a work of art **6** : a decorative pattern
[1]**des·ig·nate** \'dez-ig-ˌnāt, -nət\ *adj* : chosen for an office but not yet installed
[2]**des·ig·nate** \-ˌnāt\ *vt* **1** : INDICATE **2** : to appoint or choose by name for a special purpose **3** : to call by a name or title
designated hitter *n* : a baseball player designated at the start of the game to bat regularly in place of the pitcher
des·ig·na·tion \ˌdez-ig-'nā-shən\ *n* **1** : the act of indicating or identifying **2** : a distinguishing name, sign, or title **3** : appointment to or selection for an office or post
de·sign·ed·ly \di-'zī-nəd-lē\ *adv* : PURPOSELY
de·sign·ing \-'zī-niŋ\ *adj* : CRAFTY, SCHEMING
de·sir·a·ble \di-'zī-rə-bəl\ *adj* **1** : having pleasing qualities or properties : ATTRACTIVE **2** : worth seeking or doing as advantageous, beneficial, or wise : ADVISABLE — **de·sir·a·bil·i·ty** \-ˌzī-rə-'bil-ət-ē\ *n* — **de·sir·a·ble·ness** *n* — **de·sir·a·bly** \-'zī-rə-blē\ *adv*
[1]**de·sire** \di-'zī(ə)r\ *vb* **1** : to long for : wish earnestly **2** : to express a wish for : REQUEST
[2]**desire** *n* **1** : a strong wish : LONGING; *also* : the mental power or capacity to experience desires **2** : an expressed wish : REQUEST **3** : something desired
de·sir·ous \di-'zī(ə)r-əs\ *adj* : eagerly wishing : DESIRING
de·sist \di-'zist, -'sist\ *vi* : to cease to proceed or act
desk \'desk\ *n* **1 a** : a table, frame, or case with a flat or sloping surface esp. for writing and reading **b** : a counter at which a person performs his duties **2** : a specialized division of an organization (as a newspaper)
[1]**des·o·late** \'des-ə-lət\ *adj* **1** : lacking inhabitants and visitors : DESERTED **2** : FORSAKEN, LONELY **3 a** : showing the effects of abandonment and neglect : DILAPIDATED **b** : BARREN, LIFELESS **c** : CHEERLESS, GLOOMY — **des·o·late·ly** *adv* — **des·o·late·ness** *n*
[2]**des·o·late** \-ˌlāt\ *vt* : to make desolate
des·o·la·tion \ˌdes-ə-'lā-shən\ *n* **1** : the action of desolating **2** : the condition of being desolated : DEVASTATION, RUIN **3** : a barren wasteland **4 a** : GRIEF, SADNESS **b** : LONELINESS
[1]**de·spair** \di-'spa(ə)r\ *vi* : to lose all hope or confidence
[2]**despair** *n* **1** : utter loss of hope : feeling of complete hopelessness **2** : a cause of hopelessness
de·spair·ing \-iŋ\ *adj* : given to, arising from, or marked by despair — **de·spair·ing·ly** *adv*
des·per·a·do \ˌdes-pə-'räd-ō, -'rād-\ *n, pl* **-does** *or* **-dos** : a bold or reckless criminal
des·per·ate \'des-p(ə-)rət\ *adj* **1** : being beyond or almost beyond hope : causing despair **2** : reckless because of despair : RASH **3** : extremely intense : OVERPOWERING — **des·per·ate·ly** *adv* — **des·per·ate·ness** *n*
des·per·a·tion \ˌdes-pə-'rā-shən\ *n* **1** : a loss of hope and

surrender to misery or dread 2 : a state of hopelessness leading to extreme recklessness

de·spic·a·ble \di-'spik-ə-bəl, 'des-(,)pik-\ *adj* : deserving to be despised — **de·spic·a·ble·ness** *n* — **de·spic·a·bly** \-blē\ *adv*

de·spise \di-'spīz\ *vt* 1 : to look down on with contempt or aversion 2 : to regard as negligible, worthless, or distasteful — **de·spis·er** *n*

de·spite \di-'spīt\ *prep* : in spite of

de·spite·ful \di-'spīt-fəl\ *adj* : expressing malice or hate — **de·spite·ful·ly** \-fə-lē\ *adv* — **de·spite·ful·ness** *n*

de·spoil \di-'spȯil\ *vt* : to strip of belongings, possessions, or value : PLUNDER, PILLAGE — **de·spoil·er** *n* — **de·spoil·ment** *n*

de·spo·li·a·tion \di-,spō-lē-'ā-shən\ *n* : the act of plundering : the state of being despoiled

[1]**de·spond** \di-'spänd\ *vi* : to become discouraged or disheartened

[2]**despond** *n* : DESPONDENCY

de·spond·en·cy \di-'spän-dən-sē\ *n* : the state of being despondent : DEJECTION, DISCOURAGEMENT

de·spond·ent \-dənt\ *adj* : feeling extreme discouragement, dejection, or depression — **de·spond·ent·ly** *adv*

des·pot \'des-pət\ *n* 1 : a ruler with absolute power and authority 2 : a person exercising power abusively, oppressively, or tyrannously — **des·pot·ic** \des-'pät-ik\ *adj* — **des·pot·i·cal·ly** \-i-k(ə-)lē\ *adv* — **des·po·tism** \'des-pə-,tiz-əm\ *n*

des·sert \di-'zərt\ *n* : a course of sweet food, fruit, or cheese served at the close of a meal

des·ti·na·tion \,des-tə-'nā-shən\ *n* 1 : an act of appointing, setting aside for a purpose, or predetermining 2 : purpose for which something is destined 3 : a place which is set for the end of a journey or to which something is sent

des·tine \'des-tən\ *vt* 1 : to settle in advance 2 : to designate, assign, or dedicate in advance 3 : to be bound or directed

des·ti·ny \'des-tə-nē\ *n, pl* **-nies** 1 : something to which a person or thing is destined : FORTUNE 2 : a predetermined course of events often held to be a resistless power or agency

des·ti·tute \'des-tə-,t(y)üt\ *adj* 1 : lacking something needed or desirable 2 : extremely poor : suffering great want

des·ti·tu·tion \,des-tə-'t(y)ü-shən\ *n* : the state of being destitute; *esp* : extreme poverty

de·stroy \di-'strȯi\ *vb* 1 : to put an end to : do away with : RUIN 2 : KILL

de·stroy·er \-'strȯi(-ə)r\ *n* 1 : a destroying agent or agency 2 : a small fast warship

de·struc·ti·ble \di-'strək-tə-bəl\ *adj* : capable of being destroyed — **de·struc·ti·bil·i·ty** \-,strək-tə-'bil-ət-ē\ *n*

de·struc·tion \di-'strək-shən\ *n* 1 : the action or process of destroying something 2 : the state or fact of being destroyed : RUIN 3 : a destroying agency

de·struc·tive \di-'strək-tiv\ *adj* 1 : causing destruction : RUINOUS 2 : designed or tending to destroy — **de·struc·tive·ly** *adv* — **de·struc·tive·ness** *n*

des·ue·tude \'des-wi-,t(y)üd\ *n* : discontinuance from use or exercise : DISUSE

des·ul·to·ry \'des-əl-,tōr-ē\ *adj* : passing aimlessly from one thing or subject to another : DISCONNECTED — **des·ul·to·ri·ly** \,des-əl-'tōr-ə-lē\ *adv*

de·tach \di-'tach\ *vt* 1 : to separate esp. from a larger mass and usu. without violence or damage 2 : DISENGAGE, WITHDRAW — **de·tach·a·ble** *adj* — **de·tach·a·bly** \-ə-blē\ *adv*

de·tached \-'tacht\ *adj* 1 : not joined or connected : SEPARATE 2 : ALOOF, UNCONCERNED, IMPARTIAL

de·tach·ment \di-'tach-mənt\ *n* 1 : the action or process of detaching : SEPARATION 2 a : the dispatching of a body of troops or part of a fleet from the main body b : a portion dispatched for special service c : a small permanent military unit different in composition from normal units 3 a : indifference to worldly concerns : UNWORLDLINESS b : freedom from bias or prejudice : IMPARTIALITY

[1]**de·tail** \di-'tāl, 'dē-,\ *n* 1 a : a dealing with something item by item b : a small part : ITEM 2 a : selection (as of a group of soldiers) for some special service b : a soldier or group of soldiers appointed for special duty

[2]**detail** *vt* 1 : to report in detail 2 : ENUMERATE, SPECIFY 3 : to assign to a task — **de·tail·er** *n*

de·tailed \di-'tāld, 'dē-,\ *adj* 1 : including many details 2 : furnished with finely finished details

de·tain \di-'tān\ *vt* 1 : to hold or keep in or as if in custody 2 : to keep back (as something due) 3 : to restrain esp. from proceeding : STOP — **de·tain·ment** *n*

de·tect \di-'tekt\ *vt* : to discover the nature, existence, presence, or fact of — **de·tect·a·ble** *adj* — **de·tec·tor** \-'tek-tər\ *n*

de·tec·tion \di-'tek-shən\ *n* : the act of detecting : the state or fact of being detected : DISCOVERY

[1]**de·tec·tive** \di-'tek-tiv\ *adj* 1 : fitted for or used in detecting something 2 : of or relating to detectives

[2]**detective** *n* : an individual (as a policeman) whose business is solving crimes and catching criminals or gathering information that is not readily accessible

de·ten·tion \di-'ten-chən\ *n* : the act of detaining : the state of being detained: as a : CONFINEMENT; *esp* : temporary custody awaiting trial b : a forced delay

de·ter \di-'tər\ *vt* **de·terred**; **de·ter·ring** 1 : to turn aside, discourage, or prevent from acting (as by fear) 2 : INHIBIT — **de·ter·ment** *n*

[1]**de·ter·gent** \di-'tər-jənt\ *adj* : CLEANSING

[2]**detergent** *n* : a cleansing agent; *esp* : any of numerous synthetic organic preparations that are chemically different from soaps

de·te·ri·o·rate \di-'tir-ē-ə-,rāt\ *vb* : to make or become worse or of less value : DEGENERATE — **de·te·ri·o·ra·tion** \-,tir-ē-ə-'rā-shən\ *n*

de·ter·min·a·ble \di-'tər-mə-nə-bəl\ *adj* : capable of being determined; *esp* : ASCERTAINABLE

de·ter·mi·nant \-mə-nənt\ *n* 1 : something that determines or conditions : FACTOR 2 : a hereditary factor : GENE

de·ter·mi·nate \-mə-nət\ *adj* 1 : having fixed limits : DEFINITE 2 : definitely settled — **de·ter·mi·nate·ly** *adv*

de·ter·mi·na·tion \di-,tər-mə-'nā-shən\ *n* 1 : the act of coming to a decision; *also* : the decision or conclusion reached 2 : the act of fixing the extent, position, or character of something 3 : accurate measurement (as of length or volume) 4 : firm or fixed purpose : FIRMNESS

de·ter·mine \di-'tər-mən\ *vb* 1 a : to fix conclusively or authoritatively b : REGULATE 2 : to come to a decision : SETTLE, RESOLVE 3 : to find out the limits, nature, dimensions, or scope of : gain definite knowledge about 4 : to be the cause of or reason for : DECIDE

de·ter·mined \-mənd\ *adj* 1 : DECIDED, RESOLVED 2 : FIRM, RESOLUTE — **de·ter·mined·ly** \-mən-dlē, -mə-nəd-lē\ *adv* — **de·ter·mined·ness** \-mən(d)-nəs\ *n*

de·ter·min·er \-mə-nər\ *n* : one that determines

de·ter·min·ism \-mə-,niz-əm\ *n* : a doctrine that acts of the will, natural events, or social changes are determined by preceding causes — **de·ter·min·ist** \-mə-nəst\ *n or adj*

de·ter·rence \di-'tər-ən(t)s\ *n* : the act, process, or capacity of deterring

de·ter·rent \-ənt\ *adj* 1 : serving to deter 2 : relating to deterrence — **deterrent** *n* — **de·ter·rent·ly** *adv*

de·test \di-'test\ *vt* : to dislike intensely : LOATHE, ABHOR — **de·test·er** *n*

de·test·a·ble \di-'tes-tə-bəl\ *adj* : arousing or meriting intense dislike : ABOMINABLE — **de·test·a·ble·ness** *n* — **de·test·a·bly** \-blē\ *adv*

de·tes·ta·tion \,dē-,tes-'tā-shən\ *n* 1 : extreme hatred or dislike : LOATHING 2 : an object of hatred or contempt

de·throne \di-'thrōn\ *vt* : to remove from a throne : DEPOSE — **de·throne·ment** *n* — **de·thron·er** *n*
det·o·nate \'det-ə-ˌnāt\ *vb* : to explode or cause or explode with sudden violence — **det·o·na·tion** \ˌdet-ə-'nā-shən\ *n*
det·o·na·tor \'det-ə-ˌnāt-ər\ *n* : a device or small quantity of explosive used for detonating a high explosive
[1]**de·tour** \'dē-ˌtu̇(ə)r\ *n* : a roundabout way temporarily replacing part of a regular route
[2]**detour** *vb* **1** : to send or proceed by a detour **2** : to avoid by going around : BYPASS
de·tract \di-'trakt\ *vb* **1** : to take away : WITHDRAW, SUBTRACT **2** : DISTRACT — **de·trac·tor** \-'trak-tər\ *n*
de·trac·tion \di-'trak-shən\ *n* : a taking away of a part of the reputation or good name of a person esp. by slander
de·train \(ˈ)dē-'trān\ *vb* : to leave or cause to leave a railroad train — **de·train·ment** *n*
det·ri·ment \'de-trə-mənt\ *n* : injury or damage or its cause : HURT
det·ri·men·tal \ˌde-trə-'ment-ᵊl\ *adj* : causing detriment : HARMFUL, DAMAGING — **det·ri·men·tal·ly** \-ᵊl-ē\ *adv*
de·tri·tus \di-'trīt-əs\ *n* : fragments resulting from disintegration — **de·tri·tal** \-'trīt-ᵊl\ *adj*
deuce \'d(y)üs\ *n* **1** : a two in cards or dice **2** : a tie in tennis with each side having a score of 40 **3** : DEVIL, DICKENS — used chiefly as a mild oath
deu·te·ri·um \d(y)ü-'tir-ē-əm\ *n* : the hydrogen isotope that is of twice the mass of ordinary hydrogen and that occurs in water
de·val·ue \(ˈ)dē-'val-yü\ *vb* : to reduce the international exchange value of a currency — **de·val·u·a·tion** \(ˌ)dē-ˌval-yə-'wā-shən\ *n*
dev·as·tate \'dev-ə-ˌstāt\ *vt* **1** : to reduce to ruin : lay waste **2** : to shatter completely : DEMOLISH — **dev·as·tat·ing·ly** *adv* — **dev·as·ta·tor** \-ˌstāt-ər\ *n*
dev·as·ta·tion \ˌdev-ə-'stā-shən\ *n* : the action of devastating : the state of being devastated : DESOLATION, RUIN
de·vel·op \di-'vel-əp\ *vb* **1 a** : to unfold gradually or in detail **b** : to subject (exposed photographic material) to a chemical treatment to produce a visible image **2** : to bring out the possibilities of **3** : to make more available or usable **4** : to acquire gradually **5 a** : to go through a process of natural growth, differentiation, or evolution **b** : GROW **6** : to become apparent — **de·vel·op·a·ble** *adj*
de·vel·op·er \-'vel-ə-pər\ *n* : one that develops
de·vel·op·ment \di-'vel-əp-mənt\ *n* **1** : the act, process, or result of developing **2** : the state of being developed — **de·vel·op·men·tal** \-ˌvel-əp-'ment-ᵊl\ *adj* — **de·vel·op·men·tal·ly** \-ᵊl-ē\ *adv*
de·vi·ant \'dē-vē-ənt\ *adj* **1** : deviating esp. from some accepted norm **2** : characterized by deviation — **de·vi·ance** \-ən(t)s\ *n* — **deviant** *n*
[1]**de·vi·ate** \'dē-vē-ˌāt\ *vb* : to turn aside esp. from an established way
[2]**de·vi·ate** \-vē-ət, -vē-ˌāt\ *adj* : DEVIANT — **deviate** *n*
de·vi·a·tion \ˌdē-vē-'ā-shən\ *n* : an act or instance of deviating: as **a** : departure from an established ideology or policy (as of a political party) **b** : noticeable departure from accepted norms (as of behavior) — **de·vi·a·tion·ism** \-shə-ˌniz-əm\ *n* — **de·vi·a·tion·ist** \-sh(ə-)nəst\ *n*
de·vice \di-'vīs\ *n* **1 a** : a scheme to deceive : STRATAGEM **b** : a piece of equipment or a mechanism to serve a special purpose **2** : DESIRE, INCLINATION **3** : an emblematic design used esp. as a heraldic bearing
[1]**dev·il** \'dev-əl\ *n* **1** *often cap* : the personal supreme spirit of evil **2** : DEMON **3 a** : a wicked person **b** : a reckless or dashing person **c** : a pitiable person
[2]**devil** *vt* **dev·iled** *or* **dev·illed**; **dev·il·ing** *or* **dev·il·ling** \'dev-(ə-)liŋ\ **1** : TEASE, ANNOY **2** : to chop fine and season highly
dev·il·ish \'dev-(ə-)lish\ *adj* **1** : characteristic of or resembling the devil **2** : EXTREME, EXCESSIVE — **devilish** *adv* — **dev·il·ish·ly** *adv* — **dev·il·ish·ness** *n*
dev·il·ment \'dev-əl-mənt, -ˌment\ *n* : reckless mischief
dev·il·ry \'dev-əl-rē\ *or* **dev·il·try** \-əl-trē\ *n, pl* **-ries** *or* **-tries** : reckless unrestrained conduct : MISCHIEF
de·vi·ous \'dē-vē-əs\ *adj* **1** : deviating from a straight line : ROUNDABOUT **2 a** : ERRING **b** : not straightforward : TRICKY — **de·vi·ous·ly** *adv* — **de·vi·ous·ness** *n*
de·vise \di-'vīz\ *vt* **1 a** : INVENT **b** : PLOT **2** : to give (real estate) by will — **de·vis·er** *n*
de·vi·tal·ize \(ˈ)dē-'vīt-ᵊl-ˌīz\ *vt* : to deprive of life or vitality
de·void \di-'vȯid\ *adj* : entirely lacking : DESTITUTE
de·voir \dəv-'wär, 'dev-ˌ\ *n* **1** : DUTY **2** : a formal act of civility or respect — usu. used in pl.
de·volve \di-'välv\ *vb* : to pass by transmission or succession from one person to another
de·vote \di-'vōt\ *vt* **1** : to set apart for a special purpose (as by a vow) : DEDICATE **2** : to give up to wholly
de·vot·ed \-əd\ *adj* **1** : ZEALOUS, ARDENT, DEVOUT **2** : AFFECTIONATE, LOVING — **de·vot·ed·ly** *adv* — **de·vot·ed·ness** *n*
dev·o·tee \ˌdev-ə-'tē, -'tā\ *n* **1** : an esp. ardent adherent of a religion or deity **2** : a zealous follower, supporter, or enthusiast
de·vo·tion \di-'vō-shən\ *n* **1 a** : religious fervor : PIETY **b** : a religious exercise or practice other than the regular worship of a church **2 a** (1) : the act of devoting (2) : the quality of being devoted **b** : ardent love, affection, or dedication — **de·vo·tion·al** \-shnəl, -shən-ᵊl\ *adj* — **de·vo·tion·al·ly** \-ē\ *adv*
de·vour \di-'vau̇(ə)r\ *vt* **1** : to eat up greedily **2** : to lay waste : CONSUME **3** : to take in eagerly by the senses or mind
de·vout \di-'vau̇t\ *adj* **1** : devoted to religion or to religious duties or exercises **2** : expressing devotion or piety **3** : warmly devoted : SINCERE — **de·vout·ly** *adv* — **de·vout·ness** *n*
dew \'d(y)ü\ *n* : moisture condensed on the surfaces of cool bodies at night
dew·ber·ry \-ˌber-ē\ *n* : any of several sweet edible berries related to and resembling blackberries
dew·drop \-ˌdräp\ *n* : a drop of dew
dew·lap \'d(y)ü-ˌlap\ *n* : a hanging fold of skin under the neck of bovine animals; *also* : a similar fold on other animals including man — **dew·lapped** \-ˌlapt\ *adj*
dewy \'d(y)ü-ē\ *adj* : moist with, affected by, or suggestive of dew (as in freshness or purity) — **dew·i·ly** \'d(y)ü-ə-lē\ *adv* — **dew·i·ness** \'d(y)ü-ē-nəs\ *n*
dex·ter·i·ty \dek-'ster-ət-ē\ *n, pl* **-ties** **1** : readiness and grace in physical activity; *esp* : skill and ease in using the hands **2** : mental skill or quickness
dex·ter·ous *or* **dex·trous** \'dek-st(ə-)rəs\ *adj* **1** : skillful and competent with the hands **2** : mentally adroit and skillful : EXPERT **3** : done with skillfulness — **dex·ter·ous·ly** *adv* — **dex·ter·ous·ness** *n*
dex·trose \'dek-ˌstrōs\ *n* : a sugar that occurs in plants, fruits, and blood and may be obtained from starch
dhow \'dau̇\ *n* : an Arab sailing ship usu. having a long overhang forward and a high poop
di·a·be·tes \ˌdī-ə-'bēt-ēz, -'bēt-əs\ *n* : an abnormal condition marked by discharge of excessive amounts of urine; *esp* : an endocrine disorder in which insulin is deficient and the urine and blood contain excess sugar — **di·a·bet·ic** \ˌdī-ə-'bet-ik\ *adj or n*
di·a·bol·ic \ˌdī-ə-'bäl-ik\ *adj* : of, relating to, or characteristic of the devil : FIENDISH — **di·a·bol·i·cal** \-'bäl-i-kəl\ *adj* — **di·a·bol·i·cal·ly** \-i-k(ə-)lē\ *adv* — **di·a·bol·i·cal·ness** \-i-kəl-nəs\ *n*
di·ac·o·nate \dī-'ak-ə-nət, -ˌnāt\ *n* **1** : the office or period of office of a deacon **2** : an official body of deacons

¹di·a·crit·ic \ˌdī-ə-ˈkrit-ik\ *or* **di·a·crit·i·cal** \-ˈkrit-i-kəl\ *adj* : serving as a diacritic

²diacritic *n* : a mark accompanying a letter or combination of letters and indicating a sound value different from that given the unmarked or otherwise marked letter or combination of letters

di·a·dem \ˈdī-ə-ˌdem, -əd-əm\ *n* **1** : CROWN; *esp* : a headband worn as a badge of royalty **2** : regal power or dignity

di·aer·e·sis \dī-ˈer-ə-səs\ *n, pl* **di·aer·e·ses** \-ˈer-ə-ˌsēz\ : a mark ¨ placed over a vowel to show that it is pronounced in a separate syllable (as in *naïve* or *Brontë*)

di·ag·nose \ˈdī-əg-ˌnōs\ *vb* : to recognize (as a disease) by signs and symptoms : make a diagnosis

di·ag·no·sis \ˌdī-əg-ˈnō-səs\ *n, pl* **-no·ses** \-ˈnō-ˌsēz\ **1** : the art or act of identifying a disease from its signs and symptoms **2 a** : a careful critical study of something esp. to determine its nature or importance **b** : the conclusion reached after a critical study — **di·ag·nos·tic** \-ˈnäs-tik\ *adj* — **di·ag·nos·ti·cal·ly** \-ˈnäs-ti-k(ə-)lē\ *adv* — **di·ag·nos·ti·cian** \-ˌnäs-ˈtish-ən\ *n*

¹di·ag·o·nal \dī-ˈag-ən-ᵊl\ *adj* **1** : extending from one corner to the opposite corner in a 4-sided figure **2 a** : running in a slanting direction **b** : having diagonal markings or parts — **di·ag·o·nal·ly** \-ˈag-ən-ᵊl-ē, -ˈag-nə-lē\ *adv*

²diagonal *n* **1** : a diagonal line or plane **2 a** : a diagonal direction **b** : a diagonal row, arrangement, or pattern

¹di·a·gram \ˈdī-ə-ˌgram\ *n* : a drawing, sketch, plan, or chart that makes something clearer or easier to understand — **di·a·gram·mat·ic** \ˌdī-ə-grə-ˈmat-ik\ *or* **di·a·gram·mat·i·cal** \-ˈmat-i-kəl\ *adj* — **di·a·gram·mat·i·cal·ly** \-ˈmat-i-k(ə-)lē\ *adv*

²diagram *vt* **-gramed** *or* **-grammed**; **-gram·ing** *or* **-gram·ming** : to represent by or put into the form of a diagram

¹di·al \ˈdī(-ə)l\ *n* **1 a** : the face of a watch or clock **b** : SUNDIAL **2 a** : a face or scale upon which some measurement or other number is registered or indicated usu. by means of numbers and a pointer **b** : a disk usu. with a knob or slots that may be turned to make electrical connections (as on a telephone) or to regulate the operation of a device (as a radio) and that usu. has guiding marks around its border

²dial *vb* **di·aled** *or* **di·alled**; **di·al·ing** *or* **di·al·ling** **1** : to manipulate a telephone dial so as to call **2** : to manipulate a dial so as to operate, regulate, or select

di·a·lect \ˈdī-ə-ˌlekt\ *n* **1** : a regional variety of a language usu. transmitted orally and differing distinctively from the standard language **2** : a variety of a language used by the members of an occupational group **3** : the customary language of a social class — **dialect** *or* **di·a·lec·tal** \ˌdī-ə-ˈlek-tᵊl\ *adj* — **di·a·lec·tal·ly** \-tᵊl-ē\ *adv*

di·a·lec·tic \ˌdī-ə-ˈlek-tik\ *n* : a process or the art of reasoning through the confrontation of opposing arguments or ideas and their fusion in a truer or more comprehensive concept

di·a·logue *or* **di·a·log** \ˈdī-ə-ˌlȯg\ *n* **1 a** : a conversation between two or more persons **b** : an exchange of ideas and opinions **2** : the parts of a literary or dramatic composition that represent conversation

di·am·e·ter \dī-ˈam-ət-ər\ *n* **1** : a chord passing through the center of a figure or body **2** : the length of a straight line through the center of an object — **di·am·e·tral** \-ˈam-ə-trəl\ *adj*

di·a·met·ric \ˌdī-ə-ˈme-trik\ *adj* **1** : DIAMETRAL **2** : completely opposed or opposite — **di·a·met·ri·cal** \-ˈme-tri-kəl\ *adj* — **di·a·met·ri·cal·ly** \-tri-k(ə-)lē\ *adv*

di·a·mond \ˈdī-(ə-)mənd\ *n* **1** : native crystalline carbon that is usu. nearly colorless, that when transparent and free from flaws is highly valued as a precious stone, and that is used industrially as an abrasive powder and in rock drills **2** : a square or rhombus-shaped configuration usu. upright or otherwise clearly oriented **3** : any of a suit of playing cards marked with a red diamond **4 a** : INFIELD **b** : the entire playing field in baseball or softball

di·a·mond·back \ˈdī-(ə-)mən(d)-ˌbak\ *n* : a large and deadly rattlesnake of the southern U.S.

di·a·pa·son \ˌdī-ə-ˈpāz-ᵊn\ *n* **1** : one of two principal stops in an organ extending through the complete scale of the instrument **2** : the full range of musical tones

¹di·a·per \ˈdī-(ə-)pər\ *n* **1** : a usu. white linen or cotton fabric woven in a pattern formed by the repetition of a simple usu. geometric design **2** : a basic garment for infants consisting of a piece of absorbent material drawn up between the legs and fastened about the waist

²diaper *vt* **1** : to ornament with diaper designs **2** : to put a diaper on

di·aph·a·nous \dī-ˈaf-ə-nəs\ *adj* : so fine of texture as to be seen through — **di·aph·a·nous·ly** *adv*

di·a·phragm \ˈdī-ə-ˌfram\ *n* **1** : a body partition of muscle and connective tissue; *esp* : the partition separating the chest and abdominal cavities in mammals **2** : a thin flexible disk that vibrates (as in a microphone) — **di·a·phrag·mat·ic** \ˌdī-ə-ˌfrag-ˈmat-ik\ *adj*

di·ar·rhea *or* **di·ar·rhoea** \ˌdī-ə-ˈrē-ə\ *n* : an abnormal frequency of intestinal discharge — **di·ar·rhe·al** \-ˈrē-əl\ *or* **di·ar·rhe·ic** \-ˈrē-ik\ *adj*

di·a·ry \ˈdī-(ə-)rē\ *n, pl* **-ries** : a daily record esp. of personal experiences, observations, and thoughts; *also* : a book for keeping such private notes and records

di·as·to·le \dī-ˈas-tə-(ˌ)lē\ *n* : a rhythmically recurrent expansion; *esp* : the dilatation of the cavities of the heart during which they fill with blood — **di·a·stol·ic** \ˌdi-ə-ˈstäl-ik\ *adj*

dia·ther·my \ˈdī-ə-ˌthər-mē\ *n* : the generation of heat in tissue for medical or surgical purposes by electric currents — **dia·ther·mic** \ˌdī-ə-ˈthər-mik\ *adj*

dia·ton·ic \ˌdī-ə-ˈtän-ik\ *adj* : relating to or being a standard major or minor scale of eight tones to the octave without chromatic deviation

di·a·tribe \ˈdī-ə-ˌtrīb\ *n* : a bitter or violent attack in speech or writing : an angry criticism or denunciation

dib·ble \ˈdib-əl\ *n* : a small hand tool that is used to make holes in the ground for plants, seeds, or bulbs

¹dice \ˈdīs\ *n, pl* **dice** : a small cube marked on each face with one to six spots and used usu. in pairs in various games and in gambling

²dice *vb* **1** : to cut into small cubes **2** : to play games with dice — **dic·er** *n*

di·chot·o·my \dī-ˈkät-ə-mē\ *n, pl* **-mies** : a division or the process of dividing into two esp. mutually exclusive or contradictory groups

dick·ens \ˈdik-ənz\ *n* : DEVIL, DEUCE — used chiefly as a mild oath

dick·er \ˈdik-ər\ *vi* **dick·ered**; **dick·er·ing** \ˈdik-(ə-)riŋ\ : BARGAIN, HAGGLE — **dicker** *n*

dick·ey *or* **dicky** \ˈdik-ē\ *n, pl* **dick·eys** *or* **dick·ies** : any of various articles of clothing; *esp* : a small fabric insert worn to fill in the neckline

di·cot·y·le·don \ˌdī-ˌkät-ᵊl-ˈēd-ᵊn\ *n* : any of a group of flowering plants having an embryo with two cotyledons — **di·cot·y·le·don·ous** \-ᵊn-əs\ *adj*

¹dic·tate \ˈdik-ˌtāt\ *vb* **1** : to speak or read for a person to transcribe or for a machine to record **2** : to say or state with authority : give orders to do a certain thing

²dictate *n* : an authoritative rule, prescription, or injunction : COMMAND

dic·ta·tion \dik-ˈtā-shən\ *n* **1** : the act or process of giving arbitrary commands **2 a** : the dictating of words **b** : something that is dictated or is taken down as dictated

dic·ta·tor \ˈdik-ˌtāt-ər\ *n* **1** : a person ruling absolutely and often brutally and oppressively **2 :** one that dictates — **dic·ta·tress** \-ˌtā-trəs\ *n*

dic·ta·to·ri·al \ˌdik-tə-ˈtōr-ē-əl\ *adj* **:** of, relating to, or characteristic of a dictator or a dictatorship **:** AUTOCRATIC, ARBITRARY — **dic·ta·to·ri·al·ly** \-ē-ə-lē\ *adv*

dic·ta·tor·ship \dik-ˈtāt-ər-ˌship\ *n* **1 :** the office or term of office of a dictator **2 :** autocratic rule, control, or leadership **3 :** a government or country in which absolute power is held by a dictator or a small clique

dic·tion \ˈdik-shən\ *n* **1 :** choice of words esp. with regard to correctness, clearness, or effectiveness **:** WORDING **2 :** quality of vocal expression **:** ENUNCIATION

dic·tio·nary \ˈdik-shə-ˌner-ē\ *n, pl* **-nar·ies 1 :** a reference book containing words usu. alphabetically arranged along with information about their forms, pronunciations, functions, etymologies, meanings, and syntactical and idiomatic uses **2 :** a reference book giving for words of one language equivalents in another

dic·tum \ˈdik-təm\ *n, pl* **dic·ta** \-tə\ **1 :** an authoritative statement on some topic **:** PRONOUNCEMENT **2 :** a formal statement of an opinion

did *past of* DO

di·dac·tic \dī-ˈdak-tik\ *adj* **1 :** intended primarily to instruct rather than to entertain; *esp* **:** intended to teach a moral lesson **2 :** having or showing a tendency to instruct or lecture others — **di·dac·ti·cal** \-ti-kəl\ *adj* — **di·dac·ti·cal·ly** \-ti-k(ə-)lē\ *adv* — **di·dac·ti·cism** \-tə-ˌsiz-əm\ *n*

di·dac·tics \-tiks\ *n sing or pl* **:** systematic instruction

[1]**die** \ˈdī\ *vi* **died**; **dy·ing** \ˈdī-iŋ\ **1 :** to stop living **:** EXPIRE **2 a :** to pass out of existence **b :** to disappear or subside gradually **3 :** to long keenly or desperately **4 :** STOP

[2]**die** \ˈdī\ *n, pl* **dice** \ˈdīs\ *or* **dies** \ˈdīz\ **1** *pl dice* **:** DICE **2** *pl usu dice* **:** something determined by or as if by a cast of dice **:** CHANCE **3** *pl dies* **:** any of various tools or devices for imparting a desired shape, form, or finish to a material or for impressing an object or material

die·hard \ˈdī-ˌhärd\ *n* **:** one who resists against hopeless odds; *esp* **:** an irreconcilable opponent — **die–hard** *adj*

di·elec·tric \ˌdī-ə-ˈlek-trik\ *n* **:** a nonconductor of electric current

die·sel engine \ˌdē-zəl-, -səl-\ *n* **:** an internal-combustion engine in which air is compressed to a temperature sufficiently high to ignite fuel injected into the cylinder

[1]**di·et** \ˈdī-ət\ *n* **1 :** the food and drink that a person, animal, or group usu. takes **:** customary nourishment **2 :** the kind and amount of food selected for a person or animal for a special reason (as ill health or overweight)

[2]**diet** *vb* **:** to eat or cause to eat less or according to prescribed rules — **di·et·er** *n*

[3]**diet** *n* **:** a formal deliberative assembly; *esp* **:** any of various national or provincial legislatures

di·e·tary \ˈdī-ə-ˌter-ē\ *adj* **:** of or relating to a diet or to the rules of diet

di·e·tet·ic \ˌdī-ə-ˈtet-ik\ *adj* **:** of or relating to diet or dietetics — **di·e·tet·i·cal·ly** \-ˈtet-i-k(ə-)lē\ *adv*

di·e·tet·ics \-ˈtet-iks\ *n* **:** the science or art of applying the principles of nutrition to feeding

di·e·ti·tian *or* **di·e·ti·cian** \ˌdī-ə-ˈtish-ən\ *n* **:** a person qualified in or practicing dietetics

dif·fer \ˈdif-ər\ *vi* **dif·fered**; **dif·fer·ing** \ˈdif-(ə-)riŋ\ **1 :** to be not the same **:** be unlike **2 :** DISAGREE

dif·fer·ence \ˈdif-ərn(t)s, ˈdif-(ə-)rən(t)s\ *n* **1 :** unlikeness between two or more persons or things **2 :** the degree or amount by which things differ in quantity or measure; *esp* **:** the number that is obtained by subtracting one number from another **3 :** a disagreement in opinion **:** DISPUTE

dif·fer·ent \ˈdif-ərnt, ˈdif-(ə-)rənt\ *adj* **1 :** not of the same kind **:** UNLIKE **2 :** not the same **:** OTHER, SEPARATE

dif·fer·en·tia \ˌdif-ə-ˈren-ch(ē-)ə\ *n, pl* **-ti·ae** \-chē-ˌē, -chē-ˌī\ **:** the element, feature, or factor that distinguishes two things of the same general class

[1]**dif·fer·en·tial** \ˌdif-ə-ˈren-chəl\ *adj* **1 :** of, relating to, or constituting a distinction **:** DISTINGUISHING **2 :** making a distinction between individuals or classes — **dif·fer·en·tial·ly** \-ˈrench-(ə-)lē\ *adv*

[2]**differential** *n* **1 :** an amount or degree of difference between comparable individuals or classes **2 :** DIFFERENTIAL GEAR

differential gear *n* **:** an arrangement of gears in an automobile that allows one of the wheels imparting motion to turn (as in going around a curve) faster than the other

dif·fer·en·ti·ate \ˌdif-ə-ˈren-chē-ˌāt\ *vb* **1 :** to make or become different **2 :** to recognize or state the difference

dif·fer·en·ti·a·tion \-ˌren-chē-ˈā-shən\ *n* **:** the act or process of differentiating

dif·fer·ent·ly \ˈdif-ərnt-lē, ˈdif-(ə-)rənt-\ *adv* **1 :** in a different manner **2 :** OTHERWISE

dif·fi·cult \ˈdif-i-(ˌ)kəlt\ *adj* **1 :** hard to do, make, or carry out **:** ARDUOUS **2 a :** hard to deal with, manage, or overcome **b :** hard to understand **:** PUZZLING — **dif·fi·cult·ly** *adv*

dif·fi·cul·ty \-(ˌ)kəl-tē\ *n, pl* **-ties 1 :** difficult nature **2 :** great effort **3 :** something that is hard to do **:** OBSTACLE **4 :** a difficult or trying situation **:** TROUBLE **5 :** DISAGREEMENT

dif·fi·dence \ˈdif-əd-ən(t)s\ *n* **:** the quality or state of being diffident

dif·fi·dent \-əd-ənt\ *adj* **1 :** lacking confidence **:** TIMID **2 :** RESERVED, UNASSERTIVE — **dif·fi·dent·ly** *adv*

[1]**dif·fuse** \dif-ˈyüs\ *adj* **1 :** poured or spread out **:** not concentrated **2 :** marked by wordiness **:** VERBOSE **3 :** spreading widely or loosely **:** SCATTERED — **dif·fuse·ly** *adv* — **dif·fuse·ness** *n*

[2]**dif·fuse** \dif-ˈyüz\ *vb* **:** to pour out or spread freely — **dif·fus·er** *n*

dif·fu·sion \dif-ˈyü-zhən\ *n* **:** a diffusing or a being diffused; *also* **:** the state of being diffused

[1]**dig** \ˈdig\ *vb* **dug** \ˈdəg\; **dig·ging 1 a :** to turn up the soil (as with a spade or hoe) **b :** to hollow out or form by removing earth **2 :** to uncover or seek by turning up earth **3 :** to bring to light **:** DISCOVER **4 :** POKE, THRUST **5 :** to work hard — **dig·ger** *n*

[2]**dig** *n* **1 :** THRUST, POKE **2 :** a cutting remark **:** GIBE

[1]**di·gest** \ˈdī-ˌjest\ *n* **:** a summation or condensation of a body of information or of a literary work

[2]**di·gest** \dī-ˈjest, də-\ *vb* **1 :** to think over and arrange in the mind **:** assimilate mentally **2 :** to convert food into simpler forms that can be taken in and used by the body **3 :** to compress into a short summary **4 :** to become digested — **di·gest·er** *n*

di·gest·i·ble \dī-ˈjəs-tə-bəl, də-\ *adj* **:** capable of being digested — **di·gest·i·bil·i·ty** \(ˌ)dī-ˌjes-tə-ˈbil-ət-ē, də-\ *n*

di·ges·tion \-ˈjes-chən\ *n* **:** the process or power of digesting something and esp. food

di·ges·tive \-ˈjes-tiv\ *adj* **1 :** of or relating to digestion **2 :** having the power to cause or promote digestion

dig·gings \ˈdig-iŋz\ *n pl* **1 :** a place where ore, metals, or precious stones are dug **2 :** LODGINGS

dig·it \ˈdij-ət\ *n* **1 :** any of the arabic numerals 1 to 9 and usu. the symbol 0 **2 :** FINGER, TOE

dig·i·tal·is \ˌdij-ə-ˈtal-əs\ *n* **:** the dried leaf of the common foxglove serving as a powerful heart stimulant and a diuretic

dig·ni·fied \ˈdig-nə-ˌfīd\ *adj* **:** showing or expressing dignity

dig·ni·fy \-ˌfī\ *vt* **-fied**; **-fy·ing :** to give dignity or distinction to **:** HONOR

dig·ni·tary \ˈdig-nə-ˌter-ē\ *n, pl* **-tar·ies :** a person of high position or honor

dig·ni·ty \ˈdig-nət-ē\ *n, pl* **-ties 1 :** the quality or state of being

worthy, honored, or esteemed **2 :** high rank, office, or position **3 :** formal reserve of manner or language
di·graph \'dī-ˌgraf\ *n* **:** a group of two successive letters representing a single sound
di·gress \dī-'gres\ *vi* **:** to turn aside esp. from the main subject in writing or speaking — **di·gres·sion** \-'gresh-ən\ *n*
di·gres·sive \-'gres-iv\ *adj* **:** characterized by digressions — **di·gres·sive·ly** *adv* — **di·gres·sive·ness** *n*
dike \'dīk\ *n* **:** a bank of earth constructed to control or confine water **:** LEVEE
di·lap·i·dat·ed \də-'lap-ə-ˌdāt-əd\ *adj* **:** partly ruined or decayed
di·lap·i·da·tion \-ˌlap-ə-'dā-shən\ *n* **:** a dilapidated condition **:** partial ruin (as from neglect)
dil·a·ta·tion \ˌdil-ə-'tā-shən, ˌdī-lə-\ *n* **1 :** the condition of being stretched beyond normal dimensions esp. as a result of overwork or disease **2 :** DILATION — **dil·a·ta·tion·al** \-shnəl, -shən-ᵊl\ *adj*
di·late \dī-'lāt, 'dī-ˌ\ *vb* **:** to make or grow larger or wider
di·la·tion \dī-'lā-shən\ *n* **:** the act of dilating **:** the state of being dilated **:** EXPANSION
dil·a·to·ry \'dil-ə-ˌtōr-ē\ *adj* **1 :** tending or intended to cause delay **2 :** characterized by procrastination **:** TARDY
di·lem·ma \də-'lem-ə\ *n* **:** a choice or a situation in which one has to choose between two or more things, ways, or plans that are equally unsatisfactory **:** a difficult choice
dil·et·tante \ˌdil-ə-'tänt(-ē), -'tant(-ē)\ *n, pl* **-tantes** *or* **-tan·ti** \-'tänt-ē, -'tant-ē\ **:** a person who cultivates esp. superficially an art or branch of knowledge as a pastime — **dilettante** *adj* — **dil·et·tan·tism** \-'tän-ˌtiz-əm, -'tan-\ *n*
dil·i·gence \'dil-ə-jən(t)s\ *n* **:** careful and continued work **:** conscientious effort **:** INDUSTRY
dil·i·gent \'dil-ə-jənt\ *adj* **:** characterized by steady, earnest, and energetic application and effort **:** PAINSTAKING — **dil·i·gent·ly** *adv*
dill \'dil\ *n* **:** an herb related to the carrot with aromatic foliage and seeds used in flavoring pickles
dil·ly·dal·ly \'dil-ē-ˌdal-ē\ *vi* **:** to waste time by loitering or delay **:** DAWDLE
¹di·lute \dī-'lüt, də-\ *vt* **1 :** to make thinner or more liquid by admixture (as with water) **2 :** to diminish the strength, flavor, or brilliance of by admixture
²dilute *adj* **:** DILUTED, WEAK — **di·lute·ness** *n*
di·lu·tion \dī-'lü-shən, də-\ *n* **1 :** the act of diluting **:** the state of being diluted **2 :** something that is diluted
¹dim \'dim\ *adj* **dim·mer**; **dim·mest** **1 :** not bright or distinct **:** OBSCURE, FAINT **2 :** being without luster **:** DULL **3 :** not seeing or understanding clearly — **dim·ly** *adv* — **dim·ness** *n*
²dim *vb* **dimmed**; **dim·ming** **1 :** to make or become dim or lusterless **2 :** to reduce the light from (headlights) by switching to the low beam — **dim·mer** *n*
dime \'dīm\ *n* **:** a U.S. coin worth 1/10 dollar
di·men·sion \də-'men-chən\ *n* **1 a :** extension in one direction **b :** magnitude of extension in one direction or in all directions **:** SIZE **2 :** the range over which something extends **:** SCOPE — **di·men·sion·al** \-'mench-nəl, -'men-chən-ᵊl\ *adj*
di·min·ish \də-'min-ish\ *vb* **1 :** to make less or cause to appear less **2 :** to lessen the authority, dignity, or reputation of **:** BELITTLE **3 :** DWINDLE **4 :** TAPER — **di·min·ish·a·ble** *adj*
dim·i·nu·tion \ˌdim-ə-'n(y)ü-shən\ *n* **:** the act, process, or an instance of diminishing **:** DECREASE
¹di·min·u·tive \də-'min-yət-iv\ *n* **1 :** a diminutive word or affix **2 :** a diminutive object or individual
²diminutive *adj* **1 :** indicating small size and sometimes the state or quality of being lovable, pitiable, or contemptible **2 :** extremely small **:** TINY
dim·i·ty \'dim-ət-ē\ *n, pl* **-ties** **:** a sheer usu. corded cotton fabric of plain weave in checks or stripes
¹dim·ple \'dim-pəl\ *n* **:** a slight natural indentation in the surface of some part of the human body
²dimple *vb* **dim·pled**; **dim·pling** \-p(ə-)liŋ\ **:** to mark with or form dimples
¹din \'din\ *n* **:** a loud noise; *esp* **:** a welter of confused sounds
²din *vb* **dinned**; **din·ning** **1 :** to make or deafen with loud noise **2 :** to impress by insistent repetition
dine \'dīn\ *vb* **1 :** to eat dinner **2 :** to give a dinner to **:** FEED
din·er \'dī-nər\ *n* **1 :** one that dines **2 a :** DINING CAR **b :** a restaurant in the shape of a railroad car
di·nette \dī-'net\ *n* **:** an alcove or small room used for dining
ding \'diŋ\ *vi* **:** to make a ringing sound **:** CLANG
¹ding·dong \'diŋ-ˌdȯŋ, -ˌdäŋ\ *n* **:** the sound of repeated strokes on a bell or a similar sound
²dingdong *adj* **:** vigorously contested
din·ghy \'diŋ-(k)ē\ *n, pl* **dinghies** **1 :** a ship's small boat **2 :** a rowboat used as a tender **3 :** a rubber life raft
din·gle \'diŋ-gəl\ *n* **:** a small narrow wooded valley
din·gy \'din-jē\ *adj* **1 :** DARK, DULL **2 :** not fresh or clean **:** GRIMY — **din·gi·ly** \-jə-lē\ *adv* — **din·gi·ness** \-jē-nəs\ *n*
dining car *n* **:** a railroad car in which meals are served
din·ky \'diŋ-kē\ *adj* **:** SMALL, INSIGNIFICANT
din·ner \'din-ər\ *n* **1 :** the main meal of the day **2 :** a formal banquet
dinner jacket *n* **:** TUXEDO
di·no·saur \'dī-nə-ˌsȯr\ *n* **:** any of a group of extinct chiefly terrestrial long-tailed reptiles with limbs adapted for walking — **di·no·sau·ri·an** \ˌdī-nə-'sȯr-ē-ən\ *adj or n*

dinosaur skeleton

¹dint \'dint\ *n* **1 :** FORCE, POWER — used chiefly in the phrase *by dint of* **2 :** DENT
²dint *vt* **:** DENT
¹di·oc·e·san \dī-'äs-ə-sən\ *adj* **:** of or relating to a diocese
²diocesan *n* **:** a bishop having jurisdiction over a diocese
di·o·cese \'dī-ə-səs, -ˌsēz\ *n* **:** the district over which a bishop has authority
di·ode \'dī-ˌōd\ *n* **:** a rectifier usu. made of semiconductor material
¹dip \'dip\ *vb* **dipped**; **dip·ping** **1 a :** to plunge momentarily or partially under the surface (as of a liquid) so as to moisten, cool, or coat **b :** to thrust in a way to suggest immersion **2 :** to lift a portion of by reaching below the surface with something shaped to hold liquid **:** LADLE **3 :** to lower and then raise again **4 :** to plunge into a liquid and quickly emerge **5 a :** to drop down or out of sight esp. suddenly **b :** to decrease moderately and usu. temporarily **6 :** to reach down inside or as if inside or below a surface esp. to withdraw a part of the contents **7 :** to delve casually or tentatively into something; *esp* **:** to read superficially
²dip *n* **1 :** an act of dipping; *esp* **:** a brief plunge into the water for sport or exercise **2 :** inclination downward **:** DROP **3 :** something obtained by or used in dipping **4 :** a liquid into which something may be dipped
diph·the·ria \dif-'thir-ē-ə, dip-\ *n* **:** an acute febrile contagious bacterial disease in which the air passages become coated with a membranous layer that often obstructs breathing
diph·thong \'dif-ˌthȯŋ, 'dip-\ *n* **:** a 2-element speech sound (as *ou* in *out* and *oy* in *boy*) that begins with the tongue position

for one vowel and ends with the tongue position for another all within one syllable

di·plo·ma \də-ˈplō-mə\ *n* : an official paper bearing record of graduation from or of a degree conferred by an educational institution

di·plo·ma·cy \də-ˈplō-mə-sē\ *n* **1** : the art and practice of conducting negotiations between nations **2** : TACT

dip·lo·mat \ˈdip-lə-ˌmat\ *n* : a person employed or skilled in diplomacy

dip·lo·mat·ic \ˌdip-lə-ˈmat-ik\ *adj* **1** : of, relating to, or concerned with diplomacy or diplomats **2** : TACTFUL — **dip·lo·mat·i·cal·ly** \-ˈmat-i-k(ə-)lē\ *adv*

di·plo·ma·tist \də-ˈplō-mət-əst\ *n* : DIPLOMAT

dip·per \ˈdip-ər\ *n* **1** : one that dips; *esp* : something (as a long-handled cup) used for dipping **2** : any of several birds skilled in diving

dip·ter·an \ˈdip-tə-rən\ *adj* : of, relating to, or being a two-winged fly — **dipteran** *n*

dire \ˈdī(ə)r\ *adj* **1** : exciting horror : DREADFUL **2** : warning of disaster **3** : EXTREME

¹di·rect \də-ˈrekt, dī-\ *vt* **1** : to mark with a name and address **2** : to cause to turn, move, or point or to follow a straight course **3** : to point, extend, or project in a specified line, course, or direction **4** : to show or point out the way for **5 a** : to regulate the activities or course of **b** : to guide the organizing, supervising, or performance of **6** : to request or instruct with authority

²direct *adj* **1** : proceeding from one point to another in time or space without deviation or interruption : STRAIGHT **2 a** : stemming immediately from a source, cause, or reason **b** : operating without an intervening agency or step **c** : being or passing in a straight line of descent from parent to offspring : LINEAL **3** : NATURAL, STRAIGHTFORWARD **4 a** : effected by the action of the people or the electorate and not by representatives **b** : consisting of or reproducing the exact words of a speaker — **direct** *adv* — **di·rect·ness** *n*

di·rect·ed \-ˈrek-təd\ *adj* : proceeding in a direction designated as positive or negative

di·rec·tion \-ˈrek-shən\ *n* **1 a** : guidance or supervision of action or conduct **b** : the art and technique of directing an orchestra or theatrical production **2** : an authoritative instruction, indication, or order **3** : the line or course along which something moves, lies, or points **4** : TENDENCY, TREND

di·rec·tion·al \-shnəl, -shən-ᵊl\ *adj* **1** : relating to or indicating direction in space **2** : suitable for sending out or receiving radio signals in one direction only **3** : operating most effectively in a particular direction

¹di·rec·tive \də-ˈrek-tiv, dī-\ *adj* : serving to direct, guide, or influence

²directive *n* : a general instruction as to procedure

di·rect·ly \-ˈrek-(t)lē\ *adv* **1** : in a direct manner **2** : without delay : IMMEDIATELY

di·rec·tor \də-ˈrek-tər, dī-\ *n* : one that directs: as **a** : one of a group of persons who direct the affairs of an organized body (as a nation or corporation) **b** : one that supervises the production of a show (as for stage or screen) **c** : CONDUCTOR b — **di·rec·to·ri·al** \də-ˌrek-ˈtōr-ē-əl, (ˌ)dī-\ *adj* — **di·rec·tor·ship** \də-ˈrek-tər-ˌship, dī-\ *n*

di·rec·tor·ate \də-ˈrek-t(ə-)rət, dī-\ *n* **1** : the office of director **2** : a board of directors (as of a corporation)

di·rec·to·ry \-t(ə-)rē\ *n, pl* **-ries** : an alphabetical or classified list containing names and addresses

dire·ful \ˈdī(ə)r-fəl\ *adj* : producing dire effects — **dire·ful·ly** \-fə-lē\ *adv*

dirge \ˈdərj\ *n* : a song or hymn of lamentation; *esp* : one intended for funeral or memorial rites

dir·i·gi·ble \ˈdir-ə-jə-bəl, də-ˈrij-ə-\ *n* : AIRSHIP

dirk \ˈdərk\ *n* : a long straight-bladed dagger — **dirk** *vt*

dirt \ˈdərt\ *n* **1** : a filthy or soiling substance (as mud, dust, or grime) **2** : loose or packed earth : SOIL **3** : moral uncleanness: as **a** : OBSCENITY **b** : CORRUPTION

¹dirty \ˈdərt-ē\ *adj* **1** : not clean : FILTHY, SOILED **2** : BASE, UNFAIR **3** : INDECENT, SMUTTY **4** : FOGGY, STORMY **5** : not clear in color : DULL — **dirt·i·ly** \ˈdərt-ᵊl-ē\ *adv* — **dirt·i·ness** \ˈdərt-ē-nəs\ *n*

²dirty *vb* **dirt·ied**; **dirt·y·ing** : to make or become dirty

dis·abil·i·ty \ˌdis-ə-ˈbil-ət-ē\ *n, pl* **-ties** **1** : the condition of being disabled **2** : a source of disability; *also* : a legal disqualification

dis·able \dis-ˈā-bəl\ *vt* **dis·abled**; **dis·abling** \-b(ə-)liŋ\ **1** : to make unable or incapable : deprive of force, strength, or power of action : CRIPPLE **2** : to disqualify legally — **dis·able·ment** *n*

dis·abuse \ˌdis-ə-ˈbyüz\ *vt* : to free from error or fallacy

¹dis·ad·van·tage \ˌdis-əd-ˈvant-ij\ *n* **1** : loss or damage esp. to reputation or finances **2 a** : an unfavorable, inferior, or prejudicial condition **b** : HANDICAP

²disadvantage *vt* : to place at a disadvantage : HARM

dis·ad·van·ta·geous \(ˌ)dis-ˌad-ˌvan-ˈtā-jəs, -vən-\ *adj* : constituting a disadvantage — **dis·ad·van·ta·geous·ly** *adv* — **dis·ad·van·ta·geous·ness** *n*

dis·af·fect \ˌdis-ə-ˈfekt\ *vt* : to alienate the affection or loyalty of : cause discontent in — **dis·af·fec·tion** \-ˈfek-shən\ *n*

dis·agree \ˌdis-ə-ˈgrē\ *vi* **1** : to fail to agree **2** : to differ in opinion **3** : to be unsuitable

dis·agree·a·ble \-ˈgrē-ə-bəl\ *adj* **1** : causing discomfort : UNPLEASANT, OFFENSIVE **2** : marked by ill temper : PEEVISH — **dis·agree·a·ble·ness** *n* — **dis·agree·a·bly** \-blē\ *adv*

dis·agree·ment \-ˈgrē-mənt\ *n* **1** : the act of disagreeing **2 a** : the state of being different **b** : QUARREL

dis·al·low \ˌdis-ə-ˈlau̇\ *vt* : to refuse to admit or recognize : REJECT — **dis·al·low·ance** \-ˈlau̇-ən(t)s\ *n*

dis·ap·pear \ˌdis-ə-ˈpi(ə)r\ *vi* **1** : to pass from view suddenly or gradually **2** : to cease to be : become lost — **dis·ap·pear·ance** \-ˈpir-ən(t)s\ *n*

dis·ap·point \ˌdis-ə-ˈpȯint\ *vt* : to fail to come up to the expectation or hope of : FRUSTRATE

dis·ap·point·ed \-əd\ *adj* : defeated in expectation or hope

dis·ap·point·ment \-mənt\ *n* **1** : the act or an instance of disappointing : the state or emotion of being disappointed **2** : one that disappoints

dis·ap·pro·ba·tion \(ˌ)dis-ˌap-rə-ˈbā-shən\ *n* : the act or state of disapproving : the state of being disapproved

dis·ap·prov·al \ˌdis-ə-ˈprü-vəl\ *n* **1** : the act of disapproving **2** : unfavorable opinion or judgment : CENSURE

dis·ap·prove \-ˈprüv\ *vb* **1** : to pass unfavorable judgment on : CONDEMN **2** : to refuse approval to : REJECT **3** : to feel or express disapproval

dis·arm \(ˈ)dis-ˈärm\ *vb* **1** : to deprive of arms : take arms or weapons from **2** : to disband or esp. to reduce the size and strength of the armed forces of a country **3** : to make harmless, peaceable, or friendly : remove dislike or suspicion — **dis·ar·ma·ment** \-ˈär-mə-mənt\ *n*

dis·ar·range \ˌdis-ə-ˈrānj\ *vt* : to disturb the arrangement or order of — **dis·ar·range·ment** *n*

¹dis·ar·ray \ˌdis-ə-ˈrā\ *n* **1** : a lack of order or sequence : CONFUSION **2** : disorderly dress : DISHABILLE

²disarray *vt* **1** : to throw into disorder **2** : UNDRESS

dis·as·sem·ble \ˌdis-ə-ˈsem-bəl\ *vt* : to take apart

di·sas·ter \diz-ˈas-tər\ *n* : a sudden great misfortune; *esp* : one bringing with it destruction of life or property or causing complete ruin

di·sas·trous \-ˈas-trəs\ *adj* : accompanied by or producing suffering or disaster — **di·sas·trous·ly** *adv*

dis·avow \ˌdis-ə-ˈvau̇\ *vt* : to deny responsibility for : REPUDIATE — **dis·avow·al** \-ˈvau̇(-ə)l\ *n*

dis·band \dis-'band\ *vb* : to break up the organization of : DISPERSE — **dis·band·ment** *n*
dis·bar \dis-'bär\ *vt* **dis·barred**; **dis·bar·ring** : to deprive (a lawyer) of the rights and privileges of membership in the legal profession — **dis·bar·ment** *n*
dis·be·lief \ˌdis-bə-'lēf\ *n* : the act of disbelieving : mental rejection of a statement as untrue
dis·be·lieve \-'lēv\ *vb* **1** : to hold not to be true or real **2** : to withhold or reject belief — **dis·be·liev·er** *n*
dis·bur·den \(')dis-'bərd-ᵊn\ *vt* : to rid of a burden
dis·burse \dis-'bərs\ *vt* : to pay out : EXPEND — **dis·burs·er** *n*
dis·burse·ment \-mənt\ *n* : the act of disbursing; *also* : funds paid out
disc *var of* DISK
dis·card \dis-'kärd, 'dis-ˌ\ *vb* **1 a** : to let go a playing card from one's hand **b** : to play (a card) from a suit other than trump but different from the one led **2** : to get rid of as useless or unwanted — **dis·card** \'dis-ˌkärd\ *n*
disc brake *n* : a brake that operates by the friction of pads pressing against the sides of a rotating disk
dis·cern \dis-'ərn, diz-\ *vt* **1** : to detect with the eyes : make out : DISTINGUISH **2** : to come to know, recognize, or discriminate mentally — **dis·cern·i·ble** \-'ər-nə-bəl\ *adj* — **dis·cern·i·bly** \-blē\ *adv*
dis·cern·ing \-'ər-niŋ\ *adj* : revealing insight and understanding : DISCRIMINATING — **dis·cern·ing·ly** *adv*
dis·cern·ment \dis-'ərn-mənt, diz-\ *n* : skill in discerning or discriminating : keenness of insight
¹dis·charge \dis-'chärj, 'dis-ˌ\ *vb* **1 a** : to relieve of a charge, load, or burden : UNLOAD **b** : to throw off or deliver a charge **2** : SHOOT **3** : to set free **4** : to dismiss from service or employment **5** : to let go or let off **6** : to give forth fluid or other contents **7** : to get rid of by paying or doing — **dis·charg·er** *n*
²dis·charge \'dis-ˌchärj, dis-'\ *n* **1 a** : the act of discharging, unloading, or releasing **b** : something that discharges or releases; *esp* : a certification of release or payment **2** : a firing off **3 a** : a flowing or issuing out; *also* : a rate of flow **b** : something that is emitted **4 a** : release or dismissal esp. from an office or employment **b** : complete separation from military service **5** : a flow of electricity through a gas
dis·ci·ple \dis-'ī-pəl\ *n* **1 a** : a pupil or follower who accepts and helps to spread his master's teachings **b** : a convinced adherent **2** *cap* : a member of the Disciples of Christ — **dis·ci·ple·ship** \-ˌship\ *n*
dis·ci·pli·nar·i·an \ˌdis-ə-plə-'ner-ē-ən\ *n* : one who disciplines or enforces order — **disciplinarian** *adj*
dis·ci·plin·ary \'dis-ə-plə-ˌner-ē\ *adj* : of or relating to discipline : CORRECTIVE
¹dis·ci·pline \'dis-ə-plən\ *n* **1** : a field of study : SUBJECT **2** : training that corrects, molds, or perfects **3** : PUNISHMENT **4** : control gained by obedience or training : orderly conduct **5** : a system of rules governing conduct or practice
²discipline *vt* **1** : to punish or penalize for the sake of discipline **2** : to train or develop by instruction and exercise esp. in self-control **3 a** : to bring (a group) under control **b** : to impose order upon — **dis·ci·plin·er** *n*
disc jockey *n* : a person who conducts and announces a radio or television program of musical recordings
dis·claim \dis-'klām\ *vt* : to deny having a connection with or responsibility for : DISOWN
dis·claim·er \-'klā-mər\ *n* **1** : an act of disclaiming : a statement that disclaims : DENIAL **2** : REPUDIATION
dis·close \dis-'klōz\ *vt* : to expose to view : make known : REVEAL — **dis·clos·er** *n*
dis·clo·sure \-'klō-zhər\ *n* **1** : the act or an instance of disclosing : EXPOSURE **2** : something that is disclosed

dis·col·or \(')dis-'kəl-ər\ *vb* : to alter or change in hue or color — **dis·col·or·a·tion** \(ˌ)dis-ˌkəl-ə-'rā-shən\ *n*
dis·com·bob·u·late \ˌdis-kəm-'bäb-(y)ə-ˌlāt\ *vt* : UPSET, CONFUSE
dis·com·fit \dis-'kəm(p)-fət\ *vt* : to throw into confusion : UPSET, FRUSTRATE — **dis·com·fi·ture** \dis-'kəm(p)-fə-ˌchu̇r\ *n*
¹dis·com·fort \dis-'kəm(p)-fərt\ *vt* : to make uncomfortable or uneasy
²discomfort *n* : lack of comfort : physical or mental uneasiness : DISTRESS
dis·com·mode \ˌdis-kə-'mōd\ *vt* : to cause inconvenience to
dis·com·pose \ˌdis-kəm-'pōz\ *vt* **1** : to disturb the calmness or peace of : AGITATE **2** : DISARRANGE — **dis·com·po·sure** \-'pō-zhər\ *n*
dis·con·cert \ˌdis-kən-'sərt\ *vt* **1** : to throw into mental confusion **2** : to disturb the composure of — **dis·con·cert·ing·ly** *adv*
dis·con·nect \ˌdis-kə-'nekt\ *vt* : to undo or break the connection of — **dis·con·nec·tion** \-'nek-shən\ *n*
dis·con·nect·ed \-'nek-təd\ *adj* : not connected : INCOHERENT — **dis·con·nect·ed·ly** *adv* — **dis·con·nect·ed·ness** *n*
dis·con·so·late \dis-'kän(t)-sə-lət\ *adj* **1** : lacking consolation : hopelessly sad **2** : causing or suggestive of dejection : CHEERLESS — **dis·con·so·late·ly** *adv* — **dis·oon·so·late·ness** *n*
¹dis·con·tent \ˌdis-kən-'tent\ *adj* : DISCONTENTED
²discontent *vt* : to make discontented — **dis·con·tent·ment** *n*
³discontent *n* **1** : lack of contentment : UNEASINESS **2** : a yearning for improvement or perfection
dis·con·tent·ed \-'tent-əd\ *adj* : DISSATISFIED, MALCONTENT — **dis·con·tent·ed·ly** *adv* — **dis·con·tent·ed·ness** *n*
dis·con·tin·u·ance \ˌdis-kən-'tin-yə-wən(t)s\ *n* : the act or an instance of discontinuing
dis·con·tin·ue \ˌdis-kən-'tin-yü\ *vb* **1** : to break the continuity of : cease to operate, use, or take **2** : END
dis·con·tin·u·ous \ˌdis-kən-'tin-yə-wəs\ *adj* : not continuous : having interruptions or gaps : BROKEN — **dis·con·ti·nu·i·ty** \(ˌ)dis-ˌkänt-ᵊn-'(y)ü-ət-ē\ *n* — **dis·con·tin·u·ous·ly** *adv*
dis·cord \'dis-ˌkȯrd\ *n* : lack of agreement or harmony: **a** : DISUNITY, DISSENSION **b** : CONFLICT **c** : OPPOSITION, CONTRAST **d** (1) : a harsh combination of musical sounds (2) : DISSONANCE **e** : a harsh or unpleasant sound
dis·cord·ance \dis-'kȯrd-ᵊn(t)s\ *n* **1** : the state or an instance of being discordant **2** : DISSONANCE
dis·cord·ant \-ᵊnt\ *adj* **1 a** : being at variance : DISAGREEING **b** : QUARRELSOME **2** : relating to or producing a discord : JARRING — **dis·cord·ant·ly** *adv*
dis·co·theque \ˌdis-kə-'tek\ *n* : a usu. small intimate nightclub for dancing to recorded music
¹dis·count \'dis-ˌkau̇nt\ *n* **1** : a reduction made from a regular or list price **2** : an advance deduction of interest on money lent
²dis·count \'dis-ˌkau̇nt, dis-'\ *vt* **1 a** : to reduce or deduct from the amount of a bill, debt, or charge **b** : to sell or offer for sale at a discount **2** : to lend money on (a note) after deducting the discount **3 a** : MINIMIZE **b** : to make allowance for bias or exaggeration in **c** : to take into account (as a future event) in present calculations — **dis·count·a·ble** *adj*
dis·coun·te·nance \dis-'kau̇nt-ᵊn-ən(t)s, -'kau̇nt-nən(t)s\ *vt* **1** : EMBARRASS, DISCONCERT **2** : to look with disfavor on
dis·cour·age \dis-'kər-ij\ *vt* **1** : to lessen the courage or confidence of : DISHEARTEN **2 a** : to hinder by inspiring fear of consequences : DETER **b** : to attempt to dissuade — **dis·cour·ag·ing·ly** *adv*
dis·cour·age·ment \-'kər-ij-mənt\ *n* **1** : an act of discouraging : the state of being discouraged **2** : something that discourages
¹dis·course \'dis-ˌkōrs\ *n* **1** : verbal interchange of ideas : CONVERSATION **2** : formal and orderly and usu. extended expression of thought on a subject

²**dis·course** \dis-'\ *vi* **1 :** to express oneself in esp. oral discourse : hold forth **2 :** TALK, CONVERSE
dis·cour·te·ous \(')dis-'kərt-ē-əs\ *adj* : lacking courtesy : UNCIVIL, RUDE — **dis·cour·te·ous·ly** *adv* — **dis·cour·te·ous·ness** *n*
dis·cour·te·sy \-'kərt-ə-sē\ *n* : RUDENESS; *also* : a rude act
dis·cov·er \dis-'kəv-ər\ *vt* **dis·cov·ered**; **dis·cov·er·ing** \-'kəv-(ə-)riŋ\ **1 :** to make known or visible **2 :** to obtain sight or knowledge of for the first time : FIND — **dis·cov·er·a·ble** *adj* — **dis·cov·er·er** *n*
dis·cov·ery \dis-'kəv-(ə-)rē\ *n, pl* **-er·ies** **1 :** the act or process of discovering **2 :** something discovered
¹**dis·cred·it** \(')dis-'kred-ət\ *vt* **1 :** to refuse to accept as true or accurate : DISBELIEVE **2 :** to cause disbelief in the accuracy or authority of **3 :** to destroy the reputation of : DISGRACE
²**discredit** *n* **1 :** loss of credit or reputation **2 :** lack or loss of belief or confidence
dis·cred·it·a·ble \-ə-bəl\ *adj* : injurious to reputation — **dis·cred·it·a·bly** \-blē\ *adv*
dis·creet \dis-'krēt\ *adj* : having or showing good judgment in conduct and esp. in speech : PRUDENT; *esp* : capable of observing prudent silence — **dis·creet·ly** *adv* — **dis·creet·ness** *n*
dis·crep·an·cy \dis-'krep-ən-sē\ *n, pl* **-cies** **1 :** the quality or state of being discrepant : DIFFERENCE **2 :** an instance of being discrepant
dis·crep·ant \-ənt\ *adj* : being at variance : DISAGREEING — **dis·crep·ant·ly** *adv*
dis·crete \dis-'krēt, 'dis-,\ *adj* **1 :** individually distinct : SEPARATE **2 :** consisting of unconnected elements : DISCONTINUOUS — **dis·crete·ly** *adv* — **dis·crete·ness** *n*
dis·cre·tion \dis-'kresh-ən\ *n* **1 :** the quality of being discreet : PRUDENCE; *esp* : cautious reserve in speech **2 a :** individual choice or judgment **b :** power of free decision or latitude of choice — **dis·cre·tion·ary** \-'kresh-ə-,ner-ē\ *adj*
dis·crim·i·nate \dis-'krim-ə-,nāt\ *vb* **1 :** DISTINGUISH, DIFFERENTIATE **2 :** to make a distinction in favor of or against one person or thing as compared with others
dis·crim·i·nat·ing \-iŋ\ *adj* : marked by discrimination; *esp* : DISCERNING, JUDICIOUS — **dis·crim·i·nat·ing·ly** *adv*
dis·crim·i·na·tion \dis-,krim-ə-'nā-shən\ *n* **1 :** the act of discriminating : DIFFERENTIATION **2 :** the quality or power of finely distinguishing **3 :** distinction and esp. unjust distinction made against one person or group in favor of another — **dis·crim·i·na·tion·al** \-shnəl, -shən-ᵊl\ *adj*
dis·crim·i·na·to·ry \dis-'krim-(ə-)nə-,tōr-ē\ *adj* : marked by esp. unjust discrimination
dis·cur·sive \dis-'kər-siv\ *adj* : passing from one topic to another : RAMBLING — **dis·cur·sive·ly** *adv* — **dis·cur·sive·ness** *n*
dis·cus \'dis-kəs\ *n, pl* **dis·cus·es** : a disk (as of wood or rubber) that is hurled for distance in a track-and-field contest
dis·cuss \dis-'kəs\ *vt* **1 :** to investigate or consider carefully by presenting the various sides : debate fully and openly **2 :** to talk about
dis·cus·sant \dis-'kəs-ᵊnt\ *n* : one who takes part in a formal discussion or symposium
dis·cus·sion \dis-'kəsh-ən\ *n* **1 :** consideration of a question in open usu. informal debate **2 :** a formal treatment of a topic
¹**dis·dain** \dis-'dān\ *n* : a feeling of contempt for something regarded as beneath one : SCORN
²**disdain** *vt* **1 :** to look with scorn on **2 :** to reject or refrain from because of disdain
dis·dain·ful \-fəl\ *adj* : full of or expressing disdain : SCORNFUL — **dis·dain·ful·ly** \-fə-lē\ *adv*
dis·ease \diz-'ēz\ *n* : an alteration of the normal state of the living animal or plant body that impairs the performance of the vital functions : ILLNESS; *also* : a particular instance or kind of such alteration — **dis·eased** \-'ēzd\ *adj*
dis·em·bark \,dis-əm-'bärk\ *vb* : to go or put ashore from a ship
dis·em·body \,dis-əm-'bäd-ē\ *vt* : to deprive of bodily existence
dis·em·bow·el \,dis-əm-'baù(-ə)l\ *vt* **-eled** *or* **-elled**; **-el·ing** *or* **-el·ling** : to take out the bowels of : EVISCERATE — **dis·em·bow·el·ment** *n*
dis·en·chant \,dis-ᵊn-'chant\ *vt* : to free from enchantment : DISILLUSION — **dis·en·chant·ment** *n*
dis·en·cum·ber \,dis-ᵊn-'kəm-bər\ *vt* : to free from something that burdens or obstructs
dis·en·fran·chise \,dis-ᵊn-'fran-,chīz\ *vt* : DISFRANCHISE — **dis·en·fran·chise·ment** \-,chīz-mənt, -chəz-\ *n*
dis·en·gage \,dis-ᵊn-'gāj\ *vb* : to free or release from an engagement, entanglement, or encumbrance : EXTRICATE, DISENTANGLE; *esp* : to remove oneself from military commitments, alliances, or positions — **dis·en·gage·ment** *n*
dis·en·tan·gle \,dis-ᵊn-'taŋ-gəl\ *vb* : to free from entanglement : straighten out — **dis·en·tan·gle·ment** *n*
dis·es·tab·lish \,dis-ə-'stab-lish\ *vt* : to end the establishment of — **dis·es·tab·lish·ment** *n*
¹**dis·es·teem** \,dis-ə-'stēm\ *vt* : to regard with disfavor
²**disesteem** *n* : lack of esteem : DISFAVOR, DISREPUTE
dis·fa·vor \(')dis-'fā-vər\ *n* **1 :** DISAPPROVAL, DISLIKE **2 :** the state or fact of being deprived of favor
dis·fig·ure \dis-'fig-yər\ *vt* : to spoil the appearance of — **dis·fig·ure·ment** *n*
dis·fran·chise \(')dis-'fran-,chīz\ *vt* : to deprive of a franchise, a legal right, or a privilege or immunity; *esp* : to deprive of the right to vote — **dis·fran·chise·ment** \-,chīz-mənt, -chəz-\ *n*
dis·gorge \(')dis-'gȯrj\ *vb* **1 :** VOMIT **2 :** to discharge violently, confusedly, or as a result of force
¹**dis·grace** \dis-'grās\ *vt* : to bring reproach or shame to
²**disgrace** *n* **1 :** the condition of being out of favor : loss of respect **2 :** SHAME, DISHONOR **3 :** a cause of shame
dis·grace·ful \-fəl\ *adj* : bringing or involving shame or disgrace — **dis·grace·ful·ly** \-fə-lē\ *adv* — **dis·grace·ful·ness** *n*
dis·grun·tle \dis-'grənt-ᵊl\ *vt* **dis·grun·tled**; **dis·grun·tling** \-'grənt-liŋ, -ᵊl-iŋ\ : to put in bad humor — **dis·grun·tle·ment** *n*
¹**dis·guise** \dis-'gīz\ *vt* **1 :** to change the dress or looks of so as to conceal the identity or so as to resemble another **2 a :** HIDE, CONCEAL **b :** ALTER
²**disguise** *n* **1 :** clothing put on to conceal one's identity or counterfeit another's **2 a :** an outward form hiding or misrepresenting the true nature or identity of a person or thing **b :** PRETENSE **3 :** the act of disguising
¹**dis·gust** \dis-'gəst\ *n* : marked aversion to something distasteful or loathsome : REPUGNANCE
²**disgust** *vt* : to provoke to loathing, repugnance, or aversion : be offensive to — **dis·gust·ed** *adj*
¹**dish** \'dish\ *n* **1 :** a more or less concave vessel from which food is served **2 a :** the food served in a dish **b :** food prepared in a particular way **3 :** something resembling a dish esp. in being shallow and concave
²**dish** *vt* **1 :** to put into a dish or set of dishes **2 :** to make concave like a dish
dis·ha·bille \,dis-ə-'bēl\ *n* **1 :** the state of being dressed in a loose or careless style **2 :** UNTIDINESS, DISORDER
dish·cloth \'dish-,klȯth\ *n* : a cloth for washing dishes
dis·heart·en \(')dis-'härt-ᵊn\ *vt* : to deprive of courage and hope : DISCOURAGE
di·shev·el \dish-'ev-əl\ *vt* **di·shev·eled** *or* **di·shev·elled**; **di·shev·el·ing** *or* **di·shev·el·ling** \-'ev-(ə-)liŋ\ : to let hang or fall loosely in disorder : DISARRAY
di·shev·eled *or* **di·shev·elled** \-əld\ *adj* : marked by loose disorder or disarray
dis·hon·est \(')dis-'än-əst\ *adj* **1 :** not honest : UNTRUSTWORTHY **2 :** marked by fraud : DECEITFUL, CORRUPT — **dis·hon·est·ly** *adv*

dis·hon·es·ty \-ə-stē\ *n* : lack of honesty or integrity

¹dis·hon·or \(')dis-'än-ər\ *n* **1 a** : loss of honor or reputation **b** : something dishonorable : a cause of disgrace **2** : the act of dishonoring a piece of commercial paper

²dishonor *vt* **1** : to bring shame on : DISGRACE **2** : to refuse to accept or pay (as a bill or check)

dis·hon·or·a·ble \(')dis-'än-(ə-)rə-bəl, -'än-ər-bəl\ *adj* : not honorable : DISGRACEFUL, SHAMEFUL — **dis·hon·or·a·bly** \-blē\ *adv*

dish·wash·er \'dish-ˌwȯsh-ər, -ˌwäsh-\ *n* : a person or a machine that washes dishes

¹dis·il·lu·sion \ˌdis-ə-'lü-zhən\ *n* : DISENCHANTMENT

²disillusion *vt* **dis·il·lu·sioned; dis·il·lu·sion·ing** \-'lüzh-(ə-)niŋ\ : to free from or deprive of illusion — **dis·il·lu·sion·ment** *n*

dis·in·cli·na·tion \(ˌ)dis-ˌin-klə-'nā-shən\ *n* : an unwillingness to do something : a slight dislike or distaste

dis·in·cline \ˌdis-ᵊn-'klīn\ *vb* : to make or be unwilling

dis·in·fect \ˌdis-ᵊn-'fekt\ *vt* : to free from infection esp. by destroying harmful germs; *also* : CLEANSE — **dis·in·fec·tion** \-'fek-shən\ *n*

dis·in·fect·ant \-'fek-tənt\ *n* : an agent that frees from infection — **disinfectant** *adj*

dis·in·gen·u·ous \ˌdis-ᵊn-'jen-yə-wəs\ *adj* : lacking in candor : not frank or naïve — **dis·in·gen·u·ous·ly** *adv* — **dis·in·gen·u·ous·ness** *n*

dis·in·her·it \ˌdis-ᵊn-'her-ət\ *vt* : to prevent from inheriting property that would naturally be passed on

dis·in·te·grate \(')dis-'int-ə-ˌgrāt\ *vb* **1** : to break or decompose into constituent elements, parts, or small particles **2** : to destroy the unity or integrity of — **dis·in·te·gra·tion** \(ˌ)dis-ˌint-ə-'grā-shən\ *n*

dis·in·ter \ˌdis-ᵊn-'tər\ *vt* **1** : to take out of the grave or tomb **2** : to bring to light — **dis·in·ter·ment** *n*

dis·in·ter·est·ed \(')dis-'in-trəs-təd, -'int-ə-rəs-\ *adj* **1** : not interested **2** : free from selfish motive or interest — **dis·in·ter·est·ed·ly** *adv* — **dis·in·ter·est·ed·ness** *n*

dis·join \(')dis-'jȯin\ *vb* : SEPARATE

dis·joint \(')dis-'jȯint\ *vb* **1** : to separate the parts of **2** : to take apart or become parted at the joints

dis·joint·ed \-əd\ *adj* **1** : separated at or as if at the joint **2** : DISCONNECTED, DISORDERED; *esp* : INCOHERENT — **dis·joint·ed·ly** *adv* — **dis·joint·ed·ness** *n*

dis·junc·tion \dis-'jəŋ(k)-shən\ *n* : DISUNION, SEPARATION

dis·junc·tive \-'jəŋ(k)-tiv\ *adj* **1** : tending to disjoin **2** : expressing an alternative between the meanings of the words connected

disk *or* **disc** \'disk\ *n* **1 a** : the central part of the flower head of a typical composite plant made up of closely packed tubular flowers **b** : any of various rounded and flattened animal anatomical structures **2 a** : a thin circular object **b** *usu disc* : a phonograph record **3** *usu disc* : a tilling implement (as a harrow or plow) with sharp-edged circular concave cutting blades; *also* : one of these blades

¹dis·like \(')dis-'līk\ *vt* : to regard with dislike

²dislike *n* : a feeling of distaste or disapproval

dis·lo·cate \'dis-lō-ˌkāt, (')dis-'lō-\ *vt* **1** : to put out of place; *esp* : to displace (a bone) from normal connections **2** : DISRUPT — **dis·lo·ca·tion** \ˌdis-(ˌ)lō-'kā-shən\ *n*

dis·lodge \(')dis-'läj\ *vt* **1** : to force out of a resting place **2** : to drive from a place of hiding or defense

dis·loy·al \(')dis-'lȯi(-ə)l\ *adj* : lacking in loyalty — **dis·loy·al·ly** \-'lȯi-ə-lē\ *adv*

dis·loy·al·ty \-'lȯi(-ə)l-tē\ *n* : lack of loyalty

dis·mal \'diz-məl\ *adj* **1** : gloomy to the eye or ear : DREARY, DEPRESSING **2** : feeling gloom : DEPRESSED — **dis·mal·ly** \-mə-lē\ *adv*

dis·man·tle \(')dis-'mant-ᵊl\ *vt* **dis·man·tled; dis·man·tling** \-'mant-liŋ, -ᵊl-iŋ\ **1** : to strip of furniture and equipment **2** : to take to pieces : take apart — **dis·man·tle·ment** *n*

¹dis·may \dis-'mā\ *vt* : to cause to lose courage or resolution through alarm or fear : DAUNT

²dismay *n* **1** : sudden loss of courage or resolution from alarm or fear **2** : a feeling of alarm or disappointment

dis·mem·ber \(')dis-'mem-bər\ *vt* **dis·mem·bered; dis·mem·ber·ing** \-b(ə-)riŋ\ **1** : to cut off or separate the limbs, members, or parts of **2** : to break up or tear into pieces — **dis·mem·ber·ment** *n*

dis·miss \dis-'mis\ *vt* **1** : to send away : cause or allow to go **2** : to discharge from office, service, or employment **3** : to put aside or out of mind **4** : to refuse further judicial hearing or consideration to

dis·miss·al \-'mis-əl\ *n* : the act of dismissing : the fact or state of being dismissed

dis·mount \(')dis-'mau̇nt\ *vb* **1** : to get down from something (as a horse or bicycle) **2** : to throw down from a horse : UNHORSE **3** : to take (as a cannon) from the carriage or mountings **4** : to take apart (as a machine)

dis·obe·di·ence \ˌdis-ə-'bēd-ē-ən(t)s\ *n* : lack of obedience : neglect or refusal to obey — **dis·obe·di·ent** \-ənt\ *adj* — **dis·obe·di·ent·ly** *adv*

dis·obey \ˌdis-ə-'bā\ *vb* : to fail to obey : be disobedient

¹dis·or·der \(')dis-'ȯrd-ər\ *vt* **1** : to disturb the order of **2** : to disturb the regular or normal functions of

²disorder *n* **1 a** : lack of order **b** : a disturbing, neglecting, or breaking away from a due order **2** : an abnormal physical or mental condition : AILMENT — **dis·or·dered** \-'ȯrd-ərd\ *adj*

dis·or·der·ly \-ər-lē\ *adj* **1 a** : UNRULY, TURBULENT **b** (1) : offensive to public order or decency (2) : guilty of disorderly conduct **2** : not in an orderly condition : DISARRANGED — **dis·or·der·li·ness** *n*

dis·or·ga·nize \(')dis-'ȯr-gə-ˌnīz\ *vt* : to break up the regular arrangement or system of : throw into disorder — **dis·or·ga·ni·za·tion** \(ˌ)dis-ˌȯrg-(ə-)nə-'zā-shən\ *n*

dis·ori·ent \(')dis-'ōr-ē-ˌent\ *vt* : to cause to lose bearings — **dis·ori·en·ta·tion** \(ˌ)dis-ˌōr-ē-ən-'tā-shən\ *n*

dis·own \(')dis-'ōn\ *vt* : REPUDIATE, RENOUNCE, DISCLAIM

dis·par·age \dis-'par-ij\ *vt* **1** : to lower in rank or reputation : DEGRADE **2** : to speak slightingly of : BELITTLE — **dis·par·age·ment** *n* — **dis·par·ag·ing·ly** *adv*

dis·par·ate \dis-'par-ət, 'dis-p(ə-)rət\ *adj* : distinct in quality or character : DISSIMILAR — **dis·par·ate·ly** *adv* — **dis·par·ate·ness** *n* — **dis·par·i·ty** \dis-'par-ət-ē\ *n*

dis·pas·sion·ate \(')dis-'pash-(ə-)nət\ *adj* : not influenced by strong feeling : CALM — **dis·pas·sion·ate·ly** *adv*

¹dis·patch \dis-'pach\ *vt* **1** : to send away promptly or rapidly to a particular place or for a particular purpose **2** : to attend to or dispose of speedily **3** : to put to death — **dis·patch·er** *n*

²dispatch *n* **1 a** : the sending of a message or messenger **b** : the shipment of goods **2** : MESSAGE; *esp* : an important official message **3** : the act of putting to death **4** : a news item sent in by a correspondent to a newspaper **5** : promptness and efficiency in performing a task

dis·pel \dis-'pel\ *vt* **dis·pelled; dis·pel·ling** : to drive away by scattering : DISSIPATE

dis·pens·a·ble \dis-'pen(t)-sə-bəl\ *adj* : capable of being dispensed with : NONESSENTIAL

dis·pen·sa·ry \dis-'pen(t)s-(ə-)rē\ *n, pl* **-ries** : a place where medical or dental aid is dispensed

dis·pen·sa·tion \ˌdis-pən-'sā-shən\ *n* **1 a** : a system of rules for ordering affairs **b** : a particular arrangement or provision esp. of nature **2** : an exemption from a rule or from a vow or oath **3 a** : the act of dispensing **b** : something dispensed or distributed — **dis·pen·sa·tion·al** \-shnəl, -shən-ᵊl\ *adj*

dis·pense \dis-'pen(t)s\ *vt* **1 a** : to deal out in portions **b** : ADMINISTER **2** : to prepare and distribute (medicines) to the sick — **dis·pens·er** *n* — **dispense with** 1 : to suspend the operation of 2 : to do or get along without

dis·pers·al \dis-ˈpər-səl\ *n* : the act or result of dispersing

dis·perse \dis-ˈpərs\ *vb* 1 a : to cause to break up and go in different ways b : to cause to become spread widely c : to drive or clear away 2 : DISSEMINATE 3 : to move in different directions : SCATTER — **dis·pers·i·ble** \-ˈpər-sə-bəl\ *adj*

dis·per·sion \dis-ˈpər-zhən\ *n* 1 : the act or process of dispersing : the state of being dispersed 2 : a result or product of dispersing : something dispersed — **dis·per·sive** \-ˈpər-siv, -ziv\ *adj*

dispir·it \(ˈ)dis-ˈpir-ət\ *vt* : to deprive of cheerful spirit : DISHEARTEN — **dispir·it·ed·ly** *adv*

dis·place \(ˈ)dis-ˈplās\ *vt* 1 : to remove from a usual or proper place; *esp* : to expel or force to flee from home or homeland 2 : to take the place of : REPLACE

dis·place·ment \-ˈplās-mənt\ *n* 1 : the act of displacing : the state of being displaced 2 a : the volume or weight of a fluid (as water) displaced by a floating body (as a ship) b : the difference between the initial position of an object and any later position

[1]**dis·play** \dis-ˈplā\ *vt* 1 : to show outwardly 2 a : to spread before the view b : to set in display

[2]**display** *n* 1 : a displaying of something 2 : ostentatious show 3 : an eye-catching exhibition

dis·please \(ˈ)dis-ˈplēz\ *vb* 1 : to arouse the disapproval and dislike of 2 : to be offensive to : give displeasure

dis·plea·sure \(ˈ)dis-ˈplezh-ər\ *n* : a feeling of annoyance and dislike accompanying disapproval

dis·port \dis-ˈpōrt\ *vb* 1 a : DIVERT, AMUSE b : FROLIC 2 : DISPLAY

dis·pos·al \dis-ˈpō-zəl\ *n* 1 : an orderly distribution : ARRANGEMENT 2 : a getting rid of or putting out of the way 3 : MANAGEMENT, ADMINISTRATION 4 : the transfer of something into new hands 5 : the power to dispose of something : CONTROL, COMMAND

dis·pose \dis-ˈpōz\ *vb* 1 : to distribute and put in place : ARRANGE 2 : to give a tendency to : incline in mind — **dis·pos·a·ble** *adj* — **dispose of** 1 : to settle or determine the fate, condition, or use of : deal with conclusively 2 : to get rid of : put out of the way : finish with 3 : to transfer to the control of another

dis·po·si·tion \ˌdis-pə-ˈzish-ən\ *n* 1 : the act or power of disposing : DISPOSAL 2 : the giving up or transferring of something 3 : ARRANGEMENT 4 a : TENDENCY, INCLINATION b : natural attitude toward things

dis·pos·sess \ˌdis-pə-ˈzes\ *vt* : to deprive of the possession or occupancy of land or houses : put out : OUST — **dis·pos·ses·sion** \-ˈzesh-ən\ *n*

[1]**dis·praise** \(ˈ)dis-ˈprāz\ *vt* : to comment on with disapproval or censure

[2]**dispraise** *n* : the act of dispraising : DISPARAGEMENT

dis·proof \(ˈ)dis-ˈprüf\ *n* 1 : a proving that something is not as believed or stated 2 : evidence that disproves

dis·pro·por·tion \ˌdis-prə-ˈpōr-shən\ *n* : lack of proportion, symmetry, or proper relation : DISPARITY; *also* : an instance of such disparity — **dis·pro·por·tion·al** \-shnəl, -shən-ᵊl\ *adj* — **dis·pro·por·tion·ate** \-sh(ə-)nət\ *adj* — **dis·pro·por·tion·ate·ly** *adv*

dis·prove \(ˈ)dis-ˈprüv\ *vt* : to prove to be false : REFUTE

dis·put·a·ble \dis-ˈpyüt-ə-bəl, ˈdis-pyət-\ *adj* : open to dispute, debate, or contest — **dis·put·a·bly** \-blē\ *adv*

dis·pu·tant \dis-ˈpyüt-ᵊnt, ˈdis-pyət-ənt\ *n* : DISPUTER

dis·pu·ta·tion \ˌdis-pyə-ˈtā-shən\ *n* 1 : the act of disputing : DEBATE 2 : an oral defense of an academic thesis

dis·pu·ta·tious \ˌdis-pyə-ˈtā-shəs\ *adj* : inclined to dispute : ARGUMENTATIVE — **dis·pu·ta·tious·ness** *n*

[1]**dis·pute** \dis-ˈpyüt\ *vb* 1 : to engage in argument : DEBATE 2 : WRANGLE 3 a : to engage in controversy over : argue about b : to call into question : deny the truth or rightness of 4 a : to struggle against b : to struggle over : CONTEST — **dis·put·er** *n*

[2]**dispute** *n* 1 : verbal controversy : DEBATE 2 : QUARREL

dis·qual·i·fy \(ˈ)dis-ˈkwäl-ə-ˌfī\ *vt* 1 : to make or declare unfit or ineligible 2 : to deprive of necessary qualifications — **dis·qual·i·fi·ca·tion** \(ˌ)dis-ˌkwäl-ə-fə-ˈkā-shən\ *n*

[1]**dis·qui·et** \(ˈ)dis-ˈkwī-ət\ *vt* : to make uneasy or restless : DISTURB — **dis·qui·et·ing·ly** *adv*

[2]**disquiet** *n* : lack of peace or tranquillity : ANXIETY

dis·qui·etude \(ˈ)dis-ˈkwī-ə-ˌt(y)üd\ *n* : AGITATION, ANXIETY

dis·qui·si·tion \ˌdis-kwə-ˈzish-ən\ *n* : a formal inquiry or discussion : DISCOURSE

[1]**dis·re·gard** \ˌdis-ri-ˈgärd\ *vt* : to pay no attention to : treat as unworthy of regard or notice

[2]**disregard** *n* : the act of disregarding : the state of being disregarded : NEGLECT — **dis·re·gard·ful** \-fəl\ *adj*

dis·re·pair \ˌdis-ri-ˈpa(ə)r\ *n* : the state of being in need of repair

dis·rep·u·ta·ble \(ˈ)dis-ˈrep-yət-ə-bəl\ *adj* : not reputable : DISGRACEFUL; *esp* : having a bad reputation — **dis·rep·u·ta·ble·ness** *n* — **dis·rep·u·ta·bly** \-blē\ *adv*

dis·re·pute \ˌdis-ri-ˈpyüt\ *n* : loss or lack of reputation : low esteem : DISCREDIT

dis·re·spect \ˌdis-ri-ˈspekt\ *n* : lack of respect : DISCOURTESY — **dis·re·spect·ful** \-fəl\ *adj* — **dis·re·spect·ful·ly** \-fə-lē\ *adv*

dis·robe \(ˈ)dis-ˈrōb\ *vb* : UNDRESS

dis·rupt \dis-ˈrəpt\ *vt* 1 : to break apart : RUPTURE 2 : to throw into disorder : break up — **dis·rupt·er** *n* — **dis·rup·tion** \-ˈrəp-shən\ *n* — **dis·rup·tive** \-ˈrəp-tiv\ *adj*

dis·sat·is·fac·tion \(ˌ)dis-ˌ(s)at-əs-ˈfak-shən\ *n* : the quality or state of being dissatisfied

dis·sat·is·fy \(ˈ)dis-ˈ(s)at-əs-ˌfī\ *vt* : to fail to satisfy

dis·sect \dis-ˈekt\ *vb* 1 : to divide (as a plant or animal) into separate parts for examination and study 2 : to make a searching analysis : analyze minutely — **dis·sec·tion** \-ˈek-shən\ *n* — **dis·sec·tor** \-ˈek-tər\ *n*

dis·sect·ed \-ˈek-təd\ *adj* : cut deeply into fine lobes

dis·sem·ble \dis-ˈem-bəl\ *vb* **-bled**; **-bling** \-b(ə-)liŋ\ 1 : to hide under or put on a false appearance : conceal facts, intentions, or feelings under some pretense 2 : to put on the appearance of : SIMULATE — **dis·sem·bler** *n*

dis·sem·i·nate \dis-ˈem-ə-ˌnāt\ *vt* : to spread abroad as though sowing seed — **dis·sem·i·na·tion** \-ˌem-ə-ˈnā-shən\ *n* — **dis·sem·i·na·tor** \-ˈem-ə-ˌnāt-ər\ *n*

dis·sen·sion \dis-ˈen-chən\ *n* : disagreement in opinion : DISCORD, QUARRELING

[1]**dis·sent** \dis-ˈent\ *vi* 1 : to withhold assent 2 : to differ in opinion

[2]**dissent** *n* 1 : a difference of opinion; *esp* : religious nonconformity 2 : a written statement in which a justice disagrees with the opinion of the majority

dis·sent·er \dis-ˈent-ər\ *n* 1 : one that dissents 2 *cap* : an English Nonconformist

dis·ser·ta·tion \ˌdis-ər-ˈtā-shən\ *n* : an extended usu. written treatment of a subject; *esp* : one submitted for a doctorate

dis·ser·vice \(ˈ)dis-ˈ(s)ər-vəs\ *n* : ill service : INJURY

dis·sev·er \dis-ˈev-ər\ *vb* : to sever thoroughly : SEPARATE, DISUNITE

dis·si·dence \ˈdis-əd-ən(t)s\ *n* : DISSENT, DISAGREEMENT

dis·si·dent \-ənt\ *adj* : openly and often violently differing with an opinion or a group : DISAFFECTED — **dissident** *n*

dis·sim·i·lar \(ˈ)dis-ˈ(s)im-ə-lər\ *adj* : UNLIKE — **dis·sim·i·lar·i·ty** \(ˌ)dis-ˌ(s)im-ə-ˈlar-ət-ē\ *n* — **dis·sim·i·lar·ly** *adv*

dis·sim·u·late \(ˈ)dis-ˈim-yə-ˌlāt\ *vb* : DISSEMBLE — **dis·sim·u-**

la·tion \(ˌ)dis-ˌim-yə-'lā-shən\ *n* — **dis·sim·u·la·tor** \(')dis-'im-yə-ˌlāt-ər\ *n*

dis·si·pate \'dis-ə-ˌpāt\ *vb* **1 a :** to break up and drive off (as a crowd) **b :** to cause to spread out to the point of vanishing : DISSOLVE **2 a :** to expend aimlessly or foolishly **b :** SQUANDER **3 :** to separate into parts and scatter or vanish **4 :** to be extravagant or uncontrolled in the pursuit of pleasure; *esp* **:** to drink to excess

dis·si·pat·ed \-əd\ *adj* **:** given to or marked by dissipation — **dis·si·pat·ed·ly** *adv* — **dis·si·pat·ed·ness** *n*

dis·si·pa·tion \ˌdis-ə-'pā-shən\ *n* **:** the act of dissipating **:** the state of being dissipated

dis·so·ci·ate \(')dis-'ō-s(h)ē-ˌāt\ *vb* **1 :** to separate from association or union with another **:** DISCONNECT **2 :** DISUNITE

dis·so·ci·a·tion \(ˌ)dis-ˌō-s(h)ē-'ā-shən\ *n* **:** the act or process of dissociating **:** the state of being dissociated

dis·sol·u·ble \dis-'äl-yə-bəl\ *adj* **:** capable of being dissolved — **dis·sol·u·bil·i·ty** \dis-ˌäl-yə-'bil-ət-ē\ *n*

dis·so·lute \'dis-ə-ˌlüt\ *adj* **:** loose in morals or conduct — **dis·so·lute·ly** *adv* — **dis·so·lute·ness** *n*

dis·so·lu·tion \ˌdis-ə-'lü-shən\ *n* **1 a :** separation of a thing into component parts **b :** DECAY **2 :** the termination or breaking up of an assembly or a partnership

dis·solve \diz-'älv\ *vb* **1 :** to break up into component parts **2 :** to pass or cause to pass into solution **:** MELT, LIQUEFY **3 :** to bring to an end **:** TERMINATE **4 :** to waste or fade away as if by breaking up or melting **5 :** to be overcome emotionally **6 :** to resolve itself as if by dissolution — **dis·solv·a·ble** *adj* — **dis·solv·er** *n*

dis·so·nance \'dis-ə-nən(t)s\ *n* **1 :** a mingling of discordant sounds **2 :** lack of agreement **:** DISCORD

dis·so·nant \'dis-ə-nənt\ *adj* **1 :** marked by dissonance in sound **:** DISCORDANT **2 :** not being in harmony or agreement — **dis·so·nant·ly** *adv*

dis·suade \dis-'wād\ *vt* **:** to advise against a course of action **:** persuade or try to persuade not to do something — **dis·sua·sion** \-'wā-zhən\ *n*

[1]dis·taff \'dis-ˌtaf\ *n* **1 a :** a staff for holding the flax, tow, or wool in spinning **b :** woman's work **2 :** the female branch or side of a family

[2]distaff *adj* **:** FEMALE

[1]dis·tance \'dis-tən(t)s\ *n* **1 a :** separation in time **b :** the shortest space or amount of space between two points, lines, surfaces, or objects **c :** EXPANSE **d :** a full course **2 :** the quality or state of being distant: as **a :** spatial remoteness **b :** COLDNESS, RESERVE **c :** DIFFERENCE, DISPARITY **3 :** a distant point or region

[2]distance *vt* **:** to leave far behind **:** OUTSTRIP

dis·tant \-tənt\ *adj* **1 a :** separated in space **:** AWAY **b :** situated at a great distance **:** FAR-OFF **2 :** not close in relationship **3 :** different in kind **4 :** reserved or aloof in personal relationship **:** COLD **5 :** coming from or going to a distance — **dis·tant·ly** *adv* — **dis·tant·ness** *n*

dis·taste \(')dis-'tāst\ *n* **:** DISINCLINATION, AVERSION

dis·taste·ful \-fəl\ *adj* **1 :** unpleasant to the taste **:** LOATHSOME **2 :** OFFENSIVE, DISAGREEABLE — **dis·taste·ful·ly** \-fə-lē\ *adv* — **dis·taste·ful·ness** *n*

dis·tem·per \dis-'tem-pər\ *n* **:** a disordered or abnormal bodily state usu. of a lower animal; *esp* **:** a contagious often fatal virus disease of dogs

dis·tend \dis-'tend\ *vb* **:** to stretch out or bulge out in all directions **:** SWELL

dis·ten·si·ble \dis-'ten(t)-sə-bəl\ *adj* **:** capable of being distended

dis·ten·sion *or* **dis·ten·tion** \dis-'ten-chən\ *n* **:** the act of distending **:** the state of being distended

dis·tich \'dis-(ˌ)tik\ *n* **:** a strophic unit of two lines

dis·till \dis-'til\ *vb* **1 :** to fall or let fall in drops **2 a :** to subject to or transform by distillation **b :** to obtain by distillation **3 :** to extract the essence of **:** CONCENTRATE

dis·til·la·tion \ˌdis-tə-'lā-shən\ *n* **:** a process that consists of driving gas or vapor from liquids or solids by heating and condensing to liquid products

dis·till·er \dis-'til-ər\ *n* **:** one that distills; *esp* **:** a person whose business is distilling alcoholic liquors

dis·till·ery \dis-'til-(ə-)rē\ *n, pl* **-er·ies :** a place where distilling esp. of alcoholic liquors is carried on

dis·tinct \dis-'tiŋ(k)t\ *adj* **1 :** distinguished from others **:** SEPARATE, DIFFERENT **2 :** clearly seen, heard, or understood **:** PLAIN, UNMISTAKABLE — **dis·tinct·ly** *adv* — **dis·tinct·ness** *n*

dis·tinc·tion \dis-'tiŋ(k)-shən\ *n* **1 a :** the act of distinguishing a difference **b :** DIFFERENCE **2 :** a distinguishing quality or mark **3 a :** a special recognition **b :** a mark or sign of such recognition **4 :** HONOR

dis·tinc·tive \dis-'tiŋ(k)-tiv\ *adj* **:** clearly marking a person or a thing as different from others **:** CHARACTERISTIC — **dis·tinc·tive·ly** *adv* — **dis·tinc·tive·ness** *n*

dis·tin·guish \dis-'tiŋ-gwish\ *vb* **1 :** to recognize one thing from others by some mark or characteristic **2 :** to hear or see clearly **:** make out **:** DISCERN **3 :** to make distinctions **4 :** to set apart **:** mark as different **5 :** to separate from others by a mark of honor **:** make outstanding — **dis·tin·guish·a·ble** *adj* — **dis·tin·guish·a·bly** \-ə-blē\ *adv*

dis·tin·guished \-gwisht\ *adj* **1 :** marked by eminence, distinction, or excellence **2 :** befitting an eminent person

dis·tort \dis-'tȯrt\ *vt* **1 :** to twist out of the true meaning **:** MISREPRESENT **2 :** to twist out of a natural, normal, or original shape or condition

dis·tor·tion \dis-'tȯr-shən\ *n* **1 :** the act of distorting **2 :** the condition of being distorted or a product of distortion — **dis·tor·tion·al** \-shnəl, -shən-ᵊl\ *adj*

dis·tract \dis-'trakt\ *vt* **1 :** to turn aside **:** DIVERT; *esp* **:** to draw (the attention or mind) to a different object **2 :** to stir up or confuse with conflicting emotions or motives **:** HARASS

dis·trac·tion \dis-'trak-shən\ *n* **1 :** the act of distracting or the state of being distracted; *esp* **:** mental confusion **2 :** something that distracts; *esp* **:** AMUSEMENT — **dis·trac·tive** \-'trak-tiv\ *adj*

dis·trait \di-'strā\ *adj* **:** ABSENTMINDED, DISTRAUGHT

dis·traught \dis-'trȯt\ *adj* **1 :** agitated with doubt or mental conflict **2 :** CRAZED — **dis·traught·ly** *adv*

[1]dis·tress \dis-'tres\ *n* **1 :** great suffering of body or mind **:** PAIN, ANGUISH **2 :** MISFORTUNE, TROUBLE, SORROW **3 :** a condition of danger or desperate need

[2]distress *vt* **1 :** to subject to great strain or difficulties **2 :** to cause to worry or be troubled **:** UPSET

dis·tress·ful \-fəl\ *adj* **:** causing distress **:** full of distress — **dis·tress·ful·ly** \-fə-lē\ *adv* — **dis·tress·ful·ness** *n*

dis·trib·ute \dis-'trib-yət\ *vt* **1 :** to divide among several or many **:** APPORTION **2 :** to spread out so as to cover something **:** SCATTER **3 :** to divide or separate esp. into kinds **4 :** to market (a line of goods) in a particular area usu. as a wholesaler — **dis·trib·ut·a·ble** *adj*

dis·tri·bu·tion \ˌdis-trə-'byü-shən\ *n* **1 :** the act or process of distributing **2 :** the position, arrangement, or frequency of occurrence (as of the members of a group) over an area or throughout a space or unit of time **3 :** something distributed — **dis·tri·bu·tion·al** \-shnəl, -shən-ᵊl\ *adj*

dis·trib·u·tor \dis-'trib-yət-ər\ *n* **1 :** one that distributes **2 :** an agent or agency for marketing goods **3 :** a device for distributing electric current to the spark plugs

[1]dis·trict \'dis-(ˌ)trikt\ *n* **1 :** a territorial division marked off or defined (as for administrative or electoral purposes) **2 :** a distinctive area or region

[2]district *vt* **:** to divide or organize into districts

district attorney *n* : a public official who prosecutes cases for a state or federal government

¹dis·trust \(')dis-'trəst\ *vt* : to have no confidence in

²distrust *n* : a lack of trust or confidence : SUSPICION, WARINESS — **dis·trust·ful** \-fəl\ *adj* — **dis·trust·ful·ly** \-fə-lē\ *adv* — **dis·trust·ful·ness** *n*

dis·turb \dis-'tərb\ *vt* **1 a** : to interfere with **b** : to alter the position or arrangement of **2 a** : to destroy the tranquillity or composure of : make uneasy **b** : to throw into disorder **c** : to put to inconvenience — **dis·turb·er** *n*

dis·tur·bance \dis-'tər-bən(t)s\ *n* **1** : the act of disturbing **2** : mental confusion : UPSET **3** : public turmoil

dis·turbed \-'tərbd\ *adj* : showing symptoms of mental or emotional illness

dis·unite \ˌdish-ü-'nīt, ˌdis-yü-\ *vt* : DIVIDE, SEPARATE

dis·uni·ty \dish-'ü-nət-ē, (')dis-'yü-\ *n* : lack of unity; *esp* : DISSENSION

¹dis·use \dish-'üz, (')dis-'yüz\ *vt* : to discontinue the use or practice of

²dis·use \-'üs, -'yüs\ *n* : cessation of use or practice

di·syl·lab·ic \ˌdī-sə-'lab-ik\ *adj* : having two syllables — **di·syl·la·ble** \'dī-ˌsil-ə-bəl, (')dī-'\ *n*

¹ditch \'dich\ *n* : a long narrow excavation dug in the earth for defense, drainage, or irrigation

²ditch *vt* **1** : to enclose with a ditch **2** : to drive (a car) into a ditch **3** : to get rid of : DISCARD **4** : to make a forced landing of (an airplane) on water

dith·er \'dith-ər\ *n* : a highly nervous, excited, or agitated state — **dith·ery** \-ə-rē\ *adj*

dit·to \'dit-ō\ *n, pl* **dittos 1** : more of the same : SAME, ANOTHER — used to avoid repeating a word **2** : a mark composed of a pair of inverted commas or apostrophes used as a symbol for the word *ditto*

dit·ty \'dit-ē\ *n, pl* **ditties** : SONG; *esp* : a short simple song

di·uret·ic \ˌdī-yü-'ret-ik\ *adj* : tending to increase the flow of urine — **diuretic** *n* — **di·uret·i·cal·ly** \-'ret-i-k(ə-)lē\ *adv*

di·ur·nal \dī-'ərn-ᵊl\ *adj* **1 a** : recurring every day **b** : having a daily cycle **2** : of, relating to, or occurring in the daytime — **di·ur·nal·ly** \-ᵊl-ē\ *adv*

di·va \'dē-və\ *n, pl* **di·vas** *or* **di·ve** \-(ˌ)vā\ : PRIMA DONNA 1

di·van \'dī-ˌvan\ *n* : a large couch or sofa

¹dive \'dīv\ *vi* **dived** \'dīvd\ *or* **dove** \'dōv\; **div·ing 1 a** : to plunge into water headfirst **b** : SUBMERGE **2 a** : to descend or fall precipitously **b** : to descend in a dive **3 a** : to plunge into some matter or activity **b** : DART, LUNGE — **div·er** *n*

²dive *n* **1** : the act or an instance of diving **2** : a sharp decline **3** : a disreputable bar

di·verge \də-'vərj, dī-\ *vb* **1 a** : to move or extend in different directions from a common point : draw apart **b** : to differ in character, form, or opinion **2** : to turn aside from a path or course : DEVIATE **3** : DEFLECT

di·ver·gence \-'vər-jən(t)s\ *n* **1** : a drawing apart (as of lines extending from a common center) **2** : DIFFERENCE, DISAGREEMENT

di·ver·gent \-jənt\ *adj* **1** : diverging from each other : SPREADING **2** : differing from each other or from a standard : DEVIANT — **di·ver·gent·ly** *adv*

di·vers \'dī-vərz\ *adj* : VARIOUS

di·verse \dī-'vərs, də-, 'dī-ˌ\ *adj* **1** : differing from one another : UNLIKE **2** : having various forms or qualities — **di·verse·ly** *adv* — **di·verse·ness** *n*

di·ver·si·fy \də-'vər-sə-ˌfī, dī-\ *vb* **-fied**; **-fy·ing 1** : to make diverse : give variety to **2** : to distribute one's investments among different kinds of securities **3** : to increase the variety of the products manufactured or distributed — **di·ver·si·fi·ca·tion** \də-ˌvər-sə-fə-'kā-shən, (ˌ)dī-\ *n*

di·ver·sion \də-'vər-zhən, dī-\ *n* **1** : the act or an instance of diverting from a course, activity, or use : DEVIATION **2** : something that diverts or amuses : PASTIME — **di·ver·sion·ary** \-zhə-ˌner-ē\ *adj*

di·ver·si·ty \də-'vər-sət-ē, dī-\ *n, pl* **-ties 1** : the condition of being different or having differences **2** : an instance or a point of difference **3** : VARIETY

di·vert \də-'vərt, dī-\ *vb* **1 a** : to turn from one course or use to another : DEFLECT **b** : DISTRACT **2** : to give pleasure to

di·vest \dī-'vest, də-\ *vt* **1** : to strip esp. of clothing, ornament, or equipment **2** : to deprive esp. of a right

¹di·vide \də-'vīd\ *vb* **1 a** : to separate into two or more parts, areas, or groups **b** : to separate into classes, categories, or divisions **c** : CLEAVE, PART **2 a** : to give out in shares : DISTRIBUTE **b** : to possess or make use of in common **3** : to cause to be separate, distinct, or apart from one another **4 a** : to mark divisions on : GRADUATE **b** : to subject to mathematical division **5 a** : to become separated into parts **b** : to branch out

²divide *n* : a dividing ridge between drainage areas

di·vid·ed \-əd\ *adj* **1 a** : separated into parts or pieces **b** : having the opposing streams of traffic separated **2 a** : disagreeing with each other : DISUNITED **b** : directed or moved toward conflicting goals

div·i·dend \'div-ə-ˌdend\ *n* **1** : a sum or amount to be distributed or an individual share of such a sum **2** : BONUS **3** : a number to be divided by another

di·vid·er \də-'vīd-ər\ *n* **1** : one that divides **2** *pl* : an instrument for measuring or marking (as in dividing lines and transferring dimensions)

div·i·na·tion \ˌdiv-ə-'nā-shən\ *n* **1** : the art or practice that seeks to foresee or foretell future events or discover hidden knowledge usu. by means of augury or by the aid of supernatural powers **2** : unusual insight or intuitive perception

¹di·vine \də-'vīn\ *adj* **1 a** : of, relating to, or proceeding directly from deity **b** : being deity **2 a** : supremely good : SUPERB **b** : GODLIKE, HEAVENLY — **di·vine·ly** *adv*

²divine *n* **1** : CLERGYMAN **2** : THEOLOGIAN

³divine *vb* **1** : to discover or perceive intuitively : INFER, CONJECTURE **2** : to practice divination : PROPHESY — **di·vin·er** *n*

di·vin·ing rod \də-'vī-niŋ-ˌ\ *n* : a forked rod believed to divine the presence of water or minerals

di·vin·i·ty \də-'vin-ət-ē\ *n, pl* **-ties 1** : the quality or state of being divine : GODHEAD **2** *often cap* : a divine being; *esp* : GOD **3** : THEOLOGY

di·vis·i·ble \də-'viz-ə-bəl\ *adj* : capable of being divided or separated — **di·vis·i·bil·i·ty** \-ˌviz-ə-'bil-ət-ē\ *n*

di·vi·sion \də-'vizh-ən\ *n* **1 a** : the act or process of dividing : the state of being divided **b** : DISTRIBUTION **2** : one of the parts, sections, or groupings into which a whole is divided **3 a** : a large self-contained military unit **b (1)** : the basic naval administrative unit **(2)** : a tactical subdivision of a squadron of ships **4** : an administrative or operating unit of a governmental, business, or educational organization **5** : something that divides, separates, or marks off **6 a** : difference in opinion or interest : DISAGREEMENT **b** : the physical separation of the members of a deliberative body voting for and against a question **7** : the operation of finding how many times one number or quantity is contained in another — **di·vi·sion·al** \-'vizh-nəl, -ən-ᵊl\ *adj*

di·vi·sive \də-'vī-siv, -'viz-iv\ *adj* : creating disunity or dissension — **di·vi·sive·ly** *adv* — **di·vi·sive·ness** *n*

di·vi·sor \də-'vī-zər\ *n* : the number by which a dividend is divided

¹di·vorce \də-'vōrs\ *n* **1** : a complete legal dissolution of a marriage **2** : complete separation : SEVERANCE

²divorce *vt* **1 a** : to get rid of (one's spouse) by divorce **b** : to dissolve the marriage between (two spouses) **2** : SEPARATE, DISUNITE — **di·vorce·ment** *n*

di·vor·cée \də-ˌvōr-'sā, -'sē\ *n* : a divorced woman

div•ot \'div-ət\ *n* : a piece of turf dug from a golf fairway in making a stroke
di•vulge \də-'vəlj, dī-\ *vt* : to make public : DISCLOSE, REVEAL
diz•zi•ness \'diz-ē-nəs\ *n* : the condition of being dizzy
[1]**diz•zy** \'diz-ē\ *adj* **1 a** : having a whirling sensation in the head : GIDDY **b** : mentally confused **2 a** : causing or caused by giddiness **b** : extremely rapid — **diz•zi•ly** \'diz-ə-lē\ *adv*
[2]**dizzy** *vt* **diz•zied**; **diz•zy•ing** : to make dizzy : cause dizziness in
[1]**do** \(')dü\ *vb* **did** \(')did\; **done** \'dən\; **do•ing** \'dü-iŋ\; **does** \(')dəz\ **1 a** : to accomplish as a purposeful or willful act **b** : ACT, BEHAVE **c** : to be active or busy **d** : HAPPEN **2 a** : to work at esp. as a vocation **b** : to take appropriate action on : PREPARE **c** : to put in order (as by cleaning or arranging) **d** : DECORATE **3 a** : to get along **b** : to carry on **c** : to feel or function better **4** : to act so as to bring : RENDER **5** : to bring or come to an end : FINISH **6** : to put forth : EXERT **7** : PRODUCE **8** : to play the part of **9** : CHEAT **10 a** : TRAVERSE **b** : TOUR **c** : to travel at a speed of **11** : to serve in prison **12 a** : to serve the needs of : SUIT **b** : to answer the purpose **c** : to be fitting or proper **13** — used with *so* or a pronoun object to stand for part of a preceding predicate **14** — used as an auxiliary verb (1) before the subject in an interrogative sentence and after some adverbs, (2) in a negative statement, (3) for emphasis, and (4) as a substitute for a preceding predicate — **do away with 1** : to get rid of **2** : DESTROY, KILL — **do by** : to act toward in a specified manner — **do for** : to bring about the death or ruin of
[2]**do** \'dō\ *n* : the 1st note of the diatonic scale
do•a•ble \'dü-ə-bəl\ *adj* : capable of being done
do•cent \'dōs-ᵊnt, dō(t)-'sent\ *n* : TEACHER, LECTURER
doc•ile \'däs-əl\ *adj* : easily taught, led, or managed : TRACTABLE — **doc•ile•ly** \'däs-ə(l)-lē\ *adv* — **do•cil•i•ty** \dä-'sil-ət-ē\ *n*
[1]**dock** \'däk\ *n* : any of a genus of coarse weedy plants related to buckwheat
[2]**dock** *vt* **1** : to cut off the end of : cut short **2** : to take away a part of : make a deduction from
[3]**dock** *n* **1** : an artificial basin to receive ships that has gates to keep the water in or out **2** : a slip or waterway usu. between two piers to receive ships **3** : a wharf or platform for the loading or unloading of materials
[4]**dock** *vb* : to bring or come into dock
[5]**dock** *n* : the place in a criminal court where a prisoner stands or sits during trial
[1]**dock•et** \'däk-ət\ *n* **1 a** : a formal abridged record of the proceedings in a legal action **b** : a register of such records **2 a** : a list of legal causes to be tried **b** : a calendar of matters to be acted on : AGENDA **3** : a label attached to a parcel containing identification or directions (as for handling)
[2]**docket** *vt* **1** : to mark with an identifying statement **2** : to make a brief abstract of (as a legal matter) and inscribe it in a list **3** : to place on the docket for legal action
dock•yard \'däk-,yärd\ *n* : a storage place for naval supplies or shipbuilding materials
[1]**doc•tor** \'däk-tər\ *n* **1** : a person holding one of the highest academic degrees (as a PhD) conferred by a university **2** : one skilled or specializing in healing arts; *esp* : a physician, surgeon, dentist, or veterinarian licensed to practice his profession — **doc•tor•al** \-t(ə-)rəl\ *adj* — **doc•tor•ship** \-tər-,ship\ *n*
[2]**doctor** *vb* **doc•tored**; **doc•tor•ing** \-t(ə-)riŋ\ **1 a** : to give medical treatment to **b** : to practice medicine **c** : to restore to good condition : REPAIR **2 a** : to adapt or modify for a desired end **b** : to alter deceptively
doc•tor•ate \'däk-t(ə-)rət\ *n* : the degree, title, or rank of a doctor
doc•tri•naire \,däk-trə-'na(ə)r\ *n* : one who attempts to put an abstract theory into effect without regard to practical difficulties — **doctrinaire** *adj*
doc•trine \'däk-trən\ *n* **1** : something that is taught **2** : a principle or position or the body of principles in a branch of knowledge or system of belief : DOGMA — **doc•tri•nal** \-trən-ᵊl\ *adj* — **doc•tri•nal•ly** \-ᵊl-ē\ *adv*
[1]**doc•u•ment** \'däk-yə-mənt\ *n* : a usu. original or official written or printed paper furnishing information or used as proof of something else — **doc•u•men•tal** \,däk-yə-'ment-ᵊl\ *adj*
[2]**doc•u•ment** \'däk-yə-,ment\ *vt* : to furnish documentary evidence of — **doc•u•ment•a•ble** *adj*
[1]**doc•u•men•ta•ry** \,däk-yə-'ment-ə-rē, -'men-trē\ *adj* **1** : consisting of documents : of the nature of documents; *also* : contained or certified in writing **2** : giving a factual presentation in artistic form
[2]**documentary** *n, pl* **-ries** : a documentary presentation (as a film)
doc•u•men•ta•tion \,däk-yə-mən-'tā-shən\ *n* **1** : the providing or the using of documents in proof of something **2** : evidence in the form of documents or references (as in footnotes) to documents
dod•der \'däd-ər\ *vi* **dod•dered**; **dod•der•ing** \'däd-(ə-)riŋ\ **1** : to tremble or shake from weakness or age **2** : to progress feebly
dod•der•ing \'däd-(ə-)riŋ\ *adj* : FOOLISH, SENILE
[1]**dodge** \'däj\ *vb* **1 a** : to move suddenly aside **b** : to avoid by moving quickly aside **2** : to avoid by trickery or evasion
[2]**dodge** *n* **1** : an act of evading by sudden bodily movement **2 a** : an artful device to evade, deceive, or trick **b** : TECHNIQUE, METHOD
dodg•er \'däj-ər\ *n* **1** : one that dodges; *esp* : one who uses tricky devices **2** : a small handbill
do•do \'dōd-ō\ *n, pl* **dodoes** *or* **dodos** **1** : a heavy flightless extinct bird related to the pigeons but larger than a turkey and formerly found on some of the islands of the Indian ocean **2** : one hopelessly behind the times
doe \'dō\ *n, pl* **does** *or* **doe** : an adult female deer; *also* : the female esp. when adult of any mammal (as an antelope or hare) of which the male is called *buck*
do•er \'dü-ər\ *n* : one that does
doe•skin \'dō-,skin\ *n* : the skin of does or leather made of it; *also* : soft leather from sheepskins or lambskins
doff \'däf, 'dȯf\ *vt* **1** : to take off (one's clothes); *esp* : to take off or lift up (the hat) **2** : to rid oneself of
[1]**dog** \'dȯg\ *n* **1 a** : a variable carnivorous domesticated mammal prob. descended from the common wolf **b** : a male dog **2 a** : a worthless fellow **b** : FELLOW, CHAP **3 a** : any of various devices for holding, gripping, or fastening that consist of a spike, rod, or bar **b** : ANDIRON **4** : affected stylishness or dignity **5** *pl* : RUIN — **dog•like** *adj*
[2]**dog** *vt* **dogged**; **dog•ging** **1** : to hunt or track like a hound **2** : to worry as if by dogs : HOUND
dog•bane \'dȯg-,bān\ *n* : any of a genus of often poisonous plants with milky juice and usu. showy flowers
dog•cart \-,kärt\ *n* **1** : a cart drawn by a dog **2** : a light one-horse carriage with two seats back to back
dog•catch•er \-,kach-ər, -,kech-\ *n* : a community official assigned to catch and dispose of stray dogs
doge \'dōj\ *n* : the chief magistrate in the republics of Venice and Genoa
dog–ear \'dȯg-,i(ə)r\ *n* : the turned-down corner of a leaf of a book — **dog–ear** *vt* — **dog–eared** \-,i(ə)rd\ *adj*
dog•fight \'dȯg-,fīt\ *n* : a fight between two or more fighter planes usu. at close quarters
dog•fish \-,fish\ *n* : any of various small sharks that often appear in schools near shore
dog•ged \'dȯg-əd\ *adj* : stubbornly determined : TENACIOUS — **dog•ged•ly** *adv* — **dog•ged•ness** *n*

¹dog·ger·el \'dȯg-(ə-)rəl\ *adj* : loosely styled and irregular in measure esp. for burlesque or comic effect
²doggerel *n* : doggerel verse
¹dog·gone \'däg-'gän, 'dȯg-'gȯn\ *vb* : DAMN
²doggone *n* : DAMN
dog·gy \'dȯg-ē\ *adj* **1** : resembling a dog **2** : STYLISH, SHOWY
dog·house \'dȯg-ˌhau̇s\ *n* : a shelter for a dog — **in the doghouse** : in a state of disfavor
dog·ma \'dȯg-mə\ *n, pl* **dog·mas** **1** : something held as an established opinion; *esp* : a definite authoritative tenet **2** : a doctrine or body of doctrines concerning faith or morals laid down by a church
dog·mat·ic \dȯg-'mat-ik\ *adj* **1** : characterized by or given to the use of dogmatism **2** : of or relating to dogma — **dog·mat·i·cal·ly** \-'mat-i-k(ə-)lē\ *adv*
dog·ma·tism \'dȯg-mə-ˌtiz-əm\ *n* : positiveness in assertion of opinion esp. when unwarranted or arrogant
dog·ma·tist \-mət-əst\ *n* : one who dogmatizes
dog·ma·tize \-mə-ˌtīz\ *vb* : to speak or write dogmatically — **dog·ma·tiz·er** *n*
do–good·er \'dü-ˌgu̇d-ər\ *n* : an earnest usu. impractical and often naïve and ineffectual humanitarian or reformer
dog·trot \'dȯg-ˌträt\ *n* : a gentle trot
doi·ly \'dȯi-lē\ *n, pl* **doilies** **1** : a small napkin **2** : a small often decorative mat
do in *vt* **1** : to bring about the defeat or destruction of : RUIN **2** : KILL **3** : to wear out : EXHAUST
do·ing \'dü-iŋ\ *n* **1** : the act of performing or executing : ACTION **2** *pl* : things that are done or that occur
dol·drums \'dōl-drəmz, 'däl-\ *n pl* **1** : a spell of listlessness or despondency **2** : a part of the ocean near the equator abounding in calms and light shifting winds **3** : a state of inactivity, stagnation, or slump
¹dole \'dōl\ *n* **1 a** : a giving out of food, money, or clothing to the needy **b** : money, food, or clothing so given **2** : a grant of government funds to the unemployed
²dole *vt* **1** : to give or distribute as a charity **2** : to give or deliver in small portions : PARCEL
dole·ful \'dōl-fəl\ *adj* : full of grief : SAD — **dole·ful·ly** \-fə-lē\ *adv* — **dole·ful·ness** *n*
dole·some \'dōl-səm\ *adj* : DOLEFUL
doll \'däl, 'dȯl\ *n* **1** : a small-scale figure of a human being used esp. as a child's plaything **2** : a pretty scatterbrained young woman
dol·lar \'däl-ər\ *n* **1** : a basic monetary unit (as of the U.S. and Canada) **2** : a coin, note, or token representing one dollar
dol·lop \'däl-əp\ *n* : LUMP, BLOB
dolly \'däl-ē\ *n, pl* **doll·ies** **1** : DOLL **2** : a platform on a roller or on wheels for transporting heavy objects; *esp* : a wheeled platform for a television or motion-picture camera
dol·men \'dōl-mən, 'däl-\ *n* : a prehistoric monument consisting of two or more upright stones supporting a horizontal stone slab
do·lor \'dō-lər, 'däl-ər\ *n* : mental suffering or anguish : SORROW
do·lor·ous \'dō-lə-rəs, 'däl-ə-\ *adj* : causing, marked by, or expressive of misery or grief — **do·lor·ous·ly** *adv* — **do·lor·ous·ness** *n*
dol·phin \'däl-fən\ *n* **1** : any of various small long-nosed toothed whales **2** : PORPOISE 1
dolt \'dōlt\ *n* : a stupid fellow — **dolt·ish** \'dōl-tish\ *adj* — **dolt·ish·ly** *adv* — **dolt·ish·ness** *n*
do·main \dō-'mān\ *n* **1 a** : complete and absolute ownership of land **b** : land completely owned **2** : a territory over which dominion is exercised **3** : a sphere of influence or activity
dome \'dōm\ *n* : a large hemispherical roof or ceiling
¹do·mes·tic \də-'mes-tik\ *adj* **1** : of or relating to the household or the family **2** : of, relating to, or produced or carried on within one country **3 a** : living near or about the habitations of man **b** : DOMESTICATED, TAME **4** : devoted to home duties and pleasures — **do·mes·ti·cal·ly** \-ti-k(ə-)lē\ *adv*
²domestic *n* : a household servant
do·mes·ti·cate \də-'mes-ti-ˌkāt\ *vt* **1** : to bring into domestic use : ADOPT **2** : to fit for domestic life **3** : to adapt to life in intimate association with and to the advantage of man — **do·mes·ti·ca·tion** \də-ˌmes-ti-'kā-shən\ *n*
do·mes·tic·i·ty \ˌdō-ˌmes-'tis-ət-ē, də-\ *n, pl* **-ties** **1** : the quality or state of being domestic or domesticated **2** : domestic activities or life **3** *pl* : domestic affairs
¹dom·i·cile \'däm-ə-ˌsīl\ *n* **1** : a dwelling place : place of residence : HOME **2** : a person's fixed, permanent, and principal home for legal purposes — **dom·i·cil·i·ary** \ˌdäm-ə-'sil-ē-ˌer-ē\ *adj*
²domicile *vt* : to establish in or provide with a domicile
dom·i·nance \'däm-ə-nən(t)s\ *n* : the fact or state of being dominant; *esp* : AUTHORITY
dom·i·nant \-nənt\ *adj* **1** : commanding, controlling, or prevailing over all others **2** : overlooking and commanding from a superior elevation — **dom·i·nant·ly** *adv*
dom·i·nate \'däm-ə-ˌnāt\ *vb* **1** : RULE, CONTROL **2** : to have a commanding position or controlling power over **3** : to rise high above in a position suggesting power to dominate — **dom·i·na·tive** \-ˌnāt-iv\ *adj* — **dom·i·na·tor** \-ˌnāt-ər\ *n*
dom·i·na·tion \ˌdäm-ə-'nā-shən\ *n* **1** : supremacy or preeminence over another **2** : exercise of mastery or preponderant influence
dom·i·neer \ˌdäm-ə-'ni(ə)r\ *vb* **1** : to rule in an arrogant manner **2** : to be overbearing
dom·i·neer·ing \-iŋ\ *adj* : inclined to domineer — **dom·i·neer·ing·ly** *adv* — **dom·i·neer·ing·ness** *n*
do·mi·nie \'däm-ə-nē, 'dō-mə-\ *n* : CLERGYMAN
do·min·ion \də-'min-yən\ *n* **1** : supreme authority : SOVEREIGNTY **2** : DOMAIN **3** *often cap* : a self-governing nation of the British Commonwealth
dom·i·no \'däm-ə-ˌnō\ *n, pl* **-noes** *or* **-nos** **1** : a long loose hooded cloak usu. worn with a half mask as a masquerade costume **2 a** : a flat rectangular block whose face is divided into two equal parts that are blank or bear dots arranged as on dice faces **b** *pl* : a game played with dominoes
¹don \'dän\ *n* **1** : a Spanish nobleman or gentleman — used as a title prefixed to the Christian name **2** : a head, tutor, or fellow in a college of Oxford or Cambridge University
²don *vt* **donned**; **don·ning** : to put on : dress oneself in
do·ña \ˌdō-nyə\ *n* : a Spanish woman of rank — used as a title prefixed to the Christian name
do·nate \'dō-ˌnāt\ *vb* **1** : to make a gift of : CONTRIBUTE **2** : to make a donation — **do·na·tor** \-ˌnāt-ər\ *n*
do·na·tion \dō-'nā-shən\ *n* **1** : the action of making a gift esp. to a charity **2** : a free contribution : GIFT
¹done \'dən\ *past part of* DO
²done *adj* **1** : conformable to social convention **2** : physically exhausted : SPENT **3** : gone by : OVER **4** : doomed to failure, defeat, or death **5** : cooked sufficiently
do·nee \dō-'nē\ *n* : a recipient of a gift
don·key \'däŋ-kē, 'dəŋ-, 'dȯŋ-\ *n, pl* **donkeys** **1** : the domestic ass **2** : a stupid or obstinate person
don·nish \'dän-ish\ *adj* : of, relating to, or characteristic of a university don : PEDANTIC — **don·nish·ly** *adv* — **don·nish·ness** *n*
don·ny·brook \'dän-ē-ˌbru̇k\ *n, often cap* : an uproarious brawl
do·nor \'dō-nər\ *n* : one that gives, donates, or presents — **do·nor·ship** \-ˌship\ *n*
¹doo·dle \'düd-ᵊl\ *vb* **doo·dled**; **doo·dling** \'düd-liŋ, -ᵊl-iŋ\ : to draw or scribble aimlessly and without conscious effort while occupied with something else — **doo·dler** *n*
²doodle *n* : something produced by doodling

[1]**doom** \'düm\ *n* **1 a** : JUDGMENT, DECISION; *esp* : a judicial condemnation or sentence **b** : a final determining of what is just **2 a** : DESTINY; *esp* : unhappy destiny **b** : DEATH, RUIN

[2]**doom** *vt* **1** : to give judgment against : CONDEMN **2 a** : to fix the fate of : DESTINE **b** : to ensure the failure or destruction of

dooms·day \'dümz-ˌdā\ *n* : JUDGMENT DAY

door \'dō(ə)r\ *n* **1** : a usu. swinging or sliding barrier by which an entry is closed and opened; *also* : a similar part of a piece of furniture **2** : DOORWAY **3** : a means of access

door·jamb \-ˌjam\ *n* : an upright piece forming the side of a door opening

door·keep·er \-ˌkē-pər\ *n* : one that tends a door

door·knob \-ˌnäb\ *n* : a knob that when turned releases a door latch

door·man \-ˌman\ *n* **1** : DOORKEEPER **2** : one who tends a door (as of a hotel) and assists people by calling taxis and helping them in and out of cars

door·plate \-ˌplāt\ *n* : a plate or plaque bearing a name (as of a resident) on a door

door·post \-ˌpōst\ *n* : DOORJAMB

door·step \-ˌstep\ *n* : a step or series of steps before an outer door

door·way \-ˌwā\ *n* **1** : the opening that a door closes **2** : a means of gaining access

door·yard \-ˌyärd\ *n* : a yard outside the door of a house

[1]**dope** \'dōp\ *n* **1** : a preparation for giving a desired quality to a substance or surface **2 a** : a narcotic preparation **b** : a stupid person **3** : information esp. from a reliable source

[2]**dope** *vt* : to treat or affect with dope; *esp* : to give a narcotic to — **dop·er** *n*

dop·ey \'dō-pē\ *adj* **1** : dulled by or as if by alcohol or a narcotic **2** : DULL, STUPID — **dop·i·ness** *n*

dor·mant \'dȯr-mənt\ *adj* **1** : not active but capable of resuming activity **2 a** : sleeping or appearing to be asleep : SLUGGISH **b** : not actively growing — **dor·man·cy** \-mən-sē\ *n*

dor·mer \'dȯr-mər\ *n* : a window placed vertically in a roof; *also* : a roofed structure containing such a window

dor·mi·to·ry \'dȯr-mə-ˌtōr-ē\ *n, pl* **-ries** **1** : a room for sleeping; *esp* : a large room containing a number of beds **2** : a residence hall providing sleeping rooms

dor·mouse \'dȯ(ə)r-ˌmau̇s\ *n, pl* **dor·mice** \-ˌmīs\ : an Old World rodent that resembles a small squirrel

dor·sal \'dȯr-səl\ *adj* : relating to or situated near or on the back (as of an animal) — **dor·sal·ly** \-sə-lē\ *adv*

do·ry \'dōr-ē\ *n, pl* **dories** : a flat-bottomed boat with flaring sides

dos·age \'dō-sij\ *n* **1 a** : the giving of medicine in doses **b** : the amount of a single dose **2** : the addition of an ingredient or the application of an agent in a measured dose

[1]**dose** \'dōs\ *n* **1 a** : the measured amount of a medicine to be taken at one time **b** : the quantity of radiation administered or absorbed **2** : a portion of a substance added during a process

[2]**dose** *vt* **1** : to give medicine to **2** : to divide (as a medicine) into doses **3** : to treat with an application or agent

dos·sier \'dȯs-ˌyā\ *n* : a file of papers containing a detailed report or detailed information

[1]**dot** \'dät\ *n* **1** : a small spot : SPECK **2** : a small point made with or as if with a pen **3** : a precise point in time or space

[2]**dot** *vt* **dot·ted**; **dot·ting** **1** : to mark with a dot **2** : to cover with or as if with dots — **dot·ter** *n*

dot·age \'dōt-ij\ *n* : a state of feebleness or childishness of mind caused by or accompanying old age : SENILITY

dot·ard \'dōt-ərd\ *n* : a person in his dotage

dote \'dōt\ *vi* **1** : to be feebleminded esp. from old age **2** : to show excessive or foolish affection or fondness — **dot·er** *n* — **dot·ing·ly** *adv*

dot·ty \'dät-ē\ *adj* : mentally unbalanced : CRAZY

[1]**dou·ble** \'dəb-əl\ *adj* **1** : TWOFOLD, DUAL **2** : consisting of two members or parts **3** : being twice as great or as many **4** : folded in two **5** : having more than the usual number of floral leaves — **dou·ble·ness** *n*

[2]**double** *n* **1 a** : something twice another in size, strength, speed, quantity, or value **b** : a hit in baseball that enables the batter to reach second base **2** : COUNTERPART, DUPLICATE; *esp* : a person who closely resembles another **3** : a sharp turn : REVERSAL **4 a** : FOLD **b** : a combined bet placed on two different contests **5** *pl* : a game between two pairs of players **6** : an act of doubling in a card game

[3]**double** *adv* **1** : to twice the extent or amount : DOUBLY **2** : two together

[4]**double** *vb* **dou·bled**; **dou·bling** \'dəb-(ə-)liŋ\ **1 a** : to make or be twice as great or as many **b** : to make a call in bridge that increases the trick values and penalties of (an opponent's bid) **2 a** : to make of two thicknesses : FOLD **b** : CLENCH **c** : to become bent or folded usu. in the middle **3** : to sail around (as a cape) by reversing direction **4** : to take the place of another **5 a** : to become twice as much or as many **b** : to hit a double **6** : to turn sharply and suddenly; *esp* : to turn back on one's course — **dou·bler** *n*

double cross *n* : an act of betraying or cheating esp. an associate — **dou·ble–cross** \ˌdəb-əl-'krȯs\ *vt* — **dou·ble–cross·er** *n*

dou·ble–deal·ing \ˌdəb-əl-'dē-liŋ\ *n* : action contradictory to a professed attitude : DUPLICITY — **dou·ble–deal·er** *n* — **dou·ble–dealing** *adj*

dou·ble–deck·er \-'dek-ər\ *n* **1** : something (as a ship or bed) having two decks **2** : a sandwich having two layers

dou·ble en·ten·dre \ˌdüb-(ə-)ˌlä^n-'tä^{n}dr^ə, ˌdəb-\ *n, pl* **double entendres** *same*\ : a word or expression capable of two interpretations one of which is usu. indelicate

dou·ble·head·er \ˌdəb-əl-'hed-ər\ *n* : two games played consecutively on the same day by the same teams or by different pairs of teams

dou·ble–space \ˌdəb-əl-'spās\ *vb* : to type copy leaving every other line blank

dou·blet \'dəb-lət\ *n* **1** : a close-fitting jacket worn by men of western Europe chiefly in the 16th century **2** : one of two similar or identical things

dou·ble–talk \'dəb-əl-ˌtȯk\ *n* : language that appears to be meaningful but in fact is a mixture of sense and nonsense

dou·bly \'dəb-lē\ *adv* **1** : to twice the degree **2** : in a twofold manner

[1]**doubt** \'dau̇t\ *vb* **1** : to be uncertain about **2** : to lack confidence in : DISTRUST, FEAR **3** : to consider unlikely — **doubt·a·ble** *adj* — **doubt·er** *n*

[2]**doubt** *n* **1** : uncertainty of belief or opinion **2** : the condition of being objectively uncertain **3 a** : a lack of confidence : DISTRUST **b** : an inclination not to believe or accept

doubt·ful \'dau̇t-fəl\ *adj* **1** : not clear or certain as to fact **2** : questionable in character **3** : not settled in opinion : UNDECIDED **4** : not certain in outcome—**doubt·ful·ly** \-fə-lē\ *adv* — **doubt·ful·ness** *n*

[1]**doubt·less** \'dau̇t-ləs\ *adv* **1** : without doubt **2** : PROBABLY

[2]**doubtless** *adj* : free from doubt : CERTAIN

douche \'düsh\ *n* **1 a** : a jet of fluid (as water) directed against a part or into a cavity of the body **b** : a cleansing with a douche **2** : a device for giving douches — **douche** *vb*

dough \'dō\ *n* : a soft mass of moistened flour or meal thick enough to knead or roll; *also* : any similar soft pasty mass — **doughy** \'dō-ē\ *adj*

dough·boy \'dō-ˌbȯi\ *n* : an infantry soldier

dough·nut \-(ˌ)nət\ *n* : a small usu. ring-shaped cake fried in fat

dough·ty \'dau̇t-ē\ *adj* : being strong and valiant : BOLD — **dough·ti·ly** \'dau̇t-^{ə}l-ē\ *adv* — **dough·ti·ness** \'dau̇t-ē-nəs\ *n*

dour \'dau̇(ə)r, 'du̇(ə)r\ *adj* **1 :** STERN, HARSH **2 :** GLOOMY, SULLEN — **dour·ly** *adv* — **dour·ness** *n*
douse \'dau̇s\ *vt* **1 a :** to plunge into water **b :** to throw a liquid on : DRENCH **2 :** EXTINGUISH
[1]**dove** \'dəv\ *n* **1 :** PIGEON; *esp* : a small wild pigeon **2 :** an individual who takes a conciliatory attitude (as in a dispute) and advocates negotiations and compromise — **dov·ish** \'dəv-ish\ *adj*
[2]**dove** \'dōv\ *past of* DIVE
dove·cote \'dəv-ˌkōt, -ˌkät\ *or* **dove·cot** \-ˌkät\ *n* : a house or box with compartments for domestic pigeons
[1]**dove·tail** \'dəv-ˌtāl\ *n* : something resembling a dove's tail; *esp* : a flaring tenon and a mortise into which it fits tightly
[2]**dovetail** *vb* **1 :** to join by means of dovetails **2 :** to fit skillfully together to form a whole
dow·a·ger \'dau̇-i-jər\ *n* **1 :** a widow holding property or a title received from her deceased husband **2 :** a dignified elderly woman
dowdy \'dau̇d-ē\ *adj* : not neatly or becomingly dressed or cared for : SHABBY, UNTIDY — **dowd·i·ly** \'dau̇d-ᵊl-ē\ *adv* — **dowd·i·ness** \'dau̇d-ē-nəs\ *n*
[1]**dow·el** \'dau̇(-ə)l\ *n* : a pin or peg for fastening together two pieces (as of wood)
[2]**dowel** *vt* **-eled** *or* **-elled**; **-el·ing** *or* **-el·ling** : to fasten by or furnish with dowels
[1]**dow·er** \'dau̇(-ə)r\ *n* **1 :** the part of or interest in the real estate of a deceased husband given by law to his widow during her life **2 :** DOWRY
[2]**dower** *vt* : to supply with a dower or dowry : ENDOW
[1]**down** \'dau̇n\ *n* : an undulating usu. treeless upland with sparse soil — usu. used in pl.
[2]**down** *adv* **1 a** (1) : toward or in a lower physical position (2) : to a lying or sitting position (3) : toward or to the ground, floor, or bottom **b :** in cash **2 :** in a direction that is the opposite of up: as **a :** SOUTH **b :** away from a center **3 :** to or in a lower or worse condition, level, or status **4 :** from a past time **5 :** to or in a state of less activity **6 :** from a thinner to a thicker consistency
[3]**down** *adj* **1 a :** occupying a low position; *esp* : lying on the ground **b :** directed or going downward **c :** being at a lower level **2 a :** being in a state of reduced or low activity **b** (1) : DEPRESSED, DEJECTED (2) : SICK (3) : having a low opinion or dislike **3 :** FINISHED, DONE **4 :** being the part of a price paid at the time of purchase or delivery
[4]**down** *prep* : down along : down through : down toward : down in: down into: down on
[5]**down** *n* **1 :** a low or falling period (as in activity, emotional life, or fortunes) **2 :** one of a series of attempts to advance a football
[6]**down** *vb* : to go or cause to go or come down
[7]**down** *n* **1 :** a covering of soft fluffy feathers **2 :** something soft and fluffy like down
down·beat \'dau̇n-ˌbēt\ *n* : the downward stroke of a conductor indicating the principally accented note of a measure of music
down·cast \-ˌkast\ *adj* **1 :** DISCOURAGED, DEJECTED **2 :** directed down
down·fall \-ˌfȯl\ *n* **1 :** FALL; *esp* : a sudden or heavy fall (as of rain) **2 :** a sudden descent (as from a high position) : RUIN — **down·fall·en** \-ˌfȯ-lən\ *adj*
[1]**down·grade** \-ˌgrād\ *n* **1 :** a downward grade or slope **2 :** a decline toward a worse condition — **down·grade** \-'grād\ *adv*
[2]**down·grade** \-ˌgrād\ *vt* : to lower in grade, rank, position, or status
down·heart·ed \'dau̇n-'härt-əd\ *adj* : DEJECTED
[1]**down·hill** \-'hil\ *adv* : toward the bottom of a hill
[2]**downhill** \-ˌhil\ *adj* : sloping downhill
down·pour \-ˌpōr\ *n* : a heavy rain
[1]**down·right** \-ˌrīt\ *adv* : THOROUGHLY
[2]**downright** *adj* **1 :** ABSOLUTE, THOROUGH **2 :** PLAIN, BLUNT — **down·right·ly** *adv* — **down·right·ness** *n*
[1]**down·stairs** \'dau̇n-'sta(ə)rz\ *adv* : down the stairs : on or to a lower floor
[2]**downstairs** \-ˌsta(ə)rz\ *adj* : situated on a lower floor or on the main or ground floor
[3]**downstairs** \'dau̇n-', 'dau̇n-ˌ\ *n* : the lower floor of a building
down·stream \-'strēm\ *adv* (*or adj*) : in the direction of flow of a stream
down–to–earth \ˌdau̇n-tə-'(w)ərth\ *adj* : PRACTICAL, REALISTIC
[1]**down·town** \'dau̇n-'tau̇n\ *adv* : to, toward, or in the lower part or business center of a town or city
[2]**downtown** \-ˌtau̇n\ *adj* **1 :** situated downtown **2 :** of or relating to the business center of a town or city
[3]**downtown** \-ˌtau̇n\ *n* : an urban business center
down·trod·den \-'träd-ᵊn\ *adj* : crushed by superior power : OPPRESSED
down·turn \-ˌtərn\ *n* : a turning downward
[1]**down·ward** \'dau̇n-wərd\ *adv* **1 :** in a direction from higher to lower **2 :** from a higher to a lower condition **3 a :** from an earlier time **b :** from an ancestor or predecessor
[2]**downward** *adj* **1 :** directed toward or situated in a lower place or condition : DESCENDING **2 :** descending from a head, origin, or source — **down·ward·ly** *adv*
down·wind \'dau̇n-'wind\ *adv* (*or adj*) : in the direction that the wind is blowing : LEEWARD
downy \'dau̇-nē\ *adj* **1 a :** resembling a bird's down **b :** covered with or made of down **2 :** SOFT, SOOTHING
dow·ry \'dau̇(ə)r-ē\ *n, pl* **dowries** : the property that a woman brings to her husband in marriage
dowse \'dau̇z\ *vb* : to use a divining rod esp. to find water — **dows·er** *n*
dox·ol·o·gy \däk-'säl-ə-jē\ *n, pl* **-gies** : an expression (as a short hymn) of praise to God
doze \'dōz\ *vi* : to sleep lightly — **doze** *n* — **doz·er** *n*
doz·en \'dəz-ᵊn\ *n, pl* **dozens** *or* **dozen** : a group of twelve — **dozen** *adj* — **doz·enth** \-ᵊn(t)th\ *adj*
[1]**drab** \'drab\ *n* **1 :** SLATTERN **2 :** PROSTITUTE
[2]**drab** *adj* **1 :** of a light olive-brown color **2 :** characterized by dullness and monotony : CHEERLESS — **drab·ly** *adv* — **drab·ness** *n*
[1]**draft** \'draft, 'dráft\ *n* **1 :** the act of drawing a net; *also* : the quantity of fish taken at one drawing **2 :** the act of moving loads by drawing or pulling : PULL **3 :** the force required to pull an implement **4 a :** the act or an instance of drinking or inhaling; *also* : the portion drunk or inhaled in one such act **b :** a potion prepared for drinking : DOSE **5 a :** DELINEATION, REPRESENTATION; *esp* : a construction plan **b :** SCHEME, DESIGN **c :** a preliminary sketch, outline, or version **6 :** the act, result, or plan of drawing out or stretching **7 a :** the act of drawing (as from a cask) **b :** a portion of liquid so drawn **8 :** the depth of water a ship draws esp. when loaded **9 a :** the selection of a person esp. for compulsory military service **b :** a group of persons selected **10 a :** an order (as a check) issued by one party to another (as a bank) to pay money to a third party **b :** a heavy demand : STRAIN **11 a :** a current of air in a closed-in space **b :** a device for regulating the flow of air (as in a fireplace) — **on draft** : ready to be drawn from a receptacle
[2]**draft** *adj* **1 :** used for drawing loads **2 :** constituting a preliminary or tentative version, sketch, or outline **3 :** being on draft; *also* : DRAWN
[3]**draft** *vt* **1 :** to select usu. on a compulsory basis; *esp* : to conscript for military service **2 a :** to draw up a preliminary sketch, version, or plan of **b :** to draw up : COMPOSE, PREPARE **3 :** to draw off or away — **draft·er** *n*

draft·ee \draf-ˈtē, dráf-\ *n* : a person who is drafted esp. into the armed forces
drafts·man \ˈdraf(t)s-mən, ˈdráf(t)s-\ *n* : one who draws plans and sketches — **drafts·man·ship** \-ˌship\ *n*
drafty \ˈdraf-tē, ˈdráf-\ *adj* : relating to or exposed to a draft
¹**drag** \ˈdrag\ *n* **1** : something that is dragged, pulled, or drawn along or over a surface: as **a** : HARROW **b** : a sledge for carrying heavy loads **c** : CONVEYANCE **2 a** : something that retards motion **b** : something that hinders or obstructs progress **3** : the act or an instance of dragging or drawing
²**drag** *vb* **dragged**; **drag·ging 1 a** : to draw slowly or heavily : HAUL **b** : to move or cause to move with painful slowness or difficulty **c** : to force into or out of some situation, condition, or course of action **d** : to pass (a period of time) in lingering pain, tedium, or unhappiness **e** : PROTRACT **2** : to hang or lag behind **3** : to trail along on the ground **4** : to explore, search, or fish with a drag **5** : DRAW, PUFF
drag·gle \ˈdrag-əl\ *vb* **drag·gled**; **drag·gling** \ˈdrag-(ə-)liŋ\ **1** : to make or become wet and dirty by dragging **2** : to follow slowly : STRAGGLE
drag·net \ˈdrag-ˌnet\ *n* **1 a** : a net drawn along the bottom of a body of water : TRAWL **b** : a net used (as for capturing small game) on the ground **2** : a network of planned actions for pursuing and catching a criminal
drag·o·man \ˈdrag-ə-mən\ *n, pl* **-mans** *or* **-men** \ -mən\ : an interpreter chiefly of Arabic, Turkish, or Persian employed esp. in the Near East
drag·on \ˈdrag-ən\ *n* : a fabulous animal usu. represented as a monstrous winged and scaly serpent with a crested head and enormous claws
drag·on·fly \-ˌflī\ *n* : any of an order of large harmless insects that have four long wings and feed esp. on flies, gnats, and mosquitoes
¹**dra·goon** \drə-ˈgün\ *n* : a cavalry soldier
²**dragoon** *vt* : to force or attempt to force into submission by violent measures
¹**drain** \ˈdrān\ *vb* **1 a** : to draw off or flow off gradually or completely **b** : to exhaust physically or emotionally **2 a** : to make or become gradually dry or empty **b** : to carry away the surface water of : discharge surface or surplus water **c** : EMPTY, EXHAUST — **drain·er** *n*
²**drain** *n* **1** : a means by which liquid or other matter is drained **2 a** : the act of draining **b** : a gradual outflow or withdrawal : DEPLETION **3** : something that causes depletion : BURDEN
drain·age \ˈdrā-nij\ *n* **1** : the act, process, or mode of draining; *also* : something drained off **2** : a means for draining : DRAIN; *also* : a system of drains **3** : an area or district drained
drain·pipe \ˈdrān-ˌpīp\ *n* : a pipe for drainage
drake \ˈdrāk\ *n* : a male duck
dram \ˈdram\ *n* **1 a** : an avoirdupois weight equal to 1/16 ounce **b** : an apothecaries' weight equal to 1/8 ounce **c** : FLUIDRAM **2 a** : a small portion of something to drink **b** : a small amount
dra·ma \ˈdräm-ə, ˈdram-\ *n* **1** : a literary composition designed for theatrical performance **2** : dramatic art, literature, or affairs **3 a** : a state, situation, or series of events involving conflict of forces **b** : dramatic state, effect, or quality
dra·mat·ic \drə-ˈmat-ik\ *adj* **1** : of or relating to the drama **2 a** : VIVID **b** : striking in appearance or effect — **dra·mat·i·cal·ly** \-ˈmat-i-k(ə-)lē\ *adv*
dra·mat·ics \-iks\ *n sing or pl* **1 a** : THEATRICALS **b** : theatrical technique **2** : dramatic behavior or expression
dram·a·tist \ˈdram-ət-əst\ *n* : PLAYWRIGHT
dram·a·tize \ˈdram-ə-ˌtīz\ *vb* **1** : to adapt for or be suitable for theatrical presentation **2** : to present or represent in a dramatic manner — **dram·a·ti·za·tion** \ˌdram-ət-ə-ˈzā-shən\ *n*
dram·a·tur·gy \ˈdram-ə-ˌtər-jē, ˈdräm-\ *n* : the art or technique of dramatic composition and theatrical representation — **dram·a·tur·gic** \ˌdram-ə-ˈtər-jik, ˌdräm-\ *adj*
drank *past of* DRINK
¹**drape** \ˈdrāp\ *vb* **1** : to cover or adorn with or as if with folds of cloth **2** : to cause to hang or stretch out loosely or carelessly **3** : to arrange or become arranged in flowing lines or folds — **drap·er** *n*
²**drape** *n* **1** : a drapery esp. for a window **2** : arrangement in or of folds **3** : the cut or hang of clothing
drap·ery \ˈdrā-p(ə-)rē\ *n, pl* **-er·ies 1 a** : a decorative fabric usu. hung in loose folds and arranged in a graceful design **b** : hangings of heavy fabric for use as a curtain **2** : the draping or arranging of materials
dras·tic \ˈdras-tik\ *adj* **1** : acting rapidly or violently **2** : extreme in effect : SEVERE — **dras·ti·cal·ly** \-ti-k(ə-)lē\ *adv*
¹**draw** \ˈdrȯ\ *vb* **drew** \ˈdrü\; **drawn** \ˈdrȯn\; **draw·ing 1** : to cause to move continuously toward or after a force applied in advance : HAUL, DRAG **2 a** : to cause to go in a certain direction (as by leading) **b** : to move or go steadily or gradually **3 a** : ATTRACT, ENTICE **b** : PROVOKE, ROUSE **4** : INHALE **5 a** : to bring or pull out **b** : to force out from cover or possession **c** : to extract the essence from : STEEP **d** : EVISCERATE **6** : to require (a specified depth) to float in **7 a** : ACCUMULATE, GAIN **b** : to take money from a place of deposit **c** : WITHDRAW **d** : to receive regularly from a source **8 a** : to take (cards) from a stack or the dealer **b** : to receive or take at random **9** : to bend (a bow) by pulling back the string **10 a** : to cause to shrink or pucker : WRINKLE **b** : to change shape by or as if by pulling or stretching **11** : to leave (a contest) undecided : TIE **12 a** : to produce a likeness of by making lines on a surface **b** : to write out in due form : DRAFT **c** : to design or describe in detail : FORMULATE **13** : DEDUCE **14** : to spread or elongate (metal) by hammering or by pulling through dies **15 a** : to produce or allow a draft or current of air **b** : to swell out in a wind
²**draw** *n* **1** : the act, process, or result of drawing **2** : a lot or chance drawn at random **3** : the movable part of a drawbridge **4** : a contest left undecided or deadlocked : TIE **5** : something that draws attention or patronage
draw·back \ˈdrȯ-ˌbak\ *n* : HINDRANCE, HANDICAP
draw·bridge \-ˌbrij\ *n* : a bridge made to be wholly or partly raised up, let down, or drawn aside so as to permit or hinder passage
draw·ee \drȯ-ˈē\ *n* : the party (as a bank) ordered to pay a draft
draw·er \ˈdrȯ(-ə)r\ *n* **1** : one that draws **2** : a sliding box or receptacle (as in a table or desk) opened by pulling out and closed by pushing in **3** *pl* : an undergarment for the lower part of the body
draw·ing \ˈdrȯ-iŋ\ *n* **1** : an act or instance of drawing; *esp* : an occasion when something (as the winner of a raffle) is decided by drawing lots **2** : the act, art, or technique of representing a figure, plan, or sketch by means of lines **3** : a representation formed by drawing
drawing room *n* **1** : a formal reception room **2** : a private room on a railroad car with three berths
¹**drawl** \ˈdrȯl\ *vb* : to speak slowly with vowels greatly prolonged : utter in a slow lengthened tone — **drawl·er** *n* — **drawl·ing·ly** *adv*
²**drawl** *n* : a drawling manner of speaking
drawn butter *n* : melted butter often with seasoning
drawn·work \ˈdrȯn-ˌwərk\ *n* : decoration on cloth made by drawing out threads according to a pattern
draw on *vb* **1** : APPROACH **2** : to bring on : CAUSE
draw out *vt* **1** : REMOVE, EXTRACT **2** : to cause to speak out freely
draw·string \ˈdrȯ-ˌstriŋ\ *n* : a string, cord, or tape for use in closing a bag or controlling fullness in garments or curtains
draw up *vb* **1** : to arrange (as troops) in order **2** : to straighten to an erect posture **3** : to bring to a halt

dray \'drā\ *n* : a vehicle used to haul goods; *esp* : a strong low cart or wagon without sides

[1]dread \'dred\ *vb* 1 : to fear greatly : be apprehensive or fearful 2 : to feel extreme reluctance to meet or face

[2]dread *n* 1 : great fear esp. in the face of impending evil or harm 2 : one causing fear or awe

[3]dread *adj* 1 : causing great fear or anxiety 2 : inspiring awe

[1]dread•ful \'dred-fəl\ *adj* 1 : inspiring dread or awe : FRIGHTENING 2 : extremely distasteful, unpleasant, or shocking — **dread•ful•ly** \-f(ə-)lē\ *adv*

[2]dreadful *n* : a cheap and sensational story or periodical

dread•nought \'dred-ˌnȯt\ *n* : a battleship whose main armament consists entirely of big guns all of the same caliber

[1]dream \'drēm\ *n* 1 : a series of thoughts, images, or emotions occurring during sleep 2 a : a visionary creation of the imagination : DAYDREAM b : a state of mind in which a person is lost in fancies or reveries 3 : something notable for its beauty, excellence, or enjoyable quality 4 : a goal or purpose ardently desired : IDEAL — **dream•like** *adj*

[2]dream \'drēm\ *vb* **dreamed** \'drem(p)t, 'drēmd\ *or* **dreamt** \'drem(p)t\; **dream•ing** \'drē-miŋ\ 1 : to have a dream of 2 : to indulge in daydreams or fantasies : pass (time) in reverie or inaction 3 : to conceive as possible, fitting, or proper : IMAGINE

dream•er \'drē-mər\ *n* 1 : one that dreams 2 a : one who lives in a world of fancy and imagination b : one who has ideas or conceives projects regarded as impractical

dream•land \'drēm-ˌland\ *n* : an unreal delightful country existing only in imagination or in dreams

dream•world \-ˌwərld\ *n* : DREAMLAND; *also* : a world of illusion or fantasy

dreamy \'drē-mē\ *adj* 1 a : full of dreams b : VAGUE 2 : given to dreaming or fantasy 3 a : having the quality or characteristics of a dream b : quiet and soothing c : DELIGHTFUL, PLEASING — **dream•i•ly** \-mə-lē\ *adv* — **dream•i•ness** \-mē-nəs\ *n*

drear \'dri(ə)r\ *adj* : DREARY

drea•ry \'dri(ə)r-ē\ *adj* 1 : DOLEFUL, SAD 2 : DISMAL, GLOOMY — **drea•ri•ly** \'drir-ə-lē\ *adv* — **drea•ri•ness** \'drir-ē-nəs\ *n*

[1]dredge \'drej\ *n* 1 : a machine for removing earth usu. by buckets on an endless chain or a suction tube 2 : a barge used in dredging

[2]dredge *vb* 1 : to dig, gather, or pull out with or as if with a dredge 2 : to search with or as if with a dredge — **dredg•er** *n*

[3]dredge *vt* : to coat (food) by sprinkling (as with flour) — **dredg•er** *n*

dreg \'dreg\ *n* 1 : sediment contained in a liquid or precipitated from it : LEES — usu. used in pl. 2 : the most undesirable part — usu. used in pl.

drench \'drench\ *vt* : to wet thoroughly : SATURATE

[1]dress \'dres\ *vb* 1 a : to make or set straight b : to arrange (as troops) in a straight line and at proper intervals 2 a : to put clothes on b : to provide with clothing c : to put on or wear formal or fancy clothes 3 : to add decorative details or accessories to : EMBELLISH 4 : to put in order for use or service 5 a : to apply dressings or medicaments to b : to arrange (the hair) by combing, brushing, or curling c : to prepare (an animal) by grooming and currying d : to kill and prepare for market e : CULTIVATE, TEND; *esp* : to apply manure or fertilizer to 6 : SMOOTH, FINISH

[2]dress *n* 1 : APPAREL, CLOTHING 2 : an outer garment for a woman or child : FROCK, GOWN

[3]dress *adj* 1 : relating to or used for a dress 2 : suitable for a formal occasion 3 : requiring or permitting formal dress

dres•sage \drə-'säzh\ *n* : the execution by a horse of complex maneuvers in response to barely perceptible movements of a rider's hands, legs, and weight

dress down *vt* : to reprove severely — **dressing down** *n*

[1]dress•er \'dres-ər\ *n* 1 : a cupboard to hold dishes and cooking utensils 2 : a chest of drawers or bureau with a mirror

[2]dresser *n* : one that dresses

dress•ing \-iŋ\ *n* 1 : the act or process of one who dresses 2 a : a sauce for adding to a dish b : a seasoned mixture usu. used as a stuffing (as for poultry) 3 : material used to cover an injury

dressing gown *n* : a loose robe worn esp. while dressing or resting

dressing room *n* : a room used chiefly for dressing; *esp* : a room in a theater for changing costumes and makeup

dress•mak•er \'dres-ˌmā-kər\ *n* : one that does dressmaking

dress•mak•ing \-kiŋ\ *n* : the process or occupation of making dresses

dressy \'dres-ē\ *adj* 1 : showy in dress 2 : STYLISH, SMART

drew *past of* DRAW

[1]drib•ble \'drib-əl\ *vb* **drib•bled**; **drib•bling** \'drib-(ə-)liŋ\ 1 : to fall or flow or let fall or flow in drops or in a thin intermittent stream : TRICKLE 2 : DROOL, SLOBBER 3 : to propel by tapping, bouncing, or kicking — **drib•bler** *n*

[2]dribble *n* 1 a : a small trickling stream or flow b : a drizzling shower 2 : an act or instance of dribbling a ball or puck

drib•let \'drib-lət\ *n* 1 : a trifling sum or part : a small amount 2 : a falling drop

dri•er *also* **dry•er** \'drī(-ə)r\ *n* 1 : a substance that accelerates drying (as of oils, paints, and printing inks) 2 *usu dryer* : a device for drying

[1]drift \'drift\ *n* 1 a : the act of driving something along b : the flow of a river or ocean stream 2 a : wind-driven snow, rain, or smoke usu. near the ground surface b : a mass of matter (as sand) deposited together by or as if by wind or water c : a deposit of clay, sand, gravel, and boulders transported by a glacier or by running water from a glacier 3 a : a general underlying design or tendency b : the meaning, import, or purport of what is spoken or written

[2]drift *vb* 1 : to become or cause to be driven or carried along by a current of water, wind, or air 2 : to move or become carried along subject to no guidance or control 3 : to accumulate or cause to accumulate in a mass : be piled up in heaps by wind or water — **drift•er** *n* — **drift•ing•ly** *adv*

drift•age \'drif-tij\ *n* 1 : a drifting of some object esp. through action of wind or water 2 : something that drifts

drift•wood \'drift-ˌwu̇d\ *n* 1 : wood drifted or floated by water 2 : something that drifts aimlessly : FLOTSAM

[1]drill \'dril\ *vb* 1 : to pierce or bore with or as if with a drill 2 a : to instruct thoroughly b : to impart or communicate by repetition c : to train or exercise in military evolutions and the use of weapons — **drill•er** *n*

[2]drill *n* 1 : an instrument for making holes in hard substances by revolving or by a succession of blows 2 : the training of soldiers in military skill and discipline 3 : a physical or mental exercise regularly and repeatedly practiced

[3]drill *n* : a planting implement that opens a furrow, drops in seed, and covers it with earth

[4]drill *vt* : to sow with or as if with a drill

[5]drill *n* : a durable cotton fabric in twill weave

dril•ling \'dril-iŋ\ *n* : [5]DRILL

drill•mas•ter \'dril-ˌmas-tər\ *n* : one who drills; *esp* : an instructor in military drill

[1]drink \'driŋk\ *vb* **drank** \'draŋk\; **drunk** \'drəŋk\ *or* **drank**; **drink•ing** 1 a : to swallow liquid : IMBIBE b : to take in or suck up : ABSORB c : to take in or receive in a way suggestive of liquid being swallowed 2 : to give or join in a toast 3 : to drink alcoholic beverages

[2]drink *n* 1 a : a liquid suitable for swallowing : BEVERAGE b : alcoholic liquor 2 : a draft or portion of liquid 3 : excessive consumption of alcoholic beverages

drink·a·ble \'driŋ-kə-bəl\ *adj* : suitable or safe for drinking
drink·er \'driŋ-kər\ *n* 1 : one that drinks 2 : one that drinks alcoholic beverages esp. to excess
[1]**drip** \'drip\ *vb* **dripped** *or* **dript**; **drip·ping** 1 : to fall or let fall in drops 2 **a** : to let fall drops of moisture or liquid **b** : to overflow with or as if with moisture — **drip·per** *n*
[2]**drip** *n* 1 **a** : a falling in drops **b** : liquid that falls, overflows, or is extruded in drops 2 : the sound made by or as if by falling drops
drip–dry \'drip-'drī\ *vi* : to dry with few or no wrinkles when hung dripping wet — **drip–dry** \-ˌdrī\ *adj*
drip·ping \'drip-iŋ\ *n* : fat and juices from meat during cooking — often used in pl.
[1]**drive** \'drīv\ *vb* **drove** \'drōv\; **driv·en** \'driv-ən\; **driv·ing** \'drī-viŋ\ 1 : to urge, push, or force onward 2 **a** : to direct the movement or course of **b** : to convey or transport in a vehicle 3 : to carry along or keep in motion 4 : to carry through strongly 5 **a** : to force or compel to work or to act **b** : to project, inject, or impress forcefully 6 : to bring into a specified condition 7 : to produce by opening a way (as by drilling) 8 : to rush and press with violence 9 : to hit a golf ball from the tee
[2]**drive** *n* 1 : an act of driving: as **a** : a trip in a carriage or automobile **b** : a collecting and driving together of animals **c** : the guiding of logs downstream to a mill **d** : the act of driving a ball **e** : the flight of a ball 2 **a** : DRIVEWAY **b** : a public road for driving (as in a park) 3 **a** : an offensive or aggressive move; *esp* : a strong sustained military attack **b** : an intensive campaign 4 : the state of being hurried and under pressure 5 **a** : an urgent, basic, or instinctual need or longing **b** : dynamic quality 6 : the means for giving motion to a machine or machine part
drive–in \'drīv-ˌin\ *adj* : arranged and equipped so as to accommodate patrons while they remain in their automobiles — **drive–in** *n*
[1]**driv·el** \'driv-əl\ *vb* **driv·eled** *or* **driv·elled**; **driv·el·ing** *or* **driv·el·ling** \'driv-(ə-)liŋ\ 1 : to let saliva dribble from the mouth : SLAVER 2 : to talk or utter stupidly, carelessly, or in an infantile way — **driv·el·er** *or* **driv·el·ler** *n*
[2]**drivel** *n* : NONSENSE
driv·er \'drī-vər\ *n* : one that drives; *esp* : the operator of a motor vehicle
drive·way \'drīv-ˌwā\ *n* 1 : a road or way along which animals are driven 2 : a short private road leading from the street to a house, garage, or parking lot
[1]**driz·zle** \'driz-əl\ *vb* **driz·zled**; **driz·zling** \'driz-(ə-)liŋ\ : to rain in very small drops or lightly : SPRINKLE
[2]**drizzle** *n* : a fine mistlike rain — **driz·zly** \'driz-(ə-)lē\ *adj*
drogue \'drōg\ *n* : a small attached parachute for slowing down or stabilizing something (as an astronaut's capsule in landing)
droll \'drōl\ *adj* : having a humorous, whimsical, or odd quality — **droll·ness** \'drōl-nəs\ *n* — **drol·ly** \'drōl-lē\ *adv*
droll·ery \'drōl-(ə-)rē\ *n*, *pl* **-er·ies** 1 : something droll; *esp* : an amusing story or gesture 2 : droll behavior 3 : whimsical humor
drom·e·dary \'dräm-ə-ˌder-ē\ *n*, *pl* **-dar·ies** 1 : a camel of unusual speed bred and trained esp. for riding 2 : the one-humped camel of western Asia and northern Africa
[1]**drone** \'drōn\ *n* 1 : the stingless male bee that gathers no honey 2 : one that lives on the labors of others 3 : a pilotless airplane or ship controlled by radio signals
[2]**drone** *vb* : to make or speak with a low dull monotonous humming sound
[3]**drone** *n* : a deep monotonous sound : HUM
drool \'drül\ *vb* 1 : to let saliva or some other substance flow from the mouth : SLAVER 2 : to talk foolishly : express in a sentimental or effusive manner
[1]**droop** \'drüp\ *vb* 1 : to hang or incline downward 2 : to sink gradually 3 : to become depressed or weakened : LANGUISH 4 : to let droop
[2]**droop** *n* : the condition or appearance of drooping
droopy \'drü-pē\ *adj* 1 : drooping or tending to droop 2 : GLOOMY, DEJECTED
[1]**drop** \'dräp\ *n* 1 **a** (1) : the quantity of fluid that falls in one spherical mass (2) *pl* : a dose of medicine measured by drops **b** : a small quantity of drink **c** : the smallest practical unit of liquid measure 2 **a** : a pendent ornament attached to a piece of jewelry **b** : a small round candy 3 **a** : the act or an instance of dropping : FALL **b** : a decline in quantity or quality **c** : a descent by parachute 4 : the distance through which something drops
[2]**drop** *vb* **dropped**; **drop·ping** 1 : to fall or let fall in drops 2 **a** : to let fall **b** : LOWER 3 : SEND 4 : to let go : DISMISS 5 : to knock down : cause to fall 6 : to go lower 7 : to come or go unexpectedly or informally 8 : to pass from one state into a less active one 9 : to move downward or with a current 10 : to withdraw from participation or membership : QUIT — usu. used with *out*
drop·kick \'dräp-ˌkik\ *n* : a kick made by dropping a football to the ground and kicking it at the moment it starts to rebound — **drop–kick** *vb* — **drop–kick·er** *n*
drop·let \'dräp-lət\ *n* : a very small drop
drop·out \'dräp-ˌau̇t\ *n* : one who drops out (as from school) before achieving his goal
drop·per \'dräp-ər\ *n* 1 : one that drops 2 : a short glass tube with a rubber bulb used to measure out liquids by drops
drop·pings \'dräp-iŋz\ *n pl* : animal dung
drop·sy \'dräp-sē\ *n* : an abnormal accumulation of serous fluid in the body — **drop·si·cal** \-si-kəl\ *adj*
dross \'dräs\ *n* 1 : the scum that forms on the surface of molten metal 2 : waste or foreign matter : IMPURITY
drought *or* **drouth** \'drau̇th, 'drau̇t\ *n* 1 : lack of rain or water 2 : a long period of dry weather — **droughty** \-ē\ *adj*
drove \'drōv\ *n* 1 : a group of animals driven or moving in a body 2 : a crowd of people moving or acting together
drov·er \'drō-vər\ *n* : one that drives cattle or sheep
drown \'drau̇n\ *vb* 1 **a** : to suffocate by submersion esp. in water **b** : to become drowned 2 : to cover with water : INUNDATE 3 : OVERCOME, OVERPOWER
drowse \'drau̇z\ *vi* : DOZE — **drowse** *n*
drowsy \'drau̇-zē\ *adj* 1 : ready to fall asleep 2 : making one sleepy — **drows·i·ly** \-zə-lē\ *adv* — **drows·i·ness** \-zē-nəs\ *n*
drub \'drəb\ *vt* **drubbed**; **drub·bing** 1 : to beat severely with or as if with a stick 2 : to defeat decisively
[1]**drudge** \'drəj\ *vi* : to do hard, menial, or monotonous work — **drudg·er** *n*
[2]**drudge** *n* : a person who drudges
drudg·ery \'drəj-(ə-)rē\ *n*, *pl* **-er·ies** : tiresome or menial work
[1]**drug** \'drəg\ *n* 1 : a substance used as a medicine or in making medicines 2 : a narcotic substance or preparation
[2]**drug** *vb* **drugged**; **drug·ging** : to affect or treat with a drug; *esp* : to stupefy by a narcotic drug
drug·gist \'drəg-əst\ *n* : one who sells drugs and medicines; *also* : PHARMACIST
drug·store \'drəg-ˌstōr\ *n* : a retail shop where medicines and miscellaneous articles are sold : PHARMACY
dru·id \'drü-əd\ *n*, *often cap* : one of an ancient Celtic priesthood of Gaul, Britain, and Ireland appearing in legends as magicians and wizards — **dru·id·ic** \drü-'id-ik\ *or* **dru·id·i·cal** \-'id-i-kəl\ *adj*, *often cap* — **dru·id·ism** \'drü-ə-ˌdiz-əm\ *n*, *often cap*
[1]**drum** \'drəm\ *n* 1 : a musical percussion instrument usu. consisting of a hollow cylinder with a skin head stretched over each end that is beaten with a stick or pair of sticks in playing

2 : EARDRUM 3 : the sound of a drum; *also* : a similar sound 4 : a drum-shaped object
²**drum** *vb* **drummed**; **drum·ming** 1 : to beat a drum 2 : to sound rhythmically : THROB, BEAT 3 : to summon or enlist by or as if by beating a drum 4 : to dismiss ignominiously : EXPEL — usu. used with *out* 5 : to drive or force by steady effort or reiteration 6 : to strike or tap repeatedly so as to produce rhythmic sounds
drum·beat \-ˌbēt\ *n* : a stroke on a drum or its sound
drum·mer \ˈdrəm-ər\ *n* 1 : one that plays a drum 2 : a traveling salesman
drum·stick \ˈdrəm-ˌstik\ *n* 1 : a stick for beating a drum 2 : the lower segment of a fowl's leg
¹**drunk** \ˈdrəŋk\ *adj* 1 : having the faculties impaired by alcohol 2 : controlled by some feeling as if under the influence of alcohol 3 : of, relating to, or caused by intoxication
²**drunk** *n* 1 : a person who is drunk 2 : SPREE
drunk·ard \ˈdrəŋ-kərd\ *n* : one who is habitually drunk
drunk·en \ˈdrəŋ-kən\ *adj* 1 a : DRUNK 1 b : given to habitual excessive use of alcohol 2 : of, relating to, or resulting from intoxication 3 : unsteady or lurching as if from intoxication — **drunk·en·ly** *adv* — **drunk·en·ness** *n*
¹**dry** \ˈdrī\ *adj* 1 : free or freed from water or liquid 2 : characterized by loss or lack of water: as a : lacking precipitation and humidity b : lacking freshness : STALE 3 : not being in or under water 4 a : THIRSTY b : marked by the absence of alcoholic beverages c : no longer liquid or sticky 5 : containing or employing no liquid 6 : not giving milk 7 : lacking natural lubrication 8 : solid as opposed to liquid 9 : not warm or tender in feeling : SEVERE 10 : not yielding : BARREN 11 : marked by a matter-of-fact, ironic, or terse manner of expression 12 : UNINTERESTING, WEARISOME 13 : not sweet 14 : relating to, favoring, or practicing prohibition of alcoholic beverages — **dry·ly** *adv* — **dry·ness** *n*
²**dry** *vb* **dried**; **dry·ing** : to make or become dry
³**dry** *n, pl* **drys** : PROHIBITIONIST
dry·ad \ˈdrī-əd\ *n* : WOOD NYMPH
dry–clean \ˈdrī-ˌklēn\ *vt* : to subject to dry cleaning — **dry clean·er** \-ˌklē-nər\ *n*
dry clean·ing \-ˌklē-niŋ\ *n* : the cleansing of fabrics with organic solvents (as naphtha)
dry·er *var of* DRIER
dry goods \ˈdrī-ˌgu̇dz\ *n pl* : textiles, ready-to-wear clothing, and notions as distinguished from other goods
dry–shod \ˈdrī-ˈshäd\ *adj* : having dry shoes or feet
du·al \ˈd(y)ü-əl\ *adj* 1 : consisting of two parts or elements : having two like parts : DOUBLE 2 : having a double character or nature — **du·al·i·ty** \d(y)ü-ˈal-ət-ē\ *n* — **du·al·ly** \ˈd(y)ü-ə-lē\ *adv*
du·al·ism \ˈd(y)ü-ə-ˌliz-əm\ *n* : a doctrine that the universe is made up of or governed by two opposing principles (as good and evil) — **du·al·ist** \-ləst\ *n*
¹**dub** \ˈdəb\ *vt* **dubbed**; **dub·bing** 1 a : to confer knighthood upon b : NAME 2 : to execute poorly
²**dub** *vt* **dubbed**; **dub·bing** 1 : to add (sound effects) to a film or broadcast 2 : to transpose (recorded sound) to a new record
du·bi·e·ty \d(y)u̇-ˈbī-ət-ē\ *n, pl* **-ties** 1 : DUBIOUSNESS, UNCERTAINTY 2 : a matter of doubt
du·bi·ous \ˈd(y)ü-bē-əs\ *adj* 1 : occasioning doubt : UNCERTAIN 2 : feeling doubt : UNDECIDED 3 : of doubtful promise or uncertain outcome 4 : questionable in value, quality, or origin — **du·bi·ous·ly** *adv* — **du·bi·ous·ness** *n*
du·cal \ˈd(y)ü-kəl\ *adj* : of or relating to a duke or dukedom
duch·ess \ˈdəch-əs\ *n* 1 : the wife or widow of a duke 2 : a woman who holds a ducal title in her own right
duchy \ˈdəch-ē\ *n, pl* **duch·ies** : the territory of a duke or duchess : DUKEDOM
¹**duck** \ˈdək\ *n, pl* **duck** *or* **ducks** : any of various swimming birds related to but smaller than geese and swans
²**duck** *vb* 1 : to thrust or plunge under water 2 : to lower the head or body suddenly 3 : BOW, BOB 4 a : to move quickly : DODGE b : to evade a duty, question, or responsibility — **duck·er** *n*
³**duck** *n* 1 : a durable closely woven usu. cotton fabric 2 *pl* : clothes made of duck
duck·bill \-ˌbil\ *n* : PLATYPUS
duck·ling \-liŋ\ *n* : a young duck
duck·pin \-ˌpin\ *n* 1 : a small bowling pin shorter and wider in the middle than a tenpin 2 *pl* : a bowling game using duckpins
duct \ˈdəkt\ *n* 1 : a tube or vessel carrying a bodily fluid (as the secretion of a gland) 2 a : a pipe, tube, or channel that conveys a fluid (as air or water) b : a pipe or tubular passage for conductors (as an electric power line or telephone cables) — **duct·less** \ˈdək-tləs\ *adj*
duc·tile \ˈdək-tᵊl\ *adj* 1 : capable of being drawn out (as into a wire) or hammered thin 2 : easily led or influenced : DOCILE — **duc·til·i·ty** \ˌdək-ˈtil-ət-ē\ *n*
dud \ˈdəd\ *n* 1 *pl* a : CLOTHES b : personal belongings 2 : one that fails completely 3 : a missile that fails to explode
dude \ˈd(y)üd\ *n* 1 : an extremely fastidious man : DANDY 2 : a city man; *esp* : an Easterner in the West — **dud·ish** \-ish\ *adj* — **dud·ish·ly** *adv*
dudg·eon \ˈdəj-ən\ *n* : ill humor : RESENTMENT
¹**due** \ˈd(y)ü\ *adj* 1 : owed or owing as a debt 2 a : owed or owing as a right b : according to accepted notions or procedures : APPROPRIATE, FITTING 3 a : SUFFICIENT, ADEQUATE b : REGULAR, LAWFUL 4 : ATTRIBUTABLE, ASCRIBABLE — used with *to* 5 : having reached the date at which payment is required : PAYABLE 6 : required or expected to happen : SCHEDULED
²**due** *n* 1 : something owed : DEBT 2 *pl* : a regular or legal charge or fee
³**due** *adv* : DIRECTLY, EXACTLY
¹**du·el** \ˈd(y)ü(-ə)l\ *n* : a combat between two persons; *esp* : one fought with weapons in the presence of witnesses
²**duel** *vb* **du·eled** *or* **du·elled**; **du·el·ing** *or* **du·el·ling** : to fight in a duel — **du·el·er** *n* — **du·el·ist** \ˈd(y)ü-ə-ləst\ *n*
du·en·na \d(y)ü-ˈen-ə\ *n* 1 : an elderly woman in charge of the younger ladies in a Spanish or Portuguese family 2 : GOVERNESS, CHAPERON
du·et \d(y)ü-ˈet\ *n* : a composition for two performers
due to *prep* : because of
duf·fel bag \ˈdəf-əl-\ *n* : a large cylindrical fabric bag for personal belongings
duf·fer \ˈdəf-ər\ *n* : an incompetent or clumsy person
¹**dug** *past of* DIG
²**dug** \ˈdəg\ *n* : UDDER, BREAST; *also* : TEAT, NIPPLE
dug·out \ˈdəg-ˌau̇t\ *n* 1 : a boat made by hollowing out a large log 2 : a shelter dug in a hillside or in the ground or in the side of a trench
duke \ˈd(y)ük\ *n* 1 : a sovereign ruler of a continental European duchy 2 : a nobleman of the highest rank; *esp* : a member of the highest grade of the British peerage — **duke·dom** \-dəm\ *n*
dul·cet \ˈdəl-sət\ *adj* 1 : sweet to the ear : MELODIOUS 2 : AGREEABLE, SOOTHING
dul·ci·mer \ˈdəl-sə-mər\ *n* : a wire-stringed instrument played with light hammers held in the hands
¹**dull** \ˈdəl\ *adj* 1 : mentally slow : STUPID 2 a : slow in perception or sensibility b : lacking zest or vivacity : LISTLESS 3 : slow in action : SLUGGISH 4 : lacking sharpness of edge or point 5 : lacking brilliance or luster 6 : not resonant or ringing 7 : CLOUDY, OVERCAST 8 : TEDIOUS, UNINTERESTING 9 *of a color* : low in saturation and lightness — **dull·ness** *or* **dul·ness** \ˈdəl-nəs\ *n* — **dul·ly** \ˈdəl-(l)ē\ *adv*
²**dull** *vb* : to make or become dull

dull·ard \ˈdəl-ərd\ *n* : a person who is stupid or insensitive
du·ly \ˈd(y)ü-lē\ *adv* : in a due manner, time, or degree
dumb \ˈdəm\ *adj* **1** : lacking the power of speech **2** : not willing to speak **3** : STUPID, FOOLISH — **dumb·ly** *adv* — **dumb·ness** *n*
dumb·bell \ˈdəm-ˌbel\ *n* **1** : a weight consisting of a short bar with identical spheres or weighted disks at each end and used usu. in pairs for exercise **2** : a dull or stupid person
dumb·found *or* **dum·found** \ˌdəm-ˈfau̇nd\ *vt* : to strike dumb with astonishment
dumb show *n* : signs and gestures without words
dumb·wait·er \ˈdəm-ˈwāt-ər\ *n* **1** : a portable serving table **2** : a small elevator for conveying food and dishes or small goods from one story of a building to another
dum·dum \ˈdəm-ˌdəm\ *n* : a soft-nosed bullet that expands upon hitting an object
dum·my \ˈdəm-ē\ *n, pl* **dum·mies** **1** : a person who lacks or seems to lack the power of speech **2** : one who seems to be acting for himself but is really acting for another **3** : a stupid person **4** : an imitation of something to be used as a substitute **5 a** : an exposed hand in bridge played by one of the players in addition to his own hand **b** : a bridge player whose hand is a dummy **6** : a pattern arrangement of matter to be reproduced esp. by printing
¹dump \ˈdəmp\ *vb* **1 a** : to let fall in a heap or mass : UNLOAD **b** : to dump refuse **2** : to sell in quantity at a very low price — **dump·er** *n*
²dump *n* **1** : a place where discarded materials are dumped **2 a** : a quantity of reserve and esp. military supplies stored at one place **b** : a place where reserve materials are stored **3** : a disorderly, slovenly, or dilapidated place
dump·ling \ˈdəm-pliŋ\ *n* **1** : a small mass of dough cooked by boiling or steaming **2** : a dessert of fruit baked in biscuit dough
dumps \ˈdəm(p)s\ *n pl* : a dull gloomy state of mind
dumpy \ˈdəm-pē\ *adj* : short and thick in build : SQUAT — **dump·i·ness** *n*
¹dun \ˈdən\ *n* **1** : a pale horse usu. with dark points and dorsal stripe **2** : a variable color averaging a nearly neutral slightly brownish dark gray
²dun *vt* **dunned**; **dun·ning** **1** : to make persistent demands upon for payment **2** : to plague or pester constantly
³dun *n* **1** : a person who duns another **2** : an urgent request; *esp* : a demand for payment
dunce \ˈdən(t)s\ *n* : a dull-witted and stupid person
dun·der·head \ˈdən-dər-ˌhed\ *n* : DUNCE, BLOCKHEAD — **dun·der·head·ed** \ˌdən-dər-ˈhed-əd\ *adj*
dune \ˈd(y)ün\ *n* : a hill or ridge of sand piled up by the wind
¹dung \ˈdəŋ\ *n* : the excrement of an animal : MANURE — **dungy** \ˈdəŋ-ē\ *adj*
²dung *vt* : to fertilize or dress with manure
dun·ga·ree \ˌdəŋ-gə-ˈrē\ *n* **1** : a heavy coarse durable cotton twill; *esp* : blue denim **2** *pl* : trousers or work clothes made of dungaree
dun·geon \ˈdən-jən\ *n* : a close dark prison commonly underground
dung·hill \ˈdəŋ-ˌhil\ *n* : a manure pile
dunk \ˈdəŋk\ *vb* **1** : to dip (as bread or cake) into liquid while eating **2** : to dip or submerge temporarily in liquid **3** : to submerge oneself in water
duo \ˈd(y)ü-ō\ *n, pl* **du·os** **1** : DUET; *esp* : a composition for two performers at two pianos **2** : PAIR
du·o·de·num \ˌd(y)ü-ə-ˈdē-nəm, d(y)u̇-ˈäd-ᵊn-əm\ *n, pl* **-de·na** \-ˈdē-nə, -ᵊn-ə\ *or* **-denums** : the part of the small intestine immediately below the stomach — **du·o·de·nal** \-ˈdēn-ᵊl, -ᵊn-əl\ *adj*
¹dupe \ˈd(y)üp\ *n* : one who is easily deceived or cheated
²dupe *vt* : to make a dupe of : DECEIVE — **dup·er** *n*
¹du·plex \ˈd(y)ü-ˌpleks\ *adj* : DOUBLE, TWOFOLD; *esp* : having two parts that operate at the same time or in the same way
²duplex *n* : something duplex; *esp* : a 2-family house
¹du·pli·cate \ˈd(y)ü-pli-kət\ *adj* **1** : consisting of or existing in two corresponding or identical parts or examples **2** : being the same as another
²duplicate *n* : a thing that exactly resembles another in appearance, pattern, or content : COPY
³du·pli·cate \ˈd(y)ü-pli-ˌkāt\ *vt* **1** : to make double or twofold **2** : to make a duplicate of — **du·pli·ca·tive** \-ˌkāt-iv\ *adj*
du·pli·ca·tion \ˌd(y)ü-pli-ˈkā-shən\ *n* **1 a** : an act or process of duplicating **b** : the quality or state of being duplicated **2** : DUPLICATE, COUNTERPART
du·pli·ca·tor \ˈd(y)ü-pli-ˌkāt-ər\ *n* : one that duplicates; *esp* : a machine for making copies of typed, drawn, or printed matter
du·plic·i·ty \d(y)u̇-ˈplis-ət-ē\ *n, pl* **-ties** : deception by pretending to feel and act one way while acting another
du·ra·bil·i·ty \ˌd(y)u̇r-ə-ˈbil-ət-ē\ *n* : the quality or state of being durable
du·ra·ble \ˈd(y)u̇r-ə-bəl\ *adj* : able to last a long time — **du·ra·ble·ness** *n* — **du·ra·bly** \ˈd(y)u̇r-ə-blē\ *adv*
du·rance \ˈd(y)u̇r-ən(t)s\ *n* : IMPRISONMENT
du·ra·tion \d(y)u̇-ˈrā-shən\ *n* **1** : continuance in time **2** : the time during which something exists or lasts
du·ress \d(y)u̇-ˈres\ *n* **1** : forcible restraint or restriction **2** : compulsion by threat
dur·ing \ˌd(y)u̇r-iŋ\ *prep* **1** : throughout the duration of **2** : at some time or times in the course of
¹dusk \ˈdəsk\ *vb* : to make or become dark or gloomy
²dusk *n* **1** : the darker part of twilight esp. at night **2** : GLOOM
dusky \ˈdəs-kē\ *adj* **1** : somewhat dark in color; *esp* : having dark skin **2** : marked by slight or deficient light : SHADOWY — **dusk·i·ly** \-kə-lē\ *adv* — **dusk·i·ness** \-kē-nəs\ *n*
¹dust \ˈdəst\ *n* **1** : fine dry powdery particles of earth **2** : the earthy remains of bodies once alive; *esp* : the human corpse **3** : the surface of the ground **4 a** : something worthless **b** : a low or mean condition : state of humiliation — **dust·less** \-ləs\ *adj*
²dust *vb* **1** : to make free of dust : brush or wipe away dust **2 a** : to sprinkle with fine particles **b** : to sprinkle in the form of dust
dust·er \ˈdəs-tər\ *n* **1** : one that removes dust **2 a** : a lightweight garment to protect clothing from dust **b** : a dress-length housecoat **3** : one that scatters fine particles
dust·pan \ˈdəs(t)-ˌpan\ *n* : a shovel-shaped pan for sweepings
dusty \ˈdəs-tē\ *adj* **1** : filled or covered with dust **2** : consisting of dust : POWDERY **3** : resembling dust — **dust·i·ly** \-tə-lē\ *adv* — **dust·i·ness** \-tē-nəs\ *n*
dutch \ˈdəch\ *adv, often cap* : with each person paying his own way
Dutch \ˈdəch\ *n* : DISFAVOR, TROUBLE
du·te·ous \ˈd(y)üt-ē-əs\ *adj* : DUTIFUL, OBEDIENT — **du·te·ous·ly** *adv* — **du·te·ous·ness** *n*
du·ti·a·ble \ˈd(y)üt-ē-ə-bəl\ *adj* : subject to a duty
du·ti·ful \ˈd(y)üt-i-fəl\ *adj* **1** : filled with or motivated by a sense of duty **2** : proceeding from or expressive of a sense of duty — **du·ti·ful·ly** \-fə-lē\ *adv* — **du·ti·ful·ness** *n*
du·ty \ˈd(y)üt-ē\ *n, pl* **duties** **1** : conduct due to parents and superiors : RESPECT **2 a** : the action required by one's position or occupation **b** : assigned service or business; *esp* : active military service **3 a** : a moral or legal obligation **b** : the force of moral obligation **4** : TAX; *esp* : a tax on imports **5** : the service required (as of a machine) : USE
¹dwarf \ˈdwȯrf\ *n, pl* **dwarfs** \ˈdwȯrfs\ **1** : a person, lower animal, or plant much below normal size **2** : a small legendary manlike being usu. misshapen and ugly and skilled as an artificer — **dwarf** *adj* — **dwarf·ish** \ˈdwȯr-fish\ *adj* — **dwarf·ness** *n*

²dwarf *vb* **1** : to restrict the growth or development of : STUNT **2** : to cause to appear smaller

dwarf·ism \'dwȯr-ˌfiz-əm\ *n* : a stunted condition

dwell \'dwel\ *vi* **dwelt** \'dwelt\ *or* **dwelled** \'dweld, 'dwelt\; **dwell·ing 1** : to remain for a time **2** : to live as a resident : RESIDE **3 a** : to linger over something (as with the eyes or mind) : keep the attention directed **b** : to write or speak at length or insistently — **dwell·er** *n*

dwell·ing \'dwel-iŋ\ *n* : a building or other shelter in which people live : HOUSE

dwin·dle \'dwin-dᵊl\ *vb* **dwin·dled**; **dwin·dling** \'dwin-dliŋ, -dᵊl-iŋ\ : to make or become less : waste away

dyb·buk \'dib-ək\ *n* : a wandering soul believed in Jewish folklore to enter and possess a person

¹dye \'dī\ *n* **1** : color from dyeing **2** : a soluble or insoluble coloring matter

²dye *vb* **dyed**; **dye·ing 1** : to impart a new and often permanent color to esp. by impregnating with a dye **2** : to impart (a color) by dyeing **3** : to take up or impart color in dyeing — **dy·er** \'dī(-ə)r\ *n*

dyed–in–the–wool \ˌdīd-ᵊn-t͟hə-'wu̇l\ *adj* : THOROUGHGOING, UNCOMPROMISING

dye·ing \'dī-iŋ\ *n* : the process or art of fixing coloring matters in fibers (as of wool or cotton)

dye·stuff \-ˌstəf\ *n* : DYE 2

dy·ing \'dī-iŋ\ *adj* **1** : being about to die : being in the act of dying or dying out : EXPIRING **2** : of or relating to dying or death

dy·nam·ic \dī-'nam-ik\ *adj* **1** : of or relating to physical force or energy **2 a** : marked by continuous activity or change **b** : marked by energy : FORCEFUL — **dy·nam·i·cal** \-'nam-i-kəl\ *adj* — **dy·nam·i·cal·ly** \-i-k(ə-)lē\ *adv*

¹dy·na·mite \'dī-nə-ˌmīt\ *n* : a blasting explosive that is made of nitroglycerin absorbed in a porous material; *also* : any of various blasting explosives

²dynamite *vt* : to blow up with dynamite — **dy·na·mit·er** *n*

dy·na·mo \'dī-nə-ˌmō\ *n, pl* **-mos 1** : GENERATOR 2 **2** : a forceful energetic individual

dy·nas·ty \'dī-nə-stē, -ˌnas-tē\ *n, pl* **-ties 1** : a succession of rulers of the same line of descent **2** : a powerful group or family that maintains its position for a considerable time — **dy·nas·tic** \dī-'nas-tik\ *adj*

dys·en·tery \'dis-ᵊn-ˌter-ē\ *n* : a disease characterized by severe diarrhea with passage of mucus and blood and usu. caused by infection — **dys·en·ter·ic** \ˌdis-ᵊn-'ter-ik\ *adj*

dys·pep·sia \dis-'pep-shə, -sē-ə\ *n* : INDIGESTION

¹dys·pep·tic \-'pep-tik\ *adj* **1** : relating to or having dyspepsia **2** : GLOOMY, CROSS — **dys·pep·ti·cal·ly** \-ti-k(ə-)lē\ *adv*

²dyspeptic *n* : a person having dyspepsia

dys·pro·si·um \dis-'prō-zē-əm\ *n* : a chemical element that forms highly magnetic compounds

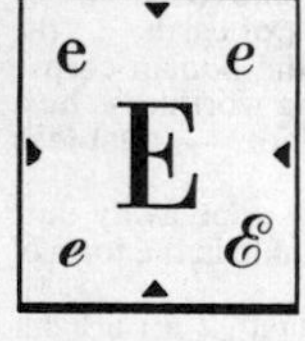

e \'ē\ *n, often cap* **1** : the 5th letter of the English alphabet **2** : the musical tone E **3** : a grade rating a student's work as poor and usu. constituting a conditional pass

¹each \'ēch\ *adj* : being one of two or more distinct individuals

²each *pron* : each one

³each *adv* : to or for each : APIECE

each other *pron* : each of two or more in reciprocal action or relation

ea·ger \'ē-gər\ *adj* : marked by keen, enthusiastic, or sharply expectant desire or interest — **ea·ger·ly** *adv* — **ea·ger·ness** *n*

ea·gle \'ē-gəl\ *n* **1** : any of various large diurnal birds of prey related to the hawks and noted for their keenness of vision and powers of flight **2** : a seal or standard or an insignia shaped like or bearing an eagle **3** : a ten-dollar gold coin of the U.S. bearing an eagle on the reverse **4** : a golf score of two strokes less than par on a hole

ea·glet \'ē-glət\ *n* : a young eagle

¹ear \'i(ə)r\ *n* **1** : the organ of hearing; *also* : the outer part of this in a vertebrate **2** : the sense or act of hearing **3** : ATTENTION; *esp* : sympathetic attention **4** : something resembling an ear in shape or position — **eared** \'i(ə)rd\ *adj* — **ear·less** \'i(ə)r-ləs\ *adj*

²ear *n* : the fruiting spike of a cereal (as Indian corn) including both the seeds and protective structures — **ear** *vi*

ear·ache \'i(ə)r-ˌāk\ *n* : an ache or pain in the ear

ear·drum \-ˌdrəm\ *n* : a thin membrane that transmits sound waves to the receptors of the ear

earl \'ərl\ *n* **1** : a great nobleman in Anglo-Saxon or medieval England **2** : a member of the British peerage ranking below a marquess and above a viscount — **earl·dom** \-dəm\ *n*

ear·lobe \'i(ə)r-ˌlōb\ *n* : the pendent part of the ear of man or some fowls

¹ear·ly \'ər-lē\ *adv* **1** : near the beginning of a period of time or of a process or series **2** : before the usual time

²early *adj* **1 a** : of, relating to, or occurring near the beginning of a period of time or of a development or series **b** : PRIMITIVE **2 a** : occurring before the usual time **b** : occurring in the near future — **ear·li·ness** *n*

¹ear·mark \'i(ə)r-ˌmärk\ *n* **1** : a mark of identification on the ear of an animal **2** : a distinguishing or identifying mark

²earmark *vt* **1** : to mark with or as if with an earmark **2** : to set aside for a specific purpose

ear·muff \-ˌməf\ *n* : one of a pair of ear coverings connected by a flexible band and worn as protection against cold

earn \'ərn\ *vt* **1** : to deserve as a result of labor or service **2** : to get for services given — **earn·er** *n*

¹ear·nest \'ər-nəst\ *n* : a serious and intent mental state

²earnest *adj* **1** : characterized by or proceeding from an intense and serious state of mind : not light or playful **2** : not trivial : IMPORTANT — **ear·nest·ly** *adv* — **ear·nest·ness** *n*

³earnest *n* **1** : something of value given by a buyer to a seller to bind a bargain **2** : a token of what is to come : PLEDGE

earn·ings \'ər-niŋz\ *n pl* **1** : something earned; *esp* : WAGES **2** : revenue after deduction of expenses

ear·phone \'i(ə)r-ˌfōn\ *n* : a device that converts electrical energy into sound waves and is worn over or inserted into the ear

ear·ring \'i(ə)r-ˌriŋ\ *n* : an ornament for the earlobe

ear·shot \-ˌshät\ *n* : the range within which the unaided voice may be heard

ear·split·ting \-ˌsplit-iŋ\ *adj* : intolerably loud or shrill

earth \'ərth\ *n* **1** : the soft or granular material composing part of the surface of the globe; *esp* : cultivable soil **2** : the sphere of mortal life as distinguished from heaven and hell **3** : areas of land as distinguished from sea and air : GROUND **4** *often cap* : the planet which we live on and which is 3d in order of distance from the sun

earth·en \'ər-thən, -t͟hən\ *adj* : made of earth or of baked clay

earth·en·ware \-ˌwa(ə)r\ *n* : articles (as utensils or ornaments) made of baked clay esp. of the coarser kinds

earth·ling \'ərth-liŋ\ *n* : an inhabitant of the earth
earth·ly \'ərth-lē\ *adj* **1** : of, relating to, or characteristic of the earth : not heavenly or spiritual **2** : POSSIBLE, IMAGINABLE — **earth·li·ness** *n*
earth·quake \'ərth-ˌkwāk\ *n* : a shaking or trembling of a portion of the earth caused by movement of rock masses or by volcanic shocks
earth·work \-ˌwərk\ *n* : an embankment or other construction of earth; *esp* : one made as a fortification
earth·worm \-ˌwərm\ *n* : a long slender worm with segmented body that lives in damp earth
earthy \'ər-thē, -t͟hē\ *adj* **1** : consisting of or resembling earth **2 a** : DOWN-TO-EARTH, PRACTICAL **b** : CRUDE, GROSS — **earth·i·ness** *n*
[1]**ease** \'ēz\ *n* **1** : freedom from pain or trouble : comfort of body or mind **2** : freedom from any sense or feeling of difficulty or embarrassment : NATURALNESS
[2]**ease** *vb* **1** : to free from something that disquiets or burdens **2** : to make less painful : ALLEVIATE **3** : to make less tight or difficult : LOOSEN, SLACKEN
ea·sel \'ē-zəl\ *n* : a frame for supporting something (as an artist's canvas)
eas·i·ly \'ēz-(ə-)lē\ *adv* **1** : in an easy manner **2** : by far
[1]**east** \'ēst\ *adv* : to or toward the east
[2]**east** *adj* **1** : situated toward or at the east **2** : coming from the east
[3]**east** *n* **1 a** : the general direction of sunrise **b** : the compass point directly opposite to west **2** *cap* : regions or countries east of a specified or implied point — **east·er·ly** \'ē-stər-lē\ *adv or adj* — **east·ward** \'ēs-twərd\ *adv or adj* — **east·wards** \-twərdz\ *adv*
east·bound \'ēs(t)-ˌbau̇nd\ *adj* : headed east
Eas·ter \'ē-stər\ *n* : a church festival observed on the first Sunday after the full moon on or next after the vernal equinox in commemoration of Christ's resurrection
east·ern \'ē-stərn\ *adj* **1** *often cap* : of, relating to, or characteristic of a region conventionally designated East **2** *cap* **a** : of, relating to, or being the Christian churches originating in the church of the Eastern Roman Empire **b** : Eastern Orthodox **3** : lying toward or coming from the east — **East·ern·er** \-stə(r)-nər\ *n* — **east·ern·most** \'ē-stərn-ˌmōst\ *adj*
Eastern Orthodox *adj* : of or consisting of the Eastern churches that form a loose federation according primacy of honor to the patriarch of Constantinople and adhering to the decisions of the first seven ecumenical councils and to one rite
easy \'ē-zē\ *adj* **1** : not hard to do or get : not difficult **2** : not severe : LENIENT **3** : COMFORTABLE **4** : showing ease : NATURAL, UNAFFECTED **5** : free from pain, trouble, or worry **6** : UNHURRIED, LEISURELY **7** : not steep or abrupt — **eas·i·ness** *n*
easy·go·ing \ˌē-zē-'gō-iŋ\ *adj* : taking life easily : CAREFREE — **easy·go·ing·ness** *n*
eat \'ēt\ *vb* **ate** \'āt\; **eat·en** \'ēt-ᵊn\; **eat·ing** **1** : to take into the mouth and swallow food : chew and swallow in turn **2** : to take a meal **3** : to destroy, use up, or waste as if by eating : wear away **4** : to affect something by gradual destruction or consumption — used with *into* — **eat·er** *n*
[1]**eat·a·ble** \'ēt-ə-bəl\ *adj* : fit to be eaten
[2]**eatable** *n* **1** : something to eat **2** *pl* : FOOD
eau de co·logne \ˌōd-ə-kə-'lōn\ *n, pl* **eaux de cologne** \ˌō(z)d-ə-\ : COLOGNE
eau–de–vie \ˌōd-ə-'vē\ *n, pl* **eaux–de–vie** \ˌō(z)d-ə-\ : BRANDY
eaves \'ēvz\ *n sing or pl* : the overhanging lower edge of a roof projecting beyond the wall of a building
eaves·drop \'ēvz-ˌdräp\ *vi* : to listen secretly to what is said in private — **eaves·drop·per** *n*
[1]**ebb** \'eb\ *n* **1** : the flowing back from the shore of water brought in by the tide **2** : a passing from a high to a low point : a time of decline
[2]**ebb** *vi* **1** : to recede from the flood state **2** : DECLINE, WEAKEN
[1]**eb·o·ny** \'eb-ə-nē\ *n, pl* **-nies** : a hard heavy wood yielded by various Old World tropical trees related to the persimmon; *also* : a tree yielding ebony
[2]**ebony** *adj* **1** : made of or resembling ebony **2** : BLACK, DARK
ebul·lient \i-'bu̇l-yənt\ *adj* **1** : BOILING, AGITATED **2** : characterized by lively or enthusiastic expression of thoughts or feelings : EXUBERANT — **ebul·lience** \-yən(t)s\ *n* — **ebul·lient·ly** *adv*
eb·ul·li·tion \ˌeb-ə-'lish-ən\ *n* : the process or state of boiling or bubbling up
ec·cen·tric \ik-'sen-trik\ *adj* **1** : not having the same center **2** : deviating from some established pattern or from conventional or accepted usage or conduct **3 a** : deviating from a circular path **b** : located elsewhere than at the geometrical center — **eccentric** *n* — **ec·cen·tri·cal·ly** \-tri-k(ə-)lē\ *adv*
ec·cen·tric·i·ty \ˌek-ˌsen-'tris-ət-ē\ *n, pl* **-ties** **1 a** : the quality or state of being eccentric **b** : deviation from an established pattern, rule, or norm; *esp* : odd or whimsical behavior **2** : the degree of deviation from a circular path
ec·cle·si·as·tic \ik-ˌlē-zē-'as-tik\ *n* : CLERGYMAN
ec·cle·si·as·ti·cal \-ti-kəl\ *or* **ec·cle·si·as·tic** \-tik\ *adj* : of or relating to the church or its organization or government — **ec·cle·si·as·ti·cal·ly** \-ti-k(ə-)lē\ *adv*
ech·e·lon \'esh-ə-ˌlän\ *n* **1 a** : a formation of units (as troops or airplanes) resembling a series of steps **b** : any of several military units **2** : one of a series of levels or grades esp. of authority or the individuals at such a level
[1]**echo** \'ek-ō\ *n, pl* **ech·oes** : the repetition of a sound caused by reflection of sound waves; *also* : the reflection of a radar signal by an object — **echo·ic** \i-'kō-ik, e-\ *adj*
[2]**echo** *vb* **1** : to resound with echoes **2** : to produce an echo : send back or repeat a sound **3** : REPEAT, IMITATE
éclair \ā-'kla(ə)r, 'ā-ˌ\ *n* : an oblong cream puff with whipped cream or custard filling
éclat \ā-'klä\ *n* **1** : brilliance esp. in performance or achievement **2** : demonstration of approval : ACCLAIM
eclec·tic \e-'klek-tik, i-\ *adj* **1** : selecting elements from various doctrines, methods, or styles **2** : composed of elements drawn from various sources — **eclectic** *n* — **eclec·ti·cal·ly** \-ti-k(ə-)lē\ *adv* — **eclec·ti·cism** \-tə-ˌsiz-əm\ *n*
[1]**eclipse** \i-'klips\ *n* **1** : a complete or partial hiding or darkening of the sun or the moon caused when the sun is obscured by the moon's passing between the sun and the earth or when the moon is obscured by its entering the shadow of the earth; *also* : the obscuring of any celestial body by another **2** : a falling into obscurity, decline, or disgrace
[2]**eclipse** *vt* **1** : to cause an eclipse of **2** : to reduce in fame **3** : to surpass greatly : OUTSHINE
eclip·tic \i-'klip-tik\ *n* : the great circle of the celestial sphere that is the apparent path of the sun among the stars
ec·logue \'ek-ˌlȯg\ *n* : a poem in which shepherds engage in dialogue
ecol·o·gy \i-'käl-ə-jē, e-\ *n* : a branch of science concerned with the interrelationship of organisms and their environments — **eco·log·i·cal** \ˌē-kə-'läj-i-kəl, ˌek-ə-\ *or* **eco·log·ic** \-ik\ *adj* — **ec·o·log·i·cal·ly** \-'läj-i-k(ə-)lē\ *adv* — **ecol·o·gist** \i-'käl-ə-jəst\ *n*
ec·o·nom·ic \ˌek-ə-'näm-ik, ˌē-kə-\ *adj* **1 a** : of or relating to the science of economics **b** : of, relating to, or based on the production, distribution, and consumption of goods and services **c** : of or relating to an economy **2** : having practical or industrial significance or uses : affecting material resources
ec·o·nom·i·cal \-'näm-i-kəl\ *adj* **1** : given to thrift : FRUGAL **2** : operating with little waste or at a saving — **ec·o·nom·i·cal·ly** \-'näm-i-k(ə-)lē\ *adv*

ec·o·nom·ics \ˌek-ə-ˈnäm-iks, ˌē-kə-\ *n* **1 :** a social science concerned chiefly with description and analysis of the production, distribution, and consumption of goods and services **2 :** economic aspect or significance — **econ·o·mist** \i-ˈkän-ə-məst\ *n*
econ·o·mize \i-ˈkän-ə-ˌmīz\ *vb* **1 :** to practice economy : be frugal **2 :** to use more economically : SAVE — **econ·o·miz·er** *n*
econ·o·my \i-ˈkän-ə-mē\ *n, pl* **-mies 1 a :** thrifty use of material resources : frugality in expenditures **b :** the efficient and sparing use of the means available for the end proposed **c :** an act of economizing **2 :** systematic arrangement : ORGANIZATION **3 :** the structure of economic life in a country, area, or period; *esp* : an economic system
ec·ru \ˈek-rü, ˈā-krü\ *adj* : BEIGE
ec·sta·sy \ˈek-stə-sē\ *n, pl* **-sies 1 :** a state of being beyond reason and self-control **2 :** a state of overwhelming emotion; *esp* : rapturous delight
ec·stat·ic \ek-ˈstat-ik\ *adj* **1 :** marked by ecstasy : full of joy and rapture **2 :** causing ecstasy — **ec·stat·i·cal·ly** \-i-k(ə-)lē\ *adv*
ec·u·men·i·cal \ˌek-yə-ˈmen-i-kəl\ *adj* **1 :** worldwide or general in extent, influence, or application **2 :** of, relating to, or representing the whole of a body of churches **3 :** promoting or tending toward worldwide Christian unity or cooperation — **ec·u·men·i·cal·ly** \-i-k(ə-)lē\ *adv* — **ec·u·me·nic·i·ty** \-mə-ˈnis-ət-ē\ *n* — **ec·u·me·nism** \ˈek-yə-mə-ˌniz-əm, e-ˈkyü-mə-\ *n*
ec·ze·ma \ig-ˈzē-mə, ˈek-sə-mə, ˈeg-zə-\ *n* : a skin inflammation marked by redness, itching, and scaly or crusted lesions — **ec·zem·a·tous** \ig-ˈzem-ət-əs, -ˈzē-mət-\ *adj*
Edam \ˈēd-əm, ˈē-ˌdam\ *n* : a Dutch pressed cheese of yellow color and mild flavor made in balls
¹ed·dy \ˈed-ē\ *n, pl* **eddies 1 :** a current of air or water running contrary to the main current; *esp* : a current moving in a circle like a whirlpool **2 :** a substance moving like an eddy
²eddy *vb* **ed·died**; **ed·dy·ing :** to move in an eddy or so as to form an eddy
edel·weiss \ˈād-ᵊl-ˌwīs\ *n* : a small perennial woolly herb that is related to the thistles and grows high in the Alps
¹edge \ˈej\ *n* **1 a :** the cutting side of a blade **b :** the sharpness of a blade **c :** penetrating power : KEENNESS **2 a :** the line where an object or surface begins or ends : VERGE, BRINK; *also* : the narrow adjacent part : BORDER **b :** the intersection of two plane faces of a solid **3 :** a favorable margin : ADVANTAGE — **edged** \ˈejd\ *adj* — **on edge :** ANXIOUS, NERVOUS
²edge *vb* **1 :** to give an edge to **2 a :** to move along gradually **b :** to advance very slowly or by short moves **3 :** to incline (a ski) sideways
edge·ways \-ˌwāz\ *or* **edge·wise** \-ˌwīz\ *adv* : with the edge foremost : SIDEWAYS
edg·ing \ˈej-iŋ\ *n* : something that forms an edge or border
edgy \ˈej-ē\ *adj* **1 :** having an edge : SHARP **2 :** being on edge : TENSE, NERVOUS, IRRITABLE
ed·i·ble \ˈed-ə-bəl\ *adj* : fit or safe to be eaten — **edible** *n* — **ed·i·ble·ness** *n*
edict \ˈē-ˌdikt\ *n* : an official public proclamation made by an authority (as a sovereign) having the force of law
ed·i·fice \ˈed-ə-fəs\ *n* : BUILDING; *esp* : a large or impressive building (as a church)
ed·i·fy \ˈed-ə-ˌfī\ *vt* **-fied**; **-fy·ing :** to instruct and improve esp. by good example : benefit morally or spiritually — **ed·i·fi·ca·tion** \ˌed-ə-fə-ˈkā-shən\ *n*
ed·it \ˈed-ət\ *vt* **1 a :** to correct, revise, and prepare esp. for publication **b :** to assemble (as a moving-picture film or tape recording) for use or publication by cutting and rearranging **2 :** to direct the publication of
edi·tion \i-ˈdish-ən\ *n* **1 a :** the form in which a text (as a printed book) is published **b :** the whole number of copies printed or published at one time **c :** one of the several issues of a newspaper for a single day **2 :** COPY, VERSION
ed·i·tor \ˈed-ət-ər\ *n* **1 :** one that edits esp. as an occupation **2 :** a person who writes editorials — **ed·i·tor·ship** \-ˌship\ *n*
¹ed·i·to·ri·al \ˌed-ə-ˈtōr-ē-əl\ *adj* **1 :** of or relating to an editor **2 :** being or resembling an editorial — **ed·i·to·ri·al·ly** *adv*
²editorial *n* : a newspaper or magazine article that gives the opinions of its editors or publishers
ed·i·to·ri·al·ize \ˌed-ə-ˈtōr-ē-ə-ˌlīz\ *vi* **1 :** to express an opinion in the form of an editorial **2 :** to introduce opinion into the reporting of facts
ed·u·ca·ble \ˈej-ə-kə-bəl\ *adj* : capable of being educated
ed·u·cate \ˈej-ə-ˌkāt\ *vt* **1 :** to provide schooling for **2 a :** to develop mentally and morally esp. by formal instruction **b :** TRAIN — **ed·u·ca·tor** \-ˌkāt-ər\ *n*
ed·u·cat·ed \-ˌkāt-əd\ *adj* **1 :** having an education; *esp* : having an education beyond the average **2 :** giving evidence of education **3 :** based on some knowledge of fact
ed·u·ca·tion \ˌej-ə-ˈkā-shən\ *n* **1 a :** the action or process of educating or of being educated **b :** the knowledge and development resulting from an educational process **2 :** the field of study that deals mainly with methods and problems of teaching — **ed·u·ca·tion·al** \-shnəl, -shən-ᵊl\ *adj* — **ed·u·ca·tion·al·ly** \-ē\ *adv*
ed·u·ca·tive \ˈej-ə-ˌkāt-iv\ *adj* **1 :** tending to educate : INSTRUCTIVE **2 :** of or relating to education
educe \i-ˈd(y)üs\ *vt* **1 :** to bring out : draw forth : ELICIT **2 :** DEDUCE — **educ·i·ble** \-ˈd(y)ü-sə-bəl\ *adj*
eel \ˈēl\ *n, pl* **eels** *or* **eel :** any of numerous long snakelike fishes with smooth slimy skin and no pelvic fins — **eel·like** *adj* — **eely** \ˈē-lē\ *adj*

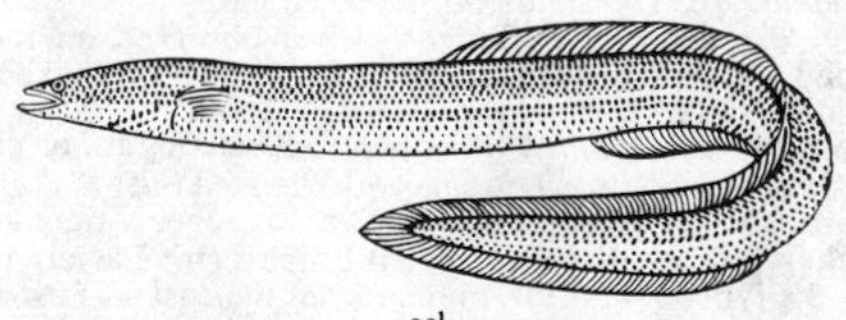
eel

ee·rie \ˈi(ə)r-ē\ *adj* **1 a :** frightening because of strangeness or gloominess **b :** arousing fear of the supernatural **2 :** STRANGE, MYSTERIOUS — **ee·ri·ly** \ˈir-ə-lē\ *adv* — **ee·ri·ness** \ˈir-ē-nəs\ *n*
ef·face \i-ˈfās\ *vt* **1 :** to wipe out : OBLITERATE **2 :** to make indistinct by or as if by rubbing out : ERASE **3 :** to make (oneself) inconspicuous or modestly unnoticeable — **ef·face·a·ble** *adj* — **ef·face·ment** *n* — **ef·fac·er** *n*
¹ef·fect \i-ˈfekt\ *n* **1 :** an event, condition, or state of affairs that is produced by a cause : the result of something that has been done or has happened : OUTCOME **2 :** FULFILLMENT, EXECUTION, OPERATION **3 :** REALITY, FACT **4 :** the act of making a particular impression **5 :** INFLUENCE **6** *pl* : GOODS, POSSESSIONS
²effect *vt* : to bring about : ACCOMPLISH — **ef·fect·er** *n*
¹ef·fec·tive \i-ˈfek-tiv\ *adj* **1 a :** producing a decided, decisive, or desired effect **b :** IMPRESSIVE, STRIKING **2 :** ready for service or action **3 :** ACTUAL **4 :** being in effect : OPERATIVE — **ef·fec·tive·ly** *adv* — **ef·fec·tive·ness** *n*
²effective *n* : one that is effective; *esp* : a soldier equipped for duty
ef·fec·tu·al \i-ˈfek-chə-wəl, -ˈfek-chəl\ *adj* : producing or able to produce a desired effect : ADEQUATE, EFFECTIVE — **ef·fec·tu·al·ness** *n*
ef·fec·tu·al·ly \i-ˈfek-chə-(wə-)lē\ *adv* **1 :** in an effectual manner **2 :** with great effect : COMPLETELY
ef·fec·tu·ate \-chə-ˌwāt\ *vt* : to bring about : EFFECT

ef·fem·i·na·cy \ə-ˈfem-ə-nə-sē\ *n* : the quality of being effeminate

ef·fem·i·nate \-nət\ *adj* 1 : marked by qualities more characteristic of and suited to women than to men : UNMANLY 2 : marked by weakness and love of ease — **ef·fem·i·nate·ly** *adv* — **ef·fem·i·nate·ness** *n*

ef·fen·di \e-ˈfen-dē\ *n* : a man of property, authority, or education in an eastern Mediterranean country

ef·fer·ent \ˈef-ə-rənt, -ˌer-ənt\ *adj* : conducting outward from a part or organ; *esp* : conveying nervous impulses to an effector — **efferent** *n* — **ef·fer·ent·ly** *adv*

ef·fer·vesce \ˌef-ər-ˈves\ *vi* 1 : to bubble, hiss, and foam as gas escapes 2 : to show liveliness or exhilaration — **ef·fer·ves·cence** \-ˈves-ᵊn(t)s\ *n* — **ef·fer·ves·cent** \-ᵊnt\ *adj* — **ef·fer·ves·cent·ly** *adv*

ef·fete \e-ˈfēt\ *adj* 1 : no longer productive 2 : worn out : EXHAUSTED; *also* : marked by weakness or decadence — **ef·fete·ly** *adv* — **ef·fete·ness** *n*

ef·fi·ca·cious \ˌef-ə-ˈkā-shəs\ *adj* : having the power to produce a desired effect — **ef·fi·ca·cious·ly** *adv* — **ef·fi·ca·cious·ness** *n*

ef·fi·ca·cy \ˈef-i-kə-sē\ *n, pl* **-cies** : power to produce effects : EFFECTIVENESS

ef·fi·cien·cy \i-ˈfish-ən-sē\ *n, pl* **-cies** 1 : the quality or degree of being efficient 2 a : efficient operation b : effective operation as measured by a comparison of production with cost (as in energy, time, and money) 3 : the ratio of the useful energy delivered by a dynamic system (as a machine) to the energy supplied to it

ef·fi·cient \i-ˈfish-ənt\ *adj* : capable of producing desired effects; *esp* : productive without waste — **ef·fi·cient·ly** *adv*

ef·fi·gy \ˈef-ə-jē\ *n, pl* **-gies** : an image or likeness esp. of a person: as a : a sculptured image on a tomb b : a crude figure representing a hated person

ef·flo·resce \ˌef-lə-ˈres\ *vi* : to burst forth : BLOOM

ef·flo·res·cence \-ˈres-ᵊn(t)s\ *n* 1 : the act, process, period, or result of developing or unfolding 2 : fullness of manifestation : CULMINATION — **ef·flo·res·cent** \-ᵊnt\ *adj*

ef·fort \ˈef-ərt\ *n* 1 : conscious exertion of power 2 : a serious attempt : TRY 3 : something produced esp. by creative or artistic exertion 4 : the force applied to a simple machine (as a lever) as distinguished from the force exerted by it against the load

ef·fort·less \-ləs\ *adj* : showing or requiring little or no effort : EASY, SMOOTH — **ef·fort·less·ly** *adv* — **ef·fort·less·ness** *n*

ef·fron·tery \i-ˈfrənt-ə-rē\ *n, pl* **-ter·ies** : shameless boldness : INSOLENCE

ef·ful·gence \i-ˈfu̇l-jən(t)s, -ˈfəl-\ *n* : radiant splendor : BRILLIANCE — **ef·ful·gent** \-jənt\ *adj*

ef·fuse \i-ˈfyüz\ *vb* 1 : to pour out (a liquid) 2 : to give off : RADIATE 3 : to flow out : EMANATE

ef·fu·sion \i-ˈfyü-zhən\ *n* 1 : an act of effusing 2 : unrestrained expression of words or feelings 3 a : escape of a fluid from containing vessels b : the fluid that escapes

ef·fu·sive \i-ˈfyü-siv\ *adj* 1 : excessively demonstrative or emotional : GUSHING 2 : characterized or formed by a nonexplosive outpouring of lava — **ef·fu·sive·ly** *adv* — **ef·fu·sive·ness** *n*

eft \ˈeft\ *n* : NEWT

egad \i-ˈgad\ *interj* — used as a mild oath

egal·i·tar·i·an \i-ˌgal-ə-ˈter-ē-ən\ *adj* : asserting, promoting, or marked by egalitarianism — **egalitarian** *n*

egal·i·tar·i·an·ism \-ē-ə-ˌniz-əm\ *n* 1 : a belief in human equality esp. in social, political, and economic affairs 2 : a social philosophy advocating the removal of inequalities among men

¹egg \ˈeg\ *vt* : to incite to action : URGE, ENCOURAGE — usu. used with *on*

²egg *n* 1 a : the hard-shelled reproductive body produced by a bird and esp. by domestic poultry b : an animal reproductive body consisting of an ovum with its nutritive and protective envelopes and being capable of development into a new individual c : OVUM 2 : something resembling an egg

egg·beat·er \-ˌbēt-ər\ *n* : a rotary beater operated by hand for beating eggs or liquids (as cream)

egg·head \-ˌhed\ *n* : INTELLECTUAL, HIGHBROW

egg·nog \-ˌnäg\ *n* : a drink consisting of eggs beaten up with sugar, milk or cream, and often alcoholic liquor

egg·plant \-ˌplant\ *n* : a widely cultivated perennial herb that is related to the potato and yields edible fruit; *also* : its usu. smooth and purple ovoid fruit

¹egg·shell \-ˌshel\ *n* : the hard exterior covering of an egg

²eggshell *adj* 1 : being thin and fragile 2 : slightly glossy

eg·lan·tine \ˈeg-lən-ˌtīn, -ˌtēn\ *n* : SWEETBRIER

ego \ˈē-gō\ *n, pl* **egos** 1 : the self as contrasted with another self or the world 2 a : EGOTISM b : SELF-ESTEEM 3 : the conscious part of the personality that is derived from the id through contacts with reality

ego·cen·tric \ˌē-gō-ˈsen-trik\ *adj* : concerned or overly concerned with the self; *esp* : SELF-CENTERED, SELFISH — **egocentric** *n*

ego·ism \ˈē-gə-ˌwiz-əm\ *n* 1 : excessive interest in oneself : a self-centered attitude 2 : EGOTISM

ego·ist \ˈē-gə-wəst\ *n* : a person whose chief interest is himself : a self-centered person — **ego·is·tic** \ˌē-gə-ˈwis-tik\ *adj* — **ego·is·ti·cal·ly** \-ˈwis-ti-k(ə-)lē\ *adv*

ego·tism \ˈē-gə-ˌtiz-əm\ *n* 1 : too frequent reference (as by use of the word *I*) to oneself 2 : an exaggerated sense of self-importance : CONCEIT 3 : EGOISM

ego·tist \ˈē-gə-təst\ *n* : a conceited person — **ego·tis·tic** \ˌē-gə-ˈtis-tik\ *or* **ego·tis·ti·cal** \-ˈtis-ti-kəl\ *adj* — **ego·tis·ti·cal·ly** \-ˈtis-ti-k(ə-)lē\ *adv*

egre·gious \i-ˈgrē-jəs\ *adj* : conspicuously bad : SHOCKING, FLAGRANT — **egre·gious·ly** *adv* — **egre·gious·ness** *n*

egress \ˈē-ˌgres\ *n* 1 : the act or right of going or coming out 2 : a place or means of going out : EXIT, OUTLET

egret \ˈē-grət, i-ˈgret, ˈē-ˌgret, ˈeg-rət\ *n* : any of various herons that bear long plumes during the breeding season

eh \ˈā, ˈe, ˈa(i)\ *interj* — used to ask for confirmation or to express inquiry

ei·der \ˈīd-ər\ *n* 1 : a large northern sea duck that is mostly white above and black below and has very soft down 2 : EIDERDOWN 1

ei·der·down \-ˌdau̇n\ *n* 1 : the down of the eider 2 : a comforter filled with eiderdown

eight \ˈāt\ *n* 1 — see NUMBER table 2 : the eighth in a set or series 3 : something having eight units or members: as a : an 8-oared racing boat or crew b : an 8-cylinder engine or automobile — **eight** *adj or pron* — **eighth** \ˈātth\ *n, pl* **eighths** \ˈāts, ˈātths\ — **eighth** *adj or adv*

eigh·teen \(ˈ)ā(t)-ˈtēn\ *n* — see NUMBER table — **eighteen** *adj or pron* — **eigh·teenth** \-ˈtēn(t)th\ *adj or n*

eighty \ˈāt-ē\ *n, pl* **eight·ies** — see NUMBER table — **eight·i·eth** \-ē-əth\ *adj or n* — **eighty** *adj or pron*

ein·stei·ni·um \īn-ˈstī-nē-əm\ *n* : a radioactive element produced artificially

¹ei·ther \ˈē-t͟hər, ˈī-\ *adj* 1 : the one and the other of two : EACH 2 : the one or the other of two

²either *pron* : the one or the other

³either *conj* — used as a function word before the first of two or more words or word groups of which the last is preceded by *or* to indicate that they represent alternatives

⁴either *adv* 1 : LIKEWISE, MOREOVER — used for emphasis after a negative 2 : for that matter — used for emphasis after an alternative following a question or conditional clause esp. where negation is implied

ejac·u·late \i-'jak-yə-ˌlāt\ *vb* **1** : to utter or eject suddenly and vigorously **2** : to eject a fluid and esp. semen — **ejac·u·la·to·ry** \-yə-lə-ˌtōr-ē\ *adj*
ejac·u·la·tion \i-ˌjak-yə-'lā-shən\ *n* **1** : an act of ejaculating; *esp* : a sudden discharging of a fluid from a duct **2** : something ejaculated; *esp* : a short sudden emotional utterance (as an exclamation)
eject \i-'jekt\ *vt* **1 a** : to drive out esp. by physical force **b** : to evict from property **2** : to throw out or off from within — **ejec·tor** \-'jek-tər\ *n*
ejec·tion \i-'jek-shən\ *n* **1** : the act of ejecting : the state of being ejected **2** : ejected matter (as from a volcano)
eke out \'ēk-\ *vt* **1 a** : SUPPLEMENT **b** : to make (a supply) last by economy **2** : to make (a living) by laborious or precarious means
ekis·tics \i-'kis-tiks\ *n* : a science dealing with human settlements and drawing on the research and experience of the architect, the engineer, the city planner, and the social scientist
[1]**elab·o·rate** \i-'lab-(ə-)rət\ *adj* **1** : planned or carried out with great care : DETAILED **2** : marked by complexity, fullness of detail, or ornateness — **elab·o·rate·ly** *adv* — **elab·o·rate·ness** *n*
[2]**elab·o·rate** \i-'lab-ə-ˌrāt\ *vb* **1** : to produce by labor **2** : to build up (complex organic compounds) from simple ingredients **3** : to work out in detail : DEVELOP **4** : to give esp. additional details — **elab·o·ra·tion** \-ˌlab-ə-'rā-shən\ *n* — **elab·o·ra·tive** \-'lab-ə-ˌrāt-iv\ *adj* — **elab·o·ra·tor** \-ˌrāt-ər\ *n*
élan \ā-'läⁿ\ *n* : SPIRIT, ARDOR, DASH
elapse \i-'laps\ *vi* : to slip or glide away : PASS
[1]**elas·tic** \i-'las-tik\ *adj* **1 a** : capable of recovering shape or size after being stretched, pressed, or squeezed together : SPRINGY **b** : capable of indefinite expansion **2** : able to recover quickly esp. from depression or fatigue **3** : FLEXIBLE, ADAPTABLE — **elas·ti·cal·ly** \-ti-k(ə-)lē\ *adv*
[2]**elastic** *n* **1 a** : an elastic fabric usu. made of yarns containing rubber **b** : something made from elastic fabric **2** : easily stretched rubber; *esp* : a rubber band
elas·tic·i·ty \i-ˌlas-'tis-ət-ē\ *n*, *pl* **-ties** : the quality or state of being elastic : RESILIENCE, ADAPTABILITY
elate \i-'lāt\ *vt* : to fill with joy or pride
elat·ed \i-'lāt-əd\ *adj* : marked by high spirits : EXULTANT — **elat·ed·ly** *adv* — **elat·ed·ness** *n*
[1]**el·bow** \'el-ˌbō\ *n* **1 a** : the joint of the arm; *also* : the outer curve of a bent arm **b** : a corresponding joint in the front limb of an animal **2** : a bend or joint resembling an elbow in shape
[2]**elbow** *vb* **1** : to push or shove aside by pushing with the elbow : JOSTLE **2** : to force or advance by or as if by pushing with the elbow
elbow grease *n* : energy vigorously exerted esp. in physical labor
el·bow·room \'el-ˌbō-ˌrüm, -ˌru̇m\ *n* **1** : room for moving the elbows freely **2** : enough space for work or operation
[1]**el·der** \'el-dər\ *n* : any of a genus of shrubs or trees of the honeysuckle family with flat clusters of small white or pink flowers and black or red drupes resembling berries
[2]**elder** *adj* **1** : of earlier birth or greater age : OLDER **2** : of or relating to earlier times : FORMER **3** : prior or superior in rank, office, or validity
[3]**elder** *n* **1** : one living in an earlier period **2** : one who is older : SENIOR **3** : a person having authority by virtue of age and experience **4** : any of various church officers — **el·der·ship** \-ˌship\ *n*
el·der·ber·ry \'el-də(r)-ˌber-ē\ *n* **1** : the edible fruit of an elder **2** : [1]ELDER
el·der·ly \'el-dər-lē\ *adj* **1** : rather old; *esp* : past middle age **2** : of, relating to, or characteristic of later life
elder statesman *n* : an eminent senior member of a group or organization; *esp* : a retired statesman who unofficially advises current leaders
el·dest \'el-dəst\ *adj* : OLDEST
El Do·ra·do \ˌel-də-'räd-ō, -'rād-\ *n* : a place of great wealth, abundance, or opportunity
[1]**elect** \i-'lekt\ *adj* **1** : carefully selected : CHOSEN **2** : chosen for eternal life through divine mercy **3** : chosen for office or position but not yet installed
[2]**elect** *n pl* : a carefully chosen group — used with *the*
[3]**elect** *vb* **1** : to select usu. by vote for an office, position, or membership **2** : CHOOSE, SELECT
elec·tion \i-'lek-shən\ *n* **1 a** : an act or process of electing; *esp* : the process of voting to choose a person to hold an office **b** : the fact of being elected **2** : predestination to eternal life **3** : the power or privilege of making a choice
elec·tion·eer \i-ˌlek-shə-'ni(ə)r\ *vi* : to work in the interest of a candidate or party in an election
[1]**elec·tive** \i-'lek-tiv\ *adj* **1** : chosen by election **2** : filled by a person who is elected and not appointed **3** : followed or taken by choice : not required — **elec·tive·ly** *adv* — **elec·tive·ness** *n*
[2]**elective** *n* : an elective course or subject in school
elec·tor \i-'lek-tər\ *n* **1** : one qualified to vote in an election **2** : one entitled by his office to participate in an election; *esp* : a member of the electoral college in the U.S.
elec·tor·al \i-'lek-t(ə-)rəl\ *adj* : of or relating to an election or electors
electoral college *n* : a body of electors; *esp* : one that elects the president and vice-president of the U.S.
elec·tor·ate \i-'lek-t(ə-)rət\ *n* : a body of people entitled to vote
elec·tric \i-'lek-trik\ *or* **elec·tri·cal** \-tri-kəl\ *adj* **1** : of, relating to, operated by, or produced by electricity **2** : ELECTRIFYING, THRILLING — **elec·tri·cal·ly** \-tri-k(ə-)lē\ *adv* — **elec·tri·cal·ness** *n*
electric chair *n* **1** : a chair used in legal electrocution **2** : the penalty of death by electrocution
electric eye *n* : PHOTOELECTRIC CELL
elec·tri·cian \i-ˌlek-'trish-ən\ *n* **1** : a specialist in electricity **2** : one who installs, operates, or repairs electrical equipment
elec·tric·i·ty \i-ˌlek-'tris-ət-ē, -'tris-tē\ *n* **1** : a fundamental phenomenon of nature consisting of negative and positive kinds composed respectively of electrons and protons, observable in the attractions and repulsions of bodies electrified by friction and in natural phenomena (as lightning), and usu. utilized as a source of energy in the form of electric currents **2** : electric current
elec·tri·fy \i-'lek-trə-ˌfī\ *vt* **-fied**; **-fy·ing** **1 a** : to charge with electricity **b** (1) : to equip for use of electric power (2) : to supply with electric power **2** : to excite intensely or suddenly : THRILL — **elec·tri·fi·ca·tion** \i-ˌlek-trə-fə-'kā-shən\ *n*
elec·tro·cute \i-'lek-trə-ˌkyüt\ *vt* : to kill by electric shock; *esp* : to execute (a criminal) in this way — **elec·tro·cu·tion** \i-ˌlek-trə-'kyü-shən\ *n*
elec·trode \i-'lek-ˌtrōd\ *n* : a conductor (as a metal or carbon) used to establish electrical contact with a nonmetallic part of a circuit (as in a storage battery, electron tube, or arc lamp)
elec·trol·y·sis \i-ˌlek-'träl-ə-səs\ *n* : the producing of chemical changes by passage of an electric current through an electrolyte with the ions carrying the current by migrating to the electrodes where they may form new substances that are given off as gases or deposited as solids
elec·tro·lyte \i-'lek-trə-ˌlīt\ *n* **1** : a nonmetallic electric conductor in which current is carried by the movement of ions with the liberation of matter at the electrodes **2** : a substance that when dissolved in a suitable solvent or when fused becomes an ionic conductor

elec·tro·lyt·ic \i-ˌlek-trə-ˈlit-ik\ *adj* : of or relating to electrolysis or an electrolyte — **elec·tro·lyt·i·cal·ly** \-i-k(ə-)lē\ *adv*
elec·tro·mag·net \i-ˌlek-trō-ˈmag-nət\ *n* : a core of magnetic material (as soft iron) surrounded by a coil of wire through which an electric current is passed to magnetize the core
elec·tro·mag·net·ic \-mag-ˈnet-ik\ *adj* **1** : of or relating to magnetism developed by a current of electricity **2** : being a wave (as a light wave) propagated by regular variations of the intensity of an associated electric and magnetic effect
elec·tro·mag·ne·tism \-ˈmag-nə-ˌtiz-əm\ *n* : magnetism developed by a current of electricity
elec·tro·mo·tive force \i-ˌlek-trə-ˌmōt-iv-\ *n* : an influence that tends to change the motion of electricity or maintain its motion against opposing forces
elec·tron \i-ˈlek-ˌträn\ *n* : a negatively charged particle that forms the part of an atom outside the nucleus and that is of the kind of particles whose flow along a conductor is an electric current
elec·tron·ic \i-ˌlek-ˈträn-ik\ *adj* **1** : of or relating to electrons **2** : of, relating to, or utilizing devices constructed or working by principles of electronics — **elec·tron·i·cal·ly** \-ˈträn-i-k(ə-)lē\ *adv*
elec·tron·ics \-ˈträn-iks\ *n* : a branch of physics that deals with the emission, behavior, and effects of electrons in vacuums and gases and with the use of electronic devices (as electron tubes, radar, radio, and television)
electron tube *n* : a device in which conduction by electrons takes place through a vacuum or a gas within a sealed glass or metal container and which has various common uses (as in radio and television) based on the controlled flow of electrons
elec·tro·type \i-ˈlek-trə-ˌtīp\ *n* **1** : a plate for use in printing made by making a mold of the matter to be printed, covering this mold with a thin shell of metal by electrolysis, and putting on a backing (as of heavy metal or plastic) **2** : a print made from an electrotype — **elec·tro·typ·er** *n*
el·ee·mos·y·nary \ˌel-i-ˈmäs-ᵊn-ˌer-ē\ *adj* : of, relating to, or supported by charity
el·e·gance \ˈel-i-gən(t)s\ *n* **1** : refined gracefulness **2** : tasteful richness of design or ornamentation
el·e·gan·cy \-gən-sē\ *n, pl* **-cies** : ELEGANCE
el·e·gant \-gənt\ *adj* **1** : marked by elegance **2** : EXCELLENT, SPLENDID — **el·e·gant·ly** *adv*
el·e·gy \ˈel-ə-jē\ *n, pl* **-gies** **1** : a poem expressing sorrow for one who is dead **2** : a poem that is sad or mournful in spirit — **el·e·gi·ac** \ˌel-ə-ˈjī-ək, i-ˈlē-jē-ˌak\ *adj* — **el·e·gize** \ˈel-ə-ˌjīz\ *vb*
el·e·ment \ˈel-ə-mənt\ *n* **1 a** : one of the four substances air, water, fire, or earth formerly believed to compose the physical universe **b** *pl* : forces of nature; *esp* : stormy or cold weather **c** : the state or sphere natural or suited to a person or an organism **2** : a constituent part: as **a** *pl* : the simplest principles of a subject of study : RUDIMENTS **b** : any of more than 100 fundamental substances that consist of atoms of only one kind **3** *pl* : the bread and wine used in the sacrament of Communion
el·e·men·tal \ˌel-ə-ˈment-ᵊl\ *adj* **1 a** : of, relating to, or being an element; *esp* : existing as an uncombined chemical element **b** : of, relating to, or being an ultimate constituent **c** : ELEMENTARY **d** : ESSENTIAL **2** : of, relating to, or resembling a great force of nature
el·e·men·ta·ry \ˌel-ə-ˈment-ə-rē, -ˈmen-trē\ *adj* **1 a** : of or relating to the simplest principles of a subject **b** : of, relating to, or teaching the basic subjects of education **2** : ELEMENTAL 1a
el·e·phant \ˈel-ə-fənt\ *n* : a huge thickset nearly hairless mammal having the snout prolonged as a trunk and two upper incisors developed into long outward-curving pointed tusks which furnish ivory
el·e·phan·tine \ˌel-ə-ˈfan-ˌtēn, -ˌtīn\ *adj* **1** : HUGE, MASSIVE **2** : CLUMSY, PONDEROUS, UNGAINLY
el·e·vate \ˈel-ə-ˌvāt\ *vb* **1** : to lift up : RAISE **2** : to raise in rank or status : EXALT **3** : to improve morally, intellectually, or culturally **4** : to raise the spirits of : ELATE
el·e·vat·ed \-ˌvāt-əd\ *adj* **1** : raised esp. above the ground **2 a** : morally or intellectually on a high plane **b** : FORMAL, DIGNIFIED
el·e·va·tion \ˌel-ə-ˈvā-shən\ *n* **1** : the height to which something is elevated: as **a** : the angular distance of a celestial object above the horizon **b** : the degree to which a gun is aimed above the horizon **c** : the height above sea level : ALTITUDE **2** : an act or instance of elevating **3 a** : something that is elevated **b** : an elevated place or station **4** : the quality or state of being elevated **5** : a scale drawing showing a vertical structural section (as of a building) as viewed horizontally
el·e·va·tor \ˈel-ə-ˌvāt-ər\ *n* **1 a** : a cage or platform and its hoisting machinery for conveying something to different levels **b** : a building for elevating, storing, discharging, and sometimes processing grain **2** : a movable surface on an airplane for producing motion up or down
elev·en \i-ˈlev-ən\ *n* **1** — see NUMBER table **2** : the eleventh in a set or series **3** : something having 11 units or members — **eleven** *adj or pron* — **elev·enth** \-ən(t)th\ *n* — **eleventh** *adj or adv*
elf \ˈelf\ *n, pl* **elves** \ˈelvz\ : a small often mischievous fairy — **elf·ish** \ˈel-fish\ *adj* — **elf·ish·ly** *adv*
elf·in \ˈel-fən\ *adj* **1** : of or relating to elves **2** : resembling an elf; *esp* : having a strange beauty or charm
elic·it \i-ˈlis-ət\ *vt* : to draw forth or bring out often by skillful questioning or discussion
elide \i-ˈlīd\ *vt* **1** : to suppress or alter by elision **2** : OMIT, IGNORE
el·i·gi·ble \ˈel-ə-jə-bəl\ *adj* : qualified to be chosen : ENTITLED — **el·i·gi·bil·i·ty** \ˌel-i-jə-ˈbil-ət-ē\ *n* — **eligible** *n* — **el·i·gi·bly** \ˈel-i-jə-blē\ *adv*
elim·i·nate \i-ˈlim-ə-ˌnāt\ *vt* **1 a** : to get rid of : EXPEL **b** : to set aside as unimportant : IGNORE **2** : to expel from the living body — **elim·i·na·tion** \i-ˌlim-ə-ˈnā-shən\ *n* — **elim·i·na·tive** \i-ˈlim-ə-ˌnāt-iv\ *adj* — **elim·i·na·tor** \-ˌnāt-ər\ *n*
eli·sion \i-ˈlizh-ən\ *n* : the omission of a final or initial sound of a word; *esp* : the omission of an unstressed vowel or syllable in a verse to achieve a uniform rhythm
elite \ā-ˈlēt\ *n* **1** : the choice part; *esp* : a socially superior group **2** : a small group exercising power by virtue of real or claimed superiority in ability or technical competence — **elite** *adj*
elix·ir \i-ˈlik-sər\ *n* **1 a** : a substance held to be capable of changing metals into gold **b** : a substance held to be capable of prolonging life indefinitely **c** : CURE-ALL **2** : a sweetened usu. alcoholic liquid used as a vehicle for medicinal agents **3** : the essential principle
elk \ˈelk\ *n, pl* **elk** *or* **elks** **1** : the largest existing deer of Europe and Asia resembling but not so large as the moose of No. America **2** : WAPITI
¹ell \ˈel\ *n* : a former English unit of length for cloth equal to 45 inches
²ell *n* : an extension at right angles to a building
el·lipse \i-ˈlips\ *n* : a closed curve of oval shape
el·lip·sis \i-ˈlip-səs\ *n, pl* **-lip·ses** \-ˈlip-ˌsēz\ **1** : the omission of one or more words that can be obviously understood and supplied to make a construction seem more complete **2** : marks or a mark (as . . . or * * * or —) used to show the omission esp. of letters or words
el·lip·tic \i-ˈlip-tik\ *or* **el·lip·ti·cal** \-ti-kəl\ *adj* **1 a** : of, relating to, or shaped like an ellipse **b** : OVAL **2** : of, relating to, or marked by ellipsis — **el·lip·ti·cal·ly** \-ti-k(ə-)lē\ *adv*

elm \'elm\ *n* : a tall shade tree with spreading branches and broad top; *also* : its wood

el·o·cu·tion \,el-ə-'kyü-shən\ *n* **1** : the art of effective public speaking **2** : a style of speaking esp. in public — **el·o·cu·tion·ary** \-shə-,ner-ē\ *adj* — **el·o·cu·tion·ist** \-sh(ə-)nəst\ *n*

[1]**elon·gate** \i-'lȯŋ-,gāt\ *vb* **1** : to extend the length of **2** : to grow in length — **elon·ga·tion** \i-,lȯŋ-'gā-shən, ,ē-\ *n*

[2]**elongate** *adj* **1** : stretched out : LENGTHENED **2** : long in proportion to width

elon·gat·ed \i-'lȯŋ-,gāt-əd\ *adj* : ELONGATE

elope \i-'lōp\ *vi* **1 a** : to run away from one's husband with a lover **b** : to run away secretly with the intention of getting married usu. without parental consent **2** : to depart secretly : slip away — **elope·ment** *n* — **elop·er** *n*

el·o·quence \'el-ə-kwən(t)s\ *n* : discourse marked by force and persuasiveness; *also* : the art or power of using such discourse

el·o·quent \-kwənt\ *adj* **1** : marked by forceful and fluent expression **2** : vividly or movingly expressive or revealing — **el·o·quent·ly** *adv*

[1]**else** \'els\ *adv* **1 a** : in a different manner or place or at a different time **b** : in an additional manner or place or at an additional time **2** : if the facts are or were different : if not : OTHERWISE

[2]**else** *adj* : OTHER: **a** : being different in identity **b** : being in addition

else·where \-,hwe(ə)r\ *adv* : in or to another place

elu·ci·date \i-'lü-sə-,dāt\ *vt* : to make clear or plain : EXPLAIN — **elu·ci·da·tion** \i-,lü-sə-'dā-shən\ *n*

elude \ē-'lüd\ *vt* : to avoid or escape by being quick, skillful, or tricky

elu·sion \ē-'lü-zhən\ *n* : an act of eluding : ESCAPE, EVASION

elu·sive \ē-'lü-siv\ *adj* **1** : tending to elude : EVASIVE **2** : hard to comprehend or define — **elu·sive·ly** *adv* — **elu·sive·ness** *n*

el·ver \'el-vər\ *n* : a young eel

elves *pl of* ELF

elv·ish \'el-vish\ *adj* : ELFISH, MISCHIEVOUS

Ely·si·um \i-'liz(h)-ē-əm\ *n* : a place or condition of ideal happiness : PARADISE — **Ely·sian** \i-'lizh-ən\ *adj*

ema·ci·ate \i-'mā-shē-,āt\ *vt* **1** : to cause to lose flesh so as to become very thin **2** : to make feeble — **ema·ci·a·tion** \i-,mā-s(h)ē-'ā-shən\ *n*

em·a·nate \'em-ə-,nāt\ *vb* **1** : to come out from a source **2** : to give out : EMIT

em·a·na·tion \,em-ə-'nā-shən\ *n* **1** : the action of emanating **2** : something that emanates or is produced by emanation — **em·a·na·tion·al** \-shnəl, -shən-^{ə}l\ *adj*

eman·ci·pate \i-'man(t)-sə-,pāt\ *vt* : to free from restraint, control, or the power of another; *esp* : to free from bondage — **eman·ci·pa·tion** \i-,man(t)-sə-'pā-shən\ *n* — **eman·ci·pa·tor** \i-'man(t)-sə-,pāt-ər\ *n*

emas·cu·late \i-'mas-kyə-,lāt\ *vt* **1** : CASTRATE **2** : to deprive of masculine vigor or spirit : WEAKEN — **emas·cu·la·tion** \i-,mas-kyə-'lā-shən\ *n*

em·balm \im-'bäm\ *vb* **1** : to treat a dead body with special preparations to preserve it from decay **2** : PERFUME **3** : to preserve in one's memory — **em·balm·er** *n* — **em·balm·ment** *n*

em·bank \im-'baŋk\ *vt* : to enclose or confine by an embankment

em·bank·ment \-mənt\ *n* **1** : the action of embanking **2** : a raised bank or wall to carry a roadway, prevent floods, or hold back water

em·bar·go \im-'bär-gō\ *n, pl* **-goes** **1** : an order of a government prohibiting the departure of commercial ships from its ports **2** : legal prohibition or restriction of commerce — **embargo** *vt*

em·bark \im-'bärk\ *vb* **1** : to go or put on board a ship or airplane **2** : to enter into some enterprise or undertaking : begin activities — **em·bar·ka·tion** \,em-,bär-'kā-shən\ *n* — **em·bark·ment** *n*

em·bar·rass \im-'bar-əs\ *vt* **1** : to hamper the freedom of movement of : IMPEDE **2** : to make confused or upset in mind : cause a feeling of uneasiness in : DISCONCERT **3** : to involve in financial difficulties — **em·bar·rass·ing·ly** *adv*

em·bar·rass·ment \-mənt\ *n* **1** : the state of being embarrassed: as **a** : confusion or discomposure of mind **b** : difficulty arising from the want of money to pay debts **2** : something that embarrasses : IMPEDIMENT

em·bas·sy \'em-bə-sē\ *n, pl* **-sies** **1** : the function or position of an ambassador **2** : the business entrusted to an ambassador **3** : the person or group of persons sent as ambassadors **4** : the residence or office of an ambassador

em·bat·tle \im-'bat-^{ə}l\ *vt* **1** : to arrange in order of battle : prepare for battle **2** : FORTIFY

em·bed \im-'bed\ *vb* **1** : to enclose closely in or as if in a surrounding mass : set solidly in or as if in a bed **2** : to become embedded

em·bel·lish \im-'bel-ish\ *vt* **1** : to make beautiful with ornamentation : DECORATE **2** : to heighten the attractiveness of by adding ornamental details — **em·bel·lish·ment** *n*

em·ber \'em-bər\ *n* **1** : a glowing piece of coal or wood from a fire; *esp* : such a piece smoldering in ashes **2** *pl* : smoldering remains of a fire

em·bez·zle \im-'bez-əl\ *vt* **em·bez·zled**; **em·bez·zling** \-'bez-(ə-)liŋ\ : to take (property entrusted to one's care) dishonestly for one's own use — **em·bez·zle·ment** *n* — **em·bez·zler** \-'bez-(ə-)lər\ *n*

em·bit·ter \im-'bit-ər\ *vt* : to make bitter or more bitter; *esp* : to arouse bitter feeling in — **em·bit·ter·ment** *n*

em·bla·zon \im-'blāz-^{ə}n\ *vt* **1** : to inscribe or ornament with markings or emblems used in heraldry **2 a** : to deck in bright colors **b** : CELEBRATE, EXTOL

em·blem \'em-bləm\ *n* **1** : an object or a likeness of an object used to suggest a thing that cannot be pictured : SYMBOL **2** : a device, symbol, design, or figure used as an identifying mark

em·blem·at·ic \,em-blə-'mat-ik\ *adj* : of, relating to, or constituting an emblem : SYMBOLIC

em·bod·i·ment \im-'bäd-i-mənt\ *n* **1** : the act of embodying : the state of being embodied **2** : a thing that embodies something

em·body \im-'bäd-ē\ *vt* **-bod·ied**; **-body·ing** **1** : to bring together so as to form a body or system **2** : to make a part of a body or system **3** : to express in a concrete or definite form **4** : to represent in visible form — **em·bod·i·er** *n*

em·bold·en \im-'bōl-dən\ *vt* : to make bold

em·bo·lism \'em-bə-,liz-əm\ *n* : obstruction of a blood vessel by a foreign or abnormal particle (as an air bubble or blood clot) during life — **em·bol·ic** \em-'bäl-ik\ *adj*

em·bon·point \äⁿ-bōⁿ-pwaⁿ\ *n* : plumpness of person : STOUTNESS

em·bo·som \im-'bu̇z-əm\ *vt* **1** : to take to one's heart : EMBRACE **2** : ENCLOSE, SHELTER

em·boss \im-'bäs, -'bȯs\ *vt* : to ornament with a pattern or design having a raised surface — **em·boss·er** *n* — **em·boss·ment** *n*

em·bou·chure \,äm-bü-'shu̇(ə)r\ *n* : the position and use of the lips in producing a musical tone on a wind instrument

em·bow·er \im-'bau̇(-ə)r\ *vt* : to shelter or enclose in or as if in a bower

[1]**em·brace** \im-'brās\ *vb* **1 a** : to clasp in the arms : HUG **b** : CHERISH, LOVE **2** : ENCIRCLE, ENCLOSE **3 a** : to take up esp. readily or gladly **b** : to avail oneself of : WELCOME **4** : to take in : INCLUDE — **em·brace·a·ble** *adj* — **em·brace·ment** *n* — **em·brac·er** *n*

[2]**embrace** *n* : a close encircling with the arms and pressure to the bosom

em·bra·sure \im-'brā-zhər\ *n* **1 :** a recess of a door or window **2 :** an opening with sides flaring outward in a wall or parapet usu. for allowing the firing of cannon

em·bro·cate \'em-brə-ˌkāt\ *vt* **:** to moisten and rub (a part of the body) with a medicinal lotion or liniment — **em·bro·ca·tion** \ˌem-brə-'kā-shən\ *n*

em·broi·der \im-'brȯid-ər\ *vb* **em·broi·dered; em·broi·der·ing** \-'brȯid-(ə-)riŋ\ **1 :** to make or fill in a design with needlework **2 :** to ornament with needlework **3 :** to add to the interest of with details far beyond the truth **:** elaborate on **:** EXAGGERATE — **em·broi·der·er** *n*

em·broi·dery \im-'brȯid-(ə-)rē\ *n, pl* **-der·ies 1 a :** the process or art of embroidering **b :** needlework done to decorate cloth **c :** embroidered work **2 :** elaboration in details esp. to add interest

em·broil \im-'brȯil\ *vt* **1 :** to throw into disorder or confusion **2 :** to involve in conflict or difficulties — **em·broil·ment** *n*

em·brown \im-'brau̇n\ *vt* **1 :** DARKEN **2 :** to make brown

em·bryo \'em-brē-ˌō\ *n, pl* **em·bry·os 1 :** a living being in its earliest stage of development **2 :** a beginning or undeveloped stage — used esp. in the phrase *in embryo*

em·bry·ol·o·gy \ˌem-brē-'äl-ə-jē\ *n* **1 :** a branch of biology dealing with embryos and their development **2 :** the features and phenomena exhibited in the formation and development of an embryo — **em·bry·o·log·ic** \ˌem-brē-ə-'läj-ik\ *or* **em·bry·o·log·i·cal** \-'läj-i-kəl\ *adj* — **em·bry·o·log·i·cal·ly** \-i-k(ə-)lē\ *adv* — **em·bry·ol·o·gist** \ˌem-brē-'äl-ə-jəst\ *n*

em·bry·on·ic \ˌem-brē-'än-ik\ *adj* **1 :** of or relating to an embryo **2 :** being in an early or undeveloped stage **:** being in embryo — **em·bry·on·i·cal·ly** \-i-k(ə-)lē\ *adv*

¹em·cee \'em-'sē\ *n* **:** MASTER OF CEREMONIES

²emcee *vb* **em·ceed; em·cee·ing :** to act as master of ceremonies

emend \ē-'mend\ *vt* **:** to correct usu. by textual alterations — **emend·a·ble** *adj*

emen·da·tion \(ˌ)ē-ˌmen-'dā-shən, ˌem-ən-\ *n* **1 :** the act of emending **2 :** an alteration designed to correct or improve

¹em·er·ald \'em-(ə-)rəld\ *n* **:** a rich green beryl prized as a gem

²emerald *adj* **:** brightly or richly green

emerge \i-'mərj\ *vi* **1 :** to rise from or as if from an enveloping fluid **:** come out into view **2 :** to become known or apparent **3 :** to rise from an obscure or inferior condition

emer·gence \i-'mər-jən(t)s\ *n* **:** the act or an instance of emerging

emer·gen·cy \i-'mər-jən-sē\ *n, pl* **-cies 1 :** an unforeseen combination of circumstances or the resulting state that calls for immediate action **2 :** a pressing need **:** EXIGENCY

emer·gent \-jənt\ *adj* **:** rising out of or as if out of a fluid

emer·i·tus \i-'mer-ət-əs\ *adj* **1 :** holding after retirement an honorary title corresponding to that held last during active service **2 :** retired from an office or position — **emeritus** *n*

emer·sion \ē-'mər-zhən\ *n* **:** an act of emerging **:** EMERGENCE

em·ery \'em-(ə-)rē\ *n* **:** a dark granular corundum used esp. in the form of powder or grains for grinding and polishing

emet·ic \i-'met-ik\ *n* **:** an agent that induces vomiting — **emetic** *adj* — **emet·i·cal·ly** \-'met-i-k(ə-)lē\ *adv*

em·i·grant \'em-i-grənt\ *n* **:** one that emigrates — **emigrant** *adj*

em·i·grate \'em-ə-ˌgrāt\ *vi* **:** to leave a place of abode or a country for life or residence elsewhere — **em·i·gra·tion** \ˌem-ə-'grā-shən\ *n*

émi·gré *or* **em·i·gré** \ˌem-ə-'grā, ˌā-mə-\ *n* **:** EMIGRANT; *esp* **:** a person who emigrates because of political conditions

em·i·nence \'em-ə-nən(t)s\ *n* **1 :** a condition or station of prominence or superiority **2** — used as a title for a cardinal **3 a :** a person of high rank or attainments **b :** a natural elevation **:** HEIGHT

em·i·nent \-nənt\ *adj* **1 :** standing above all others esp. in rank, merit, or virtue **:** NOTABLE **2 :** LOFTY, TOWERING — **em·i·nent·ly** *adv*

eminent domain *n* **:** a right of a government to take private property for public use by virtue of the superior dominion of the sovereign power over all lands within its jurisdiction

emir \i-'mi(ə)r, ā-\ *n* **:** a Muslim prince — **emir·ate** \-'mi(ə)r-ət, -ˌāt\ *n*

em·is·sary \'em-ə-ˌser-ē\ *n, pl* **-sar·ies :** one sent as the agent of another often in secret to gather information

emis·sion \ē-'mish-ən\ *n* **1 :** an act or instance of emitting **2 :** something emitted **:** DISCHARGE

emit \ē-'mit\ *vt* **emit·ted; emit·ting 1 a :** to throw or give off or out (as light) **b :** to send out **:** EJECT **2 :** to issue with authority **3 :** to give utterance to **:** EXPRESS — **emit·ter** *n*

¹emol·lient \i-'mäl-yənt\ *adj* **:** making soft or supple; *also* **:** soothing esp. to the skin or mucous membrane

²emollient *n* **:** something that softens or soothes

emol·u·ment \i-'mäl-yə-mənt\ *n* **:** profit from one's employment or from an office held **:** SALARY, WAGES

emote \i-'mōt\ *vi* **:** to give expression to emotion in or as if in a play

emo·tion \i-'mō-shən\ *n* **1 :** strong feeling **:** EXCITEMENT **2 :** a mental and bodily reaction (as anger, joy, hate, or fear) marked by strong feeling and physiological responses that prepare the body for action

emo·tion·al \i-'mō-shnəl, -shən-ᵊl\ *adj* **1 :** of or relating to the emotions **2 :** inclined to show or express emotion **:** easily moved **3 :** appealing to or arousing emotion — **emo·tion·al·ly** *adv*

em·pa·thy \'em-pə-thē\ *n* **:** the capacity for experiencing as one's own the feelings of another — **em·path·ic** \em-'path-ik\ *adj*

em·per·or \'em-pər-ər, -prər\ *n* **:** the sovereign ruler of an empire

em·pha·sis \'em(p)-fə-səs\ *n, pl* **em·pha·ses** \-fə-ˌsēz\ **1 a :** a forcefulness of expression that gives special impressiveness or importance **b :** a particular prominence given in reading or speaking to a word or syllable **2 :** special stress or insistence upon something

em·pha·size \-ˌsīz\ *vt* **:** to give emphasis to or place emphasis upon **:** STRESS

em·phat·ic \im-'fat-ik\ *adj* **1 :** uttered with or marked by emphasis **2 :** tending to express oneself in forceful speech or to take decisive action **3 :** attracting special attention **4 :** constituting or belonging to a set of verb forms in English that have the auxiliary *do* and are used rarely for emphasis and regularly to take the place of a simple verb form in questions or negative statements — **em·phat·i·cal·ly** \-'fat-i-k(ə-)lē\ *adv*

em·pire \'em-ˌpī(ə)r\ *n* **1 a** (1) **:** a major political unit with a great extent of territory or a number of territories or peoples under one sovereign authority; *esp* **:** one having an emperor as chief of state (2) **:** the territory of such a unit **b :** something held to resemble a political empire; *esp* **:** an extensive territory or enterprise under one control **2 :** imperial sovereignty, rule, or dominion

em·pir·ic \im-'pir-ik\ *n* **:** one who relies upon practical experience

em·pir·i·cal \-'pir-i-kəl\ *or* **em·pir·ic** \-'pir-ik\ *adj* **1 :** originating in or based on observation or experience **2 :** capable of being verified or disproved by observation or experiment — **em·pir·i·cal·ly** \-'pir-i-k(ə-)lē\ *adv*

em·pir·i·cism \-'pir-ə-ˌsiz-əm\ *n* **1 :** the practice of relying upon observation and experiment esp. in the natural sciences **2 :** a theory that knowledge originates in experience — **em·pir·i·cist** \-səst\ *adj or n*

em·place \im-'plās\ *vt* **:** to put into place

em·place·ment \-mənt\ *n* **1 :** a prepared position for weapons or military equipment **2 :** a putting into position **:** PLACEMENT

[1]**em·ploy** \im-'plȯi\ *vt* **1 a** : to make use of **b** : to occupy (as time) advantageously **c** : to use or engage the services of : provide with a job that pays wages or a salary **2** : to devote (as time or energy) to or direct toward a particular activity or person — **em·ploy·a·ble** *adj*

[2]**employ** *n* : the state of being employed esp. for wages or a salary

em·ploy·ee *or* **em·ploye** \im-,plȯi-'ē, (,)em-; im-'plȯi-,ē\ *n* : one employed by another usu. for wages or salary

em·ploy·er \im-'plȯi(-ə)r\ *n* : one that employs others

em·ploy·ment \im-'plȯi-mənt\ *n* **1** : USE, PURPOSE; *also* : the act of using **2 a** : the act of engaging a person for work : HIRING **b** : the work at which one is employed : OCCUPATION **c** : the state of being employed **d** : the extent or degree to which a labor force is employed

em·po·ri·um \im-'pōr-ē-əm\ *n, pl* **-ri·ums** *or* **-ria** \-ē-ə\ **1** : a place of trade : MARKETPLACE; *esp* : a commercial center **2** : a store carrying a wide variety of merchandise

em·pow·er \im-'pau̇(-ə)r\ *vt* : to give official authority or legal power to

em·press \'em-prəs\ *n* **1** : the wife or widow of an emperor **2** : a woman who holds an imperial title in her own right

em·prise \em-'prīz\ *n* : UNDERTAKING, ENTERPRISE; *esp* : a chivalric enterprise

[1]**emp·ty** \'em(p)-tē\ *adj* **1** : containing nothing **2** : UNOCCUPIED, VACANT **3** : being without reality or substance **4** : lacking in value, sense, effect, or sincerity **5** : HUNGRY — **emp·ti·ly** \-tə-lē\ *adv* — **emp·ti·ness** *n*

[2]**empty** *vb* **1** : to make empty : remove the contents of **2** : to transfer by emptying **3** : to become empty **4** : to give forth its contents (as fluid) : DISCHARGE

[3]**empty** *n, pl* **empties** : an empty container

emp·ty–hand·ed \,em(p)-tē-'han-dəd\ *adj* **1** : having nothing in the hands **2** : having acquired or gained nothing

em·pur·ple \im-'pər-pəl\ *vb* **em·pur·pled**; **em·pur·pling** \-'pər-p(ə-)liŋ\ : to tinge or color purple

em·py·re·al \,em-,pī-'rē-əl, -pə-\ *adj* **1** : of or relating to the empyrean : CELESTIAL **2** : SUBLIME

[1]**em·py·re·an** \-'rē-ən\ *adj* : EMPYREAL

[2]**empyrean** *n* **1** : the highest heaven or heavenly sphere **2** : FIRMAMENT, HEAVENS

emu \'ē-,myü\ *n* : a swift-running Australian bird with undeveloped wings that is related to but smaller than the ostrich

em·u·late \'em-yə-,lāt\ *vt* **1 a** : to strive to equal or excel **b** : IMITATE **2** : to equal or approach equality with — **em·u·la·tor** \-,lāt-ər\ *n*

em·u·la·tion \,em-yə-'lā-shən\ *n* : ambition or endeavor to equal or excel; *also* : IMITATION — **em·u·la·tive** \'em-yə-,lāt-iv\ *adj*

em·u·lous \'em-yə-ləs\ *adj* : eager or ambitious to equal or excel another — **em·u·lous·ly** *adv* — **em·u·lous·ness** *n*

emul·si·fi·er \i-'məl-sə-,fī(-ə)r\ *n* : an agent (as a soap) promoting the formation and stabilization of an emulsion

emul·si·fy \-,fī\ *vt* **-fied**; **-fy·ing** : to convert (as an oil) into an emulsion — **emul·si·fi·a·ble** *adj* — **emul·si·fi·ca·tion** \i-,məl-sə-fə-'kā-shən\ *n*

emul·sion \i-'məl-shən\ *n* **1** : a material consisting of a mixture of liquids that do not dissolve in each other and having droplets of one liquid dispersed throughout the other **2** : a light-sensitive coating on photographic plates, film, or paper consisting of particles of a silver salt suspended in a thick substance (as a gelatin solution)

en·able \in-'ā-bəl\ *vt* **en·abled**; **en·abling** \-b(ə-)liŋ\ **1 a** : to make able **b** : to make possible, practical, or easy **2** : to give legal power, capacity, or sanction to

en·act \in-'akt\ *vt* **1** : to establish by legal and authoritative act; *esp* : to make (as a bill) into law **2** : to act out : REPRESENT — **en·ac·tor** \-'ak-tər\ *n*

en·act·ment \-'ak(t)-mənt\ *n* **1** : the act of enacting : the state of being enacted **2** : LAW, STATUTE

[1]**enam·el** \in-'am-əl\ *vt* **enam·eled** *or* **enam·elled**; **enam·el·ing** *or* **enam·el·ling** \-'am-(ə-)liŋ\ **1** : to cover or inlay with enamel **2** : to form a glossy surface on

[2]**enamel** *n* **1** : a usu. opaque vitreous composition applied by fusion to the surface of metal, glass, or pottery **2** : a surface that resembles enamel **3** : a usu. glossy paint that flows out to a smooth hard coat when applied **4** : a very hard outer layer covering the crown of a tooth

enam·el·ware \-,wa(ə)r\ *n* : metal utensils (as pots and pans) coated with enamel

en·am·or \in-'am-ər\ *vt* : to inflame with love

en bloc \äⁿ-'bläk\ *adv (or adj)* : as a whole : in a mass

en·camp \in-'kamp\ *vb* **1** : to set up and occupy a camp : CAMP **2** : to place or establish in a camp

en·camp·ment \-mənt\ *n* **1** : the act of encamping : the state of being encamped **2** : CAMP

en·cap·su·late \in-'kap-sə-,lāt\ *vb* : to encase or become encased in a capsule — **en·cap·su·la·tion** \-,kap-sə-'lā-shən\ *n*

en·case \in-'kās\ *vt* : to enclose in or as if in a case — **en·case·ment** *n*

en·ceinte \äⁿ-'sant, än-\ *adj* : PREGNANT

en·ceph·a·li·tis \(,)en-,sef-ə-'līt-əs\ *n* : inflammation of the brain — **en·ceph·a·lit·ic** \-'lit-ik\ *adj*

en·chain \in-'chān\ *vt* **1** : to bind with or as if with chains **2** : to attract and hold (as the attention) — **en·chain·ment** *n*

en·chant \in-'chant\ *vt* **1** : to influence by charms and incantation : BEWITCH **2** : THRILL, ENRAPTURE

en·chant·er \-ər\ *n* : one that enchants; *esp* : SORCERER

en·chant·ing \-iŋ\ *adj* : CHARMING, ATTRACTIVE

en·chant·ment \-mənt\ *n* **1** : the act or art of enchanting : the state of being enchanted **2** : something that enchants : SPELL, CHARM

en·chant·ress \in-'chan-trəs\ *n* **1** : a woman who practices magic : SORCERESS **2** : a fascinating woman

en·chi·la·da \,en-chə-'läd-ə\ *n* : a tortilla rolled with meat filling and served with tomato sauce seasoned with chili

en·ci·pher \in-'sī-fər\ *vt* : to convert (a message) into cipher

en·cir·cle \in-'sər-kəl\ *vt* **1** : to form a circle around : SURROUND **2** : to pass completely around — **en·cir·cle·ment** *n*

en·clave \'en-,klāv, 'än-\ *n* : a territorial or culturally distinct unit enclosed within foreign territory

en·close \in-'klōz\ *vt* **1 a** : to close in : SURROUND; *esp* : to mark off (land) by or as if by a fence for one's own use **b** : to hold in : CONFINE **2** : to place in a parcel or envelope

en·clo·sure \in-'klō-zhər\ *n* **1** : the act of enclosing : the state of being enclosed **2** : an enclosed space **3** : something (as a fence) that encloses **4** : something enclosed

en·code \in-'kōd\ *vt* : to transfer from one system of communication into another; *esp* : to convert (a message) into code

en·co·mi·um \en-'kō-mē-əm\ *n, pl* **-mi·ums** *or* **-mia** \-mē-ə\ : warm or high praise esp. when formally expressed : EULOGY

en·com·pass \in-'kəm-pəs, -'käm-\ *vt* **1** : to form a circle about : ENCLOSE **2 a** : ENVELOP **b** : INCLUDE — **en·com·pass·ment** *n*

[1]**en·core** \'än-,kō(ə)r\ *n* : a demand for repetition or reappearance made by an audience; *also* : a further performance in response to such a demand

[2]**encore** *vt* : to call for a further performance or appearance of or by

[1]**en·coun·ter** \in-'kau̇nt-ər\ *vt* **en·coun·tered**; **en·coun·ter·ing** \-'kau̇nt-ə-riŋ, -'kau̇n-triŋ\ **1** : to meet as an adversary or enemy : engage in conflict with **2** : to come upon face to face : MEET **3** : to come upon unexpectedly

[2]**encounter** *n* **1 a** : a meeting between hostile factions or persons **b** : a sudden often violent clash : COMBAT **2 a** : a chance meeting **b** : a meeting face to face

en·cour·age \in-ˈkər-ij\ *vt* **1** : to inspire with courage, spirit, or hope : HEARTEN **2** : to spur on : STIMULATE **3** : to give help to : FOSTER — **en·cour·ag·ing·ly** *adv*

en·cour·age·ment \-mənt\ *n* **1** : the act of encouraging : the state of being encouraged **2** : something that encourages

en·croach \in-ˈkrōch\ *vi* **1** : to enter or force oneself gradually upon another's property or rights : TRESPASS, INTRUDE **2** : to advance beyond the usual or proper limits — **en·croach·ment** *n*

en·crust \in-ˈkrəst\ *vb* **1** : to cover, line, or overlay with a crust **2** : to form a crust

en·cum·ber \in-ˈkəm-bər\ *vt* **en·cum·bered**; **en·cum·ber·ing** \-b(ə-)riŋ\ **1** : to weigh down : BURDEN **2** : to impede or hamper the function or activity of : HINDER **3** : to burden with a legal claim (as a mortgage)

en·cum·brance \in-ˈkəm-brən(t)s\ *n* **1** : something that encumbers : LOAD, BURDEN **2** : a legal claim (as a mortgage) against property

¹en·cyc·li·cal \in-ˈsik-li-kəl\ *adj* : addressed to all the individuals of a group : GENERAL

²encyclical *n* : an encyclical letter; *esp* : a papal letter to the bishops of the church as a whole or to those in one country

en·cy·clo·pe·dia \in-ˌsī-klə-ˈpēd-ē-ə\ *n* : a work that contains information on all branches of knowledge or treats comprehensively a particular branch of knowledge usu. in articles arranged alphabetically by subject

en·cy·clo·pe·dic \-ˈpēd-ik\ *adj* **1** : of or relating to an encyclopedia **2** : covering a wide range of subjects

¹end \ˈend\ *n* **1 a** : the part of an area that lies at the boundary **b** : a point that marks the extent or limit of something **c** : the point where something ceases to exist **d** : the extreme or last part lengthwise : TIP **e** : a football lineman whose position is at the extremity of the line **2 a** : cessation of a course of action, pursuit, or activity **b** : DEATH, DESTRUCTION **c** (1) : the ultimate state (2) : RESULT, ISSUE **d** : the complex of events, parts, or sections that forms an extremity, termination, or finish **3** : something left over : REMNANT **4** : the goal toward which an agent acts or should act **5 a** : a share in an undertaking **b** : a particular phase of an undertaking or organization — **end·ed** \ˈen-dəd\ *adj*

²end *vb* **1 a** : to bring or come to an end : STOP **b** : DESTROY **2** : to make up the end of

en·dan·ger \in-ˈdān-jər\ *vt* **en·dan·gered**; **en·dan·ger·ing** \-ˈdānj-(ə-)riŋ\ : to bring into danger or peril

en·dear \in-ˈdi(ə)r\ *vt* : to cause to become dear or beloved

en·dear·ment \-mənt\ *n* : a word or an act (as a caress) showing love or affection

¹en·deav·or \in-ˈdev-ər\ *vb* **en·deav·ored**; **en·deav·or·ing** \-ˈdev-(ə-)riŋ\ : to make an effort : work for a particular end : TRY

²endeavor *n* : a serious determined effort

en·dem·ic \en-ˈdem-ik\ *adj* : restricted or peculiar to a locality or region — **en·dem·i·cal·ly** \-ˈdem-i-k(ə-)lē\ *adv* — **en·de·mic·i·ty** \ˌen-ˌdem-ˈis-ət-ē, -də-ˈmis-\ *n*

end·ing \ˈen-diŋ\ *n* **1** : CONCLUSION, END **2** : one or more sounds or letters added at the end of a word esp. in inflection

en·dive \ˈen-ˌdīv\ *n* **1** : an annual or biennial herb closely related to chicory and widely grown as a salad plant **2** : the developing crown of chicory when blanched for use as salad

end·less \ˈen-(d)ləs\ *adj* **1** : being or seeming to be without end **2** : joined at the ends : CONTINUOUS — **end·less·ly** *adv* — **end·less·ness** *n*

end man *n* : a man at each end of the line of performers in a minstrel show who engages in comic repartee with the interlocutor

end·most \ˈen(d)-ˌmōst\ *adj* : situated at the very end : FARTHEST

¹en·do·crine \ˈen-də-krən, -ˌkrīn, -ˌkrēn\ *adj* **1 a** : producing secretions that are distributed in the body by way of the bloodstream **b** : of, relating to, or resembling that of an endocrine gland **2** : HORMONAL

²endocrine *n* **1** : HORMONE **2** : an endocrine gland

en·do·cri·nol·o·gy \ˌen-də-kri-ˈnäl-ə-jē, -krī-\ *n* : a branch of knowledge dealing with the endocrine glands — **en·do·cri·no·log·i·cal** \-ˌkrin-ᵊl-ˈäj-i-kəl, -ˌkrīn-\ *adj* — **en·do·cri·nol·o·gist** \-kri-ˈnäl-ə-jəst, -krī-\ *n*

en·dorse \in-ˈdȯrs\ *vt* **1** : to write one's signature and often other matter esp. on the back of (a commercial document) for some special purpose **2** : to give one's support to : express approval of — **en·dors·er** *n*

en·dorse·ment \-mənt\ *n* **1** : the act or process of endorsing **2** : something written in the process of endorsing **3** : SANCTION, APPROVAL

en·dow \in-ˈdau̇\ *vt* **1** : to furnish with money for support or maintenance **2** : to provide or equip gratuitously

en·dow·ment \-mənt\ *n* **1** : the providing of a permanent fund for support or the fund provided **2** : a person's natural ability or talent

en·due \in-ˈd(y)ü\ *vt* : to provide with a quality or power

en·dur·ance \in-ˈd(y)u̇r-ən(t)s\ *n* **1** : PERMANENCE, DURATION **2** : the ability to withstand hardship, adversity, or stress **3** : SUFFERING, TRIAL

en·dure \in-ˈd(y)u̇(ə)r\ *vb* **1** : to continue in the same state : LAST **2 a** : to remain firm under suffering or misfortune without yielding **b** : to bear patiently : SUFFER **3** : TOLERATE, PERMIT — **en·dur·a·ble** *adj* — **en·dur·a·bly** \-ˈd(y)u̇r-ə-blē\ *adv*

en·dur·ing \-ˈd(y)u̇r-iŋ\ *adj* : LASTING, DURABLE

end·ways \ˈen-ˌdwāz\ *or* **end·wise** \-ˌdwīz\ *adv* (*or adj*) **1** : with the end forward **2** : LENGTHWISE **3** : on end : UPRIGHT

en·e·ma \ˈen-ə-mə\ *n* : the injection of liquid into the intestine by way of the anus; *also* : the material injected

en·e·my \ˈen-ə-mē\ *n, pl* **-mies** **1** : one that hates another : one that attacks or tries to harm another **2** : something that harms **3 a** : a nation with which one's own country is at war **b** : a military force, a ship, or a person belonging to such a nation

en·er·get·ic \ˌen-ər-ˈjet-ik\ *adj* : having or showing energy : ACTIVE, FORCEFUL — **en·er·get·i·cal·ly** \-ˈjet-i-k(ə-)lē\ *adv*

en·er·gize \ˈen-ər-ˌjīz\ *vb* **1** : to put forth energy : ACT **2 a** : to impart energy to **b** : to make energetic or vigorous **3** : to apply voltage to — **en·er·giz·er** *n*

en·er·gy \ˈen-ər-jē\ *n, pl* **-gies** **1** : power or capacity to be active : strength of body or mind to do things or to work **2** : natural power vigorously exerted : vigorous action **3** : the capacity for performing work

en·er·vate \ˈen-ər-ˌvāt\ *vt* : to cause to grow less in strength or vigor : WEAKEN — **en·er·va·tion** \ˌen-ər-ˈvā-shən\ *n*

en·fee·ble \in-ˈfē-bəl\ *vt* **en·fee·bled**; **en·fee·bling** \-b(ə-)liŋ\ : to make feeble — **en·fee·ble·ment** *n*

en·fi·lade \ˈen-fə-ˌlād, -ˌläd\ *n* : gunfire directed along the length of an enemy battle line

en·fold \in-ˈfōld\ *vt* **1 a** : to cover with folds : ENVELOP **b** : CONTAIN **2** : to clasp within the arms : EMBRACE

en·force \in-ˈfōrs\ *vt* **1** : FORCE, COMPEL **2** : to carry out effectively — **en·force·a·ble** *adj* — **en·force·ment** *n* — **en·forc·er** *n*

en·fran·chise \in-ˈfran-ˌchīz\ *vt* **1** : to set free (as from slavery) **2** : to admit to the privileges of a citizen; *esp* : to admit to the right of suffrage — **en·fran·chise·ment** \-ˌchīz-mənt, -chəz-\ *n*

en·gage \in-ˈgāj\ *vb* **1** : to interlock with : MESH; *also* : to cause to mesh **2** : to bind oneself to do something; *esp* : to bind by a pledge to marry **3 a** : to arrange to obtain the use or services of : HIRE **b** : ENGROSS, OCCUPY **4** : to enter into contest with **5 a** : to begin and carry on an enterprise **b** : PARTICIPATE

en·gaged \in-'gājd\ *adj* **1** : OCCUPIED, EMPLOYED, BUSY **2** : pledged to be married : BETROTHED
en·gage·ment \in-'gāj-mənt\ *n* **1 a** : the act of engaging : the state of being engaged **b** : BETROTHAL **2** : PLEDGE, OBLIGATION **3 a** : a promise to be present at a specified time and place **b** : employment esp. for a stated time **4** : the state of being in gear **5** : a hostile encounter between military forces
en·gag·ing \in-'gā-jing\ *adj* : ATTRACTIVE, PLEASING
en·gen·der \in-'jen-dər\ *vt* **en·gen·dered**; **en·gen·der·ing** \-d(ə-)riŋ\ **1** : BEGET, PROCREATE **2** : to cause to exist : PRODUCE, CREATE
en·gine \'en-jən\ *n* **1 a** : a mechanical tool (as an instrument of war or torture) **b** : a mechanical appliance **2** : a machine for converting energy into mechanical force and motion **3** : a railroad locomotive
¹en·gi·neer \ˌen-jə-'ni(ə)r\ *n* **1** : a member of a military group devoted to engineering work **2 a** : a designer or builder of engines **b** : a person who is trained in or follows as a profession a branch of engineering **c** : a person who skillfully carries out an enterprise **3** : a person who runs or supervises an engine or an apparatus
²engineer *vt* **1** : to plan, build, or manage as an engineer **2** : to guide the course of
en·gi·neer·ing \-iŋ\ *n* **1** : the art of managing engines **2** : a science by which the properties of matter and the sources of energy in nature are made useful to man
en·gorge \in-'gȯrj\ *vb* **1** : GORGE, GLUT **2** : to fill with blood : CONGEST — **en·gorge·ment** *n*
en·graft \in-'graft\ *vt* : GRAFT 1
en·grave \in-'grāv\ *vt* **1 a** : to form by incisions (as upon wood or metal) **b** : to impress deeply **2 a** : to cut figures, letters, or devices upon for printing; *also* : to print from an engraved plate **b** : PHOTOENGRAVE — **en·grav·er** *n*
en·grav·ing \in-'grā-viŋ\ *n* **1** : the art of cutting letters, pictures, or patterns in wood, stone, or metal **2** : a print made from an engraved surface
en·gross \in-'grōs\ *vt* **1 a** : to copy or write in a large hand **b** : to prepare the usu. final handwritten or printed text of (an official document) **2** : to take up the whole interest of : occupy fully : ABSORB — **en·gross·er** *n* — **en·gross·ment** *n*
en·gulf \in-'gəlf\ *vt* : to flow over and enclose; *also* : to take in (food) by such means — **en·gulf·ment** *n*
en·hance \in-'han(t)s\ *vt* : to make greater (as in value, desirability, or attractiveness) : HEIGHTEN — **en·hance·ment** *n*
en·har·mon·ic \ˌen-här-'män-ik\ *adj* : relating to a change of letter names of notes that does not change the pitch — **en·har·mon·i·cal·ly** \-i-k(ə-)lē\ *adv*
enig·ma \i-'nig-mə\ *n* : something hard to understand or explain : PUZZLE — **en·ig·mat·ic** \ˌen-ig-'mat-ik, ˌē-nig-\ *or* **en·ig·mat·i·cal** \-'mat-i-kəl\ *adj* — **en·ig·mat·i·cal·ly** \-i-k(ə-)lē\ *adv*
en·join \in-'jȯin\ *vt* **1** : to direct or impose by authoritative order **2** : FORBID, PROHIBIT
en·joy \in-'jȯi\ *vt* **1** : to take pleasure or satisfaction in **2** : to have for one's use, benefit, or lot — **en·joy·a·ble** *adj* — **en·joy·a·ble·ness** *n* — **en·joy·a·bly** \-ə-blē\ *adv*
en·joy·ment \-mənt\ *n* **1** : the condition of enjoying something : possession and use of something with satisfaction **2** : PLEASURE, SATISFACTION **3** : something that gives pleasure
en·kin·dle \in-'kin-dᵊl\ *vb* : KINDLE
en·lace \in-'lās\ *vt* **1** : ENCIRCLE, ENFOLD **2** : ENTWINE, INTERLACE
en·large \in-'lärj\ *vb* **1** : to make or grow larger : INCREASE, EXPAND **2** : ELABORATE — **en·larg·er** *n*
en·large·ment \-mənt\ *n* : an act or instance of enlarging : the state of being enlarged
en·light·en \in-'līt-ᵊn\ *vt* **en·light·ened**; **en·light·en·ing** \-'līt-niŋ, -ᵊn-iŋ\ **1** : to furnish knowledge to : INSTRUCT **2** : to give spiritual insight to — **en·light·en·ment** *n*
en·list \in-'list\ *vb* **1** : to enroll oneself or another for military or naval service; *esp* : to join one of the armed services voluntarily **2** : to obtain the help or support of; *also* : to participate heartily (as in a cause or drive) — **en·list·ment** *n*
en·list·ed \-'lis-təd\ *adj* : of, relating to, or constituting the part of a military or naval force below commissioned or warrant officers
en·liv·en \in-'lī-vən\ *vt* : to give life, action, or spirit to : ANIMATE
en masse \än-'mas, äⁿ-\ *adv* : in a body : as a whole
en·mesh \in-'mesh\ *vt* : to catch or entangle in or as if in meshes
en·mi·ty \'en-mət-ē\ *n, pl* **-ties** : ILL WILL, HATRED; *esp* : mutual hatred or ill will
en·no·ble \in-'ō-bəl\ *vt* **-bled**; **-bling** \-b(ə-)liŋ\ **1** : to make noble : ELEVATE **2** : to raise to the rank of nobility — **en·no·ble·ment** *n*
en·nui \'än-'wē\ *n* : a feeling of weariness and dissatisfaction : BOREDOM
enor·mi·ty \i-'nȯr-mət-ē\ *n, pl* **-ties** **1** : huge size **2** : great wickedness : OUTRAGEOUSNESS **3** : an outrageous act or offense
enor·mous \i-'nȯr-məs\ *adj* : extraordinarily great in size, number, or degree — **enor·mous·ly** *adv* — **enor·mous·ness** *n*
¹enough \i-'nəf\ *adj* : occurring in such quantity, quality, or scope as to fully satisfy demands or needs
²enough *adv* **1** : in sufficient amount or degree : SUFFICIENTLY **2** : FULLY, QUITE **3** : TOLERABLY
³enough *n* : a sufficient quantity
en·rage \in-'rāj\ *vt* : to fill with rage : ANGER, MADDEN
en·rapt \in-'rapt\ *adj* : RAPT, ENRAPTURED
en·rap·ture \in-'rap-chər\ *vt* **-rap·tured**; **-rap·tur·ing** \-'rap-chə-riŋ, -'rap-shriŋ\ : to fill with delight
en·rich \in-'rich\ *vt* **1** : to make rich or richer **2** : ADORN, ORNAMENT **3 a** : to make (soil) more fertile **b** : to improve (a food) in nutritive value by adding vitamins and minerals in processing — **en·rich·ment** *n*
en·roll *or* **en·rol** \in-'rōl\ *vb* **en·rolled**; **en·roll·ing** **1** : to insert, register, or enter in a list, catalog, or roll **2** : to enroll oneself or cause oneself to be enrolled — **en·roll·ment** *n*
en route \än-'rüt, en-\ *adv* : on or along the way
en·sconce \in-'skän(t)s\ *vt* **1** : to place or hide securely : CONCEAL **2** : to establish comfortably : settle snugly
en·sem·ble \än-'säm-bəl\ *n* : a group constituting a whole or producing a single effect: as **a** : SET **b** : concerted music of two or more parts or the musicians that perform it **c** : a complete set of harmonizing clothes **d** : a group of supporting performers
en·sheathe \in-'shēth\ *vt* : to cover with or as if with a sheath
en·shrine \in-'shrīn\ *vt* **1** : to enclose in or as if in a shrine **2** : to preserve or cherish as sacred
en·shroud \in-'shrau̇d\ *vt* : SHROUD
en·sign \'en(t)-sən, *in senses 1 & 2 also* 'en-ˌsīn\ *n* **1** : a flag flown as the symbol of nationality **2** : a badge of office, rank, or power **3** : a commissioned officer of the lowest rank in the navy
en·si·lage \'en(t)-sə-lij\ *n* : SILAGE
en·sile \en-'sīl\ *vt* : to prepare and store (fodder) for silage
en·slave \in-'slāv\ *vt* : to reduce to slavery : SUBJUGATE — **en·slave·ment** *n* — **en·slav·er** *n*
en·snare \in-'sna(ə)r\ *vt* : SNARE, ENTRAP
en·sue \in-'sü\ *vi* : to come after in time or as a result : FOLLOW
en·sure \in-'shu̇(ə)r\ *vt* : to make sure, certain, or safe : GUARANTEE
¹en·tail \in-'tāl\ *vt* **1** : to limit the inheritance of (property) to the owner's lineal descendants or to a class thereof **2** : to

impose, involve, or imply as a necessary accompaniment or result — **en·tail·ment** *n*

²entail \'en-ˌtāl, in-'tāl\ *n* **1 a** : an entailing esp. of lands **b** : an entailed estate **2** : the rule fixing descent by entailment

en·tan·gle \in-'taŋ-gəl\ *vt* **1** : to make tangled, complicated, or confused **2** : to involve in or as if in a tangle — **en·tan·gle·ment** *n*

en·tente \än-'tänt\ *n* **1** : an international understanding providing for a common course of action **2** : a coalition of parties to an entente

en·ter \'ent-ər\ *vb* **en·tered**; **en·ter·ing** \'ent-ə-riŋ, 'en-triŋ\ **1** : to go or come into : go or come in **2** : to pass into or through usu. by overcoming resistance : PIERCE **3** : to cause to go into or be admitted to **4** : to become a member of : JOIN **5** : to make a beginning **6** : to take part or play a part **7** : to take possession **8** : to set down in a book or list **9** : to place formally before a legal authority as a court — **en·ter·a·ble** *adj*

en·ter·prise \'ent-ə(r)-ˌprīz\ *n* **1** : a difficult, complicated, or risky project or undertaking : VENTURE **2 a** : a business organization **b** : a systematic purposeful activity **3** : readiness to engage in daring action : INITIATIVE — **en·ter·pris·er** *n*

en·ter·pris·ing \-ˌprī-ziŋ\ *adj* : marked by an independent energetic spirit and by readiness to undertake or experiment

en·ter·tain \ˌent-ər-'tān\ *vb* **1** : to receive and provide for as host : have as a guest **2** : to provide entertainment esp. for guests **3** : to have in mind : CONSIDER **4** : AMUSE, DIVERT

en·ter·tain·er \-'tā-nər\ *n* : one that entertains; *esp* : one who gives or takes part in public entertainments

en·ter·tain·ment \-'tān-mənt\ *n* **1** : provision for guests esp. in public places (as hotels and inns) **2** : AMUSEMENT, RECREATION, DIVERSION **3** : something that entertains : a means of amusement or recreation; *esp* : a public performance

en·thrall *or* **en·thral** \in-'thrȯl\ *vt* **en·thralled**; **en·thrall·ing** **1** : to hold in or reduce to slavery **2** : to hold spellbound : CHARM — **en·thrall·ment** *n*

en·throne \in-'thrōn\ *vt* **1** : to seat ceremonially on a throne **2** : to place on high : EXALT — **en·throne·ment** *n*

en·thuse \in-'th(y)üz\ *vb* **1** : to make enthusiastic **2** : to show enthusiasm

en·thu·si·asm \in-'th(y)ü-zē-ˌaz-əm\ *n* **1** : strong excitement of feeling : FERVOR **2** : something inspiring zeal or fervor

en·thu·si·ast \-zē-ˌast, -əst\ *n* : a person filled with enthusiasm

en·thu·si·as·tic \in-ˌth(y)ü-zē-'as-tik\ *adj* : filled with or marked by enthusiasm — **en·thu·si·as·ti·cal·ly** \-ti-k(ə-)lē\ *adv*

en·tice \in-'tīs\ *vt* : to attract by arousing hope or desire : TEMPT — **en·tice·ment** *n*

en·tire \in-'tī(ə)r, 'en-ˌ\ *adj* **1** : having no element or part left out **2** : COMPLETE, TOTAL, FULL **3 a** : consisting of one piece : HOMOGENOUS **b** : INTACT — **entire** *adv* — **en·tire·ly** *adv* — **en·tire·ness** *n*

en·tire·ty \in-'tī-rət-ē, -'tī(ə)rt-ē\ *n* **1** : the state of being entire or complete **2** : sum total : WHOLE

en·ti·tle \in-'tīt-ᵊl\ *vt* **en·ti·tled**; **en·ti·tling** \-'tīt-liŋ, -ᵊl-iŋ\ **1** : to give a title to : DESIGNATE **2 a** : to give a legal right to **b** : to qualify for something — **en·ti·tle·ment** *n*

en·ti·ty \'ent-ət-ē\ *n, pl* **-ti·ties** : something that has a real existence either as a thing (as a chair or a building) knowable through the senses or as a thing (as a nation or a religion) conceivable by the mind

en·tomb \in-'tüm\ *vt* : to place in a tomb : BURY — **en·tomb·ment** *n*

en·to·mol·o·gy \ˌent-ə-'mäl-ə-jē\ *n* : a branch of zoology that deals with insects — **en·to·mo·log·ic** \ˌent-ə-mə-'läj-ik\ *or* **en·to·mo·log·i·cal** \-'läj-i-kəl\ *adj* — **en·to·mo·log·i·cal·ly** \-i-k(ə-)lē\ *adv* — **en·to·mol·o·gist** \ˌent-ə-'mäl-ə-jəst\ *n*

en·tou·rage \ˌänt-ə-'räzh, ˌän-tü-\ *n* : one's attendants or associates : RETINUE

en·tr'acte \'äⁿ(n)-ˌtrakt, -ˌträkt, äⁿ(n)-'\ *n* **1** : the interval between two acts of a play **2** : a dance, piece of music, or interlude performed between two acts of a play

en·trails \'en-trəlz, -ˌtrālz\ *n pl* : internal parts : VISCERA; *esp* : INTESTINES

en·train \in-'trān\ *vb* : to put or go aboard a railroad train

¹en·trance \'en-trən(t)s\ *n* **1** : the act of entering **2** : the means or place of entry **3** : power or permission to enter : ADMISSION

²en·trance \in-'tran(t)s\ *vt* **1** : to put into a trance **2** : to fill with delight, wonder, or rapture — **en·trance·ment** *n*

en·trant \'en-trənt\ *n* : one that enters; *esp* : one that enters a contest

en·trap \in-'trap\ *vt* **1** : to catch in or as if in a trap **2** : to lure into a compromising statement or act — **en·trap·ment** *n*

en·treat \in-'trēt\ *vb* : to ask earnestly or urgently : PLEAD, BEG — **en·treat·ing·ly** *adv*

en·treaty \in-'trēt-ē\ *n, pl* **-treat·ies** : earnest request : APPEAL, PLEA

en·trée *or* **en·tree** \'än-(ˌ)trā\ *n* **1 a** : the act or manner of entering : ENTRANCE **b** : freedom of entry or access **2 a** : a dish served between the main courses **b** : the principal dish of the meal

en·trench \in-'trench\ *vb* **1 a** : to dig, place within, surround with, or occupy a trench esp. for defense **b** : to establish solidly **2** : to cut into : FURROW; *esp* : to erode downward so as to form a trench **3** : ENCROACH — used with *on* or *upon*

en·trench·ment \-mənt\ *n* **1** : the act of entrenching : the state of being entrenched **2** : DEFENSE; *esp* : a defensive work consisting of a trench and a wall of earth

en·tre·pre·neur \ˌän-trə-p(r)ə-'nər\ *n* : one who organizes, manages, and assumes the risks of a business or enterprise

en·trust \in-'trəst\ *vt* **1** : to give into the care of another (as for safekeeping) **2** : to give custody, care, or charge of something to as a trust

en·try \'en-trē\ *n, pl* **entries** **1** : the act of entering : ENTRANCE **2** : a place through which entrance is made : HALL, VESTIBULE **3 a** : the act of making (as in a book or list) a written record of something **b** : the thing thus recorded: as (1) : HEADWORD (2) : a headword with its definition or identification (3) : VOCABULARY ENTRY **4** : a person, thing, or group entered in a contest or race

en·twine \in-'twīn\ *vb* : to twine together or around

enu·mer·ate \i-'n(y)ü-mə-ˌrāt\ *vt* **1** : to ascertain the number of : COUNT **2** : to specify one after another : LIST — **enu·mer·a·ble** \-'n(y)üm-(ə-)rə-bəl\ *adj* — **enu·mer·a·tion** \-ˌn(y)ü-mə-'rā-shən\ *n* — **enu·mer·a·tive** \-'n(y)ü-mə-ˌrāt-iv, -'n(y)üm-(ə-)rət-\ *adj* — **enu·mer·a·tor** \-'n(y)ü-mə-ˌrāt-ər\ *n*

enun·ci·ate \ē-'nən(t)-sē-ˌāt\ *vb* **1** : ANNOUNCE, PROCLAIM **2** : ARTICULATE, PRONOUNCE **3** : to utter articulate sounds — **enun·ci·a·tion** \-ˌnən(t)-sē-'ā-shən\ *n* — **enun·ci·a·tor** \-'nən(t)-sē-ˌāt-ər\ *n*

en·vel·op \in-'vel-əp\ *vt* **1** : to enclose or enfold completely with or as if with a covering **2** : to mount an attack on (an enemy's flank) — **en·vel·op·ment** *n*

en·ve·lope \'en-və-ˌlōp, 'än-\ *n* **1** : something that envelops : WRAPPER **2** : a flat usu. paper container (as for a letter) **3** : the bag containing the gas in a balloon or airship

en·ven·om \in-'ven-əm\ *vt* **1** : to taint or fill with poison **2** : EMBITTER

en·vi·a·ble \'en-vē-ə-bəl\ *adj* : worthy of envy : highly desirable — **en·vi·a·ble·ness** *n* — **en·vi·a·bly** \-blē\ *adv*

en·vi·ous \'en-vē-əs\ *adj* : feeling or showing envy : caused by or proceeding from envy — **en·vi·ous·ly** *adv* — **en·vi·ous·ness** *n*

en·vi·ron \in-'vī-rən\ *vt* : ENCIRCLE, SURROUND

en·vi·ron·ment \in-'vī-rən-mənt\ *n* : something that environs : SURROUNDINGS; *esp* : the social and cultural conditions that influence the life of a person or human community — **en·vi·ron-**

mental \in-ˌvī-rən-ˈment-ᵊl\ *adj* — **en·vi·ron·men·tal·ly** \-ᵊl-ē\ *adv*
en·vi·rons \in-ˈvī-rənz, ˈen-və-\ *n pl* **1** : the districts around a city **2** : SURROUNDINGS
en·vis·age \in-ˈviz-ij\ *vt* : to have a mental picture of esp. in advance of realization : VISUALIZE
en·vi·sion \in-ˈvizh-ən\ *vt* : to picture to oneself
en·voy \ˈen-ˌvȯi, ˈän-\ *n* **1 a** : a minister plenipotentiary accredited to a foreign government who ranks between an ambassador and a minister resident **b** : a representative sent by one government to another **2** : MESSENGER, REPRESENTATIVE
¹en·vy \ˈen-vē\ *n, pl* **envies** **1** : painful or resentful awareness of an advantage enjoyed by another joined with a desire to possess the same advantage **2** : an object of envious notice or feeling
²envy *vt* **en·vied**; **en·vy·ing** : to feel envy toward or on account of — **en·vi·er** *n* — **en·vy·ing·ly** \-iŋ-lē\ *adv*
en·wrap \in-ˈrap\ *vt* **1** : ENFOLD **2** : ENVELOP **3** : ENGROSS
en·wreathe \in-ˈrēth\ *vt* : WREATHE, ENVELOP
en·zyme \ˈen-ˌzīm\ *n* : a complex organic and predominantly protein substance produced by living cells that brings about or accelerates reaction (as in the digestion of food) at body temperatures without itself being permanently altered — **en·zy·mat·ic** \ˌen-zə-ˈmat-ik\ *adj* — **en·zy·mat·i·cal·ly** \-ˈmat-i-k(ə-)lē\ *adv*
ep·au·let \ˌep-ə-ˈlet\ *n* : a shoulder ornament on a uniform esp. of a military or naval officer
épée \ˈep-ˌā, ā-ˈpā\ *n* : a fencing or dueling sword having a bowl-shaped guard and a tapering rigid blade with no cutting edge

épée

ephed·rine \i-ˈfed-rən\ *n* : a drug used in relieving hay fever, asthma, and nasal congestion
ephem·era \i-ˈfem-(ə-)rə\ *n pl* : ephemeral things
ephem·er·al \i-ˈfem-(ə-)rəl\ *adj* **1** : lasting one day only **2** : lasting a very short time — **ephem·er·al·i·ty** \i-ˌfem-ə-ˈral-ət-ē\ *n* — **ephem·er·al·ly** \i-ˈfem-(ə-)rə-lē\ *adv*
¹ep·ic \ˈep-ik\ *adj* **1** : of, relating to, or having the characteristics of an epic **2 a** : unusually long esp. in size or scope **b** : HEROIC
²epic *n* **1** : a long narrative poem in elevated style relating the deeds of a legendary or historical hero **2** : a work of art that resembles or suggests an epic **3** : a series of events or body of tradition held to form the proper subject of an epic
ep·i·cure \ˈep-i-ˌkyu̇r\ *n* : a person with sensitive and discriminating tastes in food or wine
¹ep·i·cu·re·an \ˌep-i-kyu̇-ˈrē-ən, -ˈkyu̇r-ē-\ *adj* : of, relating to, or suited to an epicure
²epicurean *n* : EPICURE
¹ep·i·dem·ic \ˌep-ə-ˈdem-ik\ *adj* **1** : affecting many individuals and esp. persons at one time **2** : excessively prevalent — **ep·i·dem·i·cal·ly** \-ˈdem-i-k(ə-)lē\ *adv* — **ep·i·de·mic·i·ty** \-ˌdem-ˈis-ət-ē\ *n*
²epidemic *n* **1** : an outbreak of epidemic disease **2** : an outbreak or product of sudden rapid spread or development
epi·der·mis \ˌep-ə-ˈdər-məs\ *n* : an outer layer esp. of skin — **epi·der·mal** \-məl\ *adj*
epi·glot·tis \ˌep-ə-ˈglät-əs\ *n* : a thin plate of flexible cartilage in front of the glottis that folds back over and protects the glottis during swallowing — **epi·glot·tal** \-ˈglät-ᵊl\ *adj*
ep·i·gram \ˈep-ə-ˌgram\ *n* **1** : a short often satirical poem ending with an ingenious turn of thought **2** : a brief witty saying
ep·i·gram·mat·ic \ˌep-i-grə-ˈmat-ik\ *adj* **1** : of, relating to, or resembling an epigram **2** : marked by or given to the use of epigrams — **ep·i·gram·mat·i·cal** \-ˈmat-i-kəl\ *adj* — **ep·i·gram·mat·i·cal·ly** \-i-k(ə-)lē\ *adv*
ep·i·lep·sy \ˈep-ə-ˌlep-sē\ *n* : a disorder marked by disturbed electrical rhythms of the central nervous system and typically manifested by convulsive attacks usu. with clouding of consciousness — **ep·i·lep·tic** \ˌep-ə-ˈlep-tik\ *adj or n*
ep·i·logue \ˈep-ə-ˌlȯg\ *n* **1** : a concluding section that rounds out the design of a literary work **2 a** : a speech often in verse addressed to the audience by an actor at the end of a play **b** : the actor speaking such an epilogue **3** : a concluding event or development
epiph·a·ny \i-ˈpif-ə-nē\ *n, pl* **-nies** : an appearance or manifestation esp. of a divine being
Epiphany *n* : January 6 observed as a church festival in commemoration of the coming of the three wise men to Jesus at Bethlehem
epis·co·pa·cy \i-ˈpis-kə-pə-sē\ *n, pl* **-cies** **1** : government of the church by bishops or by a hierarchy **2** : EPISCOPATE
epis·co·pal \i-ˈpis-kə-pəl\ *adj* **1** : of or relating to a bishop **2** : having or constituting government by bishops **3** *cap* : of or relating to the Protestant Episcopal Church representing the Anglican communion in the U.S. — **epis·co·pal·ly** \-p(ə-)lē\ *adv*
Epis·co·pa·lian \i-ˌpis-kə-ˈpāl-yən\ *n* **1** : an adherent of the episcopal form of church government **2** : a member of the Protestant Episcopal Church — **Episcopalian** *adj* — **Epis·co·pa·lian·ism** \-yə-ˌniz-əm\ *n*
epis·co·pate \i-ˈpis-kə-pət\ *n* **1** : the rank, office, or term of office of a bishop **2** : the whole body of bishops
ep·i·sode \ˈep-ə-ˌsōd\ *n* **1 a** : a developed situation integral to but separable from a continuous narrative : INCIDENT **b** : one of a series of loosely connected stories or scenes **2** : an event that is distinctive and separate esp. in history or in a life **3** : a digressive subdivision in a musical composition — **ep·i·sod·ic** \ˌep-ə-ˈsäd-ik\ *adj*
epis·tle \i-ˈpis-əl\ *n* **1** *cap* : one of the letters of the New Testament of the Bible **2** : LETTER; *esp* : a formal or elegant letter
epis·to·lary \i-ˈpis-tə-ˌler-ē\ *adj* **1** : of, relating to, or suitable to a letter **2** : contained in or carried on by letters **3** : written in the form of a series of letters
ep·i·taph \ˈep-ə-ˌtaf\ *n* : an inscription (as on a tombstone) in memory of a dead person
ep·i·the·li·um \ˌep-ə-ˈthē-lē-əm\ *n, pl* **-lia** \-lē-ə\ : a cellular membrane covering a bodily surface or lining a cavity — **ep·i·the·li·al** \-lē-əl\ *adj*
ep·i·thet \ˈep-ə-ˌthet\ *n* **1** : a characterizing word or phrase accompanying or occurring in place of the name of a person or thing **2** : a disparaging or abusive word or phrase — **ep·i·thet·ic** \ˌep-ə-ˈthet-ik\ *or* **ep·i·thet·i·cal** \-ˈthet-i-kəl\ *adj*
epit·o·me \i-ˈpit-ə-mē\ *n* **1** : a brief condensed statement of the contents of a work : SUMMARY, ABSTRACT **2** : a part that is typical of a whole : something considered to represent or embody the characteristics of something else
epit·o·mize \i-ˈpit-ə-ˌmīz\ *vt* : to make or serve as an epitome of : SUMMARIZE
ep·och \ˈep-ək, -ˌäk\ *n* : an extended period of time : ERA, AGE — **ep·och·al** \-əl\ *adj* — **ep·och·al·ly** *adv*
epon·y·mous \i-ˈpän-ə-məs, e-ˈpän-\ *adj* : of, relating to, or being the person for whom something is named or is believed to be named
ep·oxy resin \(ˌ)e-ˌpäk-sē-\ *n* : a flexible usu. thermosetting resin made by polymerization of an oxygen-containing compound and used chiefly in coatings and adhesives
equa·ble \ˈek-wə-bəl, ˈē-kwə-\ *adj* : EVEN, UNIFORM; *esp* : free

from extremes or sudden or harsh changes — **equa·bly** \-blē\ *adv*

¹equal \'ē-kwəl\ *adj* **1 a** (1) **:** of the same measure, quantity, amount, or number as another **:** LIKE (2) **:** identical in value **:** EQUIVALENT **b :** like in quality, nature, or status **c :** not varying **:** UNIFORM **2 a :** evenly balanced **b :** IMPARTIAL **3 a :** free from extremes **b :** tranquil of mind or mood **4 :** capable of meeting requirements

²equal *n* **1 :** one that is equal **2 :** an equal quantity

³equal *vt* **equaled** *or* **equalled**; **equal·ing** *or* **equal·ling** **1 :** to be equal to; *esp* **:** to be identical in value to **2 :** to produce something equal to **:** MATCH

equal·i·ty \i-'kwäl-ət-ē\ *n, pl* **-ties** **1 :** the quality or state of being equal **2 :** EQUATION 2

equal·ize \'ē-kwə-ˌlīz\ *vt* **1 :** to make equal **2 :** to make uniform; *esp* **:** to distribute evenly or uniformly **:** BALANCE — **equal·iza·tion** \ˌē-kwə-lə-'zā-shən\ *n* — **equal·iz·er** *n*

equal·ly \'ē-kwə-lē\ *adv* **1 :** in an equal manner **:** EVENLY **2 :** to an equal degree **:** ALIKE

equa·nim·i·ty \ˌē-kwə-'nim-ət-ē, ˌek-wə-\ *n* **:** evenness of mind **:** calm temper **:** COMPOSURE

equate \i-'kwāt\ *vt* **:** to make or treat as equal **:** represent or express as equal or equivalent

equa·tion \i-'kwā-zhən, -shən\ *n* **1 a :** the act or process of equating **b :** a state of being equated; *esp* **:** the regarding of two or more things as identical or similar **2 :** a statement of the equality of two mathematical expressions

equa·tor \i-'kwāt-ər, 'ē-ˌkwāt-\ *n* **:** an imaginary circle around the earth that is everywhere equally distant from the two poles and divides the earth's surface into the northern and southern hemispheres

equa·to·ri·al \ˌē-kwə-'tōr-ē-əl, ˌek-wə-\ *adj* **1 :** of, relating to, or located at the equator **2 :** of, originating in, or suggesting the region around the geographic equator

eq·uer·ry \'ek-wə-rē, i-'kwer-ē\ *n, pl* **-ries** **1 :** an officer in charge of the horses of a prince or nobleman **2 :** a personal attendant of a member of the British royal family

¹eques·tri·an \i-'kwes-trē-ən\ *adj* **1 :** of or relating to horses, horsemen, or horsemanship **2 :** mounted on horseback **3 :** representing a person on horseback **4 :** of, relating to, or composed of knights

²equestrian *n* **:** one who rides on horseback

eques·tri·enne \i-ˌkwes-trē-'en\ *n* **:** a female equestrian

equi·dis·tant \ˌē-kwə-'dis-tənt\ *adj* **:** equally distant

equi·lat·er·al \ˌē-kwə-'lat-ə-rəl, -'la-trəl\ *adj* **1 :** having all sides equal **2 :** having all the faces equal

equi·lib·ri·um \ˌē-kwə-'lib-rē-əm\ *n, pl* **-ri·ums** *or* **-ria** \-rē-ə\ **:** a static or dynamic state of balance between opposing forces or actions

equine \'ē-ˌkwīn\ *adj* **:** of, relating to, or resembling a horse or the horse family — **equine** *n* — **equine·ly** *adv*

equi·noc·tial \ˌē-kwə-'näk-shəl\ *adj* **1 :** of, relating to, or occurring at or near an equinox **2 :** of or relating to the regions or climate of the equator

equi·nox \'ē-kwə-ˌnäks\ *n* **:** either of the two times each year when the sun crosses the equator and day and night are everywhere of equal length that occur about March 21 and September 23

equip \i-'kwip\ *vt* **equipped**; **equip·ping** **1 :** to furnish for service or action **:** PREPARE **2 :** DRESS, ARRAY

eq·ui·page \'ek-wə-pij\ *n* **1 a :** material or articles used in equipment **:** OUTFIT **b :** TRAPPINGS **2 :** a horse-drawn carriage with its retinue of servants or such a carriage alone

equip·ment \i-'kwip-mənt\ *n* **1 a :** the equipping of a person or thing **b :** the state of being equipped **2 :** the set of articles or resources serving to equip a person or thing

eq·ui·poise \'ek-wə-ˌpȯiz, 'ē-kwə-\ *n* **1 :** a state of balance **:** EQUILIBRIUM **2 :** a weight used to balance another weight

equi·pol·lent \ˌē-kwə-'päl-ənt\ *adj* **1 :** equal in force, power, or validity **2 :** EQUIVALENT — **equi·pol·lence** \-ən(t)s\ *n*

eq·ui·ta·ble \'ek-wət-ə-bəl\ *adj* **1 :** having or exhibiting equity **:** JUST **2 :** existing or valid in equity as distinguished from law — **eq·ui·ta·ble·ness** *n* — **eq·ui·ta·bly** \-blē\ *adv*

eq·ui·ta·tion \ˌek-wə-'tā-shən\ *n* **:** the act or art of riding on horseback

eq·ui·ty \'ek-wət-ē\ *n, pl* **-ties** **1 :** fairness or justice in dealings between persons **2 :** a system of law originating in the English chancery supplementary to common and statute law and designed to protect rights and enforce duties fixed by substantive law **3 :** the value of an owner's interest in a property in excess of claims or liens against it

equiv·a·lent \i-'kwiv(-ə)-lənt\ *adj* **1 :** equal in force, amount, or value **2 :** like in meaning **3 :** corresponding or virtually identical in effect or function — **equiv·a·lence** \-lən(t)s\ *n* — **equivalent** *n* — **equiv·a·lent·ly** *adv*

equiv·o·cal \i-'kwiv-ə-kəl\ *adj* **1 :** having two or more possible meanings **:** AMBIGUOUS **2 :** UNCERTAIN, DOUBTFUL **3 :** SUSPICIOUS, QUESTIONABLE — **equiv·o·cal·ly** \-k(ə-)lē\ *adv* — **equiv·o·cal·ness** *n*

equiv·o·cate \i-'kwiv-ə-ˌkāt\ *vi* **1 :** to use equivocal language esp. with intent to deceive **:** LIE **2 :** to avoid committing oneself in what one says — **equiv·o·ca·tion** \i-ˌkwiv-ə-'kā-shən\ *n* — **equiv·o·ca·tor** \i-'kwiv-ə-ˌkāt-ər\ *n*

era \'ir-ə, 'er-ə\ *n* **1 :** a period of time reckoned from some special date or event **2 :** an important or distinctive period of history **3 :** one of the major divisions of geologic time

erad·i·cate \i-'rad-ə-ˌkāt\ *vt* **:** to remove by or as if by uprooting **:** ELIMINATE, EXTIRPATE — **erad·i·ca·ble** \-'rad-i-kə-bəl\ *adj* — **erad·i·ca·tion** \-ˌrad-ə-'kā-shən\ *n* — **erad·i·ca·tive** \-'rad-ə-ˌkāt-iv\ *adj* — **erad·i·ca·tor** \-ˌkāt-ər\ *n*

eras·a·ble \i-'rā-sə-bəl\ *adj* **:** capable of being erased

erase \i-'rās\ *vb* **1 :** to rub or scrape out (as something written) **2 :** to remove as if by erasing **3 :** to yield to being erased

eras·er \i-'rā-sər\ *n* **:** one that erases; *esp* **:** a sharp instrument or a piece of rubber or cloth used to erase marks

era·sure \i-'rā-shər, -zhər\ *n* **:** an act or instance of erasing

er·bi·um \'ər-bē-əm\ *n* **:** a rare metallic element that occurs with yttrium

¹ere \(ˌ)e(ə)r\ *prep* **:** ²BEFORE 2

²ere *conj* **:** ³BEFORE

¹erect \i-'rekt\ *adj* **1 a :** vertical in position **:** UPRIGHT **b :** marked by straightness of bodily posture **c :** standing up or out from the body **2 :** directed upward — **erect·ly** *adv* — **erect·ness** *n*

²erect *vt* **1 a :** to put up by the fitting together of materials **:** BUILD **b :** to fix in an upright position **c :** to cause to stand up or out **2 :** to elevate in status **3 :** ESTABLISH **4 :** to construct (as a perpendicular) upon a given base — **erec·tor** \-'rek-tər\ *n*

erec·tion \i-'rek-shən\ *n* **1 :** an erecting or a being erected **:** RAISING, BUILDING, CONSTRUCTING **2 :** something erected

ere·long \e(ə)r-'lȯŋ\ *adv* **:** before long **:** SOON

er·e·mite \'er-ə-ˌmīt\ *n* **:** HERMIT; *esp* **:** a religious recluse

er·go \'e(ə)r-ˌgō, 'ər-\ *adv* **:** THEREFORE, HENCE

er·mine \'ər-mən\ *n, pl* **ermine** *or* **ermines** **1 :** any of several weasels that assume a white winter coat usu. with more or less black on the tail **2 :** the white fur of an ermine — **er·mined** \-mənd\ *adj*

erode \i-'rōd\ *vb* **1 :** to diminish or destroy by degrees: **a :** to eat into or away by slow destruction of substance **:** CORRODE **b :** to wear away by or as if by the action of water, wind, or glacial ice **2 :** to undergo erosion — **erod·i·ble** \-'rōd-ə-bəl\ *adj*

ero·sion \i-'rō-zhən\ *n* **:** the process of eroding **:** the state of being eroded — **ero·sion·al** \-'rōzh-nəl, -'rō-zhən-ᵊl\ *adj*

erot·ic \i-ˈrät-ik\ *adj* : of, relating to, or marked by sexual love or desire — **erot·i·cal·ly** \-i-k(ə-)lē\ *adv* — **erot·i·cism** \-ˈrät-ə-ˌsiz-əm\ *n*

err \ˈe(ə)r, ˈər\ *vi* **1** : to make a mistake **2** : to violate an accepted standard of conduct : do wrong : SIN

er·rand \ˈer-ənd\ *n* : a short trip taken to attend to some business esp. for another; *also* : the object or purpose of such a trip

er·rant \ˈer-ənt\ *adj* **1** : wandering esp. in search of adventure **2 a** : straying outside the proper bounds **b** : deviating from what is true or right — **er·rant·ry** \-ən-trē\ *n*

er·ra·ta \e-ˈrät-ə, -ˈrāt-, -ˈrat-\ *n* : a list of corrigenda

er·rat·ic \ir-ˈat-ik\ *adj* **1** : having no fixed course : WANDERING **2** : marked by lack of consistency or regularity : ECCENTRIC — **er·rat·i·cal·ly** \-ˈat-i-k(ə-)lē\ *adv*

er·ra·tum \e-ˈrät-əm, -ˈrāt-, -ˈrat-\ *n, pl* **-ta** \-ə\ : CORRIGENDUM

er·ro·ne·ous \ir-ˈō-nē-əs\ *adj* : containing or characterized by error : MISTAKEN, INCORRECT — **er·ro·ne·ous·ly** *adv* — **er·ro·ne·ous·ness** *n*

er·ror \ˈer-ər\ *n* **1 a** : deviation from a code of behavior **b** : an act involving an unintentional deviation from truth or accuracy **c** : an act that through ignorance, deficiency, or accident fails to achieve what should be done **d** : a defensive misplay in baseball **2 a** : the quality or state of erring **b** : an instance of false belief **3** : something produced by mistake **4** : the difference between an observed or estimated value and the actual value — **er·ror·less** \-ləs\ *adj*

erst·while \ˈərst-ˌhwīl\ *adv* : in the past : FORMERLY — **erstwhile** *adj*

eruct \i-ˈrəkt\ *vb* : BELCH — **eruc·tate** \i-ˈrək-ˌtāt\ *vb* — **eruc·ta·tion** \i-ˌrək-ˈtā-shən, ˌē-ˌrək-\ *n*

er·u·dite \ˈer-(y)ə-ˌdīt\ *adj* : possessing or displaying erudition : LEARNED — **er·u·dite·ly** *adv*

er·u·di·tion \ˌer-(y)ə-ˈdish-ən\ *n* : extensive knowledge acquired chiefly from books : LEARNING

erupt \i-ˈrəpt\ *vb* **1 a** : to force out or release suddenly and often violently something pent up **b** : to burst forth; *also* : to break through a surface **c** : EXPLODE **2** : to break out (as with a skin eruption)

erup·tion \i-ˈrəp-shən\ *n* **1 a** : an act, process, or instance of erupting **b** : the breaking out of a rash on the skin **2** : a product (as a skin rash) of erupting — **erup·tive** \-ˈrəp-tiv\ *adj*

er·y·sip·e·las \ˌer-ə-ˈsip-(ə-)ləs, ˌir-\ *n* : an acute bacterial disease marked by fever and intense local inflammation of the skin and subcutaneous tissues

es·ca·drille \ˈes-kə-ˌdril, -ˌdrē\ *n* : a unit of a European air command containing usu. six airplanes

es·ca·late \ˈes-kə-ˌlāt\ *vb* : to increase in extent, volume, or scope — **es·ca·la·tion** \ˌes-kə-ˈlā-shən\ *n*

[1]**es·ca·la·tor** \ˈes-kə-ˌlāt-ər\ *n* : a power-driven set of stairs arranged like an endless belt that ascend or descend continuously

[2]**escalator** *adj* : providing for a periodic proportional upward or downward adjustment (as of prices or wages)

es·ca·pade \ˈes-kə-ˌpād\ *n* : a mischievous adventure : PRANK

[1]**es·cape** \is-ˈkāp\ *vb* **1 a** : to get away (as by flight) **b** : to issue from confinement **c** : to run wild from cultivation **2** : to get out of the way of : AVOID **3** : to fail to be noticed or recallable by **4** : to come out from or be uttered by involuntarily — **es·cap·er** *n*

[2]**escape** *n* **1** : an act or instance of escaping **2** : a means of escaping **3** : a cultivated plant run wild

es·cap·ee \(ˌ)es-ˌkā-ˈpē, is-ˌkā-\ *n* : one that has escaped; *esp* : an escaped prisoner

es·cap·ism \is-ˈkā-ˌpiz-əm\ *n* : habitual diversion of the mind to purely imaginative activity or entertainment in order to escape from reality or routine — **es·cap·ist** \-pəst\ *adj or n*

es·carp·ment \is-ˈkärp-mənt\ *n* **1** : a steep slope in front of a fortification **2** : a long cliff

[1]**es·cheat** \is-ˈchēt\ *n* : the reversion of property to the state when there are no persons (as heirs) legally entitled to hold it; *also* : the property that reverts

[2]**escheat** *vb* : to revert or cause to revert by escheat

es·chew \is-ˈchü\ *vt* : SHUN, AVOID

[1]**es·cort** \ˈes-ˌkȯrt\ *n* **1 a** : a person or group of persons accompanying another to give protection or show courtesy **b** : the man who goes on a date with a woman **c** : a protective screen of warships or fighter planes used to fend off enemy attack from one or more vulnerable craft **2** : accompaniment by a person or an armed protector (as a ship)

[2]**es·cort** \is-ˈkȯrt, es-ˈ, ˈes-ˌ\ *vt* : to accompany as an escort

es·cu·lent \ˈes-kyə-lənt\ *adj* : EDIBLE — **esculent** *n*

es·cutch·eon \is-ˈkəch-ən\ *n* : the usu. shield-shaped surface on which a coat of arms is shown

esoph·a·gus \i-ˈsäf-ə-gəs\ *n, pl* **-gi** \-ˌgī, -ˌjī\ : a muscular tube that leads from the pharynx to the stomach — **esoph·a·ge·al** \i-ˌsäf-ə-ˈjē-əl\ *adj*

es·o·ter·ic \ˌes-ə-ˈter-ik\ *adj* **1** : designed for, limited to, or understood by the specially initiated alone **2** : of or relating to knowledge that is restricted to a small group : RECONDITE — **es·o·ter·i·cal·ly** \-ˈter-i-k(ə-)lē\ *adv*

es·pal·ier \is-ˈpal-yər\ *n* : a plant (as a fruit tree) trained to grow flat against a support (as a wall or trellis) — **espalier** *vt*

es·pe·cial \is-ˈpesh-əl\ *adj* : SPECIAL, PARTICULAR — **es·pe·cial·ly** \-ˈpesh-(ə-)lē\ *adv*

es·pi·al \is-ˈpī(-ə)l\ *n* **1** : OBSERVATION **2** : an act of noticing : DISCOVERY

es·pi·o·nage \ˈes-pē-ə-ˌnäzh, -nij, -ˌnäj\ *n* : the practice of spying or the use of spies esp. to obtain information about the plans and activities of a foreign government

es·pla·nade \ˈes-plə-ˌnäd, -ˌnād\ *n* : a level open stretch or area; *esp* : one designed for walking or driving along a shore

es·pous·al \is-ˈpau̇-zəl\ *n* **1 a** : BETROTHAL **b** : WEDDING **c** : MARRIAGE **2** : a taking up of a cause or belief as a supporter

es·pouse \is-ˈpau̇z\ *vt* **1** : MARRY **2** : to take up the cause of : SUPPORT — **es·pous·er** *n*

es·prit \is-ˈprē\ *n* : vivacious cleverness or wit

es·prit de corps \is-ˌprēd-ə-ˈkō(ə)r\ *n* : the common spirit existing in the members of a group and inspiring enthusiasm, devotion, and strong regard for the honor of the group

es·py \is-ˈpī\ *vt* **es·pied** \-ˈpīd\; **es·py·ing** : to catch sight of

es·quire \ˈes-ˌkwī(ə)r, is-ˈ\ *n* **1** : a member of the English gentry ranking immediately below a knight **2** : a candidate for knighthood serving as attendant to a knight **3** — used as a title of courtesy usu. placed in its abbreviated form after the surname

[1]**es·say** \ˈes-ˌā, *in sense 1 also* e-ˈsā\ *n* **1** : ATTEMPT; *esp* : an initial tentative effort **2** : an analytic or interpretative literary composition usu. dealing with its subject from a limited or personal point of view

[2]**es·say** \e-ˈsā, ˈes-ˌā\ *vt* : to make an effort to perform

es·say·ist \ˈes-ˌā-əst\ *n* : a writer of essays

es·sence \ˈes-ᵊn(t)s\ *n* **1** : the basic nature of a thing : the quality or sum of qualities that make a thing what it is **2** : a substance distilled or otherwise extracted from another substance (as a plant or drug) and having the special qualities of the original substance **3** : PERFUME, SCENT

[1]**es·sen·tial** \i-ˈsen-chəl\ *adj* **1** : forming or belonging to the fundamental nature of a thing **2** : containing or having the character of a volatile essence **3** : important in the highest degree : NECESSARY — **es·sen·ti·al·i·ty** \-ˌsen-chē-ˈal-ət-ē\ *n* — **es·sen·tial·ly** \-ˈsench-(ə-)lē\ *adv* — **es·sen·tial·ness** *n*

[2]**essential** *n* : something basic, necessary, or indispensable

es·tab·lish \is-ˈtab-lish\ *vb* **1** : to make firm or stable **2** : to enact permanently **3 a** : to bring into existence : FOUND **b** : to bring about : EFFECT **4 a** : to set on a firm basis **b** : to put into a favorable position **c** : to gain full recognition or acceptance of **5** : to put beyond doubt : PROVE **6** : to become naturalized — **es·tab·lish·er** *n*

es·tab·lish·ment \is-'tab-lish-mənt\ *n* **1 a** : the act of establishing : the state or fact of being established **b** : the granting of a favorable or privileged position **2** : something (as an organized force for carrying on public or private affairs) that is established **3** : a settled place for residence or business; *also* : such a place with its grounds, buildings, furnishings, and employees **4** : an established order of society; *also* : the social, economic, and political leaders of such an order **5** : a controlling group

es·tate \is-'tāt\ *n* **1** : STATE, CONDITION **2** : social standing or rank esp. of a high order **3** : a social or political class; *esp* : one of the great classes (as the nobility, clergy, and commons) formerly vested with distinct political powers **4 a** : the nature and extent of one's interest in property (as land) **b** : POSSESSIONS, PROPERTY; *esp* : a person's property in land and tenements **c** : the assets and liabilities left by a person at death **5** : a landed property usu. with a large house on it

[1]**es·teem** \is-'tēm\ *n* : high regard

[2]**esteem** *vt* **1 a** : REGARD, CONSIDER **b** : THINK, BELIEVE **2** : to set a high value on : PRIZE

es·ter \'es-tər\ *n* : an organic compound formed by the reaction between an acid and an alcohol

es·ti·ma·ble \'es-tə-mə-bəl\ *adj* : worthy of esteem

[1]**es·ti·mate** \'es-tə-ˌmāt\ *vt* **1** : to judge or determine tentatively or approximately the value, size, or cost of **2** : to form an opinion of : JUDGE, CONCLUDE — **es·ti·ma·tor** \-ˌmāt-ər\ *n*

[2]**es·ti·mate** \'es-tə-mət\ *n* **1** : the act of appraising or valuing : CALCULATION **2** : an opinion or judgment of the nature, character, or quality of a thing **3** : a rough or approximate calculation **4** : a statement of the cost of a job

es·ti·ma·tion \ˌes-tə-'mā-shən\ *n* **1** : JUDGMENT, OPINION **2 a** : the act of estimating **b** : ESTIMATE **3** : ESTEEM, HONOR

es·trange \is-'trānj\ *vt* **1** : to remove from customary environment or associations **2** : to destroy the affection of : ALIENATE — **es·trange·ment** *n*

es·tro·gen \'es-trə-jən\ *n* : a substance (as a hormone) that promotes development of various female characteristics — **es·tro·gen·ic** \ˌes-trə-'jen-ik\ *adj* — **es·tro·gen·i·cal·ly** \-'jen-i-k(ə-)lē\ *adv*

es·tu·ary \'es-chə-ˌwer-ē\ *n, pl* **-ar·ies** : a water passage where the tide meets a river current; *esp* : an arm of the sea at the lower end of a river

et cet·era \et-'set-ə-rə, -'se-trə\ : and others esp. of the same kind : and so forth

etch \'ech\ *vt* **1** : to produce esp. on metal or glass by the corrosive action of an acid; *also* : to subject to such etching **2** : to impress sharply or clearly — **etch·er** *n*

etch·ing \'ech-iŋ\ *n* **1** : the art of producing pictures or designs by printing from an etched metal plate **2** : an impression from an etched plate

eter·nal \i-'tərn-ᵊl\ *adj* **1** : having no beginning and no end : lasting forever **2** : continuing without interruption : UNCEASING — **eter·nal·ly** *adv*

eter·ni·ty \i-'tər-nət-ē\ *n, pl* **-ties** **1** : the quality or state of being eternal **2** : infinite time **3** *pl* : AGES **4** : the state after death : IMMORTALITY **5** : a seemingly endless time

ether \'ē-thər\ *n* **1** : the upper regions of space : HEAVENS **2** : a medium formerly held to permeate all space and transmit transverse waves (as light) **3** : a light volatile flammable liquid obtained by the distillation of alcohol with sulfuric acid and used chiefly as a solvent esp. of fats and as an anesthetic

ethe·re·al \i-'thir-ē-əl\ *adj* **1** : HEAVENLY **2** : being light and airy : DELICATE — **ethe·re·al·i·ty** \i-ˌthir-ē-'al-ət-ē\ *n* — **ethe·re·al·ly** \-'thir-ē-ə-lē\ *adv*

eth·i·cal \'eth-i-kəl\ *or* **eth·ic** \-ik\ *adj* **1** : of or relating to ethics **2** : conforming to accepted and esp. professional standards of conduct **3** : sold only on a doctor's prescription — **eth·i·cal·ly** \'eth-i-k(ə-)lē\ *adv*

eth·ics \'eth-iks\ *n sing or pl* **1** : a branch of philosophy dealing with what is good and bad and with moral duty and obligation **2** : the principles of moral conduct governing an individual or a group

eth·nic \'eth-nik\ *adj* : of or relating to races or large groups of people classed according to common traits and customs — **eth·ni·cal·ly** \-ni-k(ə-)lē\ *adv*

eth·nol·o·gy \eth-'näl-ə-jē\ *n* **1** : a science that deals with the division of mankind into races and their origin, distribution, relations, and characteristics **2** : cultural anthropology — **eth·no·log·ic** \ˌeth-nə-'läj-ik\ *or* **eth·no·log·i·cal** \-'läj-i-kəl\ *adj* — **eth·no·log·i·cal·ly** \-i-k(ə-)lē\ *adv* — **eth·nol·o·gist** \eth-'näl-ə-jəst\ *n*

eth·yl \'eth-əl\ *n* : a chemical radical consisting of carbon and hydrogen

eti·ol·o·gy \ˌēt-ē-'äl-ə-jē\ *n* : the cause or origin esp. of a disease — **eti·o·log·ic** \ˌēt-ē-ə-'läj-ik\ *or* **eti·o·log·i·cal** \-'läj-i-kəl\ *adj* — **eti·o·log·i·cal·ly** \-i-k(ə-)lē\ *adv*

et·i·quette \'et-i-kət, -ˌket\ *n* : the body of rules governing the way in which people behave in social or official life or the way in which a ceremony is conducted

étude \'ā-ˌt(y)üd\ *n* **1** : a piece of music for the practice of a point of technique **2** : a composition built on a technical motive but played for its artistic value

et·y·mol·o·gy \ˌet-ə-'mäl-ə-jē\ *n, pl* **-gies** **1** : the history of a word as shown esp. by tracing its transmission from one language to another, by analyzing it into its component parts, by identifying its cognates in other languages, or by tracing it and its cognates to a common ancestral form in an ancestral language **2** : a branch of language study concerned with etymologies — **et·y·mo·log·i·cal** \-mə-'läj-i-kəl\ *adj* — **et·y·mo·log·i·cal·ly** \-'läj-i-k(ə-)lē\ *adv* — **et·y·mol·o·gist** \ˌet-ə-'mäl-ə-jəst\ *n*

eu·ca·lyp·tus \ˌyü-kə-'lip-təs\ *n, pl* **-ti** \-ˌtī, -ˌtē\ *or* **-tus·es** : any of a genus of mostly Australian evergreen trees of the myrtle family including many that are widely cultivated for their gums, resins, oils, and useful woods

Eu·cha·rist \'yü-k(ə-)rəst\ *n* : COMMUNION 2a; *esp* : a Roman Catholic sacrament renewing Christ's propitiatory sacrifice of his body and blood — **eu·cha·ris·tic** \ˌyü-kə-'ris-tik\ *adj, often cap*

eu·chre \'yü-kər\ *n* : a card game in which each player is dealt five cards and the player making trump must take three tricks to win a hand

eu·gen·ic \yu̇-'jen-ik\ *adj* **1** : relating to or fitted for the production of good offspring **2** : of or relating to eugenics — **eu·gen·i·cal·ly** \-'jen-i-k(ə-)lē\ *adv*

eu·gen·ics \yu̇-'jen-iks\ *n* : a science that deals with the improvement (as by control of human mating) of hereditary qualities of a race or breed — **eu·gen·ist** \yu̇-'jen-əst, 'yü-jə-nəst\ *n*

eu·lo·gize \'yü-lə-ˌjīz\ *vt* : to speak or write in high praise of : EXTOL — **eu·lo·gist** \-jəst\ *n* — **eu·lo·gis·tic** \ˌyü-lə-'jis-tik\ *adj* — **eu·lo·gis·ti·cal·ly** \-ti-k(ə-)lē\ *adv*

eu·lo·gy \'yü-lə-jē\ *n, pl* **-gies** **1** : a speech or a writing in praise of a person or thing; *esp* : a formal speech in praise of a dead person **2** : high praise

eu·nuch \'yü-nək\ *n* : a castrated man; *esp* : one placed in charge of a harem or employed as a chamberlain in a palace

eu·phe·mism \'yü-fə-ˌmiz-əm\ *n* : the substitution of an agreeable or inoffensive expression for one that may offend or suggest something unpleasant; *also* : the expression so substituted — **eu·phe·mis·tic** \ˌyü-fə-'mis-tik\ *adj* — **eu·phe·mis·ti·cal·ly** \-ti-k(ə-)lē\ *adv*

eu·pho·ni·ous \yu̇-ˈfō-nē-əs\ *adj* : pleasing to the ear : smooth-sounding — **eu·pho·ni·ous·ly** *adv* — **eu·pho·ni·ous·ness** *n*
eu·pho·ny \ˈyü-fə-nē\ *n, pl* **-nies** : pleasing or sweet sound; *esp* : the effect of words so combined as to please the ear — **eu·phon·ic** \yu̇-ˈfän-ik\ *adj*
eu·pho·ria \yu̇-ˈfōr-ē-ə\ *n* : an often unaccountable feeling of well-being or elation — **eu·phor·ic** \-ˈfȯr-ik, -ˈfär-\ *adj*
Eur·asian \yu̇-ˈrā-zhən, -shən\ *adj* : of or relating to Europe and Asia
eu·re·ka \yu̇-ˈrē-kə\ *interj* — used to express triumph on a discovery
eu·ro·pi·um \yu̇-ˈrō-pē-əm\ *n* : a metallic chemical element found in a sand
eu·tha·na·sia \ˌyü-thə-ˈnā-zh(ē-)ə\ *n* : the act or practice of killing (as an incurable invalid) for reasons of mercy — **eu·tha·na·sic** \-zik, -sik\ *adj*
eu·then·ics \yu̇-ˈthen-iks\ *n* : a science that deals with human improvement by control and improvement of environment — **eu·then·ic** \-ik\ *adj* — **eu·then·ist** \yu̇-ˈthen-əst, ˈyü-thə-nəst\ *n*
evac·u·ate \i-ˈvak-yə-ˌwāt\ *vb* **1** : to make empty **2** : to discharge waste matter from the body : VOID **3** : to remove something from esp. by pumping **4 a** : to remove or withdraw from a military or occupation zone or from a dangerous area **b** : VACATE — **evac·u·a·tion** \i-ˌvak-yə-ˈwā-shən\ *n* — **evac·u·a·tive** \i-ˈvak-yə-ˌwāt-iv\ *adj*
evac·u·ee \i-ˌvak-yə-ˈwē\ *n* : an evacuated person
evade \i-ˈvād\ *vb* **1** : to get away or avoid by skill or trickery **2** : to avoid facing up to **3** : BAFFLE, FOIL — **evad·a·ble** *adj* — **evad·er** *n*
eval·u·ate \i-ˈval-yə-ˌwāt\ *vt* **1** : to determine or fix the value of **2** : to examine and judge the quality or degree of — **eval·u·a·tion** \-ˌval-yə-ˈwā-shən\ *n* — **eval·u·a·tive** \-ˈval-yə-ˌwāt-iv\ *adj*
ev·a·nesce \ˌev-ə-ˈnes\ *vi* : to dissipate like vapor
ev·a·nes·cence \ˌev-ə-ˈnes-ᵊn(t)s\ *n* **1** : the process or fact of evanescing **2** : evanescent quality
ev·a·nes·cent \-ᵊnt\ *adj* : tending to vanish like vapor : not lasting : quickly passing
evan·gel \i-ˈvan-jəl\ *n* : GOSPEL
evan·gel·i·cal \ˌē-ˌvan-ˈjel-i-kəl, ˌev-ən-\ *adj* **1** : of, relating to, or in agreement with the Christian gospel esp. as it is presented in the four Gospels **2** : PROTESTANT **3** : emphasizing salvation by faith in the atoning death of Jesus Christ through personal conversion, the authority of Scripture, and the importance of preaching as contrasted with ritual **4** *often cap* : FUNDAMENTALIST **5** : EVANGELISTIC, ZEALOUS — **Evan·gel·i·cal·ism** \-i-kə-ˌliz-əm\ *n* — **evan·gel·i·cal·ly** \-i-k(ə-)lē\ *adv*
Evangelical *n* : one holding evangelical principles or belonging to an evangelical party or church
evan·ge·lism \i-ˈvan-jə-ˌliz-əm\ *n* **1** : the winning or revival of personal commitments to Christ **2** : militant or crusading zeal — **evan·ge·lis·tic** \i-ˌvan-jə-ˈlis-tik\ *adj* — **evan·ge·lis·ti·cal·ly** \-ti-k(ə-)lē\ *adv*
evan·ge·list \i-ˈvan-jə-ləst\ *n* **1** *often cap* : a writer of any of the four Gospels **2** : one who evangelizes; *esp* : a Protestant minister or layman who preaches at services of evangelism
evan·ge·lize \i-ˈvan-jə-ˌlīz\ *vb* **1** : to preach the gospel **2** : to convert to Christianity — **evan·ge·li·za·tion** \-ˌvan-jə-lə-ˈzā-shən\ *n*
evap·o·rate \i-ˈvap-ə-ˌrāt\ *vb* **1** : to change into vapor; *also* : to pass off or cause to pass off in usu. invisible minute particles **2 a** : to pass off or away : DISAPPEAR **b** : to diminish quickly **3** : to expel moisture from (as by heat) — **evap·o·ra·tion** \-ˌvap-ə-ˈrā-shən\ *n* — **evap·o·ra·tive** \-ˈvap-ə-ˌrāt-iv\ *adj* — **evap·o·ra·tor** \-ˌrāt-ər\ *n*
eva·sion \i-ˈvā-zhən\ *n* **1** : the act or an instance of evading : ESCAPE **2** : a means of evading
eva·sive \i-ˈvā-siv\ *adj* : marked by a tendency or purpose to evade : EQUIVOCAL — **eva·sive·ly** *adv* — **eva·sive·ness** *n*
eve \ˈēv\ *n* **1** : EVENING **2** : the evening or the day before a special day **3** : the period immediately preceding an event
¹even \ˈē-vən\ *adj* **1 a** : having a horizontal surface : FLAT **b** : being without break or irregularity : SMOOTH **c** : being in the same plane or line **2** : being without variation : UNIFORM **3 a** : EQUAL, FAIR **b** : SQUARE, QUITS **c** : BALANCED; *esp* : showing neither profit nor loss **4** : being exactly divisible by two **5** : EXACT, PRECISE — **even·ly** *adv* — **even·ness** *n*
²even *adv* **1 a** : PRECISELY, EXACTLY **b** : at the very same time **2 a** — used as an intensive to indicate something unexpected **b** — used as an intensive to stress the comparative degree
³even *vb* **evened; even·ing** \ˈēv-(ə-)niŋ\ : to make or become even — **even·er** \ˈēv-(ə-)nər\ *n*
even·hand·ed \ˌē-vən-ˈhan-dəd\ *adj* : FAIR, IMPARTIAL
eve·ning \ˈēv-niŋ\ *n* **1** : the latter part and close of the day and early part of the night **2** : the latter part
evening dress *n* : conventional dress for formal or semiformal evening social occasions
even·song \ˈē-vən-ˌsȯŋ\ *n, often cap* **1** : VESPERS **2** : evening prayer esp. when sung
event \i-ˈvent\ *n* **1 a** : something that happens : OCCURRENCE **b** : a noteworthy happening **c** : a social occasion or activity **2 a** : OUTCOME, RESULT **b** : CONTINGENCY, EVENTUALITY **3** : any of the contests in a program of sports — **at all events** : in any case — **in any event** : in any case
event·ful \-fəl\ *adj* **1** : full of or rich in events **2** : MOMENTOUS — **event·ful·ly** \-fə-lē\ *adv* — **event·ful·ness** *n*
even·tide \ˈē-vən-ˌtīd\ *n* : EVENING
even·tu·al \i-ˈvench-(ə-)wəl, -ˈven-chəl\ *adj* : taking place at an unspecified later time : ULTIMATE — **even·tu·al·ly** \-ē\ *adv*
even·tu·al·i·ty \i-ˌven-chə-ˈwal-ət-ē\ *n, pl* **-ties** : a possible outcome : POSSIBILITY
even·tu·ate \i-ˈven-chə-ˌwāt\ *vi* : to come out finally
ev·er \ˈev-ər\ *adv* **1** : ALWAYS **2 a** : at any time **b** : in any way **3** — used as an intensive esp. with *so*
ev·er·bloom·ing \ˌev-ər-ˈblü-miŋ\ *adj* : blooming more or less continuously throughout the growing season
ev·er·glade \ˈev-ər-ˌglād\ *n* : a low-lying tract of swampy or marshy land
¹ev·er·green \ˈev-ər-ˌgrēn\ *adj* : having foliage that remains green and functional through more than one growing season
²evergreen *n* **1** : an evergreen plant; *also* : CONIFER **2** *pl* : twigs and branches of evergreen plants used for decoration
¹ev·er·last·ing \ˌev-ər-ˈlas-tiŋ\ *adj* **1** : lasting or enduring through all time : ETERNAL **2 a** (1) : continuing long or indefinitely : PERPETUAL (2) : retaining form or color when dried **b** : TEDIOUS **3** : wearing indefinitely : DURABLE — **ev·er·last·ing·ly** *adv* — **ev·er·last·ing·ness** *n*
²everlasting *n* **1** *cap* : ²GOD — used with *the* **2** : ETERNITY **3** : a plant esp. of the daisy family with everlasting flowers; *also* : its flower
ev·er·more \ˌev-ər-ˈmō(ə)r\ *adv* : ALWAYS, FOREVER
ev·ery \ˈev-rē\ *adj* **1** : being each individual or part of a group without exception **2** : COMPLETE, ENTIRE
ev·ery·body \ˈev-ri-ˌbäd-ē\ *pron* : every person
ev·ery·day \ˈev-rē-ˌdā\ *adj* : encountered or used routinely or typically : ORDINARY
ev·ery·one \-(ˌ)wən\ *pron* : EVERYBODY
ev·ery·thing \ˈev-rē-ˌthiŋ\ *pron* **1 a** : all that exists **b** : all that relates to the subject **2** : a most important or excellent thing
ev·ery·where \-ˌhwe(ə)r\ *adv* : in every place or part
evict \i-ˈvikt\ *vt* : to put (a person) out from property by legal process — **evic·tion** \-ˈvik-shən\ *n* — **evic·tor** \-ˈvik-tər\ *n*
¹ev·i·dence \ˈev-əd-ən(t)s, -ə-ˌden(t)s\ *n* **1 a** : an outward sign : INDICATION **b** : something that furnishes proof : TESTI-

MONY; *esp* : material legally submitted to a tribunal to ascertain the truth of a matter **2** : one who bears witness; *esp* : one who voluntarily confesses a crime and testifies for the prosecution against his accomplices — **ev·i·den·tial** \ˌev-ə-'den-chəl\ *adj* — **in evidence** : to be seen : CONSPICUOUS

²evidence *vt* : to serve as or offer evidence of

ev·i·dent \'ev-əd-ənt, -ə-ˌdent\ *adj* : clear to the sight and to the mind : PLAIN — **ev·i·dent·ly** *adv*

¹evil \'ē-vəl\ *adj* **1 a** : not good morally : WICKED **b** : arising from bad character or conduct **2 a** : causing discomfort or repulsion : OFFENSIVE **b** : DISAGREEABLE **3 a** : causing harm : PERNICIOUS **b** : marked by misfortune : UNLUCKY — **evil·ly** \-və(l)-lē\ *adv*

²evil *n* **1** : something that brings sorrow, distress, or calamity **2** : the fact of suffering, misfortune, and wrongdoing — **evil·do·er** \ˌē-vəl-'dü-ər\ *n* — **evil·do·ing** \-'dü-iŋ\ *n*

evil eye *n* : an eye or glance held to be capable of inflicting harm

evil–mind·ed \ˌē-vəl-'mīn-dəd\ *adj* : having an evil disposition or evil thoughts

evince \i-'vin(t)s\ *vt* **1** : to constitute evidence of : SHOW **2** : to display clearly : REVEAL — **evinc·i·ble** \i-'vin(t)-sə-bəl\ *adj*

evis·cer·ate \i-'vis-ə-ˌrāt\ *vt* **1** : to take out the entrails of **2** : to deprive of vital content or force — **evis·cer·a·tion** \i-ˌvis-ə-'rā-shən\ *n*

evo·ca·tion \ˌē-vō-'kā-shən, ˌev-ə-\ *n* : the act or fact of evoking : SUMMONING

evoke \i-'vōk\ *vt* **1 a** : to call forth or up : SUMMON **b** : INVOKE **2** : ELICIT **3** : to re-create imaginatively — **ev·o·ca·ble** \'ev-ə-kə-bəl, i-'vō-kə-\ *adj* — **evoc·a·tive** \i-'väk-ət-iv\ *adj* — **evoc·a·tive·ly** *adv*

ev·o·lu·tion \ˌev-ə-'lü-shən\ *n* **1 a** : a process of change esp. from a lower to a higher state : GROWTH **b** : something evolved **2** : one of a set of prescribed movements **3** : the process of working out or developing **4 a** : the process by which through a series of changes or steps a living organism has acquired its distinguishing characters **b** : a theory that the various types of animals and plants have their origin in other preexisting types and that the distinguishable differences are due to modifications in successive generations — **ev·o·lu·tion·ary** \-shə-ˌner-ē\ *adj* — **ev·o·lu·tion·ism** \-shə-ˌniz-əm\ *n* — **ev·o·lu·tion·ist** \-sh(ə-)nəst\ *n or adj*

evolve \i-'välv\ *vb* **1** : to give off : EMIT **2 a** : DERIVE, EDUCE **b** : to work out : DEVELOP **c** : to produce by natural evolutionary processes **3** : to undergo evolutionary change — **evolve·ment** *n*

ewe \'yü\ *n* : the female of the sheep or a related animal esp. when mature

ew·er \'yü-ər, 'yu̇(-ə)r\ *n* : a vase-shaped pitcher or jug

ex \(ˌ)eks\ *prep* **1** : out of : FROM **2** : from a specified dam

ex·ac·er·bate \ig-'zas-ər-ˌbāt, ek-'sas-\ *vt* : to make more violent, bitter, or severe — **ex·ac·er·ba·tion** \ig-ˌzas-ər-'bā-shən, (ˌ)ek-ˌsas-\ *n*

¹ex·act \ig-'zakt\ *vt* **1** : to demand and compel peremptorily : EXTORT **2** : to call for as necessary, appropriate, or desirable — **ex·act·a·ble** *adj*

²exact *adj* **1** : showing strict, particular, and complete accordance with fact **2** : marked by thorough consideration or minute measurement of small factual details : not incomplete or approximate — **exact·ness** *n*

ex·act·ing \ig-'zak-tiŋ\ *adj* : making many or difficult demands upon a person : TRYING — **ex·act·ing·ly** *adv* — **ex·act·ing·ness** *n*

ex·ac·tion \ig-'zak-shən\ *n* **1 a** : the act or process of exacting **b** : EXTORTION **2** : something exacted; *esp* : something demanded with compelling force

ex·ac·ti·tude \ig-'zak-tə-ˌt(y)üd\ *n* : EXACTNESS

ex·act·ly \ig-'zak-(t)lē\ *adv* **1** : in an exact manner : PRECISELY **2** : quite so : just as you say — used to express agreement

ex·ag·ger·ate \ig-'zaj-ə-ˌrāt\ *vb* **1** : to enlarge a fact or statement beyond what is actual or true : OVERSTATE **2** : to enlarge or increase esp. beyond the normal — **ex·ag·ger·at·ed·ly** \-ˌrāt-əd-lē\ *adv* — **ex·ag·ger·a·tion** \-ˌzaj-ə-'rā-shən\ *n* — **ex·ag·ger·a·tor** \-'zaj-ə-ˌrāt-ər\ *n*

ex·alt \ig-'zȯlt\ *vb* **1** : to raise high : ELEVATE **2** : to raise in rank, power, or character **3** : to elevate by praise or in estimation : GLORIFY — **ex·alt·er** *n*

ex·al·ta·tion \ˌeg-ˌzȯl-'tā-shən\ *n* **1** : the act of exalting : the state of being exalted **2** : a greatly heightened sense of personal well-being, power, or importance

ex·am \ig-'zam\ *n* : EXAMINATION

ex·am·i·na·tion \ig-ˌzam-ə-'nā-shən\ *n* **1** : the act or process of examining : the state of being examined **2** : an exercise designed to examine progress or test qualification or knowledge **3** : a formal interrogation

ex·am·ine \ig-'zam-ən\ *vb* **1 a** : to look at or inspect closely **b** : to inquire into carefully : INVESTIGATE **2** : to test the condition of **3** : to question closely in order to determine progress, fitness, or knowledge — **ex·am·in·er** *n*

ex·am·ple \ig-'zam-pəl\ *n* **1** : a sample of something taken to show what the whole is like **2** : a problem to be solved in order to show how a rule works **3** : something to be imitated : MODEL **4** : punishment inflicted as a warning to others

ex·as·per·ate \ig-'zas-pə-ˌrāt\ *vt* **1** : to make angry : ENRAGE **2** : to cause irritation or annoyance to

ex·as·per·a·tion \ig-ˌzas-pə-'rā-shən\ *n* **1** : the act of exasperating : PROVOCATION **2** : the state of being exasperated : extreme irritation or annoyance : ANGER

ex ca·the·dra \ˌeks-kə-'thē-drə\ *adv* (*or adj*) : by virtue of or in the exercise of one's office

ex·ca·vate \'ek-skə-ˌvāt\ *vt* **1** : to hollow out : form a hole in **2** : to make by hollowing out **3** : to dig out and remove **4** : to uncover by digging away covering earth — **ex·ca·va·tor** \-ˌvāt-ər\ *n*

ex·ca·va·tion \ˌek-skə-'vā-shən\ *n* **1** : the act or process of excavating **2** : a hollowed-out place formed by excavating

ex·ceed \ik-'sēd\ *vb* **1** : to extend outside of **2** : to be greater than or superior to : SURPASS, PREDOMINATE **3** : to go beyond a limit set by

ex·ceed·ing \ik-'sēd-iŋ\ *adj* : exceptional in amount, quality, or degree : EXTRAORDINARY

ex·ceed·ing·ly \-lē\ *or* **ex·ceed·ing** *adv* : EXTREMELY

ex·cel \ik-'sel\ *vb* **ex·celled; ex·cel·ling** : to outdo others (as in good qualities or ability) : be better than others : SURPASS

ex·cel·lence \'ek-s(ə-)lən(t)s\ *n* **1** : the quality of being excellent **2** : an excellent or valuable quality : VIRTUE **3** : EXCELLENCY 2

ex·cel·len·cy \'ek-s(ə-)lən-sē\ *n, pl* **-cies** **1** : EXCELLENCE **2** — used as a title for high dignitaries of state (as a governor or an ambassador) and church (as a Roman Catholic archbishop or bishop)

ex·cel·lent \'ek-s(ə-)lənt\ *adj* : very good of its kind : eminently good : FIRST-CLASS — **ex·cel·lent·ly** *adv*

ex·cel·si·or \ik-'sel-sē-ər\ *n* : fine curled wood shavings used esp. for packing fragile items

¹ex·cept \ik-'sept\ *vt* : to take or leave out from a number or a whole : EXCLUDE

²except *prep* **1** : with the exclusion or exception of **2** : otherwise than : other than

³except *conj* : UNLESS

ex·cep·tion \ik-'sep-shən\ *n* **1** : the act of excepting : EXCLUSION **2** : one that is excepted **3** : something offered as objection or taken as objectionable

ex·cep·tion·a·ble \ik-'sep-sh(ə-)nə-bəl\ *adj* : likely to cause objection : OBJECTIONABLE

ex·cep·tion·al \ik-'sep-shnəl, -shən-ᵊl\ *adj* **1** : forming an exception : RARE 2 : better than average : SUPERIOR — **ex·cep·tion·al·ly** \-ē\ *adv* — **ex·cep·tion·al·ness** *n*

¹ex·cerpt \ek-'sərpt, eg-'zərpt, 'ek-ˌ, 'eg-ˌ\ *vt* : to select for quoting : EXTRACT

²ex·cerpt \'ek-ˌsərpt, 'eg-ˌzərpt\ *n* : a passage selected or copied : EXTRACT

¹ex·cess \ik-'ses, 'ek-ˌ\ *n* **1 a** : a state of surpassing limits : SUPERFLUITY **b** : something that exceeds what is usual, proper, or specified **c** : the amount or degree by which one thing or quantity exceeds another **2** : INTEMPERANCE

²excess *adj* : more than the usual, proper, or specified amount

ex·ces·sive \ik-'ses-iv\ *adj* : exceeding the usual, proper, or normal — **ex·ces·sive·ly** *adv* — **ex·ces·sive·ness** *n*

¹ex·change \iks-'chānj, 'eks-ˌ\ *n* **1** : a giving or taking one thing in return for another : TRADE **2** : the act of substituting one thing for another **3** : something offered, given, or received in an exchange **4 a** : funds payable at a distant point in foreign or domestic currency **b** (1) : interchange of two kinds of money (as money of two different countries) with allowance for difference in value (2) : the amount of one currency that will buy a given amount of another **5** : a place where things or services are exchanged: as **a** : an organized market or center for trading in securities or commodities **b** : a central office in which telephone lines are connected to permit communication

²exchange *vt* **1** : to give in exchange : TRADE, SWAP **2** : to part with for a substitute — **ex·change·a·ble** *adj* — **ex·chang·er** *n*

ex·che·quer \'eks-ˌchek-ər, iks-'\ *n* **1** : the department or office of state in Great Britain and Northern Ireland charged with the receipt and care of the national revenue **2** : TREASURY; *esp* : a national or royal treasury **3** : pecuniary resources : FUNDS

¹ex·cise \'ek-ˌsīz, -ˌsīs\ *n* : an internal tax levied on the manufacture, sale, or consumption of a commodity within a country

²ex·cise \ek-'sīz\ *vt* : to remove by cutting out — **ex·ci·sion** \-'sizh-ən\ *n*

ex·cit·a·ble \ik-'sīt-ə-bəl\ *adj* : readily roused into action or an active state — **ex·cit·a·bil·i·ty** \-ˌsīt-ə-'bil-ət-ē\ *n*

ex·cite \ik-'sīt\ *vt* **1 a** : to call to activity **b** : to rouse to feeling **2** : to kindle the emotions of : STIMULATE

ex·cit·ed \-'sīt-əd\ *adj* : having or showing strong feeling : worked up : STIRRED — **ex·cit·ed·ly** *adv*

ex·cite·ment \ik-'sīt-mənt\ *n* **1** : the act of exciting : the state of being excited **2** : something that excites or rouses

ex·cit·ing \-'sīt-iŋ\ *adj* : causing excitement : STIRRING — **ex·cit·ing·ly** *adv*

ex·claim \iks-'klām\ *vb* **1** : to cry out or speak in strong or sudden emotion **2** : to speak loudly or vehemently

ex·cla·ma·tion \ˌeks-klə-'mā-shən\ *n* **1** : a sharp or sudden utterance : OUTCRY **2** : vehement expression of protest or complaint

exclamation point *n* : a punctuation mark ! used chiefly after an interjection or exclamation to show forceful utterance or strong feeling

ex·clam·a·to·ry \iks-'klam-ə-ˌtōr-ē\ *adj* : containing, expressing, using, or relating to exclamation

ex·clude \iks-'klüd\ *vt* **1 a** : to shut out **b** : to bar from participation, consideration, or inclusion **2** : to put out : EXPEL — **ex·clud·a·ble** *adj* — **ex·clud·er** *n* — **ex·clu·sion** \-'klü-zhən\ *n*

ex·clu·sive \iks-'klü-siv\ *adj* **1** : excluding or inclined to exclude certain persons or classes (as from ownership, membership, or privileges) : catering to a special esp. fashionable class **2** : SOLE, SINGLE **3** : COMPLETE, UNDIVIDED **4** : not taking account : not inclusive — **ex·clu·sive·ly** *adv* — **ex·clu·sive·ness** *n*

ex·com·mu·ni·cate \ˌeks-kə-'myü-nə-ˌkāt\ *vt* : to bar officially from the rights of church membership — **ex·com·mu·ni·ca·tion** \-ˌmyü-nə-'kā-shən\ *n*

ex·co·ri·ate \ek-'skōr-ē-ˌāt\ *vt* : to censure scathingly — **ex·co·ri·a·tion** \(ˌ)ek-ˌskōr-ē-'ā-shən\ *n*

ex·cre·ment \'ek-skrə-mənt\ *n* : waste matter discharged from the body and esp. from the alimentary canal

ex·cres·cence \ek-'skres-ᵊn(t)s\ *n* : OUTGROWTH; *esp* : an abnormal outgrowth (as a wart) on the body

ex·cres·cent \-ᵊnt\ *adj* : being or forming an excrescence — **ex·cres·cent·ly** *adv*

ex·crete \ek-'skrēt\ *vt* : to separate and eliminate (waste) from the blood or tissues or from the active protoplasm usu. in the form of sweat or urine

ex·cre·tion \ek-'skrē-shən\ *n* **1** : the act or process of excreting **2** : excreted matter

ex·cre·to·ry \'ek-skrə-ˌtōr-ē\ *adj* : of, relating to, or functioning in excretion

ex·cru·ci·ate \ik-'skrü-shē-ˌāt\ *vt* : to subject to intense pain or mental distress — **ex·cru·ci·a·tion** \-ˌskrü-s(h)ē-'ā-shən\ *n*

ex·cru·ci·at·ing \-'skrü-shē-ˌāt-iŋ\ *adj* **1** : causing great pain or anguish : AGONIZING **2** : very intense : EXTREME — **ex·cru·ci·at·ing·ly** *adv*

ex·cul·pate \'ek-(ˌ)skəl-ˌpāt, ek-'\ *vt* : to clear from alleged fault or guilt — **ex·cul·pa·tion** \ˌek-(ˌ)skəl-'pā-shən\ *n* — **ex·cul·pa·to·ry** \ek-'skəl-pə-ˌtōr-ē\ *adj*

ex·cur·sion \ik-'skər-zhən\ *n* **1 a** : a going out or forth : EXPEDITION **b** : a usu. brief pleasure trip; *esp* : such a trip at special reduced rates **2** : deviation from a direct or proper course; *esp* : DIGRESSION **3** : a movement outward or from a mean position or axis; *also* : the distance traversed : AMPLITUDE

ex·cur·sion·ist \ik-'skərzh-(ə-)nəst\ *n* : a person who goes on an excursion

ex·cur·sive \ik-'skər-siv\ *adj* : constituting a digression : characterized by digression — **ex·cur·sive·ly** *adv* — **ex·cur·sive·ness** *n*

¹ex·cuse \ik-'skyüz\ *vt* **1** : to make apology for : try to remove blame from **2** : to accept an excuse for : PARDON **3** : to free or let off from doing something **4** : to serve as an acceptable reason or explanation for (something said or done) : JUSTIFY — **ex·cus·a·ble** *adj* — **ex·cus·a·bly** \-'skyü-zə-blē\ *adv* — **ex·cus·er** *n*

²ex·cuse \ik-'skyüs\ *n* **1** : the act of excusing **2 a** : something offered as grounds for being excused **b** : a note of explanation of an absence **3** : JUSTIFICATION, REASON

ex·ec \ig-'zek\ *n* : EXECUTIVE OFFICER

ex·e·cra·ble \'ek-si-krə-bəl\ *adj* : DETESTABLE, ABOMINABLE — **ex·e·cra·ble·ness** *n* — **ex·e·cra·bly** \-blē\ *adv*

ex·e·crate \'ek-sə-ˌkrāt\ *vt* **1** : to declare to be evil or detestable : DENOUNCE **2** : to detest utterly : ABHOR — **ex·e·cra·tion** \ˌek-sə-'krā-shən\ *n* — **ex·e·cra·tor** \'ek-sə-ˌkrāt-ər\ *n*

ex·e·cute \'ek-sə-ˌkyüt\ *vt* **1** : to put into effect : carry out : PERFORM **2** : to do what is provided or required by **3** : to put to death in compliance with a legal sentence **4** : to make or produce esp. by carrying out a design **5** : to perform what is required to give validity to — **ex·e·cut·er** *n*

ex·e·cu·tion \ˌek-sə-'kyü-shən\ *n* **1** : the act or process of executing : PERFORMANCE **2** : a putting to death as a legal penalty **3** : the act or mode or result of performance in something requiring special skill or technique **4** : effective and esp. destructive action

ex·e·cu·tion·er \-'kyü-sh(ə-)nər\ *n* : one that executes; *esp* : one who puts into effect a sentence of death

¹ex·ec·u·tive \ig-'zek-(y)ət-iv\ *adj* **1** : designed for or relating to the execution of affairs **2** : of or relating to the execution of the laws and the conduct of public affairs **3** : of or relating to an executive

²executive *n* **1** : the executive branch of a government **2** : an individual or group constituting the agency that directs an organization **3 :** one who holds a position of administrative or managerial responsibility

executive officer *n* **:** the officer second in command of a military or naval organization

ex·ec·u·tor \ig-ˈzek-(y)ət-ər, *in sense 1 also* ˈek-sə-ˌkyüt-\ *n* **1 :** one who executes something **2 :** the person designated in a will as the one to carry out its provisions

ex·ec·u·trix \ig-ˈzek-(y)ə-(ˌ)triks\ *n, pl* **ex·ec·u·trix·es** *or* **ex·ec·u·tri·ces** \-ˌzek-(y)ə-ˈtrī-ˌsēz\ **:** a female executor

ex·e·ge·sis \ˌek-sə-ˈjē-səs\ *n, pl* **-ge·ses** \-ˈjē-ˌsēz\ **:** explanation or critical interpretation of a text — **ex·e·get·ic** \-ˈjet-ik\ *or* **ex·e·get·i·cal** \-ˈjet-i-kəl\ *adj* — **ex·e·get·i·cal·ly** \-i-k(ə-)lē\ *adv*

ex·em·plar \ig-ˈzem-ˌplär, -plər\ *n* **1 a :** one that serves as a model or pattern; *esp* **:** an ideal model **b :** ARCHETYPE **2 :** a typical instance **:** EXAMPLE; *esp* **:** a typical or standard specimen

ex·em·pla·ry \ig-ˈzem-plə-rē\ *adj* **1 a :** serving as a pattern **b :** deserving imitation **:** COMMENDABLE **2 :** serving as a warning **3 :** serving as an example, instance, or illustration — **ex·em·plar·i·ly** \ˌeg-ˌzəm-ˈpler-ə-lē\ *adv* — **ex·em·pla·ri·ness** \ig-ˈzem-plə-rē-nəs\ *n*

ex·em·pli·fy \ig-ˈzem-plə-ˌfī\ *vt* **-fied; -fy·ing 1 :** to show or illustrate by example **2 :** to serve as an example of — **ex·em·pli·fi·ca·tion** \-ˌzem-plə-fə-ˈkā-shən\ *n*

¹ex·empt \ig-ˈzem(p)t\ *adj* **:** free or released from an obligation or requirement to which others are subject

²exempt *vt* **:** to make exempt **:** free from a requirement to which others are subject **:** EXCUSE

ex·emp·tion \ig-ˈzem(p)-shən\ *n* **1 :** the act of exempting **:** the state of being exempt **:** IMMUNITY **2 :** one that exempts or is exempted; *esp* **:** a source of income exempted from taxation

¹ex·er·cise \ˈek-sər-ˌsīz\ *n* **1 :** the act of bringing into play or realizing in action **:** USE **2 a :** regular or repeated use of a faculty or bodily organ **b :** bodily exertion for the sake of physical fitness **3 :** something performed or practiced in order to develop, improve, or display a specific power or skill **4 a :** a maneuver or drill carried out for training and discipline **b** *pl* **:** a program including speeches, announcements of awards and honors, and various traditional practices

²exercise *vb* **1 :** to bring to bear **:** EXERT **2 a :** to use repeatedly in order to strengthen or develop **b :** to train (as troops) by drills and maneuvers **c :** to put through exercises **:** give exercise to **3 :** to engage the attention of; *esp* **:** to cause anxiety, alarm, or indignation in **4 :** to take exercise — **ex·er·cis·a·ble** *adj* — **ex·er·cis·er** *n*

ex·ert \ig-ˈzərt\ *vt* **1 :** to put forth (as strength, force, power, or influence) **:** bring into play **2 :** to put (oneself) into action or to tiring effort

ex·er·tion \ig-ˈzər-shən\ *n* **:** the act or an instance of exerting; *esp* **:** laborious or perceptible effort

ex·e·unt \ˈek-sē-(ˌ)ənt\ — used as a stage direction to specify that all or certain named characters leave the stage

ex·ha·la·tion \ˌeks-(h)ə-ˈlā-shən\ *n* **:** an act or product of exhaling

ex·hale \eks-ˈhāl\ *vb* **1 :** to breathe out **2 :** to send forth (as gas or odor) **:** EMIT **3 :** to rise or be given off as vapor

¹ex·haust \ig-ˈzȯst\ *vb* **1 a :** to draw off or let out completely **b :** to empty by drawing something from; *esp* **:** to create a vacuum in **2 a :** to use up the whole supply of **b :** to deprive wholly of (as strength, patience, or resources) **3 a :** to develop (a subject) completely **b :** to try out the whole number of **4 :** to destroy the fertility of (soil) **5 :** to pass or flow out **:** DISCHARGE, EMPTY — **ex·haust·er** *n* — **ex·haust·i·bil·i·ty** \-ˌzȯ-stə-ˈbil-ət-ē\ *n* — **ex·haust·i·ble** \-ˈzȯ-stə-bəl\ *adj*

²exhaust *n* **1 a :** the escape of used steam or gas from an engine **b :** the gas thus escaping **2 a :** a conduit through which used gases escape **b :** an arrangement for withdrawing fumes, dusts, or odors from an enclosure

ex·haus·tion \ig-ˈzȯs-chən\ *n* **1 :** the act or process of exhausting **2 :** the state of being exhausted; *esp* **:** extreme weariness or fatigue

ex·haus·tive \ig-ˈzȯ-stiv\ *adj* **1 :** serving or tending to exhaust **2 :** testing all possibilities or considering all elements **:** THOROUGH, COMPLETE — **ex·haus·tive·ly** *adv* — **ex·haus·tive·ness** *n*

ex·haust·less \ig-ˈzȯst-ləs\ *adj* **:** INEXHAUSTIBLE

¹ex·hib·it \ig-ˈzib-ət\ *vt* **1 :** to show outwardly **:** REVEAL **2 :** to put on display **3 :** to present in legal form (as to a court) — **ex·hib·i·tor** \-ət-ər\ *n*

²exhibit *n* **1 :** an act or instance of exhibiting **2 :** something exhibited; *esp* **:** a document or material object produced and identified (as in a court) for use as evidence

ex·hi·bi·tion \ˌek-sə-ˈbish-ən\ *n* **1 :** an act or instance of exhibiting **2 :** a public showing (as of works of art, objects of manufacture, or athletic skill)

ex·hi·bi·tion·ism \-ˈbish-ə-ˌniz-əm\ *n* **1 a :** a perversion marked by a tendency to indecent exposure **b :** an act of such exposure **2 :** the act or practice of behaving so as to attract attention to oneself — **ex·hi·bi·tion·ist** \-ˈbish-(ə-)nəst\ *n* — **exhibitionist** *or* **ex·hi·bi·tion·is·tic** \-ˌbish-ə-ˈnis-tik\ *adj*

ex·hil·a·rate \ig-ˈzil-ə-ˌrāt\ *vt* **1 :** to make cheerful or jolly **2 :** to fill with a lively sense of well-being **:** INVIGORATE — **ex·hil·a·ra·tive** \-ˌrāt-iv\ *adj*

ex·hil·a·ra·tion \ig-ˌzil-ə-ˈrā-shən\ *n* **1 :** the action of exhilarating **2 :** the state or the feeling of being exhilarated **:** high spirits **:** LIVELINESS

ex·hort \ig-ˈzȯrt\ *vb* **:** to arouse by words (as of advice, encouragement, or warning) **:** urge or appeal strongly — **ex·hort·er** *n*

ex·hor·ta·tion \ˌeks-ˌȯr-ˈtā-shən, ˌegz-\ *n* **1 :** an act or instance of exhorting **2 :** a speech intended to exhort others **:** earnestly spoken words of urgent advice or warning

ex·hort·a·tive \ig-ˈzȯrt-ət-iv\ *adj* **:** serving to exhort

ex·hort·a·to·ry \-ə-ˌtōr-ē\ *adj* **:** HORTATORY

ex·hume \igz-ˈ(y)üm\ *vt* **1 :** to dig out of the ground; *esp* **:** to uncover and take out of a place of burial **:** DISINTER **2 :** to bring back from neglect or obscurity — **ex·hu·ma·tion** \ˌeks-(h)yü-ˈmā-shən\ *n* — **ex·hum·er** *n*

ex·i·gence \ˈek-sə-jən(t)s\ *n* **:** EXIGENCY

ex·i·gen·cy \ˈek-sə-jən-sē, ig-ˈzij-ən-\ *n, pl* **-cies :** a case or a state of affairs demanding immediate action or remedy **:** an urgent need

ex·i·gent \ˈek-sə-jənt\ *adj* **1 :** requiring immediate aid or action **:** URGENT **2 :** requiring or calling for much **:** DEMANDING, EXACTING — **ex·i·gent·ly** *adv*

ex·ig·u·ous \eg-ˈzig-yə-wəs\ *adj* **:** scanty in amount — **ex·i·gu·ity** \ˌek-sə-ˈgyü-ət-ē\ *n* — **ex·ig·u·ous·ly** *adv* — **ex·ig·u·ous·ness** *n*

¹ex·ile \ˈeg-ˌzīl, ˈek-ˌsīl\ *n* **1 :** forced removal or voluntary absence from one's native country; *also* **:** the state of one so absent **2 :** a person expelled from his country by authority

²exile *vt* **:** to banish or expel from one's own country or home

ex·ist \ig-ˈzist\ *vi* **1 :** to have actual being **:** be real **:** BE **2 :** to continue to be **:** LIVE **3 :** to be found **:** OCCUR

ex·ist·ence \ig-ˈzis-tən(t)s\ *n* **1 :** the fact or the state of having being or of being real **2 :** continuance in living or way of living **:** LIFE **3 :** actual occurrence **4 a :** the sum total of existing things **b :** a specific being

ex·ist·ent \-tənt\ *adj* **1 :** having being **:** EXISTING **2 :** existing now **:** EXTANT

¹ex·it \ˈeg-zət, ˈek-sət\ — used as a stage direction to specify who goes off stage

²exit *n* **1 :** a departure from a stage **2 :** the act of going out or going away **3 :** a way out of an enclosed place or space — **exit** *vi*

ex li·bris \eks-ˈlē-brəs\ *n, pl* **ex libris :** BOOKPLATE

ex·o·dus \ˈek-səd-əs\ *n* **:** a mass departure

ex of·fi·cio \ˌeks-ə-ˈfish-ē-ˌō\ *adv* (*or adj*) : by virtue or because of an office
ex·on·er·ate \ig-ˈzän-ə-ˌrāt\ *vt* : to clear from an accusation or from blame : declare innocent — **ex·on·er·a·tion** \ig-ˌzän-ə-ˈrā-shən\ *n*
ex·or·bi·tant \ig-ˈzȯr-bət-ənt\ *adj* : going beyond the limits of what is fair, reasonable, or expected : EXCESSIVE — **ex·or·bi·tance** \-bət-ən(t)s\ *n* — **ex·or·bi·tant·ly** *adv*
ex·or·cise \ˈek-ˌsȯr-ˌsīz, -sər-\ *vt* **1** : to drive (as an evil spirit) off by calling upon some holy name or by spells **2** : to free (as a person or place) from an evil spirit — **ex·or·cis·er** *n*
ex·or·cism \-ˌsiz-əm\ *n* **1** : the act or practice of exorcising **2** : a spell or formula used in exorcising — **ex·or·cist** \-ˌsist, -səst\ *n*
ex·or·di·um \eg-ˈzȯrd-ē-əm\ *n*, *pl* **-di·ums** *or* **-dia** \-ē-ə\ : a beginning or introduction esp. to a discourse or composition — **ex·or·di·al** \-ē-əl\ *adj*
ex·o·ter·ic \ˌek-sə-ˈter-ik\ *adj* **1 a** : suitable to be imparted to the public **b** : belonging to the outer or less initiate circle **2** : relating to the outside — **ex·o·ter·i·cal·ly** \-ˈter-i-k(ə-)lē\ *adv*
ex·ot·ic \ig-ˈzät-ik\ *adj* **1** : introduced from another country **2** : strikingly or excitingly different or unusual (as in color or design) — **exotic** *n* — **ex·ot·i·cal·ly** \-ˈzät-i-k(ə-)lē\ *adv* — **ex·ot·ic·ness** *n*
ex·ot·i·cism \ig-ˈzät-ə-ˌsiz-əm\ *n* **1** : the quality or state of being exotic **2** : EXOTIC
ex·pand \ik-ˈspand\ *vb* **1** : to open wide : UNFOLD **2** : to take up or to cause to take up more space : ENLARGE, SWELL **3** : to develop more fully : work out in greater detail **4** : to state in enlarged form : write out in full **5** : to increase in quantity or scope — **ex·pand·a·ble** *adj* — **ex·pand·er** *n*
ex·panse \ik-ˈspan(t)s\ *n* : the extent to which something spreads out : a wide space, area, or stretch
ex·pan·si·ble \ik-ˈspan(t)-sə-bəl\ *adj* : capable of being expanded
ex·pan·sion \ik-ˈspan-chən\ *n* **1** : the act or process of expanding **2** : the quality or state of being expanded **3** : EXPANSE **4 a** : an expanded part **b** : something that results from an act of expanding **5** : the result of an indicated operation : the expression of a function in the form of a series
ex·pan·sive \ik-ˈspan(t)-siv\ *adj* **1** : having a capacity or a tendency to expand **2** : causing or tending to cause expansion **3** : characterized by high spirits or benevolent inclinations **4** : having considerable extent — **ex·pan·sive·ly** *adv* — **ex·pan·sive·ness** *n*
ex par·te \(ˈ)eks-ˈpärt-ē\ *adj* (*or adv*) : from a one-sided or partisan point of view
ex·pa·ti·ate \ek-ˈspā-shē-ˌāt\ *vi* : to speak or write at length or in detail — **ex·pa·ti·a·tion** \(ˌ)ek-ˌspā-shē-ˈā-shən\ *n*
[1]**ex·pa·tri·ate** \ek-ˈspā-trē-ˌāt\ *vb* **1** : to drive into exile : BANISH **2** : to withdraw (oneself) from residence in or allegiance to one's native country **3** : to leave one's native country; *esp* : to renounce allegiance to one's native country — **ex·pa·tri·a·tion** \(ˌ)ek-ˌspā-trē-ˈā-shən\ *n*
[2]**ex·pa·tri·ate** \ek-ˈspā-trē-ˌāt, -trē-ət\ *adj* : living in a foreign country : EXPATRIATED — **expatriate** *n*
ex·pect \ik-ˈspekt\ *vb* **1** : to look forward **2** : to anticipate the birth of a child **3** : SUPPOSE, THINK **4** : to anticipate or look forward to the coming or occurence of **5 a** : to consider probable or certain **b** : to consider reasonable, due, or necessary **c** : to consider obligated or in duty bound — **ex·pect·a·ble** *adj* — **ex·pect·a·bly** \-ˈspek-tə-blē\ *adv*
ex·pect·ance \ik-ˈspek-tən(t)s\ *n* : EXPECTATION
ex·pect·an·cy \ik-ˈspek-tən-sē\ *n*, *pl* **-cies** **1 a** : the act or state of expecting **b** : the state of being expected **2 a** : something expected **b** : the expected amount (as of the number of years of life) based on statistical probability
ex·pect·ant \-tənt\ *adj* : characterized by or being in a state of expectation — **expectant** *n* — **ex·pect·ant·ly** *adv*
ex·pec·ta·tion \ˌek-ˌspek-ˈtā-shən\ *n* **1** : the act or state of expecting : a looking forward to or waiting for something **2** : prospect of the future : grounds for expecting something; *esp* : prospects of inheritance — usu. used in pl. **3** : something expected **4** : the product of the probability that an event will occur and the amount to be received if it does occur
ex·pec·to·rant \ik-ˈspek-tə-rənt\ *adj* : tending to promote discharge of mucus from the respiratory tract — **expectorant** *n*
ex·pec·to·rate \ik-ˈspek-tə-ˌrāt\ *vb* : to discharge (as phlegm) from the throat or lungs by coughing and spitting; *also* : SPIT — **ex·pec·to·ra·tion** \-ˌspek-tə-ˈrā-shən\ *n*
ex·pe·di·ence \ik-ˈspēd-ē-ən(t)s\ *n* : EXPEDIENCY
ex·pe·di·en·cy \ik-ˈspēd-ē-ən-sē\ *n*, *pl* **-cies** **1** : the quality or state of being suited to the end in view : suitability or convenience in a particular situation **2** : the use of means and methods advantageous to oneself without regard to principles of fairness and rightness
[1]**ex·pe·di·ent** \ik-ˈspēd-ē-ənt\ *adj* : suitable for bringing about a desired result often without regard to fairness or rightness — **ex·pe·di·ent·ly** *adv*
[2]**expedient** *n* **1** : something expedient **2** : a means to accomplish an end; *esp* : one used in place of a better means that is not available
ex·pe·dite \ˈek-spə-ˌdīt\ *vt* **1** : to carry out rapidly : execute promptly **2** : to accelerate the process or progress of : FACILITATE **3** : to send out : DISPATCH
ex·pe·dit·er \-ˌdīt-ər\ *n* : one that expedites; *esp* : one employed to ensure adequate supplies of raw materials and equipment or to coordinate the flow of materials, tools, parts, and processed goods within a plant
ex·pe·di·tion \ˌek-spə-ˈdish-ən\ *n* **1** : efficient promptness : SPEED, EXPEDITIOUSNESS **2 a** : a sending or setting forth for some object or purpose **b** : a journey or trip undertaken for a specific purpose (as for war or exploring) **c** : a group (as a military force) making such a journey
ex·pe·di·tion·ary \-ˈdish-ə-ˌner-ē\ *adj* : of, relating to, or constituting an expedition; *esp* : sent on military service abroad
ex·pe·di·tious \ˌek-spə-ˈdish-əs\ *adj* : characterized by or acting with promptness and efficiency : SPEEDY — **ex·pe·di·tious·ly** *adv* — **ex·pe·di·tious·ness** *n*
ex·pel \ik-ˈspel\ *vt* **ex·pelled**; **ex·pel·ling** **1** : to drive or force out **2** : to drive away; *esp* : DEPORT **3** : to cut off from membership — **ex·pel·la·ble** *adj*
ex·pel·lant *or* **ex·pel·lent** \ik-ˈspel-ənt\ *adj* : tending or serving to expel — **expellant** *n*
ex·pend \ik-ˈspend\ *vt* **1** : to pay out : SPEND **2** : to consume by use : use up
[1]**ex·pend·a·ble** \ik-ˈspen-də-bəl\ *adj* : that may be used up in an ordinary way or sacrificed to accomplish a mission — **ex·pend·a·bil·i·ty** \-ˌpen-də-ˈbil-ət-ē\ *n* — **ex·pend·a·bly** \-ˈpen-də-blē\ *adv*
[2]**expendable** *n* : an item of equipment or a member or unit of an armed force that is regarded as expendable
ex·pen·di·ture \ik-ˈspen-di-chər\ *n* **1** : the act or process of expending **2** : an amount (as of money or time) expended : DISBURSEMENT, EXPENSE
ex·pense \ik-ˈspen(t)s\ *n* **1 a** : something expended to secure a benefit or bring about a result **b** : financial burden or outlay : COST **2** : a cause of expenditure **3** : SACRIFICE — usu. used in the phrase *at the expense of*
ex·pen·sive \ik-ˈspen(t)-siv\ *adj* **1** : occasioning expense **2** : high-priced : DEAR — **ex·pen·sive·ly** *adv* — **ex·pen·sive·ness** *n*
[1]**ex·pe·ri·ence** \ik-ˈspir-ē-ən(t)s\ *n* **1 a** : the usu. conscious perception or apprehension of reality or of an event **b** : the

sum total of the conscious events that make up an individual life or the past of a community, nation, or mankind generally **2 a :** the actual living through an event or series of events **b :** something that one has actually done or lived through **3 a :** the skill or knowledge gained by actually doing or feeling a thing **b :** the amount or kind of work a person or animal has done or the time during which work has been done — **ex·pe·ri·en·tial** \-ˌspir-ē-ˈen-chəl\ *adj*

²experience *vt* **1 :** to have experience of : UNDERGO **2 :** to learn by experience

ex·pe·ri·enced \ik-ˈspir-ē-ən(t)st\ *adj* **:** having experience **:** made skillful or wise through experience

¹ex·per·i·ment \ik-ˈsper-ə-mənt\ *n* **1 a :** TEST, TRIAL **b :** a tentative procedure or policy **c :** an operation carried out under controlled conditions in order to discover an unknown effect or law, to test or establish a hypothesis, or to illustrate a known law **2 :** the process of testing : EXPERIMENTATION

²ex·per·i·ment \-ˌment\ *vi* **:** to make experiments — **ex·per·i·men·ta·tion** \ik-ˌsper-ə-mən-ˈtā-shən, -ˌmen-\ *n* — **ex·per·i·ment·er** *n*

ex·per·i·men·tal \ik-ˌsper-ə-ˈment-ᵊl\ *adj* **1 :** of, relating to, or based on experience : EMPIRICAL **2 :** founded on or derived from experiment **3 :** serving the ends of or used for experimentation **4 :** relating to or having the characteristics of experiment : TENTATIVE — **ex·per·i·men·tal·ly** \-ᵊl-ē\ *adv*

¹ex·pert \ˈek-ˌspərt, ik-ˈ\ *adj* **:** having, involving, or displaying special skill or knowledge derived from training or experience — **ex·pert·ly** *adv* — **ex·pert·ness** *n*

²ex·pert \ˈek-ˌspərt\ *n* **:** one who has acquired special skill in or knowledge of a subject

ex·pi·ate \ˈek-spē-ˌāt\ *vt* **1 :** to atone for : pay the penalty for **2 :** to make amends for — **ex·pi·a·ble** \-spē-ə-bəl\ *adj* — **ex·pi·a·tor** \-ˌāt-ər\ *n*

ex·pi·a·tion \ˌek-spē-ˈā-shən\ *n* **1 :** the act of making atonement **2 :** the means by which atonement is made

ex·pi·a·to·ry \ˈek-spē-ə-ˌtōr-ē\ *adj* **:** serving to expiate

ex·pi·ra·tion \ˌek-spə-ˈrā-shən\ *n* **1 :** the expelling of air from the lungs in breathing; *also* **:** air or vapor so expelled **2 :** the fact of coming to an end : TERMINATION

ex·pi·ra·to·ry \(ˈ)ek-ˈspī-rə-ˌtōr-ē\ *adj* **:** of, relating to, or used in respiratory expiration

ex·pire \ik-ˈspī(ə)r, ek-\ *vb* **1 :** DIE **2 :** to come to an end : STOP **3 a :** to emit the breath **b :** to breathe out from or as if from the lungs

ex·pi·ry \ik-ˈspī(ə)r-ē, ˈek-spə-rē\ *n, pl* **-ries 1 a :** exhalation of breath **b :** DEATH **2 :** TERMINATION; *esp* **:** the termination of a time or period fixed by law, contract, or agreement

ex·plain \ik-ˈsplān\ *vb* **1 :** to make plain or understandable **2 :** to give the reason for or cause of **3 :** to show the logical development or relationships of — **ex·plain·a·ble** *adj* — **ex·plain·er** *n*

ex·pla·na·tion \ˌek-splə-ˈnā-shən\ *n* **1 :** the act or process of explaining **2 :** something that explains : a statement that makes clear

ex·plan·a·to·ry \ik-ˈsplan-ə-ˌtōr-ē\ *adj* **:** serving to explain

ex·ple·tive \ˈek-splət-iv\ *n* **:** a usu. obscene or profane exclamatory word or phrase — **expletive** *adj*

ex·pli·cate \ˈek-splə-ˌkāt\ *vt* **:** to give a detailed explanation of — **ex·plic·a·ble** \ek-ˈsplik-ə-bəl, ˈek-(ˌ)splik-\ *adj* — **ex·pli·ca·tion** \ˌek-splə-ˈkā-shən\ *n*

ex·plic·it \ik-ˈsplis-ət\ *adj* **:** so clear in statement that there is no doubt about the meaning : fully stated — **ex·plic·it·ly** *adv* — **ex·plic·it·ness** *n*

ex·plode \ik-ˈsplōd\ *vb* **1 :** to cause to be given up or rejected : DISCREDIT **2 a :** to burst or cause to burst violently and noisily **b :** to burn suddenly so that there is a violent expansion of hot gases with great disruptive force and a loud noise; *also* **:** to undergo an atomic nuclear reaction with similar but more violent effects **3 :** to burst forth (as with anger or laughter)

¹ex·ploit \ˈek-ˌsplȯit, ik-ˈ\ *n* **:** DEED, ACT; *esp* **:** a notable or heroic act

²ex·ploit \ik-ˈsplȯit, ˈek-ˌ\ *vt* **1 :** to extract value or use from : UTILIZE **2 :** to make use of unfairly for one's own advantage — **ex·ploit·a·ble** *adj* — **ex·ploi·ta·tion** \ˌek-ˌsplȯi-ˈtā-shən\ *n* — **ex·ploit·er** *n*

ex·plo·ra·tion \ˌek-splə-ˈrā-shən\ *n* **:** the act or an instance of exploring — **ex·plor·a·tive** \ik-ˈsplōr-ət-iv\ *adj* — **ex·plor·a·to·ry** \-ə-ˌtōr-ē\ *adj*

ex·plore \ik-ˈsplō(ə)r\ *vb* **1 a :** to search through or into **b :** to examine carefully and in detail esp. for diagnostic purposes **c :** to penetrate into or range over for purposes of discovery **2 :** to make or conduct a systematic search

ex·plor·er \ik-ˈsplōr-ər\ *n* **:** one that explores; *esp* **:** a person who travels in search of geographical or scientific information

ex·plo·sion \ik-ˈsplō-zhən\ *n* **1 :** the act or an instance of exploding **2 :** a large-scale, rapid, and spectacular expansion, outbreak, or upheaval **3 :** a violent outburst of feeling

¹ex·plo·sive \ik-ˈsplō-siv\ *adj* **1 :** relating to, characterized by, or operated by explosion **2 :** tending to explode — **ex·plo·sive·ly** *adv* — **ex·plo·sive·ness** *n*

²explosive *n* **:** an explosive substance

ex·po·nent \ik-ˈspō-nənt, ˈek-ˌ\ *n* **1 :** a symbol written above and to the right of a mathematical expression to indicate the operation of raising to a power **2 a :** one that expounds or interprets **b :** one that champions or advocates

ex·po·nen·tial \ˌek-spə-ˈnen-chəl\ *adj* **1 :** of or relating to an exponent **2 :** involving a variable exponent **3 :** capable of being expressed or approximated by an exponential equation — **ex·po·nen·tial·ly** \-ˈnench-(ə-)lē\ *adv*

¹ex·port \ek-ˈspōrt, ˈek-ˌ\ *vt* **1 :** to carry away : REMOVE **2 :** to carry or send (as a commodity) to another country or place esp. for sale — **ex·port·a·ble** *adj* — **ex·por·ta·tion** \ˌek-ˌspōr-ˈtā-shən, -spər-\ *n* — **ex·port·er** *n*

²ex·port \ˈek-ˌspōrt\ *n* **1 :** something exported; *esp* **:** a commodity conveyed from one country or region to another for purposes of trade **2 :** an act of exporting : EXPORTATION

³export \ˈek-ˌ\ *adj* **1 :** of or relating to exportation or exports **2 :** intended for export

¹ex·pose \ik-ˈspōz\ *vt* **1 a :** to deprive of shelter, protection, or care **b :** to submit or subject to an action or influence; *esp* **:** to subject (a sensitive photographic film, plate, or paper) to the action of radiant energy (as light) **c :** to abandon (an infant) esp. in the open : DESERT **2 :** to lay open to view: as **a :** to offer publicly for sale **b :** to exhibit for public veneration **c :** to reveal the face of (a playing card) **3 :** to bring to light : UNMASK

²ex·po·sé \ˌek-(ˌ)spō-ˈzā\ *n* **:** an exposure of something discreditable

ex·po·si·tion \ˌek-spə-ˈzish-ən\ *n* **1 :** an explaining of the meaning or purpose of something (as a piece of writing) **2 :** a composition that explains something **3 :** a public exhibition or show — **ex·pos·i·to·ry** \ik-ˈspäz-ə-ˌtōr-ē\ *adj*

ex·pos·i·tor \ik-ˈspäz-ət-ər\ *n* **:** one that expounds or explains

ex·pos·tu·late \ik-ˈspäs-chə-ˌlāt\ *vi* **:** to reason earnestly with a person against something he has done or intends to do : REMONSTRATE — **ex·pos·tu·la·tion** \-ˌspäs-chə-ˈlā-shən\ *n* — **ex·pos·tu·la·to·ry** \-ˈspäs-chə-lə-ˌtōr-ē\ *adj*

ex·po·sure \ik-ˈspō-zhər\ *n* **1 :** the act or an instance of exposing: as **a :** disclosure to view **b :** UNMASKING **c :** an act of abandoning esp. in the open **d** (1) **:** a section of a film for a single picture (2) **:** the time during which a sensitive photographic film is exposed **2 a :** a condition or an instance of being exposed; *esp* **:** the condition of being exposed to danger (as from the elements) **b :** a position with respect to direction or to general weather conditions

ex·pound \ik-ˈspau̇nd\ *vt* **1 a :** to set forth : STATE **b :** to defend (as a theory) with argument **2 :** to make clear the meaning of : INTERPRET — **ex·pound·er** *n*

[1]**ex·press** \ik-'spres\ *adj* **1 a :** directly and distinctly stated : EXPLICIT **b :** EXACT, PRECISE **2 :** of a particular sort : SPECIAL **3 a :** traveling at high speed; *esp* : traveling with few or no stops **b :** adapted or suitable for travel at high speed

[2]**express** *adv* : by express

[3]**express** *n* **1 a :** a system for special transportation of goods at premium rates **b :** a company operating such a service or the goods or shipments so transported **2 :** an express vehicle

[4]**express** *vt* **1 a :** to represent esp. in words : STATE **b :** to give expression to the opinions, feelings, or abilities of (oneself) **c :** to represent by a sign or symbol : SYMBOLIZE **2 :** to press or squeeze out of an object **3 :** to send by express — **ex·press·er** *n* — **ex·press·i·ble** \-ə-bəl\ *adj*

ex·pres·sion \ik-'spresh-ən\ *n* **1 :** the act or process of expressing esp. in words **2 a :** a word, phrase, or sign that expresses a thought, feeling, or quality; *esp* : a significant word or phrase **b :** a mathematical symbol or a combination of symbols and signs representing a quantity or operation **3 :** a way of speaking or of singing or playing an instrument so as to show mood or feeling **4 :** LOOK, APPEARANCE **5 :** the detectable effect of a gene; *also* : EXPRESSIVITY **6 :** an act or product of pressing out — **ex·pres·sion·less** \-ləs\ *adj*

ex·pres·sion·ism \ik-'spresh-ə-ˌniz-əm\ *n* : a theory or practice in art of seeking to depict the artist's subjective responses to objects and events — **ex·pres·sion·ist** \-'spresh-(ə-)nəst\ *n or adj* — **ex·pres·sion·is·tic** \-ˌspresh-ə-'nis-tik\ *adj*

ex·pres·sive \ik-'spres-iv\ *adj* **1 :** of or relating to expression **2 :** serving to express, utter, or represent **3 :** full of expression : SIGNIFICANT — **ex·pres·sive·ly** *adv* — **ex·pres·sive·ness** *n*

ex·pres·siv·i·ty \ˌek-ˌspres-'iv-ət-ē\ *n*, *pl* **-ties :** the relative capacity of a gene to modify the organism of which it is a part

ex·press·ly \ik-'spres-lē\ *adv* **1 :** in an express manner : EXPLICITLY **2 :** for the express purpose : PARTICULARLY

ex·press·man \ik-'spres-ˌman, -mən\ *n* : a person employed in the express business

ex·press·way \-ˌwā\ *n* : a high-speed divided highway for through traffic with controlled access and grade separations at intersections

ex·pro·pri·ate \ek-'sprō-prē-ˌāt\ *vt* : to take away from a person the possession of or right to (property) — **ex·pro·pri·a·tion** \(ˌ)ek-ˌsprō-prē-'ā-shən\ *n* — **ex·pro·pri·a·tor** \ek-'sprō-prē-ˌāt-ər\ *n*

ex·pul·sion \ik-'spəl-shən\ *n* : the act of expelling : the state of being expelled — **ex·pul·sive** \-'pəl-siv\ *adj*

ex·punge \ik-'spənj\ *vt* **1 :** to blot out : rub out : ERASE **2 :** CANCEL — **ex·pung·er** *n*

ex·pur·gate \'ek-spər-ˌgāt\ *vt* : to clear of something wrong or objectionable; *esp* : to clear (as a book) of objectionable words or passages — **ex·pur·ga·tion** \ˌek-spər-'gā-shən\ *n* — **ex·pur·ga·tor** \'ek-spər-ˌgāt-ər\ *n*

[1]**ex·quis·ite** \ek-'skwiz-ət, 'ek-(ˌ)skwiz-\ *adj* **1 :** marked by flawless craftsmanship or delicate execution **2 :** keenly appreciative : DISCRIMINATING **3 :** pleasing through beauty, fitness, or perfection **4 :** ACUTE, INTENSE — **ex·quis·ite·ly** *adv* — **ex·quis·ite·ness** *n*

[2]**exquisite** *n* : one who is overly fastidious in dress or ornament : FOP

ex·tant \'ek-stənt, ek-'stant\ *adj* : currently existing : not destroyed or lost

ex·tem·po·ra·ne·ous \(ˌ)ek-ˌstem-pə-'rā-nē-əs\ *adj* **1 :** composed, performed, or uttered on the spur of the moment : IMPROMPTU **2 :** carefully prepared but delivered without notes or text **3 :** provided, made, or put to use as an expedient — **ex·tem·po·ra·ne·ous·ly** *adv* — **ex·tem·po·ra·ne·ous·ness** *n*

ex·tem·po·rary \ik-'stem-pə-ˌrer-ē\ *adj* : EXTEMPORANEOUS — **ex·tem·po·rar·i·ly** \-ˌstem-pə-'rer-ə-lē\ *adv*

ex·tem·po·re \ik-'stem-pə-(ˌ)rē\ *adv* : EXTEMPORANEOUSLY — **extempore** *adj*

ex·tem·po·rize \ik-'stem-pə-ˌrīz\ *vb* : to do, make, or utter extempore : IMPROVISE — **ex·tem·po·ri·za·tion** \ik-ˌstem-pə-rə-'zā-shən\ *n* — **ex·tem·po·riz·er** *n*

ex·tend \ik-'stend\ *vb* **1 :** to straighten out or stretch forth **2 :** to make active at full capacity **3 :** to increase the bulk of (a product) by the addition of a cheaper substance **4 a :** to make the offer of : PROFFER **b :** to make available **5 a :** to cause to reach **b :** to cause to be longer; *esp* : to prolong the time of payment of **6 a :** to cause to be of greater area or volume : ENLARGE **b :** to increase the scope, meaning, or application of : BROADEN **7 :** to stretch out in distance, space, or time : REACH **8 :** to span an interval of distance, space, or time — **ex·tend·i·ble** \-'sten-də-bəl\ *or* **ex·ten·si·ble** \-'sten(t)-sə-bəl\ *adj* — **ex·ten·si·bil·i·ty** \-ˌsten(t)-sə-'bil-ət-ē\ *n*

ex·ten·sion \ik-'sten-chən\ *n* **1 a :** the act of extending : the state of being extended **b :** something extended **2 :** the total range over which something extends : COMPASS **3 :** the property of occupying space **4 :** an increase in length of time; *esp* : a granting of extra time to fulfill an obligation **5 :** the making available of educational resources by special programs (as correspondence courses) to persons otherwise unable to take advantage of them **6 a :** a part constituting an addition **b :** a section forming an additional length **c :** an extra telephone connected to the principal line — **ex·ten·sion·al** \-'stench-nəl, -'sten-chən-ᵊl\ *adj* — **ex·ten·sion·al·ly** \-ē\ *adv*

ex·ten·sive \ik-'sten(t)-siv\ *adj* **1 :** EXTENSIONAL **2 :** having wide or considerable extent — **ex·ten·sive·ly** *adv* — **ex·ten·sive·ness** *n*

ex·tent \ik-'stent\ *n* **1 a :** the range, distance, or space over or through which something extends **b :** the point, degree, or limit to which something extends **2 :** an extended tract or region

ex·ten·u·ate \ik-'sten-yə-ˌwāt\ *vt* : DIMINISH, UNDERESTIMATE; *esp* : to represent (as a crime, fault, or mistake) as of less importance than is real or apparent : make excuses for — **ex·ten·u·a·tion** \-ˌsten-yə-'wā-shən\ *n*

[1]**ex·te·ri·or** \ek-'stir-ē-ər\ *adj* **1 :** EXTERNAL, OUTER **2 :** happening or coming from outside — **ex·te·ri·or·ly** *adv*

[2]**exterior** *n* **1 a :** an exterior part or surface : OUTSIDE **b :** outward manner or appearance **2 :** a representation of an outdoor scene

ex·ter·mi·nate \ik-'stər-mə-ˌnāt\ *vt* : to get rid of completely : ANNIHILATE — **ex·ter·mi·na·tion** \-ˌstər-mə-'nā-shən\ *n* — **ex·ter·mi·na·tor** \-'stər-mə-ˌnāt-ər\ *n*

[1]**ex·ter·nal** \ek-'stərn-ᵊl\ *adj* **1 a :** outwardly visible **b :** not intrinsic or essential : SUPERFICIAL **2 a :** of, relating to, or connected with the outside or an outer part **b :** applied or applicable to the outside **3 a** (1) **:** situated outside, apart, or beyond (2) **:** arising or acting from outside **b :** of or relating to relationships with foreign countries **c :** having existence independent of the mind : PHYSICAL — **ex·ter·nal·ly** \-ᵊl-ē\ *adv*

[2]**external** *n* : something external : an external feature or aspect — usu. used in pl.

ex·tinct \ik-'stiŋ(k)t, 'ek-ˌ\ *adj* **1 :** no longer burning : EXTINGUISHED **2 :** no longer active **3 :** no longer existing — **ex·tinc·tion** \ik-'stiŋ(k)-shən\ *n*

ex·tin·guish \ik-'stiŋ-gwish\ *vt* **1 a :** to cause to cease burning : QUENCH **b :** to cause to die out : DESTROY **c :** to dim the brightness of : ECLIPSE **2 :** to end the force or existence of — **ex·tin·guish·a·ble** *adj* — **ex·tin·guish·er** *n* — **ex·tin·guish·ment** *n*

ex·tir·pate \'ek-stər-ˌpāt, ek-'\ *vt* **1 :** to pull up by the roots **2 :** to eradicate (as by surgery) or destroy wholly — **ex·tir-**

pa·tion \ˌek-(ˌ)stər-ˈpā-shən\ *n* — **ex·tir·pa·tive** \ˈek-stər-ˌpāt-iv, ek-ˈstər-pət-\ *adj*

ex·tol \ik-ˈstōl\ *vt* **ex·tolled**; **ex·tol·ling** : to praise highly : GLORIFY — **ex·tol·ler** *n* — **ex·tol·ment** *n*

ex·tort \ik-ˈstȯrt\ *vt* : to wring (as money or a confession) from a person by the use of force or threats — **ex·tort·er** *n* — **ex·tor·tive** \-ˈstȯrt-iv\ *adj*

ex·tor·tion \ik-ˈstȯr-shən\ *n* **1** : the act or practice of extorting; *esp* : the offense committed by an official engaging in this practice **2 a** : something extorted **b** : a gross overcharge — **ex·tor·tion·er** \-ˈstȯr-sh(ə-)nər\ *n* — **ex·tor·tion·ist** \-sh(ə-)nəst\ *n*

ex·tor·tion·ate \ik-ˈstȯr-sh(ə-)nət\ *adj* **1** : characterized by extortion **2** : EXCESSIVE, EXORBITANT — **ex·tor·tion·ate·ly** *adv*

[1]**ex·tra** \ˈek-strə\ *adj* **1 a** : more than is due, usual, or necessary : ADDITIONAL **b** : subject to an additional charge **2** : SUPERIOR

[2]**extra** *n* : something extra or additional: as **a** : an added charge **b** : a special edition of a newspaper **c** : an additional worker; *esp* : one hired to act in a group scene in a motion picture or stage production

[3]**extra** *adv* : beyond the usual size, extent, or degree

[1]**ex·tract** \ik-ˈstrakt, *oftenest in sense 5* ˈek-ˌ\ *vt* **1 a** : to draw forth; *esp* : to pull out forcibly **b** : to obtain by much effort from someone unwilling **2** : to separate or otherwise obtain (as a juice or a constituent element) by physical or chemical process **3** : to separate (a metal) from an ore **4** : to determine (a mathematical root) by calculation **5** : to select (excerpts) and copy out or cite — **ex·tract·a·ble** *or* **ex·tract·i·ble** \-ə-bəl\ *adj* — **ex·trac·tor** \-ər\ *n*

[2]**ex·tract** \ˈek-ˌstrakt\ *n* **1** : a selection from a writing or discourse : EXCERPT **2** : a product (as an essence or concentrate) prepared by extracting; *esp* : a solution of essential constituents of a complex material (as meat or an aromatic plant)

ex·trac·tion \ik-ˈstrak-shən\ *n* **1** : the act or process of extracting **2** : ORIGIN, LINEAGE **3** : something extracted

ex·tra·cur·ric·u·lar \ˌek-strə-kə-ˈrik-yə-lər\ *adj* : not falling within the curriculum; *esp* : of or relating to those activities (as debating and athletics) that form part of the life of students but are not part of the courses of study

ex·tra·dite \ˈek-strə-ˌdīt\ *vt* : to cause to be delivered or given up to a different legal authority as an alleged criminal for trial — **ex·tra·dit·a·ble** *adj*

ex·tra·di·tion \ˌek-strə-ˈdish-ən\ *n* : the surrender or delivery of an alleged criminal by one authority (as a state) to another having jurisdiction to try the charge

ex·tra·dos \ˈek-strə-ˌdäs, -ˌdō; ek-ˈstrā-ˌdäs\ *n, pl* **extrados** \-ˌdōz, -ˌdäs\ *or* **ex·tra·dos·es** \-ˌdäs-əz\ : the exterior curve of an arch

ex·tra·mu·ral \ˌek-strə-ˈmyu̇r-əl\ *adj* : relating to or taking part in informal contests between teams of different schools other than varsity teams

ex·tra·ne·ous \ek-ˈstrā-nē-əs\ *adj* **1** : existing or coming from the outside **2 a** : not forming an essential or vital part : ACCIDENTAL **b** : IRRELEVANT — **ex·tra·ne·ous·ly** *adv* — **ex·tra·ne·ous·ness** *n*

ex·traor·di·nary \ik-ˈstrȯrd-ᵊn-ˌer-ē, ˌek-strə-ˈȯrd-\ *adj* **1 a** : going beyond what is usual, regular, or customary **b** : exceptional to a very marked extent : REMARKABLE **2** : employed for or sent on a special function or service — **ex·traor·di·nar·i·ly** \ik-ˌstrȯrd-ᵊn-ˈer-ə-lē, ˌek-strə-ˌȯrd-\ *adv* — **ex·traor·di·nar·i·ness** *n*

ex·trap·o·late \ik-ˈstrap-ə-ˌlāt\ *vt* : to infer (data in an unknown area or interval) from data in a known area or interval— **ex·trap·o·la·tion** \-ˌstrap-ə-ˈlā-shən\ *n*

ex·tra·sen·so·ry \ˌek-strə-ˈsen(t)s-(ə-)rē\ *adj* : extending or occurring beyond the known senses

ex·tra·ter·ri·to·ri·al \-ˌter-ə-ˈtōr-ē-əl\ *adj* **1** : located outside the territorial limits of a jurisdiction **2** : of or relating to extraterritoriality — **ex·tra·ter·ri·to·ri·al·ly** \-ē-ə-lē\ *adv*

ex·tra·ter·ri·to·ri·al·i·ty \-ˌtōr-ē-ˈal-ət-ē\ *n* : exemption from the application or jurisdiction of local law or tribunals

ex·trav·a·gance \ik-ˈstrav-i-gən(t)s\ *n* **1 a** : an extravagant act; *esp* : an excessive outlay of money **b** : something extravagant **2** : the quality or fact of being extravagant

ex·trav·a·gant \-gənt\ *adj* **1** : going beyond what is reasonable or suitable **2** : wasteful esp. of money **3** : too high : EXCESSIVE — **ex·trav·a·gant·ly** *adv*

ex·trav·a·gan·za \ik-ˌstrav-ə-ˈgan-zə\ *n* **1** : a literary or musical work marked by extreme freedom of style and structure and usu. by elements of burlesque or parody **2** : a lavish or spectacular show or event

[1]**ex·treme** \ik-ˈstrēm\ *adj* **1 a** : existing in the highest or the greatest possible degree **b** : going to great or exaggerated lengths **c** : exceeding the ordinary, usual, or expected **2** : situated at the farthest possible point from a center **3 a** : most advanced : UTMOST **b** : MAXIMUM — **ex·treme·ly** *adv* — **ex·treme·ness** *n*

[2]**extreme** *n* **1** : an extreme state or condition **2 a** : something situated at or marking one end or the other of a range **b** : the first term or the last term of a mathematical proportion **3 a** : a very pronounced or excessive degree **b** : MAXIMUM **4** : an extreme measure or expedient

ex·trem·ism \ik-ˈstrē-ˌmiz-əm\ *n* : advocacy or practice of extreme measures esp. in politics; *esp* : RADICALISM — **ex·trem·ist** \-məst\ *n or adj*

ex·trem·i·ty \ik-ˈstrem-ət-ē\ *n, pl* **-ties** **1 a** : the farthest or most remote part, section, or point **b** : a limb of the body; *esp* : a human hand or foot **2 a** : extreme danger or critical need **b** : a moment of such danger or need **3** : the utmost degree (as of emotion or pain) **4** : a drastic or desperate act or measure

ex·tri·cate \ˈek-strə-ˌkāt\ *vt* : to free or remove from an entanglement or difficulty — **ex·tri·ca·ble** \ek-ˈstrik-ə-bəl, ˈek-(ˌ)strik-\ *adj* — **ex·tri·ca·tion** \ˌek-strə-ˈkā-shən\ *n*

ex·trin·sic \ek-ˈstrin-zik, -ˈstrin(t)-sik\ *adj* **1 a** : not forming part of or belonging to a thing : EXTRANEOUS **b** : originating from or on the outside; *esp* : originating outside of but acting upon a part **2** : EXTERNAL — **ex·trin·si·cal·ly** \-zi-k(ə-)lē, -si-\ *adv*

ex·tro·ver·sion \ˌek-strə-ˈvər-zhən\ *n* : the state of an extrovert — **ex·tro·ver·sive** \-siv\ *adj* — **ex·tro·ver·sive·ly** *adv*

ex·tro·vert \ˈek-strə-ˌvərt\ *n* : a person more interested in what he does and what goes on about him than in what he thinks or imagines : one who finds most of his interests and satisfactions in external things — **ex·tro·vert·ed** \ˈek-strə-ˌvərt-əd\ *or* **extrovert** *adj*

ex·trude \ik-ˈstrüd\ *vb* **1** : to force, press, or push out **2** : to shape (as metal) by forcing through a die **3** : to become extruded — **ex·trud·er** *n*

ex·tru·sion \ik-ˈstrü-zhən\ *n* : the act or process of extruding; *also* : a form produced by this process

ex·u·ber·ant \ig-ˈzü-b(ə-)rənt\ *adj* **1** : characterized by great abundance : PLENTEOUS, LUXURIANT **2** : filled with life, vigor, and high spirits **3** : carried to or experienced in an extreme degree — **ex·u·ber·ance** \-b(ə-)rən(t)s\ *n* — **ex·u·ber·ant·ly** *adv*

ex·u·date \ˈeks-ə-ˌdāt, ˈegz-\ *n* : exuded matter

ex·ude \ig-ˈzüd\ *vb* **1** : to discharge slowly through pores or cuts : OOZE **2** : to cause to spread out in all directions — **ex·u·da·tion** \ˌeks-ə-ˈdā-shən, ˌegz-\ *n*

ex·ult \ig-ˈzəlt\ *vi* : to be extremely joyful : REJOICE — **ex·ult·ing·ly** *adv*

ex·ult·ant \ig-ˈzəlt-ᵊnt\ *adj* : filled with or expressing extreme joy : JUBILANT — **ex·ult·ant·ly** *adv*

ex·ul·ta·tion \ˌeks-(ˌ)əl-ˈtā-shən, ˌegz-\ *n* **:** the act of exulting **:** the state of being exultant

[1]**eye** \ˈī\ *n* **1 a :** an organ of sight; *esp* **:** a rounded hollow organ lined with a sensitive retina and lodged in a bony orbit in the vertebrate skull **b :** the faculty of seeing with the eyes **c :** the faculty of intellectual perception or appreciation **d :** LOOK, GLANCE **e :** STANDPOINT, JUDGMENT **2 :** something suggestive of an eye: as **a :** the hole through the head of a needle **b :** a loop to receive a hook **c :** an undeveloped bud (as on a potato) **3 :** something central **:** CENTER — **eyed** \ˈīd\ *adj* — **eye·less** \ˈī-ləs\ *adj*

[2]**eye** *vt* **eyed; eye·ing** *or* **ey·ing :** to fix the eyes on **:** watch closely

eye·ball \ˈī-ˌbȯl\ *n* **:** the vertebrate eye

eye·brow \-ˌbrau̇\ *n* **:** the ridge over the eye or hair growing on it

eye·ful \ˈī-ˌfu̇l\ *n* **1 :** a satisfying view **2 :** one that is visually attractive; *esp* **:** a strikingly beautiful woman

eye·glass \-ˌglas\ *n* **1 a :** a glass lens used to improve faulty eyesight **b** *pl* **:** GLASSES **2 :** an eyepiece esp. of a telescope or microscope

eye·let \-lət\ *n* **1 a :** a small hole designed to receive a cord or used for decoration (as in embroidery) **b :** a small usu. metal ring to reinforce an eyelet **:** GROMMET **2 :** PEEPHOLE

eye·lid \ˈī-ˌlid\ *n* **:** one of the movable lids of skin and muscle that can be closed over the eyeball

eye·sight \-ˌsīt\ *n* **:** SIGHT, VISION

eye·sore \-ˌsōr\ *n* **:** something displeasing to the sight

eye·spot \-ˌspät\ *n* **:** a simple or primitive visual organ

eye·strain \-ˌstrān\ *n* **:** weariness or a strained state of the eye

eye·tooth \-ˈtüth\ *n* **:** a canine tooth of the upper jaw

eye·wit·ness \-ˈwit-nəs\ *n* **:** a person who sees an occurrence with his own eyes and is able to give a firsthand account of it

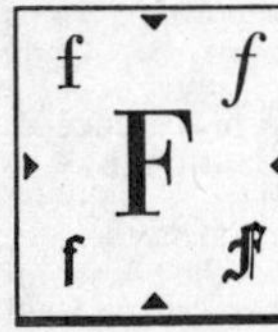

f \ˈef\ *n, often cap* **1 :** the 6th letter of the English alphabet **2 :** the musical tone F **3 :** a grade rating a student's work as failing

fa \ˈfä\ *n* **:** the 4th note of the diatonic scale

Fa·bi·an \ˈfā-bē-ən\ *adj* **1 :** CAUTIOUS, DELAYING **2 :** of, relating to, or being a society of socialists organized in England in 1884 to spread socialist principles gradually — **Fabian** *n* — **Fa·bi·an·ism** \-ə-ˌniz-əm\ *n*

[1]**fa·ble** \ˈfā-bəl\ *n* **:** a fictitious narrative or statement: as **a :** a legendary story of supernatural happenings **b :** a narration intended to teach a lesson; *esp* **:** one in which animals speak and act like human beings **c :** FALSEHOOD

[2]**fable** *vt* **fa·bled; fa·bling** \-b(ə-)liŋ\ **:** to talk or write about as if true — **fa·bler** \-b(ə-)lər\ *n*

fa·bled \ˈfā-bəld\ *adj* **1 :** FICTITIOUS **2 :** told or celebrated in fable

fab·ric \ˈfab-rik\ *n* **1 a :** STRUCTURE **b :** underlying structure **:** FRAMEWORK **2 a :** a cloth woven or knitted from natural or synthetic fibers **b :** a material that resembles cloth

fab·ri·cate \ˈfab-ri-ˌkāt\ *vt* **1 :** CONSTRUCT, MANUFACTURE **2 :** INVENT, CREATE **3 :** to make up for the purpose of deception — **fab·ri·ca·tion** \ˌfab-ri-ˈkā-shən\ *n* — **fab·ri·ca·tor** \ˈfab-ri-ˌkāt-ər\ *n*

fab·u·list \ˈfab-yə-ləst\ *n* **:** a creator or writer of fables

fab·u·lous \ˈfab-yə-ləs\ *adj* **1 :** told in or based on fable **2 :** resembling a fable esp. in exaggeration **:** being beyond belief **:** EXTRAORDINARY, WONDERFUL — **fab·u·lous·ly** *adv* — **fab·u·lous·ness** *n*

fa·cade \fə-ˈsäd\ *n* **1 :** the front of a building usu. given special architectural treatment **2 :** a false, superficial, or artificial appearance

[1]**face** \ˈfās\ *n* **1 :** the front part of the human head including the chin, mouth, nose, cheeks, eyes, and usu. the forehead **2 :** PRESENCE **3 a :** facial expression **b :** GRIMACE **4 a :** outward appearance **b :** BOLDNESS **c :** DIGNITY, PRESTIGE **5 :** a front, upper, or outer surface — **faced** \ˈfāst\ *adj*

[2]**face** *vb* **1 :** to confront brazenly **2 a :** to line near the edge esp. with a different material **b :** to cover the front or surface of **3 :** to bring face to face **4 a :** to stand or sit with the face toward **b :** to front on **5 :** to oppose firmly **6 :** to turn the face or body in a specified direction

fac·et \ˈfas-ət\ *n* **1 :** a small plane surface (as on a cut gem) **2 :** ASPECT, PHASE — **fac·et·ed** \ˈfas-ət-əd\ *adj*

fa·ce·tious \fə-ˈsē-shəs\ *adj* **1 a :** COMICAL **b :** JOCULAR **2 :** marked by unseemly jesting or ironic levity **:** FLIPPANT — **fa·ce·tious·ly** *adv* — **fa·ce·tious·ness** *n*

face–to–face \ˌfās-tə-ˈfās\ *adv* (*or adj*) **1 :** within each other's sight or presence **:** involving close contacts **:** in person **2 :** under the necessity of having to make a decision or to take action

face value *n* **1 :** the value indicated on the face (as of a bill or security) **2 :** apparent value or significance

[1]**fa·cial** \ˈfā-shəl\ *adj* **:** of or relating to the face — **fa·cial·ly** \-shə-lē\ *adv*

[2]**facial** *n* **:** a facial treatment or massage

fac·ile \ˈfas-əl\ *adj* **1 a :** easily accomplished, handled, or attained **b :** SPECIOUS, SUPERFICIAL **c :** readily manifested and often insincere **2 :** mild or yielding in disposition **:** PLIANT **3 :** READY, FLUENT — **fac·ile·ly** \-ə(l)-lē\ *adv*

fa·cil·i·tate \fə-ˈsil-ə-ˌtāt\ *vt* **:** to make easier — **fa·cil·i·ta·tion** \-ˌsil-ə-ˈtā-shən\ *n*

fa·cil·i·ty \fə-ˈsil-ət-ē\ *n, pl* **-ties 1 :** the quality of being easily performed **2 :** ease in performance **:** APTITUDE **3 :** readiness to be influenced **:** PLIANCY **4 a :** something that facilitates an action, operation, or course of conduct — usu. used in pl. **b :** something (as a hospital) that is built, installed, or established to serve a particular purpose

fac·ing \ˈfā-siŋ\ *n* **1 a :** a lining at the edge esp. of a garment **b** *pl* **:** the collar, cuffs, and trimmings of a uniform coat **2 :** an ornamental or protective layer **3 :** material for facing

fac·sim·i·le \fak-ˈsim-ə-lē\ *n* **1 :** an exact copy **2 :** the process of transmitting printed matter or still pictures by wire or radio for reproduction

fact \ˈfakt\ *n* **1 :** a thing done **:** DEED; *esp* **:** CRIME **2 :** the quality of being actual **3 a :** something that exists or occurs **:** EVENT, ACTUALITY **b :** a piece of information about such a fact

fac·tion \ˈfak-shən\ *n* **1 :** a group or combination acting together within and usu. against a larger body (as in a state, political party, or church) **:** CLIQUE **2 :** party spirit esp. when marked by dissension — **fac·tion·al** \-shnəl, -shən-ᵊl\ *adj* — **fac·tion·al·ism** \-ˌiz-əm\ *n*

fac·tious \ˈfak-shəs\ *adj* **1 :** of, relating to, or caused by faction **2 a :** inclined to faction or the formation of factions **b :** SEDITIOUS — **fac·tious·ly** *adv* — **fac·tious·ness** *n*

fac·ti·tious \fak-ˈtish-əs\ *adj* **:** not natural or genuine **:** ARTIFICIAL — **fac·ti·tious·ly** *adv* — **fac·ti·tious·ness** *n*

[1]**fac·tor** \ˈfak-tər\ *n* **1 a :** AGENT **b :** one who lends money to producers and dealers (as on the security of accounts receiv-

able) **2 :** something that actively contributes to the production of a result : INGREDIENT **3 :** GENE **4 :** any of the numbers or symbols in mathematics that when multiplied together form a product — **fac·tor·ship** \\-ˌship\\ *n*

²**factor** *vb* **fac·tored**; **fac·tor·ing** \\-t(ə-)riŋ\\ **1 :** to resolve into factors **2 :** to work as a factor — **fac·tor·a·ble** *adj*

fac·to·ry \\ˈfak-t(ə-)rē\\ *n, pl* **-ries 1 :** a trading station where resident factors trade **2 :** a building or set of buildings with facilities for manufacturing

fac·to·tum \\fak-ˈtōt-əm\\ *n* **:** an employee with numerous varied duties

fac·tu·al \\ˈfak-chə(-wə)l\\ *adj* **1 :** of or relating to facts **2 :** restricted to or based on fact — **fac·tu·al·i·ty** \\ˌfak-chə-ˈwal-ət-ē\\ *n* — **fac·tu·al·ly** \\ˈfak-chə(-wə)-lē\\ *adv* — **fac·tu·al·ness** *n*

fac·ul·ta·tive \\ˈfak-əl-ˌtāt-iv\\ *adj* **:** OPTIONAL; *also* **:** capable of more than one relationship or response — **fac·ul·ta·tive·ly** *adv*

fac·ul·ty \\ˈfak-əl-tē\\ *n, pl* **-ties 1 :** ability to do something : TALENT **2 :** one of the powers of the mind or body **3 a :** the teachers in a school or college **b :** a department of instruction in a university **4 :** the members of a profession

fad \\ˈfad\\ *n* **:** a practice or interest followed for a time with exaggerated zeal : CRAZE — **fad·dist** \\ˈfad-əst\\ *n*

fade \\ˈfād\\ *vb* **1 :** to lose freshness or vitality : WITHER **2 :** to lose or cause to lose freshness or brilliance of color **3 :** to grow dim or faint : disappear gradually

fa·er·ie \\ˈfā-(ə-)rē, ˈfa(ə)r-ē, ˈfe(ə)r-ē\\ *n, pl* **fa·er·ies 1 :** FAIRYLAND **2 :** FAIRY

¹**fag** \\ˈfag\\ *vb* **fagged**; **fag·ging 1 :** DRUDGE **2 :** to act as a fag **3 :** to tire by strenuous activity : EXHAUST

²**fag** *n* **1 :** an English public-school boy who acts as servant to another **2 :** MENIAL, DRUDGE

fag end *n* **1 :** the untwisted end of a rope **2 a :** REMNANT **b :** the extreme end

fag·ot *or* **fag·got** \\ˈfag-ət\\ *n* **:** a bundle of sticks or twigs esp. as used for fuel

fag·ot·ing *or* **fag·got·ing** \\ˈfag-ət-iŋ\\ *n* **:** an embroidery produced by tying threads in hourglass-shaped clusters

Fahr·en·heit \\ˈfar-ən-ˌhīt\\ *adj* **:** relating or conforming to a thermometric scale on which under standard atmospheric pressure the boiling point of water is at 212 degrees above the zero of the scale and the freezing point is at 32 degrees above zero — abbr. *F*

fa·ience *or* **fa·ïence** \\fā-ˈän(t)s\\ *n* **:** earthenware decorated with opaque colored glazes

¹**fail** \\ˈfāl\\ *vb* **1 a :** to lose strength : WEAKEN **b :** to die away **c :** to stop functioning **2 a :** to fall short **b :** to be or become absent or inadequate **c :** to be unsuccessful (as in passing an examination) **d :** to become bankrupt **3 :** DISAPPOINT, DESERT **4 :** NEGLECT

²**fail** *n* **:** FAILURE — usu. used in the phrase *without fail*

¹**fail·ing** \\ˈfā-liŋ\\ *n* **:** WEAKNESS, SHORTCOMING

²**failing** *prep* **:** in the absence or lack of

faille \\ˈfīl\\ *n* **:** a somewhat shiny closely woven ribbed silk, rayon, or cotton fabric

fail·ure \\ˈfāl-yər\\ *n* **1 a :** a failing to do or perform : neglect of an assigned, expected, or appropriate action **b :** a state of inability to perform a normal function adequately **2 a :** a lack of success **b :** BANKRUPTCY **3 a :** a falling short : DEFICIENCY **b :** DETERIORATION, BREAKDOWN **4 :** one that has failed

¹**faint** \\ˈfānt\\ *adj* **1 :** lacking courage and spirit : COWARDLY **2 :** being weak, dizzy, and likely to faint **3 :** lacking strength : FEEBLE **4 :** lacking distinctness : barely perceptible — **faint·ly** *adv* — **faint·ness** *n*

²**faint** *vi* **:** to lose consciousness because of a temporary decrease in the blood supply to the brain

³**faint** *n* **:** an act or condition of fainting

faint·heart·ed \\ˈfānt-ˈhärt-əd\\ *adj* **:** lacking courage or resolution : TIMID — **faint·heart·ed·ly** *adv* — **faint·heart·ed·ness** *n*

¹**fair** \\ˈfa(ə)r\\ *adj* **1 :** attractive in appearance : BEAUTIFUL **2 :** SPECIOUS **3 a :** CLEAN, PURE **b :** CLEAR, LEGIBLE **4 :** not stormy or cloudy **5 a :** marked by impartiality and honesty : JUST **b :** conforming with the rules : ALLOWED; *also* **:** being within the foul lines **c :** open to legitimate pursuit or attack **6 a :** PROMISING, LIKELY **b :** favorable to a ship's course **7 :** not dark : BLOND **8 :** ADEQUATE — **fair·ness** *n*

²**fair** *adv* **:** FAIRLY

³**fair** *n* **1 :** a gathering of buyers and sellers at a particular place and time for trade **2 :** a competitive exhibition (as of farm products) **3 :** a sale of a collection of articles usu. for a charitable purpose

fair·ground \\-ˌgraund\\ *n* **:** an area set aside for the holding of fairs and similar gatherings

fair·ly \\ˈfa(ə)r-lē\\ *adv* **1 :** HANDSOMELY, FAVORABLY **2 :** QUITE, COMPLETELY **3 :** in a fair manner : JUSTLY **4 :** MODERATELY

fair–trade \\ˈfa(ə)r-ˈtrād\\ *adj* **:** of, relating to, or being an agreement between a producer and a seller that branded merchandise will be sold at or above a specified price — **fair–trade** *vt*

fair·way \\-ˌwā\\ *n* **:** the mowed part of a golf course between a tee and a green

fairy \\ˈfa(ə)r-ē\\ *n, pl* **fair·ies :** a mythical being of folklore and romance usu. having diminutive human form and magic powers — **fairy** *adj* — **fairy·like** *adj*

fairy·land \\-ˌland\\ *n* **1 :** the land of fairies **2 :** a place of delicate beauty or magical charm

faith \\ˈfāth\\ *n* **1 a :** allegiance to duty or a person : LOYALTY **b :** fidelity to one's promises **2 a :** belief and trust in and loyalty to God **b :** firm belief in something for which there is no proof **3 :** a system of religious beliefs — **in faith :** by my faith : TRULY

¹**faith·ful** \\ˈfāth-fəl\\ *adj* **1 :** full of faith esp. in God **2 :** steadfast in keeping promises or in fulfilling duties **3 :** steady, firm, and dependable in allegiance or devotion : LOYAL **4 :** true to the facts : ACCURATE — **faith·ful·ly** \\-fə-lē\\ *adv* — **faith·ful·ness** *n*

²**faithful** *n, pl* **faith·ful** *or* **faith·fuls :** one that is faithful: as **a :** a member of a religious body **b :** a loyal follower or member

faith·less \\ˈfāth-ləs\\ *adj* **1 :** not having faith **2 :** not worthy of trust or reliance : false to promises — **faith·less·ly** *adv* — **faith·less·ness** *n*

¹**fake** \\ˈfāk\\ *vt* **1 :** to treat so as to falsify : DOCTOR **2 :** COUNTERFEIT **3 :** PRETEND, SIMULATE — **fak·er** \\ˈfā-kər\\ *n* — **fak·ery** \\-k(ə-)rē\\ *n*

²**fake** *n* **1 :** an imitation or fabrication that is passed off as genuine : FRAUD, COUNTERFEIT **2 :** IMPOSTOR, CHARLATAN

³**fake** *adj* **:** COUNTERFEIT, SHAM

fa·kir \\fə-ˈki(ə)r\\ *n* **1 :** a Muslim mendicant : DERVISH **2 :** an itinerant Hindu ascetic who performs tricks

fal·chion \\ˈfȯl-chən\\ *n* **:** a broad-bladed slightly curved medieval sword

fal·con \\ˈfal-kən, ˈfȯl-; ˈfȯ-kən\\ *n* **1 :** a hawk trained for use in falconry **2 :** any of various hawks with long wings

fal·con·er \\-kə-nər\\ *n* **:** one that hunts with hawks or breeds or trains hawks for hunting

fal·con·ry \\ˈfal-kən-rē, ˈfȯl-; ˈfȯ-kən-\\ *n* **1 :** the art of training falcons to pursue game **2 :** the sport of hunting with falcons

¹**fall** \\ˈfȯl\\ *vi* **fell** \\ˈfel\\; **fall·en** \\ˈfȯ-lən\\; **fall·ing 1 a :** to descend freely by the force of gravity **b :** to hang freely **c :** to drop oneself to a lower position **d :** to come as if by descending **2 a :** to become of lower degree or level **b :** to become uttered **c :** to become lowered **3 a :** to leave an erect position suddenly and involuntarily **b :** STUMBLE, STRAY **c :** to drop down wounded or dead; *esp* **:** to die in battle **d :** to become captured or defeated **e :** to suffer ruin or failure **4 :** to commit an immoral act; *esp* **:** to lose one's chastity **5 a :** to move or extend in a downward direction **b :** SUBSIDE, ABATE

c : to decline in quality, activity, quantity, or value d : to assume a look of shame or dejection 6 a : to occur at a certain time b : to come by chance c : DEVOLVE d : to have the proper place or station 7 : to come within the scope of something 8 : to pass from one condition of body or mind to another 9 : to set about heartily or actively — **fall flat** : to produce no response or result — **fall for** 1 : to fall in love with 2 : to become a victim of — **fall foul** 1 : to have a collision — used chiefly of ships 2 : to have a quarrel : CLASH — often used with *of* — **fall from grace** 1 : to lapse morally : SIN 2 : BACKSLIDE — **fall into line** : to comply with a certain course of action — **fall over oneself** : to display excessive eagerness — **fall short** 1 : to be deficient 2 : to fail to attain

²fall *n* 1 : the act of falling 2 a : a falling out, off, or away : DROPPING b : AUTUMN c : a thing or quantity that falls 3 a : loss of greatness : COLLAPSE b : the surrender or capture of a besieged place c : lapse or departure from innocence or goodness 4 a : the descent of land or a hill : SLOPE b : WATERFALL — usu. used in pl. 5 : a decrease in size, quantity, degree, activity, or value 6 : the distance which something falls 7 a : an act of forcing a wrestler's shoulders to the mat b : a bout of wrestling

fal·la·cious \fə-ˈlā-shəs\ *adj* 1 : embodying a fallacy 2 : MISLEADING, DELUSIVE — **fal·la·cious·ly** *adv* — **fal·la·cious·ness** *n*

fal·la·cy \ˈfal-ə-sē\ *n, pl* **-cies** 1 : a false or mistaken idea 2 : false or illogical reasoning or an instance of such reasoning

fall back *vi* : RETREAT, RECEDE

fall guy *n* 1 : one that is easily duped 2 : SCAPEGOAT

fal·li·ble \ˈfal-ə-bəl\ *adj* 1 : liable to be erroneous 2 : capable of making a mistake — **fal·li·bil·i·ty** \ˌfal-ə-ˈbil-ət-ē\ *n* — **fal·li·bly** \ˈfal-ə-blē\ *adv*

fall in *vi* : to take one's proper place in a military formation

falling star *n* : METEOR

fall out *vi* 1 : HAPPEN 2 : to have a quarrel 3 a : to leave one's place in the ranks b : to leave a building to meet a military formation

fall·out \ˈfȯl-ˌau̇t\ *n* : the often radioactive particles stirred up by or resulting from a nuclear explosion and descending through the atmosphere

¹fal·low \ˈfal-ō\ *adj* : of a light yellowish brown

²fallow *n* : usu. cultivated land allowed to lie idle during the growing season

³fallow *vt* : to till (land) without seeding

⁴fallow *adj* 1 : left untilled or unsown 2 : DORMANT, INACTIVE — **fal·low·ness** *n*

fallow deer *n* : a small European deer with broad antlers and a pale yellow coat spotted white in the summer

¹false \ˈfȯls\ *adj* 1 : not genuine 2 a : intentionally untrue b : adjusted or made so as to deceive c : tending to mislead 3 : not true 4 : not faithful or loyal : TREACHEROUS 5 : not essential to structure 6 : inaccurate in pitch 7 a : based on mistaken ideas b : inconsistent with the true facts — **false·ly** *adv* — **false·ness** *n*

²false *adv* : FAITHLESSLY, TREACHEROUSLY

false·hood \ˈfȯls-ˌhu̇d\ *n* 1 : an untrue statement : LIE 2 : absence of truth or accuracy 3 : the practice of lying

¹fal·set·to \fȯl-ˈset-ō\ *n, pl* **-tos** : an artificially high voice; *esp* : an artificial singing voice that overlaps and extends above the range of the full voice esp. of a tenor

²falsetto *adv* : in falsetto

fal·si·fy \ˈfȯl-sə-ˌfī\ *vb* **-fied; -fy·ing** 1 : to make false : change so as to deceive 2 a : to tell lies : LIE b : MISREPRESENT 3 : to prove to be false — **fal·si·fi·ca·tion** \ˌfȯl-sə-fə-ˈkā-shən\ *n* — **fal·si·fi·er** \ˈfȯl-sə-ˌfī(-ə)r\ *n*

fal·si·ty \ˈfȯl-sət-ē, -stē\ *n, pl* **-ties** 1 : something false : LIE 2 : the quality or state of being false

falt·boat \ˈfält-ˌbōt\ *n* : a small collapsible canoe made of rubberized cloth stretched over a framework

¹fal·ter \ˈfȯl-tər\ *vb* **fal·tered; fal·ter·ing** \ˈfȯl-t(ə-)riŋ\ 1 : to move unsteadily : WAVER 2 : to stumble or hesitate in speech : STAMMER 3 : to hesitate in purpose or action — **fal·ter·er** *n* — **fal·ter·ing·ly** *adv*

²falter *n* : an act or instance of faltering

fame \ˈfām\ *n* : public reputation : RENOWN

famed \ˈfāmd\ *adj* : FAMOUS, WELL-KNOWN, RENOWNED

fa·mil·ial \fə-ˈmil-yəl\ *adj* : of, relating to, or characteristic of a family

¹fa·mil·iar \fə-ˈmil-yər\ *n* 1 : an intimate associate : COMPANION 2 : a spirit held to attend and serve or guard a person 3 : one that frequents a place

²familiar *adj* 1 : closely acquainted : INTIMATE 2 : of or relating to a family 3 a : INFORMAL b : overly intimate : FORWARD, PRESUMPTUOUS 4 a : frequently seen or experienced b : of everyday occurrence 5 : having a good knowledge — **fa·mil·iar·ly** *adv*

fa·mil·iar·i·ty \fə-ˌmil-ˈyar-ət-ē, -ˌmil-ē-ˈar-\ *n, pl* **-ties** 1 : close friendship : INTIMACY 2 : close acquaintance with or knowledge of something 3 : INFORMALITY 4 : an unduly bold or forward act or expression

fa·mil·iar·ize \fə-ˈmil-yə-ˌrīz\ *vt* 1 : to make thoroughly acquainted : ACCUSTOM 2 : to make well known — **fa·mil·iar·i·za·tion** \-ˌmil-yə-rə-ˈzā-shən\ *n*

fam·i·ly \ˈfam-(ə-)lē\ *n, pl* **-lies** 1 : a group of persons of common ancestry : CLAN 2 : a group of individuals living under one roof and under one head : HOUSEHOLD 3 : a group of things having common characteristics or properties 4 : a social group composed of parents and their children 5 : a group of related plants or animals

family name *n* : SURNAME 2

fam·ine \ˈfam-ən\ *n* 1 : an extreme general scarcity of food 2 : a great shortage

fam·ish \ˈfam-ish\ *vb* 1 : STARVE 2 : to suffer or cause to suffer from extreme hunger — **fam·ish·ment** *n*

fa·mous \ˈfā-məs\ *adj* 1 : much talked about : very well known 2 : deserving to be remembered : SPLENDID, FIRST-CLASS

fa·mous·ly \ˈfā-məs-lē\ *adv* : SPLENDIDLY, EXCELLENTLY

¹fan \ˈfan\ *n* : a device (as a hand-waved triangular piece or a mechanism with blades) for producing a current of air

²fan *vb* **fanned; fan·ning** 1 : to drive away the chaff from grain by winnowing 2 : to move or impel air with a fan 3 a : to direct a current of air upon b : to stir up to activity as if by fanning : STIMULATE 4 : to spread like a fan 5 : to strike out in baseball — **fan·ner** *n*

³fan *n* 1 : an enthusiastic follower of a sport or entertainment 2 : an enthusiastic admirer (as of an athlete or movie star)

fa·nat·ic \fə-ˈnat-ik\ *adj* : marked or moved by excessive enthusiasm and intense uncritical devotion — **fanatic** *n* — **fa·nat·i·cal** \-i-kəl\ *adj* — **fa·nat·i·cal·ly** \-i-k(ə-)lē\ *adv* — **fa·nat·i·cism** \-ˈnat-ə-ˌsiz-əm\ *n*

fan·ci·er \ˈfan(t)-sē-ər\ *n* : a person who breeds or grows a particular animal or plant for points of excellence

fan·ci·ful \ˈfan(t)-si-fəl\ *adj* 1 a : full of fancy b : guided by fancy 2 : coming from the fancy rather than from the reason 3 : curiously made or shaped — **fan·ci·ful·ly** \-f(ə-)lē\ *adv*

¹fan·cy \ˈfan(t)-sē\ *n, pl* **fancies** 1 : the power of the mind to think of things not present : IMAGINATION 2 : LIKING 3 : THOUGHT, IDEA, WHIM 4 : taste or judgment esp. in art, literature, or decoration

²fancy *vt* **fan·cied; fan·cy·ing** 1 : to have a fancy for : LIKE 2 : IMAGINE 3 : to believe without evidence

³fancy *adj* 1 : based on fancy : WHIMSICAL 2 a : not plain : ORNAMENTAL b : of particular excellence 3 : executed with technical skill and superior grace — **fan·ci·ly** \ˈfan(t)-sə-lē\ *adv* — **fan·ci·ness** \-sē-nəs\ *n*

fancy dress *n* : a costume (as for a masquerade) chosen to suit the wearer's fancy — **fancy–dress** *adj*
fan·cy–free \'fan(t)-sē-ˌfrē\ *adj* : not centering the attention on any one person or thing; *esp* : not in love
fan·cy·work \-ˌwərk\ *n* : ornamental needlework
fan·dan·go \fan-'daŋ-gō\ *n, pl* **-gos** : a lively Spanish or Spanish-American dance
fan·fare \'fan-ˌfa(ə)r\ *n* **1** : a flourish of trumpets **2** : a showy outward display
fang \'faŋ\ *n* : a long sharp tooth; *esp* : a grooved or hollow tooth of a venomous snake — **fanged** \'faŋd\ *adj*
fan·light \'fan-ˌlīt\ *n* : a semicircular window with radiating sash bars like the ribs of a fan placed over a door or window
fan·tail \'fan-ˌtāl\ *n* **1** : a fan-shaped tail or end **2** : a fancy goldfish with the tail fins double **3** : an overhang at the stern of a ship
fan·ta·sia \fan-'tā-zhə, ˌfant-ə-'zē-ə\ *n* : a free instrumental composition not in strict form
fan·tas·tic \fan-'tas-tik, fən-\ *adj* **1** : produced by the fancy or resembling something produced by the fancy : IMAGINARY, UNREAL **2** : going beyond belief : incredible or hardly credible **3** : extremely individual or eccentric — **fan·tas·ti·cal·ly** \-ti-k(ə-)lē\ *adv*
fan·ta·sy \'fant-ə-sē, -ə-zē\ *n, pl* **-sies** **1** : IMAGINATION, FANCY **2** : something produced by a person's imagination; *esp* : ILLUSION **3** : FANTASIA
[1]**far** \'fär\ *adv* **far·ther** \-t͟hər\ *or* **fur·ther** \'fər-\; **far·thest** *or* **fur·thest** \-t͟həst\ **1** : at or to a considerable distance in space or time **2** : by a broad interval : WIDELY, MUCH **3** : to or at a definite distance, point, or degree **4** : to an advanced point or extent : a long way — **by far** : GREATLY — **far and away** : DECIDEDLY
[2]**far** *adj* **farther** *or* **further**; **farthest** *or* **furthest** **1 a** : very distant in space **b** : remote in time **2** : LONG **3** : the more distant of two
far·away \ˌfär-ə-ˌwā\ *adj* **1** : DISTANT **2** : DREAMY, ABSTRACTED
farce \'färs\ *n* **1** : a play made up of ridiculous and absurd situations and happenings and intended to make people laugh **2** : humor of the kind characteristic of a farce **3** : a ridiculous action, display, or pretense
far·ci·cal \'fär-si-kəl\ *adj* : of, relating to, or resembling farce : LUDICROUS, ABSURD — **far·ci·cal·i·ty** \ˌfär-si-'kal-ət-ē\ *n* — **far·ci·cal·ly** \'fär-si-k(ə-)lē\ *adv*
[1]**fare** \'fa(ə)r\ *vi* **1** : GO, TRAVEL **2** : to get along : SUCCEED **3** : EAT, DINE
[2]**fare** *n* **1** : the money a person pays to travel on a public conveyance **2** : a person paying a fare **3** : FOOD
[1]**fare·well** \fa(ə)r-'wel\ *imperative verb* : get along well — used interjectionally to or by one departing
[2]**farewell** *n* **1** : a wish of welfare at parting : GOOD-BYE **2** : an act of departure : LEAVE-TAKING
[3]**fare·well** \ˌfa(ə)r-ˌwel\ *adj* : PARTING, FINAL
far·fetched \'fär-'fecht\ *adj* : not easily or naturally deduced or introduced : IMPROBABLE
far–flung \'fär-'fləŋ\ *adj* : widely spread or distributed
fa·ri·na \fə-'rē-nə\ *n* : a fine meal (as of wheat) used chiefly for puddings or as a breakfast cereal
[1]**farm** \'färm\ *n* : a tract of land devoted to the raising of crops or livestock
[2]**farm** *vb* **1** : to devote to agriculture **2** : to engage in raising crops or livestock — **farm·er** *n*
farm·hand \'färm-ˌhand\ *n* : a farm laborer
farm·house \-ˌhaùs\ *n* : a dwelling on a farm
farm·ing \'fär-miŋ\ *n* : the occupation or business of a person who farms : AGRICULTURE
farm·stead \'färm-ˌsted\ *n* : the buildings and adjacent service areas of a farm
farm·yard \-ˌyärd\ *n* : space around or enclosed by farm buildings
far–off \'fär-'ȯf\ *adj* : remote in time or space
far–out \'fär-'aùt\ *adj* : marked by a considerable departure from the conventional or traditional : EXTREME
far–reach·ing \'fär-'rē-chiŋ\ *adj* : having a wide range, influence, or effect
far·ri·er \'far-ē-ər\ *n* : a blacksmith who shoes horses; *also* : VETERINARIAN
[1]**far·row** \'far-ō\ *vb* : to give birth to pigs
[2]**farrow** *n* : a litter of pigs
far·see·ing \'fär-'sē-iŋ\ *adj* : FARSIGHTED
far·sight·ed \-'sīt-əd\ *adj* **1** : able to see distant things more clearly than near ones **2** : JUDICIOUS, WISE, SHREWD — **far·sight·ed·ly** *adv* — **far·sight·ed·ness** *n*
[1]**far·ther** \'fär-t͟hər\ *adv* **1** : at or to a greater distance or more advanced point **2** : more completely
[2]**farther** *adj* **1** : more distant : REMOTER **2** : [2]FURTHER 2
far·ther·most \-ˌmōst\ *adj* : most distant : FARTHEST
[1]**far·thest** \'fär-t͟həst\ *adj* : most distant in space or time
[2]**farthest** *adv* **1** : to or at the greatest distance in space or time : REMOTEST **2** : to the most advanced point **3** : by the greatest degree or extent : MOST
far·thing \'fär-t͟hiŋ\ *n* : a British monetary unit equal to 1/4 of a penny; *also* : a coin representing this unit
far·thin·gale \'fär-t͟hən-ˌgāl, -t͟hiŋ-\ *n* : a support (as of hoops) worn esp. in the 16th century to swell out a skirt
fas·ci·cle \'fas-i-kəl\ *n* **1** : a small bundle or cluster (as of flowers or roots) **2** : one of the divisions of a book published in parts — **fas·ci·cled** \-kəld\ *adj* — **fas·cic·u·lar** \fə-'sik-yə-lər, fa-\ *adj*
fas·ci·nate \'fas-ᵊn-ˌāt\ *vb* **1** : to grip the attention of esp. so as to take away the power to move, act, or think for oneself **2** : to allure and hold by charming qualities : be attractive — **fas·ci·na·tion** \ˌfas-ᵊn-'ā-shən\ *n* — **fas·ci·na·tor** \'fas-ᵊn-ˌāt-ər\ *n*
fas·cism \'fash-ˌiz-əm\ *n* **1** *often cap* : the principles of an Italian political organization headed by Mussolini that governed Italy 1922–1943 **2** : a political philosophy, movement, or regime advocating nationalism and racial superiority, a centralized dictatorial regime, severe economic and social regimentation, and forcible suppression of opposition — **fas·cist** \'fash-əst\ *n or adj, often cap* — **fas·cis·tic** \fa-'shis-tik\ *adj, often cap*
Fa·sci·sta \fä-'shē-stä\ *n, pl* **Fa·sci·sti** \-(ˌ)stē\ : a member of the Italian Fascist movement
[1]**fash·ion** \'fash-ən\ *n* **1** : the make or form of something **2** : MANNER, WAY **3 a** : a prevailing custom, usage, or style **b** : the prevailing style (as in dress) during a particular time
[2]**fashion** *vt* **fash·ioned**; **fash·ion·ing** \'fash-(ə-)niŋ\ **1** : to give shape or form to : MOLD, CONSTRUCT **2** : FIT, ADAPT — **fash·ion·er** \'fash-(ə-)nər\ *n*
fash·ion·a·ble \'fash-(ə-)nə-bəl\ *adj* **1 a** : following the fashion or established style : STYLISH **b** : dressing or behaving according to fashion **2** : of or relating to the world of fashion : popular among those who conform to fashion — **fash·ion·a·ble·ness** *n* — **fash·ion·a·bly** \-blē\ *adv*
[1]**fast** \'fast\ *adj* **1 a** : firmly fixed or bound **b** : tightly shut **c** : adhering firmly **d** : UNCHANGEABLE **2** : firmly loyal : STAUNCH **3 a** : characterized by quick motion, operation, or effect: (1) : moving or able to move rapidly : SWIFT (2) : taking a comparatively short time **b** : conducive to rapidity of play or action **c** : indicating ahead of the correct time **4** : not easily disturbed **5 a** : permanently dyed **b** : proof against fading by a particular agency **6 a** : DISSIPATED, WILD **b** : daringly unconventional esp. in sexual matters
[2]**fast** *adv* **1** : in a fast or fixed manner **2** : SOUNDLY, DEEPLY **3** : SWIFTLY **4** : in a dissipated manner : RECKLESSLY

[3]**fast** *vi* **1 :** to abstain from food **2 :** to eat sparingly or abstain from some foods

[4]**fast** *n* **1 :** the act or practice of fasting **2 :** a time of fasting

fast·back \'fas(t)-ˌbak\ *n* **:** an automobile roof with a long curving downward slope to the rear; *also* **:** an automobile with such a roof

fas·ten \'fas-ᵊn\ *vb* **fas·tened**; **fas·ten·ing** \'fas-niŋ, -ᵊn-iŋ\ **1 :** to attach or join by or as if by pinning, tying, or nailing **2 :** to make fast **:** fix securely **3 :** to fix or set steadily **4 :** to become fixed or joined — **fas·ten·er** \'fas-nər, -ᵊn-ər\ *n*

fastening *n* **:** something that fastens **:** FASTENER

fas·tid·i·ous \fa-'stid-ē-əs\ *adj* **1 a :** overly difficult to please **b :** showing or demanding excessive delicacy or care **2 :** having complex nutritional requirements — **fas·tid·i·ous·ly** *adv* — **fas·tid·i·ous·ness** *n*

fast·ness \'fas(t)-nəs\ *n* **1 :** the quality or state of being fast **2 :** a fortified or secure place **:** STRONGHOLD

[1]**fat** \'fat\ *adj* **1 a :** PLUMP, FLESHY **b :** OILY, GREASY **2 :** well stocked **:** ABUNDANT **3 :** richly rewarding **:** PROFITABLE — **fat·ness** *n*

[2]**fat** *n* **1 :** animal tissue rich in greasy or oily matter **2 :** any of numerous energy-rich esters that occur naturally in animal fats and in plants and are soluble in organic solvents (as ether) but not in water **3 :** the best or richest part **4 :** excess matter

[3]**fat** *vt* **fat·ted**; **fat·ting :** to make fat **:** FATTEN

fa·tal \'fāt-ᵊl\ *adj* **1 :** causing death or ruin **:** MORTAL **2 :** determining one's fate **:** FATEFUL — **fa·tal·ly** \-ᵊl-ē\ *adv*

fa·tal·ism \'fāt-ᵊl-ˌiz-əm\ *n* **:** the belief that events are determined by fate — **fa·tal·ist** \-ᵊl-əst\ *n* — **fa·tal·is·tic** \ˌfāt-ᵊl-'is-tik\ *adj*

fa·tal·i·ty \fā-'tal-ət-ē, fə-\ *n, pl* **-ties 1 a :** the quality or state of causing death **:** DEADLINESS **b :** the quality or condition of being destined for disaster **2 :** FATE 1 **3 :** a death resulting from a disaster or accident

fat·back \'fat-ˌbak\ *n* **:** a fatty strip from the back of the hog usu. cured by salting and drying

[1]**fate** \'fāt\ *n* **1 :** a power beyond men's control that is held to determine what happens **:** DESTINY **2 :** something that happens as though determined by fate **:** FORTUNE **3 :** END, OUTCOME **4 :** DISASTER; *esp* **:** DEATH

[2]**fate** *vt* **:** DESTINE; *also* **:** DOOM

fate·ful \'fāt-fəl\ *adj* **1 :** having or marked by serious consequences **:** IMPORTANT **2 :** OMINOUS, PROPHETIC **3 :** DEADLY, DESTRUCTIVE

[1]**fa·ther** \'fäth-ər\ *n* **1 a :** a male parent **b** *cap* (1) **:** [2]GOD (2) **:** the first person of the Trinity **2 :** FOREFATHER **3 a :** one who cares for another as a father might **b :** one deserving the respect and love given to a father **4** *often cap* **:** an early Christian writer accepted by the church as an authoritative witness to its teaching and practice **5 :** ORIGINATOR, AUTHOR **6 :** PRIEST ' used esp. as a title **7 :** one of the leading men (as of a city) — usu. used in pl.

[2]**father** *vt* **fa·thered**; **fa·ther·ing** \'fäth-(ə-)riŋ\ **1 a :** BEGET **b :** to be the founder, producer, or author of **2 :** to treat or care for as a father

fa·ther·hood \'fäth-ər-ˌhu̇d\ *n* **:** the condition of being a father

fa·ther–in–law \'fäth-(ə-)rən-ˌlȯ, -ərn-ˌlȯ\ *n, pl* **fathers–in–law** \'fäth-ər-zən-\ **:** the father of one's spouse

fa·ther·land \'fäth-ər-ˌland\ *n* **1 :** one's native land or country **2 :** the native land or country of one's ancestors

fa·ther·less \-ləs\ *adj* **:** having no father **:** ORPHANED

fa·ther·ly \-lē\ *adj* **1 :** of or resembling a father **2 :** showing the affection or concern of a father — **fa·ther·li·ness** *n*

[1]**fath·om** \'fath-əm\ *n* **:** a unit of length equal to 6 feet that is used esp. for measuring the depth of water

[2]**fathom** *vb* **1 :** to measure by a sounding line **:** take soundings; *also* **:** PROBE **2 :** to penetrate and come to understand — **fath·om·a·ble** *adj*

fath·om·less \'fath-əm-ləs\ *adj* **:** incapable of being fathomed

[1]**fa·tigue** \fə-'tēg\ *n* **1 :** weariness from labor or exertion **2 a :** manual or menial work performed by military personnel **b** *pl* **:** the uniform or work clothing worn on fatigue and in the field

[2]**fatigue** *vb* **:** to weary with labor or exertion

fat·ten \'fat-ᵊn\ *vb* **fat·tened**; **fat·ten·ing** \'fat-niŋ, -ᵊn-iŋ\ **1 :** to make or become fat **2 :** to make (as land) fertile

fat·ty \'fat-ē\ *adj* **1 :** containing fat esp. in unusual amounts; *also* **:** unduly stout **:** CORPULENT **2 :** GREASY — **fat·ti·ly** \'fat-ᵊl-ē\ *adv* — **fat·ti·ness** \'fat-ē-nəs\ *n*

fa·tu·i·ty \fə-'t(y)ü-ət-ē, fa-\ *n, pl* **-ties :** FOOLISHNESS

fat·u·ous \'fach-(ə-)wəs\ *adj* **:** complacently or inanely foolish **:** SILLY — **fat·u·ous·ly** *adv* — **fat·u·ous·ness** *n*

fau·cet \'fȯ-sət, 'fäs-ət\ *n* **:** a fixture for drawing a liquid from a pipe, cask, or other vessel

[1]**fault** \'fȯlt\ *n* **1 a :** a weakness in character **:** FAILING; *esp* **:** a moral weakness less serious than a vice **b :** a physical or intellectual imperfection or impairment **c :** an error in a racket game **2 a :** MISDEMEANOR **b :** MISTAKE **3 :** responsibility for wrongdoing or failure **4 :** a fracture in the earth's crust — **at fault :** open to blame — **to a fault :** EXCESSIVELY

[2]**fault** *vb* **1 :** to commit a fault **:** ERR **2 :** to fracture so as to produce a geologic fault **3 :** to find a fault in

fault·find·er \'fȯlt-ˌfīn-dər\ *n* **:** a person who is inclined to find fault or complain — **fault·find·ing** \-diŋ\ *n or adj*

fault·less \'fȯlt-ləs\ *adj* **:** free from fault **:** PERFECT — **fault·less·ly** *adv* — **fault·less·ness** *n*

faulty \'fȯl-tē\ *adj* **:** marked by fault, blemish, or defect — **fault·i·ly** \-tə-lē\ *adv* — **fault·i·ness** \-tē-nəs\ *n*

faun \'fȯn, 'fän\ *n* **:** an ancient Italian deity of fields and herds represented as part goat and part man

fau·na \'fȯn-ə, 'fän-\ *n* **:** animals or animal life esp. of a region, period, or environment — **fau·nal** \'fȯn-ᵊl, 'fän-\ *adj* — **fau·nal·ly** \-ᵊl-ē\ *adv*

faux pas \(')fō-'pä\ *n, pl* **faux pas** \-'pä(z)\ **:** BLUNDER; *esp* **:** a social blunder

[1]**fa·vor** \'fā-vər\ *n* **1 a :** friendly regard shown toward another esp. by a superior **b :** APPROVAL, APPROBATION **c :** PARTIALITY **d :** POPULARITY **2 a :** gracious kindness; *also* **:** an act of such kindness **b** *pl* **:** effort in one's behalf or interest **:** ATTENTION **3 a :** a token of love (as a ribbon) usu. worn conspicuously **b :** a small gift or decorative item given out at a party **4 :** a special privilege or right granted or conceded **5 :** BEHALF, INTEREST — **in favor of 1 :** in accord or sympathy with **2 :** in support of

[2]**favor** *vt* **fa·vored**; **fa·vor·ing** \'fāv-(ə-)riŋ\ **1 a :** to regard or treat with favor **b** (1) **:** to do a kindness for **:** OBLIGE (2) **:** ENDOW **c :** to treat gently or carefully **:** SPARE **2 :** PREFER **3 a :** to give support to **:** SUSTAIN **b :** FACILITATE **4 :** to bear a resemblance to — **fa·vor·er** \'fā-vər-ər\ *n*

fa·vor·a·ble \'fāv-(ə-)rə-bəl, 'fā-vər-bəl\ *adj* **1 :** showing favor **:** APPROVING **2 :** HELPFUL, PROMISING, ADVANTAGEOUS — **fa·vor·a·ble·ness** *n* — **fa·vor·a·bly** \-blē\ *adv*

[1]**fa·vor·ite** \'fāv-(ə-)rət\ *n* **1 :** a person or a thing that is favored above others **2 :** the contestant in a sports competition regarded as having the best chance to win

[2]**favorite** *adj* **:** constituting a favorite; *esp* **:** best-liked

favorite son *n* **:** a candidate supported by the delegates of his state at a presidential nominating convention

fa·vor·it·ism \'fāv-(ə-)rət-ˌiz-əm\ *n* **:** unfairly favorable treatment of some to the neglect of others **:** PARTIALITY

[1]**fawn** \'fȯn, 'fän\ *vi* **1 :** to show affection — used esp. of a dog **2 :** to court favor by a cringing or flattering manner **:** GROVEL — **fawn·er** *n* — **fawn·ing·ly** *adv*

[2]**fawn** *n* **1 :** a young deer **2 :** a variable color averaging a light grayish brown

fay \'fā\ *n* **:** FAIRY, ELF — **fay** *adj*

faze \'fāz\ *vt* : to disturb the composure or courage of : DAUNT
fe·al·ty \'fē(-ə)l-tē\ *n* : LOYALTY, ALLEGIANCE
¹fear \'fi(ə)r\ *n* **1 a** : an unpleasant often strong emotion caused by expectation or awareness of danger **b** : an instance of this emotion; *esp* : a state marked by this emotion **2** : anxious concern : SOLICITUDE **3** : reverential awe esp. toward God
²fear *vb* **1** : to have a reverential awe of **2** : to be afraid of : have fear **3** : to be apprehensive — **fear·er** *n*
fear·ful \'fi(ə)r-fəl\ *adj* **1** : causing fear **2** : filled with fear **3** : showing or caused by fear **4** : extremely bad, large, or intense — **fear·ful·ly** \-fə-lē\ *adv* — **fear·ful·ness** *n*
fear·less \'fi(ə)r-ləs\ *adj* : free from fear : BRAVE — **fear·less·ly** *adv* — **fear·less·ness** *n*
fear·some \'fi(ə)r-səm\ *adj* **1** : causing fear **2** : TIMID, TIMOROUS — **fear·some·ly** *adv* — **fear·some·ness** *n*
fea·si·ble \'fē-zə-bəl\ *adj* **1** : capable of being done or carried out **2** : capable of being used or dealt with successfully : SUITABLE **3** : REASONABLE, LIKELY — **fea·si·bil·i·ty** \ˌfē-zə-'bil-ət-ē\ *n* — **fea·si·ble·ness** \'fē-zə-bəl-nəs\ *n* — **fea·si·bly** \-blē\ *adv*
¹feast \'fēst\ *n* **1 a** : an elaborate meal : BANQUET **b** : something that gives great pleasure **2** : a religious festival
²feast *vb* **1** : to eat plentifully : participate in a feast **2** : to entertain with rich and plentiful food **3** : DELIGHT
feat \'fēt\ *n* **1** : ACT, DEED **2 a** : a deed notable esp. for courage **b** : an act or product of skill, endurance, or ingenuity
¹feath·er \'fet͟h-ər\ *n* **1** : one of the light horny outgrowths that form the external covering of the body of a bird **2 a** : KIND, NATURE **b** : ATTIRE, DRESS **c** : CONDITION, MOOD — **feath·ered** \-ərd\ *adj* — **feath·er·less** \-ər-ləs\ *adj* — **a feather in one's cap** : a mark of distinction : HONOR
²feather *vb* **feath·ered**; **feath·er·ing** \'fet͟h-(ə-)riŋ\ **1** : to furnish (as an arrow) with a feather **2** : to cover, clothe, or adorn with feathers — **feather one's nest** : to provide for oneself esp. reprehensibly while in a position of trust
feath·er·bed·ding \-ˌbed-iŋ\ *n* : the requiring of an employer usu. under a union rule or safety statute to employ more workers than are needed or to limit production
feath·er·brain \'fet͟h-ər-ˌbrān\ *n* : a foolish scatterbrained person — **feath·er·brained** \ˌfet͟h-ər-'brānd\ *adj*
feath·er·edge \'fet͟h-ər-ˌej\ *n* : a very thin sharp edge; *esp* : one that is easily broken or bent over — **featheredge** *vt*
feath·er·weight \-ər-ˌwāt\ *n* **1** : a very light weight **2** : one that is very light in weight; *esp* : a boxer weighing more than 118 but not over 126 pounds
feath·ery \'fet͟h-(ə-)rē\ *adj* : resembling, suggesting, or covered with feathers
¹fea·ture \'fē-chər\ *n* **1 a** : the shape or appearance of the face **b** : a single part of the face (as the nose or the mouth) **2** : something esp. noticeable : a prominent part or detail : CHARACTERISTIC **3** : a main or outstanding attraction: as **a** : the principal motion picture on a program **b** : a special column or section in a newspaper or magazine
²feature *vb* **fea·tured**; **fea·tur·ing** \'fēch-(ə-)riŋ\ **1** : to outline or mark the features of **2** : to give special prominence to **3** : to play an important part
fe·brile \'feb-rīl, 'fēb-\ *adj* : FEVERISH
Feb·ru·ary \'feb-(y)ə-ˌwer-ē, 'feb-rə-\ *n* : the 2d month of the year
fe·ces \'fē-(ˌ)sēz\ *n pl* : bodily waste discharged through the anus : EXCREMENT — **fe·cal** \'fē-kəl\ *adj*
feck·less \'fek-ləs\ *adj* **1** : INEFFECTUAL, WEAK **2** : WORTHLESS
fe·cund \'fek-ənd, 'fēk-\ *adj* : FRUITFUL, PROLIFIC — **fe·cun·di·ty** \fi-'kən-dət-ē\ *n*
fe·cun·date \'fek-ən-ˌdāt, 'fē-kən-\ *vt* : FERTILIZE — **fe·cun·da·tion** \ˌfek-ən-'dā-shən, ˌfē-kən-\ *n*
fed·er·al \'fed-(ə-)rəl\ *adj* **1 a** : formed by a compact between political units that surrender individual sovereignty to a central authority but retain certain limited powers **b** : of or constituting a form of government in which power is distributed between a central authority and constituent territorial units **c** : of or relating to the central government of a federation **2** *often cap* : FEDERALIST **3** *often cap* : of, relating to, or loyal to the federal government or the Union armies of the U.S. in the American Civil War — **fed·er·al·ly** \-ē\ *adv*
Federal *n* **1** : a supporter of the government of the U.S. in the Civil War; *esp* : a soldier in the federal armies **2** : a federal agent or officer
federal district *n* : a district (as the District of Columbia) set apart as the seat of the central government of a federation
fed·er·al·ism \'fed-(ə-)rə-ˌliz-əm\ *n* **1 a** *often cap* : the federal principle of organization **b** : support or advocacy of this principle **2** *cap* : the principles of the Federalists
fed·er·al·ist \-ləst\ *n* **1** : an advocate of federalism; *esp, often cap* : an advocate of a federal union between the American colonies after the Revolution and of the adoption of the U.S. Constitution **2** *cap* : a member of a major political party in the early years of the U.S. favoring a strong centralized national government — **federalist** *adj, often cap*
fed·er·ate \'fed-ə-ˌrāt\ *vb* : to join in a federation
fed·er·a·tion \ˌfed-ə-'rā-shən\ *n* **1** : the act of federating; *esp* : the formation of a federal union **2 a** : a federal government **b** : a union of organizations
fed·er·a·tive \'fed-ə-ˌrāt-iv, 'fed-(ə-)rət-\ *adj* : FEDERAL
fe·do·ra \fi-'dōr-ə\ *n* : a low soft felt hat with the crown creased lengthwise
fed up *adj* : tired, sated, or disgusted beyond endurance
fee \'fē\ *n* **1 a** : an estate in land held from a feudal lord **b** : an inherited or heritable estate in land **2 a** : a fixed charge **b** : a charge for a professional service **c** : TIP — **in fee** : as a fee
fee·ble \'fē-bəl\ *adj* **1** : lacking in strength or endurance : WEAK **2** : not vigorous or loud : INEFFECTIVE, INADEQUATE — **fee·ble·ness** \-bəl-nəs\ *n* — **fee·bly** \-blē\ *adv*
fee·ble·mind·ed \ˌfē-bəl-'mīn-dəd\ *adj* : lacking normal intelligence : mentally deficient — **fee·ble·mind·ed·ness** *n*
¹feed \'fēd\ *vb* **fed** \'fed\; **feed·ing** **1 a** : to give food to **b** : to give as food **c** : to consume food : EAT **d** : PREY **2** : to furnish with something essential to growth, sustenance, or operation **3** : to supply with cues and situations that make a role more effective — **feed·er** *n*
²feed *n* **1 a** : a usu. large meal **b** : food for livestock **2 a** : material supplied (as to a furnace) **b** : a mechanism by which the action of feeding is effected
feed·back \'fēd-ˌbak\ *n* : the return to the input of a part of the output of a machine, system, or process
¹feel \'fēl\ *vb* **felt** \'felt\; **feel·ing** **1 a** : to perceive as a result of physical contact **b** : to examine or test by touching : HANDLE **2 a** : EXPERIENCE **b** : to suffer from **3** : to ascertain by cautious trial — often used with *out* **4 a** : to be aware of **b** : BELIEVE, THINK **5** : to search for something with the fingers **6** : to seem esp. to the sense of touch **7** : to have sympathy or pity
²feel *n* **1** : the sense of touch **2** : SENSATION, FEELING **3** : the quality of a thing as imparted through touch
feel·er \'fē-lər\ *n* **1** : one that feels; *esp* : a tactile process (as a tentacle) of an animal **2** : a proposal or remark made to find out the views of other people
¹feel·ing \'fē-liŋ\ *n* **1 a** : the sense of touch **b** : a sensation experienced through this sense **2 a** : an often indefinite state of mind; *also* : such a state with regard to something **b** *pl* : general emotional condition : SENSIBILITIES **3 a** : the overall quality of one's awareness **b** : conscious recognition : SENSE **4 a** : OPINION, BELIEF **b** : unreasoned attitude : SENTIMENT

5 : capacity to respond emotionally esp. with the higher emotions : SYMPATHY
[2]**feeling** *adj* : SENSITIVE; *esp* : easily moved emotionally — **feel·ing·ly** *adv* — **feel·ing·ness** *n*
feet *pl of* FOOT
feet-first \'fēt-'fərst\ *adv* : with both feet or all four feet foremost
feign \'fān\ *vb* **1** : to represent by a false appearance of : SHAM **2** : to assert as if true : PRETEND
feint \'fānt\ *n* : something feigned; *esp* : a mock blow or attack at one point in order to distract attention from the point one really intends to attack — **feint** *vi*
fe·lic·i·tate \fi-'lis-ə-ˌtāt\ *vt* : to wish joy to : CONGRATULATE — **fe·lic·i·ta·tion** \-ˌlis-ə-'tā-shən\ *n*
fe·lic·i·tous \fi-'lis-ət-əs\ *adj* **1** : suitably expressed : APT **2** : possessing a talent for apt expression — **fe·lic·i·tous·ly** *adv* — **fe·lic·i·tous·ness** *n*
fe·lic·i·ty \fi-'lis-ət-ē\ *n, pl* **-ties** **1** : the quality or state of being happy; *esp* : great happiness **2** : something that causes happiness **3** : a pleasing faculty esp. in art or language : APTNESS **4** : an apt expression
fe·line \'fē-ˌlīn\ *adj* **1 a** : of or relating to cats or the cat family **b** : resembling a cat **2 a** : SLY, TREACHEROUS **b** : STEALTHY — **feline** *n* — **fe·line·ly** *adv* — **fe·lin·i·ty** \fē-'lin-ət-ē\ *n*
[1]**fell** \'fel\ *n* : SKIN, HIDE, PELT
[2]**fell** *vt* **1 a** : to cut, beat, or knock down **b** : KILL **2** : to sew (a seam) by folding one raw edge under the other
[3]**fell** *past of* FALL
[4]**fell** *adj* : FIERCE, CRUEL; *also* : DEADLY
fel·lah \'fel-ə, fə-'lä\ *n, pl* **fel·la·hin** \ˌfel-ə-'hēn, fə-ˌlä-'hēn\ : a peasant or agricultural laborer in Arab countries (as Egypt or Syria)
[1]**fel·low** \'fel-ō\ *n* **1** : COMRADE, ASSOCIATE **2 a** : an equal in rank, power, or character : PEER **b** : one of a pair : MATE **3** : a member of an incorporated literary or scientific society **4 a** : a worthless man or boy **b** : MAN, BOY **c** : BOYFRIEND **5** : a person granted a stipend for advanced study
[2]**fellow** *adj* : being a companion, mate, or associate
fel·low·man \ˌfel-ō-'man\ *n* : a kindred human being
fel·low·ship \'fel-ō-ˌship\ *n* **1** : the condition of friendly relationship existing among persons **2** : a community of interest or feeling **3** : a group with similar interests **4 a** : the position of a fellow (as of a university) **b** : the stipend granted a fellow; *also* : a foundation providing such a stipend
fellow traveler *n* : a person who sympathizes with and often furthers the ideals and program of an organized group (as the Communist party) without joining it or regularly participating in its activities
fel·ly \'fel-ē\ *or* **fel·loe** \-ō\ *n, pl* **fellies** *or* **felloes** : the outside rim or a part of the rim of a wheel supported by the spokes
[1]**fel·on** \'fel-ən\ *n* : CRIMINAL; *esp* : one who has committed a felony
[2]**felon** *n* : a deep inflammation of the finger or toe
fel·o·ny \'fel-ə-nē\ *n, pl* **-nies** : a serious crime usu. punishable by a heavy sentence — **fe·lo·ni·ous** \fə-'lō-nē-əs\ *adj* — **fe·lo·ni·ous·ly** *adv* — **fe·lo·ni·ous·ness** *n*
[1]**felt** \'felt\ *n* **1** : a cloth made of wool and fur often mixed with natural or synthetic fibers **2** : an article (as a hat) made of felt **3** : a material resembling felt
[2]**felt** *past of* FEEL
[1]**fe·male** \'fē-ˌmāl\ *n* : a female plant or animal
[2]**female** *adj* **1 a** : of, relating to, or being the sex that bears young **b** : PISTILLATE **2** : of, relating to, or characteristic of the female sex — **fe·male·ness** *n*
[1]**fem·i·nine** \'fem-ə-nən\ *adj* **1** : of the female sex **2** : characteristic of or belonging to women : WOMANLY **3** : of, relating to, or constituting the class of words that ordinarily includes most of those referring to females — **fem·i·nine·ly** *adv*
[2]**feminine** *n* **1** : the female principle **2 a** : a word or form of the femine gender **b** : the feminine gender
fem·i·nin·i·ty \ˌfem-ə-'nin-ət-ē\ *n* : the quality or nature of the female sex
fem·i·nism \'fem-ə-ˌniz-əm\ *n* **1** : the theory of the political, economic, and social equality of the sexes **2** : organized activity on behalf of women's rights and interests — **fem·i·nist** \-nəst\ *n or adj*
fe·mur \'fē-mər\ *n, pl* **fe·murs** *or* **fem·o·ra** \'fem-(ə-)rə\ : the long bone of the thigh — **fem·o·ral** \'fem-(ə-)rəl\ *adj*
fen \'fen\ *n* : low land covered naturally in whole or in part with water
[1]**fence** \'fen(t)s\ *n* **1** : a barrier intended to prevent escape or intrusion or to mark a boundary; *esp* : such a barrier made of posts and wire or boards **2** : a person who receives stolen goods; *also* : a shop where stolen goods are disposed of — **fence·less** \-ləs\ *adj* — **on the fence** : in a state of indecision (as between two plans or policies)
[2]**fence** *vb* **1 a** : to enclose with a fence **b** : to keep in or out with a fence **2 a** : to practice fencing **b** : to use tactics of attack and defense esp. in debate resembling those of fencing — **fenc·er** *n*
fenc·ing \'fen(t)-siŋ\ *n* **1** : the art or practice of attack and defense with a sword or foil **2 a** : the fences of a property or region **b** : material used for building fences
fend \'fend\ *vb* **1** : to keep or ward off : REPEL **2** : to try to get along without help : SHIFT
fend·er \'fen-dər\ *n* : a protective device (as a guard over the wheel of a motor vehicle or a screen before an open fireplace)
fen·es·tra·tion \ˌfen-əs-'trā-shən\ *n* : the arrangement, proportioning, and design of windows and doors in a building
fen·nel \'fen-ᵊl\ *n* : a perennial European herb of the carrot family grown for its aromatic seeds
[1]**fer·ment** \(ˌ)fər-'ment\ *vb* **1** : to undergo or cause to undergo fermentation **2** : to be or cause to be in a state of agitation or intense activity : EXCITE — **fer·ment·a·ble** *adj* — **fer·ment·er** *n*
[2]**fer·ment** \'fər-ˌment\ *n* **1** : an agent capable of bringing about fermentation **2 a** : FERMENTATION 1 **b** : a state of unrest : AGITATION
fer·men·ta·tion \ˌfər-mən-'tā-shən, -ˌmen-\ *n* **1** : chemical decomposition of an organic substance (as in the souring of milk or the formation of alcohol from sugar) produced by an enzyme and often accompanied by the evolution of a gas **2** : FERMENT 2b — **fer·men·ta·tive** \(ˌ)fər-'ment-ət-iv\ *adj*
fer·mi·um \'fer-mē-əm, 'fər-\ *n* : a radioactive metallic element artificially produced (as by bombardment of plutonium with neutrons)
fern \'fərn\ *n* : any of a group of flowerless seedless vascular green plants — **fern·like** *adj* — **ferny** \'fər-nē\ *adj*
fe·ro·cious \fə-'rō-shəs\ *adj* **1** : CRUEL, SAVAGE **2** : unbearably intense — **fe·ro·cious·ly** *adv* — **fe·ro·cious·ness** *n*
fe·roc·i·ty \fə-'räs-ət-ē\ *n, pl* **-ties** : the quality or state of being ferocious
[1]**fer·ret** \'fer-ət\ *n* : a partially domesticated usu. albino European polecat used esp. for hunting rodents
[2]**ferret** *vb* **1** : to hunt game with ferrets **2 a** : to drive out of a hiding place **b** : to find and bring to light by searching — usu. used with *out* — **fer·ret·er** *n*
fer·ric \'fer-ik\ *adj* : of, relating to, or containing iron
Fer·ris wheel \'fer-əs-\ *n* : an amusement device consisting of a large upright power-driven wheel carrying seats that remain horizontal around its rim
fer·rous \'fer-əs\ *adj* : of, relating to, or containing iron
fer·rule \'fer-əl\ *n* : a metal ring or cap placed around the end of a cane or around a tool handle to prevent splitting
[1]**fer·ry** \'fer-ē\ *vb* **fer·ried**; **fer·ry·ing** **1 a** : to carry by boat over a body of water **b** : to cross by a ferry **2** : to convey from one place to another

²ferry *n, pl* **ferries** **1 :** a place where persons or things are carried across a body of water (as a river) in a boat **2 :** FERRYBOAT **3 :** an organized service and route for flying airplanes — **fer·ry·man** \-mən\ *n*

fer·ry·boat \-ˌbōt\ *n* **:** a boat used to ferry passengers, vehicles, or goods

fer·tile \ˈfərt-ᵊl\ *adj* **1 :** producing plentifully **:** PRODUCTIVE **2 :** capable of developing or reproducing — **fer·tile·ly** \-ᵊl-(l)ē\ *adv* — **fer·tile·ness** \-ᵊl-nəs\ *n* — **fer·til·i·ty** \(ˌ)fər-ˈtil-ət-ē\ *n*

fer·til·i·za·tion \ˌfərt-ᵊl-ə-ˈzā-shən\ *n* **:** an act or process of making fertile — **fer·til·i·za·tion·al** \-shnəl, -shən-ᵊl\ *adj*

fer·til·ize \ˈfərt-ᵊl-ˌīz\ *vt* **:** to make fertile; *esp* **:** to apply a fertilizer to

fer·til·iz·er \-ˌī-zər\ *n* **:** one that fertilizes; *esp* **:** a substance (as manure or a chemical mixture) used to make soil more fertile

fer·ule \ˈfer-əl\ *n* **:** a rod or ruler used to punish children

fer·ven·cy \ˈfər-vən-sē\ *n* **:** FERVOR

fer·vent \ˈfər-vənt\ *adj* **1 :** very hot **:** GLOWING **2 :** marked by great warmth of feeling **:** ARDENT — **fer·vent·ly** *adv*

fer·vid \ˈfər-vəd\ *adj* **1 :** very hot **:** BURNING **2 :** ARDENT, ZEALOUS — **fer·vid·ly** *adv* — **fer·vid·ness** *n*

fer·vor \ˈfər-vər\ *n* **1 :** intense heat **2 :** intensity of feeling **:** fervid emotion or words **:** ENTHUSIASM

fes·tal \ˈfest-ᵊl\ *adj* **:** of or relating to a feast or festival **:** FESTIVE — **fes·tal·ly** \-ᵊl-ē\ *adv*

¹fes·ter \ˈfes-tər\ *n* **:** a pus-filled sore **:** PUSTULE

²fester *vb* **fes·tered**; **fes·ter·ing** \-t(ə-)riŋ\ **1 a :** to form pus **b :** to become painful and inflamed **2 :** RANKLE

¹fes·ti·val \ˈfes-tə-vəl\ *adj* **:** of, relating to, appropriate to, or set apart as a festival

²festival *n* **1 :** a time of celebration marked by special observances **2 :** a periodic season or program of cultural events or entertainment

fes·tive \ˈfes-tiv\ *adj* **1 :** of, relating to, or suitable for a feast or festival **2 :** JOYOUS, GAY — **fes·tive·ly** *adv* — **fes·tive·ness** *n*

fes·tiv·i·ty \fes-ˈtiv-ət-ē\ *n, pl* **-ties** **1 :** FESTIVAL 1 **2 :** the quality or state of being festive **3 :** festive activity

¹fes·toon \fes-ˈtün\ *n* **1 :** a decorative chain or strip hanging between two points **2 :** a carved, molded, or painted ornament representing a decorative chain

²festoon *vt* **1 :** to hang or form festoons on **2 :** to shape into festoons

fetch \ˈfech\ *vb* **1 :** to go after and bring back **2 :** to cause to come **:** bring out **3 :** to bring as a price **:** sell for **4 :** to give by striking **5 :** ARRIVE — **fetch·er** *n*

fetch·ing \-iŋ\ *adj* **:** ATTRACTIVE, PLEASING — **fetch·ing·ly** *adv*

¹fete *or* **fête** \ˈfāt\ *n* **1 :** FESTIVAL **2 a :** a lavish often outdoor entertainment **b :** an elaborate usu. large party

²fete *or* **fête** *vt* **1 :** to honor or commemorate with a fete **2 :** to pay high honor to

fet·id \ˈfet-əd\ *adj* **:** having an offensive smell **:** STINKING — **fet·id·ly** *adv* — **fet·id·ness** *n*

fet·ish *or* **fet·ich** \ˈfet-ish, ˈfēt-\ *n* **1 :** an object (as an idol or image) believed to have supernatural or magical powers **2 :** something that is made an object of unreasoning devotion or concern — **fet·ish·ism** \-ˌiz-əm\ *n*

fet·lock \ˈfet-ˌläk\ *n* **1 :** a projection with a tuft of hair on the back of a horse's leg above the hoof **2 :** the tuft of hair growing out of the fetlock

fet·ter \ˈfet-ər\ *n* **1 :** a chain or shackle for the feet **2 :** something that confines **:** RESTRAINT — **fetter** *vt*

fet·tle \ˈfet-ᵊl\ *n* **:** a state of fitness or order **:** CONDITION

fe·tus \ˈfēt-əs\ *n* **:** an unborn or unhatched vertebrate esp. after attaining the basic structural plan of its kind — **fe·tal** \ˈfēt-ᵊl\ *adj*

feud \ˈfyüd\ *n* **:** a prolonged quarrel; *esp* **:** a lasting conflict between families or clans marked by violent attacks undertaken for revenge — **feud** *vi*

feu·dal \ˈfyüd-ᵊl\ *adj* **1 :** of, relating to, or having the characteristics of a medieval fee **2 :** of, relating to, or characteristic of feudalism — **feu·dal·ly** \-ᵊl-ē\ *adv*

feu·dal·ism \-ˌiz-əm\ *n* **:** a system of political organization prevailing in medieval Europe in which a vassal rendered service to a lord and received protection and land in return; *also* **:** a similar political or social system — **feu·dal·is·tic** \ˌfyüd-ᵊl-ˈis-tik\ *adj*

fe·ver \ˈfē-vər\ *n* **1 a :** a rise of body temperature above the normal **b :** a disease of which fever is a prominent symptom **2 a :** a state of heightened or intense emotion or activity **b :** a contagious transient enthusiasm **:** CRAZE

fe·ver·ish \ˈfēv-(ə-)rish\ *adj* **1 a :** marked by fever **b :** of, relating to, or being fever **2 :** marked by intense emotion or activity — **fe·ver·ish·ly** *adv* — **fe·ver·ish·ness** *n*

¹few \ˈfyü\ *pron* **:** not many persons or things

²few *adj* **1 :** consisting of or amounting to a small number **2 :** not many but some — **few·ness** *n*

³few *n* **1 :** a small number of units or individuals **2 :** a special limited number

¹few·er \ˈfyü-ər\ *adj* **:** not so many **:** a smaller number of

²fewer *pron* **:** a smaller number of persons or things

fez \ˈfez\ *n, pl* **fez·zes** **:** a round flat-crowned hat that usu. has a tassel, is made of red felt, and is worn by men in eastern Mediterranean countries

fi·an·cé \ˌfē-ˌän-ˈsā, fē-ˈän-ˌsā\ *n* **:** a man engaged to be married

fi·an·cée \ˌfē-ˌän-ˈsā, fē-ˈän-ˌsā\ *n* **:** a woman engaged to be married

fi·as·co \fē-ˈas-kō\ *n, pl* **-coes** **:** a complete failure

fi·at \ˈfī-ˌat, ˈfē-ˌät\ *n* **:** an authoritative and often arbitrary order or decree

¹fib \ˈfib\ *n* **:** a lie about some trivial matter

²fib *vi* **fibbed**; **fib·bing** **:** to tell a fib — **fib·ber** *n*

fi·ber *or* **fi·bre** \ˈfī-bər\ *n* **1 :** a thread or a structure or object resembling a thread: as **a :** a slender root (as of a grass) **b :** a muscle cell **c :** a slender and greatly elongated natural or synthetic unit of material (as wool, cotton, asbestos, gold, glass, or rayon) typically capable of being spun into yarn **2 a :** an element that gives texture or substance **b :** basic toughness **:** STRENGTH

fi·ber·board \ˈfī-bər-ˌbōrd\ *n* **:** a material made by compressing fibers (as of wood) into stiff sheets

fiber glass *n* **:** glass in fibrous form used in making various products (as yarn and insulation)

fi·broid \ˈfī-ˌbrȯid\ *adj* **:** resembling, forming, or consisting of fibrous tissue

fi·brous \ˈfī-brəs\ *adj* **1 :** containing, consisting of, or resembling fibers **2 :** TOUGH, STRINGY

fick·le \ˈfik-əl\ *adj* **:** not firm or steadfast in disposition or character **:** INCONSTANT — **fick·le·ness** *n*

fic·tion \ˈfik-shən\ *n* **1 :** something told or written that is not fact **:** something made up **2 :** a made-up story about real or imaginary persons or events; *also* **:** such stories as a class — **fic·tion·al** \ˈfik-shnəl, -shən-ᵊl\ *adj* — **fic·tion·al·ly** \-ē\ *adv*

fic·tion·al·ize \ˈfik-shnəl-ˌīz, -shən-ᵊl-\ *or* **fic·tion·ize** \-shə-ˌnīz\ *vt* **:** to make into fiction — **fic·tion·al·i·za·tion** \ˌfik-shnəl-ə-ˈzā-shən, -shən-ᵊl-\ *or* **fic·tion·i·za·tion** \ˌfik-shə-nə-ˈzā-shən\ *n*

fic·ti·tious \fik-ˈtish-əs\ *adj* **:** not real **:** MADE-UP, IMAGINARY — **fic·ti·tious·ly** *adv* — **fic·ti·tious·ness** *n*

¹fid·dle \ˈfid-ᵊl\ *n* **:** VIOLIN

²fiddle *vb* **fid·dled**; **fid·dling** \ˈfid-liŋ, -ᵊl-iŋ\ **1 :** to play on a fiddle **2 a :** to move the hands or fingers restlessly **b :** to spend time in aimless activity **:** PUTTER **c :** MEDDLE, TAMPER — **fid·dler** \ˈfid-lər, -ᵊl-ər\ *n*

fid·dle·stick \ˈfid-ᵊl-ˌstik\ *n* **1 :** a violin bow **2** *pl* **:** NONSENSE — used as an interjection

fi·del·i·ty \fə-ˈdel-ət-ē, fī-\ *n, pl* **-ties** **1** : the quality or state of being faithful **2** : ACCURACY

¹fidg·et \ˈfij-ət\ *n* **1** *pl* : uneasiness or restlessness as shown by nervous movements **2** : one that fidgets — **fidg·ety** \-ət-ē\ *adj*

²fidget *vb* : to move or cause to move or act nervously or restlessly

¹fi·du·cia·ry \fə-ˈd(y)ü-shē-ˌer-ē, fī-, -shə-rē\ *n, pl* **-cia·ries** **1** : one that acts as a trustee for another **2** : one that acts in a confidential capacity

²fiduciary *adj* **1** : involving a confidence or trust **2** : held or holding in trust for another

fie \ˈfī\ *interj* — used to express disgust or shock

fief \ˈfēf\ *n* : a feudal estate : FEE

¹field \ˈfēld\ *n* **1 a** : open country — usu. used in pl. **b** : a piece of open cleared or cultivated land **c** : a piece of land put to some special use or yielding some special product **d** : a place where a battle is fought : the region in which military operations are carried on **e** : an open space or expanse **2** : a sphere or range of activity or influence **3** : a background on which something is drawn, painted, or mounted **4** : an area for sports

²field *vb* **1** : to put into the field **2** : to handle a batted or thrown baseball while on defense — **field·er** *n*

³field *adj* : of or relating to a field

field event *n* : an event in a track meet other than a race

field glass *n* : a hand-held optical instrument for use outdoors usu. consisting of two telescopes on a single frame with a focusing device — usu. used in pl.

field marshal *n* : an officer (as in the British army) of the highest rank

field·piece \ˈfēld-ˌpēs\ *n* : a gun or howitzer for use in the field

fiend \ˈfēnd\ *n* **1** : DEMON, DEVIL **2** : an extremely wicked or cruel person **3 a** : a person excessively devoted to a pursuit : FANATIC **b** : a person who uses immoderate quantities of something : ADDICT

fiend·ish \ˈfēn-dish\ *adj* : extremely cruel or wicked : DIABOLICAL — **fiend·ish·ly** *adv* — **fiend·ish·ness** *n*

fierce \ˈfi(ə)rs\ *adj* **1 a** : violently hostile or aggressive in temperament **b** : PUGNACIOUS **2** : INTENSE **3** : furiously active or determined **4** : wild or menacing in aspect — **fierce·ly** *adv* — **fierce·ness** *n*

fi·ery \ˈfī-(ə-)rē\ *adj* **1 a** : consisting of fire **b** : BURNING, BLAZING **c** : FLAMMABLE **2 a** : hot like a fire **b** (1) : INFLAMED (2) : feverish and flushed **3 a** : of the color of fire : RED **b** : intensely or unnaturally red **4 a** : full of emotion or spirit **b** : IRRITABLE — **fi·eri·ness** *n*

fi·es·ta \fē-ˈes-tə\ *n* : FESTIVAL

fife \ˈfīf\ *n* : a small shrill flutelike musical instrument

fif·teen \(ˈ)fif-ˈtēn\ *n* — see NUMBER table — **fifteen** *adj or pron* — **fif·teenth** \-ˈtēn(t)th\ *adj or n*

fifth \ˈfif(t)th, ˈfift\ *n, pl* **fifths** \ˈfif(t)s, ˈfifths\ **1** — see NUMBER table **2** : a unit of measure for liquor equal to one fifth of a U.S. gallon — **fifth** *adj or adv* — **fifth·ly** *adv*

fifth column *n* : a group of secret sympathizers or supporters of a nation's enemy that engage in espionage or sabotage within the country — **fifth columnist** *n*

fif·ty \ˈfif-tē\ *n, pl* **fifties** — see NUMBER table — **fif·ti·eth** \-tē-əth\ *adj or n* — **fifty** *adj or pron*

fig \ˈfig\ *n* : the usu. edible oblong or pear-shaped fruit of a tree of the mulberry family; *also* : a tree bearing figs

¹fight \ˈfīt\ *vb* **fought** \ˈfȯt\; **fight·ing** **1 a** : to contend against another in battle or physical combat **b** : BOX **2** : to put forth a determined effort **3 a** : STRUGGLE, CONTEND **b** : to attempt to prevent the success or effectiveness of **4** : to carry on : WAGE **5** : to gain by struggle

²fight *n* **1 a** : a hostile encounter : BATTLE, COMBAT **b** : a boxing match **c** : a verbal disagreement **2** : a struggle for a goal or an objective **3** : strength or disposition for fighting

fight·er \ˈfīt-ər\ *n* : one that fights: **a** : WARRIOR **b** : BOXER **c** : an airplane of high speed and maneuverability with armament for destroying enemy aircraft

fig·ment \ˈfig-mənt\ *n* : something imagined or made up

fig·u·ra·tive \ˈfig-(y)ə-rət-iv, ˈfig-(y)ərt-iv\ *adj* **1** : representing by a figure or resemblance : EMBLEMATIC **2 a** : METAPHORICAL **b** : characterized by figures of speech — **fig·u·ra·tive·ly** *adv* — **fig·u·ra·tive·ness** *n*

¹fig·ure \ˈfig-yər, *esp Brit* ˈfig-ər\ *n* **1 a** : a number symbol : NUMERAL **b** *pl* : arithmetical calculations **c** : a written or printed character **d** : value esp. as expressed in numbers : PRICE **2 a** : the external shape or outline of something **b** : bodily shape or form esp. of a person **c** : an object noticeable only as a shape or form **3 a** : the graphic representation of a form esp. of a person **b** : a diagram or pictorial illustration of textual matter **4** : an expression (as in metaphor) that uses words in other than a plain or literal way **5** : PATTERN, DESIGN **6** : appearance made or impression produced **7** : a series of movements in a dance **8** : a prominent personality : PERSONAGE

²figure *vb* **1** : to represent by or as if by a figure or outline : PORTRAY **2** : to decorate with a pattern **3 a** : to indicate or represent by numerals **b** : REGARD, CONSIDER **4** : to be or appear important or conspicuous **5** : COMPUTE, CALCULATE — **fig·ur·er** *n*

fig·ure·head \ˈfig-(y)ər-ˌhed\ *n* **1** : a figure, statue, or bust on the bow of a ship **2** : a person who has the title but not the powers of the head of something

fig·u·rine \ˌfig-(y)ə-ˈrēn\ *n* : a small carved or molded figure

fil·a·ment \ˈfil-ə-mənt\ *n* : a single thread or a thin flexible threadlike object, process, or appendage — **fil·a·men·tous** \ˌfil-ə-ˈment-əs\ *adj*

fil·bert \ˈfil-bərt\ *n* **1** : either of two European hazels; *also* : the sweet thick-shelled nut of a filbert **2** : HAZELNUT

filch \ˈfilch\ *vt* : to steal furtively : PILFER

¹file \ˈfīl\ *n* : a usu. steel tool with sharp ridges or teeth on its surface for smoothing or rubbing down a hard substance (as metal)

file

²file *vt* : to rub, smooth, or cut away with a file

³file *vb* **1** : to arrange in order for preservation or reference **2 a** : to enter or record officially or as prescribed by law **b** : to send (copy) to a newspaper **3** : to register as a candidate esp. in a primary election

⁴file *n* **1** : a device (as a folder, case, or cabinet) by means of which papers or records may be kept in order **2** : a collection of papers or records kept in a file

⁵file *n* : a row of persons, animals, or things arranged one behind the other

⁶file *vi* : to march or proceed in file

fi·let mi·gnon \ˌfil-(ˌ)ā-mēn-ˈyōⁿ, fi-ˌlā-\ *n, pl* **filets mignons** *same or* -ˈyōⁿz\ : a fillet of beef cut from the thick end of a beef tenderloin

fil·i·al \ˈfil-ē-əl, ˈfil-yəl\ *adj* : of, relating to, or befitting a son or daughter — **fil·i·al·ly** \-ē\ *adv*

¹fil·i·bus·ter \ˈfil-ə-ˌbəs-tər\ *n* **1** : a military adventurer; *esp* : an American engaged in fomenting insurrections in Latin America in the mid-19th century **2 a** : the use of delaying tactics (as extremely long speeches) esp. in a legislative assembly **b** : an instance of this practice

²filibuster *vb* **fil·i·bus·tered**; **fil·i·bus·ter·ing** \-t(ə-)riŋ\ **1** : to carry out insurrectionist or revolutionary activities in a foreign country **2** : to engage in or subject to a filibuster — **fil·i·bus·ter·er** \-tər-ər\ *n*

fil·i·gree \'fil-ə-ˌgrē\ *n* : ornamental openwork (as of fine wire)
fil·ing \'fī-liŋ\ *n* **1** : the act of one who files **2** : a small piece scraped off by a file
[1]**fill** \'fil\ *vb* **1** : to put into as much as can be held or conveniently contained **2** : to become full **3** : SATISFY **4** : to occupy fully : take up whatever space there is **5** : to spread through **6** : to stop up (as crevices or holes) : PLUG **7 a** : to have and perform the duties of : OCCUPY **b** : to put a person in **8** : to supply according to directions — **fill·er** *n*
[2]**fill** *n* **1** : a full supply; *esp* : a quantity that satisfies or satiates **2** : material used esp. for filling a ditch or hollow in the ground
[1]**fil·let** \'fil-ət\ *n* **1** : a narrow strip of material (as a ribbon) used as a headband **2** : a piece or slice of boneless meat or fish; *esp* : the tenderloin of beef
[2]**fillet** *vt* **1** : to bind or adorn with or as if with a fillet **2** : to cut into fillets
fill·ing \'fil-iŋ\ *n* **1** : material that is used to fill something **2 a** : the yarn interlacing the warp in a fabric **b** : a food mixture used to fill pastry or sandwiches
filling station *n* : a retail station for servicing motor vehicles esp. with gasoline and oil
fil·lip \'fil-əp\ *n* **1** : a blow or gesture made by the sudden forcible straightening of a finger curled up against the thumb **2** : something tending to arouse or excite — **fillip** *vt*
fil·ly \'fil-ē\ *n, pl* **fillies** : a young female horse
[1]**film** \'film\ *n* **1** : a thin skin or membrane **2** : a thin coating or layer **3** : a flexible strip of chemically treated material used in taking pictures **4** : MOTION PICTURE
[2]**film** *vb* **1** : to cover or become covered with film **2** : to photograph on a film; *esp* : to make a motion picture of
film·dom \-dəm\ *n* **1** : the motion-picture industry **2** : the personnel of the motion-picture industry
filmy \'fil-mē\ *adj* **1** : of, resembling, or composed of film **2** : covered with a haze or film — **film·i·ness** *n*
[1]**fil·ter** \'fil-tər\ *n* **1** : a porous article or mass through which a gas or liquid is passed to separate out matter in suspension **2** : an apparatus containing a filter medium **3** : a device or material for suppressing or minimizing waves or oscillations of certain frequencies; *esp* : one (as on a camera lens) that absorbs light of certain colors
[2]**filter** *vb* **fil·tered**; **fil·ter·ing** \-t(ə-)riŋ\ **1** : to pass through a filter **2** : to remove by means of a filter
fil·ter·a·ble \'fil-t(ə-)rə-bəl\ *adj* : capable of being separated by or of passing through a filter — **fil·ter·a·bil·i·ty** \ˌfil-t(ə-)rə-'bil-ət-ē\ *n*
filth \'filth\ *n* **1** : foul or putrid matter; *esp* : loathsome dirt or refuse **2 a** : moral corruption or defilement **b** : something that tends to corrupt or defile : OBSCENITY
filthy \'fil-thē\ *adj* **1** : covered with or containing filth **2 a** : UNDERHANDED, VILE **b** : OBSCENE — **filth·i·ly** \-thə-lē\ *adv* — **filth·i·ness** \-thē-nəs\ *n*
fil·trate \'fil-ˌtrāt\ *n* : the fluid that has passed through a filter
fil·tra·tion \fil-'trā-shən\ *n* : the act or process of filtering
fin \'fin\ *n* **1** : a thin external process of an aquatic animal (as a fish) used in propelling or guiding the body **2 a** : a fin-shaped part (as on an airplane, boat, or automobile) **b** : FLIPPER 2 — **fin·like** *adj* — **finned** \'find\ *adj*
fi·na·gle \fə-'nā-gəl\ *vb* **fi·na·gled**; **fi·na·gling** \-'nā-g(ə-)liŋ\ **1** : to arrange for : WANGLE **2** : to obtain by trickery **3** : to use devious dishonest methods to achieve one's ends — **fi·na·gler** \-g(ə-)lər\ *n*
[1]**fi·nal** \'fīn-ᵊl\ *adj* **1** : not to be altered or undone : CONCLUSIVE **2** : constituting the ultimate in degree or development **3** : of or relating to the ultimate purpose or result of a process **4** : relating to or occurring at the end or conclusion — **fi·nal·ly** \'fīn-ᵊl-ē, 'fīn-lē\ *adv*
[2]**final** *n* : something final: as **a** : a deciding match, game, or trial **b** : the last examination in a course
fi·na·le \fə-'nal-ē, fi-'näl-\ *n* : the close or termination of something; *esp* : the last section of a musical composition
fi·nal·ist \'fīn-ᵊl-əst\ *n* : a contestant in the finals of a competition
fi·nal·i·ty \fī-'nal-ət-ē, fə-\ *n, pl* **-ties** **1** : the character or condition of being final, settled, or complete **2** : something final
fi·nal·ize \'fīn-ᵊl-ˌīz\ *vt* : to put in final or finished form
[1]**fi·nance** \fə-'nan(t)s, 'fī-ˌ, fī-'\ *n* **1** *pl* : liquid resources (as money) available esp. to a government or business **2** : the obtaining of funds or capital : FINANCING **3** : the system that includes the circulation of money, the granting of credit, the making of investments, and the provision of banking facilities
[2]**finance** *vt* **1 a** : to raise or provide funds or capital for **b** : to furnish with necessary funds **2** : to sell or supply on credit
finance company *n* **1** : a company that pays to the seller the cost of an article (as an automobile) purchased on the installment plan and is reimbursed with interest in installments by the purchaser **2** : a company that specializes in making small loans usu. to individuals
fi·nan·cial \fə-'nan-chəl, fī-\ *adj* : of or relating to finance or finances — **fi·nan·cial·ly** \-'nanch-(ə-)lē\ *adv*
fin·an·cier \ˌfin-ən-'si(ə)r, fə-ˌnan-, ˌfī-ˌnan-\ *n* **1** : a person skilled in managing large funds **2** : a person who invests large sums of money
finch \'finch\ *n* : any of a group of songbirds (as sparrows, linnets, or buntings) having a short stout conical bill
[1]**find** \'fīnd\ *vb* **found** \'faůnd\; **find·ing** **1** : to come upon : meet with someone or something by chance **2** : to come upon by searching or study : DISCOVER **3** : to obtain by effort or management **4** : to arrive at : REACH **5** : to make a decision and declare it **6** : to know by experience **7** : to gain or regain the use of **8** : PROVIDE, SUPPLY — **find fault** : to criticize unfavorably
[2]**find** *n* **1** : an act or instance of finding **2** : something found; *esp* : a valuable item of discovery
find·er \'fīn-dər\ *n* : one that finds; *esp* : a lens on a camera that shows the view being photographed by the camera
find·ing \'fīn-diŋ\ *n* **1 a** : the act of one that finds **b** : FIND 2 **2** : the result of a judicial proceeding or inquiry
[1]**fine** \'fīn\ *n* : a sum of money imposed as punishment for an offense — **in fine** : in short
[2]**fine** *vt* : to impose a fine on : punish by a fine
[3]**fine** *adj* **1** : free from impurity **2 a** : very thin in gauge or texture **b** : not coarse **3** : superior in quality, conception, or appearance **4** : marked by or affecting elegance or refinement — **fine·ly** *adv* — **fine·ness** *n*
[4]**fine** *adv* : FINELY
fine art *n* : art (as painting or music) concerned primarily with the creation of beautiful objects — usu. used in pl.
fin·ery \'fīn-(ə-)rē\ *n, pl* **-er·ies** : ORNAMENT, DECORATION; *esp* : showy clothing and jewels
[1]**fi·nesse** \fə-'nes\ *n* **1** : refinement or delicacy of workmanship, structure, or texture **2** : skillful handling of a situation : CUNNING, SUBTLETY
[2]**finesse** *vb* **1** : to bring about by adroit maneuvering **2** : EVADE, TRICK
[1]**fin·ger** \'fiŋ-gər\ *n* **1** : one of the five terminating members of the hand; *esp* : one other than the thumb **2 a** : something that resembles or does the work of a finger **b** : a part of a glove into which a finger is inserted — **fin·ger·like** *adj*
[2]**finger** *vb* **fin·gered**; **fin·ger·ing** \'fiŋ-g(ə-)riŋ\ **1** : to touch with the fingers : HANDLE **2** : to perform with the fingers or with a certain fingering **3** : to mark the notes of a piece of music to show what fingers are to be used **4** : to point out : IDENTIFY
fin·ger·board \'fiŋ-gər-ˌbōrd\ *n* : the part of a musical instrument against which the fingers press the strings to vary the pitch

finger bowl *n* : a basin to hold water for rinsing the fingers at table
fingering *n* **1** : the act or process of handling or touching with the fingers **2 a** : the act or method of using the fingers in playing an instrument **b** : the marking of the method of fingering
fin·ger·nail \'fiŋ-gər-ˌnāl, ˌfiŋ-gər-'\ *n* : the nail of a finger
fin·ger·print \'fiŋ-gər-ˌprint\ *n* : the pattern of marks made by pressing the tip of a finger or thumb on a surface; *esp* : an ink impression of such a pattern taken for the purpose of identification — **fingerprint** *vb*

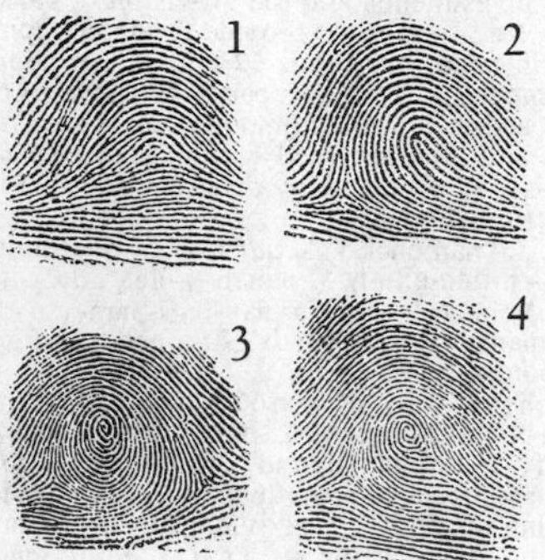

fingerprints: *1* arch, *2* loop, *3* whorl, *4* composite

fin·i·cal \'fin-i-kəl\ *adj* : FINICKY — **fin·i·cal·ly** \-k(ə-)lē\ *adv* — **fin·i·cal·ness** \-kəl-nəs\ *n*
fin·ick·ing \'fin-i-kiŋ, -kən\ *adj* : FINICKY
fin·icky \'fin-i-kē\ *adj* : excessively nice, exacting, or meticulous in taste or standards — **fin·ick·i·ness** *n*
fin·is \'fin-əs, 'fī-nəs\ *n* : END, CONCLUSION
¹fin·ish \'fin-ish\ *vb* **1 a** : to bring or come to an end : TERMINATE **b** : to use or dispose of entirely **2 a** : to bring to completion or issue : PERFECT **b** : to put a final coat or surface on **3** : to bring about the death of **4** : to come to the end of a course, task, or undertaking — **fin·ish·er** *n*
²finish *n* **1** : END, CONCLUSION **2** : the treatment given a surface or the appearance given by finishing **3** : cultivation in manners and speech : social polish
fi·nite \'fī-ˌnīt\ *adj* **1 a** : having definite or definable limits **b** : having a limited nature or existence **2** : being neither infinite nor infinitesimal **3** : showing distinction of grammatical person and number — **fi·nite·ly** *adv* — **fi·nite·ness** *n*
fin·nan had·die \ˌfin-ən-'had-ē\ *n* : smoked haddock
fin·ny \'fin-ē\ *adj* **1** : resembling or having fins **2** : of, relating to, or full of fish
fiord *var of* FJORD
fir \'fər\ *n* **1** : any of various usu. large symmetrical evergreen trees of the pine family some of which yield useful lumber or resins **2** : the wood of a fir
¹fire \'fī(ə)r\ *n* **1** : the light and heat and esp. the flame produced by burning **2** : fuel that is burning (as in a fireplace or stove) **3** : the destructive burning of something (as a building or a forest) **4** : ardent liveliness : ENTHUSIASM **5** : the discharge of firearms : SHOOTING — **on fire 1** : BURNING **2** : ARDENT, EAGER — **under fire 1** : exposed to the firing of an enemy's guns **2** : under attack
²fire *vb* **1 a** : to set on fire : IGNITE **b** : STIR, ENLIVEN **2** : to dismiss from employment : DISCHARGE **3** : to cause to explode **4 a** : to propel from or as if from a gun **b** : DISCHARGE, SHOOT **c** : LAUNCH **d** : to throw with speed : HURL **5 a** : to subject to intense heat **b** : to feed or serve the fire of **6 a** : to take fire **b** : to have the explosive charge ignite at the proper time **7 a** : to discharge a firearm **b** : to emit or let fly an object — **fir·er** *n*
fire·arm \'fī(ə)r-ˌärm\ *n* : a weapon (as a rifle or pistol) from which a shot is discharged by gunpowder
fire·ball \-ˌbȯl\ *n* **1** : a ball of fire **2** : a brilliant meteor that may trail bright sparks **3** : the highly luminous cloud of vapor and dust created by a nuclear explosion
fire·brand \-ˌbrand\ *n* **1** : a piece of burning wood **2** : a person who creates unrest or strife : AGITATOR
fire·break \-ˌbrāk\ *n* : a barrier of cleared or plowed land intended to check a forest or grass fire
fire·brick \-ˌbrik\ *n* : a brick capable of withstanding great heat and used for lining furnaces or fireplaces
fire·bug \-ˌbəg\ *n* : a person who deliberately sets destructive fires : INCENDIARY
fire·crack·er \-ˌkrak-ər\ *n* : a paper cylinder containing an explosive to be fired for noise during celebrations
fire·dog \-ˌdȯg\ *n* : ANDIRON
fire·fly \'fī(ə)r-ˌflī\ *n* : a winged nocturnal insect producing a bright soft intermittent light
fire·man \-mən\ *n* **1** : a member of a company organized to fight fires **2** : one who tends or feeds fires : STOKER
fire·place \-ˌplās\ *n* **1** : a framed rectangular opening made in a chimney to hold an open fire : HEARTH **2** : an outdoor structure of brick or stone made for an open fire
fire·plug \-ˌpləg\ *n* : a hydrant to which a large hose can be attached for drawing water to extinguish fires
fire·pow·er \-ˌpaů(-ə)r\ *n* : the relative ability to deliver gunfire or missiles on a target
¹fire·proof \-'prüf\ *adj* : proof against or resistant to fire
²fireproof *vt* : to make fireproof
fire·side \'fī(ə)r-ˌsīd\ *n* **1** : a place near the fire or hearth **2** : HOME
fire·trap \'fī(ə)r-ˌtrap\ *n* : a building or place apt to catch on fire or difficult to escape from in case of fire
fire·wa·ter \-ˌwȯt-ər, -ˌwät-\ *n* : intoxicating liquor
fire·work \-ˌwərk\ *n* : a device for producing a striking display (as of light, noise, or smoke) by the combustion of explosive or flammable compositions
¹firm \'fərm\ *adj* **1 a** : securely or solidly fixed in place **b** : SOLID, VIGOROUS **c** : having a solid or compact texture **2 a** : not subject to change or fluctuation : STEADY **b** : STEADFAST **c** : WELL-FOUNDED **3** : indicating firmness or resolution — **firm·ly** *adv* — **firm·ness** *n*
²firm *vb* **1** : to make solid or compact **2** : to become firm
³firm *n* **1** : the name under which a company does business **2** : a business partnership of two or more persons **3** : a business enterprise
fir·ma·ment \'fər-mə-mənt\ *n* : the arch of the sky : HEAVENS
¹first \'fərst\ *adj* **1** — see NUMBER table **2** : preceding all others
²first *adv* **1 a** : before any other **b** : for the first time **2** : in preference to something else : SOONER
³first *n* **1** — see NUMBER table **2** : something that is first; *esp* : the 1st gear or speed in an automotive vehicle
first aid *n* : emergency care or treatment given to an ill or injured person
first·born \'fərs(t)-'bȯrn\ *adj* : born first : ELDEST — **firstborn** *n*
first class *n* : the best or highest group in a classification — **first–class** *adj or adv*
first·hand \'fərst-'hand\ *adj* : coming directly from the original source — **firsthand** *adv*
first lady *n, often cap F&L* : the wife or hostess of the chief executive of a political unit (as a country)
first lieutenant *n* : a commissioned officer (as in the army) ranking next below a captain

first·ling \ˈfərst-liŋ\ *n* **1** : the first of a class or kind **2** : the first produce or result of something
first·ly \-lē\ *adv* : in the first place
first–rate \ˈfərst-ˈrāt\ *adj* : of the first order of size, importance, or quality — **first–rat·er** \-ˈrāt-ər\ *n*
first sergeant *n* : a master sergeant in the army
first water *n* **1** : the purest luster **2** : the highest grade, degree, or quality
firth \ˈfərth\ *n* : a narrow arm of the sea; *also* : the opening of a river into the sea
fis·cal \ˈfis-kəl\ *adj* **1** : of or relating to taxation, public revenues, or public debt **2** : of or relating to financial matters — **fis·cal·ly** \-kə-lē\ *adv*
[1]**fish** \ˈfish\ *n, pl* **fish** *or* **fish·es** **1** : an aquatic animal; *esp* : any of numerous cold-blooded water-breathing vertebrates with fins, gills, and scales **2** : the flesh of fish used as food — **fish·like** *adj*
[2]**fish** *vb* **1** : to try to catch fish **2** : to search (as with a hook) for something underwater **3** : to seek something by or as if by groping or feeling — **fish·er** *n*
fish·er·man \ˈfish-ər-mən\ *n* **1** : one who engages in fishing **2** : a ship used in commercial fishing
fish·ery \ˈfish-(ə-)rē\ *n, pl* **-er·ies** **1** : the activity or business of taking aquatic products (as fish) **2** : a place or establishment for catching fish often together with its personnel
fish·hook \ˈfish-ˌhu̇k\ *n* : a usu. barbed hook for catching fish
fish·ing *n* : the sport or business of catching fish
fish·wife \ˈfish-ˌwīf\ *n* **1** : a woman who sells fish **2** : a scurrilously abusive woman
fishy \ˈfish-ē\ *adj* **1** : of, relating to, or resembling fish **2** : inspiring doubt or suspicion : QUESTIONABLE
fis·sion \ˈfish-ən, ˈfizh-\ *n* **1** : a splitting or breaking up into parts **2** : the splitting of an atomic nucleus resulting in the release of large amounts of energy
fis·sion·a·ble \ˈfish-(ə-)nə-bəl, ˈfizh-\ *adj* : capable of undergoing fission
fission bomb *n* : ATOM BOMB
[1]**fis·sure** \ˈfish-ər\ *n* : a narrow opening or crack of some length and depth
[2]**fissure** *vb* **1** : to break into fissures **2** : CRACK, DIVIDE
fist \ˈfist\ *n* **1** : the hand clenched with fingers doubled into the palm **2** : CLUTCH, GRASP **3** : INDEX 6
fist·i·cuffs \ˈfis-ti-ˌkəfs\ *n pl* : a fight with usu. bare fists
fis·tu·la \ˈfis-chə-lə\ *n, pl* **-las** *or* **-lae** \-ˌlē, -ˌlī\ : an abnormal passage leading from an abscess or hollow organ — **fis·tu·lous** \-ləs\ *adj*
[1]**fit** \ˈfit\ *n* **1** : a sudden violent attack of a disorder **2** : a sudden outburst (as of laughter) — **by fits** *or* **by fits and starts** : in an impulsive or irregular manner
[2]**fit** *adj* **1** : adapted to an end or design : APPROPRIATE **2** : BECOMING, PROPER **3** : READY, PREPARED **4** : QUALIFIED, COMPETENT **5** : sound physically and mentally : HEALTHY — **fit·ly** *adv* — **fit·ness** *n*
[3]**fit** *vb* **fit·ted**; **fit·ting** **1** : to be suitable for or to : BEFIT **2 a** : to be correctly adjusted to or shaped for **b** : to insert or adjust until correctly in place **c** : to make a place or room for **3** : to be in agreement or accord with **4 a** : to make ready : PREPARE **b** : ADJUST **5** : SUPPLY, EQUIP **6** : to be in harmony or accord : BELONG
[4]**fit** *n* **1** : the state or manner of fitting or being fitted **2** : a piece of clothing that fits
fitch \ˈfich\ *or* **fitch·ew** \ˈfich-ü\ *n* : POLECAT 1; *also* : its fur or pelt
fit·ful \ˈfit-fəl\ *adj* : not regular : RESTLESS — **fit·ful·ly** \-fə-lē\ *adv* — **fit·ful·ness** *n*
fit·ter \ˈfit-ər\ *n* : one that fits: as **a** : a person who tries on and adjusts articles of dress **b** : a person who fits, adjusts, or assembles parts (as of machinery)

[1]**fit·ting** \ˈfit-iŋ\ *adj* : APPROPRIATE, SUITABLE — **fit·ting·ly** *adv* — **fit·ting·ness** *n*
[2]**fitting** *n* **1** : the action or act of one that fits; *esp* : a trying on of clothes being made or altered **2** : a small often standardized accessory part
five \ˈfīv\ *n* **1** — see NUMBER table **2** : the fifth in a set or series **3** : something having five units or members; *esp* : a male basketball team — **five** *adj or pron*
five–and–ten \ˌfī-vən-ˈten\ *n* : a store selling articles priced at 5 or 10 cents and other inexpensive articles
[1]**fix** \ˈfiks\ *vb* **1 a** : to make firm, stable, or fast **b** : to give a permanent or final form to **c** : AFFIX, ATTACH **2** : to hold or direct steadily **3 a** : to set or place definitely : ESTABLISH **b** : ASSIGN **4** : to set in order : ADJUST **5** : to get ready : PREPARE **6** : to make sound or whole again: **a** : REPAIR, MEND **b** : RESTORE, CURE **7** : to influence the actions, outcome, or effect of by improper or illegal methods — **fix·a·ble** *adj* — **fix·er** *n*
[2]**fix** *n* : a position of difficulty or embarrassment
fix·a·tion \fik-ˈsā-shən\ *n* : an obsessive or unhealthy preoccupation or attachment
fix·a·tive \ˈfik-sət-iv\ *n* : something that stabilizes or sets — **fixative** *adj*
fixed \ˈfikst\ *adj* **1 a** : securely placed or fastened : STATIONARY **b** (1) : NONVOLATILE (2) : COMBINED **c** : not subject to change or fluctuation : SETTLED, FINAL **d** : recurring on the same date from year to year **e** : INTENT **2** : supplied with a definite amount of something needed (as money) — **fix·ed·ly** \ˈfik-səd-lē\ *adv* — **fix·ed·ness** \ˈfik-səd-nəs\ *n*
fix·ing \ˈfik-siŋ, *2 is often* -sənz\ *n* **1** : a putting in permanent form **2** *pl* : ARRANGEMENTS, TRIMMINGS
fix·i·ty \ˈfik-sət-ē\ *n* : the quality or state of being fixed or stable
fix·ture \ˈfiks-chər\ *n* **1** : the act of fixing : the state of being fixed **2** : one firmly established in a place **3** : something attached to another thing as a permanent part
[1]**fizz** \ˈfiz\ *vi* : to make a hissing or sputtering sound
[2]**fizz** *n* **1** : a hissing sound **2** : an effervescent beverage — **fizzy** \ˈfiz-ē\ *adj*
[1]**fiz·zle** \ˈfiz-əl\ *vi* **fiz·zled**; **fiz·zling** \ˈfiz-(ə-)liŋ\ **1** : FIZZ **2** : to fail esp. after a promising start
[2]**fizzle** *n* : an abortive effort : FAILURE
fjord *or* **fiord** \fē-ˈo̊rd, ˈfyo̊rd\ *n* : a narrow inlet of the sea between cliffs or steep slopes
flab·ber·gast \ˈflab-ər-ˌgast\ *vt* : ASTOUND
flab·by \ˈflab-ē\ *adj* **1** : lacking resilience or firmness : FLACCID **2** : being weak and ineffective : FEEBLE — **flab·bi·ly** \ˈflab-ə-lē\ *adv* — **flab·bi·ness** \ˈflab-ē-nəs\ *n*
flac·cid \ˈflak-səd\ *adj* : FLABBY; *also* : deficient in turgor
flac·on \ˈflak-ən\ *n* : a small usu. ornamental bottle with a tight cap
[1]**flag** \ˈflag\ *n* : any of various monocotyledonous plants with long narrow leaves: as **a** : IRIS; *esp* : a wild iris **b** : CATTAIL
[2]**flag** *n* **1** : a hard stone that is composed of even layers and splits into flat pieces suitable for paving **2** : a thin piece of flag used for paving
[3]**flag** *n* **1** : a usu. rectangular piece of fabric of distinctive design that is used as a symbol (as of nationality) or as a signaling device and is usu. displayed hanging free from a staff or halyard to which it is attached by one edge **2** : one of the cross strokes of a musical note less than a quarter note in value
[4]**flag** *vt* **flagged**; **flag·ging** **1** : to put a flag on **2** : to signal with or as if with a flag; *esp* : to signal to stop
[5]**flag** *vi* **flagged**; **flag·ging** **1** : to be loose, yielding, or limp; *also* : to droop from lack of water **2 a** : to become feeble **b** : to decline in interest or attraction

flag·el·lant \'flaj-ə-lənt, flə-'jel-ənt\ *n* : one that whips; *esp* : a person who scourges himself as a public penance

flag·el·late \'flaj-ə-,lāt\ *vt* : to punish by whipping : WHIP — **flag·el·la·tion** \,flaj-ə-'lā-shən\ *n*

fla·geo·let \,flaj-ə-'let\ *n* : a small woodwind instrument belonging to the flute class

flag·ging \'flag-iŋ\ *n* : a pavement of flagstones

fla·gi·tious \flə-'jish-əs\ *adj* : grossly wicked : VILLAINOUS — **fla·gi·tious·ly** *adv* — **fla·gi·tious·ness** *n*

flag·man \'flag-mən\ *n* : one who signals with or as if with a flag esp. to warn of danger

flag·on \'flag-ən\ *n* : a container for liquids usu. having a handle, spout, and lid

flag·pole \'flag-,pōl\ *n* : a pole to raise a flag on

fla·grant \'flā-grənt\ *adj* : conspicuously bad : OUTRAGEOUS, NOTORIOUS — **fla·gran·cy** \-grən-sē\ *n* — **fla·grant·ly** *adv*

flag·ship \'flag-,ship\ *n* : the ship that carries the commander of a fleet or subdivision thereof and flies his flag

flag·staff \-,staf\ *n* : FLAGPOLE

flag·stone \-,stōn\ *n* : ²FLAG 2

¹flail \'flāl\ *n* : a hand threshing tool consisting of a wooden handle with a free-swinging stout short stick at the end

²flail *vb* : to strike with or as if with a flail

flair \'fla(ə)r\ *n* 1 : discriminating sense 2 : natural aptitude : BENT

flak \'flak\ *n* : antiaircraft guns or the bursting shells fired from them

¹flake \'flāk\ *n* : a thin flattened usu. loose piece : CHIP

²flake *vb* : to form or separate into flakes : make or become flaky

flaky \'flā-kē\ *adj* 1 : consisting of flakes 2 : tending to flake — **flak·i·ness** *n*

flam·beau \'flam-,bō\ *n, pl* **flam·beaux** \-,bōz\ *or* **flambeaus** : a flaming torch

flam·boy·ant \flam-'bȯi-ənt\ *adj* 1 *often cap* : characterized by waving curves suggesting flames 2 : FLORID, ORNATE; *also* : RESPLENDENT 3 : given to dashing display : SHOWY — **flam·boy·ance** \-ən(t)s\ *n* — **flam·boy·ant·ly** *adv*

flame \'flām\ *n* 1 : the glowing gaseous part of a fire 2 **a** : a state of blazing combustion **b** : a condition or appearance suggesting a flame **c** : BRILLIANCE, BRIGHTNESS 3 : burning zeal or passion 4 : SWEETHEART — **flame** *vb* — **flam·er** *n*

fla·men·co \flə-'meŋ-kō\ *n, pl* **-cos** : a vigorous rhythmic dance style of the Andalusian Gypsies

flame·proof \'flām-'prüf\ *adj* 1 : resistant to the action of flame 2 : not burning on contact with flame

flame·throw·er \-,thrō(-ə)r\ *n* : a device that expels from a nozzle a burning stream of liquid or semiliquid fuel under pressure

flam·ing \'flā-miŋ\ *adj* 1 : BLAZING 2 : suggesting a flame in brilliance or wavy outline 3 : ARDENT, PASSIONATE — **flam·ing·ly** *adv*

fla·min·go \flə-'miŋ-gō\ *n, pl* **-gos** : a long-legged and long-necked water bird with a broad bill bent downward at the end and scarlet wings

flam·ma·ble \'flam-ə-bəl\ *adj* : capable of being easily ignited and of burning with extreme rapidity — **flam·ma·bil·i·ty** \,flam-ə-'bil-ət-ē\ *n* — **flammable** *n*

flange \'flanj\ *n* : a rib or rim used for strength, for guiding, or for attachment to another object

¹flank \'flaŋk\ *n* 1 : the fleshy part of the side between the ribs and the hip; *also* : the side of a quadruped 2 **a** : SIDE **b** : the right or left of a formation

²flank *vt* 1 **a** : to attack or threaten the flank of **b** : to turn the flank of 2 : to be situated at the side of : BORDER

flank·er \'flaŋ-kər\ *n* 1 : one that flanks 2 : a football player stationed wide of the end who serves chiefly as a pass receiver

flan·nel \'flan-ᵊl\ *n* 1 **a** : a soft twilled wool or worsted fabric with a napped surface **b** : a stout cotton fabric napped on one side 2 *pl* : flannel underwear or trousers

flan·nel·ette \,flan-ᵊl-'et\ *n* : a cotton flannel napped on one or both sides

¹flap \'flap\ *n* 1 : a stroke with something broad : SLAP 2 : something broad, limber, or flat and usu. thin that hangs loose 3 : the motion of something broad and limber 4 : a state of excitement or worry

²flap *vb* **flapped**; **flap·ping** 1 : to beat with something broad and flat 2 : to move or cause to move with a beating motion 3 : to sway loosely usu. with a noise of striking

flap·jack \'flap-,jak\ *n* : GRIDDLE CAKE

flap·per \'flap-ər\ *n* 1 : one that flaps 2 : a young woman esp. of the 1920s who shows bold freedom from conventions in conduct and dress

¹flare \'fla(ə)r\ *vb* 1 : to burn with an unsteady flame 2 **a** : to shine with a sudden light **b** : to become suddenly excited or angry 3 : to open or spread outward

²flare *n* 1 : an unsteady glaring light 2 : a fire or blaze of light used to signal or illuminate; *also* : a device used to produce such a flare 3 : a spreading outward; *also* : a place or part that spreads

flare-up \-,əp\ *n* : a sudden burst (as of flame or anger)

¹flash \'flash\ *vb* 1 : to break forth in or like a sudden flame 2 : to send out in or as if in flashes 3 : to appear or pass very suddenly 4 : to make a sudden display (as of brilliance or feeling) 5 : to gleam or glow intermittently 6 : to fill by a sudden rush of water 7 : to expose to view very briefly

²flash *n* 1 **a** : a sudden burst of light **b** : a movement of a flag or light in signaling 2 : a sudden and brilliant burst (as of wit) 3 : a brief time 4 **a** : SHOW, DISPLAY; *esp* : ostentatious display **b** : one that attracts notice; *esp* : an outstanding athlete 5 : something flashed: as **a** : GLIMPSE, LOOK **b** : a first brief news report **c** : FLASHLIGHT 1 **d** : a quick-spreading flame or momentary intense outburst of radiant heat

³flash *adj* 1 : FLASHY 2 : of sudden origin and short duration

flash·back \'flash-,bak\ *n* : injection into the chronological sequence of events in a literary or theatrical work of an event of earlier occurrence

flash·bulb \-,bəlb\ *n* : an electric lamp burning metal to produce an intense flash of light for photography

flash·cube \-,kyüb\ *n* : a cube containing four flashbulbs that fits on a camera and that turns after each shot

flash·gun \'flash-,gən\ *n* : a device for holding and operating a flashbulb

flash·ing \'flash-iŋ\ *n* : sheet metal used in waterproofing roof valleys or the angle between a chimney and a roof

flash·light \'flash-,līt\ *n* 1 **a** : a sudden bright artificial light used in taking photographs **b** : a photograph taken by such a light 2 : a small battery-operated portable electric light

flashy \'flash-ē\ *adj* 1 : momentarily dazzling 2 **a** : superficially attractive : BRIGHT **b** : SHOWY — **flash·i·ly** \'flash-ə-lē\ *adv* — **flash·i·ness** \'flash-ē-nəs\ *n*

flask \'flask\ *n* : a bottle-shaped container often somewhat narrowed toward the outlet and often fitted with a closure

¹flat \'flat\ *adj* 1 : having a smooth level horizontal surface 2 : having a smooth even surface 3 : spread out on or along a surface 4 : having a broad smooth surface and little thickness 5 : DOWNRIGHT, POSITIVE 6 : FIXED, UNCHANGING 7 : EXACT 8 : DULL, UNINTERESTING, INSIPID 9 : DEFLATED — used of tires 10 **a** : lower than the true pitch **b** : lower by a half step 11 : lacking contrast 12 : free from gloss — **flat·ly** *adv* — **flat·ness** *n*

²flat *n* 1 : a level surface of land : PLAIN 2 : a flat part or surface 3 **a** : a flat note or tone **b** : a character ♭ on a line or space of the staff indicating a half step drop in pitch 4 : something flat; *esp* : a shoe or slipper having a flat heel 5 : a deflated tire

[3]**flat** *adv* : FLATLY: as **a** : on or against a flat surface **b** : EXACTLY **c** : below the true musical pitch
[4]**flat** *vb* **flat•ted**; **flat•ting** **1** : FLATTEN **2 a** : to lower in pitch esp. by a half step **b** : to sing or play below the true pitch
[5]**flat** *n* **1** : a floor or story in a building **2** : an apartment on one floor
flat•boat \'flat-ˌbōt\ *n* : a large flat-bottomed boat with square ends used for transporting heavy freight on rivers
flat•car \-ˌkär\ *n* : a railroad freight car without permanent raised sides, ends, or covering
flat•fish \-ˌfish\ *n* : any of a group of flattened bony sea fishes with both eyes on the upper side
flat•iron \'flat-ˌī(-ə)rn\ *n* : an iron for pressing clothes
flat•ten \'flat-ᵊn\ *vb* **flat•tened**; **flat•ten•ing** \'flat-niŋ, -ᵊn-iŋ\ : to make or become flat esp. in surface or position
flat•ter \'flat-ər\ *vt* **1** : to praise too much or without sincerity in order to gain some advantage or benefit for oneself or to gratify another's vanity **2** : to represent too favorably **3** : to judge (oneself) favorably or too favorably esp. in respect to an accomplishment or ability — **flat•ter•er** *n*
flat•tery \'flat-ə-rē\ *n, pl* **-ter•ies** : flattering speech or attentions : insincere or excessive praise
flat•u•lent \'flach-ə-lənt\ *adj* **1** : full of gas **2** : pretentious without real worth or substance : POMPOUS — **flat•u•lence** \-lən(t)s\ *n* — **flat•u•lent•ly** *adv*
flaunt \'flȯnt\ *vb* **1** : to wave or flutter showily **2** : to display or obtrude oneself to public notice **3** : to display ostentatiously or impudently : PARADE — **flaunt** *n*
flau•tist \'flȯt-əst, 'flau̇t-\ *n* : FLUTIST
[1]**fla•vor** \'flā-vər\ *n* **1 a** : the quality of something that affects the sense of taste : SAVOR **b** : the blend of taste and smell sensations evoked by a substance in the mouth **2** : a substance that flavors **3** : characteristic or predominant quality — **fla•vored** \-vərd\ *adj* — **fla•vor•ful** \-vər-fəl\ *adj* — **fla•vor•less** \-ləs\ *adj*
[2]**flavor** *vt* **fla•vored**; **fla•vor•ing** \'flāv-(ə-)riŋ\ : to give or add flavor to
fla•vor•ing *n* : FLAVOR 2
[1]**flaw** \'flȯ\ *n* : an imperfect part : CRACK, FAULT — **flaw•less** \-ləs\ *adj* — **flaw•less•ly** *adv* — **flaw•less•ness** *n*
[2]**flaw** *vb* **1** : to make flaws in **2** : to become defective
flax \'flaks\ *n* : a slender erect blue-flowered plant grown for its fiber and seeds; *also* : its fiber esp. prepared for spinning
flax•en \'flak-sən\ *adj* **1** : made of flax **2** : resembling flax esp. in pale soft straw color
flax•seed \'flak-ˌsēd\ *n* : the seed of flax used as a source of linseed oil and medicinally
flay \'flā\ *vt* **1** : to strip off the skin or surface of : SKIN **2** : to criticize harshly : SCOLD
flea \'flē\ *n* : any of a group of small wingless leaping blood-sucking insects
[1]**fleck** \'flek\ *vt* : STREAK, SPOT
[2]**fleck** *n* **1** : SPOT, MARK **2** : FLAKE, PARTICLE
fledg•ling \'flej-liŋ\ *n* **1** : a young bird with feathers newly developed **2** : an immature or inexperienced person
flee \'flē\ *vb* **fled** \'fled\; **flee•ing** **1 a** : to run away from danger or evil : FLY **b** : to run away from : SHUN **2** : to pass away swiftly : VANISH
[1]**fleece** \'flēs\ *n* **1** : the coat of wool covering an animal (as a sheep) **2** : a soft or woolly covering
[2]**fleece** *vt* : to strip of money or property by fraud or extortion
fleecy \'flē-sē\ *adj* : covered with, made of, or resembling fleece — **fleec•i•ness** *n*
fleer \'fli(ə)r\ *vi* : to laugh or grimace in a coarse manner : SNEER — **fleer** *n*
[1]**fleet** \'flēt\ *vi* : to fly swiftly : pass rapidly
[2]**fleet** *n* **1 a** : a group of warships under one command **b** : a country's navy **2** : a group of ships or vehicles that move together or are operated under one management
[3]**fleet** *adj* **1** : swift in motion : NIMBLE **2** : not enduring : FLEETING — **fleet•ly** *adv* — **fleet•ness** *n*
fleet admiral *n* : an admiral of the highest rank whose insignia is five stars
flesh \'flesh\ *n* **1** : the soft parts of the body of an animal; *esp* : muscular tissue **2** : parts of an animal used as food **3** : the physical being of man as distinguished from the soul **4 a** : human beings **b** : living beings **c** : STOCK, KINDRED **5** : a fleshy plant part used as food; *esp* : the fleshy part of a fruit — **fleshed** \'flesht\ *adj*
flesh•ly \'flesh-lē\ *adj* **1** : CORPOREAL, BODILY **2 a** : CARNAL, SENSUAL **b** : not spiritual : WORLDLY
flesh•pot \'flesh-ˌpät\ *n* **1** *pl* : bodily comfort : LUXURY **2** : a place of luxurious entertainment
fleshy \'flesh-ē\ *adj* **1 a** : resembling or consisting of flesh **b** : having abundant flesh; *esp* : CORPULENT **2** : SUCCULENT, PULPY — **flesh•i•ness** *n*
fleur–de–lis *or* **fleur–de–lys** \ˌflərd-ᵊl-'ē, ˌflu̇rd-\ *n, pl* **fleurs–de–lis** *or* **fleur–de–lis** *or* **fleurs–de–lys** *or* **fleur–de–lys** \ˌflərd-ᵊl-'ē(z), ˌflu̇rd-\ **1** : IRIS 2 **2** : a conventionalized iris in art and heraldry
flew *past of* FLY
flex \'fleks\ *vb* : to bend esp. repeatedly : cause flexion of
flex•i•ble \'flek-sə-bəl\ *adj* **1** : capable of being flexed : PLIANT **2** : ADAPTABLE — **flex•i•bil•i•ty** \ˌflek-sə-'bil-ət-ē\ *n* — **flex•i•bly** \'flek-sə-blē\ *adv*
flex•u•ous \'fleksh-(ə-)wəs\ *adj* **1** : having turns or windings **2** : FLEXIBLE — **flex•u•os•i•ty** \ˌflek-shə-'wäs-ət-ē\ *n* — **flex•u•ous•ly** *adv*
flex•ure \'flek-shər\ *n* **1** : the quality or state of being flexed **2** : TURN, FOLD, BEND — **flex•ur•al** \-sh(ə-)rəl\ *adj*
flib•ber•ti•gib•bet \ˌflib-ərt-ē-'jib-ət\ *n* : a silly restless person
[1]**flick** \'flik\ *n* **1** : a light sharp jerky stroke or movement **2** : a sound produced by a flick **3** : DAUB, SPLOTCH
[2]**flick** *vb* **1** : to strike lightly with a quick sharp motion **2** : FLUTTER, DART, FLIT
[1]**flick•er** \'flik-ər\ *vb* **flick•ered**; **flick•er•ing** \'flik-(ə-)riŋ\ **1 a** : to waver unsteadily : FLUTTER **b** : FLIT, DART **2** : to burn fitfully or with a fluctuating light **3** : to produce by flickering
[2]**flicker** *n* **1** : a brief interval of brightness **2** : a flickering light **3** : a brief stirring — **flick•ery** \'flik-(ə-)rē\ *adj*
flied *past of* FLY
fli•er \'flī(-ə)r\ *n* **1** : one that flies; *esp* : AVIATOR **2** : something (as an express train) that travels very fast **3** : a reckless or speculative undertaking **4** : an advertising leaflet distributed in large numbers
[1]**flight** \'flīt\ *n* **1** : an act or instance of passing through the air by the use of wings **2 a** : a passing through the air or through space outside the earth's atmosphere **b** : the distance covered in a flight **c** : swift movement **3** : an airplane making a scheduled flight **4** : a group of similar things flying through the air together **5** : a brilliant, imaginative, or unrestrained exercise or display **6** : a continuous series of stairs from one landing or floor to another
[2]**flight** *n* : an act or instance of running away
flight•less \'flīt-ləs\ *adj* : unable to fly
flighty \'flīt-ē\ *adj* : subject to flights of fancy : inclined to sudden change of mind — **flight•i•ly** \'flīt-ᵊl-ē\ *adv* — **flight•i•ness** \'flīt-ē-nəs\ *n*
flim•sy \'flim-zē\ *adj* **1 a** : lacking strength or substance **b** : of inferior materials and workmanship **2** : having little worth or plausibility — **flim•si•ly** \-zə-lē\ *adv* — **flim•si•ness** \-zē-nəs\ *n*
flinch \'flinch\ *vi* : to shrink from or as if from physical pain : WINCE — **flinch** *n* — **flinch•er** *n*
flin•ders \'flin-dərz\ *n pl* : SPLINTERS, FRAGMENTS
[1]**fling** \'fliŋ\ *vb* **flung** \'fləŋ\; **fling•ing** \'fliŋ-iŋ\ **1** : to move in

a brusque or headlong manner **2 :** to kick or plunge vigorously **3 a :** to throw or swing with force or recklessness **b :** to cast aside **:** DISCARD **4 :** to place or put suddenly and unexpectedly into a state or condition — **fling·er** \'fliŋ-ər\ *n*

²fling *n* **1 :** an act or instance of flinging **2 :** a casual try **:** ATTEMPT **3 :** a period of self-indulgence

flint \'flint\ *n* **1 :** a hard quartz that strikes fire with steel **2 :** an alloy used for striking fire in cigarette lighters

flint·lock \'flint-ˌläk\ *n* **1 :** a lock for a 17th and 18th century firearm using a flint to ignite the charge **2 :** a firearm fitted with a flintlock

flinty \'flint-ē\ *adj* **1 :** composed of or covered with flint **2 a :** notably hard **b :** UNYIELDING, STERN

¹flip \'flip\ *vb* **flipped; flip·ping 1 :** to turn by tossing **2 :** to turn quickly **3 :** FLICK, JERK **4 :** to lose self-control

²flip *n* **1 :** an act or instance of flipping **:** TOSS, FLICK **2 :** any of several mixed drinks

³flip *adj* **:** FLIPPANT, IMPERTINENT

flip·pant \'flip-ənt\ *adj* **:** treating lightly something serious or worthy of respect **:** lacking earnestness **:** SAUCY — **flip·pan·cy** \-ən-sē\ *n* — **flip·pant·ly** *adv*

flip·per \'flip-ər\ *n* **1 :** a broad flat limb (as of a seal) adapted for swimming **2 :** a flat rubber shoe with the front expanded into a paddle used in skin diving

¹flirt \'flərt\ *vi* **1 :** to move erratically **:** FLIT **2 a :** to behave amorously without serious intent **b :** TOY — **flir·ta·tion** \ˌflər-'tā-shən\ *n* — **flir·ta·tious** \-shəs\ *adj* — **flir·ta·tious·ness** *n* — **flirt·er** *n*

²flirt *n* **1 :** an act or instance of flirting **2 :** a person who flirts

flit \'flit\ *vi* **flit·ted; flit·ting :** to move or progress in quick erratic darts — **flit** *n*

flitch \'flich\ *n* **:** a side of pork cured and smoked as bacon

flit·ter \'flit-ər\ *vi* **:** FLUTTER, FLICKER

fliv·ver \'fliv-ər\ *n* **:** a small cheap usu. old automobile

¹float \'flōt\ *n* **1 :** something that floats: as **a :** a cork or bob buoying up the baited end of a fishing line **b :** a hollow ball that controls the flow or level of the liquid it floats on (as in a tank or cistern) **2 :** a vehicle with a platform used to carry an exhibit in a parade

²float *vb* **1 :** to rest or cause to rest in or on the surface of a fluid **2 a :** to drift or cause to drift on or through or as if on or through a fluid **b :** WANDER **3 :** FLOOD **4 a :** to offer (an issue of stocks or bonds) in order to finance an enterprise **b :** to finance (an enterprise) by floating an issue of stocks or bonds **c :** to arrange for — **float·er** *n*

float·ing \-iŋ\ *adj* **1 :** buoyed on or in a fluid **2 a :** not settled or committed **:** not established **b :** not funded **3 :** connected or constructed so as to operate and adjust smoothly

floc·cu·lent \'fläk-yə-lənt\ *adj* **1 :** resembling wool esp. in loose fluffy texture **2 :** covered with woolly material — **floc·cu·lence** \-lən(t)s\ *n*

¹flock \'fläk\ *n* **1 :** a group of birds or mammals assembled or herded together **2 :** a group under the guidance of a leader **3 :** a large number

²flock *vi* **:** to gather or move in a crowd

flock·ing \'fläk-iŋ\ *n* **:** a design in flock

floe \'flō\ *n* **:** a sheet or mass of floating ice

flog \'fläg\ *vt* **flogged; flog·ging :** to beat severely with a rod or whip — **flog·ger** *n*

¹flood \'fləd\ *n* **1 :** a great flow of water that rises and spreads over the land **2 :** the flowing in of the tide **3 :** an overwhelming quantity or volume

²flood *vb* **1 :** to cover or become filled with a flood **:** INUNDATE **2 :** to fill abundantly or excessively **3 :** to pour forth in a flood

¹flood·light \-ˌlīt\ *n* **1 :** artificial illumination in a broad beam **2 :** a lighting unit for projecting a beam of light

²floodlight *vt* **:** to illuminate by means of one or more floodlights

¹floor \'flō(ə)r\ *n* **1 :** the part of a room on which one stands **2 :** a ground surface **3 :** a story of a building **4 a :** a main level space (as in a legislative chamber) distinguished from a platform or gallery **b :** the right to speak from one's place in an assembly — **floor·ing** *n*

²floor *vt* **1 :** to cover with a floor or flooring **2 a :** to knock down **b :** SHOCK, OVERWHELM **c :** DEFEAT

floor·board \'flō(ə)r-ˌbōrd\ *n* **1 :** a board in a floor **2 :** the floor of an automobile

floor leader *n* **:** a member of a legislative body chosen by his party to have charge of its organization and strategy on the floor

floor·walk·er \'flō(ə)r-ˌwȯ-kər\ *n* **:** a man employed in a retail store to oversee the sales force and aid customers

flop \'fläp\ *vb* **flopped; flop·ping 1 :** to swing or bounce loosely **:** flap about **2 :** to throw oneself down heavily, clumsily, or in a completely relaxed manner **3 :** to fail completely — **flop** *n*

flop·py \'fläp-ē\ *adj* **:** tending to flop; *esp* **:** being soft and flexible

flo·ra \'flōr-ə\ *n, pl* **floras :** plants or plant life esp. of a region, period, or environment

flo·ral \'flōr-əl\ *adj* **:** of or relating to flowers or a flora — **flo·ral·ly** \-ə-lē\ *adv*

flo·res·cence \flō-'res-ᵊn(t)s, flə-\ *n* **:** a state or period of being in bloom or flourishing — **flo·res·cent** \-ᵊnt\ *adj*

flo·ret \'flōr-ət, 'flȯr-\ *n* **:** a single flower of a flower cluster

flor·id \'flȯr-əd\ *adj* **1 :** excessively flowery in style **:** ORNATE **2 :** tinged with red **:** RUDDY — **flo·rid·i·ty** \flə-'rid-ət-ē, flȯ-\ *n* — **flor·id·ly** \'flȯr-əd-lē\ *adv* — **flor·id·ness** *n*

flo·rin \'flȯr-ən\ *n* **:** a British silver coin worth two shillings

flo·rist \'flōr-əst\ *n* **:** one who deals in flowers

floss \'fläs, 'flȯs\ *n* **1 :** waste or short silk fibers that cannot be reeled **2 a :** soft thread of silk or mercerized cotton used for embroidery **b :** a lightweight wool knitting yarn **3 :** fluffy fibrous material

flossy \'fläs-ē, 'flȯs-\ *adj* **1 a :** of, relating to, or having the characteristics of floss **b :** DOWNY **2 :** STYLISH, GLAMOROUS

flo·til·la \flō-'til-ə\ *n* **:** a fleet of ships; *esp* **:** a fleet of small ships

flot·sam \'flät-səm\ *n* **:** floating wreckage of a ship or its cargo

¹flounce \'flaun(t)s\ *vi* **1 a :** to move with exaggerated jerky motions **b :** to go with sudden determination **2 :** FLOUNDER, STRUGGLE

²flounce *n* **:** an act or instance of flouncing

³flounce *n* **:** a strip of fabric attached by the upper edge

¹floun·der \'flaun-dər\ *n, pl* **flounder** *or* **flounders :** FLATFISH; *esp* **:** any of various important marine food fishes

²flounder *vi* **floun·dered; floun·der·ing** \-d(ə-)riŋ\ **1 :** to struggle to move or obtain footing **2 :** to proceed clumsily

¹flour \'flau(ə)r\ *n* **1 :** finely ground powdery meal of a cereal (as wheat) **2 :** a fine soft powder

²flour *vt* **:** to coat with flour

¹flour·ish \'flər-ish\ *vb* **1 :** to grow luxuriantly **:** THRIVE **2 a :** to achieve success **:** PROSPER **b :** to be in a state of activity or production **c :** to reach a height of development or influence **3 :** to make bold and sweeping gestures **4 :** to wield with dramatic gestures **:** BRANDISH

²flourish *n* **1 :** a period of thriving **2 a :** a florid embellishment or passage **b :** an act or instance of brandishing **:** WAVE **c :** a dramatic action

floury \'flau(ə)r-ē\ *adj* **1 :** of, relating to, or resembling flour **2 :** covered with flour

¹flout \'flaut\ *vb* **1 :** to treat with contemptuous disregard **:** SCORN **2 :** to indulge in scornful behavior — **flout·er** *n*

²flout *n* **1 :** INSULT **2 :** MOCKERY

¹flow \'flō\ *vi* **1 :** to issue or move in a stream **2 :** RISE

3 : ABOUND 4 a : to proceed smoothly and readily b : to have a smooth uninterrrupted continuity 5 : to hang loose and billowing 6 : COME, ARISE — **flow·ing·ly** *adv*

[2]**flow** *n* 1 : an act of flowing 2 : FLOOD 1, 2 3 a : a smooth uninterrupted movement b : a stream of fluid 4 : the quantity that flows in a certain time 5 : YIELD, PRODUCTION 6 : a continuous transfer of energy

[1]**flow·er** \'flau̇(-ə)r\ *n* 1 a : a plant branch modified for seed production and bearing leaves specialized into floral organs (as petals); *also* : a flowering plant b : a plant grown or esteemed for its blossoms 2 a : the best part or example b : the finest most vigorous period c : a state of blooming or flourishing — **flow·er·less** \-ləs\ *adj*

[2]**flower** *vb* 1 : to produce flowers : BLOOM 2 a : DEVELOP b : FLOURISH

flow·ered \'flau̇(-ə)rd\ *adj* 1 : having or bearing flowers 2 : decorated with flowers or flowerlike figures

flower head *n* : a very short compact cluster of small flowers suggesting a single flower

flow·er·pot \'flau̇(-ə)r-ˌpät\ *n* : a pot in which to grow plants

flow·ery \'flau̇(-ə)r-ē\ *adj* 1 : full of or covered with flowers 2 : full of fine words or phrases — **flow·er·i·ness** *n*

flown *past part of* FLY

flu \'flü\ *n* 1 : INFLUENZA 2 : any of several virus diseases marked esp. by respiratory symptoms

flub \'fləb\ *vb* **flubbed**; **flub·bing** 1 : to make a mess of : BOTCH 2 : BLUNDER — **flub** *n*

fluc·tu·ate \'flək-chə-ˌwāt\ *vi* 1 : to move up and down or back and forth like a wave 2 : to rise and fall usu. with regularity : WAVER — **fluc·tu·a·tion** \ˌflək-chə-'wā-shən\ *n*

flue \'flü\ *n* : an enclosed passageway for directing a current; *esp* : a channel in a chimney for conveying flame and smoke to the outer air

flu·ent \'flü-ənt\ *adj* 1 : capable of flowing : FLUID 2 a : ready or facile in speech b : effortlessly smooth and rapid : POLISHED — **flu·en·cy** \-ən-sē\ *n* — **flu·ent·ly** *adv*

[1]**fluff** \'fləf\ *n* 1 : NAP, DOWN 2 : something fluffy 3 : something inconsequential 4 : BLUNDER; *esp* : an actor's lapse of memory

[2]**fluff** *vb* 1 : to make or become fluffy 2 : to make a mistake : BOTCH

fluffy \'fləf-ē\ *adj* 1 a : having, covered with, or resembling fluff or down b : being light and soft or airy 2 : FATUOUS, SILLY — **fluff·i·ness** *n*

[1]**flu·id** \'flü-əd\ *adj* 1 a : capable of flowing like a liquid or gas b : likely or tending to change or move 2 : characterized by or employing a smooth easy style 3 a : available for various uses b : easily converted into cash — **flu·id·i·ty** \flü-'id-ət-ē\ *n* — **flu·id·ly** *adv* — **flu·id·ness** *n*

[2]**fluid** *n* : a substance tending to flow or conform to the outline of its container

flu·id·ounce \ˌflü-əd-'au̇n(t)s\ *n* : a unit of liquid capacity equal to 1/16 pint

flu·idram \ˌflü-ə(d)-'dram\ *n* : a unit of liquid capacity equal to 1/8 fluidounce

[1]**fluke** \'flük\ *n* 1 : the part of an anchor that fastens in the ground 2 : a barbed head (as of a harpoon) 3 : one of the lobes of a whale's tail

[2]**fluke** *n* : a stroke of luck

flume \'flüm\ *n* 1 : a ravine or gorge with a stream running through it 2 : an inclined channel for conveying water (as for power)

flum·mox \'fləm-əks, -iks\ *vt* : CONFUSE

flung *past of* FLING

flunk \'fləŋk\ *vb* 1 : to fail an examination or course 2 : to give a failing grade to — **flunk** *n*

flun·ky *or* **flun·key** \'fləŋ-kē\ *n, pl* **flunkies** *or* **flunkeys** 1 : a servant in livery; *esp* : FOOTMAN 2 : TOADY

flu·o·resce \(ˌ)flu̇(-ə)r-'es\ *vi* : to produce, undergo, or exhibit fluorescence

flu·o·res·cence \-'es-ᵊn(t)s\ *n* : emission of radiation usu. as visible light resulting from and only during the absorption of radiation from some other source; *also* : the radiation emitted — **flu·o·res·cent** \-ᵊnt\ *adj*

fluorescent lamp *n* : a tubular electric lamp in which light is produced on the inside fluorescent coating by the action of ultraviolet light

flu·o·ri·date \'flu̇r-ə-ˌdāt\ *vt* : to add a fluoride to — **flu·o·ri·da·tion** \ˌflu̇r-ə-'dā-shən\ *n*

flu·o·ride \'flu̇(-ə)r-ˌīd\ *n* : a compound of fluorine with another chemical element or radical

flu·o·rine \'flu̇(-ə)r-ˌēn, -ən\ *n* : a pale yellowish flammable irritating toxic gaseous chemical element

flu·o·ro·scope \'flu̇r-ə-ˌskōp\ *n* : an instrument for observing the internal structure of an opaque object (as the body) by means of light and shadows produced on a screen by the action of X rays — **flu·o·ro·scop·ic** \ˌflu̇r-ə-'skäp-ik\ *adj* — **flu·o·ros·co·py** \(ˌ)flu̇(-ə)r-'äs-kə-pē\ *n*

[1]**flur·ry** \'flər-ē\ *n, pl* **flurries** 1 a : a gust of wind b : a brief light snowfall 2 : nervous commotion : BUSTLE 3 : a brief outburst of activity

[2]**flurry** *vb* **flur·ried**; **flur·ry·ing** : EXCITE, FLUSTER

[1]**flush** \'fləsh\ *vb* : to begin flight or cause to begin flight suddenly

[2]**flush** *n* 1 : a sudden flow 2 : a surge of emotion 3 a : a tinge of red : BLUSH b : a fresh and vigorous state 4 : a transitory sensation of extreme heat

[3]**flush** *vb* 1 : to flow and spread suddenly and freely : RUSH 2 a : to glow brightly b : BLUSH 3 : to wash out with a rush of liquid 4 : INFLAME, EXCITE 5 : to make red or hot

[4]**flush** *adj* 1 a : filled to overflowing b : fully supplied esp. with money 2 a : full of life and vigor : LUSTY b : of a ruddy healthy color 3 : readily available : ABUNDANT 4 a : having an unbroken or even surface b : being on a level with an adjacent surface c : directly abutting or immediately adjacent d : set even with an edge of a type page or column — **flushness** *n*

[5]**flush** *adv* 1 : in a flush manner 2 : SQUARELY

[6]**flush** *vt* : to make flush

[7]**flush** *n* : a hand of playing cards all of the same suit

[1]**flus·ter** \'fləs-tər\ *vt* **flus·tered**; **flus·ter·ing** \-t(ə-)riŋ\ : to put into a state of agitated confusion : UPSET

[2]**fluster** *n* : a state of agitated confusion

flute \'flüt\ *n* 1 : a keyed woodwind instrument played by blowing across a hole near the closed end 2 a : a grooved pleat b : a rounded groove (as on a classical architectural column) — **flut·ed** *adj* — **flute·like** *adj*

flut·ing \'flüt-iŋ\ *n* : fluted material or decoration

flut·ist \'flüt-əst\ *n* : a flute player

[1]**flut·ter** \'flət-ər\ *vb* 1 : to move or cause the wings to move rapidly without flying or in short flights 2 a : to move with quick wavering or flapping motions b : to vibrate in irregular spasms 3 : to move about or behave in an agitated aimless manner — **flut·tery** \'flət-ə-rē\ *adj*

[2]**flutter** *n* 1 : an act of fluttering 2 a : a state of nervous confusion or excitement b : FLURRY, COMMOTION

[1]**flux** \'fləks\ *n* 1 : an excessive fluid discharge from the body and esp. the bowels 2 a : a flowing in b : a series of changes : a state of continuous change 3 : a substance used to promote fusion esp. of metals or minerals

[2]**flux** *vb* : to become or cause to become fluid : FUSE

[1]**fly** \'flī\ *vb* **flew** \'flü\; **flown** \'flōn\; **fly·ing** 1 a : to move in or pass through the air with wings b : to move through the air or before the wind c : to float or cause to float, wave, or soar in the air 2 a : to take flight : escape from : FLEE; *also* : AVOID, SHUN b : to fade and disappear : VANISH 3 : to move or

pass swiftly **4 :** to become expended or dissipated rapidly **5 :** to pursue or attack in flight **6** *past or past part* **flied** \ˈflīd\ **:** to hit a fly in baseball **7 a :** to operate or travel in an airplane **b :** to journey over by flying **c :** to transport by airplane

²fly *n, pl* **flies 1 :** the action or process of flying **:** FLIGHT **2 :** a horse-drawn public coach or delivery wagon **3** *pl* **:** the space over a theater stage **4 a :** a garment closing concealed by a fold of cloth extending over the fastener **b :** the outer canvas of a tent with double top **c :** the length of an extended flag from its staff or support **5 :** a baseball hit high into the air — **on the fly :** in motion: as **a :** continuously active **:** very busy **b :** while still in the air

³fly *n, pl* **flies 1 :** a winged insect **2 :** a winged or rarely wingless insect; *esp* **:** a large stout-bodied two-winged insect **3 :** a fishhook dressed to suggest an insect — **fly in the ointment :** a detracting factor or element

fly·a·ble \ˈflī-ə-bəl\ *adj* **:** suitable for flying or being flown

fly·blown \ˈflī-ˌblōn\ *adj* **:** TAINTED, SPOILED

fly casting *n* **:** the act or practice of throwing the lure in angling with artificial flies — **fly·cast·er** *n*

fly·catch·er \ˈflī-ˌkach-ər, -ˌkech-\ *n* **:** a small bird that feeds on insects that it captures in the air

¹fly·ing \ˈflī-iŋ\ *adj* **1 a :** rapidly moving **b :** HASTY **2 :** ready to move or act **:** MOBILE

²flying *n* **1 :** travel by air **2 :** the operation of an airplane

flying buttress *n* **:** a projecting arched structure to support a wall or building

flying colors *n pl* **:** complete success

flying saucer *n* **:** any of various unidentified moving objects repeatedly reported as seen in the air and usu. alleged to be saucer-shaped or disk-shaped

fly·leaf \ˈflī-ˌlēf\ *n* **:** a blank leaf at the beginning or end of a book

fly·pa·per \-ˌpā-pər\ *n* **:** paper poisoned or coated with a sticky substance for killing or catching flies

fly·speck \-ˌspek\ *n* **1 :** a speck of fly dung **2 :** something small and insignificant — **flyspeck** *vt*

fly·wheel \-ˌhwēl\ *n* **:** a heavy wheel for opposing by its inertia a fluctuation of speed in the machinery with which it revolves

¹foal \ˈfōl\ *n* **:** the young of an animal of the horse family; *esp* **:** one under one year

²foal *vb* **:** to give birth to a foal

¹foam \ˈfōm\ *n* **1 :** a light frothy mass of fine bubbles formed in or on the surface of a liquid **:** FROTH, SPUME **2 :** material (as rubber) in a lightweight cellular form

²foam *vb* **1 a :** to produce or form foam **b :** to froth at the mouth esp. in anger; *also* **:** to be angry **2 :** to gush out in foam

foamy \ˈfō-mē\ *adj* **1 :** covered with foam **:** FROTHY **2 :** full of, consisting of, or resembling foam

fob \ˈfäb\ *n* **1 :** a watch chain or ribbon; *esp* **:** one hanging from a small watch pocket near the waistband in trousers **2 :** a small ornament worn on a watch chain

fob off *vt* **1 :** to put off with a trick or excuse **2 :** to pass or offer as genuine **3 :** to put aside

fo·cal \ˈfō-kəl\ *adj* **:** of, relating to, or having a focus — **fo·cal·ly** \-kə-lē\ *adv*

¹fo·cus \ˈfō-kəs\ *n, pl* **fo·cus·es** *or* **fo·ci** \-ˌsī\ **1 :** a point at which rays (as of light, heat, or sound) converge or from which they diverge or appear to diverge; *esp* **:** the point at which an image is formed by a mirror, lens, or optical system **2 :** adjustment (as of the eye or field glasses) for distinct vision **3 :** a center of activity, attraction, or attention

²focus *vb* **fo·cused**; **fo·cus·ing 1 :** to bring or come to a focus **2 :** to cause to be concentrated **3 :** to adjust the focus of

fod·der \ˈfäd-ər\ *n* **:** coarse dry food (as cornstalks) for livestock — **fodder** *vt*

foe \ˈfō\ *n* **1 :** one who has personal enmity for another **:** ENEMY **2 :** an enemy in war **:** ADVERSARY **3 :** something prejudicial or injurious

foe·man \ˈfō-mən\ *n* **:** an enemy in war **:** FOE

¹fog \ˈfȯg, ˈfäg\ *n* **1 :** fine particles of water suspended in the lower atmosphere that differ from cloud only in being near the ground **2 :** a state of mental confusion

²fog *vb* **fogged**; **fog·ging :** to cover or become covered with or as if with fog

fog·gy \ˈfȯg-ē, ˈfäg-\ *adj* **1 :** filled or abounding with fog **2 :** MUDDLED — **fog·gi·ly** \-ə-lē\ *adv* — **fog·gi·ness** \-ē-nəs\ *n*

fog·horn \ˈfȯg-ˌhȯrn, ˈfäg-\ *n* **:** a horn sounded in foggy weather to warn ships

fo·gy \ˈfō-gē\ *n, pl* **fogies :** a person with old-fashioned ideas — usu. used with *old*

foi·ble \ˈfȯi-bəl\ *n* **:** a minor flaw or shortcoming in personal character or behavior **:** WEAKNESS

¹foil \ˈfȯil\ *vt* **1 :** to prevent from attaining an end **:** DEFEAT **2 :** to bring to naught

²foil *n* **:** a fencing weapon with a light flexible blade tapering to a blunt point

³foil *n* **1 :** a very thin sheet of metal **2 :** one that serves as a contrast to another

foist \ˈfȯist\ *vt* **:** to pass off (something false or worthless) as genuine

¹fold \ˈfōld\ *n* **1 :** an enclosure for or a flock of sheep **2 :** a group of people with a common faith, belief, or interest

²fold *vt* **:** to pen up or confine (as sheep) in a fold

³fold *vb* **1 :** to double or become doubled over itself **2 :** to clasp together **3 :** to lay one part over or against another part of something **4 :** to enclose in or as if in a fold **5 :** EMBRACE **6 :** to incorporate (a food ingredient) into a mixture by repeated overturnings without stirring or beating **7 :** FAIL, COLLAPSE

⁴fold *n* **1 :** a doubling or folding over **2 :** a part doubled or laid over another part

fold·er \ˈfōl-dər\ *n* **1 :** one that folds **2 :** a printed circular of folded sheets **3 :** a folded cover or large envelope for holding or filing loose papers

fol·de·rol \ˈfäl-də-ˌräl\ *n* **1 :** a useless trifle **2 :** NONSENSE

fo·li·a·ceous \ˌfō-lē-ˈā-shəs\ *adj* **1 :** of, relating to, or resembling a plant leaf **2 :** consisting of thin layers

fo·li·age \ˈfō-l(ē-)ij, -lyij\ *n* **:** the mass of leaves of a plant — **fo·li·aged** \-l(ē-)ijd, -lyijd\ *adj*

fo·lio \ˈfō-lē-ˌō\ *n, pl* **fo·li·os 1 :** a leaf of a manuscript or book **2 a :** the size of a piece of paper cut two from a sheet **b :** a book printed on folio pages

fo·li·ose \ˈfō-lē-ˌōs\ *adj* **:** suggesting a leaf or an arrangement of leaves

¹folk \ˈfōk\ *n, pl* **folk** *or* **folks 1 :** a group of people forming a tribe or nation; *also* **:** the largest number or most characteristic part of such a group **2 :** people in general **:** persons as a group **3 :** the persons of one's own family

²folk *adj* **:** of, relating to, or originating among the common people

folk·lore \ˈfōk-ˌlō(ə)r\ *n* **:** customs, beliefs, stories, and sayings of a people handed down from generation to generation — **folk·lor·ist** \-ˌlōr-əst\ *n*

folk song *n* **:** a song originated or traditional among the common people of a country or region — **folk singer** *n*

folksy \ˈfōk-sē\ *adj* **1 :** SOCIABLE, FRIENDLY **2 :** informal, casual, or familiar in manner or style

folk·way \ˈfōk-ˌwā\ *n* **:** a way of thinking, feeling, or acting common to a people or to a social group

fol·li·cle \ˈfäl-i-kəl\ *n* **:** a small anatomical cavity or deep narrow-mouthed depression (as from which a hair grows)

fol·low \ˈfäl-ō\ *vb* **1 :** to go or come after or behind **2 :** to take as a leader **:** OBEY **3 :** PURSUE **4 :** to proceed along **5 :** to attend upon (as a business or profession) steadily **6 :** to come after in order of rank or natural sequence **7** : to keep one's eyes or attention fixed on **8** : to result from something — **fol·low·er** *n* — **follow suit** **1** : to play a card of the same suit as the card led **2** : to follow an example set

[1]**fol·low·ing** \'fäl-ə-wiŋ\ *adj* **1** : next after : SUCCEEDING **2** : that immediately follows

[2]**following** *n* : a group of followers, adherents, or partisans

[3]**following** *prep* : subsequent to

fol·low–up \'fäl-ə-,wəp\ *n* : a system or instance of pursuing an initial effort by supplementary action

fol·ly \'fäl-ē\ *n, pl* **follies** **1** : lack of good sense **2 a** : a foolish act or idea **b** : foolish actions or conduct **3** : an excessively costly or unprofitable undertaking

fo·ment \fō-'ment\ *vt* **1** : to treat with moist heat (as for easing pain) **2** : to stir up : ROUSE, INSTIGATE — **fo·men·ta·tion** \,fō-mən-'tā-shən, -,men-\ *n* — **fo·ment·er** \fō-'ment-ər\ *n*

fond \'fänd\ *adj* **1** : FOOLISH, SILLY **2 a** : prizing highly : DESIROUS **b** : strongly attracted or predisposed **3** : TENDER, LOVING, AFFECTIONATE **4** : doted on : DEAR — **fond·ly** *adv* — **fond·ness** *n*

fon·dant \'fän-dənt\ *n* : a creamy preparation of sugar used as a basis for candies or icings

fon·dle \'fän-dᵊl\ *vt* **fon·dled**; **fon·dling** \-dliŋ, -dᵊl-iŋ\ : to touch or handle in a tender or loving manner : CARESS, PET — **fon·dler** \-dlər, -dᵊl-ər\ *n*

fon·due \fän-'d(y)ü\ *n* : a preparation of melted cheese usu. flavored with wine or brandy

[1]**font** \'fänt\ *n* **1** : a receptacle for baptismal or holy water **2** : FOUNTAIN, SOURCE

[2]**font** *n* : an assortment of type all of one size and style

food \'füd\ *n* **1 a** : material used in the body of an organism to sustain growth, repair, and vital processes and to furnish energy **b** : organic material produced by green plants and used by them as building material and as a source of energy **2** : nutriment in solid form **3** : something that nourishes, sustains, or supplies

food poisoning *n* : an acute digestive disorder caused by bacteria or their toxic products or by chemical residues in food

food·stuff \'füd-,stəf\ *n* : a substance with food value; *esp* : a specific nutrient (as protein or fat)

[1]**fool** \'fül\ *n* **1** : a person who lacks sense or judgment **2** : a person formerly kept in a noble or royal household to amuse **3** : IDIOT **4** : DUPE

[2]**fool** *vb* **1 a** : to spend time idly or aimlessly **b** : to meddle or tamper thoughtlessly or ignorantly **2** : JOKE **3** : to make a fool of : DECEIVE **4** : FRITTER — used with *away*

fool·ery \'fül-(ə-)rē\ *n, pl* **-er·ies** **1** : the habit of fooling : the behavior of a fool **2** : a foolish act : HORSEPLAY

fool·har·dy \'fül-,härd-ē\ *adj* : foolishly adventurous and bold : RASH — **fool·har·di·ly** \-,härd-ᵊl-ē\ *adv* — **fool·har·di·ness** \-,härd-ē-nəs\ *n*

fool·ish \'fü-lish\ *adj* : showing or arising from folly or lack of judgment — **fool·ish·ly** *adv* — **fool·ish·ness** *n*

fool·proof \'fül-'prüf\ *adj* : so simple, plain, or reliable as to leave no opportunity for error, misuse, or failure

fools·cap *or* **fool's cap** \'fül-,skap\ *n* : a cap or hood usu. with bells worn by jesters

[1]**foot** \'fu̇t\ *n, pl* **feet** \'fēt\ **1** : the terminal part of the leg upon which an individual stands **2** : any of various units of length; *esp* : a unit equal to 12 inches **3** : the basic unit of verse meter **4** : something resembling an animal's foot in position or use **5** : the lowest part : BOTTOM **6** : the end that is lower or opposite the head — **on foot** **1** : by walking **2** : under way : in progress

[2]**foot** *vb* **1** : DANCE **2** : to go on foot **3** : to make speed **4 a** : to add up **b** : to pay or provide for paying

foot·age \'fu̇t-ij\ *n* : length expressed in feet

foot·ball \'fu̇t-,bȯl\ *n* **1** : any of several games that are played with an inflated ball on a rectangular field having two goalposts at each end by two teams whose object is to get the ball over a goal line or between goalposts; *esp* : one played between two teams of 11 players each in which the ball is advanced by running or passing **2** : the ball used in football

foot·board \'fu̇t-,bōrd\ *n* **1** : a narrow platform on which to stand or brace the feet **2** : a board forming the foot of a bed

foot·bridge \-,brij\ *n* : a bridge for pedestrians

foot·ed \'fu̇t-əd\ *adj* **1** : having a foot or feet **2** : having such or so many feet

foot·fall \'fu̇t-,fȯl\ *n* : FOOTSTEP; *also* : the sound of a footstep

foot·gear \-,gi(ə)r\ *n* : covering (as shoes) for the feet

foot·hill \-,hil\ *n* : a hill at the foot of higher hills

foot·hold \-,hōld\ *n* **1** : a hold for the feet : FOOTING **2** : a position usable as a base for further advance

foot·ing \'fu̇t-iŋ\ *n* **1 a** : the placing of one's feet in a position to secure a firm or safe stand **b** : a place for the foot to rest on : FOOTHOLD **2** : a moving on foot : WALK, TREAD, DANCE **3 a** : position with respect to one another : STATUS **b** : BASIS **4 a** : the action of adding up a column of figures **b** : the total amount of such a column

foot·lights \'fu̇t-,līts\ *n pl* **1** : a row of lights set across the front of a stage floor **2** : the stage as a profession

foot·lock·er \-,läk-ər\ *n* : a small flat trunk designed to be placed at the foot of a bed (as in barracks)

foot·loose \-,lüs\ *adj* : having no ties : FREE, UNTRAMMELED

foot·man \'fu̇t-mən\ *n* : a male servant who attends a carriage, waits on table, admits visitors, and runs errands

foot·note \-,nōt\ *n* : a note of reference, explanation, or comment placed below the text on a printed page — **footnote** *vt*

foot·pad \-,pad\ *n* : a highwayman or robber on foot

foot·path \-,path, -,pa̐th\ *n* : a narrow path for pedestrians

foot·print \-,print\ *n* : an impression left by the foot

foot·race \-,rās\ *n* : a race run on foot

foot·sore \'fu̇t-,sō(ə)r\ *adj* : having sore or tender feet (as from much walking)

foot·step \-,step\ *n* **1 a** : a step or tread of the foot **b** : distance covered by a step **2** : the mark of the foot : TRACK **3** : a step on which to ascend or descend

foot·stool \-,stül\ *n* : a low stool to support the feet

foot·way \-,wā\ *n* : a narrow way or path for pedestrians

foot·wear \-,wa(ə)r\ *n* : FOOTGEAR

foot·work \-,wərk\ *n* : the management of the feet (as in boxing)

foo·zle \'fü-zəl\ *vt* **foo·zled**; **foo·zling** \'füz-(ə-)liŋ\ : to manage or play awkwardly : BUNGLE — **foozle** *n*

fop \'fäp\ *n* : DANDY — **fop·pish** \'fäp-ish\ *adj*

fop·pery \'fäp-(ə-)rē\ *n, pl* **fop·per·ies** **1** : FOLLY **2** : the distinguishing marks of a fop

[1]**for** \fər, (')fȯ(ə)r\ *prep* **1** — used as a function word to indicate purpose, intended destination, or object toward which one's desire or activity is directed **2** : as being **3** : because of **4 a** : in support of **b** — used as a function word to indicate appropriateness or belonging **c** — used as a function word with a following noun or pronoun to introduce an infinitive construction equivalent to a noun clause (as *that someone should* or *that he might*) **5 a** : in place of **b** : in exchange as the equivalent of **6** : in spite of **7** : CONCERNING **8** — used as a function word to indicate equality or proportion **9** — used as a function word to indicate duration of time or extent of space **10** : [2]AFTER 3b

[2]**for** *conj* : for this reason or on this ground, namely : in view of the fact that

[1]**for·age** \'fȯr-ij\ *n* **1** : food for animals esp. when taken by browsing or grazing **2** : a search for provisions

[2]**forage** *vb* **1** : to collect forage from **2** : to wander in search of provisions **3** : to get by foraging **4** : to make a search — **for·ag·er** *n*

[1]**for·ay** \'fȯr-ˌā\ *vb* : to raid esp. in search of plunder
[2]**foray** *n* : a sudden invasion or attack for war or spoils
[1]**for·bear** \fȯr-'ba(ə)r, fər-\ *vb* **-bore** \-'bō(ə)r\; **-borne** \-'bōrn\; **-bear·ing** 1 : to refrain or desist from : ABSTAIN 2 : to control oneself when provoked : be patient — **for·bear·er** *n*
[2]**forbear** *var of* FOREBEAR
for·bear·ance \fȯr-'bar-ən(t)s, fər-\ *n* 1 : the act of forbearing 2 : the quality of being forbearing : LENIENCY, PATIENCE
for·bid \fər-'bid, fȯr-\ *vt* **-bade** \-'bad, -'bād\ *or* **-bad** \-'bad\; **-bid·den** \-'bid-ᵊn\; **-bid·ding** 1 : to command against : PROHIBIT 2 a : to exclude or warn off by express command b : to bar from use 3 : to hinder or prevent as if by an effectual command — **for·bid·der** *n*
for·bid·ding \-'bid-iŋ\ *adj* : discouraging approach : frightening away : REPELLENT, DISAGREEABLE
[1]**force** \'fōrs\ *n* 1 a : strength or energy exerted or brought to bear : active power b : capacity to persuade or convince 2 a : military strength b *pl* : the whole military strength (as of a nation) c : a body of persons available for a particular end 3 : VIOLENCE, COMPULSION 4 : an influence (as a push or pull) that causes motion or a change of motion — **force·less** \-ləs\ *adj*
[2]**force** *vt* 1 : COMPEL, COERCE 2 : to make or cause through necessity 3 : to attain to or effect against resistance or inertia 4 : to achieve or win by strength in struggle or violence 5 a : to raise or accelerate to the utmost b : to produce with unnatural or unwilling effort 6 : to hasten the rate of progress or growth of — **forc·er** *n*
forced \'fōrst\ *adj* : done or produced with effort, exertion, or pressure
force·ful \'fōrs-fəl\ *adj* : possessing or filled with force — **force·ful·ly** \-fə-lē\ *adv* — **force·ful·ness** *n*
for·ceps \'fȯr-səps\ *n, pl* **forceps** : an instrument for grasping, holding, or exerting traction on objects esp. for delicate operations — **for·ceps·like** *adj*
forc·i·ble \'fōr-sə-bəl\ *adj* 1 : got, made, or done by force or violence 2 : showing force or energy — **forc·i·bly** \-blē\ *adv*
[1]**ford** \'fōrd\ *n* : a shallow part of a body of water that may be crossed by wading
[2]**ford** *vt* : to cross (a body of water) by wading — **ford·a·ble** *adj*
for·do *or* **fore·do** \fȯr-'dü, fōr-\ *vt* **-did** \-'did\; **-done** \-'dən\; **-do·ing** : to overcome with fatigue : EXHAUST
[1]**fore** \'fō(ə)r\ *adv* : in, toward, or adjacent to the front : FORWARD
[2]**fore** *adj* : being or coming before in time, order, or space
[3]**fore** *n* : a prominent place or position : FRONT
[4]**fore** *interj* — used by a golfer to warn anyone within range of the probable line of flight of his ball
fore and aft *adv* : lengthwise of a ship : from stem to stern
fore–and–aft \ˌfōr-ən-'aft\ *adj* : running in the general line of the length of a ship or other construction
[1]**fore·arm** \(')fōr-'ärm\ *vt* : to arm in advance : PREPARE
[2]**fore·arm** \'fōr-ˌärm\ *n* : the part of the arm between the elbow and the wrist
fore·bear *or* **for·bear** \'fōr-ˌba(ə)r\ *n* : ANCESTOR, FOREFATHER
fore·bode \fōr-'bōd\ *vb* 1 : FORETELL, PORTEND 2 : to have an inward and anticipatory conviction of (as misfortune) — **fore·bod·er** *n*
[1]**fore·bod·ing** \-iŋ\ *n* : an omen, prediction, or presentiment esp. of coming evil : PORTENT
[2]**foreboding** *adj* : indicative of or marked by foreboding — **fore·bod·ing·ly** *adv* — **fore·bod·ing·ness** *n*
fore·cast \'fōr-ˌkast\ *vb* **forecast** *or* **fore·cast·ed**; **fore·cast·ing** 1 : CALCULATE, PREDICT 2 : to indicate as likely to occur — **forecast** *n* — **fore·cast·er** *n*
fore·cas·tle \'fōk-səl; 'fōr-ˌkas-əl\ *n* 1 : the part of the upper deck of a ship forward of the foremast 2 : the forward part of a merchantman having crew quarters forward
fore·close \fōr-'klōz\ *vb* 1 : to shut out 2 : to take legal measures to terminate a mortgage and take possession of the mortgaged property
fore·clo·sure \-'klō-zhər\ *n* : the act of foreclosing; *esp* : the legal procedure of foreclosing a mortgage
foredo *var of* FORDO
fore·doom \fōr-'düm\ *vt* : to doom beforehand
fore·fa·ther \'fōr-ˌfäth-ər\ *n* 1 : ANCESTOR 1 2 : a person of an earlier period and common heritage
fore·fin·ger \'fōr-ˌfiŋ-gər\ *n* : the finger next to the thumb
fore·foot \-ˌfu̇t\ *n* : one of the front feet of a quadruped
fore·front \-ˌfrənt\ *n* : the foremost part or place
foregather *var of* FORGATHER
[1]**fore·go** \fōr-'gō\ *vb* **-went** \-'went\; **-gone** \-'gȯn\; **-go·ing** \-'gō-iŋ\ : to go before : PRECEDE — **fore·go·er** *n*
[2]**forego** *var of* FORGO
fore·go·ing \fōr-'gō-iŋ\ *adj* : going before; *esp* : said, written, or listed before or above
fore·gone \ˌfōr-ˌgȯn\ *adj* : determined or settled in advance
fore·ground \'fōr-ˌgrau̇nd\ *n* 1 : the part of a scene or representation that is nearest to and in front of the spectator 2 : a position of prominence : FOREFRONT
fore·hand \'fōr-ˌhand\ *n* : a stroke made with the palm of the hand turned in the direction of movement; *also* : the side on which such a stroke is made — **forehand** *adj*
fore·hand·ed \'fōr-'han-dəd\ *adj* : mindful of the future : THRIFTY, PRUDENT — **fore·hand·ed·ly** *adv* — **fore·hand·ed·ness** *n*
fore·head \'fȯr-əd, 'fär-; 'fōr-ˌhed\ *n* 1 : the part of the face above the eyes 2 : the front or forepart of something
for·eign \'fȯr-ən\ *adj* 1 : situated outside a place or country; *esp* : situated outside one's own country 2 : born in, belonging to, or characteristic of some place or country other than the one under consideration 3 : alien in character : not connected or pertinent 4 : related to or dealing with other nations 5 : occurring in an abnormal situation in the living body and commonly introduced from without — **for·eign·ness** \-ən-nəs\ *n*
for·eign·er \'fȯr-ə-nər\ *n* : a person belonging to or owing allegiance to a foreign country : ALIEN
foreign minister *n* : a governmental minister for foreign affairs
fore·know \(')fōr-'nō\ *vt* **-knew** \-'n(y)ü\; **-known** \-'nōn\; **-know·ing** : to have previous knowledge of : know beforehand — **fore·knowl·edge** \-'näl-ij\ *n*
fore·la·dy \'fōr-ˌlād-ē\ *n* : a woman who acts as a foreman
fore·land \-lənd\ *n* : PROMONTORY, HEADLAND
fore·leg \-ˌleg\ *n* : a front leg
fore·limb \-ˌlim\ *n* : an arm, fin, wing, or leg that is a foreleg or homologous to it
fore·lock \-ˌläk\ *n* : a lock of hair growing from the front of the head
fore·man \'fōr-mən\ *n* 1 : a spokesman of a jury 2 : a workman in charge of a group of workers
fore·mast \-ˌmast, -məst\ *n* : the mast nearest the bow of a ship
[1]**fore·most** \'fōr-ˌmōst\ *adj* : first in time, place, or order : most important : PREEMINENT
[2]**foremost** *adv* : in the first place
fore·name \-ˌnām\ *n* : a first name
fore·noon \'fōr-ˌnün\ *n* : MORNING
[1]**fo·ren·sic** \fə-'ren(t)-sik, -'ren-zik\ *adj* : belonging to, used in, or suitable to courts of law or to public discussion and debate — **fo·ren·si·cal·ly** \-si-k(ə-)lē, -zi-\ *adv*
[2]**forensic** *n* 1 : an argumentative exercise 2 *pl* : the art or study of argumentative discourse
fore·or·dain \ˌfōr-ȯr-'dān\ *vt* : to ordain or decree in advance — **fore·or·di·na·tion** \-ˌȯrd-ᵊn-'ā-shən\ *n*
fore·quar·ter \'fōr-ˌkwȯrt-ər\ *n* : the front half of a lateral half of the body or carcass of a quadruped

fore·run·ner \'fōr-ˌrən-ər\ *n* **1 :** one that goes or is sent before to give notice of the approach of others : HARBINGER **2 :** PREDECESSOR, ANCESTOR
fore·sail \'fōr-ˌsāl, -səl\ *n* **1 :** the lowest sail on the foremast of a square-rigged ship **2 :** the lower sail set toward the stern on the foremast of a schooner
fore·see \fōr-'sē\ *vt* **-saw** \-'sȯ\; **-seen** \-'sēn\; **-see·ing :** to see or realize beforehand : EXPECT — **fore·see·a·ble** *adj* — **fore·se·er** \-'sē-ər\ *n*
fore·shad·ow \-'shad-ō\ *vt* **:** to give a hint or suggestion of beforehand : represent beforehand
fore·sheet \'fōr-ˌshēt\ *n* **1 :** one of the sheets of a foresail **2** *pl* **:** the forward part of an open boat
fore·shore \-ˌshōr\ *n* **:** the part of a seashore between high-water and low-water marks
fore·short·en \fōr-'shȯrt-ᵊn\ *vt* **:** to shorten (a detail) in a drawing or painting so that the composition appears to have depth
fore·sight \'fōr-ˌsīt\ *n* **1 :** the act or power of foreseeing **2 :** the act of looking forward; *also* **:** a view forward **3 :** care or provision for the future : PRUDENCE — **fore·sight·ed** \-ˌsīt-əd\ *adj* — **fore·sight·ed·ly** *adv* — **fore·sight·ed·ness** *n*
fore·skin \-ˌskin\ *n* **:** a fold of skin that covers the end of the penis
for·est \'fȯr-əst\ *n* **:** a dense growth of trees and underbrush covering a large tract — **for·est·ed** \'fȯr-ə-stəd\ *adj*
fore·stall \fōr-'stȯl\ *vt* **:** to keep out, hinder, or prevent by measures taken in advance — **fore·stall·er** *n* — **fore·stall·ment** *n*
for·est·er \'fȯr-ə-stər\ *n* **1 :** a person trained in forestry **2 :** an inhabitant of a forest
for·est·ry \'fȯr-ə-strē\ *n* **:** the science of developing and caring for forests
foreswear *var of* FORSWEAR
¹fore·taste \'fōr-ˌtāst\ *n* **:** an advance indication, warning, or notion
²fore·taste \fōr-'tāst, 'fōr-ˌ\ *vt* **:** to taste beforehand : ANTICIPATE
fore·tell \fōr-'tel\ *vt* **-told** \-'tōld\; **-tell·ing :** to tell of or describe beforehand : PROPHESY
fore·thought \'fōr-ˌthȯt\ *n* **1 :** a thinking or planning out in advance : PREMEDITATION **2 :** consideration for the future — **fore·thought·ful** \-fəl\ *adj* — **fore·thought·ful·ly** \-fə-lē\ *adv* — **fore·thought·ful·ness** *n*
¹fore·to·ken \'fōr-ˌtō-kən\ *n* **:** a premonitory sign
²fore·to·ken \fōr-'tō-kən\ *vt* **fore·to·kened**; **fore·to·ken·ing** \-'tōk-(ə-)niŋ\ **:** to indicate in advance
fore·top \'fōr-ˌtäp, 'fōrt-əp\ *n* **:** the platform at the head of a ship's foremast
for·ev·er \fə-'rev-ər\ *adv* **1 :** for a limitless time : EVERLASTINGLY **2 :** at all times : ALWAYS, CONSTANTLY
for·ev·er·more \-ˌrev-ə(r)-'mō(ə)r\ *adv* **:** FOREVER
fore·warn \fōr-'wȯrn\ *vt* **:** to warn in advance
fore·wom·an \'fōr-ˌwu̇m-ən\ *n* **:** FORELADY
fore·word \'fōr-(ˌ)wərd\ *n* **:** PREFACE
¹for·feit \'fȯr-fət\ *n* **1 :** something lost by or taken away from a person because of an offense or error committed by him : PENALTY, FINE **2** *pl* **:** a game in which forfeits are exacted
²forfeit *vt* **:** to lose or lose the right to by some error, offense, or crime — **for·feit·er** *n*
for·fei·ture \'fȯr-fə-ˌchu̇r, -chər\ *n* **1 :** the act of forfeiting **2 :** something forfeited : PENALTY
for·gath·er *or* **fore·gath·er** \fȯr-'gath-ər, fōr-\ *vi* **1 :** to come together : ASSEMBLE **2 :** to meet someone usu. by chance
¹forge \'fōrj\ *n* **1 :** a furnace or a shop with its furnace where metal is heated and wrought **2 :** SMITHY
²forge *vt* **1 :** to form (as metal) by heating and hammering **2 :** SHAPE, FASHION **3 :** to make or imitate falsely esp. with intent to defraud : COUNTERFEIT
³forge *vi* **:** to move forward steadily but gradually
forg·er \'fōr-jər\ *n* **:** one that forges
forg·ery \'fōrj-(ə-)rē\ *n, pl* **-er·ies 1 :** the crime of falsely making or changing a written paper or signing someone else's name **2 :** something that has been forged
for·get \fər-'get, fȯr-\ *vb* **-got** \-'gät\; **-got·ten** \-'gät-ᵊn\ *or* **-got**; **-get·ting 1 :** to be unable to think of or recall **2 a :** to fail to become mindful at the proper time **b :** NEGLECT — **for·get·ter** *n* — **forget oneself :** to lose one's dignity, temper, or self-control
for·get·ful \-'get-fəl\ *adj* **1 :** having a poor memory **2 :** CARELESS, NEGLECTFUL — **for·get·ful·ly** \-'get-fə-lē\ *adv* — **for·get·ful·ness** *n*
forg·ing \'fōr-jiŋ\ *n* **:** a piece of forged work
for·give \fər-'giv, fȯr-\ *vb* **-gave** \-'gāv\; **-giv·en** \-'giv-ən\; **-giv·ing 1 :** to cease to feel resentment against (an offender) : PARDON **2 a :** to give up resentment of or claim to requital for **b :** to grant relief from payment of — **for·giv·a·ble** *adj* — **for·giv·er** *n*
for·give·ness \-'giv-nəs\ *n* **:** the act of forgiving : PARDON
for·giv·ing \-'giv-iŋ\ *adj* **:** showing forgiveness : inclined or ready to forgive — **for·giv·ing·ly** *adv*
for·go *or* **fore·go** \fȯr-'gō, fōr-\ *vt* **-went** \-'went\; **-gone** \-'gȯn\; **-go·ing** \-'gō-iŋ\ **:** to give up : let pass : go without
¹fork \'fȯrk\ *n* **1 :** an implement with two or more prongs used esp. for taking up (as in eating), pitching, or digging **2 :** a forked part, tool, or piece of equipment **3 a :** a dividing into branches or the place where something divides into branches **b :** a branch of a fork
²fork *vb* **1 :** to divide into two or more branches **2 :** to give the form of a fork to **3 :** to raise or pitch with a fork — **fork·er** *n*
forked \'fȯrkt, 'fȯr-kəd\ *adj* **:** having a fork : shaped like a fork
fork·lift \'fȯrk-ˌlift\ *n* **:** a machine for hoisting heavy objects by means of steel fingers inserted under the load
for·lorn \fər-'lȯrn\ *adj* **1 :** DESERTED, FORSAKEN **2 :** feeling deserted or neglected : WRETCHED **3 :** nearly hopeless — **for·lorn·ly** *adv* — **for·lorn·ness** *n*
forlorn hope *n* **1 :** a body of men selected to perform a perilous service **2 :** a desperate or extremely difficult enterprise
¹form \'fȯrm\ *n* **1 a :** the shape and structure of something as distinguished from its material **b :** a body (as of a person) esp. in its external appearance or as distinguished from the face **2 :** the essential nature of a thing **3 a :** established manner of doing or saying something **b :** a prescribed and set order of words **4 :** a printed or typed document with blank spaces for insertion of required information **5 a :** CEREMONY, CONVENTIONALITY **b :** manner or style of performing or accomplishing according to recognized standards **6 :** a long seat : BENCH **7 a :** a frame model of the human figure used for displaying clothes **b :** MOLD **8 :** the printing type or matter arranged and secured in a frame ready for printing **9 :** MODE, KIND, VARIETY **10 a :** orderly method of arrangement; *also* **:** a particular kind or instance of such arrangement **b :** the structural element, plan, or design of a work of art **c :** a bounded surface or volume **11 :** a grade in a British secondary school or in some American private schools **12 a :** a table with information on the past performances of racehorses **b** (1) **:** known ability to perform (2) **:** condition suitable for performing (as in athletic competition) **13 :** any of the different pronunciations or spellings a word may take in inflection or compounding
²form *vb* **1 :** to give form or shape to : FASHION, MAKE **2 :** TRAIN, INSTRUCT **3 :** DEVELOP, GET, CONTRACT **4 :** to make up : CONSTITUTE **5 :** to arrange in order **6 :** to take form : ARISE **7 :** to take a definite form, shape, or arrangement — **form·er** *n*
¹for·mal \'fȯr-məl\ *adj* **1 a :** CONVENTIONAL **b :** done in due or lawful form **2 a :** based on conventional forms and rules **b :** characterized by punctilious respect for form **3 :** NOMINAL — **for·mal·ly** \-mə-lē\ *adv*
²formal *n* **:** something (as a dance) formal in character
form·al·de·hyde \fȯr-'mal-də-ˌhīd, fər-\ *n* **:** a colorless gas that

has a sharp irritating odor and in solution in water is used as a disinfectant and preservative

for·mal·ism \'fȯr-mə-ˌliz-əm\ *n* : the strict observance of forms or conventions (as in religion or art) — **for·mal·ist** \-ləst\ *n* — **for·mal·is·tic** \ˌfȯr-mə-'lis-tik\ *adj*

for·mal·i·ty \fȯr-'mal-ət-ē\ *n, pl* **-ties** 1 : the quality or state of being formal 2 : compliance with formal or conventional rules : CEREMONY 3 : an established form that is required or conventional

for·mal·ize \'fȯr-mə-ˌlīz\ *vt* 1 : to give a certain or definite form to : SHAPE 2 **a** : to make formal **b** : to give formal status or approval to — **for·mal·iz·er** *n*

for·mat \'fȯr-ˌmat\ *n* : the shape, size, and general makeup of a publication

for·ma·tion \fȯr-'mā-shən\ *n* 1 : a forming of something 2 : something that is formed 3 : the manner in which a thing is formed : STRUCTURE, SHAPE 4 : an arrangement or grouping of persons, ships, or airplanes — **for·ma·tion·al** \-shnəl, -shən-ᵊl\ *adj*

for·ma·tive \'fȯr-mət-iv\ *adj* 1 : giving or capable of giving form : CONSTRUCTIVE 2 : of, relating to, or characterized by important growth or formation — **for·ma·tive·ly** *adv* — **for·ma·tive·ness** *n*

for·mer \'fȯr-mər\ *adj* 1 : coming before in time; *esp* : of, relating to, or occurring in the past 2 : preceding in place or arrangement : FOREGOING 3 : first mentioned or in order of two things mentioned or understood

for·mer·ly \-mə(r)-lē\ *adv* : at an earlier time : PREVIOUSLY

for·mi·da·ble \'fȯr-məd-ə-bəl, fȯr-'mid-\ *adj* 1 : arousing fear 2 : imposing serious difficulties or hardships 3 : tending to inspire awe or wonder — **for·mi·da·bil·i·ty** \ˌfȯr-məd-ə-'bil-ət-ē, fȯr-ˌmid-\ *n* — **for·mi·da·ble·ness** *n* — **for·mi·da·bly** \'fȯr-məd-ə-blē, fȯr-'mid-\ *adv*

form·less \'fȯrm-ləs\ *adj* : having no regular form or shape — **form·less·ly** *adv* — **form·less·ness** *n*

for·mu·la \'fȯr-myə-lə\ *n* 1 : a set form of words for use in a ceremony or ritual 2 **a** : RECIPE, PRESCRIPTION **b** : a milk mixture or substitute for a baby 3 : a group of symbols or figures joined to express a single rule or idea 4 : a prescribed or set form or method — **for·mu·la·ic** \ˌfȯr-myə-'lā-ik\ *adj* — **for·mu·la·i·cal·ly** \-'lā-ə-k(ə-)lē\ *adv*

for·mu·late \'fȯr-myə-ˌlāt\ *vt* 1 : to express in a formula 2 : to put in systematic form : state definitely and clearly — **for·mu·la·tion** \ˌfȯr-myə-'lā-shən\ *n* — **for·mu·la·tor** \'fȯr-myə-ˌlāt-ər\ *n*

for·ni·cate \'fȯr-nə-ˌkāt\ *vi* : to commit fornication — **for·ni·ca·tor** \-ˌkāt-ər\ *n*

for·ni·ca·tion \ˌfȯr-nə-'kā-shən\ *n* : human sexual intercourse other than between husband and wife

for·sake \fər-'sāk, fȯr-\ *vt* **for·sook** \-'su̇k\; **for·sak·en** \-'sā-kən\; **for·sak·ing** 1 : to give up : RENOUNCE 2 : to quit or leave entirely; *also* : DESERT

for·sooth \fər-'süth\ *adv* : in truth : INDEED

for·swear *or* **fore·swear** \fȯr-'swa(ə)r, fōr-\ *vb* **-swore** \-'swō(ə)r\; **-sworn** \-'swōrn\; **-swear·ing** 1 : to swear falsely : commit perjury 2 : to pledge oneself to give up

for·syth·ia \fər-'sith-ē-ə\ *n* : any of a genus of shrubs of the olive family widely grown for their yellow bell-shaped flowers appearing before the leaves in early spring

fort \'fōrt\ *n* 1 : a strong or fortified place; *esp* : a place surrounded with defenses and occupied by soldiers 2 : a permanent army post

¹**forte** \'fōrt, 'fȯr-ˌtā\ *n* : something in which a person excels or shows special ability : a strong point

²**for·te** \'fȯr-ˌtā, 'fȯrt-ē\ *adv* (*or adj*) : LOUDLY, POWERFULLY — used as a direction in music

forth \'fōrth\ *adv* 1 : FORWARD, ONWARD 2 : out into view : OUT

¹**forth·com·ing** \(')fōrth-'kəm-iŋ\ *adj* 1 : being about to appear : APPROACHING 2 : readily available or approachable

²**forthcoming** *n* : a coming forth : APPROACH

forth·right \'fōrth-ˌrīt\ *adj* : STRAIGHTFORWARD, DIRECT — **forth·right·ly** *adv* — **forth·right·ness** *n*

forth·with \(')fōrth-'wit͟h, -'with\ *adv* : IMMEDIATELY

for·ti·fi·ca·tion \ˌfȯrt-ə-fə-'kā-shən\ *n* 1 : the act of fortifying 2 : a construction built for the defense of a place : FORT

for·ti·fy \'fȯrt-ə-ˌfī\ *vt* **-fied**; **-fy·ing** : to make strong: as **a** : to strengthen and secure by military defenses **b** : to give physical strength, courage, or endurance to **c** : to add mental or moral strength to : ENCOURAGE **d** : to add material to for strengthening or improving : ENRICH — **for·ti·fi·er** *n*

for·ti·tude \'fȯrt-ə-ˌt(y)üd\ *n* : strength of mind that enables a person to face danger, pain, or adversity with courage

fort·night \'fōrt-ˌnīt\ *n* : the space of 14 days : two weeks

¹**fort·night·ly** \-lē\ *adj* : occurring or appearing once in a fortnight — **fortnightly** *adv*

²**fortnightly** *n, pl* **-lies** : a publication issued fortnightly

for·tress \'fȯr-trəs\ *n* : a fortified place; *esp* : a large and permanent fortification sometimes including a town

for·tu·i·tous \fȯr-'t(y)ü-ət-əs, fər-\ *adj* 1 : occurring by chance 2 : FORTUNATE — **for·tu·i·tous·ly** *adv* — **for·tu·i·tous·ness** *n*

for·tu·i·ty \-'t(y)ü-ət-ē\ *n, pl* **-ties** 1 : the quality or state of being fortuitous 2 : a chance event or occurrence

for·tu·nate \'fȯrch-(ə-)nət\ *adj* 1 : coming or happening by good luck 2 : LUCKY — **for·tu·nate·ly** *adv*

for·tune \'fȯr-chən\ *n* 1 : CHANCE, LUCK 2 : good or bad luck 3 : a person's destiny or fate 4 **a** : possession of material goods : WEALTH **b** : RICHES

fortune cookie *n* : a thin folded cookie containing a printed fortune, proverb, or humorous statement

fortune hunter *n* : a person who seeks wealth esp. by marriage

for·tune–tell·er \-ˌtel-ər\ *n* : a person who professes to foretell future events — **for·tune–tell·ing** \-ˌtel-iŋ\ *n or adj*

for·ty \'fȯrt-ē\ *n, pl* **forties** — see NUMBER table — **for·ti·eth** \-ē-əth\ *adj or n* — **forty** *adj or pron*

for·ty–nin·er \ˌfȯrt-ē-'nī-nər\ *n* : a person in California in the gold rush of 1849

forty winks *n sing or pl* : a short sleep : NAP

fo·rum \'fōr-əm\ *n* 1 **a** : the marketplace or public place of an ancient Roman city **b** : a medium of open discussion 2 : a judicial body or assembly 3 : a public assembly, lecture, or program involving audience or panel discussion

¹**for·ward** \'fȯr-wərd\ *adj* 1 : near, being at, or belonging to the front 2 **a** : strongly inclined : READY **b** : tending to push oneself : BRASH 3 : notably advanced or developed : PRECOCIOUS 4 : moving, tending, or leading toward a position in front 5 : of, relating to, or getting ready for the future — **for·ward·ly** *adv* — **for·ward·ness** *n*

²**forward** *adv* : to or toward what is before or in front

³**forward** *n* : a principally offensive player stationed at or near the front of his side or team (as in basketball or hockey)

⁴**forward** *vt* 1 : to help onward : ADVANCE 2 **a** : to send forward : TRANSMIT **b** : to send or ship onward from an intermediate post or station in transit

for·ward·er \'fȯr-wərd-ər\ *n* : one that forwards; *esp* : an agent who forwards goods

for·ward·ing \-wərd-iŋ\ *n* : the act of one that forwards; *esp* : the business of a forwarder of goods

for·wards \'fȯr-wərdz\ *adv* : FORWARD

fosse *or* **foss** \'fäs\ *n* : DITCH, MOAT

¹**fos·sil** \'fäs-əl\ *n* 1 : a trace, impression, or the remains of a plant or animal of a past age preserved in the earth's crust 2 : a person whose ideas are out-of-date

²**fossil** *adj* 1 : extracted from the earth 2 : being or resembling a fossil

fos·sil·if·er·ous \ˌfäs-ə-'lif-(ə-)rəs\ *adj* : containing fossils

¹fos·ter \'fós-tər\ *adj* : affording, receiving, or sharing nurture or parental care though not related by blood or legal ties
²foster *vt* **fos·tered**; **fos·ter·ing** \-t(ə-)riŋ\ **1** : to give parental care to : NURTURE **2** : to promote the growth or development of : ENCOURAGE — **fos·ter·er** *n*
fos·ter·ling \-tər-liŋ\ *n* : a foster child
fought *past of* FIGHT
¹foul \'faůl\ *adj* **1 a** : offensive to the senses : LOATHSOME **b** : clogged or covered with dirt **2** : morally or spiritually odious : DETESTABLE **3** : OBSCENE, ABUSIVE **4** : being wet and stormy **5 a** : TREACHEROUS, DISHONORABLE **b** : violating a rule in a game or sport **6** : marked up or defaced by changes **7** : ENTANGLED **8** : marking the bounds of a playing field; *also* : being outside the foul lines in baseball — **foul·ly** \'faů(l)-lē\ *adv* — **foul·ness** *n*
²foul *n* **1** : ENTANGLEMENT, COLLISION **2** : an infringement of the rules in a sport; *also* : a ball hit outside the foul line
³foul *adv* : FOULLY
⁴foul *vb* **1** : to make or become foul or filthy **2** : DISGRACE, DISHONOR **3 a** : to commit a foul **b** : to hit a foul ball **4** : to entangle or become entangled **5** : to collide with
fou·lard \fü-'lärd\ *n* : a lightweight silk of plain or twill weave usu. decorated with a printed pattern
foul·mouthed \'faůl-'maůthd, -'maůtht\ *adj* : given to the use of obscene, profane, or abusive language
foul play *n* : unfair play or dealing : dishonest conduct; *esp* : VIOLENCE
foul up \(')faů-'ləp\ *vb* : BUNGLE — **foul–up** \'faů-ˌləp\ *n*
¹found \'faůnd\ *past of* FIND
²found *vt* **1** : to take the first steps in building **2** : to set or ground on something solid : BASE **3** : to establish and often to provide for the future maintenance of
³found *vt* : to melt (metal) and pour into a mold
foun·da·tion \faůn-'dā-shən\ *n* **1** : the act of founding **2** : the base or basis upon which something stands or is supported **3** : funds given for the permanent support of an institution : ENDOWMENT; *also* : an organization or institution so endowed **4** : an underlying natural or prepared base or support **5** : CORSET — **foun·da·tion·al** \-shnəl, -shən-ᵊl\ *adj*
¹found·er \'faůn-dər\ *n* : one that founds or establishes
²foun·der \'faůn-dər\ *vb* **foun·dered**; **foun·der·ing** \-d(ə-)riŋ\ **1** : to become or make disabled; *esp* : to go lame **2** : to give way : COLLAPSE **3** : to sink below the surface of the water **4** : to come to grief : FAIL
³found·er *n* : one that founds metal
found·ling \'faůn-dliŋ\ *n* : an infant found after its unknown parents have abandoned it
found·ry \'faůn-drē\ *n, pl* **foundries** : an establishment where founding is carried on
fount \'faůnt\ *n* : FOUNTAIN, SOURCE
foun·tain \'faůnt-ᵊn\ *n* **1** : a spring of water issuing from the earth **2** : SOURCE **3** : an artificially produced jet of water; *also* : the structure from which it rises **4** : a reservoir containing a liquid that can be drawn off as needed
foun·tain·head \-ˌhed\ *n* : a primary source : ORIGIN
fountain pen *n* : a pen with a reservoir that automatically feeds the writing point with ink
four \'fō(ə)r\ *n* **1** — see NUMBER table **2** : the fourth in a set or series **3** : something having four units or members — **four** *adj or pron*
four–flush \'fōr-ˌfləsh\ *vi* : to make a false claim : BLUFF — **four–flush·er** *n*
four·fold \-ˌfōld, -'fōld\ *adj* **1** : having four units or members **2** : of or amounting to 400 percent — **fourfold** *adv*
four–foot·ed \-'fůt-əd\ *adj* : QUADRUPED
four–hand·ed \-'han-dəd\ *adj* : engaged in by four persons
four–in–hand \'fōr-ən-ˌhand\ *n* : a necktie tied in a slipknot with long ends overlapping vertically in front
four–post·er \-'pō-stər\ *n* : a bed with tall corner posts orig. designed to support curtains or a canopy
four·score \'fōr-ˌskōr\ *adj* : EIGHTY
four·some \'fōr-səm\ *n* **1** : a group of four persons or things **2** : a golf match between two pairs of partners
four·square \-'skwa(ə)r\ *adj* **1** : SQUARE **2** : marked by boldness and conviction : FORTHRIGHT — **foursquare** *adv*
four·teen \(')fōr(t)-'tēn\ *n* — see NUMBER table — **fourteen** *adj or pron* — **four·teenth** \-'tēn(t)th\ *adj or n*
fourth \'fōrth\ *n* **1** — see NUMBER table **2** : the 4th forward gear or speed of a motor vehicle — **fourth** *adj or adv* — **fourth·ly** *adv*
fourth estate *n, often cap F&E* : the public press
¹fowl \'faůl\ *n, pl* **fowl** *or* **fowls** **1** : BIRD; *esp* : a domestic cock or hen **2** : the flesh of fowls used as food
²fowl *vi* : to seek, catch, or kill wildfowl — **fowl·er** *n*
¹fox \'fäks\ *n, pl* **fox·es** *or* **fox** **1 a** : any of various alert carnivorous mammals of the dog family related to the wolves but smaller and with shorter legs and more pointed muzzle **b** : the fur of a fox **2** : a clever crafty person
²fox *vt* : to trick by ingenuity or cunning : OUTWIT
foxed \'fäkst\ *adj* : discolored with yellowish brown stains
fox·glove \'fäks-ˌgləv\ *n* : a common European biennial or perennial cultivated for its showy spikes of dotted white or purple tubular flowers and as a source of digitalis
fox·hole \'fäks-ˌhōl\ *n* : a pit dug hastily during combat for individual cover against enemy fire
fox·hound \-ˌhaůnd\ *n* : any of various large swift powerful hounds used in hunting foxes
foxy \'fäk-sē\ *adj* **1 a** : resembling a fox in appearance or disposition : WILY **b** : being alert and knowing : CLEVER **2** : having the color of a fox **3** : FOXED — **fox·i·ly** \-sə-lē\ *adv* — **fox·i·ness** \-sē-nəs\ *n*
foy·er \'fói(-ə)r, 'fói-ˌ(y)ā\ *n* : an anteroom or lobby esp. of a theater; *also* : an entrance hallway : VESTIBULE
fra·cas \'frā-kəs, 'frak-əs\ *n* : a noisy quarrel : BRAWL
frac·tion \'frak-shən\ *n* **1** : a numerical representation (as $\frac{3}{4}$, ⁵/₈, 3.234) of two numbers whose quotient is to be determined **2 a** : FRAGMENT **b** : PORTION, SECTION
frac·tion·al \-shnəl, -shən-ᵊl\ *adj* **1** : of, relating to, or being a fraction **2** : relatively small — **frac·tion·al·ly** \-ē\ *adv*
frac·tious \'frak-shəs\ *adj* **1** : tending to be troublesome : hard to handle or control **2** : QUARRELSOME, IRRITABLE — **frac·tious·ly** *adv* — **frac·tious·ness** *n*
¹frac·ture \'frak-chər\ *n* **1** : the act or process of breaking or the state of being broken; *esp* : the breaking of bone **2** : the result of fracturing; *esp* : an injury resulting from fracture of a bone
²fracture *vb* **frac·tured**; **frac·tur·ing** \-chə-riŋ, -shriŋ\ **1** : BREAK **2** : DESTROY **3** : to undergo fracture
frag·ile \'fraj-əl, -ˌīl\ *adj* **1** : easily broken or destroyed : DELICATE **2** : TENUOUS, SLIGHT — **fra·gil·i·ty** \frə-'jil-ət-ē\ *n*
frag·ment \'frag-mənt\ *n* : a part broken off, detached, or incomplete — **frag·ment** \-ˌment\ *vb*
frag·men·tary \'frag-mən-ˌter-ē\ *adj* : consisting of fragments : INCOMPLETE — **frag·men·tar·i·ness** *n*
fra·grance \'frā-grən(t)s\ *n* **1** : a sweet, pleasing, and often flowery or fruity odor **2** : a particular odor
fra·grant \-grənt\ *adj* : having fragrance — **fra·grant·ly** *adv*
frail \'frāl\ *adj* **1** : morally weak **2** : FRAGILE **3 a** : physically weak **b** : SLIGHT, UNSUBSTANTIAL — **frail·ly** *adv* — **frail·ness** *n*
frail·ty \'frā(-ə)l-tē\ *n, pl* **frailties** **1** : the quality or state of being frail **2** : a fault due to weakness esp. of moral character
¹frame \'frām\ *vt* **1 a** : PLAN, CONTRIVE **b** : to give expression to : FORMULATE **c** : SHAPE, CONSTRUCT **d** : to draw up **2** : to fit or adjust for a purpose **3** : to construct by fitting and uniting the parts of the skeleton of (a structure) **4** : to enclose

in a frame 5 : to make (an innocent person) appear guilty — **fram·er** *n*

²frame *n* 1 : the physical makeup of an animal and esp. a human body 2 a : an arrangement of structural parts that gives form or support to something b : a supporting or enclosing border or open case (as for a window or a picture) 3 : a particular state or disposition (as of the mind) : MOOD

³frame *adj* : having a wood frame

frame–up \ˈfrām-ˌəp\ *n* : a scheme to cause an innocent person to be accused of a crime; *also* : the action resulting from such a scheme

frame·work \ˈfrām-ˌwərk\ *n* 1 : a skeletal, openwork, or structural frame 2 : a basic structure (as of ideas)

fran·chise \ˈfran-ˌchīz\ *n* 1 : a special privilege granted to an individual or group 2 : a constitutional or statutory right or privilege; *esp* : the right to vote

fran·ci·um \ˈfran(t)-sē-əm\ *n* : a radioactive chemical element

fran·gi·ble \ˈfran-jə-bəl\ *adj* : BREAKABLE — **fran·gi·bil·i·ty** \ˌfran-jə-ˈbil-ət-ē\ *n*

¹frank \ˈfraŋk\ *adj* : free and forthright in expressing one's feelings and opinions : OUTSPOKEN, CANDID — **frank·ly** *adv* — **frank·ness** *n*

²frank *vt* : to mark (a piece of mail) with an official signature or sign indicating the right of the sender to free mailing; *also* : to mail in this manner

³frank *n* 1 : a signature, mark, or stamp on a piece of mail indicating that it can be mailed free 2 : the privilege of sending mail free of charge

Fran·ken·stein \ˈfraŋ-kən-ˌstīn, -ˌstēn\ *n* 1 : a work or agency that ruins its originator 2 : a monster in the shape of a man

frank·furt·er *or* **frank·fort·er** \ˈfraŋk-fə(r)t-ər\ *or* **frank·furt** *or* **frank·fort** \-fərt\ *n* : a seasoned beef or beef and pork sausage

frank·in·cense \ˈfraŋ-kən-ˌsen(t)s\ *n* : a fragrant resin from African or Arabian trees that is an important incense resin

fran·tic \ˈfrant-ik\ *adj* : wildly or uncontrollably excited : FRENZIED — **fran·ti·cal·ly** \-i-k(ə-)lē\ *adv*

frap·pé \fra-ˈpā\ *or* **frappe** \ˈfrap, fra-ˈpā\ *n* 1 : an iced or frozen mixture or drink 2 : a thick milk shake — **frappé** *adj*

fra·ter·nal \frə-ˈtərn-ᵊl\ *adj* 1 a : of, relating to, or involving brothers b : of, relating to, or being a fraternity or society 2 : FRIENDLY, BROTHERLY — **fra·ter·nal·ism** \-ᵊl-ˌiz-əm\ *n* — **fra·ter·nal·ly** \-ᵊl-ē\ *adv*

fra·ter·ni·ty \frə-ˈtər-nət-ē\ *n, pl* **-ties** 1 : a social, honorary, or professional organization; *esp* : a social club of male college students 2 : BROTHERLINESS, BROTHERHOOD 3 : men of the same class, profession, character, or tastes

frat·er·nize \ˈfrat-ər-ˌnīz\ *vi* 1 : to associate or mingle as brothers or friends 2 : to associate on intimate terms with citizens or troops of a hostile nation — **frat·er·ni·za·tion** \ˌfrat-ər-nə-ˈzā-shən\ *n* — **frat·er·niz·er** \ˈfrat-ər-ˌnī-zər\ *n*

frat·ri·cide \ˈfra-trə-ˌsīd\ *n* 1 : one that murders or kills his own brother or sister 2 : the act of a fratricide — **frat·ri·cid·al** \ˌfra-trə-ˈsīd-ᵊl\ *adj*

fraud \ˈfrȯd\ *n* 1 a : DECEIT, TRICKERY b : an act of deceiving or misrepresenting : TRICK 2 a : IMPOSTOR b : CHEAT

fraud·u·lent \ˈfrȯ-jə-lənt\ *adj* : characterized by, based on, or done by fraud : DECEITFUL — **fraud·u·lence** \-lən(t)s\ *n* — **fraud·u·lent·ly** *adv* — **fraud·u·lent·ness** *n*

fraught \ˈfrȯt\ *adj* : bearing promise or menace : PREGNANT

¹fray \ˈfrā\ *n* : BRAWL, FIGHT; *also* : DISPUTE

²fray *vb* 1 a : to wear (as an edge of cloth) by rubbing : FRET b : to separate the threads at the edge of c : to wear out or into shreds 2 : STRAIN, IRRITATE

fraz·zle \ˈfraz-əl\ *vb* **fraz·zled**; **fraz·zling** \ˈfraz-(ə-)liŋ\ 1 : FRAY 2 : to put in a state of extreme physical or nervous fatigue — **frazzle** *n*

freak \ˈfrēk\ *n* 1 a : WHIM b : a seemingly capricious action or event 2 : something markedly unusual or abnormal — **freak** *adj* — **freak·ish** \ˈfrē-kish\ *adj*

¹freck·le \ˈfrek-əl\ *n* : a small brownish spot in the skin — **freck·ly** \ˈfrek-(ə-)lē\ *adv*

²freckle *vb* **freck·led**; **freck·ling** \ˈfrek-(ə-)liŋ\ : to mark or become marked with freckles or small spots

¹free \ˈfrē\ *adj* 1 a : having liberty : not being a slave b : not controlled by others : INDEPENDENT c : not allowing slavery 2 : not subject to a duty, tax, or other charge 3 : released or not suffering from something unpleasant or painful 4 : given without charge 5 : made or done voluntarily 6 : LAVISH 7 : PLENTIFUL, COPIOUS 8 : not held back by fear or distrust : OPEN, FRANK 9 : not restricted by or made in accordance with conventional forms 10 : not literal or exact 11 a : not obstructed : CLEAR b : not being used or occupied c : not fastened or bound : able to act, move, or turn — **free·ly** *adv*

²free *adv* 1 : FREELY 2 : without charge

³free *vt* **freed**; **free·ing** 1 : to cause to be free : set free 2 : RELIEVE, RID 3 : DISENTANGLE, CLEAR

free·board \ˈfrē-ˌbōrd\ *n* : the vertical distance between the waterline and the deck of a ship

free·boo·ter \ˈfrē-ˌbüt-ər\ *n* : PLUNDERER, PIRATE

free·born \ˈfrē-ˈbȯrn\ *adj* 1 : not born in vassalage or slavery 2 : relating to or befitting one that is freeborn

freed·man \ˈfrēd-mən\ *n* : a man freed from slavery

free·dom \ˈfrēd-əm\ *n* 1 : the quality or state of being free : as a : liberation from slavery or restraint or from the power of another : INDEPENDENCE b : EXEMPTION, RELEASE c : EASE, FACILITY d : FRANKNESS, OUTSPOKENNESS e : unrestricted use 2 a : a political right b : FRANCHISE, PRIVILEGE

free·hand \ˈfrē-ˌhand\ *adj* : done without mechanical aids or devices : FREE — **freehand** *adv*

free·hold \-ˌhōld\ *n* : ownership of real estate for life usu. with the right of leaving it to one's heirs; *also* : an estate so owned — **free·hold·er** \-ˌhōl-dər\ *n*

free·man \ˈfrē-mən\ *n* 1 : a person enjoying civil or political liberty 2 : one having the full rights of a citizen

free·ma·son·ry \ˈfrē-ˈmās-ᵊn-rē\ *n* : natural or instinctive fellowship or sympathy

free–spo·ken \ˈfrē-ˈspō-kən\ *adj* : speaking freely : OUTSPOKEN

free·stand·ing \-ˈstan-diŋ\ *adj* : standing alone or on its own foundation

free·stone \ˈfrē-ˌstōn\ *n* 1 : a stone that may be cut freely without splitting 2 a : a fruit stone to which the flesh does not cling b : a fruit having such a stone

free·think·er \-ˈthiŋ-kər\ *n* : one who forms opinions on the basis of reason independently of authority; *esp* : one who doubts or denies religious dogma — **free·think·ing** \-kiŋ\ *n or adj*

free trade *n* : trade based upon the unrestricted international exchange of goods with tariffs used only as a source of revenue

free verse *n* : verse whose meter is irregular or whose rhythm is not metrical

free·way \ˈfrē-ˌwā\ *n* 1 : an expressway with fully controlled access 2 : a toll-free highway

free will *n* : the power of choosing without restraint of physical or divine necessity or causal law

free·will \ˌfrē-ˌwil\ *adj* : of one's own free will : VOLUNTARY

¹freeze \ˈfrēz\ *vb* **froze** \ˈfrōz\; **fro·zen** \ˈfrōz-ᵊn\; **freez·ing** 1 : to harden into or be hardened into ice or a like solid by loss of heat 2 a : to chill or become chilled with cold b : to become coldly formal in manner c : to act toward in a stiff and formal way 3 : to act on usu. destructively by frost 4 a : to adhere solidly by freezing b : to cause to grip tightly or remain in immovable contact 5 : to clog with ice 6 : to become fixed or motionless 7 : to fix at a certain stage or level

²freeze *n* 1 : a state of weather marked by low temperature

2 a : an act or instance of freezing b : the state of being frozen

freez·er \'frē-zər\ *n* : one that freezes or keeps cool; *esp* : a compartment for keeping food at a subfreezing temperature or for freezing perishable food rapidly

[1]freight \'frāt\ *n* 1 : the amount paid for carrying goods 2 : goods or cargo carried by a ship, train, truck, or airplane; *also* : the carrying of goods from one place to another by such a vehicle 3 : a train that carries freight

[2]freight *vt* 1 a : to load with goods for transportation b : BURDEN, CHARGE 2 : to transport or ship by freight

freight·er \'frāt-ər\ *n* 1 : SHIPPER 2 : a ship or airplane used chiefly to carry freight

[1]french fry \'french-\ *vt, often cap 1st F* : to fry (as strips of potato) in deep fat until brown

[2]french fry *n, often cap 1st F* : a strip of potato fried in deep fat — usu. used in pl.

French leave *n* : an informal, hasty, or secret departure

fre·net·ic \fri-'net-ik\ *adj* : FRENZIED, FRANTIC — **fre·net·i·cal·ly** \-'net-i-k(ə-)lē\ *adv*

fren·zied \'fren-zēd\ *adj* : marked by frenzy : wildly excited — **fren·zied·ly** *adv*

fren·zy \'fren-zē\ *n, pl* **frenzies** 1 : a temporary madness or violent agitation 2 : intense and usu. wild and often disorderly activity — **frenzy** *vt*

fre·quen·cy \'frē-kwən-sē\ *n, pl* **-cies** 1 : the fact or condition of occurring frequently 2 : rate of occurrence 3 : the number of cycles per second of an alternating current 4 : the number of sound waves per second produced by a sounding body 5 : the number of complete oscillations per second of an electromagnetic wave

frequency modulation *n* : modulation of the frequency of the carrier wave in accordance with the audio or video signal; *esp* : the system of broadcasting using this method of modulation — abbr. *FM*

[1]fre·quent \'frē-kwənt\ *adj* 1 : happening often or at short intervals 2 : HABITUAL, CONSTANT — **fre·quent·ly** *adv*

[2]fre·quent \frē-'kwent, 'frē-kwənt\ *vt* : to visit often : associate with, be in, or resort to habitually — **fre·quent·er** *n*

fre·quen·ta·tive \frē-'kwent-ət-iv\ *adj* : denoting repeated or recurrent action

fres·co \'fres-,kō\ *n, pl* **frescoes** *or* **frescos** 1 : the art of painting on freshly spread moist lime plaster with pigments suspended in a water vehicle 2 : a painting executed in fresco — **fresco** *vt*

[1]fresh \'fresh\ *adj* 1 a : not salt b : PURE, INVIGORATING c : fairly strong : BRISK 2 a : not altered by processing (as freezing, canning, or pickling) b (1) : full of or renewed in vigor : REFRESHED (2) : not stale, sour, or decayed (3) : not faded (4) : not worn or rumpled 3 a (1) : experienced, made, or received newly or anew (2) : ADDITIONAL, ANOTHER b : ORIGINAL, VIVID c : INEXPERIENCED, RAW d : newly or just come or arrived 4 : disposed to take liberties : IMPUDENT — **fresh·ly** *adv* — **fresh·ness** *n*

[2]fresh *adv* : just recently : FRESHLY

fresh·en \'fresh-ən\ *vb* **fresh·ened**; **fresh·en·ing** \'fresh-(ə-)niŋ\ 1 : to make or become fresh: as a : to become brisk or strong b : to make or become fresh in appearance or vitality c : to lose saltiness 2 : to come into milk — **fresh·en·er** \-(ə-)nər\ *n*

fresh·et \'fresh-ət\ *n* : a great rise or overflowing of a stream caused by heavy rains or melted snow

fresh·man \'fresh-mən\ *n* 1 : NOVICE, NEWCOMER 2 : a student in his first year (as in a college)

fresh·wa·ter \,fresh-,wȯt-ər, -,wät-\ *adj* 1 : of, relating to, or living in fresh water 2 : accustomed to navigating only in fresh waters; *also* : UNSKILLED

[1]fret \'fret\ *vb* **fret·ted**; **fret·ting** 1 : to suffer or cause to suffer emotional strain : become irritated : WORRY, VEX 2 a : to eat into or wear away : CORRODE b : FRAY c : to cause by wearing away 3 : to affect something as if by gnawing or biting : GRATE 4 : AGITATE, RIPPLE

[2]fret *n* : an irritated or worried state

[3]fret *n* : ornamental work often in relief consisting of small straight bars intersecting one another in right or oblique angles

[4]fret *n* : one of a series of ridges fixed across the fingerboard of a stringed musical instrument — **fret·ted** \'fret-əd\ *adj*

fret·ful \'fret-fəl\ *adj* 1 : disposed to fret : IRRITABLE 2 a : TROUBLED b : GUSTY — **fret·ful·ly** \-fə-lē\ *adv* — **fret·ful·ness** *n*

fret·work \-,wərk\ *n* 1 : decoration consisting of work adorned with frets 2 : ornamental openwork or work in relief

fri·a·ble \'frī-ə-bəl\ *adj* : easily crumbled or pulverized — **fri·a·bil·i·ty** \,frī-ə-'bil-ət-ē\ *n* — **fri·a·ble·ness** *n*

fri·ar \'frī(-ə)r\ *n* : a member of a mendicant religious order

[1]fric·as·see \'frik-ə-,sē\ *n* : a dish of meat (as chicken or veal) cut into pieces and stewed in a gravy

[2]fricassee *vt* **-seed**; **-see·ing** : to cook as a fricassee

fric·tion \'frik-shən\ *n* 1 a : the rubbing of one body against another b : resistance to motion between two bodies in contact 2 : the clashing between two persons or parties of opposed views : DISAGREEMENT — **fric·tion·less** \-ləs\ *adj*

fric·tion·al \'frik-shnəl, -shən-ᵊl\ *adj* 1 : of or relating to friction 2 : moved or produced by friction

Fri·day \'frīd-ē\ *n* : the 6th day of the week

fried·cake \'frīd-,kāk\ *n* : DOUGHNUT, CRULLER

friend \'frend\ *n* 1 a : one attached to another by affection or esteem b : ACQUAINTANCE 2 : one who is not hostile 3 : one who supports or favors something 4 *cap* : a member of the Society of Friends : QUAKER — **friend·less** \'fren-dləs\ *adj*

friend·ly \'fren-(d)lē\ *adj* : of, relating to, or befitting a friend: as a : showing kindly interest and goodwill b : not hostile c : serving a beneficial or helpful purpose : FAVORABLE d : COMFORTING, CHEERFUL — **friend·li·ness** *n*

friend·ship \'fren(d)-,ship\ *n* 1 : the state of being friends 2 : FRIENDLINESS

[1]frieze \'frēz, frē-'zā\ *n* : a woolen cloth with a shaggy surface

[2]frieze \'frēz\ *n* : an ornamental often sculptured band extending around something (as a building or room)

frig·ate \'frig-ət\ *n* 1 : a square-rigged warship 2 : a British or Canadian escort ship between a corvette and a destroyer in size 3 : a U.S. warship smaller than a cruiser and larger than a destroyer

[1]fright \'frīt\ *n* 1 : sudden terror : ALARM 2 : something that is ugly or shocking

[2]fright *vt* : to alarm suddenly : FRIGHTEN

fright·en \'frīt-ᵊn\ *vb* **fright·ened**; **fright·en·ing** \'frīt-niŋ, -ᵊn-iŋ\ 1 : to make afraid : TERRIFY 2 : to drive away or out by frightening 3 : to become frightened

fright·ful \'frīt-fəl\ *adj* 1 : causing fear or alarm : TERRIFYING 2 : causing shock or horror : STARTLING 3 : EXTREME — **fright·ful·ly** \-fə-lē\ *adv* — **fright·ful·ness** *n*

frig·id \'frij-əd\ *adj* 1 : intensely cold 2 : lacking warmth or ardor : INDIFFERENT — **fri·gid·i·ty** \frij-'id-ət-ē\ *n* — **frig·id·ly** *adv* — **frig·id·ness** *n*

frigid zone *n* : the area or region between the arctic circle and the north pole or between the antarctic circle and the south pole

[1]frill \'fril\ *vt* : to provide or decorate with a frill

[2]frill *n* 1 : a gathered, pleated, or ruffled edging (as of lace) 2 : an addition that is merely ornamental : something unessential — **frilly** \'fril-ē\ *adj*

fringe \'frinj\ *n* 1 : an ornamental border consisting of short threads or strips hanging from cut or raveled edges or from a separate band 2 : something resembling a fringe : BORDER 3 : something on the margin of an activity, process, or subject matter — **fringe** *vt*

fringe area *n* : a region in which reception from a broadcasting station is weak or subject to serious distortion
fringe benefit *n* : an employment benefit paid for by an employer without affecting basic wage rates
frip·pery \'frip-(ə-)rē\ *n, pl* **-per·ies** **1** : cheap showy finery **2** : affected elegance : pretentious display
frisk \'frisk\ *vb* **1** : to leap, skip, or dance in a lively or playful way : GAMBOL **2** : to search (a person) rapidly esp. for concealed weapons by running the hand over the clothing — **frisk·er** *n*
frisky \'fris-kē\ *adj* : inclined to frisk : FROLICSOME — **frisk·i·ly** \-kə-lē\ *adv* — **frisk·i·ness** \-kē-nəs\ *n*
[1]**frit·ter** \'frit-ər\ *n* : a small quantity of fried or sautéed batter often containing fruit or meat
[2]**fritter** *vb* **1** : to reduce or waste piecemeal **2** : to break into small fragments **3** : DISSIPATE, DWINDLE — **frit·ter·er** *n*
fri·vol·i·ty \friv-'äl-ət-ē\ *n, pl* **-ties** **1** : the quality or state of being frivolous **2** : a frivolous act or thing
friv·o·lous \'friv-(ə-)ləs\ *adj* **1** : of little importance : TRIVIAL **2** : lacking in seriousness : PLAYFUL — **friv·o·lous·ly** *adv* — **friv·o·lous·ness** *n*
frizz \'friz\ *vb* : to curl in small tight curls — **frizz** *n* — **frizzy** \'friz-ē\ *adj*
[1]**friz·zle** \'friz-əl\ *vb* **friz·zled**; **friz·zling** \'friz-(ə-)liŋ\ : FRIZZ, CURL — **frizzle** *n* — **friz·zly** \-(ə-)lē\ *adj*
[2]**frizzle** *vb* **1** : to fry until crisp and curled **2** : to cook with a sizzling noise
fro \'frō\ *adv* : BACK, AWAY — used in the phrase *to and fro*
frock \'fräk\ *n* **1** : a friar's habit **2 a** : an outer garment worn by men; *esp* : a loose shirt of coarse linen or cotton formerly worn by workmen **b** : a woolen jersey worn esp. by sailors **3** : a woman's or child's dress
frog \'frȯg, 'fräg\ *n* **1** : any of various smooth-skinned web-footed largely aquatic tailless agile leaping amphibians **2** : a condition in the throat that produces hoarseness **3** : an ornamental braid for fastening the front of a garment by a loop through which a button passes **4** : a device permitting the wheels on one rail of a track to cross an intersecting rail **5** : a small holder (as of metal, glass, or plastic) with perforations or spikes that is placed in a bowl or vase to keep cut flowers in position
frog·man \-ˌman, -mən\ *n* : a swimmer having equipment (as oxygen helmet and flippers) that permits an extended stay under water usu. for observation or demolition
[1]**frol·ic** \'fräl-ik\ *vi* **frol·icked**; **frol·ick·ing** **1** : to make merry **2** : to play about happily : ROMP
[2]**frolic** *n* **1** : a playful mischievous action **2** : FUN, MERRIMENT — **frol·ic·some** \-səm\ *adj*
from \(ˈ)frəm, 'främ\ *prep* **1** — used as a function word to indicate a starting point: as (1) a place where a physical movement begins (2) a starting point in a statement of limits **2** — used as a function word to indicate separation: as (1) physical separation (2) an act or condition of removal, abstention, exclusion, release, or differentiation **3** — used as a function word to indicate the source, cause, agent, or basis
frond \'fränd\ *n* : a usu. large divided leaf (as of a fern) — **frond·ed** \'frän-dəd\ *adj* — **fron·dose** \-ˌdōs\ *adj*
[1]**front** \'frənt\ *n* **1 a** : FOREHEAD; *also* : the whole face **b** : DEMEANOR, BEARING **c** : external often feigned appearance **2 a** : a region in which active warfare is taking place **b** : a sphere of active struggle or striving **3** : the side of a building containing the main entrance **4 a** : the forward part or surface **b** : FRONTAGE **5** : a position directly before or ahead of something else **6** : a person, group, or thing used to mask the identity or true character or activity of the actual controlling agent — **fron·tal** \-ᵊl\ *adj* — **fron·tal·ly** \-ᵊl-ē\ *adv*
[2]**front** *vb* **1** : FACE **2** : to serve as a front **3** : CONFRONT
[3]**front** *adj* : of, relating to, or situated at the front — **front** *adv*
front·age \'frənt-ij\ *n* **1 a** : the front face (as of a building) **b** : the direction in which something faces **2 a** : the front boundary line of a lot abutting on a street **b** : the length of such a line
fron·tier \ˌfrən-'ti(ə)r, frän-\ *n* **1** : a border between two countries **2 a** : a region that forms the margin of settled territory in a country being populated **b** : the outer limits of knowledge or achievement — **frontier** *adj*
fron·tiers·man \-'ti(ə)rz-mən\ *n* : a man living on the frontier
fron·tis·piece \'frənt-ə-ˌspēs\ *n* : an illustration preceding and usu. facing the title page of a book
[1]**frost** \'frȯst\ *n* **1** : the temperature that causes freezing **2** : a covering of minute ice crystals on a cold surface
[2]**frost** *vb* **1 a** : to cover with or as if with frost; *esp* : to put icing on (as cake) **b** : to produce a fine-grained slightly roughened surface on (as glass) **2** : to injure or kill by frost : FREEZE **3** : QUICK-FREEZE
[1]**frost·bite** \-ˌbīt\ *vt* : to blight or nip with frost
[2]**frostbite** *n* : the freezing or the local effect of a partial freezing of some part of the body
frost·ing \'frȯs-tiŋ\ *n* **1** : ICING **2** : dull finish on metal or glass
frosty \'frȯs-tē\ *adj* **1** : FREEZING **2** : covered or appearing as if covered with frost : HOARY — **frost·i·ly** \-tə-lē\ *adv* — **frost·i·ness** \-tē-nəs\ *n*
froth \'frȯth\ *n* **1** : bubbles formed in or on a liquid by fermentation or agitation **2** : something light or frivolous and of little value — **froth** *vb*
frothy \'frȯ-thē, -t͟hē\ *adj* **1** : full of or consisting of froth **2** : gaily frivolous or light — **froth·i·ly** \-thə-lē, -t͟hə-\ *adv* — **froth·i·ness** \-thē-nəs, -t͟hē-\ *n*
fro·ward \'frō-(w)ərd\ *adj* : habitually disobedient : WILLFUL — **fro·ward·ly** *adv* — **fro·ward·ness** *n*
frown \'frau̇n\ *vb* **1** : to wrinkle the forehead (as in anger, displeasure, or thought) : put on a stern look **2** : to look with disapproval **3** : to express with a frown — **frown** *n*
frow·zy *or* **frow·sy** \'frau̇-zē\ *adj* : having a slovenly or uncared-for appearance
froze *past of* FREEZE
fro·zen \'frōz-ᵊn\ *adj* **1 a** : affected or crusted over by freezing **b** : subject to long and severe cold **c** : CHILLED, REFRIGERATED **2 a** : expressing or characterized by cold unfriendliness **b** : incapable of being changed, moved, or undone : FIXED **c** : not available for present use — **fro·zen·ly** *adv* — **fro·zen·ness** \-ᵊn-(n)əs\ *n*
fruc·ti·fy \'frək-tə-ˌfī, 'fru̇k-\ *vb* **-fied**; **-fy·ing** **1** : to bear fruit **2** : to make fruitful or productive
fru·gal \'frü-gəl\ *adj* : marked by economy : THRIFTY — **fru·gal·i·ty** \frü-'gal-ət-ē\ *n* — **fru·gal·ly** *adv*
[1]**fruit** \'früt\ *n* **1 a** : a usu. useful product of plant growth **b** : the usu. edible reproductive body of a seed plant **c** : a product of fertilization in a plant; *esp* : the ripened ovary of a seed plant and its contents **2** : CONSEQUENCE, RESULT — **fruit·ed** \-əd\ *adj*
[2]**fruit** *vb* : to bear or cause to bear fruit
fruit·cake \'früt-ˌkāk\ *n* : a rich cake containing nuts, dried or candied fruits, and spices
fruit·ful \'früt-fəl\ *adj* **1** : yielding or producing fruit **2** : abundantly productive : bringing results — **fruit·ful·ly** \-fə-lē\ *adv* — **fruit·ful·ness** *n*
fru·i·tion \frü-'ish-ən\ *n* **1** : pleasurable use or possession : ENJOYMENT **2 a** : the state of bearing fruit **b** : REALIZATION, ACCOMPLISHMENT
fruit·less \'früt-ləs\ *adj* **1** : lacking or not bearing fruit **2** : productive of no good effect : UNSUCCESSFUL — **fruit·less·ly** *adv* — **fruit·less·ness** *n*
fruity \'früt-ē\ *adj* : relating to or suggesting fruit
frus·trate \'frəs-ˌtrāt\ *vt* **1** : to prevent from carrying out a purpose : DEFEAT, BLOCK **2** : to bring to nothing : NULLIFY — **frus·tra·tion** \(ˌ)frəs-'trā-shən\ *n*

[1]fry \'frī\ *vb* **fried**; **fry·ing** 1 : to cook in a pan or on a griddle over a fire esp. with the use of fat 2 : to undergo frying
[2]fry *n, pl* **fries** 1 : a dish of something fried 2 : a social gathering where fried food is eaten
[3]fry *n, pl* **fry** 1 : a young or tiny fish 2 : a young or insignificant individual
fry·er \'frī(-ə)r\ *n* : something intended for or used in frying
fuch·sia \'fyü-shə\ *n* : a shrub grown for its showy nodding flowers
fud·dle \'fəd-ᵊl\ *vt* **fud·dled**; **fud·dling** \'fəd-liŋ, -ᵊl-iŋ\ : to make confused : MUDDLE
fudge \'fəj\ *n* 1 : foolish nonsense 2 : a soft creamy candy of sugar, milk, butter, and flavoring
[1]fu·el \'fyü(-ə)l\ *n* 1 : a material used to produce heat or power by burning 2 : a material from which atomic energy can be liberated esp. in a reactor
[2]fuel *vb* **-eled** *or* **-elled**; **-el·ing** *or* **-el·ling** 1 : to provide with or take in fuel 2 : SUPPORT, STIMULATE
fu·ga·cious \fyü-'gā-shəs\ *adj* : lasting but a short time
[1]fu·gi·tive \'fyü-jət-iv\ *adj* 1 : running away or trying to escape 2 : likely to vanish suddenly : not fixed or lasting — **fu·gi·tive·ly** *adv* — **fu·gi·tive·ness** *n*
[2]fugitive *n* : one who flees or tries to escape
fugue \'fyüg\ *n* : a musical composition in which different parts successively repeat the theme — **fu·gal** \'fyü-gəl\ *adj*
füh·rer *or* **fueh·rer** \'fyu̇r-ər, 'fir-\ *n* : LEADER — used chiefly of the leader of the German Nazis
ful·crum \'fu̇l-krəm, 'fəl-\ *n, pl* **fulcrums** *or* **ful·cra** \-krə\ : the support about which a lever turns
ful·fill *or* **ful·fil** \fu̇l-'fil\ *vt* **ful·filled**; **ful·fill·ing** 1 : to put into effect 2 : to bring to an end 3 : to measure up to : SATISFY — **ful·fill·ment** *n*
[1]full \'fu̇l\ *adj* 1 : FILLED 2 a : COMPLETE b : having all the distinguishing characteristics c : being at the highest degree : MAXIMUM 3 a : plump and rounded in outline b : having an abundance of material 4 a : possessing or containing an abundance b : rich in detail 5 : satisfied esp. with food or drink 6 : having volume or depth of sound 7 : completely occupied esp. with a thought or plan — **full·ness** *also* **ful·ness** *n*
[2]full *adv* 1 a : VERY, EXTREMELY b : ENTIRELY 2 a : EXACTLY b : STRAIGHT, SQUARELY
[3]full *n* 1 a : the utmost extent b : the highest or fullest state or degree 2 : the requisite or complete amount
[4]full *vt* : to shrink and thicken (woolen cloth) by moistening, heating, and pressing — **full·er** *n*
full·back \'fu̇l-ˌbak\ *n* : an offensive football back who usu. lines up between the halfbacks
full–blood·ed \'fu̇l-'bləd-əd\ *adj* : of unmixed ancestry : PUREBRED — **full–blood·ed·ness** *n*
full–blown \-'blōn\ *adj* 1 : being at the height of bloom 2 : fully mature or developed
full–bod·ied \-'bäd-ēd\ *adj* : marked by richness and fullness
full dress *n* : the style of dress prescribed for ceremonial or formal social occasions — **full–dress** *adj*
full–fledged \'fu̇l-'flejd\ *adj* 1 : fully developed : MATURE 2 : having full plumage
full house *n* : a poker hand containing three of a kind and a pair
full moon *n* : the moon with its whole apparent disk illuminated
full–scale \'fu̇l-'skāl\ *adj* 1 : identical to an original in proportion and size 2 : involving full use of available resources
ful·ly \'fu̇l-(l)ē\ *adv* 1 : in a full manner or degree : COMPLETELY 2 : at least
ful·mi·nate \'fu̇l-mə-ˌnāt, 'fəl-\ *vb* 1 : to utter or send out censure or invective : condemn scathingly 2 : to make a sudden loud noise : EXPLODE — **ful·mi·na·tion** \ˌfu̇l-mə-'nā-shən, ˌfəl-\ *n*
ful·some \'fu̇l-səm\ *adj* : offensive esp. from insincerity or baseness of motive — **ful·some·ly** *adv* — **ful·some·ness** *n*
fum·ble \'fəm-bəl\ *vb* **fum·bled**; **fum·bling** \-b(ə-)liŋ\ 1 : to feel or grope about clumsily 2 : to handle or manage something clumsily; *esp* : to fail to hold, catch, or handle the ball properly in a game (as football) — **fumble** *n* — **fum·bler** \-b(ə-)lər\ *n*
[1]fume \'fyüm\ *n* : a usu. irritating smoke, vapor, or gas — **fumy** \'fyü-mē\ *adj*
[2]fume *vb* 1 : to treat with fumes 2 : to give off fumes 3 : to express anger or annoyance
fu·mi·gant \'fyü-mi-gənt\ *n* : a substance used for fumigation
fu·mi·gate \'fyü-mə-ˌgāt\ *vt* : to treat with fumes to disinfect or destroy pests — **fu·mi·ga·tion** \ˌfyü-mə-'gā-shən\ *n* — **fu·mi·ga·tor** \'fyü-mə-ˌgāt-ər\ *n*
fun \'fən\ *n* 1 : something that provides amusement or enjoyment 2 : AMUSEMENT, ENJOYMENT
[1]func·tion \'fəŋ(k)-shən\ *n* 1 : professional position or duties : OCCUPATION 2 : special purpose 3 : a formal ceremony or social gathering 4 : an action contributing to a larger action; *esp* : the normal contribution of a bodily part to the economy of a living organism 5 : a mathematical quantity so related to another quantity that any change in the value of one is associated with a corresponding change in the other — **func·tion·less** \-ləs\ *adj*
[2]function *vi* **func·tioned**; **func·tion·ing** \-sh(ə-)niŋ\ 1 : to have a function : SERVE 2 : to be in action : OPERATE
func·tion·al \'fəŋ(k)-shnəl, -shən-ᵊl\ *adj* 1 a : of, connected with, or being a function b : affecting functions but not structure 2 : serving in a larger whole; *also* : designed or developed chiefly from the point of view of use 3 : performing or able to perform a regular function 4 : organized by functions — **func·tion·al·ly** \-ē\ *adv*
func·tion·ary \'fəŋ(k)-shə-ˌner-ē\ *n, pl* **-ar·ies** : a person who performs a certain function; *esp* : OFFICIAL
function word *n* : a word expressing primarily grammatical relationship
[1]fund \'fənd\ *n* 1 : an available quantity : SUPPLY 2 a : a sum of money or resources the income of which is set apart for a specific objective b *pl* : available money 3 : an organization administering a special fund
[2]fund *vt* : to convert (a short-term obligation) into a long-term debt bearing a fixed interest
[1]fun·da·men·tal \ˌfən-də-'ment-ᵊl\ *adj* 1 a : serving as an original or generating source : PRIMARY b : BASIC 2 : of or relating to essential structure, function, or facts 3 : of central importance : PRINCIPAL — **fun·da·men·tal·ly** \-ᵊl-ē\ *adv*
[2]fundamental *n* : something fundamental; *esp* : one of the basic constituents essential to a thing or system
fun·da·men·tal·ism \-ᵊl-ˌiz-əm\ *n, often cap* : a Protestant religious movement emphasizing the literal infallibility of the Scriptures — **fun·da·men·tal·ist** \-ᵊl-əst\ *adj or n*
[1]fu·ner·al \'fyün-(ə-)rəl\ *adj* 1 : of, relating to, or constituting a funeral 2 : FUNEREAL 2
[2]funeral *n* 1 : the ceremonies held for a dead person usu. before burial or cremation 2 : a funeral party in transit
fu·ner·ary \'fyü-nə-ˌrer-ē\ *adj* : of, used for, or associated with burial
fu·ne·re·al \fyu̇-'nir-ē-əl\ *adj* 1 : of or relating to a funeral 2 : suggesting a funeral — **fu·ne·re·al·ly** \-ē-ə-lē\ *adv*
fun·gi·cid·al \ˌfən-jə-'sīd-ᵊl, ˌfəŋ-gə-\ *adj* : destroying or inhibiting the growth of fungi — **fun·gi·cid·al·ly** \-ᵊl-ē\ *adv* — **fun·gi·cide** \'fən-jə-ˌsīd, 'fəŋ-gə-\ *n*
fun·gous \'fəŋ-gəs\ *or* **fun·gal** \-gəl\ *adj* 1 : of, relating to, or resembling fungi 2 : caused by a fungus
fun·gus \'fəŋ-gəs\ *n, pl* **fun·gi** \'fən-ˌjī, 'fəŋ-ˌgī\ : any of a major group of lower plants that lack chlorophyll and include molds, mildews, mushrooms, and usu. bacteria — **fungus** *adj*
fu·nic·u·lar \fyu̇-'nik-yə-lər, fə-\ *n* : a cable railway ascending a mountain; *esp* : one in which an ascending car counterbalances a descending car
funk \'fəŋk\ *n* : a state of paralyzed fear : PANIC

[1]**fun•nel** \'fən-ᵊl\ *n* **1** : a utensil usu. shaped like a hollow cone with a tube extending from the point and designed to catch and direct a downward flow (as of liquid) **2** : a stack or flue for the escape of smoke or for ventilation

[2]**funnel** *vb* **1** : to pass through or as if through a funnel **2** : to move or cause to move to a focal point or into a central channel

fun•ny \'fən-ē\ *adj* **1 a** : affording light mirth and laughter : AMUSING **b** : seeking or intended to amuse **2** : QUEER **3** : involving trickery or deception — **fun•ni•ly** \'fən-ᵊl-ē\ *adv* — **fun•ni•ness** \'fən-ē-nəs\ *n*

funny bone *n* : a place at the back of the elbow where a blow compresses a nerve and causes a painful tingling sensation

[1]**fur** \'fər\ *vb* **furred**; **fur•ring** : to cover, line, trim, or clothe with fur

[2]**fur** *n* **1** : a piece of the dressed pelt of an animal used to make, trim, or line wearing apparel **2** : an article of clothing made of or with fur **3** : the hairy coat of a mammal esp. when fine, soft, and thick — **fur•less** \'fər-ləs\ *adj* — **furred** \'fərd\ *adj*

fur•be•low \'fər-bə-ˌlō\ *n* **1** : FLOUNCE, RUFFLE **2** : showy trimming

fur•bish \'fər-bish\ *vt* **1** : POLISH **2** : RENOVATE, REVIVE

fur•cate \'fər-ˌkāt\ *vi* : to branch like a fork — **furcate** *adj* — **fur•cate•ly** *adv* — **fur•ca•tion** \ˌfər-'kā-shən\ *n*

fu•ri•ous \'fyu̇r-ē-əs\ *adj* **1** : being in a fury : FIERCE, ANGRY **2** : RUSHING, VIOLENT — **fu•ri•ous•ly** *adv*

[1]**furl** \'fərl\ *vb* **1** : to wrap or roll (as a sail or a flag) close to or around something **2** : to curl or fold in furls

[2]**furl** *n* **1** : the act of furling **2** : a furled coil

fur•long \'fər-ˌlȯŋ\ *n* : a unit of distance equal to 220 yards

fur•lough \'fər-lō\ *n* : a leave of absence from duty granted esp. to a soldier — **furlough** *vt*

fur•nace \'fər-nəs\ *n* : an enclosed structure in which heat is produced (as for heating a house or melting metals)

fur•nish \'fər-nish\ *vt* **1** : to provide with what is needed; *esp* : to equip with furniture **2** : SUPPLY, GIVE — **fur•nish•er** *n*

fur•nish•ings \-nish-iŋz\ *n pl* **1** : articles or accessories of dress **2** : FURNITURE

fur•ni•ture \'fər-ni-chər\ *n* : equipment that is necessary, useful, or desirable; *esp* : movable articles (as chairs, tables, or beds) for a room

fu•ror \'fyu̇(ə)r-ˌȯr\ *n* **1** : RAGE **2** : a fashionable craze : VOGUE **3** : an outburst of public indignation or excitement

fu•rore \-ˌōr\ *n* **1** : FUROR 2 **2** : FUROR 3

fur•ri•er \'fər-ē-ər\ *n* : a person who prepares or deals in furs — **fur•ri•ery** \-ē-ə-rē\ *n*

fur•ring \'fər-iŋ\ *n* : wood or metal strips applied to a wall or ceiling to form a level surface or an air space

[1]**fur•row** \'fər-ō\ *n* **1** : a trench in the earth made by or as if by a plow **2** : something (as a groove or wrinkle) that resembles the track of a plow

[2]**furrow** *vb* **1** : to make furrows in **2** : to form furrows

fur•ry \'fər-ē\ *adj* **1** : consisting of or resembling fur **2** : covered with fur

[1]**fur•ther** \'fər-t͟hər\ *adv* **1** : [1]FARTHER 1 **2** : in addition : MOREOVER **3** : to a greater degree or extent

[2]**further** *adj* **1** : [2]FARTHER 1 **2** : going or extending beyond : ADDITIONAL

[3]**further** *vt* **fur•thered**; **fur•ther•ing** \'fərt͟h-(ə-)riŋ\ : to help forward : PROMOTE — **fur•ther•er** \'fər-t͟hər-ər\ *n*

fur•ther•ance \'fərt͟h-(ə-)rən(t)s\ *n* : the act of furthering : ADVANCEMENT

fur•ther•more \'fər-t͟hə(r)-ˌmōr\ *adv* : in addition to what precedes : BESIDES

fur•ther•most \-ˌmōst\ *adj* : most distant : FARTHEST

fur•thest \'fər-t͟həst\ *adv* (*or adj*) : FARTHEST

fur•tive \'fərt-iv\ *adj* : done by stealth : SLY, SECRET — **fur•tive•ly** *adv* — **fur•tive•ness** *n*

fu•ry \'fyu̇(ə)r-ē\ *n*, *pl* **furies** **1** : violent anger : RAGE **2** : a violently angry or spiteful person **3** : extreme fierceness or violence

furze \'fərz\ *n* : a prickly evergreen shrub of the pea family with yellow flowers

[1]**fuse** \'fyüz\ *n* **1** : a continuous train of a combustible substance enclosed in a cord or cable to transmit fire to an explosive **2** *usu* **fuze** : a mechanical or electrical detonating device for setting off the bursting charge of a projectile, bomb, or torpedo

[2]**fuse** *or* **fuze** *vt* : to equip with a fuse

[3]**fuse** *vb* **1** : to reduce to a liquid or plastic state by heat **2** : to become fluid with heat **3** : to unite by or as if by melting together : BLEND, INTEGRATE — **fus•i•bil•i•ty** \ˌfyü-zə-'bil-ət-ē\ *n* — **fus•i•ble** \'fyü-zə-bəl\ *adj*

[4]**fuse** *n* : an electrical safety device consisting of or including a wire or strip of fusible metal that melts and interrupts the circuit when the current becomes too strong

fu•see \fyü-'zē\ *n* **1** : a friction match with a bulbous head not easily blown out **2** : a red signal flare used esp. for protecting stalled trains and trucks

fu•se•lage \'fyü-sə-ˌläzh, 'fyü-zə-\ *n* : the central body portion of an airplane which holds the crew, passengers, and cargo

fu•sil•lade \'fyü-sə-ˌlād, -zə-, -ˌläd\ *n* : a number of shots fired simultaneously or in rapid succession

fu•sion \'fyü-zhən\ *n* **1** : the act or process of melting or making fluid by heat **2** : union by or as if by melting; *esp* : a merging of diverse elements into a unified whole **3** : the union of atomic nuclei to form heavier nuclei resulting in the release of enormous quantities of energy

[1]**fuss** \'fəs\ *n* **1 a** : needless bustle or excitement : COMMOTION **b** : effusive praise **2** : a state of agitation esp. over a trivial matter

[2]**fuss** *vi* **1 a** : to create or be in a state of restless activity; *esp* : to shower flattering attentions **b** : to pay undue attention to small details **2** : to become upset : WORRY — **fuss•er** *n*

fuss•budg•et \'fəs-ˌbəj-ət\ *n* : one who fusses about trifles

fussy \'fəs-ē\ *adj* **1** : IRRITABLE **2 a** : requiring or giving close attention to details **b** : FASTIDIOUS — **fuss•i•ly** \'fəs-ə-lē\ *adv* — **fuss•i•ness** \'fəs-ē-nəs\ *n*

fus•tian \'fəs-chən\ *n* **1** : a strong cotton and linen fabric **2** : pretentious writing or speech — **fustian** *adj*

fus•ty \'fəs-tē\ *adj* **1** : MOLDY, MUSTY **2** : rigidly conservative : OLD-FASHIONED — **fus•ti•ly** \-tə-lē\ *adv* — **fus•ti•ness** \-tē-nəs\ *n*

fu•tile \'fyüt-ᵊl, 'fyü-ˌtīl\ *adj* **1** : having no result or effect : USELESS **2** : UNIMPORTANT, TRIVIAL — **fu•tile•ly** \-ᵊl-(l)ē, -ˌtīl-lē\ *adv* — **fu•til•i•ty** \fyü-'til-ət-ē\ *n*

[1]**fu•ture** \'fyü-chər\ *adj* **1 a** : that is to be **b** : existing after death **2** : of, relating to, or constituting a verb tense formed in English with *will* and *shall* and expressive of time yet to come

[2]**future** *n* **1 a** : time that is to come **b** : what is going to happen **2** : expectation of advancement or development **3 a** : the future tense **b** : a verb form in the future tense

fu•tur•ism \'fyü-chə-ˌriz-əm\ *n* : a movement in art, music, and literature marked esp. by an effort to give formal expression to the dynamic energy and movement of mechanical processes — **fu•tur•ist** \'fyüch-(ə-)rəst\ *n*

fu•tur•is•tic \ˌfyü-chə-'ris-tik\ *adj* : of or relating to the future or futurism — **fu•tur•is•ti•cal•ly** \-ti-k(ə-)lē\ *adv*

fu•tu•ri•ty \fyü-'t(y)u̇r-ət-ē, -'chu̇r-\ *n*, *pl* **-ties** **1** : FUTURE **2** : the quality or state of being future **3** *pl* : future events or prospects

fuze *var of* FUSE

fuzz \'fəz\ *n* : fine light particles or fibers (as of down or fluff)

fuzzy \'fəz-ē\ *adj* **1** : covered with or resembling fuzz **2** : not clear : INDISTINCT — **fuzz•i•ly** \'fəz-ə-lē\ *adv* — **fuzz•i•ness** \'fəz-ē-nəs\ *n*

g \'jē\ *n, often cap* **1 :** the 7th letter of the English alphabet **2 :** the musical tone G **3 :** a unit of force equal to a person's weight and used to express forces he experiences (as when he is in an airplane that is pulling out of a dive or that is making a sharp turn)

gab \'gab\ *vi* **gabbed; gab·bing :** to talk idly **:** CHATTER — **gab** *n*

gab·ar·dine \'gab-ər-ˌdēn\ *n* **1 :** GABERDINE **2 a :** a firm durable twilled fabric having diagonal ribs and made of various fibers **b :** a garment of gabardine

gab·ble \'gab-əl\ *vb* **gab·bled; gab·bling** \'gab-(ə-)liŋ\ **:** to talk fast or foolishly **:** JABBER, BABBLE — **gabble** *n* — **gab·bler** \'gab-(ə-)lər\ *n*

gab·er·dine \'gab-ər-ˌdēn\ *n* **1 a :** a long smock worn chiefly by Jews in medieval times **b :** an English laborer's smock **2 :** GABARDINE

ga·ble \'gā-bəl\ *n* **:** the triangular part of an outside wall of a building that is formed by the sides of the roof sloping down from the ridgepole to the eaves; *also* **:** a similar triangular structure (as over a door or window) — **ga·bled** \-bəld\ *adj*

[1]**gad** \'gad\ *vi* **gad·ded; gad·ding :** to roam about **:** wander restlessly and without purpose — **gad·der** *n*

[2]**gad** *interj* — used as a mild oath

gad·about \'gad-ə-ˌbau̇t\ *n* **:** a person who flits about in social activity — **gadabout** *adj*

gad·fly \'gad-ˌflī\ *n* **1 :** any of various flies (as a horsefly or botfly) that bite or harass livestock **2 :** an intentionally annoying person who stimulates or provokes others esp. by persistent criticism

gadg·et \'gaj-ət\ *n* **:** CONTRIVANCE, DEVICE — **gadg·e·teer** \ˌgaj-ə-'ti(ə)r\ *n* — **gadg·et·ry** \'gaj-ə-trē\ *n*

gad·o·lin·i·um \ˌgad-ᵊl-'in-ē-əm\ *n* **:** a magnetic metallic chemical element occurring in several minerals

gad·wall \'gad-ˌwȯl\ *n, pl* **gadwalls** *or* **gadwall :** a grayish brown duck about the size of the mallard

[1]**gaff** \'gaf\ *n* **1 a :** a spear or spearhead for taking fish or turtles **b :** a handled hook for holding or lifting heavy fish **c :** a metal spur for a gamecock **2 :** the spar upon which the head of a fore-and-aft sail is extended **3 :** rough treatment **:** ABUSE

[2]**gaff** *vt* **:** to strike, take, or handle with a gaff

gaf·fer \'gaf-ər\ *n* **:** an old man

[1]**gag** \'gag\ *vb* **gagged; gag·ging 1 a :** to prevent from speaking or crying out by stopping up the mouth **b :** to prevent from speaking freely **2 :** to retch or cause to retch **3 :** to make quips

[2]**gag** *n* **1 a :** something thrust into the mouth esp. to prevent speech or outcry **b :** CLOTURE **c :** a check to free speech **2 :** a laugh-provoking remark or act **3 :** HOAX, TRICK

gage \'gāj\ *n* **1 :** a token of defiance; *esp* **:** a glove or cap cast on the ground as a pledge of combat **2 :** something deposited as a pledge **:** SECURITY

gag rule *n* **:** a rule restricting freedom of debate or expression esp. in a legislative body

gai·e·ty \'gā-ət-ē\ *n, pl* **gai·e·ties 1 :** MERRYMAKING **2 :** gay spirits or manner **3 :** FINERY

gai·ly \'gā-lē\ *adv* **:** in a gay manner

[1]**gain** \'gān\ *n* **1 :** an increase in or addition to what is of profit **2 :** the obtaining of profit or possessions **3 :** an increase in amount, magnitude, or degree

[2]**gain** *vb* **1 a :** to get possession of **:** EARN **b :** to win in competition or conflict **c :** to get by a natural development or process **:** ACHIEVE **d :** to arrive at **2 :** to increase in **3 :** to run fast **4 :** to get advantage **:** PROFIT **5 :** INCREASE — **gain·er** *n* — **gain ground :** to make progress

gain·ful \'gān-fəl\ *adj* **:** producing gain **:** PROFITABLE, PAID — **gain·ful·ly** \-fə-lē\ *adv* — **gain·ful·ness** *n*

gain·ly \'gān-lē\ *adj* **:** GRACEFUL, SHAPELY

gain·say \gān-'sā\ *vt* **gain·said** \-'sād, -'sed\; **gain·say·ing** \-'sā-iŋ\ **1 :** DENY, DISPUTE **2 :** to speak against **:** CONTRADICT — **gain·say·er** *n*

gait \'gāt\ *n* **:** manner of moving on foot; *also* **:** a particular pattern or style of such movement — **gait·ed** \-əd\ *adj*

gai·ter \'gāt-ər\ *n* **1 :** a cloth or leather leg covering reaching from the instep to ankle, mid calf, or knee **2 a :** an ankle-high shoe with elastic gores in the sides **b :** an overshoe with fabric upper

ga·la \'gā-lə, 'gal-ə\ *n* **:** a gay celebration **:** FESTIVITY — **gala** *adj*

ga·lac·tic \gə-'lak-tik\ *adj* **:** of or relating to a galaxy

gal·axy \'gal-ək-sē\ *n, pl* **gal·ax·ies 1 :** one of billions of systems each including stars, nebulae, clusters of stars, gas, and dust that make up the universe **2 :** an assemblage of brilliant or notable persons or things

gale \'gāl\ *n* **1 :** a strong current of air; *esp* **:** a wind of from 32 to 63 miles per hour **2 :** an emotional outburst

ga·le·na \gə-'lē-nə\ *n* **:** a bluish gray mineral with metallic luster consisting of sulfide of lead and constituting the principal ore of lead

[1]**gall** \'gȯl\ *n* **1 a :** BILE **b :** something bitter to endure **c :** bitterness of spirit **:** RANCOR **2 :** EFFRONTERY, IMPUDENCE

[2]**gall** *n* **1 :** a skin sore caused by chronic irritation **2 :** a cause or state of exasperation

[3]**gall** *vb* **1 a :** to fret and wear away by friction **:** CHAFE **b :** to become sore or worn by rubbing **2 :** IRRITATE, VEX **3 :** HARASS

[4]**gall** *n* **:** a swelling of plant tissue usu. due to fungi or insect parasites

[1]**gal·lant** \gə-'lant, gə-'länt, 'gal-ənt\ *n* **1 :** a young man of fashion **2 a :** a man who shows a marked fondness for the company of women and who is esp. attentive to them **b :** SUITOR

[2]**gal·lant** \'gal-ənt (*usu in sense 2b*); gə-'lant, gə-'länt (*usu in sense 3*)\ *adj* **1 :** showy in dress or bearing **:** SMART **2 a :** SPLENDID, STATELY **b :** SPIRITED, BRAVE **c :** CHIVALROUS, NOBLE **3 :** polite and attentive to women — **gal·lant·ly** *adv*

gal·lant·ry \'gal-ən-trē\ *n, pl* **-ries 1 a :** an act of marked courtesy **b :** courteous attention to a woman **2 :** conspicuous bravery

gall·blad·der \'gȯl-ˌblad-ər\ *n* **:** a membranous muscular sac in which bile from the liver is stored

gal·le·on \'gal-ē-ən\ *n* **:** a heavy square-rigged sailing ship of the 15th to early 18th centuries used for war or commerce esp. by the Spanish

gal·lery \'gal(-ə)-rē\ *n, pl* **gal·ler·ies 1 a :** a roofed promenade **:** COLONNADE **b :** an outdoor balcony **c :** a balcony in a theater, auditorium, or church; *esp* **:** the highest balcony in a theater or the people who sit in this balcony **d :** a body of spectators at a tennis or golf match **2 a :** a long narrow room, hall, or passage; *esp* **:** one having windows along one side **b :** a subterranean passageway (as in a cave or mine) **c :** a passage (as in earth or wood) made by an animal and esp. an insect **3 a :** a room or building devoted to the exhibition of works of art **b :** an institution or business exhibiting or dealing in works of art **4 :** a photographer's studio — **gal·ler·ied** \-rēd\ *adj*

gal·ley \'gal-ē\ *n, pl* **galleys 1 :** a large low usu. single-decked ship propelled by oars and sails and used in ancient times and in the Middle Ages chiefly in the Mediterranean sea **2 :** the kitchen of a ship **3 a :** an oblong tray with upright sides to hold printer's type that has been set **b :** GALLEY PROOF

galley proof *n* **:** a proof from type on a galley before it is made up in pages; *also* **:** such proofs

gal·li·cism \ˈgal-ə-ˌsiz-əm\ *n, often cap* : a characteristic French idiom, expression, or trait
gal·li·um \ˈgal-ē-əm\ *n* : a rare bluish white metallic chemical element that is hard and brittle at low temperatures but melts just above room temperature
gal·li·vant \ˈgal-ə-ˌvant\ *vi* **1** : to go about ostentatiously with members of the opposite sex **2** : to travel or roam about for pleasure
gal·lon \ˈgal-ən\ *n* : a unit of liquid capacity equal to four quarts
gal·lon·age \ˈgal-ə-nij\ *n* : amount in gallons
[1]**gal·lop** \ˈgal-əp\ *n* **1** : a springing gait of a quadruped; *esp* : a fast natural 3-beat gait of the horse **2** : a ride or run at a gallop
[2]**gallop** *vb* **1** : to move or ride at a gallop **2** : to run fast **3** : to cause to gallop — **gal·lop·er** *n*
gal·lows \ˈgal-ōz\ *n, pl* **gallows** *or* **gal·lows·es** **1** : a frame usu. of two upright posts and a traverse beam from which criminals are hanged **2** : a structure consisting of an upright frame with a crosspiece
gall·stone \ˈgȯl-ˌstōn\ *n* : a concretion formed in the gallbladder or bile passages
ga·lop \ˈgal-əp, ga-ˈlō\ *n* : a lively dance in duple measure
ga·lore \gə-ˈlō(ə)r\ *adj* : ABUNDANT, PLENTIFUL — used after the word it modifies
ga·losh \gə-ˈläsh\ *n* : a high overshoe worn esp. in snow and slush — **ga·loshed** \-ˈläsht\ *adj*
gal·van·ic \gal-ˈvan-ik\ *adj* **1** : of, relating to, or producing a direct current of electricity by chemical action **2** : STIMULATING, EXCITING — **gal·van·i·cal·ly** \-i-k(ə-)lē\ *adv*
gal·va·nism \ˈgal-və-ˌniz-əm\ *n* : a direct current of electricity produced by chemical action
gal·va·nize \ˈgal-və-ˌnīz\ *vt* **1 a** : to subject to the action of an electric current **b** : to stimulate or excite by or as if by an electric shock **2** : to coat (as iron) with zinc for protection — **gal·va·ni·za·tion** \ˌgal-və-nə-ˈzā-shən\ *n*
gam·bit \ˈgam-bət\ *n* **1** : a chess opening in which a player risks one or more minor pieces to gain an advantage in position **2** : a calculated move : STRATAGEM
[1]**gam·ble** \ˈgam-bəl\ *vb* **gam·bled**; **gam·bling** \-b(ə-)liŋ\ **1 a** : to play a game for money or other stakes **b** : to bet on an uncertain outcome **2** : to stake something on a doubtful event : BET **3** : VENTURE, HAZARD — **gam·bler** \-blər\ *n*
[2]**gamble** *n* : a risky undertaking
gam·bol \ˈgam-bəl\ *vi* **gam·boled** *or* **gam·bolled**; **gam·bol·ing** *or* **gam·bol·ling** \-b(ə-)liŋ\ : to skip about in play : FRISK — **gambol** *n*
[1]**game** \ˈgām\ *n* **1 a** : AMUSEMENT, DIVERSION **b** : FUN, SPORT **2 a** : a procedure for gaining an end **b** : a line of work : PROFESSION **3** : CONTEST **4 a** (1) : animals pursued or taken in hunting (2) : the flesh of game animals **b** : an object of ridicule or attack — often used in the phrase *fair game*
[2]**game** *vb* : to play for a stake : GAMBLE
[3]**game** *adj* : having a resolute unyielding spirit — **game·ly** *adv* — **game·ness** *n*
[4]**game** *adj* : LAME
game·cock \ˈgām-ˌkäk\ *n* : a domestic cock of a strain developed for fighting
game·keep·er \-ˌkē-pər\ *n* : one that has charge of the breeding and protection of game animals or birds on a private preserve
game·some \ˈgām-səm\ *adj* : GAY, FROLICSOME — **game·some·ly** *adv* — **game·some·ness** *n*
game·ster \ˈgām-stər\ *n* : GAMBLER
ga·mete \gə-ˈmēt, ˈgam-ˌēt\ *n* : a matured germ cell capable of uniting with another such cell to form a new plant or animal individual — **ga·met·ic** \gə-ˈmet-ik\ *adj* — **ga·met·i·cal·ly** \-ˈmet-i-k(ə-)lē\ *adv*
gam·in \ˈgam-ən\ *n* **1** : a boy who hangs out on the streets : URCHIN **2** : GAMINE 2
ga·mine \ga-ˈmēn\ *n* **1** : a girl who hangs out on the streets **2** : a playfully mischievous girl
gam·ing \ˈgā-miŋ\ *n* : the practice of gambling
gam·ma glob·u·lin \ˌgam-ə-ˈgläb-yə-lən\ *n* : a protein fraction of blood plasma rich in antibodies
gam·ma rays \ˈgam-ə-\ *n pl* : very penetrating radiation of the same nature as X rays but of shorter wavelength emitted by various radioactive atomic nuclei
gam·mer \ˈgam-ər\ *n* : an old woman
[1]**gam·mon** \ˈgam-ən\ *n* : a ham or flitch of cured bacon
[2]**gammon** *n* : deceptive talk : HUMBUG — **gammon** *vb*
gam·ut \ˈgam-ət\ *n* **1** : the whole series of recognized musical notes **2** : an entire range or series
gamy \ˈgā-mē\ *adj* **1** : GAME, PLUCKY **2** : having the flavor of game esp. when slightly tainted — **gam·i·ly** \ˈgā-mə-lē\ *adv* — **gam·i·ness** \ˈgā-mē-nəs\ *n*
gan·der \ˈgan-dər\ *n* : a male goose
[1]**gang** \ˈgaŋ\ *n* **1** : a group of persons working or going about together **2** : a group of persons associated or acting together for unlawful or antisocial purposes **3** : two or more similar implements or devices arranged to work together in order to save time and labor or to produce a unified effect
[2]**gang** *vb* **1** : to attack in a gang — usu. used with *up* **2** : to form into or move or act as a gang
gang·land \ˈgaŋ-ˌland\ *n* : the world of organized crime
gan·gling \ˈgaŋ-gliŋ, -glən\ *adj* : LANKY, SPINDLING
gan·gli·on \ˈgaŋ-glē-ən\ *n, pl* **-glia** \-glē-ə\ : a mass of neural tissue lying external to the brain or spinal cord and containing nerve cells — **gan·gli·on·ic** \ˌgaŋ-glē-ˈän-ik\ *adj*
gan·gly \ˈgaŋ-glē\ *adj* : GANGLING, LANKY
gang·plank \ˈgaŋ-ˌplaŋk\ *n* : a movable bridge used in boarding or leaving a ship at a pier
[1]**gan·grene** \ˈgaŋ-ˌgrēn, gaŋ-ˈ, ˈgan-ˌ, gan-ˈ\ *n* : local death of soft tissues due to loss of blood supply — **gan·gre·nous** \ˈgaŋ-grə-nəs\ *adj*
[2]**gangrene** *vb* : to make or become gangrenous
gang·ster \ˈgaŋ-stər\ *n* : a member of a gang of criminals : RACKETEER — **gang·ster·ism** \-stə-ˌriz-əm\ *n*
gang·way \ˈgaŋ-ˌwā\ *n* **1** : a passage into, through, or out of an enclosed place **2** : GANGPLANK **3** : a clear passage through a crowd — often used as an interjection
gan·net \ˈgan-ət\ *n* : any of several large fish-eating seabirds
gan·try \ˈgan-trē\ *n, pl* **gantries** : a frame structure on side supports over or around something
gap \ˈgap\ *n* **1** : an opening made by a break or a parting : BREACH, CLEFT **2** : a mountain pass **3** : a break or separation in continuity : a blank space
[1]**gape** \ˈgāp\ *vi* **1 a** : to open the mouth wide **b** : to open or part widely **2** : to stare openmouthed **3** : YAWN — **gap·er** *n* — **gap·ing·ly** *adv*
[2]**gape** *n* : an act or instance of gaping: as **a** : YAWN **b** : an openmouthed stare
[1]**ga·rage** \gə-ˈräzh, -ˈräj\ *n* **1** : a building where automobiles are housed **2** : a repair shop for automobiles — **ga·rage·man** \-ˌman\ *n*
[2]**garage** *vt* : to keep or put in a garage
garage sale *n* : a sale of used household items held at the seller's home
[1]**garb** \ˈgärb\ *n* **1** : style of dress **2** : CLOTHING, DRESS
[2]**garb** *vt* : CLOTHE, ARRAY
gar·bage \ˈgär-bij\ *n* : food waste : REFUSE
gar·ble \ˈgär-bəl\ *vt* **gar·bled**; **gar·bling** \-b(ə-)liŋ\ : to distort the meaning or sound of
gar·çon \gär-ˈsōⁿ\ *n, pl* **garçons** \-ˈsōⁿ(z)\ : WAITER
[1]**gar·den** \ˈgärd-ᵊn\ *n* **1** : a plot of ground where herbs, fruits, flowers, or vegetables are grown **2 a** : a public recreation

area or park; *esp* : one for the exhibition of plants or animals **b** : an open-air eating or drinking place

[2]**garden** *vb* **gar·dened**; **gar·den·ing** \'gärd-niŋ, -ᵊn-iŋ\ **1** : to lay out or work in a garden **2** : to make into a garden — **gar·den·er** \'gärd-nər, -ᵊn-ər\ *n*

[3]**garden** *adj* **1** : of, relating to, or frequenting gardens **2** : of a kind grown under cultivation esp. in the open **3** : ORDINARY, COMMONPLACE

gar·de·nia \gär-'dē-nyə\ *n* : any of various trees and shrubs with leathery leaves and fragrant white or yellow flowers; *also* : one of the flowers

[1]**gar·gle** \'gär-gəl\ *vb* **gar·gled**; **gar·gling** \-g(ə-)liŋ\ : to rinse the throat with a liquid kept in motion by air forced through it from the lungs

[2]**gargle** *n* **1** : a liquid used in gargling **2** : a gargling sound

gar·goyle \'gär-ˌgȯil\ *n* : a waterspout in the form of a grotesque human or animal figure projecting from the roof or eaves of a building — **gar·goyled** \-ˌgȯild\ *adj*

gar·ish \'ga(ə)r-ish\ *adj* **1 a** : excessively vivid : FLASHY **b** : offensively bright : GLARING **2** : tastelessly showy — **gar·ish·ly** *adv* — **gar·ish·ness** *n*

[1]**gar·land** \'gär-lənd\ *n* : a wreath or rope of leaves or flowers

[2]**garland** *vt* : to form into or deck with a garland

gar·lic \'gär-lik\ *n* : a European bulbous herb of the lily family widely grown for its pungent compound bulbs much used in cookery; *also* : one of the bulbs — **gar·licky** \-li-kē\ *adj*

[1]**gar·ment** \'gär-mənt\ *n* : an article of clothing

[2]**garment** *vt* : to clothe with or as if with a garment

gar·ner \'gär-nər\ *vt* **1** : to gather into or as if into a granary **2 a** : to acquire by effort : EARN **b** : ACCUMULATE, COLLECT

gar·net \'gär-nət\ *n* **1** : a transparent usu. red mineral used as a semiprecious stone and as an abrasive **2** : a variable color averaging a dark red

[1]**gar·nish** \'gär-nish\ *vt* **1** : DECORATE, EMBELLISH **2** : to add decorative or savory touches to (food) **3** : GARNISHEE

[2]**garnish** *n* **1** : EMBELLISHMENT, ORNAMENT **2** : a savory and usu. decorative condiment

gar·nish·ee \ˌgär-nə-'shē\ *vt* **gar·nish·eed**; **gar·nish·ee·ing** **1** : to serve with a garnishment **2** : to take (as a debtor's wages) by legal authority

gar·nish·ment \'gär-nish-mənt\ *n* **1** : GARNISH **2** : a legal warning to a party holding property of a debtor to give it to a creditor; *also* : the attachment of such property (as a bank account or pending wages) to satisfy a creditor

gar·ni·ture \'gär-ni-chər\ *n* : EMBELLISHMENT, TRIMMING

gar·ret \'gar-ət\ *n* : a room or unfinished part of a house just under the roof

[1]**gar·ri·son** \'gar-ə-sən\ *n* **1** : a military post; *esp* : a permanent military installation **2** : the troops stationed at a garrison

[2]**garrison** *vt* **1** : to furnish (as a fort or a town) with troops for defense **2** : to protect with forts and soldiers

[1]**gar·rote** *or* **ga·rotte** \gə-'rät, -'rōt\ *n* **1 a** : a method of execution by strangling with an iron collar **b** : the iron collar used **2 a** : strangulation esp. for the purpose of robbery **b** : an implement for this purpose

[2]**garrote** *or* **garotte** *vt* **1** : to execute with or as if with a garrote **2** : to strangle and rob — **gar·rot·er** *n*

gar·ru·lous \'gar-ə-ləs\ *adj* : very talkative esp. about trifles : WORDY — **gar·ru·li·ty** \gə-'rü-lət-ē\ *n* — **gar·ru·lous·ly** *adv* — **gar·ru·lous·ness** *n*

gar·ter \'gärt-ər\ *n* **1** : a band or strap worn to hold up a stocking or sock **2** *cap* **a** : the British Order of the Garter **b** : the blue velvet garter that is its badge **c** : membership in the order

[1]**gas** \'gas\ *n* **1** : a fluid (as hydrogen or air) that has neither independent shape nor volume but tends to expand indefinitely **2 a** : a gas or gaseous mixture used as a fuel or as an anesthetic **b** : a gaseous, liquid, or solid substance that can be used to produce a poisonous, asphyxiating, or irritant atmosphere **3** : GASOLINE

[2]**gas** *vb* **gassed**; **gas·sing** **1 a** : to treat chemically with gas **b** : to poison with gas **2** : to supply with gas or esp. gasoline

gas·con \'gas-kən\ *n* : a boastful swaggering person

gas·con·ade \ˌgas-kə-'nād\ *n* : BOASTING, BRAVADO — **gasconade** *vi*

gas·e·ous \'gas-ē-əs, 'gash-əs\ *adj* **1** : having the form of or being gas; *also* : of or relating to gas **2** : lacking substance or solidity

gash \'gash\ *vb* : to make a long deep cut in : CUT — **gash** *n*

gas·ket \'gas-kət\ *n* : material (as asbestos, rubber, or metal) used as packing (as for pistons or pipe joints)

gas·light \'gas-ˌlīt\ *n* **1** : light made by burning illuminating gas **2 a** : a gas flame **b** : a gas lighting fixture — **gas·light·ing** *n*

gas·lit \-ˌlit\ *adj* : illuminated by gaslight

gas·o·line *or* **gas·o·lene** \ˌgas-ə-'lēn, 'gas-ə-ˌ\ *n* : a flammable liquid made esp. by blending products from natural gas and petroleum and used as a motor fuel and cleaning fluid

gasp \'gasp\ *vb* **1** : to catch the breath with shock or other emotion **2** : to breathe laboriously : PANT **3** : to utter in a gasping manner — **gasp** *n*

gas·tric \'gas-trik\ *adj* : of, relating to, or located near the stomach

gastric juice *n* : a watery acid digestive fluid secreted by glands in the mucous membrane of the stomach

gas·tri·tis \ga-'strīt-əs\ *n* : inflammation of the stomach and esp. of its mucous membrane

gas·tron·o·my \ga-'strän-ə-mē\ *n* : the art of good eating — **gas·tro·nom·ic** \ˌgas-trə-'näm-ik\ *adj* — **gas·tro·nom·i·cal** \-'näm-i-kəl\ *adj*

gas·tro·pod \'gas-trə-ˌpäd\ *n* : any of a large class of mollusks (as snails) having a muscular ventral foot and usu. a distinct head bearing sensory organs — **gastropod** *adj*

gate \'gāt\ *n* **1** : an opening in a wall or fence **2** : a city or castle entrance often with towers or other defensive structures **3** : the frame or door that closes a gate **4** : a means of entrance or exit **5** : a door, valve, or other device for controlling the passage esp. of fluid **6** : the total admission receipts or the number of spectators at a sports event

gate·post \'gāt-ˌpōst\ *n* : the post to which a gate is hung or the one against which it closes

gate·way \-ˌwā\ *n* **1** : an opening for a gate in a wall or fence **2** : a passage into or out of a place or state

[1]**gath·er** \'gath-ər\ *vb* **gath·ered**; **gath·er·ing** \'gath-(ə-)riŋ\ **1** : to bring together : COLLECT **2 a** : PICK, HARVEST **b** : to pick up little by little **c** : to gain by gradual increase **d** : to accumulate and place in order or readiness **3 a** : to summon up **b** : to prepare (as oneself) by mustering strength **4 a** : to bring together the parts of **b** : to draw about or close to something **c** : to pull (fabric) along a line of stitching into puckers **5** : GUESS, DEDUCE **6 a** : to come together in a body **b** : to cluster around a focus of attraction **7 a** : to swell and fill with pus **b** : GROW, INCREASE — **gath·er·er** *n*

[2]**gather** *n* : a drawing together; *esp* : a puckering in cloth made by gathering

gath·er·ing *n* **1 a** : ASSEMBLY, MEETING **b** : a pus-filled swelling (as an abscess) **2** : the collecting of food and raw materials from the wild **3** : COLLECTION, COMPILATION **4** : a gather in cloth

gauche \'gōsh\ *adj* : lacking social experience or grace : CRUDE — **gauche·ness** *n*

gau·cho \'gaů-chō\ *n, pl* **gauchos** : a cowboy of the So. American pampas

gaud \'gȯd\ *n* : ORNAMENT, TRINKET

gaudy \-ē\ *adj* : ostentatiously or tastelessly ornamented — **gaud·i·ly** \-ᵊl-ē\ *adv* — **gaud·i·ness** \-ē-nəs\ *n*

[1]**gauge** \'gāj\ *n* **1 a** : measurement according to some standard

or system **b** : DIMENSIONS, SIZE **2** : an instrument for measuring, testing, or registering

²gauge *vt* **1 a** : to measure exactly the size, dimensions, or other measurable quantity of **b** : to determine the capacity or contents of **2** : ESTIMATE, JUDGE — **gauge·a·ble** *adj* — **gaug·er** *n*

gaunt \'gȯnt\ *adj* **1** : being thin and angular **2** : attenuated by suffering or weariness **3** : BARREN, DESOLATE — **gaunt·ly** *adv* — **gaunt·ness** *n*

¹gaunt·let \'gȯnt-lət\ *n* **1** : a protective glove worn with medieval armor **2** : a protective glove used in industry **3** : a challenge to combat **4** : a dress glove extending above the wrist — **gaunt·let·ed** \-lət-əd\ *adj*

²gauntlet *n* **1** : a double file of men armed with weapons (as clubs) with which to strike at an individual who is made to run between them **2** : CROSS FIRE; *also* : ORDEAL

gauze \'gȯz\ *n* **1** : a thin often transparent fabric used chiefly for clothing or draperies **2** : a loosely woven cotton surgical dressing **3** : a woven fabric of metal or plastic filaments — **gauzy** \'gȯ-zē\ *adj*

gave *past of* GIVE

gav·el \'gav-əl\ *n* : the mallet of a presiding officer or auctioneer

ga·votte \gə-'vät\ *n* : a dance of French peasant origin marked by the raising rather than sliding of the feet — **gavotte** *vi*

gawk \'gȯk\ *vi* : to gape or stare stupidly

gawky \'gȯ-kē\ *adj* : AWKWARD, CLUMSY — **gawk·i·ly** \-kə-lē\ *adv* — **gawk·i·ness** *n*

gay \'gā\ *adj* **1** : happily excited : MERRY **2 a** : BRIGHT, LIVELY **b** : brilliant in color **3** : given to social pleasures; *also* : LICENTIOUS — **gay** *adv* — **gay·ness** *n*

gaze \'gāz\ *vi* : to fix the eyes in a steady intent look — **gaze** *n* — **gaz·er** *n*

ga·zelle \gə-'zel\ *n* : any of numerous small graceful swift antelopes with soft lustrous eyes

ga·zette \gə-'zet\ *n* **1** : NEWSPAPER **2** : an official journal

gaz·et·teer \ˌgaz-ə-'ti(ə)r\ *n* : a geographical dictionary

¹gear \'gi(ə)r\ *n* **1** : CLOTHING, GARMENTS **2** : EQUIPMENT, PARAPHERNALIA **3** : the rigging of a ship or boat **4 a** (1) : a mechanism that performs a specific function in a complete machine (2) : a toothed wheel : COGWHEEL (3) : working relation or adjustment **b** : one of two or more adjustments of a motor-vehicle transmission that determine the direction of travel and the relative speed between the engine and the motion of the vehicle — **gear·less** \-ləs\ *adj*

²gear *vb* **1 a** : to provide with gearing **b** : to connect by gearing **c** : to put into gear **2 a** : to make ready for effective operation **b** : to adjust or become adjusted so as to match or blend with something **3** : to be in or come into gear

gear·ing \'gi(ə)r-iŋ\ *n* **1** : the act or process of providing or fitting with gears **2** : the parts by which motion is transmitted from one portion of machinery to another

gear·shift \'gi(ə)r-ˌshift\ *n* : a mechanism by which the transmission gears in a power-transmission system are engaged and disengaged

gee \'jē\ *imperative verb* — used as a direction to turn to the right or move ahead

geese *pl of* GOOSE

ge·gen·schein \'gā-gən-ˌshīn\ *n, often cap* : a faint light on the celestial sphere opposite the sun

Gei·ger counter \ˌgī-gər-'\ *or* **Geiger–Mül·ler counter** \-'myül-ər-ˌ, -'mil-, -'məl-\ *n* : an electronic instrument for indicating (as by clicks) the presence of cosmic rays or radioactive substances

gei·sha \'gā-shə, 'gē-\ *n, pl* **geisha** *or* **geishas** : a Japanese girl who is trained to provide entertaining company for men

gel·a·tin \'jel-ət-ᵊn\ *n* : gummy or sticky material obtained from animal tissues by boiling and used as a food, in photography, and in medicine

ge·lat·i·nous \jə-'lat-nəs, -ᵊn-əs\ *adj* **1** : resembling gelatin or jelly **2** : of, relating to, or containing gelatin

geld \'geld\ *vt* : CASTRATE; *also* : SPAY

geld·ing \'gel-diŋ\ *n* : a castrated animal; *esp* : a castrated male horse

gel·id \'jel-əd\ *adj* : extremely cold : ICY — **ge·lid·i·ty** \jə-'lid-ət-ē, jē-\ *n* — **gel·id·ly** *adv*

gem \'jem\ *n* **1 a** : JEWEL **b** : a precious or sometimes semiprecious stone cut and polished for ornament **2** : something usu. small or brief that is prized for great beauty or perfection

gen·darme \'zhän-ˌdärm, 'jän-\ *n* : one of a body of soldiers esp. in France serving as an armed police force for the maintenance of public order

gen·dar·mer·ie *or* **gen·dar·mery** \jän-'dä(r)m-ə-rē, zhän-\ *n, pl* **-mer·ies** : a body of gendarmes

gen·der \'jen-dər\ *n* **1** : SEX **2** : any of two or more classes of words (as nouns or pronouns) or of forms of words (as adjectives) in a language that are partly arbitrary but also partly based on distinguishable characteristics (as sex) and that determine agreement with and selection of other words or grammatical forms; *also* : membership of a word or a grammatical form in such a class

gene \'jēn\ *n* : one of the complex chemical units of a chromosome that transmit hereditary characters

ge·ne·al·o·gy \ˌjē-nē-'äl-ə-jē, ˌjen-ē-, -'al-\ *n, pl* **-gies** **1** : a history of the descent of a person or family from an ancestor **2** : the descent of a person or family from an ancestor : PEDIGREE, LINEAGE **3** : the study of family pedigrees — **ge·ne·a·log·i·cal** \ˌjē-nē-ə-'läj-i-kəl, ˌjen-ē-\ *adj* — **ge·ne·a·log·i·cal·ly** \-'läj-i-k(ə-)lē\ *adv* — **ge·ne·al·o·gist** \-'äl-ə-jəst, -'al-\ *n*

genera *pl of* GENUS

¹gen·er·al \'jen-(ə-)rəl\ *adj* **1** : of or relating to the whole : not local **2** : taken as a whole **3** : relating to or covering all instances or individuals of a class or group **4** : not limited in meaning : not specific or in detail **5** : common to many **6** : not special : not specialized **7** : not precise or definite **8** : superior in rank : concerned with administration or counseling

²general *n* **1** : something that involves or is applicable to the whole **2 a** : a military officer ranking above a colonel **b** (1) : a commissioned officer ranking next below a general of the army or a general of the air force (2) : a commissioned officer of the highest rank in the marine corps — **in general** : for the most part : GENERALLY

gen·er·a·lis·si·mo \ˌjen-(ə-)rə-'lis-ə-ˌmō\ *n, pl* **-mos** : the chief commander of an army : COMMANDER IN CHIEF

gen·er·al·i·ty \ˌjen-ə-'ral-ət-ē\ *n, pl* **-ties** **1** : the quality or state of being general **2 a** : GENERALIZATION 2 **b** : a vague or inadequate statement **3** : the greatest part : BULK

gen·er·al·i·za·tion \ˌjen-(ə-)rə-lə-'zā-shən\ *n* **1** : the act or process of generalizing **2** : a general statement, law, principle, or proposition

gen·er·al·ize \'jen-(ə-)rə-ˌlīz\ *vb* **1** : to make general **2** : to draw general conclusions from **3** : to reach a general conclusion esp. on the basis of particular instances **4** : to extend throughout the body — **gen·er·al·iz·er** *n*

gen·er·al·ly \'jen-(ə-)rə-lē\ *adv* : in a general manner: as **a** : in disregard of specific instances and with regard to an overall picture **b** : as a rule : USUALLY

general of the air force : a general of the highest rank in the air force whose insignia is five stars

general of the army : a general of the highest rank in the army whose insignia is five stars

gen·er·al·ship \'jen-(ə-)rəl-ˌship\ *n* **1** : office or tenure of office of a general **2** : military skill as a high commander **3** : LEADERSHIP

general store *n* : a retail store that carries a wide variety of goods but is not divided into departments
general strike *n* : a strike involving all union workers in all the trades and industries of an area
gen·er·ate \'jen-ə-,rāt\ *vt* : to bring into existence; *esp* : to originate (as electricity) by a vital or chemical process
gen·er·a·tion \,jen-ə-'rā-shən\ *n* **1** : a body of living beings constituting a single step in the line of descent from an ancestor **2** : the average span of time between the birth of parents and that of their offspring **3** : the action or process of generating
gen·er·a·tor \'jen-ə-,rāt-ər\ *n* **1** : one that generates **2** : a machine by which mechanical energy is changed into electrical energy
ge·ner·ic \jə-'ner-ik\ *adj* **1** : of, relating to, or characteristic of a whole group or class : not specific : GENERAL **2** : of, relating to, or ranking as a biological genus — **ge·ner·i·cal·ly** \-'ner-i-k(ə-)lē\ *adv*
gen·er·os·i·ty \,jen-ə-'räs-ət-ē\ *n, pl* **-ties** **1 a** : liberality in spirit or act; *esp* : liberality in giving **b** : a generous act **2** : ABUNDANCE, LARGENESS
gen·er·ous \'jen-(ə-)rəs\ *adj* **1** : free in giving or sharing : not mean or stingy : UNSELFISH **2** : HIGH-MINDED, NOBLE **3** : ABUNDANT, PLENTIFUL, AMPLE — **gen·er·ous·ly** *adv* — **gen·er·ous·ness** *n*
gen·e·sis \'jen-ə-səs\ *n, pl* **-e·ses** \-ə-,sēz\ : the origin or coming into being of something
ge·net·ic \jə-'net-ik\ *adj* **1** : of or relating to the origin, development, or causes of something **2** : of, relating to, or involving genetics — **ge·net·i·cal** \-i-kəl\ *adj* — **ge·net·i·cal·ly** \-i-k(ə-)lē\ *adv*
ge·net·ics \jə-'net-iks\ *n* : a branch of biology that deals with the heredity and variation of organisms
[1]**ge·nial** \'jē-nyəl\ *adj* **1** : favorable to growth or comfort **2** : being cheerful and cheering : KINDLY — **ge·ni·al·i·ty** \,jē-nē-'al-ət-ē, jēn-'yal-\ *n* — **ge·nial·ly** \'jē-nyə-lē\ *adv*
[2]**ge·ni·al** \jə-'nī(-ə)l\ *adj* : of or relating to the chin
ge·nie \'jē-nē\ *n, pl* **ge·nies** \-nēz\ : JINN
[1]**gen·i·tal** \'jen-ə-tᵊl\ *adj* : of or relating to reproduction or the sexual organs
[2]**genital** *n* : one of the genitalia
gen·i·ta·lia \,jen-ə-'tā-lē-ə\ *n pl* : reproductive organs; *esp* : the external genital organs
gen·i·tive \'jen-ət-iv\ *adj* : of, relating to, or constituting a grammatical case marking typically a relationship esp. of possessor or source — **genitive** *n*
ge·nius \'jē-nyəs\ *n, pl* **ge·nius·es** *or* **ge·nii** \-nē-,ī\ **1** *pl genii* : an attendant spirit of a person or place **2** : a strong leaning or inclination : PENCHANT **3 a** : a peculiar, distinctive, or identifying character or spirit **b** : the associations and traditions of a place **4** *pl genii* **a** : an elemental spirit : JINN **b** : a person who influences another for good or bad **5** *pl geniuses* **a** : a single strongly marked capacity or aptitude **b** : extraordinary intellectual power esp. as manifested in creative activity **c** : a person endowed with transcendent mental superiority; *esp* : a person with a very high intelligence quotient
gen·o·cide \'jen-ə-,sīd\ *n* : the deliberate and systematic destruction of a racial, political, or cultural group — **gen·o·cid·al** \,jen-ə-'sīd-ᵊl\ *adj*
genre \'zhä(ⁿ)n-rə, 'zhäⁿ(-ə)r\ *n* **1** : KIND, SORT **2 a** : paintings that depict scenes or events from everyday life usu. realistically; *also* : the style of painting featuring such subject matter **b** : a distinctive type or category of literary composition
gens \'jenz, 'gen(t)s\ *n, pl* **gen·tes** \'jen-,tēz, 'gen-,tās\ : a Roman clan embracing the families of the same stock in the male line
gent \'jent\ *n* : MAN, FELLOW
gen·teel \jen-'tēl\ *adj* **1 a** : ARISTOCRATIC **b** : ELEGANT, GRACEFUL **c** : STYLISH **d** : POLITE, REFINED **2 a** : maintaining the appearance of superior or middle-class social status or respectability **b** : marked by false delicacy, prudery, or affectation — **gen·teel·ly** \-'tēl-lē\ *adv* — **gen·teel·ness** *n*
gen·tian \'jen-chən\ *n* : any of various herbs with opposite smooth leaves and showy usu. blue flowers
gen·tile \'jen-,tīl\ *n* **1** *often cap* : a person who is not Jewish **2** : HEATHEN, PAGAN **3** *often cap* : a person who is not a Mormon — **gentile** *adj, often cap*
gen·til·i·ty \jen-'til-ət-ē\ *n, pl* **-ties** **1** : good birth and family **2** : the qualities characteristic of a well-bred person **3** : good manners
[1]**gen·tle** \'jent-ᵊl\ *adj* **1 a** : belonging or suitable to a family of high social station **b** : of, relating to, or characteristic of a gentleman **c** : KIND, AMIABLE **2 a** : TRACTABLE, DOCILE **b** : not harsh or stern : not violent : MILD **3** : SOFT, DELICATE **4** : MODERATE — **gen·tle·ness** *n* — **gen·tly** \'jent-lē\ *adv*
[2]**gentle** *vt* **gen·tled**; **gen·tling** \'jent-liŋ, -ᵊl-iŋ\ **1** : to make mild, docile, soft, or moderate **2** : MOLLIFY, PLACATE
gen·tle·folk \'jent-ᵊl-,fōk\ *n pl* : persons of good family and breeding
gen·tle·man \'jent-ᵊl-mən\ *n* **1** : a man of good family **2** : a well-bred man of good education and good social position **3** : MAN — used in the plural as a form of address in speaking to a group of men
gen·tle·man·ly \-lē\ *adj* : characteristic of or having the character of a gentleman — **gen·tle·man·li·ness** *n*
gentleman's agreement *n* : an agreement secured only by the honor of the participants
gen·tle·wom·an \'jent-ᵊl-,wu̇m-ən\ *n* **1** : a woman of good family or breeding **2** : a woman attending a lady of rank
gen·try \'jen-trē\ *n* **1** : people of good birth, breeding, and education : ARISTOCRACY **2** : the class of English people between the nobility and the yeomanry **3** : PEOPLE; *esp* : persons of a designated class
gen·u·flect \'jen-yə-,flekt\ *vt* : to touch the knee to the floor or ground esp. in worship — **gen·u·flec·tion** \,jen-yə-'flek-shən\ *n*
gen·u·ine \'jen-yə-wən\ *adj* **1** : being actually what it seems to be : REAL **2** : SINCERE, HONEST — **gen·u·ine·ly** *adv* — **gen·u·ine·ness** *n*
ge·nus \'jē-nəs\ *n, pl* **gen·era** \'jen-ə-rə\ **1** : a category of biological classification comprising related organisms and usu. consisting of several species **2** : a class of objects divided into several subordinate groups
ge·og·ra·pher \jē-'äg-rə-fər\ *n* : a specialist in geography
ge·o·graph·ic \,jē-ə-'graf-ik\ *adj* **1** : of or relating to geography **2** : belonging to or characteristic of a particular region — **ge·o·graph·i·cal** \-i-kəl\ *adj* — **ge·o·graph·i·cal·ly** \-i-k(ə-)lē\ *adv*
ge·og·ra·phy \jē-'äg-rə-fē\ *n, pl* **-phies** **1** : a science that deals with the natural features of the earth and its climate, products, and inhabitants **2** : the natural features of an area
ge·o·log·ic \,jē-ə-'läj-ik\ *adj* : of, relating to, or based on geology — **ge·o·log·i·cal** \-i-kəl\ *adj* — **ge·o·log·i·cal·ly** \-i-k(ə-)lē\ *adv*
ge·ol·o·gist \jē-'äl-ə-jəst\ *n* : a specialist in geology
ge·ol·o·gy \jē-'äl-ə-jē\ *n, pl* **-gies** **1** : a science that deals with the history of the earth and its life esp. as recorded in rocks **2** : the geologic features of an area
ge·o·met·ric \,jē-ə-'me-trik\ *adj* : of, relating to, or based on the methods or principles of geometry — **ge·o·met·ri·cal** \-'me-tri-kəl\ *adj*
ge·om·e·try \jē-'äm-ə-trē\ *n* : a branch of mathematics that deals with the measurement, properties, and relationships of lines, angles, surfaces, and solids
geo·pol·i·tics \,jē-ō-'päl-ə-,tiks\ *n* : a science based on the theory that domestic and foreign politics of a country are

dependent on physical geography; *also* : the physical geography of a region as affecting politics

ge·ra·ni·um \jə-ˈrā-nē-əm\ *n* : any of a widely distributed genus of herbs with usu. deeply cut leaves, regular flowers in which glands alternate with the petals, and long slender dry fruits

ger·i·at·ric \ˌjer-ē-ˈa-trik\ *adj* : of or relating to geriatrics, the aged, or the process of aging

ger·i·at·rics \ˌjer-ē-ˈa-triks\ *n* : a branch of medicine that deals with the problems and diseases of old age and aging people — **ger·i·a·tri·cian** \ˌjer-ē-ə-ˈtrish-ən\ *n*

germ \ˈjərm\ *n* **1** : a small mass of living substance capable of developing into an organism or one of its parts **2** : something that serves or may serve as an origin : RUDIMENT **3** : MICROBE

ger·man \ˈjər-mən\ *adj* : having the same parents or the same grandparents on either the maternal or paternal side

ger·mane \(ˌ)jər-ˈmān\ *adj* : having a significant connection : PERTINENT — **ger·mane·ly** *adv*

ger·ma·ni·um \(ˌ)jər-ˈmā-nē-əm\ *n* : a grayish white hard brittle chemical element that resembles silicon and is used as a semiconductor

ger·mi·cid·al \ˌjər-mə-ˈsīd-ᵊl\ *adj* : of or relating to a germicide; *also* : destroying germs

ger·mi·cide \ˈjər-mə-ˌsīd\ *n* : an agent that destroys germs

ger·mi·nate \ˈjər-mə-ˌnāt\ *vb* **1** : to cause to sprout or develop **2** : to begin to grow : SPROUT **3** : to come into being : EVOLVE — **ger·mi·na·tion** \ˌjər-mə-ˈnā-shən\ *n*

ger·on·tol·o·gy \ˌjer-ən-ˈtäl-ə-jē\ *n* : a branch of knowledge dealing with aging and the problems of the aged — **ger·on·tol·o·gist** \-jəst\ *n*

[1]ger·ry·man·der \ˌjer-ē-ˈman-dər, ˌger-\ *n* **1** : the act or method of gerrymandering **2** : a district or pattern of districts varying greatly in size or population as a result of gerrymandering

[2]gerrymander *vt* **ger·ry·man·dered**; **ger·ry·man·der·ing** \-d(ə-)riŋ\ : to divide (as a state or county) into election districts in such a way as to give one political party an advantage over its opponents

ger·und \ˈjer-ənd\ *n* **1** : a verbal noun in Latin that expresses the action of the verb as generalized or in continuance **2** : an English verbal noun in *-ing* used as a substantive and at the same time capable of taking adverbial modifiers and having an object

gest *or* **geste** \ˈjest\ *n* **1** : ADVENTURE, EXPLOIT **2** : a tale of adventures; *esp* : a romance in verse

Ge·sta·po \gə-ˈstäp-ō\ *n* : the Nazi secret-police organization operating esp. against suspected political criminals by means of terror

ges·tate \ˈjes-ˌtāt\ *vt* **1** : to carry in the uterus during pregnancy **2** : to conceive and gradually develop in the mind

ges·ta·tion \je-ˈstā-shən\ *n* **1** : the carrying of young in the uterus : PREGNANCY **2** : conception and development esp. in the mind

ges·tic·u·late \je-ˈstik-yə-ˌlāt\ *vi* : to make gestures esp. when speaking — **ges·tic·u·la·tor** \-ˌlāt-ər\ *n*

ges·tic·u·la·tion \(ˌ)jes-ˌtik-yə-ˈlā-shən\ *n* **1** : the action of making gestures **2** : GESTURE; *esp* : an expressive gesture made in showing strong feeling or in enforcing an argument

ges·tic·u·la·tive \je-ˈstik-yə-ˌlāt-iv\ *adj* : inclined to or marked by gesticulation

[1]ges·ture \ˈjes-chər\ *n* **1** : the use of motions of the limbs or body as a means of expression **2** : a movement usu. of the body or limbs that expresses or emphasizes an idea, sentiment, or attitude **3** : something said or done by way of formality or courtesy, as a symbol or token, or for its effect on the attitudes of others

[2]gesture *vb* **1** : to make a gesture **2** : to express or direct by a gesture

[1]get \(ˈ)get, *esp when unemphatic also* git\ *vb* **got** \(ˈ)gät\; **got** *or* **got·ten** \ˈgät-ᵊn\; **get·ting** **1 a** : to gain possession of (as by receiving, acquiring, earning, buying, or winning) **b** : to seek out and obtain as planned **c** : FETCH **d** : to acquire wealth **2 a** : to succeed in coming or going **b** : to cause to come or go **3** : BEGET **4 a** : to cause to be in a certain condition **b** : BECOME **c** : PREPARE **5 a** : SEIZE **b** : to move emotionally **c** : BAFFLE, PUZZLE **d** : IRRITATE **e** : HIT **f** : KILL **6 a** : to be subjected to **b** : to receive as punishment **7 a** : to find out by calculation **b** : to hear correctly **c** : UNDERSTAND **8** : PERSUADE, INDUCE **9 a** : HAVE — used in the present perfect form with present meaning **b** : to have as an obligation or necessity — used in the present perfect form with present meaning **10** : to establish communication with **11** : to be able : CONTRIVE, MANAGE **12** : to leave at once : clear out — **get ahead** : to achieve success — **get around 1** : to get the better of **2** : EVADE — **get at 1** : to reach effectively **2** : to influence corruptly **3** : to turn one's attention to **4** : to try to prove or make clear — **get away with** : to perform without suffering unpleasant consequences — **get back at** : to get even with — **get even** : to get revenge — **get even with** : to repay in kind — **get it** : to receive a scolding or punishment — **get one's goat** : to make one angry or annoyed — **get over 1** : OVERCOME **2** : to recover from — **get through 1** : to reach the end of : COMPLETE **2** : to while away — **get to 1** : BEGIN **2** : to have an effect on : INFLUENCE — **get together 1** : to bring together : ACCUMULATE **2** : to come together : ASSEMBLE **3** : to reach agreement — **get wind of** : to become aware of

[2]get \ˈget\ *n* : something begotten : OFFSPRING, PROGENY

get across *vb* : to make or become clear or convincing

get along *vi* **1 a** : PROGRESS **b** : to approach old age **2** : to meet one's needs : MANAGE **3** : to be or remain on congenial terms

get·at·a·ble \get-ˈat-ə-bəl\ *adj* : ACCESSIBLE

get·away \ˈget-ə-ˌwā\ *n* **1** : the action or fact of getting away : ESCAPE **2** : the action of starting or getting under way (as by horses in a race or an automobile starting from a dead stop)

get by *vi* **1** : to avoid failure or catastrophe : barely succeed **2** : to proceed without being discovered, criticized, or punished

get in *vt* : to allow for : INCLUDE

get off *vb* **1** : UTTER **2** : START, LEAVE **3** : to escape or help to escape **4** : to leave work with permission

get on *vi* **1** : to get along **2** : to gain knowledge or understanding

get out *vb* **1** : to bring before the public; *esp* : PUBLISH **2** : to escape or help to escape **3** : to become known : leak out

get–to·geth·er \ˈget-tə-ˌgeth-ər\ *n* : MEETING; *esp* : an informal social gathering

get up \get-ˈəp, git-\ *vb* **1 a** : to arise from bed **b** : to rise to one's feet **2** : to go ahead or faster — used as a command to a horse **3** : to make preparations for : ORGANIZE **4** : to arrange as to external appearance : DRESS

get·up \ˈget-ˌəp\ *n* **1** : general composition or structure **2** : OUTFIT, COSTUME

gew·gaw \ˈg(y)ü-ˌgȯ\ *n* : a showy trifle : BAUBLE, TRINKET

gey·ser \ˈgī-zər\ *n* : a spring that throws forth intermittent jets of heated water and steam

[1]ghast·ly \ˈgast-lē\ *adj* **1** : HORRIBLE, SHOCKING **2** : resembling a ghost : DEATHLIKE, PALE — **ghast·li·ness** *n*

[2]ghastly *adv* : in a ghastly manner

ghat \ˈgȯt\ *n* : a landing place with stairs descending to a river in India

gher·kin \ˈgər-kən\ *n* **1** : a small prickly cucumber used for pickling **2** : the immature fruit of the common cucumber

ghet·to \ˈget-ō\ *n, pl* **ghettos** *or* **ghettoes** : a quarter of a city in which Jews were formerly required to live; *also* : a quarter of a city in which members of a minority group live because of social, legal, or economic pressure

ghillie *var of* GILLIE

[1]**ghost** \'gōst\ *n* **1** : the seat of life : SOUL **2** : a disembodied soul; *esp* : the soul of a dead person believed to be an inhabitant of the unseen world or to appear to the living in bodily likeness **3** : SPIRIT, DEMON **4** : a faint shadowy trace or suggestion **5** : one who ghostwrites — **ghost·like** *adj*
[2]**ghost** *vb* **1** : to haunt like a ghost **2** : to move silently like a ghost **3** : GHOSTWRITE
ghost·ly \'gōst-lē\ *adj* **1** : of or relating to the soul : SPIRITUAL **2** : of, relating to, or having the characteristics of a ghost : SPECTRAL — **ghost·li·ness** *n*
ghost town *n* : a once flourishing town deserted or nearly so often after exhaustion of some natural resource (as gold)
ghost·write \'gōst-ˌrīt\ *vb* : to write for and in the name of another — **ghost–writ·er** *n*
ghoul \'gül\ *n* **1** : a legendary evil being that robs graves and feeds on corpses **2** : a person (as a grave robber) whose activities suggest those of a ghoul — **ghoul·ish** \'gü-lish\ *adj* — **ghoul·ish·ly** *adv* — **ghoul·ish·ness** *n*
[1]**GI** \(')jē-'ī\ *adj* **1** : provided by an official U.S. military supply department **2** : of, relating to, or characteristic of U.S. military personnel **3** : conforming to military regulations or customs
[2]**GI** *n* : a member or former member of the U.S. armed forces; *esp* : an enlisted man
[3]**GI** *vt* **GI'd**; **GI'ing** : to prepare for military inspection by cleaning
[1]**gi·ant** \'jī-ənt\ *n* **1** : a legendary being of great stature and strength and of more than mortal but less than godlike power **2 a** : a living being of great size **b** : a person of extraordinary powers **3** : something unusually large or powerful
[2]**giant** *adj* : characterized by extremely large size, proportion, or power
gi·ant·ess \'jī-ənt-əs\ *n* : a female giant; *esp* : an unusually large woman
gi·ant·ism \'jī-ənt-ˌiz-əm\ *n* : the quality or state of being a giant
gib·ber \'jib-ər\ *vi* **gib·bered**; **gib·ber·ing** \'jib-(ə-)riŋ\ : to speak rapidly, inarticulately, and often foolishly : CHATTER — **gibber** *n*
gib·ber·ish \'jib-(ə-)rish, 'gib-\ *n* : unintelligible, confused, or meaningless speech or language
[1]**gib·bet** \'jib-ət\ *n* : GALLOWS; *esp* : an upright post with a projecting arm for hanging the bodies of executed criminals as a warning
[2]**gibbet** *vt* **1 a** : to hang on a gibbet **b** : to expose to public scorn **2** : to execute by hanging
gib·bon \'gib-ən\ *n* : a manlike ape of southeastern Asia and the East Indies
[1]**gibe** \'jīb\ *vb* : to utter or reproach with taunting or sarcastic words — **gib·er** *n*
[2]**gibe** *n* : JEER, TAUNT
gib·lets \'jib-ləts\ *n pl* : the edible viscera of a fowl
gid·dy \'gid-ē\ *adj* **1** : having a feeling of whirling or reeling about : DIZZY **2** : causing dizziness **3** : not serious : lightheartedly silly : FRIVOLOUS, FICKLE — **gid·di·ly** \'gid-ᵊl-ē\ *adv* — **gid·di·ness** \'gid-ē-nəs\ *n*
gift \'gift\ *n* **1** : the act or power of giving **2** : something given : PRESENT **3** : a special ability : TALENT
gift·ed \'gif-təd\ *adj* : having great natural ability : TALENTED
[1]**gig** \'gig\ *n* **1 a** : a long light ship's boat propelled by oars, sail, or motor **b** : a rowboat designed for speed rather than for work **2** : a light 2-wheeled one-horse carriage
[2]**gig** *n* : a pronged spear for catching fish
[3]**gig** *vb* **gigged**; **gig·ging** : to spear or fish with a gig
[4]**gig** *n* : a military demerit
[5]**gig** *vt* **gigged**; **gig·ging** : to give a military gig to
gi·gan·tesque \ˌjī-ˌgan-'tesk\ *adj* : of enormous proportions
gi·gan·tic \jī-'gant-ik\ *adj* **1 a** : resembling a giant **b** : greater in size than the usual or expected **2** : extremely large or great — **gi·gan·ti·cal·ly** \-'gant-i-k(ə-)lē\ *adv*
gi·gan·tism \jī-'gan-ˌtiz-əm\ *n* : GIANTISM
[1]**gig·gle** \'gig-əl\ *vi* **gig·gled**; **gig·gling** \'gig-(ə-)liŋ\ : to laugh with repeated short catches of the breath : laugh in a silly manner — **gig·gler** \-(ə-)lər\ *n*
[2]**giggle** *n* : the act of giggling : a light silly laugh
gig·gly \'gig-(ə-)lē\ *adj* : given to giggling
gig·o·lo \'jig-ə-ˌlō\ *n, pl* **-los** **1** : a man living on the earnings of or supported by a woman **2** : a professional dancing partner or male escort
gi·got \'jig-ət, zhē-'gō\ *n, pl* **gigots** \-əts, -'gō(z)\ **1** : a leg (as of lamb) esp. when cooked **2** : a leg-of-mutton sleeve
gild \'gild\ *vt* **gild·ed** *or* **gilt** \'gilt\; **gild·ing** **1** : to cover with or as if with a thin coating of gold **2** : to give an attractive but often deceptive appearance to — **gild·er** *n* — **gild the lily** : to add unnecessary ornamentation to something beautiful in its own right
gild·ing \'gil-diŋ\ *n* **1 a** : the art or practice of coating with gold **b** : the material used **2** : a superficial coating or appearance
[1]**gill** \'jil\ *n* : a unit of liquid capacity equal to 1/4 pint
[2]**gill** \'gil\ *n* : an organ (as of a fish) for obtaining oxygen from water
gil·lie *or* **gil·ly** *or* **ghil·lie** \'gil-ē\ *n, pl* **gillies** *or* **ghillies** **1** : a male attendant on a Scottish Highland chief **2** *usu ghillie* : a low-cut shoe with decorative lacing
[1]**gilt** \'gilt\ *adj* : of the color of gold
[2]**gilt** *n* **1** : gold or something that resembles gold laid on a surface **2** : superficial brilliance
[3]**gilt** *n* : a young female swine
gilt–edged \'gilt-'ejd\ *or* **gilt–edge** \-'ej\ *adj* **1** : having a gilt edge **2** : of the best quality; *esp* : extremely safe for investment
gim·crack \'jim-ˌkrak\ *n* : a showy object of little use or value : GEWGAW — **gimcrack** *adj* — **gim·crack·ery** \-ˌkrak-(ə-)rē\ *n*
[1]**gim·let** \'gim-lət\ *n* : a small tool with a screw point, grooved shank, and cross handle for boring holes
[2]**gimlet** *adj* : having a piercing or penetrating quality
gim·mick \'gim-ik\ *n* **1** : CONTRIVANCE, GADGET; *esp* : one used in secret or for an illicit purpose **2 a** : an important feature that is not immediately apparent : CATCH **b** : a new and ingenious scheme
[1]**gimp** \'gimp\ *n* : an ornamental flat braid or round cord used as a trimming
[2]**gimp** *n* : SPIRIT, VIM
[3]**gimp** *n* : CRIPPLE; *also* : LIMP — **gimpy** \'gim-pē\ *adj*
[1]**gin** \'jin\ *n* : a mechanical tool or device: as **a** : a snare or trap for game **b** : a machine to separate seeds from cotton
[2]**gin** *vt* **ginned**; **gin·ning** **1** : SNARE **2** : to separate (cotton fiber) from seeds and waste material — **gin·ner** *n*
[3]**gin** *n* : a strong alcoholic liquor made by distilling a mash of grain with juniper berries
gin·ger \'jin-jər\ *n* **1** : any of a genus of tropical Old World herbs with pungent aromatic rhizomes used as a condiment and in medicine; *also* : this rhizome **2** : high spirit : PEP — **gin·gery** \'jinj-(ə-)rē\ *adj*
ginger ale *n* : a nonalcoholic drink flavored with ginger extract
gin·ger·bread \'jin-jər-ˌbred\ *n* **1** : a cake made with molasses and flavored with ginger **2** : tawdry, gaudy, or superfluous ornament — **gingerbread** *adj*
gin·ger·ly \'jin-jər-lē\ *adj* : very cautious or careful — **gingerly** *adv*
gin·ger·snap \-ˌsnap\ *n* : a thin brittle cookie flavored with ginger
ging·ham \'giŋ-əm\ *n* : a clothing fabric usu. of yarn-dyed cotton in plain weave
gi·raffe \jə-'raf\ *n, pl* **giraffe** *or* **giraffes** : a large fleet African ruminant mammal that is the tallest of living quadrupeds and

has a very long neck and a black-blotched coat — **gi•raff•ish** \-'raf-ish\ *adj*

gird \'gərd\ *vb* **gird•ed** *or* **girt** \'gərt\; **gird•ing** 1 : to encircle or fasten with or as if with a belt or cord : GIRDLE 2 : to clothe or invest esp. with power or authority 3 : to make or get ready : BRACE

gird•er \'gərd-ər\ *n* : a horizontal main supporting beam (as of wood or steel)

[1]**gir•dle** \'gərd-ᵊl\ *n* : something that encircles or confines: as a : a belt or sash encircling the waist b : a woman's supporting undergarment that extends from the waist to below the hips

[2]**girdle** *vt* **gir•dled**; **gir•dling** \'gərd-liŋ, -ᵊl-iŋ\ 1 : to bind or encircle with a girdle 2 : to move around : CIRCLE

girl \'gərl\ *n* 1 : a female child : young woman 2 : a female servant or employee 3 : SWEETHEART — **girl•hood** \-ˌhu̇d\ *n*

girl friend *n* 1 : a female friend 2 : a frequent or regular female companion of a boy or man 3 : a female paramour

girl•ish \'gər-lish\ *adj* : of, relating to, or having the characteristics of a girl or girlhood — **girl•ish•ly** *adv* — **girl•ish•ness** *n*

girt \'gərt\ *vt* 1 : GIRD 2 : to fasten by means of a girth

[1]**girth** \'gərth\ *n* 1 : a band or strap that encircles the body of an animal to fasten something (as a saddle) upon its back 2 : a measure around a body

[2]**girth** *vt* : to bind or fasten with a girth

gist \'jist\ *n* : the main point of a matter : ESSENCE

[1]**give** \'giv\ *vb* **gave** \'gāv\; **giv•en** \'giv-ən\; **giv•ing** 1 : to make a present of 2 a : GRANT, BESTOW b : to accord or yield to another 3 a : to put into the possession or keeping of another : HAND b : to offer to another : PROFFER c : DELIVER; *esp* : to deliver in exchange d : PAY 4 a : to present in public performance b : to present to view or observation 5 : to provide by way of entertainment 6 : to designate as a share or portion : ALLOT 7 : ATTRIBUTE, ASCRIBE 8 : to yield as a product or result : PRODUCE 9 a : to deliver by some bodily action b : to carry out (a movement of or as if of the body) : EXECUTE c : UTTER, PRONOUNCE 10 : to offer for consideration or acceptance 11 : to apply freely or fully : DEVOTE 12 : to cause to have or receive : OCCASION 13 : to make gifts or presents : CONTRIBUTE, DONATE 14 a : to yield to physical force or strain b : to collapse from the application of force or pressure — **giv•er** *n* — **give ground** : to withdraw before superior force : RETREAT — **give it to** : to attack vigorously — **give tongue** : to begin barking on the scent — **give way** 1 : RETREAT 2 : to yield oneself without restraint or control 3 a : COLLAPSE, FAIL b : CONCEDE 4 : to yield place

[2]**give** *n* 1 : capacity or tendency to yield to force or strain 2 : the quality or state of being springy

give–and–take \ˌgiv-ən-'tāk\ *n* : an exchange (as of remarks or ideas) esp. on fair or equal terms

give away \ˌgiv-ə-'wā\ *vt* 1 : to deliver (a bride) to the bridegroom at a wedding 2 a : BETRAY b : DISCLOSE, REVEAL

give•away \'giv-ə-ˌwā\ *n* 1 : an unintentional revelation or betrayal 2 : something given away free; *esp* : PREMIUM 3 : a radio or television program on which prizes are given away

giv•en \'giv-ən\ *adj* 1 : DISPOSED, INCLINED 2 : SPECIFIED, FIXED 3 : granted as true : ASSUMED 4 : EXECUTED, DATED

given name *n* : CHRISTIAN NAME

give up *vb* 1 : to hand over to another : SURRENDER 2 : to abandon (oneself) to a feeling, influence, or activity 3 : to withdraw from an activity or course of action

giz•zard \'giz-ərd\ *n* 1 : a muscular enlargement of the digestive canal (as of a bird) that follows the crop and has usu. a horny lining for grinding the food 2 : INNARDS

gla•brous \'glā-brəs\ *adj* : SMOOTH; *esp* : having a surface without hairs or projections — **gla•brous•ness** *n*

gla•cé \gla-'sā\ *adj* 1 : made or finished so as to have a smooth glossy surface 2 : coated with a glaze : CANDIED

gla•cial \'glā-shəl\ *adj* 1 a : extremely cold : FRIGID b : lacking warmth and cordiality 2 : of, relating to, or produced by glaciers — **gla•cial•ly** \-shə-lē\ *adv*

gla•cier \'glā-shər\ *n* : a large body of ice moving slowly down a slope or valley or spreading outward on a land surface

gla•cis \gla-'sē, 'glas-əs\ *n, pl* **gla•cis** \gla-'sēz\ : a slope that runs downward from the outside of a fortification

glad \'glad\ *adj* 1 a : experiencing pleasure, joy, or delight : made happy b : GRATIFIED, PLEASED c : very willing 2 : causing happiness and joy : PLEASANT 3 : full of brightness and cheerfulness — **glad•ly** *adv* — **glad•ness** *n*

glad•den \'glad-ᵊn\ *vt* **glad•dened**; **glad•den•ing** \'glad-niŋ, -ᵊn-iŋ\ : to make glad

glade \'glād\ *n* : a grassy open space in a forest

glad•i•a•tor \'glad-ē-ˌāt-ər\ *n* 1 : a person engaged in a fight to the death for public entertainment in ancient Rome 2 : a person engaging in a fierce fight or controversy — **glad•i•a•to•ri•al** \ˌglad-ē-ə-'tōr-ē-əl\ *adj*

glad•i•o•lus \ˌglad-ē-'ō-ləs\ *n, pl* **-o•li** \-'ō-(ˌ)lē, -'ō-ˌlī\ *or* **-o•lus** *or* **-o•lus•es** : any of a genus of chiefly African plants of the iris family with erect sword-shaped leaves and spikes of brilliantly colored irregular flowers arising from flattened corms

glad•some \'glad-səm\ *adj* : giving or showing joy : CHEERFUL — **glad•some•ly** *adv* — **glad•some•ness** *n*

glad•stone \'glad-ˌstōn\ *n, often cap* : a traveling bag with flexible sides on a rigid frame that opens flat into two compartments

glam•or•ize \'glam-ə-ˌrīz\ *vt* 1 : to make glamorous 2 : GLORIFY — **glam•or•i•za•tion** \ˌglam-ə-rə-'zā-shən\ *n* — **glam•or•iz•er** *n*

glam•or•ous \'glam-(ə-)rəs\ *adj* : full of glamour — **glam•or•ous•ly** *adv* — **glam•or•ous•ness** *n*

glam•our *or* **glam•or** \'glam-ər\ *n* : a romantic, exciting, and often illusory attractiveness; *esp* : alluring or fascinating personal attraction

[1]**glance** \'glan(t)s\ *vb* 1 : to strike and fly off at an angle 2 a : to give a quick or hasty look b : to refer briefly to something by way of indirect criticism or satire 3 : GLINT — **glanc•ing•ly** *adv*

[2]**glance** *n* 1 : a quick intermittent flash or gleam 2 : a deflected impact or blow 3 a : a swift movement of the eyes b : a quick or cursory look

gland \'gland\ *n* : a cell or group of cells that prepares and secretes a product for further use in the body or for elimination from the body — **gland** *adj*

glan•du•lar \'glan-jə-lər\ *adj* 1 : of, relating to, or involving glands, gland cells, or their products 2 : having the characteristics or function of a gland

[1]**glare** \'gla(ə)r\ *vb* 1 a : to shine with a harsh uncomfortably brilliant light b : to stand out offensively : OBTRUDE 2 a : to stare angrily or fiercely b : to express (as hostility) by staring angrily

[2]**glare** *n* 1 : a harsh uncomfortably bright light; *esp* : painfully bright sunlight 2 : an angry or fierce stare

glar•ing \'gla(ə)r-iŋ\ *adj* 1 : having a fixed look of hostility, fierceness, or anger 2 a : shining with or reflecting a harsh uncomfortably bright light b (1) : GARISH (2) : vulgarly ostentatious 3 : painfully obvious — **glar•ing•ly** *adv* — **glar•ing•ness** *n*

glary \'gla(ə)r-ē\ *adj* : having a dazzling brightness : GLARING

[1]**glass** \'glas\ *n* 1 a : a hard brittle usu. transparent or translucent noncrystalline inorganic substance commonly formed by melting a mixture (as of silica sand and metallic oxides) and cooling to a rigid condition b : a substance (as a rock formed by the rapid cooling of molten minerals) resembling glass 2 a : something (as a water tumbler, lens, mirror, barometer, or telescope) that is made of glass or has a glass lens b *pl* : a

pair of glass lenses used to correct defects of vision **3** : GLASSFUL

²glass *vt* : to fit or protect with glass

glass·blow·ing \-ˌblō-iŋ\ *n* : the art of shaping a mass of glass that has been softened by heat by blowing air into it through a tube — **glass·blow·er** *n*

glass·ful \ˈglas-ˌfu̇l\ *n* : the quantity held by a glass

glass·mak·ing \-ˌmā-kiŋ\ *n* : the art or process of manufacturing glass

glass·man \-ˌman\ *n* : a dealer in or maker of glass

glass·ware \-ˌwa(ə)r\ *n* : articles made of glass

glassy \ˈglas-ē\ *adj* **1** : resembling glass **2** : DULL, LIFELESS — **glass·i·ly** \ˈglas-ə-lē\ *adv* — **glass·i·ness** *n*

¹glaze \ˈglāz\ *vb* **1** : to furnish or fit with glass **2 a** : to coat with or as if with glass **b** : to apply a glaze to **3** : to give a smooth glossy surface to **4** : to become glazed — **glaz·er** *n*

²glaze *n* **1** : a smooth slippery coating of thin ice **2** : a transparent or translucent substance used as a coating (as on food or pottery) to produce a gloss

gla·zier \ˈglā-zhər\ *n* : a person who sets glass in window frames

¹gleam \ˈglēm\ *n* **1 a** : a transient subdued or partly obscured light **b** : a small bright light : GLINT **2** : a brief or faint appearance : TRACE

²gleam *vi* **1** : to shine with subdued light or moderate brightness **2** : to appear briefly or faintly

glean \ˈglēn\ *vb* **1** : to gather from a field or vineyard what has been left (as by reapers) **2** : to gather little by little : collect with patient effort — **glean·er** *n*

glean·ings \ˈglē-niŋz\ *n pl* : things acquired by gleaning

glebe \ˈglēb\ *n* : land belonging or yielding revenue to a parish church or ecclesiastical benefice

glee \ˈglē\ *n* **1** : exultant high-spirited joy : HILARITY **2** : an unaccompanied song for three or more solo usu. male voices

glee club *n* : a chorus organized for singing usu. short choral pieces

glee·ful \ˈglē-fəl\ *adj* : full of glee : MERRY — **glee·ful·ly** \-fə-lē\ *adv* — **glee·ful·ness** *n*

glee·man \ˈglē-mən\ *n* : MINSTREL

glen \ˈglen\ *n* : a small secluded narrow valley

glen·gar·ry \glen-ˈgar-ē\ *n, often cap* : a woolen cap of Scottish origin

glib \ˈglib\ *adj* : speaking or spoken with careless ease and often with little regard for truth — **glib·ly** *adv* — **glib·ness** *n*

¹glide \ˈglīd\ *vi* **1** : to move smoothly, continuously, and effortlessly **2** : to pass gradually and imperceptibly **3** : to descend smoothly without engine power sufficient for level flight

²glide *n* **1** : smooth sliding motion **2** : smooth descent without engine power

glid·er \ˈglīd-ər\ *n* : one that glides: as **a** : an aircraft without an engine **b** : a porch seat suspended from an upright framework by short chains or straps

¹glim·mer \ˈglim-ər\ *vi* **glim·mered**; **glim·mer·ing** \ˈglim-(ə-)riŋ\ : to shine faintly or unsteadily

²glimmer *n* **1 a** : a feeble or intermittent light **b** : a soft shimmer **2 a** : a dim perception or faint idea : INKLING **b** : a small amount : BIT

glim·mer·ing *n* : GLIMMER

¹glimpse \ˈglim(p)s\ *vb* : to take a brief look : see momentarily or incompletely — **glimps·er** *n*

²glimpse *n* **1** : a short hurried view **2** : a faint idea : GLIMMER

¹glint \ˈglint\ *vi* **1** : GLANCE **2** : to shine by reflection: **a** : to shine with small bright flashes **b** : GLITTER **c** : GLEAM **3** : to appear briefly or faintly

²glint *n* : a small bright flash of light : SPARKLE

glis·san·do \gli-ˈsän-dō\ *n, pl* **-di** \-(ˌ)dē\ *or* **-dos** : a rapid sliding up or down the musical scale

¹glis·ten \ˈglis-ᵊn\ *vi* **glis·tened**; **glis·ten·ing** \ˈglis-niŋ, -ᵊn-iŋ\ : to shine by reflection with a soft luster or sparkle

²glisten *n* : GLITTER, SPARKLE

glis·ter \ˈglis-tər\ *vi* **glis·tered**; **glis·ter·ing** \-t(ə-)riŋ\ : GLISTEN — **glister** *n*

¹glit·ter \ˈglit-ər\ *vi* **1 a** : to shine with brilliant or metallic luster **b** : SPARKLE **c** : to shine with a cold glassy brilliance **2** : to be brilliantly attractive esp. in a superficial way

²glitter *n* : sparkling brilliancy, showiness, or attractiveness — **glit·tery** \ˈglit-ə-rē\ *adj*

gloam·ing \ˈglō-miŋ\ *n* : TWILIGHT, DUSK

gloat \ˈglōt\ *vi* **1** : to gaze at or think about something with great self-satisfaction, gratification, or joy **2** : to linger over or dwell upon something with malicious pleasure

glob \ˈgläb\ *n* : a small drop : BLOB

glob·al \ˈglō-bəl\ *adj* **1** : SPHERICAL **2** : WORLDWIDE — **glob·al·ly** \-bə-lē\ *adv*

globe \ˈglōb\ *n* : something spherical or rounded: as **a** : a spherical representation of the earth or heavens **b** : EARTH — usu. used with *the* or *this*

glob·u·lar \ˈgläb-yə-lər\ *adj* : having the shape of a globe or globule

glob·ule \ˈgläb-yül\ *n* : a tiny globe or ball

glock·en·spiel \ˈgläk-ən-ˌs(h)pēl\ *n* : a percussion musical instrument consisting of a series of graduated metal bars tuned to the chromatic scale and played with two hammers

glom·er·ate \ˈgläm-ə-rət\ *adj* : collected into a ball, heap, or mass : CONGLOMERATE — **glom·er·a·tion** \ˌgläm-ə-ˈrā-shən\ *n*

¹gloom \ˈglüm\ *vi* **1** : to look sullen or despondent **2** : to be or become overcast

²gloom *n* **1** : partial or total darkness **2 a** : lowness of spirits : DEJECTION **b** : an atmosphere of despondency

gloomy \ˈglü-mē\ *adj* **1** : DUSKY, DIM **2** : MELANCHOLY, LOW-SPIRITED **3** : causing gloom : DISMAL — **gloom·i·ly** \-mə-lē\ *adv* — **gloom·i·ness** *n*

glo·ri·fy \ˈglōr-ə-ˌfī\ *vt* **-fied**; **-fy·ing** **1** : to make glorious by bestowing glory upon; *esp* : to elevate to celestial glory **2** : to shed radiance or splendor on **3** : to make glorious by presentation in a favorable aspect **4** : to give glory to — **glo·ri·fi·ca·tion** \ˌglōr-ə-fə-ˈkā-shən\ *n* — **glo·ri·fi·er** \ˈglōr-ə-ˌfī(-ə)r\ *n*

glo·ri·ous \ˈglōr-ē-əs\ *adj* **1 a** : possessing or deserving glory : ILLUSTRIOUS **b** : conferring glory **2** : RESPLENDENT, MAGNIFICENT **3** : DELIGHTFUL, WONDERFUL — **glo·ri·ous·ly** *adv* — **glo·ri·ous·ness** *n*

¹glo·ry \ˈglōr-ē\ *n, pl* **glories** **1 a** : praise, honor, or distinction extended by common consent : RENOWN **b** : worshipful praise, honor, and thanksgiving **2 a** : something that secures praise or renown **b** : a brilliant asset **3 a** : RESPLENDENCE, MAGNIFICENCE **b** : the splendor and beatific happiness of heaven **4** : a height of prosperity of achievement

²glory *vi* : to rejoice proudly : EXULT

¹gloss \ˈgläs, ˈglȯs\ *n* **1** : brightness from a smooth surface : LUSTER, SHEEN **2** : a deceptively attractive appearance : outward show

²gloss *vt* **1** : to give a deceptive appearance to **2** : to pass over quickly in an attempt to ignore

³gloss *n* **1** : a brief explanation (as in the margin of a text) of a difficult or obscure word or expression **2 a** : GLOSSARY **b** : an interlinear translation **c** : a continuous commentary accompanying a text

⁴gloss *vt* : to furnish glosses for

glos·sa·ry \ˈgläs-(ə-)rē, ˈglȯs-\ *n, pl* **-ries** : a list in the back of a book of the hard or unusual words found in the text; *also* : a dictionary of the special terms found in a particular field of study

glossy \ˈgläs-ē, ˈglȯs-\ *adj* : having a superficial luster or brightness — **gloss·i·ness** *n*

glot·tis \ˈglät-əs\ *n, pl* **glot·tis·es** *or* **glot·ti·des** \ˈglät-ə-ˌdēz\

: the elongated opening between the pharynx and trachea — **glot·tal** \'glät-ᵊl\ *adj*

glove \'gləv\ *n* **1 a :** a covering for the hand having separate sections for each finger **b :** GAUNTLET **2 :** a padded leather covering for the hand used in sport — **gloved** \'gləvd\ *adj*

¹glow \'glō\ *vi* **1 a :** to shine with or as if with an intense heat **b** (1) **:** to have a rich warm usu. ruddy color (2) **:** FLUSH, BLUSH **2 a :** to experience a sensation of heat **b :** to show exuberance or elation

²glow *n* **1 :** brightness or warmth of color; *esp* **:** REDNESS **2 a :** warmth of feeling or emotion **b :** a sensation of warmth **3 :** light such as is emitted by something that is intensely hot but not flaming

glow·er \'glaù(-ə)r\ *vi* **:** to look or stare with sullen annoyance or anger — **glower** *n*

glow·worm \'glō-ˌwərm\ *n* **:** an insect or insect larva that gives off light

gloze \'glōz\ *vt* **:** to make appear right or acceptable **:** GLOSS

glu·cose \'glü-ˌkōs\ *n* **1 :** a sugar known in three different forms; *esp* **:** DEXTROSE **2 :** CORN SYRUP

¹glue \'glü\ *n* **1 :** any of various strong adhesive substances; *esp* **:** a hard protein substance that absorbs water to form a viscous solution with strong adhesive properties and is obtained by cooking down animal materials (as hides or bones) **2 :** a solution of glue used to stick things together

²glue *vt* **glued; glu·ing :** to make fast with or as if with glue

glu·ey \'glü-ē\ *adj* **1 :** covered with glue **2 :** sticky like glue

glum \'gləm\ *adj* **1 :** MOROSE, SULLEN **2 :** DREARY, GLOOMY — **glum·ly** *adv* — **glum·ness** *n*

¹glut \'glət\ *vt* **glut·ted; glut·ting 1 :** to fill esp. with food to satiety **:** SATIATE **2 :** to flood with goods so that supply exceeds demand

²glut *n* **:** an excessive quantity **:** OVERSUPPLY

glu·ten \'glüt-ᵊn\ *n* **:** a tough elastic protein substance in flour esp. from wheat that holds together dough and makes it sticky — **glu·ten·ous** \'glüt-nəs, -ᵊn-əs\ *adj*

glu·ti·nous \'glüt-nəs, -ᵊn-əs\ *adj* **:** resembling glue **:** STICKY — **glu·ti·nous·ly** *adv*

glut·ton \'glət-ᵊn\ *n* **1 :** one that eats too much **2 a :** a shaggy thickset carnivorous mammal of northern Europe and Asia related to the marten and the sable **b :** WOLVERINE — **glut·ton·ous** \'glət-nəs, -ᵊn-əs\ *adj* — **glut·ton·ous·ly** *adv*

glut·tony \'glət-nē, -ᵊn-ē\ *n, pl* **-ton·ies :** excess in eating or drinking

glyc·er·in *or* **glyc·er·ine** \'glis-(ə-)rən\ *n* **:** GLYCEROL

glyc·er·ol \'glis-ə-ˌrȯl\ *n* **:** a sweet colorless syrupy alcohol usu. obtained by the hydrolysis of fats and oils and used esp. as a solvent

G–man \'jē-ˌman\ *n* **:** a special agent of the Federal Bureau of Investigation

gnarl \'närl\ *n* **:** a hard protuberance with twisted grain on a tree — **gnarled** \'närld\ *adj* — **gnarly** \'när-lē\ *adj*

gnash \'nash\ *vt* **:** to strike or grind (the teeth) together

gnat \'nat\ *n* **:** any of various small usu. biting two-winged flies

gnaw \'nȯ\ *vb* **1 a :** to bite or chew with the teeth; *esp* **:** to wear away by persistent biting or nibbling **b :** to make by gnawing **2 a :** to be a source of vexation to **:** PLAGUE **b :** to affect like gnawing **3 :** ERODE, CORRODE — **gnaw·er** *n*

gneiss \'nīs\ *n* **:** a granitelike rock in layers

gnome \'nōm\ *n* **:** a dwarf of folklore living inside the earth and guarding precious ore or treasure — **gnom·ish** \'nō-mish\ *adj*

gnu \'n(y)ü\ *n, pl* **gnu** *or* **gnus :** any of several large African antelopes with a head like that of an ox, short mane, long tail, and horns in both sexes that curve downward and outward

¹go \'gō\ *vb* **went** \'went\; **gone** \'gȯn\; **go·ing** \'gō-iŋ\; **goes** \'gōz\ **1 :** to move on a course **:** PROCEED **2 :** to move away from one point to or toward another **:** LEAVE, DEPART **3 a :** to take a certain course or follow a certain procedure **b :** to pass by a process like journeying **c** (1) **:** EXTEND, RUN (2) **:** to give access **:** LEAD **4 :** to be habitually in a certain state **5 a :** to become lost, consumed, or spent **b :** to slip away **:** ELAPSE, PASS **c :** to pass by sale **d :** to become impaired or weakened **e :** to give way under force or pressure **:** BREAK **6 a :** to take place **:** HAPPEN **b :** to be in general or on an average **c :** to become esp. as the result of a contest **7 a :** to apply oneself **b :** to put or subject oneself **8 :** to have recourse **:** RESORT **9 a :** to begin or maintain an action or motion **b :** to function properly **10 :** to have currency **:** CIRCULATE **11 a :** to be or act in accordance **b :** to come to be applied **c :** to pass by award, assignment, or lot **d :** to contribute to a result **12 a :** to be about, intending, or expecting something **b :** to come or arrive at a certain state or condition **c :** to come to be **13 a :** to be capable of passing, extending, or being contained or inserted **b :** to have a usual or proper place or position **:** BELONG **c :** to be capable of being divided **14 :** to have a tendency **:** CONDUCE **15 :** to be acceptable, satisfactory, or adequate **16 a :** to proceed along or according to **:** FOLLOW **b :** TRAVERSE **17 :** to make a wager or offer of **:** BET, BID **18 a :** to assume the function or obligation of **b :** to participate to the extent of **19 :** YIELD, WEIGH — **go at 1 :** ATTACK, ATTEMPT **2 :** UNDERTAKE — **go back on 1 :** ABANDON **2 :** BETRAY **3 :** FAIL — **go by the board :** to be discarded — **go down the line :** to give wholehearted support — **go for 1 :** to pass for or serve as **2 :** to have an interest in or liking for **:** FAVOR — **go one better :** OUTDO, SURPASS — **go over 1 :** EXAMINE **2 a :** REPEAT **b :** STUDY, REVIEW — **go places :** to be on the way to success — **go steady :** to date one person exclusively and frequently — **go through 1 :** to subject to thorough examination, consideration, or study **2 :** EXPERIENCE, UNDERGO **3 :** to carry out **:** PERFORM — **to go :** REMAINING, LEFT

²go *n, pl* **goes 1 :** the act or manner of going **2 :** the height of fashion **3 :** a turn of affairs **:** OCCURRENCE **4 :** ENERGY, VIGOR **5 :** ATTEMPT, TRY **6 :** a spell of activity — **no go :** to no avail **:** USELESS — **on the go :** constantly or restlessly active

³go *adj* **:** functioning properly

goad \'gōd\ *n* **1 :** a pointed rod used to urge an animal on **2 :** something that urges **:** SPUR — **goad** *vt*

goal \'gōl\ *n* **1 :** the terminal point of a race **2 :** the end toward which effort is directed **:** AIM **3 :** an area or object toward which play is directed in order to score; *also* **:** a successful attempt to score

goal·ie \'gō-lē\ *n* **:** a player who defends the goal in various games

goal·keep·er \'gōl-ˌkē-pər\ *n* **:** GOALIE

goal·post \-ˌpōst\ *n* **:** one of two vertical posts that with a crossbar constitute the goal in various games

goat \'gōt\ *n, pl* **goat** *or* **goats 1 :** any of various hollow-horned ruminant mammals related to the sheep but of lighter build and with backwardly arching horns, a short tail, and usu. straight hair **2 :** SCAPEGOAT — **goat·like** *adj*

goa·tee \gō-'tē\ *n* **:** a small trim pointed or tufted beard on a man's chin

¹gob \'gäb\ *n* **1 :** LUMP, MASS **2 :** a large amount — usu. used in pl.

²gob *n* **:** SAILOR

gob·bet \'gäb-ət\ *n* **:** LUMP, MASS

¹gob·ble \'gäb-əl\ *vt* **gob·bled; gob·bling** \'gäb-(ə-)liŋ\ **1 :** to swallow or eat greedily **2 :** to take eagerly **:** GRAB — usu. used with *up*

²gobble *vi* **:** to make the natural guttural noise of a male turkey — **gobble** *n*

gob·ble·dy·gook *or* **gob·ble·de·gook** \ˌgäb-əl-dē-'gük\ *n* **:** wordy and generally unintelligible jargon

gob·bler \'gäb-lər\ *n* **:** a male turkey

go–be·tween \'gō-bə-ˌtwēn\ *n* : a person who acts as a messenger or an intermediary between two parties
gob·let \'gäb-lət\ *n* : a drinking glass with a foot and stem
gob·lin \'gäb-lən\ *n* : an ugly grotesque sprite with evil or mischievous ways
go–cart \'gō-ˌkärt\ *n* **1 a** : WALKER **b** : STROLLER **2** : a light open carriage
¹god \'gäd\ *n* **1** : a being possessing more than human powers **2** : a natural or man-made physical object (as an image or idol) worshiped as divine **3** : something held to be the most important thing in existence
²God *n* : the supreme or ultimate reality; *esp* : the Being perfect in power, wisdom, and goodness whom men worship as creator and ruler of the universe
god·child \-ˌchīld\ *n* : a person for whom another person stands as sponsor at baptism and promises to see that the baptized person receives a Christian training : GODSON, GODDAUGHTER
god·daugh·ter \-ˌdȯt-ər\ *n* : a female godchild
god·dess \'gäd-əs\ *n* **1** : a female god **2** : a woman whose great charm or beauty arouses adoration
god·fa·ther \'gäd-ˌfäth-ər\ *n* : a man who stands as sponsor for a child at its baptism
god·head \-ˌhed\ *n* **1** : divine nature or essence : DIVINITY **2** *cap* **a** : ²GOD, DEITY **b** : the nature of God esp. as existing in three persons — used with *the*
god·hood \-ˌhu̇d\ *n* : DIVINITY
god·less \'gäd-ləs\ *adj* : not acknowledging a deity or divine law — **god·less·ness** *n*
god·like \-ˌlīk\ *adj* : resembling or having the qualities of God or a god : DIVINE — **god·like·ness** *n*
god·ling \-liŋ\ *n* : an inferior or local god
god·ly \-lē\ *adj* : PIOUS, DEVOUT — **god·li·ness** *n*
god·moth·er \-ˌməth-ər\ *n* : a woman who stands as sponsor for a child at its baptism
go·down \'gō-ˌdau̇n\ *n* : a warehouse in an oriental country
god·par·ent \'gäd-ˌpar-ənt, -ˌper-\ *n* : a sponsor at baptism
god·send \'gäd-ˌsend\ *n* : a desirable or needed thing or event that comes unexpectedly as if sent by God
god·son \-ˌsən\ *n* : a male godchild
God·speed \-'spēd\ *n* : a wish for success given to a person on parting
go·er \'gō(-ə)r\ *n* : one that goes
go–get·ter \'gō-ˌget-ər\ *n* : an aggressively enterprising person : HUSTLER — **go–get·ting** *adj or n*
¹gog·gle \'gäg-əl\ *vi* **gog·gled**; **gog·gling** \'gäg-(ə-)liŋ\ : to stare with wide or protuberant eyes — **gog·gler** \-(ə-)lər\ *n*
²goggle *adj* : PROTUBERANT, STARING — **gog·gly** \'gäg-(ə-)lē\ *adj*
gog·gle–eyed \ˌgäg-əl-'īd\ *adj* : having bulging or rolling eyes
gog·gles \'gäg-əlz\ *n pl* : large eyeglasses to protect the eyes (as from bright light or dust)
go in *vi* : ENTER — **go in for 1** : to make one's particular interest or specialty **2** : to take part in out of interest or liking
¹go·ing \'gō-iŋ\ *n* **1** : DEPARTURE **2** : the condition of the ground esp. for walking or driving **3** : advance toward an objective : PROGRESS
²going *adj* **1** : EXISTING, LIVING **2** : CURRENT, PREVAILING **3** : being successful and likely to continue successful
go·ings–on \ˌgō-iŋ-'zȯn, -'zän\ *n pl* : ACTIONS, EVENTS
goi·ter \'gȯit-ər\ *n* : an enlargement of the thyroid gland visible as a swelling of the front of the neck — **goi·trous** \'gȯi-trəs, 'gȯit-ə-rəs\ *adj*
gold \'gōld\ *n* **1** : a malleable ductile yellow trivalent and univalent metallic element that occurs chiefly free but also in a few minerals and is used esp. in coins and jewelry **2 a** : gold coins **b** : MONEY **3** : a variable color averaging deep yellow — **gold** *adj*
gold·brick \'gōl(d)-ˌbrik\ *n* : a person (as a soldier) who shirks assigned work — **goldbrick** *vi*
gold·en \'gōl-dən\ *adj* **1** : consisting of, relating to, or containing gold **2 a** : having the color of gold **b** : BLOND **3** : SHINING, LUSTROUS **4** : of a high degree of excellence : SUPERB **5** : FLOURISHING, PROSPEROUS **6** : radiantly youthful and vigorous **7** : FAVORABLE, ADVANTAGEOUS **8** : MELLOW, RESONANT
gold·en–ag·er \'gōl-dən-ˌāj-ər\ *n* : an elderly person usu. leading an active contented life
golden mean *n* : the medium between extremes : MODERATION
gold·en·rod \'gōl-dən-ˌräd\ *n* : any of numerous herbs related to the daisies but having tall slender stalks with many tiny usu. yellow flower heads
golden rule *n* : a rule that one should do to others as he would have others do to him
gold–filled \'gōl(d)-'fild\ *adj* : covered with a layer of gold
gold·finch \-ˌfinch\ *n* : an American finch the male of which becomes bright yellow and black in summer
gold·fish \-ˌfish\ *n* : a small usu. golden yellow or orange carp much used as an aquarium and pond fish
gold leaf *n* : a thin sheet of gold used esp. for gilding
gold·smith \'gōl(d)-ˌsmith\ *n* : one who makes or deals in articles of gold
gold standard *n* : a monetary standard under which the basic unit of currency is defined by a stated quantity of gold and which is usu. characterized by the coinage and circulation of gold
golf \'gälf, 'gȯlf\ *n* : a game played with a small ball and various clubs on a course having 9 or 18 holes
go·nad \'gō-ˌnad\ *n* : a primary sex gland : OVARY, TESTIS — **go·nad·al** \gō-'nad-ᵊl\ *adj*
gon·do·la \'gän-də-lə (*usual for sense 1*), gän-'dō-\ *n* **1** : a long narrow boat used on the canals of Venice **2** : a railroad car with no top used chiefly for hauling heavy bulk commodities **3** : an enclosure attached to the underside of an airship or balloon
gon·do·lier \ˌgän-də-'li(ə)r\ *n* : one who propels a gondola
gone \'gȯn\ *adj* **1** : ADVANCED, ABSORBED **2** : SINKING, WEAK
gon·fa·lon \'gän-fə-ˌlän\ *n* : a flag that hangs from a crosspiece or frame
gong \'gäŋ, 'gȯŋ\ *n* **1** : a metallic disk that produces a resounding tone when struck **2** : a flat saucer-shaped bell
gon·or·rhea \ˌgän-ə-'rē-ə\ *n* : a contagious inflammatory disease of the genital tract — **gon·or·rhe·al** \-'rē-əl\ *adj*
goo \'gü\ *n* : a viscid or sticky substance — **goo·ey** \'gü-ē\ *adj*
¹good \'gu̇d\ *adj* **bet·ter** \'bet-ər\; **best** \'best\ **1 a** (1) : of a favorable character or tendency (2) : BOUNTIFUL, FERTILE (3) : COMELY, ATTRACTIVE **b** (1) : SUITABLE, FIT (2) : SOUND, WHOLE (3) : not depreciated (4) : commercially reliable (5) : certain to last or live (6) : certain to pay or contribute (7) : certain to elicit a specified result **c** (1) : AGREEABLE, PLEASANT (2) : SALUTARY, WHOLESOME **d** (1) : CONSIDERABLE, AMPLE (2) : FULL **e** (1) : WELL-FOUNDED, COGENT (2) : TRUE (3) : ACTUALIZED, REAL (4) : recognized or valid esp. in law **f** (1) : ADEQUATE, SATISFACTORY (2) : conforming to a standard (3) : DISCRIMINATING, CHOICE **2 a** (1) : COMMENDABLE, VIRTUOUS, JUST (2) : RIGHT (3) : KIND, BENEVOLENT **b** : UPPER-CLASS **c** : COMPETENT, SKILLFUL **d** : LOYAL **3** : containing less fat and being less tender than higher grades — used of meat and esp. beef — **good and** : VERY, ENTIRELY
²good *n* **1 a** : something good **b** : praiseworthy character : GOODNESS **2** : PROSPERITY, BENEFIT, WELFARE **3 a** : something that has economic utility or satisfies an economic need or desire **b** *pl* : personal property (as one's clothing, furniture, automobile, or collection of rare coins) **c** *pl* : CLOTH **d** *pl* : WARES, COMMODITIES **4** : good persons — used with *the* **5** *pl* : proof of wrongdoing

³good *adv* : WELL
good–bye *or* **good–by** \gu̇d-ˈbī\ *n* : a concluding remark at parting — often used interjectionally
Good Friday *n* : the Friday before Easter observed as the anniversary of the crucifixion of Christ
good–heart·ed \ˈgu̇d-ˈhärt-əd\ *adj* : having a kindly generous disposition — **good–heart·ed·ly** *adv* — **good·heart·ed·ness** *n*
good–hu·mored \-ˈhyü-mərd, -ˈyü-\ *adj* : GOOD-NATURED, CHEERFUL — **good–hu·mored·ly** *adv* — **good–hu·mored·ness** *n*
good·ly \ˈgu̇d-lē\ *adj* **1** : of pleasing appearance **2** : LARGE, CONSIDERABLE
good–na·tured \ˈgu̇d-ˈnā-chərd\ *adj* : of a pleasant cheerful disposition — **good–na·tured·ly** *adv* — **good–na·tured·ness** *n*
good·ness \ˈgu̇d-nəs\ *n* : the quality or state of being good; *esp* : excellence of character
good–sized \ˈgu̇d-ˈsīzd\ *adj* : large enough : fairly large
good–tem·pered \-ˈtem-pərd\ *adj* : having an even temper
good·will \ˈgu̇d-ˈwil\ *n* **1** : kindly feeling : BENEVOLENCE **2** : the value of the trade a business has built up over a considerable time **3 a** : cheerful consent **b** : willing effort
goody \ˈgu̇d-ē\ *n, pl* **good·ies** : something that is particularly good to eat or otherwise attractive
goody–goody \ˌgu̇d-ē-ˈgu̇d-ē\ *adj* : affectedly good — **goody–goody** *n*
goof \ˈgüf\ *vb* : BLUNDER — **goof** *n*
go off *vi* **1** : EXPLODE **2** : to undergo decline or deterioration **3** : to follow the expected or desired course : PROCEED
goose \ˈgüs\ *n, pl* **geese** \ˈgēs\ **1 a** : any of numerous long-necked birds intermediate in size between the related swans and ducks **b** : a female goose as distinguished from a gander **2** : SIMPLETON, DOLT **3** *pl* **goos·es** : a tailor's smoothing iron with a gooseneck handle
goose·ber·ry \ˈgüs-ˌber-ē, ˈgüz-\ *n* : the acid usu. prickly fruit of any of several shrubs related to the currant
goose·flesh \ˈgüs-ˌflesh\ *n* : a roughening of the skin caused usu. by cold or fear
goose·neck \-ˌnek\ *n* : something (as a flexible jointed metal pipe) curved like the neck of a goose or U-shaped — **goose·necked** \-ˌnekt\ *adj*
goose step *n* : a straight-legged stiff-kneed step used by troops of some armies when passing in review — **goose–step** \ˈgüs-ˌstep\ *vi*
go out *vi* **1** : to go forth; *esp* : to leave one's house **2** : to become extinguished
go·pher \ˈgō-fər\ *n* **1** : a burrowing American land tortoise **2 a** : any of several burrowing American rodents with large cheek pouches **b** : a small striped ground squirrel of the prairie region of the U.S.
¹gore \ˈgō(ə)r\ *n* : BLOOD; *esp* : clotted blood
²gore *n* : a tapering or triangular piece (as of cloth in a skirt)
³gore *vt* **1** : to cut into a tapering triangular form **2** : to provide with a gore
⁴gore *vt* : to pierce or wound with a horn or tusk
¹gorge \ˈgȯrj\ *n* **1** : THROAT **2** : a narrow passage (as between two mountains) **3** : a mass of matter that chokes up a passage
²gorge *vb* : to eat greedily : stuff to capacity : GLUT — **gorg·er** *n*
gor·geous \ˈgȯr-jəs\ *adj* : resplendently beautiful — **gor·geous·ly** *adv* — **gor·geous·ness** *n*
go·ril·la \gə-ˈril-ə\ *n* : an anthropoid ape of west equatorial Africa related to but less erect and much larger than the chimpanzee
gor·man·dize \ˈgȯr-mən-ˌdīz\ *vb* : to eat greedily or ravenously — **gor·man·diz·er** *n*
gorse \ˈgȯrs\ *n* **1** : FURZE **2** : JUNIPER — **gorsy** \ˈgȯr-sē\ *adj*
gory \ˈgō(ə)r-ē\ *adj* **1** : covered with gore **2** : BLOODCURDLING, SENSATIONAL
gos·ling \ˈgäz-liŋ, ˈgȯz-, -lən\ *n* : a young goose
¹gos·pel \ˈgäs-pəl\ *n* **1 a** *often cap* : the Christian message concerning Christ, the kingdom of God, and salvation **b** *cap* : one of the first four New Testament books telling of the life, death, and resurrection of Jesus Christ; *also* : a similar apocryphal book **2** *cap* : a liturgical reading from one of the New Testament Gospels **3** : the message or teachings of a religious teacher **4** : something accepted as infallible truth or as a guiding principle
²gospel *adj* **1** : relating to or in accordance with the gospel : EVANGELICAL **2** : EVANGELISTIC **3** : of or relating to religious songs associated with evangelism and popular devotion
gos·sa·mer \ˈgäs-ə-mər, ˈgäz-\ *n* **1** : a film of cobwebs floating in air **2** : something light, delicate, or tenuous — **gossamer** *adj* — **gos·sa·mery** \-mə-rē\ *adj*
¹gos·sip \ˈgäs-əp\ *n* **1** : a person who habitually reveals personal or sensational facts **2 a** : rumor or report of an intimate nature **b** : chatty talk — **gos·sipy** \-ə-pē\ *adj*
²gossip *vi* : to relate gossip — **gos·sip·er** *n*
got *past of* GET
Goth·ic \ˈgäth-ik\ *adj* : of or relating to a style of architecture prevalent in western Europe from the middle 12th to the early 16th century
gotten *past part of* GET
¹gouge \ˈgau̇j\ *n* **1** : a chisel with a curved blade for scooping or cutting holes **2** : a hole or groove made with or as if with a gouge
²gouge *vt* **1** : to cut holes or grooves in with or as if with a gouge **2** : to force out (an eye) with the thumb **3** : to charge excessively : DEFRAUD, CHEAT — **goug·er** *n*
gou·lash \ˈgü-ˌläsh, -ˌlash\ *n* : a beef stew with onion, paprika, and caraway
gourd \ˈgōrd, ˈgu̇rd\ *n* **1** : any of a family of chiefly herbaceous tendril-bearing vines including the cucumber, melon, squash, and pumpkin **2** : the fruit of a gourd; *esp* : any of various hard-shelled inedible fruits often used for ornament or for vessels and utensils
gour·mand \ˈgu̇(ə)r-ˌmänd\ *n* **1** : one who is excessively fond of eating and drinking **2** : a luxurious eater : GOURMET — **gour·mand·ism** \ˈgu̇(ə)r-ˌmän-ˌdiz-əm, -mən-\ *n*
gour·met \-ˌmā\ *n* : a connoisseur in eating and drinking
gout \ˈgau̇t\ *n* : a disease marked by a painful inflammation and swelling of the joints — **gouty** \-ē\ *adj*
gov·ern \ˈgəv-ərn\ *vb* **1** : to exercise continuous sovereign or delegated authority over; *esp* : to control and direct the making and administration of policy in **2** : to control the speed of by automatic means **3 a** : to control, direct, or strongly influence the actions and conduct of **b** : to hold in check : RESTRAIN **4 a** : to require a word to be in a certain case or mood **b** : to require a certain case or mood **5** : to constitute a rule or law for **6** : to exercise authority : RULE — **gov·ern·a·ble** *adj*
gov·ern·ance \ˈgəv-ər-nən(t)s\ *n* : the exercise of control : GOVERNMENT
gov·ern·ess \ˈgəv-ər-nəs\ *n* : a woman who teaches and trains a child esp. in a private home
gov·ern·ment \ˈgəv-ər(n)-mənt\ *n* **1** : the act or process of governing; *esp* : authoritative direction or control **2 a** : the continuous exercise of authority over a political unit : RULE **b** : the making of policy as distinguished from the administration of policy decisions **3 a** : the organization, machinery, or agency through which a political unit exercises authority and performs functions and which is usu. classified according to the distribution of power within it **b** : the institutions, laws, and customs through which a political unit is governed **4** : the body of persons that constitutes the governing authority of a political unit — **government** *adj* — **gov·ern·men·tal** \ˌgəv-ər(n)-ˈment-ᵊl\ *adj* — **gov·ern·men·tal·ly** \-ᵊl-ē\ *adv*
gov·er·nor \ˈgəv-ə(r)-nər\ *n* **1** : one that governs: as **a** : one

that exercises authority esp. over an area or group **b** : an official elected or appointed to act as ruler, chief executive, or nominal head of a political unit (as a colony, state, or province) **c** : COMMANDANT **d** : the managing director and usu. the principal officer of an institution or organization **e** : a member of a group that directs or controls an institution or society **2** : TUTOR **3** : an attachment to a machine for automatic control of speed

gov·er·nor·ship \ˈgəv-ə(r)-nər-ˌship\ *n* **1** : the office or position of governor **2** : the term of office of a governor

gown \ˈgau̇n\ *n* **1 a** : a loose flowing outer garment formerly worn by men **b** : an official robe worn esp. by a judge, clergyman, or teacher **c** : a woman's dress; *esp* : one suitable for afternoon or evening wear **d** : a loose robe (as a dressing gown or a nightgown) **e** : a coverall worn in an operating room **2 a** : an office or profession symbolized by a distinctive robe **b** : a body of college students and faculty — **gown** *vt*

[1]**grab** \ˈgrab\ *vb* **grabbed**; **grab·bing** : to take hastily : CLUTCH, SNATCH — **grab·ber** *n*

[2]**grab** *n* **1 a** : a sudden snatch **b** : an unlawful seizure **c** : something grabbed **2** : a device for clutching an object

[1]**grace** \ˈgrās\ *n* **1 a** : help given man by God esp. in overcoming temptation or in leading a good life **b** : a state of freedom from sin and of love for God enjoyed through divine grace **c** : a virtue coming from God **2** : a short prayer at a meal asking a blessing or giving thanks **3 a** : KINDNESS, FAVOR **b** : a temporary respite granted from the performance of an obligation (as the payment of a debt) **c** : APPROVAL, ACCEPTANCE **4 a** : a charming trait or accomplishment **b** (1) : ATTRACTIVENESS, BEAUTY (2) : fitness or proportion of line or expression (3) : ease of movement : charm of bearing **5** — used as a title for a duke, a duchess, or an archbishop — **grace·ful** \-fəl\ *adj* — **grace·ful·ly** \-fə-lē\ *adv* — **grace·ful·ness** *n*

[2]**grace** *vt* **1** : HONOR **2** : ADORN, EMBELLISH

grace·less \ˈgrās-ləs\ *adj* : having no grace, charm, or elegance; *esp* : showing lack of feeling for what is fitting — **grace·less·ly** *adv* — **grace·less·ness** *n*

gra·cious \ˈgrā-shəs\ *adj* **1 a** : marked by kindness and courtesy **b** : GRACEFUL **c** : characterized by charm, good taste, and urbanity **2** : MERCIFUL, COMPASSIONATE — used conventionally of royalty and high nobility — **gra·cious·ly** *adv* — **gra·cious·ness** *n*

grack·le \ˈgrak-ᵊl\ *n* **1** : any of various Old World starlings **2** : any of several rather large American blackbirds with glossy iridescent black plumage

gra·da·tion \grā-ˈdā-shən\ *n* **1 a** : a series forming successive stages **b** : a step, degree, or stage in a series **2** : an advance by regular degrees **3** : the act or process of grading — **gra·da·tion·al** \-shnəl, -shən-ᵊl\ *adj* — **gra·da·tion·al·ly** \-ē\ *adv*

[1]**grade** \ˈgrād\ *n* **1** : a stage, step, or degree in a series, order, or ranking **2** : position in a scale of rank, quality, or order **3** : a class of things that are of the same rank, quality, or order **4 a** : a division of the school course representing a year's work **b** : the pupils in a school division **c** *pl* : the elementary school system **5** : a mark or rating esp. of accomplishment in school **6** : a standard of quality **7 a** : the degree of slope (as of a road, railroad track, or embankment) : SLOPE **b** : ground level **8** : a domestic animal with only one parent purebred

[2]**grade** *vb* **1** : to arrange in grades : SORT **2** : to make level or evenly sloping **3** : to give a grade to **4** : to assign to a grade **5** : to form a series having only slight differences

grade school *n* : a public school including the first six or the first eight grades

gra·di·ent \ˈgrād-ē-ənt\ *n* **1** : the rate of ascent or descent : INCLINATION **2** : a part (as of a road) sloping upward or downward : GRADE

grad·u·al \ˈgraj-(ə-w)əl\ *adj* **1** : proceeding by steps or degrees **2** : moving or changing by slight degrees — **grad·u·al·ly** \ˈgraj-ə-(wə-)lē\ *adv* — **grad·u·al·ness** \ˈgraj-(ə-w)əl-nəs\ *n*

[1]**grad·u·ate** \ˈgraj-ə-wət, -ˌwāt\ *n* **1** : a holder of an academic degree or diploma **2** : a graduated cup, cylinder, or flask for measuring contents

[2]**graduate** *adj* **1** : holding an academic degree or diploma **2** : of or relating to studies beyond the first or bachelor's degree

[3]**grad·u·ate** \ˈgraj-ə-ˌwāt\ *vb* **1** : to grant or receive an academic degree or diploma **2** : to admit to a particular standing or grade **3 a** : to mark with degrees of measurement **b** : to divide into grades, classes, or intervals **4** : to change gradually — **grad·u·a·tor** \-ˌwāt-ər\ *n*

grad·u·a·tion \ˌgraj-ə-ˈwā-shən\ *n* **1** : a mark on an instrument or vessel indicating degrees or quantity; *also* : these marks **2 a** : an act or process of graduating **b** : the ceremony or exercises marking the completion by a student of a course of study at a school or college : COMMENCEMENT **3** : arrangement in degrees or ranks

[1]**graft** \ˈgraft\ *vb* **1 a** : to insert a shoot from one plant into another plant so that they are joined and grow together **b** : to join one thing to another as if by grafting **2** : to gain money or advantage by dishonest means — **graft·er** *n*

[2]**graft** *n* **1 a** : a grafted plant **b** : the point of insertion of a scion upon a stock **2 a** : the act of grafting **b** : something used in grafting; as (1) : SCION (2) : living tissue used in surgical grafting **3 a** : the getting of money or advantage by dishonest means through misuse of an official position **b** : the money or advantage gained dishonestly

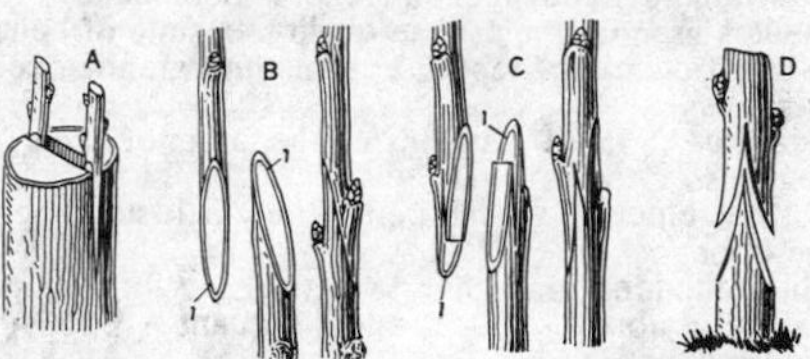

graft 1b: *A* cleft, *B* splice, *C* whip, *D* saddle, *1* cambium

Grail \ˈgrāl\ *n* : the cup or platter used according to medieval legend by Christ at the Last Supper and thereafter the object of knightly quests

[1]**grain** \ˈgrān\ *n* **1 a** : a seed or fruit of a cereal grass **b** : the seeds or fruits of various food plants and esp. the cereal grasses **c** : plants producing grain **2** : a small hard particle or crystal **3 a** : a granulated surface or appearance **b** : the outer or hair side of a skin or hide **4** : a unit of weight based on the weight of a grain of wheat **5 a** : the arrangement of fibers in wood **b** : appearance or texture due to constituent particles or fibers **6** : natural disposition : TEMPER — **grained** \ˈgrānd\ *adj* — **with a grain of salt** : SKEPTICALLY

[2]**grain** *vt* **1** : to form into grains : GRANULATE **2** : to paint in imitation of the grain of wood or stone — **grain·er** *n*

grain·field \ˈgrān-ˌfēld\ *n* : a field where grain is grown

grainy \ˈgrā-nē\ *adj* **1** : consisting of or resembling grains : GRANULAR **2** : resembling the grain of wood — **grain·i·ness** *n*

gram *or* **gramme** \ˈgram\ *n* : a metric unit of mass and weight equal to 1/1000 kilogram and nearly equal to one cubic centimeter of water at its maximum density

gram·mar \ˈgram-ər\ *n* **1** : the study of the classes of words, their inflections, and their functions and relations in the sentence **2** : the facts of language with which grammar deals **3 a** : a grammar textbook **b** : speech or writing evaluated according to its conformity to grammatical rules — **gram·mar·i·an** \grə-ˈmer-ē-ən\ *n*

grammar school *n* **1 a** : a secondary school emphasizing Latin and Greek in preparation for college **b** : a British college preparatory school **2** : an elementary school

gram·mat·i·cal \grə-'mat-i-kəl\ *adj* **1** : of or relating to grammar **2** : conforming to the rules of grammar — **gram·mat·i·cal·ly** \-k(ə-)lē\ *adv*

gra·na·ry \'grān-(ə-)rē, 'gran-\ *n, pl* **-ries** **1** : a storehouse for threshed grain **2** : a region producing grain in abundance

¹grand \'grand\ *adj* **1** : higher in rank than others of the same class : FOREMOST, PRINCIPAL **2** : great in size **3** : INCLUSIVE, COMPLETE **4 a** : marked by magnificence or splendor **b** : showing wealth or high social standing **5** : IMPRESSIVE, STATELY **6** : very good : FINE — **grand·ly** *adv* — **grand·ness** *n*

²grand *n* : GRAND PIANO

gran·dam \'gran-ˌdam, -dəm\ *or* **gran·dame** \-ˌdām, -dəm\ *n* **1** : GRANDMOTHER **2** : an old woman

grand·aunt \'gran-'dant, -'dȧnt\ *n* : an aunt of one's father or mother

grand·child \'gran(d)-ˌchīld\ *n* : a child of one's son or daughter

grand·daugh·ter \'gran-ˌdȯt-ər\ *n* : a daughter of one's son or daughter

grand duchess *n* **1** : the wife or widow of a grand duke **2** : a woman who rules a grand duchy in her own right

grand duchy *n* : the territory or dominion of a grand duke or grand duchess

grand duke *n* **1** : the sovereign duke of any of various European states **2** : a son or male descendant of a Russian czar

gran·dee \gran-'dē\ *n* : a man of elevated rank or station; *esp* : a high-ranking Spanish or Portuguese nobleman

gran·deur \'gran-jər\ *n* **1** : the quality or state of being grand : awe-inspiring magnificence **2** : something grand or conducive to grandness

grand·fa·ther \'gran(d)-ˌfät͟h-ər\ *n* : the father of one's father or mother; *also* : ANCESTOR 1

grandfather clock *n* : a tall pendulum clock standing directly on the floor

gran·dil·o·quence \gran-'dil-ə-kwən(t)s\ *n* : lofty or pompous eloquence : BOMBAST — **gran·dil·o·quent** \-kwənt\ *adj* — **gran·dil·o·quent·ly** *adv*

gran·di·ose \'gran-dē-ˌōs\ *adj* **1** : impressive because of uncommon largeness, scope, effect, or grandeur **2** : characterized by affectation of grandeur or splendor or by absurd exaggeration — **gran·di·ose·ly** *adv* — **gran·di·os·i·ty** \ˌgran-dē-'äs-ət-ē\ *n*

grand jury *n* : a jury that chiefly examines accusations of crime made against persons and if the evidence warrants makes formal charges on which the accused persons are later tried

grand·moth·er \'gran(d)-ˌmət͟h-ər\ *n* : the mother of one's father or mother; *also* : a female ancestor

grand·neph·ew \-'nef-yü\ *n* : a grandson of one's brother or sister

grand·niece \-'nēs\ *n* : a granddaughter of one's brother or sister

grand opera *n* : opera in which the plot is elaborated as in serious drama and the entire text set to music

grand·par·ent \'gran(d)-ˌpar-ənt\ *n* : a parent of one's father or mother

grand piano *n* : a piano with horizontal frame and strings

grand·son \'gran(d)-ˌsən\ *n* : a son of one's son or daughter

grand·stand \-ˌstand\ *n* : a usu. roofed stand for spectators at a racecourse or stadium

grand·un·cle \'gran-'dəŋ-kəl\ *n* : an uncle of one's father or mother

grange \'grānj\ *n* : FARM; *esp* : a farmhouse with outbuildings

gran·ite \'gran-ət\ *n* : a very hard igneous rock of visibly crystalline texture formed essentially of quartz and orthoclase or microcline and used for building and for monuments

gran·ite·ware \-ˌwa(ə)r\ *n* : enameled ironware

gran·ny *or* **gran·nie** \'gran-ē\ *n, pl* **grannies** **1** : GRANDMOTHER **2** : a fussy person

¹grant \'grant\ *vt* **1 a** : to consent to : ALLOW **b** : to permit as a right, privilege, or favor **2** : to give the possession or benefit of formally or legally **3** : to concede (something not yet proved) to be true — **grant·er** *n* — **grant·or** \'grant-ər, -ˌȯr\ *n*

²grant *n* **1** : the act of granting **2** : something granted; *esp* : a gift for a particular purpose **3 a** : a transfer of property by deed or writing **b** : the instrument by which such a transfer is made; *also* : the property so transferred

grant·ee \grant-'ē\ *n* : one to whom a grant is made

grants·man·ship \'gran(t)s-mən-ˌship\ *n* : the art of applying for and receiving grants (as for research)

gran·u·lar \'gran-yə-lər\ *adj* : consisting of or appearing to consist of granules : having a grainy texture — **gran·u·lar·i·ty** \ˌgran-yə-'lar-ət-ē\ *n*

gran·u·late \'gran-yə-ˌlāt\ *vb* **1** : to form or crystallize into grains or granules **2** : to collect into grains or granules — **gran·u·lat·ed** *adj*

gran·u·la·tion \ˌgran-yə-'lā-shən\ *n* **1** : the act or process of granulating : the condition of being granulated **2** : a product of granulating (as a tiny knot of vascular tissue in a healing wound)

gran·ule \'gran-ˌyül\ *n* : a small grain or particle

grape \'grāp\ *n* **1** : a smooth-skinned juicy greenish white to deep red or purple berry eaten dried or fresh as a fruit or fermented to produce wine **2** : a woody vine widely grown for its clustered grapes **3** : GRAPESHOT

grape·fruit \-ˌfrüt\ *n* : a large citrus fruit with a bitter yellow rind and a highly flavored somewhat acid juicy pulp

grape·shot \-ˌshät\ *n* : a cluster of small iron balls used as a cannon charge

grape·vine \-ˌvīn\ *n* **1** : GRAPE 2 **2 a** : RUMOR, REPORT; *esp* : a baseless rumor **b** (1) : an informal means of circulating information or gossip (2) : a secret source of information

¹graph \'graf\ *n* **1** : a diagram that represents change in one variable factor in comparison with that of one or more other factors **2** : the collection of all points whose coordinates satisfy a given functional relation

²graph *vt* **1** : to represent by a graph **2** : to plot upon a graph

¹graph·ic \'graf-ik\ *or* **graph·i·cal** \-i-kəl\ *adj* **1** : being written, drawn, or engraved **2 a** : described or related with vivid clarity or striking imaginative power **b** : sharply outlined or delineated **3 a** : of or relating to the pictorial arts **b** : of, relating to, or involving methods of reproduction (as painting, engraving, etching, lithography, or photography) **4** : of, relating to, or represented by a graph **5** : of or relating to writing — **graph·i·cal·ly** \-i-k(ə-)lē\ *adv* — **graph·ic·ness** *n*

²graphic *n* **1 a** : a product of graphic art **b** *pl* : the graphic media **2** : a picture, map, or graph used for illustration or demonstration

graphic arts *n pl* : the fine and applied arts of representation, decoration, and writing or printing on flat surfaces together with the techniques and crafts associated with each

graph·ite \'graf-ˌīt\ *n* : a soft black carbon with a metallic luster that conducts electricity and is used in making lead pencils, as a dry lubricant, and for electrodes — **gra·phit·ic** \gra-'fit-ik\ *adj*

grap·nel \'grap-nᵊl\ *n* : a small anchor with two or more claws used in dragging or grappling operations and for anchoring a small boat

¹grap·ple \'grap-əl\ *n* **1** : the act of grappling or seizing : GRIP, HOLD **2** : an implement used or designed for grappling; *esp* : GRAPNEL

²grapple *vb* **grap·pled**; **grap·pling** \'grap-(ə-)liŋ\ **1** : to seize or hold with or as if with a hooked implement **2** : to seize one another : struggle in or as if in a close fight **3** : to attempt to deal : COPE — **grap·pler** \-(ə-)lər\ *n*

[1]**grasp** \'grasp\ *vb* **1** : to make the motion of seizing : CLUTCH **2** : to take or seize firmly **3** : to clasp or embrace with or as if with the fingers or arms **4** : to lay hold of with the mind : COMPREHEND — **grasp·a·ble** *adj* — **grasp·er** *n*

[2]**grasp** *n* **1 a** : HANDLE **b** : EMBRACE **2** : HOLD, CONTROL **3 a** : the reach of the arms **b** : the power of seizing and holding **4** : COMPREHENSION

grasp·ing \'gras-piŋ\ *adj* : AVARICIOUS — **grasp·ing·ness** *n*

[1]**grass** \'gras\ *n* **1** : herbage suitable or used for grazing animals **2** : any of a large group of plants with jointed stems and slender leaves **3** : grass-covered land — **grass·like** *adj*

[2]**grass** *vt* : to seed to grass

grass·hop·per \'gras-ˌhäp-ər\ *n* : any of numerous plant-eating insects having the hind legs adapted for leaping

grass·land \-ˌland\ *n* : land covered naturally or under cultivation with grasses and other low-growing herbs

grass roots *n pl* : society at the local and popular level esp. in rural areas as distinguished from the centers of political leadership

grassy \'gras-ē\ *adj* **1** : containing or covered or abounding with grass **2** : resembling grass

[1]**grate** \'grāt\ *n* **1** : a frame containing parallel or crossed bars (as in a prison window) **2** : a frame or basket of iron bars for holding burning fuel (as in a furnace or a fireplace)

[2]**grate** *vb* **1** : to make into small particles by rubbing against something rough **2** : to grind or rub against something with a rasping noise **3** : to have a harsh or rasping effect — **grat·er** *n*

grate·ful \'grāt-fəl\ *adj* **1 a** : appreciative of benefits received **b** : expressing gratitude **2 a** : affording pleasure or contentment : PLEASING **b** : pleasing by reason of comfort supplied or discomfort alleviated — **grate·ful·ly** \-fə-lē\ *adv* — **grate·ful·ness** *n*

grat·i·fi·ca·tion \ˌgrat-ə-fə-'kā-shən\ *n* **1** : the act of gratifying : the state of being gratified **2** : a source of satisfaction or pleasure

grat·i·fy \'grat-ə-ˌfī\ *vt* **-fied**; **-fy·ing** **1** : to give or be a source of pleasure or satisfaction to **2** : to confer a favor on : INDULGE

grat·ing \'grāt-iŋ\ *n* : a partition, covering, or frame of parallel bars or crossbars : GRATE

gra·tis \'grāt-əs, 'grat-\ *adv* (*or adj*) : without charge or recompense : FREE

grat·i·tude \'grat-ə-ˌt(y)üd\ *n* : the state of being grateful : THANKFULNESS

gra·tu·i·tous \grə-'t(y)ü-ət-əs\ *adj* **1** : done or provided without return or expectation of return or payment; *also* : acting without compensation **2** : not called for by the circumstances : UNWARRANTED — **gra·tu·i·tous·ly** *adv* — **gra·tu·i·tous·ness** *n*

gra·tu·i·ty \grə-'t(y)ü-ət-ē\ *n, pl* **-ties** : something given freely; *esp* : something given in return for a favor or service

gra·va·men \grə-'vām-ən, -'väm-\ *n, pl* **-vamens** *or* **-va·mi·na** \-'vam-ə-nə, -'vām-, -'väm-\ : the basic or significant part of a grievance or complaint

[1]**grave** \'grāv\ *vt* **graved**; **grav·en** \'grā-vən\ *or* **graved**; **grav·ing** **1 a** : to carve or shape with a chisel : SCULPTURE **b** : to carve or cut (as letters or figures) into a hard surface : ENGRAVE **2** : to impress or fix (as a thought) deeply

[2]**grave** *n* : an excavation for burial of a body; *also* : TOMB

[3]**grave** \'grāv, *in sense 4 also* 'gräv\ *adj* **1 a** : meriting serious consideration : IMPORTANT **b** : threatening great harm or danger : MORTAL **2** : dignified in appearance or demeanor : SOLEMN, SERIOUS **3** : drab in color : SOMBER **4** : of, marked by, or being an accent mark having the form ` — **grave·ly** *adv* — **grave·ness** *n*

[4]**gra·ve** \'gräv-(ˌ)ā\ *adv* (*or adj*) : in a slow and solemn manner — used as a direction in music

[1]**grav·el** \'grav-əl\ *n* : loose rounded fragments of rock coarser than sand

[2]**gravel** *vt* **grav·eled** *or* **grav·elled**; **grav·el·ing** *or* **grav·el·ling** \'grav-(ə-)liŋ\ : to cover or spread with gravel

grav·el·ly \'grav-(ə-)lē\ *adj* **1** : of, containing, or covered with gravel **2** : having a harsh grating sound

grav·er \'grā-vər\ *n* **1** : ENGRAVER, SCULPTOR **2** : any of various cutting or shaving tools

grave·stone \'grāv-ˌstōn\ *n* : a burial monument

grave·yard \-ˌyärd\ *n* : CEMETERY

grav·id \'grav-əd\ *adj* : PREGNANT — **gra·vid·i·ty** \gra-'vid-ət-ē\ *n* — **grav·id·ly** *adv*

grav·i·tate \'grav-ə-ˌtāt\ *vi* **1** : to move or tend to move under the influence of gravitation **2** : to move toward something

grav·i·ta·tion \ˌgrav-ə-'tā-shən\ *n* **1 a** : a natural force of attraction that tends to draw bodies together **b** : the action or process of gravitating **2** : an attraction or tendency toward something — **grav·i·ta·tion·al** \-shnəl, -shən-ᵊl\ *adj* — **grav·i·ta·tion·al·ly** \-ē\ *adv* — **grav·i·ta·tive** \'grav-ə-ˌtāt-iv\ *adj*

grav·i·ty \'grav-ət-ē\ *n, pl* **-ties** **1 a** : dignity or sobriety of bearing **b** : IMPORTANCE, SIGNIFICANCE; *esp* : SERIOUSNESS **2** : WEIGHT — used chiefly in the phrase *center of gravity* **3** : the gravitational attraction of the earth's mass for bodies at or near its surface — **gravity** *adj*

gra·vure \grə-'vyu̇(ə)r, grā-\ *n* **1 a** : a process for producing an intaglio printing plate on wood or copper **b** : a gravure plate or print **2** : PHOTOGRAVURE

gra·vy \'grā-vē\ *n, pl* **gravies** **1** : a sauce made from the thickened and seasoned juices of cooked meat **2** : unearned or illicit gain : GRAFT

[1]**gray** \'grā\ *adj* **1** : of the color gray; *also* : dull in color **2** : having gray hair **3** : dull in mood or outlook : CHEERLESS, DISMAL — **gray·ness** *n*

[2]**gray** *n* **1** : something of a gray color **2** : one of the series of neutral colors ranging between black and white

[3]**gray** *vb* : to make or become gray

gray·beard \'grā-ˌbi(ə)rd\ *n* : an old man

gray·ish \'grā-ish\ *adj* **1** : somewhat gray **2** : low in saturation

gray·ling \'grā-liŋ\ *n, pl* **grayling** : any of several freshwater fishes related to the trouts and valued for food and sport

gray matter *n* : neural tissue esp. of the brain and spinal cord that contains nerve-cell bodies as well as nerve fibers and has a brownish gray color

[1]**graze** \'grāz\ *vb* **1** : to feed on growing herbage **2** : to feed or put cattle to feed on the herbage of **3** : to put to graze

[2]**graze** *vt* **1** : to rub or touch lightly in passing : touch against and glance off **2** : to scratch or scrape by rubbing against something

[3]**graze** *n* : a scraping along a surface or an abrasion made by it; *esp* : a superficial skin injury

[1]**grease** \'grēs\ *n* **1** : rendered animal fat **2** : oily matter **3** : a thick lubricant

[2]**grease** \'grēs, 'grēz\ *vt* **1** : to smear or daub with grease **2** : to lubricate with grease — **greas·er** *n*

grease·paint \'grēs-ˌpānt\ *n* : theater makeup

greasy \'grē-sē, -zē\ *adj* **1** : smeared with grease **2** : containing grease **3** : resembling grease or oil : SMOOTH, SLIPPERY — **greas·i·ly** \-sə-lē, -zə-\ *adv* — **greas·i·ness** \-sē-nəs, -zē-\ *n*

great \'grāt, *in South also* 'gre(ə)t\ *adj* **1** : large in size : not small or little **2** : large in number : NUMEROUS **3** : long continued **4** : much beyond the average or ordinary : MIGHTY, HEAVY, INTENSE **5** : EMINENT, DISTINGUISHED **6** : remarkable in knowledge of or skill in something **7** : much favored or much used **8** : EXCELLENT, FINE **9** : more distant in relationship by one generation — **great·ly** *adv* — **great·ness** *n*

great–aunt \'grāt-'ant, -'ȧnt\ *n* : GRANDAUNT

great·coat \'grāt-ˌkōt\ *n* : a heavy overcoat

great·heart·ed \'grāt-'härt-əd\ *adj* **1** : COURAGEOUS **2** : MAGNANIMOUS — **great·heart·ed·ly** *adv* — **great·heart·ed·ness** *n*

great–neph·ew \-'nef-yü\ *n* : GRANDNEPHEW

great–niece \-'nēs\ *n* : GRANDNIECE

great power *n* : one of the nations that figure most decisively in international affairs
great–un·cle \-'əŋ-kəl\ *n* : GRANDUNCLE
greave \'grēv\ *n* : armor for the leg below the knee — usu. used in pl.
grebe \'grēb\ *n* : any of a family of swimming and diving birds closely related to the loons
greed \'grēd\ *n* : excessive or blameworthy acquisitiveness : AVARICE
greedy \'grēd-ē\ *adj* **1** : having a driving appetite for food or drink : very hungry **2** : having an eager and often selfish desire or longing **3** : wanting more than one needs or more than one's fair share (as of food or wealth) — **greed·i·ly** \'grēd-ᵊl-ē\ *adv* — **greed·i·ness** \'grēd-ē-nəs\ *n*
Greek cross \'grēk-\ *n* : a cross having an upright and a transverse shaft equal in length and intersecting at their middles
Greek fire *n* : an incendiary composition of uncertain ingredients that burn in water
Greek Orthodox *adj* : Eastern Orthodox
¹green \'grēn\ *adj* **1** : of the color green **2 a** : covered by green foliage or herbage **b** : consisting of green plants or of the leafy part of a plant **3 a** : YOUTHFUL, VIGOROUS **b** : FRESH, NEW **4** : not fully grown or ripe **5** : marked by a sickly appearance **6 a** : not fully processed or treated **b** : not being in condition for a particular use or activity **7 a** : lacking training, knowledge, or experience **b** : GULLIBLE, NAÏVE — **green·ish** \'grē-nish\ *adj* — **green·ly** *adv* — **green·ness** *n*
²green *n* **1** : a color whose hue is somewhat less yellow than that of growing fresh grass or of the emerald or is that of the part of the spectrum lying between blue and yellow **2** : something of a green color **3 a** : green vegetation **b** *pl* : leafy parts of plants used for some purpose (as ornament or food) **4** : a grassy plain or plot; *esp* : a grassy area at the end of a golf fairway containing the hole into which the ball must be played — **greeny** \'grē-nē\ *adj*
green·back \'grēn-ˌbak\ *n* : a legal-tender note issued by the U.S. government; *esp* : one without gold or silver backing issued during the Civil War
green·ery \'grēn-(ə-)rē\ *n, pl* **-er·ies** : green foliage or plants : VERDURE
green·horn \'grēn-ˌhȯrn\ *n* : an inexperienced person; *esp* : one easily tricked or cheated
green·house \-ˌhau̇s\ *n* : a glassed enclosure used for the cultivation or protection of tender plants
green·sward \'grēn-ˌswȯrd\ *n* : turf green with growing grass
green thumb *n* : an unusual ability to make plants grow — **green–thumbed** \'grēn-'thəmd\ *adj*
green·wood \'grēn-ˌwu̇d\ *n* : a forest green with foliage
greet \'grēt\ *vt* **1** : to address with expressions of kind wishes : HAIL **2** : to meet or react to in a specified manner **3** : to be perceived by — **greet·er** *n*
greet·ing \'grēt-iŋ\ *n* **1** : a salutation at meeting **2** : an expression of good wishes — usu. used in pl.
gre·gar·i·ous \gri-'gar-ē-əs\ *adj* **1** : tending to associate with others of one's kind : SOCIAL **2** : habitually living or moving with others of one's own kind : tending to flock together — **gre·gar·i·ous·ly** *adv* — **gre·gar·i·ous·ness** *n*
grem·lin \'grem-lən\ *n* : a small gnome held to be responsible for malfunction of equipment esp. in an airplane
gre·nade \grə-'nād\ *n* **1** : a small bomb filled with a destructive agent (as gas, high explosive, or incendiary chemicals) and made to be hurled often by hand **2** : a container (as of glass) of volatile chemicals that can be burst by throwing (as in extinguishing a fire)
gren·a·dier \ˌgren-ə-'di(ə)r\ *n* : a member of a European regiment formerly armed with grenades
grew *past of* GROW
grey·hound \'grā-ˌhau̇nd\ *n* : a tall slender graceful smooth-coated dog noted for swiftness and keen sight and used for coursing game and racing
grid \'grid\ *n* **1** : GRATING **2** : a perforated or ridged metal plate used as a conductor in a storage battery **3** : an electron tube electrode with openings used for controlling the flow of electrons between other electrodes **4** : GRIDIRON 2
grid·dle \'grid-ᵊl\ *n* : a flat surface or pan on which food is cooked by dry heat
griddle cake *n* : a flat cake made of thin batter and cooked on both sides on a griddle
grid·iron \'grid-ˌī(-ə)rn\ *n* **1** : a grate for broiling food **2** : something consisting of or covered with a network; *esp* : a football field
grief \'grēf\ *n* **1** : deep sorrow : SADNESS, DISTRESS **2** : a cause of sorrow **3** : MISHAP, DISASTER
griev·ance \'grē-vən(t)s\ *n* **1** : a cause of distress (as an unsatisfactory working condition) affording reason for complaint or resistance **2** : the formal expression of a grievance : COMPLAINT
grieve \'grēv\ *vb* **1** : to cause grief or sorrow to : cause to suffer : DISTRESS **2** : to feel grief : SORROW — **griev·er** *n*
griev·ous \'grē-vəs\ *adj* **1** : OPPRESSIVE, ONEROUS **2** : causing or characterized by esp. severe pain, suffering, or sorrow **3** : SERIOUS, GRAVE — **griev·ous·ly** *adv* — **griev·ous·ness** *n*
grif·fin *or* **grif·fon** \'grif-ən\ *n* : a fabulous animal typically half eagle and half lion
¹grill \'gril\ *vt* **1** : to broil on a grill **2 a** : to torment as if by broiling **b** : to question intensely
²grill *n* **1** : a cooking utensil of parallel bars on which food is exposed to heat **2** : food that is broiled usu. on a grill **3** : a restaurant featuring broiled foods
grille *or* **grill** \'gril\ *n* **1** : a grating forming a barrier or screen **2** : an opening covered with a grille
grill·work \'gril-ˌwərk\ *n* : work constituting or resembling a grille
grim \'grim\ *adj* **1** : CRUEL, SAVAGE, FIERCE **2 a** : harsh and forbidding in appearance **b** : ghastly, repellent, or sinister in character **3** : UNFLINCHING, UNYIELDING — **grim·ly** *adv* — **grim·ness** *n*
grim·ace \'grim-əs, grim-'ās\ *n* : a twisting or distortion of the face or features expressive usu. of disgust or disapproval — **grimace** *vi*
grime \'grīm\ *n* : soot, smut, or dirt adhering to or embedded in a surface — **grime** *vt*
grimy \'grī-mē\ *adj* : full of or covered with grime : DIRTY — **grim·i·ness** *n*
grin \'grin\ *vi* **grinned**; **grin·ning** : to draw back the lips so as to show the teeth esp. in amusement or laughter — **grin** *n*
¹grind \'grīnd\ *vb* **ground** \'grau̇nd\; **grind·ing** **1** : to reduce to powder or small fragments by friction (as in a mill or with the teeth) **2** : to wear down, polish, or sharpen by friction : WHET **3** : to press with a grating noise : GRIT **4** : OPPRESS, HARASS **5 a** : to operate or produce by turning a crank **b** : to produce in a laborious and mechanical way **6** : to move with difficulty or friction esp. so as to make a grating noise **7** : DRUDGE; *esp* : to study hard
²grind *n* **1** : an act of grinding **2 a** : monotonous labor or routine; *esp* : intensive study **b** : a student who studies excessively **3** : the result of grinding; *esp* : the size of particle obtained by grinding
grind·er \'grīn-dər\ *n* **1 a** : MOLAR **b** *pl* : TEETH **2** : one that grinds
grind·stone \'grīn-ˌstōn\ *n* : a flat circular stone of natural sandstone that revolves on an axle and is used for grinding, shaping, or smoothing
¹grip \'grip\ *vt* **gripped**; **grip·ping** **1** : to seize firmly **2** : to hold strongly the interest of
²grip *n* **1 a** : a strong or tenacious grasp **b** : strength in gripping

c : a mode of clasping the hand by which members of a secret order recognize or greet one another d : arrangement of the hands in grasping 2 a : CONTROL, MASTERY b : mental grasp : UNDERSTANDING 3 : a part or device for gripping 4 : a part by which something is grasped; *esp* : HANDLE 5 : SUITCASE

[1]**gripe** \'grīp\ *vb* 1 : SEIZE, GRIP 2 a : AFFLICT, DISTRESS b : IRRITATE, VEX 3 : to cause or experience spasms of pain in the bowels 4 : COMPLAIN — **grip·er** *n*

[2]**gripe** *n* 1 : CLUTCH, GRASP; *also* : CONTROL, MASTERY 2 a : AFFLICTION b : COMPLAINT 3 : a spasm of intestinal pain 4 : HANDLE, GRIP 5 : a device (as a brake) for grasping or holding

grippe \'grip\ *n* : an acute febrile virus disease identical with or resembling influenza — **grippy** \'grip-ē\ *adj*

gris·ly \'griz-lē\ *adj* : HORRIBLE, GRUESOME — **gris·li·ness** *n*

grist \'grist\ *n* : grain to be ground or already ground

gris·tle \'gris-əl\ *n* : CARTILAGE — **gris·tli·ness** \'gris-(ə-)lē-nəs\ *n* — **gris·tly** \'gris-(ə-)lē\ *adj*

grist·mill \'grist-ˌmil\ *n* : a mill for grinding grain

[1]**grit** \'grit\ *n* 1 : a hard sharp granule (as of sand); *also* : material (as many abrasives) composed of such granules 2 : firmness of mind or spirit : unyielding courage

[2]**grit** *vb* **grit·ted**; **grit·ting** : to grind or cause to grind : GRATE

grits \'grits\ *n pl* : coarsely ground hulled grain

grit·ty \'grit-ē\ *adj* 1 : containing or resembling grit 2 : courageously persistent : PLUCKY — **grit·ti·ness** *n*

griz·zled \'griz-əld\ *adj* : sprinkled, streaked, or mixed with gray

[1]**griz·zly** \'griz-lē\ *adj* : GRIZZLED

[2]**grizzly** *n, pl* **grizzlies** : GRIZZLY BEAR

grizzly bear *n* : a large powerful usu. brownish yellow bear of the uplands of western No. America

groan \'grōn\ *vb* 1 : to utter a deep moan of pain, grief, or annoyance 2 : to make a harsh sound under sudden or prolonged strain — **groan** *n* — **groan·er** *n*

groat \'grōt\ *n* : a former British coin worth four pennies

gro·cer \'grō-sər\ *n* : a dealer in staple foodstuffs and household supplies

gro·cery \'grōs-(ə-)rē\ *n, pl* **-cer·ies** 1 *pl* : foodstuffs sold by a grocer 2 : a grocer's store

grog \'gräg\ *n* : alcoholic liquor; *esp* : liquor (as rum) cut with water — **grog·gery** \'gräg-ə-rē\ *n*

grog·gy \'gräg-ē\ *adj* : being weak and dazed and unsteady on the legs or in action — **grog·gi·ly** \'gräg-ə-lē\ *adv* — **grog·gi·ness** \'gräg-ē-nəs\ *n*

groin \'gròin\ *n* 1 : the fold marking the juncture of the lower abdomen and thigh; *also* : the region of this line 2 : the projecting curved line along which two intersecting structural vaults meet

grom·met \'gräm-ət, 'grəm-\ *n* 1 : a ring of rope 2 : an eyelet of firm material to strengthen or protect an opening

[1]**groom** \'grüm, 'grům\ *n* 1 : a male servant; *esp* : one in charge of horses 2 : BRIDEGROOM

[2]**groom** *vb* 1 : to clean and care for (an animal) 2 : to make neat, attractive, or acceptable : POLISH

grooms·man \'grümz-mən, 'grůmz-\ *n* : a male friend who attends a bridegroom at his wedding

groove \'grüv\ *n* 1 : a long narrow channel or depression 2 : a fixed routine : RUT — **groove** *vt* — **in the groove** : in top form

grope \'grōp\ *vb* 1 : to feel about or cast about blindly or uncertainly in search 2 : to feel one's way by groping

[1]**gross** \'grōs\ *adj* 1 a : glaringly noticeable b : OUT-AND-OUT, UTTER c : SHAMEFUL 2 a : BIG, BULKY; *esp* : excessively fat b : excessively luxuriant : RANK 3 a : GENERAL, BROAD b : consisting of an overall total exclusive of deductions 4 : EARTHY, CARNAL 5 : not fastidious in taste : UNDISCRIMINATING 6 : lacking knowledge or culture : UNREFINED 7 : COARSE, VULGAR — **gross·ly** *adv* — **gross·ness** *n*

[2]**gross** *n* : an overall total exclusive of deductions (as for taxes or expenses)

[3]**gross** *vt* : to earn (an overall total) exclusive of deductions

[4]**gross** *n, pl* **gross** : a total of 12 dozen things

gross national product *n* : the total value of the goods and services produced in a nation during a year

grot \'grät\ *n* : GROTTO

[1]**gro·tesque** \grō-'tesk\ *adj* 1 : combining (as in a painting or poem) details never found together in nature and rarely in art : using distortion and incongruity for artistic effect 2 : absurdly awkward or incongruous — **gro·tesque·ly** *adv* — **gro·tesque·ness** *n*

[2]**grotesque** *n* : something that is grotesque

grot·to \'grät-ō\ *n, pl* **grottoes** 1 : CAVE 2 : an artificial recess or structure made to resemble a natural cave

grouch \'graůch\ *n* 1 : a fit of bad temper 2 : an habitually irritable or complaining person — **grouch** *vi* — **grouch·i·ly** \'graů-chə-lē\ *adv* — **grouch·i·ness** \-chē-nəs\ *n* — **grouchy** \-chē\ *adj*

[1]**ground** \'graůnd\ *n* 1 a : the bottom of a body of water b *pl* : sediment at the bottom of a liquid : LEES 2 : a basis for belief, action, or argument 3 a : a surrounding area : BACKGROUND b : material that serves as a substratum : FOUNDATION 4 a : the surface of the earth b : an area used for a particular purpose c *pl* : the area around and belonging to a building 5 : SOIL, EARTH 6 a : an object that makes an electrical connection with the earth b : a large conducting body (as the earth) used as a common return for an electric circuit

[2]**ground** *vb* 1 : to bring to or place on the ground 2 a : to provide a reason or justification for b : to instruct in fundamentals 3 : to connect electrically with a ground 4 : to restrict to the ground 5 : to run aground 6 : to hit a grounder

[3]**ground** *past of* GRIND

ground cover *n* : low plants that cover the ground (as in a forest or as a substitute for turf); *also* : a plant used as ground cover

ground crew *n* : the mechanics and technicians who maintain and service an airplane

ground·er \'graůn-dər\ *n* : a baseball hit on the ground

ground floor *n* : the floor of a house most nearly on a level with the ground

ground glass *n* : glass with a roughened light-diffusing nontransparent surface

ground·hog \'graůnd-ˌhòg, -ˌhäg\ *n* : WOODCHUCK

ground·less \'graůn-dləs\ *adj* : being without foundation or reason — **ground·less·ly** *adv* — **ground·less·ness** *n*

ground·ling \'graůn-dliŋ\ *n* 1 a : a spectator in the pit or cheaper part of a theater b : a person of inferior taste 2 : one that lives or works on or near the ground

ground plan *n* 1 : a plan of a floor of a building 2 : a first or basic plan

ground·wa·ter \'graůnd-ˌwòt-ər, -ˌwät-\ *n* : water within the earth that supplies wells and springs

ground·work \-ˌwərk\ *n* : FOUNDATION, BASIS

[1]**group** \'grüp\ *n* 1 : two or more figures forming a complete unit in a composition 2 : a number of individuals related by a common factor (as physical association, community of interests, or blood)

[2]**group** *vb* 1 : to combine in a group 2 : to assign to a group : CLASSIFY 3 : to form a group

group·ing \'grü-piŋ\ *n* 1 : the act, process, or manner of combining in groups 2 : GROUP

[1]**grouse** \'graůs\ *n, pl* **grouse** : any of numerous plump-bodied game birds usu. protectively colored and less brilliant in plumage than the related pheasants

[2]**grouse** *vi* : COMPLAIN, GRUMBLE — **grous·er** *n*

grove \'grōv\ *n* : a small wood; *esp* : a group of trees without underbrush

grov·el \'gräv-əl, 'grəv-\ *vi* **-eled** *or* **-elled**; **-el·ing** *or* **-el·ling** \-(ə-)liŋ\ **1** : to lie or creep with the body prostrate in token of subservience or abasement **2** : to abase oneself : CRINGE — **grov·el·er** *or* **grov·el·ler** \-(ə-)lər\ *n*

grow \'grō\ *vb* **grew** \'grü\; **grown** \'grōn\; **grow·ing** **1 a** : to spring up and develop to maturity **b** : to be able to grow in some place or situation **c** : to assume some relation through or as if through a process of natural growth **2 a** : to become larger and often more complex by addition of material either by assimilation into the living organism or by accretion in a natural inorganic process (as crystallization) **b** : INCREASE, EXPAND **3 a** : RESULT, ORIGINATE **b** : to come into existence : ARISE **4 a** : to pass into a condition : BECOME **b** : to obtain influence **5** : to cause to grow : CULTIVATE, RAISE — **grow·er** *n*

grow·ing pains \'grō-iŋ-\ *n pl* : pains in the legs of growing children having no demonstrable relation to growth

growl \'grau̇l\ *vb* **1 a** : RUMBLE **b** : to utter a deep guttural threatening sound **2** : to complain angrily : GRUMBLE — **growl** *n* — **growl·er** *n*

grown \'grōn\ *adj* : fully grown : MATURE

grown–up \'grō-ˌnəp\ *adj* : ADULT — **grown–up** *n*

growth \'grōth\ *n* **1 a** : stage or condition attained in growing : SIZE **b** : a process of growing **c** : progressive development; *also* : INCREASE **2** : a result or product of growing: as **a** : vegetation or a cover of vegetation **b** : an abnormal mass of tissue (as a tumor) **3** : a producing esp. by growing

[1]**grub** \'grəb\ *vb* **grubbed**; **grub·bing** **1** : to clear or root out by digging **2** : to work hard : DRUDGE **3 a** : to dig in the ground usu. for a hidden object **b** : to search about : RUMMAGE — **grub·ber** *n*

[2]**grub** *n* **1** : a soft thick wormlike larva of an insect **2 a** : DRUDGE **b** : a slovenly person **3** : FOOD

grub·by \'grəb-ē\ *adj* **1** : DIRTY, SLOVENLY **2** : BASE, CONTEMPTIBLE — **grub·bi·ly** \'grəb-ə-lē\ *adv* — **grub·bi·ness** \'grəb-ē-nəs\ *n*

grub·stake \'grəb-ˌstāk\ *n* : supplies or funds furnished a mining prospector in return for a promise of a share in his finds — **grubstake** *vt* — **grub·stak·er** *n*

[1]**grudge** \'grəj\ *vt* : to be unwilling to give or admit : BEGRUDGE — **grudg·er** *n* — **grudg·ing·ly** *adv*

[2]**grudge** *n* : a feeling of deep-seated resentment or ill will

gru·el \'grü(-ə)l\ *n* : a thin porridge

gru·el·ing *or* **gru·el·ling** \'grü-(ə-)liŋ\ *adj* : requiring extreme effort : EXHAUSTING, PUNISHING

grue·some \'grü-səm\ *adj* : inspiring horror or repulsion : GRISLY — **grue·some·ly** *adv* — **grue·some·ness** *n*

gruff \'grəf\ *adj* **1** : rough or stern in manner, speech, or look **2** : being deep and harsh : HOARSE — **gruff·ly** *adv* — **gruff·ness** *n*

grum·ble \'grəm-bəl\ *vb* **grum·bled**; **grum·bling** \-b(ə-)liŋ\ **1** : to mutter in discontent **2 a** : GROWL **b** : RUMBLE — **grumble** *n* — **grum·bler** \-b(ə-)lər\ *n*

grump \'grəmp\ *n* **1** *pl* : a fit of ill humor **2** : a person given to complaining — **grump** *vi* — **grump·i·ly** \'grəm-pə-lē\ *adv* — **grump·i·ness** \-pē-nəs\ *n* — **grumpy** \-pē\ *adj*

[1]**grunt** \'grənt\ *vb* **1** : to make the characteristic throat sound of a hog **2** : to utter with a grunt — **grunt·er** *n*

[2]**grunt** *n* **1** : the deep short sound characteristic of a hog **2** : a sound similar to a grunt

gua·no \'gwän-ō\ *n, pl* **guanos** : a substance composed chiefly of the excrement of seabirds and used as a fertilizer

[1]**guar·an·tee** \ˌgar-ən-'tē\ *n* **1** : GUARANTOR **2** : GUARANTY 1 **3 a** : an agreement by which one party undertakes to secure another in the possession or enjoyment of something **b** : an assurance of the quality of or of the length of use to be expected from a product offered for sale often with a promise of reimbursement in case of defect or failure **4** : GUARANTY 3

[2]**guarantee** *vt* **-teed**; **-tee·ing** **1** : to undertake to answer for the debt, failure to perform, or faulty performance of (another) **2** : to undertake an obligation to establish, perform, or continue **3** : to give security to : SECURE

guar·an·tor \ˌgar-ən-'tȯ(ə)r, 'gar-ən-tər\ *n* : a person who gives a guarantee

[1]**guar·an·ty** \'gar-ən-tē\ *n, pl* **-ties** **1** : an undertaking to answer for another's failure to pay a debt or perform a duty **2** : GUARANTEE 3a **3** : something given as security : PLEDGE **4** : GUARANTOR

[2]**guaranty** *vt* **-tied**; **-ty·ing** : GUARANTEE

[1]**guard** \'gärd\ *n* **1** : a posture of defense **2 a** : the act or duty of protecting or defending **b** : PROTECTION **3 a** : a man or a body of men on sentinel duty **b** *pl* : troops attached to the person of the sovereign **c** : BRAKEMAN **4 a** : a football lineman playing between tackle and center **b** : a basketball player stationed toward the rear **5** : a protective or safety device (as on a machine)

[2]**guard** *vb* **1** : to protect from danger : DEFEND **2 a** : to watch over so as to prevent escape, disclosure, or indiscretion **b** : to attempt to prevent (an opponent) from scoring **3** : to be on guard : take precautions

guard·ed \'gärd-əd\ *adj* **1** : PROTECTED **2** : CAUTIOUS, NONCOMMITTAL — **guard·ed·ly** *adv*

guard·house \'gärd-ˌhau̇s\ *n* **1** : a building occupied by a guard or used as a headquarters by soldiers on guard duty **2** : a military jail

guard·i·an \'gärd-ē-ən\ *n* **1** : one that guards : CUSTODIAN **2** : one who has the care of the person or property of another — **guard·i·an·ship** \-ˌship\ *n*

guard of honor : a guard turned out to greet or accompany a distinguished person or to accompany the casket at a military funeral

guard·room \'gärd-ˌrüm, -ˌru̇m\ *n* **1** : a room used by a military guard while on duty **2** : a room where military prisoners are confined

guards·man \'gärdz-mən\ *n* : a member of the guards

gu·ber·na·to·ri·al \ˌgü-bə(r)-nə-'tōr-ē-əl, ˌgyü-\ *adj* : of or relating to a governor

guer·don \'gərd-ᵊn\ *n* : REWARD, RECOMPENSE

guer·ril·la *or* **gue·ril·la** \gə-'ril-ə\ *n* : a person who engages in irregular warfare esp. as a member of an independent unit carrying out harassment and sabotage — **guerrilla** *adj*

guess \'ges\ *vb* **1** : to form an opinion from little or no evidence **2** : to conjecture correctly about : DISCOVER **3** : BELIEVE, SUPPOSE — **guess** *n* — **guess·er** *n* — **guess·work** \'ges-ˌwərk\ *n*

guest \'gest\ *n* **1** : a person entertained in one's house **2** : a person to whom hospitality is extended **3** : a patron of a commercial establishment (as a hotel or restaurant)

guf·faw \(ˌ)gə-'fȯ\ *n* : a loud burst of laughter — **guffaw** *vi*

guid·ance \'gīd-ᵊn(t)s\ *n* **1** : the act or process of guiding **2** : advice on vocational or educational problems given to students

[1]**guide** \'gīd\ *n* **1 a** : one who leads or directs another in his way **b** : one who exhibits and explains points of interest **c** : something that provides a person with guiding information **d** : SIGNPOST **e** : one who directs a person in his conduct or course of life **2 a** : a contrivance for steadying or directing the motion of something **b** : a sheet or a card with projecting tab for labeling inserted in a card index to facilitate reference

[2]**guide** *vb* **1** : to act as a guide : CONDUCT **2 a** : MANAGE, DIRECT **b** : to superintend the training of

guide·book \'gīd-ˌbu̇k\ *n* : a book of information for travelers

guid·ed missile \ˌgīd-əd-\ *n* : a missile whose course toward a target may be changed (as by radio signals or a built-in target-seeking device) during flight

guide word *n* : CATCHWORD 1

guild \'gild\ *n* : an association of men with kindred pursuits or common interests or aims; *esp* : a medieval association of merchants or craftsmen

guile \'gīl\ *n* : deceitful cunning : DUPLICITY — **guile·ful** \-fəl\ *adj* — **guile·ful·ly** \-fə-lē\ *adv*

guile·less \'gīl-ləs\ *adj* : free from deceit or cunning : INNOCENT, NAÏVE — **guile·less·ly** *adv* — **guile·less·ness** *n*

guil·lo·tine \'gil-ə-ˌtēn, 'gē-(y)ə-\ *n* : a machine for cutting off a person's head by means of a heavy blade sliding in two upright grooved posts — **guillotine** *vb*

guilt \'gilt\ *n* **1** : the fact of having committed an offense and esp. one that is punishable by law **2** : BLAMEWORTHINESS **3** : a feeling of responsibility for offenses — **guilt·less** \-ləs\ *adj*

guilty \'gil-tē\ *adj* **1** : having committed a breach of conduct **2 a** : suggesting or involving guilt **b** : aware of or suffering from guilt — **guilt·i·ly** \-tə-lē\ *adv* — **guilt·i·ness** \-tē-nəs\ *n*

guin·ea \'gin-ē\ *n* **1** : a British gold coin no longer issued worth 21 shillings **2** : a unit of value equal to 21 shillings

guinea pig *n* **1** : a small stout-bodied short-eared nearly tailless rodent often kept as a pet and widely used in biological research **2** : a subject of scientific research, experimentation, or testing

guise \'gīz\ *n* **1** : a form or style of dress : COSTUME **2** : external appearance : SEMBLANCE

gui·tar \gə-'tär\ *n* : a flat-bodied musical instrument with a long fretted neck and usu. six strings plucked with a plectrum or with the fingers

gulch \'gəlch\ *n* : a deep steep-sided ravine; *esp* : one that is the bed of a stream

gulf \'gəlf\ *n* **1** : a part of an ocean or sea extending into the land **2** : a deep hollow in the earth : CHASM, ABYSS **3** : WHIRLPOOL **4** : a wide separation : an unbridgeable gap

¹gull \'gəl\ *n* : any of numerous mostly white or gray long-winged web-footed aquatic birds

²gull *vt* : to make a dupe of : DECEIVE

³gull *n* : a person easily deceived or cheated : DUPE

gul·let \'gəl-ət\ *n* : ESOPHAGUS; *also* : THROAT

gull·i·ble \'gəl-ə-bəl\ *adj* : easily deceived, cheated, or duped — **gull·i·bil·i·ty** \ˌgəl-ə-'bil-ət-ē\ *n*

gul·ly \'gəl-ē\ *n, pl* **gullies** : a trench worn in the earth by running water after rains — **gully** *vb*

gulp \'gəlp\ *vb* **1** : to swallow hurriedly or greedily or in one swallow **2** : to keep back as if by swallowing **3** : to catch the breath as if in taking a long drink — **gulp** *n*

¹gum \'gəm\ *n* : the tissue along the jaws of animals that surrounds the necks of the teeth

²gum *vt* **gummed**; **gum·ming** : to chew with the gums

³gum *n* **1** : a sticky plant exudate; *esp* : one that hardens on drying and is soluble in or swells in water and that includes substances used as emulsifiers, adhesives, and thickeners and in inks **2** : a sticky substance **3** : a tree that yields a gum **4** : the wood of a gum **5** : CHEWING GUM

⁴gum *vt* **gummed**; **gum·ming** : to smear, seal, or clog with or as if with gum

gum arabic *n* : a water-soluble gum obtained from several acacias and used esp. in adhesives, in confectionery, and in pharmacy

gum·bo \'gəm-ˌbō\ *n, pl* **gumbos** : a soup thickened with okra pods

gum·boil \'gəm-ˌbȯil\ *n* : an abscess in the gum

gum·drop \-ˌdräp\ *n* : a candy made usu. from corn syrup with gelatin or gum arabic and coated with sugar crystals

gum·my \'gəm-ē\ *adj* **1** : consisting of, containing, or covered with gum **2** : VISCOUS, STICKY — **gum·mi·ness** *n*

gump·tion \'gəm(p)-shən\ *n* **1** : shrewd common sense **2** : courageous or vigorous initiative : SPUNK

gun \'gən\ *n* **1 a** : a piece of ordnance usu. with high muzzle velocity and comparatively flat trajectory : CANNON **b** : a portable firearm (as a rifle or pistol) **c** : a device that throws a projectile **2 a** : a discharge of a gun **b** : a signal marking a beginning or ending **3** : one who is skilled with a gun **4** : something suggesting a gun in shape or function **5** : THROTTLE — **gunned** \'gənd\ *adj*

²gun *vb* **gunned**; **gun·ning** **1** : to hunt with a gun **2** : SHOOT **3** : to open up the throttle of so as to increase speed

gun·boat \'gən-ˌbōt\ *n* : a small lightly armed ship for use in shallow waters

gun·fire \-ˌfī(ə)r\ *n* : the firing of guns

gun·lock \-ˌläk\ *n* : a device on a firearm by which the charge is ignited

gun·man \-mən\ *n* : a man armed with a gun; *esp* : an armed bandit or gangster

gun·ner \'gən-ər\ *n* **1** : a soldier or airman who operates or aims a gun **2** : one that hunts with a gun

gun·nery \'gən-(ə-)rē\ *n* : the use of guns; *esp* : the science of the flight of projectiles and of the effective use of guns

gun·ny \'gən-ē\ *n, pl* **gunnies** **1** : coarse jute sacking **2** : BURLAP

gun·ny·sack \-ˌsak\ *n* : a sack made of gunny or burlap

gun·point \'gən-ˌpȯint\ *n* : the point of a gun — **at gunpoint** : under a threat of death by being shot

gun·pow·der \-ˌpau̇d-ər\ *n* : an explosive mixture of potassium nitrate, charcoal, and sulfur used in gunnery and blasting; *also* : any of various explosive powders used in guns

gun·shot \-ˌshät\ *n* **1** : shot or a projectile fired from a gun **2** : the range of a gun

gun·smith \-ˌsmith\ *n* : one whose business is the making and repair of firearms

gun·wale *or* **gun·nel** \'gən-ᵊl\ *n* : the upper edge of a ship's side

gup·py \'gəp-ē\ *n, pl* **guppies** : a small tropical fish that is frequently kept in aquariums

gur·gle \'gər-gəl\ *vi* **gur·gled**; **gur·gling** \'gər-g(ə-)liŋ\ **1** : to flow in a broken irregular current **2** : to make a sound like that of a gurgling liquid — **gurgle** *n*

gush \'gəsh\ *vb* **1** : to issue or pour forth copiously or violently : SPOUT **2** : to make an effusive display of affection or enthusiasm — **gush** *n*

gush·er \'gəsh-ər\ *n* : one that gushes; *esp* : an oil well with a copious natural flow

gushy \'gəsh-ē\ *adj* : marked by effusive sentimentality

gus·set \'gəs-ət\ *n* : a triangular insert (as in a seam of a sleeve) to give width or strength

gust \'gəst\ *n* **1** : a sudden brief rush of wind **2** : a sudden outburst : SURGE — **gusty** \'gəs-tē\ *adj*

gus·ta·to·ry \'gəs-tə-ˌtōr-ē\ *adj* : relating to, associated with, or being the sense or sensation of taste

gus·to \'gəs-ˌtō\ *n* **1** : keen and usu. vigorous enjoyment or appreciation : high relish **2** : capacity for taking delight in experience : strength of appetite

¹gut \'gət\ *n* **1 a** : VISCERA, ENTRAILS — usu. used in pl. **b** : the alimentary canal or part of it **2** *pl* : the inner essential parts **3** *pl* : COURAGE

²gut *vt* **gut·ted**; **gut·ting** **1** : EVISCERATE **2** : to destroy the inside of

gut·ter \'gət-ər\ *n* **1 a** : a trough along the eaves to catch and carry off water from a roof **b** : a low area (as at a roadside) to carry off surface water **2** : a narrow channel or groove

gut·ter·snipe \-ˌsnīp\ *n* : a person of the lowest moral or economic station; *esp* : a street urchin

gut·tur·al \'gət-ə-rəl\ *adj* **1** : formed or pronounced in the throat **2** : being or marked by an utterance that is strange, unpleasant, or disagreeable **3** : VELAR, PALATAL — **guttural** *n* — **gut·tur·al·ly** \-rə-lē\ *adv*

¹guy \'gī\ *n* : a rope, chain, or rod attached to something as a brace or guide

[2]**guy** *vt* **guyed; guy·ing :** to steady or reinforce with a guy
[3]**guy** *n* **:** MAN, FELLOW
[4]**guy** *vt* **guyed; guy·ing :** to make fun of **:** RIDICULE
guz·zle \'gəz-əl\ *vb* **guz·zled; guz·zling** \'gəz-(ə-)liŋ\ **:** to drink greedily — **guz·zler** \-(ə-)lər\ *n*
gym \'jim\ *n* **:** GYMNASIUM
gym·na·si·um *in sense 1* jim-'nā-zē-əm, *in sense 2* gim-'nä-zē-əm\ *n, pl* **-si·ums** *or* **-sia** \-zē-ə\ **1 :** a room or building for sports activities **2 :** a German secondary school preparing students for the university
gym·nast \'jim-ˌnast\ *n* **:** an expert in gymnastics
gym·nas·tics \jim-'nas-tiks\ *n sing or pl* **:** physical exercises developing or exhibiting skill, strength, and control in the use of the body — **gym·nas·tic** \-tik\ *adj*
gy·ne·col·o·gy \ˌgīn-ə-'käl-ə-jē, ˌjin-\ *n* **:** a branch of medicine that deals with women, their diseases, and their hygiene — **gy·ne·co·log·ic** \-kə-'läj-ik\ *or* **gy·ne·co·log·i·cal** \-'läj-i-kəl\ *adj* — **gy·ne·col·o·gist** \-'käl-ə-jəst\ *n*
[1]**gyp** \'jip\ *n* **1 :** CHEAT, SWINDLER **2 :** an act or instance of cheating **:** FRAUD, SWINDLE
[2]**gyp** *vb* **gypped; gyp·ping :** CHEAT, SWINDLE
gyp·sum \'jip-səm\ *n* **:** a colorless mineral that contains calcium and is used esp. as a soil improver and in making plaster of paris
Gyp·sy \'jip-sē\ *n, pl* **Gypsies :** one of a dark Caucasoid people coming orig. from India to Europe in the 14th or 15th century and living and maintaining a migratory way of life chiefly in Europe and the U.S.
gy·rate \'jī-ˌrāt\ *vi* **1 :** to revolve around a point or axis **2 :** to oscillate with or as if with a circular or spiral motion — **gy·ra·tion** \jī-'rā-shən\ *n*
gy·ro \'jī-rō\ *n, pl* **gyros 1 :** GYROSCOPE **2 :** GYROCOMPASS
gy·ro·com·pass \'jī-rō-ˌkəm-pəs, -ˌkäm-\ *n* **:** a compass in which the axis of a spinning gyroscope points to the north
gy·ro·scope \'jī-rə-ˌskōp\ *n* **:** a wheel or disk mounted to spin rapidly about an axis that is free to turn in various directions — **gy·ro·scop·ic** \ˌjī-rə-'skäp-ik\ *adj*
gyve \'jīv\ *n* **:** FETTER — usu. used in pl. — **gyve** *vt*

h \'āch\ *n, often cap* **:** the 8th letter of the English alphabet
ha \'hä\ *interj* — used to express surprise, joy, or grief or sometimes doubt or hesitation
ha·ba·ne·ra \ˌ(h)äb-ə-'ner-ə\ *n* **1 :** a Cuban dance in slow duple time **2 :** the music for the habanera
ha·be·as cor·pus \ˌhā-bē-əs-'kȯr-pəs\ *n* **1 :** any of several writs obtained for the purpose of bringing a person before a court; *esp* **:** one ordering an inquiry to determine whether or not a person has been lawfully imprisoned **2 :** the right of a citizen to obtain a writ of habeas corpus as a protection against illegal imprisonment
hab·er·dash·er \'hab-ə(r)-ˌdash-ər\ *n* **:** a dealer in men's wear (as gloves, neckties, socks, and shirts)
hab·er·dash·ery \-ˌdash-(ə-)rē\ *n, pl* **-er·ies 1 :** goods sold by a haberdasher **2 :** a haberdasher's shop
hab·er·geon \'hab-ər-jən\ *n* **1 :** a medieval jacket of mail shorter than a hauberk **2 :** HAUBERK
ha·bil·i·ment \hə-'bil-ə-mənt\ *n* **1 :** the dress characteristic of an occupation or occasion — usu. used in pl. **2 :** CLOTHES — usu. used in pl.
[1]**hab·it** \'hab-ət\ *n* **1 :** a costume characteristic of a calling, rank, or function **2 :** bodily appearance or makeup **:** PHYSIQUE **3 :** the prevailing disposition or character of a person's thoughts and feelings **:** mental makeup **4 :** a usual manner of behavior **:** CUSTOM **5 a :** a behavior pattern acquired and fixed by frequent repetition **b :** ADDICTION **6 :** characteristic mode of growth or occurrence
[2]**habit** *vt* **:** CLOTHE, DRESS
hab·it·a·ble \'hab-ət-ə-bəl\ *adj* **:** suitable or fit to live in
ha·bi·tant *n* **1** \'hab-ət-ənt\ **:** INHABITANT, RESIDENT **2** \ˌ(h)ab-i-'tä^n\ **:** a French settler or a farmer of French origin in Canada
hab·i·tat \'hab-ə-ˌtat\ *n* **1 :** the place or type of site where a plant or animal naturally or normally lives or grows **2 :** the place where something is commonly found
hab·i·ta·tion \ˌhab-ə-'tā-shən\ *n* **1 :** the act of inhabiting **:** OCCUPANCY **2 :** a dwelling place **:** RESIDENCE
hab·it–form·ing *adj* **:** inducing the formation of an addiction
ha·bit·u·al \hə-'bich-(ə-w)əl\ *adj* **1 :** according to or constituting a habit **2 :** doing or acting by force of habit **3 :** REGULAR — **ha·bit·u·al·ly** \-ē\ *adv* — **ha·bit·u·al·ness** *n*
ha·bit·u·ate \hə-'bich-ə-ˌwāt\ *vt* **:** to make used to **:** ACCUSTOM — **ha·bit·u·a·tion** \hə-ˌbich-ə-'wā-shən\ *n*
hab·i·tude \'hab-ə-ˌt(y)üd\ *n* **1 :** habitual disposition or mode of behavior or procedure **2 :** CUSTOM
ha·bi·tué \hə-'bich-ə-ˌwā\ *n* **:** one who frequents a place or type of place
ha·ci·en·da \ˌ(h)äs-ē-'en-də\ *n* **1 :** a large estate in present or formerly Spanish-speaking countries **:** PLANTATION **2 :** the main building of a farm or ranch
[1]**hack** \'hak\ *vb* **1 a :** to cut with repeated irregular or unskillful blows **b :** to sever with repeated blows **:** CHOP **2 :** to cough in a short dry manner — **hack·er** *n*
[2]**hack** *n* **1 :** an implement for hacking **2 :** NICK, NOTCH **3 :** a short dry cough **4 :** a hacking blow
[3]**hack** *n* **1 a :** a horse let out for common hire **b :** a horse worn out in service **c :** a light easy often 3-gaited saddle horse **2 a :** HACKNEY **b :** TAXICAB **3 a :** a writer who works mainly for hire **b :** one who serves a cause not out of enthusiasm or devotion but merely for reward
[4]**hack** *adj* **1 :** working for hire **2 :** done by or characteristic of a hack **3 :** HACKNEYED, TRITE
[5]**hack** *vi* **:** to operate a taxicab
hack·ie \'hak-ē\ *n* **:** a driver of a cab
[1]**hack·le** \'hak-əl\ *n* **1 :** a comb for dressing fibers (as flax or hemp) **2 :** one of the long narrow feathers on the neck or lower back of a bird **3** *pl* **a :** hairs (as on the neck of a dog) that can be erected **b :** TEMPER, DANDER
[2]**hackle** *vt* **hack·led; hack·ling** \'hak-(ə-)liŋ\ **:** to chop up or chop off roughly **:** HACK
hack·man \'hak-mən\ *n* **:** a driver of a cab
[1]**hack·ney** \'hak-nē\ *n, pl* **hack·neys 1 :** a horse suitable for ordinary riding or driving **2 :** a carriage or automobile kept for hire
[2]**hackney** *adj* **1 :** kept for public hire **2 :** HACKNEYED
[3]**hackney** *vt* **1 :** to make common or frequent use of **2 :** to make trite, vulgar, or commonplace
hack·neyed \'hak-nēd\ *adj* **:** worn out from too long or too much use **:** COMMONPLACE
hack·saw \'hak-ˌsȯ\ *n* **:** a fine-tooth saw with blade under tension in a bow-shaped frame for cutting hard materials (as metal)
hack·work \-ˌwərk\ *n* **:** literary, artistic, or professional work

done on order usu. according to formula and in conformity with commercial standards
had *past of* HAVE
had·dock \'had-ək\ *n, pl* **haddock** : an important Atlantic food fish usu. smaller than the related common cod

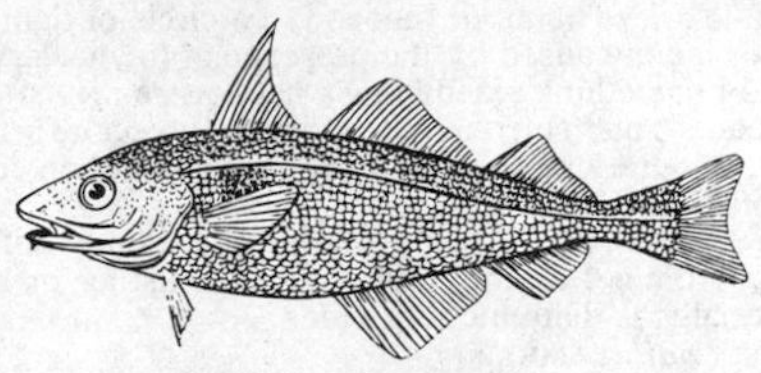
haddock

Ha·des \'hād-(,)ēz\ *n* **1** : the abode of the dead in Greek mythology **2** *often not cap* : HELL
haf·ni·um \'haf-nē-əm\ *n* : a metallic chemical element that resembles zirconium chemically and is useful because of its ready emission of electrons
[1]**haft** \'haft\ *n* : the handle of a weapon or tool (as a sword or knife)
[2]**haft** *vt* : to set in or furnish with a haft
hag \'hag\ *n* **1** : WITCH **2** : an ugly, slatternly, or evil-looking old woman
hag·gard \'hag-ərd\ *adj* : having the expression of a person who is suffering esp. from great hunger, worry, or pain or who is wasted with age : GAUNT
hag·gis \'hag-əs\ *n* : a pudding esp. popular in Scotland made of the heart, liver, and lungs of a sheep or a calf minced with suet, onions, oatmeal, and seasonings and boiled in the stomach of the animal
[1]**hag·gle** \'hag-əl\ *vb* **hag·gled**; **hag·gling** \'hag-(ə-)liŋ\ **1** : to cut roughly or clumsily : HACK **2** : to dispute or argue esp. over a bargain or a price — **hag·gler** \-(ə-)lər\ *n*
[2]**haggle** *n* : an act or instance of haggling
hag·i·og·ra·phy \,hag-ē-'äg-rə-fē, ,hā-jē-\ *n* **1** : biography of saints or venerated persons **2** : idealizing or idolizing biography — **hag·i·og·ra·pher** \-fər\ *n*
ha–ha \(')hä-'hä\ *interj* — used to express amusement or derision
[1]**hail** \'hāl\ *n* **1** : precipitation in the form of small balls or lumps usu. consisting of concentric layers of clear ice and compact snow **2** : something that gives the effect of falling hail
[2]**hail** *vb* **1** : to precipitate hail **2** : to pour down like hail **3** : to hurl forcibly
[3]**hail** *interj* — used to express acclamation
[4]**hail** *vb* **1 a** : SALUTE, GREET **b** : to greet with enthusiastic approval : ACCLAIM **2** : to greet or summon by calling **3** : to call out; *esp* : to call a greeting to a passing ship — **hail from** : to come from
[5]**hail** *n* **1** : an exclamation of greeting or acclamation **2** : a calling to attract attention **3** : hailing distance
hail–fel·low \'hāl-,fel-ō\ *or* **hail–fellow–well–met** \-,wel-'met\ *adj* : heartily informal
hail·stone \'hāl-,stōn\ *n* : a pellet of hail
hail·storm \-,stȯrm\ *n* : a storm accompanied by hail
hair \'ha(ə)r\ *n* **1 a** : a slender threadlike outgrowth of the epidermis of an animal; *esp* : one of the usu. pigmented filaments that form the characteristic coat of a mammal **b** : the hairy covering of an animal or a body part **2** : HAIRCLOTH **3 a** : a minute distance or amount : TRIFLE **b** : a precise degree : NICETY — **haired** \'ha(ə)rd\ *adj* — **hair·less** \'ha(ə)r-ləs\ *adj* — **hair·like** *adj*
[1]**hair·breadth** \'ha(ə)r-,bredth\ *or* **hairs·breadth** \'ha(ə)rz-\ *n* : a very small distance or margin
[2]**hairbreadth** *adj* : very narrow : CLOSE
hair·brush \'ha(ə)r-,brəsh\ *n* : a brush for the hair
hair·cloth \-,klȯth\ *n* : any of various stiff wiry fabrics esp. of horsehair or camel's hair used for upholstery or stiffening in garments
hair·cut \-,kət\ *n* : the act, process, or style of cutting and shaping the hair — **hair·cut·ter** *n* — **hair·cut·ting** *n*
hair·do \-,dü\ *n, pl* **hairdos** : a way of dressing a woman's hair : COIFFURE
hair·dress·er \-,dres-ər\ *n* : one who dresses or cuts women's hair — **hair·dress·ing** *n*
hair·line \-,līn\ *n* **1** : a very slender line **2** : the outline of the scalp or of the hair on the head — **hairline** *adj*
hair·pin \-,pin\ *n* **1** : a 2-pronged U-shaped pin to hold the hair in place **2** : something shaped like a hairpin; *esp* : a sharp turn in a road — **hairpin** *adj*
hair–rais·ing \-,rā-ziŋ\ *adj* : causing terror, excitement, or astonishment — **hair–rais·ing·ly** *adv*
hair shirt *n* : a shirt made of rough animal hair worn next to the skin as a penance
hair·split·ter \'ha(ə)r-,split-ər\ *n* : a person who makes unnecessarily fine distinctions in reasoning or argument — **hair·split·ting** *adj or n*
hairy \'ha(ə)r-ē\ *adj* **1** : bearing or covered with or as if with hair **2** : made of or resembling hair — **hair·i·ness** *n*
hake \'hāk\ *n* : any of several marine food fishes related to the cod
hal·berd \'hal-bərd, 'hȯl-\ *or* **hal·bert** \-bərt\ *n* : a long handled weapon used both as a spear and as a battle-ax esp. in the 15th and 16th centuries — **hal·berd·ier** \,hal-bər-'di(ə)r, ,hȯl-\ *n*
hal·cy·on \'hal-sē-ən\ *adj* **1** : CALM, PEACEFUL **2** : HAPPY, GOLDEN
[1]**hale** \'hāl\ *adj* : free from defect, disease, or infirmity : SOUND, HEALTHY
[2]**hale** *vt* **1** : HAUL, PULL **2** : to compel to go
[1]**half** \'haf, 'hȧf\ *n, pl* **halves** \'havz, 'hȧvz\ **1 a** : one of two equal parts into which a thing is divisible; *also* : a part of a thing approximately equal to the remainder **b** : half an hour **2** : one of a pair: as **a** : PARTNER **b** : SEMESTER, TERM — **by half** : by a great deal — **by halves** : in part : HALFHEARTEDLY — **in half** : into two equal or nearly equal parts
[2]**half** *adj* **1 a** : being one of two equal parts **b (1)** : amounting to nearly half **(2)** : PARTIAL, IMPERFECT **2** : of half the usual size or extent — **half·ness** *n*
[3]**half** *adv* **1 a** : to the extent of half **b** : PARTIALLY **2** : at all : by any means
half–and–half \,haf-ən-'haf, ,hȧf-ən-'hȧf\ *n* : something that is half one thing and half another; *esp* : a mixture of two malt beverages — **half–and–half** *adj or adv*
half·back \'haf-,bak, 'hȧf-\ *n* : a football back who lines up on or near either flank
half–baked \-'bākt\ *adj* **1** : imperfectly baked : UNDERDONE **2 a** : not well planned **b** : lacking judgment, intelligence, or common sense
half–breed \-,brēd\ *n* : the offspring of parents of different races; *esp* : the offspring of an American Indian and a white person — **half–breed** *adj*
half brother *n* : a brother by one parent only
half–caste \'haf-,kast, 'hȧf-\ *n* : one of mixed racial descent : HALF-BREED — **half–caste** *adj*
half cock *n* **1** : the position of the hammer of a firearm when it is partly drawn back and locked in position so that it cannot be operated by a pull on the trigger **2** : a state of inadequate preparation or mental confusion — **half–cocked** \'haf-'käkt, 'hȧf-\ *adj*

half crown *n* : a British coin worth 2*s* 6*d*
half–dollar \'haf-'däl-ər, 'häf-\ *n* **1** : a coin representing one half of a dollar **2** : the sum of fifty cents
half eagle *n* : a five-dollar gold piece issued by the U.S. 1795–1916 and in 1929
half·heart·ed \'haf-'härt-əd, 'häf-\ *adj* : lacking spirit or interest — **half·heart·ed·ly** *adv* — **half·heart·ed·ness** *n*
half hitch *n* : a simple knot so made as to be easily unfastened
half hour *n* **1** : thirty minutes **2** : the middle point of an hour — **half–hour·ly** \'haf-'aù(ə)r-lē, 'häf-\ *adv or adj*
half–knot \'haf-,nät, 'häf-\ *n* : a knot joining the ends of two cords and used in tying other knots
half–mast \'haf-'mast, 'häf-\ *n* : a point some distance but not necessarily halfway down below the top of a mast or staff or the peak of a gaff
half note *n* : a musical note of half the value of a whole note
half·pen·ny \'hāp-(ə-)nē, *US also* 'haf-,pen-ē, 'häf-\ *n, pl* **half·pence** \'hā-pən(t)s, *US also* 'haf-,pen(t)s, 'häf-\ *or* **half-pennies** **1** : a British coin representing one half of a penny **2** : the sum of half a penny **3** : a small amount
half sister *n* : a sister by one parent only
half sole *n* : a shoe sole extending from the shank forward — **half–sole** \'haf-'sōl, 'häf-\ *vt*
half sovereign *n* : a British gold coin worth ten shillings
half step *n* : the pitch interval between any two adjacent keys on a keyboard instrument
half–track \'haf-,trak, 'häf-\ *n* **1** : one of the endless-chain tracks used in place of rear wheels on a heavy-duty vehicle **2** : a motor vehicle propelled by half-tracks; *esp* : such a vehicle lightly armored for military use — **half–track** *or* **half–tracked** \-,trakt\ *adj*
half–truth \-,trüth\ *n* : a statement that is only partially true; *esp* : one that mingles truth and falsehood and is deliberately intended to deceive
half·way \-'wā\ *adj* **1** : midway between two points **2** : PARTIAL — **halfway** *adv*
half–wit \-,wit\ *n* : a foolish or imbecilic person — **half–wit·ted** \-'wit-əd\ *adj*
hal·i·but \'hal-ə-bət, 'häl-\ *n, pl* **halibut** : a marine food fish that is the largest flatfish of both the Atlantic and Pacific oceans
hal·i·to·sis \,hal-ə-'tō-səs\ *n* : a condition of having offensive breath
hall \'hòl\ *n* **1 a** : a large or imposing residence; *esp* : MANOR HOUSE **b** : a large building used for public purposes **c** : one of the buildings of a college or university set apart for a special purpose **d** : a college or a division of a college at some universities **e** : the common dining room of an English college **2** : the chief living room in a medieval castle **3 a** : the entrance room of a building : LOBBY **b** : a corridor or passage in a building **4** : a large room for assembly : AUDITORIUM **5** : a place used for public entertainment
¹hal·le·lu·jah \,hal-ə-'lü-yə\ *interj* — used to express praise, joy, or thanks
²hallelujah *n* : a shout or song of praise or thanksgiving
¹hall·mark \'hòl-,märk\ *n* **1** : a mark or device placed on an article to indicate origin, purity, or genuineness **2** : a distinguishing characteristic, trait, or feature
²hallmark *vt* : to stamp with a hallmark
hal·low \'hal-ō\ *vt* **1** : to make holy or set apart for holy use : CONSECRATE **2** : to respect greatly : VENERATE
hal·lowed \'hal-ōd, *in the Lord's Prayer also* 'hal-ə-wəd\ *adj* : CONSECRATED, SACRED
Hal·low·een \,hal-ə-'wēn, ,häl-\ *n* : October 31 observed with merrymaking and the playing of pranks by children during the evening
hal·lu·ci·na·tion \hə-,lüs-ᵊn-'ā-shən\ *n* : the perceiving of objects or the experiencing of feelings that have no cause outside one's mind esp. as the result of a mental disorder or as the effect of a drug; *also* : something so perceived or experienced — **hal·lu·ci·nate** \-'lüs-ᵊn-,āt\ *vb* — **hal·lu·ci·na·tion·al** \-,lüs-ᵊn-'ā-shnəl, -shən-ᵊl\ *adj* — **hal·lu·ci·na·to·ry** \-'lüs-ᵊn-ə-,tōr-ē\ *adj*
hall·way \'hòl-,wā\ *n* **1** : an entrance hall **2** : CORRIDOR
ha·lo \'hā-lō\ *n, pl* **halos** *or* **haloes** **1** : a circle of light around the sun or moon caused by the presence of tiny ice crystals in the air **2** : something resembling a halo: as **a** : NIMBUS **b** : a differentiated zone surrounding a central object **3** : the aura of glory, veneration, or sentiment surrounding an idealized person or thing
hal·o·gen \'hal-ə-jən\ *n* : any of the five elements fluorine, chlorine, bromine, iodine, and astatine existing in the free state normally as diatomic molecules
¹halt \'hòlt\ *adj* : LAME
²halt *vi* **1** : to walk or proceed lamely : LIMP **2** : to stand in perplexity or doubt between alternate courses : WAVER **3** : to display weakness or imperfection : FALTER
³halt *n* : STOP
⁴halt *vb* **1** : to cease marching or journeying **2** : DISCONTINUE, TERMINATE **3** : to bring to a stop : END
¹hal·ter \'hòl-tər\ *n* **1 a** : a rope or strap for leading or tying an animal **b** : HEADSTALL **2** : a rope for hanging criminals : NOOSE; *also* : death by hanging **3** : a woman's blouse that is typically held in place by straps around the neck and across the back and leaves the back, arms, and midriff bare
²halter *vt* **hal·tered**; **hal·ter·ing** \-t(ə-)riŋ\ **1 a** : to catch with or as if with a halter; *also* : to put a halter on **b** : HANG **2** : to put restraint upon : HAMPER
halt·ing \'hòl-tiŋ\ *adj* **1** : LAME, LIMPING **2** : UNCERTAIN, FALTERING — **halt·ing·ly** *adv*
halve \'hav, 'häv\ *vt* **1 a** : to divide into two equal parts **b** : to reduce to one half **c** : to share equally **2** : to play (as a hole) in the same number of strokes as one's opponent at golf
halves *pl of* HALF
hal·yard *or* **hal·liard** \'hal-yərd\ *n* : a rope or tackle for hoisting and lowering
ham \'ham\ *n* **1** *pl* : buttocks with their associated thighs **2** : a cut of meat consisting of a thigh; *esp* : one from a hog **3 a** : an unskillful but showy performer **b** : an operator of an amateur radio station — **ham** *adj*
hama·dry·ad \,ham-ə-'drī-əd\ *n* : WOOD NYMPH
ham·burg·er \'ham-,bər-gər\ *or* **ham·burg** \-,bərg\ *n* **1 a** : ground beef **b** : a cooked patty of ground beef **2** : a sandwich consisting of a patty of hamburger in a split round bun
ham·let \'ham-lət\ *n* : a small group of houses in the country
¹ham·mer \'ham-ər\ *n* **1 a** : a hand tool that consists of a solid head set crosswise on a handle and is used for pounding (as in driving nails) **b** : a power tool that substitutes a metal block or a drill for the head for pounding (as in driving posts or breaking rock) **2** : something that resembles a hammer in shape or action (as the part of a gun whose striking action causes explosion of the charge) **3** : a metal sphere usu. weighing about 16 pounds that is hurled in an athletic event — **under the hammer** : for sale at auction
²hammer *vb* **ham·mered**; **ham·mer·ing** \'ham-(ə-)riŋ\ **1** : to strike blows esp. repeatedly with or as if with a hammer : POUND **2 a** : to make repeated efforts **b** : to reiterate an opinion or attitude **3 a** : to beat, drive, or shape with repeated blows of a hammer **b** : to fasten or build with a hammer **4** : to produce or bring about as if by repeated blows — **ham·mer·er** *n*
hammer and tongs *adv* : with great force and violence
ham·mer·head \'ham-ər-,hed\ *n* **1** : the striking part of a hammer **2** : BLOCKHEAD **3** : any of various active voracious medium-sized sharks that have the eyes at the ends of lateral extensions of the flattened head

ham•mer•lock \-ˌläk\ *n* : a wrestling hold in which an opponent's arm is held bent behind his back

[1]**ham•mock** \'ham-ək\ *n* : a swinging couch or bed usu. made of netting or canvas and slung by cords from supports at each end

[2]**hammock** *n* : HUMMOCK

ham•my \'ham-ē\ *adj* : characteristic of a ham actor

[1]**ham•per** \'ham-pər\ *vt* **ham•pered**; **ham•per•ing** \-p(ə-)riŋ\ **1** : to restrict or interfere with the movement or operation of : IMPEDE, DISRUPT **2** : ENCUMBER

[2]**hamper** *n* : a large basket usu. with a cover

ham•ster \'ham(p)-stər\ *n* : any of various stocky short-tailed Old World rodents with large cheek pouches

ham•string \'ham-ˌstriŋ\ *vt* **-strung** \-ˌstrəŋ\; **-string•ing** \-ˌstriŋ-iŋ\ **1** : to cripple by cutting the leg tendons **2** : to make ineffective or powerless : CRIPPLE

[1]**hand** \'hand\ *n* **1 a** : the free end part of the forelimb when modified (as in man) for handling, grasping, and holding **b** : any of various anatomical parts that are homologous or analogous to the hand (as the hind foot of an ape or the chela of a crab) **2** : something resembling a hand: as **a** : an indicator or pointer on a dial **b** : a figure of a hand with forefinger extended to point a direction or call attention to something **c** : a cluster of bananas developed from a single flower group **3** : personal possession : CONTROL, DIRECTION **4 a** : SIDE, DIRECTION **b** : a side or aspect of an issue or argument **5** : a pledge esp. of betrothal or bestowal in marriage **6 a** : style of penmanship : HANDWRITING **b** : SIGNATURE **7 a** : SKILL, ABILITY **b** : a part or share in doing something **8** : SOURCE **9** : a round of applause **10 a** : the cards held by a player in a card game **b** : a single round in a game **11 a** : one who performs or executes a particular work **b** : a hired worker : LABORER **c** : a member of a ship's crew **d** : one skilled in a particular activity or field **12 a** : HANDIWORK **b** : style of execution : WORKMANSHIP **c** : TOUCH, FEEL — **at hand** : near in time or place — **by hand** : with the hands — **in hand** **1** : in one's possession or control **2** : in preparation — **off one's hands** : out of one's care or charge — **on all hands** *or* **on every hand** : EVERYWHERE — **on hand** **1** : in present possession **2** : about to appear : PENDING **3** : in attendance : PRESENT — **out of hand** **1** : without delay : FORTHWITH **2** : done with **3** : out of control — **to hand** **1** : into possession **2** : within reach **3** : into control or subjection

[2]**hand** *vt* **1** : to lead, guide, or assist with the hand : CONDUCT **2 a** : to give, pass, or transmit with the hand **b** : PRESENT, PROVIDE

hand•bag \'han(d)-ˌbag\ *n* **1** : TRAVELING BAG **2** : a woman's bag used for carrying small personal articles and money

hand•ball \-ˌbȯl\ *n* : a game played in a walled court or against a single wall or board by two or four players who use their hands to strike the ball

hand•bar•row \-ˌbar-ō\ *n* : a flat rectangular frame with handles at both ends that is carried by two persons

hand•bill \-ˌbil\ *n* : a small printed sheet to be distributed by hand

hand•book \-ˌbu̇k\ *n* : a small book of facts or useful information usu. about a particular subject : MANUAL

hand•car \'han(d)-ˌkär\ *n* : a small four-wheeled railroad car propelled by a hand-operated mechanism or by a small motor

hand•clasp \-ˌklasp\ *n* : HANDSHAKE

[1]**hand•craft** \-ˌkraft\ *n* : HANDICRAFT

[2]**handcraft** *vt* : to fashion by handicraft

[1]**hand•cuff** \-ˌkəf\ *vt* : to apply handcuffs to : MANACLE

[2]**handcuff** *n* : a metal fastening that can be locked around a wrist and that is usu. connected by a chain or bar with another handcuff — usu. used in pl.

hand down *vt* **1** : to transmit in succession **2** : to make official formulation of and express (the opinion of a court)

hand•ed \'han-dəd\ *adj* : having or using such or so many hands — **hand•ed•ness** *n*

hand•ful \'han(d)-ˌfu̇l\ *n, pl* **hand•fuls** \-ˌfu̇lz\ *or* **hands•ful** \'han(d)z-ˌfu̇l\ **1** : as much or as many as the hand will grasp **2** : a small quantity or number **3** : as much as one can control or manage

hand•grip \'han(d)-ˌgrip\ *n* **1** : a grasping with the hand **2** : HANDLE

hand•gun \-ˌgən\ *n* : a firearm held and fired with one hand

[1]**hand•i•cap** \'han-di-ˌkap\ *n* **1** : a race or contest in which an artificial advantage is given to or disadvantage imposed on a contestant to equalize chances of winning; *also* : the advantage given or disadvantage imposed **2** : a disadvantage that makes progress or success more difficult

[2]**handicap** *vt* **-capped**; **-cap•ping** **1 a** : to give a handicap to **b** : to assign handicaps to **2** : to put at a disadvantage

hand•i•craft \'han-di-ˌkraft\ *n* **1** : an occupation (as weaving or pottery making) requiring skill with the hands **2** : the articles fashioned by those engaged in handicraft — **hand•i•craft•er** *n* — **hand•i•crafts•man** \-ˌkraf(t)s-mən\ *n*

hand•i•ly \'han-də-lē\ *adv* : in a handy manner : EASILY, CONVENIENTLY

hand•i•ness \-dē-nəs\ *n* : the quality or state of being handy

hand in glove *or* **hand and glove** *adv* : in extremely close relationship or agreement

hand in hand *adv* : in union : CONJOINTLY

hand•i•work \'han-di-ˌwərk\ *n* **1** : work done by the hands **2** : work one has done himself

hand•ker•chief \'haŋ-kər-chəf, -ˌchēf\ *n* **1** : a small usu. square piece of cloth used for various personal purposes or as a costume accessory **2** : KERCHIEF 1

[1]**han•dle** \'han-dᵊl\ *n* **1** : a part that is designed esp. to be grasped by the hand **2** : something that resembles a handle — **han•dled** \-dᵊld\ *adj* — **off the handle** : into a state of sudden and violent anger

[2]**handle** *vb* **han•dled**; **han•dling** \-dliŋ, -dᵊl-iŋ\ **1 a** : to touch, feel, hold, or otherwise affect with the hand **b** : to manage with the hands **2 a** : to deal with in writing or speaking or in the plastic arts **b** : CONTROL, DIRECT **c** : to train and act as second for (a prizefighter) **3** : to deal with or act on **4** : to deal or trade in **5** : to act, behave, or feel in a certain way when managed or directed — **han•dler** \'han-dlər, -dᵊl-ər\ *n*

han•dle•a•ble \'han-dᵊl-ə-bəl\ *adj* : capable of being handled

han•dle•bar \'han-dᵊl-ˌbär\ *n* : a straight or bent bar with a handle (as for steering a bicycle) at each end

hand•made \'han(d)-'mād\ *adj* : made by hand and not by machine

hand•maid \-ˌmād\ *or* **hand•maid•en** \-ˌmād-ᵊn\ *n* : a female servant or attendant

hand–me–down \'han(d)-mē-ˌdau̇n\ *adj* : worn or put in use by one person or group after being discarded by another — **hand–me–down** *n*

hand on *vt* : to hand down (sense 1)

hand•out \'han-ˌdau̇t\ *n* **1** : a portion of food, clothing, or money given to or as if to a beggar **2** : an information sheet for free distribution **3** : a prepared statement released to the press

hand•pick \'han(d)-'pik\ *vt* : to select personally

hand•rail \'han-ˌdrāl\ *n* : a narrow rail for grasping with the hand as a support (as on a staircase)

hand•saw \'han(d)-ˌsȯ\ *n* : a saw used with one hand; *esp* : a woodworker's ripsaw or crosscut saw

hand•sel \'han(t)-səl\ *n* **1** : a gift made as a token of good wishes or luck esp. at the beginning of a new year **2** : EARNEST, FORETASTE

hand•shake \'han(d)-ˌshāk\ *n* : a clasping (as in greeting or farewell) of right hands by two people

hand•some \'han(t)-səm\ *adj* **1** : moderately large : SIZABLE **2** : marked by graciousness or generosity : LIBERAL **3** : having a pleasing and usu. impressive or dignified appearance — **hand•some•ly** *adv* — **hand•some•ness** *n*

hand•spring \'han(d)-ˌspriŋ\ *n* : a feat of tumbling in which the body turns forward or backward in a full circle from a standing position and lands first on the hands and then on the feet

hand•stand \-ˌstand\ *n* : a balancing position in which the body is upside down and supported on the hands

hand–to–hand \ˌhan-tə-'hand\ *adj* : being at very close quarters

hand–to–mouth \-tə-'maůth\ *adj* : having or providing nothing to spare : PRECARIOUS

hand•work \'han-ˌdwərk\ *n* : work done with the hands and not by machine

hand•writ•ing \'han-ˌdrīt-iŋ\ *n* **1** : writing done by hand; *esp* : the cast or form of writing peculiar to a particular person **2** : something written by hand : MANUSCRIPT

handy \'han-dē\ *adj* **1 a** : conveniently near **b** : convenient for use **c** : easily handled **2** : clever in using the hands

handy•man \-ˌman\ *n* : a man who does odd jobs

¹hang \'haŋ\ *vb* **hung** \'həŋ\; **hang•ing** \'haŋ-iŋ\ **1 a** : to fasten or be fastened to some elevated point without support from below : SUSPEND, DANGLE **b** : to put to death or be put to death by hanging from a rope tied round the neck **c** : to fasten so as to allow free motion upon a point of suspension **d** : to fit or fix in position or at a proper angle **e** : to adjust the hem of (a skirt) so as to hang evenly and at a proper height when worn **2** : to cover, decorate, or furnish by hanging pictures, trophies, or drapery **3** : to hold or bear in a suspended or inclined manner : DROOP **4** : to fasten to a wall **5** : to display (pictures) in a gallery **6** : to remain poised or stationary in the air **7** : to stay with persistence **8** : IMPEND **9** : DEPEND **10 a** (1) : to take hold for support : CLING (2) : to keep persistent contact **b** : to be burdensome or oppressive **c** : LEAN **11 a** : to be in suspense : suffer delay **b** : to occupy an uncertain mid-position **12** : to lean, incline, or jut over or downward **13** : to be in a state of rapt attention **14** : LINGER, LOITER **15** : to fit or fall from the figure in easy lines — **hang•a•ble** *adj* — **hang fire** : DELAY, HESITATE

²hang *n* **1** : the manner in which a thing hangs **2 a** : peculiar and significant meaning **b** : the special method of doing, using, or dealing with something : KNACK — **give a hang** *or* **care a hang** : to be concerned or worried

¹hang•ar \'haŋ-ər\ *n* : SHELTER, SHED; *esp* : a covered and usu. enclosed area for housing and repairing airplanes

²hangar *vt* : to place in a hangar

hang around *vi* **1** : to pass time or stay aimlessly : loiter idly **2** : to spend one's time in company

hang back *vi* **1** : to drag behind others **2** : to be reluctant : HESITATE, FALTER

hang•dog \'haŋ-ˌdȯg\ *adj* **1** : ASHAMED, GUILTY **2** : ABJECT, COWED

hang•er \'haŋ-ər\ *n* **1** : one that hangs or causes to be hung **2** : something that hangs, overhangs, or is suspended; *esp* : a small sword formerly used by seamen **3** : a device by which or to which something is hung or hangs: as **a** : a strap on a sword belt by which a sword or dagger can be suspended **b** : a loop (as on a collar) by which a garment is hung up **c** : a device that fits inside or around a garment (as a suit or a pair of trousers) for hanging from a hook or rod

hang•er–on \'haŋ-ə-ˌrȯn, -ˌrän\ *n, pl* **hangers–on** : one that hangs around a person, place, or institution for personal gain

hang gliding *n* : the sport of gliding down from a cliff or hill suspended from a large untethered kite

¹hang•ing \'haŋ-iŋ\ *n* **1** : an execution by strangling or breaking the neck by a suspended noose **2** : something hung: as **a** : CURTAIN — usu. used in pl. **b** : a covering (as a tapestry) for a wall — usu. used in pl. **3** : a downward slope : DECLIVITY

²hanging *adj* **1** : situated or lying on steeply sloping ground **2 a** : OVERHANGING **b** : supported only by the wall on one side **3** : adapted for sustaining a hanging object **4** : punishable by death by hanging

hang•man \'haŋ-mən\ *n* : a person who hangs condemned criminals

hang•nail \-ˌnāl\ *n* : a bit of skin hanging loose at the side or base of a fingernail

hang on *vi* **1** : to keep hold : hold onto something **2** : to persist tenaciously — **hang on to** : to hold, grip, or keep tenaciously

hang out \(')haŋ-'aůt\ *vb* **1** : to protrude in a downward direction **2** : to habitually spend one's time idly **3** : to display outside as an announcement to the public

hang•out \'haŋ-ˌaůt\ *n* : a place in which a person spends a great deal of time or which he visits regularly

hang•over \'haŋ-ˌō-vər\ *n* **1** : something (as a surviving custom) that remains from what is past **2** : disagreeable aftereffects following great excitement or excess (as in consumption of alcohol)

hang up *vb* **1 a** : to place on a hook or hanger **b** : to replace (a telephone receiver) on the cradle so that the connection is broken; *also* : to terminate a telephone conversation **2** : to stick or snag or cause to stick or snag so as to be immovable

hank \'haŋk\ *n* : COIL, LOOP, SKEIN; *esp* : a coiled or looped bundle (as of yarn)

han•ker \'haŋ-kər\ *vi* **han•kered**; **han•ker•ing** \-k(ə-)riŋ\ : to have an eager or persistent desire — **han•ker•er** *n*

han•ky–pan•ky \ˌhaŋ-kē-'paŋ-kē\ *n* : questionable or underhand activity : TRICKERY

han•som \'han(t)-səm\ *n* : a light 2-wheeled covered carriage with the driver's seat elevated behind

Ha•nuk•kah \'kän-ə-kə, 'hän-\ *n* : an 8-day Jewish holiday celebrated in November or December in commemoration of the rededication of the Temple

hao•le \'haů-(ˌ)lā\ *n* : one who is not a member of the native race of Hawaii; *esp* : WHITE

¹hap \'hap\ *n* **1** : HAPPENING **2** : CHANCE, FORTUNE

²hap *vi* **happed**; **hap•ping** : HAPPEN

¹hap•haz•ard \hap-'haz-ərd\ *n* : CHANCE, ACCIDENT, RANDOM

²haphazard *adj* : marked by lack of plan, order, or direction : AIMLESS — **haphazard** *adv* — **hap•haz•ard•ly** *adv* — **hap•haz•ard•ness** *n*

hap•less \'hap-ləs\ *adj* : having no luck : UNFORTUNATE — **hap•less•ly** *adv* — **hap•less•ness** *n*

hap•ly \'hap-lē\ *adv* : by chance, luck, or accident

hap•pen \'hap-ən\ *vi* **hap•pened**; **hap•pen•ing** \'hap-(ə-)niŋ\ **1** : to occur or come about by chance **2** : to take place **3** : to have occasion or opportunity without intention : CHANCE **4 a** : to meet or find something by chance **b** : to appear casually or by chance **5** : to come esp. by way of injury or harm

hap•pen•ing \'hap-(ə-)niŋ\ *n* **1** : OCCURRENCE **2** : an apparently aimless and pointless staged performance intended to create startling chance effects

hap•pen•stance \'hap-ən-ˌstan(t)s\ *n* : a circumstance regarded as due to chance

hap•pi•ly \'hap-ə-lē\ *adv* **1** : FORTUNATELY, LUCKILY **2** : in a happy manner or state **3** : APTLY, SUCCESSFULLY

hap•pi•ness \'hap-i-nəs\ *n* **1 a** : a state of well-being and contentment : JOY **b** : a pleasurable satisfaction **2** : APTNESS, FELICITY

hap•py \'hap-ē\ *adj* **1** : FORTUNATE, LUCKY **2** : notably well adapted or fitting : FELICITOUS **3 a** : enjoying well-being and contentment : JOYOUS **b** : expressing or suggestive of happiness : PLEASANT **c** : PLEASED, GRATIFIED

hap•py–go–lucky \ˌhap-ē-(ˌ)gō-'lək-ē\ *adj* : blithely unconcerned : CAREFREE

hara–kiri \ˌhar-i-'ki(ə)r-ē, -'kar-ē\ *n* : suicide by disembowelment

ha•rangue \hə-'raŋ\ *n* **1** : a speech addressed to a public assembly **2** : a bombastic ranting speech or writing **3** : LECTURE — **harangue** *vb*
ha•rass \hə-'ras, 'har-əs\ *vt* **1** : to tire out by persistent efforts : worry or annoy with repeated attacks **2** : to lay waste : HARRY — **ha•rass•ment** *n*
¹har•bin•ger \'här-bən-jər\ *n* : a messenger sent on ahead : one that announces or shows what is coming : FORERUNNER
²harbinger *vt* : to be a harbinger of : PRESAGE
¹har•bor \'här-bər\ *n* **1** : a place of security and comfort : REFUGE **2** : a part of a body of water protected and deep enough to furnish anchorage; *esp* : one with port facilities — **har•bor•less** \-ləs\ *adj*
²harbor *vb* **har•bored**; **har•bor•ing** \-b(ə-)riŋ\ **1 a** : to give shelter or refuge to **b** : to be the home or habitat of : CONTAIN **2** : to hold a thought or feeling of **3** : to take shelter in or as if in a harbor — **har•bor•er** *n*
har•bor•age \'här-bə-rij\ *n* : SHELTER, HARBOR
¹hard \'härd\ *adj* **1** : not easily penetrated, cut, or divided into parts : not soft **2 a** : strong in alcoholic content **b** : characterized by the presence of salts that prevent lathering with soap **3 a** : metallic as distinct from paper **b** : convertible into gold : stable in value **4 a** : physically fit **b** : HARDY **c** : free of weakness or flaw **5 a** (1) : FIRM, DEFINITE (2) : FACTUAL, ACTUAL **b** : CLOSE, SEARCHING **c** : free from sentimentality or illusion : REALISTIC **d** : OBDURATE, UNFEELING **6 a** (1) : difficult to bear or endure (2) : OPPRESSIVE, UNJUST **b** : INCORRIGIBLE, TOUGH **c** (1) : harsh, severe, or offensive in tendency or effect (2) : RESENTFUL (3) : STRICT, UNRELENTING **d** : INCLEMENT **e** (1) : intense in force, manner, or degree (2) : ARDUOUS, STRENUOUS (3) : performing or carrying on with great energy, intensity, or persistence **7 a** : characterized by sharp or harsh outline, rigid execution, and stiff drawing **b** : sharply defined : STARK **c** : lacking in shading, delicacy, or resonance **d** : sounding as in *arcing* and *geese* respectively — used of *c* and *g* **8 a** : difficult to accomplish or resolve : TROUBLESOME **b** : difficult to comprehend or explain — **hard up 1** : short of money : POOR **2** : poorly provided
²hard *adv* **1 a** : with great or utmost effort or energy : STRENUOUSLY **b** : VIOLENTLY, FIERCELY **c** : to the full extent — used in nautical directions **d** : INTENTLY **2 a** : HARSHLY, SEVERELY **b** : with rancor, bitterness, or grief **3** : TIGHTLY, FIRMLY **4** : to the point of hardness **5** : close in time or space
hard–and–fast \ˌhärd-ᵊn-'fast\ *adj* : rigidly binding : STRICT
hard•ball \'härd-ˌbȯl\ *n* : BASEBALL
hard–bit•ten \-'bit-ᵊn\ *adj* : SEASONED, TOUGH, DOGGED
hard–boiled \-'bȯild\ *adj* **1** : boiled until both white and yolk have solidified **2 a** : lacking sentiment : CALLOUS **b** : PRACTICAL, REALISTIC
hard core *n* : a usu. resistant and enduring central part; *esp* : a militant nucleus of a group — **hard–core** *adj*
hard•en \'härd-ᵊn\ *vb* **hard•ened**; **hard•en•ing** \'härd-niŋ, -ᵊn-iŋ\ **1** : to make or become hard or harder **2** : to make or become hardy or strong **3 a** : to make or become stubborn, unfeeling, or unsympathetic **b** : to become confirmed — **hard•en•er** \'härd-nər, -ᵊn-ər\ *n*
hard•hand•ed \'härd-'han-dəd\ *adj* **1** : having hands made hard by labor **2** : STRICT, OPPRESSIVE
hard•head•ed \-'hed-əd\ *adj* **1** : STUBBORN **2** : marked by sound judgment : REALISTIC — **hard•head•ed•ly** *adv*
hard•heart•ed \-'härt-əd\ *adj* : UNFEELING, PITILESS — **hard•heart•ed•ly** *adv* — **hard•heart•ed•ness** *n*
har•di•hood \'härd-ē-ˌhu̇d\ *n* **1 a** : resolute courage and fortitude **b** : disdainful insolence **2** : VIGOR, ROBUSTNESS
hard labor *n* : compulsory labor of imprisoned criminals that is a part of the prison discipline
hard•ly \'härd-lē\ *adv* **1** : with force : VIGOROUSLY **2** : SEVERELY, HARSHLY **3** : with difficulty : PAINFULLY **4** : not quite : BARELY, SCARCELY
hard•ness \-nəs\ *n* : the quality or state of being hard
hard–of–hear•ing \ˌhärd-ə(v)-'hi(ə)r-iŋ\ *adj* : of or relating to a defective but functional sense of hearing
hard•pan \'härd-ˌpan\ *n* **1** : a cemented or compacted and often clayey layer in soil that roots cannot readily penetrate **2** : a fundamental part : BEDROCK, BASIS
hard put *adj* : barely able
hard sauce *n* : a creamed mixture of butter and powdered sugar often with added cream and flavoring
hard•ship \'härd-ˌship\ *n* **1** : SUFFERING, PRIVATION **2** : something that causes or entails suffering or privation
hard•stand \-ˌstand\ *n* : a hard-surfaced area for parking an airplane
hard•tack \-ˌtak\ *n* : a hard biscuit or bread made of flour and water without salt
hard•top \-ˌtäp\ *n* : an automobile styled to resemble a convertible but having a rigid top of metal or plastic
hard•ware \-ˌwa(ə)r\ *n* : articles (as fittings, cutlery, tools, utensils, or parts of machines) made of metal
hard•wood \-ˌwu̇d\ *n* **1** : the wood of a broad-leaved usu. deciduous tree as distinguished from that of a conifer **2** : a tree that yields hardwood
hard•work•ing \-'wər-kiŋ\ *adj* : INDUSTRIOUS
har•dy \'härd-ē\ *adj* **1** : BOLD, BRAVE **2** : AUDACIOUS, BRAZEN **3 a** : inured to fatigue or hardships : ROBUST **b** : able to withstand adverse conditions (as of weather) — **har•di•ly** \'härd-ᵊl-ē\ *adv* — **har•di•ness** \'härd-ē-nəs\ *n*
hare \'ha(ə)r\ *n, pl* **hare** *or* **hares** : any of various swift timid long-eared mammals with a divided upper lip, long hind legs, a short cocked tail, and the young open-eyed and furred at birth
hare•bell \'ha(ə)r-ˌbel\ *n* : a slender herb with bright blue bell-shaped flowers
hare•brained \-'brānd\ *adj* : FLIGHTY, GIDDY
hare•lip \-'lip\ *n* : a deformity in which the upper lip is split like that of a hare — **hare•lipped** \-'lipt\ *adj*
har•em \'har-əm\ *n* **1 a** : the rooms assigned to the women in a Muslim household **b** : the women of a Muslim household **2** : a group of females associated with one male — used of polygamous animals
hark \'härk\ *vi* : to pay close attention : LISTEN
hark back *vi* : to go back to something earlier
har•le•quin \'här-li-k(w)ən\ *n* **1** *cap* : a character in comedy and pantomime with a shaved head, masked face, variegated tights, and wooden sword **2** : BUFFOON, CLOWN
har•lot \'här-lət\ *n* : PROSTITUTE
har•lot•ry \-lə-trē\ *n, pl* **-ries** : PROSTITUTION
¹harm \'härm\ *n* **1** : physical or mental damage : INJURY **2** : MISCHIEF, HURT
²harm *vt* : to cause harm to
harm•ful \'härm-fəl\ *adj* : DAMAGING, INJURIOUS — **harm•ful•ly** \-fə-lē\ *adv* — **harm•ful•ness** *n*
harm•less \-ləs\ *adj* **1** : free from harm, liability, or loss **2** : lacking capacity or intent to injure : INNOCUOUS — **harm•less•ly** *adv* — **harm•less•ness** *n*
¹har•mon•ic \här-'män-ik\ *adj* **1** : of or relating to musical harmony as opposed to melody or rhythm **2** : of an integrated nature : CONGRUOUS
²harmonic *n* **1** : a musical overtone **2** : a flutelike tone produced (as on a violin) by lightly touching a vibrating string with a finger
har•mon•i•ca \här-'män-i-kə\ *n* : a small rectangular wind instrument with free metallic reeds recessed in air slots from which tones are sounded by exhaling and inhaling
har•mon•ics \här-'män-iks\ *n* : the study of the physical characteristics of musical sounds

har·mo·ni·ous \här-'mō-nē-əs\ *adj* **1** : musically concordant **2** : having the parts agreeably related : CONGRUOUS **3** : marked by accord in sentiment or action — **har·mo·ni·ous·ly** *adv* — **har·mo·ni·ous·ness** *n*

har·mo·ni·um \-nē-əm\ *n* : a keyboard wind instrument in which the wind acts on a set of metal reeds

har·mo·nize \'här-mə-ˌnīz\ *vb* **1** : to play or sing in harmony **2** : to be in harmony **3** : to bring into harmony or agreement **4** : to provide or accompany with harmony — **har·mo·ni·za·tion** \ˌhär-mə-nə-'zā-shən\ *n*

har·mo·ny \'här-mə-nē\ *n, pl* **-nies** **1 a** : the combination of simultaneous musical notes in a chord **b** : the structure of music with respect to the composition and progression of chords **c** : the science of the structure, relation, and progression of chords **2 a** : pleasing or congruent arrangement of parts **b** : CORRESPONDENCE, ACCORD **c** : internal calm : TRANQUILLITY **3 a** : an interweaving of different accounts into a single narrative **b** : an arrangement of different accounts in parallel columns with corresponding passages side by side

[1]har·ness \'här-nəs\ *n* **1 a** (1) : the gear other than a yoke of a draft animal (2) : GEAR, EQUIPMENT **b** (1) : occupational surroundings or routine (2) : close association **2** : military equipment for horse or man

[2]harness *vt* **1 a** : to put a harness on **b** : to attach by means of a harness **2** : to tie together : YOKE **3** : to put to work : UTILIZE

[1]harp \'härp\ *n* : an instrument having strings of graded length stretched across an open triangular frame with a curving top and played by plucking with the fingers — **harp·ist** \'här-pəst\ *n*

[2]harp *vi* **1** : to play on a harp **2** : to dwell on or recur to a subject tiresomely or monotonously

har·poon \här-'pün\ *n* : a barbed spear used esp. in hunting large fish or whales — **harpoon** *vt* — **har·poon·er** *n*

harp·si·chord \'härp-si-ˌkȯrd\ *n* : a keyboard instrument resembling the grand piano and producing tones by the plucking of wire strings with quills or leather points

har·py \'här-pē\ *n, pl* **harpies** **1** : a greedy or grasping person : LEECH **2** : a shrewish woman

har·que·bus \'här-kwi-(ˌ)bəs\ *n* : a portable firearm of the 15th and 16th centuries later replaced by the musket

har·ri·dan \'har-əd-ᵊn\ *n* : a scolding old woman

[1]har·ri·er \'har-ē-ər\ *n* **1** : a hunting dog like a small foxhound used esp. for hunting rabbits **2** : a runner on a cross-country team

[2]harrier *n* **1** : one that harries **2** : any of various slender long-legged hawks

[1]har·row \'har-ō\ *n* : a cultivating implement set with spikes, spring teeth, or disks and used primarily for pulverizing and smoothing the soil

[2]harrow *vt* **1** : to cultivate with a harrow **2** : TORMENT, VEX — **har·row·er** *n*

har·ry \'har-ē\ *vt* **har·ried**; **har·ry·ing** **1** : RAID, RAVAGE, PILLAGE **2** : to torment by or as if by constant attack

harsh \'härsh\ *adj* **1** : disagreeable to the touch **2** : causing discomfort or pain **3** : unduly exacting : SEVERE **4** : aesthetically jarring — **harsh·en** \'här-shən\ *vb* — **harsh·ly** *adv* — **harsh·ness** *n*

harts·horn \'härts-ˌhȯrn\ *n* : a preparation of ammonia used as smelling salts

har·um–scar·um \ˌhar-əm-'skar-əm, ˌher-əm-'sker-\ *adj* : RECKLESS, IRRESPONSIBLE — **harum–scarum** *n* — **harum–scarum** *adv*

[1]har·vest \'här-vəst\ *n* **1** : the season when grains and fruits are gathered **2** : the gathering of a crop **3** : a ripe crop (as of grain or fruit); *also* : the quantity of a crop gathered in a single season **4** : the product or reward of effort

[2]harvest *vb* **1 a** : to gather in a crop : REAP **b** : to gather as if by harvesting **2** : to win by achievement — **har·vest·a·ble** *adj* — **har·vest·er** *n*

has *pres 3d sing of* HAVE

has–been \'haz-ˌbin\ *n* : one that has passed the peak of ability, power, effectiveness, or popularity

ha·sen·pfef·fer \'häz-ᵊn-ˌ(p)fef-ər\ *n* : a stew made of marinated rabbit meat

[1]hash \'hash\ *vt* **1 a** : to chop into small pieces **b** : CONFUSE, MUDDLE **2** : to talk about : REVIEW, CONSIDER

[2]hash *n* **1** : chopped food; *esp* : chopped meat mixed with potatoes and browned **2** : a restatement of something that is already known **3** : HODGEPODGE, JUMBLE

hash·ish \'hash-ˌēsh, -(ˌ)ish\ *n* : a narcotic preparation from hemp that is smoked, chewed, or drunk for its intoxicating effect

hasp \'hasp\ *n* : any of several devices for fastening; *esp* : a fastener esp. for a door or lid consisting of a hinged metal strap that fits over a staple and is secured by a pin or padlock

has·sle \'has-əl\ *n* **1** : a heated argument : WRANGLE **2** : a violent skirmish : FIGHT — **hassle** *vi*

has·sock \'has-ək\ *n* **1** : TUSSOCK **2 a** : a cushion to kneel on in prayer **b** : a cushion that serves as a seat or as a leg rest

[1]haste \'hāst\ *n* **1** : rapidity of motion or action : SWIFTNESS **2** : rash or headlong action : PRECIPITATENESS **3** : undue eagerness to act : URGENCY

[2]haste *vb* : to move or act swiftly : HASTEN, HURRY

has·ten \'hās-ᵊn\ *vb* **has·tened**; **has·ten·ing** \'hās-niŋ, -ᵊn-iŋ\ **1** : to urge on **2** : to speed up : ACCELERATE **3** : to move or act quickly : HURRY

hasty \'hā-stē\ *adj* **1 a** : rapid in action or movement : SPEEDY **b** : done or made in a hurry : HURRIED **2** : EAGER, IMPATIENT **3** : PRECIPITATE, RASH **4** : prone to anger : IRRITABLE — **hast·i·ly** \-stə-lē\ *adv* — **hast·i·ness** \-stē-nəs\ *n*

hat \'hat\ *n* : a covering for the head usu. having a shaped crown and brim — **hat in the ring** : an announcement of entry into a usu. political contest

hat·box \'hat-ˌbäks\ *n* : a round piece of luggage esp. for carrying hats

[1]hatch \'hach\ *n* **1** : an opening in the deck of a ship or in the floor or roof of a building; *also* : a small door or opening (as in an airplane) **2** : the covering for a hatch

[2]hatch *vb* **1 a** : to produce young by incubation **b** : INCUBATE **2** : to bring into being : ORIGINATE; *esp* : to concoct in secret **3 a** : to emerge from an egg, pupa, or chrysalis **b** : to give forth young — **hatch·a·bil·i·ty** \ˌhach-ə-'bil-ət-ē\ *n* — **hatch·a·ble** *adj*

hatch·ery \'hach-(ə-)rē\ *n, pl* **-er·ies** : a place for hatching eggs

hatch·et \'hach-ət\ *n* **1** : a short-handled ax for use with one hand that has a part opposite the blade for hammering **2** : TOMAHAWK

hatchet face *n* : a thin sharp face — **hatch·et–faced** \ˌhach-ət-'fāst\ *adj*

hatchet man *n* : one hired for murder, coercion, or unscrupulous attack

hatch·ing \'hach-iŋ\ *n* : the engraving or drawing of fine lines in close proximity chiefly to give an effect of shading; *also* : the pattern so created

hatch·ment \-mənt\ *n* : a panel on which a coat of arms of a deceased person is temporarily displayed

hatch·way \-ˌwā\ *n* : a hatch giving access to an enclosed space (as a compartment or cellar) and usu. having a ladder or stairs

[1]hate \'hāt\ *n* **1 a** : intense hostility and aversion **b** : distaste coupled with sustained ill will **c** : a very strong dislike : ANTIPATHY **2** : an object of hatred

[2]hate *vt* **1** : to feel extreme enmity toward **2 a** : to have a strong aversion to **b** : to find distasteful — **hat·er** *n*

hate·ful \'hāt-fəl\ *adj* **1** : full of hate : MALICIOUS **2** : exciting or deserving hate — **hate·ful·ly** \-fə-lē\ *adv* — **hate·ful·ness** *n*
ha·tred \'hā-trəd\ *n* **1** : HATE **2** : prejudiced hostility or animosity
hat·ter \'hat-ər\ *n* : one that makes, sells, or cleans and repairs hats
hau·berk \'hȯ-(ˌ)bərk\ *n* : a tunic of chain mail worn as defensive armor from the 12th to the 14th century
haugh·ty \'hȯt-ē\ *adj* : disdainfully proud : ARROGANT — **haugh·ti·ly** \-ᵊl-ē\ *adv* — **haugh·ti·ness** \-ē-nəs\ *n*
¹**haul** \'hȯl\ *vb* **1** : to change the course of (a ship) esp. so as to sail closer to the wind **2 a** : to exert traction : DRAW, PULL **b** : to obtain or move by hauling **c** : to transport in a vehicle **3** : HALE **4** : SHIFT — **haul·er** *n*
²**haul** *n* **1 a** : the act or process of hauling : PULL **b** : a device for hauling **2 a** : an amount collected : TAKE **b** : the fish taken in a single draft of a net **3 a** : transportation by hauling **b** : the distance or route over which a load is transported **c** : a quantity transported : LOAD
haul·age \'hȯ-lij\ *n* : the act or process of hauling
haunch \'hȯnch\ *n* **1 a** : ²HIP **b** : HINDQUARTER 2 — usu. used in pl. **2** : HINDQUARTER 1
¹**haunt** \'hȯnt\ *vb* **1 a** : to visit often : FREQUENT **b** : to continually seek the company of **c** : to stay around or persist : LINGER **2 a** : to recur constantly and spontaneously to **b** : to reappear continually in **3** : to visit or inhabit as a ghost — **haunt·ing·ly** *adv*
²**haunt** *n* : a place habitually frequented or repeatedly visited
haut·bois *or* **haut·boy** \'(h)ō-ˌbȯi\ *n, pl* **hautbois** \-ˌbȯiz\ *or* **hautboys** : OBOE
hau·teur \hō-'tər\ *n* : HAUGHTINESS, ARROGANCE
Ha·vana \hə-'van-ə\ *n* : a cigar made from Cuban tobacco
¹**have** \(')hav, (h)əv, v; *before "to" usu* 'haf\ *vb, past & past part* **had** \(')had, (h)əd, d\; *pres part* **hav·ing** \'hav-iŋ\; *pres 3d sing* **has** \(')haz, (h)əz, z, s; *before "to" usu* 'has\ **1 a** : POSSESS, OWN **b** : to hold in one's use, service, or affection or at one's disposal **c** : to consist of : CONTAIN **2** : to feel obligation or necessity in regard to **3** : to stand in relationship to **4 a** : to acquire or get possession of : OBTAIN **b** : RECEIVE **c** : ACCEPT; *esp* : to accept in marriage **5 a** : to be marked or characterized by **b** : SHOW **c** : USE, EXERCISE **6 a** : to experience esp. by submitting to, undergoing, or suffering **b** : to carry on : PERFORM, TAKE **c** : to entertain in the mind : CHERISH **7 a** : to cause to by persuasive or forceful means **b** : to cause to be **8** : ALLOW **9** : to be competent in **10 a** : to hold an advantage over **b** : TRICK, FOOL **11** : to be able to exercise **12** : BEGET, BEAR **13** : to partake of **14** : BRIBE **15** — used as an auxiliary verb with the past participle to form the present perfect, past perfect, or future perfect — **have at** \ha-'vat\ : to go at or deal with : ATTACK — **have done** : FINISH, STOP — **have it in for** \ˌhav-ət-'in-fər, -ˌfȯr\ : to intend to do harm to — **have it out** : to settle a matter of contention by discussion or a fight — **have to do with 1** : to deal with **2** : to have in the way of connection or relation with or effect on
²**have** \'hav\ *n* : one that has material wealth as distinguished from one that is poor
ha·ven \'hā-vən\ *n* **1** : HARBOR, PORT **2** : a place of safety : ASYLUM
have–not \'hav-ˌnät, -'nät\ *n* : one that is poor in material wealth as distinguished from one that is rich
hav·er·sack \'hav-ər-ˌsak\ *n* : a bag similar to a knapsack but worn over one shoulder
hav·oc \'hav-ək\ *n* **1** : wide and general destruction : DEVASTATION **2** : great confusion and disorder
¹**haw** \'hȯ\ *n* **1** : a hawthorn berry **2** : HAWTHORN
²**haw** *vi* : to utter the sound represented by *haw*
³**haw** *n* : a vocalized pause in speaking or an instance of uttering this sound
⁴**haw** *imperative verb* — used as a direction to turn to the left
Ha·wai·ian guitar \hə-ˌwä-yən-, -ˌwī-(y)ən-, -ˌwȯ-yən-\ *n* : a flat-bodied stringed musical instrument with a long fretted neck and usu. 6 to 8 strings that are plucked
¹**hawk** \'hȯk\ *n* **1** : any of numerous birds of prey including all the smaller members of this group active mostly by day **2** : an individual who takes a militant attitude (as in a dispute) and advocates immediate vigorous action — **hawk·ish** \'hȯ-kish\ *adj*
²**hawk** *vb* **1** : to hunt birds by means of a trained hawk **2** : to hunt on the wing like a hawk
³**hawk** *vt* : to offer for sale by calling out in the street
⁴**hawk** *vb* **1** : to utter a harsh guttural sound in or as if in clearing the throat **2** : to raise by hawking
⁵**hawk** *n* : an act or sound of hawking
¹**hawk·er** \'hȯ-kər\ *n* : FALCONER
²**hawker** *n* : one that hawks wares
haw·ser \'hȯ-zər\ *n* : a large rope for towing, mooring, or securing a ship
haw·thorn \'hȯ-ˌthȯrn\ *n* : any of a genus of spring-flowering spiny shrubs or small trees of the rose family with glossy and often lobed leaves, white or pink fragrant flowers, and small red fruits
¹**hay** \'hā\ *n* : herbage (as grass) mowed and cured for fodder
²**hay** *vb* **1** : to cut, cure, and store herbage for hay **2** : to feed with hay — **hay·er** *n*
hay fever *n* : an acute allergic catarrh of the mucous membranes of the eyes, nose, and throat
hay·fork \'hā-ˌfȯrk\ *n* : a hand or mechanically operated fork for loading or unloading hay
hay·loft \-ˌlȯft\ *n* : a loft for hay
hay·mow \-ˌmau̇\ *n* : a mow of or for hay
hay·rick \-ˌrik\ *n* : a large sometimes thatched outdoor stack of hay
hay·seed \-ˌsēd\ *n* **1** : clinging bits of straw or chaff from hay **2** : BUMPKIN, YOKEL
hay·wire \-ˌwī(ə)r\ *adj* **1** : hastily or shoddily made **2** : being out of order : MALFUNCTIONING **3** : emotionally or mentally upset : CRAZY
¹**haz·ard** \'haz-ərd\ *n* **1** : a game of chance played with two dice **2** : CHANCE, ACCIDENT **3** : RISK, PERIL **4** : a source of danger **5** : an obstruction on a golf course — **at hazard** : at stake
²**hazard** *vt* : VENTURE, RISK
haz·ard·ous \'haz-ərd-əs\ *adj* : DANGEROUS, RISKY — **haz·ard·ous·ly** *adv* — **haz·ard·ous·ness** *n*
¹**haze** \'hāz\ *vb* : to make or become hazy or cloudy
²**haze** *n* **1** : fine dust, smoke, or light vapor causing lack of transparency in the air **2** : vagueness of mind or mental perception
³**haze** *vt* **1** : to harass by exacting unnecessary, disagreeable, or difficult work **2 a** : to harass by banter, ridicule, or criticism **b** : to play abusive and humiliating tricks on by way of initiation — **haz·er** *n*
ha·zel \'hā-zəl\ *n* **1** : any of a genus of shrubs or small trees of the birch family bearing edible nuts enclosed in a leafy case **2** : a light brown to a strong yellowish brown — **hazel** *adj* — **ha·zel·ly** \'hāz-(ə-)lē\ *adj*
ha·zel·nut \-ˌnət\ *n* : the nut of a hazel
hazy \'hā-zē\ *adj* **1** : obscured or darkened by or as if by haze **2** : VAGUE, INDEFINITE **3** : CLOUDED — **haz·i·ly** \-zə-lē\ *adv* — **haz·i·ness** \-zē-nəs\ *n*
H–bomb \'āch-ˌbäm\ *n* : HYDROGEN BOMB
¹**he** \(')hē, ē\ *pron* **1** : that male one **2** : that one whose sex is unknown or immaterial
²**he** \'hē\ *n* : a male person or animal
¹**head** \'hed\ *n* **1** : the upper or front division of the body (as of a man or an insect) that contains the brain, the chief sense

organs, and the mouth **2 a** : MIND, UNDERSTANDING **b** : mental or emotional control : POISE **3** : the obverse of a coin **4 a** : each one among a number : INDIVIDUAL **b** *pl* **head** : a unit of number (as of livestock) **5 a** : the end that is upper or higher or opposite the foot **b** : the source of a stream **c** : either end of something (as a drum) whose two ends need not be distinguished **d** : a horizontal passage in a coal mine **6 a** : HEADMASTER **b** : a person responsible for directing the actions and duties of others : CHIEF, LEADER **7** : a compact mass of plant parts (as leaves or flowers) **8 a** : the leading element of a military column or a procession **b** : HEADWAY **9 a** : the uppermost extremity or projecting part of an object : TOP **b** : the striking part of a weapon **10** : the place of leadership or command **11** : the foam that rises on an effervescing liquid **12** : CRISIS — **off one's head** : CRAZY, DISTRACTED — **out of one's head** : DELIRIOUS — **over one's head** **1** : beyond one's comprehension **2** : so as to bypass or ignore one's superior standing or authority

²**head** *adj* **1** : of, relating to, or used for the head **2** : PRINCIPAL, CHIEF **3** : situated at the head **4** : coming from in front

³**head** *vb* **1** : to cut back or off the upper or terminal growth of (a plant or plant part) **2 a** : to provide with or form a head **b** : to form the head or top of **3** : to put oneself at the head of : act as leader to **4 a** : to get in front of so as to hinder, stop, or turn back **b** : to take a lead over (as in a race) : SURPASS **c** : to pass (a stream) by going round above the source **5 a** : to put something at the head of (as a list) **b** : to stand as the first or leading member of **6** : to take or cause to take a specified course

head·ache \ˈhed-ˌāk\ *n* **1** : pain in the head **2** : an annoying or baffling situation or problem — **head·achy** \-ˌā-kē\ *adj*

head·band \-ˌband\ *n* : a band worn on or around the head

head·board \-ˌbōrd\ *n* : a board forming the head (as of a bed)

head·cheese \-ˌchēz\ *n* : a product made from the edible parts of the head, feet, and sometimes the tongue and heart esp. of a pig cut up fine, seasoned, boiled, and pressed

head·dress \ˈhe(d)-ˌdres\ *n* : a covering or ornament for the head

head·ed \ˈhed-əd\ *adj* **1** : having a head or a heading **2** : having such a head or so many heads

head·er \ˈhed-ər\ *n* **1** : one that removes heads **2** : a fall or dive head foremost

head·first \ˈhed-ˈfərst\ *also* **head·fore·most** \-ˈfōr-ˌmōst\ *adv* : with the head foremost : HEADLONG — **headfirst** *adj*

head·gear \ˈhed-ˌgi(ə)r\ *n* **1** : a covering or protective device for the head **2** : harness for a horse's head

head·hunt·ing \-ˌhənt-iŋ\ *n* : the practice of cutting off and preserving as trophies the heads of enemies — **head·hunt·er** *n*

head·ing \ˈhed-iŋ\ *n* **1** : the compass direction in which the longitudinal axis of a ship or aircraft points **2** : something that forms or serves as a head; *esp* : an inscription, headline, or title standing at the top or beginning (as of a letter or chapter)

head·land \ˈhed-lənd, -ˌland\ *n* : a point of usu. high land jutting out into the sea : PROMONTORY

head·less \-ləs\ *adj* **1** : having no head **2** : having no chief **3** : lacking good sense or prudence : FOOLISH — **head·less·ness** *n*

head·light \-ˌlīt\ *n* : a light on the front of a vehicle

¹**head·line** \-ˌlīn\ *n* **1** : a line at the top of a page (as in a book) giving a title or heading **2** : the title over an item or article in a newspaper

²**headline** *vt* **1** : to provide with a headline **2** : to publicize highly

head·lin·er \-ˌlī-nər\ *n* : a performer whose name is given prominent billing : STAR

¹**head·long** \-ˈlȯŋ\ *adv* **1** : HEADFIRST **2** : without deliberation : RECKLESSLY **3** : without pause or delay

²**head·long** \-ˌlȯŋ\ *adj* **1** : PRECIPITATE, RASH **2** : plunging headfirst

head·man \ˈhed-ˈman, -ˌman\ *n* : one who is a leader (as of a tribe, clan, or village) : CHIEF

head·mas·ter \-ˌmas-tər\ *n* : a male head of a private school : PRINCIPAL — **head·mis·tress** \-ˌmis-trəs\ *n*

head·most \-ˌmōst\ *adj* : most advanced : LEADING

head–on \ˈhed-ˈȯn, -ˈän\ *adj* : having the head or front facing forward : front to front

head over heels *adv* **1** : in or as if in a somersault **2** : HOPELESSLY, DEEPLY

head·phone \ˈhed-ˌfōn\ *n* : an earphone held over the ear by a band worn on the head

head·piece \-ˌpēs\ *n* **1** : a protective or defensive covering for the head **2** : BRAINS, INTELLIGENCE **3** : an ornament esp. at the beginning of a chapter

head·pin \-ˌpin\ *n* : a pin that stands at the apex in a triangular arrangement of bowling pins

head·quar·ters \ˈhed-ˌkwȯrt-ərz\ *n sing or pl* **1** : a place from which a commander exercises command **2** : the administrative center of an enterprise

head·rest \-ˌrest\ *n* : a support for the head

head·set \-ˌset\ *n* : a pair of headphones

head·ship \-ˌship\ *n* : the position, office, or dignity of a head

heads·man \ˈhedz-mən\ *n* : one that beheads : EXECUTIONER

head·stall \ˈhed-ˌstȯl\ *n* : a part of a bridle or halter that encircles the head

head·stone \-ˌstōn\ *n* : a memorial stone placed at the head of a grave

head·strong \-ˌstrȯŋ\ *adj* **1** : not easily restrained : WILLFUL **2** : directed by ungovernable will

head·wait·er \-ˈwāt-ər\ *n* : the head of the dining-room staff of a restaurant or hotel

head·wa·ters \-ˌwȯt-ərz, -ˌwät-\ *n pl* : the source and upper part of a stream

head·way \-ˌwā\ *n* **1 a** : motion or rate of motion (as of a ship) in a forward direction **b** : ADVANCE, PROGRESS **2** : clear space (as under an arch) **3** : the time interval between two vehicles traveling in the same direction on the same route

head·word \-ˌwərd\ *n* **1** : a word or term placed at the beginning (as of a chapter or entry) **2** : a word qualified by a modifier

head·work \-ˌwərk\ *n* : mental work or effort : THINKING

heady \ˈhed-ē\ *adj* **1** : WILLFUL, RASH **2** : likely to make one dizzy — **head·i·ly** \ˈhed-ᵊl-ē\ *adv* — **head·i·ness** \ˈhed-ē-nəs\ *n*

heal \ˈhēl\ *vb* **1** : to make healthy or whole **2** : to return to a sound or healthy condition — **heal·er** *n*

health \ˈhelth\ *n* **1 a** : the condition of being sound in body, mind, or spirit; *esp* : freedom from physical disease or pain **b** : general functional condition of an individual **2** : flourishing condition : WELL-BEING **3** : a toast to someone's health or prosperity

health·ful \-fəl\ *adj* **1** : beneficial to health of body or mind **2** : HEALTHY — **health·ful·ly** \-fə-lē\ *adv* — **health·ful·ness** *n*

healthy \ˈhel-thē\ *adj* **1** : enjoying or typical of good health : WELL **2** : conducive to health **3 a** : PROSPEROUS, FLOURISHING **b** : not small or feeble : CONSIDERABLE — **health·i·ly** \-thə-lē\ *adv* — **health·i·ness** \-thē-nəs\ *n*

¹**heap** \ˈhēp\ *n* **1** : a collection of things thrown one on another : PILE **2** : a great number or large quantity : LOT

²**heap** *vt* **1** : to throw or lay in a heap : AMASS, PILE **2** : to cast or bestow in large quantities **3** : to fill (a measure or container) more than even full

hear \ˈhi(ə)r\ *vb* **heard** \ˈhərd\; **hear·ing** \ˈhi(ə)r-iŋ\ **1** : to perceive or apprehend by the ear; *also* : to have the power of apprehending sound **2** : to gain knowledge of by hearing : LEARN **3** : to listen to with attention : HEED **4 a** : to give a legal hearing to **b** : to take testimony from **5 a** : to get news **b** : to have knowledge or information **6** : to entertain the idea — **hear•er** *n*

hear•ing *n* **1 a** : the process, function, or power of perceiving sound; *esp* : the special sense by which noises and tones are received as stimuli **b** : EARSHOT **2 a** : opportunity to present one's case **b** : a listening to arguments **c** : a session (as of a legislative committee) in which the testimony of witnesses is heard

hear•ken \'här-kən\ *vi* **hear•kened**; **hear•ken•ing** \'härk-(ə-)niŋ\ **1** : to give ear : LISTEN **2** : to give respectful attention

hear•say \'hi(ə)r-ˌsā\ *n* **1** : something heard from another : RUMOR **2** : evidence based not on a witness's personal knowledge but on matters told him by another

hearse \'hərs\ *n* : a vehicle for conveying the dead to the grave

heart \'härt\ *n* **1 a** : a hollow muscular organ of vertebrate animals that by its rhythmic contraction acts as a pump maintaining the circulation of the blood **b** : a structure in an invertebrate animal functionally analogous to the vertebrate heart **2** : the part nearest the center **3** : the most essential part of something **4** : something resembling a heart in shape **5 a** : the whole personality including intellectual as well as emotional functions or traits **b** : human feelings : AFFECTION, KINDNESS **c** : COURAGE, SPIRIT **6** : MOOD **7** : the real meaning : hidden meaning **8** : MEMORY **9** : PERSON **10 a** : any of a suit of playing cards marked with a red heart **b** *pl* : a card game in which the object is to avoid taking tricks containing hearts — **to heart** : with deep concern

heart•ache \'härt-ˌāk\ *n* : anguish of mind : SORROW

heart•beat \-ˌbēt\ *n* : one complete pulsation of the heart

heart•break \-ˌbrāk\ *n* : crushing grief

heart•break•ing \-ˌbrā-kiŋ\ *adj* : causing intense sorrow or distress — **heart•break•ing•ly** *adv*

heart•bro•ken \-ˌbrō-kən\ *adj* : overcome by sorrow

heart•burn \-ˌbərn\ *n* : a burning discomfort behind the lower part of the sternum usu. related to spasm of the lower esophagus or the upper stomach

heart•burn•ing \-ˌbər-niŋ\ *n* : intense or rancorous jealousy or resentment

heart•ed \'härt-əd\ *adj* : having a specified kind of heart

heart•en \'härt-ᵊn\ *vt* **heart•ened**; **heart•en•ing** \'härt-niŋ, -ᵊn-iŋ\ : to cheer up : ENCOURAGE

heart•felt \'härt-ˌfelt\ *adj* : deeply felt : EARNEST

heart–free \-ˌfrē\ *adj* : not in love

hearth \'härth\ *n* **1 a** : a brick, stone, or cement area in front of a fireplace **b** : the floor of a fireplace **2** : HOME, FIRESIDE

hearth•stone \-ˌstōn\ *n* **1** : stone forming a hearth **2** : FIRESIDE

heart•i•ly \'härt-ᵊl-ē\ *adv* **1** : with sincerity, goodwill, or enthusiasm **2** : CORDIALLY **3** : COMPLETELY, THOROUGHLY

heart•land \'härt-ˌland\ *n* : a central land area; *esp* : one thought of as economically and militarily self-sufficient and able to control the landmass around it

heart•less \-ləs\ *adj* : lacking feeling : CRUEL — **heart•less•ly** *adv* — **heart•less•ness** *n*

heart•rend•ing \-ˌren-diŋ\ *adj* : causing intense grief, anguish, or distress

hearts•ease \'härts-ˌēz\ *n* : peace of mind : TRANQUILLITY

heart•sick \'härt-ˌsik\ *adj* : very despondent : DEPRESSED — **heart•sick•ness** *n*

heart•sore \-ˌsōr\ *adj* : HEARTSICK

heart–strick•en \-ˌstrik-ən\ *or* **heart–struck** \-ˌstrək\ *adj* : stricken to the heart (as with grief or dismay)

heart•string \-ˌstriŋ\ *n* : the deepest emotions or affections

heart•throb \-ˌthräb\ *n* **1** : the throb of a heart **2 a** : sentimental emotion : PASSION **b** : SWEETHEART

heart–to–heart \ˌhärt-tə-ˌhärt\ *adj* : SINCERE, FRANK

heart–whole \'härt-ˌhōl\ *adj* **1** : HEART-FREE **2** : SINCERE, GENUINE

¹hearty \'härt-ē\ *adj* **1 a** : giving unqualified support : THOROUGHGOING **b** : enthusiastically or exuberantly cordial : JOVIAL **c** : expressed unrestrainedly **2 a** : exhibiting vigorous good health **b** (1) : having a good appetite (2) : abundant and satisfying **c** : NOURISHING **3** : ENERGETIC, VIGOROUS — **heart•i•ness** *n*

²hearty *n, pl* **heart•ies** : a bold brave fellow : COMRADE; *also* : SAILOR

¹heat \'hēt\ *vb* **1** : to make or become warm or hot **2** : to make or become excited or angry

²heat *n* **1 a** : a condition of being hot : WARMTH **b** : a marked or notable degree of hotness **c** : a hot place or situation **d** : a period of heat **e** : a form of energy that causes substances to rise in temperature, fuse, evaporate, expand, or undergo any of various other changes and that flows to a body by contact with or radiation from bodies at higher temperatures **2 a** : intensity of feeling or reaction **b** : the height of an action or condition **c** : sexual excitement esp. in a female mammal **3** : pungency of flavor **4** : a single continuous effort: as **a** : a single course in a race **b** : one of several preliminary races held to eliminate less competent contenders **c** : PRESSURE, COERCION — **heat•less** \'hēt-ləs\ *adj*

heat•ed \'hēt-əd\ *adj* **1** : HOT **2** : marked by emotional heat : ANGRY

heat•ed•ly *adv* : ANGRILY

heat engine *n* : a mechanism for converting heat energy into mechanical energy

heat•er \'hēt-ər\ *n* : a device that imparts heat or holds something to be heated

heath \'hēth\ *n* **1** : any of a family of shrubby dicotyledonous and often evergreen plants that thrive on open barren usu. acid and ill-drained soil; *esp* : a low evergreen shrub with whorls of needlelike leaves and clusters of small flowers **2** : a tract of usu. level and poorly drained wasteland commonly overgrown with low shrubs — **heath•like** *adj* — **heathy** \'hē-thē\ *adj*

¹hea•then \'hē-t͟hən\ *adj* **1** : of or relating to the heathen, their religions, or their customs **2** : FOREIGN, UNCIVILIZED

²heathen *n, pl* **heathens** *or* **heathen** **1** : an unconverted member of a people or nation that does not acknowledge the God of the Bible : PAGAN **2** : an uncivilized or irreligious person — **hea•then•dom** \-dəm\ *n* — **hea•then•ism** \-t͟hə-ˌniz-əm\ *n*

hea•then•ish \'hē-t͟hə-nish\ *adj* : resembling or characteristic of heathens : BARBAROUS — **hea•then•ish•ly** *adv*

¹heath•er \'het͟h-ər\ *n* : HEATH 1 ; *esp* : a common evergreen heath of northern and alpine regions with small crowded stemless leaves and tiny usu. purplish pink flowers in one-sided spikes — **heath•ery** \'het͟h-(ə-)rē\ *adj*

²heather *adj* **1** : of, relating to, or resembling heather **2** : having flecks of various colors

heat•stroke \'hēt-ˌstrōk\ *n* : a condition marked esp. by cessation of sweating, high body temperature, and collapse that results from prolonged exposure to high temperature

heat wave *n* : a period of unusually hot weather

¹heave \'hēv\ *vb* **heaved** *or* **hove** \'hōv\; **heav•ing** **1** : to raise with an effort : LIFT **2** : THROW, CAST, HURL **3** : to utter with an effort **4** : to rise and fall repeatedly **5** : to be thrown up or raised **6** : RETCH — **heav•er** *n* — **heave in sight** : to seem to rise above the horizon and come into view — **heave to** : to bring a ship to a stop

²heave *n* **1 a** : an effort to heave or raise **b** : a forceful throw : CAST **2** : an upward motion; *esp* : a rhythmical rising (as of the chest in breathing)

heav•en \'hev-ən\ *n* **1** : the expanse of space that seems to be over the earth like a dome : FIRMAMENT — usu. used in pl. **2 a** *often cap* : the dwelling place of God and the joyful abode of the blessed dead **b :** a spiritual state of everlasting communion with God **3** *cap* **:** ²GOD **4 :** a place or condition of utmost happiness

heav·en·ly \'hev-ən-lē\ *adj* **1 :** of or relating to heaven or the heavens **2 :** DIVINE, SACRED, BLESSED **3 :** supremely delightful — **heav·en·li·ness** *n*

heav·en·ward \'hev-ən-wərd\ *adv* (*or adj*) **:** toward heaven

heav·i·ly \'hev-ə-lē\ *adv* **1 :** with or as if with weight **2 :** in a slow laborious manner **3 :** SEVERELY **4 :** THICKLY

¹**heavy** \'hev-ē\ *adj* **1 a :** having great weight or weight greater than the usual or normal **b :** weighty in proportion to bulk **:** having a high specific gravity **2 :** hard to bear; *esp* **:** GRIEVOUS **3 :** of weighty import **:** SERIOUS **4 a :** OPPRESSED, BURDENED **b :** PREGNANT; *esp* **:** approaching parturition **5 a :** slow or dull from loss of vitality or resiliency **b :** lacking sparkle or vivacity **c :** lacking mirth or gaiety **:** DOLEFUL **6 :** dulled with weariness **:** DROWSY **7 :** greater in volume or force than the average of its kind or class **8 a :** OVERCAST **b :** full of clay and inclined to hold water **c :** LOUD **d :** THICK **e :** OPPRESSIVE **f :** STEEP, ACUTE **g :** LABORIOUS, DIFFICULT **h :** of large capacity or output **9 a :** digested with difficulty because of excessive richness or seasoning **b :** not properly raised or leavened **10 :** producing goods (as coal or steel) used in the production of other goods **11 :** heavily armed or armored **12 :** ACCENTED — **heav·i·ness** *n*

²**heavy** *adv* **:** in a heavy manner **:** HEAVILY

³**heavy** *n, pl* **heav·ies 1 :** a theatrical role representing a dignified or imposing person **2 :** VILLAIN

heavy–du·ty \ˌhev-ē-'d(y)üt-ē\ *adj* **:** able or designed to withstand unusual strain

heavy–hand·ed \-'han-dəd\ *adj* **1 :** CLUMSY, UNGRACEFUL **2 :** OPPRESSIVE, HARSH — **heavy–hand·ed·ly** *adv* — **heavy–hand·ed·ness** *n*

heavy·heart·ed \-'härt-əd\ *adj* **:** SADDENED, DESPONDENT — **heavy·heart·ed·ly** *adv* — **heavy·heart·ed·ness** *n*

heavy·set \ˌhev-ē-'set\ *adj* **:** being stocky and compact and sometimes tending to stoutness in build

heavy·weight \'hev-ē-ˌwāt\ *n* **:** one above average in weight; *esp* **:** a boxer weighing over 175 pounds

He·bra·ism \'hē-brā-ˌiz-əm\ *n* **1 :** a Hebrew idiom occurring in another language **2 :** the thought, spirit, or practice characteristic of the Hebrews

He·bra·ist \-ˌbrā-əst\ *n* **:** a specialist in Hebrew and Hebraic studies

hec·a·tomb \'hek-ə-ˌtōm\ *n* **1 :** an ancient Greek and Roman sacrifice of 100 oxen or cattle **2 :** a great slaughter

heck·le \'hek-əl\ *vt* **heck·led; heck·ling** \'hek-(ə-)liŋ\ **:** to interrupt with questions or comments usu. with the intention of annoying or hindering **:** BADGER — **heck·ler** \-(ə-)lər\ *n*

hect·are \'hek-ˌta(ə)r\ *n* **:** a unit of area equal to 100 ares

hec·tic \'hek-tik\ *adj* **1 a :** characteristic of a wasting disease; *esp* **:** being a fluctuating but persistent fever (as in tuberculosis) **b :** affected by or appearing as if affected by a hectic fever; *esp* **:** FLUSHED **2 :** filled with excitement or confusion — **hec·ti·cal·ly** \-ti-k(ə-)lē\ *adv*

hec·tor \'hek-tər\ *vb* **hec·tored; hec·tor·ing** \-t(ə-)riŋ\ **1 :** to play the bully **:** SWAGGER **2 :** to intimidate by bluster or personal pressure

¹**hedge** \'hej\ *n* **1 a :** a fence or boundary formed by a dense row of shrubs or low trees **b :** BARRIER, LIMIT **2 :** a protection against financial loss **3 :** a statement that avoids a direct answer or promise

²**hedge** *vb* **1 :** to enclose or protect with or as if with a hedge **2 :** to hem in or obstruct with or as if with a barrier **:** HINDER **3 :** to protect oneself from losing by making a second balancing transaction **4 :** to avoid giving a direct or definite answer or promise — **hedg·er** *n*

³**hedge** *adj* **:** of, relating to, or designed for a hedge

hedge·hog \'hej-ˌhög, -ˌhäg\ *n* **1 :** an Old World insectivorous mammal having sharp spines mixed with the hair on its back and able to roll itself up into a spiny ball **2 :** PORCUPINE

hedge·hop \-ˌhäp\ *vi* **:** to fly an airplane so low that it is sometimes necessary to climb to avoid obstacles (as trees) — **hedge·hop·per** *n*

hedge·row \-ˌrō\ *n* **:** a row of shrubs or trees bounding or separating fields

he·do·nism \'hēd-ᵊn-ˌiz-əm\ *n* **1 :** a doctrine that pleasure or happiness is the sole or chief good in life **2 :** a way of life based on hedonism — **he·do·nist** \-ᵊn-əst\ *n* — **he·do·nis·tic** \ˌhēd-ᵊn-'is-tik\ *adj*

¹**heed** \'hēd\ *vb* **1 :** to pay attention **2 :** to concern oneself with **:** MIND

²**heed** *n* **:** ATTENTION, NOTICE

heed·ful \'hēd-fəl\ *adj* **:** taking heed **:** CAREFUL — **heed·ful·ly** \-fə-lē\ *adv* — **heed·ful·ness** *n*

heed·less \-ləs\ *adj* **:** not taking heed **:** CARELESS — **heed·less·ly** *adv* — **heed·less·ness** *n*

hee–haw \'hē-ˌhö\ *n* **1 :** the bray of a donkey **2 :** a loud rude laugh **:** GUFFAW — **hee–haw** *vi*

¹**heel** \'hēl\ *n* **1 :** the back part of the human foot behind the arch and below the ankle; *also* **:** the corresponding part of a lower vertebrate **2 a :** a part (as of a shoe) that covers the human heel **b :** a solid attachment of a shoe or boot forming the back of the sole under the heel of the foot **3 :** something resembling a heel in form, function, or position: as **a :** one of the crusty ends of a loaf of bread **b :** one of the rind ends of a cheese **4 :** a contemptible person — **heel·less** \'hēl-ləs\ *adj*

²**heel** *vt* **:** to furnish with a heel

³**heel** *vb* **:** to tilt or cause to tilt to one side **:** TIP, LIST

heel·tap \'hēl-ˌtap\ *n* **:** a small quantity of liquor remaining (as in a glass after drinking)

¹**heft** \'heft\ *n* **:** WEIGHT, HEAVINESS

²**heft** *vt* **1 :** to heave up **:** HOIST, LIFT, RAISE **2 :** to test the weight of by lifting

hefty \'hef-tē\ *adj* **1 :** quite heavy **2 :** marked by bigness, bulk, and usu. strength — **heft·i·ness** *n*

he·gem·o·ny \hi-'jem-ə-nē, 'hej-ə-ˌmō-nē\ *n* **:** preponderant influence or authority esp. of one nation over others

he·gi·ra *or* **he·ji·ra** \hi-'jī-rə, 'hej-ə-rə\ *n* **:** a journey esp. when undertaken to seek refuge away from a dangerous or undesirable environment

heif·er \'hef-ər\ *n* **:** a young cow; *esp* **:** one that has not had a calf

height \'hīt, 'hītth\ *n* **1 a :** the highest part **:** SUMMIT **b :** the highest or most advanced point **:** CLIMAX **2 a :** the distance from the bottom to the top of something standing upright **b :** the extent of elevation above a level **:** ALTITUDE **3 :** the condition of being tall or high **4 a :** an extent of land rising to a considerable degree above the surrounding country **b :** a high point or position

height·en \'hīt-ᵊn\ *vb* **height·ened; height·en·ing** \'hīt-niŋ, -ᵊn-iŋ\ **1 a :** to increase the amount or degree of **:** AUGMENT **b :** to make or become brighter or more intense **:** DEEPEN **c :** to bring out more strongly **:** point up **2 a :** to raise high or higher **:** ELEVATE **b :** to raise above the ordinary or trite

hei·nous \'hā-nəs\ *adj* **:** hatefully or shockingly evil **:** ABOMINABLE — **hei·nous·ly** *adv* — **hei·nous·ness** *n*

heir \'a(ə)r\ *n* **1 :** a person who inherits or is entitled to inherit property **2 :** a person who has legal claim to a title or a throne when the person holding it dies — **heir·ship** \-ˌship\ *n*

heir·ess \'ar-əs\ *n* **:** a female heir; *esp* **:** a female heir to great wealth

heir·loom \'a(ə)r-ˌlüm\ *n* **:** a piece of personal property handed down by inheritance; *esp* **:** a piece of intrinsic or sentimental value owned by a family for several generations

held *past of* HOLD

hel·i·cal \'hel-i-kəl, 'hē-li-\ *adj* : of, relating to, or having the form of a helix; *also* : SPIRAL 1a — **hel·i·cal·ly** \-k(ə-)lē\ *adv*

hel·i·con \'hel-ə-ˌkän, -i-kən\ *n* : a large circular bass tuba used in military bands

[1]**hel·i·cop·ter** \'hel-ə-ˌkäp-tər, 'hē-lə-\ *n* : an aircraft that is supported in the air by propellers revolving on a vertical axis

[2]**helicopter** *or* **hel·i·copt** \-ˌkäpt\ *vb* : to travel or transport by helicopter

he·lio·trope \'hēl-yə-ˌtrōp, 'hē-lē-ə-\ *n* : any of a genus of herbs or shrubs of the borage family

hel·i·port \'hel-ə-ˌpōrt, 'hē-lə-\ *n* : a landing and takeoff place for a helicopter

he·li·um \'hē-lē-əm\ *n* : a light colorless nonflammable gaseous chemical element in various natural gases

he·lix \'hē-liks\ *n, pl* **he·li·ces** \'hel-ə-ˌsēz, 'hē-lə-\ : something (as a wire coiled around a cylinder, a cone-shaped wire spring, or a corkscrew) spiral in form

hell \'hel\ *n* **1** : the abode of souls after death **2** : the place or state of punishment for the wicked after death : the home of evil spirits **3** : a place or condition of misery or wickedness **4** : something that causes torment; *esp* : a severe scolding

hell·ben·der \'hel-ˌben-dər\ *n* : a large aquatic salamander of the Ohio valley

hell–bent \-ˌbent\ *adj* **1** : stubbornly and often recklessly determined **2** : going full tilt

hell·cat \-ˌkat\ *n* **1** : WITCH 2 **2** : TORMENTOR; *esp* : SHREW

hel·le·bore \'hel-ə-ˌbōr\ *n* **1** : any of a genus of herbs of the buttercup family; *also* : its dried root formerly used in medicine **2** : a poisonous herb of the lily family; *also* : its dried root or a product of this containing alkaloids used in medicine and insecticides

Hel·le·nism \'hel-ə-ˌniz-əm\ *n* **1** : devotion to or imitation of esp. ancient Greek thought, customs, or styles **2** : Greek civilization **3** : a body of humanistic and classical ideals associated with ancient Greece

Hel·le·nist \-nəst\ *n* : a specialist in the language or culture of ancient Greece

hel·le·nize \'hel-ə-ˌnīz\ *vb, often cap* : to make or become Greek or Hellenistic in form or culture — **hel·le·ni·za·tion** \ˌhel-ə-nə-'zā-shən\ *n, often cap*

hell·gram·mite \'hel-grə-ˌmīt\ *n* : an aquatic insect larva used as bait in fishing

hel·lion \'hel-yən\ *n* : a troublesome or mischievous person

hell·ish \'hel-ish\ *adj* : of, resembling, or befitting hell : DEVILISH — **hell·ish·ly** *adv* — **hell·ish·ness** *n*

hel·lo \hə-'lō, he-\ *n, pl* **hellos** : an expression or gesture of greeting — used interjectionally in greeting, in answering the telephone, or to express surprise

[1]**helm** \'helm\ *n* : HELMET 1

[2]**helm** *n* **1** : a lever or wheel controlling the rudder of a ship for steering; *also* : the entire apparatus for steering a ship **2** : a position of control : HEAD

hel·met \'hel-mət\ *n* **1** : a covering or enclosing headpiece of ancient or medieval armor **2** : any of various protective head coverings usu. made of a hard material to resist impact **3** : something resembling a helmet — **hel·met·like** *adj*

helms·man \'helmz-mən\ *n* : the man at the helm : STEERSMAN

hel·ot \'hel-ət\ *n* : SERF, SLAVE — **hel·ot·ry** \-ə-trē\ *n*

hel·ot·ism \'hel-ət-ˌiz-əm\ *n* : SERFDOM

[1]**help** \'help\ *vb* **1 a** : to give aid or assistance **b** : to aid in doing a certain act **c** : to be of aid in putting or bringing into a certain place, position, or condition **2 a** : REMEDY, RELIEVE **b** : to get (oneself) out of a difficulty **3** : to further the advancement of : PROMOTE **4 a** : to change for the better **b** : to refrain from **c** : to keep from occurring : PREVENT **5** : to serve with food or drink esp. at a meal **6** : to appropriate for the use of (oneself) — **cannot help but** : cannot but — **so help me** : I swear it

[2]**help** *n* **1** : an act or instance of helping : AID, ASSISTANCE **2** : the state of being helped : RELIEF **3** : a person or a thing that helps **4** : a hired helper or a body of hired helpers

help·er \'hel-pər\ *n* : one that helps; *esp* : a person who helps with manual labor

help·ful \'help-fəl\ *adj* : furnishing help : ASSISTING, USEFUL — **help·ful·ly** \-fə-lē\ *adv* — **help·ful·ness** *n*

help·ing \'hel-piŋ\ *n* : a portion of food

helping verb *n* : an auxiliary verb

help·less \'help-ləs\ *adj* **1** : lacking protection or support : DEFENSELESS **2** : lacking strength or effectiveness : POWERLESS — **help·less·ly** *adv* — **help·less·ness** *n*

help·mate \'help-ˌmāt\ *n* : one who is a companion and helper; *esp* : WIFE

help·meet \-ˌmēt\ *n* : HELPMATE

[1]**hel·ter–skel·ter** \ˌhel-tər-'skel-tər\ *adv* **1** : in headlong disorder : PELL-MELL **2** : in random order : HAPHAZARDLY

[2]**helter–skelter** *n* : a disorderly confusion : TURMOIL

[3]**helter–skelter** *adj* **1** : confusedly hurried : PRECIPITATE **2** : HIT-OR-MISS, HAPHAZARD

helve \'helv\ *n* : a handle of a tool or weapon : HAFT

[1]**hem** \'hem\ *n* : a border of a garment or cloth; *esp* : one made by folding back an edge and sewing it down

[2]**hem** *vb* **hemmed**; **hem·ming** **1** : to finish with or make a hem in sewing **2** : to surround in a restrictive manner : CONFINE — **hem·mer** *n*

[3]**hem** *a throat-clearing sound*; *often read as* 'hem\ *n* : a vocalized pause in speaking — often used interjectionally to call attention or to express hesitation or doubt

[4]**hem** \'hem\ *vi* **hemmed**; **hem·ming** **1** : to utter the sound represented by *hem* **2** : EQUIVOCATE

he–man \'hē-ˌman\ *n* : an obviously strong virile man

hemi·sphere \'hem-ə-ˌsfi(ə)r\ *n* **1** : the northern or southern half of the earth divided by the equator or the eastern or western half divided by a meridian **2** : one of two half spheres formed by a plane through the sphere's center — **hemi·spher·ic** \ˌhem-ə-'sfi(ə)r-ik, -'sfer-\ *or* **hemi·spher·i·cal** \-'sfir-i-kəl, -'sfer-\ *adj*

hemi·stich \'hem-i-ˌstik\ *n* : half a poetic line usu. divided by a caesura

hem·line \'hem-ˌlīn\ *n* : the line formed by the lower edge of a dress, skirt, or coat

hem·lock \'hem-ˌläk\ *n* **1** : any of several poisonous herbs of the carrot family having finely cut leaves and small white flowers **2** : any of a genus of evergreen trees of the pine family; *also* : the soft light splintery wood of a hemlock

he·mo·glo·bin \'hē-mə-ˌglō-bən\ *n* : an iron-containing protein respiratory pigment that is the chief means of oxygen transport in the vertebrate body where it occurs in the red blood cells and is able to combine loosely with oxygen in regions (as the lungs) of high concentration and release it in regions (as the visceral tissues) of low concentration; *also* : any of various chemically or functionally similar iron-containing compounds

he·mol·y·sis \hi-'mäl-ə-səs\ *n* : a breaking down of red blood cells resulting in release of hemoglobin — **he·mo·lyt·ic** \ˌhē-mə-'lit-ik, ˌhem-ə-\ *adj* — **he·mo·lyze** \'hē-mə-ˌlīz, 'hem-ə-\ *vb*

he·mo·phil·ia \ˌhē-mə-'fil-ē-ə\ *n* : a usu. hereditary tendency to uncontrollable bleeding — **he·mo·phil·i·ac** \-ē-ˌak\ *adj or n*

hem·or·rhage \'hem-(ə-)rij\ *n* : a copious discharge of blood from the blood vessels — **hemorrhage** *vi* — **hem·or·rhag·ic** \ˌhem-ə-'raj-ik\ *adj*

hem·or·rhoid \'hem-(ə-)ˌrȯid\ *n* : a swollen mass of dilated veins situated at or just within the anus — usu. used in pl. — **hem·or·rhoid·al** \ˌhem-ə-'rȯid-ᵊl\ *adj* — **hem·or·rhoid·ec·to·my** \ˌhem-(ə-)ˌrȯi-'dek-tə-mē\ *n*

hemp \'hemp\ *n* : a tall Asiatic herb of the mulberry family widely grown for its tough bast fiber that is used esp. in cordage or for its flowers that yield hashish — **hemp·en** \'hem-pən\ *adj*

¹hem·stitch \'hem-ˌstich\ *vt* : to embroider (fabric) by drawing out parallel threads and stitching the exposed threads in groups to form various designs — **hem·stitch·er** *n*

²hemstitch *n* **1** : decorative needlework **2** : a stitch used in hemstitching

hen \'hen\ *n* **1** : a female domestic fowl esp. over a year old; *also* : a female bird **2** : the female of various mostly aquatic animals (as lobsters or fish)

hence \'hen(t)s\ *adv* **1** : from this place : AWAY **2** : from this time **3** : CONSEQUENTLY, THEREFORE

hence·forth \-ˌfōrth\ *adv* : from this point on

hence·for·ward \hen(t)s-'fȯr-wərd\ *adv* : HENCEFORTH

hench·man \'hench-mən\ *n* **1** : a trusted follower or supporter **2** : a political follower serving for his own advantage

¹hen·na \'hen-ə\ *n* **1** : an Old World tropical shrub with panicles of fragrant white flowers **2** : a reddish brown dye obtained from leaves of the henna and used esp. on hair

²henna *vt* **hen·naed** \'hen-əd\; **hen·na·ing** : to dye or tint with henna

hen·peck \'hen-ˌpek\ *vt* : to subject (one's husband) to persistent nagging and domination

hep \'hep\ *adj* : HIP

hep·a·ti·tis \ˌhep-ə-'tīt-əs\ *n* : inflammation of the liver; *also* : an acute virus disease of which this is a feature

¹her \(h)ər, ˌhər\ *adj* : of or relating to her or herself esp. as possessor, agent, or object of an action

²her \ər, (')hər\ *pron, objective case of* SHE

¹her·ald \'her-əld\ *n* **1 a** : an official at a medieval tournament **b** : an officer acting as messenger between leaders of warring parties **c** : an officer responsible for granting and registering coats of arms **2** : an official crier or messenger **3 a** : HARBINGER **b** : ANNOUNCER

²herald *vt* **1** : to give notice of : ANNOUNCE **2 a** : PUBLICIZE **b** : HAIL, GREET

he·ral·dic \he-'ral-dik\ *adj* : of or relating to heralds or heraldry — **he·ral·di·cal·ly** \-di-k(ə-)lē\ *adv*

her·ald·ry \'her-əl-drē\ *n, pl* **-ries** **1** : the art or science of a herald : the science of tracing a person's family and determining what coat of arms he is entitled to have **2** : COAT OF ARMS **3** : heraldic pomp or ceremony

herb \'(h)ərb\ *n* **1** : an annual, biennial, or perennial seed plant that does not develop persistent woody tissue but dies down at the end of a growing season **2** : a plant or plant part valued for its medicinal, savory, or aromatic qualities — **her·ba·ceous** \ˌ(h)ər-'bā-shəs\ *adj* — **herb·like** *adj* — **herby** \'(h)ər-bē\ *adj*

herb·age \'(h)ər-bij\ *n* **1** : herbaceous vegetation (as grass) esp. when used for grazing **2** : the succulent parts of herbaceous plants

¹herb·al \'(h)ər-bəl\ *n* : a book about plants esp. with reference to their medical properties

²herbal *adj* : of, relating to, or made of herbs

herb·al·ist \'(h)ər-bə-ləst\ *n* : one that collects, grows, or deals in herbs

her·bi·cide \'(h)ər-bə-ˌsīd\ *n* : an agent used to destroy or inhibit plant growth — **her·bi·cid·al** \ˌ(h)ər-bə-'sīd-ᵊl\ *adj*

her·bi·vore \'(h)ər-bə-ˌvōr\ *n* : a plant-eating animal; *esp* : UNGULATE — **her·biv·o·rous** \ˌ(h)ər-'biv-ə-rəs\ *adj*

her·cu·le·an \ˌhər-kyə-'lē-ən, ˌhər-'kyü-lē-\ *adj* : of extraordinary power, size, or difficulty

¹herd \'hərd\ *n* **1** : a number of animals of one kind kept or living together **2** : the common people : MASSES

²herd *vb* **1** : to assemble or move in a herd **2 a** : to keep or move (animals) as a herd **b** : to gather, lead, or drive as if in a herd **3** : to place or place oneself in a group : ASSOCIATE — **herd·er** *n*

herds·man \'hərdz-mən\ *n* : a manager, breeder, or tender of livestock

¹here \'hi(ə)r\ *adv* **1 a** : in or at this place **b** : NOW **2** : at or in this point or particular **3** : in the present life or state **4** : to this place **5** — used interjectionally in rebuke or encouragement

²here *n* : this place

here·about \'hir-ə-ˌbau̇t\ *or* **here·abouts** \-ˌbau̇ts\ *adv* : near or around this place : in this vicinity

¹here·af·ter \hir-'af-tər\ *adv* **1** : after this **2** : in some future time or state

²hereafter *n, often cap* **1** : FUTURE **2** : an existence beyond earthly life

here·by \hir-'bī\ *adv* : by means of this

he·red·i·tary \hə-'red-ə-ˌter-ē\ *adj* **1** : genetically transmitted or transmittable from parent to offspring **2 a** : received or passing by inheritance **b** : having title or possession through inheritance **3** : of or relating to inheritance or heredity

he·red·i·ty \hə-'red-ət-ē\ *n, pl* **-ties** **1** : the sum of the qualities and potentialities genetically derived from one's ancestors **2** : the transmission of qualities from ancestor to descendant through genes

here·in \hir-'in\ *adv* : in this

here·of \-'əv, -'äv\ *adv* : of this

here·on \-'ȯn, -'än\ *adv* : on this

her·e·sy \'her-ə-sē\ *n, pl* **-sies** **1** : religious opinion contrary to church dogma **2** : opinion or doctrine contrary to a dominant or generally accepted belief

her·e·tic \'her-ə-ˌtik\ *n* **1** : a person who believes or teaches something contrary to church dogma **2** : one that dissents from an accepted belief or doctrine

he·ret·i·cal \hə-'ret-i-kəl\ *adj* : of, relating to, or characterized by heresy : UNORTHODOX — **he·ret·i·cal·ly** \-k(ə-)lē\ *adv* — **he·ret·i·cal·ness** *n*

here·to \hir-'tü\ *adv* : to this document

here·to·fore \'hirt-ə-ˌfōr\ *adv* : up to this time : HITHERTO

here·un·der \hir-'ən-dər\ *adv* : under or in accordance with this

here·un·to \hir-'ən-tü\ *adv* : to this; *esp* : to this writing or document

here·upon \'hir-ə-ˌpȯn, -ˌpän\ *adv* : on this : immediately after this

here·with \hir-'with, -'with\ *adv* : with this : enclosed in this

her·i·ta·ble \'her-ət-ə-bəl\ *adj* **1** : capable of being inherited or of passing by inheritance **2** : HEREDITARY — **her·i·ta·bil·i·ty** \ˌher-ət-ə-'bil-ət-ē\ *n*

her·i·tage \'her-ət-ij\ *n* **1** : property that descends to an heir **2** : something transmitted by or acquired from a predecessor : LEGACY **3** : BIRTHRIGHT

her·maph·ro·dite \(ˌ)hər-'maf-rə-ˌdīt\ *n* **1** : an animal or plant having both male and female reproductive organs **2** : HOMOSEXUAL — **hermaphrodite** *adj* — **her·maph·ro·dit·ic** \(ˌ)hər-ˌmaf-rə-'dit-ik\ *adj* — **her·maph·ro·dit·i·cal·ly** \-'dit-i-k(ə-)lē\ *adv* — **her·maph·ro·dit·ism** \(ˌ)hər-'maf-rə-ˌdīt-ˌiz-əm\ *n*

her·met·ic \(ˌ)hər-'met-ik\ *adj* : AIRTIGHT; *also* : impervious to external influence — **her·met·i·cal** \-'met-i-kəl\ *adj* — **her·met·i·cal·ly** \-i-k(ə-)lē\ *adv*

her·mit \'hər-mət\ *n* **1** : one that lives in solitude esp. for religious reasons : RECLUSE **2** *obs* : BEADSMAN **3** : a spiced molasses cookie

her·mit·age \'hər-mət-ij\ *n* : the habitation of a hermit; *also* : a secluded residence : RETREAT

her·nia \'hər-nē-ə\ *n, pl* **her·ni·as** *or* **her·ni·ae** \-nē-ˌē, -nē-ˌī\ : a protrusion of an organ or part through connective tissue or through a wall of the cavity in which it is normally enclosed — **her·ni·al** \-nē-əl\ *adj* — **her·ni·ate** \-nē-ˌāt\ *vi* — **her·ni·a·tion** \ˌhər-nē-'ā-shən\ *n*

he•ro \'hē-rō\ *n, pl* **heroes** **1 a** : a mythological or legendary figure often of divine descent endowed with great strength or ability **b** : an illustrious warrior **c** : a man admired for his achievements and qualities **d** : one that shows great courage **2** : the principal male character in a literary work

he•ro•ic \hi-'rō-ik\ *adj* **1** : of, relating to, or resembling heroes esp. of antiquity **2** : exhibiting or marked by courage, daring, or desperate enterprise **3 a** : GRAND, NOBLE **b** : of impressive size, power, or effect — **he•ro•i•cal** \-'rō-i-kəl\ *adj* — **he•ro•i•cal•ly** \-i-k(ə-)lē\ *adv*

heroic couplet *n* : a rhyming couplet in iambic pentameter

he•ro•ics \hi-'rō-iks\ *n pl* : extravagant display of heroic attitudes in action or expression

heroic verse *n* : the iambic pentameter used in English poetry (as epic) during the 17th and 18th centuries

her•o•in \'her-ə-wən\ *n* : a strongly addictive narcotic made from but more potent than morphine — **her•o•in•ism** \-wə-ˌniz-əm\ *n*

her•o•ine \'her-ə-wən\ *n* **1** : a woman of courage and daring **2** : a woman admired for her achievements and qualities **3** : the chief female figure in a literary work or in an event or period

her•o•ism \'her-ə-ˌwiz-əm\ *n* **1** : heroic conduct **2** : the qualities of a hero

her•on \'her-ən\ *n* : any of various long-necked wading birds with a long tapering bill, large wings, and soft plumage

hero worship *n* **1** : veneration of a hero **2** : foolish or excessive adulation for an individual

Herr \(ˌ)he(ə)r\ *n, pl* **Her•ren** \ˌher-ən, (ˌ)he(ə)rn\ — used among German-speaking people as a title equivalent to *mister*

her•ring \'her-iŋ\ *n, pl* **herring** *or* **herrings** : a valuable soft-finned food fish abundant in the temperate and colder parts of the north Atlantic; *also* : any of various similar and related fishes

¹her•ring•bone \-ˌbōn\ *n* **1** : a pattern made up of rows of parallel lines with adjacent rows slanting in reverse directions **2** : a twilled fabric with a herringbone pattern

²herringbone *vb* **1** : to produce a herringbone pattern on a surface **2** : to arrange in a herringbone pattern

hers \'hərz\ *pron* : her one : her ones — used without a following noun as a pronoun equivalent in meaning to the adjective *her*

her•self \(h)ər-'self\ *pron* **1** : that identical female one — used reflexively, for emphasis, or in absolute constructions **2** : her normal, healthy, or sane condition or self

hertz \'he(ə)rts, 'hərts\ *n, pl* **hertz** : a unit of frequency equal to one cycle per second

hes•i•tance \'hez-ə-tən(t)s\ *n* : HESITANCY

hes•i•tan•cy \-tən-sē\ *n, pl* **-cies** **1** : the quality or state of being hesitant : INDECISION, RELUCTANCE **2** : an act or instance of hesitating

hes•i•tant \'hez-ə-tənt\ *adj* : tending to hesitate — **hes•i•tant•ly** *adv*

hes•i•tate \'hez-ə-ˌtāt\ *vi* **1** : to stop or pause because of forgetfulness, uncertainty, or indecision **2** : to hold back because of scruples : be reluctant **3** : to falter in speaking : STAMMER — **hes•i•tat•er** *n*

hes•i•ta•tion \ˌhez-ə-'tā-shən\ *n* **1** : an act or instance of hesitating **2** : STAMMERING

het•er•o•dox \'het-ə-rə-ˌdäks\ *adj* **1** : contrary to prevailing opinions, beliefs, or standards; *esp* : not orthodox in religion **2** : holding or expressing unorthodox beliefs or opinions

het•er•o•doxy \-ˌdäk-sē\ *n, pl* **-dox•ies** **1** : the quality or state of being heterodox **2** : a heterodox opinion or doctrine

het•er•o•ge•ne•ity \ˌhet-ə-rō-jə-'nē-ət-ē\ *n* : the quality or state of being heterogeneous

het•er•o•ge•neous \ˌhet-ə-rə-'jē-nē-əs\ *adj* : differing in kind : consisting of dissimilar ingredients or constituents: MIXED — **het•er•o•ge•neous•ly** *adv* — **het•er•o•ge•neous•ness** *n*

het•ero•sex•u•al \ˌhet-ə-rō-'sek-sh(ə-w)əl\ *adj* : of, relating to, or marked by sexual orientation toward members of the opposite sex — **heterosexual** *n* — **het•ero•sex•u•al•i•ty** \-ˌsek-shə-'wal-ət-ē\ *n*

het up \(')het-'əp\ *adj* : highly excited : UPSET

hew \'hyü\ *vb* **hewed**; **hewed** *or* **hewn** \'hyün\; **hew•ing** **1** : to chop down : CHOP **2** : to make or shape by or as if by cutting with an ax **3** : to conform strictly : ADHERE — **hew•er** *n*

¹hex \'heks\ *vt* **1** : to put a hex on **2** : to affect as if by an evil spell : JINX — **hex•er** *n*

²hex *n* **1** : SPELL, JINX **2** : a person who practices witchcraft

hex•a•gon \'hek-sə-ˌgän\ *n* : a polygon of six angles and six sides

hex•ag•o•nal \hek-'sag-ən-ᵊl\ *adj* : having six angles and six sides — **hex•ag•o•nal•ly** \-ᵊl-ē\ *adv*

hex•am•e•ter \hek-'sam-ət-ər\ *n* : a line consisting of six metrical feet

hex•a•pod \'hek-sə-ˌpäd\ *n* : INSECT

hey \'hā\ *interj* — used esp. to call attention or to express interrogation, surprise, or exultation

hey•day \'hā-ˌdā\ *n* : the time of greatest strength or vigor

hi \'hī(-ē)\ *interj* — used esp. as a greeting

hi•a•tus \hī-'āt-əs\ *n* **1** : a gap in space or in time; *esp* : a break occurring where a part is missing **2** : the occurrence of two vowel sounds without pause or intervening consonantal sound

hi•ba•chi \hē-'bäch-ē\ *n* : a charcoal brazier

hi•ber•nate \'hī-bər-ˌnāt\ *vi* : to pass the winter in a torpid state — **hi•ber•na•tion** \ˌhī-bər-'nā-shən\ *n* — **hi•ber•na•tor** \'hī-bər-ˌnāt-ər\ *n*

hi•bis•cus \hī-'bis-kəs, hə-\ *n* : any of a large genus of herbs, shrubs, or small trees of the mallow family with toothed leaves and large showy flowers

¹hic•cup \'hik-(ˌ)əp\ *n* : a spasmodic breathing movement checked by sudden closure of the glottis accompanied by a peculiar sound

²hiccup *vi* **hic•cuped**; **hic•cup•ing** : to make a hiccup or be affected with hiccups

hic ja•cet \(')hik-'jā-sət\ *n* : EPITAPH

hick \'hik\ *n* : an awkward provincial person

hick•ey \'hik-ē\ *n* : DEVICE, GADGET

hick•o•ry \'hik-(ə-)rē\ *n, pl* **-ries** **1 a** : any of a genus of No. American hardwood trees of the walnut family often with sweet edible nuts **b** : the usu. tough pale wood of a hickory **2** : a switch or cane (as of hickory wood) used esp. for punishing a child

hi•dal•go \hid-'al-gō\ *n, pl* **-gos** : a member of the lower nobility of Spain

¹hide \'hīd\ *vb* **hid** \'hid\; **hid•den** \'hid-ᵊn\ *or* **hid**; **hid•ing** \'hīd-iŋ\ **1** : to put or get out of sight : SECRETE **2** : to keep secret **3** : to screen from view **4** : to seek protection or evade responsibility — **hid•er** *n*

²hide *n* : the skin of an animal whether raw or dressed

³hide *vt* **hid•ed**; **hid•ing** : to give a beating to : FLOG

hide–and–seek \ˌhīd-ᵊn-'sēk\ *n* : a children's game in which one player covers his eyes and after giving the others time to hide goes looking for and tries to catch them

hide•away \'hīd-ə-ˌwā\ *n* : RETREAT, HIDEOUT

hide•bound \'hīd-ˌbau̇nd\ *adj* **1** : having a dry skin lacking in pliancy and adhering closely to the underlying flesh **2** : obstinately conservative : NARROW

hid•e•ous \'hid-ē-əs\ *adj* : horribly ugly or disgusting : FRIGHTFUL, SHOCKING — **hid•e•ous•ly** *adv* — **hid•e•ous•ness** *n*

hide•out \'hīd-ˌau̇t\ *n* : a place of refuge or concealment

hid•ing \'hīd-iŋ\ *n* : a state or place of concealment

hie \'hī\ *vb* **hied**; **hy•ing** *or* **hie•ing** : HURRY, HASTEN

hi•er•ar•chy \'hī(-ə)-ˌrär-kē\ *n, pl* **-chies** **1** : a ruling body of clergy organized into ranks each subordinate to the one above it; *esp* : the bishops of a province or nation **2** : a governing body whose members are arranged in ordered ranks; *also* : any body of persons in authority **3 a** : arrangement into a graded series **b** : persons or things arranged in ranks or classes — **hi·er·ar·chi·cal** \ˌhī(-ə)-ˈrär-ki-kəl\ *or* **hi·er·ar·chic** \-ˈrär-kik\ *adj* — **hi·er·ar·chi·cal·ly** \-ˈrär-ki-k(ə-)lē\ *adv*

hi·er·at·ic \ˌhī(-ə)-ˈrat-ik\ *adj* : SACERDOTAL — **hi·er·at·i·cal·ly** \-ˈrat-i-k(ə-)lē\ *adv*

hi·er·o·glyph \ˈhī(-ə)-rə-ˌglif\ *n* : a character used in a system of hieroglyphic writing

¹hi·er·o·glyph·ic \ˌhī(-ə)-rə-ˈglif-ik\ *adj* **1** : written in, constituting, or belonging to a system of writing mainly in pictorial characters **2** : resembling hieroglyphic in difficulty of decipherment

²hieroglyphic *n* **1** : HIEROGLYPH **2** : a system of hieroglyphic writing; *esp* : the picture script of the ancient Egyptian priesthood **3** : characters that resemble a hieroglyphic esp. in difficulty of decipherment

hi–fi \ˈhī-ˈfī\ *n* **1** : HIGH FIDELITY **2** : equipment for reproduction of sound with high fidelity

hig·gle \ˈhig-əl\ *vi* **hig·gled**; **hig·gling** \ˈhig-(ə-)liŋ\ : HAGGLE — **hig·gler** \-(ə-)lər\ *n*

hig·gle·dy–pig·gle·dy \ˌhig-əl-dē-ˈpig-əl-dē\ *adv* : in confusion : TOPSY-TURVY — **higgledy–piggledy** *adj*

¹high \ˈhī\ *adj* **1 a** : extending or raised up : ELEVATED **b** : having a specified elevation : TALL **2** : advanced toward fullness or culmination **3** : SHRILL, SHARP **4** : relatively far from the equator **5** : exalted in character : NOBLE **6** : of greater degree, size, amount, or content than average or ordinary **7** : of relatively great importance: as **a** : foremost in rank, dignity, or standing **b** : SERIOUS, GRAVE **8** : FORCIBLE, STRONG **9** : showing elation or excitement **10** : COSTLY, DEAR **11** : advanced in complexity, development, or elaboration **12** : pronounced with some part of the tongue close to the palate

²high *adv* **1** : at or to a high place, altitude, or degree **2** : RICHLY, LUXURIOUSLY

³high *n* **1** : an elevated place or region: as **a** : HILL, KNOLL **b** : SKY, HEAVEN **2** : a region of high barometric pressure **3 a** : a high point or level : HEIGHT **b** : the transmission gear of an automotive vehicle giving the highest ratio of propeller-shaft to engine-shaft speed and consequently the highest speed of travel

high·ball \ˈhī-ˌbȯl\ *n* : a drink of alcoholic liquor with water or a carbonated beverage served in a tall glass

high·born \-ˈbȯrn\ *adj* : of noble birth

high·boy \-ˌbȯi\ *n* : a high chest of drawers mounted on a base with long legs

high·bred \-ˈbred\ *adj* : coming from superior stock

high·brow \-ˌbrau̇\ *n* : a person of superior learning or culture : INTELLECTUAL — **highbrow** *adj*

high chair *n* : a child's chair with long legs, a feeding tray, and a rest for the feet

high·er education \ˌhī-ər-\ *n* : education provided by a college or university

high·er–up \ˌhī-ər-ˈəp\ *n* : a superior officer or official

high·fa·lu·tin \ˌhī-fə-ˈlüt-ᵊn\ *adj* : PRETENTIOUS, POMPOUS

high fidelity *n* : the reproduction of sound with a high degree of faithfulness to the original

high·fli·er *or* **high·fly·er** \ˈhī-ˈflī(-ə)r\ *n* **1** : an extravagant, pretentious, or excessively ambitious person **2** : an extremely orthodox or doctrinaire person

high–flown \-ˈflōn\ *adj* **1** : ELEVATED, PROUD **2** : not plain or simple : EXTRAVAGANT

high frequency *n* : a radio frequency in the range between 3 and 30 megacycles

high–grade \ˈhī-ˈgrād\ *adj* : of a grade rated as superior

high–hand·ed \-ˈhan-dəd\ *adj* : OVERBEARING, ARBITRARY — **high–hand·ed·ly** *adv* — **high–hand·ed·ness** *n*

¹high–hat \-ˈhat\ *adj* : SUPERCILIOUS, SNOBBISH

²high–hat *vt* : to treat in a high-hat manner

High Holiday *n* : either of two important Jewish holidays: **a** : ROSH HASHANAH **b** : YOM KIPPUR

high horse *n* : an arrogant mood or attitude

high jinks \-ˈjiŋ(k)s\ *n pl* : wild or boisterous behavior

high jump *n* : a jump for height in a track-and-field contest — **high jumper** *n*

¹high·land \ˈhī-lənd\ *n* : elevated or mountainous land

²highland *adj* **1** : of or relating to a highland **2** *cap* : of or relating to the Highlands of Scotland

High·land·er \-lən-dər\ *n* : an inhabitant of the Highlands of Scotland

Highland fling *n* : a lively Scottish folk dance

¹high·light \ˈhī-ˌlīt\ *n* **1 a** : one of the spots or areas on an object that reflect the most light **b** : the brightest spot (as in a painting or drawing) **2** : an event or scene of major interest

²highlight *vt* **1** : to throw a strong light on **2 a** : to center attention on : EMPHASIZE **b** : to constitute a highlight of

high·ly \ˈhī-lē\ *adv* **1** : to a high degree : very much : EXTREMELY **2** : with much approval

high mass *n, often cap H&M* : a sung mass with full ceremonials and incense and with the celebrant assisted by a deacon and subdeacon

high–mind·ed \ˈhī-ˈmīn-dəd\ *adj* : having or marked by elevated principles and feelings — **high–mind·ed·ly** *adv* — **high–mind·ed·ness** *n*

high·ness \ˈhī-nəs\ *n* **1** : the quality or state of being high **2** — used as a title for persons (as a king or prince) of exalted rank

¹high–pressure *adj* **1 a** : having or involving a high or comparatively high pressure esp. greatly exceeding that of the atmosphere **b** : having a high atmospheric pressure **2** : using or involving aggressive and insistent sales techniques

²high–pressure *vt* : to sell or influence by high-pressure tactics

high–rise \ˈhī-ˈrīz\ *adj* **1** : being multistory and equipped with elevators **2** : of, relating to, or characterized by high-rise buildings

high school *n* : a secondary school usu. comprising the 9th to 12th or 10th to 12th years of study

high seas *n pl* : the open part of a sea or ocean esp. outside territorial waters

high–sound·ing \ˈhī-ˈsau̇n-diŋ\ *adj* : POMPOUS, IMPOSING

high–spir·it·ed \ˈhī-ˈspir-ət-əd\ *adj* : characterized by a bold or lofty spirit : METTLESOME — **high–spir·it·ed·ly** *adv* — **high–spir·it·ed·ness** *n*

high–strung \-ˈstrəŋ\ *adj* : having or marked by an extremely nervous or sensitive temperament

high·tail \ˈhī-ˌtāl\ *vi* : to retreat at full speed

high–tension *adj* : having a high voltage; *also* : relating to apparatus to be used at high voltage

high–test *adj* : passing a difficult test

high tide *n* **1** : the tide when the water is at its greatest height **2** : culminating point : CLIMAX

high–toned \ˈhī-ˈtōnd\ *adj* **1** : high in social, moral, or intellectual quality **2** : PRETENTIOUS, POMPOUS

high treason *n* : TREASON

high·way \ˈhī-ˌwā\ *n* : a public road or way; *esp* : a main direct road

high·way·man \-mən\ *n* : a person who robs travelers on a highway

hi·jack *or* **high–jack** \ˈhī-ˌjak\ *vt* : to steal by stopping a vehicle on the highway; *also* : to stop and steal from (a vehicle in transit)

¹hike \ˈhīk\ *vb* **1 a** : to move or raise up **b** : to raise in amount sharply or suddenly **2** : to go on a long walk — **hik·er** *n*

²hike *n* **1** : a long walk esp. for pleasure or exercise **2** : an upward movement : RISE

hi•lar•i•ous \hil-'ar-ē-əs, hī-'lar-\ *adj* : marked by or affording hilarity — **hi•lar•i•ous•ly** *adv* — **hi•lar•i•ous•ness** *n*
hi•lar•i•ty \-ət-ē\ *n* : boisterous merriment
[1]**hill** \'hil\ *n* **1** : a usu. rounded natural elevation of land lower than a mountain **2** : an artificial heap or mound **3** : several seeds or plants planted in a group rather than a row
[2]**hill** *vt* **1** : to form into a heap **2** : to draw earth around the roots or base of — **hill•er** *n*
hill•bil•ly \'hil-,bil-ē\ *n, pl* **-lies** : a person from a mountainous backwoods area
hill•ock \'hil-ək\ *n* : a small hill — **hill•ocky** \-ə-kē\ *adj*
hill•side \'hil-,sīd\ *n* : the side of a hill
hill•top \-,täp\ *n* : the highest part of a hill
hilly \'hil-ē\ *adj* **1** : abounding in hills **2** : STEEP
hilt \'hilt\ *n* : a handle esp. of a sword or dagger — **to the hilt** : COMPLETELY
him \im, (')him\ *pron, objective case of* HE
him•self \(h)im-'self\ *pron* **1** : that identical male one : that identical one whose sex is unknown or immaterial — used reflexively, for emphasis, or in absolute constructions **2** : his normal, healthy, or sane condition or self
[1]**hind** \'hīnd\ *n* : a female red deer
[2]**hind** *adj* : located behind : REAR
[1]**hin•der** \'hin-dər\ *vb* **hin•dered**; **hin•der•ing** \-d(ə-)riŋ\ **1** : to make slow or difficult : HAMPER **2** : to hold back : CHECK
[2]**hind•er** \'hīn-dər\ *adj* : HIND
hind•most \'hīn(d)-,mōst\ *adj* : farthest to the rear
hind•quar•ter \-,kwȯrt-ər\ *n* **1** : the back half of a lateral half of the body or carcass of a quadruped **2** *pl* : the part of a quadruped lying behind the attachment of the hind legs to the trunk
hin•drance \'hin-drən(t)s\ *n* **1** : the state of being hindered **2** : the action of hindering **3** : something that hinders
hind•sight \'hīn(d)-,sīt\ *n* **1** : a rear sight of a firearm **2** : perception of the significance of an event only afterward
[1]**Hin•du** \'hin-,dü\ *n* **1** : an adherent of Hinduism **2** : a native or inhabitant of India
[2]**Hindu** *adj* : of, relating to, or characteristic of the Hindus or Hinduism
Hin•du•ism \-,iz-əm\ *n* **1** : a body of social, cultural, and religious beliefs and practices native to the Indian subcontinent; *esp* : devotion to the cult of one of the chief gods and goddesses **2** : a religious philosophy based on Hinduism
[1]**hinge** \'hinj\ *n* : a jointed piece on which one surface (as a door, gate, or lid) turns or swings on another
[2]**hinge** *vb* **1** : to attach by or furnish with hinges **2** : to hang or turn as if on a hinge : DEPEND
[1]**hint** \'hint\ *n* **1** : a slight mention : an indirect suggestion or reminder **2** : a very small amount : TRACE
[2]**hint** *vb* : to bring to mind by or give a hint — **hint•er** *n*
hin•ter•land \'hint-ər-,land\ *n* **1** : a region behind a coast **2** : a region remote from cities and towns
[1]**hip** \'hip\ *n* : the fruit of a rose consisting of a fleshy receptacle filled with achenes
[2]**hip** *n* : the part of the body that curves outward below the waist on either side formed by the side part of the pelvis and the upper part of the thigh
[3]**hip** *adj* **1** : characterized by a keen informed awareness of or interest in the newest developments **2** : WISE, ALERT
hipped \'hipt\ *adj* : having hips
hip•pie *or* **hip•py** \'hip-ē\ *n, pl* **hippies** : a young person who rejects the moves of established society, advocates a nonviolent ethic, and often uses psychedelic drugs; *also* : a long-haired unconventionally dressed young person
hip•po \'hip-ō\ *n, pl* **hippos** : HIPPOPOTAMUS
hip•po•drome \'hip-ə-,drōm\ *n* **1** : an oval stadium for horse and chariot races in ancient Greece **2** : an arena for equestrian performances
hip•po•pot•a•mus \,hip-ə-'pät-ə-məs\ *n, pl* **-mus•es** *or* **-mi** \-,mī\ : any of several large herbivorous 4-toed chiefly aquatic African mammals related to the swine and characterized by an extremely large head and mouth, very thick hairless skin, and short legs
hip roof *n* : a roof having sloping ends and sloping sides
hip•ster \'hip-stər\ *n* : a person who is unusually aware of and interested in new and unconventional patterns esp. in jazz, in the use of stimulants (as narcotics), and in exotic religion
[1]**hire** \'hī(ə)r\ *n* **1 a** : payment for temporary use **b** : payment for services : WAGES **2 a** : the act of hiring **b** : the state of being hired : EMPLOYMENT
[2]**hire** *vb* **1 a** : to engage the personal services of for a set sum **b** : to engage the temporary use of for a fixed sum **2** : to grant the personal services of for a fixed sum **3** : to take employment — **hir•er** *n* — **for hire** : available for use or service at a price
hire•ling \'hī(ə)r-liŋ\ *n* : a person who serves for wages; *esp* : one whose only interest in his work is the money he receives
hir•sute \'hər-,süt, 'hi(ə)r-\ *adj* : roughly hairy; *esp* : pubescent with coarse stiff hairs — **hir•sute•ness** *n*
[1]**his** \(h)iz, ,hiz\ *adj* : of or relating to him or himself esp. as possessor, agent, or object of an action
[2]**his** \'hiz\ *pron* : his one : his ones — used without a following noun as a pronoun equivalent in meaning to the adjective *his*
hiss \'his\ *vb* : to condemn with or make a sharp sibilant sound like that of the speech sound \s\ or that emitted by an alarmed goose or snake — **hiss** *n* — **hiss•er** *n*
hist \s *often prolonged and usu with* p *preceding and* t *following; often read as* 'hist\ *interj* — used to attract attention
his•ta•mine \'his-tə-,mēn\ *n* : a compound occurring in many animal tissues that is believed to play an important part in allergic reactions (as hives and asthma) and in certain respiratory diseases
his•to•ri•an \his-'tōr-ē-ən\ *n* **1** : a student or writer of history; *esp* : one that produces a scholarly historical study **2** : CHRONICLER
his•tor•ic \his-'tȯr-ik\ *adj* : HISTORICAL; *esp* : famous in history
his•tor•i•cal \-i-kəl\ *adj* **1 a** : of, relating to, or having the character of history; *esp* : known to be true **b** : based on history **2** : famous in history — **his•tor•i•cal•ly** \-i-k(ə-)lē\ *adv* — **his•tor•i•cal•ness** *n*
historical present *n* : the present tense used to relate past events
his•to•ry \'his-t(ə-)rē\ *n, pl* **-ries** **1** : TALE, STORY **2 a** : a chronological record of significant events with an explanation of their causes **b** : an account of a sick person's medical background **3** : a branch of knowledge that records and explains past events **4 a** : events that form the subject matter of a history **b** : past events
his•tri•on•ic \,his-trē-'än-ik\ *adj* **1** : of or relating to actors, acting, or the theater **2** : deliberately affected : THEATRICAL — **his•tri•on•i•cal•ly** \-'än-i-k(ə-)lē\ *adv*
his•tri•on•ics \-'än-iks\ *n pl* **1** : theatrical performances **2** : deliberate display of emotion for effect
[1]**hit** \'hit\ *vb* **hit**; **hit•ting** **1 a** : to strike usu. with force **b** : to make usu. forceful contact with something **2 a** : ATTACK **b** : to affect detrimentally **3** : OCCUR, HAPPEN **4 a** : COME, STUMBLE **b** : to experience or find esp. by chance **c** : to get to : REACH **d** : to reflect accurately **5** : to fire the charge in the cylinders — **hit•ter** *n*
[2]**hit** *n* **1 a** : a blow striking an object aimed at **b** : COLLISION **2 a** : a stroke of luck **b** : something that is conspicuously successful **3** : a telling remark **4** : a stroke in an athletic contest; *esp* : one in baseball enabling the batter to reach base
hit–and–miss \,hit-ᵊn-'mis\ *adj* : sometimes successful and sometimes not : HAPHAZARD

hit–and–run \-'rən\ *adj* : being or involving a motor-vehicle driver who does not stop after being involved in an accident
¹hitch \'hich\ *vb* **1** : to move by jerks **2 a** : to catch or fasten by or as if by a hook or knot **b** : to connect to or with a hitch **3** : HITCHHIKE — **hitch•er** *n*
²hitch *n* **1** : a jerky movement or pull **2** : a sudden stop : an unforeseen obstacle : HALT **3** : the connection between something towed (as a plow or trailer) and its mover (as a tractor, automobile, or animal) **4** : a knot used for a temporary fastening
hitch•hike \'hich-ˌhīk\ *vb* : to travel by or secure free rides — **hitch•hik•er** *n*
¹hith•er \'hith-ər\ *adv* : to this place
²hither *adj* : being on the near or adjacent side
hith•er•most \-ˌmōst\ *adj* : nearest on this side
hith•er•to \-ˌtü\ *adv* : up to this time
hith•er•ward \'hith-ə(r)-wərd\ *adv* : HITHER
hit off *vb* **1** : to characterize precisely and usu. satirically **2** : HARMONIZE, AGREE
hit or miss *adv* : HAPHAZARDLY — **hit–or–miss** \ˌhit-ər-'mis\ *adj*
¹hive \'hīv\ *n* **1 a** : a container for housing honeybees **b** : a colony of bees **2** : a place swarming with busy occupants — **hive•less** \-ləs\ *adj*
²hive *vb* **1 a** : to collect (as bees) into a hive **b** : to enter and take over a hive **2** : to store up in or as if in a hive
³hive *n* : an urticarial wheal
hives \'hīvz\ *n sing or pl* : an allergic disorder marked by the presence of itching wheals
ho \'hō\ *interj* — used esp. to attract attention
hoar \'hō(ə)r\ *n* : FROST 2
hoard \'hōrd\ *n* : a hidden supply or fund stored up — **hoard** *vt* — **hoard•er** *n*
hoar•frost \'hō(ə)r-ˌfrȯst\ *n* : FROST 2
hoarse \'hōrs\ *adj* **1** : harsh in sound **2** : having a rough grating voice — **hoarse•ly** *adv* — **hoarse•ness** *n*
hoary \'hōr-ē\ *adj* **1** : grayish or whitish esp. from age **2** : very old : ANCIENT — **hoar•i•ness** *n*
¹hoax \'hōks\ *vt* : to trick into believing or accepting as genuine something false and often preposterous — **hoax•er** *n*
²hoax *n* **1** : an act intended to trick or dupe **2** : something false passed off or accepted as genuine
¹hob \'häb\ *n* : MISCHIEF, TROUBLE
²hob *n* : a projection at the back or side of a fireplace on which something may be kept warm
¹hob•ble \'häb-əl\ *vb* **hob•bled**; **hob•bling** \'häb-(ə-)liŋ\ **1 a** : to move along unsteadily or with difficulty; *esp* : to limp along **b** : to cause to limp : make lame : CRIPPLE **2 a** : to keep (as a horse) from straying by joining two legs with a short length (as of rope) **b** : HAMPER, IMPEDE — **hob•bler** \-(ə-)lər\ *n*
²hobble *n* **1** : a hobbling movement **2** : something used to hobble an animal
hob•ble•de•hoy \'häb-əl-di-ˌhȯi\ *n* : an awkward gawky youth
hobble skirt *n* : a skirt very narrow at the ankles
hob•by \'häb-ē\ *n, pl* **hobbies** : an interest or activity which is outside a person's main occupation but to which he devotes much time for pleasure — **hob•by•ist** \-ē-əst\ *n*
hob•by•horse \-ē-ˌhȯrs\ *n* **1** : a stick sometimes with a horse's head on which children pretend to ride **2 a** : a toy horse **b** : ROCKING HORSE **3** : something (as a pet idea or scheme or favorite topic) to which one constantly reverts
hob•gob•lin \'häb-ˌgäb-lən\ *n* **1** : a mischievous elf or goblin **2** : BOGEY 2, BUGABOO
hob•nail \'häb-ˌnāl\ *n* : a short large-headed nail used to stud the soles of heavy shoes as a protection against wear — **hob•nailed** \-ˌnāld\ *adj*
hob•nob \-ˌnäb\ *vi* **hob•nobbed**; **hob•nob•bing** : to associate familiarly — **hob•nob•ber** *n*
ho•bo \'hō-bō\ *n, pl* **hoboes** **1** : a migratory worker **2** : TRAMP — **hobo** *vi*
Hob•son's choice \ˌhäb-sənz-\ *n* : apparently free choice with no real alternative
¹hock \'häk\ *n* : the tarsal joint or region in the hind limb of a quadruped (as the horse) corresponding to the ankle of man
²hock *n* : ¹PAWN 2
³hock *vt* : PAWN
hock•ey \'häk-ē\ *n* : a game played on a field or on ice in which two sides try to drive a ball or puck through opposite goals by hitting it with a curved or hooked stick
ho•cus \'hō-kəs\ *vt* **ho•cused** *or* **ho•cussed**; **ho•cus•ing** *or* **ho•cus•sing** **1** : DECEIVE, CHEAT **2 a** : ADULTERATE **b** : DRUG
ho•cus–po•cus \ˌhō-kəs-'pō-kəs\ *n* **1** : a set form of words used by those skilled in tricks of illusion **2** : nonsense that serves as a means of deception
hod \'häd\ *n* **1** : a long-handled wooden tray or trough used for carrying mortar or bricks on the shoulder **2** : a bucket for holding or carrying coal
hodge•podge \'häj-ˌpäj\ *n* : MIXTURE, MESS, JUMBLE
hoe \'hō\ *n* : a farm or garden tool with a thin flat blade at nearly a right angle to a long handle that is used for weeding, loosening the earth about plants, and hilling — **hoe** *vb* — **ho•er** *n*
hoe•cake \'hō-ˌkāk\ *n* : a cornmeal cake often baked on a griddle
hoe•down \-ˌdau̇n\ *n* **1** : SQUARE DANCE **2** : a gathering featuring hoedowns
¹hog \'hȯg, 'häg\ *n* **1** : a domestic swine esp. when weighing more than 120 pounds; *also* : any of various animals related to the domestic swine **2** : a selfish, gluttonous, or filthy person
²hog *vt* **hogged**; **hog•ging** : to take in excess of one's share
ho•gan \'hō-ˌgän\ *n* : an earth-covered dwelling of the Navaho Indians
hog•gish \'hȯg-ish, 'häg-\ *adj* : very selfish, gluttonous, or filthy — **hog•gish•ly** *adv* — **hog•gish•ness** *n*
hogs•head \'hȯgz-ˌhed, 'hägz-\ *n* **1** : a large cask or barrel; *esp* : one containing from 63 to 140 gallons **2** : a U.S. measure for liquids equal to 63 gallons
hog–tie \'hȯg-ˌtī, 'häg-\ *vt* **1** : to tie together the feet of **2** : to make helpless
hog•wash \-ˌwȯsh, -ˌwäsh\ *n* **1** : SWILL 1, SLOP 4a **2** : worthless or nonsensical language
hoi pol•loi \ˌhȯi-pə-'lȯi\ *n pl* : the common people : MASSES
hoise \'hȯiz\ *vt* **hoised** \'hȯizd\ *or* **hoist** \'hȯist\; **hois•ing** \'hȯi-ziŋ\ : HOIST — **hoist with one's own petard** : affected or hurt by one's own scheme
¹hoist \'hȯist\ *vb* : to raise or become raised into position by or as if by means of tackle — **hoist•er** *n*
²hoist *n* **1** : an act of hoisting : LIFT **2** : an apparatus for hoisting heavy loads
hoi•ty–toi•ty \ˌhȯit-ē-'tȯit-ē, ˌhīt-ē-'tīt-ē\ *adj* **1** : GIDDY, FLIGHTY **2** : HAUGHTY, PATRONIZING
ho•key•po•key \ˌhō-kē-'pō-kē\ *n* : HOCUS-POCUS
ho•kum \'hō-kəm\ *n* **1** : a device used (as by showmen) to evoke a desired response esp. of mirth or sentiment **2** : HOCUS-POCUS, BUNKUM
¹hold \'hōld\ *vb* **held** \'held\; **hold•ing** **1 a** : to maintain possession of : POSSESS, HAVE **b** : to retain by force **2 a** : to impose restraint upon esp. by keeping back **b** : STAY, ARREST **c** : DELAY **d** : to keep from advancing or succeeding in attack **e** : to bind legally or morally : CONSTRAIN **3 a** : to have or keep in the grasp **b** : to cause to be or remain in a particular situation, position, or relation **c** : SUPPORT, SUSTAIN **d** : to keep in custody **e** : to have in one's keeping : RESERVE **4** : BEAR, CARRY, COMPORT **5 a** : to maintain in being or action : keep up without interruption or flagging **b** : to keep the uninterrupted interest, attention, or devotion of

6 a : to receive and retain : CONTAIN, ACCOMMODATE **b :** to have in reserve **7 a :** HARBOR, ENTERTAIN **b :** CONSIDER, REGARD, JUDGE **c :** ESTEEM, VALUE **8 :** CONVOKE, CONVENE **9 a :** to have (as an office) by election or appointment **b :** to have earned or been awarded **10 :** to handle (as reins or a gun) so as to guide or manage **11 a :** to maintain position : not retreat **b** (1) **:** to continue in the same way or state : LAST (2) **:** to endure a test or trial **c :** to remain steadfast or faithful **12 :** to maintain a grasp on something : remain fastened to something **13 :** to bear or carry oneself **14 :** to be or remain valid : APPLY **15 :** to forbear an intended or threatened action : HALT, PAUSE — **hold forth :** to preach or harangue at length — **hold one's own :** to prove at least equal to opposition — **hold the bag 1 :** to be left empty-handed **2 :** to bear alone a responsibility that should have been shared by others — **hold water :** to stand up under criticism or analysis — **hold with :** to agree with or approve of

²hold *n* **1 :** STRONGHOLD **2 :** something that holds, secures, or fastens **3 :** the act or manner of holding : SEIZURE, GRASP **4 :** the authority to take or keep : POWER **5 :** something that may be grasped or held **6 :** a prolonged note or rest in music; *also* : a sign 𝄐 or 𝄑 denoting a hold

³hold *n* **1 :** the interior of a ship below decks; *esp* : the cargo deck of a ship **2 :** the cargo compartment of an airplane

hold·back \'hōl(d)-ˌbak\ *n* **1 :** a device that retains or restrains **2 a :** the act of holding back **b :** something held back

hold·er \'hōl-dər\ *n* **1 :** a person that holds: **a** (1) **:** OWNER (2) **:** TENANT **b :** a person in possession of and legally entitled to receive payment of a bill, note, or check **2 :** a device that holds

hold·ing \'hōl-diŋ\ *n* **1 a :** land held (as for farming or residence) **b :** property (as bonds or stocks) owned **2 :** a ruling of a court esp. on an issue of law raised in a case

hold out \(')hōl-'dau̇t\ *vb* **1 :** OFFER, PROFFER **2 :** REPRESENT, DESCRIBE **3 :** to remain unsubdued or operative : LAST **4 :** to refuse to come to an agreement — **hold·out** \'hōl-ˌdau̇t\ *n*

hold up \(')hōl-'dəp\ *vt* **1 :** DELAY, IMPEDE **2 :** to rob at gunpoint — **hold·up** \'hōl-ˌdəp\ *n*

hole \'hōl\ *n* **1 :** an opening into or through a thing **2 a :** a hollow place; *esp* : PIT, CAVE **b :** a deep place in a body of water **3 :** an underground habitation : BURROW **4 :** FLAW, FAULT **5 :** the unit of play from the tee to the cup in golf **6 :** a mean or dingy place **7 :** an awkward position : FIX — **hole** *vb* — **hol·ey** \'hō-lē\ *adj* — **in the hole :** in debt : ¹BEHIND 2b

hol·i·day \'häl-ə-ˌdā\ *n* **1 :** a day observed in Judaism with commemorative ceremonies **2 :** a day on which one is exempt from work; *esp* : a day marked by a general suspension of work in commemoration of an event **3 :** a period of relaxation : VACATION — **holiday** *vi*

hol·i·days \-ˌdāz\ *adv* **:** on holidays repeatedly : on any holiday

ho·li·ness \'hō-lē-nəs\ *n* **1 :** the quality or state of being holy **2** — used as a title for various high religious dignitaries

hol·lan·daise \ˌhäl-ən-'dāz\ *n* **:** a sauce made of butter, yolks of eggs, and lemon juice or vinegar

Hol·lands \'häl-ən(d)z\ *n* **:** gin made in the Netherlands

¹hol·ler \'häl-ər\ *vb* **hol·lered; hol·ler·ing** \'häl-(ə-)riŋ\ **1 :** to cry or call out (as to attract attention or in pain) : SHOUT **2 :** GRIPE, COMPLAIN

²holler *n* **1 :** SHOUT, CRY **2 :** COMPLAINT

hol·lo \'häl-ō, hä-'lō\ *or* **hol·la** \'häl-ə\ *interj* **1** — used to attract attention **2** — used as a call of encouragement or jubilation

¹hol·low \'häl-ō\ *adj* **1 :** CONCAVE, SUNKEN **2 :** having a hole inside : not solid throughout **3 :** devoid of value or significance **4 :** reverberating like a sound made in or by beating on a large empty enclosure : MUFFLED **5 :** FALSE, DECEITFUL — **hol·low·ly** *adv* — **hol·low·ness** *n*

²hollow *vb* **:** to make or become hollow

³hollow *n* **1 :** a low spot in a surface; *esp* : VALLEY **2 :** an empty space within something : HOLE

hollow ware *n* **:** vessels usu. of pottery, glass, or metal (as bowls, cups, or vases) with a significant depth and volume

hol·ly \'häl-ē\ *n, pl* **hollies :** any of a genus of trees and shrubs with thick glossy spiny-margined leaves and usu. bright red berries; *also* : the foliage or branches of a holly

hol·ly·hock \'häl-ē-ˌhäk, -ˌhȯk\ *n* **:** a tall widely grown perennial Chinese herb of the mallow family with large coarse rounded leaves and tall spikes of showy flowers

hol·mi·um \'hō(l)-mē-əm\ *n* **:** a metallic element that occurs with yttrium and forms highly magnetic compounds

hol·o·caust \'häl-ə-ˌkȯst, 'hō-lə-\ *n* **1 :** a sacrifice consumed by fire **2 :** a thorough destruction esp. by fire

hol·o·graph \'häl-ə-ˌgraf, 'hō-lə-\ *n* **:** a document wholly in the handwriting of the purported author — **holograph** *or* **hol·o·graph·ic** \ˌhäl-ə-'graf-ik, ˌhō-lə-\ *adj*

hol·ster \'hōl(t)-stər\ *n* **:** a usu. leather case for a pistol

ho·lus–bo·lus \ˌhō-ləs-'bō-ləs\ *adv* **:** all at once : ALTOGETHER

ho·ly \'hō-lē\ *adj* **1 :** set apart to the service of God or a god : SACRED **2 a :** characterized by perfection and transcendence : commanding absolute adoration and reverence **b :** spiritually pure : SAINTLY **3 a :** evoking or meriting veneration or awe **b :** being awesome, frightening, or beyond belief

ho·ly·stone \-ˌstōn\ *n* **:** a soft sandstone used to scrub a ship's decks — **holystone** *vb*

hom·age \'(h)äm-ij\ *n* **1 :** a ceremony in which a person pledged allegiance to a lord and became his vassal **2 :** something done or given as an acknowledgment of a vassal's duty to his lord **3 :** RESPECT, HONOR

hom·bre \'äm-brē, -ˌbrā\ *n* **:** GUY, FELLOW

hom·burg \'häm-ˌbərg\ *n* **:** a man's felt hat with a stiff curled brim and a high crown creased lengthwise

¹home \'hōm\ *n* **1 :** the house in which one lives or in which one's family lives **2 :** the country or place where one lives or where one's ancestors lived **3 :** the place where something is usu. or naturally found : HABITAT **4 :** a place for the care of persons unable to care for themselves **5 :** the social unit formed by a family living together in one dwelling **6 :** a dwelling house **7 :** the goal or point to be reached in some games

²home *adv* **1 :** to or at home **2 :** to a final, closed, or standard position **3 :** to a vital core

³home *vb* **1 :** to go or return home **2 :** to return home accurately from a distance

home·body \'hōm-ˌbäd-ē\ *n* **:** one whose life centers around the home

home brew *n* **:** an alcoholic beverage made at home

home·com·ing \'hōm-ˌkəm-iŋ\ *n* **1 :** a return home **2 :** the return of a group of people esp. on a special occasion to a place formerly frequented

home economics *n* **:** the study of the various arts and skills involved in the care and management of a household — **home economist** *n*

home front *n* **:** the sphere of civilian activity in war

home·grown \'hōm-'grōn\ *adj* **1 :** NATIVE, LOCAL **2 :** DOMESTIC, INDIGENOUS

home·land \'hōm-ˌland\ *n* **:** native land : FATHERLAND

home·less \'hōm-ləs\ *adj* **:** having no home

home·like \-ˌlīk\ *adj* **:** characteristic of a home: **a :** CHEERFUL, COZY **b :** SIMPLE, WHOLESOME

home·ly \'hōm-lē\ *adj* **1 :** characteristic of home life : PLAIN, SIMPLE **2 :** lacking polish or refinement : RUDE **3 :** not handsome — **home·li·ness** *n*

home·made \'hō(m)-'mād\ *adj* **:** made in the home or on the premises

home·mak·er \'hōm-ˌmā-kər\ *n* **:** one who manages a household esp. as a wife and mother — **home·mak·ing** \-kiŋ\ *n or adj*

home plate *n* : a rubber slab at the apex of a baseball diamond that a base runner must touch in order to score

hom·er \ˈhō-mər\ *n* **1** : HOMING PIGEON **2** : HOME RUN

home·room \ˈhōm-ˌrüm, -ˌru̇m\ *n* : a schoolroom where pupils of the same class report at the opening of school

home rule *n* **1** : self-government in internal affairs by the people of a dependent political unit **2** : limited autonomy in local affairs granted by a state to a county or municipality

home run *n* : a hit in baseball that enables the batter to make a complete circuit of the bases and score a run

home·sick \ˈhōm-ˌsik\ *adj* : longing for home and family while absent from them — **home·sick·ness** *n*

[1]home·spun \-ˌspən\ *adj* **1 a** : spun or made at home **b** : made of homespun **2** : SIMPLE, HOMELY

[2]homespun *n* : a loosely woven usu. woolen or linen fabric orig. made from homespun yarn

[1]home·stead \ˈhōm-ˌsted\ *n* **1 a** : the home and adjoining land occupied by a family **b** : an ancestral home **2** : a tract of land acquired from U.S. public lands by filing a record and living on and cultivating it

[2]homestead *vb* : to acquire or settle on land for use as a homestead

home·stead·er \-ˌsted-ər\ *n* : one who holds a homestead; *esp* : one who has acquired a homestead under laws authorizing the sale of public lands in parcels of 160 acres to settlers

home·stretch \-ˈstrech\ *n* **1** : the part of a racecourse between the last curve and the winning post **2** : a final stage

home·ward \-wərd\ *or* **home·wards** \-wərdz\ *adv* : toward or in the direction of home — **homeward** *adj*

home·work \-ˌwərk\ *n* : work and esp. school lessons to be done at home

hom·ey \ˈhō-mē\ *adj* : HOMELIKE, INTIMATE — **hom·ey·ness** *or* **hom·i·ness** *n*

hom·i·cid·al \ˌhäm-ə-ˈsīd-ᵊl, ˌhō-mə-\ *adj* : having or showing tendencies toward homicide : MURDEROUS — **hom·i·cid·al·ly** \-ᵊl-ē\ *adv*

hom·i·cide \ˈhäm-ə-ˌsīd, ˈhō-mə-\ *n* **1** : a person who kills another **2** : a killing of one human being by another

hom·i·ly \ˈhäm-ə-lē\ *n, pl* **-lies** **1** : SERMON **2** : a moral lecture

hom·ing pigeon \ˌhō-miŋ-\ *n* : a racing pigeon trained to return home

hom·i·ny \ˈhäm-ə-nē\ *n* : hulled corn with the germ removed

ho·mo·ge·ne·i·ty \ˌhō-mə-jə-ˈnē-ət-ē\ *n* : the quality or state of being homogeneous

ho·mo·ge·ne·ous \-ˈjē-nē-əs\ *adj* **1** : of the same or a similar kind or nature **2** : of uniform structure or composition throughout — **ho·mo·ge·ne·ous·ly** *adv* — **ho·mo·ge·ne·ous·ness** *n*

ho·mog·e·nize \hō-ˈmäj-ə-ˌnīz\ *vt* **1** : to make homogeneous **2 a** : to reduce to small particles of uniform size and distribute evenly **b** : to break up the fat globules of (milk) into very fine particles esp. by forcing through minute openings — **ho·mog·e·ni·za·tion** \-ˌmäj-ə-nə-ˈzā-shən\ *n* — **ho·mog·e·niz·er** \-ˈmäj-ə-ˌnī-zər\ *n*

hom·o·graph \ˈhäm-ə-ˌgraf, ˈhō-mə-\ *n* : one of two or more words alike in spelling but different in origin or meaning — **hom·o·graph·ic** \ˌhäm-ə-ˈgraf-ik, ˌhō-mə-\ *adj*

ho·mol·o·gous \hō-ˈmäl-ə-gəs\ *adj* **1 a** : having the same relative position, value, or structure **b** : corresponding in structure because of community of origin **c** : belonging to or consisting of a chemical series whose members exhibit homology **2** : derived from or developed in response to organisms of the same species

ho·mol·o·gy \hō-ˈmäl-ə-jē\ *n, pl* **-gies** **1** : a similarity often attributable to common origin **2 a** : structural likeness between corresponding parts of different organisms due to differentiation from a remote common ancestor **b** : structural likeness between different parts of the same individual **3** : the relation existing between chemical compounds in a series whose successive members have in composition a regular difference

hom·o·nym \ˈhäm-ə-ˌnim, ˈhō-mə-\ *n* **1** : HOMOPHONE **2** : one of two or more words spelled and pronounced alike but different in meaning

hom·o·phone \ˈhäm-ə-ˌfōn, ˈhō-mə-\ *n* : one of two or more words pronounced alike but different in meaning or derivation or spelling

ho·mo sa·pi·ens \ˌhō-mō-ˈsap-ē-ənz, -ˈsā-pē-\ *n* : MANKIND 1

ho·mo·sex·u·al \ˌhō-mə-ˈsek-sh(ə-w)əl\ *adj* : of, relating to, or exhibiting sexual desire toward a member of one's own sex — **homosexual** *n* — **ho·mo·sex·u·al·i·ty** \-ˌsek-shə-ˈwal-ət-ē\ *n*

[1]hone \ˈhōn\ *n* **1** : a fine-grit whetstone; *esp* : one for sharpening razors **2** : a tool for enlarging holes to precise measurements by means of a rotated abrasive

[2]hone *vt* : to sharpen, enlarge, or smooth with a hone

hon·est \ˈän-əst\ *adj* **1 a** : free from fraud or deception : TRUTHFUL **b** : GENUINE, REAL **c** : HUMBLE, PLAIN **2** : REPUTABLE, RESPECTABLE **3** : CREDITABLE **4 a** : marked by integrity : UPRIGHT **b** : marked by frankness or sincerity : STRAIGHTFORWARD **c** : INNOCENT, SIMPLE — **hon·est·ly** *adv*

hon·es·ty \ˈän-ə-stē\ *n* **1** : fairness and straightforwardness of conduct : INTEGRITY **2** : TRUTHFULNESS, SINCERITY

[1]hon·ey \ˈhən-ē\ *n, pl* **honeys** **1** : a thick sugary material prepared by bees from floral nectar and stored by them in a honeycomb for food **2 a** : SWEETHEART, DEAR — often used as a term of endearment **b** : something superlative **3** : SWEETNESS — **honey** *adj*

[2]honey *vb* **hon·eyed**; **hon·ey·ing** **1** : to sweeten with or as if with honey **2** : to speak ingratiatingly : FLATTER

hon·ey·bee \ˈhən-ē-ˌbē\ *n* : a social honey-producing bee; *esp* : a European bee widely kept for its honey and wax

honeybees: *1* queen, *2* drone, *3* worker

[1]hon·ey·comb \-ˌkōm\ *n* **1** : a mass of 6-sided wax cells built by honeybees in their nest to contain brood and stores of honey **2** : something that resembles a honeycomb in structure or appearance

[2]honeycomb *vb* **1** : to make or become full of holes like a honeycomb **2** : SUBVERT, WEAKEN

hon·ey·dew melon \ˌhən-ē-ˌd(y)ü-\ *n* : a pale smooth-skinned muskmelon with greenish sweet flesh

hon·ey·moon \ˈhən-ē-ˌmün\ *n* **1** : the time immediately after marriage **2** : the holiday spent by a couple after marriage — **honeymoon** *vi* — **hon·ey·moon·er** *n*

hon·ey·suck·le \-ˌsək-əl\ *n* : any of a genus of shrubs with opposite leaves and often showy flowers rich in nectar; *also* : any of various plants (as a columbine or azalea) with tubular flowers rich in nectar

honk \ˈhäŋk\ *n* : the cry of a goose; *also* : a similar sound (as of a horn) — **honk** *vb*

hon·ky–tonk \ˈhäŋ-kē-ˌtäŋk\ *n* : a cheap nightclub or dance hall : DIVE

[1]hon·or \ˈän-ər\ *n* **1 a** : good name : public esteem : REPUTATION **b** : outward respect : RECOGNITION **2** : PRIVILEGE **3** : a person of superior standing — used esp. as a title for a holder of high office **4** : one whose worth brings respect or fame

: CREDIT 5 : an evidence or symbol of distinction: as a : an exalted title or rank b : BADGE, DECORATION c : a ceremonial rite or observance d *pl* : an academic distinction conferred on a superior student e : an award in a contest or field of competition 6 : CHASTITY, PURITY 7 a : a keen sense of ethical conduct : INTEGRITY b : one's word given as a guarantee of performance 8 *pl* : social courtesies or civilities extended by a host

²**honor** *vt* **hon·ored**; **hon·or·ing** \'än-(ə-)riŋ\ 1 a : to regard or treat with honor : RESPECT b : to confer honor on 2 : to live up to or fulfill the terms of; *esp* : to accept and pay when due 3 : to salute with a bow in square dancing

hon·or·a·ble \'än-(ə-)rə-bəl\ *adj* 1 : deserving of honor 2 : performed or accompanied with marks of honor or respect 3 a : of great renown : ILLUSTRIOUS b — used as a title for children of some British noblemen and for various government officials 4 a : doing credit to the possessor b : consistent with an untarnished reputation 5 : characterized by integrity : ETHICAL — **hon·or·a·bly** \-blē\ *adv*

hon·o·rar·i·um \ˌän-ə-'rer-ē-əm\ *n, pl* **-ia** \-ē-ə\ : a reward usu. for services on which custom or propriety forbids a price to be set

hon·or·ary \'än-ə-ˌrer-ē\ *adj* 1 a : having or conferring distinction b : COMMEMORATIVE 2 a : conferred in recognition of achievement or service without the usual prerequisites or obligations b : UNPAID, VOLUNTARY — **hon·or·ar·i·ly** \ˌän-ə-'rer-ə-lē\ *adv*

hon·or·if·ic \ˌän-ə-'rif-ik\ *adj* 1 : conferring or conveying honor 2 : belonging to or constituting a class of grammatical forms used in speaking to or about a social superior

hood \'hu̇d\ *n* 1 a : a flexible covering for the head and neck b : a protective covering for the head and face 2 : an ornamental fold at the back of an academic gown or ecclesiastical vestment 3 a : something resembling a hood in form or use b : a cover for parts of mechanisms; *esp* : the movable metal covering over the engine of an automobile — **hood** *vt* — **hood·like** *adj*

hood·ed \'hu̇d-əd\ *adj* : having or shaped like a hood

hood·lum \'hüd-ləm\ *n* 1 : THUG, MOBSTER 2 : a young ruffian

hoo·doo \'hüd-ü\ *n, pl* **hoodoos** 1 : VOODOO 2 : something that brings bad luck — **hoodoo** *vt* — **hoo·doo·ism** \-ˌiz-əm\ *n*

hood·wink \'hu̇d-ˌwiŋk\ *vt* : to deceive by false appearance : impose upon

hoo·ey \'hü-ē\ *n* : NONSENSE

¹**hoof** \'hu̇f, 'hüf\ *n, pl* **hooves** \'hu̇vz, 'hüvz\ *or* **hoofs** 1 : a curved covering of horn that protects the front of or encloses the ends of the toes of some mammals and that corresponds to a nail or claw 2 : a hoofed foot esp. of a horse — **hoofed** \'hu̇ft, 'hüft, 'hu̇vd, 'hüvd\ *adj* — **on the hoof** : LIVING

²**hoof** *vb* 1 : WALK 2 : KICK, TRAMPLE 3 : to move on the feet; *esp* : DANCE

hoof·er \'hu̇f-ər, 'hü-fər\ *n* : a professional dancer

¹**hook** \'hu̇k\ *n* 1 : a curved or bent implement for catching, holding, or pulling 2 : something (as a sharp bend in a road) curved or bent like a hook 3 : a flight of a ball that deviates from a straight course in a direction opposite to the dominant hand of the player propelling it 4 : a short blow delivered with a circular motion by a boxer while the elbow remains bent and rigid — **by hook or by crook** : by any means — **off the hook** : out of trouble — **on one's own hook** : by oneself : INDEPENDENTLY

²**hook** *vb* 1 : to form into a hook : CROOK, CURVE 2 a : to seize, make fast, or connect by or as if by a hook b : to become secured or connected by or as if by a hook 3 : STEAL, PILFER 4 : to strike or pierce as if with a hook 5 : to make (as a rug) by drawing loops of thread, yarn, or cloth through a coarse fabric with a hook

hook·ah \'hu̇k-ə\ *n* : a pipe for smoking that has a long flexible tube whereby the smoke is cooled by passing through water

hook and eye *n* : a 2-part fastening device (as on a garment or a door) consisting of a wire hook that catches over a bar or into a loop of wire

hooked \'hu̇kt\ *adj* 1 : shaped like or furnished with a hook 2 : made by hooking

hook·let \'hu̇k-lət\ *n* : a small hook

hook·up \'hu̇k-ˌəp\ *n* 1 : an assemblage (as of circuits) used for a specific purpose (as in radio); *also* : the plan of such an assemblage 2 : an arrangement of mechanical parts 3 : connection often between antagonistic elements : ALLIANCE

hook·worm \-ˌwərm\ *n* : a parasitic intestinal worm having strong hooks or plates about the mouth and including serious bloodsucking pests

hooky \'hu̇k-ē\ *n* : TRUANT

hoo·li·gan \'hü-li-gən\ *n* : RUFFIAN, HOODLUM — **hoo·li·gan·ism** \-gə-ˌniz-əm\ *n*

¹**hoop** \'hu̇p, 'hüp\ *n* 1 : a circular strip used esp. for holding together the staves of containers or as a plaything 2 : a circular figure or object : RING 3 : a circle or series of circles of flexible material used to expand a woman's skirt

²**hoop** *vt* : to bind or fasten with or as if with a hoop — **hoop·er** *n*

hoop·la \'hü-ˌplä\ *n* 1 : TO-DO 2 : utterances designed to bewilder or confuse

hoop·skirt \'hu̇p-'skərt, 'hüp-\ *n* : a skirt stiffened with or as if with hoops

¹**hoot** \'hüt\ *vb* 1 : to utter a loud shout usu. in contempt 2 : to make the natural throat noise of an owl or a similar cry 3 : to assail or drive out by hooting 4 : to express in or by hoots — **hoot·er** *n*

²**hoot** *n* 1 : a sound of hooting; *esp* : the cry of an owl 2 : a very small amount

hoo·te·nan·ny \'hüt-ᵊn-ˌan-ē\ *n, pl* **-nies** : a gathering at which folk singers entertain often with the audience joining in

¹**hop** \'häp\ *vb* **hopped**; **hop·ping** 1 : to move by a quick springy leap or in a series of leaps; *esp* : to jump on one foot 2 : to jump over 3 : to get aboard by or as if by hopping 4 : to make a quick trip esp. by air

²**hop** *n* 1 a : a short brisk leap esp. on one leg b : BOUNCE, REBOUND 2 : DANCE, BALL 3 a : a flight in an airplane b : a short trip c : a free ride

³**hop** *n* 1 : a twining vine of the mulberry family with lobed leaves and pistillate flowers in cone-shaped catkins 2 *pl* : the ripe dried pistillate catkins of a hop used esp. to impart a bitter flavor to malt liquors

⁴**hop** *vt* **hopped**; **hop·ping** 1 : to flavor with hops 2 : to increase the power of beyond an original rating

¹**hope** \'hōp\ *vb* 1 : to desire with expectation of fulfillment 2 : to long for with expectation of fulfillment 3 : to expect with desire : TRUST

²**hope** *n* 1 : TRUST, RELIANCE 2 a : desire accompanied by expectation of or belief in fulfillment b : someone or something on which hopes are centered c : something hoped for

hope chest *n* : a young woman's accumulation of clothes and domestic furnishings (as silver or linen) kept in or as if in a chest in anticipation of her marriage; *also* : a chest for such an accumulation

¹**hope·ful** \'hōp-fəl\ *adj* 1 : full of or inclined to hope 2 : having qualities which inspire hope — **hope·ful·ly** \-fə-lē\ *adv* — **hope·ful·ness** *n*

²**hopeful** *n* : a person who has hopes or is considered promising esp. as a new political candidate

hope·less \'hōp-ləs\ *adj* 1 a : having no expectation of good or success : DESPAIRING b : not susceptible of remedy or cure : INCURABLE 2 a : giving no ground for hope : DESPERATE b : incapable of solution, management, or accomplishment : IMPOSSIBLE — **hope·less·ly** *adv* — **hope·less·ness** *n*

hop·lite \'häp-ˌlīt\ *n* : a heavily armed infantry soldier of ancient Greece

hop·per \'häp-ər\ *n* **1 a** : one that hops **b** : a leaping insect; *esp* : an immature hopping form of an insect **2 a** : a usu. funnel-shaped receptacle for delivering material (as grain or coal) **b** : a box in which a bill to be considered by a legislative body is dropped **c** : a tank holding liquid and having a device for releasing its contents through a pipe

hop·scotch \'häp-ˌskäch\ *n* : a child's game in which a player tosses an object (as a stone) consecutively into areas of a figure outlined on the ground and hops through the figure and back to regain the object

ho·ra \'hōr-ə\ *n* : a circle dance of Romania and Israel

horde \'hōrd\ *n* **1** : a nomadic people or tribe **2** : a great multitude : THRONG, SWARM

hore·hound \'hō(ə)r-ˌhau̇nd\ *n* : an aromatic bitter mint with hoary downy leaves; *also* : an extract or confection made from this plant

ho·ri·zon \hə-'rīz-ᵊn\ *n* **1** : the apparent junction of earth and sky **2** : the limit or range of a person's outlook or experience

[1]**hor·i·zon·tal** \ˌhȯr-ə-'zänt-ᵊl\ *adj* **1 a** : of, relating to, or situated near the horizon **b** : parallel to, in the plane of, or operating in a plane parallel to the horizon or to a base line : LEVEL **2** : consisting of individuals or groups of similar level in a hierarchy — **hor·i·zon·tal·ly** \-ᵊl-ē\ *adv*

[2]**horizontal** *n* : something (as a line or plane) that is horizontal

hor·mone \'hȯr-ˌmōn\ *n* : a product of living cells that circulates in body fluids or sap and produces a specific and usu. stimulatory effect on cells remote from its point of origin — **hor·mon·al** \-ˌmōn-ᵊl\ *adj* — **hor·mon·al·ly** \-ᵊl-ē\ *adv*

horn \'hȯrn\ *n* **1 a** : one of the hard growths of bone or a substance like bone on the head of many hoofed animals including the true permanent horns of cattle, goats, and sheep with a bony core enclosed in a sheath and the deciduous antlers of deer **b** : a hollow horn used to hold something **2** : something resembling or suggestive of a horn **3 a** : an animal's horn used as a wind instrument **b** : a brass wind instrument; *esp* : FRENCH HORN **c** : a usu. electrical device that makes a noise like that of a horn **4** : a source of strength — **horned** \'hȯrnd\ *adj* — **horn·less** \'hȯrn-ləs\ *adj* — **horn·less·ness** *n* — **horn·like** *adj*

horn·book \-ˌbu̇k\ *n* **1** : a child's primer consisting of a sheet of parchment or paper protected by a sheet of transparent horn **2** : a rudimentary treatise

hor·net \'hȯr-nət\ *n* : any of the larger social wasps

horn in *vi* : to participate without invitation or consent

horn of plenty : CORNUCOPIA

horn·pipe \'hȯrn-ˌpīp\ *n* **1** : a single reed wind instrument consisting of a wooden or bone pipe with holes at intervals and a bell and mouthpiece usu. of horn **2** : a lively folk dance of the British Isles orig. accompanied by hornpipe playing

horny \'hȯr-nē\ *adj* **1 a** : made of or as if of horn **b** (1) : resembling horn esp. in appearance or texture (2) : HARD, CALLOUS **2** : having horns

ho·rol·o·gy \hə-'räl-ə-jē\ *n* **1** : the science of measuring time **2** : the art of constructing instruments for indicating time — **hor·o·log·ic** \ˌhȯr-ə-'läj-ik\ *adj* — **hor·o·log·i·cal** \-i-kəl\ *adj* — **ho·rol·o·gist** \hə-'räl-ə-jəst\ *n*

horo·scope \'hȯr-ə-ˌskōp\ *n* : a diagram of the relative positions of planets and signs of the zodiac used by astrologers to foretell events of a person's life

hor·ren·dous \hȯ-'ren-dəs\ *adj* : DREADFUL, HORRIBLE — **hor·ren·dous·ly** *adv*

hor·ri·ble \'hȯr-ə-bəl\ *adj* **1** : marked by or conducive to horror **2** : extremely unpleasant or disagreeable — **horrible** *n* — **hor·ri·bly** \-blē\ *adv*

hor·rid \'hȯr-əd\ *adj* **1** : HIDEOUS, SHOCKING **2** : REPULSIVE, OFFENSIVE — **hor·rid·ly** *adv* — **hor·rid·ness** *n*

hor·rif·ic \hȯ-'rif-ik\ *adj* : HORRIFYING, HORRIBLE

hor·ri·fy \'hȯr-ə-ˌfī\ *vt* **-fied**; **-fy·ing** : to cause to feel horror

hor·ror \'hȯr-ər\ *n* **1 a** : painful and intense fear, dread, or dismay : CONSTERNATION **b** : intense aversion or repugnance **2 a** : the quality of inspiring horror **b** : something that inspires horror **3** *pl* : a state of extreme depression or apprehension

hors de com·bat \ˌȯrd-ə-kōⁿ-'bä\ *adv* (*or adj*) : out of combat : DISABLED

hors d'oeuvre \ȯr-'dərv\ *n* : any of various savory foods usu. served as appetizers at the beginning of a meal

[1]**horse** \'hȯrs\ *n* **1 a** : a large solid-hoofed herbivorous mammal domesticated by man since a prehistoric period and used as a beast of burden, a draft animal, or for riding **b** : a male horse : STALLION **2** : a frame that supports something (as wood while being cut or clothes while being dried) **3 horse** *pl* : CAVALRY — **from the horse's mouth** : from the original source

[2]**horse** *vb* **1** : to provide with a horse **2** : to lift, pull, or push by brute force **3** : to engage in horseplay : FOOL

[3]**horse** *adj* **1 a** : of or relating to the horse **b** : worked by horsepower **2** : large or coarse of its kind **3** : mounted on horses

[1]**horse·back** \'hȯrs-ˌbak\ *n* : the back of a horse

[2]**horseback** *adv* : on horseback

horse·car \-ˌkär\ *n* : a streetcar drawn by horses

horse·flesh \-ˌflesh\ *n* : horses for riding, driving, or racing

horse·fly \-ˌflī\ *n* : any of a family of swift usu. large two-winged flies with bloodsucking females

horse·hair \-ˌha(ə)r\ *n* **1** : the hair of a horse esp. from the mane or tail **2** : cloth made from horsehair

horse·hide \-ˌhīd\ *n* : a horse's hide or leather made from it

horse·laugh \-ˌlaf, -ˌlȧf\ *n* : a loud boisterous laugh : GUFFAW

horse·less carriage \ˌhȯrs-ləs-\ *n* : AUTOMOBILE

horse·man \'hȯrs-mən\ *n* **1 a** : a rider on horseback **b** : one skilled in managing horses **2** : a breeder or raiser of horses — **horse·man·ship** \-ˌship\ *n*

horse opera *n* : a motion picture or radio or television play usu. about western cowboys

horse·play \'hȯrs-ˌplā\ *n* : rough or boisterous play

horse·pow·er \-ˌpau̇(-ə)r\ *n* : a unit of power equal to the power necessary to raise 33,000 pounds one foot in one minute

horse·rad·ish \-ˌrad-ish\ *n* : a tall coarse white-flowered herb of the mustard family; *also* : its pungent root used as a condiment

horse sense *n* : COMMON SENSE

horse·shoe \'hȯrs(h)-ˌshü\ *n* **1** : a shoe for horses usu. consisting of a narrow plate of iron shaped to fit the rim of a horse's hoof **2** *pl* : a game like quoits played with horseshoes or with horseshoe-shaped pieces of metal — **horse·shoe** *vt* — **horse·sho·er** \-ˌshü-ər\ *n*

horse·whip \'hȯrs-ˌhwip\ *vt* : to flog with or as if with a whip made to be used on a horse

horse·wom·an \-ˌwu̇m-ən\ *n* **1** : a woman horseback rider **2** : a woman skilled in riding horseback or in caring for or managing horses

hors·ey *or* **horsy** \'hȯr-sē\ *adj* **1** : of, relating to, or suggesting a horse **2 a** : having to do with horses or horse racing **b** : characteristic of horsemen — **hors·i·ness** *n*

hor·ta·tive \'hȯrt-ət-iv\ *adj* : giving exhortation : ADVISORY — **hor·ta·tive·ly** *adv*

hor·ta·to·ry \'hȯrt-ə-ˌtōr-ē\ *adj* : HORTATIVE, EXHORTATORY

hor·ti·cul·ture \'hȯrt-ə-ˌkəl-chər\ *n* : the science and art of growing fruits, vegetables, flowers, or ornamental plants — **hor·ti·cul·tur·al** \ˌhȯrt-ə-'kəlch(-ə)-rəl\ *adj* — **hor·ti·cul·tur·al·ly** \-rə-lē\ *adv* — **hor·ti·cul·tur·ist** \-'kəlch(-ə)-rəst\ *n*

ho·san·na \hō-'zan-ə\ *interj* — used as a cry of acclamation and adoration

¹hose \'hōz\ *n, pl* **hose** *or* **hos·es** 1 *pl hose* a (1) : a cloth leg covering that sometimes covers the foot (2) : STOCKING, SOCK b (1) : a close-fitting garment covering the legs and waist (2) : short breeches reaching to the knee 2 : a flexible tube for conveying (as from a faucet) a fluid
²hose *vt* : to spray, water, or wash with a hose
ho·siery \'hōzh(-ə)-rē, 'hōz(-ə)-\ *n* : HOSE 1a
hos·pice \'häs-pəs\ *n* : an inn for travelers; *esp* : one kept by a religious order
hos·pit·a·ble \hä-'spit-ə-bəl, 'häs-(ˌ)pit-\ *adj* 1 a : showing hospitality : generous and cordial in receiving guests b : promising or suggesting generous and cordial welcome c : offering a pleasant or sustaining environment 2 : readily receptive : OPEN — **hos·pit·a·bly** \-blē\ *adv*
hos·pi·tal \'häs-ˌpit-ᵊl\ *n* 1 : an institution where the sick or injured are given medical or surgical care 2 : a repair shop for specified small objects
hos·pi·tal·i·ty \ˌhäs-pə-'tal-ət-ē\ *n, pl* **-ties** : hospitable treatment, reception, or disposition (as of visitors and guests)
hos·pi·tal·ize \'häs-ˌpit-ᵊl-ˌīz\ *vt* : to place in a hospital for care and treatment — **hos·pi·tal·i·za·tion** \ˌhäs-ˌpit-ᵊl-ə-'zā-shən\ *n*
¹host \'hōst\ *n* 1 : ARMY 2 : a great number : MULTITUDE
²host *n* 1 : one who receives or entertains guests socially or as a business 2 : a living animal or plant affording subsistence or lodgment to a parasite — **host** *vt* — **host·al** \'hōst-ᵊl\ *adj*
³host *n, often cap* : the bread or wafer consecrated in the Mass
hos·tage \'häs-tij\ *n* : a person held by one party in a conflict as a pledge that promises will be kept or terms met by the other
hos·tel \'häst-ᵊl\ *n* 1 : INN 2 : a supervised lodging for use by youth esp. on bicycling trips
hos·tel·ry \'häst-ᵊl-rē\ *n, pl* **-ries** : INN, HOTEL
host·ess \'hō-stəs\ *n* : a woman who acts as host; *esp* : one who receives and arranges for the care of patrons in a restaurant
hos·tile \'häst-ᵊl, 'häs-ˌtīl\ *adj* 1 : of or relating to an enemy 2 : marked by open antagonism : UNFRIENDLY 3 : not hospitable : FORBIDDING — **hos·tile·ly** \-ᵊl-(l)ē, -ˌtīl-lē\ *adv*
hos·til·i·ty \hä-'stil-ət-ē\ *n, pl* **-ties** 1 a : a hostile state b (1) : hostile action (2) *pl* : overt acts of warfare : WAR 2 : antagonism, opposition, or resistance in thought or principle
hos·tler \'(h)äs-lər\ *n* : one who takes care of horses or mules
hot \'hät\ *adj* 1 a : having a relatively high temperature b : capable of giving a sensation of heat or of burning, searing, or scalding 2 a : ARDENT, FIERY b : VIOLENT, RAGING c : LUSTFUL, LECHEROUS d : EAGER e : ecstatic and emotionally exciting and marked by strong rhythms and free melodic improvisations 3 : having or causing the sensation of an uncomfortable degree of body heat 4 : newly made : FRESH; *also* : close to something sought 5 a : suggestive of heat or of burning or glowing objects b : PUNGENT, PEPPERY 6 a : unusually lucky or favorable b : temporarily capable of unusual performance c : currently popular d (1) — used as a generalized term of approval (2) : ABSURD, UNBELIEVABLE 7 a : electrically energized b : RADIOACTIVE; *also* : dealing with radioactive material 8 : recently and illegally obtained — **hot·ly** *adv* — **hot·ness** *n*
hot air *n* : empty talk
hot·bed \'hät-ˌbed\ *n* 1 : a bed of soil enclosed in glass, heated usu. by fermenting manure, and used for forcing or for raising seedlings 2 : an environment that favors rapid growth or development
hot·blood \-ˌbləd\ *n* : THOROUGHBRED 1
hot–blood·ed \-'bləd-əd\ *adj* : easily roused or excited : ARDENT — **hot–blood·ed·ness** *n*
hot·box \-ˌbäks\ *n* : a journal bearing (as of a railroad car) overheated by friction
hotch·potch \'häch-ˌpäch\ *n* : HODGEPODGE
hot dog \'hät-ˌdȯg\ *n* : a cooked frankfurter usu. served in a long split roll
ho·tel \hō-'tel\ *n* : a building that provides lodging and usu. meals, entertainment, and various personal services esp. for transients : INN
¹hot·foot \'hät-ˌfu̇t\ *adv* : in haste
²hotfoot *vi* : to go hotfoot : HURRY
³hotfoot *n, pl* **hotfoots** : a practical joke in which a match is surreptitiously inserted into the side of a victim's shoe and lighted
hot·head \'hät-ˌhed\ *n* : a hotheaded person
hot·head·ed \-'hed-əd\ *adj* : HASTY, RASH, FIERY — **hot·head·ed·ly** *adv* — **hot·head·ed·ness** *n*
¹hot·house \-ˌhau̇s\ *n* : a heated glass-enclosed house for raising plants
²hothouse *adj* 1 : grown in a hothouse 2 : having the qualities of a plant raised in a hothouse; *esp* : DELICATE
hot plate *n* : a simple portable appliance for heating or for cooking
hot rod *n* : an automobile rebuilt or modified for high speed and fast acceleration — **hot–rod·der** \'hät-'räd-ər\ *n*
hot·shot \'hät-ˌshät\ *n* : a showily skillful person
hot war *n* : a conflict involving actual fighting
hot water *n* : a distressing predicament : DIFFICULTY
¹hound \'hau̇nd\ *n* 1 a : DOG b : a dog of any of various hunting breeds typically having large drooping ears and a deep voice and following their prey by scent 2 : a despicable person 3 : ADDICT, FAN
²hound *vt* : to pursue with or as if with hounds
hour \'au̇(ə)r\ *n* 1 : a time or office for daily liturgical devotion; *esp* : CANONICAL HOUR 2 : one of the 24 divisions of a day : 60 minutes 3 a : the time of day indicated by a timepiece b : the time reckoned from midnight to midnight 4 a : a customary time b : a particular time 5 : the work done or distance traveled at normal rate in an hour 6 : a class session
hour·glass \-ˌglas\ *n* : an instrument for measuring time consisting of a glass vessel with two compartments from the uppermost of which a quantity of sand, water, or mercury runs in an hour into the lower one — **hourglass** *adj*
hour·ly \'au̇(ə)r-lē\ *adj* 1 a : occurring hour by hour b : FREQUENT, CONTINUAL 2 : computed in terms of one hour — **hourly** *adv*
¹house \'hau̇s\ *n, pl* **hous·es** \'hau̇-zəz\ 1 : a building that serves as living quarters for one or more families 2 a : something that serves an animal for shelter or habitation b : a building in which something is housed 3 a : HOUSEHOLD b : FAMILY 1; *esp* : a royal or noble family 4 a : a residence for a religious community or for students b : the community or students in residence 5 a : a legislative, deliberative, or consultative assembly; *esp* : one constituting a division of a bicameral body b : the place where an assembly meets 6 a : a place of business or entertainment b : a business organization c : the audience in a theater or concert hall
²house \'hau̇z\ *vb* 1 a : to provide with living quarters or shelter b : to store in a house 2 : to encase, enclose, or shelter as if by putting in a house 3 : to take shelter : LODGE
house·boat \'hau̇s-ˌbōt\ *n* : a barge fitted for use as a dwelling or for leisurely cruising
house·break \-ˌbrāk\ *vt* : to make housebroken
house·break·ing \-ˌbrā-kiŋ\ *n* : the act of breaking into and entering a person's dwelling house with the intent of committing a felony — **house·break·er** *n*
house·bro·ken \-ˌbrō-kən\ *adj* : trained to excretory habits acceptable in indoor living
house·clean \'hau̇s-ˌklēn\ *vb* 1 : to clean a house and its furniture 2 : to clean the surfaces and furnishings of 3 : to get rid of unwanted or undesirable items or people — **house·clean·ing** *n*

house•coat \\-ˌkōt\\ *n* : a woman's usu. long-skirted informal garment for wear around the house
house•fly \\-ˌflī\\ *n* : a two-winged fly that is common about human habitations and acts as a vector of diseases (as typhoid fever)
[1]**house•hold** \\-ˌhōld\\ *n* : those who dwell under the same roof and compose a family; *also* : such a family and its servants or retainers
[2]**household** *adj* **1** : of or relating to a household : DOMESTIC **2** : FAMILIAR, COMMON
house•hold•er \\-ˌhōl-dər\\ *n* : one who occupies a dwelling alone or as the head of a household
house•keep•er \\-ˌkē-pər\\ *n* : a woman employed to keep house
house•keep•ing \\-piŋ\\ *n* : the care and management of a house and home affairs
house•less \\ˈhaủs-ləs\\ *adj* **1** : HOMELESS **2** : destitute of houses — **house•less•ness** *n*
house•lights \\-ˌlīts\\ *n pl* : the lights that illuminate the parts of a theater occupied by the audience
house•maid \\-ˌmād\\ *n* : a female servant employed to do housework
house•moth•er \\-ˌməṯẖ-ər\\ *n* : a woman acting as hostess, chaperon, and often housekeeper in a residence for young people
house•top \\-ˌtäp\\ *n* : ROOF
house•warm•ing \\-ˌwȯr-miŋ\\ *n* : a party to celebrate the taking possession of a house or premises
house•wife \\ˈhaủs-ˌwīf, *2 is often* ˈhəz-əf, ˈhəs-əf\\ *n* **1** : a married woman in charge of a household **2** : a small container for small articles (as thread) — **house•wife•li•ness** \\ˈhaủs-ˌwī-flē-nəs\\ *n* — **house•wife•ly** *adj* — **house•wif•ery** \\-ˌwī-f(ə-)rē\\ *n*
house•work \\ˈhaủs-ˌwərk\\ *n* : the work of housekeeping
[1]**hous•ing** \\ˈhaủ-ziŋ\\ *n* **1 a** : SHELTER, LODGING **b** : dwellings provided for people **2 a** : something that covers or protects **b** : a support (as a frame) for mechanical parts
[2]**housing** *n* **1** : a usu. ornamental covering for the back and sides of a horse : CAPARISON **2** *pl* : TRAPPINGS
hove *past of* HEAVE
hov•el \\ˈhəv-əl, ˈhäv-\\ *n* **1** : an open shed or shelter **2** : TABERNACLE **3** : a small mean house : HUT
hov•er \\ˈhəv-ər, ˈhäv-\\ *vb* **hov•ered**; **hov•er•ing** \\-(ə-)riŋ\\ **1 a** : to hang fluttering in the air or on the wing **b** : to remain suspended over a place or object **2 a** : to move to and fro near a place **b** : to be in a state of uncertainty, irresolution, or suspense **3** : to brood over — **hover** *n* — **hov•er•er** *n*
hov•er•craft \\-ˌkraft\\ *n* : a vehicle for traveling over land or water a short distance above the surface supported on a cushion of air produced by downwardly directed fans
[1]**how** \\(ˈ)haủ\\ *adv* **1 a** : in what manner or way **b** : with what meaning : to what effect **c** : by what name or title **d** : for what reason : WHY **2** : to what degree or extent **3** : in what state or condition **4** : at what price — **how about** : what do you say to or think of
[2]**how** *conj* : in what manner or condition
[3]**how** \\ˈhaủ\\ *n* **1** : MANNER, METHOD **2** : a question about manner or method
[1]**how•be•it** \\haủ-ˈbē-ət\\ *adv* : NEVERTHELESS
[2]**howbeit** *conj* : ALTHOUGH
how•dah \\ˈhaủd-ə\\ *n* : a seat or covered pavilion on the back of an elephant or camel
[1]**how•ev•er** \\haủ-ˈev-ər\\ *conj* : in whatever way or manner
[2]**however** *adv* **1 a** : to whatever degree or extent **b** : in whatever manner or way **2** : in spite of that : on the other hand : BUT **3** : how in the world
how•it•zer \\ˈhaủ-ət-sər\\ *n* : a short cannon used to fire projectiles at medium muzzle velocities and with relatively high trajectories
howl \\ˈhaủ(ə)l\\ *vb* **1** : to emit a loud sustained doleful sound **2** : to cry out or exclaim without restraint under strong impulse (as pain, grief, or rage) **3** : to utter with unrestrained outcry **4** : to affect, effect, or drive by adverse outcry — **howl** *n*
howl•er \\ˈhaủ-lər\\ *n* **1** : one that howls **2** : a stupid and ridiculous blunder
how•so•ev•er \\ˌhaủ-sə-ˈwev-ər\\ *adv* **1** : in whatever manner **2** : to whatever degree or extent
hoy•den \\ˈhȯid-ᵊn\\ *n* : a girl or woman of saucy, boisterous, or carefree behavior — **hoy•den•ish** \\-ish\\ *adj*
hub \\ˈhəb\\ *n* **1** : the central part of a wheel, propeller, or fan **2** : a center of activity
hub•bub \\ˈhəb-ˌəb\\ *n* **1** : a noisy confusion of sound : UPROAR **2** : TURMOIL
hu•bris \\ˈhyü-brəs\\ *n* : overweening pride or self-confidence : ARROGANCE
huck•le•ber•ry \\ˈhək-əl-ˌber-ē\\ *n* **1** : an American shrub related to the blueberry; *also* : its edible dark blue berry **2** : BLUEBERRY
huck•ster \\ˈhək-stər\\ *n* **1** : HAWKER, PEDDLER **2** : a writer of advertising esp. for radio or television
[1]**hud•dle** \\ˈhəd-ᵊl\\ *vb* **hud•dled**; **hudd•ling** \\ˈhəd-liŋ, -ᵊl-iŋ\\ **1** : to crowd, push, or pile together **2** : to gather in a group for conference : CONFER **3** : to curl up : CROUCH — **hud•dler** \\ˈhəd-lər, -ᵊl-ər\\ *n*
[2]**huddle** *n* **1** : a close-packed group : BUNCH **2** : CONFERENCE
hue \\ˈhyü\\ *n* **1** : SHAPE, ASPECT **2 a** : gradation of color **b** : a chromatic color as distinct from white, gray, and black **c** : the attribute of colors that permits them to be classed as red, yellow, green, blue, or an intermediate between any contiguous pair of these colors
hue and cry \\ˌhyü-\\ *n* **1** : a loud outcry formerly used in the pursuit of felons **2** : a clamor of pursuit or protest
[1]**huff** \\ˈhəf\\ *vb* **1** : PUFF **2 a** : BLUSTER **b** : to react indignantly **3** : to make angry : PROVOKE
[2]**huff** *n* : a fit of anger or pique
huffy \\ˈhəf-ē\\ *adj* **1** : easily offended : TOUCHY **2** : SULKY — **huff•i•ly** \\ˈhəf-ə-lē\\ *adv* — **huff•i•ness** *n*
hug \\ˈhəg\\ *vb* **hugged**; **hug•ging** **1** : to press tightly esp. in the arms : EMBRACE **2** : to hold fast : CHERISH **3** : to stay close to — **hug** *n*
huge \\ˈhyüj, ˈyüj\\ *adj* : very large or extensive: as **a** : of great size or area **b** : of sizable scale or degree **c** : of limitless scope or character — **huge•ly** *adv* — **huge•ness** *n*
hug•ger–mug•ger \\ˈhəg-ər-ˌməg-ər\\ *n* **1** : SECRECY **2** : CONFUSION, MUDDLE — **hugger–mugger** *adj*
Hu•gue•not \\ˈhyü-gə-ˌnät\\ *n* : a French Protestant of the 16th and 17th centuries
[1]**hulk** \\ˈhəlk\\ *n* **1** : a heavy clumsy ship **2** : a bulky, unwieldy, or clumsy person or thing **3 a** : the body of an old ship unfit for service or of an abandoned wreck **b** : a ship used as a prison — usu. used in pl.
[2]**hulk** *vi* : to appear impressively large : BULK
hulk•ing \\ˈhəl-kiŋ\\ *adj* : MASSIVE, HUSKY
[1]**hull** \\ˈhəl\\ *n* **1** : the outer covering of a fruit or seed **2** : the frame or body esp. of a ship or airplane
[2]**hull** *vt* : to remove the hulls of — **hull•er** *n*
hul•la•ba•loo \\ˈhəl-ə-bə-ˌlü\\ *n, pl* **-loos** : a confused noise : UPROAR
hum \\ˈhəm\\ *vb* **hummed**; **hum•ming** **1 a** : to utter a sound like that of the speech sound \\m\\ prolonged **b** : to make the natural buzzing noise of an insect in motion or a similar sound : DRONE **2** : to sing with the lips closed and without articulation **3** : to be busily active — **hum** *n* — **hum•mer** *n*
hu•man \\ˈhyü-mən, ˈyü-\\ *adj* **1** : of, relating to, or characteristic of man **2 a** : being a man **b** : consisting of men **3** : having human form or attributes — **human** *n* — **hu•man•ness** *n*
hu•mane \\hyü-ˈmān, yü-\\ *adj* **1** : marked by compassion, sympathy, or consideration for other human beings or for

animals 2 : HUMANISTIC — **hu·mane·ly** *adv* — **hu·mane·ness** *n*

hu·man·ism \'hyü-mə-ˌniz-əm, 'yü-\ *n* **1** : a revival of classical letters, an individualistic and critical spirit, and an emphasis on secular concerns characteristic of the Renaissance **2** : a doctrine or way of life centered on human interests or values — **hu·man·ist** \-nəst\ *n or adj* — **hu·man·is·tic** \ˌhyü-mə-'nis-tik, ˌyü-\ *adj*

hu·man·i·tar·i·an \(ˌ)hyü-ˌman-ə-'ter-ē-ən, (ˌ)yü-\ *n* : a person promoting human welfare and social reform : PHILANTHROPIST — **humanitarian** *adj* — **hu·man·i·tar·i·an·ism** \-ē-ə-ˌniz-əm\ *n*

hu·man·i·ty \hyü-'man-ət-ē, yü-\ *n, pl* **-ties** **1** : the quality or state of being humane **2** : the quality or state of being human **3** *pl* : the branches of learning having primarily a cultural character **4** : MANKIND 1

hu·man·ize \'hyü-mə-ˌnīz, 'yü-\ *vt* **1** : to adapt to human nature or use **2** : to make humane : CIVILIZE, REFINE — **hu·man·i·za·tion** \ˌhyü-mə-nə-'zā-shən, ˌyü-\ *n*

hu·man·kind \'hyü-mən-ˌkīnd, 'yü-\ *n* : MANKIND 1

hu·man·ly \'hyü-mən-lē, 'yü-\ *adv* **1 a** : from the viewpoint of man **b** : within the range of human capacity **2** : in a human manner

¹hum·ble \'həm-bəl, 'əm-\ *adj* **1** : modest or meek in spirit or manner : not proud or assertive **2** : expressing a spirit of deference or submission **3** : low in rank or status : UNPRETENTIOUS — **hum·bly** \-blē\ *adv*

²humble *vt* **hum·bled**; **hum·bling** \-b(ə-)liŋ\ **1** : to make humble in spirit or manner **2** : to destroy the power or prestige of — **hum·bler** \-b(ə-)lər\ *n*

hum·bug \'həm-ˌbəg\ *n* **1 a** : something designed to deceive and mislead : FRAUD **b** : CHARLATAN **2** : DRIVEL, NONSENSE — **humbug** *vb* — **hum·bug·gery** \-ˌbəg-(ə-)rē\ *n*

hum·drum \'həm-ˌdrəm\ *adj* : MONOTONOUS, DULL

hu·mer·al \'hyüm-(ə-)rəl\ *adj* : of, relating to, or used or located in the region of the humerus or shoulder — **humeral** *n*

hu·mer·us \'hyüm-(ə-)rəs\ *n, pl* **hu·meri** \'hyü-mə-ˌrī\ : the long bone of the upper arm or forelimb extending from the shoulder to the elbow

hu·mid \'hyü-məd, 'yü-\ *adj* : containing or characterized by perceptible moisture : DAMP — **hu·mid·ly** *adv*

hu·mid·i·fy \hyü-'mid-ə-ˌfī, yü-\ *vt* **-fied**; **-fy·ing** : to make (as the air of a room) humid : MOISTEN — **hu·mid·i·fi·ca·tion** \-ˌmid-ə-fə-'kā-shən\ *n* — **hu·mid·i·fi·er** *n*

hu·mid·i·ty \-'mid-ət-ē\ *n, pl* **-ties** : DAMPNESS, MOISTURE; *esp* : the amount of moisture in the air

hu·mi·dor \'hyü-mə-ˌdȯr, 'yü-\ *n* : a case usu. for storing cigars in which the air is kept properly humidified

hu·mil·i·ate \hyü-'mil-ē-ˌāt, yü-\ *vt* : to reduce to a lower position in one's own eyes or others' eyes : HUMBLE — **hu·mil·i·a·tion** \-ˌmil-ē-'ā-shən\ *n*

hu·mil·i·ty \hyü-'mil-ət-ē, yü-\ *n* : the quality or state of being humble

hum·ming·bird \'həm-iŋ-ˌbərd\ *n* : any of numerous tiny brightly colored American birds related to the swifts and having narrow swiftly beating wings, a slender bill, and a long tongue for sipping nectar

hum·mock \'həm-ək\ *n* : a rounded mound of earth : KNOLL — **hum·mocky** \-ə-kē\ *adj*

¹hu·mor \'hyü-mər, 'yü-\ *n* **1** : state of mind or disposition **2** : the amusing quality of things **3** : the power to see or tell about the amusing side of things : a keen perception of the comic or the ridiculous **4** : WHIM, FANCY **5** : something comical or amusing

²humor *vt* **hu·mored**; **hu·mor·ing** \'hyüm-(ə-)riŋ, 'yüm-\ : to comply with the wishes or mood of

hu·mor·ist \'hyüm-(ə-)rəst, 'yüm-\ *n* : a person specializing in or noted for humor

hu·mor·ous \'hyüm-(ə-)rəs, 'yüm-\ *adj* : full of, characterized by, or expressive of humor : AMUSING, DROLL — **hu·mor·ous·ly** *adv* — **hu·mor·ous·ness** *n*

¹hump \'həmp\ *n* **1** : a rounded bulge or lump (as on the back of a camel) **2** : MOUND, HUMMOCK **3** : a difficult phase — **humped** \'həm(p)t\ *adj*

²hump *vb* **1** : to exert oneself vigorously : HUSTLE **2** : to make hump-shaped : HUNCH

hump·back \'həmp-ˌbak\ *n* **1** : a humped or crooked back **2** : HUNCHBACK **3** : a large whalebone whale with very long flippers

hump·backed \-'bakt\ *or* **hump·back** \-ˌbak\ *adj* : having a humped back

hu·mus \'hyü-məs, 'yü-\ *n* : a brown or black product of partial decomposition of plant or animal matter that forms the organic portion of soil

¹hunch \'hənch\ *vb* **1** : to thrust oneself forward **2** : to assume a bent or crooked posture **3** : to thrust into a hump

²hunch *n* **1** : HUMP **2** : a strong intuitive feeling as to how something (as a course of action) will turn out

hunch·back \'hənch-ˌbak\ *n* **1** : HUMPBACK 1 **2** : a person with a humpback — **hunch·backed** \-'bakt\ *adj*

hun·dred \'hən-drəd\ *n, pl* **hundreds** *or* **hundred** **1** — see NUMBER table **2** : the number in the third decimal place to the left of the decimal point in arabic numerals **3** : a very large or indefinitely great number — **hundred** *adj*

hun·dredth \-drədth\ *n* **1** : one of 100 equal parts of something **2** : the one numbered 100 in a countable series — see NUMBER table — **hundredth** *adj*

hun·dred·weight \'hən-drəd-ˌwāt\ *n, pl* **-weight** *or* **-weights** : a unit of weight equal to 100 pounds

hung *past of* HANG

¹hun·ger \'həŋ-gər\ *n* **1** : a desire or a need for food; *also* : an uneasy feeling or weakened condition resulting from lack of food **2** : a strong desire : CRAVING — **hunger** *adj*

²hunger *vi* **hun·gered**; **hun·ger·ing** \-g(ə-)riŋ\ **1** : to feel or suffer hunger **2** : to have an eager desire

hunger strike *n* : refusal esp. by a prisoner to eat enough to sustain life

hung jury *n* : a jury that is unable to reach a unanimous verdict

hun·gry \'həŋ-grē\ *adj* **1** : feeling or showing hunger **2** : EAGER, AVID **3** : not rich or fertile : BARREN — **hun·gri·ly** \-grə-lē\ *adv* — **hun·gri·ness** \-grē-nəs\ *n*

hunk \'həŋk\ *n* : a large lump or piece

¹hunt \'hənt\ *vb* **1 a** : to pursue for food or in sport **b** : to use in hunting game **2 a** : to pursue with intent to capture **b** : to search out : SEEK **3** : to drive or chase esp. by harrying **4** : to search through in quest of prey **5** : to take part in a hunt

²hunt *n* **1** : the act, the practice, or an instance of hunting **2** : a group of hunters; *esp* : persons with horses and dogs engaged in hunting or riding to hounds

hunt·er \'hənt-ər\ *n* **1 a** : a person who hunts game **b** : a dog or horse used or trained for hunting **2** : a person who searches for something

hunt·ing \'hənt-iŋ\ *n* : the act of one that hunts; *esp* : the pursuit of game

hunt·ress \'hən-trəs\ *n* : a female hunter

hunts·man \'hən(t)s-mən\ *n* **1** : HUNTER 1a **2** : a person who manages a hunt and looks after the hounds

¹hur·dle \'hərd-ᵊl\ *n* **1** : a movable frame (as of woven twigs) used for enclosing land or livestock **2** : a barrier to be jumped in a race **3** : OBSTACLE

²hurdle *vt* **hur·dled**; **hur·dling** \'hərd-liŋ, -ᵊl-iŋ\ **1** : to leap over while running **2** : OVERCOME, SURMOUNT — **hur·dler** \'hərd-lər, -ᵊl-ər\ *n*

hur·dy–gur·dy \ˌhərd-ē-'gərd-ē\ *n, pl* **-dies** : a musical instrument in which the sound is produced by turning a crank

hurl \'hərl\ *vb* **1** : to throw violently or powerfully **2** : PITCH — **hurl·er** *n*

hur·ly–bur·ly \ˌhər-lē-ˈbər-lē\ *n, pl* **-lies** : UPROAR, TUMULT

[1]**hur·rah** \hu̇-ˈrȯ, -ˈrä\ *interj* — used to express joy, approval, or encouragement

[2]**hurrah** *n* : EXCITEMENT, FANFARE

[3]**hurrah** *vb* : to shout hurrah : CHEER

hur·ri·cane \ˈhər-ə-ˌkān, -i-kən\ *n* : a tropical cyclone with winds of 73 miles per hour or greater but rarely exceeding 150 miles per hour usu. accompanied by rain, thunder, and lightning

hurricane lamp *n* : a candlestick or an electric lamp with a glass chimney

hur·ried \ˈhər-ēd\ *adj* **1** : going or working at speed **2** : done in a hurry : HASTY — **hur·ried·ly** \-ēd-lē, -əd-\ *adv*

[1]**hur·ry** \ˈhər-ē\ *vb* **hur·ried**; **hur·ry·ing** **1 a** : to carry or cause to go with haste **b** : to move or act with haste **2 a** : to impel to greater speed : PROD **b** : EXPEDITE

[2]**hurry** *n, pl* **hurries** **1** : DISTURBANCE, COMMOTION **2** : a recurrent agitation of sound **3 a** : excessive haste : PRECIPITANCY **b** : a state of eagerness or urgency : RUSH

[1]**hurt** \ˈhərt\ *vb* **hurt**; **hurt·ing** **1 a** : to inflict with physical pain **b** : to do harm to : DAMAGE **2 a** : to cause anguish to : OFFEND **b** : HAMPER **3** : to feel or cause pain — **hurt·er** *n*

[2]**hurt** *n* **1** : a wounding blow : a cause of injury or damage **2 a** : a bodily injury or wound **b** : mental distress : SUFFERING **3** : WRONG, HARM

hurt·ful \ˈhərt-fəl\ *adj* : causing injury or suffering : DAMAGING — **hurt·ful·ly** \-fə-lē\ *adv* — **hurt·ful·ness** *n*

hur·tle \ˈhərt-ᵊl\ *vb* **hur·tled**; **hur·tling** \ˈhərt-liŋ, -ᵊl-iŋ\ **1** : to move with or as if with a rushing sound **2** : HURL, FLING

[1]**hus·band** \ˈhəz-bənd\ *n* : a married man

[2]**husband** *vt* : to manage prudently and economically : use carefully : CONSERVE — **hus·band·er** *n*

hus·band·man \ˈhəz-bən(d)-mən\ *n* : FARMER

hus·band·ry \-bən-drē\ *n* **1** : the management or judicious use of resources **2** : FARMING, AGRICULTURE

[1]**hush** \ˈhəsh\ *vb* **1** : to make quiet, calm, or still : SOOTHE **2** : to become quiet **3** : to keep from public knowledge : SUPPRESS

[2]**hush** *n* : a silence or calm esp. following noise : QUIET

[1]**husk** \ˈhəsk\ *n* **1** : a usu. thin dry outer covering of a seed or fruit **2** : an outer layer : SHELL

[2]**husk** *vt* : to strip the husk from — **husk·er** *n*

husk·ing \ˈhəs-kiŋ\ *n* : a gathering of farm families to husk corn

[1]**husky** \ˈhəs-kē\ *adj* : hoarse with or as if with emotion — **husk·i·ly** \-kə-lē\ *adv* — **husk·i·ness** \-kē-nəs\ *n*

[2]**husky** *adj* **1** : BURLY, ROBUST **2** : LARGE

[3]**husky** *n, pl* **husk·ies** : one that is husky

hus·sar \(ˌ)hə-ˈzär\ *n* : a member of any of various European military units orig. of light cavalry

hus·sy \ˈhəz-ē, ˈhəs-\ *n, pl* **hussies** **1** : a lewd or brazen woman **2** : a pert or mischievous girl

hus·tings \ˈhəs-tiŋz\ *n pl* : a place where political campaign speeches are made; *also* : the proceedings in an election campaign

hus·tle \ˈhəs-əl\ *vb* **hus·tled**; **hus·tling** \ˈhəs-(ə-)liŋ\ **1** : to push, crowd, or force forward roughly **2** : to move or work rapidly and tirelessly; *also* : to obtain by such work — **hustle** *n* — **hus·tler** \-(ə-)lər\ *n*

hut \ˈhət\ *n* : an often small and temporary dwelling or shelter : SHACK — **hut** *vb*

hutch \ˈhəch\ *n* **1 a** : a chest or compartment for storage **b** : a low cupboard usu. surmounted by open shelves **2** : a pen or coop for an animal **3** : SHACK, SHANTY

huz·zah *or* **huz·za** \(ˌ)hə-ˈzä\ *interj* — used to express joy or approbation

hy·a·cinth \ˈhī-ə-(ˌ)sin(t)th\ *n* : any of a genus of bulbous herbs of the lily family; *esp* : a common garden plant widely grown for the beauty and fragrance of its bell-shaped 6-lobed flowers — **hy·a·cin·thine** \ˌhī-ə-ˈsin(t)-thən\ *adj*

hy·brid \ˈhī-brəd\ *n* **1** : an offspring of genetically differing parents (as members of different breeds or species) **2** : something of mixed origin or composition — **hybrid** *adj* — **hy·brid·ism** \ˈhī-brə-ˌdiz-əm\ *n* — **hy·brid·i·ty** \hī-ˈbrid-ət-ē\ *n*

hy·brid·ize \ˈhī-brə-ˌdīz\ *vb* : to produce or cause to produce hybrids : INTERBREED — **hy·brid·i·za·tion** \ˌhī-brəd-ə-ˈzā-shən\ *n* — **hy·brid·iz·er** *n*

hy·dran·gea \hī-ˈdrān-jə\ *n* : any of a genus of shrubs related to the currants and having showy clusters of usu. sterile white, pink, or blue flowers

hy·drant \ˈhī-drənt\ *n* **1** : a discharge pipe with a valve and spout at which water may be drawn from a main **2** : FAUCET

hy·drate \ˈhī-ˌdrāt\ *n* **1** : a compound or complex ion formed by the union of water with some other substance **2** : HYDROXIDE

hy·drau·lic \hī-ˈdrȯ-lik\ *adj* **1** : operated, moved, or effected by means of water **2** : of or relating to hydraulics **3** : operated by the resistance offered or the pressure transmitted when a quantity of liquid is forced through a comparatively small orifice or through a tube **4** : hardening or setting under water — **hy·drau·li·cal·ly** \-li-k(ə-)lē\ *adv*

hy·drau·lics \-liks\ *n* : a science that deals with practical applications of liquid (as water) in motion

hy·dro·car·bon \ˌhī-drə-ˈkär-bən\ *n* : an organic compound (as acetylene or benzene) containing only carbon and hydrogen

hy·dro·chlo·ric acid \ˌhī-drə-ˌklōr-ik-\ *n* : an aqueous solution of hydrogen chloride that is a strong corrosive liquid acid, is normally present in dilute form in gastric juice, and is widely used in industry and in the laboratory

hy·dro·elec·tric \ˌhī-drō-i-ˈlek-trik\ *adj* : of or relating to production of electricity by waterpower — **hy·dro·elec·tric·i·ty** \-ˌlek-ˈtris-ət-ē, -ˈtris-tē\ *n*

hy·dro·foil \ˈhī-drə-ˌfȯil\ *n* **1** : a body similar to an airfoil but designed for action in or on the water **2** : a motorboat that has metal plates or fins attached by struts fore and aft for lifting the hull clear of the water as speed is attained

hy·dro·gen \ˈhī-drə-jən\ *n* : a gaseous colorless odorless highly flammable chemical element that is the lightest of the elements — **hy·drog·e·nous** \hī-ˈdräj-ə-nəs\ *adj*

hydrogen bomb *n* : a bomb whose violent explosive power is due to the sudden release of atomic energy resulting from the union of light nuclei (as of hydrogen atoms)

hydrogen peroxide *n* : an unstable liquid compound used esp. as an oxidizing and bleaching agent, an antiseptic, and a propellant

hy·drol·y·sis \hī-ˈdräl-ə-səs\ *n* : a chemical process of decomposition involving splitting of a bond and addition of the elements of water — **hy·dro·lyt·ic** \ˌhī-drə-ˈlit-ik\ *adj*

hy·drom·e·ter \hī-ˈdräm-ət-ər\ *n* : a floating instrument for determining specific gravities of liquids and hence the strength (as of alcoholic liquors, saline solutions) — **hy·dro·met·ric** \ˌhī-drə-ˈme-trik\ *adj* — **hy·drom·e·try** \hī-ˈdräm-ə-trē\ *n*

hy·dro·pho·bia \ˌhī-drə-ˈfō-bē-ə\ *n* : RABIES

[1]**hy·dro·plane** \ˈhī-drə-ˌplān\ *n* **1** : a speedboat with fins or a stepped bottom so that the hull is raised wholly or partly out of the water **2** : SEAPLANE

[2]**hydroplane** *vi* **1** : to skim over the water with the hull more or less clear of the surface **2** : to drive or ride in a hydroplane

hy·dro·pon·ics \ˌhī-drə-ˈpän-iks\ *n* : the growing of plants in nutrient solutions — **hy·dro·pon·ic** \-ik\ *adj* — **hy·dro·pon·i·cal·ly** \-ˈpän-i-k(ə-)lē\ *adv*

hy·dro·stat·ic \ˌhī-drə-ˈstat-ik\ *adj* : of or relating to liquids at rest or to the pressures they exert or transmit

hy·dro·ther·a·py \ˌhī-drō-ˈther-ə-pē\ *n* : the use of water in the treatment of disease

hy·drous \ˈhī-drəs\ *adj* : containing water usu. chemically combined

hy•drox•ide \hī-'dräk-ˌsīd\ *n* : a compound of hydroxyl with an element or radical
hy•e•na \hī-'ē-nə\ *n* : any of several large strong nocturnal carnivorous Old World mammals
hy•giene \'hī-ˌjēn\ *n* **1** : a science dealing with the establishment and maintenance of health **2** : conditions or practices (as of cleanliness) conducive to health — **hy•gi•en•ic** \ˌhī-jē-'en-ik, hī-'jen-, hī-'jēn-\ *adj* — **hy•gi•en•i•cal•ly** \-i-k(ə-)lē\ *adv* — **hy•gien•ist** \hī-'jēn-əst, -'jen-, 'hī-ˌ\ *n*
hying *pres part of* HIE
hy•me•ne•al \ˌhī-mə-'nē-əl\ *adj* : of or relating to marriage : NUPTIAL
[1]**hymn** \'him\ *n* **1** : a song of praise esp. to God : PAEAN **2** : a religious song
[2]**hymn** *vb* **hymned**; **hymn•ing** \'him-iŋ\ **1 a** : to praise or worship in hymns **b** : to sing the praises of : EXTOL **2 a** : to express in or as if in a hymn **b** : SING; *esp* : to sing hymns
hym•nal \'him-nᵊl\ *n* : a book of hymns
hy•per•ac•id \ˌhī-pər-'as-əd\ *adj* : containing more than the normal amount of acid — **hy•per•acid•i•ty** \-ə-'sid-ət-ē\ *n*
hy•per•bo•le \hī-'pər-bə-(ˌ)lē\ *n* : extravagant exaggeration used as a figure of speech
hy•per•bol•ic \ˌhī-pər-'bäl-ik\ *adj* : of, characterized by, or given to hyperbole — **hy•per•bol•i•cal** \-i-kəl\ *adj* — **hy•per•bol•i•cal•ly** \-i-k(ə-)lē\ *adv*
hy•per•crit•i•cal \ˌhī-pər-'krit-i-kəl\ *adj* : excessively critical : CAPTIOUS — **hy•per•crit•i•cal•ly** \-k(ə-)lē\ *adv*
hy•per•sen•si•tive \-'sen(t)-sət-iv\ *adj* : excessively or abnormally sensitive — **hy•per•sen•si•tive•ness** *n* — **hy•per•sen•si•tiv•i•ty** \-ˌsen(t)-sə-'tiv-ət-ē\ *n*
hy•per•son•ic \-'sän-ik\ *adj* **1** : of or relating to speed five or more times that of sound in air **2** : moving, capable of moving, or utilizing air currents that move at hypersonic speed
hy•per•ten•sion \-'ten-chən\ *n* : abnormally high blood pressure and esp. arterial blood pressure — **hy•per•ten•sive** \-'ten(t)-siv\ *adj or n*
hy•per•tro•phy \hī-'pər-trə-fē\ *n, pl* **-phies** : excessive development of a bodily part; *esp* : increase in bulk without multiplication of constituent units — **hy•per•tro•phic** \hī-'pər-trə-fik, ˌhī-pər-'träf-ik\ *adj* — **hypertrophy** *vb*
[1]**hy•phen** \'hī-fən\ *n* : a mark - used to divide or to compound words or word elements
[2]**hyphen** *vt* : to connect or mark with a hyphen
hy•phen•ate \'hī-fə-ˌnāt\ *vt* : HYPHEN
hyp•no•sis \hip-'nō-səs\ *n, pl* **-no•ses** \-'nō-ˌsēz\ : an induced state which resembles sleep but in which the subject is very responsive to suggestions of the hypnotizer
[1]**hyp•not•ic** \hip-'nät-ik\ *adj* **1** : tending to induce sleep : SOPORIFIC **2** : of or relating to hypnosis or hypnotism — **hyp•not•i•cal•ly** \-i-k(ə-)lē\ *adv*
[2]**hypnotic** *n* **1** : a sleep-inducing agent : SOPORIFIC **2** : one that is or can be hypnotized
hyp•no•tism \'hip-nə-ˌtiz-əm\ *n* **1** : the study of or act of inducing hypnosis **2** : HYPNOSIS — **hyp•no•tist** \-təst\ *n*
hyp•no•tize \-ˌtīz\ *vt* **1** : to induce hypnosis in **2** : to deaden (judgment or resistance) by or as if by hypnotic suggestion — **hyp•no•tiz•a•ble** *adj* — **hyp•no•ti•za•tion** \ˌhip-nət-ə-'zā-shən\ *n* — **hyp•no•tiz•er** *n*
hy•po•chon•dria \ˌhī-pə-'kän-drē-ə\ *n* : severe depression of mind or spirits often centered on imaginary physical ailments — **hy•po•chon•dri•ac** \-drē-ˌak\ *adj or n* — **hy•po•chon•dri•a•cal** \-kən-'drī-ə-kəl, -ˌkän-\ *adj* — **hy•po•chon•dri•a•cal•ly** \-'drī-ə-k(ə-)lē\ *adv*
hy•poc•ri•sy \hip-'äk-rə-sē\ *n, pl* **-sies** : a pretending to be what one is not or to believe what one does not; *esp* : the false assumption of an appearance of virtue or religion
hyp•o•crite \'hip-ə-ˌkrit\ *n* : one who affects virtues or qualities he does not have : DISSEMBLER — **hyp•o•crit•i•cal** \ˌhip-ə-'krit-i-kəl\ *adj* — **hyp•o•crit•i•cal•ly** \-i-k(ə-)lē\ *adv*
hy•po•der•mic \ˌhī-pə-'dər-mik\ *n* : a small syringe with a hollow needle for injecting material into or through the skin; *also* : an injection made with this
hy•pot•e•nuse \hī-'pät-ᵊn-ˌ(y)üs, -ˌ(y)üz\ *n* : the side of a right-angled triangle that is opposite the right angle
hy•poth•e•cate \hī-'päth-ə-ˌkāt\ *vb* : HYPOTHESIZE
hy•poth•e•sis \hī-'päth-ə-səs\ *n, pl* **-e•ses** \-ə-ˌsēz\ : something not proved but assumed to be true for purposes of argument or further study or investigation
hy•poth•e•size \-ˌsīz\ *vb* **1** : to make a hypothesis **2** : to adopt as a hypothesis
hy•po•thet•i•cal \ˌhī-pə-'thet-i-kəl\ *adj* **1** : involving hypothesis : ASSUMED **2** : of or depending on supposition : CONJECTURAL — **hy•po•thet•i•cal•ly** \-i-k(ə-)lē\ *adv*
hys•sop \'his-əp\ *n* : a woody European mint with pungent aromatic leaves sometimes used in folk medicine for bruises
hys•te•ria \his-'ter-ē-ə, -'tir-\ *n* **1** : a nervous disorder marked by emotional excitability **2** : unmanageable fear or emotional excess — **hys•ter•ic** \-'ter-ik\ *n* — **hysteric** *or* **hys•ter•i•cal** \-'ter-i-kəl\ *adj* — **hys•ter•i•cal•ly** \-i-k(ə-)lē\ *adv*
hys•ter•ics \his-'ter-iks\ *n sing or pl* : a fit of uncontrollable laughter or crying : HYSTERIA

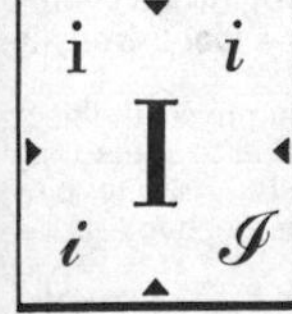

i \'ī\ *n, often cap* **1** : the 9th letter of the English alphabet **2** : the roman numeral 1
I \(')ī, ə\ *pron* : the one who is speaking or writing
iamb \'ī-ˌam\ *n* : a metrical foot consisting of one unaccented syllable followed by one accented syllable (as in *away*) — **iam•bic** \ī-'am-bik\ *adj*
ibex \'ī-ˌbeks\ *n, pl* **ibex** *or* **ibex•es** : an Old World wild goat with large curved horns
ibi•dem \'ib-ə-ˌdem, ib-'īd-əm\ *adv* : in the same place
ibis \'ī-bəs\ *n, pl* **ibis** *or* **ibis•es** : any of several wading birds related to the herons but distinguished by a long slender bill that curves downward
[1]**ice** \'īs\ *n* **1 a** : frozen water **b** : an expanse of frozen water **2** : a state of coldness (as from formality or reserve) **3** : a substance resembling ice **4** : a frozen dessert; *esp* : one containing no milk or cream
[2]**ice** *vb* **1 a** : to coat or become coated with ice : change into ice **b** : to chill with ice **c** : to supply with ice **2** : to cover with or as if with icing
ice bag *n* : a waterproof bag to hold ice for local application of cold to the body
ice•berg \'īs-ˌbərg\ *n* : a large floating mass of ice detached from a glacier
ice•boat \-ˌbōt\ *n* : a skeleton boat or frame on runners propelled on ice usu. by sails
ice•bound \-ˌbau̇nd\ *adj* : surrounded or obstructed by ice
ice•box \-ˌbäks\ *n* : REFRIGERATOR
ice•break•er \-ˌbrā-kər\ *n* **1** : a ship equipped to make and maintain a channel through ice **2** : something that breaks the ice (as at a social occasion)

ice cap *n* : a glacier forming on an extensive area of relatively level land and flowing outward from its center
ice–cold \'īs-'kōld\ *adj* : extremely cold
ice cream *n* : a frozen food containing cream or butterfat, flavoring, sweetening, and usu. eggs
ice•house \'īs-ˌhaùs\ *n* : a building for storing ice
ice•man \'īs-ˌman\ *n* : one who sells or delivers ice
ice pick *n* : a hand tool ending in a spike for chipping ice
ice–skate \'ī(s)-ˌskāt\ *vi* : to skate on ice — **ice skater** *n*
ice water *n* : chilled or iced water esp. for drinking
ichor \'īk-ˌór, 'īk-ər, 'ik-\ *n* : an ethereal fluid taking the place of blood in the veins of the ancient Greek gods — **ichor•ous** \-ə-rəs\ *adj*
ich•thy•ol•o•gy \ˌik-thē-'äl-ə-jē\ *n* : a branch of zoology that deals with fishes — **ich•thy•o•log•i•cal** \ˌik-thē-ə-'läj-i-kəl\ *adj* — **ich•thy•o•log•i•cal•ly** \-i-k(ə-)lē\ *adv* — **ich•thy•ol•o•gist** \ˌik-thē-'äl-ə-jəst\ *n*
ici•cle \'ī-ˌsik-əl\ *n* : a hanging mass of ice formed by the freezing of dripping water
ic•ing \'ī-siŋ\ *n* : a coating for baked goods usu. made from sugar and butter combined with water, milk, or egg white and flavoring
icon \'ī-ˌkän\ *n* **1** : IMAGE **2** : a conventional religious image typically painted on a small wooden panel and venerated by Eastern Christians — **icon•ic** \ī-'kän-ik\ *adj*
icon•o•clasm \ī-'kän-ə-ˌklaz-əm\ *n* : the doctrine, practice, or attitude of an iconoclast
icon•o•clast \-ˌklast\ *n* **1** : one who destroys religious images or opposes their veneration **2** : one who attacks established beliefs or institutions — **icon•o•clas•tic** \ī-ˌkän-ə-'klas-tik\ *adj*
ic•tus \'ik-təs\ *n* : the recurring stress or beat in a rhythmic or metrical series of sounds
icy \'ī-sē\ *adj* **1 a** : covered with, full of, or consisting of ice **b** : intensely cold **2** : characterized by coldness : FRIGID — **ici•ly** \-sə-lē\ *adv* — **ici•ness** \-sē-nəs\ *n*
id \'id\ *n* : the primitive undifferentiated part of the psychic apparatus that reacts blindly on a pleasure-pain level, is the seat of psychic energy, and is the ultimate source of higher psychic components (as ego and superego)
idea \ī-'dē-ə\ *n* **1** : a plan of action : INTENTION **2** : something imagined or pictured in the mind : NOTION **3** : a central meaning or purpose
[1]ide•al \ī-'dē(-ə)l\ *adj* **1** : existing only in the mind : not real **2** : embodying or symbolizing an ideal : PERFECT
[2]ideal *n* **1** : a standard of perfection, beauty, or excellence **2** : a perfect type : a model for imitation **3** : an ultimate object or aim of endeavor : GOAL
ide•al•ism \ī-'dē-(ə-)ˌliz-əm\ *n* **1** : the practice of forming or living according to ideals **2** : the ability or tendency to see things as they should be rather than as they are — **ide•al•ist** \-(ə-)ləst\ *n* — **ide•al•is•tic** \-ˌdē-(ə-)'lis-tik\ *adj* — **ide•al•is•ti•cal•ly** \-ti-k(ə-)lē\ *adv*
ide•al•ize \ī-'dē-(ə-)ˌlīz\ *vt* : to think of or represent as ideal — **ide•al•i•za•tion** \ī-ˌdē-(ə-)lə-'zā-shən\ *n*
ide•al•ly \ī-'dē-(ə-)lē\ *adv* **1** : in idea or imagination : MENTALLY **2** : conformably to an ideal : PERFECTLY
idem \'īd-ˌem\ *pron* : something previously mentioned : SAME
iden•ti•cal \ī-'dent-i-kəl, ə-\ *adj* **1** : being one and the same **2** : being essentially the same or exactly alike — **iden•ti•cal•ly** \-i-k(ə-)lē\ *adv*
iden•ti•fi•ca•tion \ī-ˌdent-ə-fə-'kā-shən, ə-\ *n* **1** : an act of identifying : the state of being identified **2** : evidence of identity
iden•ti•fy \ī-'dent-ə-ˌfī, ə-\ *vt* **-fied**; **-fy•ing** **1 a** : to cause to be or become identical **b** : ASSOCIATE **2** : to establish the identity of — **iden•ti•fi•a•ble** \-ˌfī-ə-bəl\ *adj*
iden•ti•ty \ī-'dent-ət-ē, ə-\ *n, pl* **-ties** **1** : the fact or condition of being exactly alike : SAMENESS **2** : distinctness with regard to character or appearance : INDIVIDUALITY **3** : the fact of being the same person or thing as one described or known to exist
id•e•o•gram \'id-ē-ə-ˌgram, 'īd-\ *n* **1** : a picture or symbol used in a system of writing to represent a thing or an idea but not a particular word or phrase for it **2** : a character or symbol used in a system of writing to represent an entire word without providing separate representation of the individual sounds in it
ide•ol•o•gy \ˌīd-ē-'äl-ə-jē, ˌid-\ *n, pl* **-gies** **1** : a systematic body of concepts esp. about human life or culture **2** : a manner or the content of thinking characteristic of an individual, group, or culture **3** : the integrated assertions, theories, and aims that constitute a political, social, and economic program — **ide•o•log•i•cal** \-ē-ə-'läj-i-kəl\ *adj* — **ide•o•log•i•cal•ly** \-i-k(ə-)lē\ *adv* — **ide•ol•o•gist** \-ē-'äl-ə-jəst\ *n*
ides \'īdz\ *n pl* : the 15th day of March, May, July, or October or the 13th day of any other month in the ancient Roman calendar
id•i•o•cy \'id-ē-ə-sē\ *n, pl* **-cies** **1** : extreme mental deficiency commonly due to incomplete or abnormal development of the brain **2** : something notably stupid or foolish
id•i•o•lect \'id-ē-ə-ˌlekt\ *n* : the speech pattern of one individual
id•i•om \'id-ē-əm\ *n* **1** : the language peculiar to a group **2** : the characteristic form or structure of a language **3** : an expression that cannot be understood from the meanings of its separate words but must be learned as a whole — **id•i•om•at•ic** \ˌid-ē-ə-'mat-ik\ *adj* — **id•i•om•at•i•cal•ly** \-'mat-i-k(ə-)lē\ *adv*
id•i•o•syn•cra•sy \ˌid-ē-ə-'siŋ-krə-sē\ *n, pl* **-sies** **1** : characteristic peculiarity of habitual behavior or of structure **2** : individual hypersensitiveness (as to a drug or to food) — **id•i•o•syn•crat•ic** \ˌid-ē-ō-sin-'krat-ik\ *adj* — **id•i•o•syn•crat•i•cal•ly** \-'krat-i-k(ə-)lē\ *adv*
id•i•ot \'id-ē-ət\ *n* **1** : a feebleminded person requiring complete custodial care **2** : a silly or foolish person — **idiot** *adj* — **id•i•ot•ic** \ˌid-ē-'ät-ik\ *adj* — **id•i•ot•i•cal•ly** \-'ät-i-k(ə-)lē\ *adv*
[1]idle \'īd-ᵊl\ *adj* **1** : not based on facts : WORTHLESS **2** : USELESS **3** : not employed : doing nothing **4** : LAZY — **idle•ness** *n* — **idly** \'īd-lē\ *adv*
[2]idle *vb* **idled**; **idling** \'īd-liŋ, -ᵊl-iŋ\ **1 a** : to spend time in idleness **b** : to move idly **2** : to run disconnected so that power is not used for useful work **3** : to pass in idleness : WASTE — **idler** \'īd-lər, -ᵊl-ər\ *n*
idol \'īd-ᵊl\ *n* **1** : an image of a god made or used as an object of worship **2** : one that is very greatly or excessively loved and admired
idol•a•ter \ī-'däl-ət-ər\ *n* **1** : a worshiper of idols **2** : a person that admires or loves intensely and often blindly — **idol•a•tress** \-'däl-ə-trəs\ *n*
idol•a•trous \ī-'däl-ə-trəs\ *adj* **1** : of, relating to, or having the character of idolatry **2** : given to idolatry — **idol•a•trous•ly** *adv* — **idol•a•trous•ness** *n*
idol•a•try \-trē\ *n, pl* **-tries** **1** : the worship of a physical object as a god **2** : immoderate attachment or devotion to something
idol•ize \'īd-ᵊl-ˌīz\ *vb* **1** : to worship idolatrously **2** : to love or admire to excess — **idol•i•za•tion** \ˌīd-ᵊl-ə-'zā-shən\ *n* — **idol•iz•er** *n*
idyll *or* **idyl** \'īd-ᵊl\ *n* **1 a** : a simple poetic or prose work descriptive of peaceful rustic life or pastoral scenes **b** : a romantic narrative poem **2** : a fit subject for an idyll — **idyl•lic** \ī-'dil-ik\ *adj* — **idyl•li•cal•ly** \-'dil-i-k(ə-)lē\ *adv*
[1]if \(ˌ)if, əf\ *conj* **1** : in the event that **2** : WHETHER **3** — used as a function word to introduce an exclamation expressing a wish **4** : even though
[2]if \'if\ *n* **1** : CONDITION, STIPULATION **2** : SUPPOSITION

ig·loo \'ig-lü\ *n, pl* **igloos** : an Eskimo house often made of snow blocks and in the shape of a dome
ig·ne·ous \'ig-nē-əs\ *adj* **1** : of, relating to, or resembling fire : FIERY **2** : formed by solidification of molten magma
ig·nite \ig-'nīt\ *vb* **1 a** : to set afire; *also* : KINDLE **b** : to cause (a fuel mixture) to burn **2** : to catch fire — **ig·nit·er** *or* **ig·ni·tor** \-'nīt-ər\ *n*
ig·ni·tion \ig-'nish-ən\ *n* **1** : the act or action of igniting : KINDLING **2** : the process or means (as an electric spark) of igniting a fuel mixture
ig·no·ble \ig-'nō-bəl\ *adj* **1** : of low birth : PLEBEIAN **2** : characterized by baseness or meanness — **ig·no·bly** \-blē\ *adv*
ig·no·min·i·ous \,ig-nə-'min-ē-əs\ *adj* **1** : marked by disgrace or shame : DISHONORABLE **2** : DESPICABLE **3** : HUMILIATING, DEGRADING — **ig·no·min·i·ous·ly** *adv*
ig·no·mi·ny \'ig-nə-,min-ē, ig-'näm-ə-nē\ *n, pl* **-nies** **1** : deep personal humiliation and disgrace : DISHONOR **2** : disgraceful conduct, quality, or action
ig·no·ra·mus \,ig-nə-'rā-məs\ *n, pl* **-mus·es** : an utterly ignorant person : DUNCE
ig·no·rance \'ig-nə-rən(t)s\ *n* : the state of being ignorant
ig·no·rant \-rənt\ *adj* **1** : having no knowledge or very little knowledge : not educated **2** : not knowing : UNAWARE **3** : resulting from or showing lack of knowledge — **ig·no·rant·ly** *adv*
ig·nore \ig-'nō(ə)r\ *vt* : to refuse to take notice of
igua·na \i-'gwän-ə\ *n* : a large edible tropical American lizard
ilk \'ilk\ *n* : SORT, FAMILY — used chiefly in the phrase *of that ilk*
[1]**ill** \'il\ *adj* **worse** \'wərs\; **worst** \'wərst\ **1** : showing or implying evil intention **2 a** : causing suffering or distress : DISAGREEABLE **b** (1) : not normal or sound : FAILING (2) : not in good health; *also* : NAUSEATED **3** : UNFORTUNATE, UNLUCKY **4** : UNKIND, UNFRIENDLY **5** : not right or proper
[2]**ill** *adv* **worse**; **worst** **1 a** : with displeasure **b** : HARSHLY **2** : in a reprehensible manner **3** : SCARCELY **4** : BADLY, POORLY
[3]**ill** *n* **1** : EVIL **2 a** : MISFORTUNE **b** : SICKNESS **c** : TROUBLE, AFFLICTION **3** : something that reflects unfavorably
ill–ad·vised \,il-əd-'vīzd\ *adj* : showing lack of wise and sufficient counsel or deliberation : UNWISE — **ill–ad·vis·ed·ly** \-'vī-zəd-lē\ *adv*
ill–bred \'il-'bred\ *adj* : badly brought up : IMPOLITE
il·le·gal \il-'(l)ē-gəl\ *adj* : not lawful — **il·le·gal·i·ty** \,il-ē-'gal-ət-ē\ *n* — **il·le·gal·ly** \il-'(l)ē-gə-lē\ *adv*
il·leg·i·ble \il-'(l)ej-ə-bəl\ *adj* : not legible : impossible or very hard to read — **il·leg·i·bil·i·ty** \il-,ej-ə-'bil-ət-ē\ *n* — **il·leg·i·bly** \il-'(l)ej-ə-blē\ *adv*
il·le·git·i·mate \,il-i-'jit-ə-mət\ *adj* **1** : born of a father and mother who are not married **2** : not correctly deduced or reasoned **3** : not lawful or proper — **il·le·git·i·ma·cy** \-'jit-ə-mə-sē\ *n* — **il·le·git·i·mate·ly** *adv*
ill–fat·ed \'il-'fāt-əd\ *adj* : having an evil fate : UNFORTUNATE
ill–fa·vored \-'fā-vərd\ *adj* **1** : unattractive in physical appearance; *esp* : having an ugly face **2** : OFFENSIVE
ill–got·ten \-'gät-ᵊn\ *adj* : acquired by evil means
ill–hu·mored \'il-'hyü-mərd, -'yü-\ *adj* : SURLY, IRRITABLE — **ill–hu·mored·ly** *adv*
il·lib·er·al \il-'(l)ib-(ə-)rəl\ *adj* : not liberal: as **a** : not broad-minded : BIGOTED **b** : opposed to liberalism — **il·lib·er·al·i·ty** \il-,ib-ə-'ral-ət-ē\ *n*
il·lic·it \il-'(l)is-ət\ *adj* : not permitted : UNLAWFUL — **il·lic·it·ly** *adv*
il·lim·it·a·ble \il-'(l)im-ət-ə-bəl\ *adj* : incapable of being limited : BOUNDLESS — **il·lim·it·a·bly** \-blē\ *adv*
il·lit·er·a·cy \il-'(l)it-ə-rə-sē\ *n, pl* **-cies** **1** : the quality or state of being illiterate; *esp* : inability to read or write **2** : a mistake or crudity made by one who is illiterate
il·lit·er·ate \-'(l)it-ə-rət\ *adj* **1** : having little or no education; *esp* : unable to read or write **2 a** : showing or marked by a lack of familiarity with language and literature **b** : showing ignorance of the fundamentals of a particular field of knowledge — **illiterate** *n* — **il·lit·er·ate·ly** *adv* — **il·lit·er·ate·ness** *n*
ill–man·nered \'il-'man-ərd\ *adj* : marked by bad manners : RUDE
ill–na·tured \-'nā-chərd\ *adj* : having a bad disposition : CROSS, SURLY — **ill–na·tured·ly** *adv*
ill·ness \'il-nəs\ *n* : an unhealthy condition of body or mind : SICKNESS
il·log·i·cal \il-'(l)äj-i-kəl\ *adj* : not observing the principles of logic or good reasoning — **il·log·i·cal·ly** \-i-k(ə-)lē\ *adv* — **il·log·i·cal·ness** \-kəl-nəs\ *n*
ill–starred \'il-'stärd\ *adj* : ILL-FATED, UNLUCKY
ill–tem·pered \-'tem-pərd\ *adj* : ILL-NATURED, QUARRELSOME — **ill–tem·pered·ly** *adv*
ill–treat \-'trēt\ *vt* : to treat cruelly or improperly : MALTREAT — **ill–treat·ment** *n*
il·lu·mi·nate \il-'ü-mə-,nāt\ *vt* **1 a** : to supply or brighten with light : light up **b** : ENLIGHTEN **2** : to make clear : ELUCIDATE **3** : to decorate (as a manuscript) with gold or silver or brilliant colors or with elaborate designs or miniature pictures — **il·lu·mi·na·tion** \il-,ü-mə-'nā-shən\ *n* — **il·lu·mi·na·tive** \il-'ü-mə-,nāt-iv\ *adj* — **il·lu·mi·na·tor** \-,nāt-ər\ *n*
il·lu·mine \il-'ü-mən\ *vt* : ILLUMINATE
ill–us·age \'il-'yü-sij, -zij\ *n* : harsh or abusive treatment
ill–use \-'yüz\ *vt* : MALTREAT, ABUSE
il·lu·sion \il-'ü-zhən\ *n* **1** : a misleading image presented to the eye **2** : the state or fact of being led to accept as true something unreal or imagined **3** : a mistaken idea — **il·lu·sion·ary** \-zhə-,ner-ē\ *adj*

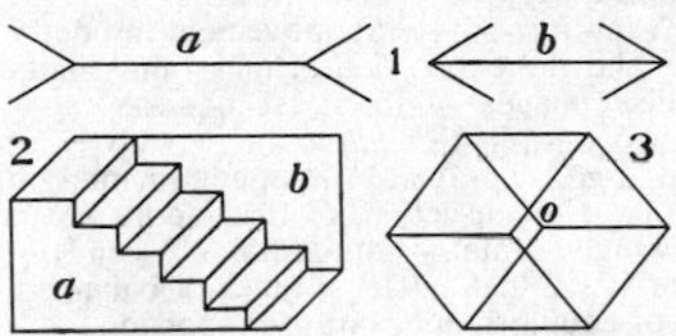

illusions 1: *1 a* equals *b* in length, *2* either side *a* or side *b* may appear nearer the observer, *3 o* may appear to be either the near or the far corner of the cube

il·lu·sive \il-'ü-siv\ *adj* : ILLUSORY
il·lu·so·ry \il-'üs(-ə)-rē, -'üz(-ə)-\ *adj* : based on or producing illusion : DECEPTIVE
il·lus·trate \'il-ə-,strāt\ *vb* **1** : to make clear esp. by giving or by serving as an example or instance **2 a** : to provide with pictures or figures intended to explain or decorate **b** : to serve to explain or decorate **3** : DEMONSTRATE — **il·lus·tra·tor** \-,strāt-ər\ *n*
il·lus·tra·tion \,il-ə-'strā-shən\ *n* **1** : the action of illustrating : the condition of being illustrated **2 a** : an example or instance intended to make something clear **b** : a picture or diagram intended to explain or decorate
il·lus·tra·tive \il-'əs-trət-iv\ *adj* : serving, tending, or designed to illustrate— **il·lus·tra·tive·ly** *adv*
il·lus·tri·ous \il-'əs-trē-əs\ *adj* : notably outstanding because of rank or achievement : EMINENT
ill will *n* : unfriendly feeling
[1]**im·age** \'im-ij\ *n* **1** : a reproduction or imitation of the form of a person or thing; *esp* : an imitation in solid form : DEVICE **2 a** : a picture of an object produced by a lens, a mirror, or an electronic system **b** : a likeness of an object produced on a photographic material **3** : exact likeness **4** : a tangible or visible representation : INCARNATION **5 a** : a mental picture of something not actually present : IMPRESSION **b** : IDEA,

CONCEPT **6 :** a vivid or graphic representation or description **7 :** something introduced to represent something else that it strikingly resembles or suggests (as the use of *sleep* for *death*) **8 :** a person strikingly like another person

²image *vt* **1 :** to describe or portray in language esp. vividly **2 :** to call up a mental picture of : IMAGINE **3 a :** REFLECT, MIRROR **b :** to make appear : PROJECT **4 a :** to create a representation of **b :** to represent symbolically

im·ag·ery \ˈim-ij-(ə-)rē\ *n, pl* **-er·ies** **1 :** the product of image makers : IMAGES; *also* : the art of making images **2 :** figurative language **3 :** mental images; *esp* : the products of imagination

imag·in·a·ble \im-ˈaj-(ə-)nə-bəl\ *adj* : capable of being imagined : CONCEIVABLE — **imag·in·a·bly** \-blē\ *adv*

imag·i·nary \im-ˈaj-ə-ˌner-ē\ *adj* : existing only in imagination : FANCIED

imag·i·na·tion \im-ˌaj-ə-ˈnā-shən\ *n* **1 :** the act or power of forming a mental image of something not present to the senses or never before wholly perceived in reality **2 a :** creative ability **b :** ability to confront and deal with a problem : RESOURCEFULNESS **3 a :** a creation of the mind; *esp* : an idealized or poetic creation **b :** fanciful or empty assumption **4 :** popular or traditional belief or conception

imag·i·na·tive \im-ˈaj-(ə-)nət-iv, -ˈaj-ə-ˌnāt-\ *adj* **1 :** of, relating to, or characterized by imagination **2 :** given to imagining : having a lively imagination **3 :** of or relating to images; *esp* : showing a command of imagery — **imag·i·na·tive·ly** *adv* — **imag·i·na·tive·ness** *n*

imag·ine \im-ˈaj-ən\ *vb* **imag·ined**; **imag·in·ing** \-ˈaj-(ə-)niŋ\ **1 :** to form a mental image of something not present : use the imagination **2 :** THINK, SUPPOSE, GUESS

im·ag·ism \ˈim-ij-ˌiz-əm\ *n* : a movement in poetry advocating free verse and the expression of ideas and emotions through clear precise images — **im·ag·ist** \-ij-əst\ *n* — **imagist** *or* **im·ag·is·tic** \ˌim-ij-ˈis-tik\ *adj*

ima·go \im-ˈā-gō, -ˈäg-ō\ *n, pl* **imagoes** *or* **ima·gi·nes** \-ˈā-gə-ˌnēz, -ˈäg-ə-\ : an insect in its final adult, sexually mature, and usu. winged state — **ima·gi·nal** \-ˈā-gən-ᵊl, -ˈäg-ən-\ *adj*

im·bal·ance \(ˈ)im-ˈbal-ən(t)s\ *n* : lack of balance : the state of being out of equilibrium or out of proportion

im·be·cile \ˈim-bə-səl, -ˌsil\ *n* **1 :** a feebleminded person; *esp* : one capable of performing routine personal care under supervision **2 :** FOOL, IDIOT — **imbecile** *or* **im·be·cil·ic** \ˌim-bə-ˈsil-ik\ *adj* — **im·be·cil·i·ty** \-ˈsil-ət-ē\ *n*

im·bibe \im-ˈbīb\ *vb* **1 :** to receive into the mind and retain **2 a :** DRINK **b :** to drink in : ABSORB — **im·bib·er** *n*

im·bri·cate \ˈim-bri-kət\ *adj* : lying lapped over each other in regular order — **im·bri·cate·ly** *adv*

im·bri·ca·tion \ˌim-brə-ˈkā-shən\ *n* **1 :** an overlapping of edges (as of tiles) **2 :** a decoration or pattern showing imbrication

im·bro·glio \im-ˈbrōl-yō\ *n, pl* **-glios** **1 :** a confused mass **2 a :** an intricate or complicated situation (as in a novel) **b :** an acutely painful or embarrassing misunderstanding : EMBROILMENT

im·brue \im-ˈbrü\ *vt* : DRENCH, STAIN

im·bue \im-ˈbyü\ *vt* **1 :** to tinge or dye deeply **2 :** to cause to become penetrated : PERMEATE

im·i·ta·ble \ˈim-ət-ə-bəl\ *adj* : capable or worthy of being imitated or copied

im·i·tate \ˈim-ə-ˌtāt\ *vt* **1 :** to follow as a pattern, model, or example **2 :** to be or appear similar to : RESEMBLE **3 :** to copy exactly : COUNTERFEIT — **im·i·ta·tor** \-ˌtāt-ər\ *n*

¹im·i·ta·tion \ˌim-ə-ˈtā-shən\ *n* **1 :** an act of imitating **2 :** something produced as a copy **3 :** a literary work designed to reproduce the style of another author

²imitation *adj* : not real

im·i·ta·tive \ˈim-ə-ˌtāt-iv\ *adj* **1 a :** marked by imitation **b :** exhibiting mimicry **2 :** inclined to imitate **3 :** imitating something superior — **im·i·ta·tive·ly** *adv* — **im·i·ta·tive·ness** *n*

im·mac·u·late \im-ˈak-yə-lət\ *adj* **1 :** having no stain or blemish : PURE **2 :** spotlessly clean — **im·mac·u·late·ly** *adv* — **im·mac·u·late·ness** *n*

im·ma·nent \ˈim-ə-nənt\ *adj* **1 :** INDWELLING; *esp* : having existence only in the mind **2 :** dwelling in nature and the souls of men — **im·ma·nence** \-nən(t)s\ *or* **im·ma·nen·cy** \-nən-sē\ *n* — **im·ma·nent·ly** *adv*

im·ma·te·ri·al \ˌim-ə-ˈtir-ē-əl\ *adj* **1 :** not consisting of matter : INCORPOREAL **2 :** of no consequence : UNIMPORTANT — **im·ma·te·ri·al·i·ty** \-ˌtir-ē-ˈal-ət-ē\ *n*

im·ma·ture \ˌim-ə-ˈt(y)u̇(ə)r\ *adj* **1 :** lacking complete development : not yet mature : YOUNG, UNRIPE **2 :** CRUDE, UNFINISHED — **immature** *n* — **im·ma·ture·ly** *adv* — **im·ma·ture·ness** *n* — **im·ma·tu·ri·ty** \-ˈt(y)u̇r-ət-ē\ *n*

im·mea·sur·a·ble \(ˈ)im-ˈezh-(ə-)rə-bəl\ *adj* : incapable of being measured : indefinitely extensive — **im·mea·sur·a·bly** \-blē\ *adv*

im·me·di·a·cy \im-ˈēd-ē-ə-sē\ *n, pl* **-cies** **1 a :** the quality or state of being immediate; *esp* : lack of an intervening object, place, time, or agent **b :** URGENCY **2 :** something that is of immediate importance

im·me·di·ate \im-ˈēd-ē-ət\ *adj* **1 :** next in line or relationship **2 :** closest in importance **3 :** acting directly and alone without anything intervening **4 :** not distant or separated : NEXT **5 :** close in time **6 :** made or done at once

im·me·di·ate·ly *adv* **1 :** with nothing between : DIRECTLY, CLOSELY **2 :** without delay : STRAIGHTWAY

im·me·mo·ri·al \ˌim-ə-ˈmōr-ē-əl\ *adj* : extending beyond the reach of memory, record, or tradition — **im·me·mo·ri·al·ly** \-ē-ə-lē\ *adv*

im·mense \im-ˈen(t)s\ *adj* **1 :** very great in size or degree : HUGE **2 :** supremely good : EXCELLENT — **im·mense·ly** *adv* — **im·mense·ness** *n*

im·men·si·ty \im-ˈen(t)-sət-ē\ *n, pl* **-ties** **1 :** the quality or state of being immense **2 :** something immense

im·merge \im-ˈərj\ *vi* : to plunge into or immerse oneself in something

im·merse \im-ˈərs\ *vt* **1 :** to plunge into something that surrounds or covers; *esp* : to plunge or dip into a fluid **2 :** to baptize by submerging in water **3 :** ENGROSS, ABSORB

im·mersed \im-ˈərst\ *adj* : growing wholly under water

im·mer·sion \im-ˈər-zhən, -shən\ *n* : an act of immersing : a state of being immersed

im·mi·grant \ˈim-i-grənt\ *n* **1 :** a person who comes to a country to become a permanent resident **2 :** a plant or animal that becomes established in an area where it was previously unknown — **immigrant** *adj*

im·mi·grate \ˈim-ə-ˌgrāt\ *vi* : to enter and usu. become established; *esp* : to come into a country of which one is not a native to take up permanent residence — **im·mi·gra·tion** \ˌim-ə-ˈgrā-shən\ *n*

im·mi·nence \ˈim-ə-nən(t)s\ *n* **1** \-nən-sē\ : the quality or state of being imminent **2 :** something imminent; *esp* : impending evil or danger

im·mi·nent \-nənt\ *adj* : ready to take place; *esp* : hanging threateningly over one's head — **im·mi·nent·ly** *adv* — **im·mi·nent·ness** *n*

im·mis·ci·ble \(ˈ)im-ˈis-ə-bəl\ *adj* : incapable of mixing — **im·mis·ci·bil·i·ty** \(ˌ)im-ˌis-ə-ˈbil-ət-ē\ *n*

im·mo·bile \(ˈ)im-ˈō-bəl\ *adj* : incapable of being moved : FIXED — **im·mo·bil·i·ty** \ˌim-(ˌ)ō-ˈbil-ət-ē\ *n*

im·mo·bi·lize \im-ˈō-bə-ˌlīz\ *vt* : to make immobile; *esp* : to prevent freedom of movement or effective use of — **im·mo·bi·li·za·tion** \im-ˌō-bə-lə-ˈzā-shən\ *n* — **im·mo·bi·liz·er** \im-ˈō-bə-ˌlī-zər\ *n*

im·mod·er·ate \(ˈ)im-ˈäd-(ə-)rət\ *adj* : lacking in moderation

: EXCESSIVE — **im·mod·er·a·cy** \-(ə-)rə-sē\ *n* — **im·mod·er·ate·ly** *adv*
im·mod·est \(ˈ)im-ˈäd-əst\ *adj* : not modest; *esp* : INDECENT — **im·mod·est·ly** *adv* — **im·mod·es·ty** \-ə-stē\ *n*
im·mo·late \ˈim-ə-ˌlāt\ *vt* **1** : to offer in sacrifice; *esp* : to kill as a sacrificial victim **2** : KILL, DESTROY — **im·mo·la·tion** \ˌim-ə-ˈlā-shən\ *n* — **im·mo·la·tor** \ˈim-ə-ˌlāt-ər\ *n*
im·mor·al \(ˈ)im-ˈȯr-əl\ *adj* : not moral : WICKED, LEWD, LICENTIOUS — **im·mor·al·ly** \-ə-lē\ *adv*
im·mor·al·ist \-ə-ləst\ *n* : an advocate of immorality
im·mo·ral·i·ty \ˌim-ˌȯ-ˈral-ət-ē, ˌim-ə-ˈral-\ *n, pl* **-ties** **1** : the quality or state of being immoral; *esp* : UNCHASTITY **2** : an immoral act or practice
[1]**im·mor·tal** \(ˈ)im-ˈȯrt-ᵊl\ *adj* **1** : exempt from death **2** : connected with or relating to immortality **3** : living or lasting forever : IMPERISHABLE — **im·mor·tal·ly** \-ᵊl-ē\ *adv*
[2]**immortal** *n* **1 a** : one exempt from death **b** *pl, often cap* : the gods of the Greek and Roman pantheon **2** : a person whose fame is lasting
im·mor·tal·i·ty \ˌim-ˌȯr-ˈtal-ət-ē\ *n* : the quality or state of being immortal: **a** : unending existence **b** : lasting fame
im·mor·tal·ize \im-ˈȯrt-ᵊl-ˌīz\ *vt* : to make immortal
im·mov·a·ble \(ˈ)im-ˈü-və-bəl\ *adj* **1 a** : incapable of being moved **b** : STATIONARY **2 a** : STEADFAST, UNYIELDING **b** : not capable of being moved in feeling : IMPASSIVE — **im·mov·a·bil·i·ty** \(ˌ)im-ˌü-və-ˈbil-ət-ē\ *n* — **im·mov·a·bly** \(ˈ)im-ˈü-və-blē\ *adv*
im·mune \im-ˈyün\ *adj* **1** : FREE, EXEMPT **2** : having a special capacity for resistance — **im·mune** *n*
im·mu·ni·ty \im-ˈyü-nət-ē\ *n, pl* **-ties** : the quality or state of being immune
im·mu·nize \ˈim-yə-ˌnīz\ *vt* : to make immune — **im·mu·ni·za·tion** \ˌim-yə-nə-ˈzā-shən\ *n*
im·mu·nol·o·gy \ˌim-yə-ˈnäl-ə-jē\ *n* : a science that deals with the phenomena and causes of immunity — **im·mu·no·log·ic** \ˌim-yə-nə-ˈläj-ik\ *or* **im·mu·no·log·i·cal** \-ˈläj-i-kəl\ *adj* — **im·mu·no·log·i·cal·ly** \-i-k(ə-)lē\ *adv* — **im·mu·nol·o·gist** \ˌim-yə-ˈnäl-ə-jəst\ *n*
im·mure \im-ˈyu̇(ə)r\ *vt* **1 a** : to enclose within or as if within walls **b** : to shut up : IMPRISON **2** : to build into a wall; *esp* : to entomb in a wall
im·mu·ta·ble \(ˈ)im-ˈyüt-ə-bəl\ *adj* : not capable or susceptible of change — **im·mu·ta·bil·i·ty** \(ˌ)im-ˌyüt-ə-ˈbil-ət-ē\ *n* — **im·mu·ta·bly** \(ˈ)im-ˈyüt-ə-blē\ *adv*
imp \ˈimp\ *n* **1** : a small demon : FIEND **2** : a mischievous child
[1]**im·pact** \im-ˈpakt\ *vt* **1 a** : to fix firmly by or as if by packing or wedging **b** : to press together **2** : to impinge upon
[2]**im·pact** \ˈim-ˌpakt\ *n* **1** : a forceful contact, collision, or onset; *also* : the impetus communicated in or as if in a collision **2** : EFFECT
im·pact·ed \im-ˈpak-təd\ *adj* : wedged between the jawbone and another tooth
im·pair \im-ˈpa(ə)r\ *vt* : to diminish in quantity, value, excellence, or strength : DAMAGE — **im·pair·ment** *n*
im·pale \im-ˈpāl\ *vt* : to pierce with or as if with something pointed; *esp* : to torture or kill by fixing on a sharp stake — **im·pale·ment** *n*
im·pal·pa·ble \(ˈ)im-ˈpal-pə-bəl\ *adj* **1** : incapable of being felt by the touch : INTANGIBLE **2** : not readily discerned or apprehended — **im·pal·pa·bil·i·ty** \(ˌ)im-ˌpal-pə-ˈbil-ət-ē\ *n* — **im·pal·pa·bly** \(ˈ)im-ˈpal-pə-blē\ *adv*
im·pan·el \im-ˈpan-ᵊl\ *vt* **-eled** *or* **-elled**; **-el·ing** *or* **-el·ling** : to enter in or on a panel or list : ENROLL
im·part \im-ˈpärt\ *vt* **1** : to give or grant from one's store or abundance : TRANSMIT **2** : to communicate the knowledge of : DISCLOSE
im·par·tial \(ˈ)im-ˈpär-shəl\ *adj* : not partial : UNBIASED — **im·par·ti·al·i·ty** \(ˌ)im-ˌpär-shē-ˈal-ət-ē, -ˌpär-ˈshal-\ *n* — **im·par·tial·ly** \(ˈ)im-ˈpärsh-(ə-)lē\ *adv*
im·pass·a·ble \(ˈ)im-ˈpas-ə-bəl\ *adj* : incapable of being passed, traversed, or circulated — **im·pass·a·bil·i·ty** \(ˌ)im-ˌpas-ə-ˈbil-ət-ē\ *n* — **im·pass·a·bly** \(ˈ)im-ˈpas-ə-blē\ *adv*
im·passe \ˈim-ˌpas\ *n* **1** : an impassable road or way **2 a** : a predicament from which there is no obvious escape **b** : DEADLOCK
im·pas·si·ble \(ˈ)im-ˈpas-ə-bəl\ *adj* **1 a** : incapable of suffering or of experiencing pain **b** : inaccessible to injury **2** : incapable of feeling : IMPASSIVE — **im·pas·si·bil·i·ty** \(ˌ)im-ˌpas-ə-ˈbil-ət-ē\ *n*
im·pas·sioned \im-ˈpash-ənd\ *adj* : filled with passion or zeal : showing great warmth or intensity of feeling
im·pas·sive \(ˈ)im-ˈpas-iv\ *adj* **1** : not feeling or not showing any emotion : CALM, UNMOVED **2** : MOTIONLESS — **im·pas·sive·ly** *adv* — **im·pas·sive·ness** *n* — **im·pas·siv·i·ty** \ˌim-ˌpas-ˈiv-ət-ē\ *n*
im·pas·to \im-ˈpas-tō, -ˈpäs-\ *n* : the thick application of a pigment to a canvas or panel in painting; *also* : the body of pigment so applied
im·pa·tience \(ˈ)im-ˈpā-shən(t)s\ *n* **1** : restlessness of spirit (as under irritation, delay, or opposition) **2** : restless or eager desire or longing
im·pa·tient \(ˈ)im-ˈpā-shənt\ *adj* **1 a** : not patient : restless or short of temper esp. under irritation, delay, or opposition **b** : INTOLERANT **2** : prompted or marked by impatience **3** : eagerly desirous : ANXIOUS — **im·pa·tient·ly** *adv*
im·peach \im-ˈpēch\ *vt* **1** : to charge (a public official) before a competent tribunal with misconduct in office **2** : to challenge the credibility or validity of — **im·peach·a·ble** *adj* — **im·peach·ment** *n*
im·pearl \im-ˈpərl\ *vt* : to form into pearls; *also* : to form of or adorn with pearls
im·pec·ca·ble \(ˈ)im-ˈpek-ə-bəl\ *adj* **1** : not capable of sinning or liable to sin **2** : free from fault or blame : FLAWLESS — **im·pec·ca·bil·i·ty** \(ˌ)im-ˌpek-ə-ˈbil-ət-ē\ *n* — **im·pec·ca·bly** \(ˈ)im-ˈpek-ə-blē\ *adv*
im·pe·cu·ni·ous \ˌim-pi-ˈkyü-nē-əs, -nyəs\ *adj* : having very little or no money usu. habitually : PENNILESS — **im·pe·cu·ni·os·i·ty** \-ˌkyü-nē-ˈäs-ət-ē\ *n* — **im·pe·cu·ni·ous·ly** \-ˈkyü-nē-əs-lē, -nyəs-\ *adv* — **im·pe·cu·ni·ous·ness** *n*
im·pede \im-ˈpēd\ *vt* : to interfere with the progress of : BLOCK, HINDER — **im·ped·er** *n*
im·ped·i·ment \im-ˈped-ə-mənt\ *n* **1** : something that impedes, hinders, or obstructs **2** : a defect in speech
im·ped·i·men·ta \im-ˌped-ə-ˈment-ə\ *n pl* : things (as baggage or supplies) that impede
im·pel \im-ˈpel\ *vt* **im·pelled**; **im·pel·ling** **1** : to urge or drive forward or into action **2** : PROPEL — **im·pel·ler** *n*
im·pend \im-ˈpend\ *vi* **1** : to hover threateningly : MENACE **2** : to be about to occur
im·pend·ing \-ˈpen-diŋ\ *adj* : threatening to occur soon : APPROACHING
im·pen·e·tra·ble \(ˈ)im-ˈpen-ə-trə-bəl\ *adj* **1 a** : incapable of being penetrated or pierced **b** : inaccessible to knowledge, reason, or sympathy **2** : incapable of being comprehended — **im·pen·e·tra·bil·i·ty** \(ˌ)im-ˌpen-ə-trə-ˈbil-ət-ē\ *n* — **im·pen·e·tra·bly** \(ˈ)im-ˈpen-ə-trə-blē\ *adv*
im·pen·i·tent \(ˈ)im-ˈpen-ə-tənt\ *adj* : not penitent : not sorry for having done wrong — **im·pen·i·tence** \-tən(t)s\ *n* — **im·pen·i·tent·ly** *adv*
[1]**im·per·a·tive** \im-ˈper-ət-iv\ *adj* **1** : expressing a command, entreaty, or exhortation **2** : having power to restrain, control, and direct : AUTHORITATIVE **3** : not to be avoided or evaded : URGENT — **im·per·a·tive·ly** *adv* — **im·per·a·tive·ness** *n*
[2]**imperative** *n* **1** : the imperative mood of a verb : a verb in this mood **2** : something that is imperative

im·per·cep·ti·ble \ˌim-pər-ˈsep-tə-bəl\ *adj* **1 :** not perceptible by a sense or by the mind **2 :** extremely slight, gradual, or subtle — **im·per·cep·ti·bly** \-blē\ *adv*

im·per·cep·tive \ˌim-pər-ˈsep-tiv\ *adj* **:** not perceptive — **im·per·cep·tive·ness** *n*

¹**im·per·fect** \(ˈ)im-ˈpər-fikt\ *adj* **1 :** not perfect **:** DEFECTIVE **2 :** of, relating to, or constituting a verb tense used to designate a continuing state or an incomplete action esp. in the past — **im·per·fect·ly** *adv* — **im·per·fect·ness** *n*

²**imperfect** *n* **:** the imperfect tense of a verb **:** a verb in this tense

im·per·fec·tion \ˌim-pər-ˈfek-shən\ *n* **:** the quality or state of being imperfect; *also* **:** FAULT, BLEMISH

im·per·fo·rate \(ˈ)im-ˈpər-f(ə-)rət\ *adj* **1 :** having no opening or aperture **2 :** lacking perforations or rouletting — **imperforate** *n*

¹**im·pe·ri·al** \im-ˈpir-ē-əl\ *adj* **1 :** of, relating to, or befitting an empire or an emperor **2 a :** SOVEREIGN **b :** REGAL, IMPERIOUS **3 :** of superior or unusual size or excellence — **im·pe·ri·al·ly** \-ē-ə-lē\ *adv*

²**imperial** *n* **:** a pointed beard growing below the lower lip

im·pe·ri·al·ism \im-ˈpir-ē-ə-ˌliz-əm\ *n* **1 :** imperial government or authority **2 :** the policy or practice of extending the power and dominion of one nation by direct territorial acquisitions or by indirect control over the political or economic life of other areas; *also* **:** advocacy of such policies or practice — **im·pe·ri·al·ist** \-ləst\ *n* — **imperialist** *or* **im·pe·ri·al·is·tic** \im-ˌpir-ē-ə-ˈlis-tik\ *adj* — **im·pe·ri·al·is·ti·cal·ly** \-ti-k(ə-)lē\ *adv*

im·per·il \im-ˈper-əl\ *vt* **-iled** *or* **-illed**; **-il·ing** *or* **-il·ling :** to bring into peril **:** ENDANGER — **im·per·il·ment** *n*

im·pe·ri·ous \im-ˈpir-ē-əs\ *adj* **1 :** COMMANDING, LORDLY **2 :** ARROGANT, DOMINEERING **3 :** IMPERATIVE, URGENT — **im·pe·ri·ous·ly** *adv*

im·per·ish·a·ble \(ˈ)im-ˈper-ish-ə-bəl\ *adj* **:** not perishable or subject to decay **:** INDESTRUCTIBLE — **im·per·ish·a·bil·i·ty** \(ˌ)im-ˌper-ish-ə-ˈbil-ət-ē\ *n* — **im·per·ish·a·ble·ness** *n* — **im·per·ish·a·bly** \(ˈ)im-ˈper-ish-ə-blē\ *adv*

im·per·ma·nent \(ˈ)im-ˈpər-mə-nənt\ *adj* **:** not permanent **:** TRANSIENT — **im·per·ma·nent·ly** *adv*

im·per·me·a·ble \(ˈ)im-ˈpər-mē-ə-bəl\ *adj* **:** not permitting passage (as of a fluid) through its substance **:** IMPERVIOUS — **im·per·me·a·bil·i·ty** \(ˌ)im-ˌpər-mē-ə-ˈbil-ət-ē\ *n* — **im·per·me·a·bly** \(ˈ)im-ˈpər-mē-ə-blē\ *adv*

im·per·son·al \(ˈ)im-ˈpərs-nəl, -ᵊn-əl\ *adj* **1 :** having no personal reference or connection **2 :** not engaging the human personality or emotions — **im·per·son·al·i·ty** \(ˌ)im-ˌpərs-ᵊn-ˈal-ət-ē\ *n* — **im·per·son·al·ize** \(ˈ)im-ˈpərs-nə-ˌlīz, -ᵊn-ə-ˌlīz\ *vt* — **im·per·son·al·ly** \-nə-lē, -ᵊn-ə-lē\ *adv*

im·per·son·ate \im-ˈpərs-ᵊn-ˌāt\ *vt* **1 :** to act the part of or pretend to be some other person **2 :** TYPIFY, EXEMPLIFY — **im·per·son·a·tion** \-ˌpərs-ᵊn-ˈā-shən\ *n* — **im·per·son·a·tor** \-ˈpərs-ᵊn-ˌāt-ər\ *n*

im·per·ti·nence \(ˈ)im-ˈpərt-ᵊn-ən(t)s\ *n* **1 :** the quality or state of being impertinent: as **a :** IRRELEVANCE, UNFITNESS **b :** INCIVILITY, INSOLENCE **2 :** something impertinent

im·per·ti·nent \-ənt\ *adj* **1 :** not pertinent **:** IRRELEVANT **2 :** not restrained within due or proper bounds **:** RUDE, INSOLENT — **im·per·ti·nent·ly** *adv*

im·per·turb·a·ble \ˌim-pər-ˈtər-bə-bəl\ *adj* **:** marked by extreme calm, impassivity, and steadiness **:** SERENE — **im·per·turb·a·bil·i·ty** \-ˌtər-bə-ˈbil-ət-ē\ *n* — **im·per·turb·a·bly** \-ˈtər-bə-blē\ *adv*

im·per·vi·ous \(ˈ)im-ˈpər-vē-əs\ *adj* **1 :** not allowing entrance or passage **:** IMPENETRABLE **2 :** not capable of being affected or disturbed — **im·per·vi·ous·ly** *adv* — **im·per·vi·ous·ness** *n*

im·pe·ti·go \ˌim-pə-ˈtē-gō, -ˈtī-\ *n* **:** an acute contagious skin disease characterized by vesicles, pustules, and yellowish crusts — **im·pe·tig·i·nous** \-ˈtij-ə-nəs\ *adj*

im·pet·u·ous \im-ˈpech-(ə-)wəs\ *adj* **1 :** marked by force and violence **2 :** marked by impulsive vehemence — **im·pet·u·os·i·ty** \im-ˌpech-ə-ˈwäs-ət-ē\ *n* — **im·pet·u·ous·ly** *adv* — **im·pet·u·ous·ness** *n*

im·pe·tus \ˈim-pət-əs\ *n* **1 a :** a driving force **:** IMPULSE **b :** INCENTIVE, STIMULUS **2 :** the property possessed by a moving body in virtue of its mass and its motion **:** MOMENTUM

im·pi·e·ty \(ˈ)im-ˈpī-ət-ē\ *n, pl* **-ties 1 a :** the quality or state of being impious **:** UNGODLINESS **b :** UNDUTIFULNESS **2 :** an impious act

im·pinge \im-ˈpinj\ *vi* **1 :** to strike or dash esp. with a sharp collision **2 :** to come into close contact **3 :** ENCROACH, INFRINGE — **im·pinge·ment** *n*

im·pi·ous \ˈim-pē-əs, (ˈ)im-ˈpī-\ *adj* **:** not pious: **a :** IRREVERENT, PROFANE **b :** UNDUTIFUL, UNFILIAL — **im·pi·ous·ly** *adv*

imp·ish \ˈim-pish\ *adj* **:** of, relating to, or befitting an imp; *esp* **:** MISCHIEVOUS — **imp·ish·ly** *adv* — **imp·ish·ness** *n*

im·plac·a·ble \(ˈ)im-ˈplak-ə-bəl, -ˈplā-kə-\ *adj* **1 :** not placable **:** not capable of being appeased, pacified, or mitigated **2 :** UNALTERABLE — **im·plac·a·bil·i·ty** \(ˌ)im-ˌplak-ə-ˈbil-ət-ē, -ˌplā-kə-\ *n* — **im·plac·a·ble·ness** \(ˈ)im-ˈplak-ə-bəl-nəs, -ˈplā-kə-\ *n* — **im·plac·a·bly** \-blē\ *adv*

im·plant \im-ˈplant\ *vt* **1 a :** to fix or set securely or deeply **b :** to set as permanent in the consciousness or habit patterns **:** INCULCATE **2 :** to insert in a living site — **im·plan·ta·tion** \ˌim-ˌplan-ˈtā-shən\ *n*

im·plau·si·ble \(ˈ)im-ˈplȯ-zə-bəl\ *adj* **:** not plausible — **im·plau·si·bil·i·ty** \(ˌ)im-ˌplȯ-zə-ˈbil-ət-ē\ *n* — **im·plau·si·bly** \(ˈ)im-ˈplȯ-zə-blē\ *adv*

¹**im·ple·ment** \ˈim-plə-mənt\ *n* **1 :** an article serving to equip **2 :** one that serves as an instrument or tool

²**im·ple·ment** \-ˌment\ *vt* **1 :** to carry out **:** FULFILL; *esp* **:** to give practical effect to by concrete measures **2 :** to provide implements for — **im·ple·men·ta·tion** \ˌim-plə-mən-ˈtā-shən, -ˌmen-\ *n*

im·pli·cate \ˈim-plə-ˌkāt\ *vt* **:** to bring into connection **:** INVOLVE

im·pli·ca·tion \ˌim-plə-ˈkā-shən\ *n* **1 a :** the act of implicating **:** the state of being implicated **b :** an incriminating involvement **2 a :** the act of implying **:** the state of being implied **b :** something implied

im·plic·it \im-ˈplis-ət\ *adj* **1 :** understood though not directly stated **2 :** COMPLETE, UNQUESTIONING — **im·plic·it·ly** *adv* — **im·plic·it·ness** *n*

im·plode \im-ˈplōd\ *vi* **:** to burst inward — **im·plo·sion** \-ˈplō-zhən\ *n* — **im·plo·sive** \-ˈplō-siv\ *adj*

im·plore \im-ˈplō(ə)r\ *vt* **1 :** to call upon in supplication **:** BESEECH **2 :** to call or pray for earnestly **:** ENTREAT

im·ply \im-ˈplī\ *vt* **im·plied**; **im·ply·ing 1 :** to include or involve as a natural or necessary though not expressly stated part or effect **2 :** to express indirectly **:** suggest rather than say plainly — **im·plied·ly** \-ˈplī(-ə)d-lē\ *adv*

im·po·lite \ˌim-pə-ˈlīt\ *adj* **:** not polite **:** RUDE — **im·po·lite·ly** *adv* — **im·po·lite·ness** *n*

im·pol·i·tic \(ˈ)im-ˈpäl-ə-ˌtik\ *adj* **:** not politic **:** UNWISE — **im·pol·i·tic·ly** *adv*

im·pon·der·a·ble \(ˈ)im-ˈpän-d(ə-)rə-bəl\ *adj* **:** incapable of being weighed or evaluated with exactness — **imponderable** *n*

¹**im·port** \im-ˈpōrt\ *vb* **1 a :** MEAN, SIGNIFY **b :** to be of importance or consequence **:** MATTER **2 :** to bring in or introduce from a foreign country; *esp* **:** to bring in goods to be resold — **im·port·a·ble** *adj* — **im·port·er** *n*

²**im·port** \ˈim-ˌpōrt\ *n* **1 :** MEANING, SIGNIFICATION **2 :** IMPORTANCE, SIGNIFICANCE **3 a :** something imported **b :** IMPORTATION

im·por·tance \im-ˈpȯrt-ᵊn(t)s, -ən(t)s\ *n* **1 :** the quality or state of being important **:** CONSEQUENCE **2 :** an important aspect or bearing **:** SIGNIFICANCE

im·por·tant \im-'pȯrt-ᵊnt, -ənt\ *adj* **1** : marked by or possessing weight or consequence : SIGNIFICANT **2** : marked by self-complacency, ostentation, or pompousness — **im·por·tant·ly** *adv*

im·por·ta·tion \,im-,pōr-'tā-shən, -pər-\ *n* **1** : the act or practice of importing **2** : something imported : IMPORT

im·por·tu·nate \im-'pȯrch-(ə-)nət\ *adj* **1** : TROUBLESOME **2** : troublesomely urgent : overly persistent in request or demand — **im·por·tu·nate·ly** *adv*

im·por·tune \,im-pər-'t(y)ün, im-'pȯr-chən\ *vb* **1** : to press, beg, or urge with troublesome persistence **2** : ANNOY, TROUBLE

im·por·tu·ni·ty \,im-pər-'t(y)ü-nət-ē\ *n, pl* **-ties** : the quality or state of being importunate : persistence in requests or demands

im·pose \im-'pōz\ *vb* **1 a** : to establish or apply as a charge or penalty : LEVY **b** : to make prevail by force **2** : to use trickery or deception to get what one wants **3** : to take unwarranted advantage of something : exploit a personal relationship

im·pos·ing \im-'pō-ziŋ\ *adj* : impressive because of size, bearing, dignity, or grandeur : COMMANDING — **im·pos·ing·ly** *adv*

im·po·si·tion \,im-pə-'zish-ən\ *n* **1** : the act of imposing **2** : something imposed: as **a** : LEVY, TAX **b** : an excessive or unduly burdensome requirement or demand **3** : DECEPTION, TRICK

im·pos·si·bil·i·ty \(,)im-,päs-ə-'bil-ət-ē\ *n, pl* **-ties** **1** : the quality or state of being impossible **2** : something impossible

im·pos·si·ble \(')im-'päs-ə-bəl\ *adj* **1 a** : incapable of being or of occurring **b** : felt to be incapable of being done, attained, or fulfilled : insuperably difficult : HOPELESS **2 a** : extremely undesirable : UNACCEPTABLE **b** : markedly difficult to deal with : OBJECTIONABLE — **im·pos·si·bly** \-blē\ *adv*

im·post \'im-,pōst\ *n* : TAX; *esp* : a customs duty

im·pos·tor \im-'päs-tər\ *n* : a person who practices deceit; *esp* : one who represents himself as being someone else

im·pos·ture \im-'päs-chər\ *n* : the act or conduct of an impostor; *esp* : fraudulent impersonation

im·po·tent \'im-pət-ənt\ *adj* **1** : not potent : lacking in power, strength, or vigor : HELPLESS **2** : unable to copulate; *also* : STERILE — usu. used of males — **im·po·tence** \-ən(t)s\ *n* — **impotent** *n* — **im·po·tent·ly** *adv*

im·pound \im-'pau̇nd\ *vt* **1** : to shut up in or as if in a pound : CONFINE **2** : to seize and hold in legal custody **3** : to collect (water) in a reservoir

im·pound·ment \-mənt\ *n* : the act of impounding : the state of being impounded

im·pov·er·ish \im-'päv-(ə-)rish\ *vt* **1** : to make poor **2** : to deprive of strength, richness, or fertility — **im·pov·er·ish·ment** *n*

im·prac·ti·ca·ble \(')im-'prak-ti-kə-bəl\ *adj* **1** : not practicable : incapable of being put into practice or use **2** : IMPASSABLE — **im·prac·ti·ca·bil·i·ty** \(,)im-,prak-ti-kə-'bil-ət-ē\ *n* — **im·prac·ti·ca·ble·ness** *n* — **im·prac·ti·ca·bly** \(')im-'prak-ti-kə-blē\ *adv*

im·prac·ti·cal \(')im-'prak-ti-kəl\ *adj* : not practical: as **a** : not wise to put into or keep in practice or effect **b** : IDEALISTIC, THEORETICAL **c** : incapable of dealing sensibly or prudently with practical matters **d** : IMPRACTICABLE — **im·prac·ti·cal·i·ty** \(,)im-,prak-ti-'kal-ət-ē\ *n* — **im·prac·ti·cal·ness** \(')im-'prak-ti-kəl-nəs\ *n*

im·pre·cate \'im-pri-,kāt\ *vb* : to invoke evil upon : CURSE — **im·pre·ca·tion** \,im-pri-'kā-shən\ *n*

im·preg·na·ble \im-'preg-nə-bəl\ *adj* : incapable of being taken by assault : UNCONQUERABLE; *also* : UNASSAILABLE — **im·preg·na·bil·i·ty** \-,preg-nə-'bil-ət-ē\ *n* — **im·preg·na·ble·ness** *n* — **im·preg·na·bly** \-'preg-nə-blē\ *adv*

im·preg·nate \im-'preg-,nāt\ *vt* **1 a** : to make pregnant **b** : to make fertile or fruitful **2** : to cause (a material or substance) to be filled, permeated, or saturated — **im·preg·na·tion** \,im-,preg-'nā-shən\ *n* — **im·preg·na·tor** \im-'preg-,nāt-ər\ *n*

im·pre·sa·rio \,im-prə-'sär-ē-,ō\ *n, pl* **-rios** **1** : the projector, manager, or conductor of an opera or concert company **2** : one who puts on or sponsors an entertainment **3** : MANAGER, PRODUCER

¹im·press \im-'pres\ *vb* **1 a** : to apply with pressure so as to imprint **b** : to produce (as a mark) by pressure **c** : to mark by or as if by pressure or stamping **2 a** : to produce a vivid impression of **b** : to affect esp. forcibly or deeply : INFLUENCE

²im·press \'im-,pres\ *n* **1 a** : a mark made by pressure : IMPRINT **b** : an image of something formed by or as if by pressure; *esp* : SEAL **c** : a product of pressure or influence **2** : a characteristic or distinctive mark : STAMP **3** : IMPRESSION, EFFECT

³im·press \im-'pres\ *vt* **1** : to seize for public service; *esp* : to force into naval service **2** : to enlist the aid or services of by strong argument or appeal

im·press·i·ble \im-'pres-ə-bəl\ *adj* : capable of being impressed : SENSITIVE

im·pres·sion \im-'presh-ən\ *n* **1 a** : a stamp, form, or figure resulting from physical contact **b** : an esp. marked influence or effect on feeling, sense, or mind **2** : a characteristic trait or feature resulting from influence **3 a** : one instance of the meeting of a printing surface and the material being printed; *also* : a single print or copy so made **b** : all the copies of a publication (as a book) printed in one continuous operation **4** : a usu. indistinct or imprecise notion or remembrance **5** : an imitation in caricature of a noted personality as a form of theatrical entertainment

im·pres·sion·a·ble \im-'presh-(ə-)nə-bəl\ *adj* : capable of being easily impressed : easily molded or influenced : PLASTIC — **im·pres·sion·a·bil·i·ty** \-,presh-(ə-)nə-'bil-ət-ē\ *n* — **im·pres·sion·a·ble·ness** *n* — **im·pres·sion·a·bly** \-'presh-(ə-)nə-blē\ *adv*

im·pres·sion·ism \im-'presh-ə-,niz-əm\ *n* **1** *often cap* : a theory or practice in modern art of depicting the natural appearances of objects by dabs or strokes of primary unmixed colors in order to simulate actual reflected light **2** : the depiction of scene, emotion, or character by details evoking impressions rather than by recreating reality — **im·pres·sion·ist** \-'presh-(ə-)nəst\ *n or adj* — **im·pres·sion·is·tic** \-,presh-ə-'nis-tik\ *adj* — **im·pres·sion·is·ti·cal·ly** \-ti-k(ə-)lē\ *adv*

im·pres·sive \im-'pres-iv\ *adj* : making or tending to make a marked impression : stirring deep feeling esp. of awe or admiration — **im·pres·sive·ly** *adv* — **im·pres·sive·ness** *n*

im·press·ment \im-'pres-mənt\ *n* : the act of seizing for public use or of impressing into public service

im·pri·ma·tur \,im-prə-'mät-ər\ *n* **1 a** : a license to print or publish **b** : official approval of a publication by a censor **2** : SANCTION, APPROVAL

¹im·print \im-'print, 'im-,\ *vt* **1 a** : to mark by or as if by pressure : STAMP, IMPRESS **b** : to add an imprint to **2** : to fix indelibly or firmly (as in the memory)

²im·print \'im-,print\ *n* : something imprinted or printed: as **a** : IMPRESS **b** : a publisher's name often with address and date of publication printed at the foot of a title page **c** : an indelible distinguishing effect or influence

im·pris·on \im-'priz-ᵊn\ *vt* **-pris·oned**; **-pris·on·ing** \-'priz-niŋ, -ᵊn-iŋ\ : to put in or as if in prison : CONFINE — **im·pris·on·ment** *n*

im·prob·a·ble \(')im-'präb-ə-bəl\ *adj* : unlikely to be true or to occur — **im·prob·a·bil·i·ty** \(,)im-,präb-ə-'bil-ət-ē\ *n* — **im·prob·a·ble·ness** *n* — **im·prob·a·bly** \(')im-'präb-ə-blē\ *adv*

im·pro·bi·ty \(')im-'prō-bət-ē, -'präb-ət-\ *n* : lack of probity or integrity : DISHONESTY

im·promp·tu \im-'präm(p)-t(y)ü\ *adj* **1** : made or done on or as if on the spur of the moment : IMPROVISED **2** : composed or uttered without previous study or preparation : EXTEMPORANEOUS — **impromptu** *adv or n*

im·prop·er \(ˈ)im-ˈpräp-ər\ *adj* **1** : not proper, fit, or suitable **2** : INCORRECT, INACCURATE **3** : not in accordance with good taste or good manners — **im·prop·er·ly** *adv* — **im·prop·er·ness** *n*

improper fraction *n* : a fraction whose numerator is equal to or larger than the denominator

im·pro·pri·e·ty \ˌim-prə-ˈprī-ət-ē\ *n, pl* **-ties** **1** : the quality or state of being improper **2** : an improper or indecorous act or remark; *esp* : an unacceptable use of a word or of language

im·prove \im-ˈprüv\ *vb* **1** : to make greater in amount or degree : INCREASE **2** : to enhance in value or quality : make or grow better **3** : to turn to good account **4** : to make useful additions or amendments — **im·prov·a·ble** *adj* — **im·prov·er** *n*

im·prove·ment \-mənt\ *n* **1** : the act or process of improving **2 a** : the state of being improved; *esp* : enhanced value or excellence **b** : an instance or result of such improvement **3** : something that increases the value esp. of real estate

im·prov·i·dent \(ˈ)im-ˈpräv-əd-ənt\ *adj* : not provident : not foreseeing or providing for the future : THRIFTLESS — **im·prov·i·dence** \-əd-ən(t)s\ *n* — **im·prov·i·dent·ly** *adv*

im·prov·i·sa·tion \im-ˌpräv-ə-ˈzā-shən, ˌim-prə-və-\ *n* **1** : the act or art of improvising **2** : something that is improvised — **im·prov·i·sa·tion·al** \-shnəl, -shən-ᵊl\ *adj*

im·pro·vise \ˌim-prə-ˈvīz\ *vb* **1** : to compose, recite, or sing on the spur of the moment : EXTEMPORIZE **2** : to make, invent, or arrange offhand — **im·pro·vis·er** *n*

im·pru·dent \(ˈ)im-ˈprüd-ᵊnt\ *adj* : not prudent : lacking discretion — **im·pru·dence** \-ᵊn(t)s\ *n* — **im·pru·dent·ly** *adv*

im·pu·dent \ˈim-pyəd-ənt\ *adj* : marked by contemptuous or cocky boldness or disregard of others : INSOLENT, DISRESPECTFUL, FORWARD — **im·pu·dence** \-ən(t)s\ *n* — **im·pu·dent·ly** *adv*

im·pugn \im-ˈpyün\ *vt* : to oppose or attack as false : call into question — **im·pugn·er** *n*

im·pulse \ˈim-ˌpəls\ *n* **1 a** : a force that starts a body into motion : IMPULSION **b** : the motion produced by such an impulsion **2** : a sudden spontaneous arousing of the mind and spirit to do something : an inclination to act **3** : a wave of excitation transmitted esp. through nerves and muscles that results in altered activity of a bodily part

im·pul·sion \im-ˈpəl-shən\ *n* **1 a** : the action of impelling : the state of being impelled **b** : an impelling force **c** : IMPETUS **2** : IMPULSE 2 **3** : COMPULSION 2

im·pul·sive \im-ˈpəl-siv\ *adj* **1** : having the power of driving or impelling **2** : acting or liable to act on impulse : moved or caused by an impulse : IMPETUOUS — **im·pul·sive·ly** *adv* — **im·pul·sive·ness** *n*

im·pu·ni·ty \im-ˈpyü-nət-ē\ *n* : exemption or freedom from punishment, harm, or loss

im·pure \(ˈ)im-ˈpyu̇(ə)r\ *adj* : not pure: as **a** : UNCHASTE, OBSCENE **b** : containing something unclean : FOUL **c** : ritually unclean **d** : marked by an intermixture of foreign elements or by substandard, incongruous, or objectionable locutions **e** : mixed with some other substance and esp. some inferior substance **f** : MIXED, BASTARD — **im·pure·ly** *adv* — **im·pure·ness** *n*

im·pu·ri·ty \(ˈ)im-ˈpyu̇r-ət-ē\ *n, pl* **-ties** **1** : the quality or state of being impure **2** : something that is impure or that makes something else impure

im·pute \im-ˈpyüt\ *vt* **1** : to lay the responsibility or blame for : CHARGE **2** : to credit to a person or a cause : ATTRIBUTE — **im·put·a·ble** *adj* — **im·pu·ta·tion** \ˌim-pyə-ˈtā-shən\ *n*

[1]**in** \(ˈ)in, ən, ᵊn\ *prep* **1 a** — used as a function word to indicate location or inclusion in space or in something immaterial **b** : INTO 1a **2** — used as a function word to indicate means **3 a** — used as a function word to indicate a qualification **b** : INTO 2a **4** — used as a function word to indicate purpose

[2]**in** \ˈin\ *adv* **1 a** : to or toward the inside **b** : to or toward some particular place **c** : at close quarters : NEAR **d** : into the midst of something **e** : to or at its proper place **f** : into line **2 a** : WITHIN **b** : in the position of insider **c** : on good terms **d** : in a position of assured success; *also* : in vogue or season **e** : at hand or on hand

[3]**in** \ˈin\ *adj* **1 a** : being inside or within **b** : being in position, operation, or power **2** : directed or bound inward : INCOMING

[4]**in** \ˈin\ *n* **1** : one who is in office or power or on the inside **2** : INFLUENCE, PULL

in- *prefix* : not : NON-, UN-

inacceptable
inaccessibility
inaccessible
inaccessibly
inaccuracy
inaccurate
inaccurately
inaction
inadequacy
inadequate
inadequately
inadequateness
inadmissibility
inadmissible
inadmissibly
inadvisability
inadvisable
inalterability
inalterable
inalterably
inapparent
inapplicability
inapplicable
inapposite
inappositely
inappositeness
inappreciative
inappreciatively
inapproachable
inappropriate
inappropriately
inappropriateness
inapt
inaptly
inaptness
inartistic
inartistically
inattentive
inattentively
inattentiveness
inaudibility
inaudible
inaudibly
inauspicious
inauspiciously
inauspiciousness
incapability
incapable
incapably
incautious
incautiously
incautiousness
incombustible
incommensurate
incommodious
incommodiously
incommodiousness
incomplete
incompletely
incompleteness
incompliant
incomprehension
incomputable
incongruent
incongruently
inconsistency
inconsonant
inconsumable
incoordinate
incorporeal
indecorous
indecorously
indecorousness
indefensibility
indefensible
indefensibly
indemonstrable
indeterminable
indigestibility
indigestible
indiscernible
indiscreet
indiscreetly
indiscreetness
indisputable
indisputably
indistinct
indistinctly
indistinctness
indistinguishable
indistinguishably
inedible
ineducable
ineffaceable
inefficacious
inefficaciously
inefficaciousness
inefficacy
inelastic
inelasticity
inequitable
inequitably
ineradicable
inexpediency
inexpedient
inexpediently
inexpensive
inexpensively
inexpensiveness
inexpressive
inexpressively
inexpressiveness
inextinguishable
infeasible
inharmonic
inharmonious
inharmoniously
inharmoniousness
inhospitable
inhospitably
injudicious
injudiciously
injudiciousness
inobservant
inoffensive
inoffensively
inoffensiveness
insensitive
insensitively
insensitiveness
insignificant
insignificantly
insincere
insincerely
insincerity
insoluble
insolubleness
insolubly
insupportable
insuppressible
insusceptibility
insusceptible

in·abil·i·ty \ˌin-ə-ˈbil-ət-ē\ *n* : the condition of being unable : lack of ability, power, or means

in ab·sen·tia \ˌin-ab-ˈsen-ch(ē-)ə\ *adv* : in one's absence

in·ac·ti·vate \(ˈ)in-ˈak-tə-ˌvāt\ *vt* : to make inactive — **in·ac·ti·va·tion** \(ˌ)in-ˌak-tə-ˈvā-shən\ *n*

in·ac·tive \(ˈ)in-ˈak-tiv\ *adj* : not active: as **a** : INDOLENT, SLUGGISH **b** : being out of use or activity **c** : relating to members of the armed forces who are not performing or available for military duties — **in·ac·tive·ly** *adv* — **in·ac·tiv·i·ty** \\ˌin-ak-ˈtiv-ət-ē\\ *n*

in·ad·ver·tence \\ˌin-əd-ˈvərt-ᵊn(t)s\\ *n* : INATTENTION; *also* : a result of inattention : OVERSIGHT

in·ad·ver·tent \\-ᵊnt\\ *adj* **1** : HEEDLESS, INATTENTIVE **2** : UNINTENTIONAL — **in·ad·ver·tent·ly** *adv*

in·alien·a·ble \\(ˈ)in-ˈāl-yə-nə-bəl, -ˈā-lē-ə-nə-\\ *adj* : not capable of being taken away, given up, or transferred — **in·alien·a·bil·i·ty** \\(ˌ)in-ˈāl-yə-nə-ˈbil-ət-ē, -ˌā-lē-ə-nə-\\ *n* — **in·alien·a·bly** \\(ˈ)in-ˈāl-yə-nə-blē, -ˈā-lē-ə-nə-\\ *adv*

in·amo·ra·ta \\(ˌ)in-ˌam-ə-ˈrät-ə\\ *n* : a woman with whom one is in love

inane \\in-ˈān\\ *adj* **1** : EMPTY, INSUBSTANTIAL **2** : lacking significance, meaning, or point : SILLY — **inane·ly** *adv* — **inane·ness** *n* — **inan·i·ty** \\-ˈan-ət-ē\\ *n*

in·an·i·mate \\(ˈ)in-ˈan-ə-mət\\ *adj* **1** : not animate: **a** : not endowed with life or spirit **b** : lacking consciousness or power of motion **2** : not animated or lively : DULL — **in·an·i·mate·ly** *adv* — **in·an·i·mate·ness** *n*

in·a·ni·tion \\ˌin-ə-ˈnish-ən\\ *n* : a weak lethargic state resulting from or as if from lack of food and water

in·ap·pre·cia·ble \\ˌin-ə-ˈprē-shə-bəl\\ *adj* : too small to be perceived : very slight — **in·ap·pre·cia·bly** \\-blē\\ *adv*

in·ap·ti·tude \\(ˈ)in-ˈap-tə-ˌt(y)üd\\ *n* : lack of aptitude

in·ar·tic·u·late \\ˌin-är-ˈtik-yə-lət\\ *adj* **1 a** : not understandable as spoken words **b** : incapable of speech esp. under stress of emotion : MUTE **c** : incapable of being expressed by speech **d** : UNSPOKEN **2** : incapable of giving coherent, clear, or effective expression to one's ideas or feelings — **in·ar·tic·u·late·ly** *adv* — **in·ar·tic·u·late·ness** *n*

in·as·much as \\ˌin-əz-ˌməch-əz\\ *conj* **1** : to the extent that **2** : in view of the fact that : SINCE

in·at·ten·tion \\ˌin-ə-ˈten-chən\\ *n* : failure to pay attention

¹in·au·gu·ral \\in-ˈȯ-gyə-rəl, -g(ə-)rəl\\ *adj* **1** : of or relating to an inauguration **2** : marking a beginning : first in a projected series

²inaugural *n* **1** : an inaugural address **2** : INAUGURATION

in·au·gu·rate \\in-ˈȯ-g(y)ə-ˌrāt\\ *vt* **1** : to introduce into office with suitable ceremonies : INSTALL **2** : to celebrate or mark the opening of **3** : to commence or enter upon : BEGIN

in·au·gu·ra·tion \\in-ˌȯ-g(y)ə-ˈrā-shən\\ *n* : an act of inaugurating; *esp* : a ceremonial introduction into office

in·board \\ˈin-ˌbōrd\\ *adv* **1** : inside the hull of a ship **2** : toward, facing, or closer to the center line of a ship or airplane fuselage — **inboard** *adj*

in·born \\ˈin-ˈbȯrn\\ *adj* **1** : born in or with one : not acquired by training or experience : NATURAL **2** : INHERITED, HEREDITARY

in·bound \\ˈin-ˈbau̇nd\\ *adj* : inward bound

in·bred \\ˈin-ˈbred\\ *adj* **1 a** : present from birth **b** : planted in by early teaching or training : INCULCATED **2** : subjected to or produced by inbreeding

in·breed·ing \\ˈin-ˌbrēd-iŋ\\ *n* : the interbreeding of closely related individuals esp. to preserve and fix desirable characters of and to eliminate unfavorable characters from a stock

in·cal·cu·la·ble \\(ˈ)in-ˈkal-kyə-lə-bəl\\ *adj* **1** : not capable of being calculated; *esp* : too large or numerous to be calculated **2** : not capable of being known in advance : UNCERTAIN — **in·cal·cu·la·bly** \\-blē\\ *adv*

in·can·des·cence \\ˌin-kən-ˈdes-ᵊn(t)s\\ *n* : a glowing condition of a body due to its high temperature

in·can·des·cent \\-ᵊnt\\ *adj* **1 a** : white or glowing with intense heat **b** : strikingly bright, radiant, or clear **c** : BRILLIANT **2 a** : of, relating to, or being light produced by incandescence **b** : producing light by incandescence — **in·can·des·cent·ly** *adv*

in·can·ta·tion \\ˌin-ˌkan-ˈtā-shən\\ *n* : a use of spells or charms spoken or sung as part of a ritual of magic; *also* : a formula of words so used

in·ca·pac·i·tate \\ˌin-kə-ˈpas-ə-ˌtāt\\ *vt* **1** : to deprive of natural capacity or power : DISABLE **2** : to make legally incapable or ineligible — **in·ca·pac·i·ta·tion** \\-ˌpas-ə-ˈtā-shən\\ *n*

in·ca·pac·i·ty \\ˌin-kə-ˈpas-ət-ē, -ˈpas-tē\\ *n, pl* **-ties** : lack of ability or power

in·car·cer·ate \\in-ˈkär-sə-ˌrāt\\ *vt* : IMPRISON, CONFINE — **in·car·cer·a·tion** \\(ˌ)in-ˌkär-sə-ˈrā-shən\\ *n*

in·car·na·dine \\in-ˈkär-nə-ˌdīn, -ˌdēn\\ *vt* : REDDEN

¹in·car·nate \\in-ˈkär-nət, -ˌnāt\\ *adj* **1** : invested with bodily esp. human nature and form **2** : EMBODIED, PERSONIFIED

²in·car·nate \\-ˌnāt\\ *vt* : to make incarnate

in·car·na·tion \\ˌin-ˌkär-ˈnā-shən\\ *n* **1** : the act of incarnating : the state of being incarnate **2** : the embodiment of a deity or spirit in an earthly form **3** : a person showing a trait or typical character to a marked degree

¹in·cen·di·ary \\in-ˈsen-dē-ˌer-ē\\ *n, pl* **-ar·ies** **1 a** : a person who maliciously sets fire to property **b** : an incendiary agent (as a bomb) **2** : a person who excites quarrels : AGITATOR

²incendiary *adj* **1** : of, relating to, or involving malicious burning of property **2** : tending to excite or inflame quarrels : INFLAMMATORY **3** : designed to kindle fires

¹in·cense \\ˈin-ˌsen(t)s\\ *n* **1** : material used to produce a fragrant odor when burned **2 a** : the perfume exhaled from some spices and gums when burned **b** : a pleasing scent

²in·cense \\in-ˈsen(t)s\\ *vt* : to inflame with anger or indignation

in·cen·tive \\in-ˈsent-iv\\ *n* : something that arouses or spurs one on to action or effort : STIMULUS — **incentive** *adj*

in·cep·tion \\in-ˈsep-shən\\ *n* : an act, process, or instance of beginning : COMMENCEMENT — **in·cep·tive** \\-ˈsep-tiv\\ *adj* — **inceptive** *n* — **in·cep·tive·ly** *adv*

in·cer·ti·tude \\(ˈ)in-ˈsərt-ə-ˌt(y)üd\\ *n* : UNCERTAINTY: **a** : absence of assurance : DOUBT, INDECISION **b** : INSECURITY, INSTABILITY

in·ces·sant \\(ˈ)in-ˈses-ᵊnt\\ *adj* : continuing without interruption : UNCEASING — **in·ces·sant·ly** *adv*

in·cest \\ˈin-ˌsest \\ *n* : sexual intercourse between persons so closely related that marriage is illegal

in·ces·tu·ous \\in-ˈses-chə-wəs\\ *adj* **1** : constituting or involving incest **2** : guilty of incest

¹inch \\ˈinch\\ *n* **1** : a measure of length that equals the twelfth part of a foot **2** : a small amount, distance, or degree **3** *pl* : STATURE, HEIGHT

²inch *vb* : to move by small degrees

in·cho·ate \\in-ˈkō-ət, ˈin-kə-ˌwāt\\ *adj* : being recently begun or only partly in existence or operation : INCIPIENT, INCOMPLETE — **in·cho·ate·ly** *adv* — **in·cho·ate·ness** *n* — **in·cho·a·tive** \\in-ˈkō-ət-iv\\ *adj* — **inchoative** *n* — **in·cho·a·tive·ly** *adv*

in·ci·dence \\ˈin(t)-səd-ən(t)s\\ *n* **1** : an act or fact of affecting : OCCURRENCE **2** : rate of occurrence or influence

¹in·ci·dent \\ˈin(t)-səd-ənt\\ *n* **1** : an occurrence that is a separate unit of experience : HAPPENING **2** : an action likely to lead to grave consequences esp. in matters diplomatic

²incident *adj* **1** : occurring or likely to occur as an esp. minor consequence or accompaniment **2** : falling or striking on something

¹in·ci·den·tal \\ˌin(t)-sə-ˈdent-ᵊl\\ *adj* **1** : occurring merely by chance or without intention **2** : being likely to happen as a chance or minor consequence — **in·ci·den·tal·ly** \\-ˈdent-lē, -ᵊl-ē\\ *adv*

²incidental *n* **1** : something that is incidental **2** *pl* : minor items (as of expense) that are not particularized

in·cin·er·ate \\in-ˈsin-ə-ˌrāt\\ *vt* : to burn to ashes — **in·cin·er·a·tion** \\(ˌ)in-ˌsin-ə-ˈrā-shən\\ *n*

in·cin·er·a·tor \\in-ˈsin-ə-ˌrāt-ər\\ *n* : one that incinerates; *esp* : a furnace or container for burning waste materials

in·cip·i·ent \\in-ˈsip-ē-ənt\\ *adj* : beginning to be or become apparent — **in·cip·i·en·cy** \\-ən-sē\\ *n* — **in·cip·i·ent·ly** *adv*

in·cise \\in-ˈsīz\\ *vt* **1** : to cut into **2** : ENGRAVE

in·ci·sion \\in-ˈsizh-ən\\ *n* : CUT, GASH; *esp* : a surgical wound

in·ci·sive \in-'sī-siv\ *adj* **1** : CUTTING, PENETRATING **2** : ACUTE, CLEAR-CUT — **in·ci·sive·ly** *adv* — **in·ci·sive·ness** *n*

in·ci·sor \in-'sī-zər\ *n* : a tooth adapted for cutting; *esp* : one of the cutting teeth in front of the canines of a mammal — **incisor** *adj*

in·ci·ta·tion \ˌin-ˌsī-'tā-shən\ *n* : INCITEMENT

in·cite \in-'sīt\ *vt* : to move to action : stir up : spur on : urge on — **in·cite·ment** *n* — **in·cit·er** *n*

in·ci·vil·i·ty \ˌin(t)-sə-'vil-ət-ē\ *n, pl* **-ties** **1** : DISCOURTESY, RUDENESS **2** : a rude or discourteous act

in·clem·ent \(')in-'klem-ənt\ *adj* **1** : harsh or severe in temper or action : UNMERCIFUL **2** : STORMY, ROUGH — **in·clem·en·cy** \-ən-sē\ *n* — **in·clem·ent·ly** *adv*

in·clin·a·ble \in-'klī-nə-bəl\ *adj* : having a tendency or inclination : DISPOSED; *also* : FAVORABLE

in·cli·na·tion \ˌin-klə-'nā-shən, ˌiŋ-\ *n* **1 a** : BOW, NOD **b** : a tilting of something **2** : PROPENSITY, BENT; *esp* : LIKING **3 a** : a departure from the true vertical or horizontal : SLANT **b** : an inclined surface : SLOPE **4** : a tendency to a particular state, character, or action — **in·cli·na·tion·al** \-shnəl, -shən-ᵊl\ *adj*

[1]**in·cline** \in-'klīn\ *vb* **1** : to bend the head or body forward : BOW **2** : to lean in one's mind : TEND **3** : to deviate from the vertical or horizontal **4** : to have influence on (as in direction, course of action, or opinion) — **in·clin·er** *n*

[2]**in·cline** \'in-ˌklīn\ *n* : an inclined plane : GRADE, SLOPE

in·clined \in-'klīnd\ *adj* **1** : having inclination, disposition, or tendency **2** : having a slant or slope

in·clude \in-'klüd\ *vt* **1** : to shut up : ENCLOSE **2** : to take in or comprise as a part of a whole **3** : to contain between — **in·clud·a·ble** *or* **in·clud·i·ble** \-'klüd-ə-bəl\ *adj* — **in·clu·sion** \-'klü-zhən\ *n*

in·clu·sive \in-'klü-siv\ *adj* **1** : INCLUDING; *esp* : including one or more limits **2** : broad in orientation, scope, or coverage — **in·clu·sive·ly** *adv* — **in·clu·sive·ness** *n*

[1]**in·cog·ni·to** \ˌin-ˌkäg-'nēt-ō, in-'käg-nə-ˌtō\ *adv* (*or adj*) : with one's identity concealed (as by a name or title not arousing special recognition)

[2]**incognito** *n, pl* **-tos** **1** : one appearing or living incognito **2** : the state or disguise of an incognito

in·co·her·ence \ˌin-kō-'hir-ən(t)s\ *n* **1** : the quality or state of being incoherent **2** : an incoherent utterance

in·co·her·ent \-ənt\ *adj* : not coherent: as **a** : not sticking closely or compactly together : LOOSE **b** : not clearly or logically connected : RAMBLING — **in·co·her·ent·ly** *adv*

in·come \'in-ˌkəm\ *n* : a gain usu. measured in money that derives from capital or labor; *also* : the amount of such gain received by an individual in a given period of time

income tax *n* : a tax on the net income of an individual or business concern

in·com·ing \'in-ˌkəm-iŋ\ *adj* : coming in

in·com·mode \ˌin-kə-'mōd\ *vt* : to give inconvenience or trouble to : DISCOMMODE

in·com·mu·ni·ca·ble \ˌin-kə-'myü-ni-kə-bəl\ *adj* : not capable of being communicated or imparted — **in·com·mu·ni·ca·bly** \-blē\ *adv*

in·com·mu·ni·ca·do \ˌin-kə-ˌmyü-nə-'käd-ō\ *adv* (*or adj*) : without means of communication with others; *also* : in solitary confinement

in·com·mu·ni·ca·tive \ˌin-kə-'myü-nə-ˌkāt-iv, -ni-kət-\ *adj* : UNCOMMUNICATIVE

in·com·pa·ra·ble \(')in-'käm-p(ə-)rə-bəl\ *adj* **1** : eminent beyond comparison : MATCHLESS **2** : not suitable for comparison — **in·com·pa·ra·bly** \-blē\ *adv*

in·com·pat·i·ble \ˌin-kəm-'pat-ə-bəl\ *adj* : incapable of or unsuitable for association — **in·com·pat·i·bil·i·ty** \-ˌpat-ə-'bil-ət-ē\ *n* — **in·com·pat·i·bly** \-'pat-ə-blē\ *adv*

in·com·pe·tent \(')in-'käm-pət-ənt\ *adj* **1** : lacking the qualities (as knowledge, skill, or ability) necessary to effective independent action **2** : not legally qualified **3** : inadequate to or unsuitable for the purpose — **in·com·pe·tence** \-ən(t)s\ *n* — **incompetent** *n* — **in·com·pe·tent·ly** *adv*

in·com·pre·hen·si·ble \ˌin-ˌkäm-prē-'hen(t)-sə-bəl\ *adj* : incapable of being comprehended : impossible to understand — **in·com·pre·hen·si·bil·i·ty** \-ˌhen(t)-sə-'bil-ət-ē\ *n* — **in·com·pre·hen·si·bly** \-'hen(t)-sə-blē\ *adv*

in·com·press·i·ble \ˌin-kəm-'pres-ə-bəl\ *adj* : incapable of or resistant to compression

in·con·ceiv·a·ble \ˌin-kən-'sē-və-bəl\ *adj* : impossible to imagine or conceive : INCREDIBLE — **in·con·ceiv·a·bil·i·ty** \-ˌsē-və-'bil-ət-ē\ *n* — **in·con·ceiv·a·ble·ness** *n* — **in·con·ceiv·a·bly** \-'sē-və-blē\ *adv*

in·con·clu·sive \ˌin-kən-'klü-siv, -ziv\ *adj* : leading to no conclusion or definite result — **in·con·clu·sive·ly** *adv* — **in·con·clu·sive·ness** *n*

in·con·gru·i·ty \ˌin-kən-'grü-ət-ē, -ˌkän-\ *n, pl* **-ties** **1** : the quality or state of being incongruous **2** : something that is incongruous

in·con·gru·ous \(')in-'käŋ-grə-wəs\ *adj* : not consistent with or suitable to the surroundings or associations : not harmonious, appropriate, or proper : out of place — **in·con·gru·ous·ly** *adv* — **in·con·gru·ous·ness** *n*

in·con·se·quen·tial \(ˌ)in-ˌkän(t)-sə-'kwen-chəl\ *adj* **1 a** : ILLOGICAL **b** : IRRELEVANT **2** : of no significance : UNIMPORTANT — **in·con·se·quen·tial·ly** \-'kwench-(ə-)lē\ *adv*

in·con·sid·er·a·ble \ˌin-kən-'sid-ər-(ə-)bəl\ *adj* : not worth considering : SLIGHT, TRIVIAL

in·con·sid·er·ate \ˌin-kən-'sid-(ə-)rət\ *adj* **1** : HEEDLESS, THOUGHTLESS **2** : careless of the rights or feelings of others — **in·con·sid·er·ate·ly** *adv* — **in·con·sid·er·ate·ness** *n*

in·con·sis·tent \ˌin-kən-'sis-tənt\ *adj* **1 a** : not being in agreement or harmony : INCOMPATIBLE **b** : containing incompatible elements **2** : not logical in thought or actions : CHANGEABLE — **in·con·sis·tent·ly** *adv*

in·con·sol·a·ble \ˌin-kən-'sō-lə-bəl\ *adj* : incapable of being consoled : not to be comforted : DISCONSOLATE — **in·con·sol·a·ble·ness** *n* — **in·con·sol·a·bly** \-blē\ *adv*

in·con·spic·u·ous \ˌin-kən-'spik-yə-wəs\ *adj* : not readily noticeable — **in·con·spic·u·ous·ly** *adv* — **in·con·spic·u·ous·ness** *n*

in·con·stant \(')in-'kän(t)-stənt\ *adj* : likely to change frequently without apparent reason : CHANGEABLE — **in·con·stan·cy** \-stən-sē\ *n* — **in·con·stant·ly** *adv*

in·con·test·a·ble \ˌin-kən-'tes-tə-bəl\ *adj* : not open to doubt or contest : INDISPUTABLE, UNQUESTIONABLE — **in·con·test·a·bly** \-blē\ *adv*

in·con·ti·nent \(')in-'känt-ᵊn-ənt\ *adj* : lacking in self-restraint esp. in the gratification of sensuous desires — **in·con·ti·nence** \-ən(t)s\ *n* — **in·con·ti·nent·ly** *adv*

in·con·tro·vert·i·ble \(ˌ)in-ˌkän-trə-'vərt-ə-bəl\ *adj* : not open to question : INDISPUTABLE — **in·con·tro·vert·i·bly** \-blē\ *adv*

[1]**in·con·ve·nience** \ˌin-kən-'vē-nyən(t)s\ *n* **1** : the quality or state of being inconvenient : lack of suitability for personal ease or comfort **2** : something inconvenient : something that disturbs or that causes discomfort or annoyance

[2]**inconvenience** *vt* : to subject to inconvenience : cause discomfort to : put to trouble : INCOMMODE

in·con·ve·nient \-nyənt\ *adj* : not convenient : causing difficulty or discomfort — **in·con·ve·nient·ly** *adv*

in·con·vert·i·ble \ˌin-kən-'vərt-ə-bəl\ *adj* : not convertible into something else

in·co·or·di·na·tion \ˌin-kō-ˌȯrd-ᵊn-'ā-shən\ *n* : lack of coordination esp. of muscular movements

[1]**in·cor·po·rate** \in-'kȯr-pə-ˌrāt\ *vb* **1** : to unite with or work into something already existent **2** : to unite or combine to

form a single body or a consistent whole **3 :** to give material form to : EMBODY **4 :** to form, form into, or become a corporation — **in·cor·po·ra·tion** \(,)in-ˌkȯr-pə-ˈrā-shən\ *n* — **in·cor·po·ra·tive** \in-ˈkȯr-pə-ˌrāt-iv, -p(ə-)rət-\ *adj* — **in·cor·po·ra·tor** \-pə-ˌrāt-ər\ *n*

²**in·cor·po·rate** \in-ˈkȯr-p(ə-)rət\ *adj* : INCORPORATED

in·cor·po·rat·ed \-pə-ˌrāt-əd\ *adj* : united in one body; *esp* : formed into a legal corporation

in·cor·rect \ˌin-kə-ˈrekt\ *adj* **1 a :** INACCURATE, FAULTY **b :** not true : WRONG **2 :** UNBECOMING, IMPROPER — **in·cor·rect·ly** *adv* — **in·cor·rect·ness** *n*

in·cor·ri·gi·ble \(ˈ)in-ˈkȯr-ə-jə-bəl\ *adj* : not to be corrected or improved: as **a :** incapable of being reformed **b :** UNRULY, UNMANAGEABLE — **in·cor·ri·gi·bil·i·ty** \(,)in-ˌkȯr-ə-jə-ˈbil-ət-ē\ *n* — **incorrigible** *n* — **in·cor·ri·gi·bly** \(ˈ)in-ˈkȯr-ə-jə-blē\ *adv*

in·cor·rupt·i·ble \ˌin-kə-ˈrəp-tə-bəl\ *adj* : not to be corrupted: as **a :** not subject to decay **b :** incapable of being bribed or morally corrupted — **in·cor·rupt·i·bil·i·ty** \-ˌrəp-tə-ˈbil-ət-ē\ *n* — **in·cor·rupt·i·bly** \-ˈrəp-tə-blē\ *adv*

¹**in·crease** \in-ˈkrēs, ˈin-ˌ\ *vb* **1 :** to make or become greater (as in size, number, value, or power) **2 :** to multiply by the production of young — **in·creas·a·ble** *adj* — **in·creas·er** *n*

²**in·crease** \ˈin-ˌkrēs, in-ˈ\ *n* **1 :** addition or enlargement in size, extent, or quantity **2 :** something (as offspring, produce, or profit) added to an original stock by enlargement or growth

in·creas·ing·ly \in-ˈkrē-siŋ-lē, ˈin-ˌkrē-\ *adv* : to an increasing degree : more and more

in·cred·i·ble \(ˈ)in-ˈkred-ə-bəl\ *adj* : too extraordinary or improbable to be believed; *also* : hard to believe — **in·cred·i·bil·i·ty** \(,)in-ˌkred-ə-ˈbil-ət-ē\ *n* — **in·cred·i·bly** \(ˈ)in-ˈkred-ə-blē\ *adv*

in·cre·du·li·ty \ˌin-kri-ˈd(y)ü-lət-ē\ *n* : the quality or state of not believing or of doubting; *also* : an instance of disbelieving

in·cred·u·lous \(ˈ)in-ˈkrej-ə-ləs\ *adj* **1 :** not credulous : tending to disbelieve : SKEPTICAL **2 :** expressing incredulity — **in·cred·u·lous·ly** *adv*

in·cre·ment \ˈiŋ-krə-mənt, ˈin-\ *n* **1 :** an increasing or growth esp. in quantity or value : ENLARGEMENT, INCREASE; *also* : QUANTITY **2 a :** something gained or added **b :** one of a series of regular consecutive additions **c :** a minute increase in quantity — **in·cre·men·tal** \ˌiŋ-krə-ˈment-ᵊl, ˌin-\ *adj*

in·crim·i·nate \in-ˈkrim-ə-ˌnāt\ *vt* : to charge with or involve in a crime or fault : ACCUSE — **in·crim·i·na·tion** \(,)in-ˌkrim-ə-ˈnā-shən\ *n* — **in·crim·i·na·to·ry** \in-ˈkrim-(ə-)nə-ˌtōr-ē\ *adj*

in·crus·ta·tion \ˌin-ˌkrəs-ˈtā-shən\ *n* **1 :** the act of encrusting : the state of being encrusted **2 :** a hard coating : CRUST **3 a :** OVERLAY **b :** INLAY

in·cu·bate \ˈiŋ-kyə-ˌbāt, ˈin-\ *vb* **1 :** to sit upon eggs to hatch them by warmth **2 :** to maintain under conditions favorable for development — **in·cu·ba·tion** \ˌiŋ-kyə-ˈbā-shən, ˌin-\ *n* — **in·cu·ba·tion·al** \-shnəl, -shən-ᵊl\ *adj* — **in·cu·ba·tive** \ˈiŋ-kyə-ˌbāt-iv, ˈin-\ *adj*

in·cu·ba·tor \ˈiŋ-kyə-ˌbāt-ər, ˈin-\ *n* : one that incubates; *esp* : an apparatus providing suitable conditions (as of warmth and moisture) for incubating something

in·cu·bus \ˈiŋ-kyə-bəs, ˈin-\ *n, pl* **-bi** \-ˌbī, -ˌbē\ **1 :** an evil spirit held to lie upon persons in their sleep **2 :** NIGHTMARE 1 **3 :** a person or thing that oppresses or burdens like a nightmare

in·cul·cate \in-ˈkəl-ˌkāt, ˈin-(ˌ)kəl-\ *vt* : to teach and impress upon the mind by frequent repetition — **in·cul·ca·tion** \ˌin-(ˌ)kəl-ˈkā-shən\ *n* — **in·cul·ca·tor** \in-ˈkəl-ˌkāt-ər, ˈin-(ˌ)kəl-\ *n*

in·cul·pate \in-ˈkəl-ˌpāt, ˈin-(ˌ)kəl-\ *vt* : INCRIMINATE — **in·cul·pa·tion** \ˌin-(ˌ)kəl-ˈpā-shən\ *n*

in·cum·ben·cy \in-ˈkəm-bən-sē\ *n, pl* **-cies** **1 :** the quality or state of being incumbent **2 :** the office or period of office of an incumbent

¹**in·cum·bent** \-bənt\ *n* : the holder of an office or position

²**incumbent** *adj* **1 :** lying or resting on something else **2 :** imposed as a duty : OBLIGATORY **3 :** bent over so as to rest on or touch an underlying surface

in·cu·nab·u·lum \ˌin-kyə-ˈnab-yə-ləm, ˌiŋ-\ *n, pl* **-la** \-lə\ : a book printed before 1501

in·cur \in-ˈkər\ *vt* **in·curred; in·cur·ring** **1 :** to meet with (as an inconvenience) **2 :** to become liable or subject to : bring down upon oneself

¹**in·cur·a·ble** \(ˈ)in-ˈkyu̇r-ə-bəl\ *adj* : not capable of being cured — **in·cur·a·bil·i·ty** \(,)in-ˌkyu̇r-ə-ˈbil-ət-ē\ *n* — **in·cur·a·bly** \(ˈ)in-ˈkyu̇r-ə-blē\ *adv*

²**incurable** *n* : a person suffering from a disease that is beyond cure

in·cu·ri·ous \(ˈ)in-ˈkyu̇r-ē-əs\ *adj* : not curious or inquisitive : UNINTERESTED — **in·cu·ri·ous·ly** *adv*

in·cur·sion \in-ˈkər-zhən\ *n* : a sudden usu. temporary invasion : RAID

in·curve \ˈin-ˌkərv\ *n* : a curving in

in·debt·ed \in-ˈdet-əd\ *adj* : being in debt : owing something (as money, gratitude, or services)

in·debt·ed·ness \-nəs\ *n* **1 :** the condition of being indebted **2 :** an amount owed

in·de·cen·cy \(ˈ)in-ˈdēs-ᵊn-sē\ *n, pl* **-cies** **1 :** lack of decency **2 :** an indecent act or word

in·de·cent \-ᵊnt\ *adj* : not decent: **a :** UNBECOMING, UNSEEMLY **b :** morally offensive — **in·de·cent·ly** *adv*

in·de·ci·pher·a·ble \ˌin-di-ˈsī-f(ə-)rə-bəl\ *adj* : that cannot be deciphered

in·de·ci·sion \ˌin-di-ˈsizh-ən\ *n* : a wavering between two or more possible courses of action : IRRESOLUTION

in·de·ci·sive \-ˈsī-siv\ *adj* **1 :** not decisive or final **2 :** characterized by indecision : HESITATING, UNCERTAIN — **in·de·ci·sive·ly** *adv* — **in·de·ci·sive·ness** *n*

in·de·clin·a·ble \ˌin-di-ˈklī-nə-bəl\ *adj* : having no grammatical inflections

in·de·co·rum \ˌin-di-ˈkōr-əm\ *n* : lack of decorum : IMPROPRIETY

in·deed \in-ˈdēd\ *adv* **1 :** in fact : in reality : TRULY — often used interjectionally to express disbelief or surprise **2 :** ADMITTEDLY, UNDENIABLY

in·de·fat·i·ga·ble \ˌin-di-ˈfat-i-gə-bəl\ *adj* : capable of working a long time without tiring : TIRELESS — **in·de·fat·i·ga·bil·i·ty** \-ˌfat-i-gə-ˈbil-ət-ē\ *n* — **in·de·fat·i·ga·bly** \-ˈfat-i-gə-blē\ *adv*

in·de·fea·si·ble \ˌin-di-ˈfē-zə-bəl\ *adj* : not capable of being abolished or annulled — **in·de·fea·si·bil·i·ty** \-ˌfē-zə-ˈbil-ət-ē\ *n* — **in·de·fea·si·bly** \-ˈfē-zə-blē\ *adv*

in·de·fin·a·ble \ˌin-di-ˈfī-nə-bəl\ *adj* : incapable of being precisely described or analyzed — **in·de·fin·a·bil·i·ty** \-ˌfī-nə-ˈbil-ət-ē\ *n* — **in·de·fin·a·ble·ness** *n* — **in·de·fin·a·bly** \-ˈfī-nə-blē\ *adv*

in·def·i·nite \(ˈ)in-ˈdef-(ə-)nət\ *adj* **1 :** not clear or fixed in meaning or details : VAGUE **2 :** not fixed or limited (as in amount or length) **3 :** being a pronoun or grammatical modifier that typically designates an unidentified or not immediately identifiable person or thing — **in·def·i·nite·ly** *adv* — **in·def·i·nite·ness** *n*

in·del·i·ble \in-ˈdel-ə-bəl\ *adj* **1 :** not capable of being erased, removed, or blotted out **2 :** making marks not easily erased — **in·del·i·bly** \-blē\ *adv*

in·del·i·ca·cy \(ˈ)in-ˈdel-i-kə-sē\ *n, pl* **-cies** **1 :** the quality or state of being indelicate : COARSENESS **2 :** an indelicate act or utterance

in·del·i·cate \-kət\ *adj* : not delicate : offensive to good manners or refined taste : IMMODEST, COARSE — **in·del·i·cate·ly** *adv* — **in·del·i·cate·ness** *n*

in·dem·ni·fy \in-ˈdem-nə-ˌfī\ *vt* **-fied; -fy·ing** **1 :** to insure or protect against loss, damage, or injury **2 :** to make compensation to for loss, damage, or injury **3 :** to make compensation for : make good — **in·dem·ni·fi·ca·tion** \-ˌdem-nə-fə-ˈkā-shən\ *n*

in·dem·ni·ty \in-ˈdem-nət-ē\ *n, pl* **-ties** **1** : protection from loss, damage, or injury : INSURANCE **2** : freedom or exemption from penalty for past offenses **3** : compensation paid for loss, damage, or injury

[1]**in·dent** \in-ˈdent\ *vt* **1** : to notch the edge of : make jagged **2** : to set (as a line of a paragraph) in from the margin

[2]**indent** *vt* **1** : to force inward so as to form a depression **2** : to form a dent in — **in·dent·er** *n*

[3]**indent** *n* : INDENTATION

in·den·ta·tion \ˌin-ˌden-ˈtā-shən\ *n* **1 a** : an angular cut in an edge : NOTCH **b** : a usu. deep recess (as in a coastline) **2 a** : the action of indenting : the state of being indented **b** : a blank or empty space produced by indenting **3** : DENT

in·den·tion \in-ˈden-chən\ *n* : an indentation esp. in printing

[1]**in·den·ture** \in-ˈden-chər\ *n* **1** : a written agreement : CONTRACT **2** : a contract that binds a person to serve another for a specified period — usu. used in pl.

[2]**indenture** *vt* : to bind (as an apprentice) by indentures

in·de·pend·ence \ˌin-də-ˈpen-dən(t)s\ *n* : the quality or state of being independent : freedom from outside control

Independence Day *n* : July 4 observed as a legal holiday in commemoration of the adoption of the Declaration of Independence in 1776

[1]**in·de·pend·ent** \ˌin-də-ˈpen-dənt\ *adj* **1** : not subject to control or rule by another : SELF-GOVERNING, FREE **2** : not having connections with another : SEPARATE **3** : not supported by or relying on another : having or providing enough money to live on **4** : not easily influenced : showing self-reliance **5** : refusing to accept help from or to come under obligation to others **6 a** : having full meaning in itself and capable of standing alone as a simple sentence : MAIN **b** : varying without respect to other variables **7** : not tied to a political party — **in·de·pend·ent·ly** *adv*

[2]**independent** *n* : one that is independent; *esp* : one not committed to a political party

in·de·scrib·a·ble \ˌin-di-ˈskrī-bə-bəl\ *adj* : incapable of being described : surpassing description — **in·de·scrib·a·bly** \-blē\ *adv*

in·de·struc·ti·ble \ˌin-di-ˈstrək-tə-bəl\ *adj* : incapable of being destroyed — **in·de·struc·ti·bil·i·ty** \-ˌstrək-tə-ˈbil-ət-ē\ *n* — **in·de·struc·ti·bly** \-ˈstrək-tə-blē\ *adv*

in·de·ter·mi·nate \ˌin-di-ˈtər-mə-nət\ *adj* **1 a** : not definitely or precisely determined : VAGUE **b** : not known in advance **2** : not leading to a definite end or result — **in·de·ter·mi·na·cy** \-mə-nə-sē\ *n* — **in·de·ter·mi·nate·ly** *adv* — **in·de·ter·mi·nate·ness** *n*

in·de·ter·mi·na·tion \-ˌtər-mə-ˈnā-shən\ *n* **1** : INDETERMINATENESS **2** : a state of mental indecision

[1]**in·dex** \ˈin-ˌdeks\ *n, pl* **in·dex·es** *or* **in·di·ces** \-də-ˌsēz\ **1** : a guide (as a table or file) for facilitating reference; *esp* : an alphabetical list of items treated in a printed work that gives with each item the page number where it may be found **2** : POINTER, INDICATOR **3** : SIGN, INDICATION, TOKEN **4** : a list of restricted or prohibited material **5** *pl usu indices* : a mathematical figure, letter, or expression (as the figure *3* in a^3) : EXPONENT **6** : a character ☞ used to direct attention

[2]**index** *vt* **1 a** : to provide with an index **b** : to list in an index **2** : to serve as an index of — **in·dex·er** *n*

index finger *n* : the finger next to the thumb

In·dia·man \ˈin-dē-ə-mən\ *n* : a large sailing ship formerly used in trade with India

In·di·an corn \ˌin-dē-ən-\ *n* **1** : a tall widely cultivated American cereal grass bearing seeds on elongated ears **2** : the ears of Indian corn; *also* : its edible seeds

Indian meal *n* : CORNMEAL

Indian summer *n* : a period of mild weather in late autumn or early winter

In·dia paper \ˌin-dē-ə-\ *n* : a thin tough opaque printing paper

in·di·cate \ˈin-də-ˌkāt\ *vt* **1 a** : to point out or point to **b** : to be a sign, symptom, or index of **2** : to state or express briefly : SUGGEST — **in·di·ca·tor** \-ər\ *n*

in·di·ca·tion \ˌin-də-ˈkā-shən\ *n* **1** : the action of indicating **2** : something that indicates : SIGN, SUGGESTION

[1]**in·dic·a·tive** \in-ˈdik-ət-iv\ *adj* **1** : of, relating to, or constituting a verb form that represents the denoted act or state as an objective fact **2** : pointing out : SUGGESTIVE — **in·dic·a·tive·ly** *adv*

[2]**indicative** *n* : the indicative mood of a verb : a verb in this mood

in·di·cia \in-ˈdish-(ē-)ə\ *n pl* **1** : distinctive marks : INDICATIONS **2** : postal markings often imprinted on mail or on labels to be affixed to mail

in·dict \in-ˈdīt\ *vt* **1** : to charge with an offense : ACCUSE **2** : to charge with a crime by the finding of a grand jury — **in·dict·a·ble** *adj*

in·dict·ment \in-ˈdīt-mənt\ *n* **1** : the act or the legal process of indicting **2** : a formal written statement drawn up by a prosecuting attorney and reported by a grand jury after an inquiry charging a person with an offense

in·dif·fer·ence \in-ˈdif-ərn(t)s, -ˈdif-(ə-)rən(t)s\ *n* **1** : the condition or the fact of being indifferent : lack of feeling for or against something **2** : lack of importance

in·dif·fer·ent \in-ˈdif-(ə-)rənt\ *adj* **1** : having no choice or preference : not interested in or concerned about something **2** : showing neither interest nor dislike **3** : neither good nor bad : MEDIOCRE **4** : of no special influence or value : not important **5** : capable of development in more than one direction — **in·dif·fer·ent·ly** *adv*

in·di·gence \ˈin-di-jən(t)s\ *n* : NEEDINESS, POVERTY

in·dig·e·nous \in-ˈdij-ə-nəs\ *adj* **1** : produced, growing, or living naturally in a particular region or environment **2** : INBORN, INNATE — **in·dig·e·nous·ly** *adv* — **in·dig·e·nous·ness** *n*

in·di·gent \ˈin-di-jənt\ *adj* : POOR, NEEDY

in·di·ges·tion \ˌin-dī-ˈjes-chən, -də-\ *n* **1** : inability to digest or difficulty in digesting something **2** : a case or attack of indigestion — **in·di·ges·tive** \-ˈjes-tiv\ *adj*

in·dig·nant \in-ˈdig-nənt\ *adj* : filled with or marked by indignation — **in·dig·nant·ly** *adv*

in·dig·na·tion \ˌin-dig-ˈnā-shən\ *n* : anger aroused by something unjust, unworthy, or mean

in·dig·ni·ty \in-ˈdig-nət-ē\ *n* **1** : an act that offends against a person's dignity or self-respect : INSULT **2** : humiliating treatment

in·di·go \ˈin-di-ˌgō\ *n, pl* **-gos** *or* **-goes** **1** : a blue dye made artificially and formerly obtained from plants and esp. indigo plants **2** : a color between blue and violet

indigo plant *n* : any of various mostly leguminous plants that yield indigo

in·di·rect \ˌin-də-ˈrekt, -dī-\ *adj* **1** : not straight : not the shortest **2** : not straightforward : ROUNDABOUT **3** : not having a plainly seen connection **4** : not straight to the point — **in·di·rect·ly** *adv* — **in·di·rect·ness** *n*

in·di·rec·tion \-ˈrek-shən\ *n* **1** : lack of straightforwardness and openness : DECEITFULNESS **2** : indirect action or procedure : DECEIT

in·dis·cre·tion \ˌin-dis-ˈkresh-ən\ *n* **1** : lack of discretion : IMPRUDENCE **2** : an indiscreet act or remark

in·dis·crim·i·nate \ˌin-dis-ˈkrim-ə-nət\ *adj* : showing lack of discrimination : not making careful distinction between persons or things — **in·dis·crim·i·nate·ly** *adv*

in·dis·pens·a·ble \ˌin-dis-ˈpen(t)-sə-bəl\ *adj* : absolutely necessary — **in·dis·pens·a·bil·i·ty** \-ˌpen(t)-sə-ˈbil-ət-ē\ *n* — **indispensable** *n* — **in·dis·pens·a·ble·ness** *n* — **in·dis·pens·a·bly** \-ˈpen(t)-sə-blē\ *adv*

in·dis·pose \\ˌin-dis-ˈpōz\\ *vt* **1** : to make unfit : DISQUALIFY **2** : to make averse : DISINCLINE

in·dis·posed \\-ˈpōzd\\ *adj* **1** : slightly ill **2** : AVERSE

in·dis·po·si·tion \\(ˌ)in-ˌdis-pə-ˈzish-ən\\ *n* **1** : a slight illness **2** : DISINCLINATION, UNWILLINGNESS

in·dis·sol·u·ble \\ˌin-dis-ˈäl-yə-bəl\\ *adj* : not capable of being dissolved, undone, broken up, or decomposed — **in·dis·sol·u·bil·i·ty** \\-ˌäl-yə-ˈbil-ət-ē\\ *n* — **in·dis·sol·u·bly** \\-ˈäl-yə-blē\\ *adv*

in·dite \\in-ˈdīt\\ *vt* **1** : to make up : COMPOSE **2** : to compose and put down in writing — **in·dit·er** *n*

in·di·um \\ˈin-dē-əm\\ *n* : a malleable fusible silvery metallic chemical element

[1]**in·di·vid·u·al** \\ˌin-də-ˈvij-(ə-w)əl\\ *adj* **1 a** : of or relating to an individual **b** : intended for one person **2** : PARTICULAR, SEPARATE **3** : having marked individuality — **in·di·vid·u·al·ly** \\-ē\\ *adv*

[2]**individual** *n* **1** : a particular being or thing as distinguished from a class, species, or collection **2** : a particular person

in·di·vid·u·al·ism \\-ˈvij-ə(-wə)-ˌliz-əm\\ *n* **1** : an ethical doctrine that the interests of the individual are primary **2 a** : a doctrine that the chief end of society is to promote the welfare of its individual members **b** : a doctrine holding that the individual has certain political or economic rights with which the state must not interfere

in·di·vid·u·al·ist \\-ləst\\ *n* **1** : a person who shows marked individuality or independence of others in thought or behavior **2** : a supporter of the doctrines of individualism — **in·di·vid·u·al·is·tic** \\-ˌvij-ə(-wə)-ˈlis-tik\\ *adj* — **in·di·vid·u·al·is·ti·cal·ly** \\-ti-k(ə-)lē\\ *adv*

in·di·vid·u·al·i·ty \\ˌin-də-ˌvij-ə-ˈwal-ət-ē\\ *n, pl* **-ties** **1** : the qualities that distinguish one person or thing from all others **2** : the condition of having separate existence **3** : INDIVIDUAL, PERSON

in·di·vid·u·al·ize \\-ˈvij-(ə-w)əl-ˌīz\\ *vt* **1** : to make individual in character **2** : to treat or notice individually : PARTICULARIZE **3** : to adapt to a particular individual

in·di·vis·i·ble \\ˌin-də-ˈviz-ə-bəl\\ *adj* : not capable of being divided or separated — **in·di·vis·i·bil·i·ty** \\-ˌviz-ə-ˈbil-ət-ē\\ *n* — **in·di·vis·i·bly** \\-ˈviz-ə-blē\\ *adv*

in·doc·tri·nate \\in-ˈdäk-trə-ˌnāt\\ *vt* **1** : to instruct esp. in fundamentals **2** : to imbue with a usu. partisan or sectarian opinion, point of view, or principle — **in·doc·tri·na·tion** \\(ˌ)in-ˌdäk-trə-ˈnā-shən\\ *n* — **in·doc·tri·na·tor** \\in-ˈdäk-trə-ˌnāt-ər\\ *n*

in·do·lent \\ˈin-də-lənt\\ *adj* : averse to exertion : LAZY, IDLE — **in·do·lence** \\-lən(t)s\\ *n* — **in·do·lent·ly** *adv*

in·dom·i·ta·ble \\in-ˈdäm-ət-ə-bəl\\ *adj* : incapable of being subdued : UNCONQUERABLE — **in·dom·i·ta·bil·i·ty** \\-ˌdäm-ət-ə-ˈbil-ət-ē\\ *n* — **in·dom·i·ta·ble·ness** *n* — **in·dom·i·ta·bly** \\-ˈdäm-ət-ə-blē\\ *adv*

in·door \\ˌin-ˌdōr\\ *adj* **1** : of or relating to the interior of a building **2** : done, living, or belonging within doors

in·doors \\(ˈ)in-ˈdō(ə)rz\\ *adv* : in or into a building

in·du·bi·ta·ble \\(ˈ)in-ˈd(y)ü-bət-ə-bəl\\ *adj* : too evident to be doubted : UNQUESTIONABLE — **in·du·bi·ta·ble·ness** *n* — **in·du·bi·ta·bly** \\-blē\\ *adv*

in·duce \\in-ˈd(y)üs\\ *vt* **1** : to lead on to do something : influence by persuasion **2** : to bring about : CAUSE **3** : to conclude or infer by reasoning from particular instances **4** : to produce (as an electric current) by induction — **in·duc·er** *n* — **in·duc·i·ble** \\-ˈd(y)ü-sə-bəl\\ *adj*

in·duce·ment \\in-ˈd(y)üs-mənt\\ *n* **1** : the act of inducing **2** : something that induces

in·duct \\in-ˈdəkt\\ *vt* **1** : to place formally in office : INSTALL **2** : to enroll into military service in accordance with a draft law — **in·duct·ee** \\(ˌ)in-ˌdək-ˈtē\\ *n*

in·duc·tance \\in-ˈdək-tən(t)s\\ *n* : a property of an electric circuit by which an electromotive force is induced in it by a variation of current either in the circuit itself or in a neighboring circuit

in·duc·tion \\in-ˈdək-shən\\ *n* **1 a** : the act or process of inducting (as into office) **b** : an initial experience : INITIATION **c** : the procedure by which a civilian is inducted into military service **2** : reasoning from particular instances to a general conclusion; *also* : the conclusion so reached **3** : the process by which an electric current, an electric charge, or magnetism is produced in a body by the proximity of an electric or magnetic field

in·duc·tive \\in-ˈdək-tiv\\ *adj* : relating to, employing, or based on induction — **in·duc·tive·ly** *adv*

in·duc·tor \\in-ˈdək-tər\\ *n* : one that inducts

in·dulge \\in-ˈdəlj\\ *vb* **1** : to be tolerant toward : give way to : HUMOR, GRATIFY **2** : to allow oneself to take pleasure — **in·dulg·er** *n*

in·dul·gence \\in-ˈdəl-jən(t)s\\ *n* **1** : a release from purgatorial punishment gained by performing pious acts authorized by the Roman Catholic Church **2 a** : the act of indulging : the state of being indulgent **b** : an indulgent act **c** : something indulged in

in·dul·gent \\-jənt\\ *adj* : indulging or characterized by indulgence : LENIENT — **in·dul·gent·ly** *adv*

[1]**in·du·rate** \\ˈin-d(y)ə-rət, in-ˈd(y)u̇r-ət\\ *adj* : physically or morally hardened

[2]**in·du·rate** \\ˈin-d(y)ə-ˌrāt\\ *vb* **1** : to make unfeeling, stubborn, or obdurate **2** : to make hardy : INURE **3** : to make fibrous or hard **4** : to grow hard : HARDEN — **in·du·ra·tion** \\ˌin-d(y)ə-ˈrā-shən\\ *n* — **in·du·ra·tive** \\ˈin-d(y)ə-ˌrāt-iv, in-ˈd(y)u̇r-ət-\\ *adj*

in·dus·tri·al \\in-ˈdəs-trē-əl\\ *adj* **1** : of, relating to, or engaged in industry **2** : characterized by highly developed industries **3** : derived from human industry **4** : used in industry — **in·dus·tri·al·ly** \\-trē-ə-lē\\ *adv*

in·dus·tri·al·ism \\-trē-ə-ˌliz-əm\\ *n* : social organization in which large-scale industries are dominant

in·dus·tri·al·ist \\-ləst\\ *n* : a person owning or engaged in the management of an industry : MANUFACTURER

in·dus·tri·al·ize \\in-ˈdəs-trē-ə-ˌlīz\\ *vb* : to make or become industrial : convert to an industrial economy — **in·dus·tri·al·i·za·tion** \\-ˌdəs-trē-ə-lə-ˈzā-shən\\ *n*

in·dus·tri·ous \\in-ˈdəs-trē-əs\\ *adj* : constantly, regularly, or habitually occupied : DILIGENT — **in·dus·tri·ous·ly** *adv* — **in·dus·tri·ous·ness** *n*

in·dus·try \\ˈin-(ˌ)dəs-trē\\ *n, pl* **-tries** **1** : diligence in an employment or pursuit **2 a** : systematic labor esp. for the creation of value **b** : a department or branch of a craft or art or of business or manufacturing; *esp* : one that employs a large number of persons and considerable capital esp. in manufacturing **c** : a distinct group of productive or profit-making enterprises **d** : manufacturing activity as a whole

in·dwell \\(ˈ)in-ˈdwel\\ *vb* : to exist within as an activating spirit, force, or principle — **in·dwell·er** *n*

ine·bri·ate \\in-ˈē-brē-ˌāt\\ *vt* : to make drunk : INTOXICATE — **ine·bri·ate** \\-brē-ət\\ *adj or n* — **ine·bri·a·tion** \\in-ˌē-brē-ˈā-shən\\ *n*

ine·bri·at·ed \\-ˌāt-əd\\ *adj* : exhilarated or confused by or as if by alcohol : INTOXICATED

in·ef·fa·ble \\(ˈ)in-ˈef-ə-bəl\\ *adj* : being beyond the power of language to describe : UNUTTERABLE — **in·ef·fa·bil·i·ty** \\(ˌ)in-ˌef-ə-ˈbil-ət-ē\\ *n* — **in·ef·fa·bly** \\(ˈ)in-ˈef-ə-blē\\ *adv*

in·ef·fec·tive \\ˌin-ə-ˈfek-tiv\\ *adj* **1** : not effective : INEFFECTUAL **2** : not efficient : INCAPABLE — **in·ef·fec·tive·ly** *adv* — **in·ef·fec·tive·ness** *n*

in·ef·fec·tu·al \\ˌin-ə-ˈfek-chə(-wə)l\\ *adj* : not producing the proper or usual effect : FUTILE — **in·ef·fec·tu·al·ly** \\-ē\\ *adv* — **in·ef·fec·tu·al·ness** *n*

in·ef·fi·cient \\ˌin-ə-ˈfish-ənt\\ *adj* **1** : not producing the effect intended or desired : INEFFICACIOUS 2 : INCAPABLE, INCOMPETENT — **in·ef·fi·cien·cy** \-'fish-ən-sē\ *n*

in·el·e·gant \(')in-'el-i-gənt\ *adj* : lacking in refinement, grace, or good taste — **in·el·e·gant·ly** *adv*

in·el·i·gi·ble \(')in-'el-ə-jə-bəl\ *adj* : not qualified to be chosen for an office — **in·el·i·gi·bil·i·ty** \(,)in-,el-ə-jə-'bil-ət-ē\ *n* — **ineligible** *n*

in·ept \in-'ept\ *adj* 1 : lacking in fitness or aptitude : UNFIT 2 : not apt for the occasion : INAPPROPRIATE 3 : lacking sense or reason : FOOLISH 4 : generally incompetent : BUNGLING — **in·ep·ti·tude** \-'ep-tə-,t(y)üd\ *n* — **in·ept·ly** *adv* — **in·ept·ness** *n*

in·equal·i·ty \,in-i-'kwäl-ət-ē\ *n* 1 : the quality of being unequal or uneven 2 : an instance of being unequal (as an irregularity in a surface)

in·eq·ui·ty \(')in-'ek-wət-ē\ *n, pl* **-ties** 1 : INJUSTICE, UNFAIRNESS 2 : an instance of injustice or unfairness

in·ert \in-'ərt\ *adj* 1 : not having the power to move itself 2 : deficient in active properties 3 : very slow to move or act : SLUGGISH — **in·ert·ly** *adv* — **in·ert·ness** *n*

in·er·tia \in-'ər-sh(ē-)ə\ *n* 1 : a property of matter by which it remains at rest or in uniform motion in the same straight line unless acted upon by some external force 2 : indisposition to motion, exertion, or change : INERTNESS — **in·er·tial** \-shəl\ *adj*

in·es·cap·a·ble \,in-ə-'skā-pə-bəl\ *adj* : incapable of being escaped : INEVITABLE — **in·es·cap·a·bly** \-blē\ *adv*

in·es·ti·ma·ble \(')in-'es-tə-mə-bəl\ *adj* 1 : incapable of being estimated or computed 2 : too valuable or excellent to be measured or appreciated — **in·es·ti·ma·bly** \-blē\ *adv*

in·ev·i·ta·ble \in-'ev-ət-ə-bəl\ *adj* : incapable of being avoided or evaded : bound to happen : CERTAIN — **in·ev·i·ta·bil·i·ty** \(,)in-,ev-ət-ə-'bil-ət-ē\ *n* — **in·ev·i·ta·ble·ness** *n* — **in·ev·i·ta·bly** \(')in-'ev-ət-ə-blē\ *adv*

in·ex·act \,in-ig-'zakt\ *adj* : not precisely correct or true : INACCURATE — **in·ex·ac·ti·tude** \-'zak-tə-,t(y)üd\ *n* — **in·ex·act·ly** *adv* — **in·ex·act·ness** *n*

in·ex·cus·a·ble \,in-ik-'skyüz-ə-bəl\ *adj* : not to be excused : not justifiable — **in·ex·cus·a·bly** \-blē\ *adv*

in·ex·haust·i·ble \,in-ig-'zò-stə-bəl\ *adj* 1 : plentiful enough not to give out or be used up : UNFAILING 2 : UNTIRING — **in·ex·haust·i·bil·i·ty** \-,zò-stə-'bil-ət-ē\ *n* — **in·ex·haust·i·bly** \-'zò-stə-blē\ *adv*

in·ex·o·ra·ble \(')in-'eks-(ə-)rə-bəl\ *adj* : not to be persuaded or moved by entreaty : RELENTLESS — **in·ex·o·ra·bil·i·ty** \(,)in-,eks-(ə-)rə-'bil-ət-ē\ *n* — **in·ex·o·ra·ble·ness** *n* — **in·ex·o·ra·bly** \(')in-'eks-(ə-)rə-blē\ *adv*

in·ex·pe·ri·ence \,in-ik-'spir-ē-ən(t)s\ *n* : lack of experience or of knowledge or proficiency gained by experience — **in·ex·pe·ri·enced** \-ən(t)st\ *adj*

in·ex·pert \(')in-'ek-,spərt\ *adj* : not expert : UNSKILLED — **in·ex·pert·ly** *adv* — **in·ex·pert·ness** *n*

in·ex·pi·a·ble \(')in-'ek-spē-ə-bəl\ *adj* : incapable of being atoned for — **in·ex·pi·a·bly** \-blē\ *adv*

in·ex·plic·a·ble \,in-ik-'splik-ə-bəl, (')in-'ek-(,)splik-\ *adj* : incapable of being explained, interpreted, or accounted for — **in·ex·plic·a·bil·i·ty** \,in-ik-,splik-ə-'bil-ət-ē, (,)in-,ek-(,)splik-ə-'bil-\ *n* — **in·ex·plic·a·ble·ness** *n* — **in·ex·plic·a·bly** \,in-ik-'splik-ə-blē, (')in-'ek-(,)splik-\ *adv*

in·ex·press·i·ble \,in-ik-'spres-ə-bəl\ *adj* : being beyond one's power to express : INDESCRIBABLE — **in·ex·press·i·bil·i·ty** \-,spres-ə-'bil-ət-ē\ *n* — **in·ex·press·i·ble·ness** *n* — **in·ex·press·i·bly** \-'spres-ə-blē\ *adv*

in ex·tre·mis \,in-ik-'strā-məs, -,mēs\ *adv* : in extreme circumstances; *esp* : at the point of death

in·ex·tric·a·ble \,in-ik-'strik-ə-bəl, (')in-'ek-(,)strik-\ *adj* 1 : forming a tangle from which one cannot free oneself 2 : not capable of being disentangled — **in·ex·tric·a·bly** \-blē\ *adv*

in·fal·li·ble \(')in-'fal-ə-bəl\ *adj* 1 : not capable of being wrong : UNERRING 2 : not liable to fail, deceive, or disappoint : SURE, CERTAIN — **in·fal·li·bil·i·ty** \(,)in-,fal-ə-'bil-ət-ē\ *n* — **in·fal·li·bly** \(')in-'fal-ə-blē\ *adv*

in·fa·mous \'in-fə-məs\ *adj* 1 : having an evil reputation 2 : DETESTABLE, DISGRACEFUL — **in·fa·mous·ly** *adv*

in·fa·my \-mē\ *n, pl* **-mies** 1 : evil reputation brought about by something grossly criminal, shocking, or brutal 2 **a** : an infamous act **b** : the state of being infamous

in·fan·cy \'in-fən-sē\ *n, pl* **-cies** 1 : early childhood 2 : a beginning or early period of existence

in·fant \'in-fənt\ *n* 1 : a child in the first period of life 2 : MINOR; *esp* : a person under the age of 21 — **infant** *adj*

in·fan·ti·cide \in-'fant-ə-,sīd\ *n* 1 : the killing of an infant 2 : one who kills an infant

in·fan·tile \'in-fən-,tīl, -təl, -,tēl\ *adj* : of, relating to, or resembling infants or infancy : CHILDISH — **in·fan·til·i·ty** \,in-fən-'til-ət-ē\ *n*

infantile paralysis *n* : POLIOMYELITIS

in·fan·til·ism \'in-fən-,tīl-,iz-əm, -təl-, -,tēl-\ *n* : retention of childish qualities in adult life

in·fan·try \'in-fən-trē\ *n, pl* **-tries** : soldiers trained, armed, and equipped to fight on foot — **in·fan·try·man** \-mən\ *n*

in·fat·u·ate \in-'fach-ə-,wāt\ *vt* : to inspire with a foolish or extravagant love or admiration — **in·fat·u·at·ed** *adj* — **in·fat·u·a·tion** \in-,fach-ə-'wā-shən\ *n*

in·fect \in-'fekt\ *vt* 1 : to contaminate with a disease-producing substance or organism 2 : to communicate a germ or disease to 3 **a** : CONTAMINATE, CORRUPT **b** : to work upon or seize upon so as to induce sympathy, belief, or support — **in·fec·tious** \-'fek-shəs\ *adj* — **in·fec·tious·ly** *adv* — **in·fec·tious·ness** *n* — **in·fec·tor** \-'fek-tər\ *n*

in·fec·tion \in-'fek-shən\ *n* 1 : an act or process of infecting 2 : the state produced by the establishment of a germ in or on a suitable host; *also* : a contagious or infectious disease 3 : an infective agent or material contaminated with an infective agent

in·fec·tive \in-'fek-tiv\ *adj* : producing or able to produce infection — **in·fec·tiv·i·ty** \(,)in-,fek-'tiv-ət-ē\ *n*

in·fe·lic·i·tous \,in-fi-'lis-ət-əs\ *adj* 1 : UNHAPPY, UNFORTUNATE 2 : not apt : not suitably chosen for the occasion — **in·fe·lic·i·tous·ly** *adv*

in·fe·lic·i·ty \-ət-ē\ *n, pl* **-ties** 1 : UNHAPPINESS, WRETCHEDNESS 2 : a lack of suitability or aptness 3 : an unsuitable or inappropriate act or utterance

in·fer \in-'fər\ *vt* **in·ferred**; **in·fer·ring** 1 : to derive as a conclusion from facts or premises 2 : GUESS, SURMISE 3 **a** : to involve as a normal outcome of thought **b** : to point out : INDICATE 4 : HINT, SUGGEST — **in·fer·a·ble** *or* **in·fer·ri·ble** \-'fər-ə-bəl\ *adj* — **in·fer·rer** *n*

in·fer·ence \'in-f(ə-)rən(t)s\ *n* 1 : the act or process of inferring 2 : something inferred

in·fe·ri·or \in-'fir-ē-ər\ *adj* 1 : situated lower down : LOWER 2 : of low or lower degree or rank 3 : of little or less importance, value, or merit — **inferior** *n* — **in·fe·ri·or·i·ty** \(,)in-,fir-ē-'ór-ət-ē\ *n* — **in·fe·ri·or·ly** *adv*

in·fer·nal \in-'fərn-ᵊl\ *adj* 1 **a** : of or relating to hell **b** : HELLISH, DIABOLICAL 2 : DAMNABLE — **in·fer·nal·ly** \-ᵊl-ē\ *adv*

in·fer·no \in-'fər-nō\ *n, pl* **-nos** : a place or a state that resembles or suggests hell esp. in intense heat or raging fire

in·fer·tile \(')in-'fərt-ᵊl\ *adj* : not fertile or productive : BARREN — **in·fer·til·i·ty** \,in-(,)fər-'til-ət-ē\ *n*

in·fest \in-'fest\ *vt* 1 : to spread or swarm in or over in a troublesome manner 2 : to live in or on as a parasite — **in·fes·ta·tion** \,in-,fes-'tā-shən\ *n* — **in·fest·er** *n*

in·fi·del \'in-fəd-ᵊl, -fə-,del\ *n* : a person who does not believe in a religion and esp. in Christianity — **infidel** *adj*

in·fi·del·i·ty \ˌin-fə-ˈdel-ət-ē, -fī-\ *n, pl* **-ties 1 :** lack of faith in a religion **2 :** unfaithfulness esp. to one's husband or wife
in·field \ˈin-ˌfēld\ *n* **:** the part of a baseball field enclosed by the three bases and home plate — **in·field·er** \-ˌfēl-dər\ *n*
in·fight·ing \ˈin-ˌfīt-iŋ\ *n* **1 :** fighting or boxing at close quarters **2 :** rough-and-tumble fighting — **in·fight·er** *n*
in·fil·trate \in-ˈfil-ˌtrāt, ˈin-(ˌ)fil-\ *vb* **1 :** to pass into or through by filtering or permeating **2 :** to enter or become established gradually or unobtrusively — **in·fil·tra·tion** \ˌin-(ˌ)fil-ˈtrā-shən\ *n* — **in·fil·tra·tor** \ˈin-(ˌ)fil-ˌtrāt-ər, in-ˈfil-\ *n*
in·fi·nite \ˈin-fə-nət\ *adj* **1 :** being without limits of any kind **:** ENDLESS **2 :** seeming to be without limits **:** VAST, INEXHAUSTIBLE **3 :** extending or lying beyond any preassigned value however large — **infinite** *n* — **in·fi·nite·ly** *adv* — **in·fi·nite·ness** *n*
in·fin·i·tes·i·mal \(ˌ)in-ˌfin-ə-ˈtes-ə-məl\ *adj* **1 :** arbitrarily small **2 :** immeasurably or incalculably small — **in·fin·i·tes·i·mal·ly** \-mə-lē\ *adv*
in·fin·i·tive \in-ˈfin-ət-iv\ *n* **:** a verb form having the characteristics of both verb and noun and in English usu. being used with *to* — **infinitive** *adj*
in·fin·i·tude \in-ˈfin-ə-ˌt(y)üd\ *n* **1 :** INFINITENESS **2 :** something infinite esp. in extent **3 :** an infinite number or quantity
in·fin·i·ty \in-ˈfin-ət-ē\ *n, pl* **-ties 1 a :** the quality of being infinite **b :** unlimited extent of time, space, or quantity **:** BOUNDLESSNESS **2 :** an indefinitely great number or amount
in·firm \in-ˈfərm\ *adj* **1 :** poor or weakened in vitality; *esp* **:** feeble from age **2 :** not solid or stable **:** INSECURE — **in·firm·ly** *adv*
in·fir·ma·ry \in-ˈfərm-(ə-)rē\ *n, pl* **-ries :** a place where the infirm or sick are lodged for care and treatment
in·fir·mi·ty \in-ˈfər-mət-ē\ *n, pl* **-ties :** the quality or state of being infirm: as **a :** FEEBLENESS, FRAILTY **b :** DISEASE, AILMENT **c :** a personal failing **:** FOIBLE
in·flame \in-ˈflām\ *vb* **1 :** to set on fire **:** KINDLE **2 a :** to excite to excessive or unnatural action or feeling **b :** to make more heated or violent **:** INTENSIFY **3 :** to cause to redden or grow hot from anger or excitement **4 :** to affect or become affected with inflammation
in·flam·ma·ble \in-ˈflam-ə-bəl\ *adj* **1 :** FLAMMABLE **2 :** easily inflamed **:** EXCITABLE — **in·flam·ma·bil·i·ty** \-ˌflam-ə-ˈbil-ət-ē\ *n* — **inflammable** *n* — **in·flam·ma·ble·ness** *n* — **in·flam·ma·bly** \-ˈflam-ə-blē\ *adv*
in·flam·ma·tion \ˌin-flə-ˈmā-shən\ *n* **1 :** the act of inflaming **:** the state of being inflamed **2 :** a bodily response to injury in which an affected area becomes red, hot, and painful and congested with blood
in·flam·ma·to·ry \in-ˈflam-ə-ˌtōr-ē\ *adj* **1 :** tending to excite anger, disorder, or tumult **:** SEDITIOUS **2 :** causing or accompanied by inflammation
in·flate \in-ˈflāt\ *vb* **1 :** to swell with air or gas **2 :** to puff up **:** ELATE **3 :** to increase abnormally — **in·flat·a·ble** *adj* — **in·fla·tor** \-ˈflāt-ər\ *n*
in·fla·tion \in-ˈflā-shən\ *n* **1 :** an act of inflating **:** the state of being inflated **2 :** an increase in the volume of money and credit relative to available goods resulting in a substantial and continuing rise in prices
in·fla·tion·ary \-shə-ˌner-ē\ *adj* **:** of, relating to, or tending to cause inflation
in·flect \in-ˈflekt\ *vb* **1 :** to turn from a direct line or course **:** CURVE **2 :** to vary a word by inflection **:** DECLINE, CONJUGATE **3 :** to vary the pitch of the voice **:** MODULATE
in·flec·tion \in-ˈflek-shən\ *n* **1 :** the act or result of curving or bending **2 :** a change in the pitch or tone of a person's voice **3 :** the change in the form of a word showing its case, gender, number, person, tense, mood, voice, or comparison — **in·flec·tion·al** \-shnəl, -shən-ᵊl\ *adj* — **in·flec·tion·al·ly** \-ē\ *adv*
in·flex·i·ble \(ˈ)in-ˈflek-sə-bəl\ *adj* **1 :** not easily bent or twisted **:** RIGID, STIFF **2 :** not easily influenced or persuaded **:** FIRM **3 :** incapable of change **:** UNALTERABLE — **in·flex·i·bil·i·ty** \(ˌ)in-ˌflek-sə-ˈbil-ət-ē\ *n* — **in·flex·i·bly** \(ˈ)in-ˈflek-sə-blē\ *adv*
in·flict \in-ˈflikt\ *vt* **1 a :** to give by striking **b :** to cause (something damaging or painful) to be endured **:** IMPOSE **2 :** AFFLICT — **in·flic·tive** \-ˈflik-tiv\ *adj*
in·flo·res·cence \ˌin-flə-ˈres-ᵊn(t)s\ *n* **:** the manner of development and arrangement of flowers on a stem; *also* **:** a flowering stem with its appendages **:** a flower cluster — **in·flo·res·cent** \-ᵊnt\ *adj*

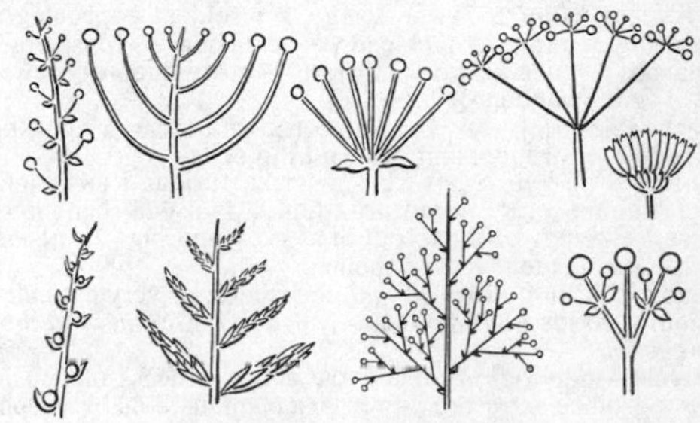

inflorescences of various forms

in·flow \ˈin-ˌflō\ *n* **1 :** the act of flowing in **2 :** something that flows in
[1]**in·flu·ence** \ˈin-ˌflü-ən(t)s\ *n* **1 :** the act or power of producing an effect without apparent exertion of force or direct exercise of command **2 :** corrupt interference with authority for personal gain **3 :** the power or capacity of causing an effect in indirect or intangible ways **:** SWAY **4 :** a person or thing that exerts influence
[2]**influence** *vt* **1 :** to affect or alter (as behavior) by indirect or intangible means **2 :** to have an effect on the condition or development of **:** MODIFY — **in·flu·enc·er** *n*
in·flu·en·tial \ˌin-flü-ˈen-chəl\ *adj* **:** having or exerting influence — **in·flu·en·tial·ly** \-ˈench-(ə-)lē\ *adv*
in·flu·en·za \ˌin-flü-ˈen-zə\ *n* **:** an acute and very contagious virus disease with sudden onset, fever, prostration, severe aches and pains, and inflammation of the respiratory tract
in·flux \ˈin-ˌfləks\ *n* **:** a flowing in **:** INFLOW
in·fold *vb* **1** \in-ˈfōld\ **:** ENFOLD **2** \ˈin-ˌfōld\ **:** to fold inward or toward one another
in·form \in-ˈfȯrm\ *vb* **1 :** to let a person know something **:** TELL **2 :** to give information so as to accuse or cast suspicion
in·for·mal \(ˈ)in-ˈfȯr-məl\ *adj* **1 :** conducted or carried out without formality or ceremony **2 :** appropriate for ordinary or casual use — **in·for·mal·i·ty** \ˌin-fȯr-ˈmal-ət-ē, -fər-\ *n* — **in·for·mal·ly** \(ˈ)in-ˈfȯr-mə-lē\ *adv*
in·form·ant \in-ˈfȯr-mənt\ *n* **:** INFORMER
in·for·ma·tion \ˌin-fər-ˈmā-shən\ *n* **1 :** the communication or reception of knowledge or intelligence **2 a :** knowledge obtained from investigation, study, or instruction **b :** INTELLIGENCE, NEWS **c :** FACTS, DATA — **in·for·ma·tion·al** \-shnəl, -shən-ᵊl\ *adj*
in·form·a·tive \in-ˈfȯr-mət-iv\ *adj* **:** imparting knowledge **:** INSTRUCTIVE — **in·form·a·tive·ly** *adv* — **in·form·a·tive·ness** *n*
in·form·a·to·ry \-mə-ˌtōr-ē\ *adj* **:** conveying information
in·formed \in-ˈfȯrmd\ *adj* **:** EDUCATED, INTELLIGENT
in·form·er \in-ˈfȯr-mər\ *n* **:** one that informs; *esp* **:** a person who informs against someone else
in·frac·tion \in-ˈfrak-shən\ *n* **:** the act of infringing **:** VIOLATION
in·fra dig \ˌin-frə-ˈdig\ *adj* **:** being beneath one's dignity **:** UNDIGNIFIED

in·fra·hu·man \ˌin-frə-ˈhyü-mən, -ˈyü-\ *adj* : less or lower than human — **infrahuman** *n*

in·fran·gi·ble \(ˈ)in-ˈfran-jə-bəl\ *adj* **1** : not capable of being broken or separated into parts **2** : not to be violated — **in·fran·gi·bil·i·ty** \(ˌ)in-ˌfran-jə-ˈbil-ət-ē\ *n* — **in·fran·gi·ble·ness** \(ˈ)in-ˈfran-jə-bəl-nəs\ *n* — **in·fran·gi·bly** \-blē\ *adv*

in·fra·red \ˌin-frə-ˈred\ *adj* : being or relating to invisible heat rays having wavelengths longer than those of red light — **infrared** *n*

in·fra·son·ic \-ˈsän-ik\ *adj* : having a frequency below the audibility range of the human ear

in·fre·quent \(ˈ)in-ˈfrē-kwənt\ *adj* **1** : seldom happening or occurring : RARE **2** : placed or occurring at considerable distances or intervals : OCCASIONAL — **in·fre·quen·cy** \-kwən-sē\ *n* — **in·fre·quent·ly** *adv*

in·fringe \in-ˈfrinj\ *vb* **1** : VIOLATE, TRANSGRESS **2** : ENCROACH — **in·fringe·ment** *n* — **in·fring·er** *n*

in·fu·ri·ate \in-ˈfyu̇r-ē-ˌāt\ *vt* : to make furious : ENRAGE — **in·fu·ri·at·ing·ly** *adv* — **in·fu·ri·a·tion** \-ˌfyu̇r-ē-ˈā-shən\ *n*

in·fuse \in-ˈfyüz\ *vt* **1** : to put in as if by pouring **2** : INSPIRE **3** : to steep (as tea) without boiling

in·fus·i·ble \(ˈ)in-ˈfyü-zə-bəl\ *adj* : incapable or very difficult of fusion — **in·fus·i·bil·i·ty** \(ˌ)in-ˌfyü-zə-ˈbil-ət-ē\ *n* — **in·fus·i·ble·ness** *n*

in·fu·sion \in-ˈfyü-zhən\ *n* **1** : the act or process of infusing **2** : a substance extracted esp. from a plant material by steeping or soaking in water

in·gath·er·ing \ˈin-ˌgath-(ə-)riŋ\ *n* **1** : COLLECTION, HARVEST **2** : ASSEMBLY

in·ge·nious \in-ˈjē-nyəs\ *adj* **1** : marked by especial aptitude at discovering, inventing, or contriving **2** : marked by originality, resourcefulness, and cleverness in conception or execution — **in·ge·nious·ly** *adv* — **in·ge·nious·ness** *n*

in·ge·nue *or* **in·gé·nue** \ˈan-jə-ˌnü, ˈaⁿ-zhə-\ *n* : a naïve girl or young woman; *esp* : an actress representing such a person

in·ge·nu·i·ty \ˌin-jə-ˈn(y)ü-ət-ē\ *n, pl* **-ties** **1 a** : skill or cleverness in devising or combining : INVENTIVENESS **b** : cleverness or aptness of design or contrivance **2** : an ingenious device or contrivance

in·gen·u·ous \in-ˈjen-yə-wəs\ *adj* **1** : STRAIGHTFORWARD, FRANK **2** : showing innocent or childlike simplicity : NAÏVE — **in·gen·u·ous·ly** *adv* — **in·gen·u·ous·ness** *n*

in·gest \in-ˈjest\ *vt* : to take in for or as if for digestion — **in·gest·i·ble** \-ˈjes-tə-bəl\ *adj* — **in·ges·tion** \-ˈjes-chən\ *n* — **in·ges·tive** \-ˈjes-tiv\ *adj*

in·gle \ˈiŋ-(g)əl\ *n* **1** : FLAME, BLAZE **2** : FIREPLACE

in·gle·nook \-ˌnu̇k\ *n* **1** : a corner by the fire or chimney **2** : a high-backed wooden settle placed close to a fireplace

in·glo·ri·ous \(ˈ)in-ˈglōr-ē-əs\ *adj* **1** : not glorious : lacking fame or honor **2** : bringing disgrace : SHAMEFUL — **in·glo·ri·ous·ly** *adv*

in·got \ˈiŋ-gət\ *n* : a mass of metal cast into a convenient shape for storage or transportation

¹in·grain \(ˈ)in-ˈgrān\ *vt* : to work indelibly into the natural texture or mental or moral constitution : IMBUE

²in·grain \ˈin-ˌgrān\ *adj* **1 a** : made of fiber that is dyed before being spun into yarn **b** : made of yarn that is dyed before being woven or knitted **2** : thoroughly worked in : INNATE — **ingrain** *n*

in·grained \ˈin-ˌgrānd, (ˈ)in-ˈ\ *adj* : worked into the grain or fiber : DEEP-SEATED

in·grate \ˈin-ˌgrāt\ *n* : an ungrateful person

in·gra·ti·ate \in-ˈgrā-shē-ˌāt\ *vt* : to gain favor or favorable acceptance for by deliberate effort — **in·gra·ti·a·tion** \-ˌgrā-shē-ˈā-shən\ *n*

in·gra·ti·at·ing \-ˌāt-iŋ\ *adj* **1** : capable of winning favor : PLEASING **2** : intended or adopted in order to gain favor : FLATTERING — **in·gra·ti·at·ing·ly** *adv*

in·grat·i·tude \(ˈ)in-ˈgrat-ə-ˌt(y)üd\ *n* : lack of gratitude or thankfulness : UNGRATEFULNESS

in·gre·di·ent \in-ˈgrēd-ē-ənt\ *n* : one of the substances that make up a mixture — **ingredient** *adj*

in·gress \ˈin-ˌgres\ *n* : ENTRANCE, ACCESS

in·grow·ing \ˈin-ˌgrō-iŋ\ *adj* : growing or tending inward

in·grown \-ˌgrōn\ *adj* : grown in; *esp* : having the free tip or edge embedded in the flesh

in·hab·it \in-ˈhab-ət\ *vt* : to live or dwell in — **in·hab·it·a·ble** *adj*

in·hab·it·ant \in-ˈhab-ət-ənt\ *n* : one who lives permanently in a place

in·hal·ant \in-ˈhā-lənt\ *n* : something (as an allergen or medicated spray) that is inhaled

in·ha·la·tion \ˌin-(h)ə-ˈlā-shən\ *n* : the act or an instance of inhaling — **in·ha·la·tion·al** \-shnəl, -shən-ᵊl\ *adj*

in·hale \in-ˈhāl\ *vb* **1** : to draw in by breathing **2** : to breathe in

in·hal·er \in-ˈhā-lər\ *n* : a device by means of which material can be inhaled

in·here \in-ˈhi(ə)r\ *vi* : to be inherent : BELONG

in·her·ent \in-ˈhir-ənt, -ˈher-\ *adj* : belonging to or being a part of the essential character of a person or thing : belonging by nature : INTRINSIC — **in·her·ence** \-ən(t)s\ *n* — **in·her·ent·ly** *adv*

in·her·it \in-ˈher-ət\ *vt* : to receive esp. from one's ancestors — **in·her·i·tor** \-ət-ər\ *n* — **in·her·i·tress** \-ə-trəs\ *or* **in·her·i·trix** \-ə-(ˌ)triks\ *n*

in·her·it·a·ble \in-ˈher-ət-ə-bəl\ *adj* : capable of being inherited : TRANSMISSIBLE — **in·her·it·a·ble·ness** *n*

in·her·it·ance \in-ˈher-ət-ən(t)s\ *n* **1** : the act of inheriting **2** : something that is or may be inherited

in·hib·it \in-ˈhib-ət\ *vt* **1** : to prohibit from doing something **2 a** : to hold in check : RESTRAIN **b** : to discourage from free or spontaneous activity : REPRESS — **in·hib·i·tive** \-ət-iv\ *adj* — **in·hib·i·tor** *or* **in·hib·it·er** \-ət-ər\ *n* — **in·hib·i·to·ry** \-ə-ˌtōr-ē\ *adj*

in·hi·bi·tion \ˌin-(h)ə-ˈbish-ən\ *n* **1 a** : the act of inhibiting : the state of being inhibited **b** : something that forbids or debars **2** : an inner impediment to free activity, expression, or functioning

in·hos·pi·tal·i·ty \(ˌ)in-ˌhäs-pə-ˈtal-ət-ē\ *n* : the quality or state of being inhospitable

in·hu·man \(ˈ)in-ˈhyü-mən, (ˈ)in-ˈyü-\ *adj* **1 a** : lacking pity or kindness : SAVAGE **b** : COLD, IMPERSONAL **c** : not worthy of or conforming to the needs of human beings **2** : of or suggesting a nonhuman class of beings — **in·hu·man·ly** *adv*

in·hu·mane \ˌin-hyü-ˈmān, ˌin-yü-\ *adj* : not humane : INHUMAN 1 — **in·hu·mane·ly** *adv*

in·hu·man·i·ty \-ˈman-ət-ē\ *n, pl* **-ties** **1** : the quality or state of being cruel or barbarous **2** : a cruel or barbarous act

in·hume \in-ˈhyüm\ *vt* : BURY, INTER

in·im·i·cal \in-ˈim-i-kəl\ *adj* **1 a** : having the disposition of an enemy : HOSTILE **b** : reflecting or indicating hostility : UNFRIENDLY **2** : HARMFUL, ADVERSE — **in·im·i·cal·ly** \-ˈim-i-k(ə-)lē\ *adv*

in·im·i·ta·ble \(ˈ)in-ˈim-ət-ə-bəl\ *adj* : not capable of being imitated : MATCHLESS — **in·im·i·ta·bil·i·ty** \(ˌ)in-ˌim-ət-ə-ˈbil-ət-ē\ *n* — **in·im·i·ta·ble·ness** \(ˈ)in-ˈim-ət-ə-bəl-nəs\ *n* — **in·im·i·ta·bly** \-blē\ *adv*

in·iq·ui·tous \in-ˈik-wət-əs\ *adj* : characterized by iniquity : WICKED — **in·iq·ui·tous·ly** *adv* — **in·iq·ui·tous·ness** *n*

in·iq·ui·ty \in-ˈik-wət-ē\ *n, pl* **-ties** **1** : gross injustice : WICKEDNESS **2** : an iniquitous act or thing : SIN

¹ini·tial \in-ˈish-əl\ *adj* **1** : of, relating to, or existing at the beginning : INCIPIENT **2** : placed or standing at the beginning : FIRST — **ini·tial·ly** \-ˈish-(ə-)lē\ *adv*

²initial *n* : the first letter of a word or name

[3]**initial** *vt* **ini·tialed** *or* **ini·tialled**; **ini·tial·ing** *or* **ini·tial·ling** \-'ish-(ə-)liŋ\ : to affix an initial to

[1]**ini·ti·ate** \in-'ish-ē-,āt\ *vt* **1** : to set going : ORIGINATE, START, BEGIN **2** : to instruct in the rudiments or principles of something : INTRODUCE **3** : to induct into membership by or as if by special rites — **ini·ti·a·tor** \-,āt-ər\ *n*

[2]**ini·tiate** \in-'ish-(ē-)ət\ *adj* : INITIATED

[3]**ini·tiate** \in-'ish-(ē-)ət\ *n* **1** : a person who is undergoing or has passed an initiation **2** : a person who is instructed or adept in a special field

ini·ti·a·tion \in-,ish-ē-'ā-shən\ *n* **1** : an initiating or a being initiated : INTRODUCTION **2** : the ceremonies with which a person is made a member of a society or club

ini·tia·tive \in-'ish-ət-iv\ *n* **1** : an introductory step or movement **2** : energy or aptitude displayed in initiation of action : ENTERPRISE **3** : a process by which laws may be introduced or enacted directly by vote of the people

ini·tia·to·ry \in-'ish-(ē-)ə-,tōr-ē\ *adj* **1** : constituting a beginning : INTRODUCTORY **2** : tending or serving to initiate

in·ject \in-'jekt\ *vt* **1 a** : to throw, drive, or force into something **b** : to force a fluid into esp. for medical purposes **2** : to introduce as an element or factor in or into some situation or subject — **in·jec·tor** \-'jek-tər\ *n*

in·jec·tion \in-'jek-shən\ *n* **1** : an act or instance of injecting (as by a syringe or pump) **2** : something (as a medication) that is injected

in·junc·tion \in-'jəŋ(k)-shən\ *n* **1** : the act or an instance of enjoining : ORDER, ADMONITION **2** : a writ granted by a court of equity requiring a party to do or refrain from doing a specified act — **in·junc·tive** \-'jəŋ(k)-tiv\ *adj*

in·jure \'in-jər\ *vt* **in·jured**; **in·jur·ing** \'inj-(ə-)riŋ\ **1 a** : to do an injustice to : WRONG **b** : to harm, impair, or tarnish the standing of **c** : to give pain to **2 a** : to inflict bodily hurt on **b** : to impair the soundness of **c** : to inflict material damage or loss on

in·ju·ri·ous \in-'jür-ē-əs\ *adj* : causing injury : HARMFUL — **in·ju·ri·ous·ly** *adv* — **in·ju·ri·ous·ness** *n*

in·ju·ry \'inj-(ə-)rē\ *n, pl* **-ries 1** : an act that damages or hurts : WRONG **2** : hurt, damage, or loss sustained

in·jus·tice \(')in-'jəs-təs\ *n* **1** : absence of justice : violation of the rights of another : UNFAIRNESS **2** : an unjust act or deed

[1]**ink** \'iŋk\ *n* : a usu. liquid and colored material for writing and printing

[2]**ink** *vt* : to put ink on — **ink·er** *n*

ink·horn \-,hórn\ *n* : a small portable bottle (as of horn) for holding ink

in·kling \'iŋ-kliŋ\ *n* **1** : HINT, INTIMATION **2** : a slight knowledge or vague notion

ink·stand \'iŋk-,stand\ *n* : INKWELL; *also* : a pen and inkwell

ink·well \-,wel\ *n* : a container for ink

inky \'iŋ-kē\ *adj* **1** : consisting of, using, or resembling ink **2** : soiled with ink **3** : of the color of ink : BLACK — **ink·i·ness** *n*

in·laid \'in-'lād\ *adj* **1** : set into a surface in a decorative design **2** : decorated with a design or material set into a surface

in·land \'in-,land, -lənd\ *n* : the interior part of a country : the land away from the coast or boundaries

[2]**inland** *adj* : of or relating to the interior of a country

[3]**inland** *adv* : into or toward the interior

in–law \'in-,lȯ\ *n* : a relative by marriage

[1]**in·lay** \(')in-'lā\ *vt* **in·laid**; **in·lay·ing** : to set into a surface or ground material for decoration or reinforcement — **in·lay·er** *n*

[2]**in·lay** \'in-,lā\ *n* **1** : inlaid work or material used in inlaying **2** : a shaped filling cemented into a tooth

in·let \'in-,let, -lət\ *n* **1** : an act of letting in **2 a** : a bay or recess in a shore; *also* : CREEK **b** : an opening for intake

in·ly \'in-lē\ *adv* **1** : INWARDLY, WITHIN **2** : INTIMATELY, THOROUGHLY

in·mate \'in-,māt\ *n* : one of a group occupying a single residence; *esp* : a person confined in an asylum, prison, or poorhouse

in me·di·as res \in-,mād-ē-,äs-'rās\ *adv* : in or into the middle of a narrative or plot

in me·mo·ri·am \,in-mə-'mōr-ē-əm\ *prep* : in memory of — used esp. in epitaphs

in·most \'in-,mōst\ *adj* : deepest within : INNERMOST

inn \'in\ *n* **1** : a public house that provides lodging and food for travelers : HOTEL **2** : TAVERN

in·nards \'in-ərdz\ *n pl* **1** : the internal organs of a man or animal; *esp* : VISCERA **2** : the internal parts of a structure or mechanism

in·nate \in-'āt, 'in-,\ *adj* **1** : existing in or belonging to an individual from birth : NATIVE **2** : belonging to the essential nature of something : INHERENT — **in·nate·ly** *adv* — **in·nate·ness** *n*

in·ner \'in-ər\ *adj* **1 a** : situated farther in **b** : near a center esp. of influence **2** : of or relating to the mind or spirit

in·ner·most \'in-ər-,mōst\ *adj* : farthest inward : INMOST

in·ner·sole \,in-ər-'sōl\ *n* : INSOLE

in·ner·vate \in-'ər-,vāt, 'in-(,)ər-\ *vt* : to supply with nerves — **in·ner·va·tion** \,in-(,)ər-'vā-shən\ *n*

in·ning \'in-iŋ\ *n* **1** : a baseball team's turn at bat ending with the 3d out; *also* : a division of a baseball game consisting of a turn at bat for each team **2** : a chance or turn for action or accomplishment

inn·keep·er \'in-,kē-pər\ *n* : the landlord of an inn

in·no·cence \'in-ə-sən(t)s\ *n* **1 a** : freedom from guilt, sin, or blame **b** : GUILELESSNESS, SIMPLICITY **c** : IGNORANCE **2** : BLUET

in·no·cent \-sənt\ *adj* **1** : free from sin : knowing nothing of evil : PURE **2** : free from guilt or blame : GUILTLESS **3** : free from evil influence or effect : HARMLESS **4** : ARTLESS, SIMPLE, UNSOPHISTICATED — **innocent** *n* — **in·no·cent·ly** *adv*

in·noc·u·ous \in-'äk-yə-wəs\ *adj* **1** : working no injury : HARMLESS **2 a** : not likely to give offense : INOFFENSIVE **b** : INSIPID, INSIGNIFICANT — **in·noc·u·ous·ly** *adv* — **in·noc·u·ous·ness** *n*

in·nom·i·nate \in-'äm-ə-nət\ *adj* : having no name : UNNAMED; *also* : ANONYMOUS

in·no·vate \'in-ə-,vāt\ *vb* **1** : to introduce as or as if new **2** : to make changes — **in·no·va·tor** \-,vāt-ər\ *n*

in·no·va·tion \,in-ə-'vā-shən\ *n* **1** : the introduction of something new **2** : a new idea, method, or device : NOVELTY

in·nu·en·do \,in-yə-'wen-dō\ *n, pl* **-dos** *or* **-does** : an oblique allusion : HINT, INSINUATION; *esp* : a veiled or equivocal reflection on character or reputation

in·nu·mer·a·ble \in-'(y)üm-(ə-)rə-bəl\ *adj* : too many to be numbered : COUNTLESS — **in·nu·mer·a·bly** \-blē\ *adv*

in·oc·u·late \in-'äk-yə-,lāt\ *vt* : to introduce something into; *esp* : to treat usu. with a serum or antibody to prevent or cure a disease — **in·oc·u·la·tion** \-,äk-yə-'lā-shən\ *n* — **in·oc·u·la·tive** \-'äk-yə-,lāt-iv\ *adj* — **in·oc·u·la·tor** \-,lāt-ər\ *n*

in·op·er·a·ble \(')in-'äp-(ə-)rə-bəl\ *adj* **1** : not suitable for surgery **2** : not operable

in·op·er·a·tive \-'äp-(ə-)rət-iv, -'äp-ə-,rāt-\ *adj* : not functioning : producing no effect — **in·op·er·a·tive·ness** *n*

in·op·por·tune \(,)in-,äp-ər-'t(y)ün\ *adj* : INCONVENIENT, UNSEASONABLE — **in·op·por·tune·ly** *adv* — **in·op·por·tune·ness** *n*

in order that *conj* : THAT

in·or·di·nate \in-'ȯrd-ən-ət, -'ȯrd-nət\ *adj* : not kept within bounds : IMMODERATE — **in·or·di·nate·ly** *adv*

in·or·gan·ic \,in-ȯr-'gan-ik\ *adj* : being or composed of matter of other than plant or animal origin : MINERAL — **in·or·gan·i·cal·ly** \-'gan-i-k(ə-)lē\ *adv*

in·pa·tient \'in-,pā-shənt\ *n* : a hospital patient who receives lodging and food as well as treatment

in·put \ˈin-ˌpu̇t\ *n* : something that is put in; *esp* : power or energy put into a machine or system
in·quest \ˈin-ˌkwest\ *n* **1** : a judicial or official inquiry or investigation esp. before a jury **2** : the finding of an inquest
in·qui·e·tude \(ˈ)in-ˈkwī-ə-ˌt(y)üd\ *n* : disturbed state : UNEASINESS, RESTLESSNESS
in·quire \in-ˈkwī(ə)r\ *vb* **1** : to ask about **2** : to make investigation or inquiry : search into : INVESTIGATE **3** : to put a question — **in·quir·er** *n* — **in·quir·ing·ly** *adv* — **inquire after** : to ask about the health of
in·qui·ry \ˈin-ˌkwī(ə)r-ē, in-ˈ; ˈin-kwə-rē, ˈiŋ-\ *n, pl* **-ries** **1 a** : the act of inquiring **b** : a request for information **2** : a search for truth or knowledge **3** : a systematic examination : INVESTIGATION
in·qui·si·tion \ˌin-kwə-ˈzish-ən\ *n* **1** : the act of inquiring **2** : a judicial or official inquiry **3 a** *cap* : a former Roman Catholic tribunal for the discovery and punishment of heresy **b** : an investigation conducted with little regard for individual rights **c** : a severe questioning — **in·qui·si·tion·al** \-ˈzish-nəl, -ən-ᵊl\ *adj*
in·quis·i·tive \in-ˈkwiz-ət-iv\ *adj* **1** : given to examination or investigation **2** : QUESTIONING; *esp* : PRYING — **in·quis·i·tive·ly** *adv* — **in·quis·i·tive·ness** *n*
in·quis·i·tor \in-ˈkwiz-ət-ər\ *n* : one who inquires or conducts an inquisition — **in·quis·i·to·ri·al** \-ˌkwiz-ə-ˈtōr-ē-əl\ *adj* — **in·quis·i·to·ri·al·ly** \-ē-ə-lē\ *adv*
in re \in-ˈrē, -ˈrā\ *prep* : in the matter of : CONCERNING, RE
in·road \ˈin-ˌrōd\ *n* **1** : a sudden hostile incursion : RAID **2** : a serious encroachment
in·rush \ˈin-ˌrəsh\ *n* : a crowding or flooding in : INFLUX
in·sane \(ˈ)in-ˈsān\ *adj* **1** : not sane : unsound in mind : MAD, CRAZY **2** : showing evidence of an unsound mind **3** : used by or for the insane **4** : FOOLISH, WILD — **in·sane·ly** *adv*
in·san·i·tary \(ˈ)in-ˈsan-ə-ˌter-ē\ *adj* : unclean enough to endanger health : CONTAMINATED
in·san·i·ty \in-ˈsan-ət-ē\ *n, pl* **-ties** **1 a** : unsoundness or derangement of the mind **b** : a mental disorder **2** : such unsoundness of mind as excuses one from criminal or civil responsibility **3 a** : extreme folly or unreasonableness **b** : something utterly foolish or unreasonable
in·sa·tia·ble \(ˈ)in-ˈsā-shə-bəl\ *adj* : incapable of being satisfied : QUENCHLESS — **in·sa·tia·bly** \-blē\ *adv*
in·sa·tiate \-ˈsā-sh(ē-)ət\ *adj* : not satiated or satisfied; *also* : INSATIABLE — **in·sa·tiate·ly** *adv*
in·scribe \in-ˈskrīb\ *vt* **1 a** : to write, engrave, or print as a lasting record **b** : ENROLL **2 a** : to write, engrave, or print characters on **b** : to autograph or address as a gift **c** : to stamp deeply : IMPRESS **3** : to dedicate (as a poem) to someone — **in·scrib·er** *n*
in·scrip·tion \in-ˈskrip-shən\ *n* **1** : something that is inscribed; *also* : TITLE, SUPERSCRIPTION **2** : the wording on a coin, medal, or seal **3** : the dedication of a book or work of art — **in·scrip·tion·al** \-shnəl, -shən-ᵊl\ *adj*
in·scru·ta·ble \in-ˈskrüt-ə-bəl\ *adj* : not readily understood : ENIGMATIC — **in·scru·ta·bil·i·ty** \-ˌskrüt-ə-ˈbil-ət-ē\ *n* — **in·scru·ta·ble·ness** \-ˈskrüt-ə-bəl-nəs\ *n* — **in·scru·ta·bly** \-blē\ *adv*
in·seam \ˈin-ˌsēm\ *n* : an inner seam of a garment or shoe
in·sect \ˈin-ˌsekt\ *n* : any of a major group of small usu. winged animals with three pairs of legs including the flies, bees, beetles, and moths
in·sec·ti·cide \in-ˈsek-tə-ˌsīd\ *n* : an agent that destroys insects — **in·sec·ti·ci·dal** \-ˌsek-tə-ˈsīd-ᵊl\ *adj*
in·sec·tiv·o·rous \ˌin-ˌsek-ˈtiv-(ə-)rəs\ *adj* : depending on insects as food
in·se·cure \ˌin(t)-si-ˈkyu̇(ə)r\ *adj* **1** : UNCERTAIN, UNSURE **2** : UNPROTECTED, UNSAFE **3** : LOOSE, SHAKY **4** : lacking stability : INFIRM **5** : beset by fear or anxiety — **in·se·cure·ly** *adv* — **in·se·cure·ness** *n* — **in·se·cu·ri·ty** \-ˈkyu̇r-ət-ē\ *n*
in·sen·sate \(ˈ)in-ˈsen-ˌsāt\ *adj* **1** : lacking animate awareness or sensation **2** : lacking sense or understanding; *also* : FOOLISH **3** : UNFEELING, BRUTAL, INHUMAN — **in·sen·sate·ly** *adv* — **in·sen·sate·ness** *n*
in·sen·si·ble \(ˈ)in-ˈsen(t)-sə-bəl\ *adj* **1** : incapable or bereft of feeling or sensation: as **a** : INANIMATE, INSENTIENT **b** : UNCONSCIOUS **c** : lacking or deprived of sensory perception **2 a** : IMPERCEPTIBLE **b** : SLIGHT, GRADUAL **3** : APATHETIC, INDIFFERENT; *also* : UNAWARE **4** : not intelligible : MEANINGLESS **5** : lacking delicacy or refinement — **in·sen·si·bil·i·ty** \(ˌ)in-ˌsen(t)-sə-ˈbil-ət-ē\ *n* — **in·sen·si·ble·ness** \(ˈ)in-ˈsen(t)-sə-bəl-nəs\ *n* — **in·sen·si·bly** \-blē\ *adv*
in·sep·a·ra·ble \(ˈ)in-ˈsep-(ə-)rə-bəl\ *adj* : incapable of being separated or disjoined — **in·sep·a·ra·bil·i·ty** \(ˌ)in-ˌsep-ə-rə-ˈbil-ət-ē\ *n* — **inseparable** *n* — **in·sep·a·ra·bly** \(ˈ)in-ˈsep-(ə-)rə-blē\ *adv*
[1]**in·sert** \in-ˈsərt\ *vb* **1** : to put or thrust in **2** : to put or introduce into the body of : INTERPOLATE **3** : to set in and make fast; *esp* : to insert by sewing between two cut edges — **in·sert·er** *n*
[2]**in·sert** \ˈin-ˌsərt\ *n* : something that is inserted or is for insertion; *esp* : written or printed material inserted (as between the leaves of a book)
in·ser·tion \in-ˈsər-shən\ *n* **1** : the act or process of inserting **2** : something that is inserted — **in·ser·tion·al** \-shnəl, -shən-ᵊl\ *adj*
[1]**in·set** \ˈin-ˌset\ *n* : something that is inset
[2]**in·set** \ˈin-ˌset, in-ˈ\ *vt* **inset** *or* **in·set·ted**; **in·set·ting** : to set in
[1]**in·shore** \ˈin-ˈshō(ə)r\ *adj* **1** : situated or carried on near shore **2** : moving toward shore
[2]**inshore** *adv* : to or toward shore
[1]**in·side** \(ˈ)in-ˈsīd, ˈin-ˌ\ *n* **1** : an inner side or surface **2 a** : inward nature, thoughts, or feeling **b** : VISCERA, ENTRAILS — usu. used in pl. — **inside** *adj*
[2]**inside** *prep* **1 a** : in or into the interior of **b** : on the inner side of **2** : before the end of : WITHIN
[3]**inside** *adv* **1** : on the inner side **2** : in or into the interior
inside of *prep* : INSIDE
in·sid·er \(ˈ)in-ˈsīd-ər\ *n* : a person who has access to confidential information
in·sid·i·ous \in-ˈsid-ē-əs\ *adj* **1 a** : awaiting a chance to entrap : TREACHEROUS **b** : harmful but enticing : SEDUCTIVE **2** : having a gradual and cumulative effect — **in·sid·i·ous·ly** *adv* — **in·sid·i·ous·ness** *n*
in·sight \ˈin-ˌsīt\ *n* **1** : the power or act of seeing into a situation : PENETRATION **2** : the act of apprehending the inner nature of things or of seeing intuitively
in·sig·nia \in-ˈsig-nē-ə\ *or* **in·sig·ne** \-(ˌ)nē\ *n, pl* **-nia** *or* **-ni·as** : a distinguishing mark esp. of authority, office, or honor : BADGE, EMBLEM
in·sig·nif·i·cance \ˌin(t)-sig-ˈnif-i-kən(t)s\ *n* : the quality or state of being insignificant
in·sin·u·ate \in-ˈsin-yə-ˌwāt\ *vt* **1 a** : to introduce (as an idea) gradually or in a subtle, indirect, or covert way **b** : HINT, IMPLY **2** : to introduce (as oneself) by stealthy, smooth, or artful means — **in·sin·u·a·tive** \-ˌwāt-iv\ *adj* — **in·sin·u·a·tor** \-ˌwāt-ər\ *n*
in·sin·u·at·ing \-ˌwāt-iŋ\ *adj* **1** : tending gradually to cause doubt, distrust, or change of outlook **2** : winning favor and confidence by imperceptible degrees — **in·sin·u·at·ing·ly** *adv*
in·sin·u·a·tion \in-ˌsin-yə-ˈwā-shən\ *n* **1** : a subtle suggestion : INNUENDO **2** : the artful pursuit of favor : INGRATIATION
in·sip·id \in-ˈsip-əd\ *adj* **1** : lacking taste or savor : TASTELESS **2** : lacking in qualities that interest, stimulate, or challenge : DULL, FLAT — **in·si·pid·i·ty** \ˌin(t)-sə-ˈpid-ət-ē\ *n* — **in·sip·id·ly** *adv*

in·sist \in-'sist\ *vb* **1** : to place special emphasis or great importance **2** : to make a demand : request urgently
in·sist·ence \in-'sis-tən(t)s\ *n* **1** : the act of insisting **2** : the quality or state of being insistent : URGENCY
in·sist·ent \-tənt\ *adj* : compelling attention : PERSISTENT — **in·sist·ent·ly** *adv*
in si·tu \in-'sī-tü\ *adv* (*or adj*) : in the natural or original position
in·so·far as \'in(t)-sə-ˌfär-əz\ *conj* : to the extent or degree that
in·sole \'in-ˌsōl\ *n* **1** : an inside sole of a shoe **2** : a loose thin strip placed inside a shoe for warmth or comfort
in·so·lence \'in(t)-sə-lən(t)s\ *n* : a haughty attitude or insulting act
in·so·lent \-lənt\ *adj* **1** : arrogant in speech or conduct **2** : exhibiting boldness or effrontery — **in·so·lent·ly** *adv*
in·solv·a·ble \(')in-'säl-və-bəl, -'sȯl-\ *adj* : admitting no solution — **in·solv·a·bly** \-blē\ *adv*
in·sol·vent \(')in-'säl-vənt\ *adj* **1** : unable or having ceased to pay debts as they fall due **2** : insufficient to pay all debts **3** : IMPOVERISHED, DEFICIENT — **in·sol·ven·cy** \-vən-sē\ *n* — **insolvent** *n*
in·som·nia \in-'säm-nē-ə\ *n* : prolonged and usu. abnormal inability to get enough sleep — **in·som·ni·ac** \-nē-ˌak\ *adj or n*
in·so·much as \'in(t)-sə-ˌməch-əz\ *conj* : inasmuch as
insomuch that \-ˌməch-t͟hət\ *conj* : to such a degree that : so that
in·sou·ci·ance \in-'sü-sē-ən(t)s\ *n* : a lighthearted unconcern : NONCHALANCE — **in·sou·ci·ant** \-ənt\ *adj* — **in·sou·ci·ant·ly** *adv*
in·spect \in-'spekt\ *vb* **1** : to examine closely (as for judging quality) **2** : to view and examine (as troops) officially
in·spec·tion \in-'spek-shən\ *n* **1** : EXAMINATION **2** : a checking or testing of an individual against established standards
in·spec·tor \in-'spek-tər\ *n* : a person employed to make inspections — **in·spec·tor·ate** \-t(ə-)rət\ *n* — **in·spec·tor·ship** \-tər-ˌship\ *n*
in·spi·ra·tion \ˌin(t)-spə-'rā-shən\ *n* **1** : INHALATION **2** : the act or power of moving the intellect or emotions **3 a** : the quality or state of being inspired **b** : something that is inspired **4** : an inspiring agent or influence — **in·spi·ra·tion·al** \-shnəl, -shən-ᵊl\ *adj* — **in·spi·ra·tion·al·ly** \-ē\ *adv* — **in·spi·ra·to·ry** \(')in-'spī-rə-ˌtōr-ē\ *adj*
in·spire \in-'spī(ə)r\ *vb* **1 a** (1) : to move or guide by divine or supernatural influence (2) : to exert an animating, enlivening, or exalting influence on **b** : AFFECT **2** : INHALE **3 a** : to communicate to an agent supernaturally **b** : AROUSE **4** : to bring about : OCCASION **5** : to spread (rumor) by indirect means or through another — **in·spir·er** *n*
in·spir·it \in-'spir-ət\ *vt* : ANIMATE, HEARTEN
in·sta·bil·i·ty \ˌin(t)-stə-'bil-ət-ē\ *n* : the quality or state of being unstable
in·sta·ble \(')in-'stā-bəl\ *adj* : UNSTABLE
in·stall *or* **in·stal** \in-'stȯl\ *vt* **in·stalled**; **in·stall·ing** **1** : to place formally in office : induct into an office, rank, or order **2** : to establish in an indicated place, condition, or status **3** : to set up for use or service — **in·stall·er** *n*
in·stal·la·tion \ˌin(t)-stə-'lā-shən\ *n* **1** : the act of installing : the state of being installed **2** : something that is installed for use **3** : a military camp, fort, or base
in·stall·ment *or* **in·stal·ment** \in-'stȯl-mənt\ *n* : INSTALLATION 1
installment *also* **instalment** *n* **1** : one of the parts into which a debt is divided when payment is made at intervals **2** : one of several parts (as of a publication) presented at intervals — **installment** *adj*
in·stance \'in(t)-stən(t)s\ *n* **1** : SUGGESTION, REQUEST **2** : EXAMPLE **3** : OCCASION, CASE — **for instance** : as an example
instance *vt* **1** : to illustrate or demonstrate by an instance **2** : to mention as a case or example : CITE
¹in·stant \'in(t)-stənt\ *n* : a very small space of time : MOMENT
²instant *adj* **1** : IMPORTUNATE, URGENT **2** : IMMEDIATE, DIRECT **3 a** : partially prepared by the manufacturer to make final preparation easy **b** : immediately soluble in water — **in·stant·ness** *n*
in·stan·ta·ne·ous \ˌin(t)-stən-'tā-nē-əs\ *adj* **1** : done, occurring, or acting without any perceptible duration of time **2** : done without any delay being introduced purposely **3** : occurring or present at a particular instant — **in·stan·ta·ne·ous·ly** *adv* — **in·stan·ta·ne·ous·ness** *n*
in·stan·ter \in-'stant-ər\ *adv* : at once : INSTANTLY
in·stant·ly \'in(t)-stənt-lē\ *adv* **1** : IMPORTUNATELY, URGENTLY **2** : without the least delay : IMMEDIATELY
in·state \in-'stāt\ *vt* : to set or establish in a rank or office : INSTALL
in sta·tu quo \in-ˌstā-tü-'kwō\ : in the former or same state
in·stead \in-'sted\ *adv* **1** : as a substitute or equivalent **2** : as an alternative to something expressed or implied : RATHER
instead of \in-ˌsted-ə(v), -ˌstid-\ *prep* : as a substitute for or alternative to
in·step \'in-ˌstep\ *n* : the arched middle part of the human foot in front of the ankle joint
in·sti·gate \'in(t)-stə-ˌgāt\ *vt* : to goad or urge forward : set on — **in·sti·ga·tion** \ˌin(t)-stə-'gā-shən\ *n* — **in·sti·ga·tive** \'in(t)-stə-ˌgāt-iv\ *adj* — **in·sti·ga·tor** \-ˌgāt-ər\ *n*
in·still \in-'stil\ *vt* **in·stilled**; **in·still·ing** **1** : to cause to enter drop by drop **2** : to impart gradually — **in·stil·la·tion** \ˌin(t)-stə-'lā-shən\ *n* — **in·still·er** *n* — **in·still·ment** *n*
¹in·stinct \'in-ˌstiŋ(k)t\ *n* **1** : a natural aptitude, impulse, or capacity **2 a** : complex but unreasoned response by an organism to environmental stimuli that is largely hereditary and unalterable **b** : behavior based on reactions below the conscious level — **in·stinc·tu·al** \in-'stiŋ(k)-chə(-wə)l\ *adj*
²in·stinct \in-'stiŋ(k)t, 'in-ˌ\ *adj* : FILLED, INFUSED
in·stinc·tive \in-'stiŋ(k)-tiv\ *adj* : of, relating to, or prompted by instinct — **in·stinc·tive·ly** *adv*
¹in·sti·tute \'in(t)-stə-ˌt(y)üt\ *vt* **1** : to set up : ESTABLISH, FOUND **2** : INAUGURATE, BEGIN
²institute *n* **1 a** : an elementary principle recognized as authoritative **b** *pl* : a collection of such principles and precepts **2 a** : an organization for the promotion of a cause : ASSOCIATION **b** : an educational institution **3** : a meeting for instruction or a brief course of such meetings
in·sti·tu·tion \ˌin(t)-stə-'t(y)ü-shən\ *n* **1** : the act of instituting : ESTABLISHMENT **2** : an established custom, practice, or law **3** : an established society or corporation; *esp* : a public one — **in·sti·tu·tion·al** \-shnəl, -shən-ᵊl\ *adj*
in·sti·tu·tion·al·ize \-'t(y)ü-shnə-ˌlīz, -shən-ᵊl-ˌīz\ *vt* **1** : to make into or treat like an institution **2** : to put in the care of an institution
in·struct \in-'strəkt\ *vt* **1** : to impart knowledge to : TEACH **2** : to give information to : INFORM **3** : to give directions or commands to
in·struct·ed \-'strək-təd\ *adj* **1** : TAUGHT, INFORMED **2** : subject to specific instructions
in·struc·tion \in-'strək-shən\ *n* **1 a** : LESSON **b** : COMMAND, ORDER **c** *pl* : an outline or manual of procedure to be followed : DIRECTIONS **2** : the action or practice of an instructor or teacher — **in·struc·tion·al** \-shnəl, -shən-ᵊl\ *adj*
in·struc·tive \in-'strək-tiv\ *adj* : giving knowledge : serving to instruct or inform — **in·struc·tive·ly** *adv*
in·struc·tor \-tər\ *n* : one that instructs : TEACHER; *esp* : a college teacher below professorial rank — **in·struc·tor·ship** \-ˌship\ *n* — **in·struc·tress** \-'strək-trəs\ *n*
in·stru·ment \'in(t)-strə-mənt\ *n* **1** : a means whereby something is achieved, performed, or furthered **2 a** : UTENSIL, IMPLEMENT, TOOL **b** : a device used to produce music **3** : a

formal legal document (as a deed) **4** : a device used in navigating an airplane

in·stru·men·tal \ˌin(t)-strə-ˈment-ᵊl\ *adj* **1** : acting as an instrument or means **2** : having to do with an instrument : designed for or performed with or on an instrument and esp. a musical instrument — **in·stru·men·tal·ly** \-ᵊl-ē\ *adv*

in·stru·men·tal·ist \-ᵊl-əst\ *n* : a player on a musical instrument

in·stru·men·tal·i·ty \ˌin(t)-strə-mən-ˈtal-ət-ē, -ˌmen-\ *n, pl* **-ties** **1** : the quality or state of being instrumental **2** : MEANS, AGENCY

in·stru·men·ta·tion \ˌin(t)-strə-mən-ˈtā-shən, -ˌmen-\ *n* **1** : the use or application of instruments for observation, measurement, or control **2** : the arrangement or composition of music for the instruments esp. of a band or orchestra **3** : instruments for a particular purpose

in·sub·or·di·nate \ˌin(t)-sə-ˈbȯrd-ᵊn-ət, -ˈbȯrd-nət\ *adj* : unwilling to submit to authority : DISOBEDIENT, REBELLIOUS — **in·sub·or·di·nate·ly** *adv* — **in·sub·or·di·na·tion** \ˌin(t)-sə-ˌbȯrd-ᵊn-ˈā-shən\ *n*

in·sub·stan·tial \ˌin(t)-səb-ˈstan-chəl\ *adj* **1** : lacking substance or reality : IMAGINARY **2** : lacking firmness or solidity — **in·sub·stan·ti·al·i·ty** \-ˌstan-chē-ˈal-ət-ē\ *n*

in·suf·fer·a·ble \(ˈ)in-ˈsəf-(ə-)rə-bəl\ *adj* : incapable of being endured : INTOLERABLE — **in·suf·fer·a·ble·ness** *n* — **in·suf·fer·a·bly** \-blē\ *adv*

in·suf·fi·cien·cy \ˌin(t)-sə-ˈfish-ən-sē\ *n, pl* **-cies** **1** : the quality or state of being insufficient **2** : something insufficient

in·suf·fi·cient \-ˈfish-ənt\ *adj* : not sufficient : INADEQUATE; *also* : INCOMPETENT — **in·suf·fi·cient·ly** *adv*

in·su·lar \ˈin(t)s-(y)ə-lər, ˈin-shə-lər\ *adj* **1** : of, relating to, or forming an island **2** : ISOLATED, DETACHED **3** : of or relating to the inhabitants of islands **4** : being isolated and illiberal : NARROW — **in·su·lar·ism** \-lə-ˌriz-əm\ *n* — **in·su·lar·i·ty** \ˌin(t)s-(y)ə-ˈlar-ət-ē, ˌin-shə-ˈlar-\ *n* — **in·su·lar·ly** *adv*

in·su·late \ˈin(t)-sə-ˌlāt\ *vt* : to place in a detached situation : ISOLATE; *esp* : to separate from conducting bodies by means of nonconductors so as to prevent transfer of electricity, heat, or sound

in·su·la·tion \ˌin(t)-sə-ˈlā-shən\ *n* **1** : the act of insulating : the state of being insulated **2** : material used in insulating

in·su·la·tor \ˈin(t)-sə-ˌlāt-ər\ *n* : one that insulates; *esp* : a material that is a poor conductor of electricity or a device made of such material

in·su·lin \ˈin(t)-s(ə-)lən\ *n* : a protein pancreatic hormone essential esp. for the metabolism of carbohydrates and used in the treatment and control of diabetes

¹in·sult \in-ˈsəlt\ *vt* **1** : to treat with insolence, indignity, or contempt : AFFRONT **2** : to make little of : BELITTLE — **in·sult·er** *n*

²in·sult \ˈin-ˌsəlt\ *n* : an act or speech showing disrespect or contempt

in·su·per·a·ble \(ˈ)in-ˈsü-p(ə-)rə-bəl\ *adj* : incapable of being surmounted, overcome, or passed over — **in·su·per·a·bly** \-blē\ *adv*

in·sur·a·ble \in-ˈshu̇r-ə-bəl\ *adj* : capable of being insured against loss, damage, or death

in·sur·ance \in-ˈshu̇r-ən(t)s\ *n* **1** : the act of insuring : the state of being insured **2 a** : the business of insuring persons or property **b** : coverage by contract whereby one party undertakes to guarantee another against loss by a specified event or peril **c** : the sum for which something is insured

in·sure \in-ˈshu̇(ə)r\ *vt* **1** : to give or procure insurance on or for **2** : to make certain : ENSURE

in·sured \-ˈshu̇(ə)rd\ *n* : a person whose life or property is insured

in·sur·er \in-ˈshu̇r-ər\ *n* : one that insures; *esp* : a company issuing insurance

in·sur·gence \in-ˈsər-jən(t)s\ *n* : UPRISING, INSURRECTION

in·sur·gen·cy \-jən-sē\ *n* **1** : the quality or state of being insurgent; *esp* : a state of revolt against a government that is less than an organized revolution **2** : INSURGENCE

¹in·sur·gent \in-ˈsər-jənt\ *n* : a person who revolts; *esp* : a rebel not recognized as a belligerent

²insurgent *adj* : rising in opposition to authority : REBELLIOUS — **in·sur·gent·ly** *adv*

in·sur·mount·a·ble \ˌin(t)-sər-ˈmau̇nt-ə-bəl\ *adj* : incapable of being surmounted : INSUPERABLE — **in·sur·mount·a·bly** \-blē\ *adv*

in·sur·rec·tion \ˌin(t)-sə-ˈrek-shən\ *n* : an act or instance of revolting against civil authority or an established government — **in·sur·rec·tion·ary** \-shə-ˌner-ē\ *adj or n* — **in·sur·rec·tion·ist** \-shə-nəst\ *n*

in·tact \in-ˈtakt\ *adj* : untouched esp. by anything that harms or diminishes : ENTIRE, UNINJURED — **in·tact·ness** *n*

in·ta·glio \in-ˈtal-yō\ *n, pl* **-glios** : an engraving or incised figure in a hard material (as stone) depressed below the surface of the material

in·take \ˈin-ˌtāk\ *n* **1** : a place where liquid or air is taken into something (as a pump) **2** : the act of taking in **3** : something taken in

in·tan·gi·ble \(ˈ)in-ˈtan-jə-bəl\ *adj* : not tangible: as **a** : incapable of being touched **b** : incapable of being thought of as matter or substance : ABSTRACT — **in·tan·gi·bil·i·ty** \(ˌ)in-ˌtan-jə-ˈbil-ət-ē\ *n* — **intangible** *n* — **in·tan·gi·bly** \(ˈ)in-ˈtan-jə-blē\ *adv*

in·te·ger \ˈint-i-jər\ *n* : a number (as 1, 2, or 3) that is not a fraction and does not include a fraction, is the negative of such a number, or is 0

¹in·te·gral \ˈint-i-grəl (*usu so in mathematics*); in-ˈteg-rəl -ˈtēg-\ *adj* **1** : essential to completeness : CONSTITUENT **2** : formed as a unit with another part **3** : composed of integral parts : INTEGRATED **4** : lacking nothing essential : ENTIRE — **in·te·gral·ly** \ˈint-i-grə-lē; in-ˈteg-rə-, -ˈtēg-\ *adv*

²integral *n* : a whole number

in·te·grate \ˈint-ə-ˌgrāt\ *vb* **1** : to form into a whole : UNITE **2** : to incorporate into a larger unit **3** : to end the segregation of and bring into common and equal membership in society or an organization — **in·te·gra·tion** \ˌint-ə-ˈgrā-shən\ *n*

in·te·gra·tion·ist \ˌint-ə-ˈgrā-sh(ə-)nəst\ *n* : a person who believes in, advocates, or practices integration

in·teg·ri·ty \in-ˈteg-rət-ē\ *n* **1** : an unimpaired condition : SOUNDNESS **2** : adherence to a code of moral, artistic, or other values **3** : the quality or state of being complete or undivided : COMPLETENESS

in·teg·u·ment \in-ˈteg-yə-mənt\ *n* : something that covers or encloses; *esp* : an enveloping layer (as a skin, membrane, or husk) of an organism or one of its parts

in·tel·lect \ˈint-ᵊl-ˌekt\ *n* **1 a** : the power of knowing **b** : the capacity for thought esp. when highly developed **2** : a person of notable intellect

in·tel·lec·tion \ˌint-ᵊl-ˈek-shən\ *n* **1** : exercise of the intellect : REASONING **2** : a specific act of the intellect : THOUGHT — **in·tel·lec·tive** \-ˈek-tiv\ *adj* — **in·tel·lec·tive·ly** *adv*

in·tel·lec·tu·al \ˌint-ᵊl-ˈek-ch(ə-w)əl\ *adj* **1 a** : having to do with the intellect or understanding **b** : performed by the intellect **2** : having intellect to a high degree : engaged in or given to learning and thinking **3** : requiring study and thought — **intellectual** *n* — **in·tel·lec·tu·al·i·ty** \-ˌek-chə-ˈwal-ət-ē\ *n* — **in·tel·lec·tu·al·ly** \-ˈek-ch(ə-w)ə-lē\ *adv*

in·tel·lec·tu·al·ism \ˌint-ᵊl-ˈek-chə(-wə)-ˌliz-əm\ *n* : devotion to the exercise of intellect or to intellectual pursuits

in·tel·li·gence \in-ˈtel-ə-jən(t)s\ *n* **1 a** : the ability to learn and understand or to deal with new or trying situations : REASON, INTELLECT **b** : mental acuteness : SHREWDNESS **2** : an agency engaged in obtaining information esp. concerning an enemy or possible enemy

intelligence quotient *n* **:** a number held to express the relative intelligence of a person and determined by dividing his mental age by his chronological age and multiplying by 100 — abbr. *IQ*
in·tel·li·gent \in-ˈtel-ə-jənt\ *adj* **:** having or showing intelligence or intellect — **in·tel·li·gent·ly** *adv*
in·tel·li·gen·tsia \in-ˌtel-ə-ˈjen(t)-sē-ə, -ˈgen(t)-\ *n* **:** intellectual people as a group **:** the educated class
in·tel·li·gi·ble \in-ˈtel-ə-jə-bəl\ *adj* **:** capable of being understood **:** COMPREHENSIBLE — **in·tel·li·gi·bil·i·ty** \-ˌtel-ə-jə-ˈbil-ət-ē\ *n* — **in·tel·li·gi·ble·ness** \-ˈtel-ə-jə-bəl-nəs\ *n* — **in·tel·li·gi·bly** \-blē\ *adv*
in·tem·per·ance \(ˈ)in-ˈtem-p(ə-)rən(t)s\ *n* **:** lack of moderation esp. in satisfying an appetite or passion; *esp* **:** habitual or excessive use of intoxicants
in·tem·per·ate \-p(ə-)rət\ *adj* **:** not temperate: as **a :** not moderate or mild **:** EXCESSIVE, EXTREME, SEVERE **b :** lacking or showing lack of restraint or self-control **c :** given to excessive use of intoxicants — **in·tem·per·ate·ly** *adv* — **in·tem·per·ate·ness** *n*
in·tend \in-ˈtend\ *vt* **:** to have in mind as a purpose or aim **:** PLAN
in·ten·dant \in-ˈten-dənt\ *n* **:** a governor or similar administrative official esp. under the French, Spanish, or Portuguese monarchies
[1]**in·tend·ed** \in-ˈten-dəd\ *adj* **1 :** INTENTIONAL **2 :** PROPOSED; *esp* **:** BETROTHED
[2]**intended** *n* **:** an affianced person **:** BETROTHED
in·tense \in-ˈten(t)s\ *adj* **1 a :** existing in an extreme degree **b :** having or showing a characteristic in extreme degree **c :** very large **:** CONSIDERABLE **2 :** strained or straining to the utmost **3 a :** feeling deeply esp. by nature or temperament **b :** deeply felt — **in·tense·ly** *adv* — **in·tense·ness** *n*
in·ten·si·fy \in-ˈten(t)-sə-ˌfī\ *vb* **-fied; -fy·ing 1 :** to make or become intense or more intensive **:** STRENGTHEN **2 :** to make or become more acute **:** SHARPEN — **in·ten·si·fi·ca·tion** \-ˌten(t)-sə-fə-ˈkā-shən\ *n* — **in·ten·si·fi·er** *n*
in·ten·si·ty \in-ˈten(t)-sət-ē\ *n, pl* **-ties 1 :** the quality or state of being intense **2 :** degree of strength, force, or energy
[1]**in·ten·sive** \in-ˈten(t)-siv\ *adj* **1 :** involving or marked by special effort **:** THOROUGH, EXHAUSTIVE **2 :** serving to give emphasis — **in·ten·sive·ly** *adv*
[2]**intensive** *n* **:** an intensive word
[1]**in·tent** \in-ˈtent\ *n* **1 :** the act, fact, or state of mind of intending **:** PURPOSE, INTENTION **2 :** MEANING, SIGNIFICANCE
[2]**intent** *adj* **1 :** directed with strained or eager attention **:** CONCENTRATED **2 a :** closely occupied **:** ENGROSSED **b :** set on some end or purpose — **in·tent·ly** *adv* — **in·tent·ness** *n*
n·ten·tion \in-ˈten-chən\ *n* **1 :** a determination to act in a certain way **2 :** an intended object **:** PURPOSE, END **3 :** IMPORT, SIGNIFICANCE
n·ten·tion·al \in-ˈtench-nəl, -ˈten-chən-ᵊl\ *adj* **:** done by intention or design **:** not accidental **:** INTENDED — **in·ten·tion·al·ly** \-ē\ *adv*
n·ter \in-ˈtər\ *vt* **in·terred; in·ter·ring :** BURY
n·ter·act \ˌint-ər-ˈakt\ *vi* **:** to act upon one another — **in·ter·ac·tion** \ˌint-ər-ˈak-shən\ *n*
n·ter alia \ˌint-ər-ˈā-lē-ə, -ˈäl-ē-ə\ *adv* **:** among other things
n·ter·breed \ˌint-ər-ˈbrēd\ *vb* **-bred** \-ˈbred\; **-breed·ing :** to breed or cause to breed together
ı·ter·ca·lary \in-ˈtər-kə-ˌler-ē\ *adj* **1 :** INTERCALATED **2 :** INTERPOLATED
·ter·ca·late \in-ˈtər-kə-ˌlāt\ *vt* **1 :** to insert (as a day) in a calendar **2 :** to insert between or among existing elements or layers — **in·ter·ca·la·tion** \-ˌtər-kə-ˈlā-shən\ *n*
·ter·cede \ˌint-ər-ˈsēd\ *vi* **1 :** to act as a go-between between parties who are unfriendly **2 :** to beg or plead in behalf of another
·ter·cept \ˌint-ər-ˈsept\ *vt* **1 :** to take or seize on the way to or before arrival at a destination **:** stop the progress of **2 :** to cut through **:** INTERSECT — **in·ter·cept·er** \-ˈsep-tər\ *n* — **in·ter·cep·tor** \-ˈsep-tər\ *n*
in·ter·cep·tion \-ˈsep-shən\ *n* **:** the act of intercepting **:** the state of being intercepted
in·ter·ces·sion \ˌint-ər-ˈsesh-ən\ *n* **:** the act of interceding **:** MEDIATION — **in·ter·ces·sor** \-ˈses-ər\ *n*
[1]**in·ter·change** \ˌint-ər-ˈchānj\ *vb* **1 :** to put each in the place of the other **2 :** EXCHANGE — **in·ter·chang·er** *n*
[2]**in·ter·change** \ˈint-ər-ˌchānj\ *n* **1 :** EXCHANGE **2 :** a highway junction that by separated levels permits passage between highways without crossing traffic streams
in·ter·change·a·ble \ˌint-ər-ˈchān-jə-bəl\ *adj* **:** capable of being interchanged; *esp* **:** permitting mutual substitution — **in·ter·change·a·bil·i·ty** \-ˌchān-jə-ˈbil-ət-ē\ *n* — **in·ter·change·a·ble·ness** \-ˈchān-jə-bəl-nəs\ *n* — **in·ter·change·a·bly** \-blē\ *adv*
in·ter·col·le·giate \ˌint-ər-kə-ˈlē-j(ē-)ət\ *adj* **:** existing or carried on between colleges
in·ter·com \ˈint-ər-ˌkäm\ *n* **:** INTERCOMMUNICATION SYSTEM
in·ter·com·mu·ni·cate \ˌint-ər-kə-ˈmyü-nə-ˌkāt\ *vi* **:** to exchange communication with one another — **in·ter·com·mu·ni·ca·tion** \-ˌmyü-nə-ˈkā-shən\ *n*
intercommunication system *n* **:** a 2-way communication system with microphone and loudspeaker at each station for localized use
in·ter·con·nect \ˌint-ər-kə-ˈnekt\ *vb* **:** to connect with one another — **in·ter·con·nec·tion** \-ˈnek-shən\ *n*
in·ter·con·ti·nen·tal \ˌint-ər-ˌkänt-ᵊn-ˈent-ᵊl\ *adj* **1 :** extending among or carried on between continents **2 :** capable of traveling between continents
in·ter·course \ˈint-ər-ˌkōrs\ *n* **1 :** connection between persons or groups **:** COMMUNICATION **2 :** COPULATION, COITUS
in·ter·cul·tur·al \ˌint-ər-ˈkəlch-(ə-)rəl\ *adj* **:** occurring between or relating to two or more cultures
in·ter·de·nom·i·na·tion·al \ˌint-ər-di-ˌnäm-ə-ˈnā-shnəl, -shən-ᵊl\ *adj* **:** involving or occurring between different denominations — **in·ter·de·nom·i·na·tion·al·ism** \-ˌiz-əm\ *n*
in·ter·de·part·men·tal \ˌint-ər-di-ˌpärt-ˈment-ᵊl, -ˌdē-\ *adj* **:** carried on between or involving different departments (as of a college) — **in·ter·de·part·men·tal·ly** \-ᵊl-ē\ *adv*
in·ter·de·pend \ˌint-ər-di-ˈpend\ *vi* **:** to depend upon one another — **in·ter·de·pend·ence** \-ˈpen-dən(t)s\ *n* — **in·ter·de·pend·en·cy** \-dən-sē\ *n* — **in·ter·de·pend·ent** \-dənt\ *adj* — **in·ter·de·pend·ent·ly** *adv*
in·ter·dict \ˌint-ər-ˈdikt\ *vt* **:** to prohibit or forbid esp. by decree — **in·ter·dic·tion** \ˌint-ər-ˈdik-shən\ *n*
in·ter·dis·ci·pli·nary \ˌint-ər-ˈdis-ə-plə-ˌner-ē\ *adj* **:** involving two or more academic disciplines
[1]**in·ter·est** \ˈin-trəst, ˈint-ə-rəst\ *n* **1 :** a right, title, or legal share in something **2 :** WELFARE, BENEFIT; *esp* **:** SELF-INTEREST **3 a :** a charge for borrowed money that is generally a percentage of the amount borrowed **b :** the return received by capital on its investment **4** *pl* **:** a group financially interested in an industry or enterprise **5 a :** readiness to be concerned with or moved by an object or class of objects **b :** the quality in a thing that arouses interest
[2]**interest** *vt* **1 :** AFFECT, CONCERN **2 :** to persuade to participate or take part **3 :** to arouse the interest of
in·ter·est·ed \-trəs-təd, -ə-ˌres-təd\ *adj* **:** having the attention occupied **:** having or showing interest — **in·ter·est·ed·ly** *adv*
interest group *n* **:** a group of persons having a common identifying interest that often provides a basis for action
in·ter·est·ing \ˈin-trəs-tiŋ, ˈint-ə-ˌres-tiŋ\ *adj* **:** holding the attention **:** arousing interest
in·ter·faith \ˈint-ər-ˌfāth\ *adj* **:** involving persons of different religious faiths
in·ter·fere \ˌint-ə(r)-ˈfi(ə)r\ *vi* **1 :** to come in collision or be in opposition **:** CLASH **2 :** to take a part in the concerns of others

3 : to act so as to augment, diminish, or otherwise affect one another 4 a : to run ahead of and provide blocking for the ballcarrier in football b : to hinder illegally an attempt of a football player to receive a pass — **in·ter·fer·er** *n*

in·ter·fer·ence \ˌint-ə(r)-ˈfir-ən(t)s\ *n* 1 : the act or process of interfering 2 : something that interferes : OBSTRUCTION

in·ter·fuse \ˌint-ər-ˈfyüz\ *vb* 1 : to combine by or as if by fusing : INTERMINGLE 2 : PERVADE, PERMEATE — **in·ter·fu·sion** \-ˈfyü-zhən\ *n*

in·ter·im \ˈin-tə-rəm, -ˌrim\ *n* : a time intervening : INTERVAL — **interim** *adj*

[1]**in·te·ri·or** \in-ˈtir-ē-ər\ *adj* 1 : lying, occurring, or functioning within the limits : INNER 2 : remote from the border or shore : INLAND — **in·te·ri·or·ly** *adv*

[2]**interior** *n* 1 : the internal or inner part of a thing 2 : the inland part (as of a country or continent) 3 : internal nature : CHARACTER 4 : the internal affairs of a state or nation — **in·te·ri·or·i·ty** \(ˌ)in-ˌtir-ē-ˈór-ət-ē\ *n*

interior decoration *n* : the art of planning the layout and furnishings of the interior of a building — **interior decorator** *n*

in·ter·ject \ˌint-ər-ˈjekt\ *vt* : to throw in between or among other things : INSERT — **in·ter·jec·tor** \-ˈjek-tər\ *n* — **in·ter·jec·to·ry** \-t(ə-)rē\ *adj*

in·ter·jec·tion \ˌint-ər-ˈjek-shən\ *n* : a word or cry expressing sudden or strong feeling and usu. lacking grammatical connection — **in·ter·jec·tion·al** \-shnəl, -shən-ᵊl\ *adj* — **in·ter·jec·tion·al·ly** \-ē\ *adv*

in·ter·lace \ˌint-ər-ˈlās\ *vb* 1 : to unite by or as if by lacing together : INTERWEAVE 2 : INTERSPERSE

in·ter·lard \ˌint-ər-ˈlärd\ *vt* : to insert or introduce at intervals : INTERSPERSE

in·ter·leaf \ˈint-ər-ˌlēf\ *n* : a usu. blank leaf inserted between two leaves of a book

in·ter·leave \ˌint-ər-ˈlēv\ *vt* : to equip with an interleaf

[1]**in·ter·line** \ˌint-ər-ˈlīn\ *vt* : to insert between lines already written or printed; *also* : to insert something between the lines of — **in·ter·lin·e·a·tion** \-ˌlin-ē-ˈā-shən\ *n*

[2]**interline** *vt* : to provide (a garment) with an interlining

in·ter·lin·e·ar \ˌint-ər-ˈlin-ē-ər\ *adj* : inserted between lines already written or printed — **in·ter·lin·e·ar·ly** *adv*

in·ter·lin·ing \ˈint-ər-ˌlī-niŋ\ *n* : a lining between the ordinary lining and the outside fabric

in·ter·link \ˌint-ər-ˈliŋk\ *vt* : to link together

in·ter·lock \ˌint-ər-ˈläk\ *vb* : to lock together : interlace firmly : UNITE

in·ter·loc·u·tor \ˌint-ər-ˈläk-yət-ər\ *n* 1 : one who takes part in dialogue or conversation 2 : a man in a minstrel show who questions the end men

in·ter·lop·er \ˌint-ər-ˈlō-pər, ˈint-ər-ˌ\ *n* : a person who intrudes or interferes wrongly or officiously : INTRUDER

in·ter·lude \ˈint-ər-ˌlüd\ *n* 1 : a performance or entertainment between the acts of a play 2 : an intervening or interruptive period, space, or event : INTERVAL 3 : a musical composition inserted between the parts of a longer composition, a drama, or a religious service

in·ter·mar·riage \ˌint-ər-ˈmar-ij\ *n* : marriage between members of different racial, social, or religious groups

in·ter·mar·ry \-ˈmar-ē\ *vi* 1 : to marry each other 2 : to become connected by intermarriage

in·ter·med·dle \ˌint-ər-ˈmed-ᵊl\ *vi* : MEDDLE, INTERFERE — **in·ter·med·dler** \-ˈmed-lər, -ᵊl-ər\ *n*

[1]**in·ter·me·di·ary** \ˌint-ər-ˈmēd-ē-ˌer-ē\ *adj* 1 : INTERMEDIATE 2 : acting as a mediator

[2]**intermediary** *n, pl* **-ar·ies** : MEDIATOR, GO-BETWEEN

[1]**in·ter·me·di·ate** \ˌint-ər-ˈmēd-ē-ət\ *adj* : being or occurring at the middle place or degree or between extremes — **in·ter·me·di·ate·ly** *adv* — **in·ter·me·di·ate·ness** *n*

[2]**intermediate** *n* 1 : an intermediate term, thing, or class 2 : MEDIATOR, GO-BETWEEN

in·ter·ment \in-ˈtər-mənt\ *n* : BURIAL

in·ter·mez·zo \ˌint-ər-ˈmet-sō, -ˈmed-zō\ *n, pl* **-zi** \-(ˌ)sē, -(ˌ)zē\ *or* **-zos** 1 : a short movement connecting major sections of an extended musical work (as a symphony) 2 : a short independent instrumental composition

in·ter·mi·na·ble \(ˈ)in-ˈtərm-(ə-)nə-bəl\ *adj* : ENDLESS; *esp* : tediously dragged out — **in·ter·mi·na·ble·ness** *n* — **in·ter·mi·na·bly** \-blē\ *adv*

in·ter·min·gle \ˌint-ər-ˈmiŋ-gəl\ *vb* : INTERMIX

in·ter·mis·sion \ˌint-ər-ˈmish-ən\ *n* 1 : INTERRUPTION 2 : a pause or interval (as between the acts of a play)

in·ter·mit \-ˈmit\ *vb* **-mit·ted**; **-mit·ting** : to stop for a time : discontinue at intervals and then continue again — **in·ter·mit·tence** \-ˈmit-ᵊn(t)s\ *n*

in·ter·mit·tent \-ˈmit-ᵊnt\ *adj* : coming and going at intervals : starting, stopping, and starting again — **in·ter·mit·tent·ly** *adv*

in·ter·mix \ˌint-ər-ˈmiks\ *vb* : to mix together — **in·ter·mix·ture** \-ˈmiks-chər\ *n*

[1]**in·tern** \ˈin-ˌtərn, in-ˈ\ *vt* : to confine or impound esp. during a war

[2]**in·tern** *or* **in·terne** \ˈin-ˌtərn\ *n* : an advanced student or graduate esp. in medicine gaining supervised practical experience (as in a hospital) — **in·tern·ship** \-ˌship\ *n*

[3]**in·tern** \ˈin-ˌtərn\ *vi* : to act as an intern

in·ter·nal \in-ˈtərn-ᵊl\ *adj* 1 a : existing or situated within the limits or surface of something b : having to do with or situated in the inside of the body 2 : relating or belonging to or existing within the mind 3 : INTRINSIC, INHERENT 4 : of or relating to the domestic affairs of a state — **in·ter·nal·i·ty** \ˌin-ˌtər-ˈnal-ət-ē\ *n* — **in·ter·nal·ly** \in-ˈtərn-ᵊl-ē\ *adv*

internal–combustion engine *n* : an engine run by a fuel mixture ignited within the engine cylinder

[1]**in·ter·na·tion·al** \ˌint-ər-ˈnash-nəl, -ən-ᵊl\ *adj* 1 : of, relating to, or affecting two or more nations 2 : of, relating to, or constituting a group having members in two or more nations — **in·ter·na·tion·al·i·ty** \-ˌnash-ə-ˈnal-ət-ē\ *n* — **in·ter·na·tion·al·ly** \-ˈnash-nə-lē, -ən-ᵊl-ē\ *adv*

[2]**in·ter·na·tion·al** \-ˈnash-nəl, -ən-ᵊl, *in sense 1 often* -ˌnash-ə-ˈnal, -ˈnäl\ *n* 1 : one of several socialist or communist organizations of international scope 2 : a labor union having locals in more than one country

in·ter·na·tion·al·ism \ˌint-ər-ˈnash-nəl-ˌiz-əm, -ˈnash-ən-ᵊl-\ *n* : a policy of political and economic cooperation among nations; *also* : an attitude favoring such a policy — **in·ter·na·tion·al·ist** \-əst\ *n or adj*

in·ter·na·tion·al·ize \-ˈnash-nəl-ˌīz, -ˈnash-ən-ᵊl-\ *vt* : to make international; *esp* : to place under international control

international law *n* : a body of rules that control or affect the rights of nations in their relations with each other

in·ter·nec·ine \ˌint-ər-ˈnes-ˌēn, -ˈnē-ˌsīn\ *adj* 1 : marked by slaughter : DEADLY 2 : of, relating to, or involving conflict within a group

in·tern·ee \ˌin-ˌtər-ˈnē\ *n* : an interned person

in·ter·nist \in-ˈtər-nəst\ *n* : a specialist in medicine as distinguished from surgery

in·tern·ment \in-ˈtərn-mənt\ *n* : the act of interning : the state of being interned

in·ter·nun·cio \ˌint-ər-ˈnən(t)-sē-ˌō\ *n* : a papal legate of lower rank than a nuncio

in·ter·of·fice \ˌint-ər-ˈóf-əs\ *adj* : functioning or communicating between the offices of an organization

in·ter·pen·e·trate \ˌint-ər-ˈpen-ə-ˌtrāt\ *vb* 1 : to penetrate between, within, or throughout : PERMEATE 2 : to penetrate mutually — **in·ter·pen·e·tra·tion** \-ˌpen-ə-ˈtrā-shən\ *n*

in·ter·plan·e·tary \ˌint-ər-ˈplan-ə-ˌter-ē\ *adj* : existing, carried on, or operating between planets

in·ter·play \ˈint-ər-ˌplā\ *n* : INTERACTION — **in·ter·play** \ˌint-ər-ˈplā\ *vi*

in·ter·po·late \in-ˈtər-pə-ˌlāt\ *vb* 1 : to alter or corrupt (as text) by inserting new or foreign matter **2** : to insert (words) into a text or into a conversation — **in·ter·po·la·tion** \-ˌtər-pə-ˈlā-shən\ *n* — **in·ter·po·la·tive** \-ˈtər-pə-ˌlāt-iv\ *adj* — **in·ter·po·la·tor** \-ˌlāt-ər\ *n*

in·ter·pose \ˌint-ər-ˈpōz\ *vb* **1 a** : to place in an intervening position **b** : to put (oneself) between : INTRUDE, INTERRUPT **2** : to introduce or throw in between the parts of a conversation or argument **3** : to be or come between; *esp* : to step in between opposing parties — **in·ter·pos·er** *n* — **in·ter·po·si·tion** \-pə-ˈzish-ən\ *n*

in·ter·pret \in-ˈtər-prət\ *vb* **1** : to explain or tell the meaning of **2** : to understand according to one's own belief, judgment, or interest **3** : to bring out the meaning or significance of by performing **4** : to act as an oral translator for speakers of different languages — **in·ter·pret·a·ble** *adj* — **in·ter·pret·er** *n* — **in·ter·pre·tive** \-prət-iv\ *adj* — **in·ter·pre·tive·ly** *adv*

in·ter·pre·ta·tion \in-ˌtər-prə-ˈtā-shən\ *n* **1** : the act or the result of interpreting : EXPLANATION **2** : an instance of artistic interpretation in performance or adaptation — **in·ter·pre·ta·tion·al** \-shnəl, -shən-ᵊl\ *adj* — **in·ter·pre·ta·tive** \-ˈtər-prə-ˌtāt-iv\ *adj* — **in·ter·pre·ta·tive·ly** *adv*

in·ter·ra·cial \ˌint-ə(r)-ˈrā-shəl\ *adj* : of, involving, or designed for members of different races

in·ter·reg·num \ˌint-ə-ˈreg-nəm\ *n, pl* **-nums** *or* **-na** \-nə\ **1** : a period between two successive reigns or regimes **2** : a lapse or pause in a continuous series

in·ter·re·late \ˌint-ə(r)-ri-ˈlāt\ *vb* : to bring into or have a mutual relationship — **in·ter·re·la·tion** \-ˈlā-shən\ *n* — **in·ter·re·la·tion·ship** \-ˌship\ *n*

in·ter·ro·gate \in-ˈter-ə-ˌgāt\ *vt* : to question formally and systematically — **in·ter·ro·ga·tion** \-ˌter-ə-ˈgā-shən\ *n* — **in·ter·ro·ga·tion·al** \-shnəl, -shən-ᵊl\ *adj* — **in·ter·ro·ga·tor** \-ˈter-ə-ˌgāt-ər\ *n*

in·ter·rog·a·tive \ˌint-ə-ˈräg-ət-iv\ *adj* : having the form or force of a question — **interrogative** *n* — **in·ter·rog·a·tive·ly** *adv*

in·ter·rog·a·to·ry \-ˈräg-ə-ˌtōr-ē\ *adj* : containing, expressing, or implying a question

in·ter·rupt \ˌint-ə-ˈrəpt\ *vb* **1** : to stop or hinder by breaking in **2** : to break the uniformity or continuity of **3** : to break in upon an action; *esp* : to break in with questions or remarks while another is speaking — **in·ter·rupt·er** *n* — **in·ter·rup·tion** \-ˈrəp-shən\ *n* — **in·ter·rup·tive** \-ˈrəp-tiv\ *adj*

in·ter·scho·las·tic \ˌint-ər-skə-ˈlas-tik\ *adj* : existing or carried on between schools

in·ter·sect \ˌint-ər-ˈsekt\ *vb* **1** : to pierce or divide by passing through or across : CROSS **2** : to meet and cross at a point

in·ter·sec·tion \ˌint-ər-ˈsek-shən\ *n* **1** : the act or process of intersecting **2** : the place or point where two or more things and esp. streets intersect

in·ter·space \ˈint-ər-ˌspās\ *n* : an intervening space

in·ter·sperse \ˌint-ər-ˈspərs\ *vt* **1** : to scatter or set here and there among others **2** : to vary with things inserted here and there — **in·ter·sper·sion** \-ˈspər-zhən\ *n*

in·ter·state \ˌint-ər-ˈstāt\ *adj* : of, connecting, or existing between two or more states esp. of the U.S.

in·ter·stel·lar \-ˈstel-ər\ *adj* : located or taking place among the stars

in·ter·stice \in-ˈtər-stəs\ *n, pl* **in·ter·stic·es** \-stə-ˌsēz, -stə-səz\ : a little space between one thing and another : CHINK, CREVICE — **in·ter·sti·tial** \ˌint-ər-ˈstish-əl\ *adj* — **in·ter·sti·tial·ly** \-ˈstish-ə-lē\ *adv*

in·ter·tid·al \-ˈtīd-ᵊl\ *adj* : of, relating to, or being the area that is above low-tide mark but exposed to tidal flooding

in·ter·twine \-ˈtwīn\ *vb* : to twine or cause to twine about one another : INTERLACE — **in·ter·twine·ment** *n*

in·ter·twist \-ˈtwist\ *vb* : INTERTWINE

in·ter·ur·ban \ˌint-ər-ˈər-bən\ *adj* : connecting cities or towns

in·ter·val \ˈint-ər-vəl\ *n* **1** : a space of time between events or states : PAUSE **2 a** : a space between things **b** : difference in pitch between tones

in·ter·vene \ˌint-ər-ˈvēn\ *vi* **1** : to happen or come in between as an unrelated event **2** : to happen or come between points of time or between events **3** : to come in or between in order to stop, settle, or change something : step in **4** : to be or lie between — **in·ter·ve·nor** \-ˈvē-nər, -ˌnȯr\ *n* — **in·ter·ven·tion** \-ˈven-chən\ *n*

in·ter·ven·tion·ism \-ˈven-chə-ˌniz-əm\ *n* : the theory or practice of intervening — **in·ter·ven·tion·ist** \-ˈvench-(ə-)nəst\ *n or adj*

in·ter·view \ˈint-ər-ˌvyü\ *n* **1** : a meeting face to face esp. for the purpose of talking or consulting with someone **2** : a meeting between a representative of a newspaper or magazine and another person in order to get news or an article to be published; *also* : the written account of such a meeting — **interview** *vt* — **in·ter·view·er** *n*

in·ter·weave \ˌint-ər-ˈwēv\ *vb* **1** : to weave together **2** : to blend or cause to blend together : INTERMINGLE — **in·ter·wo·ven** \-ˈwō-vən\ *adj*

in·tes·tate \in-ˈtes-ˌtāt, -ˈtes-tət\ *adj* **1** : not having made a will **2** : not disposed of by will — **in·tes·ta·cy** \-ˈtes-tə-sē\ *n* — **intestate** *n*

in·tes·ti·nal \in-ˈtes-tən-ᵊl\ *adj* : of, relating to, or occurring in the intestine — **in·tes·ti·nal·ly** \-ᵊl-ē\ *adv*

in·tes·tine \in-ˈtes-tən\ *n* : the tubular part of the alimentary canal that extends from the stomach to the anus

in·ti·ma·cy \ˈint-ə-mə-sē\ *n, pl* **-cies** **1** : the state of being intimate : FAMILIARITY **2** : an instance of esp. objectionable intimacy

¹in·ti·mate \ˈint-ə-ˌmāt\ *vt* **1** : ANNOUNCE, DECLARE **2** : to communicate indirectly : HINT — **in·ti·mat·er** *n* — **in·ti·ma·tion** \ˌint-ə-ˈmā-shən\ *n*

²in·ti·mate \ˈint-ə-mət\ *adj* **1** : belonging to or characterizing one's deepest nature **2** : marked by very close association or contact **3 a** : marked by a warm friendship developing through long association **b** : suggesting informal warmth or privacy **4** : of a very personal or private nature — **in·ti·mate·ly** *adv* — **in·ti·mate·ness** *n*

³in·ti·mate \ˈint-ə-mət\ *n* : an intimate friend : CONFIDANT

in·tim·i·date \in-ˈtim-ə-ˌdāt\ *vt* : to make timid or fearful; *esp* : to compel or deter by or as if by threats — **in·tim·i·da·tion** \-ˌtim-ə-ˈdā-shən\ *n* — **in·tim·i·da·tor** \-ˈtim-ə-ˌdāt-ər\ *n*

in·to \ˈin-tə, -tü\ *prep* **1 a** : to the inside of **b** — used as a function word to indicate entry, introduction, insertion, or inclusion **2 a** : to the state, condition, or form of **b** : to the occupation, action, or possession of **3** : to a position of contact with : AGAINST

in·tol·er·a·ble \(ˈ)in-ˈtäl-(ə-)rə-bəl, -ˈtäl-ər-bəl\ *adj* **1** : not tolerable : UNBEARABLE **2** : EXCESSIVE — **in·tol·er·a·ble·ness** *n* — **in·tol·er·a·bly** \-blē\ *adv*

in·tol·er·ance \(ˈ)in-ˈtäl-ə-rən(t)s\ *n* : the quality or state of being intolerant

in·tol·er·ant \-rənt\ *adj* **1** : unable to endure **2 a** : unwilling to endure **b** : unwilling to grant equality or freedom esp. in religious matters or other social rights : BIGOTED — **in·tol·er·ant·ly** *adv*

in·to·na·tion \ˌin-tə-ˈnā-shən\ *n* **1** : the act of intoning and esp. of chanting; *also* : something intoned **2** : the act of producing tones on a musical instrument esp. with regard to proper pitch **3** : the rise and fall in pitch of the voice in speech — **in·to·na·tion·al** \-shnəl, -shən-ᵊl\ *adj*

in·tone \in-ˈtōn\ *vb* : to utter in musical or prolonged tones : CHANT — **in·ton·er** *n*

in to·to \in-ˈtōt-ō\ *adv* : TOTALLY, ENTIRELY

in·tox·i·cant \in-ˈtäk-si-kənt\ *n* : something that intoxicates; *esp* : an alcoholic drink — **intoxicant** *adj*

in·tox·i·cate \in-ˈtäk-sə-ˌkāt\ *vt* **1 a** : POISON **b** : to affect by alcohol or a narcotic esp. to the point where physical and mental control is markedly diminished **2 :** to excite or elate to the point of enthusiasm or frenzy

in·tox·i·ca·tion \in-ˌtäk-sə-ˈkā-shən\ *n* **1 a :** an abnormal state that is essentially a poisoning **b :** the condition of being drunk : INEBRIATION **2 :** a strong excitement or elation

in·trac·ta·ble \(ˈ)in-ˈtrak-tə-bəl\ *adj* **1 :** not easily governed, managed, or directed **2 :** not easily relieved or cured — **in·trac·ta·bil·i·ty** \(ˌ)in-ˌtrak-tə-ˈbil-ət-ē\ *n* — **in·trac·ta·ble·ness** \(ˈ)in-ˈtrak-tə-bəl-nəs\ *n* — **in·trac·ta·bly** \-blē\ *adv*

in·tra·dos \ˈin-trə-ˌdäs, in-ˈtrā-ˌ\ *n, pl* **-dos** \-ˌdäs\ *or* **-dos·es** \-ˌdäs-əz\ : the interior curve of an arch

in·tra·mu·ral \ˌin-trə-ˈmyu̇r-əl\ *adj* : being, occurring, or undertaken within the limits usu. of a community or institution (as a school) — **in·tra·mu·ral·ly** \-ˈmyu̇r-ə-lē\ *adv*

in·tran·si·gence \in-ˈtran(t)s-ə-jən(t)s, -ˈtranz-\ *n* : the quality or state of being intransigent

in·tran·si·gent \-jənt\ *adj* **1 a :** refusing to compromise or to abandon an extreme position or attitude : UNCOMPROMISING **b :** IRRECONCILABLE **2 :** characteristic of an intransigent person — **intransigent** *n* — **in·tran·si·gent·ly** *adv*

in·tran·si·tive \(ˈ)in-ˈtran(t)s-ət-iv, -ˈtranz-\ *adj* : not transitive; *esp* : not having or containing an object required to complete its meaning — **in·tran·si·tive·ly** *adv*

in·tra·state \ˌin-trə-ˈstāt\ *adj* : existing or occurring within a state

in·tra·ve·nous \ˌin-trə-ˈvē-nəs\ *adj* : being within or entering by way of the veins — **in·tra·ve·nous·ly** *adv*

in·trep·id \in-ˈtrep-əd\ *adj* : characterized by resolute fearlessness, fortitude, and endurance — **in·tre·pid·i·ty** \ˌin-trə-ˈpid-ət-ē\ *n* — **in·trep·id·ly** *adv* — **in·trep·id·ness** *n*

in·tri·ca·cy \ˈin-tri-kə-sē\ *n, pl* **-cies** **1 :** the quality or state of being intricate **2 :** something intricate

in·tri·cate \ˈin-tri-kət\ *adj* **1 :** having many complexly interrelating parts or elements : COMPLICATED **2 :** difficult to resolve or analyze — **in·tri·cate·ly** *adv* — **in·tri·cate·ness** *n*

¹in·trigue \in-ˈtrēg\ *vb* **1 :** to make or accomplish by intrigue **2 :** PLOT, SCHEME **3 :** to arouse the interest or curiosity of — **in·trigu·er** *n*

²in·trigue \ˈin-ˌtrēg, in-ˈ\ *n* **1 :** a secret and involved stratagem : MACHINATION **2 :** a clandestine love affair

in·trin·sic \in-ˈtrin-zik, -ˈtrin(t)-sik\ *adj* **1 :** belonging to the essential nature or constitution of a thing **2 :** REAL — **in·trin·si·cal** \-zi-kəl, -si-\ *adj* — **in·trin·si·cal·ly** \-k(ə-)lē\ *adv* — **in·trin·si·cal·ness** *n*

in·tro·duce \ˌin-trə-ˈd(y)üs\ *vt* **1 :** to bring into practice or use **2 :** to lead or bring in; *esp* : to present formally **3 :** to cause to become acquainted : make known **4 :** to present or bring forward for discussion **5 :** to put in : INSERT — **in·tro·duc·er** *n*

in·tro·duc·tion \ˌin-trə-ˈdək-shən\ *n* **1 :** the action of introducing **2 :** PREFACE **3 :** a book intended for beginners in a subject **4 :** the action of making persons known to each other

in·tro·duc·to·ry \ˌin-trə-ˈdək-t(ə-)rē\ *adj* : serving to introduce : PRELIMINARY — **in·tro·duc·to·ri·ly** \-t(ə-)rə-lē\ *adv*

in·tro·mit \ˌin-trə-ˈmit\ *vt* **in·tro·mit·ted; in·tro·mit·ting** : to send or put in : INSERT — **in·tro·mis·sion** \-ˈmish-ən\ *n* — **in·tro·mit·tent** \-ˈmit-ᵊnt\ *adj* — **in·tro·mit·ter** *n*

in·tro·spec·tion \ˌin-trə-ˈspek-shən\ *n* : a reflective looking inward : an examination of one's own thoughts or feelings — **in·tro·spec·tion·al** \-shnəl, -shən-ᵊl\ *adj* — **in·tro·spec·tive** \-ˈspek-tiv\ *adj* — **in·tro·spec·tive·ly** *adv*

in·tro·vert \ˈin-trə-ˌvərt\ *n* : a person more interested in his own mental life than in the world about him — **in·tro·ver·sion** \ˌin-trə-ˈvər-zhən\ *n* — **introvert** *vt* — **in·tro·ver·tive** \ˈin-trə-ˌvərt-iv\ *adj*

in·trude \in-ˈtrüd\ *vb* **1 :** to bring in or introduce unasked **2 :** to come or go in without invitation or welcome : TRESPASS **3 :** to enter or cause to enter as if by force — **in·trud·er** *n*

in·tru·sion \in-ˈtrü-zhən\ *n* : the act of intruding : the state of being intruded

in·tru·sive \in-ˈtrü-siv, -ziv\ *adj* : characterized by intrusion; *esp* : intruding where one is not welcome or invited — **in·tru·sive·ly** *adv* — **in·tru·sive·ness** *n*

in·tu·it \in-ˈt(y)ü-ət\ *vt* : to apprehend by intuition — **in·tu·it·a·ble** \-ət-ə-bəl\ *adj*

in·tu·i·tion \ˌin-t(y)u̇-ˈish-ən\ *n* **1 :** the power of knowing immediately and without conscious reasoning **2 :** something known or understood at once and without an effort of the mind — **in·tu·i·tion·al** \-ˈish-nəl, -ən-ᵊl\ *adj*

in·tu·i·tive \in-ˈt(y)ü-ət-iv\ *adj* **1 :** knowing or understanding by intuition **2 :** known or understood by intuition — **in·tu·i·tive·ly** *adv* — **in·tu·i·tive·ness** *n*

in·tu·mesce \ˌin-t(y)u̇-ˈmes\ *vi* : ENLARGE, SWELL — **in·tu·mes·cence** \-ˈmes-ᵊn(t)s\ *n* — **in·tu·mes·cent** \-ᵊnt\ *adj*

in·un·date \ˈin-ən-ˌdāt\ *vt* : to cover with a flood : OVERFLOW — **in·un·da·tion** \ˌin-ən-ˈdā-shən\ *n* — **in·un·da·tor** \ˈin-ən-ˌdāt-ər\ *n* — **in·un·da·to·ry** \in-ˈən-də-ˌtōr-ē\ *adj*

in·ure \in-ˈ(y)u̇(ə)r\ *vb* **1 :** to make less sensitive : HARDEN **2 :** to become of advantage

in vac·uo \in-ˈvak-yə-ˌwō\ *adv* : in a vacuum

in·vade \in-ˈvād\ *vt* **1 :** to enter for conquest or plunder **2 :** to encroach upon : INFRINGE **3 :** to spread progressively over or into and usu. affect injuriously — **in·vad·er** *n*

¹in·val·id \(ˈ)in-ˈval-əd\ *adj* : having no force or effect : not valid — **in·va·lid·i·ty** \ˌin-və-ˈlid-ət-ē\ *n* — **in·val·id·ly** *adv* — **in·val·id·ness** *n*

²in·va·lid \ˈin-və-ləd\ *adj* **1 :** suffering from disease or disability : SICKLY **2 :** of, relating to, or suited to one that is sick

³invalid *like* ²\ *n* : one that is sickly or disabled — **in·va·lid·ism** \-ˌiz-əm\ *n*

⁴in·va·lid \ˈin-və-ləd, -ˌlid\ *vt* **1 :** to make sickly or disabled **2 :** to remove from active duty by reason of sickness or disability

in·val·i·date \(ˈ)in-ˈval-ə-ˌdāt\ *vt* : to make invalid; *esp* : to weaken or destroy the cogency of — **in·val·i·da·tion** \(ˌ)in-ˌval-ə-ˈdā-shən\ *n* — **in·val·i·da·tor** \in-ˈval-ə-ˌdāt-ər\ *n*

in·val·u·a·ble \(ˈ)in-ˈval-yə-(wə-)bəl\ *adj* : having value too great to be estimated : PRICELESS — **in·val·u·a·ble·ness** *n* — **in·val·u·a·bly** \-blē\ *adv*

in·var·i·a·bil·i·ty \(ˌ)in-ˌver-ē-ə-ˈbil-ət-ē\ *n* : the quality or state of being invariable

in·var·i·a·ble \(ˈ)in-ˈver-ē-ə-bəl\ *adj* : not changing or capable of change : CONSTANT — **invariable** *n* — **in·var·i·a·ble·ness** *n* — **in·var·i·a·bly** \-blē\ *adv*

in·var·i·ant \-ē-ənt\ *adj* : CONSTANT, UNCHANGING — **invariant** *n*

in·va·sion \in-ˈvā-zhən\ *n* : an act of invading; *esp* : entrance of an army into a country for conquest or plunder

in·va·sive \-ˈvā-siv\ *adj* : of, relating to, or engaged in invasion — **in·va·sive·ness** *n*

in·vec·tive \in-ˈvek-tiv\ *n* : condemnation written or spoken in a harsh or bitter tone

in·veigh \in-ˈvā\ *vi* : to protest or complain bitterly or vehemently : RAIL — **in·veigh·er** *n*

in·vei·gle \in-ˈvā-gəl, -ˈvē-\ *vt* **in·vei·gled; in·vei·gling** \-g(ə-)liŋ\ **1 :** to bring or lead by flattery : ENTICE **2 :** to acquire by ingenuity or flattery — **in·vei·gler** \-g(ə-)lər\ *n*

in·vent \in-ˈvent\ *vt* **1 a :** to think up : IMAGINE **b :** to make up : FABRICATE **2 :** to create or produce for the first time : DEVISE — **in·ven·tor** \-ˈvent-ər\ *n*

in·ven·tion \in-ˈven-chən\ *n* **1 :** INVENTIVENESS **2 :** something invented: as **a :** a product of the imagination; *esp* : a false conception **b :** a device or process originated after study and experiment **3 :** the act or process of inventing

in·ven·tive \in-ˈvent-iv\ *adj* : gifted with the skill and imagination to invent — **in·ven·tive·ly** *adv* — **in·ven·tive·ness** *n*

[1]**in·ven·to·ry** \'in-vən-ˌtōr-ē\ *n, pl* **-ries** 1 **a** : an itemized list of current assets **b** : a list of goods on hand 2 : the quantity of goods or materials on hand : STOCK 3 : the act or process of making an inventory

[2]**inventory** *vt* **-ried; -ry·ing** : to make an inventory of : CATALOG

in·ver·ness \ˌin-vər-'nes\ *n* : a loose belted coat having a cape with a close round collar

[1]**in·verse** \(')in-'vərs, 'in-ˌ\ *adj* : opposite in order, nature, or effect; *esp* : so relating two quantities that their product is a constant — **in·verse·ly** *adv*

[2]**inverse** *n* : something inverse or resulting in or from inversion

in·ver·sion \in-'vər-zhən\ *n* 1 : the act or process of inverting 2 : a reversal of position, order, or relationship

in·vert \in-'vərt\ *vt* 1 **a** : to turn inside out or upside down **b** : to turn inward 2 : to reverse the position, order, or relationship of — **in·vert·i·ble** \-ə-bəl\ *adj*

in·ver·te·brate \(')in-'vərt-ə-brət, -ˌbrāt\ *adj* : lacking a spinal column; *also* : of or relating to invertebrate animals — **invertebrate** *n*

[1]**in·vest** \in-'vest\ *vt* 1 **a** : to array in the symbols of office or honor **b** : to furnish with power or authority 2 : to cover completely : ENVELOP 3 : CLOTHE, ADORN 4 : to surround with troops or ships : BESIEGE 5 : to endow with a quality or characteristic : INFUSE

[2]**invest** *vb* 1 : to commit money in order to earn a financial return 2 : to expend for future benefits or advantages — **in·vest·a·ble** *adj* — **in·ves·tor** \-'ves-tər\ *n*

in·ves·ti·gate \in-'ves-tə-ˌgāt\ *vb* : to observe or study by close examination and systematic inquiry — **in·ves·ti·ga·tion** \-ˌves-tə-'gā-shən\ *n* — **in·ves·ti·ga·tive** \-'ves-tə-ˌgāt-iv\ *adj* — **in·ves·ti·ga·tor** \-ˌgāt-ər\ *n* — **in·ves·ti·ga·to·ry** \-'ves-ti-gə-ˌtōr-ē\ *adj*

in·ves·ti·ture \in-'ves-tə-ˌchu̇r, -chər\ *n* 1 : the action of investing a person esp. with the robes of office 2 : CLOTHING, APPAREL

[1]**in·vest·ment** \in-'ves(t)-mənt\ *n* 1 : an outer layer : ENVELOPE 2 : INVESTITURE 1 3 : BLOCKADE, SIEGE

[2]**investment** *n* : the outlay of money for income or profit; *also* : the sum invested or the property purchased

in·vet·er·ate \in-'vet-ə-rət, -'ve-trət\ *adj* 1 : firmly established by age or by being long continued 2 : HABITUAL — **in·vet·er·ate·ly** *adv*

in·vi·a·ble \(')in-'vī-ə-bəl\ *adj* : incapable of surviving — **in·vi·a·bil·i·ty** \(ˌ)in-ˌvī-ə-'bil-ət-ē\ *n*

in·vid·i·ous \in-'vid-ē-əs\ *adj* : tending to arouse dislike, ill will, or envy; *esp* : discriminating unfairly between two things — **in·vid·i·ous·ly** *adv* — **in·vid·i·ous·ness** *n*

in·vig·o·rate \in-'vig-ə-ˌrāt\ *vt* : to give life and energy to : ANIMATE — **in·vig·o·ra·tion** \-ˌvig-ə-'rā-shən\ *n* — **in·vig·o·ra·tor** \-'vig-ə-ˌrāt-ər\ *n*

in·vin·ci·bil·i·ty \(ˌ)in-ˌvin(t)-sə-'bil-ət-ē\ *n* : the quality or state of being invincible

in·vin·ci·ble \(')in-'vin(t)-sə-bəl\ *adj* : incapable of being defeated, overcome, or subdued — **in·vin·ci·ble·ness** *n* — **in·vin·ci·bly** \-blē\ *adv*

in·vi·o·la·ble \(')in-'vī-ə-lə-bəl\ *adj* 1 : too sacred to be violated 2 : incapable of being harmed or destroyed by violence — **in·vi·o·la·bil·i·ty** \(ˌ)in-ˌvī-ə-lə-'bil-ət-ē\ *n* — **in·vi·o·la·bly** \(')in-'vī-ə-lə-blē\ *adv*

in·vi·o·late \(')in-'vī-ə-lət\ *adj* : not violated; *esp* : PURE, UNPROFANED — **in·vi·o·late·ly** *adv* — **in·vi·o·late·ness** *n*

in·vis·i·ble \(')in-'viz-ə-bəl\ *adj* 1 **a** : incapable by nature of being seen **b** : inaccessible to view : HIDDEN 2 : not reflected in statistics 3 : IMPERCEPTIBLE, INCONSPICUOUS — **in·vis·i·bil·i·ty** \(ˌ)in-ˌviz-ə-'bil-ət-ē\ *n* — **invisible** *n* — **in·vis·i·ble·ness** *n* — **in·vis·i·bly** \(')in-'viz-ə-blē\ *adv*

in·vi·ta·tion \ˌin-və-'tā-shən\ *n* 1 : the act of inviting 2 : the written, printed, or spoken expression by which a person is invited — **in·vi·ta·tion·al** \-shnəl, -shən-ᵊl\ *adj*

in·vite \in-'vīt\ *vt* 1 **a** : to offer an incentive or inducement to : ENTICE **b** : to increase the likelihood of 2 **a** : to request the presence or participation of **b** : to request formally **c** : to urge politely : ENCOURAGE — **in·vit·er** *n*

in·vit·ing \ın-'vīt-iŋ\ *adj* : ATTRACTIVE, TEMPTING — **in·vit·ing·ly** *adv*

in·vo·ca·tion \ˌin-və-'kā-shən\ *n* 1 : SUPPLICATION; *esp* : a prayer at the beginning of a service 2 : a formula for conjuring : INCANTATION

[1]**in·voice** \'in-ˌvȯis\ *n* : an itemized statement furnished to a purchaser by a seller and usu. specifying the price of goods or services and the terms of sale; *also* : a shipment of goods sent with such a statement

[2]**invoice** *vt* : to submit an invoice for : BILL

in·voke \in-'vōk\ *vt* 1 : to call on for aid or protection (as in prayer) 2 : to call forth by magic : CONJURE 3 : to appeal to as an authority or for support

in·vol·un·tary \(')in-'väl-ən-ˌter-ē\ *adj* 1 : not made or done willingly or from choice : UNWILLING 2 : COMPULSORY 3 : not subject to control by the will : REFLEX — **in·vol·un·tar·i·ly** \(ˌ)in-ˌväl-ən-'ter-ə-lē\ *adv* — **in·vol·un·tar·i·ness** \(')in-'väl-ən-ˌter-ē-nəs\ *n*

in·vo·lute \'in-və-ˌlüt\ *adj* 1 : curled spirally and usu. closely 2 : INVOLVED, INTRICATE — **in·vo·lute·ly** *adv*

in·vo·lu·tion \ˌin-və-'lü-shən\ *n* 1 : the act or an instance of enfolding or entangling : INVOLVEMENT 2 : COMPLEXITY, INTRICACY — **in·vo·lu·tion·al** \-shnəl, -shən-ᵊl\ *adj* — **in·vo·lu·tion·ary** \-shə-ˌner-ē\ *adj*

in·volve \in-'välv\ *vt* 1 **a** : to draw in as a participant : ENGAGE **b** : to oblige to become associated **c** : to occupy absorbingly 2 : to make difficult : COMPLICATE 3 **a** : to have within or as part of itself : INCLUDE **b** : to require as a necessary accompaniment **c** : to have an effect on : AFFECT — **in·volve·ment** *n* — **in·volv·er** *n*

in·volved \-'välvd\ *adj* 1 : TWISTED 2 **a** : COMPLICATED, INTRICATE **b** : CONFUSED, TANGLED 3 : AFFECTED, IMPLICATED — **in·volved·ly** \-'välv-(ə-)dlē\ *adv*

in·vul·ner·a·ble \(')in-'vəl-nə-rə-bəl\ *adj* 1 : incapable of being wounded, injured, or damaged 2 : immune to or proof against attack : IMPREGNABLE — **in·vul·ner·a·bil·i·ty** \(ˌ)in-ˌvəl-nə-rə-'bil-ət-ē\ *n* — **in·vul·ner·a·ble·ness** *n* — **in·vul·ner·a·bly** \(')in-'vəl-nə-rə-blē\ *adv*

[1]**in·ward** \'in-wərd\ *adj* 1 : situated on the inside : INNER 2 **a** : MENTAL **b** : SPIRITUAL 3 : directed toward the interior

[2]**inward** *or* **in·wards** \-wərdz\ *adv* 1 : toward the inside, center, or interior 2 : toward the inner being

[3]**inward** *n* 1 : something that is inward 2 **in·wards** \'in-ərdz, -wərdz\ *pl* : INNARDS

in·ward·ly \'in-wərd-lē\ *adv* 1 : MENTALLY, SPIRITUALLY 2 **a** : INTERNALLY **b** : to oneself : PRIVATELY 3 : towards the inside

in·ward·ness \-nəs\ *n* 1 : fundamental nature or meaning 2 : absorption in one's own mental or spiritual life

in·wrought \(')in-'rȯt\ *adj* : having a decorative element worked or woven in : ORNAMENTED

io·dide \'ī-ə-ˌdīd\ *n* : a compound of iodine with another element or radical

io·dine \'ī-ə-ˌdīn, -əd-ᵊn, -ə-ˌdēn\ *n* 1 : a nonmetallic chemical element used esp. in medicine and photography 2 : a solution of iodine in alcohol used as an antiseptic

ion \'ī-ən, 'ī-ˌän\ *n* : an atom or group of atoms that carries a positive or negative electric charge as a result of having lost or gained one or more electrons

ion·ic \ī-'än-ik\ *adj* : of, relating to, or existing in the form of ions

io·ta \ī-'ōt-ə\ *n* : an infinitesimal amount : JOT

ip·so fac·to \ˌip-sō-'fak-tō\ *adv* : by the very nature of the case

iras·ci·ble \ir-ˈas-ə-bəl, ī-ˈras-\ *adj* : marked by hot temper and easily provoked anger — **iras·ci·bil·i·ty** \ir-ˌas-ə-ˈbil-ət-ē, ī-ˌras-\ *n* — **iras·ci·ble·ness** \ir-ˈas-ə-bəl-nəs, ī-ˈras-\ *n* — **iras·ci·bly** \-blē\ *adv*

irate \ī-ˈrāt\ *adj* **1** : roused to or given to ire : INCENSED **2** : arising from anger — **irate·ly** *adv* — **irate·ness** *n*

ire \ˈī(ə)r\ *n* : ANGER, WRATH — **ire** *vt* — **ire·ful** \-fəl\ *adj* — **ire·ful·ly** \-fə-lē\ *adv*

ir·i·des·cence \ˌir-ə-ˈdes-ᵊn(t)s\ *n* : a play of colors producing rainbow effects (as in mother-of-pearl) — **ir·i·des·cent** \-ᵊnt\ *adj* — **ir·i·des·cent·ly** *adv*

irid·i·um \ir-ˈid-ē-əm\ *n* : a silver-white hard brittle very heavy metallic chemical element

iris \ˈī-rəs\ *n, pl* **iris·es** *or* **iri·des** \ˈī-rə-ˌdēz, ˈir-ə-\ **1** : the opaque contractile diaphragm perforated by the pupil and forming the colored portion of the eye **2** : a plant with linear usu. basal leaves and large showy flowers

irk \ˈərk\ *vt* : to make weary, irritated, or bored : ANNOY

irk·some \ˈərk-səm\ *adj* : TIRESOME, TEDIOUS, ANNOYING — **irk·some·ly** *adv* — **irk·some·ness** *n*

¹iron \ˈī(-ə)rn\ *n* **1** : a heavy malleable ductile magnetic chiefly bivalent and trivalent silver-white metallic chemical element that readily rusts in moist air, occurs in meteorites and combined in rocks, and is vital to biological processes **2** : something made of iron; *also* : something (as handcuffs or chains) used to bind or restrain — usu. used in pl. **3** : STRENGTH, HARDNESS

²iron *adj* **1** : of, relating to, or made of iron **2** : resembling iron (as in hardness or strength) **3 a** : being strong and healthy : ROBUST **b** : INFLEXIBLE, UNRELENTING **c** : holding or binding fast

³iron *vb* **1** : to furnish or cover with iron **2 a** : to smooth or press with a heated flatiron **b** : to remove by ironing **3** : to iron clothes

iron·bound \ˈī(-ə)rn-ˈbau̇nd\ *adj* : bound with or as if with iron: as **a** : HARSH, RUGGED **b** : STERN, RIGOROUS

¹iron·clad \-ˈklad\ *adj* **1** : sheathed in iron armor **2** : RIGOROUS, EXACTING

²iron·clad \-ˌklad\ *n* : an armored naval vessel

iron curtain *n* : a political, military, and ideological barrier that cuts off and isolates an area; *esp* : one between an area under Soviet Russian control and other areas

iron·ic \ī-ˈrän-ik\ *adj* **1** : relating to, containing, or constituting irony **2** : given to irony — **iron·i·cal** \-i-kəl\ *adj* — **iron·i·cal·ly** \-i-k(ə-)lē\ *adv*

iron lung *n* : a device for artificial respiration in which rhythmic alternations in the air pressure in a chamber surrounding a patient's chest force air into and out of the lungs

iron·ware \ˈī(-ə)rn-ˌwa(ə)r\ *n* : articles made of iron

iron·work \-ˌwərk\ *n* **1** : work in iron **2** *pl* : a mill or building where iron or steel is smelted or heavy iron or steel products are made — **iron·work·er** \-ˌwər-kər\ *n*

iro·ny \ˈī-rə-nē\ *n, pl* **-nies** **1** : the humorous or sardonic use of words to express the opposite of what one really means (as when words of praise are given but blame is intended); *also* : an ironic expression or utterance **2** : incongruity between the actual result of a sequence of events and the expected result; *also* : an event or result marked by such incongruity

ir·ra·di·ate \ir-ˈād-ē-ˌāt\ *vt* **1 a** : to cast rays of light on : ILLUMINATE **b** : to enlighten intellectually or spiritually **c** : to affect or treat by exposure to radiations (as of ultraviolet light, X rays, or gamma rays) **2** : to emit like rays of light : RADIATE — **ir·ra·di·a·tion** \-ˌād-ē-ˈā-shən\ *n*

ir·rad·i·ca·ble \(ˈ)ir-ˈad-i-kə-bəl\ *adj* : impossible to eradicate : DEEP-ROOTED — **ir·rad·i·ca·bly** \-blē\ *adv*

ir·ra·tio·nal \(ˈ)ir-ˈash-nəl, -ən-ᵊl\ *adj* **1 a** : incapable of reasoning **b** : defective in mental power **2** : coming from or as if from a mind incapable of reasoning — **ir·ra·tio·nal·i·ty** \(ˌ)ir-ˌash-ə-ˈnal-ət-ē\ *n* — **ir·ra·tio·nal·ly** \(ˈ)ir-ˈash-nə-lē, -ˈash-ən-ᵊl-ē\ *adv*

ir·re·claim·a·ble \ˌir-i-ˈklā-mə-bəl\ *adj* : incapable of being reclaimed — **ir·re·claim·a·bly** \-blē\ *adv*

ir·rec·on·cil·a·ble \(ˌ)ir-ˌek-ən-ˈsī-lə-bəl, (ˈ)ir-ˈek-ən-ˌ\ *adj* : impossible to reconcile, adjust, or harmonize — **ir·rec·on·cil·a·bly** \-blē\ *adv*

ir·re·cov·er·a·ble \ˌir-i-ˈkəv-(ə-)rə-bəl\ *adj* : not capable of being recovered or rectified : IRREPARABLE — **ir·re·cov·er·a·ble·ness** *n* — **ir·re·cov·er·a·bly** \-blē\ *adv*

ir·re·deem·a·ble \ˌir-i-ˈdē-mə-bəl\ *adj* **1** : not redeemable; *esp* : not convertible into gold or silver at the will of the holder **2** : being beyond remedy : HOPELESS — **ir·re·deem·a·bly** \-blē\ *adv*

ir·re·den·tism \ˌir-i-ˈden-ˌtiz-əm\ *n* : a principle or policy directed toward the incorporation of a territory historically or ethnically part of another into that other — **ir·re·den·tist** \-ˈdent-əst\ *n or adj*

ir·re·duc·i·ble \ˌir-i-ˈd(y)ü-sə-bəl\ *adj* : not reducible — **ir·re·duc·i·bil·i·ty** \-ˌd(y)ü-sə-ˈbil-ət-ē\ *n* — **ir·re·duc·i·bly** \-ˈd(y)ü-sə-blē\ *adv*

ir·ref·ra·ga·ble \(ˈ)ir-ˈef-rə-gə-bəl\ *adj* : impossible to deny or refute : INVIOLABLE — **ir·ref·ra·ga·bly** \-blē\ *adv*

ir·re·fut·a·ble \ˌir-i-ˈfyüt-ə-bəl, (ˈ)ir-ˈef-yət-\ *adj* : not capable of being proved wrong : INDISPUTABLE — **ir·re·fut·a·bly** \-blē\ *adv*

ir·reg·u·lar \(ˈ)ir-ˈeg-yə-lər\ *adj* **1 a** : not conforming to established laws, customs, or moral principles **b** : not belonging to a recognized or organized body **2** : not conforming to the normal or usual manner of inflection **3** : lacking continuity or regularity — **ir·reg·u·lar·ly** *adv*

ir·reg·u·lar·i·ty \(ˌ)ir-ˌeg-yə-ˈlar-ət-ē\ *n, pl* **-ties** **1** : the quality or state of being irregular **2** : something (as dishonest conduct) that is irregular

ir·rel·e·vant \(ˈ)ir-ˈel-ə-vənt\ *adj* : not relevant : not applicable or pertinent : FOREIGN — **ir·rel·e·vance** \-vən(t)s\ *or* **ir·rel·e·van·cy** \-vən-sē\ *n* — **ir·rel·e·vant·ly** *adv*

ir·re·li·gious \ˌir-i-ˈlij-əs\ *adj* **1** : lacking religious emotions, doctrines, or practices **2** : indicating lack of religion — **ir·re·li·gious·ly** *adv*

ir·re·me·di·a·ble \ˌir-i-ˈmēd-ē-ə-bəl\ *adj* : INCURABLE — **ir·re·me·di·a·ble·ness** *n* — **ir·re·me·di·a·bly** \-blē\ *adv*

ir·re·mov·a·ble \ˌir-i-ˈmü-və-bəl\ *adj* : not removable

ir·rep·a·ra·ble \(ˈ)ir-ˈep-(ə-)rə-bəl\ *adj* : not capable of being repaired, recovered, regained, or remedied — **ir·rep·a·ra·ble·ness** *n* — **ir·rep·a·ra·bly** \-blē\ *adv*

ir·re·place·a·ble \ˌir-i-ˈplā-sə-bəl\ *adj* : not replaceable

ir·re·press·i·ble \ˌir-i-ˈpres-ə-bəl\ *adj* : not capable of being checked or held back — **ir·re·press·i·bil·i·ty** \-ˌpres-ə-ˈbil-ət-ē\ *n* — **ir·re·press·i·bly** \-ˈpres-ə-blē\ *adv*

ir·re·proach·a·ble \-ˈprō-chə-bəl\ *adj* : not reproachable : BLAMELESS — **ir·re·proach·a·ble·ness** *n* — **ir·re·proach·a·bly** \-blē\ *adv*

ir·re·sist·i·ble \-ˈzis-tə-bəl\ *adj* : impossible to successfully resist or oppose — **ir·re·sist·i·bly** \-blē\ *adv*

ir·res·o·lute \(ˈ)ir-ˈez-ə-ˌlüt, -lət\ *adj* : uncertain how to act or proceed : VACILLATING — **ir·res·o·lute·ly** *adv* — **ir·res·o·lute·ness** *n* — **ir·res·o·lu·tion** \(ˌ)ir-ˌez-ə-ˈlü-shən\ *n*

ir·re·spec·tive \ˌir-i-ˈspek-tiv\ *adj* : having no regard for persons, conditions, or consequences — **ir·re·spec·tive·ly** *adv*

irrespective of *prep* : without regard to

ir·re·spon·si·ble \ˌir-i-ˈspän(t)-sə-bəl\ *adj* : not responsible: as **a** : not answerable **b** : said or done with no sense of responsibility **c** : lacking a sense of responsibility **d** : unable esp. mentally or financially to bear responsibility — **ir·re·spon·si·bil·i·ty** \-ˌspän(t)-sə-ˈbil-ət-ē\ *n* — **ir·re·spon·si·bly** \-ˈspän(t)-sə-blē\ *adv*

ir·re·triev·a·ble \ˌir-i-ˈtrē-və-bəl\ *adj* : not capable of being recovered, regained, or remedied — **ir·re·triev·a·bly** \-blē\ *adv*

ir·rev·er·ence \(ˈ)ir-ˈev-(ə-)rən(t)s\ *n* **1** : lack of reverence

2 : an irreverent act or utterance
ir·rev·er·ent \-'ev-(ə-)rənt\ *adj* : showing lack of reverence : DISRESPECTFUL — **ir·rev·er·ent·ly** *adv*
ir·re·vers·i·ble \,ir-i-'vər-sə-bəl\ *adj* : incapable of being reversed — **ir·re·vers·i·bly** \-blē\ *adv*
ir·rev·o·ca·ble \(')ir-'ev-ə-kə-bəl\ *adj* : not capable of being revoked — **ir·rev·o·ca·bil·i·ty** \(,)ir-,ev-ə-kə-'bil-ət-ē\ *n* — **ir·rev·o·ca·bly** \(')ir-'ev-ə-kə-blē\ *adv*
ir·ri·gate \'ir-ə-,gāt\ *vb* 1 : to supply (as land) with water by artificial means 2 : to flush with a liquid — **ir·ri·ga·tion** \,ir-ə-'gā-shən\ *n*
ir·ri·ta·ble \'ir-ət-ə-bəl\ *adj* : capable of being irritated; *esp* : readily or easily irritated — **ir·ri·ta·bil·i·ty** \,ir-ət-ə-'bil-ət-ē\ *n* — **ir·ri·ta·ble·ness** *n* — **ir·ri·ta·bly** \'ir-ət-ə-blē\ *adv*
ir·ri·tant \'ir-ə-tənt\ *adj* : IRRITATING; *esp* : tending to produce physical irritation — **irritant** *n*
ir·ri·tate \'ir-ə-,tāt\ *vb* 1 : to excite impatience, anger, or displeasure in : ANNOY 2 a : to act as a stimulus toward : STIMULATE b : to make sore or inflamed : act as an irritant toward — **ir·ri·ta·tive** \-,tāt-iv\ *adj*
ir·ri·ta·tion \,ir-ə-'tā-shən\ *n* 1 : the act of irritating 2 : something that irritates 3 : the state of being irritated
ir·rupt \(')ir-'əpt\ *vi* 1 : to rush in forcibly or violently 2 : to increase suddenly in numbers — **ir·rup·tion** \(')ir-'əp-shən\ *n*
is *pres 3d sing of* BE
isin·glass \'īz-ᵊn-,glas, 'ī-ziŋ-\ *n* 1 : a very pure gelatin prepared from the air bladders of fishes (as sturgeons) 2 : mica in thin sheets
Is·lam \is-'läm, iz-, -'lam, 'is-,, 'iz-,\ *n* : the religious faith of Muslims; *also* : the civilization built on this faith — **Is·lam·ic** \is-'läm-ik, iz-, -'lam-\ *adj*
is·land \'ī-lənd\ *n* 1 : an area of land surrounded by water and smaller than a continent 2 : something suggesting an island by its isolated or surrounded position
is·land·er \'ī-lən-dər\ *n* : a native or inhabitant of an island
isle \'īl\ *n* : ISLAND; *esp* : a small island
is·let \'ī-lət\ *n* : a little island
ism \'iz-əm\ *n* : a distinctive doctrine, cause, or theory
iso·bar \'ī-sə-,bär\ *n* : a line drawn on a map to indicate areas having the same atmospheric pressure — **iso·bar·ic** \,ī-sə-'bär-ik, -'bar-\ *adj*
iso·late \'ī-sə-,lāt, 'is-ə-\ *vb* : to set apart from others; *also* : QUARANTINE — **iso·la·tion** \,ī-sə-'lā-shən, ,is-ə-\ *n*
iso·la·tion·ism \,ī-sə-'lā-shə-,niz-əm, ,is-ə-\ *n* : a policy of national isolation by avoiding international political and economic relations (as alliances) — **iso·la·tion·ist** \-sh(ə-)nəst\ *n or adj*
iso·mer \'ī-sə-mər\ *n* : any of two or more chemical compounds that contain the same numbers of atoms of the same elements but differ in structural arrangement and properties — **iso·mer·ic** \,ī-sə-'mer-ik\ *adj*
iso·met·rics \,ī-sə-'me-triks\ *n sing or pl* : exercise or a system of exercises in which opposing muscles are so contracted that there is little shortening but great increase in tone of muscle fibers involved
isos·ce·les \ī-'säs-ə-,lēz\ *adj* : having two equal sides
iso·tope \'ī-sə-,tōp\ *n* : any of two or more species of atoms of the same chemical element nearly identical in chemical behavior but differing in the number of neutrons — **iso·top·ic** \,ī-sə-'täp-ik, -'tō-pik\ *adj* — **iso·top·i·cal·ly** \-'täp-i-k(ə-)lē, -'tō-pi-\ *adv*
is·su·ance \'ish-ü-ən(t)s\ *n* : the act of issuing or giving out esp. officially
¹is·sue \'ish-(,)ü\ *n* 1 : the action of going, coming, or flowing out : EGRESS, EMERGENCE 2 : a means or place of going out : EXIT, OUTLET 3 : OFFSPRING, PROGENY 4 : final outcome : RESULT 5 a : a matter in dispute : a point of debate or controversy b : a final result or conclusion : DECISION 6 : a discharge (as of blood) from the body 7 : something coming forth from a specified source 8 a : the act of officially giving out (as new currency, supplies, or an order) : PUBLICATION b : the thing or the whole quantity of things given out at one time — **at issue** 1 : in a state of controversy : in disagreement 2 : under discussion or in dispute
²issue *vb* 1 a : to go, come, or flow out b : to come forth or cause to come forth : EMERGE, DISCHARGE, EMIT 2 : ACCRUE 3 : to descend from a specified parent or ancestor 4 : to be a consequence or final outcome : RESULT 5 : to appear through issuance or publication 6 : to have an outcome : result in 7 a : to put forth or distribute officially b : to send out for sale or circulation : PUBLISH — **is·su·a·ble** \'ish-ü-ə-bəl\ *adj* — **is·su·er** *n*
isth·mi·an \'is-mē-ən\ *adj* : of, relating to, or situated in or near an isthmus
isth·mus \'is-məs\ *n* : a narrow strip of land connecting two larger land areas
¹it \(')it, ət\ *pron* 1 : that one — used usu. in reference to a lifeless thing, a plant, a person or animal whose sex is unknown or disregarded, a group of individuals or things, or an abstract entity 2 — used as subject of a verb that expresses a condition or action without reference to an agent 3 a — used as anticipatory subject or object of a verb; often used to shift emphasis to a part of a statement other than the subject b — used with many verbs as a direct object with little or no meaning 4 : the general state of affairs or circumstances
²it \'it\ *n* : the player in a game who performs a function (as trying to catch others in a game of tag) essential to the nature of the game
¹ital·ic \ə-'tal-ik, i-, ī-\ *adj* : of or relating to a type style with characters that slant upward to the right (as in "*these words are italic*")
²italic *n* : an italic character or type
ital·i·cize \ə-'tal-ə-,sīz, i-, ī-\ *vt* : to print in italics : underscore with a single line
¹itch \'ich\ *vb* 1 : to have or produce an itch 2 : to cause to itch 3 : to have a strong persistent desire for something
²itch *n* 1 a : an uneasy irritating sensation in the skin usu. held to result from mild stimulation of pain receptors b : a skin disorder accompanied by an itch; *esp* : a contagious eruption caused by a mite 2 a : a restless usu. constant often compulsive desire b : LUST, PRURIENCE — **itch·i·ness** \'ich-ē-nəs\ *n* — **itchy** \-ē\ *adj*
item \'īt-əm\ *n* 1 : a separate particular in an enumeration, account, or series : ARTICLE 2 : a separate piece of news or information : a short news paragraph
item·ize \'īt-ə-,mīz\ *vt* : to set down in detail or by particulars : LIST
it·er·ate \'it-ə-,rāt\ *vt* : REITERATE, REPEAT — **it·er·a·tion** \,it-ə-'rā-shən\ *n* — **it·er·a·tive** \'it-ə-,rāt-iv, -rət-\ *adj*
itin·er·ant \ī-'tin-ə-rənt, ə-'tin-\ *adj* : traveling from place to place; *esp* : covering a circuit — **itin·er·an·cy** \-rən-sē\ *or* **itin·er·a·cy** \-rə-sē\ *n* — **itinerant** *n* — **itin·er·ant·ly** *adv*
itin·er·ary \ī-'tin-ə-,rer-ē, ə-\ *n, pl* **-ar·ies** 1 : the route of a journey 2 : a travel diary 3 : a traveler's guidebook — **itinerary** *adj*
its \(,)its, əts\ *adj* : of or relating to it or itself esp. as possessor, agent, or object of an action
it·self \it-'self, ət-\ *pron* : that identical one — used reflexively or for emphasis
ivied \'ī-vēd\ *adj* : overgrown with ivy
ivo·ry \'īv-(ə-)rē\ *n, pl* **-ries** 1 : the hard creamy-white modified dentine that composes the tusks of a tusked mammal (as an elephant) 2 : a variable color averaging a pale yellow 3 : something (as piano keys) made of ivory or of a similar substance
ivory tower *n* : a secluded place for meditation : RETREAT
ivy \'ī-vē\ *n, pl* **ivies** : a trailing woody vine with evergreen leaves and small black berries

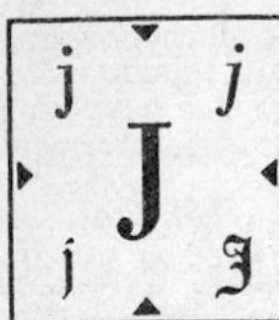

j \'jā\ *n, often cap* : the 10th letter of the English alphabet

jab \'jab\ *vb* **jabbed**; **jab·bing** : to thrust quickly or abruptly with or as if with something sharp : POKE — **jab** *n*

[1]**jab·ber** \'jab-ər\ *vb* **jab·bered**; **jab·ber·ing** \'jab-(ə-)riŋ\ : to talk or speak rapidly, indistinctly, or unintelligibly — **jab·ber·er** \'jab-ər-ər\ *n*

[2]**jabber** *n* : GIBBERISH, CHATTER

jab·ber·wocky \'jab-ər-,wäk-ē\ *n* : meaningless speech or writing

ja·bot \zha-'bō, ja-\ *n* : a ruffle of cloth or lace that falls from the collar down the front of a dress or shirt

[1]**jack** \'jak\ *n* **1** *often cap* **a** : MAN; *esp* : one of the common people **b** : SAILOR **2 a** : a device for turning a spit (as in roasting meat) **b** : any of various portable mechanisms for exerting pressure or lifting a heavy body a short distance **3** : a male ass **4 a** : something small of its kind **b** : a small target ball in lawn bowling **c** : a small national flag flown by a ship **d** (1) : a small 6-pointed metal object used in a game (2) *pl* : a game played with jacks **5** : a playing card bearing the stylized figure of a man **6** : a socket in an electric circuit used with a plug to make a connection with another circuit

[2]**jack** *vb* **1** : to hunt or fish for game at night with a jacklight **2** : to move or lift by or as if by a jack **3** : INCREASE, RAISE — **jack·er** *n*

jack·al \'jak-əl, -,ȯl\ *n* **1** : any of several Old World wild dogs smaller than the related wolves **2** : a person who performs routine or menial and often base tasks for another : LACKEY

jack·a·napes \'jak-ə-,nāps\ *n* **1** : MONKEY, APE **2** : an impudent or conceited person

jack·ass \'jak-,as\ *n* **1** : a male ass; *also* : DONKEY **2** : a stupid person : FOOL

jack·ass·ery \-,as-(ə-)rē\ *n* : a stupid or foolish act

jack·boot \'jak-,büt\ *n* **1** : a heavy military boot of glossy black leather extending above the knee **2** : a laceless military boot reaching to the calf

jack·daw \'jak-,dȯ\ *n* : a common black and gray Eurasian bird related to but smaller than the common crow

jack·et \'jak-ət\ *n* **1** : a garment for the upper body usu. having a front opening, collar, and sleeves **2** : an outer covering or casing; *esp* : a detachable outer paper wrapper on a bound book — **jack·et·ed** \-ət-əd\ *adj*

Jack Frost *n* : frost or frosty weather personified

jack–in–the–box \'jak-ən-t͟hə-,bäks\ *n, pl* **jack–in–the–boxes** *or* **jacks–in–the–box** : a small box out of which a figure (as of a clown's head) springs when the lid is raised

[1]**jack·knife** \'jak-,nīf\ *n* **1** : a large strong clasp knife for the pocket **2** : a dive in which the diver bends from the waist and touches his ankles before straightening out

[2]**jackknife** *vi* **1** : to double up like a jackknife **2** : to turn or rise and form an angle of 90 degrees or less with each other — used esp. of a pair of connected vehicles

jack·light \'jak-,līt\ *n* : a light used esp. in hunting or fishing at night

jack–of–all–trades \,jak-ə-'vȯl-,trādz\ *n, pl* **jacks–of–all–trades** : a person who can do passable work at various trades : HANDYMAN

jack–o'–lan·tern \'jak-ə-,lant-ərn\ *n* : a lantern made of a pumpkin cut to look like a human face

jack·pot \'jak-,pät\ *n* **1 a** : a large pot (as in poker) formed by the accumulation of stakes from previous play **b** (1) : a combination on a slot machine that wins a top prize or all the coins in the machine (2) : the sum so won **2** : an impressive often unexpected success or reward

jack·rab·bit \-,rab-ət\ *n* : any of several large hares of western No. America with long ears and long hind legs

jack–tar \-'tär\ *n, often cap* : SAILOR

jac·quard \'jak-,ärd\ *n, often cap* : a fabric of intricate variegated weave or pattern

[1]**jade** \'jād\ *n* **1** : a broken-down, vicious, or worthless horse **2** : a disreputable woman

[2]**jade** *vb* **1 a** : to wear out by overwork or abuse **b** : to tire by tedious tasks **2** : to become weary

[3]**jade** *n* : a tough compact usu. green gemstone that takes a high polish

jad·ed \'jād-əd\ *adj* **1** : EXHAUSTED **2** : SATIATED

[1]**jag** \'jag\ *vb* **jagged** \'jagd\; **jag·ging** : to make ragged : NOTCH

[2]**jag** *n* : a sharp projecting part : BARB

[3]**jag** *n* **1** : a small load (as of hay) **2** : a drunken spree

jag·ged \'jag-əd\ *adj* : sharply notched : ROUGH — **jag·ged·ly** *adv* — **jag·ged·ness** *n*

jag·uar \'jag-,wär, 'jag-yə-,wär\ *n* : a large cat of tropical America that is larger and stockier than the leopard and is brownish yellow or buff with black spots

jai alai \'hī-,lī, ,hī-ə-'lī\ *n* : a court game played by two or four players with a ball and a long curved wicker basket strapped to the right wrist

[1]**jail** \'jāl\ *n* : PRISON; *esp* : a building for the confinement of persons held in temporary custody

[2]**jail** *vt* : to confine in or as if in a jail

jail·bird \-,bərd\ *n* : a person confined in jail; *esp* : an habitual criminal

jail·break \-,brāk\ *n* : a forcible escape from jail

jail·er *or* **jail·or** \'jā-lər\ *n* : the keeper of a jail

jal·ap \'jal-əp, 'jäl-\ *n* : a purgative tuberous root obtained esp. from a Mexican plant related to the morning glory; *also* : a drug prepared from this

ja·lopy \jə-'läp-ē\ *n, pl* **-lop·ies** : a dilapidated old automobile

jal·ou·sie \'jal-ə-sē\ *n* **1** : a blind with adjustable horizontal slats for admitting light and air while excluding sun and rain **2** : a window made of adjustable glass louvers that control ventilation

[1]**jam** \'jam\ *vb* **jammed**; **jam·ming** **1 a** : to press into a close or tight position **b** : to cause to become wedged so as to be unworkable **c** : to block passage of : OBSTRUCT **d** : to fill full or to excess : PACK **2** : to push forcibly; *esp* : to apply the brakes suddenly with full force **3** : CRUSH, BRUISE **4** : to make unintelligible by sending out interfering signals or messages **5** : to become unworkable through the jamming of a movable part **6** : to force one's way into a restricted space — **jam·mer** *n*

[2]**jam** *n* **1 a** : an act or instance of jamming **b** : a crowded mass that impedes or blocks **2** : a difficult state of affairs

[3]**jam** *n* : a food made by boiling fruit and sugar to a thick consistency

jamb \'jam\ *n* : an upright piece forming the side of an opening (as of a door)

jam·bo·ree \,jam-bə-'rē\ *n* **1** : a large festive gathering **2** : a national or international camping assembly of boy scouts

jam session *n* : an impromptu performance by a group of jazz musicians characterized by group improvisation

[1]**jan·gle** \'jaŋ-gəl\ *vb* **jan·gled**; **jan·gling** \-g(ə-)liŋ\ **1** : to quarrel verbally **2 a** : to make a harsh or discordant sound **b** : to cause to sound harshly or inharmoniously — **jan·gler** \-g(ə-)lər\ *n*

[2]**jangle** *n* **1** : noisy quarreling **2** : discordant sound

jan·is·sary *or* **jan·i·zary** \'jan-ə-,ser-ē, -,zer-\ *n, pl* **-sar·ies** *or* **-zar·ies** *often cap* : a soldier of a select corps of Turkish troops organized in the 14th century and abolished in 1826

jan·i·tor \'jan-ət-ər\ *n* **1** : DOORKEEPER **2** : a person who has the care of a building (as a school) — **jan·i·to·ri·al** \,jan-ə-'tōr-ē-əl\ *adj* — **jan·i·tress** \'jan-ə-trəs\ *n*

Jan·u·ary \'jan-yə-,wer-ē\ *n* : the 1st month of the year

[1]**jape** \'jāp\ *vb* **1** : JOKE, FOOL **2** : MOCK — **jap·er** *n* — **jap·ery** \'jā-p(ə-)rē\ *n*
[2]**jape** *n* : JEST, GIBE
[1]**jar** \'jär\ *vb* **jarred**; **jar·ring** **1 a** : to make a harsh or discordant sound **b** : to have a harsh or disagreeable effect **2** : to undergo severe vibration **3** : to make unstable : SHAKE **4** : CLASH, QUARREL
[2]**jar** *n* **1** : a harsh sound **2** : JOLT **3** : QUARREL, DISPUTE **4** : a painful effect : SHOCK
[3]**jar** *n* **1** : a widemouthed container usu. of earthenware or glass **2** : JARFUL
jar·di·niere \ˌjärd-ᵊn-'i(ə)r\ *n* : an ornamental stand or pot for plants or flowers
jar·ful \'jär-ˌfu̇l\ *n, pl* **jarfuls** \-ˌfu̇lz\ *or* **jars·ful** \'järz-ˌfu̇l\ : the quantity held by a jar
jar·gon \'jär-gən, -ˌgän\ *n* **1 a** : confused unintelligible language **b** : a hybrid language or dialect used for communication between peoples of different speech **2** : the special vocabulary or idiom of a particular activity or group **3** : obscure and often pretentious language marked by circumlocutions and abstract words
jas·mine \'jaz-mən\ *n* : any of numerous often climbing shrubs of the olive family with extremely fragrant flowers; *also* : any of various plants noted for sweet-scented flowers
jas·per \'jas-pər\ *n* : an opaque fine-grained usu. red, yellow, or brown quartz; *esp* : green chalcedony — **jas·pery** \-pə-rē\ *adj*
[1]**jaun·dice** \'jȯn-dəs\ *n* **1** : yellowish discoloration of the skin, tissues, and body fluids caused by the deposition of bile pigments; *also* : a disease or abnormal condition marked by jaundice **2** : a state or attitude characterized by satiety, distaste, or hostility
[2]**jaundice** *vt* **1** : to affect with jaundice **2** : to affect by envy, distaste, or hostility
[1]**jaunt** \'jȯnt\ *vi* : to make a short journey for pleasure
[2]**jaunt** *n* : a short excursion for pleasure or recreation
jaun·ty \'jȯnt-ē\ *adj* : sprightly in manner or appearance : LIVELY — **jaun·ti·ly** \'jȯnt-ᵊl-ē\ *adv* — **jaun·ti·ness** \'jȯnt-ē-nəs\ *n*
jav·e·lin \'jav-(ə-)lən\ *n* **1** : a light spear **2** : a slender metal-tipped shaft of wood thrown for distance in an athletic field event
jaw \'jȯ\ *n* **1 a** : either of two cartilaginous or bony structures that support the soft parts enclosing the mouth and usu. bear teeth on their oral margin **b** : the parts constituting the walls of the mouth and serving to open and close it — usu. used in pl. **2** : one of a set of opposing parts that open and close for holding or crushing something between them — **jawed** \'jȯd\ *adj*
jaw·bone \'jȯ-'bōn, -ˌbōn\ *n* : JAW 1a; *esp* : MANDIBLE
jaw·break·er \-ˌbrā-kər\ *n* **1** : a word difficult to pronounce **2** : a round hard candy
jay \'jā\ *n* : any of several noisy birds of the crow family that are smaller and more graceful than a crow and usu. more brightly colored
jay·walk \'jā-ˌwȯk\ *vi* : to cross a street carelessly without paying attention to traffic regulations — **jay·walk·er** *n*
[1]**jazz** \'jaz\ *vt* **1** : ENLIVEN — usu. used with *up* **2** : to play in the manner of jazz
[2]**jazz** *n* **1 a** : American music characterized by group and solo improvisation, syncopated rhythms, and contrapuntal ensemble playing **b** : rhythmic popular dance music influenced by jazz **2** : empty talk : STUFF — **jazz·man** \-mən, -ˌman\ *n*
jazzy \'jaz-ē\ *adj* **1** : having the characteristics of jazz **2** : marked by unrestraint, animation, or flashiness — **jazz·i·ly** \'jaz-ə-lē\ *adv* — **jazz·i·ness** \'jaz-ē-nəs\ *n*
jeal·ous \'jel-əs\ *adj* **1** : demanding complete devotion **2** : fearful or suspicious of a rival or competitor : feeling a spiteful envy toward someone more successful than oneself **3** : suspicious that a person one loves is not faithful **4** : WATCHFUL, CAREFUL — **jeal·ous·ly** *adv*
jeal·ou·sy \'jel-ə-sē\ *n, pl* **-sies** **1** : a jealous disposition, attitude, or feeling **2** : zealous vigilance
jean \'jēn\ *n* **1** : a durable twilled cotton cloth used esp. for sportswear and work clothes **2** *pl* : pants made of jean or denim
[1]**jeer** \'ji(ə)r\ *vb* **1** : to speak or cry out in derision **2** : DERIDE, RIDICULE — **jeer·er** *n* — **jeer·ing·ly** *adv*
[2]**jeer** *n* : a jeering remark or sound : TAUNT
Je·ho·vah \ji-'hō-və\ *n* : [2]GOD
je·june \ji-'jün\ *adj* **1** : lacking nutritive value **2** : lacking interest or significance : DULL **3** : lacking maturity : CHILDISH — **je·june·ly** *adv* — **je·june·ness** *n*
jell \'jel\ *vb* **1** : to come to the consistency of jelly **2** : to take shape : CRYSTALLIZE **3** : to cause to jell
[1]**jel·ly** \'jel-ē\ *n, pl* **jellies** **1** : a food with a soft somewhat elastic consistency due usu. to the presence of gelatin or pectin; *esp* : a fruit product made by boiling sugar and the juice of fruit **2** : a substance resembling jelly in consistency
[2]**jelly** *vb* **jel·lied**; **jel·ly·ing** **1** : to make into or become jelly **2** : to set in jelly
jel·ly·fish \-ˌfish\ *n* : a free-swimming animal with a gelatinous, disk-shaped, and usu. nearly transparent body
jen·net \'jen-ət\ *n* **1** : a small Spanish horse **2** : a female donkey
jen·ny \'jen-ē\ *n, pl* **jennies** **1** : a female bird **2** : a female donkey
jeop·ar·dize \'jep-ər-ˌdīz\ *vt* : to expose to danger : IMPERIL; *also* : RISK
jeop·ar·dy \'jep-ərd-ē\ *n* **1** : exposure to death, loss, or injury : DANGER **2** : the danger that an accused person is subjected to when on trial for a criminal offense
jer·e·mi·ad \ˌjer-ə-'mī-əd, -'mī-ˌad\ *n* : a prolonged lamentation or complaint
[1]**jerk** \'jərk\ *vb* **1** : to give a sharp quick push, pull, or twist to **2 a** : to make a sudden sharp motion **b** : to move in short abrupt motions or with frequent jolts
[2]**jerk** *n* **1** : a short quick pull or twist : TWITCH **2 a** : an involuntary spasmodic muscular movement due to reflex action **b** *pl* : involuntary twitchings due to nervous excitement **3** : a stupid, foolish, or eccentric person
[3]**jerk** *vt* : to cut (meat) into long slices or strips and dry in the sun
jer·kin \'jər-kən\ *n* : a close-fitting hip-length sleeveless jacket
jerky \'jər-kē\ *adj* : moving by sudden starts and stops — **jerk·i·ly** \-kə-lē\ *adv* — **jerk·i·ness** \-kē-nəs\ *n*
jer·ry–build \'jer-ē-ˌbild\ *vt* **-built** \-ˌbilt\; **-build·ing** : to build cheaply and flimsily — **jer·ry–build·er** *n* — **jer·ry–built** \-ˌbilt\ *adj*
jer·sey \'jər-zē\ *n, pl* **jerseys** **1** : a plain knitted fabric of wool, cotton, nylon, rayon, or silk **2** : any of various close-fitting knitted garments **3** : any of a breed of small usu. fawn-colored dairy cattle noted for their rich milk
jess \'jes\ *n* : a leg strap to which the leash of a falconer's hawk is attached — **jessed** \'jest\ *adj*
[1]**jest** \'jest\ *n* **1 a** : an act intended to provoke laughter : PRANK **b** : a comic incident **2 a** : JEER **b** : a witty remark **3 a** : a frivolous mood or manner **b** : a state of gaiety and merriment **4** : LAUGHINGSTOCK
[2]**jest** *vi* : JOKE, BANTER
jest·er \'jes-tər\ *n* **1** : FOOL 2 **2** : one given to jests
Je·sus \'jē-zəs\ *n* : the founder of the Christian religion
[1]**jet** \'jet\ *n* : a compact velvet-black mineral similar to coal in composition that takes a good polish and is often used for jewelry
[2]**jet** *vb* **jet·ted**; **jet·ting** : to spout or emit in a stream : SPURT

[3]jet *n* **1 a :** a forceful rush of liquid, gas, or vapor through a narrow opening or a nozzle **b :** a nozzle for a jet of fluid (as gas or water) **2 :** a jet-propelled airplane

[4]jet *vi* **jet·ted; jet·ting :** to travel by a jet-propelled airplane

jet engine *n* **:** an engine that produces motion as a result of the rearward discharge of a jet of fluid; *esp* **:** an airplane engine having one or more exhaust nozzles for discharging rearwardly a jet of heated air and exhaust gases

jet–pro·pelled \ˌjet-prə-ˈpeld\ *adj* **:** propelled by a jet engine

jet·sam \ˈjet-səm\ *n* **:** goods thrown overboard to lighten a ship in distress; *esp* **:** such goods when washed ashore

jet set *n* **:** an international social group of wealthy individuals who frequent fashionable resorts

jet stream *n* **:** a long narrow meandering current of high-speed winds blowing from a generally westerly direction several miles above the earth's surface

[1]jet·ti·son \ˈjet-ə-sən\ *n* **:** a voluntary sacrifice of cargo to lighten a ship's load in time of distress

[2]jettison *vt* **1 a :** to throw (goods) overboard to lighten a ship in distress **b :** to drop from an airplane in flight **2 :** to cast away or aside **:** DISCARD

jet·ty \ˈjet-ē\ *n, pl* **jetties 1 :** a pier built out into the water to influence the current or to protect a harbor **2 :** a landing wharf

jeu d'es·prit \zhœ̄-des-prē\ *n, pl* **jeux d'esprit** *same*\ **:** a witty comment or composition

Jew \ˈjü\ *n* **:** one whose religion is Judaism

[1]jew·el \ˈjü(-ə)l\ *n* **1 :** an ornament of precious metal set with stones or finished with enamel and worn as an accessory of dress **2 :** one that is highly esteemed **3 :** a precious stone **:** GEM **4 :** a bearing for a pivot in a watch made of a crystal or of a precious stone

[2]jewel *vt* **-eled** *or* **-elled; -el·ing** *or* **-el·ling :** to adorn or equip with jewels

jew·el·er *or* **jew·el·ler** \ˈjü-(ə-)lər\ *n* **:** a person who makes or deals in jewelry and related articles

jew·el·ry \ˈjü(-ə)l-rē\ *n* **:** JEWELS; *esp* **:** objects of precious metal set with gems and worn for personal adornment

Jew·ess \ˈjü-əs\ *n* **:** a female Jew

Jew·ish \ˈjü-ish\ *adj* **:** of, relating to, or characteristic of the Jews — **Jew·ish·ly** *adv* — **Jew·ish·ness** *n*

Jew·ry \ˈju̇(ə)r-ē, ˈjü-rē\ *n, pl* **Jewries 1 :** a district of a city inhabited by Jews **:** GHETTO **2 :** the Jewish people

Jew's harp *or* **Jews' harp** \ˈjüz-ˌhärp\ *n* **:** a small lyre-shaped instrument that when placed between the teeth gives tones from a metal tongue struck by the finger

jib \ˈjib\ *n* **:** a triangular sail extending forward from the foremast of a ship

jibe \ˈjīb\ *vi* **:** to be in accord **:** AGREE

jif·fy \ˈjif-ē\ *n, pl* **jiffies :** MOMENT, INSTANT

[1]jig \ˈjig\ *n* **1 :** a lively springy dance in triple rhythm **2 :** TRICK, GAME **3 :** a device used to maintain mechanically the correct position of a piece of work and a tool or of parts of work during assembly

[2]jig *vb* **jigged; jig·ging :** to dance a jig

jig·ger \ˈjig-ər\ *n* **1 :** one that jigs or operates a jig **2 :** a measure used in mixing drinks that usu. holds 1½ ounces

[1]jig·gle \ˈjig-əl\ *vb* **jig·gled; jig·gling** \ˈjig-(ə-)liŋ\ **:** to move or cause to move with quick little jerks

[2]jiggle *n* **:** a jiggling motion

jig·saw \ˈjig-ˌsȯ\ *n* **:** a machine saw with a narrow blade that moves up and down for cutting curved and irregular lines or openwork patterns

jigsaw puzzle *n* **:** a puzzle consisting of small irregular pieces fitted together to form a picture

[1]jilt \ˈjilt\ *n* **:** a woman who jilts a man

[2]jilt *vt* **:** to cast (as a lover) aside unfeelingly

jim crow \ˈjim-ˈkrō\ *n, often cap J & C* **:** discrimination against the Negro by legal enforcement or traditional sanctions — **jim crow·ism** \-ˌiz-əm\ *n, often cap J & C*

jim–dan·dy \ˈjim-ˈdan-dē\ *n* **:** something excellent of its kind

[1]jim·my \ˈjim-ē\ *n, pl* **jimmies :** a short crowbar used by burglars

[2]jimmy *vt* **jim·mied; jim·my·ing :** to force open with or as if with a jimmy

jim·son·weed \ˈjim(p)-sən-ˌwēd\ *n, often cap* **:** a poisonous coarse annual weed of the nightshade family with rank-smelling foliage and large white or violet trumpet-shaped flowers

[1]jin·gle \ˈjiŋ-gəl\ *vb* **jin·gled; jin·gling** \-g(ə-)liŋ\ **1 :** to make a light clinking or tinkling sound **2 :** to rhyme or sound in a catchy repetitious manner **3 :** to cause to jingle — **jin·gler** \-g(ə-)lər\ *n*

[2]jingle *n* **1 a :** a light clinking or tinkling sound **b :** a catchy repetition of sounds in a poem **2 :** a short verse or song marked by catchy repetition — **jin·gly** \-g(ə-)lē\ *adj*

[1]jin·go \ˈjiŋ-gō\ *interj* — used as a mild oath usu. in the phrase *by jingo*

[2]jingo *n, pl* **jingoes :** one characterized by jingoism — **jin·go·ish** \-ish\ *adj*

jin·go·ism \ˈjiŋ-gō-ˌiz-əm\ *n* **:** extreme chauvinism or nationalism marked esp. by a belligerent foreign policy — **jin·go·ist** \-əst\ *n* — **jin·go·is·tic** \ˌjiŋ-gō-ˈis-tik\ *adj*

jinn \ˈjin\ *or* **jin·ni** \jə-ˈnē, ˈjin-ē\ *n, pl* **jinns** *or* **jinn :** one of a class of spirits held by the Muslims to inhabit the earth, to assume various forms, and to exercise supernatural power

jin·rik·i·sha \jin-ˈrik-ˌshȯ\ *n* **:** a small 2-wheeled covered vehicle pulled by one man and used orig. in Japan

[1]jinx \ˈjiŋ(k)s\ *n* **:** one that brings bad luck

[2]jinx *vt* **:** to foredoom to failure or misfortune

jit·ney \ˈjit-nē\ *n, pl* **jitneys :** a small bus that carries passengers over a regular route according to a flexible schedule

jit·ter·bug \ˈjit-ər-ˌbəg\ *n* **1 :** a dance in which couples two-step, balance, and twirl in standardized patterns or with vigorous acrobatics **2 :** one who dances the jitterbug — **jitterbug** *vi*

jit·ters \ˈjit-ərz\ *n pl* **:** extreme nervousness — **jit·tery** \-ə-rē\ *adj*

[1]jive \ˈjīv\ *n* **1 :** swing music or dancing performed to it **2 a :** the jargon of hipsters **b :** a special jargon of difficult or slang terms

[2]jive *vi* **:** to dance to or play jive

[1]job \ˈjäb\ *n* **1 a :** a piece of work; *esp* **:** one undertaken on order at a stated rate **b :** the object or material on which work is being done **c :** something produced by or as if by work **2 :** something done for private advantage **3 a :** something that has to be done **:** TASK **b :** a specific duty, role, or function **c :** a regular remunerative position — **job·less** \-ləs\ *adj* — **job·less·ness** *n*

[2]job *vb* **jobbed; job·bing 1 :** to do occasional pieces of work for hire **2 :** to hire or let by the job

job·ber \ˈjäb-ər\ *n* **1 :** a person who buys goods and then sells them to other dealers **:** MIDDLEMAN **2 :** a person who does work by the job

job·hold·er \ˈjäb-ˌhōl-dər\ *n* **:** one having a regular job; *esp* **:** a government employee

job lot *n* **1 :** a miscellaneous collection of goods for sale as a lot usu. to a retailer **2 :** a miscellaneous and usu. inferior collection or group

job work *n* **:** commercial printing of miscellaneous orders

[1]jock·ey \ˈjäk-ē\ *n, pl* **jockeys 1 :** one who rides a horse esp. as a professional in a race **2 :** OPERATOR

[2]jockey *vb* **jock·eyed; jock·ey·ing 1 :** to ride (a horse) as jockey **2 a :** to maneuver or manipulate by adroit or devious means **b :** to maneuver for advantage **3 :** OUTWIT, TRICK, CHEAT

jockey club *n* : an association for the promotion and regulation of horse racing
jo·cose \jō-'kōs\ *adj*. **1** : given to joking : MERRY **2** : characterized by joking : HUMOROUS — **jo·cose·ly** *adv* — **jo·cose·ness** *n*
joc·u·lar \'jäk-yə-lər\ *adj* **1** : given to jesting : MIRTHFUL **2** : said or done in jest : PLAYFUL — **joc·u·lar·ly** *adv*
joc·u·lar·i·ty \ˌjäk-yə-'lar-ət-ē\ *n, pl* **-ties** **1** : the quality or state of being jocular **2** : a jocular act or remark
joc·und \'jäk-ənd, 'jō-kənd\ *adj* : marked by or suggestive of mirth or cheerfulness : GAY — **joc·und·ly** *adv*
jodh·pur \'jäd-pər\ *n* **1** *pl* : riding breeches loose above the knee and tight-fitting below **2** : an ankle-high boot fastened with a strap that is buckled at the side
[1]**jog** \'jäg\ *vb* **jogged**; **jog·ging** **1** : to give a slight shake or push to : NUDGE **2** : to rouse to alertness **3** : to move up and down or about with a short heavy motion **4 a** : to go or cause to go at a jog **b** : to go at a slow or monotonous pace : TRUDGE — **jog·ger** *n*
[2]**jog** *n* **1** : a slight shake : PUSH **2 a** : a jogging movement, pace, or trip **b** : a horse's slow gait with marked beats
[3]**jog** *n* **1** : a projecting or retreating part of a line or surface **2** : a brief abrupt change in direction
[1]**jog·gle** \'jäg-əl\ *vb* **jog·gled**; **jog·gling** \'jäg-(ə-)liŋ\ **1** : to shake slightly **2** : to move shakily or jerkily — **jog·gler** \-(ə-)lər\ *n*
[2]**joggle** *n* : [2]JOG 2a
john·ny \'jän-ē\ *n, pl* **johnnies** : a short gown opening in the back that is used by hospital bed patients
john·ny·cake \'jän-ē-ˌkāk\ *n* : a bread made with cornmeal, flour, eggs, and milk
joie de vi·vre \ˌzhwäd-ə-'vēvrᵊ\ *n* : keen or buoyant enjoyment of life
[1]**join** \'jȯin\ *vb* **1 a** : to bring or fasten together in close physical contact **b** : to connect (as points) by a line **2** : to put or bring into close association or relationship **3 a** : to come into the company of **b** : to associate oneself with : become a member of **4 a** : to come together so as to be connected **b** : ADJOIN **5** : to take part in a collective activity
[2]**join** *n* : a point of joining : JOINT
join·er \'jȯi-nər\ *n* **1** : a person whose occupation is to construct articles by joining pieces of wood **2** : a gregarious person who joins many organizations
join·ery \'jȯin-(ə-)rē\ *n* **1** : the art or trade of a joiner **2** : things made by a joiner
[1]**joint** \'jȯint\ *n* **1** : the point of contact between elements of an animal skeleton with the parts that surround and support it **2** : a large piece of meat for roasting **3** : a place where two things or parts are joined **4 a** : a shabby or disreputable place of entertainment **b** : PLACE, ESTABLISHMENT — **joint·ed** \-əd\ *adj* — **out of joint** : DISLOCATED
[2]**joint** *adj* **1** : UNITED, COMBINED **2** : done by or shared by two or more persons **3** : sharing with another
[3]**joint** *vb* **1 a** : to unite by a joint : fit together **b** : to provide with a joint **2** : to separate the joints of — **joint·er** *n*
joint·ly \-lē\ *adv* : in a joint manner : TOGETHER
joist \'jȯist\ *n* : any of the small timbers or metal beams ranged parallel from wall to wall in a building to support the floor or ceiling
[1]**joke** \'jōk\ *n* **1 a** : something said or done to provoke laughter; *esp* : a brief oral narrative with a climactic humorous twist **b** (1) : the humorous or ridiculous element in something (2) : RAILLERY, KIDDING **c** : PRACTICAL JOKE **d** : LAUGHINGSTOCK **2 a** : something lacking substance, genuineness, or quality **b** : something presenting no difficulty
[2]**joke** *vb* **1** : to make jokes : JEST **2** : to make the object of a joke : KID — **jok·ing·ly** *adv*
jok·er \'jō-kər\ *n* **1** : a person who jokes **2** : a part (as of an agreement) meaning something quite different from what it seems to mean and changing the apparent intention of the whole **3** : an extra card used in some card games
jol·li·fi·ca·tion \ˌjäl-i-fə-'kā-shən\ *n* : a festive celebration : MERRYMAKING
jol·li·ty \'jäl-ət-ē\ *n, pl* **-ties** : GAIETY, MERRIMENT
[1]**jol·ly** \'jäl-ē\ *adj* **1 a** (1) : full of high spirits : JOYOUS (2) : given to conviviality : JOVIAL **b** : expressing, suggesting, or inspiring gaiety : CHEERFUL **2** : extremely pleasant or agreeable : SPLENDID
[2]**jolly** *vb* **jol·lied**; **jol·ly·ing** **1** : to engage in good-natured banter **2** : to put in good humor esp. in order to gain an end
Jol·ly Rog·er \ˌjäl-ē-'räj-ər\ *n* : a black flag with a white skull and crossbones
[1]**jolt** \'jōlt\ *vb* **1** : to give a quick hard knock or blow to : JAR **2** : to disturb the composure of **3** : to interfere with roughly and abruptly **4** : to move or cause to move with a sudden jerky motion — **jolt·er** *n*
[2]**jolt** *n* **1 a** : an abrupt sharp jerky blow or movement **b** : a jarring blow **2** : a sudden shock, surprise, or disappointment
jon·gleur \zhōⁿ-'glər\ *n* : an itinerant medieval minstrel
jon·quil \'jän-kwəl, 'jäŋ-\ *n* : a Mediterranean perennial bulbous herb with long linear leaves that is widely grown for its yellow or white fragrant short-tubed clustered flowers
josh \'jäsh\ *vb* : to make fun of : TEASE, JOKE — **josh·er** *n*
joss \'jäs, 'jȯs\ *n* : a Chinese idol or cult image
joss house *n* : a Chinese temple or shrine
jos·tle \'jäs-əl\ *vb* **jos·tled**; **jos·tling** \'jäs-(ə-)liŋ\ **1** : to run or knock against so as to jar : push roughly **2** : to make one's way by pushing and shoving : ELBOW
[1]**jot** \'jät\ *n* : the least bit : IOTA
[2]**jot** *vt* **jot·ted**; **jot·ting** : to write briefly or hurriedly : set down in the form of a note
jot·ting \'jät-iŋ\ *n* : a brief note : MEMORANDUM
jounce \'jau̇n(t)s\ *vb* : JOLT — **jounce** *n*
jour·nal \'jərn-ᵊl\ *n* **1 a** : a brief account of daily events **b** : a record of experiences, ideas, or reflections kept for private use **c** : a record of transactions kept by a deliberative or legislative body **2 a** : a daily newspaper **b** : a periodical dealing esp. with current events **3** : the part of a rotating shaft, axle, roll, or spindle that turns in a bearing
jour·nal·ese \ˌjərn-ᵊl-'ēz, -'ēs\ *n* : a style of writing held to be characteristic of newspapers
jour·nal·ism \'jərn-ᵊl-ˌiz-əm\ *n* **1** : the business of writing for, editing, or publishing periodicals (as newspapers) **2** : writing designed for or characteristic of newspapers or popular magazines
jour·nal·ist \-ᵊl-əst\ *n* : an editor of or writer for a periodical
jour·nal·is·tic \ˌjərn-ᵊl-'is-tik\ *adj* : of, relating to, or characteristic of journalism or journalists — **jour·nal·is·ti·cal·ly** \-ti-k(ə-)lē\ *adv*
[1]**jour·ney** \'jər-nē\ *n, pl* **journeys** : travel or passage from one place to another
[2]**journey** *vb* **jour·neyed**; **jour·ney·ing** **1** : to go on a journey : TRAVEL **2** : to travel over or through : TRAVERSE — **jour·ney·er** *n*
jour·ney·man \-mən\ *n* **1** : a worker who has learned a trade and works for another person usu. by the day **2** : an experienced reliable workman in any field
[1]**joust** \'jau̇st\ *vi* : to engage in a joust : TILT
[2]**joust** *n* : a combat on horseback between two knights with lances esp. as part of a tournament
jo·vi·al \'jō-vē-əl\ *adj* : marked by good humor : full of fun : JOLLY — **jo·vi·al·i·ty** \ˌjō-vē-'al-ət-ē\ *n* — **jo·vi·al·ly** \'jō-vē-ə-lē\ *adv*
[1]**jowl** \'jau̇l\ *n* **1** : JAW; *esp* : MANDIBLE **2** : CHEEK 1
[2]**jowl** *n* : usu. slack flesh (as a wattle) associated with the lower jaw or throat — **jowly** \-ē\ *adj*
joy \'jȯi\ *n* **1** : a feeling of great pleasure or happiness that

comes from success, good fortune, or a sense of well-being : GLADNESS **2** : something that gives great pleasure or happiness

joy·ance \'jȯi-ən(t)s\ *n* : DELIGHT, ENJOYMENT

joy·ful \'jȯi-fəl\ *adj* : experiencing, causing, or showing joy : HAPPY — **joy·ful·ly** \-fə-lē\ *adv* — **joy·ful·ness** *n*

joy·less \'jȯi-ləs\ *adj* : not feeling or causing joy : CHEERLESS — **joy·less·ly** *adv* — **joy·less·ness** *n*

joy·ous \'jȯi-əs\ *adj* : JOYFUL — **joy·ous·ly** *adv* — **joy·ous·ness** *n*

joy·ride \'jȯi-ˌrīd\ *n* : a ride taken for pleasure and often marked by reckless driving — **joy·rid·er** *n* — **joy·rid·ing** *n*

ju·bi·lant \'jü-bə-lənt\ *adj* : expressing great joy : EXULTANT — **ju·bi·lant·ly** *adv*

ju·bi·la·tion \ˌjü-bə-'lā-shən\ *n* **1** : an act of rejoicing : the state of being jubilant **2** : an expression of great joy

ju·bi·lee \'jü-bə-ˌlē\ *n* **1** : a special anniversary; *esp* : a 50th anniversary **2** : a season or occasion of celebration

Ju·da·ic \jü-'dā-ik\ *adj* : of, relating to, or characteristic of Jews or Judaism

Ju·da·ism \'jüd-ə-ˌiz-əm, 'jüd-ē-\ *n* **1** : a religion developed among the ancient Hebrews and marked by belief in one God who is creator, ruler, and redeemer of the universe and by the moral and ceremonial laws of the Old Testament and the rabbinic tradition **2** : conformity to Jewish rites, ceremonies, and practices **3** : the cultural, social, and religious beliefs and practices of the Jews **4** : the whole body of Jews

Ju·das \'jüd-əs\ *n* : TRAITOR

[1]judge \'jəj\ *vb* **1** : to form an authoritative opinion **2** : to decide as a judge : TRY **3** : to determine or pronounce after inquiry and deliberation : CONSIDER **4** : to form an estimate, conclusion, or evaluation about something : THINK — **judg·er** *n*

[2]judge *n* : one who judges: as **a** : a public official authorized to decide questions brought before a court **b** : one appointed to decide in a contest or competition : UMPIRE **c** : one who gives an authoritative opinion : CRITIC — **judge·ship** \-ˌship\ *n*

judg·ment *or* **judge·ment** \'jəj-mənt\ *n* **1 a** : the act of judging **b** : a decision or opinion given after judging **2 a** : a formal decision given by a court **b** : a court decree that a defendant has an obligation to the plaintiff for a specified amount **3** *cap* : the final judging of mankind by God **4 a** : the process of forming an opinion by discerning and comparing **b** : an opinion so formed **5** : the capacity for judging : DISCERNMENT — **judg·men·tal** \ˌjəj-'ment-ᵊl\ *adj*

Judgment Day *n* : the day of the Last Judgment

ju·di·ca·ture \'jüd-i-kə-ˌchu̇r\ *n* **1** : the administration of justice **2** : JUDICIARY 1

ju·di·cial \ju̇-'dish-əl\ *adj* **1** : of or relating to a judgment, the function of judging, the administration of justice, or the judiciary **2** : pronounced, ordered, or enforced by a court **3** : of, characterized by, or expressing judgment — **ju·di·cial·ly** \-'dish-(ə-)lē\ *adv*

ju·di·ci·ary \ju̇-'dish-ē-ˌer-ē, -'dish-ə-rē\ *n, pl* **-ar·ies** **1 a** : a system of courts of law **b** : the judges of these courts **2** : a branch of government in which judicial power is vested — **judiciary** *adj*

ju·di·cious \ju̇-'dish-əs\ *adj* : having, exercising, or characterized by sound judgment : DISCREET — **ju·di·cious·ly** *adv* — **ju·di·cious·ness** *n*

ju·do \'jüd-ō\ *n, pl* **judos** : a modern refined form of jujitsu that uses special applications of the principles of movement, balance, and leverage

ju·do·ist \'jüd-(ˌ)ō-əst\ *n* : one who is trained or skilled in judo

[1]jug \'jəg\ *n* **1 a** : a large deep usu. earthenware or glass container with a narrow mouth and a handle **b** : JUGFUL **2** : JAIL

[2]jug *vt* **jugged**; **jug·ging** : IMPRISON

jug·ful \'jəg-ˌfu̇l\ *n, pl* **jugfuls** \-ˌfu̇lz\ *or* **jugs·ful** \'jəgz-ˌfu̇l\ : the quantity held by a jug

jug·ger·naut \'jəg-ər-ˌnȯt\ *n* : a massive inexorable force or object that crushes whatever is in its path

jug·gle \'jəg-əl\ *vb* **jug·gled**; **jug·gling** \'jəg-(ə-)liŋ\ **1** : to keep several objects in motion in the air at the same time **2** : to manipulate esp. in order to achieve a desired and often fraudulent end **3** : to hold or balance insecurely — **jug·gler** \-(ə-)lər\ *n*

jug·glery \'jəg-lə-rē\ *n, pl* **-gler·ies** **1** : the art or practice of a juggler **2** : TRICKERY

jug·u·lar \'jəg-yə-lər\ *adj* : of, relating to, or situated in or on the throat or neck

juice \'jüs\ *n* **1** : the extractable fluid contents of cells or tissues **2 a** : the natural fluids of an animal body **b** : the liquid or moisture contained in something **3** : a medium (as electricity or gasoline) that supplies power — **juiced** \'jüst\ *adj* — **juice·less** \'jüs-ləs\ *adj*

juic·er \'jü-sər\ *n* : an appliance for extracting juice from fruit or vegetables

juicy \'jü-sē\ *adj* **1** : having much juice : SUCCULENT **2 a** : rich in interest : COLORFUL **b** : PIQUANT, RACY — **juic·i·ly** \-sə-lē\ *adv* — **juic·i·ness** \-sē-nəs\ *n*

ju·jit·su *or* **ju·jut·su** \jü-'jit-sü\ *n* : the Japanese art of defending oneself by grasping or striking an opponent so that his own strength and weight are used against him

ju·jube \'jü-ˌjüb\ *n* : a fruit-flavored gumdrop or lozenge

juke·box \'jük-ˌbäks\ *n* : a cabinet containing an automatic player of phonograph records that is started by inserting a coin in a slot

juke joint *n* : a small inexpensive establishment for eating, drinking, or dancing to the music of a jukebox

ju·lep \'jü-ləp\ *n* : a drink consisting of bourbon, sugar, and mint served in a frosted tumbler filled with crushed ice

Ju·ly \ju̇-'lī\ *n* : the 7th month of the year

[1]jum·ble \'jəm-bəl\ *vb* **jum·bled**; **jum·bling** \-b(ə-)liŋ\ : to mix in a confused mass

[2]jumble *n* : a disorderly mass or pile

jum·bo \'jəm-bō\ *n, pl* **jumbos** : a very large specimen of its kind

[1]jump \'jəmp\ *vb* **1 a** : to spring into the air : LEAP **b** : to give a sudden movement : START **c** : to move over a position occupied by an opponent's man in a board game **d** : SKIP **e** : to begin a forward movement — usu. used with *off* **2 a** : to rise suddenly in rank or status **b** : to undergo or cause a sudden sharp increase **3** : to make a sudden attack **4** : to bustle with activity **5 a** : to pass over by a leap **b** : BYPASS **c** : ANTICIPATE **d** : to leap aboard **6 a** : to escape from usu. in a hasty or furtive manner **b** : to abscond while at liberty under (bail) **c** : to depart from a normal course **7** : to occupy illegally **8 a** : to cause to leap **b** : to elevate in rank or status

[2]jump *n* **1 a** (1) : an act of jumping : LEAP (2) : a sports competition featuring a leap, spring, or bound (3) : a space covered by a leap **b** : a sudden involuntary movement : START **c** : a move made in a board game by jumping **2 a** : a sharp sudden increase **b** : one in a series of moves from one place to another **3** : an advantage at the start

[1]jump·er \'jəm-pər\ *n* : one that jumps

[2]jumper *n* **1** : a loose blouse or jacket worn by workmen **2** : a sleeveless one-piece dress worn usu. with a blouse **3** *pl* : a child's coverall

jump·ing–off place \ˌjəm-piŋ-'ȯf-\ *n* **1** : a remote or isolated place **2** : a place from which an enterprise is launched

jump seat *n* **1** : a movable carriage seat **2** : a folding seat between the front and rear seats of a passenger automobile

jumpy \'jəm-pē\ *adj* : NERVOUS, JITTERY — **jump·i·ness** *n*

jun·co \'jəŋ-kō\ *n, pl* **juncos** *or* **juncoes** : any of a genus of small American finches usu. with a pink bill, ashy gray head and back, and conspicuous white lateral tail feathers

junc·tion \'jəŋ(k)-shən\ *n* **1** : an act of joining : the state o

being joined **2** : a place or point of meeting **3** : something that joins
junc·ture \ˈjəŋ(k)-chər\ *n* **1** : an instance of joining : UNION **2 a** : JOINT, CONNECTION **b** : the manner of transition between two consecutive sounds in speech **3** : a point of time; *esp* : one made critical by a concurrence of circumstances — **junc·tur·al** \-chə-rəl, -shrəl\ *adj*
June \ˈjün\ *n* : the 6th month of the year
jun·gle \ˈjəŋ-gəl\ *n* **1 a** : a thick tangled mass of tropical vegetation **b** : a tract overgrown with jungle or other rank vegetation **2** : a hobo camp **3** : a place of ruthless struggle for survival — **jun·gly** \-g(ə-)lē\ *adj*
jungle gym *n* : a structure of vertical and horizontal bars for use of children at play
[1]**ju·nior** \ˈjü-nyər\ *n* **1** : a person who is younger or of lower rank than another **2** : a student in his next-to-last year before graduating from an educational institution of secondary or higher level
[2]**junior** *adj* **1 a** : YOUNGER — used chiefly to distinguish a son with the same given name as his father **b** : of more recent date **2** : lower in standing or rank **3** : of or relating to juniors in an educational institution
ju·nior·ate \ˌjü-nyə-ˌrāt, -rət\ *n* **1** : a course of high school or college study for candidates for the priesthood, brotherhood, or sisterhood; *esp* : one preparatory to the course in philosophy **2** : a seminary for juniorate training
junior college *n* : an educational institution that offers two years of studies similar to those in the first two years of a four-year college
junior high school *n* : a school usu. including the 7th, 8th, and 9th grades
junior varsity *n* : the members of a varsity squad lacking the experience or class qualification for the first team
ju·ni·per \ˈjü-nə-pər\ *n* : any of various evergreen shrubs or trees of the pine family
[1]**junk** \ˈjəŋk\ *n* **1** : hard salted beef for use on shipboard **2 a** : old iron, glass, paper, or waste : discarded articles **b** : a shoddy product : TRASH — **junk·man** \-ˌman\ *n* — **junky** \ˈjəŋ-kē\ *adj*
[2]**junk** *vt* : to get rid of as worthless : SCRAP
[3]**junk** *n* : a ship of Chinese waters with bluff lines, a high poop and overhanging stem, little or no keel, high pole masts, and a deep rudder
Jun·ker \ˈyu̇ŋ-kər\ *n* : a member of the Prussian landed aristocracy
[1]**jun·ket** \ˈjəŋ-kət\ *n* **1** : a dessert of sweetened flavored milk set in a jelly **2** : a trip made by an official at public expense
[2]**junket** *vi* **1** : FEAST, BANQUET **2** : to go on a junket
jun·ta \ˈhu̇n-tə, ˈjənt-ə\ *n* **1** : a council or committee for political or governmental purposes; *esp* : a group of persons controlling a government after a revolutionary seizure of power **2** : JUNTO
jun·to \ˈjənt-ō\ *n, pl* **juntos** : a group of persons joined for a common purpose
ju·rid·i·cal \ju̇-ˈrid-i-kəl\ *adj* **1** : of or relating to the administration of justice or the office of a judge **2** : of or relating to law or jurisprudence : LEGAL
ju·ris·dic·tion \ˌju̇r-əs-ˈdik-shən\ *n* **1** : the power, right, or authority to interpret and apply the law **2** : the authority of a sovereign power to govern or legislate **3** : the limits or territory within which authority may be exercised — **ju·ris·dic·tion·al** \-shnəl, -shən-ᵊl\ *adj* — **ju·ris·dic·tion·al·ly** \-ē\ *adv*
ju·ris·pru·dence \ˌju̇r-ə-ˈsprüd-ᵊn(t)s\ *n* **1** : a system of laws **2** : the science or philosophy of law **3** : a department of law — **ju·ris·pru·den·tial** \-sprü-ˈden-chəl\ *adj*
ju·rist \ˈju̇(ə)r-əst\ *n* : one having a thorough knowledge of law
ju·ris·tic \ju̇-ˈris-tik\ *adj* **1** : of or relating to a jurist or jurisprudence **2** : of, relating to, or recognized in law
ju·ror \ˈju̇r-ər\ *n* : a member of or a person summoned to serve on a jury
[1]**ju·ry** \ˈju̇(ə)r-ē\ *n, pl* **juries** **1** : a body of persons sworn to inquire into and test a matter submitted to them and to give their verdict according to the evidence presented **2** : a committee that judges and awards prizes at an exhibition or contest — **ju·ry·man** \-mən\ *n*
[2]**jury** *adj* : improvised for temporary use esp. in an emergency : MAKESHIFT
[1]**just** \ˈjəst\ *adj* **1 a** : having a basis in or conforming to fact or reason : REASONABLE **b** : conforming to a standard of correctness : PROPER **2 a** (1) : morally right or good : RIGHTEOUS (2) : MERITED, DESERVED **b** : legally right — **just·ly** *adv* — **just·ness** *n*
[2]**just** \(ˌ)jəst, (ˌ)jist\ *adv* **1 a** : EXACTLY, PRECISELY **b** : very recently **2 a** : by a very small margin : BARELY **b** : IMMEDIATELY, DIRECTLY **3 a** : ONLY, MERELY **b** : QUITE, VERY
jus·tice \ˈjəs-təs\ *n* **1 a** : the maintenance or administration of what is just **b** : JUDGE **c** : the administration of law **2 a** : the quality of being just, impartial, or fair **b** : RIGHTEOUSNESS **c** : the quality of conforming to law
justice of the peace : a local magistrate empowered chiefly to try minor cases, to administer oaths, and to perform marriages
jus·ti·fi·a·ble \ˈjəs-tə-ˌfī-ə-bəl\ *adj* : capable of being justified : EXCUSABLE — **jus·ti·fi·a·bly** \-blē\ *adv*
jus·ti·fi·ca·tion \ˌjəs-tə-fə-ˈkā-shən\ *n* **1** : the act, process, or state of being justified by God **2 a** : the act or an instance of justifying : VINDICATION **b** : something that justifies : DEFENSE
jus·ti·fy \ˈjəs-tə-ˌfī\ *vb* **-fied**; **-fy·ing** **1 a** : to prove or show to be just, right, or reasonable : VINDICATE **b** : to show a sufficient lawful reason for an act done **2 a** : to make righteous **b** : to release from the guilt of sin and accept as righteous **3** : to adjust or arrange exactly; *esp* : to set type so as to fill a full line — **jus·ti·fi·er** \-ˌfī(-ə)r\ *n*
jut \ˈjət\ *vb* **jut·ted**; **jut·ting** : to shoot or cause to shoot out, up, or forward : PROJECT
jute \ˈjüt\ *n* : a glossy fiber from either of two East Indian plants that is used chiefly for sacking and twine
[1]**ju·ve·nile** \ˈjü-və-ˌnīl, -vən-ᵊl\ *adj* **1** : showing incomplete development : IMMATURE, CHILDISH **2** : of, relating to, or characteristic of children or young people
[2]**juvenile** *n* **1 a** : a young person : YOUTH **b** : a book for young people **2 a** : a fledged bird not yet in adult plumage **b** : a 2-year-old racehorse **3** : an actor or actress who plays youthful parts
juvenile delinquency *n* : violation of the law or antisocial behavior by a juvenile — **juvenile delinquent** *n*
jux·ta·pose \ˈjək-stə-ˌpōz\ *vt* : to place side by side
jux·ta·po·si·tion \ˌjək-stə-pə-ˈzish-ən\ *n* : a placing or being placed side by side

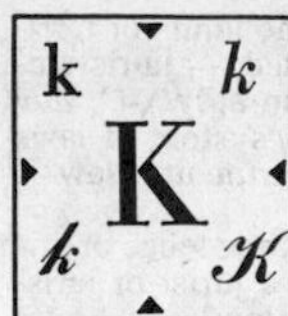

k \'kā\ *n, often cap* : the 11th letter of the English alphabet

Kaa•ba \'käb-ə\ *n* : a small stone building in the court of the Great Mosque at Mecca that contains a sacred black stone and is the goal of Islamic pilgrimage and the point toward which Muslims turn in praying

ka•bob \'kā-ˌbäb, kə-'\ *n* : cubes of meat cooked with vegetables usu. on a skewer

kaf•fee•klatsch \'kȯf-ē-ˌklach, 'käf-\ *n, often cap* : an informal social gathering for coffee and talk

kai•ser \'kī-zər\ *n* : EMPEROR; *esp* : the ruler of Germany from 1871 to 1918 — **kai•ser•dom** \-zərd-əm\ *n*

kale \'kāl\ *n* : a hardy cabbage with curled often finely cut leaves that do not form a dense head

ka•lei•do•scope \kə-'līd-ə-ˌskōp\ *n* **1** : an instrument containing loose bits of colored glass between two flat plates and two plane mirrors so placed that changes of position of the bits of glass are reflected in an endless variety of patterns **2** : a variegated changing pattern or scene — **ka•lei•do•scop•ic** \-ˌlīd-ə-'skäp-ik\ *adj*

ka•ma•ai•na \ˌkäm-ə-'ī-nə\ *n* : one who has lived in Hawaii for a long time

ka•mi•ka•ze \ˌkäm-i-'käz-ē\ *n* : a member of a corps of Japanese pilots assigned to make a crash on a target; *also* : an airplane flown in such an attack

kan•ga•roo \ˌkaŋ-gə-'rü\ *n, pl* **-roos** : any of various herbivorous leaping marsupial mammals of Australia, New Guinea, and adjacent islands with a small head, long powerful hind legs, and a long thick tail used as a support and in balancing

ka•o•lin \'kā-ə-lən\ *n* : a fine usu. white clay that is used in ceramics and refractories and as an adsorbent

ka•pok \'kā-ˌpäk\ *n* : a mass of silky fibers that clothe the seeds of the ceiba tree and are used esp. as a filling for mattresses, life preservers, and sleeping bags and as insulation

ka•put \kä-'pu̇t\ *adj* **1** : utterly defeated or destroyed **2** : made useless or unable to function **3** : hopelessly outmoded

kar•a•kul \'kar-ə-kəl\ *n* **1** : any of a breed of hardy fat-tailed Asiatic sheep with coarse wiry brown fur **2** : the tightly curled glossy black coat of the newborn lamb of a karakul valued as fur

kar•at \'kar-ət\ *n* : a unit of fineness for gold equal to $^{1}/_{24}$ part of pure gold in an alloy

ka•ra•te \kə-'rät-ē\ *n* : a Japanese system of self-defense without a weapon

kar•ma \'kär-mə\ *n, often cap* : the force generated by a person's actions held in Hinduism and Buddhism to perpetuate transmigration and to determine his destiny in his next existence

kar•roo *or* **ka•roo** \kə-'rü\ *n* : a dry tableland of southern Africa

ka•ty•did \'kāt-ē-ˌdid\ *n* : any of several large green tree-dwelling American grasshoppers

kay•ak \'kī-ˌak\ *n* **1** : an Eskimo canoe made of a frame entirely covered with skins except for a small opening in the center where one or two paddlers may sit **2** : a canvas-covered small canoe resembling a kayak

kayo \kā-'ō, 'kā-ō\ *n, pl* **kay•os** : KNOCKOUT — **kayo** *vt*

ka•zoo \kə-'zü\ *n, pl* **kazoos** : a toy musical instrument consisting of a tube with a membrane sealing one end and a side hole into which one sings or hums

[1]kedge \'kej\ *vt* : to move (a ship) by hauling on a line attached to a small anchor dropped at the distance and in the direction desired

[2]kedge *n* : a small anchor used esp. in kedging

[1]keel \'kēl\ *n* **1** : a timber or plate running lengthwise along the center of the bottom of a ship and usu. projecting from the bottom **2** : something (as the breastbone of a bird) like a ship's keel in form or use **3** : SHIP

[2]keel *vb* **1 a** : to turn over **b** : to fall in or as if in a faint — usu. used with *over* **2** : to provide with a keel

keel•haul \-ˌhȯl\ *vt* **1** : to haul under the keel of a ship as punishment or torture **2** : to rebuke severely

keel•son \'kel-sən, 'kēl-\ *n* : a structure running above and fastened to the keel of a ship in order to stiffen and strengthen its framework

[1]keen \'kēn\ *adj* **1** : having a fine edge or point : SHARP **2** : CUTTING, STINGING, SEVERE **3** : STRONG, ACUTE **4** : EAGER, ENTHUSIASTIC **5** : having or showing mental sharpness — **keen•ly** *adv* — **keen•ness** *n*

[2]keen *vb* : to lament with a keen — **keen•er** *n*

[3]keen *n* : a lamentation for the dead uttered in a loud wailing voice or in a wordless cry

[1]keep \'kēp\ *vb* **kept** \'kept\; **keep•ing** **1** : to perform as a duty : FULFILL, OBSERVE **2 a** : GUARD **b** : to take care of **3** : to continue doing something : MAINTAIN **4** : STAY, REMAIN **5** : to have in one's service or at one's disposal **6** : to preserve a record in **7** : to have on hand regularly for sale **8** : to possess permanently **9** : HOLD, DETAIN **10** : to hold back : WITHHOLD **11 a** : to cause to remain in a given place, situation, or condition **b** : to continue in an unspoiled condition **12** : REFRAIN

[2]keep *n* **1** : FORTRESS; *esp* : the strongest part of a medieval castle **2** : the means or provisions by which one is kept — **for keeps 1 a** : with the provision that one keep what he has won **b** : with deadly seriousness **2** : PERMANENTLY

keep•er \'kē-pər\ *n* : a person who watches, guards, or takes care of something : a person in charge : WARDEN, CUSTODIAN

keep•ing \'kē-piŋ\ *n* **1** : OBSERVANCE **2** : CARE, CHARGE, CUSTODY **3** : AGREEMENT, HARMONY **4** : the means by which something is kept : SUPPORT

keep•sake \'kēp-ˌsāk\ *n* : something kept or given to be kept as a memento

keg \'keg\ *n* **1** : a small cask or barrel holding 30 gallons or less **2** : the contents of a keg

keg•ler \'keg-lər\ *n* : [1]BOWLER

kelp \'kelp\ *n* **1** : any of various large brown seaweeds; *also* : a mass of these **2** : the ashes of seaweed used esp. as a source of iodine

ken \'ken\ *n* **1 a** : range of vision **b** : SIGHT, VIEW **2** : range of understanding

[1]ken•nel \'ken-[ə]l\ *n* **1** : a shelter for a dog **2** : an establishment for the breeding or boarding of dogs

[2]kennel *vb* **-neled** *or* **-nelled**; **-nel•ing** *or* **-nel•ling** : to put, keep, or take shelter in or as if in a kennel

ke•pi \'kā-pē, 'kep-ē\ *n* : a military cap with a round flat top sloping toward the front and a visor

ker•chief \'kər-chəf, -ˌchēf\ *n* **1** : a square of cloth worn by women as a head covering or around the neck **2** : HANDKERCHIEF 1

kerf \'kərf\ *n* : a slit or notch made by a saw or cutting torch

ker•mis *or* **ker•mess** \'kər-məs\ *n* **1** : an outdoor festival of the Low Countries **2** : a fair held usu. for charitable purposes

ker•nel \'kərn-[ə]l\ *n* **1 a** : the inner softer part of a seed, fruit stone, or nut **b** : a whole seed of a cereal **2** : a central or essential part : CORE

ker•o•sene *or* **ker•o•sine** \'ker-ə-ˌsēn\ *n* : a thin oil consisting of a mixture of hydrocarbons usu. obtained by distillation of petroleum and used for a fuel and as a solvent and thinner (as for paints)

ker•sey \'kər-zē\ *n* : a coarse ribbed woolen cloth for hose and work clothes

ketch \'kech\ *n* : a fore-and-aft-rigged ship similar to a yawl but with a larger mizzen and with the mizzenmast stepped farther forward

ket·tle \'ket-ᵊl\ *n* : a metallic vessel for boiling liquids; *esp* : TEAKETTLE

ket·tle·drum \-ˌdrəm\ *n* : a brass or copper kettle-shaped drum with parchment stretched across the top and capable of being tuned to definite pitches

[1]key \'kē\ *n* **1 a** : a usu. metal instrument by which the bolt of a lock is turned **b** : a device having the form or function of a key **2** : a means of gaining or preventing entrance, possession, or control **3 a** : something that gives an explanation or provides a solution **b** : a list of words or phrases giving an explanation of symbols or abbreviations **c** : an arrangement of usu. opposed characters of a group of plants or animals used for identification **d** : a map legend **4** : one of the levers with a flat surface that is pressed by a finger in operating or playing an instrument (as a typewriter, piano, or clarinet) **5** : a leading individual or principle **6** : a system of seven tones based on their relationship to a tonic **7 a** : characteristic style or tone **b** : the tone or pitch of a voice **8** : a small switch for opening or closing an electric circuit

[2]key *vb* **1 a** : to lock with a key **b** : to secure (as a pulley on a shaft) by a key **2** : to regulate the musical pitch of **3** : to make conformable : ATTUNE **4** : to make nervous or tense — usu. used with *up* **5** : to use a key

[3]key *adj* : of basic importance : FUNDAMENTAL

[4]key *n* : a low island or reef; *esp* : one of the coral islets off the southern coast of Florida

key·board \'kē-ˌbōrd\ *n* **1** : a row of keys (as on a piano) **2** : the whole arrangement of keys (as on a typewriter)

key club *n* : an informal private club serving liquor and providing entertainment

keyed \'kēd\ *adj* **1** : furnished with keys **2** : reinforced by a key or keystone

key·hole \'kē-ˌhōl\ *n* : a hole for receiving a key

[1]key·note \-ˌnōt\ *n* **1** : the first and harmonically fundamental tone of a scale **2** : the fundamental or central fact, idea, or mood

[2]keynote *vt* **1** : to set the keynote of **2** : to deliver the keynote address at — **key·not·er** *n*

keynote address *n* : an address designed to present the issues of primary interest to an assembly and often to arouse unity and enthusiasm

key·stone \'kē-ˌstōn\ *n* **1** : the wedge-shaped piece at the crown of an arch that locks the other pieces in place **2** : something on which associated things depend for support

key·way \'kē-ˌwā\ *n* : a groove or channel for a key

key word *n* : a word that is a key; *esp* : a word exemplifying the meaning or value of a letter or symbol

kha·ki \'kak-ē, 'käk-\ *n* **1** : a light yellowish brown **2 a** : a khaki-colored cloth made usu. of cotton or wool **b** : a military uniform of this cloth

[1]khan \'kän, 'kan\ *n* **1** : a Mongol leader; *esp* : one of the successors of Genghis Khan **2** : a local chieftain or man of rank in some countries of central Asia — **khan·ate** \-ˌāt\ *n*

[2]khan *n* : a building (as a caravansary) used for shelter by travelers in some Asian countries

khe·dive \kə-'dēv\ *n* : a ruler of Egypt from 1867 to 1914 governing as a viceroy of the sultan of Turkey

kib·butz \kib-'u̇ts, -'üts\ *n, pl* **kib·but·zim** \-ˌu̇t-'sēm, -ˌüt-\ : a collective farm or settlement in Israel

kib·itz·er \'kib-ət-sər\ *n* : one who looks on and often offers unwanted advice or comment esp. at a card game — **kib·itz** \-əts\ *vb*

[1]kick \'kik\ *vb* **1** : to strike out (as in defense or at a ball in games) with the foot or feet **2** : to strike, thrust, or hit violently with the foot **3** : to object strongly : PROTEST **4** : to recoil when fired **5** : to score by kicking a ball — **kick·er** *n*

[2]kick *n* **1** : a blow with the foot; *esp* : a propelling of a ball with the foot **2** : a forceful jolt or thrust suggesting a kick; *esp* : the recoil of a gun **3 a** : a feeling or expression of opposition or objection **b** : the grounds for objection **4** : a stimulating effect esp. of pleasure : THRILL

kick·back \'kik-ˌbak\ *n* **1** : a sharp violent reaction **2** : a secret return of a part of a sum received

kick·off \-ˌȯf\ *n* **1** : a kick that puts the ball into play in a football or soccer game **2** : COMMENCEMENT

kick·shaw \'kik-ˌshȯ\ *n* **1** : a fancy dish : DELICACY **2** : BAUBLE, GEWGAW

[1]kid \'kid\ *n* **1** : the young of a goat or of a related animal **2 a** : the flesh, fur, or skin of a kid **b** : something (as leather) made of kid **3** : CHILD, YOUNGSTER — **kid·dish** \'kid-ish\ *adj*

[2]kid *vb* **kid·ded**; **kid·ding** **1** : to deceive as a joke : FOOL **2** : to make fun of : TEASE — **kid·der** *n*

kid·nap \'kid-ˌnap\ *vb* **kid·napped** \-ˌnapt\ *or* **kid·naped**; **kid·nap·ping** *or* **kid·nap·ing** : to carry away a person by unlawful force or by fraud and against his will — **kid·nap·per** *or* **kid·nap·er** *n*

kid·ney \'kid-nē\ *n, pl* **kidneys** **1 a** : either of a pair of oval to bean-shaped organs situated in the body cavity near the spinal column that excrete waste products of metabolism in the form of urine **b** : an excretory organ of an invertebrate animal **2 a** : TEMPERAMENT, DISPOSITION **b** : KIND, SORT

kid·skin \'kid-ˌskin\ *n* : the skin of a young goat or leather made from or resembling this

[1]kill \'kil\ *vb* **1** : to deprive of life : put to death : SLAY **2** : DESTROY, RUIN **3** : to use up **4** : DEFEAT **5** : to mark matter for omission **6** : to hit a return (as in tennis) so hard that it cannot be played back — **kill·er** *n*

[2]kill *n* **1** : an act of killing **2 a** : an animal killed in a hunt, season, or particular period of time **b** : an enemy airplane, submarine, or ship destroyed by military action

kill·ing \'kil-iŋ\ *n* : a sudden notable gain or profit

kill·joy \'kil-ˌjȯi\ *n* : one who spoils the pleasure of others

[1]kiln \'kil(n)\ *n* : an oven, furnace, or heated enclosure for processing a substance by burning, firing, or drying

[2]kiln *vt* : to burn, fire, or dry in a kiln

ki·lo \'kē-lō, 'kil-ō\ *n, pl* **kilos** **1** : KILOGRAM **2** : KILOMETER

kilo·cy·cle \'kil-ə-ˌsī-kəl\ *n* : one thousand cycles; *esp* : one thousand cycles per second

kilo·gram \'kē-lə-ˌgram, 'kil-ə-\ *n* : the basic metric unit of mass and weight equal to 1000 grams or approximately 2.2046 pounds avoirdupois

kilo·li·ter \'kil-ə-ˌlēt-ər\ *n* : a unit of capacity equal to 1000 liters

ki·lom·e·ter \kil-'äm-ət-ər, 'kil-ə-ˌmēt-\ *n* : a unit of length equal to 1000 meters

kilo·watt \'kil-ə-ˌwät\ *n* : a unit of power equal to 1000 watts

kilt \'kilt\ *n* **1** : a knee-length pleated skirt usu. of tartan worn by men in Scotland and by Scottish regiments in the British army **2** : a garment that resembles a Scottish kilt — **kilt·ed** \'kil-təd\ *adj*

kil·ter \'kil-tər\ *n* : proper condition : ORDER

ki·mo·no \kə-'mō-nə\ *n, pl* **-nos** **1** : a loose robe with wide sleeves and a broad sash traditionally worn as an outer garment by the Japanese **2** : a loose dressing gown worn chiefly by women

[1]kin \'kin\ *n* **1** : a person's relatives : KINDRED **2** : KINSMAN

[2]kin *adj* : KINDRED, RELATED

[1]kind \'kīnd\ *n* **1 a** : a natural group : SPECIES **b** : a group united by common traits or interests : CATEGORY **c** : VARIETY **d** : a doubtful or barely admissible member of a category **2** : essential quality or character **3 a** : goods or commodities as distinguished from money **b** : the equivalent of what has been offered or received — **of a kind** **1** : of the same sort, class, or value **2** : of an imperfect or untypical quality or character : of a sort

[2]kind *adj* **1** : having the will to do good and to bring happiness to others : SYMPATHETIC, CONSIDERATE, GENTLE 2 : showing or growing out of gentleness or goodness of heart

kin·der·gar·ten \'kin-dər-ˌgärt-ᵊn, -ˌgärd-\ *n* : a school or class for very young children in which teaching is done largely through activities based on the normal aptitudes and desire of the pupils for exercise and play

kin·der·gart·ner \-ˌgärt-nər, -ˌgärd-\ *n* 1 : a kindergarten pupil 2 : a kindergarten teacher

kind·heart·ed \'kīnd-'härt-əd\ *adj* : having or showing a kind and sympathetic nature — **kind·heart·ed·ly** *adv* — **kind·heart·ed·ness** *n*

kin·dle \'kin-dᵊl\ *vb* **kin·dled**; **kin·dling** \-dliŋ, -dᵊl-iŋ\ 1 : to set on fire or take fire : start burning : LIGHT 2 : AROUSE, PROVOKE, EXCITE 3 : to begin to be excited : grow warm and animated 4 : to light up as if with flame

kin·dling \'kin-dliŋ\ *n* : easily combustible material for starting a fire

[1]**kind·ly** \'kīn-dlē\ *adj* 1 : of an agreeable or beneficial nature : PLEASANT 2 : of a sympathetic or generous nature : FRIENDLY — **kind·li·ness** *n*

[2]**kindly** *adv* 1 : READILY 2 a : SYMPATHETICALLY b : as a gesture of goodwill c : COURTEOUSLY, OBLIGINGLY

kind·ness \'kīn(d)-nəs\ *n* 1 : a kind deed : FAVOR 2 : the quality or state of being kind

[1]**kin·dred** \'kin-drəd\ *n* 1 : a group of related individuals 2 : one's relatives

[2]**kindred** *adj* : of like nature or character

ki·net·ic \kə-'net-ik, kī-\ *adj* : of or relating to the motion of material bodies and the forces and energy associated therewith

kin·folk \'kin-ˌfōk\ *n* : RELATIVES

king \'kiŋ\ *n* 1 a : a male monarch of a major territorial unit; *esp* : one who inherits his position and rules for life b : a paramount chief 2 *cap* : GOD, CHRIST 3 : one that holds a preeminent position; *esp* : a chief among competitors 4 : the principal piece in the game of chess 5 : a playing card bearing the figure of a king 6 : a checker that has been crowned

king·dom \'kiŋ-dəm\ *n* 1 : a political community or territorial unit having a monarchical form of government headed by a king or queen 2 *often cap* a : the eternal kingship of God b : the realm in which God's will is fulfilled 3 : a realm or region in which something or someone is dominant 4 : one of the three primary divisions of lifeless material, plants, and animals into which natural objects are grouped

king·fish·er \'kiŋ-ˌfish-ər\ *n* : any of a family of usu. crested and bright-colored nonpasserine birds with a short tail and a long stout sharp bill

king·ly \'kiŋ-lē\ *adj* 1 : having royal rank 2 : of, relating to, or befitting a king 3 : MONARCHICAL — **king·li·ness** *n* — **kingly** *adv*

king·pin \'kiŋ-ˌpin\ *n* 1 : any of several bowling pins: as a : HEADPIN b : the number 5 pin 2 : the chief person in a group or undertaking

King's English \ˌkiŋz-\ *n* : standard, pure, or correct English speech or usage

king·ship \'kiŋ-ˌship\ *n* 1 : the position, office, or dignity of a king 2 : the personality of a king : MAJESTY 3 : government by a king

king–size \'kiŋ-ˌsīz\ *or* **king–sized** \-ˌsīzd\ *adj* 1 : longer than the regular or standard size 2 : unusually large

[1]**kink** \'kiŋk\ *n* 1 : a short tight twist or curl 2 : QUIRK, WHIM 3 : a cramp in some part of the body 4 : an imperfection likely to cause difficulties in operation — **kinky** \'kiŋ-kē\ *adj*

[2]**kink** *vb* : to form a kink : make a kink in

kins·folk \'kinz-ˌfōk\ *n* : RELATIVES

kin·ship \'kin-ˌship\ *n* : the quality or state of being kin : RELATIONSHIP

kins·man \'kinz-mən\ *n* : RELATIVE; *esp* : a male relative

kins·wom·an \-ˌwu̇m-ən\ *n* : a female relative

ki·osk \'kē-ˌäsk, kē-'\ *n* 1 : an open summerhouse or pavilion 2 : a small light structure with one or more open sides used esp. as a newsstand or a telephone booth

kip \'kip\ *n* : the undressed hide of a young or small animal

[1]**kip·per** \'kip-ər\ *n* : a kippered herring or salmon

[2]**kipper** *vt* **kip·pered**; **kip·per·ing** \'kip-(ə-)riŋ\ : to cure by splitting, cleaning, salting, and smoking

kir·tle \'kərt-ᵊl\ *n* : a woman's dress, skirt, or petticoat

kis·met \'kiz-ˌmet, -mət\ *n, often cap* : FATE 1, 2

[1]**kiss** \'kis\ *vb* 1 : to touch with the lips as a mark of affection or greeting 2 : to touch gently or lightly — **kiss·a·ble** *adj*

[2]**kiss** *n* 1 : a caress with the lips 2 : a gentle touch or contact 3 : a bite-size candy often wrapped in paper or foil

[1]**kit** \'kit\ *n* 1 a : a collection of articles for personal use b : a set of tools or implements c : a set of parts to be assembled d : a packaged collection of related material 2 : a container (as a bag or case) for a kit

[2]**kit** *n* : a small violin

kitch·en \'kich-ən\ *n* 1 : a place (as a room) with cooking facilities 2 : the personnel that prepares, cooks, and serves food

kitchen cabinet *n* 1 : a cupboard with drawers and shelves for use in a kitchen 2 : an informal group of advisers to the head of a government

kitch·en·ette \ˌkich-ə-'net\ *n* : a small kitchen or an alcove containing cooking facilities

kitchen garden *n* : a plot in which vegetables are grown for domestic use

kitchen midden *n* : a refuse heap; *esp* : a mound marking the site of a primitive human habitation

kitchen police *n* 1 : enlisted men detailed to assist the cooks in a military mess 2 : the work done by kitchen police

kitch·en·ware \'kich-ən-ˌwa(ə)r\ *n* : hardware for use in a kitchen

kite \'kīt\ *n* 1 : any of various hawks with long narrow wings, a deeply forked tail, and feet adapted for taking insects and small reptiles as prey 2 : a light frame covered with paper or cloth and designed to be flown in the air at the end of a long string

kith \'kith\ *n* : familiar friends, neighbors, or relatives

kit·ten \'kit-ᵊn\ *n* : the young of a small mammal and esp. of a cat

kit·ten·ish \'kit-nish, -ᵊn-ish\ *adj* : resembling a kitten; *esp* : PLAYFUL — **kit·ten·ish·ly** *adv* — **kit·ten·ish·ness** *n*

[1]**kit·ty** \'kit-ē\ *n, pl* **kitties** : CAT 1a; *esp* : KITTEN

[2]**kitty** *n, pl* **kitties** 1 : a fund in a poker game made up of contributions from each pot 2 : a sum of money or a collection of goods made up of small contributions : POOL

ki·va \'kē-və\ *n* : a Pueblo Indian ceremonial structure that is usu. round and partly underground

klep·to·ma·nia \ˌklep-tə-'mā-nē-ə, -nyə\ *n* : a persistent neurotic impulse to steal esp. without economic motive — **klep·to·ma·ni·ac** \-nē-ˌak\ *adj or n*

knack \'nak\ *n* 1 : a clever way of doing something : TRICK 2 : a special ready capacity that is hard to analyze or teach

knap·sack \'nap-ˌsak\ *n* : a usu. canvas or leather bag or case strapped on the back and used esp. for carrying supplies while on a march or hike

knave \'nāv\ *n* 1 : a tricky deceitful fellow : ROGUE 2 : JACK 5

knav·ery \'nāv-(ə-)rē\ *n, pl* **-er·ies** 1 : the practices of a knave : RASCALITY 2 : a roguish or mischievous act

knav·ish \'nā-vish\ *adj* : of, relating to, or characteristic of a knave; *esp* : DISHONEST — **knav·ish·ly** *adv*

knead \'nēd\ *vt* 1 : to work and press into a mass with or as if with the hands 2 a : to form or shape as if by kneading b : to treat as if by kneading : MASSAGE — **knead·er** *n*

knee \'nē\ *n* 1 : the joint in the middle part of the leg 2 : something resembling the human knee 3 : the part of a garment covering the knee — **kneed** \'nēd\ *adj*

knee·hole \-ˌhōl\ *n* : a space (as under a desk) for the knees

kneel \'nēl\ *vi* **knelt** \'nelt\ *or* **kneeled** \'nēld\; **kneel·ing** : to bend the knee : fall or rest on the knees — **kneel·er** *n*

[1]**knell** \'nel\ *vb* 1 : to ring esp. for a death, funeral, or disaster : TOLL 2 : to sound in an ominous manner or with an ominous effect 3 : to summon, announce, or proclaim by or as if by a knell

[2]**knell** *n* 1 : a stroke or sound of a bell esp. when rung slowly for a death, funeral, or disaster 2 : a sound or other indication of a death or of the end or failure of something

knew *past of* KNOW

knick·er·bock·ers \'nik-ə(r)-ˌbäk-ərz\ *n pl* : KNICKERS

knick·ers \'nik-ərz\ *n pl* : loose-fitting short pants gathered at the knee

knick·knack \'nik-ˌnak\ *n* : a small trivial article intended for ornament

[1]**knife** \'nīf\ *n, pl* **knives** \'nīvz\ 1 a : a cutting instrument consisting of a sharp blade fastened to a handle b : a weapon resembling a knife 2 : a sharp cutting blade or tool in a machine

[2]**knife** *vt* 1 : to stab, slash, or wound with a knife 2 : to move like a knife in

[1]**knight** \'nīt\ *n* 1 a : a mounted warrior of feudal times serving a superior (as a king) b : a man honored by a sovereign for merit and in Great Britain ranking below a baronet c : a member of any of various orders or societies d : a man devoted to the service of a lady as her attendant or champion 2 : a chess piece that can move two squares in any direction to a square of the opposite color

[2]**knight** *vt* : to make a knight of : confer the rank of knight on

knight–er·rant \'nīt-'er-ənt\ *n, pl* **knights–errant** : a knight traveling in search of adventures in which to exhibit his military skill, prowess, and generosity — **knight–er·rant·ry** \-'er-ən-trē\ *n*

knight·hood \'nīt-ˌhu̇d\ *n* 1 : the rank, dignity, or profession of a knight 2 : the qualities befitting a knight : CHIVALRY 3 : knights as a class or body

knight·ly \'nīt-lē\ *adj* 1 : of, relating to, or characteristic of a knight 2 : made up of knights — **knightly** *adv*

knit \'nit\ *vb* **knit** *or* **knit·ted**; **knit·ting** 1 : to form a fabric by interlacing yarn or thread in connected loops with needles 2 : to draw or come together closely as if knitted : unite firmly 3 : WRINKLE 4 : to bind closely by a tie of any kind — **knit·ter** *n*

knit·ting \'nit-iŋ\ *n* 1 : the action or method of one that knits 2 : work done or being done by one that knits

knit·wear \'nit-ˌwa(ə)r\ *n* : knitted clothing

knob \'näb\ *n* 1 a : a rounded protuberance : LUMP b : a small rounded ornament or handle 2 : a rounded usu. isolated hill or mountain — **knobbed** \'näbd\ *adj* — **knob·by** \'näb-ē\ *adj*

[1]**knock** \'näk\ *vb* 1 a : to strike something with a sharp blow b : to drive, force, or make by so striking 2 : to collide with something 3 a : BUSTLE b : WANDER 4 : to make a pounding noise esp. as a result of abnormal ignition 5 : to find fault with

[2]**knock** *n* 1 a : a sharp blow b : a severe misfortune or hardship 2 : a pounding noise; *esp* : one in an automobile engine caused by abnormal ignition

knock·about \'näk-ə-ˌbau̇t\ *adj* 1 : suitable for rough use 2 : being noisy and rough : BOISTEROUS

knock down *vt* 1 : to dispose of to a bidder at an auction sale 2 : to take apart : DISASSEMBLE

[1]**knock·down** \'näk-ˌdau̇n\ *n* 1 : a knocking down of something or someone (as a boxer) 2 : something easily assembled or disassembled

[2]**knockdown** *adj* 1 : having such force as to strike down or overwhelm 2 : that can easily be assembled or disassembled

knock·er \'näk-ər\ *n* : one that knocks; *esp* : a device hinged to a door for use in knocking

knock–knee \'näk-'nē, -ˌnē\ *n* : a condition in which the legs curve inward at the knees — **knock–kneed** \-'nēd\ *adj*

knock out *vt* 1 : to fell (a boxing opponent) by hitting with an immobilizing blow 2 : to make inoperative, useless, or unconscious

knock·out \'näk-ˌau̇t\ *n* 1 a : the act of knocking out : the condition of being knocked out b : a blow that knocks out an opponent 2 : something sensationally striking or attractive — **knockout** *adj*

knoll \'nōl\ *n* : a small round hill : MOUND

[1]**knot** \'nät\ *n* 1 : an interlacing (as of string or ribbon) that forms a lump or knob 2 : something hard to solve : PROBLEM 3 : a bond of union; *esp* : the marriage bond 4 a : a protuberant lump or swelling in tissue b : the base of a woody branch enclosed in the stem from which it arises; *also* : its section in lumber 5 : a cluster of persons or things : GROUP 6 : an ornamental bow of ribbon : COCKADE 7 a : one nautical mile per hour b : one nautical mile

[2]**knot** *vb* **knot·ted**; **knot·ting** 1 : to tie in or with a knot : form knots in 2 : to unite closely or intricately : ENTANGLE

knot·hole \'nät-ˌhōl\ *n* : a hole in a board or tree trunk where a knot has come out

knot·ted \'nät-əd\ *adj* 1 : tied in or with a knot 2 : full of knots : GNARLED 3 : ENTANGLED, PUZZLING 4 : ornamented with knots or knobs

knot·ty \'nät-ē\ *adj* 1 : marked by or full of knots 2 : puzzling because of intricacy : COMPLEX

knotty pine *n* : pine wood with decorative distribution of knots used esp. for interior finish

knout \'nau̇t, 'nüt\ *n* : a whip for flogging criminals

know \'nō\ *vb* **knew** \'n(y)ü\; **known** \'nōn\; **know·ing** 1 a (1) : to perceive directly : have direct cognition of (2) : to have understanding of (3) : to recognize the nature of : DISCERN b (1) : to recognize as being the same as something previously known (2) : to be acquainted or familiar with 2 a : to be aware of the truth or factuality of b : to have a practical understanding of 3 : to have knowledge 4 : to be or become aware — **know·a·ble** *adj* — **know·er** *n*

know–how \'nō-ˌhau̇\ *n* : knowledge of how to do something smoothly and efficiently

know·ing \'nō-iŋ\ *adj* 1 : having or reflecting knowledge, information, or intelligence 2 : shrewdly and keenly alert : ASTUTE 3 : DELIBERATE, INTENTIONAL — **know·ing·ly** *adv*

knowl·edge \'näl-ij\ *n* 1 : understanding gained by actual experience : practical skill 2 a : the state of being aware of something or of having information b : range of information 3 : the act of understanding : clear perception of truth 4 : something learned and kept in the mind : LEARNING, ENLIGHTENMENT

knowl·edge·a·ble \'näl-i-jə-bəl\ *adj* : having or exhibiting knowledge or intelligence : WISE

know–noth·ing \'nō-ˌnəth-iŋ\ *n* : IGNORAMUS

[1]**knuck·le** \'nək-əl\ *n* : the rounded lump formed by the ends of two bones where they come together in a joint; *esp* : such a lump at a finger joint

[2]**knuckle** *vb* **knuck·led**; **knuck·ling** \'nək-(ə-)liŋ\ 1 : to place the knuckles on the ground in shooting a marble 2 : YIELD, SUBMIT — usu. used with *under* 3 : to apply oneself earnestly — usu. used with *down*

knur \'nər\ *n* : a hard excrescence : GNARL

KO \kā-'ō, 'kā-ō\ *n* : a knockout in boxing — **KO** *vt*

ko·bold \'kō-ˌbōld\ *n* 1 : a gnome that in German folklore inhabits underground places 2 : an often mischievous spirit of German folklore

Koh–i–noor \'kō-ə-ˌnu̇r\ *n* : a large diamond discovered in India and made one of the British crown jewels
kohl \'kōl\ *n* : a preparation used esp. in Arabia and Egypt to darken the edges of the eyelids
kohl•rabi \kōl-'rab-ē, -'räb-\ *n, pl* **-rab•ies** : a cabbage that forms no head but has a swollen fleshy edible stem
ko•lin•sky *or* **ko•lin•ski** \kə-'lin(t)-skē\ *n* **1** : any of several Asiatic minks **2** : the fur or pelt of a kolinsky
kol•khoz \käl-'ko̊z\ *n, pl* **kol•kho•zy** \-'ko̊-zē\ *or* **kol•khoz•es** : a collective farm of the U.S.S.R.
Kol Ni•dre \kōl-'nid-(ˌ)rā\ *n* : an Aramaic prayer chanted in the synagogue on the eve of Yom Kippur
kook \'kük\ *n* : one whose ideas or actions are considered eccentric, fantastic, or insane : SCREWBALL
kooky \'kü-kē\ *adj* : having the characteristics of a kook : CRAZY — **kook•i•ness** *n*
Ko•ran \kə-'ran\ *n* : the book composed of writings accepted by Muslims as revelations made to Muhammad by Allah — **Ko•ran•ic** \kə-'ran-ik\ *adj*
Ko•re•an \kə-'rē-ən\ *n* **1** : a native or inhabitant of Korea **2** : the language of the Korean people — **Korean** *adj*
ko•sher \'kō-shər\ *adj* **1** : sanctioned by Jewish law; *esp* : ritually fit for use **2** : selling or serving food ritually fit according to Jewish law
[1]**kow•tow** \kau̇-'tau̇, 'kau̇-ˌ\ *n* : an act of kowtowing
[2]**kowtow** *vi* **1** : to kneel and touch the forehead to the ground to show homage, worship, or deep respect **2** : to show obsequious deference
[1]**kraal** \'kro̊l, 'kräl\ *n* **1** : a village of southern African natives **2** : an enclosure for domestic animals in southern Africa
[2]**kraal** *vt* : to pen in a kraal
kraut \'krau̇t\ *n* : SAUERKRAUT
krem•lin \'krem-lən\ *n* **1** : the citadel of a Russian city **2** *cap* : the Russian government
kris \'krēs\ *n* : a Malay or Indonesian dagger with a ridged and twisting blade
Kriss Krin•gle \'kris-'kriŋ-gəl\ *n* : SANTA CLAUS
ku•dos \'k(y)ü-ˌdäs, -ˌdōs\ *n* FAME, GLORY
ku•lak \k(y)ü-'lak\ *n* : a prosperous peasant farmer in Czarist and early Soviet Russia
kul•tur \ku̇l-'tu̇(ə)r\ *n, often cap* : German culture held esp. by militant Nazi and Hohenzollern expansionists to be superior esp. in its emphasis on practical efficiency and individual subordination to the state
kum•quat \'kəm-ˌkwät\ *n* **1** : a small citrus fruit with sweet spongy rind and somewhat acid pulp used esp. for preserves **2** : tree or shrub that bears kumquats

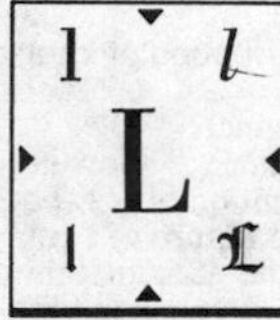

l \'el\ *n, often cap* **1** : the 12th letter of the English alphabet **2** : the roman numeral 50
la \'lä\ *n* : the 6th note of the diatonic scale
lab \'lab\ *n* : LABORATORY
[1]**la•bel** \'lā-bəl\ *n* **1** : a slip (as of paper or cloth) that is attached to something and gives an identification or description of it : TAG, STICKER **2** : a descriptive or identifying word or phrase : EPITHET
[2]**label** *vt* **la•beled** *or* **la•belled**; **la•bel•ing** *or* **la•bel•ling** \'lā-b(ə-)liŋ\ **1** : to affix a label to **2** : to describe or designate with a label — **la•bel•er** \-b(ə-)lər\ *n*
la•bi•al \'lā-bē-əl\ *adj* **1** : of or relating to the lips **2** : uttered with the participation of one or both lips — **la•bi•al•ly** \-ə-lē\ *adv*
la•bile \'lā-ˌbīl, -bəl\ *adj* **1** : characterized by a ready capability for change : ADAPTABLE **2** : readily or continually undergoing chemical or physical change : UNSTABLE — **la•bil•i•ty** \lā-'bil-ət-ē\ *n*
[1]**la•bor** \'lā-bər\ *n* **1 a** : expenditure of physical or mental effort esp. when difficult or compulsory **b** (1) : human activity that provides the goods or services in an economy (2) : the services performed by workers for wages as distinguished from those rendered by entrepreneurs for profits **c** (1) : the physical activities involved in parturition (2) : the period of such labor **2** : TASK **3** : a product of labor **4 a** : those who do labor or work for wages **b** : labor unions or their officials
[2]**labor** *vb* **la•bored**; **la•bor•ing** \-b(ə-)riŋ\ **1** : to exert one's body or mind : WORK; *esp* : to work for wages and in actual production of goods **2** : to move with great effort **3** : to suffer from some disadvantage or distress **4** : to pitch or roll heavily **5** : to treat or work out in often laborious detail
lab•o•ra•to•ry \'lab-(ə-)rə-ˌtōr-ē\ *n, pl* **-ries** : a place equipped for experimental study in a science or for testing and analysis; *also* : a place providing opportunity for experimentation, observation, or practice in a field of study — **laboratory** *adj*
labor camp *n* **1** : a penal colony where forced labor is performed **2** : a camp for migratory labor
Labor Day *n* : the 1st Monday in September observed as a legal holiday in recognition of the workingman
la•bored \'lā-bərd\ *adj* **1** : produced or performed with labor; *esp* : not freely or easily done **2** : lacking ease or spontaneity of expression
la•bor•er \'lā-bər-ər\ *n* : one that works; *esp* : a worker on jobs requiring strength rather than skill
la•bo•ri•ous \lə-'bōr-ē-əs\ *adj* **1** : INDUSTRIOUS **2** : requiring or characterized by hard or toilsome effort; *also* : LABORED — **la•bo•ri•ous•ly** *adv* — **la•bo•ri•ous•ness** *n*
la•bor•sav•ing \'lā-bər-ˌsā-viŋ\ *adj* : adapted to replace or decrease human labor and esp. manual labor
labor union *n* : an organization of workers formed to advance its members' interests in respect to wages and working conditions
la•bur•num \lə-'bər-nəm\ *n* : any of several poisonous Eurasian leguminous shrubs and trees with pendulous racemes of bright yellow flowers
lab•y•rinth \'lab-ə-ˌrin(t)th\ *n* **1** : a place constructed of or full of passageways and blind alleys so arranged as to make it difficult for a person to find his way around : MAZE **2** : something extremely complex or tortuous — **lab•y•rin•thine** \ˌlab-ə-'rin(t)-thən\ *adj*
lac \'lak\ *n* : a resinous substance secreted by a scale insect and used in the manufacture of shellac, lacquers, and sealing wax
[1]**lace** \'lās\ *n* **1** : a cord or string used for drawing together two edges (as of a garment or a shoe) **2** : an ornamental braid for trimming men's coats or uniforms **3** : a fine openwork usu. figured fabric made of thread and used chiefly for household coverings or for ornament of dress — **laced** \'lāst\ *adj*
[2]**lace** *vb* **1** : to draw together the edges of by or as if by a lace passed through eyelet holes **2 a** : to adorn with or as if with lace **b** : INTERTWINE **3** : BEAT, LASH **4 a** : to add a dash esp. of an alcoholic liquor to **b** : to give savor or zest to — **lac•er** *n*

¹lac·er·ate \'las-ə-rət\ *adj* : having the edges deeply and irregularly cut

²lac·er·ate \'las-ə-,rāt\ *vt* **1** : to tear roughly **2** : to cause sharp mental or emotional pain to : DISTRESS — **lac·er·a·tive** \-,rāt-iv\ *adj*

lac·er·a·tion \,las-ə-'rā-shən\ *n* : an act or instance of lacerating; *also* : a torn and ragged wound

lach·ry·mose \'lak-rə-,mōs\ *adj* **1** : given to tears or weeping : TEARFUL **2** : tending to cause tears : MOURNFUL — **lach·ry·mose·ly** *adv*

lac·ing \'lā-siŋ\ *n* **1** : the action of one that laces **2** : something that laces : LACE

¹lack \'lak\ *vb* **1** : to be wanting or missing **2** : to need, want, or be deficient in

²lack *n* **1** : the fact or state of being wanting or deficient **2** : something that is lacking or is needed

lack·a·dai·si·cal \,lak-ə-'dā-zi-kəl\ *adj* : lacking life, spirit, or zest : LANGUID — **lack·a·dai·si·cal·ly** \-k(ə-)lē\ *adv*

lack·ey \'lak-ē\ *n, pl* **lackeys** **1** : a liveried retainer : FOOTMAN **2** : a servile follower : TOADY

lack·lus·ter \'lak-,ləs-tər\ *adj* : lacking in sheen, radiance, or vitality : DULL

la·con·ic \lə-'kän-ik\ *adj* : sparing of words : TERSE — **la·con·i·cal·ly** \-'kän-i-k(ə-)lē\ *adv*

¹lac·quer \'lak-ər\ *n* **1** : any of numerous preparations that consist of a substance in solution (as shellac in alcohol), dry rapidly usu. by evaporation of the solvent to form a glossy film, and are used to coat objects (as wood or metal) **2** : any of various durable natural varnishes; *esp* : one from an Asiatic sumac

²lacquer *vt* **lac·quered**; **lac·quer·ing** \'lak-(ə-)riŋ\ : to coat with lacquer

lac·ri·mal \'lak-rə-məl\ *adj* : of, relating to, or being the glands that produce tears

lac·ri·ma·tion \,lak-rə-'mā-shən\ *n* : the secretion of tears esp. when abnormal or excessive

lac·ri·ma·tor *or* **lach·ry·ma·tor** \'lak-rə-,māt-ər\ *n* : TEAR GAS

la·crosse \lə-'krȯs\ *n* : a game played on a field by two teams with a hard ball and long-handled rackets

lac·tate \'lak-,tāt\ *vi* : to secrete milk — **lac·ta·tion** \lak-'tā-shən\ *n*

lac·te·al \'lak-tē-əl\ *adj* : consisting of, producing, or resembling milk

lac·tic \'lak-tik\ *adj* **1** : of or relating to milk **2** : obtained from sour milk or whey **3** : involving the production of lactic acid

lactic acid *n* : an organic acid present in cells and esp. muscle, produced from carbohydrate usu. by bacterial fermentation, and used esp. in food and medicine

la·cu·na \lə-'k(y)ü-nə\ *n, pl* **-cu·nae** \-'kyü-(,)nē, -'kü-,nī\ *or* **-cu·nas** \-'k(y)ü-nəz\ : a blank space or a missing part : GAP — **la·cu·nar** \-'k(y)ü-nər\ *adj*

la·cus·trine \lə-'kəs-trən\ *adj* : of, relating to, or growing in lakes

lacy \'lā-sē\ *adj* : resembling or consisting of lace

lad \'lad\ *n* **1** : BOY, YOUTH **2** : FELLOW, CHAP

lad·der \'lad-ər\ *n* **1** : a structure for climbing up or down that consists of two long parallel sidepieces joined at intervals by crosspieces on which one may step **2** : something that suggests a ladder in form or use **3** : a series of usu. ascending steps or stages : SCALE

lad·die \'lad-ē\ *n* : a young lad

lade \'lād\ *vb* **lad·ed** *or* **lad·en** \'lād-ᵊn\; **lad·ing** **1 a** : to put a load or burden on or in : LOAD **b** : STOW, SHIP **2** : to burden heavily : OPPRESS **3** : LADLE

la–di–da \,läd-ē-'dä\ *adj* : affectedly refined or polished

ladies' man *n* : a man who shows a marked fondness for the company of women or is esp. attentive to women

lad·ing \'lād-iŋ\ *n* **1** : the act of one that lades **2** : CARGO, FREIGHT

¹la·dle \'lād-ᵊl\ *n* : a deep-bowled long-handled spoon or dipper used esp. for taking up and conveying liquids

²ladle *vt* **la·dled**; **la·dling** \'lād-liŋ, -ᵊl-iŋ\ : to take up and convey in or as if in a ladle

la·dy \'lād-ē\ *n, pl* **la·dies** **1** : a woman of property, rank, or authority; *also* : a woman of superior social position or of refinement and gentle manners **2** : WOMAN **3** : WIFE

la·dy·bird \'lād-ē-,bərd\ *n* : LADYBUG

la·dy·bug \'lād-ē-,bəg\ *n* : any of numerous small nearly hemispherical often brightly colored beetles that usu. feed both as larvae and adults on other insects

Lady Day *n* : the feast of the Annunciation

la·dy·fin·ger \'lād-ē-,fiŋ-gər\ *n* : a small finger-shaped sponge cake

la·dy–in–wait·ing \,lād-ē-in-'wāt-iŋ\ *n, pl* **ladies–in–waiting** : a lady appointed to attend or wait on a queen or princess

la·dy·like \'lād-ē-,līk\ *adj* **1** : resembling a lady in appearance or manners : WELL-BRED **2** : suitable to a lady

la·dy·love \'lād-ē-,ləv, 'lād-ē-'\ *n* : SWEETHEART, MISTRESS

la·dy·ship \'lād-ē-,ship\ *n* : the condition of being a lady : rank of lady — used as a title for a woman having the rank of lady

la·dy's slipper *or* **lady slipper** \'lād-ē(z)-,slip-ər\ *n* : any of several No. American temperate-zone orchids with flowers whose shape suggests a slipper

¹lag \'lag\ *vb* **lagged**; **lag·ging** **1** : to stay or fall behind: as **a** : to hang back : LINGER, LOITER **b** : to move, function, or develop with comparative slowness **c** : to become retarded in attaining maximum value or development **2** : to slacken little by little : FLAG — **lag·ger** *n*

²lag *n* **1 a** : the action or condition of lagging **b** : comparative slowness or retardation **2 a** : an amount of lagging or time during which lagging continues **b** : INTERVAL

la·ger \'läg-ər\ *n* : a beer brewed by slow fermentation and stored in refrigerated cellars for maturing

lag·gard \'lag-ərd\ *adj* : lagging or tending to lag : DILATORY, SLOW — **laggard** *n* — **lag·gard·ly** *adv or adj* — **lag·gard·ness** *n*

la·gniappe \'lan-,yap, lan-'\ *n* : something given gratis or by way of good measure

la·goon \lə-'gün\ *n* : a shallow sound, channel, or pond near or communicating with a larger body of water

la·i·cal \'lā-ə-kəl\ *or* **la·ic** \'lā-ik\ *adj* : of or relating to the laity : SECULAR — **laic** *n* — **la·i·cal·ly** \'lā-ə-k(ə-)lē\ *adv*

la·i·cism \'lā-ə-,siz-əm\ *n* : a political system characterized by the exclusion of ecclesiastical control and influence

la·i·cize \'lā-ə-,sīz\ *vt* **1** : to reduce to lay status **2** : to put under the direction of or throw open to laymen — **la·i·ci·za·tion** \,lā-ə-sə-'zā-shən\ *n*

laid *past of* LAY

lain *past part of* LIE

lair \'la(ə)r\ *n* : the resting or living place of a wild animal : DEN; *also* : REFUGE, HIDEAWAY

lais·sez–faire \,les-,ā-'fa(ə)r\ *n* : a doctrine opposing governmental interference in economic affairs beyond the minimum necessary for the maintenance of peace and property rights — **laissez–faire** *adj*

la·i·ty \'lā-ət-ē\ *n, pl* **-ties** **1** : the people of a religious faith as distinguished from its clergy **2** : the mass of the people as distinguished from those of a particular profession or skill

lake \'lāk\ *n* : a considerable inland body of standing water; *also* : a pool of liquid (as lava, oil, or pitch)

lake dwelling *n* : a dwelling built on piles in a lake; *esp* : one built in prehistoric times — **lake dweller** *n*

¹lamb \'lam\ *n* **1 a** : a young sheep esp. less than one year old or without permanent teeth **b** : the young of various animals (as the smaller antelopes) **2 a** : an innocent, weak, or gentle person **b** *cap* : JESUS **3** : the flesh of a lamb used as food

[2]**lamb** *vb* **1** : to bring forth a lamb **2** : to tend (ewes) at lambing time — **lamb·er** \'lam-ər\ *n*

lam·baste *or* **lam·bast** \lam-'bāst, -'bast\ *vt* **1** : to assault violently : BEAT **2** : to thrash verbally : EXCORIATE

lam·bent \'lam-bənt\ *adj* **1** : playing lightly over a surface : FLICKERING **2** : softly radiant **3** : marked by lightness or brilliance — **lam·ben·cy** \-bən-sē\ *n*

lam·bre·quin \'lam-bər-kən, -bri-kən\ *n* : a short decorative drapery for a shelf edge or for the top of a window casing : VALANCE

lamb·skin \'lam-ˌskin\ *n* : a lamb's skin or a small fine-grade sheepskin or the leather made from either

[1]**lame** \'lām\ *adj* **1 a** : physically disabled; *also* : having a part and esp. a limb so disabled as to impair freedom of movement **b** : halting in movement : LIMPING **2** : lacking substance : UNSATISFACTORY, WEAK — **lame·ly** *adv* — **lame·ness** *n*

[2]**lame** *vt* **1** : to make lame : CRIPPLE **2** : to make weak or ineffective : DISABLE

lame duck *n* : an elected officer continuing to hold political office after his defeat and before the inauguration of a successor

[1]**la·ment** \lə-'ment\ *vb* **1** : to mourn aloud : WAIL **2** : to express sorrow for : BEWAIL

[2]**lament** *n* **1** : a crying out in grief : WAILING **2** : DIRGE, ELEGY

lam·en·ta·ble \'lam-ən-tə-bəl, lə-'ment-ə-\ *adj* **1** : that is to be regretted or lamented : DEPLORABLE **2** : expressing grief : MOURNFUL — **lam·en·ta·ble·ness** *n* — **lam·en·ta·bly** \-blē\ *adv*

lam·en·ta·tion \ˌlam-ən-'tā-shən\ *n* : an act or instance of lamenting

lam·i·na \'lam-ə-nə\ *n, pl* **-nae** \-ˌnē, -ˌnī\ *or* **-nas** **1** : a thin plate or scale **2** : BLADE 1b — **lam·i·nar** \-nər\ *adj*

[1]**lam·i·nate** \'lam-ə-ˌnāt\ *vt* **1** : to roll or compress into a thin plate **2** : to make by uniting superposed layers of one or more materials — **lam·i·na·tor** \-ˌnāt-ər\ *n*

[2]**lam·i·nate** \-nət, -ˌnāt\ *adj* **1** : consisting of laminae **2** : bearing or covered with laminae

[3]**lam·i·nate** \-nət, -ˌnāt\ *n* : a product made by laminating

lam·i·nat·ed \-ˌnāt-əd\ *adj* : composed of layers of firmly united material; *esp* : made by bonding or impregnating superposed layers of paper, wood, or fabric with resin and compressing under heat

lam·i·na·tion \ˌlam-ə-'nā-shən\ *n* **1** : the process of laminating **2** : a laminate structure **3** : LAMINA

lamp \'lamp\ *n* **1** : a vessel with a wick for burning an inflammable liquid (as oil) to produce artificial light **2** : a device for producing light or heat

lamp·black \-ˌblak\ *n* : a finely powdered deep black soot made by incomplete burning of carbon-containing material and used esp. as a pigment in paints and ink

lamp·light·er \-ˌlīt-ər\ *n* : one that lights a lamp; *esp* : a person employed to go about lighting street lights that burn gas

[1]**lam·poon** \lam-'pün\ *n* **1** : a harsh satire usu. directed against an individual **2** : a light mocking satire

[2]**lampoon** *vt* : to make (as a political opponent) the subject of a lampoon : RIDICULE — **lam·poon·er** *n*

lam·prey \'lam-prē\ *n, pl* **lampreys** : any of an order of aquatic vertebrates that resemble eels but have a large sucking mouth with no jaws

la·nai \lə-'nī, lä-\ *n* : a porch furnished for use as a living room

la·nate \'lā-ˌnāt, 'lan-ˌāt\ *adj* : covered with fine hair or filaments : WOOLLY

[1]**lance** \'lan(t)s\ *n* **1** : a weapon of war consisting of a long shaft with a sharp steel head and carried by mounted knights or light cavalry **2** : any of various sharp objects suggestive of a lance; *esp* : LANCET **3** : LANCER 1b

[2]**lance** *vt* **1** : to pierce with a lance or similar weapon **2** : to open with or as if with a lancet

lanc·er \'lan(t)-sər\ *n* **1 a** : one who carries a lance **b** : a light cavalryman armed with a lance **2** *pl* **a** : a set of five quadrilles each in a different meter **b** : the music for such dances

lan·cet \'lan(t)-sət\ *n* : a sharp-pointed and usu. 2-edged surgical instrument

lancet arch *n* : an acutely pointed arch

[1]**land** \'land\ *n* **1 a** : the solid part of the surface of the earth **b** : a portion of the earth's surface in some way distinguishable (as by natural or political boundaries, ownership, or physical quality) **c** : REALM, DOMAIN **d** *pl* : territorial possessions : REAL ESTATE **2** : the people of a country : NATION — **land·less** \'lan-dləs\ *adj*

[2]**land** *vb* **1 a** : to set or go ashore from a ship : DISEMBARK **b** : to stop at or near a place or shore **2** : to alight or cause to alight on a surface **3 a** : to bring or get to a destination : ARRIVE **b** : to reach or cause to reach a certain place or position **c** : to bring to a specified condition **4 a** : to catch with a hook and bring in **b** : GAIN, SECURE

lan·dau \'lan-ˌdau̇, -ˌdȯ\ *n* : a four-wheeled carriage with a top divided into two sections that can be lowered, thrown back, or removed

land breeze *n* : a breeze blowing toward the sea

land bridge *n* : a strip of land connecting two landmasses (as continents)

land·ed \'lan-dəd\ *adj* **1** : having an estate in land **2** : consisting of real estate

land·fall \'lan(d)-ˌfȯl\ *n* **1** : a sighting or making of land after a voyage or flight **2** : the shore or land first sighted on a voyage or flight

land grant *n* : a grant of land by a government; *esp* : one granted by the federal government to a state for the support of an agricultural and mechanical college

land·hold·er \'land-ˌhōl-dər\ *n* : a holder or owner of land — **land·hold·ing** \-diŋ\ *n*

land·ing \'lan-diŋ\ *n* **1** : the action of one that lands **2** : a place for discharging or taking on passengers and cargo **3** : the level part of a staircase at the end of a flight of stairs or connecting one flight with another

landing craft *n* : any of numerous naval craft specially designed for putting ashore troops and equipment

landing field *n* : a field where aircraft may land and take off

landing gear *n* : the undercarriage that supports the weight of an airplane when in contact with the land or water

landing net *n* : a small net with a handle used to take a hooked fish from the water

landing strip *n* : AIRSTRIP

land·la·dy \'lan(d)-ˌlād-ē\ *n* : a female landlord

land·locked \-ˌläkt\ *adj* **1** : enclosed or nearly enclosed by land **2** : confined to fresh water by some barrier

land·lord \-ˌlȯrd\ *n* **1** : the owner of property (as land) which he leases or rents to another **2** : a man who rents lodgings : INNKEEPER

land·lub·ber \-ˌləb-ər\ *n* **1** : LANDSMAN **2** : one who is unacquainted with the sea or seamanship — **land·lub·ber·ly** \-lē\ *adj*

land·mark \-ˌmärk\ *n* **1** : an object (as a stone or tree) that marks the boundary of land **2** : a conspicuous object on land that marks a course, serves as a guide, or characterizes a locality **3** : an event or development that marks a turning point or a stage

land·mass \-ˌmas\ *n* : a large area of land

land–office business *n* : extensive and rapid business

land·own·er \'land-ˌō-nər\ *n* : an owner of land — **land·own·ing** \-niŋ\ *adj*

land–poor \'lan(d)-ˌpu̇(ə)r\ *adj* : owning so much unprofitable or encumbered land as to lack funds to develop the land or pay the charges due thereon

land reform *n* : more equitable distribution of agricultural land esp. by governmental action
¹land·scape \'lan(d)-ˌskāp\ *n* **1** : a picture representing a view of natural inland scenery **2** : a portion of land that the eye can see in one glance
²landscape *vb* : to improve the natural beauties of a tract of land by grading, clearing, or gardening
landscape gardener *n* : one skilled in the development and decorative planting of gardens and grounds
land·slide \'lan(d)-ˌslīd\ *n* **1** : the slipping down of a mass of rocks or earth on a steep slope; *also* : the mass of material that slides **2** : an overwhelming material victory esp. in a political contest
lands·man \'lan(d)z-mən\ *n* : a person who lives or works on land; *esp* : one who knows little or nothing of the sea and ships
¹land·ward \'land-wərd\ *adj* : lying or being toward the land or on the side toward the land
²landward *adv* : to or toward the land
lane \'lān\ *n* **1** : a narrow passageway between fences, hedges, or buildings **2** : a relatively narrow way or track: as **a** : an ocean route for ships **b** : a strip of roadway for a single line of vehicles **c** : a bowling alley
lan·guage \'laŋ-gwij\ *n* **1 a** : the words, their pronunciation, and the methods of combining them used and understood by a large group of people **b** (1) : audible, articulate, and meaningful sound as produced by the action of the vocal organs (2) : a systematic means of communicating ideas by signs or marks with understood meanings **2 a** : form or manner of verbal expression; *esp* : STYLE **b** : the vocabulary and phraseology belonging to an art or department of knowledge **3** : the study of language esp. as a school subject
lan·guid \'laŋ-gwəd\ *adj* **1** : drooping or flagging from or as if from exhaustion : WEAK **2** : sluggish in character or disposition : LISTLESS **3** : lacking force or quickness of movement : SLOW — **lan·guid·ly** *adv* — **lan·guid·ness** *n*
lan·guish \'laŋ-gwish\ *vi* **1** : to become weak or languid **2** : to lose strength or force : waste away with longing : PINE **3** : to appeal for sympathy by putting on a weary or sorrowful look — **lan·guish·er** *n* — **lan·guish·ing** *adj* — **lan·guish·ing·ly** *adv* — **lan·guish·ment** *n*
lan·guor \'laŋ-(g)ər\ *n* **1** : weakness or weariness of body or mind **2** : a state of dreamy inactivity — **lan·guor·ous** \-(g)ə-rəs\ *adj* — **lan·guor·ous·ly** *adv*
lank \'laŋk\ *adj* **1** : SLENDER, THIN **2** : hanging straight and limp without spring or curl — **lank·ly** *adv* — **lank·ness** *n*
lanky \'laŋ-kē\ *adj* : being tall, thin, and usu. loose-jointed
lan·o·lin \'lan-ᵊl-ən\ *n* : the fatty coating of sheep's wool esp. when refined for use in ointments and cosmetics
lan·tern \'lant-ərn\ *n* **1** : a usu. portable light that has a protective transparent or translucent covering **2** : the chamber in a lighthouse containing the light **3** : PROJECTOR 2b
lantern jaw *n* **1** : an undershot jaw **2** : a long thin jaw — **lan·tern–jawed** \ˌlant-ərn-'jȯd\ *adj*
lan·yard \'lan-yərd\ *n* : a piece of rope or line for fastening something in ships
¹lap \'lap\ *n* **1** : a loose panel or hanging flap esp. of a garment **2 a** (1) : the clothing that lies on the knees, thighs, and lower part of the trunk when one sits (2) : the front part of the lower trunk and thighs of a seated person **b** : an environment of nurture **3** : CHARGE, CONTROL
²lap *vb* **lapped**; **lap·ping** **1** : FOLD **2** : WRAP **3** : to lay over or near something else so as to partly cover it
³lap *n* **1 a** : the amount by which one object overlaps or projects beyond another **b** : the part of an object that overlaps another **2 a** : one circuit around a racecourse **b** : one segment of a journey **c** : one complete turn (as of a rope around a drum)
⁴lap *vb* **lapped**; **lap·ping** **1** : to scoop up food or drink with the tip of the tongue; *also* : DEVOUR — usu. used with *up* **2** : to wash or splash gently — **lap·per** *n*
⁵lap *n* **1 a** : an act or instance of lapping **b** : the amount that can be carried to the mouth by one lick or scoop of the tongue **2** : a gentle splashing sound
lap·board \'lap-ˌbōrd\ *n* : a board used on the lap as a table or desk
lap·dog \-ˌdȯg\ *n* : a small dog that may be held in the lap
la·pel \lə-'pel\ *n* : the part of a garment that is turned back; *esp* : the fold of the front of a coat that is usu. a continuation of the collar
lap·ful \'lap-ˌfu̇l\ *n, pl* **lapfuls** \-ˌfu̇lz\ *or* **laps·ful** \'laps-ˌfu̇l\ : as much as the lap can hold or support
¹lap·i·dary \'lap-ə-ˌder-ē\ *n, pl* **-dar·ies** : a person who cuts, polishes, and engraves precious stones
²lapidary *adj* **1** : of or relating to precious stones or the art of cutting them **2** : of, relating to, or suitable for engraved inscriptions
lap·in \'lap-ən\ *n* : rabbit fur usu. sheared and dyed
la·pis la·zu·li \ˌlap-əs-'laz(h)-ə-lē\ *n* : a deep blue semiprecious stone often having sparkling bits of an iron compound
lap·pet \'lap-ət\ *n* : a fold or flap on a garment
¹lapse \'laps\ *n* **1 a** : a slight error or slip **b** : a temporary deviation or fall esp. from a higher to a lower state **2** : LOWERING, DECLINE **3 a** : the termination of a right or privilege through failure to meet requirements **b** : INTERRUPTION, DISCONTINUANCE **4** : APOSTASY **5** : a passage of time; *also* : INTERVAL
²lapse *vi* **1** : to commit apostasy **2** : to slip, pass, or fall gradually **3** : to fall into disuse **4** : to come to end : pass to someone else because of failure to meet requirements
lap·wing \'lap-ˌwiŋ\ *n* : a crested Old World plover
lar·board \'lär-bərd\ *n* : PORT — **larboard** *adj*
lar·ce·ny \'lärs-nē, -ᵊn-ē\ *n, pl* **-nies** : the unlawful taking and carrying away of personal property with intent to deprive the owner of it permanently : THEFT — **lar·ce·nous** \'lärs-nəs, -ᵊn-əs\ *adj*
larch \'lärch\ *n* **1** : any of a genus of trees of the pine family with short deciduous needles; *also* : any of several related trees **2** : the wood of a larch
¹lard \'lärd\ *vt* **1** : to insert strips of usu. pork fat into (meat) before cooking **2** : to smear with lard, fat, or grease **3** : to add to; *esp* : ENRICH
²lard *n* : a soft white solid or semisolid fat obtained by rendering fatty tissue of the hog — **lardy** \'lärd-ē\ *adj*
lar·der \'lärd-ər\ *n* : a place where foods (as meat) are kept
lar·es and pe·na·tes \ˌlar-ēz-ᵊn-pə-'nāt-ēz\ *n pl* **1** : household gods **2** : personal or household effects
large \'lärj\ *adj* : greater, bigger, more extended, or more powerful than usual — **large·ness** *n*
large·heart·ed \'lärj-'härt-əd\ *adj* : GENEROUS, SYMPATHETIC
large intestine *n* : the wide last part of the intestine that connects the small intestine with the anus and takes up water from digestive residues
large·ly \'lärj-lē\ *adv* **1** : GENEROUSLY, COMPREHENSIVELY **2** : for the most part : in the main : CHIEFLY
large–mind·ed \'lärj-'mīn-dəd\ *adj* : generous or comprehensive in outlook, range, or capacity — **large–mind·ed·ly** *adv* — **large–mind·ed·ness** *n*
large–scale \-'skāl\ *adj* : larger than others of its kind
lar·gess *or* **lar·gesse** \lär-'jes, 'lär-ˌ\ *n* **1** : liberal giving **2** : a generous gift
larg·ish \'lär-jish\ *adj* : rather large
¹lar·go \'lär-gō\ *adv* (*or adj*) : in a very slow and broad manner — used as a direction in music
²largo *n, pl* **largos** : a largo movement
lar·i·at \'lar-ē-ət\ *n* : a long light rope to catch livestock or to picket grazing animals : LASSO

[1]**lark** \'lärk\ *n* : any of various small songbirds; *esp* : SKYLARK
[2]**lark** *vi* : FROLIC, SPORT
[3]**lark** *n* : FROLIC, ROMP; *also* : PRANK
lark·spur \'lärk-ˌspər\ *n* : DELPHINIUM; *esp* : a cultivated annual delphinium grown for its flowers
lar·va \'lär-və\ *n, pl* **lar·vae** \-(ˌ)vē, -ˌvī\ **1** : the immature, wingless, and often wormlike form that hatches from the egg of many insects **2** : the early form of any animal that at birth or hatching is fundamentally unlike its parent — **lar·val** \-vəl\ *adj*
la·ryn·geal \lə-'rin-j(ē-)əl, ˌlar-ən-'jē-əl\ *adj* : of, relating to, or used on the larynx — **la·ryn·geal·ly** \-ē\ *adv*
lar·yn·gi·tis \ˌlar-ən-'jīt-əs\ *n* : inflammation of the larynx — **lar·yn·git·ic** \-'jit-ik\ *adj*
lar·ynx \'lar-iŋ(k)s\ *n, pl* **la·ryn·ges** \lə-'rin-(ˌ)jēz\ *or* **lar·ynx·es** : the modified upper part of the trachea that in man and most mammals contains the vocal cords
las·car \'las-kər\ *n* : an East Indian sailor, army servant, or native artilleryman
las·civ·i·ous \lə-'siv-ē-əs\ *adj* : LEWD, LUSTFUL — **las·civ·i·ous·ly** *adv* — **las·civ·i·ous·ness** *n*
la·ser \'lā-zər\ *n* : a device that utilizes the natural oscillations of atoms for amplifying or generating electromagnetic waves in the visible region of the spectrum
[1]**lash** \'lash\ *vb* **1** : to move violently or suddenly **2** : to strike with or as if with a whip **3** : to attack or retort verbally — **lash·er** *n*
[2]**lash** *n* **1 a** (1) : a stroke with a whip or with anything slender, pliant, and tough (2) : the flexible part of a whip; *also* : WHIP **b** : a sudden swinging blow **2** : a verbal blow
[3]**lash** *vt* : to bind with a rope, cord, or chain — **lash·er** *n*
lash·ing \-iŋ\ *n* : something used for binding, wrapping, or fastening
lass \'las\ *n* **1** : young woman : GIRL **2** : SWEETHEART
lass·ie \'las-ē\ *n* : LASS, GIRL
las·si·tude \'las-ə-ˌt(y)üd\ *n* **1** : WEARINESS, FATIGUE **2** : LISTLESSNESS, LANGUOR
las·so \'las-ō, la-'sü\ *n, pl* **lassos** *or* **lassoes** : a rope or long thong of leather with a running noose that is used esp. for catching livestock — **lasso** *vt*
[1]**last** \'last\ *vb* **1** : to continue in existence or operation : go on **2 a** : to remain valid, valuable, or important : ENDURE **b** : to manage to continue (as in a course of action) **3** : to be enough for the needs of — **last·er** *n*
[2]**last** *adj* **1 a** : following all the rest **b** : being the only remaining **2 a** : belonging to the final stage **b** : administered to the dying **3** : next before the present : LATEST **4** : least likely **5 a** : CONCLUSIVE, ULTIMATE **b** : highest in degree : SUPREME
[3]**last** *adv* **1** : at the end **2** : most lately **3** : in conclusion
[4]**last** *n* : something that is last : END
[5]**last** *n* : a wooden or metal form which is shaped like the human foot and on which a shoe is shaped or repaired
[6]**last** *vb* : to shape with a last — **last·er** *n*
last·ing \'las-tiŋ\ *adj* : existing or continuing a long while : ENDURING — **last·ing·ly** *adv* — **last·ing·ness** *n*
last·ly \'last-lē\ *adv* : in conclusion : in the last place
last word *n* **1** : the final remark in a verbal exchange **2** : the power of final decision **3** : the most advanced, up-to-date, or fashionable exemplar of its kind
lat·a·kia \ˌlat-ə-'kē-ə\ *n* : an aromatic Turkish smoking tobacco
[1]**latch** \'lach\ *vi* **1** : to catch or get hold **2** : to attach oneself
[2]**latch** *n* : a device that holds something in place by entering a notch or cavity; *esp* : a catch (as a spring bolt) that holds a door or gate closed and that sometimes is operated by a key on one side and a knob on the other
[3]**latch** *vb* : CATCH, FASTEN
latch·et \'lach-ət\ *n* : a narrow leather strap, thong, or lace that fastens a shoe or sandal on the foot
latch·key \'lach-ˌkē\ *n* : a key by which a door latch may be opened from the outside
latch·string \-ˌstriŋ\ *n* : a string on a latch that may be left hanging outside the door for raising the latch
[1]**late** \'lāt\ *adj* **1 a** : coming or remaining after the due, usual, or proper time **b** : of or relating to an advanced stage in point of time or development; *esp* : far advanced toward the close of the day or night **2 a** : living comparatively recently **b** : holding some position or relationship recently but not now **c** : made, appearing, or happening just previous to the present time — **late·ness** *n*
[2]**late** *adv* **1 a** : after the usual or proper time **b** : at or to an advanced point in time **2** : not long ago : RECENTLY — **of late** : LATELY, RECENTLY
late·com·er \'lāt-ˌkəm-ər\ *n* : one who arrives late; *also* : a recent arrival
late·ly \'lāt-lē\ *adv* : in the near past : RECENTLY
lat·en \'lāt-ᵊn\ *vb* : to grow or cause to grow late
la·ten·cy \'lāt-ᵊn-sē\ *n, pl* **-cies** : the quality or state of being latent : DORMANCY
la·tent \'lāt-ᵊnt\ *adj* : present but not visible or active — **la·tent·ly** *adv*
[1]**lat·er·al** \'lat-ə-rəl, 'la-trəl\ *adj* : of or relating to the side : situated on, directed toward, or coming from the side — **lat·er·al·ly** \-ē\ *adv*
[2]**lateral** *n* **1** : a lateral part or branch **2** : a pass in football thrown parallel to the line of scrimmage or in a direction away from the opponent's goal
la·tex \'lā-ˌteks\ *n, pl* **lat·i·ces** \'lat-ə-ˌsēz\ *or* **la·tex·es** **1** : a milky juice produced by plants esp. of the milkweed family **2** : a water emulsion of a synthetic rubber or plastic used esp. in paints and adhesives — **lat·i·cif·er·ous** \ˌlat-ə-'sif-(ə-)rəs\ *adj*
[1]**lath** \'lath\ *n, pl* **laths** \'lat͟hz, 'laths\ : a thin narrow strip of wood used esp. as a base for plaster; *also* : a building material in sheets used for the same purpose
[2]**lath** *vt* : to cover or line with laths
lathe \'lāt͟h\ *n* : a machine in which a piece of material is held and turned while being shaped by a tool
[1]**lath·er** \'lat͟h-ər\ *n* **1 a** : a foam or froth formed when a detergent (as soap) is agitated in water **b** : foam or froth from profuse sweating (as on a horse) **2** : an agitated or overwrought state : DITHER — **lath·ery** \'lat͟h-(ə-)rē\ *adj*
[2]**lather** *vb* **lath·ered**; **lath·er·ing** \'lat͟h-(ə-)riŋ\ **1 a** : to spread lather over **b** : to form a lather or a froth like lather **2** : to beat severely : FLOG — **lath·er·er** *n*
lath·ing \'lath-iŋ, 'lat͟h-\ *n* **1** : the action or process of placing laths **2** : a quantity or an installation of laths
lath·work \'lath-ˌwərk\ *n* : LATHING
Lat·in \'lat-ᵊn\ *n* **1** : the language of ancient Rome **2** : a member of any of the peoples (as the French or Spanish) whose languages derive from Latin — **Latin** *adj*
Latin cross *n* : a cross having a long upright shaft and a shorter crossbar above the middle
Lat·in·ism \'lat-ᵊn-ˌiz-əm\ *n* **1** : a word, idiom, or mode of speech derived from or imitative of Latin **2** : Latin quality, character, or mode of thought
Lat·in·ist \-ᵊn-əst\ *n* : a specialist in the Latin language or Roman culture
la·tin·i·ty \la-'tin-ət-e, lə-\ *n, often cap* **1** : a manner of speaking or writing Latin **2** : LATINISM
lat·in·i·za·tion \ˌlat-ᵊn-ə-'zā-shən\ *n* : the act or result of latinizing
lat·in·ize \'lat-ᵊn-ˌīz\ *vt, often cap* : to give Latin characteristics or forms to
lat·ish \'lāt-ish\ *adj* (*or adv*) : somewhat late
lat·i·tude \'lat-ə-ˌt(y)üd\ *n* **1 a** : angular distance north or south from the earth's equator measured in degrees **b** : a re

gion or locality as marked by its latitude **2 :** freedom from narrow restrictions — **lat·i·tu·di·nal** \ˌlat-ə-ˈt(y)üd-nəl, -^{ə}n-əl\ *adj* — **lat·i·tu·di·nal·ly** \-ē\ *adv*

lat·i·tu·di·nar·i·an \ˌlat-ə-ˌt(y)üd-^{ə}n-ˈer-ē-ən\ *n* **:** a person who is broad and liberal in his standards of religious belief and conduct — **latitudinarian** *adj* — **lat·i·tu·di·nar·i·an·ism** \-ē-ə-ˌniz-əm\ *n*

la·trine \lə-ˈtrēn\ *n* **1 :** a receptacle (as a pit in the earth) for use as a toilet **2 :** TOILET

lat·ter \ˈlat-ər\ *adj* **1 a :** more recent **:** LATER **b :** of or relating to the end **:** FINAL **2 :** of, relating to, or being the second of two things referred to

lat·ter–day \ˌlat-ər-ˌdā\ *adj* **1 :** of a later or subsequent time **2 :** of present or recent times

lat·ter·ly \ˈlat-ər-lē\ *adv* **:** LATELY, RECENTLY

lat·tice \ˈlat-əs\ *n* **1 a :** a framework or structure of crossed wood or metal strips **b :** a window, door, or gate having a lattice **2 :** a regular geometrical arrangement of points or objects over an area or in space — **lattice** *vt* — **lat·ticed** \-əst\ *adj*

lat·tice·work \ˈlat-əs-ˌwərk\ *n* **:** a lattice or work made of lattices

[1]**laud** \ˈlȯd\ *n* **:** ACCLAIM, PRAISE

[2]**laud** *vt* **:** PRAISE, EXTOL

laud·a·bil·i·ty \ˌlȯd-ə-ˈbil-ət-ē\ *n* **:** the quality or state of being laudable

laud·a·ble \ˈlȯd-ə-bəl\ *adj* **:** worthy of praise **:** COMMENDABLE — **laud·a·ble·ness** *n* — **laud·a·bly** \-blē\ *adv*

lau·da·num \ˈlȯd-nəm, -^{ə}n-əm\ *n* **1 :** a formerly used preparation of opium **2 :** a tincture of opium

lau·da·tion \lȯ-ˈdā-shən\ *n* **1 :** the act of lauding **2 :** PRAISE

lau·da·to·ry \ˈlȯd-ə-ˌtōr-ē\ *adj* **:** of, relating to, or expressing praise

[1]**laugh** \ˈlaf, ˈlȧf\ *vb* **1 a :** to show mirth, joy, or scorn with a smile and chuckle or explosive sound **b :** to become amused or derisive **2 :** to produce the sound or appearance of laughter **3 :** to utter with a laugh — **laugh·er** *n*

[2]**laugh** *n* **1 :** the act or sound of laughing **2 :** a cause for derision or merriment

laugh·a·ble \-ə-bəl\ *adj* **:** such as to provoke laughter or derision **:** RIDICULOUS — **laugh·a·ble·ness** *n* — **laugh·a·bly** \-blē\ *adv*

laugh·ing \-iŋ\ *adj* **:** fit to be treated or accompanied with laughter **:** LAUGHABLE

laugh·ing·ly \-lē\ *adv* **:** with laughter

laugh·ing·stock \ˈlaf-iŋ-ˌstäk, ˈlȧf-\ *n* **:** an object of ridicule

laugh·ter \ˈlaf-tər, ˈlȧf-\ *n* **:** the action or sound of laughing

[1]**launch** \ˈlȯnch\ *vb* **1 a :** to throw forward **:** HURL **b :** to spring forward **:** take off **c :** to send off (a self-propelled object) **d :** to set (a ship) afloat **2 a :** to put in operation **:** BEGIN **b :** to give (a person) a start **c :** to make a start **3 :** to throw oneself energetically **:** PLUNGE — **launch·er** \ˈlȯn-chər\ *n*

[2]**launch** *n* **:** an act of launching

[3]**launch** *n* **:** a small open or half-decked motorboat used for pleasure or short-distance transportation

launch·ing pad \ˈlȯn-chiŋ-\ *n* **:** a nonflammable platform from which a rocket can be launched

laun·der \ˈlȯn-dər\ *vb* **laun·dered**; **laun·der·ing** \-d(ə-)riŋ\ **1 a :** to wash (as clothes) in water **b :** to iron after washing **2 :** to wash or wash and iron clothing or household linens **3 :** to undergo washing and ironing — **laun·der·er** *n* — **laun·dress** \-drəs\ *n*

laun·dry \-drē\ *n, pl* **-dries** **1 :** clothes or linens that have been or are to be laundered **2 :** a place where laundering is done

laun·dry·man \-mən\ *n* **:** a male laundry worker — **laun·dry·wom·an** \-ˌwu̇m-ən\ *n*

lau·re·ate \ˈlȯr-ē-ət\ *n* **:** the recipient of honor for achievement in an art or science — **laureate** *adj* — **lau·re·ate·ship** \-ˌship\ *n*

lau·rel \ˈlȯr-əl\ *n* **1 :** any of a genus of trees or shrubs related to the sassafras and cinnamon; *esp* **:** a small evergreen tree of southern Europe **2 :** a crown of laurel **3 :** HONOR

la·va \ˈläv-ə, ˈlav-\ *n* **:** melted rock coming from a volcano; *also* **:** such rock that has cooled and hardened

la·vage \lə-ˈväzh\ *n* **:** WASHING; *esp* **:** the washing out (as of a wound or hollow organ) for medicinal reasons

la·va·liere *or* **la·val·liere** \ˌläv-ə-ˈli(ə)r, ˌlav-\ *n* **:** a pendant on a fine chain that is worn as a necklace

lav·a·to·ry \ˈlav-ə-ˌtōr-ē\ *n, pl* **-ries** **1 :** a vessel for washing; *esp* **:** a fixed bowl or basin with running water and drainpipe **2 :** a room with conveniences for washing and usu. with one or more toilets **3 :** WATER CLOSET

lave \ˈlāv\ *vb* **1 :** WASH **2 :** to flow along or against

lav·en·der \ˈlav-ən-dər\ *n* **1 :** a Mediterranean mint widely cultivated for its narrow aromatic leaves and lilac-purple flowers which are dried and used in sachets **2 :** a pale purple

la·ver \ˈlā-vər\ *n* **:** a large basin used for ceremonial ablutions in ancient Judaism

[1]**lav·ish** \ˈlav-ish\ *adj* **1 :** spending or giving more than is necessary **:** EXTRAVAGANT **2 :** spent, produced, or given freely — **lav·ish·ly** *adv* — **lav·ish·ness** *n*

[2]**lavish** *vt* **:** to spend or give freely **:** SQUANDER

law \ˈlȯ\ *n* **1 a :** a rule of conduct or action laid down and enforced by the supreme governing authority (as the legislature) of a community, state, or nation or established by custom **b :** the whole collection of customs and rules **c :** the control brought about by enforcing rules **2 :** a rule, principle, or formula of construction or procedure **3 :** a rule or principle stating something that always works in the same way under the same conditions **4 :** the observed regularity of nature **5** *cap* **a :** the revelation of the divine will set forth in the Old Testament of the Bible **b :** the first part of the Jewish scriptures **6 :** trial in a court to determine what is just and right according to the laws **7 :** the science that deals with laws and their interpretation and application **8 :** the profession of a lawyer **:** lawyers as a group

law–abid·ing \ˈlȯ-ə-ˌbīd-iŋ\ *adj* **:** obedient to the law

law·break·er \ˈlȯ-ˌbrā-kər\ *n* **:** a person who breaks the law — **law·break·ing** \-kiŋ\ *adj or n*

law·ful \ˈlȯ-fəl\ *adj* **1 :** permitted by law **2 :** recognized by law **:** RIGHTFUL — **law·ful·ly** \-f(ə-)lē\ *adv* — **law·ful·ness** *n*

law·giv·er \-ˌgiv-ər\ *n* **1 :** one who gives a code of laws to a people **2 :** LEGISLATOR

law·less \-ləs\ *adj* **1 :** having no laws **:** not based on or regulated by law **2 :** not controlled by law **:** UNRULY, DISORDERLY — **law·less·ly** *adv* — **law·less·ness** *n*

law·mak·er \-ˌmā-kər\ *n* **:** a person who has a part in framing laws **:** LEGISLATOR — **law·mak·ing** \-kiŋ\ *adj or n*

[1]**lawn** \ˈlȯn\ *n* **:** a fine sheer linen or cotton fabric of plain weave that is thinner than cambric — **lawny** \-ē\ *adj*

[2]**lawn** *n* **:** ground (as around a house or in a park) covered with grass that is kept mowed

lawn mower *n* **:** a machine for cutting grass on lawns

lawn tennis *n* **:** tennis played on a grass court

law·ren·ci·um \lȯ-ˈren(t)-sē-əm\ *n* **:** a short-lived radioactive element produced from californium

law·suit \ˈlȯ-ˌsüt\ *n* **:** a suit in law **:** a case before a court

law·yer \ˈlȯ-yər\ *n* **:** one whose profession is to conduct lawsuits for clients or to advise as to legal rights and obligations in other matters

lax \ˈlaks\ *adj* **1 a :** LOOSE, OPEN **b :** having loose bowels **2 :** not strict or stringent **3 a :** not tense **:** not firm or rigid **:** SLACK **b :** having an open or loose texture — **lax·ly** *adv* — **lax·ness** *n*

[1]**lax·a·tive** \ˈlak-sət-iv\ *adj* **:** having a tendency to loosen or

relax; *esp* : relieving constipation — **lax·a·tive·ly** *adv* — **lax·a·tive·ness** *n*

²laxative *n* : a usu. mild laxative drug

lax·i·ty \'lak-sət-ē\ *n* : the quality or state of being lax

¹lay \'lā\ *vb* **laid** \'lād\; **lay·ing** 1 : to beat or strike down 2 **a** : to put or set on or against a surface **b** : to place for rest or sleep; *also* : BURY 3 : to produce and deposit eggs 4 : to cause to settle or be less turbulent; *also* : CALM, ALLAY 5 : to press down smooth and even 6 **a** : to spread over a surface **b** : to place down or together in orderly sequence 7 **a** : to put and arrange dishes, linens, and silver on : SET **b** : to gather and arrange fuel for 8 : to deposit as a wager : BET 9 **a** : SET, IMPOSE **b** : to put as a burden of reproach 10 : to place or assign in one's scheme of things 11 : CONTRIVE, DEVISE 12 : to bring to a specified condition 13 : to put forward : SUBMIT 14 : to apply oneself vigorously 15 : TAKE, GRAB — **lay for** : to wait and look for a chance to attack — **lay on** : ATTACK, BEAT

²lay *n* 1 : something (as a layer) that lies or is laid 2 : the way in which a thing lies or is laid in relation to something else 3 : an egg-laying condition

³lay *past of* LIE

⁴lay *n* 1 : a simple narrative poem : BALLAD 2 : MELODY, SONG

⁵lay *adj* 1 : of or relating to the laity : not ecclesiastical 2 : of or relating to members of a religious house occupied with domestic or manual work 3 : not of or from a particular profession : NONPROFESSIONAL

lay away *vt* : to put aside for future use or delivery

lay by *vt* : to store for future use : SAVE

lay down *vt* 1 : to give up : SURRENDER 2 **a** : ESTABLISH, PRESCRIBE **b** : to assert or command dogmatically 3 : STORE, PRESERVE

lay·er \'lā-ər\ *n* 1 : one that lays 2 : one thickness, course, or fold laid or lying over or under another — **lay·ered** \'lā-ərd\ *adj*

lay·ette \lā-'et\ *n* : a complete outfit of clothing and equipment for a newborn infant

lay figure \'lā-\ *n* 1 : a jointed model of the human body used by artists to show the disposition of drapery 2 : a person of no importance or individuality : DUMMY, PUPPET

lay in *vt* : to lay by : SAVE

lay·man \'lā-mən\ *n* 1 : a person who is not a clergyman 2 : a person who is not a member of a particular profession

lay off *vb* 1 : to mark or measure off 2 : to cease to employ (a worker) usu. temporarily 3 **a** : to leave undisturbed **b** : AVOID, QUIT 4 : to stop or rest from work

lay·off \'lā-,ȯf\ *n* 1 : the act of laying off an employee or a work force 2 : a period of inactivity or idleness

lay out *vt* 1 **a** : to prepare (a corpse) for burial **b** : to knock flat or unconscious 2 : to plan in detail 3 : to mark (work) for drilling, machining, or filing 4 : ARRANGE, DESIGN 5 : SPEND

lay·out \'lā-,au̇t\ *n* 1 : ARRANGEMENT, PLAN 2 : something that is laid out 3 : the way in which a piece of printed matter is arranged 4 : a set or outfit esp. of tools

lay over *vi* : to make a temporary halt or stop

lay·over \'lā-,ō-vər\ *n* : STOPOVER

lay to *vb* : to bring (a ship) into the wind and hold stationary; *also* : to lie to

lay up *vt* 1 : to store up : lay by 2 : to disable or confine with illness or injury 3 : to take out of active service

lay·wom·an \'lā-,wu̇m-ən\ *n* : a woman who is a member of the laity

laz·ar \'laz-ər, 'lā-zər\ *n* : a person afflicted with a repulsive disease; *esp* : LEPER

laz·a·ret·to \,laz-ə-'ret-ō\ *or* **laz·a·ret** \-'ret\ *n, pl* **-rettos** *or* **-rets** 1 *usu lazaretto* : a hospital for contagious diseases 2 : a building or a ship used for detention in quarantine 3 *usu lazaret* : a space in a ship between decks used as a storeroom

laze \'lāz\ *vb* : to pass time in idleness or relaxation : IDLE

lazuli *n* : LAPIS LAZULI

la·zy \'lā-zē\ *adj* 1 : not willing to act or work : IDLE, INDOLENT 2 : SLOW, SLUGGISH — **la·zi·ly** \-zə-lē\ *adv* — **la·zi·ness** \-zē-nəs\ *n*

la·zy·bones \'lā-zē-,bōnz\ *n* : a lazy person

la·zy·ish \'lā-zē-ish\ *adj* : somewhat lazy

lazy Su·san \,lā-zē-'süz-ᵊn\ *n* : a revolving tray placed on a dining table for serving food, condiments, or relishes

lea *or* **ley** \'lē, 'lā\ *n* 1 : GRASSLAND, PASTURE 2 *usu ley* : arable land used temporarily for hay or grazing

leach \'lēch\ *vt* : to pass a liquid and esp. water through to carry off the soluble components; *also* : to dissolve out by such means

¹lead \'lēd\ *vb* **led** \'led\; **lead·ing** \'lēd-iŋ\ 1 **a** : to guide on a way esp. by going in advance : CONDUCT **b** : to direct on a course or in a direction **c** : to serve as a channel for **d** : to lie, run, or open in a specified place or direction 2 : to go through : LIVE 3 **a** : to direct the operations, activity, or performance of **b** (1) : to go at the head of (2) : to be first in or among; *also* : BEGIN, OPEN (3) : to have a margin over 4 : to begin play with 5 : to tend toward a definite result : EVENTUATE

²lead *n* 1 **a** (1) : position at the front : VANGUARD (2) : INITIATIVE (3) : the act or privilege of leading in cards; *also* : the card or suit led **b** (1) : LEADERSHIP (2) : EXAMPLE, PRECEDENT **c** : a margin or measure of advantage or superiority or position in advance 2 : one that leads: as **a** : INDICATION, CLUE **b** : a principal role in a dramatic production; *also* : one who plays such a role **c** : an introductory section of a news story; *also* : a news story of chief importance

³lead *adj* : acting or serving as a leader

⁴lead \'led\ *n* 1 : a heavy soft malleable bivalent or tetravalent bluish white metallic chemical element that is found mostly in combination and is used in pipes, cable sheaths, solder, and type metal 2 : an article made of lead; *esp* : a weight for sounding (as at sea) 3 : a thin stick of marking substance (as graphite) in or for a pencil 4 : BULLETS, PROJECTILES — **lead·less** \-ləs\ *adj*

⁵lead \'led\ *vt* 1 : to cover, line, or weight with lead 2 : to fix (window glass) in position with lead 3 : to place lead or other spacing material between the lines of (type matter) 4 : to treat or mix with lead or a lead compound

lead·en \'led-ᵊn\ *adj* 1 **a** : made of lead **b** : of the color of lead : dull gray 2 : low in quality : POOR 3 **a** : oppressively heavy **b** : SLUGGISH **c** : lacking spirit or animation : DULL — **lead·en·ness** \-ᵊn-(n)əs\ *n*

lead·er \'lēd-ər\ *n* 1 : something that leads 2 : a person that leads: as **a** : GUIDE, CONDUCTOR **b** : COMMANDER **c** : CONDUCTOR b **d** : a first or principal performer of a group — **lead·er·ship** \-,ship\ *n*

lead·ing \'lēd-iŋ\ *adj* 1 : coming or ranking first or among the first : FOREMOST 2 : exercising leadership 3 : GUIDING, DIRECTING 4 : given most prominent display

leading lady *n* : an actress who plays the leading feminine role in a play or movie

leading man *n* : an actor who plays the leading male role in a play or movie

lead·off \'lēd-,ȯf\ *n* 1 : a beginning or leading action 2 : the player who heads the batting order or bats first in any inning in baseball — **lead–off** *adj*

lead on *vt* : to entice or induce to proceed in a course esp when unwise or mistaken

lead pencil \'led-\ *n* : a pencil using graphite as the marking material

¹leaf \'lēf\ *n, pl* **leaves** \'lēvz\ 1 **a** : a usu. flat lateral outgrowth from a stem that is a unit of plant foliage and functions primarily in food manufacture by photosynthesis **b** : FOLIAGE

2 : something suggestive of a leaf: as **a** : a part of a book or folded sheet containing a page on each side **b** : the movable part of a table top **c** : a thin sheet (as of metal) : LAMINA — **leaf·less** \'lēf-ləs\ *adj* — **leaf·like** *adj*

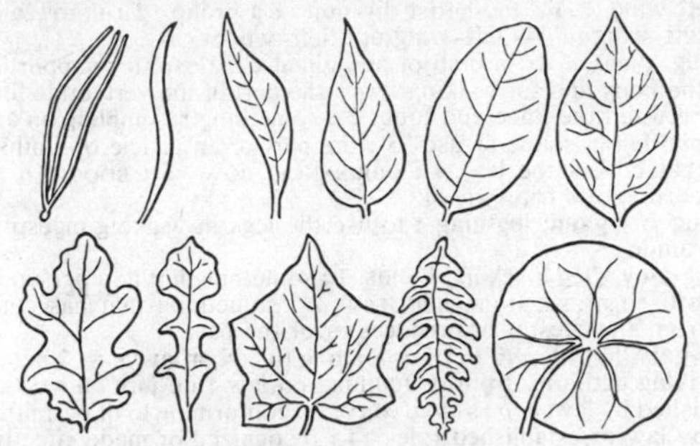
leaves of various shapes

²leaf *vb* **1** : to produce leaves **2** : to turn the pages of a book
leaf·age \'lē-fij\ *n* : FOLIAGE
leaf·let \'lēf-lət\ *n* **1** : one of the divisions of a compound leaf **2** : PAMPHLET, FOLDER
leaf mold *n* : a compost or layer composed chiefly of decayed vegetable matter
leafy \'lē-fē\ *adj* **1 a** : having or abounding in leaves **b** : consisting mostly of leaves **2** : resembling a leaf; *esp* : LAMINATE
¹league \'lēg\ *n* : any of various units of distance from about 2.4 to 4.6 statute miles
²league *n* **1 a** : an association or alliance of nations for a common purpose **b** : an association of persons or groups united for common interests or goals **2** : CLASS, CATEGORY — **league** *vb*
leagu·er \'lē-gər\ *n* : a member of a league
¹leak \'lēk\ *vb* **1 a** : to enter or escape or permit to enter or escape through an opening usu. by a fault or mistake **b** : to let a substance or light in or out through an opening **2** : to become known despite efforts at concealment **3** : to give out (information) surreptitiously
²leak *n* **1 a** : a crack or hole that usu. by mistake admits or lets escape **b** : something that permits the admission or escape of something else usu. with prejudicial effect **2** : LEAKAGE 1a
leak·age \'lē-kij\ *n* **1 a** : the act, the process, or an instance of leaking **b** : loss of electricity due esp. to faulty insulation **2** : something or the amount that leaks
leaky \'lē-kē\ *adj* : permitting fluid to leak in or out — **leak·i·ness** *n*
¹lean \'lēn\ *vb* **leaned** \'lēnd, *chiefly Brit* 'lent\; **lean·ing** \'lē-niŋ\ **1 a** : to incline, deviate, or bend from a vertical position **b** : to cast one's weight to one side for support **2** : to rely for support or inspiration **3** : to incline in opinion, taste, or desire
²lean *n* : the act or an instance of leaning : INCLINATION
³lean *adj* **1 a** : lacking or deficient in flesh **b** : containing little or no fat **2** : lacking richness, sufficiency, or productiveness **3** : characterized by economy of style or expression — **lean·ness** *n*
⁴lean *n* : the part of meat that consists principally of fat-free muscle
lean·ing \'lē-niŋ\ *n* : TENDENCY, INCLINATION
¹lean–to \'lēn-ˌtü\ *n, pl* **lean–tos** **1** : a wing or extension of a building having a lean-to roof **2** : a rough shed or shelter with a lean-to roof
²lean–to *adj* : having only one slope or pitch
¹leap \'lēp\ *vb* **leaped** *or* **leapt** \'lēpt, 'lept\; **leap·ing** \'lē-piŋ\ **1** : to spring or cause to spring free from or as if from the ground : JUMP **2 a** : to pass abruptly from one state or topic to another **b** : to act precipitately — **leap·er** *n*
²leap *n* **1 a** : an act of leaping : SPRING, BOUND **b** (1) : a place leaped over or from (2) : the distance covered by a leap **2** : a sudden transition — **by leaps and bounds** : with extraordinary rapidity
leap·frog \'lēp-ˌfrȯg, -ˌfräg\ *n* : a game in which one player bends down and another leaps over him
leap year *n* : a year containing 366 days with February 29 as the extra day
learn \'lərn\ *vb* **learned** \'lərnd, 'lərnt\; **learn·ing** **1 a** (1) : to gain knowledge or understanding of or skill in by study, instruction, or experience (2) : MEMORIZE **b** : to come to be able to **c** : to come to realize **2** : to find out : ASCERTAIN **3** : to acquire knowledge — **learn·a·ble** *adj* — **learn·er** *n*
learned *adj* **1** \'lər-nəd\ : characterized by or associated with learning : ERUDITE **2** \'lərnd, 'lərnt\ : acquired by learning — **learn·ed·ly** \'lər-nəd-lē\ *adv*
learn·ing \'lər-niŋ\ *n* **1** : the act or experience of one that learns **2** : knowledge or skill acquired by instruction or study
¹lease \'lēs\ *n* **1** : a contract by which one party conveys real estate to another for a term of years or at will usu. for a specified rent; *also* : the act of such conveyance or the term for which it is made **2** : a piece of land or property that is leased
²lease *vt* **1** : to grant by lease : LET **2** : to hold under a lease
lease·hold \'lēs-ˌhōld\ *n* **1** : a tenure by lease **2** : land held by lease — **lease·hold·er** \-ˌhōl-dər\ *n*
leash \'lēsh\ *n* **1** : a line for leading or restraining an animal **2** : a set of three animals (as dogs) — **leash** *vt*
¹least \'lēst\ *adj* **1** : lowest in importance or position **2 a** : smallest in size or degree **b** : smallest possible : SLIGHTEST
²least *n* : one that is least : something of the lowest possible value, importance, or scope — **at least** **1** : at the minimum **2** : in any case
³least *adv* : in the smallest or lowest degree
least·wise \-ˌwīz\ *adv* : at least
¹leath·er \'leth̲-ər\ *n* **1** : animal skin dressed for use **2** : something wholly or partly made of leather — **leather** *adj*
²leather *vt* **leath·ered**; **leath·er·ing** \'leth̲-(ə-)riŋ\ **1** : to cover with leather **2** : to beat with a strap : THRASH
leath·ern \'leth̲-ərn\ *adj* : made of, consisting of, or resembling leather
leath·er·neck \'leth̲-ər-ˌnek\ *n* : MARINE
leath·ery \'leth̲-(ə-)rē\ *adj* : resembling leather in appearance or texture : TOUGH
¹leave \'lēv\ *vb* **left** \'left\; **leav·ing** **1** : to allow or cause to remain behind **2** : DELIVER **3** : to have remaining (as after death or subtraction) **4** : to give by will : BEQUEATH **5** : to let stay without interference **6** : to go away **7** : to depart from
²leave *n* **1 a** : PERMISSION **b** : authorized absence from duty or employment **2** : an act of leaving : DEPARTURE
³leave *vi* **leaved**; **leav·ing** : LEAF
leaved \'lēvd\ *adj* : having leaves
¹leav·en \'lev-ən\ *n* **1** : a substance (as yeast) used to produce fermentation (as in dough) **2** : something that modifies or lightens a mass or aggregate
²leaven *vt* **leav·ened**; **leav·en·ing** \'lev-(ə-)niŋ\ **1** : to raise (dough) with a leaven **2** : to mingle or permeate with some modifying, alleviating, or vivifying element
leavening *n* : a leavening agent : LEAVEN
leave off *vb* : STOP, CEASE
leaves *pl of* LEAF
leave–tak·ing \'lēv-ˌtā-kiŋ\ *n* : DEPARTURE, FAREWELL
leav·ings \'lē-viŋz\ *n pl* : REMNANT, RESIDUE

lech•ery \'lech-(ə-)rē\ *n, pl* **-er•ies** : inordinate indulgence in sexual activity — **lecher** *n* — **lech•er•ous** \-(ə-)rəs\ *adj*
lec•tern \'lek-tərn\ *n* : a desk to support a book in a convenient position for a standing reader
lec•tor \'lek-tər\ *n* : one whose chief duty is to read the lessons in a church service
[1]**lec•ture** \'lek-chər\ *n* **1** : a discourse given before an audience or class esp. for instruction **2** : REPRIMAND, SCOLDING
[2]**lecture** *vb* **lec•tured**; **lec•tur•ing** **1** : to deliver a lecture or a course of lectures **2** : to instruct by lectures **3** : REPRIMAND, SCOLD — **lec•tur•er** *n*
led *past of* LEAD
le•der•ho•sen \'lād-ər-ˌhōz-ᵊn\ *n pl* : knee-length leather trousers worn esp. in Bavaria
ledge \'lej\ *n* **1** : a projecting ridge or raised edge along a surface : SHELF **2** : an underwater ridge or reef esp. near the shore **3** : a narrow flat surface or shelf; *esp* : one that projects (as from a wall of rock) **4** : LODE, VEIN
ledg•er \'lej-ər\ *n* : a book containing accounts to which debits and credits are posted in final form
[1]**lee** \'lē\ *n* **1** : protecting shelter **2** : the side (as of a ship) that is sheltered from the wind
[2]**lee** *adj* : of or relating to the lee
[1]**leech** \'lēch\ *n* **1** : any of numerous carnivorous or bloodsucking segmented usu. flattened freshwater worms having a sucker at each end **2** : a hanger-on who seeks advantage or gain : PARASITE
[2]**leech** *vb* **1** : to drain the substance of : EXHAUST **2** : to attach oneself to a person as a leech
leek \'lēk\ *n* : a garden herb closely related to the onion and grown for its mildly pungent leaves and thick stalk
[1]**leer** \'li(ə)r\ *vi* : to cast a sidelong glance; *esp* : to give a suggestive, knowing, or malicious look
[2]**leer** *n* : a suggestive, knowing, or malicious look
leery \'li(ə)r-ē\ *adj* : SUSPICIOUS, WARY
lees \'lēz\ *n pl* : DREGS
lee shore *n* : a shore lying off a ship's leeward side and constituting a severe danger in storm
[1]**lee•ward** \'lē-wərd, 'lü-ərd\ *adj* : situated away from the wind : DOWNWIND — **leeward** *adv*
[2]**leeward** *n* : the lee side
lee•way \'lē-ˌwā\ *n* **1** : off-course lateral movement of a ship when under way **2** : an allowable margin of freedom or variation : TOLERANCE
[1]**left** \'left\ *adj* **1** : of, relating to, or being the side of the body in which the heart is mostly located **2** : located nearer to the left side of the body than to the right; *also* : lying in the direction that an observer's left hand would naturally extend **3** *often cap* : of, adhering to, or constituted by the political Left — **left** *adv*
[2]**left** *n* **1 a** : the left hand **b** : the location or direction of or part on the left side **2** *cap* **a** : those professing views usu. characterized by desire to reform or overthrow the established order esp. in politics and usu. advocating greater freedom or well-being of the common man **b** : a radical as distinguished from a conservative position
[3]**left** *past of* LEAVE
left–hand \ˌleft-ˌhand\ *adj* **1** : situated on the left **2** : LEFT-HANDED
left–hand•ed \'left-'han-dəd\ *adj* **1** : using the left hand habitually or more easily than the right **2** : relating to, designed for, or done with the left hand **3 a** : CLUMSY, AWKWARD **b** : INSINCERE, BACKHANDED, DUBIOUS **4 a** : COUNTERCLOCKWISE **b** : having a structure involving a counterclockwise direction — **left–handed** *adv* — **left–handed•ed•ly** *adv* — **left–hand•ed•ness** *n* — **left–hand•er** \-'han-dər\ *n*
left•ist \'lef-təst\ *n* : a person who advocates or adheres to the policies of the Left
left•over \'left-ˌō-vər\ *n* : an unused or unconsumed residue; *esp* : food left over from one meal and served at another — **leftover** *adj*
left•ward \'left-wərd\ *adv* : toward or on the left — **leftward** *adj*
left wing *n* **1** : the leftist division of a group **2** : LEFT 2a — **left–wing** *adj* — **left–wing•er** \'left-ˌwiŋ-ər\ *n*
[1]**leg** \'leg\ *n* **1** : a limb of an animal used esp. for supporting the body and for walking; *esp* : the part of the vertebrate limb between the knee and foot **2** : something resembling an animal leg in shape or use **3** : the part of an article of clothing that covers the leg **4** : OBEISANCE, BOW **5** : BOOST **6** : a portion of a trip : STAGE
[2]**leg** *vi* **legged**; **leg•ging** : to use the legs in walking or esp. in running
leg•a•cy \'leg-ə-sē\ *n, pl* **-cies** **1** : something left to a person by will : INHERITANCE, BEQUEST **2** : something that has come from an ancestor or predecessor or the past
le•gal \'lē-gəl\ *adj* **1** : of or relating to law or lawyers **2 a** : deriving authority from or founded on law : de jure **b** : established by law; *esp* : STATUTORY **3** : conforming to or permitted by law or established rules **4** : recognized or made effective at law rather than in equity — **le•gal•ly** \-gə-lē\ *adv*
legal age *n* : the age at which a person enters into full adult legal rights and responsibilities (as of voting or making contracts or wills)
legal holiday *n* : a holiday established by legal authority and characterized by legal restrictions on work and transaction of official business
le•gal•ism \'lē-gə-ˌliz-əm\ *n* : strict, literal, or excessive conformity to the law or to a religious or moral code — **le•gal•ist** \-gə-ləst\ *n* — **le•gal•is•tic** \ˌlē-gə-'lis-tik\ *adj*
le•gal•i•ty \li-'gal-ət-ē\ *n, pl* **-ties** : the quality or state of being legal : LAWFULNESS
le•gal•ize \'lē-gə-ˌlīz\ *vt* : to make legal; *esp* : to give legal validity or sanction to — **le•gal•i•za•tion** \ˌlē-gə-lə-'zā-shən\ *n*
legal tender *n* : money that is legally valid for the payment of debts and that must be accepted for that purpose when offered
leg•ate \'leg-ət\ *n* : an official representative (as an ambassador or envoy)
leg•a•tee \ˌleg-ə-'tē\ *n* : a person to whom a legacy is bequeathed
le•ga•tion \li-'gā-shən\ *n* **1** : a body of deputies sent on a mission; *esp* : a diplomatic mission headed by a minister **2** : the official residence and office of a diplomatic minister to a foreign government
leg•end \'lej-ənd\ *n* **1 a** : a story coming down from the past and popularly regarded as historical although not verifiable **b** : a popular myth of recent origin **c** : a person or thing that inspires legends **2 a** : an inscription or title on an object **b** : CAPTION 2 **c** : an explanatory list of the symbols on a map or chart
leg•end•ary \'lej-ən-ˌder-ē\ *adj* : of or resembling a legend : consisting of legends
leg•end•ry \-ən-drē\ *n* : LEGENDS
leg•er•de•main \ˌlej-ərd-ə-'mān\ *n* **1** : SLEIGHT OF HAND **2** : an artful deception
legged \'leg(-ə)d\ *adj* : having legs
leg•ging *or* **leg•gin** \'leg-ən, 'leg-iŋ\ *n* : a covering for the leg usu. of leather or cloth — usu. used in pl.
leg•gy \'leg-ē\ *adj* **1 a** : having disproportionately long legs **b** : SPINDLY **2** : having attractive legs
leg•horn \'leg-ˌ(h)ȯrn, 'leg-ərn\ *n* **1 a** : a fine plaited straw made from an Italian wheat **b** : a hat of this straw **2** : any of a Mediterranean breed of small hardy fowls
leg•i•ble \'lej-ə-bəl\ *adj* : capable of being read or deciphered

: PLAIN — **leg·i·bil·i·ty** \ˌlej-ə-ˈbil-ət-ē\ *n* — **leg·i·bly** \ˈlej-ə-blē\ *adv*
le·gion \ˈlē-jən\ *n* **1** : the principal unit of the Roman army comprising 3000 to 6000 foot soldiers with cavalry **2** : ARMY 1a **3** : a very large number : MULTITUDE **4** : a national association of ex-servicemen
[1]**le·gion·ary** \ˈlē-jə-ˌner-ē\ *adj* : of, relating to, or constituting a legion
[2]**legionary** *n, pl* **-ar·ies** : LEGIONNAIRE
le·gion·naire \ˌlē-jə-ˈna(ə)r\ *n* : a member of a legion
leg·is·late \ˈlej-ə-ˌslāt\ *vb* **1** : to make or enact laws **2** : to cause, create, or bring about by legislation
leg·is·la·tion \ˌlej-ə-ˈslā-shən\ *n* **1** : the action of making laws **2** : the laws made by a legislator or legislative body
leg·is·la·tive \ˈlej-ə-ˌslāt-iv\ *adj* **1** : having the power or performing the function of legislating **2** : of or relating to a legislature or legislation — **leg·is·la·tive·ly** *adv*
leg·is·la·tor \ˈlej-ə-ˌslāt-ər\ *n* : a person who makes laws for a state or community; *esp* : a member of a legislature
leg·is·la·ture \ˈlej-ə-ˌslā-chər\ *n* : an organized body of persons having the authority to make laws for a political unit
[1]**le·git·i·mate** \li-ˈjit-ə-mət\ *adj* **1** : born of parents who are married **2** : being in accordance with law : LAWFUL **3** : being in keeping with what is right or in accordance with standards permitted **4** : of or relating to acted plays — **le·git·i·ma·cy** \-mə-sē\ *n* — **le·git·i·mate·ly** *adv*
[2]**le·git·i·mate** \-ˌmāt\ *vt* : to make lawful or legal
le·git·i·ma·tize \li-ˈjit-ə-mə-ˌtīz\ *vt* : LEGITIMATE
le·git·i·mize \li-ˈjit-ə-ˌmīz\ *vt* : LEGITIMATE
leg·less \ˈleg-ləs\ *adj* : having no legs
leg·man \ˈleg-ˌman\ *n* **1** : a newspaperman assigned usu. to gather information **2** : an assistant who gathers information and runs errands
leg–of–mut·ton \ˌleg-ə(v)-ˈmət-ᵊn\ *adj* : having the approximately triangular shape or outline of a leg of mutton
leg·ume \ˈleg-ˌyüm, li-ˈgyüm\ *n* **1** : any of a large group of plants having fruits that are dry pods and split when ripe and including important food and forage plants (as peas, beans, or clovers) **2** : the part (as seeds or pods) of a legume used as food; *also* : VEGETABLE 2 — **le·gu·mi·nous** \li-ˈgyü-mə-nəs, lē-\ *adj*
leg·work \ˈleg-ˌwərk\ *n* : the work of a legman
lei \ˈlā, ˈlā-ˌē\ *n* : a wreath or necklace usu. of flowers
lei·sure \ˈlēzh-ər, ˈlezh-\ *n* **1** : freedom provided by the cessation of activities; *esp* : time free from work or duties **2 a** : EASE **b** : CONVENIENCE — **leisure** *adj*
lei·sure·ly \-lē\ *adj* : characterized by leisure : UNHURRIED — **lei·sure·li·ness** *n* — **leisurely** *adv*
leit·mo·tiv *or* **leit·mo·tif** \ˈlīt-mō-ˌtēf\ *n* : a dominant recurring theme (as in a musical or literary work)
lem·ming \ˈlem-iŋ\ *n* : any of several small short-tailed northern rodents with furry feet and small ears
lem·on \ˈlem-ən\ *n* **1 a** : an acid fruit that is botanically a many-seeded pale yellow nearly oval berry **b** : the stout thorny citrus tree that bears this fruit **2** : DUD, FAILURE
lem·on·ade \ˌlem-ə-ˈnād\ *n* : a drink made of lemon juice, sugar, and water
lend \ˈlend\ *vb* **lent** \ˈlent\; **lend·ing** **1** : to allow the use of something on the condition that it or its equivalent be returned **2** : to give for the time being **3** : to have the quality or nature that makes suitable — **lend·er** *n*
lend–lease \ˈlen-ˈdlēs\ *n* : the transfer of goods and services to an ally to aid in a common cause with payment being made by a return of the original items or their use in the common cause or by a similar transfer of other goods and services — **lend–lease** *vt*
length \ˈleŋ(k)th\ *n* **1 a** : the longer or longest dimension of an object **b** : a measured distance or dimension **c** : the quality or state of being long **2 a** : duration or extent in time **b** : relative duration or stress of a sound **3** : the length of something taken as a unit of measure **4** : a piece constituting or usable as part of a whole or of a connected series : SECTION **5** : a vertical dimension of an article of clothing — **at length** **1** : COMPREHENSIVELY, FULLY **2** : at last : FINALLY
length·en \ˈleŋ(k)-thən\ *vb* **length·ened**; **length·en·ing** \ˈleŋ(k)th-(ə-)niŋ\ : to make or become longer
length·ways \ˈleŋ(k)th-ˌwāz\ *adv* : LENGTHWISE
length·wise \-ˌwīz\ *adv* : in the direction of the length : LONGITUDINALLY — **lengthwise** *adj*
lengthy \ˈleŋ(k)-thē\ *adj* **1** : excessively drawn out : OVERLONG **2** : EXTENDED, LONG — **length·i·ly** \-thə-lē\ *adv* — **length·i·ness** \-thē-nəs\ *n*
le·ni·en·cy \ˈlē-nē-ən-sē\ *or* **le·ni·ence** \-ən(t)s\ *n* : the quality or state of being lenient
le·ni·ent \ˈlē-nē-ənt\ *adj* : of mild and tolerant disposition or effect; *esp* : INDULGENT — **le·ni·ent·ly** *adv*
len·i·tive \ˈlen-ət-iv\ *adj* : alleviating pain or acrimony : MITIGATING — **lenitive** *n*
len·i·ty \ˈlen-ət-ē\ *n* : MILDNESS, LENIENCY
lens \ˈlenz\ *n* **1** : a piece of transparent substance (as glass) that has two opposite regular surfaces either both curved or one curved and the other plane and that is used either singly or combined in an optical instrument for forming an image by focusing rays of light **2** : a device for directing or focusing radiation (as sound waves or electrons) other than light **3** : a transparent body in the eye that focuses light rays (as upon the retina)
Lent \ˈlent\ *n* : a period of penitence and fasting observed on the 40 weekdays from Ash Wednesday to Easter by many churches
Lent·en \ˈlent-ᵊn\ *adj* : of, relating to, or suitable to Lent; *esp* : MEAGER, SOMBER
len·til \ˈlent-ᵊl\ *n* : a Eurasian annual legume widely grown for its flattened edible seeds and leafy stalks used as fodder; *also* : its seed
le·o·nine \ˈlē-ə-ˌnīn\ *adj* : of, relating to, or resembling a lion
leop·ard \ˈlep-ərd\ *n* : a large strong cat of southern Asia and Africa that is usu. tawny or buff with black spots
le·o·tard \ˈlē-ə-ˌtärd\ *n* : a close-fitting garment worn for practice or performance by dancers, acrobats, and aerialists
lep·er \ˈlep-ər\ *n* **1** : a person affected with leprosy **2** : OUTCAST
lep·re·chaun \ˈlep-rə-ˌkän\ *n* : a mischievous elf of Irish folklore usu. believed to reveal the hiding place of treasure if caught
lep·ro·sy \ˈlep-rə-sē\ *n* : a chronic bacterial disease marked by slow-growing spreading swellings accompanied by loss of sensation, wasting, and deformities
lep·rous \ˈlep-rəs\ *adj* : infected with, relating to, or resembling leprosy — **lep·rous·ly** *adv* — **lep·rous·ness** *n*
les·bi·an \ˈlez-bē-ən\ *adj, often cap* : of or relating to homosexuality between females — **lesbian** *n, often cap* — **les·bi·an·ism** \-bē-ə-ˌniz-əm\ *n*
lese maj·es·ty *or* **lèse ma·jes·té** \ˈlēz-ˈmaj-ə-stē\ *n* **1 a** : a crime committed against a sovereign power **b** : an offense violating the dignity of a ruler as the representative of a sovereign power **2** : a detraction from or affront to dignity or importance
le·sion \ˈlē-zhən\ *n* **1** : INJURY, HARM **2** : an abnormal structural change in an organ or part due to injury or disease
[1]**less** \ˈles\ *adj* **1** : of a smaller number : FEWER **2** : of lower rank, degree, or importance **3 a** : SMALLER, SLIGHTER **b** : more limited in quantity
[2]**less** *adv* : to a lesser extent or degree
[3]**less** *prep* : diminished by

⁴less *n, pl* **less** **1 :** a smaller portion or quantity **2 :** something of less importance
les·see \lə-'sē\ *n* **:** a tenant under a lease
less·en \'les-ᵊn\ *vb* **less·ened; less·en·ing** \'les-niŋ, -ᵊn-iŋ\ **:** to make or become less **:** DECREASE
¹less·er \'les-ər\ *adj* **1 :** LESS, SMALLER **2 :** INFERIOR
²lesser *adv* **:** LESS
¹les·son \'les-ᵊn\ *n* **1 :** a passage from sacred writings read in a service of worship **2 a :** a piece of instruction **:** TEACHING; *esp* **:** a reading or exercise to be studied by a pupil **b :** something learned by study or experience **3 a :** a period of instruction usu. lasting an hour or less in a single subject **b :** an instructive example; *also* **:** REPRIMAND
²lesson *vt* **les·soned; les·son·ing** \'les-niŋ, -ᵊn-iŋ\ **1 :** to give a lesson to **2 :** REBUKE
les·sor \'les-ˌȯr, le-'sȯ(ə)r\ *n* **:** one that conveys property by a lease
lest \(ˌ)lest\ *conj* **1 :** for fear that **2 :** THAT — used after an expression denoting fear or apprehension
¹let \'let\ *n* **1 :** HINDRANCE, OBSTACLE **2 :** a stroke in racket games that does not count
²let *vb* **let; let·ting** **1 :** to cause to **:** MAKE **2 a :** RENT, LEASE **b :** to assign esp. after bids **3 a :** to give opportunity to **b** — used in the imperative to introduce a request or proposal **c** — used imperatively as an auxiliary to express a warning **4 :** to free from confinement **:** RELEASE **5 :** to allow to enter, pass, or leave
let down *vb* **1 :** to fail to support **:** DESERT **2 :** DISAPPOINT **3 :** to slacken effort **:** RELAX
let·down \'let-ˌdau̇n\ *n* **1 :** DISAPPOINTMENT **2 :** a slackening of effort **:** RELAXATION
le·thal \'lē-thəl\ *adj* **1 :** of, relating to, or causing death **2 :** capable of causing death
le·thar·gic \li-'thär-jik, le-\ *adj* **1 :** of, relating to, or characterized by lethargy **:** SLUGGISH **2 :** LISTLESS — **le·thar·gi·cal·ly** \-ji-k(ə-)lē\ *adv*
leth·ar·gy \'leth-ər-jē\ *n* **1 :** abnormal drowsiness **2 :** the quality or state of being lazy or indifferent
let on *vb* **1 a :** ADMIT **b :** REVEAL, DISCLOSE **2 :** PRETEND
¹let·ter \'let-ər\ *n* **1 :** a symbol in writing or print that stands for a speech sound and constitutes a unit of an alphabet **2 :** a direct or personal written or printed message addressed to a person or organization **3** *pl* **a :** LITERATURE, BELLES LETTRES **b :** LEARNING **4 :** the strict or outward meaning **5 :** a single piece of type
²letter *vt* **1 :** PRINT **2 :** to mark with letters **:** INSCRIBE — **let·ter·er** *n*
letter carrier *n* **:** MAILMAN
let·tered \'let-ərd\ *adj* **1 a :** LEARNED, EDUCATED **b :** of, relating to, or characterized by learning **:** CULTURED **2 :** inscribed with or as if with letters
let·ter·head \'let-ər-ˌhed\ *n* **:** stationery having a printed or engraved heading; *also* **:** the heading itself
let·ter·ing \-ər-iŋ\ *n* **:** letters used in an inscription
let·ter–per·fect \ˌlet-ər-'pər-fikt\ *adj* **:** correct to the smallest detail; *esp* **:** VERBATIM
let·ter·press \'let-ər-ˌpres\ *n* **1 :** printing done directly by impressing the paper on an inked raised surface **2 :** printed reading matter **:** TEXT
letters of marque \-'märk\ **:** written authority granted to a private person by a government to seize the subjects of a foreign state or their goods; *esp* **:** a license granted to a private person to fit out an armed ship to plunder the enemy
letters pat·ent \-'pat-ᵊnt, *Brit also* 'pāt-\ *n pl* **:** a writing (as from a sovereign) that confers on a designated person a grant in a form readily open for inspection by all
let·tuce \'let-əs\ *n* **:** a common garden vegetable related to the daisies that has succulent leaves used esp. in salads
let up *vi* **1 :** to slow down **:** DIMINISH **2 :** CEASE, STOP
let-up \'let-ˌəp\ *n* **:** a lessening of effort **:** CESSATION
leu·ke·mia \lü-'kē-mē-ə\ *n* **:** a cancerous disease of warm-blooded animals (as man) in which leukocytes increase abnormally in the tissues and often in the blood — **leu·ke·mic** \-mik\ *adj* — **leu·ke·moid** \-ˌmȯid\ *adj*
leu·ko·cyte \'lü-kə-ˌsīt\ *n* **:** WHITE BLOOD CELL
¹lev·ee \'lev-ē; lə-'vē, -'vā\ *n* **1 :** a reception held by a person of distinction orig. on rising from bed **2 :** a reception usu. in honor of a particular person
²levee \'lev-ē\ *n* **1 :** an embankment or dike to prevent flooding **2 :** a river landing place **:** PIER
¹lev·el \'lev-əl\ *n* **1 :** a device for establishing a horizontal line or plane **2 :** horizontal condition; *esp* **:** a condition of liquids marked by a horizontal surface of even altitude **3 :** a horizontal position, line, or surface often taken as an index of altitude; *also* **:** a flat area of ground **4 :** height, position, rank, or size in or as if in a scale of values — **on the level :** bona fide **:** HONEST
²level *vb* **lev·eled** *or* **lev·elled; lev·el·ing** *or* **lev·el·ling** \'lev-(ə-)liŋ\ **1 :** to make (a line or surface) horizontal **:** make flat or level **2 :** AIM, DIRECT **3 :** to bring to a common level or plane **:** EQUALIZE **4 :** to lay level with the ground **:** RAZE **5 :** to attain or come to a level — **lev·el·er** *or* **lev·el·ler** \-(ə-)lər\ *n*
³level *adj* **1 :** having a flat even surface **2 :** being on a line with the floor or even ground **:** HORIZONTAL **3 a :** of the same height or rank **:** being on a line **:** EVEN **b :** UNIFORM **4 :** steady and cool in judgment — **lev·el·ly** \'lev-ə(l)-lē\ *adv* — **lev·el·ness** \-əl-nəs\ *n* — **level best :** very best
lev·el·head·ed \ˌlev-əl-'hed-əd\ *adj* **:** having sound judgment **:** SENSIBLE — **lev·el·head·ed·ness** *n*
¹lev·er \'lev-ər, 'lē-vər\ *n* **1 a :** a bar used for prying or dislodging something **b :** an instrument or agency used to achieve one's purpose **:** TOOL **2 a :** a rigid bar used to exert a pressure or sustain a weight at one point of its length by the application of a force at a second and turning at a third on a fulcrum **b :** a projecting piece by which a mechanism is operated or adjusted
²lever *vt* **lev·ered; lev·er·ing** \'lev-(ə-)riŋ, 'lēv-\ **:** to pry, raise, or move with or as if with a lever
lev·er·age \'lev-(ə-)rij, 'lēv-\ *n* **1 :** the action of a lever or the mechanical advantage gained by it **2 :** EFFECTIVENESS, POWER
le·vi·a·than \li-'vī-ə-thən\ *n* **1 :** a large sea animal **2 :** something very large, powerful, or formidable esp. of its kind — **leviathan** *adj*
lev·i·tate \'lev-ə-ˌtāt\ *vb* **:** to rise or cause to rise in the air in seeming defiance of gravitation — **lev·i·ta·tion** \ˌlev-ə-'tā-shən\ *n*
lev·i·ty \'lev-ət-ē\ *n, pl* **-ties :** excessive or unseemly lack of earnestness in conduct or character **:** FRIVOLITY
¹levy \'lev-ē\ *n, pl* **lev·ies** **1 a :** the imposition or collection of an assessment **b :** an amount levied **2 a :** the enlistment or conscription of men for military service **b :** troops raised by levy
²levy *vb* **lev·ied; lev·y·ing** **1 a :** to impose or collect by legal authority **b :** to require by authority **2 :** to enlist or conscript for military service **3 :** to carry on (war) **:** WAGE **4 :** to seize property in satisfaction of a legal claim
lewd \'lüd\ *adj* **1 :** sexually unchaste **:** LASCIVIOUS **2 :** OBSCENE, SALACIOUS — **lewd·ly** *adv* — **lewd·ness** *n*
lex·i·cog·ra·pher \ˌlek-sə-'käg-rə-fər\ *n* **:** an author or compiler of a dictionary
lex·i·cog·ra·phy \-fē\ *n* **1 :** the editing or making of a dictionary **2 :** the principles and practices of dictionary making — **lex·i·co·graph·ic** \-kō-'graf-ik\ *or* **lex·i·co·graph·i·cal** \-'graf-i-kəl\ *adj* — **lex·i·co·graph·i·cal·ly** \-i-k(ə-)lē\ *adv*

lex·i·con \'lek-sə-,kän, -si-kən\ *n, pl* **lex·i·ca** \-si-kə\ *or* **lexi·cons** : DICTIONARY

ley *var of* LEA

li·a·bil·i·ty \,lī-ə-'bil-ət-ē\ *n, pl* **-ties** 1 : the state of being liable 2 *pl* : that for which a person is liable : DEBTS 3 : something that is a drawback or disadvantage

li·a·ble \'lī-ə-bəl\ *adj* 1 : bound by law : OBLIGATED, RESPONSIBLE 2 : exposed to or likely to experience something undesirable : LIKELY 3 : SUSCEPTIBLE

li·aise \lē-'āz\ *vi* 1 : to establish liaison 2 : to act as a liaison officer

li·ai·son \'lē-ə-,zän, lē-'ā-\ *n* 1 **a** : a connecting link; *esp* : a linking or coordinating of activities **b** : AFFAIR 3a 2 : the pronunciation of an otherwise absent consonant sound at the end of the first of two consecutive words when the second begins with a vowel sound and follows without pause 3 : intercommunication esp. between parts of an armed force

li·a·na \lē-'än-ə, -'an-ə\ *or* **li·ane** \-'än, -'an\ *n* : a climbing plant that roots in the ground

li·ar \'lī(-ə)r\ *n* : one that tells lies

li·ba·tion \lī-'bā-shən\ *n* 1 : the act of pouring a liquid (as wine) esp. in honor of a god; *also* : the liquid poured out 2 : DRINK — **li·ba·tion·ary** \-shə-,ner-ē\ *adj*

¹li·bel \'lī-bəl\ *n* 1 : the action or the crime of injuring a person's reputation by means of something printed or written or by some visible representation (as a picture) 2 : a spoken or written statement or a representation that gives an unjustly unfavorable impression of a person or thing — **li·bel·ous** *or* **li·bel·lous** \-bə-ləs\ *adj*

²libel *vb* **li·beled** *or* **li·belled**; **li·bel·ing** *or* **li·bel·ling** 1 : to make libelous statements 2 : to make or publish a libel against — **li·bel·er** *or* **li·bel·ler** *n*

¹lib·er·al \'lib(-ə)-rəl\ *adj* 1 : of, relating to, or based on the liberal arts 2 **a** : marked by generosity and openhandedness **b** : AMPLE, BOUNTIFUL 3 : not literal : LOOSE 4 : BROAD-MINDED, TOLERANT; *esp* : not bound by authoritarianism, orthodoxy, or traditional forms 5 : of, favoring, or based on the principles of liberalism : not conservative — **lib·er·al·ly** \-rə-lē\ *adv*

²liberal *n* : a person who holds liberal views

liberal arts *n pl* : the studies (as language, philosophy, mathematics, history, literature, or abstract science) in a college or university intended to provide chiefly general knowledge and to develop the general intellectual capacities

lib·er·al·ism \'lib(-ə)-rə-,liz-əm\ *n* 1 : the quality or state of being liberal 2 : a political philosophy based on belief in progress, the essential goodness of man, and the autonomy of the individual and standing for the protection of political and civil liberties — **lib·er·al·ist** \-rə-ləst\ *n or adj* — **lib·er·al·is·tic** \,lib(-ə)-rə-'lis-tik\ *adj*

lib·er·al·i·ty \,lib-ə-'ral-ət-ē\ *n, pl* **-ties** 1 : the quality or state of being liberal: **a** : GENEROSITY **b** : BROAD-MINDEDNESS 2 : a liberal gift 3 : AMPLENESS, BROADNESS

lib·er·al·ize \'lib(-ə)-rə-,līz\ *vb* : to make or become liberal — **lib·er·al·i·za·tion** \,lib(-ə)-rə-lə-'zā-shən\ *n* — **lib·er·al·iz·er** *n*

lib·er·ate \'lib-ə-,rāt\ *vt* 1 : to free from bondage or restraint : set at liberty 2 : to free (as a gas) from combination — **lib·er·a·tion** \,lib-ə-'rā-shən\ *n* — **lib·er·a·tor** \'lib-ə-,rāt-ər\ *n*

lib·er·tar·i·an \,lib-ər-'ter-ē-ən\ *n* 1 : an advocate of the doctrine of free will 2 : one who upholds the principles of liberty esp. of thought and action — **libertarian** *adj* — **lib·er·tar·i·an·ism** \-ē-ə-,niz-əm\ *n*

lib·er·tine \'lib-ər-,tēn\ *n* : a person who leads a life of unrestrained dissoluteness — **libertine** *adj* — **lib·er·tin·ism** \-,tē-,niz-əm\ *n*

lib·er·ty \'lib-ərt-ē\ *n, pl* **-ties** 1 : the condition of those who are free and independent : freedom from slavery, imprisonment, or control by another 2 : power to do what one pleases : freedom from restraint 3 : permission for a sailor to go ashore off duty for a certain number of hours 4 : excessive freedom of action : the act of a person who is too free or bold or familiar — **at liberty** 1 : not confined 2 : at leisure : not busy 3 : having the right : FREE

li·bid·i·nous \lə-'bid-ᵊn-əs\ *adj* 1 : having or marked by lustful desires : LASCIVIOUS 2 : LIBIDINAL — **li·bid·i·nous·ly** *adv* — **li·bid·i·nous·ness** *n*

li·bi·do \lə-'bēd-ō, -'bīd-\ *n, pl* **-dos** 1 : emotion or psychic energy derived from primitive biological urges 2 : sexual drive — **li·bid·i·nal** \-'bid-ᵊn-əl\ *adj* — **li·bid·i·nal·ly** \-ᵊn-ə-lē\ *adv*

li·brar·i·an \lī-'brer-ē-ən\ *n* : a specialist in the care or management of a library — **li·brar·i·an·ship** \-,ship\ *n*

li·brary \'lī-,brer-ē\ *n, pl* **-brar·ies** 1 : a place in which books, manuscripts, musical scores, or other literary and artistic materials are kept for use but not for sale 2 : a collection of literary or artistic materials (as books or prints)

library paste *n* : a thick white adhesive made from starch

li·bret·tist \lə-'bret-əst\ *n* : the writer of a libretto

li·bret·to \lə-'bret-ō\ *n, pl* **-tos** *or* **-ti** \-(,)ē\ : the text of a work (as an opera) for the musical theater; *also* : a book containing such a text

lice *pl of* LOUSE

¹li·cense *or* **li·cence** \'līs-ᵊn(t)s\ *n* 1 **a** : permission to act **b** : freedom of action 2 **a** : permission granted by competent authority to engage in a business, occupation, or activity otherwise unlawful **b** : a document, plate, or tag evidencing a license granted 3 **a** : freedom that is used with irresponsibility **b** : LICENTIOUSNESS 4 : deviation from fact, form, or rule by an artist or writer for the sake of the effect gained

²license *vt* 1 : to issue a license to 2 : to permit or authorize esp. by formal license — **li·cens·a·ble** *adj*

li·cens·ee \,līs-ᵊn-'sē\ *n* : a licensed person

li·cen·ti·ate \lī-'sen-chē-ət\ *n* : one licensed (as by a university) to practice a profession

li·cen·tious \lī-'sen-chəs\ *adj* : loose and lawless in behavior; *esp* : LEWD, LASCIVIOUS — **li·cen·tious·ly** *adv* — **li·cen·tious·ness** *n*

li·chen \'lī-kən\ *n* : any of numerous complex lower plants made up of an alga and a fungus growing as a unit on a solid surface (as a rock) — **li·chen·ous** \-kə-nəs\ *adj*

lic·it \'lis-ət\ *adj* : LAWFUL — **lic·it·ly** *adv*

¹lick \'lik\ *vb* 1 **a** : to draw the tongue over **b** : to flicker over like a tongue 2 : to lap up 3 **a** : to strike repeatedly : THRASH **b** : DEFEAT

²lick *n* 1 **a** : an act or instance of licking **b** : a small amount : BIT **c** : a hasty careless effort 2 **a** : a sharp hit : BLOW **b** : OPPORTUNITY, TURN — usu. used in pl. 3 : a place (as a spring) having a deposit of salt that animals regularly lick

lick·e·ty–split \,lik-ət-ē-'split\ *adv* : at great speed

lick·spit·tle \'lik-,spit-ᵊl\ *n* : a fawning subordinate : TOADY

lic·o·rice \'lik(-ə)-rish, -rəs\ *n* 1 : a European leguminous plant 2 : the dried root of licorice; *also* : an extract from it used esp. in medicine, brewing, and confectionery

lid \'lid\ *n* 1 : a movable cover 2 : EYELID — **lid·ded** \'lid-əd\ *adj* — **lid·less** \'lid-ləs\ *adj*

¹lie \'lī\ *vi* **lay** \'lā\; **lain** \'lān\; **ly·ing** \'lī-iŋ\ 1 **a** : to be in, stay at rest in, or assume a horizontal position : RECLINE **b** : to stay in concealment or secret readiness 2 : to be in a helpless or defenseless state 3 : to have direction : EXTEND 4 **a** : to occupy a certain relative place or position **b** : to have an effect through mere presence, weight, or relative position 5 **a** : EXIST **b** : REMAIN

²lie *n* : the position in which something lies

³lie *vi* **lied**; **ly·ing** \'lī-iŋ\ 1 : to make an untrue statement with intent to deceive 2 : to create a false impression

⁴lie *n* 1 : an assertion of something known or believed by the speaker to be untrue with intent to deceive **2** : something that misleads or deceives

lied \'lēt\ *n, pl* **lie·der** \'lēd-ər\ : a German song esp. of the 19th century

lie detector *n* : an apparatus for detecting physical evidences of the tension that accompanies lying

lief \'lēv, 'lēf\ *adv* : GLADLY, WILLINGLY

[1]**liege** \'lēj\ *adj* **1** : having the right to receive service and allegiance **2** : owing or giving service to a lord

[2]**liege** *n* **1** : VASSAL **2** : a feudal superior

liege man *n* **1** : VASSAL **2** : a devoted follower

lie in *vi* : to be confined to give birth to a child

lien \'lēn, 'lē-ən\ *n* : a legal claim on the real or personal property of another person until he has met a certain obligation (as a debt or the fulfillment of a duty)

lie to *vi* : to stay stationary with head to windward

lieu·ten·an·cy \lü-'ten-ən-sē\ *n, pl* **-cies** : the office, rank, or commission of a lieutenant

lieu·ten·ant \lü-'ten-ənt\ *n* **1 a** : an officer empowered to act for a higher official **b** : a representative of another in the performance of duty **2 a (1)** : FIRST LIEUTENANT **(2)** : SECOND LIEUTENANT **b** : a commissioned officer in the navy ranking next below a lieutenant commander

lieutenant colonel *n* : a commissioned officer (as in the army) ranking next below a colonel

lieutenant commander *n* : a commissioned officer in the navy ranking next below a commander

lieutenant general *n* : a commissioned officer (as in the army) ranking next below a general

lieutenant junior grade *n* : a commissioned officer in the navy ranking next below a lieutenant

[1]**life** \'līf\ *n, pl* **lives** \'līvz\ **1 a** : the quality that distinguishes a vital and functional being from a dead body or inanimate matter **b** : a principle or force held to underlie the distinctive quality of animate beings **c** : a state of an organism characterized esp. by capacity for metabolism, growth, reaction to stimuli, and reproduction **2** : the sequence of physical and mental experiences that make up the existence of an individual **3** : BIOGRAPHY 1 **4** : spiritual existence transcending physical death **5 a** : the period during which an organism lives **b** : a specific phase or aspect of such a life **6** : a way or manner of living **7** : a vital or living being; *esp* : PERSON **8** : an animating and shaping force or principle **9** : ANIMATION, SPIRIT **10** : the period of utility, continuance, or existence of something **11** : LIVELINESS **12** : living beings (as of a kind or place) **13 a** : human activities **b** : animate activity and movement **14** : one providing interest and vigor

[2]**life** *adj* **1** : of or relating to animate being **2** : LIFELONG **3** : using a living model

life belt *n* : a life preserver in the form of a buoyant belt

life·blood \'līf-'bləd\ *n* : something that gives strength and energy : the vital force or essence

life·boat \-ˌbōt\ *n* : a strong buoyant boat esp. designed for use in saving lives at sea

life buoy *n* : a float consisting of a ring of buoyant material to support a person who has fallen into the water

life expectancy *n* : an expected number of years of life based on statistical probability

life·guard \'līf-ˌgärd\ *n* : a usu. expert swimmer employed to safeguard bathers

life insurance *n* : insurance providing for payment of a stipulated sum to a designated beneficiary upon death of the insured

life·less \'līf-ləs\ *adj* : having no life: **a** : DEAD **b** : INANIMATE **c** : lacking qualities expressive of life and vigor : DULL **d** : destitute of living beings — **life·less·ly** *adv* — **life·less·ness** *n*

life·like \'līf-ˌlīk\ *adj* : accurately representing or imitating real life — **life·like·ness** *n*

life·line \'līf-ˌlīn\ *n* : a line to which persons may cling to save or protect their lives; *esp* : one stretched along the deck or from the yards of a ship

life·long \'līf-ˌlȯŋ\ *adj* : continuing through life

life preserver *n* : a device designed to save a person from drowning by buoying up the body while in the water

lif·er \'lī-fər\ *n* : a person sentenced to life imprisonment

life raft *n* : a raft usu. made of wood or an inflatable material and designed for use by people forced into the water

life·sav·ing \'līf-ˌsā-viŋ\ *n* : the art or practice of saving or protecting lives esp. of drowning persons — **life·sav·er** \-vər\ *n* — **lifesaving** *adj*

life–size \'līf-'sīz\ *or* **life–sized** \-'sīzd\ *adj* : of natural size : of the size of the original

life·time \-ˌtīm\ *n* : the duration of an individual's existence

life vest *n* : a life preserver designed as a vest of buoyant or inflatable material

life·work \'līf-'wərk\ *n* : the entire or principal work of one's lifetime; *also* : a work extending over a lifetime

[1]**lift** \'lift\ *vb* **1** : to raise from a lower to a higher position, rate, or amount : ELEVATE **2** : to put an end to (a blockade or siege) by withdrawing investing forces **3** : REVOKE, RESCIND **4 a** : STEAL **b** : PLAGIARIZE **5** : to shift (artillery fire) usu. to a greater range **6** : to move from one place to another : TRANSPORT **7** : RISE, ASCEND **8 a** : to disperse upward **b** : to stop temporarily — **lift·er** *n*

[2]**lift** *n* **1** : the amount that may be lifted at one time : LOAD **2 a** : the action or an instance of lifting **b** : elevated carriage **3 a** : ASSISTANCE, HELP **b** : a ride along one's way **4** : one of the layers forming the heel of a shoe **5** : a rise or advance in position or condition **6** : the distance or extent to which something rises **7 a** : an apparatus for raising an automobile (as for repair) **b** : a conveyor for carrying people up or down a mountain slope **8 a** : an elevating influence **b** : an elevation of the spirits **9** : the part of the total aerodynamic force acting on an airplane or airfoil that is upward and opposes the pull of gravity

lift–off \'lift-ˌȯf\ *n* : a takeoff by an airplane or rocket

lig·a·ment \'lig-ə-mənt\ *n* **1** : a tough band of tissue that holds bones together or keeps an organ in place in the body **2** : a connecting or unifying bond : TIE — **lig·a·men·tous** \ˌlig-ə-'ment-əs\ *adj*

li·gate \'lī-ˌgāt, lī-'\ *vt* : to tie with a ligature — **li·ga·tion** \lī-'gā-shən\ *n*

lig·a·ture \'lig-ə-ˌchu̇r, -chər\ *n* **1** : a binding or tying of something **2** : something that binds or connects : BAND, BOND **3** : a thread or filament used in surgery esp. for tying blood vessels **4** : a printed or written character consisting of two or more letters or characters united

[1]**light** \'līt\ *n* **1 a** : something that makes vision possible **b** : an electromagnetic radiation visible to the human eye **2 a** : DAYLIGHT **b** : DAWN **3** : a source of light: as **a** : a heavenly body **b** : CANDLE **c** : an electric light **4 a** : spiritual illumination **b** : ENLIGHTENMENT **c** : TRUTH **5 a** : public knowledge **b** : a particular aspect or appearance presented to view **6** : a particular illumination **7 a** : WINDOW **b** : SKYLIGHT **8** *pl* : philosophy of life : STANDARDS **9** : a noteworthy person : LUMINARY **10** : a particular expression of the eye **11** : LIGHTHOUSE, BEACON; *also* : a traffic signal **12** : a flame for lighting something

[2]**light** *adj* **1** : having light : BRIGHT **2** : medium in saturation and high in lightness

[3]**light** *vb* **light·ed** *or* **lit** \'lit\; **light·ing 1** : to make or become light : BRIGHTEN **2** : to burn or cause to burn : KINDLE, IGNITE **3 a** : to conduct with a light : GUIDE **b** : ILLUMINATE

[4]**light** *adj* **1 a** : having little weight : not heavy **b** : designed to carry a comparatively small load **c** : having relatively little weight in proportion to bulk **d** : containing less than the legal

standard, or usual weight **2 a :** of little importance or seriousness : TRIVIAL **b :** not abundant : SCANTY **3 a :** easily disturbed **b :** exerting little force or pressure : GENTLE **c :** resulting from a very slight pressure : FAINT **4 :** requiring little effort **5 :** capable of moving swiftly or nimbly **6 a :** FRIVOLOUS **b :** sexually promiscuous **7 :** free from care : CHEERFUL **8 :** intended chiefly to entertain **9 :** having a comparatively low alcoholic content **10 :** well leavened **11 :** lightly armed or equipped **12 :** being coarse and sandy : easily reduced to dust **13 :** DIZZY, GIDDY **14 :** producing goods for direct consumption by the consumer **15 :** UNACCENTED **16 :** having a clear soft quality

[5]**light** *adv* **1 :** LIGHTLY **2 :** with little baggage

[6]**light** *vi* **light·ed** *or* **lit** \'lit\; **light·ing** **1 :** SETTLE, ALIGHT **2 a :** to strike or fall unexpectedly **b :** to arrive by chance : HAPPEN

[1]**light·en** \'līt-ᵊn\ *vb* **light·ened**; **light·en·ing** \'līt-niŋ, -ᵊn-iŋ\ **1 :** to make or grow light or clear : BRIGHTEN **2 :** to make or become lighter **3 :** to give out flashes of lightning — **light·en·er** \'līt-nər, -ᵊn-ər\ *n*

[2]**lighten** *vb* **light·ened**; **light·en·ing** \'līt-niŋ, -ᵊn-iŋ\ **1 :** to relieve of a burden in whole or in part **2 :** CHEER, GLADDEN **3 :** to become lighter — **light·en·er** \'līt-nər, -ᵊn-ər\ *n*

[1]**ligh·ter** \'līt-ər\ *n* **:** a large usu. flat-bottomed barge used esp. in unloading or loading ships

[2]**lighter** *vt* **:** to convey by a lighter

[3]**light·er** \'līt-ər\ *n* **:** one that lights; *esp* **:** a device for lighting

light·face \'līt-ˌfās\ *n* **:** a type having light thin lines (as in this) — **light·faced** \-'fāst\ *adj*

light–fin·gered \-'fiŋ-gərd\ *adj* **:** adroit in stealing esp. by picking pockets — **light–fin·gered·ness** *n*

light–foot·ed \-'fu̇t-əd\ *adj* **:** having a light and springy step or movement

light–head·ed \-'hed-əd\ *adj* **1 :** mentally disoriented : DIZZY **2 :** lacking in maturity or seriousness : FRIVOLOUS

light·heart·ed \-'härt-əd\ *adj* **:** free from care or anxiety : GAY — **light·heart·ed·ly** *adv* — **light·heart·ed·ness** *n*

light·house \'līt-ˌhau̇s\ *n* **:** a structure (as a tower) with a powerful light for guiding navigators at night

light·ing \'līt-iŋ\ *n* **1 a :** ILLUMINATION **b :** IGNITION **2 :** an artificial supply of light or the apparatus providing it

light·ly \'līt-lē\ *adv* **1 :** with little weight or force : GENTLY **2 :** in a small degree or amount **3 :** with little difficulty : EASILY **4 :** NIMBLY, SWIFTLY **5 :** UNCONCERNEDLY **6 :** GAILY, FRIVOLOUSLY

light–mind·ed \'līt-'mīn-dəd\ *adj* **:** lacking in seriousness : FRIVOLOUS — **light·mind·ed·ly** *adv*

[1]**light·ness** \'līt-nəs\ *n* **1 :** the quality or state of being light or lighted : ILLUMINATION **2 :** the degree to which the achromatic element of a color is nearer white than black

[2]**lightness** *n* **1 :** the quality or state of being light in weight **2 :** LEVITY **3 a :** NIMBLENESS **b :** an ease and gaiety of style or manner **4 :** DELICACY

[1]**light·ning** \'līt-niŋ\ *n* **:** the flashing of light produced by a discharge of atmospheric electricity from one cloud to another or between a cloud and the earth; *also* **:** the discharge itself

[2]**lightning** *adj* **:** moving or accomplished with the speed of lightning

lightning rod *n* **:** a metal rod set up on a building or a ship and connected with the earth or water below to decrease the chances of damage from lightning

light opera *n* **:** OPERETTA

light·proof \'līt-'prüf\ *adj* **:** impenetrable by light

lights \'līts\ *n pl* **:** the lungs esp. of a slaughtered animal

light·ship \'līt-ˌship\ *n* **:** a ship equipped with a brilliant light and moored at a place dangerous to navigation

light·some \'līt-səm\ *adj* **1 :** AIRY, NIMBLE **2 :** free from care : CHEERFUL — **light·some·ly** *adv*

light·tight \'līt-ˌtīt\ *adj* **:** LIGHTPROOF

[1]**light·weight** \'līt-ˌwāt\ *n* **1 :** one of less than average weight; *esp* **:** a boxer weighing more than 126 but not over 135 pounds **2 :** an ineffectual or poorly qualified person

[2]**lightweight** *adj* **1 :** of, relating to, or characteristic of a lightweight **2 :** having less than average weight

lig·ne·ous \'lig-nē-əs\ *adj* **:** of or resembling wood : WOODY

lig·nite \'lig-ˌnīt\ *n* **:** a usu. brownish black coal intermediate between peat and bituminous coal; *esp* **:** one in which the texture of the original wood is distinct

lik·able *or* **like·able** \'lī-kə-bəl\ *adj* **:** having qualities that bring about a favorable regard : PLEASANT, AGREEABLE — **lik·a·ble·ness** *n*

[1]**like** \'līk\ *vb* **1 :** to feel attraction toward or take pleasure in : ENJOY **2 :** to feel toward : REGARD **3 :** to wish to have : WANT **4 :** to feel inclined : CHOOSE

[2]**like** *n* **:** LIKING, PREFERENCE

[3]**like** *adj* **1 a :** the same or nearly the same (as in appearance, character, or quantity) **b :** resembling or characteristic of something — used after the word modified and in combination **2 a :** LIKELY **b :** being about or as if about — used with an infinitive

[4]**like** *prep* **1 a :** similar to **b :** typical of **2 :** in the manner of : similarly to **3 :** inclined to **4 :** such as

[5]**like** *n* **:** one that is like another : COUNTERPART

[6]**like** *conj* **1 :** in the same way that : AS **2 :** as if

like·li·hood \'lī-klē-ˌhu̇d\ *n* **:** PROBABILITY

[1]**like·ly** \'lī-klē\ *adj* **1 :** being such as to make a certain happening or result probable **2 :** seeming like the truth : BELIEVABLE **3 :** PROMISING

[2]**likely** *adv* **:** in all probability : PROBABLY

like–mind·ed \'līk-'mīn-dəd\ *adj* **:** of the same mind or habit of thought — **like–mind·ed·ly** *adv* — **like–mind·ed·ness** *n*

lik·en \'lī-kən\ *vt* **lik·ened**; **lik·en·ing** \'līk-(ə-)niŋ\ **:** to represent as like something : COMPARE

like·ness \'līk-nəs\ *n* **1 :** the quality or state of being like : RESEMBLANCE **2 :** APPEARANCE, SEMBLANCE **3 :** COPY, PORTRAIT

like·wise \'līk-ˌwīz\ *adv* **1 :** in like manner : SIMILARLY **2 :** in addition : ALSO

lik·ing \'lī-kiŋ\ *n* **:** favorable regard : FONDNESS, TASTE

li·lac \'lī-lək, -ˌlak, -ˌläk\ *n* **1 :** any of a genus of shrubs and trees of the olive family; *esp* **:** a European shrub widely grown for its showy panicles of fragrant pink, purple, or white flowers **2 :** a variable color averaging a moderate purple

[1]**lilt** \'lilt\ *vb* **1 :** to sing or play in a lively cheerful manner **2 :** to sing or speak rhythmically and with fluctuating pitch **3 :** to move in a lively springy manner

[2]**lilt** *n* **1 :** a lively and usu. gay song or tune **2 :** a rhythmical swing, flow, or cadence

[1]**lily** \'lil-ē\ *n, pl* **lil·ies** **:** any of a genus of erect perennial leafy-stemmed bulbous herbs widely grown for their showy funnel-shaped flowers; *also* **:** any of various related monocotyledonous plants

[2]**lily** *adj* **:** of, relating to, or resembling a lily

lily–liv·ered \ˌlil-ē-'liv-ərd\ *adj* **:** COWARDLY

lily of the valley **:** a low perennial herb of the lily family with usu. two large oblong leaves and a stalk of fragrant nodding bell-shaped flowers

lily pad *n* **:** a floating leaf of a water lily

lily–white \ˌlil-ē-'hwīt\ *adj* **1 :** white as a lily **2 :** FAULTLESS, PURE

li·ma bean \ˌlī-mə-\ *n* **:** any of various bush or tall-growing beans widely grown for their flat edible usu. pale green or whitish seeds; *also* **:** this seed

limb \'lim\ *n* **1 :** one of the projecting paired appendages (as wings) of an animal body used esp. for movement and grasping; *esp* **:** a leg or arm of a human being **2 :** a large primary branch of a tree **3 :** an active member or agent — **limbed** \'limd\ *adj*

[1]**lim•ber** \'lim-bər\ *adj* **:** bending easily **:** FLEXIBLE, SUPPLE — **lim•ber•ly** *adv* — **lim•ber•ness** *n*

[2]**limber** *vb* **lim•bered**; **lim•ber•ing** \-b(ə-)riŋ\ **:** to become or cause to become limber

limb•less \'lim-ləs\ *adj* **:** having no limbs

lim•bo \'lim-bō\ *n, pl* **lim•bos** **1** *often cap* **:** an abode of souls (as of unbaptized infants) barred from heaven through no fault of their own **2 a :** a place or state of confinement or oblivion **b :** an intermediate or transitional place or state

[1]**lime** \'līm\ *n* **1 :** BIRDLIME **2 :** a caustic infusible white substance that consists of calcium and oxygen, is obtained by heating limestone or shells until they crumble to powder, and is used in making cement and in fertilizer

[2]**lime** *vt* **:** to treat or cover with lime

[3]**lime** *n* **:** a fruit like the lemon but smaller and with greenish yellow rind; *also* **:** the citrus tree that bears it

lime•ade \lī-'mād\ *n* **:** a drink made of lime juice, sugar, and water

lime•kiln \'līm-,kil(n)\ *n* **:** a kiln or furnace for reducing limestone or shells to lime by burning

lime•light \-,līt\ *n* **1 :** a device formerly used for lighting of the stage producing light by means of a flame directed on a cylinder of lime; *also* **:** the light produced by this device **2 :** the center of public attention

lim•er•ick \'lim-(ə-)rik\ *n* **:** a light or humorous poem of five lines

lime•stone \'līm-,stōn\ *n* **:** a rock that is formed chiefly by accumulation of organic remains (as shells or coral), consists mainly of calcium carbonate, is extensively used in building, and yields lime when burned

[1]**lim•it** \'lim-ət\ *n* **1 a :** BOUNDARY **b** *pl* **:** BOUNDS **2 a :** something that bounds, restrains, or confines **b :** the utmost extent **3 :** LIMITATION **4 :** a prescribed maximum or minimum amount, quantity, or number

[2]**limit** *vt* **1 :** to set bounds or limits to **2 :** to curtail or reduce in quantity or extent — **lim•it•a•ble** *adj*

lim•i•ta•tion \,lim-ə-'tā-shən\ *n* **1 :** an act or instance of limiting **2 :** the quality or state of being limited **3 :** something that limits **:** BOUNDARY, RESTRAINT — **lim•i•ta•tion•al** \-shnəl, -shən-ᵊl\ *adj*

lim•it•ed \'lim-ət-əd\ *adj* **1 :** confined within limits **:** RESTRICTED **2 :** having a limited number of passengers and offering superior and faster service and transportation — **lim•it•ed•ly** *adv*

limited war *n* **:** a war with an objective less than the total defeat of the enemy

lim•it•ing \-ət-iŋ\ *adj* **:** functioning as a limit **:** RESTRICTIVE

lim•it•less \-ət-ləs\ *adj* **:** having no limits — **lim•it•less•ly** *adv* — **lim•it•less•ness** *n*

limn \'lim\ *vt* **limned**; **limn•ing** \'lim-(n)iŋ\ **1 a :** DRAW **b :** PAINT **2 a :** to outline in clear sharp detail **:** DELINEATE **b :** DESCRIBE — **limn•er** \'lim-(n)ər\ *n*

lim•ou•sine \'lim-ə-,zēn, ,lim-ə-'\ *n* **:** any of various passenger vehicles; *esp* **:** a large luxurious often chauffeur-driven sedan

[1]**limp** \'limp\ *vb* **1 :** to walk lamely **2 :** to proceed slowly or with difficulty — **limp•er** *n*

[2]**limp** *n* **:** a limping movement or gait

[3]**limp** *adj* **1 a :** having no defined shape **:** SLACK **b :** not stiff or rigid **2 a :** DROOPING, EXHAUSTED **b :** lacking in strength or firmness **:** SPIRITLESS — **limp•ly** *adv* — **limp•ness** *n*

lim•pet \'lim-pət\ *n* **:** a marine mollusk with a low conical shell that clings to rocks or timbers

lim•pid \'lim-pəd\ *adj* **1 :** TRANSPARENT **2 :** readily intelligible **:** CLEAR — **lim•pid•i•ty** \lim-'pid-ət-ē\ *n* — **lim•pid•ly** *adv*

limy \'lī-mē\ *adj* **:** containing lime or limestone

lin•age \'lī-nij\ *n* **1 :** the number of lines of printed or written matter **2 :** payment for literary matter at so much a line

linch•pin \'linch-,pin\ *n* **:** a locking pin inserted crosswise (as through the end of an axle or shaft)

lin•den \'lin-dən\ *n* **1 :** any of a genus of trees with large heart-shaped leaves and clustered yellowish flowers rich in nectar **2 :** the light fine-grained white wood of a linden; *esp* **:** BASSWOOD

[1]**line** \'līn\ *vt* **1 :** to cover the inner surface of **2 :** to put something in the inside of **:** SUPPLY **3 :** to serve as the lining of

[2]**line** *n* **1 :** THREAD, STRING, CORD, ROPE; *esp* **:** a comparatively strong slender cord **2 :** a cord, wire, or tape used in measuring and leveling **3 a :** piping for conveying a fluid (as steam or oil) **b :** wire connecting one telegraph or telephone station with another or a whole system of such wires **4 a :** a unit in the rhythmic structure of verse formed by the grouping of a number of the smallest units of the rhythm (as metrical feet) **b :** a short letter **:** NOTE **c :** the words making up a part in a drama — usu. used in pl. **5 a :** something (as a ridge or seam) that is distinct, elongated, and narrow **b :** ROUTE **6 :** a state of agreement **7 a :** a course of conduct, action, or thought; *esp* **:** a publicly proclaimed policy or viewpoint **b :** a field of activity or interest **c :** a glib often persuasive way of talking **8 a :** LIMIT, RESTRAINT **b :** FORTUNE, LUCK **9 :** any of various things arranged in or as if in a row or sequence: as **a :** FAMILY, LINEAGE **b :** a set of objects (as goods for sale) of one general kind **c :** a system of transportation; *also* **:** the company owning or operating it **d :** the football players who line up on or within one foot of the line of scrimmage **10 :** a narrow elongated mark (as one drawn by a pencil); *also* **:** EQUATOR **11 a :** a defining outline **:** CONTOUR **b :** a general plan **12 :** an indication (as of intention) based on insight or investigation — **down the line :** all the way **:** FULLY — **in line for :** due or in a position to receive — **on the line 1 :** in full view and at hazard **2 :** on the border between two categories **3 :** IMMEDIATELY

[3]**line** *vb* **1 :** to mark or cover with a line **2 :** to depict by lines **:** DRAW **3 :** to place or form a line along **4 a :** to form a line **:** form into lines **b :** ALIGN **c :** ORGANIZE

lin•e•age \'lin-ē-ij\ *n* **1 :** lineal descent from a common progenitor **2 :** a group of persons tracing descent from a common ancestor regarded as its founder

lin•e•al \'lin-ē-əl\ *adj* **1 :** LINEAR **2 a :** consisting of or being in a direct line of ancestry or descent **b :** HEREDITARY **c :** of, relating to, or dealing with a lineage — **lin•e•al•ly** \-ē-ə-lē\ *adv*

lin•e•a•ment \'lin-ē-ə-mənt\ *n* **:** one of the outlines, features, or contours of a body or figure and esp. of the face

lin•e•ar \'lin-ē-ər\ *adj* **1 a :** relating to, consisting of, or resembling a line **:** STRAIGHT **b :** involving a single dimension **c :** characterized by an emphasis on line **2 :** long and uniformly narrow — **lin•e•ar•i•ty** \,lin-ē-'ar-ət-ē\ *n* — **lin•e•ar•ly** *adv*

lin•e•a•tion \,lin-ē-'ā-shən\ *n* **1 a :** the action of marking with lines **:** DELINEATION **b :** OUTLINE **2 :** an arrangement of lines

line•man \'līn-mən\ *n* **1 :** one who sets up or repairs electric wire communication or power lines **2 :** a player in the line in football

lin•en \'lin-ən\ *n* **1 a :** cloth made of flax and noted for its strength, coolness, and luster **b :** thread or yarn spun from flax **2 :** clothing or household articles made of linen cloth or a similar fabric **3 :** paper made from linen fibers or with a linen finish — **linen** *adj*

line of duty : all that is authorized, required, or normally associated with some field of responsibility

line of scrimmage : an imaginary line in football parallel to the goal lines and passing through the ball laid on the ground preparatory to a scrimmage

[1]**lin•er** \'lī-nər\ *n* **1 :** one that makes, draws, or uses lines **2 :** something with which lines are made **3 a :** a ship belonging to a regular line of ships **b :** an airplane belonging to an airline

²liner *n* : one that lines or is used to line or back something
lines·man \'līnz-mən\ *n* **1** : LINEMAN 1 **2** : an official who assists a referee in an athletic game (as football)
line up *vb* **1** : to assume an orderly linear arrangement **2** : to put into alignment
line-up \'līn-,əp\ *n* **1** : a line of persons arranged esp. for identification by police **2 a** : a list of players taking part in a game (as of baseball) **b** : an alignment of persons or things having a common purpose or interest
ling \'liŋ\ *n* : any of various fishes (as a hake or burbot) of the cod family
lin·ger \'liŋ-gər\ *vi* **lin·gered**; **lin·ger·ing** \-g(ə-)riŋ\ **1** : to be slow in leaving or quitting a place or activity **2** : to remain alive although gradually dying **3** : to be slow to act : PROCRASTINATE — **lin·ger·er** *n* — **lin·ger·ing·ly** *adv*
lin·ge·rie \,län-jə-'rā, ,laⁿ-zhə-, ,lan-jə-, -'rē\ *n* : women's intimate apparel (as nightclothes or underwear)
lin·go \'liŋ-gō\ *n, pl* **lingoes** **1** : strange or incomprehensible language or speech; *esp* : a foreign language **2** : the special vocabulary of a particular field of interest : JARGON **3** : language characteristic of an individual
lin·gua fran·ca \,liŋ-gwə-'fraŋ-kə\ *n, pl* **lingua francas** *or* **lin·guae fran·cae** \-,gwī-'fraŋ-,kī\ **1** : a common language that consists of Italian mixed with French, Spanish, Greek, and Arabic and is spoken in Mediterranean ports **2** : any of various languages used as common or commercial tongues among speakers of different languages
lin·gual \'liŋ-gwəl\ *adj* **1 a** : of, relating to, or resembling a tongue **b** : lying near or next to the tongue **2** : produced by the tongue — **lin·gual·ly** \-gwə-lē\ *adv*
lin·guist \'liŋ-gwəst\ *n* **1** : a person skilled in languages **2** : one who specializes in linguistics
lin·guis·tic \liŋ-'gwis-tik\ *adj* : of or relating to language or linguistics — **lin·guis·ti·cal·ly** \-ti-k(ə-)lē\ *adv*
lin·guis·tics \-tiks\ *n* : the study of human speech including the units, nature, structure, and development of language, languages, or a language
lin·i·ment \'lin-ə-mənt\ *n* : a liquid preparation rubbed on the skin esp. to relieve pain
lin·ing \'lī-niŋ\ *n* **1** : material used to line esp. the inner surface of something (as a garment) **2** : the act or process of providing something with a lining
¹link \'liŋk\ *n* **1** : a connecting structure; *esp* : a single ring or division of a chain **2** : something analogous to a link of chain: as **a** : a segment of sausage in a chain **b** : a connecting element
²link *vb* : to couple or connect by a link : UNITE, JOIN — **link·er** *n*
³link *n* : a torch formerly used to light a person on his way through the streets
link·age \'liŋ-kij\ *n* **1** : the manner or style of being united **2** : the quality or state of being linked **3** : a system of links
link·boy \'liŋk-,bȯi\ *n* : an attendant formerly employed to bear a light (as a torch) for a person abroad at night
link·ing verb \'liŋ-kiŋ-\ *n* : a copulative verb
links \'liŋ(k)s\ *n pl* : a golf course
links·man \-mən\ *n* : GOLFER
lin·net \'lin-ət\ *n* : a common small Old World finch with variable plumage
li·no·le·um \lə-'nō-lē-əm, -'nōl-yəm\ *n* : a floor covering with a canvas back and a surface of hardened linseed oil and a filler (as cork dust)
lin·seed \'lin-,sēd\ *n* : FLAXSEED
linseed oil *n* : a yellowish oil obtained from flaxseed and used esp. in paint, varnish, printing ink, and linoleum
lin·sey–wool·sey \,lin-zē-'wu̇l-zē\ *n* : a coarse sturdy fabric of wool and linen or cotton
lint \'lint\ *n* **1** : linen made into a soft fleecy substance for use in surgical dressings **2** : fine ravels, fluff, or loose short fibers from yarn or fabrics **3** : fibers forming a close thick coating about cotton seeds and constituting the staple of cotton — **linty** \-ē\ *adj*
lin·tel \'lint-ᵊl\ *n* : a horizontal piece or part across the top of an opening (as of a door) that carries the weight of the structure above it
lint·er \'lint-ər\ *n* **1** : a machine for removing linters **2** *pl* : the fuzz of short fibers that adheres to cottonseed after ginning
li·on \'lī-ən\ *n, pl* **lion** *or* **lions** **1 a** : a large tawny carnivorous chiefly nocturnal cat of open or rocky areas of Africa and esp. formerly southern Asia with a tufted tail and a shaggy mane in the male **b** : any of several large wildcats; *esp* : COUGAR **2 a** : a person resembling a lion (as in courage or ferocity) **b** : a person of outstanding interest or importance — **li·on·ess** \'lī-ə-nəs\ *n* — **li·on·like** *adj*
li·on·heart·ed \,lī-ən-'härt-əd\ *adj* : having a courageous heart : BRAVE
li·on·ize \'lī-ə-,nīz\ *vt* : to treat as an object of great interest or importance — **li·on·i·za·tion** \,lī-ə-nə-'zā-shən\ *n*
¹lip \'lip\ *n* **1** : either of the two fleshy folds that surround the mouth; *also* : a part or projection suggesting such a lip **2 a** : the edge of a hollow vessel or cavity esp. where it flares slightly **b** : a short spout (as on a pitcher) **3** : EMBOUCHURE — **lip·less** \-ləs\ *adj* — **lip·like** *adj* — **lipped** \'lipt\ *adj*
²lip *adj* **1** : spoken with the lips only : INSINCERE **2** : produced with the participation of the lips : LABIAL
³lip *vt* **lipped**; **lip·ping** **1** : to touch with the lips; *esp* : KISS **2** : UTTER
lip·py \'lip-ē\ *adj* : given to insolent or argumentative answer or response : IMPUDENT
lip·read·ing \'lip-,rēd-iŋ\ *n* : the interpreting of a speaker's words without hearing his voice by watching his lip and facial movements — **lip–read** \-,rēd\ *vb* — **lip–read·er** *n*
lip service *n* : an expression of allegiance (as to a rule) without corresponding action
lip·stick \'lip-,stik\ *n* : a waxy solid colored cosmetic in stick form for the lips; *also* : a stick of such cosmetic with its case
liq·ue·fac·tion \,lik-wə-'fak-shən\ *n* **1** : the process of making or becoming liquid **2** : the state of being liquid
liq·ue·fy \'lik-wə-,fī\ *vb* **-fied**; **-fy·ing** : to reduce to a liquid state : become liquid — **liq·ue·fi·a·ble** *adj* — **liq·ue·fi·er** *n*
li·queur \li-'kər, -'k(y)u̇(ə)r\ *n* : an alcoholic beverage flavored with aromatic substances and usu. sweetened
¹liq·uid \'lik-wəd\ *adj* **1** : flowing freely like water **2** : neither solid nor gaseous **3 a** : shining clear **b** : being musical and free of harshness in sound **c** : smooth and unconstrained in movement **d** : that is without friction and like a vowel **4** : consisting of or capable of ready conversion into cash — **li·quid·i·ty** \lik-'wid-ət-ē\ *n* — **liq·uid·ly** *adv* — **liq·uid·ness** *n*
²liquid *n* **1** : a liquid substance **2** : a liquid consonant
liq·ui·date \'lik-wə-,dāt\ *vb* **1** : to pay off **2** : to settle the accounts of (as a business) and use the assets toward paying off the debts **3** : to do away with; *esp* : KILL — **liq·ui·da·tion** \,lik-wə-'dā-shən\ *n* — **liq·ui·da·tor** \'lik-wə-,dāt-ər\ *n*
liq·uid·ize \'lik-wə-,dīz\ *vt* : to cause to be liquid
¹li·quor \'lik-ər\ *n* : a liquid substance or solution; *esp* : an alcoholic beverage distilled rather than fermented
²liquor *vb* **li·quored**; **li·quor·ing** \'lik-(ə-)riŋ\ : to make or become drunk with alcoholic liquor
lisle \'līl\ *n* : a smooth tightly twisted thread usu. made of long-staple cotton
¹lisp \'lisp\ *vb* **1** : to pronounce *s* and *z* imperfectly esp. by giving them the sound of *th* **2** : to speak falteringly, childishly, or with a lisp — **lisp·er** *n*
²lisp *n* **1** : the habit or act of lisping **2** : a sound resembling a lisp
lis·some \'lis-əm\ *adj* **1** : easily flexed : LITHE **2** : NIMBLE — **lis·some·ly** *adv* — **lis·some·ness** *n*

[1]list \\'list\\ *n* **1 a :** SELVAGE **b :** a band or strip of any material (as wood) **2** *pl* **a :** an arena for jousting **b :** an arena for combat **c :** a field of competition or controversy **3 :** a streak of color (as on an animal's body) **:** STRIPE

[2]list *n* **1 a :** a simple series of names (as of persons or objects) **b :** an official roster **:** ROLL **2 :** INDEX, CATALOG

[3]list *vb* **1 a :** to make a list of **:** ENUMERATE **b :** to include on a list **:** REGISTER **2 a :** to put (oneself) down **b :** to become entered in a catalog with a selling price

[4]list *vb* **:** to lean or cause to lean to one side **:** TILT

[5]list *n* **:** a deviation from the vertical **:** TILT

lis•ten \\'lis-ᵊn\\ *vi* **lis•tened; lis•ten•ing** \\'lis-niŋ, -ᵊn-iŋ\\ **1 :** to pay attention in order to hear **2 :** to give heed **:** follow advice — **lis•ten•er** \\'lis-nər, -ᵊn-ər\\ *n*

listen in *vi* **1 :** to tune in to or monitor a broadcast **2 :** to give ear to a conversation without participating in it; *esp* **:** EAVESDROP — **lis•ten•er–in** \\ˌlis-nər-'in, -ᵊn-ər-\\ *n*

list•ing \\'lis-tiŋ\\ *n* **1 :** an act or instance of making or including in a list **2 :** something listed

list•less \\'list-ləs\\ *adj* **:** characterized by lack of inclination or impetus to exertion **:** LANGUID, SPIRITLESS — **list•less•ly** *adv* — **list•less•ness** *n*

list price *n* **:** the basic price of an item as published in a catalog, price list, or advertisement but subject to discounts (as trade)

lit *past of* LIGHT

lit•a•ny \\'lit-ᵊn-ē\\ *n, pl* **-nies :** a prayer consisting of a series of supplications and responses said alternately by a leader and a group

li•ter \\'lēt-ər\\ *n* **:** a metric unit of capacity equal to the volume of one kilogram of water at 4°C and at standard atmospheric pressure of 760 millimeters of mercury

lit•er•a•cy \\'lit-ə-rə-sē\\ *n* **:** the state of being literate **:** ability to read and write

lit•er•al \\'lit-ə-rəl\\ *adj* **1 a :** according with the letter of the scriptures **b :** adhering to fact or to the ordinary or usual meaning of a term or expression **c :** PLAIN, UNADORNED **d :** characterized by a concern mainly with facts **:** PROSAIC **2 :** of, relating to, or expressed in letters **3 :** reproduced word for word **:** EXACT, VERBATIM — **lit•er•al•ly** \\'lit-ər-(ə-)lē\\ *adv*

lit•er•al•ism \\'lit-ə-rə-ˌliz-əm, 'li-trə-\\ *n* **1 :** adherence to the explicit substance of an idea or expression **2 :** fidelity to observable fact — **lit•er•al•ist** \\-ləst\\ *n* — **lit•er•al•is•tic** \\ˌlit-ə-rə-'lis-tik, ˌli-trə-\\ *adj*

lit•er•ary \\'lit-ə-ˌrer-ē\\ *adj* **1 a :** of, relating to, or having the characteristics of letters, humane learning, or literature **b :** BOOKISH 2 **c :** of or relating to books **2 a :** well informed through reading **b :** of or relating to men of letters or writing as a profession

lit•er•ate \\'lit-ə-rət\\ *adj* **1 a :** EDUCATED, CULTURED **b :** able to read and write **2 a :** versed in literature or creative writing **:** LITERARY **b :** POLISHED, LUCID — **literate** *n* — **lit•er•ate•ly** *adv*

li•te•ra•ti \\ˌlit-ə-'rät-(ˌ)ē\\ *n pl* **1 :** the educated class **:** INTELLIGENTSIA **2 :** men of letters

lit•er•a•tim \\ˌlit-ə-'rāt-əm, -'rät-\\ *adv (or adj)* **:** letter for letter

lit•er•a•ture \\'lit-ə-rə-ˌchu̇r, -chər\\ *n* **1 :** the production of literary work esp. as an occupation **2 a :** writings in prose or verse; *esp* **:** writings having excellence of form or expression and expressing ideas of permanent or universal interest **b :** the body of writings on a particular subject **c :** printed matter (as leaflets or circulars) **3 :** the aggregate of musical compositions

lithe \\'līth, 'līth\\ *adj* **1 :** easily bent **:** FLEXIBLE **2 :** marked by effortless grace **:** LIMBER — **lithe•ly** *adv* — **lithe•ness** *n*

lithe•some \\'līth-səm, 'līth-\\ *adj* **:** LISSOME

lith•i•um \\'lith-ē-əm\\ *n* **:** a soft silver-white univalent chemical element that is the lightest metal known and is used esp. in nuclear reactions and metallurgy

[1]litho•graph \\'lith-ə-ˌgraf\\ *vt* **:** to produce, copy, or portray by lithography — **li•thog•ra•pher** \\lith-'äg-rə-fər, 'lith-ə-ˌgraf-ər\\ *n*

[2]lithograph *n* **:** a print made by lithography — **litho•graph•ic** \\ˌlith-ə-'graf-ik\\ *adj* — **litho•graph•i•cal•ly** \\-'graf-i-k(ə-)lē\\ *adv*

li•thog•ra•phy \\lith-'äg-rə-fē\\ *n* **:** the process of printing from a plane surface (as a smooth stone or metal plate) on which the image to be printed is ink-receptive and the blank area ink-repellent

lit•i•gant \\'lit-i-gənt\\ *n* **:** a party to a lawsuit

lit•i•gate \\'lit-ə-ˌgāt\\ *vb* **1 :** to carry on a legal contest by judicial process **2 :** to contest in law — **lit•i•ga•tion** \\ˌlit-ə-'gā-shən\\ *n*

li•ti•gious \\lə-'tij-əs\\ *adj* **1 a :** DISPUTATIOUS, CONTENTIOUS **b :** prone to engage in lawsuits **2 :** of or relating to litigation — **li•ti•gious•ly** *adv* — **li•ti•gious•ness** *n*

lit•mus \\'lit-məs\\ *n* **:** a coloring matter from lichens that turns red in acid solutions and blue in alkaline solutions and is used as an acid-base indicator

litmus paper *n* **:** paper impregnated with litmus

[1]lit•ter \\'lit-ər\\ *n* **1 a :** a covered and curtained couch provided with shafts and used for carrying a single passenger **b :** a device (as a stretcher) for carrying a sick or injured person **2 a :** material used as bedding for animals **b :** the uppermost layer of organic debris on the forest floor **3 :** the offspring of an animal at one birth **4 :** RUBBISH

[2]litter *vb* **1 :** to give birth to young **2 a :** to strew with litter **b :** to scatter about in disorder

lit•ter•a•teur \\ˌlit-ə-rə-'tər, ˌli-trə-\\ *n* **:** a literary man; *esp* **:** a professional writer

lit•ter•bag \\'lit-ər-ˌbag\\ *n* **:** a bag used (as in an automobile) for temporary refuse disposal

lit•ter•bug \\-ˌbəg\\ *n* **:** one that litters a public area

[1]lit•tle \\'lit-ᵊl\\ *adj* **lit•tler** \\'lit-ᵊl-ər, 'lit-lər\\ *or* **less** \\'les\\ *or* **less•er** \\'les-ər\\; **lit•tlest** \\'lit-ᵊl-əst, 'lit-ləst\\ *or* **least** \\'lēst\\ **1 :** not big: as **a :** small in size or extent **:** TINY **b :** small in comparison with related forms **c :** small in number **d :** small in condition, distinction, or scope **e :** NARROW, MEAN **f :** pleasingly small **2 :** not much: as **a :** existing only in a small amount or to a slight degree **b :** short in duration **:** BRIEF **3 :** small in importance or interest **:** TRIVIAL — **lit•tle•ness** \\'lit-ᵊl-nəs\\ *n*

[2]little *adv* **less** \\'les\\; **least** \\'lēst\\ **1 a :** in only a small quantity or degree **:** SLIGHTLY **b :** not at all **2 :** INFREQUENTLY, RARELY

[3]little *n* **1 :** a small amount or quantity **2 a :** a short time **b :** a short distance — **in little :** on a small scale; *esp* **:** in miniature

little theater *n* **:** a small theater for low-cost experimental drama designed for a relatively limited audience

[1]lit•to•ral \\'lit-ə-rəl; ˌlit-ə-'ral, -'räl\\ *adj* **:** of, relating to, or situated or growing on or near a shore esp. of the sea

[2]littoral *n* **:** a coastal region

li•tur•gi•cal \\lə-'tər-ji-kəl\\ *adj* **1 :** of, relating to, or having the characteristics of liturgy **2 :** using or favoring the use of liturgy — **li•tur•gi•cal•ly** \\-k(ə-)lē\\ *adv*

li•tur•gics \\-jiks\\ *n* **:** the study of formal public worship

lit•ur•gist \\'lit-ər-jəst\\ *n* **1 :** one who adheres to, compiles, or leads a liturgy **2 :** a specialist in liturgics

lit•ur•gy \\'lit-ər-jē\\ *n, pl* **-gies 1 :** a rite or body of rites prescribed for public worship **2** *often cap* **:** a eucharistic rite

liv•a•bil•i•ty \\ˌliv-ə-'bil-ət-ē\\ *n* **1 :** survival expectancy **:** VIABILITY **2 :** suitability for human living

liv•a•ble \\'liv-ə-bəl\\ *adj* **1 :** suitable for living in or with **2 :** ENDURABLE — **liv•a•ble•ness** *n*

[1]live \\'liv\\ *vb* **1 :** to be or continue alive **:** have life **2 :** to maintain oneself **:** SUBSIST **3 :** to conduct or pass one's life **4 :** DWELL, RESIDE **5 :** to attain eternal life **6 :** to remain in human memory or record **7 :** to have a life rich in experience

8 : COHABIT 9 : to pass through or spend the duration of 10 : ENACT, PRACTICE 11 : to exhibit vigor, gusto, or enthusiasm in

²live \'līv\ *adj* 1 : having life : LIVING 2 : abounding with life : VIVID 3 : exerting force or containing energy: as a : AFIRE, GLOWING b : carrying an electric current c : charged with explosives and containing shot or a bullet; *also* : UNEXPLODED d : rotating or imparting motion e : power-driven 4 : of continuing or current interest : UNCLOSED 5 : being in the native uncut state 6 : of bright vivid color 7 : being in play 8 a : of or involving the actual presence of real people b : broadcast directly at the time of production instead of from recorded or filmed material

lived \'līvd, 'livd\ *adj* : having a life of a specified kind or length

live·li·hood \'līv-lē-,hu̇d\ *n* : means of support or subsistence

live·long \,liv-,lȯŋ\ *adj* : WHOLE, ENTIRE

live·ly \'līv-lē\ *adj* 1 : full of life : ACTIVE 2 : KEEN, VIVID 3 : full of spirit or feeling : ANIMATED 4 : showing activity or vigor 5 : rebounding quickly — **live·li·ly** \'līv-lə-lē\ *adv* — **live·li·ness** \'līv-lē-nəs\ *n* — **lively** *adv*

liv·en \'lī-vən\ *vb* **liv·ened**; **liv·en·ing** \'līv-(ə-)niŋ\ : to make or become lively : ENLIVEN

¹liv·er \'liv-ər\ *n* 1 : a large vascular glandular organ of vertebrates that secretes bile and is a center of metabolic activity 2 : any of various large prob. digestive glands of invertebrate animals — **liv·ered** \-ərd\ *adj*

²liv·er \'liv-ər\ *n* 1 : one that lives esp. in a specified way 2 : RESIDENT

liv·er·ied \'liv-(ə-)rēd\ *adj* : wearing a livery

liv·er·ish \'liv-(ə-)rish\ *adj* 1 : suffering from liver disorder : BILIOUS 2 : CRABBED, MELANCHOLY

liv·er·wort \'liv-ər-,wərt, -,wȯrt\ *n* : any of a class of bryophytes related to and resembling the mosses but differing esp. in reproduction and development

liv·er·wurst \'liv-ə(r)-,wərst, -,wu̇rst\ *n* : a sausage consisting chiefly of liver

liv·ery \'liv-(ə-)rē\ *n, pl* **-er·ies** 1 : a special uniform worn by the servants of a wealthy household 2 : distinctive dress 3 a : the feeding, care, and stabling of horses for pay; *also* : the keeping of horses and vehicles for hire b : LIVERY STABLE

liv·ery·man \-mən\ *n* : the keeper of a livery stable

livery stable *n* : a stable where horses and vehicles are kept for hire and where stabling is provided

lives *pl of* LIFE

live steam *n* : steam direct from a boiler and under full pressure

live·stock \'līv-,stäk\ *n* : animals kept or raised for use or pleasure; *esp* : farm animals kept for use and profit

live wire *n* : an alert active aggressive person

liv·id \'liv-əd\ *adj* 1 : discolored by bruising : BLACK-AND-BLUE 2 : ASHEN, PALLID — **liv·id·ly** *adv*

¹liv·ing \'liv-iŋ\ *adj* 1 a : having life b : ACTIVE, FUNCTIONING 2 a : exhibiting the life or motion of nature : NATURAL b : LIVE 3 a : full of life or vigor b : true to life : VIVID c : suited for living 4 : VERY — used as an intensive

²living *n* 1 : the condition of being alive 2 : conduct or manner of life 3 : means of subsistence : LIVELIHOOD

living room *n* : a room in a residence used for the common social activities of the occupants

living wage *n* : a wage sufficient to provide the necessities and comforts held to comprise an acceptable standard of living

liz·ard \'liz-ərd\ *n* : any of a group of reptiles distinguished from the related snakes by a fused inseparable lower jaw, external ears, eyes with movable lids, and usu. two pairs of well differentiated functional limbs

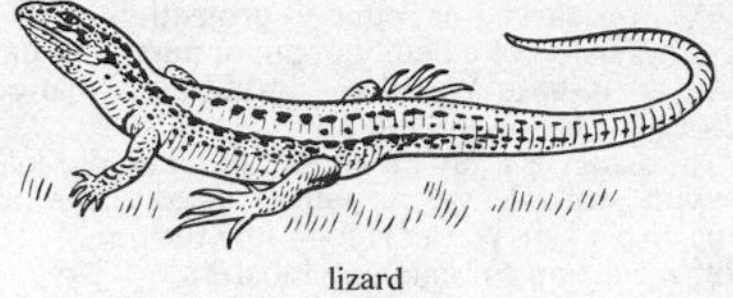

lizard

lla·ma \'läm-ə\ *n* : any of several wild and domesticated So. American ruminants related to the camels but smaller and without a hump

lla·no \'län-ō\ *n, pl* **llanos** : an open grassy plain esp. of Spanish America

lo \'lō\ *interj* — used to call attention or to express wonder or surprise

¹load \'lōd\ *n* 1 a : whatever is put on a man or pack animal to be carried : PACK b : whatever is put in a ship or vehicle or airplane for conveyance : CARGO 2 : a mass or weight supported by something 3 a : something that weighs down the mind or spirits b : a burdensome or laborious responsibility 4 : a large quantity : LOT — usu. used in pl.

²load *vb* 1 a : to put a load in or on; *also* : to receive a load b : to place in or on a means of conveyance or in a container 2 a : to encumber or oppress with something heavy, laborious, or disheartening : BURDEN b : to place as a burden or obligation 3 a : to increase the weight of by adding something heavy b : BIAS 4 : to supply in abundance or excess : HEAP 5 : to place or insert a load or as a load — **load·er** *n*

load·ed \'lōd-əd\ *adj* : having a large amount of money

load line *n* : the line on a ship indicating the depth to which it sinks in the water when properly loaded

¹loaf \'lōf\ *n, pl* **loaves** \'lōvz\ 1 : a shaped or molded mass of bread 2 : a regularly molded often rectangular mass: as a : a conical mass of sugar b : a dish (as of seasoned meat or fish) baked in the form of a loaf

²loaf *vb* 1 : to spend time in idleness : LOUNGE 2 : to pass idly

loaf·er \'lō-fər\ *n* : one that loafs : IDLER

loam \'lōm, 'lüm\ *n* : SOIL; *esp* : a soil consisting of a friable mixture of varying proportions of clay, silt, and sand — **loamy** \'lō-mē, 'lü-\ *adj*

¹loan \'lōn\ *n* 1 a : money let out at interest b : something furnished for the borrower's temporary use 2 : the grant of temporary use

²loan *vt* : to give for temporary possession or use

loan shark *n* : a person who lends money at excessive rates of interest

loan·word \'lōn-,wərd\ *n* : a word taken from another language and at least partly naturalized

loath \'lōth, 'lō*th*\ *adj* : unwilling to do something contrary to one's likes, sympathies, or ways of thinking : RELUCTANT

loathe \'lō*th*\ *vt* : to dislike greatly : feel extreme disgust for or at : DETEST

loath·ing \'lō-*th*iŋ\ *n* : extreme disgust : DETESTATION

¹loath·ly \'lō*th*-lē, 'lōth-\ *adj* : LOATHSOME, REPULSIVE

²loath·ly \'lōth-lē, 'lō*th*-\ *adv* : UNWILLINGLY

loath·some \'lōth-səm, 'lō*th*-\ *adj* : exciting loathing : DISGUSTING — **loath·some·ly** *adv* — **loath·some·ness** *n*

lob \'läb\ *vb* **lobbed**; **lob·bing** 1 : to throw, hit, or propel slowly in or as if in a high arc 2 : to move slowly and heavily — **lob** *n*

¹lob·by \'läb-ē\ *n, pl* **lob·bies** 1 : a corridor or hall connected with a larger room or series of rooms and used as a passageway or waiting room: as a : an anteroom of a legislative chamber b : a large hall serving as a foyer (as of a hotel or theater) 2 : a group of persons engaged in lobbying

²lobby *vb* **lob·bied**; **lob·by·ing** : to try to influence public officials and esp. members of a legislative body — **lob·by·ist** \-ē-əst\ *n*

lobe \'lōb\ *n* : a curved or rounded projection or division; *esp* : such a subdivision of a bodily organ or part — **lo·bar** \'lō-bər, -ˌbär\ *adj* — **lo·bate** \-ˌbāt\ *or* **lo·bat·ed** \-ˌbāt-əd\ *adj* — **lobed** \'lōbd\ *adj*

lob·ster \'läb-stər\ *n* : any of several large edible marine crustaceans with stalked eyes, a pair of large claws, and a long abdomen; *also* : SPINY LOBSTER — **lobster** *adj*

lobster pot *n* : a trap for catching lobsters

[1]**lo·cal** \'lō-kəl\ *adj* **1** : characterized by or relating to position in space **2** : characterized by, relating to, or occupying a particular place **3** : not broad or general; *esp* : involving or affecting only a small part of the body **4 a** : primarily serving the needs of a particular limited district **b** : making all the stops on a run — **lo·cal·ly** \-kə-lē\ *adv*

[2]**local** *n* : a local person or thing: as **a** : a local train or other public conveyance **b** : a local branch, lodge, or chapter (as of a labor union)

local color *n* : features and peculiarities used in a story or play that suggest a particular locality and its inhabitants

lo·cale \lō-'kal\ *n* **1** : a place or locality that is the setting for a particular event or characteristic **2** : SITE, SCENE

lo·cal·ism \'lō-kə-ˌliz-əm\ *n* **1** : the inclination to be esp. interested in the affairs of one's own locality **2** : a local manner of speech

lo·cal·i·ty \lō-'kal-ət-ē\ *n, pl* **-ties** : a particular spot, situation, or location : NEIGHBORHOOD

lo·cal·ize \'lō-kə-ˌlīz\ *vb* : to make or become local : fix in or assign or confine to a definite place or locality — **lo·cal·i·za·tion** \ˌlō-kə-lə-'zā-shən\ *n*

local option *n* : the power granted by a legislature to a political subdivision to determine by popular vote whether a law on a controversial issue is to apply locally

lo·cate \'lō-ˌkāt, lō-'\ *vb* **1** : to establish oneself or one's business : set or establish in a particular spot : STATION, SETTLE **2** : to determine or indicate the place, site, or limits of **3** : to find or fix the place of in a sequence — **lo·cat·er** *n*

lo·ca·tion \lō-'kā-shən\ *n* **1** : the process of locating **2** : SITUATION, PLACE; *esp* : a locality of or for a building **3** : a tract of land (as a mining claim) whose boundaries and purpose have been designated **4** : a place outside a studio where a motion picture is filmed — **lo·ca·tion·al** \-shnəl, -shən-ᵊl\ *adj* — **lo·ca·tion·al·ly** \-ē\ *adv*

loc·a·tive \'läk-ət-iv\ *adj* : of, relating to, or constituting a grammatical case denoting place where — **locative** *n*

loci *pl of* LOCUS

[1]**lock** \'läk\ *n* : a tuft, strand, or ringlet of hair; *also* : a cohering bunch (as of wool, cotton, or flax)

[2]**lock** *n* **1 a** : a fastening (as for a door) in which a bolt is operated (as by a key) **b** : the mechanism for exploding the charge or cartridge of a firearm **2** : an enclosure (as in a canal) with gates at each end used in raising or lowering boats as they pass from level to level

[3]**lock** *vb* **1 a** : to fasten the lock of **b** : to make or become fast with or as if with a lock **2 a** : to make secure or inaccessible by means of locks : CONFINE **b** : to hold fast or inactive : FIX **3** : to make fast by the interlacing or interlocking of parts : INTERLACE, INTERLOCK

lock·er \'läk-ər\ *n* **1** : a drawer, cabinet, compartment, or chest for personal use usu. with a lock **2** : an insulated compartment for storing frozen food at a low temperature **3** : one that locks

locker room *n* : a room devoted to storage lockers; *esp* : one in which participants in a sport have individual lockers for their clothes and special equipment and change into and out of sports costume

lock·et \'läk-ət\ *n* : a small case usu. of precious metal for a memento that is worn typically suspended from a chain or necklace

lock·jaw \'läk-ˌjȯ\ *n* : TETANUS

lock·out \'läk-ˌau̇t\ *n* : the suspension of work or closing of a plant by an employer during a labor dispute in order to make his employees accept his terms

lock·smith \'läk-ˌsmith\ *n* : one who makes or repairs locks

lock·step \'läk-ˌstep\ *n* : a mode of marching in step by a body of men moving in a very close single file

lock·up \'läk-ˌəp\ *n* : JAIL; *esp* : one where persons are detained prior to court hearing

lo·co·mo·tion \ˌlō-kə-'mō-shən\ *n* **1** : the act or power of moving from place to place **2** : TRAVEL

[1]**lo·co·mo·tive** \ˌlō-kə-'mōt-iv\ *adj* **1 a** : of, relating to, or functioning in locomotion **b** : having the ability to move independently from place to place **2** : of or relating to travel **3** : of, relating to, or being a machine that moves under its own power — **lo·co·mo·tive·ness** *n*

[2]**locomotive** *n* **1** : an engine that moves under its own power; *esp* : one that hauls cars on a railroad **2** : a school or college cheer characterized by a slow beginning and a progressive increase in speed

lo·co·mo·tor \ˌlō-kə-'mōt-ər\ *adj* **1** : LOCOMOTIVE 1 **2** : affecting or involving the locomotive organs

lo·cum te·nens \ˌlō-kəm-'tē-ˌnenz\ *n, pl* **locum te·nen·tes** \-tə-'nen-ˌtēz\ : one filling an office for a time or temporarily taking the place of another — used esp. of a doctor or clergyman

lo·cus \'lō-kəs\ *n, pl* **lo·ci** \'lō-ˌsī\ : PLACE, LOCALITY

lo·cus clas·si·cus \ˌlō-kəs-'klas-i-kəs\ *n, pl* **lo·ci clas·si·ci** \ˌlō-ˌsī-'klas-ə-ˌsī\ : a standard passage important for the elucidation of a word or subject

lo·cust \'lō-kəst\ *n* **1 a** : a migratory grasshopper often traveling in vast swarms and stripping the areas passed of vegetation **b** : CICADA **2 a** : any of various leguminous trees having hard wood **b** : the wood of a locust

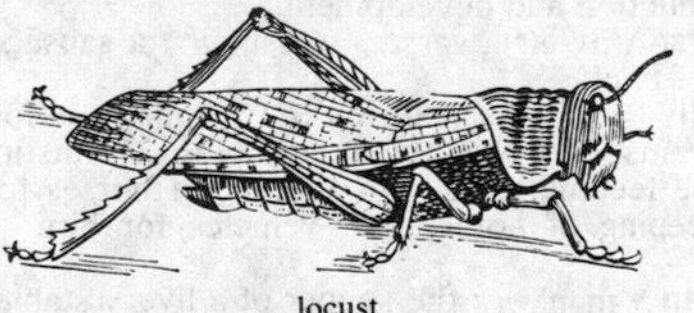
locust

lo·cu·tion \lō-'kyü-shən\ *n* **1** : a particular form of expression or a peculiarity of phrasing **2** : style of discourse : PHRASEOLOGY

lode \'lōd\ *n* **1** : a mass or strip of a mineral (as gold or copper ore) that fills a crack in rock **2** : a mass of ore in the earth or among rocks

lode·star \-ˌstär\ *n* **1** : a star that leads or guides; *esp* : NORTH STAR **2** : something that serves as a guiding star

lode·stone \-ˌstōn\ *n* **1** : an iron-containing rock with magnetic properties **2** : something that strongly attracts

[1]**lodge** \'läj\ *vb* **1 a** : to provide temporary quarters for **b** : to establish or settle oneself in a place : SLEEP, DWELL **c** : to rent lodgings to **2** : to serve as a receptacle for : CONTAIN **3** : to bring (as by throwing or thrusting) to an intended or a fixed position : come to a rest and remain **4** : to deposit for safeguard or preservation **5** : to place or vest esp. in a source, means, or agent **6** : to lay (as a complaint) before a proper authority : FILE **7** : to fall or become beaten down

[2]**lodge** *n* **1 a** : a house set apart for residence in a special season **b** : an inn or resort hotel **2** : a house on an estate orig. for the use of a gamekeeper, caretaker, or porter **3** : a den or lair esp. of a group of gregarious animals **4** : the meeting place of a branch (as of a fraternal organization); *also* : the members of such a branch

lodg·er \'läj-ər\ *n* : one that lodges; *esp* : one that occupies a rented room in another's house

lodg·ing \'läj-iŋ\ *n* **1** : DWELLING; *esp* : a temporary dwelling or sleeping place **2** : a room or suite of rooms in the house of another person rented as a dwelling place — usu. used in pl.

lodg·ment *or* **lodge·ment** \'läj-mənt\ *n* **1 a** : a lodging place : SHELTER **b** : ACCOMMODATIONS, LODGINGS **2 a** : the act, fact, or manner of lodging **b** : a placing, depositing, or coming to rest **3 a** : an accumulation or collection of something deposited in a place **b** : a place of rest or deposit

[1]loft \'lȯft\ *n* **1** : a room or floor above another : ATTIC **2 a** : a gallery in a church or hall **b** : an upper floor of a warehouse or business building esp. when not partitioned **c** : HAYLOFT

[2]loft *vb* **1** : to place, house, or store in a loft **2** : to strike or throw a ball so that it rises high in the air

lofty \'lȯf-tē\ *adj* **1** : having a haughty overbearing manner : SUPERCILIOUS **2 a** : elevated in character and spirit : NOBLE **b** : elevated in position : SUPERIOR **3 a** : rising high in the air : TOWERING **b** : REMOTE, ESOTERIC — **loft·i·ly** \-tə-lē\ *adv* — **loft·i·ness** \-tē-nəs\ *n*

[1]log \'lȯg, 'läg\ *n* **1** : a bulky piece of unshaped timber **2** : an apparatus for measuring the rate of a ship's motion through the water **3 a** : the daily record of a ship's speed and progress **b** : the full record of a ship's voyage or of an aircraft's flight **4** : a record of performance (as the operating history of an airplane or a piece of equipment, the flying time of a pilot, or a report on the construction of something) — **log** *adj*

[2]log *vb* **logged**; **log·ging** **1** : to cut trees for lumber or to clear land of trees in lumbering **2** : to enter details of or about in a log **3 a** : to move (an indicated distance) or attain (an indicated speed) as noted in a log **b** (1) : to sail a ship or fly an airplane for (an indicated distance or an indicated period of time) (2) : to have (an indicated record) to one's credit

[3]log *n* : LOGARITHM

log·a·rithm \'lȯg-ə-ˌrit͟h-əm, 'läg-\ *n* : the exponent that indicates the power to which a number is raised to produce a given number

log·a·rith·mic \ˌlȯg-ə-'rit͟h-mik, ˌläg-\ *adj* : relating to, based on, or characteristic of logarithms

log·book \'lȯg-ˌbu̇k, 'läg-\ *n* : LOG 3, 4

loge \'lōzh\ *n* **1 a** : a small compartment : BOOTH **b** : a box in a theater **2 a** : a small partitioned area **b** : the forward section of a theater mezzanine

log·ger \'lȯg-ər, 'läg-\ *n* : one engaged in logging

log·ger·head \'lȯg-ər-ˌhed, 'läg-\ *n* : any of various very large turtles; *esp* : a carnivorous sea turtle of the warmer parts of the western Atlantic — **at loggerheads** : in or into a state of quarrelsome disagreement

log·gia \'lō-jē-ə, 'lȯ-jä\ *n* : a roofed gallery open on at least one side

log·ic \'läj-ik\ *n* **1** : a science that deals with the rules and tests of sound thinking and proof by reasoning **2** : REASONING; *esp* : sound reasoning **3** : connection (as of facts or events) in a way that seems reasonable — **lo·gi·cian** \lō-'jish-ən\ *n*

log·i·cal \'läj-i-kəl\ *adj* **1** : of or relating to logic : used in logic **2** : conforming to or consistent with the rules of logic **3** : skilled in logic **4** : being in accordance with what may be reasonably expected — **log·i·cal·ly** \-k(ə-)lē\ *adv*

lo·gis·tics \lō-'jis-tiks\ *n sing or pl* : a branch of military science that deals with the transportation, quartering, and supplying of troops in military operations — **lo·gis·tic** \-tik\ *or* **lo·gis·ti·cal** \-ti-kəl\ *adj*

log·jam \'lȯg-ˌjam, 'läg-\ *n* **1** : a deadlocked jumble of logs in a watercourse **2** : DEADLOCK

log·roll·ing \'lȯg-ˌrō-liŋ, 'läg-\ *n* **1** : the rolling of logs in water by treading; *also* : a sport in which men treading logs try to dislodge one another **2** : the exchanging of assistance or favors; *esp* : the trading of votes by legislators to secure favorable action on projects of interest to each one — **log·roll·er** \-ˌrō-lər\ *n*

lo·gy \'lō-gē\ *adj* : lacking vitality : SLUGGISH — **lo·gi·ness** *n*

loin \'lȯin\ *n* **1 a** : the part of the body on each side of the spinal column and between the hip and the lower ribs **b** : a cut of meat comprising this part of one or both sides of a carcass with the adjoining half of the vertebrae included but without the flank **2** *pl* **a** : the pubic region **b** : the generative organs

loin·cloth \-ˌklȯth\ *n* : a cloth worn about the loins often as the sole article of clothing in warm climates

loi·ter \'lȯit-ər\ *vi* **1** : to interrupt or delay an errand or a journey with aimless idle stops and pauses : LINGER **2 a** : to hang around idly **b** : to lag behind — **loi·ter·er** *n*

loll \'läl\ *vb* **1** : to hang or let hang loosely or laxly : DROOP, DANGLE **2** : to recline, lean, or move in a lax, lazy, or indolent manner : LOUNGE

lol·li·pop *or* **lol·ly·pop** \'läl-ē-ˌpäp\ *n* : a lump of hard candy on the end of a stick

lone \'lōn\ *adj* **1 a** : having no company : SOLITARY **b** : preferring solitude **2** : ONLY, SOLE **3** : situated by itself : ISOLATED — **lone·ness** *n*

lone·ly \'lōn-lē\ *adj* **1** : being without company : LONE **2** : UNFREQUENTED, DESOLATE **3** : LONESOME — **lone·li·ness** *n*

lone·some \'lōn(t)-səm\ *adj* **1** : sad from lack of companionship or separation from others **2 a** : REMOTE, UNFREQUENTED **b** : LONE — **lone·some·ly** *adv* — **lone·some·ness** *n*

[1]long \'lȯŋ\ *adj* **long·er** \'lȯŋ-gər\; **long·est** \'lȯŋ-gəst\ **1 a** : extending for a considerable distance **b** : having greater length than usual **c** : having greater height than usual : TALL **d** : having a greater length than breadth : ELONGATED **e** : having a greater length than desirable or necessary **2** : having a specified length **3 a** : extending over a considerable time **b** : having a specified duration **c** : prolonged beyond the usual time : TEDIOUS **4 a** : containing many items in a series **b** : having a specified number of units **c** : consisting of a greater number or amount than usual : LARGE **5 a** : being a syllable or speech sound of relatively great duration **b** : being the member of a pair of similarly spelled vowel or vowel-containing sounds that is descended from a vowel long in duration **6** : having the capacity to reach or extend a considerable distance **7** : larger or longer than the standard **8** : extending far into the future **9** : strong in or well furnished with something — **at long last** : after a long wait : FINALLY

[2]long *adv* **1** : for or during a long time **2** : at or to a long distance : FAR **3** : for the duration of a specified period **4** : at a point of time far before or after a specified moment or event **5** : after or beyond a specified time — **as long as** *or* **so long as** **1** : in view of the fact that : SINCE **2** : PROVIDED, IF — **so long** : GOOD-BYE

[3]long *n* **1** : a long period of time **2** *pl* : long trousers — **the long and short** *or* **the long and the short** : the sum and substance : GIST

[4]long *vi* **longed**; **long·ing** \'lȯŋ-iŋ\ : to feel a strong desire or wish : YEARN

long·bow \'lȯŋ-ˌbō\ *n* : a wooden bow drawn by hand and usu. 5½ to 6 feet long

[1]long–dis·tance \-'dis-tən(t)s\ *adj* : of or relating to telephone communication with a distant point

[2]long–distance *adv* : by long-distance telephone

long distance *n* **1** : communication by long-distance telephone **2** : a telephone operator or exchange that gives long-distance connections

lon·gev·i·ty \län-'jev-ət-ē, lȯn-\ *n* **1** : a long duration of individual life **2** : length of life

long·hair \'lȯŋ-ˌha(ə)r\ *n* **1** : a person of artistic gifts or interests; *esp* : a lover of classical music **2** : an impractical intellectual — **long–hair** *or* **long–haired** \-'ha(ə)rd\ *adj*

long·hand \'lȯŋ-ˌhand\ *n* : the characters used in ordinary writing : HANDWRITING

long·head·ed \-'hed-əd\ *adj* : having unusual foresight or wisdom — **long·head·ed·ness** *n*

long·ing \'lȯŋ-iŋ\ *n* : an eager desire esp. for something unattainable : CRAVING — **long·ing·ly** *adv*

long·ish \'lȯŋ-ish\ *adj* : somewhat long

lon·gi·tude \'län-jə-ˌt(y)üd\ *n* : angular distance due east or west from a meridian and esp. from the meridian that runs between the north and south poles and passes through Greenwich, England, expressed in degrees or in time

lon·gi·tu·di·nal \ˌlän-jə-'t(y)üd-nəl, -^{ə}n-əl\ *adj* **1** : of or relating to length or the lengthwise dimension **2** : placed or running lengthwise — **lon·gi·tu·di·nal·ly** \-ē\ *adv*

long–lived \'lȯŋ-'līvd, -'livd\ *adj* : living or lasting long

long–range \-'rānj\ *adj* **1** : capable of traveling or shooting over great distances **2** : lasting over or taking into account a long period : LONG-TERM 1

long·shore·man \'lȯŋ-'shōr-mən\ *n* : a laborer at a wharf who loads and unloads cargo

long shot \'lȯŋ-ˌshät\ *n* **1** : an entry (as in a horse race) given little chance of winning **2** : a bet in which the chances of winning are slight but the possible winnings great **3** : a venture involving great risk but promising a great reward if successful — **by a long shot** : by a great deal

long·some \'lȯŋ-səm\ *adj* : tediously long — **long·some·ly** *adv* — **long·some·ness** *n*

long–suf·fer·ing \-'səf-(ə-)riŋ\ *or* **long–suf·fer·ance** \-(ə-)rən(t)s\ *n* : long and patient endurance of offense — **long–suffering** *adj*

long suit *n* **1** : a holding of more than the average number of cards in a suit **2** : the activity or quality in which a person excels

long–term \'lȯŋ-'tərm\ *adj* **1** : extending over or involving a long period of time **2** : constituting a financial obligation based on a term usu. of more than 10 years

lon·gueur \'lō^{n}-gœr\ *n, pl* **longueurs** \-gœr(z)\ : a dull and tedious passage or section

long–wind·ed \'lȯŋ-'win-dəd\ *adj* **1** : not easily subject to loss of breath **2** : tediously long in speaking or writing — **long–wind·ed·ly** *adv* — **long–wind·ed·ness** *n*

[1]look \'lu̇k\ *vb* **1** : to ascertain by the use of one's eyes **2** : to exercise the power of vision upon : EXAMINE, SEE **3** : EXPECT **4** : to express by the eyes or facial expression **5** : to have an appearance that befits or accords with **6** : to have the appearance of being : SEEM **7** : to direct one's attention or eyes **8** : to have a specified outlook **9** : to gaze in wonder or surprise : STARE **10** : to show a tendency — **look after** : to take care of : attend to — **look for 1** : to await with hope or anticipation : EXPECT **2** : to search for : SEEK — **look on** *or* **look upon** : CONSIDER, REGARD

[2]look *n* **1 a** : the action of looking **b** : GLANCE **2 a** : the expression of the countenance **b** : physical appearance; *esp* : attractive physical appearance — usu. used in pl. **3** : the state or form in which something appears : ASPECT

look·er–on \ˌlu̇k-ər-'ȯn, -'än\ *n, pl* **lookers–on** : ONLOOKER, SPECTATOR

looking glass *n* : MIRROR

look·out \'lu̇k-ˌau̇t\ *n* **1** : a person engaged in watching; *esp* : one assigned to watch (as on a ship) **2** : an elevated place or structure affording a wide view for observation **3** : a careful looking or watching **4** : VIEW, OUTLOOK **5** : a matter of care or concern

[1]loom \'lüm\ *n* : a frame or machine for weaving together threads or yarns into cloth

[2]loom *vi* **1** : to come into sight in an unnaturally large, indistinct, or distorted form **2 a** : to appear in an impressively great or exaggerated form **b** : to take shape as an impending occurrence

[1]loon \'lün\ *n* : any of several fish-eating diving birds with webbed feet, black head, and white-spotted black back

[2]loon *n* : a person of dull or disordered mind : LUNATIC

loo·ny *or* **loo·ney** \'lü-nē\ *adj* : CRAZY, FOOLISH — **loony** *n*

[1]loop \'lüp\ *n* **1** : a fold or doubling of a line leaving an aperture between the parts through which another line can be passed or into which a hook may be hooked; *also* : such a fold of cord or ribbon serving as an ornament **2** : a loop-shaped figure, bend, or course **3** : a circular airplane maneuver involving flying upside down — **for a loop** : into a state of amazement, confusion, or distress

[2]loop *vb* **1** : to make or form a loop **2 a** : to make a loop in, on, or about **b** : to fasten with a loop **3** : to execute a loop in an airplane

loop·hole \-ˌhōl\ *n* **1** : a small opening in a wall through which small firearms may be discharged **2** : a means of escape

[1]loose \'lüs\ *adj* **1 a** : not rigidly fastened or securely attached **b** : not tight-fitting **2 a** : free from a state of confinement, restraint, or obligation **b** : not brought together in a bundle, container, or binding **3** : not dense or compact in structure or arrangement **4 a** : lacking in restraint or power of restraint **b** : LEWD, UNCHASTE **5 a** : not tightly drawn or stretched : SLACK **b** : having a flexible or relaxed character **6** : lacking in precision, exactness, or care — **loose·ly** *adv* — **loose·ness** *n*

[2]loose *vb* **1 a** : to let loose : RELEASE **b** : to free from restraint **2** : to make loose : UNTIE **3** : to cast loose : DETACH **4** : to let fly : DISCHARGE, FIRE **5** : to make less rigid, tight, or strict : RELAX, SLACKEN

[3]loose *adv* : LOOSELY

loose end *n* **1** : something left hanging loose **2** : a fragment of unfinished business — **at loose ends** : uncertain of one's future course of action : UNSETTLED

loose–joint·ed \'lüs-'jȯint-əd\ *adj* : having a flexibility or lack of rigidity suggesting the absence of rigid points; *esp* : moving with unusual freedom or ease — **loose–joint·ed·ness** *n*

loos·en \'lüs-^{ə}n\ *vb* **loos·ened**; **loos·en·ing** \'lüs-niŋ, -^{ə}n-iŋ\ **1** : to release from restraint **2** : to make or become loose or looser **3** : to cause or permit to become less strict

[1]loot \'lüt\ *n* **1** : goods taken in war : SPOILS, PLUNDER **2** : something stolen or taken by force or violence **3** : the action of looting

[2]loot *vb* **1** : to plunder or sack in war **2** : to rob or steal esp. on a large scale and by violence or corruption **3** : to seize and carry away by force esp. in war — **loot·er** *n*

[1]lop \'läp\ *vt* **lopped**; **lop·ping 1 a** : to cut branches or twigs from : TRIM **b** : to cut or shear from a woody plant **2 a** : to remove superfluous parts from **b** : to eliminate as unnecessary or undesirable — usu. used with *off*

[2]lop *vi* **lopped**; **lop·ping** : to hang downward; *also* : to flop or sway loosely

[1]lope \'lōp\ *n* **1** : an easy natural gait of a horse resembling a canter **2** : an easy bounding gait (as of a wolf)

[2]lope *vi* : to go, move, or ride at a lope — **lop·er** *n*

lop–eared \'läp-'i(ə)rd\ *adj* : having ears that droop

lop·sid·ed \'läp-'sīd-əd\ *adj* **1** : leaning to one side **2** : lacking in balance, symmetry, or proportion — **lop·sid·ed·ly** *adv* — **lop·sid·ed·ness** *n*

lo·qua·cious \lō-'kwā-shəs\ *adj* : given to excessive talking : GARRULOUS — **lo·qua·cious·ly** *adv* — **lo·qua·cious·ness** *n* — **lo·quac·i·ty** \-'kwas-ət-ē\ *n*

[1]lord \'lȯrd\ *n* **1** : one having power and authority over others: **a** : a ruler to whom service and obedience are due **b** : a person from whom a feudal fee or estate is held **c** : HUSBAND **2** *cap* **a** : [2]GOD **b** : CHRIST **3** : a man of rank or high position: as **a** : a feudal tenant holding directly of the king **b** : a

British nobleman **c** *pl, cap* : the upper house of the British parliament

²lord *vi* : to play the lord : DOMINEER — used with *it*

lord·ly \ˈlȯrd-lē\ *adj* **1 a** : of, relating to, or having the characteristics of a lord : DIGNIFIED **b** : GRAND, NOBLE **2** : exhibiting pride or superiority : HAUGHTY — **lord·li·ness** *n* — **lordly** *adv*

lord·ship \ˈlȯrd-ˌship\ *n* **1** : the rank or dignity of a lord — used as a title **2** : the authority, power, or territory of a lord

Lord's Supper *n* : COMMUNION 2a

lore \ˈlō(ə)r\ *n* **1** : something that is learned: **a** : knowledge gained through study or experience **b** : traditional knowledge or belief **2** : a particular body of knowledge or tradition

lor·gnette \lȯrn-ˈyet\ *n* : a pair of eyeglasses or opera glasses with a handle

lorn \ˈlȯrn\ *adj* : FORSAKEN, DESOLATE — **lorn·ness** *n*

lor·ry \ˈlȯr-ē, ˈlär-\ *n, pl* **lorries** : a large low horse-drawn wagon without sides

lose \ˈlüz\ *vb* **lost** \ˈlȯst\; **los·ing** \ˈlü-ziŋ\ **1** : to bring to destruction **2** : to miss from one's possession or customary place **3** : to suffer deprivation of esp. in an unforeseen or accidental manner **4 a** : to suffer loss through the death or removal of or final separation from (a person) **b** : to fail to keep control of or allegiance of **5 a** : to fail to use : let slip by : WASTE **b** : to fail to win, gain, or obtain : undergo defeat **c** : to fail to catch with the senses or the mind **6** : to cause the loss of **7** : to fail to keep, sustain, or maintain **8 a** : to cause to miss one's way or bearings **b** : to make (oneself) withdrawn from immediate reality **9 a** : to wander or go astray from **b** : OUTSTRIP **10** : to fail to keep in sight or in mind **11** : to free oneself from : get rid of — **lose ground** : to suffer loss or disadvantage : fail to advance or improve — **lose one's heart** : to fall in love

los·er \ˈlü-zər\ *n* : one that loses

loss \ˈlȯs\ *n* **1 a** : the act of losing **b** : the harm or privation resulting from losing **c** : an instance of losing **2 a** : a person or thing or an amount that is lost **b** *pl* : killed, wounded, or captured soldiers **3** : failure to gain, win, obtain, or utilize; *esp* : an amount by which the cost of an article or service exceeds the selling price **4** : decrease in amount, magnitude, or degree **5** : DESTRUCTION, RUIN — **at a loss** : PUZZLED, UNCERTAIN — **for a loss** : into a state of distress

loss leader *n* : an article sold at a loss in order to draw customers

lost \ˈlȯst\ *adj* **1** : not made use of, won, or claimed **2 a** : unable to find the way **b** : no longer visible **c** : lacking assurance or self-confidence : HELPLESS **3** : ruined or destroyed physically or morally : DESPERATE **4 a** : no longer possessed **b** : no longer known **5 a** : taken away or beyond reach or attainment : DENIED **b** : HARDENED, INSENSIBLE **6** : ABSORBED, RAPT

¹lot \ˈlät\ *n* **1** : an object used as a counter in determining a question by chance **2 a** : the use of lots as a means of deciding something **b** : the choice resulting from deciding by lot **3 a** : something that comes to one by or as if by lot : SHARE **b** : one's way of life or worldly fate : FORTUNE **4** : a piece or plot of land **5** : a number of associated persons : SET **6** : a considerable quantity — often used adverbially

²lot *vb* **lot·ted**; **lot·ting** **1** : to cast or draw lots **2** : to form or divide into lots **3** : ALLOT, APPORTION

lo·thar·io \lō-ˈthar-ē-ˌō\ *n, pl* **-i·os** *often cap* : a gay seducer

lo·tion \ˈlō-shən\ *n* : a liquid preparation for cosmetic and external medicinal use

lots \ˈläts\ *adv* : MUCH

lot·tery \ˈlät-ə-rē, ˈlä-trē\ *n, pl* **-ter·ies** : a drawing of lots in which prizes are given to the winning names or numbers : a scheme for distributing prizes by chance

lo·tus *or* **lo·tos** \ˈlōt-əs\ *n* **1** : a fruit held in Greek legend to cause indolence and forgetfulness; *also* : a tree bearing this fruit **2** : any of various water lilies including several represented in ancient Egyptian and Hindu art and religious symbolism **3** : any of various erect leguminous plants including some used for hay and pasture

loud \ˈlau̇d\ *adj* **1 a** : marked by intensity or volume of sound **b** : producing a loud sound **2** : CLAMOROUS, NOISY **3** : obtrusive or offensive in color or pattern — **loud** *adv* — **loud·ly** *adv* — **loud·ness** *n*

loud·en \ˈlau̇d-ᵊn\ *vb* **loud·ened**; **loud·en·ing** \ˈlau̇d-niŋ, -ᵊn-iŋ\ : to make or become loud

loud·mouthed \ˈlau̇d-ˈmau̇t͟hd, -ˈmau̇tht\ *adj* **1** : having an offensively loud voice or a noisy blustering manner **2** : TACTLESS, INDISCREET

loud·speak·er \ˈlau̇d-ˈspē-kər\ *n* : a device similar to a telephone receiver in operation but amplifying sound

¹lounge \ˈlau̇nj\ *vb* **1** : to move or act in a lazy, slow, or listless way : LOAF **2** : to stand, sit, or lie in a slack manner — **loung·er** *n*

²lounge *n* **1 a** : a room with comfortable furniture : LIVING ROOM; *also* : LOBBY **b** : a room in a public building or vehicle often combining lounging, smoking, and toilet facilities **2** : a lounging gait or posture **3** : a long couch

lounge car *n* : a railroad passenger car with seats for lounging and facilities for serving refreshments

loup–ga·rou \ˌlü-gə-ˈrü\ *n, pl* **loups–garous** \ˌlü-gə-ˈrü(z)\ : WEREWOLF

louse \ˈlau̇s\ *n* **1** *pl* **lice** \ˈlīs\ : any of various small wingless usu. flat insects parasitic on warm-blooded animals **2** *pl* **lous·es** \ˈlau̇-səz\ : a contemptible person

louse up *vb* : to make a botch of something : BUNGLE, SPOIL

lousy \ˈlau̇-zē\ *adj* **1** : infested with lice **2 a** : MEAN, CONTEMPTIBLE **b** : miserably poor or inferior **c** : amply supplied — **lous·i·ly** \-zə-lē\ *adv* — **lous·i·ness** \-zē-nəs\ *n*

lout \ˈlau̇t\ *n* : a stupid, clownish, or awkward fellow — **lout·ish** \-ish\ *adj* — **lout·ish·ly** *adv* — **lout·ish·ness** *n*

lou·ver *or* **lou·vre** \ˈlü-vər\ *n* **1** : an opening provided with one or more slanted fixed or movable strips (as of metal or wood) to allow flow of air but to exclude rain or sun or to provide privacy; *also* : a similar device with movable strips for controlling the passage of air or light **2** : one of the slanted strips of a louver — **lou·vered** \-vərd\ *adj*

lov·a·ble \ˈləv-ə-bəl\ *adj* : having qualities that tend to make one loved : worthy of love — **lov·a·ble·ness** *n* — **lov·a·bly** \-blē\ *adv*

¹love \ˈləv\ *n* **1** : strong affection based on admiration or benevolence **2 a** : warm attachment, enthusiasm, or devotion **b** : the object of attachment or devotion **3 a** : self-sacrificing loyal concern that freely accepts another and seeks his good **b** : man's adoration of God **4 a** : attraction based on sexual desire : the ardent affection and tenderness felt by lovers **b** : an amorous episode **5** : a beloved person : DARLING **6** : a score of zero in tennis — **in love** : feeling love for and devotion toward someone

²love *vb* **1** : to hold dear : CHERISH **2 a** : to feel a lover's passion, devotion, or tenderness for **b** : CARESS **3** : to feel unselfish concern for **4** : to like or desire actively : take pleasure in **5** : to thrive in **6** : to feel affection or experience desire : be in love

love·bird \ˈləv-ˌbərd\ *n* : any of various small usu. gray or green parrots that show great affection for their mates

love knot *n* : a stylized knot sometimes used as an emblem of love

love·less \ˈləv-ləs\ *adj* **1** : being without love **2** : UNLOVING **3** : UNLOVED — **love·less·ly** *adv* — **love·less·ness** *n*

love·lorn \ˈləv-ˌlȯrn\ *adj* : deserted by one's love

love·ly \ˈləv-lē\ *adj* **1** : delicately beautiful **2** : beautiful in moral or spiritual character : GRACIOUS **3** : highly pleasing : FINE — **love·li·ness** *n*

love·mak·ing \'ləv-ˌmā-kiŋ\ *n* **1** : WOOING, COURTSHIP **2** : sexual activity

lov·er \'ləv-ər\ *n* **1 a** : a person in love; *esp* : a man in love **b** *pl* : two persons in love with each other **2** : the male partner in a sexual relationship other than that of husband and wife **3** : one who greatly enjoys or admires something : DEVOTEE

love seat *n* : a double chair, sofa, or settee for two persons

love–sick \'ləv-ˌsik\ *adj* **1** : languishing with love : YEARNING **2** : expressing a lover's longing — **love·sick·ness** *n*

lov·ing \'ləv-iŋ\ *adj* : feeling or showing love : AFFECTIONATE — **lov·ing·ly** *adv*

loving cup *n* : a large ornamental drinking vessel with two or more handles; *esp* : one given as a prize or trophy

lov·ing–kind·ness \ˌləv-iŋ-'kīn(d)-nəs\ *n* : tender and benevolent affection

[1]**low** \'lō\ *vi* : MOO

[2]**low** *n* : the deep sustained sound characteristic esp. of a cow

[3]**low** \'lō\ *adj* **1 a** : not high or tall **b** : cut far down at the neck : DÉCOLLETÉ **2 a** : situated or passing below the normal level, surface, or base of measurement **b** : marking a nadir or bottom **3** : STRICKEN, PROSTRATE **4** : not loud : SOFT **5 a** : being near the equator **b** : being near the horizon **6** : humble in status **7 a** : lacking strength, health, or vitality : WEAK **b** : lacking spirit or vivacity : DEPRESSED **8 a** : of lesser degree, size, or amount than average or ordinary **b** : less than usual in number, amount, or value **9** : falling short of some standard: as **a** : lacking dignity or elevation **b** : morally reprehensible : BASE **c** : COARSE, VULGAR **10** : not advanced in complexity, development, or elaboration **11** : UNFAVORABLE, DISPARAGING **12** : pronounced with a wide opening between the relatively flat tongue and the palate — **low** *adv* — **low·ness** *n*

[4]**low** *n* **1** : something that is low; *esp* : a region of low barometric pressure **2** : the arrangement of gears (as of an automobile) in a position to transmit the greatest power from the engine to the propeller shaft

low·born \'lō-'bȯrn\ *adj* : born in a low condition or rank

low·boy \'lō-ˌbȯi\ *n* : a chest of drawers about three feet high with long legs

low·bred \'lō-'bred\ *adj* : RUDE, VULGAR

low·brow \'lō-ˌbraů\ *n* : a person without intellectual interests or culture — **lowbrow** *adj*

low comedy *n* : comedy based on burlesque, horseplay, or slapstick rather than wit or satire

low–down \'lō-'daůn\ *adj* : CONTEMPTIBLE, DESPICABLE

low·down \-ˌdaůn\ *n* : pertinent and esp. guarded information

[1]**low·er** \'laů(-ə)r\ *vi* **1** : to look sullen : FROWN **2** : to become dark, gloomy, and threatening

[2]**lower** *n* : FROWN

[3]**low·er** \'lō(-ə)r\ *adj* **1** : relatively low in position, rank, or order **2** : constituting the popular and more representative branch of a bicameral legislative body **3** : situated or held to be situated beneath the earth's surface **4** : SOUTHERN **5** : less advanced in the scale of evolutionary development

[4]**low·er** \'lō(-ə)r\ *vb* **1** : to move down : DROP; *also* : DIMINISH **2 a** : to let descend by its own weight **b** : to make the aim lower **c** : to reduce the height of **3 a** : to reduce in value or amount **b** (1) : to bring down : DEGRADE (2) : ABASE, HUMBLE **c** : to reduce the objective of — **lower the boom** : to crack down

low·er·case \ˌlō(-ə)r-'kās\ *adj* : being a letter that belongs to or conforms to the series a, b, c, etc. rather than A, B, C, etc. — **lowercase** *n*

lower class *n* : a social class occupying a position below the middle class and having the lowest status in a society

low·er·ing \'laů-(ə-)riŋ\ *adj* **1** : FROWNING, SCOWLING **2** : OVERCAST, GLOOMY

low·er·most \'lō(-ə)r-ˌmōst\ *adj* : LOWEST

low·er world \'lō(-ə)r-\ *n* : the world of the dead or of future punishment : HADES

low·ery \'laů-(ə-)rē\ *adj* : GLOOMY, LOWERING

low frequency *n* : a frequency of a radio wave in the range between 30 and 300 kilocycles

low–grade \'lō-'grād\ *adj* **1** : being of a grade or quality rated as inferior **2** : being nearer the lower extreme of the range in which it may occur

low–key \'lō-'kē\ *adj* : of low intensity : RESTRAINED

low·land \'lō-lənd, -ˌland\ *n* : low and usu. level country — **lowland** *adj*

Low·land·er \-lən-dər, -ˌlan-\ *n* : an inhabitant of the Lowlands of Scotland

[1]**low·ly** \'lō-lē\ *adv* **1** : HUMBLY, MEEKLY **2** : in a low position, manner, or degree **3** : not loudly

[2]**lowly** *adj* **1** : HUMBLE, MEEK **2** : of or relating to a low social or economic rank **3** : low in the scale of biological or cultural evolution **4** : ranking low in some hierarchy — **low·li·ness** *n*

low–mind·ed \'lō-'mīn-dəd\ *adj* : inclined to low or unworthy things — **low–mind·ed·ly** *adv* — **low–mind·ed·ness** *n*

low–pres·sure \'lō-'presh-ər\ *adj* **1** : having, exerting, or operating under a relatively small pressure **2** : EASYGOING

low relief *n* : BAS-RELIEF

low–spir·it·ed \'lō-'spir-ət-əd\ *adj* : DEJECTED, DEPRESSED — **low–spir·it·ed·ly** *adv* — **low–spir·it·ed·ness** *n*

low tide *n* : the tide when the water is at its farthest ebb

[1]**lox** \'läks\ *n* : liquid oxygen

[2]**lox** *n, pl* **lox** *or* **lox·es** : smoked salmon

loy·al \'lȯi(-ə)l\ *adj* **1 a** : faithful in allegiance to one's lawful government **b** : faithful to a private person to whom fidelity is held to be due **2** : faithful to a cause or ideal — **loy·al·ly** \'lȯi-ə-lē\ *adv*

loy·al·ist \'lȯi-ə-ləst\ *n* : one who is or remains loyal to a political cause, party, government, or sovereign; *esp* : TORY 2

loy·al·ty \'lȯi(-ə)l-tē\ *n, pl* **-ties** : the quality or state of being loyal

loz·enge \'läz-ᵊnj\ *n* **1** : a figure with four equal sides and two acute and two obtuse angles : DIAMOND **2** : something shaped like a lozenge; *esp* : a small often medicated candy

LSD \ˌel-ˌes-'dē\ *n* : a complex organic compound that induces psychotic symptoms similar to those of schizophrenia

lu·au \'lü-ˌaů\ *n* : a Hawaiian feast

lub·ber \'ləb-ər\ *n* **1** : a big clumsy fellow **2** : an unskilled seaman — **lub·ber·li·ness** \-lē-nəs\ *n* — **lub·ber·ly** \-lē\ *adj or adv*

lube \'lüb\ *n* : LUBRICANT

lu·bri·cant \'lü-bri-kənt\ *n* : something (as a grease or oil) capable of reducing friction when applied between moving parts — **lubricant** *adj*

lu·bri·cate \'lü-brə-ˌkāt\ *vb* **1** : to make smooth or slippery **2** : to apply a lubricant to **3** : to act as a lubricant — **lu·bri·ca·tion** \ˌlü-brə-'kā-shən\ *n* — **lu·bri·ca·tor** \'lü-brə-ˌkāt-ər\ *n*

lu·bri·cious \lü-'brish-əs\ *adj* **1** : LECHEROUS; *also* : SALACIOUS **2 a** : having a smooth or slippery quality **b** : marked by uncertainty or instability : SHIFTY — **lu·bri·cious·ly** *adv* — **lu·bric·i·ty** \lü-'bris-ət-ē\ *n*

lu·bri·to·ri·um \ˌlü-brə-'tōr-ē-əm\ *n* : a station for lubricating motor vehicles

lu·cent \'lüs-ᵊnt\ *adj* **1** : glowing with light : LUMINOUS, BRIGHT **2** : CLEAR, LUCID, TRANSLUCENT — **lu·cent·ly** *adv*

lu·cid \'lü-səd\ *adj* **1 a** : suffused with light : LUMINOUS **b** : TRANSLUCENT **2** : having full use of one's faculties : clear-minded **3** : clear to the understanding : PLAIN — **lu·cid·i·ty** \lü-'sid-ət-ē\ *n* — **lu·cid·ly** *adv* — **lu·cid·ness** *n*

Lu·ci·fer \'lü-sə-fər\ *n* : DEVIL, SATAN

luck \ˈlək\ *n* **1** : whatever happens to a person apparently by chance : FORTUNE, CHANCE **2** : the accidental way events occur **3** : good fortune : SUCCESS — **luck·less** \ˈlək-ləs\ *adj*
luck·i·ly \ˈlək-ə-lē\ *adv* : by good luck : FORTUNATELY
luck·i·ness \ˈlək-ē-nəs\ *n* : the quality or state of being lucky
lucky \ˈlək-ē\ *adj* **1** : favored by luck : FORTUNATE **2** : producing a good result apparently by chance **3** : seeming to have a good influence or to bring good luck
lu·cra·tive \ˈlü-krət-iv\ *adj* : producing wealth : PROFITABLE — **lu·cra·tive·ly** *adv* — **lu·cra·tive·ness** *n*
lu·cre \ˈlü-kər\ *n* : monetary gain : PROFIT; *also* : MONEY
lu·cu·bra·tion \ˌlü-k(y)ə-ˈbrā-shən\ *n* **1** : laborious study : MEDITATION **2** : studied or pretentious expression in speech or writing
lu·di·crous \ˈlüd-ə-krəs\ *adj* **1** : amusing or laughable through obvious absurdity or incongruity **2** : meriting derisive laughter or scorn as absurdly inept, false, or foolish — **lu·di·crous·ly** *adv* — **lu·di·crous·ness** *n*
¹luff \ˈləf\ *n* : the act of sailing a ship closer to the wind
²luff *vi* : to sail nearer the wind
¹lug \ˈləg\ *vb* **lugged**; **lug·ging** **1** : DRAG, PULL **2** : to carry laboriously **3** : to introduce in a forced manner
²lug *n* : a box or basket for fruit or vegetables; *esp* : a shallow box of thin wood and standardized dimensions
³lug *n* **1** : a part (as a handle) that projects like an ear **2** : BLOCKHEAD, LOUT
lug·gage \ˈləg-ij\ *n* **1** : a traveler's belongings : BAGGAGE **2** : containers (as suitcases and traveling bags) for carrying personal belongings
lu·gu·bri·ous \lu̇-ˈg(y)ü-brē-əs\ *adj* : MOURNFUL; *esp* : exaggeratedly or affectedly mournful — **lu·gu·bri·ous·ly** *adv* — **lu·gu·bri·ous·ness** *n*
luke·warm \ˈlük-ˈwȯrm\ *adj* **1** : neither hot nor cold : moderately warm : TEPID **2** : not enthusiastic : HALFHEARTED, INDIFFERENT — **luke·warm·ly** *adv*
¹lull \ˈləl\ *vt* **1** : to cause to sleep or rest : SOOTHE **2** : to cause to relax vigilance
²lull *n* **1** : a temporary calm before or during a storm **2** : a temporary drop in activity
lul·la·by \ˈləl-ə-ˌbī\ *n, pl* **-bies** : a song to quiet children or lull them to sleep
lu·lu \ˈlü-lü\ *n* : a fixed allowance for expenses given in addition to salary
lum·ba·go \ˌləm-ˈbā-gō\ *n* : usu. painful muscular rheumatism involving the lumbar region
lum·bar \ˈləm-bər, -ˌbär\ *adj* : of or relating to the loins and esp. to the vertebrae of this region
¹lum·ber \ˈləm-bər\ *vi* **lum·bered**; **lum·ber·ing** \-b(ə-)riŋ\ : to move heavily or clumsily; *also* : RUMBLE
²lumber *n* **1** : surplus or disused articles (as furniture) that are stored away **2** : timber or logs esp. when sawed up for use — **lumber** *adj*
³lumber *vb* **lum·bered**; **lum·ber·ing** \-b(ə-)riŋ\ **1** : to clutter with or as if with lumber : ENCUMBER **2** : to heap together in disorder **3** : to cut logs : saw logs into lumber — **lum·ber·er** *n*
lumbering *adj* : heavy and awkward in movement — **lum·ber·ing·ly** *adv*
lum·ber·jack \ˈləm-bər-ˌjak\ *n* : LOGGER
lum·ber·man \-mən\ *n* : one engaged in lumbering
lum·ber·yard \-ˌyärd\ *n* : a place where a stock of lumber is kept for sale
lu·mi·nary \ˈlü-mə-ˌner-ē\ *n, pl* **-nar·ies** **1** : a very famous person **2** : a source of light; *esp* : one of the heavenly bodies — **luminary** *adj*
lu·mi·nos·i·ty \ˌlü-mə-ˈnäs-ət-ē\ *n, pl* **-ties** **1** : the quality or state of being luminous : BRIGHTNESS **2** : something luminous
lu·mi·nous \ˈlü-mə-nəs\ *adj* **1** : emitting light : SHINING **2** : LIGHTED **3** : CLEAR, INTELLIGIBLE — **lu·mi·nous·ly** *adv* — **lu·mi·nous·ness** *n*
lum·mox \ˈləm-əks\ *n* : a clumsy person
¹lump \ˈləmp\ *n* **1** : a piece or mass of irregular shape **2** : AGGREGATE, TOTALITY **3** : an abnormal swelling or growth **4** : a thickset heavy person; *esp* : one who is stupid or dull **5** *pl* **a** : BEATINGS **b** : COMEUPPANCE
²lump *adj* : not divided into parts : WHOLE
³lump *vb* **1** : to group without discrimination **2** : to make into lumps **3** : to move noisily and clumsily **4** : to become formed into lumps
⁴lump *vt* : to put up with : TOLERATE
lump·ish \ˈləm-pish\ *adj* **1** : DULL, STUPID **2** : HEAVY, AWKWARD — **lump·ish·ly** *adv* — **lump·ish·ness** *n*
lumpy \ˈləm-pē\ *adj* **1** : having or full of lumps **2** : having a thickset clumsy appearance — **lump·i·ly** \-pə-lē\ *adv* — **lump·i·ness** \-pē-nəs\ *n*
lu·na·cy \ˈlü-nə-sē\ *n, pl* **-cies** **1** : unsoundness of mind : INSANITY **2** : great foolishness : extreme folly
lu·nar \ˈlü-nər\ *adj* **1** : of or relating to the moon **2** : measured by the moon's revolution
lunar eclipse *n* : an eclipse in which the moon passes partially or wholly through the umbra of the earth's shadow
lu·nate \ˈlü-ˌnāt\ *adj* : shaped like a crescent — **lu·nate·ly** *adv*
lu·na·tic \ˈlü-nə-ˌtik\ *adj* **1** **a** : INSANE **b** : designed for insane persons **2** : wildly foolish : GIDDY — **lunatic** *n*
lunatic fringe *n* : the members of a political or social movement espousing extreme, eccentric, or fanatical views
¹lunch \ˈlənch\ *n* **1** : a light meal; *esp* : one eaten in the middle of the day **2** : the food prepared for a lunch
²lunch *vb* **1** : to eat lunch **2** : to provide lunch for — **lunch·er** *n*
lun·cheon \ˈlən-chən\ *n* : a light meal at midday; *esp* : a formal lunch
lun·cheon·ette \ˌlən-chə-ˈnet\ *n* : a place where light lunches are sold
lunch·room \ˈlənch-ˌrüm, -ˌru̇m\ *n* **1** : a restaurant specializing in food that is ready to serve or that can be quickly prepared **2** : a room (as in a school) where lunches brought from home may be eaten
lu·nette \lü-ˈnet\ *n* : something (as a window or a space over a doorway) that is shaped like a crescent
lung \ˈləŋ\ *n* **1** : one of the usu. paired thoracic organs that form the special breathing apparatus of air-breathing vertebrates **2** : a device (as an iron lung) to promote and facilitate breathing
¹lunge \ˈlənj\ *vb* **1** : to thrust or push with a lunge **2** : to make a stretching thrust or a forceful forward movement
²lunge *n* **1** : a sudden stretching thrust or pass (as with a sword or foil) **2** : the act of striding or leaping suddenly forward
¹lung·er \ˈlən-jər\ *n* : one that lunges
²lung·er \ˈləŋ-ər\ *n* : one suffering from a chronic disease of the lungs; *esp* : a tubercular person
lunk·head \ˈləŋk-ˌhed\ *n* : a dull-witted person : DOLT — **lunk·head·ed** \-ˈhed-əd\ *adj*
lu·nule \ˈlü-nyül\ *n* : a crescent-shaped body part or marking; *esp* : the whitish mark at the base of a fingernail
lu·pine \ˈlü-pən\ *n* : a leguminous plant with long clusters of pealike flowers
¹lurch \ˈlərch\ *n* **1** : a sudden roll of a ship to one side **2** : a sudden swaying or tipping movement; *also* : a staggering gait
²lurch *vi* : to roll or tip abruptly : PITCH; *also* : STAGGER
¹lure \ˈlu̇(ə)r\ *n* **1** **a** : an inducement to pleasure or gain : ENTICEMENT **b** : APPEAL, ATTRACTION **2** : a decoy for attracting animals to capture; *esp* : an artificial bait used for catching fish
²lure *vt* : to tempt with a promise of pleasure or gain : ENTICE — **lur·er** *n*
lu·rid \ˈlu̇r-əd\ *adj* **1** : wan and ghastly pale in appearance

: LIVID 2 : shining with the red glow of fire seen through smoke or cloud 3 a : causing horror or revulsion : GRUESOME b : highly colored : SENSATIONAL — **lu·rid·ly** *adv* — **lu·rid·ness** *n*

lurk \'lərk\ *vi* 1 a : to lie in ambush : SKULK b : to move furtively or inconspicuously : SNEAK c : to persist in staying 2 : to lie concealed; *esp* : to constitute a latent threat — **lurk·er** *n*

lus·cious \'ləsh-əs\ *adj* 1 : having a delicious taste or smell : SWEET 2 : having sensual appeal : SEDUCTIVE 3 : richly luxurious or appealing to the senses; *also* : FLORID — **lus·cious·ly** *adv* — **lus·cious·ness** *n*

¹lush \'ləsh\ *adj* 1 : producing or covered with luxuriant growth 2 a : THRIVING b : characterized by abundance : PLENTIFUL 3 a : SAVORY, DELICIOUS b : OPULENT, SUMPTUOUS — **lush·ly** *adv* — **lush·ness** *n*

²lush *n* : an habitual heavy drinker : DRUNKARD

¹lust \'ləst\ *n* 1 a : sexual desire b : intense or unrestrained sexual desire : LASCIVIOUSNESS 2 : an intense longing : CRAVING

²lust *vi* : to have an intense desire or need; *esp* : to have a strong sexual desire

lus·ter *or* **lus·tre** \'ləs-tər\ *n* 1 : a shine or sheen esp. from reflected light : GLOSS; *esp* : the appearance of the surface of a mineral with respect to its reflecting qualities 2 : BRIGHTNESS, GLITTER 3 : GLORY, SPLENDOR 4 : a surface on pottery sometimes iridescent and always metallic in appearance — **lus·ter·less** \-ləs\ *adj*

lus·ter·ware \-ˌwa(ə)r\ *n* : pottery decorated by applying to the glaze metallic compounds which become iridescent metallic films in the process of firing

lust·ful \'ləst-fəl\ *adj* : excited by lust : LECHEROUS — **lust·ful·ly** \-fə-lē\ *adv* — **lust·ful·ness** *n*

lus·tral \'ləs-trəl\ *adj* : PURIFICATORY

lus·trous \'ləs-trəs\ *adj* 1 : having a gloss : SHINING 2 : radiant in character or reputation : ILLUSTRIOUS — **lus·trous·ly** *adv* — **lus·trous·ness** *n*

lusty \'ləs-tē\ *adj* : full of vitality : VIGOROUS, ROBUST — **lust·i·ly** \-tə-lē\ *adv* — **lust·i·ness** \-tē-nəs\ *n*

lu·ta·nist *or* **lu·te·nist** \'lüt-ᵊn-əst, 'lüt-nəst\ *n* : a lute player

lute \'lüt\ *n* : a stringed musical instrument with a pear-shaped body and a fretted fingerboard played by plucking the strings with the fingers

Lu·ther·an \'lü-th(ə-)rən\ *n* : a member of a Protestant denomination adhering to the doctrines of Martin Luther

lut·ist \'lüt-əst\ *n* : a lute player

lux·u·ri·ant \(ˌ)ləg-'zhu̇r-ē-ənt, (ˌ)lək-'shu̇r-\ *adj* 1 a : yielding abundantly : PRODUCTIVE b : characterized by abundant growth : LUSH 2 a : exuberantly rich and varied : PROFUSE b : excessively elaborate : FLORID — **lux·u·ri·ance** \-ən(t)s\ *n* — **lux·u·ri·ant·ly** *adv*

lux·u·ri·ate \-ē-ˌāt\ *vi* 1 : to grow profusely : PROLIFERATE 2 : to indulge oneself luxuriously : REVEL

lux·u·ri·ous \(ˌ)ləg-'zhu̇r-ē-əs, (ˌ)lək-'shu̇r-\ *adj* 1 : of or relating to unrestrained gratification of the senses : VOLUPTUOUS 2 a : fond of luxury or self-indulgence : SYBARITIC b : characterized by opulence or rich abundance; *esp* : excessively ornate — **lux·u·ri·ous·ly** *adv* — **lux·u·ri·ous·ness** *n*

lux·u·ry \'ləksh-(ə-)rē, 'ləgzh-\ *n, pl* **-ries** 1 : liberal use or possession of costly food, dress, or anything that pleases a person's appetite or desire : great ease or comfort : rich surroundings 2 a : something desirable but costly or hard to get b : something adding to pleasure or comfort but not absolutely necessary — **luxury** *adj*

ly·cée \lē-'sā\ *n* : a French public secondary school that prepares for the university

ly·ce·um \lī-'sē-əm, 'lī-sē-\ *n* 1 : a hall for public lectures or discussions 2 : an association providing public lectures, concerts, and entertainments

lych–gate \'lich-ˌgāt\ *n* : a roofed gate in a churchyard under which a bier rests during the initial part of the burial service

lye \'lī\ *n* : a white crystalline corrosive alkaline substance used for scouring and in making soap

¹ly·ing \'lī-iŋ\ *pres part of* LIE

²lying *adj* : UNTRUTHFUL, FALSE

ly·ing–in \ˌlī-iŋ-'in\ *n, pl* **lyings–in** *or* **lying–ins** : the state attending and consequent to childbirth : CONFINEMENT — **lying–in** *adj*

lymph \'lim(p)f\ *n, pl* **lymphs** \'lim(p)fs, 'lim(p)s\ : a pale fluid that consists of a liquid portion resembling blood plasma and containing white blood cells, circulates in lymphatic vessels, and bathes the cells of the body — **lymph** *adj* — **lym·phat·ic** \lim-'fat-ik\ *adj*

lynch \'linch\ *vt* : to put to death by mob action without legal sanction or due process of law — **lynch·er** *n*

lynch law *n* : the punishment of presumed crimes or offenses usu. by death without due process of law

lynx \'liŋ(k)s\ *n, pl* **lynx** *or* **lynx·es** : any of several wildcats with relatively long legs, short stubby tail, mottled coat, and often tufted ears; *esp* : a large No. American cat with soft fur and large padded feet

lynx–eyed \'liŋ(k)s-'īd\ *adj* : having sharp sight

lyre \'lī(ə)r\ *n* : a stringed musical instrument of the harp class used by the ancient Greeks

¹lyr·ic \'lir-ik\ *adj* 1 : of or relating to a lyre 2 : resembling a song in form, feeling, or literary quality : expressing a poet's own feeling : not narrative or dramatic 3 : having a light flexible quality esp. adapted for singing songs

²lyric *n* 1 : a lyric composition; *esp* : a lyric poem 2 *pl* : the words of a popular song

lyr·i·cal \'lir-i-kəl\ *adj* 1 : resembling a song in mood or suggestion or emotional expression 2 : unrestrained or rhapsodic in expressing enthusiasm, delight, or praise — **lyr·i·cal·ly** \-k(ə-)lē\ *adv*

lyr·i·cism \'lir-ə-ˌsiz-əm\ *n* 1 : the quality or character of being lyric 2 : a style or quality expressing personal emotion in poetry or the other arts

lyr·i·cist \'lir-ə-səst\ *n* : a writer of lyrics

lyr·ist *n* 1 \'lī(ə)r-əst\ : a player on the lyre 2 \'lir-əst\ : LYRICIST

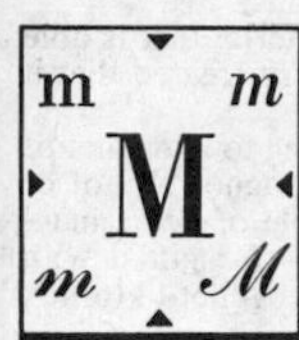

m \'em\ *n, often cap* **1 :** the 13th letter of the English alphabet **2 :** the roman numeral 1000
ma \'mä, 'mȯ\ *n, pl* **mas :** MOTHER
ma·ca·bre \mə-'käb(-rə)\ *adj* **1 :** having death as a subject : including a representation of death personified **2 a :** GRISLY, GRUESOME **b :** tending to produce horror in a beholder : HORRIBLE — **ma·ca·bre·ly** \-'käb-rə-lē\ *adv*
mac·ad·am \mə-'kad-əm\ *n* **1 :** a roadway or pavement of small closely packed broken stone **2 :** the broken stone used in macadamizing
mac·ad·am·ize \mə-'kad-ə-,mīz\ *vt* **:** to construct or surface (as a road) by packing a layer of small broken stone on a well-drained earth roadbed
ma·caque \mə-'kak, -'käk\ *n* **:** any of several short-tailed monkeys of Asia and the East Indies
mac·a·ro·ni \,mak-ə-'rō-nē\ *n, pl* **-nis** *or* **-nies 1 :** a food made chiefly of semolina paste dried in the form of slender tubes **2 a :** one of a class of young men in the 18th century who affected foreign ways **b :** DANDY, FOP
mac·a·roon \,mak-ə-'rün\ *n* **:** a small cake made of egg whites, sugar, and ground almonds or coconut
ma·caw \mə-'kȯ\ *n* **:** any of numerous parrots of South and Central America including some of the largest and showiest
¹mace \'mās\ *n* **1 :** a heavy spiked club used as a weapon in the Middle Ages for breaking armor **2 :** an ornamental staff borne as a symbol of authority (as before a public official or a legislative body)
²mace *n* **:** a spice consisting of the dried outer fibrous covering of the nutmeg
mac·er·ate \'mas-ə-,rāt\ *vb* **1 :** to waste away or cause to waste away **2 :** to cause to become soft or separated into constituent elements by or as if by steeping in fluid — **mac·er·a·tion** \,mas-ə-'rā-shən\ *n*
ma·chete \mə-'shet-ē\ *n* **:** a large heavy knife used for cutting sugarcane and underbrush and as a weapon

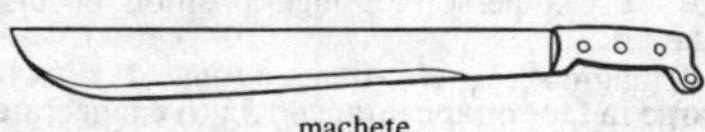
machete

mach·i·nate \'mak-ə-,nāt\ *vb* **:** CONTRIVE, PLOT; *esp* **:** to plot or scheme to do harm — **mach·i·na·tor** \-,nāt-ər\ *n*
mach·i·na·tion \,mak-ə-'nā-shən\ *n* **:** a scheme or plot to accomplish some usu. evil end — usu. used in pl.
ma·chine \mə-'shēn\ *n* **1 a :** VEHICLE, CONVEYANCE; *esp* **:** AUTOMOBILE **b :** a combination of parts that transmit forces, motion, and energy in a way that accomplishes some desired work **c :** an instrument (as a lever or pulley) designed to transmit or modify the application of power, force, or motion **2 a :** a person or organization that acts like a machine **b :** a combination of persons acting together for a common end together with the means they use; *esp* **:** a highly organized group that under the leadership of a boss or a small clique controls the policies and activities of a political party — **ma·chine·like** *adj*
machine *adj* **1 :** characterized by the widespread use of machinery **2 :** produced by or as if by machinery
machine *vt* **:** to shape or finish by machine-operated tools — **ma·chin·a·ble** *adj*
machine gun *n* **:** an automatic gun usu. having a cooling device and being capable of continuous firing — **ma·chine–gun** \mə-'shēn-,gən\ *vb* — **machine gunner** *n*
ma·chin·ery \mə-'shēn-(ə-)rē\ *n* **1 :** MACHINES **2 :** the working parts of a machine or instrument having moving parts **3 :** the organization or system by which something is done or carried on
machine shop *n* **:** a workshop in which metal articles are machined and assembled
machine tool *n* **:** a machine (as a lathe or drill) that is operated by power and is partly or wholly automatic
ma·chin·ist \mə-'shē-nəst\ *n* **:** a person who makes or works on machines and engines
mack·er·el \'mak-(ə-)rəl\ *n, pl* **-el** *or* **-els :** a No. Atlantic food fish that is green with blue bars above and silvery below
mackerel sky *n* **:** a sky covered with rows of clouds resembling the patterns on a mackerel's back
mack·i·naw \'mak-ə-,nȯ\ *n* **1 :** a flat-bottomed boat with pointed prow and square stern formerly much used on the upper Great Lakes **2 :** a short heavy woolen plaid coat reaching to about mid-thigh
mack·in·tosh *or* **mac·in·tosh** \'mak-ən-,täsh\ *n* **:** a lightweight waterproof fabric
mac·ro·cosm \'mak-rə-,käz-əm\ *n* **:** the great world **:** UNIVERSE — **mac·ro·cos·mic** \,mak-rə-'käz-mik\ *adj*
ma·cron \'māk-,rän, 'mak-\ *n* **:** a mark ¯ placed over a vowel (as in \māk\) to show that the vowel is long
mac·ro·scop·ic \,mak-rə-'skäp-ik\ *adj* **1 :** large enough to be observed by the naked eye **2 :** considered in terms of large units or elements
mac·u·la·tion \,mak-yə-'lā-shən\ *n* **:** the arrangement of spots and markings on an animal or plant
mad \'mad\ *adj* **1 :** disordered in mind **:** INSANE **2 :** being rash and foolish **3 :** FURIOUS, ENRAGED **4 :** FRANTIC **5 :** carried away by enthusiasm **6 :** wildly gay **7 :** affected with rabies **:** RABID **8 :** ANGRY, DISPLEASED
mad·am \'mad-əm\ *n, pl* **mes·dames** \mā-'däm\ — used as a form of polite address to a woman
ma·dame \mə-'dam, *before a surname also* ,mad-əm\ *n, pl* **mes·dames** \mā-'däm\ **:** MISTRESS — used as a title equivalent to *Mrs.* for a married woman not of English-speaking nationality
mad·cap \'mad-,kap\ *adj* **:** WILD, RECKLESS — **madcap** *n*
mad·den \'mad-ᵊn\ *vt* **:** to make mad **:** ENRAGE
mad·den·ing \'mad-niŋ, -ᵊn-iŋ\ *adj* **:** INFURIATING, IRRITATING — **mad·den·ing·ly** *adv*
mad·der \'mad-ər\ *n* **:** a Eurasian herb with spear-shaped leaves, small yellowish flowers followed by berries, and red fleshy roots used to make a dye; *also* **:** its root or a dye prepared from it
mad·ding \'mad-iŋ\ *adj* **1 :** acting as if mad **:** FRENZIED **2 :** MADDENING
made *past of* MAKE
Ma·dei·ra \mə-'dir-ə, -'der-\ *n* **:** an amber-colored dessert wine of the Madeira islands; *also* **:** a similar wine made elsewhere
ma·de·moi·selle \,mad(-ə)-mə-'zel, -mwə-'zel; mam-'zel\ *n, pl* **ma·de·moi·selles** \-'zelz\ *or* **mes·de·moi·selles** \,mād(-ə)-mə-'zel, -mwə-'zel\ **:** an unmarried girl or woman — used as a title equivalent to *Miss* for an unmarried woman not of English-speaking and esp. of French nationality
made–up \'mād-'əp\ *adj* **1 :** marked by the use of makeup **2 :** fancifully conceived or falsely devised **3 :** fully manufactured
mad·house \'mad-,hau̇s\ *n* **1 :** a place where insane persons are detained and treated **2 :** a place of bewildering uproar or confusion
mad·ly \'mad-lē\ *adv* **:** in a mad manner
mad·man \'mad-,man\ *n* **:** a man who is or acts as if insane **:** LUNATIC — **mad·wom·an** \-,wu̇m-ən\ *n*
mad·ness \'mad-nəs\ *n* **:** the quality or state of being mad: as **a :** INSANITY **b :** extreme folly **c :** FRENZY, RAGE
ma·dras \mə-'dras, 'mad-rəs\ *n* **:** a fine usu. corded or striped cotton fabric
mad·ri·gal \'mad-ri-gəl\ *n* **1 a :** a short love poem suitable for

a musical setting **b** : a musical setting for a madrigal **2** : a complex 16th century part-song — **mad·ri·gal·ist** \-gə-ləst\ *n*

mael·strom \'māl-strəm\ *n* **1** : a whirlpool of great force and violence dangerous to ships **2** : a great tumult : TURMOIL

mae·sto·so \mī-'stō-sō\ *adv (or adj)* : so as to be majestic and stately — used as a direction in music

mae·stro \'mī-strō\ *n, pl* **mae·stros** \-strōz\ *or* **mae·stri** \-ˌstrē\ : a master in an art; *esp* : an eminent composer, conductor, or teacher of music

Mae West \'mā-'west\ *n* : an inflatable life vest

Ma·fia \'mäf-ē-ə, 'maf-\ *n* **1** : a Sicilian secret terrorist society **2** : a secret criminal organization held to control illicit activities (as racketeering) throughout the world

mag·a·zine \'mag-ə-ˌzēn, ˌmag-ə-'\ *n* **1** : a storehouse or warehouse esp. for military supplies **2** : a place for keeping gunpowder in a fort or ship **3** : a publication usu. containing stories, articles, or poems and issued periodically (as weekly or monthly) **4** : a supply chamber: as **a** : a chamber in a gun for holding cartridges **b** : a chamber for film on a camera or motion-picture projector

ma·gen·ta \mə-'jent-ə\ *n* : a deep purplish red

mag·got \'mag-ət\ *n* **1** : a soft-bodied legless grub that is the larva of a two-winged fly (as the housefly) **2** : a fantastic idea : WHIM — **mag·goty** \-ət-ē\ *adj*

ma·gi \'mā-ˌjī\ *n pl, often cap* : the three wise men from the East who paid homage to the infant Jesus

¹mag·ic \'maj-ik\ *n* **1** : the art of persons who claim to be able to do things by the help of supernatural creatures or by their own knowledge of nature's secrets **2 a** : something that charms **b** : seemingly hidden or secret power **3** : SLEIGHT OF HAND

²magic *adj* **1** : of or relating to magic **2 a** : having seemingly supernatural qualities or powers **b** : ENCHANTING — **mag·i·cal** \'maj-i-kəl\ *adj* — **mag·i·cal·ly** \-k(ə-)lē\ *adv*

ma·gi·cian \mə-'jish-ən\ *n* **1** : a person skilled in magic; *esp* : SORCERER **2** : a performer of sleight of hand

magic lantern *n* : an early type of slide projector

mag·is·te·ri·al \ˌmaj-ə-'stir-ē-əl\ *adj* **1** : AUTHORITATIVE, COMMANDING **2** : of or relating to a magistrate or his office or duties — **mag·is·te·ri·al·ly** \-ē-ə-lē\ *adv*

mag·is·tra·cy \'maj-ə-strə-sē\ *n, pl* **-cies** **1** : the state of being a magistrate **2** : the office, power, or dignity of a magistrate **3** : a body of magistrates

mag·is·tral \'maj-e-strəl\ *adj* : MAGISTERIAL 1 — **mag·is·tral·ly** \-strə-lē\ *adv*

mag·is·trate \'maj-ə-ˌstrāt, -strət\ *n* : an official entrusted with administration of the laws: as **a** : a local official exercising administrative and often judicial functions **b** : a local judiciary official having jurisdiction in some criminal cases

mag·na cum lau·de \ˌmäg-nə-ˌku̇m-'lau̇d-ə, -'lau̇d-ē; ˌmag-nə-ˌkəm-'lȯd-ē\ *adv (or adj)* : with great academic distinction

mag·na·nim·i·ty \ˌmag-nə-'nim-ət-ē\ *n, pl* **-ties** **1 a** : nobility of character : HIGH-MINDEDNESS **b** : GENEROSITY **2** : a magnanimous act

mag·nan·i·mous \mag-'nan-ə-məs\ *adj* **1** : showing or suggesting a lofty and courageous spirit : NOBLE **2** : GENEROUS, FORGIVING — **mag·nan·i·mous·ly** *adv* — **mag·nan·i·mous·ness** *n*

mag·nate \'mag-ˌnāt, -nət\ *n* : a person of rank, power, influence, or distinction (as in an industry)

mag·ne·sia \mag-'nē-shə, -'nē-zhə\ *n* : a white highly infusible earthy solid that consists of magnesium and oxygen and is used in refractories, fertilizers, and rubber and as an antacid and mild laxative — **mag·ne·sian** \-shən, -zhən\ *adj*

mag·ne·sium \mag-'nē-zē-əm, -zhəm\ *n* : a silver-white metallic element that is lighter than aluminum, is easily worked, burns with a dazzling light, and is used in making lightweight alloys

mag·net \'mag-nət\ *n* **1** : a piece of some material that is able to attract iron; *esp* : a mass of iron or steel so treated that it has this property **2** : something that attracts

mag·net·ic \mag-'net-ik\ *adj* **1 a** : of or relating to a magnet or magnetism **b** : having the properties of a magnet **2** : of or relating to the earth's magnetism **3** : capable of being magnetized **4** : working by magnetic attraction **5** : gifted with great power to attract — **mag·net·i·cal·ly** \-'net-i-k(ə-)lē\ *adv*

magnetic needle *n* : a narrow strip of magnetized steel that is free to swing horizontally or vertically to show the direction of the earth's magnetism and that is the essential part of a compass

magnetic north *n* : the northerly direction in the earth's magnetic field indicated by the north-seeking pole of the horizontal magnetic needle

magnetic tape *n* : a ribbon of thin paper or plastic coated for use in magnetic recording

mag·ne·tism \'mag-nə-ˌtiz-əm\ *n* **1 a** : the property of attracting certain metals or producing a magnetic field as shown by a magnet, a magnetized material, or a conductor carrying an electric current **b** : the science that deals with magnetic occurrences or conditions **2** : the power to attract or charm others

mag·ne·tize \'mag-nə-ˌtīz\ *vt* **1** : to cause to be magnetic : make into a magnet **2** : CHARM, CAPTIVATE — **mag·ne·tiz·a·ble** *adj* — **mag·ne·ti·za·tion** \ˌmag-nət-ə-'zā-shən\ *n*

mag·ne·to \mag-'nēt-ō\ *n, pl* **-tos** : a small electric generator using permanent magnets; *esp* : one used to produce sparks in an internal-combustion engine

mag·ni·fi·ca·tion \ˌmag-nə-fə-'kā-shən\ *n* **1** : the act of magnifying : the state of being magnified **2** : the apparent enlargement of an object by an optical instrument

mag·nif·i·cence \mag-'nif-ə-sən(t)s\ *n* : the quality or state of being magnificent : SPLENDOR, GRANDEUR

mag·nif·i·cent \-sənt\ *adj* **1** : having grandeur and beauty : SPLENDID **2** : EXALTED, NOBLE — **mag·nif·i·cent·ly** *adv*

mag·nif·i·co \mag-'nif-i-ˌkō\ *n, pl* **-coes** *or* **-cos** **1** : a nobleman of Venice **2** : a person of high position or distinguished appearance

mag·ni·fy \'mag-nə-ˌfī\ *vb* **-fied**; **-fy·ing** **1** : EXTOL, LAUD **2** : to enlarge in fact or appearance **3** : to exaggerate in importance — **mag·ni·fi·er** *n*

mag·ni·fy·ing glass *n* : a lens that magnifies an object seen through it

mag·nil·o·quent \mag-'nil-ə-kwənt\ *adj* : speaking in a high-flown or bombastic manner : GRANDILOQUENT — **mag·nil·o·quence** \-kwən(t)s\ *n* — **mag·nil·o·quent·ly** *adv*

mag·ni·tude \'mag-nə-ˌt(y)üd\ *n* **1 a** : greatness esp. in size or extent : BIGNESS **b** : spatial quality : SIZE **c** : QUANTITY, NUMBER **d** : a numerical measure of size or quantity **2** : greatness in influence or effect **3** : degree of brightness; *esp* : a number representing the relative brightness of a star on a scale on which the fainter stars are indicated by higher numbers

mag·no·lia \mag-'nōl-yə\ *n* : any of a genus of No. American and Asiatic shrubs and trees with usu. showy white, yellow, rose, or purple flowers appearing in early spring

mag·num opus \ˌmag-nəm-'ō-pəs\ *n* : a great work; *esp* : a literary or artistic masterpiece

mag·pie \'mag-ˌpī\ *n* **1** : any of numerous noisy birds related to the jays but having a long tapered tail and black-and-white plumage **2** : a person who chatters constantly

ma·ha·ra·ja *or* **ma·ha·ra·jah** \ˌmä-hə-'räj-ə, -'räzh-ə\ *n* : a Indian prince ranking above a raja

ma·ha·ra·ni *or* **ma·ha·ra·nee** \-'rän-ē\ *n* **1** : the wife of a maharaja **2** : an Indian princess ranking above a rani

ma·hat·ma \mə-'hät-mə, -'hat-\ *n* : a person revered f

high-mindedness, wisdom, and selflessness — used as a title of honor esp. by Hindus

ma·hog·a·ny \mə-'häg-ə-nē\ *n, pl* **-nies** : any of various tropical trees with reddish wood used in furniture; *esp* : an American evergreen tree or its durable lustrous reddish brown wood

ma·hout \mə-'hau̇t\ *n* : a keeper and driver of an elephant

maid \'mād\ *n* **1** : an unmarried girl or woman; *esp* : a young unmarried woman **2** : a female servant

¹maid·en \'mād-ᵊn\ *n* **1** : a young unmarried girl or woman **2** : VIRGIN

²maiden *adj* **1 a** : UNMARRIED **b** : VIRGIN **2** : of, relating to, or befitting a maiden **3** : FIRST, EARLIEST **4** : INTACT, FRESH

maid·en·hair \'mād-ᵊn-,ha(ə)r\ *n* : a fern with slender stems and delicate much-divided often feathery leaves

maid·en·hood \-,hu̇d\ *n* : the condition or time of being a maiden

maid·en·ly \-lē\ *adj* : of or relating to a maiden or maidenhood — **maid·en·li·ness** *n*

maiden name *n* : the surname of a woman before she is married

maid–in–wait·ing *n, pl* **maids–in–waiting** : a young woman of a queen's or princess's household appointed to attend her

maid of honor **1** : an unmarried woman usu. of noble birth who attends a queen or princess **2** : an unmarried woman serving as the principal female attendant of a bride at her wedding

maid·ser·vant \'mād-,sər-vənt\ *n* : a female servant

¹mail \'māl\ *n* **1** : matter (as letters or parcels) sent under public authority from one person to another through the agency of the post office **2** : the whole system used in the public sending and delivery of letters and parcels **3** : something that comes in the mail; *esp* : the contents of a single delivery **4** : a conveyance (as a train, truck, or boat) that carries mail

²mail *vt* : to send by mail : POST — **mail·a·ble** *adj* — **mail·er** *n*

³mail *n* : a flexible network of small metal rings linked together for use as armor

mail·box \'māl-,bäks\ *n* **1** : a public box for the collection of mail **2** : a private box for the delivery of mail

mailed \'māld\ *adj* : protected or armed with or as if with mail

mail·man \'māl-,man\ *n* : a man who delivers mail or who collects mail from public mailboxes

mail order *n* : an order for goods that is received and filled by mail — **mail–or·der** \'māl-,ȯrd-ər\ *adj*

mail–order house *n* : a retail establishment whose business is conducted by mail

maim \'mām\ *vt* **1** : to commit mayhem upon **2** : to mutilate, disfigure, or wound seriously : CRIPPLE — **maim·er** *n*

¹main \'mān\ *n* **1** : physical strength : FORCE — used in the phrase *with might and main* **2 a** : MAINLAND **b** : HIGH SEAS **3** : a principal pipe, duct, or circuit of a utility system — **in the main** : for the most part

²main *adj* **1 a** : OUTSTANDING, CONSPICUOUS **b** : CHIEF, PRINCIPAL **2** : fully exerted : SHEER **3** : being a clause that is capable of standing alone as a simple sentence but actually is part of a larger sentence that includes also a subordinate clause or another main clause

main·land \'mān-,land, -lənd\ *n* : a continent or the main part of a continent as distinguished from an offshore island or sometimes from a cape or a peninsula — **main·land·er** \-,lan-dər, -lən-\ *n*

main·ly \'mān-lē\ *adv* : for the most part : CHIEFLY

main·mast \'mān-,mast, -məst\ *n* : the principal mast of a sailing ship

main·sail \'mān-,sāl, 'mān(t)-səl\ *n* : the principal sail on the mainmast

main·sheet \'mān-,shēt\ *n* : a rope by which the mainsail is trimmed and secured

main·spring \-,spriŋ\ *n* **1** : the principal spring in a mechanism esp. of a watch or clock **2** : the chief motive, cause, or force underlying or responsible for an action

main·stay \-,stā\ *n* **1** : the large strong rope running from the maintop of a ship usu. to the foot of the foremast **2** : a chief support

main stem *n* : the main street of a city or town

main·stream \'mān-,strēm\ *n* : a prevailing current or direction of activity or influence

main·tain \mān-'tān, mən-\ *vt* **1** : to keep in an existing state; *esp* : to keep in a state of good repair or efficiency **2** : to uphold and defend against opposition or danger **3** : to continue in : carry on **4 a** : to provide for : SUPPORT **b** : SUSTAIN **5** : to affirm in or as if in argument : ASSERT — **main·tain·a·ble** *adj* — **main·tain·er** *n*

main·te·nance \'mānt-nən(t)s, -ᵊn-ən(t)s\ *n* **1** : the act of maintaining : the state of being maintained **2** : something that maintains or supports; *esp* : a supply of necessities and conveniences **3** : the upkeep of property or machinery

mai·son·ette \,māz-ᵊn-'et\ *n* **1** : a small house **2** : an apartment often of two stories

maî·tre d'hô·tel \,mā-trə-(,)dō-'tel\ *n, pl* **maîtres d'hôtel** *same*\ **1** : MAJORDOMO **2** : HEADWAITER

maize \'māz\ *n* : INDIAN CORN

ma·jes·tic \mə-'jes-tik\ *adj* : being stately and dignified : NOBLE — **ma·jes·ti·cal·ly** \-ti-k(ə-)lē\ *adv*

maj·es·ty \'maj-ə-stē\ *n, pl* **-ties** **1** : sovereign power, authority, or dignity; *also* : the person of a sovereign — used as a title for a king, queen, emperor, or empress **2 a** : royal bearing or quality : GRANDEUR **b** : greatness of quality or character

ma·jol·i·ca \mə-'jäl-i-kə\ *n* : any of several faiences; *esp* : an Italian tin-glazed pottery

¹ma·jor \'mā-jər\ *adj* **1 a** : greater in dignity, rank, or importance **b** : greater in number, quantity, or extent **2** : having attained majority **3 a** : having half steps between the 3d and 4th and the 7th and 8th degrees **b** : based on a major scale **4** : involving risk to life : SERIOUS **5** : of or relating to an academic major

²major *n* **1** : a person having attained majority **2** : a major musical interval, scale, key, or mode **3** : a commissioned officer (as in the army) ranking next below a lieutenant colonel **4 a** : an academic subject chosen by a student as a field of specialization **b** : a student specializing in such a field

³major *vi* **ma·jored**; **ma·jor·ing** \'māj-(ə-)riŋ\ : to pursue an academic major

ma·jor·do·mo \,mā-jər-'dō-mō\ *n, pl* **-mos** **1** : a man in charge of a great household and esp. of a royal establishment : a head steward **2** : BUTLER, STEWARD

ma·jor·ette \,mā-jə-'ret\ *n* : DRUM MAJORETTE

major general *n* : a commissioned officer (as in the army) ranking next below a lieutenant general

ma·jor·i·ty \mə-'jȯr-ət-ē\ *n, pl* **-ties** **1 a** : the age at which one is given full civil rights; *esp* : the age of 21 **b** : the status of one who has attained this age **2 a** : a number greater than half of a total **b** : the amount by which such a greater number exceeds the smaller number **c** : the preponderant quantity or share **3** : the group or party that makes up the greater part of a whole body of persons **4** : the military office or rank of a major

majority rule *n* : a political principle providing that a majority of an organized group shall have the power to make decisions binding upon the whole group

major league *n* : a league in the highest class of U.S. professional baseball; *also* : a league of major importance in another sport (as hockey)

major party *n* : a political party strong enough to win control of a government periodically and when defeated to be the principal opposition to the party in power

[1]make \'māk\ *vb* **made** \'mād\; **mak·ing** **1 a** : to seem to begin an action **b** : to act so as to appear **2 a** : to cause to be undergone **b** : to cause to exist, occur, or appear : CREATE **c** : to create for some purpose or goal **3 a** : to form or shape out of material : FASHION **b** : to put together out of components : CONSTRUCT, BUILD **c** : to comprise or become combined into a whole : CONSTITUTE **4** : to frame or formulate in the mind **5 a** : to decide by computation or estimation **b** : to regard as being : CONSIDER **c** : UNDERSTAND **6** : to set in order : PREPARE **7** : to cause to be or become **8 a** : ENACT, ESTABLISH **b** : to execute in an appropriate manner **c** : SET, NAME **9** : to complete (an electric circuit) **10 a** : to carry out a specified action : UNDERTAKE, PERFORM **b** : FOLLOW, TRAVERSE **11** : to cause to act in some manner : COMPEL **12** : to cause or assure the success of **13** : to amount to in significance **14** : REACH, ATTAIN **15 a** : to gain by or as if by working **b** : to acquire by effort **c** : to score in a game or sport **16** : CATCH — **mak·er** *n* — **make away with 1** : to carry off **2** : KILL, DESTROY — **make believe** : FEIGN, PRETEND — **make good 1** : to make complete : FULFILL **2** : to make up for a deficiency **3** : SUCCEED — **make love** : WOO, COURT — **make sail 1** : to raise or spread sail **2** : to set out on a voyage — **make time 1** : to travel fast **2** : to gain time — **make way** : to open or give room for passing or entering

[2]**make** *n* **1** : the way in which a thing is made : manner of construction **2** : the type or process of making or manufacturing **3** : the completion of an electric circuit

[1]**make–be·lieve** \'māk-bə-ˌlēv\ *n* : a pretending to believe (as in the play of children) : PRETENSE

[2]**make–believe** *adj* **1** : PRETENDED, IMAGINARY **2** : INSINCERE

make–do \'māk-ˌdü\ *adj* : MAKESHIFT — **make–do** *n*

make out *vb* **1** : to draw up in writing **2** : to find or grasp the meaning of : UNDERSTAND **3** : to represent as being **4** : DISCERN **5** : SUCCEED, PROSPER

make over *vt* **1** : to transfer the title of : CONVEY **2** : REMODEL

make·shift \'māk-ˌshift\ *n* : a temporary expedient : SUBSTITUTE — **makeshift** *adj*

make up *vb* **1 a** : CONSTRUCT, COMPOSE **b** : to combine to produce a whole : COMPRISE **2** : INVENT, CONCOCT **3** : to compensate for a deficiency **4** : to become reconciled **5 a** : to put on costumes or makeup (as for a play) **b** : to apply cosmetics

make·up \'māk-ˌəp\ *n* **1** : the way the parts or elements of something are put together : composition or manner of composition **2** : materials (as wigs or cosmetics) used in making up or in special costuming

mak·ing \'mā-kiŋ\ *n* **1** : the action of one that makes **2** : a process or means of advancement or success **3** : material from which something can be developed **4** *for cigarette materials usu* 'mā-kənz\ *pl* : the materials from which something can be made

mal·adapt·ed \ˌmal-ə-'dap-təd\ *adj* : poorly suited to a particular use, purpose, or situation

mal·ad·just·ed \ˌmal-ə-'jəs-təd\ *adj* : poorly or inadequately adjusted; *esp* : lacking harmony with one's environment — **mal·ad·just·ment** *n*

mal·ad·min·is·ter \ˌmal-əd-'min-ə-stər\ *vt* : to administer badly — **mal·ad·min·is·tra·tion** \-ˌmin-ə-'strā-shən\ *n*

mal·adroit \ˌmal-ə-'drȯit\ *adj* : not adroit : AWKWARD, CLUMSY — **mal·adroit·ly** *adv* — **mal·adroit·ness** *n*

mal·a·dy \'mal-əd-ē\ *n, pl* **-dies** : a disease or disorder of the body or mind : AILMENT

mal·aise \ma-'lāz\ *n* : an indefinite feeling of bodily or mental disorder

mal·a·mute *or* **mal·e·mute** \'mal-ə-ˌmyüt\ *n* : a sled dog of northern No. America

mal·a·prop·ism \'mal-ə-ˌpräp-ˌiz-əm\ *n* **1** : a usu. humorous misuse of a word esp. for one of similar sound by someone unaware of the error **2** : an example of malapropism

mal·ap·ro·pos \ˌmal-ˌap-rə-'pō\ *adv* : in an inappropriate or inopportune way — **malapropos** *adj*

ma·lar·ia \mə-'ler-ē-ə\ *n* : a disease marked by recurring chills and fever and caused by a parasite carried by a mosquito — **ma·lar·i·al** \-ē-əl\ *adj* — **ma·lar·i·ous** \-ē-əs\ *adj*

ma·lar·key \mə-'lär-kē\ *n* : insincere or foolish talk : BUNKUM

mal·con·tent \ˌmal-kən-'tent\ *adj* : dissatisfied with the existing state of affairs : DISCONTENTED — **malcontent** *n*

mal de mer \ˌmal-də-'me(ə)r\ *n* : SEASICKNESS

[1]**male** \'māl\ *adj* **1 a** : of, relating to, or being the sex that fathers young **b** : STAMINATE **2 a** : of, relating to, or characteristic of the male sex **b** : made up of males — **male·ness** *n*

[2]**male** *n* : a male plant or animal

mal·e·dic·tion \ˌmal-ə-'dik-shən\ *n* : a prayer for harm to befall someone : CURSE

mal·e·fac·tor \'mal-ə-ˌfak-tər\ *n* **1** : one guilty of a crime or offense **2** : EVILDOER

ma·lef·i·cent \mə-'lef-ə-sənt\ *adj* : working or productive of harm or evil : HARMFUL — **ma·lef·i·cence** \-sən(t)s\ *n*

ma·lev·o·lent \mə-'lev-ə-lənt\ *adj* : having or showing ill will toward others : SPITEFUL — **ma·lev·o·lence** \-'lev-ə-lən(t)s\ *n* — **ma·lev·o·lent·ly** *adv*

mal·fea·sance \(')mal-'fēz-ᵊn(t)s\ *n* : wrongful conduct esp. by a public official

mal·for·ma·tion \ˌmal-fȯr-'mā-shən\ *n* : an irregular, anomalous, abnormal, or faulty formation or structure

mal·formed \(')mal-'fȯrmd\ *adj* : marked by malformation

mal·func·tion \(')mal-'fəŋ(k)-shən\ *vi* : to fail to operate in the normal or usual manner — **malfunction** *n*

mal·ice \'mal-əs\ *n* : ILL WILL; *esp* : the deliberate intention of doing unjustified harm for the satisfaction of doing it

ma·li·cious \mə-'lish-əs\ *adj* **1** : feeling strong ill will : being mean and spiteful **2** : done or carried on with malice or caused by malice — **ma·li·cious·ly** *adv* — **ma·li·cious·ness** *n*

[1]**ma·lign** \mə-'līn\ *adj* **1** : moved by ill will toward others : MALEVOLENT **2** : operating so as to injure or hurt

[2]**malign** *vt* : to utter injurious or false reports about : speak evil of : DEFAME

ma·lig·nan·cy \mə-'lig-nən-sē\ *n, pl* **-cies** **1** : the quality or state of being malignant **2** : a malignant tumor

ma·lig·nant \-nənt\ *adj* **1 a** : evil in influence or effect : INJURIOUS **b** : MALEVOLENT, MALICIOUS **2** : tending or likely to produce death esp. through being dispersed and growing throughout the body — **ma·lig·nant·ly** *adv*

ma·lig·ni·ty \mə-'lig-nət-ē\ *n, pl* **-ties** **1** : the quality or state of being malignant : MALIGNANCY **2** : something (as an act or an event) that is malignant

ma·li·hi·ni \ˌmäl-ē-'hē-nē\ *n* : a newcomer to Hawaii

ma·lin·ger \mə-'liŋ-gər\ *vi* **ma·lin·gered**; **ma·lin·ger·ing** \-g(ə-)riŋ\ : to pretend incapacity (as illness) so as to avoid duty or work — **ma·lin·ger·er** *n*

mal·i·son \'mal-ə-sən, -zən\ *n* : MALEDICTION, CURSE

mall \'mȯl, 'mal\ *n* : a shaded walk : PROMENADE

mal·lard \'mal-ərd\ *n, pl* **mallard** *or* **mallards** : a common and widely distributed wild duck of the northern hemisphere that is ancestral to the domestic ducks

mal·le·a·ble \'mal-ē-ə-bəl, 'mal-(y)ə-bəl\ *adj* **1** : capable of being beaten out, extended, or shaped by hammer blows or by the pressure of rollers **2** : ADAPTABLE, PLIABLE — **mal·le·a·bil·i·ty** \ˌmal-ē-ə-'bil-ət-ē, ˌmal-(y)ə-'bil-\ *n*

mal·let \'mal-ət\ *n* **1** : a hammer usu. having a barrel-shaped head of wood; *esp* : a tool with a short handle and a large head used for driving another tool (as a chisel) **2** : a long-handled club with a cylindrical head used in playing croquet **3** : a polo stick

mal·low \'mal-ō\ *n* : any of a genus of herbs with lobed or dissected leaves, usu. showy flowers, and a disk-shaped frui

malm•sey \'mä(l)m-zē\ *n, pl* **malmseys** *often cap* : a sweet aromatic wine orig. produced in Greece
mal•nour•ished \(')mal-'nər-isht\ *adj* : poorly nourished
mal•nu•tri•tion \,mal-n(y)ù-'trish-ən\ *n* : faulty and esp. inadequate nutrition
mal•oc•clu•sion \,mal-ə-'klü-zhən\ *n* : faulty coming together of teeth in biting
mal•odor•ous \(')mal-'ōd-ə-rəs\ *adj* : bad-smelling
mal•prac•tice \(')mal-'prak-təs\ *n* **1** : violation of professional standards esp. by negligence or improper conduct **2** : an injurious, negligent, or improper practice
1malt \'mȯlt\ *n* **1** : grain and esp. barley softened by steeping in water, allowed to germinate, and used chiefly in brewing and distilling **2** : MALTED MILK — **malt** *adj* — **malty** \'mȯl-tē\ *adj*
2malt *vb* **1** : to convert into malt **2** : to make or treat with malt or malt extract **3** : to become malt
malt•ed milk \,mȯl-təd-\ *n* **1** : a soluble powder prepared from dried milk and malted cereals **2** : a beverage made by dissolving malted milk in a liquid (as milk)
Mal•tese cross \mȯl-,tēz-\ *n* : a cross with four arms of equal size that increase in width toward the outward ends
mal•treat \(')mal-'trēt\ *vt* : to treat unkindly or roughly : ABUSE — **mal•treat•ment** *n*
mam•bo \'mäm-bō\ *n, pl* **mambos** : a dance of Haitian origin related to the rumba — **mambo** *vi*
mam•ma *or* **ma•ma** \'mäm-ə\ *n* : MOTHER
mam•mal \'mam-əl\ *n* : any of a class of higher vertebrates comprising man and all other animals that nourish their young with milk secreted by mammary glands and have the skin usu. more or less covered with hair — **mam•ma•li•an** \mə-'mā-lē-ən, ma-'mā-\ *adj or n*
mam•ma•ry \'mam-ə-rē\ *adj* : of, relating to, or being the glands that in female mammals secrete milk
mam•mon \'mam-ən\ *n, often cap* : an often personified devotion to material possessions; *also* : WEALTH
1mam•moth \'mam-əth\ *n* **1** : any of numerous large hairy extinct elephants with very long upward-curving tusks **2** : something immense of its kind : GIANT
2mammoth *adj* : of very great size : GIGANTIC
mam•my \'mam-ē\ *n, pl* **mammies** **1** : MAMMA **2** : a Negro woman serving as a nurse to white children esp. formerly in the southern states of the U.S.
1man \'man\ *n, pl* **men** \'men\ **1 a** : a human being; *esp* : an adult male human **b** : the human race : MANKIND **c** : HUSBAND, LOVER **d** : any member of the natural family to which human beings belong including both human beings and extinct related forms known only from fossils **e** : one possessing in high degree the qualities considered distinctive of manhood **2 a** : VASSAL **b** : an adult male servant **c** *pl* : the working force as distinguished from the employer **3** : an indefinite person **4** : one of the pieces with which various games (as chess) are played
2man *vt* **manned**; **man•ning** **1 a** : to supply with men (as for management or operation) **b** : to station members of a ship's crew at **2** : to furnish with strength : BRACE
ma•na \'män-ə\ *n* **1** : the power of the elemental forces of nature embodied in an object or person **2** : PRESTIGE
man–about–town \,man-ə-,baüt-'taün\ *n, pl* **men–about–town** \,men-\ : a worldly and socially active man
1man•a•cle \'man-i-kəl\ *n* **1** : a shackle for the hand or wrist : HANDCUFF — usu. used in pl. **2** : something that restrains or restricts
2manacle *vt* **-cled**; **-cling** \-k(ə-)liŋ\ **1** : to put manacles on **2** : RESTRAIN
man•age \'man-ij\ *vb* **1** : to oversee and make decisions about : DIRECT **2** : to make responsive or submissive : HANDLE, MANIPULATE **3** : to treat with care : use to best advantage : HUSBAND **4** : to succeed in one's purpose : get along : CONTRIVE
man•age•a•ble \'man-ij-ə-bəl\ *adj* : capable of being managed — **man•age•a•bil•i•ty** \,man-ij-ə-'bil-ət-ē\ *n*
man•age•ment \'man-ij-mənt\ *n* **1** : the act or art of managing : CONTROL, DIRECTION **2** : skillfulness in managing **3** : the collective body of those who manage an enterprise
man•ag•er \'man-ij-ər\ *n* : one that manages: as **a** : a person who conducts business or household affairs with economy and care **b** : a person whose work or profession is management **c** : a person who directs a team or an athlete — **man•a•ger•i•al** \,man-ə-'jir-ē-əl\ *adj*
ma•ña•na \mən-'yän-ə\ *n* : an indefinite time in the future — **mañana** *adv*
man–at–arms \,man-ət-'ärmz\ *n, pl* **men–at–arms** \,men-\ : SOLDIER; *esp* : a heavily armed mounted soldier
man•ci•ple \'man(t)-sə-pəl\ *n* : a steward or purveyor esp. for a college or monastery
man•da•mus \man-'dā-məs\ *n* : a writ issued by a superior court commanding that a specified official act or duty be performed
1man•da•rin \'man-d(ə-)rən\ *n* **1** : a public official under the Chinese Empire of any of nine superior grades **2** : a small spiny Chinese orange tree with yellow to reddish orange loose-skinned fruits; *also* : its fruit
2mandarin *adj* : of, relating to, or typical of a mandarin
man•da•tary \'man-də-,ter-ē\ *n, pl* **-tar•ies** : MANDATORY
1man•date \'man-,dāt\ *n* **1 a** : an authoritative command, instruction, or direction **b** : authorization or approval given to a representative esp. by voters **2 a** : a commission granted by the League of Nations to a member nation to administer a conquered territory as guardian on behalf of the League **b** : a mandated territory
2mandate *vt* : to administer or assign under a mandate
1man•da•to•ry \'man-də-,tōr-ē\ *adj* **1** : containing or constituting a command : OBLIGATORY **2** : of, relating to, or holding a League of Nations mandate
2mandatory *n, pl* **-ries** : one given a mandate
man•di•ble \'man-də-bəl\ *n* **1** : JAW 1a; *esp* : a lower jaw **2** : either the upper or lower segment of the bill of a bird — **man•dib•u•lar** \man-'dib-yə-lər\ *adj*
man•do•lin \,man-də-'lin, 'man-dᵊl-ən\ *n* : a musical instrument of the lute family that has a pear-shaped body and fretted neck and four to six pairs of strings — **man•do•lin•ist** \,man-də-'lin-əst\ *n*
man•drag•o•ra \man-'drag-ə-rə\ *n* : MANDRAKE 1
man•drake \'man-,drāk\ *n* **1** : a Mediterranean herb of the nightshade family with a large forked root superstitiously credited with human and medicinal attributes **2** : MAYAPPLE
mane \'mān\ *n* **1** : long heavy hair growing about the neck of some mammals (as a horse) **2** : long heavy hair on a person's head — **maned** \'mānd\ *adj*
man–eat•er \'man-,ēt-ər\ *n* : one (as a cannibal, shark, or tiger) that has or is thought to have an appetite for human flesh — **man–eat•ing** \-,ēt-iŋ\ *adj*
ma•nege \ma-'nezh\ *n* **1** : a school for teaching horsemanship **2** : the art of horsemanship or of training horses
ma•nes \'män-,ās, 'mā-,nēz\ *n pl, often cap* : the spirits of the dead and gods of the lower world in ancient Roman belief
1ma•neu•ver \mə-'n(y)ü-vər\ *n* **1 a** : a planned movement of troops or ships **b** : an armed forces training exercise; *esp* : an extensive exercise involving large-scale deployment of military or naval forces **2** : a skillful physical movement or procedure **3** : a clever often evasive move or action : a shift of position to gain a tactical end
2maneuver *vb* **1** : to move (as troops or ships) in a maneuver **2** : to perform a maneuver **3** : to guide with adroitness and design : HANDLE, MANIPULATE **4** : to use stratagems

: SCHEME — **ma·neu·ver·a·bil·i·ty** \-ˌn(y)üv-(ə-)rə-ˈbil-ət-ē\ *n* — **ma·neu·ver·a·ble** \-ˈn(y)üv-(ə-)rə-bəl\ *adj*

man·ful \ˈman-fəl\ *adj* : showing courage and resolution : BRAVE — **man·ful·ly** \-fə-lē\ *adv* — **man·ful·ness** *n*

man·ga·nese \ˈmaŋ-gə-ˌnēz, -ˌnēs\ *n* : a grayish white usu. hard and brittle metallic element that resembles iron but is not magnetic

mange \ˈmānj\ *n* : any of several persistent contagious skin diseases marked esp. by itching and loss of hair in domestic animals and sometimes man; *esp* : one caused by a minute parasitic mite

man·gel–wur·zel \ˈmaŋ-gəl-ˌwər-zəl\ *n* : a large coarse yellow to reddish orange beet extensively grown as food for cattle

man·ger \ˈmān-jər\ *n* : a trough or open box for livestock feed or fodder

[1]**man·gle** \ˈmaŋ-gəl\ *vt* **man·gled**; **man·gling** \-g(ə-)liŋ\ **1** : to cut, bruise, or hack with repeated blows or strokes **2** : to spoil or injure in making or performing — **man·gler** \-g(ə-)lər\ *n*

[2]**mangle** *n* : a machine for ironing laundry by passing it between heated rollers

[3]**mangle** *vt* **man·gled**; **man·gling** \-g(ə-)liŋ\ : to press or smooth with a mangle — **man·gler** \-g(ə-)lər\ *n*

man·go \ˈmaŋ-gō\ *n, pl* **mangoes** *or* **mangos** : a yellowish red tropical fruit with a firm skin, hard central stone, and juicy aromatic mildly acid pulp; *also* : the evergreen tree of the sumac family that bears this fruit

man·grove \ˈman-ˌgrōv, ˈmaŋ-\ *n* : any of various tropical maritime trees or shrubs that throw out many prop roots and form dense masses

mangy \ˈmān-jē\ *adj* **1** : affected with or resulting from mange **2** : having many worn-out or bare spots : SHABBY, SEEDY — **mang·i·ness** *n*

man·han·dle \ˈman-ˌhan-dᵊl\ *vt* **1** : to move or manage by human force **2** : to handle roughly

man·hole \ˈman-ˌhōl\ *n* : a hole (as in a pavement, tank, or boiler) through which a man may go

man·hood \-ˌhu̇d\ *n* **1** : manly qualities : COURAGE, VIRILITY **2** : the condition of being an adult male **3** : adult males : MEN

man–hour *n* : a unit of one hour's work by one man used esp. as a basis for wages and cost accounting

man·hunt \ˈman-ˌhənt\ *n* : an organized hunt for a person and esp. for one charged with a crime

ma·nia \ˈmā-nē-ə, -nyə\ *n* **1** : MADNESS; *esp* : insanity characterized by uncontrollable emotion or excitement **2** : excessive or unreasonable enthusiasm : CRAZE

[1]**ma·ni·ac** \ˈmā-nē-ˌak\ *adj* **1** : affected with or suggestive of madness **2** : characterized by ungovernable excitement or frenzy : FRANTIC — **ma·ni·a·cal** \mə-ˈnī-ə-kəl\ *adj* — **ma·ni·a·cal·ly** \-k(ə-)lē\ *adv*

[2]**maniac** *n* **1** : LUNATIC, MADMAN **2** : a person characterized by an uncontrollable enthusiasm for something

man·ic \ˈman-ik\ *adj* : affected with, relating to, or resembling mania — **manic** *n*

man·ic–de·pres·sive \ˌman-ik-di-ˈpres-iv\ *adj* : characterized by alternating mania and depression — **manic–depressive** *n*

[1]**man·i·cure** \ˈman-ə-ˌkyu̇(ə)r\ *n* **1** : MANICURIST **2** : a treatment for the care of the hands and nails

[2]**manicure** *vt* **1** : to give a manicure to **2** : to trim closely and evenly

man·i·cur·ist \-ˌkyu̇r-əst\ *n* : a person who gives manicures

[1]**man·i·fest** \ˈman-ə-ˌfest\ *adj* : readily perceived by the senses or by the mind : OBVIOUS — **man·i·fest·ly** *adv*

[2]**manifest** *vt* : to show plainly : make evident : DISPLAY

[3]**manifest** *n* : a list (as of cargo or passengers) esp. for a ship or plane

man·i·fes·ta·tion \ˌman-ə-fə-ˈstā-shən, -ˌfes-ˈtā-\ *n* **1 a** : the act, process, or an instance of manifesting : EXPRESSION **b** : something that manifests : EVIDENCE **2** : a public demonstration of power and purpose

man·i·fes·to \ˌman-ə-ˈfes-tō\ *n, pl* **-tos** *or* **-toes** : a public declaration of policy, purpose, or views

[1]**man·i·fold** \ˈman-ə-ˌfōld\ *adj* **1** : of many and various kinds **2** : including or uniting various features : MULTIFARIOUS **3** : consisting of or operating many of one kind joined together — **man·i·fold·ly** *adv* — **man·i·fold·ness** *n*

[2]**manifold** *n* : something that is manifold: as **a** : a whole consisting of many diverse elements **b** : a pipe fitting having several outlets for connecting one pipe with others

[3]**manifold** *vb* **1** : to make many or several copies **2** : MULTIPLY

man·i·kin *or* **man·ni·kin** \ˈman-i-kən\ *n* **1** : MANNEQUIN **2** : a little man : DWARF, PYGMY

ma·nila \mə-ˈnil-ə\ *adj* **1** : made of manila paper **2** *often cap* : made from Manila hemp

Manila hemp *n* : a tough fiber from a Philippine banana plant used esp. for cordage

manila paper *n, often cap M* : a tough brownish paper made orig. from Manila hemp and used esp. as a wrapping paper

man in the street : an average or ordinary man

ma·nip·u·late \mə-ˈnip-yə-ˌlāt\ *vt* **1** : to treat or operate with the hands or by mechanical means esp. with skill **2 a** : to manage or utilize skillfully **b** : to manage artfully or fraudulently **c** : to influence (as prices of stocks) by artificial means **d** : to play upon or control by artful, unfair, or insidious means — **ma·nip·u·la·tion** \-ˌnip-yə-ˈlā-shən\ *n* — **ma·nip·u·la·tor** \-ˈnip-yə-ˌlāt-ər\ *n*

man·kind *n* **1** \ˈman-ˈkīnd, -ˌkīnd\ : the human race : the totality of human beings **2** \-ˌkīnd\ : men as distinguished from women

man·like \ˈman-ˌlīk\ *adj* : resembling or characteristic of a man : MANNISH

man·li·ness \ˈman-lē-nəs\ *n* : manly conduct or character

man·ly \ˈman-lē\ *adj* **1** : having qualities appropriate to a man : BRAVE, RESOLUTE **2** : befitting a man

man–made \ˈman-ˈmād\ *adj* : made by man rather than nature; *also* : SYNTHETIC

man·na \ˈman-ə\ *n* **1** : food miraculously supplied to the Israelites in the wilderness **2** : something likened to the biblical manna esp. in being much needed and joyfully received

manned \ˈmand\ *adj* : carrying or performed by a man

man·ne·quin \ˈman-i-kən\ *n* **1** : an artist's, tailor's, or dressmaker's jointed figure of the human body; *also* : a form representing the human figure used esp. for displaying clothes **2** : a woman who models clothing : MODEL

man·ner \ˈman-ər\ *n* **1 a** : KIND **b** : SORTS **2 a** : a way of acting or proceeding **b** : HABIT, CUSTOM **c** : STYLE **3 a** *pl* : social conduct or rules of conduct as shown in the prevalent customs : MORES **b** *pl* : characteristic or habitual deportment : BEHAVIOR **c** : BEARING, AIR

man·nered \ˈman-ərd\ *adj* **1** : having manners of a specified kind **2** : having an artificial character

man·ner·ism \ˈman-ə-ˌriz-əm\ *n* **1** : affected use of a particular style or manner : ARTIFICIALITY **2** : a peculiarity of action, bearing, or treatment

man·ner·ly \ˈman-ər-lē\ *adj* : showing good manners : POLITE — **man·ner·li·ness** *n* — **mannerly** *adv*

man·nish \ˈman-ish\ *adj* **1** : resembling or suggesting a man rather than a woman **2** : suitable to or characteristic of a man rather than a woman — **man·nish·ly** *adv* — **man·nish·ness** *n*

man–of–war \ˌman-ə(v)-ˈwȯ(ə)r\ *n, pl* **men–of–war** \ˌmen-\ : WARSHIP

man·or \ˈman-ər\ *n* : a usu. large landed estate; *esp* : one granted by a sovereign to a feudal lord with rights over land and tenants — **ma·no·ri·al** \mə-ˈnōr-ē-əl\ *adj* — **ma·no·ri·al·ism** \-ē-ə-ˌliz-əm\ *n*

manor house *n* : the house of the lord of a manor

man power *n* **1 :** power available from or supplied by the physical effort of man **2** *usu* **man•pow•er** \'man-ˌpau̇(-ə)r\ **:** the total supply of persons available and fitted for service (as military or industrial)
man•sard \'man-ˌsärd, -sərd\ *n* **:** a roof having two slopes on all sides with the lower slope steeper than the upper one
manse \'man(t)s\ *n* **:** the residence of a clergyman; *esp* **:** the house of a Presbyterian clergyman
man•ser•vant \'man-ˌsər-vənt\ *n, pl* **men•ser•vants** \'men-ˌsər-vən(t)s\ **:** a male servant
man•sion \'man-chən\ *n* **:** a large imposing residence
man–size \'man-ˌsīz\ *or* **man–sized** \-ˌsīzd\ *adj* **1 :** suitable for or requiring a man **2 :** LARGE-SCALE
man•slaugh•ter \'man-ˌslȯt-ər\ *n* **:** the unlawful killing of a person without intent to do so
man•slay•er \-ˌslā-ər\ *n* **:** one who slays a man
man•sue•tude \'man(t)-swi-ˌt(y)üd, man-'sü-ə-ˌt(y)üd\ *n* **:** the quality or state of being gentle **:** MEEKNESS, TAMENESS
man•ta \'mant-ə\ *n* **:** a square piece of cloth or blanket used in southwestern U.S. and Latin America as a cloak or shawl
man•teau \man-'tō\ *n* **:** a loose cloak, coat, or robe
man•tel \'mant-ᵊl\ *n* **1 :** the beam, stone, arch, or shelf above a fireplace **2 :** the finish around a fireplace
man•telet \'mant-lət\ *n* **:** a very short cape or cloak
man•tel•piece \'mant-ᵊl-ˌpēs\ *n* **1 :** a mantel with its side elements **2 :** the shelf of a mantel
man•til•la \man-'tē-(y)ə, -'til-ə\ *n* **1 :** a light scarf worn over the head and shoulders esp. by Spanish and Latin American women **2 :** a short light cape or cloak
man•tis \'mant-əs\ *n, pl* **man•tis•es** *or* **man•tes** \'man-ˌtēz\ **:** any of various insects related to the grasshoppers and roaches that feed upon other insects and clasp the prey in forelimbs held up as if in prayer
[1]man•tle \'mant-ᵊl\ *n* **1 :** a loose sleeveless outer garment **:** CLOAK **2 :** something that covers or envelops **3 :** a lacy sheath that gives light by incandescence when placed over a flame
[2]mantle *vt* **man•tled**; **man•tling** \'mant-liŋ, -ᵊl-iŋ\ **:** to cover or envelop with or as if with a mantle
man•tra \'man-trə\ *n* **:** a mystical formula of invocation or incantation (as in Hinduism)
man•trap \'man-ˌtrap\ *n* **:** a trap for catching men **:** SNARE
man•tua \'manch-(ə-)wə\ *n* **:** a usu. loose-fitting gown worn esp. in the 17th and 18th centuries
[1]man•u•al \'man-yə(-wə)l\ *adj* **1 a :** of, relating to, or involving the hands **b :** worked by hand **2 :** requiring or using physical skill and energy — **man•u•al•ly** \-ē\ *adv*
[2]manual *n* **1 :** a book capable of being conveniently handled; *esp* **:** HANDBOOK **2 :** the set movements in the handling of a weapon during a military drill or ceremony
manual training *n* **:** a course of training to develop skill in using the hands and to teach practical arts (as woodworking)
man•u•fac•to•ry \ˌman-(y)ə-'fak-t(ə-)rē\ *n, pl* **-ries :** FACTORY
[1]man•u•fac•ture \ˌman-(y)ə-'fak-chər\ *n* **1 :** something made from raw materials **2 :** the process of making wares by hand or by machinery esp. when carried on systematically with division of labor **3 :** the act or process of producing something
[2]manufacture *vt* **-fac•tured**; **-fac•tur•ing** \-'fak-chə-riŋ, -'fak-shriŋ\ **1 :** to make into a product suitable for use **2 :** to make from raw materials by hand or by machinery **3 :** INVENT, FABRICATE — **man•u•fac•tur•ing** *n*
man•u•fac•tur•er \-'fak-chər-ər, -'fak-shrər\ *n* **:** one that manufactures; *esp* **:** an employer of workers in manufacturing
man•u•mis•sion \ˌman-yə-'mish-ən\ *n* **:** emancipation from slavery
man•u•mit \ˌman-yə-'mit\ *vt* **-mit•ted**; **-mit•ting :** to set free; *esp* **:** to release from slavery
[1]ma•nure \mə-'n(y)u̇(ə)r\ *vt* **:** to enrich (land) by the application of manure — **ma•nur•er** *n*
[2]manure *n* **:** material that fertilizes land; *esp* **:** the dung of livestock — **ma•nu•ri•al** \mə-'n(y)u̇r-ē-əl\ *adj*
[1]man•u•script \'man-yə-ˌskript\ *adj* **:** written by hand or typed
[2]manuscript *n* **1 :** a written or typewritten composition or document **2 :** writing as opposed to print
[1]many \'men-ē\ *adj* **more** \'mō(ə)r\; **most** \'mōst\ **1 :** consisting of or amounting to a large but indefinite number **2 :** being one of a large but indefinite number — **as many :** the same in number
[2]many *pron* **:** a large number of persons or things
[3]many *n* **:** a large but indefinite number
many•fold \ˌmen-ē-'fōld\ *adv* **:** by many times
many–sid•ed \ˌmen-ē-'sīd-əd\ *adj* **1 :** having many sides or aspects **2 :** having many interests or aptitudes **:** VERSATILE — **many•sid•ed•ness** *n*
[1]map \'map\ *n* **1 :** a drawing or picture showing features of the surface of the earth, another planet, or the moon **2 :** a drawing or picture of the sky showing the position of stars and planets
[2]map *vt* **mapped**; **map•ping 1 :** to study and make a map of **2 :** to chart the course of **:** plan in detail — **map•per** *n*
ma•ple \'mā-pəl\ *n* **:** any of a genus of trees or shrubs with opposite leaves and a 2-winged dry fruit; *also* **:** the hard light-colored close-grained wood of a maple
maple sugar *n* **:** a brown sugar made by boiling maple syrup
maple syrup *n* **:** syrup made by concentrating the sap of maples and esp. the sugar maple
ma•quis \ma-'kē, mä-\ *n, pl* **ma•quis** \-'kē(z)\ *often cap* **:** a guerrilla fighter in the French underground during World War II
mar \'mär\ *vt* **marred**; **mar•ring :** to make a blemish on **:** DAMAGE, SPOIL
ma•ra•ca \mə-'räk-ə, -'rak-\ *n* **:** a dried gourd or a rattle like a gourd that contains dried seeds or pebbles and is used as a percussion instrument
mar•a•schi•no \ˌmar-ə-'skē-nō, -'shē-\ *n, often cap* **1 :** a sweet liqueur distilled from the fermented juice of a bitter wild cherry **2 :** a usu. large cherry preserved in true or imitation maraschino
mar•a•thon \'mar-ə-ˌthän\ *n* **1 :** a long-distance race; *esp* **:** a footrace run on an open course of 26 miles 385 yards **2 :** an endurance contest — **marathon** *adj*
ma•raud \mə-'rȯd\ *vb* **:** to roam about and raid in search of plunder — **ma•raud•er** *n*
[1]mar•ble \'mär-bəl\ *n* **1 a :** limestone that is more or less crystallized by natural alteration, is capable of taking a high polish, and is used in architecture and sculpture **b :** something made from marble; *esp* **:** a piece of sculpture **2 a :** a little ball (as of glass) used in various games **b** *pl* **:** a children's game played with these little balls
[2]marble *vt* **mar•bled**; **mar•bling** \-b(ə-)liŋ\ **:** to give a veined or mottled appearance to (as by staining)
[3]marble *adj* **:** made of, resembling, or suggestive of marble
mar•ble•ize \'mär-bə-ˌlīz\ *vt* **:** MARBLE
mar•bling \'mär-b(ə-)liŋ\ *n* **1 :** coloration or markings resembling or suggestive of marble **2 :** an intermixture of fat through the lean of a cut of meat
mar•bly \'mär-b(ə-)lē\ *adj* **:** MARBLE
[1]mar•cel \mär-'sel\ *n* **:** a deep soft wave made in the hair by the use of a heated curling iron
[2]marcel *vt* **mar•celled**; **mar•cel•ling :** to make a marcel in
[1]march \'märch\ *n* **:** a border region **:** FRONTIER
[2]march *vi* **:** to have common borders or frontiers
[3]march *vb* **1 :** to move along with a steady regular stride esp. in step with others **2 a :** to move in a direct purposeful manner **:** PROCEED **b :** ADVANCE — **march•er** *n*

⁴march *n* **1 a :** the action of marching **b :** the distance covered within a specific period of time by marching **c :** a regular even step used in marching **2 :** forward movement : PROGRESS **3 :** a musical composition in duple rhythm (as 4/4 time) with a strongly accentuated beat suitable to accompany marching

March \'märch\ *n* **:** the 3d month of the year

mar·chio·ness \'mär-sh(ə-)nəs\ *n* **1 :** the wife or widow of a marquess **2 :** a woman who holds the rank of a marquess in her own right

march·pane \'märch-ˌpān\ *n* **:** MARZIPAN

march–past \'märch-ˌpast\ *n* **:** a marching by esp. of troops in review

Mar·di Gras \ˌmärd-ē-'grä\ *n* **:** the Tuesday before Ash Wednesday often observed with parades and merrymaking

mare \'ma(ə)r\ *n* **:** the female of a member of the horse family

mare's nest *n* **1 :** something that is thought wonderful at first but turns out to be imaginary or false **2 :** a situation or condition of great confusion : a hopeless tangle

mare's tail *n* **:** a cirrus cloud that has a long slender flowing appearance

mar·ga·rine \'märj-(ə-)rən, 'märj-ə-ˌrēn\ *n* **:** a food product made from usu. vegetable oils and skimmed milk often with vitamins A and D added and used as a spread and a cooking fat

¹mar·gin \'mär-jən\ *n* **1 :** the part of a page outside the main body of printed or written matter **2 :** BORDER, EDGE **3 a :** a spare amount (as of time or money) allowed for use if needed **b :** the limit below which economic activity cannot be continued under normal conditions **4 :** the difference which exists between net selling price and cost — **mar·gined** \-jənd\ *adj*

²margin *vt* **1 :** to provide with an edging or border **2 :** BORDER

mar·gin·al \'märj-nəl, -ən-ᵊl\ *adj* **1 :** written or printed in the margin of a page or sheet **2 :** of, relating to, or situated at a margin or border **3 a :** close to the lower limit of qualification or acceptability **b :** yielding a supply of goods which when marketed at existing price levels will barely cover the cost of production; *also* **:** relating to or derived from goods produced and marketed with such result — **mar·gin·al·i·ty** \ˌmär-jə-'nal-ət-ē\ *n* — **mar·gin·al·ly** \'märj-nə-lē, -ən-ᵊl-ē\ *adv*

mar·gi·na·lia \ˌmär-jə-'nā-lē-ə\ *n pl* **:** marginal notes

mari·gold \'mar-ə-ˌgōld, 'mer-\ *n* **:** any of a genus of tropical American herbs related to the daisies and grown for their showy yellow or red and yellow flower heads

mar·i·jua·na *or* **mar·i·hua·na** \ˌmar-ə-'(h)wän-ə\ *n* **:** a narcotic product of hemp

ma·rim·ba \mə-'rim-bə\ *n* **:** a primitive xylophone with resonators beneath each bar; *also* **:** a modern form of this instrument

ma·ri·na \mə-'rē-nə\ *n* **:** a dock or basin providing secure moorings for motorboats and yachts and often offering other facilities

¹mar·i·nade \ˌmar-ə-'nād\ *vt* **:** MARINATE

²marinade *n* **:** a brine or pickle in which meat or fish is soaked to enrich its flavor

mar·i·nate \'mar-ə-ˌnāt\ *vt* **:** to steep (as meat or fish) in a marinade

¹ma·rine \mə-'rēn\ *adj* **1 a :** of or relating to the sea **b :** of or relating to the navigation of the sea : NAUTICAL **c :** of or relating to the commerce of the sea : MARITIME **2 :** of or relating to marines

²marine *n* **1 :** the mercantile and naval shipping of a country **2 :** one of a class of soldiers serving on shipboard or in close association with a naval force; *esp* **:** a member of the U.S. Marine Corps

marine glue *n* **:** a water-insoluble adhesive

mar·i·ner \'mar-ə-nər\ *n* **:** one who navigates or assists in navigating a ship : SAILOR

mar·i·o·nette \ˌmar-ē-ə-'net, ˌmer-\ *n* **:** a puppet moved by strings or by hand

mar·i·tal \'mar-ət-ᵊl\ *adj* **:** of or relating to marriage : CONJUGAL — **mar·i·tal·ly** *adv*

mar·i·time \'mar-ə-ˌtīm\ *adj* **1 :** of or relating to navigation or commerce on the sea **2 :** bordering on or living or situated near the ocean **3 :** having characteristics controlled primarily by oceanic winds and air masses

mar·jo·ram \'märj-(ə-)rəm\ *n* **:** any of various usu. fragrant and aromatic mints sometimes used in cookery

¹mark \'märk\ *n* **1 :** a border territory : MARCH **2 a :** something (as a line, notch, or fixed object) designed to record position **b :** a conspicuous object serving as a guide for travelers **c** (1) **:** something aimed at : TARGET, GOAL (2) **:** the question under discussion **d :** an object of ridicule or abuse : BUTT **e :** the starting line or position in a track event **f :** a standard of performance, quality, or condition : NORM, RECORD **3 a :** SIGN, INDICATION **b :** a characteristic or distinguishing trait or quality **c :** a cross made in place of a signature **d :** a written or printed symbol **e :** a symbol (as a brand or label) used for identification or for indication of ownership or quality **f :** a symbol (as a number or letter) representing an estimation of the quality of work or conduct : GRADE **4 :** an impression (as a scar, scratch, or stain) made on a surface **5 :** a lasting or strong impression **6 :** ATTENTION, NOTICE **7 :** IMPORTANCE, DISTINCTION

²mark *vt* **1 a :** to fix or trace out the bounds of by or as if by a mark **b :** to set apart by a line or boundary **c :** CHART **2 a :** to designate as if by a mark **b :** to make a mark or notation on **c :** to furnish with natural marks **d :** to label so as to indicate price or quality **3 a :** to make note of in writing : JOT **b :** to indicate by a mark or symbol; *also* **:** RECORD **c :** to determine the value of by means of marks or symbols : GRADE **4 :** CHARACTERIZE, DISTINGUISH **5 :** to take notice of : OBSERVE — **mark time 1 :** to keep the time of a marching step by moving the feet alternately without advancing **2 :** to function or operate without making progress

mark down *vt* **:** to put a lower price on

mark·down \'märk-ˌdau̇n\ *n* **1 :** a lowering of price **2 :** the amount by which an original selling price is reduced

marked \'märkt\ *adj* **1 :** having marks **2 :** having a distinctive character : NOTICEABLE **3 a :** enjoying fame or notoriety **b :** being an object of attack, suspicion, or vengeance — **mark·ed·ly** \'mär-kəd-lē\ *adv*

mark·er \'mär-kər\ *n* **1 :** one that marks **2 :** something used for marking

¹mar·ket \'mär-kət\ *n* **1 a :** a meeting together of people to buy and sell **b :** a public place where a market is held **c :** a retail establishment usu. of a specified kind **2 a :** a geographical area of demand for commodities **b :** an opportunity for selling **3 :** the area of economic activity in which buyers and sellers come together and the forces of supply and demand affect prices

²market *vb* **1 :** to deal in a market **2 :** to offer for sale in a market : SELL — **mar·ke·teer** \ˌmär-kə-'ti(ə)r\ *or* **mar·ket·er** *n* — **mar·ket·ing** *n*

mar·ket·a·ble \'mär-kət-ə-bəl\ *adj* **1 :** fit to be offered for sale in a market **2 :** wanted by purchasers : SALABLE — **mar·ket·a·bil·i·ty** \ˌmär-kət-ə-'bil-ət-ē\ *n*

market garden *n* **:** a plot in which vegetables are raised for market — **market gardener** *n* — **market gardening** *n*

mar·ket·place \'mär-kət-ˌplās\ *n* **1 :** an open square or place in a town where markets or public sales are held **2 :** the world of trade or economic activity

market price *n* **:** a price actually given or obtainable in current market dealings

market research *n* **:** the gathering of factual information as to consumer preferences for goods and services

market value *n* : the value of a commodity determined by current market prices
mark·ing \'mär-kiŋ\ *n* **1** : the act, process, or an instance of making or giving a mark **2** : a mark made
marks·man \'märks-mən\ *n* : one that shoots at a mark; *esp* : a person skilled at target shooting — **marks·man·ship** \-,ship\ *n*
mark up *vt* : to put a higher price on
mark·up \'märk-,əp\ *n* **1** : a raising of price **2** : an amount added to the cost price of an article to determine the selling price
[1]**marl** \'märl\ *n* : a loose or crumbling earthy deposit that contains a substantial amount of calcium carbonate — **marly** \'mär-lē\ *adj*
[2]**marl** *vt* : to dress (land) with marl
mar·lin \'mär-lən\ *n* : a large oceanic sport fish
mar·line \'mär-lən\ *n* : a small loosely twisted line of two strands used for seizing and as a covering for wire rope
mar·line·spike \'mär-lən-,spīk\ *n* : a pointed iron tool used to separate strands of rope or wire (as in splicing)
mar·ma·lade \'mär-mə-,lād\ *n* : a clear jelly holding in suspension pieces of fruit and fruit rind
mar·mo·re·al \mär-'mōr-ē-əl\ *adj* : of, relating to, or resembling marble or a marble statue
mar·mo·set \'mär-mə-,set\ *n* : any of numerous soft-furred bushy-tailed So. and Central American monkeys with claws instead of nails except on the great toe
mar·mot \'mär-mət\ *n* : a stout-bodied short-legged burrowing No. American rodent
[1]**ma·roon** \mə-'rün\ *vt* **1** : to put ashore and abandon on a desolate island or coast **2** : to leave isolated and helpless
[2]**maroon** *n* : a variable color averaging a dark red
mar·plot \'mär-,plät\ *n* : one who frustrates or ruins a plan or undertaking by his meddling
mar·quee \mär-'kē\ *n* **1** : a large field tent set up for an outdoor party, reception, or exhibition **2** : a canopy usu. of metal and glass projecting over an entrance
mar·quess \'mär-kwəs\ *n* **1** : a nobleman of hereditary rank in Europe and Japan **2** : a member of the British peerage ranking below a duke and above an earl
mar·que·try \'mär-kə-trē\ *n, pl* **-tries** : decoration in which elaborate patterns are formed by the insertion of pieces of wood, shell, or ivory into a wood veneer that is then applied to a piece of furniture
mar·quis \'mär-kwəs, mär-'kē\ *n, pl* **mar·quises** \-kwə-səz, -'kēz\ : MARQUESS
mar·quise \mär-'kēz\ *n, pl* **mar·quises** \-'kēz(-əz)\ : MARCHIONESS
mar·qui·sette \,mär-k(w)ə-'zet\ *n* : a sheer meshed fabric
mar·riage \'mar-ij\ *n* **1 a** : the state of being married **b** : the mutual relation of husband and wife : WEDLOCK **c** : the institution whereby a man and a woman are joined in a special social and legal relationship for the purpose of making a home and raising a family **2** : an act of marrying; *esp* : the wedding ceremony and attendant festivities or formalities **3** : an intimate or close union — **mar·riage·a·ble** *adj*
marriage of convenience : a marriage contracted for social, political, or economic advantage
mar·ried \'mar-ēd\ *adj* **1** : united in marriage : WEDDED **2** : of or relating to marriage : CONNUBIAL
mar·row \'mar-ō\ *n* **1** : a soft vascular tissue that fills the cavities of most bones **2** : the inmost, best, or essential part — **mar·row·less** \-ō-ləs\ *adj* — **mar·rowy** \'mar-ə-wē\ *adj*
mar·row·bone \'mar-ə-,bōn\ *n* **1** : a bone (as a shinbone) rich in marrow **2** *pl* : KNEES
mar·ry \'mar-ē\ *vb* **mar·ried**; **mar·ry·ing** **1 a** : to join as husband and wife according to law or custom **b** : to give in marriage **c** : to take as husband or wife **d** : to take a spouse : WED **2** : to unite in close and usu. permanent relation
marsh \'märsh\ *n* : an area of soft wet land usu. overgrown by grasses and sedges
[1]**mar·shal** \'mär-shəl\ *n* **1 a** : a high official in a medieval royal household **b** : a person who arranges and directs ceremonies **2** : a general officer of the highest rank in some military forces **3 a** : a federal official in a U.S. judicial district having duties similar to those of a sheriff **b** : a municipal official having similar duties
[2]**marshal** *vt* **-shaled** *or* **-shalled**; **-shal·ing** *or* **-shal·ling** \'märsh-(ə-)liŋ\ **1** : to arrange in proper position, rank, or order **2** : to lead with ceremony : USHER
marsh·mal·low \'märsh-,mel-ō, -,mal-\ *n* : a sweetened pasty confection made from corn syrup, sugar, albumen, and gelatin beaten to a light creamy consistency
marshy \'mär-shē\ *adj* **1** : resembling or constituting marsh **2** : of or relating to marshes — **marsh·i·ness** *n*
[1]**mar·su·pi·al** \mär-'sü-pē-əl\ *adj* : of, relating to, or being a marsupial
[2]**marsupial** *n* : any of an order of lowly mammals comprising kangaroos, opossums, and related animals that have a pouch on the abdomen of the female containing the teats and serving to carry the young
mart \'märt\ *n* : a trading place : MARKET
mar·ten \'märt-ᵊn\ *n, pl* **marten** *or* **martens** : a slim flesh-eating mammal larger than the related weasels; *also* : its soft gray or brown fur
mar·tial \'mär-shəl\ *adj* **1** : of, relating to, or suited for war or a warrior **2** : of or relating to an army or to military life — **mar·tial·ly** \-shə-lē\ *adv*
martial law *n* **1** : the law applied in occupied territory by the military forces of the occupying power **2** : the established law of a country administered by military forces in an emergency when civilian law enforcement agencies are unable to maintain public order and safety
mar·tin \'märt-ᵊn\ *n* : any of various swallows and flycatchers
mar·ti·net \,märt-ᵊn-'et\ *n* : a strict disciplinarian
mar·tin·gale \'märt-ᵊn-,gāl\ *n* : a strap connecting a horse's girth to the bit or reins so as to hold down its head
[1]**mar·tyr** \'märt-ər\ *n* **1** : a person who suffers death rather than give up his religion **2** : one who sacrifices his life or something of great value for the sake of principle or devotion to a cause **3** : a great or constant sufferer — **mar·tyr·i·za·tion** \,märt-ə-rə-'zā-shən\ *n* — **mar·tyr·ize** \'märt-ə-,rīz\ *vb*
[2]**martyr** *vt* **1** : to put to death for adhering to a belief **2** : TORTURE
mar·tyr·dom \'märt-ərd-əm\ *n* **1** : the sufferings and death of a martyr **2** : TORTURE
[1]**mar·vel** \'mär-vəl\ *n* : something that causes wonder or astonishment
[2]**marvel** *vb* **mar·veled** *or* **mar·velled**; **mar·vel·ing** *or* **mar·vel·ling** \'märv-(ə-)liŋ\ : to become filled with surprise, wonder, or astonishment
mar·vel·ous *or* **mar·vel·lous** \'märv-(ə-)ləs\ *adj* **1** : causing wonder : ASTONISHING **2** : having the characteristics of a miracle **3** : of the highest kind or quality : SPLENDID — **mar·vel·ous·ly** *adv* — **mar·vel·ous·ness** *n*
Marx·ism \'märk-,siz-əm\ *n* : the political and economic doctrines developed by Karl Marx and Friedrich Engels — **Marx·ist** \-səst\ *n or adj*
mar·zi·pan \'märt-sə-,pän, 'mär-zə-,pan\ *n* : a confection of almond paste, sugar, and whites of eggs
mas·cara \ma-'skar-ə\ *n* : a cosmetic for coloring the eyelashes and eyebrows
mas·cot \'mas-,kät\ *n* : a person, animal, or object believed to bring good luck
[1]**mas·cu·line** \'mas-kyə-lən\ *adj* **1** : of the male sex **2** : characteristic of or belonging to men : MANLY **3** : of, relating to, or constituting the class of words that ordinarily includes

most of those referring to males **4 :** having or occurring in a stressed final syllable — **mas·cu·line·ly** *adv* — **mas·cu·line·ness** *n* — **mas·cu·lin·i·ty** \ˌmas-kyə-ˈlin-ət-ē\ *n*

²masculine *n* **1 :** a word or form of the masculine gender **2 :** the masculine gender

ma·ser \ˈmā-zər\ *n* **:** a device that utilizes the natural oscillations of atoms or molecules for amplifying or generating electromagnetic waves

¹mash \ˈmash\ *n* **1 :** crushed malt or grain meal steeped and stirred in hot water to produce wort **2 :** a mixture of ground feeds for livestock **3 :** a soft pulpy mass

²mash *vt* **1 :** to reduce to a soft pulpy state by beating or pressure **:** SMASH **2 :** to subject (as crushed malt) to the action of water with heating and stirring in preparing wort — **mash·er** *n*

¹mask \ˈmask\ *n* **1 :** a cover for the face used for disguise or protection **2 :** a device usu. covering the mouth and nose either to aid in or prevent the inhaling of something (as a gas or spray) **3 :** a covering (as of gauze) for the mouth and nose to prevent infective droplets from being blown into the air **4 :** something that disguises or conceals **:** CLOAK, PRETENSE **5 :** one that wears a mask **:** MASKER **6 :** a sculptured face or face and neck or a copy of a face made by means of a mold in plaster or wax **7 :** the face of a mammal (as a fox or dog) **8 :** a dramatic entertainment **:** MASQUE

²mask *vb* **1 :** to take part in a masquerade **2 :** to put on or wear a mask **3 :** CONCEAL, DISGUISE **4 :** to cover for protection

masked \ˈmaskt\ *adj* **1 :** wearing or using a mask **2 :** marked by or requiring the wearing of masks **3 :** CONCEALED, HIDDEN

mask·er \ˈmas-kər\ *n* **:** a person who wears a mask; *esp* **:** a participant in a masquerade

ma·son \ˈmās-ᵊn\ *n* **:** a person who builds or works with stone, brick, or cement

ma·son jar \ˌmās-ᵊn-\ *n* **:** a widemouthed jar used for home canning

ma·son·ry \ˈmās-ᵊn-rē\ *n, pl* **-ries 1 :** the art, trade, or occupation of a mason **2 :** the work done by a mason **3 :** something built of stone, brick, or concrete

masque \ˈmask\ *n* **1 :** MASQUERADE **2 :** a short allegorical dramatic entertainment of the 16th and 17th centuries performed by masked actors

masqu·er \ˈmas-kər\ *n* **:** MASKER

¹mas·quer·ade \ˌmas-kə-ˈrād\ *n* **1 a :** a social gathering of persons wearing masks and often fantastic costumes **b :** a costume for wear at such a gathering **2 :** an action or appearance that is mere disguise or outward show **:** POSE

²masquerade *vi* **1 a :** to disguise oneself or go about disguised **b :** to take part in a masquerade **2 :** to assume the appearance of something one is not **:** POSE — **mas·quer·ad·er** *n*

¹mass \ˈmas\ *n* **1** *cap* **:** a sequence of prayers and ceremonies forming the eucharistic office esp. of the Roman Catholic Church **2** *often cap* **:** a celebration of the Eucharist **3 :** a musical setting for parts of the Mass

²mass *n* **1 a :** a quantity of matter or the form of matter that holds or clings together in one body **b :** greatness of size **:** BULK, MAGNITUDE **c :** the principal part **:** main body **2 :** the quantity of matter in a body as measured by its inertia **3 :** a large quantity, amount, or number **4 a :** a large body of persons in a compact group **b** *pl* **:** the body of ordinary or common people as contrasted with the elite

³mass *vb* **:** to form or collect into a mass

⁴mass *adj* **1 a :** of, relating to, or designed for the mass of the people **b :** participated in by or affecting a large number of individuals **c :** LARGE-SCALE, WHOLESALE **2 :** viewed as a whole **:** TOTAL

¹mas·sa·cre \ˈmas-i-kər\ *vt* **-cred; -cring** \-k(ə-)riŋ\ **:** to kill in a massacre **:** SLAUGHTER — **mas·sa·crer** \-i-kər-ər, -i-krər\ *n*

²massacre *n* **1 :** the violent, cruel, and indiscriminate killing of a number of persons **2 :** a slaughter of animals in large numbers

¹mas·sage \mə-ˈsäzh, -ˈsäj\ *n* **:** treatment for remedial or hygienic purposes by rubbing, stroking, kneading, or tapping

²massage *vt* **:** to subject to massage — **mas·sag·er** *n*

mas·seur \ma-ˈsər\ *n* **:** a man who practices massage

mas·seuse \-ˈsə(r)z, -ˈsüz\ *n* **:** a woman who practices massage

mas·sif \ma-ˈsēf\ *n* **:** a principal mountain mass

mas·sive \ˈmas-iv\ *adj* **1 :** forming or consisting of a large mass: **a :** WEIGHTY, HEAVY **b :** impressively large or ponderous **2 a :** large, solid, or heavy in structure **b :** large in scope or degree — **mas·sive·ly** *adv* — **mas·sive·ness** *n*

mass medium *n, pl* **mass media :** a medium of communication (as newspapers, radio, or television) that is designed to reach the mass of the people

mass meeting *n* **:** a large or general assembly of people esp. for discussion of a public question

mass–pro·duce \ˌmas-prə-ˈd(y)üs\ *vt* **:** to produce in quantity usu. by machinery — **mass production** *n*

massy \ˈmas-ē\ *adj* **:** having bulk and weight or substance **:** MASSIVE

¹mast \ˈmast\ *n* **1 :** a long pole or spar that rises from the keel or deck of a ship and supports the yards, booms, sails, and rigging **2 :** a vertical or nearly vertical tall pole (as a post on a lifting crane) — **mast·ed** \ˈmas-təd\ *adj* — **before the mast :** in the position of a common sailor

²mast *vt* **:** to furnish with a mast

³mast *n* **:** nuts (as acorns) accumulated on the forest floor and often serving as food for animals (as hogs)

¹mas·ter \ˈmas-tər\ *n* **1 a :** a male teacher **b :** a person holding an academic degree higher than a bachelor's but lower than a doctor's **c** *often cap* **:** a revered religious leader **d :** an independent workman of proved proficiency; *esp* **:** one employing journeymen and apprentices **e :** an artist or performer of consummate skill **2 a :** one having authority over another **b :** VICTOR, SUPERIOR **c :** a person licensed to command a merchant ship **d :** an owner esp. of a slave or animal **e :** EMPLOYER **f :** the male head of a household **3 :** a youth or boy too young to be called *mister* — used as a title **4 :** a presiding officer in an institution or society (as a college)

²master *vt* **mas·tered; mas·ter·ing** \-t(ə-)riŋ\ **1 :** OVERCOME, SUBDUE **2 :** to become skilled or proficient in or in the use of

³master *adj* **1 :** being a master **2 :** GOVERNING, MAIN, PRINCIPAL **3 :** controlling the operation of other mechanisms **4 :** establishing a standard (as of dimension or weight) for reference

mas·ter–at–arms \ˌmas-tər-ət-ˈärmz\ *n, pl* **masters–at–arms :** a petty officer charged with maintaining discipline aboard ship

master chief petty officer *n* **:** a noncommissioned officer in the navy of the highest enlisted rank

mas·ter·ful \ˈmas-tər-fəl\ *adj* **1 :** inclined to take control or dominate **2 :** having or showing the technical or artistic skill of a master — **mas·ter·ful·ly** \-fə-lē\ *adv* — **mas·ter·ful·ness** *n*

master key *n* **:** a key designed to open several different locks

mas·ter·ly \ˈmas-tər-lē\ *adj* **:** suitable to or resembling a master; *esp* **:** showing superior knowledge or skill — **mas·ter·li·ness** *n* — **masterly** *adv*

mas·ter·mind \-ˌmīnd\ *n* **:** a person who supplies the directing or creative intelligence for a project — **mastermind** *vt*

master of ceremonies 1 : a person who determines the forms to be observed on a public occasion or acts as host at a formal event **2 :** a person who acts as host for a variety program (as on television)

mas·ter·piece \ˈmas-tər-ˌpēs\ *n* **1 :** a piece of work presented by a journeyman to a guild as evidence of qualification for the rank of master **2 :** a work done with extraordinary skill; *esp* **:** a supreme intellectual or artistic achievement

master race *n* : a people held to be racially preeminent and hence fitted to rule or enslave other peoples
master sergeant *n* : a noncommissioned officer ranking in the army next below a sergeant major and in the air force next below a senior master sergeant
mas·ter·ship \'mas-tər-,ship\ *n* **1** : the authority or control of a master **2** : the office or position of a master **3** : the proficiency of a master
mas·ter·stroke \-,strōk\ *n* : a masterly performance or move
mas·ter·work \-,wərk\ *n* : MASTERPIECE
mas·tery \'mas-t(ə-)rē\ *n, pl* **-ter·ies** **1** : the position or authority of a master : MASTERSHIP **2** : VICTORY, ASCENDANCY, SUPERIORITY **3** : skill or knowledge that makes one master of something : COMMAND
mast·head \'mast-,hed\ *n* **1** : the top of a mast **2 a** : the printed matter in a newspaper or periodical that gives the title and pertinent details of ownership, advertising rates, and subscription rates **b** : the name of a newspaper displayed on the top of the first page
mas·ti·cate \'mas-tə-,kāt\ *vb* : CHEW — **mas·ti·ca·tion** \,mas-tə-'kā-shən\ *n* — **mas·ti·ca·tor** \'mas-tə-,kāt-ər\ *n* — **mas·ti·ca·to·ry** \'mas-ti-kə-,tōr-ē\ *adj*
mas·tiff \'mas-təf\ *n* : a large powerful deep-chested smooth-coated dog used chiefly as a watchdog and guard dog
mas·to·don \'mas-tə-,dän\ *n* : any of numerous huge extinct mammals related to the mammoths and existing elephants — **mas·to·don·ic** \,mas-tə-'dän-ik\ *adj* — **mas·to·dont** \'mas-tə-,dänt\ *adj or n*
mas·toid \'mas-,tȯid\ *n* : a bony prominence behind the ear; *also* : an infection of this area — **mastoid** *adj*
¹mat \'mat\ *n* **1 a** : a piece of coarse fabric made of woven or braided rushes, straw, or wool **b** : a piece of material in front of a door to wipe the shoes on **c** : a piece of material (as leather, woven straw, or cloth) used under a dish or vase or as an ornament **d** : a pad or cushion for gymnastics or wrestling **2** : something made up of many intertwined or tangled strands
²mat *vb* **mat·ted**; **mat·ting** **1** : to provide with a mat or matting **2** : to form into a tangled mass
³mat *adj* : lacking or deprived of luster or gloss
⁴mat *n* **1** : a border going around a picture between picture and frame or serving as the frame **2** : a dull finish or a roughened surface (as in gilding or painting)
mat·a·dor \'mat-ə-,dȯ(ə)r\ *n* : a bullfighter who finally kills the bull with a sword thrust
¹match \'mach\ *n* **1 a** : a person or thing that is equal or similar to another **b** : a thing that is exactly like another **c** : one that is able to cope with another **2** : two persons or things that go well together **3 a** : MARRIAGE **b** : a person to be considered as a marriage partner **4** : a contest between two or more parties
²match *vb* **1** : to meet usu. successfully as a competitor **2 a** : to place in competition with **b** : to provide with a worthy competitor **3** : to join or give in marriage **4 a** : to make or find the equal or the like of **b** : to make correspond **c** : to be the same or suitable to one another : be or make a match **5 a** : to flip or toss (coins) and compare exposed faces **b** : to toss coins with (another)
³match *n* : a short slender piece of wood or other material tipped with a mixture that ignites when subjected to friction
match·book \'mach-,bu̇k\ *n* : a small folder containing rows of paper matches
match·less \'mach-ləs\ *adj* : having no equal : better than any other — **match·less·ly** *adv*
match·lock \'mach-,läk\ *n* : an old form of gunlock in which the charge was lighted by a cord match; *also* : a gun equipped with such a lock
match·mak·er \-,mā-kər\ *n* : one that arranges a match; *esp* : one that arranges marriages — **match·mak·ing** *n*
match·wood \-,wu̇d\ *n* : small pieces of wood
¹mate \'māt\ *vt* : CHECKMATE
²mate *n* : CHECKMATE
³mate *n* **1 a** : ASSOCIATE, COMPANION **b** : an assistant to a more skilled workman : HELPER **2** : a deck officer on a merchant ship ranking below the captain **3** : one of a pair: as **a** : either member of a married couple **b** : either member of a breeding pair of animals **c** : either of two matched objects
⁴mate *vb* **1** : to join or fit together **2 a** : to bring together as mates **b** : to provide a mate for
⁵ma·té *or* **ma·te** \'mä-,tā\ *n* : an aromatic beverage made from the leaves and shoots of a So. American holly; *also* : these leaves and shoots
¹ma·te·ri·al \mə-'tir-ē-əl\ *adj* **1 a** : relating to, derived from, or consisting of matter; *esp* : PHYSICAL **b** : BODILY **2 a** : having real importance or great consequence **b** : ESSENTIAL, RELEVANT, PERTINENT **3** : relating to or concerned with physical rather than spiritual or intellectual things — **ma·te·ri·al·i·ty** \-,tir-ē-'al-ət-ē\ *n* — **ma·te·ri·al·ly** \-'tir-ē-ə-lē\ *adv* — **ma·te·ri·al·ness** *n*
²material *n* **1** : the elements, constituents, or substance of which something is composed or can be made **2 a** : apparatus necessary for doing or making something **b** : MATÉRIEL
ma·te·ri·al·ism \mə-'tir-ē-ə-,liz-əm\ *n* **1 a** : a theory that matter is the only reality and that everything can be explained as either being or coming from matter **b** : a doctrine that the only or the highest values lie in material well-being and material progress **2** : a preoccupation with material rather than intellectual or spiritual things — **ma·te·ri·al·ist** \-ē-ə-ləst\ *n or adj* — **ma·te·ri·al·is·tic** \-,tir-ē-ə-'lis-tik\ *adj* — **ma·te·ri·al·is·ti·cal·ly** \-'lis-ti-k(ə-)lē\ *adv*
ma·te·ri·al·ize \mə-'tir-ē-ə-,līz\ *vb* **1 a** : to make material : give form and substance to **b** : to cause to appear in bodily form **2** : to assume bodily form **3 a** : to come into existence : become realized fact **b** : to put in an appearance; *esp* : to appear suddenly — **ma·te·ri·al·i·za·tion** \-,tir-ē-ə-lə-'zā-shən\ *n* — **ma·te·ri·al·iz·er** *n*
ma·te·ria med·i·ca \mə-,tir-ē-ə-'med-i-kə\ *n* **1** : substances used in the composition of medical remedies : DRUGS, MEDICINE **2** : a branch of medical science that deals with the sources, nature, properties, and preparation of drugs
ma·té·ri·el *or* **ma·te·ri·el** \mə-,tir-ē-'el\ *n* : equipment, apparatus, and supplies used by an organization or institution
ma·ter·nal \mə-'tərn-ᵊl\ *adj* **1** : of, relating to, or characteristic of a mother : MOTHERLY **2 a** : related through a mother **b** : derived or received from a mother — **ma·ter·nal·ly** \-ᵊl-ē\ *adv*
ma·ter·ni·ty \mə-'tər-nət-ē\ *n, pl* **-ties** **1** : the state of being a mother : MOTHERHOOD **2** : motherly character or qualities : MOTHERLINESS
math \'math\ *n* : MATHEMATICS
math·e·mat·i·cal \,math-ə-'mat-i-kəl\ *adj* **1** : of, relating to, or according with mathematics **2** : very exact : PRECISE **3** : possible but highly improbable — **math·e·mat·i·cal·ly** \-i-k(ə-)lē\ *adv*
math·e·ma·ti·cian \,math-(ə-)mə-'tish-ən\ *n* : a specialist or expert in mathematics
math·e·mat·ics \,math-ə-'mat-iks\ *n* : the science of numbers and their operations, interrelations, and combinations and of space configurations and their structure and measurement
mat·i·nee *or* **mat·i·née** \,mat-ᵊn-'ā\ *n* : a musical or dramatic performance or a social event (as a reception) held in the daytime and esp. in the afternoon
mat·ins \'mat-ᵊnz\ *n pl, often cap* : the service of morning prayer in churches of the Anglican communion
ma·tri·arch \'mā-trē-,ärk\ *n* : a woman who rules a family, group, or state; *esp* : a mother who is head and ruler of her family and descendants — **ma·tri·ar·chal** \,mā-trē-'är-kəl\ *adj*

ma·tri·ar·chate \-ˌär-kət, -ˌkāt\ *n* : a family, group, or state governed by a matriarch

ma·tri·ar·chy \-ˌär-kē\ *n, pl* **-chies** 1 : MATRIARCHATE 2 : a system of social organization in which descent and inheritance are traced through the female line

ma·tri·cide \ˈma-trə-ˌsīd, ˈmā-\ *n* 1 : murder of a mother by her child 2 : one that murders his mother — **ma·tri·ci·dal** \ˌma-trə-ˈsīd-ᵊl, ˌmā-\ *adj*

ma·tric·u·late \mə-ˈtrik-yə-ˌlāt\ *vb* : to enroll as a member of a body and esp. of a college or university — **ma·tric·u·la·tion** \-ˌtrik-yə-ˈlā-shən\ *n*

ma·tri·lin·e·al \ˌma-trə-ˈlin-ē-əl, ˌmā-\ *adj* : relating to, based on, or tracing descent through the maternal line — **ma·tri·lin·e·al·ly** \-ē-ə-lē\ *adv*

mat·ri·mo·ni·al \ˌma-trə-ˈmō-nē-əl\ *adj* : of or relating to matrimony — **mat·ri·mo·ni·al·ly** \-nē-ə-lē\ *adv*

mat·ri·mo·ny \ˈma-trə-ˌmō-nē\ *n, pl* **-nies** : the union of man and woman as husband and wife : MARRIAGE

ma·trix \ˈmā-triks\ *n, pl* **ma·tri·ces** \ˈmā-trə-ˌsēz, ˈma-\ *or* **ma·trix·es** \ˈmā-trik-səz\ 1 : something within which something else originates or develops 2 : something (as a mold) that gives form, foundation, or origin to something else (as molten metal) enclosed in it

ma·tron \ˈmā-trən\ *n* 1 : a married woman usu. marked by dignified maturity or social distinction 2 : a woman supervisor (as in a school or police station)

ma·tron·ly \-lē\ *adj* : of or resembling a matron : suitable for a matron

matron of honor : a married woman serving as the principal wedding attendant of a bride

[1]**mat·ter** \ˈmat-ər\ *n* 1 a : a subject of interest or concern (as a topic under consideration or a cause of disagreement or dispute) b : something to be dealt with : AFFAIR, CONCERN c : a condition affecting a person or thing usu. unfavorably 2 : the material of thought or discourse esp. as contrasted with its form 3 a : the substance of which a physical object is composed : something that occupies space and has weight b : material substance of a particular kind or function c : PUS 4 : a more or less definite amount or quantity 5 : something written or printed 6 : MAIL

[2]**matter** *vi* 1 : to be of importance : SIGNIFY 2 : to form or discharge pus : SUPPURATE

matter of course : something that may be expected as a natural or logical result of something else — **mat·ter–of–course** \ˌmat-ər-ə(v)-ˈkōrs\ *adj*

mat·ter–of–fact \ˌmat-ər-ə-ˈfakt\ *adj* : adhering to or concerned with fact; *esp* : not fanciful or imaginative : PRACTICAL, COMMONPLACE — **mat·ter–of–fact·ly** *adv* — **mat·ter–of–fact·ness** *n*

mat·ting \ˈmat-iŋ\ *n* 1 : material for mats 2 : MATS

mat·tock \ˈmat-ək\ *n* : a long-handled digging tool combining an adz blade with either an ax blade or a pick

mat·tress \ˈma-trəs\ *n* 1 : a fabric case filled with resilient material used either alone as a bed or on a bedstead 2 : an inflatable airtight sack for use as a mattress

mat·u·rate \ˈmach-ə-ˌrāt\ *vb* : MATURE

mat·u·ra·tion \ˌmach-ə-ˈrā-shən\ *n* : the process of becoming mature

[1]**ma·ture** \mə-ˈt(y)u̇(ə)r\ *adj* 1 : based on slow careful consideration 2 a : fully grown and developed : ADULT, RIPE b : having attained a final or desired state 3 : of or relating to a condition of full development 4 : due for payment — **ma·ture·ly** *adv* — **ma·ture·ness** *n*

[2]**mature** *vb* 1 : to bring to maturity or completion 2 : to become fully developed or ripe 3 : to become due

ma·tu·ri·ty \mə-ˈt(y)u̇r-ət-ē\ *n* 1 : the quality or state of being mature; *esp* : full development 2 : the date when an obligation (as a bond or note) becomes due

ma·tu·ti·nal \ˌmach-u̇-ˈtīn-ᵊl, mə-ˈt(y)üt-ᵊn-əl\ *adj* : of, relating to, or occurring in the morning : EARLY — **ma·tu·ti·nal·ly** \-ē\ *adv*

mat·zo \ˈmät-sə, ˌ-sō\ *n, pl* **mat·zoth** *or* **mat·zos** \-səz, -səs, -ˌsōz, -ˌsōs, -ˌsōth\ 1 : unleavened bread traditionally eaten at the Passover 2 : a wafer of matzo

matzo ball *n* : a small dumpling made from matzo meal

maud·lin \ˈmȯd-lən\ *adj* 1 : weakly and excessively sentimental 2 : drunk enough to be tearfully silly

[1]**maul** \ˈmȯl\ *n* : a heavy hammer often with a wooden head used esp. for driving wedges or posts

[2]**maul** *vt* 1 : BEAT, BRUISE 2 : to injure by beating : MANGLE 3 : to handle roughly — **maul·er** *n*

maun·der \ˈmȯn-dər\ *vi* **maun·dered**; **maun·der·ing** \-d(ə-)riŋ\ 1 : to wander slowly and idly 2 : to speak disconnectedly or without apparent plan or purpose

mau·so·le·um \ˌmȯ-sə-ˈlē-əm\ *n, pl* **-le·ums** *or* **-lea** \-ˈlē-ə\ : a large tomb; *esp* : a usu. stone building for the entombment of the dead above ground

mauve \ˈmōv\ *n* : a moderate purple, violet, or lilac color

mav·er·ick \ˈmav-(ə-)rik\ *n* 1 : an unbranded range animal; *esp* : a motherless calf 2 : a person who refuses to follow the leadership of his political party or conform with his group and sets an independent course

ma·vis \ˈmā-vəs\ *n* : an Old World thrush

maw \ˈmȯ\ *n* 1 : the receptacle into which food is taken by swallowing: a : STOMACH b : CROP 2 : the throat, gullet, or jaws esp. of a voracious carnivore

mawk·ish \ˈmȯ-kish\ *adj* 1 : having an insipid often unpleasant taste 2 : marked by sickly sentimentality — **mawk·ish·ly** *adv* — **mawk·ish·ness** *n*

max·il·la \mak-ˈsil-ə\ *n, pl* **max·il·lae** \-ˈsil-(ˌ)ē\ *or* **max·il·las** : JAW; *esp* : an upper jaw — **max·il·lary** \ˈmak-sə-ˌler-ē\ *adj or n*

max·im \ˈmak-səm\ *n* 1 : a general truth, fundamental principle, or rule of conduct 2 : a proverbial saying

max·i·mal \ˈmak-s(ə-)məl\ *adj* : MAXIMUM — **max·i·mal·ly** *adv*

max·i·mize \ˈmak-sə-ˌmīz\ *vb* 1 : to raise to the highest degree 2 : to assign maximum importance to 3 : to interpret something in the broadest sense — **max·i·miz·er** *n*

max·i·mum \ˈmak-s(ə-)məm\ *n, pl* **max·i·mums** *or* **max·i·ma** \-sə-mə\ 1 a : the greatest quantity or value attainable or attained b : the period of highest, greatest, or utmost development 2 : an upper limit allowed by authority — **maximum** *adj*

may \(ˈ)mā\ *auxiliary verb, past* **might** \(ˈ)mīt\; *pres sing & pl* **may** 1 a : have permission to b : be in some degree likely to 2 — used to express a wish or desire 3 — used to express purpose, contingency, or concession

May \ˈmā\ *n* : the 5th month of the year

may·ap·ple \ˈmā-ˌap-əl\ *n* : a No. American woodland herb related to the barberries that has a poisonous rootstock, leaves up to one foot in diameter, and a single large waxy white flower followed by a yellow egg-shaped berry; *also* : its edible but insipid fruit

may·be \ˈmā-bē\ *adv* : PERHAPS

May·day \mā-ˈdā, ˈmā-ˌ\ — an international radio telephone signal word used as a distress call

may·flow·er \ˈmā-ˌflau̇(-ə)r\ *n* : any of various spring-blooming plants (as the trailing arbutus, hepatica, or several No. American anemones)

may·hap \ˈmā-ˌhap, mā-ˈ\ *adv* : PERHAPS

may·hem \ˈmā-ˌhem, ˈmā-əm\ *n* 1 : willful and permanent crippling, mutilation, or disfigurement of any part of the body 2 : needless or willful damage

may·on·naise \ˈmā-ə-ˌnāz, ˌmā-ə-ˈ\ *n* : a dressing (as for salads) consisting chiefly of yolk of egg, vegetable oil, and vinegar or lemon juice

may·or \'mā-ər\ *n* : an official elected to act as chief executive or nominal head of a city or borough — **may·or·al** \'mā-ə-rəl\ *adj*

may·or·al·ty \'mā-ə-rəl-tē\ *n, pl* **-ties** : the office or the term of office of a mayor

may·pole \'mā-ˌpōl\ *n, often cap* : a tall flower-wreathed pole forming a center for May Day sports and dances

May·tide \'mā-ˌtīd\ *or* **May·time** \-ˌtīm\ *n* : the month of May

maze \'māz\ *n* : a confusing intricate network of passages : LABYRINTH

ma·zur·ka \mə-'zər-kə\ *n* **1** : a Polish dance in moderate triple measure **2** : music for the mazurka usu. in moderate 3/4 or 3/8 time

mazy \'mā-zē\ *adj* : resembling a maze in confusing turns and windings

me \(')mē\ *pron, objective case of* I

mead \'mēd\ *n* : a fermented drink made of water, honey, malt, and yeast

mead·ow \'med-ō\ *n* : land in or mainly in grass; *esp* : a tract of moist low-lying usu. level grassland

mead·ow·lark \-ˌlärk\ *n* : any of several No. American songbirds largely brown and buff above with a yellow breast bearing a black crescent

mea·ger *or* **mea·gre** \'mē-gər\ *adj* **1** : having little flesh : THIN **2** : lacking richness, strength, or comparable qualities : INADEQUATE — **mea·ger·ly** *adv* — **mea·ger·ness** *n*

¹meal \'mēl\ *n* **1** : the food eaten or prepared for eating at one time **2** : the act or time of eating a meal

²meal *n* **1** : usu. coarsely ground seeds of a cereal; *esp* : CORNMEAL **2** : something like meal esp. in texture

meal·time \'mēl-ˌtīm\ *n* : the usual time at which a meal is served

meal·worm \-ˌwərm\ *n* : a small brownish worm that is the larva of various beetles and that lives in grain products and is often raised as food for insectivorous animals

mealy \'mē-lē\ *adj* **1** : being soft, dry, and crumbly **2** : containing meal **3** : covered with fine granules or with flecks (as of color) **4** : MEALYMOUTHED

mealy·bug \'mē-lē-ˌbəg\ *n* : any of numerous destructive scale insects with a white powdery covering

mealy·mouthed \ˌmē-lē-'mau̇t͟hd, -'mau̇tht\ *adj* : smooth, plausible, and insincere in speech; *also* : affectedly unwilling to use strong or coarse language

¹mean \'mēn\ *adj* **1** : of low birth or station : HUMBLE **2** : ORDINARY, INFERIOR **3** : POOR, SHABBY **4** : not honorable or worthy : UNKIND, WICKED **5** : STINGY, MISERLY **6** : SPITEFUL, MALICIOUS **7** : of vicious or troublesome disposition **8** : UNWELL, INDISPOSED

²mean *vb* **meant** \'ment\; **mean·ing** \'mē-niŋ\ **1 a** : to have in the mind as a purpose : INTEND **b** : to intend for a particular purpose, use, or destination **2** : to serve to convey, show, or indicate : SIGNIFY **3** : to be of a specified degree of importance — **mean business** : to be in earnest

³mean *n* **1** : a middle point between extremes **2 a** : AVERAGE 1 **b** : the average of the two extremes of a range of values **c** : either of the middle two terms of a proportion **3** *pl* : something by the use or help of which a desired end is accomplished or furthered **4** *pl* : resources available for disposal; *esp* : WEALTH — **by all means** : without fail : CERTAINLY — **by any means** : in any way : at all — **by means of** : through the use of — **by no means** : not at all : certainly not

⁴mean *adj* **1** : holding a middle position : INTERMEDIATE **2** : being the mean of a set of values : AVERAGE

¹me·an·der \mē-'an-dər\ *n* **1** : a turn or winding of a stream **2** : a winding path or course

²meander *vi* **-dered**; **-der·ing** \-d(ə-)riŋ\ **1** : to follow a winding or intricate course **2** : to wander aimlessly : RAMBLE

¹mean·ing \'mē-niŋ\ *n* **1 a** : the sense one intends to convey esp. by language : PURPORT **b** : the sense that is conveyed **2** : INTENT, PURPOSE **3** : intent to convey information : SIGNIFICANCE

²meaning *adj* : SIGNIFICANT, EXPRESSIVE — **mean·ing·ly** *adv*

mean·ing·ful \-fəl\ *adj* : having a meaning or purpose; *esp* : full of meaning : SIGNIFICANT — **mean·ing·ful·ly** \-fə-lē\ *adv* — **mean·ing·ful·ness** *n*

mean·ing·less \'mē-niŋ-ləs\ *adj* **1** : lacking sense or significance **2** : lacking motive — **mean·ing·less·ly** *adv* — **mean·ing·less·ness** *n*

mean·ly \'mēn-lē\ *adv* **1** : in a poor, humble, or shabby manner **2** : in an ungenerous or ignoble manner

mean·ness \'mēn-nəs\ *n* **1** : the quality or state of being low in station or ignoble in conduct **2** : a mean act

means test \'mēnz-\ *n* : an examination of a person's financial state to determine his eligibility to receive unemployment insurance or public assistance benefits

¹mean·time \'mēn-ˌtīm\ *n* : the intervening time

²meantime *adv* : MEANWHILE

¹mean·while \-ˌhwīl\ *n* : MEANTIME

²meanwhile *adv* : during the intervening time

mea·sles \'mē-zəlz\ *n sing or pl* : an acute contagious virus disease marked by fever and red spots on the skin

mea·sly \'mēz-(ə-)lē\ *adj* : contemptibly small or insignificant

mea·sur·a·ble \'mezh-(ə-)rə-bəl\ *adj* : capable of being measured — **mea·sur·a·bil·i·ty** \ˌmezh-(ə-)rə-'bil-ət-ē\ *n* — **mea·sur·a·bly** \'mezh-(ə-)rə-blē\ *adv*

¹mea·sure \'mezh-ər\ *n* **1 a** : a moderate extent or degree **b** : AMOUNT, EXTENT, DEGREE **2 a** : the dimensions, capacity, or quantity of something as fixed by measuring **b** : something (as a yardstick or cup) used in measuring **c** : a unit used in measuring **d** : a system of measuring **3** : the act or process of measuring **4 a** : DANCE; *esp* : a stately dance **b** : rhythmic structure or movement in music or poetry : METER, CADENCE **c** : the part of a musical staff between two adjacent bars; *also* : the group or grouping of beats between these bars **5** : a basis or standard of comparison : CRITERION **6** : an action planned or taken as a means to an end; *esp* : a legislative bill or act

²measure *vb* **mea·sured**; **mea·sur·ing** \'mezh-(ə-)riŋ\ **1** : to select or regulate with caution : GOVERN **2 a** : to mark or fix in multiples of a specific unit **b** : to allot or apportion in measured amounts **3** : to determine the dimensions, extent, or amount of **4 a** : ESTIMATE **b** : to bring into comparison **5** : to serve as a measure of **6** : to turn out to be of a certain measurement (as in length or breadth) — **mea·sur·er** *n*

mea·sured \-ərd\ *adj* **1 a** : regulated or determined by a standard **b** : being slow and steady : EVEN **2** : DELIBERATE, CALCULATED **3** : RHYTHMICAL, METRICAL

mea·sure·less \-ər-ləs\ *adj* : being without measure : IMMEASURABLE

mea·sure·ment \'mezh-ər-mənt\ *n* **1** : the act or process of measuring **2** : a figure, extent, or amount obtained by measuring : DIMENSION

meat \'mēt\ *n* **1 a** : FOOD; *esp* : solid food as distinguished from drink **b** : the edible part of something as distinguished from the husk, shell, or other covering **2** : animal and esp. mammal tissue used as food

meat·ball \-ˌbȯl\ *n* : a small ball of chopped or ground meat

meat·man \-ˌman\ *n* : BUTCHER

meaty \'mēt-ē\ *adj* **1** : full of meat : FLESHY **2** : rich in matter for thought : SUBSTANTIAL — **meat·i·ness** *n*

mec·ca \'mek-ə\ *n, often cap* : a place considered extremely desirable esp. by a particular group of people

¹me·chan·ic \mi-'kan-ik\ *adj* : of or relating to manual work or skill

²mechanic *n* : a manual worker : ARTISAN; *esp* : a repairer of machines

me·chan·i·cal \-'kan-i-kəl\ *adj* **1 a** : of or relating to machinery **b** : made or operated by a machine or tool **2** : of or relating to mechanics or artisans **3** : done as if by machine : IMPERSONAL **4** : relating to or in accordance with the principles of mechanics **5** : relating to a process that involves a purely physical change — **me·chan·i·cal·ly** \-i-k(ə-)lē\ *adv*

mechanical drawing *n* : a method of drawing that makes use of such instruments as compasses, squares, and triangles in order to insure mathematical precision; *also* : a drawing so made

mech·a·ni·cian \ˌmek-ə-'nish-ən\ *n* : MECHANIC, MACHINIST

me·chan·ics \mi-'kan-iks\ *n sing or pl* **1** : a branch of physical science that deals with energy and forces and their effect on bodies **2** : the practical application of mechanics to the making or operation of machines **3** : mechanical or functional details

mech·a·nism \'mek-ə-ˌniz-əm\ *n* **1** : a machine or mechanical device **2 a** : the parts by which a machine operates as a mechanical unit **b** : the parts or steps that make up a process or activity **3** : the doctrine that natural processes (as of life) are orderly and wholly subject to natural law **4** : the fundamental physical or chemical processes involved in or responsible for a natural phenomenon (as an action or reaction) — **mech·a·nist** \-nəst\ *n*

mech·a·nis·tic \ˌmek-ə-'nis-tik\ *adj* **1** : mechanically determined **2** : of or relating to the doctrine of mechanism — **mech·a·nis·ti·cal·ly** \-ti-k(ə-)lē\ *adv*

mech·a·nize \'mek-ə-ˌnīz\ *vt* **1** : to make mechanical; *esp* : to make automatic **2 a** : to equip with machinery esp. to replace human or animal labor **b** : to equip (a military force) with armed and armored motor-driven vehicles — **mech·a·ni·za·tion** \ˌmek-ə-nə-'zā-shən\ *n*

med·al \'med-ᵊl\ *n* : a piece of metal often in the form of a coin issued to commemorate a person or event or as an award

med·al·ist *or* **med·al·list** \-ᵊl-əst\ *n* **1** : a designer or maker of medals **2** : a recipient of a medal

me·dal·lion \mə-'dal-yən\ *n* **1** : a large medal **2** : something (as a tablet or panel bearing a figure in relief or a design on wallpaper) resembling a large medal

med·dle \'med-ᵊl\ *vi* **med·dled** \-ᵊld\; **med·dling** \'med-liŋ, -ᵊl-iŋ\ : to interfere without right or propriety — **med·dler** \'med-lər, -ᵊl-ər\ *n*

med·dle·some \'med-ᵊl-səm\ *adj* : given to meddling : INTRUSIVE — **med·dle·some·ness** *n*

media *pl of* MEDIUM

me·di·al \'mēd-ē-əl\ *adj* **1 a** : MEDIAN **b** : extending toward the middle **2** : situated between the beginning and the end of a word **3** : ORDINARY, AVERAGE — **medial** *n* — **me·di·al·ly** \-ə-lē\ *adv*

¹me·di·an \'mēd-ē-ən\ *n* **1** : a median part **2** : a value in a series below and above which there are an equal number of values

²median *adj* **1** : being in the middle or in an intermediate position **2** : relating to or constituting a median

me·di·ate \'mēd-ē-ˌāt\ *vb* : to act as an intermediary (as in settling a dispute or in carrying out a process) — **me·di·a·tion** \ˌmēd-ē-'ā-shən\ *n* — **me·di·a·tor** \'mēd-ē-ˌāt-ər\ *n*

med·ic \'med-ik\ *n* : one engaged in medical work

med·i·ca·ble \'med-i-kə-bəl\ *adj* : CURABLE, REMEDIABLE — **med·i·ca·bly** \-blē\ *adv*

med·ic·aid \'med-i-ˌkād\ *n* : a program of providing medical aid designed for people unable to afford regular medical services and financed by the federal and state governments

med·i·cal \'med-i-kəl\ *adj* : of or relating to the science or practice of medicine or the treatment of disease — **med·i·cal·ly** \-k(ə-)lē\ *adv*

me·dic·a·ment \mi-'dik-ə-mənt\ *n* : a medicine or healing application

med·i·care \'med-i-ˌke(ə)r\ *n* : a government program of medical care esp. for the aged

med·i·cate \'med-ə-ˌkāt\ *vt* **1** : to treat with medicine **2** : to add a medicinal substance to

med·i·ca·tion \ˌmed-ə-'kā-shən\ *n* **1** : the act or process of medicating **2** : a medicinal substance : MEDICAMENT

me·dic·i·nal \mə-'dis-nəl, -ᵊn-əl\ *adj* : tending or used to relieve or cure disease or pain — **me·dic·i·nal·ly** *adv*

med·i·cine \'med-ə-sən\ *n* **1** : a substance or preparation used in treating disease **2** : a science or art that deals with the prevention, cure, or easing of disease; *esp* : the part of this that is the business of the physician as distinguished from the surgeon **3** : an object held to give control over natural or magical forces; *also* : a magical power or rite

medicine man *n* : a person among primitive peoples believed to be able to cure diseases by potions and charms

medicine show *n* : a traveling show using entertainers to attract a crowd that may buy remedies or nostrums

med·i·co \'med-i-ˌkō\ *n, pl* **-cos** : a medical practitioner : PHYSICIAN; *also* : a medical student

me·di·e·val \ˌmēd-ē-'ē-vəl, ˌmed-\ *adj* : of, relating to, or characteristic of the Middle Ages

me·di·e·val·ism \-və-ˌliz-əm\ *n* **1** : medieval quality, character, or state **2** : devotion to the institutions, arts, and practices of the Middle Ages — **me·di·e·val·ist** \-ləst\ *n*

me·di·o·cre \ˌmēd-ē-'ō-kər\ *adj* : of moderate or low quality : ORDINARY

me·di·oc·ri·ty \ˌmēd-ē-'äk-rət-ē\ *n, pl* **-ties** **1** : the quality or state of being mediocre **2** : a mediocre person

med·i·tate \'med-ə-ˌtāt\ *vb* **1 a** : to reflect on or muse over : CONTEMPLATE **b** : to engage in contemplation or reflection **2** : INTEND, PURPOSE — **med·i·ta·tor** \-ˌtāt-ər\ *n*

med·i·ta·tion \ˌmed-ə-'tā-shən\ *n* : the act or process of meditating : serious contemplation or reflection

med·i·ta·tive \'med-ə-ˌtāt-iv\ *adj* : inclined or given to meditation — **med·i·ta·tive·ly** *adv*

¹me·di·um \'mēd-ē-əm\ *n, pl* **me·di·ums** *or* **me·dia** \'mēd-ē-ə\ **1** : something that is between or in the middle; *also* : a middle condition or degree **2** : a means of effecting or conveying something; *esp* : a substance through which a force acts or through which something is transmitted **3** : a channel (as newspapers, radio, or television) of communication **4 a** : GO-BETWEEN, INTERMEDIARY **b** : a person through whom others seek to communicate with the spirits of the dead **5 a** : a surrounding substance **b** : a condition in which something may function or flourish **6** : a nutrient system for the artificial cultivation of organisms (as bacteria) or cells **7** : a liquid with which paint is mixed by a painter

²medium *adj* : intermediate in amount, quality, position, or degree

medium of exchange : something commonly accepted in exchange for goods and services and recognized as representing a standard of value

med·ley \'med-lē\ *n, pl* **medleys** **1** : MIXTURE; *esp* : a confused mixture **2** : a musical composition made up of parts from other pieces

me·dul·la \mə-'dəl-ə\ *n, pl* **-dul·las** *or* **-dul·lae** \-'dəl-(ˌ)ē\ **1** : MARROW 1 **2** : the inner or deep part of an animal or plant structure — **med·ul·lary** \'med-ᵊl-ˌer-ē\ *adj*

medulla ob·lon·ga·ta \-ˌäb-ˌlȯŋ-'gät-ə\ *n* : the somewhat pyramidal last part of the vertebrate brain continuous posteriorly with the spinal cord

meed \'mēd\ *n* : something deserved or earned : REWARD

meek \'mēk\ *adj* **1** : enduring injury with patience and without resentment : MILD **2** : lacking spirit or self-assurance : HUMBLE — **meek·ly** *adv* — **meek·ness** *n*

meer·schaum \'mi(ə)r-shəm, -ˌshȯm\ *n* : a pipe made of a light white clayey material

[1]**meet** \'mēt\ *vb* **met** \'met\; **meet·ing** **1** : to come upon or across **2 a** : to approach from different directions **b** : to come into contact and join or cross **3 a** : to go to the place where a person or thing is or will be **b** : to become acquainted **c** : to make the acquaintance of **4 a** : to come together as opponents **b** : to struggle against : OPPOSE **c** : to cope with : MATCH **d** : EXPERIENCE, ENDURE **5** : to come together for a common purpose : ASSEMBLE **6** : to become one : UNITE **7** : to become noticed by **8 a** : to conform to or comply with : SATISFY **b** : to pay fully : DISCHARGE, FULFILL

[2]**meet** *n* : an assembly or meeting esp. to engage in a competitive sport

[3]**meet** *adj* : SUITABLE, PROPER — **meet·ly** *adv*

meet·ing \'mēt-iŋ\ *n* **1** : the act of persons or things that meet **2** : a coming together of a number of persons usu. at a stated time and place and for a known purpose : ASSEMBLY, GATHERING **3** : an assembly for religious worship **4** : the place where two things come together : JUNCTION

meet·ing·house \-ˌhau̇s\ *n* : a building used for public assembly and esp. for Protestant worship

mega·cy·cle \'meg-ə-ˌsī-kəl\ *n* : one million cycles per second

meg·a·lo·ma·nia \ˌmeg-ə-lō-'mā-nē-ə, -nyə\ *n* : a disorder of mind marked by feelings of personal omnipotence and grandeur — **meg·a·lo·ma·ni·ac** \-'mā-nē-ˌak\ *adj or n* — **meg·a·lo·ma·ni·a·cal** \-mə-'nī-ə-kəl\ *or* **meg·a·lo·man·ic** \-'man-ik\ *adj*

meg·a·lop·o·lis \ˌmeg-ə-'läp-ə-ləs\ *n* **1** : a very large city **2** : a thickly populated region centering in a metropolis or embracing several metropolises — **meg·a·lo·pol·i·tan** \ˌmeg-ə-lō-'päl-ət-^{ə}n\ *n or adj*

mega·phone \'meg-ə-ˌfōn\ *n* : a cone-shaped device used to intensify or direct the voice — **mega·phon·ic** \ˌmeg-ə-'fän-ik\ *adj*

mega·ton \'meg-ə-ˌtən\ *n* : an explosive force equal to that of one million tons of TNT

me·grim \'mē-grəm\ *n* **1** : a dizzy disordered state; *esp* : MIGRAINE **2 a** : WHIM, FANCY **b** *pl* : low spirits : mental depression

Mei·ster·sing·er \'mī-stər-ˌsiŋ-ər, -stər-ˌziŋ-\ *n, pl* **-sing·er** \-ˌziŋ-ər\ *or* **-sing·ers** \-ˌsiŋ-ərz\ : a member of any of various German guilds formed chiefly in the 15th and 16th centuries by workingmen for the cultivation of poetry and music

mel·an·cho·lia \ˌmel-ən-'kō-lē-ə\ *n* : a mental condition characterized by extreme depression, bodily complaints, and often hallucinations and delusions — **mel·an·cho·li·ac** \-lē-ˌak\ *n*

mel·an·chol·ic \ˌmel-ən-'käl-ik\ *adj* **1** : inclined to or affected with melancholy **2** : affected with or relating to melancholia **3** : tending to depress the spirits — **mel·an·chol·i·cal·ly** \-'käl-i-k(ə-)lē\ *adv*

[1]**mel·an·choly** \'mel-ən-ˌkäl-ē\ *n, pl* **-chol·ies** : depression of spirits : DEJECTION, SADNESS

[2]**melancholy** *adj* **1 a** : depressed in spirits : DEJECTED, SAD **b** : PENSIVE **2 a** : DEPRESSING, DISMAL **b** : causing sadness : LAMENTABLE

mé·lange \mā-'lä^{n}zh, -'länj\ *n* : a mixture or medley esp. of incongruous elements

mel·ba toast \ˌmel-bə-\ *n* : very thin bread toasted till crisp

[1]**meld** \'meld\ *vb* : to show or announce for a score in a card game

[2]**meld** *n* : a card or combination of cards that is or can be melded

me·lee \'mā-ˌlā, mā-'lā\ *n* : a confused fight or struggle; *esp* : a hand-to-hand fight among a number of persons

me·lio·rate \'mēl-yə-ˌrāt\ *vb* : to make or become better : IMPROVE — **me·lio·ra·tion** \ˌmēl-yə-'rā-shən\ *n* — **me·lio·ra·tive** \'mēl-yə-ˌrāt-iv\ *adj* — **me·lio·ra·tor** \-ˌrāt-ər\ *n*

mel·lif·lu·ous \me-'lif-lə-wəs, mə-\ *adj* : smoothly or sweetly flowing — **mel·lif·lu·ous·ly** *adv* — **mel·lif·lu·ous·ness** *n*

[1]**mel·low** \'mel-ō\ *adj* **1 a** : tender and sweet because of ripeness **b** : well aged and pleasingly mild **2** : made gentle by age or experience **3** : of soft and loamy consistency **4** : being clear, full, and pure : not coarse or rough — **mel·low·ly** *adv* — **mel·low·ness** *n*

[2]**mellow** *vb* : to make or become mellow

me·lo·de·on \mə-'lōd-ē-ən\ *n* : a small reed organ in which a suction bellows draws air inward through the reeds

me·lod·ic \mə-'läd-ik\ *adj* : of or relating to melody : MELODIOUS — **me·lod·i·cal·ly** \-'läd-i-k(ə-)lē\ *adv*

me·lo·di·ous \mə-'lōd-ē-əs\ *adj* **1** : pleasing to the ear because of a succession of sweet sounds : TUNEFUL **2** : of, relating to, or producing melody — **me·lo·di·ous·ly** *adv* — **me·lo·di·ous·ness** *n*

mel·o·dist \'mel-əd-əst\ *n* : a composer or singer of melodies

melo·dra·ma \'mel-ə-ˌdräm-ə, -ˌdram-\ *n* **1 a** : an extravagantly theatrical play in which action and plot predominate over characterization **b** : a dramatic category constituted by such plays **2** : melodramatic events or behavior — **melo·dra·ma·tist** \-'dram-ət-əst, -'dräm-\ *n*

melo·dra·mat·ic \ˌmel-ə-drə-'mat-ik\ *adj* **1** : of or relating to melodrama **2** : resembling or suitable for melodrama : SENSATIONAL — **melo·dra·mat·i·cal·ly** \-i-k(ə-)lē\ *adv*

melo·dra·mat·ics \-'mat-iks\ *n sing or pl* : melodramatic conduct

mel·o·dy \'mel-əd-ē\ *n, pl* **-dies** **1** : pleasing succession of sounds : TUNEFULNESS **2** : a rhythmical series of musical tones of a given key so arranged as to make a pleasing effect **3** : the leading part in a harmonic composition

mel·on \'mel-ən\ *n* : any of certain gourds (as a muskmelon or watermelon) usu. eaten raw as fruits

[1]**melt** \'melt\ *vb* **1** : to change from a solid to a liquid state usu. through the application of heat **2** : DISSOLVE **3** : to grow less : disappear as if by dissolving **4** : to make or become gentle : SOFTEN **5** : to lose distinct outline or shape : BLEND, MERGE — **melt·a·bil·i·ty** \ˌmel-tə-'bil-ət-ē\ *n* — **melt·a·ble** *adj* — **melt·er** *n*

[2]**melt** *n* : a melted substance

[3]**melt** *n* : SPLEEN 1

melt·ing pot *n* **1** : a container capable of withstanding great heat in which something is melted : CRUCIBLE **2 a** : a place (as a city or country) in which various nationalities or races live together and gradually blend into one community **b** : the population of such a place

mel·ton \'melt-^{ə}n\ *n* : a smooth heavy woolen cloth with a short nap used for overcoats

melt·wa·ter \'melt-ˌwȯt-ər, -ˌwät-\ *n* : water derived from the melting of ice and snow

mem·ber \'mem-bər\ *n* **1** : a part (as an arm, leg, leaf, or branch) of the body of a person, lower animal, or plant **2** : one of the individuals or units belonging to or forming part of a group or organization **3** : a part of a whole: as **a** : a part of a structure (as a building) **b** : either of the equated elements in a mathematical equation

mem·ber·ship \-ˌship\ *n* **1** : the state or status of being a member **2** : the body of members

mem·brane \'mem-ˌbrān\ *n* : a thin soft pliable sheet or layer esp. of animal or plant origin — **mem·bra·na·ceous** \ˌmem-brə-'nā-shəs\ *adj* — **mem·braned** \'mem-ˌbrānd\ *adj* — **mem·bra·nous** \'mem-brə-nəs, mem-'brā-\ *adj* — **mem·bra·nous·ly** *adv*

me·men·to \mi-'ment-ō\ *n, pl* **-tos** *or* **-toes** : something that serves as a reminder : SOUVENIR

me·men·to mo·ri \mi-ˌment-ō-'mōr-ē, -'mōr-ˌī, -'mȯr-\ *n, pl* **memento mori** : a reminder (as a representation of a human skull) of mortality

memo \'mem-ō\ *n, pl* **mem·os** : MEMORANDUM

mem·oir \'mem-ˌwär\ *n* **1 a** : a narrative of a personal experience **b** : AUTOBIOGRAPHY — usu. used in pl. **c** : BIOGRAPHY **2** : ACCOUNT, REPORT

mem·o·ra·bil·ia \ˌmem-ə-rə-ˈbil-ē-ə\ *n pl* : things worthy of remembrance; *also* : a record of such things

mem·o·ra·ble \ˈmem-(ə-)rə-bəl\ *adj* : worth remembering : NOTABLE — **mem·o·ra·bly** \-blē\ *adv*

mem·o·ran·dum \ˌmem-ə-ˈran-dəm\ *n, pl* **-dums** *or* **-da** \-də\ **1 a** : an informal record or communication **b** : a written reminder **2** : an informal written note of a transaction or proposed legal instrument

[1]**me·mo·ri·al** \mə-ˈmōr-ē-əl\ *adj* : serving to preserve the memory of a person or an event — **me·mo·ri·al·ly** \-ē-ə-lē\ *adv*

[2]**memorial** *n* **1** : something that keeps alive the memory of a person or event; *esp* : MONUMENT **2 a** : RECORD, MEMOIR **b** : a statement of facts accompanying a petition or remonstrance to a government official

Memorial Day *n* : May 30 observed as a legal holiday in commemoration of dead servicemen

me·mo·ri·al·ize \mə-ˈmōr-ē-ə-ˌlīz\ *vt* **1** : to address or petition (as a government official) by a memorial **2** : COMMEMORATE

mem·o·rize \ˈmem-ə-ˌrīz\ *vt* : to commit to memory : learn by heart — **mem·o·ri·za·tion** \ˌmem-(ə-)rə-ˈzā-shən\ *n* — **mem·o·riz·er** *n*

mem·o·ry \ˈmem-(ə-)rē\ *n, pl* **-ries** **1 a** : the power or process of recalling what has been learned and retained **b** : the store of things learned and retained as evidenced by recall and recognition **2** : commemorative remembrance **3 a** : something remembered **b** : the time within which past events can be or are remembered

mem·sa·hib \ˈmem-ˌsä-ˌ(h)ib\ *n* : a white foreign woman of some social status living in India; *esp* : the wife of a British official in India under British rule

men *pl of* MAN

[1]**men·ace** \ˈmen-əs\ *n* **1** : a show of intention to inflict harm : THREAT **2 a** : someone or something that represents a threat : DANGER **b** : an annoying person : NUISANCE

[2]**menace** *vb* **1** : to make a show of intention to harm **2** : to appear likely to cause harm : ENDANGER — **men·ac·ing·ly** *adv*

mé·nage \mā-ˈnäzh\ *n* : a domestic establishment : HOUSEHOLD

me·nag·er·ie \mə-ˈnaj-ə-rē\ *n* **1** : a place where animals are kept and trained esp. for exhibition **2** : a collection of wild or foreign animals kept esp. for exhibition

[1]**mend** \ˈmend\ *vb* **1 a** : to improve in manners or morals : REFORM **b** : to put into good shape or working order again : REPAIR **2** : to become corrected or improved **3** : to improve in health; *also* : HEAL — **mend·er** *n*

[2]**mend** *n* **1** : an act of mending : REPAIR **2** : a mended place — **on the mend** : IMPROVING

men·da·cious \men-ˈdā-shəs\ *adj* : given to falsehood : LYING, UNTRUTHFUL; *also* : FALSE — **men·da·cious·ly** *adv* — **men·da·cious·ness** *n*

men·dac·i·ty \men-ˈdas-ət-ē\ *n, pl* **-ties** : the quality or state of being mendacious; *also* : LIE

men·di·can·cy \ˈmen-di-kən-sē\ *n* **1** : the condition of being a beggar **2** : the act or practice of begging

men·di·cant \-kənt\ *n* **1** : BEGGAR; *esp* : one who lives by begging **2** : a member of a religious order combining monastic life and outside religious activity and orig. owning neither personal nor community property : FRIAR — **mendicant** *adj*

men·folk \ˈmen-ˌfōk\ *or* **men·folks** \-ˌfōks\ *n pl* **1** : men in general **2** : the men of a family or community

men·ha·den \men-ˈhād-ᵊn, mən-\ *n, pl* **-den** : a fish of the herring family found along the Atlantic coast of the U.S. and used for bait or converted into oil and fertilizer

[1]**me·ni·al** \ˈmē-nē-əl, -nyəl\ *adj* **1** : of, relating to, or suitable for servants **2** : HUMBLE, SERVILE — **me·ni·al·ly** *adv*

[2]**menial** *n* : a domestic servant or retainer

men·in·gi·tis \ˌmen-ən-ˈjīt-əs\ *n* : inflammation of the membranes enclosing the brain and spinal cord; *also* : a usu. bacterial disease in which this occurs — **men·in·git·ic** \-ˈjit-ik\ *adj*

meno·pause \ˈmen-ə-ˌpȯz\ *n* : the period of natural cessation of menstruation usu. between the ages of 45 and 50 — **meno·paus·al** \ˌmen-ə-ˈpȯ-zəl\ *adj*

menservants *pl of* MANSERVANT

men·ses \ˈmen-ˌsēz\ *n pl* : the menstruous flow

men·stru·al \ˈmen(t)-strə(-wə)l\ *adj* **1** : of or relating to menstruation **2** : MONTHLY

men·stru·ate \ˈmen(t)-strə-ˌwāt, ˈmen-ˌstrāt\ *vi* : to undergo menstruation

men·stru·a·tion \ˌmen(t)-strə-ˈwā-shən, men-ˈstrā-shən\ *n* : a discharging of blood, secretions, and tissue debris from the uterus that recurs at approximately monthly intervals in breeding-age primate females that are not pregnant; *also* : PERIOD 5b — **men·stru·ous** \ˈmen(t)-strə(-wə)s\ *adj*

men·su·ra·ble \ˈmen(t)-sə-rə-bəl, ˈmen-chə-\ *adj* : MEASURABLE — **men·su·ra·bil·i·ty** \ˌmen(t)-sə-rə-ˈbil-ət-ē, ˌmen-chə-\ *n* — **men·su·ra·ble·ness** *n*

men·su·ra·tion \ˌmen(t)-sə-ˈrā-shən, ˌmen-chə-\ *n* : the process or art of measuring

men·tal \ˈment-ᵊl\ *adj* **1 a** : of or relating to the mind **b** : carried on or experienced in the mind **c** : relating to spirit or idea as opposed to matter **2 a** : of, relating to, or affected by a disorder of the mind **b** : intended for the care or treatment of persons affected by mental disorders — **men·tal·ly** \-ᵊl-ē\ *adv*

men·tal·i·ty \men-ˈtal-ət-ē\ *n, pl* **-ties** **1** : mental power or capacity : INTELLIGENCE **2** : mode of thinking

men·thol \ˈmen-ˌthȯl, -ˌthōl\ *n* : a white crystalline soothing substance from oils of mint

men·tho·lat·ed \ˈmen(t)-thə-ˌlāt-əd\ *adj* : treated with or containing menthol

[1]**men·tion** \ˈmen-chən\ *n* : a brief reference to something : a passing remark

[2]**mention** *vt* **men·tioned**; **men·tion·ing** \ˈmench-(ə-)niŋ\ : to refer to : discuss or speak about briefly — **men·tion·a·ble** \ˈmench-(ə-)nə-bəl\ *adj* — **men·tion·er** \-(ə-)nər\ *n*

men·tor \ˈmen-ˌtȯ(ə)r, ˈment-ər\ *n* : a wise and faithful adviser or teacher

menu \ˈmen-yü, ˈmān-\ *n* : a list of dishes served at a meal; *also* : the dishes served

me·ow \mē-ˈau̇\ *n* : the cry of a cat — **meow** *vb*

me·phit·ic \mə-ˈfit-ik\ *adj* : foul-smelling

mer·can·tile \ˈmər-kən-ˌtēl, -ˌtīl\ *adj* **1** : of or relating to merchants, trade, or commerce **2** : of, relating to, or having the characteristics of mercantilism

Mer·ca·tor projection \ˌmər-ˌkāt-ər-\ *n* : a map projection in which the meridians are drawn parallel to each other and the parallels of latitude are straight lines whose distance from each other increases with their distance from the equator

[1]**mer·ce·nary** \ˈmərs-ᵊn-ˌer-ē\ *n, pl* **-nar·ies** : one that serves merely for wages; *esp* : a soldier hired by a foreign country to fight in its army

[2]**mercenary** *adj* **1** : doing something only for the pay or reward **2** : greedy for money

mer·cer·ize \ˈmər-sə-ˌrīz\ *vt* : to treat (cotton fiber or fabrics) with a chemical so that the fibers are strengthened, take dyes better, and often acquire a sheen

[1]**mer·chan·dise** \ˈmər-chən-ˌdīz, -ˌdīs\ *n* : the commodities or goods that are bought and sold in trade : WARES

[2]**merchandise** \-ˌdīz\ *vb* : to buy and sell : TRADE; *esp* : to try to further sales or the use of merchandise or services by attractive presentation and publicity — **mer·chan·dis·er** *n*

[1]**mer·chant** \ˈmər-chənt\ *n* **1** : a buyer and seller of commodities for profit; *esp* : one who carries on trade on a large scale or with foreign countries **2** : the operator of a retail business : STOREKEEPER

²merchant *adj* **1 :** of, relating to, or used in commerce **2 :** of or relating to a merchant marine
mer·chant·a·ble \-ə-bəl\ *adj* **:** of commercial quality **:** SALABLE
mer·chant·man \-mən\ *n* **:** a ship used in commerce
merchant marine *n* **1 :** the commercial shipping of a nation **2 :** the personnel of a merchant marine
mer·ci·ful \'mər-si-fəl\ *adj* **:** having, showing, or disposed to mercy **:** COMPASSIONATE — **mer·ci·ful·ly** \-f(ə-)lē\ *adv*
mer·ci·less \'mər-si-ləs\ *adj* **:** having no mercy **:** PITILESS — **mer·ci·less·ly** *adv* — **mer·ci·less·ness** *n*
¹mer·cu·ri·al \(ˌ)mər-'kyu̇r-ē-əl\ *adj* **1 :** characterized by rapid and unpredictable changeableness of mood **2 :** of, relating to, or containing the element mercury — **mer·cu·ri·al·ly** \-ē-ə-lē\ *adv* — **mer·cu·ri·al·ness** *n*
²mercurial *n* **:** a drug or chemical containing mercury
mer·cu·ry \'mər-kyə-rē\ *n, pl* **-ries 1 :** a heavy silver-white metallic element that is liquid at ordinary temperatures **2 :** the column of mercury in a thermometer or barometer
mer·cy \'mər-sē\ *n, pl* **mercies 1 :** compassion or forbearance shown to one (as an offender or adversary) having no claim to kindness **2 :** a fortunate circumstance **3 :** compassion shown to victims of misfortune
¹mere \'mi(ə)r\ *n* **:** a sheet of standing water **:** POOL
²mere *adj* **:** being only this and nothing else **:** nothing more than — **mere·ly** *adv*
mer·e·tri·cious \ˌmer-ə-'trish-əs\ *adj* **:** attracting by a display of showy but superficial and tawdry charms **:** falsely attractive — **mer·e·tri·cious·ly** *adv* — **mer·e·tri·cious·ness** *n*
merge \'mərj\ *vb* **1 :** to be or cause to be swallowed up or absorbed in or within something else **:** MINGLE, BLEND **2 :** COMBINE, UNITE
merg·er \'mər-jər\ *n* **:** the action or result of merging; *esp* **:** the combination of two or more business firms into one
me·rid·i·an \mə-'rid-ē-ən\ *n* **1 :** the highest point attained **:** ZENITH, CULMINATION **2 :** an imaginary circle on the earth's surface passing through the north and south poles and any given place — **meridian** *adj*
me·ringue \mə-'raŋ\ *n* **1 :** a dessert topping baked from a mixture of beaten egg white and sugar **2 :** a shell made of meringue and filled with fruit or ice cream
me·ri·no \mə-'rē-nō\ *n, pl* **-nos 1 :** any of a breed of fine-wooled white sheep producing a heavy fleece of exceptional quality **2 :** a soft wool or wool and cotton fabric resembling cashmere **3 :** a fine wool and cotton yarn — **merino** *adj*
¹mer·it \'mer-ət\ *n* **1 :** the condition or fact of deserving well or ill **:** DESERT **2 :** WORTH, EXCELLENCE **3 :** a praiseworthy quality **:** VIRTUE
²merit *vb* **:** to earn by service or performance **:** DESERVE
mer·i·to·ri·ous \ˌmer-ə-'tōr-ē-əs\ *adj* **:** deserving reward or honor **:** PRAISEWORTHY — **mer·i·to·ri·ous·ly** *adv* — **mer·i·to·ri·ous·ness** *n*
merit system *n* **:** a system by which appointments and promotions are based on competence rather than political favoritism
mer·maid \'mər-ˌmād\ *n* **:** an imaginary sea creature usu. represented with a woman's body and a fish's tail
mer·man \-ˌman, -mən\ *n, pl* **mer·men** \-ˌmen, -mən\ **:** an imaginary sea creature usu. represented with a man's body and a fish's tail
mer·ri·ment \'mer-i-mənt\ *n* **:** GAIETY, MIRTH, FUN
mer·ry \'mer-ē\ *adj* **1 :** full of good humor and good spirits **:** MIRTHFUL **2 :** marked by gaiety or festivity — **mer·ri·ly** \'mer-ə-lē\ *adv* — **mer·ri·ness** \'mer-ē-nəs\ *n*
mer·ry–an·drew \ˌmer-ē-'an-ˌdrü\ *n* **:** CLOWN, BUFFOON
mer·ry–go–round \'mer-ē-gō-ˌrau̇nd\ *n* **1 :** a circular revolving platform fitted with seats and figures of animals on which people sit for a ride **2 :** a rapid round of activities **:** WHIRL
mer·ry·mak·ing \-ˌmā-kiŋ\ *n* **1 :** gay or festive activity **:** MERRIMENT, FESTIVITY **2 :** a festive or convivial occasion — **mer·ry·mak·er** *n*
me·sa \'mā-sə\ *n* **:** a flat-topped hill or small plateau with steep sides
més·al·liance \ˌmā-ˌzal-'yäⁿs\ *n, pl* **-liances** \-'yäⁿs(-əz)\ **:** a marriage with a person of inferior social position
mesdames *pl of* MADAM *or of* MADAME
mesdemoiselles *pl of* MADEMOISELLE
¹mesh \'mesh\ *n* **1 :** one of the open spaces formed by the threads of a net or the wires of a sieve or screen **2 a :** NET, NETWORK **b :** a fabric of open texture with evenly spaced small holes **3 :** WEB, SNARE — usu. used in pl. **4 :** the coming or fitting together of the teeth of two gears — **meshed** \'mesht\ *adj*
²mesh *vb* **1 :** to catch in or as if in a mesh **:** ENTANGLE **2 :** to make into a net or network **3 :** to fit together **:** INTERLOCK
mesh·work \'mesh-ˌwərk\ *n* **:** MESHES, NETWORK
mes·mer·ism \'mez-mə-ˌriz-əm, 'mes-\ *n* **:** HYPNOTISM — **mes·mer·ic** \mez-'mer-ik, me-'smer-\ *adj* — **mes·mer·ist** \'mez-mə-rəst, 'mes-\ *n*
mes·mer·ize \'mez-mə-ˌrīz, 'mes-\ *vt* **1 :** HYPNOTIZE **2 :** SPELLBIND, FASCINATE — **mes·mer·iz·er** *n*
mes·quite \mə-'skēt, me-\ *n* **:** a spiny deep-rooted leguminous tree or shrub of the southwestern U.S. and Mexico bearing pods rich in sugar and important as a livestock feed
¹mess \'mes\ *n* **1 a :** a quantity of food **b :** a dish of soft or liquid food **2 :** a group of people and esp. of military personnel who regularly eat together; *also* **:** the meal they eat or the place where they eat **3 a :** a confused heap **b :** a state of confusion or disorder
²mess *vb* **1 a :** to supply with meals **b :** to take meals with a mess **2 :** to make dirty or untidy **:** DISARRANGE; *also* **:** BUNGLE **3 :** INTERFERE, MEDDLE **4 :** PUTTER
mes·sage \'mes-ij\ *n* **1 :** a communication in writing, in speech, or by signals **2 :** a messenger's errand or function
messeigneurs *pl of* MONSEIGNEUR
mes·sen·ger \'mes-ᵊn-jər\ *n* **:** one who bears a message or does an errand: as **a :** a dispatch bearer esp. in military service **b :** an employee who carries messages
mes·si·ah \mə-'sī-ə\ *n* **1** *cap* **a :** the expected king and deliverer of the Jews **b :** JESUS **2 :** a professed or accepted leader of some hope or cause — **mes·si·ah·ship** \-ˌship\ *n* — **mes·si·an·ic** \ˌmes-ē-'an-ik\ *adj*
messieurs *pl of* MONSIEUR
mess jacket *n* **:** a man's short tight jacket
mess kit *n* **:** a kit consisting of a metal dish and eating utensils for use by soldiers and campers
mess·mate \'mes-ˌmāt\ *n* **:** a member of a group who eat regularly together (as in a ship's mess)
messy \'mes-ē\ *adj* **:** marked by confusion, disorder, or dirt **:** UNTIDY — **mess·i·ly** \'mes-ə-lē\ *adv* — **mess·i·ness** \'mes-ē-nəs\ *n*
mes·ti·zo \me-'stē-zō\ *n, pl* **-zos :** a person of mixed blood; *esp* **:** one of mixed European and American Indian ancestry
met *past of* MEET
me·tab·o·lism \mə-'tab-ə-ˌliz-əm\ *n* **1 a :** the sum of the processes in the building up and destruction of protoplasm incidental to life **b :** the sum of the processes by which a particular substance is handled in the living body **2 :** METAMORPHOSIS 3 — **met·a·bol·ic** \ˌmet-ə-'bäl-ik\ *adj* — **me·tab·o·lize** \mə-'tab-ə-ˌlīz\ *vb*
¹met·al \'met-ᵊl\ *n* **1 :** any of various substances (as gold, tin, copper, or bronze) that have a more or less shiny appearance, are good conductors of electricity and heat, are opaque, can be melted, and are usu. capable of being drawn into a wire or hammered into a thin sheet **2 :** any of more than three fourths of the chemical elements that exhibit the properties of a metal, typically are crystalline solids, and have atoms that readily

lose electrons **3 a :** METTLE **b :** the material or substance out of which a person or thing is made — **metal** *adj*

²**metal** *vt* **-aled** *or* **-alled**; **-al·ing** *or* **-al·ling** : to cover or furnish with metal

me·tal·lic \mə-ˈtal-ik\ *adj* **1 :** of, relating to, or being a metal **2 :** containing or made of metal **3 :** HARSH, GRATING — **me·tal·li·cal·ly** \-ˈtal-i-k(ə-)lē\ *adv*

met·al·lize \ˈmet-ᵊl-ˌīz\ *vt* : to treat or combine with a metal

met·al·lur·gy \ˈmet-ᵊl-ˌər-jē\ *n* : the science of extracting metals from their ores, refining them, and preparing them for use — **met·al·lur·gi·cal** \ˌmet-ᵊl-ˈər-ji-kəl\ *adj* — **met·al·lur·gist** \ˈmet-ᵊl-ˌər-jəst\ *n*

met·al·ware \ˈmet-ᵊl-ˌwa(ə)r, -ˌwe(ə)r\ *n* : metal utensils for household use

met·al·work \ˈmet-ᵊl-ˌwərk\ *n* **1 :** the process or occupation of making things from metal **2 :** work and esp. artistic work made of metal — **met·al·work·er** \-ˌwər-kər\ *n* — **met·al·work·ing** \-kiŋ\ *n*

met·a·mor·phose \ˌmet-ə-ˈmȯr-ˌfōz, -ˌfōs\ *vb* : to change or cause to change in form : undergo metamorphosis

met·a·mor·pho·sis \-ˈmȯr-fə-səs\ *n, pl* **-pho·ses** \-fə-ˌsēz\ **1 :** a change of form, structure, or substance esp. by witchcraft or magic **2 :** a striking alteration in appearance, character, or circumstances **3 :** a fundamental and usu. rather abrupt change in the form and often the habits of an animal that occurs during the transformation of a larva into an adult

met·a·phor \ˈmet-ə-ˌfȯ(ə)r, -fər\ *n* : a figure of speech in which a word or phrase denoting one kind of object or idea is used in place of another to suggest a similarity between them (as in *the ship plows the sea*) — **met·a·phor·i·cal** \ˌmet-ə-ˈfȯr-i-kəl\ *adj* — **met·a·phor·i·cal·ly** \-i-k(ə-)lē\ *adv*

met·a·phys·i·cal \ˌmet-ə-ˈfiz-i-kəl\ *adj* **1 :** of, relating to, or based on metaphysics **2 :** SUPERNATURAL **3 :** highly abstract or difficult to understand **4 :** of or relating to poetry esp. of the early 17th century that is marked by subtle and elaborate metaphors — **met·a·phys·i·cal·ly** \-ˈfiz-i-k(ə-)lē\ *adv*

met·a·phy·si·cian \-fə-ˈzish-ən\ *n* : a student of or specialist in metaphysics

met·a·phys·ics \ˌmet-ə-ˈfiz-iks\ *n* : the part of philosophy concerned with the study of the ultimate causes and the underlying nature of things

me·tas·ta·sis \mə-ˈtas-tə-səs\ *n, pl* **-ta·ses** \-tə-ˌsēz\ : transfer of a disease-producing agency from its original site to another part of the body; *also* : a secondary growth of a malignant tumor — **met·a·stat·ic** \ˌmet-ə-ˈstat-ik\ *adj* — **met·a·stat·i·cal·ly** \-ˈstat-i-k(ə-)lē\ *adv*

me·tas·ta·size \mə-ˈtas-tə-ˌsīz\ *vi* : to spread by metastasis

mete \ˈmēt\ *vt* : to assign by measure : ALLOT, APPORTION

me·tem·psy·cho·sis \mə-ˌtem(p)-si-ˈkō-səs, ˌmet-əm-ˌsī-\ *n* : the passing of the soul at death into another body either human or animal

me·te·or \ˈmēt-ē-ər\ *n* : one of the small particles of matter in the solar system observable directly only when it falls into the earth's atmosphere where the heat of friction may cause it to glow brightly for a short time; *also* : the streak of light produced by the passage of a meteor

me·te·or·ic \ˌmēt-ē-ˈȯr-ik\ *adj* **1 :** of or relating to a meteor **2 :** resembling a meteor in speed or in sudden and temporary brilliance

me·te·or·ite \ˈmēt-ē-ə-ˌrīt\ *n* : a meteor that reaches the surface of the earth

me·te·or·oid \-ˌrȯid\ *n* : a meteoric particle in interplanetary space

me·te·o·rol·o·gy \ˌmēt-ē-ə-ˈräl-ə-jē\ *n* : a science that deals with the atmosphere and its phenomena and with weather and weather forecasting — **me·te·o·ro·log·ic** \ˌmēt-ē-ˌȯr-ə-ˈläj-ik\ *or* **me·te·o·ro·log·i·cal** \-ˈläj-i-kəl\ *adj* — **me·te·o·rol·o·gist** \ˌmēt-ē-ə-ˈräl-ə-jəst\ *n*

¹**me·ter** \ˈmēt-ər\ *n* **1 :** a systematically arranged and measured rhythm in verse **2 :** the basic rhythmical pattern of note values, accents, and beats per measure in music

²**meter** *n* : a measure of length that is equal to 39.37 inches and is the basis of the metric system

³**meter** *n* : an instrument for measuring and sometimes recording the amount of something

⁴**meter** *vt* **1 :** to measure by means of a meter **2 :** to supply in a measured or regulated amount

meth·ane \ˈmeth-ˌān\ *n* : an odorless flammable gas consisting of carbon and hydrogen produced by decomposition of organic matter in marshes and mines and by distillation

meth·od \ˈmeth-əd\ *n* **1 a :** a regular way of doing something **b :** a systematic plan or procedure for doing something **2 a :** orderly arrangement **b :** REGULARITY, ORDERLINESS

me·thod·i·cal \mə-ˈthäd-i-kəl\ *adj* **1 :** characterized by or performed or arranged by method or order **2 :** habitually following a method : SYSTEMATIC — **me·thod·i·cal·ly** \-i-k(ə-)lē\ *adv* — **me·thod·i·cal·ness** *n*

Meth·od·ist \ˈmeth-əd-əst\ *n* : a member of a Protestant denomination adhering to the doctrines of John Wesley — **Meth·od·ism** \-ə-ˌdiz-əm\ *n* — **Methodist** *adj*

meth·od·ize \ˈmeth-ə-ˌdīz\ *vt* : to reduce to method : SYSTEMATIZE

meth·od·ol·o·gy \ˌmeth-ə-ˈdäl-ə-jē\ *n, pl* **-gies** : a body of methods and rules followed in a science or discipline — **meth·od·o·log·i·cal** \ˌmeth-əd-ᵊl-ˈäj-i-kəl\ *adj* — **meth·od·ol·o·gist** \ˌmeth-ə-ˈdäl-ə-jəst\ *n*

me·tic·u·los·i·ty \mə-ˌtik-yə-ˈläs-ət-ē\ *n* : METICULOUSNESS

me·tic·u·lous \mə-ˈtik-yə-ləs\ *adj* : extremely or excessively careful in small details — **me·tic·u·lous·ly** *adv* — **me·tic·u·lous·ness** *n*

mé·tier \mā-ˈtyā\ *n* : an area of activity in which one is expert or successful : FORTE

me–too \ˈmē-ˈtü\ *adj* : marked by similarity to or acceptance of successful or persuasive policies or practices of a political rival — **me–too·ism** \-ˌiz-əm\ *n*

met·ric \ˈme-trik\ *adj* **1 :** of or relating to measurement; *esp* : of, relating to, or based on the metric system **2 :** of or relating to poetic or musical meter : METRICAL

met·ri·cal \ˈme-tri-kəl\ *adj* **1 a :** of or relating to meter (as in poetry or music) **b :** arranged in meter **2 :** of or relating to measurement or the metric system : METRIC — **met·ri·cal·ly** \-k(ə-)lē\ *adv*

metric system *n* : a decimal system of weights and measures in which the meter is the unit of length and the kilogram is the unit of weight

met·ro \ˈme-trō\ *n, pl* **metros** : SUBWAY

met·ro·nome \ˈme-trə-ˌnōm\ *n* : an instrument that produces a regularly repeated tick used esp. to help a music student play in exact time — **met·ro·nom·ic** \ˌme-trə-ˈnäm-ik\ *adj* — **met·ro·nom·i·cal·ly** \-ˈnäm-i-k(ə-)lē\ *adv*

me·trop·o·lis \mə-ˈträp-(ə-)ləs\ *n* **1 :** the mother city or country of a colony **2 a :** the chief or capital city of a country, state, or region **b :** a large or important city **3 :** a principal seat or center of an activity

met·ro·pol·i·tan \ˌme-trə-ˈpäl-ət-ᵊn\ *adj* **1 :** of, relating to, or characteristic of a metropolis **2 :** of, relating to, or constituting a region made up of a city and the densely populated surrounding areas socially and economically integrated with it

met·tle \ˈmet-ᵊl\ *n* **1 :** quality of temperament or disposition **2 a :** SPIRIT, ARDOR **b :** STAMINA — **on one's mettle** : aroused to do one's best

met·tle·some \-ᵊl-səm\ *adj* : full of mettle : SPIRITED, FIERY

mew \ˈmyü\ *vt* : to shut up : CONFINE

mewl \ˈmyül\ *vi* : to cry weakly : WHIMPER

mez·za·nine \ˈmez-ᵊn-ˌēn\ *n* **1 :** a low story between two main

stories of a building often projecting in the form of a balcony **2** : the lowest balcony in a theater or its first few rows
mez·zo–so·prano \ˌmet-sō-sə-ˈpran-ō, ˌme(d)z-ō-, -ˈprän-\ *n* : a woman's voice having a full deep quality between that of the soprano and contralto; *also* : a singer having such a voice
mez·zo·tint \ˈmet-sō-ˌtint, ˈme(d)z-ō-\ *n* : a process of engraving on copper or steel by scraping or burnishing a roughened surface to produce light and shade; *also* : an engraving produced by this process
mi \ˈmē\ *n* : the 3d note of the diatonic scale
mi·as·ma \mī-ˈaz-mə\ *n, pl* **-mas** *or* **-ma·ta** \-mət-ə\ **1** : a vaporous exhalation (as of a swamp) formerly believed to cause disease **2** : a harmful influence or atmosphere — **mi·as·mal** \-məl\ *or* **mi·as·mat·ic** \ˌmī-əz-ˈmat-ik\ *or* **mi·as·mic** \mī-ˈaz-mik\ *adj*
mi·ca \ˈmī-kə\ *n* : any of various silicon-containing minerals that may be separated easily into thin and often somewhat flexible and transparent sheets — **mi·ca·ceous** \mī-ˈkā-shəs\ *adj*
mice *pl of* MOUSE
Mick·ey Finn \ˌmik-ē-ˈfin\ *n* : a drink of liquor doctored with a drug
mi·crobe \ˈmī-ˌkrōb\ *n* : MICROORGANISM, GERM — **mi·cro·bi·al** \mī-ˈkrō-bē-əl\ *or* **mi·cro·bic** \-bik\ *adj*
mi·cro·copy \ˈmī-krō-ˌkäp-ē\ *n* : a photographic copy in which printed or drawn matter is reduced in size — **microcopy** *vb*
mi·cro·cosm \ˈmī-krə-ˌkäz-əm\ *n* : a little world; *esp* : an individual man or a community that is a miniature universe or a world in itself — **mi·cro·cos·mic** \ˌmī-krə-ˈkäz-mik\ *adj*
mi·cro·film \ˈmī-krə-ˌfilm\ *n* : a film bearing a photographic record on a reduced scale of graphic matter (as printing) — **microfilm** *vb*
mi·crom·e·ter \mī-ˈkräm-ət-ər\ *n* : an instrument used with a telescope or microscope for measuring very small distances
mi·cron \ˈmī-ˌkrän\ *n* : one thousandth of a millimeter
mi·cron·ize \ˈmī-krə-ˌnīz\ *vt* : to pulverize extremely fine
mi·cro·or·ga·nism \ˌmī-krō-ˈór-gə-ˌniz-əm\ *n* : an organism (as a bacterium) of microscopic or less than microscopic size
mi·cro·phone \ˈmī-krə-ˌfōn\ *n* : an instrument used in increasing or transmitting sounds; *esp* : one used in radio and television to receive sound and convert it into electrical waves
mi·cro·scope \ˈmī-krə-ˌskōp\ *n* **1** : an optical instrument consisting of a lens or a combination of lenses for making enlarged or magnified images of minute objects **2** : an instrument using radiations other than light for making enlarged images of minute objects
mi·cro·scop·ic \ˌmī-krə-ˈskäp-ik\ *or* **mi·cro·scop·i·cal** \-ˈskäp-i-kəl\ *adj* **1** : of, relating to, or involving the use of the microscope **2** : resembling a microscope : able to see very tiny objects **3** : able to be seen only through a microscope : very small — **mi·cro·scop·i·cal·ly** \-ˈskäp-i-k(ə-)lē\ *adv*
¹mid \ˈmid\ *adj* **1** : being the part in the middle or midst **2** : occupying a middle position **3** : uttered with the tongue midway between its highest and its lowest elevation
²mid \(ˌ)mid\ *prep* : AMID
mid·day \ˈmid-ˌdā, -ˈdā\ *n* : the middle part of the day : NOON — **midday** *adj*
mid·den \ˈmid-ᵊn\ *n* : a refuse heap
¹mid·dle \ˈmid-ᵊl\ *adj* **1** : equally distant from the extremes : CENTRAL **2** : being at neither extreme : INTERMEDIATE **3** : typically asserting that a person or thing both performs and is affected by the action represented
²middle *n* **1** : a middle part, point, or position **2** : WAIST **3** : the position of being among or in the midst of something
middle age *n* : the period of life from about 40 to about 60 — **mid·dle–aged** \ˌmid-ᵊl-ˈājd\ *adj*
Middle Ages *n pl* : the period of European history from about A.D. 500 to about 1500
mid·dle·brow \ˈmid-ᵊl-ˌbraů\ *n* : a person who is moderately but not highly cultivated — **middlebrow** *adj*
middle class *n* : a social class occupying a position between the upper class and the lower class
mid·dle–class \ˌmid-ᵊl-ˈklas\ *adj* : of or relating to the middle class
middle distance *n* **1** : a part of a picture or scene between the foreground and the background **2** : any footrace distance from 400 meters and 440 yards to 1500 meters and one mile
mid·dle·man \ˈmid-ᵊl-ˌman\ *n* : an intermediary or agent between two parties; *esp* : a dealer or agent intermediate between the producer of goods and the retailer or the consumer
mid·dle·most \-ˌmōst\ *adj* : MIDMOST
mid·dle–of–the–road \ˌmid-ᵊl-əv-t͟hə-ˈrōd\ *adj* : standing for or following a course of action midway between extremes; *esp* : being neither liberal nor conservative in politics — **mid·dle–of–the–road·er** *n*
middle term *n* : the term of a syllogism that occurs in both premises
mid·dle·weight \ˈmid-ᵊl-ˌwāt\ *n* : one of average weight; *esp* : a boxer weighing more than 147 but not over 160 pounds
¹mid·dling \ˈmid-liŋ, -lən\ *adj* : of middle, medium, or moderate size, degree, or quality — **middling** *adv*
²middling *n* **1** : any of various commodities of medium quality or size **2** *pl* : a granular product of grain milling; *esp* : a wheat milling by-product used in animal feeds
mid·dy \ˈmid-ē\ *n, pl* **mid·dies** **1** : MIDSHIPMAN **2** : a loosely fitting blouse for women and children with a collar cut wide and square in the back
midge \ˈmij\ *n* : a very small fly : GNAT
midg·et \ˈmij-ət\ *n* : an individual much smaller than the usual or typical — **midget** *adj* — **midg·et·ism** \-ət-ˌiz-əm\ *n*
mid·land \ˈmid-lənd, -ˌland\ *n* : the interior or central region of a country
mid·line \-ˌlīn\ *n* : a median line
mid·most \ˈmid-ˌmōst\ *adj* **1** : being in the exact middle **2** : INNERMOST — **midmost** *adv or n*
mid·night \-ˌnīt\ *n* : the middle of the night; *esp* : 12 o'clock at night — **midnight** *adj* — **mid·night·ly** *adv or adj*
midnight sun *n* : the sun above the horizon at midnight in the arctic or antarctic summer
mid·point \ˈmid-ˌpȯint\ *n* : a point at or near the center or middle
mid·riff \-ˌrif\ *n* **1** : DIAPHRAGM 1 **2** : the middle region of the human torso
mid·ship·man \ˈmid-ˌship-mən, (ˈ)mid-ˈship-\ *n* : a student naval officer ranking above a master chief petty officer and below a warrant officer
mid·ships \ˈmid-ˌships\ *adv* : AMIDSHIPS
¹midst \ˈmidst\ *n* **1** : the interior or central part or point : MIDDLE **2** : a position among the members of a group **3** : the condition of being surrounded or beset
²midst \(ˌ)midst\ *prep* : AMID
mid·stream \ˈmid-ˈstrēm\ *n* : the middle of a stream
mid·sum·mer \ˈmid-ˈsəm-ər\ *n* **1** : the middle of summer **2** : the summer solstice
¹mid·way \ˈmid-ˌwā\ *n* : an avenue (as at a carnival) for concessions and light amusements
²mid·way \-ˌwā, -ˈwā\ *adv (or adj)* : in the middle of the way or distance : HALFWAY
mid·week \ˈmid-ˌwēk\ *n* : the middle of the week — **midweek** *adj* — **mid·week·ly** *adj or adv*
mid·wife \-ˌwīf\ *n* : a woman who helps other women in childbirth — **mid·wife·ry** \-ˌwī-f(ə-)rē\ *n*
mid·win·ter \-ˈwint-ər\ *n* **1** : the middle of winter **2** : the winter solstice
mid·year \-ˌyi(ə)r\ *n* **1 a** : the middle of a calendar year **b** : the

middle of an academic year **2** : a midyear examination — **midyear** *adj*
mien \'mēn\ *n* : look, appearance, or bearing esp. as showing mood or personality : DEMEANOR
¹miff \'mif\ *n* **1** : a fit of ill humor **2** : a trivial quarrel
²miff *vt* : to put into an ill humor : OFFEND
¹might \(')mīt\ *past of* MAY — used as an auxiliary verb to express permission, probability, possibility in the past, or a present condition contrary to fact
²might \'mīt\ *n* : power to do something : FORCE
might·i·ly \'mīt-ᵊl-ē\ *adv* **1** : in a mighty manner : VIGOROUSLY **2** : very much
¹mighty \'mīt-ē\ *adj* **1** : having might : POWERFUL, STRONG **2** : done by might : showing great power **3** : great or imposing in size or extent — **might·i·ness** *n*
²mighty *adv* : VERY, EXTREMELY
mi·gnon·ette \,min-yə-'net\ *n* : a garden plant with long spikes of small fragrant greenish white flowers
mi·graine \'mī-,grān\ *n* : a condition marked by recurrent severe headache often with nausea and vomiting — **mi·grain·ous** \-,grā-nəs\ *adj*
mi·grant \'mī-grənt\ *n* : a person, animal, or plant that migrates — **migrant** *adj*
mi·grate \'mī-,grāt\ *vi* **1** : to move from one country, place, or locality to another **2** : to pass usu. periodically from one region or climate to another for feeding or breeding — **mi·gra·tion** \mī-'grā-shən\ *n*
mi·gra·to·ry \'mī-grə-,tōr-ē\ *adj* : of, relating to, or characterized by migration
mi·ka·do \mə-'käd-ō\ *n, pl* **-dos** : an emperor of Japan
mike \'mīk\ *n* : MICROPHONE
milch \'milk, 'milch\ *adj* : giving milk : kept for milk production
mild \'mīld\ *adj* **1** : gentle in nature or behavior **2** : moderate in action or effect : not strong **3** : TEMPERATE — **mild·ly** *adv* — **mild·ness** *n*
¹mil·dew \'mil-,d(y)ü\ *n* : a superficial usu. whitish growth produced on organic matter or living plants by fungi; *also* : a fungus producing mildew — **mil·dewy** \-,d(y)ü-ē\ *adj*
²mildew *vb* : to affect with or become affected with mildew
mile \'mīl\ *n* **1** : a unit of measure equal to 5280 feet **2** : a unit of measure equal to about 6076 feet
mile·age \'mī-lij\ *n* **1** : an allowance for traveling expenses at a certain rate per mile **2** : distance or distance covered in miles **3 a** : the number of miles that something (as a car or tire) will travel before wearing out **b** : USEFULNESS, PROFIT
mile·post \'mīl-,pōst\ *n* : a post indicating the distance in miles to a stated place
mil·er \'mī-lər\ *n* : a man or a horse that competes in mile races
mile·stone \'mīl-,stōn\ *n* **1** : a stone serving as a milepost **2** : an important point in progress or development
mi·lieu \mēl-'yə(r), -'yü\ *n* : ENVIRONMENT, SETTING
mil·i·tant \'mil-ə-tənt\ *adj* **1** : engaged in warfare : FIGHTING **2** : aggressively active esp. in a cause — **mil·i·tan·cy** \-tən-sē\ *n* — **militant** *n* — **mil·i·tant·ly** *adv*
mil·i·tar·i·ly \,mil-ə-'ter-ə-lē\ *adv* **1** : in a military manner **2** : from a military standpoint
mil·i·ta·rism \'mil-ə-tə-,riz-əm\ *n* **1 a** : control or domination by a military class **b** : exaltation of military virtues and ideals **2** : a policy of aggressive military preparedness — **mil·i·ta·rist** \-rəst\ *n* — **mil·i·ta·ris·tic** \,mil-ə-tə-'ris-tik\ *adj* — **mil·i·ta·ris·ti·cal·ly** \-'ris-ti-k(ə-)lē\ *adv*
mil·i·ta·rize \'mil-ə-tə-,rīz\ *vt* **1** : to equip with military forces and defenses **2** : to give a military character to — **mil·i·ta·ri·za·tion** \,mil-ə-t(ə-)rə-'zā-shən\ *n*
¹mil·i·tary \'mil-ə-,ter-ē\ *adj* **1** : of, relating to, or characteristic of soldiers, arms, or war **2** : carried on or supported by armed force **3** : of or relating to the army
²military *n, pl* **military** **1** : ARMED FORCES **2** : military persons; *esp* : army officers
military police *n* : a branch of an army that exercises guard and police functions
mil·i·tate \'mil-ə-,tāt\ *vi* : to have weight or effect : OPERATE
mi·li·tia \mə-'lish-ə\ *n* : a body of citizens with some military training who are called to active duty only in an emergency — **mi·li·tia·man** \-mən\ *n*
¹milk \'milk\ *n* **1** : a fluid secreted by the mammary glands of females for the nourishment of their young **2** : a liquid (as a plant juice) resembling milk
²milk *vb* **1** : to draw milk from the breasts or udder of **2** : to draw or yield milk **3** : to draw something from as if by milking; *esp* : to draw unreasonable or excessive profit or advantage from — **milk·er** *n*
milk·maid \'milk-,mād\ *n* : DAIRYMAID
milk·man \-,man, -mən\ *n* : a man who sells or delivers milk
milk of magnesia : a milk-white liquid preparation of magnesium in water used as a laxative and as a medicine to counteract acidity
milk shake *n* : a drink made of milk, a flavoring syrup, and sometimes ice cream shaken or mixed thoroughly
milk·sop \'milk-,säp\ *n* : a timid unmanly man or boy : MOLLYCODDLE
milk tooth *n* : one of the first temporary teeth of a young mammal that in man number 20
milk·weed \'milk-,wēd\ *n* : any of various related herbs and shrubs with milky juice and flowers usu. in dense clusters
milky \'mil-kē\ *adj* **1** : resembling milk in color or consistency **2** : MILD, TIMID **3** : consisting of, containing, or full of milk — **milk·i·ness** *n*
Milky Way *n* : a broad luminous irregular band of light that stretches across the sky and is caused by the light of a vast multitude of faint stars
¹mill \'mil\ *n* **1** : a building with machinery for grinding grain into flour **2** : a machine used in treating (as by grinding, crushing, stamping, cutting, or finishing) raw material **3** : a building or group of buildings with machinery for manufacturing
²mill *vb* **1** : to subject to an operation or process in a mill **2** : to hit out hard with the fists : SLUG **3** : to move about in a circle or in a disorderly eddying mass **4** : to undergo milling
³mill *n* : one tenth of a cent
mill·dam \'mil-,dam\ *n* : a dam to make a millpond; *also* : MILLPOND
mil·le·nar·i·an \,mil-ə-'ner-ē-ən\ *adj* **1** : of or relating to 1000 years **2** : of or relating to belief in the millennium — **millenarian** *n* — **mil·le·nar·i·an·ism** \-ē-ə-,niz-əm\ *n*
¹mil·le·nary \'mil-ə-,ner-ē, mə-'len-ə-rē\ *n, pl* **-nar·ies** **1** : a thousand units or things **2** : 1000 years : MILLENNIUM
²millenary *adj* : relating to or consisting of 1000
mil·len·ni·al·ism \mə-'len-ē-ə-,liz-əm\ *n* : MILLENARIANISM — **mil·len·ni·al·ist** \-ē-ə-ləst\ *n*
mil·len·ni·um \mə-'len-ē-əm\ *n, pl* **-nia** \-ē-ə\ *or* **-ni·ums** **1 a** : a period of 1000 years **b** : a 1000th anniversary or its celebration **2 a** : the thousand years mentioned in Revelation 20 during which holiness is to prevail and Christ is to reign on earth **b** : a period of great happiness or of perfection in human existence — **mil·len·ni·al** \-ē-əl\ *adj*
mill·er \'mil-ər\ *n* **1** : one that operates a mill; *esp* : one that grinds grain into flour **2** : a moth whose wings are covered with powdery dust
mil·let \'mil-ət\ *n* **1** : any of several small-seeded annual cereal and forage grasses; *esp* : one with small shiny whitish seeds **2** : the seed of a millet
mil·li·gram \'mil-ə-,gram\ *n* : a weight equal to 1/1000 gram
mil·li·me·ter \'mil-ə-,mēt-ər\ *n* : a measure of length equal to 1/1000 meter

mil·li·ner \'mil-ə-nər\ *n* **:** a person who designs, makes, trims, or sells women's hats
mil·li·nery \'mil-ə-ˌner-ē\ *n* **1 :** women's hats **2 :** the business or work of a milliner
mill·ing \'mil-iŋ\ *n* **:** a corrugated edge on a coin
mil·lion \'mil-yən\ *n, pl* **millions** *or* **million 1** — see NUMBER table **2 :** a very large or indefinitely great number — **million** *adj* — **mil·lionth** \-yən(t)th\ *adj or n*
mil·lion·aire \ˌmil-yə-'na(ə)r, 'mil-yə-ˌ\ *n* **:** one whose wealth is estimated at a million or more (as of dollars)
mill·pond \'mil-ˌpänd\ *n* **:** a pond produced by damming a stream to produce a head of water for operating a mill
mill·race \-ˌrās\ *n* **:** a canal in which water flows to and from a mill wheel; *also* **:** the current that drives the wheel
mill·stone \-ˌstōn\ *n* **1 :** either of two circular stones used for grinding a substance (as grain) **2 a :** something that grinds or crushes **b :** a heavy burden
mill·stream \-ˌstrēm\ *n* **:** the stream in a millrace
mill wheel *n* **:** a waterwheel that drives a mill
mill·wright \'mil-ˌrīt\ *n* **:** one whose occupation is planning and building mills or setting up their machinery
¹mime \'mīm, 'mēm\ *n* **1 :** MIMIC 2 **2 a :** an ancient play or skit representing scenes from life usu. in a ridiculous manner **b :** an actor in such a performance **3 :** the art of portraying a character or of narration by body movement **:** PANTOMIME
²mime *vb* **1 :** to act a part with mimic gesture and action usu. without words **2 :** to imitate closely **:** MIMIC **3 :** to act out in the manner of a mime — **mim·er** *n*
mim·e·o·graph \'mim-ē-ə-ˌgraf\ *n* **:** a machine for making copies of typewritten or written matter by means of a stencil — **mimeograph** *vb*
mi·me·sis \mə-'mē-səs, mī-'mē-\ *n* **:** IMITATION, MIMICRY
mi·met·ic \-'met-ik\ *adj* **1 :** IMITATIVE **2 :** relating to, characterized by, or exhibiting mimicry — **mi·met·i·cal·ly** \-'met-i-k(ə-)lē\ *adv*
¹mim·ic \'mim-ik\ *adj* **1 a :** IMITATIVE **b :** IMITATION, MOCK **2 :** of or relating to mime or mimicry
²mimic *n* **1 :** MIME 2b **2 :** one that mimics
³mimic *vt* **mim·icked** \-ikt\; **mim·ick·ing 1 :** to imitate closely **:** APE **2 :** to ridicule by imitation **3 :** SIMULATE
mim·ic·ry \'mim-i-krē\ *n, pl* **-ries :** the action, art, or an instance of mimicking
mi·mo·sa \mə-'mō-sə, mī-\ *n* **:** any of a genus of leguminous trees, shrubs, and herbs of warm regions with small white or pink flowers in ball-shaped heads
min·a·ret \ˌmin-ə-'ret\ *n* **:** a tall slender tower of a mosque from a balcony of which the people are called to prayer
min·a·to·ry \'min-ə-ˌtōr-ē, 'mī-nə-\ *adj* **:** THREATENING, MENACING
¹mince \'min(t)s\ *vb* **1 :** to cut into very small pieces **:** HASH **2 :** to utter with affectation **3 :** to restrain (words) within the bounds of politeness or decorum **4 :** to walk with short steps in a prim affected manner — **minc·er** *n*
²mince *n* **:** small bits into which something is chopped; *esp* **:** MINCEMEAT
mince·meat \'min(t)s-ˌmēt\ *n* **1 :** minced meat **2 :** a finely chopped mixture of ingredients (as raisins, apples, or spices) with or without meat
mince pie *n* **:** a pie made of mincemeat
minc·ing \'min(t)-siŋ\ *adj* **:** affectedly dainty or delicate — **minc·ing·ly** *adv*
¹mind \'mīnd\ *n* **1 :** MEMORY, RECOLLECTION **2 :** the element or complex of elements in an individual that feels, perceives, thinks, wills, and esp. reasons **3 :** INTENTION, DESIRE **4 :** the normal or healthy condition of the mental faculties **5 :** OPINION, VIEW **6 :** CHOICE, LIKING
²mind *vb* **1 a :** to attend to closely **b :** to pay attention to **:** HEED **c :** OBEY **2 :** NOTICE **3 a :** to be bothered about **b :** DISLIKE **4 a :** to be careful **:** SEE **b :** to be cautious about **:** watch out for **5 :** to take charge of **:** TEND — **mind·er** *n*
mind·ed \'mīn-dəd\ *adj* **1 :** having a specified kind of mind — usu. used in combination **2 :** DISPOSED, INCLINED
mind·ful \'mīn(d)-fəl\ *adj* **:** bearing in mind **:** AWARE, HEEDFUL — **mind·ful·ly** \-fə-lē\ *adv* — **mind·ful·ness** *n*
mind·less \'mīn-(d)ləs\ *adj* **:** lacking mind or consciousness; *esp* **:** UNINTELLIGENT — **mind·less·ly** *adv* — **mind·less·ness** *n*
mind reader *n* **:** one who professes or is held to be able to perceive another's thought without normal means of communication — **mind reading** *n*
mind's eye *n* **:** the mental faculty of conceiving imaginary or recollected scenes
¹mine \'mīn\ *pron* **:** my one **:** my ones — used without a following noun as a pronoun equivalent in meaning to the adjective *my*
²mine *n* **1 :** a pit or tunnel from which minerals (as coal, gold, or diamonds) are taken **2 :** a deposit of ore **3 :** a subterranean passage under an enemy position **4 a :** a charge buried in the ground and set to explode when disturbed (as by an enemy soldier or vehicle) **b :** an explosive charge placed in a case and sunk in the water to sink enemy ships **5 :** a rich source of supply
³mine *vb* **1 :** to dig a mine **2 :** to obtain from a mine **3 :** to work in a mine **4 a :** to burrow in the earth **:** dig or form mines under a place **b :** to lay military mines in or under
mine·lay·er \'mīn-ˌlā-ər\ *n* **:** a naval vessel for laying underwater mines
min·er \'mī-nər\ *n* **:** one that mines; *esp* **:** a person who works in a mine
¹min·er·al \'min-(ə-)rəl\ *n* **1 :** a naturally occurring crystalline element or compound (as diamond or quartz) that has a definite chemical composition and results from processes other than those of plants and animals **2 :** any of various naturally occurring substances (as ore, coal, salt, sand, stone, petroleum, natural gas, or water) obtained for man's use usu. from the ground
²mineral *adj* **1 :** of, relating to, or having the characteristics of a mineral **:** INORGANIC **2 :** containing mineral salts or gases
min·er·al·o·gy \ˌmin-ə-'räl-ə-jē, -'ral-\ *n* **:** a science that collects and studies facts about minerals — **min·er·al·og·i·cal** \ˌmin-(ə-)rə-'läj-i-kəl\ *adj* — **min·er·al·o·gist** \ˌmin-ə-'räl-ə-jəst, -'ral-\ *n*
mineral water *n* **:** water naturally or artificially impregnated with mineral salts or gases
min·e·stro·ne \ˌmin-ə-'strō-nē, -'strōn\ *n* **:** a rich thick vegetable soup with dried beans, macaroni, vermicelli, or similar ingredients
mine·sweep·er \'mīn-ˌswē-pər\ *n* **:** a warship designed for removing or neutralizing mines by dragging
min·gle \'miŋ-gəl\ *vb* **min·gled**; **min·gling** \-g(ə-)liŋ\ **1 a :** to bring or combine together or with something else **:** MIX **b :** to become mingled **2 :** to come in contact **:** ASSOCIATE
¹min·i·a·ture \'min-ē-ə-ˌchu̇r, 'min-i-ˌchu̇r, -chər\ *n* **1 :** something much smaller than the usual size; *esp* **:** a copy on a much reduced scale **2 :** the art of painting miniatures **3 :** a very small portrait or painting (as on ivory or metal) — **min·i·a·tur·ist** \-ˌchu̇r-əst\ *n*
²miniature *adj* **:** very small **:** represented on a small scale
min·i·a·tur·ize \-ˌchu̇r-ˌīz, -chər-\ *vt* **:** to design or construct in small size — **min·i·a·tur·i·za·tion** \ˌmin-ē-ə-ˌchu̇r-ə-'zā-shən, ˌmin-i-ˌchu̇r-, -chər-\ *n*
min·i·fy \'min-ə-ˌfī\ *vt* **-fied**; **-fy·ing :** to make small or smaller **:** LESSEN
min·im \'min-əm\ *n* **1 :** something very minute **2 :** a single downward stroke in penmanship
min·i·mal \'min-ə-məl\ *adj* **:** relating to or being a minimum **:** LEAST — **min·i·mal·ly** \-mə-lē\ *adv*

min·i·mize \'min-ə-ˌmīz\ *vt* **1** : to make as small as possible : reduce to a minimum **2 a** : to place a low estimate on **b** : BELITTLE, DISPARAGE — **min·i·mi·za·tion** \ˌmin-ə-mə-'zā-shən\ *n*

min·i·mum \'min-ə-məm\ *n, pl* **-ma** \-mə\ *or* **-mums** **1** : the least quantity assignable, admissible, or possible **2** : the lowest degree or amount reached or recorded — **minimum** *adj*

minimum wage *n* : a wage fixed by legal authority or by contract as the least that will provide the minimum standard of living necessary for employee health, well-being, and efficiency

min·ing \'mī-niŋ\ *n* : the process or business of working mines

min·ion \'min-yən\ *n* **1** : a servile dependent **2** : FAVORITE, IDOL **3** : a subordinate official

¹min·is·ter \'min-ə-stər\ *n* **1** : AGENT **2 a** : one officiating or assisting at the administration of a sacrament **b** : a Protestant clergyman **c** : a person exercising the functions of a clergyman **3** : a high government official entrusted with the management of a division of governmental activities **4 a** : a diplomatic representative (as an ambassador) accredited to the court or seat of government of a foreign state **b** : a diplomatic representative ranking below an ambassador and usu. accredited to states of less importance

²minister *vi* **min·is·tered**; **min·is·ter·ing** \-st(ə-)riŋ\ : to give aid : SERVE

min·is·te·ri·al \ˌmin-ə-'stir-ē-əl\ *adj* **1** : of or relating to a minister or ministry **2 a** : prescribed by law as part of the duties of an administrative office **b** : done in obedience to a legal order without exercise of personal judgment or discretion — **min·is·te·ri·al·ly** \-ē-ə-lē\ *adv*

min·is·trant \'min-ə-strənt\ *adj* : serving as a minister — **ministrant** *n*

min·is·tra·tion \ˌmin-ə-'strā-shən\ *n* : the act or process of ministering

min·is·try \'min-ə-strē\ *n, pl* **-tries** **1** : MINISTRATION **2** : the office, duties, or functions of a minister **3** : the body of ministers of religion : CLERGY **4** : AGENCY 2, INSTRUMENTALITY **5** : the period of service or office of a minister or ministry **6** *often cap* **a** : the body of ministers governing a nation or state from which a smaller cabinet is sometimes selected **b** : the group of ministers constituting a cabinet **7 a** : a government department presided over by a minister **b** : the building in which the business of a ministry is transacted

mink \'miŋk\ *n, pl* **mink** *or* **minks** \'miŋ(k)s\ : any of several slender-bodied mammals resembling the related weasels, having partially webbed feet and a somewhat bushy tail, and living near water; *also* : the soft typically dark brown fur of this animal

min·ne·sing·er \'min-i-ˌsiŋ-ər, 'min-ə-ˌziŋ-\ *n* : one of a class of German lyric poets and musicians of the 12th to the 14th centuries

min·now \'min-ō\ *n, pl* **minnows** *or* **minnow** : any of various small freshwater bottom-feeding fish (as the dace or shiner) related to the carps

¹mi·nor \'mī-nər\ *adj* **1 a** : inferior in dignity, rank, or importance **b** : inferior in number, quantity, or extent **2** : not having attained majority **3 a** : having the 3d, 6th, and sometimes the 7th degrees lowered by a half step **b** : based on a minor scale **4** : not involving risk to life : not serious **5** : of or relating to an academic minor

²minor *n* **1** : a person who has not attained majority **2** : a minor musical interval, scale, key, or mode **3** : an academic subject chosen by a student as a secondary field of specialization; *also* : a student specializing in such a field

³minor *vi* : to pursue an academic minor

mi·nor·i·ty \mə-'nȯr-ət-ē, mī-\ *n, pl* **-ties** **1 a** : the period before attainment of majority **b** : the state of being a legal minor **2** : the smaller in number of two groups constituting a whole; *esp* : a group having less than the number of votes necessary for control **3** : a part of a population differing from other groups in some characteristics and often subjected to differential treatment

minor league *n* : a league of professional clubs in a sport (as baseball) other than the recognized major leagues

minor party *n* : a political party whose strength in elections is so small as to prevent its gaining control of a government except in rare and exceptional circumstances

min·ster \'min(t)-stər\ *n* **1** : a church attached to a monastery **2** : a large or important church

min·strel \'min(t)-strəl\ *n* **1** : a medieval musical entertainer; *esp* : a singer of verses to the accompaniment of a harp **2 a** : MUSICIAN **b** : POET **3 a** : one of a troupe of performers typically giving a program of Negro melodies and jokes and usu. blacked in imitation of Negroes **b** : a performance by a troupe of minstrels

min·strel·sy \-sē\ *n, pl* **-sies** **1** : the singing and playing of a minstrel **2** : a body of minstrels **3** : a collection of songs or verse

¹mint \'mint\ *n* **1** : a place where coins are made **2** : a place where something is manufactured **3** : a vast sum or amount

²mint *vt* **1 a** : to make (money) out of metal : COIN **b** : to convert (a metal) into coin **2** : FABRICATE, INVENT — **mint·er** *n*

³mint *adj* : unmarred as if fresh from a mint

⁴mint *n* **1** : any of a family of herbs and shrubs (as basil, rosemary, and salvia) with square stems, opposite aromatic leaves, commonly 2-lipped flowers; *esp* : one (as peppermint or spearmint) that is fragrant and yields a flavoring oil **2** : a piece of candy flavored with mint

mint·age \'mint-ij\ *n* **1** : the action or process of minting coins **2** : coins produced by minting **3** : the cost of manufacturing coins

min·u·et \ˌmin-yə-'wet\ *n* **1** : a slow graceful dance consisting of forward balancing, bowing, and toe pointing **2** : music for or in the rhythm of a minuet

¹mi·nus \'mī-nəs\ *prep* : diminished by

²minus *n* **1** : a negative quantity **2** : DEFICIENCY, DEFECT

³minus *adj* **1** : algebraically negative **2** : falling low in a specified range

¹min·us·cule \'min-əs-ˌkyül, min-'əs-\ *n* : a lowercase letter

²minuscule *adj* : very small

¹min·ute \'min-ət\ *n* **1** : the 60th part of an hour of time or of a degree **2** : MOMENT **3 a** : a brief note of instructions or recommendations written on a document **b** : an official memorandum authorizing or recommending some action **4** *pl* : a series of brief notes taken to provide a record of the proceedings of a meeting

²minute *vt* **1 a** : to write in or in the form of a minute **b** : to write a minute on **2** : to make notes or a brief summary of

³mi·nute \mī-'n(y)üt, mə-\ *adj* **1** : very small : INFINITESIMAL **2** : of small importance : TRIFLING **3** : marked by close attention to details — **mi·nute·ness** *n*

mi·nute·ly \mī-'n(y)üt-lē, mə-\ *adv* **1** : into very small pieces **2** : in a minute manner or degree

min·ute·man \'min-ət-ˌman\ *n* : a member of a group of armed men pledged to take the field at a minute's notice during and immediately before the American Revolution

mi·nu·tia \mə-'n(y)ü-sh(ē-)ə, mī-\ *n, pl* **-ti·ae** \-shē-ˌē\ : a minute or minor detail — usu. used in pl.

minx \'miŋ(k)s\ *n* : a pert girl

mir·a·cle \'mir-i-kəl\ *n* **1** : an extraordinary event taken to manifest a supernatural work of God **2** : an extremely outstanding or unusual event, thing, or accomplishment

mi·rac·u·lous \mə-'rak-yə-ləs\ *adj* **1** : of the nature of a miracle : SUPERNATURAL **2** : resembling a miracle : MARVELOUS **3** : working or able to work miracles — **mi·rac·u·lous·ly** *adv* — **mi·rac·u·lous·ness** *n*

mi·rage \mə-'räzh\ *n* **1** : an optical effect that is sometimes seen at sea, in the desert, or over a hot pavement, that may have the appearance of a pool of water or a mirror in which distant objects are seen inverted, and that is caused by the bending or reflection of rays of light by a layer of heated air of varying density **2 :** something illusory like a mirage

[1]**mire** \'mī(ə)r\ *n* **1 :** MARSH, BOG **2 :** heavy often deep mud slush, or dirt

[2]**mire** *vb* **1 a :** to sink or stick fast in mire **b :** ENTANGLE, INVOLVE **2 :** to soil with mud, slush, or dirt

[1]**mir·ror** \'mir-ər\ *n* **1 :** a glass backed with a reflecting substance (as mercury) **2 :** a smooth or polished surface that reflects an image **3 :** something that reflects a true likeness or gives a true description **:** PATTERN, MODEL

[2]**mirror** *vt* **:** to reflect in or as if in a mirror

mirth \'mərth\ *n* **:** gladness or gaiety as shown by or accompanied with laughter

mirth·ful \-fəl\ *adj* **:** full of, expressing, or producing mirth — **mirth·ful·ly** \-fə-lē\ *adv* — **mirth·ful·ness** *n*

miry \'mī(ə)r-ē\ *adj* **1 :** MARSHY, BOGGY **2 :** MUDDY, SLUSHY

mis·ad·ven·ture \,mis-əd-'ven-chər\ *n* **:** MISFORTUNE, MISHAP

mis·al·li·ance \,mis-ə-'lī-ən(t)s\ *n* **:** an improper or unsuitable alliance esp. in marriage

mis·an·thrope \'mis-ᵊn-,thrōp\ *n* **:** a person who dislikes and distrusts mankind

mis·an·thro·py \mis-'an(t)-thrə-pē\ *n* **:** a dislike or hatred of mankind — **mis·an·throp·ic** \,mis-ᵊn-'thräp-ik\ *adj* — **mis·an·throp·i·cal·ly** \-'thräp-i-k(ə-)lē\ *adv*

mis·ap·ply \,mis-ə-'plī\ *vt* **:** to apply wrongly — **mis·ap·pli·ca·tion** \,mis-,ap-lə-'kā-shən\ *n*

mis·ap·pre·hend \,mis-,ap-ri-'hend\ *vt* **:** MISUNDERSTAND — **mis·ap·pre·hen·sion** \-'hen-chən\ *n*

mis·ap·pro·pri·ate \,mis-ə-'prō-prē-,āt\ *vt* **:** to appropriate wrongly; *esp* **:** to take dishonestly for one's own use — **mis·ap·pro·pri·a·tion** \-,prō-prē-'ā-shən\ *n*

mis·be·got·ten \,mis-bi-'gät-ᵊn\ *adj* **:** unlawfully or irregularly begotten **:** ILLEGITIMATE

mis·be·have \,mis-bi-'hāv\ *vi* **:** to behave badly — **mis·be·hav·ior** \-'hāv-yər\ *n*

mis·be·lief \,mis-bə-'lēf\ *n* **:** a mistaken or false belief

mis·be·liev·er \-'lē-vər\ *n* **:** one who is held to have false beliefs esp. in religion

mis·brand \(')mis-'brand\ *vt* **:** to brand falsely or in a misleading way

mis·cal·cu·late \(')mis-'kal-kyə-,lāt\ *vb* **:** to calculate wrongly — **mis·cal·cu·la·tion** \,mis-,kal-kyə-'lā-shən\ *n*

mis·call \(')mis-'kȯl\ *vt* **:** to call by a wrong name

mis·car·riage \mis-'kar-ij\ *n* **1 :** MISMANAGEMENT; *esp* **:** a failure or blunder in the administration of justice **2 a :** a failure (as of a letter) to arrive **b :** a failure (as of goods) to carry properly **3 :** the accidental separation of an unborn child from the body of its mother before it is capable of living independently **:** loss of a child through premature birth

mis·car·ry \mis-'kar-ē\ *vi* **1 :** to have a miscarriage **:** give birth prematurely **2 :** to fail of the intended purpose **:** go wrong or go amiss

mis·cast \(')mis-'kast\ *vt* **:** to cast in an unsuitable role

mis·ceg·e·na·tion \(,)mis-,ej-ə-'nā-shən, ,mis-i-jə-'nā-\ *n* **:** a mixture of races; *esp* **:** marriage or cohabitation between a white person and a member of another race

mis·cel·la·ne·ous \,mis-ə-'lā-nē-əs\ *adj* **1 :** consisting of numerous things of different sorts **:** MIXED **2 a :** marked by an interest in unrelated topics or subjects **b :** having the characteristics of a patchwork — **mis·cel·la·ne·ous·ly** *adv* — **mis·cel·la·ne·ous·ness** *n*

mis·cel·la·nist \'mis-ə-,lā-nəst\ *n* **:** a writer of miscellanies

mis·cel·la·ny \-nē\ *n, pl* **-nies 1 :** a mixture of various things **2** *pl* **:** separate studies or writings collected in one book

mis·chance \(')mis-'chan(t)s\ *n* **1 :** bad luck **2 :** a piece of bad luck **:** MISHAP

mis·chief \'mis-chəf\ *n* **1 :** injury or damage caused by a human agency **2 :** a source of harm, evil, or irritation; *esp* **:** a person who causes mischief **3 a :** action that annoys **b :** mischievous quality

mis·chie·vous \'mis-chə-vəs\ *adj* **1 :** causing mischief **:** intended to do harm **2 a :** causing or tending to cause petty injury or annoyance **b :** irresponsibly playful **3 :** showing a spirit of mischief — **mis·chie·vous·ly** *adv* — **mis·chie·vous·ness** *n*

mis·ci·ble \'mis-ə-bəl\ *adj* **:** capable of being mixed; *esp* **:** soluble in each other — **mis·ci·bil·i·ty** \,mis-ə-'bil-ət-ē\ *n*

mis·con·ceive \,mis-kən-'sēv\ *vt* **:** to interpret incorrectly **:** MISJUDGE — **mis·con·ceiv·er** *n* — **mis·con·cep·tion** \-'sep-shən\ *n*

[1]**mis·con·duct** \(')mis-'kän-(,)dəkt\ *n* **1 :** bad management **2 :** improper or unlawful behavior

[2]**mis·con·duct** \,mis-kən-'dəkt\ *vt* **1 :** MISMANAGE **2 :** to behave (oneself) badly

mis·con·struc·tion \,mis-kən-'strək-shən\ *n* **:** the act, the process, or an instance of misconstruing

mis·con·strue \,mis-kən-'strü\ *vt* **:** to construe wrongly **:** MISINTERPRET

mis·count \(')mis-'kau̇nt\ *vb* **:** to count incorrectly **:** MISCALCULATE — **miscount** *n*

mis·cre·ant \'mis-krē-ənt\ *n* **:** VILLAIN, SCOUNDREL, RASCAL — **miscreant** *adj*

[1]**mis·cue** \(')mis-'kyü\ *n* **1 :** a stroke (as in billiards) in which the cue slips **2 :** MISTAKE, SLIP

[2]**miscue** *vi* **1 :** to make a miscue **2 a :** to miss a stage cue **b :** to answer a wrong cue

mis·deal \(')mis-'dēl\ *vb* **-dealt** \-'delt\; **-deal·ing** \-'dē-liŋ\ **:** to deal wrongly — **misdeal** *n*

mis·deed \(')mis-'dēd\ *n* **:** a wrong deed

mis·de·mean·or \,mis-də-'mē-nər\ *n* **1 :** a crime less serious than a felony **2 :** MISDEED

mis·di·rect \,mis-də-'rekt, -dī-\ *vt* **:** to direct incorrectly — **mis·di·rec·tion** \-'rek-shən\ *n*

mis·do·ing \(')mis-'dü-iŋ\ *n* **1 :** WRONGDOING **2 :** MISDEED — **mis·do·er** \-'dü-ər\ *n*

mis·doubt \(')mis-'dau̇t\ *vt* **1 :** to doubt the reality or truth of **2 :** SUSPECT, FEAR — **misdoubt** *n*

mise-en-scène \,mē-,zäⁿ-'sen\ *n, pl* **mise-en-scènes** \-'sen(z)\ **1 :** the setting of a play **2 :** physical setting **:** ENVIRONMENT

mi·ser \'mī-zər\ *n* **:** a mean grasping person; *esp* **:** one who lives miserably in order to hoard his wealth

mis·er·a·ble \'miz-ər-bəl, 'miz-(ə-)rə-bəl\ *adj* **1 a :** wretchedly deficient or meager **b :** causing great discomfort or unhappiness **2 :** extremely poor or unhappy **:** WRETCHED **3 :** PITIFUL, LAMENTABLE **4 :** SHAMEFUL, DISCREDITABLE — **miserable** *n* — **mis·er·a·ble·ness** *n* — **mis·er·a·bly** \-blē\ *adv*

mi·ser·ly \'mī-zər-lē\ *adj* **:** of, relating to, or characteristic of a miser **:** GRASPING — **mi·ser·li·ness** *n*

mis·ery \'miz-(ə-)rē\ *n, pl* **-er·ies 1 :** a state of great suffering and want due to poverty or affliction **2 :** a circumstance, thing, or place that causes suffering or discomfort **3 :** a state of great unhappiness and emotional distress

mis·fea·sance \mis-'fēz-ᵊn(t)s\ *n* **:** the performance of a lawful action in an illegal or improper manner

mis·file \(')mis-'fīl\ *vt* **:** to file in an inappropriate place

mis·fire \(')mis-'fī(ə)r\ *vi* **1 :** to have the explosive or propulsive charge fail to ignite at the proper time **2 :** to fail to fire **3 :** to miss an intended effect — **misfire** *n*

mis·fit \(')mis-'fit\ *n* **1 :** something that fits badly **2 :** a person poorly adjusted to his environment

mis·for·tune \mis-'fȯr-chən\ *n* **1 :** bad fortune **:** ill luck **2 :** an unfortunate condition or event **:** DISASTER, MISHAP

mis·give \(ˈ)mis-ˈgiv\ *vb* **-gave** \-ˈgāv\; **-giv·en** \-ˈgiv-ən\; **-giv·ing** 1 : to suggest doubt or fear to 2 : to be fearful or apprehensive

mis·giv·ing \-ˈgiv-iŋ\ *n* : a feeling of doubt or suspicion esp. concerning a future event

mis·gov·ern \-ˈgəv-ərn\ *vt* : to govern badly — **mis·gov·ern·ment** \-ər(n)-mənt\ *n*

mis·guide \(ˈ)mis-ˈgīd\ *vt* : to lead astray : MISDIRECT — **mis·guid·ance** \-ˈgīd-ᵊn(t)s\ *n* — **mis·guid·er** *n*

mis·han·dle \(ˈ)mis-ˈhan-dᵊl\ *vt* 1 : to treat roughly : MALTREAT 2 : to manage wrongly

mis·hap \ˈmis-ˌhap, mis-ˈ\ *n* : an unfortunate accident

mish·mash \ˈmish-ˌmash, -ˌmäsh\ *n* : HODGEPODGE, JUMBLE

mis·in·form \ˌmis-ᵊn-ˈfȯrm\ *vt* : to give untrue or misleading information to — **mis·in·for·ma·tion** \ˌmis-ˌin-fər-ˈmā-shən\ *n*

mis·in·ter·pret \ˌmis-ᵊn-ˈtər-prət\ *vt* : to understand or explain wrongly — **mis·in·ter·pre·ta·tion** \-ˌtər-prə-ˈtā-shən\ *n*

mis·judge \(ˈ)mis-ˈjəj\ *vb* : to judge wrongly or unjustly — **mis·judg·ment** *n*

mis·lay \(ˈ)mis-ˈlā\ *vt* **-laid** \-ˈlād\; **-lay·ing** : to put in a place later forgotten : LOSE

mis·lead \(ˈ)mis-ˈlēd\ *vt* **-led** \-ˈled\; **-lead·ing** : to lead in a wrong direction or into a mistaken action or belief — **misleading** *adj*

mis·like \(ˈ)mis-ˈlīk\ *vt* : DISLIKE — **mislike** *n*

mis·man·age \(ˈ)mis-ˈman-ij\ *vt* : to manage badly or improperly — **mis·man·age·ment** *n*

mis·match \(ˈ)mis-ˈmach\ *vt* : to match (as in marriage) unsuitably or badly — **mismatch** *n*

mis·mate \(ˈ)mis-ˈmāt\ *vt* : to mate unsuitably

mis·name \(ˈ)mis-ˈnām\ *vt* : to name incorrectly : MISCALL

mis·no·mer \(ˈ)mis-ˈnō-mər\ *n* : a wrong or unsuitable name

mi·sog·a·mist \mə-ˈsäg-ə-məst\ *n* : one who hates marriage — **mi·sog·a·my** \-ˈsäg-ə-mē\ *n*

mi·sog·y·nist \mə-ˈsäj-ə-nəst\ *n* : one who hates or distrusts women — **mis·o·gyn·ic** \ˌmis-ə-ˈjin-ik, -ə-ˈgī-nik\ *adj*

mi·sog·y·ny \mə-ˈsäj-ə-nē\ *n* : a hatred of women

mis·place \(ˈ)mis-ˈplās\ *vt* 1 : to put in a wrong place 2 : MISLAY — **mis·place·ment** *n*

mis·play \(ˈ)mis-ˈplā\ *n* : a wrong or unskillful play — **misplay** *vt*

mis·print \(ˈ)mis-ˈprint\ *vt* : to print incorrectly — **misprint** \ˈmis-ˌprint, (ˈ)mis-ˈ\ *n*

mis·pro·nounce \ˌmis-prə-ˈnau̇n(t)s\ *vt* : to pronounce incorrectly or in a way regarded as incorrect — **mis·pro·nun·ci·a·tion** \-ˌnən(t)-sē-ˈā-shən\ *n*

mis·quote \(ˈ)mis-ˈkwōt\ *vt* : to quote incorrectly — **mis·quo·ta·tion** \ˌmis-kwō-ˈtā-shən\ *n*

mis·read \(ˈ)mis-ˈrēd\ *vt* **-read** \-ˈred\; **-read·ing** \-ˈrēd-iŋ\ 1 : to read incorrectly 2 : to misinterpret in or as if in reading

mis·rep·re·sent \ˌmis-ˌrep-ri-ˈzent\ *vt* : to give a false or misleading representation of — **mis·rep·re·sen·ta·tion** \(ˌ)mis-ˌrep-ri-ˌzen-ˈtā-shən\ *n*

¹mis·rule \(ˈ)mis-ˈrül\ *vt* : to rule or govern badly

²misrule *n* 1 : the action of misruling : the state of being misruled 2 : DISORDER, ANARCHY

¹miss \ˈmis\ *vb* 1 : to fail to hit, catch, reach, or get 2 : ESCAPE, AVOID 3 : to leave out : OMIT 4 : to discover or feel the absence of 5 : to fail to understand, sense, or experience 6 : MISFIRE

²miss *n* 1 **a** : a failure to reach a desired goal (as a target) **b** : a failure to attain a result 2 : MISFIRE

³miss *n* 1 **a** — used as a title before the name of an unmarried woman or girl **b** — used before the name of a place or of a line of activity or before some epithet to form a title for a girl who represents the thing indicated 2 : young lady — used without a name as a conventional term of address to a young woman 3 : a young unmarried woman or girl

mis·sal \ˈmis-əl\ *n* : a book containing the prayers to be said or sung in the Mass during the year

mis·send \(ˈ)mis-ˈsend\ *vt* : to send incorrectly

mis·shape \(ˈ)mis(h)-ˈshāp\ *vt* : to shape badly : DEFORM — **mis·shap·en** \-ˈshā-pən\ *adj*

mis·sile \ˈmis-əl\ *n* : an object (as a stone, arrow, artillery shell, bullet, or rocket) that is thrown or projected usu. so as to strike something at a distance; *esp* : GUIDED MISSILE

mis·sile·man \-mən\ *n* : one who helps to design, build, or operate guided missiles

mis·sile·ry \-rē\ *n* 1 : MISSILES; *esp* : GUIDED MISSILES 2 : the science dealing with the design, manufacture, and use of guided missiles

miss·ing \ˈmis-iŋ\ *adj* : ABSENT; *also* : LOST

missing link *n* 1 : an absent member needed to complete a series 2 : a hypothetical intermediate form between man and his presumed simian progenitors

mis·sion \ˈmish-ən\ *n* 1 **a** : a ministry commissioned by a religious organization to propagate its faith or carry on humanitarian work **b** : a mission establishment 2 **a** : a group sent to a foreign country to conduct diplomatic or political negotiations **b** : a team of military or technical specialists or cultural leaders sent to a foreign country 3 : a task or function assigned or undertaken; *esp* : an official assignment — **mission** *adj*

¹mis·sion·ary \ˈmish-ə-ˌner-ē\ *adj* 1 : relating to, engaged in, or devoted to missions 2 : characteristic of a missionary

²missionary *n, pl* **-ar·ies** : one sent to spread a religious faith among unbelievers

mis·sion·er \ˈmish-ə-nər\ *n* : MISSIONARY

mis·sive \ˈmis-iv\ *n* : a written communication : LETTER

mis·spell \(ˈ)mis-ˈspel\ *vt* : to spell incorrectly

mis·spell·ing \-ˈspel-iŋ\ *n* : an incorrect spelling

mis·spend \(ˈ)mis-ˈspend\ *vt* **-spent** \-ˈspent\; **-spend·ing** : WASTE, SQUANDER

mis·state \(ˈ)mis-ˈstāt\ *vt* : to state incorrectly — **mis·state·ment** *n*

mis·step \(ˈ)mis-ˈstep\ *n* 1 : a wrong step 2 : a mistake in judgment or action : BLUNDER

missy \ˈmis-ē\ *n* : a young girl : MISS

¹mist \ˈmist\ *n* 1 : water in the form of particles floating in the air or falling as fine rain 2 : something that blurs or hinders vision : HAZE, FILM 3 : a cloud of small particles or objects suggestive of a mist — **mist·like** *adj*

²mist *vb* 1 : to be or become misty 2 : to become dim or blurred 3 : to cover with mist

¹mis·take \mə-ˈstāk\ *vb* **mis·took** \-ˈstu̇k\; **mis·tak·en** \-ˈstā-kən\; **mis·tak·ing** 1 : to choose wrongly 2 **a** : to understand wrongly : MISINTERPRET **b** : to estimate incorrectly 3 : to identify wrongly — **mis·tak·en·ly** *adv* — **mis·tak·er** *n*

²mistake *n* 1 : a wrong judgment : MISUNDERSTANDING 2 : a wrong action or statement : BLUNDER

mis·ter \ˈmis-tər\ *n* 1 **a** — used as a title before the name of a man or a designation of occupation or office and usu. written *Mr.* or in the plural *Messrs.* **b** — used before the name of a place or of a line of activity or before some epithet to form a title for a male representing the thing indicated 2 : SIR — used without a name as a conventional term of address to a man

mis·tle·toe \ˈmis-əl-ˌtō\ *n* : a green plant with yellowish flowers and waxy white berries that grows on the branches and trunks of trees

mis·tral \ˈmis-trəl, mi-ˈsträl\ *n* : a violent cold dry northerly wind of southern Europe

mis·treat \(ˈ)mis-ˈtrēt\ *vt* : to treat badly : ABUSE — **mis·treat·ment** *n*

mis·tress \ˈmis-trəs; *in contracted form "Mrs."* ˌmis-əz, -əs\ *n* 1 : a woman (as the head of a household or school) who ha power, authority, or ownership like that of a master **2 :** something personified as female that rules or directs **3 :** a woman with whom a man cohabits without benefit of marriage **4 —** used formerly as a title before the name of a woman

mis·tri·al \(ˈ)mis-ˈtrī(-ə)l\ *n* **:** a trial that is void because of some error or serious prejudicial misconduct in the proceedings

¹mis·trust \(ˈ)mis-ˈtrəst\ *n* **:** a lack of confidence **:** DISTRUST — **mis·trust·ful** \-fəl\ *adj* — **mis·trust·ful·ly** \-fə-lē\ *adv* — **mis·trust·ful·ness** *n*

²mistrust *vb* **1 :** SUSPECT **2 :** to lack confidence in

misty \ˈmis-tē\ *adj* **1 :** full of mist **2 :** blurred by or as if by mist **3 :** VAGUE, INDISTINCT — **mist·i·ly** \-tə-lē\ *adv* — **mist·i·ness** \-tē-nəs\ *n*

mis·un·der·stand \(ˌ)mis-ˌən-dər-ˈstand\ *vt* **-stood** \-ˈstu̇d\; **-stand·ing 1 :** to fail to understand **2 :** to interpret incorrectly

mis·un·der·stand·ing \-ˈstan-diŋ\ *n* **1 :** a mistake of meaning **:** MISINTERPRETATION **2 :** QUARREL

mis·us·age \(ˈ)mis-ˈyü-sij, -ˈyü-zij, mish-ˈü-\ *n* **1 :** bad treatment **:** ABUSE **2 :** wrong or improper use

¹mis·use \(ˈ)mis-ˈyüz, mish-ˈüz\ *vt* **1 :** to use incorrectly **:** MISAPPLY **2 :** ABUSE, MISTREAT

²mis·use \(ˈ)mis-ˈyüs, mish-ˈüs\ *n* **:** incorrect or improper use **:** MISAPPLICATION

mite \ˈmīt\ *n* **1 :** any of various tiny animals that are related to the ticks and spiders, often live on plants, animals, and stored foods, and include important disease vectors **2 :** a very small coin or sum of money **3 :** a very small object or creature

¹mi·ter *or* **mi·tre** \ˈmīt-ər\ *n* **1 :** a high pointed headdress worn by a bishop or abbot in church ceremonies **2 :** a joint or corner made by cutting two pieces of wood at an angle and fitting the cut edges together

²miter *or* **mitre** *vt* **mi·tered** *or* **mi·tred**; **mi·ter·ing** *or* **mi·tring** \ˈmīt-ə-riŋ\ **1 :** to match or fit together in a miter joint **2 :** to bevel the ends of for making a miter joint

mit·i·gate \ˈmit-ə-ˌgāt\ *vt* **:** to make less severe — **mit·i·ga·ble** \ˈmit-i-gə-bəl\ *adj* — **mit·i·ga·tion** \ˌmit-ə-ˈgā-shən\ *n* — **mit·i·ga·tor** \ˈmit-ə-ˌgāt-ər\ *n* — **mit·i·ga·to·ry** \ˈmit-i-gə-ˌtōr-ē\ *adj*

mitt \ˈmit\ *n* **1 :** a woman's glove that leaves the fingers uncovered **2 :** MITTEN **3 :** a baseball glove (as for a catcher)

mit·ten \ˈmit-ᵊn\ *n* **:** a covering for the hand and wrist having a separate section for the thumb only

¹mix \ˈmiks\ *vb* **1 :** to make into one mass by stirring together **:** BLEND **2 :** to make by blending different things **3 :** to become one mass through blending **4 :** to associate with others on friendly terms **5 :** CONFUSE — **mix·er** *n*

²mix *n* **:** MIXTURE; *esp* **:** a commercially prepared mixture of food ingredients

mixed \ˈmikst\ *adj* **1 :** combining characteristics of more than one kind; *esp* **:** combining features of two or more systems **2 :** made up of or involving individuals or items or more than one kind: as **a :** made up of or involving persons differing in race, national origin, religion, or class **b :** made up of or involving individuals of both sexes **3 :** including or accompanied by inconsistent or incompatible elements **4 :** CROSSBRED

mix·ture \ˈmiks-chər\ *n* **1 :** the act, the process, or an instance of mixing **2 a :** something mixed or being mixed **:** a product of mixing **b :** a cloth made of thread of different colors **c :** a preparation consisting of two or more ingredients or kinds **3 :** the relative proportion of the elements in a mixture **4 :** two or more substances mixed together but not chemically united and not necessarily present in definite proportions

mix–up \ˈmiks-ˌəp\ *n* **1 :** an instance of confusion **2 :** CONFLICT, FIGHT

miz·zen *or* **miz·en** \ˈmiz-ᵊn\ *n* **1 :** a fore-and-aft sail set on the mizzenmast **2 :** MIZZENMAST

miz·zen·mast \-ˌmast, -məst\ *n* **:** the mast aft or next aft of the mainmast in a ship

mne·mon·ic \ni-ˈmän-ik\ *adj* **1 :** assisting or intended to assist memory **2 :** of or relating to memory — **mne·mon·i·cal·ly** \-ˈmän-i-k(ə-)lē\ *adv*

¹moan \ˈmōn\ *n* **1 :** a low drawn-out sound indicative of pain or grief **2 :** a sound like a moan

²moan *vb* **1 :** to utter a moan **2 :** COMPLAIN, LAMENT **3 :** to utter with moans

moat \ˈmōt\ *n* **:** a deep wide trench around the walls of a castle or fortress that is usu. filled with water **:** DITCH

¹mob \ˈmäb\ *n* **1 :** the common usu. uncultured mass of people; *esp* **:** the lower classes of a city **2 :** a large disorderly crowd often tending to violent and illegal action **3 a :** a criminal gang **b :** SET 2

²mob *vt* **mobbed**; **mob·bing :** to crowd about and attack or annoy

¹mo·bile \ˈmō-bəl, -ˌbēl, -ˌbīl\ *adj* **1 :** MOVABLE **2 :** changing quickly in expression **:** FLUID **3 :** capable of being readily moved **4 :** MIGRATORY **5 :** providing opportunity for or characterized by movement from one class or group to another — **mo·bil·i·ty** \mō-ˈbil-ət-ē\ *n*

²mo·bile \-ˌbēl\ *n* **:** an artistic structure (as of cardboard or sheet metal) that has parts moved by a current of air or by machinery or that is itself suspended (as by a wire) so as to move in a current of air

mo·bi·lize \ˈmō-bə-ˌlīz\ *vb* **1 :** to put into movement or circulation **2 :** to assemble and make ready for action **:** MARSHAL — **mo·bi·li·za·tion** \ˌmō-b(ə-)lə-ˈzā-shən\ *n*

mob·oc·ra·cy \mä-ˈbäk-rə-sē\ *n* **1 :** rule by the mob **2 :** the mob as a ruling class **3 :** rule by gangsters — **mob·o·crat** \ˈmäb-ə-ˌkrat\ *n* — **mob·o·crat·ic** \ˌmäb-ə-ˈkrat-ik\ *adj*

mob·ster \ˈmäb-stər\ *n* **:** a member of a criminal gang

moc·ca·sin \ˈmäk-ə-sən\ *n* **1 :** a soft leather shoe without a heel and with the sole and sides made of one piece joined on top by a seam to a U-shaped piece across the front **2 :** WATER MOCCASIN

¹mock \ˈmäk\ *vb* **1 :** to laugh at scornfully **:** RIDICULE **2 :** DEFY, DISREGARD **3 :** to make fun of by mimicking — **mock·er** *n* — **mock·ing·ly** *adv*

²mock *n* **1 :** an act of mocking **:** JEER **2 :** an object of ridicule

³mock *adj* **:** not real **:** SHAM

mock·ery \ˈmäk-(ə-)rē\ *n, pl* **-er·ies 1 :** insulting or contemptuous action or speech **2 :** someone or something that is laughed at **3 :** an insincere or a poor imitation **4 :** ridiculously useless or unsuitable action

mock–he·ro·ic \ˌmäk-hi-ˈrō-ik\ *adj* **:** ridiculing or burlesquing the heroic style or heroic character or action

mock·ing·bird \ˈmäk-iŋ-ˌbərd\ *n* **:** a songbird of the southern U.S. remarkable for its exact imitations of the notes of other birds

mock–up \ˈmäk-ˌəp\ *n* **:** a full-sized structural model built accurately to scale chiefly for study, testing, or display

¹mode \ˈmōd\ *n* **1 :** ²MOOD **2 a :** a particular form or variety of something **b :** a form or manner of expression **:** STYLE **c :** a manner of doing something — **mod·al** \ˈmōd-ᵊl\ *adj*

²mode *n* **:** a prevailing fashion or style of dress or behavior

¹mod·el \ˈmäd-ᵊl\ *n* **1 a :** a small but exact copy of something **b :** a pattern or figure of something to be made **2 :** a person who sets a good example **3 a :** a person or thing that serves as an artist's pattern; *esp* **:** a person who poses for an artist **b :** a person who wears in the presence of customers garments that are for sale **:** MANNEQUIN **4 :** a type or design of product (as a car or airplane) **5 a :** a description or analogy used to help visualize something (as an atom) that cannot be directly observed **b :** a system of assumptions, data, and inferences used to describe mathematically an object or state of affairs **6 :** a description of a possible or imaginary system

[2]**model** *vb* **mod·eled** *or* **mod·elled**; **mod·el·ing** *or* **mod·el·ling** \-ᵊl-iŋ, 'mäd-liŋ\ 1 : to plan or shape after a pattern 2 : to make a model : MOLD 3 : to act or serve as a model — **mod·el·er** *or* **mod·el·ler** \-ᵊl-ər, 'mäd-lər\ *n*

[3]**model** *adj* 1 : serving as or worthy of being a pattern 2 : being a miniature representation of something

[1]**mod·er·ate** \'mäd-(ə-)rət\ *adj* 1 : neither too much nor too little : not extreme 2 : avoiding extremes of behavior 3 : REASONABLE, CALM 4 a : avoiding extremes of view, program, and tactics esp. in politics and usu. inclined to compromise b : not extremely partisan 5 : neither very good nor very bad : MEDIOCRE, ORDINARY 6 : not expensive : reasonable in price — **mod·er·ate·ly** *adv* — **mod·er·ate·ness** *n*

[2]**mod·er·ate** \'mäd-ə-ˌrāt\ *vb* 1 : to make or become less violent, severe, or intense 2 : to preside over or act as chairman of a meeting

[3]**mod·er·ate** \'mäd-(ə-)rət\ *n* : one holding moderate views or belonging to a moderate group (as in politics or religion)

mod·er·a·tion \ˌmäd-ə-'rā-shən\ *n* 1 : the action of moderating 2 : the condition of being moderate or of keeping within proper bounds

mod·er·a·tor \'mäd-ə-ˌrāt-ər\ *n* 1 : one that moderates 2 : a presiding officer — **mod·er·a·tor·ship** \-ˌship\ *n*

[1]**mod·ern** \'mäd-ərn\ *adj* 1 : of, relating to, or characteristic of the present or the immediate past : CONTEMPORARY 2 : of or relating to the period from about 1500 to the present — **mo·der·ni·ty** \mə-'dər-nət-ē, mä-\ *n* — **mod·ern·ly** *adv* — **mod·ern·ness** *n*

[2]**modern** *n* : a person of modern times or with modern views

mod·ern·ism \'mäd-ər-ˌniz-əm\ *n* : a modern practice; *esp* : a modern usage, expression, or characteristic — **mod·ern·ist** \-nəst\ *n or adj* — **mod·ern·is·tic** \ˌmäd-ər-'nis-tik\ *adj*

mod·ern·ize \'mäd-ər-ˌnīz\ *vb* : to make or become modern : make conform to present usage, style, or taste — **mod·ern·i·za·tion** \ˌmäd-ər-nə-'zā-shən\ *n* — **mod·ern·iz·er** *n*

mod·est \'mäd-əst\ *adj* 1 : having a moderate opinion of one's own good qualities and abilities : not boastful 2 : showing moderation in size, scope, or aim : not excessive 3 : pure in thought, conduct, and dress : DECENT — **mod·est·ly** *adv*

mod·es·ty \'mäd-ə-stē\ *n* : the quality of being modest; *esp* : freedom from conceit or impropriety

mod·i·cum \'mäd-i-kəm, 'mōd-\ *n* : a limited quantity : a small amount

mod·i·fi·ca·tion \ˌmäd-ə-fə-'kā-shən\ *n* 1 : the act of modifying : the state of being modified 2 : QUALIFICATION, LIMITATION 3 : partial alteration

mod·i·fi·er \'mäd-ə-ˌfī(-ə)r\ *n* : one that modifies; *esp* : a word (as an adjective or adverb) joined to another word to limit or qualify its meaning

mod·i·fy \'mäd-ə-ˌfī\ *vb* **-fied**; **-fy·ing** 1 a : to make changes in : ALTER b : to become modified 2 : to lower or reduce in extent or degree : MODERATE 3 : to limit in meaning : QUALIFY — **mod·i·fi·a·ble** *adj* — **mod·i·fi·a·ble·ness** *n*

mod·ish \'mōd-ish\ *adj* : FASHIONABLE, STYLISH — **mod·ish·ly** *adv* — **mod·ish·ness** *n*

mo·diste \mō-'dēst\ *n* : a fashionable dressmaker

mod·u·lar \'mäj-ə-lər\ *adj* : of, relating to, or based on a module

mod·u·late \'mäj-ə-ˌlāt\ *vb* 1 : to adjust or regulate to a certain proportion; *esp* : to soften or tone down 2 : to tune to a key or pitch 3 : to vary the frequency, amplitude, or phase of a carrier wave for the transmission of intelligence (as in radio or television) 4 : to pass from one musical key to another usu. in a gradual movement and esp. by a melodious progression of chords — **mod·u·la·tor** \-ˌlāt-ər\ *n* — **mod·u·la·to·ry** \-lə-ˌtōr-ē\ *adj*

mod·u·la·tion \ˌmäj-ə-'lā-shən\ *n* : an action of modulating : the extent or degree by which something is modulated

mod·ule \'mäj-ül\ *n* 1 : a standard or unit of measurement 2 : a usu. packaged functional subassembly of parts (as for an electronic device)

mo·dus vi·ven·di \ˌmō-dəs-vi-'ven-dē\ *n* : a usu. temporary working arrangement or compromise pending or in place of a permanent settlement of matters in dispute

mo·gul \'mō-(ˌ)gəl, mō-'gəl\ *n* : a great personage : MAGNATE — **mogul** *adj*

mo·hair \'mō-ˌha(ə)r\ *n* : a fabric or yarn made wholly or in part of the long silky hair of the Angora goat; *also* : the hair of this goat

moi·e·ty \'mȯi-ət-ē\ *n, pl* **-ties** 1 : one of two equal parts : HALF 2 : approximately a half

[1]**moil** \'mȯil\ *vi* : to work hard : DRUDGE — **moil·er** *n*

[2]**moil** *n* 1 : hard work : DRUDGERY 2 : CONFUSION, TURMOIL

moi·ré \mȯ-'rā, mwä-\ *or* **moire** *same, or* 'mȯi(ə)r, 'mwär\ *n* : a fabric (as silk) having a watered appearance — **moiré** *adj*

moist \'mȯist\ *adj* : slightly wet : not completely dry : DAMP — **moist·ly** *adv* — **moist·ness** *n*

moist·en \'mȯis-ᵊn\ *vb* **moist·ened**; **moist·en·ing** \-ᵊn-iŋ, 'mȯis-niŋ\ : to make or become moist — **moist·en·er** \'mȯis-ᵊn-ər, 'mȯis-nər\ *n*

mois·ture \'mȯis-chər\ *n* : the small amount of liquid that causes moistness : dampness in the air or on a surface

[1]**mo·lar** \'mō-lər\ *n* : one of the broad teeth adapted to grinding food and located in the back of the jaw

[2]**molar** *adj* 1 : able or fitted to grind 2 : of or relating to a molar

mo·las·ses \mə-'las-əz\ *n* : a thick brown syrup that is separated from raw sugar in sugar manufacture

[1]**mold** \'mōld\ *n* : light rich crumbly earth containing decayed organic matter (as leaves or manure)

[2]**mold** *n* 1 : distinctive nature or character : TYPE 2 : the frame on or around which an object is constructed 3 a : a cavity in which something is shaped b : something shaped in a mold

[3]**mold** *vb* 1 : to knead into shape 2 : to form or become formed in or as if in a mold — **mold·a·ble** *adj* — **mold·er** *n*

[4]**mold** *n* : an often woolly surface growth of fungus esp. on damp or decaying organic matter; *also* : a fungus that produces mold

[5]**mold** *vi* : to become moldy

mold·board \'mōl(d)-ˌbōrd\ *n* : a curved iron plate attached above the plowshare of a plow to lift and turn the soil

mol·der \'mōl-dər\ *vi* **mol·dered**; **mol·der·ing** \-d(ə-)riŋ\ : to crumble into particles

mold·ing \'mōl-diŋ\ *n* 1 : the act or work of a person who molds 2 : an object produced by molding 3 : a strip of material having a shaped surface and used (as on a wall or the edge of a table) as a decoration

moldings 3

moldy \'mōl-dē\ *adj* 1 : of, resembling, or covered with a mold 2 : being old and moldering — **mold·i·ness** *n*

[1]**mole** \'mōl\ *n* : a small usu. brown and sometimes protruding permanent spot on the skin

[2]**mole** *n* : a small burrowing mammal with tiny eyes, concealed ears, and soft fur

[3]**mole** *n* 1 : a heavy masonry structure built in the sea as a breakwater or pier 2 : the harbor formed by a mole

mo·lec·u·lar \mə-'lek-yə-lər\ *adj* 1 : relating to molecules 2 : produced by or consisting of molecules

mol·e·cule \'mäl-i-ˌkyül\ *n* 1 : the smallest portion of a sub stance retaining all the properties of the substance in a mass 2 : a very small bit : PARTICLE

mole·hill \'mōl-,hil\ *n* 1 : a little ridge of earth thrown up by a mole 2 : an unimportant obstacle

mole·skin \-,skin\ *n* : the skin of the mole used as fur

mo·lest \mə-'ləst\ *vt* 1 : to annoy, disturb, or persecute esp. with hostile intent or injurious effect 2 : to take indecent liberties with — **mo·les·ta·tion** \,mōl-,es-'tā-shən, ,mäl-\ *n* — **mo·lest·er** *n*

moll \'mäl\ *n* : a girl friend esp. of a gangster

mol·li·fy \'mäl-ə-,fī\ *vt* **-fied**; **-fy·ing** 1 : CALM, QUIET 2 : APPEASE, PACIFY — **mol·li·fi·ca·tion** \,mäl-ə-fə-'kā-shən\ *n*

mol·lusk *or* **mol·lusc** \'mäl-əsk\ *n* : any of a large phylum of invertebrate animals (as snails or clams) with a soft body lacking segments and usu. enclosed in a calcareous shell — **mol·lus·can** \mə-'ləs-kən, mä-\ *adj*

[1]**mol·ly·cod·dle** \'mäl-ē-,käd-ᵊl\ *n* : a person who is used to being coddled or petted; *esp* : a pampered man or boy

[2]**mollycoddle** *vt* **-cod·dled**; **-cod·dling** \-,käd-liŋ, -ᵊl-iŋ\ : CODDLE, PAMPER — **mol·ly·cod·dler** \-,käd-lər, -ᵊl-ər\ *n*

Mol·o·tov cocktail \,mäl-ə-,tȯf-, ,mō-lə-\ *n* : a crude hand grenade made of a bottle filled with a flammable liquid (as gasoline) and fitted with a wick or saturated rag taped to the bottom and ignited at the moment of hurling

[1]**molt** \'mōlt\ *vb* : to shed hair, feathers, outer skin, or horns periodically with the cast-off parts being replaced by a new growth — **molt·er** *n*

[2]**molt** *n* : the act or process of molting

mol·ten \'mōlt-ᵊn\ *adj* : melted esp. by intense heat

mo·ly \'mō-lē\ *n* : a mythical herb with black root, white flowers, and magic powers

mo·lyb·de·num \mə-'lib-də-nəm\ *n* : a white metallic element used in steel alloys to give greater strength and hardness

mo·ment \'mō-mənt\ *n* 1 : a minute portion or point of time : INSTANT 2 : IMPORTANCE, CONSEQUENCE

mo·men·tar·i·ly \,mō-mən-'ter-ə-lē\ *adv* 1 : for a moment 2 : INSTANTLY 3 : at any moment

mo·men·tary \'mō-mən-,ter-ē\ *adj* : lasting only a moment : SHORT-LIVED, TRANSITORY

mo·ment·ly \'mō-mənt-lē\ *adv* : MOMENTARILY

moment of truth 1 : the final sword thrust in a bullfight 2 : a moment of crisis on whose outcome much or everything depends

mo·men·tous \mō-'ment-əs\ *adj* : very important : CONSEQUENTIAL — **mo·men·tous·ly** *adv* — **mo·men·tous·ness** *n*

mo·men·tum \mō-'ment-əm\ *n*, *pl* **-men·ta** \-'ment-ə\ *or* **-men·tums** : a property of a moving body that determines the length of time required to bring it to rest when under the action of a constant force or moment : the product of the mass of a body and its velocity; *also* : IMPETUS

mon·arch \'män-ərk, -,ärk\ *n* : a person who reigns over a kingdom or empire usu. for life and by hereditary succession: **a** : one having sovereign power and exercising effective control over the government **b** : one acting primarily as chief of state and exercising only limited powers — **mo·nar·chal** \mə-'när-kəl, mä-\ *or* **mo·nar·chi·al** \-kē-əl\ *adj*

mo·nar·chi·cal \mə-'när-ki-kəl, mä-\ *or* **mo·nar·chic** \-'när-kik\ *adj* 1 : of, resembling, or having the powers of a monarch 2 : having the form of a monarchy 3 : favoring monarchism

mon·ar·chism \'män-ər-,kiz-əm\ *n* 1 : the principles of monarchical government 2 : belief in or support of the principles of monarchical government — **mon·ar·chist** \-kəst\ *n*

mon·ar·chy \'män-ər-kē\ *n*, *pl* **-chies** 1 : undivided or absolute rule by one person 2 : a nation or country having a monarch as chief of state 3 : a form of government characterized by a usu. hereditary chief of state with life tenure and powers varying from nominal to absolute

mon·as·tery \'män-ə-,ster-ē\ *n*, *pl* **-ter·ies** : an establishment in which a community of religious persons and esp. monks live and carry on their work

mo·nas·tic \mə-'nas-tik\ *adj* 1 : of or relating to monks or monasteries 2 : separated from worldly affairs — **monastic** *n* — **mo·nas·ti·cal·ly** \-ti-k(ə-)lē\ *adv*

mo·nas·ti·cism \mə-'nas-tə-,siz-əm\ *n* : the life or state of monks : the system or practice of living apart from the rest of the world for religious reasons esp. as members of a secluded community

mon·au·ral \(')män-'ȯ-rəl\ *adj* : MONOPHONIC — **mon·au·ral·ly** \-rə-lē\ *adv*

Mon·day \'mən-dē\ *n* : the 2d day of the week

mon·e·tary \'män-ə-,ter-ē, 'mən-\ *adj* 1 : of or relating to coinage or currency 2 : of or relating to money : PECUNIARY

monetary unit *n* : the standard unit of value of a currency

mon·e·tize \'män-ə-,tīz, 'mən-\ *vt* 1 **a** : to establish as the standard of a national currency **b** : to establish as legal tender 2 : to coin into money — **mon·e·ti·za·tion** \,män-ət-ə-'zā-shən, ,mən-\ *n*

mon·ey \'mən-ē\ *n*, *pl* **mon·eys** *or* **mon·ies** \-ēz\ 1 : something generally accepted as a medium of exchange, a measure of value, or a means of payment: as **a** : officially coined or stamped metal currency **b** : paper money **c** : an amount or a sum of money 2 : wealth reckoned in terms of money 3 : a form or denomination of coin or paper money 4 : the 1st, 2d, and 3d place in a horse or dog race 5 : persons or interests possessing or controlling great wealth — **mon·ey·lend·er** \-,len-dər\ *n*

mon·ey·bags \-,bagz\ *n sing or pl* : a wealthy person

money changer *n* : one whose business is the exchanging of kinds or denominations of currency

mon·eyed *or* **mon·ied** \'mən-ēd\ *adj* 1 : having money : WEALTHY 2 : consisting in or derived from money

mon·ey–mak·er \'mən-ē-,mā-kər\ *n* 1 : one who accumulates wealth 2 : a plan or product that produces profit — **mon·ey·mak·ing** \-kiŋ\ *adj or n*

money order *n* : an order purchased at a post office, bank, or express or telegraph office directing another office to pay to a named payee a specified sum of money equal to the purchaser's deposit at the issuing office

mon·ger \'məŋ-gər\ *n* 1 : a dealer in some commodity — usu. used in combination 2 : one dealing in or promoting something petty or discreditable

mon·grel \'məŋ-grəl, 'mäŋ-\ *n* 1 : the offspring of parents of different breeds (as of dogs); *esp* : one of uncertain ancestry 2 : a person or thing of mixed origin — **mongrel** *or* **mon·grel·ly** \-grə-lē\ *adj* — **mon·grel·ism** \-grə-,liz-əm\ *n* — **mon·grel·i·za·tion** \,məŋ-grə-lə-'zā-shən, ,mäŋ-\ *n* — **mon·grel·ize** \'məŋ-grə-,līz, 'mäŋ-\ *vt*

mo·nism \'mō-,niz-əm, 'män-,iz-\ *n* : a view that a complex entity (as the universe) is basically one — **mo·nist** \'mō-nəst, 'män-əst\ *n* — **mo·nis·tic** \mō-'nis-tik, mä-\ *or* **mo·nis·ti·cal** \-ti-kəl\ *adj*

[1]**mon·i·tor** \'män-ət-ər\ *n* 1 **a** : a student appointed to assist a teacher **b** : a person or thing that warns or instructs **c** : one that monitors or is used in monitoring; *esp* : a receiver used to view the picture being picked up by a television camera 2 : a heavily armored warship formerly used in coastal operations that has a very low freeboard and one or more revolving gun turrets — **mon·i·to·ri·al** \,män-ə-'tōr-ē-əl\ *adj* — **mon·i·tor·ship** \'män-ət-ər-,ship\ *n* — **mon·i·tress** \'män-ə-trəs\ *n*

[2]**monitor** *vt* **mon·i·tored**; **mon·i·tor·ing** \'män-ət-ə-riŋ, 'män-ə-triŋ\ : to watch, observe, or check esp. for a special purpose: as **a** : to check (a radio or television signal or program) by means of a receiver for quality of transmission **b** : to check (a radio or television broadcast or a telephone conversation) for military, political or criminal significance **c** : to test for intensity of radioactivity

mon·i·to·ry \'män-ə-ˌtōr-ē\ *adj* : giving admonition : WARNING

monk \'məŋk\ *n* **1** : a member of a religious order of men taking vows of poverty, chastity, and obedience and living in community under a rule **2** : a member of a religious community of men **3** : a man who renounces the world for ascetic reasons — **monk·hood** \-ˌhu̇d\ *n*

[1]**mon·key** \'məŋ-kē\ *n, pl* **monkeys** **1** : a primate mammal other than man; *esp* : any of the smaller longer-tailed primates as contrasted with the apes **2 a** : a mischievous child : IMP **b** : a ludicrous figure : DUPE — **mon·key·ish** \-kē-ish\ *adj*

[2]**monkey** *vi* **mon·keyed**; **mon·key·ing** **1** : to act in a grotesque or mischievous manner **2** : TRIFLE, MEDDLE

mon·key·shine \'məŋ-kē-ˌshīn\ *n* : a mischievous trick : PRANK

monkey wrench *n* : a wrench with one fixed and one adjustable jaw at right angles to a straight handle

monk·ish \'məŋ-kish\ *adj* **1** : of or relating to monks **2** : having features attributed to a monk or monasticism — **monk·ish·ly** *adv* — **monk·ish·ness** *n*

monks·hood \'məŋ(k)s-ˌhu̇d\ *n* : a poisonous Eurasian herb related to the buttercups and often cultivated for its showy hood-shaped white or purplish flowers

mono·chrome \'män-ə-ˌkrōm\ *n* : a painting, drawing, or photograph in a single hue — **monochrome** *adj*

mon·o·cle \'män-i-kəl\ *n* : an eyeglass for one eye — **mon·o·cled** \-kəld\ *adj*

mono·cul·ture \'män-ə-ˌkəl-chər\ *n* : the cultivation of a single product to the exclusion of other uses of land

mon·o·dy \'män-əd-ē\ *n, pl* **-dies** : ELEGY, DIRGE — **mo·nod·ic** \mə-'näd-ik\ *adj* — **mon·o·dist** \'män-əd-əst\ *n*

mo·nog·a·mous \mə-'näg-ə-məs\ *adj* : of, relating to, or practicing monogamy — **mo·nog·a·mous·ly** *adv* — **mo·nog·a·mous·ness** *n*

mo·nog·a·my \mə-'näg-ə-mē\ *n* : marriage with but one person at a time — **mo·nog·a·mist** \-məst\ *n*

mono·gram \'män-ə-ˌgram\ *n* : an identifying symbol usu. made up of the combined initials of a person's name — **mono·gram** *vt* — **mono·grammed** \-ˌgramd\ *adj*

mono·graph \'män-ə-ˌgraf\ *n* : a learned treatise on a particular subject; *esp* : a scholarly or scientific paper printed in a journal or as a pamphlet

mono·lin·gual \ˌmän-ə-'liŋ-gwəl\ *adj* : expressed in or knowing or using only one language

mon·o·lith \'män-ᵊl-ˌith\ *n* **1** : a single great stone often in the form of a monument or column **2** : something (as a political organization or a social structure) held to be a single massive whole exhibiting solid uniformity — **mon·o·lith·ic** \ˌmän-ᵊl-'ith-ik\ *adj*

mon·o·logue *or* **mon·o·log** \'män-ᵊl-ˌȯg\ *n* **1** : a dramatic scene in which one person speaks alone **2** : a drama performed by one actor **3** : a literary composition (as a poem) in the form of a soliloquy **4** : a long speech monopolizing a conversation — **mon·o·logu·ist** \'män-ᵊl-ˌȯg-əst\ *n*

mono·ma·nia \ˌmän-ə-'mā-nē-ə, -'mā-nyə\ *n* **1** : mental derangement restricted to one idea or group of ideas **2** : excessive concentration on a single object or idea — **mono·ma·ni·ac** \-'mā-nē-ˌak\ *n or adj*

mo·nom·e·ter \mə-'näm-ət-ər\ *n* : a line consisting of one metrical foot

mono·phon·ic \ˌmän-ə-'fän-ik\ *adj* : of or relating to sound transmission, recording, or reproduction involving a single transmission path

mon·oph·thong \'män-ə(f)-ˌthȯŋ\ *n* : a vowel sound that throughout its duration has a single constant articulatory position — **mon·oph·thon·gal** \ˌmän-ə(f)-'thȯŋ-(g)əl\ *adj*

mono·plane \'män-ə-ˌplān\ *n* : an airplane with only one main supporting surface

mo·nop·o·list \mə-'näp-ə-ləst\ *n* : one who has a monopoly or favors monopoly

mo·nop·o·lis·tic \mə-ˌnäp-ə-'lis-tik\ *adj* : tending toward or having the characteristics of monopoly — **mo·nop·o·lis·ti·cal·ly** \-'lis-ti-k(ə-)lē\ *adv*

mo·nop·o·lize \mə-'näp-ə-ˌlīz\ *vt* : to acquire or have a monopoly of — **mo·nop·o·li·za·tion** \-ˌnäp-ə-lə-'zā-shən\ *n* — **mo·nop·o·liz·er** *n*

mo·nop·o·ly \mə-'näp-(ə-)lē\ *n, pl* **-lies** **1 a** : exclusive ownership or control through legal privilege, command of supply, or concerted action **b** : exclusive possession **2** : an instance of monopoly **3** : a commodity controlled by one party **4** : a person or group having a monopoly

mono·rail \'män-ə-ˌrāl\ *n* : a single rail serving as a track for cars that are balanced upon it or suspended from it

mono·syl·la·ble \'män-ə-ˌsil-ə-bəl, ˌmän-ə-'\ *n* : a word of one syllable — **mono·syl·lab·ic** \ˌmän-ə-sə-'lab-ik\ *adj* — **mono·syl·lab·i·cal·ly** \-'lab-i-k(ə-)lē\ *adv*

mono·the·ism \'män-ə-(ˌ)thē-ˌiz-əm\ *n* : a doctrine or belief that there is only one deity — **mono·the·ist** \-ˌthē-əst\ *n* — **mono·the·is·tic** \ˌmän-ə-thē-'is-tik\ *adj*

mono·tone \'män-ə-ˌtōn\ *n* **1** : a succession of syllables, words, or sentences on one unvaried key or pitch **2** : a single unvaried musical tone **3 a** : tedious sameness of tone or style **b** : sameness of color **4** : a person not able to produce musical intervals properly with the voice — **monotone** *adj* — **mono·ton·ic** \ˌmän-ə-'tän-ik\ *adj* — **mono·ton·i·cal·ly** \-'tän-i-k(ə-)lē\ *adv*

mo·not·o·nous \mə-'nät-ᵊn-əs, -'nät-nəs\ *adj* **1** : uttered or sounded in one unvarying tone **2** : tediously uniform or unvarying — **mo·not·o·nous·ly** *adv* — **mo·not·o·nous·ness** *n*

mo·not·o·ny \mə-'nät-ᵊn-ē, -'nät-nē\ *n, pl* **-nies** **1** : sameness of tone or sound **2** : lack of variety; *esp* : tiresome sameness

mon·ox·ide \mə-'näk-ˌsīd\ *n* : an oxide containing only one oxygen atom in the molecule

Mon·roe Doctrine \mən-ˌrō-\ *n* : a statement of U.S. foreign policy proclaimed in 1823 by President James Monroe expressing opposition to extension of European control or influence in the western hemisphere

mon·sei·gneur \ˌmō^{n}-ˌsān-'yər\ *n, pl* **mes·sei·gneurs** \ˌmā-ˌsān-'yər(z)\ : a French dignitary — used as a title preceding a title of office or rank

mon·sieur \məs(h)-'yə(r), mə-'si(ə)r\ *n, pl* **mes·sieurs** *same, or with* z *added*\ — used as a title equivalent to *Mister* and prefixed to the name of a Frenchman

mon·si·gnor \män-'sē-nyər\ *n, pl* **mon·si·gnors** *or* **mon·si·gno·ri** \ˌmän-ˌsēn-'yōr-ē\ : a Roman Catholic prelate — used as a title

mon·soon \män-'sün\ *n* **1** : a wind in the Indian ocean and southern Asia that blows from the southwest from April to October and from the northeast from October to April **2** : the rainy season that accompanies the southwest monsoon in India and adjacent areas

[1]**mon·ster** \'män(t)-stər\ *n* **1** : an animal or plant of abnormal form or structure **2** : a creature of strange or horrible form **3** : one unusually large for its kind **4** : an extremely wicked or cruel person

[2]**monster** *adj* : very large : ENORMOUS

mon·strance \'män(t)-strən(t)s\ *n* : a vessel in which the consecrated Host is exposed for the adoration of the faithful

mon·stros·i·ty \män-'sträs-ət-ē\ *n, pl* **-ties** **1** : the condition of being monstrous **2** : something monstrous : MONSTER

mon·strous \'män(t)-strəs\ *adj* **1** : being great or overwhelming in size : GIGANTIC **2** : having the qualities or appearance of a monster **3 a** : very ugly or vicious : HORRIBLE **b** : shockingly wrong or ridiculous **4** : deviating greatly from the natural form or character — **mon·strous·ly** *adv* — **mon·strous·ness** *n*

mon·tage \män-'täzh\ *n* **1** : a composite photograph made by combining several separate pictures **2** : an artistic composition made up of several different kinds of items (as strips of newspaper, pictures, bits of wood) arranged together

month \'mən(t)th\ *n, pl* **months** \'mən(t)s, 'mən(t)ths\ : one of the 12 portions into which the year is divided

[1]**month·ly** \'mən(t)th-lē\ *adj* **1** : occurring, done, produced, or issued every month **2** : computed in terms of one month **3** : lasting a month — **monthly** *adv*

[2]**monthly** *n, pl* **monthlies 1** : a monthly periodical **2** *pl* : a menstrual period

mon·u·ment \'män-yə-mənt\ *n* **1** : something that serves as a memorial; *esp* : a building, pillar, stone, or statue provided in memory of a person or event **2** : a work, saying, or deed that lasts or that is worth preserving **3** : a boundary marker (as a stone) **4** : a natural feature or historic site set aside and maintained by the government as public property

mon·u·men·tal \,män-yə-'ment-ᵊl\ *adj* **1** : serving as or resembling a monument : MASSIVE; *also* : OUTSTANDING **2** : of, relating to, or suitable for a monument **3** : very great : COLOSSAL — **mon·u·men·tal·ly** \-ᵊl-ē\ *adv*

moo \'mü\ *vi* : to make the natural throat noise of a cow : LOW — **moo** *n*

[1]**mood** \'müd\ *n* : a state or frame of mind : DISPOSITION

[2]**mood** *n* : a distinction of form of a verb to express whether its action or state is conceived as fact or in some other manner (as wish)

moody \'müd-ē\ *adj* **1** : subject to moods; *esp* : subject to fits of depression or bad temper **2** : expressing a moody state of mind — **mood·i·ly** \'müd-ᵊl-ē\ *adv* — **mood·i·ness** \'müd-ē-nəs\ *n*

moon \'mün\ *n* **1** : the celestial body that revolves around the earth **2** : SATELLITE 2a

moon·beam \-,bēm\ *n* : a ray of light from the moon

moon·calf \-,kaf, -,káf\ *n* **1** : MONSTER 1 **2** : a foolish or absentminded person : SIMPLETON

moon·light \-,līt\ *n* : the light of the moon

moon·light·er \-,līt-ər\ *n* : a person holding a second job in addition to a regular one — **moon·light·ing** *n*

moon·lit \-,lit\ *adj* : lighted by the moon

moon·scape \'mün-,skāp\ *n* : the surface of the moon as seen or as pictured

moon·shine \-,shīn\ *n* **1** : MOONLIGHT **2** : empty talk : NONSENSE **3** : intoxicating liquor; *esp* : illegally distilled corn whiskey — **moon·shin·er** *n*

moon·stone \-,stōn\ *n* : a transparent or translucent mineral with a pearly greenish or bluish luster that is a variety of feldspar and is used in jewelry

moon·struck \-,strək\ *adj* **1** : mentally unbalanced **2** : romantically sentimental

[1]**moor** \'mu̇(ə)r\ *n* : an area of open wasteland that is usu. infertile or wet and peaty

[2]**moor** *vb* : to secure or fasten with cables, lines, or anchors — **moor·age** \-ij\ *n*

moor·ing \'mu̇(ə)r-iŋ\ *n* **1** : a place where or an object to which a craft can be made fast **2** : a device (as a chain or line) by which an object is moored

moor·land \'mu̇(ə)r-lənd, -,land\ *n* : land consisting of moors

moose \'müs\ *n, pl* **moose 1** : a large ruminant mammal related to the typical deers and found in forested parts of Canada and the northern U.S. **2** : ELK 1

[1]**moot** \'müt\ *vt* **1** : to bring up for discussion : BROACH **2** : DEBATE

[2]**moot** *adj* **1** : DEBATABLE **2** : of no practical significance

moot court *n* : a mock court in which students of law argue hypothetical cases for practice

[1]**mop** \'mäp\ *n* **1 a** : an implement for cleaning made of a bundle of cloth or yarn fastened to a handle **b** : a device consisting of a sponge fastened to a handle **2** : something resembling a mop

[2]**mop** *vb* **mopped; mop·ping** : to wipe or clean with or as if with a mop — **mop·per** *n*

[1]**mope** \'mōp\ *vb* : to be or pass in a dull and dispirited state — **mop·er** *n*

[2]**mope** *n* **1** : a dull listless person **2** *pl* : low spirits : BLUES

mo·ped \'mō-,ped\ *n* : a small lightweight low-powered motorcycle that can be pedaled

mop·pet \'mäp-ət\ *n* : a young child

mop up *vb* **1** : to clean up by or as if by mopping **2** : to eliminate remaining resistance **3** : to finish a task

mop–up \'mäp-,əp\ *n* : a final clearance or disposal

mo·raine \mə-'rān\ *n* : an accumulation of earth and stones deposited by a glacier — **mo·rain·al** \-'rān-ᵊl\ *adj* — **mo·rain·ic** \-'rā-nik\ *adj*

[1]**mor·al** \'mȯr-əl\ *adj* **1 a** : of or relating to principles of right and wrong in behavior : ETHICAL **b** : expressing or teaching a conception of right behavior **c** : conforming to a standard of right behavior : VIRTUOUS, GOOD **d** : capable of right and wrong action **2** : probable but not proved : VIRTUAL — **mor·al·ly** \-ə-lē\ *adv*

[2]**moral** *n* **1** : the inner meaning of or lesson to be learned from a story or an experience **2** *pl* : moral teachings or principles **3** *pl* : moral conduct

mo·rale \mə-'ral\ *n* : the mental and emotional condition (as of enthusiasm, spirit, loyalty) of an individual or a group with regard to the function or tasks at hand

mor·al·ist \'mȯr-ə-ləst\ *n* **1** : one who moralizes; *esp* : a person who teaches, studies, or points out morals **2** : one who leads a moral life

mor·al·is·tic \,mȯr-ə-'lis-tik\ *adj* **1** : teaching or pointing out morals : MORALIZING **2** : narrowly conventional in morals — **mor·al·is·ti·cal·ly** \-'lis-ti-k(ə-)lē\ *adv*

mo·ral·i·ty \mə-'ral-ət-ē\ *n, pl* **-ties 1** : moral quality or character : VIRTUE **2** : moral conduct : MORALS **3** : a system of morals : principles of conduct

mor·al·ize \'mȯr-ə-,līz\ *vb* **1** : to explain in a moral sense : draw a moral from **2** : to make moral or morally better **3** : to make moral reflections : talk or write in a moralistic way — **mor·al·i·za·tion** \,mȯr-ə-lə-'zā-shən\ *n* — **mor·al·iz·er** *n*

mo·rass \mə-'ras\ *n* : MARSH, SWAMP — **mo·rassy** \-'ras-ē\ *adj*

mor·a·to·ri·um \,mȯr-ə-'tōr-ē-əm\ *n, pl* **-ri·ums** *or* **-ria** \-ē-ə\ **1** : a legally authorized period of delay in the performance of a legal obligation and esp. the payment of a debt **2** : a temporary ban or suspension

mor·bid \'mȯr-bəd\ *adj* **1 a** : of, relating to, or characteristic of disease **b** : not healthful : DISEASED **2** : characterized by gloomy or unwholesome ideas or feelings — **mor·bid·ly** *adv* — **mor·bid·ness** *n*

mor·bid·i·ty \mȯr-'bid-ət-ē\ *n, pl* **-ties 1** : the quality or state of being morbid **2** : the relative incidence of disease

mor·dant \'mȯrd-ᵊnt\ *adj* : biting and caustic in thought, manner, or style : INCISIVE — **mor·dan·cy** \-ᵊn-sē\ *n* — **mor·dant·ly** *adv*

[1]**more** \'mō(ə)r\ *adj* **1** : greater in amount or degree **2** : ADDITIONAL, FURTHER

[2]**more** *adv* **1 a** : in addition **b** : MOREOVER **2** : to a greater or higher degree — often used with an adjective or adverb to form the comparative

[3]**more** *n* **1** : a greater amount or number **2 a** : an additional amount **b** : additional persons or things

mo·rel·lo \mə-'rel-ō\ *n* : a cultivated sour cherry with dark red fruit

more·over \mōr-'ō-vər\ *adv* : in addition to what has been said

mo·res \'mȯ(ə)r-,āz, -,ēz\ *n pl* **1** : the fixed morally binding customs of a particular group **2** : CUSTOMS, CONVENTIONS

mor·ga·nat·ic marriage \,mȯr-gə-,nat-ik-\ *n* : a marriage between a person of royal or noble rank and a commoner who does not assume the superior partner's rank and whose children do not succeed to the title or inheritance of the parent of superior rank

morgue \ˈmȯrg\ *n* **1 :** a place where the bodies of persons found dead are kept usu. for identification until released for burial **2 :** a department of a newspaper where reference material is filed

mor·i·bund \ˈmȯr-ə-(ˌ)bənd\ *adj* **:** being in a dying state — **mor·i·bun·di·ty** \ˌmȯr-ə-ˈbən-dət-ē\ *n*

Mor·mon \ˈmȯr-mən\ *n* **:** a member of the Church of Jesus Christ of Latter-Day Saints — **Mormon** *adj* — **Mor·mon·ism** \ˈmȯr-mə-ˌniz-əm\ *n*

morn \ˈmȯrn\ *n* **1 :** DAWN **2 :** MORNING

morn·ing \ˈmȯr-niŋ\ *n* **1 a :** DAWN **b :** the time from sunrise to noon **c :** the time from midnight to noon **2 :** the first or early part

morning glory *n* **:** any of various usu. twining plants with showy trumpet-shaped flowers that usu. close when the sun is high

morn·ings \ˈmȯr-niŋz\ *adv* **:** in the morning repeatedly

morning sickness *n* **:** nausea on arising usu. associated with early pregnancy

mo·roc·co \mə-ˈräk-ō\ *n* **:** a fine leather made of goat skins tanned with sumac

mo·ron \ˈmōr-ˌän\ *n* **1 :** a feebleminded person having a potential mental age of between eight and twelve years and being capable of doing routine work under supervision **2 :** a very stupid person — **mo·ron·ic** \mə-ˈrän-ik\ *adj* — **mo·ron·i·cal·ly** \-ˈrän-i-k(ə-)lē\ *adv*

mo·rose \mə-ˈrōs\ *adj* **1 :** having a sullen and gloomy disposition **2 :** marked by or expressive of gloom — **mo·rose·ly** *adv* — **mo·rose·ness** *n*

mor·phia \ˈmȯr-fē-ə\ *n* **:** MORPHINE

mor·phine \ˈmȯr-ˌfēn\ *n* **:** a bitter white crystalline habit-forming drug made from opium and used to deaden pain and to induce sleep

mor·phol·o·gy \mȯr-ˈfäl-ə-jē\ *n* **1 a :** a branch of biology that deals with the form and structure of animals and plants **b :** the form and structure of an organism or any of its parts **2 :** the part of grammar dealing with word formation and including inflection, derivation, and the formation of compounds **3 a :** a study of structure or form **b :** STRUCTURE, FORM — **mor·pho·log·i·cal** \ˌmȯr-fə-ˈläj-i-kəl\ *adj* — **mor·pho·log·i·cal·ly** \-i-k(ə-)lē\ *adv* — **mor·phol·o·gist** \mȯr-ˈfäl-ə-jəst\ *n*

mor·ris \ˈmȯr-əs\ *n* **:** a vigorous English dance performed by men wearing costumes and bells

mor·ris chair \ˌmȯr-əs-\ *n* **:** an easy chair with adjustable back and removable cushions

mor·row \ˈmär-ō\ *n* **:** the next following day

Morse code \ˈmȯrs-\ *n* **:** either of two codes consisting of dots and dashes or long and short sounds used for transmitting messages by audible or visual signals

mor·sel \ˈmȯr-səl\ *n* **1 :** a small piece of food **:** BITE **2 :** a small quantity **:** a little piece

¹mor·tal \ˈmȯrt-ᵊl\ *adj* **1 :** capable of causing death **:** FATAL **2 a :** subject to death **b :** very tedious or prolonged **3 :** unrelentingly hostile **:** IMPLACABLE **4 :** very great, intense, or severe **5 :** HUMAN **6 :** of, relating to, or connected with death — **mor·tal·ly** \-ᵊl-ē\ *adv*

²mortal *n* **:** a human being

mor·tal·i·ty \mȯr-ˈtal-ət-ē\ *n, pl* **-ties 1 :** the quality or state of being mortal **2 a :** the number of deaths in a given time or place **b :** the ratio of deaths to population **3 a :** failure in and withdrawal or elimination from an activity **b :** the rate of failure and withdrawal from an activity

mortality table *n* **:** a table of mortality statistics over a number of years used chiefly by insurance companies in computing premiums

¹mor·tar \ˈmȯrt-ər\ *n* **1 :** a strong bowl-shaped container in which substances are pounded or rubbed with a pestle **2 :** a muzzle-loading cannon that has a tube short in relation to its caliber and is used to throw projectiles at high angles

²mortar *n* **:** a plastic building material (as one made of lime and cement mixed with sand and water) that hardens and is spread between bricks or stones to hold them together — **mortar** *vt*

mor·tar·board \ˈmȯrt-ər-ˌbōrd\ *n* **1 :** a board for holding mortar while it is being applied **2 :** an academic cap with a broad projecting square top

¹mort·gage \ˈmȯr-gij\ *n* **1 :** a conditional conveyance of rights to a piece of property usu. as security for the payment of a loan or debt and with the rights reverting to the mortgagor upon payment or performance according to stipulated terms **2 :** the formal document by which a mortgage is made

²mortgage *vt* **:** to subject to or as if to a mortgage

mort·gag·ee \ˌmȯr-gi-ˈjē\ *n* **:** a person to whom property is mortgaged

mort·ga·gor \ˌmȯr-gi-ˈjȯ(ə)r\ *n* **:** a person who mortgages his property

mor·ti·cian \mȯr-ˈtish-ən\ *n* **:** UNDERTAKER

mor·ti·fi·ca·tion \ˌmȯrt-ə-fə-ˈkā-shən\ *n* **1 :** the overcoming or disciplining of bodily passions and appetites through penance and self-denial **2 :** humiliation or shame caused by something that wounds one's pride **3 :** NECROSIS, GANGRENE

mor·ti·fy \ˈmȯrt-ə-ˌfī\ *vb* **-fied; -fy·ing 1 :** to subdue or deaden the body or bodily appetites through mortification **2 :** to subject to humiliation or shame **3 :** to become necrotic or gangrenous

mor·tise \ˈmȯrt-əs\ *n* **:** a hole cut in a piece of wood or other material into which another piece fits so as to form a joint

¹mor·tu·ary \ˈmȯr-chə-ˌwer-ē\ *n, pl* **-ar·ies :** a place in which dead bodies are kept until burial

²mortuary *adj* **:** of or relating to death or the burial of the dead

mo·sa·ic \mō-ˈzā-ik\ *n* **1 :** a surface decoration made by inlaying small pieces of variously colored material to form pictures or patterns; *also* **:** the process of making it **2 :** a picture or design made in mosaic **3 :** something resembling a mosaic — **mosaic** *adj*

mo·sa·icist \-ˈzā-ə-səst\ *n* **:** one who makes mosaics

mosque \ˈmäsk\ *n* **:** a Muslim place of worship

mos·qui·to \mə-ˈskēt-ō\ *n, pl* **-toes :** any of numerous two-winged flies having females with a proboscis adapted to puncture the skin of animals and suck the blood — **mos·qui·to·ey** \-ˈskēt-ə-wē\ *adj*

mosquito net *n* **:** a net for keeping out mosquitoes

moss \ˈmȯs\ *n* **:** any of a class of plants without flowers but with small leafy often tufted stems growing in patches and bearing sex organs at the tip — **moss·like** *adj*

moss·back \-ˌbak\ *n* **:** one who is far behind the times **:** an extremely conservative person **:** FOGY — **moss–backed** \-ˌbakt\ *adj*

mossy \ˈmȯ-sē\ *adj* **1 :** covered with moss or something like moss **2 :** resembling moss

¹most \ˈmōst\ *adj* **1 :** the majority of **2 :** greatest in quantity, extent, or degree

²most *adv* **1 :** to the greatest or highest degree — often used with an adjective or adverb to form the superlative **2 :** to a very great degree

³most *n* **:** the greatest amount, number, or part

⁴most *adv* **:** ALMOST

most·ly \ˈmōst-lē\ *adv* **:** for the greatest part **:** MAINLY

mote \ˈmōt\ *n* **:** a small particle **:** SPECK

mo·tel \mō-ˈtel\ *n* **:** a building or group of buildings used as a hotel in which the rooms are directly accessible from an outdoor parking area for automobiles

mo·tet \mō-ˈtet\ *n* **:** a polyphonic choral composition on a sacred text usu. without accompaniment

moth \'mȯth\ *n, pl* **moths** \'mȯt͟hz, 'mȯths\ : a usu. night-flying insect with mostly feathery antennae and a stouter body, duller coloring, and proportionately smaller wings than the related butterflies; *esp* : a small pale insect whose larvae eat wool, fur, and feathers

moth•ball \'mȯth-,bȯl\ *n* : a ball (as of naphthalene) used to keep moths out of clothing

moth–eat•en \'mȯth-,ēt-ᵊn\ *adj* **1** : eaten into by moths **2** : resembling cloth eaten into by moths

[1]**moth•er** \'mət͟h-ər\ *n* **1 a** : a female parent **b** (1) : a woman in authority; *esp* : the superior of a religious community of women (2) : an old or elderly woman **2** : SOURCE, ORIGIN — **moth•er•hood** \-,hu̇d\ *n* — **moth•er•less** \-ləs\ *adj* — **moth•er•less•ness** *n*

[2]**mother** *adj* **1 a** : of, relating to, or being a mother **b** : being in the relation of a mother to others **2** : derived from or as if from one's mother **3** : acting as or providing parental stock — used without reference to sex

[3]**mother** *vt* **moth•ered**; **moth•er•ing** \'mət͟h-(ə-)riŋ\ : to be or act as mother to

[4]**mother** *n* : a slimy mass of yeast cells and bacteria that forms on the surface of fermenting alcoholic liquids and is added to wine or cider to produce vinegar

moth•er•house \'mət͟h-ər-,hau̇s\ *n* **1** : the convent in which the superior of a religious community resides **2** : the original convent of a religious community

Mother Hub•bard \,mət͟h-ər-'həb-ərd\ *n* : a loose usu. shapeless dress

moth•er–in–law \'mət͟h-ər(-ə)n-,lȯ\ *n, pl* **moth•ers–in–law** \-ər-zən-,lȯ\ : the mother of one's husband or wife

moth•er•land \'mət͟h-ər-,land\ *n* **1** : the land of origin of something **2** : FATHERLAND

moth•er•ly \'mət͟h-ər-lē\ *adj* **1** : of, relating to, or characteristic of a mother **2** : resembling a mother : MATERNAL — **moth•er•li•ness** *n*

moth•er–of–pearl \,mət͟h-ər-ə(v)-'pərl\ *n* : the hard pearly iridescent substance forming the inner layer of a mollusk shell

mother tongue *n* **1** : one's native language **2** : a language from which another language derives

mother wit *n* : natural wit or intelligence

mo•tif \mō-'tēf\ *n* **1** : a usu. recurring element in a work of art; *esp* : a dominant idea or central theme **2** : a feature in a decoration or design

mo•tile \'mōt-ᵊl, 'mō-,tīl\ *adj* : exhibiting or being capable of movement — **mo•til•i•ty** \mō-'til-ət-ē\ *n*

[1]**mo•tion** \'mō-shən\ *n* **1** : a formal proposal for action made in a deliberative assembly **2** : an act, process, or instance of changing place : MOVEMENT — **mo•tion•less** \-ləs\ *adj* — **mo•tion•less•ly** *adv* — **mo•tion•less•ness** *n*

[2]**motion** *vb* **mo•tioned**; **mo•tion•ing** \'mō-sh(ə-)niŋ\ : to direct or signal by a movement or gesture

motion picture *n* **1** : a series of pictures projected on a screen in rapid succession with objects shown in successive positions slightly changed so as to produce the optical effect of a continuous picture in which the objects move **2** : a representation of a story or other subject matter by means of motion pictures

motion sickness *n* : sickness induced by motion (as in travel by air, car, or ship) and characterized by nausea

mo•ti•vate \'mōt-ə-,vāt\ *vt* : to provide with a motive : INDUCE — **mo•ti•va•tion** \,mōt-ə-'vā-shən\ *n* — **mo•ti•va•tion•al** \-shnəl, -shən-ᵊl\ *adv*

[1]**mo•tive** \'mōt-iv, *2 is also* mō-'tēv\ *n* **1** : something (as a need or desire) that leads or influences a person to do something **2** : a fragment of a musical theme recurring again and again and often elaborated or developed — **mo•tive•less** \-ləs\ *adj*

[2]**motive** *adj* : of or relating to motion or the causing of motion

[1]**mot•ley** \'mät-lē\ *adj* **1** : having various colors **2** : of various mixed kinds or parts

[2]**motley** *n* **1** : an old English woolen fabric of mixed colors **2 a** : a garment of motley constituting the characteristic dress of a court jester **b** : JESTER, FOOL **3** : a mixture of diverse elements

[1]**mo•tor** \'mōt-ər\ *n* **1** : a small compact engine **2** : INTERNAL-COMBUSTION ENGINE; *esp* : a gasoline engine **3** : MOTOR VEHICLE; *esp* : AUTOMOBILE **4** : a rotating machine that transforms electrical energy into mechanical energy

[2]**motor** *vi* : to travel by automobile

mo•tor•boat \'mōt-ər-,bōt\ *n* : a boat propelled by a motor

mo•tor•cade \'mōt-ər-,kād\ *n* : a procession of motor vehicles

mo•tor•car \-,kär\ *n* : AUTOMOBILE

motor court *n* : MOTEL

mo•tor•cy•cle \'mōt-ər-,sī-kəl\ *n* : a 2-wheeled motor vehicle — **motorcycle** *vi* — **mo•tor•cy•clist** \-,sī-k(ə-)ləst\ *n*

mo•tor•ist \'mōt-ə-rəst\ *n* : a person who travels by automobile; *esp* : one who drives an automobile

mo•tor•ize \'mōt-ə-,rīz\ *vt* **1** : to equip with a motor **2** : to equip with motor-driven vehicles for transportation — **mo•tor•i•za•tion** \,mōt-ə-rə-'zā-shən\ *n*

mo•tor•man \'mōt-ər-mən\ *n* : an operator of a motor-driven vehicle (as a streetcar or a subway train)

motor pool *n* : a group of governmental motor vehicles controlled by a single agency and dispatched for use as needed

motor scooter *n* : a low 2- or 3-wheeled automotive vehicle resembling a child's scooter but having a seat

motor vehicle *n* : an automotive vehicle not operated on rails; *esp* : one with rubber tires for use on highways

mot•tle \'mät-ᵊl\ *n* **1** : a colored spot **2** : a pattern of colored spots or blotches — **mottle** *vt* — **mot•tled** \-ᵊld\ *adj* — **mot•tler** \'mät-lər, -ᵊl-ər\ *n*

mot•to \'mät-ō\ *n, pl* **mottoes** **1** : a sentence, phrase, or word inscribed on something as suitable to its character or use **2** : a short expression of a guiding rule of conduct : MAXIM

moue \'mü\ *n* : a little grimace : POUT

[1]**mound** \'mau̇nd\ *n* : a small hill or heap of dirt (as made by man to mark a grave or to serve as a fort)

[2]**mound** *vt* : to form into a mound

[1]**mount** \'mau̇nt\ *n* : a high hill : MOUNTAIN — used esp. before a proper name

[2]**mount** *vb* **1** : RISE, ASCEND; *also* : CLIMB **2** : to get up onto something; *esp* : to get astride a horse **3** : to furnish (as troops) with riding animals or vehicles **4** : to increase rapidly in amount **5 a** : to prepare for use or display by fastening in proper position on a support **b** : to prepare (a specimen) for examination or display **6** : to furnish with scenery, properties, and costumes **7** : to post as a means of defense or observation **8** : to place (as artillery) in position — **mount•er** *n*

[3]**mount** *n* **1** : something upon which a person or thing is mounted : SUPPORT: as **a** : a jewelry setting **b** : a glass slide with its accessories on which objects are placed for examination with a microscope **2** : a means of conveyance; *esp* : SADDLE HORSE — **mount•a•ble** *adj*

moun•tain \'mau̇nt-ᵊn\ *n* **1** : a land mass that is higher than a hill **2** : a great mass or vast number

moun•tain•eer \,mau̇nt-ᵊn-'i(ə)r\ *n* **1** : a person who lives in the mountains **2** : a mountain climber — **mountaineer** *vi*

moun•tain•ous \'mau̇nt-ᵊn-əs, 'mau̇nt-nəs\ *adj* **1** : having many mountains **2** : resembling a mountain esp. in size : HUGE — **moun•tain•ous•ly** *adv* — **moun•tain•ous•ness** *n*

mountain range *n* : a series of mountains or mountain ridges closely related in direction and position

moun•tain•side \'mau̇nt-ᵊn-,sīd\ *n* : the side of a mountain

moun•tain•top \-,täp\ *n* : the summit of a mountain

moun•te•bank \'mau̇nt-i-,baŋk\ *n* **1** : a person who sells quack medicines from a platform (as at fairs and carnivals) **2** : a

boastful pretender : CHARLATAN — **moun·te·bank·ery** \-ˌbaŋ-k(ə-)rē\ *n*
Mount·ie \ˈmau̇nt-ē\ *n* : a member of the Royal Canadian Mounted Police
mount·ing \ˈmau̇nt-iŋ\ *n* **1** : the act of a person who mounts **2** : something that serves as a mount : SUPPORT
mourn \ˈmōrn\ *vb* : to feel or show grief or sorrow; *esp* : to grieve over someone's death — **mourn·er** *n* — **mourn·ing·ly** *adv*
mourn·ful \ˈmōrn-fəl\ *adj* **1** : expressing sorrow : SORROWFUL **2** : full of sorrow : SAD **3** : causing sorrow : SADDENING — **mourn·ful·ly** \-fə-lē\ *adv* — **mourn·ful·ness** *n*
mourn·ing \ˈmōr-niŋ\ *n* **1** : the act of sorrowing **2 a** : an outward sign (as black clothes or a veil) of grief for a person's death **b** : a period of time during which signs of grief are shown — **in mourning** : showing the outward signs and observing the conventions of mourning
mourning dove *n* : a wild dove of the U.S. with a mournful cry
[1]**mouse** \ˈmau̇s\ *n, pl* **mice** \ˈmīs\ **1** : any of numerous small rodents with pointed snout, rather small ears, elongated body, and slender tail **2** : a person without spirit or courage
[2]**mouse** \ˈmau̇z\ *vb* **1** : to hunt for mice **2** : to search or move slyly **3** : to move about softly like a mouse **4** : to discover by painstaking search
mous·er \ˈmau̇-zər\ *n* : a catcher of mice and rats; *esp* : a cat proficient at mousing
mousse \ˈmüs\ *n* : a light spongy food; *esp* : a dessert of sweetened and flavored whipped cream or thin cream and gelatin frozen without stirring
mous·tache \ˈməs-ˌtash, (ˌ)məs-ˈ\ *n* **1** : the hair growing on the human upper lip **2** : hair or bristles about the mouth of a lower animal
mousy *or* **mous·ey** \ˈmau̇-sē, -zē\ *adj* : of, relating to, or suggestive of mice: as **a** : QUIET **b** : TIMID, COLORLESS
[1]**mouth** \ˈmau̇th\ *n, pl* **mouths** \ˈmau̇t͟hz, ˈmau̇ths\ **1 a** : the opening through which food passes into the body of an animal **b** : the cavity that encloses in the typical vertebrate the tongue, gums, and teeth **2** : GRIMACE **3** : something that resembles a mouth esp. in affording entrance or exit **4** : the place where a stream enters a larger body of water — **mouthed** \ˈmau̇t͟hd, ˈmau̇tht\ *adj*
[2]**mouth** \ˈmau̇t͟h\ *vb* **1 a** : SPEAK, UTTER **b** : to utter loudly or pompously : RANT **c** : to repeat without comprehension or sincerity **2** : to take into the mouth — **mouth·er** *n*
mouth·ful \ˈmau̇th-ˌfu̇l\ *n* : as much as the mouth will hold; *also* : the amount put into the mouth at one time
mouth organ *n* : HARMONICA
mouth·part \ˈmau̇th-ˌpärt\ *n* : a structure or appendage near the mouth
mouth·piece \-ˌpēs\ *n* **1** : something placed at or held in the mouth **2** : a part (as of an instrument) to which the mouth is held **3** : one that expresses another's views : SPOKESMAN
mouth·wash \-ˌwȯsh, -ˌwäsh\ *n* : a usu. antiseptic liquid preparation for cleaning the mouth and teeth
[1]**mov·a·ble** *or* **move·a·ble** \ˈmü-və-bəl\ *adj* **1** : capable of being moved : not fixed **2** : changing from one date to another — **mov·a·bil·i·ty** \ˌmü-və-ˈbil-ət-ē\ *n* — **mov·a·ble·ness** *n* — **mov·a·bly** \ˈmü-və-blē\ *adv*
[2]**movable** *or* **moveable** *n* : a piece of property (as an article of furniture) that can be moved
[1]**move** \ˈmüv\ *vb* **1** : to change the place or position of : SHIFT **2** : to go or shift continuously from one place to another **3** : to set in motion **4 a** : to cause a person to act or decide : PERSUADE **b** : to take action : ACT **5** : to affect the feelings of **6 a** : to propose something formally in a deliberative assembly **b** : to present a motion or make an appeal **7** : to change hands or cause to change hands through sale or rental **8 a** : to change residence **b** : to change place or position : STIR **9** : to cause to operate or function : ACTUATE **10** : PROGRESS, ADVANCE **11** : to carry on one's way of life or activity **12** : to go away : DEPART **13** : to transfer a piece in a game (as chess or checkers) from one place to another **14** : to evacuate or cause to evacuate
[2]**move** *n* **1 a** : the act of moving a piece in a game **b** : the turn of a player to move **2 a** : a step taken to gain an objective : MANEUVER **b** : the action of moving : MOVEMENT **c** : a change of residence or location
move·less \ˈmüv-ləs\ *adj* : MOTIONLESS, FIXED — **move·less·ly** *adv* — **move·less·ness** *n*
move·ment \ˈmüv-mənt\ *n* **1 a** : the act or process of moving : an instance or manner of moving **b** : ACTION, ACTIVITY **2** : TENDENCY, TREND **3 a** : a series of actions taken by a body of persons to bring about an objective **b** : the body of persons taking part in a series of actions **4** : a mechanical arrangement (as of wheels) for causing a particular motion (as in a clock or watch) **5 a** : RHYTHM, METER; *also* : CADENCE, TEMPO **b** : a section of a longer piece of music **6** : an emptying of the bowels or the matter emptied
mov·er \ˈmü-vər\ *n* : one that moves or sets in motion; *esp* : a person or company that moves the belongings of others from one home or place of business to another
mov·ie \ˈmü-vē\ *n* **1** : MOTION PICTURE **2** *pl* : a showing of a motion picture **3** *pl* : the motion-picture industry
mov·ing \ˈmü-viŋ\ *adj* **1** : changing place or position **2** : causing motion or action **3** : having the power to affect the feelings or sympathies — **mov·ing·ly** *adv*
moving picture *n* : MOTION PICTURE
moving staircase *n* : ESCALATOR
[1]**mow** \ˈmau̇\ *n* : the part of a barn where hay or straw is stored
[2]**mow** \ˈmō\ *vb* **mowed**; **mowed** *or* **mown** \ˈmōn\; **mow·ing** **1** : to cut down with a scythe or machine **2** : to cut the standing herbage from **3** : to kill or destroy in great numbers **4** : to overcome decisively : ROUT — **mow·er** *n*
mow·ing machine \ˌmō-iŋ-\ *n* : an implement with blades for cutting standing grass or grain
[1]**much** \ˈməch\ *adj* **more** \ˈmō(ə)r\; **most** \ˈmōst\ : great in quantity, amount, extent, or degree
[2]**much** *adv* **more**; **most** **1 a** : to a great degree or extent : CONSIDERABLY **b** (1) : FREQUENTLY, OFTEN (2) : LONG **2** : APPROXIMATELY, NEARLY
[3]**much** *n* **1** : a great quantity, amount, extent, or degree **2** : something considerable or impressive
mu·ci·lage \ˈmyü-s(ə-)lij\ *n* : an aqueous solution of a gum or similar substance used esp. as an adhesive
mu·ci·lag·i·nous \ˌmyü-sə-ˈlaj-ə-nəs\ *adj* **1** : STICKY, VISCID **2** : producing or full of mucilage — **mu·ci·lag·i·nous·ly** *adv*
muck \ˈmək\ *n* **1** : soft moist barnyard manure **2** : DIRT, FILTH **3 a** : dark highly organic soil **b** : MIRE, MUD — **mucky** \ˈmək-ē\ *adj*
muck·rak·er \ˈmək-ˌrā-kər\ *n* : one of a group of writers noted for seeking out and exposing real or alleged abuses (as graft or corruption) in American business, government, and society at the beginning of the 20th century — **muck·rake** \-ˌrāk\ *vb*
mu·cous \ˈmyü-kəs\ *adj* **1** : of, relating to, or resembling mucus **2** : secreting or containing mucus
mu·cus \ˈmyü-kəs\ *n* : a slimy slippery protective secretion of membranes lining various bodily cavities — **mu·coid** \-ˌkȯid\ *adj*
mud \ˈməd\ *n* : soft wet earth
[1]**mud·dle** \ˈməd-ᵊl\ *vb* **mud·dled**; **mud·dling** \ˈməd-liŋ, -ᵊl-iŋ\ **1** : CONFUSE, STUPEFY **2** : to mix up confusedly **3** : to think or act in a confused way : BUNGLE — **mud·dler** \ˈməd-lər, -ᵊl-ər\ *n*
[2]**muddle** *n* **1** : a state of confusion **2** : a confused mess

mud·dle·head·ed \ˌməd-ᵊl-ˈhed-əd\ *adj* **1** : mentally confused **2** : BUNGLING, INEPT — **mud·dle·head·ed·ness** *n*

1**mud·dy** \ˈməd-ē\ *adj* **1** : filled or covered with mud **2** : resembling mud **3** : not clear or bright : DULL, CLOUDY **4** : CONFUSED, MUDDLED — **mud·di·ly** \ˈməd-ᵊl-ē\ *adv* — **mud·di·ness** \ˈməd-ē-nəs\ *n*

2**muddy** *vt* **mud·died**; **mud·dy·ing** **1** : to soil or stain with or as if with mud **2** : to make turbid **3** : to make cloudy or dull **4** : CONFUSE

mud·guard \ˈməd-ˌgärd\ *n* : a guard over a wheel of a vehicle to catch or deflect mud

mud·sling·ing \ˈməd-ˌsliŋ-iŋ\ *n* : the use of abusive tactics (as invective or slander) esp. in a political campaign — **mud·sling·er** *n*

mu·ez·zin \m(y)ü-ˈez-ᵊn\ *n* : a Muslim crier who calls the hours of daily prayers

1**muff** \ˈməf\ *n* : a soft thick cover into which both hands may be thrust for protection from cold

2**muff** *n* : a bungling performance; *esp* : a failure to hold a ball in attempting a catch — **muff** *vb*

muf·fin \ˈməf-ən\ *n* : a bread made of egg batter or yeast dough and baked in a small cup-shaped container

muf·fle \ˈməf-əl\ *vt* **muf·fled**; **muf·fling** \ˈməf-(ə-)liŋ\ **1** : to wrap up so as to conceal or protect or to prevent seeing, hearing, or speaking **2** : to deaden the sound of

muf·fler \ˈməf-lər\ *n* **1** : a scarf for the neck **2** : something that deadens noises; *esp* : a device attached to the exhaust system of an automobile

muf·ti \ˈməf-tē\ *n* : ordinary clothes when worn by one usu. dressed in a uniform

1**mug** \ˈməg\ *n* **1** : a usu. large metal or earthenware cylindrical drinking cup **2** : the face or mouth of a person **3** : THUG

2**mug** *vb* **mugged**; **mug·ging** **1** : to make faces esp. in order to attract the attention of an audience **2** : PHOTOGRAPH; *esp* : to take a police photograph of

3**mug** *vb* : to attack from behind esp. by seizing the throat and usu. with intent to rob

mug·ger \ˈməg-ər\ *n* : a person who attacks from behind

mug·gy \ˈməg-ē\ *adj* : being warm, damp, and stifling — **mug·gi·ly** \ˈməg-ə-lē\ *adv* — **mug·gi·ness** \ˈməg-ē-nəs\ *n*

mug·wump \ˈməg-ˌwəmp\ *n* : a person who is undecided or neutral in politics

Mu·ham·mad·an \mō-ˈham-əd-ən, mü-\ *n* : MUSLIM — **Muhammadan** *adj* — **Mu·ham·mad·an·ism** \-əd-ə-ˌniz-əm\ *n*

muk·luk \ˈmək-ˌlək\ *n* **1** : an Eskimo boot of sealskin or reindeer skin **2** : a boot with a soft leather sole worn over several pairs of socks

mu·lat·to \m(y)u̇-ˈlat-ō\ *n, pl* **-toes** *or* **-tos** **1** : a person with one Negro and one white parent **2** : a person of mixed white and Negro descent

mul·ber·ry \ˈməl-ˌber-ē\ *n* : any of a genus of trees with edible usu. purple fruits resembling berries; *also* : the fruit

mulch \ˈməlch\ *n* : a protective covering (as of sawdust, compost, or paper) used on the ground esp. to reduce evaporation, prevent erosion, control weeds, or enrich the soil; *also* : the material used — **mulch** *vt*

mulct \ˈməlkt\ *vt* **1** : to punish by a fine **2 a** : to defraud esp. of money : SWINDLE **b** : to obtain (as money) by fraud, duress, or theft

1**mule** \ˈmyül\ *n* **1** : a hybrid between a horse and a donkey; *esp* : the offspring of a male donkey and a mare **2** : a very stubborn person

2**mule** *n* : a slipper without sidepieces

mule skinner *n* : a driver of mules

mu·le·teer \ˌmyü-lə-ˈti(ə)r\ *n* : a driver of mules

mul·ish \ˈmyü-lish\ *adj* : STUBBORN, INFLEXIBLE — **mul·ish·ly** *adv* — **mul·ish·ness** *n*

1**mull** \ˈməl\ *vb* : to consider at length : PONDER

2**mull** *vt* : to sweeten, spice, and heat

mul·let \ˈməl-ət\ *n, pl* **mullet** *or* **mullets** **1** : any of a family of largely gray food fishes **2** : any of a family of moderate-sized usu. red or golden fishes with two barbels on the chin

mul·li·gan \ˈməl-i-gən\ *n* : a stew basically of vegetables and meat or fish

mul·li·ga·taw·ny \ˌməl-i-gə-ˈtȯ-nē\ *n* : a soup usu. of chicken stock seasoned with curry

mul·lion \ˈməl-yən\ *n* : a slender vertical bar between units of windows, doors, or screens — **mullion** *vt*

mul·ti·col·ored \ˌməl-ti-ˈkəl-ərd\ *adj* : having many colors

mul·ti·far·i·ous \ˌməl-tə-ˈfar-ē-əs\ *adj* : of various kinds : being many and varied — **mul·ti·far·i·ous·ly** *adv* — **mul·ti·far·i·ous·ness** *n*

mul·ti·fold \ˈməl-ti-ˌfōld\ *adj* : MANIFOLD

mul·ti·form \ˈməl-tə-ˌfȯrm\ *adj* : having many forms, shapes, or appearances

mul·ti·lat·er·al \ˌməl-ti-ˈlat-ə-rəl, -ˈla-trəl\ *adj* **1** : having many sides **2** : participated in by more than two nations or parties — **mul·ti·lat·er·al·ly** \-ē\ *adv*

mul·ti·mil·lion·aire \ˌməl-ti-ˌmil-yə-ˈna(ə)r, -ˈmil-yə-ˌ\ *n* : a person worth several million dollars

mul·ti·par·tite \ˌməl-ti-ˈpär-ˌtīt\ *adj* : having numerous members or signatories

1**mul·ti·ple** \ˈməl-tə-pəl\ *adj* : containing or consisting of more than one : MANIFOLD

2**multiple** *n* **1** : the product of a quantity by an integer **2** : a group with respect to its divisions or parts

multiple–choice *adj* : having several answers given from which the correct one is to be chosen

mul·ti·pli·ca·tion \ˌməl-tə-plə-ˈkā-shən\ *n* **1** : the act or process of multiplying **2** : a mathematical operation that consists of adding an integer to itself a specified number of times — **mul·ti·plic·a·tive** \ˌməl-tə-ˈplik-ət-iv, ˈməl-tə-plə-ˌkāt-\ *adj* — **mul·ti·plic·a·tive·ly** *adv*

mul·ti·plic·i·ty \ˌməl-tə-ˈplis-ət-ē\ *n, pl* **-ties** **1** : the quality or state of being multiple or various **2** : a great number

mul·ti·ply \ˈməl-tə-ˌplī\ *vb* **-plied**; **-ply·ing** **1 a** : to increase in number : make or become more numerous **b** : BREED, PROPAGATE **2** : to find the product of numbers by means of multiplication : perform the operation of multiplication — **mul·ti·pli·er** *n*

mul·ti·ra·cial \ˌməl-tē-ˈrā-shəl, -ˌtī-\ *adj* : composed of, relating to, or representing various races

mul·ti·stage \ˌməl-ti-ˌstāj\ *adj* : operating in or involving two or more steps or stages

mul·ti·sto·ry \ˌməl-ti-ˌstōr-ē\ *adj* : having several stories

mul·ti·tude \ˈməl-tə-ˌt(y)üd\ *n* : a countless number of things or people : HOST

mul·ti·tu·di·nous \ˌməl-tə-ˈt(y)üd-nəs, -ᵊn-əs\ *adj* : consisting of a great multitude — **mul·ti·tu·di·nous·ly** *adv* — **mul·ti·tu·di·nous·ness** *n*

mul·ti·ver·si·ty \ˌməl-ti-ˈvər-sət-ē, -ˈvər-stē\ *n, pl* **-ties** : a very large university with many component schools, colleges, or divisions, with widely diverse functions, and with a large staff engaged in activities other than instruction and esp. in administration

mul·ti·vol·ume \ˌməl-ti-ˈväl-yəm, -ˌtī-\ *or* **mul·ti·vol·umed** \-yəmd\ *adj* : comprising several volumes

1**mum** \ˈməm\ *adj* : SILENT — often used interjectionally

2**mum** *n* : CHRYSANTHEMUM

mum·ble \ˈməm-bəl\ *vb* **mum·bled**; **mum·bling** \-b(ə-)liŋ\ **1** : to speak indistinctly usu. with lips partly closed : MUTTER **2** : to chew gently with closed lips or with little use of the lips — **mumble** *n* — **mum·bler** \-b(ə-)lər\ *n* — **mum·bling·ly** *adv*

mum·ble·ty–peg \ˈməm-bəl-(tē-)ˌpeg\ *n* : a game in which the players try to flip a knife from various positions so that the blade will stick into the ground

mum·bo jum·bo \ˌməm-bō-ˈjəm-bō\ *n* **1** : an object of superstitious homage and fear **2 a** : a complicated ritual with elaborate trappings **b** : complicated activity or language that obscures and confuses
mum·mer \ˈməm-ər\ *n* **1** : a person who masks and engages in merrymaking (as at Christmastide) **2** : an actor esp. in a pantomime
mum·mery \ˈməm-ə-rē\ *n, pl* **-mer·ies** **1** : a performance by mummers **2** : a ridiculous or pompous ceremony
mum·mi·fy \ˈməm-i-ˌfī\ *vb* **-fied**; **-fy·ing** **1** : to embalm and dry as a mummy **2** : to dry up like the skin of a mummy : SHRIVEL — **mum·mi·fi·ca·tion** \ˌməm-i-fə-ˈkā-shən\ *n*
mum·my \ˈməm-ē\ *n, pl* **mummies** : a body embalmed for burial in the manner of the ancient Egyptians
mumps \ˈməm(p)s\ *n sing or pl* : an acute contagious virus disease marked by fever and by swelling esp. of salivary glands
munch \ˈmənch\ *vb* : to chew with a crunching sound — **munch·er** *n*
mun·dane \ˌmən-ˈdān, ˈmən-ˌ\ *adj* : of or relating to the world : WORLDLY — **mun·dane·ly** *adv*
mu·nic·i·pal \myu̇-ˈnis-ə-pəl\ *adj* **1** : of or relating to the internal affairs of a nation **2** : of or relating to a municipality — **mu·nic·i·pal·ly** \-p(ə-)lē\ *adv*
mu·nic·i·pal·i·ty \myu̇-ˌnis-ə-ˈpal-ət-ē\ *n, pl* **-ties** : a primarily urban political unit (as a city or town) having corporate status and usu. powers of self-government
mu·nif·i·cent \myu̇-ˈnif-ə-sənt\ *adj* : extremely liberal in giving : very generous — **mu·nif·i·cence** \-sən(t)s\ *n* — **mu·nif·i·cent·ly** *adv*
mu·ni·tions \myu̇-ˈnish-ənz\ *n pl* : military supplies, equipment, or provisions; *esp* : AMMUNITION — **mu·ni·tion** \-ˈnish-ən\ *vt*
mun·tin \ˈmənt-ᵊn\ *or* **munt·ing** \-ᵊn, -iŋ\ *n* : a strip separating panes of glass in a sash
¹**mu·ral** \ˈmyu̇r-əl\ *adj* **1** : of or relating to a wall **2** : applied to and made a part of a wall surface
²**mural** *n* : a mural painting — **mu·ral·ist** \-ə-ləst\ *n*
¹**mur·der** \ˈmərd-ər\ *n* : the crime of unlawfully killing a person esp. with deliberate intent or design
²**murder** *vb* **mur·dered**; **mur·der·ing** \ˈmərd-(ə-)riŋ\ **1** : to kill a human being unlawfully and esp. with deliberate intent or design : commit murder **2** : to spoil by performing in a wretched manner : MANGLE — **mur·der·er** *n* — **mur·der·ess** \ˈmərd-ə-rəs\ *n*
mur·der·ous \ˈmərd-(ə-)rəs\ *adj* **1** : resulting in or likely to result in murder **2** : having or appearing to have the purpose of murder — **mur·der·ous·ly** *adv* — **mur·der·ous·ness** *n*
murk \ˈmərk\ *n* : DARKNESS, GLOOM; *also* : FOG
murky \ˈmər-kē\ *adj* **1** : marked by darkness, gloominess, or pbscurity **2** : FOGGY, MISTY — **murk·i·ly** \-kə-lē\ *adv* — **murk·i·ness** \-kē-nəs\ *n*
mur·mur \ˈmər-mər\ *n* **1** : a muttered complaint : GRUMBLE **2** : a low indistinct sound **3** : an abnormal heart sound occurring when the heart is disordered in function or structure — **murmur** *vb* — **mur·mur·er** *n*
mur·mur·ous \ˈmərm-(ə-)rəs\ *adj* : filled with or characterized by murmurs — **mur·mur·ous·ly** *adv*
mur·rain \ˈmər-ən\ *n* : a pestilence or plague esp. of domestic animals
mus·ca·tel \ˌməs-kə-ˈtel\ *n* : a sweet dessert wine
¹**mus·cle** \ˈməs-əl\ *n* **1 a** : a body tissue consisting of long cells that contract when stimulated and produce motion **b** : an organ that is essentially a mass of muscle tissue attached at either end to a fixed point and that by contracting moves or checks the movement of a body part **2** : muscular strength : BRAWN
²**muscle** *vi* **mus·cled**; **mus·cling** \ˈməs-(ə-)liŋ\ : to force one's way
mus·cle–bound \ˈməs-əl-ˌbau̇nd\ *adj* : having some of the muscles abnormally enlarged and lacking in elasticity (as from excessive athletic exercise)
mus·cu·lar \ˈməs-kyə-lər\ *adj* **1 a** : of, relating to, or constituting muscle **b** : performed by the muscles **2 a** : having well-developed muscles **b** : of or relating to physical strength : STRONG — **mus·cu·lar·i·ty** \ˌməs-kyə-ˈlar-ət-ē\ *n* — **mus·cu·lar·ly** *adv*
mus·cu·la·ture \ˈməs-kyə-lə-ˌchu̇(ə)r\ *n* : the muscles of the body or of one of its parts
¹**muse** \ˈmyüz\ *vb* : to consider carefully : PONDER, MEDITATE — **mus·er** *n* — **mus·ing·ly** *adv*
²**muse** *n* : a source of inspiration; *esp* : a guiding genius
mu·sette \myü-ˈzet\ *n* : a small knapsack with a shoulder strap used esp. by soldiers for carrying provisions and personal belongings
mu·se·um \myu̇-ˈzē-əm, ˈmyü-ˌ\ *n* : a building or part of a building in which are displayed objects of permanent interest in one or more of the arts or sciences
¹**mush** \ˈməsh\ *n* **1** : cornmeal boiled in water **2** : something soft and spongy or shapeless **3** : insipid sentimentality or courting
²**mush** *vi* : to travel over snow with a sled drawn by dogs — often used as a command to a dog team — **mush·er** *n*
³**mush** *n* : a hike across snow with a dog team
¹**mush·room** \ˈməsh-ˌrüm, -ˌru̇m\ *n* : the fleshy usually caplike fruiting body of various fungi esp. when edible
²**mushroom** *adj* **1** : springing up suddenly or multiplying rapidly **2** : having the shape of a mushroom
³**mushroom** *vi* : to spring up suddenly or multiply rapidly
mushy \ˈməsh-ē\ *adj* **1** : soft like mush **2** : weakly sentimental — **mush·i·ly** \ˈməsh-ə-lē\ *adv* — **mush·i·ness** \ˈməsh-ē-nəs\ *n*
mu·sic \ˈmyü-zik\ *n* **1 a** : the art of combining tones so that they are pleasing, expressive, or intelligible **b** : compositions made according to the rules of music **c** : the score of music compositions inscribed on paper **2** : sounds that have rhythm, harmony, and melody; *also* : an agreeable sound **3** : punishment for a misdeed
¹**mu·si·cal** \ˈmyü-zi-kəl\ *adj* **1 a** : of or relating to music **b** : having the pleasing harmonious qualities of music : MELODIOUS **2** : having an interest in or talent for music **3** : set to or accompanied by music **4** : of or relating to musicians or music lovers — **mu·si·cal·i·ty** \ˌmyü-zi-ˈkal-ət-ē\ *n* — **mu·si·cal·ly** \ˈmyü-zi-k(ə-)lē\ *adv*
²**musical** *n* : a film or theatrical production consisting of musical numbers and dialogue that develop the plot of an underlying story
mu·si·cale \ˌmyü-zi-ˈkal\ *n* : a usu. private social gathering featuring a concert of music
music box *n* : a box or case enclosing an apparatus that reproduces music mechanically when activated by clockwork
music hall *n* : a vaudeville theater
mu·si·cian \myu̇-ˈzish-ən\ *n* : one skilled in music; *esp* : a composer or professional performer of music — **mu·si·cian·ly** *adj* — **mu·si·cian·ship** \-ˌship\ *n*
mu·si·col·o·gy \ˌmyü-zi-ˈkäl-ə-jē\ *n* : a study of music as a branch of knowledge or field of research — **mu·si·co·log·i·cal** \-zi-kə-ˈläj-i-kəl\ *adj* — **mu·si·col·o·gist** \-zi-ˈkäl-ə-jəst\ *n*
musk \ˈməsk\ *n* : a substance of penetrating persistent odor obtained esp. from a small Asiatic deer and used as a perfume fixative
mus·kel·lunge \ˈməs-kə-ˌlənj\ *n, pl* **muskellunge** : a large North American pike prized as a sport fish
mus·ket \ˈməs-kət\ *n* : a large-caliber usu. muzzle-loading military shoulder firearm with smooth bore
mus·ke·teer \ˌməs-kə-ˈti(ə)r\ *n* : a soldier armed with a musket
mus·ket·ry \ˈməs-kə-trē\ *n, pl* **-ries** : small-arms fire
musk·mel·on \ˈməsk-ˌmel-ən\ *n* : a small round to oval and

sometimes ridged melon that is related to the cucumber and has usu. sweet edible green or orange flesh

musk·rat \'məsk-ˌrat\ *n, pl* **muskrat** *or* **muskrats** : a No. American aquatic rodent with a long scaly tail, webbed hind feet, and dark glossy brown fur; *also* : its fur or pelt

musky \'məs-kē\ *adj* : having an odor of or resembling musk — **musk·i·ness** *n*

Mus·lim \'məz-ləm, 'mu̇s-\ *n* : an adherent of Islam — **Muslim** *adj*

mus·lin \'məz-lən\ *n* : a cotton fabric of plain weave

¹muss \'məs\ *n* : DISORDER, CONFUSION

²muss *vt* : to make untidy : RUMPLE

mus·sel \'məs-əl\ *n* **1** : an edible saltwater 2-valved mollusk with a long dark shell **2** : any of numerous 2-valved freshwater mollusks of the central U.S. having shells with pearly inner linings

mussy \'məs-ē\ *adj* : DISORDERED, SOILED, RUMPLED — **muss·i·ly** \'məs-ə-lē\ *adv* — **muss·i·ness** \'məs-ē-nəs\ *n*

¹must \məs(t), 'məst\ *auxiliary verb, pres & past all persons* **must 1 a** : is commanded or requested to **b** : is urged to **2 a** : is compelled, required, or obliged to **b** : is determined to **3** : is inferred by reasoning or supposed to

²must \'məst\ *n* : something necessary, required, or indispensable

³must *n* : the expressed juice of fruit (as grapes) before and during fermentation

mus·tach·io \(ˌ)məs-'tash-(ē-ˌ)ō, -'täsh-\ *n, pl* **-ios** : MOUSTACHE; *esp* : a large moustache — **mus·tach·ioed** \-(ē-ˌ)ōd\ *adj*

mus·tang \'məs-ˌtaŋ\ *n* : the small hardy naturalized horse of the western plains directly descended from horses brought in by the Spaniards; *also* : BRONCO

mus·tard \'məs-tərd\ *n* **1** : a pungent yellow powder of the seeds of a common mustard used as a condiment or in medicine **2** : any of several yellow-flowered herbs related to the turnips and cabbages

¹mus·ter \'məs-tər\ *vb* **mus·tered**; **mus·ter·ing** \-t(ə-)riŋ\ **1** : to enlist or enroll a person in military service **2 a** : to assemble (as troops or a ship's company) for roll call or inspection **b** : ASSEMBLE, CONGREGATE **3** : to collect and display **4** : to amount to : COMPRISE

²muster *n* **1 a** : an act of assembling; *esp* : a formal military inspection **b** : critical examination **2** : an assembled group : COLLECTION

muster out *vt* : to discharge from service

musty \'məs-tē\ *adj* **1 a** : impaired by damp or mildew : MOLDY **b** : tasting or smelling of damp and decay **2 a** : TRITE, STALE **b** : OUT-OF-DATE, ANTIQUATED — **must·i·ly** \-tə-lē\ *adv* — **must·i·ness** \-tē-nəs\ *n*

mu·ta·ble \'myüt-ə-bəl\ *adj* **1** : prone to change : INCONSTANT **2 a** : capable of change in form or nature **b** : capable of or liable to mutation — **mu·ta·bil·i·ty** \ˌmyüt-ə-'bil-ət-ē\ *n* — **mu·ta·ble·ness** *n* — **mu·ta·bly** \'myüt-ə-blē\ *adv*

mu·tate \'myü-ˌtāt\ *vb* : to undergo or cause to undergo mutation

mu·ta·tion \myü-'tā-shən\ *n* **1** : a basic alteration : CHANGE **2 a** : a sudden and relatively permanent change in a hereditary character **b** : an individual or strain resulting from mutation — **mu·ta·tion·al** \-shnəl, -shən-ᵊl\ *adj* — **mu·ta·tion·al·ly** \-ē\ *adv* — **mu·ta·tive** \'myü-ˌtāt-iv, 'myüt-ət-iv\ *adj*

mu·ta·tis mu·tan·dis \mü-ˌtät-əs-mü-'tän-dəs\ *adv* : with the necessary changes having been made

¹mute \'myüt\ *adj* **1** : unable to speak : DUMB **2** : marked by absence of speech **3** : not pronounced : SILENT — **mute·ly** *adv* — **mute·ness** *n* — **mut·ism** \'myüt-ˌiz-əm\ *n*

²mute *n* **1** : a person who cannot or does not speak **2** : a device on a musical instrument that deadens, softens, or muffles its tone

³mute *vt* **1** : to muffle or reduce the sound of **2** : to tone down (a color)

mu·ti·late \'myüt-ᵊl-ˌāt\ *vt* **1 a** : to deprive of an essential part (as a limb) : CRIPPLE, MAIM **b** : to cut off or permanently destroy the use of (as a limb) **2** : to cut up or alter radically so as to make imperfect — **mu·ti·la·tion** \ˌmyüt-ᵊl-'ā-shən\ *n* — **mu·ti·la·tor** \'myüt-ᵊl-ˌāt-ər\ *n*

mu·ti·neer \ˌmyüt-ᵊn-'i(ə)r\ *n* : one that mutinies

mu·ti·nous \'myüt-ᵊn-əs, 'myüt-nəs\ *adj* **1 a** : disposed to or in a state of mutiny : REBELLIOUS **b** : TURBULENT, UNRULY **2** : of, relating to, or constituting mutiny — **mu·ti·nous·ly** *adv* — **mu·ti·nous·ness** *n*

mu·ti·ny \'myüt-ᵊn-ē, 'myüt-nē\ *n, pl* **-nies 1** : willful refusal to obey constituted authority; *esp* : revolt by a military group against a superior officer **2** : an act or instance of mutiny — **mutiny** *vi*

mutt \'mət\ *n* : MONGREL, CUR

mut·ter \'mət-ər\ *vb* **1** : to utter indistinctly or with a low voice and lips partly closed **2** : to murmur complainingly or angrily : GRUMBLE — **mutter** *n* — **mut·ter·er** *n*

mut·ton \'mət-ᵊn\ *n* : the flesh of a mature sheep — **mut·tony** \-ē\ *adj*

mut·ton·chops \-ˌchäps\ *n pl* : side-whiskers that are narrow at the temple and broad and round by the lower jaws

mu·tu·al \'myü-chə-wəl, -chəl\ *adj* **1 a** : given and received in equal amount **b** : having the same feelings one for the other **2** : participated in, shared, or enjoyed by two or more at the same time : JOINT **3** : organized in such a way that the members share in the profits, benefits, expenses, and liabilities — **mu·tu·al·i·ty** \ˌmyü-chə-'wal-ət-ē\ *n* — **mu·tu·al·ly** \'myü-chə-(wə-)lē\ *adv*

mutual fund *n* : an investment company that invests money of its shareholders in a usu. diversified group of securities of other corporations

muu·muu \'mü-mü\ *n* : a loose dress of Hawaiian origin for informal wear

mu·zhik \mü-'zhēk, -'zhik\ *n* : a Russian peasant

¹muz·zle \'məz-əl\ *n* **1** : the projecting jaws and nose of an animal : SNOUT **2** : a fastening or covering for the mouth of an animal used to prevent eating or biting **3** : the open end of a weapon from which the missile is discharged

²muzzle *vt* **muz·zled**; **muz·zling** \'məz-(ə-)liŋ\ **1** : to fit with a muzzle **2** : to prevent free or normal expression by : GAG — **muz·zler** \'məz-(ə-)lər\ *n*

muz·zle–load·er \ˌməz-ə(l)-'lōd-ər\ *n* : a gun that is loaded through the muzzle — **muz·zle–load·ing** *adj*

muz·zy \'məz-ē\ *adj* **1** : muddled or confused in mind : DULL **2** : BLURRED — **muz·zi·ly** \'məz-ə-lē\ *adv* — **muz·zi·ness** \'məz-ē-nəs\ *n*

my \(')mī, mə\ *adj* : of or relating to me or myself esp. as possessor, agent, or object of an action

my·col·o·gy \mī-'käl-ə-jē\ *n* **1** : a branch of botany dealing with fungi **2** : fungal life — **my·co·log·i·cal** \ˌmī-kə-'läj-i-kəl\ *adj* — **my·col·o·gist** \mī-'käl-ə-jəst\ *n*

my·na *or* **my·nah** \'mī-nə\ *n* : any of various Asiatic starlings; *esp* : a dark brown slightly crested bird of southeastern Asia

my·o·pia \mī-'ō-pē-ə\ *n* : NEARSIGHTEDNESS, SHORTSIGHTEDNESS — **my·o·pic** \-'ōp-ik, -'äp-\ *adj* — **my·o·pi·cal·ly** \-i-k(ə-)lē\ *adv*

¹myr·i·ad \'mir-ē-əd\ *n* **1** : ten thousand **2** : an indefinitely large number

²myriad *adj* : consisting of a very great but indefinite number

myr·mi·don \'mər-mə-ˌdän, 'mər-məd-ən\ *n* **1** : a loyal follower or retainer **2** : a subordinate who unquestioningly or pitilessly executes orders

myrrh \'mər\ *n* : a brown slightly bitter aromatic plant gum obtained from African and Arabian trees and used esp. in perfumes or formerly in incense

myr·tle \ˈmərt-ᵊl\ *n* **1 :** a common evergreen bushy shrub of southern Europe with oval to lance-shaped shining leaves, fragrant white or rosy flowers, and black berries **2 a :** any of the family of chiefly tropical shrubs or trees to which the common myrtle belongs **b :** any of several plants of other families; *esp* **:** the common periwinkle

my·self \mī-ˈself, mə-\ *pron* **1 :** that identical one that is I — used reflexively, for emphasis, or in absolute constructions **2 :** my normal, healthy, or sane condition or self

mys·te·ri·ous \mis-ˈtir-ē-əs\ *adj* **:** of or relating to mystery **:** containing, suggesting, or implying a mystery **:** SECRET — **mys·te·ri·ous·ly** *adv* — **mys·te·ri·ous·ness** *n*

mys·tery \ˈmis-t(ə-)rē\ *n, pl* **-ter·ies** **1 a :** a religious truth known by revelation alone **b :** any of the 15 events (as the Nativity, the Crucifixion, or the Assumption) serving as a subject for meditation during the saying of the rosary **2 a :** something not understood or beyond understanding **:** ENIGMA **b :** the special practices peculiar to an occupation or a body of people **c :** a piece of fiction dealing with a mysterious crime **3 :** mysterious quality or character

[1]mys·tic \ˈmis-tik\ *adj* **1 :** MYSTICAL 1 **2 :** of or relating to mysteries or magical rites **:** OCCULT **3 :** of or relating to mysticism or mystics **4 a :** MYSTERIOUS **b :** MAGICAL

[2]mystic *n* **:** a person who seeks direct knowledge of God through contemplation and prayer

mys·ti·cal \ˈmis-ti-kəl\ *adj* **1 :** having a spiritual meaning or reality that is neither apparent to the senses nor obvious to the intelligence **2 :** of, relating to, or resulting from an individual's direct communion with God or ultimate reality **3 :** MYSTIC 2 — **mys·ti·cal·ly** \-ti-k(ə-)lē\ *adv*

mys·ti·cism \ˈmis-tə-ˌsiz-əm\ *n* **1 :** the experience of mystical union or direct communion with ultimate reality reported by mystics **2 :** the belief that direct knowledge of God or of spiritual truth can be achieved by personal insight and inspiration **3 :** vague guessing or speculation; *also* **:** a belief without a sound basis **:** GUESS

mys·ti·fy \ˈmis-tə-ˌfī\ *vb* **-fied; -fy·ing** **1 :** to make obscure or difficult to understand **2 :** PERPLEX, BEWILDER — **mys·ti·fi·ca·tion** \ˌmis-tə-fə-ˈkā-shən\ *n*

mys·tique \mi-ˈstēk\ *n* **:** a set of beliefs and attitudes developing around an object or associated with a particular group **:** CULT

myth \ˈmith\ *n* **1 :** a usu. legendary narrative that presents part of the beliefs of a people or explains a practice, belief, or natural phenomenon **2 :** PARABLE, ALLEGORY **3 a :** a person or thing having only an imaginary existence **b :** a belief that supports the practices and institutions of a group and is held uncritically by its members **c :** a belief concerning a visionary ideal **4 :** the whole body of myths

myth·i·cal \ˈmith-i-kəl\ *adj* **1 :** based on, described in, or constituting a myth **2 :** IMAGINARY, INVENTED — **myth·i·cal·ly** \-i-k(ə-)lē\ *adv*

my·thol·o·gy \mith-ˈäl-ə-jē\ *n, pl* **-gies** **1 :** a body of myths; *esp* **:** the myths dealing with the gods and heroes of a people **2 :** a branch of knowledge that deals with myth — **myth·o·log·i·cal** \ˌmith-ə-ˈläj-i-kəl\ *adj*

my·thos \ˈmī-ˌthäs, ˈmith-ˌäs\ *n* **:** a pattern of beliefs expressing often symbolically the characteristic or prevalent attitudes in a group or culture

n \ˈen\ *n, often cap* **1 :** the 14th letter of the English alphabet **2 :** an unspecified quantity

nab \ˈnab\ *vt* **nabbed; nab·bing** **1 :** to seize and take into custody **:** ARREST, APPREHEND **2 :** to seize suddenly **:** snatch away

na·bob \ˈnā-ˌbäb\ *n* **1 :** a provincial governor of the Mogul empire in India **2 :** a man of great wealth or prominence

na·celle \nə-ˈsel\ *n* **:** an enclosed shelter on an aircraft for an engine or sometimes for crew

na·cre \ˈnā-kər\ *n* **:** MOTHER-OF-PEARL — **na·cred** \-kərd\ *adj* — **na·cre·ous** \-krē-əs, -k(ə-)rəs\ *adj*

na·dir \ˈnā-ˌdi(ə)r, ˈnād-ər\ *n* **1 :** the point of the celestial sphere that is directly opposite the zenith and vertically downward from the observer **2 :** the lowest point

[1]nag \ˈnag\ *n* **:** HORSE; *esp* **:** one that is old or in poor condition

[2]nag *vb* **nagged; nag·ging** **1 :** to find fault incessantly **:** COMPLAIN **2 :** to irritate by constant scolding or urging **3 :** to be a continuing source of annoyance — **nag·ger** *n*

na·if \nä-ˈēf\ *adj* **:** NAÏVE

[1]nail \ˈnāl\ *n* **1 a :** a horny sheath protecting the end of each finger and toe in man and most other primates **b :** a corresponding structure (as a claw) terminating a digit **2 :** a slender usu. pointed and headed fastener to be pounded in

[2]nail *vt* **1 :** to fasten with or as if with a nail **2 :** to fix (as the eyes) in steady attention **3 :** CATCH, TRAP; *esp* **:** to detect and expose so as to discredit — **nail·er** *n*

nail·brush \ˈnāl-ˌbrəsh\ *n* **:** a small firm-bristled brush for cleaning the hands and esp. the fingernails

nail down *vt* **:** to settle or establish clearly and unmistakably

nain·sook \ˈnān-ˌsu̇k\ *n* **:** a soft lightweight muslin

na·ïve \nä-ˈēv\ *adj* **1 :** marked by unaffected simplicity **:** ARTLESS, INGENUOUS **2 :** showing lack of informed judgment; *esp* **:** CREDULOUS — **na·ïve·ly** *adv* — **na·ïve·ness** *n*

na·ïve·té \(ˌ)nä-ˌē-və-ˈtā, nä-ˈē-və-ˌ\ *n* **1 :** the quality or state of being naïve **2 :** a naïve remark or action

na·ive·ty \nä-ˈē-vət-ē, -ˈēv-tē\ *n* **:** NAÏVETÉ

na·ked \ˈnā-kəd, *esp South* ˈnek-əd\ *adj* **1 :** having no clothes on **:** NUDE **2 :** lacking a usual or natural covering (as of foliage or feathers) **3 :** lacking embellishment of any kind **:** PLAIN, UNADORNED **4 :** not aided by artificial means — **na·ked·ly** *adv* — **na·ked·ness** *n*

nam·by–pam·by \ˌnam-bē-ˈpam-bē\ *adj* **1 :** lacking in character or substance **:** INSIPID **2 :** WEAK, INDECISIVE — **namby–pamby** *n*

[1]name \ˈnām\ *n* **1 :** a word or combination of words by which a person or thing is regularly known **2 :** a descriptive often disparaging epithet **3 :** REPUTATION; *esp* **:** a distinguished reputation **4 :** FAMILY, CLAN **5 :** semblance as opposed to reality

[2]name *vt* **1 :** to give a name to **:** CALL **2 a :** to mention or identify by name **b :** to accuse by name **3 :** to nominate for office **:** APPOINT **4 :** to decide upon **:** CHOOSE **5 :** to speak about **:** MENTION — **nam·er** *n*

[3]name *adj* **1 :** of, relating to, or bearing a name **2 :** having an established reputation

name·a·ble \ˈnā-mə-bəl\ *adj* **1 :** capable of being named **:** IDENTIFIABLE **2 :** worthy of being named **:** MEMORABLE

name day *n* **:** the day of the saint whose name one bears

name·less \ˈnām-ləs\ *adj* **1 :** having no name **2 :** not marked with a name **3 :** not known by name **:** UNKNOWN, ANONYMOUS **4 :** not to be described — **name·less·ly** *adv* — **name·less·ness** *n*

name•ly \'nām-lē\ *adv* : that is to say
name•plate \-ˌplāt\ *n* : a plate or plaque bearing a name (as of a resident or proprietor)
name•sake \'nām-ˌsāk\ *n* : one that has the same name as another; *esp* : one named after another
nan•keen \nan-'kēn\ *n* : a durable brownish yellow cotton fabric orig. woven by hand in China
¹nap \'nap\ *vi* **napped; nap•ping** **1** : to sleep briefly esp. during the day : DOZE **2** : to be off guard
²nap *n* : a short sleep esp. during the day : SNOOZE
³nap *n* : a hairy or downy surface on a woven fabric — **nap•less** \'nap-ləs\ *adj* — **napped** \'napt\ *adj* — **nap•py** \'nap-ē\ *adj*
⁴nap *vt* **napped; nap•ping** : to raise a nap on (fabric or leather)
na•palm \'nā-ˌpäm, -ˌpälm\ *n* **1** : a thickener used in jelling gasoline esp. for incendiary bombs and flamethrowers **2** : fuel jelled with napalm
nape \'nāp, 'nap\ *n* : the back of the neck
na•pery \'nā-p(ə-)rē\ *n* : household linen esp. for the table
naph•tha \'naf-thə, 'nap-\ *n* **1** : PETROLEUM **2** : any of various volatile often flammable liquid hydrocarbon mixtures used chiefly as solvents and diluents
naph•tha•lene \-ˌlēn\ *n* : a crystalline hydrocarbon usu. obtained by distillation of coal tar and used in chemical manufacture and as a moth repellent — **naph•tha•le•nic** \ˌnaf-thə-'lēn-ik, ˌnap-, -'len-\ *adj*
nap•kin \'nap-kən\ *n* **1** : a piece of material (as cloth or paper) used at table to wipe the lips or fingers and protect the clothes **2** : a small cloth or towel
na•po•leon \nə-'pōl-yən, -'pō-lē-ən\ *n* : an oblong pastry consisting of layers of puff paste with a filling of cream, custard, or jelly
nar•cis•sism \'när-sə-ˌsiz-əm\ *n* : undue dwelling on one's own self or attainments — **nar•cis•sist** \'när-sə-səst\ *n or adj* — **nar•cis•sis•tic** \ˌnär-sə-'sis-tik\ *adj*
nar•cis•sus \när-'sis-əs\ *n, pl* **-cissus** *or* **-cis•sus•es** \-'sis-ə-səz\ *or* **-cis•si** \-'sis-ˌī, -(ˌ)ē\ : DAFFODIL; *esp* : one whose flowers have a short tube and are usu. borne separately
nar•co•sis \när-'kō-səs\ *n, pl* **-co•ses** \-'kō-ˌsēz\ : a state of stupor, unconsciousness, or arrested activity produced by the influence of chemicals (as narcotics)
¹nar•cot•ic \när-'kät-ik\ *n* **1** : a drug (as opium) that in moderate doses dulls the senses, relieves pain, and induces sleep but in excessive doses causes stupor, coma, or convulsions **2** : something that soothes, relieves, or lulls
²narcotic *adj* **1** : having the properties of or yielding a narcotic **2** : of or relating to narcotics or to their use or addicts — **nar•cot•i•cal•ly** \-'kät-i-k(ə-)lē\ *adv*
nar•co•tize \'när-kə-ˌtīz\ *vt* **1 a** : to treat with or subject to a narcotic **b** : to put into a state of narcosis **2** : to soothe to unconsciousness or unawareness
nard \'närd\ *n* : a fragrant ointment of the ancients
na•ris \'nar-əs\ *n, pl* **na•res** \'na(ə)r-(ˌ)ēz\ : any of the openings of the nose or nasal cavity of a vertebrate
nar•rate \'nar-ˌāt, na-'rāt\ *vt* : to recite the details of (as a story) : give an account of : RELATE, TELL — **nar•ra•tor** *or* **nar•rat•er** \'nar-ˌāt-ər, na-'rāt-\ *n*
nar•ra•tion \na-'rā-shən, nə-\ *n* **1** : the act or process or an instance of narrating **2** : STORY, NARRATIVE — **nar•ra•tion•al** \-shnəl, -shən-ᵊl\ *adj*
nar•ra•tive \'nar-ət-iv\ *n* **1** : something (as a story or an account of a series of events) that is narrated **2** : the art or practice of narration — **narrative** *adj* — **nar•ra•tive•ly** *adv*
¹nar•row \'nar-ō\ *adj* **1 a** : of slender width **b** : of less than standard width **2** : limited in size or scope : RESTRICTED **3 a** : not liberal in views or disposition : PREJUDICED **b** : interpreted or interpreting strictly **4 a** : barely sufficient : CLOSE **b** : barely successful **5** : minutely precise : METICULOUS — **nar•row•ly** *adv* — **nar•row•ness** *n*
²narrow *n* : a narrow part or passage; *esp* : a strait connecting two bodies of water — usu. used in pl.
³narrow *vb* : to lessen in width or extent : CONTRACT, RESTRICT
nar•row–mind•ed \ˌnar-ō-'mīn-dəd\ *adj* : lacking in tolerance or breadth of vision : ILLIBERAL, BIGOTED — **nar•row–mind•ed•ly** *adv* — **nar•row–mind•ed•ness** *n*
nar•thex \'när-ˌtheks\ *n* **1** : the portico of an ancient church **2** : a vestibule leading to the nave of a church
nar•whal \'när-ˌ(h)wäl, 'när-wəl\ *n* : an arctic sea animal about 20 feet long that is related to the dolphin and in the male has a long twisted ivory tusk
¹na•sal \'nā-zəl\ *n* **1** : a nasal part **2** : a nasal consonant or vowel
²nasal *adj* **1** : of or relating to the nose **2 a** : uttered with the mouth passage closed and the nose passage open **b** : uttered with the nose passage as well as the mouth passage open **c** : characterized by resonance produced through the nose — **na•sal•i•ty** \nā-'zal-ət-ē\ *n* — **na•sal•ly** \'nā-zə-lē\ *adv*
na•sal•ize \'nā-zə-ˌlīz\ *vb* **1** : to make nasal **2** : to speak in a nasal manner — **na•sal•i•za•tion** \ˌnā-zə-lə-'zā-shən\ *n*
nas•cent \'nas-ᵊnt, 'nās-\ *adj* : coming into existence : beginning to develop — **nas•cence** \-ᵊn(t)s\ *n*
na•so•pha•ryn•geal \ˌnā-zō-fə-'rin-j(ē-)əl, -ˌfar-ən-'jē-əl\ *adj* : of or relating to the nose and pharynx or the nasopharynx
na•so•phar•ynx \-'far-iŋ(k)s\ *n* : the upper part of the pharynx continuous with the nasal passages
nas•tur•tium \nə-'stər-shəm, na-\ *n* : any of a genus of watery-stemmed herbs with showy spurred flowers and pungent seeds
nas•ty \'nas-tē\ *adj* **1** : very dirty or foul : FILTHY **2** : INDECENT, VILE **3** : DISAGREEABLE **4** : MEAN, ILL-NATURED **5** : DISHONORABLE **6** : HARMFUL, DANGEROUS — **nas•ti•ly** \-tə-lē\ *adv* — **nas•ti•ness** \-tē-nəs\ *n*
na•tal \'nāt-ᵊl\ *adj* **1** : NATIVE **2** : of or relating to birth
na•tal•i•ty \nā-'tal-ət-ē, nə-\ *n* : BIRTHRATE
na•ta•tion \nā-'tā-shən, na-\ *n* : the action or art of swimming
na•ta•to•ri•al \ˌnāt-ə-'tōr-ē-əl, ˌnat-\ *or* **na•ta•to•ry** \'nāt-ə-ˌtōr-ē, 'nat-\ *adj* **1** : of or relating to swimming **2** : adapted to or characterized by swimming
na•ta•to•ri•um \ˌnāt-ə-'tōr-ē-əm, ˌnat-\ *n* : a swimming pool esp. indoors
na•tion \'nā-shən\ *n* **1 a** : NATIONALITY 4a **b** : a politically organized nationality **c** : a community of people composed of one or more nationalities with its own territory and government **d** : a usu. large and independent territorial division containing a body of people of one or more nationalities **2** : a tribe or federation of tribes (as of American Indians)
¹na•tion•al \'nash-nəl, -ən-ᵊl\ *adj* **1** : of or relating to a nation **2** : comprising or characteristic of a nationality **3** : FEDERAL 1c
²national *n* **1** : one who is under the protection of a nation without regard to the more formal status of citizen or subject **2** : an organization (as a labor union) having local units throughout a nation
national anthem *n* : a song or hymn officially adopted and played or sung on formal occasions as a mark of loyalty to the nation
National Guard *n* : a militia force recruited by each state, equipped by the federal government, and jointly maintained subject to the call of either
national income *n* : the total earnings from a nation's current production including wages of employees, interest, rental income, and business profits after taxes
na•tion•al•ism \'nash-nəl-iz-əm, -ən-ᵊl-\ *n* : loyalty and devotion to a nation esp. as expressed in an exalting of one nation above all others with primary emphasis on promotion of its culture and interests

na·tion·al·ist \-nəl-əst, -ən-ᵊl-əst\ *n* **1 :** an advocate of or believer in nationalism **2** *cap* **:** a member of a political party or group advocating national independence or strong national government — **nationalist** *adj, often cap* — **na·tion·al·is·tic** \ˌnash-nəl-ˈis-tik, -ən-ᵊl-ˈis-\ *adj*

na·tion·al·i·ty \ˌnash-(ə-)ˈnal-ət-ē\ *n, pl* **-ties** **1 :** national character **2 a :** national status; *esp* **:** a legal relationship involving allegiance of an individual and his protection by the state **b :** membership in a particular nation **3 :** political independence or existence as a separate nation **4 a :** a people having a common origin, tradition, and language and capable of forming or actually constituting a state **b :** an ethnic group within a larger unit (as a nation)

na·tion·al·ize \ˈnash-nəl-ˌīz, -ən-ᵊl-\ *vt* **1 :** to make national **:** make a nation of **2 :** to remove from private ownership and place under government control — **na·tion·al·i·za·tion** \ˌnash-nəl-ə-ˈzā-shən, ˌnash-ən-ᵊl-\ *n*

na·tion·al·ly \ˈnash-nəl-ē, -ən-ᵊl-ē\ *adv* **:** by or with regard to a nation as a whole **:** throughout a nation

national park *n* **:** an area of special scenic, historical, or scientific importance set aside and maintained by a national government esp. for recreation or study

na·tion·hood \ˈnā-shən-ˌhu̇d\ *n* **:** the quality or state of being a nation

na·tion·wide \ˌnā-shən-ˈwīd\ *adj* **:** extending throughout a nation

¹na·tive \ˈnāt-iv\ *adj* **1 :** INBORN, NATURAL **2 :** born in a particular place or country **3 :** belonging to a person because of the place or circumstances of his birth **4 :** grown, produced, or having its origin in a particular region **:** INDIGENOUS **5 :** occurring in nature **:** not artificially prepared — **na·tive·ly** *adv* — **na·tive·ness** *n*

²native *n* **1 :** one born or reared in a particular place **2 a :** an original or indigenous inhabitant **b :** something indigenous to a particular locality **3 :** a local resident; *esp* **:** a person who has lived all his life in a place

na·tiv·i·ty \nə-ˈtiv-ət-ē, nā-\ *n, pl* **-ties** **1** *cap* **:** the birth of Christ **2** *cap* **:** CHRISTMAS 1 **3 :** the process or circumstances of being born **:** BIRTH **4 :** a horoscope at or of the time of one's birth

nat·ty \ˈnat-ē\ *adj* **:** trimly neat and tidy **:** SMART — **nat·ti·ly** \ˈnat-ᵊl-ē\ *adv* — **nat·ti·ness** \ˈnat-ē-nəs\ *n*

¹nat·u·ral \ˈnach-(ə-)rəl\ *adj* **1 :** born in or with one **:** INNATE **2 :** being such by nature **:** BORN **3 :** born of unmarried parents **:** ILLEGITIMATE **4 :** existing or used in or produced by nature **5 :** having or showing qualities held to be part of the nature of man **:** HUMAN **6 :** of or relating to nature **:** conforming to the laws of nature or of the physical world **7 :** not made or altered by man **8 :** marked by simplicity and sincerity **:** not affected **9 :** closely resembling the object imitated **:** LIFELIKE **10 :** having neither sharps nor flats in the key signature or having a sharp or a flat changed in pitch by a natural sign — **nat·u·ral·ness** *n*

²natural *n* **1 :** IDIOT **2 a :** a character ♮ placed on a line or space of the musical staff to nullify the effect of a preceding sharp or flat **b :** a note or tone affected by the natural sign **3 a :** one having natural skills, talents, or abilities **b :** one obviously suitable for a specific purpose

natural gas *n* **:** gas issuing from the earth's crust through natural openings or bored wells; *esp* **:** a combustible mixture of hydrocarbons and esp. methane used chiefly as a fuel and raw material

natural history *n* **:** the study of natural objects esp. from an amateur or popular point of view

nat·u·ral·ism \ˈnach-(ə-)rə-ˌliz-əm\ *n* **1 :** action, inclination, or thought based only on natural desires and instincts **2 :** a theory denying a supernatural explanation of the origin and development of the universe and holding that scientific laws account for everything in nature **3 :** realism in art or literature; *esp* **:** a theory in literature emphasizing scientific observation of life without idealization or the avoidance of the ugly

nat·u·ral·ist \-ləst\ *n* **1 :** one that advocates or practices naturalism **2 :** a student of natural history; *esp* **:** a field biologist — **naturalist** *adj*

nat·u·ral·is·tic \ˌnach-(ə-)rə-ˈlis-tik\ *adj* **:** of, characterized by, or according with naturalism — **nat·u·ral·is·ti·cal·ly** \-ti-k(ə-)lē\ *adv*

nat·u·ral·ize \ˈnach-(ə-)rə-ˌlīz\ *vb* **1 :** to introduce into common use or into the vernacular **2 :** to become or cause to become established as if native **3 :** to bring into conformity with nature **4 :** to confer the rights of a national on; *esp* **:** to admit to citizenship — **nat·u·ral·i·za·tion** \ˌnach-(ə-)rə-lə-ˈzā-shən\ *n*

natural law *n* **:** a body of law or a specific principle held to be derived from nature and binding upon human society in the absence of or in addition to positive law

nat·u·ral·ly \ˈnach-(ə-)rə-lē, ˈnach-ər-lē\ *adv* **1 :** by nature **:** by natural character or ability **2 :** according to the usual course of things **:** as might be expected **3 a :** without artificial aid **b :** without affectation **4 :** with truth to nature **:** REALISTICALLY

natural resource *n* **:** something (as a mineral, waterpower source, forest, or kind of animal) that occurs in nature and is of value to human life

natural science *n* **:** a science (as physics, chemistry, or biology) that deals with matter, energy, and their interrelations and transformations or with objectively measurable phenomena

natural selection *n* **:** a natural process that tends to cause the survival of individuals or groups best adjusted to the conditions under which they live and that is equally important for the perpetuation of desirable genetic qualities and for the elimination of those that are undesirable

na·ture \ˈnā-chər\ *n* **1 :** the peculiar quality or character or basic constitution of a person or thing **2 :** general character **:** KIND, SORT **3 :** DISPOSITION, TEMPERAMENT **4** *often cap* **:** a power or set of forces thought of as controlling the universe **5 :** natural feeling esp. as shown in one's attitude toward others **6 :** man's native state **:** primitive life **7 :** the whole physical universe **8 :** the physical workings or drive of an organism **9 :** natural scenery

¹naught \ˈnȯt, ˈnät\ *pron* **:** NOTHING

²naught *n* **1 a :** NOTHING **b :** NOTHINGNESS, NONEXISTENCE **2 :** the arithmetical symbol 0

³naught *adj* **:** of no importance **:** INSIGNIFICANT

naugh·ty \ˈnȯt-ē, ˈnät-\ *adj* **1 :** guilty of disobedience or misbehavior **2 :** lacking in taste or propriety — **naugh·ti·ly** \ˈnȯt-ᵊl-ē, ˈnät-\ *adv* — **naugh·ti·ness** \ˈnȯt-ē-nəs, ˈnät-\ *n*

nau·sea \ˈnȯ-zē-ə, -shə\ *n* **1 :** a stomach distress with distaste for food and an urge to vomit **2 :** extreme disgust

nau·se·ate \ˈnȯ-z(h)ē-ˌāt, -s(h)ē-\ *vb* **:** to affect or become affected with nausea — **nau·se·at·ing** *adj* — **nau·se·at·ing·ly** \-ˌāt-iŋ-lē\ *adv*

nau·seous \ˈnȯ-shəs, ˈnȯ-zē-əs\ *adj* **1 :** NAUSEATED **2 :** NAUSEATING — **nau·seous·ly** *adv* — **nau·seous·ness** *n*

nautch \ˈnȯch\ *n* **:** an entertainment in India consisting chiefly of dancing by professional dancing girls

nau·ti·cal \ˈnȯt-i-kəl\ *adj* **:** of or relating to seamen, navigation, or ships — **nau·ti·cal·ly** \-k(ə-)lē\ *adv*

nautical mile *n* **:** MILE 2

nau·ti·lus \ˈnȯt-ᵊl-əs\ *n, pl* **-lus·es** *or* **-li** \-ᵊl-ˌī\ **:** a mollusk of the So. Pacific and Indian oceans having a spiral chambered shell pearly on the inside

na·val \ˈnā-vəl\ *adj* **1 :** of or relating to a navy or warships **2 :** possessing a navy

naval stores *n pl* **:** products (as pitch, turpentine, or rosin) obtained from resinous conifers (as pines)

¹nave \ˈnāv\ *n* **:** the hub of a wheel

[2]**nave** *n* : the main part of the interior of a church; *esp* : the long central hall in a cruciform church
na•vel \'nā-vəl\ *n* : a depression in the middle of the abdomen marking the point of attachment of fetus and mother
nav•i•ga•ble \'nav-i-gə-bəl\ *adj* **1** : deep enough and wide enough to afford passage to ships **2** : capable of being steered — **nav•i•ga•bil•i•ty** \ˌnav-i-gə-'bil-ət-ē\ *n* — **nav•i•ga•bly** \'nav-i-gə-blē\ *adv*
nav•i•gate \'nav-ə-ˌgāt\ *vb* **1 a** : to travel by water **b** : to sail over, on, or through **2 a** : to direct one's course in a ship or aircraft **b** : to steer, direct, or control the course of (as a boat or aircraft) **3 a** : to get about : MOVE; *esp* : WALK **b** : to make one's way on, about, or through — **nav•i•ga•tor** \-ˌgāt-ər\ *n*
nav•i•ga•tion \ˌnav-ə-'gā-shən\ *n* **1** : the act or practice of navigating **2** : the science of getting ships or airplanes from place to place; *esp* : the method of determining position, course, and distance traveled **3** : ship traffic or commerce — **nav•i•ga•tion•al** \-shnəl, -shən-ᵊl\ *adj*
na•vy \'nā-vē\ *n, pl* **navies** **1** : a group of ships : FLEET **2** : a nation's ships of war **3** *often cap* : the complete naval establishment of a nation including yards, stations, ships, and personnel
navy yard *n* : a naval shore station with facilities for building, equipping, and repairing warships
[1]**nay** \'nā\ *adv* **1** : NO **2** : not merely this but also : not only so but
[2]**nay** *n* **1** : DENIAL, REFUSAL **2 a** : a negative reply or vote **b** : one who votes no
Na•zi \'nät-sē, 'nat-\ *n* **1** : a member of a German fascist party controlling Germany from 1933 to 1945 under Adolf Hitler **2** *often not cap* : one held to resemble a German Nazi — **nazi** *adj, often cap* — **Na•zism** \'nät-ˌsiz-əm, 'nat-\ *or* **Na•zi•ism** \-sē-ˌiz-əm\ *n*
Ne•an•der•thal \nē-'an-dər-ˌt(h)ȯl, nā-'än-dər-ˌtäl\ *adj* : of, relating to, or being an extinct primitive Old World man
neap tide \'nēp-\ *n* : a tide of minimum range occurring at the first and the third quarters of the moon
[1]**near** \'ni(ə)r\ *adv* **1** : at, within, or to a short distance or time **2** : ALMOST, NEARLY **3** : CLOSELY
[2]**near** *prep* : close to
[3]**near** *adj* **1** : closely related or associated **2 a** : not far distant in time, place, or degree **b** : barely avoided **c** : coming close : failing or missing by very little **3 a** : being the closer of two **b** : being the left-hand one of a pair **4** : DIRECT, SHORT **5** : STINGY **6 a** : closely resembling a prototype **b** : approximating the genuine — **near•ly** *adv* — **near•ness** *n*
[4]**near** *vb* : to draw near : APPROACH
near•by \ni(ə)r-'bī, 'ni(ə)r-ˌ\ *adv (or adj)* : close at hand
near•sight•ed \'ni(ə)r-'sīt-əd\ *adj* : able to see near things more clearly than distant ones : MYOPIC — **near•sight•ed•ly** *adv* — **near•sight•ed•ness** *n*
[1]**neat** \'nēt\ *n, pl* **neat** : the common domestic bovine (as a cow, bull, or ox)
[2]**neat** *adj* **1** : not mixed or diluted : STRAIGHT **2** : marked by tasteful simplicity **3 a** : PRECISE, SYSTEMATIC **b** : marked by skill or ingenuity : ADROIT **4** : being orderly and clean : TIDY **5** : CLEAR, NET — **neat•ly** *adv* — **neat•ness** *n*
neat•herd \'nēt-ˌhərd\ *n* : COWHERD, HERDSMAN
neat's–foot oil \'nēts-ˌfu̇t-\ *n* : a pale yellow fatty oil made esp. from the bones of cattle and used chiefly for dressing leather
neb \'neb\ *n* **1 a** : the beak of a bird or tortoise : BILL **b** : NOSE, SNOUT **2** : NIB, TIP
neb•bish \'neb-ish\ *n* : a timid, meek, or ineffectual person
neb•u•la \'neb-yə-lə\ *n, pl* **-las** *or* **-lae** \-ˌlē\ **1** : any of many immense bodies of highly rarefied gas or dust in interstellar space **2** : GALAXY — **neb•u•lar** \-lər\ *adj*
neb•u•lize \'neb-yə-ˌlīz\ *vt* : to reduce to a fine spray — **neb•u•liz•er** *n*
neb•u•los•i•ty \ˌneb-yə-'läs-ət-ē\ *n, pl* **-ties** **1** : the quality or state of being nebulous **2** : nebulous matter : NEBULA
neb•u•lous \'neb-yə-ləs\ *adj* **1** : HAZY, INDISTINCT, VAGUE **2** : of, relating to, or resembling a nebula : NEBULAR — **neb•u•lous•ly** *adv* — **neb•u•lous•ness** *n*
[1]**nec•es•sary** \'nes-ə-ˌser-ē\ *adj* **1 a** : of an inevitable nature : INESCAPABLE **b** : logically unavoidable : CERTAIN **c** : PREDETERMINED **d** : COMPULSORY **2** : positively needed : INDISPENSABLE — **nec•es•sar•i•ly** \ˌnes-ə-'ser-ə-lē\ *adv*
[2]**necessary** *n, pl* **-sar•ies** : an indispensable item : ESSENTIAL
ne•ces•si•tate \ni-'ses-ə-ˌtāt\ *vt* : to make necessary : make inevitable or unavoidable : DEMAND, REQUIRE, COMPEL — **ne•ces•si•ta•tion** \-ˌses-ə-'tā-shən\ *n*
ne•ces•si•tous \ni-'ses-ət-əs\ *adj* **1** : hard up : NEEDY **2** : forced by necessity : NECESSARY — **ne•ces•si•tous•ly** *adv* — **ne•ces•si•tous•ness** *n*
ne•ces•si•ty \ni-'ses-ət-ē\ *n, pl* **-ties** **1** : very great need of help or relief **2** : a very necessary thing : something badly needed **3** : lack of necessary things : WANT, POVERTY **4** : conditions that cannot be changed
[1]**neck** \'nek\ *n* **1** : the part of the body connecting the head and the trunk **2** : the part of a garment covering or nearest to the neck **3** : something like a neck in shape or position : a relatively narrow part **4** : a narrow margin esp. of victory — **necked** \'nekt\ *adj* — **neck and neck** : so nearly equal (as in a race) that one cannot be said to be ahead of the other : very close
[2]**neck** *vb* : to kiss and caress amorously
neck•band \'nek-ˌband\ *n* **1** : a band worn around the neck **2 a** : a part of a garment that encircles the neck **b** : a part of a shirt to which the collar is attached
neck•er•chief \'nek-ər-chəf, -ˌchēf\ *n* : a square of cloth worn folded about the neck like a scarf
neck•lace \'nek-ləs\ *n* : an ornament (as a string of beads) worn around the neck
neck•line \-ˌlīn\ *n* : the outline of the neck opening of a garment
neck•piece \-ˌpēs\ *n* : an article of apparel (as a fur scarf) worn about the neck
neck•tie \-ˌtī\ *n* : a narrow length of material worn about the neck and tied in front; *esp* : FOUR-IN-HAND
neck•wear \-ˌwa(ə)r\ *n* : articles (as scarves or neckties) for wear around the neck
ne•crol•o•gy \nə-'kräl-ə-jē, ne-\ *n, pl* **-gies** **1** : a list of the recently dead **2** : OBITUARY — **nec•ro•log•i•cal** \ˌnek-rə-'läj-i-kəl\ *adj* — **ne•crol•o•gist** \nə-'kräl-ə-jəst, ne-\ *n*
nec•ro•man•cer \'nek-rə-ˌman(t)-sər\ *n* : one that practices necromancy : MAGICIAN, SORCERER, WIZARD
nec•ro•man•cy \-sē\ *n* **1** : the art or practice of conjuring up the spirits of the dead for purposes of magically revealing the future or influencing the course of events **2** : MAGIC, SORCERY
ne•crop•o•lis \nə-'kräp-ə-ləs, ne-\ *n, pl* **-lis•es** *or* **-les** \-ˌlēz\ : CEMETERY; *esp* : a large elaborate cemetery of an ancient city
ne•cro•sis \nə-'krō-səs, ne-\ *n, pl* **-cro•ses** \-'krō-ˌsēz\ : usu. local death of body tissue — **ne•crot•ic** \-'krät-ik\ *adj*
nec•tar \'nek-tər\ *n* **1 a** : the drink of the Greek and Roman gods **b** : a delicious drink **2** : a sweet liquid secreted by plants that is the chief raw material of honey — **nec•tar•ous** \-t(ə-)rəs\ *adj*
nec•tar•ine \ˌnek-tə-'rēn\ *n* : a smooth-skinned peach; *also* : a tree producing this fruit
née *or* **nee** \'nā\ *adj* : BORN — used to identify a woman by her maiden family name
[1]**need** \'nēd\ *n* **1** : necessary duty : OBLIGATION **2** : a lack of something requisite, desirable, or useful **3** : a condition re-

quiring supply or relief **4 :** want of the means of subsistence **:** POVERTY

[2]**need** *vb* **1 :** to be in want **2 :** to have cause or occasion for **:** REQUIRE **3 a :** to be under obligation or necessity **b —** used as an auxiliary verb

need·ful \'nēd-fəl\ *adj* **:** NECESSARY, REQUISITE — **need·ful·ly** \-fə-lē\ *adv* — **need·ful·ness** *n*

[1]**nee·dle** \'nēd-ᵊl\ *n* **1 a :** a small slender usu. steel instrument having an eye for thread at one end and used for sewing **b :** a slender hollow instrument for introducing material into or removing material from the body **2 :** a slender usu. sharp-pointed indicator on a dial **3 a :** a needle-shaped leaf (as of a pine) **b :** a slender piece of jewel, steel, wood, or fiber with a rounded tip used in a phonograph to transmit vibrations from the record

[2]**needle** *vb* **nee·dled**; **nee·dling** \'nēd-liŋ, -ᵊl-iŋ\ **1 :** to sew with or as if with a needle **2 :** to pierce with or as if with a needle **3 :** PROD, GOAD; *esp* **:** to incite to action by repeated gibes — **nee·dler** \'nēd-lər, -ᵊl-ər\ *n*

nee·dle·point \'nēd-ᵊl-,pȯint\ *n* **1 :** lace worked with a needle over a paper pattern **2 :** embroidery done on canvas usu. in simple even stitches across counted threads — **needlepoint** *adj*

need·less \'nēd-ləs\ *adj* **:** UNNECESSARY — **need·less·ly** *adv* — **need·less·ness** *n*

nee·dle·wom·an \'nēd-ᵊl-,wu̇m-ən\ *n* **:** a woman who does needlework; *esp* **:** SEAMSTRESS

nee·dle·work \-,wərk\ *n* **:** work done with a needle; *esp* **:** work (as embroidery) other than plain sewing

needs \'nēdz\ *adv* **:** of necessity **:** NECESSARILY

needy \'nēd-ē\ *adj* **:** being in want **:** very poor — **need·i·ness** *n*

ne'er–do–well \'ne(ə)rd-ü-,wel\ *n* **:** an idle worthless person — **ne'er–do–well** *adj*

ne·far·i·ous \ni-'far-ē-əs\ *adj* **:** flagrantly wicked or impious **:** EVIL — **ne·far·i·ous·ly** *adv* — **ne·far·i·ous·ness** *n*

ne·gate \ni-'gāt\ *vt* **1 :** to deny the existence or truth of **2 :** to cause to be ineffective or invalid

ne·ga·tion \ni-'gā-shən\ *n* **1 a :** the action of negating **:** DENIAL **b :** a negative doctrine or statement **2 :** something that is the opposite of something positive **:** CONTRADICTION — **ne·ga·tion·al** \-shnəl, -shən-ᵊl\ *adj*

[1]**neg·a·tive** \'neg-ət-iv\ *adj* **1 :** marked by denial, prohibition, or refusal **2 a :** lacking positive qualities **b :** opposing constructive treatment or development **3 a :** less than zero **b :** taken in a direction opposite to one chosen as positive **4 a :** of, being, or relating to electricity of a kind of which the electron is the elementary unit and which predominates in a hard rubber rod after being rubbed with wool **b :** having more electrons than protons **5 :** not affirming the presence of what is sought or suspected to be present **6 :** having the light and dark parts in approximately inverse order to those of the original photographic subject — **neg·a·tive·ly** *adv* — **neg·a·tive·ness** *n* — **neg·a·tiv·i·ty** \,neg-ə-'tiv-ət-ē\ *n*

[2]**negative** *n* **1 a :** a proposition by which something is denied or contradicted **b :** a reply that indicates the withholding of assent **:** REFUSAL **2 :** something that is the opposite or negation of something else **3 a :** an expression (as the word *no*) of negation or denial **b :** a negative number **4 :** the side that upholds the contradictory proposition in a debate **5 :** a negative photographic image on transparent material

[3]**negative** *vt* **1 a :** to refuse to accept or approve **b** (1) **:** to vote against (2) **:** VETO **2 :** DISPROVE **3 :** DENY, CONTRADICT

neg·a·tiv·ism \'neg-ət-iv-,iz-əm\ *n* **:** an attitude of skepticism and denial of nearly everything affirmed or suggested by others — **neg·a·tiv·ist** \-iv-əst\ *n* — **neg·a·tiv·is·tic** \,neg-ət-iv-'is-tik\ *adj*

[1]**ne·glect** \ni-'glekt\ *vt* **1 :** to give little attention or respect to **:** DISREGARD **2 :** to leave undone or unattended to esp. through carelessness

[2]**neglect** *n* **1 :** an act or instance of neglecting something **2 :** the condition of being neglected

ne·glect·ful \ni-'glekt-fəl\ *adj* **:** given to neglecting **:** CARELESS, HEEDLESS — **ne·glect·ful·ly** \-fə-lē\ *adv* — **ne·glect·ful·ness** *n*

neg·li·gee \,neg-lə-'zhā\ *n* **1 :** a woman's long flowing dressing gown **2 :** carelessly informal or incomplete attire

neg·li·gence \'neg-li-jən(t)s\ *n* **1 a :** the quality or state of being negligent **b :** failure to exercise the care that a prudent person usu. exercises **2 :** an act or instance of negligence

neg·li·gent \-jənt\ *adj* **1 :** marked by or given to neglect **2 :** chargeable with negligence — **neg·li·gent·ly** *adv*

neg·li·gi·ble \'neg-li-jə-bəl\ *adj* **:** fit to be neglected or disregarded **:** TRIFLING — **neg·li·gi·bly** \-blē\ *adv*

ne·go·tia·ble \ni-'gō-sh(ē-)ə-bəl\ *adj* **:** capable of being negotiated — **ne·go·tia·bil·i·ty** \-,gō-sh(ē-)ə-'bil-ət-ē\ *n*

ne·go·tiant \ni-'gō-sh(ē-)ənt\ *n* **:** NEGOTIATOR

ne·go·ti·ate \ni-'gō-shē-,āt\ *vb* **1 :** to confer with another so as to arrive at the settlement of some matter; *also* **:** to arrange for or bring about by such conference **2 :** to transfer to another by delivery or endorsement in return for equivalent value **3 :** to get through, around, or over successfully — **ne·go·ti·a·tion** \-,gō-s(h)ē-'ā-shən\ *n* — **ne·go·ti·a·tor** \-'gō-shē-,āt-ər\ *n*

Ne·gro \'nē-grō, *esp South* 'nig-rō\ *n, pl* **Negroes 1 :** a member of the black race of mankind distinguished from members of other races by classification according to physical features but without regard to language or culture; *esp* **:** a member of a people belonging to the African branch of the black race **2 :** a person of Negro ancestry — **Negro** *adj* — **ne·groid** \'nē-,grȯid\ *n or adj, often cap*

ne·gus \'nē-gəs\ *n* **:** a beverage of wine, hot water, sugar, lemon juice, and nutmeg

neigh \'nā\ *vi* **:** to make the loud prolonged cry of a horse — **neigh** *n*

[1]**neigh·bor** \'nā-bər\ *n* **1 :** one living or located near another **2 :** FELLOWMAN — often used as a term of address

[2]**neighbor** *vt* **neigh·bored**; **neigh·bor·ing** \-b(ə-)riŋ\ **:** to be next to or near to **:** border on

neigh·bor·hood \'nā-bər-,hu̇d\ *n* **1 :** the quality or state of being neighbors **:** NEARNESS **2 a :** a place or region near **:** VICINITY **b :** an approximate amount, extent, or degree **3 a :** the people living near one another **b :** a section lived in by neighbors and usu. having distinguishing characteristics

neigh·bor·ly \-lē\ *adj* **:** of, relating to, or characteristic of congenial neighbors; *esp* **:** FRIENDLY — **neigh·bor·li·ness** *n*

[1]**nei·ther** \'nē-t͟hər, 'nī-\ *pron* **:** not the one and not the other

[2]**neither** *conj* **1 :** both not **:** equally not **2 :** also not

[3]**neither** *adj* **:** not either

nem·e·sis \'nem-ə-səs\ *n, pl* **-e·ses** \-ə-,sēz\ **1 a :** one that inflicts retribution or vengeance **b :** a formidable and usu. victorious rival **2 a :** an act or effect of retribution **b :** BANE 2, CURSE

neo·clas·sic \,nē-ō-'klas-ik\ *adj* **:** of or relating to a revival or adaptation of the classical style esp. in literature, art, or music — **neo·clas·si·cal** \-'klas-i-kəl\ *adj* — **neo·clas·si·cism** \-'klas-ə-,siz-əm\ *n*

neo·co·lo·nial·ism \-kə-'lō-nyə-,liz-əm, -nē-ə-,liz-\ *n* **:** the economic and political policies by which a great power indirectly maintains or extends its influence over other areas or peoples

neo·dym·i·um \,nē-ō-'dim-ē-əm\ *n* **:** a metallic chemical element

ne·ol·o·gism \nē-'äl-ə-,jiz-əm\ *n* **:** a new word or expression — **ne·ol·o·gist** \-jəst\ *n* — **ne·ol·o·gis·tic** \-,äl-ə-'jis-tik\ *adj*

ne·ol·o·gy \-jē\ *n* **:** the use of a new word or expression or of an established word in a new or different sense

ne·on \'nē-,än\ *n* **:** a colorless odorless inert gaseous chemical element found in minute amounts in air and used in electric lamps

neo·na·tal \ˌnē-ō-ˈnāt-ᵊl\ *adj* : of, relating to, or affecting the newborn — **neo·na·tal·ly** \-ᵊl-ē\ *adv* — **neo·nate** \ˈnē-ə-ˌnāt\ *n*
ne·o·phyte \ˈnē-ə-ˌfīt\ *n* **1** : a new convert : PROSELYTE **2** : BEGINNER, NOVICE
ne·o·plasm \ˈnē-ə-ˌplaz-əm\ *n* : a new growth of tissue serving no physiologic function : TUMOR — **ne·o·plas·tic** \ˌnē-ə-ˈplas-tik\ *adj*
ne·pen·the \nə-ˈpen(t)-thē\ *n* : a potion used by the ancients to dull pain and sorrow — **ne·pen·the·an** \-thē-ən\ *adj*
neph·ew \ˈnef-yü\ *n* : a son of one's brother, sister, brother-in-law, or sister-in-law
ne·phri·tis \ni-ˈfrīt-əs\ *n* : inflammation of the kidneys
ne plus ul·tra \ˌnē-ˌpləs-ˈəl-trə\ *n* : the highest point capable of being attained : ACME
nep·o·tism \ˈnep-ə-ˌtiz-əm\ *n* : favoritism (as in the distribution of political offices) shown to a relative
nep·tu·ni·um \nep-ˈt(y)ü-nē-əm\ *n* : a radioactive metallic chemical element that is similar to uranium and is obtained in nuclear reactors as a by-product in the production of plutonium
ner·va·tion \ˌnər-ˈvā-shən\ *n* : an arrangement or system of nerves; *also* : VENATION
[1]**nerve** \ˈnərv\ *n* **1** : one of the filamentous bands of nervous tissue connecting parts of the nervous system with the other organs and conducting nervous impulses **2 a** : power of endurance or control **b** (1) : BOLDNESS, DARING (2) : BRASS, GALL **3 a** : a sore or sensitive point **b** *pl* : nervous disorganization or collapse : HYSTERIA **4** : VEIN 2b, 2c — **nerve** *adj* — **nerved** \ˈnərvd\ *adj*
[2]**nerve** *vt* : to give strength or courage to
nerve gas *n* : a war gas damaging esp. to the nervous and respiratory systems
nerve·less \ˈnərv-ləs\ *adj* **1** : destitute of strength or courage : FEEBLE **2** : showing control : not nervous : POISED — **nerve·less·ly** *adv* — **nerve·less·ness** *n*
nerve–rack·ing *or* **nerve–wrack·ing** \ˈnərv-ˌrak-iŋ\ *adj* : extremely trying on the nerves
nerv·ous \ˈnər-vəs\ *adj* **1** : marked by vigor of thought, feeling, or style **2 a** : of, relating to, or composed of neurons **b** : of or relating to the nerves; *also* : originating in or affected by the nerves **3 a** : easily excited or irritated : JUMPY **b** : TIMID, APPREHENSIVE — **nerv·ous·ly** *adv* — **nerv·ous·ness** *n*
nervous breakdown *n* **1** : NEURASTHENIA **2** : a case of neurasthenia
nervy \ˈnər-vē\ *adj* **1 a** : showing calm courage : BOLD **b** : marked by impudence or presumption : BRASH **2** : EXCITABLE, NERVOUS — **nerv·i·ness** *n*
ne·science \ˈnesh-(ē-)ən(t)s, ˈnēsh-\ *n* : lack of knowledge or awareness : IGNORANCE — **ne·scient** *adj*
ness \ˈnes\ *n* : CAPE, PROMONTORY
Nes·sel·rode \ˈnes-əl-ˌrōd\ *n* : a mixture of candied fruits, nuts, and maraschino used in puddings, pies, and ice cream
[1]**nest** \ˈnest\ *n* **1 a** : a bed or receptacle prepared by a bird for its eggs and young **b** : a place where eggs are laid and hatched **2 a** : a place of rest, retreat, or lodging **b** : DEN, HANGOUT **3** : the occupants or frequenters of a nest **4 a** : a group of similar things : AGGREGATION **b** : HOTBED 2 **5** : a group of objects made to fit close together or one within another
[2]**nest** *vb* **1** : to build or occupy a nest **2** : to fit compactly together or within one another
nest egg *n* **1** : a natural or artificial egg left in a nest to induce a fowl to continue to lay there **2** : a fund of money accumulated as a reserve
nes·tle \ˈnes-əl\ *vb* **nes·tled**; **nes·tling** \ˈnes-(ə-)liŋ\ **1** : to settle snugly or comfortably **2 a** : to settle, shelter, or house as if in a nest **b** : to press closely and affectionately : CUDDLE — **nes·tler** \-(ə-)lər\ *n*
nest·ling \ˈnest-liŋ\ *n* : a young bird not yet able to leave the nest
[1]**net** \ˈnet\ *n* **1 a** : a meshed fabric twisted, knotted, or woven together at regular intervals **b** : something made of net; *esp* : a device for catching fish, birds, or insects **2** : an entrapping situation **3** : a network of lines, fibers, or figures
[2]**net** *vt* **net·ted**; **net·ting** **1** : to cover or enclose with or as if with a net **2** : to catch in or as if in a net — **net·ter** *n*
[3]**net** *adj* : free from all charges or deductions
[4]**net** *vt* **net·ted**; **net·ting** : to gain or produce as profit : CLEAR
[5]**net** *n* : a net amount, profit, weight, or price
neth·er \ˈneth-ər\ *adj* : situated down or below : LOWER
neth·er·most \-ˌmōst\ *adj* : LOWEST
neth·er·world \-ˌwərld\ *n* **1** : the world of the dead **2** : UNDERWORLD 4
net·ting \ˈnet-iŋ\ *n* **1** : NETWORK **2** : the act or process of making a net or network **3** : the act, process, or right of fishing with a net
[1]**net·tle** \ˈnet-ᵊl\ *n* : any of various coarse herbs with stinging hairs
[2]**nettle** *vt* **net·tled**; **net·tling** \ˈnet-liŋ, -ᵊl-iŋ\ **1** : to strike or sting with or as if with nettles **2** : PROVOKE, VEX
nettle rash *n* : an eruption on the skin caused by or resembling the condition produced by stinging with nettles
net·tle·some \ˈnet-ᵊl-səm\ *adj* : causing vexation : IRRITATING
net·work \ˈnet-ˌwərk\ *n* **1** : a fabric or structure of cords or wires that cross at regular intervals and are knotted or secured at the crossings **2** : a system of lines, channels, or other elements resembling a network **3** : an interconnected or interrelated chain, group, or system; *esp* : a group of radio or television stations linked by wire or radio relay
neu·ral \ˈn(y)u̇r-əl\ *adj* **1** : of, relating to, or involving a nerve or the nervous system **2** : DORSAL — **neu·ral·ly** \-ə-lē\ *adv*
neu·ral·gia \n(y)u̇-ˈral-jə\ *n* : acute pain that follows the course of a nerve; *also* : a condition marked by such pain — **neu·ral·gic** \-jik\ *adj*
neur·as·the·nia \ˌn(y)u̇r-əs-ˈthē-nē-ə\ *n* : a state in which one is tense and irritable, esp. subject to fatigue, and troubled by headache and often ill-defined circulatory or digestive distress — **neur·as·then·ic** \-ˈthen-ik\ *adj or n*
neu·ri·tis \n(y)u̇-ˈrīt-əs\ *n* : inflammation of a nerve — **neu·rit·ic** \-ˈrit-ik\ *adj or n*
neu·rol·o·gy \n(y)u̇-ˈräl-ə-jē\ *n* : the scientific study of the nervous system — **neu·ro·log·i·cal** \ˌn(y)u̇r-ə-ˈläj-i-kəl\ *or* **neu·ro·log·ic** \-ˈläj-ik\ *adj* — **neu·rol·o·gist** \n(y)u̇-ˈräl-ə-jəst\ *n*
neu·ron \ˈn(y)ü-ˌrän\ *n* : a grayish or reddish granular cell with specialized processes that is the fundamental functional unit of nervous tissue — **neu·ro·nal** \ˈn(y)u̇r-ən-ᵊl, n(y)u̇-ˈrōn-ᵊl\ *or* **neu·ron·ic** \n(y)u̇-ˈrän-ik\ *adj*
neu·ro·sis \n(y)u̇-ˈrō-səs\ *n, pl* **-ro·ses** \-ˈrō-ˌsēz\ : a functional nervous disorder without demonstrable physical lesion
[1]**neu·rot·ic** \n(y)u̇-ˈrät-ik\ *adj* : of, relating to, constituting, or affected with neurosis — **neu·rot·i·cal·ly** \-ˈrät-i-k(ə-)lē\ *adv*
[2]**neurotic** *n* : an emotionally unstable person or one affected with a neurosis
[1]**neu·ter** \ˈn(y)üt-ər\ *adj* **1** : of, relating to, or constituting the class of words that ordinarily includes most of those referring to things that are neither male nor female **2** : lacking sex organs; *also* : having imperfectly developed sex organs
[2]**neuter** *n* **1 a** : a word or form of the neuter gender **b** : the neuter gender **2** : one that is neutral **3 a** : WORKER 2 **b** : a spayed or castrated animal
[3]**neuter** *vt* : CASTRATE, ALTER
[1]**neu·tral** \ˈn(y)ü-trəl\ *adj* **1** : not engaged on either side; *esp* : not aligned with a political or ideological grouping **2** : of or relating to a neutral state or power **3 a** : neither one thing nor the other : MIDDLING **b** (1) : ACHROMATIC (2) : not decided

in color : nearly achromatic **c** : neither acid nor basic — **neu·tral·ly** \-trə-lē\ *adv*

²neutral *n* **1** : one that is neutral **2** : a neutral color **3** : a position of disengagement (as of gears)

neu·tral·ism \'n(y)ü-trə-ˌliz-əm\ *n* : a policy or the advocacy of neutrality esp. in international affairs — **neu·tral·ist** \-ləst\ *n* — **neu·tral·is·tic** \ˌn(y)ü-trə-'lis-tik\ *adj*

neu·tral·i·ty \n(y)ü-'tral-ət-ē\ *n* **1** : the quality or state of being neutral **2** : the condition of being neutral in time of war that gives immunity from invasion or from use by belligerents

neu·tral·ize \'n(y)ü-trə-ˌlīz\ *vt* **1** : to make chemically neutral **2** : to destroy the effectiveness of : NULLIFY **3** : to invest with neutrality under international law — **neu·tral·i·za·tion** \ˌn(y)ü-trə-lə-'zā-shən\ *n* — **neu·tral·iz·er** *n*

neu·tri·no \n(y)ü-'trē-nō\ *n, pl* **-nos** : an uncharged elementary particle having a mass less than 1/10 that of the electron

neu·tron \'n(y)ü-ˌträn\ *n* : an uncharged elementary particle that has a mass nearly equal to that of the proton and is present in all known atomic nuclei except the hydrogen nucleus

nev·er \'nev-ər\ *adv* **1** : not ever : at no time **2** : not in any degree, way, or condition

nev·er·more \ˌnev-ər-'mō(ə)r\ *adv* : never again

nev·er–nev·er land \ˌnev-ər-'nev-ər-\ *n* : an ideal or imaginary place

nev·er·the·less \ˌnev-ər-t͟hə-'les\ *adv* : in spite of that : HOWEVER

ne·vus \'nē-vəs\ *n, pl* **ne·vi** \-ˌvī\ : a congenital pigmented area on the skin : BIRTHMARK

¹new \'n(y)ü\ *adj* **1** : not old : RECENT, MODERN **2** : not the same as the former : taking the place of one that came before **3** : recently discovered, recognized, or learned about **4** : not formerly known or experienced **5** : not accustomed **6** : beginning as a repetition of some previous act or thing **7** : REFRESHED, REGENERATED **8** : being in a position or place for the first time — **new·ness** *n*

²new *adv* : NEWLY, RECENTLY

new·born \-'bȯrn\ *adj* **1** : recently born **2** : born anew : REBORN

new·com·er \-ˌkəm-ər\ *n* **1** : one recently arrived **2** : BEGINNER, NOVICE

New Deal *n* **1** : the legislative and administrative program of President F. D. Roosevelt designed to promote economic recovery and social reform during the 1930s **2** : the period of the New Deal — **New Deal·er** \-'dē-lər\ *n*

new·el \'n(y)ü-əl\ *n* **1** : an upright post about which the steps of a circular staircase wind **2** : a post at the foot of a straight stairway or one at a landing

new·fan·gled \'n(y)ü-'faŋ-gəld\ *adj* : of the newest style

new–fash·ioned \-'fash-ənd\ *adj* **1** : made in a new fashion or form **2** : UP-TO-DATE

new·found \-'fau̇nd\ *adj* : newly found

new·ish \'n(y)ü-ish\ *adj* : rather new

new·ly \'n(y)ü-lē\ *adv* **1** : LATELY, RECENTLY **2** : ANEW, AFRESH

new·ly·wed \-ˌwed\ *n* : one recently married

new moon *n* **1** : the phase of the moon with its dark side toward the earth **2** : the thin crescent moon seen for a few days after the new moon phase

news \'n(y)üz\ *n* **1** : a report of recent events : TIDINGS **2 a** : material reported in a newspaper or news periodical or on a newscast **b** : matter that is newsworthy

news agency *n* : an organization that supplies news to subscribing newspapers, periodicals, and newscasters

news·boy \-ˌbȯi\ *n* : a person who delivers or sells newspapers

news·cast \-ˌkast\ *n* : a radio or television broadcast of news — **news·cast·er** *n*

news conference *n* : PRESS CONFERENCE

news·let·ter \'n(y)üz-ˌlet-ər\ *n* : a newspaper containing news or information of interest chiefly to a special group

news·man \-mən, -ˌman\ *n* : one who gathers, reports, or comments on the news : REPORTER, CORRESPONDENT

news·mon·ger \-ˌməŋ-gər, -ˌmäŋ-\ *n* : GOSSIP

news·pa·per \'n(y)üz-ˌpā-pər\ *n* **1** : a paper that is printed and distributed usu. daily or weekly and contains news, opinions, features, and advertising **2** : NEWSPRINT

news·pa·per·man \-ˌman\ *n* : one who owns or is employed by a newspaper; *esp* : one who writes or edits copy for a newspaper

news·print \'n(y)üz-ˌprint\ *n* : cheap machine-finished paper made chiefly from wood pulp and used mostly for newspapers

news·reel \-ˌrēl\ *n* : a short motion picture dealing with current events

news·stand \-ˌstand\ *n* : a place where newspapers and periodicals are sold

news·wor·thy \-ˌwər-t͟hē\ *adj* : sufficiently interesting to the general public to warrant reporting (as in a newspaper)

newsy \'n(y)ü-zē\ *adj* : filled with news; *esp* : CHATTY

newt \'n(y)üt\ *n* : any of various small salamanders that live mostly in water

New World *n* : the western hemisphere; *esp* : the continental landmass of No. and So. America

New Year \'n(y)ü-ˌyi(ə)r\ *n* **1** : NEW YEAR'S DAY; *also* : the first days of the year **2** : ROSH HASHANAH

New Year's Day *n* : January 1 observed as a legal holiday

¹next \'nekst\ *adj* : immediately preceding or following : NEAREST

²next *adv* **1** : in the time, place, or order nearest or immediately succeeding **2** : on the first occasion to come

³next *prep* : next to

next of kin : one or more persons in the nearest degree of relationship to another person

¹next to *prep* : immediately following : adjacent to

²next to *adv* : very nearly : ALMOST

nex·us \'nek-səs\ *n, pl* **nex·us·es** \-sə-səz\ *or* **nex·us** : CONNECTION, LINK

ni·a·cin \'nī-ə-sən\ *n* : NICOTINIC ACID

nib \'nib\ *n* **1** : BILL, BEAK **2 a** : the sharpened point of a quill pen **b** : a pen point **3** : a small pointed or projecting part

¹nib·ble \'nib-əl\ *vb* **nib·bled**; **nib·bling** \'nib-(ə-)liŋ\ **1** : to bite or chew gently or bit by bit **2** : to make cautious attempts — **nib·bler** \-(ə-)lər\ *n*

²nibble *n* **1** : an act of nibbling; *esp* : a small or cautious bite **2** : a very small quantity

nibs \'nibz\ *n sing or pl* : an important or self-important person — used chiefly in the phrase *his nibs*

nice \'nīs\ *adj* **1** : showing fastidious or finicky tastes : REFINED **2** : marked by or demanding delicate discrimination or treatment **3 a** : PLEASING, AGREEABLE **b** : well-executed **4 a** : socially acceptable : WELL-BRED **b** : VIRTUOUS, RESPECTABLE — **nice·ly** *adv* — **nice·ness** *n*

nice–nel·ly \'nīs-'nel-ē\ *adj, often cap 2d N* **1** : PRUDISH **2** : EUPHEMISTIC — **nice nelly** *n, often cap 2d N* — **nice–nel·ly·ism** \-ˌiz-əm\ *n, often cap 2d N*

ni·ce·ty \'nī-sət-ē\ *n, pl* **-ties** **1** : a dainty, delicate, or elegant thing **2** : a small point : a fine detail **3** : careful attention to details : EXACTNESS **4** : the point at which a thing is at its best

niche \'nich\ *n* **1** : a recess in a wall esp. for a statue **2** : a place, use, or work for which a person is best fitted

¹nick \'nik\ *n* **1** : a small groove : NOTCH **2** : CHIP **3** : the final critical moment

²nick *vb* **1** : to make a nick in : NOTCH, CHIP **2** : to make petty attacks : SNIPE

¹nick·el \'nik-əl\ *n* **1** : a silver-white hard malleable ductile metallic chemical element that is capable of a high polish, resistant to corrosion, and used chiefly in alloys and as a catalyst **2 a** : the U.S. 5-cent piece regularly containing 25 percent nickel and 75 percent copper **b** : five cents

²nick·el *vt* **-eled** *or* **-elled**; **-el·ing** *or* **-el·ling** \'nik-(ə-)liŋ\ : to plate with nickel
nick·el·ode·on \ˌnik-ə-'lōd-ē-ən\ *n* **1** : a theater presenting entertainment for an admission price of five cents **2** : JUKEBOX
nickel silver *n* : a silver-white alloy of copper, zinc, and nickel
nick·er \'nik-ər\ *vi* **nick·ered**; **nick·er·ing** \'nik-(ə-)riŋ\ : NEIGH, WHINNY — **nicker** *n*
¹nick·name \'nik-ˌnām\ *n* **1** : a usu. descriptive name given instead of or in addition to the one belonging to an individual **2** : a familiar form of a proper name
²nickname *vt* : to give a nickname to — **nick·nam·er** *n*
nic·o·tine \'nik-ə-ˌtēn\ *n* : a poisonous alkaloid that is the chief active principle of tobacco and is used as an insecticide
nic·o·tin·ic \ˌnik-ə-'tē-nik, -'tin-ik\ *adj* : of or relating to nicotine or nicotinic acid
nicotinic acid *n* : an organic acid of the vitamin B complex found widely in animals and plants and used esp. against pellagra
nic·ti·tate \'nik-tə-ˌtāt\ *vi* : WINK — **nic·ti·ta·tion** \ˌnik-tə-'tā-shən\ *n*
niece \'nēs\ *n* : a daughter of one's brother, sister, brother-in-law, or sister-in-law
nif·ty \'nif-tē\ *adj* : FINE, SWELL — **nifty** *n*
nig·gard \'nig-ərd\ *n* : a meanly covetous and stingy person : MISER — **niggard** *adj*
nig·gard·li·ness \'nig-ərd-lē-nəs\ *n* : the quality or state of being niggardly
nig·gard·ly \-lē\ *adj* **1** : grudgingly reluctant to spend or grant : STINGY **2** : characteristic of a niggard : SCANTY — **niggardly** *adv*
nig·gling \'nig-(ə-)liŋ\ *adj* **1** : PETTY **2** : demanding meticulous care — **niggling** *n* — **nig·gling·ly** *adv*
¹nigh \'nī\ *adv* **1** : near in place, time, or relationship **2** : NEARLY, ALMOST
²nigh *adj* **1** : CLOSE, NEAR **2** : being on the left side
³nigh *prep* : NEAR
night \'nīt\ *n* **1** : the time between dusk and dawn when there is no sunlight **2** : the beginning of darkness : NIGHTFALL **3** : the darkness of night — **night** *adj*
night–blind \-ˌblīnd\ *adj* : afflicted with night blindness
night blindness *n* : reduced visual capacity in faint light (as at night)
night·cap \'nīt-ˌkap\ *n* **1** : a cloth cap worn with nightclothes **2** : a usu. alcoholic drink taken at bedtime
night·clothes \-ˌklō(t͟h)z\ *n pl* : garments worn in bed
night·club \-ˌkləb\ *n* : a place of entertainment open at night usu. serving food and liquor, having a floor show, and providing music and space for dancing
night crawler *n* : EARTHWORM; *esp* : a large earthworm found on the soil surface at night
night·dress \'nīt-ˌdres\ *n* **1** : NIGHTGOWN **2** : NIGHTCLOTHES
night·fall \-ˌfȯl\ *n* : the coming of night
night·gown \-ˌgau̇n\ *n* : a long loose garment worn in bed
night·hawk \-ˌhȯk\ *n* **1** : any of several birds that resemble the related whippoorwill **2** : a person who habitually stays up late at night
night·ie \'nīt-ē\ *n* : a nightgown for a woman or a child
night·in·gale \'nīt-ᵊn-ˌgāl\ *n* : any of several Old World thrushes noted for the sweet usu. nocturnal song of the male
night latch *n* : a door lock having a spring bolt operated from the outside by a key and from the inside by a knob
night letter *n* : a telegram sent at night at a reduced rate per word for delivery the following morning
night·long \'nīt-ˌlȯŋ\ *adj* : lasting the whole night
night·long \-'lȯŋ\ *adv* : through the whole night
night·ly \'nīt-lē\ *adj* **1** : of or relating to the night or every night **2** : happening, done, or produced by night or every night — **nightly** *adv*
night·mare \-ˌma(ə)r\ *n* **1** : a frightening dream accompanied by a sense of oppression or suffocation that usu. awakens the sleeper **2** : an experience, situation, or object having the monstrous character of a nightmare or producing a feeling of anxiety or terror — **night·mar·ish** \-ish\ *adj*
night owl *n* : a person who keeps late hours at night
night rider *n* : a member of a secret band who ride masked at night doing acts of violence for the purpose of punishing or terrorizing
night–robe \'nīt-ˌrōb\ *n* : NIGHTGOWN
nights \'nīts\ *adv* : in the nighttime repeatedly
night·shade \'nīt-ˌshād\ *n* : any of a family of herbs, shrubs, and trees having alternate leaves, usu. white, yellow, or purple flowers, and fruits that are berries and including many poisonous forms (as belladonna) and important food plants (as the potato, tomato, and eggplant)
night·shirt \-ˌshərt\ *n* : a nightgown resembling a shirt
night·stick \-ˌstik\ *n* : a policeman's club
night·tide \'nīt-ˌtīd\ *n* : NIGHTTIME
night·time \'nīt-ˌtīm\ *n* : the time from dusk to dawn
night·walk·er \-ˌwȯ-kər\ *n* : a person who roves about at night esp. with criminal or immoral intent
nil \'nil\ *n* : NOTHING, ZERO — **nil** *adj*
nim·ble \'nim-bəl\ *adj* **1** : quick and light in motion : AGILE **2** : quick in understanding and learning : CLEVER — **nim·ble·ness** *n* — **nim·bly** \-blē\ *adv*
nim·bus \'nim-bəs\ *n, pl* **nim·bi** \-ˌbī, -ˌbē\ *or* **nim·bus·es** **1** : an indication (as a circle) of radiant light or glory about the head of a drawn or sculptured divinity, saint, or sovereign **2 a** : a rain cloud that is of uniform grayness and extends over the entire sky **b** : a cloud from which rain is falling
nim·rod \'nim-ˌräd\ *n, often cap* : HUNTER
nin·com·poop \'nin-kəm-ˌpüp\ *n* : FOOL, SIMPLETON
nine \'nīn\ *n* **1** — see NUMBER table **2** : the ninth in a set or series **3** : something having nine units or members; *esp* : a baseball team — **nine** *adj or pron* — **to the nines** : to the highest point : to perfection
nine days' wonder *n* : something that creates a short-lived sensation
nine·pence \'nīn-pən(t)s, *US also* -ˌpen(t)s\ *n* : the sum of nine usu. British pennies
nine·pins \'nīn-ˌpinz\ *n pl* : tenpins played without the headpin
nine·teen \(')nīn(t)-'tēn\ *n* — see NUMBER table — **nineteen** *adj or pron* — **nine·teenth** \-'tēn(t)th\ *adj or n*
nine·ty \'nīnt-ē\ *n, pl* **nineties** — see NUMBER table — **nine·ti·eth** \-ē-əth\ *adj or n* — **ninety** *adj or pron*
nin·ny \'nin-ē\ *n, pl* **ninnies** : FOOL, SIMPLETON
nin·ny·ham·mer \'nin-ē-ˌham-ər\ *n* : NINNY
ninth \'nīn(t)th\ *n, pl* **ninths** \'nīn(t)s, 'nīn(t)ths\ — see NUMBER table — **ninth** *adj or adv*
ni·o·bi·um \nī-'ō-bē-əm\ *n* : a lustrous platinum-gray ductile metallic chemical element that is used in alloys
¹nip \'nip\ *vb* **nipped**; **nip·ping** **1** : to catch hold of and squeeze tightly between two surfaces, edges, or points **2 a** : to sever by or as if by pinching sharply : CLIP **b** : to destroy the growth, progress, maturing, or fulfillment of **3** : to injure or make numb with cold : CHILL **4** : SNATCH, STEAL
²nip *n* **1** : something that nips: as **a** : a sharp stinging cold **b** : a biting or pungent flavor : TANG **2** : the act of nipping : PINCH, BITE **3** : a small portion : BIT
³nip *n* : a small quantity of liquor
⁴nip *vi* **nipped**; **nip·ping** : to take liquor in nips : TIPPLE
nip and tuck \ˌnip-ən-'tək\ *adj* (*or adv*) : so close that the lead or advantage shifts rapidly from one contestant to another
nip·per \'nip-ər\ *n* **1** : a device (as pincers) for nipping — usu. used in pl. **2** : CHELA

nip·ple \'nip-əl\ *n* **1 :** the protuberance of a mammary gland upon which the ducts open and from which milk is drawn **2 :** something resembling a nipple; *esp* **:** the rubber mouthpiece of a baby's nursing bottle

nip·py \'nip-ē\ *adj* **:** CHILLY, CHILLING

nir·va·na \ni(ə)r-'vän-ə\ *n, often cap* **1 :** the final freeing of a soul from all that enslaves it; *esp* **:** the supreme happiness that according to Hinduism and Buddhism comes when all passion, hatred, and delusion die out and the soul is released from the necessity of further purification **2 :** a place or state of oblivion to care, pain, or external reality

ni·sei \(')nē-'sā\ *n, pl* **nisei :** a son or daughter of immigrant Japanese parents who is born and educated in America

Nis·sen hut \,nis-ᵊn-\ *n* **:** a prefabricated shelter of corrugated iron with cement floor shaped like a cylinder on edge

nit \'nit\ *n* **:** the egg of a louse or similar insect; *also* **:** the insect itself when young

ni·ter \'nīt-ər\ *n* **1 :** POTASSIUM NITRATE **2 :** SODIUM NITRATE

nit–pick·ing \'nit-,pik-iŋ\ *n* **:** minute and usu. unjustified criticism

[1]**ni·trate** \'nī-,trāt\ *n* **1 :** a salt or ester of nitric acid **2 :** sodium nitrate or potassium nitrate used as a fertilizer

[2]**nitrate** *vt* **:** to treat or combine with nitric acid or a nitrate — **ni·tra·tion** \nī-'trā-shən\ *n*

ni·tric acid \,nī-trik-\ *n* **:** a corrosive liquid acid used esp. as an oxidizing agent, in nitrations, and in making fertilizers, explosives, and dyes

ni·tro·gen \'nī-trə-jən\ *n* **:** a colorless tasteless odorless gaseous chemical element that usu. has a valence of 3 or 5, constitutes 78 percent of the atmosphere by volume, and is a constituent of all living tissues — **ni·trog·e·nous** \nī-'träj-ə-nəs\ *adj*

ni·tro·glyc·er·in *or* **ni·tro·glyc·er·ine** \,nī-trō-'glis-(ə-)rən\ *n* **:** a heavy oily explosive poisonous liquid used in making dynamite and in medicine

nit·ty–grit·ty \'nit-ē-,grit-ē, ,nit-ē-'\ *n* **:** the actual state of things **:** what is ultimately essential and true

nit·wit \'nit-,wit\ *n* **:** a scatterbrained or stupid person

[1]**no** \(')nō\ *adv* **1** — used as a function word to express the negative of an alternative choice or possibility **2 :** in no respect or degree — used in comparisons **3 :** not so — used to express negation, dissent, denial, or refusal **4** — used with a following adjective to imply a meaning expressed by the opposite positive statement **5** — used as a function word to emphasize a following negative or to introduce a more emphatic, explicit, or comprehensive statement **6** — used as an interjection to express surprise, doubt, or incredulity

[2]**no** *adj* **1 a :** not any **b :** hardly any **:** very little **2 :** not a **:** quite other than a

[3]**no** \'nō\ *n, pl* **noes** *or* **nos** \'nōz\ **1 :** an act or instance of refusing or denying by the use of the word *no* **:** DENIAL **2 a :** a negative vote or decision **b** *pl* **:** persons voting in the negative

nob·by \'näb-ē\ *adj* **:** of the first quality or style **:** SMART

no·bel·i·um \nō-'bel-ē-əm\ *n* **:** a radioactive chemical element produced artificially

No·bel prize \(,)nō-,bel-\ *n* **:** any of various annual prizes (as in peace, literature, medicine) established by the will of Alfred Nobel for the encouragement of persons who work for the interests of humanity

no·bil·i·ary \nō-'bil-ē-,er-ē\ *adj* **:** of or relating to the nobility

no·bil·i·ty \nō-'bil-ət-ē\ *n, pl* **-ties 1 :** the quality or state of being noble **2 :** noble rank **3 :** the class or group of nobles

[1]**no·ble** \'nō-bəl\ *adj* **1 a :** possessing outstanding qualities **:** ILLUSTRIOUS **b :** FAMOUS, NOTABLE **2 :** of high birth or exalted rank **:** ARISTOCRATIC **3 a :** possessing very high or excellent qualities or properties **b :** very good or excellent **4 :** grand or impressive esp. in appearance **5 :** possessing, characterized by, or arising from superiority of mind or character **:** MAGNANIMOUS **6 :** chemically inert or inactive esp. toward oxygen — **no·ble·ness** *n* — **no·bly** \-blē\ *adv*

[2]**noble** *n* **1 :** a person of noble rank or birth **2 :** an old English gold coin equivalent to 8*s* 6*d*

no·ble·man \'nō-bəl-mən\ *n* **:** a member of the nobility **:** PEER — **no·ble·wom·an** \-,wu̇m-ən\ *n*

no·blesse oblige \nō-,bles-ə-'blēzh\ *n* **:** the obligation of honorable, generous, and responsible behavior associated with high rank or birth

[1]**nobody** \'nō-,bäd-ē, -bəd-ē\ *pron* **:** no person **:** not anybody

[2]**nobody** *n, pl* **no·bod·ies :** a person of no importance

noct·am·bu·la·tion \(,)näk-,tam-byə-'lā-shən\ *or* **noct·am·bu·lism** \näk-'tam-byə-,liz-əm\ *n* **:** SOMNAMBULISM — **noct·am·bu·list** \-ləst\ *n*

noc·tur·nal \näk-'tərn-ᵊl\ *adj* **1 :** of, relating to, or occurring in the night **2 :** active at night — **noc·tur·nal·ly** \-ᵊl-ē\ *adv*

noc·turne \'näk-,tərn\ *n* **:** a work of art dealing with night; *esp* **:** a dreamy pensive composition for the piano

noc·u·ous \'näk-yə-wəs\ *adj* **:** likely to cause injury **:** HARMFUL — **noc·u·ous·ly** *adv*

[1]**nod** \'näd\ *vb* **nod·ded; nod·ding 1 :** to bend the head downward or forward (as in bowing or going to sleep or as a way of answering "yes"); *also* **:** to cause (the head) to move in this way **2 :** to move up and down **3 :** to show by a nod of the head **4 :** to let one's attention lapse for a moment **:** make a slip or an error — **nod·der** *n*

[2]**nod** *n* **:** the action of nodding

nod·dle \'näd-ᵊl\ *n* **:** HEAD

nod·dy \'näd-ē\ *n, pl* **noddies 1 :** a stupid person **2 :** any of several stout-bodied terns of warm seas

node \'nōd\ *n* **1 :** an entangling complication (as in a drama) **2 a :** thickened or swollen enlargement (as of a rheumatic joint) **b :** a discrete mass of one kind of tissue enclosed in tissue of a different kind **3 a :** a point at which subsidiary parts originate or center **b :** a point on a stem at which a leaf is inserted — **nod·al** \'nōd-ᵊl\ *adj* — **nod·ed** *adj*

nod·u·lar \'näj-ə-lər\ *adj* **:** of, relating to, characterized by, or occurring in the form of nodules

nod·ule \'näj-ül\ *n* **:** a small lump or swelling

no·el \nō-'el\ *n* **1 :** a Christmas carol **2** *cap* **:** the Christmas season

nog·gin \'näg-ən\ *n* **1 :** a small mug or cup **2 :** a small quantity of drink usu. equivalent to a gill **3 :** a person's head

[1]**no–good** \,nō-,gu̇d\ *adj* **:** having no worth, use, or chance of success

[2]**no–good** \'nō-,gu̇d\ *n* **:** a no-good person or thing

[1]**noise** \'nȯiz\ *n* **1 :** loud, confused, or senseless shouting or outcry **2 a :** SOUND; *esp* **:** one that lacks agreeable musical quality or is noticeably loud, harsh, or discordant **b :** an unwanted signal in an electronic communication system

[2]**noise** *vt* **:** to spread by rumor or report

noise·less \'nȯiz-ləs\ *adj* **:** making or causing no noise — **noise·less·ly** *adv* — **noise·less·ness** *n*

noise·mak·er \-,mā-kər\ *n* **:** one that makes noise; *esp* **:** a device used to make noise at parties

noi·some \'nȯi-səm\ *adj* **1 :** NOXIOUS, UNWHOLESOME **2 :** offensive to the senses (as smell) **:** DISGUSTING — **noi·some·ly** *adv* — **noi·some·ness** *n*

noisy \'nȯi-zē\ *adj* **1 :** making noise **2 :** full of or characterized by noise — **nois·i·ly** \-zə-lē\ *adv* — **nois·i·ness** \-zē-nəs\ *n*

no·mad \'nō-,mad\ *n* **1 :** a member of a people that has no fixed residence but wanders from place to place **2 :** an individual who roams about aimlessly — **nomad** *or* **no·mad·ic** \nō-'mad-ik\ *adj* — **no·mad·ism** \'nō-,mad-,iz-əm\ *n*

no–man's–land \'nō-,manz-,land\ *n* **1 :** an area of unowned, unclaimed, or uninhabited land **2 :** an unoccupied area be tween opposing troops **3** : an area of anomalous, ambiguous, or indefinite character

nom de guerre \ˌnäm-di-ˈge(ə)r\ *n, pl* **noms de guerre** \ˌnäm(z)-di-\ : PSEUDONYM

nom de plume \ˌnäm-di-ˈplüm\ *n, pl* **noms de plume** \ˌnäm(z)-di-\ : PEN NAME

no·men \ˈnō-mən\ *n, pl* **nom·i·na** \ˈnäm-ə-nə, ˈnō-mə-\ : the second of the three usual names of an ancient Roman

no·men·cla·ture \ˈnō-mən-ˌklā-chər\ *n* **1** : NAME, DESIGNATION **2** : a system of terms used in a particular science, discipline, or art

nom·i·nal \ˈnäm-ən-ᵊl\ *adj* **1** : of, relating to, or being a noun or a word or expression taking a noun construction **2 a** : of, relating to, or constituting a name **b** : bearing the name of a person **3 a** : existing in name or form only **b** : very small : TRIFLING, INSIGNIFICANT — **nom·i·nal·ly** \-ᵊl-ē\ *adv*

nom·i·nate \ˈnäm-ə-ˌnāt\ *vt* : to choose as a candidate for election, appointment, or honor; *esp* : to propose for office — **nom·i·na·tor** \-ˌnāt-ər\ *n*

nom·i·na·tion \ˌnäm-ə-ˈnā-shən\ *n* **1** : the act, process, or an instance of nominating **2** : the state of being nominated

nom·i·na·tive \ˈnäm-(ə-)nət-iv\ *adj* : of, relating to, or constituting a grammatical case marking typically the subject of a verb — **nominative** *n*

nom·i·nee \ˌnäm-ə-ˈnē\ *n* : a person nominated for an office, duty, or position

non- \(ˈ)nän, ˌnän\ *prefix* : not : reverse of : absence of

nonabrasive
nonabsorbent
nonabstainer
nonacademic
nonacceptance
nonacid
nonactive
nonadaptive
nonadherence
nonadhesive
nonadjacent
nonadjustable
nonadministrative
nonadmission
nonaggression
nonagreement
nonagricultural
nonalcoholic
nonalphabetic
nonanalytic
nonappearance
nonaquatic
nonaqueous
nonaromatic
nonassessable
nonathletic
nonattributive
nonauthoritative
nonautomatic
nonautomotive
nonbasic
nonbearing
nonbeing
nonbeliever
nonbelligerent
nonbiting
nonbreakable
nonburning
nonbusiness
noncaking
noncalcareous
noncanonical
noncarbohydrate
noncarnivorous
noncash
noncellular
nonchargeable
non-Christian
noncitizen
nonclassical
nonclerical
nonclinical
nonclotting
noncoercive
noncollapsible
noncollectible
noncollegiate
noncombat
noncombining
noncombustible
noncommercial
noncommunicable
noncommunication
noncompensating
noncompetent
noncompeting
noncompetitive
noncomplementary
noncompliance
noncomplying
noncompound
noncompressible
nonconclusive
nonconcurrent
noncondensing
nonconditioned
nonconducting
nonconfidence
nonconflicting
nonconformance
nonconforming
noncongenital
nonconscious
nonconstitutional
nonconstructive
nonconsumable
noncontact
noncontagious
noncontemporary
noncontentious
noncontiguous
noncontinuous
noncontraband
noncontradictory
noncontributing
noncontrolled
noncontrolling
noncontroversial
nonconvertible
noncooperation
noncorporate
noncorrodible
noncorroding
noncorrosive
noncovered
noncreative
noncriminal
noncritical
noncrystalline
noncultivated
noncumulative
noncurrent
noncyclic
nondeductible
nondeferrable
nondefining
nondegenerate
nondelivery
nondemocratic
nondenominational
nondepartmental
nondeposition
nonderivative
nondestructive
nondetonating
nondevelopment
nondifferentiation
nondigestible
nondirectional
nondirective
nondisclosure
nondiscrimination
nondiscriminatory
nondiscursive
nondisqualifying
nondistinctive
nondistribution
nondivided
nondocumentary
nondollar
nondomesticated
nondramatic
nondrying
nondurable
nondynastic
nonecclesiastical
noneconomic
noneducational
noneffective
noneffervescent
nonelastic
nonelective
nonelectric
noneligible
nonemotional
nonempirical
nonenforceable
nonenforcement
nonentanglement
nonepiscopal
noneruptive
nonessential
nonethical
nonexchangeable
nonexclusive
nonexempt
nonexistence
nonexistent
nonexpendable
nonexplosive
nonexportation
nonextant
nonfarm
nonfat
nonfatal
nonfattening
nonfebrile
nonfederal
nonfederated
nonfeeding
nonferrous
nonfiction
nonfictional
nonfigurative
nonfilamentous
nonfinancial
nonfissionable
nonflagellated
nonflammable
nonflowering
nonfluency
nonflying
nonforfeiture
nonfraternal
nonfreezing
nonfulfillment
nonfunctional
nongaseous
nongenetic
nongovernmental
nongregarious
nonhardy
nonharmonic
nonhereditary
nonhistorical
nonhomogeneous
nonhomologous
nonhuman
nonidentical
nonidentity
nonimmigrant
nonimmune
nonimportation
nonindustrial
noninfectious
noninflammable
noninflammatory
noninstitutional
noninstructional
nonintegrated
nonintellectual
nonintercourse
noninterference
nonintersecting
nonintervention
noninterventionist
nonintoxicating
noninvolvement
nonirritating
nonlegal
nonlethal
nonlife
nonlinear
nonliquid
nonliterary
nonliterate
nonliturgical
nonlocal
nonlogical
nonluminous
nonmagnetic
nonmailable
nonmalignant
nonmalleable
nonman
nonmarketable
nonmaterial
nonmechanical
nonmechanistic
nonmember
nonmembership
nonmetered
nonmetrical
nonmigratory
nonmilitary
nonmoney
nonmoral
nonmotile
nonmoving
nonnational
nonnative
nonnatural
nonnecessity
nonnegotiable
nonnitrogenous
nonobjective
nonobligatory
nonobservance
nonoccurrence
nonofficial
nonoily
nonoperating
nonorganic
nonorthodox
nonparallel
nonparalytic
nonparasitic
nonparticipant
nonparticipating
nonparty
nonpasserine
nonpaternity
nonpathogenic
nonpaying
nonpayment
nonpecuniary
nonperformance
nonperishable
nonpermanent
nonpersistent
nonpersonal
nonphysical
nonpoisonous
nonpolar
nonpolitical
nonporous
nonpossession
nonpractical
nonpredicative
nonpregnant
nonprinting
nonproducer
nonprofessional
nonprogressive
nonproprietary
nonprotein
nonproven
nonpublic
nonpungent
nonquota
nonrabbinic
nonracial
nonradical
nonradioactive
nonrandom
nonrated
nonrational
nonreactive
nonreader
nonrealistic
nonreciprocal
nonrecognition
nonrecourse
nonrecoverable
nonrecurrent
nonrecurring
nonreducing
nonrefillable
nonregistered
nonregulation
nonreligious
nonremovable
nonrenewable
nonrepayable
nonrepresentational
nonrepresentative
nonresidential
nonrestraint
nonrestricted
nonretractile
nonretroactive
nonreturnable
nonrevenue
nonreversible
nonrhetorical
nonrigid
nonrotating
nonruminant
nonsalable
nonscheduled
nonscientific
nonscientist
nonseasonal
nonsecret
nonsecretory
nonsectarian
nonsegregated
nonselective
non-self-governing
nonsensitive
nonsensuous
nonsexual
nonshrinkable
nonsignificant
nonsinkable
nonsmoker
nonsocial
nonsolid
nonspatial
nonspeaking
nonspecialized
nonspecific
nonspectacular
nonspectral
nonspeculative
nonstaining
nonstarter
nonstationary

nonstatistical
nonstellar
nonstrategic
nonstriated
nonstriker
nonstructural
nonsubscriber
nonsuccess
nonsurgical
nonsustaining
nonsyllabic
nonsymbolic
nonsymmetrical
nontaxable
nontechnical
nontemporal
nonterritorial
nontheatrical
nontheistic
nonthermal
nontidal
nontoxic
nontraditional
nontransferable
nontransparency
nontransparent
nontransposing
nontropical
nontuberculous
nontypical
nonunderstandable
nonuniform
nonuniformity
nonuser
nonutilitarian
nonvariant
nonvascular
nonvegetative
nonvenomous
nonviable
nonvibratory
nonviolation
nonviscous
nonvisual
nonvocal
nonvocational
nonvolatile
nonvoluntary
nonvoter
nonvoting
nonwhite
nonworker
nonworking
nonwoven
nonzero

non·age \ˈnän-ij, ˈnō-nij\ *n* **1** : MINORITY 1 **2 a** : a period of youth **b** : IMMATURITY

no·na·ge·nar·i·an \ˌnō-nə-jə-ˈner-ē-ən, ˌnän-ə-\ *n* : a person who is 90 or more but less than 100 years old — **nonagenarian** *adj*

non·aligned \ˌnän-ə-ˈlīnd\ *adj* : not allied with other states or governments and esp. with one of the great powers

non·align·ment \-ˈlīn-mənt\ *n* : the condition of a state or government that is nonaligned

[1]**nonce** \ˈnän(t)s\ *n* : the one, particular, or present occasion, purpose, or use

[2]**nonce** *adj* : occurring, used, or made only once or for a special occasion

non·cha·lance \ˌnän-shə-ˈlän(t)s\ *n* : the state of being nonchalant

non·cha·lant \-ˈlänt\ *adj* : having a confident and easy manner; *esp* : unconcerned about drawing attention to oneself — **non·cha·lant·ly** *adv*

non·com \ˈnän-ˌkäm\ *n* : NONCOMMISSIONED OFFICER

non·com·bat·ant \ˌnän-kəm-ˈbat-ᵊnt, (ˈ)nän-ˈkäm-bət-ənt\ *n* : a member (as a chaplain) of the armed forces whose duties do not include fighting; *also* : CIVILIAN — **noncombatant** *adj*

non·com·mis·sioned officer \ˌnän-kə-ˌmish-ənd-\ *n* : a subordinate officer in a branch of the armed forces appointed from enlisted personnel and holding one of various grades (as staff sergeant)

non·com·mit·tal \ˌnän-kə-ˈmit-ᵊl\ *adj* : not telling or showing what a person thinks or has decided — **non·com·mit·tal·ly** \-ᵊl-ē\ *adv*

non–Com·mu·nist \(ˈ)nän-ˈkäm-yə-nəst\ *adj* : not Communist : being other than Communist

non com·pos men·tis \ˌnän-ˌkäm-pəs-ˈment-əs, ˌnōn-\ *adj* : not of sound mind

non·con·duc·tor \ˌnän-kən-ˈdək-tər\ *n* : a substance that conducts heat, electricity, or sound only in very small degree

non·con·form·ist \ˌnän-kən-ˈfȯr-məst\ *n* **1** *often cap* : a person who does not conform to an established church and esp. the Church of England **2** : a person who does not conform to a generally accepted pattern of thought or action — **nonconformist** *adj, often cap*

non·con·for·mi·ty \-ˈfȯr-mət-ē\ *n* **1** : failure or refusal to conform to an established church **2** : refusal to conform to conventional rules or customs

non·con·trib·u·to·ry \ˌnän-kən-ˈtrib-yə-ˌtōr-ē\ *adj* : paid for entirely by an employer : not involving payments by employees

non·de·script \ˌnän-di-ˈskript\ *adj* : belonging or appearing to belong to no particular class or kind : not easily described — **nondescript** *n*

non·du·ra·ble goods \(ˌ)nän-ˌd(y)u̇r-ə-bəl-\ *n pl* : articles (as clothing or food) usable only for a short time or only once

[1]**none** \ˈnən\ *pron* **1** : not any **2** : not one **3** : not any such thing or person

[2]**none** *adv* : by no means : not at all

non·en·ti·ty \nä-ˈnent-ət-ē\ *n, pl* **-ti·ties 1** : something that does not exist or exists only in the imagination **2** : one of no consequence or significance

nones \ˈnōnz\ *n pl* : the 9th day before the ides according to ancient Roman reckoning

none·such \ˈnən-ˌsəch\ *n* : a person or thing without an equal — **nonesuch** *adj*

none·the·less \ˌnən-t͟hə-ˈles\ *adv* : NEVERTHELESS

non·in·tox·i·cant \ˌnän-in-ˈtäk-si-kənt\ *adj* : not intoxicating — **nonintoxicant** *n*

non·ir·ri·gat·ed \(ˈ)nän-ˈir-ə-ˌgāt-əd\ *adj* : not irrigated

non·ju·ror \(ˈ)nän-ˈju̇r-ər\ *n* : a person refusing to take an oath esp. of allegiance, supremacy, or abjuration — **non·jur·ing** \-ˈju̇(ə)r-iŋ\ *adj*

non·liv·ing \(ˈ)nän-ˈliv-iŋ\ *adj* : not having or characterized by life

non·met·al \(ˈ)nän-ˈmet-ᵊl\ *n* : a chemical element (as carbon or nitrogen) that lacks metallic properties

non·me·tal·lic \ˌnän-mə-ˈtal-ik\ *adj* **1** : not metallic **2** : of, relating to, or being a nonmetal

[1]**non·pa·reil** \ˌnän-pə-ˈrel\ *adj* : having no equal : PEERLESS

[2]**nonpareil** *n* **1** : an individual of unequaled excellence : PARAGON **2** : a small flat disk of chocolate covered with white sugar pellets

non·par·ti·san \(ˈ)nän-ˈpärt-ə-zən\ *adj* : not partisan; *esp* : free from party affiliation, bias, or designation — **non·par·ti·san·ship** \-ˌship\ *n*

[1]**non·plus** \(ˈ)nän-ˈpləs\ *n, pl* **non·plus·es** *or* **non·plus·ses** : a state of bafflement or perplexity : QUANDARY

[2]**nonplus** *vt* **non·plussed**; **non·plus·sing** : to cause to be at a loss as to what to say, think, or do : PERPLEX

non·pro·duc·tive \ˌnän-prə-ˈdək-tiv\ *adj* **1** : failing to produce or yield : UNPRODUCTIVE **2** : not directly productive — **non·pro·duc·tive·ness** *n*

non·prof·it \(ˈ)nän-ˈpräf-ət\ *adj* : not conducted or maintained for the purpose of making a profit

non·pro·lif·er·a·tion \ˌnän-prə-ˌlif-ə-ˈrā-shən\ *adj* : providing for the end of further spread (as of nuclear arms)

non·res·i·dent \(ˈ)nän-ˈrez-əd-ənt, -ə-ˌdent\ *adj* : not living in a specified or implied place — **nonresident** *n*

non·re·sis·tance \ˌnän-ri-ˈzis-tən(t)s\ *n* : the principles or practice of passive submission to authority even when unjust or oppressive — **non·re·sis·tant** \-tənt\ *adj*

non·re·stric·tive \ˌnän-ri-ˈstrik-tiv\ *adj* **1** : not serving or tending to restrict **2** : not limiting the reference of the word or phrase modified

non·sense \ˈnän-ˌsen(t)s, ˈnän(t)-sən(t)s\ *n* **1** : foolish or meaningless words or actions **2** : things of no importance or value : TRIFLES — **non·sen·si·cal** \(ˈ)nän-ˈsen(t)-si-kəl\ *adj* — **non·sen·si·cal·ly** \-k(ə-)lē\ *adv* — **non·sen·si·cal·ness** *n*

non se·qui·tur \(ˈ)nän-ˈsek-wət-ər\ *n* : an inference that does not follow from the premises

non·sked \(ˈ)nän-ˈsked\ *n* : a nonscheduled airline or transport plane

non·skid \(ˈ)nän-ˈskid\ *adj* : having the tread corrugated or specially constructed to resist skidding

non·stan·dard \(ˈ)nän-ˈstan-dərd\ *adj* **1** : not standard **2** : not conforming in pronunciation, grammatical construction, idiom or choice of word to the usage generally characteristic of educated native speakers of the language

non·stop \(ˈ)nän-ˈstäp\ *adj* : done or made without a stop — **nonstop** *adv*

non·sup·port \ˌnän(t)-sə-ˈpōrt\ *n* : failure to support; *esp* : failure on the part of one under obligation to provide maintenance

non–U \(ˈ)nän-ˈyü\ *adj* : not characteristic of the upper classes

non·union \(ˈ)nän-ˈyü-nyən\ *adj* **1 :** not belonging to a trade union **2 :** not recognizing or favoring trade unions or their members

non·vi·o·lence \(ˈ)nän-ˈvī-ə-lən(t)s\ *n* **:** abstention on principle from violence; *also* **:** the principle of such abstention — **non·vi·o·lent** \-lənt\ *adj*

¹noo·dle \ˈnüd-ᵊl\ *n* **:** a stupid person **:** SIMPLETON

²noodle *n* **:** a food like macaroni but shaped into long flat strips and made with egg — usu. used in pl.

nook \ˈnu̇k\ *n* **1 :** an interior angle or corner formed usu. by two walls **2 :** a sheltered or hidden place **:** a corner set apart from its surroundings

noon \ˈnün\ *n* **:** the middle of the day **:** 12 o'clock in the daytime — **noon** *adj*

noon·day \-ˌdā\ *n* **:** MIDDAY

no one *pron* **:** NOBODY

noon·tide \ˈnün-ˌtīd\ *n* **1 :** the time of noon **2 :** the highest or culminating point

noon·time \-ˌtīm\ *n* **:** the time of noon

¹noose \ˈnüs\ *n* **:** a loop with a running knot that binds closer the more it is drawn

²noose *vt* **:** to catch or fasten with or as if with a noose

nor \nər, (ˈ)nȯ(ə)r\ *conj* **:** and not — used esp. to introduce and negate the second member and each later member of a series of items of which the first is preceded by *neither*

norm \ˈnȯrm\ *n* **:** AVERAGE, STANDARD; *esp* **:** a set standard of development or achievement usu. derived from the average or median achievement of a large group

¹nor·mal \ˈnȯr-məl\ *adj* **1 :** constituting or not deviating from a norm, rule, or principle **:** REGULAR **2 :** occurring naturally **3 a :** of, relating to, or characterized by average intelligence or development **b :** free from disorder of body or mind **:** SOUND, SANE — **nor·mal·cy** \-sē\ *n* — **nor·mal·i·ty** \nȯr-ˈmal-ət-ē\ *n* — **nor·mal·ly** \ˈnȯr-mə-lē\ *adv*

²normal *n* **1 :** one (as a line or person) that is normal **2 :** the usual condition, level, or quantity **:** AVERAGE

nor·mal·ize \ˈnȯr-mə-ˌlīz\ *vt* **:** to make normal or average — **nor·mal·i·za·tion** \ˌnȯr-mə-lə-ˈzā-shən\ *n*

normal school *n* **:** a usu. two-year school for training chiefly elementary teachers

¹north \ˈnȯrth; *in compounds, as "northeast", also* (ˈ)nȯr *esp by seamen*\ *adv* **:** to or toward the north

²north *adj* **1 :** situated toward or at the north **2 :** coming from the north

³north *n* **1 a :** the direction to the left of one facing east **b :** the compass point directly opposite to south **2** *cap* **:** regions or countries north of a specified or implied point — **north·er·ly** \ˈnȯr-t͟hər-lē\ *adv or adj* — **north·ern** \-t͟hə(r)n\ *adj* — **North·ern·er** \-t͟hə(r)-nər\ *n* — **north·ern·most** \-t͟hə(r)n-ˌmōst\ *adj* — **north·ward** \ˈnȯrth-wərd\ *adv or adj* — **north·wards** \-wərdz\ *adv*

north·bound \ˈnȯrth-ˌbau̇nd\ *adj* **:** headed north

north·east \nȯrth-ˈēst\ *n* **1 a :** the general direction between north and east **b :** the compass point midway between north and east **2** *cap* **:** regions or countries northeast of a specified or implied point — **northeast** *adj or adv* — **north·east·er·ly** \-ˈē-stər-lē\ *adv or adj* — **north·east·ern** \-ˈē-stərn\ *adj*

north·east·er \nȯrth-ˈē-stər\ *n* **:** a storm or strong wind from the northeast

north·er \ˈnȯr-t͟hər\ *n* **:** a storm or wind coming from the north

northern hemisphere *n* **:** the half of the earth that lies north of the equator

northern lights *n pl* **:** AURORA BOREALIS

north·ing \ˈnȯr-thiŋ, -t͟hiŋ\ *n* **1 :** difference in latitude to the north from the last preceding point of reckoning **2 :** northerly progress

north·land \ˈnȯrth-ˌland, -lənd\ *n, often cap* **:** land in the north **:** the north of a country or region

north pole *n, often cap N & P* **:** the northernmost point of the earth

North Star *n* **:** the star toward which the northern end of the earth's axis very nearly points

north·west \nȯrth-ˈwest\ *n* **1 a :** the general direction between north and west **b :** the compass point midway between north and west **2** *cap* **:** regions or countries northwest of a specified or implied point — **northwest** *adj or adv* — **north·west·er·ly** \-ˈwes-tər-lē\ *adv or adj* — **north·west·ern** \-tərn\ *adj*

nos *pl of* NO

¹nose \ˈnōz\ *n* **1 a :** the part of the face that bears the nostrils and covers the anterior part of the nasal cavity; *also* **:** this part together with the nasal cavity **b :** the vertebrate olfactory organ **2 :** the sense of smell **3 :** something (as a point, edge, or projecting front part) that resembles a nose — **nosed** *adj*

²nose *vb* **1 :** to detect by or as if by smell **:** SCENT **2 a :** to push or move with the nose **b :** to touch or rub with the nose **:** NUZZLE **3 :** to defeat by a narrow margin in a contest **4 :** to search impertinently **:** PRY **5 :** to move ahead slowly or cautiously

nose·bleed \-ˌblēd\ *n* **:** a bleeding from the nose

nose cone *n* **:** a protective cone constituting the forward end of a rocket or missile

nose dive *n* **1 :** the downward nose-first plunge of a flying object (as an airplane) **2 :** a sudden extreme drop — **nose–dive** \ˈnōz-ˌdīv\ *vi*

nose·gay \ˈnōz-ˌgā\ *n* **:** a small bunch of flowers **:** POSY

nose·piece \-ˌpēs\ *n* **1 :** a piece of armor for protecting the nose **2 :** a fitting at the lower end of a microscope tube to which the objectives are attached

no–show \nō-ˈshō\ *n* **:** a person who reserves space esp. on an airplane but neither uses nor cancels the reservation

nos·tal·gia \nä-ˈstal-jə, nə-\ *n* **:** a wistful yearning for something past or irrecoverable — **nos·tal·gic** \-jik\ *adj* — **nos·tal·gi·cal·ly** \-ji-k(ə-)lē\ *adv*

nos·tril \ˈnäs-trəl\ *n* **:** an external naris usu. with the adjoining nasal wall and passage

nos·trum \ˈnäs-trəm\ *n* **1 :** a medicine of secret composition recommended esp. by its preparer **2 :** a questionable remedy or scheme **:** PANACEA

nosy *or* **nos·ey** \ˈnō-zē\ *adj* **:** of prying or inquisitive disposition or quality **:** INTRUSIVE — **nos·i·ly** \-zə-lē\ *adv* — **nos·i·ness** \-zē-nəs\ *n*

not \(ˈ)nät\ *adv* **1** — used as a function word to make negative a group of words or a word **2** — used as a function word to stand for the negative of a preceding group of words

no·ta be·ne \ˌnōt-ə-ˈben-ē\ — used to call attention to something important

no·ta·bil·i·ty \ˌnōt-ə-ˈbil-ət-ē\ *n, pl* **-ties 1 :** the quality or state of being notable **2 :** a notable or prominent person

¹no·ta·ble \ˈnōt-ə-bəl\ *adj* **1 :** worthy of note **:** REMARKABLE **2 :** DISTINGUISHED, PROMINENT — **no·ta·bly** \-blē\ *adv*

²notable *n* **:** a person of note or of great reputation **:** NOTABILITY

no·tar·i·al \nō-ˈter-ē-əl\ *adj* **:** of, relating to, or done by a notary public — **no·tar·i·al·ly** \-ē-ə-lē\ *adv*

no·ta·rize \ˈnōt-ə-ˌrīz\ *vt* **:** to make legally authentic through the use of the powers granted to a notary public — **no·ta·ri·za·tion** \ˌnōt-ə-rə-ˈzā-shən\ *n*

no·ta·ry public \ˌnōt-ə-rē-\ *n, pl* **no·ta·ries public** *or* **notary publics :** a public official who attests or certifies writings (as deeds) to make them legally authentic

no·tate \ˈnō-ˌtāt\ *vt* **:** to put into notation

no·ta·tion \nō-ˈtā-shən\ *n* **1 :** the act of noting **2 :** ANNOTATION, NOTE **3 :** the act, process, or method of representing data symbolically by marks, signs, figures, or characters; *also* **:** a system of symbols (as letters, numerals, or musical notes) used in such notation — **no·ta·tion·al** \-shnəl, -shən-ᵊl\ *adj*

¹notch \'näch\ *n* **1 a** : a V-shaped indentation **b** : any of several rounded indentations cut symmetrically on the fore edge of a book to facilitate reference **2** : a narrow pass between mountains : GAP **3** : DEGREE, STEP

²notch *vt* **1** : to cut or make notches in **2** : to score or record by or as if by cutting a series of notches

¹note \'nōt\ *vt* **1 a** : to notice or observe with care **b** : to record or preserve in writing **2** : to make special mention of : REMARK — **not·er** *n*

²note *n* **1 a** : a musical sound **b** : a cry, call, or sound esp. of an animal **c** : a special and often emotional tone of voice **2 a** : MEMORANDUM **b** : a brief and informal record **c** : a written or printed comment or explanation **d** : a short informal letter **e** : a formal diplomatic or official communication **f (1)** : a written promise to pay **(2)** : a piece of paper money **3** : a character in music that by its shape shows the length of time a tone is to be held and by its place on the staff shows the pitch of a tone **4** : MOOD, QUALITY, CHARACTERISTIC **5 a** : REPUTATION, DISTINCTION **b** : NOTICE, HEED, OBSERVATION

note·book \'nōt-,bu̇k\ *n* : a book for notes or memoranda

not·ed \'nōt-əd\ *adj* : specially marked or noticed : well-known and highly regarded : FAMOUS — **not·ed·ly** *adv*

note·less \'nōt-ləs\ *adj* **1** : not noticed : UNDISTINGUISHED **2** : UNMUSICAL, VOICELESS

note·wor·thy \'nōt-,wər-t͟hē\ *adj* : worthy of note : REMARKABLE — **note·wor·thi·ness** *n*

¹noth·ing \'nəth-iŋ\ *pron* **1** : not anything **2** : one of no interest, value, or consequence — **nothing doing** : by no means : definitely no

²nothing *adv* : not at all : in no degree

³nothing *n* **1 a** : something that does not exist **b** : absence of magnitude : ZERO **2** : something of little or no worth or importance — **noth·ing·ness** *n*

¹no·tice \'nōt-əs\ *n* **1 a** : warning or intimation of something : ANNOUNCEMENT **b** : notification by one of the parties to an agreement usu. of intent to terminate it at a specified time **c** : the condition of being warned or notified **2 a** : ATTENTION, HEED **b** : polite or favorable attention : CIVILITY **3** : a written or printed announcement **4** : a short critical account

²notice *vt* **1** : to make mention of : remark on **2** : to take notice or note of : OBSERVE, MARK

no·tice·a·ble \'nōt-ə-sə-bəl\ *adj* **1** : worthy of notice **2** : capable of being or likely to be noticed — **no·tice·a·bly** \-blē\ *adv*

no·ti·fi·ca·tion \,nōt-ə-fə-'kā-shən\ *n* **1** : the act or an instance of notifying; *esp* : the act of giving official notice or information **2** : written or printed matter that gives notice

no·ti·fy \'nōt-ə-,fī\ *vt* **-fied; -fy·ing 1** : to give notice of : report the occurrence of **2** : to give notice to — **no·ti·fi·er** *n*

no·tion \'nō-shən\ *n* **1 a** : IDEA, CONCEPTION **b** : a belief held : OPINION, VIEW **c** : WHIM, FANCY **2** *pl* : small useful articles (as pins, needles, or thread)

no·tion·al \'nō-shnəl, -shən-ᵊl\ *adj* **1** : existing in idea only : IMAGINARY, UNREAL **2** : inclined to foolish or visionary fancies or moods

no·to·ri·e·ty \,nōt-ə-'rī-ət-ē\ *n, pl* **-ties 1** : the quality or state of being notorious **2** : a notorious person

no·to·ri·ous \nō-'tōr-ē-əs\ *adj* : generally known and talked of; *esp* : widely and unfavorably known — **no·to·ri·ous·ly** *adv* — **no·to·ri·ous·ness** *n*

¹not·with·stand·ing \,nät-with-'stan-diŋ, -wit͟h-\ *prep* : in spite of

²notwithstanding *adv* : NEVERTHELESS, HOWEVER

³notwithstanding *conj* : ALTHOUGH

nou·gat \'nü-gət\ *n* : a confection of nuts or fruit pieces in a sugar paste

noun \'nau̇n\ *n* : a word that is the name of a subject of discourse (as a person or place)

nour·ish \'nər-ish\ *vt* : to cause to grow or to survive in a healthy state: as **a** : to provide with nutriment : FEED **b** : SUPPORT, CHERISH, MAINTAIN — **nour·ish·er** *n*

nour·ish·ing \-iŋ\ *adj* : giving nourishment : NUTRITIOUS

nour·ish·ment \-mənt\ *n* **1** : something that nourishes : NUTRIMENT **2** : the act of nourishing : the state of being nourished

nou·veau riche \,nü-,vō-'rēsh\ *n, pl* **nou·veaux riches** *same*\ : a person newly rich : PARVENU

no·va \'nō-və\ *n, pl* **novas** *or* **no·vae** \-(,)vē\ : a star that suddenly increases greatly in brightness and then within a few months or years grows dim again

¹nov·el \'näv-əl\ *adj* **1** : having no precedent **2** : STRANGE, UNUSUAL

²novel *n* : a prose narrative longer than a short story that usu. portrays imaginary characters and events — **nov·el·is·tic** \,näv-ə-'lis-tik\ *adj*

nov·el·ette \,näv-ə-'let\ *n* : a brief novel or long short story

nov·el·ist \'näv-(ə-)ləst\ *n* : a writer of novels

nov·el·ize \'näv-ə-,līz\ *vt* : to convert into the form of a novel — **nov·el·i·za·tion** \,näv-ə-lə-'zā-shən\ *n*

no·vel·la \nō-'vel-ə\ *n, pl* **no·vel·le** \-'vel-ē\ : a story with a compact and pointed plot

nov·el·ty \'näv-əl-tē\ *n, pl* **-ties 1** : something new or unusual **2** : the quality or state of being novel : NEWNESS **3** : a small manufactured article intended mainly for personal or household adornment — usu. used in pl.

No·vem·ber \nō-'vem-bər\ *n* : the 11th month of the year

no·ve·na \nō-'vē-nə\ *n, pl* **-nas** *or* **-nae** \-(,)nē\ : a Roman Catholic devotion in which prayers are said for the same intention on nine successive days

nov·ice \'näv-əs\ *n* **1** : a new member of a religious order who is preparing to take the vows of religion **2** : one who has no previous training or experience in a specific field or activity : BEGINNER

no·vi·tiate \nō-'vish-ət\ *n* **1** : the period or state of being a novice **2** : a house where novices are trained

¹now \(')nau̇\ *adv* **1 a** : at the present time or moment **b** : in the time immediately before the present **c** : in the time immediately to follow : FORTHWITH **2** — used with the sense of present time weakened or lost (as to express command, introduce an important point, or indicate a transition) **3** : SOMETIMES **4** : under the present circumstances **5** : at the time referred to

²now *conj* : seeing that at or by this time : SINCE

³now \'nau̇\ *n* : the present time or moment : PRESENT

⁴now \'nau̇\ *adj* : of or relating to the present time : EXISTING

now·a·days \'nau̇-(ə-),dāz\ *adv* : at the present time

no·way \'nō-,wā\ *or* **no·ways** \-,wāz\ *adv* : NOWISE

no·where \'nō-,hwe(ə)r\ *adv* **1** : not in or at any place **2** : to no place — **nowhere** *n*

nowhere near *adv* : not nearly

no·wise \'nō-,wīz\ *adv* : in no way : not at all

nox·ious \'näk-shəs\ *adj* : harmful or injurious esp. to health or morals : UNWHOLESOME, PERNICIOUS — **nox·ious·ly** *adv* — **nox·ious·ness** *n*

noz·zle \'näz-əl\ *n* : a projecting part with an opening that usu. serves as an outlet; *esp* : a short tube with a taper or constriction used on a hose or pipe to direct or speed up a flow of fluid

nth \'en(t)th\ *adj* **1** : numbered with an unspecified or indefinitely large ordinal number **2** : EXTREME, UTMOST

nu·ance \'n(y)ü-,än(t)s, -,äⁿs, n(y)ü-'\ *n* : a shade of difference : a delicate gradation or variation (as in color, tone, or meaning)

nub \'nəb\ *n* **1** : KNOB, LUMP **2** : GIST, POINT

nub·bin \'nəb-ən\ *n* **1** : a small or imperfect ear of Indian corn *also* : any small shriveled or undeveloped fruit **2** : a small and usu. projecting part or bit **3** : NUB 2

nub·ble \'nəb-əl\ *n* : a small knob or lump — **nub·bly** \'nəb-(ə-)lē\ *adj*

nu·bile \'n(y)ü-bəl, -ˌbīl\ *adj* : of marriageable condition or age — **nu·bil·i·ty** \n(y)ü-'bil-ət-ē\ *n*

nu·cle·ar \'n(y)ü-klē-ər\ *adj* **1** : of, relating to, or constituting a nucleus (as of a cell) **2** : of, relating to, or utilizing the atomic nucleus, atomic energy, the atom bomb, or atomic power

nuclear energy *n* : ATOMIC ENERGY

nu·cle·ic acid \n(y)ü-ˌklē-ik-\ *n* : any of various acids composed of a sugar or derivative of a sugar, phosphoric acid, and a base and found esp. in cell nuclei

nu·cle·us \'n(y)ü-klē-əs\ *n, pl* **-clei** \-klē-ˌī\ : a central point, group, or mass of something: as **a** : a part of a cell that contains chromosomes and is the seat of the mechanisms of heredity **b** : the central part of an atom that comprises nearly all of the atomic mass

[1]**nude** \'n(y)üd\ *adj* : BARE, NAKED, UNCLOTHED — **nude·ly** *adv* — **nude·ness** *n* — **nu·di·ty** \'n(y)üd-ət-ē\ *n*

[2]**nude** *n* **1** : a nude human figure esp. as depicted in art **2** : the condition of being nude

nudge \'nəj\ *vt* : to touch or push gently; *esp* : to seek the attention of by a push of the elbow — **nudge** *n* — **nudg·er** *n*

nud·ism \'n(y)ü-ˌdiz-əm\ *n* : the cult or practice of living unclothed — **nud·ist** \'n(y)üd-əst\ *n*

nu·ga·to·ry \'n(y)ü-gə-ˌtōr-ē\ *adj* **1** : INCONSEQUENTIAL, WORTHLESS **2** : having no force : INOPERATIVE

nug·get \'nəg-ət\ *n* **1** : a solid lump usu. of precious metal **2** : something like a gold nugget

nui·sance \'n(y)üs-ᵊn(t)s\ *n* : an annoying or troublesome person or thing; *also* : an act or practice that constitutes a continuous invasion of the legal rights of another

nuisance tax *n* : an excise tax collected in small amounts directly from the consumer

null \'nəl\ *adj* **1** : having no legal or binding force : INVALID, VOID **2** : amounting to nothing : NIL **3** : having no value : INSIGNIFICANT

nul·li·fi·ca·tion \ˌnəl-ə-fə-'kā-shən\ *n* : the act of nullifying : the state of being nullified — **nul·li·fi·ca·tion·ist** \-sh(ə-)nəst\ *n*

nul·li·fy \'nəl-ə-ˌfī\ *vt* **-fied; -fy·ing** : to make null or valueless; *also* : ANNUL — **nul·li·fi·er** *n*

nul·li·ty \'nəl-ət-ē\ *n, pl* **-ties** **1** : the quality or state of being null; *esp* : legal invalidity **2** : something null; *esp* : an act with no legal effect

numb \'nəm\ *adj* **1** : devoid of sensation esp. from cold **2** : devoid of emotion : INDIFFERENT — **numb** *vt* — **numb·ly** *adv* — **numb·ness** *n*

[1]**num·ber** \'nəm-bər\ *n* **1 a** : the sum of units : total of individual items **b** : a group or aggregate not specifically enumerated **2 a** : the state of being numerable : the possibility of being counted **b** : the characteristic common to all collections whose members can be matched unit by unit : the property involved in seeing things as units subject to separating **3 a** : a unit belonging to a mathematical system and subject to its laws **b** *pl* : ARITHMETIC **4** : a distinction of word form to denote reference to one or more than one; *also* : a form or group of forms so distinguished **5** : a symbol (as a character, letter, or word) used to represent a mathematical number; *also* : such a number used to identify or designate **6** *pl* : regular count esp. of syllables in poetry : METER; *also* : metrical verse **7** : a member of a sequence or series **8** *pl* : a form of lottery in which bets are placed on numbers regularly published for other purposes — **by the numbers** **1** : in unison to a specific count or cadence **2** : in a systematic, routine, or mechanical manner

[2]**number** *vb* **num·bered; num·ber·ing** \-b(ə-)riŋ\ **1** : COUNT, ENUMERATE **2** : to claim as part of a total : INCLUDE **3** : to restrict to a definite number **4** : to assign a number to **5** : to comprise in number **6** : to comprise a total number — **num·ber·a·ble** *adj* — **num·ber·er** *n*

num·ber·less \'nəm-bər-ləs\ *adj* : too many to count : INNUMERABLE

nu·mer·a·ble \'n(y)üm-(ə-)rə-bəl\ *adj* : capable of being counted

nu·mer·al \'n(y)üm-(ə-)rəl\ *n* **1** : a symbol representing a number **2** *pl* : numbers designating by year a school or college class that are awarded for distinction in an extracurricular activity

nu·mer·ate \'n(y)ü-mə-ˌrāt\ *vt* : ENUMERATE

nu·mer·a·tion \ˌn(y)ü-mə-'rā-shən\ *n* **1** : the act or process or a system or instance of enumeration **2** : the reading in words of numbers expressed by numerals

nu·mer·a·tor \'n(y)ü-mə-ˌrāt-ər\ *n* : the part of a fraction written above the line that signifies the number of parts of the denominator taken

nu·mer·i·cal \n(y)u̇-'mer-i-kəl\ *adj* : of or relating to number : denoting a number or expressed in numbers — **nu·mer·i·cal·ly** \-k(ə-)lē\ *adv*

nu·mer·ol·o·gy \ˌn(y)ü-mə-'räl-ə-jē\ *n* : the study of the occult significance of numbers — **nu·mer·ol·o·gist** \-jəst\ *n*

nu·mer·ous \'n(y)üm-(ə-)rəs\ *adj* **1** : consisting of or including a great number **2** : of or relating to a great number : MANY — **nu·mer·ous·ly** *adv* — **nu·mer·ous·ness** *n*

nu·mis·mat·ic \ˌn(y)ü-məz-'mat-ik, -məs-\ *adj* **1** : of or relating to numismatics **2** : of or relating to coins — **nu·mis·mat·i·cal·ly** \-'mat-i-k(ə-)lē\ *adv*

nu·mis·mat·ics \-iks\ *n* : the study or collection of monetary objects (as coins, tokens, medals, or paper money) — **nu·mis·ma·tist** \n(y)ü-'miz-mət-əst\ *n*

num·skull \'nəm-ˌskəl\ *n* : a stupid person : DUNCE

nun \'nən\ *n* : a woman belonging to a religious order; *esp* : one under solemn vows of poverty, chastity, and obedience

nun·cio \'nən(t)-sē-ˌō, 'nu̇n(t)-\ *n, pl* **-ci·os** : a papal legate of the highest rank permanently accredited to a civil government

nun·cu·pa·tive \'nən-kyu̇-ˌpāt-iv, ˌnən-'kyü-pət-\ *adj* : not written : ORAL

nun·nery \'nən-(ə-)rē\ *n, pl* **-ner·ies** : a convent of nuns

[1]**nup·tial** \'nəp-shəl\ *adj* : of or relating to marriage or a wedding

[2]**nuptial** *n* : MARRIAGE, WEDDING — usu. used in pl.

[1]**nurse** \'nərs\ *n* **1 a** : a woman who has the care of a young child **b** : one that fosters or advises **2** : one skilled or trained in caring for the sick or infirm esp. under the supervision of a physician

[2]**nurse** *vb* **1** : to feed at the breast : SUCKLE **2** : REAR, EDUCATE **3 a** : to manage with care or economy **b** : to take charge of and watch over **4** : to care for as a nurse **5** : to hold in one's memory or consideration **6** : to treat with special care **7** : to act or serve as a nurse

nurse·maid \'nərs-ˌmād\ *n* : a girl employed to look after children

nurs·ery \'nərs-(ə-)rē\ *n, pl* **-er·ies** **1 a** : a child's bedroom **b** : a place where children are temporarily cared for in their parents' absence **2** : something that fosters, develops, or promotes **3** : a place where plants (as trees or shrubs) are grown for transplanting

nurs·ery·maid \-(ə-)rē-ˌmād\ *n* : NURSEMAID

nurs·ery·man \-mən\ *n* : a man who keeps or works in a plant nursery

nursery rhyme *n* : a tale in rhymed verse for children

nursery school *n* : a school for children usu. under five years of age

nurs·ing bottle \ˌnər-siŋ-\ *n* : a bottle with a rubber nipple used for feeding a baby

TABLE OF NUMBERS

CARDINAL NUMBERS[1]

NAME	SYMBOL *arabic*	SYMBOL *roman*[2]
naught *or* zero *or* cipher	0	
one	1	I
two	2	II
three	3	III
four	4	IV
five	5	V
six	6	VI
seven	7	VII
eight	8	VIII
nine	9	IX
ten	10	X
eleven	11	XI
twelve	12	XII
thirteen	13	XIII
fourteen	14	XIV
fifteen	15	XV
sixteen	16	XVI
seventeen	17	XVII
eighteen	18	XVIII
nineteen	19	XIX
twenty	20	XX
twenty-one	21	XXI
twenty-two	22	XXII
twenty-three	23	XXIII
twenty-four	24	XXIV
twenty-five	25	XXV
twenty-six	26	XXVI
twenty-seven	27	XXVII
twenty-eight	28	XXVIII
twenty-nine	29	XXIX
thirty	30	XXX
thirty-one *etc*	31	XXXI
forty	40	XL
fifty	50	L
sixty	60	LX
seventy	70	LXX
eighty	80	LXXX
ninety	90	XC
one hundred	100	C
one hundred and one *or* one hundred one *etc*	101	CI
two hundred	200	CC
three hundred	300	CCC
four hundred	400	CD
five hundred	500	D
six hundred	600	DC
seven hundred	700	DCC
eight hundred	800	DCCC
nine hundred	900	CM
one thousand *or* ten hundred *etc*	1,000	M
two thousand *etc*	2,000	MM
five thousand	5,000	$\overline{V}$
ten thousand	10,000	$\overline{X}$
one hundred thousand	100,000	$\overline{C}$
one million	1,000,000	$\overline{M}$

ORDINAL NUMBERS[3]

NAME	SYMBOL
first	1st
second	2d *or* 2nd
third	3d *or* 3rd
fourth	4th
fifth	5th
sixth	6th
seventh	7th
eighth	8th
ninth	9th
tenth	10th
eleventh	11th
twelfth	12th
thirteenth	13th
fourteenth	14th
fifteenth	15th
sixteenth	16th
seventeenth	17th
eighteenth	18th
nineteenth	19th
twentieth	20th
twenty-first	21st
twenty-second	22d *or* 22nd
twenty-third	23d *or* 23rd
twenty-fourth	24th
twenty-fifth	25th
twenty-sixth	26th
twenty-seventh	27th
twenty-eighth	28th
twenty-ninth	29th
thirtieth	30th
thirty-first *etc*	31st
fortieth	40th
fiftieth	50th
sixtieth	60th
seventieth	70th
eightieth	80th
ninetieth	90th
hundredth *or* one hundredth	100th
hundred and first *or* one hundred and first *etc*	101st
two hundredth	200th
three hundredth	300th
four hundredth	400th
five hundredth	500th
six hundredth	600th
seven hundredth	700th
eight hundredth	800th
nine hundredth	900th
thousandth *or* one thousandth	1,000th
two thousandth *etc*	2,000th
five thousandth	5,000th
ten thousandth	10,000th
hundred thousandth *or* one hundred thousandth	100,000th
millionth *or* one millionth	1,000,000th

[1]The cardinal numbers are used in simple counting or in answer to "how many?" The words for these numbers may be used as nouns (he counted to *twelve*), as pronouns (*twelve* were found), or as adjectives (*twelve* boys).
[2]The roman numerals are written either in capitals or in lowercase letters.
[3]The ordinal numbers are used to show the order of succession in which such items as names, objects, and periods of time are considered (the *twelfth* month; the *fourth* row of seats; the *18th* century).

nurs·ling \ˈnərs-liŋ\ *n* **1** : one that is solicitously cared for **2** : a nursing child

[1]**nur·ture** \ˈnər-chər\ *n* **1** : TRAINING, UPBRINGING **2** : something that nourishes : FOOD **3** : the influences that modify the expression of the genetic potentialities of an organism

[2]**nurture** *vt* **nur·tured**; **nur·tur·ing** \ˈnərch-(ə-)riŋ\ **1** : to supply with nourishment **2** : EDUCATE **3** : to further the development of : FOSTER

[1]**nut** \ˈnət\ *n* **1** : a hard-shelled dry fruit or seed with a separable rind or shell and an inner kernel; *also* : this kernel **2** : a perforated block usu. of metal that has an internal screw thread and is used on a bolt or screw for tightening or holding something **3** : the ridge in a musical instrument over which the strings pass on the upper end of the fingerboard **4 a** : a foolish, eccentric, or crazy person **b** : ENTHUSIAST — **nut·like** *adj*

[2]**nut** *vi* **nut·ted**; **nut·ting** : to gather or seek nuts

nut·crack·er \ˈnət-ˌkrak-ər\ *n* : an instrument for cracking the shells of nuts

nut·hatch \ˈnət-ˌhach\ *n* : any of various small birds that creep on tree trunks in search of food and resemble titmice

nut·let \ˈnət-lət\ *n* **1** : a small nut **2** : a small fruit similar to a nut

nut·meg \ˈnət-ˌmeg\ *n* **1** : the aromatic seed of a tree grown in the East and West Indies and Brazil; *also* : this tree **2** : a spice consisting of ground nutmeg seeds

nut·pick \-ˌpik\ *n* : a small sharp-pointed table implement for extracting the kernels from nuts

nu·tria \ˈn(y)ü-trē-ə\ *n* **1** : COYPU 1 **2** : the durable usu. light brown fur of the coypu

[1]**nu·tri·ent** \ˈn(y)ü-trē-ənt\ *adj* : furnishing nourishment

[2]**nutrient** *n* : a nutritive substance or ingredient

nu·tri·ment \ˈn(y)ü-trə-mənt\ *n* : something that nourishes or promotes growth and repairs the natural wastage of organic life

nu·tri·tion \n(y)u̇-ˈtrish-ən\ *n* : the act or process of nourishing or being nourished; *esp* : the processes by which an animal or plant takes in and utilizes food substances — **nu·tri·tion·al** \-ˈtrish-nəl, -ən-^{ə}l\ *adj* — **nu·tri·tion·al·ly** \-ē\ *adv*

nu·tri·tion·ist \-ˈtrish-(ə-)nəst\ *n* : a specialist in the study of nutrition

nu·tri·tious \n(y)u̇-ˈtrish-əs\ *adj* : NOURISHING — **nu·tri·tious·ly** *adv* — **nu·tri·tious·ness** *n*

nu·tri·tive \ˈn(y)ü-trət-iv\ *adj* **1** : of or relating to nutrition **2** : NUTRITIOUS — **nu·tri·tive·ly** *adv*

nuts \ˈnəts\ *adj* **1** : ENTHUSIASTIC, KEEN **2** : CRAZY, DEMENTED

nut·shell \ˈnət-ˌshel\ *n* : the shell of a nut — **in a nutshell** : in a small compass

nut·ty \ˈnət-ē\ *adj* **1** : containing or suggesting nuts (as in flavor) **2** : ECCENTRIC; *also* : mentally unbalanced — **nut·ti·ness** *n*

nuz·zle \ˈnəz-əl\ *vb* **nuz·zled**; **nuz·zling** \ˈnəz-(ə-)liŋ\ **1** : to push or rub with the nose **2** : to lie close : NESTLE

ny·lon \ˈnī-ˌlän\ *n* **1** : any of numerous strong tough elastic synthetic materials used esp. in textiles and plastics **2** *pl* : stockings made of nylon — **nylon** *adj*

nymph \ˈnim(p)f\ *n*, *pl* **nymphs** \ˈnim(p)fs, ˈnim(p)s\ : any of various immature insects; *esp* : a larval insect that differs chiefly in size and degree of differentiation from the adult — **nymph·al** \ˈnim(p)-fəl\ *adj*

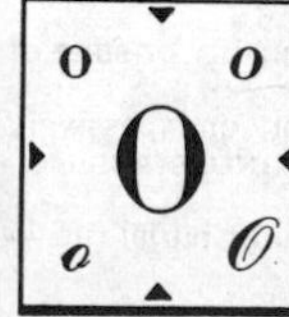

o \ˈō\ *n*, *often cap* **1** : the 15th letter of the English alphabet **2** : ZERO

oaf \ˈōf\ *n* : a stupid or awkward person — **oaf·ish** \ˈō-fish\ *adj* — **oaf·ish·ly** *adv* — **oaf·ish·ness** *n*

oak \ˈōk\ *n*, *pl* **oaks** *or* **oak** **1** : any of various trees or shrubs closely related to the beech and chestnut and having a rounded one-seeded thin-shelled nut **2** : the usu. tough hard durable wood of the oak much used for furniture and flooring — **oak** *adj* — **oak·en** \ˈō-kən\ *adj*

oa·kum \ˈō-kəm\ *n* : hemp or jute fiber impregnated with tar or a tar derivative and used in caulking seams and packing joints

oar \ˈō(ə)r\ *n* **1** : a long slender broad-bladed wooden implement for propelling or steering a boat **2** : OARSMAN — **oared** \ˈō(ə)rd\ *adj*

oar·lock \ˈō(ə)r-ˌläk\ *n* : a usu. U-shaped device for holding an oar in place

oars·man \ˈō(ə)rz-mən\ *n* : one who rows esp. in a racing crew

oa·sis \ō-ˈā-səs\ *n*, *pl* **oa·ses** \-ˈā-ˌsēz\ : a fertile or green area in an arid region

oat \ˈōt\ *n* **1** : a cereal grass that is widely grown for its seed which is used for human food and livestock feed **2** *pl* : a crop or plot of the oat; *also* : oat seed

oat·cake \-ˌkāk\ *n* : a thin flat oatmeal cake

oat·en \ˈōt-^{ə}n\ *adj* : of or relating to oats, oat straw, or oatmeal

oath \ˈōth\ *n*, *pl* **oaths** \ˈōt͟hz, ˈōths\ **1** : a solemn appeal to God or to some revered person or thing to bear witness to the truth of one's word or the sacredness of a promise **2** : a careless or profane use of a sacred name

oat·meal \ˈōt-ˌmēl, ōt-ˈ\ *n* : oats husked and crushed into course meal or flattened into flakes; *also* : porridge made from such meal or flakes

ob·bli·ga·to \ˌäb-lə-ˈgät-ō\ *n*, *pl* **-gatos** : a prominent accompanying part usu. played by a solo instrument; *also* : any accompanying part

ob·du·ra·cy \ˈäb-d(y)ə-rə-sē\ *n*, *pl* **-cies** : the quality or state or an instance of being obdurate

ob·du·rate \ˈäb-d(y)ə-rət\ *adj* **1 a** : hardened in feelings **b** : stubbornly persistent in wrongdoing **2** : resisting change : UNYIELDING — **ob·du·rate·ly** *adv*

obe·di·ence \ō-ˈbēd-ē-ən(t)s\ *n* **1** : an act or instance of obeying **2** : the quality or state of being obedient

obe·di·ent \-ənt\ *adj* : submissive to the restraint or command of authority — **obe·di·ent·ly** *adv*

obei·sance \ō-ˈbās-^{ə}n(t)s, -ˈbēs-\ *n* **1** : a movement of the body made in token of respect or submission : BOW **2** : DEFERENCE, HOMAGE — **obei·sant** \-^{ə}nt\ *adj*

ob·e·lisk \ˈäb-ə-ˌlisk\ *n* : a 4-sided pillar that tapers toward the top and ends in a pyramid

obese \ō-ˈbēs\ *adj* : excessively fat — **obe·si·ty** \ō-ˈbē-sət-ē\ *n*

obey \ō-ˈbā\ *vb* **obeyed**; **obey·ing** **1** : to follow the commands or guidance of **2** : to comply with : EXECUTE **3** : to behave obediently

ob·fus·cate \ˈäb-fə-ˌskāt, äb-ˈfəs-ˌkāt\ *vt* **1** : to make dark or obscure **2** : CONFUSE — **ob·fus·ca·tion** \ˌäb-(ˌ)fəs-ˈkā-shən\ *n*

obi \ˈō-bē\ *n* : a broad sash worn with a Japanese kimono

obit \ō-ˈbit, ˈō-bət\ *n* : OBITUARY

obi·ter dic·tum \ˌō-bət-ər-ˈdik-təm\ *n*, *pl* **obiter dic·ta** \-tə\ : an incidental remark or observation

obit·u·ary \ə-ˈbich-ə-ˌwer-ē\ *n*, *pl* **-ar·ies** : a notice of a person's death usu. with a short biographical account — **obituary** *adj*

[1]**ob·ject** \'äb-jikt\ *n* **1 a :** something that may be seen or felt **b :** something that may be perceived or examined mentally **2 :** something that arouses an emotional response (as of affection, hatred, or pity) **3 :** AIM, PURPOSE **4 a :** a noun or noun equivalent denoting someone or something that the action of a verb is directed toward **b :** a noun or noun equivalent in a prepositional phrase — **ob·ject·less** \'äb-jik-tləs\ *adj*

[2]**ob·ject** \əb-'jekt\ *vb* **1 :** to offer or cite as an objection **2 :** to state one's opposition to or oppose something **3 :** to feel distaste for or disapproval of something — **ob·jec·tor** \-'jek-tər\ *n*

ob·jec·ti·fy \əb-'jek-tə-ˌfī\ *vt* **-fied; -fy·ing :** to make objective — **ob·jec·ti·fi·ca·tion** \-ˌjek-tə-fə-'kā-shən\ *n*

ob·jec·tion \əb-'jek-shən\ *n* **1 :** an act of objecting **2 :** a reason for or feeling of disapproval

ob·jec·tion·a·ble \-sh(ə-)nə-bəl\ *adj* **:** arousing objection **:** DISPLEASING, OFFENSIVE — **ob·jec·tion·a·ble·ness** *n* — **ob·jec·tion·a·bly** \-blē\ *adv*

[1]**ob·jec·tive** \əb-'jek-tiv\ *adj* **1 :** of or relating to an object or end **2 :** existing outside and independent of the mind **3 :** treating or dealing with facts without distortion by personal feelings or prejudices **4 :** of, relating to, or constituting a grammatical case marking typically the object of a verb or preposition — **ob·jec·tive·ly** *adv* — **ob·jec·tive·ness** *n* — **ob·jec·tiv·i·ty** \(ˌ)äb-ˌjek-'tiv-ət-ē\ *n*

[2]**objective** *n* **1 :** something toward which effort is directed **:** GOAL **2 :** the objective case; *also* **:** a word in the objective case **3 :** a lens or system of lenses (as in a microscope) that forms an image of an object

object lesson \'äb-jikt-\ *n* **:** a lesson taught by means of illustrative objects or concrete examples; *also* **:** something that teaches by a concrete example

ob·jet d'art \ˌȯb-ˌzhā-'där\ *n, pl* **ob·jets d'art** *same*\ **:** an article of artistic worth; *also* **:** CURIO

ob·jur·gate \'äb-jər-ˌgāt\ *vt* **:** to denounce or reproach harshly — **ob·jur·ga·tion** \ˌäb-jər-'gā-shən\ *n* — **ob·jur·ga·to·ry** \əb-'jər-gə-ˌtōr-ē\ *adj*

[1]**ob·late** \äb-'lāt, 'äb-ˌ\ *adj* **:** flattened or depressed at the poles

[2]**ob·late** \'äb-ˌlāt\ *n* **:** a layman living in a monastery under a modified rule and without vows

obla·tion \ə-'blā-shən\ *n* **:** a religious offering

ob·li·gate \'äb-lə-ˌgāt\ *vt* **:** to bring under obligation **:** bind legally or morally

ob·li·ga·tion \ˌäb-lə-'gā-shən\ *n* **1 :** an act of obligating oneself to a course of action **2 a :** something (as the constraining power of a promise or contract) that binds one to a course of action **b :** something one is bound to do **:** DUTY **3 a :** INDEBTEDNESS **b :** money committed to a particular purpose

oblig·a·to·ry \ə-'blig-ə-ˌtōr-ē, 'äb-li-gə-\ *adj* **:** legally or morally binding **:** REQUIRED

oblige \ə-'blīj\ *vb* **1 :** FORCE, COMPEL **2 a :** to bind by a favor **b :** to do a favor for or do something as a favor

oblig·ing \ə-'blī-jiŋ\ *adj* **:** willing to do favors **:** ACCOMMODATING — **oblig·ing·ly** *adv* — **oblig·ing·ness** *n*

[1]**oblique** \ō-'blēk, -'blīk\ *adj* **1 :** neither perpendicular nor parallel **:** INCLINED **2 :** not straightforward **:** INDIRECT, DEVIOUS — **oblique·ly** *adv* — **oblique·ness** *n*

[2]**oblique** *adv* **:** at a 45 degree angle

obliq·ui·ty \ō-'blik-wət-ē\ *n, pl* **-ties :** the quality or state of being oblique

oblit·er·ate \ə-'blit-ə-ˌrāt\ *vt* **1 :** to make undecipherable or imperceptible by wiping out or covering over **2 :** to remove from recognition or memory **:** destroy all trace of **3 :** CANCEL — **oblit·er·a·tion** \-ˌblit-ə-'rā-shən\ *n*

obliv·i·on \ə-'bliv-ē-ən\ *n* **1 :** an act or instance of forgetting **2 :** the quality or state of being forgotten

obliv·i·ous \-ē-əs\ *adj* **:** lacking memory or mindful attention **:** FORGETFUL, UNAWARE — **obliv·i·ous·ly** *adv* — **obliv·i·ous·ness** *n*

ob·long \'äb-ˌlȯŋ\ *adj* **:** longer in one direction than in the other with opposite sides parallel **:** RECTANGULAR — **oblong** *n*

ob·lo·quy \'äb-lə-kwē\ *n, pl* **-quies 1 :** strongly condemnatory utterance or language **2 :** bad repute **:** DISGRACE

ob·nox·ious \äb-'näk-shəs\ *adj* **:** OFFENSIVE, REPUGNANT — **ob·nox·ious·ly** *adv* — **ob·nox·ious·ness** *n*

oboe \'ō-bō\ *n* **:** a woodwind musical instrument in the form of a slender cone-shaped tube with holes and keys that is played by blowing into a reed mouthpiece — **obo·ist** \-(ˌ)bō-əst\ *n*

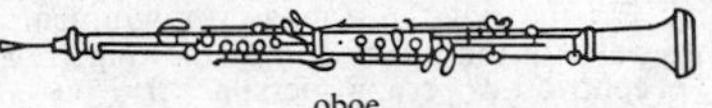
oboe

ob·scene \äb-'sēn\ *adj* **1 :** disgusting to the senses **:** REPULSIVE **2 :** deeply offensive to morality or decency; *esp* **:** designed to incite to lust or depravity — **ob·scene·ly** *adv*

ob·scen·i·ty \-'sen-ət-ē\ *n, pl* **-ties 1 :** the quality or state of being obscene **2 :** something that is obscene

ob·scur·ant \äb-'skyu̇r-ənt, əb-\ *or* **ob·scu·ran·tic** \ˌäb-skyə-'rant-ik\ *adj* **:** tending to make obscure — **ob·scu·ra·tion** \ˌäb-skyə-'rā-shən\ *n*

ob·scu·ran·tism \äb-'skyu̇r-ən-ˌtiz-əm, ˌäb-skyu̇-'ran-\ *n* **1 :** opposition to the spread of knowledge **2 :** deliberate vagueness or abstruseness — **ob·scu·ran·tist** \-ən-təst, -'rant-əst\ *n or adj*

[1]**ob·scure** \äb-'skyu̇(ə)r\ *adj* **1 :** lacking or inadequately supplied with light **:** DIM, GLOOMY **2 a :** withdrawn from the centers of human activity **:** REMOTE **b :** not readily understood or not clearly expressed **:** ABSTRUSE **c :** lacking showiness or prominence **:** HUMBLE **d :** not distinct **:** FAINT — **ob·scure·ly** *adv* — **ob·scure·ness** *n*

[2]**obscure** *vt* **1 :** to make dark, dim, or indistinct **2 :** to conceal or hide by or as if by covering

ob·scu·ri·ty \-'skyu̇r-ət-ē\ *n, pl* **-ties 1 :** the quality or state of being obscure **2 :** one that is obscure

ob·se·qui·ous \əb-'sē-kwē-əs, äb-\ *adj* **:** humbly or excessively attentive (as to a person in authority) **:** FAWNING, SERVILE — **ob·se·qui·ous·ly** *adv* — **ob·se·qui·ous·ness** *n*

ob·se·quy \'äb-sə-kwē\ *n, pl* **-quies :** a funeral or burial rite — usu. used in pl.

ob·serv·a·ble \əb-'zər-və-bəl\ *adj* **1 :** necessarily or customarily observed **2 :** capable of being observed **:** DETECTABLE, NOTICEABLE — **ob·serv·a·bly** \-blē\ *adv*

ob·serv·ance \əb-'zər-vən(t)s\ *n* **1 :** a customary practice or ceremony **2 :** an act or instance of following a custom, rule, or law **3 :** an act or instance of noticing

ob·serv·ant \-vənt\ *adj* **1 :** paying strict attention **:** WATCHFUL **2 :** careful in observing **:** MINDFUL **3 :** quick to observe **:** KEEN — **ob·serv·ant·ly** *adv*

ob·ser·va·tion \ˌäb-sər-'vā-shən, -zər-\ *n* **1 :** an act or the power of seeing or fixing the mind upon something **2 :** the gathering of information (as for scientific studies) by noting facts or occurrences **3 a :** a conclusion drawn from observing **:** VIEW **b :** REMARK, COMMENT **4 :** the fact of being observed — **observation** *adj* — **ob·ser·va·tion·al** \-shnəl, -shən-ᵊl\ *adj*

ob·serv·a·to·ry \əb-'zər-və-ˌtōr-ē\ *n, pl* **-ries :** a place or institution given over to or equipped for observation of natural phenomena (as in astronomy)

ob·serve \əb-'zərv\ *vb* **1 :** to conform one's action or practice to **2 :** CELEBRATE **3 :** to see or sense esp. through directed careful analytic attention **:** WATCH **4 :** to come to realize or know esp. through consideration of noted facts **:** PERCEIVE **5 :** to utter as a remark **6 :** to make a scientific observation on — **ob·serv·ing·ly** *adv*

ob·serv·er \əb-ˈzər-vər\ *n* : one that observes; *esp* : a representative sent to observe but not participate officially in an activity

ob·sess \əb-ˈses, äb-\ *vt* : to preoccupy intensely or abnormally

ob·ses·sion \äb-ˈsesh-ən, əb-\ *n* : a persistent disturbing preoccupation with an often unreasonable idea or feeling; *also* : an emotion or idea causing such a preoccupation — **ob·ses·sion·al** \-ˈsesh-nəl, -ən-ᵊl\ *adj* — **ob·ses·sion·al·ly** \-ē\ *adv* — **ob·ses·sive** \-ˈses-iv\ *adj* — **ob·ses·sive·ly** *adv*

ob·sid·i·an \əb-ˈsid-ē-ən\ *n* : a dark-colored natural glass formed by the cooling of molten lava

ob·so·les·cent \ˌäb-sə-ˈles-ᵊnt\ *adj* : going out of use : becoming obsolete — **ob·so·lesce** \-ˈles\ *vi* — **ob·so·les·cence** \-ˈles-ᵊn(t)s\ *n* — **ob·so·les·cent·ly** *adv*

ob·so·lete \ˌäb-sə-ˈlēt\ *adj* : no longer in use : DISUSED: **a** : OUTMODED **b** : VESTIGIAL — **ob·so·lete·ly** *adv* — **ob·so·lete·ness** *n*

ob·sta·cle \ˈäb-sti-kəl\ *n* : something that stands in the way or opposes : HINDRANCE, OBSTRUCTION

ob·stet·ri·cal \əb-ˈste-tri-kəl\ *adj* : of or relating to childbirth or obstetrics — **ob·stet·ri·cal·ly** \-tri-k(ə-)lē\ *adv*

ob·ste·tri·cian \ˌäb-stə-ˈtrish-ən\ *n* : a physician specializing in obstetrics

ob·stet·rics \əb-ˈste-triks\ *n* : a branch of medical science that deals with childbirth and with the care of women before, during, and after this

ob·sti·na·cy \ˈäb-stə-nə-sē\ *n, pl* **-cies** **1** : the quality or state of being obstinate **2** : an instance of being obstinate

ob·sti·nate \ˈäb-stə-nət\ *adj* **1** : clinging to an opinion, purpose, or course in spite of reason, arguments, or persuasion **2** : not easily subdued, remedied, or removed — **ob·sti·nate·ly** *adv* — **ob·sti·nate·ness** *n*

ob·strep·er·ous \əb-ˈstrep-(ə-)rəs, äb-\ *adj* **1** : uncontrollably noisy : CLAMOROUS **2** : stubbornly defiant : UNRULY — **ob·strep·er·ous·ly** *adv* — **ob·strep·er·ous·ness** *n*

ob·struct \əb-ˈstrəkt\ *vt* **1** : to block or close up by an obstacle **2** : to hinder from passage, action, or operation : IMPEDE **3** : to cut off from sight — **ob·struc·tive** \-ˈstrək-tiv\ *adj or n* — **ob·struc·tor** \-tər\ *n*

ob·struc·tion \əb-ˈstrək-shən\ *n* **1** : an act of obstructing : the state of being obstructed **2** : something that obstructs : HINDRANCE

ob·struc·tion·ist \əb-ˈstrək-sh(ə-)nəst\ *n* : a person who hinders progress esp. in a legislative body — **ob·struc·tion·ism** \-shə-ˌniz-əm\ *n*

ob·tain \əb-ˈtān\ *vb* **1** : to gain or attain usu. by planning or effort **2** : to be generally recognized or established : PREVAIL — **ob·tain·a·ble** *adj* — **ob·tain·er** *n*

ob·trude \əb-ˈtrüd\ *vb* **1** : to thrust out **2** : to thrust forward or call to notice without warrant or request **3** : to thrust oneself upon attention — **ob·trud·er** *n* — **ob·tru·sion** \-ˈtrü-zhən\ *n*

ob·tru·sive \əb-ˈtrü-siv\ *adj* : inclined to obtrude : FORWARD — **ob·tru·sive·ly** *adv* — **ob·tru·sive·ness** *n*

ob·tuse \äb-ˈt(y)üs\ *adj* **1** : lacking sharpness or quickness of wit : DULL, INSENSITIVE **2 a** : exceeding 90 degrees but less than 180 degrees **b** : not pointed or acute : BLUNT — **ob·tuse·ly** *adv* — **ob·tuse·ness** *n*

¹ob·verse \äb-ˈvərs, ˈäb-ˌ\ *adj* **1** : facing the observer or opponent **2** : having the base narrower than the top **3** : being a counterpart or complement — **ob·verse·ly** *adv*

²ob·verse \ˈäb-ˌvərs, äb-ˈ\ *n* **1** : the side of something (as a coin or medal) bearing the principal design or lettering **2** : a front or principal surface **3** : COUNTERPART

ob·vi·ate \ˈäb-vē-ˌāt\ *vt* : to anticipate and dispose of beforehand : make unnecessary — **ob·vi·a·tion** \ˌäb-vē-ˈā-shən\ *n*

ob·vi·ous \ˈäb-vē-əs\ *adj* : easily discovered, seen, or understood : PLAIN — **ob·vi·ous·ly** *adv* — **ob·vi·ous·ness** *n*

oc·a·ri·na \ˌäk-ə-ˈrē-nə\ *n* : a simple wind instrument usu. of terra-cotta and with a mouthpiece and holes that may be opened or closed by the finger to vary the pitch

¹oc·ca·sion \ə-ˈkā-zhən\ *n* **1** : a favorable opportunity or circumstance **2** : a state of affairs that provides a ground or reason **3** : an occurrence or condition that brings something about; *esp* : the immediate inciting circumstance as distinguished from fundamental cause **4** : a time at which something happens **5** : a need arising from a particular circumstance : EXIGENCY **6** *pl* : AFFAIRS, BUSINESS **7** : a special event or ceremony : CELEBRATION

²occasion *vt* **oc·ca·sioned**; **oc·ca·sion·ing** \-ˈkāzh-(ə-)niŋ\ : to give occasion to : CAUSE

oc·ca·sion·al \ə-ˈkāzh-nəl, -ən-ᵊl\ *adj* **1** : happening or met with now and then **2** : used or meant for a special occasion — **oc·ca·sion·al·ly** \-ē\ *adv*

Oc·ci·dent \ˈäk-səd-ənt, -sə-ˌdent\ *n* : WEST 2

oc·ci·den·tal \ˌäk-sə-ˈdent-ᵊl\ *adj, often cap* : of or relating to the Occident — **oc·ci·den·tal·ly** \-ᵊl-ē\ *adv*

oc·clude \ə-ˈklüd, ä-\ *vb* **1** : to stop up : OBSTRUCT **2** : to shut in or out **3** : to take up and hold by absorption or adsorption **4** : to come together with opposing surfaces in contact — **oc·clud·ent** \-ˈklüd-ᵊnt\ *adj* — **oc·clu·sive** \-ˈklü-siv\ *adj*

oc·clu·sion \ə-ˈklü-zhən\ *n* : the act of occluding : the state of being occluded

oc·cult \ə-ˈkəlt, ä-\ *adj* **1** : not revealed : SECRET, HIDDEN **2** : ABSTRUSE, MYSTERIOUS **3** : of or relating to supernatural agencies, their effects, or knowledge of them — **oc·cult·ly** *adv*

oc·cult·ism \ə-ˈkəl-ˌtiz-əm, ä-\ *n* : a belief in or study of supernatural powers and the possibility of subjecting them to human control — **oc·cult·ist** \-təst\ *n*

oc·cu·pan·cy \ˈäk-yə-pən-sē\ *n, pl* **-cies** : the act of occupying : the state of being occupied

oc·cu·pant \-pənt\ *n* : one that occupies something or takes or has possession of it

oc·cu·pa·tion \ˌäk-yə-ˈpā-shən\ *n* **1** : an activity in which one engages; *esp* : one's business or vocation **2 a** : the taking possession of property : OCCUPANCY **b** : the taking possession or holding and controlling of an area by a foreign military force — **oc·cu·pa·tion·al** \-shnəl, -shən-ᵊl\ *adj* — **oc·cu·pa·tion·al·ly** \-ē\ *adv*

occupational therapy *n* : therapy by means of activity; *esp* : creative activity prescribed for its effect in promoting recovery or rehabilitation — **occupational therapist** *n*

oc·cu·py \ˈäk-yə-ˌpī\ *vt* **-pied**; **-py·ing** **1 a** : to engage the attention or energies of **b** : to fill up (an extent in space or time) **2** : to take or hold possession of **3** : to reside in as an owner or tenant — **oc·cu·pi·er** *n*

oc·cur \ə-ˈkər\ *vi* **oc·curred**; **oc·cur·ring** **1** : to be found or met with : APPEAR **2** : to take place **3** : to come to mind : suggest itself

oc·cur·rence \ə-ˈkər-ən(t)s\ *n* **1** : something that takes place; *esp* : something that happens unexpectedly **2 a** : the action or process of taking place **b** : the action or process of coming into view : APPEARANCE

ocean \ˈō-shən\ *n* **1** : the whole body of salt water that covers nearly three fourths of the surface of the earth **2** : one of the large bodies of water into which the great ocean is divided **3** : an unlimited space or quantity — **oce·an·ic** \ˌō-shē-ˈan-ik\ *adj*

ocean·ar·i·um \ˌō-shə-ˈnar-ē-əm, -ˈner-\ *n* : a large marine aquarium

ocean·go·ing \ˈō-shən-ˌgō-iŋ\ *adj* : of, relating to, or suitable for travel on the ocean

ocean·og·ra·phy \ˌō-shə-ˈnäg-rə-fē\ *n* : a science that deals with the ocean and its phenomena — **ocean·og·ra·pher** \-fər\

n — **ocean·o·graph·ic** \ˌō-shə-nə-ˈgraf-ik\ *adj* — **ocean·o·graph·i·cal·ly** \-ˈgraf-i-k(ə-)lē\ *adv*

oc·e·lot \ˈäs-ə-ˌlät, ˈō-sə-\ *n* : a medium-sized American wildcat ranging from Texas to Patagonia and having a tawny yellow or grayish coat marked with black

ocher *or* **ochre** \ˈō-kər\ *n* **1** : an earthy usu. red or yellow and often impure iron ore used as a pigment **2** : the color of ocher and esp. of yellow ocher — **ocher·ous** \ˈō-k(ə-)rəs\ *or* **ochre·ous** \ˈō-k(ə-)rəs, -krē-əs\ *adj*

o'clock \ə-ˈkläk\ *adv* : according to the clock

oc·ta·gon \ˈäk-tə-ˌgän\ *n* : a polygon of eight angles and eight sides — **oc·tag·o·nal** \äk-ˈtag-ən-ᵊl\ *adj* — **oc·tag·o·nal·ly** \-ᵊl-ē\ *adv*

oc·tane number \ˈäk-ˌtān-\ *n* : a number that is used to measure or indicate the antiknock properties of a liquid motor fuel and that increases as the likelihood of knocking decreases

oc·tave \ˈäk-tiv, -təv\ *n* **1** : a stanza or poem of eight lines **2 a** : a musical interval embracing eight degrees **b** : a tone or note at this interval **c** : the whole series of notes, tones, or keys within this interval **3** : a group of eight

octave

oc·ta·vo \äk-ˈtā-vō, -ˈtäv-ō\ *n, pl* **-vos** : the size of a piece of paper cut eight from a sheet; *also* : a book, a page, or paper of this size

oc·tet \äk-ˈtet\ *n* **1** : a musical composition for eight voices or eight instruments; *also* : the performers of such a composition **2** : a group or set of eight

Oc·to·ber \äk-ˈtō-bər\ *n* : the 10th month of the year

oc·to·ge·nar·i·an \ˌäk-tə-jə-ˈner-ē-ən\ *n* : a person who is 80 or more but less than 90 years old

oc·to·pus \ˈäk-tə-pəs\ *n, pl* **-pus·es** *or* **-pi** \-ˌpī\ **1** : any of various sea mollusks having round the front of the head eight muscular arms with two rows of suckers which hold objects (as its prey) **2** : something suggestive of an octopus; *esp* : a powerful grasping organization with many branches

oc·to·roon \ˌäk-tə-ˈrün\ *n* : a person of one-eighth Negro ancestry

oc·to·syl·lab·ic \ˌäk-tə-sə-ˈlab-ik\ *adj* : having eight syllables : composed of verses having eight syllables — **octosyllabic** *n*

oc·u·lar \ˈäk-yə-lər\ *adj* **1** : of or relating to the eye or the eyesight **2** : obtained or perceived by the sight : VISUAL

oc·u·list \-ləst\ *n* **1** : OPHTHALMOLOGIST **2** : OPTOMETRIST

odd \ˈäd\ *adj* **1** : being only one of a pair or set **2 a** : not divisible by two without leaving a remainder **b** : somewhat more than the number mentioned **3** : additional to or apart from what is usual, planned on, or taken into account : RANDOM, CASUAL, OCCASIONAL **4** : not usual or conventional : STRANGE — **odd·ly** *adv* — **odd·ness** *n*

odd·ball \-ˌbȯl\ *n* : one whose behavior is eccentric

odd·i·ty \ˈäd-ət-ē\ *n, pl* **-ties** **1** : one that is odd : ECCENTRICITY **2** : the quality or state of being odd

odd·ment \ˈäd-mənt\ *n* : something left over : REMNANT

odds \ˈädz\ *n pl* **1** : DIFFERENCE; *esp* : a difference by which one thing is favored over another **2** : an equalizing allowance made to a bettor or contestant believed to have a smaller chance of winning **3** : DISAGREEMENT, QUARRELING

odds and ends *n pl* : miscellaneous things or matters : ODDMENTS, REMNANTS

odds–on \ˈäd-ˈzȯn, -ˈzän\ *adj* : having or viewed as having a better than even chance to win

ode \ˈōd\ *n* : a lyric poem characterized usu. by elevation of feeling and style, varying length of line, and complexity of stanza forms

odi·ous \ˈōd-ē-əs\ *adj* : causing or deserving hatred or repugnance — **odi·ous·ly** *adv* — **odi·ous·ness** *n*

odi·um \ˈōd-ē-əm\ *n* **1** : the condition of being generally hated and condemned usu. for despicable conduct : merited loathing **2** : the disgrace or shame attached to something considered hateful or low

odom·e·ter \ō-ˈdäm-ət-ər\ *n* : an instrument for measuring the distance traversed (as by a vehicle)

odor \ˈōd-ər\ *n* **1** : a quality of something that stimulates the nasal sensory organs that receive smell : SCENT; *also* : the resulting sensation : SMELL **2 a** : a predominant quality : FLAVOR **b** : REPUTE, ESTIMATION — **odored** \-ərd\ *adj* — **odor·less** \-ər-ləs\ *adj*

odor·ant \ˈōd-ə-rənt\ *n* : an odorous substance

odor·if·er·ous \ˌōd-ə-ˈrif-(ə-)rəs\ *adj* **1 a** : producing an odorous substance **b** : ODOROUS **2** : morally offensive — **odor·if·er·ous·ly** *adv* — **odor·if·er·ous·ness** *n*

odor·ous \ˈōd-ə-rəs\ *adj* : having an odor — **odor·ous·ly** *adv* — **odor·ous·ness** *n*

od·ys·sey \ˈäd-ə-sē\ *n, pl* **-seys** : a long wandering usu. marked by many changes of fortune

of \əv, ˈəv, ˈäv\ *prep* **1 a** : from as a consequence **b** : by as author or doer **c** : as experienced or performed by **2** : having as its material, parts, or contents **3** — used as a function word to indicate the whole that includes the part denoted by the preceding word **4 a** : CONCERNING **b** : in respect to **5** : possessed by : belonging to **6** : specified as **7** : having as its object **8** : having as a distinctive quality or possession

[1]**off** \ˈȯf\ *adv* **1 a** : from a place or position **b** : away from land **c** : into an unconscious state **2 a** : so as not to be supported or covering or enclosing or attached **b** : so as to be divided **3** : to a state of discontinuance or exhaustion or completion **4** : in absence from or suspension of regular work or service **5** : at a distance in space or time

[2]**off** \(ˈ)ȯf\ *prep* **1** : away from; *esp* : from a place or situation on **2** : at the expense of **3 a** : not now engaged in **b** : below the usual standard or level of

[3]**off** \(ˈ)ȯf\ *adj* **1** : more removed or distant **2 a** : started on the way **b** : CANCELED **c** : not operating **d** : not placed so as to permit operation **3 a** : not corresponding to fact : INCORRECT **b** : POOR, SUBNORMAL **c** : not entirely sane : ECCENTRIC **d** : REMOTE, SLIGHT **4 a** : spent off duty **b** : SLACK **5** : INFERIOR **6** : CIRCUMSTANCED

of·fal \ˈȯ-fəl, ˈäf-əl\ *n* : the waste or by-product of a process; *esp* : the viscera and trimmings of a butchered animal removed in dressing

[1]**off·beat** \ˈȯf-ˌbēt\ *n* : the unaccented part of a musical measure

[2]**offbeat** *adj* : ECCENTRIC, UNCONVENTIONAL

off–col·or \ˈȯf-ˈkəl-ər\ *or* **off–col·ored** \-ərd\ *adj* **1** : not having the right or standard color **2** : of doubtful propriety : RISQUÉ

of·fend \ə-ˈfend\ *vb* **1 a** : to transgress the moral or divine law : SIN **b** : to violate the law : do wrong **2 a** : to cause difficulty, discomfort, or injury **b** : to cause dislike, anger, or vexation **3** : to cause pain to **4** : to cause to feel vexed or resentful esp. by hurting pride or self-respect — **of·fend·er** *n*

of·fense *or* **of·fence** \ə-ˈfen(t)s, *esp for 2* ˈäf-ˌen(t)s\ *n* **1** : something that outrages the moral or physical senses : NUISANCE **2 a** : the act of attacking : ASSAULT **b** : the side that is attacking in a contest or battle **3 a** : the act of displeasing or affronting **b** : the state of being insulted or morally outraged **4 a** : SIN, MISDEED **b** : an infraction of law : CRIME — **of·fense·less** \-ləs\ *adj*

[1]**of·fen·sive** \ə-ˈfen(t)-siv\ *adj* **1** : relating to or made or suited

for attack 2 : causing unpleasant sensations 3 : causing displeasure or resentment : INSULTING — **of·fen·sive·ly** *adv* — **of·fen·sive·ness** *n*

²offensive *n* 1 : the act, attitude, or position of an attacking party 2 : ATTACK

¹of·fer \'òf-ər\ *vb* **of·fered**; **of·fer·ing** \-(ə-)riŋ\ 1 : to present as an act of worship : SACRIFICE 2 a : to present for acceptance or rejection : TENDER b : to propose as payment : BID 3 a : PROPOSE, SUGGEST b : to declare one's readiness or willingness 4 a : to put up b : THREATEN

²offer *n* 1 : PROPOSAL 2 : a price named by one proposing to buy : BID 3 : ATTEMPT, TRY

of·fer·ing \'òf-(ə-)riŋ\ *n* 1 a : the act of one who offers b : a sacrifice ceremonially offered as a part of worship c : a contribution to the support of a church 2 : something offered for sale 3 : a course of instruction or study

of·fer·to·ry \'òf-ə(r)-,tōr-ē\ *n, pl* **-ries** 1 : the presentation of the offerings of the congregation at public worship 2 : the musical accompaniment played or sung during an offertory

off·hand \'òf-'hand\ *adv (or adj)* : without previous thought or preparation : EXTEMPORE

off·hand·ed \-'han-dəd\ *adj* : OFFHAND — **off·hand·ed·ly** *adv* — **off·hand·ed·ness** *n*

of·fice \'òf-əs\ *n* 1 : a special duty, charge, or position; *esp* : a position of authority in government 2 : a prescribed form or service of worship 3 a : an assigned or assumed duty, task, or role b : FUNCTION 4 : a place where a business is transacted or a service is supplied: as a : a place in which record keeping and clerical work are performed b : the directing headquarters of an enterprise or organization c : the place in which a professional man (as a physician or lawyer) conducts his business

office boy *n* : a boy employed for odd jobs in a business office

of·fice·hold·er \-,hōl-dər\ *n* : one holding a public office

¹of·fi·cer \'òf-ə-sər\ *n* 1 : a policeman or other person charged with the enforcement of law 2 : one who holds an office of trust, authority, or command 3 : one who holds a commission in the armed forces

²officer *vt* 1 : to furnish with officers 2 : to command or direct as an officer

¹of·fi·cial \ə-'fish-əl\ *n* : one who holds an office : OFFICER

²official *adj* 1 : of or relating to an office, position, or trust 2 : holding an office 3 : AUTHORIZED, AUTHORITATIVE 4 : befitting or characteristic of a person in office : FORMAL — **of·fi·cial·ly** \-'fish-(ə-)lē\ *adv*

of·fi·cial·dom \ə-'fish-əl-dəm\ *n* : officials as a class

of·fi·cial·ism \-'fish-ə-,liz-əm\ *n* : lack of flexibility and initiative combined with excessive adherence to regulations (as in the behavior of government officials)

of·fi·ci·ant \ə-'fish-ē-ənt\ *n* : an officiating clergyman

of·fi·ci·ate \ə-'fish-ē-,āt\ *vi* 1 : to perform a ceremony, function, or duty 2 : to act in an official capacity; *esp* : to preside as an officer — **of·fi·ci·a·tion** \-,fish-ē-'ā-shən\ *n*

of·fi·cious \ə-'fish-əs\ *adj* : volunteering one's services where they are neither asked nor needed : MEDDLESOME — **of·fi·cious·ly** *adv* — **of·fi·cious·ness** *n*

off·ing \'òf-iŋ\ *n* 1 : the part of the deep sea seen from the shore 2 : the near or foreseeable future

off·ish \'òf-ish\ *adj* : inclined to be formal, stiff, or aloof in manner — **off·ish·ly** *adv* — **off·ish·ness** *n*

off·print \'òf-,print\ *n* : a separately printed excerpt (as from a magazine)

¹off·set \'òf-,set\ *n* 1 : an abrupt bend in an object by which one part is turned aside out of line 2 : a printing process in which an inked impression is first made on a rubber-blanketed cylinder and then transferred to the paper being printed

²off·set \'òf-,set, *1 is also* òf-'\ *vb* **-set**; **-set·ting** 1 a : to place over against : BALANCE b : to compensate for : COUNTERBALANCE 2 : to form an offset in

off·shoot \'òf-,shüt\ *n* 1 : a branch of a main stem esp. of a plant 2 a : a lateral branch (as of a mountain range) b : a collateral or derived branch, descendant, or member

¹off·shore \'òf-'shō(ə)r\ *adv* : from the shore : at a distance from the shore

²off·shore \'òf-,\ *adj* 1 : coming or moving away from the shore 2 a : situated off the shore and esp. within a zone extending three miles from low-water line b : distant from the shore

off side *adv (or adj)* : illegally in advance of the ball or puck

off·spring \'òf-,spriŋ\ *n, pl* **offspring** : the progeny of an animal or plant : YOUNG

off·stage \-'stāj\ *adv (or adj)* : off or away from the stage

off–the–record *adj* : given or made in confidence and not for publication

off–white \'òf-'hwīt\ *n* : a yellowish or grayish white

off year *n* 1 : a year in which no major election is held 2 : a year of diminished activity or production

oft \'òft\ *adv* : OFTEN

of·ten \'ò-fən, 'òf-tən\ *adv* : many times : FREQUENTLY

of·ten·times \-,tīmz\ *or* **oft·times** \'òf(t)-,tīmz\ *adv* : OFTEN

¹ogle \'ō-gəl\ *vb* **ogled**; **ogling** \-g(ə-)liŋ\ : to glance or stare in a flirtatious way — **ogler** \-g(ə-)lər\ *n*

²ogle *n* : an amorous or coquettish glance

ogre \'ō-gər\ *n* 1 : a hideous giant of fairy tales and folklore that feeds on human beings : MONSTER 2 : a dreaded person or object — **ogre·ish** \'ō-g(ə-)rish\ *adj* — **ogress** \'ō-g(ə-)rəs\ *n*

¹oh \(')ō\ *interj* — used to express various emotions (as astonishment, pain, or desire)

²oh \'ō\ *n* : ZERO

ohm \'ōm\ *n* : the mks unit of electric resistance equal to the resistance of a circuit in which a potential difference of one volt produces a current of one ampere — **ohm·ic** \'ō-mik\ *adj*

¹oil \'òil\ *n* 1 a : any of numerous combustible usu. liquid substances from plant, animal, or mineral sources that are soluble in ether but not in water b : PETROLEUM 2 : a substance of oily consistency 3 a : artists' colors made with oil b : a painting done in oil — **oil** *adj*

²oil *vt* : to treat, furnish, or lubricate with oil

oil·cloth \'òil-,klòth\ *n* : cloth treated with oil or paint and used for table and shelf coverings

oil·er \'òi-lər\ *n* : one that oils; *esp* : a receptacle or device for applying oil

oil field *n* : a region rich in petroleum deposits

oil·skin \'òil-,skin\ *n* 1 : an oiled waterproof cloth used for coverings and garments 2 : an oilskin raincoat 3 *pl* : an oilskin suit of coat and trousers

oil slick *n* : a film of oil floating on water

oil·stone \'òil-,stōn\ *n* : a whetstone for use with oil

oil well *n* : a well from which petroleum is obtained

oily \'òi-lē\ *adj* 1 : of or relating to oil 2 : covered or impregnated with oil : GREASY 3 : excessively smooth or suave in manner : UNCTUOUS — **oil·i·ness** *n*

oint·ment \'òint-mənt\ *n* : a semisolid usu. greasy and medicated preparation for application to the skin

¹OK *or* **okay** \ō-'kā\ *adv (or adj)* : all right

²OK *or* **okay** *vt* **OK'd** *or* **okayed**; **OK'·ing** *or* **okay·ing** : APPROVE, AUTHORIZE

³OK *or* **okay** *n* : APPROVAL, ENDORSEMENT

okra \'ō-krə\ *n* : a tall annual plant related to the hollyhocks and grown for its edible green pods which are used esp. in soups and stews; *also* : these pods

¹old \'ōld\ *adj* 1 a : dating from the remote past : ANCIENT b : persisting from an earlier time : of long standing 2 : having existed for a specified period of time 3 : of, relating to, or originating in a past era : ANTIQUE 4 a : advanced in years or age b : showing the characteristics of age 5 : FORMER 6 a : showing the effects of time or use : WORN, AGED b : no longer in use : DISCARDED

²**old** *n* : old or earlier time

old country *n* : an emigrant's country of origin; *esp* : EUROPE

old·en \'ōl-dən\ *adj* : of or relating to a bygone era : ANCIENT

old–fash·ioned \'ōl(d)-'fash-ənd\ *adj* 1 : of, relating to, or characteristic of a past era : ANTIQUATED 2 : adhering to customs of a past era : CONSERVATIVE

old guard *n, often cap O & G* : the conservative or reactionary members esp. of a political party

old hand *n* : VETERAN

old·ish \'ōl-dish\ *adj* : somewhat old or elderly

old–line \'ōl-'(d)līn\ *adj* 1 : ORIGINAL, ESTABLISHED 2 : adhering to old policies or practices : CONSERVATIVE

old maid *n* 1 : SPINSTER 2 2 : a prim nervous fussy person — **old–maid·ish** \'ōl(d)-'mād-ish\ *adj*

old man *n* 1 a : HUSBAND b : FATHER 2 *cap* : one in authority; *esp* : COMMANDING OFFICER

old master *n* 1 : a superior artist or craftsman of established reputation; *esp* : a distinguished painter of the 16th, 17th, or early 18th century 2 : a work by an old master

old school *n* : adherents to the policies and practices of the past

old·ster \'ōl(d)-stər\ *n* : an old or elderly person

old–time \'ōl(d)-ˌtīm\ *adj* : of, relating to, or characteristic of an earlier period

old–tim·er \-'tī-mər\ *n* 1 : VETERAN 2 : OLDSTER

old wives' tale *n* : a traditional tale or bit of lore (as a superstitious notion)

Old World *n* : the eastern hemisphere; *esp* : the continent of Europe

old–world \'ōl-'(d)wərld\ *adj* : OLD-FASHIONED, PICTURESQUE

ole·ag·i·nous \ˌō-lē-'aj-ə-nəs\ *adj* : resembling or having the properties of oil; *also* : containing or producing oil — **ole·ag·i·nous·ly** *adv* — **ole·ag·i·nous·ness** *n*

ole·an·der \'ō-lē-ˌan-dər\ *n* : a poisonous evergreen shrub of the dogbane family often grown for its showy fragrant white to red flowers

oleo \'ō-lē-ˌō\ *n, pl* **ole·os** : MARGARINE

oleo·mar·ga·rine \ˌō-lē-ō-'märj-(ə-)rən, -'märj-ə-ˌrēn\ *n* : MARGARINE

ol·fac·tion \äl-'fak-shən, ōl-\ *n* : the sense of smell : the act or process of smelling

ol·fac·to·ry \äl-'fak-t(ə-)rē, ōl-\ *adj* : of, relating to, or concerned with the sense of smell

ol·i·garch \'äl-ə-ˌgärk\ *n* : a member of an oligarchy

ol·i·gar·chy \-ˌgär-kē\ *n, pl* **-chies** 1 : a government in which the power is in the hands of a few persons 2 : a state having an oligarchy; *also* : the group of persons holding power in such a state — **ol·i·gar·chic** \ˌäl-ə-'gär-kik\ *or* **ol·i·gar·chi·cal** \-ki-kəl\ *adj*

ol·i·gop·o·ly \ˌäl-i-'gäp-ə-lē\ *n, pl* **-lies** : a market situation in which a few producers control the demand from a large number of buyers

olio \'ō-lē-ˌō\ *n, pl* **oli·os** : HODGEPODGE, MEDLEY

ol·ive \'äl-iv\ *n* : an Old World evergreen tree grown for its fruit that is an important food and source of oil; *also* : this fruit

olive branch *n* 1 : a branch of the olive tree esp. when used as a symbol of peace 2 : an offer or gesture of conciliation or goodwill

om·buds·man \'äm- bu̇dz-mən, 'óm-, -bədz-; äm-'bu̇dz-, óm-\ *n, pl* **-men** \-mən\ : a government official appointed to receive and investigate complaints made by individuals against abuses or capricious acts of public officials

om·elet \'äm-(ə-)lət\ *n* : eggs beaten with milk or water, cooked without stirring until set, and folded over

omen \'ō-mən\ *n* : an event or phenomenon believed to be a sign or warning of some future occurrence : PORTENT

om·i·nous \'äm-ə-nəs\ *adj* : being or showing an omen; *esp* : foretelling evil : THREATENING — **om·i·nous·ly** *adv* — **om·i·nous·ness** *n*

omis·si·ble \ō-'mis-ə-bəl\ *adj* : that may be omitted

omis·sion \ō-'mish-ən\ *n* 1 : something neglected or left undone 2 : the act of omitting : the state of being omitted

omis·sive \ō-'mis-iv\ *adj* : failing or neglecting to do : OMITTING — **omis·sive·ly** *adv*

omit \ō-'mit\ *vt* **omit·ted**; **omit·ting** 1 : to leave out or leave unmentioned 2 : to fail to perform : leave undone : NEGLECT

¹**om·ni·bus** \'äm-ni-(ˌ)bəs\ *n* : a usu. automotive public vehicle designed to carry a comparatively large number of passengers : BUS

²**omnibus** *adj* : of, relating to, or providing for many things or classes at once

om·ni·far·i·ous \ˌäm-nə-'far-ē-əs, -'fer-\ *adj* : of all varieties, forms, or kinds

om·nip·o·tence \äm-'nip-ət-ən(t)s\ *n* : the quality or state of being omnipotent

om·nip·o·tent \-ət-ənt\ *adj* 1 *often cap* : ALMIGHTY 1 2 : having virtually unlimited authority or influence — **omnipotent** *n* — **om·nip·o·tent·ly** *adv*

om·ni·pres·ent \ˌäm-ni-'prez-ᵊnt\ *adj* : present in all places at all times — **om·ni·pres·ence** \-ᵊn(t)s\ *n*

om·ni·scient \äm-'nish-ənt\ *adj* 1 : having infinite awareness, understanding, and insight 2 : possessed of universal or complete knowledge — **om·ni·science** \-ən(t)s\ *n* — **om·ni·scient·ly** *adv*

om·ni·um–gath·er·um \ˌäm-nē-əm-'gath-ə-rəm\ *n* : a miscellaneous collection of a variety of things or persons : HODGEPODGE

om·niv·o·rous \äm-'niv-(ə-)rəs\ *adj* 1 : feeding on both animal and vegetable substances 2 : avidly taking in everything as if devouring or consuming — **om·niv·o·rous·ly** *adv* — **om·niv·o·rous·ness** *n*

¹**on** \(')ón, (')än\ *prep* 1 : in or to a position over and in contact with 2 : touching the surface of 3 : AT, TO 4 : at or toward as an object 5 : IN, ABOARD 6 — used to indicate a basis, source, or standard of computation 7 : ABOUT, CONCERNING 8 : connected with as a member or participant 9 : with regard to 10 : in a state or process of 11 : during or at the time of 12 : through the agency of 13 : following in series

²**on** \'ón, 'än\ *adv* 1 a : in or into a position of contact with an upper surface b : in or into a position of being attached to or covering a surface 2 a : forward in space, time, or action : ONWARD b : in continuance or succession 3 : into operation or a position permitting operation

³**on** \'ón, 'än\ *adj* 1 : engaged in an activity or function (as a dramatic role) 2 a (1) : OPERATING (2) : placed so as to permit operation b : taking place 3 : PLANNED

¹**once** \'wən(t)s\ *adv* 1 : one time and no more 2 : at any one time : under any circumstances : EVER 3 : at some indefinite time in the past : FORMERLY 4 : by one degree of relationship

²**once** *n* : one single time : one time at least — **at once** 1 : at the same time : SIMULTANEOUSLY 2 : IMMEDIATELY

³**once** *conj* : at the moment when

once–over \'wən(t)s-ˌō-vər\ *n* : a swift examination or survey

on·com·ing \'ón-ˌkəm-iŋ, 'än-\ *adj* : coming on : APPROACHING

¹**one** \'wən\ *adj* 1 : being a single unit or thing — see NUMBER table 2 a : being one in particular b : being preeminently what is indicated 3 a : being the same in kind or quality b : not divided : UNITED

²**one** *pron* 1 a : a single member or specimen of a usu. specified class or group b : a person in general : SOMEBODY 2 — used for *I* or *we*

³**one** *n* 1 : the number denoting unity 2 : the first in a set or series 3 : a single person or thing

one another *pron* : EACH OTHER
one•ness \'wən-nəs\ *n* : the quality or state or fact of being one: as **a** : SINGLENESS **b** : WHOLENESS, INTEGRITY **c** : HARMONY **d** : SAMENESS, IDENTITY **e** : UNITY, UNION
on•er•ous \'än-ə-rəs, 'ō-nə-\ *adj* : involving, imposing, or constituting a burden : TROUBLESOME — **on•er•ous•ly** *adv* — **on•er•ous•ness** *n*
one•self \(,)wən-'self\ *pron* **1** : a person's self : one's own self — used reflexively as object of a preposition or verb or for emphasis in various constructions **2** : one's normal, healthy, or sane condition or self
one–sid•ed \'wən-'sīd-əd\ *adj* **1 a** : having or occurring on one side only **b** : having one side prominent or more developed **c** : UNEQUAL **2** : limited to or favoring one side : PARTIAL — **one–sid•ed•ly** *adv* — **one–sid•ed•ness** *n*
one–step \'wən-,step\ *n* : a ballroom dance marked by quick walking steps backward and forward in 2/4 time — **one–step** *vi*
one•time \'wən-,tīm\ *adj* : FORMER, SOMETIME
one–to–one \,wən-tə-'wən\ *adj* : pairing each element of a class uniquely with an element of another class
one–way \'wən-'wā\ *adj* : that moves in, allows movement in, or functions in only one direction
on•go•ing \'ȯn-,gō-iŋ, 'än-\ *adj* : continuously moving forward : GROWING
on•ion \'ən-yən\ *n* : a widely grown Asiatic herb of the lily family with pungent edible bulbs; *also* : its bulb
on•ion•skin \-,skin\ *n* : a thin strong translucent paper of very light weight
on•look•er \'ȯn-,lu̇k-ər, 'än-\ *n* : one that looks on : SPECTATOR — **on•look•ing** *adj*
¹on•ly \'ōn-lē\ *adj* **1** : unquestionably the best : PEERLESS **2** : alone in its class or kind : SOLE
²only *adv* **1 a** : as a single fact or instance and nothing more or different : MERELY **b** : EXCLUSIVELY, SOLELY **2** : at the very least **3** : with nevertheless the final result **4** : as recently as : in the immediate past
³only *conj* **1** : with this sole restriction **2** : were it not that
on•o•mat•o•poe•ia \,än-ə-,mat-ə-'pē-(y)ə\ *n* **1** : formation of words in imitation of natural sounds (as *buzz* or *hiss*) **2** : the use of words whose sound suggests the sense — **on•o•mat•o•poe•ic** \-'pē-ik\ *or* **on•o•mat•o•po•et•ic** \-pō-'et-ik\ *adj*
on•rush \'ȯn-,rəsh, 'än-\ *n* : a rushing forward or onward
on•set \-,set\ *n* **1** : ATTACK **2** : BEGINNING
on•shore \'ȯn-,shōr, 'än-\ *adj* : moving toward the shore — **on•shore** \'ȯn-', 'än-'\ *adv*
on side *adv (or adj)* : not off side : in a position legally to receive the ball or puck
on•slaught \'än-,slȯt, 'ȯn-\ *n* : an esp. fierce attack
on–stream \'ȯn-'strēm, 'än-\ *adv* : in or into operation
on•to \'ȯn-tə, 'än-, -tü\ *prep* : to a position or point on
onus \'ō-nəs\ *n* **1 a** : BURDEN **b** : a disagreeable necessity : OBLIGATION **2** : BLAME
¹on•ward \'ȯn-wərd, 'än-\ *adv* : toward or at a point lying ahead in space or time : FORWARD
²onward *adj* : directed or moving onward : FORWARD
on•yx \'än-iks\ *n* : chalcedony with straight parallel alternating bands of color
oo•dles \'üd-ᵊlz\ *n pl* : a great quantity : LOT
oo•long \'ü-,lȯŋ\ *n* : a tea partially fermented before drying that combines characteristics of black and green teas
oomph \'u̇m(p)f\ *n* **1** : personal charm or magnetism : GLAMOUR **2** : SEX APPEAL **3** : VITALITY, ENTHUSIASM
¹ooze \'üz\ *n* **1** : a soft deposit (as of mud, slime, or shells) esp. on the bottom of a body of water **2** : soft wet plastic ground : MUD, SLIME
²ooze *vb* **1** : to pass or flow slowly through or as if through small openings **2** : to move slowly or imperceptibly **3** : to give off : EXUDE
³ooze *n* **1** : the action of oozing **2** : something that oozes
oozy \'ü-zē\ *adj* **1** : containing or composed of ooze **2** : exuding moisture : SLIMY
opac•i•ty \ō-'pas-ət-ē\ *n, pl* **-ties** **1** : the quality or state of being opaque **2** : obscurity of meaning **3** : mental dullness
opal \'ō-pəl\ *n* : a mineral that is a hydrated amorphous silica softer and less dense than quartz and typically with an iridescent play of colors
opal•es•cent \,ō-pə-'les-ᵊnt\ *adj* : having a play of colors like an opal — **opal•esce** \-'les\ *vi* — **opal•es•cence** \-'les-ᵊn(t)s\ *n*
opal•ine \'ō-pə-,līn, -,lēn\ *adj* : resembling opal : OPALESCENT
opaque \ō-'pāk\ *adj* **1** : not transmitting light rays : being neither transparent nor translucent **2 a** : not easily understood : OBSCURE **b** : lacking mental clarity : OBTUSE — **opaque•ly** *adv* — **opaque•ness** *n*
ope \'ōp\ *vb* : OPEN
¹open \'ō-pən\ *adj* **1 a** : permitting passage or access : not shut or shut up : not stopped or clogged **b** : having openings or spaces **2 a** : not enclosed or covered : BARE **b** : not protected against something : LIABLE **c** : not secret : exposed to general knowledge : PUBLIC; *also* : not secretive **3 a** : free to the use, entry, or participation of all **b** : easy to enter, get through, or see; *also* : free from hampering restraints or controls **c** : available or ready for use or operation **4** : not snowy or stormy **5** : not drawn together : not folded or contracted : spread out **6 a** : not finally decided or settled **b** : receptive to appeals or ideas : RESPONSIVE **7** : having components separated by a space in writing or printing — **open•ly** *adv* — **open•ness** *n*
²open *vb* **opened** \'ō-pənd\; **open•ing** \'ōp-(ə-)niŋ\ **1 a** : to change or move from a shut condition : UNFASTEN, UNCLOSE **b** : to make or become open by or as if by clearing away obstacles **c** : to make an opening or openings in **d** : to spread out : UNFOLD **2** : to make or become functional **3** : to give access **4** : to enter upon : BEGIN, START **5** : to speak out — **open•er** *n*
³open *n* **1** : OPENING **2 a** : open and unobstructed space or water **b** : OUTDOORS
open air *n* : space where air is unconfined; *esp* : OUT-OF-DOORS
open–air \,ō-pən-'a(ə)r\ *adj* : OUTDOOR
open–and–shut *adj* : perfectly simple : OBVIOUS
open door *n* : a policy giving opportunity for commercial intercourse with a country to all nations on equal terms — **open–door** *adj*
open–eyed \-'īd\ *adj* **1** : having the eyes open **2** : WATCHFUL, DISCERNING, ALERT
open•hand•ed \-'han-dəd\ *adj* : generous in giving : LIBERAL — **open•hand•ed•ly** *adv* — **open•hand•ed•ness** *n*
open•heart•ed \-'härt-əd\ *adj* : FRANK, GENEROUS — **open•heart•ed•ly** *adv* — **open•heart•ed•ness** *n*
open–hearth \-,härth\ *adj* : being or relating to a process of making steel in a furnace that reflects heat from the roof onto the material
open house *n* : ready and usu. informal hospitality or entertainment for all comers; *also* : an occasion devoted to this
open•ing \'ōp-(ə-)niŋ\ *n* **1** : an act or instance of making or becoming open **2** : something that is open : an open place or span : APERTURE, HOLE **3** : something that constitutes a beginning **4 a** : OCCASION, CHANCE **b** : an opportunity for employment
open letter *n* : a letter of protest or appeal intended for the general public and printed in a newspaper or periodical
open–mind•ed \,ō-pən-'mīn-dəd\ *adj* : receptive of arguments or ideas : not prejudiced — **open–mind•ed•ly** *adv* — **open–mind•ed•ness** *n*
open•mouthed \-'mau̇t͟hd, -'mau̇tht\ *adj* **1** : having the mouth wide open **2** : struck with amazement or wonder — **open•mouthed•ly** \-'mau̇-t͟həd-lē, -'mau̇th-tlē\ *adv*

open sea *n* : the part of the sea not enclosed between headlands or included in narrow straits : the main sea

open secret *n* : something supposedly secret but in fact generally known

open ses·a·me \ˌō-pən-ˈses-ə-mē\ *n* : something that unfailingly brings about a desired end

open shop *n* : an establishment employing and retaining on the payroll members and nonmembers of a labor union

open·work \ˈō-pən-ˌwərk\ *n* : something made or work done so as to show openings through the substance — **openwork** *or* **open–worked** \ˌō-pən-ˈwərkt\ *adj*

[1]**opera** *pl of* OPUS

[2]**op·era** \ˈäp-(ə-)rə\ *n* : a drama set to music and made up of vocal pieces with orchestral accompaniment and orchestral overtures and interludes

op·er·a·ble \ˈäp-(ə-)rə-bəl\ *adj* **1** : fit, possible, or desirable to use : PRACTICABLE **2** : suitable for surgical treatment — **op·er·a·bly** \-blē\ *adv*

opera glass *n* : a small binocular similar to a field glass and adapted for use at the opera — often used in pl.

opera hat *n* : a man's collapsible top hat consisting usu. of a dull silky fabric stretched over a steel frame

op·er·ate \ˈäp-ə-ˌrāt\ *vb* **1** : to perform or cause to perform an appointed function **2** : to produce an effect **3** : to carry on the activities of; *esp* : MANAGE **4** : to perform surgery

op·er·at·ic \ˌäp-ə-ˈrat-ik\ *adj* : of, relating to, resembling, or suitable to opera — **op·er·at·i·cal·ly** \-ˈrat-i-k(ə-)lē\ *adv*

op·er·a·tion \ˌäp-ə-ˈrā-shən\ *n* **1** : the act, process, method, or result of operating **2** : a functioning; *esp* : the quality or state of being functional or operative **3** : a surgical procedure **4** : a process (as addition or multiplication) of deriving one mathematical expression from others according to a rule **5 a** : a military or naval action, mission, or maneuver including its planning and execution **b** *pl* : the office of an airfield which controls flying from the field — **op·er·a·tion·al** \-shnəl, -shən-ᵊl\ *adj*

[1]**op·er·a·tive** \ˈäp-(ə-)rət-iv, ˈäp-ə-ˌrāt-\ *adj* **1** : producing an appropriate effect : EFFICACIOUS **2** : exerting force or influence : OPERATING **3 a** : having to do with physical operations **b** : WORKING **4** : based on or consisting of operation — **op·er·a·tive·ly** *adv* — **op·er·a·tive·ness** *n*

[2]**operative** *n* : OPERATOR

op·er·a·tor \ˈäp-ə-ˌrāt-ər\ *n* **1** : one that operates **2** : a shrewd person who knows how to circumvent restrictions or difficulties

op·er·et·ta \ˌäp-ə-ˈret-ə\ *n* : a light musical-dramatic production having usu. a romantic plot and containing spoken dialogue and dancing scenes — **op·er·et·tist** \-ˈret-əst\ *n*

oph·thal·mic \äf-ˈthal-mik, äp-\ *adj* : of, relating to, or situated near the eye : OCULAR

oph·thal·mol·o·gist \ˌäf-ˌthal-ˈmäl-ə-jəst, ˌäp-\ *n* : a physician specializing in ophthalmology

oph·thal·mol·o·gy \-jē\ *n* : a branch of medical science dealing with the structure, functions, and diseases of the eye — **oph·thal·mo·log·ic** \(ˌ)äf-ˌthal-mə-ˈläj-ik, (ˌ)äp-\ *or* **oph·thal·mo·log·i·cal** \-ˈläj-i-kəl\ *adj* — **oph·thal·mo·log·i·cal·ly** \-i-k(ə-)lē\ *adv*

[1]**opi·ate** \ˈō-pē-ət, -ˌāt\ *adj* **1** : containing or mixed with opium **2 a** : inducing sleep : NARCOTIC **b** : causing dullness or inaction

[2]**opiate** *n* **1** : a preparation or derivative of opium; *also* : NARCOTIC 1 **2** : something that induces rest or inaction or quiets uneasiness

opine \ō-ˈpīn\ *vb* **1** : to state as an opinion **2** : to form or express opinions

opin·ion \ə-ˈpin-yən\ *n* **1** : a belief stronger than an impression but less strong than positive knowledge **2** : a judgment about a person or thing **3** : a formal statement by an expert after careful study

opin·ion·at·ed \-yə-ˌnāt-əd\ *adj* : adhering unduly to personal opinions or preconceived notions — **opin·ion·at·ed·ly** *adv* — **opin·ion·at·ed·ness** *n*

opin·ion·a·tive \-ˌnāt-iv\ *adj* **1** : of, relating to, or consisting of opinion **2** : OPINIONATED

opi·um \ˈō-pē-əm\ *n* : a bitter brownish addictive narcotic drug that is the dried juice of the opium poppy — **opium** *adj*

opium poppy *n* : an annual poppy grown since antiquity for opium, for its edible oily seeds, and for its showy flowers

opos·sum \(ə-)ˈpäs-əm\ *n* : any of various American marsupials; *esp* : a common omnivorous largely nocturnal and arboreal mammal of the eastern U.S.

[1]**op·po·nent** \ə-ˈpō-nənt\ *n* : a person or thing that opposes another person or thing : RIVAL, ANTAGONIST

[2]**opponent** *adj* **1** : ANTAGONISTIC **2** : OPPOSITE

op·por·tune \ˌäp-ər-ˈt(y)ün\ *adj* : SUITABLE, TIMELY — **op·por·tune·ly** *adv* — **op·por·tune·ness** *n*

op·por·tun·ism \-ˈt(y)ü-ˌniz-əm\ *n* : the art, policy, or practice of taking advantage of opportunities or circumstances esp. with little regard for principles or ultimate consequences — **op·por·tun·ist** \-nəst\ *n or adj* — **op·por·tu·nis·tic** \-t(y)ü-ˈnis-tik\ *adj*

op·por·tu·ni·ty \ˌäp-ər-ˈt(y)ü-nət-ē\ *n, pl* **-ties** **1** : a favorable juncture of circumstances, time, and place **2** : a chance for advancement or progress

op·pos·a·ble \ə-ˈpō-zə-bəl\ *adj* **1** : capable of being resisted **2** : capable of being placed opposite something else and esp. in a position for grasping — **op·pos·a·bil·i·ty** \ə-ˌpō-zə-ˈbil-ət-ē\ *n*

op·pose \ə-ˈpōz\ *vt* **1** : to place opposite or against something esp. so as to provide resistance, counterbalance, or contrast **2** : to offer resistance to : strive against — **op·pos·er** *n*

[1]**op·po·site** \ˈäp-ə-zət\ *n* : something that is opposite

[2]**opposite** *adj* **1** : set over against something that is at the other end or side **2 a** : OPPOSED, HOSTILE **b** : diametrically different : CONTRARY **3** : contrarily turned or moving — **op·po·site·ly** *adv* — **op·po·site·ness** *n*

[3]**opposite** *adv* : on opposite sides

[4]**opposite** *prep* **1** : across from and usu. facing or on the same level with **2** : in a role complementary to

op·po·si·tion \ˌäp-ə-ˈzish-ən\ *n* **1** : a setting opposite or being set opposite **2** : resistant or contrary action or condition **3** : something that opposes; *esp* : a body of persons opposing something — **op·po·si·tion·al** \-ˈzish-nəl, -ən-ᵊl\ *adj*

op·press \ə-ˈpres\ *vt* **1** : to weigh down : burden in spirit as if with weight **2** : to crush by harsh rule : treat cruelly or with too great severity — **op·pres·sor** \-ˈpres-ər\ *n*

op·pres·sion \ə-ˈpresh-ən\ *n* **1 a** : unjust or cruel exercise of authority or power **b** : something that so oppresses **2** : a sense of heaviness or obstruction in the body or mind : DEPRESSION

op·pres·sive \ə-ˈpres-iv\ *adj* **1** : unreasonably burdensome or severe **2** : TYRANNICAL **3** : overpowering or depressing to the spirit or senses — **op·pres·sive·ly** *adv* — **op·pres·sive·ness** *n*

op·pro·bri·ous \ə-ˈprō-brē-əs\ *adj* **1** : expressive of opprobrium : SCURRILOUS **2** : deserving of opprobrium — **op·pro·bri·ous·ly** *adv* — **op·pro·bri·ous·ness** *n*

op·pro·bri·um \-brē-əm\ *n* **1** : something that brings disgrace **2** : public disgrace or ill repute that follows from conduct considered grossly wrong or vicious : INFAMY

opt \ˈäpt\ *vi* : to make a choice

op·ta·tive \ˈäp-tət-iv\ *adj* : expressing desire or wish

op·tic \ˈäp-tik\ *adj* : of or relating to vision or the eye

op·ti·cal \ˈäp-ti-kəl\ *adj* **1** : relating to optics **2** : OPTIC — **op·ti·cal·ly** \-k(ə-)lē\ *adv*

op·ti·cian \äp-ˈtish-ən\ *n* **1** : a maker of or dealer in optical

items and instruments **2** : one that grinds spectacle lenses to prescription and dispenses spectacles
op·tics \'äp-tiks\ *n* : a science that deals with the nature and properties of light and the effects that it undergoes and produces
op·ti·mal \'äp-tə-məl\ *adj* : most desirable or satisfactory : OPTIMUM — **op·ti·mal·ly** \-mə-lē\ *adv*
op·ti·mism \'äp-tə-,miz-əm\ *n* **1** : a doctrine that this world is the best possible world **2** : an inclination to put the most favorable construction on actions and happenings or to anticipate the best possible outcome — **op·ti·mist** \-məst\ *n or adj* — **op·ti·mis·tic** \,äp-tə-'mis-tik\ *or* **op·ti·mis·ti·cal** \-ti-kəl\ *adj* — **op·ti·mis·ti·cal·ly** \-ti-k(ə-)lē\ *adv*
op·ti·mum \'äp-tə-məm\ *n, pl* **-ma** \-mə\ **1** : the amount or degree of something that is most favorable to some end **2** : greatest degree attained under implied or specified conditions — **optimum** *adj*
op·tion \'äp-shən\ *n* **1 a** : the power or right to choose **b** : a right to buy or sell something at a specified price during a specified period **2** : something offered for choice
op·tion·al \'äp-shnəl, -shən-ᵊl\ *adj* : permitting a choice : not compulsory — **op·tion·al·ly** \-ē\ *adv*
op·tom·e·trist \äp-'täm-ə-trəst\ *n* : a specialist in optometry
op·tom·e·try \-trē\ *n* : the art or profession of examining the eye for defects and faults of refraction and prescribing correctional lenses or exercises but not drugs or surgery — **op·to·met·ric** \,äp-tə-'me-trik\ *or* **op·to·met·ri·cal** \-tri-kəl\ *adj*
op·u·lence \'äp-yə-lən(t)s\ *n* **1** : WEALTH, RICHES **2** : PLENTY, PROFUSION
op·u·lent \-lənt\ *adj* : marked by opulence: as **a** : WEALTHY **b** : richly abundant : PROFUSE; *also* : amply fashioned : LUSH — **op·u·lent·ly** *adv*
opus \'ō-pəs\ *n, pl* **opera** \'ō-pə-rə, 'äp-ə-\ : WORK; *esp* : a musical composition or set of compositions
or \ər, (,)ȯ(ə)r\ *conj* — used as a function word to indicate an alternative
or·a·cle \'ȯr-ə-kəl\ *n* **1 a** : a person (as a priestess of ancient Greece) through whom a deity is held to speak **b** : a shrine in which a deity so reveals hidden knowledge or the divine purpose **c** : an answer or revelation given by an oracle **2 a** : a person giving wise or authoritative decisions or opinions **b** : an authoritative or wise expression or answer
orac·u·lar \ȯ-'rak-yə-lər\ *adj* **1** : of, relating to, or being an oracle **2** : resembling an oracle in wisdom, solemnity, or obscurity — **orac·u·lar·i·ty** \-,rak-yə-'lar-ət-ē\ *n* — **orac·u·lar·ly** *adv*
oral \'ōr-əl, 'ȯr-\ *adj* **1 a** : uttered by the mouth or in words : SPOKEN **b** : using speech or the lips **2** : of, relating to, given through, or situated near the mouth — **oral·ly** \-ə-lē\ *adv*
or·ange \'ȯr-inj\ *n* **1 a** : a globose berry with a reddish yellow rind and a sweet edible pulp **b** : any of various rather small evergreen citrus trees whose fruits are oranges **2** : any of a group of colors that lie midway between red and yellow in hue — **orange** *adj*
or·ange·ade \,ȯr-inj-'ād\ *n* : a drink made of orange juice, sugar, and water
or·ange pe·koe \,ȯr-inj-'pēk-(,)ō\ *n* : a tea formerly made from the tiny leaf and end bud of the spray; *also* : India or Ceylon tea of good quality
or·ange·ry \'ȯr-inj-(ə-)rē, 'är-\ *n, pl* **-ries** : a protected place (as a greenhouse) for raising oranges in cool climates
orang·u·tan *or* **orang·ou·tan** \ə-'raŋ-ə-,taŋ, -,tan\ *n* : a largely herbivorous and arboreal anthropoid ape of Borneo and Sumatra about two thirds as large as the gorilla
orate \ȯ-'rāt\ *vi* : to speak in a declamatory or grandiloquent manner : HARANGUE
ora·tion \ə-'rā-shən\ *n* : an elaborate discourse delivered in a formal and dignified manner usu. on some special occasion
or·a·tor \'ȯr-ət-ər\ *n* : one that delivers an oration; *also* : a public speaker noted for skill and power in speaking
or·a·tor·i·cal \,ȯr-ə-'tȯr-i-kəl\ *adj* : of, relating to, or characteristic of an orator or oratory — **or·a·tor·i·cal·ly** \-k(ə-)lē\ *adv*
or·a·to·rio \,ȯr-ə-'tōr-ē-,ō\ *n, pl* **-ri·os** : a vocal and orchestral work usu. on a scriptural subject
¹or·a·to·ry \'ȯr-ə-,tōr-ē\ *n, pl* **-ries** : a place of prayer; *esp* : a private or institutional chapel
²oratory *n* **1** : the art of an orator **2** : oratorical language or presentations
orb \'ȯrb\ *n* : a spherical body; *esp* : a heavenly body (as a planet)
or·bic·u·lar \ȯr-'bik-yə-lər\ *adj* : SPHERICAL, CIRCULAR
¹or·bit \'ȯr-bət\ *n* **1** : the bony socket of the eye **2** : a path described by one body or object in its revolution about another **3** : range or sphere of activity — **or·bit·al** \-ᵊl\ *adj*
²orbit *vb* **1** : to revolve in an orbit around : CIRCLE **2** : to send up and make revolve in an orbit **3** : to travel in circles — **or·bit·er** *n*
or·chard \'ȯr-chərd\ *n* : a planting of fruit trees or nut trees; *also* : the trees of such a planting — **or·chard·ist** \-əst\ *n* — **or·chard·man** \-mən, -,man\ *n*
or·ches·tra \'ȯr-kə-strə\ *n* **1** : a group of instrumentalists including esp. string players organized to perform ensemble music **2** : a front part of a theater; *esp* : the forward section of seats on the main floor of a theater
or·ches·tral \ȯr-'kes-trəl\ *adj* : of, relating to, or composed for an orchestra — **or·ches·tral·ly** \-trə-lē\ *adv*
or·ches·trate \'ȯr-kə-,strāt\ *vt* : to compose or arrange (music) for an orchestra; *also* : to provide (as a ballet) with such music — **or·ches·tra·tion** \,ȯr-kə-'strā-shən\ *n* — **or·ches·tra·tor** \'ȯr-kə-,strāt-ər\ *n*
or·chid \'ȯr-kəd\ *n* : any of a large family of perennial plants that have usu. showy 3-petaled flowers with the middle petal enlarged into a lip and differing from the others in shape and color; *also* : its flower
or·dain \ȯr-'dān\ *vb* **1** : to admit to the Christian ministry or priesthood by the ritual of a church : confer holy orders upon **2** : to establish or order by appointment, decree, or law : ENACT, DECREE; *esp* : DESTINE — **or·dain·er** *n* — **or·dain·ment** *n*
or·deal \ȯr-'dēl\ *n* **1** : a primitive method of determining guilt or innocence by submitting the accused to dangerous or painful tests believed to be under supernatural control **2** : a severe trial or experience
¹or·der \'ȯrd-ər\ *n* **1 a** : a group of people united in some way (as by living under the same religious rules, by having won the same distinction, or by loyalty to common interests and obligations) **b** : the badge or insignia of such an order **c** : a military decoration **2 a** : any of the several grades of the Christian ministry **b** *pl* : ORDINATION **3 a** : a rank, class, or special group in a community or society **b** : a class grouped according to quality, value, or natural characteristics **4 a** : the arrangement or sequence of objects in position or of events in time **b** : the prevailing mode or arrangement of things **c** : regular or harmonious arrangement; *also* : a condition characterized by such an arrangement **5 a** : a customary or prescribed mode of procedure (as in debate or religious ritual) **b** : the rule of law or proper authority **c** : a specific rule, regulation, or authoritative direction : COMMAND **6 a** : a style of building **b** : an architectural column with its related structures forming the unit of a style **7** : state or condition esp. with regard to functioning or repair **8 a** : a written direction to pay money to someone **b** : a commission to purchase, sell, or supply goods or to perform work **c** : goods or items bought or sold — **in order to** : for the purpose of
²order *vb* **or·dered**; **or·der·ing** \'ȯrd-(ə-)riŋ\ **1** : to put in order

: ARRANGE; *also* : REGULATE 2 : to give an order to or for 3 : to give or place an order — **or·der·er** *n*

[1]**or·der·ly** \'ȯrd-ər-lē\ *adj* 1 a : arranged according to some order or pattern b : not marked by disorder : TIDY; *also* : METHODICAL c : governed by law or system : REGULATED 2 : well-behaved : PEACEFUL — **or·der·li·ness** *n* — **orderly** *adv*

[2]**orderly** *n, pl* **-lies** 1 : a soldier who attends a superior officer to convey messages and perform various services 2 : a hospital attendant who does general work

or·di·nal \'ȯrd-nəl, -ᵊn-əl\ *adj* : of a specified order or rank (as sixth) in a series

ordinal number *n* : a number designating the place (as first, second, third) occupied by an item in an ordered sequence — see NUMBER table

or·di·nance \'ȯrd-nən(t)s, 'ȯrd-ᵊn-ən(t)s\ *n* 1 : an authoritative decree or direction : ORDER 2 : a law enacted by governmental authority; *esp* : a municipal regulation 3 : a prescribed usage, practice, or ceremony

or·di·nand \,ȯrd-ᵊn-'and\ *n* : a person being ordained

[1]**or·di·nary** \'ȯrd-ᵊn-,er-ē\ *n, pl* **-nar·ies** 1 : a prelate (as the bishop of a diocese) exercising jurisdiction over a territory or group by virtue of his office 2 *often cap* : the parts of the mass that do not vary from day to day 3 : regular or customary condition or course of things

[2]**ordinary** *adj* 1 : to be expected : ROUTINE, NORMAL 2 a : of common quality, rank, or ability b : POOR, INFERIOR c : lacking in refinement — **or·di·nar·i·ly** \,ȯrd-ᵊn-'er-ə-lē\ *adv* — **or·di·nar·i·ness** \'ȯrd-ᵊn-,er-ē-nəs\ *n*

or·di·na·tion \,ȯrd-ᵊn-'ā-shən\ *n* : the act of ordaining : the state of being ordained

ord·nance \'ȯrd-nən(t)s\ *n* 1 a : military supplies including weapons, ammunition, vehicles, and equipment b : a service of the army in charge of ordnance 2 : CANNON, ARTILLERY

or·dure \'ȯr-jər\ *n* : EXCREMENT

ore \'ō(ə)r\ *n* : a mineral containing a constituent for which it is mined and worked

oreg·a·no \ə-'reg-ə-,nō\ *n, pl* **-nos** : a bushy perennial mint used as a seasoning and a source of aromatic oil

or·gan \'ȯr-gən\ *n* 1 a : a wind instrument consisting of sets of pipes made to sound by compressed air and controlled by keyboards and producing a variety of musical effects b : an instrument in which the sounds of the pipe organ are approximated by means of electronic devices c : any of various similar cruder instruments 2 : a differentiated animal or plant structure consisting of cells and tissues and performing some specific function 3 : a means of performing some function or accomplishing some end 4 : a publication (as a newspaper or magazine) serving the interests of a special group

or·gan·dy \'ȯr-gən-dē\ *n, pl* **-dies** : a very fine transparent muslin with a stiff finish

or·gan·ic \ȯr-'gan-ik\ *adj* 1 a : of, relating to, or arising in a bodily organ b : affecting the structure of the organism 2 a (1) : of, relating to, or derived from living organisms (2) : relating to or produced with fertilizer of plant or animal origin without the use of chemically formulated fertilizers and pesticides b (1) : of, relating to, or containing carbon compounds (2) : of, relating to, or dealt with by a branch of chemistry concerned with the carbon compounds of living beings and most other carbon compounds 3 a : forming an integral element of a whole b : having systematic coordination of parts : ORGANIZED — **or·gan·i·cal·ly** \-i-k(ə-)lē\ *adv*

or·ga·nism \'ȯr-gə-,niz-əm\ *n* : an individual constituted to carry on the activities of life by means of organs separate in function but mutually dependent : a living person, plant, or animal — **or·ga·nis·mal** \,ȯr-gə-'niz-məl\ *or* **or·ga·nis·mic** \-mik\ *adj* — **or·ga·nis·mi·cal·ly** \-mi-k(ə-)lē\ *adv*

or·gan·ist \'ȯr-gə-nəst\ *n* : one who plays an organ

or·ga·ni·za·tion \,ȯrg-(ə-)nə-'zā-shən\ *n* 1 : the act or process of organizing or of being organized 2 : the condition or manner of being organized 3 a : ASSOCIATION, SOCIETY b : an administrative body or its personnel : MANAGEMENT; *also* : such a body with other groups directed and supervised by it — **or·ga·ni·za·tion·al** \-shnəl, -shən-ᵊl\ *adj* — **or·ga·ni·za·tion·al·ly** \-ē\ *adv*

organization man *n* : a man who subordinates individualism to conformity with the standards and requirements of an organization

or·ga·nize \'ȯr-gə-,nīz\ *vb* 1 : to develop an organic structure : undergo or cause to undergo organization 2 : to arrange to form into a complete and functioning whole 3 a : to set up an administrative structure for b : to persuade to associate in an organization; *esp* : UNIONIZE 4 : to arrange by systematic planning and united effort 5 : to form or join in an organization; *esp* : to join in a union

or·ga·niz·er \-,nī-zər\ *n* : one that organizes

or·gan·za \ȯr-'gan-zə\ *n* : a sheer dress fabric resembling organdy and usu. made of silk, rayon, or nylon

or·gasm \'ȯr-,gaz-əm\ *n* : the climax of sexual excitement in coitus — **or·gas·mic** \ȯr-'gaz-mik\ *or* **or·gas·tic** \-'gas-tik\ *adj*

or·gi·as·tic \,ȯr-jē-'as-tik\ *adj* : of, relating to, or marked by orgies — **or·gi·as·ti·cal·ly** \-ti-k(ə-)lē\ *adv*

or·gu·lous \'ȯr-gyə-ləs\ *adj* : PROUD, HAUGHTY

or·gy \'ȯr-jē\ *n, pl* **orgies** 1 : drunken revelry 2 : an excessive indulgence in an activity

ori·el \'ōr-ē-əl\ *n* : a large bay window projecting from a wall and supported by a corbel or bracket

[1]**ori·ent** \'ōr-ē-ənt, -ē-,ent\ *adj* : LUSTROUS, SPARKLING

[2]**ori·ent** \-,ent\ *vt* 1 : to set or arrange in a definite position esp. in relation to the points of the compass 2 a : to set right by adjusting to facts or principles b : to acquaint with an existing situation or environment

Ori·ent \-ənt, -,ent\ *n* : EAST; *esp* : the countries of eastern Asia

ori·en·tal \,ōr-ē-'ent-ᵊl\ *adj, often cap* : of or relating to the Orient — **ori·en·tal·ly** \-ᵊl-ē\ *adv*

ori·en·tate \'ōr-ē-ən-,tāt, -ē-,en-\ *vb* 1 : ORIENT 2 : to face east

ori·en·ta·tion \,ōr-ē-ən-'tā-shən, -ē-,en-\ *n* : the act or process of orienting : the state of being oriented — **ori·en·ta·tion·al** \-shnəl, -shən-ᵊl\ *adj*

or·i·fice \'ȯr-ə-fəs\ *n* : an opening (as a vent, mouth, hole, or aperture) through which something may pass — **or·i·fi·cial** \,ȯr-ə-'fish-əl\ *adj*

ori·flamme \'ȯr-ə-,flam\ *n* : a brightly colored banner used as a standard or ensign in battle

ori·ga·mi \,ȯr-ə-'gäm-ē\ *n* : the art or process of Japanese paper folding

or·i·gin \'ȯr-ə-jən\ *n* 1 : ANCESTRY, PARENTAGE 2 a : rise, beginning, or derivation from a source b : primary source or cause

[1]**orig·i·nal** \ə-'rij-ən-ᵊl, -'rij-nəl\ *n* 1 a : that from which a copy, reproduction, or translation is made b : a work composed firsthand 2 : a person who is original in thought or action

[2]**original** *adj* 1 : of or relating to the origin or beginning : FIRST, EARLIEST 2 a : having spontaneous origin : not copied, reproduced, or translated b : constituting that from which a copy, reproduction, or translation is made 3 : independent and creative in thought or action : INVENTIVE — **orig·i·nal·ly** \-ē\ *adv*

orig·i·nal·i·ty \ə-,rij-ə-'nal-ət-ē\ *n* 1 : the quality or state of being original : FRESHNESS, NOVELTY 2 : the power or ability to think, to act, or to do something in ways that are new

orig·i·nate \ə-'rij-ə-,nāt\ *vb* 1 : to bring into existence : cause to be : give rise to : INITIATE 2 : to take or have origin : come into existence — **orig·i·na·tion** \ə-,rij-ə-'nā-shən\ *n* — **orig·i·na·tor** \ə-'rij-ə-,nāt-ər\ *n*

orig·i·na·tive \ə-ˈrij-ə-ˌnāt-iv\ *adj* : having ability to originate : CREATIVE — **orig·i·na·tive·ly** *adv*
ori·ole \ˈōr-ē-ˌōl\ *n* **1** : any of a family of usu. brightly colored Old World passerine birds related to the crows **2** : any of a family of New World passerine birds of which the males are usu. black and yellow or orange and the females chiefly greenish or yellowish
or·i·son \ˈȯr-ə-sən\ *n* : PRAYER
or·mo·lu \ˈȯr-mə-ˌlü\ *n* : a brass made to imitate gold and used for decorative purposes
[1]**or·na·ment** \ˈȯr-nə-mənt\ *n* **1** : something that adorns or adds beauty : DECORATION, EMBELLISHMENT **2** : the act of adorning : addition or inclusion of something that beautifies : ORNAMENTATION
[2]**or·na·ment** \-ˌment\ *vt* : to provide with ornament : EMBELLISH, ADORN, DECORATE
[1]**or·na·men·tal** \ˌȯr-nə-ˈment-ᵊl\ *adj* : of, relating to, or serving as ornament — **or·na·men·tal·ly** \-ᵊl-ē\ *adv*
[2]**ornamental** *n* : a decorative object; *esp* : a plant cultivated for its beauty rather than for use
or·na·men·ta·tion \ˌȯr-nə-mən-ˈtā-shən, -ˌmen-\ *n* **1** : the act or process of ornamenting : the state of being ornamented **2** : a decorative device; *also* : ORNAMENTS
or·nate \ȯr-ˈnāt\ *adj* **1** : marked by elaborate rhetoric or florid style **2** : elaborately or excessively decorated — **or·nate·ly** *adv* — **or·nate·ness** *n*
or·nery \ˈȯrn-(ə-)rē, ˈän-\ *adj* : having an irritable disposition : CANTANKEROUS — **or·ner·i·ness** *n*
or·ni·thol·o·gy \ˌȯr-nə-ˈthäl-ə-jē\ *n* : a branch of zoology dealing with birds — **or·ni·tho·log·i·cal** \(ˌ)ȯr-ˌnith-ə-ˈläj-i-kəl\ *or* **or·ni·tho·log·ic** \-ˈläj-ik\ *adj* — **or·ni·tho·log·i·cal·ly** \-i-k(ə-)lē\ *adv* — **or·ni·thol·o·gist** \ˌȯr-nə-ˈthäl-ə-jəst\ *n*
oro·tund \ˈȯr-ə-ˌtənd\ *adj* **1** : marked by fullness, strength, and clarity of sound : SONOROUS **2** : POMPOUS, BOMBASTIC — **oro·tun·di·ty** \ˌȯr-ə-ˈtən-dət-ē\ *n*
[1]**or·phan** \ˈȯr-fən\ *n* **1** : a child deprived by death of one or usu. both parents **2** : a motherless young animal — **orphan** *adj* — **or·phan·hood** \-ˌhu̇d\ *n*
[2]**orphan** *vt* **or·phaned**; **or·phan·ing** \ˈȯrf-(ə-)niŋ\ : to cause to become an orphan : deprive of parents
or·phan·age \ˈȯrf-(ə-)nij\ *n* : an institution for the care of orphans
or·ris \ˈȯr-əs\ *n* : a European iris with a fragrant rootstock used esp. in perfume and sachet powder; *also* : its rootstock
or·ris·root \-ˌrüt, -ˌru̇t\ *n* : the rootstock of an orris
orth·odon·tia \ˌȯr-thə-ˈdän-ch(ē-)ə\ *n* : ORTHODONTICS
orth·odon·tics \-ˈdänt-iks\ *n* : a branch of dentistry dealing with irregularities of the teeth and their correction — **orth·odon·tic** \-ˈdänt-ik\ *adj* — **orth·odon·tist** \-ˈdänt-əst\ *n*
or·tho·dox \ˈȯr-thə-ˌdäks\ *adj* **1** : holding established beliefs esp. in religion **2** : approved as measuring up to some standard : USUAL, CONVENTIONAL
or·tho·doxy \-ˌdäk-sē\ *n, pl* **-dox·ies** **1** : the quality or state of being orthodox **2** : an orthodox belief or practice
or·tho·epy \ˈȯr-thə-ˌwep-ē, ȯr-ˈthō-ə-pē\ *n* : the customary pronunciation of a language — **or·tho·ep·ic** \ˌȯr-thə-ˈwep-ik\ *adj* — **or·tho·ep·i·cal·ly** \-ˈwep-i-k(ə-)lē\ *adv* — **or·tho·ep·ist** \ˈȯr-thə-ˌwep-əst, ȯr-ˈthō-ə-pəst\ *n*
or·thog·ra·phy \ȯr-ˈthäg-rə-fē\ *n, pl* **-phies** **1 a** : the writing of words with the proper letters according to standard usage **b** : a manner of representing the sounds of a language by written or printed symbols **2** : the study of letters and spelling — **or·tho·graph·ic** \ˌȯr-thə-ˈgraf-ik\ *or* **or·tho·graph·i·cal** \-ˈgraf-i-kəl\ *adj*
or·tho·pe·dic \ˌȯr-thə-ˈpēd-ik\ *adj* **1** : of or relating to orthopedics **2** : marked by deformities or crippling — **or·tho·pe·di·cal·ly** \-ˈpēd-i-k(ə-)lē\ *adv*
or·tho·pe·dics \-ˈpēd-iks\ *n* : the correction or prevention of skeletal deformities — **or·tho·pe·dist** \-ˈpēd-əst\ *n*
or·to·lan \ˈȯrt-ᵊl-ən\ *n* **1** : a European bunting valued as a table delicacy **2** : BOBOLINK
Os·car \ˈäs-kər\ *n* : a golden statuette awarded for achievement in motion pictures; *also* : any similar award
os·cil·late \ˈäs-ə-ˌlāt\ *vi* **1 a** : to swing backward and forward like a pendulum : VIBRATE **b** : to move or travel back and forth between two points **2** : to vary between opposing beliefs, feelings, or theories **3** : to vary above and below a mean value **4** : to increase and decrease in magnitude or reverse direction periodically — **os·cil·la·to·ry** \ä-ˈsil-ə-ˌtōr-ē\ *adj*
os·cil·la·tion \ˌäs-ə-ˈlā-shən\ *n* **1** : the act or fact of oscillating : VIBRATION **2** : VARIATION, FLUCTUATION **3** : a flow of electricity changing periodically from a maximum to a minimum; *esp* : a flow periodically changing direction **4** : a single swing or change (as of an oscillating body) from one extreme limit to the other
os·cil·la·tor \ˈäs-ə-ˌlāt-ər\ *n* : one that oscillates
os·cil·la·to·ry \ä-ˈsil-ə-ˌtōr-ē\ *adj* : characterized by oscillation
os·cil·lo·scope \ä-ˈsil-ə-ˌskōp\ *n* : an instrument in which the variations in a fluctuating electrical quantity appear temporarily as visible waves of light
os·cu·late \ˈäs-kyə-ˌlāt\ *vb* : KISS — **os·cu·la·tion** \ˌäs-kyə-ˈlā-shən\ *n* — **os·cu·la·to·ry** \ˈäs-kyə-lə-ˌtōr-ē\ *adj*
osier \ˈō-zhər\ *n* **1** : any of various willows with pliable twigs used esp. in making baskets and furniture; *also* : a twig from an osier — **osier** *adj*
os·mi·um \ˈäz-mē-əm\ *n* : a hard brittle blue-gray or blue-black metallic element with a high melting point that is the heaviest metal known and that is used esp. as a catalyst and in hard alloys
os·mose \ˈäs-ˌmōs, ˈäz-\ *vb* **1** : to subject to osmosis **2** : to diffuse by osmosis
os·mo·sis \äs-ˈmō-səs, äz-\ *n* **1** : a diffusion through a partially permeable membrane typically separating a solvent and a solution that tends to equalize their concentrations **2** : a process of absorption or diffusion suggestive of the flow of osmotic action — **os·mot·ic** \-ˈmät-ik\ *adj*
os·prey \ˈäs-prē\ *n, pl* **ospreys** : a large brown and white hawk that feeds on fish
os·si·fi·ca·tion \ˌäs-ə-fə-ˈkā-shən\ *n* **1 a** : formation of or conversion into bone or a bony substance **b** : an area of ossified tissue **2** : a state of being callous or conventional in outlook — **os·sif·i·ca·to·ry** \ä-ˈsif-i-kə-ˌtōr-ē\ *adj*
os·si·fy \ˈäs-ə-ˌfī\ *vb* **-fied**; **-fy·ing** **1** : to become or change into bone or bony tissue **2** : to become or make callous or conventional
os·su·ary \ˈäsh-ə-ˌwer-ē\ *n, pl* **-ar·ies** : a depository for the bones of the dead
os·ten·si·ble \ä-ˈsten(t)-sə-bəl\ *adj* : open to view : shown outwardly : DECLARED, PROFESSED, APPARENT — **os·ten·si·bly** \-blē\ *adv*
os·ten·ta·tion \ˌäs-tən-ˈtā-shən\ *n* : pretentious or excessive display : unnecessary show
os·ten·ta·tious \-shəs\ *adj* : marked by or fond of unnecessary display — **os·ten·ta·tious·ly** *adv* — **os·ten·ta·tious·ness** *n*
os·te·o·path \ˈäs-tē-ə-ˌpath\ *n* : a practitioner of osteopathy
os·te·op·a·thy \ˌäs-tē-ˈäp-ə-thē\ *n* : a system of treating diseases that places emphasis on manipulation esp. of bones but does not exclude other treatment (as the use of medicine and surgery) — **os·te·o·path·ic** \ˌäs-tē-ə-ˈpath-ik\ *adj* — **os·te·o·path·i·cal·ly** \-ˈpath-i-k(ə-)lē\ *adv*
os·tra·cism \ˈäs-trə-ˌsiz-əm\ *n* : exclusion by general consent from common privileges or social acceptance
os·tra·cize \-ˌsīz\ *vt* **1** : to exile by ostracism **2** : to exclude from a group by common consent
os·trich \ˈäs-trich, ˈȯs-\ *n* : a swift-footed 2-toed flightless bird

of Africa and Arabia with valuable wing and tail plumes that is the largest of existing birds

[1]**oth·er** \'əth-ər\ *adj* **1 a :** being the one (as of two or more) left **b :** being the ones distinct from those first mentioned **c :** SECOND **2 :** not the same **:** DIFFERENT **3 :** ADDITIONAL **4 :** recently past

[2]**other** *pron* **1 :** remaining one **:** remaining ones **2 :** a different or additional one

[3]**other** *adv* **:** OTHERWISE

oth·er·wise \-ˌwīz\ *adv* **1 :** in a different way **:** DIFFERENTLY **2 :** in different circumstances **3 :** in other respects — **otherwise** *adj*

oth·er·world \'əth-ər-ˌwərld\ *n* **:** a world beyond death or beyond present reality

oth·er·world·ly \-ˌwərl-(d)lē\ *adj* **1 a :** of or relating to a world other than the actual world **b :** concerned with or devoted to preparing for a world to come **2 :** devoted to highly intellectual, imaginative, or idealistic pursuits — **oth·er·world·li·ness** *n*

oti·ose \'ō-shē-ˌōs, 'ōt-ē-\ *adj* **1 :** being at leisure **:** IDLE **2 :** STERILE **3 :** USELESS, FUNCTIONLESS

ot·ter \'ät-ər\ *n, pl* **otter** *or* **otters** **1 :** any of several aquatic fish-eating mammals that are related to the weasels and minks and that have webbed and clawed feet and dark brown fur **2 :** the fur or pelt of an otter

ot·to·man \'ät-ə-mən\ *n, pl* **-mans :** an upholstered often overstuffed seat or couch usu. without a back; *also* **:** an overstuffed footstool

ou·bli·ette \ˌü-blē-'et\ *n* **:** a dungeon with an opening only at the top

ouch \'auch\ *interj* — used to express sudden pain or displeasure

ought \'ot\ *auxiliary verb* — used to express moral obligation, advisability, natural expectation, or logical consequence

ounce \'aun(t)s\ *n* **1 :** a unit of weight equal to 1/12 pound troy **2 :** a unit of weight equal to 1/16 pound avoirdupois

our \är, (')au̇(ə)r\ *adj* **:** of or relating to us or ourselves or ourself esp. as possessors or possessor, agents or agent, or objects or object of an action

ours \(')au̇(ə)rz, ärz\ *pron* **:** our one **:** our ones — used without a following noun as a pronoun equivalent in meaning to the adjective *our*

our·self \är-'self, au̇(ə)r-\ *pron* **:** MYSELF — used (as by a sovereign or writer) to refer to the single-person subject when *we* is used instead of *I*

our·selves \-'selvz\ *pron* **1 :** those identical ones that are we — used reflexively, for emphasis, or in absolute constructions **2 :** our normal, healthy, or sane condition or selves

oust \'au̇st\ *vt* **:** to force or drive out (as from office or from possession of something) **:** EXPEL

oust·er \'au̇s-tər\ *n* **:** the act or an instance of ousting **:** EXPULSION

[1]**out** \'au̇t\ *adv* **1 :** in a direction away from the inside or the center **2 :** away from home, business, or usual or proper place **3 :** into a state of loss or deprivation **4 :** beyond control, possession, or occupation **5 :** into a state of vexation or disagreement **6 a :** beyond the limits of existence, continuance, or supply **b :** to extinction, exhaustion, or completion **7 a :** in or into the open **b :** ALOUD **8** — used as an intensive with numerous verbs **9 a :** so as to retire a batter or base runner **b :** so as to be retired

[2]**out** *vi* **:** to become known

[3]**out** *adj* **1 a :** not being in power **b :** not successful in reaching base **2 :** directed outward or serving to direct something outward **:** OUTGOING

[4]**out** \(')au̇t\ *prep* **1 :** out through **2 :** outward along or on

[5]**out** \'au̇t\ *n* **1 :** one who is out of power **2 a :** the retiring of a batter or base runner in baseball **b :** a player so retired **3 :** a way of escaping from an embarrassing situation or a difficulty

out–and–out \ˌau̇t-ᵊn-'(d)au̇t\ *adj* **1 :** OPEN, UNDISGUISED **2 :** COMPLETE, THOROUGHGOING

out·bal·ance \(')au̇t-'bal-ən(t)s\ *vt* **:** OUTWEIGH

out·bid \-'bid\ *vt* **-bid**; **-bid·ding :** to make a higher bid than

[1]**out·board** \'au̇t-ˌbōrd\ *adj* **1 :** situated outboard **2 :** having, using, or limited to the use of an outboard motor

[2]**outboard** *adv* **1 :** outside the line of a ship's hull **:** away from the center line of a ship **2 :** in a position closer or closest to either of the wing tips of an airplane

outboard motor *n* **:** a small internal-combustion engine with propeller attached for mounting at the stern of a small boat

out·bound \'au̇t-ˌbau̇nd\ *adj* **:** outward bound

out·brave \(')au̇t-'brāv\ *vt* **:** to face or resist defiantly

out·break \'au̇t-ˌbrāk\ *n* **1 :** a sudden or violent breaking out **:** a sudden increase of activity or currency **2 :** something that breaks out: as **a :** EPIDEMIC **b :** INSURRECTION, REVOLT

out·build·ing \'au̇t-ˌbil-diŋ\ *n* **:** a building separate from and smaller than the main one

out·burst \-ˌbərst\ *n* **1 :** ERUPTION; *esp* **:** a violent expression of feeling **2 :** a surge of activity or growth

out·cast \-ˌkast\ *n* **:** one who is cast out by society **:** PARIAH — **outcast** *adj*

out·caste \-ˌkast\ *n* **:** a Hindu who has been ejected from his caste for violation of its customs or rules; *also* **:** one who has no caste

out·class \(')au̇t-'klas\ *vt* **:** to excel or surpass so decisively as to appear of a higher class

out·come \'au̇t-ˌkəm\ *n* **:** final consequence **:** RESULT

[1]**out·crop** \'au̇t-ˌkräp\ *n* **1 :** a coming out of bedrock or of an unconsolidated deposit to the surface of the ground **2 :** the part of a rock formation that appears at the surface of the ground

[2]**out·crop** \'au̇t-'kräp\ *vi* **:** to come to the surface **:** APPEAR

out·cry \'au̇t-ˌkrī\ *n* **:** a loud cry **:** CLAMOR

out·dat·ed \(')au̇t-'dāt-əd\ *adj* **:** OBSOLETE

out·dis·tance \(')au̇t-'dis-tən(t)s\ *vt* **:** to go far ahead of (as in a race) **:** OUTSTRIP

out·do \(')au̇t-'dü\ *vt* **-did** \-'did\; **-done** \-'dən\; **-do·ing** \-'dü-iŋ\ **:** to go beyond in action or performance **:** EXCEL, SURPASS

out·door \ˌau̇t-ˌdōr\ *adj* **1 :** of or relating to the outdoors **2 :** performed outdoors **3 :** not enclosed **:** having no roof

[1]**out·doors** \(')au̇t-'dō(ə)rz\ *adv* **:** outside a building **:** in or into the open air

[2]**outdoors** *n* **1 :** the open air **2 :** the world away from human habitations

out·er \'au̇t-ər\ *adj* **1 :** EXTERNAL, OBJECTIVE **2 a :** situated farther out **b :** being away from a center

out·er·most \-ˌmōst\ *adj* **:** farthest out

outer space *n* **:** SPACE; *esp* **:** the region beyond the solar system

out·face \(')au̇t-'fās\ *vt* **1 :** to stare down **2 :** to confront unflinchingly **:** DEFY

out·fall \'au̇t-ˌfȯl\ *n* **:** the outlet of a river, stream, lake, drain, or sewer

out·field \-ˌfēld\ *n* **:** the part of a baseball field beyond the infield and between the foul lines — **out·field·er** *n*

out·fight \(')au̇t-'fīt\ *vt* **-fought** \-'fȯt\; **-fight·ing :** to surpass in fighting **:** DEFEAT

[1]**out·fit** \'au̇t-ˌfit\ *n* **1 :** the articles forming the equipment or apparel for some purpose or occasion **2 :** a group of persons working together or associated in the same undertaking

[2]**outfit** *vt* **1 :** to furnish with an outfit **:** EQUIP **2 :** SUPPLY — **out·fit·ter** *n*

out·flank \(')au̇t-'flaŋk\ *vt* **:** to get around the flank of (an opposing force)

out·foot \(')au̇t-'fu̇t\ *vt* **:** to outdo in speed **:** OUTSTRIP

out·fox \(')au̇t-'fäks\ *vt* **:** OUTSMART

out·gen·er·al \-'jen-(ə-)rəl\ *vt* **-gen·er·aled** *or* **-gen·er·alled**;

-gen·er·al·ing *or* **-gen·er·al·ling** : to surpass in generalship : OUTMANEUVER
out·go \ˈau̇t-ˌgō\ *n, pl* **outgoes** : EXPENDITURE, OUTLAY
out·go·ing \ˈau̇t-ˌgō-iŋ\ *adj* **1 a** : going out : DEPARTING **b** : retiring or withdrawing from a place or position **2** : FRIENDLY, RESPONSIVE
out·grow \(ˈ)au̇t-ˈgrō\ *vt* **-grew** \-ˈgrü\; **-grown** \-ˈgrōn\; **-grow·ing** **1** : to grow faster than **2** : to grow too large or too mature for
out·growth \ˈau̇t-ˌgrōth\ *n* **1** : a product of growing out : PROCESS 4, OFFSHOOT **2** : CONSEQUENCE, BY-PRODUCT
out·guess \(ˈ)au̇t-ˈges\ *vt* : ANTICIPATE, OUTWIT
out·house \ˈau̇t-ˌhau̇s\ *n* : OUTBUILDING; *esp* : an outdoor toilet
out·ing \ˈau̇t-iŋ\ *n* **1** : an excursion usu. with a picnic **2** : a brief stay or trip in the open
out·land·er \ˈau̇t-ˌlan-dər\ *n* : FOREIGNER, ALIEN, STRANGER
out·land·ish \(ˈ)au̇t-ˈlan-dish\ *adj* **1** : of or relating to another country **2** : of foreign appearance or manner : BIZARRE **3** : remote from civilization — **out·land·ish·ly** *adv* — **out·land·ish·ness** *n*
out·last \(ˈ)au̇t-ˈlast\ *vt* : to last longer than : SURVIVE
[1]**out·law** \ˈau̇t-ˌlȯ\ *n* **1** : a person excluded from the benefit or protection of the law **2 a** : a lawless person or a fugitive from the law **b** : a person or organization under a ban or disability — **outlaw** *adj*
[2]**outlaw** *vt* **1 a** : to deprive of the benefit and protection of law **b** : to make illegal **2** : to place under a ban or disability — **out·law·ry** \ˈau̇t-ˌlȯ-rē\ *n*
out·lay \ˈau̇t-ˌlā\ *n* **1** : the act of laying out or spending **2** : EXPENDITURE, PAYMENT
out·let \ˈau̇t-ˌlet, -lət\ *n* **1** : a place or opening through which something is let out : EXIT, VENT **2** : a means of release or satisfaction for an emotion or impulse **3** : a market for a product : an agency (as a store or a dealer) through which a product is marketed
[1]**out·line** \ˈau̇t-ˌlīn\ *n* **1** : a line that traces or forms the outer limits of an object or figure and shows its shape **2** : a drawing or picture giving only the outlines of something **3** : SUMMARY, SYNOPSIS **4** : a condensed treatment of a subject : DIGEST
[2]**outline** *vt* **1** : to draw the outline of **2** : to indicate the principal features or different parts of
out·live \(ˈ)au̇t-ˈliv\ *vt* : to live longer than : SURVIVE
out·look \ˈau̇t-ˌlu̇k\ *n* **1 a** : a place offering a view **b** : a view from a particular place **2** : STANDPOINT **3** : the prospect for the future
out·ly·ing \ˈau̇t-ˌlī-iŋ\ *adj* : remote from a center or main body
out·ma·neu·ver \ˌau̇t-mə-ˈn(y)ü-vər\ *vt* **1** : to defeat by more skillful maneuvering **2** : to surpass in maneuvering
out·match \(ˈ)au̇t-ˈmach\ *vt* : to prove superior to : OUTDO
out·mod·ed \(ˈ)au̇t-ˈmōd-əd\ *adj* **1** : not in style **2** : no longer acceptable or usable
out·most \ˈau̇t-ˌmōst\ *adj* : farthest out : OUTERMOST
out·num·ber \(ˈ)au̇t-ˈnəm-bər\ *vt* : to exceed in number
out of *prep* **1 a** (1) : from within to the outside of (2) — used as a function word to indicate a change in quality, state, or form **b** (1) : beyond the range or limits of (2) : from among **2** : in or into a state of deprivation or lack of **3** : because of : FROM **4** — used as a function word to indicate the constituent material, basis, or source
out–of–bounds \ˌau̇t-ə(v)-ˈbau̇n(d)z\ *adv* (*or adj*) : outside the prescribed area of play
out–of–date \ˌau̇t-ə(v)-ˈdāt\ *adj* : OUTMODED, OBSOLETE
out–of–door \ˌau̇t-ə(v)-ˈdō(ə)r\ *or* **out–of–doors** \-ˈdō(ə)rz\ *adj* : OUTDOOR
out–of–doors *n* : OUTDOORS
out–of–the–way \ˌau̇t-ə(v)-t͟hə-ˈwā\ *adj* **1** : being off the beaten track **2** : not commonly found or met : UNUSUAL
out·pa·tient \ˈau̇t-ˌpā-shənt\ *n* : a patient not an inmate of a hospital who visits it for diagnosis or treatment — **outpatient** *adj*
out·play \(ˈ)au̇t-ˈplā\ *vt* : to play more skillfully than : EXCEL
out·point \-ˈpȯint\ *vt* : to win more points than
out·post \ˈau̇t-ˌpōst\ *n* **1** : a soldier or group of soldiers stationed at some distance from a military force or a camp as a guard against enemy attack **2** : the position occupied by an outpost **3** : a settlement on a frontier; *also* : an outlying settlement
out·pour·ing \ˈau̇t-ˌpōr-iŋ\ *n* **1** : something that pours out or is poured out : OUTFLOW **2** : OUTBURST
out·put \-ˌpu̇t\ *n* : the amount produced or able to be produced usu. in a stated time by a man, machine, factory, or industry : PRODUCTION, YIELD
[1]**out·rage** \ˈau̇t-ˌrāj\ *n* **1** : an act of violence or brutality **2** : INJURY, INSULT
[2]**outrage** *vt* **1 a** : RAPE **b** : to subject to violent injury or gross insult **2** : to arouse anger or extreme resentment in
out·ra·geous \au̇t-ˈrā-jəs\ *adj* : being beyond all bounds of decency or justice : extremely offensive, insulting, or shameful : SHOCKING — **out·ra·geous·ly** *adv* — **out·ra·geous·ness** *n*
out·rank \(ˈ)au̇t-ˈraŋk\ *vt* : to rank higher than : exceed in importance
ou·tré \ü-ˈtrā\ *adj* : violating convention or propriety : BIZARRE
out·reach \(ˈ)au̇t-ˈrēch\ *vb* **1** : to surpass in reach : EXCEED **2** : to get the better of by trickery : OVERREACH
out·ride \(ˈ)au̇t-ˈrīd\ *vt* **-rode** \-ˈrōd\; **-rid·den** \-ˈrid-ᵊn\; **-rid·ing** \-ˈrīd-iŋ\ : to ride better, faster, or farther than : OUTSTRIP
out·rid·er \ˈau̇t-ˌrīd-ər\ *n* **1** : a mounted attendant **2** : FORERUNNER, HARBINGER
out·rig·ger \ˈau̇t-ˌrig-ər\ *n* **1 a** : a projecting frame on a float attached to the side of a canoe or boat to prevent upsetting **b** : a projecting support for an oarlock; *also* : a boat so equipped **2** : a projecting frame to support the elevator or tail planes of an airplane or the rotor of a helicopter

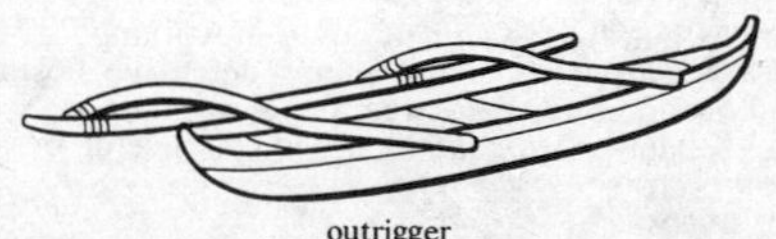
outrigger

[1]**out·right** \(ˈ)au̇t-ˈrīt\ *adv* **1 a** : in entirety : COMPLETELY **b** : UNRESERVEDLY **2** : on the spot : INSTANTANEOUSLY
[2]**out·right** \ˈau̇t-ˌrīt\ *adj* **1** : going to the full extent : THOROUGHGOING **2** : given without reservation
out·run \(ˈ)au̇t-ˈrən\ *vt* **-ran** \-ˈran\; **-run**; **-run·ning** : to run faster than; *also* : EXCEED
out·sell \-ˈsel\ *vt* **-sold** \-ˈsōld\; **-sell·ing** **1** : to exceed in sales **2** : to surpass in selling
out·set \ˈau̇t-ˌset\ *n* : BEGINNING, START
out·shine \(ˈ)au̇t-ˈshīn\ *vt* **-shone** \-ˈshōn\; **-shin·ing** **1 a** : to shine brighter than **b** : to exceed in splendor or showiness **2** : OUTDO, SURPASS
out·shoot \-ˈshüt\ *vt* **-shot** \-ˈshät\; **-shoot·ing** **1** : to surpass in shooting or making shots **2** : to shoot or go beyond
[1]**out·side** \(ˈ)au̇t-ˈsīd, ˈau̇t-ˌ\ *n* **1** : a place or region beyond an enclosure or boundary **2** : an outer side or surface **3** : the utmost limit or extent
[2]**outside** *adj* **1** : of, relating to, or being on or toward the outer side or surface **2 a** : situated or performed outside a particular place **b** : connected with or giving access to the outside **3** : MAXIMUM **4 a** : not included or originating in a particular group or organization **b** : not belonging to one's regular occupation or duties **5** : barely possible : REMOTE

³outside *adv* : on or to the outside : OUTDOORS
⁴outside *prep* **1** : on or to the outside of **2** : beyond the limits of
outside of *prep* **1** : OUTSIDE **2** : BESIDES
out·sid·er \(ˈ)au̇t-ˈsīd-ər\ *n* : a person who does not belong to a particular group
out·sit \-ˈsit\ *vt* **-sat** \-ˈsat\; **-sit·ting** : to remain sitting or in session longer than or beyond the time of
¹out·size \ˈau̇t-ˌsīz\ *n* : an unusual size; *esp* : a size larger than the standard
²outsize *adj* : unusually large or heavy
out·skirts \ˈau̇t-ˌskərts\ *n pl* : the outlying parts of a place or town : BORDERS
out·smart \(ˈ)au̇t-ˈsmärt\ *vt* : to get the better of; *esp* : OUTWIT
out·soar \-ˈsō(ə)r\ *vt* : to soar beyond or above
out·spo·ken \au̇t-ˈspō-kən\ *adj* : direct and open in speech or expression : FRANK — **out·spo·ken·ness** *n*
out·spread \au̇t-ˈspred\ *vt* **-spread**; **-spread·ing** : to spread out : EXTEND — **out·spread** \ˈau̇t-ˌspred\ *adj*
out·stand·ing \au̇t-ˈstan-diŋ\ *adj* **1 a** : UNPAID **b** : CONTINUING, UNRESOLVED **c** : publicly issued and sold **2 a** : standing out from a group : CONSPICUOUS **b** : DISTINGUISHED, EMINENT — **out·stand·ing·ly** *adv*
out·sta·tion \ˈau̇t-ˌstā-shən\ *n* : a remote or outlying station
out·stay \(ˈ)au̇t-ˈstā\ *vt* **1** : to stay beyond or longer than **2** : to surpass in staying power
out·stretch \au̇t-ˈstrech\ *vt* : to stretch out : EXTEND
out·strip \au̇t-ˈstrip\ *vt* **1** : to go faster or farther than **2 a** : EXCEL **b** : EXCEED
¹out·ward \ˈau̇t-wərd\ *adj* **1** : moving or directed toward the outside or away from a center **2** : showing outwardly
²outward *or* **out·wards** \-wərdz\ *adv* : toward the outside
out·ward·ly \ˈau̇t-wərd-lē\ *adv* : on the outside : in outward appearance : SUPERFICIALLY
out·wear \(ˈ)au̇t-ˈwa(ə)r\ *vt* **-wore** \-ˈwō(ə)r\; **-worn** \-ˈwōrn\; **-wear·ing** : to wear or last longer than
out·weigh \-ˈwā\ *vt* : to exceed in weight, value, or importance
out·wit \au̇t-ˈwit\ *vt* : to get the better of by superior cleverness : OUTSMART
¹out·work \(ˈ)au̇t-ˈwərk\ *vt* : to outdo in working
²out·work \ˈau̇t-ˌwərk\ *n* : a minor defensive position constructed outside a fortified area
out·worn \(ˈ)au̇t-ˈwōrn\ *adj* : no longer useful or accepted : OUT-OF-DATE
ova *pl of* OVUM
¹oval \ˈō-vəl\ *adj* : having the shape of an egg; *also* : broadly elliptical
²oval *n* : an oval figure or object
ova·ry \ˈōv-(ə-)rē\ *n, pl* **-ries** **1** : the typically paired essential female reproductive organ that produces eggs and in vertebrates female sex hormones **2** : the enlarged rounded part of the pistil or gynoecium of a flowering plant that bears the ovules and consists of one or more carpels — **ovar·i·an** \ō-ˈvar-ē-ən\ *adj*
ova·tion \ō-ˈvā-shən\ *n* **1** : a ceremony honoring a Roman general who had won a victory less important than one for which a triumph was granted **2** : an expression or demonstration of popular acclaim
ov·en \ˈəv-ən\ *n* : a heated chamber (as in a stove) for baking, heating, or drying
ov·en·bird \-ˌbərd\ *n* : an American warbler that builds a dome-shaped nest on the ground
¹over \ˈō-vər\ *adv* **1 a** : across a barrier or intervening space **b** : in a direction down or forward and down **c** : across the brim **d** : so as to bring the underside up **e** : from a vertical to a prone or inclined position **f** : from one person or side to another **2 a** : ACROSS **b** : to agreement or concord **3** : beyond some quantity, limit, or norm often by a specified amount or to a specified degree; *also* : in or to excess : EXCESSIVELY **4** : so as to cover the whole surface **5** : at an end **6 a** : THROUGH; *also* : THOROUGHLY **b** : once more : AGAIN
²over *prep* **1** : higher than : ABOVE **2 a** : having authority, power, or jurisdiction in regard to **b** : having superiority, advantage, or preference in comparison to **3** : more than **4 a** : upon or down upon esp. so as to cover **b** : throughout the area of **c** : along the length of **d** : through a review or examination of **5 a** : moving above and across **b** : to or on the other side of **c** : off or down from **6** : THROUGHOUT, DURING **7 a** — used as a function word to indicate an object of concern or an activity **b** : on account of **8** : by or through the medium of
³over *adj* **1** : COVERING, OUTER **2 a** : EXCESSIVE **b** : having or showing an excess or surplus usu. of a specified amount or degree
over- *prefix* **1** : so as to exceed or surpass **2** : excessive

overabundance	**overenthusiastic**	**overprice**
overabundant	**overestimate**	**overproduce**
overactive	**overestimation**	**overproduction**
overambitious	**overexcite**	**overproportion**
overanxious	**overexert**	**overprotect**
overbid	**overexertion**	**overprotection**
overbold	**overextend**	**overprotective**
overbuild	**overfatigued**	**overproud**
overbuy	**overfeed**	**overrate**
overcapitalize	**overfill**	**overrefinement**
overcareful	**overgenerous**	**overripe**
overcautious	**overgraze**	**oversell**
overcompensation	**overhasty**	**oversensitive**
overcompensatory	**overheat**	**oversensitiveness**
overconfidence	**overindulge**	**oversimplification**
overconfident	**overindulgence**	**oversimplify**
overconscientious	**overindulgent**	**overspecialization**
overcooked	**overissue**	**overspecialize**
overcritical	**overlarge**	**overspend**
overcrowd	**overlearn**	**overstock**
overdecorated	**overliberal**	**overstrict**
overdevelop	**overload**	**oversubtle**
overdevelopment	**overlong**	**oversupply**
overdosage	**overman**	**overtax**
overdose	**overmodest**	**overtired**
overdress	**overnice**	**overtrain**
overeager	**overpay**	**overuse**
overeat	**overpopulate**	**overvalue**
overemphasis	**overpopulation**	**overzealous**
overemphasize	**overpraise**	

over·act \ˌō-vər-ˈakt\ *vb* **1** : to exaggerate or overdo in acting **2** : to act more than is necessary — **over·ac·tion** \-ˈak-shən\ *n*
over against *prep* : opposed to : contrasted with
¹over·age \ˌō-vər-ˈāj\ *adj* **1** : too old to be useful **2** : older than is normal for one's position, function, or grade
²over·age \ˈōv-(ə-)rij\ *n* : SURPLUS, EXCESS
¹over·all \ˌō-vər-ˈȯl\ *adv* : as a whole : GENERALLY
²overall *adj* : including everything
over·alls \ˈō-vər-ˌȯlz\ *n pl* : loose trousers made of strong material usu. with a bib and shoulder straps and worn esp. by workmen
over·arm \ˈō-vər-ˌärm\ *adj* : done with the arm raised above the shoulder
over·awe \ˌō-vər-ˈȯ\ *vt* : to restrain or subdue by awe
over·bal·ance \-ˈbal-ən(t)s\ *vb* **1** : to have greater weight or greater importance than : OUTWEIGH **2** : to lose or cause to lose balance
over·bear \-ˈba(ə)r\ *vb* **-bore** \-ˈbō(ə)r\; **-borne** \-ˈbōrn\; **-bear·ing** **1** : to bear or carry down (as by too much weight) : OVERBURDEN **2** : to domineer over **3** : to bear fruit or offspring to excess
over·bear·ing \-ˈba(ə)r-iŋ\ *adj* : acting in a proud or domineering way toward other people : ARROGANT — **over·bear·ing·ly** *adv*

over•blown \-'blōn\ *adj* **1** : excessively large of girth : FAT **2** : INFLATED, PRETENTIOUS
over•board \'ō-vər-ˌbōrd\ *adv* **1** : over the side of a ship into the water **2** : to extremes of enthusiasm **3** : into discard : ASIDE
over•bur•den \ˌō-vər-'bərd-ᵊn\ *vt* : to burden too heavily
¹**over•cast** \ˌō-vər-'kast, 'ō-vər-ˌ\ *vt* **-cast**; **-cast•ing** : DARKEN, OVERSHADOW
²**over•cast** \'ō-vər-ˌkast, ˌō-vər-'\ *adj* : clouded over : GLOOMY
³**over•cast** \'ō-vər-ˌkast\ *n* : COVERING; *esp* : a covering of clouds over the sky
over•charge \ˌō-vər-'chärj\ *vb* **1** : to charge too much **2** : to fill or load too full — **over•charge** \'ō-vər-ˌchärj\ *n*
over•cloud \ˌō-vər-'klaůd\ *vt* : to overspread with clouds : DARKEN
over•coat \'ō-vər-ˌkōt\ *n* : a warm coat worn over indoor clothing
over•come \ˌō-vər-'kəm\ *vt* **-came** \-'kām\; **-come**; **-com•ing** **1** : to get the better of : CONQUER **2** : to make helpless or exhausted
over•do \-'dü\ *vb* **-did** \-'did\; **-done** \-'dən\; **-do•ing** \-'dü-iŋ\ **1 a** : to do too much **b** : to tire oneself **2** : EXAGGERATE **3** : to cook too long
over•draft \'ō-vər-ˌdraft, -ˌdråft\ *n* : an overdrawing of a bank account; *also* : the amount overdrawn
over•draw \ˌō-vər-'drȯ\ *vb* **-drew** \-'drü\; **-drawn** \-'drȯn\; **-draw•ing** **1** : to draw checks on (a bank account) for more than the balance **2** : EXAGGERATE, OVERSTATE **3** : to make an overdraft
over•due \-'d(y)ü\ *adj* **1** : unpaid when due **2** : delayed beyond an appointed time
over•ex•pose \-ik-'spōz\ *vt* : to expose excessively; *esp* : to expose (photographic material) for a longer time than is needed — **over•ex•po•sure** \-'spō-zhər\ *n*
¹**over•flow** \-'flō\ *vb* **1** : to cover with or as if with water : INUNDATE **2** : to flow over the brim or top of **3** : to flow over bounds
²**over•flow** \'ō-vər-ˌflō\ *n* **1** : a flowing over : FLOOD **2** : something that flows over : SURPLUS **3** : an outlet or receptacle for surplus liquid
over•grow \ˌō-vər-'grō\ *vb* **-grew** \-'grü\; **-grown** \-'grōn\; **-grow•ing** **1** : to grow over so as to cover **2** : to grow beyond or rise above : OUTGROW **3** : to grow excessively **4** : to become grown over — **over•growth** \'ō-vər-ˌgrōth\ *n*
over•grown \ˌō-vər-'grōn\ *adj* : grown unusually or too big
¹**over•hand** \'ō-vər-ˌhand\ *adj* **1** : made with the hand brought down from above **2** : played with the hand downward or inward toward the body — **overhand** *adv* — **over•hand•ed** \ˌō-vər-'han-dəd\ *adv*
²**overhand** *n* : an overhand stroke (as in tennis)
¹**over•hang** \'ō-vər-ˌhaŋ, ˌō-vər-'\ *vb* **-hung** \-ˌhəŋ, -'həŋ\; **-hang•ing** \-ˌhaŋ-iŋ, -'haŋ-\ **1** : to jut, project, or be suspended over **2** : to hang over threateningly
²**over•hang** \'ō-vər-ˌhaŋ\ *n* : a part that overhangs
over•haul \ˌō-vər-'hȯl\ *vt* **1** : to make a thorough examination of and the necessary repairs and adjustments on (as a car) **2** : OVERTAKE — **over•haul** \'ō-vər-ˌhȯl\ *n*
¹**over•head** \ˌō-vər-'hed\ *adv* : above one's head : ALOFT
²**over•head** \'ō-vər-ˌhed\ *adj* **1** : operating or lying above **2** : of or relating to business expense
³**over•head** \'ō-vər-ˌhed\ *n* : business expenses not chargeable to a particular part of the work or product
over•hear \ˌō-vər-'hi(ə)r\ *vb* **-heard** \-'hərd\; **-hear•ing** \-'hi(ə)r-iŋ\ : to hear without the speaker's knowledge or intention
over•joy \ˌō-vər-'jȯi\ *vt* : to fill with great joy
over•kill \ˌō-vər-'kil\ *vt* : to obliterate (a target) with more nuclear force than required — **over•kill** \'ō-vər-ˌkil\ *n*
over•land \'ō-vər-ˌland, -lənd\ *adv* (*or adj*) : by, on, or across land
over•lap \ˌō-vər-'lap\ *vb* **1** : to lap over **2** : to have something in common or in common with — **over•lap** \'ō-vər-ˌlap\ *n*
¹**over•lay** \ˌō-vər-'lā\ *vt* **-laid** \-'lād\; **-lay•ing** **1 a** : to lay or spread over or across something : SUPERIMPOSE **b** : to lay or spread something over or across : COVER **2** : OVERLIE
²**over•lay** \'ō-vər-ˌlā\ *n* : something (as a veneer on wood) that is overlaid
over•leap \ˌō-vər-'lēp\ *vt* **1** : to leap over or across **2** : to defeat (oneself) by going too far
over•lie \ˌō-vər-'lī\ *vt* **-lay** \-'lā\; **-lain** \-'lān\; **-ly•ing** \-'lī-iŋ\ : to lie over or upon
over•look \ˌō-vər-'lůk\ *vt* **1** : to look over : INSPECT **2 a** : to look down upon from above **b** : to rise above or afford a view of **3 a** : to fail to see : MISS **b** : to pass over : IGNORE **c** : EXCUSE **4** : to watch over : SUPERVISE
over•lord \'ō-vər-ˌlȯrd\ *n* **1** : a lord who has supremacy over other lords **2** : an absolute or supreme ruler — **over•lord•ship** \-ˌship\ *n*
over•ly \'ō-vər-lē\ *adv* : EXCESSIVELY, TOO
over•mas•ter \ˌō-vər-'mas-tər\ *vt* : OVERPOWER, SUBDUE
over•match \ˌō-vər-'mach\ *vt* **1** : to be more than a match for : DEFEAT **2** : to match with a superior opponent
¹**over•much** \ˌō-vər-'məch\ *adj* (*or adv*) : too much
²**over•much** \'ō-vər-ˌməch\ *n* : too great an amount : EXCESS
¹**over•night** \ˌō-vər-'nīt\ *adv* **1** : on or during the evening or night **2** : SUDDENLY
²**overnight** *adj* : of, lasting, or staying the night
¹**over•pass** \ˌō-vər-'pas\ *vt* **1** : to pass across, over, or beyond : CROSS; *also* : SURPASS **2** : TRANSGRESS **3** : DISREGARD, IGNORE
²**over•pass** \'ō-vər-ˌpas\ *n* : a crossing (as by means of a bridge) of two highways or of a highway and pedestrian path or railroad at different levels; *also* : the upper level of such a crossing
over•per•suade \ˌō-vər-pər-'swād\ *vt* : to persuade to act contrary to conviction or preference — **over•per•sua•sion** \-'swā-zhən\ *n*
over•play \ˌō-vər-'plā\ *vt* **1 a** : to present (as a dramatic role) extravagantly : EXAGGERATE **b** : OVEREMPHASIZE **2** : to rely too much on the strength of
over•plus \'ō-vər-ˌpləs\ *n* : SURPLUS
over•pow•er \ˌō-vər-'paů(-ə)r\ *vt* **1** : to overcome by superior force : DEFEAT **2** : OVERWHELM — **over•pow•er•ing•ly** *adv*
¹**over•print** \ˌō-vər-'print\ *vt* : to print over with something additional
²**over•print** \'ō-vər-ˌprint\ *n* : something added by overprinting; *esp* : a printed marking added to a postage or revenue stamp esp. to alter the original or to commemorate a special event
over•reach \ˌō-və(r)-'rēch\ *vb* **1** : to reach above or beyond : OVERTOP **2** : to defeat (oneself) by seeking to do or gain too much **3 a** : to go to excess **b** : EXAGGERATE
over•ride \-'rīd\ *vt* **-rode** \-'rōd\; **-rid•den** \-'rid-ᵊn\; **-rid•ing** \-'rīd-iŋ\ **1 a** : to ride over or across **b** : TRAMPLE **2** : to ride (as a horse) too much or too hard **3 a** : to prevail over : DOMINATE **b** : to set aside : annul by a contrary decision
over•rule \-'rül\ *vt* **1** : to decide against **2** : to reverse or set aside (a decision or ruling made by a lesser authority)
over•run \-'rən\ *vt* **-ran** \-'ran\; **-run**; **-run•ning** **1** : to run over : OVERSPREAD **2** : to trample down **3** : INFEST **4** : to win over and occupy the positions of **5** : to run further than : go beyond : EXCEED
over•sea \ˌō-vər-'sē, 'ō-vər-ˌ\ *adj* (*or adv*) : OVERSEAS
over•seas \-'sēz, -ˌsēz\ *adv* : beyond or across the sea : ABROAD — **overseas** *adj*
over•see \ˌō-vər-'sē\ *vt* **-saw** \-'sȯ\; **-seen** \-'sēn\; **-see•ing**

1 : SURVEY, WATCH 2 a : INSPECT, EXAMINE b : SUPERINTEND, SUPERVISE, MANAGE

over•seer \'ō-və(r)-ˌsi(ə)r, -ˌsē-ər, ˌō-və(r)-'\ *n* : SUPERINTENDENT, SUPERVISOR

over•shad•ow \ˌō-vər-'shad-ō\ *vt* 1 : to cast a shadow over : DARKEN 2 : to exceed in importance : OUTWEIGH

over•shoe \'ō-vər-ˌshü\ *n* : a protective outer shoe; *esp* : GALOSH

over•shoot \ˌō-vər-'shüt\ *vt* **-shot** \-'shät\; **-shoot•ing** 1 : to pass swiftly beyond; *also* : to miss by going beyond 2 : to shoot over or beyond so as to miss

over•shot \'ō-vər-ˌshät\ *adj* : having the upper jaw extending beyond the lower

over•sight \'ō-vər-ˌsīt\ *n* 1 : the act or duty of overseeing : SUPERVISION 2 : an omission or error resulting from carelessness or haste

[1]**over•size** \'ō-vər-ˌsīz\ *n* : a size larger than the usual or normal size

[2]**over•size** \ˌō-vər-'sīz\ *or* **over•sized** \-'sīzd\ *adj* : being of more than ordinary size

over•sleep \-'slēp\ *vi* **-slept** \-'slept\; **-sleep•ing** : to sleep beyond the usual time for waking or beyond the time set for getting up

over•spread \ˌō-vər-'spred\ *vt* **-spread**; **-spread•ing** : to spread over or above — **over•spread** \'ō-vər-ˌspred\ *n*

over•state \ˌō-vər-'stāt\ *vt* : to state in too strong terms : EXAGGERATE — **over•state•ment** *n*

over•stay \-'stā\ *vt* : to stay beyond the time or the limits of

over•step \-'step\ *vt* : to step over or beyond : EXCEED

over•strung \-'strəŋ\ *adj* : too highly strung : too sensitive

over•stuffed \-'stəft\ *adj* 1 : stuffed too full 2 : covered completely and deeply with upholstery

over•sub•scribe \-səb-'skrīb\ *vt* : to subscribe for more of than is available, asked for, or offered for sale

overt \ō-'vərt, 'ō-(ˌ)vərt\ *adj* : open to view : not secret — **overt•ly** *adv*

over•take \ˌō-vər-'tāk\ *vt* **-took** \-'tu̇k\; **-tak•en** \-'tā-kən\; **-tak•ing** 1 a : to catch up with b : to catch up with and pass by 2 : to come upon suddenly

over•throw \-'thrō\ *vt* **-threw** \-'thrü\; **-thrown** \-'thrōn\; **-throw•ing** 1 : to thrust or knock over : UPSET 2 : to bring down : DEFEAT — **over•throw** \'ō-vər-ˌthrō\ *n*

over•time \'ō-vər-ˌtīm\ *n* 1 : time in excess of a set limit; *esp* : working time in excess of a standard day or week 2 : the wage paid for overtime work — **overtime** *adv* (*or adj*)

over•tone \'ō-vər-ˌtōn\ *n* 1 : one of the higher tones in a complex musical tone 2 : a secondary effect, quality, or meaning : SUGGESTION

over•top \ˌō-vər-'täp\ *vt* 1 : to rise above the top of : surpass in height 2 : to rise above in power 3 : SURPASS

over•ture \'ō-və(r)-ˌchu̇r, -chər\ *n* 1 : an opening offer : a first proposal 2 : an orchestral composition that is the introduction to an oratorio, opera, or dramatic work; *also* : a composition in this style for concert performance

over•turn \ˌō-vər-'tərn\ *vb* 1 : to turn over : UPSET 2 : OVERTHROW, DESTROY — **over•turn** \'ō-vər-ˌtərn\ *n*

over•view \'ō-vər-ˌvyü\ *n* : an overall view

over•ween•ing \ˌō-vər-'wē-niŋ\ *adj* 1 : ARROGANT, PRESUMPTUOUS 2 : EXAGGERATED, IMMODERATE — **over•ween•ing•ly** *adv*

over•weigh \ˌō-vər-'wā\ *vt* 1 : to exceed in weight : OVERBALANCE 2 : to weigh down : OPPRESS

over•weight \'ō-vər-ˌwāt, *2 is usu* ˌō-vər-'\ *n* 1 : weight over and above what is required or allowed 2 : excessive or burdensome weight; *esp* : bodily weight in excess of what is held normal to one's age, height, and build — **over•weight** \ˌō-vər-'\ *adj*

over•whelm \ˌō-vər-'hwelm\ *vt* 1 : OVERTHROW, UPSET 2 a : to cover over completely : SUBMERGE b : to overcome completely : CRUSH — **over•whelm•ing•ly** *adv*

over•wind \ˌō-vər-'wīnd\ *vt* **-wound** \-'wau̇nd\; **-wind•ing** : to wind too much

over•win•ter \ˌō-vər-'wint-ər\ *vi* : to spend or survive the winter

over•work \ˌō-vər-'wərk\ *vb* 1 : to work or cause to work too hard or long or to exhaustion 2 : to decorate all over 3 a : to work too much on : OVERDO b : to make excessive use of — **overwork** *n*

over•write \ˌō-və(r)-'rīt\ *vb* **-wrote** \-'rōt\; **-writ•ten** \-'rit-ᵊn\; **-writ•ing** \-'rīt-iŋ\ 1 : to write over the surface of 2 : to write in inflated or pretentious style 3 : to write too much

over•wrought \ˌō-və(r)-'ro̊t\ *adj* 1 : extremely excited : AGITATED 2 : elaborated to excess : OVERDONE

ovip•a•rous \ō-'vip-(ə-)rəs\ *adj* : producing eggs that develop and hatch outside the maternal body — **ovip•a•rous•ly** *adv*

ovoid \'ō-ˌvo̊id\ *or* **ovoi•dal** \ō-'vo̊id-ᵊl\ *adj* : shaped like an egg — **ovoid** *n*

ovule \'ō-vyül\ *n* 1 : any of the bodies in a plant ovary that after fertilization become seeds 2 : a small egg; *esp* : one in an early stage of growth — **ovu•lar** \-vyə-lər\ *adj*

ovum \'ō-vəm\ *n, pl* **ova** \-və\ : a female gamete : an egg cell

owe \'ō\ *vb* 1 : to have or bear (an emotion or attitude) to someone or something 2 a (1) : to be under obligation to pay or repay in return for something received : be indebted in the sum of (2) : to be under obligation to render (as duty or service) b : to be indebted to or for c : to be in debt

ow•ing \'ō-iŋ\ *adj* : due to be paid : OWED

owing to *prep* : because of

owl \'au̇l\ *n* : any of an order of birds of prey with large head and eyes, short hooked bill, strong talons, and more or less nocturnal habits

owl•et \'au̇-lət\ *n* : a young or small owl

owl•ish \'au̇-lish\ *adj* : resembling or suggesting an owl (as in solemnity or appearance of wisdom) — **owl•ish•ly** *adv* — **owl•ish•ness** *n*

[1]**own** \'ōn\ *adj* : belonging to oneself or itself — usu. used following a possessive case or pronoun

[2]**own** *vb* 1 a : to have or hold as property : POSSESS b : to have legal title to 2 : ACKNOWLEDGE, ADMIT 3 : CONFESS — **own•er** *n* — **own•er•ship** \'ō-nər-ˌship\ *n*

[3]**own** *pron* : one or ones belonging to oneself — used after a possessive and without a following noun as a pronoun equivalent in meaning to the adjective *own*—**on one's own** 1 : being without outside help or control : INDEPENDENT 2 : on one's own initiative : INDEPENDENTLY

own up *vi* : CONFESS

ox \'äks\ *n, pl* **ox•en** \'äk-sən\ : the common large domestic bovine mammal kept for milk, draft, and meat; *esp* : an adult castrated male

ox•blood \'äks-ˌbləd\ *n* : a moderate reddish brown

ox•bow \-ˌbō\ *n* 1 : a U-shaped collar worn by a draft ox 2 : a U-shaped bend in a river — **oxbow** *adj*

ox•cart \-ˌkärt\ *n* : a cart drawn by oxen

ox•ford \'äks-fərd\ *n* : a low shoe laced or tied over the instep

ox•i•da•tion \ˌäk-sə-'dā-shən\ *n* 1 : the process of oxidizing 2 : the state or result of being oxidized — **ox•i•da•tive** \'äk-sə-ˌdāt-iv\ *adj*

ox•ide \'äk-ˌsīd\ *n* : a compound of oxygen with an element or radical

ox•i•dize \'äk-sə-ˌdīz\ *vb* : to combine with oxygen — **ox•i•diz•er** *n*

ox•tail \'äks-ˌtāl\ *n* : the tail of cattle; *esp* : the skinned tail used for soup

oxy•acet•y•lene \ˌäk-sē-ə-'set-ᵊl-ən, -ᵊl-ˌēn\ *adj* : of, relating to, or utilizing a mixture of oxygen and acetylene

ox•y•gen \'äk-si-jən\ *n* : a chemical element that is found fre as a colorless tasteless odorless gas in the atmosphere of which it forms about 21 percent or combined in water, that is capable of combining with all elements except the inert gases, that is active in physiological processes, and that is involved esp. in combustion processes — **ox·y·gen·ic** \ˌäk-si-ˈjen-ik\ *adj*

oxygen mask *n* : a device worn over the nose and mouth (as by airmen at high altitudes) through which oxygen is supplied from a storage tank

oxygen tent *n* : a canopy which can be placed over a bedfast person and within which a flow of oxygen can be maintained

oys·ter \ˈȯi-stər\ *n* : any of various marine bivalve mollusks having a rough irregular shell and including important edible shellfish

oyster bed *n* : a place where oysters grow or are cultivated

oyster cracker *n* : a small salted cracker

oys·ter·man \-mən\ *n* : a gatherer, opener, breeder, or seller of oysters

ozone \ˈō-ˌzōn\ *n* **1** : a form of oxygen that has three atoms in the molecule, is a faintly blue irritating gas with a pungent odor, is generated usu. in dilute form by a silent electric discharge in oxygen or air, and is used esp. in disinfection and deodorization and in oxidation and bleaching **2** : pure and refreshing air — **ozo·nic** \ō-ˈzō-nik\ *adj* — **ozo·nif·er·ous** \ˌō-(ˌ)zō-ˈnif-(ə-)rəs\ *adj*

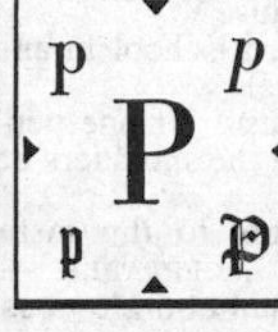

p \ˈpē\ *n, often cap* : the 16th letter of the English alphabet

pa \ˈpä, ˈpȯ\ *n* : FATHER

pab·u·lum \ˈpab-yə-ləm\ *n* : FOOD; *esp* : a suspension or solution of nutrients suitable for absorption

[1]**pace** \ˈpās\ *n* **1** : rate of moving or progressing esp. on foot **2 a** : a manner of walking : TREAD **b** : GAIT; *esp* : a horse's gait in which the legs on the same side move together

[2]**pace** *vb* **1 a** : to walk with slow or measured tread **b** : to move along : PROCEED **2** : to go or cover at a pace — used of a horse **3** : to measure by or in paces **4** : to set or regulate the pace of; *also* : LEAD, PRECEDE — **pac·er** *n*

pace·mak·er \ˈpās-ˌmā-kər\ *n* : one that sets the pace for another

pach·y·derm \ˈpak-i-ˌdərm\ *n* : any of various thick-skinned hoofed mammals (as an elephant or a rhinoceros) — **pach·y·der·mal** \ˌpak-i-ˈdər-məl\ *adj* — **pach·y·der·ma·tous** \-mət-əs\ *adj*

pach·ys·an·dra \ˌpak-ə-ˈsan-drə\ *n* : any of a genus of low evergreen plants used as a ground cover

pa·cif·ic \pə-ˈsif-ik\ *adj* **1** : making or suitable to make peace **2** : having a mild and calm nature : PEACEABLE — **pa·cif·i·cal·ly** \-ˈsif-i-k(ə-)lē\ *adv*

pac·i·fi·ca·tion \ˌpas-ə-fə-ˈkā-shən\ *n* : the act or process of pacifying : the state of being pacified

pac·i·fi·er \ˈpas-ə-ˌfī(-ə)r\ *n* **1** : one that pacifies **2** : a usu. nipple-shaped device for babies to suck or bite upon

pac·i·fism \ˈpas-ə-ˌfiz-əm\ *n* : opposition to war or violence as a means of settling disputes — **pac·i·fist** \-fəst\ *n* — **pacifist** *or* **pac·i·fis·tic** \ˌpas-ə-ˈfis-tik\ *adj*

pac·i·fy \ˈpas-ə-ˌfī\ *vt* **-fied; -fy·ing 1** : to ease the anger, agitation, or distress of : SOOTHE **2** : to restore to a peaceful state : SETTLE, SUBDUE

[1]**pack** \ˈpak\ *n* **1 a** : a bundle arranged for convenience in carrying esp. on the back **b** : a group or pile of related objects or these together with their container **2** : a large amount or number : HEAP **3** : an act or instance or a method of packing; *also* : arrangement in a pack **4** : a group or band of persons or animals **5** : absorbent material used therapeutically (as for checking bleeding or applying medication or moisture) — **pack** *adj*

[2]**pack** *vb* **1 a** : to place articles in (as for transportation or storage) **b** : to arrange closely and securely in a container or bundle **2** : to crowd together so as to fill full : CRAM **3** : to fill or cover so as to prevent passage (as of air or steam) **4** : to send or go away without ceremony **5** : to transport in packs (as on the back of an animal) **6** : WEAR, CARRY

[3]**pack** *vt* : to bring together or make up fraudulently to secure a favorable vote

[1]**pack·age** \ˈpak-ij\ *n* **1 a** : a small or moderate-sized pack : PARCEL **b** : a single item or set of a product uniformly wrapped or sealed for sale **2** : a covering wrapper or container **3** : something (as a group of related things offered as a whole) resembling a package

[2]**package** *vt* : to make into or enclose in a package

pack·er \ˈpak-ər\ *n* : one that packs; *esp* : a dealer who prepares and packs foods for the market

pack·et \ˈpak-ət\ *n* **1 a** : a small group, cluster, or mass **b** : a small bundle or parcel **2** : a passenger boat carrying mail and cargo on a regular schedule

pack·ing·house \ˈpak-iŋ-ˌhau̇s\ *n* : an establishment for processing and packing foodstuffs and esp. meat and its by-products

pack·sad·dle \ˈpak-ˌsad-ᵊl\ *n* : a saddle that supports the load on the back of a pack animal

pact \ˈpakt\ *n* : [4]COMPACT; *esp* : an international treaty

[1]**pad** \ˈpad\ *n* **1 a** : a cushioned or cushioning part or thing : CUSHION **b** : a piece of material saturated with ink for inking the surface of a rubber stamp **2 a** : the hairy foot of some mammals **b** : the cushioned thickening of the underside of the toes of some mammals **3** : a floating leaf of a water plant **4** : TABLET 1b **5** : LAUNCHING PAD

[2]**pad** *vt* **pad·ded; pad·ding 1** : to furnish with a pad or padding **2** : to expand with superfluous or insignificant matter

[3]**pad** *vb* **pad·ded; pad·ding 1** : to traverse or go on foot **2** : to move along with a muffled step

[4]**pad** *n* : a soft muffled or slapping sound

padding *n* : material with which something is padded

[1]**pad·dle** \ˈpad-ᵊl\ *n* **1** : an implement with a flat blade to propel and steer a small craft (as a canoe) **2** : an implement used for stirring, mixing, or beating **3** : one of the broad boards at the circumference of a paddle wheel or waterwheel

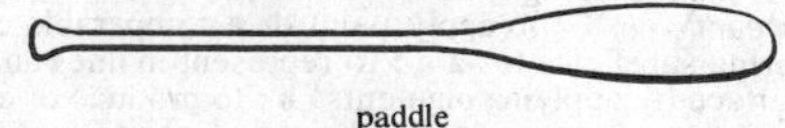

paddle

[2]**paddle** *vb* **pad·dled; pad·dling** \ˈpad-liŋ, -ᵊl-iŋ\ **1** : to go, propel, or transport by or as if by means of a paddle or paddle wheel **2** : to beat or stir by or as if by a paddle

[3]**paddle** *vi* **pad·dled; pad·dling** \ˈpad-liŋ, -ᵊl-iŋ\ **1** : to move the hands or feet about in shallow water **2** : TODDLE

pad·dler \ˈpad-lər, -ᵊl-ər\ *n* : one that paddles

paddle wheel *n* : a wheel with blades around its rim used to propel a boat

pad•dock \'pad-ək, -ik\ *n* : a usu. enclosed area used esp. for pasturing or exercising animals; *esp* : an enclosure where racehorses are saddled and paraded before a race

pad•dy \'pad-ē\ *n, pl* **paddies** 1 : RICE 2 : wet land in which rice is grown

pad•dy wagon \'pad-ē-\ *n* : PATROL WAGON

pad•lock \'pad-ˌläk\ *n* : a removable lock with a hinged bow-shaped piece attached at one end so that the other end can be passed through a staple (as on a hasp) and then snapped into a catch in the lock — **padlock** *vt*

pa•dre \'päd-(ˌ)rā, -rē\ *n* 1 : PRIEST 2 : a military chaplain

pae•an \'pē-ən\ *n* : a joyously exultant song or hymn of praise, tribute, thanksgiving, or triumph

pa•gan \'pā-gən\ *n* 1 : HEATHEN 1 2 : an irreligious person — **pagan** *adj* — **pa•gan•ism** \'pā-gə-ˌniz-əm\ *n*

[1]**page** \'pāj\ *n* 1 : a youth being trained for the medieval rank of knight; *also* : a youth attendant on a person of rank 2 : one employed (as by a hotel) esp. to deliver messages

[2]**page** *vt* : to summon by repeatedly calling out the name of

[3]**page** *n* : one side of a printed or written leaf; *also* : the entire leaf

[4]**page** *vt* : to number or mark the pages of

pag•eant \'paj-ənt\ *n* 1 : an elaborate exhibition or spectacle 2 : an entertainment consisting of loosely linked scenes or tableaux based on history or legend 3 : ostentatious pomp and display

pag•eant•ry \'paj-ən-trē\ *n, pl* **-ries** 1 : PAGEANTS; *also* : the presentation of pageants 2 : splendid or ostentatious display : SPECTACLE

pag•i•na•tion \ˌpaj-ə-'nā-shən\ *n* 1 : the paging of written or printed matter 2 : the number and arrangement of pages (as of a book) or an indication of these

pa•go•da \pə-'gōd-ə\ *n* : a Far Eastern tower usu. with roofs curving upward at the division of each of several stories and erected as a temple or memorial

paid *past of* PAY

pail \'pāl\ *n* 1 : a usu. cylindrical vessel with a handle : BUCKET 2 : PAILFUL

pail•ful \-ˌfu̇l\ *n, pl* **pail•fuls** \-ˌfu̇lz\ *or* **pails•ful** \'pālz-ˌfu̇l\ : the quantity held by a pail

[1]**pain** \'pān\ *n* 1 : PUNISHMENT 2 **a** : usu. localized physical suffering associated with disease, injury, or other bodily disorder; *also* : a basic bodily sensation induced by a noxious stimulus and characterized by physical discomfort (as pricking, throbbing, or aching) **b** : acute mental or emotional distress : GRIEF 3 *pl* : care or effort taken for the accomplishment of something — **pain** *adj* — **pain•less** \-ləs\ *adj* — **pain•less•ly** *adv* — **pain•less•ness** *n*

[2]**pain** *vb* 1 : to cause pain in or to : HURT 2 : to give or experience pain

pain•ful \'pān-fəl\ *adj* 1 **a** : feeling or giving pain **b** : ANNOYING, IRKSOME, VEXATIOUS 2 : requiring or involving effort or careful diligence — **pain•ful•ly** \-fə-lē\ *adv* — **pain•ful•ness** *n*

pains•tak•ing \'pānz-ˌtā-kiŋ\ *adj* : marked by diligent care and effort — **pains•tak•ing•ly** *adv*

[1]**paint** \'pānt\ *vb* 1 : to apply paint or a comparable covering or coloring substance to 2 **a** : to represent in lines and colors on a surface by applying pigments **b** : to produce or evoke as if by painting 3 : to practice the art of painting 4 : to use cosmetics

[2]**paint** *n* 1 : MAKEUP; *esp* : a cosmetic to add color 2 **a** : a mixture of a pigment and a suitable liquid to form a thin closely adherent coating when spread on a surface in a thin coat **b** : an applied coating of paint

paint•brush \-ˌbrəsh\ *n* : a brush for applying paint

paint•er \'pānt-ər\ *n* : one that paints; *esp* : an artist who paints — **paint•er•ly** \-lē\ *adj*

paint•ing \'pānt-iŋ\ *n* 1 : a product of painting; *esp* : a painted work of art 2 : the art or occupation of painting

[1]**pair** \'pa(ə)r\ *n, pl* **pairs** 1 : two corresponding things either naturally matched or intended to be used together 2 : a single thing composed of two connected corresponding parts 3 : a set of two people or animals

[2]**pair** *vb* 1 : to make a pair of or arrange in pairs 2 : to become grouped or separated into pairs

pais•ley \'pāz-lē\ *adj, often cap* : made typically of soft wool with colorful curved abstract figures — **paisley** *n*

pa•ja•mas \pə-'jäm-əz, -'jam-\ *n pl* : a loose usu. 2-piece lightweight suit designed for sleeping or lounging

[1]**pal** \'pal\ *n* : PARTNER; *esp* : a close friend

[2]**pal** *vi* **palled**; **pal•ling** : to be or become pals

pal•ace \'pal-əs\ *n* 1 : the official residence of a sovereign 2 **a** : a large stately house **b** : a large public building (as for a legislature, court, or governor) **c** : a showy place for public amusement or refreshment

pal•a•din \'pal-əd-ən\ *n* 1 : a knightly supporter of a medieval prince 2 : an outstanding protagonist of a cause

pa•laes•tra \pə-'les-trə\ *n, pl* **-trae** \-(ˌ)trē\ : a school in ancient Greece or Rome for sports (as wrestling)

pal•an•quin \ˌpal-ən-'kēn\ *n* : a conveyance usu. for one person consisting of an enclosed litter carried on the shoulders of men by means of poles

pal•at•a•ble \'pal-ət-ə-bəl\ *adj* 1 : agreeable to the taste : SAVORY 2 : agreeable to the mind : ACCEPTABLE — **pal•at•a•bil•i•ty** \ˌpal-ət-ə-'bil-ət-ē\ *n* — **pal•at•a•ble•ness** \'pal-ət-ə-bəl-nəs\ *n* — **pal•at•a•bly** \-blē\ *adv*

pal•a•tal \'pal-ət-ᵊl\ *adj* : of or relating to the palate

pal•ate \'pal-ət\ *n* 1 : the roof of the mouth separating the mouth from the nasal cavity 2 **a** : the sense of taste **b** : intellectual relish or taste

pa•la•tial \pə-'lā-shəl\ *adj* 1 : of, relating to, or being a palace 2 : suitable to a palace : MAGNIFICENT — **pa•la•tial•ly** \-shə-lē\ *adv* — **pa•la•tial•ness** *n*

pa•lat•i•nate \pə-'lat-ᵊn-ət\ *n* : the territory of a palatine

[1]**pal•a•tine** \'pal-ə-ˌtīn\ *adj* 1 : of or relating to a palace : PALATIAL 2 **a** : possessing royal privileges **b** : of or relating to a palatine or a palatinate

[2]**palatine** *n* 1 : a high officer of an imperial palace 2 : a feudal lord having sovereign power within his domains

[1]**pa•lav•er** \pə-'lav-ər, -'läv-\ *n* 1 : a long parley : TALK 2 **a** : idle talk : CHATTER **b** : misleading or beguiling speech

[2]**palaver** *vi* : to talk at length and usu. obscurely or idly

[1]**pale** \'pāl\ *adj* 1 **a** : light in color or shade **b** : not having the warm skin color of a person in good health : PALLID, WAN 2 : not bright or brilliant : DIM — **pale•ly** *adv* — **pale•ness** *n*

[2]**pale** *vb* : to make or become pale

[3]**pale** *vt* : to enclose with pales : FENCE

[4]**pale** *n* 1 : a stake or picket of a fence or palisade 2 : an enclosed place; *also* : territory within clearly marked bounds or under a particular jurisdiction 3 : limits within which one is protected or privileged

pale•face \-ˌfās\ *n* : a white person : CAUCASIAN

pa•le•on•tol•o•gy \ˌpā-lē-än-'täl-ə-jē\ *n* : a science dealing with the life of past geological periods as known esp. from fossil remains — **pa•le•on•to•log•i•cal** \-ˌänt-ᵊl-'äj-i-kəl\ *or* **pa•le•on•to•log•ic** \-'äj-ik\ *adj* — **pa•le•on•tol•o•gist** \-än-'täl-ə-jəst\ *n*

pal•ette \'pal-ət\ *n* 1 : a thin oval or rectangular board or tablet with a hole for the thumb at one end by which a painter holds it and on which he lays and mixes pigments 2 : the set of colors put on the palette

pal•frey \'pȯl-frē\ *n, pl* **palfreys** : a saddle horse; *esp* : one suitable for a lady

pal•imp•sest \'pal-əm(p)-ˌsest\ *n* : writing material (as a parchment) used again after earlier writing has been erased

al·ing \'pā-liŋ\ *n* **1** : PALE, PICKET **2 a** : material for pales **b** : a fence of pales
pal·i·sade \,pal-ə-'sād\ *n* **1** : a stout high fence of stakes esp. for defense **2** : a line of bold cliffs
palisade *vt* : to surround or fortify with palisades
pall \'pȯl\ *n* **1** : a heavy cloth covering for a coffin, hearse, or tomb **2** : something that covers, darkens, or produces a gloomy effect
pall *vi* : to become dull or uninteresting : lose the ability to give pleasure
al·la·di·um \pə-'lād-ē-əm\ *n* : a silver-white ductile malleable metallic chemical element that is used esp. as a catalyst and in alloys
all·bear·er \'pȯl-,bar-ər\ *n* : a person who attends the coffin at a funeral
pal·let \'pal-ət\ *n* : a straw-filled tick or mattress; *also* : any small, hard, or temporary bed
pallet *n* **1** : a flat-bladed implement for forming, beating, or rounding clay or glass **2** : PALETTE 1
al·li·ate \'pal-ē-,āt\ *vt* **1** : to ease without curing **2** : to cover by excuses and apologies : EXCUSE — **pal·li·a·tion** \,pal-ē-'ā-shən\ *n* — **pal·li·a·tor** \'pal-ē-,āt-ər\ *n*
al·li·a·tive \'pal-ē-,āt-iv, 'pal-yət-\ *adj* : serving to palliate — **palliative** *n* — **pal·li·a·tive·ly** *adv*
al·lid \'pal-əd\ *adj* : deficient in color : WAN — **pal·lid·i·ty** \pa-'lid-ət-ē\ *n* — **pal·lid·ly** *adv* — **pal·lid·ness** *n*
al·lor \'pal-ər\ *n* : deficiency of color esp. of the face : PALENESS
palm \'päm, 'pälm\ *n* **1** : any of a group of mostly tropical trees, shrubs, or vines usu. with a simple but often tall stem topped by a crown of large leaves **2 a** : a palm leaf esp. when carried as a symbol of victory **b** : an emblem of success or triumph; *also* : VICTORY, HONORS — **palm-like** *adj*
palm *n* : the under part of the hand between the fingers and the wrist
palm *vt* **1** : to conceal in or pick up stealthily with the hand **2** : to impose by fraud
al·mate \'pal-,māt, 'pä(l)m-,āt\ *adj* : resembling a hand with the fingers spread — **pal·mate·ly** *adv* — **pal·ma·tion** \pal-'mā-shən, pä(l)-'mā-\ *n*
alm·er \'päm-ər, 'päl-mər\ *n* : a person wearing two crossed palm leaves as a sign of his pilgrimage to the Holy Land
al·met·to \pal-'met-ō\ *n, pl* **-tos** *or* **-toes** : any of several usu. low-growing palms with fan-shaped leaves
alm·ist·ry \'päm-ə-strē, 'päl-mə-\ *n* : the practice of reading a person's character or future from the markings on his palms — **palm·ist** \'päm-əst, 'päl-məst\ *n*
alm Sunday *n* : the Sunday before Easter celebrated in commemoration of Christ's triumphal entry into Jerusalem
almy \'päm-ē, 'päl-mē\ *adj* **1** : abounding in or bearing palms **2** : FLOURISHING, PROSPEROUS
al·o·mi·no \,pal-ə-'mē-nō\ *n, pl* **-nos** : a slender-legged short-bodied horse of a light tan or cream color with lighter mane and tail
al·pa·ble \'pal-pə-bəl\ *adj* **1** : capable of being touched or felt : TANGIBLE **2** : easily perceptible : NOTICEABLE **3** : easily understood or recognized : MANIFEST — **pal·pa·bil·i·ty** \,pal-pə-'bil-ət-ē\ *n* — **pal·pa·bly** \'pal-pə-blē\ *adv*
al·pate \'pal-,pāt\ *vt* : to examine by touch esp. medically — **pal·pa·tion** \pal-'pā-shən\ *n*
al·pi·tate \'pal-pə-,tāt\ *vi* : to beat rapidly and strongly : THROB, QUIVER
al·pi·ta·tion \,pal-pə-'tā-shən\ *n* : an act or instance of palpitating
al·sy \'pȯl-zē\ *n* **1** : PARALYSIS **2** : a condition marked by uncontrollable tremor of the body or a part — **palsy** *vt*
al·ter \'pȯl-tər\ *vi* **pal·tered**; **pal·ter·ing** \-t(ə-)riŋ\ **1** : to act insincerely : EQUIVOCATE **2** : HAGGLE, CHAFFER — **pal-ter·er** *n*
pal·try \'pȯl-trē\ *adj* **1** : INFERIOR, TRASHY **2** : MEAN, DESPICABLE **3** : TRIVIAL — **pal·tri·ness** *n*
pam·pa \'pam-pə\ *n, pl* **pampas** \-pəz, -pəs\ : an extensive generally grass-covered plain of So. America
pam·per \'pam-pər\ *vt* **pam·pered**; **pam·per·ing** \'pam-p(ə-)riŋ\ : to treat with extreme or excessive care and attention — **pam·per·er** *n*
pam·phlet \'pam(p)-flət\ *n* : an unbound printed publication with no cover or a paper cover
[1]**pam·phle·teer** \,pam(p)-flə-'ti(ə)r\ *n* : a writer of pamphlets usu. attacking something or urging a cause
[2]**pamphleteer** *vi* : to write and publish pamphlets
[1]**pan** \'pan\ *n* : a usu. broad, shallow, and open container for domestic use; *also* : something resembling such a container
[2]**pan** *vb* **panned**; **pan·ning** **1** : to wash earthy material in a pan in searching for gold **2 a** : to yield precious metal in panning **b** : to turn out; *esp* : SUCCEED **3** : to criticize severely
pan·a·cea \,pan-ə-'sē-ə\ *n* : a remedy for all ills or difficulties : CURE-ALL
pan·a·ma \'pan-ə-,mä, -,mȯ\ *n, often cap* : a lightweight hat hand-plaited of narrow strips from the young leaves of a tropical American tree
Pan–Amer·i·can \,pan-ə-'mer-ə-kən\ *adj* : of, relating to, or involving the republics of No. and So. America
pan·cake \'pan-,kāk\ *n* **1** : GRIDDLE CAKE **2** : a horizontal landing of an airplane with little run along the ground
pan·chro·mat·ic \,pan-krō-'mat-ik\ *adj* : sensitive to light of all colors in the visible spectrum
pan·cre·as \'paŋ-krē-əs, 'pan-\ *n* : a large compound gland of vertebrates that lies near the stomach and secretes digestive enzymes and the hormone insulin — **pan·cre·at·ic** \,paŋ-krē-'at-ik, ,pan-\ *adj*
pan·da \'pan-də\ *n* : a large black-and-white mammal of Tibet resembling a bear but related to the raccoon; *also* : a smaller reddish related animal resembling the raccoon
pan·dem·ic \pan-'dem-ik\ *n* : an outbreak of disease occurring over a wide area and affecting many people— **pandemic** *adj*
pan·de·mo·ni·um \,pan-də-'mō-nē-əm\ *n* : a wild uproar : TUMULT; *also* : a wildly riotous place
[1]**pan·der** \'pan-dər\ *or* **pan·der·er** \-dər-ər\ *n* **1 a** : a go-between in love intrigues **b** : a man who solicits clients for a prostitute **2** : someone who caters to or exploits the weaknesses of others
[2]**pander** *vi* **pan·dered**; **pan·der·ing** \-d(ə-)riŋ\ : to act as a pander
pan·dow·dy \pan-'dau̇d-ē\ *n, pl* **-dies** : a deep-dish apple dessert spiced, sweetened, and covered with a rich crust
pane \'pān\ *n* **1** : a section or side of something (as a facet of a gem) **2** : one of the compartments of a window or door consisting of a sheet of glass in a frame; *also* : the sheet of glass in such a frame
pan·e·gyr·ic \,pan-ə-'jir-ik, -'jī-rik\ *n* : a formal speech or writing in praise of someone or something; *also* : formal or elaborate praise
[1]**pan·el** \'pan-ᵊl\ *n* **1 a** : a schedule containing names of persons summoned as jurors; *also* : JURY 1 **b** : a group of persons taking part in a discussion or a quiz program **2** : a separate or distinct part of a surface: as **a** : a usu. rectangular and sunken or raised section of a surface (as of a door, wall, or ceiling) set off by a margin **b** : a section of a switchboard; *also* : a mount for controls (as of an electrical device) **3** : a thin flat piece of wood on which a picture is painted
[2]**panel** *vt* **-eled** *or* **-elled**; **-el·ing** *or* **-el·ling** : to furnish or decorate with panels
paneling *n* : decorative wood panels

pan·el·ist \'pan-ᵊl-əst\ *n* : a member of a panel for discussion or entertainment

pang \'paŋ\ *n* : a sudden sharp attack or spasm (as of pain or emotional distress)

[1]**pan·han·dle** \'pan-ˌhan-dᵊl\ *n* : a narrow projection of a larger territory (as a state)

[2]**panhandle** *vb* **-dled; -dling** \-dliŋ, -dᵊl-iŋ\ : to approach people on the street and beg for money — **pan·han·dler** \-dlər\ *n*

[1]**pan·ic** \'pan-ik\ *n* : a sudden overpowering fright — **panic** *adj* — **pan·icky** \'pan-i-kē\ *adj* — **pan·ic–strick·en** \'pan-ik-ˌstrik-ən\ *adj*

[2]**panic** *vb* **pan·icked** \-ikt\; **pan·ick·ing 1** : to affect or be affected with panic **2** : to produce demonstrative appreciation on the part of

pan·i·cle \'pan-i-kəl\ *n* : a loosely branched often pyramidal flower cluster (as of the oat) — **pan·i·cled** \-kəld\ *adj* — **pa·nic·u·late** \pa-'nik-yə-lət\ *adj*

pan·nier \'pan-yər\ *n* : a large basket; *esp* : one of wicker carried on the back

pan·o·ply \'pan-ə-plē\ *n, pl* **-plies 1 a** : a full suit of armor **b** : ceremonial attire **2** : something forming a protective covering **3** : a magnificently impressive array or display — **pan·o·plied** \-plēd\ *adj*

pan·o·rama \ˌpan-ə-'ram-ə, -'räm-\ *n* **1** : a picture exhibited a part at a time by being unrolled before the spectator **2 a** : an unobstructed view in every direction **b** : a comprehensive presentation of a subject — **pan·o·ram·ic** \-'ram-ik\ *adj*

pan·sy \'pan-zē\ *n, pl* **pansies** : a low-growing garden herb related to the violet; *also* : its showy flower

[1]**pant** \'pant\ *vb* **1 a** : to breathe hard or quickly : GASP **b** : to make a throbbing or puffing sound **c** : to progress with panting **2** : to long eagerly **3** : to utter with panting

[2]**pant** *n* : a panting breath or sound

pan·ta·lets *or* **pan·ta·lettes** \ˌpant-ᵊl-'ets\ *n pl* : long drawers with a ruffle at the bottom of each leg formerly worn by women and girls

pan·ta·loons \ˌpant-ᵊl-'ünz\ *n pl* : close-fitting trousers of the 19th century having straps that pass under the insteps

pan·the·ism \'pan(t)-thē-ˌiz-əm\ *n* : a doctrine that equates God with the forces and laws of the universe — **pan·the·ist** \-thē-əst\ *n* — **pan·the·is·tic** \ˌpan(t)-thē-'is-tik\ *adj*

pan·the·on \'pan(t)-thē-ˌän\ *n* **1** : a temple dedicated to all the gods **2** : a building serving as the burial place of or containing memorials to famous dead **3** : the gods of a people; *esp* : the gods officially recognized

pan·ther \'pan(t)-thər\ *n* : a large wild cat (as the leopard or cougar)

pant·ie *or* **panty** \'pant-ē\ *n, pl* **pant·ies** : a woman's or child's undergarment covering the lower trunk and made with closed crotch and short legs — usu. used in pl.

pan·to·mime \'pant-ə-ˌmīm\ *n* **1** : PANTOMIMIST **2** : a performance in which a story is told primarily by expressive bodily or facial movements of the performers **3** : conveyance of information by bodily or facial movements — **pantomime** *vb* — **pan·to·mim·ic** \ˌpant-ə-'mim-ik\ *adj*

pan·to·mim·ist \'pant-ə-ˌmim-əst, -ˌmīm-\ *n* : an actor or dancer in or a composer of pantomimes

pan·try \'pan-trē\ *n, pl* **pantries** : a small room in which food and dishes are kept or from which food is brought to the table

pants \'pan(t)s\ *n pl* **1** : TROUSERS **2** : UNDERPANTS; *esp* : PANTIE

panty hose *n* : a one-piece undergarment for women combining hosiery and panties

pap \'pap\ *n* : soft food for infants or invalids

pa·pa \'päp-ə\ *n* : FATHER

pa·pa·cy \'pā-pə-sē\ *n, pl* **-cies 1** : the office of pope **2** : a line of popes **3** : the term of a pope's reign **4** *cap* : the government of the Roman Catholic Church

pa·pal \'pā-pəl\ *adj* : of or relating to the pope or the papac

pa·paw *n* **1** \pə-'pȯ\ : PAPAYA **2** \'päp-ȯ, 'pȯp-\ : a No American tree with purple flowers and a yellow edible fruit *also* : its fruit

pa·pa·ya \pə-'pī-ə\ *n* : a tropical American tree with larg yellow black-seeded edible fruit; *also* : its fruit

[1]**pa·per** \'pā-pər\ *n* **1 a** : a sheet of usu. vegetable fibers lai down on a fine screen from a water suspension **b** : a sheet o piece of paper **2** : a piece of paper containing a written o printed statement **3** : a paper container or wrapper **4** : NEWSPAPER **5** : WALLPAPER — **on paper** : in theory

[2]**paper** *vb* **pa·pered; pa·per·ing** \'pā-p(ə-)riŋ\ : to cover or lin with paper; *esp* : to apply wallpaper to — **pa·per·er** *n*

[3]**paper** *adj* **1** : of, relating to, or made of paper **2** : of or relat ing to clerical work or written communication

pa·per·hang·er \-ˌhaŋ-ər\ *n* : one that applies wallpaper — **pa·per·hang·ing** \-ˌhaŋ-iŋ\ *n*

paper tiger *n* : one that appears strong and powerful but i really weak and ineffectual

pa·per·weight \'pā-pər-ˌwāt\ *n* : an object used to hold dow loose papers by its weight

pa·pery \'pā-p(ə-)rē\ *adj* : resembling paper in thinness o consistency — **pa·per·i·ness** *n*

pa·pier–mâ·ché \ˌpā-pər-mə-'shā, -ma-\ *n* : a light stron molding material of wastepaper pulped with glue and othe additives — **papier–mâché** *adj*

pa·pil·la \pə-'pil-ə\ *n, pl* **-pil·lae** \-'pil-(ˌ)ē, -ˌī\ : a small pro jecting bodily structure that suggests a nipple — **pap·il·la·r** \'pap-ə-ˌler-ē, pə-'pil-ə-rē\ *adj* — **pap·il·late** \'pap-ə-ˌlā pə-'pil-ət\ *adj* — **pap·il·lose** \'pap-ə-ˌlōs, pə-'pil-ˌōs\ *adj*

pa·pist \'pā-pəst\ *n, often cap* : ROMAN CATHOLIC — usu. use disparagingly — **papist** *adj* — **pa·pist·ry** \-pə-strē\ *n*

pa·poose \pa-'püs, pə-\ *n* : a No. American Indian infant

pa·pri·ka \pə-'prē-kə, pa-\ *n* : a mild red condiment made fro the fruit of some sweet peppers

pa·py·rus \pə-'pī-rəs\ *n, pl* **-rus·es** *or* **-ri** \-(ˌ)rē, -ˌrī\ **1** : a ta sedge of the Nile valley **2** : paper made from the pith of th papyrus plant **3** : a writing on or written scroll of papyrus

par \'pär\ *n* **1** : a stated value (as of a security) **2** : commo level : EQUALITY **3** : an accepted standard (as of physic condition or health) **4** : the score standard set for each ho of a golf course — **par** *adj*

par·a·ble \'par-ə-bəl\ *n* : a short simple story illustrating moral or spiritual truth

pa·rab·o·la \pə-'rab-ə-lə\ *n* : the curve formed by the interse tion of a cone with a plane parallel to one of its sides — **par·a·bol·ic** \ˌpar-ə-'bäl-ik\ *adj* — **par·a·bol·i·cal·ly** \-'bä i-k(ə-)lē\ *adv*

[1]**par·a·chute** \'par-ə-ˌshüt\ *n* **1** : a folding umbrella-shape device of light fabric used esp. for making a safe descent fro an airplane **2** : something suggestive of a parachute in form use, or operation

[2]**parachute** *vb* : to convey or descend by means of a parachu

par·a·chut·ist \'par-ə-ˌshüt-əst\ *n* : one that descends b parachute

[1]**pa·rade** \pə-'rād\ *n* **1** : pompous show or display **2** : a cere monial formation of a body of troops before a superior offic **3** : a public procession **4** : a place of promenade; *also* : thos who promenade

[2]**parade** *vb* **1 a** : to cause to maneuver or march **b** : to marc in a procession **2** : PROMENADE **3** : to exhibit ostentatious : show off — **pa·rad·er** *n*

par·a·digm \'par-ə-ˌdīm, -ˌdim\ *n* **1** : MODEL, PATTERN **2** : conjugation or declension showing a word in all its inflection forms — **par·a·dig·mat·ic** \ˌpar-ə-dig-'mat-ik\ *adj*

par·a·dise \'par-ə-ˌdīs, -ˌdīz\ *n* **1** *often cap* : HEAVEN **2** : place or state of bliss

par·a·di·si·a·cal \ˌpar-ə-də-'sī-ə-kəl\ *or* **par·a·dis·i·ac** \-'diz-

ˌak\ *adj* : of, relating to, or resembling paradise — **par·a·di·si·a·cal·ly** \-də-ˈsī-ə-k(ə-)lē\ *adv*

par·a·dox \ˈpar-ə-ˌdäks\ *n* **1 a** : a statement that seems to contradict common sense and yet is perhaps true **b** : a self-contradictory statement that at first seems true **2** : something (as a person, condition, or act) with seemingly contradictory qualities or phases — **par·a·dox·i·cal** \ˌpar-ə-ˈdäk-si-kəl\ *adj* — **par·a·dox·i·cal·ly** \-k(ə-)lē\ *adv* — **par·a·dox·i·cal·ness** *n*

par·af·fin \ˈpar-ə-fən\ *n* : a waxy substance used esp. in coating and sealing and in candles — **par·af·fin·ic** \ˌpar-ə-ˈfin-ik\ *adj*

par·a·gon \ˈpar-ə-ˌgän, -gən\ *n* : a model of excellence or perfection

¹**par·a·graph** \ˈpar-ə-ˌgraf\ *n* **1 a** : a subdivision of a piece of writing or a speech that consists of one or more sentences and develops in an organized manner one point of a subject or gives the words of one speaker **b** : a short written article (as in a newspaper) that is complete in one undivided section **2** : a character ¶ used as a reference mark or to indicate the beginning of a paragraph — **par·a·graph·ic** \ˌpar-ə-ˈgraf-ik\ *adj*

²**paragraph** *vb* **1** : to divide into paragraphs **2** : to write paragraphs esp. as a paragrapher

par·a·graph·er \ˈpar-ə-ˌgraf-ər\ *n* : a writer of paragraphs esp. for the editorial page of a newspaper

par·al·lax \ˈpar-ə-ˌlaks\ *n* : the apparent displacement or the difference in apparent direction of an object as seen from two different points not on a straight line with the object — **par·al·lac·tic** \ˌpar-ə-ˈlak-tik\ *adj*

¹**par·al·lel** \ˈpar-ə-ˌlel\ *adj* **1 a** : extending in the same direction, everywhere equidistant, and not meeting **b** : everywhere equally distant **2 a** : marked by likeness or correspondence : SIMILAR, ANALOGOUS **b** : having corresponding syntactical elements

²**parallel** *n* **1 a** : a parallel line, curve, or surface **b** : one of the imaginary circles on the surface of the earth paralleling the equator and marking the latitude **c** : a character ‖ used as a reference mark **2 a** : something equal or similar in all essential particulars : COUNTERPART **b** : SIMILARITY, ANALOGUE

³**parallel** *vt* **1** : to indicate similarity or analogy of : COMPARE **2 a** : to show something equal to : MATCH **b** : to correspond to **3** : to extend, run, or move in a direction parallel to

par·al·lel·o·gram \ˌpar-ə-ˈlel-ə-ˌgram\ *n* : a quadrilateral whose opposite sides are parallel and equal

pa·ral·y·sis \pə-ˈral-ə-səs\ *n, pl* **-y·ses** \-ə-ˌsēz\ **1** : complete or partial loss of function esp. when involving motion or sensation in a part of the body **2** : loss of the ability to move or act — **par·a·lyt·ic** \ˌpar-ə-ˈlit-ik\ *adj or n*

par·a·lyze \ˈpar-ə-ˌlīz\ *vt* **1** : to affect with paralysis **2** : to make powerless, ineffective, or unable to act or function

pa·ram·e·ter \pə-ˈram-ət-ər\ *n* : a characteristic element or constant factor — **para·met·ric** \ˌpar-ə-ˈme-trik\ *adj*

par·a·mount \ˈpar-ə-ˌmaůnt\ *adj* : superior to all others : SUPREME

par·amour \ˈpar-ə-ˌmůr\ *n* : an illicit lover; *esp* : MISTRESS

par·a·noia \ˌpar-ə-ˈnȯi-ə\ *n* : a mental disorder marked by delusions and irrational suspicion — **par·a·noi·ac** \-ˈnȯi-ˌak, -ˈnȯi-ik\ *adj or n* — **par·a·noid** \ˈpar-ə-ˌnȯid\ *adj or n*

par·a·pet \ˈpar-ə-pət, -ˌpet\ *n* **1** : a wall of earth or stone to protect soldiers : BREASTWORK **2** : a low wall or railing to protect the edge of a platform, roof, or bridge

par·aph \ˈpar-əf\ *n* : a flourish at the end of a signature sometimes meant to safeguard against forgery

par·a·pher·na·lia \ˌpar-ə-fə(r)-ˈnāl-yə\ *n sing or pl* **1** : personal belongings **2** : FURNISHINGS, APPARATUS

¹**par·a·phrase** \ˈpar-ə-ˌfrāz\ *n* : a restatement of a text, passage, or work giving the meaning in another form

²**paraphrase** *vb* : to make a paraphrase of : give the meaning of something in different words — **par·a·phras·er** *n*

par·a·ple·gia \ˌpar-ə-ˈplē-j(ē-)ə\ *n* : paralysis of the lower trunk and legs — **par·a·ple·gic** \-jik\ *adj or n*

par·a·site \ˈpar-ə-ˌsīt\ *n* **1** : a person who lives at the expense of another **2** : an organism living in or on another organism usu. to its harm — **par·a·sit·ic** \ˌpar-ə-ˈsit-ik\ *adj* — **par·a·sit·i·cal·ly** \-i-k(ə-)lē\ *adv* — **par·a·sit·ism** \ˈpar-ə-ˌsīt-ˌiz-əm\ *n*

par·a·sit·ize \ˈpar-ə-sə-ˌtīz, -ˌsīt-ˌīz\ *vt* : to infest or live on or with as a parasite

par·a·sol \ˈpar-ə-ˌsȯl\ *n* : a lightweight umbrella used as a protection against the sun

para·thi·on \ˌpar-ə-ˈthī-ən, -ˌän\ *n* : a highly toxic insecticide

para·troops \ˈpar-ə-ˌtrüps\ *n pl* : troops trained and equipped to parachute from an airplane — **para·troop** \-ˌtrüp\ *adj* — **para·troop·er** \-ˌtrü-pər\ *n*

para·ty·phoid \ˌpar-ə-ˈtī-ˌfȯid\ *n* : a food poisoning resembling typhoid fever

par·boil \ˈpär-ˌbȯil\ *vt* **1** : to boil briefly usu. before cooking in another manner **2** : OVERHEAT

¹**par·cel** \ˈpär-səl\ *n* **1** : FRAGMENT, PORTION **2** : a tract or plot of land **3** : a company, collection, or group of persons, animals, or things : LOT **4** : a wrapped bundle : PACKAGE

²**parcel** *vt* **par·celed** *or* **par·celled**; **par·cel·ing** *or* **par·cel·ling** \ˈpär-s(ə-)liŋ\ **1** : to divide into parts : DISTRIBUTE **2** : to make up into a parcel : WRAP

parch \ˈpärch\ *vb* **1** : to toast under dry heat **2** : to dry up : shrivel with heat

parch·ment \ˈpärch-mənt\ *n* **1** : the skin of a sheep or goat prepared for use as a writing material **2** : a parchment manuscript; *also* : an academic diploma

¹**par·don** \ˈpärd-ᵊn\ *n* **1 a** : the excusing of an offense without exacting a penalty **b** : remission of the legal penalties of an offense **2** : excuse for a fault or discourtesy — **par·don·a·ble** \ˈpärd-nə-bəl, -ᵊn-ə-bəl\ *adj* — **par·don·a·bly** \-blē\ *adv*

²**pardon** *vt* **par·doned**; **par·don·ing** \ˈpärd-niŋ, -ᵊn-iŋ\ **1** : to free from penalty **2** : to allow (an offense) to pass without punishment : FORGIVE

pare \ˈpa(ə)r\ *vt* **1** : to cut or shave off the outside or the ends of **2** : to diminish gradually by or as if by paring

par·e·go·ric \ˌpar-ə-ˈgȯr-ik\ *n* : an alcoholic preparation of opium and camphor used esp. to relieve pain

par·ent \ˈpar-ənt\ *n* **1 a** : one that begets or brings forth offspring **b** : an animal or plant regarded in relation to its offspring **2** : the material, source, or originator of something — **parent** *adj*

par·ent·age \-ənt-ij\ *n* **1** : descent from parents or ancestors : LINEAGE **2** : DERIVATION, ORIGIN

pa·ren·tal \pə-ˈrent-ᵊl\ *adj* : of, typical of, or being parents — **pa·ren·tal·ly** \-ᵊl-ē\ *adv*

pa·ren·the·sis \pə-ˈren(t)-thə-səs\ *n, pl* **-the·ses** \-thə-ˌsēz\ **1 a** : an amplifying or explanatory word, phrase, or sentence inserted in a passage from which it is usu. set off by punctuation **b** : DIGRESSION **2** : one of a pair of marks ( ) used to enclose a parenthetic expression or to group a symbolic unit in a mathematical expression — **par·en·thet·ic** \ˌpar-ən-ˈthet-ik\ *or* **par·en·thet·i·cal** \-ˈthet-i-kəl\ *adj* — **par·en·thet·i·cal·ly** \-i-k(ə-)lē\ *adv*

pa·ren·the·size \pə-ˈren(t)-thə-ˌsīz\ *vt* : to make a parenthesis of

par·ent·hood \ˈpar-ənt-ˌhůd\ *n* : the position, function, or standing of a parent

pa·re·sis \pə-ˈrē-səs, ˈpar-ə-\ *n, pl* **-re·ses** \-ˈrē-ˌsēz, -ə-ˌsēz\ : a usu. partial paralysis; *also* : a syphilitic disorder marked by mental and paralytic symptoms — **pa·ret·ic** \pə-ˈret-ik\ *adj or n*

par ex·cel·lence \ˌpär-ˌek-sə-ˈläⁿs\ *adv* (*or adj*) : in the highest degree : PREEMINENTLY

par·fait \pär-ˈfā\ *n* **1** : a flavored custard containing whipped cream and syrup frozen without stirring **2** : a cold dessert made of layers of fruit, syrup, ice cream, and whipped cream

pa·ri·ah \pə-ˈrī-ə\ *n* : OUTCAST

pa·ri·etal \pə-ˈrī-ət-ᵊl\ *adj* : of, relating to, or forming the walls of an anatomical structure

pari–mu·tu·el \ˌpar-i-ˈmyü-chə-wəl, -chəl\ *n* : a system of betting on a race in which those who bet on the winners of the first three places share the total stakes minus a percentage for the management

par·ing \ˈpa(ə)r-iŋ\ *n* **1** : the act of cutting away an edge or surface **2** : something pared off

par·ish \ˈpar-ish\ *n* **1** : a section of a diocese in charge of a priest or minister; *also* : the persons who live in such a section **2** : the members of any church **3** : a civil division of the state of Louisiana corresponding to a county in other states

pa·rish·io·ner \pə-ˈrish-(ə-)nər\ *n* : a member or resident of a parish

par·i·ty \ˈpar-ət-ē\ *n, pl* **-ties** : the quality or state of being equal or equivalent

[1]park \ˈpärk\ *n* **1 a** : a piece of ground in or near a city or town kept as a place of beauty and recreation **b** : an area maintained in its natural state as a public property **2** : a space occupied by military animals, vehicles, or materials **3** : an enclosed arena esp. for ball games

[2]park *vb* **1** : to leave a vehicle temporarily on a public way or in a place reserved for the purpose **2** : to set and leave temporarily

par·ka \ˈpär-kə\ *n* : a hooded fur pullover garment for arctic wear; *also* : a garment of similar style made of windproof fabric for sports or military wear

park·way \ˈpärk-ˌwā\ *n* : a broad landscaped thoroughfare

par·lance \ˈpär-lən(t)s\ *n* : manner or mode of speech : IDIOM

[1]par·lay \ˈpär-ˌlā, -lē\ *vt* : to bet in a parlay; *esp* : to multiply by or as if by so betting

[2]parlay *n* : a series of bets in which the original stake plus its winnings are risked on the successive wagers

[1]par·ley \ˈpär-lē\ *vi* **par·leyed**; **par·ley·ing** : to speak with another : CONFER; *esp* : to discuss terms with an enemy

[2]parley *n, pl* **parleys** : DISCUSSION, CONVERSATION; *esp* : a conference with an enemy

par·lia·ment \ˈpär-lə-mənt, ˈpärl-yə-\ *n* **1** : a formal conference on public affairs **2** : an assembly that constitutes the supreme legislative body of a country (as the United Kingdom) — **par·lia·men·ta·ry** \ˌpär-lə-ˈment-ə-rē, ˌpärl-yə-, -ˈmen-trē\ *adj*

par·lia·men·tar·i·an \ˌpär-lə-ˌmen-ˈter-ē-ən, -mən-, ˌpärl-yə-\ *n* **1** *often cap* : an adherent of the parliament in opposition to the king during the English Civil War **2** : an expert in parliamentary procedure

par·lor \ˈpär-lər\ *n* **1** : a room used primarily for conversation or the reception of guests **2** : any of various business places

par·lous \ˈpär-ləs\ *adj* : full of danger or risk : PRECARIOUS — **par·lous·ly** *adv*

pa·ro·chi·al \pə-ˈrō-kē-əl\ *adj* **1** : of or relating to a parish **2** : confined as if within the borders of a parish : NARROW, PROVINCIAL — **pa·ro·chi·al·ism** \-kē-ə-ˌliz-əm\ *n*

par·o·dy \ˈpar-əd-ē\ *n, pl* **-dies** **1** : a literary or musical work in which the style of an author or work is closely imitated for comic effect or in ridicule **2** : a feeble or ridiculous imitation — **par·o·dist** \-əd-əst\ *n* — **parody** *vt*

[1]pa·role \pə-ˈrōl\ *n* **1** : a promise confirmed by a pledge; *esp* : the promise of a prisoner of war to fulfill stated conditions in consideration of his release **2** : a conditional release of a prisoner before his sentence has expired

[2]parole *vt* : to release (a prisoner) on parole — **pa·rol·ee** \pə-ˌrō-ˈlē, ˌpar-ə-ˈlē\ *n*

par·ox·ysm \ˈpar-ək-ˌsiz-əm\ *n* **1** : a fit, attack, or sudden increase of violence of a disease that occurs at intervals **2** : a sudden violent emotion or action — **par·ox·ys·mal** \ˌpar-ək-ˈsiz-məl\ *adj*

par·quet \pär-ˈkā\ *n* **1** : a flooring of parquetry **2** : the lower floor of a theater esp. in front of the balcony

par·que·try \ˈpär-kə-trē\ *n, pl* **-tries** : a patterned wood inlay used esp. for floors

par·ra·keet \ˈpar-ə-ˌkēt\ *n* : any of numerous usu. small slender parrots with a long graduated tail

par·ri·cide \ˈpar-ə-ˌsīd\ *n* **1** : one that murders his father or mother or a close relative **2** : the act of a parricide — **par·ri·cid·al** \ˌpar-ə-ˈsīd-ᵊl\ *adj*

[1]par·rot \ˈpar-ət\ *n* **1** : a bright-colored tropical bird with a strong hooked bill **2** : a person who repeats words mechanically and without understanding

[2]parrot *vt* : to repeat by rote

par·ry \ˈpar-ē\ *vb* **par·ried**; **par·ry·ing** **1** : to ward off a weapon or blow : turn aside skillfully **2** : to evade esp. by an adroit answer — **parry** *n*

parse \ˈpärs, ˈpärz\ *vb* **1** : to analyze a sentence by naming its parts and their relations to each other **2** : to give the part of speech of a word and explain its relation to other words in a sentence

par·si·mo·ni·ous \ˌpär-sə-ˈmō-nē-əs\ *adj* : excessively frugal : STINGY, NIGGARDLY — **par·si·mo·ni·ous·ly** *adv* — **par·si·mo·ni·ous·ness** *n*

par·si·mo·ny \ˈpär-sə-ˌmō-nē\ *n* : extreme frugality : STINGINESS

pars·ley \ˈpär-slē\ *n, pl* **parsleys** : a garden plant widely grown for its finely divided leaves which are used as a flavoring or garnish

pars·nip \ˈpär-snəp\ *n* : a garden plant with a long white root used as a vegetable; *also* : this root

par·son \ˈpärs-ᵊn\ *n* **1** : a minister in charge of a parish : RECTOR **2** : CLERGYMAN; *esp* : a Protestant pastor

par·son·age \ˈpär-snij, ˈpärs-ᵊn-ij\ *n* : the house provided by a church for its pastor

[1]part \ˈpärt\ *n* **1 a** : a division or portion of a whole **b** : the melody or score for a particular voice or instrument **c** : a constituent member of a machine or apparatus; *also* : a spare piece or member **2** : DUTY, FUNCTION **3** : one of the opposing sides in a conflict **4 a** : an actor's lines in a play **b** : the role of a character in a play **5** : the line where the hair is divided in combing

[2]part *vb* **1 a** : to separate from or take leave of someone **b** : to take leave of one another **2** : to go away : DEPART **3** : to become separated, detached, or broken **4** : to give up possession or control **5 a** : to divide into parts or shares **b** : to separate by combing on each side of a line **6** : SEPARATE, SUNDER

par·take \pär-ˈtāk, pər-\ *vi* **par·took** \-ˈtu̇k\; **par·tak·en** \-ˈtā-kən\; **par·tak·ing** **1 a** : to take a part or share **b** : PARTICIPATE **2** : to have some of the qualities or attributes of something — **par·tak·er** *n*

par·the·no·gen·e·sis \ˌpär-thə-nō-ˈjen-ə-səs\ *n, pl* **-gen·e·ses** \-ə-ˌsēz\ : development of a new individual from an unfertilized egg — **par·the·no·ge·net·ic** \-jə-ˈnet-ik\ *adj* — **par·the·no·ge·net·i·cal·ly** \-ˈnet-i-k(ə-)lē\ *adv*

par·tial \ˈpär-shəl\ *adj* **1** : inclined to favor one side or party over another : BIASED **2** : markedly or excessively fond of someone or something **3** : of or relating to a part rather than the whole — **par·tial·ly** \ˈpärsh-(ə-)lē\ *adv*

par·ti·al·i·ty \ˌpär-shē-ˈal-ət-ē, pär-ˈshal-\ *n, pl* **-ties** **1** : the quality or state of being partial : BIAS **2** : a special taste or liking

par·tic·i·pant \pər-ˈtis-ə-pənt, pär-\ *n* : one that participates

par·tic·i·pate \pər-ˈtis-ə-ˌpāt, pär-\ *vi* : to take part or have share in something (as an activity) usu. in common with others — **par·tic·i·pa·tion** \-ˌtis-ə-ˈpā-shən\ *n*

par·ti·cip·i·al \ˌpärt-ə-ˈsip-ē-əl\ *adj* : of, relating to, or formed with or from a participle — **par·ti·cip·i·al·ly** \-ē-ə-lē\ *adv*
par·ti·ci·ple \ˈpärt-ə-ˌsip-əl\ *n* : a word having the characteristics of both verb and adjective
par·ti·cle \ˈpärt-i-kəl\ *n* **1** : one of the minute subdivisions of matter (as a molecule, atom, electron) **2 a** : a minute quantity or fragment **b** : the smallest possible portion or amount of something
par·ti–col·ored \ˌpärt-ē-ˈkəl-ərd\ *adj* : showing different colors or tints
[1]**par·tic·u·lar** \pə(r)-ˈtik-yə-lər\ *adj* **1** : of or relating to a single person or thing **2** : of or relating to details : MINUTE **3** : distinctive among others : SPECIAL **4 a** : attentive to details : EXACT **b** : hard to please : EXACTING, FASTIDIOUS
[2]**particular** *n* : an individual fact, detail, or item — **in particular 1** : ESPECIALLY, PARTICULARLY **2** : in detail : INDIVIDUALLY
par·tic·u·lar·i·ty \-ˌtik-yə-ˈlar-ət-ē\ *n, pl* **-ties 1 a** : a minute detail : PARTICULAR **b** : an individual characteristic : PECULIARITY **2** : the quality or state of being particular as opposed to universal **3** : attentiveness to detail : EXACTNESS, FASTIDIOUSNESS
par·tic·u·lar·ize \-ˈtik-yə-lə-ˌrīz\ *vb* : to go into details : state in detail : SPECIFY — **par·tic·u·lar·i·za·tion** \-ˌtik-yə-lə-rə-ˈzā-shən\ *n*
par·tic·u·lar·ly \-ˈtik-yə-lər-lē\ *adv* **1** : in a particular manner **2** : to an unusual degree : ESPECIALLY
[1]**part·ing** \ˈpärt-iŋ\ *n* **1** : SEPARATION, DIVISION **2** : a place where a division or separation occurs **3** : LEAVE-TAKING
[2]**parting** *adj* **1** : DEPARTING **2** : serving to divide : SEPARATING **3** : given, taken, or performed at parting
par·ti·san \ˈpärt-ə-zən\ *n* **1** : a person who takes the part of another; *esp* : a devoted adherent to the cause of another **2** : a member of a guerrilla force within enemy lines who impedes the enemy by sabotage and raids — **partisan** *adj* — **par·ti·san·ship** \-ˌship\ *n*
par·tite \ˈpär-ˌtīt\ *adj* : divided into a usu. specified number of parts
par·ti·tion \pər-ˈtish-ən, pär-\ *n* **1 a** : the action of parting : DIVISION **b** : separation of a class or whole into constituent elements; *esp* : the division of a united territory among two or more governments **2** : an interior dividing wall **3** : PART, SECTION — **partition** *vt* — **par·ti·tion·er** \-ˈtish-(ə-)nər\ *n*
par·ti·tive \ˈpärt-ət-iv\ *adj* **1** : of, relating to, or denoting a part **2** : serving to indicate that of which a part is specified
part·ly \ˈpärt-lē\ *adv* : in some measure or degree : PARTIALLY
[1]**part·ner** \ˈpärt-nər\ *n* **1 a** : one that is associated in action with another : COLLEAGUE **b** : either of a couple who dance together **c** : one of two or more persons who play together in a game against an opposing side **d** : HUSBAND, WIFE **2** : a member of a partnership
[2]**partner** *vt* : to join as partner : act as partner to
part·ner·ship \ˈpärt-nər-ˌship\ *n* : the state of being a partner : PARTICIPATION
part of speech : a traditional class of words distinguished according to the kind of idea denoted and the function performed in a sentence
partook *past of* PARTAKE
par·tridge \ˈpär-trij\ *n, pl* **partridge** *or* **par·tridg·es** : any of several stout-bodied game birds
part–song \ˈpärt-ˌsȯŋ\ *n* : a song consisting of two or more voice parts
par·tu·ri·tion \ˌpärt-ə-ˈrish-ən\ *n* : the act or process of giving birth to offspring
par·ty \ˈpärt-ē\ *n, pl* **parties 1** : a person or group taking one side of a question **2** : a group of persons organized for the purpose of influencing or directing the policies of a government **3** : a person or group participating in an action, affair, or transaction **4** : a particular individual : PERSON **5** : a detail of soldiers **6** : a social gathering — **party** *adj*
par·ve·nu \ˈpär-və-ˌn(y)ü\ *n* : one who has recently or suddenly risen to wealth or power and has not yet secured the social position appropriate to it : UPSTART — **parvenu** *adj*
pa·sha \ˈpäsh-ə, pə-ˈshä\ *n* : a man (as formerly a governor in Turkey) of high rank
[1]**pass** \ˈpas\ *vb* **1** : MOVE, PROCEED **2 a** : to go away : DEPART **b** : DIE — often used with *on* or *away* **3** : to go by or move past **4 a** : to go across, over, or through **b** : to go unchallenged **5 a** : to change or transfer ownership **b** : to go from the control or possession of one person or group to that of another **6 a** : HAPPEN, OCCUR **b** : to take place as a mutual exchange or transaction **7 a** : to secure the approval of a legislative body **b** : to go through or allow to go through an inspection, test, or course of study successfully **8** : to be held or regarded **9** : to decline to bid, bet, or draw an additional card in a card game **10** : to go beyond; *esp* : SURPASS **11** : to leave out in an account or narration **12 a** : UNDERGO **b** : to cause or permit to elapse : SPEND **13 a** : to put in circulation **b** : to transfer from one person to another **c** : to transfer the ball or puck to another player **14** : VOID **15** : to permit to reach first base on a base on balls — **pass·er** *n* — **pass muster** : to pass an inspection or examination — **pass the buck** : to shift a responsibility to someone else — **pass the hat** : to take up a collection of money
[2]**pass** *n* : a gap in a mountain range
[3]**pass** *n* **1** : the act or an instance of passing : PASSAGE **2** : ACCOMPLISHMENT **3** : a state of affairs : CONDITION **4** : a written authorization to leave, enter, or move about freely **5** : a transfer of a ball or a puck from one player to another on the same team **6** : BASE ON BALLS **7** : a refusal to bid, bet, or draw an additional card in a card game **8** : EFFORT, TRY; *esp* : an amorous approach
pass·a·ble \ˈpas-ə-bəl\ *adj* **1** : capable of being passed, crossed, or traveled on **2** : barely good enough : TOLERABLE — **pass·a·bly** \-blē\ *adv*
pas·sage \ˈpas-ij\ *n* **1** : the action or process of passing from one place or condition to another **2** : something (as a road, channel, or corridor) giving passage or access **3 a** : VOYAGE, JOURNEY **b** : a privilege of conveyance as a passenger **4** : the passing of a legislative measure or law : ENACTMENT **5** : a usu. brief portion (as of a written work or speech)
pas·sage·way \-ˌwā\ *n* : a road or way by which a person or thing may pass : PASSAGE
pass·book \ˈpas-ˌbu̇k\ *n* : BANKBOOK
pas·sé \pa-ˈsā\ *adj* : behind the times : OUTMODED
pas·sen·ger \ˈpas-ᵊn-jər\ *n* : a traveler in a public or private conveyance
pass·er·by \ˌpas-ər-ˈbī\ *n, pl* **pass·ers·by** \-ərz-\ : one who passes by
pas·ser·ine \ˈpas-ə-ˌrīn\ *adj* : of or relating to the great group of birds comprising singing birds that perch — **passerine** *n*
[1]**pass·ing** \ˈpas-iŋ\ *n* : the act of one that passes or causes to pass; *esp* : DEATH — **in passing** : PARENTHETICALLY
[2]**passing** *adj* **1** : going by or past **2** : having a brief duration **3** : marked by haste or inattention : SUPERFICIAL **4** : given on satisfactory completion of an examination or course of study
[3]**passing** *adv* : to a surpassing degree : EXCEEDINGLY
pas·sion \ˈpash-ən\ *n* **1** *often cap* : the sufferings of Christ between the night of the Last Supper and his death **2 a** *pl* : the emotions as distinguished from reason **b** : violent, intense, or overmastering feeling **3 a** : ardent affection : LOVE **b** : a strong liking for some activity, object, or concept **c** : sexual desire **d** : an object of desire or deep interest — **pas·sion·al** \-ᵊl\ *adj* — **pas·sion·less** \-ləs\ *adj*
pas·sion·ate \ˈpash-(ə-)nət\ *adj* **1 a** : easily aroused to anger **b** : filled with anger : ANGRY **2** : capable of, affected by, or

expressing intense feeling 3 : strongly affected with sexual desire — **pas·sion·ate·ly** *adv* — **pas·sion·ate·ness** *n*

[1]**pas·sive** \'pas-iv\ *adj* 1 a : not active but acted upon : receptive to or affected by outside force, agency, or influence b : of, relating to, or constituting a verb form or voice indicating that the person or thing represented by the grammatical subject is subjected to or affected by the action represented by the verb 2 : receiving or enduring without resistance : SUBMISSIVE — **pas·sive·ly** *adv* — **pas·sive·ness** *n* — **pas·siv·i·ty** \pa-'siv-ət-ē\ *n*

[2]**passive** *n* : the passive voice; *also* : a verb form in the passive voice

pass·key \'pas-,kē\ *n* 1 : a key for opening two or more locks 2 : SKELETON KEY

pass off *vt* 1 : to make public or offer for sale with intent to deceive 2 : to give a false identity or character to

pass out *vi* : to lose consciousness

Pass·over \'pas-,ō-vər\ *n* : a Jewish holiday celebrated in March or April in commemoration of the liberation of the Hebrews from slavery in Egypt

pass·port \'pas-,pōrt\ *n* : an official document issued to a citizen about to travel abroad that requests protection for him in foreign countries

pass up *vt* : DECLINE, REJECT

pass·word \'pas-,wərd\ *n* : a word or phrase that must be spoken by a person before he is allowed to pass a guard

[1]**past** \'past\ *adj* 1 a : AGO b : just gone by or elapsed 2 : having existed or taken place in a period before the present : BYGONE 3 : of, relating to, or constituting a verb tense that in English is usu. formed by internal vowel change (as in *sang*) or by the addition of a suffix (as in *laughed*) and that expresses elapsed time

[2]**past** *prep* 1 a : beyond the age for or of b : AFTER 2 a : at the farther side of : BEYOND b : in a course or direction going close to and then beyond 3 : beyond the range, scope, or sphere of

[3]**past** *n* 1 a : time gone by b : something that happened or was done in the past 2 : a verb form in the past tense 3 : a past life that is secret or questionable

[4]**past** *adv* : so as to reach and go beyond a point near at hand

[1]**paste** \'pāst\ *n* 1 a : DOUGH b : a smooth food product made by evaporation or grinding 2 : a preparation of flour and water or starch and water used for sticking things together 3 : a very brilliant glass used for the manufacture of artificial gems

[2]**paste** *vt* 1 : to cause to adhere by paste : STICK 2 : to cover with or as if with something pasted on

[3]**paste** *vt* : to hit hard

paste·board \-,bōrd\ *n* 1 : a stiff material made of sheets of paper pasted together 2 : cardboard of medium thickness

[1]**pas·tel** \pa-'stel\ *n* 1 : a paste made of ground color and used for making crayons; *also* : a crayon made of such paste 2 : a drawing in pastel 3 : any of various pale or light colors

[2]**pastel** *adj* 1 a : of or relating to a pastel b : made with pastels 2 : pale and light in color

pas·tern \'pas-tərn\ *n* : the part of the foot of a horse between the fetlock and the joint at the hoof

pas·teur·i·za·tion \,pas-chə-rə-'zā-shən, ,pas-tə-\ *n* : partial sterilization of a substance and esp. a fluid (as milk) at a temperature and period of exposure that destroys objectionable organisms without major chemical alteration of the substance

pas·teur·ize \'pas-chə-,rīz, 'pas-tə-\ *vt* : to subject to pasteurization — **pas·teur·iz·er** *n*

pas·tiche \pa-'stēsh\ *n* : a composition (as in literature or music) made up of selections from different works : POTPOURRI

pas·tille \pa-'stēl\ *n* 1 : a small mass of aromatic paste for fumigating or scenting the air of a room 2 : an aromatic or medicated lozenge : TROCHE

pas·time \'pas-,tīm\ *n* : something that serves to make time pass agreeably : DIVERSION

past·i·ness \'pā-stē-nəs\ *n* : the quality or state of being pasty

pas·tor \'pas-tər\ *n* : a minister or priest in charge of a church or parish

[1]**pas·to·ral** \'pas-t(ə-)rəl\ *adj* 1 a : of or relating to shepherds or rural life b : devoted to or based on livestock raising c : RURAL d : portraying the life of shepherds or country people esp. in an idealized and conventionalized manner 2 : of or relating to spiritual care or to the pastor of a church — **pas·to·ral·ly** \-t(ə-)rə-lē\ *adv* — **pas·to·ral·ness** *n*

[2]**pas·to·ral** \'pas-t(ə-)rəl\ *n* 1 : a letter addressed by a bishop to his diocese 2 a : a literary work dealing with shepherds or rural life in a usu. artificial manner b : pastoral poetry or drama c : a rural picture or scene

pas·tor·ate \'pas-t(ə-)rət\ *n* : the office, duties, or term of service of a pastor

past·ry \'pā-strē\ *n, pl* **pastries** 1 : sweet baked goods (as cakes, puffs, or tarts) made of dough or having a crust made of enriched dough 2 : a piece of pastry

pas·tur·age \'pas-chə-rij\ *n* : PASTURE

[1]**pas·ture** \'pas-chər\ *n* 1 : plants (as grass) for the feeding esp. of grazing animals 2 : land or a plot of land used for grazing

[2]**pasture** *vb* 1 : GRAZE 2 : to feed (as cattle) on pasture 3 : to use as pasture — **pas·tur·er** *n*

[1]**pas·ty** \'pas-tē\ *n, pl* **pasties** : PIE 1; *esp* : a meat pie

[2]**pasty** \'pā-stē\ *adj* : resembling paste; *esp* : pallid and unhealthy in appearance

[1]**pat** \'pat\ *n* 1 : a light blow esp. with the hand or a flat instrument 2 : a light tapping often rhythmical sound 3 : something (as butter) shaped into a small flat usu. square individual portion

[2]**pat** *vb* **pat·ted**; **pat·ting** 1 : to strike lightly with a flat instrument : strike or beat gently 2 : to flatten, smooth, or put into place or shape with light blows (as of the hand) 3 : to stroke or tap gently with the hand to soothe, caress, or show approval 4 : to walk or run with a light beating sound

[3]**pat** *adv* : in a pat manner : APTLY, PROMPTLY

[4]**pat** *adj* 1 a : exactly suited to the purpose or occasion : APT, OPPORTUNE b : too exactly suitable : CONTRIVED 2 : learned, mastered, or memorized exactly 3 : FIRM, UNYIELDING

[1]**patch** \'pach\ *n* 1 : a piece of material used to mend or cover a hole, a torn place, or a weak spot 2 : a small piece (as of cloth) worn on the face to cover a defect or to attract attention 3 : a small piece : SCRAP 4 a : a small area or plot distinguished from its surroundings b : a spot of color : BLOTCH

[2]**patch** *vt* 1 : to mend, cover, or fill up a hole or weak spot in 2 a : to make of patches or fragments b : to mend or put together esp. hastily or clumsily c : SETTLE, ADJUST — usu used with *up*

patch·work \-,wərk\ *n* 1 : something composed of miscellaneous or incongruous parts : HODGEPODGE 2 : pieces of cloth of various colors and shapes sewed together usu. in a pattern — **patchwork** *adj*

patchy \'pach-ē\ *adj* : consisting of or marked by patches : resembling patchwork : SPOTTY

[1]**pate** \'pāt\ *n* : HEAD; *esp* : the crown of the head — **pat·ed** \'pāt-əd\ *adj*

[2]**pâ·té** \pä-'tā\ *n* 1 : a meat or fish pie or patty 2 : a spread of finely mashed seasoned and spiced meat

pat·en \'pat-ᵊn\ *n* 1 : a plate of precious metal for the eucharistic bread 2 : PLATE 3 : a thin disk (as of metal)

[1]**pat·ent** *5, 6 are* 'pat-ᵊnt, 'pāt-; *1–4 are* 'pat-\ *adj* 1 : open to public inspection — used chiefly in the phrase *letters patent* 2 : PATENTED 3 : of, relating to, or concerned with the granting of patents esp. for inventions 4 : marketed as

proprietary commodity **5** : OPEN, UNOBSTRUCTED **6** : EVIDENT, OBVIOUS — **pat·en·cy** \-ᵊn-sē\ *n* — **pat·ent·ly** *adv*

²pat·ent \'pat-ᵊnt\ *n* **1** : an official document conferring a right or privilege **2 a** : a writing securing to an inventor for a term of years the exclusive right to make, use, or sell his invention **b** : the right so granted **3** : PRIVILEGE, LICENSE

³pat·ent *vt* : to secure by patent — **pat·ent·a·ble** *adj*

pat·en·tee \ˌpat-ᵊn-'tē\ *n* : one to whom a grant is made or a privilege secured by patent

pa·ter·fa·mil·i·as \ˌpāt-ər-fə-'mil-ē-əs\ *n* **1** : the male head of a household **2** : the father of a family

pa·ter·nal \pə-'tərn-ᵊl\ *adj* **1** : of or relating to a father : FATHERLY **2** : received or inherited from one's father **3** : related through the father — **pa·ter·nal·ly** \-ᵊl-ē\ *adv*

pa·ter·nal·ism \-ᵊl-ˌiz-əm\ *n* : the principle or practice of governing or of exercising authority (as over a group of employees) in a manner suggesting the care and control exercised by a father over his children — **pa·ter·nal·ist** \-ᵊl-əst\ *adj or n* — **pa·ter·nal·is·tic** \-ˌtərn-ᵊl-'is-tik\ *adj*

pa·ter·ni·ty \pə-'tər-nət-ē\ *n* **1** : the quality or state of being a father **2** : origin or descent from a father

path \'path, 'path\ *n, pl* **paths** \'pat͟hz, 'paths, 'pat͟hz, 'paths\ **1** : a trodden way **2 a** : the way traversed by something : COURSE, ROUTE **b** : a way of life, conduct, or thought

pa·thet·ic \pə-'thet-ik\ *adj* **1** : evoking tenderness, pity, or sorrow : PITIABLE **2** : marked by sorrow or melancholy : SAD — **pa·thet·i·cal·ly** \-'thet-i-k(ə-)lē\ *adv*

path·find·er \'path-ˌfīn-dər, 'path-\ *n* : one that discovers a way; *esp* : one that explores untraveled regions to mark out a new route

path·less \-ləs\ *adj* : UNTROD, TRACKLESS

path·o·gen \'path-ə-jən\ *n* : a specific cause (as a bacterium or virus) of disease — **path·o·gen·ic** \ˌpath-ə-'jen-ik\ *adj* — **path·o·ge·nic·i·ty** \-jə-'nis-ət-ē\ *n*

path·o·log·i·cal \ˌpath-ə-'läj-i-kəl\ *or* **path·o·log·ic** \-ik\ *adj* **1** : of or relating to pathology **2** : altered or caused by disease — **path·o·log·i·cal·ly** \-'läj-i-k(ə-)lē\ *adv*

pa·thol·o·gist \pə-'thäl-ə-jəst, pa-\ *n* : a specialist in pathology and esp. in tissue pathology

pa·thol·o·gy \-jē\ *n* **1** : the study of the essential nature of diseases **2** : something abnormal; *esp* : the structural and functional deviations from the normal that constitute disease or characterize a particular disease

pa·thos \'pā-ˌthäs\ *n* **1** : an element in experience or in artistic representation evoking pity or compassion **2** : an emotion of sympathetic pity

path·way \'path-ˌwā, 'path-\ *n* : PATH, COURSE

pa·tience \'pā-shən(t)s\ *n* : the capacity, habit, or fact of being patient

pa·tient \'pā-shənt\ *adj* **1** : bearing pains or trials calmly or without complaint **2** : manifesting forbearance under provocation or strain **3** : not hasty or impetuous **4** : steadfast despite opposition, difficulty, or adversity — **pa·tient·ly** *adv*

patient *n* : an individual awaiting or under medical care and treatment

pat·i·na \'pat-ə-nə, pə-'tē-nə\ *n, pl* **patinas** *or* **pat·i·nae** \'pat-ə-ˌnē, -ˌnī\ : a usu. green film formed on copper and bronze by long exposure to moist air

pat·io \'pat-ē-ˌō, 'pät-\ *n, pl* **-i·os** **1** : COURTYARD; *esp* : an inner court open to the sky **2** : an often paved recreation area that adjoins a dwelling

pa·tois \'pa-ˌtwä\ *n, pl* **patois** \-ˌtwäz\ **1 a** : a dialect other than the standard or literary dialect **b** : illiterate or provincial speech **2** : JARGON 2

pa·tri·arch \'pā-trē-ˌärk\ *n* **1 a** : a man revered as father or founder **b** : a venerable old man **2** : an ecclesiastical dignitary (as the bishop of an Eastern Orthodox see) — **pa·tri·ar·chal** \ˌpā-trē-'är-kəl\ *adj*

pa·tri·cian \pə-'trish-ən\ *n* **1** : a person of high birth : ARISTOCRAT **2** : a person of breeding and cultivation — **patrician** *adj*

pat·ri·mo·ny \'pa-trə-ˌmō-nē\ *n, pl* **-nies** : something inherited or derived from one's father or ancestors : HERITAGE — **pat·ri·mo·ni·al** \ˌpa-trə-'mō-nē-əl\ *adj*

pa·tri·ot \'pā-trē-ət\ *n* : a person who loves his country

pa·tri·ot·ic \ˌpā-trē-'ät-ik\ *adj* **1** : inspired by patriotism **2** : befitting or characteristic of a patriot — **pa·tri·ot·i·cal·ly** \-'ät-i-k(ə-)lē\ *adv*

pa·tri·ot·ism \'pā-trē-ə-ˌtiz-əm\ *n* : love of one's own country and devotion to its welfare

pa·tris·tic \pə-'tris-tik\ *adj* : of or relating to the church fathers or their writings

¹pa·trol \pə-'trōl\ *n* : the action of going the rounds (as of an area) for the purpose of observation or of the maintenance of security; *also* : a person or group performing such an action

²patrol *vb* **pa·trolled**; **pa·trol·ling** : to carry out a patrol or a patrol of — **pa·trol·ler** *n*

pa·trol·man \-mən\ *n* : one who patrols; *esp* : a policeman assigned to a beat

patrol wagon *n* : an enclosed police truck used to carry prisoners

pa·tron \'pā-trən\ *n* **1** : a person chosen as a special guardian, protector, or supporter **2** : one who gives of his means or uses his influence to help an individual, an institution, or a cause **3** : a regular client or customer — **pa·tron·ess** \-trə-nəs\ *n*

pat·ron·age \'pa-trə-nij, 'pā-\ *n* **1** : the support or influence of a patron **2** : the trade of customers **3** : the power to distribute government jobs

pa·tron·ize \'pā-trə-ˌnīz, 'pa-\ *vt* **1** : to act as a patron to or of : FAVOR, SUPPORT **2** : to treat with a superior air : be condescending toward **3** : to do business with — **pa·tron·iz·ing·ly** *adv*

pat·ro·nym·ic \ˌpa-trə-'nim-ik\ *n* : a name derived from that of the father or a paternal ancestor usu. by the addition of a prefix or suffix (as in *MacDonald,* son of Donald, or *Johnson,* son of John) — **patronymic** *adj*

pa·troon \pə-'trün\ *n* : the proprietor of a manorial estate esp. in New York or New Jersey granted by the Dutch

¹pat·ter \'pat-ər\ *vb* **1** : to say or speak in a rapid or mechanical manner **2** : to talk glibly and volubly

²patter *n* **1** : a specialized lingo : CANT **2** : extremely rapid talk

³patter *vb* **1** : to strike or pat rapidly and repeatedly **2** : to run with quick light-sounding steps

¹pat·tern \'pat-ərn\ *n* **1** : a form or model proposed for imitation : EXEMPLAR **2** : something designed or used as a model for making things **3** : SPECIMEN, SAMPLE **4 a** : an artistic or mechanical design **b** : form or style in literary or musical composition **5** : a natural or chance configuration

²pattern *vt* : to make or fashion according to a pattern

pat·ty \'pat-ē\ *n, pl* **patties** **1** : a little pie **2 a** : a small flat cake of chopped food **b** : a small flat candy

pau·ci·ty \'pò-sət-ē\ *n* **1** : smallness of number : FEWNESS **2** : smallness of quantity : DEARTH

paunch \'pònch\ *n* **1** : the belly together with its contents **2** : POTBELLY

paunchy \'pòn-chē\ *adj* : having a potbelly — **paunch·i·ness** *n*

pau·per \'pò-pər\ *n* : a very poor person; *esp* : one supported by charity — **pau·per·ism** \-pə-ˌriz-əm\ *n* — **pau·per·ize** \-ˌrīz\ *vt*

¹pause \'pòz\ *n* **1** : a temporary stop **2 a** : a break in a verse **b** : a brief suspension of the voice to indicate the limits and relations of sentences and their parts **3** : temporary inaction often because of doubt or uncertainty **4 a** : the sign 𝄐 or 𝄑 placed over or under a musical note, chord, or rest to indicate that it is to be prolonged **b** : a mark (as a period or comma)

used in writing or printing to indicate or correspond to a pause of voice **5 :** a reason or cause for pausing
[2]pause *vi* **1 :** to stop temporarily **:** HESITATE **2 :** to linger for a time
pave \'pāv\ *vt* **1 :** to lay or cover with material (as stone or concrete) that makes a firm level surface for travel **2 :** to cover firmly and solidly as if with paving material — **pave the way :** to prepare a smooth easy way **:** facilitate the development
pave•ment \'pāv-mənt\ *n* **1 :** a paved surface (as of a street) **2 :** the material with which something is paved
pa•vil•ion \pə-'vil-yən\ *n* **1 :** a usu. large tent with a peaked or rounded top **2 :** a lightly constructed ornamented building serving as a shelter in a park, garden, or athletic field **3 :** a part of a building projecting from the main body of the structure **4 :** a building either partly or completely detached from the main building or main group of buildings
pav•ing \'pā-viŋ\ *n* **:** PAVEMENT
[1]paw \'pȯ\ *n* **1 :** the foot of a quadruped (as a lion or dog) having claws; *also* **:** the foot of an animal **2 :** a human hand esp. when large or clumsy
[2]paw *vb* **1 :** to feel or touch clumsily, amorously, or rudely **2 :** to touch or strike with a paw **3 :** to scrape or beat upon with a hoof **4 :** to flail at or grab for wildly
[1]pawn \'pȯn\ *n* **1 :** something deposited with another as security for a loan **:** PLEDGE **2 :** the state of being pledged
[2]pawn *vt* **:** to deposit in pledge or as security **:** STAKE — **pawn•er** *n*
[3]pawn *n* **1 :** a chessman of the least value **2 :** one used to further the purposes of another
pawn•bro•ker \-ˌbrō-kər\ *n* **:** one who loans money on the security of personal property pledged in his keeping — **pawn•bro•king** \-kiŋ\ *n*
pawn•shop \'pȯn-ˌshäp\ *n* **:** a pawnbroker's shop
[1]pay \'pā\ *vb* **paid** \'pād\; **pay•ing 1 :** to give money esp. in return for services received or for something bought **2 :** to discharge a debt **3 :** to get even with **4 :** to give or offer freely **5 :** to return value or profit **6 :** to be worth the effort or pains required **7 :** to make slack (as a rope) and allow to run out — usu. used with *out*
[2]pay *n* **1 a :** the act or fact of paying or being paid **:** PAYMENT **b :** the status of being paid by an employer **:** EMPLOY **2 :** something paid; *esp* **:** WAGES, SALARY
[3]pay *adj* **1 :** containing or leading to something precious or valuable (as gold or oil) **2 :** equipped with a coin slot for receiving a fee for use **3 :** requiring payment
pay•a•ble \'pā-ə-bəl\ *adj* **:** that may, can, or must be paid; *esp* **:** DUE
pay•check \'pā-ˌchek\ *n* **1 :** a check in payment of wages or salary **2 :** WAGES, SALARY
pay dirt *n* **1 :** earth or ore that yields a profit to a miner **2 :** a useful or remunerative discovery or object
pay•ee \pā-'ē\ *n* **:** one to whom money is or is to be paid
pay•er \'pā-ər\ *n* **:** one that pays; *esp* **:** the maker of a bill or note
pay•load \'pā-ˌlōd\ *n* **:** something (as cargo, passengers, instruments, or explosives) carried by a vehicle, missile, or rocket in addition to what is necessary for its operation
pay•mas•ter \'pā-ˌmas-tər\ *n* **:** an officer or agent of an employer whose duty it is to pay salaries or wages
pay•ment \-mənt\ *n* **1 :** the act of paying **2 :** money given to discharge a debt **3 :** PAY
pay off *vt* **1 :** to pay in full often through small payments made at intervals **2 :** to take revenge on
pay•off \'pā-ˌȯf\ *n* **1 :** payment at the outcome of an enterprise **2 :** the climax of an incident or enterprise
pay•roll \-ˌrōl\ *n* **:** a list of persons entitled to receive pay with the amounts due to each; *also* **:** the amount of money necessary to pay those on such a list
pay up *vb* **:** to pay in full esp. debts that are overdue
pea \'pē\ *n* **1 :** a variable annual leguminous vine grown for its rounded smooth or wrinkled edible protein-rich seeds **2 :** the seed of the pea
peace \'pēs\ *n* **1 :** a state of tranquillity or quiet; *esp* **:** a state of security or order protected by law or custom **2 :** freedom from disquieting or oppressive thoughts or emotions **3 :** harmony in personal relations **4 a :** a state or period of concord between governments **b :** a pact or agreement to end hostilities
peace•a•ble \'pē-sə-bəl\ *adj* **1 :** inclined toward peace **:** not quarrelsome **2 :** PEACEFUL — **peace•a•bly** \-blē\ *adv*
peace corps *n* **:** a body of trained personnel sent out as volunteers to assist underdeveloped nations
peace•ful \'pēs-fəl\ *adj* **1 :** PEACEABLE 1 **2 :** untroubled by conflict, agitation, or commotion **:** QUIET, TRANQUIL **3 :** devoid of violence or force — **peace•ful•ly** \-fə-lē\ *adv* — **peace•ful•ness** *n*
peaceful coexistence *n* **:** a living together in peace rather than in constant hostility
peace•mak•er \'pēs-ˌmā-kər\ *n* **:** a person who arranges a peace **:** one who settles an argument or stops a fight — **peace•mak•ing** \-kiŋ\ *n or adj*
peace•time \-ˌtīm\ *n* **:** a time when a nation is not at war
[1]peach \'pēch\ *n* **1 :** a low spreading tree related to the plums and cherries that is grown for its sweet juicy fruit; *also* **:** its fruit **2 :** one likened to a peach in sweetness, beauty, or excellence
[2]peach *vi* **:** to turn informer **:** BLAB
peachy \'pē-chē\ *adj* **1 :** resembling a peach **2 :** unusually fine **:** DANDY
[1]pea•cock \'pē-ˌkäk\ *n* **1 :** a male peafowl having long tail coverts which can be spread at will displaying brilliant colors **2 :** one making a proud display of himself
[2]peacock *vi* **:** to make a vainglorious display **:** STRUT
pea•fowl \-ˌfau̇l\ *n* **:** a very large domesticated Asiatic pheasant
pea•hen \'pē-ˌhen, -'hen\ *n* **:** a female peafowl
[1]peak \'pēk\ *n* **1 :** a pointed or projecting part (as of a garment); *esp* **:** the visor of a cap or hat **2 :** PROMONTORY **3 :** a sharp or pointed ridge or end **4 a :** the top of a hill or mountain ending in a point **b :** a whole hill or mountain esp. when isolated **5 :** the narrow part of a ship's bow or stern or the part of the hold in it **6 :** the highest level or greatest degree of development esp. as represented on a graph **7 :** a point formed by the hair on the forehead
[2]peak *vb* **:** to come or cause to come to a peak, point, or maximum
[3]peak *adj* **:** being at or reaching the maximum
peaked *adj* **1** \'pēkt, 'pē-kəd\ **:** having a peak **:** POINTED **2** \'pē-kəd\ **:** sharp and lean in figure or features **:** THIN, SICKLY
[1]peal \'pēl\ *n* **1 a :** the loud ringing of bells **b :** a set of tuned bells **2 :** a loud sound or succession of sounds
[2]peal *vb* **:** to emit peals or in peals
pea•nut \'pē-(ˌ)nət\ *n* **1 :** a low-branching widely cultivated leguminous annual herb with showy yellow flowers and pods that ripen underground; *also* **:** this pod or one of the oily edible seeds it contains **2 :** an insignificant or tiny person **3** *pl* **:** a trifling amount
pear \'pa(ə)r\ *n* **:** a fleshy fruit that usu. tapers toward the stem end; *also* **:** a tree related to the apple that bears pears
pearl \'pərl\ *n* **1 :** a dense usu. lustrous body formed of concentric layers of nacre as an abnormal growth within the shell of some mollusks and used as a gem **2 :** something resembling a pearl (as in shape, color, or value) **3 :** a nearly neutral slightly bluish medium gray

pearly \ˈpər-lē\ *adj* : resembling, containing, or adorned with pearls or mother-of-pearl

peas·ant \ˈpez-ᵊnt\ *n* **1** : a European small farmer or farm laborer; *also* : a member of a similar agricultural class elsewhere **2** : an uncouth person or one of low social status

peas·ant·ry \ˈpez-ᵊn-trē\ *n* : a body of peasants

peat \ˈpēt\ *n* **1** : TURF 2b **2** : a dark vegetable matter resulting from partial decomposition in water of various plants and esp. some mosses — **peaty** \ˈpēt-ē\ *adj*

[1]**peb·ble** \ˈpeb-əl\ *n* **1** : a small usu. round stone esp. when worn by the action of water **2** : an irregular, crinkled, or grainy surface — **peb·bly** \ˈpeb-(ə-)lē\ *adj*

[2]**pebble** *vt* **peb·bled**; **peb·bling** \ˈpeb-(ə-)liŋ\ **1** : to pelt with pebbles **2** : to pave or cover with pebbles or something resembling pebbles **3** : to treat (as leather) so as to produce a rough and irregularly indented surface

pe·can \pi-ˈkän, -ˈkan\ *n* : a large hickory of the south central U.S.; *also* : its edible oblong nut

pec·ca·dil·lo \ˌpek-ə-ˈdil-(ˌ)ō\ *n, pl* **-loes** *or* **-los** : a slight offense or fault

pec·ca·ry \ˈpek-ə-rē\ *n, pl* **-ries** : either of two largely nocturnal gregarious American chiefly tropical mammals resembling but smaller than the related pigs

[1]**peck** \ˈpek\ *n* **1** : a unit of dry capacity equal to 1/4 bushel **2** : a large quantity : great deal

[2]**peck** *vb* **1** : to strike with the bill : thrust the beak into **2** : to pick up with the bill **3** : to strike at or pick up something with or as if with a bill **4** : to bite daintily : NIBBLE — **peck·er** *n*

[3]**peck** *n* **1** : an impression or hole made by pecking **2** : a quick sharp stroke

pec·tic \ˈpek-tik\ *adj* : of, relating to, or derived from pectin

pec·tin \ˈpek-tən\ *n* : any of various water-soluble substances in plant tissues that yield a gel which is the basis of fruit jellies; *also* : a commercial product rich in pectins — **pec·tin·ous** \-tə-nəs\ *adj*

pec·to·ral \ˈpek-t(ə-)rəl\ *adj* **1** : of, relating to, or situated in, near, or on the chest **2** : coming from the breast or heart as the seat of emotion : SUBJECTIVE

pec·u·late \ˈpek-yə-ˌlāt\ *vt* : EMBEZZLE — **pec·u·la·tion** \ˌpek-yə-ˈlā-shən\ *n* — **pec·u·la·tor** \ˈpek-yə-ˌlāt-ər\ *n*

pe·cu·liar \pi-ˈkyül-yər\ *adj* **1** : belonging exclusively to one person or group **2** : characteristic of one only : DISTINCTIVE **3** : different from the usual or normal: **a** : SPECIAL, PARTICULAR **b** : ODD, CURIOUS, ECCENTRIC — **pe·cu·liar·ly** *adv*

pe·cu·li·ar·i·ty \pi-ˌkyü-lē-ˈar-ət-ē, -ˌkyül-ˈyar-\ *n, pl* **-ties** **1** : the quality or state of being peculiar **2** : a distinguishing characteristic **3** : ODDITY, QUIRK

pe·cu·ni·ary \pi-ˈkyü-nē-ˌer-ē\ *adj* **1** : consisting of money : taken or given in money **2** : of or relating to money : MONETARY — **pe·cu·niar·i·ly** \-ˌkyün-ˈyer-ə-lē, -ˌkyü-nē-ˈer-\ *adv*

ped·a·gog·ics \ˌped-ə-ˈgäj-iks\ *n* : PEDAGOGY

ped·a·gogue \ˈped-ə-ˌgäg\ *n* **1** : a teacher of children : SCHOOLMASTER **2** : a dull, formal, and pedantic teacher

ped·a·go·gy \ˈped-ə-ˌgō-jē, -ˌgäj-ē\ *n* : the art, science, or profession of teaching; *esp* : EDUCATION 2 — **ped·a·gog·ic** \ˌped-ə-ˈgäj-ik\ *or* **ped·a·gog·i·cal** \-ˈgäj-i-kəl\ *adj* — **ped·a·gog·i·cal·ly** \-i-k(ə-)lē\ *adv*

[1]**ped·al** \ˈped-ᵊl\ *n* **1** : a lever acted on by the foot in the playing of musical instruments **2** : a foot lever or treadle by which a part is activated in a mechanism

[2]**pedal** *adj* : of or relating to the foot

[3]**pedal** *vb* **ped·aled**; **ped·al·ing** \ˈped-ᵊl-iŋ, ˈped-liŋ\ **1** : to use or work the pedals of something **2** : to ride a bicycle

pedal pushers *n pl* : women's and girls' calf-length trousers

ped·ant \ˈped-ᵊnt\ *n* **1** : a person who shows off his learning **2** : a formal unimaginative teacher who emphasizes petty details — **pe·dan·tic** \pə-ˈdant-ik\ *adj* — **pe·dan·ti·cal·ly** \-ˈdant-i-k(ə-)lē\ *adv*

ped·ant·ry \ˈped-ᵊn-trē\ *n, pl* **-ries** **1** : pedantic presentation or application of knowledge or learning **2** : an instance of pedantry

ped·dle \ˈped-ᵊl\ *vb* **ped·dled**; **ped·dling** \ˈped-liŋ, -ᵊl-iŋ\ **1** : to travel about esp. from house to house with wares for sale **2** : to sell or offer for sale from place to place usu. in small quantities : HAWK **3** : to seek to disseminate — **ped·dler** *or* **ped·lar** \ˈped-lər\ *n*

ped·es·tal \ˈped-əst-ᵊl\ *n* **1** : the support or foot of a column; *also* : the base of any upright structure (as a vase, lamp, or statue) **2** : a position of high regard : the state of being held in exceptionally high esteem

[1]**pe·des·tri·an** \pə-ˈdes-trē-ən\ *adj* **1** : UNIMAGINATIVE, COMMONPLACE **2 a** : going or performed on foot **b** : of or relating to walking

[2]**pedestrian** *n* : a person going on foot : WALKER

pe·des·tri·an·ism \-ˌiz-əm\ *n* **1 a** : the practice of walking **b** : fondness for walking **2** : the quality or state of being unimaginative or commonplace

pe·di·a·tri·cian \ˌpēd-ē-ə-ˈtrish-ən\ *n* : a specialist in pediatrics

pe·di·at·rics \ˌpēd-ē-ˈa-triks\ *n* : a branch of medicine dealing with the child, its development, care, and diseases — **pe·di·at·ric** \-trik\ *adj*

ped·i·gree \ˈped-ə-ˌgrē\ *n* **1** : a register of a line of ancestors **2 a** : an ancestral line : LINEAGE **b** : the origin and history of something (as a document, a collector's coin or stamp) **3 a** : distinguished ancestry **b** : recorded purity of breed of an individual or strain — **ped·i·greed** \-ˌgrēd\ *adj*

ped·i·ment \ˈped-ə-mənt\ *n* : a usu. triangular space forming the gable of a 2-pitched roof in classic architecture; *also* : a similar form used as a decoration (as over a door or a window)

pediments

pe·dom·e·ter \pi-ˈdäm-ət-ər\ *n* : an instrument that measures the distance one covers in walking

pe·dun·cle \ˈpē-ˌdəŋ-kəl, pi-ˈ\ *n* : a narrow supporting stalk

[1]**peek** \ˈpēk\ *vi* **1 a** : to look furtively **b** : to peer through a crack or hole or from a place of concealment **2** : to take a brief look : GLANCE

[2]**peek** *n* : a brief or surreptitious look

[1]**peel** \ˈpēl\ *vb* **1** : to strip off the skin, bark, or rind of **2** : to strip or tear off **3 a** : to come off **b** : to lose the skin, bark, or rind — **peel·er** *n*

[2]**peel** *n* : a skin or rind esp. of a fruit

peel·ing \ˈpē-liŋ\ *n* : a peeled-off piece or strip (as of skin or rind)

peen \ˈpēn\ *n* : the usu. hemispherical or wedge-shaped end of the head of a hammer opposite the face

[1]**peep** \ˈpēp\ *vi* **1** : to utter a feeble shrill sound as of a bird newly hatched : CHEEP **2** : to speak with a small weak voice : utter the slightest sound — **peep·er** *n*

[2]**peep** *n* **1** : a feeble shrill sound : CHEEP **2** : a slight utterance esp. of complaint or protest

[3]**peep** *vb* **1 a** : to peer through a crevice **b** : to look cautiously or slyly **2** : to begin to emerge from concealment : show slightly **3** : to cause (as the head of one peeping) to protrude slightly — **peep·er** *n*

[4]**peep** *n* **1** : the first glimpse or faint appearance **2** : a brief or furtive look

peep·hole \ˈpēp-ˌhōl\ *n* : a hole or crevice to peep through

[1]**peer** \ˈpi(ə)r\ *n* **1** : one that is of equal standing with another

: EQUAL 2 : NOBLE 1 — **peer·age** \'pi(ə)r-ij\ *n* — **peer·ess** \'pir-əs\ *n*

²**peer** *vi* 1 : to look narrowly or curiously; *esp* : to look searchingly at something difficult to discern 2 : to come slightly into view

peer·less \'pi(ə)r-ləs\ *adj* : having no equal : MATCHLESS, INCOMPARABLE — **peer·less·ly** *adv* — **peer·less·ness** *n*

¹**peeve** \'pēv\ *vt* : to make peevish or resentful : ANNOY, IRRITATE

²**peeve** *n* 1 : a peevish mood : a feeling of resentment 2 : a particular grievance : GRUDGE

pee·vish \'pē-vish\ *adj* 1 : cross and complaining in temperament or mood : FRETFUL, IRRITABLE 2 : perversely obstinate : CONTRARY 3 : marked by ill temper — **pee·vish·ly** *adv* — **pee·vish·ness** *n*

pee·wee \'pē-(,)wē\ *n* : something or someone diminutive or tiny — **peewee** *adj*

¹**peg** \'peg\ *n* 1 : a small usu. cylindrical pointed or tapered piece (as of wood) used esp. to pin down or fasten things or to fit into or close holes : PIN, PLUG 2 : a projecting piece used as a support or boundary marker 3 : a step or degree esp. in estimation 4 : THROW

²**peg** *vb* **pegged**; **peg·ging** 1 a : to fasten or mark with pegs b : to pin down : RESTRICT c : to fix or hold (as prices) at a predetermined level d : to place in a definite category 2 : THROW 3 : to work steadily and diligently 4 : to move along vigorously or hastily : HUSTLE

peg–top \'peg-'täp\ *or* **peg–topped** \-'täpt\ *adj* : wide at the top and narrow at the bottom

pei·gnoir \pān-'wär\ *n* : a woman's loose negligee or dressing gown

pe·jor·a·tive \pi-'jör-ət-iv, 'pej-(ə-)rət-\ *adj* : having a tendency to make or become worse : DEPRECIATORY, DISPARAGING — **pe·jor·a·tive·ly** *adv*

Pe·king·ese *or* **Pe·kin·ese** \,pē-kən-'ēz, -kiŋ-, -'ēs\ *n, pl* **Pekingese** *or* **Pekinese** : any of a Chinese breed of small short-legged dogs with a broad flat face and a profuse long soft coat

pe·lag·ic \pə-'laj-ik\ *adj* : of, relating to, or living or occurring in the open sea : OCEANIC

pelf \'pelf\ *n* : MONEY, RICHES

pel·i·can \'pel-i-kən\ *n* : any of a genus of large web-footed birds with a very large bill bearing a pouch in which fish are caught

pe·lisse \pə-'lēs\ *n* 1 : a long cloak or coat made of fur or lined or trimmed with fur 2 : a woman's loose lightweight cloak with wide collar and fur trimming

pel·lag·ra \pə-'lag-rə, -'lāg-\ *n* : a disease marked by skin and digestive disorders and nervous symptoms and associated with a deficient diet — **pel·lag·rous** \-rəs\ *adj*

pel·let \'pel-ət\ *n* 1 : a little ball (as of food, medicine, or debris) 2 a : BULLET b : a piece of small shot

pell–mell \'pel-'mel\ *adv* 1 : in confusion or disorder 2 : in confused or headlong haste — **pell–mell** *adj or n*

pel·lu·cid \pə-'lü-səd\ *adj* 1 : extremely clear : LIMPID, TRANSPARENT 2 : extremely easy to understand — **pel·lu·cid·ly** *adv* — **pel·lu·cid·ness** *n*

¹**pelt** \'pelt\ *n* : a usu. undressed skin with its hair, wool, or fur

²**pelt** *vt* : to strip off the skin of

³**pelt** *vb* 1 : to strike with or deliver a succession of blows or missiles 2 : HURL, THROW 3 : to beat or dash repeatedly against something 4 : to move rapidly and vigorously or with pounding blows or thuds — **pelt·er** *n*

⁴**pelt** *n* 1 : a persistent falling or beating (as of rain, hail, or sleet) 2 : a rapid pace or speed — used esp. in the phrase *full pelt*

pel·vic \'pel-vik\ *adj* : of, relating to, or located in or near the pelvis — **pelvic** *n*

pel·vis \'pel-vəs\ *n, pl* **pel·vis·es** *or* **pel·ves** \'pel-,vēz\ : a basin-shaped structure in the skeleton of many vertebrates consisting chiefly of the two large bones of the hip

pem·mi·can \'pem-i-kən\ *n* : a concentrated food used by No. American Indians consisting of dried lean meat pounded fine and mixed with melted fat

¹**pen** \'pen\ *n* 1 : a small enclosure for animals 2 : a small place of confinement or storage

²**pen** *vt* **penned**; **pen·ning** : to shut in a pen

³**pen** *n* 1 : an instrument with a split point to hold ink used in writing; *also* : a fluid-using writing instrument 2 a : a writing instrument regarded as a means of expression b : WRITER

⁴**pen** *vt* **penned**; **pen·ning** : WRITE, INDITE

pe·nal \'pēn-ᵊl\ *adj* : of, relating to, or involving punishment, penalties, or punitive institutions — **pe·nal·ly** \-ᵊl-ē\ *adv*

pe·nal·ize \'pēn-ᵊl-,īz, 'pen-\ *vt* 1 : to subject to a penalty 2 : to place at a disadvantage : HANDICAP — **pe·nal·i·za·tion** \,pēn-ᵊl-ə-'zā-shən, ,pen-\ *n*

pen·al·ty \'pen-ᵊl-tē\ *n, pl* **-ties** 1 : punishment for a crime or offense 2 : something forfeited when a person fails to do what he agreed to do 3 : disadvantage, loss, or hardship due to some action or condition

pen·ance \'pen-ən(t)s\ *n* 1 : an act of self-abasement, mortification, or devotion performed to show sorrow or repentance for sin 2 : a sacrament in the Roman Catholic and Eastern churches consisting in repentance or contrition for sin, confession to a priest, satisfaction as imposed by the confessor, and absolution

pence \'pen(t)s\ *pl of* PENNY

pen·chant \'pen-chənt\ *n* : a strong leaning : LIKING

¹**pen·cil** \'pen(t)-səl\ *n* 1 : an artist's individual skill or style 2 a : an implement for writing, drawing, or marking consisting of or containing a slender cylinder or strip of a solid marking substance b : a small medicated or cosmetic roll or stick

²**pencil** *vt* **-ciled** *or* **-cilled**; **-cil·ing** *or* **-cil·ling** \-s(ə-)liŋ\ : to mark, draw, or write with or as if with a pencil

pen·dant \'pen-dənt\ *n* : something that hangs down esp. as an ornament

pen·den·cy \'pen-dən-sē\ *n* : the state of being pending

pen·dent *or* **pen·dant** \'pen-dənt\ *adj* 1 : supported from above : SUSPENDED 2 : jutting or leaning over : OVERHANGING 3 : remaining undetermined : PENDING — **pen·dent·ly** *adv*

¹**pend·ing** \'pen-diŋ\ *prep* 1 : DURING 2 : while awaiting

²**pending** *adj* : not yet decided

pen·du·lous \'pen-jə-ləs\ *adj* 1 : suspended so as to swing freely 2 : inclined or hanging downward : DROOPING — **pen·du·lous·ly** *adv* — **pen·du·lous·ness** *n*

pen·du·lum \'pen-jə-ləm, -dyə-ləm, -dᵊl-əm\ *n* : a body suspended from a fixed point so as to swing freely to and fro under the action of gravity

pen·e·tra·bil·i·ty \,pen-ə-trə-'bil-ət-ē\ *n* : the quality or state of being penetrable or being able to penetrate

pen·e·tra·ble \'pen-ə-trə-bəl\ *adj* : capable of being penetrated — **pen·e·tra·ble·ness** *n* — **pen·e·tra·bly** \-blē\ *adv*

pen·e·trate \'pen-ə-,trāt\ *vb* 1 a : to pass into or through b : to enter by overcoming resistance : PIERCE 2 a : to see into or through b : to discover the inner contents or meaning of 3 : to affect deeply the senses or feelings 4 : to diffuse through : PERMEATE

pen·e·trat·ing *adj* 1 : BITING, SHARP 2 : ACUTE, DISCERNING — **pen·e·trat·ing·ly** \-,trāt-iŋ-lē\ *adv*

pen·e·tra·tion \,pen-ə-'trā-shən\ *n* 1 : the act or process of penetrating 2 a : the depth to which something penetrates b : the power to penetrate; *esp* : the ability to discern deeply and acutely

pen·e·tra·tive \'pen-ə-,trāt-iv\ *adj* : tending or able to penetrate — **pen·e·tra·tive·ly** *adv* — **pen·e·tra·tive·ness** *n*

pen·guin \'pen-gwən, 'peŋ-\ *n* : any of various erect short-legged aquatic birds of the southern hemisphere with the wings reduced to flippers and used in swimming

pen·hold·er \'pen-ˌhōl-dər\ *n* : a holder or handle for a pen

pen·i·cil·lin \ˌpen-ə-'sil-ən\ *n* : an antibiotic produced by a green mold and used against bacteria

pen·in·su·la \pə-'nin(t)-sə-lə, -'nin-chə-lə\ *n* : a portion of land nearly surrounded by water; *also* : a piece of land jutting out into the water — **pen·in·su·lar** \-lər\ *adj*

pe·nis \'pē-nəs\ *n, pl* **pe·nes** \'pē-ˌnēz\ *or* **pe·nis·es** : a male organ of copulation

pen·i·tence \'pen-ə-tən(t)s\ *n* : sorrow for one's sins or faults : REPENTANCE

[1]**pen·i·tent** \-tənt\ *adj* : feeling or expressing pain or sorrow for sins or offenses : REPENTANT — **pen·i·tent·ly** *adv*

[2]**penitent** *n* : a person who repents of sin

pen·i·ten·tial \ˌpen-ə-'ten-chəl\ *adj* : of or relating to penitence or penance — **pen·i·ten·tial·ly** \-'tench-(ə-)lē\ *adv*

[1]**pen·i·ten·tia·ry** \ˌpen-ə-'tench-(ə-)rē\ *n, pl* **-ries** : a state or federal prison

[2]**penitentiary** *adj* : of, relating to, or incurring confinement in a penitentiary

pen·knife \'pen-ˌnīf\ *n* : a small pocketknife

pen·man \'pen-mən\ *n* **1 a** : COPYIST, SCRIBE **b** : one who is expert in penmanship **2** : AUTHOR

pen·man·ship \'pen-mən-ˌship\ *n* **1** : the art or practice of writing with the pen **2** : quality or style of handwriting

pen name *n* : an author's pseudonym

pen·nant \'pen-ənt\ *n* **1 a** : any of various nautical flags tapering usu. to a point or swallowtail and used for identification or signaling **b** : a long narrow flag or banner that tapers to a point **2** : a flag emblematic of championship

pen·ni·less \'pen-i-ləs, 'pen-ᵊl-əs\ *adj* : having no money at all : very poor

pen·non \'pen-ən\ *n* **1 a** : a long usu. triangular or swallow-tailed streamer typically attached to the head of a lance as an ensign **b** : PENNANT 1a **2** : a flag of any shape : BANNER

pen·ny \'pen-ē\ *n, pl* **pen·nies** \-ēz\ *or* **pence** \'pen(t)s\ **1 a** : a British monetary unit equal to 1/240 pound or 1/12 shilling **b** : a coin representing this unit **2** *pl pennies* : a cent of the U.S. or Canada **3** : a piece or sum of money

pen·ny pinch·er \'pen-ē-ˌpin-chər\ *n* : a stingy person — **pen·ny–pinch·ing** \-chiŋ\ *adj or n*

pen·ny·weight \'pen-ē-ˌwāt\ *n* : a unit of troy weight equal to 24 grains or 1/20 troy ounce

pen·ny–wise \-ˌwīz\ *adj* : wise or prudent only in small matters

pen·ny·worth \'pen-ē-ˌwərth\ *n, pl* **-worth** *or* **-worths** : a penny's worth : as much as a penny will buy

pe·nol·o·gy \pi-'näl-ə-jē\ *n* : a branch of criminology dealing with prison management and the treatment of offenders — **pe·no·log·i·cal** \ˌpēn-ᵊl-'äj-i-kəl\ *adj* — **pe·nol·o·gist** \pi-'näl-ə-jəst\ *n*

pen pal *n* : a friend made and kept through correspondence often without any face-to-face acquaintance

[1]**pen·sion** \'pen-chən\ *n* : a fixed sum paid regularly to a person; *esp* : one paid to a person following his retirement or to his surviving dependents — **pen·sion·less** \'pen-chən-ləs\ *adj*

[2]**pension** *vt* **pen·sioned**; **pen·sion·ing** \'pench-(ə-)niŋ\ : to grant or pay a pension to

pen·sion·er \'pench-(ə-)nər\ *n* : a person who receives or lives on a pension

pen·sive \'pen(t)-siv\ *adj* **1** : musingly or dreamily thoughtful **2** : suggestive of sad thoughtfulness : MELANCHOLY — **pen·sive·ly** *adv* — **pen·sive·ness** *n*

pent \'pent\ *adj* : shut up : CONFINED

pen·ta·gon \'pent-i-ˌgän\ *n* : a polygon of five angles and five sides — **pen·tag·o·nal** \pen-'tag-ən-ᵊl\ *adj*

pen·tam·e·ter \pen-'tam-ət-ər\ *n* : a line consisting of five metrical feet

Pen·te·cost \'pent-i-ˌkȯst, -ˌkäst\ *n* : the 7th Sunday after Easter observed as a church festival in commemoration of the descent of the Holy Spirit on the apostles

Pen·te·cos·tal \ˌpent-i-'käst-ᵊl, -'kȯst-\ *adj* **1** : of, relating to, or suggesting Pentecost **2** : of, relating to, or constituting any of various usu. fundamentalist sects that are ardently evangelistic — **Pentecostal** *n* — **Pen·te·cos·tal·ism** \-ˌiz-əm\ *n*

pent·house \'pent-ˌhau̇s\ *n* **1** : a roof or a shed attached to and sloping from a wall or building **2** : a structure (as an apartment) built on the roof of a building

pe·nult \'pē-ˌnəlt\ *n* : the next to the last syllable of a word

pen·ul·ti·mate \pi-'nəl-tə-mət\ *adj* **1** : next to the last **2** : of or relating to a penult — **penultimate** *n* — **pen·ul·ti·mate·ly** *adv*

pen·um·bra \pə-'nəm-brə\ *n, pl* **-brae** \-(ˌ)brē, -ˌbrī\ *or* **-bras** : the partial shadow surrounding a perfect shadow (as in an eclipse) — **pen·um·bral** \-brəl\ *adj*

pe·nu·ri·ous \pə-'n(y)u̇r-ē-əs\ *adj* **1** : marked by or suffering from penury **2** : given to or marked by extreme stinting frugality — **pe·nu·ri·ous·ly** *adv* — **pe·nu·ri·ous·ness** *n*

pen·u·ry \'pen-yə-rē\ *n* **1** : extreme poverty : PRIVATION **2** : absence of resources : SCANTINESS

pe·on \'pē-ˌän, -ən\ *n* **1** : a member of the landless laboring class in Spanish America **2** : a person held in compulsory servitude to work out an indebtedness **3** : DRUDGE, MENIAL — **pe·on·age** \'pē-ə-nij\ *n*

pe·o·ny \'pē-ə-nē, 'pī-nē\ *n, pl* **-nies** : a garden plant with large usu. double flowers of red, pink, or white

[1]**peo·ple** \'pē-pəl\ *n, pl* **people** **1** *pl* : human beings : PERSONS — often used in compounds instead of *persons* **2** *pl* : the members of a family : KINDRED; *also* : ANCESTORS **3** *pl* : the mass of a community as distinguished from a special class **4** *pl* **peoples** : a body of persons united by a common culture, tradition, or sense of kinship, typically having common language, institutions, and beliefs, and often politically organized **5** : a body of enfranchised citizens : ELECTORATE

[2]**people** *vt* **peo·pled**; **peo·pling** \'pē-p(ə-)liŋ\ **1** : to supply or fill with people **2** : to dwell in : INHABIT

[1]**pep** \'pep\ *n* : brisk energy or initiative and high spirits

[2]**pep** *vt* **pepped**; **pep·ping** : to inject pep into : STIMULATE

[1]**pep·per** \'pep-ər\ *n* **1 a** : a pungent product from the fruit of an East Indian climbing shrub used as a condiment and in medicine and consisting of the entire dried berry or the dried seeds divested of membranes and pulp **b** : the plant that yields pepper **c** : any of several somewhat similar products obtained from other plants **2** : a plant related to the tomato and widely grown for its hot or mild sweet fruit used as a vegetable or in salads and pickles; *also* : this fruit — **pepper** *adj*

[2]**pepper** *vt* **pep·pered**; **pep·per·ing** \'pep-(ə-)riŋ\ **1 a** : to sprinkle or season with or as if with pepper **b** : to shower with missiles (as shot) **2** : to hit with rapid repeated blows **3** : to sprinkle as pepper is sprinkled

pep·per·corn \'pep-ər-ˌkȯrn\ *n* : a dried berry of the East Indian pepper

pep·per·mint \-(ˌ)mint\ *n* **1** : a pungent and aromatic mint with dark green lanceolate leaves and whorls of small pink flowers in spikes **2** : candy flavored with peppermint

pep·pery \'pep-(ə-)rē\ *adj* **1** : of, relating to, or having the qualities of pepper : HOT, PUNGENT **2** : having a hot temper : TOUCHY **3** : FIERY, STINGING

pep·py \'pep-ē\ *adj* : full of pep — **pep·pi·ness** *n*

pep·sin \'pep-sən\ *n* **1** : an enzyme of the stomach that begins the digestion of most proteins **2** : a preparation of pepsin used medicinally

pep·tic \'pep-tik\ *adj* **1** : relating to or promoting digestion **2** : resulting from the action of digestive juices

per \(ˈ)pər\ *prep* **1 :** by the means or agency of **2 :** to or for each **3 :** as indicated by : according to

per·ad·ven·ture \ˈpər-əd-ˌven-chər, ˈper-\ *n* : DOUBT, CHANCE

per·am·bu·late \pə-ˈram-byə-ˌlāt\ *vb* **1 :** to travel over or through esp. on foot : TRAVERSE **2 :** STROLL, RAMBLE — **per·am·bu·la·tion** \-ˌram-byə-ˈlā-shən\ *n*

per·am·bu·la·tor \pə-ˈram-byə-ˌlāt-ər\ *n* : one that perambulates

per an·num \(ˌ)pər-ˈan-əm\ *adv* : in or for each year : ANNUALLY

per·cale \(ˌ)pər-ˈkāl, -ˈkal\ *n* : a fine closely woven cotton cloth variously finished for clothing, sheeting, and industrial uses

per cap·i·ta \(ˌ)pər-ˈkap-ət-ə\ *adv (or adj)* : per unit of population : by or for each person

per·ceiv·a·ble \pər-ˈsē-və-bəl\ *adj* : PERCEPTIBLE, INTELLIGIBLE — **per·ceiv·a·bly** \-blē\ *adv*

per·ceive \pər-ˈsēv\ *vt* **1 :** to attain awareness or understanding of **2 :** to become aware of through the senses and esp. through sight — **per·ceiv·er** *n*

¹per·cent \pər-ˈsent\ *adv* : in the hundred : of each hundred

²percent *n, pl* **percent 1 :** one part in a hundred : HUNDREDTH **2 :** PERCENTAGE

³percent *adj* : reckoned on the basis of a whole divided into one hundred parts

per·cent·age \pər-ˈsent-ij\ *n* **1 a :** a part of a whole expressed in hundredths **b :** the result obtained by multiplying a number by a percentage **2 :** a share of winnings or profits

per·cen·tile \pər-ˈsen-ˌtīl\ *n* : a measure widely used in educational testing that expresses an individual's standing in terms of the percentage of people falling below him

per·cep·ti·ble \pər-ˈsep-tə-bəl\ *adj* : capable of being perceived — **per·cep·ti·bil·i·ty** \-ˌsep-tə-ˈbil-ət-ē\ *n* — **per·cep·ti·bly** \-ˈsep-tə-blē\ *adv*

per·cep·tion \pər-ˈsep-shən\ *n* **1 a :** a result of perceiving : OBSERVATION, DISCERNMENT **b :** a mental image : CONCEPT **2 :** awareness of the elements of environment through physical sensation **3 a :** INSIGHT **b :** a capacity for comprehension

per·cep·tive \pər-ˈsep-tiv\ *adj* **1 :** responsive to sensory stimulus : DISCERNING **2 a :** capable of or exhibiting keen perception : OBSERVANT **b :** characterized by sympathetic understanding or insight — **per·cep·tive·ly** *adv* — **per·cep·tive·ness** *n* — **per·cep·tiv·i·ty** \(ˌ)pər-ˌsep-ˈtiv-ət-ē\ *n*

per·cep·tu·al \(ˌ)pər-ˈsep-chə-wəl\ *adj* : of, relating to, or involving sensory stimulus as opposed to abstract concept — **per·cep·tu·al·ly** \-wə-lē\ *adv*

¹perch \ˈpərch\ *n* **1 :** a bar or peg on which something is hung **2 a :** a roost for a bird **b :** a resting place or vantage point : SEAT **c :** EMINENCE

²perch *vb* **1 :** to place on a perch, a height, or precarious spot **2 :** to alight, settle, or rest on or as if on a perch

³perch *n, pl* **perch** *or* **perch·es :** either of two small freshwater spiny-finned food fishes; *also* : any of various fishes resembling or related to these

per·chance \pər-ˈchan(t)s\ *adv* : PERHAPS, POSSIBLY

per·cip·i·ent \pər-ˈsip-ē-ənt\ *adj* : capable of or characterized by perception : DISCERNING — **per·cip·i·ence** \-ē-ən(t)s\ *n*

per·co·late \ˈpər-kə-ˌlāt\ *vb* **1 :** to trickle or filter through a permeable substance **2 :** to prepare (coffee) in a percolator — **per·co·la·tion** \ˌpər-kə-ˈlā-shən\ *n*

per·co·la·tor \ˈpər-kə-ˌlāt-ər\ *n* : one that percolates; *esp* : a coffeepot in which boiling water rising through a tube is repeatedly deflected downward through a perforated basket containing the ground coffee beans

per·cuss \pər-ˈkəs\ *vt* : to tap sharply; *esp* : to practice percussion on

per·cus·sion \pər-ˈkəsh-ən\ *n* **1 :** the act of tapping sharply: as **a :** the striking of a percussion cap so as to set off the charge in a firearm **b :** the beating or striking of a musical instrument **2 :** musical instruments sounded by striking

percussion cap *n* : a small cap or container of explosive to be fired by a sharp forceful blow

¹per di·em \(ˌ)pər-ˈdē-əm\ *adv* : by the day : for each day — **per diem** *adj*

²per diem *n* : a sum (as for traveling expenses) computed by the day

per·di·tion \pər-ˈdish-ən\ *n* **1 :** eternal damnation **2 :** HELL

per·e·gri·nate \ˈper-ə-grə-ˌnāt\ *vb* : to travel esp. on foot : WALK — **per·e·gri·na·tion** \ˌper-ə-grə-ˈnā-shən\ *n*

per·e·grine \ˈper-ə-grən, -ˌgrēn\ *adj* : having a tendency to wander : ROVING

pe·remp·to·ry \pə-ˈrem(p)-t(ə-)rē\ *adj* **1 a :** putting an end to or precluding a right of action, debate, or delay **b :** ABSOLUTE, FINAL **2 :** expressive of urgency or command : IMPERATIVE **3 a :** marked by self-assurance : POSITIVE **b :** DECISIVE **4 :** HAUGHTY, DICTATORIAL, MASTERFUL — **pe·remp·to·ri·ly** \-t(ə-)rə-lē\ *adv* — **pe·remp·to·ri·ness** \-t(ə-)rē-nəs\ *n*

pe·ren·ni·al \pə-ˈren-ē-əl\ *adj* **1 :** present at all seasons of the year **2 :** continuing to live from year to year **3 a :** PERSISTENT, ENDURING **b :** continuing without interruption : CONSTANT **c :** regularly repeated : RECURRENT — **perennial** *n* — **pe·ren·ni·al·ly** \-ē-ə-lē\ *adv*

¹per·fect \ˈpər-fikt\ *adj* **1 a :** being entirely without fault or defect : FLAWLESS **b :** satisfying all requirements : ACCURATE **c :** corresponding to an ideal standard **2 :** faithfully reproducing the original **3 a :** PURE, TOTAL **b :** lacking in no essential detail : COMPLETE **c :** of an extreme kind : UNMITIGATED **4 :** of, relating to, or constituting a verb form or verbal that expresses an action or state completed at the time of speaking or at a time spoken of — **per·fect·ness** *n*

²per·fect \pər-ˈfekt, ˈpər-fikt\ *vt* **1 :** to make perfect : IMPROVE, REFINE **2 :** to bring to final form : COMPLETE — **per·fect·er** *n*

³per·fect \ˈpər-fikt\ *n* **1 :** the perfect tense **2 :** a verb form in the perfect tense

per·fect·i·ble \pər-ˈfek-tə-bəl, ˈpər-fik-\ *adj* : capable of improvement or perfection — **per·fect·i·bil·i·ty** \pər-ˌfek-tə-ˈbil-ət-ē, ˌpər-fik-\ *n*

per·fec·tion \pər-ˈfek-shən\ *n* **1 :** the quality or state of being perfect: as **a :** FLAWLESSNESS **b :** COMPLETENESS **c :** MATURITY **d :** SAINTLINESS **2 a :** an exemplification of supreme excellence **b :** an unsurpassable degree of accuracy or excellence **3 :** the act or process of perfecting

per·fec·tion·ist \pər-ˈfek-sh(ə-)nəst\ *n* : a person who will not accept or be content with anything less than perfection — **perfectionist** *or* **per·fec·tion·is·tic** \-ˌfek-shə-ˈnis-tik\ *adj*

per·fect·ly \ˈpər-fik-(t)lē\ *adv* **1 :** in a perfect manner **2 :** to an adequate extent : QUITE

per·fer·vid \ˌpər-ˈfər-vəd\ *adj* : extremely fervent

per·fid·i·ous \(ˌ)pər-ˈfid-ē-əs\ *adj* : of, relating to, or characterized by perfidy — **per·fid·i·ous·ly** *adv* — **per·fid·i·ous·ness** *n*

per·fi·dy \ˈpər-fəd-ē\ *n, pl* **-dies :** the quality or state of being faithless or disloyal : TREACHERY

per·fo·rate \ˈpər-fə-ˌrāt\ *vb* : to make a hole through : PIERCE; *esp* : to make a line of holes to facilitate separation — **per·fo·rate** \ˈpər-f(ə-)rət, -fə-ˌrāt\ *adj* — **per·fo·ra·tion** \ˌpər-fə-ˈrā-shən\ *n* — **per·fo·ra·tor** \ˈpər-fə-ˌrāt-ər\ *n*

per·force \pər-ˈfōrs\ *adv* : by force of circumstances or of necessity : WILLY-NILLY

per·form \pər-ˈfȯrm\ *vb* **1 :** to adhere to the terms of : FULFILL **2 a :** to carry out : DO **b :** ACT, FUNCTION **3 a :** to do in a formal manner or according to prescribed ritual **b :** to give a performance or a rendition of : PRESENT, PLAY — **per·form·er** *n*

per·form·ance \pər-ˈfȯr-mən(t)s\ *n* **1 a :** the execution of an action **b :** something accomplished : DEED, FEAT **2 :** the fulfillment of an obligation, claim, promise, or request : IMPLEMENTATION 3 a : the action of representing a character in a play b : a public presentation or exhibition 4 a : the ability to perform : EFFICIENCY b : the manner in which a mechanism performs

per·form·ing \-'fȯr-miŋ\ *adj* : of, relating to, or constituting an art that involves public performance

[1]**per·fume** \'pər-ˌfyüm, (ˌ)pər-'\ *n* 1 : the scent of something usu. sweet-smelling 2 : a preparation used for scenting

[2]**per·fume** \(ˌ)pər-'fyüm, 'pər-ˌ\ *vt* : to fill or impregnate with an odor (as of flowers) : SCENT

per·fum·er \pə(r)-'fyü-mər\ *n* : one that makes or sells perfumes

per·fum·ery \pə(r)-'fyüm-(ə-)rē\ *n, pl* **-er·ies** : the products made by a perfumer

per·func·to·ry \pər-'fəŋ(k)-t(ə-)rē\ *adj* 1 : characterized by routine or superficiality : MECHANICAL 2 : lacking in interest or enthusiasm : APATHETIC, INDIFFERENT — **per·func·to·ri·ly** \-t(ə-)rə-lē\ *adv* — **per·func·to·ri·ness** \-t(ə-)rē-nəs\ *n*

per·go·la \'pər-gə-lə, pər-'gō-\ *n* : a structure consisting of posts supporting an open roof in the form of a trellis

per·haps \pər-'(h)aps, 'praps\ *adv* : possibly but not certainly : MAYBE

per·i·gee \'per-ə-(ˌ)jē\ *n* : the point at which an orbiting object is nearest the body (as the earth or moon) being orbited

[1]**per·il** \'per-əl\ *n* 1 : exposure to the risk of being injured, destroyed, or lost 2 : something that imperils : RISK

[2]**peril** *vt* : to expose to danger : HAZARD

per·il·ous \'per-ə-ləs\ *adj* : full of or involving peril : HAZARDOUS — **per·il·ous·ly** *adv* — **per·il·ous·ness** *n*

pe·rim·e·ter \pə-'rim-ət-ər\ *n* : the outer boundary of a body or figure

[1]**pe·ri·od** \'pir-ē-əd\ *n* 1 : an utterance from one full stop to another : SENTENCE 2 a : the full pause with which a sentence closes b : END, STOP 3 : a punctuation mark . used chiefly to mark the end of a declarative sentence or an abbreviation 4 : the completion of a cycle, a series of events, or a single action : CONCLUSION 5 a : a portion or division of time in which something comes to an end and is ready to begin again b : a single cyclic occurrence of menstruation 6 : a chronological division : STAGE 7 : one of the divisions of the academic day

[2]**period** *adj* : of, relating to, or representing a particular historical period

pe·ri·od·ic \ˌpir-ē-'äd-ik\ *adj* 1 a : occurring at regular intervals b : happening repeatedly : RECURRENT 2 : consisting of or containing a series of repeated stages : CYCLIC 3 : of or relating to a sentence that has no trailing elements following full grammatical statement of the essential idea

[1]**pe·ri·od·i·cal** \ˌpir-ē-'äd-i-kəl\ *adj* 1 : PERIODIC 1 2 a : published with a fixed interval between the issues or numbers b : published in, characteristic of, or connected with a periodical — **pe·ri·od·i·cal·ly** \-k(ə-)lē\ *adv*

[2]**periodical** *n* : a periodical publication

pe·ri·od·ic·i·ty \ˌpir-ē-ə-'dis-ət-ē\ *n, pl* **-ties** : the quality, state, or fact of being regularly recurrent

per·i·pa·tet·ic \ˌper-ə-pə-'tet-ik\ *adj* : moving about from place to place : ITINERANT — **per·i·pa·tet·i·cal·ly** \-'tet-i-k(ə-)lē\ *adv*

pe·riph·er·al \pə-'rif-(ə-)rəl\ *adj* : of, relating to, located in, or forming a periphery — **pe·riph·er·al·ly** \-ē\ *adv*

pe·riph·ery \pə-'rif-(ə-)rē\ *n, pl* **-er·ies** 1 : the boundary of a rounded figure : PERIMETER 2 a : the outer or outermost part of something as distinguished from its more internal regions or center b : an area lying beyond the strict limits of a thing

pe·riph·ra·sis \pə-'rif-rə-səs\ *n, pl* **-ra·ses** \-rə-ˌsēz\ : CIRCUMLOCUTION

per·i·phras·tic \ˌper-ə-'fras-tik\ *adj* : of, relating to, or characterized by periphrasis — **per·i·phras·ti·cal·ly** \-ti-k(ə-)lē\ *adv*

peri·scope \'per-ə-ˌskōp\ *n* : a tubular optical instrument containing lenses and mirrors by which an observer (as on a submerged submarine) obtains an otherwise obstructed field of view — **peri·scop·ic** \ˌper-ə-'skäp-ik\ *adj*

per·ish \'per-ish\ *vi* : to pass away completely : become destroyed or ruined : DIE

per·ish·a·bil·i·ty \ˌper-ish-ə-'bil-ət-ē\ *n* : the quality or condition of being perishable

per·ish·a·ble \'per-ish-ə-bəl\ *adj* : liable to spoil or decay — **perishable** *n*

per·i·stal·sis \ˌper-ə-'stȯl-səs, -'stal-\ *n, pl* **-stal·ses** \-ˌsēz\ : successive waves of involuntary contraction passing along the walls of the intestine and forcing the contents onward — **per·i·stal·tic** \-'stȯl-tik, -'stal-\ *adj* — **per·i·stal·ti·cal·ly** \-ti-k(ə-)lē\ *adv*

peri·style \'per-ə-ˌstīl\ *n* 1 : a row of columns surrounding a building or court 2 : an open space enclosed by a row of columns

per·i·to·ni·tis \ˌper-ət-ᵊn-'īt-əs\ *n* : inflammation of the membrane lining the cavity of the abdomen

per·i·wig \'per-i-ˌwig\ *n* : WIG

[1]**per·i·win·kle** \'per-i-ˌwiŋ-kəl\ *n* : a creeping plant widely grown as a ground cover and for its usu. blue flowers

[2]**periwinkle** *n* : any of numerous small edible littoral marine snails

per·jure \'pər-jər\ *vt* **per·jured**; **per·jur·ing** \'pərj-(ə-)riŋ\ : to make (oneself) guilty of perjury

per·jur·er \'pər-jər-ər\ *n* : a person guilty of perjury

per·ju·ry \'pərj-(ə-)rē\ *n, pl* **-ries** : violation of an oath by knowingly swearing to what is untrue : false swearing

perk \'pərk\ *vb* 1 : to lift quickly, saucily, or alertly 2 : to smarten one's appearance — **perk up** : to be or become lively : regain vigor or cheerfulness

perky \'pər-kē\ *adj* : JAUNTY, SAUCY, LIVELY — **perk·i·ly** \-kə-lē\ *adv* — **perk·i·ness** \-kē-nəs\ *n*

per·ma·frost \'pər-mə-ˌfrȯst\ *n* : a permanently frozen layer at variable depth below the earth's surface in frigid regions

per·ma·nence \'pər-mə-nən(t)s\ *n* : the quality or state of being permanent

per·ma·nen·cy \-nən-sē\ *n, pl* **-cies** : PERMANENCE

[1]**per·ma·nent** \'pər-mə-nənt\ *adj* : lasting or intended to last for a very long time : not temporary : not changing — **per·ma·nent·ly** *adv*

[2]**permanent** *n* : a long-lasting hair wave produced by mechanical and chemical means

per·me·a·bil·i·ty \ˌpər-mē-ə-'bil-ət-ē\ *n, pl* **-ties** : the quality or state of being permeable

per·me·a·ble \'pər-mē-ə-bəl\ *adj* : having pores or openings that permit liquids or gases to pass through

per·me·ance \'pər-mē-ən(t)s\ *n* : PERMEATION

per·me·ate \'pər-mē-ˌāt\ *vb* 1 : to pass through something which has pores or small openings or is of loose texture : seep through 2 : to spread throughout : PERVADE — **per·me·a·tion** \ˌpər-mē-'ā-shən\ *n*

per·mis·si·ble \pər-'mis-ə-bəl\ *adj* : that may be permitted : ALLOWABLE — **per·mis·si·bil·i·ty** \-ˌmis-ə-'bil-ət-ē\ *n* — **per·mis·si·bly** \-'mis-ə-blē\ *adv*

per·mis·sion \pər-'mish-ən\ *n* 1 : the act of permitting 2 : the consent of a person in authority : LEAVE, AUTHORIZATION

per·mis·sive \pər-'mis-iv\ *adj* 1 : granting or tending to grant permission : ALLOWING 2 : not forbidden : ALLOWABLE, OPTIONAL — **per·mis·sive·ly** *adv* — **per·mis·sive·ness** *n*

[1]**per·mit** \pər-'mit\ *vb* **per·mit·ted**; **per·mit·ting** 1 : to consent to expressly or formally : give permission 2 : to make possible : give an opportunity : ALLOW — **per·mit·ter** *n*

[2]**per·mit** \'pər-ˌmit, pər-'\ *n* : a written statement of permission given by one having authority : LICENSE

per·mu·ta·tion \ˌpər-myü-ˈtā-shən\ *n* **1 :** a thorough change in character or condition : TRANSFORMATION **2 a :** the act or process of changing the order of a set of objects **b :** an ordered arrangement of a set of objects — **per·mu·ta·tion·al** \-shnəl, -shən-ᵊl\ *adj*

per·ni·cious \pər-ˈnish-əs\ *adj* : very destructive or injurious — **per·ni·cious·ly** *adv* — **per·ni·cious·ness** *n*

per·ora·tion \ˌper-ər-ˈā-shən\ *n* **1 :** the concluding part of a discourse and esp. an oration **2 :** a highly rhetorical speech

per·ox·ide \pə-ˈräk-ˌsīd\ *n* **1 :** an oxide containing a high proportion of oxygen; *esp* : a compound in which oxygen is held to be joined to oxygen **2 :** HYDROGEN PEROXIDE

[1]**per·pen·dic·u·lar** \ˌpər-pən-ˈdik-yə-lər\ *adj* **1 a :** exactly vertical or upright **b :** being at right angles to a given line or plane **2 :** extremely steep : PRECIPITOUS — **per·pen·dic·u·lar·i·ty** \-ˌdik-yə-ˈlar-ət-ē\ *n* — **per·pen·dic·u·lar·ly** *adv*

[2]**perpendicular** *n* : a line at right angles to the plane of the horizon or to another line or surface

per·pe·trate \ˈpər-pə-ˌtrāt\ *vt* : to be guilty of doing or performing : COMMIT — **per·pe·tra·tion** \ˌpər-pə-ˈtrā-shən\ *n* — **per·pe·tra·tor** \ˈpər-pə-ˌtrāt-ər\ *n*

per·pet·u·al \pər-ˈpech-(ə-w)əl\ *adj* **1 a :** continuing forever : EVERLASTING **b** (1) : valid for all time (2) : holding for life or for an unlimited time **2 :** occurring continually : indefinitely long-continued : CONSTANT — **per·pet·u·al·ly** \-ē\ *adv*

per·pet·u·ate \pər-ˈpech-ə-ˌwāt\ *vt* : to make perpetual or cause to last indefinitely — **per·pet·u·a·tion** \-ˌpech-ə-ˈwā-shən\ *n* — **per·pet·u·a·tor** \-ˈpech-ə-ˌwāt-ər\ *n*

per·pe·tu·i·ty \ˌpər-pə-ˈt(y)ü-ət-ē\ *n, pl* **-ties 1 :** perpetual existence or duration **2 :** endless time : ETERNITY

per·plex \pər-ˈpleks\ *vt* **1 :** to disturb mentally; *esp* : CONFUSE, BEWILDER **2 :** to make intricate or involved : COMPLICATE

per·plexed \-ˈplekst\ *adj* **1 :** filled with uncertainty : PUZZLED **2 :** full of difficulty : COMPLICATED — **per·plexed·ly** \-ˈplek-səd-lē, -ˈpleks-tlē\ *adv*

per·plex·i·ty \pər-ˈplek-sət-ē\ *n, pl* **-ties 1 :** the state of being perplexed : BEWILDERMENT **2 :** something that perplexes **3 :** ENTANGLEMENT

per·qui·site \ˈpər-kwə-zət\ *n* **1 :** a profit made from one's employment in addition to one's regular pay; *esp* : such a profit when expected or promised **2 :** TIP

per se \(ˌ)pər-ˈsā\ *adv* : by, of, or in itself or oneself or themselves : as such : INTRINSICALLY

per·se·cute \ˈpər-si-ˌkyüt\ *vt* **1 :** to harass in a manner to injure, grieve, or afflict; *esp* : to cause to suffer because of belief **2 :** to annoy with persistent or urgent approaches : PESTER — **per·se·cu·tion** \ˌpər-si-ˈkyü-shən\ *n* — **per·se·cu·tor** \ˈpər-si-ˌkyüt-ər\ *n* — **per·se·cu·to·ry** \-kyü-ˌtōr-ē\ *adj*

per·se·ver·ance \ˌpər-sə-ˈvir-ən(t)s\ *n* : the action, condition, or an instance of persevering : STEADFASTNESS

per·se·vere \ˌpər-sə-ˈvi(ə)r\ *vi* : to keep at something in spite of difficulties, opposition, or discouragement

per·se·ver·ing \-ˈvi(ə)r-iŋ\ *adj* : showing perseverance : PERSISTENT — **per·se·ver·ing·ly** *adv*

per·si·flage \ˈpər-sə-ˌfläzh, ˈper-\ *n* : frivolous or lightly derisive talk or manner of treating a subject

per·sim·mon \pər-ˈsim-ən\ *n* **1 :** a tree related to the ebony **2 :** the usu. orange edible fruit of a persimmon that resembles a plum

per·sist \pər-ˈsist, -ˈzist\ *vi* **1 :** to go on resolutely in spite of opposition, warnings, or pleas : PERSEVERE **2 :** to last on and on : continue to exist

per·sist·ence \pər-ˈsis-tən(t)s, -ˈzis-\ *n* **1 :** the act or fact of persisting **2 :** the quality of being persistent : the power of going on in spite of difficulties : PERSEVERANCE

per·sist·en·cy \-tən-sē\ *n* : PERSISTENCE, LASTINGNESS

per·sist·ent \-tənt\ *adj* **1 :** continuing, existing, or acting for a long or longer than usual time **2 :** DOGGED, TENACIOUS — **per·sist·ent·ly** *adv*

per·snick·e·ty \pər-ˈsnik-ət-ē\ *adj* : fussy about small details

per·son \ˈpərs-ᵊn\ *n* **1 :** a human being : INDIVIDUAL — used in combination esp. by those who prefer to avoid *man* in compounds (as *chairperson*) applicable to both sexes **2 :** CHARACTER, GUISE **3 :** one of the three modes of being in the Godhead as understood by Trinitarians **4 :** the body of a human being **5 a :** the individual personality of a human being : SELF **b :** bodily presence **6 :** reference of a segment of discourse to the speaker, to one spoken to, or to one spoken of as indicated by means of certain pronouns

per·son·a·ble \ˈpərs-nə-bəl, -ᵊn-ə-bəl\ *adj* : pleasing in appearance : attractive in looks and manner — **per·son·a·ble·ness** *n*

per·son·age \ˈpərs-nij, -ᵊn-ij\ *n* **1 :** a person of rank or distinction : a famous person **2 :** a character in a book or play

[1]**per·son·al** \ˈpərs-nəl, -ᵊn-əl\ *adj* **1 :** of, relating to, or belonging to a person : PRIVATE **2 a :** done in person or proceeding from a single person **b :** carried on between individuals directly **3 :** relating to the person or body **4 :** closely related to an individual : INTIMATE **5 :** denoting grammatical person

[2]**personal** *n* : a short newspaper paragraph relating to a person or group or to personal matters

per·son·al·i·ty \ˌpərs-ᵊn-ˈal-ət-ē\ *n, pl* **-ties 1 :** the state of being a person **2 :** the totality of characteristics or traits of a person that makes him different from other persons : INDIVIDUALITY **3 :** pleasing qualities of character **4 :** a person who has strongly marked qualities **5 :** a personal remark : a slighting reference to a person

per·son·al·ize \ˈpərs-nə-ˌlīz, -ᵊn-ə-\ *vt* **1 :** PERSONIFY **2 :** to make personal or individual; *esp* : to mark as belonging to a particular person

per·son·al·ly \ˈpərs-nə-lē, -ᵊn-ə-\ *adv* **1 :** in person **2 :** as a person : in personality **3 :** for oneself : as far as oneself is concerned

per·son·al·ty \ˈpərs-nəl-tē, -ᵊn-əl-\ *n, pl* **-ties :** personal property

per·so·na non gra·ta \pər-ˌsō-nə-ˌnän-ˈgrat-ə, -ˈgrät-\ *n, pl* **per·so·nae non gra·tae** \-nē-ˌnän-ˈgrat-ē, -ˌnī-ˌnän-ˈgrat-ˌī, -ˈgrät-\ : an unacceptable person

per·son·ate \ˈpərs-ᵊn-ˌāt\ *vt* **1 :** IMPERSONATE, REPRESENT **2 :** to invest with personality or personal characteristics — **per·son·a·tion** \ˌpərs-ᵊn-ˈā-shən\ *n* — **per·son·a·tive** \ˈpərs-ᵊn-ˌāt-iv\ *adj* — **per·son·a·tor** \-ˌāt-ər\ *n*

per·son·i·fi·ca·tion \pər-ˌsän-ə-fə-ˈkā-shən\ *n* **1 :** the act of personifying **2 :** an imaginary being thought of as representing a thing or an idea **3 :** EMBODIMENT, INCARNATION **4 :** a figure of speech in which a lifeless object or abstract quality is spoken of as if alive

per·son·i·fi·er \pər-ˈsän-ə-ˌfī(-ə)r\ *n* : one that personifies

per·son·i·fy \-ˌfī\ *vt* **-fied; -fy·ing 1 :** to think of or represent as a person **2 :** to represent in a physical form **3 :** to serve as the perfect type or example of

per·son·nel \ˌpərs-ᵊn-ˈel\ *n* **1 :** a body of employees **2 :** a division of an organization concerned with personnel

[1]**per·spec·tive** \pər-ˈspek-tiv\ *n* **1 :** the art or technique of painting or drawing a scene so that objects in it have apparent depth and distance **2 :** the power to see or think of things in their true relationship to each other **3 :** the true relationship of objects or events to one another

[2]**perspective** *adj* : of, relating to, or seen in perspective — **per·spec·tive·ly** *adv*

per·spi·ca·cious \ˌpər-spə-ˈkā-shəs\ *adj* : having or showing keen understanding or discernment — **per·spi·ca·cious·ly** *adv*

per·spi·cac·i·ty \ˌpər-spə-ˈkas-ət-ē\ *n* : the quality or state of being perspicacious : acuteness of understanding or discernment

per·spi·cu·i·ty \ˌpər-spə-ˈkyü-ət-ē\ *n* : the quality of being easily understandable : clearness of expression or thought

per·spic·u·ous \pər-ˈspik-yə-wəs\ *adj* **1** : plain to the understanding : CLEAR **2** : expressing oneself clearly — **per·spic·u·ous·ly** *adv*

per·spi·ra·tion \ˌpər-spə-ˈrā-shən\ *n* **1** : the act or process of perspiring **2** : a saline fluid secreted by the sweat glands : SWEAT — **per·spi·ra·to·ry** \pər-ˈspī-rə-ˌtōr-ē\ *adj*

per·spire \pər-ˈspī(ə)r\ *vi* : SWEAT

per·suade \pər-ˈswād\ *vt* : to win over to a belief or to a course of action by argument or earnest request : induce to do or believe something — **per·suad·er** *n*

per·sua·sion \pər-ˈswā-zhən\ *n* **1** : the act of persuading **2** : the power or ability to persuade : persuasive quality **3** : the state of being persuaded **4** : a way of believing : BELIEF; *esp* : a system of religious beliefs

per·sua·sive \pər-ˈswā-siv, -ziv\ *adj* : tending to persuade : having the power or effect of persuading — **per·sua·sive·ly** *adv* — **per·sua·sive·ness** *n*

pert \ˈpərt\ *adj* **1 a** : saucily free and forward : IMPUDENT **b** : being trim and chic : JAUNTY **c** : piquantly stimulating **2** : LIVELY, VIVACIOUS — **pert·ly** *adv* — **pert·ness** *n*

per·tain \pər-ˈtān\ *vi* **1** : to belong to a person or thing as a part, quality, or function **2** : to refer or relate to a person or thing

per·ti·na·cious \ˌpərt-ᵊn-ˈā-shəs\ *adj* **1** : holding strongly to an opinion, purpose, or course of action **2** : stubbornly or annoyingly persistent — **per·ti·na·cious·ly** *adv* — **per·ti·nac·i·ty** \ˌpərt-ᵊn-ˈas-ət-ē\ *n*

per·ti·nent \ˈpərt-ᵊn-ənt\ *adj* : having to do with the subject or matter that is being considered : being to the point — **per·ti·nence** \-ᵊn-ən(t)s\ *or* **per·ti·nen·cy** \-ᵊn-ən-sē\ *n* — **per·ti·nent·ly** *adv*

per·turb \pər-ˈtərb\ *vt* **1** : to disturb greatly in mind : DISQUIET **2** : to throw into confusion : AGITATE — **per·turb·a·ble** *adj*

per·tur·ba·tion \ˌpərt-ər-ˈbā-shən, ˌpər-ˌtər-\ *n* **1** : the action of perturbing : the state of being perturbed **2** : a cause of worry or disquiet — **per·tur·ba·tion·al** \-shnəl, -shən-ᵊl\ *adj*

pe·ruke \pə-ˈrük\ *n* : WIG

pe·rus·al \pə-ˈrü-zəl\ *n* : the action of perusing

pe·ruse \pə-ˈrüz\ *vt* : READ; *esp* : to read carefully or thoroughly — **pe·rus·er** *n*

per·vade \pər-ˈvād\ *vt* : to spread or become diffused throughout every part of — **per·va·sion** \-ˈvā-zhən\ *n* — **per·va·sive** \-ˈvā-siv, -ziv\ *adj* — **per·va·sive·ly** *adv* — **per·va·sive·ness** *n*

per·verse \(ˌ)pər-ˈvərs, ˈpər-ˌ\ *adj* **1** : turned away from what is right or good : CORRUPT **2 a** : obstinate in opposing what is right, reasonable, or accepted : WRONGHEADED **b** : arising from or showing stubbornness or obstinacy **3** : marked by peevishness or petulance : CRANKY — **per·verse·ly** *adv* — **per·verse·ness** *n*

per·ver·sion \pər-ˈvər-zhən\ *n* **1** : the action of perverting : the condition of being perverted **2** : a perverted form **3** : abnormal sexual behavior

per·ver·si·ty \pər-ˈvər-sət-ē\ *n, pl* **-ties** : the quality, state, or an instance of being perverse

¹per·vert \pər-ˈvərt\ *vt* **1 a** : to cause to turn aside or away from what is good or true or morally right : CORRUPT **b** : to cause to turn aside or away from what is generally done or accepted : MISDIRECT **2 a** : to divert to a wrong end or purpose : MISUSE **b** : to twist the meaning or sense of : MISINTERPRET — **per·vert·er** *n*

²per·vert \ˈpər-ˌvərt\ *n* : one that is perverted; *esp* : one given to some form of sexual perversion

per·vert·ed \pər-ˈvərt-əd\ *adj* **1** : TWISTED, CORRUPT **2** : marked by perversion — **per·vert·ed·ly** *adv* — **per·vert·ed·ness** *n*

per·vi·ous \ˈpər-vē-əs\ *adj* : allowing entrance or passage : PERMEABLE — **per·vi·ous·ness** *n*

pes·ky \ˈpes-kē\ *adj* : ANNOYING, TROUBLESOME, VEXATIOUS

pes·si·mism \ˈpes-ə-ˌmiz-əm\ *n* **1** : an inclination to emphasize adverse aspects, conditions, and possibilities or to expect the worst possible outcome **2** : a belief that evil is more common or powerful than good — **pes·si·mist** \-məst\ *n*

pes·si·mis·tic \ˌpes-ə-ˈmis-tik\ *adj* **1** : lacking in hope that one's troubles will end or that success or happiness will come : GLOOMY **2** : having the belief that evil is more common or powerful than good — **pes·si·mis·ti·cal·ly** \-ti-k(ə-)lē\ *adv*

pest \ˈpest\ *n* **1** : an epidemic disease with a high mortality; *esp* : PLAGUE **2** : something resembling a pest in destructiveness; *esp* : a plant or animal detrimental to man **3** : one that pesters or annoys : NUISANCE

pes·ter \ˈpes-tər\ *vt* **pes·tered**; **pes·ter·ing** \-t(ə-)riŋ\ : ANNOY, BOTHER

pest·hole \ˈpest-ˌhōl\ *n* : a place in which pestilences are common

pest·house \-ˌhau̇s\ *n* : a shelter or hospital for those infected with a contagious or epidemic disease

pes·ti·cide \ˈpes-tə-ˌsīd\ *n* : an agent used to destroy pests — **pes·ti·cid·al** \ˌpes-tə-ˈsīd-ᵊl\ *adj*

pes·tif·er·ous \pe-ˈstif-(ə-)rəs\ *adj* **1** : dangerous to society : PERNICIOUS **2** : carrying or propagating infection **3** : ANNOYING, TROUBLESOME

pes·ti·lence \ˈpes-tə-lən(t)s\ *n* : a contagious or infectious epidemic disease that is virulent and devastating; *esp* : BUBONIC PLAGUE

pes·ti·lent \-lənt\ *adj* **1** : dangerous or destructive to life : DEADLY; *also* : being or conveying a pestilence **2** : harmful or dangerous to society : PERNICIOUS **3** : VEXING, IRRITATING

pes·ti·len·tial \ˌpes-tə-ˈlen-chəl\ *adj* : causing or likely to cause pestilence : PESTILENT

pes·tle \ˈpes-əl\ *n* : a usu. club-shaped implement for pounding or grinding substances in a mortar — **pestle** *vt*

¹pet \ˈpet\ *n* **1** : a domesticated animal kept for pleasure rather than utility **2 a** : a pampered and usu. spoiled child **b** : a person who is treated with unusual kindness or consideration : DARLING

²pet *adj* **1** : kept or treated as a pet **2** : expressing fondness or endearment **3** : FAVORITE

³pet *vb* **pet·ted**; **pet·ting** **1** : to stroke in a gentle or loving manner **2** : to treat with unusual kindness and consideration : PAMPER **3** : to engage in amorous embracing, caressing, and kissing — **pet·ter** *n*

⁴pet *n* : a fit of peevishness, sulkiness, or anger

pet·al \ˈpet-ᵊl\ *n* : one of the often brightly colored modified leaves making up the corolla of a flower — **pet·aled** *or* **pet·alled** \-ᵊld\ *adj* — **pet·al·less** \-ᵊl-(l)əs\ *adj* — **pet·al·like** \-ᵊl-ˌ(l)īk\ *adj*

pe·tard \pə-ˈtär(d)\ *n* : a case containing an explosive to break down a door or gate or breach a wall

pe·ter \ˈpēt-ər\ *vi* : to diminish gradually and come to an end : give out

pet·i·ole \ˈpet-ē-ˌōl\ *n* : a stalk that supports a leaf — **pet·i·o·lar** \ˌpet-ē-ˈō-lər\ *adj* — **pet·i·o·late** \ˈpet-ē-ə-ˌlāt\ *or* **pet·i·oled** \ˈpet-ē-ˌōld\ *adj*

pe·tite \pə-ˈtēt\ *adj* : small and trim of figure : LITTLE — **pe·tite·ness** *n*

pe·tit four \ˌpet-ē-ˈfō(ə)r\ *n, pl* **petits fours** *or* **petit fours** \-ē-ˈfō(ə)rz\ : a small frosted and ornamented cake cut from pound or sponge cake

¹pe·ti·tion \pə-ˈtish-ən\ *n* **1** : an earnest request : ENTREATY **2** : a formal written request made to a superior or authority **3** : something asked or requested

²petition *vb* **pe·ti·tioned**; **pe·ti·tion·ing** \-ˈtish-(ə-)niŋ\ : to make a request to or for : SOLICIT; *esp* : to make a formal written request — **pe·ti·tion·er** \-ˈtish-(ə-)nər\ *n*

pet·rel \'pe-trəl\ *n* : any of various small long-winged seabirds that fly far from land

pet·ri·fac·tion \ˌpe-trə-'fak-shən\ *n* **1** : the process of petrifying or state of being petrified **2** : something that is petrified

pet·ri·fi·ca·tion \ˌpe-trə-fə-'kā-shən\ *n* : PETRIFACTION

pet·ri·fy \'pe-trə-ˌfī\ *vb* **-fied**; **-fy·ing** **1** : to convert into stony material **2** : to make or become rigid or inactive

pet·ro·la·tum \ˌpe-trə-'lāt-əm\ *n* : a tasteless, odorless, and oily or greasy substance from petroleum that is used esp. in ointments and dressings

pe·tro·le·um \pə-'trō-lē-əm, -'trōl-yəm\ *n* : an oily flammable liquid widely distributed in the upper strata of the earth that is the source of gasoline and lubricants and a major industrial raw material

[1]**pet·ti·coat** \'pet-ē-ˌkōt\ *n* **1 a** : an outer skirt formerly worn by women and small children **b** : a skirt worn under a dress or outer skirt **2 a** : a garment characteristic or typical of women **b** : WOMAN **3** : something (as a valance) resembling a petticoat

[2]**petticoat** *adj* : FEMALE

pet·ti·fog \'pet-ē-ˌfȯg, -ˌfäg\ *vi* **-fogged**; **-fog·ging** **1** : to engage in legal trickery **2** : to quibble over insignificant details : CAVIL — **pet·ti·fog·ger** *n* — **pet·ti·fog·gery** \-ˌfȯg-(ə-)rē, -ˌfäg-\ *n*

pet·tish \'pet-ish\ *adj* : FRETFUL, PEEVISH — **pet·tish·ly** *adv* — **pet·tish·ness** *n*

pet·ty \'pet-ē\ *adj* **1** : having secondary rank or importance : MINOR, SUBORDINATE **2** : having little or no importance or significance **3** : marked by or reflective of narrow interests and sympathies : SMALL-MINDED — **pet·ti·ly** \'pet-ᵊl-ē\ *adv* — **pet·ti·ness** \'pet-ē-nəs\ *n*

petty officer *n* : an enlisted man in the navy of any of the three lowest noncommissioned ranks

pet·u·lant \'pech-ə-lənt\ *adj* : characterized by temporary or capricious ill humor : PEEVISH — **pet·u·lance** \-lən(t)s\ *n* — **pet·u·lant·ly** *adv*

pe·tu·nia \pə-'t(y)ü-nyə\ *n* : a garden plant with showy funnel-shaped flowers

pew \'pyü\ *n* : one of the benches with backs fixed in rows in a church

pew·ter \'pyüt-ər\ *n* **1** : any of various tin-based alloys usu. with lead and sometimes also with varying amounts of copper or antimony **2** : wares (as table utensils) of pewter — **pewter** *adj*

pha·e·ton \'fā-ət-ᵊn\ *n* **1** : a light 4-wheeled horse-drawn vehicle **2** : an open automobile with two cross seats

pha·lanx \'fā-ˌlaŋ(k)s\ *n, pl* **pha·lanx·es** *or* **pha·lan·ges** \fə-'lan-(ˌ)jēz, fā-\ : a group or body (as of troops) in a compact formation

phal·a·rope \'fal-ə-ˌrōp\ *n* : any of various small shorebirds

phal·lus \'fal-əs\ *n, pl* **phal·li** \'fal-ˌī, -ˌē\ *or* **phal·lus·es** **1** : a symbol or representation of the male organ of generation **2** : PENIS — **phal·lic** \'fal-ik\ *adj*

phan·tasm \'fan-ˌtaz-əm\ *n* **1** : a product of fantasy: as **a** : delusive appearance : ILLUSION **b** : GHOST, SPECTER **c** : a figment of the imagination : FANTASY **2** : a deceptive or illusory appearance of a thing — **phan·tas·mal** \fan-'taz-məl\ *adj* — **phan·tas·mic** \-'taz-mik\ *adj*

phan·tas·ma·go·ria \(ˌ)fan-ˌtaz-mə-'gōr-ē-ə\ *n* **1** : a constantly shifting complex succession of things seen or imagined **2** : a scene that constantly changes or fluctuates — **phan·tas·ma·go·ric** \-'gōr-ik\ *adj*

[1]**phan·tom** \'fant-əm\ *n* **1 a** : something (as a specter) apparent to sense but with no substantial existence : APPARITION **b** : something elusive or visionary : WILL-O'-THE-WISP **c** : an object of continual dread or abhorrence : BUGBEAR **2** : something existing in appearance only **3** : a representation of something abstract, ideal, or incorporeal

[2]**phantom** *adj* : of the nature of, suggesting, or being a phantom : ILLUSORY

phar·aoh \'fe(ə)r-ō, 'fā(ə)r-ō\ *n, often cap* : a ruler of ancient Egypt

phar·i·sa·ic \ˌfar-ə-'sā-ik\ *adj* : PHARISAICAL

phar·i·sa·i·cal \-'sā-ə-kəl\ *adj* : marked by hypocritical censorious self-righteousness — **phar·i·sa·i·cal·ly** \-k(ə-)lē\ *adv*

phar·i·see \'far-ə-(ˌ)sē\ *n* **1** *cap* : a member of a Jewish sect of New Testament times noted for strict observance of rites and ceremonies of the written law and for insistence on the validity of the oral tradition **2** : a pharisaical person

[1]**phar·ma·ceu·ti·cal** \ˌfär-mə-'süt-i-kəl\ *or* **phar·ma·ceu·tic** \-'süt-ik\ *adj* **1** : of or relating to pharmacy or pharmacists **2** : MEDICINAL — **phar·ma·ceu·ti·cal·ly** \-i-k(ə-)lē\ *adv*

[2]**pharmaceutical** *n* : a pharmaceutical preparation : a medicinal material or product

phar·ma·cist \'fär-mə-səst\ *n* : one skilled or engaged in pharmacy

phar·ma·col·o·gy \ˌfär-mə-'käl-ə-jē\ *n* **1** : the science of drugs esp. as related to their use in medicine **2** : the properties and reactions of drugs — **phar·ma·co·log·i·cal** \-kə-'läj-i-kəl\ *or* **phar·ma·co·log·ic** \-'läj-ik\ *adj* — **phar·ma·co·log·i·cal·ly** \-i-k(ə-)lē\ *adv* — **phar·ma·col·o·gist** \-'käl-ə-jəst\ *n*

phar·ma·co·poe·ia *or* **phar·ma·co·pe·ia** \ˌfär-mə-kə-'pē-(y)ə\ *n* **1** : a book describing drugs, chemicals, and medicinal preparations **2** : a collection or stock of drugs — **phar·ma·co·poe·ial** \-(y)əl\ *adj*

phar·ma·cy \'fär-mə-sē\ *n, pl* **-cies** **1** : the art, practice, or profession of preparing and dispensing drugs **2** : DRUGSTORE

phar·ynx \'far-iŋ(k)s\ *n, pl* **pha·ryn·ges** \fə-'rin-(ˌ)jēz\ : the space just behind the mouth into which the nostrils, esophagus, and trachea open — **pha·ryn·geal** \fə-'rin-j(ē-)əl, ˌfar-ən-'jē-əl\ *adj*

phase \'fāz\ *n* **1** : the apparent shape of the moon or a planet at any time in its series of changes with respect to illumination **2 a** : a stage or interval in a development or cycle **b** : an aspect or part under consideration — **pha·sic** \'fā-zik\ *adj*

pheas·ant \'fez-ᵊnt\ *n, pl* **pheasant** *or* **pheasants** : any of numerous large long-tailed brilliantly colored Old World birds related to the domestic fowl many of which are reared as ornamental or game birds

pheasant

phe·no·bar·bi·tal \ˌfē-nō-'bär-bə-ˌtȯl\ *n* : a crystalline barbiturate drug used as a hypnotic and sedative

phe·nol \'fē-ˌnōl, fi-'\ *n* : a caustic poisonous crystalline acidic compound present in coal tar and wood tar that in dilute solution is used as a disinfectant — **phe·no·lic** \fi-'nō-lik, -'näl-ik\ *adj*

phe·nom·e·nal \fi-'näm-ən-ᵊl\ *adj* **1** : of, relating to, or being a phenomenon **2** : EXTRAORDINARY, REMARKABLE — **phe·nom·e·nal·ly** \-ᵊl-ē\ *adv*

phe·nom·e·non \fi-'näm-ə-ˌnän, -nən\ *n, pl* **-na** \-nə, -ˌnä\ *or* **-nons** **1** : an observable fact or event **2** : a fact or event that can be scientifically described and explained **3** *pl phenomenons* : an exceptional person, thing, or event : PRODIGY

phi·al \'fī(-ə)l\ *n* : VIAL
phi·lan·der \fə-'lan-dər\ *vi* **phi·lan·dered**; **phi·lan·der·ing** \-d(ə-)riŋ\ : to make love frivolously : FLIRT — **phi·lan·der·er** \-dər-ər\ *n*
phil·an·throp·ic \ˌfil-ən-'thräp-ik\ *adj* : of, relating to, or characterized by philanthropy : BENEVOLENT, CHARITABLE — **phil·an·throp·i·cal** \-'thräp-i-kəl\ *adj* — **phil·an·throp·i·cal·ly** \-i-k(ə-)lē\ *adv*
phi·lan·thro·pist \fə-'lan(t)-thrə-pəst\ *n* : one who practices philanthropy
phi·lan·thro·py \-pē\ *n, pl* **-pies** **1** : goodwill to fellowmen; *esp* : active effort to promote human welfare **2** : a philanthropic act or gift or an organization distributing or supported by philanthropic funds
phil·a·tel·ic \ˌfil-ə-'tel-ik\ *adj* : of or relating to philately — **phil·a·tel·i·cal·ly** \-'tel-i-k(ə-)lē\ *adv*
phi·lat·e·ly \fə-'lat-ᵊl-ē\ *n* : the collection and study of postage and imprinted stamps — **phi·lat·e·list** \-ᵊl-əst\ *n*
phi·lip·pic \fə-'lip-ik\ *n* : a discourse or declamation full of acrimonious invective : TIRADE
phil·is·tine \'fil-ə-ˌstēn; fə-'lis-tən, -ˌtēn\ *n, often cap* : a materialistic person; *esp* : one who takes an attitude of smug indifference to art and literature and the cultural values they represent — **philistine** *adj* — **phil·is·tin·ism** \-ˌiz-əm\ *n*
phil·o·den·dron \ˌfil-ə-'den-drən\ *n, pl* **-drons** *or* **-dra** \-drə\ : any of various arums grown for their showy often variegated foliage
phi·lol·o·gy \fə-'läl-ə-jē\ *n* **1** : the study of literature and of relevant disciplines **2** : LINGUISTICS; *esp* : historical and comparative linguistics — **phil·o·log·i·cal** \ˌfil-ə-'läj-i-kəl\ *adj* — **phil·o·log·i·cal·ly** \-'läj-i-k(ə-)lē\ *adv* — **phi·lol·o·gist** \fə-'läl-ə-jəst\ *n*
phi·los·o·pher \fə-'läs-ə-fər\ *n* **1 a** : SCHOLAR, THINKER **b** : a student of philosophy **2** : a person whose philosophical perspective enables him to meet trouble with fortitude and resignation
phil·o·soph·ic \ˌfil-ə-'säf-ik\ *adj* **1** : of, relating to, or based on philosophy **2** : characterized by the attitude of a philosopher; *esp* : calm in face of trouble : TEMPERATE — **phil·o·soph·i·cal** \-'säf-i-kəl\ *adj* — **phil·o·soph·i·cal·ly** \-i-k(ə-)lē\ *adv*
phi·los·o·phize \fə-'läs-ə-ˌfīz\ *vi* **1** : to reason in the manner of a philosopher **2** : to expound a superficial philosophy : MORALIZE — **phi·los·o·phiz·er** *n*
phi·los·o·phy \fə-'läs-ə-fē\ *n, pl* **-phies** **1** : the study of the nature of knowledge and existence and the principles of moral and esthetic value **2** : the philosophical teachings or principles of a man or group of men **3** : the general principles of a field of study **4** : wisdom or insight applied to life itself **5** : sciences and liberal arts exclusive of medicine, law, and theology
phil·ter *or* **phil·tre** \'fil-tər\ *n* **1** : a potion, drug, or charm held to have the power to excite sexual passion **2** : a potion credited with magical power
phle·bi·tis \fli-'bīt-əs\ *n* : inflammation of a vein
phle·bot·o·my \fli-'bät-ə-mē\ *n* : the letting of blood in the treatment of disease — **phle·bot·o·mist** \-məst\ *n* — **phle·bot·o·mize** \-ˌmīz\ *vt*
phlegm \'flem\ *n* **1** : viscid mucus secreted in abnormal quantity in the respiratory passages **2 a** : dull or apathetic coldness or indifference **b** : intrepid coolness : CALMNESS
phleg·mat·ic \fleg-'mat-ik\ *adj* : not easily excited or aroused : slow to respond — **phleg·mat·i·cal·ly** \-i-k(ə-)lē\ *adv*
phlo·em \'flō-ˌem\ *n* : a vascular tissue of higher plants that transports dissolved food material, contains sieve tubes, and lies mostly external to the cambium
phlox \'fläks\ *n, pl* **phlox** *or* **phlox·es** : any of a genus of American annual or perennial herbs with showy red, purple, white, or variegated flowers
pho·bia \'fō-bē-ə\ *n* : an unreasonable persistent fear of a particular thing — **pho·bic** \'fō-bik, 'fäb-ik\ *adj*
¹phone \'fōn\ *n* **1** : EARPHONE **2** : TELEPHONE
²phone *vb* : TELEPHONE
pho·neme \'fō-ˌnēm\ *n* : a member of the set of the smallest units of speech that serve to distinguish one utterance from another
pho·ne·mic \fə-'nē-mik\ *adj* **1** : of, relating to, or having the characteristics of a phoneme **2** : constituting different phonemes — **pho·ne·mi·cal·ly** \-mi-k(ə-)lē\ *adv*
pho·net·ic \fə-'net-ik\ *adj* **1 a** : of or relating to spoken language or speech sounds **b** : of or relating to the science of phonetics **2** : representing the phenomena of speech — **pho·net·i·cal** \-'net-i-kəl\ *adj* — **pho·net·i·cal·ly** \-i-k(ə-)lē\ *adv*
pho·net·ics \fə-'net-iks\ *n* **1** : the study and systematic classification of the sounds made in spoken utterance **2** : the system of speech sounds of a language or group of languages — **pho·ne·ti·cian** \ˌfō-nə-'tish-ən\ *n*
phon·ic \'fän-ik\ *adj* **1** : of, relating to, or producing sound **2** : of or relating to the sounds of speech or to phonics — **phon·i·cal·ly** \-i-k(ə-)lē\ *adv*
phon·ics \'fän-iks\ *n* : a method of teaching beginners to read and pronounce words by learning the phonetic value of letters, letter groups, and esp. syllables
pho·no·graph \'fō-nə-ˌgraf\ *n* : an instrument for reproducing sounds by means of the vibration of a stylus or needle following a spiral groove on a revolving disc — **pho·no·graph·ic** \ˌfō-nə-'graf-ik\ *adj* — **pho·no·graph·i·cal·ly** \-i-k(ə-)lē\ *adv*
pho·nol·o·gy \fō-'näl-ə-jē\ *n* : the science of speech sounds including esp. the history and theory of sound changes in a language or in two or more related languages — **pho·no·log·i·cal** \ˌfōn-ᵊl-'äj-i-kəl\ *adj* — **pho·no·log·i·cal·ly** \-k(ə-)lē\ *adv* — **pho·nol·o·gist** \fō-'näl-ə-jəst\ *n*
¹pho·ny *or* **pho·ney** \'fō-nē\ *adj* : FALSE, SPURIOUS, COUNTERFEIT; *esp* : falsely pretentious — **pho·ni·ly** \'fōn-ᵊl-ē\ *adv* — **pho·ni·ness** \'fō-nē-nəs\ *n*
²phony *or* **phoney** *n, pl* **phonies** *or* **phoneys** : FAKE
phos·phate \'fäs-ˌfāt\ *n* **1** : an effervescent drink of carbonated water flavored with fruit syrup **2** : a phosphatic material used for fertilizers
phos·phat·ic \fäs-'fat-ik, -'fāt-\ *adj* : of, relating to, or containing phosphoric acid or phosphates
phos·pho·res·cence \ˌfäs-fə-'res-ᵊn(t)s\ *n* : the property of emitting light without easily perceptible heat shown by phosphorus or living organisms (as various bacteria and fungi); *also* : the light so produced — **phos·pho·res·cent** \-ᵊnt\ *adj*
phos·phor·ic acid \fäs-ˌfȯr-ik-\ *n* : an oxygen-containing acid of phosphorus; *esp* : a syrupy or crystalline acid used in making fertilizers and as a flavoring in soft drinks
phos·pho·rus \'fäs-f(ə-)rəs\ *n* **1** : a phosphorescent substance; *esp* : one that glows in the dark **2** : a poisonous active chemical element usu. obtained in the form of waxy disagreeable-smelling crystals that glow in moist air — **phosphoric** *adj* — **phos·pho·rous** \'fäs-f(ə-)rəs; fäs-'fōr-əs\ *adj* — **phosphorus** *adj*
pho·to \'fōt-ō\ *n, pl* **photos** : PHOTOGRAPH — **photo** *vb* — **photo** *adj*
pho·to·cell \'fōt-ə-ˌsel\ *n* : PHOTOELECTRIC CELL
pho·to·copy \'fōt-ə-ˌkäp-ē\ *n* : a photographic reproduction of graphic matter — **photocopy** *vb*
pho·to·elec·tric \ˌfōt-ō-ə-'lek-trik\ *adj* : relating to or utilizing any of various electrical effects due to the interaction of light with matter
photoelectric cell *n* : a cell in which variations of light are converted into corresponding variations in an electric current
pho·to·en·grave \ˌfōt-ō-in-'grāv\ *vt* : to make a photoengraving of — **pho·to·en·grav·er** *n*

pho·to·en·grav·ing \-'grā-viŋ\ *n* : a process by which an etched printing plate is made from a photograph or drawing; *also* : a print made from such a plate
photo finish *n* : a race finish in which contestants are so close that a photograph of them as they cross the finish line has to be examined to determine the winner
pho·to·flash \'fōt-ə-,flash\ *n* : FLASHBULB
pho·to·gen·ic \,fōt-ə-'jen-ik, -'jēn-\ *adj* : suitable for being photographed esp. from the artistic point of view : photographing well — **pho·to·gen·i·cal·ly** \-i-k(ə-)lē\ *adv*
pho·to·graph \'fōt-ə-,graf\ *n* : a picture or likeness obtained by photography — **photograph** *vb* — **pho·tog·ra·pher** \fə-'täg-rə-fər\ *n*
pho·tog·ra·phy \fə-'täg-rə-fē\ *n* : the art or process of producing images on a sensitized surface (as a film or plate) by the action of light or other radiant energy — **pho·to·graph·ic** \,fōt-ə-'graf-ik\ *adj* — **pho·to·graph·i·cal·ly** \-i-k(ə-)lē\ *adv*
pho·to·mi·cro·graph \,fōt-ə-'mī-krə-,graf\ *n* : a photograph of a magnified image of a small object — **pho·to·mi·cro·graph·ic** \-,mī-krə-'graf-ik\ *adj* — **pho·to·mi·crog·ra·phy** \-mī-'kräg-rə-fē\ *n*
pho·to·mu·ral \-'myu̇r-əl\ *n* : an enlarged photograph usu. several yards long used on walls esp. as decoration
pho·ton \'fō-,tän\ *n* : a quantum of radiant energy
pho·to·play \'fōt-ə-,plā\ *n* : MOTION PICTURE 2
pho·to·sen·si·tive \,fōt-ə-'sen(t)-sət-iv, -'sen(t)-stiv\ *adj* : sensitive or sensitized to the action of radiant energy and esp. light — **pho·to·sen·si·tiv·i·ty** \-,sen(t)-sə-'tiv-ət-ē\ *n* — **pho·to·sen·si·ti·za·tion** \-,sen(t)-sət-ə-'zā-shən\ *n*
pho·to·syn·the·sis \,fōt-ə-'sin(t)-thə-səs\ *n* : formation of carbohydrates in the chlorophyll-containing tissues of plants exposed to light — **pho·to·syn·the·size** \-,sīz\ *vi* — **pho·to·syn·thet·ic** \-sin-'thet-ik\ *adj* — **pho·to·syn·thet·i·cal·ly** \-'thet-i-k(ə-)lē\ *adv*
phras·al \'frā-zəl\ *adj* : of, relating to, or consisting of a phrase — **phras·al·ly** \-zə-lē\ *adv*
[1]**phrase** \'frāz\ *n* **1** : a characteristic manner of expression : DICTION **2** : a brief expression; *esp* : one commonly used **3** : a group of two or more grammatically related words that form a sense unit expressing a thought
[2]**phrase** *vt* : to express in words or in appropriate or telling terms : WORD
phra·se·ol·o·gy \,frā-zē-'äl-ə-jē\ *n* **1** : manner of organizing words and phrases into longer elements : DICTION, STYLE **2** : choice of words : VOCABULARY
phras·ing \'frā-ziŋ\ *n* **1** : style of expression : PHRASEOLOGY **2** : the act, method, or result of grouping notes into musical phrases
phre·net·ic \fri-'net-ik\ *adj* : FRENETIC
phre·nol·o·gy \fri-'näl-ə-jē\ *n* : the study of the conformation of the skull as indicative of mental faculties and character — **phren·o·log·i·cal** \,fren-ᵊl-'äj-i-kəl, ,frēn-\ *adj* — **phre·nol·o·gist** \fri-'näl-ə-jəst\ *n*
phy·lac·tery \fə-'lak-t(ə-)rē\ *n, pl* **-ter·ies** **1** : one of two small square leather boxes containing slips inscribed with scripture passages and traditionally worn on the left arm and forehead by Jewish men during morning weekday prayers **2** : AMULET
phy·lum \'fī-ləm\ *n, pl* **phy·la** \-lə\ : a group (as of people or languages) apparently of common origin; *also* : a major division of the plant or animal kingdom — **phy·lar** \-lər\ *adj*
[1]**phys·ic** \'fiz-ik\ *n* : a remedy for disease; *esp* : CATHARTIC, PURGATIVE
[2]**physic** *vt* **phys·icked** \-ikt\; **phys·ick·ing** \-i-kiŋ\; **phys·ics** *or* **phys·icks** : to treat with or administer medicine to; *esp* : PURGE
phys·i·cal \'fiz-i-kəl\ *adj* **1** : of or relating to nature or the laws of nature **2** : of or relating to material things : not mental or spiritual **3** : of or relating to natural science **4** : of or relating to physics **5** : of or relating to the body : BODILY; *also* : preoccupied with the body or its needs — **phys·i·cal·ly** \-k(ə-)lē\ *adv*
physical science *n* : the natural sciences (as mineralogy or astronomy) that deal primarily with nonliving materials
phy·si·cian \fə-'zish-ən\ *n* : a person skilled in the art of healing; *esp* : a doctor of medicine
phys·i·cist \'fiz-ə-səst\ *n* : a specialist in the science of physics
phys·ics \'fiz-iks\ *n* **1** : a science that deals with the phenomena of inanimate matter and motion and includes consideration of mechanics, heat, light, electricity, sound, and nuclear phenomena **2** : physical composition, properties, or processes
phys·i·og·no·my \,fiz-ē-'äg)-nə-mē\ *n, pl* **-mies** **1** : the art of discovering temperament and character from outward appearance **2** : the facial features held to show qualities of mind or character **3** : external aspect; *also* : inner character or quality revealed outwardly — **phys·i·og·nom·ic** \-ē-ə(g)-'näm-ik\ *or* **phys·i·og·nom·i·cal** \-'näm-i-kəl\ *adj* — **phys·i·og·nom·i·cal·ly** \-i-k(ə-)lē\ *adv*
phys·i·og·ra·phy \,fiz-ē-'äg-rə-fē\ *n* : geography dealing with physical features of the earth — **phys·i·og·ra·pher** \-rə-fər\ *n* — **phys·io·graph·ic** \,fiz-ē-ə-'graf-ik\ *adj*
phys·i·o·log·i·cal \,fiz-ē-ə-'läj-i-kəl\ *or* **phys·i·o·log·ic** \-'läj-ik\ *adj* **1** : of, relating to, or affecting physiology **2** : characteristic of healthy or normal physiology — **phys·i·o·log·i·cal·ly** \-i-k(ə-)lē\ *adv*
phys·i·ol·o·gy \,fiz-ē-'äl-ə-jē\ *n* **1** : a branch of biology dealing with the processes, activities, and phenomena incidental to and characteristic of life or of living matter **2** : the organic processes and phenomena of an organism or any of its parts or of a particular bodily process — **phys·i·ol·o·gist** \-jəst\ *n*
phys·io·ther·a·py \,fiz-ē-ō-'ther-ə-pē\ *n* : treatment of disease by physical means (as massage or exercise)
phy·sique \fə-'zēk\ *n* : the build of a person's body : physical constitution
[1]**pi** \'pī\ *n, pl* **pis** \'pīz\ **1** : the symbol π denoting the ratio of the circumference of a circle to its diameter **2** : the ratio itself having a value to eight decimal places of 3.14159265
[2]**pi** *n, pl* **pies** : type or type matter that is spilled, mixed, or incorrectly distributed
[3]**pi** *vb* **pied**; **pi·ing** **1** : to spill or throw (type or type matter) into disorder **2** : to become pied
pi·a·nis·si·mo \,pē-ə-'nis-ə-,mō\ *adv* (*or adj*) : very softly — used as a direction in music
pi·an·ist \pē-'an-əst, 'pē-ə-nəst\ *n* : a person who plays the piano
pi·ano \pē-'an-ō\ *n, pl* **-an·os** : a musical percussion instrument having steel-wire strings that sound when struck by felt-covered hammers operated from a keyboard
pi·an·o·forte \pē-'an-ə-,fōrt, -,fȯrt-ē\ *n* : PIANO
pi·az·za \pē-'az-ə, *1 is usu* -'at-sə, -'ät-\ *n, pl* **piazzas** *or* **pi·az·ze** \-'at-(,)sā, -'ät-\ **1** : an open square esp. in an Italian town **2** : an arcaded and roofed gallery
pi·broch \'pē-,bräk\ *n* : a set of martial or mournful variations for the Scottish bagpipe
pic·a·resque \,pik-ə-'resk\ *adj* : of or relating to rogues or rascals; *also* : of or relating to a type of fiction of Spanish origin dealing with rogues and vagabonds
[1]**pic·a·yune** \,pik-ē-'(y)ün\ *n* : something trivial
[2]**picayune** *adj* : having little value : PALTRY; *also* : PETTY, SMALL-MINDED
pic·ca·lil·li \,pik-ə-'lil-ē\ *n* : a pungent relish of chopped vegetables and spices
pic·co·lo \'pik-ə-,lō\ *n, pl* **-los** : a small shrill flute pitched an octave higher than the ordinary flute — **pic·co·lo·ist** \-əst\ *n*
[1]**pick** \'pik\ *vb* **1** : to strike or work on (as for piercing, breaking, or denting) with a pointed tool; *also* : to move, alter, or

form by such action **2 a :** to clear away (something) or free from something by or as if by plucking **b :** to gather or move by plucking **c :** to handle or operate by plucking something; *also* **:** to pluck at **3 :** to look over and choose or separate **:** CULL, SELECT **4 :** to steal or pilfer from **5 :** PROVOKE **6 :** to eat sparingly or in a finicky manner **7 :** to unlock without a key — **pick·er** *n* — **pick on 1 :** TEASE, HARASS **2 :** to single out esp. for some unpleasant task

²pick *n* **1 :** a blow or stroke with a pointed instrument **2 a :** the act or privilege of choosing or selecting **:** CHOICE **b :** the best or choicest one

³pick *n* **1 :** PICKAX **2 :** any of several slender pointed implements for picking or chipping **3 :** PLECTRUM

pick·a·nin·ny *or* **pic·a·nin·ny** \ˈpik-ə-ˌnin-ē, ˌpik-ə-ˈ\ *n, pl* **-nies :** a Negro child

pick·ax *or* **pick·axe** \ˈpik-ˌaks\ *n* **:** a heavy tool with a wooden handle and a curved or straight blade pointed at one or both ends that is used esp. in loosening or breaking up soil or rock

picked \ˈpikt\ *adj* **:** fit or ready for use **:** CHOICE

pick·er·el \ˈpik-(ə-)rəl\ *n, pl* **pickerel** *or* **pickerels :** any of several comparatively small pikes; *also* **:** WALLEYE 2

¹pick·et \ˈpik-ət\ *n* **1 :** a pointed stake or post (as for a fence) **2 :** a soldier or a detachment of soldiers posted to guard an army from surprise attack **3 :** a person posted by a labor organization at a place of work where there is a strike

²picket *vb* **1 :** to enclose, fence, or fortify with pickets **2 :** to guard with or post as a picket **3 :** TETHER **4 a :** to post pickets or act as a picket at **b :** to serve as a picket — **pick·et·er** *n*

pick·ings \ˈpik-iŋz, -ənz\ *n pl* **1 :** something available or left over; *esp* **:** eatable remains **2 :** yield or return for effort expended

¹pick·le \ˈpik-əl\ *n* **1 :** a bath for preserving or cleaning; *esp* **:** a brine or vinegar solution in which foods are preserved **2 :** a difficult situation **:** PLIGHT **3 :** an article of food (as a cucumber) preserved in brine or vinegar

²pickle *vt* **pick·led**; **pick·ling** \ˈpik-(ə-)liŋ\ **:** to treat, preserve, or clean in or with a pickle

pick out *vt* **1 a :** SELECT, CHOOSE **b :** DISTINGUISH **2 :** to play the notes of by ear or one by one

pick·pock·et \ˈpik-ˌpäk-ət\ *n* **:** one who steals from pockets

pick up *vb* **1 a :** to take hold of and lift **b :** to take in or into a vehicle **2 a :** to acquire casually, irregularly, or at a bargain **b :** to strike up a casual acquaintance with and persuade to accompany esp. for purposes of lovemaking **3 :** to bring within range of sight or hearing **4 :** to gather or regain speed, vigor, or activity

pick·up \ˈpik-ˌəp\ *n* **1 a :** a revival of activity **b :** ACCELERATION **2 :** a temporary chance acquaintance **3 :** a light truck having an open body with low sides

¹pic·nic \ˈpik-(ˌ)nik\ *n* **1 :** an excursion or outing with food usu. taken along and eaten in the open **2 :** something pleasant or easy

²picnic *vi* **pic·nicked**; **pic·nick·ing :** to go on a picnic **:** eat in picnic fashion — **pic·nick·er** *n*

pi·cot \ˈpē-kō, pē-ˈ\ *n* **:** one of a series of small ornamental loops forming an edging on ribbon or lace

pic·to·ri·al \pik-ˈtōr-ē-əl\ *adj* **1 :** of or relating to a painter, a painting, or the painting or drawing of pictures **2 a :** consisting of pictures **b :** illustrated by pictures **3 :** having the qualities of a picture — **pic·to·ri·al·ly** \-ē-ə-lē\ *adv*

¹pic·ture \ˈpik-chər\ *n* **1 :** a representation made on a surface (as by painting, drawing, or photography) **2 a :** a very vivid or graphic description **b :** a presentation of a problem or situation or the matter presented **3 a :** an exact likeness **:** SEMBLANCE **b :** a tangible or visible representation **:** EMBODIMENT **4 a :** a transitory visible image (as on a television screen) **b :** MOTION PICTURE — **picture** *adj*

²picture *vt* **pic·tured**; **pic·tur·ing** \ˈpik-chə-riŋ, ˈpik-shriŋ\ **1 :** to make a picture of (as by drawing) **:** DEPICT **2 :** to describe vividly **3 :** to form a mental image of **:** IMAGINE

pic·tur·esque \ˌpik-chə-ˈresk\ *adj* **1 :** resembling a picture **:** suggesting or suitable for a painted scene **2 :** CHARMING, QUAINT — **pic·tur·esque·ly** *adv* — **pic·tur·esque·ness** *n*

pid·dle \ˈpid-ᵊl\ *vi* **pid·dled**; **pid·dling** \ˈpid-liŋ, -ᵊl-iŋ\ **:** to act or work idly **:** DAWDLE

pid·dling \ˈpid-lən, -ᵊl-ən, -liŋ, -ᵊl-iŋ\ *adj* **:** TRIVIAL, PALTRY

pid·gin \ˈpij-ən\ *n* **:** a simplified speech used for communication between people with different languages; *esp* **:** an English-based pidgin used in the Orient

pie \ˈpī\ *n* **1 :** a dish consisting of a pastry crust and a filling (as of fruit or meat) **2 :** a layer cake with a thick filling (as of jam or custard)

¹pie·bald \ˈpī-ˌbȯld\ *adj* **:** of two colors; *esp* **:** spotted or blotched with black and white

²piebald *n* **:** a piebald animal (as a horse)

¹piece \ˈpēs\ *n* **1 :** a part cut, torn, or broken from a thing **:** FRAGMENT **2 :** one of a group, set, or mass of things **3 :** a portion marked off **4 :** a single item, example, or instance **5 :** a definite quantity or size in which an article is made for sale or use **6 :** a finished product **:** something made, composed, or written **7 :** COIN **8 :** FIREARM — **of a piece :** ALIKE, UNIFORM, CONSISTENT

²piece *vt* **1 :** to repair, renew, or complete by adding pieces **:** PATCH **2 :** to join into a whole — **piec·er** *n*

pièce de ré·sis·tance \pē-ˌes-də-rə-ˌzē-ˈstän(t)s\ *n, pl* **pièces de ré·sis·tance** *same*\ **1 :** the chief dish of a meal **2 :** an outstanding item

¹piece·meal \ˈpēs-ˌmēl\ *adv* **1 :** one piece at a time **:** GRADUALLY **2 :** in pieces or fragments **:** APART

²piecemeal *adj* **:** done, made, or accomplished piece by piece or in a fragmentary way **:** GRADUAL

piece·work \-ˌwərk\ *n* **:** work done and paid for by the piece — **piece·work·er** \-ˌwər-kər\ *n*

pied \ˈpīd\ *adj* **:** of two or more colors in blotches **:** PARTI-COLORED

pie·plant \ˈpī-ˌplant\ *n* **:** garden rhubarb

pier \ˈpi(ə)r\ *n* **1 :** a support for a bridge span **2 :** a structure built out into the water for use as a landing place or walk or to protect or form a harbor **3 :** a single pillar or a structure used to support something

pierce \ˈpi(ə)rs\ *vb* **1 :** to run into or through as a pointed weapon does **:** STAB **2 :** to make a hole through **:** PERFORATE **3 :** to force or make a way into or through something **4 :** to penetrate with the eye or mind **:** DISCERN **5 :** to penetrate so as to move or touch the emotions of — **pierc·ing·ly** *adv*

pier glass *n* **:** a tall mirror; *esp* **:** one designed to occupy the wall space between windows

pies *pl of* PI *or of* PIE

pi·e·ty \ˈpī-ət-ē\ *n, pl* **-ties 1 :** the quality or state of being pious: as **a :** fidelity to natural obligations (as to parents) **b :** dutifulness in religion **:** DEVOUTNESS **2 :** an act inspired by piety

¹pif·fle \ˈpif-əl\ *vi* **pif·fled**; **pif·fling** \ˈpif-(ə-)liŋ\ **:** to talk or act in a trivial, inept, or ineffective way **:** TRIFLE

²piffle *n* **:** trifling talk or action

¹pig \ˈpig\ *n* **1 :** a young swine not yet sexually mature **2 :** PORK **3 :** one resembling a pig **4 :** a casting of metal (as iron or lead) run directly from the smelting furnace into a mold — **pig** *adj*

²pig *vb* **pigged**; **pig·ging :** to live like a pig

pi·geon \ˈpij-ən\ *n* **1 :** any of numerous birds with a stout body, usu. short legs, and smooth and compact plumage; *esp* **:** a domesticated bird **2 :** an easy mark **:** DUPE

¹pi·geon·hole \-ˌhōl\ *n* **1 :** a hole or small place for pigeons to nest 2 : a small open compartment (as in a desk or cabinet) for keeping letters or papers

²**pigeonhole** *vt* : to place in or as if in the pigeonhole of a desk: as **a** : to lay aside : SHELVE **b** : to assign to a category : CLASSIFY

pi·geon–toed \ˌpij-ən-'tōd\ *adj* : having the toes turned in

pig·gish \'pig-ish\ *adj* : resembling a pig esp. in greed, dirtiness, or stubbornness — **pig·gish·ly** *adv*

pig·gy·back \'pig-ē-ˌbak\ *adv* (*or adj*) **1** : on the back or shoulders **2** : on a railroad flatcar

pig·head·ed \'pig-'hed-əd\ *adj* : OBSTINATE, STUBBORN

¹**pig·ment** \'pig-mənt\ *n* **1** : a substance that imparts black or white or a color to other materials; *esp* : a powdered substance mixed with a liquid in which it is relatively insoluble to impart color **2** : a natural coloring matter in animals and plants — **pig·men·tary** \-mən-ˌter-ē\ *adj*

²**pig·ment** \-mənt, -ˌment\ *vt* : to color with or as if with pigment

pig·men·ta·tion \ˌpig-mən-'tā-shən, -ˌmen-\ *n* : coloration with or deposition of pigment; *esp* : an excessive deposition of bodily pigment

pig·nut \'pig-ˌnət\ *n* : any of several bitter-flavored hickory nuts; *also* : a tree bearing these

pig·pen \-ˌpen\ *n* **1** : PIGSTY **2** : a dirty place

pig·skin \-ˌskin\ *n* **1** : the skin of a swine or leather made of it **2 a** : a jockey's saddle **b** : FOOTBALL 2

pig·sty \'pig-ˌstī\ *n* : a pen for pigs

pig·tail \-ˌtāl\ *n* : a tight braid of hair

¹**pike** \'pīk\ *n* : a sharp point or spike; *also* : the tip of a spear — **piked** \'pīkt\ *adj*

²**pike** *n, pl* **pike** *or* **pikes** : a large slender greedy freshwater food fish; *also* : any of various related or similar fishes

³**pike** *n* : a long wooden shaft with a pointed steel head formerly used as a weapon by infantry

⁴**pike** *n* : TURNPIKE

pik·er \'pī-kər\ *n* **1** : one who does things in a small way or on a small scale **2** : TIGHTWAD, CHEAPSKATE

pike·staff \'pīk-ˌstaf\ *n* : the shaft of a soldier's pike

pi·laf *or* **pi·laff** \pi-'läf\ *or* **pi·lau** \pi-'lō, -'lȯ, *South often* 'pər-lü, -lō\ *n* : a dish made of rice with meat and seasoning

pi·las·ter \'pī-ˌlas-tər\ *n* : an upright rectangular slightly projecting architectural member that ornaments or helps to support a wall

pil·chard \'pil-chərd\ *n* : a fish resembling the related herring and occurring in great schools along the coasts of Europe; *also* : any of several related fishes

¹**pile** \'pīl\ *n* : a long slender column (as of wood or steel) driven into the ground to carry a vertical load

²**pile** *n* **1 a** : a quantity of things heaped together **b** : a heap of wood for burning a corpse or a sacrifice : PYRE **2** : a great amount (as of money)

³**pile** *vb* **1** : to lay or place something in a pile : STACK **2** : to heap in abundance : LOAD **3** : to move or press forward in or as if in a mass : CROWD

⁴**pile** *n* : a velvety surface produced on textile by an extra set of filling yarns that form raised loops which are cut and sheared

pi·le·ate \'pī-lē-ˌāt\ *or* **pi·le·at·ed** \-ˌāt-əd\ *adj* : having a cap or crest

piled \'pīld\ *adj* : having a pile

pil·fer \'pil-fər\ *vb* **pil·fered**; **pil·fer·ing** \-f(ə-)riŋ\ : to steal articles of small value or in small amounts at a time — **pil·fer·age** \-f(ə-)rij\ *n* — **pil·fer·er** *n*

pil·grim \'pil-grəm\ *n* **1** : one who journeys in alien lands : WAYFARER **2** : one who travels to a shrine or holy place as a devotee **3** *cap* : one of the English colonists founding the first permanent settlement in New England at Plymouth in 1620

pil·grim·age \'pil-grə-mij\ *n* : a journey of a pilgrim esp. to a shrine or a sacred place — **pilgrimage** *vi*

pil·ing \'pī-liŋ\ *n* : a structure of piles; *also* : PILES

pill \'pil\ *n* : medicine in a small rounded mass to be swallowed whole

¹**pil·lage** \'pil-ij\ *n* : the act of looting or plundering esp. in war

²**pillage** *vb* : to take booty : PLUNDER, LOOT — **pil·lag·er** *n*

pil·lar \'pil-ər\ *n* **1** : a comparatively slender upright support (as for a roof) **2** : a column or shaft standing alone (as for a monument) **3** : something suggesting a pillar : a main support — **pil·lared** \-ərd\ *adj* — **from pillar to post** : from one place or one situation to another

pill·box \'pil-ˌbäks\ *n* **1** : a small usu. shallow round box for pills **2** : a small low concrete emplacement for machine guns and antitank weapons **3** : a small round hat without a brim; *esp* : a woman's shallow hat with a flat crown and straight sides

¹**pil·lion** \'pil-yən\ *n* **1** : a cushion or pad placed behind a saddle for an extra rider **2** : a passenger's saddle (as on a motorcycle)

²**pillion** *adv* : on or as if on a pillion

pil·lo·ry \'pil-(ə-)rē\ *n, pl* **-ries** **1** : a device for publicly punishing offenders that consists of a wooden frame with holes in which the head and hands can be locked **2** : a means for exposing to public scorn or ridicule — **pillory** *vt*

¹**pil·low** \'pil-ō\ *n* : a support for the head of a person lying down that consists usu. of a bag filled with resilient material (as feathers or sponge rubber)

²**pillow** *vb* **1** : to rest or lay on or as if on a pillow **2** : to serve as a pillow for

pil·low·case \-ˌkās\ *n* : a removable covering for a pillow

¹**pi·lot** \'pī-lət\ *n* **1 a** : one employed to steer a ship **b** : a person qualified and usu. licensed to conduct a ship into and out of a port or in specified waters **2** : GUIDE, LEADER **3** : one who flies or is qualified to fly an airplane — **pi·lot·less** \-ləs\ *adj*

²**pilot** *vt* **1** : CONDUCT, GUIDE **2 a** : to direct the navigation of **b** : to act as pilot of : FLY

³**pilot** *adj* **1** : serving on a small scale as a guiding or tracing device or an activating or auxiliary unit **2** : serving on a small scale as a testing or trial device or unit

pilot biscuit *n* : HARDTACK

pi·lot·house \'pī-lət-ˌhau̇s\ *n* : an enclosed place forward on the upper deck of a ship that shelters the steering gear and the helmsman

pi·men·to \pə-'ment-ō\ *n, pl* **-tos** *or* **-to** **1** : PIMIENTO **2** : ALLSPICE

pi·mien·to \pə-'ment-ō, pəm-'yent-\ *n, pl* **-tos** : any of various thick-fleshed sweet peppers of mild flavor used esp. as a source of paprika

¹**pimp** \'pimp\ *n* : PROCURER, PANDER

²**pimp** *vi* : to act as a pimp

pim·per·nel \'pim-pər-ˌnel\ *n* : any of a genus of herbs of the primrose family; *esp* : one whose scarlet, white, or purplish flowers close at the approach of rainy or cloudy weather

pim·ple \'pim-pəl\ *n* : a small inflamed swelling of the skin often containing pus : PUSTULE — **pim·pled** \-pəld\ *adj* — **pim·ply** \-p(ə-)lē\ *adj*

¹**pin** \'pin\ *n* **1 a** : a piece of wood or metal used esp. for fastening separate articles together or as a support by which one article may be suspended from another **b** : one of the pieces constituting the target in various games (as bowling) **c** : the staff of the flag marking a hole on a golf course **2 a** : a small pointed piece of wire with a head used esp. for fastening cloth or paper **b** : an ornament or emblem fastened to clothing with a pin **3** : LEG **4** : something of small value : TRIFLE

²**pin** *vt* **pinned**; **pin·ning** **1 a** : to fasten, join, or pierce with a pin **b** : to hold or fix as if with a pin **2 a** : ATTACH, HANG **b** : to assign the blame or responsibility for

pin·a·fore \ˈpin-ə-ˌfōr\ *n* : a low-necked sleeveless apron worn esp. by children
pince–nez \paⁿs-ˈnā, pan(t)s-\ *n, pl* **pince–nez** \-ˈnā(z)\ : eyeglasses clipped to the nose by a spring
pin·cer \ˈpin-chər, ˈpin(t)-sər\ *n* **1** *pl* : an instrument having two short handles and two grasping jaws working on a pivot and used for gripping things **2** : a claw (as of a lobster) resembling pincers — **pin·cer·like** *adj*
[1]pinch \ˈpinch\ *vb* **1 a** : to squeeze between the finger and thumb or between the jaws of an instrument **b** : to squeeze or compress painfully **c** : to cause to appear thin or shrunken **2** : to subject to or practice strict economy **3** : NARROW, TAPER — **pinch·er** *n*
[2]pinch *n* **1 a** : a critical time or point : EMERGENCY **b** : a hurtful pressure or stress : HARDSHIP **2 a** : an act of pinching : SQUEEZE **b** : as much as may be taken between the finger and thumb
pinch hitter *n* **1** : a baseball player sent in to bat for another esp. in an emergency when a hit is much needed **2** : a person called upon to do another's work in an emergency — **pinch–hit** \ˈpinch-ˈhit\ *vi*
pin·cush·ion \ˈpin-ˌku̇sh-ən\ *n* : a small cushion in which pins may be stuck
[1]pine \ˈpīn\ *vi* **1** : to lose vigor, health, or weight through grief, worry, or other distress **2** : to have a continuing fruitless desire : YEARN
[2]pine *n* **1** : any of a genus of coniferous evergreen trees having slender elongated needles and including valuable timber trees as well as many ornamentals **2** : the straight-grained white or yellow usu. durable and resinous wood of a pine — **piny** *or* **pin·ey** \ˈpī-nē\ *adj*
pine·ap·ple \ˈpīn-ˌap-əl\ *n* : a tropical plant bearing an edible juicy fruit; *also* : this fruit
pin·feath·er \ˈpin-ˌfet͟h-ər\ *n* : a new feather just breaking through the skin — **pin·feath·ered** \-ərd\ *adj*
ping \ˈpiŋ\ *n* **1** : a sharp sound like that of a bullet striking **2** : ignition knock — **ping** *vi*
pin·hole \ˈpin-ˌhōl\ *n* : a small hole made by, for, or as if by a pin
[1]pin·ion \ˈpin-yən\ *n* : the terminal section of a bird's wing; *also* : WING — **pin·ioned** \-yənd\ *adj*
[2]pinion *vt* **1** : to disable or restrain by binding the arms **2** : to bind fast : SHACKLE
[3]pinion *n* : a gear with a small number of teeth designed to mesh with a larger wheel or rack
[1]pink \ˈpiŋk\ *vt* **1** : PIERCE, STAB **2 a** : to perforate in an ornamental pattern **b** : to cut a saw-toothed edge on
[2]pink *n* **1** : any of various plants with narrow leaves often grown for their showy flowers **2** : the highest degree
[3]pink *adj* **1** : of the color pink **2** : holding moderately radical and usu. socialistic political or economic views — **pink·ly** *adv* — **pink·ness** *n*
[4]pink *n* **1** : any of a group of colors bluish red to red in hue, of medium to high lightness, and of low to moderate saturation **2 a** : the scarlet color of a fox hunter's coat; *also* : a coat of this color **b** *pl* : light-colored trousers formerly worn by army officers **3** : a person who holds moderately radical political or economic views
pink·eye \ˈpiŋk-ˌī\ *n* : an acute highly contagious eye inflammation
pink·ish \ˈpiŋ-kish\ *adj* : somewhat pink — **pink·ish·ness** *n*
pin·nace \ˈpin-əs\ *n* **1** : a light sailing ship used largely as a tender **2** : any of various ship's boats
pin·na·cle \ˈpin-i-kəl\ *n* **1** : an upright structure (as on a tower) generally ending in a small spire **2** : a lofty peak : a pointed summit **3** : the summit or highest point of achievement or development
pin·nate \ˈpin-ˌāt\ *adj* : resembling a feather esp. in having similar parts arranged on opposite sides of an axis — **pin·nate·ly** *adv* — **pin·na·tion** \pin-ˈā-shən\ *n*
pi·noch·le \ˈpē-ˌnək-əl\ *n* : a card game played with a 48-card pack
[1]pin·point \ˈpin-ˌpȯint\ *vt* **1** : to locate or determine with precision **2** : to cause to stand out conspicuously : HIGHLIGHT
[2]pinpoint *adj* **1** : extremely fine or precise **2** : located, fixed, or directed with extreme precision
pin·prick \ˈpin-ˌprik\ *n* **1** : a small puncture made by or as if by a pin **2** : a petty irritation or annoyance — **pinprick** *vb*
pin·stripe \ˈpin-ˌstrīp\ *n* : a narrow stripe on a fabric; *also* : a suit with such stripes — **pin–striped** \-ˌstrīpt\ *adj*
pint \ˈpīnt\ *n* **1** : any of various units of capacity equal to ½ quart **2** : a pint vessel
[1]pin·to \ˈpin-tō\ *n* : a spotted horse or pony
[2]pinto *adj* : MOTTLED, PIED
pin·up \ˈpin-ˌəp\ *n* **1** : a photograph of a pinup girl **2** : an accessory (as a lamp) attached to a wall
pinup girl *n* : a girl whose glamorous qualities make her a suitable subject for a display photograph
pin·wale \ˈpin-ˌwāl\ *adj* : made with narrow wales
pin·wheel \-ˌhwēl\ *n* **1** : a toy consisting of lightweight vanes that revolve at the end of a stick **2** : a fireworks device in the form of a revolving wheel of colored fire
[1]pi·o·neer \ˌpī-ə-ˈni(ə)r\ *n* **1** : a member of a unit of military engineers **2 a** : a person who goes before opening up new ways (as of thought or activity) **b** : one of the first to settle in an area : COLONIST — **pioneer** *adj*
[2]pioneer *vb* **1** : to act as a pioneer **2** : to open or prepare for others to follow; *esp* : SETTLE **3** : to originate or take part in the development of something new
pi·os·i·ty \pī-ˈäs-ət-ē\ *n, pl* **-ties** : an exaggerated or superficial piousness
pi·ous \ˈpī-əs\ *adj* **1 a** : showing reverence for deity and devotion to divine worship : DEVOUT **b** : marked by conspicuous display of religion **2** : SACRED, RELIGIOUS **3** : showing loyal reverence for a person or thing : DUTIFUL **4 a** : marked by sham or hypocrisy **b** : marked by self-conscious virtue — **pi·ous·ly** *adv* — **pi·ous·ness** *n*
[1]pip \ˈpip\ *n* **1** : a disease of birds **2** : a usu. minor human ailment
[2]pip *n* : a dot or spot (as on dice or playing cards) to indicate numerical value
[3]pip *n* : a small fruit seed
[4]pip *vb* **pipped**; **pip·ping** : [1]PEEP 1
[1]pipe \ˈpīp\ *n* **1 a** : a musical instrument consisting of a tube played by forcing a blast of air through it **b** : BAGPIPE — usu. used in pl. **2** : a long tube or hollow body used esp. to conduct a substance (as water, steam, or gas) **3** : a tube with a small bowl at one end used for smoking tobacco — **pipe·less** \-ləs\ *adj*
[2]pipe *vb* **1** : to play on a pipe **2** : to speak in or have a high shrill tone **3** : to convey by or as if by pipes — **pip·er** *n*
pipe·line \-ˌlīn\ *n* **1** : a line of pipe with pumps, valves, and control devices for conveying liquids, gases, or finely divided solids **2** : a direct channel for information
pip·ing \ˈpī-piŋ\ *n* **1** : the music of or as if of a pipe **2** : a quantity or system of pipes **3** : a narrow decorative fold stitched in seams or along edges (as of clothing)
piping hot *adj* : very hot
pip·kin \ˈpip-kən\ *n* : a small earthenware or metal pot usu. with a horizontal handle
pip·pin \ˈpip-ən\ *n* **1** : any of numerous yellowish apples **2** : a highly admired or very admirable person or thing
pip–squeak \ˈpip-ˌskwēk\ *n* : a small or insignificant person
pi·quant \ˈpē-kənt\ *adj* **1** : agreeably stimulating to the palate : PUNGENT **2** : engagingly provocative; *also* : having a lively arch charm — **pi·quan·cy** \-kən-sē\ *n* — **pi·quant·ly** *adv* — **pi·quant·ness** *n*

[1]**pique** \'pēk\ *n* : offense taken by one slighted or disdained; *also* : a fit of resentment

[2]**pique** *vt* **1** : to arouse anger or resentment in : IRRITATE; *esp* : to offend by slighting **2** : to excite or arouse by a provocation, challenge, or rebuff

[3]**pi·qué** *or* **pi·que** \pi-'kā, 'pē-ˌ\ *n* : a durable ribbed fabric of cotton, rayon, or silk

pi·quet \pi-'kā, pik-'et\ *n* : a two-handed card game played with 32 cards

pi·ra·cy \'pī-rə-sē\ *n, pl* **-cies** **1** : robbery on the high seas **2** : the unauthorized use of another's production or invention esp. in infringement of a copyright

[1]**pi·rate** \'pī-rət\ *n* : a person who commits piracy and esp. robbery on the high seas — **pi·rat·i·cal** \pə-'rat-i-kəl, pī-\ *adj* — **pi·rat·i·cal·ly** \-'rat-i-k(ə-)lē\ *adv*

[2]**pirate** *vt* : to take or appropriate by piracy

pir·ou·ette \ˌpir-ə-'wet\ *n* : a rapid whirling about of the body; *esp* : a full turn on the toe or ball of one foot in ballet — **pirouette** *vi*

pis *pl of* PI

pis·ca·to·ry \'pis-kə-ˌtōr-ē\ *adj* : of, relating to, or dependent on fishermen or fishing — **pis·ca·to·ri·al** \ˌpis-kə-'tōr-ē-əl\ *adj*

pis·mire \'pis-ˌmī(ə)r, 'piz-\ *n* : ANT

pis·tach·io \pə-'stash-(ē-ˌ)ō, -'stäsh-\ *n, pl* **-ios** : a small tree of the sumac family whose fruit contains a greenish edible seed; *also* : its seed

pis·til \'pist-ᵊl\ *n* : the female reproductive organ of a flower

pis·til·late \'pis-tə-ˌlāt\ *adj* : having pistils

pis·tol \'pist-ᵊl\ *n* : a short firearm intended to be aimed and fired with one hand — **pistol** *vt*

pis·tol–whip \'pist-ᵊl-ˌhwip\ *vt* : to beat with a pistol

pis·ton \'pis-tən\ *n* : a sliding piece moved by or moving against fluid pressure that usu. consists of a short cylinder fitting within a cylindrical vessel along which it moves back and forth

[1]**pit** \'pit\ *n* **1** : a hole, shaft, or cavity in the ground **2** : an area set off from and often sunken below adjacent areas **3 a** : a hollowed or indented area esp. in the surface of the body **b** : an indented scar (as from a boil)

[2]**pit** *vb* **pit·ted**; **pit·ting** **1 a** : to put into or store in a pit **b** : to make pits in; *esp* : to scar with pits **2** : to set (as gamecocks) into or as if into a pit to fight; *also* : to set into opposition or rivalry **3** : to become marked with pits

[3]**pit** *n* : the stone of a fruit (as the cherry)

[4]**pit** *vt* **pit·ted**; **pit·ting** : to remove the pit from

pit–a–pat \ˌpit-i-'pat\ *adv (or adj)* : PITTER-PATTER — **pit–a–pat** *n* — **pit–a–pat** *vi*

[1]**pitch** \'pich\ *n* **1** : a dark sticky substance obtained as a residue in the distillation of organic materials (as tars) **2** : resin from various conifers

[2]**pitch** *vb* **1** : to erect and fix firmly in place **2** : THROW, TOSS, FLING; *also* : to deliver a baseball to a batter **3 a** : to cause to be at a particular level **b** : to incline or cause to incline at a particular angle **4 a** : to fall precipitately or headlong **b** : to have the bow alternately plunge precipitately down and rise abruptly up **c** : BUCK 1

[3]**pitch** *n* **1** : the action or a manner of pitching **2** : SLOPE; *also* : degree of slope **3** : a high point : ZENITH **4** : the property of a tone that is determined by the frequency of the sound waves producing it : highness or lowness of sound **5** : a high-pressure sales talk **6 a** : the delivery of a baseball by a pitcher to a batter **b** : a baseball so thrown — **pitched** \'picht\ *adj*

[1]**pitch·er** \'pich-ər\ *n* : a container for holding and pouring liquids that usu. has a lip or spout and a handle

[2]**pitcher** *n* : one that pitches esp. in a baseball game

pitch·fork \'pich-ˌfȯrk\ *n* : a usu. long-handled fork used in pitching hay or grain — **pitchfork** *vt*

pitch in *vi* : to begin to work energetically

pitchy \'pich-ē\ *adj* **1** : full of pitch : TARRY **2** : of, relating to, or having the qualities of pitch

pit·e·ous \'pit-ē-əs\ *adj* : arousing or deserving pity or compassion — **pit·e·ous·ly** *adv* — **pit·e·ous·ness** *n*

pit·fall \'pit-ˌfȯl\ *n* **1** : TRAP, SNARE; *esp* : a pit flimsily covered or camouflaged and used to capture and hold animals or men **2** : a hidden danger or difficulty

pith \'pith\ *n* **1 a** : a central strand of spongy tissue in the stems of most vascular plants that prob. functions chiefly in storage **b** : any of various loose spongy internal tissues or parts **2** : the essential part : CORE — **pith** *adj*

pithy \'pith-ē\ *adj* **1** : consisting of or filled with pith **2** : having substance and point : tersely cogent — **pith·i·ly** \'pith-ə-lē\ *adv* — **pith·i·ness** \'pith-ē-nəs\ *n*

piti·a·ble \'pit-ē-ə-bəl\ *adj* **1** : deserving or exciting pity : LAMENTABLE **2** : pitifully insignificant or scanty — **piti·a·ble·ness** *n* — **piti·a·bly** \-blē\ *adv*

pit·i·ful \'pit-i-fəl\ *adj* **1** : arousing pity or sympathy **2** : deserving pitying contempt : PITIABLE — **pit·i·ful·ly** \-f(ə-)lē\ *adv*

pit·i·less \'pit-i-ləs, 'pit-ᵊl-əs\ *adj* : devoid of pity : MERCILESS — **pit·i·less·ly** *adv* — **pit·i·less·ness** *n*

pit·tance \'pit-ᵊn(t)s\ *n* : a small portion, amount, or allowance

pit·ter–pat·ter \'pit-ər-ˌpat-ər, 'pit-ē-ˌpat-\ *n* : a rapid succession of light sounds or beats — **pit·ter–pat·ter** \ˌpit-ər-', ˌpit-ē-'\ *adv (or adj)* — **pitter–patter** *like adv*\ *vi*

pi·tu·i·tary \pə-'t(y)ü-ə-ˌter-ē\ *adj* : of, relating to, or being a small oval endocrine gland attached to the brain — **pituitary** *n*

pit viper *n* : any of a family of mostly New World venomous snakes with a sensory pit on each side of the head and hollow perforated fangs

[1]**pity** \'pit-ē\ *n* **1 a** : sympathetic sorrow for one suffering, distressed, or unhappy : COMPASSION **b** : capacity to feel pity **2** : something to be regretted

[2]**pity** *vb* **pit·ied**; **pit·y·ing** : to feel pity or pity for

[1]**piv·ot** \'piv-ət\ *n* **1** : a shaft or pin on which something turns **2** : something upon which something else turns or depends : a central member, part, or point

[2]**pivot** *vb* **1** : to turn on or as if on a pivot **2** : to provide with, mount on, or attach by a pivot **3** : to cause to pivot

piv·ot·al \'piv-ət-ᵊl\ *adj* **1** : of, relating to, or functioning as a pivot **2** : vitally important : CRUCIAL — **piv·ot·al·ly** \-ᵊl-ē\ *adv*

pix·ie *or* **pixy** \'pik-sē\ *n, pl* **pix·ies** : a mischievous sprite or fairy — **pix·ie·ish** \-sē-ish\ *adj*

plac·a·ble \'plak-ə-bəl, 'plā-kə-\ *adj* : easily placated : TOLERANT, TRACTABLE — **plac·a·bil·i·ty** \ˌplak-ə-'bil-ət-ē, ˌplā-kə-\ *n* — **plac·a·bly** \'plak-ə-blē, 'plā-kə-\ *adv*

[1]**plac·ard** \'plak-ˌärd, -ərd\ *n* : a notice posted or carried in a public place : POSTER

[2]**placard** *vt* **1** : to post placards on or in **2** : to announce by or as if by posting

pla·cate \'plā-ˌkāt, 'plak-ˌāt\ *vt* : to calm the anger of esp. by concessions : SOOTHE, APPEASE — **pla·ca·tion** \plā-'kā-shən, pla-\ *n* — **pla·ca·tive** \'plā-ˌkāt-iv, 'plak-ˌāt-\ *adj* — **pla·ca·to·ry** \'plā-kə-ˌtōr-ē, 'plak-ə-\ *adj*

[1]**place** \'plās\ *n* **1 a** : physical extension : SPACE **b** : a particular but often unspecified location in space : LOCALITY; *also* : an inhabited area (as a city or village) **2 a** : a building in which people live : a dwelling or residence often together with its grounds : HOMESTEAD **b** : a building or part of a building or sometimes an outside area designed for or devoted to a particular purpose **3** : an identifiable or differentiated part of something : SPOT **4** : position in some ordering: as **a** : relative position in a scale or sequence : DEGREE **b** : a leading position at the conclusion of a competition **5** : suitable or assigned location or situation: as **a** : accommodation occu-

pied by or available for occupancy of one person **b** : space or situation customarily or formerly occupied **c** : a situation of employment : JOB; *also* : official position — **place·less** \'plās-ləs\ *adj*

²**place** *vb* **1** : to distribute in an orderly manner : ARRANGE **2 a** : to put in or direct to a particular place **b** : to present for consideration **c** : to put in a particular state **3** : to appoint to a position; *esp* : to find employment or a home for **4 a** : to assign to or hold a position in a series : RANK **b** : ESTIMATE **c** : to identify by association **5** : to give an order for **6** : to come in second in a horse race — **place·a·ble** \'plā-sə-bəl\ *adj*

pla·ce·bo \plə-'sē-bō\ *n, pl* **-bos** : an inert medication used for psychological reasons or as a control

place·ment \'plās-mənt\ *n* : an act or instance of placing; *esp* : the assignment of a person to a suitable place (as a class in school or a job)

pla·cen·ta \plə-'sent-ə\ *n* : the vascular organ in most mammals by which the fetus is joined to the maternal uterus and nourished — **pla·cen·tal** \-'sent-ᵊl\ *adj or n* — **plac·en·ta·tion** \ˌplas-ᵊn-'tā-shən\ *n*

plac·er \'plas-ər\ *n* : an alluvial or glacial deposit containing particles of valuable mineral (as gold) — **placer miner** *n* — **placer mining** *n*

plac·id \'plas-əd\ *adj* **1** : UNDISTURBED, PEACEFUL **2** : COMPLACENT — **pla·cid·i·ty** \pla-'sid-ət-ē, plə-\ *n* — **plac·id·ly** \'plas-əd-lē\ *adv* — **plac·id·ness** *n*

plack·et \'plak-ət\ *n* : a slit or opening in a garment (as a skirt) often forming the closure

pla·gia·rism \'plā-jə-ˌriz-əm\ *n* **1** : an act of plagiarizing **2** : something plagiarized — **pla·gia·rist** \-rəst\ *n*

pla·gia·rize \'plā-jə-ˌrīz\ *vb* : to steal and pass off as one's own the work of another — **pla·gia·riz·er** *n*

¹**plague** \'plāg\ *n* **1** : a disastrous evil or destructively numerous influx; *also* : a cause or occasion of annoyance **2** : an epidemic disease causing a high rate of mortality : PESTILENCE; *esp* : a virulent contagious bacterial disease occurring in several forms (as bubonic plague)

²**plague** *vt* **1** : to strike or afflict with or as if with disease, calamity, or natural evil **2** : TEASE, TORMENT — **plagu·er** *n*

plaid \'plad\ *n* **1** : a rectangular length of tartan worn over the left shoulder by men and women as part of the Scottish national costume **2 a** : TARTAN 2 **b** : a fabric with a pattern of tartan or imitative of tartan **3 a** : TARTAN 1 **b** : a pattern of unevenly spaced repeated stripes crossing at right angles — **plaid** *adj* — **plaid·ed** \-əd\ *adj*

¹**plain** \'plān\ *n* : an extensive area of level or rolling treeless country; *also* : a broad unbroken expanse

²**plain** *adj* **1 a** : lacking ornament : UNDECORATED **b** : having no pattern **2** : free of added or extraneous matter : PURE **3** : free of impediments to view : UNOBSTRUCTED **4 a** : clear to the mind or senses **b** : marked by candor : BLUNT **5 a** : of common or average attainments or status : neither notable nor lowly : ORDINARY **b** : free from complexity : SIMPLE; *also* : containing or using only simple wholesome ingredients **c** : lacking beauty or ugliness : HOMELY — **plain·ly** *adv* — **plain·ness** \'plān-nəs\ *n*

³**plain** *adv* : in a plain manner

plain·clothes·man \'plān-'klō(th)z-mən, -ˌman\ *n* : a police officer who does not wear a uniform while on duty : DETECTIVE

plains·man \'plānz-mən\ *n* : an inhabitant of plains

plain·spo·ken \'plān-'spō-kən\ *adj* : speaking or spoken plainly and esp. bluntly

plaint \'plānt\ *n* **1** : LAMENTATION, WAIL **2** : PROTEST, COMPLAINT

plain·tiff \'plānt-əf\ *n* : the complaining party in a lawsuit : one who begins a lawsuit to enforce his claims

plain·tive \'plānt-iv\ *adj* : expressive of suffering or woe : MELANCHOLY — **plain·tive·ly** *adv* — **plain·tive·ness** *n*

¹**plait** \'plāt, 'plat\ *n* **1** : PLEAT **2** : a usu. flat braid (as of hair or straw)

²**plait** *vt* **1** : PLEAT 1 **2 a** : to interweave the strands or locks of : BRAID **b** : to make by plaiting — **plait·er** *n*

¹**plan** \'plan\ *n* **1** : a drawing or diagram showing the parts or outline of something **2** : a method or scheme of acting, doing, or arranging **3** : INTENT, AIM

²**plan** *vb* **planned**; **plan·ning** **1** : to form a plan of or for : arrange the parts or details of in advance **2** : to have in mind : INTEND; *also* : to make plans — **plan·ner** *n*

¹**plane** \'plān\ *vt* : to make smooth or even esp. with a plane; *also* : to remove by planing — **plan·er** *n*

²**plane** *n* : any of a genus of trees with large palmately lobed leaves and flowers in globose heads

³**plane** *n* : a tool for smoothing or shaping a wood surface

⁴**plane** *n* **1 a** : a surface such that any two included points can be joined by a straight line lying wholly within the surface **b** : a flat or level material surface **2** : a level of existence, consciousness, or development **3 a** : one of the main supporting surfaces of an airplane **b** : AIRPLANE

⁵**plane** *adj* **1** : lacking elevations or depressions : FLAT, LEVEL **2** : of, relating to, or dealing with planes

plan·et \'plan-ət\ *n* : a heavenly body except a comet or meteor that revolves about the sun; *also* : such a body revolving about the sun of another solar system

plan·e·tar·i·um \ˌplan-ə-'ter-ē-əm\ *n, pl* **-i·ums** *or* **-ia** \-ē-ə\ **1** : a model or representation of the solar system **2 a** : an optical device to project various celestial images and effects **b** : a building or room housing such a device

plan·e·tary \'plan-ə-ˌter-ē\ *adj* **1 a** : of or relating to a planet **b** : having a motion like that of a planet **2** : GLOBAL, WORLDWIDE

¹**plank** \'plaŋk\ *n* **1** : a heavy thick board **2** : an article in the platform of a political party

²**plank** *vt* **1** : to cover or floor with planks **2** : to set down forcefully **3** : to cook and serve on a board

plank·ing *n* : a quantity or covering of planks

plank·ton \'plaŋ(k)-tən, -ˌtän\ *n* : the passively floating or weakly swimming animal and plant life of a body of water — **plank·ton·ic** \plaŋ(k)-'tän-ik\ *adj*

¹**plant** \'plant\ *vb* **1 a** : to put or set in the ground to grow **b** : IMPLANT **2 a** : to cause to become established **b** : to stock or provide with something usu. to grow or increase **3 a** : to place or fix in the ground **b** : to place firmly or forcibly **4** : to hide, place secretly, or prearrange with intent to mislead **5** : to plant something — **plant·a·ble** \-ə-bəl\ *adj*

²**plant** *n* **1** : any of a kingdom of living beings typically lacking locomotive movement or obvious nervous or sensory organs and possessing cellulose cell walls and capacity for indefinite growth **2 a** : the land, buildings, and equipment esp. of an industrial business **b** : a factory or workshop for the manufacture of a product **3** : an act of planting **4** : something or someone planted — **plant·like** *adj*

¹**plan·tain** \'plant-ᵊn\ *n* : any of several common short-stemmed weedy herbs with spikes of tiny greenish flowers

²**plantain** *n* : a banana plant with large greenish starchy fruit that is eaten cooked and is a staple food in the tropics; *also* : this fruit

plan·ta·tion \plan-'tā-shən\ *n* **1** : a usu. large group of plants and esp. trees under cultivation **2** : a settlement in a new country or region : COLONY **3** : a planted area; *esp* : an agricultural estate worked by resident labor

plant·er \'plant-ər\ *n* **1** : one that plants or cultivates; *esp* : an owner or operator of a plantation **2** : one who settles or founds a colony **3** : a container in which ornamental plants are grown

plaque \'plak\ *n* **1** : an ornamental brooch; *esp* : the badge of an honorary order **2 :** a flat thin piece (as of metal) used for decoration; *also* **:** a commemorative or identifying inscribed tablet

plash \'plash\ *n* **:** SPLASH — **plash** *vb*

plas·ma \'plaz-mə\ *n* **1 a :** the fluid part of blood, lymph, or milk as distinguished from suspended material **b :** PROTOPLASM **2 :** a gas in a highly ionized condition — **plas·mat·ic** \plaz-'mat-ik\ *adj*

[1]**plas·ter** \'plas-tər\ *n* **1 :** a medicated or protective dressing consisting of a film (as of cloth or plastic) spread with an often medicated substance that clings to the skin **2 :** a pasty composition (as of lime, water, and sand) that hardens on drying and is used for coating walls and ceilings — **plas·tery** \-t(ə-)rē\ *adj*

[2]**plaster** *vb* **plas·tered; plas·ter·ing** \-t(ə-)riŋ\ **1 :** to apply or to overlay or cover with plaster **2 :** to apply a plaster to **3 :** to cover over or conceal as if with a coat of plaster **4 :** to fasten with or as if with paste **:** stick tightly **5 :** to affix to or place upon esp. conspicuously or in quantity — **plas·ter·er** \-tər-ər\ *n*

plaster of par·is \-'par-əs\ *often cap 2d P* **:** a white powder made from gypsum and used chiefly for casts and molds in the form of a quick-setting paste with water

[1]**plas·tic** \'plas-tik\ *adj* **1 :** FORMATIVE, CREATIVE **2 a :** capable of being molded or modeled **b :** capable of usu. adaptive change **3 :** characterized by or using modeling **4 :** SCULPTURAL **5 :** made or consisting of a plastic — **plas·ti·cal·ly** \-ti-k(ə-)lē\ *adv* — **plas·tic·i·ty** \plas-'tis-ət-ē\ *n*

[2]**plastic** *n* **:** a plastic substance; *esp* **:** any of numerous organic synthetic or processed materials that can be formed into objects, films, or filaments

plastic surgery *n* **:** surgery concerned with the repair or restoration of lost, injured, or deformed parts of the body — **plastic surgeon** *n*

[1]**plat** \'plat\ *n* **1 :** a small piece of ground **:** PLOT **2 :** a plan or map of a piece of land (as a town) with lots and landmarks marked out

[2]**plat** *vt* **plat·ted; plat·ting :** to make a plat of

[1]**plate** \'plāt\ *n* **1 :** a flat, thin, and usu. smooth piece of material: as **a :** metal in sheets usu. thicker than 1/4 inch **b :** a thin layer of one metal deposited on another usu. by electrical means **c :** a rubber slab at the apex of a baseball diamond that must be touched by a base runner in order to score **2 :** precious metal; *esp* **:** silver bullion **3 a :** domestic hollow ware usu. of or plated with precious metal (as silver) **b :** a shallow usu. circular dish **4 a :** a flat piece or surface on which something (as letters or a design) is or is to be embossed or incised **b :** the molded metal or plastic cast of a page of type to be printed from **c :** a sheet of material (as glass) coated with a light-sensitive photographic emulsion **5 :** the part of a denture that bears the teeth and fits to the mouth **6 :** a full-page illustration often on special paper — **plate·like** *adj*

[2]**plate** *vt* **1 :** to cover or equip with plate: as **a :** to arm with armor plate **b :** to cover with an adherent layer (as of metal) **c :** to deposit (as a layer of metal) on a surface **2 :** to make a printing surface from or for

pla·teau \pla-'tō, 'pla-,\ *n, pl* **plateaus** *or* **pla·teaux** \-'tōz, -,tōz\ **1 :** a usu. large relatively level land area raised above adjacent land on at least one side **2 :** a relatively stable level, period, or condition

plate·ful \'plāt-,fu̇l\ *n, pl* **platefuls** \-,fu̇lz\ **:** a quantity to fill a plate

plat·en \'plat-ᵊn\ *n* **1 :** a flat plate of metal that exerts or receives pressure; *esp* **:** one in some printing presses that presses the paper against the type **2 :** the roller of a typewriter

plat·form \'plat-,fȯrm\ *n* **1 :** a declaration of principles; *esp* **:** a declaration of principles and policies adopted by a political party or a candidate **2 :** a horizontal flat surface usu. higher than the adjoining area; *esp* **:** a raised flooring (as for speakers or performers)

plat·ing *n* **1 :** the act or process of covering esp. with metal plate **2 :** a coating of metal plates or plate

plat·i·num \'plat-nəm, -ᵊn-əm\ *n* **:** a heavy precious grayish white ductile malleable metallic element that is used esp. in chemical ware and apparatus, as a catalyst, and in jewelry

plat·i·tude \'plat-ə-,t(y)üd\ *n* **1 :** the quality or state of being dull or insipid **:** TRITENESS **2 :** a flat, trite, or weak remark — **plat·i·tu·di·nous** \,plat-ə-'t(y)üd-nəs, -ᵊn-əs\ *adj*

pla·ton·ic \plə-'tän-ik, plā-\ *adj* **:** of or relating to love freed from sexual desire — **pla·ton·i·cal·ly** \-'tän-i-k(ə-)lē\ *adv*

Pla·to·nism \'plāt-ᵊn-,iz-əm\ *n* **:** the philosophy of Plato stressing esp. that actual things and ideas (as of truth or beauty) are only copies of transcendent ideas which are the objects of true knowledge — **Pla·to·nist** \-ᵊn-əst\ *n*

pla·toon \plə-'tün\ *n* **:** a subdivision of a military company normally consisting of a headquarters and two or more squads

platoon sergeant *n* **:** SERGEANT FIRST CLASS

plat·ter \'plat-ər\ *n* **:** a large plate used esp. for serving meat

plat·y·pus \'plat-i-pəs, -,pu̇s\ *n* **:** a small aquatic egg-laying mammal of southern and eastern Australia and Tasmania with a fleshy bill resembling that of a duck, webbed feet, and a broad flattened tail

plau·dit \'plȯd-ət\ *n* **1 :** an act or round of applause **2 :** enthusiastic approval

plau·si·bil·i·ty \,plȯ-zə-'bil-ət-ē\ *n, pl* **-ties 1 :** the quality or state of being plausible **2 :** something plausible

plau·si·ble \'plȯ-zə-bəl\ *adj* **1 :** apparently reasonable or worthy of belief **2 :** seemingly trustworthy **:** inspiring confidence **:** PERSUASIVE — **plau·si·bly** \'plȯ-zə-blē\ *adv*

[1]**play** \'plā\ *n* **1 a :** a brisk handling or using (as of a weapon) **b :** the conduct, course, or action of or a particular act or maneuver in a game **c :** recreational activity; *esp* **:** the spontaneous activity of children **d :** JEST; *also* **:** a playing on words **e :** GAMBLING, GAMING **2 a :** a way or manner of acting or proceeding **b :** OPERATION, ACTIVITY **c :** brisk, fitful, or light movement **d :** free or unimpeded motion (as of a part of a machine); *also* **:** freedom for such motion **e :** scope or opportunity for action **3 a :** the stage representation of an action or story **b :** a dramatic composition **:** DRAMA — **in play :** in condition or position to be legitimately played

[2]**play** *vb* **1 a :** to move swiftly, aimlessly, or lightly; *also* **:** to move freely **b :** to treat or behave frivolously or lightly or without due consideration or respect sometimes with an ulterior motive **c :** to make use of double meaning or of the similarity of sound of two words usu. for humorous effect **d :** to take advantage **e :** to finger or trifle with something **f :** to discharge in a stream **2 a :** to engage in sport or recreation and esp. in spontaneous activity for amusement **b :** to imitate in playing **c :** to take part or engage in (as a game) **d :** to contend against in a game **e :** to bet on **:** WAGER **3 a :** to perform on a musical instrument **b :** to produce music **4 :** to be performed **5 a :** ACT, BEHAVE; *esp* **:** to conduct oneself in a particular way **b :** to perform on or as if on the stage; *also* **:** to act the part of **c :** to put or keep in action **d :** to do for amusement or from mischief; *also* **:** to bring about **:** WREAK — **play·a·ble** \-ə-bəl\ *adj* — **play·er** \'plā-ər\ *n* — **play ball :** COOPERATE

play·act·ing \'plā-,ak-tiŋ\ *n* **1 :** performance in theatrical productions **2 :** insincere or artificial behavior

play·back \'plā-,bak\ *n* **:** an act of reproducing a sound recording often immediately after recording

play·bill \-,bil\ *n* **:** a poster advertising the performance of a play and usu. the cast of players; *also* **:** a theater program

play·boy \-,bȯi\ *n* **:** a man whose chief interest is the pursuit of pleasure

played out *adj* **1 :** worn out or used up **2 :** tired out **:** SPENT

play·fel·low \'plā-ˌfel-ō\ *n* : PLAYMATE
play·ful \-fəl\ *adj* 1 : full of play : SPORTIVE 2 : HUMOROUS, JOCULAR — **play·ful·ly** \-fə-lē\ *adv* — **play·ful·ness** *n*
play·go·er \-ˌgō(-ə)r\ *n* : a person who frequently attends plays
play·ground \-ˌgraund\ *n* : a piece of ground used for games and recreation esp. by children
play·house \-ˌhau̇s\ *n* 1 : THEATER 2 : a small house for children to play in
playing card *n* : one of a set of cards marked to show its rank and suit and used in playing various games
play·let \'plā-lət\ *n* : a short play
play·mate \-ˌmāt\ *n* : a companion in play
play–off \'plā-ˌȯf\ *n* : a contest or series of contests to break a tie or determine a championship
play out *vb* 1 : to perform to the end 2 : to use up or become used up : FINISH, EXHAUST 3 : UNREEL, UNFOLD
play·pen \'plā-ˌpen\ *n* : a portable enclosure in which a baby or young child may play
play·thing \-ˌthiŋ\ *n* : TOY
play·wright \'plā-ˌrīt\ *n* : a person who writes plays
plaza \'plaz-ə, 'pläz-\ *n* : a public square in a city or town
plea \'plē\ *n* 1 : a defendant's answer to a plantiff's declaration or to a criminal charge 2 : something offered as an excuse 3 : an earnest entreaty : APPEAL
plead \'plēd\ *vb* **plead·ed** \'plēd-əd\ *or* **pled** \'pled\; **plead·ing** 1 : to argue a case in a court of law 2 : to answer to a charge or indictment 3 **a** : to argue for or against a claim **b** : to entreat or appeal earnestly : IMPLORE 4 : to offer in defense, apology, or excuse — **plead·a·ble** \'plēd-ə-bəl\ *adj* — **plead·er** *n*
pleas·ance \'plez-ᵊn(t)s\ *n* : a pleasing place (as a charming vista); *esp* : a private formal garden attached to a mansion
pleas·ant \'plez-ᵊnt\ *adj* 1 : giving pleasure : AGREEABLE 2 : having or characterized by pleasing manners, behavior, or appearance — **pleas·ant·ly** *adv* — **pleas·ant·ness** *n*
pleas·ant·ry \-ᵊn-trē\ *n, pl* **-ries** 1 : agreeable playfulness esp. in conversation 2 **a** : a humorous act or speech : JEST **b** : a light or casual polite remark
please \'plēz\ *vb* 1 : to afford or give pleasure or satisfaction : GRATIFY 2 : to feel the desire or inclination : LIKE 3 : to be willing to — usu. used in the imperative to express a polite command or request
pleas·ing \'plē-ziŋ\ *adj* : giving pleasure : AGREEABLE — **pleas·ing·ly** \-ziŋ-lē\ *adv* — **pleas·ing·ness** *n*
plea·sur·a·ble \'plezh-(ə-)rə-bəl\ *adj* : GRATIFYING, PLEASANT — **plea·sur·a·bil·i·ty** \ˌplezh-(ə-)rə-'bil-ət-ē\ *n* — **plea·sur·a·ble·ness** \'plezh-(ə-)rə-bəl-nəs\ *n* — **plea·sur·a·bly** \-blē\ *adv*
plea·sure \'plezh-ər, 'plāzh-\ *n* 1 : DESIRE, INCLINATION 2 : a state of gratification : ENJOYMENT 3 : a source of delight or joy
¹pleat \'plēt\ *vt* 1 : FOLD; *esp* : to arrange in pleats 2 : PLAIT 2 —**pleat·ed** *adj* — **pleat·er** *n*
²pleat *n* : a fold (as in cloth) made by doubling material over on itself
pleb \'pleb\ *n* : PLEBEIAN
plebe \'plēb\ *n* : a freshman at a military or naval academy
ple·be·ian \pli-'bē-(y)ən\ *n* 1 : a member of the Roman plebs 2 : one of the common people — **ple·be·ian·ism** \-(y)ə-ˌniz-əm\ *n*
plebeian *adj* 1 : of or relating to plebeians 2 : crude or coarse in manner or style : COMMON — **ple·be·ian·ly** *adv*
pleb·i·scite \'pleb-ə-ˌsīt, -sət\ *n* : a popular vote by which the people of an entire country or a district indicate their wishes on a measure officially submitted to them
plec·trum \'plek-trəm\ *n, pl* **plec·tra** \-trə\ *or* **plectrums** : a small thin piece (as of ivory or metal) used to pluck a stringed instrument
¹pledge \'plej\ *n* 1 **a** : something given as security for the performance of an act **b** : a token, sign, or earnest of something else 2 **a** : TOAST 3 **b** : a binding promise or agreement 3 **a** : a person pledged to join an organization (as a fraternity) **b** : a gift pledged (as to a charity)
²pledge *vt* 1 : to make a pledge of; *esp* : to deposit in pledge or pawn 2 : to drink the health of : TOAST 3 : to bind by a pledge 4 : to promise by a pledge — **pledg·ee** \ple-'jē\ *n* — **pledg·er** \'plej-ər\ *n* — **pledg·or** \'plej-ər, ple-'jȯ(ə)r\ *n*
ple·na·ry \'plē-nə-rē, 'plen-ə-\ *adj* 1 : COMPLETE, FULL 2 : including all entitled to attend
plen·i·po·ten·tia·ry \ˌplen-ə-pə-'tench-(ə-)rē, -'ten-chē-ˌer-ē\ *n, pl* **-ries** : a person and esp. a diplomatic agent invested with full power to transact any business — **plenipotentiary** *adj*
plen·i·tude \'plen-ə-ˌt(y)üd\ *or* **plent·i·tude** \'plen(t)-ə-\ *n* : the quality or state of being full; *also* : ABUNDANCE
plen·te·ous \'plent-ē-əs\ *adj* 1 : ABUNDANT, PLENTIFUL 2 : yielding abundantly : FRUITFUL — **plen·te·ous·ly** *adv*
plen·ti·ful \'plent-i-fəl\ *adj* 1 : containing or yielding plenty : FRUITFUL 2 : characterized by, constituting, or existing in plenty : NUMEROUS, ABUNDANT — **plen·ti·ful·ly** \-fə-lē\ *adv* — **plen·ti·ful·ness** *n*
¹plen·ty \'plent-ē\ *n* 1 : a full or abundant supply : a sufficient number or amount 2 : PLENTIFULNESS, ABUNDANCE
²plenty *adj* : PLENTIFUL, ABUNDANT, AMPLE
³plenty *adv* : ABUNDANTLY, QUITE
plen·um \'plen-əm, 'plēn-əm\ *n, pl* **plenums** *or* **ple·na** \-ə\ : a general assembly of all members of a public body
pleth·o·ra \'pleth-ə-rə\ *n* 1 : a bodily condition characterized by an excess of blood 2 : SUPERFLUITY, EXCESS — **ple·thor·ic** \plə-'thȯr-ik\ *adj*
pleu·ri·sy \'plu̇r-ə-sē\ *n* : inflammation of the membrane that lines the chest usu. with fever, painful breathing, and coughing — **pleu·rit·ic** \plü-'rit-ik\ *adj*
plex·us \'plek-səs\ *n, pl* **plex·us·es** *or* **plex·us** \-səs, -ˌsüs\ : an interlacing network esp. of blood vessels or nerves
pli·a·ble \'plī-ə-bəl\ *adj* 1 : capable of being bent or folded without damage : FLEXIBLE 2 : easily influenced — **pli·a·bil·i·ty** \ˌplī-ə-'bil-ət-ē\ *n* — **pli·a·bly** \'plī-ə-blē\ *adv*
pli·an·cy \'plī-ən-sē\ *n* : the quality or state of being pliant
pli·ant \'plī-ənt\ *adj* 1 : readily yielding without breaking : FLEXIBLE 2 : easily influenced : PLIABLE, YIELDING 3 : ADAPTABLE — **pli·ant·ly** *adv*
pli·ers \'plī(-ə)rz\ *n pl* : a small pincers with long jaws for holding small objects or for bending and cutting wire
¹plight \'plīt\ *vt* : to put or give in pledge : ENGAGE — **plight·er** *n*
²plight *n* : CONDITION, STATE; *esp* : bad state or condition
plinth \'plin(t)th\ *n* 1 : the lowest part of the base of an architectural column 2 : a block used as a base (as for a statue or vase)
plod \'pläd\ *vi* **plod·ded**; **plod·ding** 1 : to walk heavily or slowly : TRUDGE 2 : to work or study laboriously : DRUDGE — **plod** *n* — **plod·der** *n* — **plod·ding·ly** \-iŋ-lē\ *adv*
plop \'pläp\ *vb* **plopped**; **plop·ping** 1 : to make or move with a sound like that of something dropping into water 2 : to allow the body to drop heavily 3 : to set, drop, or throw heavily — **plop** *n*
¹plot \'plät\ *n* 1 : a small area of ground : LOT 2 : GROUND PLAN 3 : the plan or main story of a literary work 4 : a secret plan for accomplishing a usu. evil or unlawful end : INTRIGUE 5 : a graphic representation : CHART, DIAGRAM
²plot *vb* **plot·ted**; **plot·ting** 1 **a** : to make a plot, map, or plan of **b** : to mark or note on or as if on a map or chart 2 : to plan or contrive esp. secretly : CONSPIRE, SCHEME — **plot·ter** *n*
plov·er \'pləv-ər, 'plō-vər\ *n, pl* **plover** *or* **plovers** : any of numerous shorebirds differing from the related sandpipers in having shorter and stouter bills

[1]**plow** *or* **plough** \'plau̇\ *n* **1 :** an implement used to cut, lift, and turn over soil **2 :** any of various devices (as for spreading or opening something) that operate like a plow; *esp* **:** SNOWPLOW

[2]**plow** *or* **plough** *vb* **1 :** to open, break up, or work with a plow **2 a :** to cleave the surface of or move through like a plow cutting the soil **b :** to proceed steadily and laboriously **:** PLOD — **plow·a·ble** \-ə-bəl\ *adj* — **plow·er** \'plau̇(-ə)r\ *n*

plow·boy \'plau̇-ˌbȯi\ *n* **:** a boy who guides a plow or leads the horse drawing it

plow·man \-mən\ *n* **1 :** a man who guides a plow **2 :** a farm laborer

plow·share \-ˌshe(ə)r\ *n* **:** the part of a plow that cuts the earth

[1]**pluck** \'plək\ *vt* **1 a :** to pull or pick off or out **b :** to remove something and esp. hair or feathers from by or as if by plucking **2 :** ROB, FLEECE **3 :** to move or separate forcibly **:** TUG, SNATCH **4 :** to pick, pull, or grasp at; *also* **:** to play (an instrument) in this manner — **pluck·er** *n*

[2]**pluck** *n* **1 :** an act or instance of plucking **:** a sharp pull **:** TUG **2 :** SPIRIT, COURAGE, RESOLUTION

plucky \'plək-ē\ *adj* **:** COURAGEOUS, RESOLUTE — **pluck·i·ly** \'plək-ə-lē\ *adv* — **pluck·i·ness** \'plək-ē-nəs\ *n*

[1]**plug** \'pləg\ *n* **1 a :** a piece (as of wood or metal) used to stop or fill a hole **:** STOPPER **b :** an obtruding or obstructing mass of material (as in rock or tissue) felt to resemble a stopper **2 :** a poor or worn-out horse **3 :** a device for making an electrical connection by insertion into an interrupted circuit **4 :** a piece of favorable publicity usu. placed in general material

[2]**plug** *vb* **plugged**; **plug·ging 1 :** to stop, make tight, or secure with or as if with a plug **2 :** to hit with a bullet **:** SHOOT **3 :** to advertise or publicize insistently **4 :** to become plugged — usu. used with *up* — **plug·ger** *n*

plug hat *n* **:** a man's stiff hat (as a bowler or top hat)

plum \'pləm\ *n* **1 a :** any of numerous trees and shrubs related to the peach and cherries and having globular to oval smooth-skinned fruits with oblong seeds **b :** the edible fruit of a plum **2 a :** RAISIN **b :** SUGARPLUM **3 :** something excellent or superior; *esp* **:** something given as recompense for service — **plum·like** *adj*

plum·age \'plü-mij\ *n* **:** the feathers of a bird

[1]**plumb** \'pləm\ *n* **:** a weight often of lead used on a line esp. to determine a vertical direction or distance — **out of plumb** *or* **off plumb :** out of vertical or true

[2]**plumb** *adv* **1 :** straight down or up **:** VERTICALLY **2 :** DIRECTLY, EXACTLY

[3]**plumb** *vb* **1 :** to sound, adjust, or test with a plumb **2 :** to examine and determine hidden aspects of **:** FATHOM

[4]**plumb** *adj* **1 :** exactly vertical or true **2 :** DOWNRIGHT, COMPLETE

plumb·er \'pləm-ər\ *n* **:** one that fits or repairs water and gas pipes and fixtures

plumb·ing \'pləm-iŋ\ *n* **1 :** a plumber's occupation or trade **2 :** the apparatus (as pipes and fixtures) concerned in the distribution and use of water in a building

[1]**plume** \'plüm\ *n* **:** a feather of a bird; *esp* **:** a large conspicuous or showy feather — **plumy** \'plü-mē\ *adj*

[2]**plume** *vt* **1 :** to provide or deck with plumes **2 :** to pride (oneself) on something **3 :** to dress the feathers of **:** PREEN

[1]**plum·met** \'pləm-ət\ *n* **:** PLUMB; *also* **:** a line with a plumb at one end

[2]**plummet** *vi* **:** to fall perpendicularly or sharply and abruptly

[1]**plump** \'pləmp\ *vb* **1 :** to drop, sink, or come in contact suddenly or heavily **2 :** to favor someone or something strongly — used with *for*

[2]**plump** *adv* **1 :** with a sudden or heavy drop **2 :** STRAIGHT, DIRECTLY

[3]**plump** *n* **:** a sudden plunge, fall, or blow; *also* **:** the sound accompanying such an act

[4]**plump** *adj* **:** having a full rounded usu. pleasing form — **plump·ness** *n*

[5]**plump** *vb* **:** to make or become plump

plum pudding *n* **:** a boiled or steamed pudding containing fruits (as raisins) and usu. rich in fat

[1]**plun·der** \'plən-dər\ *vb* **plun·dered**; **plun·der·ing** \-d(ə-)riŋ\ **:** to rob esp. openly and by force (as in an invasion or raid) **:** PILLAGE — **plun·der·er** \-dər-ər\ *n*

[2]**plunder** *n* **1 :** an act of plundering **:** PILLAGING **2 :** something taken by force or theft **:** LOOT

[1]**plunge** \'plənj\ *vb* **1 :** to cause to penetrate or enter something quickly and forcibly **2 :** to thrust or cast oneself into or as if into water **:** DIVE **3 a :** to throw oneself or move suddenly and sharply forward and downward **b :** to move rapidly or suddenly downward **4 a :** to rush or act with reckless haste; *also* **:** to bring to a usu. unpleasant state or course of action suddenly or unexpectedly **b :** to speculate or gamble recklessly

[2]**plunge** *n* **:** an act or instance of plunging **:** a sudden dive, leap, or rush

plung·er \'plən-jər\ *n* **1 :** a person (as a diver or a reckless gambler) that plunges **2 a :** a device (as a piston in a pump) that acts with a plunging motion **b :** a rubber suction cup on a handle used to free plumbing traps and waste outlets of obstructions

plunk \'pləŋk\ *vb* **1 :** to make or cause to make a hollow metallic sound **2 :** to drop heavily or suddenly

plu·per·fect \plü-'pər-fikt\ *adj* **:** of, relating to, or constituting a verb tense that denotes an action or state as completed at or before a past time spoken of — **pluperfect** *n*

plu·ral \'plu̇r-əl\ *adj* **1 :** of, relating to, or constituting a word form used to denote more than one **2 :** relating to, consisting of, or containing more than one — **plural** *n* — **plu·ral·ly** \-ə-lē\ *adv*

plu·ral·i·ty \plu̇-'ral-ət-ē\ *n, pl* **-ties 1 :** the state of being plural or numerous **2 :** the greater number or part **3 a :** the fact of being chosen by the voters out of three or more candidates or measures when no one of them obtains more than half the total vote **b :** the excess of the number of votes received by one candidate over another

plu·ral·ize \'plu̇r-ə-ˌlīz\ *vt* **:** to make plural or express in the plural form — **plu·ral·i·za·tion** \ˌplu̇r-ə-lə-'zā-shən\ *n*

[1]**plus** \'pləs\ *prep* **1 :** increased by **2 :** WITH

[2]**plus** *n* **1 :** an added quantity **2 :** a positive factor or quality **:** ADVANTAGE **3 :** SURPLUS

[3]**plus** *adj* **1 :** requiring addition **2 :** having, receiving, or being in addition **3 a :** falling high in a specified range **b :** greater than that specified

[1]**plush** \'pləsh\ *n* **:** a fabric with an even pile longer and less dense than velvet pile — **plushy** \-ē\ *adj*

[2]**plush** *adj* **1 :** relating to, resembling, or made of plush **2 :** notably luxurious or satisfactory

plu·toc·ra·cy \plü-'täk-rə-sē\ *n, pl* **-cies 1 :** government by the wealthy **2 :** a controlling class of rich men — **plu·to·crat** \'plüt-ə-ˌkrat\ *n* — **plu·to·crat·ic** \ˌplüt-ə-'krat-ik\ *adj* — **plu·to·crat·i·cal·ly** \-'krat-i-k(ə-)lē\ *adv*

plu·to·ni·um \plü-'tō-nē-əm\ *n* **:** a radioactive metallic chemical element that is formed by decay of neptunium and found in minute quantities in pitchblende and that is fissionable to yield atomic energy

plu·vi·al \'plü-vē-əl\ *adj* **1 :** of or relating to rain **2 :** characterized by or resulting from the action of abundant rain

[1]**ply** \'plī\ *n, pl* **plies :** one of the folds, thicknesses, layers, or strands of which something (as yarn or plywood) is made up

[2]**ply** *vb* **plied**; **ply·ing 1 a :** to use or wield diligently **b :** to practice or perform diligently **2 :** to keep supplying to; *also* **:** to press or harass with something **3 :** to go or travel regularly

ply·wood \ˈplī-ˌwu̇d\ *n* : a structural material consisting of thin sheets of wood glued or cemented together

pneu·mat·ic \n(y)u̇-ˈmat-ik\ *adj* **1** : of, relating to, or using air, wind, or other gas **2** : moved or worked by air pressure **3** : adapted for holding or inflated with compressed air — **pneu·mat·i·cal·ly** \-ˈmat-i-k(ə-)lē\ *adv*

pneu·mo·nia \n(y)u̇-ˈmō-nyə\ *n* : an inflammatory disease of the lungs

[1]poach \ˈpōch\ *vt* : to cook in simmering liquid

[2]poach *vb* : to hunt or fish unlawfully usu. on private property — **poach·er** *n*

pock \ˈpäk\ *n* : a small swelling on the skin similar to a pimple (as in chicken pox or small pox); *also* : the scar it leaves — **pock** *vt* — **pocky** \-ē\ *adj*

[1]pock·et \ˈpäk-ət\ *n* **1 a** : a small bag carried by a person : PURSE **b** : a small bag open at the top or side inserted in a garment **2** : supply of money : MEANS **3** : RECEPTACLE, CONTAINER **4 a** : a small isolated area or group **b** : a small body of ore

[2]pocket *vt* **1 a** : to put or enclose in or as if in one's pocket **b** : to appropriate to one's own use esp. dishonestly **2** : to put up with : ACCEPT

[3]pocket *adj* : small enough to be carried in the pocket

pocket billiards *n* : POOL 2

pock·et·book \ˈpäk-ət-ˌbu̇k\ *n* **1 a** (1) : a pocket-size container for money and personal papers : WALLET (2) : PURSE **b** : HANDBAG 2 **2 a** : financial resources : INCOME **b** : economic interests

pock·et·ful \ˈpäk-ət-ˌfu̇l\ *n, pl* **pocketfuls** \-ˌfu̇lz\ *or* **pock·ets·ful** \-əts-ˌfu̇l\ : as much or as many as the pocket will contain

pock·et·knife \ˈpäk-ət-ˌnīf\ *n* : a knife with a folding blade to be carried in the pocket

pock·mark \ˈpäk-ˌmärk\ *n* : the depressed scar left by a pock esp. of smallpox — **pockmark** *vt*

pod \ˈpäd\ *n* **1** : a dry dehiscent fruit; *esp* : LEGUME **2** : an anatomical pouch **3** : a streamlined compartment under the wings or fuselage of an airplane used as a container (as for fuel or a jet engine)

podgy \ˈpäj-ē\ *adj* : PUDGY

po·di·a·try \pə-ˈdī-ə-trē\ *n* : CHIROPODY — **po·di·a·trist** \-trəst\ *n*

po·di·um \ˈpōd-ē-əm\ *n, pl* **-di·ums** *or* **-dia** \-ē-ə\ **1** : a dais esp. for an orchestral conductor **2** : LECTERN

po·em \ˈpō-əm, -ˌem\ *n* **1** : a composition in verse **2** : a piece of poetry communicating to the reader the sense of a complete experience **3** : a creation, experience, or object likened to a poem

po·e·sy \ˈpō-ə-zē, -sē\ *n, pl* **-sies** **1 a** : a body of poems : POEM **b** : POETRY **2** : poetic inspiration

po·et \ˈpō-ət\ *n* **1** : one who writes poetry **2** : a creative artist of great imaginative and expressive gifts and special sensitivity to his medium

po·et·as·ter \ˈpō-ət-ˌas-tər\ *n* : an inferior poet : VERSIFIER

po·et·ess \ˈpō-ət-əs\ *n* : a female poet

po·et·ic \pō-ˈet-ik\ *adj* **1 a** : of, relating to, or characteristic of poets or poetry **b** : given to writing poetry **2** : written in verse

po·et·i·cal \pō-ˈet-i-kəl\ *adj* **1** : POETIC **2** : beyond or above the truth of history or nature : IDEALIZED — **po·et·i·cal·ly** \-k(ə-)lē\ *adv* — **po·et·i·cal·ness** \-kəl-nəs\ *n*

po·et·ics \pō-ˈet-iks\ *n* **1 a** : a treatise on poetry or aesthetics **b** : poetic theory or practice **2** : poetic feelings or utterances

po·et·ry \ˈpō-ə-trē\ *n* **1 a** : VERSE **b** : the productions of a poet : POEMS **2** : writing in language chosen and arranged to create a specific emotional response through meaning, sound, and rhythm **3 a** : a quality that stirs the imagination **b** : a quality of spontaneity and grace

po·grom \pō-ˈgräm, ˈpō-grəm\ *n* : an organized massacre of helpless people and esp. of Jews

poi \ˈpȯi\ *n, pl* **poi** *or* **pois** : a Hawaiian food made of cooked taro root pounded to a paste and often fermented

poi·gnant \ˈpȯi-nyənt\ *adj* **1** : PUNGENT **2 a** (1) : painfully affecting the feelings : PIERCING (2) : deeply affecting : TOUCHING **b** : CUTTING, INCISIVE **3 a** : pleasurably stimulating **b** : being to the point : APT — **poi·gnan·cy** \-nyən-sē\ *n* — **poi·gnant·ly** *adv*

poin·set·tia \pȯin-ˈset-ē-ə, -ˈset-ə\ *n* : a showy Mexican and So. American spurge with tapering scarlet bracts that grow like petals about its small yellow flowers

[1]point \ˈpȯint\ *n* **1 a** (1) : an individual detail : ITEM (2) : a distinguishing detail : CHARACTERISTIC **b** : the most important essential in a discussion or matter **c** : EFFECTIVENESS, COGENCY, FORCE **2** : an end or object to be achieved : PURPOSE **3 a** : a narrowly localized place having a precisely indicated position **b** : a particular place : LOCALITY **c** (1) : an exact moment (2) : a time interval immediately before something indicated : VERGE **d** (1) : a particular step, stage, or degree in development (2) : a definite position in a scale **4** : the terminal usu. sharp or narrowly rounded part of something (as a fin, sword, or pencil) : TIP **5 a** : a projecting usu. tapering piece of land or a sharp prominence **b** *pl* : terminal bodily projections esp. when differing from the rest of the body in color **6** : a short musical phrase; *esp* : a phrase in contrapuntal music **7 a** : a very small mark **b** (1) : PUNCTUATION MARK; *esp* : PERIOD (2) : a decimal mark **8 a** : one of the 32 pointed marks indicating direction on a mariner's compass **b** : the difference of 11¼ degrees between two such adjacent points **9 a** : NEEDLEPOINT 1 **b** : lace made with a bobbin **10** : one of 12 spaces marked off on each side of a backgammon board **11 a** : a unit of counting (as in the scoring of a game or contest) **b** : a unit of academic credit — **in point** : RELEVANT, PERTINENT — **to the point** : RELEVANT, PERTINENT, APT

[2]point *vb* **1 a** : to furnish with a point **b** : to give added force, emphasis, or piquancy to **2 a** : PUNCTUATE **b** : to separate (a decimal fraction) from an integer by a decimal point **3 a** : to direct someone's attention to **b** : to indicate the position or direction of something (as by the finger or by the nose of a dog) **4** : to turn, face, or cause to be turned in a particular direction : AIM **5** : to indicate the fact or probability of something specified

point–blank \ˈpȯint-ˈblaŋk\ *adj* **1** : so close to a target that a missile fired will travel in a straight line to the mark **2** : DIRECT, BLUNT — **point–blank** *adv*

point·ed \ˈpȯint-əd\ *adj* **1 a** : having a point **b** : having a crown tapering to a point **2 a** : PERTINENT, TERSE **b** : aimed at a particular person or group **3** : CONSPICUOUS, MARKED — **point·ed·ly** *adv* — **point·ed·ness** *n*

point·er \ˈpȯint-ər\ *n* **1** : one that furnishes with points **2** : one that points out; *esp* : a rod used to direct attention **3** : a large strong slender smooth-haired hunting dog that hunts by scent and indicates the presence of game by pointing **4** : a useful suggestion or hint : TIP

poin·til·lism \ˈpwa^n(n)-tē-ˌiz-əm\ *n* : the practice or technique of applying dots of color to a surface so that from a distance they blend together — **poin·til·list** \-tē-əst\ *n* — **poin·til·lis·tic** \ˌpwa^n(n)-tē-ˈis-tik\ *adj*

point·less \ˈpȯint-ləs\ *adj* **1** : without a point **2** : devoid of meaning : SENSELESS **3** : devoid of effectiveness : FLAT — **point·less·ly** *adv* — **point·less·ness** *n*

point of no return **1** : the point in the flight of an aircraft beyond which the remaining fuel will be insufficient for a return to the starting point and the craft must proceed **2** : a critical point at which turning back or reversal is not possible

[1]poise \ˈpȯiz\ *vb* **1 a** : BALANCE; *esp* : to hold or carry in equilibrium **b** : to hold or be supported or suspended without motion in a steady position **2 :** to hold or carry (the head) in a particular way **3 :** to put into readiness : BRACE **4 :** HOVER

²poise *n* **1 :** BALANCE, EQUILIBRIUM **2 a** (1) **:** self-possessed composure, assurance, and dignity (2) **:** TRANQUILLITY, CALM, SERENITY **b :** a particular way of carrying oneself : BEARING, CARRIAGE

¹poi·son \'pȯiz-ᵊn\ *n* **1 :** a substance that through its chemical action is able to kill, injure, or impair an organism **2 a :** something destructive or harmful **b :** an object of aversion or abhorrence

²poison *vb* **poi·soned; poi·son·ing** \'pȯiz-niŋ, -ᵊn-iŋ\ **1 a :** to injure or kill with poison **b :** to treat, taint, or impregnate with poison **2 :** to exert a baneful influence on : CORRUPT — **poi·son·er** \'pȯiz-nər, -ᵊn-ər\ *n*

³poison *adj* **1 :** POISONOUS, VENOMOUS **2 :** POISONED

poison ivy *n* **:** a usu. climbing plant of the sumac family that has shiny 3-parted leaves and may irritate the skin of one who touches it

poi·son·ous \'pȯiz-nəs, -ᵊn-əs\ *adj* **:** having the properties or effects of poison : VENOMOUS — **poi·son·ous·ly** *adv*

¹poke \'pōk\ *vb* **1 a** (1) **:** PROD, JAB, THRUST (2) **:** to urge or stir by prodding or jabbing **b** (1) **:** PIERCE, STAB (2) **:** to produce by piercing, stabbing, or jabbing **c** (1) **:** HIT, PUNCH (2) **:** to deliver (a blow) with the fist **2 a :** to cause to project **b :** to thrust forward obtrusively or suddenly **3 a :** to look about or through something without system : RUMMAGE **b :** MEDDLE **4 :** to move or act slowly or aimlessly : DAWDLE — **poke fun at :** RIDICULE, MOCK

²poke *n* **1 :** a quick thrust : JAB **2 :** a blow with the fist : PUNCH

¹pok·er \'pō-kər\ *n* **:** one that pokes; *esp* **:** a metal rod for stirring a fire

²po·ker \'pō-kər\ *n* **:** any of several card games in which a player bets on the value of his hand to win a pool

poker hands, in descending value: *1* royal flush, *2* straight flush, *3* four of a kind, *4* full house, *5* flush, *6* straight, *7* three of a kind, *8* two pairs, *9* one pair

poky *or* **pok·ey** \'pō-kē\ *adj* **1 :** being small and cramped **2 :** SHABBY, DULL **3 :** annoyingly slow — **pok·i·ness** \-kē-nəs\ *n*

po·lar \'pō-lər\ *adj* **1 :** of or relating to a geographical pole or the region around it; *also* **:** coming from or having the characteristics of such a region **2 :** of or relating to one or more poles (as of a magnet) **3 :** serving as a guide

po·lar·i·ty \pō-'lar-ət-ē, pə-\ *n, pl* **-ties 1 :** the quality or condition of having poles **2 :** the particular state either positive or negative with reference to magnetic or electrical poles

po·lar·i·za·tion \ˌpō-lə-rə-'zā-shən\ *n* **1 :** the action of polarizing or state of being polarized **2 :** concentration about opposing extremes

po·lar·ize \'pō-lə-ˌrīz\ *vb* **1 :** to cause to undergo polarization **2 :** to give polarity to **3 :** to become polarized — **po·lar·iz·a·ble** \-ˌrī-zə-bəl\ *adj* — **po·lar·iz·er** *n*

¹pole \'pōl\ *n* **:** a long slender usu. cylindrical piece of material (as wood or metal)

²pole *vb* **1 :** to act upon, impel, or push with a pole **2 a :** to propel a boat with a pole **b :** to use ski poles to gain speed — **pol·er** *n*

³pole *n* **1 :** either end of an axis of a sphere and esp. of the earth's axis **2 a :** either of two related opposites **b :** a point of guidance or attraction **3 a :** one of the two terminals of an electric cell, battery, or dynamo **b :** one of two or more regions in a magnetized body at which the magnetism seems to be concentrated

pole·ax \'pōl-ˌaks\ *n* **:** a battle-ax with short handle and cutting edge or point opposite the blade

pole·cat \'pōl-ˌkat\ *n, pl* **polecats** *or* **polecat 1 :** a European carnivorous mammal of which the ferret is considered a domesticated variety **2 :** SKUNK

po·lem·ic \pə-'lem-ik\ *n* **1 a :** an aggressive attack on or refutation of the opinions or principles of another **b :** the art or practice of disputation or controversy — usu. used in pl. **2 :** an aggressive controversialist : DISPUTANT **3** *pl* **:** the branch of Christian theology devoted to the refutation of errors — **polemic** *or* **po·lem·i·cal** \-'lem-i-kəl\ *adj* — **po·lem·i·cal·ly** \-i-k(ə-)lē\ *adv* — **po·lem·i·cist** \-'lem-ə-səst\ *n*

pole·star \'pōl-ˌstär\ *n* **1 :** a directing principle : GUIDE **2 :** a center of attraction

pole vault *n* **:** a track-and-field event in which each contestant uses a pole to vault for height over a crossbar — **pole–vault** \'pōl-ˌvȯlt\ *vi* — **pole–vault·er** *n*

¹po·lice \pə-'lēs\ *n, pl* **police 1 :** the department of government concerned primarily with maintenance of public order and safety, enforcement of laws, and prevention, detection, and prosecution of public nuisances and crimes **2** *pl* **:** POLICEMEN **3 a :** the action or process of cleaning and putting in order **b :** military personnel detailed to perform this function

²police *vt* **1 :** to control, regulate, or keep in order by use of or as of police **2 :** to make clean and put in order : clean up **3 :** to supervise the operation, execution, or administration of

po·lice·man \pə-'lēs-mən\ *n* **:** a member of a police force — **po·lice·wom·an** \-ˌwu̇m-ən\ *n*

¹pol·i·cy \'päl-ə-sē\ *n, pl* **-cies 1 :** prudence or wisdom in the management of affairs : SAGACITY **2 :** a course of action selected in light of given conditions to guide and determine decisions

²policy *n, pl* **-cies :** a writing embodying a contract of insurance

pol·i·cy·hold·er \-ˌhōl-dər\ *n* **:** one granted an insurance policy

po·lio \'pō-lē-ˌō\ *n* **:** POLIOMYELITIS — **polio** *adj*

po·lio·my·e·li·tis \ˌpō-lē-ˌō-ˌmī-ə-'līt-əs\ *n* **:** an acute infectious virus disease marked by inflammation of nerve cells in the spinal cord accompanied by fever and often paralysis and atrophy of muscles — **po·lio·my·e·lit·ic** \-'lit-ik\ *adj*

¹pol·ish \'päl-ish\ *vb* **1 :** to make smooth and glossy usu. by rubbing **2 :** to smooth or refine in manners or condition **3 :** to bring to a highly developed, finished, or refined state : PERFECT — **pol·ish·er** *n*

²polish *n* **1 a :** a smooth glossy surface : LUSTER **b :** REFINEMENT, CULTURE **c :** a state of high development or refinement **2 :** the action or process of polishing **3 :** a preparation used in polishing

polish off *vt* **:** to dispose of rapidly or completely

po·lite \pə-'līt\ *adj* **1 :** of, relating to, or having the characteristics of advanced culture **2 a :** showing or characterized by correct social usage **b :** marked by consideration, tact, deference, or courtesy : COURTEOUS — **po·lite·ly** *adv* — **po·lite·ness** *n*

pol·i·tic \'päl-ə-ˌtik\ *adj* **1 :** characterized by shrewdness **2 :** sagacious in promoting a policy **3 :** shrewdly tactful

po·lit·i·cal \pə-'lit-i-kəl\ *adj* **:** of or relating to government or politics — **po·lit·i·cal·ly** \-k(ə-)lē\ *adv*

pol·i·ti·cian \ˌpäl-ə-'tish-ən\ *n* **:** a person actively engaged in government or politics

pol·i·tics \'päl-ə-ˌtiks\ *n sing or pl* **1 :** the art or science of government, of guiding or influencing governmental policy, or of winning and holding control over a government **2 :** political affairs or business; *esp* : competition between groups or individuals for power and leadership **3** : political opinions

pol·i·ty \'päl-ət-ē\ *n, pl* **-ties 1** : a form of political organization **2** : a politically organized unit

pol·ka \'pōl-kə\ *n* : a vivacious couple dance of Bohemian origin; *also* : music for this dance — **polka** *vi*

pol·ka dot \'pō-kə-ˌdät\ *n* : a dot in a pattern of regularly distributed dots in textile design

[1]**poll** \'pōl\ *n* **1** : HEAD **2 a** : the casting or recording of the votes of a body of persons **b** : the place where votes are cast or recorded — usu. used in pl. **3 a** : a questioning or canvassing of persons to obtain information or opinions to be analyzed **b** : the information so obtained

[2]**poll** *vb* **1** : to cut off or cut short a growth or part of : CROP, SHEAR **2** : to receive and record the votes of **3** : to receive (as votes) in an election **4** : to question or canvass in a poll **5** : to cast one's vote at a poll — **poll·ee** \pō-'lē\ *n* — **poll·er** \'pō-lər\ *n*

pol·lack *or* **pol·lock** \'päl-ək\ *n, pl* **pollack** *or* **pollacks** *or* **pollock** *or* **pollocks** : a commercially important north Atlantic food fish resembling the related cods

pol·len \'päl-ən\ *n* : a mass of male spores of a seed plant appearing usu. as a fine dust — **pollen** *adj* — **pol·lin·ic** \pä-'lin-ik\ *adj*

pol·li·nate \'päl-ə-ˌnāt\ *vt* : to place pollen on the stigma of — **pol·li·na·tion** \ˌpäl-ə-'nā-shən\ *n*

pol·li·na·tor \'päl-ə-ˌnāt-ər\ *n* : an agent that pollinates flowers

pol·li·wog *or* **pol·ly·wog** \'päl-ē-ˌwäg\ *n* : TADPOLE

poll·ster \'pōl-stər\ *n* : one that conducts a poll or compiles data obtained by a poll

pol·lute \pə-'lüt\ *vt* : to make impure : CONTAMINATE — **pol·lu·tion** \pə-'lü-shən\ *n*

po·lo \'pō-lō\ *n* : a game played by teams of players on horseback using mallets with long flexible handles to drive a wooden ball — **po·lo·ist** \'pō-lə-wəst\ *n*

po·lo·ni·um \pə-'lō-nē-əm\ *n* : a radioactive metallic chemical element that emits a helium nucleus to form an isotope of lead

[1]**pol·troon** \päl-'trün\ *n* : a spiritless coward : CRAVEN

[2]**poltroon** *adj* : characterized by complete cowardice

pol·troon·ery \-'trün-(ə-)rē\ *n* : COWARDICE

poly·cen·trism \ˌpäl-i-'sen-ˌtriz-əm\ *n* : the doctrine of a plurality of centers of Communist thought and leadership

poly·clin·ic \ˌpäl-i-'klin-ik\ *n* : a clinic or hospital treating diseases of many sorts

po·lyg·a·mous \pə-'lig-ə-məs\ *adj* **1** : of, relating to, or being a marriage form in which a spouse of either sex has more than one mate at one time **2** : having more than one spouse or mate at one time — **po·lyg·a·mist** \-məst\ *n* — **po·lyg·a·mous·ly** *adv* — **po·lyg·a·my** \-mē\ *n*

pol·y·glot \'päl-i-ˌglät\ *adj* **1** : speaking or writing several languages **2** : containing matter in or composed of elements from several languages — **polyglot** *n*

pol·y·gon \'päl-i-ˌgän\ *n* : a closed plane figure bounded by straight lines — **po·lyg·o·nal** \pə-'lig-ən-ᵊl\ *adj*

pol·y·mer \'päl-ə-mər\ *n* : a substance formed by union of small molecules of the same kind — **pol·y·mer·ic** \ˌpäl-ə-'mer-ik\ *adj*

pol·y·no·mi·al \ˌpäl-i-'nō-mē-əl\ *n* : an algebraic expression having two or more terms

pol·yp \'päl-əp\ *n* **1** : an animal (as a coral) having a hollow cylindrical body closed and attached at one end **2** : a projecting mass of overgrown membrane — **pol·yp·oid** \'päl-ə-ˌpȯid\ *adj*

pol·y·phon·ic \ˌpäl-i-'fän-ik\ *adj* : of, relating to, or marked by polyphony — **pol·y·phon·i·cal·ly** \-'fän-i-k(ə-)lē\ *adv*

po·lyph·o·ny \pə-'lif-ə-nē\ *n* : music consisting of two or more melodically independent but harmonizing voice parts

poly·syl·lab·ic \ˌpäl-i-sə-'lab-ik\ *adj* : having many syllables; *esp* : having more than three syllables — **poly·syl·lab·i·cal·ly** \-'lab-i-k(ə-)lē\ *adv* — **poly·syl·la·ble** \'päl-i-ˌsil-ə-bəl, ˌpäl-i-'\ *n*

pol·y·tech·nic \ˌpäl-i-'tek-nik\ *adj* : relating to or devoted to instruction in many technical arts or applied sciences

poly·the·ism \'päl-i-(ˌ)thē-ˌiz-əm\ *n* : belief in or worship of more than one god — **poly·the·ist** \-ˌthē-əst\ *adj or n* — **poly·the·is·tic** \ˌpäl-i-thē-'is-tik\ *adj*

po·made \pō-'mād, -'mäd\ *n* : a perfumed unguent esp. for the hair or scalp — **pomade** *vt*

po·man·der \'pō-ˌman-dər, pō-'\ *n* : a mixture of aromatic substances enclosed in a perforated bag or box and formerly carried as a guard against infection

pome·gran·ate \'päm-(ə-)ˌgran-ət, 'pəm-ˌgran-\ *n* : a thick-skinned reddish berry about the size of an orange having many seeds in a crimson pulp of acid flavor; *also* : a tropical Old World tree bearing pomegranates

[1]**pom·mel** \'pəm-əl, 'päm-\ *n* **1** : the knob on the hilt of a sword or saber **2** : the protuberance at the front and top of a saddlebow

[2]**pom·mel** \'pəm-əl\ *vt* **-meled** *or* **-melled; -mel·ing** *or* **-mel·ling** \'pəm-(ə-)liŋ\ : PUMMEL

pomp \'pämp\ *n* **1** : a show of magnificence : SPLENDOR **2** : an ostentatious act or display

pom·pa·dour \'päm-pə-ˌdōr\ *n* : a style of dressing the hair high over the forehead; *also* : hair dressed in this style

pom·pa·no \'päm-pə-ˌnō, 'pəm-\ *n, pl* **-nos** : a food fish of the southern Atlantic and Gulf coasts

pom·pon \'päm-ˌpän\ *n* **1** : an ornamental ball or tuft used on clothing, caps, and fancy costumes **2** : a chrysanthemum or dahlia with small rounded flower heads

pom·pos·i·ty \päm-'päs-ət-ē\ *n, pl* **-ties 1** : POMPOUSNESS **2** : a pompous gesture, habit, or action

pomp·ous \'päm-pəs\ *adj* **1** : making an appearance of importance or dignity **2** : SELF-IMPORTANT **3** : excessively elevated or ornate — **pomp·ous·ly** *adv* — **pomp·ous·ness** *n*

pon·cho \'pän-chō\ *n, pl* **ponchos 1** : a cloak resembling a blanket with a slit in the middle for the head **2** : a waterproof garment resembling a poncho worn chiefly as a raincoat

pond \'pänd\ *n* : a small body of water

pon·der \'pän-dər\ *vb* **pon·dered; pon·der·ing** \'pän-d(ə-)riŋ\ : to consider carefully — **pon·der·er** \-dər-ər\ *n*

pon·der·a·ble \'pän-d(ə-)rə-bəl\ *adj* : capable of being weighed or appraised : APPRECIABLE

pon·der·ous \'pän-d(ə-)rəs\ *adj* **1** : very heavy **2** : heavy because of weight and size **3** : not light or lively : DULL — **pon·der·ous·ly** *adv* — **pon·der·ous·ness** *n*

pon·gee \pän-'jē, 'pän-ˌ\ *n* : a thin soft tan fabric

pon·iard \'pän-yərd\ *n* : a slender dagger

pon·tiff \'pänt-əf\ *n* : BISHOP; *esp* : POPE

[1]**pon·tif·i·cal** \pän-'tif-i-kəl\ *adj* : of or relating to a pontiff — **pon·tif·i·cal·ly** \-k(ə-)lē\ *adv*

[2]**pontifical** *n* : episcopal attire; *esp* : the insignia of the episcopal order worn by a prelate when celebrating a pontifical service — usu. used in pl.

[1]**pon·tif·i·cate** \pän-'tif-i-kət, -'tif-ə-ˌkāt\ *n* : the office or term of office of a pontiff

[2]**pon·tif·i·cate** \-'tif-ə-ˌkāt\ *vi* : to speak pompously or dogmatically — **pon·tif·i·ca·tor** \-ˌkāt-ər\ *n*

pon·toon \pän-'tün\ *n* **1** : a flat-bottomed boat; *esp* : a flat-bottomed boat or portable float used in building a floating temporary bridge **2** : a float of an airplane

po·ny \'pō-nē\ *n, pl* **ponies 1** : a small horse; *esp* : one of any of several breeds of very small stocky animals **2** : a small glass for an alcoholic drink or the amount it will hold **3** : a literal translation of a foreign language text; *esp* : one used illegitimately by students in preparing or reciting lessons

po·ny·tail \ˈpō-nē-ˌtāl\ *n* : a style of arranging hair to resemble the tail of a pony; *also* : hair arranged in this style
poo·dle \ˈpüd-ᵊl\ *n* : any of an old breed of active intelligent heavy-coated solid-colored dogs
pooh \ˈpü, ˈpu̇\ *interj* — used to express contempt, disapproval, or impatience
pooh–pooh \ˈpü-pü, pü-ˈpü\ *vb* **1** : to express contempt or impatience **2** : DERIDE, SCORN
¹pool \ˈpül\ *n* **1** : a small and rather deep natural or artificial body of usu. fresh water **2** : a small body of standing liquid : PUDDLE
²pool *n* **1** : all the money bet on the result of an event **2** : a game of billiards played on a pool table having 6 pockets **3 a** : a common fund for buying or selling **b** : a combination between competing firms for mutual profit **4** : a readily available supply
³pool *vt* : to contribute to a common fund or effort
poop \ˈpüp\ *n* : an enclosed superstructure at the stern of a ship above the main deck
poop deck *n* : a partial deck above a ship's main afterdeck
¹poor \ˈpu̇(ə)r\ *adj* **1** : lacking riches : NEEDY **2** : SCANTY, INSUFFICIENT **3** : not good in quality or workmanship **4** : FEEBLE **5** : lacking fertility **6** : UNFAVORABLE, UNCOMFORTABLE **7** : lacking in signs of wealth or good taste **8** : not efficient or capable : not satisfactory **9** : worthy of pity or sympathy — **poor·ness** *n*
²poor *n pl* : the class of poor people
poor·house \-ˌhau̇s\ *n* : a place maintained at public expense to house needy or dependent persons
poor·ly \-lē\ *adj* : somewhat ill : INDISPOSED
poor–spir·it·ed \-ˈspir-ət-əd\ *adj* : lacking zest, confidence, or courage — **poor–spir·it·ed·ly** *adv* — **poor–spir·it·ed·ness** *n*
¹pop \ˈpäp\ *vb* **popped**; **pop·ping** **1** : to burst or cause to burst with a pop **2** : to go, come, push, or enter quickly or unexpectedly **3** : to shoot with a gun **4** : to stick out **5** : to cause to burst open **6** : to hit a pop fly — **pop the question** : to propose marriage
²pop *n* **1** : a sharp explosive sound **2** : a shot from a gun **3** : a flavored carbonated beverage
³pop *adv* : like or with a pop : SUDDENLY
pop·corn \ˈpäp-ˌkȯrn\ *n* : an Indian corn whose kernels burst open to form a white starchy mass when heated
pope \ˈpōp\ *n, often cap* : the head of the Roman Catholic Church
pop·ery \ˈpō-p(ə-)rē\ *n* : ROMAN CATHOLICISM — usu. used disparagingly
pop fly *n* : a short high fly in baseball
pop·gun \ˈpäp-ˌgən\ *n* : a toy gun for shooting pellets with compressed air
pop·in·jay \ˈpäp-ən-ˌjā\ *n* : a vain talkative thoughtless person
pop·lar \ˈpäp-lər\ *n* : any of a genus of slender quick-growing trees (as an aspen or cottonwood) of the willow family
pop·lin \ˈpäp-lən\ *n* : a strong fabric in plain weave with crosswise ribs
pop off \(ˈ)päp-ˈȯf\ *vi* **1 a** : to leave suddenly **b** : to die unexpectedly **2** : to talk thoughtlessly and often loudly or angrily
pop·over \ˈpäp-ˌō-vər\ *n* : a quick bread made from a thin batter of eggs, milk, and flour which bakes into a hollow shell
pop·per \ˈpäp-ər\ *n* : one that pops; *esp* : a utensil for popping corn
pop·py \ˈpäp-ē\ *n, pl* **poppies** : any of a genus of chiefly annual or perennial herbs with milky juice, showy regular flowers, and capsular fruits including one that is the source of opium and several that are grown as ornamentals
pop·py·cock \ˈpäp-ē-ˌkäk\ *n* : empty talk : NONSENSE
pop·u·lace \ˈpäp-yə-ləs\ *n* **1** : the common people : MASSES **2** : POPULATION
pop·u·lar \ˈpäp-yə-lər\ *adj* **1** : of, relating to, or coming from the whole body of people **2** : suitable to the majority: as **a** : easy to understand **b** : suited to the means of the majority : INEXPENSIVE **3** : having general currency : PREVALENT **4** : commonly liked or approved — **pop·u·lar·ly** *adv*
pop·u·lar·i·ty \ˌpäp-yə-ˈlar-ət-ē\ *n* : the quality or state of being popular
pop·u·lar·i·za·tion \ˌpäp-yə-lə-rə-ˈzā-shən\ *n* **1** : the act of popularizing : the state of being popularized **2** : something that is popularized
pop·u·lar·ize \ˈpäp-yə-lə-ˌrīz\ *vt* : to make popular — **pop·u·lar·iz·er** *n*
pop·u·late \ˈpäp-yə-ˌlāt\ *vt* : to furnish or provide with inhabitants : PEOPLE
pop·u·la·tion \ˌpäp-yə-ˈlā-shən\ *n* **1** : the whole number of people or inhabitants in a country or region **2** : the act or process of populating **3** : a group of items from which samples are taken for statistical measurement
pop·u·lous \ˈpäp-yə-ləs\ *adj* : densely populated — **pop·u·lous·ly** *adv* — **pop·u·lous·ness** *n*
por·ce·lain \ˈpōr-s(ə-)lən\ *n* : a fine ceramic ware that is hard, translucent, white, and nonporous, usu. consists essentially of kaolin, quartz, and feldspar, and is used for dishes, dentures, and chemical utensils — **por·ce·lain·like** *adj*
porch \ˈpōrch\ *n* **1** : a covered entrance to a building usu. with a separate roof **2** : VERANDA 2
por·cine \ˈpȯr-ˌsīn\ *adj* : of, relating to, or suggesting swine
por·cu·pine \ˈpȯr-kyə-ˌpīn\ *n* : any of various rather large rodents with stiff sharp easily detachable bristles mingled with the hair
¹pore \ˈpō(ə)r\ *vi* : to gaze, study, or think long or earnestly
²pore *n* : a tiny opening or space (as in the skin or the soil) often giving passage to a fluid — **pored** \ˈpōrd\ *adj*
pork \ˈpōrk\ *n* : the fresh or salted flesh of swine dressed for food
pork·er \ˈpōr-kər\ *n* : HOG; *esp* : a young pig suitable for use as fresh pork
por·nog·ra·phy \pȯr-ˈnäg-rə-fē\ *n* : pictures or writings describing erotic behavior and intended to cause sexual excitement — **por·nog·ra·pher** \-fər\ *n* — **por·no·graph·ic** \ˌpȯr-nə-ˈgraf-ik\ *adj* — **por·no·graph·i·cal·ly** \-ˈgraf-i-k(ə-)lē\ *adv*
po·ros·i·ty \pə-ˈräs-ət-ē, pōr-ˈäs-\ *n, pl* **-ties** **1** : the quality or state of being porous **2** : PORE
po·rous \ˈpōr-əs\ *adj* **1** : full of pores **2** : capable of absorbing liquids : permeable to fluids
por·phy·ry \ˈpȯr-f(ə-)rē\ *n, pl* **-ries** : a dark red or purple rock with white crystals embedded in it — **por·phy·rit·ic** \ˌpȯr-fə-ˈrit-ik\ *adj*
por·poise \ˈpȯr-pəs\ *n* **1** : any of several small gregarious blunt-snouted whales **2** : any of several dolphins
por·ridge \ˈpȯr-ij\ *n* : a soft food made by boiling meal of grains or legumes in milk or water until thick
por·rin·ger \ˈpȯr-ən-jər\ *n* : a low one-handled metal bowl or cup for children
¹port \ˈpōrt\ *n* **1** : a place where ships may ride secure from storms **2 a** : a harbor town or city where ships may take on or discharge cargo **b** : AIRPORT
²port *n* **1** : an opening (as in machinery) for intake or exhaust of a fluid **2** : PORTHOLE
³port *n* : the manner in which one bears himself
⁴port *n* : the left side of a ship or airplane looking forward — **port** *adj*
⁵port *vt* : to turn or put (a helm or rudder) to the left
⁶port *n* : a fortified sweet wine of rich taste and aroma
por·ta·ble \ˈpōrt-ə-bəl\ *adj* : capable of being carried : easily moved from one place to another — **por·ta·bil·i·ty** \ˌpōrt-ə-ˈbil-ət-ē\ *n*
¹por·tage \ˈpōrt-ij, *2 is also* pȯr-ˈtäzh\ *n* **1** : the labor of carrying

or transporting **2 :** the carrying of boats or goods overland from one body of water to another; *also* **:** a regular route for such carrying

²portage *vb* **1 :** to carry over a portage **2 :** to move gear over a portage

por·tal \'pōrt-ᵊl\ *n* **:** DOOR, GATE, ENTRANCE; *esp* **:** a grand or imposing one

port·cul·lis \pōrt-'kəl-əs\ *n* **:** a grating at the gateway of a castle or fortress that can be lowered to prevent entrance

porte co·chere \ˌpōrt-kō-'she(ə)r\ *n* **:** a roofed structure extending from the entrance of a building over an adjacent driveway and sheltering those getting in or out of vehicles

porte–mon·naie \'pōrt-ˌmən-ē\ *n* **:** a small pocketbook or purse

por·tend \pȯr-'tend\ *vt* **:** to give a sign or warning of beforehand

por·tent \'pȯ(ə)r-ˌtent\ *n* **1 :** a sign or warning that foreshadows something usu. evil **2 :** prophetic indication or significance

por·ten·tous \pȯr-'tent-əs\ *adj* **1 :** of, relating to, or constituting a portent **:** THREATENING **2 :** eliciting amazement or wonder **:** PRODIGIOUS **3 :** self-consciously weighty **:** POMPOUS — **por·ten·tous·ly** *adv* — **por·ten·tous·ness** *n*

por·ter \'pōrt-ər\ *n* **1 :** one who carries burdens; *esp* **:** one employed to carry baggage for patrons at a hotel or transportation terminal **2 :** an attendant in a railroad car **3 :** a dark heavy ale that is weaker than stout

por·ter·house \-ˌhau̇s\ *n* **:** a choice beefsteak with a large piece of tenderloin on a T-shaped bone

port·fo·lio \pōrt-'fō-lē-ˌō\ *n, pl* **-li·os 1 :** a case for carrying papers or drawings **2 :** the office and functions of a minister of state or member of a cabinet **3 :** the securities held by an investor or a financial house

port·hole \'pōrt-ˌhōl\ *n* **:** an opening (as a window) in the side of a ship or airplane

por·ti·co \'pōrt-i-ˌkō\ *n, pl* **-coes** *or* **-cos 1 :** a covered walk **2 :** a row of columns supporting a roof around or at the entrance of a building

por·ti·ere \ˌpōrt-ē-'e(ə)r, pōr-'ti(ə)r\ *n* **:** a curtain hanging across a doorway

¹por·tion \'pōr-shən\ *n* **1 a :** an individual's share of something **b :** DOWRY **2 :** one's lot, fate, or fortune **3 a :** a part of a whole **b :** a limited amount or quantity

²portion *vt* **por·tioned; por·tion·ing** \-sh(ə-)niŋ\ **1 :** to divide into portions **:** DISTRIBUTE **2 :** to allot or give as a portion **:** DOWER

por·tion·less \-shən-ləs\ *adj* **:** having no portion

port·ly \'pōrt-lē\ *adj* **:** heavy or rotund of body **:** CORPULENT — **port·li·ness** *n*

¹port·man·teau \pōrt-'man-tō\ *n, pl* **-teaus** *or* **-teaux** \-tōz\ **:** TRAVELING BAG, SUITCASE

²portmanteau *adj* **:** combining more than one use or quality

port of entry 1 : a place where foreign goods may be cleared through a customhouse **2 :** a place where an alien may enter a country

por·trait \'pōr-trət, -ˌtrāt\ *n* **1 :** a pictorial representation (as a painting) of a person usu. showing his face **2 :** a graphic portrayal in words

por·trai·ture \'pōr-trə-ˌchu̇r, -chər\ *n* **1 :** the making of portraits **:** PORTRAYAL **2 :** PORTRAIT

por·tray \pōr-'trā\ *vt* **1 :** to make a picture of **2 a :** to describe in words **b :** to play the role of **:** ENACT — **por·tray·er** *n*

por·tray·al \-'trā(-ə)l\ *n* **1 :** the act or process of portraying **:** REPRESENTATION **2 :** PORTRAIT

¹pose \'pōz\ *vb* **1 a :** to hold or cause to hold a special posture or attitude usu. for artistic purposes **b :** to affect an attitude or character **2 :** to put forth **:** PROPOUND

²pose *n* **1 :** a sustained posture; *esp* **:** one assumed for artistic effect **2 :** an assumed attitude; *esp* **:** AFFECTATION

¹pos·er \'pō-zər\ *n* **:** a puzzling or baffling question

²poser *n* **:** a person who poses

po·seur \pō-'zər\ *n* **:** one who habitually pretends to be what he is not **:** an affected person

pos·it \'päz-ət\ *vt* **:** to assume the existence of **:** POSTULATE

¹po·si·tion \pə-'zish-ən\ *n* **1 a :** an arranging in order **b :** the manner in which something is placed or arranged **c :** POSTURE **2 :** the stand taken on a question **3 a :** the point or area occupied by a physical object **b :** situation in an ordered arrangement **4 a :** social or official rank or status **b :** EMPLOYMENT, JOB **c :** a situation that confers advantage or preference — **po·si·tion·al** \-'zish-nəl, -ən-ᵊl\ *adj*

²position *vt* **po·si·tioned; po·si·tion·ing** \-'zish-(ə-)niŋ\ **:** to put in proper position

¹pos·i·tive \'päz-ət-iv, 'päz-tiv\ *adj* **1 a :** formally laid down or imposed **:** PRESCRIBED **b :** expressed clearly or definitely **:** PEREMPTORY **c :** fully assured **:** CONFIDENT **2 a :** of the degree of comparison expressed by the unmodified and uninflected form of an adjective or adverb **b :** definite, accurate, or certain in its action **c :** INCONTESTABLE, UNQUALIFIED **3 a :** not fictitious **:** REAL **b :** active in the social or economic sphere **4 a :** having rendition of light and shade similar in tone to the tones of the original subject **b :** being real and numerically greater than zero **5 a :** of, being, or relating to electricity of a kind that predominates in a glass rod after being rubbed with silk **b :** charged with positive electricity **:** having a deficiency of electrons **6 a :** marked by or indicating agreement or affirmation **b :** affirming the presence of what is sought or suspected to be present — **pos·i·tive·ness** *n*

²positive *n* **:** something positive: as **a :** the positive degree or a positive form in a language **b :** a positive photograph or a print from a negative

positive law *n* **:** law established or recognized by governmental authority

pos·i·tive·ly \-lē, *2 is often* ˌpäz-ə-'tiv-lē\ *adv* **1 :** in a positive manner **:** so as to be positive **2 :** EXTREMELY, CERTAINLY, ABSOLUTELY

pos·i·tron \'päz-ə-ˌträn\ *n* **:** a positively charged particle having the same mass and magnitude of charge as the electron

pos·se \'päs-ē\ *n* **:** a force of men called upon by a sheriff to aid him in his duty (as pursuit of a criminal)

pos·sess \pə-'zes\ *vt* **1 a :** to have and hold as property **:** OWN **b :** to have as an attribute, knowledge, or skill **2 a :** to take into one's possession **b :** to enter into and control firmly **:** DOMINATE

pos·ses·sion \pə-'zesh-ən\ *n* **1 a :** the act of possessing or holding as one's own **:** OWNERSHIP **b :** control or occupancy of property without regard to ownership **2 :** something that is held as one's own property **3 :** domination by an idea or influence from outside oneself — **pos·ses·sion·al** \-'zesh-nəl, -ən-ᵊl\ *adj*

pos·ses·sive \pə-'zes-iv\ *adj* **1 :** of, relating to, or constituting a grammatical case that denotes ownership **2 :** showing possession or the desire to possess or keep — **possessive** *n* — **pos·ses·sive·ly** *adv* — **pos·ses·sive·ness** *n*

pos·ses·sor \pə-'zes-ər\ *n* **:** one that possesses

pos·set \'päs-ət\ *n* **:** a hot drink of sweetened and spiced milk curdled with ale or wine

pos·si·bil·i·ty \ˌpäs-ə-'bil-ət-ē\ *n, pl* **-ties 1 :** the condition or fact of being possible **2 :** something possible

pos·si·ble \'päs-ə-bəl\ *adj* **1 :** being within the limits of one's ability **:** being something that can be done or brought about **2 :** being something that may or may not occur **3 :** ALLOWABLE, PERMITTED **4 :** able or fitted to be or to become

pos·si·bly \-blē\ *adv* **1 :** by possible means **:** by any possibility **2 :** PERHAPS, MAYBE

pos·sum \ˈpäs-əm\ *n* : OPOSSUM

¹post \ˈpōst\ *n* : a piece of timber or metal fixed firmly in an upright position esp. as a stay or support : PILLAR, COLUMN

²post *vt* **1** : to fasten to a place used for public notices **2** : to publish or announce by or as if by a notice **3** : to forbid persons from entering or using by putting up warning notices

³post *vb* **1** : to ride or travel with haste : HURRY **2** : MAIL **3** : to make familiar with a subject : INFORM

⁴post *adv* : with post-horses : EXPRESS

⁵post *n* **1 a** : the place at which a soldier is stationed; *esp* : a sentry's beat or station **b** : a station or task to which anyone is assigned **c** : a place to which troops are assigned : CAMP **2** : an office or position to which a person is appointed **3** : a trading settlement or station

⁶post *vt* **1** : to station in a given place **2** : to put up as security

post·age \ˈpō-stij\ *n* : the charge fixed by law for carrying something (as a letter or parcel) by mail

post·al \ˈpōst-ᵊl\ *adj* : of or relating to the mails or to the post office

postal card *n* : POSTCARD

post·card \ˈpōs(t)-ˌkärd\ *n* : a card on which a message may be written for mailing without an envelope

post chaise *n* : a carriage usu. having a closed body on four wheels and seating two to four persons

post·clas·si·cal \(ˈ)pōs(t)-ˈklas-i-kəl\ *adj* : of or relating to a period following the classical

post·con·so·nan·tal \ˌpōs(t)-ˌkän(t)-sə-ˈnant-ᵊl\ *adj* : immediately following a consonant

post·date \(ˈ)pōs(t)-ˈdāt\ *vt* **1** : to date with a date later than that of execution **2** : to follow in time

post·er \ˈpō-stər\ *n* **1** : a notice or advertisement to be posted in a public place **2** : a person who posts such notices

¹pos·te·ri·or \pō-ˈstir-ē-ər, pä-\ *adj* **1** : later in time **2** : situated behind or toward the back — **pos·te·ri·or·ly** *adv*

²posterior \pä-ˈstir-ē-ər, pō-\ *n* : the hinder parts of the body; *esp* : BUTTOCKS

pos·ter·i·ty \pä-ˈster-ət-ē\ *n* **1** : the offspring of one progenitor to the furthest generation : DESCENDANTS **2** : all future generations : future time

pos·tern \ˈpōs-tərn, ˈpäs-\ *n* **1** : a back door or gate **2** : a private or side entrance or way — **postern** *adj*

post exchange *n* : a store at a military post that sells to military personnel and authorized civilians

¹post·grad·u·ate \(ˈ)pōs(t)-ˈgraj-ə-wət, -ˌwāt\ *adj* : GRADUATE 2

²postgraduate *n* : a student continuing his education after graduation from high school or college

post·haste \ˈpōst-ˈhāst\ *adv* : with great speed : in great haste

post–horse \ˈpōst-ˌhȯrs\ *n* : a horse for use esp. by couriers or mail carriers

post·hu·mous \ˈpäs-chə-məs\ *adj* **1** : born after the death of the father **2** : published after the death of the author **3** : following or occurring after one's death — **post·hu·mous·ly** *adv*

pos·til·ion *or* **pos·til·lion** \pō-ˈstil-yən\ *n* : one who rides on the left-hand horse of a pair drawing a coach

post·lude \ˈpōst-ˌlüd\ *n* : a closing piece of music; *esp* : an organ voluntary at the end of a church service

post·man \ˈpōs(t)-mən, -ˌman\ *n* : MAILMAN

¹post·mark \-ˌmärk\ *n* : a mark officially put on a piece of mail; *esp* : one canceling the postage stamp and giving the date and place of sending

²postmark *vt* : to put a postmark on

post·mas·ter \-ˌmas-tər\ *n* : one who has charge of a post office

postmaster general *n, pl* **postmasters general** : an official in charge of a national post office department

post·me·rid·i·an \ˌpōs(t)-mə-ˈrid-ē-ən\ *adj* : occurring after noon

post me·ri·di·em \-ˈrid-ē-əm, -ē-ˌem\ *adj* : POSTMERIDIAN

post·mis·tress \ˈpōs(t)-ˌmis-trəs\ *n* : a woman in charge of a post office

post·mor·tem \pōs(t)-ˈmȯrt-əm\ *adj* **1 a** : occurring after death **b** : of or relating to a postmortem examination **2** : following the event — **postmortem** *n*

postmortem examination *n* : an examination of a dead body esp. to determine the cause of death

post·na·sal \(ˈ)pōs(t)-ˈnā-zəl\ *adj* : lying or occurring posterior to the nose — **postnasal** *n*

post·na·tal \(ˈ)pōs(t)-ˈnāt-ᵊl\ *adj* : subsequent to birth; *also* : of or relating to a newborn child — **post·na·tal·ly** \-ᵊl-ē\ *adv*

post office *n* **1** : a government department handling the transmission of mail **2** : a local branch of a post office

post·op·er·a·tive \(ˈ)pōst-ˈäp-(ə-)rət-iv, -ˈäp-ə-ˌrāt-\ *adj* : following a surgical operation — **post·op·er·a·tive·ly** *adv*

post·paid \ˈpōs(t)-ˈpād\ *adv* : with postage paid by the sender and not chargeable to the receiver

post·pone \pōs(t)-ˈpōn\ *vt* : to hold back to a later time : put off — **post·pone·ment** \-mənt\ *n*

post road *n* : a road over which mail is carried

post·script \ˈpō(s)-ˌskript\ *n* : a note or series of notes added at the end of a letter, article, or book

pos·tu·lant \ˈpäs-chə-lənt\ *n* : a person admitted to a religious house as a probationary candidate for membership

¹pos·tu·late \ˈpäs-chə-ˌlāt\ *vt* : to claim as true : assume as a postulate or axiom

²pos·tu·late \-lət,-ˌlāt\ *n* : a hypothesis advanced as an essential basis of a system of thought or premise of a train of reasoning

¹pos·ture \ˈpäs-chər\ *n* **1** : the position or bearing of the body or of a body part **2** : relative place or position : SITUATION **3** : frame of mind : ATTITUDE — **pos·tur·al** \-chə-rəl\ *adj*

²posture *vb* : to assume or cause to assume a given posture; *esp* : to strike a pose for effect — **pos·tur·er** *n*

post·war \ˈpōst-ˈwȯ(ə)r\ *adj* : of, relating to, or being a period after a war

po·sy \ˈpō-zē\ *n, pl* **posies** **1** : a brief sentiment, motto, or legend **2** : a bunch of flowers : FLOWER, BOUQUET, NOSEGAY

¹pot \ˈpät\ *n* **1 a** : a rounded metal or earthen container used chiefly for domestic purposes **b** : the quantity held by a pot **2** : an enclosed framework for catching fish or lobsters **3 a** : a large quantity or sum **b** : the total of the bets at stake at one time **4** : RUIN, DETERIORATION

²pot *vt* **pot·ted**; **pot·ting** **1** : to preserve in a sealed pot, jar, or can **2** : to plant or grow in a pot **3** : to shoot with a potshot

po·ta·ble \ˈpōt-ə-bəl\ *adj* : suitable for drinking — **po·ta·bil·i·ty** \ˌpōt-ə-ˈbil-ət-ē\ *n*

pot·ash \ˈpät-ˌash\ *n* **1** : potassium carbonate esp. from wood ashes **2** : potassium or a potassium compound esp. as used in agriculture or industry

po·tas·si·um \pə-ˈtas-ē-əm\ *n* : a silver-white soft light low-melting univalent metallic chemical element that occurs abundantly in nature esp. combined in minerals

potassium nitrate *n* : a soluble salt that occurs in some soils and is used in making gunpowder, in preserving meat, and in medicine

po·ta·tion \pō-ˈtā-shən\ *n* **1** : a usu. alcoholic drink or brew **2 a** : the act of drinking **b** : DRAFT 4a

po·ta·to \pə-ˈtāt-ō\ *n, pl* **-toes** **1** : SWEET POTATO **2 a** : an erect American herb of the nightshade family widely cultivated as a vegetable crop **b** : its edible starchy tuber

pot·bel·ly \ˈpät-ˌbel-ē\ *n* **1** : an enlarged, swollen, or protruding abdomen **2** : a stove with a bulging body — **pot·bel·lied** \-ēd\ *adj*

pot·boil·er \-ˌbȯi-lər\ *n* : a usu. inferior work of art or literature produced only to earn money

po·ten·cy \ˈpōt-ᵊn-sē\ *n, pl* **-cies** : the quality or condition of being potent; *esp* : power to bring about a certain result

po·tent \'pōt-ᵊnt\ *adj* **1 :** having or wielding force, authority, or influence : POWERFUL **2 :** producing an effect **3 a :** chemically or medicinally effective **b :** rich in a characteristic constituent : STRONG **4 :** able to copulate — **po·tent·ly** *adv*

po·ten·tate \'pōt-ᵊn-ˌtāt\ *n* **:** one who wields controlling power : SOVEREIGN

[1]**po·ten·tial** \pə-'ten-chəl\ *adj* **:** capable of becoming real : POSSIBLE — **po·ten·tial·ly** \-'tench-(ə-)lē\ *adv*

[2]**potential** *n* **1 :** something that can develop or become actual : POSSIBILITY **2 :** the degree of electrification with reference to a standard (as that of the earth)

po·ten·ti·al·i·ty \pə-ˌten-chē-'al-ət-ē\ *n, pl* **-ties 1 :** the ability to develop or to come into existence **2 :** POTENTIAL 1

[1]**poth·er** \'päth̲-ər\ *n* **1 a :** a noisy disturbance **b :** FUSS **2 :** a choking cloud of dust or smoke **3 :** mental turmoil

[2]**pother** *vb* **poth·ered; poth·er·ing** \'päth̲-(ə-)riŋ\ **:** to put into or be in a pother

pot·herb \'pät-ˌ(h)ərb\ *n* **:** an herb whose leaves or stems are boiled for use as greens

pot·hole \-ˌhōl\ *n* **:** a large pit or hole (as in the bed of a river or in a road surface)

pot·hunt·er \-ˌhənt-ər\ *n* **:** one who hunts game for food — **pot–hunt·ing** \-ˌhənt-iŋ\ *n*

po·tion \'pō-shən\ *n* **:** DRINK, DOSE; *esp* **:** a dose of a liquid medicine or poison

pot·latch \'pät-ˌlach\ *n* **:** a ceremonial feast of northwest coast Indians in which the host distributes gifts lavishly and the guests must reciprocate

pot·luck \'pät-'lək\ *n* **:** the regular meal available to a guest for whom no special preparations have been made

pot·pie \'pät-'pī\ *n* **:** meat or fowl stew served with a crust or dumplings

pot·pour·ri \ˌpō-pu̇-'rē\ *n* **1 :** a jar of flower petals and spices used for scent **2 :** a miscellaneous collection : MEDLEY

pot·sherd \'pät-ˌshərd\ *n* **:** a pottery fragment

pot·shot \-ˌshät\ *n* **1 :** a shot taken in a casual manner or at an easy target **2 :** a critical remark made in a random or sporadic manner — **potshot** *vb*

pot·tage \'pät-ij\ *n* **:** a thick soup of vegetables or vegetables and meat

[1]**pot·ter** \'pät-ər\ *n* **:** one that makes pottery

[2]**potter** *vi* **:** PUTTER — **pot·ter·er** *n*

pot·tery \'pät-ə-rē\ *n, pl* **-ter·ies 1 :** a place where earthen vessels are made **2 :** the art of the potter : CERAMICS **3 :** ware made usu. from clay

pot·ty \'pät-ē\ *n, pl* **potties :** a small child's pot for urinating or defecating

pot·ty–chair \-ˌche(ə)r\ *n* **:** a small chair with an open seat under which a potty is placed for use by a small child

[1]**pouch** \'pau̇ch\ *n* **1 :** a small drawstring bag carried on the person **2 :** a bag of small or moderate size for storing or transporting goods **3 :** an anatomical structure in the form of a bag or sac; *esp* **:** one in which a marsupial carries her young — **pouched** \'pau̇cht\ *adj*

[2]**pouch** *vb* **:** to put or form into or as if into a pouch

pouchy \'pau̇-chē\ *adj* **:** having, tending to have, or resembling a pouch

poult \'pōlt\ *n* **:** a young fowl; *esp* **:** a young turkey

poul·ter·er \'pōl-tər-ər\ *n* **:** one that deals in poultry

poul·tice \'pōl-təs\ *n* **:** a soft usu. heated and often medicated mass spread on cloth and applied to sores or other lesions — **poultice** *vt*

poul·try \'pōl-trē\ *n* **:** domesticated birds kept for eggs or meat

poul·try·man \-mən\ *n* **1 :** one that raises domestic fowls esp. on a commercial scale **2 :** a dealer in poultry or poultry products

pounce \'pau̇n(t)s\ *vi* **1 :** to swoop down on and seize something with or as if with talons **2 :** to make an abrupt assault or approach — **pounce** *n*

[1]**pound** \'pau̇nd\ *n* **1 :** any of various units of mass and weight; *esp* **:** a unit in general use among English-speaking peoples equal to 16 ounces **2 :** the basic monetary unit of the United Kingdom

[2]**pound** *vb* **1 :** to reduce to powder or pulp by beating **2 a :** to strike heavily or repeatedly **b :** to produce by means of repeated vigorous strokes **c :** DRIVE **3 :** to move along heavily or persistently

[3]**pound** *n* **:** an act or sound of pounding

[4]**pound** *n* **:** an enclosure for animals; *esp* **:** a public enclosure for stray or unlicensed animals

pound cake *n* **:** a rich cake made with a large amount of eggs and shortening in proportion to the flour used

[1]**pound·er** \'pau̇n-dər\ *n* **:** one that pounds

[2]**pounder** *n* **:** one having a specified weight or value in pounds

[1]**pour** \'pō(ə)r\ *vb* **1 :** to flow or to cause to flow in a stream **2 a :** to let loose something without restraint : express freely **b :** to supply or produce copiously **3 :** to rain very hard — **pour·a·ble** \-ə-bəl\ *adj* — **pour·er** *n*

[2]**pour** *n* **:** the action of pouring; *esp* **:** a heavy fall of rain

[1]**pout** \'pau̇t\ *vb* **1 :** to show displeasure by thrusting out the lips **2 :** SULK — **pout·er** *n*

[2]**pout** *n* **1 :** a protrusion of the lips expressive of displeasure **2** *pl* **:** a fit of bad humor

pov·er·ty \'päv-ərt-ē\ *n* **1 :** the state of being poor : lack of money or material possessions : WANT **2 :** SCARCITY, DEARTH **3 a :** debility due to malnutrition **b :** lack of fertility

pov·er·ty–strick·en \-ˌstrik-ən\ *adj* **:** afflicted with poverty : very poor : DESTITUTE

[1]**pow·der** \'pau̇d-ər\ *n* **1 :** dry material made up of fine particles; *also* **:** a medicinal or cosmetic preparation in this form **2 :** any of various solid explosives used chiefly in gunnery and blasting

[2]**powder** *vb* **1 :** to sprinkle or cover with or as if with powder **2 :** to reduce to powder or become powder **3 :** to apply cosmetic powder — **pow·der·er** \-ər-ər\ *n*

pow·dery \'pau̇d-ə-rē\ *adj* **1 a :** resembling or consisting of powder **b :** easily reduced to powder : CRUMBLING **2 :** covered with or as if with powder : DUSTY

[1]**pow·er** \'pau̇(-ə)r\ *n* **1 a :** possession of control, authority, or influence over others **b :** one having such power; *esp* **:** a sovereign state **2 a :** ability to act or do **b :** legal or official authority, capacity, or right **3 a :** physical might **b :** mental or moral efficacy **4 :** the number of times as indicated by an exponent a number is to be multiplied by itself **5 a :** force or energy that is or can be applied to work; *esp* **:** mechanical or electrical force or energy **b :** the time rate at which work is done or energy emitted or transferred **6 :** MAGNIFICATION 2

[2]**power** *adj* **:** relating to, supplying, or utilizing power; *esp* **:** utilizing mechanical or electrical energy

[3]**power** *vt* **:** to supply with power

pow·er·ful \'pau̇(-ə)r-fəl\ *adj* **:** full of or having power, strength, or influence : STRONG, MIGHTY, EFFECTIVE — **pow·er·ful·ly** \-f(ə-)lē\ *adv*

pow·er·house \'pau̇(-ə)r-ˌhau̇s\ *n* **1 :** a building in which electric power is generated **2 :** a source of power, energy, or influence **3 :** one having unusual strength or energy

pow·er·less \'pau̇(-ə)r-ləs\ *adj* **1 :** lacking power, force, or energy : unable to produce an effect **2 :** lacking authority to act — **pow·er·less·ness** *n*

pow·wow \'pau̇-ˌwau̇\ *n* **1 :** a No. American Indian medicine man **2 a :** a No. American Indian ceremony (as for victory in war) **b :** a conference with an Indian leader or group **3 a :** a noisy gathering **b :** a meeting for discussion — **powwow** *vi*

pox \'päks\ *n* **:** any of various usu. virus diseases (as smallpox or syphilis) that cause eruptions on the skin

prac·ti·ca·ble \ˈprak-ti-kə-bəl\ *adj* **1** : capable of being done, put into practice, or accomplished : FEASIBLE **2** : USABLE — **prac·ti·ca·bil·i·ty** \ˌprak-ti-kə-ˈbil-ət-ē\ *n* — **prac·ti·ca·bly** \ˈprak-ti-kə-blē\ *adv*

prac·ti·cal \ˈprak-ti-kəl\ *adj* **1** : actively engaged in an action or occupation **2 a** : of, relating to, or manifested in practice or action **b** : being such in practice or effect : VIRTUAL **3** : capable of being put to use or account : USEFUL **4 a** : disposed to action as opposed to speculation or theorizing **b** (1) : qualified by practice or practical training (2) : designed to supplement theoretical training by experience — **prac·ti·cal·i·ty** \ˌprak-ti-ˈkal-ət-ē\ *n* — **prac·ti·cal·ness** \ˈprak-ti-kəl-nəs\ *n*

practical joke *n* : a joke turning on something done rather than said; *esp* : a trick played on a person — **practical joker** *n*

prac·ti·cal·ly \ˈprak-ti-k(ə-)lē\ *adv* **1** : REALLY, ACTUALLY **2** : by experience or experiment **3** : to all practical purposes though not absolutely **4** : NEARLY, ALMOST **5** : within limits of usefulness

[1]**prac·tice** *or* **prac·tise** \ˈprak-təs\ *vb* **1 a** : to perform or work at repeatedly so as to become proficient **b** : to train by repeated exercises **2 a** : to carry out : APPLY **b** : to do or perform often, customarily, or habitually **c** : to be professionally engaged in — **prac·tic·er** *n*

[2]**practice** *n* **1 a** : actual performance or application **b** : a repeated or customary action **c** : the usual way of doing something **2 a** : systematic exercise for proficiency **b** : the condition of being proficient through systematic exercise **3 a** : the exercise of a profession **b** : a professional business

prac·ticed *or* **prac·tised** \ˈprak-təst\ *adj* **1** : EXPERIENCED, SKILLED **2** : learned by practice

prac·ti·tion·er \prak-ˈtish-(ə-)nər\ *n* : a person who practices a profession and esp. law or medicine

prag·mat·ic \prag-ˈmat-ik\ *adj* **1** : concerned with practical affairs often to the exclusion of intellectual or artistic matters **2** : PRACTICAL — **prag·mat·i·cal·ly** \-i-k(ə-)lē\ *adv*

prag·ma·tism \ˈprag-mə-ˌtiz-əm\ *n* : a practical approach to problems and affairs — **prag·ma·tist** \-mət-əst\ *adj or n*

prai·rie \ˈpre(ə)r-ē\ *n* : a tract of grassland; *esp* : a large area of level or rolling land (as in the central U.S.) with deep fertile soil, a cover of tall coarse grasses, and few trees

prairie schooner *n* : a covered wagon used by pioneers in cross-country travel

[1]**praise** \ˈprāz\ *vb* **1** : to express approval : COMMEND **2** : to glorify esp. by ascription of perfections : WORSHIP — **prais·er** *n*

[2]**praise** *n* **1** : an act of praising : COMMENDATION **2** : WORSHIP

praise·wor·thy \-ˌwər-thē\ *adj* : worthy of praise : LAUDABLE — **praise·wor·thi·ly** \-thə-lē\ *adv* — **praise·wor·thi·ness** \-thē-nəs\ *n*

pra·line \ˈprä-ˌlēn, ˈprā-\ *n* : a candy of nut kernels embedded in boiled brown sugar or maple sugar

prance \ˈpran(t)s\ *vi* **1** : to spring from the hind legs or move by so doing **2** : to ride on a prancing horse **3 a** : SWAGGER **b** : CAPER — **prance** *n* — **pranc·er** \ˈpran(t)-sər\ *n* — **pranc·ing·ly** \-siŋ-lē\ *adv*

[1]**prank** \ˈpraŋk\ *n* : a playful or mischievous act : PRACTICAL JOKE, TRICK — **prank·ish** \ˈpraŋ-kish\ *adj* — **prank·ish·ly** *adv* — **prank·ish·ness** *n*

[2]**prank** *vt* : to dress or adorn (oneself) gaily or showily

prank·ster \ˈpraŋ(k)-stər\ *n* : a player of pranks

pra·seo·dym·i·um \ˌprā-zē-ō-ˈdim-ē-əm\ *n* : a yellowish white metallic chemical element used chiefly in the form of its salts in coloring glass greenish yellow

[1]**prate** \ˈprāt\ *vb* : to talk long and idly : speak foolishly : CHATTER, BABBLE — **prat·er** *n* — **prat·ing·ly** \ˈprāt-iŋ-lē\ *adv*

[2]**prate** *n* : an act of prating : idle or foolish talk

prat·fall \ˈprat-ˌfȯl\ *n* : a fall on the buttocks

[1]**prat·tle** \ˈprat-ᵊl\ *vb* **prat·tled**; **prat·tling** \ˈprat-liŋ, -ᵊl-iŋ\ **1** : PRATE **2** : to utter meaningless sounds suggestive of the chatter of children **3** : BABBLE — **prat·tler** \ˈprat-lər, -ᵊl-ər\ *n*

[2]**prattle** *n* **1** : trifling or empty talk **2** : a sound that is meaningless, repetitive, and suggestive of the chatter of children

prau \ˈprau̇\ *n* : any of several usu. undecked Indonesian boats propelled by sails, oars, or paddles

prawn \ˈprȯn\ *n* : any of numerous widely distributed edible crustaceans resembling shrimps

pray \ˈprā\ *vb* **1** : ENTREAT, IMPLORE **2** : to get or bring by praying **3** : to make entreaty or supplication : PLEAD **4** : to address God with adoration, confession, supplication, or thanksgiving

[1]**prayer** \ˈpra(-ə)r\ *n* **1** : the act or practice of praying to God **2 a** : a supplication or expression addressed to God **b** : an earnest request or wish : PLEA **3** : a religious service consisting chiefly of prayers **4** : a set form of words used in praying

[2]**pray·er** \ˈprā-ər\ *n* : one that prays : SUPPLIANT

prayer book *n* : a book containing prayers and often other forms and directions for worship

prayer·ful \ˈpra(ə)r-fəl\ *adj* **1** : given to or characterized by prayer : DEVOUT **2** : EARNEST — **prayer·ful·ly** \-fə-lē\ *adv* — **prayer·ful·ness** *n*

preach \ˈprēch\ *vb* **1 a** : to deliver a sermon : utter publicly **b** : to set forth in a sermon **2** : to urge acceptance or abandonment of an idea or course of action : ADVOCATE; *esp* : to exhort in an officious or tiresome manner — **preach·er** *n* — **preach·ing·ly** \ˈprē-chiŋ-lē\ *adv*

preach·ment \ˈprēch-mənt\ *n* **1** : the act or practice of preaching **2** : SERMON, EXHORTATION; *esp* : a tedious or unwelcome exhortation

pre·am·ble \ˈprē-ˌam-bəl\ *n* **1** : an introductory statement **2** : an introductory fact or circumstance : PRELIMINARY; *esp* : one indicating what is to follow

pre·ar·range \ˌprē-ə-ˈrānj\ *vt* : to arrange beforehand — **pre·ar·range·ment** \-mənt\ *n*

pre·as·signed \ˌprē-ə-ˈsīnd\ *adj* : assigned beforehand

pre·can·cer·ous \(ˈ)prē-ˈkan(t)s-(ə-)rəs\ *adj* : likely to become cancerous

pre·car·i·ous \pri-ˈkar-ē-əs\ *adj* **1** : DUBIOUS **2 a** : dependent on chance circumstances, unknown conditions, or uncertain developments **b** : characterized by a lack of security or stability that threatens with danger — **pre·car·i·ous·ly** *adv* — **pre·car·i·ous·ness** *n*

pre·cau·tion \pri-ˈkȯ-shən\ *n* **1** : care taken in advance : FORESIGHT **2** : a measure taken beforehand to prevent harm or secure good : SAFEGUARD — **pre·cau·tion·ary** \-shə-ˌner-ē\ *adj*

pre·cede \pri-ˈsēd\ *vb* **1** : to surpass in rank, dignity, or importance **2** : to be, go, or come before or in front of in position or time **3** : to cause to be preceded : PREFACE

prec·e·dence \ˈpres-əd-ən(t)s, pri-ˈsēd-ᵊn(t)s\ *or* **prec·e·den·cy** \-ən-sē, -ᵊn-sē\ *n* **1** : the act or fact of preceding **2** : PRIORITY, PREFERENCE

prec·e·dent \ˈpres-əd-ənt\ *n* : something that may serve as an example or rule to authorize or justify a similar future act or statement

pre·ced·ing \pri-ˈsēd-iŋ\ *adj* : going before : PREVIOUS

pre·cen·tor \pri-ˈsent-ər\ *n* : a leader of the singing of a choir or congregation

pre·cept \ˈprē-ˌsept\ *n* : a command or principle intended as a general rule of action

pre·cep·tor \pri-ˈsep-tər, ˈprē-ˌ\ *n* : TEACHER, TUTOR — **pre·cep·to·ri·al** \pri-ˌsep-ˈtōr-ē-əl, ˌprē-\ *adj* — **pre·cep·tor·ship** \pri-ˈsep-tər-ˌship, ˈprē-ˌ\ *n* — **pre·cep·tress** \-trəs\ *n*

pre·cinct \ˈprē-ˌsiŋ(k)t\ *n* **1** : an administrative subdivision (as of a city) : DISTRICT **2** : the enclosure bounded by the walls or limits of a building or place **3** *pl* : the region immediately surrounding a place : ENVIRONS **4** : BOUNDARY

pre·ci·os·i·ty \ˌpres(h)-ē-'äs-ət-ē\ *n, pl* **-ties** : fastidious refinement esp. in language

[1]**pre·cious** \'presh-əs\ *adj* **1** : of great value or high price **2** : highly esteemed or cherished **3** : excessively refined : AFFECTED **4** : GREAT, THOROUGHGOING — **pre·cious·ly** *adv* — **pre·cious·ness** *n*

[2]**precious** *adv* : EXTREMELY, VERY

prec·i·pice \'pres-ə-pəs\ *n* **1** : a very steep or overhanging place (as the face of a cliff) **2** : the brink of disaster

pre·cip·i·tance \pri-'sip-ət-ən(t)s\ *n* : rash haste : PRECIPITANCY

pre·cip·i·tan·cy \-ən-sē\ *n, pl* **-cies** : precipitate action : PRECIPITATION

pre·cip·i·tant \-ənt\ *adj* : PRECIPITATE — **pre·cip·i·tant·ly** *adv* — **pre·cip·i·tant·ness** *n*

[1]**pre·cip·i·tate** \pri-'sip-ə-ˌtāt\ *vb* **1 a** : to throw violently : HURL **b** : to fall headlong **c** : to fall or come suddenly into some condition **2 a** : to move, urge, or press on with haste or violence **b** : to bring on abruptly **3 a** : to separate or cause to separate from solution or suspension **b** : to fall as rain, snow, or hail — **pre·cip·i·ta·tor** \-ˌtāt-ər\ *n*

[2]**pre·cip·i·tate** \pri-'sip-ət-ət, -ə-ˌtāt\ *n* : a usu. solid substance separated from a solution or suspension by chemical or physical change

[3]**pre·cip·i·tate** \pri-'sip-ət-ət\ *adj* **1** : exhibiting violent or unwise speed : RASH **2 a** : falling, flowing, or rushing with steep descent **b** : PRECIPITOUS — **pre·cip·i·tate·ly** *adv* — **pre·cip·i·tate·ness** *n*

pre·cip·i·ta·tion \pri-ˌsip-ə-'tā-shən\ *n* **1** : the quality or state of being precipitate : HASTE **2** : the process of precipitating or of forming a precipitate **3 a** : a deposit on the earth of hail, mist, rain, sleet, or snow; *also* : the quantity of water deposited **b** : PRECIPITATE

pre·cip·i·tous \pri-'sip-ət-əs\ *adj* **1 a** : steep like a precipice **b** : having precipices **2** : falling very quickly : very rapid **3** : SUDDEN, RASH — **pre·cip·i·tous·ly** *adv* — **pre·cip·i·tous·ness** *n*

pré·cis \prā-'sē, 'prā-(ˌ)sē\ *n, pl* **pré·cis** \-'sēz, -(ˌ)sēz\ : a concise summary of essential points, statements, or facts

pre·cise \pri-'sīs\ *adj* **1** : exactly or sharply defined or stated **2** : very exact : ACCURATE **3** : clear and sharp in enunciation : DISTINCT **4** : strictly conforming to rule or convention **5** : distinguished from every other : VERY — **pre·cise·ly** *adv* — **pre·cise·ness** *n*

pre·ci·sion \pri-'sizh-ən\ *n* : the quality or state of being precise : EXACTNESS — **pre·ci·sion·ist** \-'sizh-(ə-)nəst\ *n*

pre·clude \pri-'klüd\ *vt* : to make impossible or ineffectual : keep from taking place : PREVENT — **pre·clu·sion** \-'klü-zhən\ *n* — **pre·clu·sive** \-'klü-siv\ *adj* — **pre·clu·sive·ly** *adv*

pre·co·cious \pri-'kō-shəs\ *adj* **1** : exceptionally early in development or occurrence **2** : exhibiting mature qualities at an unusually early age — **pre·co·cious·ly** *adv* — **pre·co·cious·ness** *n* — **pre·coc·i·ty** \pri-'käs-ət-ē\ *n*

pre·con·ceive \ˌprē-kən-'sēv\ *vt* : to form an opinion of prior to actual knowledge or experience — **pre·con·cep·tion** \-'sep-shən\ *n*

pre·con·cert·ed \ˌprē-kən-'sərt-əd\ *adj* : arranged or agreed upon in advance

pre·con·di·tion \ˌprē-kən-'dish-ən\ *vt* : to put in proper or desired condition or frame of mind in advance

pre·con·scious \(')prē-'kän-chəs\ *adj* : not present in consciousness but capable of being readily recalled — **pre·con·scious·ly** *adv*

pre·cur·sor \pri-'kər-sər, 'prē-ˌ\ *n* **1** : one that precedes and indicates the approach of another : FORERUNNER **2** : PREDECESSOR

pre·cur·so·ry \pri-'kərs-(ə-)rē\ *adj* : having the character of a precursor : PRELIMINARY, PREMONITORY

pre·da·cious *or* **pre·da·ceous** \pri-'dā-shəs\ *adj* : living by preying on others : PREDATORY

pre·date \(')prē-'dāt\ *vt* : ANTEDATE

pre·da·tion \pri-'dā-shən\ *n* : the act of preying or plundering : DEPREDATION — **pred·a·tor** \'pred-ət-ər\ *n*

pred·a·to·ry \'pred-ə-ˌtōr-ē\ *adj* **1** : of, relating to, or marked by plundering **2** : disposed to exploit others **3** : preying upon other animals — **pred·a·to·ri·ly** \ˌpred-ə-'tōr-ə-lē\ *adv*

pred·e·ces·sor \'pred-ə-ˌses-ər, 'prēd-\ *n* : one that precedes; *esp* : a person who has held a position or office before another

pre·des·ti·nate \prē-'des-tə-ˌnāt\ *vt* : to foreordain to an earthly or eternal destiny by divine decree

pre·des·ti·na·tion \(ˌ)prē-ˌdes-tə-'nā-shən\ *n* : the act of predestinating : the state of being predestinated

pre·des·tine \(')prē-'des-tən\ *vt* : to destine, decree, determine, appoint, or settle beforehand; *esp* : PREDESTINATE

pre·de·ter·mine \ˌprēd-i-'tər-mən\ *vt* **1 a** : FOREORDAIN, PREDESTINE **b** : to determine or settle beforehand **2** : to impose a direction or tendency on beforehand — **pre·de·ter·mi·na·tion** \-ˌtər-mə-'nā-shən\ *n*

pred·i·ca·ble \'pred-i-kə-bəl\ *adj* : capable of being predicated or affirmed

pre·dic·a·ment \pri-'dik-ə-mənt\ *n* : a difficult, perplexing, or trying situation : FIX

[1]**pred·i·cate** \'pred-i-kət\ *n* : the part of a sentence or clause that expresses what is said of the subject — **pred·i·ca·tive** \'pred-i-kət-iv, 'pred-ə-ˌkāt-\ *adj* — **pred·i·ca·tive·ly** *adv*

[2]**pred·i·cate** \'pred-ə-ˌkāt\ *vt* **1** : AFFIRM, DECLARE **2** : to assert to be a quality or property **3** : BASE, FOUND **4** : IMPLY

pred·i·ca·tion \ˌpred-ə-'kā-shən\ *n* : an act or instance of predicating

pre·dict \pri-'dikt\ *vt* : to declare in advance : foretell on the basis of observation, experience, or scientific reasoning — **pre·dict·a·ble** \-'dik-tə-bəl\ *adj* — **pre·dict·a·bly** \-blē\ *adv*

pre·dic·tion \pri-'dik-shən\ *n* **1** : an act of predicting **2** : something that is predicted : FORECAST — **pre·dic·tive** \-'dik-tiv\ *adj* — **pre·dic·tive·ly** *adv*

pre·di·gest \ˌprēd-ī-'jest, ˌprēd-ə-\ *vt* : to subject to predigestion

pre·di·ges·tion \-'jes(h)-chən\ *n* : artificial partial digestion of food for use in illness or impaired digestion

pred·i·lec·tion \ˌpred-ᵊl-'ek-shən, ˌprēd-\ *n* : an inclination in favor of something in advance of knowledge of it : PREFERENCE, PARTIALITY

pre·dis·pose \ˌprēd-is-'pōz\ *vt* : to dispose in advance : make susceptible : INCLINE

pre·dis·po·si·tion \ˌprē-ˌdis-pə-'zish-ən\ *n* : a condition of being predisposed : INCLINATION

pre·dom·i·nance \pri-'däm-ə-nən(t)s\ *n* : the quality or state of being predominant : PREVALENCE

pre·dom·i·nant \-nənt\ *adj* : having superior strength, influence, or authority : PREVAILING — **pre·dom·i·nant·ly** *adv*

pre·dom·i·nate \pri-'däm-ə-ˌnāt\ *vb* **1** : to exert controlling power or influence : PREVAIL, DOMINATE **2** : to hold advantage in numbers or quantity : PREPONDERATE — **pre·dom·i·na·tion** \-ˌdäm-ə-'nā-shən\ *n*

pre·em·i·nence \prē-'em-ə-nən(t)s\ *n* : the quality or state of being preeminent : SUPERIORITY

pre·em·i·nent \-nənt\ *adj* : having paramount rank, dignity, or importance : OUTSTANDING, SUPREME — **pre·em·i·nent·ly** *adv*

pre·empt \prē-'em(p)t\ *vt* **1** : to settle upon (as public land) with the right to purchase before others; *also* : to take by such a right **2** : to take before someone else can : APPROPRIATE — **pre·emp·tion** \-'em(p)-shən\ *n* — **pre·emp·tive** \-'em(p)-tiv\ *adj* — **pre·emp·tive·ly** *adv* — **pre·emp·tor** \-tər\ *n*

preen \'prēn\ *vb* **1** : to trim or dress with the bill **2** : to dress or smooth oneself up : PRIMP **3** : to indulge oneself in pride : congratulate oneself : GLOAT

pre·ex·ist \ˌprē-ig-ˈzist\ *vb* : to exist earlier or before something
pre·ex·ist·ence \-ˈzis-tən(t)s\ *n* : existence in a former state or previous to something else; *esp* : existence of the soul before its union with the body — **pre·ex·ist·ent** \-tənt\ *adj*
pre·fab \(ˈ)prē-ˈfab, ˈprē-ˌ\ *n* : a prefabricated structure
pre·fab·ri·cate \(ˈ)prē-ˈfab-rə-ˌkāt\ *vt* : to fabricate the parts of at a factory for rapid assembly elsewhere — **pre·fab·ri·ca·tion** \ˌprē-ˌfab-rə-ˈkā-shən\ *n*
¹pref·ace \ˈpref-əs\ *n* **1** : the introductory remarks of a speaker or author : PROLOGUE **2** : PRELIMINARY
²preface *vb* **1** : to make introductory remarks : say or write as a preface **2** : PRECEDE, HERALD **3** : to introduce by or begin with a preface **4** : to locate in front of **5** : to be a preliminary to — **pref·ac·er** *n*
pref·a·to·ry \ˈpref-ə-ˌtōr-ē\ *adj* : of, relating to, or constituting a preface : INTRODUCTORY, PRELIMINARY
pre·fect \ˈprē-ˌfekt\ *n* **1** : a presiding or chief officer or magistrate **2** : a student monitor in some usu. private schools
pre·fec·ture \ˈprē-ˌfek-chər\ *n* **1** : the office or term of office of a prefect **2** : the district governed by a prefect
pre·fer \pri-ˈfər\ *vt* **pre·ferred**; **pre·fer·ring** **1** : to choose or esteem above another **2** : to present for action or consideration — **pre·fer·rer** *n*
pref·er·a·ble \ˈpref-(ə-)rə-bəl, ˈpref-ər-bəl\ *adj* : worthy to be preferred : more desirable — **pref·er·a·bly** \-blē\ *adv*
pref·er·ence \ˈpref-ərn(t)s, ˈpref-(ə-)rən(t)s\ *n* **1 a** : the act of preferring : the state of being preferred **b** : the power or opportunity of choosing **2** : one that is preferred : FAVORITE, CHOICE **3** : the act, fact, or principle of giving advantages to some over others — **pref·er·en·tial** \ˌpref-ə-ˈren-chəl\ *adj* — **pref·er·en·tial·ly** \-ˈrench-(ə-)lē\ *adv*
pre·fer·ment \pri-ˈfər-mənt\ *n* **1** : advancement or promotion in dignity, office, or station **2** : a position or office of honor or profit
pre·fig·ure \(ˈ)prē-ˈfig-yər, *esp Brit* -ˈfig-ər\ *vt* **1** : to show, suggest, or announce by an antecedent type, image, or likeness **2** : to picture or imagine beforehand : FORESEE — **pre·fig·u·ra·tion** \(ˌ)prē-ˌfig-(y)ə-ˈrā-shən\ *n* — **pre·fig·u·ra·tive** \(ˈ)prē-ˈfig-(y)ə-rət-iv, -ˈfig-(y)ərt-iv\ *adj*
¹pre·fix \ˈprē-ˌfiks, prē-ˈ\ *vt* : to place in front : add as a prefix
²pre·fix \ˈprē-ˌfiks\ *n* : an affix occurring at the beginning of a word — **pre·fix·al** \ˈprē-ˌfik-səl, prē-ˈ\ *adj* — **pre·fix·al·ly** \-sə-lē\ *adv*
pre·for·ma·tion \ˌprē-fȯr-ˈmā-shən\ *n* : previous formation
preg·na·ble \ˈpreg-nə-bəl\ *adj* : capable of being taken or captured : VULNERABLE
preg·nan·cy \ˈpreg-nən-sē\ *n, pl* **-cies** : the condition or quality of being pregnant : GESTATION
preg·nant \ˈpreg-nənt\ *adj* **1** : containing unborn young **2** : abounding in fancy, wit, or resourcefulness : INVENTIVE **3** : rich in significance or implication : MEANINGFUL **4** : containing the germ or shape of future events — **preg·nant·ly** *adv*
pre·heat \(ˈ)prē-ˈhēt\ *vt* : to heat beforehand; *esp* : to heat (an oven) to a designated temperature before placing food therein
pre·hen·sile \prē-ˈhen(t)-səl\ *adj* : adapted for grasping esp. by wrapping around
pre·hen·sion \-ˈhen-chən\ *n* : the act of taking hold, seizing, or grasping
pre·his·tor·ic \ˌprē-(h)is-ˈtȯr-ik\ *adj* : of, relating to, or existing in times antedating written history — **pre·his·tor·i·cal** \-i-kəl\ *adj* — **pre·his·tor·i·cal·ly** \-i-k(ə-)lē\ *adv*
pre·his·to·ry \(ˈ)prē-ˈhis-t(ə-)rē\ *n* : a history of the antecedents of an event or situation — **pre·his·to·ri·an** \ˌprē-(h)is-ˈtōr-ē-ən\ *n*
pre·judge \(ˈ)prē-ˈjəj\ *vt* : to judge before hearing or before full and sufficient examination — **pre·judg·ment** \-ˈjəj-mənt\ *n*
¹prej·u·dice \ˈprej-əd-əs\ *n* **1** : DAMAGE; *esp* : detriment to one's legal rights or claims **2 a** (1) : preconceived judgment or opinion (2) : a favoring or dislike of something without just grounds or before sufficient knowledge **b** : an irrational attitude of hostility directed against an individual, a group, or a race
²prejudice *vt* **1** : to injure or damage by some judgment or action esp. at law **2** : to cause to have prejudice : BIAS
prej·u·di·cial \ˌprej-ə-ˈdish-əl\ *adj* **1** : tending to injure or impair : DETRIMENTAL **2** : leading to premature judgment or unwarranted opinion — **prej·u·di·cial·ly** \-ˈdish-(ə-)lē\ *adv* — **prej·u·di·cial·ness** \-ˈdish-əl-nəs\ *n*
prel·a·cy \ˈprel-ə-sē\ *n, pl* **-cies** **1** : the office or dignity of a prelate **2** : the whole body of prelates **3** : episcopal church government
prel·ate \ˈprel-ət\ *n* : a high-ranking clergyman (as a bishop)
¹pre·lim·i·nary \pri-ˈlim-ə-ˌner-ē\ *n, pl* **-nar·ies** : something that precedes the main business or event
²preliminary *adj* : preceding the main discourse or business : INTRODUCTORY — **pre·lim·i·nar·i·ly** \-ˌlim-ə-ˈner-ə-lē\ *adv*
¹prel·ude \ˈprel-ˌyüd, ˈprā-ˌlüd\ *n* **1** : an introductory performance, action, or event **2 a** : a musical section or movement introducing the theme or chief subject **b** : a short musical piece (as an organ solo) played at the beginning of a church service
²prelude *vb* **1** : to give, play, or serve as a prelude **2** : FORESHADOW — **pre·lud·er** *n*
pre·ma·ture \ˌprē-mə-ˈt(y)u̇(ə)r, -ˈchu̇(ə)r\ *adj* : happening, arriving, existing, or performed before the proper or usual time — **premature** *n* — **pre·ma·ture·ly** *adv*
pre·med·i·cal \(ˈ)prē-ˈmed-i-kəl\ *adj* : preceding and preparing for the professional study of medicine
pre·med·i·tate \pri-ˈmed-ə-ˌtāt, ˈprē-\ *vt* : to think about and plan beforehand — **pre·med·i·tat·ed·ly** \-ˌtāt-əd-lē\ *adv* — **pre·med·i·ta·tion** \pri-ˌmed-ə-ˈtā-shən, ˌprē-\ *n*
¹pre·mier \pri-ˈm(y)i(ə)r; ˈprē-mē-ər, ˈprem-ē-\ *adj* : first in position, rank, or importance : PRINCIPAL
²premier *n* : the chief minister of government : the prime minister — **pre·mier·ship** \-ˌship\ *n*
¹pre·miere \pri-ˈmye(ə)r, -ˈmi(ə)r\ *n* : a first performance or exhibition
²premiere *adj* : OUTSTANDING, CHIEF
¹prem·ise \ˈprem-əs\ *n* **1** : a proposition assumed as a basis of argument or inference **2** *pl* : matters previously stated **3** *pl* **a** : a tract of land with the buildings thereon **b** : a building or part of a building usu. with its grounds or other appurtenances
²premise *vt* **1** : to set forth beforehand as introductory or as postulated : POSTULATE **2** : to offer as a premise in an argument
¹pre·mi·um \ˈprē-mē-əm\ *n* **1 a** : a reward or recompense for a particular act **b** : a sum over and above a regular price or a face or par value **c** : something given free or at a reduced price with the purchase of a product or service **2** : the amount paid for a contract of insurance **3** : a high value or a value in excess of that normally or usu. expected
²premium *adj* : of exceptional quality, value, or price
pre·mo·ni·tion \ˌprē-mə-ˈnish-ən, ˌprem-ə-\ *n* **1** : previous warning or notice : FOREWARNING **2** : anticipation of an event without conscious reason : PRESENTIMENT — **pre·mon·i·to·ry** \prē-ˈmän-ə-ˌtōr-ē\ *adj*
pre·na·tal \(ˈ)prē-ˈnāt-ᵊl\ *adj* : occurring or existing before birth — **pre·na·tal·ly** \-ᵊl-ē\ *adv*
pren·tice \ˈprent-əs\ *n* : APPRENTICE 1, LEARNER — **prentice** *adj*
pre·oc·cu·pied \prē-ˈäk-yə-ˌpīd\ *adj* **1** : lost in thought : ENGROSSED **2** : already occupied
pre·oc·cu·py *vt* **-pied**; **-py·ing** **1** \prē-ˈäk-yə-ˌpī\ : to engage or engross the attention of beforehand or preferentially **2** \(ˈ)prē-\ : to take possession of or fill beforehand or before another — **pre·oc·cu·pa·tion** \(ˌ)prē-ˌäk-yə-ˈpā-shən\ *n*

pre·op·er·a·tive \(')prē-'äp-(ə-)rət-iv, -'äp-ə-,rāt-\ *adj* : occurring during the period preceding a surgical operation — **pre·op·er·a·tive·ly** *adv*

pre·or·dain \,prē-ȯr-'dān\ *vt* : to decree in advance : FOREORDAIN — **pre·or·di·na·tion** \(,)prē-,ȯrd-ᵊn-'ā-shən\ *n*

¹prep \'prep\ *n* : PREPARATORY SCHOOL

²prep *vb* **prepped**; **prep·ping** 1 : to attend preparatory school 2 : to engage in preparatory study or training 3 : to get ready : PREPARE

prep·a·ra·tion \,prep-ə-'rā-shən\ *n* 1 : the action or process of making something ready for use or service or of getting ready for some occasion, test, or duty 2 : a state of being prepared : READINESS 3 : a preparatory act or measure 4 : something that is prepared

pre·par·a·to·ry \pri-'par-ə-,tōr-ē\ *adj* : preparing or serving to prepare for something : INTRODUCTORY, PRELIMINARY

preparatory school *n* : a usu. private school preparing students primarily for college

pre·pare \pri-'pa(ə)r\ *vb* 1 : to make or get ready 2 : to put together : COMPOUND — **pre·par·er** *n*

pre·par·ed·ness \pri-'par-əd-nəs, -'pa(ə)rd-\ *n* : the quality or state of being prepared; *esp* : a state of adequate preparation for war

pre·pay \(')prē-'pā\ *vt* **pre·paid**; **pre·pay·ing** : to pay or pay the charge on in advance — **pre·pay·ment** \-'pā-mənt\ *n*

pre·pon·der·ance \pri-'pän-d(ə-)rən(t)s\ *n* 1 : a superiority in weight or in power, importance, or strength 2 : a superiority or excess in number or quantity

pre·pon·der·ant \pri-'pän-d(ə-)rənt\ *adj* 1 : outweighing others: PREDOMINANT 2 : having greater frequency or prevalence — **pre·pon·der·ant·ly** *adv*

pre·pon·der·ate \pri-'pän-də-,rāt\ *vi* 1 : to exceed in weight, power, or importance : PREDOMINATE 2 : to exceed in numbers

prep·o·si·tion \,prep-ə-'zish-ən\ *n* : a linguistic form that combines with a noun or pronoun to form a phrase — **prep·o·si·tion·al** \-'zish-nəl, -ən-ᵊl\ *adj* — **prep·o·si·tion·al·ly** \-ē\ *adv*

pre·pos·sess \,prē-pə-'zes\ *vt* 1 : to cause to be preoccupied with an idea, belief, or attitude 2 : to influence beforehand; *esp* : to move to a favorable opinion beforehand

pre·pos·sess·ing *adj* : tending to create a favorable impression : ATTRACTIVE

pre·pos·ses·sion \,prē-pə-'zesh-ən\ *n* 1 : an attitude, belief, or impression formed beforehand : PREJUDICE 2 : an exclusive concern with one idea or object

pre·pos·ter·ous \pri-'päs-t(ə-)rəs\ *adj* : contrary to nature, reason, or common sense : ABSURD — **pre·pos·ter·ous·ly** *adv* — **pre·pos·ter·ous·ness** *n*

pre·puce \'prē-,pyüs\ *n* : FORESKIN — **pre·pu·tial** \prē-'pyü-shəl\ *n*

pre·req·ui·site \(')prē-'rek-wə-zət\ *n* : something that is required beforehand or is necessary as a preliminary to something else — **prerequisite** *adj*

pre·rog·a·tive \pri-'räg-ət-iv\ *n* : a superior privilege or advantage; *esp* : a right attached to an office, rank, or status

¹pres·age \'pres-ij\ *n* 1 : something that foreshadows or portends a future event : OMEN 2 : FOREBODING, PRESENTIMENT

²pres·age \'pres-ij, pri-'sāj\ *vt* 1 : to give an omen or warning of : FORESHADOW 2 : FORETELL, PREDICT

pres·by·ter \'prez-bət-ər, 'pres-\ *n* 1 : a member of the governing body of an early Christian church 2 : a Christian priest

Pres·by·te·ri·an \,prez-bə-'tir-ē-ən, ,pres-\ *adj* 1 *often not cap* : characterized by a system of representative governing councils of ministers and elders 2 : of, relating to, or constituting a Protestant Christian church that is presbyterian in government and traditionally Calvinistic in doctrine — **Presbyterian** *n* — **Pres·by·te·ri·an·ism** \-ē-ə-,niz-əm\ *n*

pres·by·tery \'prez-bə-,ter-ē, 'pres-\ *n*, *pl* **-ter·ies** : a ruling body in presbyterian churches consisting of the ministers and representative elders from congregations within a district

pre·school \'prē-'skül\ *adj* : of, relating to, or constituting the period in a child's life from infancy to the age of five or six

pre·science \'prēsh-(ē-)ən(t)s, 'presh-\ *n* : foreknowledge of events: a : omniscience with regard to the future b : FORESIGHT — **pre·scient** \-(ē-)ənt\ *adj* — **pre·scient·ly** *adv*

pre·scribe \pri-'skrīb\ *vb* 1 a : to lay down as a guide, direction, or rule of action : ORDAIN b : to specify with authority 2 : to order or direct the use of something as a remedy — **pre·scrib·er** *n*

pre·scrip·tion \pri-'skrip-shən\ *n* 1 : the action of prescribing 2 : a written direction or order for the preparation and use of a medicine; *also* : a medicine prescribed — **pre·scrip·tive** \-'skrip-tiv\ *adj* — **pre·scrip·tive·ly** *adv*

pres·ence \'prez-ᵊn(t)s\ *n* 1 : the fact or condition of being present 2 : the part of space within one's immediate vicinity 3 : one that is present 4 : the bearing or air of a person; *esp* : stately or distinguished bearing 5 : something held to be present

¹pres·ent \'prez-ᵊnt\ *n* : something presented : GIFT

²pre·sent \pri-'zent\ *vt* 1 a : to bring or introduce into the presence of someone b : to bring (as a play) before the public c : to introduce (one person) formally to another 2 : to make a gift to 3 : to give or bestow formally 4 : to lay (a charge) against a person 5 : to offer to view : DISPLAY, SHOW 6 : to aim, point, or direct (as a weapon) so as to face something or in a particular direction — **pre·sent·er** *n*

³pres·ent \'prez-ᵊnt\ *adj* 1 : now existing or in progress 2 a : being in view or at hand b : existing in something mentioned or under consideration 3 : of, relating to, or constituting a verb tense that expresses present time or the time of speaking

⁴pres·ent \'prez-ᵊnt\ *n* 1 *pl* : the present words or statements; *esp* : the legal instrument in which these words are used 2 : a verb form in the present tense 3 : the present time

pre·sent·a·ble \pri-'zent-ə-bəl\ *adj* 1 : capable of being presented 2 : being in condition to be seen or inspected esp. by the critical

pre·sen·ta·tion \,prē-,zen-'tā-shən, ,prez-ᵊn-\ *n* 1 : the act of presenting 2 : something presented: as a : something offered or given : GIFT b : something set forth for the attention of the mind — **pre·sen·ta·tion·al** \-shnəl, -shən-ᵊl\ *adj*

pres·ent–day \,prez-ᵊnt-,dā\ *adj* : now existing or occurring : CURRENT

pre·sen·ti·ment \pri-'zent-ə-mənt\ *n* : a feeling that something will or is about to happen : PREMONITION

pres·ent·ly \'prez-ᵊnt-lē\ *adv* 1 : before long : SOON 2 : at the present time : NOW

pre·sent·ment \pri-'zent-mənt\ *n* : the act of presenting

pres·er·va·tion \,prez-ər-'vā-shən\ *n* : the act of preserving : the state of being preserved

¹pre·serv·a·tive \pri-'zər-vət-iv\ *adj* : having the power of preserving

²preservative *n* : something that preserves; *esp* : an additive used to protect against decay, discoloration, or spoilage

¹pre·serve \pri-'zərv\ *vt* 1 : to keep safe from harm or destruction : PROTECT 2 a : to keep alive, intact, or free from decay or decomposition b : to keep up : MAINTAIN, RETAIN 3 : to prepare (as by canning or pickling) for future use — **pre·serv·a·ble** \-'zər-və-bəl\ *adj* — **pre·serv·er** *n*

²preserve *n* 1 : fruit canned or made into jams or jellies or cooked whole or in large pieces with sugar so as to keep its shape — often used in pl. 2 : an area restricted for the protection and preservation of natural resources (as animals and trees) 3 : something regarded as reserved for certain persons

pre·set \(ˈ)prē-ˈset\ *vt* : to set beforehand

pre·side \pri-ˈzīd\ *vi* **1** : to occupy the place of authority : act as chairman **2** : to exercise guidance or control

pres·i·den·cy \ˈprez-əd-ən-sē, ˈprez-dən-; ˈprez-ə-ˌden(t)-sē\ *n, pl* **-cies** **1** : the office or term of a president **2** : the jurisdiction or function of a president

pres·i·dent \ˈprez-əd-ənt, ˈprez-dənt, ˈprez-ə-ˌdent\ *n* **1** : one who presides over a meeting or assembly **2** : the chief officer of a corporation, institution, or organization **3 a** : an elected official serving as both chief of state and chief political executive **b** : an elected official having the position of chief of state but usu. only minimal political powers — **pres·i·den·tial** \ˌprez-ə-ˈden-chəl\ *adj*

pre·sort \(ˈ)prē-ˈsȯrt\ *vt* : to sort (outgoing mail) by zip code usu. before delivery to a post office

[1]**press** \ˈpres\ *n* **1** : a crowded condition : CROWD, THRONG **2** : an apparatus or machine for exerting pressure (as for shaping material, extracting liquid, drilling, or preventing something from warping) **3** : CLOSET **4** : an act of pressing or pushing : PRESSURE **5** : the properly smoothed and creased condition of a freshly pressed garment **6 a** : PRINTING PRESS **b** : the act or the process of printing **c** : a printing or publishing establishment **7 a** : the gathering and publishing of news : JOURNALISM **b** : newspapers, periodicals, and often radio and television news broadcasting

[2]**press** *vb* **1** : to act upon through steady pushing or thrusting force exerted in contact : SQUEEZE **2 a** : ASSAIL **b** : OPPRESS **3 a** : to squeeze so as to force out the juice or contents of **b** : to squeeze out **4 a** : to flatten out or smooth by bearing down upon; *esp* : to smooth by ironing **b** : to squeeze with an apparatus into a desired shape **5** : to urge strongly or forcefully : CONSTRAIN **6 a** : to present earnestly or insistently : STRESS **b** : to follow through (a course of action) **7** : to clasp in affection or courtesy : EMBRACE **8 a** : to crowd closely : MASS **b** : to force or push one's way **9** : to seek urgently : CONTEND — **press·er** *n*

[3]**press** *vt* : to force into service esp. in the army or navy : IMPRESS

press agent *n* : an agent employed to establish and maintain good public relations through publicity

press conference *n* : an interview given by a public figure to newsmen by appointment

press·ing *adj* **1** : urgently important : CRITICAL **2** : EARNEST, WARM

press·man \ˈpres-mən, -ˌman\ *n* : an operator of a press; *esp* : the operator of a printing press

press·room \ˈpres-ˌrüm, -ˌrům\ *n* : a room in a printing plant containing the printing presses

[1]**pres·sure** \ˈpresh-ər\ *n* **1 a** : the action of pressing **b** : the condition of being pressed **2 a** : a painful feeling of weight or burden : OPPRESSION, DISTRESS **b** : a burdensome or restricting force or influence **3 a** : the action of a force against an opposing force **b** : the force exerted over a surface divided by its area **c** : ELECTROMOTIVE FORCE **4** : the stress of matters demanding attention : URGENCY

[2]**pressure** *vt* **pres·sured**; **pres·sur·ing** \ˈpresh-(ə-)riŋ\ **1** : to apply pressure to : CONSTRAIN **2** : PRESSURIZE **3** : to cook in a pressure cooker

pressure cooker *n* : a utensil for quick cooking or preserving of foods by means of steam under pressure

pres·sur·ize \ˈpresh-ə-ˌrīz\ *vt* **1** : to maintain near-normal atmospheric pressure in (as an airplane cabin) during high-level flight **2** : to apply pressure to **3** : to design to withstand pressure — **pres·sur·i·za·tion** \ˌpresh-ə-rə-ˈzā-shən\ *n* — **pres·sur·iz·er** *n*

pres·ti·dig·i·ta·tion \ˌpres-tə-ˌdij-ə-ˈtā-shən\ *n* : SLEIGHT OF HAND, LEGERDEMAIN — **pres·ti·dig·i·ta·tor** \-ˈdij-ə-ˌtāt-ər\ *n*

pres·tige \pre-ˈstēzh, -ˈstēj\ *n* **1** : importance or estimation in the eyes of people : high standing : REPUTE **2** : commanding position in men's minds : ASCENDANCY — **pres·ti·gious** \-ˈstij-əs\ *adj* — **pres·ti·gious·ly** *adv* — **pres·ti·gious·ness** *n*

pres·to \ˈpres-tō\ *adv (or adj)* : at once : QUICKLY

pre·sume \pri-ˈzüm\ *vb* **1** : to undertake without leave or clear justification : DARE, VENTURE **2** : to suppose to be true without proof **3** : to act or behave boldly without reason for doing so; *esp* : to take liberties — **pre·sum·a·ble** \-ˈzü-mə-bəl\ *adj* — **pre·sum·a·bly** \-blē\ *adv* — **pre·sum·er** *n*

pre·sum·ing *adj* : PRESUMPTUOUS — **pre·sum·ing·ly** \-ˈzü-miŋ-lē\ *adv*

pre·sump·tion \pri-ˈzəm(p)-shən\ *n* **1** : presumptuous attitude or conduct : AUDACITY **2 a** : strong grounds for believing something to be so in spite of lack of proof **b** : a conclusion reached on strong grounds of belief

pre·sump·tive \-ˈzəm(p)-tiv\ *adj* **1** : giving grounds for reasonable opinion or belief **2** : based on probability or presumption — **pre·sump·tive·ly** *adv*

pre·sump·tu·ous \pri-ˈzəm(p)-ch(ə-w)əs\ *adj* : overstepping due bounds : taking liberties : OVERWEENING — **pre·sump·tu·ous·ly** *adv* — **pre·sump·tu·ous·ness** *n*

pre·sup·pose \ˌprē-sə-ˈpōz\ *vt* : to suppose beforehand : take for granted — **pre·sup·po·si·tion** \(ˌ)prē-ˌsəp-ə-ˈzish-ən\ *n*

pre·tend \pri-ˈtend\ *vb* **1** : to hold out the appearance of being, possessing, or performing : PROFESS **2 a** : to make believe : feign an action, part, or role in a play **b** : to hold out, represent, or assert falsely **3** : to put in a claim (as to a throne or title) — **pre·tend·er** *n*

pre·tense *or* **pre·tence** \ˈprē-ˌten(t)s, pri-ˈ\ *n* **1** : a claim made or implied and usu. not supported by fact **2 a** : mere ostentation : PRETENTIOUSNESS **b** : a pretentious act or assertion **3** : an attempt to attain a condition or quality **4** : professed rather than real intention or purpose : PRETEXT **5** : MAKE-BELIEVE, FICTION **6** : false show : SIMULATION

pre·ten·sion \pri-ˈten-chən\ *n* **1** : PRETEXT **2** : PRETENSE 1; *also* : an effort to establish a claim made or implied **3** : a claim for or right to attention or honor because of merit **4** : PRETENTIOUSNESS, VANITY

pre·ten·tious \-chəs\ *adj* **1** : making or having claims esp. as to excellence or worth : SHOWY, OSTENTATIOUS **2** : making demands on one's skill, ability, or means : AMBITIOUS — **pre·ten·tious·ly** *adv* — **pre·ten·tious·ness** *n*

pret·er·it *or* **pret·er·ite** \ˈpret-ə-rət\ *adj* : of, relating to, or constituting a verb tense that indicates action in the past without reference to duration, continuance, or repetition — **preterit** *n*

pre·ter·mit \ˌprēt-ər-ˈmit\ *vt* **-mit·ted**; **-mit·ting** **1** : to let pass without mention or notice : OMIT **2** : to leave undone : NEGLECT **3** : to break off : SUSPEND — **pre·ter·mis·sion** \-ˈmish-ən\ *n*

pre·ter·nat·u·ral \ˌprēt-ər-ˈnach-(ə-)rəl\ *adj* **1** : not conforming to what is natural or regular in nature : ABNORMAL **2** : inexplicable by ordinary means — **pre·ter·nat·u·ral·ly** \-ˈnach-(ə-)rə-lē, -ˈnach-ər-lē\ *adv*

pre·text \ˈprē-ˌtekst\ *n* : something (as a claimed intent or motive) put forward in order to conceal a real intent, motive, or state of affairs

pret·ti·fy \ˈprit-i-ˌfī, ˈpu̇rt-\ *vt* **-fied**; **-fy·ing** : to make pretty — **pret·ti·fi·ca·tion** \ˌprit-i-fə-ˈkā-shən, ˌpu̇rt-\ *n*

[1]**pret·ty** \ˈprit-ē, ˈpu̇rt-\ *adj* **1 a** : ARTFUL, CLEVER **b** : PAT, APT **2** : pleasing by delicacy or grace esp. of appearance or sound **3** : FINE, GOOD — often used ironically **4** : moderately large : CONSIDERABLE — **pret·ti·ly** \ˈprit-ᵊl-ē, ˈpu̇rt-\ *adv* — **pret·ti·ness** \ˈprit-ē-nəs, ˈpu̇rt-\ *n* — **pret·ty·ish** \-ē-ish\ *adj*

[2]**pret·ty** \ˌpu̇rt-ē, pərt-ē (*unstressed* pərt-), ˌprit-ē\ *adv* : in some degree : MODERATELY

[3]**pretty** *like* [1]\ *n, pl* **pretties** **1** : a pretty person or thing **2** *pl* : dainty clothes

pret·zel \'pret-səl\ *n* : a brittle, glazed and salted, and usu. twisted cracker

pre·vail \pri-'vāl\ *vi* 1 : to gain ascendancy through strength or superiority : TRIUMPH 2 : to be or become effective or effectual 3 : to urge successfully 4 : to be frequent : PREDOMINATE 5 : to be or continue in use or fashion : PERSIST

pre·vail·ing *adj* 1 : having superior force or influence 2 a : most frequent b : generally current : COMMON — **pre·vail·ing·ly** \-'vā-liŋ-lē\ *adv*

prev·a·lent \'prev-(ə-)lənt\ *adj* 1 : being in ascendancy : DOMINANT 2 : generally or widely accepted, practiced, or favored : WIDESPREAD — **prev·a·lence** \-(ə-)lən(t)s\ *n* — **prev·a·lent·ly** *adv*

pre·var·i·cate \pri-'var-ə-ˌkāt\ *vi* : to deviate from the truth : EQUIVOCATE — **pre·var·i·ca·tion** \-ˌvar-ə-'kā-shən\ *n* — **pre·var·i·ca·tor** \-'var-ə-ˌkāt-ər\ *n*

pre·vent \pri-'vent\ *vt* : to keep from happening, acting, or succeeding : HINDER, STOP — **pre·vent·a·ble** \-ə-bəl\ *adj* — **pre·vent·er** *n*

pre·vent·a·tive \-'vent-ət-iv\ *adj or n* : PREVENTIVE

pre·ven·tion \pri-'ven-chən\ *n* : the act of preventing or hindering

¹pre·ven·tive \-'vent-iv\ *n* : something that prevents; *esp* : something used to prevent disease

²preventive *adj* : devoted to, concerned with, or undertaken for prevention — **pre·ven·tive·ly** *adv* — **pre·ven·tive·ness** *n*

¹pre·view \'prē-ˌvyü\ *vt* : to view or to show in advance

²preview *n* : an advance showing or viewing: as a : a showing of snatches from a motion picture advertised for appearance in the near future b : a statement giving advance information c : a preliminary survey

pre·vi·ous \'prē-vē-əs\ *adj* 1 : going before in time or order : PRECEDING 2 : acting too soon : PREMATURE — **pre·vi·ous·ly** *adv* — **pre·vi·ous·ness** *n*

previous to *prep* : prior to : BEFORE

pre·vi·sion \prē-'vizh-ən\ *n* 1 : FORESIGHT, PRESCIENCE 2 : FORECAST, PREDICTION

pre·war \'prē-'wȯ(ə)r\ *adj* : occurring or existing before a war

¹prey \'prā\ *n* 1 : an animal taken by a predator as food 2 : a person that is helpless or unable to resist attack : VICTIM 3 : the act or habit of preying

²prey *vi* 1 : to raid for booty 2 : to seize and devour something as prey 3 : to have an injurious, destructive, or wasting effect — **prey·er** *n*

¹price \'prīs\ *n* 1 : the amount of money given or demanded for a specified thing 2 : the cost at which something is obtainable

²price *vt* 1 : to set a price on 2 : to ask the price of 3 : to drive by raising prices excessively — **pric·er** *n*

price·less \'prīs-ləs\ *adj* 1 : having a value beyond any price : INVALUABLE 2 : surprisingly amusing or odd

¹prick \'prik\ *n* 1 : a mark or shallow hole made by a pointed instrument 2 : a pointed instrument or part 3 : an instance of pricking; *also* : the sensation of being pricked

²prick *vb* 1 a : to pierce slightly with a sharp point b : to have or cause a pricking sensation 2 : to cause to feel anguish, grief, or remorse 3 : to urge on a horse with spurs 4 : to mark or outline with or as if with pricks 5 : to direct forward or upward : make or become erect — **prick up one's ears** : to listen intently

prick·er \'prik-ər\ *n* : BRIAR, PRICKLE, THORN

¹prick·le \'prik-əl\ *n* 1 : a fine sharp projection (as on a plant) 2 : a prickling sensation

²prickle *vb* **prick·led**; **prick·ling** \'prik-(ə-)liŋ\ 1 : to prick lightly 2 : TINGLE

prick·ly \'prik-lē\ *adj* 1 : full of or covered with prickles 2 : PRICKING, STINGING — **prick·li·ness** *n*

¹pride \'prīd\ *n* 1 : the quality or state of being proud: as a : excessive self-esteem : CONCEIT b : a reasonable or justifiable self-respect c : delight or elation arising from some act or possession 2 : proud or disdainful behavior or treatment : DISDAIN 3 a : the best part or condition : PRIME b : something that is or is fit to be a source of pride 4 : a company of lions

²pride *vt* : to indulge in pride : PLUME

pride·ful \'prīd-fəl\ *adj* : full of pride: as a : HAUGHTY b : ELATED — **pride·ful·ly** \-fə-lē\ *adv* — **pride·ful·ness** *n*

prie–dieu \prēd-'yə(r)\ *n, pl* **prie–dieux** \-'yə(r)(z)\ : a small kneeling bench designed for use by a person at prayer and fitted with a raised shelf on which the elbows or a book may be rested

priest \'prēst\ *n* : a person who has the authority to conduct religious rites; *esp* : a clergyman ranking below a bishop and above a deacon — **priest·ess** \'prē-stəs\ *n*

priest·hood \'prēst-ˌhu̇d, 'prē-ˌstu̇d\ *n* 1 : the office, dignity, or status of a priest 2 : the whole group of priests

priest·ly \'prēst-lē\ *adj* 1 : of or relating to a priest or the priesthood 2 : characteristic of or befitting a priest — **priest·li·ness** *n*

prig \'prig\ *n* : a person who offends or irritates others by a too careful or rigid observance of niceties and proprieties (as of speech or manners) — **prig·gery** \'prig-ə-rē\ *n* — **prig·gish** \'prig-ish\ *adj* — **prig·gish·ly** *adv* — **prig·gish·ness** *n*

prim \'prim\ *adj* : very or excessively formal and precise (as in conduct or dress) — **prim·ly** *adv* — **prim·ness** *n*

pri·ma·cy \'prī-mə-sē\ *n, pl* **-cies** 1 : the condition of being first (as in time, place, or rank) 2 : the office, status, or dignity of a bishop of the highest rank

pri·ma don·na \ˌprim-ə-'dän-ə, ˌprē-mə-\ *n, pl* **prima donnas** 1 : a principal female singer (as in an opera) 2 : an extremely sensitive, vain, or undisciplined person

¹pri·ma fa·cie \ˌprī-mə-'fā-shə, -s(h)ē\ *adv* : at first view : on the first appearance

²prima facie *adj* 1 : APPARENT, EVIDENT 2 : legally sufficient to establish a fact or a case unless disproved

pri·mal \'prī-məl\ *adj* 1 : ORIGINAL, PRIMITIVE 2 : first in importance : CHIEF

pri·mar·i·ly \prī-'mer-ə-lē\ *adv* : in the first place : ORIGINALLY; *also* : FUNDAMENTALLY

¹pri·mary \'prī-ˌmer-ē, 'prīm-(ə-)rē\ *adj* 1 a : first in order of time or development : INITIAL, PRIMITIVE b : not derived from or dependent on something else c : coming before and usu. preparatory for something else 2 a : of first rank, importance, or value : CHIEF b : BASIC, FUNDAMENTAL c : of, relating to, or constituting the strongest of the three or four degrees of stress d : not derivable from other colors 3 : expressive of present or future time

²primary *n, pl* **-mar·ies** 1 : something that is primary: as a : a planet as distinguished from its satellites b : a primary quill or feather c : any of a set of colors (as red, yellow, or blue) from which all other colors may be derived 2 : an election in which voters select party candidates for political office, choose party officials, or select delegates for a party convention

primary cell *n* : a cell that converts chemical energy into electrical energy by irreversible chemical reactions

pri·mate \'prī-ˌmāt *or esp for 1* -mət\ *n* 1 : a bishop or archbishop governing or having highest status in a district, nation, or church 2 : any of the group of mammals that includes man, the apes, and monkeys

¹prime \'prīm\ *n* 1 : the first part : earliest stage 2 : the most active, thriving, or successful stage or period (as of one's life) 3 : the chief or best individual or part : PICK

²prime *adj* 1 : first in time : ORIGINAL 2 a : having no factor except itself and one b : having no common factor except one 3 a : first in rank, authority, or significance : PRINCIPAL b : first in excellence, quality, or value c : of the highest grade regularly marketed — used of meat and esp. beef — **prime•ly** *adv* — **prime•ness** *n*

³prime *vt* 1 : to prepare for firing by supplying with priming or a primer 2 : to apply (as in painting) a first color, coating, or preparation to 3 : to put into working order by filling or charging with something 4 : to instruct beforehand : COACH

¹prim•er \'prim-ər, *esp Brit* 'prī-mər\ *n* 1 : a small book for teaching children to read 2 : a small introductory book on a subject

²prim•er \'prī-mər\ *n* 1 : a device (as a cap, tube, or wafer) containing a substance that ignites an explosive charge and that is itself ignited by friction, percussion, or electricity 2 : PRIMING

pri•me•val \prī-'mē-vəl\ *adj* : of or relating to the earliest ages : PRIMITIVE — **pri•me•val•ly** \-və-lē\ *adv*

prim•ing *n* 1 : the explosive used in priming a charge 2 : the material used in priming a surface

¹prim•i•tive \'prim-ət-iv\ *adj* 1 : not derived : ORIGINAL, PRIMARY 2 a : of or relating to the earliest age or period : PRIMEVAL b : little evolved and closely approximating an early ancestral type 3 a : of or relating to a relatively simple people or culture b : marked by the style, simplicity, or crudity held to characterize simple people c : lacking formal or technical training : SELF-TAUGHT; *also* : produced by a self-taught artist — **prim•i•tive•ly** *adv* — **prim•i•tive•ness** *n*

²primitive *n* 1 : something primitive; *esp* : a primitive idea, term, or proposition 2 a (1) : an artist of an early period of a culture or artistic movement (2) : a later imitator or follower of such an artist b : a work of art produced by a primitive artist 3 : a member of a primitive people

pri•mo•gen•i•tor \,prī-mō-'jen-ət-ər\ *n* : ANCESTOR, FOREFATHER

pri•mo•gen•i•ture \-'jen-ə-,chu̇r, -'jen-i-chər\ *n* 1 : the state of being the firstborn among the children of a pair of parents 2 : an exclusive right of inheritance belonging to the eldest son

pri•mor•di•al \prī-'mȯrd-ē-əl\ *adj* 1 a : first created or developed : PRIMEVAL b : earliest formed in the growth of an individual or organ : PRIMITIVE 2 : FUNDAMENTAL, PRIMARY — **pri•mor•di•al•ly** \-ē-ə-lē\ *adv*

primp \'primp\ *vb* : to dress, adorn, or arrange in a careful or finicky manner

prim•rose \'prim-,rōz\ *n* : any of several low herbs with clusters of showy variously colored flowers

prince \'prin(t)s\ *n* 1 a : MONARCH, KING b : the ruler of a principality or state 2 : a male member of a royal family; *esp* : a son of the king 3 : a nobleman of varying rank 4 : a person of high standing in his class or profession — **prince•dom** \-dəm\ *n* — **prince•ship** \-,ship\ *n*

prince•ling \'prin(t)s-liŋ\ *n* : a petty prince

prince•ly \'prin(t)s-lē\ *adj* 1 : of or relating to a prince : ROYAL 2 : befitting a prince : NOBLE, MAGNIFICENT — **prince•li•ness** *n*

¹prin•cess \'prin(t)-səs, 'prin-,ses, prin-'ses\ *n* 1 : a female member of a royal family; *esp* : a daughter or granddaughter of a sovereign 2 : the consort of a prince

²princess *like* ¹\ *or* **prin•cesse** \prin-'ses\ *adj* : close-fitting and usu. with gores from neck to flaring hemline

¹prin•ci•pal \'prin(t)-sə-pəl\ *adj* : most important, consequential, or influential : CHIEF — **prin•ci•pal•ly** \-pə-lē\ *adv*

²principal *n* 1 a : a chief or head man or woman b : the head of a school c : one who employs another to act for him 2 : a capital sum placed at interest, due as a debt, or used as a fund — **prin•ci•pal•ship** \-,ship\ *n*

prin•ci•pal•i•ty \,prin(t)-sə-'pal-ət-ē\ *n, pl* **-ties** : the position, territory, or jurisdiction of a prince

prin•ci•ple \'prin(t)-sə-pəl\ *n* 1 a : a comprehensive and fundamental law, doctrine, or assumption b : a rule or code of conduct; *also* : habitual devotion to right principles c : the laws or facts of nature underlying the working of an artificial device 2 a : a primary source : ORIGIN b : an underlying faculty or endowment 3 : a constituent that exhibits or imparts a characteristic quality

prink \'priŋk\ *vb* : PRIMP — **prink•er** *n*

¹print \'print\ *n* 1 : a mark made by pressure : IMPRESSION 2 : a device or instrument for impressing or forming a print 3 a : printed state or form b : printed matter c : printed letters : TYPE 4 a : a copy made by printing (as from a photographic negative) b : cloth with a pattern applied by printing; *also* : an article of such cloth — **in print** : procurable from the publisher — **out of print** : not procurable from the publisher

²print *vb* 1 a : to make an impression in or on b : to cause (as a mark) to be stamped c : to produce impressions with a relief surface (as type or a plate) d : to impress (a surface) with a design by pressure 2 : to publish in printed form 3 : to write in unconnected letters like those made by a printing press 4 : to make (a positive picture) on a sensitized photographic surface 5 : to reproduce by printing — **print•er** *n*

print•a•ble \'print-ə-bəl\ *adj* 1 : capable of being printed or of being printed from 2 : worthy or fit to be published — **print•a•bil•i•ty** \,print-ə-'bil-ət-ē\ *n*

printer's devil *n* : an apprentice in a printing office

print•ing *n* 1 : reproduction in printed form 2 : the art, practice, or business of a printer 3 : IMPRESSION 3b

printing press *n* : a machine that produces printed copies (as by letterpress); *esp* : one that is power driven

print•out \'print-,au̇t\ *n* : a printed record produced automatically (as by a computer)

¹pri•or \'prī(-ə)r\ *n* : the superior of a religious house

²prior *adj* 1 : earlier in time or order 2 : taking precedence logically or in importance or value

pri•or•ess \'prī-ə-rəs\ *n* : a nun corresponding in rank to a prior

pri•or•i•ty \prī-'ȯr-ət-ē\ *n, pl* **-ties** : the quality or state of coming before another in time or importance

prior to *prep* : in advance of : BEFORE

pri•o•ry \'prī-(ə-)rē\ *n, pl* **-ries** : a religious house under a prior or prioress

prism \'priz-əm\ *n* 1 : a solid whose ends are similar, equal, and parallel polygons and whose faces are parallelograms 2 : a 3-sided glass or crystal object of prism shape that breaks up light into rainbow colors

pris•mat•ic \priz-'mat-ik\ *adj* 1 : relating to, resembling, or constituting a prism 2 : formed by refraction of light through a transparent prism 3 : highly colored : BRILLIANT — **pris•mat•i•cal•ly** \-'mat-i-k(ə-)lē\ *adv*

pris•on \'priz-ᵊn\ *n* : a place or state of confinement esp. for criminals

pris•on•er \'priz-nər, -ᵊn-ər\ *n* : a person kept under involuntary restraint, confinement, or custody; *esp* : one in prison

pris•sy \'pris-ē\ *adj* : being prim and precise : FINICKY — **pris•si•ly** \'pris-ə-lē\ *adv* — **pris•si•ness** \'pris-ē-nəs\ *n*

pris•tine \'pris-,tēn\ *adj* : of or relating to the earliest period or condition : ORIGINAL, PRIMITIVE; *esp* : having the purity or freshness of the original state

pri•va•cy \'prī-və-sē\ *n, pl* **-cies** 1 : the condition of being apart from company or observation : SECLUSION 2 : SECRECY

¹pri•vate \'prī-vət\ *adj* 1 : belonging to, concerning, or reserved for the use of a particular person or group : not public 2 a : offering privacy : SECLUDED b : not publicly known : SECRET 3 : not holding public office or employment 4 : not under public control — **pri•vate•ly** *adv*

²private *n* : an enlisted man in the army ranking above a recruit and below a private first class — **in private** : PRIVATELY, SECRETLY

¹pri•va•teer \,prī-və-'ti(ə)r\ *n* 1 : an armed private ship commissioned to cruise against the commerce or warships of an enemy **2 :** the commander or one of the crew of a privateer — **pri•va•teers•man** \-'ti(ə)rz-mən\ *n*

[2]**privateer** *vi* **:** to cruise in or as a privateer

private first class *n* **:** an enlisted man in the army ranking above a private and below a corporal

pri•va•tion \prī-'vā-shən\ *n* **1 :** an act or instance of depriving **:** DEPRIVATION **2 :** the state of being deprived esp. of what is needed for existence **:** WANT

pri•va•tism \'prī-və-ˌtiz-əm\ *n* **:** the attitude of being uncommitted to or avoiding involvement in anything beyond one's immediate interests

[1]**priv•a•tive** \'priv-ət-iv\ *n* **:** a privative term, expression, or proposition; *also* **:** a privative prefix or suffix

[2]**privative** *adj* **:** constituting or predicating privation or absence of a quality — **priv•a•tive•ly** *adv*

priv•et \'priv-ət\ *n* **:** a nearly evergreen shrub of the olive family with small white flowers that is widely used for hedges

[1]**priv•i•lege** \'priv(-ə)-lij\ *n* **:** a right or immunity granted as a benefit, advantage, or favor; *esp* **:** one attached specif. to a position or an office

[2]**privilege** *vt* **:** to grant a privilege to

priv•i•leged \-lijd\ *adj* **1 :** having or enjoying one or more privileges **2 :** not subject to disclosure in a court of law

priv•i•ly \'priv-ə-lē\ *adv* **:** PRIVATELY, SECRETLY

[1]**privy** \'priv-ē\ *adj* **1 :** belonging or relating to a person in his individual rather than his official capacity **2 :** WITHDRAWN, PRIVATE **3 :** sharing in a secret

[2]**privy** *n, pl* **priv•ies :** a small building without plumbing that is used as a toilet; *also* **:** TOILET 2b

[1]**prize** \'prīz\ *n* **1 :** something won or to be won in competition or in contests of chance; *also* **:** a premium given as an inducement to buy **2 :** something exceptionally desirable

[2]**prize** *adj* **1 a :** awarded a prize **b :** awarded as a prize **2 :** outstanding of its kind

[3]**prize** *vt* **1 :** to estimate the value of **:** RATE **2 :** to value highly **:** ESTEEM

[4]**prize** *n* **1 :** something taken by force, stratagem, or threat; *esp* **:** property lawfully captured in time of war **2 :** an act of capturing or taking; *esp* **:** the wartime capture of a ship and its cargo at sea

[5]**prize** *vt* **:** to press, force, or move with or as if with a lever **:** PRY

prize•fight \'prīz-ˌfīt\ *n* **:** a contest between professional boxers for pay — **prize•fight•er** \-ər\ *n* — **prize•fight•ing** \-iŋ\ *n*

[1]**pro** \'prō\ *n, pl* **pros** \'prōz\ **1 :** a favorable argument or piece of evidence **2 :** the affirmative position or one holding it

[2]**pro** *adv* **:** on the affirmative side

[3]**pro** *n or adj* **:** PROFESSIONAL

prob•a•bil•i•ty \ˌpräb-ə-'bil-ət-ē\ *n, pl* **-ties 1 :** the quality, state, or degree of being probable **2 :** something probable

prob•a•ble \'präb-ə-bəl\ *adj* **1 :** supported by evidence strong enough to make it likely though not certain to be true **2 :** likely to happen or to have happened **:** being such as may or might be real or true — **prob•a•bly** \'präb-ə-blē, 'präb-lē\ *adv*

[1]**pro•bate** \'prō-ˌbāt\ *n* **1 :** proof before a probate court that the last will and testament of a deceased person is genuine **2 :** judicial determination of the validity of a will

[2]**probate** *vt* **:** to establish (a will) by probate as genuine and valid

pro•ba•tion \prō-'bā-shən\ *n* **1 :** subjection of an individual to a period of testing and trial to ascertain fitness (as for a job) **2 :** the suspending of a convicted offender's sentence during good behavior under the supervision of a probation officer — **pro•ba•tion•al** \-shnəl, -shən-ᵊl\ *adj* — **pro•ba•tion•al•ly** \-ē\ *adv* — **pro•ba•tion•ary** \-shə-ˌner-ē\ *adj*

pro•ba•tion•er \prō-'bā-sh(ə-)nər\ *n* **:** a person (as a new student nurse or a convict on a suspended sentence) who is undergoing probation

[1]**probe** \'prōb\ *n* **1 :** a slender instrument for examining a cavity (as a wound) **2 :** an information-gathering device sent high into the air or into outer space **3 :** a penetrating investigation

[2]**probe** *vb* **1 :** to examine with or as if with a probe **2 :** to investigate thoroughly **3 :** to make an exploratory investigation — **prob•er** *n*

pro•bi•ty \'prō-bət-ē\ *n* **:** adherence to the highest principles and ideals **:** UPRIGHTNESS

[1]**prob•lem** \'präb-ləm\ *n* **1 :** a question raised for inquiry, consideration, or solution **2 a :** an intricate unsettled question **b :** a source of perplexity or vexation

[2]**problem** *adj* **1 :** dealing with a problem of human conduct or social relationship **2 :** difficult to deal with

prob•lem•at•ic \ˌpräb-lə-'mat-ik\ *or* **prob•lem•at•i•cal** \-'mat-i-kəl\ *adj* **:** having the nature of a problem **:** difficult and uncertain **:** PUZZLING — **prob•lem•at•i•cal•ly** \-i-k(ə-)lē\ *adv*

pro•bos•cis \prə-'bäs-əs\ *n, pl* **-bos•cis•es :** the trunk of an elephant; *also* **:** a long, flexible, or prominent snout or nose

pro•ce•dure \prə-'sē-jər\ *n* **1 :** a particular often prescribed manner or method of proceeding in a process or a course of action **2 :** an action or series of actions **:** the continuance or progress of a process or action — **pro•ce•dur•al** \prə-'sēj-(ə-)rəl\ *adj* — **pro•ce•dur•al•ly** \-ē\ *adv*

pro•ceed \prō-'sēd, prə-\ *vi* **1 :** to come forth from a source **:** ISSUE **2 a :** to continue after a pause or interruption **b :** to go on in an orderly regulated way **3 a :** to begin and carry on an action, process, or movement **b :** to be in the process of being accomplished **4 :** to move along a course

pro•ceed•ing *n* **1 :** PROCEDURE **2** *pl* **:** EVENTS, HAPPENINGS **3 a** *pl* **:** legal action **:** LITIGATION **b :** a suit or action at law **4 :** AFFAIR, TRANSACTION **5** *pl* **:** an official record of things said or done

pro•ceeds \'prō-ˌsēdz\ *n pl* **:** the total amount or the profit arising from a business deal **:** RETURN

[1]**proc•ess** \'präs-ˌes, 'prōs-, -əs\ *n, pl* **proc•ess•es** \-ˌes-əz, -ə-səz, -ə-ˌsēz\ **1 a :** PROGRESS, ADVANCE **b :** something going on **:** PROCEEDING **2 a :** a natural phenomenon marked by gradual changes that lead toward a particular result **b :** a series of actions, operations, or changes conducing to an end **3 a :** the proceedings or manner of proceeding in a legal action **b :** a legal summons or writ used by a court to compel the appearance of the defendant or compliance with its orders **4 :** a prominent or projecting bodily part **:** OUTGROWTH

[2]**process** *vt* **:** to subject to a special process or treatment (as in the course of manufacture) — **proc•es•sor** \-ˌes-ər, -ə-sər, -ə-ˌsȯr\ *n*

[3]**process** *adj* **:** treated or made by a special process esp. when involving synthesis or artificial modification

pro•ces•sion \prə-'sesh-ən\ *n* **1 :** continuous forward movement **:** PROGRESSION **2 :** a group of individuals moving along in an orderly often ceremonial way

[1]**pro•ces•sion•al** \prə-'sesh-nəl, -ən-ᵊl\ *n* **:** a hymn sung during a procession (as of a choir entering the church at the beginning of a service); *also* **:** a ceremonial procession

[2]**processional** *adj* **:** of, relating to, or moving in a procession — **pro•ces•sion•al•ly** \-ē\ *adv*

pro•claim \prō-'klām\ *vt* **:** to announce publicly **:** DECLARE — **pro•claim•er** *n*

proc•la•ma•tion \ˌpräk-lə-'mā-shən\ *n* **1 :** the action of proclaiming **:** an official publication **2 :** something proclaimed

pro•cliv•i•ty \prō-'kliv-ət-ē\ *n, pl* **-ties :** a tendency or inclination of the mind or temperament **:** DISPOSITION

pro•con•sul \(')prō-'kän(t)-səl\ *n* **:** an administrator in a modern colony, dependency, or occupied area — **pro•con•sul•ar** \-s(ə-)lər\ *adj* — **pro•con•sul•ate** \-s(ə-)lət\ *n* — **pro•con•sul•ship** \-səl-ˌship\ *n*

pro•cras•ti•nate \prə-'kras-tə-ˌnāt\ *vb* **1 :** to put off repeatedly

2 : to keep postponing something supposed to be done — **pro·cras·ti·na·tion** \-ˌkras-tə-ˈnā-shən\ *n* — **pro·cras·ti·na·tor** \-ˈkras-tə-ˌnāt-ər\ *n*

pro·cre·ate \ˈprō-krē-ˌāt\ *vb* : to beget or bring forth offspring : REPRODUCE — **pro·cre·a·tion** \ˌprō-krē-ˈā-shən\ *n* — **pro·cre·a·tive** \ˈprō-krē-ˌāt-iv\ *adj* — **pro·cre·a·tor** \-ˌāt-ər\ *n*

pro·crus·te·an \prə-ˈkrəs-tē-ən\ *adj, often cap* : marked by arbitrary often ruthless disregard of individual differences or special circumstances

proc·tor \ˈpräk-tər\ *n* : SUPERVISOR, MONITOR; *esp* : one appointed to supervise students (as at an examination) — **proctor** *vb*

pro·cum·bent \prō-ˈkəm-bənt\ *adj* : lying face down

pro·cur·a·ble \prə-ˈkyu̇r-ə-bəl\ *adj* : capable of being procured

proc·u·ra·tor \ˈpräk-yə-ˌrāt-ər\ *n* : one that manages another's affairs : AGENT

pro·cure \prə-ˈkyu̇(ə)r\ *vb* **1 a** : to get possession of : OBTAIN **b** : to make women available for promiscuous sexual intercourse **2** : to bring about : ACHIEVE — **pro·cure·ment** \-mənt\ *n*

pro·cur·er \-ˈkyu̇r-ər\ *n* : one that procures; *esp* : PANDER — **pro·cur·ess** \-ˈkyu̇(ə)r-əs\ *n*

[1]**prod** \ˈpräd\ *vt* **prod·ded**; **prod·ding** **1 a** : to thrust a pointed instrument into : PRICK **b** : to incite to action : STIR **2** : to poke or stir as if with a prod — **prod·der** *n*

[2]**prod** *n* **1** : a pointed instrument used to prod **2** : an incitement to act

[1]**prod·i·gal** \ˈpräd-i-gəl\ *adj* **1** : recklessly extravagant **2** : WASTEFUL, LAVISH — **prod·i·gal·i·ty** \ˌpräd-ə-ˈgal-ət-ē\ *n* — **prod·i·gal·ly** \ˈpräd-i-g(ə-)lē\ *adv*

[2]**prodigal** *n* : a person who spends prodigally : SPENDTHRIFT, WASTREL

pro·di·gious \prə-ˈdij-əs\ *adj* **1** : exciting amazement or wonder **2** : extraordinary in bulk, quantity, or degree : ENORMOUS — **pro·di·gious·ly** *adv* — **pro·di·gious·ness** *n*

prod·i·gy \ˈpräd-ə-jē\ *n, pl* **-gies** **1** : an amazing instance, deed, or performance **2** : a highly gifted or precocious person

[1]**pro·duce** \prə-ˈd(y)üs\ *vb* **1** : to offer to view or notice : EXHIBIT **2** : to give birth or rise to : YIELD **3** : to extend in length, area, or volume **4** : to present to the public on the stage or screen or over radio or television **5** : to give being, form, or shape to : MAKE; *esp* : MANUFACTURE **6** : to accrue or cause to accrue **7** : to produce something — **pro·duc·er** *n*

[2]**pro·duce** \ˈpräd-ˌüs, ˈprōd-, -ˌyüs\ *n* **1** : something produced **2** : agricultural products; *esp* : fresh fruits and vegetables as distinguished from staple crops (as grain)

pro·duced \prə-ˈd(y)üst\ *adj* : disproportionately elongated

pro·duc·i·ble \prə-ˈd(y)ü-sə-bəl\ *adj* : capable of being produced

prod·uct \ˈpräd-(ˌ)əkt\ *n* **1** : the number or expression resulting from the multiplication of two or more numbers or expressions **2** : something produced **3** : the amount, quantity, or total produced

pro·duc·tion \prə-ˈdək-shən\ *n* **1 a** : something produced : PRODUCT **b** (1) : a literary or artistic work (2) : a work presented on the stage or screen or over the air **2 a** : the act or process of producing **b** : the making of goods available for human wants **3** : total output

pro·duc·tive \prə-ˈdək-tiv\ *adj* **1** : having the power to produce esp. in abundance **2** : effective in or bringing about a production **3** : yielding or furnishing results, benefits, or profits **4 a** : effecting or contributing to effect production **b** : yielding or devoted to the satisfaction of wants or the creation of utilities — **pro·duc·tive·ly** *adv* — **pro·duc·tive·ness** *n* — **pro·duc·tiv·i·ty** \(ˌ)prō-ˌdək-ˈtiv-ət-ē, ˌpräd-(ˌ)ək-\ *n*

prof·a·na·tion \ˌpräf-ə-ˈnā-shən, ˌprō-fə-\ *n* : the act of profaning

pro·fan·a·to·ry \prō-ˈfan-ə-ˌtōr-ē, -ˈfā-nə-\ *adj* : tending to profane : DESECRATING

[1]**pro·fane** \prō-ˈfān\ *vt* **1** : to violate or treat with irreverence, abuse, or contempt : DESECRATE **2** : to put to a wrong, unworthy, or vulgar use : DEBASE — **pro·fan·er** *n*

[2]**profane** *adj* **1** : not concerned with religion or religious purposes : SECULAR **2** : not holy because unconsecrated, impure, or defiled : UNSANCTIFIED **3** : serving to debase or defile what is holy : IRREVERENT — **pro·fane·ly** *adv* — **pro·fane·ness** \-ˈfān-nəs\ *n*

pro·fan·i·ty \prō-ˈfan-ət-ē\ *n, pl* **-ties** **1 a** : the quality or state of being profane **b** : the use of profane language **2** : profane language

pro·fess \prə-ˈfes\ *vt* **1 a** : to receive formally into a religious community following a novitiate by acceptance of the required vows **b** : to take (vows) as a member of a religious community or order **2 a** : to declare openly or freely **b** : PRETEND, CLAIM **3** : to confess one's faith in or allegiance to **4** : to practice or claim to be versed in (a calling or profession)

pro·fessed \-ˈfest\ *adj* **1** : openly declared whether truly or falsely **2** : having taken the vows of a religious order

pro·fess·ed·ly \prə-ˈfes-əd-lē, -ˈfest-lē\ *adv* **1** : AVOWEDLY **2** : ALLEGEDLY

pro·fes·sion \prə-ˈfesh-ən\ *n* **1** : the act of taking the vows of a religious community **2** : an act of openly declaring or publicly claiming a belief, faith, or opinion : PROTESTATION **3** : an avowed religious faith **4 a** : a calling requiring specialized knowledge and academic preparation **b** : a principal calling, vocation, or employment **c** : the whole body of persons engaged in a calling

[1]**pro·fes·sion·al** \prə-ˈfesh-nəl, -ən-ᵊl\ *adj* **1 a** : of, relating to, or characteristic of a profession **b** : engaged in one of the learned professions **2** : participating for gain or livelihood in an activity or field of endeavor often engaged in by amateurs **3** : following a line of conduct as though it were a profession — **pro·fes·sion·al·ly** \-ē\ *adv*

[2]**professional** *n* : one that engages in a pursuit or activity professionally

pro·fes·sion·al·ism \-ˌiz-əm\ *n* **1** : the conduct, aims, or qualities that characterize or mark a profession or a professional person **2** : the following of a profession (as athletics) for gain or livelihood

pro·fes·sor \prə-ˈfes-ər\ *n* **1** : a faculty member of the highest academic rank at an institution of higher education **2** : a teacher at a university, college, or sometimes secondary school — **pro·fes·so·ri·al** \ˌprō-fə-ˈsōr-ē-əl, ˌpräf-ə-\ *adj* — **pro·fes·so·ri·al·ly** \-ē-ə-lē\ *adv* — **pro·fes·sor·ship** \prə-ˈfes-ər-ˌship\ *n*

[1]**prof·fer** \ˈpräf-ər\ *vt* **prof·fered**; **prof·fer·ing** \ˈpräf-(ə-)riŋ\ : to present for acceptance : TENDER, OFFER

[2]**proffer** *n* : OFFER, SUGGESTION

pro·fi·cien·cy \prə-ˈfish-ən-sē\ *n, pl* **-cies** **1** : advancement in knowledge or skill **2** : the quality or state of being proficient

pro·fi·cient \prə-ˈfish-ənt\ *adj* : well advanced in an art, occupation, or branch of knowledge : ADEPT

[1]**pro·file** \ˈprō-ˌfīl\ *n* **1** : a representation of something in outline; *esp* : a human head or face represented or seen in a side view **2** : an outline seen or represented in sharp relief : CONTOUR **3** : a concise biographical sketch

[2]**profile** *vt* : to represent in profile : draw or write a profile of

[1]**prof·it** \ˈpräf-ət\ *n* **1** : a valuable return : GAIN **2** : the excess of the selling price of goods over their cost — **prof·it·less** \-ləs\ *adj*

[2]**profit** *vb* **1** : to be of service or advantage : AVAIL **2** : to derive benefit : GAIN **3** : BENEFIT

prof·it·a·ble \ˈpräf-ət-ə-bəl, ˈpräf-tə-bəl\ *adj* : affording profits : USEFUL, LUCRATIVE — **prof·it·a·ble·ness** \ˈpräf-ət-ə-bəl-nəs ˈpräf-tə-bəl-\ *n* — **prof·it·a·bly** \-blē\ *adv*

prof·i·teer \ˌpräf-ə-ˈti(ə)r\ *n* : one who makes an unreasonable profit esp. on the sale of essential goods during an emergency — **profiteer** *vi*

prof·li·ga·cy \ˈpräf-li-gə-sē\ *n* : the quality or state of being profligate

prof·li·gate \ˈpräf-li-gət\ *adj* **1** : completely given up to dissipation and licentiousness **2** : wildly extravagant : PRODIGAL — **profligate** *n* — **prof·li·gate·ly** *adv*

pro·found \prə-ˈfau̇nd\ *adj* **1 a** : having intellectual depth and insight **b** : difficult to fathom or understand **2 a** : extending far below the surface **b** : coming from, reaching to, or situated at a depth : DEEP-SEATED **3 a** : characterized by intensity of feeling or quality **b** : all encompassing : COMPLETE — **pro·found·ly** *adv* — **pro·found·ness** \-ˈfau̇n(d)-nəs\ *n*

pro·fun·di·ty \prə-ˈfən-dət-ē\ *n, pl* **-ties** **1 a** : intellectual depth **b** : something profound or abstruse **2** : the quality or state of being very profound or deep

pro·fuse \prə-ˈfyüs\ *adj* **1** : pouring forth liberally : EXTRAVAGANT **2** : exhibiting great abundance : BOUNTIFUL — **pro·fuse·ly** *adv* — **pro·fuse·ness** *n*

pro·fu·sion \prə-ˈfyü-zhən\ *n* **1** : profuse or lavish expenditure **2** : lavish display : ABUNDANCE

pro·gen·i·tor \prō-ˈjen-ət-ər\ *n* **1** : a direct ancestor : FOREFATHER **2** : ORIGINATOR, PRECURSOR

prog·e·ny \ˈpräj-ə-nē\ *n, pl* **-nies** : DESCENDANTS, CHILDREN, OFFSPRING

prog·na·thous \ˈpräg-nə-thəs, präg-ˈnā-\ *adj* : having the jaws projecting beyond the upper part of the face — **prog·na·thism** \-ˌthiz-əm\ *n*

prog·no·sis \präg-ˈnō-səs\ *n, pl* **-no·ses** \-ˈnō-ˌsēz\ **1** : a forecast of the course of a disease; *also* : the outlook given by such a forecast **2** : FORECAST, PROGNOSTICATION

prog·nos·tic \präg-ˈnäs-tik\ *n* **1** : something that foretells : OMEN **2** : PROGNOSTICATION, PROPHECY — **prognostic** *adj*

prog·nos·ti·cate \präg-ˈnäs-tə-ˌkāt\ *vt* **1** : to foretell from signs or symptoms : PREDICT, PROPHESY **2** : PRESAGE — **prog·nos·ti·ca·tor** \-ˌkāt-ər\ *n*

prog·nos·ti·ca·tion \(ˌ)präg-ˌnäs-tə-ˈkā-shən\ *n* **1** : an indication in advance : FORETOKEN **2** : an act, the fact, or the power of prognosticating : FORECAST

[1]**pro·gram** \ˈprō-ˌgram, -grəm\ *n* **1** : a brief statement or written outline of something (as a concert or play) **2** : PERFORMANCE **3** : a plan of action **4** : a sequence of coded instructions for a computer

[2]**program** *vt* **pro·grammed** *or* **pro·gramed** \-ˌgramd, -grəmd\; **pro·gram·ming** *or* **pro·gram·ing** **1 a** : to arrange or furnish a program of or for : BILL **b** : to enter in a program **2** : to provide (an electronic computer) with a program — **pro·gram·mer** *n*

[1]**prog·ress** \ˈpräg-rəs, -ˌres, *chiefly Brit* ˈprō-ˌgres\ *n* **1 a** : a royal journey or tour **b** : an official journey or circuit **c** : a journeying forward : TOUR **2** : a forward or onward movement : ADVANCE **3** : gradual betterment; *esp* : the progressive development of mankind

[2]**pro·gress** \prə-ˈgres\ *vi* **1** : to move forward : PROCEED **2** : to develop to a higher, better, or more advanced stage

pro·gres·sion \prə-ˈgresh-ən\ *n* **1** : the action of progressing or moving forward **2** : a continuous and connected series — **pro·gres·sion·al** \-ˈgresh-nəl, -ən-ᵊl\ *adj*

[1]**pro·gres·sive** \prə-ˈgres-iv\ *adj* **1 a** : of, relating to, or characterized by progress or progression **b** : gradually increasing : GRADUATED **2** : moving forward or onward : ADVANCING **3** : increasing in extent or severity — **pro·gres·sive·ly** *adv* — **pro·gres·sive·ness** *n*

[2]**progressive** *n* **1 a** : one that is progressive **b** : one believing in moderate political change and social improvement by governmental action **2** *cap* : a member of a Progressive Party (as in the presidential campaigns of 1912, 1924, and 1948) in the U.S.

pro·hib·it \prō-ˈhib-ət\ *vt* **1** : to forbid by authority **2 a** : to prevent from doing something **b** : to make impossible

pro·hi·bi·tion \ˌprō-ə-ˈbish-ən\ *n* **1** : the act of prohibiting **2** : an order to restrain or stop **3** : the forbidding by law of the sale and sometimes the manufacture and transportation of alcoholic liquors as beverages

pro·hi·bi·tion·ist \-ˈbish-(ə-)nəst\ *n* : a person who is in favor of prohibiting the manufacture and sale of alcoholic liquors as beverages

pro·hib·i·tive \prō-ˈhib-ət-iv\ *adj* : serving or tending to prohibit — **pro·hib·i·tive·ly** *adv*

pro·hib·i·to·ry \prō-ˈhib-ə-ˌtōr-ē\ *adj* : PROHIBITIVE

[1]**proj·ect** \ˈpräj-ˌekt, -ikt\ *n* **1** : a specific plan or design : SCHEME **2** : a planned undertaking **3** : a group of houses or apartment buildings constructed and arranged according to a single plan

[2]**pro·ject** \prə-ˈjekt\ *vb* **1** : to devise in the mind : DESIGN **2** : to throw or cast forward **3** : to stick out or cause to protrude **4** : to cause (light or shadow) to fall into space or (an image) upon a surface **5** : to reproduce (as a point, line, or area) on a surface by motion in a prescribed direction

pro·ject·a·ble \prə-ˈjek-tə-bəl\ *adj* : capable of being projected

[1]**pro·jec·tile** \prə-ˈjek-tᵊl\ *n* **1** : a body projected by external force and continuing in motion by its own inertia; *esp* : a missile for a weapon (as a firearm or cannon) **2** : a self-propelling weapon (as a guided missile)

[2]**projectile** *adj* **1** : projecting or impelling forward **2** : capable of being thrust forward

pro·jec·tion \prə-ˈjek-shən\ *n* **1** : the act of throwing or shooting forward : EJECTION **2** : the forming of a plan : SCHEMING **3 a** : a jutting out **b** : a part that juts out **4** : the display of motion pictures by projecting an image from them upon a screen **5** : an estimate of future possibilities based on a current trend — **pro·jec·tion·al** \-shnəl, -shən-ᵊl\ *adj*

pro·jec·tion·ist \-sh(ə-)nəst\ *n* : one that makes projections; *esp* : one that operates a motion-picture projector or television equipment

pro·jec·tive \prə-ˈjek-tiv\ *adj* : jutting out : PROJECTING

pro·jec·tor \prə-ˈjek-tər\ *n* **1** : one that plans a project; *esp* : PROMOTER **2** : one that projects: as **a** : a device for projecting a beam of light **b** : an optical instrument or machine for projecting an image or pictures upon a surface

[1]**pro·le·tar·i·an** \ˌprō-lə-ˈter-ē-ən\ *n* : a member of the proletariat

[2]**proletarian** *adj* : of, relating to, or representative of the proletariat

pro·le·tar·i·at \ˌprō-lə-ˈter-ē-ət\ *n, pl* **proletariat** : the working class : wage earners

pro·lif·er·ate \prə-ˈlif-ə-ˌrāt\ *vi* : to grow or increase by rapid production of new units (as cells or offspring) — **pro·lif·er·a·tion** \-ˌlif-ə-ˈrā-shən\ *n* — **pro·lif·er·a·tive** \-ˈlif-ə-ˌrāt-iv\ *adj*

pro·lif·ic \prə-ˈlif-ik\ *adj* **1** : producing young or fruit abundantly : REPRODUCTIVE **2** : highly inventive : PRODUCTIVE **3** : causing fruitfulness : characterized by fruitfulness — **pro·lif·i·cal·ly** \-ˈlif-i-k(ə-)lē\ *adv* — **pro·lif·ic·ness** *n*

pro·lix \prō-ˈliks, ˈprō-(ˌ)liks\ *adj* : continued or drawn out too long (as by too many words) : WORDY, LONG-WINDED — **pro·lix·i·ty** \prō-ˈlik-sət-ē\ *n* — **pro·lix·ly** \prō-ˈliks-lē, ˈprō-(ˌ)liks-\ *adv*

pro·logue \ˈprō-ˌlȯg\ *n* **1** : the preface or introduction to a literary work **2 a** : a speech often in verse addressed to the audience by an actor at the beginning of a play **b** : the actor speaking such a prologue **3** : an introductory or preceding event or development

pro·long \prə-ˈlȯŋ\ *vt* **1 :** to make longer than usual : continue or lengthen in time **2 :** to lengthen in extent or range

pro·lon·ga·tion \(ˌ)prō-ˌlȯŋ-ˈgā-shən\ *n* **1 :** a lengthening in space or time **2 :** something that prolongs or is prolonged

prom \ˈpräm\ *n* **:** an often formal dance given by a high school or college class

[1]**prom·e·nade** \ˌpräm-ə-ˈnād, -ˈnäd\ *n* **1 :** a leisurely walk for pleasure or display **2 :** a place for strolling **3 :** an opening grand march at a formal ball

[2]**promenade** *vb* **1 :** to take or go on a promenade **2 :** to walk about in or on — **prom·e·nad·er** *n*

Pro·me·the·an \prə-ˈmē-thē-ən\ *adj* **:** daringly original or creative

pro·me·thi·um \-thē-əm\ *n* **:** a metallic chemical element obtained as a fission product of uranium or from neutron-irradiated neodymium

prom·i·nence \ˈpräm-ə-nən(t)s\ *n* **1 :** the quality, state, or fact of being prominent or conspicuous **2 :** something prominent **:** PROJECTION

prom·i·nent \-nənt\ *adj* **1 :** standing out or projecting beyond a surface or line **:** PROTUBERANT **2 :** readily noticeable **:** CONSPICUOUS **3 :** NOTABLE, EMINENT — **prom·i·nent·ly** *adv*

prom·is·cu·i·ty \ˌpräm-is-ˈkyü-ət-ē, (ˌ)prō-ˌmis-\ *n, pl* **-ties** **1 :** a miscellaneous mixture or mingling of persons or things **2 :** promiscuous sexual behavior

pro·mis·cu·ous \prə-ˈmis-kyə-wəs\ *adj* **1 :** composed of all sorts of persons and things **2 :** not restricted to one person or class; *esp* **:** not restricted to one sexual partner **3 :** HAPHAZARD, IRREGULAR — **pro·mis·cu·ous·ly** *adv* — **pro·mis·cu·ous·ness** *n*

[1]**prom·ise** \ˈpräm-əs\ *n* **1 :** a statement assuring someone that the person making the statement will do or not do something **:** PLEDGE **2 :** something promised **3 :** a cause or ground for hope or expectation esp. of success or distinction

[2]**promise** *vb* **1 a :** to engage to do, bring about, or provide **b :** to tell as a promise **c :** to make a promise **2 :** to suggest beforehand **:** FORETOKEN — **prom·is·er** \ˈpräm-ə-sər\ *or* **prom·i·sor** \ˌpräm-ə-ˈsȯ(ə)r\ *n*

prom·is·ing *adj* **:** full of promise **:** giving hope or assurance (as of success) — **prom·is·ing·ly** \-ə-siŋ-lē\ *adv*

prom·is·so·ry \ˈpräm-ə-ˌsōr-ē\ *adj* **:** containing or conveying a promise or assurance

prom·on·to·ry \ˈpräm-ən-ˌtōr-ē\ *n, pl* **-ries** **:** a high point of land or rock jutting out into a body of water **:** HEADLAND

pro·mote \prə-ˈmōt\ *vt* **1 :** to advance in position, rank, or honor **:** ELEVATE **2 :** to contribute to the growth, success, or development of **:** FURTHER **3 :** to take the first steps in organizing (as a business)

pro·mot·er \prə-ˈmōt-ər\ *n* **:** one that promotes: as **a :** one who assumes the financial responsibilities of a sporting event **b :** a person who alone or with others organizes a business undertaking

pro·mo·tion \prə-ˈmō-shən\ *n* **1 :** the act or fact of being raised in position or rank **2 :** the act of furthering the growth or development of something — **pro·mo·tion·al** \-shnəl, -shən-ᵊl\ *adj*

[1]**prompt** \ˈpräm(p)t\ *vt* **1 :** to move to action **:** CAUSE **2 :** to remind of something forgotten or poorly learned (as by suggesting the next few words in a speech) **3 :** SUGGEST, INSPIRE

[2]**prompt** *adj* **1 a :** being ready and quick as occasion demands **b :** PUNCTUAL **2 :** performed readily or immediately — **prompt·ly** *adv* — **prompt·ness** *n*

prompt·er \ˈpräm(p)-tər\ *n* **:** a person who reminds another of the words to be spoken next (as in a play)

promp·ti·tude \ˈpräm(p)-tə-ˌt(y)üd\ *n* **:** the quality or habit of being prompt **:** PROMPTNESS

prom·ul·gate \ˈpräm-əl-ˌgāt; prō-ˈməl-\ *vt* **:** to make known by open declaration **:** PROCLAIM — **prom·ul·ga·tion** \ˌpräm-əl-ˈgā-shən, ˌprō-(ˌ)məl-\ *n* — **prom·ul·ga·tor** \ˈpräm-əl-ˌgāt-ər, prō-ˈməl-\ *n*

prone \ˈprōn\ *adj* **1 :** having a tendency or inclination **:** DISPOSED **2 a :** lying belly or face downward **b :** not erect **:** lying flat or prostrate — **prone·ness** \ˈprōn-nəs\ *n*

prong \ˈprȯŋ\ *n* **1 :** a tine of a fork **2 :** a slender pointed or projecting part (as of a tooth or an antler) — **pronged** \ˈprȯŋd\ *adj*

pro·noun \ˈprō-ˌnau̇n\ *n* **:** a word that is used as a substitute for a noun

pro·nounce \prə-ˈnau̇n(t)s\ *vb* **1 :** to declare officially or solemnly **2 :** to assert as an opinion **3 :** to utter the sounds of **:** speak aloud; *esp* **:** to say or speak correctly — **pro·nounce·a·ble** \-ˈnau̇n(t)-sə-bəl\ *adj*

pro·nounced \-ˈnau̇n(t)st\ *adj* **:** strongly marked **:** DECIDED — **pro·nounc·ed·ly** \-ˈnau̇n(t)-səd-lē\ *adv*

pro·nounce·ment \prə-ˈnau̇n(t)s-mənt\ *n* **1 :** a usu. formal declaration of opinion **2 :** an authoritative announcement

pron·to \ˈprän-ˌtō\ *adv* **:** QUICKLY, PROMPTLY

pro·nun·ci·a·men·to \prō-ˌnən(t)-sē-ə-ˈment-ō\ *n, pl* **-tos** *or* **-toes** **:** PROCLAMATION, MANIFESTO

pro·nun·ci·a·tion \prə-ˌnən(t)-sē-ˈā-shən\ *n* **:** the act or manner of pronouncing something

[1]**proof** \ˈprüf\ *n* **1 a :** evidence of truth or correctness **b :** a test to find out or show the essential facts or truth **2 a :** an impression (as from type) taken for correction or examination **b :** a test photographic print made from a negative **3 :** alcoholic content (as of a beverage) indicated by a number that is about twice the percent by volume of alcohol present

[2]**proof** *adj* **1 :** designed for or successful in repelling, resisting, or withstanding — usu. used in combination **2 :** used in proving or testing or as a standard of comparison

proof·read \ˈprüf-ˌrēd\ *vb* **:** to read and make corrections (as in printer's proof)

proof·read·er \-ˌrēd-ər\ *n* **:** a person who reads and makes corrections in printer's proof

[1]**prop** \ˈpräp\ *n* **:** something that props or sustains **:** SUPPORT

[2]**prop** *vt* **propped; prop·ping** **1 a :** to hold up or keep from falling or slipping by placing something under or against **b :** to support by placing against something **2 :** SUSTAIN, STRENGTHEN

[3]**prop** *n* **:** PROPERTY 5

[4]**prop** *n* **:** PROPELLER

prop·a·gan·da \ˌpräp-ə-ˈgan-də, ˌprō-pə-\ *n* **:** the spreading of ideas, information, or rumor for the purpose of helping or injuring a cause or the ideas, facts, or allegations so spread — **prop·a·gan·dist** \-dəst\ *n*

prop·a·gan·dize \-ˌdīz\ *vb* **1 :** to spread propaganda **2 :** to influence or attempt to influence by propaganda

prop·a·gate \ˈpräp-ə-ˌgāt\ *vb* **1 :** to reproduce or increase by sexual or asexual means **:** MULTIPLY **2 :** to cause to spread out and affect a greater number or greater area **3 :** PUBLICIZE **4 :** TRANSMIT **5 :** INCREASE, EXTEND — **prop·a·ga·ble** \-gə-bəl\ *adj* — **prop·a·ga·tive** \-ˌgāt-iv\ *adj* — **prop·a·ga·tor** \-ˌgāt-ər\ *n*

prop·a·ga·tion \ˌpräp-ə-ˈgā-shən\ *n* **:** the act or process of propagating: as **a :** an increasing (as of a kind of organism) numerically **b :** the spreading of something (as a belief) abroad or into new regions **:** DISSEMINATION — **prop·a·ga·tion·al** \-shnəl, -shən-ᵊl\ *adj*

pro·pane \ˈprō-ˌpān\ *n* **:** a heavy flammable gas found in petroleum and natural gas and used as a fuel

pro·pel \prə-ˈpel\ *vt* **pro·pelled; pro·pel·ling** **1 :** to push or drive usu. forward or onward **2 :** to give an impelling motive to **:** urge ahead

[1]**pro·pel·lant** *or* **pro·pel·lent** \-ˈpel-ənt\ *adj* **:** capable of propelling

[2]**propellant** *n* **:** something that propels: as **a :** an explosive for

propelling projectiles **b** : fuel plus oxidizer used by a rocket engine **c** : a gas in a specially made bottle for expelling the contents when the pressure is released
pro·pel·ler \prə-'pel-ər\ *n* : a device consisting of a hub fitted with revolving blades that imparts motion to a vehicle (as a motorboat or an airplane)
pro·pen·si·ty \prə-'pen(t)-sət-ē\ *n, pl* **-ties** : a natural inclination or liking : BENT
prop·er \'präp-ər\ *adj* **1** : marked by suitability, rightness, or appropriateness : FIT **2 a** : appointed for the liturgy of a particular day **b** : belonging to one : OWN **3** : belonging characteristically to a species or individual : PECULIAR **4** : strictly limited to a specified thing, place, or idea **5 a** : strictly accurate : CORRECT **b** : strictly decorous : GENTEEL
prop·er·ly \'präp-ər-lē\ *adv* **1** : in a suitable or fit manner **2** : strictly in accordance with fact : CORRECTLY
prop·er·tied \'präp-ərt-ēd\ *adj* : owning property and esp. much property
prop·er·ty \'präp-ərt-ē\ *n, pl* **-ties** **1** : a special quality or characteristic of a thing : a quality or attribute common to all things called by the same name **2** : anything that is owned (as land, goods, or money) **3** : a piece of real estate with or without a structure on it **4** : OWNERSHIP **5** : an article to be used on the stage during a play except artificial scenery or actors' costumes
proph·e·cy \'präf-ə-sē\ *n, pl* **-cies** **1** : the work or revelation of an inspired prophet **2** : the foretelling of the future **3** : something foretold of the future : PREDICTION
proph·e·sy \'präf-ə-,sī\ *vb* **-sied**; **-sy·ing** **1 a** : to speak or write as a prophet **b** : to utter by divine inspiration **2** : FORETELL, PREDICT — **proph·e·si·er** \-,sī(-ə)r\ *n*
proph·et \'präf-ət\ *n* **1** : a person who declares publicly a message that he believes has been divinely inspired **2** : one gifted with more than ordinary spiritual and moral insight; *esp* : an inspired poet **3** : one who foretells future events **4** : an effective or leading spokesman for a cause, doctrine, or group — **proph·et·ess** \-ət-əs\ *n*
pro·phet·ic \prə-'fet-ik\ *adj* **1** : of, relating to, or characteristic of a prophet or prophecy **2** : foretelling events : PREDICTIVE — **pro·phet·i·cal·ly** \-i-k(ə-)lē\ *adv*
pro·phy·lac·tic \,prō-fə-'lak-tik\ *adj* **1** : guarding from or preventing disease **2** : tending to prevent or ward off : PREVENTIVE — **pro·phy·lac·ti·cal·ly** \-ti-k(ə-)lē\ *adv*
pro·pin·qui·ty \prō-'piŋ-kwət-ē\ *n* **1** : nearness of blood : KINSHIP **2** : nearness in place or time
pro·pi·ti·ate \prō-'pish-ē-,āt\ *vt* : to gain or regain the favor or goodwill of : APPEASE, CONCILIATE — **pro·pi·ti·a·tion** \-,pish-ē-'ā-shən\ *n* — **pro·pi·ti·a·tor** \-'pish-ē-,āt-ər\ *n* — **pro·pi·ti·a·to·ry** \-'pish-(ē-)ə-,tōr-ē\ *adj*
pro·pi·tious \prə-'pish-əs\ *adj* **1** : favorably disposed **2** : of good omen : PROMISING **3** : likely to produce good results : OPPORTUNE — **pro·pi·tious·ly** *adv* — **pro·pi·tious·ness** *n*
prop·jet engine \,präp-,jet-\ *n* : TURBO-PROPELLER ENGINE
pro·po·nent \prə-'pō-nənt\ *n* : one who argues in favor of something : ADVOCATE
[1]**pro·por·tion** \prə-'pōr-shən\ *n* **1** : the size, number, or amount of one thing or group of things as compared to the size, number, or amount of another thing or group of things **2** *pl* : the length and width or length, breadth, and height : DIMENSIONS **3** : a balanced or pleasing arrangement **4** : fair or just share
[2]**proportion** *vt* **-tioned**; **-tion·ing** \-sh(ə-)niŋ\ **1** : to adjust (a part or thing) in size relative to other parts or things **2** : to make the parts of harmonious or symmetrical
pro·por·tion·al \prə-'pōr-shnəl, -shən-ᵊl\ *adj* **1 a** : being in proportion : PROPORTIONATE **b** : having the same or a constant ratio **2** : regulated or determined in size or degree with reference to proportions — **pro·por·tion·al·i·ty** \-,pōr-shə-'nal-ət-ē\ *n* — **pro·por·tion·al·ly** \-'pōr-shnə-lē, -shən-ᵊl-ē\ *adv*
pro·por·tion·ate \prə-'pōr-sh(ə-)nət\ *adj* : being in proportion — **pro·por·tion·ate·ly** *adv*
pro·pos·al \prə-'pō-zəl\ *n* **1** : an act of putting forward or stating something for consideration **2 a** : something proposed : SUGGESTION **b** : OFFER; *esp* : an offer of marriage
pro·pose \prə-'pōz\ *vb* **1** : to offer for consideration or discussion : SUGGEST **2** : to make plans : INTEND **3** : to offer as a toast : suggest drinking to **4** : NAME, NOMINATE **5** : to make an offer of marriage — **pro·pos·er** *n*
prop·o·si·tion \,präp-ə-'zish-ən\ *n* **1** : something proposed or offered for consideration or acceptance : PROPOSAL **2** : an expression in language or signs of something that can be either true or false **3** : a project or situation requiring action : AFFAIR, UNDERTAKING — **prop·o·si·tion·al** \-'zish-nəl, -ən-ᵊl\ *adj*
pro·pound \prə-'paund\ *vt* : to offer for consideration : PROPOSE — **pro·pound·er** *n*
[1]**pro·pri·e·tary** \prə-'prī-ə-,ter-ē\ *n, pl* **-tar·ies** **1** : a body of proprietors **2** : a proprietary medicine
[2]**proprietary** *adj* **1** : of, relating to, or characteristic of a proprietor **2** : made and marketed by one having the exclusive right to manufacture and sell **3** : privately owned and managed
pro·pri·e·tor \prə-'prī-ət-ər\ *n* : one who holds something as his property or possession : OWNER — **pro·pri·e·tor·ship** \-,ship\ *n* — **pro·pri·e·tress** \-'prī-ə-trəs\ *n*
pro·pri·e·ty \prə-'prī-ət-ē\ *n, pl* **-ties** **1** : the quality or state of being proper **2** : correctness in manners or behavior : POLITENESS **3** *pl* : the rules and customs of polite society
pro·pul·sion \prə-'pəl-shən\ *n* **1** : the action or process of propelling **2** : something that propels
pro·pul·sive \-'pəl-siv\ *adj* : tending or having power to propel
pro ra·ta \(')prō-'rāt-ə, -'rät-ə\ *adv* : according to share or liability : PROPORTIONATELY — **pro rata** *adj*
pro·rate \(')prō-'rāt\ *vb* : to divide, distribute, or assess proportionately — **pro·ra·tion** \prō-'rā-shən\ *n*
pro·rogue \prə-'rōg\ *vb* : to suspend or end a legislative session — **pro·ro·ga·tion** \,prōr-ō-'gā-shən\ *n*
pro·sa·ic \prō-'zā-ik\ *adj* **1 a** : characteristic of prose as distinguished from poetry : FACTUAL **b** : DULL, UNIMAGINATIVE **2** : belonging to the everyday world : COMMONPLACE — **pro·sa·i·cal·ly** \-'zā-ə-k(ə-)lē\ *adv*
pro·sce·ni·um \prō-'sē-nē-əm\ *n* : the wall that separates the stage from the auditorium and provides the arch that frames it
pro·scribe \prō-'skrīb\ *vt* **1** : to put outside the protection of the law : OUTLAW **2** : to condemn or forbid as harmful : PROHIBIT — **pro·scrib·er** *n* — **pro·scrip·tion** \-'skrip-shən\ *n* — **pro·scrip·tive** \-'skrip-tiv\ *adj* — **pro·scrip·tive·ly** *adv*
[1]**prose** \'prōz\ *n* **1** : the ordinary language of men in speaking or writing **2** : a prosaic style, quality, character, or condition : ORDINARINESS, MATTER-OF-FACTNESS — **prose** *adj*
[2]**prose** *vi* **1** : to write prose **2** : to write or speak in a dull prosy manner
pros·e·cute \'präs-i-,kyüt\ *vb* **1** : to follow up to the end : keep at : persist in **2** : to seek to punish through an appeal to the courts : carry on a legal action against an accused person to prove his guilt — **pros·e·cu·tion** \,präs-i-'kyü-shən\ *n* — **pros·e·cu·tor** \'präs-i-,kyüt-ər\ *n*
[1]**pros·e·lyte** \'präs-ə-,līt\ *n* : a new convert : NEOPHYTE
[2]**proselyte** *vb* **1** : to convert from one religion, belief, or party to another **2** : to recruit members esp. by the offer of special inducements — **pros·e·ly·tism** \-,līt-,iz-əm, -lə-,tiz-\ *n*
pros·e·ly·tize \-lə-,tīz\ *vb* : PROSELYTE
pros·i·ness \'prō-zē-nəs\ *n* : the quality or state of being prosy
pro·sit \'prō-zət, -sət\ *or* **prost** \'prōst\ *interj* — used to wish good health esp. before drinking

pros·o·dist \ˈpräs-əd-əst\ *n* : a specialist in prosody
pros·o·dy \ˈpräs-əd-ē\ *n, pl* **-dies** : the study of versification and esp. of metrical structure — **pro·sod·ic** \prə-ˈsäd-ik\ *adj* — **pro·sod·i·cal** \-ˈsäd-i-kəl\ *adj* — **pro·sod·i·cal·ly** \-i-k(ə-)lē\ *adv*
[1]**pros·pect** \ˈpräs-ˌpekt\ *n* **1 a** : an extensive view **b** : SURVEY **2** : something extended to the view : SCENE **3 a** : act of looking forward : ANTICIPATION **b** : a mental picture of something to come : VISION **c** : something that is awaited or expected : POSSIBILITY **4 a** : a potential buyer or customer **b** : a candidate or a person likely to become a candidate
[2]**prospect** *vb* : to explore an area esp. for mineral deposits — **pros·pec·tor** \-ˌpek-tər\ *n*
pro·spec·tive \prə-ˈspek-tiv, ˈpräs-ˌpek-\ *adj* **1** : likely to come about : EXPECTED **2** : likely to be or become — **pro·spec·tive·ly** *adv*
pro·spec·tus \prə-ˈspek-təs, prä-\ *n, pl* **pro·spec·tus·es** : a printed statement describing an enterprise and distributed to prospective investors
pros·per \ˈpräs-pər\ *vb* **pros·pered**; **pros·per·ing** \-p(ə-)riŋ\ **1** : SUCCEED; *esp* : to succeed financially **2** : FLOURISH, THRIVE **3** : to cause to succeed or thrive
pros·per·i·ty \prä-ˈsper-ət-ē\ *n* : the condition of being successful or thriving; *esp* : economic well-being
pros·per·ous \ˈpräs-p(ə-)rəs\ *adj* **1** : marked by success or economic well-being **2** : FLOURISHING — **pros·per·ous·ly** *adv* — **pros·per·ous·ness** *n*
pros·tate \ˈpräs-ˌtāt\ *n* : a glandular body about the base of the male urethra — **prostate** *adj*
[1]**pros·ti·tute** \ˈpräs-tə-ˌt(y)üt\ *vt* : to devote to corrupt or unworthy purposes : DEBASE
[2]**prostitute** *n* : a woman who engages in promiscuous sexual intercourse esp. for money : WHORE
pros·ti·tu·tion \ˌpräs-tə-ˈt(y)ü-shən\ *n* **1** : the acts or practices of a prostitute **2** : the state of being prostituted : DEBASEMENT
[1]**pros·trate** \ˈpräs-ˌtrāt\ *adj* **1 a** : stretched out with face on the ground (as in adoration or submission) **b** : extended in a horizontal position : FLAT **2** : lacking in vitality or will : OVERCOME
[2]**prostrate** *vt* **1** : to throw or put into a prostrate position **2** : to reduce to submission, helplessness, or exhaustion
pros·tra·tion \prä-ˈstrā-shən\ *n* **1** : the act of assuming or state of being in a prostrate position **2** : complete physical or mental exhaustion : COLLAPSE
prosy \ˈprō-zē\ *adj* **1** : PROSAIC **2** : TEDIOUS
pro·tag·o·nist \prō-ˈtag-ə-nəst\ *n* **1** : one who takes the leading part in a drama, novel, or story **2** : the leader of a cause : CHAMPION
pro·te·an \ˈprōt-ē-ən\ *adj* : readily assuming different shapes or roles
pro·tect \prə-ˈtekt\ *vt* **1** : to cover or shield from injury or destruction : GUARD **2** : to save from contingent financial loss
pro·tec·tion \prə-ˈtek-shən\ *n* **1** : the act of protecting : the state of being protected **2 a** : one that protects **b** : the oversight or support of one that is smaller and weaker **3** : the freeing of the producers of a country from foreign competition by high duties on foreign goods — **pro·tec·tive** \-ˈtek-tiv\ *adj* — **pro·tec·tive·ly** *adv*
pro·tec·tion·ist \-sh(ə-)nəst\ *n* : an advocate of government economic protection for domestic producers through restrictions on foreign competitors — **pro·tec·tion·ism** \-shə-ˌniz-əm\ *n* — **protectionist** *adj*
pro·tec·tor \prə-ˈtek-tər\ *n* **1 a** : one that protects : GUARDIAN **b** : a device used to prevent injury : GUARD **2** : REGENT
pro·tec·tor·ate \prə-ˈtek-t(ə-)rət\ *n* **1** : government by a protector **2** : the relationship of superior authority assumed by one state over a dependent one; *also* : the dependent state in such a relationship
pro·té·gé \ˈprōt-ə-ˌzhā\ *n* : a person under the care and protection of someone influential who intends to further his career
pro·tein \ˈprō-ˌtēn, ˈprōt-ē-ən\ *n* : any of a great class of chemicals that contain carbon, hydrogen, nitrogen, oxygen, and sometimes other elements, are present in all living matter, and are an essential food item — **pro·tein·aceous** \ˌprō-ˌtē-ˈnā-shəs, ˌprōt-ē-ə-ˈnā-\ *adj*
pro tem \prō-ˈtem\ *adv* : for the time being
pro tem·po·re \prō-ˈtem-pə-rē\ *adv* : for the present : TEMPORARILY
[1]**pro·test** \ˈprō-ˌtest\ *n* **1** : a formal declaration of opinion and usu. of objection or complaint **2** : a complaint, objection, or display of unwillingness or disapproval
[2]**pro·test** \prə-ˈtest\ *vb* **1 a** : to make solemn declaration of : ASSERT **b** : to make a protestation **2 a** : to make a protest against **b** : to object strongly
prot·es·tant \ˈprät-əs-tənt, *2 is also* prə-ˈtes-\ *n* **1** *cap* **a** : a member or adherent of one of the Christian churches deriving from the Reformation **b** : a Christian not of a Catholic or Eastern church **2** : one who makes or enters a protest — **protestant** *adj, often cap* — **Prot·es·tant·ism** \ˈprät-əs-tənt-ˌiz-əm\ *n*
prot·es·ta·tion \ˌprät-əs-ˈtā-shən, ˌprō-ˌtes-\ *n* : the act of protesting : a solemn declaration or avowal
pro·to·col \ˈprōt-ə-ˌkȯl\ *n* **1** : an original draft, minute, or record of a document or transaction : MEMORANDUM **2** : a code of diplomatic or military etiquette and precedence
pro·ton \ˈprō-ˌtän\ *n* : an elementary particle that is present in all atomic nuclei and carries a positive charge of electricity — **pro·ton·ic** \prō-ˈtän-ik\ *adj*
pro·to·plasm \ˈprōt-ə-ˌplaz-əm\ *n* : the complex colloidal largely protein substance of plant and animal cells — **pro·to·plas·mic** \ˌprōt-ə-ˈplaz-mik\ *adj*
pro·to·type \ˈprōt-ə-ˌtīp\ *n* **1** : an original model on which something is patterned **2** : an individual that exhibits the essential features of a later type
pro·to·zo·an \ˌprōt-ə-ˈzō-ən\ *n* : any of a great group of lowly animals that are essentially single cells — **protozoan** *or* **pro·to·zo·al** \-ˈzō-əl\ *adj* — **pro·to·zo·ic** \-ˈzō-ik\ *adj*
pro·tract \prō-ˈtrakt\ *vt* **1** : to prolong in time or space **2** : to lay down the lines and angles of with scale and protractor : PLOT — **pro·trac·tion** \-ˈtrak-shən\ *n* — **pro·trac·tive** \-ˈtrak-tiv\ *adj*
pro·trac·tor \prō-ˈtrak-tər\ *n* **1** : one that protracts, prolongs, or delays **2** : an instrument for laying down and measuring angles that is used in drawing and plotting
pro·trude \prō-ˈtrüd\ *vb* **1** : to stick out or cause to stick out : PROJECT **2** : to jut out from the surroundings — **pro·tru·si·ble** \-ˈtrü-sə-bəl\ *adj*
pro·tru·sion \prō-ˈtrü-zhən\ *n* **1** : the act of protruding : the state of being protruded **2** : something that protrudes
pro·tu·ber·ance \prō-ˈt(y)ü-b(ə-)rən(t)s\ *n* **1** : the quality or state of being protuberant **2** : something that is protuberant : BULGE
pro·tu·ber·ant \-b(ə-)rənt\ *adj* : bulging beyond the surrounding surface : PROMINENT — **pro·tu·ber·ant·ly** *adv*
proud \ˈpraůd\ *adj* **1** : feeling or showing pride: as **a** : having or displaying excessive self-esteem **b** : much pleased : EXULTANT **c** : having proper self-respect **2** : MAGNIFICENT, GLORIOUS **3** : VIGOROUS, SPIRITED — **proud·ly** *adv*
prove \ˈprüv\ *vb* **proved**; **proved** *or* **prov·en** \ˈprü-vən\; **prov·ing** **1** : to try or ascertain by an experiment or a standard **2 a** : to establish the truth or validity of by evidence or demonstration **b** : to check the correctness of (as an arithmetic operation) **3** : to ascertain the genuineness of : VERIFY; *esp* : to obtain probate of (a will) **4** : to turn out esp. after trial or test — **prov·a·ble** \ˈprü-və-bəl\ *adj*

prov·en·der \ˈpräv-ən-dər\ *n* **1 :** dry food for domestic animals : FEED **2 :** FOOD, VICTUALS
prov·erb \ˈpräv-ˌərb\ *n* : a brief popular saying or maxim
pro·ver·bi·al \prə-ˈvər-bē-əl\ *adj* **1 :** of, relating to, or resembling a proverb **2 :** commonly spoken of — **pro·ver·bi·al·ly** \-bē-ə-lē\ *adv*
pro·vide \prə-ˈvīd\ *vb* **1 :** to take precautionary measures **2 :** to make a proviso or condition : STIPULATE **3 :** to supply what is needed for sustenance or support **4 a :** OUTFIT, EQUIP **b :** to supply for use : YIELD — **pro·vid·er** *n*
pro·vid·ed *conj* : on condition : IF — sometimes followed by *that*
prov·i·dence \ˈpräv-əd-ən(t)s, -ə-ˌden(t)s\ *n* **1 a** *often cap* : divine guidance or care **b** *cap* : God conceived as the power sustaining and guiding human destiny **2 :** the quality or state of being provident : PRUDENCE
prov·i·dent \-əd-ənt, -ə-ˌdent\ *adj* **1 :** making provision for the future : PRUDENT **2 :** FRUGAL, SAVING — **prov·i·dent·ly** *adv*
prov·i·den·tial \ˌpräv-ə-ˈden-chəl\ *adj* **1 :** of, relating to, or determined by Providence **2 :** occurring by or as if by an intervention of Providence : FORTUNATE — **prov·i·den·tial·ly** \-ˈdench-(ə-)lē\ *adv*
prov·ince \ˈpräv-ən(t)s\ *n* **1 :** a usu. large administrative district or division of a country **2** *pl* : all of a country except the metropolis **3 :** proper or appropriate business or scope : SPHERE
¹pro·vin·cial \prə-ˈvin-chəl\ *n* **1 :** one living in or coming from a province **2 :** a person with a local or limited point of view
²provincial *adj* **1 :** of, relating to, or coming from a province **2 :** limited in outlook : SECTIONAL, NARROW — **pro·vin·ci·al·i·ty** \-ˌvin-chē-ˈal-ət-ē\ *n* — **pro·vin·cial·ly** \-ˈvinch-(ə-)lē\ *adv*
pro·vin·cial·ism \prə-ˈvin-chə-ˌliz-əm\ *n* **1 :** a dialectal or local word, phrase, or idiom **2 :** the quality or state of being provincial
¹pro·vi·sion \prə-ˈvizh-ən\ *n* **1 a :** the act or process of providing **b :** a measure taken beforehand : PREPARATION **2 :** a stock of needed materials or supplies; *esp* : a stock of food — usu. used in pl. **3 :** STIPULATION, PROVISO
²provision *vt* **pro·vi·sioned**; **pro·vi·sion·ing** \-ˈvizh-(ə-)niŋ\ : to supply with provisions
pro·vi·sion·al \prə-ˈvizh-nəl, -ən-ᵊl\ *adj* : serving for the time being : TEMPORARY, TENTATIVE — **pro·vi·sion·al·ly** \-ē\ *adv*
pro·vi·so \prə-ˈvī-zō\ *n*, *pl* **-sos** *or* **-soes 1 :** a sentence or clause in a legal document in which a condition is stated **2 :** a conditional stipulation : PROVISION
prov·o·ca·tion \ˌpräv-ə-ˈkā-shən\ *n* : the act of provoking; *also* : something that provokes, arouses, or stimulates
pro·voc·a·tive \prə-ˈväk-ət-iv\ *adj* : serving or tending to provoke, excite, or stimulate — **pro·voc·a·tive·ly** *adv* — **pro·voc·a·tive·ness** *n*
pro·voke \prə-ˈvōk\ *vt* **1 :** to arouse to action or feeling; *esp* : to excite to anger **2 :** to bring about : stir up : EVOKE
pro·vok·ing \-ˈvō-kiŋ\ *adj* : causing mild anger : ANNOYING — **pro·vok·ing·ly** \-kiŋ-lē\ *adv*
pro·vost \ˈprō-ˌvōst, ˈpräv-əst, *before "marshal" often* ˈprō-vō\ *n* **1 :** the chief dignitary of a collegiate or cathedral chapter **2 :** a chief magistrate or a high-ranking administrative officer (as in a university)
provost marshal *n* : the head of the military police of a command
prow \ˈprau̇\ *n* : the bow of a ship : STEM
prow·ess \ˈprau̇-əs\ *n* **1 :** distinguished bravery; *esp* : military valor and skill **2 :** extraordinary ability
prowl \ˈprau̇l\ *vb* **1 :** to move about or wander stealthily in the manner of a wild beast seeking prey **2 :** to roam over in a predatory manner — **prowl** *n* — **prowl·er** *n*
prox·i·mate \ˈpräk-sə-mət\ *adj* **1 a :** very near **b :** soon forthcoming **2 :** next preceding or following — **prox·i·mate·ly** *adv*
prox·im·i·ty \präk-ˈsim-ət-ē\ *n* : the quality or state of being proximate
proxy \ˈpräk-sē\ *n*, *pl* **prox·ies :** authority held by one person to act for another (as in voting); *also* : a written paper giving a person such authority — **proxy** *adj*
prude \ˈprüd\ *n* : a person and esp. a woman who is exaggeratedly or affectedly modest in speech, behavior, and dress and is oversensitive to slight violations of accepted rules of decorous behavior — **prud·ish** \ˈprüd-ish\ *adj* — **prud·ish·ly** *adv* — **prud·ish·ness** *n*
pru·dence \ˈprüd-ᵊn(t)s\ *n* **1 :** the ability to govern and discipline oneself by the use of reason **2 :** sagacity or shrewdness in the management of affairs : DISCRETION **3 :** skill and good judgment in the use of resources : ECONOMY, FRUGALITY **4 :** CAUTION, CIRCUMSPECTION
pru·dent \-ᵊnt\ *adj* **1 :** FORESIGHTED, WISE **2 :** shrewd in the management of practical affairs **3 :** CIRCUMSPECT, DISCREET **4 :** PROVIDENT, FRUGAL — **pru·dent·ly** *adv*
pru·den·tial \prü-ˈden-chəl\ *adj* **1 :** of, relating to, or resulting from prudence **2 :** using prudence — **pru·den·tial·ly** \-chə-lē\ *adv*
prud·ery \ˈprüd-(ə-)rē\ *n*, *pl* **-er·ies 1 :** the quality or state of being prudish : exaggerated or priggish modesty **2 :** a prudish remark or act
¹prune \ˈprün\ *n* : a plum dried or capable of drying without fermentation
²prune *vb* **1 :** to cut off the dead or unwanted parts of a usu. woody plant **2 a :** to cut down or reduce by eliminating superfluous or unwanted matter : RETRENCH **b :** to remove as superfluous — **prun·er** *n*
pru·ri·ent \ˈpru̇r-ē-ənt\ *adj* : having or revealing indecent desires or thoughts : LEWD — **pru·ri·ence** \-ē-ən(t)s\ *n* — **pru·ri·ent·ly** *adv*
¹pry \ˈprī\ *vi* **pried**; **pry·ing :** to look closely or inquisitively : PEER; *esp* : to make a presumptuous inquiry — **pry** *n*
²pry *vt* **pried**; **pry·ing 1 :** to raise, move, or pull apart with a pry or lever : PRIZE **2 :** to extract, detach, or open with difficulty
³pry *n* **1 :** a tool for prying **2 :** LEVERAGE
pry·ing *adj* : impertinently or officiously inquisitive or interrogatory — **pry·ing·ly** \-iŋ-lē\ *adv*
psalm \ˈsäm, ˈsälm\ *n* : a sacred song or poem
psalm·ist \-əst\ *n* : a writer or composer of psalms
Psal·ter \ˈsȯl-tər\ *n* : a collection of Psalms for liturgical or devotional use
pseu·do \ˈsüd-ō\ *adj* : SHAM, FEIGNED, SPURIOUS
pseu·do·nym \ˈsüd-ᵊn-ˌim\ *n* : a fictitious name; *esp* : PEN NAME
pshaw \ˈshȯ\ *interj* — used to express irritation, disapproval, contempt, or disbelief
psy·che \ˈsī-kē\ *n* : SOUL, SELF; *also* : MIND
psy·che·del·ic \ˌsī-kə-ˈdel-ik\ *adj* **1 :** of, relating to, or being drugs (as LSD) capable of producing abnormal psychic effects and sometimes psychic states resembling mental illness **2 :** imitating or reproducing effects (as distorted or bizarre images) resembling those produced by psychedelic drugs
psy·chi·a·try \sə-ˈkī-ə-trē, sī-\ *n* : a branch of medicine that deals with mental, emotional, or behavioral disorders — **psy·chi·at·ric** \ˌsī-kē-ˈa-trik\ *adj* — **psy·chi·at·ri·cal·ly** \-trik(ə-)lē\ *adv* — **psy·chi·a·trist** \sə-ˈkī-ə-trəst, sī-\ *n*
¹psy·chic \ˈsī-kik\ *adj* **1 :** of or relating to the psyche **2 :** not physical; *esp* : not to be explained by knowledge of natural laws **3 :** sensitive to influences or forces supposedly exerted from beyond the natural world — **psy·chi·cal** \-ki-kəl\ *adj* — **psy·chi·cal·ly** \-ki-k(ə-)lē\ *adv*
²psychic *n* : a person (as a medium) apparently sensitive to nonphysical forces
psy·cho·anal·y·sis \ˌsī-kō-ə-ˈnal-ə-səs\ *n*, *pl* **-y·ses** \-ˌsēz\ : a method of explaining and treating psychic and esp. emotional

disorders that emphasizes the importance of the patient's talking freely about himself while under treatment and esp. about early childhood memories and experiences and about his dreams — **psy·cho·an·a·lyst** \-'an-ᵊl-əst\ *n* — **psy·cho·an·a·lyt·ic** \-ˌan-ᵊl-'it-ik\ *or* **psy·cho·an·a·lyt·i·cal** \-'it-i-kəl\ *adj* — **psy·cho·an·a·lyt·i·cal·ly** \-'it-i-k(ə-)lē\ *adv* — **psy·cho·an·a·lyze** \-'an-ᵊl-ˌīz\ *vb*

psy·cho·log·i·cal \ˌsī-kə-'läj-i-kəl\ *adj* **1 a :** of or relating to psychology **b :** MENTAL **2 :** directed toward or intended to influence the will or mind — **psy·cho·log·i·cal·ly** \-i-k(ə-)lē\ *adv*

psy·chol·o·gy \sī-'käl-ə-jē\ *n, pl* **-gies 1 :** the science or study of mind and behavior **2 :** the mental or behavioral characteristics of an individual or group — **psy·chol·o·gist** \-jəst\ *n*

psy·cho·path \'sī-kə-ˌpath\ *n* **:** a person lacking in mental stability and defective in social orientation often to the point of delinquency — **psy·cho·path·ic** \ˌsī-kə-'path-ik\ *adj*

psy·cho·sis \sī-'kō-səs\ *n, pl* **-cho·ses** \-'kō-ˌsēz\ **:** fundamental lasting mental derangement characterized by defective or lost contact with reality — **psy·chot·ic** \-'kät-ik\ *adj or n* — **psy·chot·i·cal·ly** \-'kät-i-k(ə-)lē\ *adv*

psy·cho·so·mat·ic \ˌsī-kə-sə-'mat-ik\ *adj* **:** of, relating to, or resulting from the interaction and interdependence of mental and bodily phenomena — **psy·cho·so·mat·i·cal·ly** \-'mat-i-k(ə-)lē\ *adv*

pto·maine \'tō-ˌmān, tō-'\ *n* **:** any of various organic compounds formed by the action of putrefactive bacteria on nitrogenous matter

ptomaine poisoning *n* **:** food poisoning caused usu. by bacteria or bacterial products

pu·ber·ty \'pyü-bərt-ē\ *n* **:** the condition of being or the period of becoming first capable of reproducing sexually — **pu·ber·tal** \-bərt-ᵊl\ *adj*

¹pub·lic \'pəb-lik\ *adj* **1 a :** of, relating to, or affecting all the people **b :** GOVERNMENTAL **c :** relating to or engaged in the service of the community or nation **2 a :** of or relating to mankind in general **:** UNIVERSAL **b :** GENERAL, POPULAR **3 :** of or relating to business or community interests as opposed to private affairs **:** SOCIAL **4 :** devoted to the general welfare **5 :** accessible to or shared by all members of the community **6 a :** exposed to general view **:** OPEN **b :** WELL-KNOWN, PROMINENT **c :** PERCEPTIBLE, MATERIAL — **pub·lic·ly** *adv*

²public *n* **1 :** a place accessible or visible to the public **2 :** the people as a whole **:** POPULACE **3 :** a particular group of people

pub·li·ca·tion \ˌpəb-lə-'kā-shən\ *n* **1 :** the act or process or an instance of publishing **2 :** a published work

public house *n* **:** INN, HOSTELRY

pub·li·cist \'pəb-lə-səst\ *n* **:** one that publicizes; *esp* **:** PRESS AGENT

pub·lic·i·ty \(ˌ)pə-'blis-ət-ē\ *n* **1 :** the condition of being public or publicly known **2 :** ADVERTISING; *esp* **:** information with a news value designed to further the interests of a place, person, or cause **3 :** an action that gains public attention; *also* **:** the attention so gained

pub·li·cize \'pəb-lə-ˌsīz\ *vt* **:** to give publicity to **:** ADVERTISE

public school *n* **1 :** any of various select endowed British schools that give a liberal education and prepare students for the universities **2 :** an elementary or secondary school maintained by a local government

pub·lic–spir·it·ed \ˌpəb-lik-'spir-ət-əd\ *adj* **:** motivated by devotion to the general or national welfare

public television *n* **:** television that provides cultural, informational, and instructional programs for the public and that does not carry advertising

pub·lish \'pəb-lish\ *vb* **1 :** to make generally known **:** make public announcement of **2 a :** to produce or release for publication; *esp* **:** PRINT **b :** to issue the work of (an author) **3 :** to have one's work accepted for publication — **pub·lish·a·ble** \-ə-bəl\ *adj* — **pub·lish·er** \-ər\ *n*

¹puck \'pək\ *n* **:** a mischievous sprite **:** HOBGOBLIN

²puck *n* **:** a vulcanized rubber disk used in ice hockey

¹puck·er \'pək-ər\ *vb* **puck·ered; puck·er·ing** \'pək-(ə-)riŋ\ **:** to contract into folds or wrinkles

²pucker *n* **:** a fold or wrinkle in a normally even surface — **puck·ery** \'pək-(ə-)rē\ *adj*

puck·ish \'pək-ish\ *adj* **:** IMPISH, WHIMSICAL — **puck·ish·ly** *adv* — **puck·ish·ness** *n*

pud·ding \'pu̇d-iŋ\ *n* **1 :** a boiled or baked soft food usu. with a cereal base **2 :** a dessert of a soft, spongy, or thick creamy consistency **3 :** a dish often containing suet or having a suet crust and orig. boiled in a bag

¹pud·dle \'pəd-ᵊl\ *n* **:** a very small pool of usu. dirty or muddy water

²puddle *vt* **pud·dled; pud·dling** \'pəd-liŋ, -ᵊl-iŋ\ **1 :** to make muddy or turbid **:** MUDDLE **2 :** to convert (melted pig iron) into wrought iron by stirring in the presence of an oxidizer **3 :** to strew with puddles — **pud·dler** \-lər, -ᵊl-ər\ *n*

pudgy \'pəj-ē\ *adj* **:** short and plump **:** CHUBBY — **pudg·i·ness** *n*

pu·eb·lo \pü-'eb-lō, pyü-\ *n, pl* **pueblos :** an Indian village of Arizona or New Mexico consisting of flat-roofed stone or adobe houses joined in groups sometimes several stories high

pu·er·ile \'pyu̇(-ə)r-əl, -ˌīl\ *adj* **1 :** JUVENILE **2 :** CHILDISH, SILLY — **pu·er·il·i·ty** \ˌpyu̇(-ə)r-'il-ət-ē\ *n*

¹puff \'pəf\ *vb* **1 a** (1) **:** to blow in short gusts (2) **:** to exhale forcibly **b :** to breathe hard **:** PANT **c :** to emit, propel, blow, or expel by or as if by small whiffs or clouds (as of smoke) **:** WAFT **2 a :** to speak or act in a scornful, conceited, or exaggerated manner **b :** to make proud or conceited **:** ELATE **c :** to praise extravagantly; *esp* **:** ADVERTISE **3 a :** to distend or become distended with or as if with air or gas **:** SWELL, INFLATE **b :** to open or appear in or as if in a puff — **puff·er** *n*

²puff *n* **1 a :** an act or instance of puffing **:** WHIFF, GUST **b :** a slight explosive sound accompanying a puff **c :** a perceptible cloud (as of smoke or steam) emitted in a puff **2 :** a light pastry that rises high in baking **3 a :** a slight swelling **:** PROTUBERANCE **b :** a fluffy mass: as (1) **:** a small fluffy pad for applying cosmetic powder (2) **:** a soft loose roll of hair (3) **:** a quilted bed covering **4 :** a commendatory notice or review — **puff·i·ness** \'pəf-ē-nəs\ *n* — **puffy** \'pəf-ē\ *adj*

pug \'pəg\ *n* **1 :** a small sturdy compact dog of Asiatic origin with a close coat, tightly curled tail, and broad wrinkled face **2 a :** a short nose turned up at the tip **b :** a close knot or coil of hair **:** BUN

pu·gi·list \'pyü-jə-ləst\ *n* **:** FIGHTER; *esp* **:** a professional boxer — **pu·gi·lism** \-ˌliz-əm\ *n* — **pu·gi·lis·tic** \ˌpyü-jə-'lis-tik\ *adj*

pug·na·cious \ˌpəg-'nā-shəs\ *adj* **:** having a quarrelsome or belligerent nature — **pug·na·cious·ly** *adv* — **pug·na·cious·ness** *n* — **pug·nac·i·ty** \-'nas-ət-ē\ *n*

puis·sance \'pwis-ᵊn(t)s, 'pyü-ə-sən(t)s\ *n* **:** STRENGTH, POWER — **puis·sant** \-ᵊnt, -sənt\ *adj* — **puis·sant·ly** *adv*

puk·ka \'pək-ə\ *adj* **:** GENUINE, AUTHENTIC; *also* **:** FIRST-CLASS, COMPLETE

pul·chri·tude \'pəl-krə-ˌt(y)üd\ *n* **:** physical comeliness **:** BEAUTY — **pul·chri·tu·di·nous** \ˌpəl-krə-'t(y)üd-ᵊn-əs\ *adj*

pule \'pyül\ *vi* **:** WHINE, WHIMPER

¹pull \'pu̇l\ *vb* **1 a :** to separate forcibly from a natural or firm attachment **:** PLUCK, EXTRACT **b :** to remove something by or as if by pulling **2 a :** to exert force upon so as to cause or tend to cause motion toward the force **b :** to stretch (cooling candy) repeatedly **c :** to strain by stretching abnormally **d** (1) **:** to use force in drawing, dragging, or tugging (2) **:** MOVE (3) **:** to take a drink (4) **:** to draw hard in smoking **e :** to work (an oar) by drawing back strongly **3 :** to draw apart **:** REND, TEAR **4 :** to print a proof from by impression **5 :** REMOVE **6 :** to bring (a weapon) into the open **7 :** to carry out with skill or daring **:** COMMIT **8 :** to draw the support or attention of

: ATTRACT 9 : to feel or express strong sympathy : ROOT — **pull·er** *n* — **pull oneself together** : to regain one's self-possession — **pull one's leg** : to deceive someone playfully : HOAX — **pull stakes** *or* **pull up stakes** : to move out : LEAVE — **pull strings** *or* **pull wires** : to exert secret influence or control — **pull together** : to work in harmony : COOPERATE

²pull *n* **1 a** : the act or an instance of pulling **b** : a draft of liquid : an inhalation of smoke **c** : the effort expended in moving **d** : force required to overcome resistance to pulling **2 a** : ADVANTAGE **b** : special influence **3** : PROOF 2a **4** : a device for pulling something or for operating by pulling **5** : a force that attracts, compels, or influences : ATTRACTION

pull away *vi* : to draw oneself back or away : WITHDRAW, ESCAPE

pull down *vt* **1** : DEMOLISH, DESTROY **2 a** : to bring to a lower level : REDUCE **b** : to depress in health, strength, or spirits **3** : to draw as wages or salary

pul·let \'pu̇l-ət\ *n* : a young hen; *esp* : a hen of the common fowl less than a year old

pul·ley \'pu̇l-ē\ *n, pl* **pulleys** **1** : a small wheel with a grooved rim used singly with a rope or chain to change the direction and point of application of a pulling force and in combinations to increase the applied force esp. for lifting weights; *also* : the simple machine constituted by such a pulley with ropes **2** : a wheel used to transmit power by means of a band, belt, cord, rope, or chain

pull in *vb* **1** : CHECK, RESTRAIN **2** : ARREST **3** : to arrive at a destination : come to a stop

Pull·man \'pu̇l-mən\ *n* : a railroad passenger car with specially comfortable furnishings; *esp* : SLEEPING CAR

pull off *vt* : to accomplish successfully esp. against odds

pull out \(')pu̇l-'au̇t\ *vi* **1** : LEAVE, DEPART **2** : WITHDRAW

¹pull·over \ˌpu̇l-ˌō-vər\ *adj* : put on by being pulled over the head

²pull·over \'pu̇l-ˌō-vər\ *n* : a pullover garment

pull through *vb* : to help through or to survive a dangerous or difficult period or situation

pull up *vb* **1** : CHECK, REBUKE **2** : to bring or come to a stop : HALT **3** : to draw even with others in a race

pul·mo·nary \'pu̇l-mə-ˌner-ē, 'pəl-\ *adj* **1** : relating to or associated with the lungs **2** : carried on by the lungs

pul·mo·tor \'pu̇l-ˌmōt-ər, 'pəl-\ *n* : a respiratory apparatus for pumping oxygen or air into and out of the lungs (as of an asphyxiated person)

¹pulp \'pəlp\ *n* **1** : the soft juicy or fleshy part of a fruit or vegetable **2** : the soft sensitive tissue that fills the central cavity of a tooth **3** : a material prepared by chemical or mechanical means chiefly from wood but also from other materials (as rags) and used in making paper and cellulose products **4** : a magazine or book using rough-surfaced paper made of wood pulp and often dealing with sensational material

²pulp *vb* : to form into a pulp : make or become pulpy

pul·pit \'pu̇l-ˌpit\ *n* **1** : an elevated platform or high reading desk used in preaching or conducting a worship service **2** : the preaching profession; *also* : a post in it

pulp·wood \'pəlp-ˌwu̇d\ *n* : a wood (as of aspen, hemlock, pine, or spruce) used in making pulp for paper

pulpy \'pəl-pē\ *adj* : resembling or consisting of pulp — **pulp·i·ness** *n*

pul·sate \'pəl-ˌsāt\ *vi* : to expand and contract in a rhythmic manner : throb rhythmically : BEAT

pul·sa·tion \ˌpəl-'sā-shən\ *n* : pulsating movement or action (as of an artery); *also* : a single throb of such movement

¹pulse \'pəls\ *n* **1** : a regular throbbing caused in the arteries by the contractions of the heart **2 a** : rhythmical beating, vibrating, or sounding **b** : BEAT, THROB **3** : a transient variation of a quantity (as electrical current or voltage) whose value is normally constant

²pulse *vb* **1** : to exhibit a pulse or pulsation : THROB **2** : to drive by or as if by a pulsation **3** : to cause to pulsate

pul·ver·ize \'pəl-və-ˌrīz\ *vb* **1** : to reduce or become reduced (as by beating or grinding) into a powder or dust **2** : to demolish as if by pulverizing : SMASH, ANNIHILATE — **pul·ver·i·za·tion** \ˌpəl-və-rə-'zā-shən\ *n* — **pul·ver·iz·er** *n*

pu·ma \'p(y)ü-mə\ *n* : COUGAR

pum·ice \'pəm-əs\ *n* : a volcanic glass full of cavities and very light in weight used esp. in powder form for smoothing and polishing

pum·mel \'pəm-əl\ *vb* **-meled** *or* **-melled**; **-mel·ing** *or* **-mel·ling** : POUND, BEAT, THUMP

¹pump \'pəmp\ *n* : a device that raises, transfers, or compresses fluids or that reduces the density of gases esp. by suction or pressure or both

²pump *vb* **1** : to raise, transfer, or compress by means of a pump **2** : to free (as from water or air) by the use of a pump **3** : to fill by means of a pump **4** : to draw, force, or drive onward in the manner of a pump **5** : to move up and down like a pump handle **6** : to spurt out intermittently **7** : to subject to persistent questioning to find out something; *also* : to draw out by such questioning — **pump·er** *n*

³pump *n* : a low shoe not fastened on and gripping the foot chiefly at the toe and heel

pum·per·nick·el \'pəm-pər-ˌnik-əl\ *n* : a dark coarse somewhat sour rye bread

pump·kin \'pəŋ-kən, 'pəm(p)-kən\ *n* **1** : the usu. round deep yellow fruit of a vine of the gourd family widely used as food **2** : a usu. hairy prickly vine that produces pumpkins

¹pun \'pən\ *n* : the humorous use of a word in such a way as to suggest different meanings or applications or of words having the same or nearly the same sound but different meanings

²pun *vi* **punned**; **pun·ning** : to make puns

¹punch \'pənch\ *vb* **1 a** : PROD, POKE **b** : to drive or herd (cattle) **2 a** : to strike with a forward thrust of the fist **b** : to drive or push forcibly by or as if by a punch; *esp* : to press so as to activate **3** : to emboss, cut, perforate, or make with a punch **4** : to strike or press sharply — **punch·er** *n*

²punch *n* **1** : the action of punching **2** : a quick blow with or as if with the fist **3** : energy that commands attention : effective force

³punch *n* : a tool or machine for piercing, cutting (as a hole or notch), forming, driving the head of a nail below a surface or a bolt out of a hole, or impressing a design in a softer material

⁴punch *n* : a drink made of various and usu. many ingredients and often flavored with wine or distilled liquor

pun·cheon \'pən-chən\ *n* : a large cask of varying capacity

punch in *vi* : to record the time of one's arrival or beginning work by punching a time clock

punch out *vi* : to record the time of one's stopping work or departure by punching a time clock

punc·til·io \ˌpəŋ(k)-'til-ē-ˌō\ *n, pl* **-i·os** **1** : a nice detail of conduct in a ceremony or in observance of a code **2** : careful observance of forms (as in social conduct)

punc·til·i·ous \-ē-əs\ *adj* : marked by precise exact accordance with the details of codes or conventions — **punc·til·i·ous·ly** *adv* — **punc·til·i·ous·ness** *n*

punc·tu·al \'pəŋ(k)-chə-wəl\ *adj* **1** : PUNCTILIOUS **2** : acting or habitually acting at an appointed time or at a regularly scheduled time : PROMPT — **punc·tu·al·i·ty** \ˌpəŋ(k)-chə-'wal-ət-ē\ *n* — **punc·tu·al·ly** \'pəŋ(k)-chə-wə-lē\ *adv* — **punc·tu·al·ness** \-wəl-nəs\ *n*

punc·tu·ate \'pəŋ(k)-chə-ˌwāt\ *vb* **1** : to mark or divide with punctuation marks **2** : to break into or interrupt at intervals

punc·tu·a·tion \ˌpəŋ(k)-chə-'wā-shən\ *n* : the act, practice, or system of inserting standardized marks or signs in written matter to clarify the meaning and separate structural units

¹punc·ture \'pəŋ(k)-chər\ *n* **1** : the act of puncturing **2** : a hole or a narrow wound resulting from puncturing **3 :** a minute depression

[2]**puncture** *vb* **punc·tured**; **punc·tur·ing** \'pəŋ(k)-chə-riŋ, 'pəŋ(k)-shriŋ\ **1 :** to pierce with a pointed instrument or object **2 :** to suffer a puncture of **3 :** to become punctured **4 :** to make useless or absurd as if by a puncture

pun·dit \'pən-dət\ *n* **:** a wise or learned man **:** AUTHORITY

pun·gen·cy \'pən-jən-sē\ *n* **:** the quality or state of being pungent

pun·gent \'pən-jənt\ *adj* **1 :** having a stiff and sharp point **2 :** sharply stimulating to the mind **3 :** causing a sharp or irritating sensation; *esp* **:** ACRID — **pun·gent·ly** *adv*

pun·ish \'pən-ish\ *vb* **1 :** to cause to suffer pain or loss of freedom or privileges for an offense committed **:** CHASTISE **2 :** to inflict punishment for (as a crime) **3 :** to deal with or handle severely or roughly **4 :** to inflict punishment — **pun·ish·a·bil·i·ty** \ˌpən-ish-ə-'bil-ət-ē\ *n* — **pun·ish·a·ble** \'pən-ish-ə-bəl\ *adj*

pun·ish·ment \'pən-ish-mənt\ *n* **1 :** the act of punishing **:** the state or fact of being punished **2 :** the penalty for a fault or crime **3 :** severe, rough, or disastrous treatment

pu·ni·tive \'pyü-nət-iv\ *adj* **1 :** of or relating to punishment or penalties **2 :** intended to inflict punishment

[1]**punk** \'pəŋk\ *adj* **:** very poor in quality **:** BAD, MISERABLE

[2]**punk** *n* **1 :** wood so decayed as to be dry, crumbly, and useful for tinder **2 :** a dry spongy substance prepared from fungi and used to ignite fuses esp. of fireworks

pun·ster \'pən(t)-stər\ *n* **:** one who is given to making puns

[1]**punt** \'pənt\ *n* **:** a long narrow flat-bottomed boat with square ends usu. propelled with a pole

[2]**punt** *vb* **1 :** to propel by pushing with a pole against the bottom of a body of water **2 :** to go boating in a punt

[3]**punt** *vb* **1 :** to kick a football dropped from the hands before it touches the ground **2 :** to punt a ball

[4]**punt** *n* **:** the act or an instance of punting a ball

punt·er \'pənt-ər\ *n* **:** one that punts

pu·ny \'pyü-nē\ *adj* **:** slight or inferior in power, size, or importance **:** WEAK — **pu·ni·ness** *n*

[1]**pup** \'pəp\ *n* **:** a young dog; *also* **:** one of the young of various animals (as seals)

[2]**pup** *vi* **pupped**; **pup·ping :** to give birth to pups

pu·pa \'pyü-pə\ *n, pl* **pu·pae** \-(ˌ)pē, -ˌpī\ *or* **pupas :** an insect (as a bee, moth, or beetle) in an intermediate stage of its growth when it is in a case or cocoon — **pu·pal** \'pyü-pəl\ *adj*

[1]**pu·pil** \'pyü-pəl\ *n* **1 :** a child or young person in school or in the charge of a tutor **:** STUDENT **2 :** one who has been taught or influenced by a person of fame or distinction **:** DISCIPLE

[2]**pupil** *n* **:** the contractile usu. round aperture in the iris of the eye — **pu·pil·ar** \-pə-lər\ *adj* — **pu·pil·lary** \-ˌler-ē\ *adj*

pu·pil·age *or* **pu·pil·lage** \'pyü-pə-lij\ *n* **:** the state or period of being a pupil

pup·pet \'pəp-ət\ *n* **1 :** a small-scale figure of a living being (as a human) often made with jointed limbs and moved by hand or by strings or wires **2 :** DOLL 1 **3 :** one (as a person or a government) whose acts are controlled by an outside force or influence

pup·pe·teer \ˌpəp-ə-'ti(ə)r\ *n* **:** one who manipulates puppets or marionettes

pup·py \'pəp-ē\ *n, pl* **puppies 1 :** a young domestic dog; *esp* **:** one less than a year old **2 :** a silly or ill-bred young man — **pup·py·ish** \-ē-ish\ *adj*

pur·blind \'pər-ˌblīnd\ *adj* **1 :** partly blind **2 :** lacking in vision, insight, or understanding **:** OBTUSE — **pur·blind·ly** *adv* — **pur·blind·ness** \-ˌblīn(d)-nəs\ *n*

[1]**pur·chase** \'pər-chəs\ *vt* **1 a :** to obtain by paying money or its equivalent **:** BUY **b :** to obtain by labor, danger, or sacrifice **:** EARN **2 :** to apply a device for obtaining a mechanical advantage to (as something to be moved); *also* **:** to move by a purchase — **pur·chas·a·ble** \-chə-sə-bəl\ *adj* — **pur·chas·er** *n*

[2]**purchase** *n* **1 :** an act or instance of purchasing **2 :** something purchased **3 :** a mechanical hold or advantage applied to the raising or moving of heavy bodies **4 :** a secure hold, grasp, or place to stand

pure \'pyù(ə)r\ *adj* **1 :** not mixed with anything else **:** free from everything that might taint, alter, or lower the quality **2 :** free from sin or moral guilt; *esp* **:** marked by chastity **3 :** nothing other than **:** MERE, SHEER, ABSOLUTE **4 :** ABSTRACT, THEORETICAL — **pure·ness** *n*

pure·bred \-'bred\ *adj* **:** bred from members of a recognized breed, strain, or kind without admixture of other blood over many generations — **pure·bred** \-ˌbred\ *n*

[1]**pu·ree** \pyù-'rā, -'rē\ *n* **1 :** a paste or thick liquid suspension usu. produced by rubbing cooked food through a sieve **2 :** a thick soup having pureed vegetables as a base

[2]**puree** *vt* **pu·reed**; **pu·ree·ing :** to boil soft and then rub through a sieve

pure·ly \'pyù(ə)r-lē\ *adv* **1 :** without admixture of anything injurious or foreign **2 :** MERELY, SOLELY **3 :** CHASTELY, INNOCENTLY **4 :** COMPLETELY

pur·ga·tion \ˌpər-'gā-shən\ *n* **:** the act or result of purging

[1]**pur·ga·tive** \'pər-gət-iv\ *adj* **:** purging or tending to purge; *esp* **:** causing a usu. marked looseness of the bowels

[2]**purgative** *n* **:** a purgative medicine

pur·ga·to·ri·al \ˌpər-gə-'tōr-ē-əl\ *adj* **1 :** cleansing of sin **:** EXPIATORY **2 :** of or relating to purgatory

pur·ga·to·ry \'pər-gə-ˌtōr-ē\ *n, pl* **-ries 1 :** an intermediate state after death for expiatory purification **2 :** a place or state of temporary punishment

[1]**purge** \'pərj\ *vb* **1 :** to cleanse or purify by separating and carrying off impurities; *esp* **:** to remove sin or guilt from **2 :** to have or cause vigorous and usu. repeated evacuation of the bowels **3 :** to get rid of (as disloyal or suspect elements) by a purge — **purg·er** *n*

[2]**purge** *n* **1 a :** an act or instance of purging **b :** a ridding of persons regarded as treacherous or disloyal **2 :** something that purges; *esp* **:** PURGATIVE

pu·ri·fi·ca·tion \ˌpyùr-ə-fə-'kā-shən\ *n* **:** an act or instance of purifying or of being purified

pu·ri·fi·ca·tor \'pyùr-ə-fə-ˌkāt-ər\ *n* **1 :** PURIFIER **2 :** a linen cloth used to wipe the chalice after celebration of the Eucharist

pu·rif·i·ca·to·ry \pyùr-'if-i-kə-ˌtōr-ē, 'pyùr-ə-fə-kə-\ *adj* **:** serving, tending, or intended to purify

pu·ri·fy \'pyùr-ə-ˌfī\ *vb* **-fied**; **-fy·ing 1 :** to make pure **:** free from anything alien, extraneous, improper, corrupting, or damaging **2 :** to grow or become pure or clean — **pu·ri·fi·er** \-ˌfī(-ə)r\ *n*

pur·ism \'pyù(ə)r-ˌiz-əm\ *n* **:** rigid adherence to or insistence on nicety esp. in use of words — **pur·ist** \-əst\ *n* — **pu·ris·tic** \pyùr-'is-tik\ *adj*

pu·ri·tan \'pyùr-ət-ᵊn\ *n* **1** *cap* **:** a member of a 16th and 17th century Protestant group in England and New England opposing as unscriptural many traditional customs of the Church of England **2 :** one who practices or preaches or follows a stricter moral code than that which prevails — **puritan** *adj, often cap* — **pu·ri·tan·i·cal** \ˌpyùr-ə-'tan-i-kəl\ *adj* — **pu·ri·tan·i·cal·ly** \-k(ə-)lē\ *adv* — **pu·ri·tan·ism** \'pyùr-ət-ᵊn-ˌiz-əm\ *n, often cap*

pu·ri·ty \'pyùr-ət-ē\ *n* **:** the quality or state of being pure: as **a :** freedom from impurities **:** CLEANNESS **b :** freedom from guilt or sin **c :** freedom from all elements considered linguistically or stylistically inappropriate

[1]**purl** \'pərl\ *n* **:** a stitch in knitting

[2]**purl** *vb* **:** to knit in purl stitch

[3]**purl** *n* **1 :** a purling or swirling stream or rill **2 :** a gentle murmur or movement (as of purling water)

⁴purl *vi* **1 :** EDDY, SWIRL **2 :** to make a soft murmuring sound like that of a purling stream

pur·lieu \'pərl-ˌyü\ *n* **1 a :** a place of resort **:** HAUNT **b** *pl* **:** BOUNDS **2 a :** an outlying or adjacent district **b** *pl* **:** ENVIRONS

pur·loin \(ˌ)pər-'lȯin, 'pər-ˌ\ *vb* **:** STEAL, FILCH — **pur·loin·er** *n*

¹pur·ple \'pər-pəl\ *adj* **1 :** of the color purple **2 :** highly rhetorical **:** ORNATE

²purple *n* **1 :** any of various colors that fall about midway between red and blue in hue **2 a :** cloth dyed purple **b :** a garment of purple cloth; *esp* **:** a robe worn as an emblem of rank or authority **3 :** imperial or regal rank or power **:** exalted station

³purple *vb* **pur·pled; pur·pling** \'pər-p(ə-)liŋ\ **:** to turn purple

pur·plish \'pər-p(ə-)lish\ *adj* **:** somewhat purple

¹pur·port \'pər-ˌpōrt\ *n* **:** meaning conveyed, professed, or implied **:** IMPORT; *also* **:** SUBSTANCE, GIST

²pur·port \(ˌ)pər-'pōrt\ *vt* **:** to give the impression of being **:** CLAIM, PROFESS

pur·port·ed *adj* **:** REPUTED, RUMORED — **pur·port·ed·ly** *adv*

¹pur·pose \'pər-pəs\ *n* **1 a :** something set up as an end to be attained **:** INTENTION **b :** RESOLUTION, DETERMINATION **2 :** an object or result aimed at or achieved **3 :** a subject under discussion — **pur·pose·ful** \-fəl\ *adj* — **pur·pose·ful·ly** \-fə-lē\ *adv* — **pur·pose·ful·ness** \-fəl-nəs\ *n* — **pur·pose·less** \-ləs\ *adj* — **on purpose :** by intent **:** INTENTIONALLY

²purpose *vt* **:** to propose as an aim to oneself **:** INTEND

pur·pose·ly \'pər-pəs-lē\ *adv* **:** with a deliberate or express purpose **:** INTENTIONALLY

pur·pos·ive \'pər-pə-siv\ *adj* **1 :** serving or effecting a useful end though not clearly as a result of design **2 :** having or tending to fulfill a conscious purpose or design **:** PURPOSEFUL — **pur·pos·ive·ly** *adv* — **pur·pos·ive·ness** *n*

purr \'pər\ *n* **:** a low vibratory murmur typical of a cat apparently contented or pleased — **purr** *vb*

¹purse \'pərs\ *n* **1 a :** a small receptacle (as a wallet) esp. to carry money **b :** a receptacle (as a pouch) shaped like a purse **2 a :** RESOURCES, FUNDS **b :** a sum of money offered as a prize or present

²purse *vt* **1 :** to put into a purse **2 :** PUCKER, KNIT

purse–proud \-ˌpraủd\ *adj* **:** proud because of one's wealth

purs·er \'pər-sər\ *n* **:** an official on a ship who keeps accounts and attends to the comfort and welfare of passengers

pur·su·ance \pər-'sü-ən(t)s\ *n* **:** the act of pursuing or carrying out

pursuant to *prep* **:** in carrying out **:** in conformance to **:** according to

pur·sue \pər-'sü\ *vb* **1 :** to follow in order to overtake and capture or destroy **2 :** to try to obtain or accomplish **:** SEEK **3 :** to proceed along **:** FOLLOW **4 :** to engage in **:** PRACTICE **5 :** HARASS, HAUNT **6 :** COURT, WOO — **pur·su·er** *n*

pur·suit \pər-'süt\ *n* **1 :** the act of pursuing **2 :** an activity that one engages in esp. as a vocation **:** OCCUPATION

pur·sui·vant \'pər-s(w)i-vənt\ *n* **1 :** an officer of arms ranking below a herald but having similar duties **2 :** FOLLOWER, ATTENDANT

pu·ru·lent \'pyủr-(y)ə-lənt\ *adj* **:** containing, consisting of, or accompanied by the formation of pus — **pu·ru·lence** \-lən(t)s\ *n*

pur·vey \(ˌ)pər-'vā, 'pər-ˌ\ *vt* **:** to supply (as provisions) usu. as a business — **pur·vey·ance** \-ən(t)s\ *n*

pur·vey·or \-ər\ *n* **:** a person who supplies esp. provisions **:** CATERER

pur·view \'pər-ˌvyü\ *n* **1 :** the range or limit of authority, competence, responsibility, concern, or intention **2 :** range of vision, understanding, or cognizance

pus \'pəs\ *n* **:** thick opaque usu. yellowish white fluid matter formed by suppuration (as in an abscess) and containing white blood cells, tissue debris, and microorganisms

push \'pủsh\ *vb* **1 a :** to press against with force in order to drive or impel **b :** to move away or ahead by pressure without striking **2 :** to thrust forward, downward, or outward **3 a :** to press or urge forward **b :** to prosecute with vigor or effectiveness — **push·er** *n*

²push *n* **1 :** a vigorous advance against obstacles (as a military offensive) **2 :** a condition or occasion of stress **:** EMERGENCY **3 :** an act of pushing: as **a :** a sudden thrust **:** SHOVE **b :** a steady application of physical force in a direction away from the body exerting it **c :** a stimulating effect or action

push–but·ton \ˌpủsh-ˌbət-ᵊn\ *adj* **:** using or dependent on complex and more or less automatic mechanisms

push·cart \'pủsh-ˌkärt\ *n* **:** a cart or barrow pushed by hand

push·ing *adj* **1 :** ENTERPRISING, ENERGETIC **2 :** tactlessly forward or officious

push·over \'pủsh-ˌō-vər\ *n* **1 :** an opponent easy to defeat or a victim capable of no effective resistance **2 :** someone unwilling or unable to resist the power of a particular attraction or appeal **3 :** something accomplished without difficulty **:** SNAP

pushy \'pủsh-ē\ *adj* **:** aggressive often to an objectionable degree **:** FORWARD — **push·i·ly** \'pủsh-ə-lē\ *adv* — **push·i·ness** \'pủsh-ē-nəs\ *n*

pu·sil·la·nim·i·ty \ˌpyü-sə-lə-'nim-ət-ē\ *n* **:** the quality or state of being pusillanimous **:** COWARDLINESS

pu·sil·lan·i·mous \ˌpyü-sə-'lan-ə-məs\ *adj* **1 :** lacking in manly strength or spirit **:** COWARDLY **2 :** indicative of or resulting from lack of courage and weakness of spirit — **pu·sil·lan·i·mous·ly** *adv*

puss \'pủs\ *n* **1 :** CAT **2 :** GIRL

¹pussy \'pủs-ē\ *n, pl* **puss·ies :** PUSS

²pus·sy \'pəs-ē\ *adj* **:** full of or resembling pus

puss·y·foot \'pủs-ē-ˌfủt\ *vi* **1 :** to tread or move warily or stealthily **2 :** to refrain from committing oneself **:** HEDGE

pus·tule \'pəs-chül\ *n* **1 :** a small elevation of the skin having an inflamed base and containing pus **2 :** a small elevation resembling a pimple or blister

put \'pủt\ *vb* **put; put·ting 1 a :** to place in or move into a particular position or relationship **b :** to throw with an overhand pushing motion **c :** to bring into a specified state or condition **2 a :** to cause to endure or suffer something **b :** IMPOSE, INFLICT **c :** to apply to some end **3 :** to set before one for judgment or decision (as by a formal vote) **4 :** to give expression to esp. in intelligible language **:** TRANSLATE **5 a :** to devote or urge to an activity or end **b :** INVEST **6 a :** to give as an estimate **b :** ATTACH, ATTRIBUTE **c :** IMPUTE **7 :** to commence a voyage; *also* **:** to take a course — **put forth 1 :** to bring into action **:** EXERT **2 :** to produce or send out by growth **3 :** to start out — **put forward :** PROPOSE — **put in mind :** REMIND — **put to it :** to give difficulty to

put across *vt* **:** to achieve or convey successfully

pu·ta·tive \'pyüt-ət-iv\ *adj* **:** commonly accepted or supposed **:** REPUTED — **pu·ta·tive·ly** *adv*

put·out \'pủt-ˌaủt\ *n* **:** the retiring of a base runner or batter in baseball

pu·tre·fac·tion \ˌpyü-trə-'fak-shən\ *n* **1 :** the decomposing of organic matter **2 :** the state of being putrefied **:** CORRUPTION — **pu·tre·fac·tive** \-'fak-tiv\ *adj*

pu·tre·fy \'pyü-trə-ˌfī\ *vb* **-fied; -fy·ing :** to make or become putrid **:** DECOMPOSE, ROT

pu·trid \'pyü-trəd\ *adj* **1 a :** being in a state of putrefaction **:** ROTTEN **b :** characteristic of putrefaction **:** FOUL **2 a :** morally corrupt **b :** totally disagreeable or objectionable **:** VILE — **pu·trid·i·ty** \pyü-'trid-ət-ē\ *n* — **pu·trid·ly** \'pyü-trəd-lē\ *adv* — **pu·trid·ness** *n*

putsch \'pủch\ *n* **:** a secretly plotted and suddenly executed attempt to overthrow a government

putt \'pət\ *n* **:** a golf stroke made on the green to cause the ball to roll into or near the hole — **putt** *vb*

put·tee \ˌpə-'tē, pủ-; 'pət-ē\ *n* **1 :** a cloth strip wrapped around the leg from ankle to knee 2 : a leather legging secured by a strap or catch or by laces

[1]put·ter \'pu̇t-ər\ *n* : one that puts

[2]putt·er \'pət-ər\ *n* : a golf club used in putting

[3]put·ter \'pət-ər\ *vi* 1 : to move or act aimlessly or idly : DAWDLE 2 : to work at random : TINKER — **put·ter·er** \-ər-ər\ *n*

put through *vt* : to carry to a successful conclusion

[1]put·ty \'pət-ē\ *n, pl* **putties** : a cement usu. made of whiting and boiled linseed oil beaten or kneaded to the consistency of dough and used in fastening glass in sashes

[2]putty *vt* **put·tied**; **put·ty·ing** : to cement or seal up with putty

put up \(')pu̇t-'əp\ *vb* 1 a : to prepare for later use; *esp* : CAN b : to put away out of use 2 : to start (game) from cover 3 : to nominate for election 4 : to offer for public sale 5 : to give or obtain food and shelter : LODGE 6 : BUILD, ERECT 7 : to carry on 8 : to make available : PAY — **put up to** : INCITE, INSTIGATE — **put up with** : TOLERATE, ENDURE

put–up \ˌpu̇t-ˌəp\ *adj* : arranged secretly beforehand

[1]puz·zle \'pəz-əl\ *vb* **puz·zled**; **puz·zling** \'pəz-(ə-)liŋ\ 1 : to confuse the understanding of : PERPLEX, BEWILDER 2 : to solve with difficulty or ingenuity 3 : to be uncertain as to action or choice 4 : to attempt a solution of a puzzle — **puz·zler** \-(ə-)lər\ *n*

[2]puzzle *n* 1 : the state of being puzzled : PERPLEXITY 2 a : something that puzzles b : a question, problem, or contrivance designed for testing ingenuity

puz·zle·ment \'pəz-əl-mənt\ *n* 1 : the state of being puzzled : PERPLEXITY 2 : PUZZLE 2

pyg·my \'pig-mē\ *n, pl* **pygmies** : a person or thing very small for its kind : DWARF — **pygmy** *adj*

py·lon \'pī-ˌlän, -lən\ *n* 1 : a usu. massive gateway; *esp* : an ancient Egyptian one composed of two flat-topped pyramids and a crosspiece 2 : a tower for supporting either end of a wire over a long span 3 : a projection (as a post or tower) marking a prescribed course of flight for an airplane

py·or·rhea \ˌpī-ə-'rē-ə\ *n* : a pussy inflammation of the sockets of the teeth leading usu. to loosening of the teeth — **py·or·rhe·al** \-'rē-əl\ *adj*

[1]pyr·a·mid \'pir-ə-ˌmid\ *n* 1 : a massive structure built esp. in ancient Egypt that usu. has a square base and four triangular faces meeting at a point and contains tombs 2 : something felt to resemble a pyramid (as in shape or in broad-based organization) 3 : a polyhedron having for its base a plane figure with three or more angles and for its sides three or more triangles that meet to form the vertex — **py·ram·i·dal** \pə-'ram-əd-ᵊl, ˌpir-ə-'mid-ᵊl\ *adj* — **py·ram·i·dal·ly** \-ē\ *adv* — **pyr·a·mid·i·cal** \ˌpir-ə-'mid-i-kəl\ *adj*

[2]pyramid *vb* 1 : to increase rapidly and progressively step by step on a broad base 2 : to arrange or build up as if on the base of a pyramid

pyre \'pī(ə)r\ *n* : a combustible heap for burning a dead body as a funeral rite; *also* : a pile of material to be burned

py·ro·ma·nia \ˌpī-rō-'mā-nē-ə, -nyə\ *n* : a compulsive urge to start fires — **py·ro·ma·ni·ac** \-nē-ˌak\ *n* — **py·ro·ma·ni·a·cal** \-mə-'nī-ə-kəl\ *adj*

py·ro·tech·nic \ˌpī-rə-'tek-nik\ *n* 1 *pl* : the art of making or the manufacture and use of fireworks 2 *pl* a : materials (as fireworks) for flares or signals b : a display of fireworks 3 : a spectacular display (as of oratory) — usu. used in pl. — **py·ro·tech·ni·cal** \-ni-kəl\ *or* **pyrotechnic** *adj* — **py·ro·tech·ni·cal·ly** \-ni-k(ə-)lē\ *adv* — **py·ro·tech·nist** \-'tek-nəst\ *n*

py·thon \'pī-ˌthän, -thən\ *n* : a large constricting snake (as a boa); *esp* : any of an Old World genus including the largest recent snakes

pyx \'piks\ *n* : a small round case used to carry the Eucharist to the sick

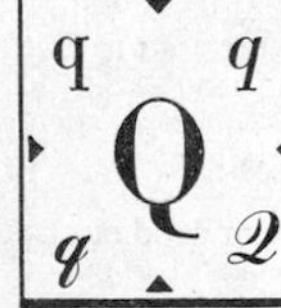

q \'kyü\ *n, often cap* : the 17th letter of the English alphabet

[1]quack \'kwak\ *vi* : to make the characteristic cry of a duck

[2]quack *n* : a cry made by or as if by quacking

[3]quack *n* 1 : a pretender to medical skill 2 : CHARLATAN — **quackery** \'kwak-(ə-)rē\ *n* — **quack·ish** \'kwak-ish\ *adj*

[4]quack *adj* : of, relating to, or characteristic of a quack; *esp* : pretending to cure diseases

quack·sal·ver \'kwak-ˌsal-vər\ *n* : CHARLATAN, QUACK

[1]quad \'kwäd\ *n* : QUADRANGLE

[2]quad *n* : QUADRUPLET

quad·ran·gle \'kwäd-ˌraŋ-gəl\ *n* 1 : QUADRILATERAL 2 a : a quadrilateral enclosure esp. when surrounded by buildings b : the buildings enclosing a quadrangle — **qua·dran·gu·lar** \kwä-'draŋ-gyə-lər\ *adj*

quad·rant \'kwäd-rənt\ *n* 1 : an instrument for measuring altitudes (as in astronomy or surveying) 2 : an arc of 90° : one quarter of a circle 3 : any of the four quarters into which something is divided by two real or imaginary lines that intersect each other at right angles — **qua·dran·tal** \kwä-'drant-ᵊl\ *adj*

qua·drat·ic \kwä-'drat-ik\ *adj* : involving no higher power of terms than a square — **quadratic** *n*

qua·dren·ni·al \kwä-'dren-ē-əl\ *adj* 1 : consisting of or lasting for four years 2 : occurring or being done every four years — **qua·dren·ni·al·ly** \-ē-ə-lē\ *adv*

[1]quad·ri·lat·er·al \ˌkwäd-rə-'lat-ə-rəl, -'la-trəl\ *adj* : having four sides

[2]quadrilateral *n* : a plane figure of four sides and four angles

qua·drille \kwä-'dril, k(w)ə-\ *n* : a square dance for four couples or music for this dance

quad·ri·par·tite \ˌkwäd-rə-'pär-ˌtīt\ *adj* 1 : consisting of four parts 2 : shared by four parties or persons

qua·droon \kwä-'drün\ *n* : a person of one-fourth Negro ancestry

quad·ru·ped \'kwäd-rə-ˌped\ *n* : an animal having four feet — **quadruped** *or* **qua·dru·pe·dal** \kwä-'drü-pəd-ᵊl, ˌkwäd-rə-'ped-\ *adj*

[1]qua·dru·ple \kwä-'drüp-ᵊl, -'drəp-; 'kwäd-rəp-\ *vb* **qua·dru·pled**; **qua·dru·pling** \-(ə-)liŋ\ : to make or become four times as great or as many

[2]quadruple *adj* 1 : having four units or members 2 : being four times as great or as many — **quadruple** *n*

qua·drup·let \kwä-'drəp-lət, -'drüp-; 'kwäd-rəp-\ *n* 1 : one of four offspring born at one birth 2 : a combination of four of a kind

[1]qua·dru·pli·cate \kwä-'drü-pli-kət\ *adj* 1 : repeated four times 2 : FOURTH

[2]qua·dru·pli·cate \-plə-ˌkāt\ *vt* 1 : QUADRUPLE 2 : to provide in quadruplicate — **qua·dru·pli·ca·tion** \(ˌ)kwä-ˌdrü-plə-'kā-shən\ *n*

[3]qua·dru·pli·cate \kwä-'drü-pli-kət\ *n* 1 : one of four like things 2 : four copies all alike

[1]quaff \'kwäf, 'kwaf\ *vb* : to drink deeply or repeatedly

[2]quaff *n* : a deep drink

quag·gy \ˈkwag-ē, ˈkwäg-\ *adj* **1** : BOGGY, MARSHY **2** : FLABBY, YIELDING

quag·mire \ˈkwag-ˌmī(ə)r, ˈkwäg-\ *n* : soft miry land that shakes or yields under the foot

qua·hog \ˈkwō-ˌhȯg, ˈk(w)ō-, -ˌhäg\ *n* : a round thick-shelled American clam

¹quail \ˈkwāl\ *n, pl* **quail** *or* **quails** : any of various game birds related to the grouse

²quail *vi* : to lose courage : shrink fearfully : COWER

quaint \ˈkwānt\ *adj* : unusual or different in character or appearance : ODD; *esp* : pleasingly old-fashioned or unfamiliar — **quaint·ly** *adv* — **quaint·ness** *n*

¹quake \ˈkwāk\ *vi* **1** : to shake or vibrate usu. from shock or instability **2** : to tremble or shudder usu. from cold or fear

²quake *n* : a shaking or trembling; *esp* : EARTHQUAKE

quak·er \ˈkwā-kər\ *n* **1** : one that quakes **2** *cap* : FRIEND 4 — **Quak·er·ism** \-kə-ˌriz-əm\ *n*

qual·i·fi·ca·tion \ˌkwäl-ə-fə-ˈkā-shən\ *n* **1** : the act or an instance of qualifying **2** : the state of being qualified **3 a** : a special skill, knowledge, or ability that fits a person for a particular work or position : FITNESS **b** : a condition that must be complied with (as for the attainment of a privilege) **4** : something that qualifies : LIMITATION

qual·i·fied \ˈkwäl-ə-ˌfīd\ *adj* **1** : having the necessary skill, knowledge, or ability to do something : FITTED **2** : limited or modified in some way

qual·i·fi·er \-ˌfī(-ə)r\ *n* : one that qualifies

qual·i·fy \ˈkwäl-ə-ˌfī\ *vb* **-fied**; **-fy·ing** **1 a** : to reduce from a general to a particular or restricted form : MODIFY **b** : to make less harsh or strict : MODERATE **c** : to limit the meaning of (as a noun) **2** : to characterize by naming an attribute : DESCRIBE **3 a** : to fit by training, skill, or ability for a special purpose **b** : to declare competent or adequate : CERTIFY, LICENSE **4** : to be fit (as for an office); *also* : to demonstrate the necessary ability (as in a race)

qual·i·ta·tive \ˈkwäl-ə-ˌtāt-iv\ *adj* : of, relating to, or involving quality or kind — **qual·i·ta·tive·ly** *adv*

qual·i·ty \ˈkwäl-ət-ē\ *n, pl* **-ties** **1 a** : peculiar and essential character : NATURE **b** : an inherent feature : PROPERTY **2 a** : degree of excellence : GRADE **b** : superiority in kind **3** : social status : RANK **4** : a distinguishing attribute : CHARACTERISTIC

qualm \ˈkwäm, ˈkwȯm\ *n* **1** : a sudden attack of illness, faintness, or nausea **2** : a sudden fear or misgiving **3** : a feeling of doubt or hesitation in matters of conscience : SCRUPLE — **qualmy** \-ē\ *adj*

qualm·ish \-ish\ *adj* **1 a** : feeling qualms : NAUSEATED **b** : overly scrupulous : SQUEAMISH **2** : of, relating to, or producing qualms — **qualm·ish·ly** *adv*

quan·da·ry \ˈkwän-d(ə-)rē\ *n, pl* **-ries** : a state of perplexity or doubt : DILEMMA

quan·ti·ta·tive \ˈkwän(t)-ə-ˌtāt-iv\ *adj* : of, relating to, or involving quantity — **quan·ti·ta·tive·ly** *adv*

quan·ti·ty \ˈkwän(t)-ət-ē\ *n, pl* **-ties** **1 a** : an indefinite amount or number **b** : a determinate or estimated amount **c** : a considerable amount or number — often used in pl. **2** : the aspect in which a thing is measurable in terms of degree or magnitude

quan·tum \ˈkwänt-əm\ *n, pl* **quan·ta** \ˈkwänt-ə\ **1** : QUANTITY, AMOUNT **2** : one of the very small parcels into which many forms of energy are subdivided

¹quar·an·tine \ˈkwȯr-ən-ˌtēn\ *n* **1 a** : a term during which a ship arriving in port and suspected of carrying contagious disease is forbidden contact with the shore **b** : a restraint upon the activities or movements of persons or the transport of goods designed to prevent the spread of disease or pests **2** : a place (as a hospital) where individuals under quarantine are kept **3** : a state of enforced isolation — **quar·an·tin·a·ble** *adj*

²quarantine *vt* **1** : to detain in or exclude by quarantine **2** : to isolate from normal relations or intercourse

¹quar·rel \ˈkwȯr(-ə)l\ *n* **1** : a ground of dispute or complaint **2** : DISAGREEMENT, ALTERCATION; *esp* : an angry dispute

²quarrel *vi* **-reled** *or* **-relled**; **-rel·ing** *or* **-rel·ling** **1** : to find fault : CAVIL **2** : to contend or dispute actively : SQUABBLE — **quar·rel·er** *or* **quar·rel·ler** *n*

quar·rel·some \ˈkwȯr(-ə)l-səm\ *adj* : apt or disposed to quarrel : CONTENTIOUS — **quar·rel·some·ly** *adv*

¹quar·ry \ˈkwȯr-ē\ *n, pl* **quarries** **1** : the object of a chase; *esp* : game hunted with hawks **2** : PREY

²quarry *n, pl* **quarries** : an open excavation usu. for obtaining building stone, slate, or limestone

³quarry *vt* **quar·ried**; **quar·ry·ing** **1** : to dig or take from or as if from a quarry **2** : to make a quarry in — **quar·ri·er** *n*

quart \ˈkwȯrt\ *n* **1** : a measure of capacity that equals two pints **2** : a vessel or measure having a capacity of one quart

¹quar·ter \ˈkwȯrt-ər\ *n* **1** : one of four equal parts into which something is divisible **2** : a unit (as of weight or length) that equals one fourth of some larger unit **3** : something that is or approximates one fourth of something else: as **a** : a coin worth a fourth of a dollar **b** : one of the four equal parts into which the playing time of some games is divided **4** : someone or something (as a place, direction, or group) not definitely or implicitly specified **5 a** : a particular division or district of a city **b** *pl* : living accommodations : LODGING **6** : MERCY — **at close quarters** : at close range or in immediate contact

²quarter *vb* **1** : to divide into four essentially equal parts **2** : to provide with or occupy a lodging

quar·ter·back \-ˌbak\ *n* : an offensive football back who calls the signals and directs the offensive play of his team

quar·ter·deck \-ˌdek\ *n* **1** : the stern area of a ship's upper deck **2** : a part of a naval vessel set aside for ceremonial and official use

quarter horse *n* : an alert stocky muscular horse capable of high speed for short distances and of great endurance under the saddle

¹quar·ter·ly \ˈkwȯrt-ər-lē\ *adv* : at 3-month intervals

²quarterly *adj* : coming during or at the end of each 3-month interval

³quarterly *n, pl* **-lies** : a periodical published four times a year

quar·ter·mas·ter \ˈkwȯrt-ər-ˌmas-tər\ *n* **1** : a petty officer who attends to a ship's steering and signals **2** : an army officer responsible for the clothing and subsistence of a body of troops

quarter note *n* : a musical note equal in time value to a fourth of a whole note

quar·ter·staff \-ˌstaf\ *n* : a long stout staff formerly used as a weapon

quar·tet \kwȯr-ˈtet\ *n* **1** : a musical composition for four instruments or voices **2** : a group or set of four

quar·to \ˈkwȯrt-ō\ *n, pl* **quartos** **1** : the size of a piece of paper cut four from a sheet **2** : a book printed on quarto pages

quartz \ˈkwȯrts\ *n* : a common mineral consisting of silica often found in the form of colorless transparent crystals

¹quash \ˈkwäsh, ˈkwȯsh\ *vt* : to set aside or make void by judicial action

²quash *vt* : to suppress or extinguish completely : QUELL

¹qua·si \ˈkwā-ˌzī, -ˌsī; ˈkwäz-ē\ *adv* : in some sense or degree : SEEMINGLY

²quasi *adj* : having or legally regarded as having a likeness to something else

quat·rain \ˈkwä-ˌtrān\ *n* : a unit or group of four lines of verse

qua·ver \ˈkwā-vər\ *vb* **qua·vered**; **qua·ver·ing** \ˈkwāv-(ə-)riŋ\ **1** : TREMBLE, SHAKE **2** : TRILL **3** : to utter sound in tremulous uncertain tones — **quaver** *n* — **qua·ver·ing·ly** *adv* — **qua·very** \ˈkwāv-(ə-)rē\ *adj*

quay \ˈkē, ˈk(w)ā\ *n* : a paved bank or a solid artificial landing place beside navigable water for convenience in loading and unloading ships

quean \'kwēn\ *n* : a disreputable woman

quea·sy \'kwē-zē\ *adj* **1** : full of doubt : HAZARDOUS **2 a** : causing nausea **b** : NAUSEATED **3 a** : causing uneasiness **b** (1) : DELICATE, SQUEAMISH (2) : ill at ease — **quea·si·ly** \-zə-lē\ *adv* — **quea·si·ness** \-zē-nəs\ *n*

[1]**queen** \'kwēn\ *n* **1** : the wife or widow of a king **2** : a female monarch **3 a** : a woman eminent in rank, power, or attractions **b** : an attractive girl or woman; *esp* : a beauty contest winner **4** : a chess piece that can move as either a rook or a bishop and is the most privileged piece in the set **5** : a playing card bearing the stylized figure of a queen **6** : the fertile fully developed female of social bees, ants, and termites whose function is to lay eggs — **queen·dom** \-dəm\ *n* — **queen·like** *adj* — **queen·li·ness** \-lē-nəs\ *n* — **queen·ly** *adv or adj*

[2]**queen** *vb* **1 a** : to act like a queen **b** : to put on airs **2** : to become or promote to a queen in chess

queen consort *n, pl* **queens consort** : the wife of a reigning king

queen mother *n* : a dowager queen who is mother of the reigning sovereign

[1]**queer** \'kwi(ə)r\ *adj* **1 a** : differing from what is usual or normal : ODD **b** : ECCENTRIC, UNCONVENTIONAL **2** : QUESTIONABLE, SUSPICIOUS **3** : not quite well : QUEASY — **queer·ish** \-ish\ *adj* — **queer·ly** *adv* — **queer·ness** *n*

[2]**queer** *adv* : QUEERLY

[3]**queer** *vt* **1** : to spoil the effect or success of : DISRUPT **2** : to put or get into an embarrassing or disadvantageous situation

quell \'kwel\ *vt* **1** : to put down : SUPPRESS **2** : QUIET, PACIFY — **quell·er** *n*

quench \'kwench\ *vt* **1 a** : to put out : EXTINGUISH **b** : to put out the fire or light of **2** : SUBDUE, OVERCOME **3** : DESTROY **4** : SLAKE, SATISFY **5** : to cool (as heated steel) suddenly by immersion esp. in water or oil — **quench·a·ble** *adj* — **quench·er** *n* — **quench·less** \'kwench-ləs\ *adj*

quer·u·lous \'kwer-(y)ə-ləs\ *adj* **1** : habitually complaining : CAPTIOUS **2** : FRETFUL, WHINING — **quer·u·lous·ly** *adv* — **quer·u·lous·ness** *n*

[1]**que·ry** \'kwi(ə)r-ē\ *n, pl* **queries** **1** : QUESTION, INQUIRY **2** : a question in the mind : DOUBT

[2]**query** *vt* **que·ried**; **que·ry·ing** **1** : to put as a question **2** : to ask questions about esp. in order to resolve a doubt **3** : to ask questions of esp. with a desire for authoritative information

[1]**quest** \'kwest\ *n* **1** : an act or instance of seeking **2 a** : PURSUIT, SEARCH **b** : a chivalrous enterprise in medieval romance

[2]**quest** *vb* **1** : to go on a quest : SEEK **2** : to search for : PURSUE **3** : to ask for : DEMAND

[1]**ques·tion** \'kwes-chən\ *n* **1 a** (1) : an interrogative expression often used to test knowledge (2) : an interrogative sentence or clause **b** : a subject or aspect in dispute or open for discussion : ISSUE **c** : a subject or point of debate or a proposition to be voted on in a meeting **d** : the specific point at issue **2 a** : an act or instance of asking : INQUIRY **b** : OBJECTION, DISPUTE **c** : CHANCE, POSSIBILITY

[2]**question** *vb* **1 a** : to ask questions of or about **b** : INQUIRE **2** : CROSS-EXAMINE **3 a** : DOUBT, DISPUTE **b** : to subject to analysis : EXAMINE — **ques·tion·er** *n* — **ques·tion·ing·ly** *adv*

ques·tion·a·ble \'kwes-chə-nə-bəl\ *adj* **1** : affording reason for being doubted, questioned, or challenged : not certain or exact : PROBLEMATIC **2** : attended by well-grounded suspicions of being immoral, crude, false, or unsound : DUBIOUS — **ques·tion·a·bly** \-blē\ *adv*

question mark *n* : a punctuation mark ? used chiefly at the end of a sentence to indicate a direct question

ques·tion·naire \ˌkwes-chə-'na(ə)r\ *n* : a set of questions to be asked of a number of persons usu. in order to gather statistics (as on opinions, facts, or knowledge)

[1]**queue** \'kyü\ *n* **1** : a taillike braid of hair usu. worn hanging at the back of the head **2** : a line esp. of persons or vehicles

[2]**queue** *vb* **queued**; **queu·ing** *or* **queue·ing** : to line up or wait in a queue

[1]**quib·ble** \'kwib-əl\ *n* **1** : an evasion of or shift from the point : EQUIVOCATION **2** : a minor objection or criticism

[2]**quibble** *vi* **quib·bled**; **quib·bling** \'kwib-(ə-)liŋ\ **1** : to evade the issue : EQUIVOCATE **2 a** : CAVIL, CARP **b** : BICKER — **quib·bler** \-(ə-)lər\ *n*

[1]**quick** \'kwik\ *adj* **1** : RAPID, SPEEDY: as **a** : fast in understanding, thinking, or learning : mentally agile **b** : reacting with speed and sensitivity **c** : aroused immediately and intensely **d** : fast in development or occurrence **e** : marked by speed, readiness, or promptness of physical movement **2** : turning or bending at a sharp angle — **quick·ly** *adv* — **quick·ness** *n*

[2]**quick** *adv* : QUICKLY

[3]**quick** *n* **1** : a very sensitive area of flesh (as under a fingernail) **2** : the very center of something : HEART

quick bread *n* : a bread made with a leavening agent that permits immediate baking of the dough or batter mixture

quick·en \'kwik-ən\ *vb* **quick·ened**; **quick·en·ing** \'kwik-(ə-)niŋ\ **1 a** : to make or become alive : REVIVE **b** : to cause to be enlivened : STIMULATE **2** : to make or become more rapid : HASTEN, ACCELERATE **3** : to show vitality or animation **4** : to shine more brightly — **quick·en·er** *n*

quick–freeze \'kwik-'frēz\ *vt* **-froze** \-'frōz\; **-fro·zen** \-'frōz-ᵊn\; **-freez·ing** : to freeze (food) for preservation so rapidly that ice crystals formed are too small to rupture the cells and the natural juices and flavor are preserved

quick·ie \'kwik-ē\ *n* : something done or made in a hurry

quick·sand \'kwik-ˌsand\ *n* : a deep mass of loose sand mixed with water into which heavy objects sink

quick·sil·ver \-ˌsil-vər\ *n* : MERCURY 1

quick·step \-ˌstep\ *n* : a spirited march tune

quick–tem·pered \'kwik-'tem-pərd\ *adj* : easily angered : IRASCIBLE

quick–wit·ted \-'wit-əd\ *adj* : quick in perception and understanding : mentally alert — **quick–wit·ted·ness** *n*

quid \'kwid\ *n* : a cut or wad of something chewable

quid pro quo \ˌkwid-ˌprō-'kwō\ *n* : an equivalent something (as a gift, privilege, or action) in return

qui·es·cent \kwī-'es-ᵊnt, kwē-\ *adj* **1** : being at rest : INACTIVE, MOTIONLESS **2** : causing no trouble or symptoms — **qui·es·cence** \-ᵊn(t)s\ *n* — **qui·es·cent·ly** *adv*

[1]**qui·et** \'kwī-ət\ *n* : the quality or state of being quiet : TRANQUILLITY — **on the quiet** : in a secretive manner

[2]**quiet** *adj* **1 a** : marked by little or no motion or activity : CALM **b** : GENTLE, EASYGOING **c** : UNDISTURBED **d** : enjoyed in peace and relaxation **2 a** : free from noise or uproar : STILL **b** : UNOBTRUSIVE, CONSERVATIVE **3** : RETIRED, SECLUDED — **qui·et·ly** *adv* — **qui·et·ness** *n*

[3]**quiet** *adv* : QUIETLY

[4]**quiet** *vb* **1** : to cause to be quiet : CALM **2** : to become quiet — **qui·et·er** *n*

qui·e·tude \'kwī-ə-ˌt(y)üd\ *n* : TRANQUILLITY, QUIETNESS, REPOSE

qui·e·tus \kwī-'ēt-əs\ *n* **1** : a final freeing from something (as a debt or life itself) **2** : something that quiets or represses **3** : a state or period of inactivity

quill \'kwil\ *n* **1 a** : the hollow horny barrel of a feather; *also* : one of the large stiff feathers of the wing or tail **b** : one of the hollow sharp spines of a porcupine or hedgehog **2** : an article made from or resembling the quill of a feather; *esp* : a writing implement formed by cutting a nib on the base of the quill of a stiff feather

[1]**quilt** \'kwilt\ *n* : a bed coverlet having two layers of cloth

filled with wool, cotton, or down held in place by usu. patterned stitching

[2]**quilt** *vb* **1 a :** to fill, pad, or line like a quilt **b :** to stitch, sew, or cover with lines or patterns like those used in quilts **2 :** to make quilts

quilt·ing \'kwil-tiŋ\ *n* **1 :** the process of quilting **2 :** material that is quilted or used for making quilts

quince \'kwin(t)s\ *n* **:** the fruit of an Asiatic tree of the rose family that resembles a hard-fleshed yellow apple and is used esp. for marmalade, jelly, and preserves; *also* **:** this tree

qui·nine \'kwī-ˌnīn\ *n* **:** a bitter crystalline alkaloid from cinchona bark used in medicine esp. against malaria; *also* **:** a salt of this

quin·quen·ni·al \kwin-'kwen-ē-əl\ *adj* **1 :** consisting of or lasting for five years **2 :** occurring or being done every five years — **quinquennial** *n* — **quin·quen·ni·al·ly** \-ē-ə-lē\ *adv*

quin·sy \'kwin-zē\ *n* **:** a severe inflammation of the throat or adjacent parts with swelling and fever

quint \'kwint\ *n* **:** QUINTUPLET

quin·tes·sence \kwin-'tes-ᵊn(t)s\ *n* **1 :** the purest form of something **2 :** the most highly perfected type or example — **quint·es·sen·tial** \ˌkwint-ə-'sen-chəl\ *adj*

quin·tet \kwin-'tet\ *n* **1 :** a musical composition for five instruments or voices **2 :** a group or set of five

[1]**quin·tu·ple** \kwin-'t(y)üp-əl, -'təp-; 'kwint-əp-\ *adj* **1 :** having five units or members **2 :** being five times as great or as many — **quintuple** *n*

[2]**quintuple** *vb* **quin·tu·pled**; **quin·tu·pling** \-(ə-)liŋ\ **:** to make or become five times as great or as many

quin·tup·let \kwin-'təp-lət, -'t(y)üp-; 'kwint-əp-\ *n* **1 :** a combination of five of a kind **2 :** one of five offspring born at one birth

[1]**quip** \'kwip\ *n* **1 :** a clever usu. taunting remark **:** GIBE **2 :** a witty or funny observation or response **3 :** something strange or eccentric **:** ODDITY — **quip·ster** \-stər\ *n*

[2]**quip** *vb* **quipped**; **quip·ping** **1 :** to make quips **:** GIBE **2 :** to jest or gibe at

quire \'kwī(ə)r\ *n* **:** a collection of 24 or sometimes 25 sheets of paper of the same size and quality

quirk \'kwərk\ *n* **:** a peculiar trait **:** MANNERISM

quirt \'kwərt\ *n* **:** a riding whip with a short handle and a rawhide lash

quis·ling \'kwiz-liŋ\ *n* **:** a traitor who collaborates with the invaders of his country esp. by serving in a puppet government

[1]**quit** \'kwit\ *adj* **:** released from obligation, charge, or penalty **:** ABSOLVED; *esp* **:** FREE

[2]**quit** *vb* **quit**; **quit·ting** **1 :** to make full payment to or for **:** REPAY **2 :** ACQUIT **3 a :** to depart from or out of **b :** to bring (as a way of thought, acting, or living) to an end **:** RELINQUISH, ABANDON, FORSAKE **c :** to give up (an action, activity, or employment) **:** LEAVE **4 :** to admit defeat **:** SURRENDER

quite \'kwīt\ *adv* **1 :** COMPLETELY, WHOLLY **2 :** to an extreme **:** POSITIVELY **3 :** to a considerable extent **:** RATHER

quits \'kwits\ *adj* **:** even or equal with another (as by repaying a debt or returning a favor)

quit·tance \'kwit-ᵊn(t)s\ *n* **1 :** discharge from a debt or an obligation **2 :** RECOMPENSE, REQUITAL

quit·ter \'kwit-ər\ *n* **:** one that shirks or gives up too easily; *esp* **:** COWARD, DEFEATIST

[1]**quiv·er** \'kwiv-ər\ *n* **1 :** a case for carrying arrows **2 :** the arrows in a quiver

[2]**quiver** *vb* **quiv·ered**; **quiv·er·ing** \'kwiv-(ə-)riŋ\ **:** to move with a slight trembling motion

[3]**quiver** *n* **:** the act or action of quivering **:** TREMOR

quix·ot·ic \kwik-'sät-ik\ *adj* **:** idealistic to an impractical degree — **quix·ot·i·cal·ly** \-'sät-i-k(ə-)lē\ *adv* — **quix·o·tism** \'kwik-sə-ˌtiz-əm\ *n*

[1]**quiz** \'kwiz\ *n, pl* **quiz·zes** **1 :** an eccentric person **2 :** a practical joke **3 :** a short oral or written test

[2]**quiz** *vt* **quizzed**; **quiz·zing** **1 :** to make fun of **:** MOCK **2 :** to look at inquisitively **3 :** to question closely **:** EXAMINE — **quiz·zer** *n*

quiz·zi·cal \'kwiz-i-kəl\ *adj* **1 :** slightly eccentric **:** ODD **2 :** BANTERING, TEASING **3 :** QUESTIONING, INQUISITIVE — **quiz·zi·cal·ly** \-k(ə-)lē\ *adv*

quoit \'kwāt, 'k(w)öit\ *n* **1 :** a flattened ring of iron or circle of rope used in a throwing game to encircle a fixed peg **2** *pl* **:** a game played with quoits

quon·dam \'kwän-dəm, -ˌdam\ *adj* **:** FORMER, SOMETIME

quo·rum \'kwōr-əm\ *n* **:** the number of officers or members of a body that when duly assembled is legally competent to transact business

quo·ta \'kwōt-ə\ *n* **:** a proportional part or share; *esp* **:** the share or proportion assigned to each member of a body

quot·a·ble \'kwōt-ə-bəl\ *adj* **:** fit for or worth quoting

quo·ta·tion \kwō-'tā-shən\ *n* **1 :** something that is quoted; *esp* **:** a passage referred to or repeated **2 :** the act or process of quoting

quotation mark *n* **:** one of a pair of punctuation marks " " or " " or ' ' or ' ' used chiefly to indicate the beginning and the end of a quotation in which the exact phraseology of another or of a text is directly cited

[1]**quote** \'kwōt\ *vb* **1 a :** to speak or write (a passage) from another usu. with credit acknowledgment **b :** to repeat a passage from esp. as authority or illustration **2 :** to cite in illustration **3 a :** to name (the current price) of a commodity, stock, or bond **b :** to give exact information on

[2]**quote** *n* **1 :** QUOTATION **2 :** QUOTATION MARK

quo·tid·i·an \kwō-'tid-ē-ən\ *adj* **1 :** DAILY **2 :** COMMONPLACE, ORDINARY

quo·tient \'kwō-shənt\ *n* **:** the number resulting from the division of one number by another

r \'är\ *n, often cap* **:** the 18th letter of the English alphabet

[1]**rab·bet** \'rab-ət\ *n* **:** a groove or recess cut in the edge or face of a surface esp. to receive the edge of another surface

[2]**rabbet** *vt* **1 :** to cut a rabbet in **2 :** to join the edges of by a rabbet

rab·bi \'rab-ˌī\ *n* **1 :** MASTER, TEACHER — used as a term of address for Jewish religious leaders **2 :** a Jew trained professionally and ordained as the official leader of a Jewish congregation — **rab·bin·ic** \rə-'bin-ik, ra-\ *adj* — **rab·bin·i·cal** \-'bin-i-kəl\ *adj*

rab·bin·ate \'rab-ə-nət, -ˌnāt\ *n* **1 :** the office or tenure of a rabbi **2 :** a group of rabbis

rab·bit \'rab-ət\ *n* **:** a small long-eared burrowing mammal related to the hare; *also* **:** its pelt

rab·ble \'rab-əl\ *n* **1 :** MOB **2 :** a body of people looked down upon as ignorant and disorderly

rab·id \'rab-əd\ *adj* **1 :** extremely violent **:** FURIOUS **2 :** going to extreme lengths in expressing or pursuing a feeling, interest, or opinion **3 :** affected with rabies — **rab·id·ly** *adv* — **rab·id·ness** *n*

ra·bies \'rā-bēz\ *n* **:** an acute deadly virus disease transmitted by the bite of a rabid animal — **ra·bic** \-bik\ *adj*

rac·coon \ra-'kün\ *n, pl* **raccoon** *or* **raccoons :** a small tree-dwelling gray mammal of No. America that has a bushy ringed tail; *also* **:** its pelt

[1]**race** \'rās\ *n* **1 :** a strong or rapid current of water; *also* **:** the channel or passage for such a current **2 a :** a set course or duration of time **b :** the course of life **3 a :** a contest in speed **b :** a contest involving progress toward a goal

[2]**race** *vb* **1 :** to run in a race **2 :** to go, move, or drive at top speed or out of control **3 :** to engage in a race with

[3]**race** *n* **1 a :** a group of people of common ancestry or stock **b :** one of the three, four, or five primary divisions commonly recognized in mankind and based on readily observed traits (as skin color) that are transmitted by heredity **c :** MANKIND **2 :** a group of individuals within a biological species able to breed together

race·course \'rās-ˌkōrs\ *n* **:** a course for racing

race·horse \-ˌhȯrs\ *n* **:** a horse bred or kept for racing

ra·ceme \rā-'sēm\ *n* **:** a flower cluster consisting of a long axis bearing flowers on short stems in succession toward the apex — **rac·e·mose** \'ras-ə-ˌmōs, rā-'sē-\ *adj*

ra·cial \'rā-shəl\ *adj* **1 :** of, relating to, or based on race **2 :** existing or occurring between human races — **ra·cial·ly** \-shə-lē\ *adv*

rac·i·ly \'rā-sə-lē\ *adv* **:** in a racy manner

rac·i·ness \-sē-nəs\ *n* **:** the quality or state of being racy

rac·ism \'rā-ˌsiz-əm\ *n* **:** belief that some races of men are by nature superior to others; *also* **:** discrimination based upon such belief — **rac·ist** \'rā-səst\ *n*

[1]**rack** \'rak\ *n* **1 :** an instrument of torture on which a body is stretched **2 :** a framework, stand, or grating on or in which articles are placed **3 :** a bar with teeth on one face for gearing with a pinion or worm gear

[2]**rack** *vt* **1 :** to torture on the rack **2 :** to cause to suffer torture, pain, or anguish **3 :** to stretch or strain violently

[1]**rack·et** \'rak-ət\ *n* **:** a usu. long-handled implement used for hitting a ball or shuttlecock that consists of an open oval frame strung with a netting (as of nylon)

[2]**racket** *n* **1 :** confused clattering noise **:** DIN **2 :** a dishonest scheme; *esp* **:** one for obtaining money by cheating or through threats of violence

[3]**racket** *vi* **:** to move with or make a racket

rack·e·teer \ˌrak-ə-'ti(ə)r\ *n* **:** a person engaged in a racket — **racketeer** *vi*

ra·con·teur \ˌrak-ˌän-'tər\ *n* **:** one who excels in telling anecdotes

racy \'rā-sē\ *adj* **1 :** having the distinctive quality of something in its original or most characteristic form **2 a :** full of zest or vigor **:** LIVELY **b :** PIQUANT, PUNGENT **c :** RISQUÉ, SUGGESTIVE

ra·dar \'rā-ˌdär\ *n* **:** a device that sends out a powerful beam of radio waves that when reflected back to it from a distant object indicate the position and direction of motion of the object — **ra·dar·man** \-mən, -ˌman\ *n*

[1]**ra·di·al** \'rād-ē-əl\ *adj* **:** arranged or having parts arranged like rays from a common center — **ra·di·al·ly** \-ē-ə-lē\ *adv*

[2]**radial** *n* **:** a pneumatic tire in which the cords of the reinforcing fabric run at right angles to the line of the tread

ra·di·ance \'rād-ē-ən(t)s\ *n* **:** radiant quality or state

ra·di·ant \'rād-ē-ənt\ *adj* **1 :** vividly bright and shining **:** GLOWING **2 :** beaming with happiness **3 :** emitted or transmitted by radiation — **ra·di·ant·ly** *adv*

radiant energy *n* **:** energy transmitted in the form of electromagnetic waves

ra·di·ate \'rād-ē-ˌāt\ *vb* **1 :** to send out rays **:** shine brightly **2 :** to issue in rays **3 :** to spread out from or as if from a center — **ra·di·a·tion** \ˌrād-ē-'ā-shən\ *n*

ra·di·a·tor \'rād-ē-ˌāt-ər\ *n* **:** a device for heating a room or for cooling (as an automobile engine) by radiation

[1]**rad·i·cal** \'rad-i-kəl\ *adj* **1 :** of or relating to the origin **:** FUNDAMENTAL **2 a :** EXTREME **b :** of, relating to, or constituting a political group associated with views, practices, and policies of extreme change — **rad·i·cal·ism** \'rad-i-kə-ˌliz-əm\ *n* — **rad·i·cal·ly** \-k(ə-)lē\ *adv* — **rad·i·cal·ness** *n*

[2]**radical** *n* **1 :** one who is radical **2 :** a group of atoms that is replaceable by a single atom and is capable of remaining unchanged during a series of reactions **3 a :** the indicated root of a mathematical expression **b :** the sign $\sqrt{}$ placed before an expression in mathematics to indicate that its root is to be extracted

radii *pl of* RADIUS

[1]**ra·dio** \'rād-ē-ˌō\ *n, pl* **ra·di·os 1 :** the sending or receiving of messages or effects and esp. sound by means of electric waves without a connecting wire **2 :** a radio receiving set **3 :** the radio broadcasting industry — **radio** *adj*

[2]**radio** *vb* **1 :** to send or communicate by radio **2 :** to send a radio message to

ra·dio·ac·tive \ˌrād-ē-ō-'ak-tiv\ *adj* **:** of, caused by, or exhibiting radioactivity — **ra·dio·ac·tive·ly** *adv*

ra·dio·ac·tiv·i·ty \-ˌak-'tiv-ət-ē\ *n* **:** the property possessed by some elements (as uranium) of spontaneously emitting rays of radiant energy by the disintegration of the nuclei of atoms

radio astronomy *n* **:** astronomy dealing with electromagnetic radio waves received from outside the earth's atmosphere — **radio astronomer** *n*

ra·dio·car·bon \ˌrād-ē-ō-'kär-bən\ *n* **:** CARBON 14

ra·dio·gram \'rād-ē-ō-ˌgram\ *n* **1 :** RADIOGRAPH **2 :** a message transmitted by radiotelegraphy

[1]**ra·dio·graph** \-ˌgraf\ *n* **:** a picture produced on a sensitive surface by a form of radiation other than light; *esp* **:** an X-ray photograph

[2]**radiograph** *vt* **:** to make a radiograph of

ra·dio·iso·tope \ˌrād-ē-ō-'ī-sə-ˌtōp\ *n* **:** a radioactive isotope

ra·di·ol·o·gy \ˌrād-ē-'äl-ə-jē\ *n* **:** the science of radioactive substances and high-energy radiations; *esp* **:** the use of radiant energy in medicine — **ra·dio·log·ic** \ˌrād-ē-ə-'läj-ik\ *adj* — **ra·dio·log·i·cal** \-'läj-i-kəl\ *adj* — **ra·di·ol·o·gist** \ˌrād-ē-'äl-ə-jəst\ *n*

ra·dio·tel·e·graph \ˌrād-ē-ō-'tel-ə-ˌgraf\ *n* **:** wireless telegraphy — **ra·dio·te·leg·ra·phy** \-tə-'leg-rə-fē\ *n*

ra·dio·tel·e·phone \-'tel-ə-ˌfōn\ *n* **:** a telephone that utilizes radio waves wholly or partly instead of connecting wires

radio telescope *n* : a radio receiver-antenna combination used for observation in radio astronomy
rad·ish \'rad-ish\ *n* : a pungent fleshy root usu. eaten raw; *also* : a plant of the mustard family whose roots are radishes
ra·di·um \'rād-ē-əm\ *n* : a metallic chemical element that emits radiant energy by the disintegration of the nuclei of atoms, and is used chiefly in luminous materials and in the treatment of cancer
ra·di·us \'rād-ē-əs\ *n, pl* **-dii** \-ē-ˌī\ **1** : a line segment extending from the center of a circle or sphere to the curve or surface **2** : a circular area defined by a radius
ra·don \'rā-ˌdän\ *n* : a heavy radioactive gaseous chemical element formed by disintegration of radium
raf·fia \'raf-ē-ə\ *n* : fiber from stalks of leaves of a Madagascar palm used esp. for baskets and hats
[1]**raf·fle** \'raf-əl\ *n* : a lottery in which the prize is won by one of numerous persons buying chances
[2]**raffle** *vt* **raf·fled**; **raf·fling** \'raf-(ə-)liŋ\ : to dispose of by a raffle
[1]**raft** \'raft\ *n* **1** : a collection of logs or timber fastened together for conveyance by water **2** : a flat structure for support or transportation on water
[2]**raft** *vb* **1** : to transport or move in or by means of a raft **2** : to make into a raft
[3]**raft** *n* : a large amount
raf·ter \'raf-tər\ *n* : one of the usu. sloping timbers that support a roof
[1]**rag** \'rag\ *n* **1 a** : a waste or worn piece of cloth **b** *pl* : shabby or tattered clothing **2** : something felt to resemble a rag of cloth
[2]**rag** *vt* **ragged** \'ragd\; **rag·ging** **1** : to rail at : SCOLD **2** : TEASE, HARASS
rag·a·muf·fin \'rag-ə-ˌməf-ən\ *n* : a ragged often disreputable person; *esp* : a poorly clothed often dirty child
[1]**rage** \'rāj\ *n* **1** : violent and uncontrolled anger : FURY **2** : CRAZE, VOGUE
[2]**rage** *vi* **1** : to be in a rage **2** : to be in tumult **3** : to prevail uncontrollably
rag·ged \'rag-əd\ *adj* **1 a** : torn or worn to or as if to tatters **b** : wearing tattered clothes **2** : executed in an irregular or uneven manner — **rag·ged·ly** *adv* — **rag·ged·ness** *n*
rag·lan \'rag-lən\ *n* : a loose overcoat having sleeves that extend to the neckline with slanted seams from the underarm to the neck
ra·gout \ra-'gü\ *n* : a highly seasoned meat stew with vegetables
rag·time \'rag-ˌtīm\ *n* **1** : musical rhythm in which the melody has the accented notes falling on beats that are not usu. accented **2** : music with ragtime rhythm
rag·weed \'rag-ˌwēd\ *n* : any of various weedy herbs that produce highly allergenic pollen
[1]**raid** \'rād\ *n* : a sudden usu. surprise attack or invasion
[2]**raid** *vt* : to make a raid on — **raid·er** *n*
[1]**rail** \'rāl\ *n* **1 a** : a bar extending from one post or support to another and serving as a guard or barrier **b** : RAILING **2 a** : a bar of rolled steel forming a track for wheeled vehicles **b** : RAILROAD
[2]**rail** *n, pl* **rails** *or* **rail** : any of a family of small wading birds related to the cranes
[3]**rail** *vi* : REVILE, SCOLD — **rail·er** *n*
rail·ing \'rā-liŋ\ *n* : a barrier of rails and their supports
rail·lery \'rā-lə-rē\ *n, pl* **-ler·ies** **1** : BANTER **2** : JEST
[1]**rail·road** \'rāl-ˌrōd\ *n* : a permanent road having a line of rails fixed to ties and laid on a roadbed and providing a track for cars drawn by locomotives or propelled by self-contained motors; *also* : such a road and its assets constituting a single property
[2]**railroad** *vb* **1 a** : to transport by railroad **b** : to work for a railroad company **2 a** : to push through hastily **b** : to convict with undue haste and by means of false charges or insufficient evidence — **rail·road·er** *n*
rail·way \'rāl-ˌwā\ *n* **1** : RAILROAD; *esp* : a railroad operating with light equipment or within a small area **2** : a line of track providing a runway for wheels
rai·ment \'rā-mənt\ *n* : CLOTHING, GARMENTS
[1]**rain** \'rān\ *n* **1** : water falling in drops condensed from vapor in the atmosphere; *also* : the descent of such water **2** : a heavy fall of particles or bodies — **rain·less** \-ləs\ *adj*
[2]**rain** *vb* **1** : to fall as water in drops from the clouds **2** : to send down rain **3** : to fall like rain **4** : to bestow abundantly
rain·bow \-ˌbō\ *n* : an arc or circle of colors that is formed opposite the sun by the refraction and reflection of the sun's rays in raindrops, spray, or mist
rain·coat \-ˌkōt\ *n* : a coat of waterproof or water-resistant material
rain·drop \-ˌdräp\ *n* : a drop of rain
rain·fall \-ˌfȯl\ *n* **1** : a fall of rain **2** : amount of precipitation
rain·proof \-'prüf\ *adj* : impervious to rain
rain·storm \-ˌstȯrm\ *n* : a storm of or with rain
rainy \'rā-nē\ *adj* : having much rain : SHOWERY
[1]**raise** \'rāz\ *vb* **1** : to cause to rise : LIFT **2** : AWAKEN, AROUSE **3 a** : to set upright by lifting or building **b** : to place higher in rank or dignity : ELEVATE **c** : END **4** : COLLECT **5 a** : to foster the growth and development of : GROW, REAR **b** : to bring up (a child) **6** : to give rise to : PROVOKE **7** : to bring up for consideration or debate **8 a** : INCREASE **b** : to increase the amount of a poker bet or a partner's bridge bid **9** : to make light and porous **10** : to cause (an elevated injury) to form on the skin — **rais·er** *n*
[2]**raise** *n* **1** : an act of raising or lifting **2 a** : an increase in amount (as of a bet or bid) **b** : an increase in pay
rai·sin \'rāz-^{ə}n\ *n* : a grape usu. of a special type dried for food
rai·son d'être \ˌrā-ˌzō^{n}-'detr^{ə}\ *n* : reason or justification for existence
ra·ja *or* **ra·jah** \'räj-ə\ *n* : an Indian prince
[1]**rake** \'rāk\ *n* : a long-handled garden tool having a bar with teeth or prongs
[2]**rake** *vt* **1** : to gather, loosen, or smooth with or as if with a rake **2** : to sweep the length of esp. with gunfire — **rak·er** *n*
[3]**rake** *n* : a slant or slope away from the perpendicular
[4]**rake** *n* : a dissolute person : LIBERTINE
rake–off \'rāk-ˌȯf\ *n* : an often unlawful commission or profit received by one party in a business deal
rak·ish \'rā-kish\ *adj* **1** : having a smart stylish appearance suggestive of speed **2** : negligent of convention or formality : JAUNTY — **rak·ish·ly** *adv* — **rak·ish·ness** *n*
[1]**ral·ly** \'ral-ē\ *vb* **ral·lied**; **ral·ly·ing** **1 a** : to bring together for a common purpose **b** : to bring back to order **2** : to rouse for action or from depression or weakness **3** : to come together to renew an effort **4** : RECOVER, REBOUND
[2]**rally** *n, pl* **rallies** **1** : the action of rallying **2** : a mass meeting intended to arouse group enthusiasm
[3]**rally** *vt* **ral·lied**; **ral·ly·ing** : BANTER, TEASE
[1]**ram** \'ram\ *n* **1** : a male sheep **2** : BATTERING RAM
[2]**ram** *vb* **rammed**; **ram·ming** **1** : to strike or strike against with violence : CRASH **2** : to force in, down, or together by or as if by driving or pressing **3** : to force passage or acceptance of — **ram·mer** *n*
[1]**ram·ble** \'ram-bəl\ *vb* **ram·bled**; **ram·bling** \-b(ə-)liŋ\ : to move aimlessly from place to place : WANDER
[2]**ramble** *n* : a leisurely excursion; *esp* : an aimless walk
ram·bler \'ram-blər\ *n* **1** : one that rambles **2** : a climbing rose with small flowers in large clusters
ram·bunc·tious \ram-'bəŋ(k)-shəs\ *adj* : UNRULY — **ram·bunc·tious·ly** *adv* — **ram·bunc·tious·ness** *n*

ram·ie \ˈram-ē, ˈrā-mē\ *n* : a strong lustrous textile fiber from an Asiatic nettle
ram·i·fi·ca·tion \ˌram-ə-fə-ˈkā-shən\ *n* **1** : the act or process of branching **2** : BRANCH, OFFSHOOT **3** : OUTGROWTH, CONSEQUENCE
ram·i·fy \ˈram-ə-ˌfī\ *vb* **-fied**; **-fy·ing** : to spread out or split up into branches or divisions
ramp \ˈramp\ *n* : a sloping passage or roadway connecting different levels
[1]**ram·page** \ˈram-ˌpāj, (ˈ)ram-ˈ\ *vi* : to rush wildly about
[2]**ram·page** \ˈram-ˌpāj\ *n* : a course of violent, riotous, or reckless action or behavior
ram·pant \ˈram-pənt, -ˌpant\ *adj* : unchecked in growth or spread — **ram·pan·cy** \-pən-sē\ *n* — **ram·pant·ly** *adv*
ram·part \ˈram-ˌpärt, -pərt\ *n* : a broad embankment raised as a fortification or protective barrier
ram·rod \ˈram-ˌräd\ *n* **1** : a rod for ramming home the charge in a muzzle-loading firearm **2** : a cleaning rod for small arms
ram·shack·le \ˈram-ˌshak-əl\ *adj* : appearing ready to collapse : RICKETY
ran *past of* RUN
[1]**ranch** \ˈranch\ *n* **1** : an establishment for the grazing and rearing of horses, cattle, or sheep **2** : a farm devoted to a specialty
[2]**ranch** *vb* : to live or work or raise livestock on a ranch
ranch·er \ˈran-chər\ *n* : one who owns or operates or works on a ranch
ran·cid \ˈran(t)-səd\ *adj* **1** : having a rank smell or taste typical of decomposed oil or fat **2** : RANK, ROTTEN — **ran·cid·i·ty** \ran-ˈsid-ət-ē\ *n* — **ran·cid·ness** *n*
ran·cor \ˈraŋ-kər\ *n* : strong ill will : intense hatred — **ran·cor·ous** \-k(ə-)rəs\ *adj* — **ran·cor·ous·ly** *adv*
[1]**ran·dom** \ˈran-dəm\ *n* : a haphazard course — **at random** : without definite aim, direction, rule, or method
[2]**random** *adj* **1** : lacking a definite plan, purpose, or pattern **2** : having a definite and esp. an equal probability of occurring — **ran·dom·ly** *adv* — **ran·dom·ness** *n*
rang *past of* RING
[1]**range** \ˈrānj\ *n* **1** : a series of things in a line : ROW **2** : a cooking stove **3 a** : a place that may be ranged over **b** : open land over which livestock may roam and feed **4** : the act of ranging about **5 a** (1) : the horizontal distance to which a projectile can be propelled (2) : the maximum distance a vehicle can travel without refueling **b** : a place where shooting is practiced; *also* : a course over which missiles are tested **6** : the space or extent included, covered, or used : SCOPE
[2]**range** *vb* **1 a** : to set in a row or in the proper order **b** : to place among others in a position or situation **2** : to rove over or through : roam freely **3 a** : to correspond in direction or line **b** : to extend in a particular direction **4** : to vary within limits
rang·er \ˈrān-jər\ *n* **1** : an officer charged with patrolling and protecting a forest **2** : one that ranges **3 a** : one of a body of troops who range over a region **b** : a soldier trained in close-range fighting and raiding tactics
rangy \ˈrān-jē\ *adj* : being long-limbed and slender — **rang·i·ness** *n*
ra·ni *or* **ra·nee** \rä-ˈnē\ *n* : an Indian queen : a rajah's wife
[1]**rank** \ˈraŋk\ *adj* **1** : strong and vigorous and usu. coarse in growth **2** : unpleasantly strong-smelling : FOUL — **rank·ly** *adv* — **rank·ness** *n*
[2]**rank** *n* **1** : ROW, SERIES **2** : a line of soldiers ranged side by side **3** *pl* : a group of individuals classed together **4** : relative position or order : STANDING **5** : official grade or status (as in the army or navy) **6** : position in regard to merit **7** : high social position **8** *pl* : the body of enlisted men in an army
[3]**rank** *vb* **1** : to arrange in lines or in a regular formation **2** : to determine the relative position of : RATE **3** : to take or have a position in relation to others : be in a class
rank and file *n* **1** : the enlisted men of an armed force **2** : the ordinary body of an organization or society as distinguished from the leaders
rank·ing \ˈraŋ-kiŋ\ *adj* : having a high position: as **a** : FOREMOST **b** : being next to the chairman in seniority
ran·kle \ˈraŋ-kəl\ *vb* **ran·kled**; **ran·kling** \-k(ə-)liŋ\ **1** : to cause anger, irritation, or deep bitterness **2** : to cause resentment or bitterness in : irritate deeply
ran·sack \ˈran-ˌsak, (ˈ)ran-ˈ\ *vt* : to search thoroughly : RUMMAGE; *esp* : to search through and rob — **ran·sack·er** *n*
[1]**ran·som** \ˈran(t)-səm\ *n* **1** : a consideration (as money) paid or demanded for the freedom of a captured person **2** : the act of ransoming
[2]**ransom** *vt* : to free from captivity or punishment by paying a price — **ran·som·er** *n*
rant \ˈrant\ *vb* **1** : to talk noisily, excitedly, or wildly **2** : to scold violently — **rant·er** *n*
[1]**rap** \ˈrap\ *n* : a sharp blow or knock
[2]**rap** *vb* **rapped**; **rap·ping** **1** : to give a quick sharp blow : KNOCK **2** : to utter suddenly with force
ra·pa·cious \rə-ˈpā-shəs\ *adj* **1** : excessively grasping or covetous **2** : living on prey : PREDATORY **3** : RAVENOUS, VORACIOUS — **ra·pa·cious·ly** *adv* — **ra·pa·cious·ness** *n* — **ra·pac·i·ty** \-ˈpas-ət-ē\ *n*
[1]**rape** \ˈrāp\ *vt* : to commit rape on : RAVISH — **rap·er** *n* — **rap·ist** \ˈrā-pəst\ *n*
[2]**rape** *n* **1** : a seizing by force **2** : sexual intercourse with a woman carried out without her consent and esp. by force
[1]**rap·id** \ˈrap-əd\ *adj* : marked by a fast rate of motion, activity, succession, or occurrence : SWIFT — **rap·id·ly** *adv* — **rap·id·ness** *n*
[2]**rapid** *n* : a part of a river where the current is fast and the surface is usu. broken by obstructions — usu. used in pl.
ra·pid·i·ty \rə-ˈpid-ət-ē, ra-\ *n* : SWIFTNESS, SPEED
ra·pi·er \ˈrā-pē-ər\ *n* : a straight 2-edged sword with a narrow pointed blade

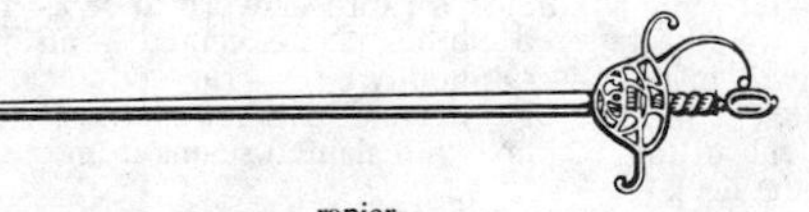
rapier

rap·ine \ˈrap-ən\ *n* : PILLAGE, PLUNDER
rap·port \ra-ˈpō(ə)r\ *n* : harmonious accord or relation that makes communication possible or easy
rap·scal·lion \rap-ˈskal-yən\ *n* : RASCAL, SCAMP
rapt \ˈrapt\ *adj* **1** : carried away with emotion : ENRAPTURED **2** : wholly absorbed : ENGROSSED — **rapt·ly** *adv* — **rapt·ness** *n*
rap·ture \ˈrap-chər\ *n* : a state of being carried away by joy or delight or love — **rap·tur·ous** \ˈrap-chə-rəs, ˈrap-shrəs\ *adj* — **rap·tur·ous·ly** *adv* — **rap·tur·ous·ness** *n*
[1]**rare** \ˈra(ə)r\ *adj* : cooked a short time : UNDERDONE
[2]**rare** *adj* **1** : not thick or dense : THIN **2** : unusually fine : EXCELLENT, SPLENDID **3** : seldom occurring or found : very uncommon : INFREQUENT — **rare·ness** *n*
rare·bit \ˈra(ə)r-bət\ *n* : WELSH RABBIT
rar·e·fac·tion \ˌrar-ə-ˈfak-shən\ *n* : the act or process of rarefying : the state of being rarefied
rar·e·fy \ˈrar-ə-ˌfī\ *vb* **-fied**; **-fy·ing** : to make or become thin, porous, or less dense
rare·ly \ˈra(ə)r-lē\ *adv* **1** : not often : SELDOM **2** : with rare skill : EXCELLENTLY **3** : UNUSUALLY
rar·i·ty \ˈrar-ət-ē\ *n, pl* **-ties** **1** : the quality, state, or fact of being rare **2** : someone or something rare

ras·cal \'ras-kəl\ *n* **1** : a mean, unprincipled, or dishonest person : ROGUE **2** : a mischievous person : IMP

ras·cal·i·ty \ra-'skal-ət-ē\ *n, pl* **-ties** : the act, actions, or character of a rascal

ras·cal·ly \'ras-kə-lē\ *adj* : of or characteristic of a rascal — **rascally** *adv*

¹rash \'rash\ *adj* **1** : being too hasty in speech or action or in making decisions **2** : showing undue disregard for consequences : RECKLESS — **rash·ly** *adv* — **rash·ness** *n*

²rash *n* : a breaking out of the skin with red spots (as in measles) : ERUPTION

rash·er \'rash-ər\ *n* : a thin slice of bacon or ham cut for broiling or frying

¹rasp \'rasp\ *vb* **1** : to rub with or as if with a rough file **2** : to grate harshly upon : IRRITATE **3** : to speak or utter in a grating tone

²rasp *n* : a coarse file with cutting points instead of lines

rasp·ber·ry \'raz-,ber-ē, -b(ə-)rē\ *n* **1 a** : any of various black or red edible berries produced by some brambles **b** : a bramble that bears raspberries **2** : a sound of contempt made by protruding the tongue between the lips and expelling air forcibly to produce a vibration

raspy \'ras-pē\ *adj* **1** : GRATING, HARSH **2** : IRRITABLE

¹rat \'rat\ *n* **1** : a scaly-tailed gnawing rodent larger than the mouse **2** : a person who deserts a cause or betrays his fellows

²rat *vi* **rat·ted**; **rat·ting** **1** : to desert or inform on one's associates **2** : to catch or hunt rats

ratch·et \'rach-ət\ *n* : a mechanism that consists of a bar or wheel having inclined teeth into which a pawl drops so as to allow motion in one direction only

¹rate \'rāt\ *vt* : to scold violently : BERATE

²rate *n* **1** : reckoned value : VALUATION **2 a** : a fixed ratio between two things **b** : a charge, payment, or price fixed according to a ratio, scale, or standard **3 a** : a quantity, amount, or degree of something measured per unit of something else **b** : an amount of payment or charge based on another amount **4** : relative condition or quality : CLASS — **at any rate** : in any case : at least

³rate *vb* **1** : CONSIDER, REGARD **2** : to set an estimate or value on **3** : to determine the rank, class, or position of : assign to a rank or class : GRADE **4** : to have a rating or rank : be classed **5** : to set a rate on **6** : to be qualified for — **rat·er** *n*

rath·er \'rath-ər, 'räth-\ *adv* **1** : more willingly : PREFERABLY **2** : on the contrary : INSTEAD **3** : more exactly : more properly : with better reason **4** : SOMEWHAT

rat·i·fy \'rat-ə-,fī\ *vt* **-fied**; **-fy·ing** : to approve and sanction formally : CONFIRM — **rat·i·fi·ca·tion** \,rat-ə-fə-'kā-shən\ *n* — **rat·i·fi·er** *n*

rat·ing \'rāt-iŋ\ *n* **1 a** : a classification according to grade or rank **b** : a naval specialist classification **2** : a relative estimate or evaluation : STANDING

ra·tio \'rā-shō, -shē-,ō\ *n, pl* **ra·tios** **1** : a fixed or approximate relation in number, quantity, or degree between things or to another thing **2** : the quotient of one quantity divided by another

rat·i·o·ci·na·tion \,rat-ē-,ōs-ᵊn-'ā-shən, ,rash-ē-, -ē-,äs-\ *n* : the process of exact thinking : REASONING — **rat·i·o·ci·nate** \-'ōs-ᵊn-,āt, -'äs-\ *vi* — **rat·i·o·ci·na·tive** \-,āt-iv\ *adj* — **rat·i·o·ci·na·tor** \-,āt-ər\ *n*

¹ra·tion \'rash-ən, 'rā-shən\ *n* **1 a** : a food allowance for one day **b** : FOOD, PROVISIONS, DIET — usu. used in pl. **2** : SHARE, ALLOTMENT

²ration *vt* **ra·tioned**; **ra·tion·ing** \'rash-(ə-)niŋ, 'rāsh-\ **1** : to supply with rations **2 a** : to distribute or allot as a ration **b** : to use or allot sparingly

¹ra·tio·nal \'rash-nəl, -ən-ᵊl\ *adj* **1** : having reason or understanding **2** : relating to, based on, or agreeable to reason; *also* : SANE — **ra·tio·nal·i·ty** \,rash-ə-'nal-ət-ē\ *n* — **ra·tio·nal·ly** \'rash-nə-lē, -ən-ᵊl-ē\ *adv*

²rational *n* : something rational

ra·tio·nale \,rash-ə-'nal\ *n* : a fundamental explanation or underlying reason : BASIS

ra·tio·nal·ism \'rash-nə-,liz-əm, -ən-ᵊl-,iz-\ *n* **1** : a theory that reason is a source of knowledge superior to and independent of sense perceptions **2** : a view that reason is the final judge of truth — **ra·tio·nal·ist** \-nə-ləst, -ən-ᵊl-əst\ *n* — **rationalist** *or* **ra·tio·nal·is·tic** \,rash-nə-'lis-tik, -ən-ᵊl-'is-\ *adj*

ra·tio·nal·ize \'rash-nə-,līz, -ən-ᵊl-,īz\ *vb* : to bring into accord with reason or cause something to seem reasonable: as **a** : to account for on the basis of known phenomena **b** : to attribute rational and creditable motives to (as actions or beliefs) without analyzing underlying motives — **ra·tio·nal·i·za·tion** \,rash-nə-lə-'zā-shən, -ən-ᵊl-ə-\ *n*

rat·line \'rat-lən\ *n* : one of the small transverse ropes attached to the shrouds of a ship so as to form the steps of a rope ladder

rat·tan \ra-'tan, rə-\ *n* : a climbing palm with very long tough stems used esp. for walking sticks and wickerwork

¹rat·tle \'rat-ᵊl\ *vb* **rat·tled**; **rat·tling** \'rat-liŋ, -ᵊl-iŋ\ **1** : to make or cause to make a rapid succession of short sharp noises **2 a** : to move with a clatter or rattle **b** : to say, perform, or affect in a brisk lively fashion **3** : to disturb the composure of : UPSET

²rattle *n* **1** : a series of short sharp sounds : CLATTER **2** : a device (as a toy) for making a rattling sound **3** : a rattling organ at the end of a rattlesnake's tail made up of horny joints

rat·tler \'rat-lər, -ᵊl-ər\ *n* : RATTLESNAKE

rat·tle·snake \'rat-ᵊl-,snāk\ *n* : any of various venomous American snakes having at the end of the tail horny interlocking joints that rattle when shaken

rat·tle·trap \-,trap\ *n* : something rattly or rickety; *esp* : an old car — **rattletrap** *adj*

rat·tly \'rat-lē, -ᵊl-ē\ *adj* : likely to rattle : making a rattle

rau·cous \'rȯ-kəs\ *adj* **1** : disagreeably harsh or strident **2** : boisterously disorderly — **rau·cous·ly** *adv* — **rau·cous·ness** *n*

rau·wol·fia \raů-'wůl-fē-ə, rȯ-\ *n* : a medicinal extract from the root of an Indian tree; *also* : this tree

¹rav·age \'rav-ij\ *n* **1** : an act or practice of ravaging **2** : damage resulting from ravaging

²ravage *vb* **1** : to lay waste : PLUNDER **2** : DESTROY, RUIN — **rav·ag·er** *n*

rave \'rāv\ *vb* **1** : to talk irrationally in or as if in delirium **2** : to speak or utter with extreme enthusiasm — **rav·er** *n*

rav·el \'rav-əl\ *vb* **-eled** *or* **-elled**; **-el·ing** *or* **-el·ling** \'rav-(ə-)liŋ\ **1** : to separate or undo the texture of : UNRAVEL, FRAY **2** : to undo the intricacies of : DISENTANGLE — **ravel** *n* — **rav·el·er** *or* **rav·el·ler** \-(ə-)lər\ *n*

¹ra·ven \'rā-vən\ *n* : a glossy black bird about two feet long of northern regions that is related to the crow

²raven *adj* : of the color or glossy sheen of the raven

rav·en·ing \'rav-(ə-)niŋ\ *adj* : GREEDY, RAPACIOUS

rav·en·ous \'rav-ə-nəs\ *adj* **1** : RAPACIOUS, VORACIOUS **2** : very eager for food, satisfaction, or gratification — **rav·en·ous·ly** *adv* — **rav·en·ous·ness** *n*

ra·vine \rə-'vēn\ *n* : a small narrow steep-sided valley larger than a gully and smaller than a canyon

rav·i·o·li \,rav-ē-'ō-lē\ *n pl* : little cases of dough containing a savory filling

rav·ish \'rav-ish\ *vt* **1** : to seize and take away by violence **2** : to transport with emotion **3** : RAPE **4** : PLUNDER, ROB — **rav·ish·er** *n*

rav·ish·ing \'rav-i-shiŋ\ *adj* : unusually attractive, pleasing, or striking — **rav·ish·ing·ly** *adv*

¹raw \'rȯ\ *adj* **1** : not cooked **2** : being in or nearly in the natural state : not processed **3** : having the surface abraded or chafed **4 a :** lacking experience or understanding : GREEN **b :** VULGAR, COARSE **5 :** disagreeably damp or cold — **raw·ly** *adv* — **raw·ness** *n*

2raw *n* : a raw place or state; *esp* : NUDITY

raw·boned \ˈrȯ-ˈbōnd\ *adj* : having little flesh : GAUNT

raw·hide \ˈrȯ-ˌhīd\ *n* **1 :** untanned cattle skin **2 :** a whip of untanned hide

1ray \ˈrā\ *n* : any of numerous flat broad fishes that live on the sea bottom and have their eyes on the upper surface of their bodies and the tail long and narrow

2ray *n* **1 a :** one of the lines of light that appear to radiate from a bright object **b :** a thin beam of radiant energy (as light) **2 :** light cast by rays : RADIANCE **3 :** a thin line suggesting a ray **4 :** a plant or animal structure resembling a ray **5 :** PARTICLE, TRACE

ray·on \ˈrā-ˌän\ *n* : a smooth textile fiber made from cellulosic material

raze \ˈrāz\ *vt* : to utterly destroy by or as if by laying level with the ground : DEMOLISH, OBLITERATE

ra·zor \ˈrā-zər\ *n* : a sharp cutting instrument used esp. to shave off hair — **razor** *adj*

ra·zor–backed \ˌrā-zər-ˈbakt\ *or* **ra·zor·back** \ˈrā-zər-ˌbak\ *adj* : having a sharp narrow back

razz \ˈraz\ *vt* : to banter mockingly : RIDICULE, TEASE, KID

1re \ˈrā\ *n* : the 2d note of the diatonic scale

2re \(ˈ)rā, (ˈ)rē\ *prep* : with regard to : in re

re- \(ˈ)rē *before* ˈ*-stressed syll,* (ˌ)rē *before* ˌ*-stressed syll,* ˌrē *before unstressed syll*\ *prefix* **1 :** again : anew **2 :** back : backward

reabsorb
reabsorption
reaccommodate
reacquire
reactuate
readapt
readdress
readjust
readjustable
readjustment
readmission
readmit
readmittance
readopt
readoption
reaffirm
reaffirmation
realign
realignment
reallocate
reallocation
reanalysis
reanalyze
reanimate
reanimation
reannex
reannexation
reappear
reappearance
reapplication
reapply
reappoint
reappointment
reapportion
reapportionment
reappraisal
reappraise
rearm
rearmament
rearouse
rearrange
rearrangement
rearrest
reascend
reassail
reassemble
reassembly
reassert
reassertion
reassess
reassessment
reassign
reassignment
reassort
reassortment
reassume
reassumption
reattach
reattachment
reattack
reattain
reattainment
reattempt
reauthorization
reauthorize
reawake
reawaken
rebaptism
rebaptize
rebid
rebind
reboil
rebroadcast
reburial
rebury
recalculate
recalculation
recapitalization
recapitalize
recapture
recast
rechannel
recharge
recharter
recheck
rechristen
reclean
recoal
recoat
recoin
recolonization
recolonize
recolor
recomb
recombination
recombine
recommence
recommencement
recommission
recompile
recomplete
recompletion
recompose
recompound
recompress
recompression
recomputation
recompute
reconceive
reconcentrate
reconcentration
reconception
recondensation
recondense
reconfine
reconfirm
reconfirmation
reconnect
reconquer
reconquest
reconsecrate
reconsecration
reconsign
reconsignment
reconstructible
reconstructive
reconsult
reconsultation
recontact
recontaminate
recontamination
recontract
reconvene
reconvert
recook
recopy
recouple
recross
recrystallization
recrystallize
recurve
recut
redecorate
redecoration
rededicate
rededication
redefine
redefinition
redeliver
redelivery
redemand
redemandable
redeploy
redeposit
redesign
redetermination
redetermine
redevelop
redeveloper
redevelopment
redifferentiation
redigest
redigestion
redip
rediscount
rediscover
rediscovery
redispose
redisposition
redissolve
redistill
redistillation
redistribute
redistribution
redo
redomesticate
redraft
redraw
redrawer
reduplicate
reduplication
reduplicative
reecho
reeducative
reelect
reelection
reeligibility
reeligible
reembark
reembodiment
reembody
reemerge
reemergence
reemergent
reemission
reemphasis
reemphasize
reemploy
reemployment
reenact
reenactment
reenlist
reenlistment
reenter
reentry
reequip
reestablish
reestablishment
reevaluate
reevaluation
reevaporation
reevoke
reexamination
reexamine
reexchange
reexport
reexportation
reexporter
reface
refashion
refasten
refight
refigure
refilm
refilter
refinance
refind
refinish
refix
refloat
reflourish
reflow
reflower
refly
refocus
refold
reforge
reformulate
reformulation
refortify
refound
reframe
refreeze
refront
refuel
refurnish
regather
regild
regive
reglaze
reglow
reglue
regrade
regrind
regroup
regrow
regrowth
rehammer
rehandle
rehear
rehearing
reheat
rehouse
reimpose
reimposition
reincarnate
reincorporate
reinsert
reinsertion
reinterpret
reinterpretation
reintroduce
reintroduction
reinvasion
reinvest
reinvestment
reinvigorate
reinvigoration
reissue
rejudge
rekindle
reknit
relearn
relet
reletter
relight
reload
relocate
relocation
remake
remanufacture
remarry
remelt
remigrate
remigration
remilitarization
remilitarize
remix
remold
remonetization
rename
renegotiate
renegotiation
renominate
renomination
renumber
reoccupy
reopen
reordination
reorient
reorientate
reorientation
repack
repackage
repaint
repass
repeople
rephotograph
rephrase
replant
replay
reprice
reprint
reprocess
republication
republish
repurchase
reradiate
reread
rerecord
reroll
reroller
resaw
resay
rescore
rescreen
reseal
reseat
reseed
resell
resensitize
reset
resettle
resettlement
resew
reshape
reship
reshipment
reshow
reshuffle
resilver
resitting
resmooth
resow
respell
respring
restaff
restage
restate
restatement
restimulate
restock
restraighten
restrengthen
restrike
restring
resubmission
resubmit
resummon
resupply
resurface
resurvey

resynthesis
resynthesize
retaste
retell
retest
rethink
retool
retrack
retrain
retransmission
retransmit
retraverse
retrial
reunification
reunify
reunite
reuse
revaluation
revalue
reverification
reverify
revictual
revisit
rewarm
rewash
rewater
reweave
rewed
reweigh
reweld
rewind
rewire
rework

[1]**reach** \ˈrēch\ *vb* **1 a** : to stretch out : EXTEND **b** : to attempt to grasp something with or as if with the hand **c** : to touch or grasp by extending a part of the body or an object **2** : to go as far as **3** : to arrive at : come to **4** : to communicate with **5** : to hand over : PASS — **reach·a·ble** *adj* — **reach·er** *n*

[2]**reach** *n* **1 a** : the action or an act of reaching **b** : the ability to stretch (as an arm) so as to touch or obtain something **c** : COMPREHENSION, RANGE **2** : an unbroken stretch or expanse; *esp* : a straight portion of a stream or river

re·act \rē-ˈakt\ *vb* **1** : to exert a reciprocal or counteracting force or influence **2** : to act or behave in response; *also* : to respond to a stimulus **3** : to act in opposition to a force or influence **4** : to undergo or make undergo chemical reaction

re–act \(ˈ)rē-ˈakt\ *vt* : to act or perform a second time

re·ac·tion \rē-ˈak-shən\ *n* **1 a** : the act or process or an instance of reacting **b** : tendency toward a former esp. outmoded political or social order or policy **2** : bodily, mental, or emotional response to or activity aroused by a stimulus **3** : chemical transformation or change — **re·ac·tion·al** \-shnəl, -shən-ᵊl\ *adj* — **re·ac·tion·al·ly** \-ē\ *adv*

[1]**re·ac·tion·ary** \rē-ˈak-shə-ˌner-ē\ *adj* : relating to, marked by, or favoring esp. political reaction

[2]**reactionary** *n, pl* **-ar·ies** : a reactionary person

re·ac·ti·vate \(ˈ)rē-ˈak-tə-ˌvāt\ *vb* : to make or become activated again — **re·ac·ti·va·tion** \(ˌ)rē-ˌak-tə-ˈvā-shən\ *n*

re·ac·tive \rē-ˈak-tiv\ *adj* : reacting or tending to react — **re·ac·tive·ly** *adv* — **re·ac·tiv·i·ty** \(ˌ)rē-ˌak-ˈtiv-ət-ē\ *n*

re·ac·tor \rē-ˈak-tər\ *n* **1** : one that reacts **2** : an apparatus in which a chain reaction of fissionable material is initiated and controlled

[1]**read** \ˈrēd\ *vb* **read** \ˈred\; **read·ing** \ˈrēd-iŋ\ **1 a** (1) : to go over systematically by sight or touch to take in and understand the meaning of (as letters or symbols); *esp* : to perform such an action with written matter (2) : to utter aloud the words represented by (written matter) **b** : to learn from what one has seen or found in writing or printing **2** : to interpret the meaning or significance of **3 a** : to attribute meaning or interpretation to : UNDERSTAND **b** : to put or attribute as an assumption or conjecture **4** : INDICATE **5** : to pursue a course of study **6** : to consist of specific words, phrases, or symbols — **read·a·bil·i·ty** \ˌrēd-ə-ˈbil-ət-ē\ *n* — **read·a·ble** *adj* — **read·a·ble·ness** *n* — **read·a·bly** \ˈrēd-ə-blē\ *adv* — **read·er** *n*

[2]**read** \ˈred\ *adj* : taught or informed by reading

read·i·ly \ˈred-ᵊl-ē\ *adv* : in a ready manner: as **a** : WILLINGLY **b** : SPEEDILY **c** : EASILY

read·i·ness \ˈred-ē-nəs\ *n* : the quality or state of being ready

read·ing \ˈrēd-iŋ\ *n* **1 a** : material read or for reading **b** : extent of material read **2 a** : a particular version **b** : something that is registered (as on a gauge) **3** : a particular interpretation or performance

read out \(ˈ)rēd-ˈau̇t\ *vt* : to drive out officially : EXPEL

[1]**ready** \ˈred-ē\ *adj* **1** : prepared for use or action **2** : APT, LIKELY **3** : WILLING **4** : QUICK, PROMPT **5** : AVAILABLE, HANDY **6** : notably dexterous, adroit, or skilled

[2]**ready** *vt* **read·ied**; **read·y·ing** : to make ready

ready–made \ˌred-ē-ˈmād\ *adj* **1** : made beforehand for general sale **2** : lacking individuality : COMMONPLACE

re·agent \rē-ˈā-jənt\ *n* : a substance that takes part in or brings about a particular chemical reaction

re·al \ˈrē(-ə)l\ *adj* **1** : of, relating to, or constituting fixed, permanent, or immovable things (as lands, houses, or fixtures) **2 a** : not artificial, fraudulent, illusory, or apparent : GENUINE **b** : occurring in fact **c** (1) : necessarily existent (2) : FUNDAMENTAL, ESSENTIAL — **re·al·ness** *n*

real estate *n* : property in houses and land

re·al·ism \ˈrē-ə-ˌliz-əm\ *n* **1** : the disposition to see situations or difficulties in the light of facts and to deal with them practically **2** : the representation in literature and art of things as they are in life — **re·al·ist** \-ləst\ *n*

re·al·is·tic \ˌrē-ə-ˈlis-tik\ *adj* **1** : true to life or nature **2** : having or showing an inclination to face facts and to deal with them sensibly — **re·al·is·ti·cal·ly** \-ti-k(ə-)lē\ *adv*

re·al·i·ty \rē-ˈal-ət-ē\ *n, pl* **-ties** **1** : actual existence : GENUINENESS **2** : someone or something real or actual **3** : the characteristic of being true to life or to fact

re·al·ize \ˈrē-ə-ˌlīz\ *vt* **1** : to make actual : ACCOMPLISH **2** : to convert into money **3** : to bring or get by sale, investment, or effort : GAIN **4** : to be aware of : UNDERSTAND — **re·al·iz·a·ble** *adj* — **re·al·i·za·tion** \ˌrē-ə-lə-ˈzā-shən\ *n* — **re·al·iz·er** *n*

re·al·ly \ˈrē-(ə-)lē\ *adv* **1 a** : in reality : ACTUALLY **b** : UNQUESTIONABLY, TRULY **2** : INDEED

realm \ˈrelm\ *n* **1** : KINGDOM **2** : SPHERE, DOMAIN

re·al·ty \ˈrē(-ə)l-tē\ *n, pl* **-ties** : REAL ESTATE

[1]**ream** \ˈrēm\ *n* **1** : a quantity of paper being 20 quires or variously 480, 500, or 516 sheets **2** : a great amount — usu. used in pl.

[2]**ream** *vt* **1** : to widen the opening of (a hole) : COUNTERSINK **2** : to shape, enlarge, or dress (a hole) with a reamer **3** : to remove by reaming

ream·er \ˈrē-mər\ *n* : a rotating tool with cutting edges for enlarging or shaping a hole

reap \ˈrēp\ *vb* **1 a** : to cut or clear with a sickle, scythe, or reaping machine **b** : to gather by so cutting : HARVEST **2** : to gain as a reward

reap·er \ˈrē-pər\ *n* : one that reaps; *esp* : a machine for reaping grain

[1]**rear** \ˈri(ə)r\ *vb* **1** : to erect by building : CONSTRUCT **2 a** : to raise upright **b** : to rise high **c** : to rise up on the hind legs **3 a** : to undertake the breeding and raising of **b** : to bring up (a person)

[2]**rear** *n* **1** : the back part of something: as **a** : the unit (as of an army) or area farthest from the enemy **b** : BUTTOCKS **2** : the space or position at the back

[3]**rear** *adj* : being at the back

rear admiral *n* : a commissioned officer in the navy ranking next below a vice admiral

rear·most \ˈri(ə)r-ˌmōst\ *adj* : farthest in the rear

[1]**rear·ward** \ˈri(ə)r-wərd\ *adj* **1** : located at, near, or toward the rear **2** : directed toward the rear : BACKWARD — **rear·ward·ly** *adv*

[2]**rearward** *adv* : at, near, or toward the rear : BACKWARD

[1]**rea·son** \ˈrēz-ᵊn\ *n* **1 a** : a statement offered in explanation or justification **b** : a rational ground or motive **c** : the thing that makes some fact intelligible : CAUSE **2 a** : the power of comprehending, inferring, or thinking esp. in orderly logical ways : INTELLIGENCE **b** : SANITY — **within reason** : within reasonable limits — **with reason** : with good cause : JUSTIFIABLY

[2]**reason** *vb* **rea·soned**; **rea·son·ing** \ˈrēz-niŋ, -ᵊn-iŋ\ **1** : to talk persuasively or to present reasons in order to cause a change of mind **2 a** : to use one's reason or to think in a logical way or manner **b** : to state, formulate, or conclude by use of reason

rea·son·a·ble \ˈrēz-nə-bəl, -ᵊn-ə-bəl\ *adj* **1 a** : agreeable to reason **b** : not extreme or excessive : MODERATE **c** : INEXPENSIVE **2 a** : having the faculty of reason : RATIONAL **b** : possessing sound judgment — **rea·son·a·ble·ness** *n* — **rea·son·a·bly** \-blē\ *adv*

rea·son·ing *n* **1 :** the use of reason **2 :** ARGUMENT

re·as·sur·ance \ˌrē-ə-ˈshu̇r-ən(t)s\ *n* **:** the action of reassuring **:** the state of being reassured

re·as·sure \ˌrē-ə-ˈshu̇(ə)r\ *vt* **1 :** to assure anew **2 :** to restore to confidence **3 :** to insure anew

¹re·bate \ˈrē-ˌbāt, ri-ˈ\ *vt* **:** to make a rebate of **:** give as a rebate — **re·bat·er** *n*

²re·bate \ˈrē-ˌbāt\ *n* **:** a return of a portion of a payment

¹reb·el \ˈreb-əl\ *adj* **1 :** of or relating to rebels **2 :** REBELLIOUS

²rebel *n* **:** one who rebels or participates in a rebellion

³re·bel \ri-ˈbel\ *vi* **re·belled; re·bel·ling 1 :** to oppose or resist authority or control **2 :** to renounce and resist by force the authority of one's government

re·bel·lion \ri-ˈbel-yən\ *n* **1 :** opposition to one in authority or dominance **2 :** open defiance of or resistance to an established government through uprising or revolt

re·bel·lious \ri-ˈbel-yəs\ *adj* **1 :** engaged in rebellion **2 :** inclined to resist or disobey authority **:** INSUBORDINATE — **re·bel·lious·ly** *adv* — **re·bel·lious·ness** *n*

re·birth \(ˈ)rē-ˈbərth\ *n* **1 :** a new or second birth **2 :** RENAISSANCE, REVIVAL

re·born \(ˈ)rē-ˈbȯrn\ *adj* **:** born again **:** REVIVED

¹re·bound \ˈrē-ˈbau̇nd, ri-\ *vi* **1 :** to spring back on striking something **2 :** to recover from setback or frustration

²re·bound \ˈrē-ˌbau̇nd, ri-ˈ\ *n* **1 a :** the action of rebounding **b :** an upward leap or movement **2 :** a basketball or hockey puck that rebounds **3 :** an immediate spontaneous reaction to setback or frustration

¹re·buff \ri-ˈbəf\ *vt* **1 :** SNUB **2 :** to drive or beat back

²rebuff *n* **1 :** an abrupt refusal to meet an advance or offer **:** SNUB **2 :** a sharp check **:** REPULSE

re·build \(ˈ)rē-ˈbild\ *vb* **-built** \-ˈbilt\; **-build·ing 1 a :** to make extensive repairs to **b :** to restore to a previous state **2 :** REMODEL **3 :** to build again

re·buke \ri-ˈbyük\ *vt* **:** to scold or criticize sharply **:** REPRIMAND — **rebuke** *n* — **re·buk·er** *n*

re·bus \ˈrē-bəs\ *n* **:** a representation of words or syllables by pictures; *also* **:** a riddle made up of such pictures or symbols

re·but \ri-ˈbət\ *vt* **re·but·ted; re·but·ting 1 :** to contradict or oppose by formal argument, plea, or contrary proof **2 :** to expose the falsity of **:** REFUTE — **re·but·ta·ble** *adj*

re·but·tal \ri-ˈbət-ᵊl\ *n* **:** the act of rebutting; *also* **:** argument or proof that rebuts

re·cal·ci·trance \ri-ˈkal-sə-trən(t)s\ *or* **re·cal·ci·tran·cy** \-trən-sē\ *n* **:** the state of being recalcitrant

re·cal·ci·trant \-trənt\ *adj* **1 :** obstinately defiant of authority or restraint **2 :** not responsive to handling or treatment — **recalcitrant** *n*

¹re·call \ri-ˈkȯl\ *vt* **1 a :** to ask or order to come back **b :** to bring back to mind **2 :** CANCEL, REVOKE **3 :** RESTORE, REVIVE — **re·call·a·ble** *adj*

²re·call \ri-ˈkȯl, ˈrē-ˌ\ *n* **1 :** a summons to return **2 :** the right or procedure by which an official may be removed by popular vote **3 :** remembrance of what has been learned or experienced **4 :** the act of revoking

re·cant \ri-ˈkant\ *vb* **:** to withdraw or repudiate a statement of opinion or belief formally and publicly **:** RENOUNCE — **re·can·ta·tion** \ˌrē-ˌkan-ˈtā-shən\ *n*

¹re·cap \(ˈ)rē-ˈkap\ *vt* **re·capped; re·cap·ping :** to cement, mold, and vulcanize a strip of rubber upon the surface of the tread of (a worn automobile tire)

²re·cap \ˈrē-ˌkap\ *n* **:** a recapped tire

re·ca·pit·u·late \ˌrē-kə-ˈpich-ə-ˌlāt\ *vb* **:** to repeat briefly **:** SUMMARIZE

re·ca·pit·u·la·tion \-ˌpich-ə-ˈlā-shən\ *n* **:** a concise summary

re·cede \ri-ˈsēd\ *vi* **1 a :** to move back or away **:** WITHDRAW **b :** to slant backward **2 :** to grow less **:** CONTRACT

¹re·ceipt \ri-ˈsēt\ *n* **1 :** RECIPE **2 :** the act or process of receiving **3 :** something received — usu. used in pl. **4 :** a writing acknowledging the receiving of goods or money

²receipt *vt* **1 :** to give a receipt for or acknowledge the receipt of **2 :** to mark as paid

re·ceiv·a·ble \ri-ˈsē-və-bəl\ *adj* **1 :** capable of being received **2 :** subject to call for payment

re·ceive \ri-ˈsēv\ *vb* **1 :** to take or get something that is given, paid, or sent **2 :** to permit to enter one's household or company **:** WELCOME, GREET **3 :** to hold a reception **4 :** to undergo or be subjected to (an experience or treatment) **5 :** to change incoming radio waves into sounds or pictures

re·ceiv·er \ri-ˈsē-vər\ *n* **:** one that receives: as **a :** a person appointed to take control of property that is involved in a lawsuit **b :** an apparatus for receiving and converting an electrical signal into a visible or audible effect

re·ceiv·er·ship \-ˌship\ *n* **1 :** the office or function of a receiver **2 :** the state of being in the hands of a receiver

re·cen·cy \ˈrēs-ᵊn-sē\ *n* **:** RECENTNESS

re·cent \ˈrēs-ᵊnt\ *adj* **1 :** of or relating to a time not long past **2 :** having lately appeared or come into existence **:** NEW, FRESH — **re·cent·ly** *adv* — **re·cent·ness** *n*

re·cep·ta·cle \ri-ˈsep-ti-kəl\ *n* **1 :** something used to receive and contain smaller objects **:** CONTAINER **2 :** the enlarged end of a stalk bearing a flower **3 :** an electrical fitting containing the live parts of a circuit

re·cep·tion \ri-ˈsep-shən\ *n* **1 :** the act or process of receiving **2 :** a social gathering

re·cep·tion·ist \ri-ˈsep-sh(ə-)nəst\ *n* **:** one employed to greet callers

re·cep·tive \ri-ˈsep-tiv\ *adj* **1 :** able or inclined to receive ideas **2 :** able to receive and transmit stimuli **:** SENSORY — **re·cep·tive·ly** *adv* — **re·cep·tive·ness** *n* — **re·cep·tiv·i·ty** \ˌrē-ˌsep-ˈtiv-ət-ē, ri-\ *n*

re·cep·tor \ri-ˈsep-tər\ *n* **:** a cell or group of cells that receives stimuli **:** SENSE ORGAN

¹re·cess \ˈrē-ˌses, ri-ˈ\ *n* **1 :** a hidden, secret, or secluded place **2 a :** a space or little hollow set back **:** INDENTATION **b :** ALCOVE **3 :** a suspension of business or procedure; *esp* **:** a brief period for relaxation between class or study periods of a school day

²recess *vb* **1 :** to put into a recess **2 :** to make a recess in **3 :** to interrupt for or take a recess

re·ces·sion \ri-ˈsesh-ən\ *n* **1 :** the act or fact of receding or withdrawing **2 :** a downward turn in business activity; *also* **:** the period of such a downward turn

re·ces·sion·al \ri-ˈsesh-nəl, -ən-ᵊl\ *n* **1 :** a hymn or musical piece at the conclusion of a service or program **2 :** a return processional

re·ces·sive \ri-ˈses-iv\ *adj* **:** tending to go back **:** RECEDING — **re·ces·sive·ly** *adv* — **re·ces·sive·ness** *n*

rec·i·pe \ˈres-ə-(ˌ)pē\ *n* **1 :** PRESCRIPTION 2 **2 :** a set of instructions for making something (as a food dish) from various ingredients **3 :** method of procedure

re·cip·i·ent \ri-ˈsip-ē-ənt\ *n* **:** one that receives — **recipient** *adj*

re·cip·ro·cal \ri-ˈsip-rə-kəl\ *adj* **1 :** done or felt equally by both sides **2 :** related to each other in such a way that one completes the other or is the equivalent of the other — **re·cip·ro·cal·ly** \-k(ə-)lē\ *adv*

re·cip·ro·cate \ri-ˈsip-rə-ˌkāt\ *vb* **1 :** to give and take mutually **:** EXCHANGE **2 :** to make a return for something **3 :** to move forward and backward alternately — **re·cip·ro·ca·tion** \-ˌsip-rə-ˈkā-shən\ *n* — **re·cip·ro·ca·tor** \-ˈsip-rə-ˌkāt-ər\ *n*

rec·i·proc·i·ty \ˌres-ə-ˈpräs-ət-ē\ *n, pl* **-ties 1 :** mutual dependence, cooperation, or exchange between persons, groups, or states **2 :** international policy by which special commercial advantages are granted to one country in return for special advantages granted by another

re·cit·al \ri-ˈsīt-ᵊl\ *n* **1** : a reciting of something; *esp* : a story told in detail **2** : a program of one kind of music **3** : a public performance by pupils (as music or dancing pupils) — **re·cit·al·ist** \-ᵊl-əst\ *n*

rec·i·ta·tion \ˌres-ə-ˈtā-shən\ *n* **1** : an enumeration or telling in detail **2** : the act or an instance of reading or repeating aloud esp. publicly **3 a** : a student's oral reply to questions **b** : a class period

re·cite \ri-ˈsīt\ *vb* **1** : to repeat from memory or read aloud publicly **2 a** : to give a detailed narration of **b** : STATE **3** : to answer (as to a teacher) questions about a lesson — **re·cit·er** *n*

reck·less \ˈrek-ləs\ *adj* **1 a** : marked by lack of caution : RASH **b** : IRRESPONSIBLE, WILD **2** : CARELESS, NEGLIGENT — **reck·less·ly** *adv* — **reck·less·ness** *n*

reck·on \ˈrek-ən\ *vb* **reck·oned**; **reck·on·ing** \ˈrek-(ə-)niŋ\ **1 a** : COUNT, COMPUTE **b** : to estimate by calculation **2** : CONSIDER, REGARD **3** : to make up or settle an account **4** : DEPEND — **reck·on·er** \-(ə-)nər\ *n* — **reckon with** : to take into account — **reckon without** : to fail to take into account

reck·on·ing *n* **1** : the act or an instance of reckoning: as **a** : ACCOUNT, BILL **b** : COMPUTATION **c** : calculation of a ship's position **2** : a settling of accounts

re·claim \ri-ˈklām\ *vt* **1** : to recall from wrong or improper conduct : REFORM **2** : to alter from an undesirable or uncultivated state **3** : to obtain from a waste product or by-product : RECOVER — **re·claim·a·ble** *adj* — **re·claim·er** *n*

rec·la·ma·tion \ˌrek-lə-ˈmā-shən\ *n* : the act or process of reclaiming : the state of being reclaimed

re·cline \ri-ˈklīn\ *vb* **1** : to lean or cause to lean backwards **2** : REPOSE, LIE

rec·luse \ˈrek-ˌlüs, ri-ˈklüs\ *n* : a person (as a hermit) who lives away from others — **re·clu·sive** \ri-ˈklü-siv\ *adj*

rec·og·ni·tion \ˌrek-ig-ˈnish-ən, ˌrek-əg-\ *n* **1** : the act of recognizing **2** : special attention or notice **3** : formal acknowledgment of the political existence of a government or nation

rec·og·niz·a·ble \ˈrek-ig-ˌnī-zə-bəl, ˈrek-əg-\ *adj* : capable of being recognized — **rec·og·niz·a·bly** \-blē\ *adv*

re·cog·ni·zance \ri-ˈkäg-nə-zən(t)s, -ˈkän-ə-\ *n* : a recorded legal promise to do something (as to appear in court or to keep the peace)

rec·og·nize \ˈrek-ig-ˌnīz, ˈrek-əg-\ *vt* **1** : to know and remember upon seeing **2** : to consent to admit : ACKNOWLEDGE **3** : to take approving notice of **4** : to acknowledge acquaintance with **5** : to acknowledge as entitled to be heard at a meeting **6** : to grant diplomatic recognition to

¹re·coil \ri-ˈkȯil\ *vi* **1 a** : to fall back under pressure **b** : to shrink back **2** : to spring back to or as if to a starting point

²re·coil \ri-ˈkȯil, ˈrē-ˌ\ *n* : the act or action of recoiling (as by a discharged gun or a spring)

rec·ol·lect \ˌrek-ə-ˈlekt\ *vb* : to recall to mind : REMEMBER

rec·ol·lec·tion \ˌrek-ə-ˈlek-shən\ *n* **1** : the action or power of recalling to mind : REMEMBRANCE **2** : something recalled to the mind

rec·om·mend \ˌrek-ə-ˈmend\ *vt* **1** : to make a statement in praise of; *esp* : to endorse as fit, worthy, or competent **2** : ADVISE, COUNSEL **3** : to cause to receive favorable attention — **rec·om·mend·er** *n*

rec·om·men·da·tion \ˌrek-ə-mən-ˈdā-shən, -ˌmen-\ *n* **1** : the act of recommending **2** : something that recommends **3** : a thing or course of action recommended

rec·om·pense \ˈrek-əm-ˌpen(t)s\ *vt* : to give compensation to or for : REPAY, PAY — **recompense** *n*

rec·on·cil·a·bil·i·ty \ˌrek-ən-ˌsī-lə-ˈbil-ət-ē\ *n* : the quality or state of being reconcilable

rec·on·cil·a·ble \ˌrek-ən-ˈsī-lə-bəl\ *adj* : capable of being reconciled — **rec·on·cil·a·ble·ness** *n*

rec·on·cile \ˈrek-ən-ˌsīl\ *vt* **1** : to make friendly again **2** : SETTLE, ADJUST **3** : to make agree **4** : to cause to submit or to accept : make content — **rec·on·cile·ment** *n* — **rec·on·cil·er** *n* — **rec·on·cil·i·a·tion** \ˌrek-ən-ˌsil-ē-ˈā-shən\ *n*

rec·on·dite \ˈrek-ən-ˌdīt, ri-ˈkän-\ *adj* **1** : incomprehensible to one of ordinary understanding or knowledge : DEEP **2** : little known : OBSCURE — **rec·on·dite·ly** *adv* — **rec·on·dite·ness** *n*

re·con·di·tion \ˌrē-kən-ˈdish-ən\ *vt* : to restore to good condition (as by repairing or replacing parts)

re·con·nais·sance \ri-ˈkän-ə-zən(t)s\ *n* : a preliminary survey to gain information; *esp* : an exploratory military survey of enemy territory

re·con·noi·ter \ˌrē-kə-ˈnȯit-ər, ˌrek-ə-\ *vb* : to make a reconnaissance; *esp* : to survey in preparation for military action

re·con·sid·er \ˌrē-kən-ˈsid-ər\ *vb* : to consider again esp. with a view to change or reversal — **re·con·sid·er·a·tion** \-ˌsid-ə-ˈrā-shən\ *n*

re·con·sti·tute \(ˈ)rē-ˈkän(t)-stə-ˌt(y)üt\ *vt* : to restore to a former condition by adding water

re·con·struct \ˌrē-kən-ˈstrəkt\ *vt* : REBUILD, REMODEL

re·con·struc·tion \ˌrē-kən-ˈstrək-shən\ *n* **1 a** : the action of reconstructing : the state of being reconstructed **b** *often cap* : the reorganization and reestablishment of the seceded states in the Union after the American Civil War **2** : something reconstructed

¹re·cord \ri-ˈkȯrd\ *vb* **1 a** : to set down in writing **b** (1) : to register permanently (2) : INDICATE, READ **2** : to cause (as sound or visual images) to be registered (as on a phonograph disc or magnetic tape) in reproducible form **3** : to give evidence of

²rec·ord \ˈrek-ərd, -ˌȯrd\ *n* **1** : the state or fact of being recorded **2** : something that records; *esp* : an official written account of proceedings **3 a** : the known facts regarding someone **b** : an attested top performance **4** : something on which sound or visual images have been recorded for later reproduction

re·cord·er \ri-ˈkȯrd-ər\ *n* **1** : a person or device that records **2** : a municipal judge with criminal and sometimes limited civil jurisdiction **3** : an early vertical flute

re·cord·ing \ri-ˈkȯrd-iŋ\ *n* : RECORD 4

¹re·count \ri-ˈkau̇nt\ *vt* : to relate in detail : NARRATE

²re·count \(ˈ)rē-ˈkau̇nt\ *vt* : to count again

³re·count \ˈrē-ˌkau̇nt, (ˈ)rē-ˈ\ *n* : a second or fresh count

re·coup \ri-ˈküp\ *vt* **1** : to make up for : RECOVER **2** : REIMBURSE, COMPENSATE — **re·coup·ment** *n*

re·course \ˈrē-ˌkōrs, ri-ˈ\ *n* **1** : a turning for assistance or protection **2** : a source of help or strength : RESORT

re·cov·er \ri-ˈkəv-ər\ *vb* **-cov·ered**; **-cov·er·ing** \-ˈkəv-(ə-)riŋ\ **1** : to get back : REGAIN **2** : to bring back to normal position or condition **3 a** : to make up for **b** : to gain by legal process; *also* : to recover damages at law **4** : RECLAIM **5** : to regain health, consciousness, or self-control — **re·cov·er·a·ble** \-ˈkəv-(ə-)rə-bəl\ *adj*

re·cov·ery \ri-ˈkəv-(ə-)rē\ *n*, *pl* **-er·ies** : the act or process or an instance of recovering

¹rec·re·ant \ˈrek-rē-ənt\ *adj* **1** : crying for mercy : COWARDLY **2** : unfaithful to duty or allegiance

²recreant *n* **1** : COWARD **2** : DESERTER, APOSTATE

rec·re·ate \ˈrek-rē-ˌāt\ *vt* : to give new life or freshness to — **rec·re·a·tive** \-ˌāt-iv\ *adj*

re–cre·ate \ˌrē-krē-ˈāt\ *vt* : to create anew — **re–cre·a·tion** \-ˈā-shən\ *n* — **re–cre·a·tive** \-ˈāt-iv\ *adj*

rec·re·a·tion \ˌrek-rē-ˈā-shən\ *n* : refreshment of strength and spirits after toil; *also* : a means of refreshment or diversion — **rec·re·a·tion·al** \-shnəl, -shən-ᵊl\ *adj*

re·crim·i·nate \ri-ˈkrim-ə-ˌnāt\ *vi* **1** : to make a retaliatory charge against an accuser **2** : to retort bitterly — **re·crim·i-**

na·tion \-ˌkrim-ə-ˈnā-shən\ *n* — **re·crim·i·na·to·ry** \-ˈkrim-ə-nə-ˌtōr-ē\ *adj*

[1]**re·cruit** \ri-ˈkrüt\ *n* : a newcomer to a field or activity; *esp* : an enlisted man of the lowest rank in the army

[2]**recruit** *vb* **1 a** : to form or strengthen with new members **b** : to secure the services of : ENGAGE **2** : REPLENISH **3** : to restore or increase the health, vigor, or intensity of — **re·cruit·er** *n* — **re·cruit·ment** \-ˈkrüt-mənt\ *n*

rec·tan·gle \ˈrek-ˌtaŋ-gəl\ *n* : a parallelogram all of whose angles are right angles

rec·tan·gu·lar \rek-ˈtaŋ-gyə-lər\ *adj* : having a flat surface shaped like a rectangle

rec·ti·fi·er \ˈrek-tə-ˌfī(-ə)r\ *n* : one that rectifies

rec·ti·fy \ˈrek-tə-ˌfī\ *vt* **-fied**; **-fy·ing** **1** : to set right : REMEDY **2** : to correct by removing errors : ADJUST **3** : to convert (an alternating current) into a direct current — **rec·ti·fi·ca·tion** \ˌrek-tə-fə-ˈkā-shən\ *n*

rec·ti·lin·e·ar \ˌrek-tə-ˈlin-ē-ər\ *adj* **1** : moving in, being in, or forming a straight line **2** : characterized by straight lines — **rec·ti·lin·e·ar·ly** *adv*

rec·ti·tude \ˈrek-tə-ˌt(y)üd\ *n* **1** : STRAIGHTNESS **2** : moral integrity : RIGHTEOUSNESS

rec·to \ˈrek-tō\ *n, pl* **rectos** : a right-hand page

rec·tor \ˈrek-tər\ *n* **1** : a clergyman in charge of a church or parish **2** : the head of a university or school

rec·to·ry \ˈrek-t(ə-)rē\ *n, pl* **-ries** : a rector's residence

rec·tum \ˈrek-təm\ *n, pl* **rectums** *or* **rec·ta** \-tə\ : the last part of the intestine linking the colon to the anus — **rec·tal** \-tᵊl\ *adj*

re·cum·ben·cy \ri-ˈkəm-bən-sē\ *n* : recumbent position

re·cum·bent \-bənt\ *adj* **1** : RESTING **2** : lying down — **re·cum·bent·ly** *adv*

re·cu·per·ate \ri-ˈk(y)ü-pə-ˌrāt\ *vb* : to get back : RECOVER; *esp* : to regain health or strength — **re·cu·per·a·tion** \-ˌk(y)ü-pə-ˈrā-shən\ *n*

re·cu·per·a·tive \ri-ˈk(y)ü-pə-ˌrāt-iv, -p(ə-)rət-\ *adj* : of, relating to, or promoting recuperation

re·cur \ri-ˈkər\ *vi* **re·curred**; **re·cur·ring** **1** : to go or come back in thought or discussion **2** : to come again into the mind **3** : to occur or appear again — **re·cur·rence** \-ˈkər-ən(t)s\ *n*

re·cur·rent \ri-ˈkər-ənt\ *adj* **1** : returning from time to time : RECURRING **2** : running or turning back in direction — **re·cur·rent·ly** *adv*

[1]**red** \ˈred\ *adj* **1** : of the color red **2 a** : inciting or endorsing radical social or political change esp. by force **b** : COMMUNIST **c** : of or relating to the U.S.S.R. or a Communist country — **red·ly** *adv* — **red·ness** *n*

[2]**red** *n* **1** : a color whose hue resembles that of blood or the ruby **2** : one that is of a red or reddish color **3 a** : REVOLUTIONARY **b** *cap* : COMMUNIST **4** : the condition of showing a loss

red·breast \ˈred-ˌbrest\ *n* : ROBIN

red·cap \-ˌkap\ *n* : a baggage porter at a railroad station

red·coat \ˈred-ˌkōt\ *n* : a British soldier esp. during the Revolutionary War

red·den \ˈred-ᵊn\ *vb* **red·dened**; **red·den·ing** \ˈred-niŋ, -ᵊn-iŋ\ : to make or become red or reddish; *esp* : BLUSH

red·dish \ˈred-ish\ *adj* : somewhat red — **red·dish·ness** *n*

re·deem \ri-ˈdēm\ *vt* **1** : to buy back : REPURCHASE **2 a** : RANSOM **b** : LIBERATE **c** : to free from the bondage of sin **3** : to regain (a pledge) by payment of an amount secured thereby **4 a** : to atone for : EXPIATE **b** : to offset the bad effect of : RETRIEVE **5** : to make good : FULFILL — **re·deem·a·ble** *adj* — **re·deem·er** *n*

re·demp·tion \ri-ˈdem(p)-shən\ *n* : the act or process or an instance of redeeming — **re·demp·tion·al** \-shnəl, -shən-ᵊl\ *adj* — **re·demp·tive** \-ˈdem(p)-tiv\ *adj*

red–hand·ed \ˈred-ˈhan-dəd\ *adv (or adj)* : in the act of committing a crime or misdeed

red·head \ˈred-ˌhed\ *n* : a person having red hair

red–hot \ˈred-ˈhät\ *adj* **1** : glowing red with heat **2** : exhibiting or marked by intense emotion, enthusiasm, or energy **3** : FRESH, NEW

re·di·rect \ˌrēd-ə-ˈrekt, ˌrē-(ˌ)dī-\ *vt* : to change the course or direction of — **re·di·rec·tion** \-ˈrek-shən\ *n*

re·dis·trict \(ˈ)rē-ˈdis-(ˌ)trikt\ *vt* : to divide anew into districts; *esp* : to revise the legislative districts of

red–let·ter \ˈred-ˈlet-ər\ *adj* : memorable esp. in a happy or joyful way

red·o·lence \ˈred-ᵊl-ən(t)s\ *n* **1** : the quality or state of being redolent **2** : SCENT, AROMA

red·o·lent \-ənt\ *adj* **1** : exuding fragrance : AROMATIC **2 a** : full of a specified fragrance : SCENTED **b** : EVOCATIVE, REMINISCENT — **red·o·lent·ly** *adv*

re·doubt \ri-ˈdau̇t\ *n* : a small often temporary fortification (as for defending a hilltop)

re·doubt·a·ble \ri-ˈdau̇t-ə-bəl\ *adj* : arousing fear or dread

re·dound \ri-ˈdau̇nd\ *vi* : to become reflected back esp. so as to bring credit or discredit : have a result or effect

[1]**re·dress** \ri-ˈdres\ *vt* **1** : to set (as a wrong) right : REMEDY, RELIEVE **2** : to correct or amend the faults of

[2]**re·dress** \ri-ˈdres, ˈrē-ˌ\ *n* **1 a** : relief from distress **b** : means or possibility of seeking a remedy **2** : compensation for wrong or loss **3 a** : an act or instance of redressing **b** : CORRECTION, RETRIBUTION

red·skin \ˈred-ˌskin\ *n* : a No. American Indian

re·duce \ri-ˈd(y)üs\ *vb* **1** : to diminish in size, amount, extent, or number; *esp* : to lose weight by dieting **2** : to bring to a specified state or condition **3** : to force to surrender **4 a** : to bring to a systematic form or character **b** : to become converted or equated **5** : to correct (as a fracture) by bringing displaced or broken parts back into normal position **6 a** : to lower in grade or rank **b** : to lower in condition or status **c** : to diminish in strength or intensity — **re·duc·er** *n* — **re·duc·i·bil·i·ty** \-ˌd(y)ü-sə-ˈbil-ət-ē\ *n* — **re·duc·i·ble** \-ˈd(y)ü-sə-bəl\ *adj* — **re·duc·i·bly** \-blē\ *adv*

re·duc·tion \ri-ˈdək-shən\ *n* **1** : the act or process of reducing : the state of being reduced **2 a** : the amount by which something is reduced in price **b** : something made by reducing — **re·duc·tion·al** \-shnəl, -shən-ᵊl\ *adj* — **re·duc·tive** \-ˈdək-tiv\ *adj*

re·dun·dan·cy \ri-ˈdən-dən-sē\ *n, pl* **-cies** **1** : the quality or state of being redundant : SUPERFLUITY **2** : PROFUSION, ABUNDANCE **3** : superfluous repetition : PROLIXITY

re·dun·dant \ri-ˈdən-dənt\ *adj* : exceeding what is necessary or normal; *esp* : characterized by or containing more words than necessary — **re·dun·dant·ly** *adv*

red·wood \ˈred-ˌwu̇d\ *n* : a tall coniferous timber tree of California; *also* : its light durable brownish red wood

reed \ˈrēd\ *n* **1 a** : any of various slender tall grasses growing esp. in wet areas **b** : a stem or a growth or mass of reeds **2** : a musical instrument made of the hollow joint of a plant **3** : an elastic tongue of cane, wood, or metal by which tones are produced in organ pipes and certain other wind instruments — **reedy** \ˈrēd-ē\ *adj*

re·ed·u·cate \(ˈ)rē-ˈej-ə-ˌkāt\ *vt* : to train again; *esp* : to rehabilitate through education — **re·ed·u·ca·tion** \(ˌ)rē-ˌej-ə-ˈkā-shən\ *n*

[1]**reef** \ˈrēf\ *n* **1** : a part of a sail taken in or let out in regulating size **2** : the reduction in sail area made by reefing

[2]**reef** *vt* **1** : to reduce the area of (a sail) by rolling or folding a portion **2** : to lower or bring inboard (a spar)

[3]**reef** *n* : a chain of rocks or ridge of sand at or near the surface of water

[1]**reef·er** \ˈrē-fər\ *n* **1** : one that reefs **2** : a close-fitting thick jacket

[2]**reefer** *n* : a marijuana cigarette
[1]**reek** \'rēk\ *n* : a strong or disagreeable fume or odor
[2]**reek** *vi* **1 a** : to have a strong or unpleasant smell **b** : to be unpleasantly or strongly permeated **2** : to give a strong impression
[1]**reel** \'rēl\ *n* **1** : a revolvable device on which something flexible is wound **2** : a quantity of something wound on a reel
[2]**reel** *vb* **1** : to wind upon or as if upon a reel **2** : to draw (as a fish) by reeling a line **3** : to wind or turn a reel
[3]**reel** *vi* **1 a** : to whirl around **b** : to be in a whirl **2** : to give way : fall back : WAVER **3** : to stagger or sway dizzily
[4]**reel** *n* : a reeling motion
[5]**reel** *n* : a lively Scottish-Highland dance or its music
reel off *vt* **1** : to recite fluently **2** : to cover or traverse with seeming ease
reeve \'rēv\ *vt* **rove** \'rōv\ *or* **reeved**; **reev•ing 1** : to pass (as a rope) through a hole or opening **2** : to rig for operation by passing a rope through
re•fec•tion \ri-'fek-shən\ *n* **1** : refreshment of mind, spirit, or body; *esp* : NOURISHMENT **2 a** : the taking of refreshment **b** : food and drink together : REPAST
re•fec•to•ry \ri-'fek-t(ə-)rē\ *n, pl* **-ries** : a dining hall esp. in a monastery
re•fer \ri-'fər\ *vb* **re•ferred**; **re•fer•ring 1** : to place in a certain class so far as cause, relationship, or source is concerned **2** : to send or direct to some person or place for treatment, help, or information **3** : to go for information, advice, or aid **4** : to have relation or connection : RELATE **5** : to submit or hand over to someone else **6** : to direct attention : make reference — **ref•er•a•ble** \'ref-(ə-)rə-bəl, ri-'fər-ə-\ *adj* — **re•fer•rer** *n*
[1]**ref•er•ee** \ˌref-ə-'rē\ *n* **1** : an attorney or person to whom a legal matter is referred for investigation and report or for settlement **2** : a sports official usu. having final authority in administering a game
[2]**referee** *vb* **-eed**; **-ee•ing** : to act or supervise as a referee
ref•er•ence \'ref-ərn(t)s, 'ref-(ə-)rən(t)s\ *n* **1** : the act of referring or consulting **2** : a bearing on a matter : RELATION **3** : something that refers: as **a** : ALLUSION, MENTION **b** : a sign or indication referring a reader to another passage or book **c** : consultation of sources of information **4 a** : a person to whom inquiries as to character or ability can be made **b** : a written recommendation of a person for employment
ref•er•en•dum \ˌref-ə-'ren-dəm\ *n, pl* **-da** \-də\ *or* **-dums** : the principle or practice of submitting to popular vote legislative measures; *also* : a vote on a measure so submitted
[1]**re•fill** \(')rē-'fil\ *vb* : to fill again — **re•fill•a•ble** *adj*
[2]**re•fill** \'rē-ˌfil\ *n* : a new or fresh supply of something
re•fine \ri-'fīn\ *vb* **1** : to come or bring to a pure state **2** : IMPROVE, PERFECT **3** : to free from what is coarse, vulgar, or uncouth **4** : to make improvement by introducing subtleties — **re•fin•er** *n*
re•fined \ri-'fīnd\ *adj* **1** : freed from impurities : PURE **2** : WELL-BRED, CULTURED **3** : SUBTLE
re•fine•ment \ri-'fīn-mənt\ *n* **1** : the action or process of refining **2** : the quality or state of being refined : CULTIVATION **3 a** : a refined feature or method **b** : SUBTLETY **c** : a contrivance or device intended to improve or perfect
re•fin•ery \ri-'fīn-(ə-)rē\ *n, pl* **-er•ies** : a building and equipment for refining or purifying metals, oil, or sugar
re•fit \(')rē-'fit\ *vb* **re•fit•ted**; **re•fit•ting** : to get ready for use again — **re•fit** \'rē-ˌfit, (')rē-'\ *n*
re•flect \ri-'flekt\ *vb* **1** : to bend or throw back waves of light, sound, or heat **2** : to give back an image or likeness of as if by a mirror **3** : to bring as a result **4** : to cast reproach or blame **5** : to think seriously and carefully : MEDITATE — **re•flec•tion** \ri-'flek-shən\ *n* — **re•flec•tor** \-'flek-tər\ *n*
re•flec•tive \ri-'flek-tiv\ *adj* **1** : capable of reflecting light, images, or sound waves **2** : marked by reflection : THOUGHTFUL **3** : of, relating to, or caused by reflection — **re•flec•tive•ly** *adv* — **re•flec•tive•ness** *n*
[1]**re•flex** \'rē-ˌfleks\ *n* : an automatic and usu. inborn response to a stimulus not involving higher mental centers
[2]**reflex** *adj* **1** : bent, turned, or directed back : REFLECTED **2** : of, relating to, or produced by a neural reflex — **re•flex•ly** *adv*
[1]**re•flex•ive** \ri-'flek-siv\ *adj* **1** : directed or turned back upon itself **2** : of, relating to, or constituting an action directed back upon the doer or the grammatical subject — **re•flex•ive•ly** *adv* — **re•flex•ive•ness** *n* — **re•flex•iv•i•ty** \ˌrē-ˌflek-'siv-ət-ē, ri-\ *n*
[2]**reflexive** *n* : a reflexive pronoun or verb
re•for•est \(')rē-'fȯr-əst\ *vt* : to renew forest cover on by seeding or planting — **re•for•es•ta•tion** \(ˌ)rē-ˌfȯr-ə-'stā-shən\ *n*
[1]**re•form** \ri-'fȯrm\ *vb* **1** : to make better or improve by removal of faults **2** : to correct or improve one's own character or habits — **re•form•a•ble** *adj*
[2]**reform** *n* **1** : amendment of what is bad or corrupt **2** : a removal or correction of an abuse, a wrong, or errors
ref•or•ma•tion \ˌref-ər-'mā-shən\ *n* **1** : the act of reforming : the state of being reformed **2** *cap* : a 16th century religious movement marked by the establishment of the Protestant churches — **ref•or•ma•tion•al** \-shnəl, -shən-ᵊl\ *adj*
re•for•ma•tive \ri-'fȯr-mət-iv\ *adj* : tending or disposed to reform
[1]**re•form•a•to•ry** \ri-'fȯr-mə-ˌtōr-ē\ *adj* : REFORMATIVE
[2]**reformatory** *n, pl* **-ries** : a penal institution for reforming young or first offenders or women
re•form•er \ri-'fȯr-mər\ *n* **1** : one that works for or urges reform **2** *cap* : a leader of the Protestant Reformation
re•form•ism \ri-'fȯr-ˌmiz-əm\ *n* : a doctrine, policy, or movement of reform — **re•form•ist** \-məst\ *n*
re•fract \ri-'frakt\ *vt* : to subject to refraction
re•frac•tion \ri-'frak-shən\ *n* : the bending of a ray when it passes slantwise from one medium into another in which its speed is different (as when light passes from air into water)
re•frac•tive \ri-'frak-tiv\ *adj* : of, relating to, or active in refraction — **re•frac•tiv•i•ty** \ˌrē-ˌfrak-'tiv-ət-ē, ri-\ *n*
re•frac•to•ry \ri-'frak-t(ə-)rē\ *adj* **1** : resisting control or authority : STUBBORN **2** : difficult to fuse, corrode, or draw out; *esp* : capable of enduring high temperature — **re•frac•to•ri•ly** \-t(ə-)rə-lē\ *adv* — **re•frac•to•ri•ness** \-t(ə-)rē-nəs\ *n*
[1]**re•frain** \ri-'frān\ *vi* : to hold oneself back : restrain oneself
[2]**refrain** *n* : a regularly recurring phrase or verse esp. at the end of each stanza of a poem or song
re•fresh \ri-'fresh\ *vb* **1** : to restore strength and animation to : REVIVE **2** : to restore or maintain by renewing supply : REPLENISH **3** : to restore water to **4** : to take refreshment — **re•fresh•er** *n*
re•fresh•ment \ri-'fresh-mənt\ *n* **1** : the act of refreshing : the state of being refreshed **2 a** : something that refreshes **b** *pl* : a light meal : LUNCH
re•frig•er•ate \ri-'frij-ə-ˌrāt\ *vt* : to make or keep cold or cool; *esp* : to freeze or chill (food) for preservation — **re•frig•er•a•tion** \ri-ˌfrij-ə-'rā-shən\ *n*
re•frig•er•a•tor \ri-'frij-ə-ˌrāt-ər\ *n* : a cabinet or room for keeping articles (as food) cool
ref•uge \'ref-(ˌ)yüj\ *n* **1** : shelter or protection from danger or distress **2** : a place that provides shelter or protection
ref•u•gee \ˌref-yu̇-'jē\ *n* : a person who flees for safety esp. to a foreign country
re•ful•gence \ri-'fu̇l-jən(t)s, -'fəl-\ *n* : a radiant or resplendent quality or state — **re•ful•gent** \-jənt\ *adj*
[1]**re•fund** \ri-'fənd, 'rē-ˌfənd\ *vt* : to return (money) in restitution or repayment — **re•fund•a•ble** *adj*

²re·fund \'rē-ˌfənd\ *n* **1** : the act of refunding **2** : a sum refunded
re·fur·bish \(ˈ)rē-'fər-bish\ *vt* : to brighten or freshen up : RENOVATE — **re·fur·bish·ment** *n*
re·fus·al \ri-'fyü-zəl\ *n* **1** : the act of refusing **2** : the opportunity or right of refusing or taking before others
¹re·fuse \ri-'fyüz\ *vb* **1** : to decline to accept : REJECT **2** : to decline to do, give, or grant : DENY — **re·fus·er** *n*
²ref·use \'ref-ˌyüs, -ˌyüz\ *n* : TRASH, GARBAGE, RUBBISH
ref·u·ta·tion \ˌref-yu̇-'tā-shən\ *n* : the act or process of refuting : DISPROOF
re·fute \ri-'fyüt\ *vt* : to prove wrong by argument or evidence : show to be false — **re·fut·er** *n*
re·gain \ri-'gān\ *vt* **1** : to gain or get again : get back **2** : to get back to : reach again
re·gal \'rē-gəl\ *adj* **1** : of, relating to, or suitable for a king **2** : of notable excellence or magnificence : SPLENDID — **re·gal·i·ty** \ri-'gal-ət-ē\ *n* — **re·gal·ly** *adv*
re·gale \ri-'gāl\ *vb* **1** : to treat or entertain sumptuously or agreeably **2** : to feast oneself : FEED — **re·gale·ment** *n*
re·ga·lia \ri-'gāl-yə\ *n sing or pl* **1** : the emblems and symbols (as the crown and scepter) of royalty **2** : the insignia of an office or order **3** : special dress : FINERY
¹re·gard \ri-'gärd\ *n* **1 a** : CONSIDERATION, HEED **b** : LOOK, GAZE **2 a** : the worth or estimation in which something is held **b** (1) : a feeling of respect and affection : ESTEEM (2) *pl* : friendly greetings implying such feeling **3** : an aspect to be taken into consideration
²regard *vt* **1** : to pay attention to **2 a** : to show respect or consideration for **b** : to hold in high esteem **3** : to look at steadily or attentively **4** : to take into consideration or account **5** : to relate to **6** : to think of : look upon — **as regards** : with respect to : REGARDING
re·gard·ful \ri-'gärd-fəl\ *adj* **1** : HEEDFUL, OBSERVANT **2** : full or expressive of regard or respect : RESPECTFUL — **re·gard·ful·ly** *adv* — **re·gard·ful·ness** *n*
re·gard·ing \ri-'gärd-iŋ\ *prep* : CONCERNING
¹re·gard·less \ri-'gärd-ləs\ *adj* : having or taking no regard or heed : HEEDLESS, CARELESS — **re·gard·less·ly** *adv* — **re·gard·less·ness** *n*
²regardless *adv* : despite everything
re·gat·ta \ri-'gät-ə, -'gat-\ *n* : a rowing, speedboat, or sailing race or a series of such races
re·gen·cy \'rē-jən-sē\ *n, pl* **-cies** **1** : the office, jurisdiction, or government of a regent or body of regents **2** : the period of rule of a regent or body of regents
¹re·gen·er·ate \ri-'jen-(ə-)rət\ *adj* : REGENERATED; *esp* : spiritually reborn or converted — **re·gen·er·ate·ly** *adv* — **re·gen·er·ate·ness** *n*
²re·gen·er·ate \ri-'jen-ə-ˌrāt\ *vb* **1** : to cause to be reborn spiritually **2** : to reform completely in character and habits **3** : to generate or produce anew; *esp* : to renew (a lost or damaged body part) by a new growth of tissue **4** : to give new life to : REVIVE — **re·gen·er·a·tor** \-ˌrāt-ər\ *n*
re·gen·er·a·tion \ri-ˌjen-ə-'rā-shən, ˌrē-\ *n* : an act or the process of regenerating : the state of being regenerated
re·gen·er·a·tive \ri-'jen-ə-ˌrāt-iv\ *adj* **1** : of, relating to, or marked by regeneration **2** : tending to regenerate
re·gent \'rē-jənt\ *n* **1** : one who governs a kingdom during the minority, absence, or disability of the sovereign **2** : a member of a governing board (as of a state university) — **regent** *adj*
reg·i·cide \'rej-ə-ˌsīd\ *n* **1** : one who kills a king **2** : the killing of a king — **reg·i·cid·al** \ˌrej-ə-'sīd-ᵊl\ *adj*
re·gime \rā-'zhēm, ri-\ *n* **1** : REGIMEN 1 **2** : a form of government or administration
reg·i·men \'rej-ə-mən, 'rezh-ə-\ *n* **1** : a systematic course of treatment **2** : GOVERNMENT, RULE
¹reg·i·ment \'rej-(ə-)mənt\ *n* : a military unit consisting of a variable number of units (as battalions) — **reg·i·men·tal** \ˌrej-ə-'ment-ᵊl\ *adj* — **reg·i·men·tal·ly** \-ᵊl-ē\ *adv*
²reg·i·ment \'rej-ə-ˌment\ *vt* **1** : to organize rigidly esp. for the sake of regulation or control **2** : to subject to order or uniformity — **reg·i·men·ta·tion** \ˌrej-ə-mən-'tā-shən, -ˌmen-\ *n*
reg·i·men·tals \ˌrej-ə-'ment-ᵊlz\ *n pl* **1** : a regimental uniform **2** : military dress
re·gion \'rē-jən\ *n* **1** : an often indefinitely bounded part, portion, or area; *also* : VICINITY **2** : a sphere of activity or interest : FIELD
re·gion·al \'rēj-nəl, -ən-ᵊl\ *adj* **1** : of, relating to, or characteristic of a region **2** : affecting a particular region : LOCALIZED — **re·gion·al·ly** \-ē\ *adv*
¹reg·is·ter \'rej-ə-stər\ *n* **1 a** : a written record or list containing regular entries of items or details **b** : a book for such a record **2** : a device (as in a floor or wall) usu. with a grille and shutters that regulates the flow of heated air from a furnace **3** : a part of the range of a human voice or a musical instrument comprising tones similarly produced or of the same quality **4** : a mechanical device which records items
²register *vb* **reg·is·tered**; **reg·is·ter·ing** \-st(ə-)riŋ\ **1 a** : to make or secure official entry of in a register : RECORD **b** : to enroll formally esp. as a voter or student **c** : to record automatically : INDICATE **2** : to make or adjust so as to correspond exactly **3** : to secure special protection for (a piece of mail) by prepayment of a fee **4** : to convey by expression and bodily movements alone
³register *n* : REGISTRAR
reg·is·trar \'rej-ə-ˌsträr\ *n* : an official recorder or keeper of records
reg·is·tra·tion \ˌrej-ə-'strā-shən\ *n* **1** : an act or the fact of registering **2** : an entry in a register **3** : the number of individuals registered : ENROLLMENT **4** : a document certifying an act of registering
reg·is·try \'rej-ə-strē\ *n, pl* **-tries** **1** : ENROLLMENT, REGISTRATION **2** : a place of registration **3** : an official record book or an entry in one
reg·nant \'reg-nənt\ *adj* **1** : exercising rule : REIGNING **2** : having the chief power : DOMINANT
¹re·gress \'rē-ˌgres\ *n* **1** : WITHDRAWAL **2** : RETROGRESSION
²re·gress \ri-'gres\ *vb* : to go or cause to go back esp. to a former level or condition — **re·gres·sion** \-'gresh-ən\ *n* — **re·gres·sive** \-'gres-iv\ *adj* — **re·gres·sor** \-'gres-ər\ *n*
¹re·gret \ri-'gret\ *vb* **re·gret·ted**; **re·gret·ting** **1 a** : to mourn the loss or death of **b** : to miss poignantly **2** : to be keenly sorry for **3** : to experience regret — **re·gret·ta·ble** *adj* — **re·gret·ta·bly** \-'gret-ə-blē\ *adv* — **re·gret·ter** *n*
²regret *n* **1** : sorrow aroused by circumstances beyond one's power to remedy **2 a** : an expression of distressing emotion (as sorrow or disappointment) **b** *pl* : a note politely declining an invitation — **re·gret·ful** \-'gret-fəl\ *adj* — **re·gret·ful·ly** \-fə-lē\ *adv* — **re·gret·ful·ness** *n*
¹reg·u·lar \'reg-yə-lər\ *adj* **1** : belonging to a religious order **2 a** : formed, built, arranged, or ordered according to an established rule, law, principle, or type **b** : symmetrical or even in form **3 a** : ORDERLY, METHODICAL **b** : recurring or functioning at fixed or uniform intervals **4 a** : undeviating in conformance to a set standard **b** : conforming to the normal or usual manner of inflection **5** : of, relating to, or constituting a permanent standing army — **reg·u·lar·i·ty** \ˌreg-yə-'lar-ət-ē\ *n* — **reg·u·lar·ly** *adv*
²regular *n* : one who is regular: as **a** : one of the regular clergy **b** : a soldier in a regular army **c** : a player on an athletic team who usu. starts every game
reg·u·late \'reg-yə-ˌlāt\ *vt* **1 a** : to govern or direct according to rule **b** : to bring under the control of law or constituted authority **2** : to reduce to order, method, or uniformity **3** : to adjust so as to work accurately or regularly — **reg·u·la·tive**

\-ˌlāt-iv\ *adj* — **reg·u·la·tor** \-ˌlāt-ər\ *n* — **reg·u·la·to·ry** \-lə-ˌtōr-ē\ *adj*

¹reg·u·la·tion \ˌreg-yə-ˈlā-shən\ *n* **1 :** the act of regulating **:** the state of being regulated **2 a :** an authoritative rule dealing with details of procedure **b :** a rule or order having the force of law issued by an executive authority

²regulation *adj* **:** prescribed by regulations

re·gur·gi·tate \(ˈ)rē-ˈgər-jə-ˌtāt\ *vb* **:** to throw or be thrown back or out again — **re·gur·gi·ta·tion** \(ˌ)rē-ˌgər-jə-ˈtā-shən\ *n*

re·ha·bil·i·tate \ˌrē-(h)ə-ˈbil-ə-ˌtāt\ *vt* **1 :** to restore to a former capacity **:** REINSTATE **2 :** to restore to good condition again — **re·ha·bil·i·ta·tion** \-ˌbil-ə-ˈtā-shən\ *n* — **re·ha·bil·i·ta·tive** \-ˈbil-ə-ˌtāt-iv\ *adj*

re·hash \(ˈ)rē-ˈhash\ *vt* **:** to present or use (as an argument) again in another form without substantial change or improvement — **re·hash** \ˈrē-ˌhash\ *n*

re·hears·al \ri-ˈhər-səl\ *n* **:** a rehearsing of something: as **a :** a private performance or practice session preparatory to a public appearance **b :** a practice exercise **:** TRIAL

re·hearse \ri-ˈhərs\ *vb* **1 a :** to say again **:** REPEAT **b :** to recount in order **:** ENUMERATE **2 a :** to practice for public performance **b :** to train or make proficient by rehearsal **3 :** to engage in a rehearsal — **re·hears·er** *n*

Reichs·tag \ˈrīks-ˌtäg, -ˌtäk\ *n* **:** the lower house of the legislature of the German Empire and of the succeeding Republic

¹reign \ˈrān\ *n* **1 :** the authority or rule of a sovereign **2 :** the time during which a sovereign reigns

²reign *vi* **1 :** to possess or exercise sovereign power **:** RULE **2 :** to be predominant or prevalent

re·im·burse \ˌrē-əm-ˈbərs\ *vt* **:** to pay back **:** REPAY — **re·im·burs·a·ble** *adj* — **re·im·burse·ment** *n*

¹rein \ˈrān\ *n* **1 :** a line or strap fastened to a bit on each side for controlling an animal — usu. used in pl. **2 a :** a restraining influence **:** CHECK **b :** controlling or guiding power **3 :** complete freedom **:** SCOPE — usu. used in the phrase *give rein to*

²rein *vb* **:** to check, control, or stop by or as if by reins

re·in·car·na·tion \(ˌ)rē-ˌin-ˌkär-ˈnā-shən\ *n* **:** a rebirth of a soul in a new human body

rein·deer \ˈrān-ˌdi(ə)r\ *n* **:** any of several large deer of northern regions used as meat and draft animals

re·in·force \ˌrē-ən-ˈfōrs\ *vt* **1 :** to strengthen with new force, assistance, material, or support **2 :** to strengthen with additional troops or ships — **re·in·force·ment** \-mənt\ *n* — **re·in·forc·er** *n*

re·in·state \ˌrē-ən-ˈstāt\ *vt* **:** to place again in possession or in a former position, condition, or capacity — **re·in·state·ment** *n*

re·it·er·ate \rē-ˈit-ə-ˌrāt\ *vt* **:** to say or do over again or repeatedly — **re·it·er·a·tion** \(ˌ)rē-ˌit-ə-ˈrā-shən\ *n* — **re·it·er·a·tive** \rē-ˈit-ə-ˌrāt-iv, -rət-\ *adj* — **re·it·er·a·tive·ly** *adv* — **re·it·er·a·tive·ness** *n*

¹re·ject \ri-ˈjekt\ *vt* **1 :** to refuse to acknowledge, believe, or receive **2 :** to throw away as useless or unsatisfactory **3 :** to refuse to grant or consider

²re·ject \ˈrē-ˌjekt\ *n* **:** a rejected person or thing

re·jec·tion \ri-ˈjek-shən\ *n* **1 :** the action of rejecting **:** the state of being rejected **2 :** something rejected

re·joice \ri-ˈjȯis\ *vb* **1 :** to give joy to **:** GLADDEN **2 :** to feel joy or great delight — **re·joic·er** *n* — **re·joic·ing·ly** *adv*

re·joic·ing \-ˈjȯi-siŋ\ *n* **1 :** the action of one that rejoices **2 :** an instance, occasion, or expression of joy **:** FESTIVITY

re·join *vt* **1** \(ˈ)rē-ˈjȯin\ **:** to join again **:** return to **2** \ri-\ **:** to say as an answer **:** REPLY

re·join·der \ri-ˈjȯin-dər\ *n* **:** REPLY; *esp* **:** an answer to a reply

re·ju·ve·nate \ri-ˈjü-və-ˌnāt\ *vt* **:** to make young or youthful again **:** give new vigor to — **re·ju·ve·na·tion** \-ˌjü-və-ˈnā-shən\ *n* — **re·ju·ve·na·tor** \-ˈjü-və-ˌnāt-ər\ *n*

¹re·lapse \ri-ˈlaps\ *n* **:** a relapsing; *esp* **:** a recurrence of illness after a period of improvement

²relapse *vi* **1 :** to slip or fall back into a former worse state **2 :** SINK, SUBSIDE **3 :** BACKSLIDE — **re·laps·er** *n*

re·lat·a·ble \ri-ˈlāt-ə-bəl\ *adj* **:** capable of being related

re·late \ri-ˈlāt\ *vb* **1 :** to give an account of **:** NARRATE **2 :** to show or establish a relationship between **3 :** to have relationship or connection **:** REFER **4 :** to have meaningful social relationships

re·lat·ed \-ˈlāt-əd\ *adj* **:** belonging to the same group on the basis of known or determinable qualities; *also* **:** belonging to the same family by blood or marriage

re·la·tion \ri-ˈlā-shən\ *n* **1 :** the act of telling or recounting **:** ACCOUNT **2 :** CONNECTION, RELATIONSHIP **3 a :** a related person **:** RELATIVE **b :** relationship by blood or marriage **:** KINSHIP **4 :** REFERENCE, RESPECT **5 a :** the state of being mutually or reciprocally interested (as in social or commercial matters) **b** *pl* (1) **:** DEALINGS, AFFAIRS (2) **:** INTERCOURSE — **re·la·tion·al** \-shnəl, -shən-ᵊl\ *adj*

re·la·tion·ship \-shən-ˌship\ *n* **:** the state or character of being related or interrelated

¹rel·a·tive \ˈrel-ət-iv\ *n* **1 :** a word referring grammatically to an antecedent **2 :** a thing having a relation to or connection with or necessary dependence upon another thing **3 :** an individual connected with another by ancestry or affinity

²relative *adj* **1 :** introducing a subordinate clause that qualifies an expressed or implied antecedent; *also* **:** introduced by such a connective **2 :** RELEVANT, PERTINENT **3 :** not absolute or independent **:** COMPARATIVE — **rel·a·tive·ly** *adv* — **rel·a·tive·ness** *n*

rel·a·tiv·i·ty \ˌrel-ə-ˈtiv-ət-ē\ *n* **1 :** the quality or state of being relative; *esp* **:** dependence on something else **2 :** a theory formulated by Albert Einstein and leading to the assertion of the equivalence of mass and energy and of the increase of the mass of a body with increased velocity — **rel·a·tiv·is·tic** \ˌrel-ət-iv-ˈis-tik\ *adj*

re·la·tor \ri-ˈlāt-ər\ *n* **:** one that relates **:** NARRATOR

re·lax \ri-ˈlaks\ *vb* **1 :** to make or become less tense or rigid **:** SLACKEN, EASE **2 :** to make or become less severe or stringent **3 :** to seek rest or recreation — **re·lax·er** *n*

re·lax·a·tion \ˌrē-ˌlak-ˈsā-shən, ri-\ *n* **:** the act or fact of relaxing **:** the state of being relaxed

¹re·lay \ˈrē-ˌlā\ *n* **1 :** a fresh supply (as of horses or men) arranged to relieve others at various stages **2 :** a race between teams in which each team member covers a specified portion of the course **3 :** an electromagnetic device for remote or automatic control of other devices (as switches) in the same or a different circuit **4 :** the act of passing along by stages; *also* **:** one of such stages

²re·lay \ˈrē-ˌlā, ri-ˈlā\ *vt* **re·layed; re·lay·ing 1 a :** to place or dispose in relays **b :** to provide with relays **2 :** to pass along by relays

¹re·lease \ri-ˈlēs\ *vt* **1 :** to set free from restraint or confinement **2 :** to relieve from something that holds, burdens, or oppresses **3 :** RELINQUISH **4 :** to give permission for publication, performance, exhibition, or sale of at a specified date — **re·leas·a·bil·i·ty** \-ˌlē-sə-ˈbil-ət-ē\ *n* — **re·leas·a·ble** *adj* — **re·leas·er** *n*

²release *n* **1 :** relief or deliverance from sorrow, suffering, or trouble **2 a :** a discharge from an obligation (as a debt) **b :** a document embodying a release **3 :** the act or an instance of liberating or freeing **4 :** the state of being freed **5 :** a device adapted to hold or release a mechanism as required **6 a :** the act of permitting performance or publication **b :** the matter released

rel·e·gate \ˈrel-ə-ˌgāt\ *vt* **1 :** EXILE, BANISH **2 :** to remove or dismiss to a less important or prominent place **3 :** to refer or hand over for decision or carrying out — **rel·e·ga·tion** \ˌrel-ə-ˈgā-shən\ *n*

re·lent \ri-ˈlent\ *vi* **1 :** to become less severe, harsh, or strict **2 :** to let up : SLACKEN

re·lent·less \-ləs\ *adj* **:** mercilessly hard or harsh — **re·lent·less·ly** *adv* — **re·lent·less·ness** *n*

rel·e·vance \ˈrel-ə-vən(t)s\ *n* **:** relation to the matter at hand : PERTINENCE

rel·e·vant \-vənt\ *adj* **:** having something to do with the case being considered : PERTINENT — **rel·e·vant·ly** *adv*

re·li·a·ble \ri-ˈlī-ə-bəl\ *adj* **:** suitable or fit to be relied on : DEPENDABLE — **re·li·a·bil·i·ty** \ri-ˌlī-ə-ˈbil-ət-ē\ *n* — **re·li·a·ble·ness** *n* — **re·li·a·bly** \-ˈlī-ə-blē\ *adv*

re·li·ance \ri-ˈlī-ən(t)s\ *n* **1 :** the act of relying **2 :** the condition or attitude of one who relies : DEPENDENCE **3 :** something or someone relied on

re·li·ant \-ənt\ *adj* **:** having reliance on something or someone : TRUSTING — **re·li·ant·ly** *adv*

rel·ic \ˈrel-ik\ *n* **1 a :** an object venerated because of association with a saint or martyr **b :** SOUVENIR, MEMENTO **2** *pl* **:** REMAINS, RUINS **3 :** a trace of some past or outmoded practice, custom, or belief : VESTIGE

rel·ict \ˈrel-ikt\ *n* **1 :** WIDOW **2 :** a persistent remnant of an otherwise extinct flora or fauna

re·lief \ri-ˈlēf\ *n* **1 a :** removal or lightening of something oppressive, painful, or distressing **b :** aid in the form of money or necessities for the indigent, aged, or handicapped **c :** military assistance to a post or force in extreme danger **2 a :** release from sentry or other duty **b :** one that takes the place of another on duty **3 :** projection from the background (as in sculpture) : sharpness of outline **4 :** the elevations or inequalities of a land surface

re·lieve \ri-ˈlēv\ *vb* **1 :** to bring or give relief wholly or partly from a burden, pain, discomfort, or trouble **2 :** to release from a post or duty esp. by taking the place of **3 :** to take away the sameness or monotony of **4 :** to put or stand out in relief — **re·liev·er** *n*

re·li·gion \ri-ˈlij-ən\ *n* **1 a (1) :** the service and worship of God or the supernatural **(2) :** belief in or devotion to religious faith or observance **b :** the state of a religious **2 :** a set or system of religious attitudes, beliefs, and practices **3 :** a cause, principle, or system of beliefs held to with ardor and faith

¹re·li·gious \ri-ˈlij-əs\ *adj* **1 a :** devoted to God or to the powers or principles believed to govern life **b :** belonging to a religious order **2 :** of or relating to religion **3 :** DEPENDABLE, FAITHFUL — **re·li·gious·ly** *adv* — **re·li·gious·ness** *n*

²religious *n, pl* **religious :** a member of a religious order

re·lin·quish \ri-ˈliŋ-kwish\ *vt* **1 :** to withdraw or retreat from : ABANDON **2 :** RENOUNCE **3 :** to let go of : RELEASE — **re·lin·quish·ment** *n*

rel·i·quary \ˈrel-ə-ˌkwer-ē\ *n, pl* **-quar·ies :** a small box or shrine in which sacred relics are kept

¹rel·ish \ˈrel-ish\ *n* **1 :** a pleasing appetizing taste **2 :** a small bit added for flavor : DASH **3 :** personal liking **4 :** keen enjoyment of food or of anything **5 :** a highly seasoned sauce (as of pickles or mustard) eaten with other food to add flavor

²relish *vt* **1 :** to add relish to **2 :** to be pleased or gratified by **3 :** to eat with pleasure — **rel·ish·a·ble** *adj*

re·live \(ˈ)rē-ˈliv\ *vb* **:** to experience again in imagination

re·luc·tance \ri-ˈlək-tən(t)s\ *n* **1 :** the quality or state of being reluctant **2 :** the opposition offered by a magnetic substance to magnetic flux

re·luc·tan·cy \-tən-sē\ *n, pl* **-cies :** RELUCTANCE 1

re·luc·tant \-tənt\ *adj* **1 :** UNWILLING **2 :** showing hesitation or unwillingness — **re·luc·tant·ly** *adv*

re·ly \ri-ˈlī\ *vi* **re·lied; re·ly·ing 1 :** to have confidence : TRUST **2 :** to be dependent : COUNT

¹re·main \ri-ˈmān\ *vi* **1 a :** to be a part not destroyed, taken, or used up **b :** to be something yet to be shown, done, or treated : have yet **2 :** to stay behind **3 :** to continue unchanged

²remain *n* **1 :** a remaining part or trace — usu. used in pl. **2** *pl* **:** writings left unpublished at a writer's death **3** *pl* **:** a dead body

re·main·der \ri-ˈmān-dər\ *n* **1 a :** a remaining group, part, or trace **b :** the number left after a subtraction **2 :** a book sold at a reduced price by the publisher after sales have slowed

re·mand \ri-ˈmand\ *vt* **:** to order back; *esp* **:** to return to custody pending trial or for further detention

¹re·mark \ri-ˈmärk\ *vb* **1 :** to take notice of : OBSERVE **2 :** to express as an observation or comment : SAY

²remark *n* **1 :** the act of remarking : NOTICE **2 :** mention of that which deserves attention or notice **3 :** an expression of opinion or judgment

re·mark·a·ble \ri-ˈmär-kə-bəl\ *adj* **1 :** worthy of being or likely to be noticed **2 :** UNCOMMON, EXTRAORDINARY — **re·mark·a·ble·ness** *n* — **re·mark·a·bly** \-blē\ *adv*

re·mar·riage \(ˈ)rē-ˈmar-ij\ *n* **:** a second or later marriage

re·me·di·al \ri-ˈmēd-ē-əl\ *adj* **:** intended to remedy or improve — **re·me·di·al·ly** \-ē-ə-lē\ *adv*

¹rem·e·dy \ˈrem-əd-ē\ *n, pl* **-dies 1 :** a medicine or treatment that cures or relieves **2 :** something that corrects an evil, rights a wrong, or makes up for a loss

²remedy *vt* **-died; -dy·ing :** to provide or serve as a remedy for : RELIEVE

re·mem·ber \ri-ˈmem-bər\ *vb* **-bered; -ber·ing** \-b(ə-)riŋ\ **1 :** to bring to mind or think of again **2 a :** to keep in mind for attention or consideration **b :** REWARD **3 :** to retain in the memory **4 :** to convey greetings from **5 :** COMMEMORATE — **re·mem·ber·a·ble** \-b(ə-)rə-bəl\ *adj* — **re·mem·ber·er** *n*

re·mem·brance \ri-ˈmem-brən(t)s\ *n* **1 :** the act of remembering **2 :** something remembered **3 :** something (as a souvenir) that brings to mind **4** *pl* **:** GREETINGS

re·mind \ri-ˈmīnd\ *vt* **:** to put in mind of something : cause to remember — **re·mind·er** *n*

rem·i·nisce \ˌrem-ə-ˈnis\ *vi* **:** to indulge in reminiscence

rem·i·nis·cence \ˌrem-ə-ˈnis-ᵊn(t)s\ *n* **1 :** a recalling or telling of a past experience **2** *pl* **:** an account of one's memorable experiences

rem·i·nis·cent \-ᵊnt\ *adj* **1 :** of or relating to reminiscence : indulging in reminiscence **2 :** that reminds one (as of something seen or known before)

re·miss \ri-ˈmis\ *adj* **1 :** negligent in the performance of work or duty : CARELESS **2 :** showing neglect or inattention : LAX — **re·miss·ly** *adv* — **re·miss·ness** *n*

re·mis·si·ble \ri-ˈmis-ə-bəl\ *adj* **:** that may be forgiven — **re·mis·si·bly** \-blē\ *adv*

re·mis·sion \ri-ˈmish-ən\ *n* **:** the act or process of remitting

re·mit \ri-ˈmit\ *vb* **re·mit·ted; re·mit·ting 1 a :** to release from the guilt or penalty of : PARDON **b :** to refrain from exacting **c :** to give relief from (suffering) **2 :** to submit or refer for consideration, judgment, decision, or action **3 :** to send (money) esp. in payment **4 :** MODERATE — **remit** *n* — **re·mit·ment** *n* — **re·mit·ta·ble** *adj* — **re·mit·ter** *n*

re·mit·tal \ri-ˈmit-ᵊl\ *n* **:** REMISSION

re·mit·tance \ri-ˈmit-ᵊn(t)s\ *n* **1 :** a sending (as of money or bills) esp. to a distance **2 :** money sent esp. in payment

rem·nant \ˈrem-nənt\ *n* **1 :** something that remains or is left over **2 :** a surviving trace

re·mod·el \(ˈ)rē-ˈmäd-ᵊl\ *vt* **:** to alter the structure of

re·mon·strance \ri-ˈmän(t)-strən(t)s\ *n* **:** an act or instance of remonstrating : EXPOSTULATION

re·mon·strant \-strənt\ *adj* **:** vigorously objecting or opposing — **remonstrant** *n* — **re·mon·strant·ly** *adv*

re·mon·strate \ri-ˈmän-ˌstrāt\ *vb* **:** to plead in opposition to something : speak in reproof : OBJECT, PROTEST

re·morse \ri-ˈmȯrs\ *n* **:** a gnawing distress arising from a sense of guilt for past wrongs : SELF-REPROACH

re·morse·ful \-fəl\ *adj* : springing from or marked by remorse — **re·morse·ful·ly** \-fə-lē\ *adv* — **re·morse·ful·ness** *n*
re·morse·less \-ləs\ *adj* : being without remorse : MERCILESS — **re·morse·less·ly** *adv* — **re·morse·less·ness** *n*
re·mote \ri-'mōt\ *adj* **1** : far off in place or time : not near or recent **2** : OUT-OF-THE-WAY, SECLUDED **3** : not closely connected or related **4** : not obvious or striking : SLIGHT **5** : APART, ALOOF **6** : operated or operating from a distance — **re·mote·ly** *adv* — **re·mote·ness** *n*
¹re·mount \(')rē-'mau̇nt\ *vb* : to mount again
²re·mount \'rē-ˌmau̇nt, (')rē-'\ *n* : a fresh horse to take the place of one disabled or exhausted
re·mov·a·ble \ri-'mü-və-bəl\ *adj* : capable of being removed — **re·mov·a·ble·ness** *n* — **re·mov·a·bly** \-blē\ *adv*
re·mov·al \ri-'mü-vəl\ *n* : the act of removing : the fact of being removed
¹re·move \ri-'müv\ *vb* **1 a** : to change or cause to change to another location, position, station, or residence **b** : to go away **2** : to move by lifting, pushing aside, or taking away or off; *also* : to yield to being so moved **3** : to dismiss from office **4** : ELIMINATE — **re·mov·er** *n*
²remove *n* **1** : REMOVAL; *esp* : MOVE 2C **2 a** : a distance or interval separating one thing from another **b** : a degree or stage of separation
re·moved \ri-'müvd\ *adj* **1** : far away : DISTANT **2** : distant in relationship
re·mu·ner·ate \ri-'myü-nə-ˌrāt\ *vt* : to pay an equivalent to for a service, loss, or expense : RECOMPENSE — **re·mu·ner·a·tor** \-ˌrāt-ər\ *n* — **re·mu·ner·a·to·ry** \ri-'myü-nə-rə-ˌtōr-ē\ *adj*
re·mu·ner·a·tion \ri-ˌmyü-nə-'rā-shən\ *n* **1** : an act or fact of remunerating **2** : something that remunerates
re·mu·ner·a·tive \ri-'myü-nə-ˌrāt-iv\ *adj* **1** : serving to remunerate **2** : affording remuneration : PROFITABLE — **re·mu·ner·a·tive·ly** *adv* — **re·mu·ner·a·tive·ness** *n*
Re·nais·sance \ˌren-ə-'sän(t)s, -'zän(t)s\ *n* **1** : the movement or period in Europe between the 14th and 17th centuries marked by a humanistic revival of classical influence in the arts and literature and by the beginnings of modern science **2** *often not cap* : a movement or period marked by a revival of vigorous artistic and intellectual activity
re·nal \'rēn-ᵊl\ *adj* : of, relating to, or located in or near the kidneys
re·nas·cence \ri-'nas-ᵊn(t)s, -'nās-\ *n, often cap* : RENAISSANCE — **re·nas·cent** \-ᵊnt\ *adj*
rend \'rend\ *vb* **rent** \'rent\; **rend·ing** **1** : to remove from place by violence : WREST **2** : to split or tear apart or in pieces by violence
ren·der \'ren-dər\ *vt* **ren·dered**; **ren·der·ing** \-d(ə-)riŋ\ **1** : DELIVER, GIVE **2** : to melt down : extract by heating **3** : to give up : SURRENDER **4** : to give in return **5** : to present a statement of : bring to one's attention **6** : to cause to be or become : MAKE **7** : FURNISH, CONTRIBUTE **8** : PRESENT, PERFORM **9** : TRANSLATE — **ren·der·a·ble** \-d(ə-)rə-bəl\ *adj* — **ren·der·er** *n*
¹ren·dez·vous \'rän-di-ˌvü, -dā-\ *n, pl* **ren·dez·vous** \-ˌvüz\ **1 a** : a place appointed for assembling or meeting **b** : a place of popular resort : HAUNT **2** : an appointed meeting
²rendezvous *vb* **ren·dez·voused** \-ˌvüd\; **ren·dez·vous·ing** \-ˌvü-iŋ\; **ren·dez·vouses** \-ˌvüz\ : to come or bring together at a rendezvous
ren·di·tion \ren-'dish-ən\ *n* : the act or result of rendering
ren·e·gade \'ren-i-ˌgād\ *n* : a deserter from one faith, cause, or allegiance to another
re·nege \ri-'nig, -'neg, -'nēg, -'nāg\ *vi* **1** : to violate a rule in a card game by failing to follow suit when able **2** : to go back on a promise or commitment — **re·neg·er** *n*
re·new \ri-'n(y)ü\ *vt* **1** : to make new again : restore to freshness or vigor **2** : to restore to existence : REESTABLISH, RECREATE **3** : to do or make again **4** : to begin again : RESUME **5** : to put in a fresh supply of : REPLACE **6** : to grant or obtain an extension of : continue in force for a fresh period — **re·new·a·ble** *adj* — **re·new·er** *n*
re·new·al \ri-'n(y)ü-əl\ *n* **1** : the act of renewing : the state of being renewed **2** : something renewed
re·nounce \ri-'nau̇n(t)s\ *vt* **1** : to give up, abandon, or resign usu. by formal declaration **2** : to refuse further to follow, obey, or recognize : REPUDIATE — **re·nounce·ment** *n* — **re·nounc·er** *n*
ren·o·vate \'ren-ə-ˌvāt\ *vt* : to make like new again : restore to a former state or to good condition — **ren·o·va·tion** \ˌren-ə-'vā-shən\ *n* — **ren·o·va·tor** \'ren-ə-ˌvāt-ər\ *n*
re·nown \ri-'nau̇n\ *n* : a state of being widely acclaimed and highly honored : FAME
re·nowned \-'nau̇nd\ *adj* : having renown : CELEBRATED
¹rent \'rent\ *n* : a periodic payment made by a tenant to the owner for the possession and use of real property — **for rent** : available for use or service at a price
²rent *vb* **1** : to take and hold property under an agreement to pay rent **2** : to grant the possession and enjoyment of for rent : LET **3** : to be for rent — **rent·a·ble** *adj*
³rent *past of* REND
⁴rent *n* **1** : an opening made by or as if by rending **2** : an act or instance of rending
¹rent·al \'rent-ᵊl\ *n* **1** : an amount paid or collected as rent **2** : an act of renting
²rental *adj* : of, relating to, or available for rent
rent·er \'rent-ər\ *n* : one that rents; *esp* : TENANT
re·nun·ci·a·tion \ri-ˌnən(t)-sē-'ā-shən\ *n* : the act or practice of renouncing — **re·nun·ci·a·tive** \-'nən(t)-sē-ˌāt-iv\ *adj* — **re·nun·ci·a·to·ry** \-sē-ə-ˌtōr-ē\ *adj*
¹re·or·der \(')rē-'ȯrd-ər\ *vb* **1** : REORGANIZE **2** : to place a reorder
²reorder *n* : an order like a previous order from the same supplier
re·or·ga·ni·za·tion \(ˌ)rē-ˌȯrg-(ə-)nə-'zā-shən\ *n* : the act of reorganizing : the state of being reorganized
re·or·ga·nize \(')rē-'ȯr-gə-ˌnīz\ *vb* : to organize again or anew — **re·or·ga·niz·er** *n*
¹re·pair \ri-'pa(ə)r\ *vi* : to betake oneself : GO
²repair *vb* **1 a** : to restore by replacing a part or putting together what is torn or broken : MEND **b** : to restore to a sound or healthy state : RENEW **2** : to make good : REMEDY — **re·pair·a·ble** *adj* — **re·pair·er** *n*
³repair *n* **1** : the action or process of repairing **2** : the result of repairing **3** : good or sound condition **4** : condition with respect to soundness or need of repairing
re·pair·man \-'pa(ə)r-ˌman, -'pe(ə)r-\ *n* : one whose occupation is making repairs
rep·a·ra·ble \'rep-(ə-)rə-bəl\ *adj* : capable of being repaired
rep·a·ra·tion \ˌrep-ə-'rā-shən\ *n* **1** : a making amends for a wrong or injury done **2** : the amends made for a wrong or injury; *esp* : money paid (as by one country to another) in compensation (as for damages in war)
rep·ar·tee \ˌrep-ər-'tē\ *n* : a clever witty reply; *also* : the making of such replies
re·past \ri-'past\ *n* : MEAL, FEAST
re·pay \(')rē-'pā\ *vb* **-paid**; **-pay·ing** **1** : to pay back **2** : to make return payment or requital — **re·pay·a·ble** *adj* — **re·pay·ment** *n*
re·peal \ri-'pēl\ *vt* : REVOKE, ANNUL; *esp* : to do away with by legislative enactment — **repeal** *n* — **re·peal·a·ble** *adj* — **re·peal·er** *n*
¹re·peat \ri-'pēt\ *vt* **1 a** : to say or state again **b** : to say over from memory : RECITE **2** : to make, do, or perform again — **re·peat·a·ble** *adj* — **re·peat·er** *n*

²re·peat \ri-ˈpēt, ˈrē-ˌ\ *n* **1 :** the act of repeating **2 :** something repeated or to be repeated

re·peat·ed \ri-ˈpēt-əd\ *adj* **:** done or happening again and again **:** FREQUENT — **re·peat·ed·ly** *adv*

re·pel \ri-ˈpel\ *vb* **re·pelled**; **re·pel·ling** **1 a :** to drive back **:** REPULSE **b :** to fight against **:** RESIST **2 :** to turn away **:** REJECT **3 :** to drive away **:** DISCOURAGE **4 :** to cause aversion **:** DISGUST — **re·pel·ler** *n*

re·pel·lent \-ənt\ *adj* **1 :** serving or tending to drive away or ward off **2 :** arousing aversion or disgust **:** REPULSIVE — **re·pel·len·cy** \-ən-sē\ *n* — **repellent** *n* — **re·pel·lent·ly** *adv*

re·pent \ri-ˈpent\ *vb* **1 :** to feel sorrow for one's sin and determine to do what is right **2 :** to feel sorry for or dissatisfied with something one has done **:** REGRET — **re·pent·er** *n*

re·pent·ance \ri-ˈpent-ᵊn(t)s\ *n* **:** a feeling of regret for something done or said; *esp* **:** regret or sorrow for sin

re·pent·ant \ri-ˈpent-ᵊnt\ *adj* **:** feeling or showing repentance — **re·pent·ant·ly** *adv*

re·per·cus·sion \ˌrē-pər-ˈkəsh-ən, ˌrep-ər-\ *n* **1 :** REFLECTION, REVERBERATION **2 a :** a reciprocal action or effect **b :** a widespread, indirect, or unforeseen effect of an act, action, or event — **re·per·cus·sive** \-ˈkəs-iv\ *adj*

rep·er·toire \ˈrep-ə(r)-ˌtwär\ *n* **1 :** a list or supply of dramas, operas, pieces, or parts that a company or person is prepared to perform **2 :** a supply of skills, devices, or expedients possessed by a person

rep·er·to·ry \ˈrep-ə(r)-ˌtōr-ē\ *n, pl* **-ries** **1 :** a stock or store of something **:** COLLECTION **2 :** REPERTOIRE

rep·e·ti·tion \ˌrep-ə-ˈtish-ən\ *n* **1 :** the act or an instance of repeating **2 :** the fact of being repeated **3 :** something repeated

rep·e·ti·tious \-ˈtish-əs\ *adj* **:** marked by repetition; *esp* **:** tediously repeating — **rep·e·ti·tious·ly** *adv* — **rep·e·ti·tious·ness** *n*

re·pet·i·tive \ri-ˈpet-ət-iv\ *adj* **:** REPETITIOUS — **re·pet·i·tive·ly** *adv* — **re·pet·i·tive·ness** *n*

re·pine \ri-ˈpīn\ *vi* **1 :** to feel or express dejection or discontent **2 :** to wish discontentedly — **re·pin·er** *n*

re·place \ri-ˈplās\ *vt* **1 :** to put back in a proper or former place **2 :** to take the place of **:** SUPPLANT **3 :** to fill the place of **:** supply an equivalent for — **re·place·a·ble** *adj*

re·place·ment \-mənt\ *n* **1 :** the act of replacing **:** the state of being replaced **2 :** one that replaces another

re·plen·ish \ri-ˈplen-ish\ *vt* **:** to fill again **:** bring back to a condition of being full or complete — **re·plen·ish·er** *n* — **re·plen·ish·ment** *n*

re·plete \ri-ˈplēt\ *adj* **1 :** filled to capacity **:** FULL; *esp* **:** full of food **2 :** fully supplied or provided

re·ple·tion \ri-ˈplē-shən\ *n* **:** the condition of being replete

rep·li·ca \ˈrep-li-kə\ *n* **1 :** a close reproduction or facsimile esp. by the maker of the original **2 :** COPY, DUPLICATE

¹re·ply \ri-ˈplī\ *vb* **re·plied**; **re·ply·ing** **:** to say or do in answer or response — **re·pli·er** *n*

²reply *n, pl* **replies** **:** ANSWER, RESPONSE

¹re·port \ri-ˈpōrt\ *n* **1 a :** common talk **:** an account spread by common talk **:** RUMOR **b :** FAME, REPUTATION **2 :** a usu. detailed account or statement **3 :** an explosive noise

²report *vb* **1 :** to give an account (as of an incident or of one's activities) **2 :** to give an account of in a newspaper article **3 :** to make a charge of misconduct against **4 :** to present oneself **5 :** to make known to the proper authorities — **re·port·a·ble** *adj*

re·port·ed·ly \ri-ˈpōrt-əd-lē\ *adv* **:** according to report

re·port·er \ri-ˈpōrt-ər\ *n* **:** one that reports: as **a :** one employed by a newspaper or magazine to gather and write news **b :** one that broadcasts news — **rep·or·to·ri·al** \ˌrep-ə(r)-ˈtōr-ē-əl, ˌrēp-\ *adj* — **rep·or·to·ri·al·ly** \-ē-ə-lē\ *adv*

¹re·pose \ri-ˈpōz\ *vt* **1 :** to place unquestioningly **:** SET **2 :** to place for control, management, or use

²repose *vb* **1 :** to lay at rest **:** put in a restful position **2 :** to lie at rest **:** take rest

³repose *n* **1 :** a state of resting after exertion or strain; *esp* **:** rest in sleep **2 :** CALM, PEACE **3 :** cessation or absence of activity, movement, or animation

re·pose·ful \ri-ˈpōz-fəl\ *adj* **:** full of repose **:** QUIET — **re·pose·ful·ly** \-fə-lē\ *adv* — **re·pose·ful·ness** *n*

re·pos·i·to·ry \ri-ˈpäz-ə-ˌtōr-ē\ *n, pl* **-ries** **1 :** a place or container where something is deposited or stored **2 :** a person to whom something is confided or entrusted

re·pos·sess \ˌrē-pə-ˈzes\ *vt* **:** to regain possession of — **re·pos·ses·sion** \-ˈzesh-ən\ *n*

rep·re·hend \ˌrep-ri-ˈhend\ *vt* **:** to voice disapproval of **:** CENSURE

rep·re·hen·si·ble \ˌrep-ri-ˈhen(t)-sə-bəl\ *adj* **:** worthy of or deserving censure or reprehension **:** CULPABLE — **rep·re·hen·si·ble·ness** *n* — **rep·re·hen·si·bly** \-blē\ *adv*

rep·re·hen·sion \-ˈhen-chən\ *n* **:** the act of reprehending **:** REPROOF — **rep·re·hen·sive** \-ˈhen(t)-siv\ *adj*

rep·re·sent \ˌrep-ri-ˈzent\ *vt* **1 :** to present a picture, image, or likeness of **:** PORTRAY **2 :** to serve as a sign or symbol of **3 a :** to take the place of in some respect **b :** to act for or in the place of (as in a legislative body) **4 :** to describe as having a specified character or quality **5 :** to serve as a specimen, example, or instance of — **rep·re·sent·a·ble** *adj* — **rep·re·sent·er** *n*

rep·re·sen·ta·tion \ˌrep-ri-ˌzen-ˈtā-shən\ *n* **1 :** one that represents: as **a :** an artistic likeness or image **b :** a sign or symbol of something **c :** a statement or account of an opinion or of a fact made to influence opinion or action **2 :** a usu. formal protest **3 :** the act or action of representing **4 :** the body of persons representing a constituency — **rep·re·sen·ta·tion·al** \-shnəl, -shən-ᵊl\ *adj*

¹rep·re·sen·ta·tive \ˌrep-ri-ˈzent-ət-iv\ *adj* **1 :** serving to represent **2 :** standing or acting for another esp. through delegated authority **3 :** of, based upon, or constituting a government in which the many are represented by persons chosen from among them usu. by election **4 :** TYPICAL, CHARACTERISTIC — **rep·re·sen·ta·tive·ly** *adv* — **rep·re·sen·ta·tive·ness** *n*

²representative *n* **1 :** a typical example of a group, class, or quality **:** SPECIMEN **2 :** one that represents another or others **:** DELEGATE, AGENT; *esp* **:** one representing a district or a state in a legislative body usu. as a member of a lower house

re·press \ri-ˈpres\ *vt* **1 :** to check by or as if by pressure **:** CURB **2 :** to hold in by self-control **3 :** to put down by force **:** SUBDUE **4 :** to exclude from consciousness — **re·pres·sive** \-ˈpres-iv\ *adj* — **re·pres·sive·ly** *adv* — **re·pres·sive·ness** *n* — **re·pres·sor** \-ˈpres-ər\ *n*

re·pres·sion \ri-ˈpresh-ən\ *n* **:** the act of repressing **:** the state of being repressed

¹re·prieve \ri-ˈprēv\ *vt* **1 :** to delay the punishment of **2 :** to give relief or deliverance to for a time

²reprieve *n* **1 a :** the act of reprieving **:** the state of being reprieved **b :** a formal temporary suspension of the execution of a sentence **2 :** a temporary respite

¹rep·ri·mand \ˈrep-rə-ˌmand\ *n* **:** a severe or formal reproof

²reprimand *vt* **:** to reprove severely and esp. officially

re·pri·sal \ri-ˈprī-zəl\ *n* **:** an act of retaliation esp. in war

¹re·proach \ri-ˈprōch\ *n* **1 a :** a cause or occasion of blame, discredit, or disgrace **b :** DISCREDIT, DISGRACE **2 :** the act or action of reproaching **:** REBUKE — **re·proach·ful** \-fəl\ *adj* — **re·proach·ful·ly** \-fə-lē\ *adv* — **re·proach·ful·ness** *n*

²reproach *vt* **1 :** to utter a reproach to **:** find fault with **:** blame for a mistake or failure **2 :** to bring into discredit — **re·proach·a·ble** *adj* — **re·proach·er** *n* — **re·proach·ing·ly** *adv*

¹rep·ro·bate \ˈrep-rə-ˌbāt\ *vt* **:** to condemn as unworthy or evil — **rep·ro·ba·tion** \ˌrep-rə-ˈbā-shən\ *n* — **rep·ro·ba·tive** \ˈrep-rə-ˌbāt-iv\ *adj*

[2]**reprobate** *adj* : morally abandoned : DEPRAVED
[3]**reprobate** *n* : a reprobate person
re·pro·duce \\,rē-prə-'d(y)üs\\ *vb* **1** : to produce again or anew **2** : to produce offspring — **re·pro·duc·er** *n* — **re·pro·duc·i·bil·i·ty** \\-,d(y)ü-sə-'bil-ət-ē\\ *n* — **re·pro·duc·i·ble** \\-'d(y)ü-sə-bəl\\ *adj*
re·pro·duc·tion \\,rē-prə-'dək-shən\\ *n* **1** : the act or process of reproducing; *esp* : the process by which plants and animals give rise to offspring **2** : something reproduced : COPY
re·pro·duc·tive \\,rē-prə-'dək-tiv\\ *adj* : of, relating to, capable of, or concerned with reproduction — **re·pro·duc·tive·ly** *adv* — **re·pro·duc·tive·ness** *n* — **re·pro·duc·tiv·i·ty** \\-,dək-'tiv-ət-ē\\ *n*
re·proof \\ri-'prüf\\ *n* : censure for a fault : REBUKE
re·prove \\ri-'prüv\\ *vt* **1** : to administer a rebuke to : SCOLD **2** : to express disapproval of : CENSURE, CONDEMN — **re·prov·er** *n*
rep·tile \\'rep-tᵊl, -,tīl\\ *n* : any of a group of air-breathing scaly vertebrates including alligators, lizards, snakes, and turtles
rep·til·i·an \\rep-'til-ē-ən\\ *adj* : of, relating to, or resembling reptiles — **reptilian** *n*
re·pub·lic \\ri-'pəb-lik\\ *n* **1 a** : a government having a chief of state who is not a monarch and who is usu. a president **b** : a political unit having such a form of government **2 a** : a government in which supreme power resides in a body of citizens entitled to vote and is exercised by elected officers and representatives responsible to them **b** : a political unit (as a nation) having such a form of government
[1]**re·pub·li·can** \\ri-'pəb-li-kən\\ *adj* **1 a** : of, relating to, or having the characteristics of a republic **b** : favoring, supporting, or advocating a republic **2** *cap* : of, relating to, or constituting one of the two major political parties in the U.S. evolving in the mid-19th century — **re·pub·li·can·ism** \\-kə-,niz-əm\\ *n*
[2]**republican** *n* **1** : one that favors or supports a republican form of government **2** *cap* : a member of a republican party and esp. of the Republican party of the U.S.
re·pu·di·ate \\ri-'pyüd-ē-,āt\\ *vt* **1** : to refuse to have anything to do with : DISOWN **2** : to refuse to accept, acknowledge, or pay — **re·pu·di·a·tion** \\-,pyüd-ē-'ā-shən\\ *n* — **re·pu·di·a·tor** \\-'pyüd-ē-,āt-ər\\ *n*
re·pug·nance \\ri-'pəg-nən(t)s\\ *n* : deep-rooted dislike
re·pug·nant \\-nənt\\ *adj* **1** : CONTRARY, INCOMPATIBLE **2** : DISTASTEFUL, REPULSIVE
[1]**re·pulse** \\ri-'pəls\\ *vt* **1** : to drive or beat back : REPEL **2** : to repel by discourtesy, coldness, or denial : REBUFF **3** : to cause repulsion in : DISGUST
[2]**repulse** *n* **1** : REBUFF, REJECTION **2** : the action of repelling an attacker : the fact of being repelled
re·pul·sion \\ri-'pəl-shən\\ *n* **1** : the action of repulsing : the state of being repulsed **2** : the action of repelling : the force with which bodies, particles, or like forces repel one another **3** : a feeling of aversion : REPUGNANCE
re·pul·sive \\ri-'pəl-siv\\ *adj* **1** : tending or serving to repulse **2** : arousing aversion or disgust — **re·pul·sive·ly** *adv* — **re·pul·sive·ness** *n*
rep·u·ta·ble \\'rep-yət-ə-bəl\\ *adj* : having a good reputation : RESPECTED — **rep·u·ta·bly** *adv*
rep·u·ta·tion \\,rep-yə-'tā-shən\\ *n* **1** : overall quality or character as seen or judged by people in general **2** : good name : a place in public esteem **3** : FAME
[1]**re·pute** \\ri-'pyüt\\ *vt* : SUPPOSE, BELIEVE, CONSIDER
[2]**repute** *n* **1** : the character or status commonly ascribed to one : REPUTATION **2** : FAME, NOTE
re·put·ed \\ri-'pyüt-əd\\ *adj* **1** : having repute **2** : popularly supposed — **re·put·ed·ly** *adv*
[1]**re·quest** \\ri-'kwest\\ *n* **1** : an asking for something : PETITION, ENTREATY **2** : something asked for **3** : the condition of being requested **4** : DEMAND
[2]**request** *vt* **1** : to make a request to or of **2** : to ask for — **re·quest·er** *n*
req·ui·em \\'rek-wē-əm, 'rā-kwē-\\ *n* **1** : a mass for a dead person; *also* : a musical setting for such a mass **2** : a musical service or hymn in honor of the dead
re·quire \\ri-'kwī(ə)r\\ *vt* **1** : ORDER, COMMAND **2** : to call for : NEED
re·quire·ment \\-mənt\\ *n* **1** : something (as a condition or quality) required **2** : NECESSITY, NEED
req·ui·site \\'rek-wə-zət\\ *adj* : REQUIRED, NEEDFUL — **requisite** *n* — **req·ui·site·ness** *n*
[1]**req·ui·si·tion** \\,rek-wə-'zish-ən\\ *n* **1** : an authoritative or formal demand or application **2** : the condition of being demanded or put into use
[2]**requisition** *vt* **-si·tioned**; **-si·tion·ing** \\-'zish-(ə-)niŋ\\ : to make a requisition for
re·quit·al \\ri-'kwīt-ᵊl\\ *n* **1** : the act or action of requiting : the state of being requited **2** : something given in requital
re·quite \\ri-'kwīt\\ *vt* **1 a** : to make return for : REPAY **b** : to make retaliation for : AVENGE **2** : to make return to for a benefit or service or for an injury — **re·quit·er** *n*
[1]**re·run** \\(')rē-'rən\\ *vt* : to run again or anew
[2]**re·run** \\'rē-,rən, (')rē-'\\ *n* : the act or action or an instance of rerunning; *esp* : presentation of a motion-picture film or television program after its first run
re·sale \\'rē-,sāl, (')rē-'\\ *n* : the act or an instance of selling again
re·scind \\ri-'sind\\ *vt* **1** : to make void : ANNUL, CANCEL **2** : REPEAL — **re·scind·er** *n*
re·scis·sion \\ri-'sizh-ən\\ *n* : an act of rescinding
re·script \\'rē-,skript\\ *n* : an official or authoritative order, decree, edict, or announcement
res·cue \\'res-kyü\\ *vt* : to free from confinement, danger, or evil : SAVE — **rescue** *n* — **res·cu·er** *n*
re·search \\ri-'sərch, 'rē-,\\ *n* **1** : careful or diligent search **2** : studious inquiry or examination; *esp* : investigation or experimentation aimed at the discovery and interpretation of new knowledge — **research** *vb* — **re·search·er** *n*
re·sem·blance \\ri-'zem-blən(t)s\\ *n* **1** : the quality or state of resembling : SIMILARITY; *also* : a point of likeness **2** : REPRESENTATION, IMAGE
re·sem·ble \\ri-'zem-bəl\\ *vt* **-bled**; **-bling** \\-b(ə-)liŋ\\ : to be like or similar to
re·sent \\ri-'zent\\ *vt* : to feel or express annoyance or ill will over
re·sent·ful \\-fəl\\ *adj* **1** : full of resentment : inclined to resent **2** : caused or marked by resentment — **re·sent·ful·ly** \\-fə-lē\\ *adv* — **re·sent·ful·ness** *n*
re·sent·ment \\-mənt\\ *n* : a feeling of indignant displeasure at something regarded as a wrong, insult, or injury
re·ser·pine \\ri-'sər-pən, -'zər-\\ *n* : a drug obtained esp. from rauwolfia and used similarly
res·er·va·tion \\,rez-ər-'vā-shən\\ *n* **1** : the act of reserving **2** : an arrangement to have something (as a hotel room or train seat) held for one's use **3** : something reserved for a special use **4** : a limiting condition : EXCEPTION
[1]**re·serve** \\ri-'zərv\\ *vt* **1** : to keep in store for future or special use **2** : to retain or hold over to a future time or place : DEFER **3** : to arrange to have set aside and held for one's use **4** : to set or have set aside or apart
[2]**reserve** *n* **1** : something stored or available for future use : STOCK **2 a** : military forces withheld or available for later decisive use — usu. used in pl. **b** : the military forces of a country not part of the regular services; *also* : RESERVIST **c** : a tract set apart : RESERVATION **3** : an act of reserving : EXCEPTION **4** : restraint, closeness, or caution in one's words and bearing **5** : money or its equivalent kept in hand or set apart usu. to meet liabilities

re·served \ri-'zərvd\ *adj* **1** : restrained in words and actions **2** : kept or set apart or aside for future or special use — **re·serv·ed·ly** \-'zər-vəd-lē\ *adv* — **re·serv·ed·ness** \-vəd-nəs\ *n*
re·serv·ist \ri-'zər-vəst\ *n* : a member of a military reserve
res·er·voir \'rez-ə(r)v-ˌwär, -ə(r)v-ˌ(w)ȯr\ *n* : a place where something is kept in store; *esp* : an artificial lake where water is collected and kept in quantity for use
re·side \ri-'zīd\ *vi* **1** : to dwell permanently or continuously : have a fixed abode **2** : to be present as an element, quality, or right — **re·sid·er** *n*
res·i·dence \'rez-əd-ən(t)s, -ə-ˌden(t)s\ *n* **1** : the act or fact of residing in a place as a dweller or in discharge of a duty **2** : the place where one actually lives **3 a** : DWELLING **b** : a unit of housing provided for students **4** : the period or duration of abode in a place
res·i·den·cy \'rez-əd-ən-sē, -ə-ˌden(t)-\ *n*, *pl* **-cies** **1** : a usu. official place of residence **2** : a territorial unit in which a political resident exercises authority **3** : a period of advanced resident training esp. in a medical specialty
[1]**res·i·dent** \'rez-əd-ənt, -ə-ˌdent\ *adj* **1** : living in a place for some length of time : RESIDING **2** : living in a place while discharging official duties **3** : PRESENT, INHERENT **4** : not migratory
[2]**resident** *n* **1** : one who resides in a place **2** : a diplomatic agent exercising authority in a protected state **3** : one (as a physician) serving a residency
res·i·den·tial \ˌrez-ə-'den-chəl\ *adj* **1** : used as a residence or by residents **2** : adapted to or occupied by residences **3** : of or relating to residence or residences
[1]**re·sid·u·al** \ri-'zij-(ə-w)əl\ *adj* : being or active as a residue : left over — **re·sid·u·al·ly** \-ē\ *adv*
[2]**residual** *n* **1** : a residual product, substance, or result **2** : a payment (as to an actor or writer) for each rerun after an initial showing (as of a television tape)
re·sid·u·ary \ri-'zij-ə-ˌwer-ē\ *adj* : of, relating to, disposing of, or constituting a residue
res·i·due \'rez-ə-ˌd(y)ü\ *n* : whatever remains after a part is taken, set apart, or lost : REMNANT, REMAINDER
re·sid·u·um \ri-'zij-ə-wəm\ *n*, *pl* **-ua** \-wə\ : something residual : RESIDUE, REMAINDER
re·sign \ri-'zīn\ *vb* **1** : to give up by a formal or official act **2** : to give up an office or position **3** : to commit or give over or up : submit or yield deliberately — **re·sign·er** *n*
res·ig·na·tion \ˌrez-ig-'nā-shən\ *n* **1 a** : an act of resigning **b** : a letter or written statement that gives notice of this act **2** : the quality or state of being resigned
re·signed \ri-'zīnd\ *adj* : submitting patiently : SUBMISSIVE, UNCOMPLAINING — **re·sign·ed·ly** \-'zī-nəd-lē\ *adv* — **re·sign·ed·ness** \-'zī-nəd-nəs\ *n*
re·sil·ience \ri-'zil-yən(t)s\ *or* **re·sil·ien·cy** \-yən-sē\ *n* **1** : the ability of a body to rebound, recoil, or resume its original size and shape after being compressed, bent, or stretched : ELASTICITY **2** : the ability to recover from or adjust to misfortune or change
re·sil·ient \-yənt\ *adj* : having resilience: as **a** : capable of withstanding shock without permanent deformation or rupture **b** : SPRINGY **c** : tending to recover readily from fatigue or depression — **re·sil·ient·ly** *adv*
res·in \'rez-ᵊn\ *n* **1** : a substance obtained from the gum or sap of some trees and used chiefly in varnishes, plastics, and medicine **2** : a synthetic product comparable to resin — **res·in·ous** \-əs\ *adj*
re·sist \ri-'zist\ *vb* **1** : to withstand the force or effect of **2** : to exert oneself to check or defeat **3** : to exert force in opposition — **re·sist·er** *n*
re·sist·ance \ri-'zis-tən(t)s\ *n* **1** : an act or instance of resisting **2** : the ability to resist **3** : an opposing force **4** : the opposition offered by a body or substance to the passage through it of a steady electric current
re·sist·ant \-tənt\ *adj* : giving or capable of resistance
re·sist·i·ble \ri-'zis-tə-bəl\ *adj* : capable of being resisted
re·sist·less \ri-'zist-ləs\ *adj* **1** : IRRESISTIBLE **2** : offering no resistance — **re·sist·less·ly** *adv* — **re·sist·less·ness** *n*
re·sis·tor \ri-'zis-tər\ *n* : a device offering electrical resistance
re·sol·u·ble \ri-'zäl-yə-bəl\ *adj* : SOLUBLE
res·o·lute \'rez-ə-ˌlüt\ *adj* **1** : marked by firm determination : RESOLVED **2** : BOLD, STEADY — **res·o·lute·ly** *adv* — **res·o·lute·ness** *n*
res·o·lu·tion \ˌrez-ə-'lü-shən\ *n* **1** : the act or process of resolving **2** : the act of answering : SOLVING **3 a** : something that is resolved **b** : firmness of resolve **4** : a formal expression of the opinion, will, or intent of an official body or assembled group
[1]**re·solve** \ri-'zälv\ *vb* **1 a** : to break up or separate into component parts **b** : to reduce by analysis **2 a** : to clear up : DISPEL **b** : to find an answer or solution to **3** : to reach a decision about : DETERMINE, DECIDE **4** : to declare or decide by a formal resolution and vote — **re·solv·a·ble** *adj* — **re·solv·er** *n*
[2]**resolve** *n* **1** : something resolved : DETERMINATION, RESOLUTION **2** : fixity of purpose
re·solved \ri-'zälvd\ *adj* : DETERMINED, RESOLUTE — **re·solv·ed·ly** \-'zäl-vəd-lē\ *adv*
res·o·nance \'rez-ᵊn-ən(t)s\ *n* **1** : the quality or state of being resonant **2** : the intensification and enriching of a musical tone by supplementary vibration
res·o·nant \-ᵊn-ənt\ *adj* **1** : continuing to sound : ECHOING **2** : of, relating to, or showing resonance **3** : intensified and enriched by resonance — **res·o·nant·ly** *adv*
res·o·na·tor \-ᵊn-ˌāt-ər\ *n* : something that resounds or exhibits resonance
[1]**re·sort** \ri-'zȯrt\ *n* **1 a** : one that is looked to for help : REFUGE, RESOURCE **b** : RECOURSE **2 a** : frequent, habitual, or general visiting **b** (1) : a frequently visited place (2) : a place providing recreation and entertainment esp. to vacationers
[2]**resort** *vi* **1** : to go esp. frequently or habitually : REPAIR **2** : to have recourse
re·sound \ri-'zau̇nd\ *vb* **1** : to become filled with sound : REVERBERATE **2 a** : to sound loudly **b** : to sound or utter in full resonant tones **3** : to become renowned **4** : to extol loudly or widely : CELEBRATE
re·sound·ing \-'zau̇n-diŋ\ *adj* **1** : RESONATING, RESONANT **2 a** : impressively sonorous **b** : EMPHATIC, UNEQUIVOCAL — **re·sound·ing·ly** *adv*
re·source \'rē-ˌsōrs, -ˌzōrs, ri-'\ *n* **1** : a new or a reserve source of supply or support **2** *pl* : a usable stock or supply **3** : the possibility of relief or recovery **4** : the ability to meet and handle situations : RESOURCEFULNESS
re·source·ful \-fəl\ *adj* : able to meet situations — **re·source·ful·ly** \-fə-lē\ *adv* — **re·source·ful·ness** *n*
[1]**re·spect** \ri-'spekt\ *n* **1** : a relation to or concern with something usu. specified : REFERENCE **2 a** : deferential regard : ESTEEM **b** : the quality or state of being esteemed : HONOR **c** *pl* : expressions of respect or deference **3** : PARTICULAR, DETAIL
[2]**respect** *vt* **1 a** : to consider worthy of high regard : ESTEEM **b** : to refrain from interfering with **2** : to have reference to : CONCERN — **re·spect·er** *n*
re·spect·a·bil·i·ty \ri-ˌspek-tə-'bil-ət-ē\ *n* : the quality or state of being respectable
re·spect·a·ble \ri-'spek-tə-bəl\ *adj* **1** : worthy of respect : ESTIMABLE **2** : decent or correct in character or behavior : PROPER **3 a** : fair in size or quantity **b** : moderately good : TOLERABLE **4** : fit to be seen : PRESENTABLE — **re·spect·a·ble·ness** *n* — **re·spect·a·bly** \-blē\ *adv*

re·spect·ful \ri-ˈspekt-fəl\ *adj* : marked by or showing respect or deference — **re·spect·ful·ly** \-fə-lē\ *adv* — **re·spect·ful·ness** *n*

re·spect·ing \-ˈspek-tiŋ\ *prep* : CONCERNING

re·spect·ive \ri-ˈspek-tiv\ *adj* **1** : PARTIAL **2** : PARTICULAR, SEVERAL — **re·spect·ive·ness** *n*

re·spect·ive·ly \-lē\ *adv* : as relating to each : each in the order given

res·pi·ra·tion \ˌres-pə-ˈrā-shən\ *n* **1** : an act or the process of breathing **2** : an energy-yielding oxidation in living matter — **res·pi·ra·tion·al** \-shnəl, -shən-ᵊl\ *adj*

res·pi·ra·tor \ˈres-pə-ˌrāt-ər\ *n* **1** : a device covering the mouth or nose esp. to prevent the inhalation of harmful vapors **2** : a device used in the rhythmic forcing of air into and out of the lungs of one whose breathing has stopped

res·pi·ra·to·ry \ˈres-p(ə-)rə-ˌtōr-ē, ri-ˈspī-rə-\ *adj* : of or relating to respiration or the organs of respiration

re·spire \ri-ˈspī(ə)r\ *vb* : BREATHE

res·pite \ˈres-pət\ *n* **1** : a temporary delay : POSTPONEMENT; *esp* : REPRIEVE 1b **2** : an interval of rest or relief

re·splen·dence \ri-ˈsplen-dən(t)s\ *n* : the quality or state of being resplendent — **re·splen·den·cy** \-dən-sē\ *n*

re·splen·dent \-dənt\ *adj* : shining brilliantly : LUSTROUS — **re·splen·dent·ly** *adv*

re·spond \ri-ˈspänd\ *vi* **1** : to say something in return : make an answer **2** : to react esp. favorably in response **3** : to be answerable

re·spon·dent \ri-ˈspän-dənt\ *n* : one who responds; *esp* : one who answers in various legal proceedings — **respondent** *adj*

re·sponse \ri-ˈspän(t)s\ *n* **1** : the act of replying : ANSWER **2** : something constituting a reply or reaction

re·spon·si·bil·i·ty \ri-ˌspän(t)-sə-ˈbil-ət-ē\ *n, pl* **-ties** **1** : the quality or state of being responsible : ACCOUNTABILITY **2** : something for which one is responsible

re·spon·si·ble \ri-ˈspän(t)-sə-bəl\ *adj* **1** : liable to be called upon to give satisfaction (as for losses or misdeeds) : ANSWERABLE **2** : able to fulfill one's obligations : TRUSTWORTHY, RELIABLE **3** : requiring a person to take charge of or be trusted with important matters **4** : able to choose for oneself between right and wrong — **re·spon·si·ble·ness** *n* — **re·spon·si·bly** \-blē\ *adv*

re·spon·sive \ri-ˈspän(t)-siv\ *adj* **1** : giving response : ANSWERING **2** : quick to respond or react sympathetically : SENSITIVE **3** : using responses — **re·spon·sive·ly** *adv* — **re·spon·sive·ness** *n*

¹rest \ˈrest\ *n* **1** : REPOSE, SLEEP **2 a** : freedom from activity **b** : a state of motionlessness or inactivity **3** : a place for resting or lodging **4 a (1)** : a silence in music equivalent in duration to a note of the same name **(2)** : a character representing such a silence **b** : a brief pause in reading **5** : something used for support

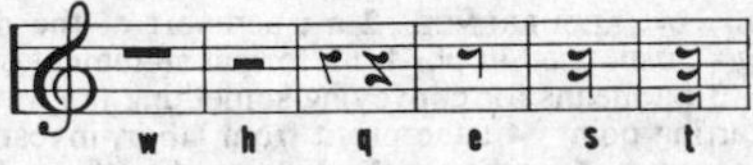

rests 4a (2) : *w* whole, *h* half, *q* quarters, *e* eighth, *s* sixteenth, *t* thirty-second

²rest *vb* **1 a** : to get rest by lying down : SLEEP; *also* : to give rest to **b** : to lie dead **2** : to refrain from work or activity **3** : to place or be placed for or as if for support **4 a** : to remain for action or accomplishment **b** : DEPEND **c** : to fix or be fixed in trust or confidence

³rest *n* : something that is left over or behind : REMAINDER — used with *the*

res·tau·rant \ˈres-t(ə-)rənt, -tə-ˌränt\ *n* : a public eating place

res·tau·ra·teur \ˌres-tə-rə-ˈtər\ *n* : a restaurant keeper

rest·ful \ˈrest-fəl\ *adj* **1** : giving rest **2** : giving a feeling of rest : QUIET — **rest·ful·ly** \-fə-lē\ *adv* — **rest·ful·ness** *n*

res·ti·tu·tion \ˌres-tə-ˈt(y)ü-shən\ *n* : the restoring of something to its rightful owner or the giving of an equivalent (as for loss or damage)

res·tive \ˈres-tiv\ *adj* **1** : BALKY **2** : fidgeting about : UNEASY — **res·tive·ly** *adv* — **res·tive·ness** *n*

rest·less \ˈrest-ləs\ *adj* **1** : being without rest : giving no rest **2** : finding no rest or sleep : UNEASY **3** : never resting or settled : always moving — **rest·less·ly** *adv* — **rest·less·ness** *n*

res·to·ra·tion \ˌres-tə-ˈrā-shən\ *n* **1** : an act of restoring : the condition of being restored **2** : something that is restored; *esp* : a representation or reconstruction of the original form (as of a fossil or a building)

¹re·stor·a·tive \ri-ˈstōr-ət-iv\ *adj* : of or relating to restoration; *esp* : having power to restore — **re·stor·a·tive·ly** *adv* — **re·stor·a·tive·ness** *n*

²restorative *n* : something that serves to restore to consciousness or health

re·store \ri-ˈstō(ə)r\ *vt* **1** : to give back : RETURN **2** : to put or bring back into existence or use **3** : to bring back to or put back into a former or original state : RENEW; *esp* : RECONSTRUCT **4** : to put again in possession of something — **re·stor·er** *n*

re·strain \ri-ˈstrān\ *vt* **1 a (1)** : to prevent from doing something **(2)** : CURB, REPRESS **b** : to limit, restrict, or keep under control **2** : to deprive of liberty; *esp* : to place under arrest or restraint — **re·strain·a·ble** *adj* — **re·strain·er** *n*

re·strained \ri-ˈstrānd\ *adj* : marked by restraint : DISCIPLINED — **re·strain·ed·ly** \-ˈstrā-nəd-lē\ *adv*

re·straint \ri-ˈstrānt\ *n* **1** : the act of restraining : the state of being restrained **2** : a means of restraining : a restraining force or influence **3** : control over one's thoughts or feelings : RESERVE, CONSTRAINT

re·strict \ri-ˈstrikt\ *vt* **1** : to confine within bounds : RESTRAIN **2** : to place under restrictions as to use — **re·strict·ed** *adj* — **re·strict·ed·ly** *adv*

re·stric·tion \ri-ˈstrik-shən\ *n* **1** : something (as a law or rule) that restricts **2** : an act of restricting : the condition of being restricted

re·stric·tive \ri-ˈstrik-tiv\ *adj* **1** : serving or tending to restrict **2** : limiting the reference of a modified word or phrase — **restrictive** *n* — **re·stric·tive·ly** *adv* — **re·stric·tive·ness** *n*

¹re·sult \ri-ˈzəlt\ *vi* **1** : to come about as an effect **2** : to end as an effect : FINISH

²result *n* : something that results as a consequence, issue, or conclusion; *also* : beneficial or tangible effect — **re·sult·ful** \-fəl\ *adj* — **re·sult·less** \-ləs\ *adj*

¹re·sult·ant \ri-ˈzəlt-ᵊnt\ *adj* : derived from or resulting from something else — **re·sult·ant·ly** *adv*

²resultant *n* : something that results : OUTCOME

¹re·sume \ri-ˈzüm\ *vb* **1** : to take again : occupy again **2** : to begin again or go back to (as after an interruption)

²ré·su·mé *or* **re·su·me** \ˈrez-ə-ˌmā\ *n* : a summing up : SUMMARY

re·sump·tion \ri-ˈzəm(p)-shən\ *n* : the action of resuming

re·sur·gence \ri-ˈsər-jən(t)s\ *n* : a rising again into life, activity, or prominence — **re·sur·gent** \-jənt\ *adj*

res·ur·rect \ˌrez-ə-ˈrekt\ *vt* **1** : to raise from the dead : bring back to life **2** : to bring to view or into use again

res·ur·rec·tion \ˌrez-ə-ˈrek-shən\ *n* **1 a** *cap* : the rising of Christ from the dead **b** *often cap* : the rising again to life of all the human dead before the final judgment **2** : RESURGENCE, REVIVAL — **res·ur·rec·tion·al** \-shnəl, -shən-ᵊl\ *adj*

re·sus·ci·tate \ri-ˈsəs-ə-ˌtāt\ *vb* : to revive from apparent death or from unconsciousness; *also* : REVITALIZE — **re·sus·ci·ta·tion** \-ˌsəs-ə-ˈtā-shən\ *n* — **re·sus·ci·ta·tive** \-ˈsəs-ə-ˌtāt-iv\ *adj* — **re·sus·ci·ta·tor** \-ˌtāt-ər\ *n*

[1]**re·tail** \'rē-ˌtāl, ri-'\ *vb* **1 a :** to sell in small quantities **b :** to sell directly to the ultimate consumer **2 :** TELL, RETELL — **re·tail·er** *n*

[2]**re·tail** \'rē-ˌtāl\ *n* **:** the sale of commodities or goods in small quantities directly to consumers — **retail** *adj or adv*

re·tain \ri-'tān\ *vt* **1 a :** to keep in possession or use **b :** to keep in pay or in one's service; *esp* **:** to employ by paying a retainer **2 :** to hold secure or intact

[1]**re·tain·er** \ri-'tā-nər\ *n* **:** a fee paid (as to a lawyer) to secure services

[2]**retainer** *n* **1 :** one that retains **2 :** a servant or follower in a wealthy household

[1]**re·take** \(')rē-'tāk\ *vt* **-took** \-'tu̇k\; **-tak·en** \-'tā-kən\; **-tak·ing :** to take again; *esp* **:** to photograph again

[2]**re·take** \'rē-ˌtāk\ *n* **:** a second photographing or photograph

re·tal·i·ate \ri-'tal-ē-ˌāt\ *vi* **:** to return like for like; *esp* **:** to get revenge — **re·tal·i·a·tion** \-ˌtal-ē-'ā-shən\ *n* — **re·tal·i·a·tive** \-'tal-ē-ˌāt-iv\ *adj* — **re·tal·ia·to·ry** \-'tal-yə-ˌtōr-ē\ *adj*

re·tard \ri-'tärd\ *vt* **:** to slow up **:** keep back **:** HINDER, DELAY — **re·tard·er** *n*

re·tard·ant \ri-'tärd-ᵊnt\ *adj* **:** serving or tending to retard — **retardant** *n*

re·tar·da·tion \ˌrē-ˌtär-'dā-shən\ *n* **1 :** an act or instance of retarding **2 :** the extent to which something is retarded **3 :** an abnormal slowness esp. of mental or bodily development

re·tard·ed \ri-'tärd-əd\ *adj* **:** showing developmental retardation

retch \'rech, *Brit* 'rēch\ *vb* **:** VOMIT; *also* **:** to try to vomit

re·ten·tion \ri-'ten-chən\ *n* **1 :** the act of retaining **:** the state of being retained **2 :** power of retaining **:** RETENTIVENESS **3 :** something retained

re·ten·tive \ri-'tent-iv\ *adj* **:** having ability to retain; *esp* **:** having a good memory — **re·ten·tive·ly** *adv* — **re·ten·tive·ness** *n*

ret·i·cence \'ret-ə-sən(t)s\ *n* **:** the quality or state of being secretive or reticent

ret·i·cent \-sənt\ *adj* **1 :** inclined to be silent or secretive **:** UNCOMMUNICATIVE **2 :** restrained in expression or presentation — **ret·i·cent·ly** *adv*

ret·i·na \'ret-ᵊn-ə\ *n, pl* **retinas** *or* **ret·i·nae** \-ᵊn-ˌē\ **:** the sensory membrane that lines the eye and receives the image formed by the lens — **ret·i·nal** \-ᵊn-əl\ *adj*

ret·i·nue \'ret-ᵊn-ˌ(y)ü\ *n* **:** the body of retainers who follow a distinguished person **:** SUITE

re·tire \ri-'tī(ə)r\ *vb* **1 :** to withdraw or cause to withdraw from action or danger **:** RETREAT **2 :** to withdraw esp. for privacy **3 :** to withdraw or cause to withdraw from one's position or occupation **4 :** to go to bed **5 :** to withdraw from circulation **:** RECALL **6 :** to cause to be out in baseball

re·tired \ri-'tī(ə)rd\ *adj* **1 :** QUIET, HIDDEN, SECRET **2 :** withdrawn from active duties or business **3 :** received by or due to a person who has retired

re·tire·ment \ri-'tī(ə)r-mənt\ *n* **:** an act of retiring **:** the state of being retired

re·tir·ing \ri-'tī(ə)r-iŋ\ *adj* **:** RESERVED, SHY — **re·tir·ing·ly** *adv* — **re·tir·ing·ness** *n*

[1]**re·tort** \ri-'tȯrt\ *vb* **1 :** to answer back **:** reply angrily or sharply **2 :** to reply (as to an argument) with a counter argument

[2]**retort** *n* **:** a quick, witty, or cutting reply

[3]**re·tort** \ri-'tȯrt, 'rē-ˌ\ *n* **:** a vessel in which substances are distilled or decomposed by heat

re·touch \(')rē-'təch\ *vt* **:** to touch up; *esp* **:** to alter (as a photographic negative) in order to produce a more desirable appearance — **re·touch** \'rē-ˌtəch, (')rē-'\ *n* — **re·touch·er** \(')rē-'təch-ər\ *n*

re·trace \(')rē-'trās\ *vt* **:** to trace again or back

re·tract \ri-'trakt\ *vt.* **1 :** to draw or pull back or in **2 :** to take back (as an offer, a statement, or an accusation) **:** WITHDRAW, DISAVOW — **re·tract·a·ble** *adj*

re·trac·tile \ri-'trak-tᵊl, -ˌtīl\ *adj* **:** capable of being drawn back or in — **re·trac·til·i·ty** \ˌrē-ˌtrak-'til-ət-ē\ *n*

re·trac·tion \ri-'trak-shən\ *n* **1 :** RECANTATION; *esp* **:** a statement made by one retracting **2 :** an act of retracting **:** the state of being retracted **3 :** the ability to retract

re·tread \(')rē-'tred\ *vt* **re·tread·ed; re·tread·ing :** to put a new tread upon the bare cord fabric of (a worn pneumatic tire)

[1]**re·treat** \ri-'trēt\ *n* **1 a :** an act or process of withdrawing esp. from what is difficult, dangerous, or disagreeable **b :** a signal for retreating **c :** a military flag-lowering ceremony **2 :** a place of privacy or safety **:** REFUGE **3 :** a period of group withdrawal for prayer, meditation, and instruction under a director

[2]**retreat** *vi* **1 :** to make a retreat **:** WITHDRAW **2 :** to slope backward

re·trench \ri-'trench\ *vb* **1 :** to cut down (as expenses) **:** REDUCE **2 :** to reduce expenses **:** ECONOMIZE — **re·trench·ment** *n*

ret·ri·bu·tion \ˌre-trə-'byü-shən\ *n* **:** something given in payment for an offense **:** PUNISHMENT

re·trib·u·tive \ri-'trib-yət-iv\ *adj* **:** of, relating to, or marked by retribution — **re·trib·u·tive·ly** *adv*

re·trib·u·to·ry \-yə-ˌtōr-ē\ *adj* **:** RETRIBUTIVE

re·triev·al \ri-'trē-vəl\ *n* **1 :** an act or process of retrieving **2 :** possibility of being retrieved or of recovering

[1]**re·trieve** \ri-'trēv\ *vb* **1 :** to find and bring in killed or wounded game **2 :** RECOVER, RESTORE — **re·triev·a·ble** *adj*

[2]**retrieve** *n* **1 :** RETRIEVAL **2 :** the successful return of a ball that is difficult to reach or control (as in tennis)

re·triev·er \ri-'trē-vər\ *n* **:** one that retrieves; *esp* **:** a medium-sized dog used esp. for retrieving game

ret·ro·ac·tive \ˌre-trō-'ak-tiv\ *adj* **:** intended to apply or take effect at a date in the past — **ret·ro·ac·tive·ly** *adv*

[1]**ret·ro·grade** \'re-trə-ˌgrād\ *adj* **:** going or inclined to go backward or from a better to a worse state

[2]**retrograde** *vi* **1 :** to go back **:** RETREAT **2 :** to decline to a worse condition

ret·ro·gress \ˌre-trə-'gres\ *vi* **:** to move backward; *esp* **:** to revert to an earlier, lower, or less specialized state or condition — **ret·ro·gres·sion** \-'gresh-ən\ *n*

ret·ro·spect \'re-trə-ˌspekt\ *n* **:** a looking back on things past **:** a thinking of past events

ret·ro·spec·tion \ˌre-trə-'spek-shən\ *n* **1 :** the act or power of recalling the past **2 :** a review of past events

ret·ro·spec·tive \-'spek-tiv\ *adj* **1 :** of, relating to, characteristic of, or given to retrospection **2 :** affecting things past **:** RETROACTIVE — **ret·ro·spec·tive·ly** *adv*

[1]**re·turn** \ri-'tərn\ *vb* **1 :** to come or go back **2 :** REPLY, ANSWER **3 :** to make (as a report) officially by submitting a statement **4 :** to elect to office **5 :** to bring, carry, send, or put back **:** RESTORE **6 :** to bring in (as profit) **:** YIELD **7 :** REPAY **8 :** to send or say in response or reply — **re·turn·er** *n*

[2]**return** *n* **1 a :** the act of coming back to or from a place or condition **b :** RECURRENCE **2 a :** a report of the results of balloting — usu. used in pl. **b :** a formal statement of taxable income **3 :** a means for conveying something (as water) back to its starting point **4 :** the profit from labor, investment, or business **:** YIELD **5 a :** the act of returning something **b :** something returned **6 a :** something given in repayment or reciprocation **b :** ANSWER, RETORT

[3]**return** *adj* **:** played, delivered, or given in return

re·turn·a·ble \ri-'tər-nə-bəl\ *adj* **1 :** that may be returned **2 :** that must be returned

re·turn·ee \ri-ˌtər-'nē\ *n* **:** one who returns

re·union \(')rē-'yü-nyən\ *n* **1 :** the act of reuniting **:** the state of being reunited **2 :** a reuniting of persons after separation

rev \'rev\ *vb* **revved; rev·ving :** to operate or cause to operate at an increasing speed of revolution

re·vamp \(ˈ)rē-ˈvamp\ *vt* **1** : RENOVATE, RECONSTRUCT **2** : to work over : REVISE
re·veal \ri-ˈvēl\ *vt* **1** : to make known : DIVULGE **2** : to show plainly : DISPLAY — **re·veal·a·ble** *adj* — **re·veal·er** *n*
rev·eil·le \ˈrev-ə-lē\ *n* : a signal sounded at about sunrise on a bugle or drum to call soldiers or sailors to duty
¹rev·el \ˈrev-əl\ *vi* **-eled** *or* **-elled**; **-el·ing** *or* **-el·ling** \ˈrev-(ə-)liŋ\ **1** : to take part in a revel : ROISTER **2** : to take intense satisfaction — **rev·el·er** *or* **rev·el·ler** \-(ə-)lər\ *n*
²revel *n* : a noisy or merry celebration
rev·e·la·tion \ˌrev-ə-ˈlā-shən\ *n* **1** : an act of revealing **2** : something that is revealed; *esp* : an enlightening or astonishing disclosure
rev·el·ry \ˈrev-əl-rē\ *n, pl* **-ries** : boisterous merrymaking
¹re·venge \ri-ˈvenj\ *vt* **1** : to inflict injury in return for **2** : to avenge for a wrong done — **re·veng·er** *n*
²revenge *n* **1** : an act or instance of revenging **2** : a desire to repay injury for injury **3** : an opportunity for getting satisfaction
re·venge·ful \-fəl\ *adj* : full of or prone to revenge — **re·venge·ful·ly** \-fə-lē\ *adv* — **re·venge·ful·ness** *n*
rev·e·nue \ˈrev-ə-ˌn(y)ü\ *n* **1** : the income from an investment **2** : the income that a government collects for public use **3** : the income produced by a given source
re·ver·ber·ant \ri-ˈvər-b(ə-)rənt\ *adj* : REVERBERATING — **re·ver·ber·ant·ly** *adv*
re·ver·ber·ate \ri-ˈvər-bə-ˌrāt\ *vi* : RESOUND, ECHO — **re·ver·ber·a·tion** \-ˌvər-bə-ˈrā-shən\ *n*
re·vere \ri-ˈvi(ə)r\ *vt* : to show devotion and honor to : regard with reverence
¹rev·er·ence \ˈrev-(ə-)rən(t)s\ *n* **1 a** : honor or respect felt or shown : DEFERENCE **b** : a feeling of worshipful respect : VENERATION **2** : a gesture of respect (as a bow)
²reverence *vt* : to regard or treat with reverence
rev·er·end \ˈrev-(ə-)rənd\ *adj* **1** : worthy of reverence : REVERED **2** — used as a title for members of the clergy
rev·er·ent \ˈrev-(ə-)rənt\ *adj* : very respectful : showing reverence — **rev·er·ent·ly** *adv*
rev·er·en·tial \ˌrev-ə-ˈren-chəl\ *adj* : REVERENT — **rev·er·en·tial·ly** \-ˈrench-(ə-)lē\ *adv*
rev·er·ie *or* **rev·ery** \ˈrev-(ə-)rē\ *n, pl* **-er·ies** **1** : DAYDREAM **2** : the condition of being lost in thought
re·vers \ri-ˈvi(ə)r, -ˈve(ə)r\ *n, pl* **re·vers** \-ˈvi(ə)rz, -ˈve(ə)rz\ : a lapel esp. on a woman's garment
re·vers·al \ri-ˈvər-səl\ *n* : an act or the process of reversing
¹re·verse \ri-ˈvərs\ *adj* **1** : opposite or contrary to a previous or normal condition **2** : acting or operating in a manner contrary to the usual **3** : effecting reverse movement — **re·verse·ly** *adv*
²reverse *vb* **1** : to turn completely about or upside down or inside out **2 a** : to overthrow or set aside (a legal decision) by a contrary decision **b** : to change to the contrary **3 a** : to go or cause to go in the opposite direction **b** : to put (as a car) into reverse — **re·vers·er** *n*
³reverse *n* **1** : something directly contrary to something else : OPPOSITE **2** : an act or instance of reversing; *esp* : a change for the worse **3** : the back part of something **4 a** : a gear that reverses something; *also* : the whole mechanism brought into play when such a gear is used **b** : movement in reverse
re·vers·i·bil·i·ty \ri-ˌvər-sə-ˈbil-ət-ē\ *n* : the quality or state of being reversible
re·vers·i·ble \ri-ˈvər-sə-bəl\ *adj* : capable of being reversed or of reversing — **re·vers·i·bly** \-blē\ *adv*
re·ver·sion \ri-ˈvər-zhən\ *n* **1** : a right of future possession (as of property or a title) **2** : an act or the process of returning (as to a former condition); *also* : a product of reversion
re·vert \ri-ˈvərt\ *vi* **1** : to come or go back **2** : to undergo reversion — **re·vert·er** *n* — **re·vert·i·ble** \-ˈvərt-ə-bəl\ *adj*
¹re·view \ri-ˈvyü\ *n* **1 a** : a formal military inspection **b** : a military ceremony honoring a person or an event **2** : a general survey **3** : an act of inspecting or examining **4** : judicial reexamination of the proceedings of a lower court **5 a** : a critical evaluation (as of a book or play) **b** : a magazine devoted chiefly to reviews and essays **6** : renewed study of material previously studied **7** : REVUE
²review *vb* **1** : to look at a thing again : study or examine again; *esp* : to reexamine judicially **2** : to make a formal inspection of (as troops) **3** : to give a criticism of (as a book or play) **4** : to look back on — **re·view·er** *n*
re·vile \ri-ˈvīl\ *vb* : to abuse verbally : rail at — **re·vile·ment** *n* — **re·vil·er** *n*
re·vis·a·ble \ri-ˈvī-zə-bəl\ *adj* : capable of being revised
¹re·vise \ri-ˈvīz\ *vt* **1** : to look over again in order to correct or improve **2** : to make a new, amended, improved, or up-to-date version or arrangement of — **re·vis·er** *or* **re·vi·sor** \-ˈvī-zər\ *n*
²re·vise \ˈrē-ˌvīz, ri-ˈ\ *n* : an act of revising : REVISION
re·vi·sion \ri-ˈvizh-ən\ *n* **1** : an act of revising **2** : a revised version — **re·vi·sion·ary** \-ˈvizh-ə-ˌner-ē\ *adj*
re·vi·so·ry \ri-ˈvīz-(ə-)rē\ *adj* : having the power or purpose to revise
re·vi·tal·i·za·tion \(ˌ)rē-ˌvīt-ᵊl-ə-ˈzā-shən\ *n* **1** : an act or instance of revitalizing **2** : something revitalized
re·vi·tal·ize \(ˈ)rē-ˈvīt-ᵊl-ˌīz\ *vt* : to give new life or vigor to
re·viv·al \ri-ˈvī-vəl\ *n* **1** : a reviving of interest (as in art, literature, or religion) **2** : a new publication or presentation (as of a book or play) **3** : a renewed flourishing **4** : an evangelistic meeting or series of meetings
re·vive \ri-ˈvīv\ *vb* **1** : to bring back or come back to life, consciousness, or activity : make or become fresh or strong again **2** : to bring back into use — **re·viv·er** *n*
re·viv·i·fy \rē-ˈviv-ə-ˌfī\ *vt* **-fied**; **-fy·ing** : to give new life to : REVIVE — **re·viv·i·fi·ca·tion** \-ˌviv-ə-fə-ˈkā-shən\ *n*
rev·o·ca·ble \ˈrev-ə-kə-bəl\ *adj* : capable of being revoked
rev·o·ca·tion \ˌrev-ə-ˈkā-shən\ *n* : an act or instance of revoking
re·voke \ri-ˈvōk\ *vb* **1** : to put an end to (as a law, order, or privilege) by withdrawing, repealing, or canceling : ANNUL **2** : to renege in cards
¹re·volt \ri-ˈvōlt\ *vb* **1** : to renounce allegiance or subjection (as to a government) : REBEL **2** : to experience or cause to experience disgust or shock — **re·volt·er** *n*
²revolt *n* : REBELLION, INSURRECTION
re·volt·ing \-ˈvōl-tiŋ\ *adj* : extremely offensive : NAUSEATING — **re·volt·ing·ly** *adv*
rev·o·lu·tion \ˌrev-ə-ˈlü-shən\ *n* **1** : the action by a celestial body of going round in an orbit **2** : CYCLE **3** : ROTATION **4** : a sudden, radical, or complete change; *esp* : the overthrow of one government and the substitution of another by the governed
¹rev·o·lu·tion·ary \-shə-ˌner-ē\ *adj* **1** : of, relating to, or constituting a revolution **2** : tending to or promoting revolution **3** : RADICAL, EXTREMIST
²revolutionary *n, pl* **-ar·ies** : REVOLUTIONIST
rev·o·lu·tion·ist \ˌrev-ə-ˈlü-sh(ə-)nəst\ *n* **1** : one engaged in a revolution **2** : an adherent or advocate of revolutionary doctrines — **revolutionist** *adj*
rev·o·lu·tion·ize \-shə-ˌnīz\ *vt* : to change fundamentally or completely (as by a revolution) — **rev·o·lu·tion·iz·er** *n*
re·volve \ri-ˈvälv\ *vb* **1** : to turn over at length in the mind **2 a** : to go round or cause to go round in an orbit **b** : to turn round on or as if on an axis : ROTATE — **re·volv·a·ble** *adj*
re·volv·er \ri-ˈväl-vər\ *n* : a handgun with a cylinder of several chambers
re·vue \ri-ˈvyü\ *n* : a theatrical production consisting typically of brief often satirical sketches and songs
re·vul·sion \ri-ˈvəl-shən\ *n* **1** : a sudden or strong reaction or

change 2 : a sense of utter repugnance : REPULSION — **re·vul·sive** \-'vəl-siv\ *adj*

[1]**re·ward** \ri-'wȯrd\ *vt* 1 : to give a reward to or for 2 : RECOMPENSE — **re·ward·a·ble** *adj* — **re·ward·er** *n*

[2]**reward** *n* : something given or offered in return for a service; *esp* : money offered for the return of something lost or stolen or for the capture of a criminal

re·word \(')rē-'wərd\ *vt* : to state in different words

re·write \(')rē-'rīt\ *vt* **-wrote** \-'rōt\; **-writ·ten** \-'rit-ᵊn\; **-writ·ing** 1 : to write over again esp. in a different form 2 : REVISE — **re·write** \'rē-ˌrīt\ *n* — **re·writ·er** *n*

rhap·so·dize \'rap-sə-ˌdīz\ *vi* : to speak or write rhapsodically — **rhap·so·dist** \-səd-əst\ *n*

rhap·so·dy \'rap-səd-ē\ *n, pl* **-dies** 1 : a written or spoken expression of extravagant praise or ecstasy 2 : a musical composition of irregular form — **rhap·sod·ic** \rap-'säd-ik\ *or* **rhap·sod·i·cal** \-i-kəl\ *adj* — **rhap·sod·i·cal·ly** \-i-k(ə-)lē\ *adv*

rhe·ni·um \'rē-nē-əm\ *n* : a rare heavy hard silvery white metallic chemical element

rhe·o·stat \'rē-ə-ˌstat\ *n* : a resistor for regulating the flow of electric current

rhe·sus \'rē-səs\ *n* : a pale brown Indian monkey

rhet·o·ric \'ret-ə-rik\ *n* 1 : the art of speaking or writing effectively; *also* : the study or application of the principles and rules of composition 2 a : skill in the effective use of speech b : insincere or grandiloquent language

rhe·tor·i·cal \ri-'tȯr-i-kəl\ *adj* 1 a : of, relating to, or dealing with rhetoric b : used solely for rhetorical effect 2 : using rhetoric; *esp* : GRANDILOQUENT — **rhe·tor·i·cal·ly** \-k(ə-)lē\ *adv* — **rhe·tor·i·cal·ness** *n*

rhet·o·ri·cian \ˌret-ə-'rish-ən\ *n* 1 a : a master or teacher of rhetoric b : ORATOR 2 : an eloquent or grandiloquent writer or speaker

rheum \'rüm\ *n* : a watery discharge from the mucous membranes esp. of the eyes or nose — **rheumy** \'rü-mē\ *adj*

rheu·mat·ic \rü-'mat-ik\ *adj* : of, relating to, characteristic of, or affected with rheumatism — **rheu·mat·i·cal·ly** \-'mat-i-k(ə-)lē\ *adv*

rheu·ma·tism \'rü-mə-ˌtiz-əm\ *n* : a disorder marked by inflammation or pain in muscles or joints

Rh factor \ˌär-'āch-\ *n* : a substance present in the red blood cells capable of inducing dangerous reactions

rhine·stone \'rīn-ˌstōn\ *n* : a brilliant colorless imitation diamond made usu. of glass or paste

rhi·noc·er·os \rī-'näs-(ə-)rəs\ *n, pl* **-er·os·es** *or* **-er·os** : a large thick-skinned three-toed plant-eating mammal of Africa and Asia that is related to the horse and has one or two heavy upright horns on the snout

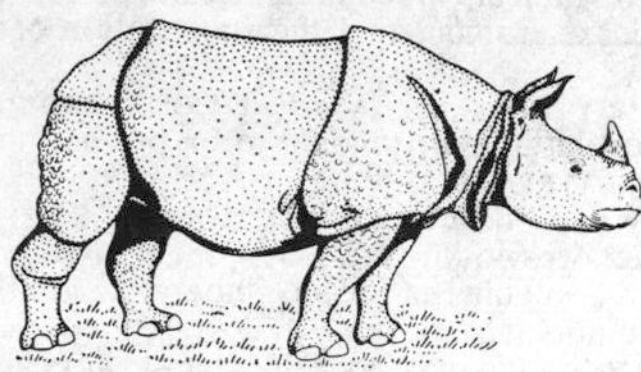

rhinoceros

rhi·zome \'rī-ˌzōm\ *n* : a usu. horizontal underground plant stem that produces shoots above and roots below

rho·di·um \'rōd-ē-əm\ *n* : a white hard ductile metallic chemical element

rho·do·den·dron \ˌrōd-ə-'den-drən\ *n* : any of various shrubs or trees related to the heath family

rhom·boid \'räm-ˌbȯid\ *n* : a parallelogram in which the angles are oblique and adjacent sides are unequal — **rhomboid** *adj* — **rhom·boi·dal** \räm-'bȯid-ᵊl\ *adj*

rhom·bus \'räm-bəs\ *n, pl* **rhom·bus·es** *or* **rhom·bi** \-ˌbī\ : a parallelogram having the sides equal and the angles usu. oblique

rhu·barb \'rü-ˌbärb\ *n* : a plant related to buckwheat that has broad green leaves borne on thick juicy pinkish stems often used for food

[1]**rhyme** \'rīm\ *n* 1 : correspondence in terminal sounds of two or more words or lines of verse 2 a : rhyming verse b : a composition in verse that rhymes

[2]**rhyme** *vb* 1 : to make rhymes : put into rhyme; *also* : to compose rhyming verse 2 : to end in syllables that rhyme — **rhym·er** *n*

rhythm \'rith-əm\ *n* 1 : a flow of rising and falling sounds in language 2 : a movement or activity in which some action or element recurs regularly — **rhyth·mic** \'rith-mik\ *or* **rhyth·mi·cal** \-mi-kəl\ *adj* — **rhyth·mi·cal·ly** \-mi-k(ə-)lē\ *adv*

[1]**rib** \'rib\ *n* 1 : one of the paired curved bony rods that are joined to the spinal column, stiffen the walls of the body of most vertebrates, and protect the viscera 2 : something resembling a rib in shape or function 3 : an elongated ridge

[2]**rib** *vt* **ribbed**; **rib·bing** : to furnish or enclose with ribs

[3]**rib** *vt* **ribbed**; **rib·bing** : to poke fun at : KID

rib·ald \'rib-əld\ *adj* 1 : CRUDE, OFFENSIVE 2 : characterized by or using broad indecent humor — **rib·ald·ry** \-əl-drē\ *n*

rib·bon \'rib-ən\ *n* 1 : a narrow usu. closely woven strip of decorative fabric (as silk) used esp. for trimming or for tying or ornamenting packages 2 : a narrow strip of inked fabric (as in a typewriter) 3 : TATTER, SHRED — usu. used in pl. — **rib·bon·like** *adj*

ri·bo·fla·vin \ˌrī-bə-'flā-vən\ *n* : a growth-promoting member of the vitamin B complex occurring in milk and in liver

rice \'rīs\ *n, pl* **rice** : an annual cereal grass widely grown in warm wet areas for its seed that is used esp. for food; *also* : this seed

rich \'rich\ *adj* 1 : possessing or controlling great wealth : WEALTHY 2 : having high value; *also* : COSTLY, SUMPTUOUS 3 a : abundantly supplied with some usu. desirable quality or thing b : highly productive : FRUITFUL, FERTILE c : containing much seasoning, fat, or sugar — **rich·ly** *adv* — **rich·ness** *n*

rich·es \'rich-əz\ *n pl* : things that make one rich : WEALTH

rick \'rik\ *n* : a stack or pile (as of hay or grain) in the open air

rick·ets \'rik-əts\ *n* : a children's disease marked esp. by soft and deformed bones and caused by inadequate vitamin D

rick·ety \'rik-ət-ē\ *adj* 1 : affected with rickets 2 : feeble in the joints 3 : DILAPIDATED, SHAKY

rick·sha *or* **rick·shaw** \'rik-ˌshȯ\ *n* : JINRIKISHA

[1]**ric·o·chet** \'rik-ə-ˌshā, *Brit also* -ˌshet\ *n* : a glancing rebound (as of a bullet off a flat surface)

[2]**ricochet** *vi* **-cheted** *or* **-chet·ted**; **-chet·ing** *or* **-chet·ting** : to skip with or as if with glancing rebounds

rid \'rid\ *vt* **rid**; **rid·ding** : to make free : RELIEVE — often used in the phrase *be rid of* or *get rid of*

rid·dance \'rid-ᵊn(t)s\ *n* : the act of ridding : the state of being rid of

[1]**rid·dle** \'rid-ᵊl\ *n* : a puzzling question posed as a problem to be solved or guessed : CONUNDRUM

[2]**riddle** *vb* **rid·dled**; **rid·dling** \'rid-liŋ, -ᵊl-iŋ\ 1 : to find the solution of a riddle or mystery 2 : to speak in riddles or set forth a riddle — **rid·dler** \-lər, -ᵊl-ər\ *n*

[3]**riddle** *n* : a coarse sieve (as for ashes)

[4]**riddle** *vt* 1 : to sift or separate with or as if with a riddle 2 : to fill full of holes so as to make like a riddle

[1]**ride** \'rīd\ *vb* **rode** \'rōd\; **rid·den** \'rid-ᵊn\; **rid·ing** \'rīd-iŋ\ 1 a : to go or be carried along on an animal's back or on or in a conveyance (as a boat, automobile, or airplane) b : to sit on and control so as to be carried along 2 a : to be supported and usu. carried along by b : to float at anchor c : to remain

afloat through : SURVIVE 3 a : to convey in or as if in a vehicle : give a ride to b : to function as a means of conveyance 4 a : to torment by constant nagging or teasing : HARASS b : OBSESS, OPPRESS — **ride for a fall** : to court disaster — **ride roughshod over** : to treat with disdain or abuse

²ride *n* 1 : an act of riding; *esp* : a trip on horseback or by vehicle 2 : a way (as a road or path) for riding 3 : a mechanical device (as at an amusement park) for riding on 4 : a means of transportation

rid•er \'rīd-ər\ *n* 1 : one that rides 2 a : an addition to a document often attached on a separate piece of paper b : an additional clause often dealing with an unrelated subject attached to a bill during its passage through a lawmaking body — **rid•er•less** \-ləs\ *adj*

¹ridge \'rij\ *n* 1 : a range of hills or mountains 2 : a raised line or strip 3 : the line made where two sloping surfaces come together

²ridge *vb* : to form into or extend in ridges

ridge•pole \'rij-ˌpōl\ *n* : the highest horizontal timber in a sloping roof to which the upper ends of the rafters are fastened

ridgy \'rij-ē\ *adj* : having or rising in ridges

¹rid•i•cule \'rid-ə-ˌkyül\ *n* : the act of exposing to laughter

²ridicule *vt* : to make fun of : DERIDE — **rid•i•cul•er** *n*

ri•dic•u•lous \rə-'dik-yə-ləs\ *adj* : arousing or deserving ridicule : ABSURD, PREPOSTEROUS — **ri•dic•u•lous•ly** *adv* — **ri•dic•u•lous•ness** *n*

rife \'rīf\ *adj* 1 : WIDESPREAD, PREVALENT 2 : ABOUNDING — **rife•ly** *adv*

riff•raff \'rif-ˌraf\ *n* 1 a : disreputable persons b : RABBLE 2 : REFUSE, RUBBISH — **riffraff** *adj*

¹ri•fle \'rī-fəl\ *vb* **ri•fled**; **ri•fling** \-f(ə-)liŋ\ 1 : to ransack esp. with the intent to steal 2 : to steal and carry away — **ri•fler** \-f(ə-)lər\ *n*

²rifle *vt* **ri•fled**; **ri•fling** \-f(ə-)liŋ\ : to cut spiral grooves into the bore of

³rifle *n* 1 a : a weapon with a rifled bore intended to be fired from the shoulder b : a rifled artillery piece 2 *pl* : a body of soldiers armed with rifles

ri•fle•man \'rī-fəl-mən\ *n* 1 : a soldier armed with a rifle 2 : a person skilled in shooting with a rifle

¹rift \'rift\ *n* 1 : an opening made by splitting or separation : CLEFT, FISSURE, CREVASSE 2 : ESTRANGEMENT, BREACH

²rift *vb* : CLEAVE, DIVIDE, SPLIT

¹rig \'rig\ *vt* **rigged**; **rig•ging** 1 : to fit out (as a ship) with rigging 2 : CLOTHE, DRESS 3 : to furnish with special gear : EQUIP 4 : to set up or fit up often as a makeshift

²rig *n* 1 : the distinctive shape, number, and arrangement of sails and masts of a ship 2 : EQUIPAGE; *esp* : a carriage with its horse 3 : DRESS, CLOTHING 4 : tackle, equipment, or machinery fitted for a specified purpose

³rig *vt* **rigged**; **rig•ging** 1 : to manipulate or control usu. by deceptive or dishonest means 2 : to fix in advance for a desired result

rig•ger \'rig-ər\ *n* 1 : one that rigs 2 : a ship of a specified rig

rig•ging \'rig-iŋ\ *n* 1 a : the lines and chains used aboard a ship esp. in working sail and supporting masts and spars b : a similar network (as in theater scenery) used for support and manipulation 2 : TACKLE, GEAR

¹right \'rīt\ *adj* 1 : RIGHTEOUS, UPRIGHT 2 : being in accordance with what is just, good, or proper 3 a : agreeable to a standard b : conforming to facts or truth : CORRECT 4 : SUITABLE, APPROPRIATE 5 : STRAIGHT 6 : GENUINE, REAL 7 a : of, relating to, situated on, or being the side of the body which is away from the heart and on which the hand is stronger and more skilled in most people b : located in the same relative position as the right of the body when facing in the same direction as the observer : RIGHT-HAND 8 : of, relating to, or constituting the principal or more prominent side of an object — **right•ness** *n*

²right *n* 1 : qualities that together constitute the ideal of moral propriety 2 : something to which one has a just claim 3 : something that one may properly claim as due 4 : the cause of truth or justice 5 : the location or direction of or something situated on or toward the right side 6 a : the true account or correct interpretation b : the quality or state of being factually correct 7 *often cap* : political conservatives; *also* : the beliefs they hold — **by rights** : with reason or justice : PROPERLY — **to rights** : into proper order

³right *adv* 1 : according to right 2 : EXACTLY, PRECISELY 3 : in a suitable, proper, or desired manner 4 : in a direct line or course 5 : according to fact or truth : TRULY 6 a : all the way b : COMPLETELY 7 : IMMEDIATELY 8 : EXTREMELY, VERY 9 : on or to the right

⁴right *vb* 1 a : to relieve from wrong b : JUSTIFY, VINDICATE 2 a : to adjust or restore to the proper state or condition b : to bring or restore to an upright position 3 : to become upright

right angle *n* : the angle bounded by two lines perpendicular to each other

righ•teous \'rī-chəs\ *adj* 1 : acting rightly : UPRIGHT 2 : according to what is right — **righ•teous•ly** *adv* — **righ•teous•ness** *n*

right•ful \'rīt-fəl\ *adj* 1 : JUST, EQUITABLE 2 : having a just or legally enforceable claim : LEGITIMATE 3 : FITTING, PROPER 4 : held by right or just claim : LEGAL — **right•ful•ly** \-fə-lē\ *adv* — **right•ful•ness** *n*

right–hand \ˌrīt-ˌhand\ *adj* 1 : situated on the right 2 : RIGHT-HANDED 3 : chiefly relied on

right–hand•ed \'rīt-'han-dəd\ *adj* 1 : using the right hand more skillfully or freely than the left 2 : done or made with or for the right hand 3 : having or moving with a clockwise turn or twist — **right–hand•ed•ly** *or* **right–hand•ed** *adv* — **right–hand•ed•ness** *n*

right•ly \'rīt-lē\ *adv* 1 : FAIRLY, JUSTLY 2 : PROPERLY, FITLY 3 : CORRECTLY, EXACTLY

right•ward \-wərd\ *adv* : toward or on the right — **rightward** *adj*

rig•id \'rij-əd\ *adj* 1 : lacking flexibility : STIFF, HARD 2 : STRICT — **ri•gid•i•ty** \rə-'jid-ət-ē\ *n* — **rig•id•ly** *adv* — **rig•id•ness** *n*

rig•ma•role \'rig-ə-mə-ˌrōl, 'rig-mə-\ *n* 1 : confused or meaningless talk 2 : a complex and ritualistic procedure

rig•or \'rig-ər\ *n* 1 a : harsh inflexibility : the quality of being unyielding : SEVERITY, STRICTNESS b : an act or instance of strictness or severity 2 : a tremor caused by a chill 3 : a condition that makes life difficult or uncomfortable; *esp* : extremity of cold 4 : strict precision : EXACTNESS

rig•or•ous \'rig-(ə-)rəs\ *adj* 1 : exercising or favoring rigor : very strict 2 : marked by extremes of temperature or climate : HARSH, SEVERE 3 : scrupulously accurate : PRECISE — **rig•or•ous•ly** *adv* — **rig•or•ous•ness** *n*

rile \'rīl\ *vt* 1 : ROIL 1 2 : to make angry

rill \'ril\ *n* : a very small brook

¹rim \'rim\ *n* 1 a : the outer often curved or circular edge or border of something b : BRINK 2 : the outer part of a wheel — **rim•less** \-ləs\ *adj*

²rim *vb* **rimmed**; **rim•ming** 1 : to furnish with a rim : serve as a rim for : BORDER 2 : to run around the rim of

rime \'rīm\ *n* 1 : FROST 2 2 : an accumulation of granular ice tufts on objects that resembles frost in appearance but is formed from fog or cloud

rimy \'rī-mē\ *adj* : covered with rime : FROSTY

rind \'rīnd\ *n* : a usu. hard or tough outer layer

¹ring \'riŋ\ *n* 1 : a circular band for holding, connecting, hanging, or pulling or for packing or sealing 2 : a circlet usu. of precious metal worn on the finger 3 : something circular in shape **4 a :** a space for exhibitions or competitions **b :** PRIZEFIGHTING **5 :** a combination of persons for a selfish and often corrupt purpose (as to control a market) — **ringed** \'riŋd\ *adj* — **ring·like** *adj*

²ring *vb* **1 :** to place or form a ring around : ENCIRCLE **2 :** to provide with a ring **3 :** to throw a ring over (the mark) in a game (as quoits) **4 :** to form or take the shape of a ring

³ring *vb* **rang** \'raŋ\; **rung** \'rəŋ\; **ring·ing** \'riŋ-iŋ\ **1 :** to sound clearly and resonantly when struck **2 :** to cause (as a metallic body) to sound esp. by striking **3 :** to cause something (as a bell) to ring **4 a :** to make (a sound) by ringing **b :** to announce by or as if by ringing **5 :** to sound loudly **6 :** to repeat often or loudly or earnestly **7 a :** to summon esp. by bell **b :** to call on the telephone — **ring a bell :** to arouse a response

⁴ring *n* **1 :** a set of bells **2 :** a clear resonant sound made by or as if by vibrating metal **3 :** resonant tone : SONORITY **4 :** a sound or character expressive of some particular quality **5 a :** the act or an instance of ringing **b :** a telephone call

¹ring·er \'riŋ-ər\ *n* **1 :** one that sounds esp. by ringing **2 a :** one that enters a competition under false representations **b :** one that strongly resembles another

²ringer *n* **:** one that encircles or puts a ring around

ring·lead·er \'riŋ-ˌlēd-ər\ *n* **:** a leader esp. of a group engaged in an improper enterprise

ring·let \'riŋ-lət\ *n* **:** CURL; *esp* **:** a long curl of hair

ring·mas·ter \'riŋ-ˌmas-tər\ *n* **:** one in charge of performances in a ring (as of a circus)

ring·worm \-ˌwərm\ *n* **:** a contagious skin disease caused by fungi

rink \'riŋk\ *n* **1 :** a level extent of ice marked off for skating or various games **2 :** an enclosure for roller-skating

¹rinse \'rin(t)s\ *vt* **1 a :** to cleanse (as from soap used in washing) by clear water **b :** to treat (hair) with a rinse **2 :** to wash lightly or in water only — **rins·er** *n*

²rinse *n* **1 :** the act or process of rinsing **2 a :** liquid used for rinsing **b :** a solution that temporarily tints hair

¹ri·ot \'rī-ət\ *n* **1 a :** public violence, tumult, or disorder **b :** a tumultuous disturbance of the public peace by three or more persons assembled together **2 :** a random or disorderly profusion esp. of color **3 :** something or someone wildly amusing

²riot *vb* **1 :** REVEL **2 :** to create or engage in a riot **3 :** to waste or spend recklessly — **ri·ot·er** *n*

ri·ot·ous \'rī-ət-əs\ *adj* **1 :** ABUNDANT, EXUBERANT **2 a :** of the nature of a riot : TURBULENT **b :** participating in riot — **ri·ot·ous·ly** *adv* — **ri·ot·ous·ness** *n*

¹rip \'rip\ *vb* **ripped**; **rip·ping 1 :** to tear or split apart or open **2 :** to saw or split (wood) with the grain **3 :** to slash or slit with or as if with a sharp blade **4 :** to rush headlong

²rip *n* **:** a rent made by ripping : TEAR

ri·par·i·an \rə-'per-ē-ən, rī-\ *adj* **:** of or relating to the bank of a stream or lake

ripe \'rīp\ *adj* **1 :** fully grown and developed : MATURE **2 :** fully prepared : READY — **ripe·ly** *adv* — **ripe·ness** *n*

rip·en \'rī-pən\ *vb* **rip·ened**; **rip·en·ing** \'rīp-(ə-)niŋ\ **:** to grow or make ripe — **rip·en·er** \'rīp-(ə-)nər\ *n*

ri·poste \ri-'pōst\ *n* **1 :** a fencer's quick return thrust following a parry **2 :** a quick retort **3 :** a retaliatory maneuver or measure — **riposte** *vi*

rip·ple \'rip-əl\ *vb* **rip·pled**; **rip·pling** \'rip-(ə-)liŋ\ **1 :** to become lightly ruffled or covered with small waves **2 :** to stir up small waves on **3 :** to flow with a light rise and fall of sound or inflection **4 :** to impart a wavy motion or appearance to — **ripple** *n* — **rip·pler** \-(ə-)lər\ *n*

rip–roar·ing \'rip-'rōr-iŋ\ *adj* **:** noisily excited or exciting

rip·saw \'rip-ˌsȯ\ *n* **:** a coarse-toothed saw for cutting wood in the direction of the grain

¹rise \'rīz\ *vi* **rose** \'rōz\; **ris·en** \'riz-ᵊn\; **ris·ing** \'rī-ziŋ\ **1 a :** to get up esp. from lying, kneeling, or sitting **b :** to get up from sleep or from one's bed **2 :** to return from death **3 :** to take up arms **4 :** to end a session : ADJOURN **5 :** to appear above the horizon **6 a :** to move upward : ASCEND **b :** to extend upward **7 :** to swell in size or volume **8 a :** to become heartened or elated **b :** to increase in intensity **9 a :** to attain a higher rank or position **b :** to increase in quantity or number **c :** to increase in price or be marked by increasing prices **10 :** to come about : HAPPEN, ORIGINATE

²rise \'rīz\ *n* **1 :** an act of rising : a state of being risen **2 :** BEGINNING, ORIGIN **3 :** the distance or elevation of one point above another **4 :** the amount of an increase (as in number, volume, price, value, or rate) **5 a :** an upward slope **b :** a spot higher than surrounding ground **6 :** an irritated or angry reaction

ris·er \'rī-zər\ *n* **1 :** one that rises (as from sleep) **2 :** the upright member between two stair treads

ris·i·bil·i·ty \ˌriz-ə-'bil-ət-ē\ *n, pl* **-ties :** the ability or inclination to laugh — often used in pl.

ris·i·ble \'riz-ə-bəl\ *adj* **1 :** able or disposed to laugh **2 :** FUNNY **3 :** relating to or used in laughter

¹risk \'risk\ *n* **1 :** possibility of loss or injury : PERIL **2 :** the chance of loss or the perils to a person or thing that is insured

²risk *vt* **1 :** to expose to hazard or danger **2 :** to incur the risk or danger of — **risk·er** *n*

risky \'ris-kē\ *adj* **:** attended with risk or danger : HAZARDOUS — **risk·i·ness** *n*

ris·qué \ri-'skā\ *adj* **:** verging on impropriety or indecency

rite \'rīt\ *n* **1 a :** a prescribed form for a ceremony **b :** LITURGY **2 :** a ceremonial act or action

¹rit·u·al \'rich-(ə-w)əl\ *adj* **1 :** of or relating to rites or a ritual **2 :** according to religious law or social custom — **rit·u·al·ly** \-ē\ *adv*

²ritual *n* **1 :** an established form for a ceremony **2 a :** ritual observance; *esp* **:** a system of rites **b :** a ceremonial act or action

rit·u·al·ism \-ˌiz-əm\ *n* **1 :** the use of ritual **2 :** excessive devotion to ritual — **rit·u·al·ist** \-əst\ *n* — **rit·u·al·is·tic** \ˌrich-(ə-w)əl-'is-tik\ *adj* — **rit·u·al·is·ti·cal·ly** \-ti-k(ə-)lē\ *adv*

ritzy \'rit-sē\ *adj* **1 :** ostentatiously smart **2 :** SNOBBISH

¹ri·val \'rī-vəl\ *n* **1 a :** one of two or more striving to reach or obtain that which only one can possess **b :** one who tries to excel **2 :** one that equals another in desired qualities : PEER

²rival *adj* **:** having the same pretensions or claims

³rival *vt* **-valed** *or* **-valled**; **-val·ing** *or* **-val·ling** \'rīv-(ə-)liŋ\ **1 :** to be in competition with **2 :** to strive to equal or excel **3 :** EQUAL, MATCH

ri·val·ry \'rī-vəl-rē\ *n, pl* **-ries :** COMPETITION

rive \'rīv\ *vb* **rived** \'rīvd\; **riv·en** \'riv-ən\; **riv·ing** \'rī-viŋ\ **1 a :** to tear apart : REND **b :** SPLIT, CLEAVE **2 a :** to divide into pieces : SHATTER **b :** FRACTURE

riv·er \'riv-ər\ *n* **1 :** a natural stream of water larger than a brook or creek **2 :** a large stream : copious flow

riv·er·side \-ˌsīd\ *n* **:** the side or bank of a river

¹riv·et \'riv-ət\ *n* **:** a headed pin or bolt of metal used for uniting two or more pieces by passing the shank through a hole in each piece and then beating or pressing down the plain end so as to make a second head

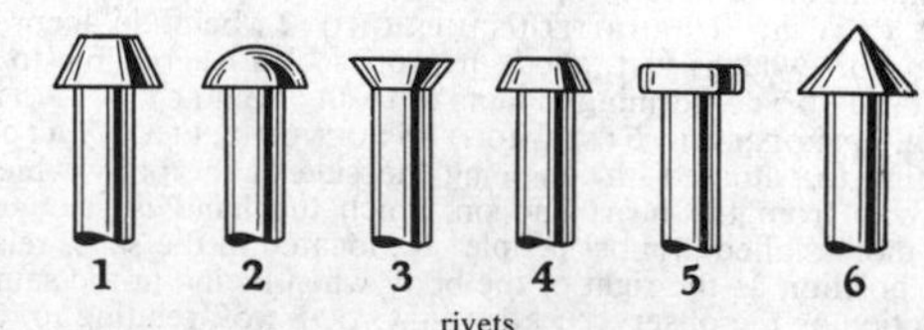

rivets

²rivet *vt* : to fasten with or as if with rivets — **riv·et·er** *n*
riv·u·let \'riv-(y)ə-lət\ *n* : a small stream
¹roach \'rōch\ *n, pl* **roach** : a European freshwater fish
²roach *n* : COCKROACH
road \'rōd\ *n* **1** : a place less enclosed than a harbor where ships may ride at anchor — often used in pl. **2** : an open way for vehicles, persons, and animals **3** : ROUTE, PATH **4** : RAILWAY
road·a·bil·i·ty \ˌrōd-ə-'bil-ət-ē\ *n* : the qualities (as steadiness and balance) desirable in an automobile on the road
road·bed \'rōd-ˌbed\ *n* **1** : the foundation of a road or railroad **2** : the part of the surface of a road traveled by vehicles
¹road·side \-ˌsīd\ *n* : the strip of land along a road
²roadside *adj* : situated at the side of a road
road·stead \-ˌsted\ *n* : ROAD 1
road·ster \'rōd-stər\ *n* **1** : a light horse for driving or riding **2** : an open automobile with one cross seat
road·way \'rōd-ˌwā\ *n* **1 a** : the strip of land over which a road passes **b** : ROAD; *esp* : ROADBED 2 **2** : the part of a bridge used by vehicles
roam \'rōm\ *vb* : to go or go over from place to place with no fixed purpose or direction : WANDER — **roam·er** *n*
¹roan \'rōn\ *adj* : having a base color (as black, red, or brown) muted and lightened by white hairs
²roan *n* **1** : an animal (as a horse) with a roan coat **2** : the color of a roan horse
¹roar \'rō(ə)r\ *vb* **1** : to utter or emit a loud prolonged sound **2 a** : to make or emit a loud confused sound **b** : to laugh loudly **3** : to be boisterous or disorderly **4** : to cause to roar
²roar *n* **1 a** : the deep cry of a wild beast **b** : a loud deep cry **2** : a loud continuous confused sound
¹roast \'rōst\ *vb* **1** : to cook by exposing to dry heat (as in an oven or before a fire) **2** : to criticize severely
²roast *n* **1** : a piece of meat roasted or suitable for roasting **2** : an outing at which food is roasted (as before an open fire)
³roast *adj* : ROASTED
roast·er \'rō-stər\ *n* **1** : one that roasts; *esp* : a usu. covered pan for roasting meat **2** : something (as a chicken) of a size or kind suitable for roasting
rob \'räb\ *vb* **robbed**; **rob·bing** **1 a** : to take something away from a person or place by force, threat, stealth, or trickery **b** : to commit robbery : STEAL **2 a** : to deprive of something due, expected, or desired **b** : to withhold unjustly or injuriously — **rob·ber** *n*
rob·bery \'räb-(ə-)rē\ *n, pl* **-ber·ies** : the act or practice of robbing; *esp* : larceny from the person or presence of another by violence or threat
¹robe \'rōb\ *n* **1** : a long loose or flowing garment: as **a** : one used for ceremonial occasions or as a symbol of office or profession **b** : an easy garment (as a dressing gown) replacing outer garments for informal wear **2** : a covering or wrap for the lower body
²robe *vb* **1** : to clothe, invest, or cover with or as if with a robe **2** : to put on a robe; *also* : DRESS
rob·in \'räb-ən\ *n* **1** : a small European thrush with yellowish red throat and breast **2** : a large No. American thrush with grayish upperparts and reddish breast
ro·bot \'rō-ˌbät\ *n* **1 a** : a machine that looks and acts like a human being **b** : an efficient but insensitive person **2** : an automatic apparatus **3** : something run by automatic controls
ro·bust \rō-'bəst, 'rō-ˌ\ *adj* : being strong and vigorously healthy — **ro·bust·ly** *adv* — **ro·bust·ness** *n*
¹rock \'räk\ *vb* **1** : to move back and forth as in a cradle **2** : to sway or cause to sway back and forth
²rock *n* : a rocking movement
³rock *n* **1** : a large mass of stone forming a cliff, promontory, or peak **2** : solid mineral deposits **3** : something (as a support or refuge) like a rock in firmness — **on the rocks** **1** : in or into a state of destruction or wreckage **2** : on ice cubes
rock bottom *n* : the lowest or most fundamental part or level — **rock–bottom** *adj*
rock·bound \'räk-'baund\ *adj* : fringed, surrounded, or covered with rocks : ROCKY
rock·er \'räk-ər\ *n* **1** : a curving piece of wood or metal on which an object (as a cradle) rocks **2** : a device that works with a rocking motion
rock·et \'räk-ət\ *n* **1** : a firework consisting of a case containing a combustible composition that is propelled through the air by the reaction resulting from the rearward discharge of the gases liberated by combustion **2** : a jet engine that operates on the same principle as the firework rocket but carries the oxygen needed for burning its fuel **3** : a rocket-propelled bomb, missile, or projectile
rock·et·ry \'räk-ə-trē\ *n* : the study of, experimentation with, or use of rockets
rock·ing chair \'räk-iŋ-\ *n* : a chair mounted on rockers
rocking horse *n* : a toy horse mounted on rockers
rock salt *n* : common salt in large crystals or masses
rock wool *n* : a woollike insulation made from molten rock or slag
¹rocky \'räk-ē\ *adj* **1** : abounding in or consisting of rocks **2** : difficult to impress or affect: as **a** : INSENSITIVE **b** : STEADFAST
²rocky *adj* **1** : UNSTABLE, WOBBLY **2** : physically upset : UNWELL — **rock·i·ness** *n*
rod \'räd\ *n* **1** : a straight slender stick or bar: as **a** : a stick used to punish; *also* : PUNISHMENT **b** : a bar for measuring **c** : a staff carried as a badge of office (as of marshal) **2 a** : a unit of length **b** : a square rod — **rod·less** \-ləs\ *adj* — **rod·like** *adj*
rode *past of* RIDE
ro·dent \'rōd-ᵊnt\ *n* : any of a group of relatively small gnawing mammals (as mice, squirrels, or beavers)
ro·deo \'rōd-ē-ˌō, rə-'dā-ō\ *n, pl* **-de·os** **1** : ROUNDUP 1 **2** : an exhibition featuring cowboy skills (as riding and roping)
rod·o·mon·tade \ˌräd-ə-mən-'tād, ˌrōd-\ *n* : vain boasting or bluster — **rodomontade** *adj*
¹roe \'rō\ *n, pl* **roe** *or* **roes** **1** : a small nimble European deer **2** : DOE
²roe *n* : the eggs of a fish esp. while still bound together in a membrane
roe·buck \'rō-ˌbək\ *n* : a male roe deer
roent·gen ray \'rent-gən-ˌrā, 'rənt-, -jən-\ *n, often cap 1st R* : X RAY
rog·er \'räj-ər\ *interj* — used esp. in radio and signaling to indicate that a message has been received and understood
¹rogue \'rōg\ *n* **1** : a worthless, dishonest, or unprincipled person : KNAVE, SCOUNDREL **2** : a pleasantly mischievous individual : SCAMP — **rogu·ish** \'rō-gish\ *adj* — **rogu·ish·ly** *adv* — **rogu·ish·ness** *n*
²rogue *adj* : being vicious and destructive
rogu·ery \'rō-g(ə-)rē\ *n, pl* **-er·ies** : the practices of a rogue
roil \'rȯil, *2 is also* 'rīl\ *vt* **1** : to make cloudy or muddy by stirring up sediment **2** : to rouse the temper of
rois·ter \'rȯi-stər\ *vi* **rois·tered**; **rois·ter·ing** \-st(ə-)riŋ\ : to engage in noisy revelry — **rois·ter·er** *n*
role \'rōl\ *n* **1 a** : a character assigned or assumed **b** : a part played by an actor or singer **2** : FUNCTION
¹roll \'rōl\ *n* **1 a** : a written document that may be rolled up : SCROLL **b** : an official list esp. of members of a body (as a legislative body) **2** : something that is rolled or rounded as if rolled **3** : something that rolls : ROLLER
²roll *vb* **1 a** : to move by turning over and over on a surface without sliding **b** : to move about or as if about an axis or point **2 a** : to put a wrapping around **b** : to form into a ball or

roll 3 : to make smooth, even, or compact with or as if with a roller 4 a : to move on rollers or wheels b : to begin operating or moving 5 a : to sound with a full reverberating tone or with a continuous beating sound b : to utter with a trill 6 : to luxuriate in an abundant supply 7 : ELAPSE, PASS 8 : to flow in a continuous stream 9 : to have an undulating contour 10 : to move with a side-to-side sway : ROCK

³roll *n* 1 a : a sound produced by rapid strokes on a drum b : a sonorous and often rhythmical flow of speech c : a heavy reverberating sound 2 : a rolling movement or an action or process involving such movement; *esp* : a swaying or side-to-side movement

roll call *n* : the act of calling off a list of names (as for checking attendance); *also* : a time for a roll call

roll·er \ˈrō-lər\ *n* 1 a : a revolving cylinder over or on which something is moved or which is used to press, shape, or smooth something b : a rod on which something (as a map) is rolled up c : a small wheel (as of a roller skate) 2 : a long heavy wave on the sea

roller skate *n* : a set of two pairs of wheels in a frame that fits the sole of a boot for gliding over a hard flat surface; *also* : a boot with wheels attached — **roller–skate** *vi*

rol·lick \ˈräl-ik\ *vi* : to move or behave in a carefree joyous manner : FROLIC — **rollick** *n* — **rol·lick·ing** *adj*

roll·ing pin \ˈrō-liŋ-\ *n* : a cylinder for rolling out dough

¹ro·man \ˈrō-mən\ *n* : roman letters or type

²roman *adj* 1 : UPRIGHT — used of numbers and letters whose capital forms are modeled on ancient Roman inscriptions 2 *cap* : of or relating to the Roman Catholic Church

Roman candle *n* : a cylindrical firework that discharges at intervals balls or stars of fire

Roman Catholic *adj* : of or relating to the body of Christians in communion with the pope having a hierarchy under the pope and a liturgy centered in the mass — **Roman Catholic** *n* — **Roman Catholicism** *n*

¹ro·mance \rō-ˈman(t)s, ˈrō-ˌ\ *n* 1 a : a medieval tale based on legend, chivalric love and adventure, and the supernatural b : a prose narrative dealing with heroic, adventurous, or mysterious events remote in time or place c : a love story 2 : a love affair

²romance *vb* 1 : to exaggerate or invent detail or incident 2 a : to entertain romantic thoughts or ideas b : to carry on a love affair with

¹ro·man·tic \rō-ˈmant-ik\ *adj* 1 a : of, relating to, or resembling a romance b : not factual : IMAGINARY 2 a : IMPRACTICAL, VISIONARY b *often cap* : of, relating to, or exhibiting romanticism 3 : having a strong emotional or imaginative appeal or association 4 : of, relating to, or associated with love — **ro·man·ti·cal·ly** \-i-k(ə-)lē\ *adv*

²romantic *n* 1 : a romantic person, trait, or component 2 *often cap* : ROMANTICIST

ro·man·ti·cism \rō-ˈmant-ə-ˌsiz-əm\ *n* 1 : the quality or state of being romantic 2 *often cap* : a literary, artistic, and philosophical movement marked esp. by an emphasis on the imagination and emotions — **ro·man·ti·cist** \-səst\ *n, often cap*

¹romp \ˈrämp\ *n* : boisterous play : FROLIC

²romp *vi* : to play in a boisterous manner : FROLIC

romp·er \ˈräm-pər\ *n* 1 : one that romps 2 : a child's one-piece garment with the lower part shaped like bloomers

rood \ˈrüd\ *n* 1 : CROSS, CRUCIFIX 2 : any of various units of land area; *esp* : a British unit equal to 1/4 acre

¹roof \ˈrüf, ˈru̇f\ *n* 1 : the upper covering part of a building 2 : something resembling a roof in form, position, or function — **roof·less** \-ləs\ *adj* — **roof·like** *adj*

²roof *vt* : to cover with or as if with a roof

roof·ing \ˈrü-fiŋ, ˈru̇f-iŋ\ *n* : material for a roof

roof·top \ˈrüf-ˌtäp, ˈru̇f-\ *n* : ROOF

roof·tree \-ˌtrē\ *n* : RIDGEPOLE

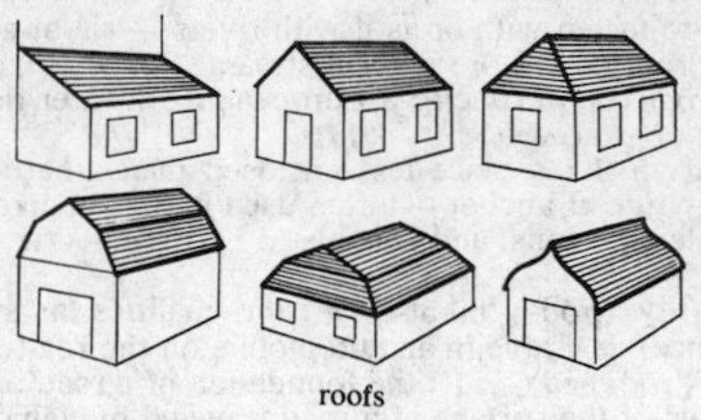
roofs

¹rook \ˈru̇k\ *n* : a common Old World gregarious bird resembling the related American crow

²rook *vt* : to defraud by cheating or swindling

³rook *n* : a chess piece that can move parallel to the sides of the board across any number of unoccupied squares

rook·ie \ˈru̇k-ē\ *n* : RECRUIT; *also* : NOVICE

¹room \ˈrüm, ˈru̇m\ *n* 1 : unoccupied area : SPACE 2 : a delimited space : COMPASS 3 a : a partitioned part of the inside of a building b : the people in a room 4 : OPPORTUNITY, CHANCE

²room *vb* : to provide with or occupy lodgings

room·er \ˈrü-mər, ˈru̇m-ər\ *n* : LODGER

room·ette \rü-ˈmet, ru̇m-ˈet\ *n* : a small private single room on a railroad sleeping car

room·ful \ˈrüm-ˌfu̇l, ˈru̇m-\ *n, pl* **roomfuls** \-ˌfu̇lz\ *or* **rooms·ful** \ˈrümz-ˌfu̇l, ˈru̇mz-\ : as much or as many as a room will hold; *also* : the persons or objects in a room

room·mate \ˈrüm-ˌmāt, ˈru̇m-\ *n* : one of two or more persons occupying the same room

roomy \ˈrü-mē, ˈru̇m-ē\ *adj* : having plenty of room : SPACIOUS — **room·i·ness** *n*

¹roost \ˈrüst\ *n* 1 : PERCH 2 : a place where birds roost

²roost *vb* : to settle on or as if on a roost : PERCH

roost·er \ˈrü-stər\ *n* : an adult male domestic fowl

¹root \ˈrüt, ˈru̇t\ *n* 1 a : the leafless usu. underground part of a seed plant that functions as an organ of absorption, aeration, and food storage or as a means of anchorage and support b : a subterranean plant part esp. when fleshy and edible 2 : something (as the basal part of a tooth or hair) that resembles a root 3 a : an original cause or quality : SOURCE b : an underlying support : BASIS c : the essential core : HEART 4 : a number that when taken as a factor an indicated number of times gives a specified number — **root·ed** \-əd\ *adj* — **root·less** \-ləs\ *adj* — **root·like** *adj*

²root *vb* 1 a : to form roots b : to fix or become fixed by or as if by roots 2 : to remove altogether often by force

³root *vb* 1 : to turn up or dig in the earth with the snout 2 : to poke or dig about

⁴root \ˈrüt\ *vi* 1 : to applaud noisily : CHEER 2 : to encourage or lend support — **root·er** *n*

root·let \ˈrüt-lət, ˈru̇t-\ *n* : a small root

root·stock \-ˌstäk\ *n* : a rootlike underground stem

¹rope \ˈrōp\ *n* 1 a : a large stout cord of strands (as of fiber or wire) twisted or braided together b : a hangman's noose 2 : a row or string of things united by or as if by braiding, twining, or threading 3 *pl* : special techniques or procedures

²rope *vb* 1 : to bind, fasten, or tie with a rope or cord 2 : to set off or divide by a rope 3 : LASSO — **rop·er** *n*

ropy \ˈrō-pē\ *adj* 1 : capable of being drawn into a sticky thread 2 : resembling rope — **rop·i·ness** *n*

ro·sa·ry \ˈrōz-(ə-)rē\ *n, pl* **-ries** 1 : a string of beads used in counting prayers esp. of the Roman Catholic rosary 2 *often cap* : a Roman Catholic devotion consisting of meditation on usu. five sacred mysteries during recitation of Ave Marias

¹rose *past of* RISE

²rose \ˈrōz\ *n* 1 a : any of various usu. prickly shrubs with divided leaves and showy flowers b : the flower of a rose

2 : something resembling a rose in form 3 : a variable color averaging a moderate purplish red — **rose·like** *adj*
³rose *adj* 1 : of, relating to, resembling, or used for the rose 2 : of the color rose
ro·se·ate \'rō-zē-ət, -zē-ˌāt\ *adj* 1 : resembling a rose esp. in color 2 : overly optimistic — **ro·se·ate·ly** *adv*
rose·mary \'rōz-ˌmer-ē\ *n* : a fragrant shrubby mint of southern Europe and Asia Minor used in cookery and in making perfumes
ro·sette \rō-'zet\ *n* 1 : an ornament resembling a rose usu. gathered or pleated and worn as a badge of office, as evidence of having won a decoration, or as trimming 2 : a disk of foliage or a floral design used as a decorative motif
rose·wood \'rōz-ˌwu̇d\ *n* : any of various tropical trees yielding valuable cabinet woods of a dark red or purplish color streaked and variegated with black
Rosh Ha·sha·nah \ˌrōsh-(h)ə-'shō-nə\ *n* : the Jewish New Year observed as a religious holiday in September or October
ros·in \'räz-ᵊn\ *n* : a brittle resin that is obtained from pine trees and is used in making varnish and on violin bows
ros·ter \'räs-tər\ *n* : a list usu. of personnel : ROLL
ros·trum \'räs-trəm\ *n, pl* **rostrums** *or* **ros·tra** \-trə\ : a stage or platform for public speaking
rosy \'rō-zē\ *adj* 1 a : of the color rose b : having a rosy complexion : BLOOMING c : BLUSHING 2 : characterized by or tending to promote optimism — **ros·i·ly** \-zə-lē\ *adv* — **ros·i·ness** \-zē-nəs\ *n*
¹rot \'rät\ *vb* **rot·ted**; **rot·ting** : to undergo decomposition
²rot *n* 1 : the process of rotting : the state of being rotten 2 : a disease marked by the breaking down of tissue
¹ro·ta·ry \'rōt-ə-rē\ *adj* 1 : turning on an axis like a wheel 2 : having an important part that turns on an axis
²rotary *n, pl* **-ries** 1 : a rotary machine 2 : a road junction formed around a central circle
ro·tat·a·ble \'rō-ˌtāt-ə-bəl\ *adj* : capable of being rotated
ro·tate \'rō-ˌtāt\ *vb* 1 : to turn or cause to turn about an axis or a center : REVOLVE 2 : to do or cause to do something in turn : ALTERNATE — **ro·ta·tor** \-ˌtāt-ər\ *n*
ro·ta·tion \rō-'tā-shən\ *n* 1 a : the act of rotating b : one complete turn 2 : return or succession in a series — **ro·ta·tion·al** \-shnəl, -shən-ᵊl\ *adj*
ro·ta·to·ry \'rōt-ə-ˌtōr-ē\ *adj* 1 : of, relating to, or producing rotation 2 : occurring in rotation
rote \'rōt\ *n* 1 : the use of memory usu. with little intelligence 2 : routine or repetition carried out mechanically or without understanding
ro·to·gra·vure \ˌrōt-ə-grə-'vyu̇(ə)r\ *n* : a process by which pictures and text are printed from etched plates affixed to the rollers of a rotary printing press
ro·tor \'rōt-ər\ *n* 1 : a part that revolves in a stationary part 2 : a complete system of more or less horizontal rotating blades supporting an aircraft in flight
rot·ten \'rät-ᵊn\ *adj* 1 : having rotted : PUTRID, UNSOUND 2 : morally corrupt 3 : extremely unpleasant or inferior — **rot·ten·ly** *adv* — **rot·ten·ness** *n*
ro·tund \rō-'tənd, 'rō-ˌ\ *adj* 1 : marked by roundness : ROUNDED 2 : FULL, SONOROUS 3 : PLUMP, CHUBBY — **ro·tun·di·ty** \rō-'tən-dət-ē\ *n*
ro·tun·da \rō-'tən-də\ *or* **ro·ton·da** \-'tän-\ *n* 1 : a round building; *esp* : one covered by a dome 2 : a large round room
roué \rü-'ā\ *n* : DEBAUCHEE, RAKE
rouge \'rüzh, 'rüj\ *n* 1 : any of various cosmetics to color the cheeks or lips red 2 : a red powder used in polishing glass, metal, or gems and as a pigment — **rouge** *vb*
¹rough \'rəf\ *adj* 1 a : marked by inequalities or projections on the surface : COARSE b : covered with or made up of coarse and often shaggy hair or bristles c (1) : having an uneven or bumpy surface (2) : difficult to travel over or penetrate : WILD 2 a : TURBULENT, TEMPESTUOUS b (1) : characterized by harshness, violence, or force (2) : DIFFICULT, TRYING 3 a : coarse or rugged in character or appearance b : marked by a lack of refinement : UNCOUTH 4 a : CRUDE, UNFINISHED b : executed hastily, tentatively, or imperfectly — **rough·ly** *adv* — **rough·ness** *n*
²rough *n* 1 : uneven ground covered with high grass esp. along a golf fairway 2 : something in a crude, unfinished, or preliminary state; *also* : such a state 3 : ROWDY, TOUGH
³rough *vt* 1 : ROUGHEN 2 : MANHANDLE, BEAT 3 a : to shape, make, or dress in a rough or preliminary way b : to indicate the chief lines of — **rough·er** *n* — **rough it** : to live under primitive conditions
rough·age \'rəf-ij\ *n* : coarse bulky food (as bran) that by its bulk stimulates the activity of the intestines
rough–and–ready \ˌrəf-ən-'red-ē\ *adj* : crude in nature, method, or manner but effective in action or use
rough–and–tum·ble \-ən-'təm-bəl\ *n* : a rough disorderly unrestrained struggle — **rough–and–tumble** *adj*
¹rough·cast \'rəf-ˌkast\ *n* : a rough model
²roughcast *vt* **-cast**; **-cast·ing** : to shape or form roughly
rough·dry \-'drī\ *vt* : to dry (laundry) without smoothing or ironing — **roughdry** *adj*
rough·en \'rəf-ən\ *vb* **rough·ened**; **rough·en·ing** \'rəf-(ə-)niŋ\ : to make or become rough
rough·hew \'rəf-'hyü\ *vt* **-hewed**; **-hewed** *or* **-hewn** \-'hyün\; **-hew·ing** 1 : to hew (as timber) coarsely without smoothing or finishing 2 : to form crudely
rough·house \'rəf-ˌhau̇s\ *n* : violence or rough boisterous play esp. among occupants of a room — **rough·house** \-ˌhau̇s, -ˌhau̇z\ *vb* — **rough·house** \-ˌhau̇s\ *adj*
rough·neck \'rəf-ˌnek\ *n* : ROWDY, TOUGH
rough·shod \-'shäd\ *adj* : shod with calked shoes
rou·lette \rü-'let\ *n* 1 : a gambling game in which a revolving wheel is used 2 : a toothed wheel or disk for making rows of dots or small holes — **roulette** *vt*
¹round \'rau̇nd\ *adj* 1 a : having every part of the surface or circumference equidistant from the center : SPHERICAL, CIRCULAR b : CYLINDRICAL c : having a curved outline 2 : PLUMP, SHAPELY 3 a : COMPLETE, FULL b : approximately correct; *esp* : exact only to a specific decimal c : AMPLE, LARGE 4 : BLUNT, OUTSPOKEN 5 : moving in or forming a circle 6 : curved or predominantly curved rather than angular — **round·ly** *adv* — **round·ness** *n*
²round *adv* : AROUND
³round \(')rau̇nd\ *prep* : AROUND
⁴round \'rau̇nd\ *n* 1 : something (as a circle, globe, or ring) round 2 a : a rung of a ladder or a chair b : a rounded molding 3 a : a circling or circuitous path or course b : motion in a circle or a curving path 4 : a route or circuit habitually covered : a series of customary calls or stops 5 : a drink of liquor apiece served at one time to each person in a group 6 : a sequence of recurring routine or repetitive actions or events 7 : a period of time that recurs in a fixed pattern 8 a : one shot fired by a weapon or by each man in a military unit b : a unit of ammunition consisting of the parts necessary to fire one shot 9 : a period of time or a unit of play in a contest or game 10 : an outburst of applause 11 : a cut of beef esp. between the rump and the lower leg 12 : a rounded or curved part — **in the round** 1 : FREESTANDING 2 : with a center stage surrounded by an audience on all sides
⁵round \'rau̇nd\ *vb* 1 a : to make round b : to become round, plump, or shapely 2 a : to go around b : to pass part way around 3 : ENCIRCLE, ENCOMPASS 4 : COMPLETE, FINISH 5 : to express as a round number 6 : to follow a winding course
¹round·about \'rau̇n-də-ˌbau̇t\ *n* : a circuitous route
²round·about \ˌrau̇n-də-'bau̇t\ *adj* : CIRCUITOUS, INDIRECT
roun·de·lay \'rau̇n-də-ˌlā\ *n* 1 : a simple song with refrain

2 : a poem with a refrain recurring frequently or at fixed intervals

round·house \'raund-,haus\ *n* **1** : a circular building for housing and repairing locomotives **2** : a cabin or apartment on the stern of a quarterdeck

round·ish \'raun-dish\ *adj* : somewhat round

round table *n* : a meeting of a group of persons for discussion of questions of mutual interest; *also* : the persons so meeting

round trip *n* : a trip to a place and back

round up *vt* **1** : to collect (cattle) by means of a roundup **2** : to gather in or bring together

round·up \'raun-,dəp\ *n* **1** : the gathering together of cattle on the range by riding around them and driving them in **2** : a gathering together of scattered persons or things **3** : SUMMARY, RÉSUMÉ

¹rouse \'rauz\ *vb* **1** : to arouse or become aroused from or as if from sleep : AWAKEN **2** : to stir up : EXCITE

²rouse *n* : an act or instance of rousing

rous·ing \'rau-ziŋ\ *adj* **1 a** : EXCITING, STIRRING **b** : BRISK, LIVELY **2** : EXCEPTIONAL, SUPERLATIVE

roust·about \'rau-stə-,baut\ *n* : one who does heavy unskilled labor (as a deckhand or longshoreman, a laborer in an oil field)

¹rout \'raut\ *n* **1** : MOB, THRONG; *esp* : RABBLE **2** : DISTURBANCE **3** : a fashionable gathering : RECEPTION

²rout *vb* **1** : to search haphazardly : RUMMAGE **2** : to find or bring to light esp. with difficulty **3** : to gouge out **4** : to cause to emerge esp. from bed : ROUSE

³rout *n* **1** : a state of wild confusion and disorderly retreat **2** : a disastrous defeat

⁴rout *vt* **1** : to disorganize or defeat completely; *esp* : to put to precipitate flight **2** : to drive out : DISPEL

¹route \'rüt, 'raut\ *n* **1** : a means of access : CHANNEL **2** : an established, selected, or assigned course of travel

²route *vt* **1** : to send, forward, or transport by a certain route **2** : to arrange and direct the course of procedure of (as a series of operations in a factory)

route·man \-mən, -,man\ *n* : one who sells or makes deliveries on an assigned route

¹rou·tine \rü-'tēn\ *n* **1** : a regular or customary course of procedure **2** : a reiterated speech or formula **3** : a fixed piece of entertainment often repeated : ACT

²routine *adj* **1** : COMMONPLACE, UNINSPIRED **2** : of, relating to, or in accordance with established procedure — **rou·tine·ly** *adv*

¹rove \'rōv\ *vb* : to wander through or over : ROAM

²rove *past of* REEVE

¹ro·ver \'rō-vər\ *n* : PIRATE

²rov·er \'rō-vər\ *n* : WANDERER, ROAMER

¹row \'rō\ *vb* **1** : to propel a boat by means of oars **2** : to compete against in rowing **3** : to transport in or as if in a boat propelled by oars — **row·er** *n*

²row *n* : an act or instance of rowing

³row *n* **1** : a number of objects in an orderly series or sequence **2** : WAY, STREET

⁴row \'rau\ *n* : a noisy disturbance or quarrel : BRAWL

⁵row \'rau\ *vi* : to engage in a row : FIGHT, QUARREL

row·boat \'rō-,bōt\ *n* : a boat designed to be rowed

¹row·dy \'raud-ē\ *adj* : coarse or boisterous in behavior : ROUGH — **row·di·ness** *n* — **row·dy·ish** \-ē-ish\ *adj* — **row·dy·ism** \-ē-,iz-əm\ *n*

²rowdy *n, pl* **rowdies** : a rowdy person : TOUGH

row·el \'rau(-ə)l\ *n* : a revolving disk at the end of a spur with sharp marginal points for goading a horse

roy·al \'rȯi(-ə)l\ *adj* **1** : of or relating to a king or sovereign : REGAL **2** : suitable for royalty — **roy·al·ly** \'rȯi-ə-lē\ *adv*

roy·al·ist \'rȯi-ə-ləst\ *n* **1** : a supporter of a king **2** : an adherent or advocate of monarchy — **royalist** *adj*

roy·al·ty \'rȯi(-ə)l-tē\ *n, pl* **-ties** **1** : royal status or power : SOVEREIGNTY **2** : regal character or bearing **3 a** : persons of royal lineage **b** : a person of royal rank **4 a** : a share of the product or profit reserved by the grantor esp. of an oil or mining lease **b** : a payment made to the owner of a patent or copyright for the use of it

¹rub \'rəb\ *vb* **rubbed**; **rub·bing** **1 a** : to move along the surface of a body with pressure : GRATE **b** : to fret or chafe with friction **2** : to treat in any of various ways by rubbing

²rub *n* **1 a** : OBSTRUCTION, DIFFICULTY **b** : something grating to the feelings (as a gibe or sarcasm) **2** : the application of friction with pressure : RUBBING

¹rub·ber \'rəb-ər\ *n* **1 a** : one that rubs **b** : an instrument or object (as a rubber eraser) used in rubbing, polishing, scraping, or cleaning **c** : something that prevents rubbing or chafing **2** : a flexible waterproof elastic substance made from the milky juice of various tropical plants or synthetically **3** : something made of or resembling rubber — **rub·ber·ize** \'rəb-ə-,rīz\ *vb* — **rub·ber·like** *adj* — **rub·bery** \'rəb-(ə-)rē\ *adj*

²rubber *n* : an odd game or hand played to determine the winner of a tie

rub·bish \'rəb-ish\ *n* : useless waste or rejected matter : TRASH

rub·ble \'rəb-əl\ *n* **1** : waterworn or rough broken stones or bricks used in coarse masonry **2** : a mass made up of rough irregular pieces

ru·bi·cund \'rü-bi-(,)kənd\ *adj* : RED, RUDDY — **ru·bi·cun·di·ty** \,rü-bi-'kən-dət-ē\ *n*

ru·bid·i·um \rü-'bid-ē-əm\ *n* : a soft silvery metallic chemical element

ru·bric \'rü-brik\ *n* : a rule esp. for the conduct of a religious service — **rubric** *or* **ru·bri·cal** \-bri-kəl\ *adj*

ru·by \'rü-bē\ *n, pl* **rubies** : a precious stone that is a deep red corundum

rud·der \'rəd-ər\ *n* : a flat piece of wood or metal attached to the stern of a boat for steering it; *also* : a similar piece attached to the rear of an aircraft

rud·dy \'rəd-ē\ *adj* **1** : having a healthy reddish color **2** : RED, REDDISH — **rud·di·ly** \'rəd-ᵊl-ē\ *adv* — **rud·di·ness** \'rəd-ē-nəs\ *n*

rude \'rüd\ *adj* **1** : being in a rough or unfinished state : CRUDE **2** : lacking refinement, delicacy, or culture : UNCOUTH **3** : DISCOURTEOUS **4** : FORCEFUL, ABRUPT — **rude·ly** *adv* — **rude·ness** *n*

ru·di·ment \'rüd-ə-mənt\ *n* **1** : a basic principle or element or a fundamental skill — usu. used in pl. **2** : something not fully formed or developed — **ru·di·men·ta·ry** \,rüd-ə-'ment-ə-rē, -'men-trē\ *adj*

¹rue \'rü\ *vt* : to feel penitence, remorse, or regret for

²rue *n* : REGRET, SORROW

³rue *n* : a woody perennial herb with yellow flowers, a strong smell, and bitter-tasting leaves

rue·ful \'rü-fəl\ *adj* **1** : exciting pity or sympathy : PITIABLE **2** : MOURNFUL, REGRETFUL — **rue·ful·ly** \-fə-lē\ *adv* — **rue·ful·ness** *n*

ruff \'rəf\ *n* **1** : a wheel-shaped stiff collar worn by men and women of the late 16th and early 17th centuries **2** : a fringe of long hairs or feathers growing around or on the neck — **ruffed** \'rəft\ *adj*

ruf·fi·an \'rəf-ē-ən\ *n* : a brutal cruel fellow — **ruffian** *adj* — **ruf·fi·an·ism** \-ē-ə-,niz-əm\ *n*

¹ruf·fle \'rəf-əl\ *vb* **ruf·fled**; **ruf·fling** \'rəf-(ə-)liŋ\ **1 a** : to disturb the smoothness of : ROUGHEN **b** : TROUBLE, VEX **2** : to erect (as feathers) in or like a ruff **3** : to make into a ruffle

²ruffle *n* **1** : RIPPLE **2 a** : a strip of fabric gathered or pleated on one edge **b** : RUFF 2

³ruffle *n* : a low vibrating drumbeat

rug \'rəg\ *n* **1** : a piece of thick heavy fabric usu. with a nap or pile used as a floor covering **2** : a floor mat of an animal pelt **3** : a lap robe

rug·ged \'rəg-əd\ *adj* **1** : having a rough uneven surface

: JAGGED 2 : TURBULENT, STORMY 3 : showing signs of strength : STURDY 4 a : AUSTERE, STERN b : COARSE, RUDE 5 : presenting a severe test of ability, stamina, or resolution — **rug·ged·ly** *adv* — **rug·ged·ness** *n*

¹ru·in \'rü-ən\ *n* 1 : physical, moral, economic, or social collapse 2 : the remains of something destroyed — usu. used in pl. 3 : a cause of destruction 4 : a ruined person or thing

²ruin *vt* 1 : to reduce to ruins : DEVASTATE 2 a : to damage irreparably b : BANKRUPT, IMPOVERISH

ru·in·a·tion \ˌrü-ə-'nā-shən\ *n* : RUIN, DESTRUCTION

ru·in·ous \'rü-ə-nəs\ *adj* 1 : RUINED, DILAPIDATED 2 : causing ruin : DESTRUCTIVE — **ru·in·ous·ly** *adv*

¹rule \'rül\ *n* 1 a : a guide or principle for conduct or action : REGULATION b : the laws laid down by the founder of a religious order 2 a : a generally prevailing quality, state, or mode b : a regulating principle 3 : the exercise of authority or control : DOMINION 4 : a strip of material marked off in units used for measuring or ruling off lengths

²rule *vb* 1 a : CONTROL, DIRECT b : GUIDE, MANAGE 2 a : to exercise authority or power over : GOVERN b : to be preeminent in : DOMINATE 3 : to declare authoritatively; *esp* : to lay down a legal rule 4 : to mark with lines drawn along or as if along the straight edge of a ruler

rul·er \'rü-lər\ *n* 1 : SOVEREIGN 2 : RULE 4

rum \'rəm\ *n* 1 : a liquor distilled from a fermented cane product (as molasses) 2 : alcoholic liquor

rum·ba \'rəm-bə, 'rům-\ *n* : a Cuban Negro dance or an imitation of it

¹rum·ble \'rəm-bəl\ *vb* **rum·bled**; **rum·bling** \-b(ə-)liŋ\ 1 : to make a low heavy rolling sound 2 : to travel with a low reverberating sound

²rumble *n* : a low heavy continuous reverberating sound

¹ru·mi·nant \'rü-mə-nənt\ *n* : a ruminant mammal

²ruminant *adj* 1 : chewing the cud 2 : of or relating to a group of hoofed mammals (as sheep, giraffes, deer, and camels) that chew the cud — **ru·mi·nant·ly** *adv*

ru·mi·nate \'rü-mə-ˌnāt\ *vb* 1 : to engage in contemplation : MUSE, MEDITATE 2 : to chew the cud — **ru·mi·na·tion** \ˌrü-mə-'nā-shən\ *n* — **ru·mi·na·tive** \'rü-mə-ˌnāt-iv\ *adj*

¹rum·mage \'rəm-ij\ *n* : a thorough search esp. among a confusion of objects or into every section

²rummage *vb* : to poke around in all corners looking for something

rum·my \'rəm-ē\ *n* : a card game in which each player tries to be the first to assemble all of his cards in groups of three or more

¹ru·mor \'rü-mər\ *n* 1 : common talk or opinion : HEARSAY 2 : a statement or report current without known authority for its truth

²rumor *vt* : to tell or spread by rumor

rump \'rəmp\ *n* 1 : the back part of an animal's body 2 : a cut of beef between the loin and round 3 : a small fragment remaining after the separation of the larger part of a group or an area — **rumped** \'rəm(p)t\ *adj*

rum·ple \'rəm-pəl\ *vt* **rum·pled**; **rum·pling** \-p(ə-)liŋ\ 1 : WRINKLE, CRUMPLE 2 : to make unkempt : TOUSLE

rum·pus \'rəm-pəs\ *n* : DISTURBANCE, FRACAS

¹run \'rən\ *vb* **ran** \'ran\; **run**; **run·ning** 1 a : to go faster than a walk b : FLEE, RETREAT, ESCAPE 2 a : to move freely about at will b : to sail in the same direction as the wind blows c : ROAM, ROVE 3 a : to go or cause to go rapidly or hurriedly : HASTEN b : to do or accomplish something by or as if by running 4 a : to contend in a race b : to enter an election 5 a : to move on or as if on wheels : GLIDE b : to roll forward rapidly or freely 6 : to go back and forth : PLY 7 : to migrate or move in schools; *esp* : to ascend a river to spawn 8 : FUNCTION, OPERATE 9 : to continue in force or operation 10 : to pass into a specified condition 11 a : to move as a fluid : FLOW b : MELT, FUSE c : to spread out : DISSOLVE d : to discharge a fluid 12 a : to develop rapidly in a specific direction b : to tend to develop a specified quality or feature 13 a : EXTEND b : to go back c : to be in a certain form or expression or order of succession 14 a : to occur persistently : RECUR b : to play on a stage a number of successive days or nights 15 : to be current : CIRCULATE 16 : TRACE 17 a : to pass over or traverse b : to slip through or past 18 a : to cause to penetrate or enter b : STITCH c : to cause to pass : LEAD d : to cause to collide e : SMUGGLE 19 : to cause to pass lightly or quickly over, along, or into something 20 a : to cause or allow to go in a specified manner or direction b : to carry on : MANAGE 21 a : to flow with b : CONTAIN, ASSAY 22 : to make oneself liable to : INCUR 23 : to permit charges to accumulate before settling — **run·ner** *n*

²run *n* 1 a : an act or the action of running : continued rapid movement b : a fast gallop c : a migrating of fish; *also* : fish migrating esp. to spawn d : a running race e : a score made in baseball by a base runner reaching home plate 2 : something that flows in the course of an operation or during a particular time 3 a : the horizontal distance from one point to another b : general tendency or direction 4 a : a continuous series esp. of things of identical or similar sort b : sudden heavy demands from depositors, creditors, or customers 5 : the quantity of work turned out in a continuous operation 6 : the usual or normal kind 7 a : the distance covered in a period of continuous traveling or sailing b : regular course : TRIP c : freedom of movement in or access to a place or area 8 a : a way, track, or path frequented by animals b : an enclosure for livestock where they may feed or exercise 9 a : an inclined course (as for skiing) b : a track or guide on which something runs 10 : a ravel in a knitted fabric

run·around \'rən-ə-ˌraůnd\ *n* : deceptive or delaying action esp. in response to a request

¹run·away \'rən-ə-ˌwā\ *n* 1 : FUGITIVE 2 : the act of running away out of control; *also* : a running horse out of control

²runaway *adj* 1 : running away : FUGITIVE 2 : accomplished by elopement or during flight 3 : won by or having a long lead 4 : subject to uncontrolled changes

run down *vb* 1 : to collide with and knock down 2 a : to chase until exhausted or captured b : to find by search : trace the source of 3 : DISPARAGE 4 : to cease to operate because of the exhaustion of motive power 5 : to deteriorate in physical condition

run–down \'rən-'daůn\ *adj* 1 : being in poor repair : DILAPIDATED 2 : being in poor health 3 : completely unwound

rune \'rün\ *n* 1 : one of the characters of an alphabet used by the Germanic peoples from about the 3d to the 13th centuries 2 : mystic utterance or inscription 3 : a Finnish or Old Norse poem — **ru·nic** \'rü-nik\ *adj*

¹rung *past part of* RING

²rung \'rəŋ\ *n* 1 a : a rounded part placed as a crosspiece between the legs of a chair b : one of the crosspieces of a ladder 2 : a stage in an ascent : DEGREE

run·let \'rən-lət\ *n* : RUNNEL

run·nel \'rən-ᵊl\ *n* : RIVULET

run·ner–up \'rən-ər-ˌəp\ *n* : the competitor in a contest that finishes next to the winner

¹run·ning \'rən-iŋ\ *adj* 1 : FLUID, RUNNY 2 : INCESSANT, CONTINUOUS 3 : measured in a straight line 4 : FLOWING, CURSIVE 5 : initiated or performed while running or with a running start 6 : fitted or trained for running

²running *adv* : in succession : CONSECUTIVELY

run·ny \'rən-ē\ *adj* : having a tendency to run

run off *vb* 1 : to produce by a printing press 2 : to cause to be run or played to a finish 3 : to steal (as cattle) by driving away 4 : to run away — **run off with** : to carry off : STEAL

run·off \'rən-ˌȯf\ *n* : a final contest to decide a previous indecisive contest or series of contests
run on *vb* **1** : CONTINUE **2** : to talk or narrate at length **3** : to place or add (as an entry in a dictionary) at the end of a paragraphed item
[1]**run–on** \'rən-'ȯn, -'än\ *adj* : continuing without rhetorical pause from one line of verse into another
[2]**run–on** \'rən-ˌȯn, -ˌän\ *n* : something (as a dictionary entry) that is run on
run out *vi* **1** : to come to an end : EXPIRE **2** : to become exhausted or used up : FAIL **3** : to use up the available supply
run over *vb* **1** : OVERFLOW **2** : to exceed a limit **3** : to go over, examine, repeat, or rehearse quickly **4** : to collide with, knock down, and often drive over
runt \'rənt\ *n* : an unusually small person or animal
run·way \'rən-ˌwā\ *n* **1** : RUN 8 **2** : an artificially surfaced strip of ground on a landing field for the landing and takeoff of airplanes **3** : a support (as a track, pipe, or trough) on which something runs
[1]**rup·ture** \'rəp-chər\ *n* **1** : a breaking or tearing apart **2** : HERNIA
[2]**rupture** *vb* **rup·tured**; **rup·tur·ing** \-chə-riŋ, -shriŋ\ **1** : to part by violence : BREAK **2** : to produce a rupture in **3** : to have a rupture
ru·ral \'ru̇r-əl\ *adj* : of or relating to the country, country people or life, or agriculture
ruse \'rüs, 'rüz\ *n* : a deceptive stratagem : ARTIFICE
[1]**rush** \'rəsh\ *n* : any of various marsh plants with hollow stems
[2]**rush** *vb* **1** : to move forward, progress, or act with haste or eagerness or without preparation **2** : to push or impel on or forward with speed or violence **3** : to perform in a short time or at high speed **4** : ATTACK, CHARGE — **rush·er** *n*
[3]**rush** *n* **1 a** : a violent forward motion **b** : ATTACK, ONSET **2** : a burst of activity, productivity, or speed **3** : a thronging of people usu. to a new place and in search of wealth **4** : a round of attention usu. involving extensive social activity
[4]**rush** *adj* : requiring or marked by special speed or urgency
rusk \'rəsk\ *n* : a sweet or plain bread baked, sliced, and baked again until dry and crisp
rus·set \'rəs-ət\ *n* **1** : a variable reddish brown or yellowish brown color **2** : any of various winter apples with rough russet skins — **russet** *adj*
rust \'rəst\ *n* **1** : the reddish brittle coating formed on metal (as iron) esp. when chemically attacked by moist air **2** : any of numerous destructive diseases of plants marked by reddish brown spots **3** : a strong reddish brown — **rust** *vb*
[1]**rus·tic** \'rəs-tik\ *adj* **1** : of, relating to, or suitable for the country : RURAL **2** : made of the rough limbs of trees **3** : AWKWARD, BOORISH **4** : PLAIN, SIMPLE — **rus·ti·cal·ly** \-ti-k(ə-)lē\ *adv* — **rus·tic·i·ty** \ˌrəs-'tis-ət-ē\ *n*
[2]**rustic** *n* : an inhabitant of a rural area
rus·ti·cate \'rəs-ti-ˌkāt\ *vb* : to go into or reside in the country
[1]**rus·tle** \'rəs-əl\ *vb* **rus·tled**; **rus·tling** \'rəs-(ə-)liŋ\ **1** : to make or cause to make a rustle **2** : to act or move with energy or speed **3** : to get by rustling; *esp* : FORAGE **4** : to steal (as cattle) from the range — **rus·tler** \'rəs-(ə-)lər\ *n*
[2]**rustle** *n* : a quick succession or confusion of small sounds
rust·proof \'rəst-'prüf\ *adj* : incapable of rusting
rusty \'rəs-tē\ *adj* **1** : affected by or as if by rust **2** : inept and slow through lack of practice or old age **3** : of the color rust — **rust·i·ly** \'rəs-tə-lē\ *adv* — **rust·i·ness** \-tē-nəs\ *n*
[1]**rut** \'rət\ *n* : a state of sexual excitement esp. in the male deer
[2]**rut** *vi* **rut·ted**; **rut·ting** : to be in or enter a state of rut
[3]**rut** *n* **1** : a track worn by a wheel or by habitual passage **2** : a usual or fixed practice : a regular course; *esp* : a monotonous routine — **rut·ty** \'rət-ē\ *adj*
[4]**rut** *vt* **rut·ted**; **rut·ting** : to make a rut in : FURROW
ru·ta·ba·ga \ˌrüt-ə-'bā-gə, ˌru̇t-, -'beg-ə\ *n* : a turnip with a very large yellowish root
ruth \'rüth\ *n* **1** : compassion for the misery of another : PITY **2** : sorrow for one's own faults : REMORSE
ru·the·ni·um \rü-'thē-nē-əm\ *n* : a hard brittle grayish rare metallic chemical element
ruth·less \'rüth-ləs\ *adj* : having no ruth : MERCILESS, CRUEL — **ruth·less·ly** *adv* — **ruth·less·ness** *n*
rye \'rī\ *n* **1** : a hardy annual cereal grass widely grown for grain and as a cover crop; *also* : its seeds **2** : whiskey distilled from rye or from rye and malt

s \'es\ *n, often cap* **1** : the 19th letter of the English alphabet **2** : a grade rating a student's work as satisfactory
Sab·bath \'sab-əth\ *n* **1** : the 7th day of the week observed from Friday evening to Saturday evening as a day of rest and worship by Jews and some Christians **2** : the day of the week (as among Christians) set aside in a religion for rest and worship
[1]**sa·ber** *or* **sa·bre** \'sā-bər\ *n* : a cavalry sword with a curved blade, thick back, and guard

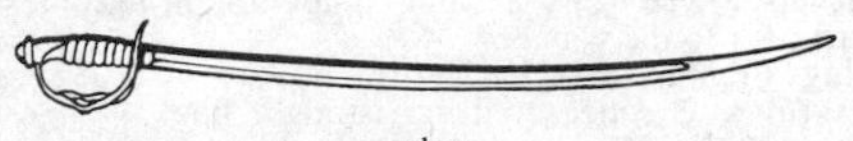

saber

[2]**saber** *or* **sabre** *vt* **sa·bered** *or* **sa·bred**; **sa·ber·ing** *or* **sa·bring** \-b(ə-)riŋ\ : to strike, cut, or kill with a saber
Sa·bin vaccine \'sā-bən-\ *n* : a polio vaccine that contains living attenuated virus and is taken by mouth
sa·ble \'sā-bəl\ *n, pl* **sable** *or* **sables** **1 a** : the color black **b** : black clothing worn in mourning — usu. used in pl. **2 a** : a carnivorous mammal of northern Europe and Asia related to the martens and valued for its soft rich brown fur; *also* : a related animal **b** : the fur or pelt of a sable
sa·bot \sa-'bō, 'sab-ō\ *n* : a wooden shoe worn in various European countries
[1]**sab·o·tage** \'sab-ə-ˌtäzh\ *n* **1** : destruction of an employer's property (as tools or materials) or the hindering of manufacturing by discontented workmen **2** : destructive or obstructive action carried on by enemy agents or sympathizers to hinder a nation's war or defense effort
[2]**sabotage** *vt* : to practice sabotage on : WRECK, DESTROY
sab·o·teur \ˌsab-ə-'tər\ *n* : a person who commits sabotage
sac \'sak\ *n* : a pouch within an animal or plant often containing a fluid — **sac·cate** \'sak-ˌāt\ *adj* — **sac·like** *adj*
sac·cha·rin \'sak-(ə-)rən\ *n* : a very sweet white coal tar derivative that is used as a calorie-free sweetener
sac·cha·rine \'sak-ə-rən\ *adj* : overly or ingratiatingly sweet
sac·er·do·tal \ˌsas-ər-'dōt-ᵊl, ˌsak-ər-\ *adj* : PRIESTLY — **sac·er·do·tal·ly** \-ᵊl-ē\ *adv* — **sac·er·do·tal·ism** \-ᵊl-ˌiz-əm\ *n* — **sac·er·do·tal·ist** \-ᵊl-əst\ *n*
sa·chem \'sā-chəm\ *n* : a No. American Indian chief
sa·chet \sa-'shā\ *n* : a small bag that contains a perfumed

powder and is used (as in a closet) to scent clothes and linens

[1]**sack** \'sak\ *n* **1 a :** a large bag made of coarse strong material **b :** a small container made of light material (as paper) **2 :** the amount contained in a sack **3 a :** a woman's loose-fitting dress **b :** a short usu. loose-fitting coat for women and children **4 :** DISMISSAL — usu. used with *get* or *give* **5 :** BED

[2]**sack** *vt* **1 :** to put in a sack **2 :** to dismiss esp. summarily

[3]**sack** *n* **:** a usu. dry white wine imported to England from the south of Europe esp. during the 16th and 17th centuries

[4]**sack** *n* **:** the plundering of a captured town

[5]**sack** *vt* **1 :** to plunder after capture **2 :** PILLAGE, LOOT

sack·cloth \'sak-ˌklȯth\ *n* **1 :** coarse cloth for sacks **2 :** a garment of sackcloth worn as a sign of mourning or penitence

sack coat *n* **:** a man's jacket with a straight unfitted back

sack·ing \'sak-iŋ\ *n* **:** strong coarse cloth (as burlap) from which sacks are made

sac·ra·ment \'sak-rə-mənt\ *n* **1 :** a formal religious act that is sacred as a sign or symbol of a spiritual reality; *esp* **:** one instituted by Jesus Christ as a means of grace **2 :** the elements of the Eucharist — **sac·ra·men·tal** \ˌsak-rə-'ment-ᵊl\ *adj* — **sac·ra·men·tal·ly** \-ᵊl-ē\ *adv*

sa·cred \'sā-krəd\ *adj* **1 :** set apart in honor of someone (as a god) **2 :** HOLY **3 :** RELIGIOUS **4 :** requiring or deserving to be held in highest esteem and protected from violation or encroachment — **sa·cred·ly** *adv* — **sa·cred·ness** *n*

[1]**sac·ri·fice** \'sak-rə-ˌfīs, -fəs\ *n* **1 :** an act of offering to deity something precious; *esp* **:** the killing of a victim on an altar **2 :** something offered in sacrifice **3 :** a destroying or yielding of something for the sake of something else; *also* **:** something so given up **4 :** loss of something and esp. of a profit **5 :** a play in baseball (as a bunt or a fly) in which the base runner is advanced when the batter is put out

[2]**sac·ri·fice** \-ˌfīs\ *vb* **1 :** to offer as a sacrifice or perform sacrificial rites **2 :** to give up for the sake of something else **3 :** to sell at a loss **4 :** to make a sacrifice in baseball — **sac·ri·fic·er** *n*

sacrifice fly *n* **:** an outfield fly in baseball caught by a fielder after which a base runner scores

sac·ri·fi·cial \ˌsak-rə-'fish-əl\ *adj* **:** of or relating to sacrifice — **sac·ri·fi·cial·ly** \-'fish-ə-lē\ *adv*

sac·ri·lege \'sak-rə-lij\ *n* **1 :** theft or violation of something consecrated to God **2 :** gross misuse or disrespect of something sacred or precious — **sac·ri·le·gious** \ˌsak-rə-'lij-əs, -'lē-jəs\ *adj* — **sac·ri·le·gious·ly** *adv*

sac·ris·tan \'sak-rə-stən\ *n* **:** an officer of a church in charge of the sacristy; *also* **:** SEXTON

sac·ris·ty \-rə-stē\ *n, pl* **-ties :** a room in a church where sacred utensils and vestments are kept **:** VESTRY

sac·ro·sanct \'sak-rō-ˌsaŋ(k)t\ *adj* **:** SACRED, INVIOLABLE

sad \'sad\ *adj* **1 :** affected with or expressive of grief or unhappiness **2 a :** causing or associated with grief or unhappiness **b :** DISMAYING, DEPLORABLE — **sad·ly** *adv*

sad·den \'sad-ᵊn\ *vb* **sad·dened; sad·den·ing** \'sad-niŋ, -ᵊn-iŋ\ **:** to make or become sad

[1]**sad·dle** \'sad-ᵊl\ *n* **1 a :** a girthed usu. padded and leather-covered seat for a rider on horseback; *also* **:** a comparable part of a driving harness **b :** a seat esp. on a bicycle **2 :** a ridge connecting two higher land elevations **3 :** a cut of meat consisting of both sides of the unsplit back of a carcass including both loins **4 :** something that resembles a saddle in shape, position, or use; *esp* **:** a support for an object

[2]**saddle** *vb* **sad·dled; sad·dling** \'sad-liŋ, -ᵊl-iŋ\ **1 :** to put a saddle on **2 :** ENCUMBER, BURDEN

sad·dle·bag \'sad-ᵊl-ˌbag\ *n* **:** a large pouch carried hanging from one side of a saddle or over the rear wheel of a bicycle or motorcycle and usu. one of a pair

sad·dle·bow \-ˌbō\ *n* **:** the arch in or the pieces forming the front of a saddle

sad·dler \'sad-lər\ *n* **:** one that makes, repairs, or sells horse equipment (as saddles)

sad·dlery \'sad-lə-rē, 'sad-ᵊl-rē\ *n, pl* **-dler·ies :** the trade, articles of trade, or shop of a saddler

sad·dle·tree \'sad-ᵊl-ˌtrē\ *n* **:** the frame of a saddle

sad·iron \'sad-ˌī(-ə)rn\ *n* **:** a flatiron pointed at both ends and having a removable handle

sad·ism \'sād-ˌiz-əm, 'sad-\ *n* **1 :** an abnormal condition in which a person takes pleasure in hurting another; *also* **:** an unwholesome love of cruelty **2 :** excessive cruelty — **sad·ist** \-əst\ *n* — **sa·dis·tic** \sə-'dis-tik, sā-\ *adj* — **sa·dis·ti·cal·ly** \-ti-k(ə-)lē\ *adv*

sad·ness \'sad-nəs\ *n* **:** the quality, state, or fact of being sad

sa·fa·ri \sə-'fär-ē, -'far-\ *n, pl* **-ris 1 :** the caravan and equipment of a hunting expedition esp. in eastern Africa **2 a :** a hunting expedition in eastern Africa **b :** JOURNEY, TRIP

[1]**safe** \'sāf\ *adj* **1 :** freed from harm or risk **:** UNHURT **2 a :** secure from threat of danger, harm, or loss **b :** successful in reaching base in baseball **3 :** affording safety from danger **4 :** not threatening danger **:** HARMLESS **5 a :** CAUTIOUS **b :** TRUSTWORTHY, RELIABLE — **safe·ly** *adv* — **safe·ness** *n*

[2]**safe** *n* **:** a container to keep articles (as valuables) safe

safe–con·duct \'sāf-'kän-(ˌ)dəkt\ *n* **1 :** protection given a person passing through a military zone or occupied area **2 :** a document authorizing safe-conduct

safe–deposit box *n* **:** a box (as in the vault of a bank) for safe storage of valuables — called also *safety-deposit box*

[1]**safe·guard** \'sāf-ˌgärd\ *n* **:** something that protects **:** DEFENSE

[2]**safeguard** *vt* **:** to make safe or secure **:** PROTECT

safe·keep·ing \'sāf-'kē-piŋ\ *n* **:** a keeping or being kept in safety **:** PROTECTION, CARE, CUSTODY

safe·ty \'sāf-tē\ *n, pl* **safeties 1 :** the condition of being safe from hurt, injury, or loss **:** SECURITY **2 :** a protective device to prevent inadvertent or hazardous operation of something (as a pistol or a machine) **3 a :** a football play in which the ball is downed by the offensive team behind its own goal line **b :** a defensive football back who plays the deepest position

saf·fron \'saf-rən\ *n* **:** an aromatic deep orange powder from the flower of a crocus used to color and flavor foods

[1]**sag** \'sag\ *vi* **sagged; sag·ging 1 :** to droop, sink, or settle from or as if from pressure or loss of tautness **2 :** to lose firmness, resiliency, or vigor **3 :** to fall from a thriving state

[2]**sag** *n* **:** a sagging part or area; *also* **:** an instance or amount of sagging

sa·ga \'säg-ə\ *n* **1 :** an Icelandic prose narrative of historic or legendary figures and events of Norway and Iceland **2 :** a modern heroic narrative resembling the Icelandic saga

sa·ga·cious \sə-'gā-shəs\ *adj* **:** of keen and farsighted understanding and judgment **:** DISCERNING — **sa·ga·cious·ly** *adv* — **sa·ga·cious·ness** *n* — **sa·gac·i·ty** \-'gas-ət-ē\ *n*

sag·a·more \'sag-ə-ˌmōr\ *n* **:** an Indian chief under a sachem

[1]**sage** \'sāj\ *adj* **:** WISE, PRUDENT — **sage·ly** *adv*

[2]**sage** *n* **:** a man of profound and scholarly wisdom; *also* **:** a mature or venerable man of sound judgment

[3]**sage** *n* **1 :** a mint with grayish green aromatic leaves used esp. in flavoring meats; *also* **:** a plant belonging to the same genus as this mint and including several grown as ornamentals for their showy flowers **2 :** SAGEBRUSH

sage·brush \'sāj-ˌbrəsh\ *n* **:** any of several low shrubby No. American plants related to the daisies; *esp* **:** a common plant with a bitter juice and an odor like a sage that is widespread on alkaline plains of the western U.S.

sa·go \'sā-gō\ *n, pl* **sagos :** a dry granulated or powdered starch prepared from the pith of an East Indian palm

sa·hib \'sä-ˌ(h)ib,—ˌ(h)ēb, ˌsä-'\ *n* **:** SIR, MASTER — used esp. among Hindus and Muslims in colonial India when addressing or speaking of a European of some social or official status

said \'sed\ *adj* **:** AFOREMENTIONED

¹sail \'sāl, *as last element in compounds often* səl\ *n* **1 a :** a usu. rectangular or triangular piece of fabric (as canvas) by means of which wind is used to propel a ship through water; *also* **:** the sails of a ship **b** *pl usu* **sail :** a ship equipped with sails **2 :** something like a sail in function or form **3 :** a passage by a sailing ship

²sail *vb* **1 a :** to travel on water by sailboat; *also* **:** to travel or begin a journey by water **b :** to move or pass over by ship **c :** to function in sailing; *also* **:** to handle or manage the sailing of **2 :** to move or cause to move in a manner suggesting a ship under sail **3 :** to attack something with gusto

sail·boat \'sāl-ˌbōt\ *n* **:** a boat equipped with sails

sail·cloth \-ˌklȯth\ *n* **:** a heavy canvas used esp. for sails and tents

sail·or \'sā-lər\ *n* **:** one that sails: as **a :** a member of a ship's crew **b :** SEAMAN 2 **c :** a traveler by water

saint \'sānt; *when a name follows* (ˌ)sānt *or* (*not shown below*) sənt\ *n* **1 :** a holy and godly person; *esp* **:** one who is canonized **2 :** a person who is sweet-tempered, self-sacrificing, and righteous

saint·ed \'sānt-əd\ *adj* **1 :** befitting or relating to a saint **2 :** attained to or worthy of sainthood

saint·hood \'sānt-ˌhu̇d\ *n* **1 :** the quality or state of being a saint **2 :** SAINTS

saint·ly \'sānt-lē\ *adj* **:** relating to, resembling, or befitting a saint **:** HOLY — **saint·li·ness** *n*

¹sake \'sāk\ *n* **1 :** END, PURPOSE **2 :** GOOD, ADVANTAGE

²sa·ke *or* **sa·ki** \'säk-ē\ *n* **:** a Japanese alcoholic beverage of fermented rice usu. served hot

sa·laam \sə-'läm\ *n* **1 :** a salutation or ceremonial greeting in the East **2 :** an obeisance performed by bowing very low and placing the right palm on the forehead — **salaam** *vb*

sal·a·ble *or* **sale·a·ble** \'sā-lə-bəl\ *adj* **1 :** fit to be sold **2 :** likely to be bought **:** easy to sell — **sal·a·bil·i·ty** \ˌsā-lə-'bil-ət-ē\ *n*

sa·la·cious \sə-'lā-shəs\ *adj* **1 :** arousing sexual desire or imagination **:** LASCIVIOUS **2 :** LECHEROUS, LUSTFUL — **sa·la·cious·ly** *adv* — **sa·la·cious·ness** *n*

sal·ad \'sal-əd\ *n* **1 :** a cold dish usu. of raw green vegetables served with oil, vinegar, and seasonings **2 :** a cold dish (as of meat, shellfish, fruit, or vegetables served singly or in combinations) with a dressing

salad days *n pl* **:** time of youthful inexperience or indiscretion

sal·a·man·der \'sal-ə-ˌman-dər\ *n* **:** any of an order of amphibians superficially resembling lizards but scaleless and covered with a soft moist skin

sa·la·mi \sə-'läm-ē\ *n* **:** highly seasoned sausage of pork and beef often dried for storage

sal·a·ried \'sal-(ə-)rēd\ *adj* **:** receiving or yielding a salary

sal·a·ry \'sal-(ə-)rē\ *n, pl* **-ries :** fixed compensation paid regularly for work or services **:** STIPEND

sale \'sāl\ *n* **1 :** the act of selling; *esp* **:** the transfer of ownership of property from one person to another for a price **2 :** availability for purchase — usu. used in the phrases *for sale* and *on sale* **3 :** public disposal to the highest bidder **:** AUCTION **4 :** a selling of goods at bargain prices **5** *pl* **a :** the business of selling **b :** gross receipts

sales·clerk \'sālz-ˌklərk\ *n* **:** a salesman or saleswoman in a store

sales·man \'sālz-mən\ *n* **:** one that sells either in a territory or in a store — **sales·man·ship** \-ˌship\ *n* — **sales·wom·an** \-ˌwu̇m-ən\ *n*

sa·lience \'sāl-yən(t)s, 'sā-lē-ən(t)s\ *or* **sa·lien·cy** \-yən-sē, -lē-ən-\ *n, pl* **sa·lienc·es** *or* **sa·lien·cies 1 :** the quality or state of being salient **2 :** a striking point or feature **:** HIGHLIGHT

¹sa·lient \'sāl-yənt, 'sā-lē-ənt\ *adj* **1 :** moving by leaps or springs **:** JUMPING **2 :** jetting upward **3 a :** projecting beyond a line, surface, or level **:** PROTUBERANT **b :** standing out conspicuously **:** PROMINENT, STRIKING — **sa·lient·ly** *adv*

²salient *n* **:** an outwardly projecting part of a fortification, trench system, or line of defense

¹sa·line \'sā-ˌlēn, -ˌlīn\ *adj* **1 :** consisting of or containing salt **2 :** of, relating to, or resembling salt **:** SALTY — **sa·lin·i·ty** \sā-'lin-ət-ē, sə-\ *n*

²saline *n* **1 :** a metallic salt esp. with a cathartic action **2 :** a saline solution

sa·li·va \sə-'lī-və\ *n* **:** a liquid secreted into the mouth that helps digestion

sal·i·vary \'sal-ə-ˌver-ē\ *adj* **:** of or relating to saliva or the glands that secrete it; *esp* **:** producing or carrying saliva

Salk vaccine \'sȯ(l)k-\ *n* **:** a polio vaccine that contains virus inactivated with formaldehyde and is given by injection

sal·low \'sal-ō\ *adj* **:** of a grayish greenish yellow color — **sal·low·ish** \'sal-ə-wish\ *adj* — **sal·low·ness** \'sal-ō-nəs\ *n*

¹sal·ly \'sal-ē\ *n, pl* **sallies 1 :** an action of rushing or bursting forth; *esp* **:** a sortie of besieged troops upon the attackers **2 a :** a brief outbreak **:** OUTBURST **b :** a witty or imaginative saying **:** QUIP **3 :** an excursion usu. off the beaten track

²sally *vi* **sal·lied**; **sal·ly·ing 1 :** to leap out or burst forth suddenly **2 :** to set out **:** DEPART

salm·on \'sam-ən\ *n, pl* **salmon 1 a :** a large soft-finned game fish of the northern Atlantic related to the trouts and chars and noted as a table fish **b :** any of various related fishes; *esp* **:** any of a genus of fishes that breed in rivers tributary to the northern Pacific **2 :** a strong yellowish pink — **salmon** *adj* — **salm·on·oid** \'sam-ə-ˌnȯid\ *adj or n*

sa·lon \sa-'lōⁿ, sə-'län\ *n* **1 :** an elegant apartment or living room (as in a fashionable French home) **2 :** a fashionable assemblage of notables held by custom at the home of a prominent person **3 a :** a hall for exhibition of art **b :** an annual exhibition of such works **4 :** a stylish business establishment or shop

sa·loon \sə-'lün\ *n* **1 :** an elaborately decorated public apartment or hall (as a large cabin for social use of a ship's passengers) **2 :** a place in which alcoholic beverages are sold and consumed **:** BARROOM

sal soda \'sal-'sōd-ə\ *n* **:** a transparent crystalline hydrated sodium carbonate used in washing and bleaching textiles

¹salt \'sȯlt\ *n* **1 a :** a crystalline compound that is the chloride of sodium, abundant in nature, and used esp. for seasoning or preserving food **b** *pl* **:** a mineral or saline mixture used as a laxative or cathartic **c :** a compound formed usu. by the action of an acid on metal **2 a :** an element that gives savor, piquancy, or zest **:** FLAVOR **b :** sharpness of wit **:** PUNGENCY **c :** EARTHINESS **d :** RESERVE, SKEPTICISM — often used in the phrase *with a grain of salt* **e :** the sprinkling of people thought to set a model of excellence for or to give tone to the rest — usu. used in the phrase *salt of the earth* **3 :** SAILOR

²salt *vt* **1 :** to treat, preserve, flavor, or supply with salt; *esp* **:** to sprinkle with or as if with salt **2 :** to give flavor or piquancy to — **salt·er** *n*

³salt *adj* **1 a :** SALINE, SALTY **b :** being or inducing one of the four basic taste sensations **2 :** cured or seasoned with salt **:** SALTED **3 :** overflowed with salt water **4 :** SHARP, PUNGENT — **salt·ness** *n*

sal·ta·tion \sal-'tā-shən, sȯl-\ *n* **1 a :** the action of leaping or jumping **b :** DANCING **2 :** an abrupt change esp. in the course of evolution

sal·ta·to·ry \'sal-tə-ˌtōr-ē, 'sȯl-\ *adj* **1 :** of or relating to dancing **2 :** proceeding by leaps rather than by gradual transitions

salt away *vt* **:** to lay away safely **:** SAVE

salt·cel·lar \'sȯlt-ˌsel-ər\ *n* **:** a small vessel for holding salt at table

sal·tine \sȯl-'tēn\ *n* **:** a thin crisp cracker sprinkled with salt

salt·ish \'sȯl-tish\ *adj* **:** somewhat salty

salt·pe·ter \'sȯlt-'pēt-ər\ *n* **:** a chemical salt found in the earth and used in explosives, in fertilizers, and in curing meat

salt·shak·er \-ˌshā-kər\ *n* : a container with a perforated top for sprinkling salt

salt·wa·ter \ˌsȯlt-ˌwȯt-ər, -ˌwät-\ *adj* : relating to, living in, or consisting of salt water

salty \ˈsȯl-tē\ *adj* **1** : of, seasoned with, or containing salt : tasting of or like salt **2** : smacking of the sea or nautical life **3 a** : PIQUANT **b** : EARTHY, RACY — **salt·i·ness** *n*

sa·lu·bri·ous \sə-ˈlü-brē-əs\ *adj* : favorable to or promoting health : HEALTHFUL — **sa·lu·bri·ous·ly** *adv* — **sa·lu·bri·ous·ness** *n* — **sa·lu·bri·ty** \-brət-ē\ *n*

sal·u·tary \ˈsal-yə-ˌter-ē\ *adj* **1** : promoting health : CURATIVE **2** : producing a beneficial effect

sal·u·ta·tion \ˌsal-yə-ˈtā-shən\ *n* **1** : an expression of greeting, goodwill, or courtesy by word, gesture, or ceremony **2** : the word or phrase of greeting (as *Gentlemen* or *Dear Sir*) that conventionally comes immediately before the body of a letter — **sal·u·ta·tion·al** \-shnəl, -shən-ᵊl\ *adj*

sa·lu·ta·to·ri·an \sə-ˌlüt-ə-ˈtōr-ē-ən\ *n* : the graduating student usu. second highest in rank who gives the salutatory oration

¹sa·lu·ta·to·ry \sə-ˈlüt-ə-ˌtōr-ē\ *adj* : expressing salutations or welcome

²salutatory *n, pl* **-ries** : a salutatory oration delivered at the commencement exercises of an educational institution

¹sa·lute \sə-ˈlüt\ *vb* **1** : to address with expressions of kind wishes, courtesy, or honor or with a sign of respect, courtesy, or goodwill : GREET **2 a** : to honor by a conventional military or naval ceremony **b** : to show respect and recognition to (a military superior) by assuming a prescribed position **c** : PRAISE — **sa·lut·er** *n*

²salute *n* **1** : GREETING, SALUTATION **2 a** : a sign, token, or ceremony (as a kiss or a bow) expressing goodwill, compliment, or respect **b** : the position of the hand or weapon or the entire attitude of a person saluting a superior

¹sal·vage \ˈsal-vij\ *n* **1** : money paid for saving a wrecked or endangered ship or its cargo or passengers **2 a** : the act of saving a ship **b** : the saving of possessions in danger of being lost **3** : something that is saved or recovered (as from a wreck or fire)

²salvage *vt* : to rescue or save esp. from wreckage or ruin — **sal·vage·a·ble** *adj* — **sal·vag·er** *n*

sal·va·tion \sal-ˈvā-shən\ *n* **1** : the saving of a person from the power and effects of sin **2** : the saving from danger or evil **3** : something that saves

¹salve \ˈsav, ˈsȧv\ *n* **1** : a healing ointment **2** : an influence or agency that remedies or soothes **3** : something (as praise or flattery) laid on like a salve

²salve *vt* : to ease or soothe with or as if with a salve

sal·ver \ˈsal-vər\ *n* : a tray esp. for serving food or beverages

sal·vo \ˈsal-vō\ *n, pl* **salvos** *or* **salvoes** **1** : a simultaneous discharge of two or more guns at the same target or as a salute **2** : a sudden burst (as of cheers)

sa·mar·i·tan \sə-ˈmar-ət-ᵊn, -ˈmer-\ *n, often cap* : one ready and generous in helping those in distress — **samaritan** *adj, often cap*

sa·mar·i·um \sə-ˈmer-ē-əm, -ˈmar-\ *n* : a pale gray lustrous metallic chemical element

sam·ba \ˈsam-bə, ˈsäm-\ *n* : a Brazilian dance characterized by a dip and spring upward with a bending of the knee at each beat of the music — **samba** *vi*

¹same \ˈsām\ *adj* **1 a** : resembling in every relevant respect **b** : conforming in every respect **2 a** : being one without addition, change, or discontinuance : IDENTICAL **b** : being the one under discussion or already referred to **3** : corresponding so closely as to be indistinguishable : COMPARABLE

²same *pron* **1** : something identical with or similar to another **2** : something previously defined or described

³same *adv* : in the same manner

same·ness \ˈsām-nəs\ *n* **1** : the quality or state of being the same : IDENTITY **2** : MONOTONY, UNIFORMITY

sam·ite \ˈsam-ˌīt, ˈsā-ˌmīt\ *n* : a rich medieval silk fabric interwoven with gold or silver

sam·o·var \ˈsam-ə-ˌvär\ *n* : an urn with a spigot at its base used esp. in Russia to boil water for tea

sam·pan \ˈsam-ˌpan\ *n* : a flat-bottomed Chinese skiff usu. propelled by two short oars

¹sam·ple \ˈsam-pəl\ *n* **1** : a representative part or a single item from a larger whole or group presented for inspection or shown as evidence of quality : SPECIMEN **2** : a part of a statistical population whose properties are studied to gain information about the whole

²sample *vt* **sam·pled**; **sam·pling** \-p(ə-)liŋ\ **1** : to take a sample of; *esp* : to judge the quality of by a sample : TEST **2** : to present a sample of

¹sam·pler \ˈsam-plər\ *n* : a decorative piece of needlework typically having letters or verses embroidered on it in various stitches as an example of skill

²sampler *n* **1** : one that collects or examines samples **2** : something containing representative specimens or selections

san·a·to·ri·um \ˌsan-ə-ˈtōr-ē-əm\ *n, pl* **-ri·ums** *or* **-ria** \-ē-ə\ : an establishment for the care and treatment esp. of convalescents or the chronically ill

sanc·ti·fy \ˈsaŋ(k)-ti-ˌfī\ *vt* **-fied**; **-fy·ing** **1** : to set apart as sacred : CONSECRATE **2** : to make free from sin : PURIFY **3** : to give moral or social sanction to — **sanc·ti·fi·ca·tion** \ˌsaŋ(k)-ti-fə-ˈkā-shən\ *n* — **sanc·ti·fi·er** *n*

sanc·ti·mo·ni·ous \ˌsaŋ(k)-tə-ˈmō-nē-əs\ *adj* : affecting piousness : hypocritically devout — **sanc·ti·mo·ni·ous·ly** *adv* — **sanc·ti·mo·ni·ous·ness** *n*

sanc·ti·mo·ny \ˈsaŋ(k)-tə-ˌmō-nē\ *n* : assumed or hypocritical holiness

¹sanc·tion \ˈsaŋ(k)-shən\ *n* : explicit or official permission or ratification : APPROBATION

²sanction *vt* **sanc·tioned**; **sanc·tion·ing** \-sh(ə-)niŋ\ **1** : RATIFY, VALIDATE **2** : to give effective approval or consent to : PERMIT

sanc·ti·ty \ˈsaŋ(k)-tət-ē\ *n, pl* **-tities** **1** : HOLINESS, GODLINESS **2 a** : INVIOLABILITY, SACREDNESS **b** *pl* : sacred objects, obligations, or rights

sanc·tu·ary \ˈsaŋ(k)-chə-ˌwer-ē\ *n, pl* **-ar·ies** **1** : a holy or sacred place **2** : a building or room for religious worship **3** : the most sacred part (as near the altar) of a place of worship **4** : a refuge for wildlife where predators are controlled and hunting is illegal **5 a** : a place of refuge and protection **b** : safety or protection afforded by a sanctuary

sanc·tum \ˈsaŋ(k)-təm\ *n, pl* **sanctums** **1** : a sacred place **2** : a study, office, or place where one is free from intrusion

¹sand \ˈsand\ *n* **1 a** : a loose granular material resulting from the disintegration of rocks **b** : soil containing 85 percent or more of sand and a maximum of 10 percent of clay **2** : a tract, region, or deposit of sand : BEACH — often used in pl. **3** : firm resolution : COURAGE, BOLDNESS

²sand *vt* **1** : to sprinkle with sand **2** : to add sand to **3** : to smooth by grinding or rubbing esp. with sandpaper

san·dal \ˈsan-dᵊl\ *n* **1** : a shoe consisting of a sole strapped to the foot **2** : a low-cut shoe that fastens by an ankle strap **3** : a strap to hold on a slipper or low shoe **4** : a rubber overshoe cut very low — **san·daled** *or* **san·dalled** \-dᵊld\ *adj*

sand·bank \ˈsan(d)-ˌbaŋk\ *n* : a deposit of sand in a mound, hillside, bar, or shoal

sand·bar \-ˌbär\ *n* : a ridge of sand formed in water by tides or currents

¹sand·blast \-ˌblast\ *n* : a stream of sand projected by air or steam for engraving, cutting, or cleaning glass or stone or for removing scale from metals

²sandblast *vt* : to engrave, cut, or clean with a high-velocity stream of sand — **sand·blast·er** *n*

sand·hog \'sand-,hȯg, -,häg\ *n* : a laborer who works in a caisson in driving underwater tunnels

sand·man \'san(d)-,man\ *n* : the genie of folklore who makes children sleepy supposedly by sprinkling sand in their eyes

[1]**sand·pa·per** \-,pā-pər\ *n* : paper covered on one side with abrasive material (as sand) glued fast and used for smoothing and polishing

[2]**sandpaper** *vt* : to rub with sandpaper

sand·pip·er \-,pī-pər\ *n* : any of numerous small shorebirds distinguished from the related plovers chiefly by the longer and soft-tipped bill

sand·stone \'san(d)-,stōn\ *n* : a sedimentary rock consisting of usu. quartz sand united by a natural cement

[1]**sand·wich** \'san-,(d)wich\ *n* **1** : two or more slices of bread with a filling (as of meat, cheese, or savory mixture) spread between them **2** : something resembling a sandwich

[2]**sandwich** *vt* **1** : to insert between two or more things **2** : to make a place for : CROWD

sandy \'san-dē\ *adj* : consisting of, containing, or sprinkled with sand

sane \'sān\ *adj* : mentally sound and healthy; *also* : RATIONAL, SENSIBLE — **sane·ly** *adv* — **sane·ness** *n*

sang *past of* SING

sang·froid \'säⁿ-'frwä\ *n* : self-possession or imperturbability esp. under strain

san·gui·nary \'saŋ-gwə-,ner-ē\ *adj* **1** : BLOODTHIRSTY, MURDEROUS **2** : attended by bloodshed : BLOODY

san·guine \'saŋ-gwən\ *adj* **1 a** : BLOODRED **b** : RUDDY **2** : SANGUINARY 1 **3** : having a bodily conformation and temperament marked by sturdiness, high color, and cheerfulness **4** : CONFIDENT, OPTIMISTIC — **san·guine·ly** *adv*

san·guin·e·ous \san-'gwin-ē-əs\ *adj* **1** : BLOODRED **2** : of, relating to, or involving bloodshed : BLOODTHIRSTY

san·i·tar·i·um \,san-ə-'ter-ē-əm\ *n*, *pl* **-i·ums** *or* **-ia** \-ē-ə\ : SANATORIUM

san·i·tary \'san-ə-,ter-ē\ *adj* **1** : of or relating to health : HYGIENIC **2** : free from filth, infection, or dangers to health — **san·i·tar·i·ly** \,san-ə-'ter-ə-lē\ *adv*

san·i·ta·tion \,san-ə-'tā-shən\ *n* **1** : the act or process of making sanitary **2** : the promotion of hygiene and prevention of disease by maintenance of sanitary conditions

san·i·ty \'san-ət-ē\ *n* : the quality or state of being sane

sank *past of* SINK

sans \(,)sanz\ *prep* : WITHOUT

San·ta Claus \'sant-ə-,klȯz, 'sant-ē-\ *n* : the gift-giving and holiday spirit of Christmas personified as a fat, jolly old man in a red suit who distributes toys to children at Christmas

[1]**sap** \'sap\ *n* **1** : the fluid part of a plant; *esp* : a watery solution that circulates through a vascular plant **2** : VITALITY **3** : a foolish gullible person

[2]**sap** *n* : a trench built out to a point beneath an enemy's fortifications

[3]**sap** *vt* **sapped**; **sap·ping** **1 a** : to attack, pierce, or undermine by a sap **b** : to destroy by undermining **2** : to weaken gradually

sap·head \'sap-,hed\ *n* : a weak-minded or foolish person : SAP — **sap·head·ed** \-'hed-əd\ *adj*

sa·pi·ence \'sā-pē-ən(t)s, 'sap-ē-\ *n* : WISDOM, SAGENESS

sa·pi·ent \'sā-pē-ənt, 'sap-ē-\ *adj* : WISE, DISCERNING — **sa·pi·ent·ly** *adv*

sap·ling \'sap-liŋ\ *n* : a young tree usu. not over four inches in diameter at breast height

sa·por \'sā-pər\ *n* : the property of something that stimulates the sense of taste : FLAVOR — **sa·por·ous** \-pə-rəs\ *adj*

sap·phire \'saf-,ī(ə)r\ *n* : a hard transparent bright blue precious stone — **sapphire** *adj*

sap·py \'sap-ē\ *adj* **1** : abounding with sap **2** : containing much sapwood **3 a** : foolishly sentimental : MAWKISH **b** : lacking in good sense : SILLY — **sap·pi·ness** *n*

sap·wood \'sap-,wu̇d\ *n* : the younger softer physiologically active outer portion of wood that is more permeable, less durable, and usu. lighter in color than the heartwood

sar·casm \'sär-,kaz-əm\ *n* **1** : a cutting remark : a bitter rebuke **2** : the use of sharp, stinging remarks expressing contempt and often made in the form of irony

sar·cas·tic \sär-'kas-tik\ *adj* **1** : having the habit of sarcasm **2** : containing sarcasm — **sar·cas·ti·cal·ly** \-ti-k(ə-)lē\ *adv*

sar·coph·a·gus \sär-'käf-ə-gəs\ *n*, *pl* **-gi** \-,gī, -,jī\ *or* **-gus·es** : a stone coffin; *esp* : one exposed to view in the open air or in a tomb

sar·dine \sär-'dēn\ *n*, *pl* **sardines** : any of several small or immature fishes of the herring family; *esp* : the young of the European pilchard when of a size suitable for preserving for food

sar·don·ic \sär-'dän-ik\ *adj* : bitterly scornful : MOCKING, SNEERING — **sar·don·i·cal·ly** \-'dän-i-k(ə-)lē\ *adv*

sar·sa·pa·ril·la \,sas-(ə-)pə-'ril-ə, ,särs-\ *n* **1 a** : any of various tropical American smilaxes **b** : the dried roots of a sarsaparilla plant used esp. as a flavoring **2** : a sweetened carbonated beverage flavored chiefly with birch oil and sassafras

sar·to·ri·al \sär-'tōr-ē-əl\ *adj* : of or relating to a tailor or tailored clothes and esp. men's clothes — **sar·to·ri·al·ly** \-ē-ə-lē\ *adv*

[1]**sash** \'sash\ *n* : a broad band (as of silk) worn around the waist or over the shoulder

[2]**sash** *n*, *pl* **sash** *or* **sash·es** : the framework in which panes of glass are set in a window or door; *also* : the movable part of a window

sa·shay \sa-'shā, sī-\ *vi* **1** : to strut or move about in an ostentatious manner **2** : to proceed diagonally or sideways

[1]**sass** \'sas\ *n* : impudent speech

[2]**sass** *vt* : to talk impudently or disrespectfully to

sas·sa·fras \'sas-(ə-),fras\ *n* : a tall eastern No. American tree of the laurel family with mucilaginous twigs and leaves; *also* : its dried root bark used esp. in medicine or as flavoring

sassy \'sas-ē\ *adj* : SAUCY, IMPUDENT

sat *past of* SIT

Sa·tan \'sāt-ᵊn\ *n* : DEVIL 1 — **sa·tan·ic** \sə-'tan-ik, sā-\ *adj* — **sa·tan·i·cal·ly** \-'tan-i-k(ə-)lē\ *adv*

satch·el \'sach-əl\ *n* : a small bag of leather or heavy cloth for carrying clothes or books

sate \'sāt\ *vt* **1** : to cloy with overabundance : GLUT **2** : to appease (as a thirst or violent emotion) by indulging to the full

sa·teen \sa-'tēn\ *n* : a cotton fabric finished with a glossy surface to resemble satin

sat·el·lite \'sat-ᵊl-,īt\ *n* **1** : an obsequious follower or dependent **2 a** : a celestial body orbiting another of larger size **b** : a man-made object or vehicle intended to orbit the earth, the moon, or another celestial body — **satellite** *adj*

sa·tia·ble \'sā-shə-bəl\ *adj* : capable of being appeased or satisfied

[1]**sa·tiate** \'sā-sh(ē-)ət\ *adj* : SATIATED

[2]**sa·ti·ate** \'sā-shē-,āt\ *vt* **1** : to satisfy fully **2** : GLUT, SURFEIT — **sa·ti·a·tion** \,sā-s(h)ē-'ā-shən\ *n*

sa·ti·e·ty \sə-'tī-ət-ē\ *n* **1** : FULLNESS, REPLETION **2** : the revulsion or disgust of overindulgence or excess

sat·in \'sat-ᵊn\ *n* : a fabric (as of silk) with smooth lustrous face and dull back — **satin** *adj*

sat·in·et *or* **sat·in·ette** \,sat-ᵊn-'et\ *n* : a usu. thin silk satin

sat·in·wood \'sat-ᵊn-,wu̇d\ *n* **1** : a hard yellowish brown wood with a satiny luster **2** : a tree yielding satinwood

sat·iny \'sat-ᵊn-ē\ *adj* : having the soft lustrous smoothness of satin : resembling satin

sat·ire \'sa-,tī(ə)r\ *n* **1** : a literary work holding up human vices and follies to ridicule or scorn **2** : biting wit, irony, or sarcasm used to expose and discredit vice or folly — **sa·tir·ic** \sə-'tir-ik\ *or* **sa·tir·i·cal** \-'tir-i-kəl\ *adj* — **sa·tir·i·cal·ly** \-i-k(ə-)lē\ *adv*

sat·i·rist \'sat-ə-rəst\ *n* : one (as a writer) that satirizes

sat·i·rize \-,rīz\ *vb* **1** : to utter or write satires **2** : to censure or ridicule by means of satire

sat·is·fac·tion \,sat-əs-'fak-shən\ *n* **1** : the payment through penance of the temporal punishment incurred by a sin **2 a** : fulfillment of a need or want **b** : the quality or state of being satisfied : CONTENTMENT **c** : a cause or means of enjoyment : GRATIFICATION **3** : compensation for a loss or injury : RESTITUTION **4** : convinced assurance or certainty

sat·is·fac·to·ry \,sat-əs-'fak-t(ə-)rē\ *adj* : sufficient or adequate to satisfy : meeting what is asked or demanded — **sat·is·fac·to·ri·ly** \-t(ə-)rə-lē\ *adv* — **sat·is·fac·to·ri·ness** \-t(ə-)rē-nəs\ *n*

sat·is·fy \'sat-əs-,fī\ *vb* **-fied; -fy·ing** **1 a** : to carry out the terms of (as a contract) : DISCHARGE **b** : to meet a financial obligation to : PAY **2** : INDEMNIFY **3 a** : to make happy : PLEASE **b** : to gratify to the full : APPEASE **4 a** : CONVINCE **b** : to put an end to : DISPEL **5 a** : FULFILL, MEET **b** : to make true by fulfilling a condition — **sat·is·fy·ing·ly** *adv*

sa·trap \'sā-,trap, 'sa-\ *n* : a subordinate ruler; *esp* : a petty tyrant

sa·tra·py \'sā-trə-pē, 'sa-, -,trap-ē\ *n, pl* **-pies** : the territory or jurisdiction of a satrap

sat·u·ra·ble \'sach-(ə-)rə-bəl\ *adj* : capable of saturation — **sat·u·ra·bil·i·ty** \,sach-(ə-)rə-'bil-ət-ē\ *n*

sat·u·rate \'sach-ə-,rāt\ *vt* **1** : to treat, furnish, or charge with something to the point where no more can be absorbed, dissolved, or retained **2 a** : to infuse thoroughly or cause to be pervaded : STEEP **b** : to fill completely : IMBUE — **sat·u·ra·tor** \-,rāt-ər\ *n*

sat·u·ra·tion \,sach-ə-'rā-shən\ *n* : the act of saturating : the state of being saturated

Sat·ur·day \'sat-ərd-ē\ *n* : the 7th day of the week

sat·ur·na·lia \,sat-ər-'nāl-yə\ *n sing or pl* : an unrestrained often licentious celebration — **sat·ur·na·lian** \-yən\ *adj*

sat·ur·nine \'sat-ər-,nīn\ *adj* : having a sullen or sardonic aspect : GLOOMY, GRAVE — **sat·ur·nine·ly** *adv*

sa·tyr \'sāt-ər, 'sat-\ *n* **1** : a forest god in Greek mythology often represented as having ears and tail of a horse or goat and given to boisterous pleasures **2** : a man of lustful or lecherous habits

[1]**sauce** \'sȯs, *4 is usu* 'sas\ *n* **1** : a condiment or relish for food; *esp* : a fluid or semisolid accompaniment of food : DRESSING **2** : something that adds zest or piquancy **3** : stewed or canned fruit eaten with other food or as a dessert **4** : SASS

[2]**sauce** \'sȯs, *2 usu* 'sas\ *vt* **1** : to give zest or piquancy to **2** : to be rude or impudent to

sauce·pan \'sȯs-,pan\ *n* : a small deep cooking pan with a handle

sau·cer \'sȯ-sər\ *n* **1** : a small round shallow dish in which a cup is set at table **2** : something like a saucer esp. in shape

saucy \'sas-ē *also* 'sȯs-ē\ *adj* **1** : BOLD, IMPUDENT **2** : IRREPRESSIBLE, PERT **3** : SMART, TRIM — **sauc·i·ly** \-ə-lē\ *adv* — **sauc·i·ness** \-ē-nəs\ *n*

sau·er·kraut \'sau̇(-ə)r-,krau̇t\ *n* : finely cut cabbage fermented in brine

saun·ter \'sȯnt-ər, 'sänt-\ *vi* : to walk along in an idle or leisurely manner : STROLL — **saunter** *n* — **saun·ter·er** *n*

sau·sage \'sȯ-sij\ *n* : highly seasoned minced meat (as pork) usu. stuffed in casings; *also* : a roll of such meat in a casing

[1]**sau·té** \sȯ-'tā, sō-\ *n* : a sautéed dish — **sauté** *adj*

[2]**sauté** *vt* **sau·téed** *or* **sau·téd**; **sau·té·ing** : to fry in shallow fat

sau·terne \sō-'tərn, sȯ-, -'te(ə)rn\ *n* : a semisweet golden-colored table wine

[1]**sav·age** \'sav-ij\ *adj* **1 a** : not domesticated or not under human control **b** : FERAL, WILD **2** : CRUEL, FEROCIOUS **3 a** : PRIMITIVE **b** : UNCIVILIZED, RUDE — **sav·age·ly** *adv* — **sav·age·ness** *n*

[2]**savage** *n* **1** : a person belonging to a primitive society **2** : a brutal person **3** : a rude or unmannerly person

[3]**savage** *vt* : to attack or treat violently or brutally

sav·age·ry \'sav-ij-(ə-)rē\ *n, pl* **-ries** **1** : savage disposition or action : CRUELTY **2** : the state or condition of being savage

sa·vant \sa-'vänt, -'vä^n; 'sav-ənt\ *n* : a man of learning : SCHOLAR

[1]**save** \'sāv\ *vb* **1 a** : to deliver from sin **b** : to rescue or deliver from danger or harm **c** : to preserve or guard from injury, destruction, or loss **2** : to put away as a store or reserve : ACCUMULATE **3 a** : to make unnecessary : AVOID **b** : to prevent an opponent from scoring or winning **4** : MAINTAIN, PRESERVE **5 a** : to put by money **b** : ECONOMIZE — **sav·a·ble** *or* **save·a·ble** *adj* — **sav·er** *n*

[2]**save** *n* : a play that prevents an opponent from scoring or winning; *also* : a game that has been saved

[3]**save** \(,)sāv\ *prep* : EXCEPT

[4]**save** \(,)sāv\ *conj* **1** : [1]BUT 2b **2** : UNLESS

[1]**sav·ing** \'sā-viŋ\ *n* **1** : the act of rescuing **2 a** : something saved **b** *pl* : money saved over a period of time

[2]**saving** *adj* **1** : ECONOMICAL, THRIFTY **2** : making up for something : COMPENSATING

[3]**saving** *prep* **1** : EXCEPT, SAVE **2** : without disrespect to

[4]**saving** *conj* : EXCEPT, SAVE

sav·ior *or* **sav·iour** \'sāv-yər\ *n* **1** : one that saves from danger or destruction **2** *cap* : one who brings salvation; *esp* : JESUS

sa·voir faire \,sav-,wär-'fa(ə)r\ *n* : ability to do or say the right or graceful thing : TACT

[1]**sa·vor** \'sā-vər\ *n* **1** : the taste and odor of something **2** : a distinctive quality : SMACK — **sa·vor·less** \-ləs\ *adj*

[2]**savor** *vb* **sa·vored**; **sa·vor·ing** \'sāv-(ə-)riŋ\ **1** : to have a specified smell or quality : SMACK **2** : to give flavor to : SEASON **3 a** : to have experience of : TASTE **b** : to taste or smell with pleasure : RELISH **c** : to delight in : ENJOY — **sa·vor·er** *n*

sa·vory \'sāv-(ə-)rē\ *adj* : pleasing to the taste or smell : APPETIZING — **sa·vor·i·ness** *n*

[1]**saw** *past of* SEE

[2]**saw** \'sȯ\ *n* **1** : a hand or power tool used to cut hard material (as wood, metal, or bone) and made of a toothed blade or disk **2** : a machine mounting a saw

[3]**saw** *vb* **sawed** \'sȯd\; **sawed** *or* **sawn** \'sȯn\; **saw·ing** **1** : to cut or form by cutting with a saw **2** : to slice as though with a saw **3** : to make motions as though using a saw — **saw·er** \'sȯ(-ə)r\ *n*

[4]**saw** *n* : a common saying : PROVERB

saw·buck \'sȯ-,bək\ *n* : SAWHORSE

saw·dust \'sȯ-(,)dəst\ *n* : dust or fine particles of wood made by a saw in cutting

sawed–off \'sȯd-'ȯf\ *adj* **1** : having an end sawed off **2** : being of less than average height

saw·horse \'sȯ-,hȯrs\ *n* : a frame or rack on which wood is rested while being sawed by hand

saw·mill \-,mil\ *n* : a mill or machine for sawing logs

saw·yer \'sȯ-yər\ *n* : one that saws something and esp. timber

sax·o·phone \'sak-sə-,fōn\ *n* : a wind instrument with reed mouthpiece, curved conical metal tube, and finger keys — **sax·o·phon·ist** \-,fō-nəst\ *n*

[1]**say** \'sā\ *vt* **said** \'sed\; **say·ing** \'sā-iŋ\; **says** \'sez\ **1 a** : to express in words : STATE **b** : to state as opinion or belief : DECLARE **2 a** : UTTER, PRONOUNCE **b** : RECITE, REPEAT **3** : INDICATE, SHOW — **say·er** \'sā-ər\ *n*

[2]**say** *n* **1** : an expression of opinion **2** : the power to decide or help decide

[3]**say** *adv* **1** : ABOUT, APPROXIMATELY **2** : for example : AS

say·able \'sā-ə-bəl\ *adj* **1** : capable of being said **2** : capable of being spoken effectively or easily

say·ing \'sā-iŋ\ *n* : something frequently said : PROVERB, SAW

say–so \'sā-ˌsō\ *n* **1 a** : one's bare word or assurance **b** : an authoritative pronouncement **2** : a right of final decision

¹scab \'skab\ *n* **1** : a disease of plants or animals characterized by crusted lesions **2** : a crust of hardened blood and serum over a wound **3 a** : a contemptible person **b** : a worker who replaces a union worker during a strike

²scab *vi* **scabbed**; **scab·bing** **1** : to become covered with a scab **2** : to act as a scab

scab·bard \'skab-ərd\ *n* : a sheath for a sword, dagger, or bayonet — **scabbard** *vt*

scab·by \'skab-ē\ *adj* **1 a** : covered with or full of scabs **b** : diseased with scab **2** : MEAN, CONTEMPTIBLE

scad \'skad\ *n* **1** : a large number or quantity **2** *pl* : a great abundance

scaf·fold \'skaf-əld, -ˌōld\ *n* **1 a** : a temporary or movable platform for workmen (as bricklayers, painters, or miners) **b** : a platform on which a criminal is executed (as by hanging or beheading) **c** : a platform at a height above ground or floor level **2** : a supporting framework

scaf·fold·ing \-əl-diŋ, -ˌōl-\ *n* : a system of scaffolds; *also* : materials for scaffolds

scal·a·ble \'skā-lə-bəl\ *adj* : capable of being scaled

scal·a·wag \'skal-i-ˌwag\ *n* : SCAMP, REPROBATE

¹scald \'skòld\ *vb* **1** : to burn with or as if with hot liquid or steam **2 a** : to subject to the action of boiling water or steam **b** : to bring to a temperature just below the boiling point **3** : SCORCH

²scald *n* **1** : an injury to the body caused by scalding **2** : an act or process of scalding

¹scale \'skāl\ *n* **1 a** : either pan of a weighing device **b** : BALANCE — usu. used in pl. **2** : a device for weighing

²scale *vb* **1** : to weigh in scales **2** : to have a specified weight

³scale *n* **1** : one of the small rigid flattened plates forming an outer covering on the body esp. of a fish or reptile **2** : a small thin part or structure suggesting a fish scale **3** : SCALE INSECT **4** : a thin layer, coating, or incrustation forming esp. on metal (as iron) — **scaled** \'skāld\ *adj* — **scale·less** \'skāl-ləs\ *adj* — **scale·like** *adj*

⁴scale *vb* **1** : to remove scale or the scales from **2** : to take off in scales or thin layers **3** : to form scale on **4** : to come off in or shed scales : FLAKE **5** : to become encrusted with scale **6** : to throw (a flat object) so as to sail in air or skip on water

⁵scale *n* **1** : something graduated esp. when used as a measure or rule **2** : a basis for a system of numbering **3** : a graduated series **4** : the size of a picture, plan, or model of a thing in proportion to the size of the thing itself **5** : a relative size or degree **6** : a standard by which something can be measured or judged **7** : a graduated series of tones going up or down in pitch according to a specified scheme of intervals

⁶scale *vb* **1** : to climb by or as if by means of a ladder : SURMOUNT **2 a** : to arrange in a graduated series **b** : to measure by or as if by a scale **c** : to make, regulate, or estimate according to a rate or standard

scale insect *n* : any of numerous small insects that live on plants and have scale-covered females

scal·lion \'skal-yən\ *n* : an onion without an enlarged bulb

¹scal·lop \'skäl-əp, 'skal-\ *n* **1 a** : any of a family of marine bivalve mollusks with the shell radially ribbed **b** : a large edible muscle of a scallop **2** : one of a continuous series of circle segments or angular projections forming a border

²scallop *vt* **1** : to bake in a sauce usu. covered with seasoned bread or cracker crumbs **2 a** : to shape, cut, or finish in scallops **b** : to form scallops in — **scal·lop·er** *n*

¹scalp \'skalp\ *n* : the part of the skin and flesh of the head usu. covered with hair

²scalp *vb* **1 a** : to deprive of the scalp **b** : to remove an upper or better part from **2** : to obtain speculatively and resell at greatly increased prices — **scalp·er** *n*

scal·pel \'skal-pəl, skal-'pel\ *n* : a small straight thin-bladed knife used esp. in surgery

scaly \'skā-lē\ *adj* **1 a** : covered with, composed of, or rich in scale or scales **b** : FLAKY **2** : DESPICABLE, POOR **3** : infested with scale insects — **scal·i·ness** *n*

¹scamp \'skamp\ *n* **1** : RASCAL, ROGUE **2** : an impish or playful young person

²scamp *vt* : to perform in a hasty, neglectful, or imperfect manner : SKIMP

scam·per \'skam-pər\ *vi* **scam·pered**; **scam·per·ing** \-p(ə-)riŋ\ : to run nimbly and playfully about — **scamper** *n*

scam·pi \'skam-pē\ *n, pl* **scampi** : SHRIMP; *esp* : large shrimp prepared with a garlic-flavored sauce

scan \'skan\ *vb* **scanned**; **scan·ning** **1 a** : to read or mark verses so as to show metrical structure **b** : to conform to a metrical pattern **2 a** : to examine intensively **b** : to make a wide sweeping search of **c** : to look through or over hastily — **scan** *n*

scan·dal \'skan-dᵊl\ *n* **1** : DISGRACE, DISHONOR **2** : malicious or defamatory gossip

scan·dal·ize \'skan-də-ˌlīz\ *vt* **1** : to speak falsely or maliciously of : MALIGN **2** : to offend the moral sense of : SHOCK — **scan·dal·iz·er** *n*

scan·dal·mon·ger \'skan-dᵊl-ˌməŋ-gər, -ˌmäŋ-\ *n* : a person who spreads scandal

scan·dal·ous \'skan-d(ə-)ləs\ *adj* **1** : DEFAMATORY, LIBELOUS **2** : offensive to propriety or morality : SHOCKING — **scan·dal·ous·ly** *adv*

scan·di·um \'skan-dē-əm\ *n* : a white metallic chemical element

scan·sion \'skan-chən\ *n* : the analysis of verse to show its meter

¹scant \'skant\ *adj* **1 a** : barely or scarcely sufficient; *esp* : not quite coming up to a stated measure **b** : lacking in amplitude or quantity : MEAGER, SCANTY **2** : having a small or insufficient supply — **scant·ly** *adv*

²scant *vt* **1** : to provide with a meager or inadequate portion or allowance : STINT **2** : to make small, narrow, or meager : SKIMP **3** : to provide an incomplete supply of : WITHHOLD **4** : to give scant attention to : SLIGHT

scant·ling \'skant-liŋ, -lən\ *n* : a small piece of lumber; *esp* : one of the upright pieces in the frame of a house

scanty \'skant-ē\ *adj* **1** : barely enough : lacking size or extent **2** : less than is needed : INSUFFICIENT — **scant·i·ly** \'skant-ᵊl-ē\ *adv* — **scant·i·ness** \'skant-ē-nəs\ *n*

scape·goat \'skāp-ˌgōt\ *n* : a person or thing bearing the blame for others

scape·grace \-ˌgrās\ *n* : an incorrigible rascal

¹scar \'skär\ *n* **1** : a mark remaining after injured tissue has healed **2** : a lasting moral or emotional injury — **scar·less** \-ləs\ *adj*

²scar *vb* **scarred**; **scar·ring** **1** : to mark with or form a scar **2** : to do lasting injury to **3** : to become scarred

scar·ab \'skar-əb\ *n* **1** : a large black or nearly black beetle **2** : an ornament or a gem made to represent a scarab

¹scarce \'skers, 'skars\ *adj* **1** : deficient in quantity or number : not plentiful or abundant **2** : not provided in sufficient abundance to be free : UNCOMMON, RARE — **scarce·ly** *adv*

²scarce *adv* : SCARCELY, HARDLY

scar·ci·ty \'sker-sət-ē, 'skar-\ *n, pl* **-ties** : the quality or condition of being scarce : a very small supply

¹scare \'ske(ə)r, 'ska(ə)r\ *vb* **1** : to frighten suddenly : ALARM **2** : to become scared

²scare *n* **1** : a sudden fright **2** : a widespread state of alarm

scare·crow \'ske(ə)r-ˌkrō, 'ska(ə)r-\ *n* **1 a** : an object usu.

suggesting a human figure that is set up to scare birds away from crops **b** : something frightening but harmless **2** : a skinny or ragged person

scarf \'skärf\ *n, pl* **scarves** \'skärvz\ *or* **scarfs** \'skärfs\ : a broad band (as of cloth) worn about the shoulders, around the neck, over the head, or about the waist

scar·i·fy \'skar-ə-,fī\ *vt* **-fied; -fy·ing** **1** : to make scratches or small cuts in : wound superficially **2** : to lacerate the feelings of : FLAY — **scar·i·fi·ca·tion** \,skar-ə-fə-'kā-shən\ *n*

scar·la·ti·na \,skär-lə-'tē-nə\ *n* : a usu. mild scarlet fever — **scar·la·ti·nal** \-'tēn-ᵊl\ *adj*

¹scar·let \'skär-lət\ *n* **1** : scarlet cloth or clothes **2** : a bright red

²scarlet *adj* : of the color scarlet

scarlet fever *n* : an acute contagious disease caused by a streptococcus and marked by fever, inflammation of the nose, throat, and mouth, toxemia, and a red rash

scary \'ske(ə)r-ē, 'ska(ə)r-\ *adj* **1** : causing fright : ALARMING **2** : easily scared : TIMID **3** : SCARED, FRIGHTENED

scat \'skat\ *n* : jazz singing with nonsense syllables

¹scathe \'skāth\ *n* : HARM, INJURY — **scathe·less** \-ləs\ *adj*

²scathe *vt* **1** : to do harm to : INJURE; *esp* : SCORCH, SEAR **2** : to assail with withering denunciation

scath·ing \'skā-thiŋ\ *adj* : bitterly severe — **scath·ing·ly** *adv*

scat·ter \'skat-ər\ *vb* **1** : to cause to separate widely **2** : to distribute irregularly **3** : to sow broadcast : STREW **4** : to separate from each other and go in various directions **5** : to occur or fall irregularly or at random — **scat·ter·er** *n*

scat·ter·brain \-,brān\ *n* : a giddy heedless person incapable of concentration — **scat·ter·brained** \-,brānd\ *adj*

¹scat·ter·ing \-ər-iŋ\ *n* **1** : an act or process in which something scatters or is scattered **2** : something scattered; *esp* : a small number or quantity interspersed here and there

²scattering *adj* **1** : going in various directions **2** : found or placed far apart and in no order — **scat·ter·ing·ly** *adv*

scav·enge \'skav-inj\ *vb* **1** : to remove dirt or refuse from an area **2** : to salvage usable material from what has been discarded

scav·en·ger \'skav-ən-jər\ *n* **1** : one that scavenges **2** : an organism that feeds habitually on refuse or carrion

sce·nar·io \sə-'nar-ē-,ō\ *n, pl* **-i·os** **1 a** : an outline or synopsis of a play **b** : the libretto of an opera **2** : the story or the plot of a motion picture

sce·nar·ist \-'nar-əst\ *n* : a writer of scenarios

scene \'sēn\ *n* **1** : one of the subdivisions of a play: as **a** : a division of an act presenting continuous action in one place **b** : a single situation or unit of dialogue in a play **c** : a motion picture or television episode or sequence **2 a** : a stage setting **b** : a view or sight having pictorial quality **3** : the place of an occurrence or action : LOCALE **4** : an exhibition of anger or indecorous behavior — **behind the scenes** **1** : out of public view : in secret **2** : in a position to see or control the hidden workings

scen·ery \'sēn-(ə-)rē\ *n* **1** : the painted scenes or hangings and accessories used on a theater stage **2** : a picturesque view or landscape

scene·shift·er \'sēn-,shif-tər\ *n* : a worker who moves the scenes in a theater

sce·nic \'sē-nik\ *adj* **1** : of or relating to the stage, a stage setting, or stage representation **2** : of or relating to natural scenery **3** : representing graphically an action, event, or episode

¹scent \'sent\ *vb* **1 a** : SMELL **b** : to get or have an inkling of **2** : to imbue or fill with odor

²scent *n* **1 a** : an odor left by an animal on a surface passed over; *also* : a course of pursuit or discovery **b** : a characteristic or particular and usu. agreeable odor **2 a** : sense of smell **b** : power of detection : NOSE **3** : INKLING, INTIMATION **4** : PERFUME 2

scent·ed \'sent-əd\ *adj* : having scent; *esp* : PERFUMED

scent·less \'sent-ləs\ *adj* : lacking scent; *esp* : ODORLESS

scep·ter \'sep-tər\ *n* : a staff or baton borne by a sovereign as an emblem of authority

¹sched·ule \'skej-ül, -əl, *Canad also* 'shej-, *Brit usu* 'shed-yül\ *n* **1 a** : a written or printed list, catalog, or inventory **b** : TIMETABLE **2** : PROGRAM, AGENDA

²schedule *vt* **1** : to place in or as if in a schedule **2** : to make a schedule of

sche·mat·ic \ski-'mat-ik\ *adj* : of, relating to, or forming a scheme, plan, or diagram : DIAGRAMMATIC — **schematic** *n* — **sche·mat·i·cal·ly** \-'mat-i-k(ə-)lē\ *adv*

sche·ma·tize \'skē-mə-,tīz\ *vt* : to form or form into a scheme or systematic arrangement

¹scheme \'skēm\ *n* **1** : a graphic sketch or outline **2** : a concise statement or table : EPITOME **3** : a plan or program of action; *esp* : a crafty or secret one **4** : a systematic or organized design

²scheme *vb* **1** : to form a scheme for **2** : to form plans; *also* : to engage in intrigue : PLOT — **schem·er** *n*

schem·ing \'skē-miŋ\ *adj* : given to forming schemes; *esp* : shrewdly devious and intriguing

schism \'siz-əm, 'skiz-\ *n* **1** : DIVISION, SEPARATION; *also* : lack of harmony : DISCORD **2 a** : formal division in or separation from a church or religious body **b** : the offense of promoting schism

¹schis·mat·ic \s(k)iz-'mat-ik\ *n* : one who takes part in schism

²schismatic *adj* : of, relating to, or guilty of schism

schiz·o·phre·nia \,skit-sə-'frē-nē-ə\ *n* : a mental disorder marked by loss of contact with environment and by personality disintegration — **schiz·o·phren·ic** \-'fren-ik\ *adj or n*

schol·ar \'skäl-ər\ *n* **1** : one who attends a school or studies under a teacher : PUPIL **2 a** : one who has done advanced study in a special field **b** : a learned person **3** : a holder of a scholarship

schol·ar·ly \-ər-lē\ *adj* : characteristic of or suitable to learned persons : LEARNED, ACADEMIC

schol·ar·ship \-ər-,ship\ *n* **1** : money given to a student to help him pay for his education **2** : the character, qualities, or attainments of a scholar : LEARNING

scho·las·tic \skə-'las-tik\ *adj* **1** : excessively subtle : PEDANTIC **2** : of or relating to schools or scholars — **scho·las·ti·cal·ly** \-ti-k(ə-)lē\ *adv*

¹school \'skül\ *n* **1 a** : a place or establishment for teaching and learning; *also* : SCHOOLHOUSE **b** : the students or students and teachers of a school **c** : a session of school **2** : persons holding the same opinions and beliefs or accepting the same intellectual methods or leadership **3** : a faculty or division within an institution of higher learning devoted to teaching, study, and research in a particular field of knowledge

²school *vt* : TEACH, TRAIN; *esp* : to drill in or habituate to something

³school *n* : a large number of aquatic animals of one kind (as bass) swimming together

school·bag \'skül-,bag\ *n* : a bag for carrying schoolbooks and school supplies

school·book \'skül-,bu̇k\ *n* : a school textbook

school·house \-,hau̇s\ *n* : a building used as a school

school·ing \'skü-liŋ\ *n* **1** : instruction in school : EDUCATION **2** : the training of an animal and esp. a horse to service

school·mas·ter \'skül-,mas-tər\ *n* : a male schoolteacher

school·mate \-,māt\ *n* : a school companion

school·mis·tress \-,mis-trəs\ *n* : a woman schoolteacher

school·room \-,rüm, -,ru̇m\ *n* : CLASSROOM

school·teach·er \-,tē-chər\ *n* : a person who teaches in a school

school·work \\-ˌwərk\\ *n* : lessons done in classes at school or assigned to be done at home

school·yard \\-ˌyärd\\ *n* : the playground of a school

schoo·ner \\ˈskü-nər\\ *n* **1** : a fore-and-aft rigged ship with two or more masts **2** : a large tall glass (as for beer)

schwa \\ˈshwä\\ *n* : an unstressed vowel that is the usual sound of the first and last vowels of the English word *America*

sci·at·i·ca \\sī-ˈat-i-kə\\ *n* : pain along the course of a sciatic nerve esp. in the back of the thigh; *also* : pain in or near the hips

sci·ence \\ˈsī-ən(t)s\\ *n* **1 a** : a department of systematized knowledge that is an object of study; *esp* : one of the natural sciences **b** : something (as a sport or technique) that may be studied or learned like systematized knowledge **2** : knowledge covering general truths or the operation of general laws esp. as obtained and tested through the scientific method

sci·en·tif·ic \\ˌsī-ən-ˈtif-ik\\ *adj* : of, relating to, or exhibiting the methods or principles of science — **sci·en·tif·i·cal·ly** \\-ˈtif-i-k(ə-)lē\\ *adv*

sci·en·tist \\ˈsī-ən-təst\\ *n* : one learned in science and esp. natural science : a scientific investigator

scim·i·tar \\ˈsim-ət-ər, -ə-ˌtär\\ *n* : a saber that has a curved blade with the edge on the convex side

scin·til·la \\sin-ˈtil-ə\\ *n* : IOTA, TRACE

scin·til·late \\ˈsint-ᵊl-ˌāt\\ *vi* **1** : to give off sparks : SPARK **2 a** : to emit quick flashes as if throwing off sparks **b** : SPARKLE, TWINKLE **3** : to perform with dazzling brilliance — **scin·til·lant** \\-ᵊl-ənt\\ *adj* — **scin·til·la·tion** \\ˌsint-ᵊl-ˈā-shən\\ *n*

sci·on \\ˈsī-ən\\ *n* **1** : a detached living portion of a plant joined to a stock in grafting **2** : DESCENDANT, CHILD

¹scis·sor \\ˈsiz-ər\\ *n* : SCISSORS

²scissor *vt* : to cut, cut up, or cut off with scissors or shears

scis·sors \\ˈsiz-ərz\\ *n sing or pl* : a cutting instrument having two blades so fastened together that the sharp edges slide past each other

scissors kick *n* : a swimming kick (as in a sidestroke) in which the legs move like scissors

scle·ro·sis \\sklə-ˈrō-səs\\ *n* : a usu. pathological hardening of tissue (as of an artery)

¹scoff \\ˈskäf, ˈskȯf\\ *n* : an expression of scorn, derision, or contempt : GIBE

²scoff *vb* : to show or treat with contempt by derisive acts or language : MOCK — **scoff·er** *n*

¹scold \\ˈskōld\\ *n* **1** : one addicted to abusive ribald speech **2** : one that scolds habitually or persistently

²scold *vb* **1** : to find fault noisily **2** : to rebuke severely or angrily — **scold·er** *n*

sconce \\ˈskän(t)s\\ *n* : a candlestick or group of candlesticks mounted on a plaque and fastened to a wall

scone \\ˈskōn, ˈskän\\ *n* : a quick bread usu. made with oatmeal or barley flour and baked on a griddle

¹scoop \\ˈsküp\\ *n* **1 a** : a large shovel (as for shoveling coal) **b** : a tool or utensil shaped like a shovel for digging into a soft substance and lifting out a portion **c** : a small tool of similar shape for cutting or gouging **2** : an act or the action of scooping : a motion made with or as if with a scoop **3 a** : the amount held by a scoop **b** : a hole made by scooping **4** : information of immediate interest; *also* : BEAT 4

²scoop *vt* **1** : to take out or up or empty with or as if with a scoop **2** : to make hollow : dig out **3** : to report a news item in advance of — **scoop·er** *n*

scoot \\ˈsküt\\ *vi* : to go suddenly and swiftly : DART — **scoot** *n*

¹scope \\ˈskōp\\ *n* **1** : space or opportunity for unhampered action or thought : chance to develop **2** : extent covered, reached, or viewed : RANGE

²scope *n* : an instrument (as a microscope or radarscope) for viewing

¹scorch \\ˈskȯrch\\ *vb* **1 a** : to burn superficially usu. to the point of changing color, texture, or flavor **b** : to parch and discolor with or as if with intense heat **2** : to distress or embarrass with usu. sarcastic censure **3** : to travel at great and usu. excessive speed

²scorch *n* : a result of scorching

scorch·er \\ˈskȯr-chər\\ *n* : one that scorches; *esp* : a very hot day

¹score \\ˈskō(ə)r\\ *n, pl* **scores** *or* **score** **1** : TWENTY **2** : a line made with or as if with a sharp instrument **3 a** : a reckoning kept by making marks on a tally **b** : ACCOUNT **c** : amount due : INDEBTEDNESS **4** : an obligation or injury kept in mind for requital **5 a** : REASON, GROUND **b** : SUBJECT, TOPIC **6** : a musical composition in written or printed notation **7** : a number expressing accomplishment (as in a game or test) or quality (as of a product); *also* : RATING — **score·less** \\-ləs\\ *adj*

²score *vb* **1 a** : to record by or as if by notches on a tally **b** : to keep score in a game or contest **2** : to mark with lines, grooves, scratches, or notches **3** : BERATE, SCOLD **4** : to gain or tally in or as if in a game **5** : to determine the merit of : GRADE **6 a** : to gain or have the advantage **b** : to be successful — **scor·er** *n*

¹scorn \\ˈskȯrn\\ *n* **1** : an emotion involving both anger and disgust : vigorous contempt **2** : an object of extreme disdain, contempt, or derision

²scorn *vb* **1** : to reject with bitter or angry contempt **2** : to refuse because of scorn : DISDAIN — **scorn·er** *n*

scorn·ful \\ˈskȯrn-fəl\\ *adj* : full of scorn : CONTEMPTUOUS — **scorn·ful·ly** \\-fə-lē\\ *adv* — **scorn·ful·ness** *n*

scor·pi·on \\ˈskȯr-pē-ən\\ *n* **1** : a spiderlike animal having an elongated body and a narrow segmented tail with a venomous sting at the tip **2** : something that incites to action like a sting

scotch \\ˈskäch\\ *vt* **1** : to injure so as to make temporarily harmless **2** : to stamp out : CRUSH; *esp* : to end decisively by demonstrating the falsity of

¹Scotch \\ˈskäch\\ *adj* : FRUGAL

²Scotch *n* : whiskey distilled in Scotland esp. from barley

scot–free \\ˈskät-ˈfrē\\ *adj* : completely free from obligation, harm, or penalty

scoun·drel \\ˈskau̇n-drəl\\ *n* : a mean worthless fellow : VILLAIN — **scoundrel** *adj* — **scoun·drel·ly** \\-drə-lē\\ *adj*

¹scour \\ˈskau̇(ə)r\\ *vb* **1** : to move about or through quickly esp. in search **2** : to examine minutely and rapidly — **scour·er** *n*

²scour *vb* **1 a** : to rub hard for the purpose of cleansing **b** : to remove by rubbing hard and washing **2** : to free from foreign matter or impurities by or as if by washing **3** : to suffer from diarrhea or dysentery — **scour·er** *n*

¹scourge \\ˈskərj\\ *n* **1** : WHIP, LASH **2 a** : an instrument of punishment or criticism **b** : a cause of widespread or great affliction

²scourge *vt* **1** : to whip severely : FLOG **2** : to subject to affliction : DEVASTATE — **scourg·er** *n*

¹scout \\ˈskau̇t\\ *vb* **1** : to go about and observe in search of information : RECONNOITER, SPY **2 a** : to make a search **b** : to find by searching

²scout *n* **1** : the act or an instance of scouting : RECONNAISSANCE **2 a** : one sent to obtain information and esp. to reconnoiter in war **b** : WATCHMAN, LOOKOUT **3** : a member of either the Boy Scouts of America or the Girl Scouts of the United States of America **4** : FELLOW, GUY

³scout *vb* : SCORN, SCOFF

scout·mas·ter \\ˈskau̇t-ˌmas-tər\\ *n* : the leader of a band of scouts and esp. of a troop of boy scouts

scow \\ˈskau̇\\ *n* : a large flat-bottomed boat with broad square ends

¹scowl \\ˈskau̇l\\ *vb* **1** : to draw down the forehead in a frowning expression of displeasure **2** : to exhibit or express with a threatening aspect — **scowl·er** *n*

[2]**scowl** *n* : a facial expression of displeasure : FROWN
[1]**scrab·ble** \'skrab-əl\ *vb* **scrab·bled**; **scrab·bling** \'skrab-(ə-)liŋ\ **1** : SCRAWL, SCRIBBLE **2** : to scratch or scrape with hands or paws; *also* : SCRAMBLE **3** : to struggle by or as if by scraping or scratching — **scrab·bler** \-(ə-)lər\ *n*
[2]**scrabble** *n* : an act or instance of scrabbling
scrag·gy \'skrag-ē\ *adj* **1** : ROUGH, JAGGED **2** : being lean and long : SCRAWNY
scram \'skram\ *vi* **scrammed**; **scram·ming** : to go away at once
scram·ble \'skram-bəl\ *vb* **scram·bled**; **scram·bling** \-b(ə-)liŋ\ **1** : to clamber clumsily around **2** : to move or act urgently or unceremoniously in trying to win or escape something **3** : SPRAWL, STRAGGLE **4 a** : to toss or mix together : JUMBLE **b** : to prepare (eggs) by stirring during cooking — **scramble** *n* — **scram·bler** \-b(ə-)lər\ *n*
[1]**scrap** \'skrap\ *n* **1** *pl* : fragments of discarded or leftover food **2** : a small bit : FRAGMENT **3** : discarded or waste metal for reprocessing
[2]**scrap** *vt* **scrapped**; **scrap·ping** **1** : to break up into scrap **2** : to discard as worthless
[3]**scrap** *adj* : made up of scraps; *also* : constituting scrap
[4]**scrap** *n* : QUARREL, FIGHT
[5]**scrap** *vi* **scrapped**; **scrap·ping** : QUARREL, FIGHT — **scrap·per** *n*
scrap·book \'skrap-ˌbu̇k\ *n* : a blank book for mementos (as clippings and pictures)
[1]**scrape** \'skrāp\ *vb* **1 a** : to remove by repeated strokes of an edged tool **b** : to clean or smooth by rubbing with an edged tool or abrasive **2** : to move along or over something with a grating noise : GRATE; *also* : to damage by such an action **3 a** : to gather with difficulty and little by little **b** : to barely get by — **scrap·er** *n*
[2]**scrape** *n* **1 a** : the act or process of scraping **b** : a sound, mark, or injury made by scraping **2** : a bow made by drawing back the foot **3** : a disagreeable predicament
scrap·ple \'skrap-əl\ *n* : a seasoned mush of meat scraps and cornmeal set in a mold and served sliced and fried
[1]**scrap·py** \'skrap-ē\ *adj* : consisting of scraps : FRAGMENTARY
[2]**scrappy** *adj* **1** : QUARRELSOME **2** : aggressive and determined in spirit — **scrap·pi·ness** *n*
[1]**scratch** \'skrach\ *vb* **1** : to dig, rub, or mar with or as if with the claws or nails **2 a** : SCRAPE 3 **b** : to make a living by hard work and saving **3** : to write or draw on a surface esp. hastily or carelessly : SCRAWL **4** : to cancel or erase by or as if by scraping away **5 a** : to use the claws or nails in digging, tearing, or wounding **b** : to scrape or rub oneself (as to relieve itching) **6** : to make a thin grating sound — **scratch·er** *n*
[2]**scratch** *n* **1 a** : an act or sound of scratching **b** : a mark (as a line) or injury made by scratching **2 a** : the line from which contestants start in a race **b** : NOTHING **3** : satisfactory condition or performance
scratchy \'skrach-ē\ *adj* **1** : likely to scratch or irritate : PRICKLY **2** : making a scratching noise **3** : marked or made with scratches **4** : uneven in quality : RAGGED — **scratch·i·ly** \'skrach-ə-lē\ *adv* — **scratch·i·ness** \'skrach-ē-nəs\ *n*
scrawl \'skrȯl\ *vb* : to write or draw awkwardly, hastily, or carelessly : SCRIBBLE — **scrawl** *n* — **scrawl·er** *n* — **scrawly** \'skrȯ-lē\ *adj*
scraw·ny \'skrȯ-nē\ *adj* : ill-nourished : SKINNY — **scraw·ni·ness** *n*
[1]**scream** \'skrēm\ *vb* **1** : to cry out, sound, or utter loudly and shrilly **2** : to produce or give a vivid, startling, or alarming effect or expression — **scream·er** *n*
[2]**scream** *n* **1** : a loud shrill prolonged cry or noise **2** : one that provokes screams of laughter
scream·ing·ly \'skrē-miŋ-lē\ *adv* : to an extreme degree
screech \'skrēch\ *vb* **1** : to utter or utter with a shrill harsh cry : make an outcry usu. in terror or pain **2** : to make a sound like a screech — **screech·er** *n*
[2]**screech** *n* **1** : a shrill harsh cry usu. expressing pain or terror **2** : a sound like a screech
screed \'skrēd\ *n* : a lengthy discourse
[1]**screen** \'skrēn\ *n* **1** : a device or partition used to hide, restrain, protect, or decorate; *also* : something that serves to shelter, protect, or conceal **2** : a sieve or perforated material set in a frame and used for separating finer parts from coarser parts (as of sand) **3 a** : a surface upon which pictures appear (as in movies or television) **b** : the motion-picture industry
[2]**screen** *vb* **1** : to guard from injury or danger **2** : to shelter, protect, or separate with or as if with a screen **3** : to provide with a screen and esp. with screening to keep out insects **4** : to present (as a motion-picture film) on a screen — **screen·a·ble** *adj* — **screen·er** *n*
[1]**screw** \'skrü\ *n* **1 a** : a simple machine consisting of a spirally grooved solid cylinder and a correspondingly grooved cylindrical hollow part into which it fits **b** : a nail-shaped or rod-shaped metal piece with a spiral groove and a slotted or recessed head used for fastening pieces of solid material together **2 a** : a screw-shaped form : SPIRAL **b** : a turn of a screw; *also* : a twist like the turn of a screw **c** : a screw-shaped device (as a corkscrew) **3** : a sharp bargainer **4** : a wheellike device with a central hub and radiating blades for propelling vehicles (as motorboats or airplanes) **5** : THUMBSCREW 2 — **screw·like** *adj*
[2]**screw** *vb* **1 a** (1) : to attach, fasten, or close by means of a screw (2) : to operate, tighten, or adjust by means of a screw **b** : to move or cause to move spirally as a screw does; *also* : to close or set in position by such an action **2 a** : to twist out of shape **b** : SQUINT **3** : to increase in amount or capability
[1]**screw·ball** \'skrü-ˌbȯl\ *n* : a whimsical, eccentric, or crazy person
[2]**screwball** *adj* : crazily eccentric or whimsical
screw·driv·er \'skrü-ˌdrī-vər\ *n* : a tool for turning screws
scrib·ble \'skrib-əl\ *vb* **scrib·bled**; **scrib·bling** \'skrib-(ə-)liŋ\ : to write or draw hastily or carelessly — **scribble** *n*
scrib·bler \'skrib-lər\ *n* **1** : one that scribbles **2** : a minor or inferior author
[1]**scribe** \'skrīb\ *n* **1 a** : an official or public secretary or clerk **b** : a copier of manuscripts **2** : AUTHOR; *esp* : JOURNALIST
[2]**scribe** *vt* : to mark or make by cutting or scratching with a pointed instrument
scrib·er \'skrī-bər\ *n* : a sharp-pointed tool for marking off material (as wood or metal) to be cut
scrim \'skrim\ *n* : a light coarse usu. cotton fabric of open weave
[1]**scrim·mage** \'skrim-ij\ *n* **1** : a confused fight : SCUFFLE **2 a** : the interplay between two football teams that begins with the snap of the ball **b** : practice play between a team's squads
[2]**scrimmage** *vi* : to take part in a scrimmage
scrimp \'skrimp\ *vb* **1** : to make too small, short, or scanty **2** : to be frugal : ECONOMIZE — **scrimpy** \'skrim-pē\ *adj*
scrip \'skrip\ *n* **1** : a document showing that the holder or bearer is entitled to something (as stock or land) **2** : paper currency or a token issued for temporary use in an emergency
script \'skript\ *n* : something written (as lines for a play or broadcast)
scrip·tur·al \'skrip-chə-rəl, 'skrip-shrəl\ *adj* : of, relating to, or being in accordance with a sacred writing; *esp* : BIBLICAL — **scrip·tur·al·ly** \-ē\ *adv*
scrip·ture \'skrip-chər\ *n* **1 a** *cap* : BIBLE — often used in pl. **b** : the sacred writings of a religion **2** : a body of writings considered as authoritative
scriv·e·ner \'skriv-(ə-)nər\ *n* : a professional copyist or writer
scroll \'skrōl\ *n* **1** : a roll (as of paper or parchment) providing a writing surface; *also* : one on which something is written or

engraved 2 : a spiral or coiled ornamental form suggesting a loosely or partly rolled scroll

scrooge \ˈskrüj\ *n, often cap* : a miserly person

scro·tum \ˈskrōt-əm\ *n, pl* **scro·ta** \ˈskrōt-ə\ *or* **scro·tums** : the external pouch that in most mammals contains the testes — **scro·tal** \ˈskrōt-ᵊl\ *adj*

scrounge \ˈskraůnj\ *vb* **1** : to engage in or collect by or as if by foraging **2** : CADGE, WHEEDLE — **scroung·er** *n*

¹scrub \ˈskrəb\ *n* **1 a** : a stunted tree or shrub **b** : vegetation consisting chiefly of or a tract covered with scrubs **2** : a usu. inferior domestic animal of mixed or unknown parentage **3 a** : a person of insignificant size or standing **b** : a player not belonging to the first team — **scrub** *adj*

²scrub *vb* **scrubbed**; **scrub·bing** **1 a** : to rub hard in cleaning or washing; *also* : to wash thoroughly **b** : to remove by or as if by scrubbing **2** : to subject to friction : RUB — **scrub·ber** *n*

³scrub *n* **1** : an act or instance of scrubbing **2** : one that scrubs

scrub·by \ˈskrəb-ē\ *adj* **1** : inferior in size or quality : STUNTED **2** : covered with or consisting of vegetational scrub **3** : lacking distinction : SHABBY

scruff \ˈskrəf\ *n* : the loose skin of the back of the neck : NAPE

scrump·tious \ˈskrəm(p)-shəs\ *adj* : DELIGHTFUL, EXCELLENT

scrunch \ˈskrənch\ *vb* **1 a** : CRUNCH, CRUSH, CRUMPLE **b** : to make or move with a crunching sound **2** : CROUCH, SQUEEZE

¹scru·ple \ˈskrü-pəl\ *n* : a tiny part or quantity

²scruple *n* **1** : an ethical consideration or principle that makes one uneasy or inhibits action **2** : SCRUPULOUSNESS

³scruple *vi* **scru·pled**; **scru·pling** \-p(ə-)liŋ\ : to have scruples

scru·pu·lous \ˈskrü-pyə-ləs\ *adj* : full of or having scruples : PUNCTILIOUS — **scru·pu·lous·ly** *adv* — **scru·pu·lous·ness** *n*

scru·ti·nize \ˈskrüt-ᵊn-ˌīz\ *vb* : to examine very closely or critically : INSPECT — **scru·ti·niz·er** *n*

scru·ti·ny \ˈskrüt-ᵊn-ē, ˈskrüt-nē\ *n, pl* **-nies** **1** : a searching study, inquiry, or inspection : EXAMINATION **2** : a searching look

scu·ba \ˈsk(y)ü-bə\ *n* : an apparatus used for breathing while swimming under water

¹scud \ˈskəd\ *vi* **scud·ded**; **scud·ding** : to move or run swiftly esp. as if driven forward

²scud *n* **1** : the act of scudding **2** : loose vapory clouds driven by wind

¹scuff \ˈskəf\ *vb* **1** : to scrape the feet in walking : SHUFFLE **2** : to become rough or scratched through wear

²scuff *n* **1** : a noise or act of scuffing **2** : a flat-soled house slipper

scuf·fle \ˈskəf-əl\ *vb* **scuf·fled**; **scuf·fling** \ˈskəf-(ə-)liŋ\ **1** : to struggle in a confused way at close quarters **2** : to move with a quick shuffling gait; *also* : SCUFF — **scuffle** *n* — **scuf·fler** \-(ə-)lər\ *n*

¹scull \ˈskəl\ *n* **1 a** : an oar used at the stern of a boat to propel it forward with a crosswise motion **b** : one of a pair of short oars for use by one person **2** : a boat usu. for racing propelled by one or more pairs of sculls

²scull *vb* : to propel a boat by sculls — **scull·er** *n*

scul·lery \ˈskəl-(ə-)rē\ *n, pl* **-ler·ies** : a room for cleaning and storing dishes and culinary utensils, washing vegetables, and similar domestic work

scul·lion \ˈskəl-yən\ *n* : a kitchen helper

sculpt \ˈskəlpt\ *vb* : CARVE, SCULPTURE

sculp·tor \ˈskəlp-tər\ *n* : one that sculptures — **sculp·tress** \-trəs\ *n*

sculp·tur·al \ˈskəlp-chə-rəl, ˈskəlp-shrəl\ *adj* : of, relating to, or resembling sculpture — **sculp·tur·al·ly** \-ē\ *adv*

¹sculp·ture \ˈskəlp-chər\ *n* **1** : the act, process, or art of carving or cutting hard materials or modeling plastic materials into works of art **2** : work produced by sculpture; *also* : a piece of such work

²sculpture *vb* : to represent or produce by or subject to sculpture; *also* : to adorn with sculpture

¹scum \ˈskəm\ *n* **1 a** : extraneous matter or impurities risen to or formed on the surface of a liquid **b** : a slimy coating esp. on stagnant water **2 a** : foul or worthless things **b** : the lowest class : RABBLE — **scum·my** \ˈskəm-ē\ *adj*

²scum *vi* **scummed**; **scum·ming** : to form or become covered with or as if with scum

scup·per \ˈskəp-ər\ *n* : an opening in the bulwarks of a boat through which water drains overboard

scurf \ˈskərf\ *n* **1** : thin dry scales given off by the skin **2** : a scaly deposit or covering — **scurfy** \ˈskər-fē\ *adj*

scur·ri·lous \ˈskər-ə-ləs\ *adj* **1 a** : using or given to the language of low buffoonery **b** : being vulgar and evil : LOW **2** : containing low obscenities or coarse abuse — **scur·ril·i·ty** \skə-ˈril-ət-ē\ *n* — **scur·ri·lous·ly** *adv* — **scur·ri·lous·ness** *n*

scur·ry \ˈskər-ē\ *vi* **scur·ried**; **scur·ry·ing** : to move briskly : SCAMPER — **scurry** *n*

¹scur·vy \ˈskər-vē\ *adj* : MEAN, DESPICABLE — **scur·vi·ly** \-və-lē\ *adv* — **scur·vi·ness** \-vē-nəs\ *n*

²scurvy *n* : a deficiency disease marked by spongy gums, loosened teeth, and bleeding into the tissues

scutch·eon \ˈskəch-ən\ *n* : ESCUTCHEON

¹scut·tle \ˈskət-ᵊl\ *n* : a metal pail for carrying coal

²scuttle *n* : a small opening (as in the side or deck of a ship or the roof of a house) furnished with a lid; *also* : its lid

³scuttle *vt* **scut·tled**; **scut·tling** \ˈskət-liŋ, -ᵊl-iŋ\ : to sink (a boat) intentionally by cutting holes or by opening valves to let in water; *also* : to injure or end by a deliberate act

⁴scuttle *vi* **scut·tled**; **scut·tling** \ˈskət-liŋ, -ᵊl-iŋ\ : SCURRY

scut·tle·butt \ˈskət-ᵊl-ˌbət\ *n* : RUMOR, GOSSIP

¹scythe \ˈsīth\ *n* : an implement used for mowing (as grass) and composed of a long curving blade fastened at an angle to a long handle; *also* : its blade

²scythe *vt* : to cut with or as if with a scythe : MOW

sea \ˈsē\ *n* **1 a** : a great body of salty water **b** : OCEAN **2** : rough water : a heavy swell or wave **3** : something suggesting the sea (as in vastness) **4** : the seafaring life — **sea** *adj* — **at sea** **1** : on the sea; *esp* : on a sea voyage **2** : LOST, BEWILDERED — **to sea** : to or upon the open waters of the sea

sea·bird \ˈsē-ˌbərd\ *n* : a bird (as a gull or albatross) frequenting the open ocean

sea·board \ˈsē-ˌbōrd\ *n* : SEACOAST; *also* : the country bordering a seacoast — **seaboard** *adj*

sea·borne \-ˌbōrn\ *adj* **1** : borne over or upon the sea **2** : engaged in or carried on by overseas shipping

sea breeze *n* : a breeze blowing inland from the sea

sea change *n* **1** : a change brought about by the sea **2** : TRANSFORMATION

sea·coast \ˈsē-ˌkōst\ *n* : the shore or border of the land adjacent to the sea

sea dog *n* : a veteran sailor

sea·far·er \ˈsē-ˌfar-ər\ *n* : MARINER

sea·far·ing \-ˌfar-iŋ\ *n* **1** : traveling over the sea **2** : the occupation of a sailor — **seafaring** *adj*

sea·food \ˈsē-ˌfüd\ *n* : edible marine fish and shellfish

sea·go·ing \-ˌgō-iŋ\ *adj* : adapted or used for sea travel; *also* : SEAFARING

sea horse *n* : a small long-snouted fish that is covered with bony plates and has a head suggestive of a horse's head

¹seal \ˈsēl\ *n, pl* **seals** **1** : any of numerous large marine mammals chiefly of cold regions with limbs adapted for swimming **2** : the pelt of a seal

²seal *vi* : to hunt seals — **seal·er** *n*

³seal *n* **1** : a device with a raised design that can be pressed or stamped (as into paper or wax) to form a mark; *also* : a piece of wax or a wafer bearing such an impressed mark or the mark itself **2** : a usu. ornamental adhesive stamp that may be used to close a letter or package **3 a :** something (as a pledge) that makes safe or secure **b :** a closure that can be opened only by breaking or tearing **c :** a tight and perfect closure; *also* **:** a device or an arrangement of material designed to produce such a closure — **under seal :** with an authenticating seal affixed

4seal *vt* **1 :** to mark with or certify or authenticate by or as if by a seal **2 :** to close or make fast with or as if with a seal often to prevent or disclose tampering **3 :** to determine finally and irrevocably — **seal·er** *n*

sea legs *n* **:** bodily adjustment to the motion of a ship at sea

sea level *n* **:** the height of the surface of the sea midway between the average high and low tides

seal·skin \'sēl-ˌskin\ *n* **1 :** the fur or pelt of a fur seal **2 :** a garment (as a coat) of sealskin — **sealskin** *adj*

1seam \'sēm\ *n* **1 :** the joining or the mark made by the joining of two pieces or edges of material by sewing **2 a :** GROOVE, FURROW, WRINKLE **b :** a layer or stratum (as of mineral) between distinctive layers — **seam·less** \-ləs\ *adj*

2seam *vt* **1 :** to join by or as if by sewing **2 :** to mark with lines suggesting seams **:** FURROW — **seam·er** *n*

sea·man \'sē-mən\ *n* **1 :** SAILOR, MARINER **2 :** an enlisted man in the navy ranking next below a petty officer third class

seaman apprentice *n* **:** an enlisted man in the navy ranking next below a seaman

seaman recruit *n* **:** an enlisted man in the navy of the lowest rank

sea·man·ship \'sē-mən-ˌship\ *n* **:** the art or skill of handling, working, and navigating a ship

seam·stress \'sēm(p)-strəs\ *n* **:** a woman who sews esp. for a living

seamy \'sē-mē\ *adj* **1 :** having or showing seams **2 :** less pleasing or presentable **:** WORSE — **seam·i·ness** *n*

sé·ance \'sā-ˌän(t)s, -ˌäⁿs\ *n* **1 :** a meeting for discussion **:** SESSION **2 :** a spiritualist meeting

sea·plane \'sē-ˌplān\ *n* **:** an airplane designed to take off from and land on the water

sea·port \-ˌpōrt\ *n* **:** a port, harbor, or town accessible to seagoing ships

1sear \'si(ə)r\ *vb* **1 :** to cause withering or drying **:** PARCH, SHRIVEL **2 :** to burn, scorch, or injure with or as if with sudden application of intense heat; *also* **:** to brown the surface of quickly in cooking

2sear *n* **:** a mark or scar left by searing

1search \'sərch\ *vb* **1 a :** to go through or look carefully and thoroughly in an effort to find or discover **b :** to examine or explore with painstaking care often with a particular objective in view **:** PROBE **2 :** to find or come to know by or as if by careful investigation or scrutiny — **search·a·ble** *adj* — **search·er** *n* — **search·ing·ly** *adv*

2search *n* **1 a :** an act of searching **b :** an act of boarding and inspecting a ship on the high seas **2 :** a person or party that searches

search·light \'sərch-ˌlīt\ *n* **1 :** an apparatus for projecting a beam of light; *also* **:** a beam of light projected by it **2 :** FLASHLIGHT 2

sea·scape \'sē-ˌskāp\ *n* **1 :** a view of the sea **2 :** a picture representing a scene at sea

sea·shore \'sē-ˌshōr\ *n* **:** land adjacent to the sea **:** SEACOAST

sea·sick \-ˌsik\ *adj* **:** nauseated by or as if by the motion of a ship — **sea·sick·ness** *n*

sea·side \'sē-ˌsīd\ *n* **:** country adjacent to the sea **:** SEASHORE

1sea·son \'sēz-ᵊn\ *n* **1 :** a suitable or natural time or occasion **2 a :** a period of the year associated with some recurrent phenomenon or activity **b :** one of the four quarters into which the year is commonly divided — **in season 1 :** at the right or fitting time **2 :** in a state or at the stage of greatest fitness (as for eating); *also* **:** proper or legal to take by hunting or fishing — **out of season :** not in season; *esp* **:** available at other than the usual local season

2season *vb* **sea·soned**; **sea·son·ing** \'sēz-niŋ, -ᵊn-iŋ\ **1 :** to give food better flavor or more zest by adding seasoning; *also* **:** to add seasoning **2 a :** to treat so as to be fit for use; *esp* **:** to prepare (lumber) for use by controlled drying **b :** to make fit by experience **3 :** to become seasoned

sea·son·a·ble \'sēz-nə-bəl, -ᵊn-ə-bəl\ *adj* **1 :** occurring in good or proper time **:** OPPORTUNE **2 :** suitable to the season or circumstances **:** TIMELY — **sea·son·a·bly** \-blē\ *adv*

sea·son·al \'sēz-nəl, -ᵊn-əl\ *adj* **:** of, relating to, or restricted to a particular season — **sea·son·al·ly** \-ē\ *adv*

sea·son·ing \'sēz-niŋ, -ᵊn-iŋ\ *n* **:** something that serves to season; *esp* **:** an ingredient (as a condiment, spice, or herb) added to food primarily for savor

1seat \'sēt\ *n* **1 :** a place on or at which a person sits; *also* **:** something (as a chair) intended to be sat in or on **2 :** a place or area where something is situated or centered; *esp* **:** a place (as a capital city) from which authority is exercised — **seat·ed** \-əd\ *adj*

2seat *vb* **1 :** to cause to sit or assist in finding a seat **2 :** to provide seats for — **seat·er** *n*

1sea·ward \'sē-wərd\ *adv* (*or adj*) **:** toward the sea

2seaward *n* **:** the direction or side away from land and toward the open sea

sea·way \-ˌwā\ *n* **:** a deep inland waterway that admits ocean shipping

sea·weed \-ˌwēd\ *n* **:** a plant growing in the sea; *esp* **:** a marine alga (as a kelp)

sea·wor·thy \-ˌwər-t͟hē\ *adj* **:** fit or safe for a sea voyage — **sea·wor·thi·ness** *n*

se·ba·ceous \si-'bā-shəs\ *adj* **:** of, relating to, or secreting fatty material

se·cede \si-'sēd\ *vi* **:** to withdraw from an organization or communion (as a nation, church, or political party)

se·ces·sion \si-'sesh-ən\ *n* **:** the act of seceding **:** a formal withdrawal — **se·ces·sion·ist** \-'sesh-(ə-)nəst\ *n*

se·clude \si-'klüd\ *vt* **1 :** to withhold from free intercourse **:** make inaccessible **2 :** to shut away **:** SCREEN, ISOLATE

se·clud·ed \-əd\ *adj* **1 :** screened or hidden from view **:** SEQUESTERED **2 :** living in seclusion **:** SOLITARY

se·clu·sion \si-'klü-zhən\ *n* **1 :** the act of secluding **:** the condition of being secluded **2 :** a secluded or isolated place — **se·clu·sive** \-'klü-siv, -ziv\ *adj* — **se·clu·sive·ly** *adv* — **se·clu·sive·ness** *n*

1sec·ond \'sek-ənd\ *adj* **1** — see NUMBER table **2 :** next to the first in time, order, or importance **3 :** ALTERNATE, OTHER **4 :** resembling or suggesting a prototype **:** ANOTHER — **second** *adv* — **sec·ond·ly** *adv*

2second *n* **1 a** — see NUMBER table **b :** one next after the first in time, order, or importance **2 :** one who assists or supports another (as in a duel or prizefight) **3 :** an inferior or flawed article (as of merchandise) **4 :** the second gear or speed in an automotive vehicle

3second *n* **1 :** the 60th part of a minute of time or of a degree **2 :** an instant of time **:** MOMENT

4second *vt* **1 :** to give support or encouragement to **:** ASSIST **2 :** to endorse (a motion or a nomination) so that it may be debated or voted on — **sec·ond·er** *n*

1sec·ond·ary \'sek-ən-ˌder-ē\ *adj* **1 a :** of second rank, importance, or value **b :** of, relating to, or constituting the second strongest of the three or four degrees of stress **2 a :** of, relating to, or being a second order or stage in a sequence or series **b :** intermediate between elementary and collegiate — **sec·ond·ar·i·ly** \ˌsek-ən-'der-ə-lē\ *adv*

2secondary *n, pl* **-ar·ies :** one that is secondary

sec·ond–class \ˌsek-ᵊŋ-'klas, -ən(d)-\ *adj* **1 :** INFERIOR, MEDIOCRE **2 :** socially or economically deprived

¹sec·ond·hand \ˌsek-ən(d)-ˈhand\ *adj* **1** : not original : taken from someone else **2** : not new : having had a previous owner **3** : selling used goods
²secondhand *adv* : in a secondhand condition; *esp* : INDIRECTLY
second lieutenant *n* : a commissioned officer (as in the army) ranking next below a first lieutenant
sec·ond–rate \ˌsek-ən-ˈ(d)rāt\ *adj* : of second or inferior quality or value : MEDIOCRE — **sec·ond–rat·er** \-ˈ(d)rāt-ər\ *n*
se·cre·cy \ˈsē-krə-sē\ *n, pl* **-cies 1** : the habit or practice of keeping secrets : SECRETIVENESS **2** : the quality or state of being hidden or concealed
¹se·cret \ˈsē-krət\ *adj* **1 a** : hidden or kept from knowledge or view **b** : working in secret as a spy or detective : UNDERCOVER **2** : remote from human resort or notice : SECLUDED **3** : revealed only to the initiated : ESOTERIC — **se·cret·ly** *adv*
²secret *n* **1 a** : something kept hidden or unexplained : MYSTERY **b** : something kept from the knowledge of others or shared only confidentially with a few **2** : a secret condition or place : SECRECY **3** : something taken to be a specific or key to a desired end
sec·re·tar·i·at \ˌsek-rə-ˈter-ē-ət\ *n* **1** : the office of a secretary **2 a** : an office housing a clerical staff **b** : the clerical staff of an organization **3** : the administrative department of a governmental organization
sec·re·tary \ˈsek-rə-ˌter-ē\ *n, pl* **-tar·ies 1** : a confidential clerk **2** : an officer of a business corporation or society who has charge of the correspondence and records **3** : a government official in charge of the affairs of a department **4** : a writing desk — **sec·re·tar·i·al** \ˌsek-rə-ˈter-ē-əl\ *adj*
secretary–general *n, pl* **secretaries–general** : a principal administrative officer
¹se·crete \si-ˈkrēt\ *vb* : to produce and give off a secretion
²se·crete \si-ˈkrēt, ˈsē-krət\ *vt* : to deposit or conceal in a hiding place
se·cre·tion \si-ˈkrē-shən\ *n* **1** : a concealing or hiding of something **2 a** : the act or process of secreting **b** : a product of glandular activity; *esp* : one (as a hormone or enzyme) that performs a specific useful function in the organism
se·cre·tive \ˈsē-krət-iv, si-ˈkrēt-\ *adj* : disposed to secrecy or concealment : not frank or open — **se·cre·tive·ly** *adv* — **se·cre·tive·ness** *n*
se·cre·to·ry \si-ˈkrēt-ə-rē\ *adj* : of, relating to, or active in secretion
sect \ˈsekt\ *n* **1 a** : a dissenting religious body **b** : a religious denomination **2** : a group adhering to a distinctive doctrine or to a leader
¹sec·tar·i·an \sek-ˈter-ē-ən\ *adj* **1** : of, relating to, or characteristic of a sect or sectarian **2** : limited in character or scope — **sec·tar·i·an·ism** \-ē-ə-ˌniz-əm\ *n*
²sectarian *n* **1** : a member of a sect **2** : a narrow or bigoted person
¹sec·tion \ˈsek-shən\ *n* **1 a** : the action or an instance of cutting or separating by cutting **b** : a part set off by or as if by cutting : PORTION, SLICE **2** : a distinct part or portion of a writing **3** : the profile of something as it would appear if cut through by an intersecting plane **4** : a distinct part of an area, community, or group of people
²section *vb* **sec·tioned**; **sec·tion·ing** \-sh(ə-)niŋ\ : to cut or separate or become cut or separated into sections
sec·tion·al \ˈsek-shnəl, -shən-ᵊl\ *adj* **1 a** : of or relating to a section **b** : local or regional rather than general in character **2** : consisting of or divided into sections — **sec·tion·al·ly** \-ē\ *adv*
sec·tion·al·ism \ˈsek-shnə-ˌliz-əm, -shən-ᵊl-ˌiz-\ *n* : an exaggerated devotion to the interests of a region
sec·tor \ˈsek-tər\ *n* **1** : the part of a circle included between two radii **2** : an area assigned to a military commander to defend **3** : a distinctive part (as of an economy)
sec·to·ri·al \sek-ˈtōr-ē-əl\ *adj* : of, relating to, or constituting a sector
¹sec·u·lar \ˈsek-yə-lər\ *adj* **1** : of or relating to the worldly or temporal : not religious or ecclesiastical **2** : of or relating to clergy not belonging to a religious order — **sec·u·lar·ly** *adv*
²secular *n* : LAYMAN
sec·u·lar·ism \-lə-ˌriz-əm\ *n* : indifference to or exclusion of religion — **sec·u·lar·ist** \-rəst\ *n* — **secularist** *or* **sec·u·lar·is·tic** \ˌsek-yə-lə-ˈris-tik\ *adj*
sec·u·lar·ize \ˈsek-yə-lə-ˌrīz\ *vt* : to make secular — **sec·u·lar·i·za·tion** \ˌsek-yə-lə-rə-ˈzā-shən\ *n* — **sec·u·lar·iz·er** *n*
¹se·cure \si-ˈkyu̇(ə)r\ *adj* **1** : easy in mind : CONFIDENT **2 a** : free from danger **b** : free from risk of loss **c** : affording safety : INVIOLABLE **d** : TRUSTWORTHY, DEPENDABLE **3** : ASSURED, CERTAIN — **se·cure·ly** *adv* — **se·cure·ness** *n*
²secure *vb* **1 a** : to relieve from exposure to danger : make safe : GUARD, SHIELD **b** : to give pledge of payment to (a creditor) or of (an obligation) **2** : to make fast : SEAL **3 a** : to get secure possession of : PROCURE **b** : to bring about : EFFECT
se·cu·ri·ty \si-ˈkyu̇r-ət-ē\ *n, pl* **-ties 1** : the quality or state of being secure: as **a** : freedom from danger : SAFETY **b** : freedom from fear or anxiety **2** : something given, deposited, or pledged to make certain the fulfillment of an obligation **3** *pl* : stock or bond certificates **4** : something that secures
se·dan \si-ˈdan\ *n* **1** : a portable often covered chair borne on poles by two men **2 a** : an enclosed automobile usu. with front and back seats **b** : a motorboat with one passenger compartment
se·date \si-ˈdāt\ *adj* : QUIET, STAID, SOBER — **se·date·ly** *adv* — **se·date·ness** *n*
¹sed·a·tive \ˈsed-ət-iv\ *adj* : tending to calm, moderate, or relieve tension — **se·da·tion** \si-ˈdā-shən\ *n*
²sedative *n* : a sedative agent or drug
sed·en·tary \ˈsed-ᵊn-ˌter-ē\ *adj* **1** : not migratory : SETTLED **2** : doing or requiring much sitting
sedge \ˈsej\ *n* : any of a family of usu. tufted marsh plants differing from the related grasses in having achenes and solid stems — **sedgy** \ˈsej-ē\ *adj*
sed·i·ment \ˈsed-ə-mənt\ *n* **1** : the matter that settles to the bottom of a liquid : DREGS **2** : material (as stones and sand) deposited by water, wind, or glaciers — **sed·i·ment** \-ˌment\ *vb* — **sed·i·men·ta·ry** \ˌsed-ə-ˈment-ə-rē, -ˈmen-trē\ *adj*
se·di·tion \si-ˈdish-ən\ *n* : incitement of resistance to or of insurrection against lawful authority
se·di·tious \si-ˈdish-əs\ *adj* **1** : disposed to arouse, take part in, or be guilty of sedition **2** : of or relating to sedition — **se·di·tious·ly** *adv* — **se·di·tious·ness** *n*
se·duce \si-ˈd(y)üs\ *vt* **1** : to persuade to disobedience or disloyalty **2** : to lead astray **3** : to entice into unchastity **4** : ATTRACT — **se·duc·er** *n* — **se·duc·tion** \-ˈdək-shən\ *n*
se·duc·tive \si-ˈdək-tiv\ *adj* : ALLURING, TEMPTING — **se·duc·tive·ly** *adv* — **se·duc·tive·ness** *n*
sed·u·lous \ˈsej-ə-ləs\ *adj* : diligent in application or pursuit : ASSIDUOUS — **sed·u·lous·ly** *adv* — **sed·u·lous·ness** *n*
¹see \ˈsē\ *vb* **saw** \ˈsȯ\; **seen** \ˈsēn\; **see·ing** \ˈsē-iŋ\ **1 a** : to perceive by the eye or have the power of sight **b** : to give or pay attention **c** : to look about **2 a** : to have experience of : UNDERGO **b** : to come to know : DISCOVER **3 a** : to form a mental picture of : VISUALIZE **b** : to perceive the meaning or importance of : UNDERSTAND **c** : to be aware of : RECOGNIZE **d** : to imagine as a possibility : SUPPOSE **4 a** : to make investigation or inquiry : EXAMINE, WATCH **b** (1) : READ (2) : to read of **c** : to attend as a spectator **5 a** : to take care of : provide for **b** : to make sure **6 a** : to regard as : JUDGE **b** : to prefer to have **c** : to find acceptable or attractive **7 a** : to call on : VISIT **b** (1) : to keep company with esp. in courtship or dating (2) : to grant an interview to : RECEIVE **8** : ACCOM-

PANY, ESCORT **9** : to meet (a bet) in poker or to equal the bet of (a player) : CALL

²see *n* **1** : the city in which a bishop's church is located **2** : the jurisdiction of a bishop : DIOCESE

¹seed \'sēd\ *n, pl* **seed** *or* **seeds** **1 a** : the grains or ripened ovules of plants used for sowing **b** : the fertilized ripened ovule of a flowering plant containing an embryo and capable normally of germination to produce a new plant; *also* : a propagative plant structure (as a spore or small dry fruit) **2** : PROGENY, DESCENDANTS **3** : a source of development or growth — **seed** *adj* — **seed·ed** \-əd\ *adj* — **seed·like** *adj*

²seed *vb* **1** : PLANT, SOW **2** : to bear or shed seeds **3** : to remove seeds from

seed·er \'sēd-ər\ *n* **1** : a machine for planting or sowing seeds **2** : a device for seeding fruit

seed·less \'sēd-ləs\ *adj* : having no seeds

seed·ling \-liŋ\ *n* **1** : a plant grown from seed **2** : a young plant; *esp* : a tree smaller than a sapling — **seedling** *adj*

seed pearl *n* : a very small and often irregular pearl

seed·time \'sēd-ˌtīm\ *n* : the season for sowing

seedy \'sēd-ē\ *adj* **1 a** : containing or full of seeds **b** : containing many small similar inclusions **2** : inferior in condition or quality: as **a** : SHABBY, RUN-DOWN **b** : somewhat disreputable : SQUALID **c** : slightly unwell : DEBILITATED — **seed·i·ly** \'sēd-ᵊl-ē\ *adv* — **seed·i·ness** \'sēd-ē-nəs\ *n*

see·ing \'sē-iŋ\ *conj* : in view of the fact that

seek \'sēk\ *vb* **sought** \'sȯt\; **seek·ing** **1** : to resort to : go to **2 a** : to go in search of : look for **b** : to make a search or inquiry **c** : to try to discover **3** : to ask for : REQUEST **4** : to try to acquire or gain : aim at **5** : to make an attempt : TRY — **seek·er** *n*

seem \'sēm\ *vi* **1 a** (1) : to give the impression of being : APPEAR (2) : to pretend to be : FEIGN **b** : to appear to the observation or understanding **c** : to appear to one's own mind or opinion **2** : to give evidence of existing or being present

¹seem·ing \'sē-miŋ\ *n* : external appearance as distinguished from true character : LOOK

²seeming *adj* : apparent on superficial view : OSTENSIBLE — **seem·ing·ly** *adv*

seem·ly \'sēm-lē\ *adj* **1** : good-looking : HANDSOME, ATTRACTIVE **2** : conventionally proper **3** : suited to the occasion, purpose, or person : FIT — **seem·li·ness** *n* — **seem·ly** *adv*

see out *vt* : to continue with until the end : FINISH

seep \'sēp\ *vi* : to flow or pass slowly through fine pores or small openings : OOZE

seep·age \'sē-pij\ *n* **1** : the process of seeping : OOZING **2** : a quantity of fluid that has seeped through porous material

seer \'si(ə)r, *esp for 1 also* 'sē-ər\ *n* **1** : one that sees **2** : one that predicts events or developments : PROPHET

seer·ess \'si(ə)r-əs\ *n* : a female seer : PROPHETESS

seer·suck·er \'si(ə)r-ˌsək-ər\ *n* : a light fabric of linen, cotton, or rayon usu. striped and slightly puckered

see·saw \'sē-ˌsȯ\ *n* **1** : a contest or struggle in which now one side now the other has the lead **2 a** : a game in which children ride on opposite ends of a plank balanced in the middle so that one end goes up as the other goes down **b** : the plank so used — **seesaw** *adj* — **seesaw** *vb*

seethe \'sēt͟h\ *vb* **1** : BOIL, STEW **2** : to soak or saturate in a liquid **3 a** : to be in a state of rapid agitated movement **b** : to churn or foam as if boiling **4** : to suffer violent internal excitement

seg·ment \'seg-mənt\ *n* **1** : any of the parts into which a thing is divided or naturally separates : SECTION, DIVISION **2** : a part cut off from a geometrical figure (as a circle or sphere) by a line or plane — **seg·ment** \'seg-ˌment\ *vb* — **seg·men·tary** \'seg-mən-ˌter-ē\ *adj*

seg·re·gate \'seg-ri-ˌgāt\ *vb* : to separate or set apart from others : ISOLATE; *esp* : to separate by races — **seg·re·ga·tive** \-ˌgāt-iv\ *adj*

seg·re·ga·tion \ˌseg-ri-'gā-shən\ *n* **1** : the act or process of segregating : the state of being segregated **2** : the separation or isolation of a race, class, or ethnic group by discriminatory means

seg·re·ga·tion·ist \-sh(ə-)nəst\ *n* : an advocate of segregation esp. of races

sei·gneur \sān-'yər\ *n, often cap* : LORD, SEIGNIOR

sei·gnior \sān-'yȯ(ə)r\ *n* : a man of rank or authority; *esp* : the feudal lord of a manor

sei·gniory *or* **sei·gnory** \'sān-yə-rē\ *n, pl* **-gnior·ies** *or* **-gnor·ies** : the territory of a lord : DOMAIN

sei·gno·ri·al \sān-'yōr-ē-əl\ *adj* : of, relating to, or befitting a seignior : MANORIAL

¹seine \'sān\ *n* : a large fishing net kept hanging vertically in the water by weights and floats

²seine *vb* : to fish with or catch with a seine — **sein·er** *n*

seis·mic \'sīz-mik, 'sīs-\ *adj* : of, subject to, or caused by an earthquake or an artificially produced earth vibration

seis·mo·graph \'sīz-mə-ˌgraf, 'sīs-\ *n* : an apparatus for recording the intensity, direction, and duration of earthquakes or similar vibrations of the ground — **seis·mo·graph·ic** \ˌsīz-mə-'graf-ik, ˌsīs-\ *adj* — **seis·mog·ra·phy** \sīz-'mäg-rə-fē, sīs-\ *n*

seize \'sēz\ *vb* **1** : to take possession of by force **2** : to take hold of suddenly or with force : CLUTCH **3** : UNDERSTAND, COMPREHEND **4** : to take prisoner : ARREST **5** : to attack or overwhelm suddenly (as with fever) — **seiz·er** *n*

seiz·ing \'sē-ziŋ\ *n* **1** : the operation of fastening together or lashing with small rope or cord **2 a** : the cord used in seizing **b** : the fastening so made

sei·zure \'sē-zhər\ *n* **1** : the act or process of seizing : the state of being seized **2** : a sudden attack (as of disease) : FIT

sel·dom \'sel-dəm\ *adv* : in few instances : RARELY

¹se·lect \sə-'lekt\ *adj* **1** : chosen from a number or group by fitness or preference **2 a** : of special value or excellence : SUPERIOR, CHOICE **b** : exclusively or fastidiously chosen often with regard to social, economic, or cultural characteristics **3** : judicious or restrictive in choice : DISCRIMINATING

²select *vb* : to take by preference from a number or group : pick out : CHOOSE — **se·lec·tor** \-'lek-tər\ *n*

se·lec·tion \sə-'lek-shən\ *n* **1** : the act or process of selecting : the state of being selected **2** : one that is selected : CHOICE; *also* : a collection of selected things **3** : a natural or artificial process that prevents or tends to prevent some individuals or groups of organisms from surviving and propagating and allows others to do so

se·lec·tive \sə-'lek-tiv\ *adj* : of, relating to, or characterized by selection : selecting or tending to select — **se·lec·tive·ly** *adv* — **se·lec·tive·ness** *n* — **se·lec·tiv·i·ty** \si-ˌlek-'tiv-ət-ē, ˌsē-\ *n*

se·lect·man \sə-'lek(t)-ˌman, -mən; -ˌlek(t)-'man\ *n* : one of a board of town officials elected annually in some of the New England states

se·le·ni·um \sə-'lē-nē-əm\ *n* : a nonmetallic chemical element that varies in electrical conductivity with the intensity of its illumination and is used in electronic devices

¹self \'self\ *pron* : MYSELF, HIMSELF, HERSELF

²self *adj* **1** : having a single character or quality throughout; *esp* : having one color only **2** : of the same kind (as in color, material, or pattern) as something with which it is used

³self \'self\ *n, pl* **selves** \'selvz\ **1** : a person regarded as an individual apart from everyone else **2** : a particular side of a person's character **3** : personal interest or advantage

self- *comb form* **1** : oneself : itself **2** : of oneself or itself **3** : by oneself; *also* : automatic **4** : to, for, or toward oneself

self-abandoned
self-abasement
self-abnegating
self-abnegation
self-absorbed
self-absorption
self-accusation
self-acting
self-addressed
self-adjusting
self-administered
self-advancement
self-aggrandizement
self-analysis
self-appointed
self-approbation
self-assertion
self-assertive
self-assurance
self-assured
self-awareness
self-betrayal
self-charging
self-closing
self-complacency
self-complacent
self-conceit
self-concern
self-concerned
self-condemnation
self-condemned
self-confidence
self-confident
self-constituted
self-contempt
self-created
self-criticism
self-deception
self-dedication
self-defeating
self-defense
self-delusion
self-denial
self-denying
self-dependence
self-depreciation
self-destruction
self-determined
self-development
self-devotion
self-devouring
self-directed
self-discipline
self-discovery
self-distrust
self-doubt
self-driven
self-educated
self-effacement
self-effacing
self-esteem
self-evident
self-examination
self-explanatory
self-glorification
self-glory
self-gratification
self-hardening
self-help
self-hypnosis
self-immolation
self-imposed
self-improvement
self-inclusive
self-induced
self-indulgence
self-inflicted
self-instructed
self-justification
self-knowledge
self-limiting
self-locking
self-love
self-lubricating
self-luminous
self-mastery
self-observation
self-operating
self-originated
self-perpetuating
self-pity
self-possessed
self-possession
self-praise
self-preservation
self-pride
self-proclaimed
self-propelled
self-propelling
self-protection
self-recording
self-registering
self-regulating
self-reliance
self-reliant
self-renunciation
self-reproach
self-respecting
self-restraint
self-rewarding
self-sacrifice
self-sacrificing
self-satisfaction
self-satisfied
self-satisfying
self-sealing
self-sufficiency
self-sufficient
self-sufficing
self-supporting
self-sustained
self-sustaining
self-taught
self-winding

self-ac·quired \\ˌself-ə-ˈkwī(ə)rd\\ *adj* : acquired by oneself or for one's own use and benefit
self-ap·plause \\ˌself-ə-ˈplȯz\\ *n* : an expression or feeling of approval of oneself
self-as·sert·ing \\ˌself-ə-ˈsərt-iŋ\\ *adj* **1** : asserting oneself or one's own rights or claims **2** : putting oneself forward in a confident or arrogant manner
self-cen·tered \\ˈself-ˈsent-ərd\\ *adj* : interested chiefly in one's own self : SELFISH — **self-cen·tered·ness** *n*
self-com·mand \\ˌself-kə-ˈmand\\ *n* : control of one's own behavior and emotions : SELF-CONTROL
self-com·posed \\ˌself-kəm-ˈpōzd\\ *adj* : having control over one's emotions : CALM — **self-com·pos·ed·ly** \\-ˈpō-zəd-lē\\ *adv*
self-con·fessed \\-kən-ˈfest\\ *adj* : openly acknowledged
self-con·scious \\ˈself-ˈkän-chəs\\ *adj* **1** : aware of oneself as an individual **2** : uncomfortably conscious of oneself as an object of the observation of others : ill at ease — **self-con·scious·ly** *adv* — **self-con·scious·ness** *n*
self-con·sist·ent \\ˌself-kən-ˈsis-tənt\\ *adj* : having each part logically consistent with the rest — **self-con·sist·en·cy** \\-tən-sē\\ *n*
self-con·tained \\ˌself-kən-ˈtānd\\ *adj* **1** : sufficient in itself **2 a** : showing self-command **b** : formal and reserved in manner **3** : complete in itself
self-con·tra·dic·to·ry \\ˌself-ˌkän-trə-ˈdik-t(ə-)rē\\ *adj* : consisting of two contradictory members or parts
self-con·trol \\ˌself-kən-ˈtrōl\\ *n* : control over one's own impulses, emotions, or acts — **self-con·trolled** \\-ˈtrōld\\ *adj*
self-de·ter·mi·na·tion \\ˌself-di-ˌtər-mə-ˈnā-shən\\ *n* **1** : the act or power of deciding things for oneself **2** : determination by the people of a territorial unit of their own future political status — **self-de·ter·min·ing** \\-ˈtər-mə-niŋ\\ *adj*
self-em·ployed \\ˌself-im-ˈplȯid\\ *adj* : earning income directly from one's own business, trade, or profession rather than as salary or wages from an employer — **self-em·ploy·ment** \\-ˈplȯi-mənt\\ *n*
self-ex·pres·sion \\ˌself-ik-ˈspresh-ən\\ *n* : the expression of one's own personality — **self-ex·pres·sive** \\-ˈspres-iv\\ *adj*
self-gov·ern·ment \\ˈself-ˈgəv-ər(n)-mənt\\ *n* : government of a political unit by action of its own people — **self-gov·erned** \\-ˈgəv-ərnd\\ *adj* — **self-gov·ern·ing** \\-ər-niŋ\\ *adj*
self-im·por·tance \\ˌself-ᵊm-ˈpȯrt-ᵊn(t)s, -ən(t)s\\ *n* **1** : an exaggerated estimate of one's own importance : SELF-CONCEIT **2** : arrogant or pompous bearing or behavior — **self-im·por·tant** \\-ᵊnt, -ənt\\ *adj* — **self-im·por·tant·ly** *adv*
self-in·crim·i·na·tion \\ˌself-in-ˌkrim-ə-ˈnā-shən\\ *n* : incrimination of oneself; *esp* : the giving of evidence or answering of questions the tendency of which would be to subject one to criminal prosecution — **self-in·crim·i·nat·ing** \\-ˈkrim-ə-ˌnāt-iŋ\\ *adj*
self-in·ter·est \\ˈself-ˈin-trəst, -ˈint-ə-rəst\\ *n* **1** : one's own interest or advantage **2** : a concern for one's own advantage and well-being — **self-in·ter·est·ed** \\-əd\\ *adj*
self·ish \\ˈsel-fish\\ *adj* **1** : concerned excessively or exclusively with oneself : seeking or concentrating on one's own advantage, pleasure, or well-being without regard for others **2** : arising from concern with one's own welfare or advantage in disregard of others — **self·ish·ly** *adv* — **self·ish·ness** *n*
self·less \\ˈself-ləs\\ *adj* : having or showing no concern for self : UNSELFISH — **self·less·ly** *adv* — **self·less·ness** *n*
self-made \\ˈself-ˈmād\\ *adj* **1** : made by oneself or itself **2** : raised from poverty or obscurity by one's own efforts
self-opin·ion·at·ed \\ˌself-ə-ˈpin-yə-ˌnāt-əd\\ *adj* **1** : CONCEITED **2** : stubbornly holding to one's own opinion
self-por·trait \\ˈself-ˈpōr-trət, -ˌtrāt\\ *n* : a portrait of oneself done by oneself
self-re·gard \\ˌself-ri-ˈgärd\\ *n* **1** : regard for or consideration of oneself or one's own interests **2** : SELF-RESPECT — **self-re·gard·ing** \\-iŋ\\ *adj*
self-re·spect \\ˌself-ri-ˈspekt\\ *n* **1** : a proper respect for oneself as a human being **2** : regard for one's own standing or position — **self-re·spect·ing** \\-ˈspek-tiŋ\\ *adj*
self-righ·teous \\ˈself-ˈrī-chəs\\ *adj* : convinced of one's own righteousness esp. in contrast with the actions and beliefs of others — **self-righ·teous·ly** *adv* — **self-righ·teous·ness** *n*
self-ris·ing \\ˈself-ˈrī-ziŋ\\ *adj* : rising without the use of leaven
self·same \\ˈself-ˌsām\\ *adj* : precisely the same : IDENTICAL
self-seek·er \\ˈself-ˈsē-kər\\ *n* : one that seeks only or mainly his own advantage or pleasure — **self-seek·ing** \\-kiŋ\\ *adj*
self-ser·vice \\ˈself-ˈsər-vəs\\ *n* : the serving of oneself (as in a cafeteria or supermarket) with things to be paid for at a cashier's desk usu. upon leaving — **self-service** *adj*
self-start·er \\ˈself-ˈstärt-ər\\ *n* : a more or less automatic attachment for starting an internal-combustion engine
self-styled \\ˈself-ˈstīld\\ *adj* : called by oneself
self-will \\ˈself-ˈwil\\ *n* : stubborn or willful adherence to one's own desires or ideas : OBSTINACY — **self-willed** \\-ˌwild\\ *adj*
¹sell \\ˈsel\\ *vb* **sold** \\ˈsōld\\; **sell·ing** **1** : to deliver up in violation of duty, trust, or loyalty : BETRAY **2 a** : to give in exchange esp. for money; *also* : to give in exchange foolishly or dishonorably **b** : to work at or deal in the sale of : have or offer for sale; *also* : to achieve the sale of **3 a** : to find buyers : be bought **b** : to be for sale **4 a** : to make acceptable, believable, or desirable by persuasion **b** : to bring around to a favorable way of thinking **c** : to gain acceptance or approval — **sell·a·ble** *adj* — **sell short** : to underestimate the ability, strength, or importance of

²sell *n* **1 :** a deliberate deception : HOAX **2 :** the act or a type of selling : SALESMANSHIP
sell·er \'sel-ər\ *n* **1 :** one that offers for sale or makes a sale **2 :** a product selling well or to a specified extent
sell out *vb* **1 :** to dispose of all of one's goods by sale **2 :** to betray one's cause or associates
sell·out \'sel-ˌau̇t\ *n* **1 :** the act or an instance of selling out **2 :** a performance or exhibition for which all seats are sold
selt·zer \'selt-sər\ *n* **:** an artificially prepared water containing carbon dioxide
sel·vage *or* **sel·vedge** \'sel-vij\ *n* **:** the edge of cloth so woven that it will not ravel
selves *pl of* SELF
se·man·tic \si-'mant-ik\ *adj* **1 :** of or relating to meaning in language **2 :** of or relating to semantics — **se·man·ti·cal·ly** \-'mant-i-k(ə-)lē\ *adv*
se·man·ti·cist \si-'mant-ə-səst\ *n* **:** a specialist in semantics
se·man·tics \si-'mant-iks\ *n* **:** the study of meanings; *esp* **:** the historical and psychological study and the classification of changes in the meaning of words or forms viewed as factors in linguistic development
¹sem·a·phore \'sem-ə-ˌfōr\ *n* **1 :** an apparatus for visual signaling (as by the position of one or more movable arms) **2 :** a system of visual signaling by two flags held one in each hand

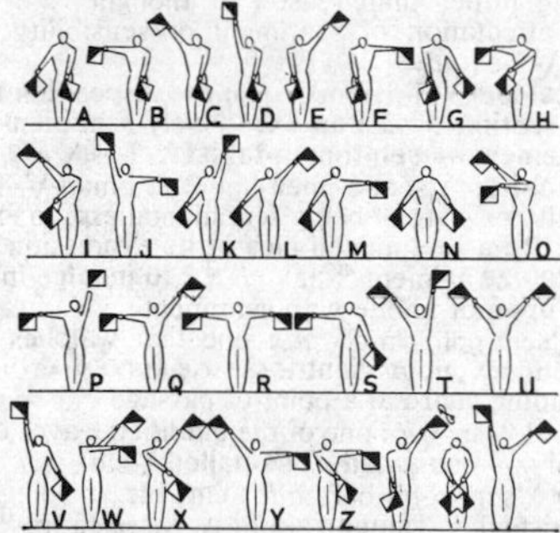

semaphore 2: alphabet (plus last three positions: error, break, numerals follow)

²semaphore *vb* **:** to signal by or as if by semaphore
sem·blance \'sem-blən(t)s\ *n* **1 :** outward appearance **2 :** LIKENESS, IMAGE
se·men \'sē-mən\ *n, pl* **sem·i·na** \'sem-ə-nə\ *or* **semens :** a viscid whitish fluid of the male reproductive tract consisting of spermatozoa suspended in secretions of accessory glands
se·mes·ter \sə-'mes-tər\ *n* **:** one of two usu. 18-week terms into which an academic year is usu. divided
semi- *prefix* **1 :** precisely half of **2 :** half in quantity or value; *also* **:** half of or occurring halfway through a specified period **3 :** partly **:** incompletely **4 :** partial **:** incomplete **5 :** having some of the characteristics of

semiannual	**semi–independent**	**semiprofessional**
semiautomatic	**semilegendary**	**semireligious**
semiautonomous	**semiliquid**	**semiskilled**
semicircle	**semiliterate**	**semisoft**
semicircular	**semimonthly**	**semisolid**
semicivilized	**semiofficial**	**semisweet**
semiconscious	**semipermanent**	**semitransparent**
semidarkness	**semipolitical**	**semitropical**
semidivine	**semiprecious**	**semiweekly**
semiformal	**semipro**	**semiyearly**

semi·co·lon \'sem-i-ˌkō-lən\ *n* **:** a punctuation mark ; used esp. in a coordinating function between major sentence elements
semi·con·duc·tor \ˌsem-i-kən-'dək-tər, ˌsem-ˌī\ *n* **1 :** a substance whose electrical conductivity is between that of a conductor and an insulator **2 :** a device (as a transistor or diode) made of semiconductor material that is used to control the flow of electricity (as in a television)
¹semi·fi·nal \ˌsem-i-'fīn-ᵊl\ *adj* **:** being next to the last in an elimination tournament
²semi·fi·nal \'sem-i-ˌfīn-ᵊl\ *n* **:** a semifinal match or round — **semi·fi·nal·ist** \ˌsem-i-'fīn-ᵊl-əst\ *n*
semi·flu·id \ˌsem-i-'flü-əd, ˌsem-ˌī-\ *adj* **:** having the qualities of both a fluid and a solid : VISCOUS
semi·lu·nar \ˌsem-i-'lü-nər, ˌsem-ˌī-\ *adj* **:** shaped like a crescent
sem·i·nar \'sem-ə-ˌnär\ *n* **1 :** a course of study pursued by a group of advanced students doing original research under a professor and exchanging results and discussions **2 :** a meeting of a seminar; *also* **:** a room for such meetings
sem·i·nar·i·an \ˌsem-ə-'ner-ē-ən\ *n* **:** a student in a seminary esp. of the Roman Catholic Church
sem·i·nary \'sem-ə-ˌner-ē\ *n, pl* **-nar·ies 1 :** an institution of secondary education; *esp* **:** an academy for girls **2 :** an institution for training clergymen
semi·pri·vate \ˌsem-i-'prī-vət, ˌsem-ˌī-\ *adj* **:** shared with only one or a few others
Se·mit·ic \sə-'mit-ik\ *adj* **:** JEWISH
sem·pi·ter·nal \ˌsem-pi-'tərn-ᵊl\ *adj* **:** EVERLASTING — **sem·pi·ter·nal·ly** \-ᵊl-ē\ *adv*
sen·ate \'sen-ət\ *n* **1 :** the higher chamber in some bicameral legislatures **2 :** the hall or chamber in which a senate meets
sen·a·tor \'sen-ət-ər\ *n* **:** a member of a senate — **sen·a·tor·ship** \-ˌship\ *n*
sen·a·to·ri·al \ˌsen-ə-'tōr-ē-əl\ *adj* **:** of, relating to, or befitting a senator or a senate
send \'send\ *vb* **sent** \'sent\; **send·ing 1 :** to cause to go; *esp* **:** to drive or propel physically **2 :** to cause to happen or occur **3 :** to have an agent, order, or request go or be transmitted; *esp* **:** to transmit an order or request to come or return **4 :** to put or bring into a certain condition — **send·er** *n* — **send packing :** to send off roughly or in disgrace
send–off \'send-ˌȯf\ *n* **:** a demonstration of goodwill and enthusiasm for the beginning of a new venture
se·nile \'sēn-ˌīl, 'sen-\ *adj* **:** of or relating to old age : resulting from old age; *also* **:** having infirmities associated with old age
se·nil·i·ty \si-'nil-ət-ē\ *n* **:** the quality or state of being senile; *esp* **:** the physical and mental infirmity of old age
¹se·nior \'sē-nyər\ *n* **1 :** a person who is older or of higher rank than another **2 :** a student in his last year before graduating from a school of secondary or higher level
²senior *adj* **1 a :** OLDER — used chiefly to distinguish a father with the same given name as his son **b :** earliest in date of origin **2 :** higher in standing or rank **3 :** of or relating to seniors in an educational institution
senior chief petty officer *n* **:** a noncommissioned officer in the navy ranking next below a master chief petty officer
se·nior·i·ty \sēn-'yȯr-ət-ē, -'yär-\ *n* **1 :** the quality or state of being senior : PRIORITY **2 :** a privileged status attained by length of service
senior master sergeant *n* **:** a noncommissioned officer in the air force ranking next below a chief master sergeant
sen·na \'sen-ə\ *n* **1 :** CASSIA 2; *esp* **:** one used medicinally **2 :** the dried leaflets of various cassias used as a purgative
sen·sa·tion \sen-'sā-shən, sən-\ *n* **1 a :** awareness (as of noise or heat) or a mental process (as seeing, hearing, or smelling) due to stimulation of a sense organ **b :** an indefinite bodily feeling **c :** something that causes or is the object of sensation

2 **a** : a state of excited interest or feeling **b** : a cause of such excitement

sen·sa·tion·al \-shnəl, -shən-ᵊl\ *adj* **1** : of or relating to sensation or the senses **2** : arousing or tending to arouse (as by lurid details) a quick, intense, and usu. superficial interest, curiosity, or emotional reaction **3** : exceedingly or unexpectedly excellent or great — **sen·sa·tion·al·ly** \-ē\ *adv*

sen·sa·tion·al·ism \-ˌiz-əm\ *n* : the use or effect of sensational subject matter or treatment

¹sense \'sen(t)s\ *n* **1 a** : the faculty of perceiving by means of sense organs **b** : a specialized animal function or mechanism (as sight, hearing, smell, taste, or touch) basically involving interaction of a stimulus and a sense organ **2** : a particular sensation or kind or quality of sensation **3** : AWARENESS, CONSCIOUSNESS **4** : intellectual appreciation **5** : INTELLIGENCE, JUDGMENT; *esp* : good judgment **6** : good reason or excuse **7** : MEANING; *esp* : one of the meanings a word may bear **8** : IMPORT, INTENTION

²sense *vt* **1 a** : to perceive by the senses **b** : to be or become conscious of **2** : GRASP, COMPREHEND

sense·less \'sen(t)s-ləs\ *adj* : destitute of, deficient in, or contrary to sense: as **a** : UNCONSCIOUS **b** : FOOLISH, STUPID **c** : PURPOSELESS, MEANINGLESS — **sense·less·ly** *adv*

sense organ *n* : a bodily structure affected by a stimulus (as heat or sound waves) in such a manner as to activate associated sensory nerve fibers to convey impulses to the central nervous system where they are interpreted as corresponding sensations

sen·si·bil·i·ty \ˌsen(t)-sə-'bil-ət-ē\ *n, pl* **-ties** **1** : ability to receive sensations : SENSITIVENESS **2** : peculiar susceptibility to a pleasurable or painful impression (as a slight or unkindness) — often used in pl. **3** : awareness of and responsiveness toward something (as emotion in another) **4** : refined sensitiveness in emotion and taste

sen·si·ble \'sen(t)-sə-bəl\ *adj* **1 a** : capable of being perceived by the senses or by reason or understanding **b** : of a significant size, amount, or degree **2** : capable of receiving sense impressions **3** : COGNIZANT, AWARE **4** : having or containing good sense or reason : REASONABLE — **sen·si·ble·ness** *n* — **sen·si·bly** \-blē\ *adv*

sen·si·tive \'sen(t)-sət-iv, 'sen(t)-stiv\ *adj* **1** : subject to excitement by or responsive to stimuli **2** : easily or strongly affected or hurt; *esp* : HYPERSENSITIVE **3 a** : capable of indicating minute differences : DELICATE **b** : readily affected or changed by various agents or causes (as light or mechanical shock) **4** : concerned with or involving highly classified government information — **sen·si·tive·ly** *adv* — **sen·si·tive·ness** *n*

sen·si·tiv·i·ty \ˌsen(t)-sə-'tiv-ət-ē\ *n, pl* **-ties** : the quality or state of being sensitive: as **a** : the capacity of an organism or sense organ to respond to stimulation **b** : HYPERSENSITIVITY

sen·si·tize \'sen(t)-sə-ˌtīz\ *vb* : to make or become sensitive or hypersensitive — **sen·si·ti·za·tion** \ˌsen(t)-sət-ə-'zā-shən\ *n* — **sen·si·tiz·er** \'sen(t)-sə-ˌtī-zər\ *n*

sen·sor \'sen-ˌsȯr, 'sen(t)-sər\ *n* : a device that responds to a physical stimulus and transmits a resulting impulse

sen·so·ry \'sen(t)s-(ə-)rē\ *adj* **1** : of or relating to sensation or to the senses **2** : conveying nerve impulses from the sense organs : AFFERENT

sen·su·al \'sench-(ə-)wəl\ *adj* **1** : SENSORY **2** : relating to or consisting in the gratification of the senses or the indulgence of appetite : FLESHLY **3 a** : devoted to or preoccupied with the senses or appetites **b** : VOLUPTUOUS **c** : deficient in moral, spiritual, or intellectual interests : WORLDLY; *esp* : IRRELIGIOUS — **sen·su·al·i·ty** \ˌsen-chə-'wal-ət-ē\ *n* — **sen·su·al·ly** \'sench-(ə-)wə-lē\ *adv*

sen·su·al·ism \'sench-(ə-)wə-ˌliz-əm\ *n* : SENSUALITY

sen·su·ous \'sench-(ə-)wəs\ *adj* **1** : having to do with the senses or with things perceived by the senses **2** : characterized by sense impressions or imagery addressing the senses **3** : highly susceptible to influence through the senses — **sen·su·ous·ly** *adv* — **sen·su·ous·ness** *n*

sent *past of* SEND

¹sen·tence \'sent-ᵊn(t)s, -ᵊnz\ *n* **1 a** : JUDGMENT 2a; *esp* : one formally pronounced by a court in a criminal proceeding and specifying the punishment to be inflicted **b** : the punishment so imposed **2** : a grammatically self-contained speech unit that expresses an assertion, a question, a command, a wish, or an exclamation

²sentence *vt* **1** : to pronounce sentence on **2** : to condemn to a specified punishment

sen·ten·tious \sen-'ten-chəs\ *adj* **1** : being concise and forceful : PITHY **2** : containing, using, or inclined to use high-sounding empty phrases or pompous sayings — **sen·ten·tious·ly** *adv* — **sen·ten·tious·ness** *n*

sen·tient \'sen-ch(ē-)ənt\ *adj* : capable of feeling : conscious of sense impressions — **sen·tience** \-ch(ē-)ən(t)s\ *n*

sen·ti·ment \'sent-ə-mənt\ *n* **1 a** : an attitude, thought, or judgment prompted by feeling **b** : OPINION **2 a** : EMOTION **b** : refined feeling : delicate sensibility **c** : emotional idealism **d** : a romantic or nostalgic feeling

sen·ti·men·tal \ˌsent-ə-'ment-ᵊl\ *adj* **1 a** : marked or governed by feeling, sensibility, or emotional idealism **b** : resulting from feeling rather than reason or thought **2** : having an excess or affectation of sentiment or sensibility — **sen·ti·men·tal·ly** \-ᵊl-ē\ *adv*

sen·ti·men·tal·ism \-ᵊl-ˌiz-əm\ *n* **1** : the disposition to favor or indulge in sentiment **2** : an excessively sentimental conception or statement — **sen·ti·men·tal·ist** \-ᵊl-əst\ *n*

sen·ti·men·tal·i·ty \ˌsent-ə-ˌmen-'tal-ət-ē, -mən-\ *n, pl* **-ties** **1** : the quality or state of being sentimental esp. to excess or in affectation **2** : a sentimental idea or its expression

sen·ti·men·tal·ize \-'ment-ᵊl-ˌīz\ *vb* **1** : to indulge in sentiment **2** : to look upon or imbue with sentiment

sen·ti·nel \'sent-nəl, -ᵊn-əl\ *n* : one that watches or guards

sen·try \'sen-trē\, *n, pl* **sentries** : GUARD, WATCH; *esp* : a soldier standing guard at a point of passage

se·pal \'sēp-əl, 'sep-\ *n* : one of the modified leaves comprising a flower calyx — **se·paled** *or* **se·palled** \-əld\ *adj*

sep·a·ra·ble \'sep-(ə-)rə-bəl\ *adj* : capable of being separated or distinguished — **sep·a·ra·bil·i·ty** \ˌsep-(ə-)rə-'bil-ət-ē\ *n*

¹sep·a·rate \'sep-ə-ˌrāt\ *vb* **1 a** : to set or keep apart : DISCONNECT, DISUNITE **b** : to make a distinction between : DISTINGUISH **c** : SORT **d** : to disperse in space or time : SCATTER **2** : to sever contractual relations with : DISCHARGE **3** : to block off : SEGREGATE **4** : to isolate from a mixture **5** : to become divided or detached : come apart **6 a** : to break off an association : WITHDRAW **b** : to cease to be or live together **7** : to go in different directions

²sep·a·rate \'sep-(ə-)rət\ *adj* **1** : not connected : not united or associated **2** : divided from another or others **3** : being apart from others : ISOLATED **4** : relating to one only : not shared **5** : SINGLE, PARTICULAR — **sep·a·rate·ly** *adv* — **sep·a·rate·ness** *n*

sep·a·ra·tion \ˌsep-ə-'rā-shən\ *n* **1** : the act or process of separating : the state of being separated **2 a** : a point, line, or means of division **b** : an intervening space : GAP

sep·a·rat·ist \'sep(-ə)-rət-əst\ *n* : one that favors separation (as from a political or religious body) — **sep·a·rat·ism** \-rə-ˌtiz-əm\ *n*

sep·a·ra·tive \'sep-ə-ˌrāt-iv, 'sep-(ə-)rət-\ *adj* : tending toward, causing, or expressing separation

sep·a·ra·tor \'sep-ə-ˌrāt-ər\ *n* : one that separates; *esp* : a device for separating cream from milk

se·pia \'sē-pē-ə\ *n* : a brownish gray to dark brown

sep·sis \'sep-səs\ *n, pl* **sep·ses** \'sep-ˌsēz\ : a poisoned condition resulting from the spread of bacteria or their poisonous products from a center of infection

Sep·tem·ber \sep-'tem-bər, səp-\ *n* : the 9th month of the year

sep·tic \'sep-tik\ *adj* **1** : PUTREFACTIVE **2** : relating to or characteristic of sepsis

septic tank *n* : a tank in which the solid matter of continuously flowing sewage is disintegrated by bacteria

sep·tu·a·ge·nar·i·an \sep-,t(y)ü-ə-jə-'ner-ē-ən, ,sep-tə-wə-jə-\ *n* : a person who is 70 or more but less than 80 years old — **septuagenarian** *adj*

Sep·tu·a·gint \sep-'t(y)ü-ə-jənt, 'sep-tə-wə-,jint\ *n* : a Greek version of the Old Testament used by Greek-speaking Christians

[1]**sep·ul·cher** *or* **sep·ul·chre** \'sep-əl-kər\ *n* : a place of burial : TOMB

[2]**sepulcher** *or* **sepulchre** *vt* **-chered** *or* **-chred**; **-cher·ing** *or* **-chring** \-k(ə-)riŋ\ : BURY, ENTOMB

se·pul·chral \sə-'pəl-krəl\ *adj* **1** : of or relating to burial, the grave, or monuments to the dead **2** : DISMAL, GLOOMY — **se·pul·chral·ly** \-krə-lē\ *adv*

sep·ul·ture \'sep-əl-,chu̇r\ *n* **1** : BURIAL **2** : SEPULCHER

se·quel \'sē-kwəl\ *n* **1** : an event that follows or comes afterward : RESULT **2** : a book that continues a story begun in another

se·quence \'sē-kwən(t)s, -,kwen(t)s\ *n* **1** : a continuous or connected series **2** : order of succession **3 a** : CONSEQUENCE, RESULT **b** : a subsequent development **4** : continuity of progression

se·quent \'sē-kwənt\ *adj* : following in time or as an effect — **sequent** *n*

se·quen·tial \si-'kwen-chəl\ *adj* : SEQUENT

se·ques·ter \si-'kwes-tər\ *vt* **se·ques·tered**; **se·ques·ter·ing** \-t(ə-)riŋ\ **1** : to set apart : SEGREGATE, WITHDRAW **2** : to take custody of (as personal property) until a demand is satisfied

se·ques·trate \si-'kwes-,trāt\ *vt* : CONFISCATE

se·ques·tra·tion \,sē-kwəs-'trā-shən, si-,kwes-\ *n* : the act of sequestering : the state of being sequestered

se·quin \'sē-kwən\ *n* : a spangle used as an ornament on clothes

se·quoia \si-'kwȯi-ə\ *n* : either of two huge coniferous California trees of the pine family

sera *pl of* SERUM

se·ra·glio \sə-'ral-yō\ *n, pl* **-glios** : HAREM 1a

ser·aph \'ser-əf\ *n, pl* **ser·a·phim** \-ə-,fim\ *or* **seraphs** : an angel of a very high order — **seraph** *adj* — **se·raph·ic** \sə-'raf-ik\ *adj* — **se·raph·i·cal·ly** \-'raf-i-k(ə-)lē\ *adv*

sere \'si(ə)r\ *adj* : dried up : WITHERED

[1]**ser·e·nade** \,ser-ə-'nād\ *n* : a complimentary vocal or instrumental performance; *esp* : one given outdoors at night for a woman

[2]**serenade** *vb* : to entertain with or perform a serenade — **ser·e·nad·er** *n*

ser·en·dip·i·ty \,ser-ən-'dip-ət-ē\ *n* : the gift of finding valuable or agreeable things not sought for

se·rene \sə-'rēn\ *adj* **1 a** : being clear and free of storms **b** : shining bright and steady **2** : marked by utter calm : TRANQUIL **3** : AUGUST — used as part of a title — **se·rene·ly** *adv*

se·ren·i·ty \sə-'ren-ət-ē\ *n* : the quality or state of being serene

serf \'sərf\ *n* : a member of a servile feudal class bound to the soil and more or less subject to the will of his lord — **serf·dom** \-dəm\ *n*

serge \'sərj\ *n* : a durable twilled fabric having a smooth clear face and a diagonal rib on the front and the back

ser·geant \'sär-jənt\ *n* **1** : a police officer ranking in the U.S. just below captain or sometimes lieutenant and in England just below inspector **2** : a noncommissioned officer in the army ranking next below a staff sergeant

sergeant first class *n* : a noncommissioned officer in the army ranking next below a master sergeant

sergeant major *n, pl* **sergeants major** *or* **sergeant majors** **1** : a noncommissioned officer (as in the army) serving as chief enlisted assistant in a headquarters **2** : a noncommissioned officer in the army of the highest enlisted rank

[1]**se·ri·al** \'sir-ē-əl\ *adj* **1** : of, consisting of, or arranged in a series, rank, or row **2** : appearing in parts or numbers that follow regularly — **se·ri·al·ly** \-ē-ə-lē\ *adv*

[2]**serial** *n* **1** : a work appearing (as in a magazine or on television) in parts at intervals **2** : one part of a serial work : INSTALLMENT — **se·ri·al·ist** \-ē-ə-ləst\ *n*

se·ri·al·ize \'sir-ē-ə-,līz\ *vt* : to arrange or publish in serial form — **se·ri·al·i·za·tion** \,sir-ē-ə-lə-'zā-shən\ *n*

se·ries \'si(ə)r-(,)ēz\ *n, pl* **series** **1 a** : a number of things or events of the same class coming one after another **b** : a group with an order of arrangement exhibiting progression **2** : the indicated sum of a sequence of numbers **3** : a succession of volumes or issues published with related subjects or authors, similar format and price, or continuous numbering **4** : a group of successive coordinate sentence elements joined together — **in series** : in a serial arrangement

se·rio·com·ic \,sir-ē-ō-'käm-ik\ *adj* : having a mixture of the serious and the comic

se·ri·ous \'sir-ē-əs\ *adj* **1** : thoughtful or subdued in appearance or manner : SOBER **2 a** : requiring much thought or work **b** : of or relating to a matter of importance **3** : not joking or trifling : EARNEST **4 a** : not easily answered or solved **b** : having important or dangerous possible consequences — **se·ri·ous·ly** *adv* — **se·ri·ous·ness** *n*

ser·mon \'sər-mən\ *n* **1** : a public speech usu. by a clergyman giving religious instruction or exhortation **2 a** : a lecture on conduct or duty **b** : an annoying harangue

ser·mon·ize \'sər-mə-,nīz\ *vb* **1** : to compose or deliver a sermon : PREACH **2** : to discourse didactically or dogmatically

se·rous \'sir-əs\ *adj* : of, relating to, resembling, or producing serum; *esp* : of thin watery constitution

ser·pent \'sər-pənt\ *n* **1** : SNAKE; *esp* : a large snake **2** : DEVIL 1 **3** : a subtle treacherous malicious person

ser·pen·tine \'sər-pən-,tēn, -,tīn\ *adj* **1** : of or resembling a serpent **2** : subtly wily or tempting : DIABOLIC **3** : winding or turning one way and another : SINUOUS

[1]**ser·rate** \sə-'rāt, 'ser-,āt\ *vt* : to put notches in

[2]**serrate** *or* **ser·rat·ed** \sə-'rāt-əd, 'ser-,āt-\ *adj* : having a saw-toothed edge

ser·ried \'ser-ēd\ *adj* : crowded or pressed together : COMPACT — **ser·ried·ly** *adv* — **ser·ried·ness** *n*

se·rum \'sir-əm\ *n, pl* **serums** *or* **se·ra** \'sir-ə\ : the watery portion of an animal fluid (as blood) remaining after coagulation; *esp* : blood serum that contains specific immune bodies (as antitoxins) — **se·ral** \'sir-əl\ *adj*

ser·vant \'sər-vənt\ *n* : one that serves others; *esp* : one that performs household or personal services

[1]**serve** \'sərv\ *vb* **1 a** : to be a servant : ATTEND **b** : to give the service and respect due to (a superior); *also* : WORSHIP **c** : to comply with the commands or demands of : GRATIFY **d (1)** : to work through or perform a term of service esp. in the army or navy **(2)** : to put in : SPEND **2 a** : to officiate as a clergyman or priest **b** : to assist as server at mass **3 a** : to be of use : answer a purpose **b** : BENEFIT **c** : to be favorable, opportune, or convenient **d** : to prove adequate or satisfactory : SUFFICE **e** : to hold an office : discharge a duty or function **4 a** : to help persons to foods (as at a table or counter) **b** : to set out portions of food or drink **5 a** : to furnish or supply with something (as heat or light) needed or desired **b** : to wait on customers **c** : to furnish professional services to **6** : to make a serve (as in tennis) **7** : to treat or act toward in a specified way : REQUITE

²serve *n* : the act of putting the ball or shuttlecock in play (as in tennis or badminton)
serv·er \'sər-vər\ *n* **1** : one that serves food or drink **2** : the player who puts a ball in play **3** : something (as a tray) used in serving food or drink
¹ser·vice \'sər-vəs\ *n* **1** : the occupation or function of serving; *esp* : employment as a servant **2 a** : the work or action performed by one that serves **b** : HELP, USE, BENEFIT **c** : contribution to the welfare of others **d** : disposal for use **3 a** : a form followed in worship or in a religious ceremony **b** : a meeting for worship **4** : the act of serving: as **a** : a helpful act : good turn **b** : useful labor that does not produce a tangible commodity — usu. used in pl. **c** : SERVE **5** : a set of articles for a particular use **6 a** : an administrative division (as of a government) **b** : a nation's military forces or one of these forces **7** : a facility supplying some public demand; *esp* : one providing maintenance and repair
²service *adj* **1** : of or relating to the armed services **2** : used in serving or supplying **3** : intended for everyday use : DURABLE **4** : providing services (as repairs or maintenance)
³service *vt* : to perform services for : repair or provide maintenance for
ser·vice·a·ble \'sər-və-sə-bəl\ *adj* **1** : HELPFUL, USEFUL **2** : wearing well in use — **ser·vice·a·bil·i·ty** \ˌsər-və-sə-'bil-ət-ē\ *n* — **ser·vice·a·ble·ness** *n*
ser·vice·man \'sər-vəs-ˌman, -mən\ *n* **1** : a male member of the armed forces **2** : a man employed to repair or maintain equipment
service station *n* : FILLING STATION
ser·vile \'sər-vəl, -ˌvīl\ *adj* **1** : of or befitting a slave or an enslaved or menial class **2** : lacking spirit or independence : SUBMISSIVE — **ser·vil·i·ty** \(ˌ)sər-'vil-ət-ē\ *n*
ser·vi·tor \'sər-vət-ər\ *n* : a male servant
ser·vi·tude \'sər-və-ˌt(y)üd\ *n* : the state of subjection to another that constitutes or resembles slavery or serfdom
ses·a·me \'ses-ə-mē\ *n* : an East Indian annual erect hairy herb; *also* : its small somewhat flat seeds used as a source of oil and a flavoring agent
ses·qui·cen·ten·ni·al \ˌses-kwi-sen-'ten-ē-əl\ *n* : a 150th anniversary or its celebration — **sesquicentennial** *adj*
ses·sile \'ses-əl, -ˌīl\ *adj* : attached by the base
ses·sion \'sesh-ən\ *n* **1** : a meeting or series of meetings of a body (as a court or legislature) for the transaction of business **2** : the period between the first and last of a series of meetings of a legislative or judicial body **3** : the period during the year or day in which a school conducts classes **4** : a meeting or period devoted to a particular activity
ses·tet \se-'stet\ *n* : a stanza or poem of six lines
¹set \'set\ *vb* **set**; **set·ting** **1 a** : to cause to sit **b** : to place in or on a seat **2** : to give (a fowl) eggs to hatch or provide (eggs) with suitable conditions for hatching **3** : to put or fix in any place, condition, or position **4** : to direct with fixed attention **5** : to cause to assume a specified condition, relation, or occupation **6** : to appoint or assign an office or duty : POST, STATION **7** : FIX, SETTLE **8 a** : to establish as the highest level or best performance **b** : to furnish as a pattern or model **9 a** : to put in order for immediate use **b** : to compose (type) for printing : put into type **10** : to wave, curl, or arrange (hair) by wetting and drying **11 a** : to adorn with something affixed or infixed : STUD, DOT **b** : to fix in a setting or frame **12** : to become or cause to become firm or solid **13** : to pass below the horizon : go down **14** : to apply oneself to some activity **15** : to become whole by knitting **16** : to defeat (a contract) esp. in bridge — **set about** : to begin to do — **set aside** **1** : DISCARD **2** : RESERVE, SAVE **3** : DISMISS **4** : ANNUL, OVERRULE — **set at** : ATTACK, ASSAIL — **set forth** **1** : PUBLISH **2** : to give an account or statement of **3** : to start out on a journey : set out — **set forward** **1** : FURTHER **2** : to set out on a journey : START — **set upon** : to attack with violence : ASSAULT
²set *adj* **1** : INTENT, DETERMINED **2** : PITCHED **3** : PRESCRIBED, SPECIFIED **4** : INTENTIONAL, PREMEDITATED **5** : reluctant to change : OBSTINATE **6 a** : IMMOVABLE, RIGID **b** : BUILT-IN **7** : SETTLED, PERSISTENT **8 a** : PREPARED, READY **b** : poised to start running or to dive in at the instant the signal is given
³set *n* **1** : the act or action of setting : the condition of being set **2** : a number of persons or things of the same kind that belong, are associated, or are used together **3** : DIRECTION, COURSE **4** : form or carriage of the body or of its parts **5** : the manner of fitting or of being placed or suspended **6** : an artificial setting for a scene of a play or motion picture **7** : a group of tennis games in which one side wins at least six and at least two more than an opponent
set·back \'set-ˌbak\ *n* **1** : a checking of progress **2** : an unexpected reverse
set down *vt* **1** : to cause to sit down : SEAT **2** : to place at rest on a surface or on the ground **3** : to cause or allow to get off a vehicle : DELIVER **4** : to put in writing **5 a** : REGARD, CONSIDER **b** : ATTRIBUTE
set in *vb* **1** : INSERT; *esp* : to stitch (a small part) within a large article **2** : to enter upon a particular state **3** : to set to work
set off *vb* **1 a** : to show up by contrast **b** : ADORN, EMBELLISH **c** : to set apart : make distinct or outstanding **2** : OFFSET, COMPENSATE **3 a** : to set in motion : cause to begin **b** : to cause to explode **4** : to measure off on a surface : lay off **5** : to start out on a course or a journey
set·off \'set-ˌȯf\ *n* : something that is set off against another
set on *vb* **1** : ATTACK **2 a** : to urge (as a dog) to attack or pursue **b** : to incite to action : INSTIGATE **c** : to set to work **3** : to go on : ADVANCE
set out *vb* **1** : to recite, describe, or state in detail **2** : to lay out the plan of **3** : to begin with a definite purpose : INTEND **4** : to start out on a course, a journey, or a career
set·tee \se-'tē\ *n* **1** : a long seat with a back **2** : a medium-sized sofa with arms and a back
set·ter \'set-ər\ *n* **1** : one that sets — often used in combination **2** : a large long-coated hunting dog
set·ting \'set-iŋ\ *n* **1** : the manner, position, or direction in which something is set **2** : the frame or bed in which a gem is set **3 a** : BACKGROUND, ENVIRONMENT **b** : the time and place within which a scene of a play or motion picture is enacted **4** : the music composed for a poem or other text **5** : the articles of tableware required for setting a place at table **6** : a batch of eggs for incubation
¹set·tle \'set-ᵊl\ *n* : a wooden bench with arms, a high solid back, and an enclosed foundation
²settle *vb* **set·tled**; **set·tling** \'set-liŋ, -ᵊl-iŋ\ **1** : to place so as to stay **2 a** : to establish residence in : COLONIZE **b** : to make one's home **3 a** : to cause to pack down or to become compact by sinking : sink gradually or to the bottom **b** : to clarify by causing dregs or impurities to sink **c** : to become clear by depositing a constituent as sediment **4 a** : to make or become quiet or orderly **b** : to take up an ordered or stable life **5 a** : to fix or resolve conclusively **b** : to establish or secure permanently **6** : to arrange in a desired position **7 a** : to make or arrange for final disposition of **b** : to bestow or give possession of legally **c** : to pay in full **8** : to adjust differences or accounts
set·tle·ment \'set-ᵊl-mənt\ *n* **1** : the act or process of settling **2** : an amount bestowed by a settlement **3 a** : a place or region newly settled **b** : a small village **4** : an institution providing various community services to people in a crowded part of a city **5** : an agreement composing differences
set·tler \'set-lər, -ᵊl-ər\ *n* : a person who settles in a new region

set to *vi* **1 :** to begin actively and earnestly **2 :** to begin fighting
set–to \'set-ˌtü\ *n, pl* **set–tos** \-ˌtüz\ **:** a usu. brief and vigorous contest (as a bout or an argument)
set up *vb* **1 :** to raise to and place in a high position **2 :** to make (a loud noise) with the voice **3 a :** ELATE, GRATIFY **b :** to make proud or vain **4 a :** to put forward or extol as a model **b :** to claim (oneself) to be **5 a :** to place upright **:** ERECT **b :** to assemble the parts of and erect **6 a :** FOUND, INAUGURATE **b :** to put in operation as a way of living or a means of livelihood **c :** to come into active operation or use **7 a :** to treat to (drinks) **b :** to treat (someone) to something
set•up \'set-ˌəp\ *n* **:** the way in which something is set up **:** ORGANIZATION, ARRANGEMENT
sev•en \'sev-ən\ *n* **1** — see NUMBER table **2 :** the seventh in a set or series **3 :** something having seven units or members — **seven** *adj or pron*
sev•en•teen \ˌsev-ən-'tēn\ *n* — see NUMBER table — **seventeen** *adj or pron* — **sev•en•teenth** \-'tēn(t)th\ *adj or n*
sev•enth \'sev-ən(t)th\ *n, pl* **sev•enths** \'sev-ən(t)s, -ən(t)ths\ — see NUMBER table — **seventh** *adj or adv*
sev•en•ty \'sev-ən-tē\ *n, pl* **-ties** — see NUMBER table — **sev•en•ti•eth** \-tē-əth\ *adj or n* — **seventy** *adj or pron*
sev•er \'sev-ər\ *vb* **sev•ered**; **sev•er•ing** \'sev-(ə-)riŋ\ **1 :** to put or keep apart **:** DIVIDE; *esp* **:** to part by violence (as by cutting) **2 :** to come or break apart — **sev•er•a•ble** \'sev-(ə-)rə-bəl\ *adj*
[1]**sev•er•al** \'sev-(ə-)rəl\ *adj* **1 a :** separate or distinct from one another **:** DIFFERENT **b :** PARTICULAR, RESPECTIVE **2 a :** more than one **b :** more than two but fewer than many — **sev•er•al•ly** \-ē\ *adv*
[2]**several** *pron* **:** an indefinite number more than two and fewer than many
sev•er•ance \'sev-(ə-)rən(t)s\ *n* **:** the act or process of severing **:** the state of being severed
se•vere \sə-'vi(ə)r\ *adj* **1 a :** strict in judgment, discipline, or government **b :** of a strict or stern bearing or manner **:** AUSTERE **2 :** rigorous in restraint, punishment, or requirement **:** STRINGENT **3 :** sober or restrained in decoration or manner **:** PLAIN **4 a :** inflicting physical discomfort or hardship **:** HARSH **b :** inflicting pain or distress **:** GRIEVOUS **5 :** requiring great effort **:** ARDUOUS **6 :** of a great degree **:** MARKED, SERIOUS — **se•vere•ly** *adv* — **se•vere•ness** *n*
se•ver•i•ty \sə-'ver-ət-ē\ *n, pl* **-ties** **:** the quality or state of being severe
sew \'sō\ *vb* **sewed**; **sewn** \'sōn\ *or* **sewed**; **sew•ing** **1 :** to unite or fasten by stitches made with a flexible thread or filament **2 :** to close or enclose by sewing **3 :** to practice or engage in working with needle and thread
sew•age \'sü-ij\ *n* **:** refuse liquids or waste matter carried off by sewers
[1]**sew•er** \'sō(-ə)r\ *n* **:** one that sews
[2]**sew•er** \'sü-ər, 'sů(-ə)r\ *n* **:** a covered usu. underground passage to carry off water and sewage
sew•er•age \'sü-ə-rij, 'sů(-ə)r-ij\ *n* **1 :** SEWAGE **2 :** the removal and disposal of sewage and surface water by sewers **3 :** a system of sewers
sew•ing \'sō-iŋ\ *n* **1 :** the act, method, or occupation of one that sews **2 :** material that has been or is to be sewed
sex \'seks\ *n* **1 :** either of two divisions of organisms distinguished respectively as male and female **2 :** the sum of the structural, functional, and behavioral peculiarities of living beings that are ultimately related to reproduction by two interacting parents and that serve to distinguish males and females **3 :** sexual activity or intercourse
sex•a•ge•nar•i•an \ˌsek-sə-jə-'ner-ē-ən\ *n* **:** a person who is 60 or more but less than 70 years old — **sexagenarian** *adj*
sex appeal *n* **:** personal appeal or physical attractiveness for members of the opposite sex
sexed \'sekst\ *adj* **:** having sex or sexual instincts
sex•ism \'sek-siz-əm\ *n* **:** prejudice or discrimination based on sex; *esp* **:** discrimination against women — **sex•ist** \'sek-səst\ *adj* or *n*
sex•tant \'sek-stənt\ *n* **:** an instrument for measuring altitudes of celestial bodies from a moving ship or airplane
sex•tet \sek-'stet\ *n* **1 :** a musical composition for six instruments or voices **2 :** a group or set of six
sex•ton \'sek-stən\ *n* **:** a church officer or employee whose duties include care of the buildings and property and the ringing of the bell for services
[1]**sex•tu•ple** \sek-'st(y)üp-əl, -'stəp-; 'sek-stəp-\ *adj* **1 :** having six units or members **2 :** being six times as great or as many — **sextuple** *n*
[2]**sextuple** *vb* **sex•tu•pled**; **sex•tu•pling** \-(ə-)liŋ\ **:** to make or become six times as much or as many
sex•tup•let \sek-'stəp-lət, -'st(y)üp-; 'sek-stəp-\ *n* **1 :** a combination of six of a kind **2 :** one of six offspring born at one birth
sex•u•al \'sek-sh(ə-w)əl\ *adj* **1 :** of, relating to, or associated with sex or the sexes **2 :** having or involving sex — **sex•u•al•i•ty** \ˌsek-shə-'wal-ət-ē\ *n* — **sex•u•al•ly** \'sek-shə-wə-lē, 'seksh-(ə-)lē\ *adv*
shab•by \'shab-ē\ *adj* **1 a :** threadbare and faded from wear **b :** ill kept **:** DILAPIDATED **2 :** clothed with worn or seedy garments **3 a :** MEAN, DESPICABLE **b :** UNGENEROUS, UNFAIR **c :** inferior in quality — **shab•bi•ly** \'shab-ə-lē\ *adv* — **shab•bi•ness** \'shab-ē-nəs\ *n*
shack \'shak\ *n* **1 :** HUT, SHANTY **2 :** a room or similar enclosed structure for a particular person or use
[1]**shack•le** \'shak-əl\ *n* **1 :** something (as a manacle or fetter) that confines the legs or arms **2 :** something that checks or prevents free action as if by fetters — usu. used in pl. **3 :** a device for making something fast or secure
[2]**shackle** *vt* **shack•led**; **shack•ling** \'shak-(ə-)liŋ\ **1 a :** to bind with shackles **b :** to make fast with a shackle **2 :** to deprive of freedom of action by means of restrictions or handicaps **:** HINDER, IMPEDE — **shack•ler** \-(ə-)lər\ *n*
shad \'shad\ *n, pl* **shad** **:** any of several deep-bodied food fishes that are closely related to the herrings but ascend rivers in the spring to spawn
[1]**shade** \'shād\ *n* **1 a :** partial darkness caused by interception of the rays of light **b :** relative obscurity or retirement **2 a :** shelter (as by foliage) from the heat and glare of sunlight **b :** a place sheltered from the sun **3 :** an evanescent or unreal appearance **4** *pl* **:** the shadows that gather as darkness comes on **5 :** a disembodied spirit **:** GHOST **6 :** something that intercepts or shelters from light, sun, or heat **7 a :** a color having some black in it **b :** a color slightly different from the one under consideration **8 :** a minute difference or variation
[2]**shade** *vb* **1 a :** to shelter or screen by intercepting radiated light or heat **b :** to cover with a shade **2 :** to hide partly by or as if by a shadow **3 :** to darken with or as if with a shadow **4 :** to cast into the shade **:** OBSCURE **5 :** to add shading to **6 :** to change by gradual transition or qualification — **shad•er** *n*
shad•ing \'shād-iŋ\ *n* **:** the filling up within outlines that represents the effect of darkness in a picture or drawing
[1]**shad•ow** \'shad-ō\ *n* **1 :** shade within defined bounds **2 :** a reflected image **3 :** shelter from danger or observation **4 a :** an imperfect and faint representation **b :** IMITATION, COPY **5 :** the image made by an obscured space on a surface that cuts across it usu. representing in silhouette the form of the interposed body **6 :** PHANTOM **7** *pl* **:** DARKNESS **8 :** a shaded or darker portion of a picture **9 :** a form without substance **:** VESTIGE **10 :** a small degree or portion **:** TRACE **11 :** a gloomy influence
[2]**shadow** *vb* **1 a :** to cast a shadow upon **b :** to cast a gloom

over : CLOUD **2** : to represent or indicate obscurely or faintly **3** : to follow esp. secretly : TRAIL **4** : to shade off **5** : to become overcast with or as if with shadows — **shad·ow·er** \'shad-ə-wər\ *n*

[3]**shadow** *adj* **1** : having form without substance **2** : having an indistinct pattern

shad·owy \'shad-ə-wē\ *adj* **1 a** : of the nature of or resembling a shadow : UNSUBSTANTIAL **b** : INDISTINCT, VAGUE **2** : being in or obscured by shadow **3** : SHADY 1

shady \'shād-ē\ *adj* **1** : producing or affording shade **2** : sheltered from the sun's rays **3 a** : of questionable merit **b** : DISREPUTABLE — **shad·i·ly** \'shād-ᵊl-ē\ *adv* — **shad·i·ness** \'shād-ē-nəs\ *n*

shaft \'shaft\ *n, pl* **shafts** \'shaf(t)s, *in sense 3 also* 'shavz\ **1 a** : the long handle of a weapon (as a spear) **b** : SPEAR, LANCE **2 a** : the slender stem of an arrow **b** : ARROW **3** : POLE; *esp* : one of two poles between which a horse is hitched to pull a vehicle **4** : a narrow beam of light **5** : something suggestive of the shaft of an arrow or spear : a long slender part esp. when round **6** : the handle of a tool **7** : a tall monument (as a column) **8** : a vertical opening or passage through the floors of a building **9** : a commonly cylindrical bar used to support rotating pieces or to transmit power or motion by rotation **10** : a vertical or inclined opening for finding or mining ore, raising water, or ventilating underground workings

shag \'shag\ *n* **1 a** : a shaggy tangled mass or covering **b** : long coarse or matted fiber or nap **2** : a strong coarse tobacco cut into fine shreds

shag·gy \'shag-ē\ *adj* **1 a** : covered with or consisting of long, coarse, or matted hair or thick, tangled, or unkempt vegetation **b** : having a rough or hairy nap, texture, or surface **2** : UNKEMPT — **shag·gi·ly** \'shag-ə-lē\ *adv* — **shag·gi·ness** \'shag-ē-nəs\ *n*

shah \'shä, 'shȯ\ *n* : the sovereign of Iran

[1]**shake** \'shāk\ *vb* **shook** \'shu̇k\; **shak·en** \'shā-kən\; **shak·ing** **1** : to move irregularly to and fro : QUIVER, TREMBLE **2** : to become unsteady : TOTTER **3** : to brandish, wave, or flourish often in a threatening manner **4** : to cause to move in a quick jerky manner **5** : to free oneself from **6** : to cause to waver : WEAKEN **7** : to dislodge or eject by quick jerky movements **8** : to clasp (hands) in greeting or as a sign of goodwill or agreement **9** : to stir the feelings of : UPSET — **shak·a·ble** *or* **shake·a·ble** *adj*

[2]**shake** *n* **1** : an act of shaking **2 a** : a blow or shock that upsets the equilibrium or disturbs the balance of something **b** : EARTHQUAKE **3** : something produced by shaking **4** : a wavering, quivering, or alternating motion caused by a blow or shock **5** : TRILL **6** : a very brief period of time : INSTANT **7** : [3]DEAL 2 **8** : a shingle split from a piece of log usu. three to four feet long — **no great shakes** : of no great importance

shake·down \'shāk-ˌdau̇n\ *n* : an act or instance of shaking someone down; *esp* : EXTORTION

shake down *vb* : to obtain money from in a dishonest or illegal manner

shak·er \'shā-kər\ *n* **1** : one that shakes **2** *cap* : a member of a millenarian sect originating in England in 1747 — **Shaker** *adj*

shake up *vt* **1** : to jar by or as if by a physical shock **2** : to effect an extensive and often drastic reorganization of

shake–up \'shāk-ˌəp\ *n* : an act or instance of shaking up; *esp* : an extensive and often drastic reorganization

shako \'shak-ō, 'shāk-\ *n, pl* **shak·os** *or* **shak·oes** : a stiff military cap with a high crown and plume

shaky \'shā-kē\ *adj* **1 a** : lacking stability **b** : lacking in firmness **c** : lacking in authority or reliability : QUESTIONABLE **2 a** : somewhat unsound in health **b** : characterized by shaking : TREMBLING **3** : easily shaken : RICKETY — **shak·i·ly** \-kə-lē\ *adv* — **shak·i·ness** \-kē-nəs\ *n*

shale \'shāl\ *n* : a rock that is formed by the consolidation of clay, mud, or silt, has a finely layered structure, and splits easily

shall \shəl, (')shal\ *auxiliary verb, past* **should** \shəd, (')shu̇d\; *pres sing & pl* **shall** **1 a** — used to express a command or exhortation **b** — used in laws, regulations, or directives to express what is mandatory **2 a** — used to express what is inevitable or likely to happen in the future **b** — used to express simple futurity **3** — used to express determination

shal·lop \'shal-əp\ *n* : a small open boat propelled by oars or sails and used chiefly in shallow waters

[1]**shal·low** \'shal-ō\ *adj* **1** : having little depth **2** : lacking intellectual depth — **shal·low·ly** *adv*

[2]**shallow** *n* : a shallow place or area in a body of water — usu. used in pl.

[1]**sham** \'sham\ *n* **1** : HOAX **2** : cheap falseness : HYPOCRISY **3** : a decorative piece of cloth simulating an article of personal or household linen and used in place of or over it **4** : an imitation or counterfeit purporting to be genuine **5** : a person who shams

[2]**sham** *vb* **shammed**; **sham·ming** : to act intentionally so as to give a false impression of being : COUNTERFEIT, FEIGN

[3]**sham** *adj* : FALSE: as **a** : FEIGNED, PRETENDED **b** : made or used as an imitation

[1]**sham·ble** \'sham-bəl\ *vi* **sham·bled**; **sham·bling** \-b(ə-)liŋ\ : to walk awkwardly with dragging feet : SHUFFLE

[2]**shamble** *n* : a shambling gait

sham·bles \'sham-bəlz\ *n sing or pl* : a place or scene of slaughter or destruction

[1]**shame** \'shām\ *n* **1 a** : a painful emotion caused by consciousness of guilt, shortcoming, impropriety, or disgrace **b** : the susceptibility to such emotion **2** : DISHONOR, DISGRACE **3 a** : something that brings strong regret, censure, or reproach **b** : a cause of feeling shame

[2]**shame** *vt* **1** : to bring shame to : DISGRACE **2** : to put to shame by outdoing **3** : to cause to feel shame **4** : to force by causing to feel guilty

shame·faced \'shām-'fāst\ *adj* **1** : showing modesty : MODEST, SHY, BASHFUL **2** : ASHAMED — **shame·fac·ed·ly** \-'fā-səd-lē, -'fāst-lē\ *adv* — **shame·fac·ed·ness** \-'fā-səd-nəs, -'fās(t)-nəs\ *n*

shame·ful \'shām-fəl\ *adj* **1** : bringing shame : DISGRACEFUL **2** : arousing the feeling of shame : INDECENT — **shame·ful·ly** \-fə-lē\ *adv* — **shame·ful·ness** *n*

shame·less \'shām-ləs\ *adj* **1** : having no shame : BRAZEN **2** : showing lack of shame : DISGRACEFUL — **shame·less·ly** *adv*

[1]**sham·poo** \sham-'pü\ *vt* **1** : to wash (as the hair) with soap and water or with a special preparation **2** : to wash the hair of **3** : to wash or clean (as a rug or upholstery) with soap or a dry-cleaning preparation — **sham·poo·er** *n*

[2]**shampoo** *n, pl* **shampoos** **1** : an act or instance of shampooing **2** : a preparation used in shampooing

sham·rock \'sham-ˌräk\ *n* : a plant with three leaflets used as a floral emblem by the Irish

shang·hai \shaŋ-'hī\ *vt* **shang·haied**; **shang·hai·ing** **1** : to make helpless (as by drugs or alcohol) and put on a ship as a sailor **2** : to put by deceit or force into a place of detention

shank \'shaŋk\ *n* **1 a** : the part of the leg between the knee and the ankle in man or the corresponding part in various other vertebrates **b** : a cut of meat from usu. the upper part of a leg **2** : a straight narrow usu. essential part of an object **3** : a part of a tool that connects the acting part with a part (as a handle) by which it is held or moved **4 a** : the latter part of a period of time **b** : the early or main part of a period of time

shan·tung \(')shan-'təŋ\ *n* : a fabric in plain weave having a slightly irregular surface

shan·ty \'shant-ē\ *n, pl* **shanties** : a small roughly built shelter or dwelling : HUT

¹shape \'shāp\ *vb* **1** : FORM, CREATE; *esp* : to give a particular form or shape to **2** : to fashion (as a garment) by a pattern **3** : DEVISE, PLAN **4** : to embody in definite form **5** : to make fit for : ADAPT, ADJUST **6** : to determine or direct the course of (as a person's life) **7** : to take on or approach a definite form : DEVELOP — often used with *up* — **shap·er** *n*

²shape *n* **1 a** : the visible characteristic of a particular thing **b** : spatial form **c** : a standard or universally recognized spatial form **2** : bodily contour esp. of the trunk : FIGURE **3 a** : PHANTOM, APPARITION **b** : assumed appearance : GUISE **4** : form of embodiment **5** : definite form and arrangement **6** : something having a particular form **7** : the condition in which someone or something exists at a particular time — **shaped** \ˌshāpt\ *adj*

shape·less \'shāp-ləs\ *adj* **1** : having no definite shape **2 a** : deprived of usual or normal shape : MISSHAPEN **b** : not shapely

shape·ly \'shāp-lē\ *adj* : having a regular or pleasing shape — **shape·li·ness** *n*

shard \'shärd\ *n* : a broken piece : FRAGMENT

¹share \'she(ə)r\ *n* **1 a** : a portion belonging to, due to, or contributed by an individual **b** : a fair portion **2** : any of the equal portions or interests into which the property of a corporation is divided

²share *vb* **1** : to divide and distribute in shares : APPORTION — usu. used with *out* **2** : to partake of, use, experience, or enjoy with others **3 a** : to give or be given a share in **b** : to take a share : PARTAKE — used with *in* — **shar·er** *n*

³share *n* : PLOWSHARE

share·crop \-ˌkräp\ *vb* : to farm or produce as a sharecropper

share·crop·per \-ˌkräp-ər\ *n* : a farmer who works land for a landlord in return for a share of the value of the crop

share·hold·er \-ˌhōl-dər\ *n* : STOCKHOLDER

¹shark \'shärk\ *n* : any of numerous mostly rather large and typically gray marine fishes that are mostly active, voracious, and rapacious predators

²shark *n* **1** : a greedy crafty person who takes advantage of the needs of others **2** : a person who excels esp. in a particular line

shark·skin \-ˌskin\ *n* **1** : the hide of a shark or leather made from it **2** : a fabric (as of cotton or rayon) woven from strands of many fine threads and having a sleek appearance and silky feel

¹sharp \'shärp\ *adj* **1** : adapted to cutting or piercing: as **a** : having a thin keen edge or fine point **b** : briskly cold : NIPPING **2 a** : keen in intellect : QUICK-WITTED **b** : keen in perception : ACUTE, VIGILANT **c** : keen in attention to one's own interest sometimes to the point of being unethical **3** : keen in spirit or action: as **a** : EAGER, BRISK **b** : capable of acting or reacting strongly; *esp* : CAUSTIC **4** : SEVERE, HARSH: as **a** : inclined to or marked by irritability or anger **b** : causing intense mental or physical distress **c** : cutting in language or import **5 a** : having a strong odor or flavor **b** : ACRID **c** : having a strong piercing sound **6 a** : terminating in a point or edge **b** : involving an abrupt change in direction **c** : clear in outline or detail : DISTINCT **d** : set forth with clarity and distinctness **7 a** : higher by a half step **b** : higher than the true pitch **8** : STYLISH, DRESSY — **sharp·ly** *adv* — **sharp·ness** *n*

²sharp *vb* : to raise in pitch esp. by a half step

³sharp *adv* **1** : in a sharp manner : SHARPLY **2** : PRECISELY, EXACTLY

⁴sharp *n* **1** : a musical note or tone one half step higher than a specified note or tone; *also* : a character ♯ on a line or space of the staff indicating such a note or tone **2** : a real or self-styled expert; *also* : SHARPER

sharp·en \'shär-pən\ *vb* **sharp·ened**; **sharp·en·ing** \'shärp-(ə-)niŋ\ : to make or become sharp or sharper — **sharp·en·er** \-(ə-)nər\ *n*

sharp·er \'shär-pər\ *n* : CHEAT, SWINDLER

sharp–eyed \'shärp-'īd\ *adj* : having keen sight; *also* : keen in observing or penetrating

sharp·ie *or* **sharpy** \'shär-pē\ *n, pl* **sharp·ies** **1** : SHARPER **2** : a person who is exceptionally keen or alert

sharp·shoot·er \'shärp-ˌshüt-ər\ *n* : one skilled in shooting : a good marksman — **sharp·shoot·ing** \-ˌshüt-iŋ\ *n*

sharp–tongued \-'təŋd\ *adj* : having a sharp tongue

sharp–wit·ted \-'wit-əd\ *adj* : having or showing a quick keen mind

¹shat·ter \'shat-ər\ *vb* **1** : to dash, burst, or part violently into fragments : break at once into pieces **2** : to damage badly

²shatter *n* : FRAGMENT, SHRED

shat·ter·proof \ˌshat-ər-'prüf\ *adj* : made so as not to shatter

¹shave \'shāv\ *vb* **shaved**; **shaved** *or* **shav·en** \'shā-vən\; **shav·ing** **1** : to cut or pare off by means of an edged instrument (as a razor); *esp* : to remove hair close to the skin with a razor **2** : to make bare or smooth by cutting the hair from **3** : to cut off closely **4** : to cut off thin slices from (as a board with a plane) **5** : to pass close to : skim along or near the surface of with or without touching

²shave *n* **1** : any of various tools for shaving or cutting thin slices **2** : an act or process of shaving **3** : an act of passing very near to so as almost to graze

shav·er \'shā-vər\ *n* **1** : one that shaves; *esp* : an electric-powered razor **2** : BOY, YOUNGSTER

shav·ing \'shā-viŋ\ *n* **1** : the act of one that shaves **2** : something shaved off

shawl \'shȯl\ *n* : a square or oblong piece of woven or knitted fabric used esp. by women as a loose covering for the head or shoulders

¹she \(')shē\ *pron* : that female one

²she \'shē\ *n* : a female person or animal

sheaf \'shēf\ *n, pl* **sheaves** \'shēvz\ **1** : a bundle of stalks and ears of grain **2** : something resembling or suggesting a sheaf of grain — **sheaf·like** *adj*

¹shear \'shi(ə)r\ *vb* **sheared**; **sheared** *or* **shorn** \'shōrn\; **shear·ing** **1** : to cut the hair or wool from : CLIP, SHAVE **2** : to deprive of by or as if by cutting off **3** : to cut or cut through with or as if with shears **4** : to become divided under the action of a shear — **shear·er** *n*

²shear *n* **1** : a cutting implement similar or identical to a pair of scissors but typically larger — usu. used in pl.; *also* : one blade of a pair of shears **2** : any of various cutting machines operating by the action of opposed cutting edges of metal — usu. used in pl.

sheath \'shēth\ *n, pl* **sheaths** \'shēt͟hz, 'shēths\ **1** : a case for a blade (as of a knife) **2** : a covering esp. of an anatomical structure suggesting a sheath in form or use

sheathe \'shēt͟h\ *vt* **1** : to put into or as if into a sheath **2** : to encase or cover with something (as thin boards or sheets of metal) that protects — **sheath·er** \'shē-t͟hər, -thər\ *n*

sheath·ing \'shē-t͟hiŋ, -thiŋ\ *n* : material used to sheathe something

sheave \'shiv, 'shēv\ *n* : a grooved wheel : PULLEY

¹shed \'shed\ *vb* **shed**; **shed·ding** **1** : to pour forth or down esp. in drops **2** : to cause to flow from a cut or wound **3** : to spread abroad : DIFFUSE **4** : to throw off **5 a** : to cast aside or let fall (some natural covering) **b** : to rid oneself of : DISCARD — **shed·der** *n*

²shed *n* **1** : a slight structure built for shelter or storage **2** : a single-storied building with one or more sides unenclosed

sheen \'shēn\ *n* **1** : subdued shininess of surface : LUSTER **2** : GLOSS, GLITTER

sheep \'shēp\ *n, pl* **sheep** **1** : any of a genus of ruminant mammals related to the goats but stockier and lacking a beard in the male; *esp* : one long domesticated for its flesh, wool, and other products **2** : one that is like a sheep (as in being timid, defenseless, or easily led) **3** : SHEEPSKIN — **sheep** *adj*

sheep•fold \'shēp-ˌfōld\ *n* : a pen or shelter for sheep
sheep•ish \'shē-pish\ *adj* **1** : resembling a sheep in meekness, stupidity, or timidity **2** : embarrassed by consciousness of a fault — **sheep•ish•ly** *adv* — **sheep•ish•ness** *n*
sheep's eye *n* : a shy, longing, and usu. amorous glance — usu. used in pl.
sheep•skin \'shēp-ˌskin\ *n* **1** : the skin of a sheep or leather prepared from it; *also* : PARCHMENT **2** : DIPLOMA
[1]**sheer** \'shi(ə)r\ *adj* **1** : very thin or transparent **2 a** : UNQUALIFIED, UTTER **b** : taken or acting apart from everything else **3** : very steep : being almost straight up and down — **sheer•ly** *adv* — **sheer•ness** *n*
[2]**sheer** *adv* **1** : ALTOGETHER, COMPLETELY **2** : PERPENDICULARLY
[3]**sheer** *vi* : to deviate from a course : SWERVE
[1]**sheet** \'shēt\ *n* **1** : a broad piece of cloth; *esp* : an oblong of usu. linen or cotton cloth used as an article of bedding next to the person **2** : a usu. rectangular piece of paper (as for writing or printing) **3** : a broad expanse or surface of something **4** : a portion of something that is thin in comparison to its length and breadth
[2]**sheet** *vt* **1** : to cover with a sheet **2** : to furnish with sheets
[3]**sheet** *n* **1** : a rope or chain that regulates the angle at which a sail is set in relation to the wind **2** *pl* : the spaces at either end of an open boat not occupied by thwarts
sheet•ing \'shēt-iŋ\ *n* : material in the form of sheets or suitable for forming into sheets
sheikh *or* **sheik** \'shēk, *for 1 also* 'shāk & 'shīk\ *n* **1** : an Arab chief **2** *usu sheik* : a man supposed to be irresistibly attractive to romantic young women — **sheik•dom** \-dəm\ *n*
shelf \'shelf\ *n, pl* **shelves** \'shelvz\ **1 a** : a thin flat usu. long and narrow piece of material (as of wood or glass) fastened horizontally (as on a wall) at a distance from the floor to hold objects **b** : the contents of a shelf **2** : something resembling a shelf: as **a** : a sandbank or ledge of rocks usu. partially submerged **b** : a flat projecting layer of rock — **shelf•like** *adj* — **on the shelf** : in a state of inactivity or uselessness
[1]**shell** \'shel\ *n* **1 a** : a hard rigid usu. largely calcareous covering of an animal (as a turtle, oyster, or beetle) **b** : the outer covering of an egg and esp. of a bird's egg **c** : the outer covering of a nut, fruit, or seed esp. when hard or toughly fibrous **2** : shell material or shells esp. of mollusks; *also* : a shell-bearing mollusk **3** : something that resembles a shell: as **a** : a framework or exterior structure **b** : a casing without substance **c** : an edible case for holding a filling **4** : an impersonal manner that conceals the presence or absence of feeling **5** : a narrow light racing boat propelled by one or more oarsmen **6 a** : a hollow projectile for cannon containing an explosive bursting charge **b** : a metal or paper case which holds the charge of powder and shot or bullet used with breech-loading small arms — **shell** *adj* — **shelled** \'sheld\ *adj*
[2]**shell** *vb* **1 a** : to remove from a natural enclosing cover (as a shell or husk) : SHUCK **b** : to remove the grains from (as an ear of Indian corn) **2** : to throw or shoot shells at, upon, or into : BOMBARD **3** : to fall out of the pod or husk
[1]**shel•lac** \shə-'lak\ *n* **1** : purified lac **2** : a preparation of lac dissolved in alcohol and used in filling wood or as a varnish
[2]**shellac** *vt* **shel•lacked**; **shel•lack•ing** **1** : to coat or treat with shellac **2** : to defeat decisively
shell•fish \'shel-ˌfish\ *n* : an aquatic invertebrate animal with a shell; *esp* : an edible mollusk or crustacean
shell shock *n* : a nervous disorder appearing in soldiers exposed to modern warfare — **shell–shock** \'shel-ˌshäk\ *vt*
[1]**shel•ter** \'shel-tər\ *n* **1** : something that covers or affords protection : a means or place of protection **2** : the state of being covered and protected — **shel•ter•less** \-ləs\ *adj*
[2]**shelter** *vb* **shel•tered**; **shel•ter•ing** \-t(ə-)riŋ\ **1** : to constitute or provide a shelter for : PROTECT **2** : to place under shelter or protection **3** : to take shelter — **shel•ter•er** *n*
shelve \'shelv\ *vb* **1** : to furnish with shelves **2** : to place on a shelf **3 a** : to put on the shelf : DISMISS **b** : to put aside temporarily or permanently **4** : to slope in a formation like a shelf
shelv•ing \'shel-viŋ\ *n* **1** : material for shelves **2** : SHELVES
she•nan•i•gan \shə-'nan-i-gən\ *n* **1** : an underhand trick **2 a** : tricky or questionable conduct **b** : high-spirited or mischievous activity — usu. used in pl.
[1]**shep•herd** \'shep-ərd\ *n* **1** : a man who tends and guards sheep **2** : PASTOR
[2]**shepherd** *vt* **1** : to tend as a shepherd **2** : to guide or guard in the manner of a shepherd
shep•herd•ess \'shep-ərd-əs\ *n* : a woman or girl who tends sheep
sher•bet \'shər-bət\ *n* **1** : a cooling drink of sweetened and diluted fruit juice **2** : a water ice with milk, egg white, or gelatin added
sher•iff \'sher-əf\ *n* : an important official of a county charged primarily with judicial duties
sher•ry \'sher-ē\ *n, pl* **sherries** : a fortified wine with a distinctive nutty flavor
shib•bo•leth \'shib-ə-ləth, -ˌleth\ *n* **1 a** : CATCHWORD, SLOGAN **b** : a use of language that is distinctive of a particular group **2** : a custom or usage that is a criterion for distinguishing members of one group
[1]**shield** \'shēld\ *n* **1** : a broad piece of defensive armor carried on the arm **2** : one that protects or defends : DEFENSE
[2]**shield** *vt* **1** : to cover with or as if with a shield **2** : to cut off from observation : HIDE
[1]**shift** \'shift\ *vb* **1** : to exchange for or replace by another : CHANGE **2 a** : to change the place, position, or direction of : MOVE **b** : to make a change in place, position, or direction **c** : to change the gear rotating the transmission shaft of an automobile **3** : to change phonetically **4** : to get along : MANAGE
[2]**shift** *n* **1 a** : a means or device for effecting an end **b** : a deceitful scheme : DODGE **c** : an expedient tried in difficult circumstances : EXTREMITY **2** : a woman's slip or chemise **3** : a change in direction **4** : a change in place or position **5** : a group who work together in alternation with other groups; *also* : the period during which one such group works **6** : a removal from one person or thing to another : TRANSFER **7** : GEARSHIFT
shift•less \'shift-ləs\ *adj* **1** : lacking in resourcefulness : INEFFICIENT **2** : lacking in ambition or incentive : LAZY
shifty \'shif-tē\ *adj* **1 a** : given to deception, evasion, or fraud : TRICKY **b** : capable of evasive movement : ELUSIVE **2** : indicative of a tricky nature — **shift•i•ly** \-tə-lē\ *adv* — **shift•i•ness** \-tē-nəs\ *n*
shil•le•lagh \shə-'lā-lē\ *n* : CUDGEL, CLUB
shil•ling \'shil-iŋ\ *n* **1 a** : a British monetary unit equal to 12 pence or 1/20 pound **b** : a coin representing this unit **2** : a unit of value equal to 1/20 pound and a corresponding coin in any of several countries in or formerly in the British Commonwealth **3** : any of several early American coins
[1]**shil•ly–shal•ly** \'shil-ē-ˌshal-ē\ *n* : INDECISION, IRRESOLUTION
[2]**shilly–shally** *vi* **shil•ly–shal•lied**; **shil•ly–shal•ly•ing** **1** : to show hesitation or lack of decisiveness : VACILLATE **2** : to waste time : DAWDLE
[1]**shim•mer** \'shim-ər\ *vi* **shim•mered**; **shim•mer•ing** \'shim-(ə-)riŋ\ **1** : to shine with a wavering light : GLIMMER **2** : to appear in a constantly changing wavy form
[2]**shimmer** *n* **1** : a wavering light : subdued sparkle or sheen : GLIMMER **2** : a wavering image or effect esp. when produced by heat waves — **shim•mery** \'shim-(ə-)rē\ *adj*
shim•my \'shim-ē\ *n, pl* **shimmies** **1** : a jazz dance characterized by a shaking of the body from the shoulders down **2** : an abnormal vibration esp. in the front wheels of an automobile — **shimmy** *vi*

[1]**shin** \'shin\ *n* : the front part of the leg below the knee
[2]**shin** *vb* **shinned; shin·ning** : to climb by moving oneself along alternately with the arms or hands and legs
shin·bone \'shin-'bōn, -ˌbōn\ *n* : TIBIA
shin·dig \'shin-ˌdig\ *n* : a festive occasion
[1]**shine** \'shīn\ *vb* **shone** \'shōn\ *or* **shined; shin·ing 1** : to send out rays of light **2** : to be bright by reflection of light : GLEAM **3** : to show brilliance : be eminent or distinguished **4** : to have a bright glowing appearance **5** : to be conspicuously evident or clear **6** : to throw or flash the light of **7** : to make bright by polishing
[2]**shine** *n* **1** : brightness caused by the emission of light **2** : brightness caused by the reflection of light : LUSTER **3** : BRILLIANCE, SPLENDOR **4** : fair weather : SUNSHINE **5** : TRICK, CAPER — usu. used in pl. **6** : LIKING, FANCY **7** : a polish given to shoes
shin·er \'shī-nər\ *n* **1** : one that shines **2** : a small silvery fish **3** : a black eye
[1]**shin·gle** \'shiŋ-gəl\ *n* **1** : a small thin piece of building material (as of wood or a composition of asbestos) for laying in overlapping rows as a covering for the roof or sides of a building **2** : a small signboard **3** : a woman's haircut with the hair trimmed short from the back of the head to the nape
[2]**shingle** *vt* **shin·gled; shin·gling** \-g(ə-)liŋ\ **1** : to cover with or as if with shingles **2** : to bob and shape (the hair) in a shingle
[3]**shingle** *n* **1** : coarse pebbly gravel on the seashore **2** : a place (as a beach) strewn with shingle
shin·ing \'shī-niŋ\ *adj* **1** : giving forth or reflecting light **2** : BRIGHT, RESPLENDENT **3** : having a distinguished quality
shin·ny \'shin-ē\ *vi* **shin·nied; shin·ny·ing** : SHIN
Shin·to \'shin-ˌtō\ *n* : a religious cult of Japan consisting chiefly in the reverence of the spirits of natural forces, emperors, and heroes — **Shin·to·ism** \-ˌiz-əm\ *n* — **Shin·to·ist** \-əst\ *n or adj*
shiny \'shī-nē\ *adj* **1** : bright in appearance : GLITTERING, POLISHED **2** : rubbed or worn smooth — **shin·i·ness** *n*
[1]**ship** \'ship\ *n* **1 a** : a large seagoing boat **b** : a sailing boat having a bowsprit and usu. three square-rigged masts **2** : BOAT; *esp* : one propelled by power or sail **3** : a ship's crew **4** : AIRSHIP, AIRPLANE
[2]**ship** *vb* **shipped; ship·ping 1 a** : to place or receive on board a ship for transportation by water **b** : to cause to be transported **2** : to put in place for use **3** : to take into a ship or boat **4** : to take (as water) over the side **5** : to engage to serve on shipboard
ship biscuit *n* : HARDTACK
ship·board \'ship-ˌbōrd\ *n* **1** : the side of a ship **2** : SHIP
ship·build·er \'ship-ˌbil-dər\ *n* : one who designs or builds ships — **ship·build·ing** \-diŋ\ *n*
ship·mate \-ˌmāt\ *n* : a fellow sailor
ship·ment \'ship-mənt\ *n* **1** : the act or process of shipping **2** : the goods shipped
ship·per \'ship-ər\ *n* : one that sends goods by any form of conveyance
ship·ping \'ship-iŋ\ *n* **1** : the body of ships in one place or belonging to one port or country **2** : the act or business of one that ships
ship·shape \'ship-'shāp\ *adj* : TRIM, TIDY
ship·worm \'ship-ˌwərm\ *n* : any of various long-bodied marine clams that resemble worms, burrow in submerged wood, and damage wharf piles and wooden ships
[1]**ship·wreck** \-ˌrek\ *n* **1** : a wrecked ship or its parts : WRECKAGE **2** : the destruction or loss of a ship
[2]**shipwreck** *vt* **1 a** : to cause to experience shipwreck **b** : RUIN **2** : to destroy (a ship) by grounding or foundering
ship·yard \-ˌyärd\ *n* : a place where ships are built or repaired
shire \'shī(ə)r, *in place-name compounds* ˌshi(ə)r, shər\ *n* : a county in Great Britain
shirk \'shərk\ *vb* **1** : to evade the performance of an obligation **2** : AVOID — **shirk·er** *n*
shirr \'shər\ *vt* **1** : to draw (as cloth) together in a shirring **2** : to bake (eggs removed from the shell) until set
shirr·ing \'shər-iŋ\ *n* : a decorative gathering (as of cloth) made by drawing up the material along two or more parallel lines of stitching
shirt \'shərt\ *n* **1** : a loose cloth garment usu. having a collar, sleeves, a front opening, and a tail long enough to be tucked inside trousers or a skirt **2** : UNDERSHIRT
shirt·front \-ˌfrənt\ *n* : the front of a shirt; *esp* : DICKEY
shirt·ing \'shərt-iŋ\ *n* : fabric suitable for shirts
[1]**shiv·er** \'shiv-ər\ *n* : one of the small pieces into which a brittle thing is broken by sudden violence
[2]**shiver** *vb* **shiv·ered; shiv·er·ing** \'shiv-(ə-)riŋ\ : to break into many small pieces : SHATTER
[3]**shiver** *vi* **shiv·ered; shiv·er·ing** \'shiv-(ə-)riŋ\ : to undergo trembling (as from cold or fear) : QUIVER
[4]**shiver** *n* : an instance of shivering : TREMBLE
shiv·ery \'shiv-(ə-)rē\ *adj* **1** : characterized by shivers : TREMULOUS **2** : causing shivers
[1]**shoal** \'shōl\ *adj* : SHALLOW
[2]**shoal** *n* **1** : a shallow place in a body of water (as the sea or a river) **2** : a sandbank or sandbar that makes the water shallow
shoat \'shōt\ *n* : a young hog usu. less than one year old
[1]**shock** \'shäk\ *n* : a pile of sheaves of grain or stalks of Indian corn set up in a field with the butt ends down
[2]**shock** *n* **1** : the impact or encounter of individuals or groups in combat **2** : a violent shake or jar : CONCUSSION **3 a** : a disturbance in the equilibrium or permanence of something **b** : a sudden or violent disturbance in the mental or emotional faculties **4** : a state of profound bodily depression associated with reduced blood volume and pressure and caused usu. by severe esp. crushing injuries, hemorrhage, or burns **5** : sudden stimulation of the nerves and convulsive contraction of the muscles caused by the discharge of electricity through the animal body **6** : an attack of apoplexy or heart disease
[3]**shock** *vt* **1 a** : to strike with surprise, terror, horror, or disgust **b** : to subject to the action of an electrical discharge **2** : to drive into or out of by or as if by a shock
[4]**shock** *n* : a thick bushy mass (as of hair)
shock·ing \'shäk-iŋ\ *adj* : extremely startling and offensive — **shock·ing·ly** *adv*
[1]**shod·dy** \'shäd-ē\ *n* **1** : a fabric often of inferior quality manufactured wholly or partly from reclaimed wool **2** : inferior, imitation, or pretentious articles or matter
[2]**shoddy** *adj* **1** : made of shoddy **2 a** : cheaply imitative : vulgarly pretentious **b** : hastily or poorly done : INFERIOR **c** : SHABBY — **shod·di·ly** \'shäd-ᵊl-ē\ *adv* — **shod·di·ness** \'shäd-ē-nəs\ *n*
[1]**shoe** \'shü\ *n* **1** : an outer covering for the human foot usu. made of leather with a thick or stiff sole and an attached heel **2** : HORSESHOE **3** : the part of a brake that presses on the wheel of a vehicle **4** : the outside casing of an automobile tire
[2]**shoe** *vt* **shod** \'shäd\; **shoe·ing 1** : to furnish with a shoe or shoes **2** : to cover for protection, strength, or ornament
shoe·horn \'shü-ˌhȯrn\ *n* : a curved piece (as of horn, wood, or metal) to aid in slipping on a shoe
shoe·lace \-ˌlās\ *n* : a lace or string for fastening a shoe
shoe·mak·er \-ˌmā-kər\ *n* : one whose business is selling or repairing shoes
shoe·string \-ˌstriŋ\ *n* **1** : SHOELACE **2** : a small or barely adequate amount of money or capital
shoe tree *n* : a foot-shaped device for inserting in a shoe to preserve its shape
shone *past of* SHINE
shoo \'shü\ *vt* : to scare, drive, or send away by or as if by crying *shoo*

shook *past of* SHAKE
[1]**shoot** \'shüt\ *vb* **shot** \'shät\; **shoot·ing** **1 a :** to let fly or cause to be driven forward with force **b :** to cause an engine or weapon to discharge a missile **2 :** to strike with a missile esp. from a bow or gun; *esp* **:** to wound or kill with a missile discharged from a firearm **3 :** to push or slide into or out of a fastening **4 :** to set off **:** DETONATE, IGNITE **5 a :** to push or thrust forward usu. abruptly or swiftly **b :** to grow or sprout by or as if by putting forth shoots **c :** DEVELOP, MATURE **6 a :** to go or pass rapidly and precipitately **b :** to pass swiftly along **c :** to stream out suddenly **:** SPURT **7 a :** to take a picture of **:** PHOTOGRAPH **b :** to film a scene — **shoot·er** *n*
[2]**shoot** *n* **1 a :** the aerial part of a plant **:** a stem with its leaves and appendages; *also* **:** a branch or part of a plant developed from a single bud **b :** OFFSHOOT **2 :** a shooting match **3 a :** a motion or movement of rapid thrusting **b :** TWINGE
shoot·ing star \ˌshüt-iŋ-\ *n* **:** METEOR
[1]**shop** \'shäp\ *n* **1 :** a retail store **2 :** a place where things are made or worked on **:** FACTORY, MILL **3 a :** a school laboratory equipped for instruction in manual arts **b :** the art or science of working with tools and machinery
[2]**shop** *vb* **shopped**; **shop·ping :** to examine goods or services with intent to buy or in search of the best buy
shop·keep·er \'shäp-ˌkē-pər\ *n* **:** STOREKEEPER
shop·lift·er \'shäp-ˌlif-tər\ *n* **:** a thief who steals merchandise on display in stores — **shop·lift·ing** \-tiŋ\ *n*
shop·per \'shäp-ər\ *n* **:** one that shops
shop·worn \'shäp-ˌwōrn\ *adj* **1 :** faded, soiled, or impaired by remaining too long in a store **2 :** BEDRAGGLED, JADED
[1]**shore** \'shō(ə)r\ *n* **:** the land bordering a usu. large body of water; *esp* **:** COAST
[2]**shore** *vt* **:** to give support to **:** BRACE
[3]**shore** *n* **:** a prop or support placed beneath or against something to support it
shore·bird \-ˌbərd\ *n* **:** any of a group of birds that frequent the seashore
shorn *past part of* SHEAR
[1]**short** \'shȯrt\ *adj* **1 :** not tall or long **2 a :** not extended in time **:** BRIEF **b :** not retentive **c :** seeming to pass quickly **3 :** limited in distance **4 a :** not coming up to a measure or requirement **:** INSUFFICIENT **b :** not reaching far enough **5 a :** ABRUPT, CURT **b :** quickly provoked **6 :** containing or cooked with shortening **7 :** consisting of or relating to the sale of securities or commodities that the seller does not possess or has not contracted for at the time of the sale
[2]**short** *adv* **1 :** in a curt manner **2 :** BRIEFLY **3 :** at a disadvantage **:** UNAWARES **4 :** so as to interrupt **5 :** ABRUPTLY, SUDDENLY **6 :** at some point before a goal or limit aimed at **7 :** by or as if by a short sale
[3]**short** *n* **1 :** the sum and substance **:** UPSHOT **2 :** something that is shorter than the usual or regular length **3** *pl* **a :** knee-length or less than knee-length trousers **b :** short underpants — **in short :** by way of summary **:** BRIEFLY
short·age \'shȯrt-ij\ *n* **:** a lack in the amount needed **:** DEFICIT
short·cake \'shȯrt-ˌkāk\ *n* **1 :** a crisp and often unsweetened biscuit or cookie **2 :** a dessert made of usu. short biscuit spread with sweetened fruit
short·change \-'chānj\ *vt* **1 :** to give less than the correct amount of change to **2 :** to deprive of something due **:** CHEAT
short circuit *n* **:** a connection of comparatively low resistance accidentally or intentionally made between points in an electric circuit — **short–cir·cuit** \'shȯrt-'sər-kət\ *vb*
short·com·ing \'shȯrt-ˌkəm-iŋ, (')shȯrt-'\ *n* **:** DEFICIENCY, DEFECT, FAULT
short·cut \-ˌkət\ *n* **1 :** a route more direct than that usu. taken **2 :** a quicker way of doing something
short·en \'shȯrt-ᵊn\ *vb* **short·ened**; **short·en·ing** \'shȯrt-niŋ, -ᵊn-iŋ\ **:** to make or become short or shorter — **short·en·er** \'shȯrt-nər, -ᵊn-ər\ *n*
short·en·ing \'shȯrt-niŋ, -ᵊn-iŋ\ *n* **:** an edible fat (as butter or lard) used for cooking (as in making biscuit or pastry)
short·hand \'shȯrt-ˌhand\ *n* **:** a method of writing rapidly by substituting characters, abbreviations, or symbols for letters, words, or phrases **:** STENOGRAPHY — **shorthand** *adj*
short·hand·ed \-'han-dəd\ *adj* **:** short of the regular or necessary number of people
short·horn \'shȯrt-ˌhȯrn\ *n* **:** any of a breed of red, roan, or white cattle originating in the north of England
short–lived \'shȯrt-'līvd, -'livd\ *adj* **:** not living or lasting long
short·ly \'shȯrt-lē\ *adv* **1 a :** in a few words **:** BRIEFLY **b :** in an abrupt manner **:** CURTLY **2 a :** in a short time **:** SOON **b :** at a short interval
short·ness \'shȯrt-nəs\ *n* **:** the quality or state of being short
short·sight·ed \'shȯrt-'sīt-əd\ *adj* **1 :** NEARSIGHTED, MYOPIC **2 :** characterized by lack of foresight — **short·sight·ed·ly** *adv* — **short·sight·ed·ness** *n*
short·stop \'shȯrt-ˌstäp\ *n* **:** a baseball player defending the area on the third-base side of second base
short story *n* **:** an invented prose narrative usu. dealing with a few characters and aiming at developing a single episode or creating a single mood
short–tem·pered \'shȯrt-'tem-pərd\ *adj* **:** easily angered
short–term \-'tərm\ *adj* **1 :** occurring over or involving a relatively short period of time **2 :** of or relating to a financial transaction based on a term usu. of less than a year
short·wave \-'wāv\ *n* **:** a radio wave of 60-meter wavelength or less used esp. in long-distance broadcasting
[1]**shot** \'shät\ *n* **1 a :** an action of shooting **b :** a directed propelling of a missile (as an arrow, stone, or rocket); *esp* **:** a directed discharge of a gun or cannon **c :** a stroke or throw in a game **d :** a setting off of an explosive **e :** an injection of something (as a medicine or antibody) into the body **2 a** *pl* **shot :** something propelled by shooting; *esp* **:** small lead or steel pellets esp. forming a charge for a shotgun **b :** a metal sphere that is thrown for distance **3 a :** the distance that a missile is or can be thrown **b :** RANGE, REACH **4 :** a charge to be paid **5 :** one that shoots **6 a :** ATTEMPT, TRY **b :** GUESS, CONJECTURE **c :** CHANCE **7 :** a remark so directed as to have telling effect **8 a :** PHOTOGRAPH **b :** a single sequence of a motion picture or a television program shot by one camera without interruption **9 a :** a single drink of liquor **b :** a portion (as of medicine) taken at one time
[2]**shot** *adj* **1 a :** having contrasting and changeable color effects that react varyingly to dyes **:** IRIDESCENT **b :** suffused or streaked with a color **c :** PERMEATED **2 :** reduced to a state of ruin, prostration, or uselessness
shot·gun \'shät-ˌgən\ *n* **:** a gun with a smooth bore used to fire small shot at short range
shot put *n* **:** a field event consisting in throwing the shot for distance — **shot–put·ter** \-ˌpu̇t-ər\ *n* — **shot–put·ting** \-ˌpu̇t-iŋ\ *n*
should \shəd, (')shu̇d\ *past of* SHALL — used as an auxiliary verb to express (1) condition or possibility, (2) obligation or propriety, (3) futurity from the point of view in the past, (4) what is probable or expected, and (5) politeness in softening a request or assertion
[1]**shoul·der** \'shōl-dər\ *n* **1 a :** the laterally projecting part of the human body formed of the bones and joints by which the arm is connected with the trunk together with the muscles covering these **b :** the corresponding but usu. less projecting part of a lower vertebrate **2 :** a part or projection resembling a human shoulder
[2]**shoulder** *vb* **shoul·dered**; **shoul·der·ing** \-d(ə-)riŋ\ **1 :** to push or thrust with the shoulder **:** JOSTLE **2 a :** to place or bear on the shoulder **b :** to assume the burden or responsibility of
shoulder blade *n* **:** the flat triangular bone at the back of the shoulder

[1]**shout** \'shaůt\ *vb* **1** : to utter a sudden loud cry **2** : to utter in a loud voice — **shout•er** *n*
[2]**shout** *n* : a loud cry or call
[1]**shove** \'shəv\ *vb* **1** : to push with steady force **2** : to push carelessly or rudely — **shov•er** *n* — **shove off 1** : to move away from shore by pushing **2** : to set out : DEPART
[2]**shove** *n* : an act or instance of shoving
[1]**shov•el** \'shəv-əl\ *n* **1** : an implement consisting of a plate or scoop attached to a long handle used for lifting and throwing loose material (as snow, earth, grain, or coal) **2** : SHOVELFUL
[2]**shovel** *vb* **-eled** *or* **-elled**; **-el•ing** *or* **-el•ling** \'shəv-(ə-)liŋ\ **1** : to take up and throw with a shovel **2** : to dig or clean out with a shovel **3** : to throw or convey roughly or in the mass as if with a shovel
[1]**show** \'shō\ *vb* **showed**; **shown** \'shōn\ *or* **showed**; **show•ing** **1** : to place in sight : DISPLAY **2** : REVEAL **3** : GRANT, BESTOW **4** : TEACH, INSTRUCT **5** : PROVE **6** : DIRECT, USHER, GUIDE **7** : APPEAR **8** : to be noticeable **9** : to be third in a horse race
[2]**show** *n* **1** : a demonstrative display **2 a** : a false semblance : PRETENSE **b** : a more or less true appearance of something : SIGN **c** : an impressive display **d** : OSTENTATION **3** : CHANCE **4** : something exhibited esp. for wonder or ridicule : SPECTACLE **5** : a public presentation: as **a** : a theatrical presentation **b** : a radio or television program **c** : ENTERTAINMENT 3 **6** : third place at the finish of a horse race
show•boat \'shō-ˌbōt\ *n* **1** : a river steamboat containing a theater and carrying a troupe of actors to give plays at river communities **2** : one who tries to attract attention by conspicuous behavior
show•case \-ˌkās\ *n* : a glass case or box to display and protect wares in a store or articles in a museum
show•down \-ˌdaůn\ *n* : the final settlement of a contested issue; *also* : the test of strength by which a contested issue is resolved
[1]**show•er** \'shaů(-ə)r\ *n* **1 a** : a fall of rain of short duration **b** : a like fall of sleet, hail, or snow **2** : something resembling a rain shower **3** : a party given by friends who bring gifts often of a particular kind **4** : a bath in which water is showered on the person — **show•ery** \-ē\ *adj*
[2]**shower** *vb* **1** : to rain or fall in or as if in a shower **2** : to bathe in a shower **3** : to wet copiously (as with water) in a spray, fine stream, or drops **4** : to give in abundance
[3]**show•er** \'shō(-ə)r\ *n* : one that shows : EXHIBITOR
show•ing \'shō-iŋ\ *n* **1** : an act of putting something on view : DISPLAY, EXHIBITION **2** : PERFORMANCE, RECORD
show•man \'shō-mən\ *n* **1** : the producer of a theatrical show **2** : a person having a sense or knack for dramatization or visual effectiveness — **show•man•ship** \-ˌship\ *n*
show off *vb* **1** : to display proudly **2** : to seek to attract attention by conspicuous behavior
show–off \'shō-ˌȯf\ *n* **1** : the act of showing off **2** : one that shows off
show up *vb* **1** : to reveal the true nature of : EXPOSE **2** : ARRIVE
showy \'shō-ē\ *adj* **1** : making an attractive show : STRIKING **2** : OSTENTATIOUS, GAUDY — **show•i•ly** \'shō-ə-lē\ *adv* — **show•i•ness** \'shō-ē-nəs\ *n*
shrap•nel \'shrap-nᵊl\ *n, pl* **shrapnel** **1** : a projectile that consists of a case provided with a powder charge and a large number of usu. lead balls and is exploded in flight **2** : bomb, mine, or shell fragments
[1]**shred** \'shred\ *n* : a long narrow strip cut or torn off
[2]**shred** *vb* **shred•ded**; **shred•ding** **1** : to cut or tear into shreds **2** : to break up into shreds — **shred•der** *n*
shrew \'shrü\ *n* **1** : a very small mouselike mammal **2** : a woman who scolds or quarrels constantly
shrewd \'shrüd\ *adj* **1 a** : SEVERE, HARD **b** : BITING, PIERCING **2** : marked by cleverness, discernment, or sagacity : ASTUTE — **shrewd•ly** *adv* — **shrewd•ness** *n*
shrew•ish \'shrü-ish\ *adj* : ILL-TEMPERED, SCOLDING, INTRACTABLE — **shrew•ish•ly** *adv* — **shrew•ish•ness** *n*
[1]**shriek** \'shrēk\ *vb* **1** : to utter a loud shrill sound **2** : to cry out in a high-pitched voice : SCREECH **3** : to utter with a shriek or sharply and shrilly
[2]**shriek** *n* **1** : a shrill usu. wild or involuntary cry **2** : a sound like a shriek
shrike \'shrīk\ *n* : any of numerous usu. largely gray or brownish singing birds that feed chiefly on insects and often impale their prey on thorns
[1]**shrill** \'shril\ *vb* : to utter or emit an acute piercing sound
[2]**shrill** *adj* **1** : having or emitting a sharp high-pitched tone or sound : PIERCING **2** : accompanied by sharp high-pitched sounds or cries **3** : having an intense or vivid effect on the senses — **shrill** *adv* — **shrill•ness** *n* — **shril•ly** \'shril-lē\ *adv*
shrimp \'shrimp\ *n, pl* **shrimp** *or* **shrimps** **1** : any of numerous small mostly marine crustaceans related to the lobsters and having a long slender body, compressed abdomen, and long legs **2** : a very small or puny person or thing
[1]**shrine** \'shrīn\ *n* **1** : the tomb of a saint; *also* : a place where devotion is paid to a saint or deity **2** : SANCTUARY **3** : a place or object hallowed because of its associations
[2]**shrine** *vt* : ENSHRINE
[1]**shrink** \'shriŋk\ *vb* **shrank** \'shraŋk\; **shrunk** \'shrəŋk\; **shrink•ing** **1** : to contract or curl up the body or part of it : HUDDLE, COWER **2 a** : to contract or cause to contract to a less extent or compass **b** : to become or cause to become smaller or more compacted (as from heat or melting) **c** : to lose substance or weight **d** : to lessen in value : DWINDLE **3** : to draw back — **shrink•a•ble** *adj* — **shrink•er** *n*
[2]**shrink** *n* : the act of shrinking
shrink•age \'shriŋ-kij\ *n* **1** : the act or process of shrinking **2** : the amount lost by shrinkage
shrink•ing violet \ˌshriŋ-kiŋ-\ *n* : a bashful or retiring person; *esp* : one who shrinks from public recognition of his merit
shrive \'shrīv\ *vb* **shrived** *or* **shrove** \'shrōv\; **shriv•en** \'shriv-ən\ *or* **shrived**; **shriv•ing** \'shrī-viŋ\ **1** : to hear the confession of and administer the sacrament of penance to : PARDON **2** : to confess one's sins esp. to a priest
shriv•el \'shriv-əl\ *vb* **-eled** *or* **-elled**; **-el•ing** *or* **-el•ling** \'shriv-(ə-)liŋ\ **1** : to draw into wrinkles esp. with a loss of moisture **2** : to reduce or become reduced to inanition, helplessness, or inefficiency
[1]**shroud** \'shraůd\ *n* **1** : burial garment : WINDING-SHEET **2** : something that covers, screens, or guards **3** : one of the ropes leading usu. in pairs from a ship's masthead to give lateral support to the mast
[2]**shroud** *vt* **1 a** : to cut off from view : SCREEN **b** : to veil under another appearance **2** : to dress for burial
shrub \'shrəb\ *n* : a low usu. several-stemmed woody plant
shrub•bery \'shrəb-(ə-)rē\ *n* : a planting or growth of shrubs
shrub•by \'shrəb-ē\ *adj* **1** : consisting of or covered with shrubs **2** : resembling a shrub
[1]**shrug** \'shrəg\ *vb* **shrugged**; **shrug•ging** : to raise or draw in the shoulders esp. to express lack of interest or dislike
[2]**shrug** *n* **1** : an act of shrugging **2** : a woman's small waist-length or shorter jacket
shrug off *vt* **1** : to brush aside : MINIMIZE **2** : to shake off **3** : to remove (a garment) by wriggling out
shrunk•en \'shrəŋ-kən\ *adj* **1** : that has diminished or contracted esp. in size or value **2** : that has been subjected to a shrinking process
[1]**shuck** \'shək\ *n* : SHELL, HUSK
[2]**shuck** *vt* **1** : to strip of shucks **2** : to peel off
[1]**shud•der** \'shəd-ər\ *vi* **shud•dered**; **shud•der•ing** \'shəd-

(ə-)riŋ\ 1 : to tremble convulsively (as with fear, horror, or aversion) : SHIVER 2 : QUIVER

²**shudder** *n* : an act of shuddering : TREMOR — **shud·dery** \-ə-rē\ *adj*

shuf·fle \'shəf-əl\ *vb* **shuf·fled**; **shuf·fling** \'shəf-(ə-)liŋ\ 1 : to mix in a mass confusedly : JUMBLE 2 : to put or thrust aside or under cover 3 a : to mix (as a pack of cards) with the purpose of causing a later appearance in random order b : to move about, back and forth, or from one place to another : SHIFT 4 a : to move (as the feet) by sliding along or dragging back and forth without lifting b : to perform (as a dance) with a dragging sliding step — **shuffle** *n* — **shuf·fler** \-(ə-)lər\ *n*

shun \'shən\ *vt* **shunned**; **shun·ning** : to avoid deliberately and esp. habitually — **shun·ner** *n*

shun·pik·ing \'shən-,pī-kiŋ\ *n* : the practice of avoiding superhighways esp. for the pleasure of driving on back roads

¹**shunt** \'shənt\ *vb* 1 : to turn off to one side : SHIFT; *esp* : to switch (as a train) from one track to another 2 : to travel back and forth — **shunt·er** *n*

²**shunt** *n* : a means or mechanism for turning or thrusting aside

shut \'shət\ *vb* **shut**; **shut·ting** 1 : to close or become closed by bringing openings or covering parts together 2 : to forbid entrance to or passage to or from : BAR 3 : to hold within limits by or as if by enclosure : hem in : IMPRISON 4 : to cease or cause to cease or suspend operation

shut·down \'shət-,daủn\ *n* : a temporary or permanent ending of an activity (as work in a factory)

shut–in \,shət-,in\ *adj* : confined by illness or incapacity — **shut–in** \'shət-,in\ *n*

¹**shut·ter** \'shət-ər\ *n* 1 : one that shuts 2 : a usu. movable cover or screen for a window or door 3 : the part of a camera that opens and closes to expose the film

²**shutter** *vt* : to close with or by shutters

¹**shut·tle** \'shət-ᵊl\ *n* 1 : an instrument used in weaving to carry the thread back and forth from side to side through the threads that run lengthwise 2 a : a going back and forth regularly over a specified and often short route by a vehicle b : a vehicle used in a shuttle

²**shuttle** *vb* **shut·tled**; **shut·tling** \'shət-liŋ, -ᵊl-iŋ\ 1 : to move or travel back and forth frequently 2 : to move by or as if by a shuttle

shut·tle·cock \'shət-ᵊl-,käk\ *n* : a light feathered object (as of cork or plastic) used in badminton

shut up *vb* 1 : to cause (a person) to stop talking 2 : to cease writing or speaking

¹**shy** \'shī\ *adj* 1 : easily frightened : TIMID 2 : disposed to avoid a person or thing : DISTRUSTFUL 3 : hesitant in committing oneself : CHARY 4 : marked by sensitive diffidence : BASHFUL 5 a : very light : SCANT b : DEFICIENT, LACKING

²**shy** *vi* **shied**; **shy·ing** 1 : to draw back in sudden dislike or distaste 2 : to start suddenly aside through fright or alarm

³**shy** *n, pl* **shies** : a sudden start aside (as of a horse)

shy·ly \'shī-lē\ *adv* : in a shy manner

shy·ness \'shī-nəs\ *n* : the quality or state of being shy

shy·ster \'shī-stər\ *n* : an unscrupulous lawyer or politician

si \'sē\ *n* : the 7th note of the diatonic scale : TI

Si·a·mese twin \,sī-ə-,mēz-, -,mēs-\ *n* : either of a pair of congenitally united twins in man or lower animals

¹**sib·i·lant** \'sib-ə-lənt\ *adj* : having, containing, or producing the sound of or a sound resembling that of the *s* or the *sh* in *sash*

²**sibilant** *n* : a sibilant speech sound (as English \s\, \z\, \sh\, \zh\, \ch (= tsh)\, or \j (= dzh)\)

sib·yl \'sib-əl\ *n, often cap* 1 : any of several ancient prophetesses 2 a : a female prophet b : FORTUNE-TELLER — **sib·yl·line** \'sib-ə-,līn\ *adj*

sick \'sik\ *adj* 1 a (1) : affected with disease or ill health : AILING (2) : of, relating to, or intended for use in sickness b : NAUSEATED, QUEASY 2 : spiritually or morally unsound or corrupt 3 a : sickened by strong emotion (as shame or fear) b : SATIATED, SURFEITED c : depressed and longing for something 4 : mentally or emotionally unsound or disordered 5 : deficient or declining in vigor or condition — **sick·ly** *adv*

sick·en \'sik-ən\ *vb* **sick·ened**; **sick·en·ing** \'sik-(ə-)niŋ\ : to make or become sick

sick·ish \'sik-ish\ *adj* 1 : somewhat nauseated : QUEASY 2 : somewhat sickening — **sick·ish·ly** *adv*

sick·le \'sik-əl\ *n* : an agricultural implement consisting of a curved metal blade with a short handle — **sickle** *adj*

sick·ly \'sik-lē\ *adj* 1 : somewhat unwell; *also* : habitually or often ailing 2 : produced by or associated with sickness 3 : producing or tending to sickness 4 : appearing as if sick: a : LANGUID, PALE b : WRETCHED, UNEASY c : lacking in vigor : WEAK 5 : MAWKISH — **sick·li·ly** \'sik-lə-lē\ *adv* — **sick·li·ness** \'sik-lē-nəs\ *n*

sick·ness \'sik-nəs\ *n* 1 : ill health : ILLNESS 2 : a specific disease : MALADY 3 : NAUSEA

¹**side** \'sīd\ *n* 1 : the right or left part of the trunk or wall of the body; *also* : the entire right or left half of the animal body 2 : a place, space, or direction with respect to a center line (as of an aisle, river, or street) 3 : a surface forming a border or face of an object 4 : an outer portion of a thing considered as facing in a particular direction 5 : a slope or declivity of a hill or ridge 6 a : a bounding line of a geometrical figure b : one of the surfaces that delimit a solid; *esp* : one of the longer surfaces c : either surface of a thin object 7 : the space beside one 8 : the attitude or activity of one person or group with respect to another : PART 9 : a body of partisans or contestants 10 : a line of descent traced through either parent 11 : an aspect or part of something held to be contrasted with some other aspect or part

²**side** *adj* 1 : of, relating to, or situated on the side 2 a : directed toward or from the side b : in addition to or secondary to something primary c : additional to the main portion

³**side** *vb* 1 : to take sides : join or form sides 2 : to furnish with sides or siding

⁴**side** *n* : swaggering or arrogant manner : PRETENTIOUSNESS

side·board \'sīd-,bōrd\ *n* : a piece of dining-room furniture for holding articles of table service

side·burns \'sīd-,bərnz\ *n pl* : short side-whiskers worn with a smooth chin

sid·ed \'sīd-əd\ *adj* : having sides often of a specified number or kind

side–glance \'sīd-,glan(t)s\ *n* 1 : a glance directed to the side 2 : a passing allusion : an indirect or slight reference

side·light \-,līt\ *n* : incidental or additional information

side·line \-,līn\ *n* 1 : a business or activity pursued in addition to one's regular occupation 2 : the standpoint of persons not immediately participating or concerned — usu. used in pl.

¹**side·long** \'sīd-,lȯŋ\ *adv* 1 : OBLIQUELY, SIDEWAYS 2 : on the side

²**sidelong** *adj* 1 : lying or inclining to one side : SLANTING 2 a : directed to one side b : indirect rather than straightforward

side·piece \'sīd-,pēs\ *n* : a piece contained in or forming the side of something

si·de·re·al \sī-'dir-ē-əl\ *adj* 1 : of or relating to the stars or constellations 2 : measured by the apparent motion of fixed stars

side·show \'sīd-,shō\ *n* 1 : a minor show offered in addition to a main exhibition (as of a circus) 2 : an incidental diversion

side·split·ting \-,split-iŋ\ *adj* : extremely funny : HILARIOUS

side·step \'sīd-,step\ *vb* 1 : to avoid by a step to the side 2 : to avoid meeting issues : EVADE

side·stroke \-,strōk\ *n* : a stroke made by a swimmer while lying on his side in which the arms are moved without breaking water while the legs do a scissors kick

side·swipe \-ˌswīp\ *vt* : to strike with a glancing blow along the side

¹side·track \-ˌtrak\ *n* : SIDING

²sidetrack *vt* **1** : to transfer from a main railroad line to a siding **2** : to turn aside from a main purpose or use; *also* : to divert to a subordinate position

side·walk \ˈsīd-ˌwȯk\ *n* : a usu. paved walk for pedestrians at the side of a street

side·wall \-ˌwȯl\ *n* **1** : a wall forming the side of something **2** : the side of an automotive tire between the tread shoulder and the rim bead

side·ward \-wərd\ *or* **side·wards** \-wərdz\ *adv* (*or adj*) : toward the side

side·way \-ˌwā\ *adv* (*or adj*) : SIDEWAYS

side·ways \-ˌwāz\ *adv* (*or adj*) **1** : from one side **2** : with one side forward **3** : toward one side; *also* : ASKANCE

side–whis·kers \ˈsīd-ˌhwis-kərz\ *n pl* : whiskers on the side of the face usu. worn long with the chin shaven

side·wise \-ˌwīz\ *adv* (*or adj*) : SIDEWAYS

sid·ing \ˈsīd-iŋ\ *n* **1** : a short railroad track connected with the main track by switches at one or more places **2** : material (as boards or metal pieces) used to cover the outside walls of frame buildings

si·dle \ˈsīd-ᵊl\ *vb* **si·dled**; **si·dling** \ˈsīd-liŋ, -ᵊl-iŋ\ **1** : to go or move with one side foremost esp. in a furtive advance **2** : to cause to move or turn sideways — **sidle** *n*

siege \ˈsēj\ *n* **1** : a military blockade of a fortified place **2** : a continued attempt to gain possession of something **3** : a persistent attack (as of illness)

si·er·ra \sē-ˈer-ə\ *n* **1** : a range of mountains esp. with jagged peaks **2** : the country about a sierra

si·es·ta \sē-ˈes-tə\ *n* : an afternoon nap or rest

¹sieve \ˈsiv\ *n* : a device with meshes or perforations through which finer particles of a mixture of various sizes are passed to separate them from coarser ones or through which the liquid is drained from liquid-containing material

²sieve *vb* : to put through a sieve : SIFT

sift \ˈsift\ *vb* **1 a** : to put through a sieve **b** : to separate by putting through a sieve **2 a** : to screen out the valuable or good : SELECT **b** : to study or investigate thoroughly : PROBE **3** : to scatter by or as if by sifting **4** : to pass through or as if through a sieve — **sift·er** *n*

sigh \ˈsī\ *vb* **1** : to take a deep audible breath (as in weariness or grief) **2** : to make a sound like sighing **3** : GRIEVE, YEARN **4** : to express by sighs — **sigh** *n* — **sigh·er** \ˈsī(-ə)r\ *n*

¹sight \ˈsīt\ *n* **1** : something that is seen : SPECTACLE **2** : a thing that is worth seeing **3** : the process, power, or function of seeing; *esp* : the animal sense of which the eye is the receptor organ and by which the position, shape, and color of objects are perceived **4 a** : INSPECTION, PERUSAL **b** : VIEW, GLIMPSE **5** : the range of vision **6** : a device (as a small metal bead on a gun barrel) that aids the eye in aiming or in determining the direction of an object

²sight *vb* **1** : to get sight of **2** : to look at through or as if through a sight **3** : to aim by means of sights **4** : to look carefully in a particular direction

sight·ed \ˈsīt-əd\ *adj* : having sight

sight·less \ˈsīt-ləs\ *adj* : lacking sight : BLIND — **sight·less·ness** *n*

sight·ly \ˈsīt-lē\ *adj* **1** : pleasing to the sight : HANDSOME **2** : affording a good view — **sight·li·ness** *n*

sight–read \ˈsīt-ˌrēd\ *vb* **sight–read** \-ˌred\; **sight–read·ing** \-ˌrēd-iŋ\ : to read a foreign language or perform music without previous preparation or study — **sight reader** \-ˌrēd-ər\ *n*

¹sight–see·ing \ˈsīt-ˌsē-iŋ\ *adj* : engaged in, devoted to, or used for seeing things and places of interest

²sight–seeing *n* : the act or pastime of seeing places of interest — **sight·seer** \ˈsīt-ˌsē-ər, -ˌsi(-ə)r\ *n*

¹sign \ˈsīn\ *n* **1 a** : a motion or gesture by which a thought is expressed or a command made known **b** : SIGNAL 1a **2** : a mark having a conventional meaning and used in place of words or to represent a complex notion; *also* : SYMBOL **3** : one of the 12 divisions of the zodiac **4 a** : a lettered board or other display used to identify or advertise a place of business **b** : a posted command, warning, or direction **c** : SIGNBOARD **5 a** : something that serves to indicate the presence or existence of something : TOKEN **b** : PRESAGE, PORTENT

²sign *vb* **1 a** : to place a sign upon **b** : to represent or indicate by a sign **2** : to affix a signature to : write one's name on something in token of assent, responsibility, or obligation **3** : to communicate by making a sign **4** : to hire by securing the signature of — **sign·er** *n*

¹sig·nal \ˈsig-nᵊl\ *n* **1 a** : an act, event, or watchword that serves to start some action **b** : something that incites to action **2** : a sound or gesture made to give warning or command **3** : an object placed to convey notice or warning **4** : the message, sound, or effect transmitted in electronic communication (as radio or television)

²signal *vb* **-naled** *or* **-nalled**; **-nal·ing** *or* **-nal·ling** **1** : to notify by a signal **2** : to communicate by signals **3** : to make or send a signal — **sig·nal·er** *n*

³signal *adj* **1** : distinguished from the ordinary : OUTSTANDING **2** : used in signaling — **sig·nal·ly** \-nᵊl-ē\ *adv*

sig·nal·ize \ˈsig-nᵊl-ˌīz\ *vt* **1** : to make conspicuous : DISTINGUISH **2** : to point out carefully or distinctly **3** : to make signals to : SIGNAL; *also* : INDICATE — **sig·nal·i·za·tion** \ˌsig-nᵊl-ə-ˈzā-shən\ *n*

sig·na·to·ry \ˈsig-nə-ˌtōr-ē\ *n*, *pl* **-ries** : a signer with another or others; *esp* : a government bound with others by a signed convention — **signatory** *adj*

sig·na·ture \ˈsig-nə-ˌchu̇r, -chər\ *n* **1** : the name of a person written with his own hand **2** : a tune, musical number, or sound effect or in television a characteristic title or picture used to identify a program, entertainer, or orchestra

sign·board \ˈsīn-ˌbōrd\ *n* : a board bearing a notice or sign

sig·net \ˈsig-nət\ *n* **1** : a seal used in place of a signature on a document **2** : the impression made by or as if by a signet **3** : a small intaglio seal (as in a finger ring)

signet ring *n* : a finger ring engraved with a signet

sig·ni·fi·a·ble \ˈsig-nə-ˌfī-ə-bəl\ *adj* : capable of being represented by a sign or symbol

sig·nif·i·cance \sig-ˈnif-i-kən(t)s\ *n* **1 a** : something signified **b** : SUGGESTIVENESS **2** : IMPORTANCE, CONSEQUENCE

sig·nif·i·cant \-kənt\ *adj* **1** : having meaning : SUGGESTIVE, EXPRESSIVE **2** : suggesting or containing a disguised or special meaning **3 a** : IMPORTANT, WEIGHTY **b** : probably caused by something other than mere chance **c** : DISTINCTIVE — **sig·nif·i·cant·ly** *adv*

sig·ni·fi·ca·tion \ˌsig-nə-fə-ˈkā-shən\ *n* **1** : a signifying by signs esp. to convey meaning **2** : IMPORT

sig·nif·i·ca·tive \sig-ˈnif-ə-ˌkāt-iv\ *adj* **1** : INDICATIVE **2** : SIGNIFICANT, SUGGESTIVE — **sig·nif·i·ca·tive·ly** *adv*

sig·ni·fi·er \ˈsig-nə-ˌfī(-ə)r\ *n* : one that signifies : SIGN

sig·ni·fy \ˈsig-nə-ˌfī\ *vb* **-fied**; **-fy·ing** **1** : MEAN, DENOTE **2** : to show esp. by a conventional token (as word, signal, or gesture) **3** : to have significance or importance

sign language *n* : a system of hand gestures used for communication by the deaf or by people speaking different languages

sign·post \ˈsīn-ˌpōst\ *n* : a post with a sign on it to direct travelers

Sikh \ˈsēk\ *n* : an adherent of a monotheistic religion of India founded about 1500 by a Hindu under Islamic influence and marked by rejection of idolatry and caste — **Sikh** *adj* — **Sikh·ism** \-ˌiz-əm\ *n*

si·lage \'sī-lij\ *n* : fodder converted into succulent feed for livestock through processes of anaerobic acid fermentation (as in a silo)

[1]**si·lence** \'sī-lən(t)s\ *n* **1** : forbearance from speech or noise — often used interjectionally **2** : absence of sound or noise **3** : absence of mention: **a** : OBLIVION, OBSCURITY **b** : SECRECY

[2]**silence** *vt* **1** : to stop the noise or speech of : reduce to silence **2** : to restrain from expression : SUPPRESS **3** : to cause to cease hostile firing by return fire or by destroying

si·lent \'sī-lənt\ *adj* **1** : making no utterance: **a** : MUTE, SPEECHLESS **b** : indisposed to speak : TACITURN **2** : free from sound or noise : STILL **3** : performed or borne without utterance : UNSPOKEN **4 a** : making no mention **b** : INACTIVE; *esp* : taking no active part in the conduct of a business **5** : UNPRONOUNCED — **si·lent·ly** *adv*

[1]**sil·hou·ette** \,sil-ə-'wet\ *n* **1** : a drawing or cutout of the outline of an object filled in with black; *esp* : a profile portrait of this kind **2** : characteristic shape of an object (as an airplane) seen or as if seen against the light

[2]**silhouette** *vt* : to represent by a silhouette; *also* : to project upon a background like a silhouette

sil·i·ca \'sil-i-kə\ *n* : a mineral that consists of silicon and oxygen and is found as quartz and opal

sil·i·cate \'sil-i-kət, 'sil-ə-,kāt\ *n* : a compound regarded as formed from silica and any of various oxides of metals

si·li·ceous *or* **si·li·cious** \sə-'lish-əs\ *adj* : of, relating to, or containing silica or a silicate

sil·i·con \'sil-i-kən, 'sil-ə-,kän\ *n* : a nonmetallic chemical element that occurs combined as the most abundant element next to oxygen in the earth's crust

sil·i·cone \'sil-ə-,kōn\ *n* : an organic silicon compound obtained as oil, grease, or plastic

sil·i·co·sis \,sil-ə-'kō-səs\ *n* : a disease of the lungs marked by fibrosis and shortness of breath and caused by prolonged inhaling of silica dusts — **sil·i·cot·ic** \-'kät-ik\ *adj or n*

silk \'silk\ *n* **1** : a fine continuous protein fiber produced by various insect larvae usu. for cocoons; *esp* : a lustrous tough elastic fiber produced by silkworms and used for textiles **2 a** : thread, yarn, or fabric made from silk **b** : a garment of silk — **silk** *adj*

silk·en \'sil-kən\ *adj* **1** : made or consisting of silk **2 a** : resembling silk esp. in soft lustrous smoothness **b** : smoothly agreeable : HARMONIOUS; *also* : INGRATIATING **3 a** : dressed in silk **b** : LUXURIOUS

silk hat *n* : a hat with a tall cylindrical crown and a silk-plush finish worn by men as a dress hat

silk·worm \'silk-,wərm\ *n* : a moth larva that spins a large amount of strong silk in constructing its cocoon; *esp* : the rough wrinkled hairless yellowish caterpillar of an Asiatic moth long grown as a source of silk

silky \'sil-kē\ *adj* **1** : SILKEN **2** : having or covered with fine soft hairs, plumes, or scales — **silk·i·ness** *n*

sill \'sil\ *n* : a horizontal piece (as a timber) that forms the lowest member of a framework or supporting structure (as of a house or bridge): as **a** : the horizontal member at the base of a window **b** : the timber or stone at the foot of a door

sil·ly \'sil-ē\ *adj* **1** : weak in intellect : FOOLISH **2** : contrary to reason : ABSURD **3** : TRIFLING, FRIVOLOUS — **sil·li·ly** \'sil-ə-lē\ *adv* — **sil·li·ness** \'sil-ē-nəs\ *n* — **silly** *n or adv*

si·lo \'sī-lō\ *n, pl* **silos** : a trench, pit, or esp. a tall cylinder (as of wood or concrete) usu. sealed to exclude air and used for making and storing silage

[1]**silt** \'silt\ *n* **1** : fine earth; *esp* : particles of such soil floating in rivers, ponds, or lakes **2** : a deposit of sediment (as by a river) — **silty** \'sil-tē\ *adj*

[2]**silt** *vb* : to become or make choked, obstructed, or covered with silt — **silt·a·tion** \sil-'tā-shən\ *n*

[1]**sil·ver** \'sil-vər\ *n* **1** : a white ductile and malleable metallic chemical element that takes a high polish, is usu. univalent in compounds, and has the highest thermal and electric conductivity of any substance **2 a** : coin made of silver **b** : articles (as tableware) made of or plated with silver **3** : a grayish white color

[2]**silver** *adj* **1** : relating to, made of, or yielding silver **2** : SILVERY 1

[3]**silver** *vt* **sil·vered**; **sil·ver·ing** \'silv-(ə-)riŋ\ **1** : to cover with or as if silver **2** : to give a silvery appearance to — **sil·ver·er** \'sil-vər-ər\ *n*

silver nitrate *n* : an irritant compound that is used as a chemical reagent, in photography, and in medicine esp. as an antiseptic

sil·ver·smith \'sil-vər-,smith\ *n* : a person who makes articles of silver

sil·ver–tongued \,sil-vər-'təŋd\ *adj* : ELOQUENT

sil·ver·ware \'sil-vər-,wa(ə)r\ *n* : articles (as knives, forks, and spoons) made of silver, silver-plated metal, or stainless steel

sil·very \'silv-(ə-)rē\ *adj* **1 a** : having a soft clear ring like that of struck silver **b** : having the white lustrous sheen of silver **2** : containing or consisting of silver — **sil·ver·i·ness** *n*

[1]**sim·i·an** \'sim-ē-ən\ *adj* : of, relating to, or resembling monkeys or apes

[2]**simian** *n* : MONKEY, APE

sim·i·lar \'sim-ə-lər\ *adj* **1** : marked by correspondence or resemblance **2** : not differing in shape but only in size or position — **sim·i·lar·ly** *adv*

sim·i·lar·i·ty \,sim-ə-'lar-ət-ē\ *n, pl* **-ties** **1** : the quality or state of being similar **2** : a point in which things are similar

sim·i·le \'sim-ə-(,)lē\ *n* : a figure of speech in which things different in kind or quality are compared by the use of the word *like* or *as* (as in *cheeks like roses*)

si·mil·i·tude \sə-'mil-ə-,t(y)üd\ *n* **1 a** : COUNTERPART, DOUBLE **b** : a visible likeness : IMAGE **2** : an imaginative comparison **3** : SIMILARITY

sim·mer \'sim-ər\ *vb* **sim·mered**; **sim·mer·ing** \'sim-(ə-)riŋ\ **1** : to stew gently below or just at the boiling point **2 a** : to be in a state of incipient development : FERMENT **b** : to be in inward turmoil — **simmer** *n*

si·mo·nize \'sī-mə-,nīz\ *vt* : to polish with or as if with wax

si·mo·ny \'sī-mə-nē, 'sim-ə-\ *n* : the buying or selling of a church office

[1]**sim·per** \'sim-pər\ *vi* **sim·pered**; **sim·per·ing** \-p(ə-)riŋ\ : to smile in a foolish affected manner — **sim·per·er** \-pər-ər\ *n*

[2]**simper** *n* : a simpered smile : SMIRK

[1]**sim·ple** \'sim-pəl\ *adj* **1** : free from guile or vanity **2 a** : of humble origin **b** : deficient in education, experience, or intelligence **3** : free from complexity or complications: as **a** : free from elaboration or showiness **b** : not mixed or compounded with anything else **c** : consisting of only one main clause and no subordinate clauses **d** : not compound **4 a** : UNMIXED, SHEER **b** : unlikely to cause difficulty because of complexity or obscurity : STRAIGHTFORWARD, EASY — **sim·ple·ness** *n*

[2]**simple** *n* **1 a** : a person of humble station **b** : an ignorant or mentally retarded person **2** : a medicinal plant **3** : something incapable of further subdivision : a simple component

sim·ple·mind·ed \,sim-pəl-'mīn-dəd\ *adj* : devoid of subtlety; *also* : FOOLISH — **sim·ple·mind·ed·ly** *adv* — **sim·ple·mind·ed·ness** *n*

sim·ple·ton \'sim-pəl-tən\ *n* : a person lacking in common sense

sim·plex \'sim-,pleks\ *adj* : SIMPLE, SINGLE

sim·plic·i·ty \sim-'plis-ət-ē\ *n, pl* **-ties** **1** : the quality or state of being simple and esp. not compounded **2** : lack of subtlety : freedom from pretense or guile : HONESTY, STRAIGHTFORWARDNESS **3 a** : directness or clarity of expression **b** : restraint in ornamentation : PLAINNESS **4** : FOLLY, SILLINESS

sim·pli·fy \'sim-plə-ˌfī\ *vt* **-fied**; **-fy·ing** : to make simple or simpler — **sim·pli·fi·ca·tion** \ˌsim-plə-fə-'kā-shən\ *n* — **sim·pli·fi·er** \'sim-plə-ˌfī(-ə)r\ *n*
sim·ply \'sim-plē\ *adv* **1 a** : without ambiguity : CLEARLY **b** : without embellishment : PLAINLY **c** : DIRECTLY, CANDIDLY **2 a** : MERELY, SOLELY **b** : LITERALLY, REALLY
sim·u·la·crum \ˌsim-yə-'lāk-rəm, -'lak-\ *n, pl* **-cra** \-rə\ **1** : IMAGE, REPRESENTATION **2** : an insubstantial form or semblance of something : SHADOW; *also* : TRACE
sim·u·late \'sim-yə-ˌlāt\ *vt* : to give the appearance or effect of — **sim·u·la·tive** \-ˌlāt-iv\ *adj* — **sim·u·la·tor** \-ˌlāt-ər\ *n*
sim·u·la·tion \ˌsim-yə-'lā-shən\ *n* **1** : the act or process of simulating **2** : a sham object : COUNTERFEIT
si·mul·ta·ne·ous \ˌsī-məl-'tā-nē-əs\ *adj* : existing or occurring at the same time : COINCIDENT — **si·mul·ta·ne·i·ty** \-tə-'nē-ət-ē\ *n* — **si·mul·ta·ne·ous·ly** *adv* — **si·mul·ta·ne·ous·ness** *n*
¹sin \'sin\ *n* **1 a** : an offense against God **b** : a weakened state of human nature in which the self is estranged from God **2** : MISDEED, FAULT
²sin *vi* **sinned**; **sin·ning** : to commit a sin
¹since \(')sin(t)s\ *adv* **1** : from a definite past time until now **2** : before the present time : AGO **3** : after a time in the past
²since *prep* : from or after a specified time in the past
³since *conj* **1** : at a time or times in the past after or later than **2** : from the time in the past when **3** : in view of the fact that
sin·cere \sin-'si(ə)r\ *adj* : being the same in fact as in appearance: as **a** : free from dissimulation : HONEST **b** : free from adulteration : PURE **c** : true to self or nature : GENUINE — **sin·cere·ly** *adv* — **sin·cere·ness** *n* — **sin·cer·i·ty** \-'ser-ət-ē, -'sir-\ *n*
si·ne·cure \'sī-ni-ˌkyu̇r, 'sin-i-\ *n* : an office or position that requires little or no work
si·ne die \ˌsī-nē-'dī-ˌē, ˌsin-ē-'dē-ˌā\ *adv* : INDEFINITELY
si·ne qua non \ˌsin-ē-ˌkwä-'nōn, ˌsī-nē-ˌkwā-'nän\ *n* : something absolutely essential or indispensable
sin·ew \'sin-yü, 'sin-ü\ *n* **1** : TENDON; *esp* : one dressed for use as a cord or thread **2 a** : solid resilient strength : POWER **b** : the chief supporting force — usu. used in pl.
sin·ewy \'sin-(y)ə-wē\ *adj* **1** : full of sinews : TOUGH, STRINGY **2** : STRONG, POWERFUL
sin·ful \'sin-fəl\ *adj* : marked by or full of sin : WICKED — **sin·ful·ly** \-fə-lē\ *adv* — **sin·ful·ness** *n*
sing \'siŋ\ *vb* **sang** \'saŋ\ *or* **sung** \'səŋ\; **sung**; **sing·ing** \'siŋ-iŋ\ **1 a** : to produce musical sounds by means of the voice **b** : to utter with musical sounds; *also* : CHANT, INTONE **2** : to make pleasing musical sounds **3** : to make a slight shrill sound **4 a** : to tell a story in poetry : relate in verse **b** : to express vividly and enthusiastically **5** : HUM, BUZZ, RING **6** : to act on or affect by singing **7 a** : to call aloud : cry out **b** : to divulge information or give evidence
¹singe \'sinj\ *vb* **singed** \'sinjd\; **singe·ing** \'sin-jiŋ\ : to burn superficially or lightly : SCORCH; *esp* : to remove hair, down, or fuzz from usu. by passing briefly over a flame
²singe *n* : a slight burn : SCORCH
sing·er \'siŋ-ər\ *n* : one that sings
sing·ing bird \'siŋ-iŋ-\ *n* **1** : SONGBIRD 1 **2** : a passerine bird
¹sin·gle \'siŋ-gəl\ *adj* **1** : UNMARRIED **2** : being alone : being the only one **3** : having only one part or feature **4** : engaged in man to man **5** : designed for the use of one person or family only — **sin·gle·ness** *n*
²single *n* **1** : a separate individual person or thing **2** : a hit in baseball that enables the batter to reach first base **3** *pl* : a game (as of tennis) between two players
³single *vb* **sin·gled**; **sin·gling** \'siŋ-g(ə-)liŋ\ **1** : to select or distinguish (a person or thing) from a number or group **2** : to hit a single
sin·gle–breast·ed \ˌsiŋ-gəl-'bres-təd\ *adj* : having a center closing with one row of buttons and no lap
sin·gle–hand·ed \ˌsiŋ-gəl-'han-dəd\ *adj* **1** : managed or done by one person or with one hand **2** : working alone : lacking help — **sin·gle–hand·ed·ly** *adv* — **sin·gle–hand·ed·ness** *n*
sin·gle–heart·ed \-'härt-əd\ *adj* : characterized by sincerity and unity of purpose — **sin·gle–heart·ed·ly** *adv*
sin·gle–mind·ed \-'mīn-dəd\ *adj* **1** : SINCERE, SINGLE-HEARTED **2** : having one overriding purpose — **sin·gle–mind·ed·ly** *adv* — **sin·gle–mind·ed·ness** *n*
sin·gle·ton \'siŋ-gəl-tən\ *n* : a playing card that is the only one of its suit orig. held in a hand
sin·gle·tree \-(ˌ)trē\ *n* : WHIFFLETREE
sin·gly \'siŋ-g(ə-)lē\ *adv* **1** : by or with oneself : INDIVIDUALLY **2** : SINGLE-HANDEDLY
¹sing·song \'siŋ-ˌsȯŋ\ *n* : a monotonous rhythm or a monotonous rise and fall of pitch; *also* : speech or voice marked by this
²singsong *adj* : having a monotonous cadence or rhythm
sin·gu·lar \'siŋ-gyə-lər\ *adj* **1 a** : of or relating to a separate person or thing : INDIVIDUAL **b** : of, relating to, or constituting a word form denoting one person, thing, or instance **c** : of or relating to a single instance or to something considered by itself **2 a** : distinguished by superiority : EXCEPTIONAL **b** : of unusual quality : UNIQUE **3** : being at variance with others : PECULIAR — **singular** *n* — **sin·gu·lar·ly** *adv*
sin·gu·lar·i·ty \ˌsiŋ-gyə-'lar-ət-ē\ *n, pl* **-ties** **1** : the quality or state of being singular **2** : something that is singular : PECULIARITY, ECCENTRICITY
sin·is·ter \'sin-əs-tər\ *adj* **1** : singularly evil or productive of evil : BAD, CORRUPTIVE **2** : presaging or leading to ill fortune or trouble : OMINOUS — **sin·is·ter·ly** *adv* — **sin·is·ter·ness** *n*
¹sink \'siŋk\ *vb* **sank** \'saŋk\ *or* **sunk** \'səŋk\; **sunk**; **sink·ing** **1 a** : to move or cause to move downward usu. so as to be submerged or swallowed up **b** : to descend gradually lower and lower **c** : to fall to a lower level **2** : to lessen in amount or intensity: as **a** : to make or become less active or vigorous **b** : to fall to or into an inferior status (as of quality, worth, or number) : RETROGRESS, DECLINE **c** : to fail in strength, spirits, or health esp. from some burdening pressure **d** : RESTRAIN, SUBORDINATE **3 a** : to penetrate or cause to penetrate **b** : to become absorbed; *also* : to be taken in so as to be apprehended and retained **4** : to form by digging or boring usu. in the earth **5 a** : INVEST **b** : to spend or invest unwisely or without expectation of a return — **sink·a·ble** *adj*
²sink *n* **1 a** : CESSPOOL **b** : SEWER **c** : a stationary basin for washing (as in a kitchen) connected with a drain and usu. a water supply **2** : a place where vice, corruption, or evil collect **3** : a depression in the land surface
sink·er \'siŋ-kər\ *n* **1** : one that sinks; *esp* : a weight for sinking a line or net **2** : DOUGHNUT
sin·less \'sin-ləs\ *adj* : free from sin : IMPECCABLE, HOLY
sin·ner \'sin-ər\ *n* : one that sins
sin·u·os·i·ty \ˌsin-yə-'wäs-ət-ē\ *n, pl* **-ties** **1** : the quality or state of being sinuous **2** : something that is sinuous
sin·u·ous \'sin-yə-wəs\ *adj* **1 a** : of a serpentine or wavy form : WINDING **b** : marked by strong lithe movements **2** : INTRICATE, COMPLEX — **sin·u·ous·ly** *adv* — **sin·u·ous·ness** *n*
si·nus \'sī-nəs\ *n* : CAVITY, HOLLOW: as **a** : a narrow passage by which pus is discharged **b** : any of several cavities in the skull mostly communicating with the nostrils **c** : a space forming a channel (as for the passage of blood)
¹sip \'sip\ *vb* **sipped**; **sip·ping** **1** : to drink in small quantities or little by little **2** : to take sips from : TASTE — **sip·per** *n*
²sip *n* **1** : the act of sipping **2** : a small amount taken by sipping
¹si·phon \'sī-fən\ *n* **1** : a tube bent to form two legs of unequal length by which a liquid can be transferred to a lower level over an intermediate elevation by the pressure of the atmosphere in forcing the liquid up the shorter branch of the tube

immersed in it while the excess of weight of the liquid in the longer branch when once filled causes a continuous flow **2** *usu* **sy·phon** : a bottle for holding carbonated water that is driven out through a bent tube in its neck by the pressure of the gas when a valve in the tube is opened

²siphon *vb* **si·phoned**; **si·phon·ing** \'sī-f(ə-)niŋ\ : to draw off or pass off by or as if by a siphon

sir \(')sər\ *n* **1** : a man entitled to be addressed as *sir* — used as a title before the given name of a knight or baronet **2 a** — used as a usu. respectful form of address **b** *cap* — used as a conventional form of address in the salutation of a letter

¹sire \'sī(ə)r\ *n* **1** : FATHER **2** : the male parent of an animal and esp. of a domestic animal

²sire *vt* **1** : BEGET, PROCREATE — used esp. of domestic animals **2** : to bring into being : ORIGINATE

¹si·ren \'sī-rən, *for 2 also* sī-'rēn\ *n* **1** : a woman who is insidiously seductive : TEMPTRESS **2** : a device often electrically operated for producing a penetrating warning sound

²si·ren \'sī-rən\ *adj* : of or relating to a siren : ENTICING

sir·loin \'sər-ˌlòin\ *n* : a cut of meat and esp. of beef from the part of the hindquarter just in front of the round

si·roc·co \sə-'räk-ō\ *n, pl* **-cos** **1** : a hot dust-laden wind from the Libyan desert that blows on the northern Mediterranean coast **2** : a hot southerly wind

sir·ree \(ˌ)sər-'ē\ *n* : SIR — used as an emphatic form usu. after *yes* or *no*

si·sal \'sī-səl, -zəl\ *n* **1** : a strong durable white fiber used for cordage **2** : a widely grown West Indian agave whose leaves yield sisal

sis·si·fied \'sis-i-ˌfīd\ *adj* : SISSY

sis·sy \'sis-ē\ *n, pl* **sissies** : an effeminate man or boy; *also* : a timid or cowardly person — **sissy** *adj*

¹sis·ter \'sis-tər\ *n* **1 a** : a female person or lower animal viewed in relation to another person or animal having one or both parents in common **b** : SISTER-IN-LAW **c** : a kinswoman by blood **2** *often cap* : a member of a religious society of women : NUN **3 a** : a woman related to another by a common tie or interest **b** : one having similar characteristics to another

²sister *adj* : having or suggesting the relationship of a sister

sis·ter·hood \-ˌhu̇d\ *n* **1 a** : the state of being a sister **b** : sisterly relationship **2** : a community or society of sisters

sis·ter–in–law \'sis-t(ə-)rən-ˌlò, -tərn-ˌlò\ *n, pl* **sis·ters–in–law** \-tər-zən-\ **1** : the sister of one's spouse **2 a** : the wife of one's brother **b** : the wife of one's spouse's brother

sis·ter·ly \'sis-tər-lē\ *adj* : of, relating to, or having the characteristics of a sister — **sisterly** *adv*

sit \'sit\ *vb* **sat** \'sat\; **sit·ting** **1 a** : to rest upon the buttocks or haunches; *also* : to cause (as oneself) thus to rest : SEAT **b** : PERCH, ROOST **c** : to keep one's seat upon **d** : to provide seats or seating room for **2** : to occupy a place as a member of an official body **3** : to hold a session **4** : to cover eggs for hatching : BROOD **5 a** : to pose for a portrait or photograph **b** : to serve as a model **6** : to lie or hang relative to a wearer **7** : to lie or rest in any condition **8** : to have a location **9** : to remain inactive **10** : BABY-SIT — **sit on** **1** : to hold deliberations concerning **2** : REPRESS, SQUELCH **3** : to delay action or decision concerning : SUPPRESS — **sit on one's hands** **1** : to withhold applause **2** : to fail to take action — **sit pretty** : to be in a highly favorable situation — **sit tight** : to maintain one's position without change

sit–down \'sit-ˌdau̇n\ *n* : a strike in which the workers stop work and refuse to leave their places of employment

site \'sīt\ *n* **1 a** : local position (as of a building, town, or monument) **b** : a space of ground occupied or to be occupied by a building **2** : the place or scene of something

sit–in \'sit-ˌin\ *n* **1** : SIT-DOWN **2** : an act of occupying seats in a racially segregated establishment in organized protest against discrimination

sit·ter \'sit-ər\ *n* : one that sits; *esp* : BABY-SITTER

¹sit·ting \'sit-iŋ\ *n* **1** : an act of one that sits; *esp* : a single occasion of continuous sitting **2** : SETTING 6 **3** : SESSION

²sitting *adj* **1** : that is setting **2** : easily hit **3 a** : used in or for sitting **b** : performed while sitting

sitting duck *n* : an easy or defenseless target

sitting room *n* : LIVING ROOM

¹sit·u·ate \'sich-ə-wət, -ˌwāt\ *adj* : having its site : LOCATED

²sit·u·ate \'sich-ə-ˌwāt\ *vt* : to place in a site or situation

sit·u·at·ed \-ˌwāt-əd\ *adj* **1** : LOCATED **2** : CIRCUMSTANCED, FIXED

sit·u·a·tion \ˌsich-ə-'wā-shən\ *n* **1 a** : the way in which something is placed in relation to its surroundings **b** : SITE **2 a** : position or place of employment : POST, JOB **b** : position in life : STATUS **3** : position with respect to conditions and circumstances **4 a** : relative position or combination of circumstances at a certain moment **b** : a particular or striking complex of affairs at a stage in the action of a narrative or drama — **sit·u·a·tion·al** \-shnəl, -shən-ᵊl\ *adj*

si·tus \'sīt-əs\ *n* : the place where something exists or originates

six \'siks\ *n* **1** — see NUMBER table **2** : the sixth in a set or series **3** : something having six units or members; *esp* : a 6-cylinder engine or automobile — **six** *adj or pron* — **at sixes and sevens** : in disorder : CONFUSED

six·pence \'siks-pən(t)s, *US also* -ˌpen(t)s\ *n* : the sum of six pence; *also* : a coin representing six pence or half a shilling

six·pen·ny \-pə-nē, *US also* -ˌpen-ē\ *adj* **1** : of the value of or costing sixpence **2** : of trifling worth : CHEAP, TRASHY

six·teen \(')siks-'tēn\ *n* — see NUMBER table — **sixteen** *adj or pron* — **six·teenth** \-'tēn(t)th\ *adj or n*

sixth \'siks(t)th, 'sikst\ *n* — see NUMBER table — **sixth** *adj or adv* — **sixth·ly** \-lē\ *adv*

sixth sense *n* : a keen intuitive power

six·ty \'sik-stē\ *n, pl* **sixties** — see NUMBER table — **six·ti·eth** \-stē-əth\ *adj or n* — **sixty** *adj or pron*

siz·a·ble *or* **size·a·ble** \'sī-zə-bəl\ *adj* : fairly large : CONSIDERABLE — **siz·a·ble·ness** *n* — **siz·a·bly** \-blē\ *adv*

¹size \'sīz\ *n* **1 a** : physical magnitude, extent, or bulk : relative or proportionate dimensions **b** : BIGNESS **2** : one of a series of graduated measures esp. of manufactured articles (as of clothing) conventionally identified by numbers or letters **3** : character or status of a person or thing esp. with reference to importance, merit, or correspondence to needs **4** : actual state of affairs : true condition

²size *vb* **1** : to make a particular size : bring to proper or suitable size **2** : to arrange, grade, or classify according to size

³size *n* : a gluey material (as a preparation of glue, flour, varnish, or resins) used for filling the pores in a surface (as of plaster), as a stiffener (as of fabric), or as an adhesive for applying color or leaf to book edges or covers

⁴size *vt* : to apply size to

⁵size *adj* : SIZED

sized \'sīzd\ *adj* **1** : having a specified size or bulk **2** : arranged or adjusted according to size

size up *vb* **1** : to form a judgment of **2** : to equal in size or some particular : measure up — often used with *to* or *with*

siz·ing \'sī-ziŋ\ *n* : ³SIZE

siz·zle \'siz-əl\ *vb* **siz·zled**; **siz·zling** \'siz-(ə-)liŋ\ **1** : to burn up or sear with a hissing sound **2** : to make a hissing sound in or as if in burning or frying **3** : to seethe with deeply felt anger or resentment — **sizzle** *n* — **siz·zler** \-(ə-)lər\ *n*

skald \'skòld, 'skäld\ *n* : an ancient Scandinavian poet or writer of history — **skald·ic** \-ik\ *adj*

¹skate \'skāt\ *n* : any of numerous rays with broadly developed pectoral fins

[2]**skate** *n* **1 :** a metal runner on a frame that fits the sole of a boot for use in gliding over ice; *also* **:** a boot with runner attached **2 :** ROLLER SKATE — **skate** *vi* — **skat•er** *n*
skate•board \ˈskāt-ˌbōrd\ *n* **:** a narrow board mounted on roller-skate wheels — **skate•board•er** *n*
skein \ˈskān\ *n* **1** *or* **skean** *or* **skeane** \ˈskān\ **:** a looped length of yarn or thread put up in a loose twist after it is taken from the reel **2 :** something suggesting the twists or coils of a skein **:** TANGLE
skel•e•tal \ˈskel-ət-ᵊl\ *adj* **:** of, relating or attached to, forming, or resembling a skeleton — **skel•e•tal•ly** \-ᵊl-ē\ *adv*
[1]**skel•e•ton** \ˈskel-ət-ᵊn\ *n* **1 :** a usu. rigid supporting or protecting structure or framework of an organism; *esp* **:** the bony or sometimes cartilaginous framework supporting the soft tissues and protecting the internal organs of a vertebrate (as a fish or man) **2 :** something reduced to its minimum form or essential parts **3 :** an emaciated person or animal **4 :** something forming a structural framework **5 :** something shameful and kept secret (as in a family)
[2]**skeleton** *adj* **:** of, consisting of, or resembling a skeleton
skel•e•ton•ize \ˈskel-ət-ᵊn-ˌīz\ *vt* **:** to produce in or reduce to skeleton form
skeleton key *n* **:** a key made to open many locks
skep•tic \ˈskep-tik\ *n* **1 :** an adherent or advocate of skepticism **2 :** a person disposed to skepticism esp. regarding religion or religious principles
skep•ti•cal \-ti-kəl\ *adj* **:** relating to, characteristic of, or marked by skepticism — **skep•ti•cal•ly** \-k(ə-)lē\ *adv*
skep•ti•cism \ˈskep-tə-ˌsiz-əm\ *n* **1 a :** the doctrine that true knowledge or knowledge in a particular area is uncertain **b :** the method of suspended judgment, systematic doubt, or criticism characteristic of skeptics **2 :** an attitude of doubt esp. concerning basic religious principles
[1]**sketch** \ˈskech\ *n* **1 a :** a rough drawing representing the chief features of an object or scene and often made as a preliminary study **b :** a tentative draft (as for a literary work) **2 :** a brief description or outline **3 a :** a short literary composition somewhat resembling the short story and the essay but intentionally slight in treatment and familiar in tone **b :** a slight theatrical piece having a single scene; *esp* **:** a comic vaudeville act
[2]**sketch** *vb* **1 :** to make a sketch, rough draft, or outline of **2 :** to draw or paint sketches — **sketch•er** *n*
sketch•book \ˈskech-ˌbu̇k\ *n* **:** a book of or for sketches
sketchy \ˈskech-ē\ *adj* **1 :** of the nature of a sketch **:** roughly outlined **2 :** wanting in completeness, clearness, or substance **:** SLIGHT, VAGUE — **sketch•i•ly** \ˈskech-ə-lē\ *adv* — **sketch•i•ness** \ˈskech-ē-nəs\ *n*
[1]**skew** \ˈskyü\ *vb* **1 :** to take an oblique course **:** move or turn aside **:** TWIST, SWERVE **2 :** to make, set, or cut on the skew **3 :** to distort from a true value or symmetrical form
[2]**skew** *adj* **1 a :** set, placed, or running obliquely to something else **b :** neither parallel nor intersecting **2 :** ASYMMETRICAL
[1]**skew•er** \ˈskyü-ər, ˈskyu̇(-ə)r\ *n* **:** a pin for keeping meat in form while roasting or for holding small pieces of meat and vegetables for broiling
[2]**skewer** *vt* **:** to fasten or pierce with or as if with a skewer
[1]**ski** \ˈskē\ *n, pl* **skis :** one of a pair of narrow strips (as of wood) worn by people for gliding over snow or water
[2]**ski** *vi* **skied; ski•ing :** to glide on skis — **ski•er** *n*
[1]**skid** \ˈskid\ *n* **1 :** a log or plank for supporting something (as above the ground) **2 :** one of the logs, planks, or rails along or on which something heavy is rolled or slid **3 :** a device placed under a carriage wheel to prevent its turning **:** DRAG **4 :** a runner used as part of the landing gear of an airplane or helicopter **5 :** the act of skidding **:** SLIDE
[2]**skid** *vb* **skid•ded; skid•ding 1 :** to slow or halt by a skid **2 :** to haul along, slide, hoist, or store on skids **3 :** to slide without rotating **4 a :** to fail to grip the roadway; *esp* **:** to slip sideways on the road **b :** to slide sideways away from the center of curvature when turning **c :** SLIDE, SLIP **5 :** to fall rapidly, steeply, or far
skiff \ˈskif\ *n* **:** a small open boat
skill \ˈskil\ *n* **1 :** ability or dexterity that comes from training or practice **2 a :** a particular art or science **b :** a developed or acquired ability **:** ACCOMPLISHMENT
skilled \ˈskild\ *adj* **:** having or requiring skill
skil•let \ˈskil-ət\ *n* **:** a frying pan
skill•ful *or* **skil•ful** \ˈskil-fəl\ *adj* **1 :** having or displaying skill **:** EXPERT, DEXTEROUS **2 :** accomplished with skill — **skill•ful•ly** \-fə-lē\ *adv* — **skill•ful•ness** *n*
[1]**skim** \ˈskim\ *vb* **skimmed; skim•ming 1 :** to take off from the top of a liquid; *also* **:** to remove (scum or cream) from **2 :** to read, study, or examine superficially and rapidly **3 :** to pass swiftly or lightly over
[2]**skim** *n* **1 :** a thin layer, coating, or film **2 :** the act of skimming **3 :** something skimmed; *esp* **:** SKIM MILK
[3]**skim** *adj* **1 :** SKIMMED **2 :** made of skim milk
skim•mer \ˈskim-ər\ *n* **:** one that skims; *esp* **:** a flat perforated scoop or spoon used for skimming
skim milk *n* **:** milk from which the cream has been taken
skimp \ˈskimp\ *vb* **1 :** to give insufficient or barely sufficient attention or effort to or funds for **:** SCAMP **2 :** to save by or as if by skimping **:** SCRIMP
skimpy \ˈskim-pē\ *adj* **:** deficient (as in supply) esp. through skimping **:** SCANTY — **skimp•i•ly** \-pə-lē\ *adv* — **skimp•i•ness** \-pē-nəs\ *n*
[1]**skin** \ˈskin\ *n* **1 a :** the integument of an animal and esp. of a fur-bearing animal when separated from the body **b :** a sheet of parchment or vellum made from a hide **2 a :** the external limiting layer of an animal body esp. when forming a tough but flexible cover; *also* **:** the 2-layered tissue of which this is formed in a vertebrate **b :** an outer or surface layer (as a rind) **3 :** the life or physical well-being of a person — **skin•less** \-ləs\ *adj* — **skinned** \ˈskind\ *adj*
[2]**skin** *vb* **skinned; skin•ning 1 :** to cover or become covered with or as if with skin **2 a :** to strip, scrape, or rub off the skin of **b :** to strip or peel off **3 a :** CHEAT, FLEECE **b :** DEFEAT **c :** CENSURE, REPRIMAND **4 a :** to climb or descend **b :** to pass or get by with scant room to spare
skin–deep \ˈskin-ˈdēp\ *adj* **1 :** as deep as the skin **2 :** not thorough or lasting in impression **:** SUPERFICIAL
skin dive *vi* **:** to swim deep below the surface of water with a face mask and flippers and with or without a portable breathing device — **skin diver** *n*
skin•flint \ˈskin-ˌflint\ *n* **:** a miserly person
skin•ner \ˈskin-ər\ *n* **1 a :** one that deals in skins, pelts, or hides **b :** one that removes, cures, or dresses skins **2 :** a driver of draft animals and esp. of mules
skin•ny \ˈskin-ē\ *adj* **1 :** resembling skin **:** MEMBRANOUS **2 :** very thin **:** LEAN, EMACIATED — **skin•ni•ness** *n*
skin•tight \ˈskin-ˈtīt\ *adj* **:** closely fitted to the figure
[1]**skip** \ˈskip\ *vb* **skipped; skip•ping 1 a :** to move or proceed with leaps and bounds **:** CAPER **b :** to bound or cause to bound off one point after another **:** RICOCHET **c :** to leap over lightly and nimbly **2 :** to leave or leave from hurriedly or secretly **3 a :** to pass over or omit (as an interval, item, or step) **b :** to omit or cause to omit a grade in school in advancing to the next **c :** to pass over without notice or mention **d :** to fail to attend **e :** MISFIRE 1
[2]**skip** *n* **1 a :** a light bounding step **b :** a gait composed of alternating hops and steps **2 :** an act of omission or the thing omitted
[1]**skip•per** \ˈskip-ər\ *n* **:** one that skips
[2]**skipper** *n* **:** the master of a ship; *esp* **:** the master of a fishing, small trading, or pleasure boat

skirl \'skərl, 'skirl\ *n* : the shrill tone of a bagpipe — **skirl** *vb*

[1]**skir·mish** \'skər-mish\ *n* **1** : a minor fight in war usu. incidental to larger movements **2** : a brisk preliminary conflict

[2]**skirmish** *vi* **1** : to engage in a skirmish **2** : to search about (as for supplies) — **skir·mish·er** *n*

[1]**skirt** \'skərt\ *n* **1 a** : a free hanging part of a garment extending from the waist down **b** : a separate free hanging garment for women and girls covering the body from the waist down **2** *pl* : the outlying parts of a town or city : OUTSKIRTS **3** : a part or attachment serving as a rim, border, or edging

[2]**skirt** *vb* **1** : to form or run along the edge of : BORDER **2** : to provide a skirt or border for **3 a** : to go or pass around or about; *esp* : to go around or keep away from in order to avoid danger or discovery **b** : to evade or miss by a narrow margin **4** : to be, lie, or move along an edge, border, or margin

skirt·ing \-iŋ\ *n* **1** : BORDER, EDGING **2** : fabric (as wool) suitable for skirts

skit \'skit\ *n* **1** : a satirical or humorous story or sketch; *esp* : a sketch included in a dramatic performance (as a review) **2** : a short serious dramatic piece; *esp* : one done by amateurs

skit·ter \'skit-ər\ *vb* : to glide or skip lightly or quickly : skim along a surface

skit·tish \'skit-ish\ *adj* **1** : lively or frisky in action : CAPRICIOUS **2** : easily frightened : RESTIVE **3** : COY, BASHFUL — **skit·tish·ly** *adv* — **skit·tish·ness** *n*

skit·tle \'skit-ᵊl\ *n* **1** *pl* : a form of ninepins that sometimes uses wooden disks instead of balls **2** : one of the pins used in skittles

skiv·vy \'skiv-ē\ *n, pl* **skivvies** : underwear consisting of shorts and a collarless short-sleeved pullover — usu. used in pl.

ski·wear \'skē-ˌwa(ə)r\ *n* : clothing suitable for wear while skiing

skul·dug·gery *or* **skull·dug·gery** \ˌskəl-'dəg-(ə-)rē\ *n, pl* **-geries** : underhanded or unscrupulous behavior : DISHONESTY

[1]**skulk** \'skəlk\ *vi* **1** : to move in a stealthy or furtive manner : SNEAK **2** : to hide or conceal oneself from cowardice or fear or with treacherous intent — **skulk·er** *n*

[2]**skulk** *n* : SKULKER

skull \'skəl\ *n* **1** : the vertebrate head skeleton that forms a bony or cartilaginous case enclosing the brain and chief sense organs and supporting the jaws **2** : the seat of understanding or intelligence : MIND

skull·cap \'skəl-ˌkap\ *n* : a close-fitting cap; *esp* : a light cap without brim for indoor wear

skunk \'skəŋk\ *n, pl* **skunks** **1** : any of various common omnivorous black-and-white New World mammals related to the weasels and having glands near the anus from which a secretion of pungent and offensive odor is ejected when the animal is startled **2** : an obnoxious person

sky \'skī\ *n, pl* **skies** **1** : the upper atmosphere that constitutes an apparent great vault or arch over the earth : FIRMAMENT **2** : HEAVEN 2 **3** : WEATHER, CLIMATE

sky·div·ing \'skī-ˌdī-viŋ\ *n* : the sport of jumping from an airplane (as at an altitude of 6000 feet) and executing various body maneuvers before pulling the rip cord of a parachute — **sky diver** *n*

sky–high \'skī-'hī\ *adv* (*or adj*) **1 a** : high into the air **b** : to a high level or degree **2** : in an enthusiastic manner **3** : to bits : APART **4** : EXORBITANTLY

[1]**sky·lark** \'skī-ˌlärk\ *n* : a common Old World lark that sings as it rises in almost perpendicular flight

[2]**skylark** *vi* : to play wild boisterous pranks : FROLIC — **sky·lark·er** *n*

sky·light \'skī-ˌlīt\ *n* : a window or group of windows in a roof or ceiling

sky·line \-ˌlīn\ *n* **1** : the line where earth and sky or water and sky seem to meet : HORIZON **2** : an outline against the sky

[1]**sky·rock·et** \'skī-ˌräk-ət\ *n* : ROCKET 1

[2]**skyrocket** *vb* **1** : to shoot up abruptly **2** : to cause to rise or increase abruptly and rapidly

sky·scrap·er \'skī-ˌskrā-pər\ *n* : a very tall building

sky·ward \'skī-wərd\ *adv* (*or adj*) **1** : toward the sky **2** : UPWARD

sky·writ·ing \'skī-ˌrīt-iŋ\ *n* : writing formed in the sky by means of a visible substance (as smoke) emitted from an airplane — **sky·writ·er** \-ˌrīt-ər\ *n*

slab \'slab\ *n* **1** : a thick plate or slice (as of stone, wood, or bread) **2** : the outside piece cut from a log in squaring it

[1]**slack** \'slak\ *adj* **1** : not using due diligence, care, or dispatch : NEGLIGENT **2 a** : characterized by slowness, sluggishness, or lack of energy **b** : moderate in some quality; *esp* : moderately warm **3 a** : not tight : not tense or taut : RELAXED **b** : lacking in firmness : WEAK, SOFT **4** : wanting in activity : DULL — **slack·ly** *adv* — **slack·ness** *n*

[2]**slack** *vb* **1 a** : to be or become slack or negligent in performing or doing **b** : LESSEN, MODERATE **2** : to shirk or evade work or duty **3** : LOOSEN **4 a** : to cause to abate **b** : SLAKE 2

[3]**slack** *n* **1** : cessation in movement or flow **2** : a part of something that hangs loose without strain **3** *pl* : trousers esp. for casual wear **4** : a dull season or period : LULL

slack·en \'slak-ən\ *vb* **slack·ened**; **slack·en·ing** \'slak-(ə-)niŋ\ **1** : to make or become less active : slow up : MODERATE, RETARD **2** : to make less taut **3** : to become negligent

slack·er \'slak-ər\ *n* : one who shirks work or evades an obligation esp. for military service in time of war

slag \'slag\ *n* **1** : waste left after the melting of ores and the separation of the metal from them **2** : volcanic lava resembling cinders — **slag·gy** \'slag-ē\ *adj*

slain *past part of* SLAY

slake \'slāk, *2 is also* 'slak\ *vb* **1** : to relieve or satisfy with water or liquid : QUENCH **2** : to cause (lime) to heat and crumble by treatment with water : HYDRATE

sla·lom \'släl-əm\ *n* : skiing in a zigzag course between upright obstacles

[1]**slam** \'slam\ *n* : the winning of all or all but one of the tricks of a deal in bridge

[2]**slam** *vb* **slammed**; **slam·ming** **1** : to strike or beat hard **2** : to shut forcibly and noisily : BANG **3** : to set or slap down violently or noisily **4** : to make a banging noise **5** : to criticize harshly

[3]**slam** *n* **1** : a heavy impact **2 a** : a noisy violent closing **b** : a banging noise esp. from the slamming of a door **3** : a cutting or violent criticism

[1]**slan·der** \'slan-dər\ *n* **1** : the utterance of false charges or misrepresentations which defame and damage another's reputation **2** : a false and defamatory oral statement about a person — **slan·der·ous** \-d(ə-)rəs\ *adj* — **slan·der·ous·ly** *adv*

[2]**slander** *vt* **slan·dered**; **slan·der·ing** \-d(ə-)riŋ\ : to utter slander against : DEFAME — **slan·der·er** \-dər-ər\ *n*

slang \'slaŋ\ *n* **1** : language peculiar to a particular group, trade, or pursuit **2** : an informal nonstandard vocabulary composed typically of coinages, arbitrarily changed words, and extravagant, forced, or facetious figures of speech — **slang** *adj*

slangy \'slaŋ-ē\ *adj* **1** : of, relating to, or constituting slang : containing slang **2** : addicted to the use of slang — **slang·i·ly** \'slaŋ-ə-lē\ *adv* — **slang·i·ness** \'slaŋ-ē-nəs\ *n*

[1]**slant** \'slant\ *vb* **1** : to turn or incline from a straight line or a level : SLOPE **2** : to interpret or present in accordance with a special viewpoint

[2]**slant** *n* **1** : a slanting direction, line, or plane : SLOPE **2** : something that slants **3** : a way of looking at something : a peculiar or personal point of view, attitude, or opinion **4** : GLANCE, LOOK — **slant** *adj*

slant·ways \'slant-ˌwāz\ *adv* : SLANTWISE

ə abut ᵊ kitten ər further a back ā bake ä cot, cart aù out ch chin e less ē easy g gift i trip ī life

slant·wise \-ˌwīz\ *adv (or adj)* : so as to slant : at a slant : in a slanting direction or position

¹slap \ˈslap\ *n* **1** : a quick sharp blow esp. with the open hand; *also* : a noise suggesting that of a slap **2** : REBUFF, INSULT

²slap *vb* **slapped**; **slap·ping** **1 a** : to strike with or as if with the open hand **b** : to make a sound like that of slapping **2** : to put, place, or throw with careless haste or force **3** : INSULT

³slap *adv* : DIRECTLY, SMACK

slap·dash \ˈslap-ˌdash, -ˈdash\ *adv (or adj)* : in a slipshod manner : HAPHAZARD; *also* : HASTILY

slap·stick \ˈslap-ˌstik\ *n* : comedy stressing farce and horseplay — **slapstick** *adj*

¹slash \ˈslash\ *vb* **1** : to cut by sweeping and aimless blows : GASH **2** : to whip or strike with or as if with a cane **3** : to criticize without mercy **4** : to cut slits in (as a skirt) to reveal a color beneath **5** : to reduce sharply : CUT — **slash·er** *n*

²slash *n* **1** : an act or result of slashing: as **a** : a long cut or stroke made by slashing **b** : an ornamental slit in a garment **c** : a sharp reduction **2** : an open debris-strewn tract in a forest; *also* : the debris in such a tract

slat \ˈslat\ *n* : a thin narrow flat strip of wood, plastic, or metal — **slat·ted** \ˈslat-əd\ *adj*

¹slate \ˈslāt\ *n* **1** : a fine-grained and usu. bluish gray rock that is formed by compression of shales or other rocks and that splits readily into thin layers or plates and is used esp. for roofing and blackboards; *also* : a piece of this (as a shingle) dressed for use **2** : a tablet of material (as slate) used for writing on **3** : something (as deeds, events, or a list of candidates) recorded or made public as if written on a slate — **slate** *adj* — **slate·like** *adj*

²slate *vt* **1** : to cover with slate or a slatelike substance **2** : to register or schedule on or as if on a slate — **slat·er** *n*

slat·tern \ˈslat-ərn\ *n* : an untidy slovenly woman — **slat·tern·ly** \-lē\ *adj or adv*

slaty \ˈslāt-ē\ *adj* : of, containing, or characteristic of slate; *also* : gray like slate

¹slaugh·ter \ˈslȯt-ər\ *n* **1** : the act of killing; *esp* : the butchering of livestock for market **2** : destruction of human lives in battle : CARNAGE

²slaughter *vt* **1** : to kill (an animal) for food : BUTCHER **2** : to kill ruthlessly or in large numbers — **slaugh·ter·er** *n*

slaugh·ter·house \ˈslȯt-ər-ˌhau̇s\ *n* : an establishment where animals are butchered

¹slave \ˈslāv\ *n* **1** : a person held in servitude as the property of another **2** : a person who has lost control of himself and is dominated by something or someone **3** : DRUDGE, TOILER — **slave** *adj*

²slave *vi* : to work like a slave : DRUDGE

slave·hold·er \ˈslāv-ˌhōl-dər\ *n* : an owner of slaves — **slave·hold·ing** \-diŋ\ *adj or n*

¹slav·er \ˈslav-ər, ˈslāv-\ *vi* **slav·ered**; **slav·er·ing** \-(ə-)riŋ\ : DROOL, SLOBBER

²slav·er \ˈslā-vər\ *n* : a person or ship engaged in the slave trade

slav·ery \ˈslāv-(ə-)rē\ *n* **1** : DRUDGERY, TOIL **2 a** : the state of being a slave : SERVITUDE **b** : the practice of slaveholding

slav·ey \ˈslā-vē\ *n, pl* **slaveys** : DRUDGE; *esp* : a maid of all work

slav·ish \ˈslā-vish\ *adj* **1** : of or characteristic of a slave : SERVILE **2** : lacking in independence or originality esp. of thought — **slav·ish·ly** *adv* — **slav·ish·ness** *n*

slaw \ˈslȯ\ *n* : COLESLAW

slay \ˈslā\ *vb* **slew** \ˈslü\; **slain** \ˈslān\; **slay·ing** : to put to death violently : KILL — **slay·er** *n*

slea·zy \ˈslē-zē, ˈslā-\ *adj* **1** : not firmly or closely woven : FLIMSY **2** : made carelessly of inferior material : SHODDY — **slea·zi·ly** \-zə-lē\ *adv* — **slea·zi·ness** \-zē-nəs\ *n*

¹sled \ˈsled\ *n* : a vehicle on runners adapted esp. for sliding on snow

²sled *vb* **sled·ded**; **sled·ding** : to ride or carry on a sled or sleigh — **sled·der** *n*

¹sledge \ˈslej\ *n* : SLEDGEHAMMER

²sledge *n* : a vehicle with low runners that is used for transporting loads esp. over snow or ice

³sledge *vb* : to travel with or transport on a sledge

sledge·ham·mer \ˈslej-ˌham-ər\ *n* : a large heavy hammer usu. wielded with both hands — **sledgehammer** *adj or vb*

¹sleek \ˈslēk\ *vb* **1** : to make or become sleek **2** : to cover up : gloss over

²sleek *adj* **1 a** : smooth and glossy as if polished **b** : having a smooth healthy well-groomed look **2** : having a prosperous air : THRIVING — **sleek·ly** *adv* — **sleek·ness** *n*

¹sleep \ˈslēp\ *n* **1** : the natural periodic suspension of consciousness during which the powers of the body are restored **2** : a state resembling sleep: as **a** : a state of torpid inactivity **b** : DEATH; *also* : TRANCE, COMA — **sleep·like** *adj*

²sleep *vb* **slept** \ˈslept\; **sleep·ing** **1** : to rest or be in a state of sleep **2** : to have sexual relations **3** : to get rid of or spend in or by sleep **4** : to provide sleeping space for

sleep·er \ˈslē-pər\ *n* **1** : one that sleeps **2** : a piece of timber, stone, or steel on or near the ground to support a superstructure, keep railroad rails in place, or receive floor joists **3** : SLEEPING CAR **4** : something unpromising or unnoticed that suddenly attains prominence or value

sleep·ing bag \ˈslē-piŋ-\ *n* : a bag usu. waterproof and warmly lined or padded to sleep in outdoors

sleeping car *n* : a railroad passenger car having berths for sleeping

sleep·less \ˈslēp-ləs\ *adj* **1** : not able to sleep : INSOMNIAC **2** : affording no sleep **3** : unceasingly alert or active — **sleep·less·ly** *adv* — **sleep·less·ness** *n*

sleep·walk·er \ˈslēp-ˌwȯ-kər\ *n* : one that walks in his sleep : SOMNAMBULIST — **sleep·walk·ing** \-kiŋ\ *n*

sleepy \ˈslē-pē\ *adj* **1** : ready to fall asleep : DROWSY **2** : quietly inactive : DULL, LETHARGIC — **sleep·i·ly** \-pə-lē\ *adv* — **sleep·i·ness** \-pē-nəs\ *n*

¹sleet \ˈslēt\ *n* **1** : partly frozen rain : a mixture of rain and snow **2** : the icy coating formed by freezing rain : GLAZE

²sleet *vi* : to shower sleet

sleeve \ˈslēv\ *n* **1** : the part of a garment covering the arm **2** : something like a sleeve in shape or use; *esp* : a tubular part fitting over another part — **sleeved** \ˈslēvd\ *adj* — **sleeve·less** \ˈslēv-ləs\ *adj*

¹sleigh \ˈslā\ *n* : a vehicle on runners used for transporting persons or goods on snow or ice

²sleigh *vi* : to drive or travel in a sleigh

sleight \ˈslīt\ *n* **1** : deceitful craftiness : CUNNING; *also* : STRATAGEM **2** : DEXTERITY, SKILL

sleight of hand **1** : skill and dexterity esp. in juggling or conjuring tricks **2** : a conjuring or juggling trick requiring sleight of hand

slen·der \ˈslen-dər\ *adj* **1 a** : spare in frame or flesh; *esp* : gracefully slight **b** : small in circumference in proportion to length or height **2** : limited or inadequate in amount : MEAGER — **slen·der·ly** *adv* — **slen·der·ness** *n*

¹sleuth \ˈslüth\ *n* : DETECTIVE

²sleuth *vi* : to act as a detective

¹slew \ˈslü\ *past of* SLAY

²slew *n* : a large number : LOT

¹slice \ˈslīs\ *n* **1** : a thin flat piece cut from something **2** : a spatula or knife with wedge-shaped blade **3** : a flight of a ball (as in golf) that curves in the direction of the dominant hand of the player propelling it

²slice *vb* **1 a** : to cut with or as if with a knife **b** : to cut into slices **2** : to hit (a ball) so that a slice results — **slic·er** *n*

¹slick \ˈslik\ *vt* **:** to make sleek or smooth
²slick *adj* **1 a :** having a smooth surface **:** SLIPPERY **b :** GLIB, TRITE **2 a :** characterized by subtlety or nimble wit **:** CLEVER; *esp* **:** WILY **b :** DEFT, SKILLFUL — **slick·ly** *adv* — **slick·ness** *n*
³slick *n* **1 :** something that is smooth or slippery; *esp* **:** a smooth patch of water covered with a film of oil **2 :** a popular magazine printed on coated stock
slick·er \ˈslik-ər\ *n* **1 :** a long loose raincoat often of oilskin or plastic **2 :** a sly clever tricky person
¹slide \ˈslīd\ *vb* **slid** \ˈslid\; **slid·ing** \ˈslīd-iŋ\ **1 a :** to move or cause to move smoothly over a surface **:** GLIDE, SLIP **b :** to coast on snow or ice **2 :** to slip and fall by a loss of footing, balance, or support **3 a :** to move or pass smoothly and easily **b :** to move, pass, or put stealthily or imperceptibly
²slide *n* **1 :** the act or motion of sliding **2 :** a loosened mass that slides **3 a :** a surface down which a person or thing slides **b :** something (as a cover for an opening) that operates or adjusts by sliding **4 a :** a transparent picture or image that can be thrown on a screen by means of a projecting device **b :** a glass plate on which is placed an object to be examined under a microscope
slide fastener *n* **:** ZIPPER
slid·er \ˈslīd-ər\ *n* **:** one that slides or operates a slide
slide rule *n* **:** an instrument consisting in its simple form of a ruler and a medial slide graduated with similar logarithmic scales labeled with the corresponding antilogarithms and used for rapid calculation

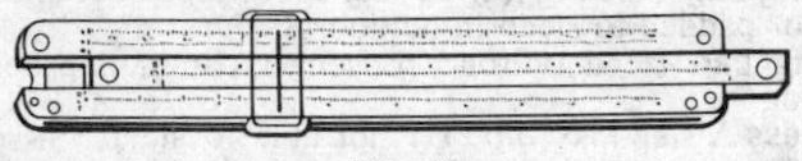

slide rule

¹slight \ˈslīt\ *adj* **1 a :** having a slim or delicate build **:** not stout or massive in body **b :** lacking in strength or substance **:** FLIMSY, FRAIL **c :** deficient in weight, solidity, or importance **:** TRIVIAL **2 :** small of its kind or in amount **:** SCANTY, MEAGER — **slight·ly** *adv* — **slight·ness** *n*
²slight *vt* **:** to treat as slight or unimportant: as **a :** to treat with disdain or discourteous indifference **b :** to perform or attend to carelessly and inadequately
³slight *n* **1 :** an act or an instance of slighting **2 :** a humiliating discourtesy
slight·ing \ˈslīt-iŋ\ *adj* **:** characterized by disregard or disrespect **:** DISPARAGING — **slight·ing·ly** *adv*
¹slim \ˈslim\ *adj* **1 :** of small diameter or thickness in proportion to the height or length **:** SLENDER **2 a :** inferior in quality or amount **b :** SCANTY — **slim·ly** *adv* — **slim·ness** *n*
²slim *vb* **slimmed; slim·ming :** to make or become slender
slime \ˈslīm\ *n* **1 :** soft moist earth or clay; *esp* **:** sticky slippery mud **2 :** a soft slippery substance; *esp* **:** a skin secretion (as of a slug or catfish)
slimy \ˈslī-mē\ *adj* **1 :** of, relating to, or resembling slime **:** VISCOUS; *also* **:** covered with or yielding slime **2 :** VILE, OFFENSIVE — **slim·i·ly** \-mə-lē\ *adv* — **slim·i·ness** \-mē-nəs\ *n*
¹sling \ˈsliŋ\ *vt* **slung** \ˈsləŋ\; **sling·ing** \ˈsliŋ-iŋ\ **1 :** to toss casually or forcibly **:** FLING **2 :** to throw with a sling — **sling·er** \ˈsliŋ-ər\ *n*
²sling *n* **:** a slinging or hurling of or as if of a missile
³sling *n* **1 a :** a device for throwing something (as stones) that usu. consists of a short strap with strings fastened to its ends and is whirled round to discharge its missile **b :** SLINGSHOT **2 a :** a usu. looped line (as of rope) used to hoist, lower, support, or carry something; *esp* **:** a hanging bandage suspended from the neck to support an arm or hand **b :** a device for enclosing material to be hoisted by a tackle or crane
⁴sling *vt* **slung** \ˈsləŋ\; **sling·ing** \ˈsliŋ-iŋ\ **1 :** to put in or move or support with a sling **2 :** to cause to become suspended
sling·shot \ˈsliŋ-ˌshät\ *n* **:** a forked stick with an elastic band attached for shooting small stones
slink \ˈsliŋk\ *vb* **slunk** \ˈsləŋk\; **slink·ing :** to move or go stealthily **:** creep along (as in fear or shame)
slinky \ˈsliŋ-kē\ *adj* **1 :** stealthily quiet **2 :** sleek and sinuous in outline
¹slip \ˈslip\ *vb* **slipped; slip·ping 1 a :** to move easily and smoothly **:** SLIDE **b :** to move or place quietly or stealthily **:** STEAL **c :** to pass without being noted or used **2 a :** to get away from **:** ELUDE; *also* **:** to free from **:** SHED **b :** to escape the attention of; *also* **:** to utter or become uttered inadvertently or casually **c :** to let loose or let go of; *also* **:** to cause to slide open **:** RELEASE, DISENGAGE **3 a :** to slide out of place, away from a support, or from one's grasp; *also* **:** to slide so as to fall or lose balance **b :** to cause to slide esp. in putting, passing, or inserting easily or quickly **c :** to move sideways or aside; *also* **:** DISLOCATE **d :** to fail to progress or hold normally from or as if from sliding **4 :** to fall from some level or standard (as of conduct or activity) usu. gradually
²slip *n* **1 a :** a sloping ramp that extends out into the water and serves for landing or repairing ships **b :** a ship's berth between two piers **2 :** the act or an instance of departing secretly or hurriedly **3 :** a mistake in judgment, policy, or procedure **:** BLUNDER, MISSTEP **4 :** the act or an instance of slipping down or out of place: as **a :** a sudden mishap **b :** a fall from some level or standard **:** DECLINE **5 a :** an undergarment made in dress length with shoulder straps **b :** PILLOWCASE
³slip *n* **1 :** a small shoot or twig cut for planting or grafting **:** CUTTING **2 a :** a long narrow strip of material **b :** a piece of paper used for a memorandum or record **3 :** a young and slender person
⁴slip *vt* **slipped; slip·ping :** to take cuttings from (a plant)
slip·knot \ˈslip-ˌnät\ *n* **:** a knot that slips along a line around which it is made
slip·per \ˈslip-ər\ *n* **:** a light low shoe without laces that is easily slipped on or off — **slip·pered** \-ərd\ *adj*
slip·pery \ˈslip-(ə-)rē\ *adj* **1 :** having a surface smooth enough to cause one to slide or lose one's hold **:** deficient in friction **2 :** not worthy of trust **:** UNRELIABLE — **slip·per·i·ness** *n*
slip·shod \ˈslip-ˈshäd\ *adj* **:** very careless **:** SLOVENLY
slip·stick \ˈslip-ˌstik\ *n* **:** SLIDE RULE
slip up *vi* **:** to make a mistake **:** BLUNDER
slip·up \ˈslip-ˌəp\ *n* **1 :** MISTAKE **2 :** MISCHANCE
¹slit \ˈslit\ *vt* **slit; slit·ting 1 a :** to make a slit in **:** SLASH **b :** to cut off or away **:** SEVER **2 :** to cut into long narrow strips
²slit *n* **:** a long narrow cut or opening — **slit** *adj*
slith·er \ˈslith-ər\ *vb* **slith·ered; slith·er·ing** \ˈslith-(ə-)riŋ\ **1 :** to slide or cause to slide on or as if on a loose gravelly surface **2 :** to slip or slide like a snake
¹sliv·er \ˈsliv-ər\ *n* **:** a long slender piece cut or torn off
²sliver *vb* **sliv·ered; sliv·er·ing** \ˈsliv-(ə-)riŋ\ **:** to cut or form into slivers **:** SPLINTER
slob \ˈsläb\ *n* **:** a slovenly or boorish person
¹slob·ber \ˈsläb-ər\ *vb* **slob·bered; slob·ber·ing** \ˈsläb-(ə-)riŋ\ **1 :** to let saliva or liquid dribble from the mouth **:** DROOL **2 :** to show feeling to excess **:** GUSH — **slob·ber·er** *n*
²slobber *n* **1 :** dripping saliva **2 :** silly excessive show of feeling — **slob·bery** \ˈsläb-(ə-)rē\ *adj*
sloe \ˈslō\ *n* **:** the tart bluish black globular fruit of the blackthorn; *also* **:** BLACKTHORN 1
slog \ˈsläg\ *vb* **slogged; slog·ging 1 :** to hit hard **:** BEAT **2 :** to plod or work doggedly on — **slog·ger** *n*
slo·gan \ˈslō-gən\ *n* **1 :** a word or phrase that calls to battle **:** WAR CRY **2 :** a word or phrase used by a party, a group, or a business to attract attention

sloop \ˈslüp\ *n* : a sailing boat with one mast and a fore-and-aft mainsail and jib

¹slop \ˈsläp\ *n* **1** : soft mud : SLUSH **2** : thin tasteless drink or liquid food — usu. used in pl. **3** : liquid spilled or splashed **4 a** : food waste (as garbage) or a thin gruel fed to animals **b** : excreted body waste — usu. used in pl.

²slop *vb* **slopped**; **slop•ping** **1** : to spill on or over **2** : to feed slop to **3** : to behave or deal with in a sloppy manner

¹slope \ˈslōp\ *adj* : SLANTING, SLOPING

²slope *vb* : to take a slanting direction : give a slant to

³slope *n* **1** : ground that forms a natural or artificial incline **2** : upward or downward slant or inclination or degree of slant **3** : the part of a continent draining to a particular ocean

slop•py \ˈsläp-ē\ *adj* **1 a** : wet so as to spatter easily : SLUSHY **b** : wet with or as if with something slopped over **2** : SLOVENLY, CARELESS **3** : disagreeably effusive — **slop•pi•ly** \ˈsläp-ə-lē\ *adv* — **slop•pi•ness** \ˈsläp-ē-nəs\ *n*

slosh \ˈsläsh\ *vb* **1** : to flounder through or splash about in or with water, mud, or slush **2** : to move with a splashing motion

¹slot \ˈslät\ *n* : a long narrow opening, groove, or passage

²slot *vt* **slot•ted**; **slot•ting** : to cut a slot in

sloth \ˈslȯth, ˈslōth\ *n* **1** : INDOLENCE, LAZINESS **2** : any of several slow-moving mammals of Central and So. America that are related to the armadillos and live in trees where they hang back downward and feed on leaves, shoots, and fruits

sloth•ful \-fəl\ *adj* : LAZY, SLUGGISH, INDOLENT — **sloth•ful•ly** \-fə-lē\ *adv* — **sloth•ful•ness** *n*

slot machine *n* : a machine whose operation is begun when a coin is dropped into a slot

¹slouch \ˈslau̇ch\ *n* **1** : an awkward, lazy, or incompetent person **2** : a gait or posture characterized by ungainly stooping of head and shoulders

²slouch *vi* : to walk with or assume a slouch — **slouch•er** *n*

slouchy \ˈslau̇-chē\ *adj* : slouching or slovenly esp. in appearance — **slouch•i•ly** \-chə-lē\ *adv* — **slouch•i•ness** \-chē-nəs\ *n*

¹slough *n* **1** \ˈslü *also* ˈslau̇\ : a wet and marshy or muddy place (as a swamp) **2** \ˈslau̇ *also* ˈslü\ : a discouraged, degraded, or dejected state

²slough *or* **sluff** \ˈsləf\ *n* **1** : the cast-off skin of a snake **2** : something that may be shed or cast off

³slough *or* **sluff** \ˈsləf\ *vb* **1** : to cast off or become cast off: as **a** : to cast off one's skin or dead tissue from living tissue **b** : to get rid of or discard as irksome, objectionable, or disadvantageous **2** : to crumble slowly and fall away

¹slov•en \ˈsləv-ən\ *n* : one habitually negligent of neatness or cleanliness esp. in dress or person

²sloven *adj* : SLOVENLY

slov•en•ly \ˈsləv-ən-lē\ *adj* **1 a** : untidy esp. in dress or person **b** : lazily slipshod **2** : characteristic of a sloven — **slov•en•li•ness** *n* — **slovenly** *adv*

¹slow \ˈslō\ *adj* **1 a** : mentally dull : STUPID **b** : naturally inert or sluggish **2 a** : lacking in readiness, promptness, or willingness **b** : not hasty or precipitate **3 a** : moving, flowing, or proceeding without speed or at less than usual speed **b** : not vigorous or active; *also* : taking place at a low rate or over a considerable period of time **4** : having qualities that hinder or stop rapid progress or action **5 a** : registering behind or below what is correct **b** : that is behind the time at a specified time or place **6** : lacking in activity or liveliness — **slow•ly** *adv* — **slow•ness** *n*

²slow *adv* : SLOWLY

³slow *vb* : to make or go slow or slower

slow•poke \ˈslō-ˌpōk\ *n* : a very slow person

slow–wit•ted \-ˈwit-əd\ *adj* : SLOW 1 a

sludge \ˈsləj\ *n* **1** : MUD, MIRE **2** : a muddy or slushy mass, deposit, or sediment; *esp* : precipitated solid matter produced by water and sewage treatment processes

¹slue \ˈslü\ *vb* : to turn, twist, or swing about esp. out of a course : VEER

²slue *n* : an act or instance of or the position attained by sluing

¹slug \ˈsləg\ *n* **1** : SLUGGARD **2** : any of numerous chiefly terrestrial mollusks that are closely related to the land snails but long and wormlike and with only a rudimentary shell or none

²slug *n* **1** : a small piece of shaped metal: as **a** : a musket ball or bullet **b** : a metal disk for insertion in a slot machine in place of a coin **2** : a single drink of liquor : SHOT

³slug *n* : a heavy blow esp. with the fist

⁴slug *vb* **slugged**; **slug•ging** : to strike heavily with or as if with the fist or a bat — **slug•ger** *n*

slug•gard \ˈsləg-ərd\ *n* : an habitually lazy person — **sluggard** *adj*

slug•gish \ˈsləg-ish\ *adj* : slow and inactive in movement or reaction by habit or condition — **slug•gish•ly** *adv* — **slug•gish•ness** *n*

¹sluice \ˈslüs\ *n* **1** : an artificial passage for water with a gate for controlling its flow or changing its direction **2** : a body of water held back by a gate or a stream flowing through a gate **3** : a device (as a water gate) for controlling the flow of water **4** : a channel that carries off surplus water **5** : a long inclined trough (as for floating logs to a sawmill)

²sluice *vt* **1** : to draw off by or through a sluice **2 a** : to wash with or in water running through or from a sluice **b** : DRENCH, FLUSH

¹slum \ˈsləm\ *n* : a thickly populated section esp. of a city marked by crowding, dirty run-down housing, and generally wretched living conditions

²slum *vi* **slummed**; **slum•ming** : to visit slums esp. out of curiosity or for pleasure — **slum•mer** *n*

¹slum•ber \ˈsləm-bər\ *vi* **slum•bered**; **slum•ber•ing** \-b(ə-)riŋ\ **1** : to sleep usu. lightly **2** : to lie dormant or latent — **slum•ber•er** *n*

²slumber *n* **1 a** : act of slumbering : SLEEP **b** : light sleep : DOZE **2** : LETHARGY, TORPOR

slum•ber•ous *or* **slum•brous** \ˈsləm-b(ə-)rəs\ *adj* **1** : SLEEPY, SOMNOLENT **2** : inviting slumber : SOPORIFIC

slum•lord \ˈsləm-ˌlȯrd\ *n* : a landlord who receives unusually high profits from substandard properties

¹slump \ˈsləmp\ *vi* **1** : to drop or slide down suddenly : COLLAPSE **2** : to assume a drooping posture or carriage : SLOUCH **3** : to fall off sharply

²slump *n* : a marked or sustained decline esp. in economic activity or prices

slung *past of* SLING

slunk *past of* SLINK

¹slur \ˈslər\ *vb* **slurred**; **slur•ring** **1 a** : to slide or slip over without due mention, consideration, or emphasis **b** : to perform hurriedly : SKIMP **2** : to perform (successive musical notes of different pitch) in a smooth or connected manner **3** : to speak indistinctly usu. as a result of carelessness or haste

²slur *n* **1 a** : a curved line ‿ or ⁀ connecting notes to be sung or performed without a break **b** : the combination of two or more slurred tones **2** : a slurring manner of speech

³slur *vb* **slurred**; **slur•ring** **1** : to cast aspersions upon : DISPARAGE **2** : OBSCURE **3** : to slip so as to cause a slur

⁴slur *n* **1** : ASPERSION, CALUMNY **2** : REPROACH, STIGMA

slush \ˈsləsh\ *n* **1** : partly melted or watery snow **2** : soft mud : MIRE **3** : RUBBISH, DRIVEL

slushy \ˈsləsh-ē\ *adj* : full of or resembling slush

slut \ˈslət\ *n* **1** : a slovenly woman : SLATTERN **2** : a lewd woman; *esp* : PROSTITUTE — **slut•tish** \ˈslət-ish\ *adj* — **slut•tish•ly** *adv* — **slut•tish•ness** *n*

sly \ˈslī\ *adj* **1 a** : artfully cunning : CRAFTY **b** : SECRETIVE, FURTIVE **2** : lightly mischievous : ROGUISH — **sly•ly** *adv* — **sly•ness** *n* — **on the sly** : FURTIVELY

[1]**smack** \'smak\ *n* **1 :** characteristic or perceptible taste or flavor **2 :** a small quantity
[2]**smack** *vi* **:** to have a flavor, trace, or suggestion
[3]**smack** *vb* **1 :** to close and open (lips) noisily esp. in eating **2 :** to kiss usu. loudly **3 :** to make or give a smack
[4]**smack** *n* **1 :** a quick sharp noise made by rapidly compressing and opening the lips **2 :** a loud kiss **3 :** a sharp slap or blow
[5]**smack** *adv* **:** in a square and sharp manner **:** DIRECTLY
[6]**smack** *n* **:** a sailing ship used chiefly in coasting and fishing
smack·ing \'smak-iŋ\ *adj* **:** BRISK, LIVELY
[1]**small** \'smȯl\ *adj* **1 :** little in size **2 :** few in numbers or members **3 :** little in amount **4 :** not very much **5 :** UNIMPORTANT **6 :** operating on a limited scale **7 :** GENTLE, SOFT **8 :** not generous **:** MEAN **9 :** made up of small units **10 :** HUMBLE, MODEST **11 :** HUMILIATED, HUMBLED **12 :** LOWERCASE — **small·ness** *n*
[2]**small** *adv* **1 :** in or into small pieces **2 :** without force or loudness **3 :** in a small manner
[3]**small** *n* **1 :** a part smaller and esp. narrower than the remainder **2** *pl* **:** small-sized products
small arm *n* **:** a firearm fired while held in the hands
small intestine *n* **:** the long narrow first part of the intestine that extends from the stomach to the large intestine and is the chief seat of digestion and absorption of food
small·ish \'smȯ-lish\ *adj* **:** somewhat small
small–mind·ed \'smȯl-'mīn-dəd\ *adj* **:** having narrow interests, sympathies, or outlook; *also* **:** typical of a small-minded person — **small–mind·ed·ly** *adv* — **small–mind·ed·ness** *n*
small·pox \'smȯl-ˌpäks\ *n* **:** an acute contagious virus disease marked by fever and skin eruption with pustules, sloughing, and scar formation
small–scale \-'skāl\ *adj* **:** small in scope; *esp* **:** small in output or operation
small–time \'smȯl-'tīm\ *adj* **:** insignificant in performance and standing **:** SMALL-SCALE, MINOR — **small–tim·er** \-'tī-mər\ *n*
[1]**smart** \'smärt\ *vi* **1 :** to cause or feel a sharp stinging pain **2 :** to feel or endure distress, remorse, or embarrassment
[2]**smart** *adj* **1 :** causing smarting **:** STINGING **2 :** marked by forceful activity or vigorous strength **3 :** BRISK, SPIRITED **4 a :** mentally alert **:** BRIGHT **b :** sharp in scheming **:** SHREWD **5 a :** WITTY, CLEVER **b :** PERT, SAUCY **6 a :** stylish or elegant in dress or appearance **b :** SOPHISTICATED **c :** FASHIONABLE — **smart·ly** *adv* — **smart·ness** *n*
[3]**smart** *adv* **:** SMARTLY
[4]**smart** *n* **1 :** a smarting pain; *esp* **:** a stinging local pain **2 :** poignant grief or remorse
smart al·eck \'smärt-ˌal-ik, -ˌel-\ *n* **:** an offensively conceited and bumptious person
smart·en \'smärt-ᵊn\ *vb* **smart·ened; smart·en·ing** \'smärt-niŋ, -ᵊn-iŋ\ **1 :** to make smart or smarter **:** SPRUCE, FRESHEN **2 :** to make or become more alert
[1]**smash** \'smash\ *vb* **1 :** to break in pieces by violence **:** SHATTER **2 :** to drive, throw, or move violently esp. with a destructive effect **3 :** to destroy utterly **:** WRECK **4 :** to go to pieces suddenly **:** COLLAPSE — **smash·er** *n*
[2]**smash** *n* **1 a :** a smashing blow or attack **b :** a hard overhand stroke (as in tennis) **2 :** the condition of being smashed **3 a :** the action or sound of smashing; *esp* **:** a wreck due to collision **:** CRASH **b :** utter collapse **:** RUIN; *esp* **:** BANKRUPTCY **4 :** a striking success **:** HIT
smash·up \'smash-ˌəp\ *n* **1 :** a complete collapse **2 :** a destructive collision of motor vehicles
smat·ter·ing \'smat-ə-riŋ\ *n* **1 :** superficial piecemeal knowledge **2 :** a small scattered number
[1]**smear** \'smi(ə)r\ *n* **1 :** a spot made by or as if by an oily or sticky substance **:** SMUDGE **2 :** a usu. unsubstantiated charge or accusation
[2]**smear** *vt* **1 a :** to spread or daub with something oily or sticky **b :** to spread over a surface **2 :** to stain, smudge, or dirty by or as if by smearing; *also* **:** to blacken the reputation of **3 :** to obliterate or blur by or as if by smearing — **smear·er** *n*
smeary \'smi(ə)r-ē\ *adj* **1 :** SMEARED **2 :** liable to cause smears
[1]**smell** \'smel\ *vb* **smelled** \'smeld\ *or* **smelt** \'smelt\; **smell·ing 1 :** to get the odor or scent of through stimuli affecting the olfactory sense organs of the nose **2 :** to detect or become aware of as if by the sense of smell **3 :** to exercise the sense of smell **4 a :** to have or give forth an odor **b :** to give off a suggestion of something and esp. of something unwholesome or evil — **smell·er** *n*
[2]**smell** *n* **1 a :** the process or power of smelling **b :** the special sense concerned with the perception of odor **2 :** the property of a thing that affects the olfactory organs **:** ODOR **3 :** a pervading quality **:** AURA **4 :** an act of smelling
smell·ing salts \'smel-iŋ-\ *n pl* **:** a usu. scented aromatic preparation used as a stimulant and restorative
smelly \'smel-ē\ *adj* **:** having a smell and esp. a bad smell
[1]**smelt** \'smelt\ *n, pl* **smelts** *or* **smelt :** any of several very small food fishes of coastal or fresh waters that resemble and are related to the trout
[2]**smelt** *vt* **:** to melt or fuse (as ore) usu. in order to separate the metal **:** REFINE, REDUCE
smelt·er \'smel-tər\ *n* **:** one that smelts: **a :** a worker in or an owner of a smeltery **b** *or* **smelt·ery** \-t(ə-)rē\ **:** an establishment for smelting
smi·lax \'smī-ˌlaks\ *n* **1 :** any of various mostly climbing and prickly plants related to the lilies **2 :** a delicate greenhouse twining plant related to the garden asparagus
[1]**smile** \'smīl\ *vb* **1 :** to have, produce, or exhibit a smile **2 a :** to look with amusement or ridicule **b :** to be propitious or agreeable **3 :** to express by a smile — **smil·er** *n* — **smil·ing·ly** *adv*
[2]**smile** *n* **:** a change of facial expression in which the eyes brighten and the lips curve slightly upward esp. in expression of amusement, pleasure, approval, or sometimes scorn
smirch \'smərch\ *vt* **1 :** to make dirty, stained, or discolored esp. by smearing with something that soils **2 :** to bring discredit or disgrace on — **smirch** *n*
smirk \'smərk\ *vi* **:** to smile in an affected manner — **smirk** *n*
smite \'smīt\ *vb* **smote** \'smōt\; **smit·ten** \'smit-ᵊn\ *or* **smote; smit·ing** \'smīt-iŋ\ **1 :** to strike sharply or heavily esp. with the hand or a hand weapon **2 a :** to kill or injure by smiting **b :** to attack or afflict suddenly and injuriously **3 :** to affect like a sudden hard blow — **smit·er** \'smīt-ər\ *n*
smith \'smith\ *n* **1 :** a worker in metals **:** BLACKSMITH **2 :** MAKER — often used in combination
smith·er·eens \ˌsmith-ə-'rēnz\ *n pl* **:** FRAGMENTS, BITS
smithy \'smith-ē, 'smith-\ *n, pl* **smith·ies :** the workshop of a smith
[1]**smock** \'smäk\ *n* **:** a light loose garment worn usu. over regular clothing for protection from dirt
[2]**smock** *vt* **:** to embroider or shirr with smocking
smock·ing \'smäk-iŋ\ *n* **:** a decorative embroidery or shirring made by gathering cloth in regularly spaced round tucks
smog \'smäg\ *n* **:** a fog made heavier and darker by smoke and chemical fumes — **smog·gy** \'smäg-ē\ *adj*
[1]**smoke** \'smōk\ *n* **1 a :** the gas of burning organic materials (as coal, wood, or tobacco) made visible by small particles of carbon **b :** a suspension of solid or liquid particles in a gas **2 :** a mass or column of smoke **3 :** fume or vapor often resulting from the action of heat on moisture **4 :** something of little substance, permanence, or value **5 :** something that obscures **6 :** something to smoke (as a cigarette); *also* **:** the smoking of this — **smoke·less** \-ləs\ *adj* — **smoke·like** *adj*
[2]**smoke** *vb* **1 a :** to emit or exhale smoke **b :** to emit excessive smoke **2 :** to inhale and exhale the fumes of burning tobacco

or something like tobacco; *also* : to use in smoking 3 : to act on with smoke: as a : to drive away by smoke b : to blacken or discolor with smoke c : to cure by exposure to smoke
smoke·house \'smōk-ˌhau̇s\ *n* : a building where meat or fish is cured by means of dense smoke
smoke out *vt* 1 : to drive out by or as if by smoke 2 : to bring to public knowledge
smok·er \'smō-kər\ *n* 1 : one that smokes 2 : an informal social gathering for men
smoke·stack \'smōk-ˌstak\ *n* : a chimney or funnel through which smoke and gases are discharged (as from a ship)
smoky \'smō-kē\ *adj* 1 : emitting smoke esp. in large quantities 2 : resembling or suggestive of smoke 3 : filled with or darkened by smoke
[1]**smol·der** *or* **smoul·der** \'smōl-dər\ *n* : a slow smoky fire
[2]**smolder** *or* **smoulder** *vi* **smol·dered** *or* **smoul·dered**; **smol·der·ing** *or* **smoul·der·ing** \-d(ə-)riŋ\ 1 : to burn sluggishly with smoke and usu. without flame 2 : to exist in a state of suppressed activity; *also* : to indicate a suppressed emotion
[1]**smooth** \'smüth\ *adj* 1 a : having a continuous even surface : not rough b : being without hairs or projections : GLABROUS c : causing no resistance to sliding 2 : free from obstacles or difficulties 3 : even and uninterrupted in flow or flight 4 : plausibly flattering : INGRATIATING 5 a : SERENE, EQUABLE b : AMIABLE, COURTEOUS 6 : not sharp or acid : BLAND — **smooth·ly** *adv* — **smooth·ness** *n*
[2]**smooth** *vt* 1 : to make smooth 2 a : to free from what is harsh or disagreeable : POLISH b : SOOTHE 3 : to minimize (as a fault) in order to allay ill will : PALLIATE 4 : to free from obstruction or difficulty 5 : to cause to lie evenly and in order
smor·gas·bord \'smȯr-gəs-ˌbō̇rd\ *n* : a luncheon or supper buffet offering a large variety of foods and dishes
smote *past of* SMITE
[1]**smoth·er** \'sməth-ər\ *n* 1 : a dense cloud (as of fog, foam, or dust) 2 : a confused multitude of things : WELTER
[2]**smother** *vb* **smoth·ered**; **smoth·er·ing** \'sməth-(ə-)riŋ\ 1 a : to overcome by depriving of air or exposing to smoke or fumes : SUFFOCATE b : to prevent the development or activity of 2 : to become suffocated 3 a : to cover up : SUPPRESS b : to overlay thickly : BLANKET c : OVERWHELM d : CONQUER
[1]**smudge** \'sməj\ *vb* 1 a : to make a smudge on b : to soil as if by smudging 2 : to smoke or protect by a smudge 3 : to make a smudge or become smudged
[2]**smudge** *n* 1 a : a blurry spot or streak : SMEAR b : STAIN 2 : a fire made to smoke (as for driving away mosquitoes or protecting fruit from frost) — **smudg·i·ly** \'sməj-ə-lē\ *adv*
smug \'sməg\ *adj* : highly self-satisfied : COMPLACENT — **smug·ly** *adv* — **smug·ness** *n*
smug·gle \'sməg-əl\ *vb* **smug·gled**; **smug·gling** \'sməg-(ə-)liŋ\ 1 : to export or import secretly and unlawfully esp. to avoid paying duty 2 : to take, bring, or introduce secretly or stealthily — **smug·gler** \'sməg-lər\ *n*
[1]**smut** \'smət\ *vb* **smut·ted**; **smut·ting** 1 : to stain, taint, or affect with smut 2 : to become affected by smut
[2]**smut** *n* 1 : matter that soils or blackens; *esp* : a particle of soot 2 : any of various destructive diseases of plants and esp. of cereal grasses caused by parasitic fungi that transform plant organs (as seeds) into dark masses of spores; *also* : a fungus causing a smut 3 : obscene or indecent language or matter
smut·ty \'smət-ē\ *adj* 1 : soiled or tainted with smut 2 : affected with smut fungus 3 : OBSCENE, INDECENT
snack \'snak\ *n* : a light meal : LUNCH
snaf·fle \'snaf-əl\ *n* : a simple jointed bit for a bridle
[1]**snag** \'snag\ *n* 1 : a stump or stub of a tree branch esp. when embedded under water 2 : a concealed or unexpected difficulty or hindrance — **snag·gy** \'snag-ē\ *adj*
[2]**snag** *vt* **snagged**; **snag·ging** 1 a : to catch and usu. damage on or as if on a snag b : to halt or impede as if by catching on a snag 2 : to catch or obtain by quick action
snag·gle·tooth \'snag-əl-ˌtüth\ *n* : an irregular, broken, or projecting tooth — **snag·gle·toothed** \ˌsnag-əl-'tütht\ *adj*
snail \'snāl\ *n* 1 : a gastropod mollusk esp. when having an external enclosing spiral shell 2 : a slow-moving person or thing
[1]**snake** \'snāk\ *n* 1 : any of numerous limbless reptiles with a long tapering body and often salivary glands modified to produce venom which is injected through grooved or tubular fangs 2 : a despicable or treacherous person — **snake·like** *adj*
[2]**snake** *vb* 1 : to crawl or move sinuously, silently, or secretly 2 : to move (as logs) by dragging
snaky \'snā-kē\ *adj* 1 : of or resembling a snake 2 : abounding in snakes — **snak·i·ly** \-kə-lē\ *adv*
[1]**snap** \'snap\ *vb* **snapped**; **snap·ping** 1 a : to make a sudden closing of the jaws : seize something sharply with the mouth b : to grasp at something eagerly c : to take possession of promptly and decisively 2 : to speak or utter sharply or irritably 3 a : to break or break apart suddenly esp. with a sharp sound b : to give way or cause to give way suddenly under stress c : to bring to a sudden end 4 : to make or cause to make a sharp or crackling sound 5 a : to close or fit in place with an abrupt movement b : to put into or remove from a position by a sudden movement or with a snapping sound c : to close by means of snaps or fasteners 6 : FLASH 7 a : to act or be acted upon with snap b : to put (a football) in play c : to take a snapshot of
[2]**snap** *n* 1 : an abrupt closing (as of the mouth in biting or of scissors in cutting); *esp* : a biting or snatching with the teeth or jaws 2 : something that is easy and presents no problems : CINCH 3 : a small amount : BIT 4 a : a sudden snatching at something b : a quick short movement c : a sudden sharp breaking 5 : a sound made by snapping something 6 : a sudden interval of harsh weather 7 : a catch or fastening that closes or locks with a click 8 : a thin brittle cookie 9 : SNAPSHOT 10 a : ENERGY b : SMARTNESS, SNAPPINESS c : RESILIENCE 11 : an act or instance of snapping a football
[3]**snap** *adj* 1 : made suddenly or without deliberation 2 : shutting or fastening with a click or by means of a device that snaps 3 : unusually easy
snap·drag·on \'snap-ˌdrag-ən\ *n* : any of several garden plants having showy white, crimson, or yellow 2-lipped flowers
snap·per \'snap-ər\ *n* : something that snaps
snap·pish \'snap-ish\ *adj* 1 : marked by snapping irritable speech : IRASCIBLE 2 : inclined to bite — **snap·pish·ly** *adv* — **snap·pish·ness** *n*
snap·py \'snap-ē\ *adj* 1 : SNAPPISH 2 a : LIVELY b : briskly cold c : STYLISH, SMART
snap·shot \'snap-ˌshät\ *n* : a casual photograph made by rapid exposure usu. with a small hand-held camera
[1]**snare** \'sna(ə)r\ *n* 1 : a trap often consisting of a noose for catching small animals or birds 2 : something by which one is entangled, trapped, or deceived
[2]**snare** *vt* 1 : to capture or entangle by or as if by use of a snare 2 : to win or attain by skillful or deceptive maneuvers
[1]**snarl** \'snärl\ *n* 1 : a tangle esp. of hairs or thread : KNOT 2 : a tangled situation : COMPLICATION
[2]**snarl** *vb* : to get into a tangle
[3]**snarl** *vb* 1 : to growl with a snapping or gnashing of teeth 2 : to give vent to anger in surly language 3 : to utter with a snarl
[4]**snarl** *n* : a surly angry growl
[1]**snatch** \'snach\ *vb* 1 : to seize or try to seize something quickly or suddenly 2 : to grasp or take suddenly or hastily : GRAB — **snatch·er** *n*
[2]**snatch** *n* 1 : a snatching at or of something 2 : a brief opportune period 3 : something brief, fragmentary, or hurried

[1]**sneak** \ˈsnēk\ *vb* **1 :** to go stealthily or furtively : SLINK **2 :** to put, bring, or take in a furtive or sly manner
[2]**sneak** *n* **1 :** a person who acts in a stealthy, furtive, or sly manner **2 :** the act or an instance of sneaking
sneak•er \ˈsnē-kər\ *n* **1 :** one that sneaks **2 :** a usu. canvas sports shoe with a pliable rubber sole
sneak•ing \-kiŋ\ *adj* **1 :** FURTIVE, UNDERHAND **2 :** not openly expressed as if something to be ashamed of
sneaky \ˈsnē-kē\ *adj* **:** marked by stealth, furtiveness, or slyness — **sneak•i•ly** \-kə-lē\ *adv* — **sneak•i•ness** \-kē-nəs\ *n*
[1]**sneer** \ˈsni(ə)r\ *vi* **1 :** to smile or laugh with facial contortions that express scorn or contempt **2 :** to speak or write in a scornfully jeering manner — **sneer•er** *n*
[2]**sneer** *n* **:** a sneering expression or remark
[1]**sneeze** \ˈsnēz\ *vi* **:** to make a sudden violent spasmodic audible expiration of breath — **sneez•er** *n*
[2]**sneeze** *n* **:** an act or fact of sneezing
snick \ˈsnik\ *n* **:** a cutting or clicking noise
[1]**snick•er** \ˈsnik-ər\ *or* **snig•ger** \ˈsnig-ər\ *vi* **:** to laugh in a slight, covert, or partly suppressed manner : TITTER
[2]**snicker** *or* **snigger** *n* **:** an act or sound of snickering
snide \ˈsnīd\ *adj* **1 :** MEAN, LOW **2 :** slyly disparaging
sniff \ˈsnif\ *vb* **1 :** to draw air audibly up the nose **2 :** to show or express disdain or scorn **3 :** to smell or take by inhalation through the nose : INHALE **4 :** to detect by or as if by smelling — **sniff** *n*
[1]**snif•fle** \ˈsnif-əl\ *vi* **snif•fled**; **snif•fling** \ˈsnif-(ə-)liŋ\ **1 :** to sniff repeatedly **2 :** to speak with or as if with sniffling
[2]**sniffle** *n* **1 :** an act or sound of sniffling **2** *pl* **:** a head cold marked by nasal discharge
[1]**snip** \ˈsnip\ *n* **1 :** a small piece that is snipped off; *also* : FRAGMENT **2 :** an act or sound of snipping **3 :** an impertinent person : MINX
[2]**snip** *vb* **snipped**; **snip•ping :** to cut or cut off with or as if with shears or scissors; *esp* : to clip suddenly or by bits
[1]**snipe** \ˈsnīp\ *n, pl* **snipes** *or* **snipe :** any of several game birds esp. of marshy areas that resemble the related woodcocks
[2]**snipe** *vb* **1 :** to shoot at an exposed enemy from a concealed position usu. at long range **2 :** to aim a carping or snide attack — **snip•er** *n*
snip•py \ˈsnip-ē\ *adj* **1 :** SHORT-TEMPERED, SNAPPISH **2 :** unduly brief or curt **3 :** putting on airs — **snip•pi•ness** *n*
snitch \ˈsnich\ *vb* **1 :** INFORM, TATTLE **2 :** to take by stealth; *esp* : PILFER — **snitch•er** *n*
sniv•el \ˈsniv-əl\ *vi* **-eled** *or* **-elled**; **-el•ing** *or* **-el•ling** \ˈsniv-(ə-)liŋ\ **1 :** to run at the nose **2 :** to snuff mucus up the nose audibly : SNUFFLE **3 :** to cry or whine with snuffling — **sniv•el•er** \-(ə-)lər\ *n*
snob \ˈsnäb\ *n* **1 :** one who blatantly imitates, fawningly admires, or vulgarly seeks association with those of higher status than himself **2 :** one who looks down upon those he regards as inferior to himself
snob•bery \ˈsnäb-(ə-)rē\ *n* **:** snobbish conduct : SNOBBISHNESS
snob•bish \ˈsnäb-ish\ *adj* **:** characteristic of or befitting a snob — **snob•bish•ly** *adv* — **snob•bish•ness** *n*
snood \ˈsnüd\ *n* **:** a net or fabric bag for confining a woman's hair pinned or tied on at the back of the head
[1]**snoop** \ˈsnüp\ *vi* **:** to look or pry esp. in a sneaking or meddlesome manner — **snoop•er** *n*
[2]**snoop** *n* **:** one that snoops
snooty \ˈsnüt-ē\ *adj* **:** haughtily contemptuous : SNOBBISH — **snoot•i•ly** \ˈsnüt-ᵊl-ē\ *adv* — **snoot•i•ness** \ˈsnüt-ē-nəs\ *n*
[1]**snooze** \ˈsnüz\ *vi* **:** to take a nap : DOZE — **snooz•er** *n*
[2]**snooze** *n* **:** a short sleep : NAP
snore \ˈsnō(ə)r\ *vi* **:** to breathe during sleep with a rough hoarse noise — **snore** *n* — **snor•er** *n*
snor•kel \ˈsnȯr-kəl\ *n* **:** a tube used by swimmers for breathing with the head under water
[1]**snort** \ˈsnȯrt\ *vb* **1 :** to force air violently through the nose with a rough harsh sound **2 :** to express scorn, anger, indignation, or surprise by a snort — **snort•er** *n*
[2]**snort** *n* **1 :** an act or sound of snorting **2 :** a drink of usu. straight liquor taken in one draft
snout \ˈsnaůt\ *n* **1 a :** a long projecting nose or muzzle (as of a swine) **b :** the human nose esp. when large or grotesque **2 :** something resembling a snout — **snout•ed** \-əd\ *adj*
[1]**snow** \ˈsnō\ *n* **1 a :** small white crystals of frozen water formed directly from the water vapor of the air **b :** a fall of snow crystals : a mass of snow crystals fallen to earth **2 :** something resembling snow — **snowy** \ˈsnō-ē\ *adj*
[2]**snow** *vb* **1 :** to fall or cause to fall in or as snow **2 :** to cover, shut in, or imprison with or as if with snow
[1]**snow•ball** \-ˌbȯl\ *n* **:** a round mass of snow pressed or rolled together
[2]**snowball** *vb* **1 :** to throw snowballs at **2 :** to increase or expand at a rapidly accelerating rate
snow•bound \-ˈbaůnd\ *adj* **:** shut in or blockaded by snow
snow•drift \-ˌdrift\ *n* **:** a bank of drifted snow
snow•drop \-ˌdräp\ *n* **:** an early-blooming European plant of the amaryllis family that bears nodding white flowers
snow•fall \-ˌfȯl\ *n* **1 :** a fall of snow **2 :** the amount of snow that falls in a single storm or in a given period
snow•plow \ˈsnō-ˌplaů\ *n* **:** any of various devices used for clearing away snow
[1]**snow•shoe** \-ˌshü\ *n* **:** a light oval wooden frame strung with thongs that is attached to the foot to enable a person to walk on soft snow without sinking
[2]**snowshoe** *vi* **:** to travel on snowshoes
snow•storm \-ˌstȯrm\ *n* **:** a storm of falling snow
[1]**snub** \ˈsnəb\ *vt* **snubbed**; **snub•bing 1 :** to check or stop with a cutting reply : REBUKE **2 :** to slow up or check the motion of **3 :** to treat with contempt or neglect : slight deliberately **4 :** to extinguish by stubbing — **snub•ber** *n*
[2]**snub** *n* **:** an act or an instance of snubbing; *esp* : REBUFF
[3]**snub** *or* **snubbed** \ˈsnəbd\ *adj* **:** BLUNT, STUBBY
snub–nosed \ˈsnəb-ˈnōzd\ *adj* **:** having a stubby and usu. slightly turned-up nose
[1]**snuff** \ˈsnəf\ *n* **:** the charred part of a candlewick
[2]**snuff** *vt* **1 :** to cut or pinch off the snuff of (a candle) so as to brighten the light **2 :** EXTINGUISH — **snuff•er** *n*
[3]**snuff** *vb* **1 :** to draw forcibly through or into the nostrils **2 :** to sniff inquiringly
[4]**snuff** *n* **:** the act of snuffing : SNIFF
[5]**snuff** *n* **:** a preparation of pulverized tobacco to be chewed, placed against the gums, or inhaled through the nostrils — **up to snuff :** in good shape
[1]**snuf•fle** \ˈsnəf-əl\ *vb* **snuf•fled**; **snuf•fling** \ˈsnəf-(ə-)liŋ\ **1 :** to snuff or sniff usu. audibly and repeatedly **2 :** to breathe through an obstructed nose with a sniffing sound **3 :** WHINE
[2]**snuffle** *n* **:** the sound made in snuffling
snug \ˈsnəg\ *adj* **1 a :** TRIM, NEAT **b :** fitting closely and comfortably **2 :** enjoying or affording warm secure shelter and comfort : COZY **3 :** SECRETED, CONCEALED — **snug** *adv* — **snug•ly** *adv* — **snug•ness** *n*
snug•gle \ˈsnəg-əl\ *vb* **snug•gled**; **snug•gling** \ˈsnəg-(ə-)liŋ\ **1 :** to curl up comfortably or cozily : CUDDLE **2 :** to draw close esp. for comfort or in affection : NESTLE
[1]**so** \(ˈ)sō\ *adv* **1 a :** in a manner or way that is indicated or suggested **b :** in the same manner or way : ALSO **c :** SUBSEQUENTLY, THEN **2 a :** to an indicated or suggested extent or degree or way **b :** to a great extent or degree : VERY, EXTREMELY **c :** to a definite but unspecified extent or degree **d :** most certainly : INDEED **3 :** for a reason that has just been stated : THEREFORE
[2]**so** \(ˈ)sō\ *conj* **1 a :** with the result that **b :** in order that —

often followed by *that* **2** : provided that — often preceded by *just* **3** : for that reason : THEREFORE

³so \'sō\ *adj* **1** : conforming with actual facts : TRUE **2** : marked by a definite order

⁴so \'sō\ *n, pl* **sos** : SOL

¹soak \'sōk\ *vb* **1 a** : to remain steeping in liquid (as water) **b** : to place in a medium (as liquid) to wet or as if to wet thoroughly : SUBMERGE, STEEP **2** : to penetrate or affect the mind or feelings **3 a** : to extract by or as if by steeping **b** : to levy an exorbitant charge against **4** : to draw in by or as if by suction or absorption — **soak·er** *n*

²soak *n* **1** : the act or process of soaking : the state of being soaked **2** : DRUNKARD

so–and–so \'sō-ən-ˌsō\ *n, pl* **so–and–sos** \-ən-ˌsōz\ : an unnamed or unspecified person or thing

¹soap \'sōp\ *n* : a substance that is usu. made by the action of alkali on fat, dissolves in water, and is used for washing — **soap·less** \-ləs\ *adj* — **soap·mak·ing** \-ˌmā-kiŋ\ *n*

²soap *vt* : to rub soap over or into

soap·box \-ˌbäks\ *n* **1** : a box for soap **2** : an improvised platform used by a spontaneous or informal orator — **soapbox** *adj*

soap opera *n* : a radio or television serial drama performed usu. on a daytime commercial program

soap·stone \'sōp-ˌstōn\ *n* : a soft stone having a soapy feel and containing talc

soap·suds \-ˌsədz\ *n pl* : SUDS

soapy \'sō-pē\ *adj* **1** : smeared with or full of soap **2** : containing or combined with soap **3 a** : resembling or having the qualities of soap **b** : UNCTUOUS, SUAVE

soar \'sō(ə)r\ *vi* **1 a** : to fly aloft or about **b** : to sail or hover in the air often at a great height : GLIDE **2 a** : to move upward in position or status : RISE **b** : to ascend to a higher or more exalted level **3** : to rise to majestic stature — **soar·er** *n*

¹sob \'säb\ *vb* **sobbed**; **sob·bing** **1** : to weep with heavings of the chest or with catching in the throat **2** : to bring about by sobbing **3** : to make a sound like that of sobbing; *also* : to utter with sobs

²sob *n* **1** : an act of sobbing **2** : a sound of or like that of sobbing

¹so·ber \'sō-bər\ *adj* **1 a** : sparing or temperate esp. in the use of food and drink **b** : not drunk **2** : being gravely or earnestly thoughtful in character or demeanor : SERIOUS, SOLEMN **3** : subdued in tone or color **4** : not fanciful or emotional : well balanced — **so·ber·ly** *adv* — **so·ber·ness** *n*

²sober *vb* **so·bered**; **so·ber·ing** \-b(ə-)riŋ\ : to make or become sober

so·bri·e·ty \sə-'brī-ət-ē\ *n* : the quality or state of being sober

so·bri·quet \'sō-bri-ˌkā, -ˌket\ *n* : a fanciful name or epithet

so–called \'sō-'kȯld\ *adj* : commonly or popularly but often inaccurately so termed

soc·cer \'säk-ər\ *n* : a football game with 11 players on a side in which a round inflated ball is advanced esp. by kicking

so·cia·bil·i·ty \ˌsō-shə-'bil-ət-ē\ *n, pl* **-ties** : the quality or state of being sociable : AFFABILITY; *also* : the act or an instance of being sociable

¹so·cia·ble \'sō-shə-bəl\ *adj* **1** : inclined to seek or enjoy companionship : AFFABLE, FRIENDLY **2** : conducive to friendliness or pleasant social relations — **so·cia·ble·ness** *n* — **so·cia·bly** \-blē\ *adv*

²sociable *n* : an informal gathering for sociability and frequently a special activity or interest

¹so·cial \'sō-shəl\ *adj* **1 a** : marked by, devoted to, or engaged in for sociability **b** : SOCIABLE **2 a** : naturally living or growing in groups or communities **b** : tending to form cooperative and interdependent relationships with one's fellows **3** : of or relating to human society, the interaction of the group and its members, and the welfare of these members **4** : of, relating to, or based on rank in a particular society; *also* : of or relating to fashionable society **5** : SOCIALIST

²social *n* : SOCIABLE

so·cial·ism \'sō-shə-ˌliz-əm\ *n* : any of various economic and political theories or social systems based on collective or governmental ownership and administration of the means of production and distribution of goods — **so·cial·ist** \'sōsh-(ə-)ləst\ *n* — **socialist** *or* **so·cial·is·tic** \ˌsō-shə-'lis-tik\ *adj*

so·cial·ite \'sō-shə-ˌlīt\ *n* : a person prominent in fashionable society

so·ci·al·i·ty \ˌsō-shē-'al-ət-ē\ *n, pl* **-ties** **1** : SOCIABILITY **2** : the tendency to associate with one's fellows or to form social groups

so·cial·ize \'sō-shə-ˌlīz\ *vb* **1** : to make social; *esp* : to train so as to develop the qualities essential to group living **2** : to adapt to social needs and uses **3** : to regulate according to the theory or practice of socialism : place under social control **4** : to take part in the social life around one — **so·cial·i·za·tion** \ˌsō-shə-lə-'zā-shən\ *n*

so·cial·ly \'sōsh-(ə-)lē\ *adv* **1** : in a social manner **2** : with respect to society **3** : by society

¹so·ci·e·ty \sə-'sī-ət-ē\ *n, pl* **-ties** **1** : companionship with one's fellows : COMPANY **2** : the social order or community life considered as a system within which the individual lives **3** : people in general **4** : an association of persons for some purpose **5** : a part of a community regarded as a unit distinguished by common interests or standards; *esp* : the group or set of fashionable persons — **so·ci·e·tal** \-ət-ᵊl\ *adj*

²society *adj* : of, relating to, or characteristic of fashionable society

so·ci·ol·o·gy \ˌsō-sē-'äl-ə-jē, -shē-\ *n* : the science of society, social institutions, and social relationships — **so·ci·o·log·ic** \-ə-'läj-ik\ *or* **so·ci·o·log·i·cal** \-ə-'läj-i-kəl\ *adj* — **so·ci·o·log·i·cal·ly** \-ə-'läj-i-k(ə-)lē\ *adv* — **so·ci·ol·o·gist** \-'äl-ə-jəst\ *n*

¹sock \'säk\ *n, pl* **socks** **1** *or pl* **sox** \'säks\ : a knitted or woven covering for the foot usu. extending above the ankle and sometimes to the knee **2** : comic drama

²sock *vb* : to hit, strike, or apply forcefully : deliver a blow

³sock *n* : a vigorous or violent blow : PUNCH

sock·et \'säk-ət\ *n* : an opening or hollow that receives and holds something

¹sod \'säd\ *n* **1** : TURF 1 **2** : one's native land

²sod *vt* **sod·ded**; **sod·ding** : to cover with sod or turfs

so·da \'sōd-ə\ *n* **1 a** : SODIUM CARBONATE **b** : SODIUM BICARBONATE **c** : SODIUM HYDROXIDE **d** : sodium oxide **e** : SODIUM — used in combination **2 a** : SODA WATER **b** : a sweet drink consisting of soda water, flavoring, and often ice cream

soda pop *n* : a bottled soft drink consisting of soda water with added flavoring and a sweet syrup

soda water *n* **1** : a beverage consisting of water highly charged with carbonic acid gas **2** : SODA POP

sod·den \'säd-ᵊn\ *adj* **1** : dull or lacking in expression; *also* : TORPID, UNIMAGINATIVE **2 a** : heavy with moisture : SOAKED, SATURATED **b** : heavy or doughy because of imperfect cooking — **sod·den·ly** *adv* — **sod·den·ness** \-ᵊn-(n)əs\ *n*

so·di·um \'sōd-ē-əm\ *n* : a soft waxy silver-white metallic element chemically very active and found abundantly in nature always in combination

sodium bicarbonate *n* : a white crystalline weakly alkaline salt used esp. in cooking, fire extinguishers, and medicine

sodium carbonate *n* : a carbonate of sodium used esp. in washing and bleaching textiles

sodium chloride *n* : SALT 1a

sodium hydroxide *n* : a white brittle solid that is a strong caustic base used esp. in making soap, rayon, and paper and in bleaching

sodium nitrate *n* : a deliquescent crystalline salt found in crude form in Chile and used as a fertilizer and an oxidizing agent and in curing meat

so·ev·er \sō-'ev-ər\ *adv* **1** : to any possible or known extent **2** : of any or every kind that may be specified — used after a noun modified as by *any, no,* or *what*

so·fa \'sō-fə\ *n* : a long upholstered seat usu. with arms and a back and often convertible into a bed

soft \'sȯft\ *adj* **1** : having a pleasing, comfortable, or soothing quality or effect: as **a** : causing little distress or anguish : MILD **b** : not harsh or inclement : gentle in action **c** : pleasing to the ear : melodious and quiet in pitch or volume **d** : not bright or glaring : subdued and with little contrast **e** : demanding little effort : EASY **f** : smooth or delicate in appearance or texture **g** : pleasingly mild in taste or odor; *esp* : free from excessive pungency, acidity, or acridity **2 a** : having a mild gentle nature : DOCILE **b** : lacking in strength or vigor : unfit for prolonged exertion or severe stress : FEEBLE **c** : weak or deficient mentally **d** : defective in firmness or resolution **e** : advocating or being a moderate or conciliatory policy **3** : yielding to physical pressure : COMPRESSIBLE, MALLEABLE; *also* : relatively lacking in hardness **4** : gently or gradually curved or rounded : not harsh or jagged **5** : sounding as in *ace* and *gem* respectively — used of *c* and *g* **6 a** : deficient in or free from substances (as calcium and magnesium salts) that prevent lathering of soap **b** : containing no alcohol — **soft·ly** *or* **soft** *adv* — **soft·ness** *n*

soft·ball \'sȯf(t)-ˌbȯl\ *n* : a game resembling baseball played with a ball larger and softer than a baseball; *also* : the ball used in this game

soft–boiled \-'bȯild\ *adj* : lightly boiled so that the contents are only partly coagulated

soft coal *n* : bituminous coal

soft·en \'sȯ-fən\ *vb* **soft·ened; soft·en·ing** \'sȯf-(ə-)niŋ\ **1** : to make or become soft or softer **2** : to impair the strength or resistance of — **soft·en·er** \'sȯf-(ə-)nər\ *n*

soft·heart·ed \'sȯft-'härt-əd\ *adj* : emotionally responsive : SYMPATHETIC, TENDER — **soft·heart·ed·ly** *adv* — **soft·heart·ed·ness** *n*

soft–ped·al \'sȯf(t)-'ped-ᵊl\ *vt* : to refrain from emphasizing

soft–soap \'sȯf(t)-'sōp\ *vb* : to soothe or coax with flattery

soft–spo·ken \'sȯf(t)-'spō-kən\ *adj* : speaking softly : having a mild or gentle voice : SUAVE

softy \'sȯf-tē\ *n, pl* **soft·ies** **1** : a silly or sentimental person **2** : WEAKLING

sog·gy \'säg-ē\ *adj* **1** : saturated or heavy with water or moisture : SOAKED, SODDEN **2** : heavily dull : PONDEROUS — **sog·gi·ly** \'säg-ə-lē\ *adv* — **sog·gi·ness** \'säg-ē-nəs\ *n*

soi–di·sant \ˌswäd-ē-'zäⁿ\ *adj* : SELF-STYLED, SO-CALLED — usu. used disparagingly

¹soil \'sȯil\ *vb* : to make or become dirty or corrupt

²soil *n* **1 a** : SOILAGE, STAIN **b** : moral defilement : CORRUPTION **2** : something that soils or pollutes

³soil *n* **1** : firm land : EARTH **2** : the loose surface material of the earth in which plants grow **3** : COUNTRY, LAND **4** : the agricultural life or calling **5** : a medium in which something may take root and grow

soil·age \'sȯi-lij\ *n* : the act of soiling : the condition of being soiled

soi·ree *or* **soi·rée** \swä-'rā\ *n* : an evening party or reception

¹so·journ \'sō-ˌjərn, sō-'\ *n* : a temporary stay

²sojourn *vi* : to stay as a temporary resident : STOP — **so·journ·er** *n*

sol \'sōl\ *n* : the 5th note of the diatonic scale

Sol \'säl\ *n* : SUN

¹sol·ace \'säl-əs\ *n* : alleviation of grief or anxiety or a source of this

²solace *vt* **1** : to give solace to : CONSOLE **2** : to make cheerful : DIVERT **3** : ALLAY, SOOTHE — **sol·ac·er** *n*

so·lar \'sō-lər\ *adj* **1** : of, derived from, or relating to the sun **2** : measured by the earth's course in relation to the sun **3** : produced or operated by the action of the sun's light or heat; *also* : utilizing the sun's rays

so·lar·i·um \sō-'lar-ē-əm\ *n, pl* **-ia** \-ē-ə\ : a room exposed to the sun (as for treatment of illness)

solar plexus *n* **1** : a network of nerves situated behind the stomach **2** : the pit of the stomach

solar system *n* : the sun and the planets, asteroids, comets, and meteors that revolve around it

sold *past of* SELL

¹sol·der \'säd-ər, 'sȯd-\ *n* **1** : a metal or metallic alloy used when melted to join metallic surfaces **2** : something that unites or cements

²solder *vb* **sol·dered; sol·der·ing** \-(ə-)riŋ\ **1** : to unite or repair with solder **2** : to bring into or restore to firm union **3** : to become joined or renewed by or as if by the use of solder — **sol·der·er** *n*

¹sol·dier \'sōl-jər\ *n* **1** : a person in military service usu. as an enlisted man or woman **2** : a worker in a cause **3** : SHIRKER, LOAFER — **sol·dier·ly** \-lē\ *adj*

²soldier *vi* **sol·diered; sol·dier·ing** \'sōlj-(ə-)riŋ\ **1** : to serve as or act like a soldier **2** : to make a show of activity while really loafing

soldier of fortune : one who follows a military career wherever there is promise of profit, adventure, or pleasure

sol·diery \'sōlj-(ə-)rē\ *n, pl* **-dier·ies** **1 a** : a body of soldiers **b** : SOLDIERS, MILITARY **2** : the profession or technique of soldiering

¹sole \'sōl\ *n* **1** : the undersurface of a foot **2** : the part of footwear on which the sole of the foot rests **3** : the bottom or lower part of something — **soled** \'sōld\ *adj*

²sole *vt* : to furnish with a sole

³sole *n* : any of a family of small-mouthed flatfishes having reduced fins and small closely set eyes

⁴sole *adj* **1** : having no companion : ALONE **2 a** : having no sharer **b** : being the only one **3** : functioning independently and without assistance or interference **4** : belonging exclusively or otherwise limited to the one person, unit, or group named

sol·e·cism \'säl-ə-ˌsiz-əm, 'sō-lə-\ *n* **1** : an ungrammatical combination of words in a sentence **2** : a breach of etiquette or decorum

sole·ly \'sō(l)-lē\ *adv* **1** : without another : SINGLY, ALONE **2** : EXCLUSIVELY, ENTIRELY

sol·emn \'säl-əm\ *adj* **1** : celebrated with religious rites or ceremony : SACRED **2** : FORMAL, STATELY **3** : done or made seriously and thoughtfully **4** : GRAVE, SOBER **5** : SOMBER — **so·lem·ni·ty** \sə-'lem-nət-ē\ *n* — **sol·emn·ly** *adv*

sol·em·nize \'säl-əm-ˌnīz\ *vt* **1** : to observe or honor with solemnity **2** : to perform with pomp or ceremony; *esp* : to celebrate (a marriage) with religious rites **3** : to make solemn : DIGNIFY — **sol·em·ni·za·tion** \ˌsäl-əm-nə-'zā-shən\ *n*

soli *pl of* SOLO

so·lic·it \sə-'lis-ət\ *vb* **1** : BEG, ENTREAT; *esp* : to approach with a request or plea **2** : to appeal for **3 a** : to entice or lure esp. into evil **b** : to accost a man for immoral purposes — **so·lic·i·ta·tion** \-ˌlis-ə-'tā-shən\ *n*

so·lic·i·tor \sə-'lis-ət-ər\ *n* **1** : one that solicits (as contributions to charity) **2** : LAWYER; *esp* : a legal official of a city or state

so·lic·i·tous \sə-'lis-ət-əs\ *adj* **1** : full of concern or fears : APPREHENSIVE **2** : anxiously willing : EAGER **3** : meticulously careful — **so·lic·i·tous·ly** *adv* — **so·lic·i·tous·ness** *n*

so·lic·i·tude \sə-'lis-ə-ˌt(y)üd\ *n* : the state of being solicitous : ANXIETY; *also* : excessive care or attention

¹sol·id \'säl-əd\ *adj* **1 a** : having an interior filled with matter : not hollow **b** : written as one word without a hyphen **c** : not interrupted **2 :** having, involving, or dealing with three dimensions or with solids **3 a :** not loose or spongy : COMPACT **b :** neither gaseous nor liquid : HARD, RIGID **4 :** of good substantial quality or kind: as **a :** SOUND **b :** STURDY **c :** EXCELLENT **5 :** UNANIMOUS, UNITED **6 a :** thoroughly dependable : RELIABLE; *also* : well established financially **b :** serious in purpose or character **7 :** of one substance or character — **solid** *adv* — **sol·id·ly** *adv* — **sol·id·ness** *n*

[2]**solid** *n* **1 :** a geometrical figure (as a cube or sphere) having three dimensions **2 :** a solid substance

sol·i·dar·i·ty \ˌsäl-ə-ˈdar-ət-ē\ *n, pl* **-ties :** community of interests, objectives, or standards in a group

so·lid·i·fi·ca·tion \sə-ˌlid-ə-fə-ˈkā-shən\ *n* **:** an act or instance of solidifying : the condition of being solidified

so·lid·i·fy \sə-ˈlid-ə-ˌfī\ *vb* **-fied; -fy·ing :** to make or become solid, compact, or hard

so·lid·i·ty \sə-ˈlid-ət-ē\ *n* **:** the quality or state of being solid

sol·id–state \ˈsäl-əd-ˈstāt\ *adj* **:** using electronic circuitry containing semiconductors instead of electron tubes

so·lil·o·quize \sə-ˈlil-ə-ˌkwīz\ *vi* **:** to utter a soliloquy : talk to oneself — **so·lil·o·quiz·er** *n*

so·lil·o·quy \sə-ˈlil-ə-kwē\ *n, pl* **-quies 1 :** the act of talking to oneself **2 :** a dramatic monologue that gives the illusion of being a series of unspoken thoughts

sol·i·taire \ˈsäl-ə-ˌta(ə)r\ *n* **1 :** a single gem (as a diamond) set alone **2 :** a card game played by one person alone

[1]**sol·i·tary** \ˈsäl-ə-ˌter-ē\ *adj* **1 :** all alone **2 :** seldom visited : LONELY **3 :** being the only one : SOLE **4 :** growing or living alone — **sol·i·tar·i·ness** *n*

[2]**solitary** *n, pl* **-tar·ies :** one who lives or seeks to live a solitary life : RECLUSE, HERMIT

sol·i·tude \ˈsäl-ə-ˌt(y)üd\ *n* **1 :** the quality or state of being alone or remote from society : SECLUSION, LONELINESS **2 :** a lonely place (as a desert)

[1]**so·lo** \ˈsō-lō\ *n, pl* **solos 1** *or pl* **so·li** \ˈsō-(ˌ)lē\ **a :** a musical composition for a single voice or instrument with or without accompaniment **b :** the featured part of a concerto or similar work **2 :** an action in which there is only one performer (as in a dance or airplane flight)

[2]**solo** *adv (or adj)* **:** without a companion : ALONE

[3]**solo** *vi* **:** to perform by oneself; *esp* : to fly solo in an airplane

so·lo·ist \ˈsō-lə-wəst, -ˌlō-əst\ *n* **:** one who performs a solo

so·lon \ˈsō-lən, -ˌlän\ *n* **1 :** a wise and skillful lawgiver **2 :** a member of a legislative body

so long \sō-ˈlȯŋ\ *interj* — used to express good-bye or farewell

sol·stice \ˈsäl-stəs, ˈsōl-, ˈsȯl-\ *n* **1 :** the point in the apparent path of the sun at which the sun is farthest from the equator either north or south **2 :** the time of the sun's passing a solstice which occurs on June 22d to begin summer in the northern hemisphere and on December 22d to begin winter in the northern hemisphere — **sol·sti·tial** \säl-ˈstish-əl, sōl-, sȯl-\ *adj*

sol·u·bil·i·ty \ˌsäl-yə-ˈbil-ət-ē\ *n, pl* **-ties 1 :** the quality or state of being soluble **2 :** the amount of a substance that will dissolve in a given amount of another substance

sol·u·ble \ˈsäl-yə-bəl\ *adj* **1 a :** capable of being dissolved in a fluid **b :** EMULSIFIABLE **2 :** capable of being solved or explained : SOLVABLE — **sol·u·ble·ness** *n* — **sol·u·bly** \-blē\ *adv*

so·lu·tion \sə-ˈlü-shən\ *n* **1 a :** an act or process of solving **b :** an answer to a problem : EXPLANATION **2 a :** an act or the process by which a solid, liquid, or gaseous substance is uniformly mixed with a liquid or sometimes a gas or solid **b :** a typically liquid uniform mixture formed by the process of solution **c :** the condition of being dissolved **d :** a liquid containing a dissolved substance

solv·a·ble \ˈsäl-və-bəl, ˈsȯl-\ *adj* **:** capable of being solved

solve \ˈsälv, ˈsȯlv\ *vt* **:** to find a solution for

sol·ven·cy \ˈsäl-vən-sē, ˈsȯl-\ *n, pl* **-cies :** the quality or state of being solvent

[1]**sol·vent** \-vənt\ *adj* **1 :** able to pay all legal debts **2 :** dissolving or able to dissolve — **sol·vent·ly** *adv*

[2]**solvent** *n* **1 :** a usu. liquid substance capable of dissolving or dispersing one or more other substances **2 :** something that provides a solution

som·ber *or* **som·bre** \ˈsäm-bər\ *adj* **1 :** so shaded as to be dark and gloomy **2 :** GRAVE, MELANCHOLY **3 :** dull or dark colored — **som·ber·ly** *adv* — **som·ber·ness** *n*

som·bre·ro \səm-ˈbre(ə)r-ō, säm-\ *n, pl* **-ros :** a high-crowned hat of felt or straw with a very wide brim worn esp. in the Southwest and Mexico

[1]**some** \ˈsəm *or, for 2b, without stress*\ *adj* **1 :** being one unknown, undetermined, or unspecified unit or thing **2 a :** being one, a part, or an unspecified number of something (as a class or group) named or implied **b :** being of an unspecified amount or number **3 :** worthy of notice or consideration **4 :** being at least one and sometimes all of

[2]**some** \ˈsəm\ *pron* **1 :** some one among a number **2 :** one indeterminate quantity, portion, or number as distinguished from the rest

[3]**some** \ˈsəm, ˌsəm\ *adv* **1 :** ABOUT **2 :** SOMEWHAT

[1]**some·body** \ˈsəm-ˌbäd-ē, -bəd-\ *pron* **:** one or some person of no certain or known identity

[2]**somebody** *n* **:** a person of position or importance

some·day \ˈsəm-ˌdā\ *adv* **:** at some future time

some·how \ˈsəm-ˌhau̇\ *adv* **:** in one way or another not known or designated : by some means

some·one \-(ˌ)wən\ *pron* **:** SOMEBODY

som·er·sault \ˈsəm-ər-ˌsȯlt\ *n* **:** a leap or roll in which a person turns his heels over his head — **somersault** *vi*

som·er·set \-ˌset\ *n or vi* **:** SOMERSAULT

[1]**some·thing** \ˈsəm(p)-thiŋ\ *pron* **1 a :** some undetermined or unspecified thing **b :** some thing not remembered or immaterial **2 :** some definite but not specified thing **3 :** a person or thing of consequence

[2]**something** *adv* **1 :** in some degree : SOMEWHAT **2 :** EXTREMELY

[1]**some·time** \ˈsəm-ˌtīm\ *adv* **1 :** at some time in the future **2 :** at some not specified or definitely known point of time

[2]**sometime** *adj* **:** FORMER, LATE

some·times \ˈsəm-ˌtīmz, (ˌ)səm-ˈ\ *adv* **:** at times : now and then : OCCASIONALLY

some·way \ˈsəm-ˌwā\ *adv* **:** in some way : SOMEHOW

[1]**some·what** \-ˌhwät, -ˌhwət, (ˌ)səm-ˈ\ *pron* **1 :** something (as an amount or degree) indefinite or unspecified **2 :** one having a character, quality, or nature to some extent

[2]**somewhat** *adv* **:** in some degree or measure : SLIGHTLY

[1]**some·where** \ˈsəm-ˌhwe(ə)r\ *adv* **1 :** in, at, or to a place unknown or unspecified **2 :** APPROXIMATELY

[2]**somewhere** *n* **:** an undetermined or unnamed place

som·nam·bu·lism \säm-ˈnam-byə-ˌliz-əm\ *n* **:** a sleep or somnolent state in which acts (as walking) are performed; *also* : actions performed in this state — **som·nam·bu·list** \-ləst\ *n* — **som·nam·bu·lis·tic** \(ˌ)säm-ˌnam-byə-ˈlis-tik\ *adj*

som·no·lence \ˈsäm-nə-lən(t)s\ *n* **:** DROWSINESS, SLEEPINESS

som·no·lent \-lənt\ *adj* **:** DROWSY — **som·no·lent·ly** *adv*

son \ˈsən\ *n* **1 a :** a male offspring esp. of human beings **b :** a male descendant — usu. used in pl. **2** *cap* **:** the second person of the Trinity **3 :** a person closely associated with or deriving from a formative agent (as a nation, school, or race)

so·nant \ˈsō-nənt\ *adj* **:** VOICED — used of speech sounds — **sonant** *n*

so·nar \ˈsō-ˌnär\ *n* **:** an apparatus that detects the presence and location of submerged objects (as submarines) by reflected vibrations

so·na·ta \sə-ˈnät-ə\ *n* **:** an instrumental musical composition typically of three or four movements in contrasting rhythms and keys

song \ˈsȯŋ\ *n* **1 :** the act or art of singing **2 :** poetical composition : POETRY 3 : a short musical composition of words and music 4 : a small amount — **song·book** \-ˌbu̇k\ *n*

song·bird \-ˌbərd\ *n* 1 : a bird that utters a succession of musical tones 2 : SINGING BIRD 2

song·ster \ˈsȯŋ(k)-stər\ *n* : one skilled in song : a man that sings — **song·stress** \-strəs\ *n*

son·ic \ˈsän-ik\ *adj* 1 : utilizing, produced by, or relating to sound waves 2 : of, relating to, or being the speed of sound in air — **son·i·cal·ly** \ˈsän-i-k(ə-)lē\ *adv*

son–in–law \ˈsən-ən-ˌlȯ\ *n, pl* **sons–in–law** \ˈsən-zən-\ : the husband of one's daughter

son·net \ˈsän-ət\ *n* : a poem of 14 lines usu. in iambic pentameter rhyming according to a prescribed scheme

son·ne·teer \ˌsän-ə-ˈti(ə)r\ *n* : a writer of sonnets

so·nor·i·ty \sə-ˈnȯr-ət-ē\ *n, pl* **-ties** 1 : the quality or state of being sonorous : RESONANCE 2 : a sonorous tone or speech

so·no·rous \sə-ˈnōr-əs, ˈsän-ə-rəs\ *adj* 1 : producing sound (as when struck) 2 : full or loud in sound : RESONANT 3 : imposing or impressive in effect or style — **so·no·rous·ly** *adv* — **so·no·rous·ness** *n*

soon \ˈsün\ *adv* 1 : before long : without undue time lapse 2 : PROMPTLY, SPEEDILY 3 : before the usual time 4 : READILY, WILLINGLY

soot \ˈsu̇t, ˈsət, ˈsüt\ *n* : a black substance that is formed by combustion, rises in fine particles, and adheres to the sides of the chimney or pipe conveying the smoke; *esp* : the fine powder consisting chiefly of carbon that colors smoke

soothe \ˈsüt͟h\ *vb* 1 a : to please by or as if by attention or concern : PLACATE b : RELIEVE, ALLEVIATE 2 : to bring comfort, solace, or reassurance

sooth·ing \ˈsü-t͟hiŋ\ *adj* : tending to calm or allay; *also* : having a sedative effect — **sooth·ing·ly** *adv* — **sooth·ing·ness** *n*

sooth·say·er \ˈsüth-ˌsā-ər\ *n* : a person who claims to foretell events — **sooth·say·ing** \-ˌsā-iŋ\ *n*

sooty \ˈsu̇t-ē, ˈsət-, ˈsüt-\ *adj* 1 a : of, relating to, or producing soot b : soiled with soot 2 : of the color of soot

[1]**sop** \ˈsäp\ *n* : a bribe, gift, or gesture for pacifying or winning favor

[2]**sop** *vt* **sopped**; **sop·ping** 1 a : to steep or dip in or as if in liquid b : to wet thoroughly : SOAK 2 : to mop up (as water) 3 : to give a bribe or conciliatory gift to

soph·ism \ˈsäf-ˌiz-əm\ *n* : an unsound misleading argument that on the surface seems reasonable

soph·ist \ˈsäf-əst\ *n* : one who argues by the use of sophisms

so·phis·tic \sə-ˈfis-tik\ *or* **so·phis·ti·cal** \-ti-kəl\ *adj* : being clever and subtle but misleading

[1]**so·phis·ti·cate** \sə-ˈfis-tə-ˌkāt\ *vt* 1 : to alter deceptively; *esp* : ADULTERATE 2 : to deprive of genuineness, naturalness, or simplicity; *esp* : to deprive of naïveté and make worldly-wise : DISILLUSION — **so·phis·ti·ca·tion** \-ˌfis-tə-ˈkā-shən\ *n*

[2]**so·phis·ti·cate** \-ˈfis-ti-kət, -tə-ˌkāt\ *n* : a sophisticated person

so·phis·ti·cat·ed \-tə-ˌkāt-əd\ *adj* 1 : not in a natural, pure, or original state : ADULTERATED 2 : deprived of native or original simplicity: as a : highly complicated : COMPLEX b : WORLDLY-WISE, KNOWING 3 : devoid of grossness : SUBTLE: as a : finely experienced and aware b : intellectually appealing

soph·ist·ry \ˈsäf-ə-strē\ *n, pl* **-ries** : deceptively subtle reasoning or argumentation

soph·o·more \ˈsäf-ᵊm-ˌōr, ˈsäf-ˌmōr\ *n* : a student in his second year at a college or secondary school

soph·o·mor·ic \ˌsäf-ə-ˈmōr-ik\ *adj* 1 : of, relating to, or characteristic of a sophomore 2 : being conceited and overconfident of knowledge but poorly informed and immature

[1]**sop·o·rif·ic** \ˌsäp-ə-ˈrif-ik, ˌsōp-\ *adj* 1 a : causing or tending to cause sleep b : tending to dull awareness or alertness 2 : of, relating to, or characterized by sleepiness or lethargy

[2]**soporific** *n* : a soporific agent or drug

sop·ping \ˈsäp-iŋ\ *adj* : wet through : SOAKING

[1]**so·prano** \sə-ˈpran-ō, -ˈprän-\ *n, pl* **-pran·os** 1 : the highest voice part in 4-part mixed harmony 2 : the highest singing voice 3 : a singer with a soprano voice

[2]**soprano** *adj* 1 : of or relating to the soprano voice or part 2 : having a high range

sor·cer·er \ˈsȯrs(-ə)-rər\ *n* : a person who practices sorcery : WIZARD — **sor·cer·ess** \-rəs\ *n*

sor·cery \ˈsȯrs(-ə)-rē\ *n, pl* **-cer·ies** : the use of power gained from the assistance or control of evil spirits esp. for divining

sor·did \ˈsȯrd-əd\ *adj* 1 : DIRTY, FILTHY 2 : marked by baseness or grossness : VILE 3 : MISERLY, NIGGARDLY, COVETOUS — **sor·did·ly** *adv* — **sor·did·ness** *n*

[1]**sore** \ˈsō(ə)r\ *adj* 1 a : causing pain or distress b : painfully sensitive : TENDER c : hurt or inflamed so as to be or seem painful 2 : attended by difficulties, hardship, or exertion 3 : ANGERED, VEXED — **sore·ness** *n*

[2]**sore** *n* 1 : a localized sore spot on the body; *esp* : one (as an ulcer) with the tissues broken and usu. infected 2 : a source of pain or vexation : AFFLICTION

[3]**sore** *adv* : SORELY

sore·head \-ˌhed\ *n* : a person easily angered or disgruntled — **sorehead** *or* **sore·head·ed** \-ˈhed-əd\ *adj*

sore·ly \-lē\ *adv* : in a sore manner : PAINFULLY, SEVERELY

sor·ghum \ˈsȯr-gəm\ *n* : a tall variable Old World tropical grass grown widely for its edible seed, for forage, or for its sweet juice which yields a syrup

so·ror·i·ty \sə-ˈrȯr-ət-ē\ *n, pl* **-ties** : a club of girls or women esp. at a college

[1]**sor·rel** \ˈsȯr-əl, ˈsär-\ *n* 1 : an animal (as a horse) of a sorrel color 2 : a brownish orange to light brown

[2]**sorrel** *n* : any of various plants with sour juice; *esp* : [1]DOCK

[1]**sor·row** \ˈsär-ō\ *n* 1 a : sadness or anguish due to loss (as of something loved) b : a cause of grief or sadness 2 : CONTRITION, REPENTANCE

[2]**sorrow** *vi* : to feel or express sorrow : GRIEVE

sor·row·ful \-fəl\ *adj* 1 : full of or marked by sorrow 2 : expressive of or inducing sorrow — **sor·row·ful·ly** \-fə-lē\ *adv* — **sor·row·ful·ness** *n*

sor·ry \ˈsär-ē\ *adj* 1 : feeling sorrow, regret, or penitence 2 : MOURNFUL, SAD 3 : inspiring sorrow, pity, scorn, or ridicule : WRETCHED — **sor·ri·ness** \ˈsär-ē-nəs\ *n*

[1]**sort** \ˈsȯrt\ *n* 1 : a group set up on the basis of any characteristic in common : CLASS 2 : a number of things used together : SET, SUIT 3 : method or manner of acting : WAY, MANNER 4 : general character or disposition; *also* : PERSON, INDIVIDUAL — **after a sort** : in a rough or haphazard way — **of sorts** *or* **of a sort** : of an inconsequential or mediocre quality — **out of sorts** 1 : out of temper : IRRITABLE 2 : not well

[2]**sort** *vb* : to put in a certain place or rank according to kind, class, or nature : CLASSIFY — **sort·a·ble** *adj* — **sort·er** *n*

sor·tie \ˈsȯrt-ē, sȯr-ˈtē\ *n* 1 : a sudden issuing of troops from a defensive position against the enemy : SALLY 2 : one mission or attack by a single plane — **sortie** *vi*

sort of *adv* : to a moderate degree : RATHER

SOS \ˌes-(ˌ)ō-ˈes\ *n* 1 : an internationally recognized signal of distress in radio code . . . – – – . . . used esp. by ships calling for help 2 : a call or request for help or rescue

[1]**so–so** \ˈsō-ˈsō\ *adv* : TOLERABLY, PASSABLY

[2]**so–so** *adj* : neither very good nor very bad : MIDDLING

sot \ˈsät\ *n* : an habitual drunkard

sot·tish \ˈsät-ish\ *adj* : resembling a sot : STUPID; *also* : DRUNKEN — **sot·tish·ly** *adv* — **sot·tish·ness** *n*

sot·to vo·ce \ˌsät-ō-ˈvō-chē\ *adv* (*or adj*) 1 : under the breath : in an undertone; *also* : PRIVATELY 2 : very softly

sou·brette \sü-ˈbret\ *n* : a coquettish maid or frivolous young woman in comedies; *also* : an actress who plays such a part

souf·flé \sü-ˈflā\ *n* : a delicate spongy hot dish lightened in baking by stiffly beaten egg whites
sough \ˈsəf, ˈsaů\ *vi* : to make a moaning or sighing sound — **sough** *n*
sought *past of* SEEK
[1]**soul** \ˈsōl\ *n* **1** : the spiritual part of man believed to give life to his body and in many religions regarded as immortal **2 a** : man's moral and emotional nature **b** : spiritual force : FERVOR **3** : the essential part of something **4** : the moving spirit : LEADER **5** : EMBODIMENT **6** : a human being : PERSON **7** : a disembodied spirit **8** : a strong positive feeling (as of intense sensitivity and emotional fervor) conveyed esp. by American Negro performers
[2]**soul** *adj* : of, relating to, or characteristic of American Negroes or their culture
soul·ful \-fəl\ *adj* : full of or expressing feeling or emotion — **soul·ful·ly** \-fə-lē\ *adv* — **soul·ful·ness** *n*
soul·less \ˈsōl-ləs\ *adj* : having no soul or no greatness or nobleness of mind or feeling — **soul·less·ly** *adv*
[1]**sound** \ˈsaůnd\ *adj* **1** : free from flaw, defect, or decay **2** : not diseased or weak : HEALTHY **3** : SOLID, FIRM **4** : STABLE **5** : not faulty : VALID, RIGHT **6** : showing good sense : WISE **7** : HONORABLE, HONEST **8** : THOROUGH **9** : UNDISTURBED, DEEP — **sound·ly** *adv* — **sound·ness** *n*
[2]**sound** *adv* : SOUNDLY
[3]**sound** *n* **1 a** : the sensation experienced through the sense of hearing **b** : a particular auditory impression : NOISE, TONE **c** : mechanical energy that is transmitted by longitudinal waves in a material medium (as air) and is the objective cause of hearing **2 a** : one of the noises that together make up human speech **b** : a sequence of spoken noises **3 a** : meaningless noise **b** : impression conveyed : IMPORT, IMPLICATION **4** : hearing distance : EARSHOT
[4]**sound** *vb* **1 a** : to make or cause to make a sound **b** : RESOUND **c** : to give a summons by sound **2** : to put into words : VOICE **3 a** : to make known : PROCLAIM **b** : to order, signal, or indicate by a sound **4** : to make or convey an impression : SEEM **5** : to examine by causing to emit sounds — **sound·a·ble** *adj* — **sound·er** *n*
[5]**sound** *n* **1** : a long passage of water that is wider than a strait and often connects two larger bodies of water or forms a channel between the mainland and an island **2** : the air bladder of a fish
[6]**sound** *vb* **1 a** : to measure the depth of (as with a sounding line) : FATHOM **b** : to look into or investigate the possibility **2** : to try to find out the views or intentions of : PROBE **3** : to dive down suddenly
sound·ing \ˈsaůn-diŋ\ *adj* **1** : SONOROUS 2 **2** : HIGH-SOUNDING
sound·less \ˈsaůn-dləs\ *adj* : SILENT — **sound·less·ly** *adv*
[1]**soup** \ˈsüp\ *n* **1** : a liquid food with a meat, fish, or vegetable stock as a base and often containing pieces of solid food **2** : something having or suggesting the consistency of soup (as a heavy fog) **3** : an unfortunate predicament
[2]**soup** *vt* : to increase the power or efficiency of — **souped–up** \ˈsüpt-ˈəp\ *adj*
soup·çon \süp-ˈsōⁿ, ˈsüp-ˌsän\ *n* : a little bit : TRACE
soupy \ˈsü-pē\ *adj* **1** : having the consistency of soup **2** : densely foggy or cloudy
[1]**sour** \ˈsaů(ə)r\ *adj* **1** : having an acid or tart taste **2 a** : having undergone a usu. acid fermentation **b** : indicative of decay : PUTRID **3** : UNPLEASANT, DISAGREEABLE **4** : acid in reaction — **sour·ish** \-ish\ *adj* — **sour·ly** *adv* — **sour·ness** *n*
[2]**sour** *n* **1** : something sour **2** : the primary taste sensation produced by acid stimuli
[3]**sour** *vb* : to become or make sour
source \ˈsōrs\ *n* **1** : the point of origin of a stream of water : FOUNTAINHEAD **2 a** : a generative force : CAUSE **b** (1) : a point of origin (2) : one that initiates : AUTHOR; *also* : PROTOTYPE, MODEL (3) : one that supplies information **3** : a firsthand document or primary reference work
sour·dough \ˈsaů(ə)r-ˌdō\ *n* **1** : a leaven of dough in which fermentation is active **2** : an old-time prospector in Alaska or northwestern Canada
sour grapes *n pl* : disparagement of something unattainable
[1]**souse** \ˈsaůs\ *vb* **1** : PICKLE **2 a** : to plunge in liquid : IMMERSE **b** : DRENCH, SATURATE **3** : to make or become drunk
[2]**souse** *n* **1** : something pickled; *esp* : seasoned and chopped pork trimmings, fish, or shellfish **2** : an act of sousing : WETTING **3** : an habitual drunkard
sou·tane \sü-ˈtän, -ˈtan\ *n* : CASSOCK
[1]**south** \ˈsaůth; *in compounds, as "southwest", also* (ˈ)saů *esp by seamen*\ *adv* : to or toward the south
[2]**south** *adj* **1** : situated toward or at the south **2** : coming from the south
[3]**south** *n* **1 a** : the direction to the right of one facing east **b** : the compass point directly opposite to north **2** *cap* : regions or countries south of a specified or implied point; *esp* : the part of the U.S. that lies south of the Mason-Dixon line, the Ohio river, and the southern boundaries of Missouri and Kansas — **south·er·ly** \ˈsət͟h-ər-lē\ *adv or adj* — **south·ern** \ˈsət͟h-ərn\ *adj* — **South·ern·er** \ˈsət͟h-ə(r)-nər\ *n* — **south·ern·most** \-ərn-ˌmōst\ *adj* — **south·ward** \ˈsaůth-wərd\ *adv or adj* — **south·wards** \-wərdz\ *adv*
south·east \saůth-ˈēst\ *n* **1 a** : the general direction between south and east **b** : the compass point midway between south and east **2** *cap* : regions or countries southeast of a specified or implied point — **southeast** *adj or adv* — **south·east·er·ly** \-ˈē-stər-lē\ *adv or adj* — **south·east·ern** \-ˈē-stərn\ *adj*
south·east·er \saůth-ˈē-stər\ *n* : a storm, strong wind, or gale coming from the southeast
southern hemisphere *n* : the half of the earth that lies south of the equator
south·land \ˈsaůth-ˌland, -lənd\ *n, often cap* : land in the south : the south of a country or region
south pole *n, often cap S & P* : the southernmost point of the earth
south·west \saůth-ˈwest\ *n* **1 a** : the general direction between south and west **b** : the compass point midway between south and west **2** *cap* : regions or countries southwest of a specified or implied point — **southwest** *adj or adv* — **south·west·er·ly** \-ˈwes-tər-lē\ *adv or adj* — **south·west·ern** \-ˈwes-tərn\ *adj*
sou·ve·nir \ˈsü-və-ˌni(ə)r, ˌsü-və-ˈ\ *n* : something that serves as a reminder : MEMENTO, REMEMBRANCE
sou'·west·er \saů-ˈwes-tər\ *n* **1** : a long oilskin coat worn esp. at sea during stormy weather **2** : a waterproof hat with wide slanting brim longer in back than in front
[1]**sov·er·eign** \ˈsäv-(ə-)rən, ˈsäv-ərn, ˈsəv-\ *n* **1 a** : a person, body of persons, or a state possessing sovereignty; *esp* : a monarch exercising supreme authority in a state **b** : one that exercises supreme authority within a limited sphere **c** : an acknowledged leader : ARBITER **2** : a British gold coin no longer issued worth 1 pound sterling
[2]**sovereign** *adj* **1** : CHIEF, HIGHEST **2** : supreme in power or authority **3** : having independent authority **4 a** : EFFECTUAL **b** : EXCELLENT
sov·er·eign·ty \-tē\ *n, pl* **-ties** **1** : the condition of being sovereign or a sovereign **2 a** : supreme power esp. over a politically organized unit **b** : freedom from external control **3** : one that is sovereign; *esp* : an autonomous state
[1]**so·vi·et** \ˈsō-vē-ˌet, -ət, ˈsäv-ē-\ *n* **1** : an elected governmental council in a Communist country **2** *pl, cap* : the people and esp. the political and military leaders of the U.S.S.R.
[2]**soviet** *adj* **1** : of, relating to, or organized on the basis of soviets **2** *usu cap* : of or relating to the U.S.S.R.
[1]**sow** \ˈsaů\ *n* : an adult female swine
[2]**sow** \ˈsō\ *vb* **sowed**; **sown** \ˈsōn\ *or* **sowed**; **sow·ing** **1 a** : to

plant seed for growth esp. by scattering **b** : to strew with or as if with seed **2** : to set in motion : FOMENT **3** : to spread abroad : DISPERSE, DISSEMINATE — **sow·er** \'sō(-ə)r\ *n*

sox *pl of* SOCK

soy \'sȯi\ *n* **1** : a Chinese and Japanese sauce made from soybeans fermented in brine **2** : SOYBEAN

soy·bean \'sȯi-'bēn, -ˌbēn\ *n* : a hairy annual Asiatic legume widely grown for its oil-rich and protein-rich edible seeds and for forage and soil improvement; *also* : its seed

spa \'spä, 'spȯ\ *n* **1 a** : a mineral spring **b** : a resort with mineral springs **2** : a fashionable resort or hotel

¹space \'spās\ *n* **1** : a period of time; *also* : its duration **2 a** : a limited extent in one, two, or three dimensions : DISTANCE, AREA, VOLUME **b** : an extent set apart or available **3** : the region beyond the earth's atmosphere **4** : a blank area separating words or lines **5 a** : LINAGE 1 **b** : broadcast time available esp. to advertisers **6** : accommodations on a public vehicle

²space *vt* : to place at intervals or arrange with space between

space·craft \'spās-ˌkraft\ *n* : SPACESHIP

space·less \'spās-ləs\ *adj* **1** : having no limits : BOUNDLESS **2** : occupying no space

space·man \'spās-ˌman\ *n* : one concerned with traveling beyond the earth's atmosphere

space·ship \'spās(h)-ˌship\ *n* : a vehicle designed to operate outside the earth's atmosphere

space station *n* : a manned artificial satellite designed for a fixed orbit about the earth and to serve as a base (as for the refueling of spaceships or launching of missiles)

space suit *n* : a suit with air supply and provisions to make life in free space possible for its wearer

spac·ing \'spā-siŋ\ *n* **1** : an arrangement in space **2 a** : SPACE **b** : the distance between any two objects in a usu. regularly arranged series

spa·cious \'spā-shəs\ *adj* **1** : vast or ample in extent : ROOMY **2** : large or magnificent in scale : EXPANSIVE — **spa·cious·ly** *adv* — **spa·cious·ness** *n*

¹spade \'spād\ *n* **1** : an implement for turning soil that resembles a shovel, is adapted for being pushed into the ground with the foot, and has a heavy usu. flat blade **2** : a spade-shaped instrument

²spade *vb* : to dig with or use a spade — **spad·er** *n*

³spade *n* : any of a suit of playing cards marked with a black figure resembling an inverted heart with a short stem at the bottom

spade·work \-ˌwərk\ *n* **1** : work done with the spade **2** : the hard plain preliminary drudgery in any undertaking

spa·ghet·ti \spə-'get-ē\ *n* : a dough made chiefly from wheat flour and formed in thin solid strings

¹span \'span\ *n* **1** : an English unit of length equal to 9 inches **2** : an extent, stretch, reach, or spread between two limits: as **a** : a limited space of time **b** : the spread of an arch, beam, truss, or girder from one support to another; *also* : the portion thus extended

²span *vt* **spanned**; **span·ning** **1 a** : to measure by or as if by the hand with fingers and thumb extended **b** : MEASURE **2 a** : to reach or extend across **b** : to place or construct a span over

³span *n* : a pair of animals (as mules) driven together

¹span·gle \'spaŋ-gəl\ *n* **1** : a small piece of shining metal or plastic used for ornamentation esp. on dresses **2** : a small glittering object

²spangle *vb* **span·gled**; **span·gling** \'spaŋ-g(ə-)liŋ\ **1** : to set or sprinkle with or as if with spangles : adorn with small brilliant objects **2** : to glitter as if covered with spangles : SPARKLE

span·iel \'span-yəl\ *n* **1** : any of numerous small or medium-sized mostly short-legged dogs usu. having long wavy hair, feathered legs and tail, and large drooping ears **2** : a cringing fawning person

Span·ish fly \ˌspan-ish-\ *n* : a green European beetle containing a substance irritating to the skin; *also* : a dried preparation of these beetles

spank \'spaŋk\ *vt* : to strike esp. on the buttocks usu. with the open hand — **spank** *n*

spank·ing \'spaŋ-kiŋ\ *adj* **1** : remarkable of its kind **2** : moving with a quick, lively pace : BRISK, LIVELY

¹spar \'spär\ *n* : a stout rounded wood or metal piece (as a mast, boom, or yard) used to support sail rigging

²spar *vi* **sparred**; **spar·ring** **1** : to engage in a practice or exhibition bout of boxing **2** : SKIRMISH, WRANGLE

¹spare \'spa(ə)r\ *vb* **1** : to forbear to destroy, punish, or harm : be lenient **2** : to refrain from attacking or reprimanding with necessary or salutary severity **3** : to relieve of the necessity of doing or undergoing something : EXEMPT **4** : to refrain from : AVOID **5** : to use frugally **6 a** : to give up as not strictly needed **b** : to have left over or as margin

²spare *adj* **1** : not being used; *esp* : held for emergency use **2** : being over and above what is needed : SUPERFLUOUS **3** : not liberal or profuse : SPARING **4** : somewhat thin **5** : not abundant or plentiful : SCANTY — **spare·ly** *adv* — **spare·ness** *n*

³spare *n* **1** : a spare or duplicate piece or part (as an automobile tire) **2** : the knocking down of all the bowling pins with the first 2 balls

spare·ribs \'spa(ə)r-ˌ(r)ibz\ *n pl* : a cut of pork ribs separated from the bacon strip

spar·ing \'spa(ə)r-iŋ\ *adj* **1** : tending to save; *esp* : FRUGAL **2** : MEAGER, SCANTY — **spar·ing·ly** *adv*

¹spark \'spärk\ *n* **1 a** : a small particle of a burning substance **b** : a hot glowing particle struck from a larger mass; *esp* : one heated by friction **2** : a luminous electrical discharge of very short duration between two conductors **3** : SPARKLE, FLASH **4** : something that sets off a sudden force **5** : a latent particle capable of growth or developing : GERM

²spark *vb* **1 a** : to throw out or produce sparks : SPARKLE **b** : to flash or fall like sparks **2** : to respond with enthusiasm **3** : to set off in a burst of activity : ACTIVATE **4** : to stir to activity : INCITE, STIMULATE — **spark·er** *n*

³spark *n* **1** : a foppish young man : GALLANT **2** : LOVER, BEAU

⁴spark *vb* : WOO, COURT — **spark·er** *n*

¹spar·kle \'spär-kəl\ *vi* **spar·kled**; **spar·kling** \-k(ə-)liŋ\ **1 a** : to throw out sparks **b** : to shine as if throwing out sparks : GLISTEN **2** : to perform brilliantly **3** : EFFERVESCE **4** : to become lively or animated

²sparkle *n* **1** : a little spark : SCINTILLATION **2** : the quality of sparkling **3 a** : ANIMATION, LIVELINESS **b** : EFFERVESCENCE

spar·kler \'spär-klər\ *n* : one that sparkles: as **a** : DIAMOND **b** : a firework that throws off brilliant sparks on burning

spark plug *n* **1** : a part that fits into the cylinder head of an internal-combustion engine and produces the spark for combustion **2** : one that initiates or gives impetus to an undertaking — **spark·plug** \'spärk-ˌpləg\ *vt*

spar·row \'spar-ō\ *n* : any of several small dull singing birds related to the finches

sparse \'spärs\ *adj* : not thickly grown or settled — **sparse·ly** *adv* — **sparse·ness** *n* — **spar·si·ty** \'spär-sət-ē\ *n*

¹Spar·tan \'spärt-ᵊn\ *n* : a person of great courage and fortitude

²Spartan *adj* **1** : marked by strict self-discipline and avoidance of comfort and luxury **2** : undaunted by pain or danger

spasm \'spaz-əm\ *n* **1** : an involuntary and abnormal muscular contraction **2** : a sudden violent and temporary effort or emotion

spas·mod·ic \spaz-'mäd-ik\ *adj* **1** : relating to or affected or characterized by spasm **2** : acting or proceeding fitfully : INTERMITTENT **3** : subject to outbursts of emotional excitement : EXCITABLE — **spas·mod·i·cal·ly** \-'mäd-i-k(ə-)lē\ *adv*

¹spas·tic \'spas-tik\ *adj* **1** : of, relating to, or characterized by

spasm 2 : suffering from spastic paralysis — **spas·ti·cal·ly** \-ti-k(ə-)lē\ *adv* — **spas·tic·i·ty** \spa-'stis-ət-ē\ *n*
[2]**spastic** *n* : one suffering from spastic paralysis
[1]**spat** \'spat\ *past of* SPIT
[2]**spat** *n, pl* **spat** *or* **spats** : a young bivalve mollusk (as an oyster) — usu. used collectively
[3]**spat** *n* : a cloth or leather gaiter covering the instep and ankle
[4]**spat** *n* **1** : a brief petty quarrel : DISPUTE **2** : a sound like that of rain falling in large drops
[5]**spat** *vb* **spat·ted; spat·ting** **1** : to quarrel pettily or briefly **2** : to strike with a sound like that of rain falling in large drops
spa·tial \'spā-shəl\ *adj* : relating to, occupying, or of the nature of space — **spa·ti·al·i·ty** \ˌspā-shē-'al-ət-ē\ *n* — **spa·tial·ly** \'spāsh-(ə-)lē\ *adv*
[1]**spat·ter** \'spat-ər\ *vb* **1** : to splash with or as if with a liquid; *also* : to soil or spot in this way **2** : to scatter by splashing **3** : to injure by aspersion : DEFAME **4 a** : to spurt forth in scattered drops **b** : to drop with a sound like rain
[2]**spatter** *n* **1** : the act or noise of spattering : the state of being spattered **2 a** : a drop or splash spattered on something : a spot or stain due to spattering **b** : a small number or quantity
spat·u·la \'spach-ə-lə\ *n* : a flat thin usu. metal implement that resembles a knife and is used esp. for spreading or mixing soft substances, scooping, or lifting
spat·u·late \'spach-ə-lət\ *adj* : shaped like a spatula
spav·in \'spav-ən\ *n* : a bony enlargement of the hock of a horse associated with strain — **spav·ined** \-ənd\ *adj*
[1]**spawn** \'spȯn\ *vb* **1 a** : to produce or deposit eggs or spawn — used of an aquatic animal **b** : to induce (fish) to spawn **2** : to bring forth : GENERATE **3** : to produce young esp. in large numbers — **spawn·er** *n*
[2]**spawn** *n* **1** : the eggs of aquatic animals (as fishes or oysters) that lay many small eggs **2** : PRODUCT, OFFSPRING; *also* : offspring produced in large quantities
spay \'spā\ *vt* : to remove the ovaries of (a female animal)
speak \'spēk\ *vb* **spoke** \'spōk\; **spo·ken** \'spō-kən\; **speak·ing** **1** : to utter words with the ordinary voice : TALK **2** : to utter by means of words **3** : to address a gathering **4** : to mention in speech or writing **5** : to carry a meaning as if by speech **6** : to make a natural or characteristic sound **7** : to use in talking — **speak·er** *n* — **speak for** **1** : to speak in behalf of : represent the opinions of **2** : to apply for : CLAIM — **speak out** **1** : to speak loudly and distinctly **2** : to speak freely — **speak to** : REPROVE, REBUKE — **speak up** : to speak out
speak·easy \'spēk-ˌē-zē\ *n* : a place where alcoholic drinks are illegally sold
speak·ing \'spē-kiŋ\ *adj* **1** : highly significant or expressive : ELOQUENT **2** : STRIKING, FAITHFUL
[1]**spear** \'spi(ə)r\ *n* **1** : a thrusting or throwing weapon with long shaft and sharp head or blade **2** : a sharp-pointed instrument with barbs used in spearing fish **3** : SPEARMAN
[2]**spear** *vb* **1** : to pierce or strike with or as if with a spear **2** : to thrust with or as if with a spear — **spear·er** *n*
[3]**spear** *n* : a usu. young blade, shoot, or sprout (as of grass)
[1]**spear·head** \'spi(ə)r-ˌhed\ *n* **1** : the sharp-pointed head of a spear **2** : a leading element, force, or influence (as in an attack, drive, or enterprise)
[2]**spearhead** *vt* : to serve as leader or leading element of
spear·man \'spi(ə)r-mən\ *n* : one armed with a spear
spear·mint \-ˌmint, -mənt\ *n* : a common mint grown for flavoring and esp. for its aromatic oil
spe·cial \'spesh-əl\ *adj* **1 a** : distinguished by some unusual quality **b** : regarded with particular flavor **2 a** : PECULIAR, UNIQUE **b** : of, relating to, or constituting a species : SPECIFIC **3** : ADDITIONAL, EXTRA **4** : designed for a particular purpose or occasion — **special** *n* — **spe·cial·ly** \'spesh-(ə-)lē\ *adv*
spe·cial·ist \'spesh-(ə-)ləst\ *n* **1** : one who devotes himself to a special occupation or branch of learning **2** : any of six enlisted ranks in the army corresponding to the ranks of corporal through sergeant major — **specialist** *or* **spe·cial·is·tic** \ˌspesh-ə-'lis-tik\ *adj*
spe·ci·al·i·ty \ˌspesh-ē-'al-ət-ē\ *n, pl* **-ties** **1** : a special mark or quality **2** : a special object or class of objects **3 a** : a special aptitude or skill **b** : a particular occupation or branch of learning
spe·cial·i·za·tion \ˌspesh-(ə-)lə-'zā-shən\ *n* : a making or becoming specialized
spe·cial·ize \'spesh-ə-ˌlīz\ *vb* **1** : to make particular mention of : PARTICULARIZE **2** : to apply or direct to a specific end or use **3** : to concentrate one's efforts in a special activity or field **4** : to undergo specialization; *esp* : to change adaptively
spe·cial·ty \'spesh-əl-tē\ *n, pl* **-ties** **1** : a distinctive mark or quality **2 a** : a special object or class of objects; *esp* : a product of a special kind or of special excellence **b** : the state of being special, distinctive, or peculiar **3** : something in which one specializes or has special knowledge
spe·cie \'spē-shē, -sē\ *n* : money in coin esp. of gold or silver
spe·cies \'spē-(ˌ)shēz, -(ˌ)sēz\ *n, pl* **species** **1** : a class of individuals with common qualities and a common name : KIND, SORT **2** : a taxonomic group comprising closely related organisms potentially able to breed with one another
spec·i·fi·a·ble \'spes-ə-ˌfī-ə-bəl\ *adj* : capable of being specified
[1]**spe·cif·ic** \spi-'sif-ik\ *adj* **1** : of, relating to, or constituting a species **2** : PARTICULAR, ACTUAL, EXACT **3** : having a unique relation to something; *esp* : exerting a distinctive and usu. a causative or curative influence — **spe·cif·i·cal·ly** \-'sif-i-k(ə-)lē\ *adv* — **spec·i·fic·i·ty** \ˌspes-ə-'fis-ət-ē\ *n*
[2]**specific** *n* **1 a** : something peculiarly adapted to a purpose or use **b** : a drug or remedy specific for a particular disease **2 a** : a characteristic quality or trait **b** : DETAILS, PARTICULARS **c** *pl* : SPECIFICATION 2a
spec·i·fi·ca·tion \ˌspes-(ə-)fə-'kā-shən\ *n* **1** : the act or process of specifying **2 a** (1) : a detailed precise presentation of something or of a plan or proposal for something — often used in pl. (2) : a written description of an invention for which a patent is sought **b** : a single item in such a detailed presentation
specific gravity *n* : the ratio of the weight of a volume of a substance to the weight of an equal volume of some other substance taken as the standard which is water for solids and liquids and air or hydrogen for gases
spec·i·fy \'spes-ə-ˌfī\ *vt* **-fied; -fy·ing** **1** : to name or state explicitly or in detail **2** : to include as an item in a specification
spec·i·men \'spes-ə-mən\ *n* **1** : an item or part typical of a group or whole : SAMPLE **2** : SORT, INDIVIDUAL
spe·cious \'spē-shəs\ *adj* : apparently but not really fair, just, or right — **spe·cious·ly** *adv* — **spe·cious·ness** *n*
[1]**speck** \'spek\ *n* **1** : a small discoloration or spot esp. from dirt or decay **2** : BIT, PARTICLE
[2]**speck** *vt* : to produce specks on or in
[1]**speck·le** \'spek-əl\ *n* : a little speck
[2]**speckle** *vt* **speck·led; speck·ling** \'spek-(ə-)liŋ\ **1** : to mark with speckles **2** : to be distributed in or on like speckles
specs \'speks\ *n pl* : GLASS 2b
spec·ta·cle \'spek-ti-kəl\ *n* **1 a** : something exhibited to view as unusual, notable, or entertaining; *esp* : an impressive public display **b** : an object of curiosity or contempt **2** *pl* : GLASS 2b
spec·ta·cled \-kəld\ *adj* **1** : having or wearing spectacles **2** : having markings suggesting a pair of spectacles
[1]**spec·tac·u·lar** \spek-'tak-yə-lər, spək-\ *adj* : of, relating to, or constituting a spectacle — **spec·tac·u·lar·ly** *adv*
[2]**spectacular** *n* : something that is spectacular
spec·ta·tor \'spek-ˌtāt-ər, spek-'\ *n* : one who looks on or watches : ONLOOKER — **spectator** *adj*
spec·ter *or* **spec·tre** \'spek-tər\ *n* **1** : a visible disembodied spirit : GHOST **2** : something that haunts or perturbs the mind

spec·tral \'spek-trəl\ *adj* **1 :** of, relating to, or suggesting a specter : GHOSTLY **2 :** of, relating to, or made by a spectrum
spec·tro·graph \'spek-trə-ˌgraf\ *n* **:** an apparatus for dispersing radiation into a spectrum and photographing or mapping the spectrum — **spec·tro·graph·ic** \ˌspek-trə-'graf-ik\ *adj* — **spec·tro·graph·i·cal·ly** \-'graf-i-k(ə-)lē\ *adv*
spec·tro·scope \'spek-trə-ˌskōp\ *n* **:** any of various instruments for forming and examining spectra — **spec·tro·scop·ic** \ˌspek-trə-'skäp-ik\ *adj* — **spec·tro·scop·i·cal·ly** \-'skäp-i-k(ə-)lē\ *adv* — **spec·tros·co·pist** \spek-'träs-kə-pəst\ *n* — **spec·tros·co·py** \-pē\ *n*
spec·trum \'spek-trəm\ *n, pl* **spec·tra** \-trə\ *or* **spectrums** **1 a :** a series of colors formed when a beam of white light is dispersed (as by passing through a prism) so that the component waves are arranged in the order of their wavelengths from red continuing through orange, yellow, green, blue, indigo, and violet **b :** a series of radiations arranged in regular order according to some varying characteristic esp. wavelength **2 :** a continuous sequence or range
spec·u·late \'spek-yə-ˌlāt\ *vi* **1 a :** to meditate on or ponder a subject : REFLECT **b :** to think or theorize about something in which evidence is too slight for certainty to be reached **2 :** to assume a business risk in hope of gain; *esp* **:** to buy or sell in expectation of profiting from market fluctuations — **spec·u·la·tion** \ˌspek-yə-'lā-shən\ *n* — **spec·u·la·tive** \'spek-yə-lət-iv, -ˌlāt-\ *adj* — **spec·u·la·tive·ly** *adv* — **spec·u·la·tor** \-ˌlāt-ər\ *n*
speech \'spēch\ *n* **1 a :** the communication or expression of thoughts in spoken words **b :** CONVERSATION **2 a :** something that is spoken **b :** a public discourse **3 a :** LANGUAGE, DIALECT **b :** an individual manner or style of speaking **4 :** the power of expressing or communicating thoughts by speaking
speech·less \'spēch-ləs\ *adj* **1 :** lacking or deprived of the power of speaking **2 :** not speaking for a time : SILENT
[1]**speed** \'spēd\ *n* **1 a :** the act or state of moving swiftly : SWIFTNESS **b :** rate of motion : VELOCITY **2 :** swiftness or rate of performance or action : QUICKNESS **3 :** a transmission gear in automotive vehicles
[2]**speed** *vb* **sped** \'sped\ *or* **speed·ed**; **speed·ing** **1 a :** to make haste **b :** to go or drive at excessive or illegal speed **2 :** to move, work, or take place faster : ACCELERATE **3 a :** to cause to move quickly : HASTEN **b :** to wish Godspeed to **c :** to increase the speed of : ACCELERATE — **speed·er** *n*
[3]**speed** *adj* **:** of, relating to, or regulating speed
speed·boat \'spēd-ˌbōt\ *n* **:** a fast launch or motorboat
speed·i·ly \'spēd-ᵊl-ē\ *adv* **1 :** RAPIDLY, QUICKLY **2 :** PROMPTLY, SOON
speed·om·e·ter \spi-'däm-ət-ər\ *n* **1 :** an instrument that measures speed **2 :** an instrument that both measures speed and records distance traveled
speed·ster \'spēd-stər\ *n* **:** one that speeds or is capable of great speed
speed·up \'spēd-ˌəp\ *n* **:** ACCELERATION
speed·way \'spēd-ˌwā\ *n* **1 :** a road on which more than ordinary speed is allowed **2 :** a racecourse for motor vehicles
speed·well \'spēd-ˌwel\ *n* **:** a low creeping perennial European herb with small bluish flowers
speedy \'spēd-ē\ *adj* **:** rapid in motion : FAST, SWIFT — **speed·i·ness** *n*
[1]**spell** \'spel\ *n* **1 a :** a spoken word or form of words believed to have magic power : INCANTATION **b :** a state of enchantment **2 :** a strong compelling influence or attraction
[2]**spell** *vt* **:** to put under a spell : BEWITCH
[3]**spell** *vb* **spelled** \'speld, 'spelt\; **spell·ing** **1 :** to read or discern slowly and with difficulty **2 a :** to name, write, or print the letters of in order **b :** to constitute the letters of **3 :** MEAN, SIGNIFY **4 :** to form words with letters
[4]**spell** *vb* **spelled** \'speld\; **spell·ing** **1 :** to take the place of for a time : RELIEVE **2 :** to allow an interval of rest to : REST
[5]**spell** *n* **1 :** one's turn at work **2 :** a period spent in a job or occupation **3 a :** a short period of time **b :** a stretch of a specified type of weather **4 :** a period of bodily or mental distress or disorder : ATTACK, FIT
spell·bind \'spel-ˌbīnd\ *vt* **-bound** \-ˌbau̇nd\; **-bind·ing** **:** to hold by or as if by a spell : FASCINATE
spell·bind·er \-ˌbīn-dər\ *n* **:** a speaker of compelling eloquence
spell·bound \-'bau̇nd\ *adj* **:** ENTRANCED, FASCINATED
spell·er \'spel-ər\ *n* **1 :** one who spells words **2 :** a book with exercises for teaching spelling
spell·ing \'spel-iŋ\ *n* **:** the forming of words from letters according to accepted usage; *also* **:** the letters composing a word
spell out *vt* **:** to make very explicit or emphatic
spe·lunk·er \spi-'ləŋ-kər, 'spē-ˌ\ *n* **:** one who makes a hobby of exploring caves
spe·lunk·ing \-kiŋ\ *n* **:** the practice of exploring caves
spend \'spend\ *vb* **spent** \'spent\; **spend·ing** **1 :** to use up or pay out : EXPEND **2 a :** to wear out : EXHAUST **b :** to consume wastefully : SQUANDER **3 :** to cause or permit to elapse : PASS **4 :** to make use of : EMPLOY, OCCUPY — **spend·er** *n*
spend·thrift \'spen(d)-ˌthrift\ *n* **:** one who spends lavishly or wastefully — **spendthrift** *adj*
spent \'spent\ *adj* **1 :** used up : CONSUMED **2 :** drained of energy or effectiveness : EXHAUSTED
sperm \'spərm\ *n, pl* **sperm** *or* **sperms** **1 :** SEMEN **2 :** a male gamete
sper·ma·to·zo·on \ˌspər-mət-ə-'zō-ˌän, (ˌ)spər-ˌmat-, -'zō-ən\ *n, pl* **-zoa** \-'zō-ə\ **:** a male germ cell — **sper·ma·to·zo·al** \-'zō-əl\ *adj*
sperm whale *n* **:** a large whale with conical teeth and no whalebone
spew \'spyü\ *vb* **:** to pour forth : VOMIT — **spew·er** *n*
sphere \'sfi(ə)r\ *n* **1 a :** the apparent surface of the heavens of which half forms the dome of the visible sky **b :** a globe representing the earth **2 a :** a globular body : BALL **b :** a surface all points of which are equally distant from a center; *also* **:** the space enclosed by such a surface **3 :** natural, normal, or proper place; *esp* **:** social order or rank **4 :** a field or range of influence or significance : PROVINCE
spher·i·cal \'sfir-i-kəl, 'sfer-\ *adj* **1 :** having the form of a sphere or of one of its segments **2 :** relating to or dealing with a sphere or its properties — **spher·i·cal·ly** \-k(ə-)lē\ *adv*
sphe·roid \'sfi(ə)r-ˌȯid, 'sfe(ə)r-\ *n* **:** a figure resembling a flattened sphere — **sphe·roi·dal** \sfir-'ȯid-ᵊl\ *adj*
sphinc·ter \'sfiŋ(k)-tər\ *n* **:** a muscular ring surrounding and able to contract or close a bodily opening
sphinx \'sfiŋ(k)s\ *n* **1 :** a person whose character, motives, or feelings are enigmatic **2 :** an ancient Egyptian image in the form of a recumbent lion having a man's head, a ram's head, or a hawk's head
[1]**spice** \'spīs\ *n* **1 :** any of various aromatic plant products (as pepper or nutmeg) used to season or flavor foods **2 :** something that gives zest or relish **3 :** a pungent or fragrant odor
[2]**spice** *vt* **:** to season with or as if with spices
spick–and–span \ˌspik-ən-'span\ *adj* **1 :** FRESH, BRAND-NEW **2 :** spotlessly clean and neat
spic·ule \'spik-yül\ *n* **:** a slender pointed body esp. of bony material
spicy \'spī-sē\ *adj* **1 :** having the quality, flavor, or fragrance of spice **2 :** producing or abounding in spices **3 :** KEEN, ZESTFUL **4 :** PIQUANT, RACY; *esp* **:** somewhat scandalous or salacious — **spic·i·ly** \-sə-lē\ *adv* — **spic·i·ness** \-sē-nəs\ *n*
spi·der \'spīd-ər\ *n* **1 :** any of an order of arachnids having a body with two main divisions, four pairs of walking legs, and two or more pairs of abdominal organs for spinning threads of silk used in making cocoons for their eggs, nests for them-

selves, or webs for entangling their prey 2 : a cast-iron frying pan

spi·dery \'spīd-ə-rē\ *adj* 1 : resembling a spider; *also* : long and thin like the legs of a spider 2 : resembling the web of a spider 3 : full of spiders

¹spiel \'spēl\ *vb* : to talk volubly or perfunctorily — **spiel·er** *n*

²spiel *n* : voluble mechanical often extravagant talk

spiffy \'spif-ē\ *adj* : fine looking : SMART

spig·ot \'spig-ət, 'spik-ət\ *n* 1 : a pin or peg used to stop the vent in a cask 2 : FAUCET

¹spike \'spīk\ *n* 1 : a very large nail 2 : any of various pointed projections (as on the sole of a shoe to prevent slipping)

²spike *vt* 1 : to fasten or furnish with spikes 2 : to suppress or block completely : QUASH 3 : to pierce or impale with or on a spike 4 : to add alcohol or liquor to (a drink)

³spike *n* 1 : an ear of grain 2 : a long cluster of usu. stemless flowers

spiked \'spīkt\ *adj* 1 a : bearing ears b : having a spiky inflorescence 2 : SPIKY

spiky \'spī-kē\ *adj* 1 : resembling a spike : POINTED 2 : furnished or armed with spikes

¹spill \'spil\ *vb* **spilled** \'spild, 'spilt\; **spill·ing** 1 : to cause (blood) to flow 2 a : to cause or allow accidentally or unintentionally to fall, flow, or run out b : to fall or run out so as to be lost or wasted 3 : to throw off or out 4 : to let out : DIVULGE — **spill·a·ble** *adj*

²spill *n* 1 : an act or instance of spilling; *esp* : a fall from a horse or vehicle 2 : something spilled 3 : SPILLWAY

spill·age \'spil-ij\ *n* 1 : the act or process of spilling 2 : the quantity that spills

spill·way \'spil-ˌwā\ *n* : a passage for surplus water to run over or around a dam or similar obstruction

spilth \'spilth\ *n* 1 : an act or instance of spilling 2 a : something spilled b : REFUSE, RUBBISH

¹spin \'spin\ *vb* **spun** \'spən\; **spin·ning** 1 : to draw out and twist into yarn or thread 2 a : to produce by drawing out and twisting fibers b : to form threads or a web or cocoon by extruding a viscous rapidly hardening fluid 3 a : to revolve rapidly : GYRATE b : to be dizzy : feel as if turning rapidly 4 : to cause to whirl : TWIRL 5 a : to extend to great length : PROLONG b : to make up with the imagination 6 : to move swiftly on wheels or in a vehicle — **spin·ner** *n*

²spin *n* 1 a : the act of spinning or twirling something b : whirling motion imparted by spinning : rapid rotation c : an excursion in a vehicle esp. on wheels 2 : a mental whirl or state of confusion

spin·ach \'spin-ich\ *n* : a potherb of the goosefoot family widely grown for its edible leaves

spi·nal \'spīn-ᵊl\ *adj* 1 : of, relating to, or situated near the backbone 2 : of, relating to, or affecting the spinal cord — **spi·nal·ly** \-ᵊl-ē\ *adv*

spinal column *n* : the axial skeleton of the trunk and tail of a vertebrate that consists of a jointed series of vertebrae enclosing and protecting the spinal cord

spinal cord *n* : the cord of nervous tissue that extends from the brain along the back in the cavity of the spinal column, gives off the spinal nerves, and not only carries impulses to and from the brain but also serves as a center for initiating and coordinating many reflex acts

spin·dle \'spin-dᵊl\ *n* 1 : a round stick with tapered ends used to form and twist the yarn in hand spinning 2 : a turned part of a piece of furniture 3 : a slender pin or rod which turns or on which something else turns

spin·dling \'spin-(d)liŋ, 'spin-dᵊl-iŋ\ *adj* : being long or tall and thin and usu. feeble or frail

spin·dly \'spin-(d)lē, 'spin-dᵊl-ē\ *adj* : SPINDLING

spine \'spīn\ *n* 1 a : SPINAL COLUMN b : something resembling a spinal column or constituting a central axis or chief support 2 : a stiff pointed process; *esp* : one on a plant that is a modified leaf or leaf part — **spiny** \'spī-nē\ *adj* — **spin·i·ness** *n*

spine·less \'spīn-ləs\ *adj* : lacking courage or strength of character : WEAK

spin·et \'spin-ət\ *n* 1 : a small harpsichord similar to the virginal 2 : a small upright piano

spin·ning wheel \'spin-iŋ-\ *n* : a small domestic hand-driven or foot-driven machine for spinning yarn or thread in which a wheel drives a single spindle

spin·ster \'spin(t)-stər\ *n* 1 : a woman whose occupation is to spin 2 : an unmarried woman; *esp* : a woman past the common age for marrying or one who seems unlikely to marry — **spin·ster·hood** \-ˌhu̇d\ *n* — **spin·ster·ish** \-st(ə-)rish\ *adj*

spiny lobster *n* : an edible crustacean distinguished from the related true lobster by the simple unenlarged first pair of legs and by the spiny carapace

¹spi·ral \'spī-rəl\ *adj* 1 a : winding around a center or pole and gradually receding from or approaching it b : HELICAL c : of, relating to, or resembling a spiral 2 : advancing to higher levels through a series of cyclical movements — **spi·ral·ly** \-rə-lē\ *adv*

²spiral *n* 1 : a single turn or coil in a spiral object 2 : something having a spiral form 3 : a continuously spreading and accelerating increase or decrease

³spiral *vb* **-raled** *or* **-ralled**; **-ral·ing** *or* **-ral·ling** 1 : to move in a spiral course 2 : to form into a spiral

¹spire \'spī(ə)r\ *n* 1 : a slender tapering blade or stalk (as of grass) 2 : a sharp pointed tip 3 : STEEPLE

²spire *n* 1 : SPIRAL 2 : COIL

¹spir·it \'spir-ət\ *n* 1 : a life-giving force; *esp* : a force within man held to endow his body with life, energy, and power : SOUL 2 *cap* : the active presence of God in human life : the third person of the Trinity 3 : SPECTER, GHOST 4 : MOOD, DISPOSITION 5 : mental vigor or animation : VIVACITY 6 : real meaning or intention 7 : an emotion, frame of mind, or inclination governing one's actions 8 : PERSON 9 : distilled alcoholic liquor — usu. used in pl.

²spirit *vt* 1 : ANIMATE, ENCOURAGE 2 : to carry off or convey secretly or mysteriously

spir·it·ed \'spir-ət-əd\ *adj* : full of spirit, courage, or energy : LIVELY, ANIMATED — **spir·it·ed·ly** *adv* — **spir·it·ed·ness** *n*

spir·it·less \'spir-ət-ləs\ *adj* : lacking animation, cheerfulness, or courage — **spir·it·less·ly** *adv* — **spir·it·less·ness** *n*

¹spir·i·tu·al \'spir-ich-(ə-w)əl\ *adj* 1 : of, relating to, or consisting of spirit : not bodily or material 2 a : RELIGIOUS b : ecclesiastical rather than lay or temporal 3 : related or joined in spirit : having a spiritual rather than physical relationship 4 a : of or relating to supernatural beings b : SPIRITUALISTIC — **spir·i·tu·al·ly** \-ē\ *adv* — **spir·i·tu·al·ness** *n*

²spiritual *n* : a Negro religious song esp. of the southern U.S. usu. of a deeply emotional character

spir·i·tu·al·ism \'spir-ich-(ə-w)ə-ˌliz-əm\ *n* 1 : a belief that the spirits of the dead communicate with the living 2 *cap* : a movement comprising religious organizations emphasizing spiritualism — **spir·i·tu·al·ist** \-ləst\ *n*, *often cap* — **spir·i·tu·al·is·tic** \ˌspir-ich-(ə-w)ə-'lis-tik\ *adj*

spir·i·tu·al·i·ty \ˌspir-ich-ə-'wal-ət-ē\ *n* 1 : sensitivity or attachment to religious values 2 : the quality or state of being spiritual

spir·i·tu·al·ize \'spir-ich-(ə-w)ə-ˌlīz\ *vt* 1 : to make spiritual esp. by freeing from worldly influences 2 : to give a spiritual meaning to or understand in a spiritual sense — **spir·i·tu·al·i·za·tion** \ˌspir-ich-(ə-w)ə-lə-'zā-shən\ *n*

spir·i·tu·ous \'spir-ich-(ə-w)əs\ *adj* : containing or impregnated with distilled alcohol

spi·ro·chete *or* **spi·ro·chaete** \'spī-rə-ˌkēt\ *n* : any of various spiral bacteria including one that causes syphilis

¹spit \'spit\ *n* **1 :** a slender pointed rod for holding meat over a fire **2 :** a small point of land running into a body of water
²spit *vt* **spit·ted; spit·ting :** to fix on or as if on a spit
³spit *vb* **spit** *or* **spat** \'spat\; **spit·ting 1 a :** to eject saliva from the mouth : EXPECTORATE **b :** to express by or as if by spitting or make a spitting sound **2 a :** to give off usu. briskly or vigorously : EMIT **b :** to rain or snow in flurries
⁴spit *n* **1 a :** SALIVA **b :** the act of spitting **2 :** perfect likeness
¹spite \'spīt\ *n* **:** petty ill will or malice with the disposition to irritate, annoy, or thwart — **in spite of :** in defiance or contempt of : NOTWITHSTANDING
²spite *vt* **1 :** to treat maliciously (as by shaming or thwarting) **2 :** ANNOY, OFFEND
spite·ful \'spīt-fəl\ *adj* **:** filled with or showing spite : MALICIOUS — **spite·ful·ly** \-fə-lē\ *adv* — **spite·ful·ness** *n*
spit·fire \'spit-,fī(ə)r\ *n* **:** a quick-tempered person
spit·tle \'spit-ᵊl\ *n* **:** SALIVA
spit·toon \spi-'tün\ *n* **:** a receptacle for spit
¹splash \'splash\ *vb* **1 a :** to strike or move through a liquid or semifluid substance and cause it to move and scatter roughly **b :** to wet or soil by dashing water or mud on : SPATTER; *also* **:** to cause to soil something by splashing **2 :** to make a splashing sound (as in falling or moving) **3 a :** to spread or scatter like a splashed liquid **b :** to display prominently
²splash *n* **1 :** splashed material; *also* **:** a spot or daub from or as if from splashed liquid **2 :** the sound or action of splashing **3 :** a vivid impression created esp. by ostentatious activity or appearance; *also* **:** an ostentatious display
splash·down \'splash-,daùn\ *n* **:** the landing of a manned spacecraft in the ocean
splat·ter \'splat-ər\ *vb* **:** SPATTER — **splatter** *n*
¹splay \'splā\ *vb* **1 :** to spread out : EXPAND **2 :** to make or become slanting
²splay *n* **:** SPREAD, EXPANSION
³splay *adj* **1 :** turned outward **2 :** AWKWARD, UNGAINLY
spleen \'splēn\ *n* **1 :** a vascular organ near the stomach of most vertebrates concerned esp. with the storage, formation, and destruction of blood cells **2 :** SPITE, MALICE
splen·did \'splen-dəd\ *adj* **1 :** possessing or displaying splendor: as **a :** SHINING, BRILLIANT **b :** SHOWY, MAGNIFICENT **2 :** ILLUSTRIOUS, GRAND **3 :** EXCELLENT — **splen·did·ly** *adv*
splen·dif·er·ous \splen-'dif-(ə-)rəs\ *adj* **1 :** SPLENDID **2 :** deceptively splendid — **splen·dif·er·ous·ly** *adv*
splen·dor \'splen-dər\ *n* **1 a :** great brightness or luster : BRILLIANCY **b :** sumptuous display or ceremonial : MAGNIFICENCE, POMP **2 :** something splendid or contributing to splendor — **splen·dor·ous** \-d(ə-)rəs\ *adj*
sple·net·ic \spli-'net-ik\ *adj* **1 :** SPLENIC **2 :** marked by bad temper, malevolence, or spite — **sple·net·i·cal·ly** \spli-'net-i-k(ə-)lē\ *adv*
sple·nic \'splen-ik\ *adj* **:** of, relating to, or located in the spleen
¹splice \'splīs\ *vt* **1 :** to unite (as two ropes) by weaving the strands together **2 :** to unite (as rails or timbers) by lapping the ends together and making them fast — **splic·er** *n*
²splice *n* **:** a joining or joint made by splicing
¹splint \'splint\ *n* **1 :** a thin strip of wood interwoven with others in caning **2 :** SPLINTER **3 :** material or a device used to protect and immobilize a body part (as a broken arm)
²splint *vt* **:** to support and immobilize with or as if with a splint
¹splin·ter \'splint-ər\ *n* **1 a :** a thin piece split or torn off lengthwise : SLIVER **b :** a small jagged particle **2 :** a group or faction broken away from a parent body — **splinter** *adj* — **splin·tery** \'splint-ə-rē\ *adj*
²splinter *vb* **:** to divide or break into splinters
¹split \'split\ *vb* **split; split·ting 1 a :** to divide lengthwise usu. along a grain or seam or by layers : CLEAVE **b :** to separate the parts of by interposing something **2 a :** to tear or break apart : BURST **b :** to affect as if by breaking up or tearing apart : SHATTER **3 :** to divide into parts or portions: as **a :** to divide between individuals : SHARE **b :** to divide into factions, parties, or groups **c :** to mark (a ballot) or cast (a vote) for candidates of different parties **d :** to divide (stock) by issuing a larger number of shares to existing shareholders usu. without increase in total par value — **split·ter** *n*
²split *n* **1 :** a product or result of splitting: as **a :** a narrow break made by or as if by splitting : CRACK **b :** a part split off or made thin by splitting **c :** a group or faction formed by splitting **2 :** the act or process of splitting : DIVISION; *esp* **:** a dividing into divergent or antagonistic elements **3 :** the feat of lowering oneself to the floor or leaping into the air with the legs extended in a straight line and in opposite directions
³split *adj* **:** divided by or as if by splitting; *also* **:** prepared for use by splitting
splotch \'splăch\ *n* **:** BLOTCH, SPOT — **splotch** *vt* — **splotchy** \'splăch-ē\ *adj*
¹splurge \'splərj\ *n* **:** a showy display
²splurge *vi* **1 :** to make a splurge **2 :** to indulge oneself extravagantly
¹splut·ter \'splət-ər\ *n* **1 :** a confused noise (as of hasty speaking) **2 :** a splashing or sputtering sound — **splut·tery** \'splət-ə-rē\ *adj*
²splutter *vb* **1 :** to make a noise as if spitting **2 :** to speak or utter hastily and confusedly — **splut·ter·er** *n*
¹spoil \'spȯil\ *n* **1 a :** plunder taken from an enemy in war or a victim in robbery : LOOT **b :** public offices made the property of a successful party — usu. used in pl. **c :** something won usu. by effort or skill : PREY **2 :** PLUNDERING, SPOLIATION
²spoil *vb* **spoiled** \'spȯild, 'spȯilt\ *or* **spoilt** \'spȯilt\; **spoil·ing 1 :** DESPOIL, PILLAGE, ROB **2 a :** to damage seriously : RUIN **b :** to impair the quality or effect of **c :** to decay or lose freshness, value, or usefulness usu. through being kept too long **3 :** to damage the disposition or character of by pampering **4 :** to have an eager desire — **spoil·er** *n*
spoil·age \'spȯi-lij\ *n* **1 :** the act or process of spoiling **2 :** something spoiled or wasted **3 :** loss by spoilage
¹spoke \'spōk\ *past of* SPEAK
²spoke *n* **1 a :** one of the small radiating bars inserted in the hub of a wheel to support the rim **b :** something resembling the spoke of a wheel **2 :** a rung of a ladder
³spoke *vt* **:** to furnish with or as if with spokes
a manner — used in combination
spokes·man \'spōks-mən\ *n* **:** a person who speaks as a representative of another person or of a group
spo·ken \'spō-kən\ *adj* **1 a :** delivered by word of mouth : ORAL **b :** used in speaking : UTTERED **2 :** speaking in (such)
spokes·wom·an \-,wùm-ən\ *n* **:** a female spokesman
spo·li·a·tion \,spō-lē-'ā-shən\ *n* **:** the act of plundering : the state of being plundered esp. in war — **spo·li·a·tor** \'spō-lē-,āt-ər\ *n*
¹sponge \'spənj\ *n* **1 a :** an elastic porous mass of interlacing horny fibers that forms the internal skeleton of various marine animals and is able when wetted to absorb water; *also* **:** a piece of this material or of a porous rubber or cellulose product of similar properties used esp. for cleaning **b :** any of a phylum of lowly aquatic animals that are essentially double-walled cell colonies and permanently attached as adults **2 :** one who lives upon others : SPONGER
²sponge *vb* **1 a :** to cleanse, wipe, or moisten with or as if with a sponge **b :** to erase or destroy with or as if with a sponge **2 :** to absorb with or as if with or like a sponge **3 :** to get something from or live on another by imposing on hospitality or good nature — **spong·er** *n*
sponge cake *n* **:** a cake made without shortening
spongy \'spən-jē\ *adj* **:** resembling a sponge in appearance or absorbency : not firm or solid — **spong·i·ness** *n*

¹spon·sor \'spän(t)-sər\ *n* **1 :** a person who takes the responsibility for some other person or thing **2 :** GODPARENT **3 :** a person or an organization that pays for or plans and carries out a project or activity; *esp* **:** one that pays the cost of a radio or television program usu. in return for limited advertising time during its course — **spon·sor·ship** \-ˌship\ *n*
²sponsor *vt* **:** to be or stand sponsor for
spon·ta·ne·i·ty \ˌspänt-ə-'nē-ət-ē, -'nā-\ *n* **1 :** the quality or state of being spontaneous **2 :** spontaneous action or movement
spon·ta·ne·ous \spän-'tā-nē-əs\ *adj* **1 :** done, said, or produced freely and naturally **2 :** acting or taking place without external force, cause, or influence — **spon·ta·ne·ous·ly** *adv*
spontaneous combustion *n* **:** a bursting into flame of combustible material through heat produced within itself by chemical action (as oxidation)
¹spoof \'spüf\ *vt* **1 :** DECEIVE, HOAX **2 :** to make good-natured fun of
²spoof *n* **1 :** HOAX, DECEPTION **2 :** a light amiable takeoff
spook \'spük\ *n* **:** GHOST, SPECTER
spooky \'spü-kē\ *adj* **1 :** relating to, resembling, or suggesting spooks **2 :** NERVOUS, SKITTISH — **spook·i·ness** *n*
spool \'spül\ *n* **1 :** a cylinder which has a rim or ridge at each end and usu. a hollow center and on which thread, wire, or tape is wound **2 :** material wound on a spool
¹spoon \'spün\ *n* **1 :** an implement that consists of a small shallow bowl with a handle and is used esp. in eating and cooking **2 :** something that resembles a spoon in shape (as a usu. metal or shell fishing lure)
²spoon *vb* **1 :** to take up and usu. transfer in or as if in a spoon **2 :** to make love esp. in a silly demonstrative way
spoon·ful \'spün-ˌfu̇l\ *n*, *pl* **spoonfuls** \-ˌfu̇lz\ *or* **spoons·ful** \'spünz-ˌfu̇l\ **:** as much as a spoon can hold
spoor \'spu̇(ə)r, 'spō(ə)r\ *n* **:** a track or trail esp. of a wild animal
spo·rad·ic \spə-'rad-ik\ *adj* **:** occurring occasionally, singly, or in scattered instances **:** SEPARATE, ISOLATED — **spo·rad·i·cal·ly** \-'rad-i-k(ə-)lē\ *adv*
spore \'spō(ə)r\ *n* **:** a primitive usu. one-celled resistant or reproductive body produced by plants and some lower animals — **spored** \'spōrd\ *adj* — **spo·rif·er·ous** \spə-'rif-(ə-)rəs\ *adj*
spor·ran \'spȯr-ən\ *n* **:** a pouch of skin with the hair or fur on that is worn in front of the kilt by Highlanders in full dress
¹sport \'spōrt\ *vb* **1 a :** to amuse oneself **:** FROLIC **b :** to engage in a sport **2 :** to speak or act in jest or mockingly **:** TRIFLE **3 :** to make usu. ostentatious display of **:** show off **4 :** to deviate or vary abruptly from type **:** MUTATE
²sport *n* **1 a :** a source of diversion **:** RECREATION **b :** physical activity engaged in for pleasure **2 a :** PLEASANTRY, JEST **b :** MOCKERY, DERISION **3 a :** something tossed or driven about in or as if in play **b :** LAUGHINGSTOCK, BUTT **4 a :** SPORTSMAN **b :** a person devoted to a gay easy life; *also* **:** one inclined to be venturesome **5 :** an individual exhibiting a sudden deviation from type usu. as a result of mutation
³sport *or* **sports** \'spōrts\ *adj* **:** of, relating to, or suitable for sport
sport·ful \'spōrt-fəl\ *adj* **1 :** PLAYFUL, FROLICSOME **2 :** done in sport — **sport·ful·ly** \-fə-lē\ *adv* — **sport·ful·ness** *n*
sport·ive \'spōrt-iv\ *adj* **:** PLAYFUL, FROLICSOME, MERRY — **sport·ive·ly** *adv* — **sport·ive·ness** *n*
sports·man \'spōrts-mən\ *n* **1 :** a person who engages in or is interested in sports and esp. outdoor sports **2 :** a person who is fair and generous and a good loser and a graceful winner — **sports·man·like** *adj* — **sports·man·ly** \-lē\ *adj* — **sports·man·ship** \-ˌship\ *n* — **sports·wom·an** \-ˌwu̇m-ən\ *n*
sports·wear \-ˌwa(ə)r\ *n* **:** clothes suitable for engaging in or watching sports
sporty \'spōrt-ē\ *adj* **1 :** characteristic of a sportsman **2 a :** notably gay or dissipated **:** FAST **b :** FLASHY, SHOWY **3 :** SPORT — **sport·i·ly** \'spōrt-ᵊl-ē\ *adv* — **sport·i·ness** \'spōrt-ē-nəs\ *n*
¹spot \'spät\ *n* **1 :** a blemish or stain on character or reputation **:** FAULT **2 a :** a small area visibly different (as in color, finish, or material) from the surrounding area **b :** an area marred or marked (as by dirt); *also* **:** a circumscribed surface lesion of disease (as measles) **3 a :** a small quantity or amount **b :** a small or particular place or extent of space **4 a :** a particular position (as in an organization or on a program) **b :** a position usu. of difficulty or embarrassment
²spot *vb* **spot·ted**; **spot·ting** **1 :** to mark or mar with or as if with spots **:** STAIN, BLEMISH **2 :** to single out **:** IDENTIFY, DETECT; *also* **:** to locate precisely **3 a :** to lie or occur at intervals in or on **b :** to place at intervals or in a desired spot **4 :** to remove spots from — **spot·ta·ble** *adj*
³spot *adj* **1 :** being, originating, or done on the spot or in or for a particular spot **2 a :** paid out upon delivery **b :** broadcast between scheduled programs **3 :** made at random or restricted to a few places or instances
spot-check \'spät-ˌchek\ *vb* **:** to sample or investigate quickly or at random **:** make a spot check
spot·less \'spät-ləs\ *adj* **:** free from spot or blemish **:** immaculately clean or pure — **spot·less·ly** *adv*
¹spot·light \'spät-ˌlīt\ *n* **1 a :** a projected spot of light used to illuminate something (as a person on the stage) brilliantly **b :** conspicuous public notice **2 :** a light designed to direct a narrow intense beam of light on a small area
²spotlight *vt* **:** to illuminate with or as if with a spotlight
spot·ted \'spät-əd\ *adj* **1 a :** marked with spots **b :** SULLIED, TARNISHED **2 :** accompanied by an eruption
spot·ter \'spät-ər\ *n* **1 :** one that makes, applies, or removes spots **2 :** one that keeps watch **:** OBSERVER; *esp* **:** a civilian watcher whose duty is to report all approaching airplanes
spot·ty \'spät-ē\ *adj* **1 :** marked with spots **:** SPOTTED **2 :** lacking uniformity esp. in quality **:** UNEVEN — **spot·ti·ly** \'spät-ᵊl-ē\ *adv* — **spot·ti·ness** \'spät-ē-nəs\ *n*
spouse \'spau̇s\ *n* **:** a married person **:** HUSBAND, WIFE
¹spout \'spau̇t\ *vb* **1 :** to eject (as liquid) in a stream or jet; *also* **:** to release material in this manner **2 :** to speak or utter readily, volubly, and at length **3 :** to issue with force or in a jet **:** SPURT — **spout·er** *n*
²spout *n* **1 :** a tube, pipe, or hole through which liquid spouts **2 :** a jet of liquid; *esp* **:** WATERSPOUT
¹sprain \'sprān\ *n* **1 :** a sudden or violent twist or wrench of a joint with stretching or tearing of ligaments **2 :** a sprained condition
²sprain *vt* **:** to subject to sprain
sprat \'sprat\ *n* **:** a small European herring closely related to the common herring; *also* **:** a small or young herring
sprawl \'sprȯl\ *vb* **1 :** to creep or clamber awkwardly **2 :** to lie or sit with arms and legs spread out **3 :** to spread or cause to spread out irregularly or awkwardly — **sprawl** *n*
¹spray \'sprā\ *n* **:** a usu. flowering branch or shoot or an arrangement of these
²spray *n* **1 :** water flying in small drops or particles blown from waves or thrown up by a waterfall **2 a :** a jet of vapor or finely divided liquid (as from an atomizer) **b :** a device (as an atomizer or sprayer) by which a spray is dispersed or applied
³spray *vb* **1 :** to scatter or let fall in a spray **2 :** to project spray on or into — **spray·er** *n*
¹spread \'spred\ *vb* **spread**; **spread·ing** **1 a :** to open or expand over a larger area **b :** to stretch out **:** EXTEND **2 a :** SCATTER, STREW **b :** to distribute over a period or among a group **c :** to apply on a surface **d :** COVER, OVERLAY **e** (1) **:** to prepare or furnish for dining **:** SET (2) **:** SERVE **3 a :** to become or cause to become disseminated or widely known **b :** to extend the range or incidence of **4 :** to stretch or move apart — **spread·er** *n*

²**spread** *n* **1 a :** the act or process of spreading **b :** extent of spreading **2 :** something spread out: as **a :** EXPANSE **b :** a prominent display in a periodical **3 :** something spread on or over a surface: as **a :** a food to be spread on bread or crackers **b :** a sumptuous meal **:** FEAST **c :** a cloth cover for a table or bed **4 :** distance between two points **:** GAP
spree \'sprē\ *n* **:** an unrestrained indulgence in or outburst of an activity; *esp* **:** a drunken revel
sprig \'sprig\ *n* **:** a small shoot **:** TWIG
spright·ly \'sprīt-lē\ *adj* **:** marked by a gay lightness and liveliness — **spright·li·ness** *n*
¹**spring** \'spriŋ\ *vb* **sprang** \'spraŋ\ *or* **sprung** \'sprəŋ\; **sprung**; **spring·ing** \'spriŋ-iŋ\ **1 a** (1) **:** DART, SHOOT (2) **:** to be resilient or elastic; *also* **:** to move by elastic force **b :** to become warped **2 :** to issue with speed and force or as a stream **3 a :** to grow as a plant **b :** to issue by birth or descent **c :** to come into being **:** ARISE **4 a :** to make a leap or series of leaps **b :** to jump up suddenly **5 :** to stretch out in height **:** RISE **6 a :** SPLIT, CRACK **b :** to undergo the opening of (a leak) **7 :** to cause to operate suddenly **8 :** to produce or disclose suddenly or unexpectedly — **spring·er** \'spriŋ-ər\ *n*
²**spring** *n* **1 a :** a source of supply; *esp* **:** a source of water issuing from the ground **b :** an ultimate source esp. of action or motion **2 a :** the season between winter and summer **b :** a time or season of growth or development **3 :** an elastic body or device that recovers its original shape when released after being distorted **4 a :** the act or an instance of leaping up or forward **:** BOUND **b :** capacity for springing **:** RESILIENCE
spring·board \'spriŋ-ˌbōrd\ *n* **1 :** a flexible board usu. secured at one end and used for gymnastic stunts or diving **2 :** a point of departure
springe \'sprinj\ *n* **:** SNARE, TRAP
spring·tide \'spriŋ-ˌtīd\ *n* **:** SPRINGTIME
spring tide *n* **:** a greater than usual tide occurring at each new moon and full moon
spring·time \'spriŋ-ˌtīm\ *n* **:** the season of spring
springy \'spriŋ-ē\ *adj* **:** having an elastic quality **:** RESILIENT — **spring·i·ness** *n*
¹**sprin·kle** \'spriŋ-kəl\ *vb* **sprin·kled**; **sprin·kling** \-k(ə-)liŋ\ **1 :** to scatter in drops or particles **2 a :** to scatter over or at intervals in or among **b :** to wet lightly **3 :** to rain lightly in scattered drops — **sprin·kler** \-k(ə-)lər\ *n*
²**sprinkle** *n* **1 :** the act or an instance of sprinkling; *esp* **:** a light rain **2 :** SPRINKLING
sprin·kling \'spriŋ-kliŋ\ *n* **:** a limited quantity or amount
¹**sprint** \'sprint\ *vi* **:** to run at top speed esp. for a short distance — **sprint·er** *n*
²**sprint** *n* **1 :** the act or an instance of sprinting **2 :** DASH 6b
sprite \'sprīt\ *n* **1 :** a disembodied spirit **2 a :** ELF, FAIRY **b :** an elfish person
sprock·et \'spräk-ət\ *n* **1 :** a projection on the rim of a wheel shaped so as to interlock with the links of a chain **2 :** a wheel having sprockets
¹**sprout** \'spraůt\ *vb* **1 :** to send out new growth **2 :** to grow rapidly **3 :** to cause to sprout
²**sprout** *n* **:** SHOOT 1a; *esp* **:** a young shoot (as from a seed)
¹**spruce** \'sprüs\ *n* **:** any of a genus of evergreen trees of the pine family with a conical head of dense foliage and with soft light wood; *also* **:** its wood
²**spruce** *adj* **:** neat or smart in appearance **:** TRIM
³**spruce** *vb* **:** to make or make oneself spruce
sprung *past of* SPRING
spry \'sprī\ *adj* **:** vigorously active **:** CHIPPER, NIMBLE, BRISK — **spry·ly** *adv* — **spry·ness** *n*
spud \'spəd\ *n* **1 :** a tool or device (as for digging, lifting, or cutting) combining the characteristics of spade and chisel **2 :** POTATO
¹**spume** \'spyüm\ *n* **:** frothy matter on liquids **:** FOAM, SCUM — **spu·mous** \'spyü-məs\ *adj* — **spumy** \'spyü-mē\ *adj*
²**spume** *vi* **:** FROTH, FOAM
spun *past of* SPIN
spunk \'spəŋk\ *n* **:** SPIRIT, PLUCK
spunky \'spəŋ-kē\ *adj* **:** full of spunk **:** SPIRITED — **spunk·i·ly** \-kə-lē\ *adv* — **spunk·i·ness** \-kē-nəs\ *n*
¹**spur** \'spər\ *n* **1 a :** a pointed device secured to a rider's heel and used to urge the horse **b** *pl* **:** recognition for achievement **2 :** a goad to action **:** STIMULUS **3 :** a stiffly projecting part or process (as on the leg of a cock or on some flowers) **4 :** a ridge that extends laterally from a mountain **5 :** a railroad track diverging from a main line — **on the spur of the moment :** on hasty impulse
²**spur** *vb* **spurred**; **spur·ring** **1 :** to urge a horse on with spurs **2 :** INCITE, STIMULATE
spurge \'spərj\ *n* **:** any of a family of mostly shrubby plants with a bitter milky juice and often showy bracts surrounding insignificant flowers
spu·ri·ous \'spyůr-ē-əs\ *adj* **:** not genuine or authentic **:** FALSE, COUNTERFEIT — **spu·ri·ous·ly** *adv* — **spu·ri·ous·ness** *n*
¹**spurn** \'spərn\ *vt* **1 :** to kick aside **2 :** to reject or thrust aside with disdain or contempt — **spurn·er** *n*
²**spurn** *n* **1 :** KICK **2 :** disdainful rejection
spurred \'spərd\ *adj* **1 :** wearing spurs **2 :** having one or more spurs
¹**spurt** \'spərt\ *n* **:** a brief burst of increased effort or activity
²**spurt** *vi* **:** to make a spurt
³**spurt** *vb* **1 :** to gush forth **:** SPOUT **2 :** SQUIRT
⁴**spurt** *n* **:** a sudden gush **:** JET
sput·nik \'spůt-nik, 'spət-\ *n* **:** SATELLITE 2b
¹**sput·ter** \'spət-ər\ *vb* **1 :** to spit or squirt particles of food or saliva noisily from the mouth **2 :** to speak or utter hastily or explosively in confusion or excitement **3 :** to make explosive popping sounds — **sput·ter·er** *n*
²**sputter** *n* **:** the act or sound of sputtering
spu·tum \'sp(y)üt-əm\ *n, pl* **spu·ta** \-ə\ **:** material expectorated and made up of saliva and mucous discharges from the respiratory passages
¹**spy** \'spī\ *vb* **spied**; **spy·ing** **1 :** to watch, inspect, or examine secretly **:** act as a spy **2 :** to catch sight of **:** SEE
²**spy** *n, pl* **spies** **1 :** one that watches the conduct of others esp. in secret **2 :** a person who tries secretly to obtain information for one country in the territory of another usu. hostile country
spy·glass \'spī-ˌglas\ *n* **:** a small telescope
squab \'skwäb\ *n, pl* **squabs** *or* **squab :** a fledgling bird; *esp* **:** a fledgling pigeon about four weeks old
¹**squab·ble** \'skwäb-əl\ *n* **:** a noisy quarrel usu. over trifles
²**squabble** *vi* **squab·bled**; **squab·bling** \'skwäb-(ə-)liŋ\ **:** to quarrel noisily and to no purpose **:** WRANGLE
squad \'skwäd\ *n* **1 :** a small organized group of military personnel; *esp* **:** a tactical unit that can be easily directed in the field **2 :** a small group engaged in a common effort or occupation
squad·ron \'skwäd-rən\ *n* **:** any of several units of military organization
squal·id \'skwäl-əd\ *adj* **1 :** marked by filthiness and degradation from neglect or poverty **2 :** morally debased **:** SORDID — **squal·id·ly** *adv* — **squal·id·ness** *n*
¹**squall** \'skwȯl\ *vb* **:** to cry out raucously **:** SCREAM
²**squall** *n* **1 :** a raucous cry **2 :** SQUAWK
³**squall** *n* **1 :** a sudden violent wind often with rain or snow **2 :** a short-lived commotion
squally \'skwȯ-lē\ *adj* **:** marked by squalls **:** GUSTY, STORMY
squal·or \'skwäl-ər\ *n* **:** the quality or state of being squalid
squan·der \'skwän-dər\ *vb* **squan·dered**; **squan·der·ing** \-d(ə-)riŋ\ **:** to spend extravagantly or wastefully
¹**square** \'skwa(ə)r\ *n* **1 :** an instrument having at least one right angle and two straight edges used to lay out or test right

angles 2 : a rectangle with all four sides equal 3 : any of the quadrilateral spaces marked out on a board for playing games 4 : the product of a number multiplied by itself 5 a : an open place or area formed at the meeting of two or more streets b : BLOCK 5b, 5c

[2]**square** *adj* 1 a : having four equal sides and four right angles b : forming a right angle 2 : multiplied by itself 3 a : of a shape suggesting strength and solidity b : rectangular and equilateral in section c : having a rectangular rather than curving outline 4 a : converted from a linear unit into a square unit of area having the same length of side b : being of a specified length in each of two equal dimensions 5 a : exactly adjusted : well made b : JUST, FAIR c : leaving no balance : SETTLED d : TIED e : SUBSTANTIAL, SATISFYING — **square·ly** *adv* — **square·ness** *n*

[3]**square** *vb* 1 : to make square : form with four equal sides and right angles or with right angles and straight lines or with flat surfaces 2 : to bring to a right angle 3 a : to multiply (a number) by itself b : to find a square equal in area to 4 : to agree or make agree : HARMONIZE 5 : BALANCE, SETTLE

square dance *n* : a dance for four couples who form a hollow square — **square dancer** *n* — **square dancing** *n*

square–rigged \ˈskwa(ə)r-ˈrigd\ *adj* : having the principal sails extended on yards fastened to the masts horizontally and at their center

square root *n* : a factor of a number that when squared gives the number

[1]**squash** \ˈskwäsh\ *vb* 1 : to press or beat into a pulp or a flat mass : CRUSH 2 : to put down : SUPPRESS, SQUELCH

[2]**squash** *n* 1 : the sudden fall of a heavy soft body or the sound of such a fall 2 : a crushed mass 3 : SQUASH RACQUETS

[3]**squash** *n, pl* **squash·es** *or* **squash** : a fruit of any of various widely grown plants of the gourd family that are used esp. as vegetables; *also* : a plant that bears squashes

squash racquets *n* : a game played in a 4-wall court with a racket and a rubber ball

squashy \ˈskwäsh-ē\ *adj* : easily squashed : SOFT

[1]**squat** \ˈskwät\ *vb* **squat·ted**; **squat·ting** 1 : to sit or cause (oneself) to sit on one's haunches or heels 2 : to occupy land as a squatter 3 : CROUCH, COWER

[2]**squat** *n* 1 : the act of squatting 2 : a squatting posture

[3]**squat** *adj* 1 : CROUCHING 2 : low to the ground; *also* : being short and thick — **squat·ly** *adv* — **squat·ness** *n*

squat·ter \ˈskwät-ər\ *n* 1 : one that squats 2 a : one that settles on land without right or title or payment of rent b : one that settles on public land under government regulation with the purpose of acquiring title

squat·ty \ˈskwät-ē\ *adj* : SQUAT, THICKSET

squaw \ˈskwȯ\ *n* : an American Indian woman

[1]**squawk** \ˈskwȯk\ *vi* 1 : to utter a harsh abrupt scream 2 : to complain or protest loudly or vehemently — **squawk·er** *n*

[2]**squawk** *n* 1 : a harsh abrupt scream 2 : a noisy complaint

[1]**squeak** \ˈskwēk\ *vb* 1 : to make a short shrill cry or noise 2 : to pass, succeed, or win by a narrow margin

[2]**squeak** *n* 1 : a sharp shrill cry or sound 2 : ESCAPE — **squeaky** \ˈskwē-kē\ *adj*

[1]**squeal** \ˈskwēl\ *vb* 1 : to make a shrill cry or noise 2 a : to turn informer b : COMPLAIN, PROTEST 3 : to utter with or as if with a squeal — **squeal·er** *n*

[2]**squeal** *n* : a shrill sharp cry or noise

squea·mish \ˈskwē-mish\ *adj* 1 a : easily nauseated : QUEASY b : affected with nausea : NAUSEATED 2 a : easily shocked or disgusted : PRUDISH b : excessively fastidious or scrupulous in conduct or belief — **squea·mish·ly** *adv* — **squea·mish·ness** *n*

squee·gee \ˈskwē-ˌjē\ *n* : a blade of leather or rubber set on a handle and used for spreading or wiping liquid material on, across, or off a surface (as a window) — **squeegee** *vt*

[1]**squeeze** \ˈskwēz\ *vb* 1 a : to exert pressure esp. on opposite sides of : COMPRESS b : to extract or emit under pressure c : to force or thrust by compression : CROWD 2 a : to extort money, goods, or services from b : to cause hardship to 3 : to gain or win by a narrow margin — **squeez·er** *n*

[2]**squeeze** *n* 1 a : an act or instance of squeezing : COMPRESSION b : HANDCLASP; *also* : EMBRACE 2 : financial pressure caused by narrowing margins (as between costs and selling price) or by shortages

[1]**squelch** \ˈskwelch\ *n* 1 : a sound of or as if of semiliquid matter under suction 2 : a retort that silences an opponent

[2]**squelch** *vb* 1 a : to fall or stamp on so as to crush b : to completely suppress : QUELL, SILENCE 2 : to emit or cause to emit a sucking sound 3 : to splash through water, slush, or mire — **squelch·er** *n*

squib \ˈskwib\ *n* 1 a : a small firecracker b : a broken firecracker that burns out with a fizz 2 : a short humorous or satiric writing or speech

squid \ˈskwid\ *n, pl* **squid** *or* **squids** : any of numerous 10-armed mollusks with a long tapered body, a fin on each side, and usu. a slender internal chitinous support

squint \ˈskwint\ *vi* 1 a : to look or peer obliquely b : to be cross-eyed 2 : to look or peer with eyes partly closed — **squint** *n or adj* — **squinty** \-ē\ *adj*

[1]**squire** \ˈskwī(ə)r\ *n* 1 : one who bears the shield or armor of a knight 2 a : a male attendant on a great personage b : GALLANT, ESCORT 3 a : a member of the British gentry ranking below a knight and above a gentleman b : an owner of a country estate

[2]**squire** *vt* : to attend as a squire or escort

squirm \ˈskwərm\ *vi* : to twist about like an eel or a worm — **squirmy** \ˈskwər-mē\ *adj*

squir·rel \ˈskwər(-ə)l\ *n, pl* **squirrels** *also* **squirrel** 1 : any of various small or medium-sized rodents; *esp* : one with a long bushy tail and strong hind legs adapted to leaping from branch to branch 2 : the fur of a squirrel

[1]**squirt** \ˈskwərt\ *vb* : to come forth, drive, or eject in a sudden rapid stream : SPURT

[2]**squirt** *n* 1 a : an instrument (as a syringe) for squirting a liquid b : a small quick stream : JET c : the action of squirting 2 : an impudent youngster

[1]**stab** \ˈstab\ *n* 1 : a wound produced by a pointed weapon 2 : a thrust of a pointed weapon 3 : EFFORT, TRY

[2]**stab** *vb* **stabbed**; **stab·bing** 1 : to wound or pierce by the thrust of a pointed weapon 2 : THRUST, DRIVE 3 : to thrust or give a wound with or as if with a pointed weapon — **stab·ber** *n*

sta·bil·i·ty \stə-ˈbil-ət-ē\ *n, pl* **-ties** : the quality, state, or degree of being stable

sta·bi·lize \ˈstā-bə-ˌlīz\ *vb* : to make or become stable, steadfast, or firm; *also* : to hold steady — **sta·bi·li·za·tion** \ˌstā-bə-lə-ˈzā-shən\ *n*

sta·bi·liz·er \ˈstā-bə-ˌlī-zər\ *n* : one that stabilizes; *esp* : a fixed surface for stabilizing the motion of an airplane

[1]**sta·ble** \ˈstā-bəl\ *n* 1 : a building in which domestic animals are sheltered and fed; *esp* : such a building having stalls or compartments 2 a : the racehorses of one owner b : a group of athletes (as boxers) under one management — **sta·ble·man** \-mən, -ˌman\ *n*

[2]**stable** *vb* **sta·bled**; **sta·bling** \-b(ə-)liŋ\ : to put, keep, or live in or as if in a stable

[3]**stable** *adj* 1 a : firmly established : FIXED, STEADFAST b : not changing or fluctuating : UNVARYING c : ENDURING, PERMANENT 2 : steady in purpose : CONSTANT 3 a : designed so as to develop forces that restore the original condition when disturbed from a condition of equilibrium or steady motion b : able to resist alteration in chemical, physical, or biological properties — **sta·bly** \-b(ə-)lē\ *adv*

sta·bling *n* : accommodation for animals in a building
stac·ca·to \stə-'kät-ō\ *adj* **1 a** : cut short or apart in performing : DISCONNECTED **b** : marked by short clear-cut playing or singing of tones or chords **2** : ABRUPT, DISJOINTED — **staccato** *adv* — **staccato** *n*
¹stack \'stak\ *n* **1** : a large usu. conical pile (as of hay, straw, or grain) **2** : an orderly pile of objects usu. one on top of the other **3** : a vertical pipe for carrying off smoke or vapor : CHIMNEY, SMOKESTACK **4 a** : a rack with shelves for storing books **b** *pl* : the part of a library in which books are stored in racks
²stack *vb* : to arrange in or form a stack : PILE — **stack·er** *n*
sta·di·um \'stād-ē-əm\ *n* : a large usu. unroofed building with tiers of seats for spectators at sports events
¹staff \'staf\ *n, pl* **staffs** \'stafs\ *or* **staves** \'stāvz, 'stāvz\ **1 a** : a pole, stick, rod, or bar used as a support or as a sign of authority; *also* : the long handle of a weapon (as a lance or pike) **b** : CLUB, CUDGEL **2** : something that props or sustains **3** : the five horizontal lines with their spaces on which music is written **4** *pl staffs* **a** : a group of persons serving as assistants to or employees under a chief **b** : a group of officers or aides appointed to assist a civil executive or commanding officer **c** : military officers not eligible for operational command but having administrative duties
²staff *vt* : to supply with a staff or with workers
staff sergeant *n* : a noncommissioned officer ranking in the army next below a sergeant first class and in the air force next below a technical sergeant
¹stag \'stag\ *n, pl* **stag** *or* **stags** **1** : an adult male of various large deer **2 a** : a social gathering of men only **b** : a man who attends a dance or party unaccompanied by a woman
²stag *adj* : restricted to men : intended or suitable for a gathering of men only — **stag** *adv*
¹stage \'stāj\ *n* **1** : one of the horizontal levels into which a structure is divisible: as **a** : a floor of a building **b** : a shelf or layer esp. as one of a series **c** : any of the levels attained by a river above an arbitrary zero point **2** : a raised platform on which an orator may speak or a play may be presented **3 a** : a center of attention : scene of action **b** : the theatrical profession or art **4** : a division or a dividing point: as **a** : a stopping place esp. for a stagecoach providing fresh horses and refreshments **b** : the distance between stopping places in a journey **c** : a degree of advance attained (as in a process or undertaking) **d** : one complete process or step in a sequential or recurrent activity **5** : STAGECOACH **6** : a propulsion unit in a rocket with its own fuel and containers — **on the stage** : in or into the acting profession
²stage *vt* : to produce or show publicly on or as if on the stage
stage·coach \-ˌkōch\ *n* : a horse-drawn passenger and mail coach running on a regular schedule between established stops
stage·craft \-ˌkraft\ *n* : the effective management of theatrical devices or techniques
stage·hand \'stāj-ˌhand\ *n* : a stage worker who handles scenery, properties, or lights
stage·struck \'stāj-ˌstrək\ *adj* : fascinated by the stage
¹stag·ger \'stag-ər\ *vb* **stag·gered**; **stag·ger·ing** \'stag-(ə-)riŋ\ **1 a** : to move unsteadily from side to side as if about to fall : REEL **b** : to cause to reel or totter **2 a** : to begin to doubt and waver : become less confident **b** : to cause to doubt, waver, or hesitate **3** : to place or arrange in a zigzag or alternate but regular way — **stag·ger·er** \'stag-ər-ər\ *n*
²stagger *n* **1** *pl* : an abnormal condition of domestic mammals and birds associated with damage to the central nervous system and marked by incoordination and a reeling unsteady gait **2** : a reeling or unsteady gait or stance
stag·ing \'stā-jiŋ\ *n* **1** : SCAFFOLDING **2** : the putting of a play on the stage
stag·nant \'stag-nənt\ *adj* **1** : not flowing in a current or stream : MOTIONLESS; *also* : STALE **2** : DULL, INACTIVE — **stag·nan·cy** \-nən-sē\ *n* — **stag·nant·ly** *adv*
stag·nate \'stag-ˌnāt\ *vi* : to be or become stagnant — **stag·na·tion** \stag-'nā-shən\ *n*
stagy \'stā-jē\ *adj* : of or resembling the stage; *esp* : theatrical or artificial in manner
¹staid \'stād\ *adj* **1** : SETTLED, FIXED **2** : GRAVE, SEDATE — **staid·ly** *adv* — **staid·ness** *n*
²staid *past of* STAY
¹stain \'stān\ *vb* **1** : to soil or discolor esp. in spots **2** : to suffuse with color (as by dyeing) : TINGE **3 a** : to taint with guilt, vice, or corruption **b** : to bring reproach on — **stain·a·ble** *adj* — **stain·er** *n*
²stain *n* **1** : a soiled or discolored spot **2** : a taint of guilt : STIGMA **3** : a preparation (as of dye or pigment) used in staining — **stain·less** \'stān-ləs\ *adj* — **stain·less·ly** *adv*
stainless steel *n* : steel alloyed with chromium and highly resistant to stain, rust, and corrosion
stair \'sta(ə)r\ *n* **1** : a series of steps or flights of steps for passing from one level to another — often used in pl. **2** : one step of a stairway
stair·case \-ˌkās\ *n* : a flight of stairs with the supporting framework, casing, and balusters
stair·way \-ˌwā\ *n* : one or more flights of stairs usu. with landings to pass from one level to another
¹stake \'stāk\ *n* **1** : a pointed piece (as of wood) driven or to be driven into the ground esp. as a marker or support **2 a** : a post to which a person is bound for execution by burning **b** : execution by burning at a stake **3 a** : something that is staked for gain or loss **b** : the prize in a contest **c** : an interest or share in a commercial venture **4** : GRUBSTAKE — **at stake** : at issue : in jeopardy
²stake *vt* **1 a** : to mark the limits of by stakes **b** : to tether to a stake **c** : to fasten up or support (as plants) with stakes **2 a** : BET, HAZARD **b** : to back financially; *esp* : GRUBSTAKE
sta·lac·tite \stə-'lak-ˌtīt\ *n* : a deposit of calcium carbonate resembling an icicle hanging from the roof or sides of a cavern
sta·lag·mite \stə-'lag-ˌmīt\ *n* : a deposit like an inverted stalactite found on the floor of a cave
¹stale \'stāl\ *adj* **1** : tasteless, unpleasant, or unwholesome from age **2** : tedious from familiarity **3** : impaired in vigor or effectiveness — **stale·ly** \'stāl-lē\ *adv* — **stale·ness** *n*
²stale *vb* : to make or become stale
¹stalk \'stȯk\ *vb* **1** : to hunt stealthily; *also* : to cover (an area) in stalking prey **2** : to walk with haughty or pompous bearing
²stalk *n* **1** : the act of stalking **2** : a stalking gait
³stalk *n* : a plant stem; *also* : any slender upright supporting or connecting part — **stalked** \'stȯkt\ *adj* — **stalk·less** \'stȯk-ləs\ *adj*
¹stall \'stȯl\ *n* **1 a** : a compartment for a domestic animal in a stable or barn **b** : a space set off (as for parking a motor vehicle) **2** : a seat in the chancel of a church with back and sides wholly or partly enclosed **3** : a booth, stand, or counter at which articles are displayed for sale
²stall *vb* **1** : to put into or keep in a stall **2** : to bring or come to a standstill unintentionally
³stall *n* : a ruse to deceive or delay
⁴stall *vb* : to hold off, divert, or delay by evasion or deception
stal·lion \'stal-yən\ *n* : a male horse
¹stal·wart \'stȯl-wərt\ *adj* **1** : STOUT, STURDY **2** : VALIANT, RESOLUTE — **stal·wart·ly** *adv* — **stal·wart·ness** *n*
²stalwart *n* **1** : a stalwart person **2** : an unwavering partisan (as in politics)
sta·men \'stā-mən\ *n* : an organ of a flower that produces pollen — **sta·mi·nate** \'stā-mə-nət, 'stam-ə-\ *adj*
stam·i·na \'stam-ə-nə\ *n* : VIGOR, ENDURANCE
¹stam·mer \'stam-ər\ *vb* **stam·mered**; **stam·mer·ing** \'stam-

(ə-)riŋ\ : to make or utter with involuntary stops and repetitions in speaking — **stam·mer·er** \-ər-ər\ *n*

²stammer *n* : an act or instance of stammering

¹stamp \'stamp; *1b & 2 are also* 'stämp\ *vb* **1 a :** to pound or crush with a heavy instrument **b :** to strike or beat forcibly with the bottom of the foot **c :** to extinguish or destroy by or as if by stamping with the foot **2 :** to walk heavily or noisily **3 a :** IMPRESS, IMPRINT **b :** to attach a stamp to **4 :** to form with a stamp or die **5 :** CHARACTERIZE — **stamp·er** *n*

²stamp *n* **1 :** a device or instrument for stamping **2 :** the impression or mark made by stamping **3 :** a distinctive character, indication, or mark **4 :** the act of stamping **5 :** a paper or a mark put on a thing to show that a required charge (as a tax) has been paid

¹stam·pede \stam-'pēd\ *n* **1 :** a wild headlong rush or flight of frightened animals **2 :** a mass movement of people at a common impulse

²stampede *vb* **1 :** to run away or cause (as cattle) to run away in panic **2 :** to act together or cause to act together suddenly and without thought

stance \'stan(t)s\ *n* **1 :** way of standing or being placed : POSTURE **2 :** intellectual or emotional attitude

stanch \'stònch, 'stänch\ *vt* : to stop the flowing of; *also* : to stop the flow of blood from (a wound) — **stanch·er** *n*

stan·chion \'stan-chən\ *n* : an upright bar, post, or support

¹stand \'stand\ *vb* **stood** \'stu̇d\; **stand·ing 1 a :** to support oneself on the feet in an erect position **b :** to be a specified height when fully erect **c :** to rise to one's feet **2 a :** to take up or maintain a usu. specified position or posture **b :** to maintain one's position **3 a :** to be firm and steadfast in support or opposition **b :** to be in a particular state or situation **4 :** to hold a course at sea **5 a :** to rest, remain, or set upright on a base or lower end **b :** to occupy a place or location **6 a :** to remain stationary or inactive **b :** to remain in effect **7 :** to exist in a definite form **8 a :** to endure or undergo successfully : BEAR, WITHSTAND **b :** to submit to **9 :** to perform the duty of **10 :** to pay for — **stand·er** *n* — **stand by :** to be or remain present, available, or loyal to — **stand for 1 :** to be a symbol for : REPRESENT **2 :** to put up with : PERMIT

²stand *n* **1 :** an act or instance of stopping or staying in one place: as **a :** a halt for defense or resistance **b :** a stop made to give a theatrical performance **2 a :** a place or post where one stands **b :** a position esp. with respect to an issue **3 a :** the place occupied by a witness testifying in court **b :** a tier of seats for spectators — usu. used in pl. **c :** a raised platform (as for a speaker) **4 :** a small often open-air structure for a small retail business **5 :** a support (as a rack or table) on or in which something may be placed **6 :** a group of plants growing in a continuous area

¹stan·dard \'stan-dərd\ *n* **1 a :** a figure adopted as an emblem by an organized body of people **b :** the personal flag of the ruler of a state **2 a :** something set up by authority or by general consent as a rule for measuring or as a model **b :** the basis of value in a monetary system **3 :** a structure that serves as a support

²standard *adj* **1 a :** constituting or conforming to a standard established by law or custom **b :** being sound and usable but not of special or the highest quality **2 :** regularly and widely used **3 :** having recognized and permanent value **4 :** substantially uniform and well established by usage in the speech and writing of the educated and widely recognized as acceptable and authoritative

stan·dard–bear·er \-ˌbar-ər\ *n* **1 :** one that bears a standard or banner **2 :** the leader of an organization or movement

stan·dard·ize \'stan-dər-ˌdīz\ *vt* : to compare with or bring into conformity with a standard — **stan·dard·i·za·tion** \ˌstan-dərd-ə-'zā-shən\ *n*

standard of living : the necessities, comforts, and luxuries that a person or group is accustomed to

standard time *n* : the time established by law or by general usage over a region or country

stand by *vi* **1 :** to be present; *also* : to remain apart or aloof **2 :** to be or to get ready to act

stand·by \'stan(d)-ˌbī\ *n* : one available or to be relied upon esp. in emergencies

stand·ee \stan-'dē\ *n* : one who occupies standing room

stand in *vi* : to act as a stand-in

stand–in \'stan-ˌdin\ *n* **1 :** someone employed to occupy an actor's place while lights and camera are readied **2 :** SUBSTITUTE

¹stand·ing \'stan-diŋ\ *adj* **1 :** upright on the feet or base : ERECT **2 a :** not flowing : STAGNANT **b :** remaining at the same level, degree, or amount for an indeterminate period **c :** continuing in existence or use indefinitely : PERMANENT **3 :** done from a standing position

²standing *n* **1 :** the action or position of one that stands **2 :** DURATION; *esp* : length of service or experience esp. as determining status **3 :** position or comparative rank (as in society, a profession, or a competitive activity); *also* : good reputation

stand·off \'stan-ˌdòf\ *n* **1 :** a standing off; *esp* : ALOOFNESS **2 a :** a counterbalancing effect **b :** TIE, DRAW, DEADLOCK

stand·off·ish \stan-'dò-fish\ *adj* : lacking cordiality

stand out *vi* **1 a :** to appear as if in relief : PROJECT **b :** to be prominent or conspicuous **2 :** to be stubborn in resolution or resistance

stand·pat \'stan(d)-ˌpat\ *adj* : stubbornly conservative — **stand·pat·ter** \-ˌpat-ər\ *n*

stand·pipe \-ˌpīp\ *n* : a high vertical pipe or reservoir for water used to deliver water at uniform pressure

stand·point \-ˌpòint\ *n* : a position from which objects or principles are viewed and according to which they are compared and judged

stand·still \-ˌstil\ *n* : a state marked by absence of motion or activity : STOP

stand up *vb* **1 :** to remain sound and intact **2 :** to fail to keep an appointment with — **stand up for :** DEFEND

stank *past of* STINK

stan·za \'stan-zə\ *n* : a division of a poem consisting of a series of lines arranged together in a usu. recurring pattern of meter and rhyme — **stan·za·ic** \stan-'zā-ik\ *adj*

staph·y·lo·coc·cus \ˌstaf-ə-lō-'käk-əs\ *n, pl* **-coc·ci** \-'käk-ˌ(s)ī, -(ˌ)(s)ē\ : any of various spherical bacteria including some that cause purulent infections

¹sta·ple \'stā-pəl\ *n* **1 :** a U-shaped piece of metal usu. with sharp points to be driven into a surface to hold something (as a hook, rope, or wire) **2 :** a U-shaped piece of thin wire to be driven through papers and bent over at the ends to fasten them together or to be driven through thin material to fasten it to something else

²staple *vt* **sta·pled; sta·pling** \-p(ə-)liŋ\ : to fasten with staples

³staple *n* **1 :** a place of supply : SOURCE **2 :** a chief commodity or product of a place **3 a :** something in widespread and constant use or demand **b :** the sustaining or principal element : SUBSTANCE **4 :** raw material **5 :** textile fiber (as wool or rayon) of relatively short length that when spun and twisted forms a yarn rather than a filament

⁴staple *adj* **1 :** used, needed, or enjoyed constantly usu. by many individuals **2 :** produced regularly or in large quantities **3 :** PRINCIPAL, CHIEF

sta·pler \'stā-plər\ *n* : a device that staples

¹star \'stär\ *n* **1 :** any natural luminous body visible in the sky except a planet, satellite, comet, or meteor; *esp* : a self-luminous gaseous celestial body (as the sun) of great mass whose shape is usu. spheroidal and whose size may be as small as the earth or larger than the earth's orbit **2 a :** a planet or a configuration of the planets that is held in astrology to influence

one's destiny or fortune — usu. used in pl. **b** : FORTUNE, FAME **3** : a conventional figure with five or more points that represents or resembles a star; *esp* : ASTERISK **4 a** : the principal member of a theatrical or operatic company **b** : an outstandingly talented performer — **star•like** *adj*
[2]star *vb* **starred**; **star•ring 1** : to sprinkle or adorn with stars **2 a** : to mark with a star as being superior **b** : to mark with an asterisk **3** : to present in the role of a star **4** : to play the most prominent or important role **5** : to perform outstandingly
[3]star *adj* **1** : of, relating to, or being a star **2** : being of outstanding excellence : PREEMINENT
[1]star•board \'stär-bərd\ *n* : the right side of a ship or airplane looking forward
[2]starboard *vt* : to turn or put (a helm or rudder) to the right
[3]starboard *adj* : of, relating to, or situated to starboard
[1]starch \'stärch\ *vt* : to stiffen with or as if with starch
[2]starch *n* **1** : a white odorless tasteless granular or powdery complex carbohydrate that is the chief storage form of carbohydrate in plants, is an important foodstuff, and is used also in adhesives and sizes, in laundering, and in pharmacy and medicine **2** : a stiff formal manner — **starchy** \'stär-chē\ *adj*
star•dom \'stärd-əm\ *n* **1** : the status or position of a star **2** : a body of stars
[1]stare \'sta(ə)r\ *vb* **1** : to look fixedly often with wide-open eyes **2** : to show oneself conspicuously **3** : to have an effect upon by looking fixedly at a person — **star•er** *n*
[2]stare *n* : the act or an instance of staring
star•fish \'stär-ˌfish\ *n* : a star-shaped sea animal that feeds on mollusks
star•gaze \-ˌgāz\ *vi* **1** : to gaze at stars **2** : to stare absent-mindedly : DAYDREAM
star•gaz•er \-ˌgā-zər\ *n* : one that gazes at the stars: as **a** : ASTROLOGER **b** : ASTRONOMER
[1]stark \'stärk\ *adj* **1** : STRONG, ROBUST **2 a** : rigid in or as if in death **b** : UNBENDING, STRICT **3** : SHEER, UTTER **4 a** : BARREN, DESOLATE **b** (1) : having few or no ornaments : BARE (2) : HARSH, UNADORNED **5** : sharply delineated — **stark•ly** *adv* — **stark•ness** *n*
[2]stark *adv* **1** : STARKLY **2** : WHOLLY, ABSOLUTELY
star•less \'stär-ləs\ *adj* : being without stars and esp. visible stars
star•let \-lət\ *n* : a young movie actress being coached and publicized for starring roles
star•light \-ˌlīt\ *n* : the light given by the stars
star•ling \'stär-liŋ\ *n* : any of a family of usu. dark gregarious passerine birds; *esp* : a dark brown or in summer glossy greenish black European bird naturalized and often a pest in the U.S.
star•lit \'stär-ˌlit\ *adj* : lighted by the stars
starred \'stärd\ *adj* **1** : adorned with or as if with stars **2** : marked with or having the shape of a star **3** : affected in fortune by the stars
star•ry \'stär-ē\ *adj* **1** : adorned with stars **2** : of, relating to, or consisting of the stars : STELLAR **3** : shining like stars : SPARKLING **4** : having parts arranged like the rays of a star
star–span•gled \'stär-ˌspaŋ-gəld\ *adj* : studded with stars
[1]start \'stärt\ *vb* **1** : to move suddenly and sharply : react with a quick involuntary movement **2 a** : to issue with sudden force **b** : to come into being, activity, or operation : BEGIN **3** : to seem to protrude : PROTRUDE **4** : to become or cause to become loosened or forced out of place **5 a** : to begin a course or journey **b** : to range from a specified initial point **6** : to be or cause to be a participant in a game or contest **7** : to cause to leave a place of concealment : FLUSH **8** : to bring up for consideration or discussion **9** : to bring into being **10** : to begin the use or employment of **11 a** : to cause to move, act, or operate **b** : to care for during early stages **12** : to perform the first stages or actions of — **start•er** \'stärt-ər\ *n*
[2]start *n* **1 a** : a quick involuntary bodily reaction **b** : a brief and sudden action or movement **c** : a sudden capricious impulse or outburst **2** : a beginning of movement, activity, or development **3** : a place of beginning
[1]star•tle \'stärt-ᵊl\ *vb* **star•tled**; **star•tling** \'stärt-liŋ, -ᵊl-iŋ\ **1** : to move or jump suddenly as in surprise or alarm **2** : to frighten suddenly and usu. not seriously **3** : to cause to start
[2]startle *n* : a sudden mild shock (as of surprise or alarm)
star•tling *adj* : causing a momentary fright, surprise, or astonishment — **star•tling•ly** *adv*
star•va•tion \stär-'vā-shən\ *n* : the act or an instance of starving : the state of being starved
starve \'stärv\ *vb* **1** : to die or suffer greatly from lack of food **2** : to suffer or perish or cause to suffer or perish from deprivation **3 a** : to kill or subdue with hunger **b** : to deprive of nourishment **c** : to cause to capitulate as if by depriving of nourishment
starve•ling \-liŋ\ *n* : one thin and weakened by or as if by lack of food
[1]stash \'stash\ *vt* : to store in a usu. secret place for future use
[2]stash *n* **1** : hiding place : CACHE **2** : something stored or hidden away
[1]state \'stāt\ *n* **1 a** : mode or condition of being **b** (1) : condition of mind or temperament (2) : a condition of abnormal tension or excitement **2 a** : social position; *esp* : high rank **b** (1) : elaborate or luxurious style of living (2) : formal dignity : POMP **3** : ESTATE 3 **4 a** : a politically organized body of people usu. occupying a definite territory; *esp* : one that is sovereign **b** : the political organization of such a body of people **5** : the operations or concerns of the government of a country **6** : one of the constituent units of a nation having a federal government **7** : the territory of a state — **state•hood** \-ˌhu̇d\ *n* — **state•less** \-ləs\ *adj*
[2]state *adj* **1** : suitable or used for ceremonial or formal occasions **2** : of or relating to a national state or to a constituent state of a federal government **3** : GOVERNMENTAL
[3]state *vt* **1** : to set by regulation or authority **2** : to express the particulars of esp. in words; *also* : to express in words
state•craft \'stāt-ˌkraft\ *n* : the art of conducting state affairs
state•house \-ˌhau̇s\ *n* : the building in which a state legislature sits
state•ly \'stāt-lē\ *adj* **1 a** : HAUGHTY, UNAPPROACHABLE **b** : marked by lofty or imposing dignity **2** : impressive in size or proportions — **state•li•ness** *n* — **stately** *adv*
state•ment \'stāt-mənt\ *n* **1** : the act or process of stating or presenting orally or on paper **2** : something stated: as **a** : a report of facts or opinions **b** : a single declaration or remark **3** : a brief summarized record of a financial account
state•room \'stāt-ˌrüm, -ˌru̇m\ *n* : a private room on a ship or on a railroad car
states•man \'stāts-mən\ *n* : a person engaged in fixing the policies and conducting the affairs of a government; *esp* : one having unusual wisdom in such matters — **states•man•like** *adj* — **states•man•ly** \-lē\ *adj* — **states•man•ship** \-ˌship\ *n*
state•wide \'stāt-'wīd\ *adj* : including all parts of a state
[1]stat•ic \'stat-ik\ *adj* **1** : exerting force by reason of weight alone without motion **2** : of or relating to bodies at rest or forces in equilibrium **3** : showing little change **4 a** : characterized by a lack of movement, animation, or progression **b** : producing an effect of repose or quiescence **5** : STATIONARY **6** : of, relating to, producing, or being stationary charges of electricity (as those produced by friction or induction) **7** : of, relating to, or caused by radio static — **stat•i•cal•ly** \'stat-i-k(ə-)lē\ *adv*
[2]static *n* : disturbing effects produced in a radio or television receiver by atmospheric or electrical disturbances
[1]sta•tion \'stā-shən\ *n* **1** : the place or position in which something or someone stands or is assigned to stand or remain

2 : the act or manner of standing : POSTURE 3 : a stopping place: as a : a regular stopping place in a transportation route b : a building at such a stopping place : DEPOT 4 a : a post or sphere of duty or occupation b : a stock farm or ranch of Australia or New Zealand 5 : STANDING, RANK 6 : a place established to provide a public service 7 : a complete assemblage of radio or television equipment for transmitting or receiving

[2]**station** *vt* **sta·tioned**; **sta·tion·ing** \'stā-sh(ə-)niŋ\ : to assign to or set in a station or position : POST

sta·tion·ary \'stā-shə-ˌner-ē\ *adj* 1 : fixed in a station, course, or mode : IMMOBILE 2 : unchanging in condition : STABLE

sta·tion·er \'stā-sh(ə-)nər\ *n* : one that sells stationery

sta·tion·ery \'stā-shə-ˌner-ē\ *n* 1 : materials (as paper, pens, and ink) for writing or typing 2 : letter paper usu. accompanied with matching envelopes

station wagon *n* : an automobile that has an interior longer than a sedan's, one or more rear seats readily lifted out or folded to facilitate light trucking, and no separate luggage compartment

sta·tis·tic \stə-'tis-tik\ *n* : a single term or datum in a collection of statistics

stat·is·ti·cian \ˌstat-ə-'stish-ən\ *n* : one versed in or engaged in compiling statistics

sta·tis·tics \stə-'tis-tiks\ *n sing or pl* : a branch of mathematics dealing with the collection, analysis, interpretation, and presentation of masses of numerical data; *also* : a collection of such numerical data — **sta·tis·ti·cal** \-'tis-ti-kəl\ *adj* — **sta·tis·ti·cal·ly** \-ti-k(ə-)lē\ *adv*

stat·u·ary \'stach-ə-ˌwer-ē\ *n*, *pl* **-ar·ies** 1 a : a branch of sculpture treating of figures in the round b : a collection of statues 2 : SCULPTOR — **statuary** *adj*

stat·ue \'stach-ü\ *n* : a likeness (as of a person or animal) sculptured, modeled, or cast in a solid substance

stat·u·esque \ˌstach-ə-'wesk\ *adj* : resembling a statue esp. in well-proportioned or massive dignity

stat·u·ette \ˌstach-ə-'wet\ *n* : a small statue

stat·ure \'stach-ər\ *n* 1 : natural height (as of a person) in an upright position 2 : quality or status gained by growth, development, or achievement

sta·tus \'stāt-əs, 'stat-\ *n* 1 : position or rank in relation to others : STANDING 2 : CONDITION, SITUATION

sta·tus quo \ˌstāt-əs-'kwō, ˌstat-\ *n* : the existing state of affairs

stat·ute \'stach-üt, -ət\ *n* : a law enacted by the legislative branch of a government

statute mile *n* : MILE 1

stat·u·to·ry \'stach-ə-ˌtōr-ē\ *adj* 1 : of, relating to, or of the nature of a statute 2 : fixed by statute 3 : punishable by statute

staunch \'stönch, 'stänch\ *adj* 1 a : WATERTIGHT, SOUND b : strongly built : SUBSTANTIAL 2 : steadfast in loyalty or principle — **staunch·ly** *adv* — **staunch·ness** *n*

[1]**stave** \'stāv\ *n* 1 : a wooden stick 2 : one of the narrow strips of wood or narrow iron plates placed edge to edge to form the sides, covering, or lining of a vessel (as a barrel) or structure 3 : STANZA

[2]**stave** *vb* **staved** *or* **stove** \'stōv\; **stav·ing** 1 : to break in the staves of (a cask) 2 : to smash a hole in; *also* : to crush or break inward 3 : to drive or thrust away

stave off *vt* : to ward or fend off

staves *pl of* STAFF

[1]**stay** \'stā\ *n* : a strong rope or wire used to steady or brace something (as a mast)

[2]**stay** *vb* : to fasten (as a smokestack) with stays

[3]**stay** *vb* **stayed** \'stād\ *or* **staid** \'stād\; **stay·ing** 1 : to stop going forward : PAUSE 2 : to continue in a place or condition : REMAIN 3 : to stand firm 4 : to take up residence : LODGE 5 : WAIT, DELAY 6 : to last out (as a race) 7 : CHECK, HALT

[4]**stay** *n* 1 : the action of halting : the state of being stopped 2 : a residence or sojourn in a place

[5]**stay** *n* 1 a : something that serves as a prop : SUPPORT b : a thin firm strip (as of whalebone, steel, or plastic) used for stiffening a garment (as a corset) or part (as a shirt collar) 2 : a corset stiffened with stays — usu. used in pl.

[6]**stay** *vt* 1 : to provide physical or moral support for : SUSTAIN 2 : to fix on as a foundation : GROUND, REST

stead \'sted\ *n* 1 : ADVANTAGE, SERVICE 2 : the office, place, or function ordinarily occupied or carried out by someone or something else

stead·fast \'sted-ˌfast\ *adj* 1 a : firmly fixed in place b : not subject to change 2 : firm in belief, determination, or adherence : LOYAL — **stead·fast·ly** *adv* — **stead·fast·ness** *n*

[1]**steady** \'sted-ē\ *adj* 1 a : firm in position : FIXED b : direct or sure in movement : UNFALTERING 2 a : REGULAR, UNIFORM b : not fluctuating or varying widely 3 a : not easily moved or upset : RESOLUTE b : constant in feeling, principle, purpose, or attachment : DEPENDABLE c : not given to dissipation or disorderly behavior : SOBER — **stead·i·ly** \'sted-ᵊl-ē\ *adv* — **stead·i·ness** \'sted-ē-nəs\ *n*

[2]**steady** *vb* **stead·ied**; **stead·y·ing** : to make, keep, or become steady

[3]**steady** *adv* 1 : in a steady manner : STEADILY 2 : on the course set — used as a direction to the helmsman of a ship

steak \'stāk\ *n* 1 a : a slice of meat cut from a fleshy part of a beef carcass b : a similar slice of a specified meat other than beef 2 : a cross-section slice of a large fish (as salmon)

[1]**steal** \'stēl\ *vb* **stole** \'stōl\; **sto·len** \'stō-lən\; **steal·ing** 1 : to come or go secretly, unobtrusively, gradually, or unexpectedly 2 a : to take and carry away without right and with intent to keep the property of another : ROB b : to appropriate entirely to oneself or beyond one's proper share 3 a : to move, convey, or introduce secretly : SMUGGLE b : to accomplish or get in a concealed or unobserved manner 4 : to gain a base in baseball by running without the aid of a hit or an error — **steal·er** *n*

[2]**steal** *n* 1 : the act or an instance of stealing 2 : something offered or purchased at a low price : BARGAIN

stealth \'stelth\ *n* 1 : the act or action of going or proceeding furtively, secretly, or imperceptibly 2 : FURTIVENESS, SLYNESS

stealthy \'stel-thē\ *adj* 1 : slow, deliberate, and secret in action or character 2 : intended to escape observation : FURTIVE — **stealth·i·ly** \-thə-lē\ *adv* — **stealth·i·ness** \-thē-nəs\ *n*

[1]**steam** \'stēm\ *n* 1 a : the invisible vapor into which water is converted when heated to the boiling point b : the mist formed by the condensation on cooling of water vapor 2 a : water vapor kept under pressure so as to supply energy for heating, cooking, or mechanical work; *also* : the power so generated b : driving force : POWER c : emotional tension

[2]**steam** *vb* 1 : to rise or pass off as vapor 2 : to give off steam or vapor 3 : to move or travel by or as if by the agency of steam 4 : to be angry : BOIL 5 : to expose to the action of steam (as for softening or cooking)

steam·er \'stē-mər\ *n* 1 : a vessel in which something is steamed 2 a : a ship propelled by steam b : an engine, machine, or vehicle operated by steam

steam fitter *n* : one that installs or repairs equipment (as steam pipes) for heating, ventilating, or refrigerating systems — **steam fitting** *n*

steam·ship \'stēm-ˌship\ *n* : STEAMER 2a

steamy \'stē-mē\ *adj* : consisting of, characterized by, or full of steam — **steam·i·ly** \-mə-lē\ *adv*

steed \'stēd\ *n* : HORSE; *esp* : a spirited horse

[1]**steel** \'stēl\ *n* 1 : commercial iron that contains carbon in any amount up to about 1.7 percent as an essential alloying constituent and is distinguished from cast iron by its malleability and lower carbon content 2 : an instrument or implement of

or characteristically of steel **3 :** a hard cold quality characteristic of steel

[2]steel *vt* **1 :** to overlay, point, or edge with steel **2 a :** to cause to resemble steel **b :** to fill with resolution or determination

[3]steel *adj* **1 :** made of or resembling steel **2 :** of or relating to the production of steel

steel wool *n* **:** an abrasive material composed of long fine steel shavings and used esp. for scouring and burnishing

steel·work \'stēl-ˌwərk\ *n* **1 :** work in steel **2** *pl* **:** an establishment where steel is made — **steel·work·er** \-ˌwər-kər\ *n*

steely \'stē-lē\ *adj* **1 :** made of steel **2 :** resembling steel

steel·yard \'stēl-ˌyärd\ *n* **:** a balance on which something to be weighed is hung from the shorter arm of a lever and is balanced by a weight that slides along the longer arm which is marked with a scale

[1]steep \'stēp\ *adj* **1 :** making a large angle with the plane of the horizon **:** almost perpendicular **2 :** being or characterized by a very rapid decline or increase **3 :** difficult to accept, meet, or perform **:** EXCESSIVE — **steep·ly** *adv* — **steep·ness** *n*

[2]steep *vb* **1 a :** to soak in a liquid (as for softening, bleaching, or extracting a flavor) at a temperature under the boiling point **b :** to undergo the process of soaking in a liquid **2 :** BATHE, WET **3 :** to saturate with or subject thoroughly to

steep·en \'stē-pən\ *vb* **:** to make or become steeper

stee·ple \'stē-pəl\ *n* **:** a tall structure usu. having a small spire at the top and surmounting a church tower; *also* **:** a church tower — **stee·pled** \-pəld\ *adj*

stee·ple·chase \'stē-pəl-ˌchās\ *n* **:** a cross-country race by horsemen; *also* **:** a race over a course obstructed by obstacles (as hedges, walls, or hurdles) — **stee·ple·chas·er** \-ˌchā-sər\ *n*

stee·ple·jack \-ˌjak\ *n* **:** one whose work is building smokestacks, towers, or steeples or climbing up the outside of such structures to paint and make repairs

[1]steer \'sti(ə)r\ *n* **:** a domestic bull castrated before sexual maturity; *esp* **:** a young ox being raised for beef

[2]steer *vb* **1 :** to direct the course or the course of **:** GUIDE **2 :** to set and hold to (a course) **3 :** to pursue a course of action **4 :** to be subject to guidance — **steer·a·ble** *adj* — **steer·er** *n*

[3]steer *n* **:** a hint as to procedure **:** TIP

steer·age \'sti(ə)r-ij\ *n* **1 :** the act or practice of steering; *also* **:** DIRECTION **2 :** a section in a passenger ship for passengers paying the lowest fares

steers·man \'sti(ə)rz-mən\ *n* **:** one who steers **:** HELMSMAN

stein \'stīn\ *n* **:** an earthenware mug esp. for beer

stel·lar \'stel-ər\ *adj* **1 a :** of or relating to the stars **:** ASTRAL **b :** composed of stars **2 :** of or relating to a theatrical or film star **3 a :** LEADING, PRINCIPAL **b :** OUTSTANDING

[1]stem \'stem\ *n* **1 a :** the main shaft of a plant **b :** a plant part that supports another **2 :** the prow of a ship **3 :** a line of ancestry **:** STOCK **4 :** the part of an inflected word that remains unchanged throughout an inflection **5 :** something resembling the stem of a plant — **stem·less** \-ləs\ *adj*

[2]stem *vt* **stemmed; stem·ming 1 :** to make headway against (as an adverse tide, current, or wind) **2 :** to go counter to

[3]stem *vb* **stemmed; stem·ming 1 :** to have or trace an origin or development **:** DERIVE **2 :** to remove the stem from

[4]stem *vb* **stemmed; stem·ming 1 :** to stop, check, or restrain by or as if by damming; *also* **:** to become checked or stanched **2 a :** to turn (skis) in stemming **b :** to retard oneself by forcing the heel of one ski or of both skis outward from the line of progress

[1]stemmed \'stemd\ *adj* **:** having a stem

[2]stemmed *adj* **:** having the stem removed

stench \'stench\ *n* **:** an extremely disagreeable smell **:** STINK

[1]sten·cil \'sten(t)-səl\ *n* **1 :** an impervious material (as a sheet of paper, thin wax, or woven fabric) perforated with lettering or a design through which a substance (as ink, paint, or metallic powder) is forced onto a surface to be printed **2 :** a pattern, design, or print produced by means of a stencil

FRAGILE

stencil

[2]stencil *vt* **-ciled** *or* **-cilled; -cil·ing** *or* **-cil·ling** \-s(ə-)liŋ\ **1 :** to produce by stencil **2 :** to mark or paint with a stencil

ste·nog·ra·pher \stə-'näg-rə-fər\ *n* **1 :** a writer of shorthand **2 :** one employed chiefly to take and transcribe dictation

ste·nog·ra·phy \-fē\ *n* **1 :** the art or process of writing in shorthand **2 :** shorthand esp. written from dictation or oral discourse **3 :** the making of shorthand notes and subsequent transcription of them — **sten·o·graph·ic** \ˌsten-ə-'graf-ik\ *adj* — **sten·o·graph·i·cal·ly** \-'graf-i-k(ə-)lē\ *adv*

sten·to·ri·an \sten-'tōr-ē-ən\ *adj* **:** extremely loud

[1]step \'step\ *n* **1 :** a rest for the foot in ascending or descending: as **a :** STAIR **b :** a ladder rung **2 a (1) :** an advance or movement made by raising the foot and bringing it down elsewhere **(2) :** a combination of foot or foot and body movements constituting a unit or a repeated pattern **(3) :** manner of walking **:** STRIDE **b :** FOOTPRINT **c :** the sound of a footstep **3 a :** the space passed over in one step **b :** a short distance **c :** the height of one stair **4** *pl* **:** COURSE, WAY **5 a :** a degree, grade, or rank in a scale **b :** a stage in a process **6 :** an action, proceeding, or measure often occurring as one in a series **7 :** pace with another **8 :** a steplike offset or part usu. occurring in a series — **step·like** *adj* — **stepped** \'stept\ *adj*

[2]step *vb* **stepped; step·ping 1 a :** to move or take by raising the foot and bringing it down elsewhere or by moving each foot in succession **b :** DANCE **2 a :** to go or traverse on foot **:** WALK **b :** to move briskly **3 :** to press down with the foot **4 :** to come as if at a single step **5 :** to erect by fixing the lower end in a step **6 :** to measure by steps **7 :** to make steps in **8 :** to construct or arrange in or as if in steps

step·broth·er \'step-ˌbrət͟h-ər\ *n* **:** a son of one's stepparent by a former marriage

step·child \'step-ˌchīld\ *n* **:** a child of one's wife or husband by a former marriage

step·daugh·ter \-ˌdȯt-ər\ *n* **:** a daughter of one's wife or husband by a former marriage

step down *vb* **:** to give up a position

step·fa·ther \'step-ˌfät͟h-ər\ *n* **:** the husband of one's mother by a subsequent marriage

step–in \'step-ˌin\ *n* **1 :** an article of clothing that is put on by being stepped into **2** *pl* **:** a woman's brief panties

step·lad·der \'step-ˌlad-ər\ *n* **:** a portable set of steps with a hinged frame for steadying

step·moth·er \-ˌmət͟h-ər\ *n* **:** the wife of one's father by a subsequent marriage

step out *vi* **1 :** to go away from a place usu. for a short distance and for a short time **2 :** to go or march at a vigorous pace

step·par·ent \'step-ˌpar-ənt\ *n* **:** the husband or wife of one's mother or father by a subsequent marriage

steppe \'step\ *n* **:** dry usu. rather level predominantly grass-covered land in regions of wide temperature range (as in southeastern Europe and parts of Asia)

step·per \'step-ər\ *n* **:** one that steps

step·sis·ter \'step-ˌsis-tər\ *n* **:** a daughter of one's stepparent by a former marriage

step·son \-ˌsən\ *n* **:** a son of one's husband or wife by a former marriage

step up *vb* **1 :** to increase, augment, or advance **2 :** to come forward **3 :** to receive a promotion — **step–up** \'step-ˌəp\ *adj*

step·wise \'step-ˌwīz\ *adj* **:** marked by steps **:** GRADUAL

ster·eo \'ster-ē-ˌō, 'stir-\ *n* **1 :** STEREOTYPE **2 a :** a stereoscopic method, system, or effect **b :** a stereoscopic photograph **3 a :** stereophonic reproduction **b :** a stereophonic sound system — **stereo** *adj*

ster·e·o·phon·ic \ˌster-ē-ə-'fän-ik, ˌstir-\ *adj* **:** giving, relating to, or constituting a three-dimensional effect of reproduced sound

ster·e·o·scope \'ster-ē-ə-ˌskōp, 'stir-\ *n* **:** an optical instrument with two eyeglasses for helping the observer to combine the images of two pictures taken from points of view a little way apart and thus to get the effect of solidity or depth

ster·e·o·scop·ic \ˌster-ē-ə-'skäp-ik, ˌstir-\ *adj* **1 :** of or relating to the stereoscope **2 :** characterized by stereoscopy — **ster·e·o·scop·i·cal·ly** \-'skäp-i-k(ə-)lē\ *adv*

ster·e·os·co·py \ˌster-ē-'äs-kə-pē, ˌstir-\ *n* **:** the seeing of objects in three dimensions

[1]**ster·e·o·type** \'ster-ē-ə-ˌtīp, 'stir-\ *n* **1 :** a plate made by molding a matrix of a printing surface and making from this a cast in type metal **2 :** something conforming to a fixed or general pattern and lacking individual distinguishing qualities

[2]**stereotype** *vt* **1 :** to make a stereotype from **2 a :** to repeat without variation **b :** to develop a mental stereotype about — **ster·e·o·typ·er** *n*

ster·e·o·typed \-ˌtīpt\ *adj* **:** repeated by rote or without variation **:** lacking originality

ster·ile \'ster-əl\ *adj* **1 :** not able to bear fruit, crops, or offspring **:** not fertile **:** BARREN **2 :** free from living organisms and esp. microorganisms **3 :** deficient in ideas or originality — **ste·ril·i·ty** \stə-'ril-ət-ē\ *n*

ster·il·ize \'ster-ə-ˌlīz\ *vt* **:** to make sterile: as **a :** to deprive of the power of reproducing or germinating **b :** to make powerless or useless **c :** to free from living organisms (as bacteria) — **ster·il·i·za·tion** \ˌster-ə-lə-'zā-shən\ *n* — **ster·il·iz·er** \'ster-ə-ˌlī-zər\ *n*

[1]**ster·ling** \'stər-liŋ\ *n* **1 :** British money **2 :** sterling silver

[2]**sterling** *adj* **1 :** of, relating to, or calculated in terms of British sterling **2 a :** having a fixed standard of purity usu. defined legally as represented by an alloy of 925 parts of silver with 75 parts of copper **b :** made of sterling silver **3 :** conforming to the highest standard

[1]**stern** \'stərn\ *adj* **1 :** hard and severe in nature or manner **2 :** not inviting or attractive **:** FORBIDDING, GRIM **3 :** showing severity **:** HARSH **4 :** STOUT, RESOLUTE — **stern·ly** *adv* — **stern·ness** *n*

[2]**stern** *n* **1 :** the rear end of a boat **2 :** a hinder or rear part

ster·num \'stər-nəm\ *n, pl* **sternums** *or* **ster·na** \-nə\ **:** a compound ventral bone or cartilage connecting the ribs of the two sides — **ster·nal** \'stərn-ᵊl\ *adj*

ster·to·rous \'stərt-ə-rəs\ *adj* **:** characterized by a harsh snoring or gasping sound — **ster·to·rous·ly** *adv* — **ster·to·rous·ness** *n*

steth·o·scope \'steth-ə-ˌskōp, 'steth-\ *n* **:** an instrument used for listening to sounds produced in the body and esp. in the chest

ste·ve·dore \'stē-və-ˌdōr\ *n* **:** a person whose work is to load and unload boats in port — **stevedore** *vb*

[1]**stew** \'st(y)ü\ *vb* **1 :** to boil slowly **:** cook in liquid over a low heat **:** SIMMER **2 :** to become agitated or worried **:** FRET

[2]**stew** *n* **1 :** food (as meat with vegetables) prepared by slow boiling **2 :** a state of excitement, worry, or confusion

stew·ard \'st(y)ü-ərd, 'st(y)u̇(-ə)rd\ *n* **1 a :** a person appointed to manage the domestic and business affairs of a large household or estate **b :** one actively concerned with the direction of the affairs of an organization (as a church or club) **2 a :** a person employed to supervise the provision and distribution of food (as on a ship) **b :** a worker who serves and attends the needs of passengers (as on a train or ship) — **stew·ard·ess** \-əs\ *n* — **stew·ard·ship** \-ˌship\ *n*

[1]**stick** \'stik\ *n* **1 :** a cut or broken branch or twig esp. when dry and dead **2 :** a long slender piece of wood **3 :** something like a stick in shape, origin, or use **4 :** a person who is dull, stiff, and lifeless **5** *pl* **:** remote or rural districts

[2]**stick** *vb* **stuck** \'stək\; **stick·ing** **1 a :** PIERCE, STAB **b :** to kill by piercing **2 :** to cause (as a pointed instrument) to penetrate — used with *in, into,* or *through* **3 a :** to fasten by thrusting in **b :** IMPALE **c :** to push out, up, or under **4 :** to put or set in a specified place or position **5 :** to attach by or as if by causing to adhere to a surface **6 :** to halt the movement or action of **7 :** BAFFLE, STUMP **8 a :** CHEAT, DEFRAUD **b :** to saddle with something disadvantageous or disagreeable **9 :** to hold to something firmly by or as if by adhesion **10 a :** to remain in a place, situation, or environment **b :** to hold fast or adhere resolutely **:** CLING **c :** to keep close in a chase or competition **11 a :** to become blocked, wedged, or jammed **b :** to be unable to proceed through fear or scruple **12 :** PROJECT, PROTRUDE

[3]**stick** *n* **:** a thrust with a pointed instrument **:** STAB

stick·er \'stik-ər\ *n* **1 :** one (as a brier or knife) that pierces with a point **2 a :** one that adheres (as a bur) or causes adhesion (as glue) **b :** a slip of paper with gummed back

stick·le \'stik-əl\ *vi* **stick·led**; **stick·ling** \'stik-(ə-)liŋ\ **1 :** to contend esp. stubbornly and usu. on insufficient grounds **2 :** to feel often excessive scruples

stick·ler \'stik-(ə-)lər\ *n* **:** one who insists on exactitude or rigid propriety (as of conduct or dress)

stick out *vb* **1 a :** PROJECT **b :** to be conspicuous **2 :** to be persistent **3 :** to put up with **:** ENDURE

stick·pin \'stik-ˌpin\ *n* **:** an ornamental pin worn in a necktie

stick up *vt* **:** to rob at the point of a gun — **stick·up** \'stik-ˌəp\ *n*

sticky \'stik-ē\ *adj* **1 a :** ADHESIVE, GLUEY, VISCOUS **b :** coated with a sticky substance **2 :** HUMID, MUGGY **3 :** tending to stick — **stick·i·ly** \'stik-ə-lē\ *adv* — **stick·i·ness** \'stik-ē-nəs\ *n*

[1]**stiff** \'stif\ *adj* **1 a :** not easily bent **:** RIGID **b :** lacking in normal or usual suppleness or mobility **2 a :** FIRM, RESOLUTE **b :** STUBBORN, UNYIELDING **c :** PROUD **d :** formally reserved in manner; *also* **:** lacking in ease or grace **3 :** hard fought **4 a :** exerting great force **:** STRONG, VIGOROUS **b :** POTENT **5 a :** HARSH, SEVERE **b :** difficult to do or cope with; *also* **:** RUGGED **6 :** EXPENSIVE, STEEP — **stiff·ly** *adv* — **stiff·ness** *n*

[2]**stiff** *adv* **1 :** STIFFLY **2 :** to an extreme degree **:** INTENSELY

[3]**stiff** *n* **1 :** CORPSE **2 :** PERSON, FELLOW, MAN

stiff·en \'stif-ən\ *vb* **stiff·ened**; **stiff·en·ing** \'stif-(ə-)niŋ\ **:** to make or become stiff or stiffer — **stiff·en·er** \-(ə-)nər\ *n*

stiff–necked \'stif-'nekt\ *adj* **:** arrogantly stubborn

sti·fle \'stī-fəl\ *vb* **sti·fled**; **sti·fling** \-f(ə-)liŋ\ **1 a :** to kill by depriving of or die from lack of oxygen or air **b :** to smother by or as if by depriving of air **2 a :** to keep in check by deliberate effort **:** REPRESS **b :** to restrain firmly or forcibly **:** DETER

stig·ma \'stig-mə\ *n, pl* **stig·ma·ta** \stig-'mät-ə, 'stig-mət-ə\ *or* **stigmas** **1 a :** a mark of shame or discredit **:** STAIN **b :** an identifying mark or characteristic; *esp* **:** a specific diagnostic sign of a disease **2** *stigmata pl* **:** bodily marks or pains resembling the wounds of the crucified Christ **3 :** the part of the pistil of a flower which receives the pollen grains and on which they germinate — **stig·mat·ic** \stig-'mat-ik\ *adj*

stig·ma·tize \'stig-mə-ˌtīz\ *vt* **:** to mark with a stigma; *esp* **:** to describe or identify in opprobrious terms

stile \'stīl\ *n* **:** a step or set of steps for passing over a fence or wall; *also* **:** TURNSTILE

sti·let·to \stə-'let-ō\ *n, pl* **-tos** *or* **-toes** **1 :** a slender dagger with a blade thick in proportion to its breadth **2 :** a pointed instrument for piercing holes for eyelets or embroidery

[1]**still** \'stil\ *adj* **1 a :** MOTIONLESS **b :** of, relating to, or being an ordinary photograph as distinguished from a motion picture **2 a :** uttering no sound **:** QUIET **b :** SUBDUED, MUTED

3 **a** : CALM, TRANQUIL **b** : free from noise or turbulence : PEACEFUL — **still·ness** *n*

[2]**still** *vb* **1 a** : ALLAY, CALM **b** : SETTLE **2** : to make or become motionless or silent : QUIET

[3]**still** *adv* **1** : without motion **2** — used as a function word to indicate the continuance of an action or condition **3** : in spite of that : NEVERTHELESS **4 a** : EVEN **b** : in addition : YET

[4]**still** *n* **1** : QUIET, SILENCE **2** : a still photograph; *esp* : one of actors or scenes of a motion picture

[5]**still** *n* **1** : DISTILLERY **2** : apparatus used in distillation

still·born \'stil-'bȯrn\ *adj* **1** : dead at birth **2** : failing from the start : ABORTIVE — **still·born** \-ˌbȯrn\ *n*

still life *n, pl* **still lifes** : a picture consisting predominantly of inanimate objects

[1]**stil·ly** \'stil-lē\ *adv* : CALMLY, QUIETLY

[2]**stilly** \'stil-ē\ *adj* : STILL

stilt \'stilt\ *n* **1** : one of two poles each with a rest or strap for the foot used to elevate the wearer above the ground in walking **2** : a pile or post serving as one of the supports of a structure above ground or water level

stilt·ed \'stil-təd\ *adj* **1** : raised on or as if on stilts **2** : stiffly formal : not easy and natural

stim·u·lant \'stim-yə-lənt\ *n* **1** : an agent (as a drug) that temporarily increases the functional activity of an organism or any of its parts **2** : STIMULUS **3** : an alcoholic beverage — **stimulant** *adj*

stim·u·late \-ˌlāt\ *vb* **1** : to make active or more active : ANIMATE, AROUSE **2** : to act toward as a physiological stimulus or stimulant — **stim·u·la·tion** \ˌstim-yə-'lā-shən\ *n* — **stim·u·la·tive** \'stim-yə-ˌlāt-iv\ *adj* — **stim·u·la·tor** \-ˌlāt-ər\ *n* — **stim·u·la·to·ry** \-lə-ˌtōr-ē\ *adj*

stim·u·lus \'stim-yə-ləs\ *n, pl* **-li** \-ˌlī, -ˌlē\ : something that rouses or incites to activity : INCENTIVE

[1]**sting** \'stiŋ\ *vb* **stung** \'stəŋ\; **sting·ing** \'stiŋ-iŋ\ **1 a** : to prick painfully esp. with a sharp or poisonous process **b** : to affect with or feel sharp, quick, and usu. burning pain or smart **2** : to cause to suffer acutely **3** : OVERCHARGE, CHEAT

[2]**sting** *n* **1 a** : the act of stinging **b** : a wound or pain caused by or as if by stinging **2** : STINGER 2 **3** : a stinging element, force, or quality — **sting·less** \'stiŋ-ləs\ *adj*

sting·er \'stiŋ-ər\ *n* **1** : one that stings; *esp* : a sharp blow or remark **2** : a sharp organ of offense and defense (as of a bee or scorpion) usu. adapted to wound by piercing and injecting a poisonous secretion

stin·gy \'stin-jē\ *adj* **1** : not generous or liberal : sparing or scant in giving or spending **2** : SCANTY, MEAGER — **stin·gi·ly** \-jə-lē\ *adv* — **stin·gi·ness** \-jē-nəs\ *n*

[1]**stink** \'stiŋk\ *vb* **stank** \'staŋk\ *or* **stunk** \'stəŋk\; **stunk**; **stink·ing** **1** : to give forth or cause to have a strong and offensive smell **2** : to be offensive or have something to an offensive degree **3** : to be of wretchedly poor quality — **stink·er** *n*

[2]**stink** *n* **1** : a strong offensive odor : STENCH **2** : a public outcry against something offensive

[1]**stint** \'stint\ *vb* **1** : to limit in share or portion : cut short in amount **2** : to be sparing or frugal

[2]**stint** *n* **1** : RESTRAINT, LIMITATION **2** : a definite quantity of work assigned

sti·pend \'stī-ˌpend, -pənd\ *n* : a fixed sum of money paid periodically for services or to defray expenses

[1]**sti·pen·di·ary** \stī-'pen-dē-ˌer-ē\ *adj* : receiving or compensated by wages or salary

[2]**stipendiary** *n, pl* **-ar·ies** : one who receives a stipend

[1]**stip·ple** \'stip-əl\ *vt* **stip·pled**; **stip·pling** \'stip-(ə-)liŋ\ **1** : to engrave by means of dots and flicks **2 a** : to depict (as in paint or ink) by small short touches that together produce an even or softly graded shadow **b** : to apply (as paint) by repeated small touches — **stip·pler** \-(ə-)lər\ *n*

[2]**stipple** *n* : production of gradation of light and shade in graphic art by stippling; *also* : the effect produced

stip·u·late \'stip-yə-ˌlāt\ *vb* : to make an agreement or arrange as part of an agreement; *esp* : to demand or insist on as a condition in an agreement

stip·u·la·tion \ˌstip-yə-'lā-shən\ *n* **1** : an act of stipulating **2** : something stipulated; *esp* : a condition required as part of an agreement

[1]**stir** \'stər\ *vb* **stirred**; **stir·ring** **1 a** : to make or cause to make an esp. slight movement or change of position **b** : to disturb the quiet of : AGITATE **2 a** : to disturb the relative position of the particles or parts of esp. by a continued circular movement; *also* : to treat something thus **b** : to mix by or as if by stirring **3** : BESTIR, EXERT **4** : to bring into notice or debate : RAISE **5 a** : to rouse to activity : INCITE, QUICKEN **b** : to call forth (as a memory) **6** : to be active or busy — **stir·rer** *n*

[2]**stir** *n* **1 a** : a state of disturbance, agitation, or activity **b** : widespread notice and discussion : IMPRESSION **2 a** : a slight movement **b** : a stirring movement

stir·ring \'stər-iŋ\ *adj* **1** : ACTIVE, BUSTLING **2** : ROUSING, INSPIRING

stir·rup \'stər-əp\ *n* : either of a pair of small light frames often of metal hung by straps from a saddle and used as a support for the foot of a horseback rider

[1]**stitch** \'stich\ *n* **1** : a local sharp and sudden pain esp. in the side **2 a** : one in-and-out movement of a threaded needle in sewing, embroidering, or suturing **b** : a portion of thread left in the material after one stitch **3** : a single loop of thread or yarn around an implement (as a knitting needle or crochet hook) **4** : a series of stitches **5** : a method of stitching — **in stitches** : in a state of uncontrollable laughter

[2]**stitch** *vb* **1 a** : to join with or as if with stitches **b** : to make, mend, or decorate with or as if with stitches **2** : to unite by means of staples **3** : to do needlework : SEW — **stitch·er** *n*

stoat \'stōt\ *n* : the European ermine esp. in its brown summer coat

[1]**stock** \'stäk\ *n* **1 a** : STUMP **b** (1) : something without life or consciousness (2) : a dull, stupid, or lifeless person **2** : a supporting framework or part: as **a** *pl* : a timber frame with holes to contain the feet or feet and hands of an offender undergoing public punishment **b** : the wooden part by which a rifle or shotgun is held during firing **c** : the butt of an implement **3 a** : the original (as a man, race, or language) from which others derive : SOURCE **b** : individuals or a group of common ancestry : FAMILY, LINEAGE, STRAIN **4 a** (1) : the equipment of an establishment (2) : farm animals : LIVESTOCK **b** : a store or supply accumulated; *esp* : the inventory of goods of a merchant or manufacturer **5** : the sum of money invested in a large business **6** : raw material **7 a** : the estimation in which one is held **b** : confidence placed in one **8** : the production and presentation of plays by a repertory company

[2]**stock** *vb* **1** : to fit to or with a stock **2 a** : to provide with or acquire stock or a stock **b** : to procure or keep a stock of **3** : to use (land) for pasture or put (livestock) on land to graze

[3]**stock** *adv* : COMPLETELY — usu. used in combination

[4]**stock** *adj* **1 a** : kept regularly in stock **b** : commonly used or brought forward : STANDARD **2 a** : kept for breeding purposes **b** : devoted to or used or intended for livestock

[1]**stock·ade** \stä-'kād\ *n* : an enclosure of posts and stakes for defense or confinement

[2]**stockade** *vt* : to fortify or surround with a stockade

stock·bro·ker \'stäk-ˌbrō-kər\ *n* : one that executes orders to buy and sell securities

stock exchange *n* **1** : a place where organized trading in securities is conducted **2** : an association of people organized to provide a market among themselves for the purchase and sale of securities

stock·hold·er \ˈstäk-ˌhōl-dər\ *n* : an owner of stocks
stock·i·net \ˌstäk-ə-ˈnet\ *n* : a soft elastic usu. cotton fabric used esp. for bandages and infants' wear
stock·ing \ˈstäk-iŋ\ *n* **1** : a usu. knit close-fitting covering for the foot and leg **2** : SOCK — **stock·inged** \-iŋd\ *adj*
stock·man \ˈstäk-mən, -ˌman\ *n* : one occupied as an owner or worker in the raising of livestock
stock market *n* **1** : STOCK EXCHANGE 1 **2** : a market for stocks or for a particular stock
stock·pile \ˈstäk-ˌpīl\ *n* : a reserve supply esp. of something essential — **stockpile** *vb*
stock·room \-ˌrüm, -ˌrům\ *n* : a storage place for supplies or goods used in a business
stock–still \-ˈstil\ *adj* : very still : MOTIONLESS
stocky \ˈstäk-ē\ *adj* : compact, sturdy, and relatively thick in build : THICKSET — **stock·i·ly** \ˈstäk-ə-lē\ *adv* — **stock·i·ness** \ˈstäk-ē-nəs\ *n*
stock·yard \ˈstäk-ˌyärd\ *n* : a yard for stock; *esp* : one in which livestock are kept temporarily for slaughter, market, or shipping
stodgy \ˈstäj-ē\ *adj* **1** : having a thick gluey consistency : HEAVY **2** : moving in a slow plodding way esp. as a result of physical bulkiness **3** : having no excitement or interest : PROSAIC, DULL, COMMONPLACE **4** : extremely old-fashioned in attitude or outlook **5** : DRAB, DOWDY — **stodg·i·ly** \ˈstäj-ə-lē\ *adv* — **stodg·i·ness** \ˈstäj-ē-nəs\ *n*
sto·gie *or* **sto·gy** \ˈstō-gē\ *n, pl* **stogies** : an inexpensive slender cylindrical cigar
¹sto·ic \ˈstō-ik\ *n* : one who appears or claims to be indifferent to pleasure or pain
²stoic *adj* : indifferent to pleasure or pain — **sto·i·cal** \ˈstō-i-kəl\ *adj* — **sto·i·cal·ly** \-i-k(ə-)lē\ *adv*
sto·i·cism \ˈstō-ə-ˌsiz-əm\ *n* : indifference to pleasure or pain
stoke \ˈstōk\ *vb* **1** : to stir up or tend (as a fire) : supply (as a furnace) with fuel **2** : to stir up a fire : tend the fires of furnaces **3** : to feed (as oneself) abundantly
stok·er \ˈstō-kər\ *n* **1** : one that tends a furnace; *esp* : one that tends a ship's steam boiler **2** : a machine for feeding a fire
¹stole *past of* STEAL
²stole \ˈstōl\ *n* **1** : a long loose garment : ROBE **2** : a long narrow band worn around the neck by bishops and priests and over the left shoulder by deacons in ceremonies **3** : a long wide scarf or similar covering worn by women usu. across the shoulders
stolen *past part of* STEAL
stol·id \ˈstäl-əd\ *adj* : having or expressing little or no sensibility : not easily aroused or excited : UNEMOTIONAL — **sto·lid·i·ty** \stä-ˈlid-ət-ē\ *n* — **stol·id·ly** \ˈstäl-əd-lē\ *adv*
¹stom·ach \ˈstəm-ək, -ik\ *n* **1 a** : a pouch of the vertebrate alimentary canal into which food goes for further mixing and digestion after passing from the mouth by way of the esophagus and which communicates posteriorly with the duodenum **b** : an analogous cavity in an invertebrate animal **c** : the part of the body that contains the stomach : BELLY, ABDOMEN **2 a** : desire for food caused by hunger : APPETITE **b** : INCLINATION, DESIRE — **stomach** *adj*
²stomach *vt* : to bear without overt reaction or resentment
stom·ach·ache \-ˌāk\ *n* : pain in or in the region of the stomach
stom·a·cher \ˈstəm-ə-kər, -i-kər, -chər\ *n* : the front of a bodice usu. appearing between the laces of an outer garment (as in 16th century costume)
¹stomp \ˈstämp\ *vb* : STAMP — **stomp·er** *n*
²stomp *n* : STAMP 4
¹stone \ˈstōn\ *n* **1** : earth or mineral matter hardened in a mass **2** : a piece of rock not as fine as gravel **3** : rock used as a material esp. for building **4** : a piece of rock used for some special purpose (as for a monument at a grave) **5** : JEWEL, GEM **6** : a hard stony seed or one (as of a plum) enclosed in a stony cover **7** *pl usu* **stone** : any of various units of weight; *esp* : an official British unit equal to 14 pounds
²stone *vt* **1** : to hurl stones at; *esp* : to kill by hitting with stones **2** : to remove the stones of (a fruit) **3 a** : to rub, scour, or polish (as leather or machined metal) with a stone **b** : to sharpen with a whetstone — **ston·er** *n*
³stone *adj* : of, relating to, or made of stone
stone–broke \ˈstōn-ˈbrōk\ *adj* : completely broke : lacking funds
stone·cut·ter \-ˌkət-ər\ *n* : one that cuts, carves, or dresses stone — **stone·cut·ting** \-ˌkət-iŋ\ *n*
stone·ma·son \ˈstōn-ˌmās-ᵊn\ *n* : a mason who builds with stone — **stone·ma·son·ry** \-rē\ *n*
stone·work \-ˌwərk\ *n* **1** : a structure or part built of stone : MASONRY **2** : the shaping, preparation, or setting of stone
stony \ˈstō-nē\ *adj* **1** : abounding in or having the nature of stone : ROCKY **2 a** : insensitive as stone : PITILESS, HARDHEARTED **b** : manifesting no movement or reaction : DUMB, EXPRESSIONLESS — **ston·i·ly** \ˈstōn-ᵊl-ē\ *adv*
stood *past of* STAND
stooge \ˈstüj\ *n* **1** : an actor who usu. by asking questions prepares the way for a principal comedian's jokes **2** : one who slavishly follows or serves another — **stooge** *vi*
stool \ˈstül\ *n* **1 a** : a seat without back or arms supported by three or four legs or by a central pedestal **b** : FOOTSTOOL **2** : a discharge of fecal matter
¹stoop \ˈstüp\ *vb* **1** : to bend down or over **2** : to carry the head and shoulders or the upper part of the body bent forward **3** : to descend to doing something that is beneath one : degrade or debase oneself **4** : to descend swiftly on prey : SWOOP
²stoop *n* **1 a** : an act of bending the body forward **b** : a temporary or habitual forward bend of the back and shoulders **2** : a lowering of oneself either in condescension or in submission
³stoop *n* : a porch, platform, entrance stairway, or small veranda at a house door
¹stop \ˈstäp\ *vb* **stopped**; **stop·ping** **1** : to close an opening by filling or blocking it : PLUG **2** : CHECK, RESTRAIN **3** : to halt the movement or progress of **4** : to instruct one's banker not to honor or pay **5** : to come to an end : cease activity or operation **6** : to make a visit : STAY, TARRY
²stop *n* **1 a** : CESSATION, END **b** : a pause or breaking off in speech **2** : a graduated set of organ pipes of like kind and tone quality **3 a** : something that impedes, obstructs, or brings to a halt : IMPEDIMENT, OBSTACLE **b** : STOPPER **4** : a device for arresting or limiting motion **5** : the act of stopping : the state of being stopped : CHECK **6 a** : a halt in a journey : STAY **b** : a stopping place **7** — used in telegrams and cables to indicate a period
³stop *adj* : serving to stop : designed to stop
stop·gap \ˈstäp-ˌgap\ *n* : something that fills a gap : a temporary substitute or expedient : MAKESHIFT
stop·over \ˈstäp-ˌō-vər\ *n* **1** : a stop at an intermediate point in one's journey **2** : a stopping place on a journey
stop·page \ˈstäp-ij\ *n* : the act of stopping : the state of being stopped : HALT, OBSTRUCTION
¹stop·per \ˈstäp-ər\ *n* **1** : one that brings to a halt : CHECK **2** : one that closes, shuts, or fills up; *esp* : something (as a bung or cork) used to plug an opening
²stopper *vt* : to close or secure with or as if with a stopper
stop·watch \ˈstäp-ˌwäch\ *n* : a watch having a hand that can be started and stopped at will for exact timing (as of a race)
stor·a·ble \ˈstōr-ə-bəl\ *adj* : that may be stored — **storable** *n*
stor·age \ˈstōr-ij\ *n* **1 a** : space or a place for storing **b** : an amount stored **2 a** : the act of storing : the state of being stored **b** : the price charged for storing something
storage battery *n* : a connected group of cells that converts chemical energy into electrical energy by reversible chemical

reactions and that may be recharged by passing a current through it in the direction opposite to that of its discharge

[1]**store** \'stō(ə)r\ *vt* **1** : FURNISH, SUPPLY **2** : to lay away : ACCUMULATE **3** : to deposit in a place (as a warehouse) for safekeeping or disposal **4** : to provide storage room for

[2]**store** *n* **1** *pl* : accumulated supplies (as of food) **2** : something stored : STOCK **3** : a place where goods are sold : SHOP **4** : VALUE, IMPORTANCE — **in store** : in readiness for use

[3]**store** *adj* : purchased from a store : not made to order or homemade

store•house \'stō(ə)r-ˌhau̇s\ *n* **1** : a building for storing goods **2** : an abundant supply or source

store•keep•er \-ˌkē-pər\ *n* **1** : one who is in charge of stores **2** : one who keeps a store or shop

store•room \-ˌrüm, -ˌru̇m\ *n* : a room for the storing of goods or supplies

[1]**sto•ried** \'stōr-ēd\ *adj* : having an interesting history : celebrated in story or history

[2]**storied** *or* **sto•reyed** *adj* : having stories

stork \'stȯrk\ *n* : any of various large mostly Old World wading birds having a long stout bill and being related to the herons

[1]**storm** \'stȯrm\ *n* **1** : a disturbance of the atmosphere attended by wind and usu. by rain, snow, hail, sleet, or thunder and lightning **2** : a disturbed or agitated state : a sudden or violent commotion **3** : a heavy discharge of objects (as missiles) or actions (as blows) **4** : a tumultuous outburst **5** : a violent assault on a defended position

[2]**storm** *vb* **1 a** : to blow with violence **b** : to rain, hail, snow, or sleet heavily **2** : to attack by storm **3** : to show violent emotion : RAGE **4** : to rush about violently

storm•bound \-ˌbau̇nd\ *adj* : cut off from outside communication by a storm or its effects : stopped or delayed by storms

stormy \'stȯr-mē\ *adj* **1** : relating to, characterized by, or indicative of a storm **2** : marked by turmoil or fury : PASSIONATE, TURBULENT — **storm•i•ly** \-mə-lē\ *adv* — **storm•i•ness** \-mē-nəs\ *n*

[1]**sto•ry** \'stōr-ē\ *n, pl* **stories** **1 a** : an account of incidents or events **b** : ANECDOTE **2 a** : a fictional narrative shorter than a novel; *esp* : SHORT STORY **b** : the plot of a narrative or dramatic work **3** : a widely circulated rumor **4** : LIE, FALSEHOOD **5** : LEGEND, ROMANCE **6** : a news article or broadcast

[2]**story** *vt* **sto•ried**; **sto•ry•ing** : to adorn with a story or a scene from history

[3]**story** *or* **sto•rey** *n, pl* **stories** *or* **storeys** **1** : a set of rooms on one floor level of a building **2** : a horizontal division of a building's exterior

sto•ry•book \'stōr-ē-ˌbu̇k\ *n* : a book of stories (as for children)

sto•ry•tell•er \-ˌtel-ər\ *n* : a teller of stories — **sto•ry•tell•ing** \-ˌtel-iŋ\ *adj or n*

stoup \'stüp\ *n* : a container for beverages (as a large glass or a tankard)

[1]**stout** \'stau̇t\ *adj* **1** : strong of character: as **a** : BRAVE, BOLD **b** : FIRM, DETERMINED **2** : physically or materially strong: **a** : STURDY, VIGOROUS **b** : STAUNCH, ENDURING **c** : SOLID, SUBSTANTIAL **3** : FORCEFUL **4 a** : bulky in body : THICKSET **b** : CORPULENT, FAT, FLESHY — **stout•ish** \-ish\ *adj* — **stout•ly** *adv* — **stout•ness** *n*

[2]**stout** *n* **1** : a heavy-bodied dark brew made with roasted malt and hops **2 a** : a fat person **b** : a clothing size designed for the large figure

stout•en \'stau̇t-ᵊn\ *vb* **stout•ened**; **stout•en•ing** \'stau̇t-niŋ, -ᵊn-iŋ\ : to make or become stout

stout•heart•ed \'stau̇t-'härt-əd\ *adj* : COURAGEOUS, BOLD, BRAVE — **stout•heart•ed•ly** *adv* — **stout•heart•ed•ness** *n*

[1]**stove** \'stōv\ *n* **1** : an apparatus that burns fuel or uses electricity to provide heat (as for cooking or heating) **2** : KILN

[2]**stove** *past of* STAVE

stove•pipe \'stōv-ˌpīp\ *n* **1** : a metal pipe for carrying off smoke from a stove **2** : a tall silk hat

stow \'stō\ *vt* **1** : HOUSE, LODGE **2** : to put away : STORE **3 a** : to dispose in an orderly fashion : ARRANGE, PACK **b** : LOAD **4** : to cram in (food)

stow•age \'stō-ij\ *n* **1 a** : an act or process of stowing **b** : goods stowed or to be stowed **2 a** : storage capacity **b** : a place for storage **3** : STORAGE

stow away *vi* : to secrete oneself aboard a vehicle as a means of obtaining transportation

stow•away \'stō-ə-ˌwā\ *n* : one who stows away : an unregistered passenger

[1]**strad•dle** \'strad-ᵊl\ *vb* **strad•dled**; **strad•dling** \'strad-liŋ, -ᵊl-iŋ\ **1** : to part the legs wide : stand, sit, or walk with the legs wide apart; *esp* : to sit astride **2** : to stand, sit, or be astride of **3** : SPRAWL **4** : to be noncommittal : favor or seem to favor two apparently opposite sides — **strad•dler** \'strad-lər, -ᵊl-ər\ *n*

[2]**straddle** *n* **1** : the act or position of one that straddles **2** : a noncommittal or equivocal position

strafe \'strāf\ *vt* : to fire upon (as ground troops) at close range and esp. with machine guns from low-flying airplanes

strag•gle \'strag-əl\ *vi* **strag•gled**; **strag•gling** \'strag-(ə-)liŋ\ **1** : to wander from the direct course or way : ROVE, STRAY **2** : to trail off from others of its kind : spread out irregularly or scatteringly — **strag•gler** \-(ə-)lər\ *n*

strag•gly \'strag-(ə-)lē\ *adj* : spread out or scattered irregularly

[1]**straight** \'strāt\ *adj* **1 a** : free from curves, bends, angles, or irregularities **b** : generated by a point moving continuously in the same direction **2** : DIRECT, UNINTERRUPTED: as **a** : lying along or holding to a direct or proper course or method **b** : CANDID, FRANK **c** : coming directly from a trustworthy source **d** : having the elements in an order **e** : UPRIGHT, VERTICAL **3 a** : JUST, VIRTUOUS **b** : properly ordered or arranged **4** : not modified : UNMIXED — **straight•ness** *n*

[2]**straight** *adv* : in a straight manner, course, or line

[3]**straight** *n* **1** : something that is straight **2** : a combination of five cards in sequence in a poker hand

[1]**straight•away** \'strāt-ə-ˌwā\ *adj* **1** : proceeding in a straight line : STRAIGHTFORWARD **2** : IMMEDIATE

[2]**straightaway** *n* : a straight course: as **a** : the straight part of a closed racecourse : STRETCH **b** : a straight and unimpeded stretch of road or way

[3]**straight•away** \ˌstrāt-ə-'wā\ *adv* : without hesitation or delay

straight•edge \'strāt-ˌej\ *n* : a bar or piece of wood, metal, or plastic with a straight edge for testing straight lines and surfaces or drawing straight lines

straight•en \'strāt-ᵊn\ *vb* **straight•ened**; **straight•en•ing** \'strāt-niŋ, -ᵊn-iŋ\ **1** : to make or become straight **2** : to put in order — **straight•en•er** \'strāt-nər, -ᵊn-ər\ *n*

[1]**straight•for•ward** \(')strāt-'fȯr-wərd\ *adv* : in a straightforward manner

[2]**straightforward** *adj* **1** : proceeding in a straight course or manner : DIRECT, UNDEVIATING **2 a** : OUTSPOKEN, CANDID **b** : CLEAR-CUT, PRECISE — **straight•for•ward•ly** *adv* — **straight•for•ward•ness** *n*

straight•way \'strāt-ˌwā, -'wā\ *adv* **1** : in a direct course : DIRECTLY **2** : IMMEDIATELY, FORTHWITH

[1]**strain** \'strān\ *n* **1 a** : LINEAGE, ANCESTRY **b** : a group of presumed common ancestry that is physiologically but usu. not morphologically distinct **c** : KIND, SORT **2 a** : inherited or inherent character, quality, or disposition **b** : TRACE, STREAK **3 a** : TUNE, AIR **b** : a passage of verbal or musical expression **4 a** : the general tone of an utterance (as a song or speech) or of a course of action or conduct **b** : MOOD, TEMPER

[2]**strain** *vb* **1 a** : to draw tight : cause to clasp firmly **b** : to stretch to maximum extension and tautness **2 a** : to exert (as oneself) to the utmost : STRIVE **b** : to injure or undergo injury

by overuse, misuse, or excessive pressure **c** : to cause a change of form or size in (a body) by application of external force **3** : to squeeze or clasp tightly: as **a** : HUG **b** : CONSTRICT **4 a** : to pass or cause to pass through or as if through a strainer : FILTER **b** : to remove by straining **5** : to stretch beyond a proper limit **6** : to make great difficulty or resistance : BALK

³**strain** *n* **1** : an act of straining or the condition of being strained: as **a** : excessive physical or mental tension **b** : bodily injury from excessive tension, effort, or use; *esp* : one resulting from a wrench or twist and involving undue stretching of muscles or ligaments **c** : deformation of a material body under the action of applied forces **2** : a degree or intensity reached only by straining

strained \ˈstrānd\ *adj* **1** : FORCED **2** : pushed by antagonism near to open conflict

strain·er \ˈstrā-nər\ *n* : one that strains; *esp* : a device (as a screen, sieve, or filter) to retain solid pieces while a liquid passes through

¹**strait** \ˈstrāt\ *adj* **1** : DISTRESSFUL, DIFFICULT **2** : LIMITED, STRAITENED — **strait·ly** *adv* — **strait·ness** *n*

²**strait** *n* **1 a** : a comparatively narrow passageway connecting two large bodies of water — often used in pl. **b** : ISTHMUS **2** : a situation of perplexity or distress : DIFFICULTY, NEED

strait·en \ˈstrāt-ᵊn\ *vt* **strait·ened**; **strait·en·ing** \ˈstrāt-niŋ, -ᵊn-iŋ\ **1 a** : to make strait or narrow **b** : to hem in : squeeze together : CONFINE **2** : to subject to distress, privation, or deficiency : limit or restrict esp. in resources

strait·jack·et *or* **straight·jack·et** \ˈstrāt-ˌjak-ət\ *n* : a cover or garment of strong material (as canvas) used to bind the body and esp. the arms closely in restraining a violent prisoner or patient

strait·laced *or* **straight·laced** \ˈstrāt-ˈlāst\ *adj* : excessively strict in manners, morals, or opinion

¹**strand** \ˈstrand\ *n* : the land bordering a body of water : SHORE

²**strand** *vb* **1** : to run, drive, or cause to drift onto a strand : run aground : BEACH **2** : to leave in a strange or an unfavorable place esp. without funds or means to depart

³**strand** *n* **1** : one of the threads, strings, or wires twisted to make a cord, rope, or cable; *also* : the rope, cord, or cable into which these strands are twisted **2** : an elongated or twisted and plaited body resembling a rope **3** : one of the elements interwoven in a complex whole

⁴**strand** *vt* **1** : to form (as a rope) from strands **2** : to play out, twist, or arrange in a strand

strange \ˈstrānj\ *adj* **1** : of or relating to some other person or place **2** : exciting surprise or wonder because not usual : UNACCOUNTABLE, QUEER **3** : UNFAMILIAR **4** : ill at ease : SHY — **strange·ly** *adv* — **strange·ness** *n*

strang·er \ˈstrān-jər\ *n* **1** : one who is strange: as **a** : FOREIGNER **b** : GUEST, VISITOR, INTRUDER **c** : a person or thing that is unknown or with whom one is unacquainted **d** : one who does not belong to or is kept from the activities of a group **2** : one ignorant of or unacquainted with someone or something

stran·gle \ˈstraŋ-gəl\ *vb* **stran·gled**; **stran·gling** \-g(ə-)liŋ\ **1** : to choke to death by squeezing the throat **2** : to cause (someone or something) to stifle, choke, or suffocate **3** : to become strangled — **stran·gler** \-g(ə-)lər\ *n*

stran·gle·hold \ˈstraŋ-gəl-ˌhōld\ *n* **1** : a wrestling hold by which one's opponent is choked **2** : a force or influence that chokes or suppresses freedom of movement or expression

stran·gu·late \ˈstraŋ-gyə-ˌlāt\ *vb* **1** : STRANGLE, CONSTRICT **2** : to become constricted so as to stop circulation

stran·gu·la·tion \ˌstraŋ-gyə-ˈlā-shən\ *n* **1** : an act or process of strangling or strangulating **2** : the state of being strangled or strangulated

¹**strap** \ˈstrap\ *n* : a narrow usu. flat strip or thong of a flexible material and esp. leather used variously (as for securing, holding together, or wrapping)

²**strap** *vt* **strapped**; **strap·ping** **1 a** : to secure with or attach by means of a strap **b** : BIND, CONSTRICT; *also* : to support (as a sprained joint) with strips of adhesive plaster **2** : to beat or punish with a strap **3** : STROP

strap·less \ˈstrap-ləs\ *adj* : having no strap; *esp* : made or worn without shoulder straps

strap·ping \ˈstrap-iŋ\ *adj* : having a vigorously sturdy constitution : ROBUST

strat·a·gem \ˈstrat-ə-jəm\ *n* **1 a** : an artifice or trick in war for deceiving and outwitting the enemy **b** : a cleverly contrived trick or scheme for gaining an end **2** : skill in ruses or trickery

stra·te·gic \strə-ˈtē-jik\ *adj* **1** : of, relating to, or marked by strategy **2 a** : important in strategy **b** : required for the conduct of war **c** : of great importance within an integrated whole or to a planned effect **3** : designed or trained to strike an enemy at the sources of his power — **stra·te·gi·cal** \-ji-kəl\ *adj* — **stra·te·gi·cal·ly** \-k(ə-)lē\ *adv*

strat·e·gist \ˈstrat-ə-jəst\ *n* : one skilled in strategy

strat·e·gy \ˈstrat-ə-jē\ *n, pl* **-gies** **1** : the science and art of employing the political, economic, psychological, and military forces of a country so as to support adopted policies in peace or war **2** : the science and art of military command exercised to meet the enemy in combat under advantageous conditions **3 a** : a careful plan or method : a clever stratagem **b** : the art of devising or employing plans or stratagems toward a goal

strat·i·fy \ˈstrat-ə-ˌfī\ *vb* **-fied**; **-fy·ing** **1** : to form, deposit, or arrange in strata **2** : to become arranged in strata — **strat·i·fi·ca·tion** \ˌstrat-ə-fə-ˈkā-shən\ *n*

strat·o·sphere \ˈstrat-ə-ˌsfi(ə)r\ *n* : a portion of the earth's atmosphere from about 7 to 37 miles above the earth's surface — **strat·o·spher·ic** \ˌstrat-ə-ˈsfi(ə)r-ik, -ˈsfer-\ *adj*

stra·tum \ˈstrāt-əm, ˈstrat-\ *n, pl* **stra·ta** \-ə\ **1** : a layer of a substance; *esp* : one having parallel layers of other kinds lying above or below or both above and below it **2 a** : a stage of historical or cultural development **b** : a level of society comprised of persons of the same or similar social, economic, or cultural status

¹**straw** \ˈstrȯ\ *n* **1** : stalks of grain after threshing; *also* : a dry coarse stem esp. of a cereal grass **2 a** (1) : something of small worth or significance : TRIFLE (2) : something too insubstantial to provide support or help in a desperate situation (3) : a slight fact that is an indication of a coming event **b** : CHAFF 2 **3** : a prepared tube for sucking up a beverage

²**straw** *adj* **1 a** : made of straw **b** : of, relating to, or used for straw **2** : of little or no value : WORTHLESS

straw·ber·ry \ˈstrȯ-ˌber-ē, -b(ə-)rē\ *n* : an edible juicy red pulpy fruit of a low herb of the rose family with white flowers and long slender runners; *also* : this plant — **strawberry** *adj*

¹**stray** \ˈstrā\ *vi* **1** : to wander from company, restraint, or proper limits : ROAM **2 a** : to wander from a direct course or at random : DEVIATE, MEANDER **b** : ERR, SIN — **stray·er** *n*

²**stray** *n* **1** : a domestic animal wandering at large or lost **2** : a person or thing that strays : a detached individual

³**stray** *adj* **1** : WANDERING **2** : occurring at random or as detached individuals : SCATTERED, OCCASIONAL, INCIDENTAL

¹**streak** \ˈstrēk\ *n* **1** : a line or mark of a different color or texture from the ground : STRIPE **2 a** : a narrow band of light **b** : a lightning bolt **3 a** : TRACE, STRAIN **b** : a brief run (as of luck) **c** : a consecutive series **4** : a narrow layer

²**streak** *vb* **1** : to make streaks on or in **2** : to move swiftly

streaky \ˈstrē-kē\ *adj* **1** : marked with streaks **2** : VARIABLE, UNRELIABLE — **streak·i·ness** *n*

¹**stream** \ˈstrēm\ *n* **1** : a body of running water (as a river or brook) flowing on the earth; *also* : a body of flowing fluid (as water or gas) **2 a** : a steady succession **b** : a constantly renewed supply **c** : a continuous moving procession **3** : an

unbroken flow (as of gas or particles of matter)
[2]stream *vb* **1 a :** to flow or cause to flow in or as if in a stream **b :** to leave a bright trail **2 a :** to exude a bodily fluid profusely **b :** to become saturated **3 :** to trail out at full length **4 :** to pour in large numbers **5 :** to display fully extended
stream·er \'strē-mər\ *n* **1 a :** a flag that streams in the wind; *esp* **:** PENNANT **b :** a long narrow wavy strip like or suggesting a banner floating in the wind **c :** a newspaper headline that runs across the entire sheet **2** *pl* **:** AURORA BOREALIS
stream·line \'strēm-'līn, -ˌlīn\ *vt* **1 :** to design or construct with a contour for decreasing resistance to motion through water or air or as if for this purpose **2 :** to bring up to date **:** MODERNIZE **3 :** to make simpler or more efficient
stream·lined \-'līnd, -ˌlīnd\ *adj* **1 a :** contoured to reduce resistance to motion through water or air or as if for this purpose **b :** SIMPLIFIED, COMPACT **2 :** MODERNIZED
street \'strēt\ *n* **1 a :** a thoroughfare esp. in a city, town, or village **b :** the part of a street reserved for vehicles **c :** a thoroughfare with abutting property **2 :** the people occupying property on a street
street·car \'strēt-ˌkär\ *n* **:** a vehicle on rails used primarily for transporting passengers and typically operating on city streets
strength \'streŋ(k)th\ *n* **1 :** the quality or state of being strong **:** inherent power **2 :** power to resist force **:** SOLIDITY, TOUGHNESS **3 :** power of resisting attack **:** IMPREGNABILITY **4 :** legal, logical, or moral force **5 a :** degree of potency of effect or of concentration **b :** intensity of light, color, sound, or odor **6 :** force as measured in numbers **7 :** one regarded as embodying or affording force or firmness **:** SUPPORT
strength·en \'streŋ(k)-thən\ *vb* **strength·ened; strength·en·ing** \'streŋ(k)th-(ə-)niŋ\ **:** to make or become stronger — **strength·en·er** \'streŋ(k)th-(ə-)nər\ *n*
stren·u·ous \'stren-yə-wəs\ *adj* **1 a :** vigorously active **:** ENERGETIC **b :** FERVENT, ZEALOUS **2 :** marked by or calling for energy or stamina **:** ARDUOUS — **stren·u·ous·ly** *adv*
strep·to·coc·cus \ˌstrep-tə-'käk-əs\ *n, pl* **strep·to·coc·ci** \-'käk-ˌ(s)ī, -(ˌ)(s)ē\ **:** any of various nonmotile mostly parasitic spherical bacteria that occur in pairs or chains and include important pathogens of man and domestic animals
strep·to·my·cin \-'mīs-ᵊn\ *n* **:** an antibiotic base produced by a soil microorganism and used esp. in the treatment of tuberculosis
[1]stress \'stres\ *n* **1 a :** constraining force or influence **b :** a force that tends to distort a body **c :** a factor that induces bodily or mental tension and may be a factor in disease causation; *also* **:** a state of tension resulting from a stress **2 :** EMPHASIS, WEIGHT **3 :** intensity of utterance given to a speech sound, syllable, or word **4 :** relative force or prominence of sound in verse; *also* **:** a syllable having this stress — **stress·less** \-ləs\ *adj*
[2]stress *vt* **1 :** ACCENT **2 :** to subject to physical stress **3 :** to lay stress on **:** EMPHASIZE
[1]stretch \'strech\ *vb* **1 :** to extend (as one's limbs or body) in a reclining position **2 :** to reach out **3 a :** to extend in length or breadth or both **:** SPREAD **b :** to extend over a continuous period **4 :** to cause the limbs of (a person) to be pulled esp. in torture **5 :** to draw up (one's body) from a cramped, stooping, or relaxed position **6 :** to pull taut **7 a :** to enlarge or distend esp. by force **b :** STRAIN **8 :** to cause to reach or continue **9 :** to extend often unduly the scope or meaning of **10 :** to become extended without breaking — **stretch·a·bil·i·ty** \ˌstrech-ə-'bil-ət-ē\ *n* — **stretch·a·ble** *adj*
[2]stretch *n* **1 a :** an exercise of something (as the imagination or understanding) beyond ordinary or normal limits **b :** an extension of the scope or application of something **2 :** the extent to which something may be stretched **3 :** the act of stretching **:** the state of being stretched **4 a :** an extent in length or area **b :** a continuous period of time **5 :** a walk to relieve fatigue **6 :** a term of imprisonment **7 a :** either of the straight sides of a racecourse; *esp* **:** HOMESTRETCH **b :** a final stage **8 :** the capacity for being stretched **:** ELASTICITY
[3]stretch *adj* **:** easily stretched **:** ELASTIC
stretch·er \'strech-ər\ *n* **1 :** one that stretches **2 :** a litter (as of canvas) for carrying a disabled or dead person

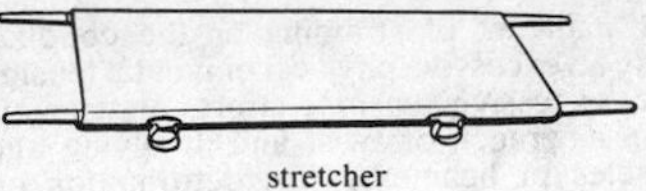
stretcher

strew \'strü\ *vt* **strewed; strewed** *or* **strewn** \'strün\; **strew·ing 1 :** to spread (as seeds or flowers) by scattering **2 :** to cover by or as if by scattering something over or on **3 :** to become dispersed over **4 :** to spread abroad **:** DISSEMINATE
stria \'strī-ə\ *n, pl* **stri·ae** \'strī-ˌē\ **1 :** a minute groove or channel **2 :** a narrow line or band (as of color) esp. when one of a series of parallel grooves or lines
stri·at·ed \'strī-ˌāt-əd\ *adj* **:** marked with lines, bands, or grooves — **stri·a·tion** \strī-'ā-shən\ *n*
strick·en \'strik-ən\ *adj* **1 :** hit or wounded by or as if by a missile **2 :** afflicted with disease, misfortune, or sorrow
strict \'strikt\ *adj* **1 :** permitting no evasion or escape **2 a :** inflexibly maintained or adhered to **:** COMPLETE, ABSOLUTE **b** (1) **:** rigorously conforming to principle or to a norm (2) **:** severe in discipline **3 :** EXACT, PRECISE — **strict·ly** *adv* — **strict·ness** \'strik(t)-nəs\ *n*
stric·ture \'strik-chər\ *n* **1 :** an abnormal narrowing of a bodily passage; *also* **:** the narrowed part **2 :** something that closely restrains or limits **:** RESTRICTION **3 :** an adverse criticism
[1]stride \'strīd\ *vb* **strode** \'strōd\; **strid·den** \'strid-ᵊn\; **strid·ing** \'strīd-iŋ\ **1 :** to move over, through, or along with or as if with long measured steps **2 :** to take a very long step **3 :** BESTRIDE, STRADDLE — **strid·er** \'strīd-ər\ *n*
[2]stride *n* **1 :** a step or the distance covered by a step **2 :** an act or manner of progressing on foot **:** way of striding **3 :** a stage of progress **:** ADVANCE
stri·dent \'strīd-ᵊnt\ *adj* **:** harsh sounding **:** GRATING; *also* **:** SHRILL — **stri·den·cy** \-ᵊn-sē\ *n* — **stri·dent·ly** *adv*
strife \'strīf\ *n* **1 :** bitter sometimes violent conflict or dissension **2 :** an act of contention **:** FIGHT, STRUGGLE
[1]strike \'strīk\ *vb* **struck** \'strək\; **struck; strik·ing** \'strī-kiŋ\ **1 :** to take a course **:** GO **2 a :** to deliver a stroke, blow, or thrust **:** HIT **b :** to drive or remove by or as if by a blow **3 :** to come into contact or collision with **:** COLLIDE **4 :** to remove or cancel with or as if with a stroke of the pen **5 :** to lower, take down, or take apart **6 a :** to indicate or become indicated by a clock, bell, or chime **b :** to indicate by sounding **7 :** to pierce or penetrate or to cause to pierce or penetrate **8 :** to make a military attack **:** FIGHT **9 :** to seize the bait **10 :** to stop work in order to force an employer to comply with demands **11 :** to make a beginning **:** LAUNCH **12 :** to afflict suddenly **:** lay low **13 a :** to bring into forceful contact **b :** to thrust suddenly **c :** to fall on **d :** to become audible to **14 a :** to affect with a mental or emotional state or a strong emotion **b :** to affect a person with (a strong emotion) **c :** to cause to become by or as if by a sudden blow **d :** to produce by stamping with a die or punch **e :** to cause to ignite by friction **15 :** to agree on the terms of **16 a :** to occur to **b :** to appear to **c :** to make a strong impression on **:** IMPRESS **17 :** to arrive at by computation **18 a :** to come to **b :** to run across **19 :** to take on **:** ASSUME — **strik·er** *n*
[2]strike *n* **1 :** an act or instance of striking **2 a :** a work stoppage by a body of workers to force an employer to comply with demands **b :** a temporary stoppage of activities in protest against an act or condition **3 :** a pull on a line by a fish in

striking 4 : a stroke of good luck; *esp* : a discovery of a valuable mineral deposit 5 : a pitched baseball recorded against a batter 6 : an act or instance of knocking down all the bowling pins with the first ball 7 : a military attack

strike·break·er \'strīk-ˌbrā-kər\ *n* : a person hired to help break up a strike of workmen

strike out *vb* 1 : to make an out in baseball by a strikeout 2 : to enter upon a course of action 3 : to set out vigorously

strike·out \'strīk-ˌau̇t\ *n* : an out in baseball resulting from a batter's being charged with three strikes

strike up *vb* 1 : to begin or cause to begin to sing or play or to be sung or played 2 : to cause to begin

strike zone *n* : the area (as between the knees and shoulders of a batter in his natural stance) over home plate through which a pitched baseball must pass to be called a strike

strik·ing \'strī-kiŋ\ *adj* : REMARKABLE, IMPRESSIVE — **strik·ing·ly** \-kiŋ-lē\ *adv*

[1]**string** \'striŋ\ *n* 1 : a small cord used to bind, fasten, or tie 2 : a thin tough plant structure; *esp* : the fiber connecting the halves of a bean pod 3 **a** : the gut or wire cord of a musical instrument **b** *pl* (1) : the stringed instruments of an orchestra (2) : the players of such instruments 4 **a** : a group of objects threaded on a string **b** : a series of things arranged in or as if in a line 5 : a group of players ranked according to skill or proficiency 6 : SUCCESSION, SEQUENCE 7 *pl* **a** : contingent conditions or obligations **b** : CONTROL, DOMINATION — **string·less** \'striŋ-ləs\ *adj*

[2]**string** *vb* **strung** \'strəŋ\; **string·ing** \'striŋ-iŋ\ 1 **a** : to equip with strings **b** : to tune the strings of 2 : to make tense 3 **a** : to thread on or as if on a string **b** : to thread with objects **c** : to tie, hang, or fasten with string 4 : to hang by the neck 5 : to remove the strings of 6 **a** : to extend or stretch like a string **b** : to set out in a line or series **c** : to move, progress, or lie in a string **d** : to form into strings 7 : FOOL, HOAX

string along *vb* 1 : to go along : AGREE 2 : to keep dangling or waiting 3 : DECEIVE, FOOL

strin·gent \'strin-jənt\ *adj* 1 : TIGHT, CONSTRICTED 2 : marked by rigor, strictness, or severity esp. with regard to rule or standard — **strin·gen·cy** \-jən-sē\ *n* — **strin·gent·ly** *adv*

string·er \'striŋ-ər\ *n* 1 : one that strings 2 : a long horizontal member in a framed structure or a bridge

stringy \'striŋ-ē\ *adj* 1 **a** : containing, consisting of, or resembling fibrous matter or a string **b** : lean and sinewy in build : WIRY 2 : capable of being drawn out to form a string : ROPY 3 : not compact — **string·i·ness** *n*

[1]**strip** \'strip\ *vb* **stripped** \'stript\; **strip·ping** 1 **a** : to remove clothing, covering, or surface matter from **b** : to remove (as clothing) from a person : UNDRESS **c** : SKIN, PEEL 2 : to divest of honors, privileges, or functions 3 **a** : to remove extraneous or superficial matter from **b** : to remove furniture, equipment, or accessories from 4 : PLUNDER, SPOIL 5 : to make bare or clear (as by cutting or grazing) — **strip·per** *n*

[2]**strip** *n* 1 : a long narrow piece or area 2 : AIRSTRIP

[1]**stripe** \'strīp\ *n* : a stroke or blow with a rod or lash

[2]**stripe** *n* 1 : a line or long narrow section differing in color or texture from parts adjoining 2 **a** : a piece of braid (as on the sleeve) to indicate military rank or length of service **b** : CHEVRON 3 : a distinct variety or sort : TYPE

[3]**stripe** *vt* : to make stripes on or variegate with stripes

striped \'strīpt, 'strī-pəd\ *adj* : having stripes or streaks

strip·ling \'strip-liŋ\ *n* : a youth just passing from boyhood to manhood

strive \'strīv\ *vi* **strove** \'strōv\; **striv·en** \'striv-ən\ *or* **strived**; **striv·ing** \'strī-viŋ\ 1 : to struggle in opposition : CONTEND 2 : to devote serious effort or energy : ENDEAVOR

stro·bo·scope \'strō-bə-ˌskōp\ *n* : an instrument for determining speeds of rotation or frequencies of vibration by means of a rapidly flashing light that illuminates an object intermittently — **stro·bo·scop·ic** \ˌstrō-bə-'skäp-ik\ *adj*

strode *past of* STRIDE

[1]**stroke** \'strōk\ *vt* : to rub gently in one direction; *also* : CARESS — **strok·er** *n*

[2]**stroke** *n* 1 : the act of striking; *esp* : a blow with a weapon or implement 2 : a single unbroken movement; *esp* : one of a series of repeated or to-and-fro movements 3 : a striking of the ball in a game 4 : a sudden action or process producing an impact or unexpected result 5 : APOPLEXY 6 **a** : one of a series of propelling movements against a resisting medium **b** : an oarsman who sets the tempo for a crew 7 **a** : a vigorous or energetic effort **b** : a delicate or clever touch in a narrative, description, or construction 8 **a** : the sound of a bell being struck **b** : PULSATION, BEAT 9 **a** : a mark made by a single movement of a tool **b** : one of the lines of a letter of the alphabet

stroll \'strōl\ *vb* 1 : to walk in a leisurely or idle manner : RAMBLE 2 : to walk at leisure along or about — **stroll** *n*

stroll·er \'strō-lər\ *n* 1 : one that strolls 2 : a wheeled seat in which a baby may be pushed

strong \'strȯŋ\ *adj* **strong·er** \'strȯŋ-gər\; **strong·est** \'strȯŋ-gəst\ 1 : having or marked by great physical power : ROBUST 2 : having moral or intellectual power 3 : having great resources (as of wealth) 4 : of a specified number 5 : effective or efficient esp. in a specified direction 6 : FORCEFUL, COGENT 7 : not mild or weak : INTENSE 8 : moving with rapidity or force 9 : ARDENT, ZEALOUS 10 **a** : able to withstand stress : not easily injured : SOLID **b** : not easily subdued or taken 11 : well established : FIRM 12 : having an offensive or intense odor or flavor : RANK — **strong** *adv* — **strong·ly** *adv*

strong·box \-ˌbäks\ *n* : a strongly made container for valuables

strong·hold \-ˌhōld\ *n* : a fortified place : FORTRESS

strong–mind·ed \-'mīn-dəd\ *adj* : markedly independent in thought and judgment — **strong–mind·ed·ly** *adv*

stron·tium \'strän-ch(ē-)əm, 'stränt-ē-əm\ *n* : a soft malleable ductile metallic element occurring only in combination

[1]**strop** \'sträp\ *n* : STRAP; *esp* : a usu. leather band for sharpening a razor

[2]**strop** *vt* **stropped**; **strop·ping** : to sharpen (a razor) on a strop

stro·phe \'strō-fē\ *n* : a division of a poem : STANZA — **stroph·ic** \'sträf-ik, 'strō-fik\ *adj*

strove *past of* STRIVE

struck \'strək\ *adj* : closed or affected by a labor strike

struc·tur·al \'strək-chə-rəl, 'strək-shrəl\ *adj* 1 : of, relating to, or affecting structure 2 : used or formed for use in construction — **struc·tur·al·ly** \-ē\ *adv*

struc·ture \'strək-chər\ *n* 1 : the action of building : CONSTRUCTION 2 **a** : something constructed **b** : something made up of interdependent parts in a definite pattern of organization 3 : manner of construction : MAKEUP 4 : the arrangement or relationship of elements (as particles, parts, or organs) in a substance, body, or system — **struc·ture·less** \-ləs\ *adj*

[1]**strug·gle** \'strəg-əl\ *vi* **strug·gled**; **strug·gling** \'strəg-(ə-)liŋ\ 1 : to make violent strenuous efforts against opposition : STRIVE 2 : to proceed with difficulty or with great effort

[2]**struggle** *n* 1 : a violent effort or exertion 2 : CONTEST, STRIFE

strum \'strəm\ *vb* **strummed**; **strum·ming** : to play on a musical instrument by brushing the strings with the fingers

strum·pet \'strəm-pət\ *n* : PROSTITUTE, HARLOT

strung *past of* STRING

[1]**strut** \'strət\ *vb* **strut·ted**; **strut·ting** 1 : to walk with a stiff proud gait 2 : to parade (as clothes) with a show of pride

[2]**strut** *n* 1 : a bar or brace to resist pressure in the direction of its length 2 : a pompous step or walk

strych·nine \'strik-ˌnīn, -nən, -ˌnēn\ *n* : a bitter poisonous alkaloid obtained from some plants and used as an economic poison (as for rodents) and medicinally as a stimulant

[1]**stub** \'stəb\ *n* 1 : STUMP 1b 2 : something having or worn to

a short or blunt shape: as **a** : a pen with a short blunt nib **b** : a short part left after a larger part has been broken off or used up **3 a** : a small part of a check kept as a record of the contents of the check **b** : the part of a ticket returned to the user

²stub *vt* **stubbed**; **stub·bing** **1** : to extinguish (as a cigarette) by crushing **2** : to strike (as one's toe) against an object

stub·ble \'stəb-əl\ *n* **1** : the stem ends of herbaceous plants and esp. cereal grasses remaining attached to the soil after harvest **2** : a rough surface or growth resembling stubble; *esp* : a short growth of beard — **stub·bly** \'stəb-(ə-)lē\ *adj*

stub·born \'stəb-ərn\ *adj* **1 a** : having a firm idea or purpose : DETERMINED **b** : hard to convince, persuade, or move to action : OBSTINATE **2** : done or continued in an obstinate or persistent manner **3** : difficult to handle, manage, or treat — **stub·born·ly** *adv* — **stub·born·ness** *n*

stub·by \'stəb-ē\ *adj* **1** : resembling a stub esp. in shortness and broadness **2** : abounding with stubs : BRISTLY

¹stuc·co \'stək-ō\ *n*, *pl* **stuccos** *or* **stuccoes** : a plaster used to cover exterior walls or ornament interior walls

²stucco *vt* : to coat or decorate with stucco

stuck *past of* STICK

stuck–up \'stək-'əp\ *adj* : CONCEITED, SELF-IMPORTANT

¹stud \'stəd\ *n* **1** : one of the smaller uprights in the framing of the walls of a building to which sheathing, paneling, or laths are fastened : SCANTLING **2** : a removable device like a button used as a fastener or ornament **3** : a piece (as a rod or pin) projecting from a machine and serving chiefly as a support or axis

²stud *vt* **stud·ded**; **stud·ding** **1** : to furnish (a building or wall) with studs **2** : to adorn, cover, or protect with studs **3** : to set (a place or thing) with a number of prominent objects

stud·ding \'stəd-iŋ\ *n* **1** : material for studs **2** : STUDS

stu·dent \'st(y)üd-ᵊnt, *esp South* -ənt\ *n* **1** : LEARNER, SCHOLAR; *esp* : one who attends a school or college **2** : one who studies

stud·ied \'stəd-ēd\ *adj* **1** : KNOWLEDGEABLE, LEARNED **2** : carefully considered or prepared : THOUGHTFUL **3** : produced or marked by conscious design or premeditation

stu·dio \'st(y)üd-ē-ˌō\ *n*, *pl* **-di·os** **1 a** : the working place of an artist **b** : a place for the study of an art **2** : a place where motion pictures are made **3** : a place maintained and equipped for the transmission of radio or television programs

stu·di·ous \'st(y)üd-ē-əs\ *adj* **1** : given to or concerned with study **2** : marked by purposeful diligence : EARNEST — **stu·di·ous·ly** *adv* — **stu·di·ous·ness** *n*

¹study \'stəd-ē\ *n*, *pl* **stud·ies** **1** : a state of contemplation : REVERIE **2 a** : application of the mind to the acquisition of knowledge often about a particular field or topic **b** : a careful examination or analysis of something; *also* : a report or publication on such a study **3** : a building or room devoted to study or literary pursuits **4** : PURPOSE, INTENT **5 a** : a branch or department of learning : SUBJECT **b** : the activity or work of a student **6** : a usu. preliminary or elementary artistic production concerned esp. with problems of technique

²study *vb* **stud·ied**; **stud·y·ing** **1** : to engage in study or the study of **2** : ENDEAVOR, TRY **3** : to develop a plan for : DESIGN **4** : to consider attentively or in detail esp. with the intent of fixing in the mind or of appraising

¹stuff \'stəf\ *n* **1** : materials, supplies, or equipment used in various activities: as **a** : a person's or a family's movable possessions (as household goods or baggage) **b** : material to be manufactured, wrought, or used in construction **c** : a finished textile suitable for clothing; *esp* : wool or worsted material **2 a** : writing, discourse, or ideas often of little or transitory worth **b** : actions or talk of a particular and often objectionable kind **3 a** : an aggregate of matter **b** : matter of a particular kind often unspecified **4 a** : fundamental material **b** : subject matter **5** : special knowledge or capability

²stuff *vb* **1 a** : to fill by or as if by packing things in : CRAM **b** : to eat gluttonously : GORGE, SURFEIT **c** : to fill with a stuffing **d** : to stop up : PLUG **e** : to fill with ideas or information **2** : to put or push into something esp. carelessly or casually : cause to enter or fill : THRUST, PRESS **3** : to fill (a ballot box) with fraudulent votes — **stuff·er** *n*

stuffed shirt \ˌstəft-\ *n* : a smug, conceited, and usu. pompous and inflexibly conservative person

stuff·ing \'stəf-iŋ\ *n* : material used to stuff something; *esp* : a seasoned mixture used to stuff meat or poultry

stuffy \'stəf-ē\ *adj* **1** : SULLEN, ILL-HUMORED **2 a** : oppressive to the breathing : CLOSE **b** : stuffed or choked up **3** : DULL, STODGY **4** : narrowly inflexible in standards of conduct — **stuff·i·ly** \'stəf-ə-lē\ *adv* — **stuff·i·ness** \'stəf-ē-nəs\ *n*

stul·ti·fy \'stəl-tə-ˌfī\ *vt* **-fied**; **-fy·ing** **1** : to cause to appear or be stupid, foolish, or absurdly illogical **2** : to make futile or useless esp. through weakening or repressive influences — **stul·ti·fi·ca·tion** \ˌstəl-tə-fə-'kā-shən\ *n*

stum·ble \'stəm-bəl\ *vi* **stum·bled**; **stum·bling** \-b(ə-)liŋ\ **1** : to trip in walking or running; *also* : to walk unsteadily **2 a** : to blunder morally **b** : to speak or act in a blundering or clumsy manner **3** : to come or happen unexpectedly or by chance — **stumble** *n* — **stum·bler** \-b(ə-)lər\ *n* — **stum·bling·ly** *adv*

¹stump \'stəmp\ *n* **1 a** : the base of a bodily part (as an arm or leg) remaining after the rest is removed **b** : the part of a plant and esp. a tree remaining attached to the root after the top is cut off **2** : STUB 2 **3** : a place or occasion for political public speaking

²stump *vb* **1 a** : STUB 2 **b** : to walk or walk over heavily or clumsily **2 a** : CHALLENGE, DARE **b** : PERPLEX, CONFOUND **3** : to clear (land) of stumps **4** : to go about making political speeches or supporting a cause — **stump·er** *n*

stumpy \'stəm-pē\ *adj* **1** : full of stumps **2** : being short and thick : SQUAT

stun \'stən\ *vt* **stunned**; **stun·ning** **1** : to make senseless or dizzy by or as if by a blow **2** : BEWILDER, STUPEFY — **stun** *n*

stung *past of* STING

stunk *past of* STINK

stun·ning \'stən-iŋ\ *adj* **1** : tending or able to stupefy or bewilder **2** : strikingly lovely or pleasing — **stun·ning·ly** *adv*

¹stunt \'stənt\ *vt* : to hinder the normal growth of : DWARF

²stunt *n* : an unusual or difficult feat performed or undertaken usu. to gain attention or publicity

³stunt *vi* : to perform stunts

stu·pe·fy \'st(y)ü-pə-ˌfī\ *vt* **-fied**; **-fy·ing** **1** : to make stupid, dull, or numb by or as if by drugs **2** : ASTONISH, BEWILDER — **stu·pe·fac·tion** \ˌst(y)ü-pə-'fak-shən\ *n*

stu·pen·dous \st(y)ù-'pen-dəs\ *adj* : stupefying or amazing esp. because of great size or height — **stu·pen·dous·ly** *adv* — **stu·pen·dous·ness** *n*

stu·pid \'st(y)ü-pəd\ *adj* **1 a** : slow of mind : OBTUSE **b** : UNTHINKING, IRRATIONAL **2 a** : dulled in feeling or sensation : TORPID **b** : incapable of feeling or sensation **3** : marked by or resulting from dullness : SENSELESS **4** : DREARY, BORING — **stu·pid·ly** *adv* — **stu·pid·ness** *n*

stu·pid·i·ty \st(y)ù-'pid-ət-ē\ *n*, *pl* **-ties** **1** : the quality or state of being stupid **2** : something (as an idea or act) that is stupid

stu·por \'st(y)ü-pər\ *n* **1** : a condition characterized by great dulling or suspension of sense or feeling **2** : a state of extreme apathy or torpor resulting often from stress or shock — **stu·por·ous** \-p(ə-)rəs\ *adj*

stur·dy \'stərd-ē\ *adj* **1 a** : firmly built or made : STOUT **b** : HARDY **c** : sound in design or execution : SUBSTANTIAL **2 a** : marked by or reflecting physical strength or vigor : ROBUST **b** : FIRM, RESOLUTE — **stur·di·ly** \'stərd-ᵊl-ē\ *adj* — **stur·di·ness** \'stərd-ē-nəs\ *n*

stur·geon \'stər-jən\ *n* : any of various usu. large long-bodied fishes that have a thick skin with rows of bony plates and ar valued for their flesh and esp. for their roe which is made into caviar

[1]**stut·ter** \'stət-ər\ *vb* : to speak or utter with spasmodic repetition as a result of excitement or impediment — **stut·ter·er** \'stət-ər-ər\ *n*

[2]**stutter** *n* **1** : an act or instance of stuttering **2** : a speech impediment involving stuttering

[1]**sty** \'stī\ *n, pl* **sties** \'stīz\ **1** : a pen or enclosed housing for swine **2** : a filthy, low, or vicious place

[2]**sty** *or* **stye** \'stī\ *n, pl* **sties** *or* **styes** \'stīz\ : an inflamed swelling of a skin gland on the edge of an eyelid

[1]**style** \'stīl\ *n* **1** : a slender pointed instrument or process; *esp* : STYLUS **2** : mode of expressing thought in language; *esp* : one characteristic of an individual, period, school, or nation **3** : the custom or plan followed in spelling, capitalization, punctuation, and typographic arrangement and display **4** : mode of address : TITLE **5 a** (1) : manner or method of acting or performing esp. as sanctioned by some standard (2) : a distinctive or characteristic manner **b** : a fashionable manner or mode **c** : overall excellence, skill, or grace in performance, manner, or appearance — **style·less** *adj*

[2]**style** *vt* **1** : NAME, CALL **2 a** : to cause to conform to a customary style **b** : to design and make in accord with the prevailing mode — **styl·er** *n*

styl·ish \'stī-lish\ *adj* : having style; *esp* : conforming to current fashion — **styl·ish·ly** *adv* — **styl·ish·ness** *n*

styl·ist \'stī-ləst\ *n* **1** : a master or model of style; *esp* : a writer or speaker eminent in matters of style **2** : one who develops, designs, or advises on styles — **sty·lis·tic** \stī-'lis-tik\ *adj* — **sty·lis·ti·cal·ly** \-ti-k(ə-)lē\ *adv*

styl·ize \'stīl-,īz\ *vt* : to conform to a style : CONVENTIONALIZE; *esp* : to represent or design according to a style or stylistic pattern rather than according to nature — **styl·i·za·tion** \,stī-lə-'zā-shən\ *n* — **styl·iz·er** *n*

sty·lus \'stī-ləs\ *n, pl* **sty·li** \'stīl-,ī\ **1** : an instrument for writing or marking **2** : a phonograph needle

[1]**sty·mie** \'stī-mē\ *n* **1** : a position in golf when the ball nearer the hole lies in the line of play of another ball **2** : a thoroughly distressing and thwarting situation

[2]**stymie** *vt* **sty·mied**; **sty·mie·ing** : BLOCK, CHECK

styp·tic \'stip-tik\ *adj* : tending to contract or bind : ASTRINGENT; *esp* : tending to check bleeding — **styptic** *n*

sua·sion \'swā-zhən\ *n* : the act of influencing or persuading

suave \'swäv\ *adj* : persuasively pleasing : smoothly polite and agreeable — **suave·ly** *adv* — **suav·i·ty** \'swäv-ət-ē\ *n*

[1]**sub** \'səb\ *n* : SUBSTITUTE

[2]**sub** *vi* **subbed**; **sub·bing** : to act as a substitute

[3]**sub** *n* : SUBMARINE

sub- \'səb, ,səb\ *prefix* **1** : under : beneath : below **2** : subordinate : secondary **3** : subordinate portion of : subdivision of **4** : with repetition of a process described in a simple verb so as to form, stress, or deal with subordinate parts or relations **5** : somewhat **6** : falling nearly in the category of : bordering upon

subacid
subacute
subadult
subagency
subagent
subangular
subaquatic
subaqueous
subarctic
subarea
subarid
subatmospheric
subaverage
subbasement
subbituminous
subcaliber
subcaption
subcartilaginous
subcaste
subcaudal
subcellar
subcentral
subchairman
subchief
subcircular
subcivilized
subclass
subclassification
subclassify
subclause
subclinical
subcollegiate
subcolumnar
subcommission
subconic
subcortical
subcrescentic
subcrystalline
subcylindrical
subdeacon
subdean
subdentate
subdepot
subdimension
subdorsal
subeffective
subelliptic
subentry
subepidermal
subequal
subequatorial
suberect
subesophageal
subessential
subfamily
subfauna
subflora
subfossil
subfunctional
subgenus
subgroup
subhorizontal
subhuman
subhumid
subindex
subinterval
subintestinal
subirrigate
subkingdom
sublabial
sublateral
sublethal
sublingual
subliterate
sublunar
submature
submaximal
submetallic
subminimal
subneural
subnutrition
suboblique
suboceanic
subocular
subopaque
subopposite
suboptimal
suborbicular
subovoid
subparagraph
subparallel
subpermanent
subplot
subpolar
subpotent
subprincipal
subprofessional
subrational
subrecent
subregion
subrigid
subroutine
subsaline
subsaturated
subscience
subsense
subserous
subsexual
subshining
subsize
subsocial
subspace
subspecialty
subspecies
subspherical
substage
subsurface
subsystem
subtemperate
subterminal
subtetanic
subthreshold
subtidal
subtopic
subtotal
subtreasury
subtype
subunit
subvisible
subvocal

[1]**sub·al·tern** \sə-'bȯl-tərn\ *adj* : of low or lower rank

[2]**subaltern** *n* : SUBORDINATE; *esp* : a commissioned officer in the British army below the rank of captain

sub·as·sem·bly \,səb-ə-'sem-blē\ *n* : an assembled unit designed to be incorporated with other units in a finished product

sub·com·mit·tee \'səb-kə-,mit-ē\ *n* : a subdivision of a committee usu. organized for a specific purpose

[1]**sub·con·scious** \'səb-'kän-chəs\ *adj* : existing in the mind but not immediately available to consciousness — **sub·con·scious·ly** *adv* — **sub·con·scious·ness** *n*

[2]**subconscious** *n* : the mental activities just below the threshold of consciousness

sub·con·ti·nent \'səb-'känt-ᵊn-ənt, -'känt-nənt\ *n* : a large landmass (as Greenland) smaller than any of the usu. recognized continents; *also* : a major subdivision of a continent — **sub·con·ti·nen·tal** \,səb-,känt-ᵊn-'ent-ᵊl\ *adj*

sub·cu·ta·ne·ous \,səb-kyu̇-'tā-nē-əs\ *adj* : being, living, used, or made under the skin — **sub·cu·ta·ne·ous·ly** *adv*

sub·di·vide \,səb-də-'vīd\ *vb* **1** : to divide the parts of into more parts **2** : to divide into several parts; *esp* : to divide (a tract of land) into building lots — **sub·di·vi·sion** \,səb-də-'vizh-ən, 'səb-də-,\ *n*

sub·due \səb-'d(y)ü\ *vt* **1** : to conquer and bring into subjection : VANQUISH **2** : to bring under control or into order : CURB **3** : to reduce the intensity or degree of — **sub·du·er** *n*

sub·freez·ing \'səb-'frē-ziŋ\ *adj* : lower than is required to produce freezing

sub·head \'səb-,hed\ *or* **sub·head·ing** \-iŋ\ *n* **1** : a heading of a subdivision **2** : a subordinate caption or title

sub·ja·cent \,səb-'jās-ᵊnt\ *adj* : lying under or below; *also* : lower than though not directly below

[1]**sub·ject** \'səb-jikt\ *n* **1** : one that is placed under authority or control: as **a** : one subject to a monarch and governed by his law **b** : one who lives in the territory of, enjoys the protection of, and owes allegiance to a sovereign power or state **2 a** : a department of knowledge or learning **b** : an individual that is studied or experimented on **c** : something concerning which something is said or done **3** : a noun or noun equivalent about which something is stated by the predicate

[2]**subject** *adj* **1** : owing obedience or allegiance to the dominion of another **2 a** : EXPOSED, LIABLE **b** : PRONE, DISPOSED **3** : CONDITIONAL, CONTINGENT

[3]**sub·ject** \səb-'jekt\ *vt* **1 a** : to bring under control or do-

minion : SUBJUGATE **b** : to make amenable to the discipline and control of a superior **2 a** : to make liable : PREDISPOSE **b** : to make accountable : SUBMIT **3** : to cause to undergo or submit to : EXPOSE — **sub·jec·tion** \səb-ˈjek-shən\ *n*

sub·jec·tive \səb-ˈjek-tiv\ *adj* **1** : of, relating to, or being a subject **2** : of, relating to, or arising within one's self or mind in contrast to what is outside : PERSONAL — **sub·jec·tive·ly** *adv* — **sub·jec·tiv·i·ty** \(ˌ)səb-ˌjek-ˈtiv-ət-ē\ *n*

subject matter *n* : matter presented for consideration in discussion, thought, or study

sub·join \(ˌ)səb-ˈjȯin\ *vt* : ANNEX, APPEND

sub·ju·gate \ˈsəb-jə-ˌgāt\ *vt* **1** : to force to submit to control and governance : MASTER **2** : to bring into servitude : ENSLAVE — **sub·ju·ga·tion** \ˌsəb-jə-ˈgā-shən\ *n* — **sub·ju·ga·tor** \ˈsəb-jə-ˌgāt-ər\ *n*

1sub·junc·tive \səb-ˈjəŋ(k)-tiv\ *adj* : of, relating to, or constituting a verb form that represents a denoted act or state not as fact but as contingent or possible or viewed emotionally (as with doubt or desire)

2subjunctive *n* : the subjunctive mood of a verb : a verb in this mood

sub·lease \ˈsəb-ˈlēs\ *n* : a lease by a tenant of part or all of leased premises to another person — **sublease** *vb*

sub·let \ˈsəb-ˈlet\ *vb* **sub·let**; **sub·let·ting** **1** : to lease or rent all or part of a leased or rented property **2** : SUBCONTRACT

sub·li·mate \ˈsəb-lə-ˌmāt\ *vt* **1** : to cause to sublime **2** : to direct the energy of (desires and impulses) from a lower to a higher level — **sub·li·ma·tion** \ˌsəb-lə-ˈmā-shən\ *n*

1sub·lime \sə-ˈblīm\ *vb* **1** : to pass from a solid to a gaseous state on heating and back to solid form on cooling without apparently passing through a liquid state; *also* : to release or purify by such action **2** : to make finer or more worthy : convert into something better — **sub·lim·er** *n*

2sublime *adj* **1 a** : lofty, grand, or exalted in thought, expression, or manner **b** : of outstanding spiritual, intellectual, or moral worth **2** : inspiring awe : SOLEMN — **sub·lime·ly** *adv*

sub·lim·i·nal \ˈsəb-ˈlim-ən-ᵊl\ *adj* : existing or functioning outside the area of conscious awareness — **sub·lim·i·nal·ly** \-ᵊl-ē\ *adv*

sub·lim·i·ty \sə-ˈblim-ət-ē\ *n*, *pl* **-ties** **1** : something sublime or exalted **2** : the quality or state of being sublime

sub·ma·chine gun \ˌsəb-mə-ˈshēn-ˌgən\ *n* : a lightweight automatic or semiautomatic portable firearm fired from the shoulder or hip

sub·mar·gin·al \ˈsəb-ˈmärj-nəl, -ən-ᵊl\ *adj* **1** : located near or beneath a margin or a marginal structure **2** : less than marginal; *esp* : inadequate for some end or use

1sub·ma·rine \ˈsəb-mə-ˌrēn, ˌsəb-mə-ˈ\ *adj* : being, acting, or growing under water esp. in the sea

2submarine *n* : something (as an explosive mine) that functions or operates underwater; *esp* : a naval vessel designed for undersea operations

sub·ma·rin·er \ˈsəb-mə-ˌrē-nər, ˌsəb-mə-ˈ; ˌsəb-ˈmar-ə-\ *n* : a crewman of a submarine

sub·merge \səb-ˈmərj\ *vb* **1** : to put under or plunge into water **2** : to cover or become covered with or as if with water : INUNDATE — **sub·mer·gence** \-ˈmər-jən(t)s\ *n* — **sub·merg·i·ble** \-ˈmər-jə-bəl\ *adj*

sub·merse \səb-ˈmərs\ *vt* : SUBMERGE — **sub·mer·sion** \-ˈmər-zhən\ *n*

1sub·mers·i·ble \səb-ˈmər-sə-bəl\ *adj* : SUBMERGIBLE

2submersible *n* : a boat capable of submerging : SUBMARINE

sub·mis·sion \səb-ˈmish-ən\ *n* **1** : an act of submitting something (as for consideration, inspection, or comment) **2** : the condition of being submissive, humble, or compliant **3** : an act of submitting to the authority or control of another

sub·mis·sive \-ˈmis-iv\ *adj* : inclined or willing to submit to others : YIELDING, MEEK — **sub·mis·sive·ly** *adv*

sub·mit \səb-ˈmit\ *vb* **sub·mit·ted**; **sub·mit·ting** **1** : to give over or leave to the judgment or approval of someone else : REFER **2** : to subject to a process or practice **3** : to put forward as an opinion, reason, or idea : AFFIRM **4** : to yield to power or authority : SURRENDER

1sub·nor·mal \ˈsəb-ˈnȯr-məl\ *adj* : falling below what is normal — **sub·nor·mal·i·ty** \ˌsəb-nȯr-ˈmal-ət-ē\ *n* — **sub·nor·mal·ly** \ˈsəb-ˈnȯr-mə-lē\ *adv*

2subnormal *n* : one that is below normal; *esp* : a person of subnormal intelligence

1sub·or·di·nate \sə-ˈbȯrd-ᵊn-ət, -ˈbȯrd-nət\ *adj* **1** : placed in or occupying a lower class or rank : INFERIOR **2** : submissive to or controlled by authority **3 a** : of, relating to, or constituting a clause that functions as a noun, adjective, or adverb **b** : grammatically subordinating — **sub·or·di·nate·ly** *adv* — **sub·or·di·nate·ness** *n*

2subordinate *n* : one that is subordinate

3sub·or·di·nate \sə-ˈbȯrd-ᵊn-ˌāt\ *vt* : to make subordinate — **sub·or·di·na·tion** \-ˌbȯrd-ᵊn-ˈā-shən\ *n*

sub·orn \sə-ˈbȯrn\ *vt* : to induce secretly to do an improper or unlawful thing and esp. to commit perjury — **sub·or·na·tion** \ˌsəb-ˌȯr-ˈnā-shən\ *n* — **sub·orn·er** \sə-ˈbȯr-nər\ *n*

1sub·poe·na \sə-ˈpē-nə\ *n* : a writ commanding a person designated in it to appear in court under a penalty for failure to appear

2subpoena *vt* **-naed**; **-na·ing** : to serve with or summon by a writ of subpoena

sub ro·sa \ˌsəb-ˈrō-zə\ *adv* : in confidence : SECRETLY

sub·scribe \səb-ˈskrīb\ *vb* **1 a** : to sign (one's name or a document) usu. to indicate consent to, obligation by, or approval or awareness of something written **b** : to signify adherence or approval by or as if by signing one's name **2 a** : to pledge payment of (as a sum of money) over one's signature **b** : to agree to contribute to something; *also* : to make an agreed contribution **3 a** : to enter one's name for a publication or service; *also* : to receive a periodical or service regularly on order **b** : to make a signed application for securities of a new offering — **sub·scrib·er** *n*

sub·script \ˈsəb-ˌskript\ *n* : a distinguishing symbol or letter immediately below or below and to the right or left of another written character — **subscript** *adj*

sub·scrip·tion \səb-ˈskrip-shən\ *n* **1** : an act or instance of subscribing **2 a** : something that is subscribed **b** : an amount obtained by subscription

sub·se·quent \ˈsəb-si-kwənt, -sə-ˌkwent\ *adj* : following in time, order, or place : SUCCEEDING — **sub·se·quence** \-sə-ˌkwen(t)s, -si-kwən(t)s\ *n* — **subsequent** *n* — **sub·se·quent·ly** \-ˌkwent-lē, -kwənt-\ *adv* — **sub·se·quent·ness** \-ˌkwent-, -kwənt-\ *n*

sub·serve \səb-ˈsərv\ *vt* **1** : to serve as an instrument or means of **2** : to promote the welfare or purposes of

sub·ser·vi·ence \səb-ˈsər-vē-ən(t)s\ *n* **1** : a subservient or subordinate place or function **2** : obsequious servility

sub·ser·vi·ent \-ənt\ *adj* **1** : useful in an inferior capacity **2** : obsequiously servile — **sub·ser·vi·ent·ly** *adv*

sub·side \səb-ˈsīd\ *vi* **1** : to sink or fall to the bottom : SETTLE **2** : to tend downward : DESCEND, SINK **3** : to let oneself settle down : SINK **4** : to become quiet or less : ABATE — **sub·sid·ence** \səb-ˈsīd-ᵊn(t)s, ˈsəb-səd-ən(t)s\ *n*

1sub·sid·i·ary \səb-ˈsid-ē-ˌer-ē\ *adj* **1 a** : furnishing aid or support : AUXILIARY **b** : of secondary importance : TRIBUTARY **2** : of, relating to, affected by, or constituting a subsidy

2subsidiary *n*, *pl* **-ar·ies** : one that is subsidiary; *esp* : a company wholly controlled by another

sub·si·dize \ˈsəb-sə-ˌdīz, -zə-\ *vt* : to aid or furnish with a subsidy — **sub·si·di·za·tion** \ˌsəb-səd-ə-ˈzā-shən, ˌsəb-zəd-\ *n*

sub·si·dy \ˈsəb-səd-ē, -zəd-\ *n*, *pl* **-dies** : a grant or gift esp. of money; *esp* : a grant by a government to a private person or company or to another government to assist an enterprise advantageous to the public

sub·sist \səb-'sist\ *vi* **1** : to have or continue to have existence **2** : to receive maintenance (as food and clothing) : LIVE

sub·sist·ence \səb-'sis-tən(t)s\ *n* **1 a** : real being : EXISTENCE **b** : CONTINUATION, PERSISTENCE **2 a** : means of subsisting **b** : the minimum (as of food and shelter) necessary to support life — **sub·sist·ent** \-tənt\ *adj*

sub·soil \'səb-,sȯil\ *n* : a layer of weathered material that lies just under the surface soil

sub·son·ic \'səb-'sän-ik\ *adj* **1** : of, relating to, or being a speed less than that of sound in air **2** : moving, capable of moving, or utilizing air currents moving at a subsonic speed **3** : INFRASONIC

sub·stance \'səb-stən(t)s\ *n* **1 a** : essential nature : ESSENCE **b** : the fundamental or essential part, quality, or import **2 a** : physical material from which something is made or which has discrete existence **b** : matter of particular or definite chemical constitution **3** : material possessions : PROPERTY

sub·stan·dard \'səb-'stan-dərd\ *adj* : falling short of a standard or norm

sub·stan·tial \səb-'stan-chəl\ *adj* **1 a** : existing as or in substance : MATERIAL **b** : not illusory : REAL **c** : IMPORTANT, ESSENTIAL **2** : having substance: as **a** : ample to satisfy and nourish **b** : possessed of means : WELL-TO-DO **c** : considerable in quantity : significantly large **d** : well and sturdily built **3** : being largely but not wholly that specified — **sub·stan·ti·al·i·ty** \-,stan-chē-'al-ət-ē\ *n* — **sub·stan·tial·ly** \-'stanch-(ə-)lē\ *adv*

sub·stan·ti·ate \səb-'stan-chē-,āt\ *vt* **1** : to provide evidence for : PROVE **2** : to give substance or body to : EMBODY — **sub·stan·ti·a·tion** \-,stan-chē-'ā-shən\ *n*

¹sub·stan·tive \'səb-stən-tiv\ *n* : NOUN; *also* : a word or phrase used as a noun — **sub·stan·ti·val** \,səb-stən-'tī-vəl\ *adj*

²substantive *adj* **1 a** : of, relating to, or constituting something real or independent **b** : belonging to the substance of a thing : not external, derivative, or accidental : ESSENTIAL **c** : expressing existence **2** : having the function of a grammatical substantive **3** : considerable in amount or numbers : SUBSTANTIAL **4** : creating and defining rights and duties — **sub·stan·tive·ly** *adv* — **sub·stan·tive·ness** *n*

sub·sta·tion \'səb-,stā-shən\ *n* : a station subordinate to another station (as a post-office branch)

¹sub·sti·tute \'səb-stə-,t(y)üt\ *n* : a person or thing that takes the place of another — **substitute** *adj*

²substitute *vb* **1** : to put in the place of another : EXCHANGE **2** : to serve as a substitute : REPLACE — **sub·sti·tu·tion** \,səb-stə-'t(y)ü-shən\ *n* — **sub·sti·tu·tion·al** \-shnəl, -shən-ᵊl\ *adj* — **sub·sti·tu·tion·al·ly** \-ē\ *adv* — **sub·sti·tu·tion·ary** \-shə-,ner-ē\ *adj*

sub·stra·tum \'səb-,strāt-əm, -,strat-\ *n* : the layer or structure lying underneath

sub·struc·ture \'səb-,strək-chər\ *n* : FOUNDATION, GROUNDWORK

sub·sume \səb-'süm\ *vt* : to classify within a larger category or under a general principle — **sub·su·ma·tion** \,səb-sü-'mā-shən\ *n* — **sub·sump·tion** \səb-'səm(p)-shən\ *n*

sub·tend \səb-'tend\ *vt* **1 a** : to be opposite to **b** : to extend under and mark off **2** : to underlie so as to include

sub·ter·fuge \'səb-tər-,fyüj\ *n* : a device (as a plan or trick) used to avoid some unpleasant circumstance (as to escape blame) : a deceptive evasion

sub·ter·ra·ne·an \,səb-tə-'rā-nē-ən\ *or* **sub·ter·ra·ne·ous** \-nē-əs\ *adj* **1** : being, living, or operating under the surface of the earth **2** : existing or working in secret : HIDDEN — **sub·ter·ra·ne·an·ly** *adv*

sub·tile \'sət-ᵊl, 'səb-tᵊl\ *adj* **1** : SUBTLE, ELUSIVE **2** : CUNNING, CRAFTY — **sub·tile·ly** \'sət-lē, -ᵊl-(l)ē; 'səb-tə-lē\ *adv* — **sub·tile·ness** \'sət-ᵊl-nəs, 'səb-tᵊl-\ *n*

sub·ti·tle \'səb-,tīt-ᵊl\ *n* **1** : a secondary or explanatory title **2** : a printed statement or fragment of dialogue appearing on the screen between the scenes of a silent motion picture or appearing as a translation at the bottom of the screen during the scenes — **subtitle** *vt*

sub·tle \'sət-ᵊl\ *adj* **1 a** : DELICATE, ELUSIVE **b** : difficult to understand or distinguish : OBSCURE **2 a** : marked by insight and sensitivity : PERCEPTIVE **b** : SKILLFUL, EXPERT; *also* : cleverly made or contrived : INGENIOUS **3 a** : WILY, DEVIOUS, ARTFUL **b** : INSIDIOUS — **sub·tle·ness** *n* — **sub·tly** \'sət-lē, -ᵊl-(l)ē\ *adv*

sub·tle·ty \'sət-ᵊl-tē\ *n, pl* **-ties** **1** : the quality or state of being subtle **2** : something subtle; *esp* : a fine distinction

sub·tract \səb-'trakt\ *vb* : to take away by deducting : perform a subtraction — **sub·tract·er** *n*

sub·trac·tion \səb-'trak-shən\ *n* **1** : an act or instance of subtracting **2** : the operation of deducting one number from another

sub·trac·tive \-'trak-tiv\ *adj* **1** : tending to subtract **2** : constituting or involving subtraction

sub·tra·hend \'səb-trə-,hend\ *n* : a number that is to be subtracted from a minuend

sub·trop·i·cal \'səb-'träp-i-kəl\ *adj* : of, relating to, or being the regions bordering on the tropical zone

sub·urb \'səb-,ərb\ *n* **1 a** : an outlying part of a city or town **b** : a smaller community adjacent to a city **2** *pl* : the residential area adjacent to a city or large town; *also* : ENVIRONS — **sub·ur·ban** \sə-'bər-bən\ *adj or n*

sub·ur·ban·ite \sə-'bər-bə-,nīt\ *n* : a dweller in the suburbs

sub·ven·tion \səb-'ven-chən\ *n* : financial support esp. in the form of an endowment or a subsidy

sub·ver·sion \səb-'vər-zhən\ *n* : the act of subverting : the state of being subverted — **sub·ver·sive** \-'vər-siv, -ziv\ *adj or n* — **sub·ver·sive·ly** *adv*

sub·vert \səb-'vərt\ *vt* **1** : to overturn or overthrow from the foundation : RUIN **2** : to undermine the morals, allegiance, or faith of : CORRUPT — **sub·vert·er** *n*

sub·way \'səb-,wā\ *n* : an underground way; *also* : a usu. electric underground railway

suc·ce·dent \sək-'sēd-ᵊnt\ *adj* : SUCCEEDING, SUBSEQUENT

suc·ceed \sək-'sēd\ *vb* **1 a** : to come next after another in possession of an office or estate; *esp* : to inherit sovereignty **b** : to follow after another in order **2** : to turn out well : be successful — **suc·ceed·er** *n*

suc·cess \sək-'ses\ *n* **1 a** : degree or measure of succeeding **b** : a favorable termination of a venture **c** : the gaining of wealth, favor, or eminence **2** : one that succeeds

suc·cess·ful \-fəl\ *adj* **1** : resulting or terminating in success **2** : gaining or having gained success — **suc·cess·ful·ly** \-fə-lē\ *adv* — **suc·cess·ful·ness** *n*

suc·ces·sion \sək-'sesh-ən\ *n* **1** : the order, action, or right of succeeding to a throne, title, or property **2** : a repeated following of one person or thing after another **3** : a number of persons or things that follow one after another — **suc·ces·sion·al** \-'sesh-nəl, -ən-ᵊl\ *adj* — **suc·ces·sion·al·ly** \-ē\ *adv*

suc·ces·sive \sək-'ses-iv\ *adj* : following in succession or serial order : following each other without interruption — **suc·ces·sive·ly** *adv* — **suc·ces·sive·ness** *n*

suc·ces·sor \sək-'ses-ər\ *n* : one that follows; *esp* : one who succeeds to a throne, title, estate, or office

suc·cinct \(,)sək-'siŋ(k)t, sə-'siŋ(k)t\ *adj* : CONCISE, TERSE — **suc·cinct·ly** *adv* — **suc·cinct·ness** *n*

¹suc·cor \'sək-ər\ *n* : AID, HELP, RELIEF

²succor *vt* : to go to the aid of (one in want or distress)

suc·co·tash \'sək-ə-,tash\ *n* : beans and kernels of sweet corn cooked together

suc·cu·lence \'sək-yə-lən(t)s\ *n* : the state of being succulent

suc·cu·lent \-lənt\ *adj* 1 a : full of juice : JUICY b : having fleshy tissues designed to conserve moisture 2 : full of vitality, freshness, or richness — **suc·cu·lent·ly** *adv*

suc·cumb \sə-ˈkəm\ *vi* 1 : to yield to superior strength or force or overpowering appeal or desire 2 : to cease to exist

[1]**such** \(ˈ)səch, (ˌ)sich\ *adj* 1 a : of a kind or character to be indicated or suggested b : having a quality to a degree to be indicated 2 : having a quality already specified 3 : of the same class, type, or sort : SIMILAR 4 : so great : so remarkable — **such and such** 1 : not named or specified 2 : something unspecified

[2]**such** *pron* 1 : such a person or thing 2 : someone or something stated, implied, or exemplified

[3]**such** *adv* 1 : to such a degree : SO 2 : ESPECIALLY, VERY

[1]**such·like** \ˈsəch-ˌlīk\ *adj* : of like kind : SIMILAR

[2]**suchlike** *pron* : someone or something of the same sort : a similar person or thing

[1]**suck** \ˈsək\ *vb* 1 a : to draw in (liquid) or draw liquid from by movements of the mouth b : to draw milk from a breast or udder with the mouth c (1) : to consume by applying the lips or tongue to (2) : to apply the mouth to in the manner of a child sucking the breast 2 : to take something in or up or remove something from by or as if by suction 3 : to make or cause to make a sound or motion like that of sucking

[2]**suck** *n* 1 : the act of sucking 2 : a sucking movement or force

suck·er \ˈsək-ər\ *n* 1 : one that sucks 2 : a person who is easily deceived or tricked 3 : a part of an animal's body used for sucking or for clinging by suction 4 : any of numerous freshwater fishes related to the carps but having usu. thick soft lips for sucking in food 5 : a secondary shoot from the roots or lower part of a plant 6 : LOLLIPOP

suck·le \ˈsək-əl\ *vt* **suck·led**; **suck·ling** \ˈsək-(ə-)liŋ\ 1 a : to give milk to from the breast or udder b : to bring up : NOURISH 2 : to draw milk from the breast or udder of

suck·ling \ˈsək-liŋ\ *n* : a young unweaned mammal

su·crose \ˈsü-ˌkrōs\ *n* : cane or beet sugar

suc·tion \ˈsək-shən\ *n* 1 : the act or process of sucking 2 a : the action of exerting a force upon something by means of reduced air pressure over part of its surface so that the normal air pressure on another part of its surface pushes or tends to push it toward the region of reduced pressure b : force so exerted — **suc·tion·al** \-shən-ᵊl\ *adj*

sud·den \ˈsəd-ᵊn\ *adj* 1 a : happening or coming quickly and unexpectedly b : come upon unexpectedly c : ABRUPT, STEEP 2 : marked by or showing hastiness : RASH 3 : made or brought about in a short time : PROMPT — **sud·den·ly** *adv* — **sud·den·ness** \ˈsəd-ᵊn-(n)əs\ *n*

[1]**suds** \ˈsədz\ *n pl* : soapy water esp. when frothy; *also* : the froth on soapy water

[2]**suds** *vb* 1 : to wash in suds 2 : to form suds

sudsy \ˈsəd-zē\ *adj* : full of suds : FROTHY, FOAMY

sue \ˈsü\ *vb* 1 : to pay court or suit to : WOO 2 : to seek justice from a person by bringing a legal action 3 : to make a request or application — usu. used with *for* or *to* — **su·er** *n*

suede *or* **suède** \ˈswād\ *n* 1 : leather with a napped surface 2 : a cloth fabric finished with a nap to simulate suede

su·et \ˈsü-ət\ *n* : the hard fat about the kidneys and loins in beef and mutton that yields tallow

suf·fer \ˈsəf-ər\ *vb* **suf·fered**; **suf·fer·ing** \ˈsəf-(ə-)riŋ\ 1 : to feel or endure pain 2 : EXPERIENCE, UNDERGO 3 : to bear loss or damage 4 : ALLOW, PERMIT — **suf·fer·er** *n*

suf·fer·ance \ˈsəf-(ə-)rən(t)s\ *n* 1 : consent or sanction implied by a lack of interference or failure to enforce a prohibition 2 : power or ability to endure

suf·fer·ing *n* : PAIN, HARDSHIP

suf·fice \sə-ˈfīs\ *vb* 1 : to meet or satisfy a need : be sufficient 2 : to be competent or capable 3 : to be enough for

suf·fi·cien·cy \sə-ˈfish-ən-sē\ *n, pl* **-cies** 1 : sufficient means to meet one's needs : COMPETENCY 2 : the quality or state of being sufficient : ADEQUACY

suf·fi·cient \sə-ˈfish-ənt\ *adj* : enough to meet the needs of a situation or a proposed end — **suf·fi·cient·ly** *adv*

[1]**suf·fix** \ˈsəf-ˌiks\ *n* : an affix occurring at the end of a word — **suf·fix·al** \-ˌik-səl\ *adj* — **suf·fix·less** \-ˌiks-ləs\ *adj*

[2]**suf·fix** \ˈsəf-ˌiks, (ˌ)sə-ˈfiks\ *vt* : to attach as a suffix

suf·fo·cate \ˈsəf-ə-ˌkāt\ *vb* 1 a : to stop the breath of (as by strangling or asphyxiation) b : to deprive of oxygen : distress by want of cool fresh air 2 : to impede or stop the development of 3 : to be or become suffocated; *esp* : to die or suffer from lack of breathable air — **suf·fo·cat·ing·ly** *adv* — **suf·fo·ca·tion** \ˌsəf-ə-ˈkā-shən\ *n*

suf·fra·gan \ˈsəf-ri-gən\ *n* : an assistant bishop; *esp* : one not having the right of succession — **suffragan** *adj*

suf·frage \ˈsəf-rij\ *n* 1 : VOTE 2 : the right of voting : FRANCHISE; *also* : the exercise of such right

suf·frag·ette \ˌsəf-ri-ˈjet\ *n* : a woman who advocates suffrage for her sex

suf·frag·ist \ˈsəf-ri-jəst\ *n* : one who advocates extension of suffrage esp. to women

suf·fuse \sə-ˈfyüz\ *vt* : to spread over or through in the manner of fluid or light : FLUSH, FILL — **suf·fu·sion** \-ˈfyü-zhən\ *n*

[1]**sug·ar** \ˈshu̇g-ər\ *n* 1 : a sweet crystallizable material that consists wholly or essentially of sucrose, is colorless or white when pure, and is obtained commercially from sugarcane or sugar beet 2 : any of various water-soluble compounds that vary widely in sweetness and comprise the simpler carbohydrates

[2]**sugar** *vb* **sug·ared**; **sug·ar·ing** \ˈshu̇g-(ə-)riŋ\ 1 : to mix, cover, or sprinkle with sugar 2 : to make something less hard to take or bear : SWEETEN 3 : to change to crystals of sugar

sugar beet *n* : a white-rooted beet grown for the sugar in its roots

sug·ar·cane \ˈshu̇g-ər-ˌkān\ *n* : a stout tall perennial grass that has broad leaves and a large terminal panicle and is widely grown in warm regions as a source of sugar

sug·ar·coat \ˌshu̇g-ər-ˈkōt\ *vt* 1 : to coat with sugar 2 : to make attractive or agreeable on the surface

sug·ar·plum \ˈshu̇g-ər-ˌpləm\ *n* : a round piece of candy

sug·ary \ˈshu̇g-(ə-)rē\ *adj* 1 : containing, resembling, or tasting of sugar 2 : cloyingly sweet : SENTIMENTAL

sug·gest \sə(g)-ˈjest\ *vt* 1 a : to put (as a thought, plan, or desire) into a person's mind b : to propose as an idea or possibility 2 : to call to mind through close association

sug·gest·i·ble \sə(g)-ˈjes-tə-bəl\ *adj* : easily influenced by suggestion — **sug·gest·i·bil·i·ty** \-ˌjes-tə-ˈbil-ət-ē\ *n*

sug·ges·tion \sə(g)-ˈjes-chən\ *n* 1 a : the act or process of suggesting b : something suggested 2 a : the process by which one thought leads to another esp. through association of ideas b : a means or process of influencing attitudes and behavior hypnotically 3 : a slight indication : TRACE

sug·ges·tive \sə(g)-ˈjes-tiv\ *adj* 1 a : giving a suggestion : INDICATIVE b : full of suggestions : PROVOCATIVE c : stirring mental associations : EVOCATIVE 2 : suggesting or tending to suggest something improper or indecent : RISQUÉ — **sug·ges·tive·ly** *adv* — **sug·ges·tive·ness** *n*

su·i·ci·dal \ˌsü-ə-ˈsīd-ᵊl\ *adj* 1 : relating to or of the nature of suicide 2 : marked by an impulse to commit suicide 3 a : very dangerous to life b : destructive of one's own interests — **su·i·ci·dal·ly** \-ᵊl-ē\ *adv*

su·i·cide \ˈsü-ə-ˌsīd\ *n* 1 a : the act of taking one's own life voluntarily b : ruin of one's own interests 2 : one that commits or attempts suicide

sui ge·ner·is \ˌsü-ˌī-ˈjen-ə-rəs\ *adj* : constituting a class alone : UNIQUE, PECULIAR

[1]**suit** \ˈsüt\ *n* 1 : an action or process in a court for enforcing a right or claim 2 : an act or instance of suing or seeking by

entreaty : APPEAL; *esp* : COURTSHIP **3** : a number of things used together : SET **4** : a set of garments: as **a** : an outer costume of two or more pieces **b** : a costume to be worn for a special purpose or under particular conditions **5** : all the playing cards of one kind in a pack

²suit *vb* **1** : ACCORD, AGREE **2** : to be appropriate or satisfactory **3** : to outfit with clothes : DRESS **4** : ACCOMMODATE, ADAPT **5 a** : to be proper for : BEFIT **b** : to be becoming to **6** : to meet the needs or desires of

suit·a·ble \'süt-ə-bəl\ *adj* **1** : adapted to a use or purpose **2** : satisfying propriety : PROPER **3** : CAPABLE, QUALIFIED — **suit·a·bil·i·ty** \ˌsüt-ə-'bil-ət-ē\ *n* — **suit·a·ble·ness** \'süt-ə-bəl-nəs\ *n* — **suit·a·bly** \-blē\ *adv*

suit·case \'süt-ˌkās\ *n* : TRAVELING BAG; *esp* : a rigid flat rectangular one

suite \'swēt, *2c is also* 'süt\ *n* **1** : RETINUE; *esp* : the personal staff accompanying a ruler, diplomat, or dignitary on official business **2** : a group of things forming a unit or constituting a collection : SET: as **a** : a group of rooms occupied as a unit : APARTMENT **b** (1) : a modern instrumental composition in a number of usu. descriptive movements (2) : an orchestral concert arrangement in suite form of material drawn from a longer work (as a ballet) **c** : a set of matched furniture

suit·ing \'süt-iŋ\ *n* : fabric for suits of clothes

suit·or \'süt-ər\ *n* **1** : one that petitions or entreats : PLEADER **2** : a party to a suit at law **3** : one who courts a woman or seeks to marry her

sul·fa \'səl-fə\ *adj* **1** : related chemically to sulfanilamide **2** : of, relating to, or employing sulfa drugs

sul·fa·nil·a·mide \ˌsəl-fə-'nil-ə-ˌmīd, -məd\ *n* : a sulfur-containing organic compound used in the treatment of various infections

sul·fate *or* **sul·phate** \'səl-ˌfāt\ *n* : a salt or ester of sulfuric acid

sul·fide *or* **sul·phide** \'səl-ˌfīd\ *n* : a compound of sulfur with an element or radical

sul·fur *or* **sul·phur** \'səl-fər\ *n* : a nonmetallic element that occurs either free or combined esp. in nature, is a constituent of proteins, exists in several forms including yellow crystals, and is used esp. in the chemical and paper industries, in rubber vulcanization, and in medicine for treating skin diseases

sul·fu·re·ous \ˌsəl-'fyu̇r-ē-əs\ *adj* : SULFUROUS

sul·fu·ric *or* **sul·phu·ric** \ˌsəl-'fyu̇(ə)r-ik\ *adj* : of, relating to, or containing sulfur esp. in a higher valence

sulfuric acid *n* : a heavy corrosive oily strong acid that is colorless when pure and is a vigorous oxidizing and dehydrating agent

sul·fu·rous *or* **sul·phu·rous** \'səl-f(y)ə-rəs, *also esp for 1* ˌsəl-'fyu̇r-əs\ *adj* **1** : of, relating to, or containing sulfur **2 a** : of, relating to, or dealing with the fire of hell : INFERNAL **b** : FIERY, INFLAMED **c** : PROFANE, BLASPHEMOUS

¹sulk \'səlk\ *vi* : to be moodily silent or ill-humored : nurse a grievance

²sulk *n* **1** : the state of one sulking — often used in pl. **2** : a sulky mood or spell

¹sulky \'səl-kē\ *adj* **1** : inclined to sulk : given to fits of sulking **2** : DISCONTENTED, GLOOMY — **sulk·i·ly** \-kə-lē\ *adv* — **sulk·i·ness** \-kē-nəs\ *n*

²sulky *n, pl* **sulk·ies** : a light 2-wheeled vehicle having a seat for the driver only and usu. no body

sul·len \'səl-ən\ *adj* **1 a** : gloomily or resentfully silent or repressed : not sociable **b** : suggesting a sullen state : LOWERING **2** : dull or somber in sound or color **3** : DISMAL, GLOOMY — **sul·len·ly** *adv* — **sul·len·ness** *n*

sul·ly \'səl-ē\ *vb* **sul·lied**; **sul·ly·ing** : to make or become soiled or tarnished : SMIRCH

sul·tan \'səlt-ᵊn\ *n* : a king or sovereign esp. of a Muslim state

sul·tana \ˌsəl-'tan-ə\ *n* **1** : a female member of a sultan's family; *esp* : a sultan's wife **2 a** : a pale yellow seedless grape grown for raisins and wine **b** : the raisin of this grape

sul·tan·ate \'səlt-ᵊn-ˌāt\ *n* **1** : the office, dignity, or power of a sultan **2** : a state or country governed by a sultan

sul·try \'səl-trē\ *adj* **1** : very hot and humid **2** : burning hot **3** : SENSUAL, VOLUPTUOUS — **sul·tri·ness** \-trē-nəs\ *n*

¹sum \'səm\ *n* **1** : an indefinite or specified amount of money **2** : the whole amount : AGGREGATE **3 a** : EPITOME, SUMMARY **b** : GIST **4 a** : the result of adding numbers **b** : a problem in arithmetic

²sum *vb* **summed**; **sum·ming** **1** : to calculate the sum of : COUNT **2** : to reach a sum : AMOUNT — usu. used with *to* **3** : SUMMARIZE — usu. used with *up*

su·mac *or* **su·mach** \'s(h)ü-ˌmak\ *n* : any of a genus of trees, shrubs, and woody vines with feathery compound leaves turning to brilliant red in autumn and spikes or loose clusters of red or whitish berries

sum·ma cum lau·de \ˌsu̇m-ə-ˌku̇m-'lau̇d-ə, -'lau̇d-ē; ˌsəm-ə-ˌkəm-'lȯd-ē\ *adv (or adj)* : with highest academic distinction

sum·ma·rize \'səm-ə-ˌrīz\ *vb* **1** : to tell in or reduce to a summary **2** : to make a summary — **sum·ma·ri·za·tion** \ˌsəm-ə-rə-'zā-shən\ *n* — **sum·ma·riz·er** *n*

¹sum·ma·ry \'səm-ə-rē\ *adj* **1** : expressing or covering the main points briefly : CONCISE **2** : done without delay or formality — **sum·mar·i·ly** \(ˌ)sə-'mer-ə-lē, 'səm-ə-rə-lē\ *adv*

²summary *n, pl* **-ries** : an abstract, abridgment, or compendium esp. of a preceding discourse : RECAPITULATION

sum·ma·tion \(ˌ)sə-'mā-shən\ *n* **1** : the act or process of forming a sum : ADDITION **2** : SUM, TOTAL **3** : a final part of an argument reviewing points made and expressing conclusions

¹sum·mer \'səm-ər\ *n* **1 a** : the season between spring and autumn **b** : the warmer half of the year **2** : YEAR **3** : a time or season of fulfillment

²summer *vb* : to pass the summer

sum·mer·house \'səm-ər-ˌhau̇s\ *n* : a rustic covered structure in a garden or park to provide a cool shady retreat in summer

sum·mer·time \-ˌtīm\ *n* : the summer season or a period like summer

sum·mery \'səm-ə-rē\ *adj* : of, resembling, or fit for summer

sum·mit \'səm-ət\ *n* **1** : TOP, APEX; *esp* : the highest point (as of a mountain) **2** : the highest degree **3** : the highest level

sum·mon \'səm-ən\ *vt* **1** : to issue a call to convene : CONVOKE **2** : to command by service of a summons to appear in court **3** : to send for : CALL **4** : to call forth or arouse — **sum·mon·er** *n*

¹sum·mons \'səm-ənz\ *n, pl* **sum·mons·es** **1** : the act of summoning; *esp* : a call by authority to appear at a place named or to attend to some duty **2** : a warning or notice to appear in court **3** : a call, signal, or knock that summons

²summons *vt* : SUMMON 2

sum·mum bo·num \ˌsu̇m-əm-'bō-nəm, ˌsəm-\ *n* : the supreme or greatest good

sump \'səmp\ *n* : a pit or reservoir serving as a receptacle or as a drain for fluids

sump·tu·ary \'səm(p)-chə-ˌwer-ē\ *adj* : designed to regulate personal expenditures and esp. to prevent extravagance

sump·tu·ous \'səm(p)-chə-wəs, -chəs\ *adj* : involving large expense — **sump·tu·ous·ly** *adv* — **sump·tu·ous·ness** *n*

¹sun \'sən\ *n* **1 a** : the luminous celestial body around which the planets revolve and from which they receive heat and light **b** : a celestial body like the sun **2** : the heat or light radiated from the sun : SUNSHINE **3** : one resembling the sun usu. in brilliance **4** : the rising or setting of the sun

²sun *vb* **sunned**; **sun·ning** **1** : to expose to or as if to the rays of the sun **2** : to sun oneself

sun·bath \'sən-ˌbath, -ˌbȧth\ *n* : exposure to sunlight or a sunlamp

sun·bathe \-ˌbāt͟h\ *vi* : to take a sunbath — **sun·bath·er** *n*

sun·beam \-ˌbēm\ *n* : a ray of sunlight

sun·bon·net \-ˌbän-ət\ *n* : a woman's bonnet with a wide brim framing the face and usu. a ruffle at the back to protect the neck from the sun

¹sun·burn \-ˌbərn\ *vb* **1** : to burn or discolor by the sun **2** : to cause or undergo sunburn

²sunburn *n* : a skin inflammation caused by excessive exposure to sunlight

sun·burst \'sən-ˌbərst\ *n* **1** : a burst of sunlight esp. through a break in the clouds **2** : a representation of a sun surrounded by rays

sun·dae \'sən-dē\ *n* : a portion of ice cream served with topping (as crushed fruit, syrup, or nuts)

¹Sun·day \'sən-dē\ *n* : the 1st day of the week : the Christian Sabbath

²Sunday *adj* **1** : of, relating to, or associated with Sunday **2** : BEST **3** : AMATEUR, DILETTANTE

sun·der \'sən-dər\ *vt* **sun·dered**; **sun·der·ing** \-d(ə-)riŋ\ : to break or force apart or in two : sever esp. with violence

sun·di·al \'sən-ˌdī(-ə)l\ *n* : a device to show the time of day by the position of the shadow cast on a plate or disk typically by an upright pin

sun·down \-ˌdau̇n\ *n* : SUNSET

sun·dries \'sən-drēz\ *n pl* : miscellaneous small articles or items

¹sun·dry \'sən-drē\ *adj* : MISCELLANEOUS, SEVERAL, VARIOUS

²sundry *pron* : an indeterminate number

sun·fast \'sən-ˌfast \ *adj* : resistant to fading by sunlight

sun·fish \-ˌfish\ *n* **1** : a large sea fish with a very deep, short, and flat body, high fins, and a small mouth **2** : any of a family of American freshwater fishes that are related to the perches and usu. have a deep compressed body and metallic luster

sun·flow·er \-ˌflau̇(-ə)r\ *n* : any of a genus of tall herbs related to the daisies that are often grown for their showy yellow-petaled flower heads and for their oil-rich seeds

sung *past of* SING

sun·glass·es \'sən-ˌglas-əz\ *n pl* : glasses to protect the eyes from the sun

sunk *past of* SINK

sunk·en \'səŋ-kən\ *adj* **1** : SUBMERGED **2** : fallen in : HOLLOW **3 a** : lying in a depression **b** : constructed below the general floor level

sun·lamp \'sən-ˌlamp\ *n* : an electric lamp designed to emit radiation of wavelengths from ultraviolet to infrared

sun·less \'sən-ləs\ *adj* : lacking sunshine : CHEERLESS, DARK

sun·light \-ˌlīt\ *n* : the light of the sun : SUNSHINE

sun·lit \-ˌlit\ *adj* : lighted by or as if by the sun

sun·ny \'sən-ē\ *adj* **1** : bright with sunshine **2** : MERRY, BRIGHT, CHEERFUL — **sun·ni·ness** \'sən-ē-nəs\ *n*

sun·rise \'sən-ˌrīz\ *n* **1** : the apparent rising of the sun above the horizon **2** : the time at which the sun rises

sun·set \-ˌset\ *n* **1** : the apparent descent of the sun below the horizon; *also* : the accompanying atmospheric effects **2** : the time at which the sun sets

sun·shade \-ˌshād\ *n* : something used as a protection from the sun's rays: as **a** : PARASOL **b** : AWNING

sun·shine \-ˌshīn\ *n* **1 a** : the sun's light or direct rays **b** : the warmth and light given by the sun's rays **c** : a spot or surface on which the sun's light shines **2** : something that radiates warmth, cheer, or happiness — **sun·shiny** \-ˌshī-nē\ *adj*

sun·spot \-ˌspät\ *n* : one of the dark spots that appear from time to time on the sun's surface

sun·stroke \-ˌstrōk\ *n* : heatstroke caused by direct exposure to the sun

sun·suit \-ˌsüt\ *n* : an outfit worn usu. for sunbathing and play

sun·tan \-ˌtan\ *n* **1** : a browning of the skin from exposure to the rays of the sun **2** *pl* : a tan-colored summer uniform

sun·up \'sən-ˌəp\ *n* : SUNRISE

¹sun·ward \-wərd\ *or* **sun·wards** \-wərdz\ *adv* : toward the sun

²sunward *adj* : facing the sun

¹sup \'səp\ *vb* **supped**; **sup·ping** : to take or drink in swallows or gulps

²sup *n* : a mouthful esp. of liquor or broth : SIP; *also* : a small quantity of liquid

³sup *vi* **supped**; **sup·ping** **1** : to eat the evening meal **2** : to make one's supper — used with *on* or *off*

¹su·per \'sü-pər\ *n* **1 a** : a supernumerary actor **b** : SUPERINTENDENT, SUPERVISOR **2** : a removable upper story of a beehive **3** : a superfine grade or extra large size

²super *adj* **1** : very good **2** : very large or powerful : GREAT — **super** *adv*

super- *prefix* **1** : over and above : higher in quantity, quality, or degree than : more than **2** : in addition : extra **3** : exceeding a norm **4** : in excessive degree or intensity **5** : surpassing all or most others of its kind **6** : situated or placed above, on, or at the top of **7** : next above or higher **8** : more inclusive than **9** : superior in status or position

superacid	**supermicroscope**	**supersized**
superalkaline	**supernormal**	**superspectacle**
superbomb	**superorder**	**superspeed**
superclass	**superorganism**	**superstate**
supercritical	**superparasitism**	**superstratum**
superduty	**superpatriot**	**superstrength**
supereminent	**superpatriotism**	**supersubtle**
superendurance	**superpersonal**	**supersubtlety**
superfamily	**superphylum**	**supersystem**
superfine	**superphysical**	**supertanker**
supergalaxy	**superpower**	**supertax**
supergene	**superrace**	**supertemporal**
superglacial	**supersalesman**	**supertower**
supergovernment	**supersalesmanship**	**supervoltage**
superindividual	**supersecret**	**superwoman**
superinfection	**supersensory**	**superzealot**
superliner	**supersize**	

su·per·a·ble \'sü-p(ə-)rə-bəl\ *adj* : capable of being overcome or conquered : SURMOUNTABLE — **su·per·a·ble·ness** *n*

su·per·abound \ˌsü-pər-ə-'bau̇nd\ *vi* : to abound or prevail greatly or to excess

su·per·abun·dant \-'bən-dənt\ *adj* : more than ample : EXCESSIVE — **su·per·abun·dance** \-dən(t)s\ *n* — **su·per·abun·dant·ly** *adv*

su·per·an·nu·ate \ˌsü-pər-'an-yə-ˌwāt\ *vb* **1 a** : to make or declare obsolete or out-of-date **b** : to retire and pension because of age or infirmity **2** : to become retired or antiquated — **su·per·an·nu·a·tion** \-ˌan-yə-'wā-shən\ *n*

su·per·an·nu·at·ed \-'an-yə-ˌwāt-əd\ *adj* **1** : too old or outmoded for work or use **2** : retired on a pension

su·perb \su̇-'pərb\ *adj* **1** : MAJESTIC, NOBLE **2** : RICH, SUMPTUOUS **3** : of supreme excellence or beauty

su·per·car·go \ˌsü-pər-'kär-gō\ *n* : an officer on a merchant ship in charge of the commercial concerns of the voyage

su·per·cil·i·ous \ˌsü-pər-'sil-ē-əs\ *adj* : haughtily contemptuous — **su·per·cil·i·ous·ly** *adv* — **su·per·cil·i·ous·ness** *n*

su·per·ego \ˌsü-pər-'ē-gō\ *n* : a largely unconscious part of the psyche that aids in character formation by reflecting parental conscience and the rules of society

su·per·er·o·ga·tion \ˌsü-pər-ˌer-ə-'gā-shən\ *n* : the act of performing more than is required by duty, obligation, or need

su·per·e·rog·a·to·ry \ˌsü-pər-i-'räg-ə-ˌtōr-ē\ *adj* **1** : observed or performed to an extent not demanded or needed **2** : SUPERFLUOUS, NONESSENTIAL

su·per·fi·cial \ˌsü-pər-'fish-əl\ *adj* **1 a** : of or relating to a surface **b** : situated on or near or affecting only the surface **2** : concerned only with the obvious or apparent : not profound or thorough : SHALLOW — **su·per·fi·ci·al·i·ty** \-ˌfish-ē-'al-ət-ē\ *n* — **su·per·fi·cial·ly** \-'fish-(ə-)lē\ *adv* — **su·per·fi·cial·ness** \-'fish-əl-nəs\ *n*

su·per·flu·i·ty \ˌsü-pər-ˈflü-ət-ē\ *n, pl* **-ties** **1** : EXCESS, OVERSUPPLY **2** : something unnecessary or more than enough
su·per·flu·ous \sü-ˈpər-flə-wəs\ *adj* : exceeding what is sufficient or necessary : EXTRA — **su·per·flu·ous·ly** *adv*
su·per·high·way \ˌsü-pər-ˈhī-ˌwā\ *n* : a broad highway designed for high-speed traffic
su·per·hu·man \-ˈhyü-mən, -ˈyü-\ *adj* **1** : being above the human : DIVINE **2** : exceeding normal human power, size, or capability : HERCULEAN — **su·per·hu·man·ly** *adv*
su·per·im·pose \ˌsü-pər-im-ˈpōz\ *vt* : to place or lay over or above something — **su·per·im·pos·a·ble** \-ˈpō-zə-bəl\ *adj*
su·per·in·cum·bent \-in-ˈkəm-bənt\ *adj* : lying or resting and usu. exerting pressure on something else
su·per·in·tend \ˌsü-pər-in-ˈtend, ˌsü-prin-\ *vt* : to have or exercise the charge and oversight of : DIRECT
su·per·in·tend·ence \-ˈten-dən(t)s\ *or* **su·per·in·tend·en·cy** \-dən-sē\ *n* : the act, duty, or office of superintending
su·per·in·tend·ent \-ˈten-dənt\ *n* : a person who oversees or manages something
¹su·pe·ri·or \sü-ˈpir-ē-ər\ *adj* **1** : situated higher up or sometimes anterior or dorsal to something else : UPPER **2 a** : of higher rank, quality, or importance **b** : greater in quantity or numbers **3** : courageously or serenely indifferent **4 a** : excellent of its kind : BETTER **b** : affecting or assuming an air of superiority : SUPERCILIOUS **5** : more comprehensive — **su·pe·ri·or·i·ty** \-ˌpir-ē-ˈȯr-ət-ē\ *n* — **su·pe·ri·or·ly** *adv*
²superior *n* **1** : one who is above another in rank, station, or office; *esp* : the head of a religious house or order **2** : one that surpasses another in quality or merit
su·per·ja·cent \ˌsü-pər-ˈjās-ᵊnt\ *adj* : lying above or upon
¹su·per·la·tive \sü-ˈpər-lət-iv\ *adj* **1** : of, relating to, or constituting the degree of grammatical comparison that denotes an extreme or unsurpassed level or extent **2** : surpassing all others : SUPREME **3** : EXAGGERATED, EXCESSIVE — **su·per·la·tive·ly** *adv* — **su·per·la·tive·ness** *n*
²superlative *n* **1** : the superlative degree or a superlative form in a language **2** : the superlative or utmost degree of something : ACME; *also* : something that is superlative
su·per·man \ˈsü-pər-ˌman\ *n* : a man with superhuman physical, mental, or spiritual powers
su·per·mar·ket \-ˌmär-kət\ *n* : a self-service retail market selling foods and household merchandise
su·per·nal \sü-ˈpərn-ᵊl\ *adj* **1** : being or coming from on high : HEAVENLY **2** : LOFTY, ETHEREAL — **su·per·nal·ly** \-ᵊl-ē\ *adv*
su·per·nat·u·ral \ˌsü-pər-ˈnach-(ə-)rəl\ *adj* **1** : of or relating to an order of existence beyond the visible observable universe **2 a** : departing from what is usual or normal esp. so as to appear to transcend the laws of nature **b** : attributed to a supernormal agency (as a ghost or spirit) — **supernatural** *n* — **su·per·nat·u·ral·ly** \-ˈnach-(ə-)rə-lē, -ˈnach-ər-lē\ *adv*
¹su·per·nu·mer·ary \ˌsü-pər-ˈn(y)ü-mə-ˌrer-ē\ *adj* **1** : exceeding the stated or prescribed number **2** : SUPERFLUOUS
²supernumerary *n, pl* **-ar·ies** **1** : a supernumerary person or thing **2** : an actor employed to play a small usu. nonspeaking part (as in a mob scene or spectacle)
su·per·pose \ˌsü-pər-ˈpōz\ *vt* : to place or lay over or above another esp. so as to coincide — **su·per·po·si·tion** \-pə-ˈzish-ən\ *n*
su·per·scribe \ˈsü-pər-ˌskrīb\ *vt* : to write or engrave on the top or outside; *esp* : to write (as a name or address) on the outside or cover of
su·per·script \ˈsü-pər-ˌskript\ *n* : a distinguishing symbol or letter written immediately above or above and to the right or left of another character — **superscript** *adj*
su·per·scrip·tion \ˌsü-pər-ˈskrip-shən\ *n* **1** : the act of superscribing **2** : something superscribed on something else
su·per·sede \ˌsü-pər-ˈsēd\ *vt* **1** : to force out of use as inferior **2** : to take the place, room, or position of **3** : to displace in favor of another : SUPPLANT — **su·per·sed·er** *n* — **su·per·se·dure** \-ˈsē-jər\ *n*
su·per·sen·si·tive \-ˈsen(t)-sət-iv, -ˈsen(t)-stiv\ *adj* : HYPERSENSITIVE — **su·per·sen·si·tive·ness** *n*
su·per·son·ic \ˌsü-pər-ˈsän-ik\ *adj* **1** : having a frequency above the human ear's audibility limit **2** : utilizing, produced by, or relating to supersonic waves or vibrations **3** : of, being, or relating to speeds from one to five times the speed of sound in air **4** : moving, capable of moving, or utilizing air currents moving at supersonic speed — **su·per·son·i·cal·ly** \-ˈsän-i-k(ə-)lē\ *adv*
su·per·sti·tion \ˌsü-pər-ˈstish-ən\ *n* **1** : beliefs or practices resulting from ignorance, fear of the unknown, or trust in magic or chance **2** : an irrationally abject attitude of mind toward nature, the unknown, or God resulting from superstition — **su·per·sti·tious** \-ˈstish-əs\ *adj* — **su·per·sti·tious·ly** *adv* — **su·per·sti·tious·ness** *n*
su·per·struc·ture \ˈsü-pər-ˌstrək-chər\ *n* : something built upon an underlying or more fundamental base — **su·per·struc·tur·al** \-ˌstrək-chə-rəl, -ˌstrək-shrəl\ *adj*
su·per·vene \ˌsü-pər-ˈvēn\ *vi* : to take place as an additional, adventitious, or unlooked-for development — **su·per·ve·nience** \-ˈvē-nyən(t)s\ *n* — **su·per·ve·nient** \-nyənt\ *adj* — **su·per·ven·tion** \-ˈven-chən\ *n*
su·per·vise \ˈsü-pər-ˌvīz\ *vt* : SUPERINTEND, OVERSEE — **su·per·vi·sion** \ˌsü-pər-ˈvizh-ən\ *n*
su·per·vi·sor \ˈsü-pər-ˌvī-zər\ *n* : one that supervises; *esp* : an administrative officer in charge of a business, government, or school unit or operation — **su·per·vi·so·ry** \ˌsü-pər-ˈvīz-(ə-)rē\ *adj*
su·pine \sü-ˈpīn\ *adj* **1** : lying on the back or with the face upward **2** : showing mental or moral slackness : ABJECT
sup·per \ˈsəp-ər\ *n* **1** : the evening meal when dinner is taken at midday **2** : refreshments served late in the evening esp. at a social gathering
sup·plant \sə-ˈplant\ *vt* **1** : to take the place of (another) esp. by force or treachery **2 a** : to root out and supply a substitute for **b** : to gain the place of esp. by reason of superior excellence or power — **sup·plan·ta·tion** \sə-ˌplan-ˈtā-shən\ *n*
¹sup·ple \ˈsəp-əl\ *adj* **1 a** : adapting easily and often obsequiously to the wishes of others **b** : readily adaptable to new situations **2 a** : capable of being bent or folded without creases or breaks : PLIANT **b** : able to bend or twist with ease and grace : LIMBER — **sup·ple·ness** *n*
²supple *vt* **sup·pled**; **sup·pling** \ˈsəp-(ə-)liŋ\ : to make supple
¹sup·ple·ment \ˈsəp-lə-mənt\ *n* : something that supplies a want or makes an addition — **sup·ple·men·tal** \ˌsəp-lə-ˈment-ᵊl\ *adj*
²sup·ple·ment \ˈsəp-lə-ˌment\ *vt* : to add to : COMPLETE
sup·ple·men·ta·ry \ˌsəp-lə-ˈment-ə-rē, -ˈmen-trē\ *adj* : added as a supplement : ADDITIONAL
¹sup·pli·ant \ˈsəp-lē-ənt\ *n* : one who supplicates
²suppliant *adj* : BESEECHING, IMPLORING
sup·pli·cant \ˈsəp-li-kənt\ *n* : one who supplicates : SUPPLIANT — **supplicant** *adj* — **sup·pli·cant·ly** *adv*
sup·pli·cate \ˈsəp-lə-ˌkāt\ *vb* **1** : to make a humble entreaty; *esp* : to pray to God **2** : to ask earnestly and humbly : BESEECH — **sup·pli·ca·tion** \ˌsəp-lə-ˈkā-shən\ *n*
¹sup·ply \sə-ˈplī\ *vt* **sup·plied**; **sup·ply·ing** **1** : to add as a supplement **2 a** : to provide for : SATISFY **b** : to provide or furnish with : AFFORD **c** : to satisfy the needs or wishes of — **sup·pli·er** \-ˈplī(-ə)r\ *n*
²supply *n, pl* **supplies** **1 a** : the quantity or amount (as of a commodity) needed or available **b** : PROVISIONS, STORES — usu. used in pl. **2** : the act or process of filling a want or need : PROVISION **3** : the quantities of goods or services offered for sale at a particular time or at one price
¹sup·port \sə-ˈpōrt\ *vt* **1** : to endure bravely or quietly : BEAR

2 a (1) : to promote the interests or cause of (2) : to uphold or defend as valid or right : ADVOCATE (3) : to argue or vote for b : ASSIST, HELP c : to act with (a star actor) d : SUBSTANTIATE, VERIFY 3 : to pay the costs of : MAINTAIN 4 a : to hold up or in position or serve as a foundation or prop for b : to maintain (the price of a commodity) at a high level by purchases or loans 5 : to keep (something) going : SUSTAIN — **sup·port·a·ble** *adj* — **sup·port·er** *n*

²**support** *n* 1 : the act or process of supporting : the condition of being supported 2 : one that supports

sup·port·ive \sə-'pōrt-iv\ *adj* : furnishing or intended to furnish support

sup·pose \sə-'pōz\ *vb* 1 : to take as true or as a fact for the sake of argument : lay down as a hypothesis 2 : to hold as an opinion : BELIEVE 3 : CONJECTURE, OPINE

sup·posed \sə-'pōzd\ *adj* : BELIEVED; *also* : mistakenly believed : IMAGINED — **sup·pos·ed·ly** \-'pō-zəd-lē\ *adv*

sup·po·si·tion \ˌsəp-ə-'zish-ən\ *n* 1 : something that is supposed : HYPOTHESIS 2 : the act of supposing

sup·pos·i·ti·tious \sə-ˌpäz-ə-'tish-əs\ *adj* : of the nature of a supposition : HYPOTHETICAL — **sup·pos·i·ti·tious·ly** *adv*

sup·pos·i·to·ry \sə-'päz-ə-ˌtōr-ē\ *n, pl* **-ries** : a solid but readily meltable cone or cylinder of usu. medicated material for insertion into a bodily passage or cavity (as the rectum)

sup·press \sə-'pres\ *vt* 1 : to put down by authority or force : SUBDUE 2 a : to keep from being known b : to stop the publication or circulation of 3 a : to exclude from consciousness b : to keep from giving vent to : CHECK 4 a : to restrain from a usual course or action : HALT b : to inhibit the growth or development of : STUNT — **sup·pres·sion** \-'presh-ən\ *n*

sup·pu·rate \'səp-yə-ˌrāt\ *vi* : to form or give off pus — **sup·pu·ra·tion** \ˌsəp-yə-'rā-shən\ *n* — **sup·pu·ra·tive** \'səp-yə-ˌrāt-iv\ *adj*

su·prem·a·cy \sü-'prem-ə-sē\ *n, pl* **-cies** : the quality or state of being supreme; *also* : supreme authority or power

su·preme \sü-'prēm\ *adj* 1 : highest in rank or authority 2 : highest in degree or quality 3 : ULTIMATE, FINAL — **su·preme·ly** *adv* — **su·preme·ness** *n*

Supreme Being *n* : ²GOD

sur·cease \'sər-ˌsēs, (ˌ)sər-'\ *n* : CESSATION; *esp* : a temporary respite or end

¹**sur·charge** \'sər-ˌchärj\ *vt* 1 a : OVERCHARGE b : to charge an extra fee 2 : OVERLOAD 3 : to mark a new denomination figure or a surcharge on (a stamp)

²**surcharge** *n* 1 : an additional tax or charge 2 : an excessive load or burden 3 a : an overprint on a stamp; *esp* : one that alters the denomination b : a stamp bearing such an overprint

sur·cin·gle \'sər-ˌsiŋ-gəl\ *n* : a belt, band, or girth passing around the body of a horse to bind a saddle or pack fast

sur·coat \'sər-ˌkōt\ *n* : an outer coat or cloak; *esp* : a tunic worn over armor

¹**sure** \'shu̇(ə)r\ *adj* 1 : firmly established : STEADFAST 2 : RELIABLE, TRUSTWORTHY 3 : ASSURED, CONFIDENT 4 : admitting of no doubt : CERTAIN 5 a : bound to happen : INEVITABLE b : DESTINED, BOUND — **sure·ness** *n* — **for sure** : without doubt : with certainty — **to be sure** 1 : SURELY, CERTAINLY 2 : ADMITTEDLY

²**sure** *adv* : SURELY

sure·fire \-'fī(ə)r\ *adj* : certain to get results : DEPENDABLE

sure·ly \'shu̇(ə)r-lē\ *adv* 1 a : with assurance : CONFIDENTLY b : without doubt : CERTAINLY 2 : INDEED, REALLY — often used as an intensive

sure·ty \'shu̇r-ət-ē, 'shu̇(ə)rt-ē\ *n, pl* **sureties** 1 : sure knowledge : CERTAINTY 2 : a formal engagement (as a pledge) for the fulfillment of an undertaking : GUARANTEE 3 : one who assumes legal liability for the debt, default, or failure in duty of another — **sure·ty·ship** \-ˌship\ *n*

surf \'sərf\ *n* 1 : the swell of the sea that breaks upon the shore 2 : the foam, splash, and sound of breaking waves

¹**sur·face** \'sər-fəs\ *n* 1 : the outside of an object or body 2 : the external aspect of something — **surface** *adj*

²**surface** *vb* 1 : to give a surface to : make smooth 2 : to come to the surface — **sur·fac·er** *n*

surf·board \'sərf-ˌbōrd\ *n* : a buoyant board used in the sport of riding the surf — **surfboard** *vi* — **surf·board·er** *n*

¹**sur·feit** \'sər-fət\ *n* 1 : an overabundant supply : EXCESS 2 : an intemperate indulgence in something (as food or drink) 3 : disgust caused by excess : SATIETY

²**surfeit** *vb* : to feed, supply, or indulge to the point of surfeit

¹**surge** \'sərj\ *vi* 1 : to rise and fall actively : TOSS 2 : to rise and move or roll forward in or as if in waves or billows

²**surge** *n* 1 : a swelling, rolling, or sweeping forward like that of a wave 2 : a large wave or billow : SWELL 3 : a transient sudden rise of current in an electrical circuit

sur·geon \'sər-jən\ *n* : a physician who specializes in surgery

sur·gery \'sərj-(ə-)rē\ *n, pl* **-ger·ies** 1 : a branch of medicine concerned with the correction of physical defects, the repair and healing of injuries, and the treatment of diseased conditions esp. through instrumental procedures 2 : work done by a surgeon 3 : a room or area where surgery is performed

sur·gi·cal \'sər-ji-kəl\ *adj* : of, relating to, or associated with surgeons or surgery — **sur·gi·cal·ly** \-k(ə-)lē\ *adv*

sur·ly \'sər-lē\ *adj* : ILL-NATURED, CRABBED, DISAGREEABLE — **sur·li·ness** *n*

¹**sur·mise** \sər-'mīz\ *vb* : to imagine or infer on slight grounds

²**sur·mise** \sər-'mīz, 'sər-ˌ\ *n* : a thought or idea based on scanty evidence : CONJECTURE

sur·mount \sər-'mau̇nt\ *vt* 1 : to rise superior to : OVERCOME 2 : to get to the top of : CLIMB 3 : to stand or lie at the top of : CROWN — **sur·mount·a·ble** *adj*

¹**sur·name** \'sər-ˌnām\ *n* 1 : an added name : NICKNAME 2 : the name borne in common by members of a family

²**surname** *vt* : to give a surname to

sur·pass \sər-'pas\ *vt* 1 : to be greater, better, or stronger than : EXCEED 2 : to go beyond the reach, powers, or capacity of — **sur·pass·a·ble** *adj*

sur·plice \'sər-pləs\ *n* : a loose white tunic worn at service by a clergyman or choir member

sur·plus \'sər-(ˌ)pləs\ *n* 1 : the amount that remains when use or need is satisfied : EXCESS 2 : an excess of receipts over disbursements — **surplus** *adj*

¹**sur·prise** \sə(r)-'prīz\ *n* 1 a : an attack made without warning b : a taking unawares 2 : something that surprises 3 : the state of being surprised : ASTONISHMENT

²**surprise** *vt* 1 : to attack unexpectedly; *also* : to capture by an unexpected attack 2 : to take unawares : come upon unexpectedly 3 : to bring about or obtain by a taking unawares 4 : to strike with wonder or amazement because unexpected

sur·pris·ing \-'prī-ziŋ\ *adj* : ASTONISHING, AMAZING — **sur·pris·ing·ly** *adv*

sur·re·al \sə-'rē(-ə)l\ *adj* : having the intense irrational reality of a dream; *also* : SURREALISTIC

sur·re·al·ism \sə-'rē-ə-ˌliz-əm\ *n* : a modern movement in art and literature that purports to express subconscious mental activities through fantastic or incongruous imagery or unnatural juxtapositions and combinations — **sur·re·al·ist** \-ləst\ *n or adj* — **sur·re·al·is·tic** \-ˌrē-ə-'lis-tik\ *adj* — **sur·re·al·is·ti·cal·ly** \-ti-k(ə-)lē\ *adv*

¹**sur·ren·der** \sə-'ren-dər\ *vb* **sur·ren·dered**; **sur·ren·der·ing** \-d(ə-)riŋ\ 1 : to give over to the power, control, or possession of another esp. under compulsion 2 a : to give oneself up into the power of another esp. as a prisoner b : to give oneself over to something (as an influence or course of action)

²**surrender** *n* : the giving of oneself or something into the power of another person or thing

sur·rep·ti·tious \ˌsər-əp-'tish-əs\ *adj* : done, made, or acquire by stealth : CLANDESTINE, STEALTHY — **sur•rep•ti•tious•ly** *adv* — **sur•rep•ti•tious•ness** *n*

sur•rey \'sər-ē\ *n, pl* **surreys** : a four-wheel two-seated horse-drawn pleasure carriage

sur•ro•gate \'sər-ə-,gāt, -gət\ *n* **1** : DEPUTY, SUBSTITUTE **2** : a local judicial officer in some states having probate jurisidction

¹sur•round \sə-'raủnd\ *vt* : to enclose on all sides : ENCIRCLE

²surround *n* : something (as a border or edging) that surrounds

sur•round•ings \-'raủn-diŋz\ *n pl* : the circumstances, conditions, or objects by which one is surrounded : ENVIRONMENT

sur•tax \'sər-,taks\ *n* : an additional tax over and above a general tax

sur•veil•lance \sər-'vā-lən(t)s, -'vāl-yən(t)s\ *n* : close watch

¹sur•vey \sər-'vā, 'sər-,\ *vt* **sur•veyed**; **sur•vey•ing** **1** : to look over and examine closely **2** : to determine the form, extent, and position of (a piece of land) **3** : to view or study as a whole : make a survey of — **sur•vey•or** \sər-'vā-ər\ *n*

²sur•vey \'sər-,vā, sər-'\ *n, pl* **surveys** **1** : the action or an instance of surveying **2** : something that is surveyed **3** : a careful examination to learn certain facts **4** : a history or description that covers a large subject briefly **5 a** : the process of determining and making a record of the outline, measurements, and position of any part of the earth's surface **b** : an organization engaged in surveying **6** : a measured plan and description (as of a portion of land or of a road)

sur•vey•ing \sər-'vā-iŋ\ *n* : the occupation of a surveyor; *esp* : the branch of mathematics that teaches the art of measuring and representing the earth's surface accurately

sur•viv•al \sər-'vī-vəl\ *n* **1** : a living or continuing longer than another or beyond something **2** : one that survives

sur•vive \sər-'vīv\ *vb* **1** : to remain alive or in existence : live on **2** : to remain alive after the death of **3** : to continue to exist or live after — **sur•vi•vor** \-'vī-vər\ *n*

sus•cep•ti•bil•i•ty \sə-,sep-tə-'bil-ət-ē\ *n, pl* **-ties** : the quality or state of being susceptible

sus•cep•ti•ble \sə-'sep-tə-bəl\ *adj* **1** : capable of submitting to an action, process, or operation **2** : open, subject, or unresistant to some stimulus, influence, or agency **3** : IMPRESSIONABLE — **sus•cep•ti•ble•ness** *n* — **sus•cep•ti•bly** \-blē\ *adv*

¹sus•pect \'səs-,pekt, sə-'spekt\ *adj* : regarded with suspicion

²sus•pect \'səs-,pekt\ *n* : one who is suspected

³sus•pect \sə-'spekt\ *vb* **1** : to have doubts of : DISTRUST **2** : to believe it possible or likely that a person is guilty on slight evidence or without proof **3** : to imagine to be or be true, likely, or probable : SURMISE **4** : to be suspicious

sus•pend \sə-'spend\ *vb* **1** : to bar temporarily from any privilege or office **2 a** : to stop or do away with for a time : WITHHOLD **b** : to defer on specified conditions **3** : to cease for a time from operation or activity **4 a** : HANG; *esp* : to hang so as to be free on all sides except at the point of support **b** : to keep from falling or sinking through the action of some force (as buoyancy) that opposes gravity

sus•pend•er \sə-'spen-dər\ *n* **1** : one that suspends **2** : one of two supporting bands worn across the shoulders to support trousers, skirt, or belt — usu. used in pl.

sus•pense \sə-'spen(t)s\ *n* **1** : temporary cessation : SUSPENSION **2** : mental uncertainty: **a** : ANXIETY **b** : a pleasurable excitement produced by a story or play as to its outcome **3** : the state of being undecided — **sus•pense•ful** \-fəl\ *adj*

sus•pen•sion \sə-'spen-chən\ *n* **1** : the act of suspending or the state or period of being suspended **2** : the act of hanging : the state of being hung **3** : the state of a substance when its particles are mixed with but undissolved in a fluid or solid; *also* : a substance in this state **4** : something suspended **5** : a device by which something is suspended

sus•pen•sive \sə-'spen(t)-siv\ *adj* **1** : stopping temporarily : SUSPENDING **2** : characterized by suspense, suspended judgment, or indecisiveness **3** : characterized by suspension

¹sus•pen•so•ry \sə-'spen(t)s-(ə-)rē\ *adj* **1 a** : SUSPENDED **b** : fitted or serving to suspend something **2** : temporarily leaving undetermined : SUSPENSIVE 1

²suspensory *n, pl* **-ries** : something that suspends or holds up

sus•pi•cion \sə-'spish-ən\ *n* **1** : the act or an instance of suspecting or being suspected **2** : a feeling that something is wrong without definite evidence **3** : a slight touch or trace

sus•pi•cious \sə-'spish-əs\ *adj* **1** : tending to arouse suspicion : QUESTIONABLE **2** : disposed to suspect : DISTRUSTFUL **3** : indicative of suspicion — **sus•pi•cious•ly** *adv* — **sus•pi•cious•ness** *n*

sus•pire \sə-'spī(ə)r\ *vi* : to draw a long deep breath : SIGH — **sus•pi•ra•tion** \,səs-pə-'rā-shən\ *n*

sus•tain \sə-'stān\ *vt* **1** : to give support or relief to **2** : to supply with sustenance : NOURISH **3** : to keep going : PROLONG **4** : to support the weight of : CARRY **5** : to buoy up **6 a** : to bear up under : ENDURE **b** : RECEIVE, UNDERGO **7 a** : to support as true, legal, or just **b** : to allow or admit as valid **8** : PROVE, CONFIRM — **sus•tain•a•ble** *adj* — **sus•tain•er** *n*

sus•te•nance \'səs-tə-nən(t)s\ *n* **1 a** : means of support, maintenance, or subsistence **b** : FOOD; *also* : NOURISHMENT **2** : the act of sustaining : the state of being sustained; *esp* : a supplying with the necessaries of life **3** : something that gives support, endurance, or strength

su•sur•ra•tion \,sü-sə-'rā-shən\ *n* : MURMUR

¹su•ture \'sü-chər\ *n* **1 a** : a strand or fiber used to sew parts of the living body; *also* : a stitch made with this **b** : the act or process of sewing with sutures **2** : a seam or line along which two things or parts are joined by or as if by sewing

²suture *vt* : to unite, close, or secure with sutures

su•zer•ain \'süz-(ə-)rən, 'süz-ə-,rān\ *n* **1** : a feudal lord : OVERLORD **2** : a state controlling the foreign relations of another but allowing it internal sovereignty — **su•zer•ain•ty** \-tē\ *n*

svelte \'svelt\ *adj* **1 a** : SLENDER, LITHE **b** : having clean lines : SLEEK **2** : URBANE, SUAVE — **svelte•ly** *adv* — **svelte•ness** *n*

¹swab \'swäb\ *n* **1 a** : MOP; *esp* : a yarn mop **b** : a wad of absorbent material esp. for applying medication or for removing material (as from a wound or lesion) **2** : SAILOR, GOB

²swab *vt* **swabbed**; **swab•bing** : to use a swab on

swab•ber \'swäb-ər\ *n* **1** : one that swabs **2** : SWAB

swad•dle \'swäd-ᵊl\ *vt* **swad•dled**; **swad•dling** \'swäd-liŋ, -ᵊl-iŋ\ **1 a** : to wrap (an infant) with swaddling clothes **b** : SWATHE, ENVELOP **2** : RESTRAIN, RESTRICT

swaddling clothes *n pl* **1** : narrow strips of cloth wrapped around an infant to restrict movement **2** : limitations or restrictions imposed upon the immature or inexperienced

swag \'swag\ *n* **1 a** : something hanging in a curve between two points : FESTOON **b** : a suspended cluster **2 a** : goods acquired by unlawful means : LOOT **b** : SPOILS, PROFITS

swage \'swāj, 'swej\ *n* : a tool used by workers in metals for shaping their work — **swage** *vt*

¹swag•ger \'swag-ər\ *vi* **swag•gered**; **swag•ger•ing** \'swag-(ə-)riŋ\ **1** : to conduct oneself in an arrogant or superciliously pompous manner; *esp* : to walk with an air of overbearing self-confidence **2** : BOAST, BRAG

²swagger *n* : an act or instance of swaggering

³swagger *adj* : marked by elegance or showiness : SMART

swain \'swān\ *n* **1** : RUSTIC, PEASANT; *esp* : SHEPHERD **2** : a male admirer or suitor

¹swal•low \'swäl-ō\ *n* : any of a family of small long-winged migratory passerine birds that are noted for their graceful flight and have usu. a deeply forked tail

²swallow *vb* **1 a** : to take into the stomach through the mouth and throat **b** : to perform the actions used in swallowing something **2** : to envelop or take in as if by swallowing **3** : to accept without question, protest, or resentment **4** : to take back : RETRACT **5** : to keep from expressing or showing : REPRESS — **swal•low•er** \'swäl-ə-wər\ *n*

[3]**swallow** *n* **1 :** an act of swallowing **2 :** an amount that can be swallowed at one time

swal·low·tail \'swäl-ō-ˌtāl\ *n* **1 :** a deeply forked and tapering tail (as of a swallow) **2 :** TAILCOAT **3 :** any of various large butterflies with the border of the hind wing drawn out into a process resembling a tail — **swal·low–tailed** \ˌswäl-ō-'tāld\ *adj*

swam *past of* SWIM

[1]**swamp** \'swämp\ *n* **:** wet spongy land or a tract of this often partially or intermittently covered with water and usu. overgrown with shrubs and trees — **swamp·land** \-ˌland\ *n*

[2]**swamp** *vb* **1 a :** to cause to capsize in water or fill with water and sink **b :** to fill with or as if with water : SUBMERGE **2 :** to open by removing underbrush and debris **3 :** OVERWHELM

swan \'swän\ *n* **:** any of various heavy-bodied long-necked mostly pure white aquatic birds related to the geese

[1]**swank** \'swaŋk\ *vi* **:** to show off : SWAGGER

[2]**swank** *n* **1 :** PRETENTIOUSNESS, SWAGGER **2 :** ELEGANCE

[3]**swank** *or* **swanky** \'swaŋ-kē\ *adj* **1 :** characterized by showy display : OSTENTATIOUS **2 :** fashionably elegant : SMART — **swank·i·ly** \'swaŋ-kə-lē\ *adv* — **swank·i·ness** \-kē-nəs\ *n*

[1]**swap** \'swäp\ *vb* **swapped**; **swap·ping :** to give in exchange

[2]**swap** *n* **:** EXCHANGE, TRADE

sward \'swȯrd\ *n* **:** the grassy surface of land : TURF

[1]**swarm** \'swȯrm\ *n* **1 :** a great number of honeybees emigrating together from a hive in company with a queen to start a new colony elsewhere; *also* **:** a colony of honeybees settled in a hive **2 :** an extremely large number massed together and usu. in motion : MULTITUDE

[2]**swarm** *vb* **1 :** to form and depart from a hive in a swarm **2 :** to migrate, move, or gather in a swarm : THRONG **3 :** to contain or fill with a swarm : TEEM — **swarm·er** *n*

swart \'swȯrt\ *adj* **:** SWARTHY — **swart·ness** *n*

swar·thy \'swȯr-t͟hē, -thē\ *adj* **:** of a dark color, complexion, or cast : DUSKY — **swarth·i·ness** *n*

[1]**swash** \'swäsh\ *n* **1 :** a dashing of water against or upon something **2 :** SWAGGER

[2]**swash** *vb* **1 :** BLUSTER, SWAGGER **2 :** to make violent noisy movements **3 :** to move with a splashing sound

swash·buck·ler \-ˌbək-lər\ *n* **:** a boasting soldier or blustering daredevil — **swash·buck·ling** \-ˌbək-liŋ\ *adj or n*

swas·ti·ka \'swäs-ti-kə, swä-'stē-kə\ *n* **:** a symbol or ornament in the form of a Greek cross with the ends of the arms extended at right angles all in the same rotary direction

swat \'swät\ *vb* **swat·ted**; **swat·ting :** to hit with a quick hard blow — **swat** *n* — **swat·ter** *n*

swatch \'swäch\ *n* **1 a :** a sample piece (as of fabric) or a collection of samples **b :** a characteristic specimen **2 :** PATCH **3 :** a small collection

swath \'swäth, 'swȯth\ *or* **swathe** \'swät͟h, 'swȯt͟h, 'swāt͟h\ *n* **1 :** the sweep of a scythe or machine in mowing or the path cut in one course **2 :** a row of cut grain or grass

[1]**swathe** \'swät͟h, 'swȯt͟h, 'swāt͟h\ *vt* **1 :** to bind, wrap, or swaddle with or as if with a bandage **2 :** ENVELOP

[2]**swathe** \'swät͟h, 'swȯt͟h, 'swāt͟h\ *or* **swath** \'swät͟h, 'swäth, 'swȯt͟h, 'swȯth\ *n* **1 :** a band used in swathing **2 :** an enveloping medium

[1]**sway** \'swā\ *vb* **1 a :** to swing or cause to swing slowly back and forth from a base or pivot **b :** to move gently from an upright to a leaning position **2 :** to hold sway : act as ruler or governor **3 :** to fluctuate or veer between one point, position, or opinion and another **4 :** to cause to turn aside : DEFLECT, DIVERT **5 :** to exert a guiding or controlling influence upon

[2]**sway** *n* **1 :** the action or an instance of swaying or of being swayed **:** an oscillating, fluctuating, or sweeping motion **2 a :** a controlling force or influence **b :** sovereign power

swear \'swa(ə)r\ *vb* **swore** \'swō(ə)r\; **sworn** \'swōrn\; **swear·ing 1 :** to utter or take solemnly (an oath) **2 a :** to assert as true or promise under oath **b :** to assert or promise emphatically or earnestly **3 a :** to administer an oath to **b :** to bind by an oath **4 :** to bring into a specified state by swearing **5 :** to take an oath **6 :** to use profane or obscene language : CURSE — **swear·er** *n* — **swear by 1 :** to take an oath by **2 :** to place great confidence in — **swear for :** to answer for : GUARANTEE — **swear off :** RENOUNCE

swear in *vt* **:** to induct into office by administration of an oath

swear out *vt* **:** to procure (a warrant for arrest) by making a sworn accusation

[1]**sweat** \'swet\ *vb* **sweat** *or* **sweat·ed**; **sweat·ing 1 :** to give off perceptible salty moisture through the openings of the sweat glands : PERSPIRE **2 :** to give off or cause to give off moisture **3 :** to collect drops of moisture **4 a :** to work so hard that one perspires : TOIL **b :** to undergo anxiety or mental distress **5 :** to soak with sweat **6 :** to get rid of or lose by perspiring **7 :** to drive hard : OVERWORK

[2]**sweat** *n* **1 :** hard work : DRUDGERY **2 :** fluid excreted from the sweat glands of the skin : PERSPIRATION **3 :** moisture issuing from or gathering in drops on a surface **4 :** the condition of one sweating or sweated **5 :** a state of anxiety or impatience

sweat·band \'swet-ˌband\ *n* **:** a usu. leather band lining the inner edge of a hat or cap to prevent sweat damage

sweat·er \'swet-ər\ *n* **1 :** one that sweats or causes sweating **2 :** a knitted or crocheted jacket or pullover

sweat·shop \'swet-ˌshäp\ *n* **:** a shop or factory in which workers are employed for long hours at low wages and under unhealthy conditions

sweaty \'swet-ē\ *adj* **1 :** wet or stained with or smelling of sweat **2 :** causing sweat — **sweat·i·ly** \'swet-ᵊl-ē\ *adv* — **sweat·i·ness** \'swet-ē-nəs\ *n*

[1]**sweep** \'swēp\ *vb* **swept** \'swept\; **sweep·ing 1 a :** to remove from a surface with or as if with a broom or brush **b :** to remove or take with a single continuous forceful action **c :** to drive or carry along with irresistible force **2 a :** to clean with or as if with a broom or brush **b :** to clear by repeated and forcible action **c :** to move across or along swiftly, violently, or overwhelmingly **d :** to win an overwhelming victory in or on **3 :** to touch in passing with a swift continuous movement **4 :** to go with stately or sweeping movements **5 :** to cover the entire range of **6 :** to move or extend in a wide curve or range — **sweep·er** *n*

[2]**sweep** *n* **1 :** something that sweeps or works with a sweeping motion **2 a :** an act or instance of sweeping; *esp* **:** a clearing out or away with or as if with a broom **b :** an overwhelming victory (as the winning of all the contests or prizes in a competition) **3 a :** a movement of great range and force **b :** a curving or circular course or line **c :** the compass of a sweeping movement : SCOPE **d :** a broad extent

[1]**sweep·ing** \'swē-piŋ\ *n* **1 :** the act or action of one that sweeps **2** *pl* **:** things collected by sweeping : REFUSE

[2]**sweeping** *adj* **1 a :** moving or extending in a wide curve or over a wide area **b :** having a curving line or form **2 a :** EXTENSIVE **b :** INDISCRIMINATE

sweep·stakes \'swēp-ˌstāks\ *n, pl* **sweepstakes 1 :** a race or contest in which the entire prize may be awarded to the winner; *esp* **:** a horse race in which the stakes are contributed at least in part by the owners of the horses **2 :** any of various lotteries

[1]**sweet** \'swēt\ *adj* **1 a :** pleasing to the taste **b :** being or inducing the one of the four basic taste sensations that is typically induced by table sugar and is mediated esp. by receptors at the front of the tongue **c :** having a relatively large sugar content **2 a :** pleasing to the mind or feelings : AGREEABLE **b :** marked by gentle good humor or kindliness **c :** FRAGRANT **d :** delicately pleasing to the ear or eye **e :** CLOYING, SACCHARINE **3 :** much loved : DEAR **4 a :** not sour or rancid

: not decaying or stale : WHOLESOME **b** : not salt or salted : FRESH **c** : free from excessive acidity **d** : free from noxious gases and odors — **sweet·ish** \-ish\ *adj* — **sweet·ly** *adv* — **sweet·ness** *n* — **sweet on** : in love with

²sweet *adv* : SWEETLY

³sweet *n* **1** : something that is sweet to the taste; *esp* : a food (as a candy or preserve) having a high sugar content **2** : a sweet taste sensation **3** : a pleasant or gratifying experience, possession, or state **4** : DARLING

sweet·bread \'swēt-ˌbred\ *n* : the thymus or pancreas esp. of a young animal used as food

sweet·bri·er \-ˌbrī(-ə)r\ *n* : a thorny Old World rose with fragrant white to deep rosy pink single flowers

sweet corn *n* : an Indian corn with kernels containing much sugar and adapted for table use when immature

sweet·en \'swēt-ᵊn\ *vb* **sweet·ened**; **sweet·en·ing** \'swēt-niŋ, -ᵊn-iŋ\ : to make or become sweet — **sweet·en·er** \'swēt-nər, -ᵊn-ər\ *n*

sweet·en·ing *n* **1** : the act or process of making sweet **2** : something that sweetens

sweet·heart \'swēt-ˌhärt\ *n* **1** : DARLING **2** : LOVER

sweet·meat \'swēt-ˌmēt\ *n* : a food rich in sugar: as **a** : a candied or crystallized fruit **b** : CANDY

sweet pea *n* : a garden plant with slender climbing stems and large fragrant flowers; *also* : its flower

sweet potato *n* **1** : a tropical vine related to the morning glory with variously shaped leaves and purplish flowers; *also* : its large sweet and nutritious tuberous root that is cooked and eaten as a vegetable **2** : OCARINA

sweet tooth *n* : a craving or fondness for sweet food

¹swell \'swel\ *vb* **swelled**; **swelled** *or* **swol·len** \'swō-lən\; **swell·ing** **1 a** : to expand or distend abnormally esp. by internal pressure or growth **b** : to increase in size, number, or intensity **c** : to form a bulge or rounded elevation **2** : to fill or become filled with pride and arrogance **3** : to fill or become filled with emotion

²swell *n* **1 a** : the condition of being protuberant **b** : a rounded elevation **2** : a long often massive crestless wave or succession of waves **3** : a gradual increase and decrease of the loudness of a musical sound **4 a** : a person dressed in the height of fashion **b** : a person of high social position or outstanding competence

³swell *adj* **1** : STYLISH, FASHIONABLE **2** : EXCELLENT

swell·ing \'swel-iŋ\ *n* **1** : something that is swollen; *esp* : an abnormal bodily protuberance or localized enlargement **2** : the condition of being swollen

¹swel·ter \'swel-tər\ *vb* **swel·tered**; **swel·ter·ing** \'swel-t(ə-)riŋ\ **1** : to suffer, sweat, or be faint from heat **2** : to oppress with heat

²swelter *n* **1** : a state of oppressive heat **2** : an excited or overwrought state of mind

swel·ter·ing *adj* : oppressively hot — **swel·ter·ing·ly** *adv*

swept *past of* SWEEP

¹swerve \'swərv\ *vb* : to turn aside suddenly from a straight line or course

²swerve *n* : an act or instance of swerving

¹swift \'swift\ *adj* **1** : moving or capable of moving with great speed **2** : occurring suddenly or within a very short time **3** : quick to respond — **swift·ly** *adv* — **swift·ness** *n*

²swift *adv* : SWIFTLY

³swift *n* : any of numerous small and usu. sooty black birds that are related to the hummingbirds but superficially resemble swallows

¹swig \'swig\ *n* : a quantity drunk at one time : DRAFT

²swig *vb* **swigged**; **swig·ging** : to drink in gulps

¹swill \'swil\ *vb* **1** : WASH, DRENCH **2** : to drink great drafts of **3** : to feed (as a pig) with swill — **swill·er** *n*

²swill *n* **1** : food for animals (as swine) composed of edible refuse mixed with liquid **2** : GARBAGE, REFUSE **3** : a draft of liquor

¹swim \'swim\ *vb* **swam** \'swam\; **swum** \'swəm\; **swim·ming** **1 a** : to move through water by natural means (as the action of limbs, fins, or tail) **b** : to move quietly and smoothly : GLIDE **2 a** : to float on or in or be covered with or as if with a liquid **b** : to experience or suffer from or as if from vertigo **3** : to surmount difficulties **4** : to cross by propelling oneself through water — **swim·ma·ble** *adj* — **swim·mer** *n*

²swim *n* **1** : an act or period of swimming **2** : a temporary dizziness or unconsciousness **3** : the main current of activity

swim·ming \'swim-iŋ\ *adj* : marked by, adapted to, or used in or for swimming

swim·ming·ly \-iŋ-lē\ *adv* : very well : SPLENDIDLY

¹swin·dle \'swin-dᵊl\ *vb* **swin·dled**; **swin·dling** \-dliŋ, -dᵊl-iŋ\ : to obtain money or property from by fraud or deceit : DEFRAUD — **swin·dler** \-dlər, -dᵊl-ər\ *n*

²swindle *n* : an act or instance of swindling : FRAUD

swine \'swīn\ *n, pl* **swine** **1** : any of a family of stout-bodied short-legged omnivorous hoofed mammals with a thick bristly skin and a long mobile snout; *esp* : a domesticated animal derived from the European wild boar and widely raised for meat **2** : a contemptible person

¹swing \'swiŋ\ *vb* **swung** \'swəŋ\; **swing·ing** \'swiŋ-iŋ\ **1 a** : to wield with a sweep or flourish **b** : to cause to sway to and fro or turn on an axis; *also* : to face or move in another direction **2 a** : to hang or be hung so as to permit swaying or turning **b** : to die by hanging **c** : to move freely to and fro from or rotate about a point of suspension **d** : to hang freely from a support **e** : to shift or fluctuate between extremes **3** : to handle successfully : MANAGE **4** : to play or sing (as a melody) in the style of swing music : perform swing music **5 a** : to move along rhythmically **b** : to start up in a smooth vigorous manner **c** : to hit at something with a sweeping movement — **swing·a·ble** \'swiŋ-ə-bəl\ *adj*

²swing *n* **1** : an act of swinging **2** : a swinging movement, blow, or rhythm: as **a** : a regular to-and-fro movement of or as if of a suspended body **b** : a steady pulsing rhythm (as in poetry or music) **c** : a repeated shifting from one condition, form, or position to another **3** : the distance through which something swings **4** : a swinging seat usu. hung by overhead ropes **5** : a curving course or outline or one beginning and ending at the same point **6** : a style of jazz in which the melody is freely interpreted and improvised on by the individual players within a steadily maintained and usu. lively rhythm — **swing** *adj*

swin·ish \'swī-nish\ *adj* : of, suggesting, or befitting swine : BEASTLY — **swin·ish·ly** *adv* — **swin·ish·ness** *n*

¹swipe \'swīp\ *n* : a strong sweeping blow

²swipe *vb* **1** : to strike or wipe with a sweeping motion **2** : SNATCH, PILFER

¹swirl \'swərl\ *n* **1** : a whirling mass or motion : EDDY **2** : whirling confusion **3** : a twisting shape or mark

²swirl *vb* **1** : to move with or pass in a swirl **2** : to be marked with or arranged in swirls **3** : to cause to swirl

¹swish \'swish\ *vb* : to make, move, or strike with a rustling or hissing sound — **swish·ing·ly** *adv*

²swish *n* : a prolonged hissing sound (as of a whip cutting the air) or a light sweeping or rustling sound (as of silk in friction)

Swiss \'swis\ *n* **1** *often not cap* : a fine sheer cotton fabric often with raised dots orig. made in Switzerland **2** : a mild elastic hard cheese with large holes — **Swiss** *adj*

¹switch \'swich\ *n* **1** : a slender flexible whip, rod, or twig **2** : an act of switching: as **a** : a blow with a switch **b** : a shift from one to another **3 a** : a device made usu. of two movable rails and necessary connections and designed to turn a locomotive or train from one track to another **b** : a railroad siding **4** : a device for making, breaking, or changing the connections in an electrical circuit 5 : a strand of added or artificial hair used in some coiffures

²switch *vb* 1 : to strike or whip with or as if with a switch 2 : to lash from side to side : WHISK 3 : to turn, shift, or change by operating a switch 4 : to change one for another : EXCHANGE — **switch•er** *n*

switch•board \'swich-ˌbōrd\ *n* : an apparatus (as in a telephone exchange) consisting of a panel on which are mounted electric switches so arranged that a number of circuits may be connected, combined, and controlled

switch•man \'swich-mən\ *n* : one who attends a railroad switch

¹swiv•el \'swiv-əl\ *n* : a device joining two parts so that one or both can pivot freely (as on a bolt or pin)

²swivel *vb* **-eled** *or* **-elled**; **-el•ing** *or* **-el•ling** \'swiv-(ə-)liŋ\ : to turn on or as if on a swivel

swollen *past part of* SWELL

¹swoon \'swün\ *vi* 1 : FAINT 2 : to drift or fade imperceptibly

²swoon *n* 1 : a partial or total loss of consciousness; *also* : a dazed enraptured state 2 : a languorous drift

¹swoop \'swüp\ *vb* 1 : to descend or pounce suddenly like a hawk attacking its prey 2 : SNATCH

²swoop *n* : an act or instance of swooping

sword \'sōrd\ *n* 1 : a weapon having a long usu. sharp-pointed and sharp-edged blade 2 : something that kills or punishes as effectively as a sword 3 : military power or the use of it : WAR — **sword•like** *adj*

sword•fish \'sōrd-ˌfish\ *n* : a very large sea food fish having a long swordlike beak formed by the bones of the upper jaw

swordfish

sword•play \-ˌplā\ *n* : the art or skill of using a sword esp. in fencing

swords•man \'sōrdz-mən\ *n* : one skilled in the use of the sword : FENCER

swore *past of* SWEAR

sworn *past part of* SWEAR

swum *past part of* SWIM

swung *past of* SWING

syb•a•rite \'sib-ə-ˌrīt\ *n* : VOLUPTUARY — **syb•a•rit•ic** \ˌsib-ə-'rit-ik\ *adj* — **syb•a•rit•i•cal•ly** \-'rit-i-k(ə-)lē\ *adv*

syc•a•more \'sik-ə-ˌmōr\ *n* 1 : a Eurasian maple with yellow flowers in long clusters 2 : a large spreading American plane tree with light-brown flaky bark and round fruits like buttons

syc•o•phant \'sik-ə-fənt\ *n* : a servile self-seeking flatterer : PARASITE — **syc•o•phan•cy** \-fən-sē\ *n* — **syc•o•phan•tic** \ˌsik-ə-'fant-ik\ *adj*

syl•la•bary \'sil-ə-ˌber-ē\ *n, pl* **-bar•ies** : a series or set of written characters each one of which is used to represent a syllable

syl•lab•ic \sə-'lab-ik\ *adj* 1 : of, relating to, or denoting syllables 2 *of a consonant* : not accompanied in the same syllable by a vowel 3 : characterized by distinct enunciation or separation of syllables — **syl•lab•i•cal•ly** \-'lab-i-k(ə-)lē\ *adv*

syl•lab•i•ca•tion \sə-ˌlab-ə-'kā-shən\ *n* : the forming of syllables : the division of words into syllables — **syl•lab•i•cate** \-'lab-ə-ˌkāt\ *vb*

syl•lab•i•fy \sə-'lab-ə-ˌfī\ *vt* **-fied**; **-fy•ing** : to form or divide into syllables

¹syl•la•ble \'sil-ə-bəl\ *n* 1 : a unit of spoken language that consists of one or more vowel sounds alone or of a syllabic consonant alone or of either with one or more consonant sounds preceding or following 2 : one or more letters (as *syl, la,* and *ble*) in a word (as *syl•la•ble*) usu. set off from the rest of the word by a centered dot or a hyphen and treated as guides to hyphenation at the end of a line

²syllable *vt* **syl•la•bled**; **syl•la•bling** \-b(ə-)liŋ\ : to express or utter in syllables

syl•la•bus \-bəs\ *n, pl* **-bi** \-ˌbī, -ˌbē\ *or* **-bus•es** : a summary outline (as of a discourse or course of study)

syl•lo•gism \'sil-ə-ˌjiz-əm\ *n* 1 : a brief form for stating an argument from the general to the particular that consists of two statements and a conclusion that must be true if these two statements are true 2 : deductive reasoning — **syl•lo•gis•tic** \ˌsil-ə-'jis-tik\ *adj*

syl•lo•gize \'sil-ə-ˌjīz\ *vb* : to reason by means of syllogisms

sylph \'silf\ *n* 1 : an imaginary aerial spirit 2 : a slender graceful woman — **sylph•like** *adj*

syl•van \'sil-vən\ *adj* 1 a : living or located in the woods or forest b : of, relating to, or characteristic of the woods or forest 2 : abounding in woods or trees : WOODED

sym•bol \'sim-bəl\ *n* 1 : something that stands for something else; *esp* : something concrete that represents or suggests another thing that cannot in itself be represented or visualized : EMBLEM 2 : a letter, character, or sign used (as to represent a quantity, position, relationship, direction, or something to be done) instead of a word or group of words

sym•bol•ic \sim-'bäl-ik\ *or* **sym•bol•i•cal** \-'bäl-i-kəl\ *adj* 1 : of, relating to, or using symbols or symbolism 2 : having the function or significance of a symbol — **sym•bol•i•cal•ly** \-i-k(ə-)lē\ *adv*

sym•bol•ism \'sim-bə-ˌliz-əm\ *n* 1 : the art or practice of using symbols or indicating symbolically (as in art or literature) esp. by means of visible or sensuous representations 2 : a system of symbols or representations

sym•bol•ist \-ləst\ *n* 1 : a user of symbols or symbolism (as in artistic expression) 2 : an expert in the interpretation or explication of symbols

sym•bol•ize \'sim-bə-ˌlīz\ *vb* 1 : to serve as a symbol of : TYPIFY 2 : to use symbols : represent by a symbol or set of symbols — **sym•bol•i•za•tion** \ˌsim-bə-lə-'zā-shən\ *n*

sym•met•ri•cal \sə-'me-tri-kəl\ *or* **sym•met•ric** \-trik\ *adj* : having, involving, or exhibiting symmetry — **sym•met•ri•cal•ly** \-tri-k(ə-)lē\ *adv*

sym•me•try \'sim-ə-trē\ *n, pl* **-tries** 1 : balanced proportions; *also* : beauty of form arising from balanced proportions 2 : correspondence in size, shape, and relative position of parts on opposite sides of a dividing line or median plane or about a center or axis

sym•pa•thet•ic \ˌsim-pə-'thet-ik\ *adj* 1 : existing or operating through an affinity, interdependence, or mutual association 2 : not discordant or antagonistic: as a : appropriate to one's mood or disposition : CONGENIAL b : favorably impressed or inclined c : marked by kindly or pleased appreciation 3 : given to or arising from sympathy, compassion, friendliness, and sensitivity to others — **sym•pa•thet•i•cal•ly** \-'thet-i-k(ə-)lē\ *adv*

sym•pa•thize \'sim-pə-ˌthīz\ *vi* 1 : to react or respond in sympathy 2 a : to share in some distress, suffering, or grief b : to express sympathy 3 : to be in accord with something; *also* : to approve and foster the policies of a group without total commitment — **sym•pa•thiz•er** *n*

sym•pa•thy \'sim-pə-thē\ *n, pl* **-thies** 1 : a relationship between persons or things wherein whatever affects one similarly affects the other 2 a : inclination to think or feel alike : emotional or intellectual accord forming a bond of goodwill b : tendency to favor or support 3 : the act of or capacity for entering into or sharing the feelings or interests of another

sym•pho•ny \'sim(p)-fə-nē\ *n, pl* **-nies** 1 : harmony of sounds

2 : a large and complex composition for a full orchestra 3 : a large orchestra of a kind that plays symphonies — **sym·phon·ic** \sim-'fän-ik\ *adj*

sym·po·si·um \sim-'pō-zē-əm, -zh(ē-)əm\ *n, pl* **-sia** \-zē-ə, -zh(ē-)ə\ *or* **-si·ums** 1 : a meeting at which several speakers deliver short addresses on a topic or on related topics and which may be followed by group discussion 2 a : a collection of opinions on a subject b : DISCUSSION

symp·tom \'sim(p)-təm\ *n* 1 : a change in an organism indicative of disease or physical abnormality; *esp* : one (as headache) that is directly perceptible only to the individual affected 2 : INDICATION, SIGN, TRACE — **symp·tom·at·ic** \ˌsim(p)-tə-'mat-ik\ *adj*

syn·a·gogue *or* **syn·a·gog** \'sin-ə-ˌgäg\ *n* 1 : a Jewish congregation 2 : the house of worship and communal center of a Jewish congregation

[1]**sync** \'siŋk\ *n* : SYNCHRONIZATION, SYNCHRONISM

[2]**sync** *vb* **synced** \'siŋ(k)t\; **sync·ing** \'siŋ-kiŋ\ : SYNCHRONIZE

syn·chro·nism \'siŋ-krə-ˌniz-əm, 'sin-\ *n* 1 : the quality or state of being synchronous 2 : chronological arrangement of historical events and personages so as to indicate coincidence or coexistence — **syn·chro·nis·tic** \ˌsiŋ-krə-'nis-tik, ˌsin-\ *adj*

syn·chro·nize \'siŋ-krə-ˌnīz, 'sin-\ *vb* 1 : to happen at the same time : agree in time 2 : to cause to agree in time : represent, arrange, or tabulate according to dates or time 3 : to make (as two gears) synchronous in operation — **syn·chro·ni·za·tion** \ˌsiŋ-krə-nə-'zā-shən, ˌsin-\ *n*

syn·chro·nous \'siŋ-krə-nəs, 'sin-\ *adj* 1 : happening or existing at the same time : SIMULTANEOUS 2 : working, moving, or occurring together at the same rate and at the proper time with respect to each other; *esp* : having the same period and phase — **syn·chro·nous·ly** *adv*

syn·co·pate \'siŋ-kə-ˌpāt, 'sin-\ *vt* 1 a : to shorten or produce by syncope b : to cut short : CLIP, ABBREVIATE 2 : to modify or affect (musical rhythm) by syncopation — **syn·co·pa·tor** \-ˌpāt-ər\ *n*

syn·co·pa·tion \ˌsiŋ-kə-'pā-shən, ˌsin-\ *n* 1 : a temporary displacement of the regular metrical accent in music caused typically by stressing the weak beat 2 : a syncopated rhythm, passage, or dance step

syn·co·pe \'siŋ-kə-(ˌ)pē, 'sin-\ *n* : the loss of one or more sounds or letters in the interior of a word (as *fo'c'sle* from *forecastle*)

[1]**syn·di·cate** \'sin-di-kət\ *n* 1 : an association of persons officially authorized to undertake some duty or negotiate some business 2 a : a group of persons or concerns who combine to carry out a particular transaction b : CARTEL 3 : a business concern that sells materials for publication in a number of newspapers or periodicals simultaneously

[2]**syn·di·cate** \'sin-də-ˌkāt\ *vb* 1 : to subject to or manage as a syndicate 2 : to sell (as a cartoon) to a publication syndicate 3 : to unite to form a syndicate — **syn·di·ca·tion** \ˌsin-də-'kā-shən\ *n* — **syn·di·ca·tor** \'sin-də-ˌkāt-ər\ *n*

syn·er·gism \'sin-ər-ˌjiz-əm\ *n* : cooperative action of discrete agencies such that the total effect is greater than the sum of the effects taken independently — **syn·er·gist** \-jəst\ *n* — **syn·er·gis·tic** \ˌsin-ər-'jis-tik\ *adj* — **syn·er·gis·ti·cal·ly** \-ti-k(ə-)lē\ *adv*

syn·od \'sin-əd\ *n* 1 : an ecclesiastical assembly or council 2 : a group assembled (as for consultation) : MEETING, CONVENTION — **syn·od·al** \-əd-ᵊl\ *adj*

syn·o·nym \'sin-ə-ˌnim\ *n* 1 : one of two or more words of the same language that have the same or nearly the same meaning in some or all senses 2 : a symbolic or figurative name — **syn·o·nym·i·ty** \ˌsin-ə-'nim-ət-ē\ *n*

syn·on·y·mous \sə-'nän-ə-məs\ *adj* : having the character of a synonym — **syn·on·y·mous·ly** *adv*

syn·on·y·my \-mē\ *n, pl* **-mies** 1 a : the study or discrimination of synonyms b : a list or collection of synonyms often defined and discriminated from each other 2 : the quality or state of being synonymous

syn·op·sis \sə-'näp-səs\ *n, pl* **-op·ses** \-'äp-ˌsēz\ : a condensed statement or outline (as of a narrative or treatise) : SUMMARY

syn·op·tic \sə-'näp-tik\ *adj* 1 : affording a general view of a whole 2 : manifesting or characterized by comprehensiveness or breadth of view 3 : affording or sharing the same or a common view — **syn·op·ti·cal** \-ti-kəl\ *adj* — **syn·op·ti·cal·ly** \-ti-k(ə-)lē\ *adv*

syn·tac·tic \sin-'tak-tik\ *adj* : of, relating to, or according to the rules of syntax — **syn·tac·ti·cal** \-ti-kəl\ *adj* — **syn·tac·ti·cal·ly** \-ti-k(ə-)lē\ *adv*

syn·tax \'sin-ˌtaks\ *n* 1 : connected or orderly system or arrangement 2 a : the way in which words are put together to form phrases, clauses, or sentences b : the part of grammar dealing with this

syn·the·sis \'sin(t)-thə-səs\ *n, pl* **-the·ses** \-thə-ˌsēz\ : the composition or combination of parts or elements so as to form a whole — **syn·the·sist** \-səst\ *n*

syn·the·size \-ˌsīz\ *vt* : to combine or produce by synthesis — **syn·the·siz·er** *n*

[1]**syn·thet·ic** \sin-'thet-ik\ *adj* 1 : of or relating to synthesis 2 : produced artificially : MAN-MADE: a : produced only by chemical means : not found in nature b : made to substitute for or imitate a natural substance — **syn·thet·i·cal·ly** \-'thet-i-k(ə-)lē\ *adv*

[2]**synthetic** *n* : a product of chemical synthesis

syph·i·lis \'sif-(ə-)ləs\ *n* : a chronic contagious usu. venereal and sometimes congenital disease caused by a spirochete and marked by a clinical course in three stages extending over many years — **syph·i·lit·ic** \ˌsif-ə-'lit-ik\ *adj or n*

sy·phon *var of* SIPHON

[1]**sy·ringe** \sə-'rinj, 'sir-inj\ *n* : a device used to inject fluids into or withdraw them from the body or its cavities

[2]**syringe** *vt* : to irrigate or cleanse with or as if with a syringe

syr·up \'sər-əp, 'sir-əp\ *n* 1 : a thick sticky solution of sugar and water often flavored or medicated 2 : the concentrated juice of a fruit or plant — **syr·upy** \-ē\ *adj*

sys·tem \'sis-təm\ *n* 1 a : a group of objects or units so combined as to form a whole and work, function, or move interdependently and harmoniously b (1) : a body that functions as a whole (2) : a group of bodily organs that together carry on one or more vital functions c : a particular form of societal organization 2 a : an organized set of doctrines or principles usu. designed to explain the ordering or functioning of some whole b : a scheme or method of governing or arranging : a method of procedure or classification 3 : regular method or order — **sys·tem·less** \-ləs\ *adj*

sys·tem·at·ic \ˌsis-tə-'mat-ik\ *adj* 1 : relating to or forming a system 2 : presented or formulated as a system : SYSTEMATIZED 3 a : methodical in procedure or plan b : carried on or acting with thoroughness or persistency — **sys·tem·at·i·cal** \-'mat-i-kəl\ *adj* — **sys·tem·at·i·cal·ly** \-i-k(ə-)lē\ *adv*

sys·tem·a·tize \'sis-tə-mə-ˌtīz\ *vt* : to make into or arrange according to a system — **sys·tem·a·ti·za·tion** \ˌsis-tə-mət-ə-'zā-shən\ *n* — **sys·tem·a·tiz·er** \'sis-tə-mə-ˌtī-zər\ *n*

sys·tem·ic \sis-'tem-ik\ *adj* : of, relating to, or common to a system; *esp* : of or relating to the body as a whole — **sys·tem·i·cal·ly** \-'tem-i-k(ə-)lē\ *adv*

sys·tem·ize \'sis-tə-ˌmīz\ *vt* : SYSTEMATIZE — **sys·tem·i·za·tion** \ˌsis-tə-mə-'zā-shən\ *n*

systems analysis *n* : the act, process, or profession of studying an activity (as a procedure, a business, or a physiological function) typically by mathematical means in order to determine its desired or essential end and how this may most efficiently be attained

sys·to·le \'sis-tə-(ˌ)lē\ *n* : a rhythmically recurrent contraction; *esp* : the contraction of the heart by which the circulation is kept up — **sys·tol·ic** \sis-'täl-ik\ *adj*

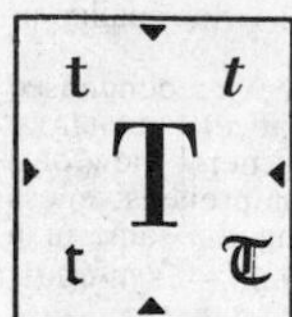

t \'tē\ *n, often cap* : the 20th letter of the English alphabet — **to a T** : PRECISELY, EXACTLY
't \t\ *pron* : IT
¹tab \'tab\ *n* **1 a** : a short projecting device: as (1) : a small hand grip (2) : a projection from a card used as an aid in filing **b** : a small insert, addition, or remnant **c** : APPENDAGE, EXTENSION; *esp* : one of a series of small pendants forming a decorative border or edge of a garment **2 a** : SURVEILLANCE, WATCH **b** : a creditor's statement : BILL, CHECK
²tab *vt* **tabbed**; **tab·bing** **1** : to furnish or ornament with tabs **2** : to single out : DESIGNATE
tab·ard \'tab-ərd\ *n* **1** : a tunic worn by a knight over his armor and emblazoned with his arms **2** : a herald's official cape or coat emblazoned with his lord's arms
tab·by \'tab-ē\ *n, pl* **tabbies** **1** : a plain silk taffeta esp. with moiré finish **2 a** : a domestic cat with a gray or tawny coat striped and mottled with black **b** : a female cat
tab·er·na·cle \'tab-ər-ˌnak-əl\ *n* **1 a** *often cap* : a tent sanctuary used by the Israelites during the Exodus **b** : a dwelling place **2** : an ornamental locked box fixed to the middle of the altar and used for reserving bread consecrated at Mass **3** : a house of worship
¹ta·ble \'tā-bəl\ *n* **1** : TABLET 1a **2 a** : a piece of furniture consisting of a smooth flat slab fixed on legs **b** (1) : FOOD, FARE (2) : an act of assembling to eat : MEAL **c** : a group of people assembled at or as if at a table **3 a** : a systematic arrangement of data for ready reference **b** : LIST
²table *vt* **ta·bled**; **ta·bling** \-b(ə-)liŋ\ : to remove (a parliamentary motion) from consideration indefinitely
tab·leau \'tab-ˌlō, tab-'lō\ *n, pl* **tableaus** *or* **tab·leaux** \-ˌlōz, -'lōz\ : a lifelike representation of a scene or event by an appropriate grouping of persons who remain silent and motionless
ta·ble·cloth \'tā-bəl-ˌklȯth\ *n* : a covering spread over a dining table before the places are set
ta·ble d'hôte \ˌtäb-əl-'dōt, ˌtab-\ *n* : a complete meal of several courses offered in a restaurant or hotel at a fixed price
ta·ble·land \'tā-bə(l)-ˌland\ *n* : PLATEAU
ta·ble·spoon \'tā-bəl-ˌspün\ *n* **1** : a spoon of a size convenient for serving rather than eating food **2** : TABLESPOONFUL
ta·ble·spoon·ful \ˌtā-bəl-'spün-ˌfu̇l, 'tā-bəl-ˌ\ *n, pl* **-spoonfuls** \-ˌfu̇lz\ *or* **-spoons·ful** \-'spünz-ˌfu̇l, -ˌspünz-\ : as much as a tablespoon can hold
tab·let \'tab-lət\ *n* **1 a** : a flat slab or plaque suited for or bearing an inscription **b** : a collection of sheets of writing paper glued together at one edge **2 a** : a compressed or molded block of a solid material : CAKE **b** : a small mass of medicated material usu. in the shape of a disk
ta·ble·top \'tā-bəl-ˌtäp\ *n* : the top of a table — **tabletop** *adj*
ta·ble·ware \'tā-bəl-ˌwa(ə)r\ *n* : utensils (as of china, glass, or silver) for table use
¹tab·loid \'tab-ˌlȯid\ *adj* : condensed into small scope
²tabloid *n* : a newspaper about half the page size of an ordinary newspaper that contains news esp. of a sensational nature and much photographic matter
¹ta·boo *or* **ta·bu** \ta-'bü, tə-\ *adj* : prohibited by a taboo
²taboo *or* **tabu** *n, pl* **taboos** *or* **tabus** **1** : a prohibition against touching, saying, or doing something on pain of immediate harm from a mysterious superhuman force **2** : a prohibition imposed by social custom
³taboo *or* **tabu** *vt* : to place under a taboo
ta·bor \'tā-bər\ *n* : a small drum with one head used to accompany a pipe played by the same person
tab·u·lar \'tab-yə-lər\ *adj* **1** : having a flat surface **2** : arranged or entered in a table — **tab·u·lar·ly** *adv*
tab·u·late \'tab-yə-ˌlāt\ *vt* : to put into tabular form — **tab·u·la·tion** \ˌtab-yə-'lā-shən\ *n* — **tab·u·la·tor** \'tab-yə-ˌlāt-ər\ *n*
ta·chom·e·ter \tə-'käm-ət-ər\ *n* : a device for indicating speed of rotation
tac·it \'tas-ət\ *adj* **1** : expressed or carried on without words or speech **2** : implied or indicated but not actually expressed — **tac·it·ly** *adv* — **tac·it·ness** *n*
tac·i·turn \'tas-ə-ˌtərn\ *adj* : habitually or temperamentally disinclined to talk — **tac·i·tur·ni·ty** \ˌtas-ə-'tər-nət-ē\ *n*
¹tack \'tak\ *n* **1** : a small short sharp-pointed nail usu. with a broad flat head **2 a** : the direction a ship is sailing as shown by the way the sails are trimmed; *also* : the run of a ship as trimmed in one way **b** : a change of course from one tack to another **3** : a zigzag movement on land **4** : a course or method of action **5** : a slight or temporary sewing or fastening
²tack *vb* **1** : ATTACH; *esp* : to fasten or affix with tacks **2** : to join in a slight or hasty manner **3** : to add as a supplement **4** : to change the direction of a sailing ship from one tack to another **5 a** : to follow a zigzag course **b** : to modify one's policy or an attitude abruptly — **tack·er** *n*
¹tack·le \'tak-əl, *by seamen often* 'tāk-\ *n* **1** : a set of the equipment used in a particular activity : GEAR **2 a** : a ship's rigging **b** : an assemblage of ropes and pulleys arranged to gain mechanical advantage for hoisting and pulling **3 a** : the act or an instance of tackling **b** : a football lineman who lines up inside the end
²tackle *vb* **tack·led**; **tack·ling** \'tak-(ə-)liŋ\ **1** : HARNESS **2 a** : to seize, take hold of, or grapple with esp. with the intention of stopping or subduing **b** : to seize and throw down or stop in football **3** : to set about dealing with — **tack·ler** \-(ə-)lər\ *n*
¹tacky \'tak-ē\ *adj* : barely sticky to the touch : ADHESIVE
²tacky *adj* **1 a** : characteristic of or suitable for a low-class person **b** : SHABBY, SEEDY **2** : marked by lack of style or good taste : DOWDY
tact \'takt\ *n* : a keen understanding of how to act in getting along with others; *esp* : the ability to deal with others without offending them
tact·ful \'takt-fəl\ *adj* : having or showing tact — **tact·ful·ly** \-fə-lē\ *adv* — **tact·ful·ness** *n*
tac·tic \'tak-tik\ *n* **1** : a method of employing forces in combat **2** : a planned action or maneuver for accomplishing an end
tac·ti·cal \'tak-ti-kəl\ *adj* **1 a** : of or relating to combat tactics **b** : of, relating to, or designed for air attack in close support of friendly ground forces **2 a** : of or relating to small-scale actions serving a larger purpose **b** : adroit in planning or maneuvering — **tac·ti·cal·ly** \-k(ə-)lē\ *adv*
tac·ti·cian \tak-'tish-ən\ *n* : one skilled in tactics
tac·tics \'tak-tiks\ *n sing or pl* **1 a** : the science and art of disposing and maneuvering forces in combat **b** : the art or skill of employing available means to accomplish an end **2** : a system or mode of procedure
tac·tile \'tak-tᵊl, -ˌtīl\ *adj* : of, relating to, or perceptible through the sense of touch — **tac·til·i·ty** \tak-'til-ət-ē\ *n*
tact·less \'takt-ləs\ *adj* : having or showing no tact — **tact·less·ly** *adv* — **tact·less·ness** *n*
tad·pole \'tad-ˌpōl\ *n* : a larval aquatic frog or toad typically having a long tail, rounded body, and gills
taf·fe·ta \'taf-ət-ə\ *n* : a crisp plain-woven lustrous fabric of various fibers used esp. for women's clothing
taff·rail \'taf-ˌrāl, -rəl\ *n* : the rail around the stern of a ship
taf·fy \'taf-ē\ *n, pl* **taffies** : a candy usu. of molasses or brown sugar boiled and pulled until porous and light-colored
¹tag \'tag\ *n* **1** : a loose hanging piece of cloth : TATTER **2** : a metal or plastic binding on an end of a shoelace **3** : a piece of hanging or attached material **4 a** : a brief quotation used for rhetorical emphasis or sententious effect **b** : a hackneyed saying **5** : a descriptive or identifying phrase or epithet
²tag *vb* **tagged**; **tag·ging** **1** : to provide or mark with or as if

with a tag 2 : to attach as an addition : APPEND 3 : to follow closely and persistently

³tag *n* : a children's game in which one player chases the others and tries to touch one of them

⁴tag *vt* **tagged**; **tag·ging** : to touch in or as if in a game of tag

¹tail \ˈtāl\ *n* 1 : the rear end or a process or prolongation of the rear end of the body of an animal 2 : something resembling an animal's tail 3 *pl* **a** : TAILCOAT **b** : full evening dress for men 4 : the back, last, lower, or inferior part of something; *esp* : the reverse of a coin 5 : a spy (as a detective) who follows someone 6 : the trail of a fugitive in flight — **tailed** \ˈtāld\ *adj* — **tail·less** \ˈtāl-ləs\ *adj* — **tail·like** *adj*

²tail *adj* 1 : being at the rear 2 : coming from the rear

³tail *vb* 1 **a** : to fasten by or at the tail, stern, or rear **b** : to connect end to end 2 : ²DOCK 1 3 **a** : to make or furnish with a tail **b** : to follow or be drawn behind like a tail 4 : to follow closely for purposes of observation : SHADOW 5 : to grow progressively smaller, fainter, or more scattered : SUBSIDE

tail·board \-ˌbōrd\ *n* : TAILGATE

tail·coat \-ˈkōt\ *n* : a man's full-dress coat with two long tapering skirts at the back

tail end *n* 1 : the hindmost end 2 : the concluding period

¹tail·gate \ˈtāl-ˌgāt\ *n* : a board at the back end of a vehicle (as a station wagon) that can be let down for loading and unloading

²tailgate *vb* : to drive dangerously close behind another vehicle

tail·light \ˈtāl-ˌlīt\ *n* : a red warning light mounted at the rear of a vehicle

¹tai·lor \ˈtā-lər\ *n* : one whose occupation is making or altering men's or women's outer garments

²tailor *vt* 1 **a** : to make or fashion as the work of a tailor **b** : to make or adapt to suit a special need or purpose 2 : to fit with clothes 3 : to style (as women's garments) with trim lines and hand finishing like that of a tailor's work on men's garments

tai·lor·ing \ˈtā-lə-riŋ\ *n* 1 **a** : the business or occupation of a tailor **b** : the work or workmanship of a tailor 2 : the making or adapting of something to suit a particular purpose

tai·lor–made \ˌtā-lər-ˈmād\ *adj* : made or seeming to have been made to suit a particular need

tail pipe *n* : the pipe discharging the exhaust gases from the muffler of an automotive engine

¹taint \ˈtānt\ *vt* 1 : to touch or affect slightly with something bad 2 : to affect with putrefaction 3 : CORRUPT

²taint *n* 1 : a trace of decay : STAIN, BLEMISH 2 : a contaminating influence — **taint·less** \-ləs\ *adj*

¹take \ˈtāk\ *vb* **took** \ˈtu̇k\; **tak·en** \ˈtā-kən\; **tak·ing** 1 : to lay hold of : GRASP 2 : CAPTURE 3 : WIN 4 : to get possession of (as by buying or capturing) 5 : to seize and affect suddenly 6 : CHARM, DELIGHT 7 : EXTRACT 8 : REMOVE, SUBTRACT; *also* : to put an end to (as life) 9 : to find out by testing or examining 10 : SELECT, CHOOSE 11 : ASSUME 12 : ABSORB 13 : to be affected by : CONTRACT 14 : ACCEPT, FOLLOW 15 : to introduce into the body 16 **a** : to submit to **b** : WITHSTAND 17 : to subscribe for 18 : UNDERSTAND 19 : FEEL 20 : to be formed or used with 21 : CONVEY, CONDUCT, CARRY 22 **a** : to avail oneself of **b** : to proceed to occupy 23 : NEED, REQUIRE 24 : to obtain an image or copy of 25 : to set out to make, do, or perform — often used with *on* 26 : to have effect (as by adherence or absorption) 27 : to betake oneself — **take advantage of** 1 : to use to advantage : profit by 2 : to impose upon : EXPLOIT — **take after** 1 : to take as an example : FOLLOW 2 : to look like : RESEMBLE — **take amiss** : to impute a bad meaning or intention to : be offended by — **take care** : to be careful : exercise caution or prudence — **take care of** : to attend to or provide for the needs, operation, or treatment of — **take effect** 1 : to become operative 2 : to produce a result as expected or intended : be effective — **take for** : to suppose to be; *esp* : to suppose mistakenly to be — **take for granted** 1 : to assume as true, real, or expected 2 : to value too lightly — **take hold** : to become attached or established — **take into account** : to make allowance for — **take part** : JOIN, PARTICIPATE, SHARE — **take place** : HAPPEN, OCCUR

²take *n* 1 : an act or the action of taking (as by seizing, accepting, or coming into possession) 2 : something that is taken: **a** : money received : PROCEEDS, RECEIPTS **b** : SHARE, CUT **c** : the quantity (as of game) taken at one time : CATCH 3 : mental response or reaction

take back *vt* : RETRACT, WITHDRAW

take down *vb* 1 **a** : to pull to pieces **b** : DISASSEMBLE 2 : to lower the spirit or vanity of : HUMBLE 3 : to write down 4 : to become seized or attacked esp. by illness

¹take·down \ˈtāk-ˌdau̇n\ *adj* : constructed so as to be readily taken apart

²takedown *n* : the action or an act of taking down

take–home pay \ˈtāk-ˌhōm-\ *n* : the part of gross salary or wages remaining after deductions

take in *vt* 1 : to draw into a smaller compass: **a** : FURL **b** : to make (a garment) smaller by enlarging seams or tucks 2 **a** : to receive as a guest or inmate **b** : to give shelter to 3 : to receive (work) into one's house to be done for pay 4 : to encompass within fixed limits : COMPRISE, INCLUDE 5 : ATTEND 6 : to receive into the mind : PERCEIVE, COMPREHEND 7 : to impose upon : CHEAT, DECEIVE

taken *past part of* TAKE

take off *vb* 1 : REMOVE 2 : RELEASE 3 : to omit or withold from service owed or from time being spent (as at one's occupation) 4 **a** : to copy from an original : REPRODUCE **b** : MIMIC 5 : to take away : DETRACT 6 **a** : to start off or away : set out **b** : to branch off (as from a main stream or stem) **c** : to begin a leap or spring **d** : to leave the surface : begin flight

take·off \ˈtāk-ˌȯf\ *n* : an act or instance of taking off

take on *vb* 1 : to engage with as an opponent 2 : ENGAGE, HIRE 3 : to assume or acquire (as an appearance or quality) as or as if one's own 4 : to show one's feelings esp. of grief or anger in a demonstrative way

take out *vb* 1 : to remove by cleansing 2 : to find release for : EXPEND 3 : to conduct or escort into the open or to a public entertainment 4 : to take as an equivalent in another form 5 : to obtain from the proper authority 6 : to start on a course

take·out \ˈtāk-ˌau̇t\ *n* : the action or an act of taking out

take over *vb* : to assume control or possession of or responsibility for something

take–over \ˈtāk-ˌō-vər\ *n* : the action or an act of taking over

take up *vb* 1 : to remove by lifting or pulling up 2 : to accept or adopt for the purpose of assisting 3 : to take or accept (as a belief, idea, or practice) as one's own 4 : to pull up or pull in so as to tighten or to shorten 5 : to respond favorably to (as a bet, challenge, or proposal) 6 : to make a beginning where another has left off

take–up \ˈtāk-ˌəp\ *n* : the action of taking up

¹tak·ing \ˈtā-kiŋ\ *n* 1 : a state of violent agitation and distress 2 *pl* : receipts esp. of money : PROFIT

²taking *adj* : ATTRACTIVE, CAPTIVATING

talc \ˈtalk\ *n* : a soft mineral consisting of a basic silicate of magnesium that is usu. whitish, greenish, or grayish with a soapy feel and occurs in flaky, granular, or fibrous masses

tal·cum powder \ˈtal-kəm-\ *n* : a toilet powder composed of perfumed talc or talc and a mild antiseptic

tale \ˈtāl\ *n* 1 : an oral relation or recital 2 : a story about an imaginary event 3 : a false story : LIE 4 : a piece of harmful gossip 5 **a** : COUNT, TALLY **b** : a number of things taken together : TOTAL

tale·bear·er \-ˌbar-ər\ *n* : one that spreads gossip, scandal, or idle rumors : GOSSIP — **tale·bear·ing** *adj or n*

tal·ent \ˈtal-ənt\ *n* 1 : the natural endowments of a person

2 a : a special often creative or artistic aptitude b : general intelligence or mental power : ABILITY 3 : persons of talent in a field or activity — **tal·ent·ed** *adj*

tal·is·man \'tal-əs-mən, -əz-\ *n, pl* **talismans** : a ring or stone carved with symbols and believed to have magical powers

¹talk \'tók\ *vb* 1 : to deliver or express in speech : UTTER 2 : to make the subject of conversation or discourse : DISCUSS 3 : to influence, affect, or cause by talking 4 : to use (a language) for conversing or communicating 5 a : to express or exchange ideas by means of spoken words : CONVERSE b : to convey information or communication any way (as with signs or sounds) c : to use speech 6 a : to speak idly : PRATE b : GOSSIP c : to reveal secret or confidential information 7 : to give a talk : LECTURE — **talk·er** *n*

²talk *n* 1 : the act or an instance of talking : SPEECH 2 : a way of speaking : LANGUAGE 3 : pointless or fruitless discussion : VERBIAGE 4 : a formal discussion, negotiation, or exchange of views : CONFERENCE 5 : RUMOR, GOSSIP 6 : the topic of interested comment, conversation, or gossip 7 : an analysis or discussion presented in an informal manner

talk·a·tive \'tó-kət-iv\ *adj* : fond of talking — **talk·a·tive·ness** *n*

talk down *vb* : to speak in a condescending fashion

talk·ing–to \-,tü\ *n* : SCOLDING

talk out *vt* : to clarify or settle by oral discussion

talk up *vt* : to discuss favorably : ADVOCATE

talky \'tó-kē\ *adj* 1 : given to talking : TALKATIVE 2 : containing too much talk

tall \'tól\ *adj* 1 a : great in stature or height b : of a specified height 2 a : large or formidable in amount, extent, or degree b : GRANDILOQUENT, HIGH-FLOWN c : INCREDIBLE, IMPROBABLE — **tall** *adv* — **tall·ness** *n*

tall·ish \'tó-lish\ *adj* : rather tall

tal·low \'tal-ō\ *n* : the white nearly tasteless solid rendered fat of cattle and sheep used chiefly in soap, margarine, candles, and lubricants — **tal·lowy** \'tal-ə-wē\ *adj*

¹tal·ly \'tal-ē\ *n, pl* **tallies** 1 : a device for recording business transactions; *esp* : a rod notched with marks representing numbers that serves as a record of a transaction and of the amount due or paid 2 a : a reckoning or recorded account; *also* : a total recorded b : a score or point made (as in a game) 3 a : a part that corresponds to an opposite or companion member : COMPLEMENT b : CORRESPONDENCE, AGREEMENT

²tally *vb* **tal·lied**; **tal·ly·ing** 1 : to keep a reckoning of : COUNT 2 : to make a tally : SCORE 3 : MATCH, AGREE

tal·ly·ho \,tal-ē-'hō\ *n, pl* **tallyhos** 1 : a call of a huntsman at sight of the fox 2 : a four-horse coach used for show and sport

Tal·mud \'täl-,mu̇d, 'tal-məd\ *n* : the authoritative body of Jewish tradition — **tal·mu·dic** \tal-'m(y)üd-ik, -'məd-\ *adj, often cap* — **tal·mud·ist** \'täl-,mu̇d-əst, 'tal-məd-\ *n, often cap*

tal·on \'tal-ən\ *n* : the claw of an animal and esp. of a bird of prey — **tal·oned** \-ənd\ *adj*

tam \'tam\ *n* : TAM-O'-SHANTER

tam·a·ble *or* **tame·a·ble** \'tā-mə-bəl\ *adj* : capable of being tamed

ta·ma·le \tə-'mäl-ē\ *n* : ground meat seasoned usu. with chili, rolled in cornmeal dough, wrapped in corn husks, and steamed

tam·a·rack \'tam-ə-,rak\ *n* : any of several American larches; *also* : their wood

tam·a·rind \'tam-ə-,rind\ *n* : a tropical tree with hard yellowish wood and feathery leaves; *also* : its acid brown fruit

tam·bour \'tam-,bu̇r\ *n* 1 : ¹DRUM 1 2 a : an embroidery frame; *esp* : a set of two interlocking hoops between which cloth is stretched before stitching b : embroidery made on a tambour frame

tam·bou·rine \,tam-bə-'rēn\ *n* : a shallow one-headed drum with loose metallic disks at the sides played by shaking, striking with the hand, or rubbing with the thumb

¹tame \'tām\ *adj* 1 : reduced from a state of native wildness esp. so as to be tractable and useful to man : DOMESTICATED 2 : made docile and submissive : SUBDUED 3 : lacking spirit, zest, or interest : INSIPID — **tame·ly** *adv* — **tame·ness** *n*

²tame *vb* 1 a : to make or become tame b : to subject to cultivation 2 : HUMBLE, SUBDUE 3 : to tone down : SOFTEN — **tam·er** *n*

tame·less \'tām-ləs\ *adj* : not tamed or tamable

tam–o'–shan·ter \'tam-ə-,shant-ər\ *n* : a cap of Scottish origin with a tight headband, wide flat circular crown, and usu. a pompon in the center

tamp \'tamp\ *vt* : to drive in or down by a succession of light or medium blows : COMPACT — **tamp·er** *n*

tam·per \'tam-pər\ *vi* **tam·pered**; **tam·per·ing** \-p(ə-)riŋ\ 1 : to use underhand or improper methods (as bribery) 2 a : to interfere so as to cause a weakening or change for the worse b : to try foolish or dangerous experiments : MEDDLE

¹tan \'tan\ *vb* **tanned**; **tan·ning** 1 : to convert (hide) into leather esp. by treatment with an infusion of tannin-rich bark 2 : to make or become tan or brown esp. by exposure to the sun 3 : THRASH, WHIP

²tan *n* 1 : TANBARK 2 : a tanning material or its active agent (as tannin) 3 : a brown color imparted to the skin by exposure to the sun or weather 4 : a variable color averaging a light yellowish brown

³tan *adj* : of the color tan

tan·bark \'tan-,bärk\ *n* : bark rich in tannin that is used in tanning

¹tan·dem \'tan-dəm\ *n* 1 : a 2-seated carriage drawn by horses harnessed one before the other; *also* : a team so harnessed 2 : a bicycle for two persons sitting one behind the other

²tandem *adv (or adj)* : one after or behind another

¹tang \'taŋ\ *n* 1 : a projecting part (as on a knife, file, or sword) to connect with the handle 2 a : a sharp distinctive often lingering flavor b : a pungent odor 3 a : a faint suggestion : TRACE b : a distinguishing characteristic that sets apart or gives a special individuality — **tanged** \'taŋd\ *adj*

²tang *vb* : CLANG, RING

³tang *n* : a sharp twanging sound

¹tan·gent \'tan-jənt\ *adj* 1 : TOUCHING; *esp* : meeting a curve or surface and not cutting it if extended 2 : diverging from an original purpose or course : IRRELEVANT

²tangent *n* 1 : a tangent line, curve, or surface 2 : an abrupt change of course : DIGRESSION

tan·gen·tial \tan-'jen-chəl\ *adj* 1 : TANGENT 2 : acting along or lying in a tangent 3 : DIVERGENT, DIGRESSIVE — **tan·gen·tial·ly** \-'jench-(ə-)lē\ *adv*

tan·ger·ine \'tan-jə-,rēn\ *n* : a deep orange loose-skinned citrus fruit

tan·gi·bil·i·ty \,tan-jə-'bil-ət-ē\ *n, pl* **-ties** : the quality or state of being tangible

¹tan·gi·ble \'tan-jə-bəl\ *adj* 1 a : capable of being perceived esp. by the sense of touch : PALPABLE b : substantially real : MATERIAL 2 : capable of being appraised — **tan·gi·ble·ness** *n* — **tan·gi·bly** \-blē\ *adv*

²tangible *n* : something tangible; *esp* : a tangible asset

¹tan·gle \'taŋ-gəl\ *vb* **tan·gled**; **tan·gling** \-g(ə-)liŋ\ 1 : to make or become involved so as to hamper or embarrass : be or become entangled 2 : to twist or become twisted together into a mass hard to straighten out again : ENTANGLE

²tangle *n* 1 : a tangled twisted mass (as of vines) confusedly interwoven : SNARL 2 : a complicated or confused state or condition 3 : DISPUTE, ARGUMENT

tan·gle·ment \'taŋ-gəl-mənt\ *n* : ENTANGLEMENT

tan·gly \'taŋ-g(ə-)lē\ *adj* : full of tangles or knots : INTRICATE

¹tan·go \'taŋ-gō\ *n, pl* **tangos** 1 : a ballroom dance of Spanish-American origin 2 : music for the tango in moderate duple

time with dotted and syncopated rhythm
²tango *vi* : to dance the tango
tangy \'taŋ-ē\ *adj* : having or suggestive of a tang
¹tank \'taŋk\ *n* **1** : a usu. large receptacle for holding, transporting, or storing liquids **2** : an enclosed heavily armed and armored combat vehicle supported, driven, and steered by endless-belt treads
²tank *vt* : to place, store, or treat in a tank
tank•ard \'taŋ-kərd\ *n* : a tall one-handled drinking vessel; *esp* : a silver or pewter mug with a lid
tank•er \'taŋ-kər\ *n* **1 a** : a boat fitted with tanks for carrying liquid in bulk **b** : a vehicle (as a truck or trailer) on which a tank is mounted to carry liquids **2** : a cargo airplane for transporting fuel
tan•ner \'tan-ər\ *n* : one that tans hides
tan•nery \'tan-(ə-)rē\ *n*, *pl* **tan•ner•ies** : a place where tanning is carried on
tan•nic acid \,tan-ik-\ *n* : TANNIN
tan•nin \'tan-ən\ *n* : any of various substances of plant origin used in tanning and dyeing, in inks, and as an astringent
tan•ta•lize \'tant-ᵊl-,īz\ *vb* : to tease or torment by or as if by presenting something desirable to the view but continually keeping it out of reach — **tan•ta•liz•er** *n*
tan•ta•liz•ing \-,ī-ziŋ\ *adj* : possessing a quality that arouses or stimulates desire or interest : mockingly out of reach — **tan•ta•liz•ing•ly** *adv*
tan•ta•lum \'tant-ᵊl-əm\ *n* : a hard ductile gray-white acid-resisting metallic chemical element
tan•ta•mount \'tant-ə-,maùnt\ *adj* : equal in value, meaning, or effect
tan•trum \'tan-trəm\ *n* : a fit of bad temper
Tao•ism \'taù-,iz-əm, 'daù-\ *n* : a religion developed from a Chinese mystic philosophy and Buddhist religion — **Tao•ist** \-əst\ *adj or n* — **Tao•is•tic** \taù-'is-tik, daù-\ *adj*
¹tap \'tap\ *n* **1 a** : FAUCET, COCK, SPIGOT **b** : liquor drawn through a tap **2** : the procedure of removing fluid from a container or cavity by tapping **3** : a tool for forming an internal screw thread **4** : an intermediate point in an electric circuit where a connection may be made — **on tap 1** : ready to be drawn **2** : on hand : AVAILABLE
²tap *vt* **tapped**; **tap•ping 1** : to release or cause to flow by piercing or by drawing a plug from the containing vessel or cavity **2 a** : to pierce so as to let out or draw off a fluid **b** : to draw from or upon **c** : to connect into (a telephone or telegraph wire) to get information or to connect into (an electrical circuit) — **tap•per** *n*
³tap *vb* **tapped**; **tap•ping 1** : to strike or cause to strike lightly esp. with a slight sound **2** : to make or produce by repeated light blows **3** : to repair by putting a half sole on — **tap•per** *n*
⁴tap *n* **1** : a light usu. audible blow; *also* : its sound **2** : a small metal plate for the sole or heel of a shoe
tap dance *n* : a step dance tapped out audibly with the feet — **tap–dance** \'tap-,dan(t)s\ *vi* — **tap dancer** *n* — **tap dancing** *n*
¹tape \'tāp\ *n* **1** : a narrow band of woven fabric **2** : a narrow flexible strip or band **3** : MAGNETIC TAPE
²tape *vt* **1** : to fasten, tie, bind, cover, or support with tape **2** : to measure with a tape measure **3** : to record on magnetic tape
tape measure *n* : a tape marked off usu. in inches and used for measuring
¹ta•per \'tā-pər\ *n* **1** : a long waxed wick; *also* : a slender candle **2 a** : gradual diminution of thickness, diameter, or width in an elongated object **b** : a gradual decrease
²taper *vb* **ta•pered**; **ta•per•ing** \-p(ə-)riŋ\ **1** : to make or become gradually smaller toward one end **2** : to diminish gradually
tape–re•cord \,tāp-ri-'kȯrd\ *vt* : to make a recording of on magnetic tape — **tape recorder** *n* — **tape recording** *n*
taper off *vb* : to stop gradually
tap•es•try \'tap-ə-strē\ *n*, *pl* **-tries** : a heavy decorative fabric used esp. as a wall hanging or furniture covering
tape•worm \'tāp-,wərm\ *n* : a long flat segmented worm that is parasitic when adult in the intestine of vertebrates
tap•i•o•ca \,tap-ē-'ō-kə\ *n* : a usu. granular preparation of cassava starch used esp. in puddings and as a thickening in liquid foods
ta•pir \'tā-pər\ *n*, *pl* **tapir** *or* **tapirs** : any of several large inoffensive chiefly nocturnal hoofed mammals of South America and southeast Asia
tap•room \'tap-,rüm, -,rùm\ *n* : BARROOM
tap•root \-,rüt, -,rùt\ *n* : a large strong root that grows vertically downward and gives off small lateral roots
taps \'taps\ *n sing or pl* : the last bugle call at night blown as a signal that lights are to be put out; *also* : a similar call blown at military funerals and memorial services
tap•ster \'tap-stər\ *n* : one employed to dispense liquors in a barroom
¹tar \'tär\ *n* : a dark usu. odorous viscous liquid obtained by destructive distillation of organic material (as wood, coal, or peat)
²tar *vt* **tarred**; **tar•ring** : to treat or smear with or as if with tar
³tar *n* : SEAMAN, SAILOR
tar•an•tel•la \,tar-ən-'tel-ə\ *n* : a vivacious folk dance of southern Italy in ⁶⁄₈ time
ta•ran•tu•la \tə-'ranch-(ə-)lə, -'rant-ᵊl-ə\ *n* **1** : a large European spider whose bite was once thought to cause an uncontrollable desire to dance **2** : any of a family of large hairy American spiders that are mostly rather sluggish and essentially harmless to man
tar•boosh \tär-'büsh\ *n* : a usu. red hat similar to the fez used alone or as part of a turban and worn esp. by Muslim men
tar•dy \'tärd-ē\ *adj* **1** : moving slowly : SLUGGISH **2** : LATE; *also* : DILATORY — **tar•di•ly** \'tärd-ᵊl-ē\ *adv* — **tar•di•ness** \'tärd-ē-nəs\ *n*
¹tare \'ta(ə)r\ *n* **1** : VETCH; *also* : its seed **2** : a weed of grainfields mentioned in the Bible
²tare *n* : a deduction of weight made to allow for the weight of a container or vehicle — **tare** *vt*
tar•get \'tär-gət\ *n* **1** : a mark to shoot at **2** : an object of ridicule or criticism **3** : a goal to be achieved : OBJECTIVE
tar•iff \'tar-əf\ *n* **1 a** : a schedule of duties imposed by a government on imported or in some countries exported goods **b** : a duty or rate of duty imposed in such a schedule **2** : a schedule of rates or charges
tarn \'tärn\ *n* : a small mountain lake or pool
¹tar•nish \'tär-nish\ *vb* **1** : to make or become dull, dim, or discolored **2** : IMPAIR, SULLY
²tarnish *n* **1** : tarnished condition **2** : a surface film (as of oxide or sulfide) formed or deposited in tarnishing
ta•ro \'tär-ō, 'tar-\ *n*, *pl* **taros** : a plant of the arum family grown throughout the tropics for its edible starchy tuberous rootstocks; *also* : this rootstock
tarp \'tärp\ *n* : TARPAULIN
tar•pau•lin \tär-'pȯ-lən, 'tär-pə-\ *n* : waterproofed material and esp. canvas used in sheets for protecting exposed objects
tar•pon \'tär-pən\ *n*, *pl* **tarpon** *or* **tarpons** : a large silvery sport fish common off the Florida coast
¹tar•ry \'tar-ē\ *vi* **tar•ried**; **tar•ry•ing 1** : to be tardy : DELAY, LINGER **2** : to abide or stay in or at a place : SOJOURN
²tar•ry \'tär-ē\ *adj* : of, resembling, or covered with tar
¹tart \'tärt\ *adj* **1** : agreeably sharp to the taste : pleasantly acid **2** : BITING, CAUSTIC — **tart•ly** *adv* — **tart•ness** *n*
²tart *n* **1** : a small pie or pastry shell containing jelly, custard, or fruit **2** : PROSTITUTE
tar•tan \'tärt-ᵊn\ *n* **1** : a plaid textile design of Scottish origin usu. distinctively patterned to designate a clan **2** : a fabric or

garment with tartan design

¹tar·tar \'tärt-ər\ *n* **1 :** a substance consisting essentially of cream of tartar found in the juice of grapes and deposited in wine casks as a reddish crust or sediment **2 :** an incrustation on the teeth consisting of saliva, food residue, and various calcium salts

²tartar *n* **:** a bad-tempered or unexpectedly formidable person

task \'task\ *n* **:** a piece of work esp. as assigned by another

task force *n* **:** a temporary grouping esp. of armed forces units to accomplish a particular objective

task·mas·ter \'task-ˌmas-tər\ *n* **:** one that imposes a task or burdens another with labor

¹tas·sel \'tas-əl, 'täs-, 'tȯs-\ *n* **1 :** a hanging ornament made of a bunch of cords of even length fastened at one end **2 :** something resembling a tassel; *esp* **:** the terminal male inflorescence of Indian corn

²tassel *vb* **-seled** *or* **-selled; -sel·ing** *or* **-sel·ling** \-(ə-)liŋ\ **:** to adorn with or put forth tassels

¹taste \'tāst\ *vb* **1 :** EXPERIENCE, UNDERGO **2 :** to try or determine the flavor of something by taking a little into the mouth **3 a :** to eat or drink esp. in small quantities **b :** to experience slightly **4 :** to perceive or recognize as if by the sense of taste **5 :** to have a specific flavor — **tast·er** *n*

²taste *n* **1 a :** a small amount tasted **b :** a small sample of experience **2 :** the one of the special senses that perceives and distinguishes the sweet, sour, bitter, or salty quality of a dissolved substance and is mediated by receptors in the taste buds of the tongue **3 a :** the objective quality of a dissolved substance perceptible to the sense of taste **b :** a complex sensation resulting from usu. combined stimulation of the senses of taste, smell, and touch **:** FLAVOR **4 :** the distinctive quality of an experience **5 :** individual preference **:** INCLINATION **6 a :** critical judgment, discernment, or appreciation **b :** manner or aesthetic quality indicative of discernment or appreciation

taste·ful \'tāst-fəl\ *adj* **:** having, showing, or conforming to good taste — **taste·ful·ly** \-fə-lē\ *adv* — **taste·ful·ness** *n*

taste·less \'tāst-ləs\ *adj* **1 :** lacking flavor **:** FLAT, INSIPID **2 :** not having or showing good taste — **taste·less·ly** *adv* — **taste·less·ness** *n*

tasty \'tā-stē\ *adj* **1 :** pleasing to the taste **:** SAVORY **2 :** TASTEFUL — **tast·i·ly** \-stə-lē\ *adv* — **tast·i·ness** \-stē-nəs\ *n*

tat \'tat\ *vb* **tat·ted; tat·ting :** to work at or make by tatting

¹tat·ter \'tat-ər\ *n* **1 :** a part torn and left hanging **:** SHRED **2** *pl* **:** tattered clothing **:** RAGS

²tatter *vb* **:** to make or become ragged

tat·ter·de·ma·lion \ˌtat-ərd-i-'māl-yən\ *n* **:** a person dressed in ragged clothing **:** RAGAMUFFIN

tat·tered \'tat-ərd\ *adj* **1 :** wearing ragged clothes **2 :** torn in shreds **:** RAGGED; *also* **:** DILAPIDATED

tat·ting \'tat-iŋ\ *n* **1 :** a delicate handmade lace formed usu. by looping and knotting with a single thread and a small shuttle **2 :** the act or process of making tatting

¹tat·tle \'tat-ᵊl\ *vb* **tat·tled; tat·tling** \'tat-liŋ, -ᵊl-iŋ\ **1 :** CHATTER, PRATTLE **2 :** to tell secrets **:** BLAB

²tattle *n* **1 :** idle talk **:** CHATTER **2 :** GOSSIP, TALEBEARING

tat·tler \'tat-lər, -ᵊl-ər\ *n* **:** TATTLETALE

tat·tle·tale \'tat-ᵊl-ˌtāl\ *n* **:** one that tattles **:** INFORMER

¹tat·too \ta-'tü\ *n, pl* **tattoos 1 :** a call sounded shortly before taps as notice to go to quarters **2 :** a rapid rhythmic rapping

²tattoo *n* **:** an indelible mark or figure fixed upon the body by insertion of pigment under the skin or by production of scars

³tattoo *vt* **1 :** to mark or color (the skin) with tattoos **2 :** to mark the skin with (a tattoo) — **tat·too·er** *n*

taught *past of* TEACH

¹taunt \'tȯnt\ *vt* **:** to reproach or challenge in a mocking or insulting manner **:** jeer at — **taunt·er** *n* — **taunt·ing·ly** *adv*

²taunt *n* **:** a sarcastic or jeering challenge or insult

taupe \'tōp\ *n* **:** a brownish gray

taut \'tȯt\ *adj* **1 a :** tightly drawn **:** not slack **b :** HIGH-STRUNG, TENSE **2 a :** kept in proper order or condition **b :** not loose or flabby **:** FIRM — **taut·ly** *adv* — **taut·ness** *n*

tau·tol·o·gy \tȯ-'täl-ə-jē\ *n, pl* **-gies :** needless repetition of an idea, statement, or word; *also* **:** an instance of such repetition — **tau·to·log·i·cal** \ˌtȯt-ᵊl-'äj-i-kəl\ *adj* — **tau·tol·o·gous** \tȯ-'täl-ə-gəs\ *adj*

tav·ern \'tav-ərn\ *n* **1 :** an establishment where alcoholic liquors are sold to be drunk on the premises **2 :** INN

taw \'tȯ\ *n* **1 :** a marble used as a shooter **2 :** the line from which players shoot at marbles

taw·dry \'tȯd-rē\ *adj* **:** cheap and gaudy in appearance and quality — **taw·dri·ly** \-rə-lē\ *adv* — **taw·dri·ness** \-rē-nəs\ *n*

¹taw·ny \'tȯ-nē\ *adj* **:** of the color tawny

²tawny *n, pl* **tawnies :** a brownish orange to light brown color

¹tax \'taks\ *vt* **1 :** to levy a tax on **2 :** to call to account for something **:** CENSURE **3 :** to make onerous and rigorous demands upon **:** subject to excessive stress — **tax·a·bil·i·ty** \ˌtak-sə-'bil-ət-ē\ *n* — **tax·a·ble** *adj* — **tax·er** *n*

²tax *n* **1 a :** a charge usu. of money imposed by authority upon persons or property for public purposes **b :** a sum levied on members of an organization to defray expenses **2 :** something (as an effort or duty) that makes heavy demands **:** STRAIN

tax·a·tion \tak-'sā-shən\ *n* **1 :** the action of taxing; *esp* **:** the imposition of taxes **2 :** revenue obtained from taxes

¹taxi \'tak-sē\ *n, pl* **tax·is** \-sēz\ **:** TAXICAB; *also* **:** a similarly operated boat or airplane

²taxi *vb* **tax·ied; taxi·ing** *or* **taxy·ing; tax·is** \-sēz\ *or* **tax·ies 1 a :** to ride in a taxicab **b :** to transport by taxi **2 :** to go at low speed along the surface of the ground

taxi·cab \'tak-sē-ˌkab\ *n* **:** an automobile that carries passengers for a fare usu. determined by the distance traveled and often shown by a meter

tax·i·der·my \'tak-sə-ˌdər-mē\ *n* **:** the art of preparing, stuffing, and mounting skins of animals — **tax·i·der·mic** \ˌtak-sə-'dər-mik\ *adj* — **tax·i·der·mist** \'tak-sə-ˌdər-məst\ *n*

tax·on·o·my \tak-'sän-ə-mē\ *n* **:** CLASSIFICATION; *esp* **:** orderly classification of plants and animals according to their presumed natural relationships — **tax·o·nom·ic** \ˌtak-sə-'näm-ik\ *adj* — **tax·on·o·mist** \tak-'sän-ə-məst\ *n*

tax·pay·er \'taks-ˌpā-ər\ *n* **:** one that pays or is liable for a tax

TB \(')tē-'bē\ *n* **:** TUBERCULOSIS

tea \'tē\ *n* **1 a :** the cured leaves and leaf buds of a shrub grown mainly in China, Japan, India, and Ceylon; *also* **:** this shrub **b :** an aromatic beverage prepared from tea by steeping in boiling water **2 a :** a late afternoon serving of tea and a light meal **b :** a party or reception at which tea is served

teach \'tēch\ *vb* **taught** \'tȯt\; **teach·ing 1 :** to assist in learning how to do something **:** show how **2 :** to guide the studies of **:** INSTRUCT **3 :** to give lessons in **:** instruct pupils in **4 :** to be a teacher **5 :** to cause to learn **:** cause to know the consequences of an action

teach·a·ble \'tē-chə-bəl\ *adj* **1 :** capable of being taught; *esp* **:** apt and willing to learn **2 :** well adapted for use in teaching — **teach·a·bil·i·ty** \ˌtē-chə-'bil-ət-ē\ *n*

teach·er \'tē-chər\ *n* **:** one that teaches; *esp* **:** one whose occupation is to instruct

teach·ing \'tē-chiŋ\ *n* **1 :** the act, practice, or profession of a teacher **2 :** something taught; *esp* **:** DOCTRINE

tea·cup \'tē-ˌkəp\ *n* **:** a cup usu. of less than 8-oz. capacity used with a saucer for hot beverages

tea·cup·ful \-ˌfu̇l\ *n, pl* **-cupfuls** \-ˌfu̇lz\ *or* **-cups·ful** \-ˌkəps-ˌfu̇l\ **:** as much as a teacup can hold

teak \'tēk\ *n* **:** a tall East Indian timber tree of the vervain family; *also* **:** its hard durable yellowish brown wood

tea·ket·tle \'tē-ˌket-ᵊl\ *n* **:** a covered kettle with a handle and spout for boiling water

teal \'tēl\ *n, pl* **teal** *or* **teals** : any of several small short-necked river ducks of Europe and America

¹team \'tēm\ *n* **1** : two or more draft animals harnessed to the same vehicle or implement **2** : a number of persons associated together in work or activity: as **a** : a group on one side in a match **b** : CREW, GANG

²team *vb* **1** : to yoke or join in a team **2** : to haul with or drive a team **3** : to form a team

team•mate \'tēm-ˌmāt\ *n* : a fellow member of a team

team•ster \'tēm(p)-stər\ *n* : one who drives a team or truck esp. as an occupation

team•work \'tēm-ˌwərk\ *n* : the work or activity of a number of persons acting in close association as members of a unit

tea•pot \'tē-ˌpät\ *n* : a vessel with a spout for brewing and serving tea

¹tear \'ti(ə)r\ *n* : a drop of the salty liquid that keeps the eye and the inner eyelids moist — **teary** \'ti(ə)r-ē\ *adj*

²tear \'ta(ə)r\ *vb* **tore** \'tō(ə)r\; **torn** \'tōrn\; **tear•ing** **1** : to separate or pull apart by force : REND; *also* : LACERATE **2** : to divide or disrupt by the pull of contrary forces **3** : to remove by force : WRENCH **4** : to effect by force or violent means **5** : to move or act with violence, haste, or force — **tear•er** *n*

³tear \'ta(ə)r\ *n* **1 a** : the act of tearing **b** : damage from being torn; *esp* : a torn place **2 a** : a hurried pace **b** : SPREE

tear•ful \'ti(ə)r-fəl\ *adj* : flowing with, accompanied by, or causing tears — **tear•ful•ly** \-fə-lē\ *adv* — **tear•ful•ness** *n*

tear gas *n* : a solid, liquid, or gaseous substance that on dispersion in the atmosphere blinds the eyes with tears

tea•room \'tē-ˌrüm, -ˌrům\ *n* : a small restaurant serving light meals

¹tease \'tēz\ *vt* **1** : to disentangle and lay parallel by combing or carding **2 a** : to annoy persistently : PESTER, TORMENT **b** : TANTALIZE — **teas•er** *n*

²tease *n* **1** : the act of teasing : the state of being teased **2** : one that teases

tea•sel *or* **tea•zel** *or* **tea•zle** \'tē-zəl\ *n* **1** : any of a genus of Old World prickly herbs; *esp* : one with flower heads covered with stiff hooked bracts **2 a** : a dried flower head of the fuller's teasel used to raise a nap on woolen cloth **b** : a wire substitute for the fuller's teasel

tea•spoon \'tē-ˌspün, -'spün\ *n* **1** : a small spoon used esp. for eating soft foods and stirring beverages **2** : TEASPOONFUL

tea•spoon•ful \-ˌfu̇l\ *n, pl* **-spoonfuls** \-ˌfu̇lz\ *or* **-spoons•ful** \-ˌspünz-ˌfu̇l, -'spünz-\ : as much as a teaspoon can hold

teat \'tit, 'tēt\ *n* : NIPPLE

tech•nic \'tek-nik, tek-'nēk\ *n* : TECHNIQUE 1

tech•ni•cal \'tek-ni-kəl\ *adj* **1 a** : having special usu. practical knowledge esp. of a mechanical or scientific subject **b** : marked by or characteristic of specialization **2** : of or relating to a particular subject; *esp* : of or relating to a practical subject organized on scientific principles **3** : existing by application of the laws or rules **4** : of or relating to technique — **tech•ni•cal•ly** \-k(ə-)lē\ *adv*

tech•ni•cal•i•ty \ˌtek-nə-'kal-ət-ē\ *n, pl* **-ties** **1** : the quality or state of being technical **2** : something technical; *esp* : a detail meaningful only to a specialist

technical sergeant *n* : a noncommissioned officer in the air force ranking next below a master sergeant

tech•ni•cian \tek-'nish-ən\ *n* : a person skilled in the technical details or in the technique of a subject, art, or occupation

tech•nique \tek-'nēk\ *n* **1** : the manner in which technical details are treated (as by a writer) or basic physical movements are used (as by a dancer); *also* : ability in such treatment or use **2 a** : technical methods esp. in scientific research **b** : a method of accomplishing a desired aim

tech•no•log•i•cal \ˌtek-nə-'läj-i-kəl\ *or* **tech•no•log•ic** \-'läj-ik\ *adj* : of, relating to, or characterized or caused by technology — **tech•no•log•i•cal•ly** \-läj-i-k(ə-)lē\ *adv*

tech•nol•o•gist \tek-'näl-ə-jəst\ *n* : a specialist in technology

tech•nol•o•gy \-jē\ *n, pl* **-gies** **1** : applied science **2** : a technical method of achieving a practical purpose

te•dious \'tēd-ē-əs, 'tē-jəs\ *adj* : tiresome because of length or dullness : BORING — **te•dious•ly** *adv* — **te•dious•ness** *n*

te•di•um \'tēd-ē-əm\ *n* : the quality or state of being tedious : TEDIOUSNESS; *also* : BOREDOM

¹tee \'tē\ *n* : the area from which a golf ball is struck in starting play on a hole; *also* : a tiny mound or a small peg with concave top on which the ball is set to be struck

²tee *vb* **teed**; **tee•ing** **1** : to place (a ball) on a tee — often used with *up* **2** : to drive a golf ball from a tee; *also* : BEGIN, START — usu. used with *off*

teem \'tēm\ *vi* **1** : to become filled to overflowing : ABOUND **2** : to be present in large quantity

teen•age \'tēnˌāj\ *or* **teen•aged** \-ˌājd\ *adj* : of, being, or relating to people in their teens

teen•a•ger \-ˌā-jər\ *n* : a person in his teens

teens \'tēnz\ *n pl* **1** : the numbers 13 through 19; *esp* : the years 13 through 19 in a lifetime or century **2** : TEENAGERS

tee•ter \'tēt-ər\ *vi* **1 a** : to move unsteadily : WOBBLE **b** : WAVER, VACILLATE **2** : SEESAW — **teeter** *n*

teeth *pl of* TOOTH

teethe \'tē<u>th</u>\ *vi* : to cut one's teeth : grow teeth

tee•to•tal•er *or* **tee•to•tal•ler** \'tē-'tōt-ᵊl-ər\ *n* : a person who completely abstains from alcoholic liquor

tee•to•tal•ism \-ᵊl-ˌiz-əm\ *n* : the principle or practice of complete abstinence from alcoholic drinks

tele•cast \'tel-i-ˌkast\ *vb* **telecast**; **tele•cast•ing** : to broadcast by television — **telecast** *n* — **tele•cast•er** *n*

tele•com•mu•ni•ca•tion \ˌtel-i-kə-ˌmyü-nə-'kā-shən\ *n* : communication at a distance (as by cable, radio, telegraph, telephone, or television)

tel•e•gram \'tel-ə-ˌgram\ *n* : a message sent by telegraph

¹tel•e•graph \-ˌgraf\ *n* : an apparatus for communication at a distance by coded signals; *esp* : an apparatus, system, or process for communication at a distance by electric transmission of such signals over wire — **tel•e•graph•ic** \ˌtel-ə-'graf-ik\ *adj* — **tel•e•graph•i•cal•ly** \-'graf-i-k(ə-)lē\ *adv*

²telegraph *vt* **1 a** : to send by or as if by telegraph **b** : to send a telegram to **c** : to send (as flowers or money) by means of a telegraphic order **2** : to make known by signs esp. unknowingly and in advance — **te•leg•ra•pher** \tə-'leg-rə-fər\ *n* — **te•leg•ra•phist** \-fəst\ *n*

te•leg•ra•phy \tə-'leg-rə-fē\ *n* : the use or operation of a telegraph apparatus or system

tel•e•me•ter \'tel-ə-ˌmēt-ər\ *n* : an electrical apparatus for measuring something (as pressure, speed, or temperature), transmitting the result esp. by radio to a distant station, and there indicating the measurement — **tel•e•met•ric** \ˌtel-ə-'me-trik\ *adj* — **tel•e•met•ri•cal•ly** \-tri-k(ə-)lē\ *adv* — **te•lem•e•try** \tə-'lem-ə-trē\ *n*

te•lep•a•thy \tə-'lep-ə-thē\ *n* : apparent communication from one mind to another otherwise than through the channels of sense — **tel•e•path•ic** \ˌtel-ə-'path-ik\ *adj* — **tel•e•path•i•cal•ly** \-'path-i-k(ə-)lē\ *adv*

¹tel•e•phone \'tel-ə-ˌfōn\ *n* : an instrument for reproducing sounds at a distance; *esp* : an instrument for receiving and reproducing the sound of the human voice transmitted from a distance over wires by means of electricity

²telephone *vb* **1** : to communicate by telephone **2** : to send by telephone **3** : to speak to by telephone

tel•e•phon•ic \ˌtel-ə-'fän-ik\ *adj* **1** : conveying sound to a distance **2** : of, relating to, or conveyed by telephone

te•leph•o•ny \tə-'lef-ə-nē, 'tel-ə-ˌfō-\ *n* : the use or operation of an apparatus for transmission of sounds between widely removed points with or without connecting wires

tele•pho•to \ˌtel-ə-'fōt-ō\ *adj* : being a camera lens designed to give a large image of a distant object

[1]**tel·e·scope** \'tel-ə-ˌskōp\ *n* : a usu. tubular optical instrument for viewing distant objects and esp. the heavenly bodies by means of the refraction of light rays through a lens or the reflection of light rays by a concave mirror

[2]**telescope** *vb* **1** : to slide or pass or cause to slide or pass one within another like the cylindrical sections of a hand telescope **2** : to run together in order to shorten or simplify : COMPRESS

tel·e·scop·ic \ˌtel-ə-'skäp-ik\ *adj* **1** : of, with, or relating to a telescope **2** : seen or discoverable only by a telescope **3** : able to discern objects at a distance : FARSEEING **4** : having parts that telescope — **tel·e·scop·i·cal·ly** \-'skäp-i-k(ə-)lē\ *adv*

tele·view \'tel-ə-ˌvyü\ *vi* : to observe or watch by means of a television receiver — **tele·view·er** *n*

tel·e·vise \'tel-ə-ˌvīz\ *vt* : to pick up and usu. to broadcast (as a baseball game) by television

tel·e·vi·sion \'tel-ə-ˌvizh-ən\ *n* **1** : an electronic system of transmitting transient images of fixed or moving objects together with sound over a wire or through space by apparatus that converts light and sound into electrical waves and reconverts them into visible light rays and audible sound **2** : a television receiving set **3 a** : the television broadcasting industry **b** : television as a medium of communication

tell \'tel\ *vb* **told** \'tōld\; **tell·ing** **1** : COUNT, ENUMERATE **2 a** : to relate in detail : NARRATE **b** : SAY, UTTER **3 a** : to make known : DIVULGE, REVEAL **b** : to express in words **4** : to report to : INFORM **5** : ORDER, DIRECT **6** : to ascertain by observing : find out **7** : to act as a talebearer **8** : to have a marked effect **9** : EVIDENCE, INDICATE

tell·er \'tel-ər\ *n* **1** : one that relates or communicates **2** : a person who counts votes (as in a legislative body) **3** : a bank employee who receives and pays out money

tell·ing \'tel-iŋ\ *adj* : producing a marked effect : EFFECTIVE

tell off *vt* : REPRIMAND, SCOLD

[1]**tell·tale** \'tel-ˌtāl\ *n* **1 a** : TALEBEARER, INFORMER **b** : an outward sign : INDICATION **2** : a device for indicating or recording something

[2]**telltale** *adj* : INFORMING, REVEALING

tel·lu·ri·um \tə-'lu̇r-ē-əm\ *n* : a chemical element that resembles selenium and sulfur in properties

te·mer·i·ty \tə-'mer-ət-ē\ *n* : unreasonable or foolhardy contempt of danger or opposition : RASHNESS

[1]**tem·per** \'tem-pər\ *vb* **tem·pered**; **tem·per·ing** \'tem-p(ə-)riŋ\ **1** : MODERATE, SOFTEN **2** : to control by reducing : SUBDUE **3** : to bring to the desired consistency or texture **4** : to bring (as steel) to the desired hardness by heating and cooling **5** : to be or become tempered — **tem·per·a·ble** *adj*

[2]**temper** *n* **1** : characteristic tone : TREND, TENDENCY **2** : high quality of mind or spirit : COURAGE, METTLE **3** : the state of a substance with respect to certain desired qualities (as hardness, elasticity, or workability) **4 a** : a characteristic cast of mind or state of feeling : DISPOSITION **b** : calmness of mind : COMPOSURE **c** : state of feeling or frame of mind at a particular time **d** : a state of anger **e** : a proneness to anger

tem·pera \'tem-pə-rə\ *n* : a process of painting in which an albuminous or colloidal medium is employed as a vehicle instead of oil

tem·per·a·ment \'tem-p(ə-)rə-mənt\ *n* **1** : characteristic or habitual inclination or mode of emotional response **2** : excessive sensitiveness or irritability

tem·per·a·men·tal \ˌtem-p(ə-)rə-'ment-ᵊl\ *adj* **1** : of, relating to, or arising from temperament **2 a** : marked by excessive sensitivity and impulsive changes of mood : HIGH-STRUNG, EXCITABLE **b** : UNPREDICTABLE, CAPRICIOUS — **tem·per·a·men·tal·ly** \-ᵊl-ē\ *adv*

tem·per·ance \'tem-p(ə-)rən(t)s\ *n* **1** : moderation in action, thought, or feeling : RESTRAINT **2** : habitual moderation in the indulgence of the appetites or passions; *esp* : moderation in or abstinence from the use of intoxicating drink

tem·per·ate \'tem-p(ə-)rət\ *adj* **1** : marked by moderation: as **a** : not excessive or extreme **b** : moderate in satisfying one's needs or desires **c** : moderate in the use of liquor **d** : marked by self-control : RESTRAINED **2** : having, found in, or associated with a moderate climate — **tem·per·ate·ly** *adv* — **tem·per·ate·ness** *n*

temperate zone *n, often cap T & Z* : the area or region between the tropic of Cancer and the arctic circle or between the tropic of Capricorn and the antarctic circle

tem·per·a·ture \'tem-pər-ˌchu̇r, 'tem-p(ə-)rə-ˌchu̇r, -chər\ *n* **1** : the degree of hotness or coldness of something (as air, water, or the body) as shown by a thermometer **2** : FEVER

tem·pered \'tem-pərd\ *adj* **1** : having a particular kind of temper **2** : brought to the desired state (as of hardness, toughness, or flexibility) **3** : qualified, lessened, or diluted by the mixture or influence of an additional ingredient

tem·pest \'tem-pəst\ *n* **1** : an extensive violent wind; *esp* : one accompanied by rain, hail, or snow **2** : a violent commotion

tem·pes·tu·ous \tem-'pes-chə-wəs\ *adj* : VIOLENT, STORMY — **tem·pes·tu·ous·ly** *adv* — **tem·pes·tu·ous·ness** *n*

tem·plate *or* **tem·plet** \'tem-plət\ *n* : a gauge, pattern, or mold used as a guide to the form of a piece being made

[1]**tem·ple** \'tem-pəl\ *n* **1** : an edifice for the worship of a deity **2** : a place devoted to a special or exalted purpose — **tem·pled** \-pəld\ *adj*

[2]**temple** *n* : the flattened space on each side of the forehead of man and some other mammals

tem·po \'tem-pō\ *n, pl* **tem·pi** \-(ˌ)pē\ *or* **tempos** **1** : the rate of speed of a musical piece or passage indicated by one of a series of directions **2** : rate of motion or activity : PACE

[1]**tem·po·ral** \'tem-p(ə-)rəl\ *adj* **1** : of or relating to time as opposed to eternity : TEMPORARY **2 a** : of or relating to earthly life **b** : of or relating to lay or secular concerns — **tem·po·ral·ly** \-ē\ *adv*

[2]**temporal** *adj* : of or relating to the temples or to the sides of the skull behind the orbits — **tem·po·ral·ly** \-ē\ *adv*

tem·po·rary \'tem-pə-ˌrer-ē\ *adj* : lasting for a time only : IMPERMANENT — **tem·po·rar·i·ly** \ˌtem-pə-'rer-ə-lē\ *adv* — **tem·po·rar·i·ness** \'tem-pə-ˌrer-ē-nəs\ *n*

tem·po·rize \'tem-pə-ˌrīz\ *vi* **1** : to act to suit the time or occasion : yield to current or dominant opinion : COMPROMISE **2** : to draw out negotiations so as to gain time — **tem·po·ri·za·tion** \ˌtem-pə-rə-'zā-shən\ *n* — **tem·po·riz·er** *n*

tempt \'tem(p)t\ *vt* **1** : to entice to do wrong by promise of pleasure or gain : allure into evil : SEDUCE **2 a** : to try presumptuously : PROVOKE **b** : to risk the dangers of **3 a** : to induce to do something : INCITE **b** : to cause to be strongly inclined : almost move or persuade — **tempt·a·ble** *adj*

temp·ta·tion \tem(p)-'tā-shən\ *n* **1** : the act of tempting : the state of being tempted esp. to evil : ENTICEMENT **2** : something tempting

tempt·er \'tem(p)-tər\ *n* : one that tempts or entices — **tempt·ress** \-trəs\ *n*

tempt·ing \'tem(p)-tiŋ\ *adj* : ALLURING, ENTICING — **tempt·ing·ly** *adv*

ten \'ten\ *n* **1** — see NUMBER table **2** : the tenth in a set or series **3** : something having ten units or members **4** : a ten-dollar bill **5** : the number in the second decimal place to the left of the decimal point in arabic numerals — **ten** *adj or pron*

ten·a·bil·i·ty \ˌten-ə-'bil-ət-ē\ *n* : the quality or state of being tenable

ten·a·ble \'ten-ə-bəl\ *adj* : capable of being held, maintained, or defended : DEFENSIBLE, REASONABLE — **ten·a·ble·ness** *n* — **ten·a·bly** \-blē\ *adv*

te·na·cious \tə-'nā-shəs\ *adj* **1 a** : not easily pulled apart : COHESIVE, TOUGH **b** : tending to adhere to another substance : STICKY **2 a** : holding fast or tending to hold fast : PERSIST-

ENT, STUBBORN **b** : RETENTIVE — **te·na·cious·ly** *adv* — **te·na·cious·ness** *n*

te·nac·i·ty \tə-'nas-ət-ē\ *n* : the quality or state of being tenacious

ten·an·cy \'ten-ən-sē\ *n, pl* **-cies** : the temporary possession or occupancy of property that belongs to another; *also* : the period of such occupancy or possession

[1]**ten·ant** \'ten-ənt\ *n* **1 a** : the owner or possessor of property **b** : one who occupies or has temporary possession of property of another; *esp* : one who rents or leases (as a house) from a landlord **2** : DWELLER, OCCUPANT — **ten·ant·less** \-ləs\ *adj*

[2]**tenant** *vt* : to hold or occupy as a tenant : INHABIT — **ten·ant·a·ble** *adj*

ten–cent store \'ten-'sent-\ *n* : FIVE-AND-TEN

Ten Commandments *n pl* : the commandments of God given to Moses on Mount Sinai

[1]**tend**\'tend\ *vb* **1** : to pay attention **2** : to take care of : attend to (as plants) : CULTIVATE **3** : to have charge of as caretaker or overseer **4** : to manage or superintend the operation of

[2]**tend** *vi* **1** : to move or turn in a certain direction : LEAD **2** : to have a tendency : be likely

tend·en·cy \'ten-dən-sē\ *n, pl* **-cies 1 a** : direction or approach toward a place, object, effect, or limit **b** : INCLINATION, BENT **c** : proneness to a particular kind of thought or action **2** : the purposeful trend of something written or said : AIM

[1]**ten·der** \'ten-dər\ *adj* **1 a** : having a soft or yielding texture : easily broken, cut, or damaged : DELICATE, FRAGILE **b** : easily chewed : SUCCULENT **2 a** : physically weak : not able to endure hardship **b** : IMMATURE, YOUNG **c** : incapable of resisting cold **3** : marked by, responding to, or expressing the softer emotions : FOND, LOVING **4 a** : showing care : CONSIDERATE, SOLICITOUS **b** : highly susceptible to impressions or emotions : IMPRESSIONABLE **5 a** : appropriate or conducive to a delicate or sensitive constitution or character : GENTLE, MILD **b** : delicate or soft in quality or tone **6 a** : sensitive to touch : easily hurt **b** : sensitive to injury or insult : TOUCHY **c** : demanding careful and sensitive handling : TICKLISH — **ten·der·ly** *adv* — **ten·der·ness** *n*

[2]**tend·er** \'ten-dər\ *n* : one that tends or takes care: as **a** : a ship employed (as to supply provisions) to attend other ships **b** : a boat that carries passengers or freight between shore and a larger ship **c** : a vehicle attached to a locomotive for carrying a supply of fuel and water

[3]**ten·der** *n* **1** : an offer of money in satisfaction of a debt **2** : an offer or proposal made for acceptance; *esp* : an offer of a bid for a contract **3** : something that may by law be offered in payment; *esp* : MONEY

[4]**ten·der** *vt* **ten·dered**; **ten·der·ing** \-d(ə-)riŋ\ **1** : to make a tender of **2** : to present for acceptance : PROFFER

ten·der·foot \'ten-dər-ˌfu̇t\ *n, pl* **-feet** \-ˌfēt\ **1** : a person who is not hardened to a rough out-of-door life; *esp* : a newcomer in a recent settlement (as on a frontier) **2** : a boy scout or girl scout of the beginning class

ten·der·heart·ed \ˌten-dər-'härt-əd\ *adj* : easily moved to love, pity, or sorrow : COMPASSIONATE, IMPRESSIONABLE — **ten·der·heart·ed·ly** *adv* — **ten·der·heart·ed·ness** *n*

ten·der·ize \'ten-də-ˌrīz\ *vt* : to make (meat) tender — **ten·der·i·za·tion** \ˌten-də-rə-'zā-shən\ *n* — **ten·der·iz·er** *n*

ten·der·loin \'ten-dər-ˌlȯin\ *n* : a strip of tender meat on each side of the backbone : a fillet of beef or pork

ten·di·nous \'ten-də-nəs\ *adj* **1** : of, relating to, or resembling a tendon **2** : consisting of tendons : SINEWY

ten·don \'ten-dən\ *n* : a tough cord or band of fibrous tissue connecting a muscle to some other part (as a bone) and transmitting the force exerted by the muscle

ten·dril \'ten-drəl\ *n* : a slender spirally coiling sensitive organ serving to attach a plant to its support — **ten·driled** *or* **ten·drilled** \-drəld\ *adj* — **ten·dril·ly** \-drə-lē\ *adj* — **ten·dril·ous** \-drə-ləs\ *adj*

ten·e·brous \'ten-ə-brəs\ *adj* : shut off from the light : GLOOMY, OBSCURE

ten·e·ment \'ten-ə-mənt\ *n* **1** : land or property treated in law like land that is held by one person from another : HOLDING **2 a** : a house used as a dwelling : RESIDENCE **b** : APARTMENT, FLAT **c** : TENEMENT HOUSE

tenement house *n* : an apartment building; *esp* : one barely meeting minimum standards of sanitation, safety, and comfort and housing poorer families

ten·et \'ten-ət\ *n* : a principle, belief, or doctrine generally held to be true; *esp* : one held in common by members of an organization, group, or profession

ten·fold \'ten-ˌfōld, -'fōld\ *adj* **1** : having 10 units or members **2** : of or amounting to 1000 percent — **tenfold** *adv*

ten·nis \'ten-əs\ *n* : a game that is played with rackets and a light elastic ball on a level court divided by a low net

ten·on \'ten-ən\ *n* : a projecting part in a piece of material (as wood) for insertion into a mortise to make a joint

[1]**ten·or** \'ten-ər\ *n* **1** : the general drift of something spoken or written : PURPORT **2** : the voice part next to the lowest in 4-part harmony **3** : the highest natural adult male voice **4** : a continuance in a course, movement, or activity

[2]**tenor** *adj* **1** : of or relating to the tenor in music **2** : close in range to a tenor voice

ten·pin \'ten-ˌpin\ *n* **1** : a bottle-shaped bowling pin **2** *pl* : a bowling game using 10 tenpins and a large ball

[1]**tense** \'ten(t)s\ *n* : distinction of form of a verb to indicate the time of the action or state

[2]**tense** *adj* **1** : stretched tight : made taut : RIGID **2 a** : feeling or showing nervous tension : HIGH-STRUNG **b** : marked by strain or suspense **3** : produced with the speech muscles in a relatively tense state — **tense·ly** *adv* — **tense·ness** *n*

[3]**tense** *vb* : to make or become tense

ten·sile \'ten(t)-səl, 'ten-ˌsīl\ *adj* : of or relating to tension

ten·sion \'ten-chən\ *n* **1 a** : the act or action of stretching or the condition or degree of being stretched to stiffness : TAUTNESS **b** : STRESS 1c **2 a** : a state of mental unrest often with signs of physiological stress **b** : a state of latent hostility or opposition between individuals or groups

ten·sion·less \'ten-chən-ləs\ *adj* : free from tension

ten·si·ty \'ten(t)-sət-ē\ *n* : TENSENESS

[1]**tent** \'tent\ *n* **1** : a collapsible shelter (as of canvas) stretched and sustained by poles and used esp. (as by campers) as temporary housing **2** : something that resembles a tent or that serves as a shelter; *esp* : a canopy or enclosure placed over the head and shoulders to retain medicinal vapors or oxygen administered

[2]**tent** *vb* **1** : to live or lodge in a tent **2** : to cover with or as if with a tent — **tent·er** *n*

ten·ta·cle \'tent-i-kəl\ *n* : one of the long flexible processes usu. about the head or mouth of an animal (as a worm or fish) used esp. for feeling, grasping, or handling — **ten·ta·cled** \-kəld\ *adj* — **ten·tac·u·lar** \ten-'tak-yə-lər\ *adj*

ten·ta·tive \'tent-ət-iv\ *adj* **1** : not fully worked out or developed : not final : PROVISIONAL, TEMPORARY **2** : HESITANT, UNCERTAIN — **ten·ta·tive·ly** *adv* — **ten·ta·tive·ness** *n*

tenth \'ten(t)th\ *n* **1** — see NUMBER table **2** : one of 10 equal parts of something **3** : the one numbered 10 in a countable series — **tenth** *adj or adv*

ten·u·ous \'ten-yə-wəs\ *adj* **1** : not dense : RARE **2** : not thick : SLENDER **3** : having little substance or strength : FLIMSY, WEAK — **te·nu·i·ty** \te-'n(y)ü-ət-ē, tə-\ *n* — **ten·u·ous·ly** *adv* — **ten·u·ous·ness** *n*

ten·ure \'ten-yər\ *n* **1** : the act, right, manner, or term of holding something (as real property, a position, or an office) **2** : GRASP, HOLD — **ten·ur·i·al** \te-'nyu̇r-ē-əl\ *adj*

te·pee \'tē-(ˌ)pē\ *n* : a conical tent usu. of skins used by some American Indians
tep·id \'tep-əd\ *adj* **1** : moderately warm : LUKEWARM **2** : lacking enthusiasm or conviction : HALFHEARTED — **te·pid·i·ty** \tə-'pid-ət-ē, te-\ *n* — **tep·id·ly** *adv* — **tep·id·ness** *n*
ter·bi·um \'tər-bē-əm\ *n* : a usu. trivalent metallic chemical element
ter·cen·ten·a·ry \ˌtər-ˌsen-'ten-ə-rē, (')tər-'sent-ᵊn-ˌer-ē\ *n, pl* **-ries** : a 300th anniversary or its celebration — **tercentenary** *adj*
te·re·do \tə-'rēd-ō\ *n, pl* **-re·dos** *or* **-red·i·nes** \-'red-ᵊn-ˌēz\ : SHIPWORM
ter·gi·ver·sate \'tər-ji-(ˌ)vər-ˌsāt\ *vi* **1** : to change one's mind about or desert something (as a cause or party) **2** : to use subterfuges : EQUIVOCATE — **ter·gi·ver·sa·tion** \ˌtər-ji-(ˌ)vər-'sā-shən\ *n* — **ter·gi·ver·sa·tor** \'tər-ji-(ˌ)vər-ˌsāt-ər\ *n*
¹term \'tərm\ *n* **1 a** : a time or date that is a boundary between periods or is assigned to a particular purpose (as payment of rent or interest) **b** : END, LIMIT **2** : a limited or definite extent of time esp. as fixed by law, custom, or some recurrent phenomenon **3** : the time for which something lasts : DURATION **4** *pl* : provisions determining the nature and scope of something and esp. of an agreement **5 a** : a word or expression that has a precise meaning in some uses or is peculiar to a particular field **b** *pl* : diction of a specified kind **6 a** : a mathematical expression connected with another by a plus or minus sign **b** : an element of a fraction or proportion or of a series or sequence **7** *pl* **a** : mutual relationship : FOOTING **b** : AGREEMENT, CONCORD — **in terms of** : with respect to
²term *vt* : to apply a term to : CALL, NAME
ter·ma·gant \'tər-mə-gənt\ *n* : an overbearing quarrelsome woman : SHREW
¹ter·mi·nal \'tər-mən-ᵊl\ *adj* **1 a** : of or relating to an end, extremity, boundary, or terminus **b** : growing at the end of a branch or stem **2** : of, relating to, or occurring in a term or each term **3 a** : occurring at or constituting the end of a period or series : CONCLUDING **b** : limited but complete in itself
²terminal *n* **1** : a part that forms the end **2** : a terminating usu. ornamental detail : FINIAL **3** : a device attached to the end (as of a wire) for convenience in making electrical connections **4 a** : either end of a carrier line (as a railroad or shipping line) with its handling and storage facilities, offices, and stations; *also* : a freight or passenger station **b** : TERMINUS
ter·mi·nate \'tər-mə-ˌnāt\ *vb* **1 a** : to bring to or come to an end : CLOSE **b** : to form the conclusion of : form an ending **2** : to serve as a limit to : BOUND **3** : to extend only to a limit (as a point or line); *esp* : to reach a terminus — **ter·mi·na·ble** \-mə-nə-bəl\ *adj* — **ter·mi·na·tive** \-ˌnāt-iv\ *adj* — **ter·mi·na·tor** \-ˌnāt-ər\ *n*
ter·mi·na·tion \ˌtər-mə-'nā-shən\ *n* **1** : end in time or existence : CONCLUSION **2** : a limit in space or extent : BOUND **3** : the last part of a word : SUFFIX **4** : the act of terminating — **ter·mi·na·tion·al** \-shnəl, -shən-ᵊl\ *adj*
ter·mi·nol·o·gy \ˌtər-mə-'näl-ə-jē\ *n, pl* **-gies** : the technical or special terms or expressions used in a business, art, science, or special subject — **ter·mi·no·log·i·cal** \ˌtərm-nə-'läj-i-kəl, ˌtər-mən-ᵊl-'äj-\ *adj*
ter·mi·nus \'tər-mə-nəs\ *n, pl* **-ni** \-ˌnī\ *or* **-nus·es** **1** : final goal : finishing point **2** : a post or stone marking a boundary **3 a** : either end of a transportation line or travel route **b** : the station or the town or city at such a place : TERMINAL
ter·mite \'tər-ˌmīt\ *n* : any of an order of pale-colored soft-bodied social insects that feed on wood
tern \'tərn\ *n* : any of numerous sea gulls that are smaller and slenderer in body and bill than typical gulls and have narrower wings, often forked tails, black cap, and white body
terp·si·cho·re·an \ˌtərp-(ˌ)sik-ə-'rē-ən\ *adj* : of or relating to dancing
¹ter·race \'ter-əs\ *n* **1 a** : a flat roof or open platform : BALCONY, DECK **b** : a relatively level paved or planted area adjoining a building **2** : a raised embankment with the top leveled; *also* : one of a series of banks or ridges formed in a slope to conserve moisture and soil for agriculture **3 a** (1) : a row of houses on raised ground or a sloping site (2) : a group of such houses **b** : a strip of park in the middle of a street **c** : STREET
²terrace *vt* : to make into a terrace or supply with terraces
ter·ra–cot·ta \ˌter-ə-'kät-ə\ *n, pl* **terra–cottas** **1** : a glazed or unglazed fired earthenware **2** : a brownish orange
ter·ra fir·ma \-'fər-mə\ *n* : dry land : solid ground
ter·rain \tə-'rān\ *n* : the surface features of a tract of land
ter·ra·pin \'ter-ə-pən\ *n* : any of various edible No. American turtles living in fresh or brackish water
ter·res·tri·al \tə-'res-t(r)ē-əl\ *adj* **1 a** : of or relating to the earth or its inhabitants **b** : mundane in scope or character : PROSAIC **2** : of or relating to land as distinct from air or water **3** : living on or in or growing from land — **terrestrial** *n* — **ter·res·tri·al·ly** \-ē\ *adv*
ter·ri·ble \'ter-ə-bəl\ *adj* **1** : causing terror or awe : FEARFUL, DREADFUL **2 a** : hard to bear usu. because of excess of some quality **b** : very bad or extremely unpleasant **c** : of notably inferior quality — **ter·ri·bly** \-blē\ *adv*
ter·ri·er \'ter-ē-ər\ *n* : any of various usu. small dogs orig. used by hunters to dig for small game and engage the quarry underground or drive it out
ter·rif·ic \tə-'rif-ik\ *adj* **1** : TERRIBLE, FRIGHTFUL **2** : EXTRAORDINARY, ASTOUNDING; *esp* : TREMENDOUS **3** : unusually fine : MAGNIFICENT — **ter·rif·i·cal·ly** \-'rif-i-k(ə-)lē\ *adv*
ter·ri·fy \'ter-ə-ˌfī\ *vb* **-fied**; **fy·ing** : to fill with or move to some action by terror — **ter·ri·fy·ing·ly** *adv*
ter·ri·to·ri·al \ˌter-ə-'tōr-ē-əl\ *adj* **1 a** : of or relating to territory **b** *often cap* : of or relating to all or any of the territories of the U.S. **2** : organized primarily for territorial defense — **ter·ri·to·ri·al·ly** \-ē-ə-lē\ *adv*
ter·ri·to·ry \'ter-ə-ˌtōr-ē\ *n, pl* **-ries** **1 a** : a geographical area belonging to or under the jurisdiction of a government **b** : an administrative subdivision of a country (as the U.S.S.R.) **c** : a part of the U.S. not included within any state but organized with a separate legislature **d** : a geographical area dependent upon an external government but having some degree of autonomy **2 a** : an indeterminate geographical area **b** : a field of knowledge or interest **3** : an assigned area
ter·ror \'ter-ər\ *n* **1** : a state of intense fear **2 a** : a cause of fear or anxiety **b** : an appalling person or thing; *esp* : BRAT **3** : the use of violence and brutality esp. as a political weapon
ter·ror·ism \'ter-ər-ˌiz-əm\ *n* : the systematic use of terror esp. as a means of keeping or gaining control of a government — **ter·ror·ist** \-ər-əst\ *adj or n*
ter·ror·ize \'ter-ər-ˌīz\ *vt* **1** : to fill with terror or anxiety **2** : to coerce by threat or violence — **ter·ror·i·za·tion** \ˌter-ər-ə-'zā-shən\ *n*
ter·ry \'ter-ē\ *n, pl* **terries** : an absorbent fabric with a loose pile of uncut loops
terse \'tərs\ *adj* : using as few words as possible without loss of force or clearness — **terse·ly** *adv* — **terse·ness** *n*
ter·ti·ary \'tər-shē-ˌer-ē\ *adj* **1 a** : of 3d rank, importance, or value **b** : of, relating to, or constituting the 3d strongest of three or four degrees of stress **2** : occurring in or being a 3d stage
tes·sel·late \'tes-ə-ˌlāt\ *vt* : to form into or adorn with mosaic — **tes·sel·la·tion** \ˌtes-ə-'lā-shən\ *n*
¹test \'test\ *n* **1 a** : a critical examination, observation, or evaluation : TRIAL **b** : something that tries quality or resistance **2** : a means of testing: as **a** : a procedure, reaction, or reagent used to identify or differentiate something **b** : an examination (as in a school) intended to determine factual

knowledge or acquired skill or sometimes intelligence, capacities, or aptitudes **3** : a result of or rating based on a test
[2]**test** *vb* **1** : to put to test or proof : TRY **2 a** : to undergo a test **b** : to achieve a rating on the basis of tests **3** : to use tests as a means of analysis or diagnosis — **test·a·ble** *adj*
tes·ta·ment \'tes-tə-mənt\ *n* **1** *cap* : either of two chief divisions of the Bible **2 a** : a tangible proof or tribute **b** : an expression of conviction : CREDO **3** : a legal instrument by which a person determines the disposition of his property after his death — **tes·ta·men·ta·ry** \ˌtes-tə-'ment-ə-rē, -'men-trē\ *adj*
tes·tate \'tes-ˌtāt, -tət\ *adj* : having left a will
tes·ta·tor \'tes-ˌtāt-ər, te-'stāt-\ *n* : a person who leaves a will in force at his death — **tes·ta·trix** \te-'stā-triks\ *n*
[1]**tes·ter** \'tē-stər, 'tes-\ *n* : a canopy over a bed, pulpit, or altar
[2]**test·er** \'tes-tər\ *n* : one that tests
tes·ti·cle \'tes-ti-kəl\ *n* : TESTIS — **tes·tic·u·lar** \te-'stik-yə-lər\ *adj*
tes·ti·fy \'tes-tə-ˌfī\ *vb* **-fied**; **-fy·ing** **1** : to make a solemn statement of what is personally known or believed to be true **2** : to give outward proof : serve as a sign — **tes·ti·fi·er** *n*
[1]**tes·ti·mo·ni·al** \ˌtes-tə-'mō-nē-əl\ *adj* : being a testimonial; *also* : expressive of appreciation or esteem
[2]**testimonial** *n* **1** : an indication of worth or quality: as **a** : an endorsement of a product or service **b** : a character reference : letter of recommendation **2** : an expression of appreciation
tes·ti·mo·ny \'tes-tə-ˌmō-nē\ *n*, *pl* **-nies** **1 a** : evidence based on observation or knowledge : authoritative evidence **b** : a solemn declaration usu. made orally by a witness under oath in response to interrogation by a lawyer or authorized public official **2** : an open acknowledgment or profession (as of religious experience)
tes·tis \'tes-təs\ *n*, *pl* **tes·tes** \'tes-ˌtēz\ : a male reproductive gland
test tube *n* : a usu. plain tube of thin glass closed at one end and used esp. in chemistry and biology
tes·ty \'tes-tē\ *adj* **1** : easily annoyed : IRRITABLE **2** : marked by impatience or ill humor : EXASPERATED — **tes·ti·ly** \-tə-lē\ *adv* — **tes·ti·ness** \-tē-nəs\ *n*
te·tan·ic \te-'tan-ik\ *adj* : of, relating to, or being tetanus or tetany — **te·tan·i·cal·ly** \-'tan-i-k(ə-)lē\ *adv*
tet·a·nus \'tet-ᵊn-əs\ *n* : a disease caused by bacterial poisons and marked by violent muscular spasm esp. of the jaw
[1]**tête–à–tête** \ˌtāt-ə-'tāt\ *adv* : face to face : PRIVATELY
[2]**tête–à–tête** *n* **1** : a private conversation between two persons **2** : a seat for two persons facing each other
[3]**tête–à–tête** *adj* : being face to face : PRIVATE
[1]**teth·er** \'teth-ər\ *n* **1** : a line (as of rope or chain) by which an animal is fastened so as to restrict its range **2** : the limit of one's strength or resources : SCOPE
[2]**tether** *vt* **teth·ered**; **teth·er·ing** \'teth-(ə-)riŋ\ : to fasten or restrain by or as if by a tether
te·tral·o·gy \te-'träl-ə-jē, -'tral-\ *n*, *pl* **-gies** : a series of four connected works (as operas or novels)
te·tram·e·ter \te-'tram-ət-ər\ *n* : a line consisting of four metrical feet
text \'tekst\ *n* **1 a** : the original written or printed words and form of a literary work **b** : an edited or emended copy of an original work **2 a** : the main body of printed or written matter on a page **b** : the principal part of a book exclusive of front and back matter **3 a** : a passage of Scripture chosen for the subject of a sermon; *also* : a passage providing a basis (as for a speech) **b** : a source of information or authority **c** : a subject on which one writes or speaks : THEME, TOPIC **4** : TEXTBOOK
text·book \'teks(t)-ˌbu̇k\ *n* : a book used in the study of a subject; *esp* : one that presents the principles of a subject and is used as a basis of instruction
tex·tile \'tek-ˌstīl, 'teks-tᵊl\ *n* **1** : CLOTH 1; *esp* : a woven or knit cloth **2** : a fiber, filament, or yarn used in making cloth — **textile** *adj*
tex·tu·al \'teks-ch(ə-w)əl\ *adj* : of, relating to, or based on a text — **tex·tu·al·ly** \-ē\ *adv*
[1]**tex·ture** \'teks-chər\ *n* **1** : something (as cloth or a web) formed by or as if by weaving **2 a** : the structure, feel, and appearance of a textile that result from the kind and arrangement of its threads **b** : similar qualities dependent on the nature and arrangement of the constituent particles of a substance **3** : an essential or identifying part or quality — **tex·tur·al** \-chə-rəl\ *adj*
[2]**texture** *vt* : to give a particular and esp. a rough texture to
thal·li·um \'thal-ē-əm\ *n* : a poisonous metallic chemical element resembling lead in physical properties
than \t̲h̲ən, (')t̲h̲an\ *conj* **1** — used after a comparative adjective or adverb to introduce the second part of a comparison expressing inequality **2** — used after *other* or a word of similar meaning to express a difference of kind, manner, or identity
thane \'thān\ *n* **1** : THEGN **2** : a Scottish feudal lord
[1]**thank** \'thaŋk\ *n* **1** *pl* : kindly or grateful thoughts : GRATITUDE **2** : an expression of gratitude — usu. used in pl.; often used in an utterance containing no verb and serving as an ordinarily courteous and informal expression of gratitude
[2]**thank** *vt* **1** : to express gratitude to **2** : to hold responsible
thank·ful \'thaŋk-fəl\ *adj* **1** : conscious of benefit received **2** : expressive of thanks **3** : well pleased : GLAD — **thank·ful·ly** \-fə-lē\ *adv* — **thank·ful·ness** *n*
thank·less \'thaŋk-ləs\ *adj* **1** : not expressing or feeling gratitude : UNGRATEFUL **2** : not likely to obtain thanks : UNAPPRECIATED — **thank·less·ly** *adv* — **thank·less·ness** *n*
thanks·giv·ing \thaŋ(k)s-'giv-iŋ\ *n* **1** : the act of giving thanks **2** : a prayer expressing gratitude **3** *cap* : the 4th Thursday in November observed as a legal holiday for public thanksgiving to God
[1]**that** \(')t̲h̲at\ *pron*, *pl* **those** \(')t̲h̲ōz\ **1 a** : the person, thing, or idea indicated, mentioned, or understood from the situation **b** : the one, kind, or thing specified as follows **2 a** : the one farther away or less immediately under observation **b** : the former one
[2]**that** *adj*, *pl* **those** **1** : being the one specified or understood **2** : the farther away or less immediately under observation or discussion
[3]**that** \t̲h̲ət, (ˌ)t̲h̲at\ *conj* **1 a** (1) — used to introduce a noun clause serving esp. as the subject or object of a verb or as a predicate nominative (2) — used to introduce a subordinate clause that modifies a noun or adjective or is in apposition with a noun **b** — used to introduce an exclamatory clause expressing surprise, sorrow, or indignation **2 a** — used alone or after *so* or *in order* to introduce a subordinate clause expressing purpose **b** — used to introduce an exclamatory clause expressing a wish **3** — used to introduce a subordinate clause expressing a reason **4** — used esp. after an expression including the word *so* or *such* to introduce a subordinate clause expressing result
[4]**that** \t̲h̲ət, (ˌ)t̲h̲at\ *pron* **1** — used to introduce a relative clause and to serve as a substitute within that clause for the substantive modified by that clause **2** : at which : in which : on which : by which : with which : to which
[5]**that** \'t̲h̲at\ *adv* : to such an extent
[1]**thatch** \'thach\ *vt* : to cover with or as if with thatch
[2]**thatch** *n* : a plant material (as straw) for use as roofing (as for a house); *also* : a cover (as a roof) of thatch or as if of thatch
[1]**thaw** \'tho̊\ *vb* **1** : to melt or cause to melt : reverse the effect of freezing **2 a** : to become so warm or mild as to melt ice or snow **b** : to recover from chilling **3** : to grow less cold or reserved in manner : become more friendly
[2]**thaw** *n* **1** : the action, fact, or process of thawing **2** : a

warmth of weather sufficient to thaw ice

[1]**the** \t͟hə, *before vowel sounds usu* t͟hē\ *definite article* **1 a :** that (one) or those (ones) previously mentioned or clearly understood from the context or situation **b :** that unique (one) **:** that (one) existing as only one at a time **c :** that (one) or those (ones) near in space, time, or thought **d :** that (one) or those (ones) best known to the speaker or writer or to the hearer or reader **e :** MY, YOUR, HIS, HER, ITS, OUR, THEIR, ONE'S **f** (1) **:** in, to, or for each (2) **:** EACH, EVERY **g :** that (one) or those (ones) considered best, most typical, or most worth singling out **2 a :** any (one) typical of or standing for an entire class so named **b :** that which is **3 :** all those that are

[2]**the** *adv* **1 :** than before **:** than otherwise — used before a comparative **2 a :** to what extent **b :** to that extent

the·a·ter *or* **the·a·tre** \'thē-ət-ər\ *n* **1 :** a building or area for dramatic performances or for showing motion pictures **2 :** a place resembling a theater in form or use; *esp* **:** a room often with rising tiers of seats for assemblies (as for a lecture) **3 :** a place of enactment of significant events or action **4 a :** dramatic literature or performance **b :** dramatic effectiveness

the·at·ri·cal \thē-'a-tri-kəl\ *adj* **1 :** of or relating to the theater or the presentation of plays **2 :** marked by pretense or artificiality of emotion **:** not natural and simple **:** SHOWY — **the·at·ri·cal·ism** \-kə-ˌliz-əm\ *n* — **the·at·ri·cal·i·ty** \-ˌa-trə-'kal-ət-ē\ *n* — **the·at·ri·cal·ly** \-'a-tri-k(ə-)lē\ *adv*

the·at·ri·cals \thē-'a-tri-kəlz\ *n pl* **:** the performance of plays; *also* **:** the arts of acting and stagecraft

theft \'theft\ *n* **:** the act of stealing **:** LARCENY

thegn \'thān\ *n* **:** a free retainer of an Anglo-Saxon lord; *esp* **:** one holding lands of the king and performing military service

their \t͟hər, (ˌ)t͟he(ə)r\ *adj* **:** of or relating to them or themselves esp. as possessors, agents, or objects of an action

theirs \'t͟he(ə)rz\ *pron* **:** their one **:** their ones— used without a following noun as a pronoun equivalent in meaning to the adjective *their*

the·ism \'thē-ˌiz-əm\ *n* **:** belief in the existence of a god or gods; *esp* **:** belief in the existence of God as creator and ruler of the universe — **the·ist** \'thē-əst\ *n* — **the·is·tic** \thē-'is-tik\ *adj* — **the·is·ti·cal·ly** \-ti-k(ə-)lē\ *adv*

them \(t͟h)əm, (')t͟hem\ *pron, objective case of* THEY

theme \'thēm\ *n* **1 :** a subject of discourse, of artistic representation, or of musical composition **2 :** a written exercise **:** COMPOSITION — **the·mat·ic** \thi-'mat-ik\ *adj* — **the·mat·i·cal·ly** \-'mat-i-k(ə-)lē\ *adv*

them·selves \t͟həm-'selvz, t͟hem-\ *pron* **1 :** those identical ones that are they — used reflexively, for emphasis, or in absolute constructions **2 :** their normal, healthy, or sane condition or selves

[1]**then** \(ˌ)t͟hen\ *adv* **1 :** at that time **2 :** soon after that **3 a :** following next after in order **b :** in addition **:** BESIDES **4 a :** in that case **b :** according to that **c :** as it appears **d :** as a necessary consequence

[2]**then** \'t͟hen\ *n* **:** that time

[3]**then** \'t͟hen\ *adj* **:** existing or acting at or belonging to the time mentioned

thence \'t͟hen(t)s, 'then(t)s\ *adv* **1 :** from that place **2 :** from that fact or circumstance **:** THEREFROM

thence·forth \-ˌfōrth\ *adv* **:** from that time forward

thence·for·ward \t͟hen(t)s-'fȯr-wərd, then(t)s-\ *adv* **:** onward from that place or time **:** THENCEFORTH

the·oc·ra·cy \thē-'äk-rə-sē\ *n, pl* **-cies 1 :** government of a country by officials regarded as divinely guided **2 :** a country governed by a theocracy — **theo·crat** \'thē-ə-ˌkrat\ *n* — **the·o·crat·ic** \ˌthē-ə-'krat-ik\ *adj* — **the·o·crat·i·cal·ly** \-'krat-i-k(ə-)lē\ *adv*

the·o·lo·gian \ˌthē-ə-'lō-jən\ *n* **:** a specialist in theology

the·o·log·i·cal \ˌthē-ə-'läj-i-kəl\ *adj* **:** of or relating to theology — **the·o·log·i·cal·ly** \-k(ə-)lē\ *adv*

the·ol·o·gy \thē-'äl-ə-jē\ *n, pl* **-gies :** the study and interpretation of religious faith, practice, and experience; *esp* **:** thought about God and his relation to the world

the·o·rem \'thē-ə-rəm, 'thi(-ə)r-əm\ *n* **1 :** a statement in mathematics that has been or is to be proved **2 :** an idea accepted or proposed as a demonstrable truth **:** PROPOSITION

the·o·ret·i·cal \ˌthē-ə-'ret-i-kəl\ *adj* **1 a :** relating to or having the character of theory **:** ABSTRACT **b :** confined to theory or speculation **:** SPECULATIVE **2 :** given to or skilled in theorizing **3 :** existing only in theory **:** HYPOTHETICAL — **the·o·ret·i·cal·ly** \-i-k(ə-)lē\ *adv*

the·o·rist \'thē-ə-rəst, 'thi(-ə)r-əst\ *n* **:** a person that theorizes

the·o·rize \'thē-ə-ˌrīz\ *vi* **:** to form a theory — **the·o·riz·er** *n*

the·o·ry \'thē-ə-rē, 'thi(-ə)r-ē\ *n, pl* **-ries 1 :** the general or abstract principles of a body of fact, a science, or an art **2 :** a plausible or scientifically acceptable general principle or body of principles offered to explain phenomena **3 a :** a hypothesis assumed for the sake of argument or investigation **b :** SUPPOSITION, CONJECTURE **4 :** abstract thought **:** SPECULATION

ther·a·peu·tic \ˌther-ə-'pyüt-ik\ *adj* **:** of, relating to, or dealing with healing and esp. with remedies for diseases **:** MEDICINAL — **ther·a·peu·ti·cal·ly** \-'pyüt-i-k(ə-)lē\ *adv*

ther·a·peu·tics \-'pyüt-iks\ *n* **:** a branch of medical science dealing with the use of remedies

ther·a·pist \'ther-ə-pəst\ *n* **:** one specializing in therapy; *esp* **:** a person trained in methods of treatment and rehabilitation other than the use of drugs or surgery

ther·a·py \'ther-ə-pē\ *n, pl* **-pies :** therapeutic treatment of bodily, mental, or social disorders or maladjustment

[1]**there** \'t͟ha(ə)r\ *adv* **1 :** in or at that place — often used interjectionally **2 :** to or into that place **:** THITHER **3 :** at that point or stage **4 :** in that matter, respect, or relation **5 —** used interjectionally to express satisfaction, approval, soothing, or defiance

[2]**there** \(ˌ)t͟ha(ə)r, *1 is also* t͟hər\ *pron* **1 —** used as a function word to introduce a sentence or clause esp. when the verb has no complement **2 —** used as an indefinite substitute for a name

[3]**there** *like*[1]\ *n* **1 :** that place or position **2 :** that point

[4]**there** *like*[1]\ *adj* — used for emphasis esp. after a demonstrative pronoun or a noun modified by a demonstrative adjective

there·abouts *or* **there·about** \ˌt͟har-ə-'baủt(s)\ *adv* **1 :** near that place or time **2 :** near that number, degree, or quantity

there·af·ter \t͟har-'af-tər\ *adv* **:** after that

there·at \-'at\ *adv* **1 :** at that place **2 :** at that occurrence **:** on that account

there·by \t͟ha(ə)r-'bī\ *adv* **1 :** by that **:** by that means **2 :** connected with or with reference to that

there·for \-'fȯ(ə)r\ *adv* **:** for or in return for that

there·fore \'t͟ha(ə)r-ˌfōr\ *adv* **1 a :** for that reason **:** CONSEQUENTLY **b :** because of that **2 :** to that end

there·from \t͟ha(ə)r-'frəm, -'främ\ *adv* **:** from that or it

there·in \t͟har-'in\ *adv* **1 :** in or into that place, time, or thing **2 :** in that particular or respect

there·of \-'əv, -'äv\ *adv* **1 :** of that or it **2 :** from that cause or particular **:** THEREFROM

there·on \-'ȯn, -'än\ *adv* **:** on that

there·to \t͟ha(ə)r-'tü\ *adv* **:** to that

there·to·fore \'t͟hart-ə-ˌfōr\ *adv* **:** up to that time

there·un·der \t͟har-'ən-dər\ *adv* **:** under that

there·upon \'t͟har-ə-ˌpȯn, -ˌpän\ *adv* **1 :** on that matter **:** THEREON **2 :** THEREFORE **3 :** immediately after that **:** at once

there·with \t͟ha(ə)r-'wit͟h, -'with\ *adv* **:** with that

there·with·al \'t͟ha(ə)r-wə-ˌt͟hȯl, -ˌthȯl\ *adv* **:** THEREWITH

ther·mal \'thər-məl\ *adj* **:** of, relating to, or caused by heat **:** WARM, HOT — **ther·mal·ly** \-mə-lē\ *adv*

ther·mo·dy·nam·ics \ˌther-mə-dī-'nam-iks\ *n* **:** physics that deals with the mechanical action or relations of heat — **ther-**

mo·dy·nam·ic \-ik\ *adj* — **ther·mo·dy·nam·i·cal·ly** \-'nam-i-k(ə-)lē\ *adv*

ther·mom·e·ter \thə(r)-'mäm-ət-ər\ *n* : an instrument for measuring temperature commonly by means of the expansion or contraction of mercury or alcohol as indicated by its rise or fall in a thin glass tube alongside a numbered scale — **ther·mo·met·ric** \ˌthər-mə-'me-trik\ *adj*

ther·mo·nu·cle·ar \ˌthər-mō-'n(y)ü-klē-ər\ *adj* **1** : of or relating to the transformations in the nucleus of atoms of low atomic weight (as hydrogen) that require a very high temperature (as in the hydrogen bomb or in the sun) **2** : of, utilizing, or relating to a thermonuclear bomb

ther·mo·plas·tic \ˌthər-mə-'plas-tik\ *adj* : having the property of softening or fusing when heated and of hardening again when cooled

ther·mo·set·ting \'thər-mō-ˌset-iŋ\ *adj* : having the property of becoming permanently rigid when heated or cured

ther·mo·stat \'thər-mə-ˌstat\ *n* : an automatic device for regulating temperature (as of a heating system); *also* : a device for actuating fire alarms or for controlling automatic sprinklers — **ther·mo·stat·ic** \ˌthər-mə-'stat-ik\ *adj* — **ther·mo·stat·i·cal·ly** \-'stat-i-k(ə-)lē\ *adv*

the·sau·rus \thi-'sȯr-əs\ *n, pl* **-sau·ri** \-'sȯr-ˌī\ *or* **-sau·rus·es** : a book of words; *esp* : a dictionary of synonyms

these *pl of* THIS

the·sis \'thē-səs\ *n, pl* **the·ses** \'thē-ˌsēz\ **1** : a proposition to be proved or advanced without proof : HYPOTHESIS **2** : the first stage of a dialectical process **3** : a dissertation embodying results of original research; *esp* : one written by a candidate for an academic degree

¹thes·pi·an \'thes-pē-ən\ *adj, often cap* : relating to the drama

²thespian *n* : ACTOR

thew \'th(y)ü\ *n* : MUSCLE, SINEW — usu. used in pl.

they \(')t̲hā\ *pron* **1** : those ones — used as 3d person pronoun serving as the plural of *he, she,* or *it* or referring to a group of two or more individuals not all of the same sex **2** : PEOPLE 1

thi·a·mine \'thī-ə-ˌmēn\ *also* **thi·a·min** \-mən\ *n* : a vitamin essential to normal metabolism and nerve function

¹thick \'thik\ *adj* **1 a** : having or being of relatively great depth or extent from one surface to its opposite **b** : heavily built : THICKSET **2 a** : close-packed : DENSE **b** : occurring in large numbers : NUMEROUS **c** : viscous in consistency **d** : SULTRY, STUFFY **e** : marked by haze, fog, or mist **f** : impenetrable to the eye : PROFOUND **g** : extremely intense **3** : measuring in thickness **4 a** : imperfectly articulated : INDISTINCT **b** : PRONOUNCED **c** : producing inarticulate speech **5** : OBTUSE, STUPID **6** : associated on close terms : INTIMATE **7** : exceeding bounds of propriety or fitness : EXCESSIVE — **thick·ish** \-ish\ *adj* — **thick·ly** *adv*

²thick *n* **1** : the most crowded or active part **2** : the part of greatest thickness

³thick *adv* : THICKLY

thick·en \'thik-ən\ *vb* **thick·ened**; **thick·en·ing** \'thik-(ə-)niŋ\ **1 a** : to make or become thick, dense, or viscous in consistency **b** : to make or become close or compact **2** : to add to the depth or diameter of **3 a** : to make inarticulate : BLUR **b** : to grow blurred or obscure **4** : to grow broader or bulkier **5** : to grow complicated or keen — **thick·en·er** *n*

thick·en·ing *n* **1** : the act of making or becoming thick **2** : something used to thicken **3** : a thickened part or place

thick·et \'thik-ət\ *n* : a thick usu. circumscribed growth of shrubbery, small trees, or underbrush

thick·head·ed \'thik-'hed-əd\ *adj* **1** : having a thick head **2** : STUPID

thick·ness \'thik-nəs\ *n* **1** : the quality or state of being thick **2** : the smallest of three dimensions **3** : viscous consistency **4** : the thick part of something **5** : CONCENTRATION, DENSITY **6** : DULLNESS, STUPIDITY **7** : LAYER, PLY, SHEET

thick·set \'thik-'set\ *adj* **1** : closely placed or planted **2** : of short stout build : STOCKY

thick–skinned \-'skind\ *adj* **1** : having a thick skin **2** : CALLOUS, INSENSITIVE

thief \'thēf\ *n, pl* **thieves** \'thēvz\ : one that steals — **thiev·ish** \'thē-vish\ *adj* — **thiev·ish·ly** *adv* — **thiev·ish·ness** *n*

thieve \'thēv\ *vb* : STEAL, ROB

thiev·ery \'thēv-(ə-)rē\ *n, pl* **-er·ies** : the action of stealing

thigh \'thī\ *n* : the segment of the vertebrate hind limb extending from the hip to the knee

thim·ble \'thim-bəl\ *n* **1** : a cap or cover used in sewing to protect the finger that pushes the needle **2** : a grooved ring of thin metal used to fit in a loop in a wire or rope **3** : fixed or movable ring, tube, or lining in a hole

thim·ble·ful \-ˌfu̇l\ *n* **1** : as much as a thimble will hold **2** : a very small quantity

¹thin \'thin\ *adj* **1 a** : having little extent from one surface to its opposite **b** : measuring little in cross section or diameter **2** : not dense in arrangement or distribution **3** : not well fleshed : LEAN **4 a** : more fluid or rarefied than normal **b** : having less than the usual number : SCANTY **5** : lacking substance or strength **6** : somewhat feeble, shrill, and lacking in resonance — **thin·ly** *adv* — **thin·ness** *n* — **thin·nish** \'thin-ish\ *adj*

²thin *adv* : THINLY

³thin *vb* **thinned**; **thin·ning** : to make or become thin or thinner

thing \'thiŋ\ *n* **1 a** : a matter of concern : AFFAIR **b** *pl* : state of affairs in general or within a specified or implied sphere **c** : a particular state of affairs : SITUATION **d** : EVENT, CIRCUMSTANCE **2 a** : DEED, ACT, ACCOMPLISHMENT **b** : a product of work or activity **c** : the aim of effort or activity **3 a** : a separate and distinct item or object : ENTITY; *esp* : a tangible object **b** : an inanimate object distinguished from a living being **4 a** *pl* : POSSESSIONS, EFFECTS **b** : an article of clothing **c** *pl* : equipment or utensils esp. for a particular purpose **5** : an object or entity not precisely designated or capable of being designated **6 a** : DETAIL, POINT **b** : a material or substance of a specified kind **7 a** : a spoken or written observation or point **b** : IDEA, NOTION **c** : a piece of news or information **8** : INDIVIDUAL; *esp* : PERSON **9** : the proper or fashionable way of behaving, talking, or dressing **10** : a mild obsession

think \'thiŋk\ *vb* **thought** \'thȯt\; **think·ing** **1** : to form or have in the mind **2** : INTEND, PLAN **3 a** : to have as an opinion : BELIEVE **b** : to regard as : CONSIDER **4** : to reflect on : PONDER **5** : to call to mind : REMEMBER **6** : to form a mental picture of **7** : to subject to the processes of logical thought **8** : to exercise the powers of judgment, conception, or inference : REASON **9 a** : to have the mind engaged in reflection : MEDITATE **b** : to consider the suitability **10** : to have a view or opinion **11** : to have concern **12** : EXPECT, SUSPECT — **think·a·ble** *adj* — **think·er** *n*

thin·ner \'thin-ər\ *n* : one that thins; *esp* : a volatile liquid (as turpentine) used to thin paint

thin–skinned \'thin-'skind\ *adj* **1** : having a thin skin or rind **2** : unduly susceptible to criticism or insult : TOUCHY

¹third \'thərd\ *adj* **1 a** — see NUMBER table **b** : next after the second in time, order, or importance **2** : being one of three equal parts of something — **third** *adv* — **third·ly** *adv*

²third *n* **1** — see NUMBER table **2** : one of three equal parts of something **3** : the third gear or speed of an automotive vehicle **4** : one next after a second in time, order, or importance

third degree *n* : severe or brutal treatment of a prisoner in order to get an admission

third–rate \'thərd-'rāt\ *adj* : of third quality or value; *esp* : worse than second-rate — **third–rat·er** \-'rāt-ər\ *n*

third world *n, often cap T & W* : a group of nations esp. in Africa and Asia aligned with neither the Communist nor non-Communist blocs

[1]**thirst** \ˈthərst\ *n* **1 :** a feeling of dryness in the mouth and throat associated with a desire for liquids; *also* **:** the bodily condition that induces this **2 :** an ardent desire

[2]**thirst** *vi* **1 :** to feel thirsty **:** suffer thirst **2 :** to have a vehement desire **:** CRAVE

thirsty \ˈthər-stē\ *adj* **1 a :** feeling thirst **b :** deficient in moisture **:** PARCHED **c :** highly absorbent **2 :** having a strong desire — **thirst·i·ly** \-stə-lē\ *adv* — **thirst·i·ness** \-stē-nəs\ *n*

thir·teen \ˌthər(t)-ˈtēn, ˈthər(t)-\ *n* — see NUMBER table — **thirteen** *adj or pron* — **thir·teenth** \-ˈtēn(t)th\ *adj or n*

thir·ty \ˈthərt-ē\ *n, pl* **thirties 1** — see NUMBER table **2** *pl* **:** the numbers 30 to 39; *esp* **:** the years 30 to 39 in a lifetime or century **3 :** a mark or sign of completion — **thir·ti·eth** \-ē-əth\ *n or adj* — **thirty** *adj or pron*

[1]**this** \(ˈ)t͟his\ *pron, pl* **these** \(ˈ)t͟hēz\ **1 :** the person, thing, or idea present or near in place, time, or thought, or just mentioned **2 a :** the one nearer or more immediately under observation **b :** the latter one

[2]**this** *adj, pl* **these 1 :** being the one present or near in place, time, or thought, or just mentioned **2 :** the nearer at hand or more immediately under observation or discussion

[3]**this** \ˈt͟his\ *adv* **:** to the degree or extent indicated by something immediately present

this·tle \ˈthis-əl\ *n* **:** any of various prickly plants related to the daisies — **this·tly** \ˈthis-(ə-)lē\ *adj*

this·tle·down \-ˌdau̇n\ *n* **:** the down from the ripe flower head of a thistle

[1]**thith·er** \ˈthit͟h-ər, ˈt͟hit͟h-\ *adv* **:** to that place **:** THERE

[2]**thither** *adj* **:** being on the other and farther side **:** more remote

thith·er·to \-ˌtü\ *adv* **:** until that time

thith·er·ward \-wərd\ *adv* **:** toward that place **:** THITHER

thong \ˈthȯŋ\ *n* **:** a strip of leather used esp. for fastening

tho·rax \ˈthōr-ˌaks\ *n, pl* **tho·rax·es** *or* **tho·ra·ces** \ˈthōr-ə-ˌsēz, ˈthȯr-\ **1 :** the part of the body of a mammal between the neck and the abdomen; *also* **:** its cavity in which the heart and lungs lie **2 :** the middle of the three chief divisions of the body of an insect — **tho·rac·ic** \thə-ˈras-ik\ *adj*

tho·ri·um \ˈthōr-ē-əm\ *n* **:** a radioactive metallic chemical element that occurs combined in minerals

thorn \ˈthȯrn\ *n* **1 :** a woody plant bearing sharp processes (as briers, prickles, or spines); *esp* **:** HAWTHORN **2 :** a sharp rigid process on a plant; *esp* **:** one that is a short, rigid, sharp-pointed, and leafless branch **3 :** something that causes distress or irritation — **thorned** *adj* — **thorn·less** \ˈthȯrn-ləs\ *adj*

thorny \ˈthȯr-nē\ *adj* **1 :** full of or covered with thorns **:** SPINY **2 :** DIFFICULT, TRYING — **thorn·i·ness** *n*

thor·ough \ˈthər-ō\ *adj* **1 :** being such to the fullest degree **:** EXHAUSTIVE, DETAILED, COMPLETE **2 :** careful about detail **:** PAINSTAKING — **thor·ough·ly** *adv* — **thor·ough·ness** *n*

[1]**thor·ough·bred** \-ˌbred\ *adj* **1 :** thoroughly trained or skilled **2 :** bred from the best blood through a long line **:** PUREBRED **3** *cap* **:** of, relating to, or being a member of the Thoroughbred breed of horses **4 a :** marked by high-spirited grace and elegance **b :** of the best quality or highest worth **:** FIRST-CLASS

[2]**thoroughbred** *n* **1** *cap* **:** any of an English breed of light speedy horses kept chiefly for racing and originating from crosses between English mares of uncertain ancestry and Arab stallions **2 :** a purebred or pedigreed animal **3 :** a person of sterling qualities

thor·ough·fare \-ˌfa(ə)r\ *n* **:** a way for passage: as **a :** public way connecting two streets **b :** a main road **:** a busy street

thor·ough·go·ing \ˌthər-ə-ˈgō-iŋ\ *adj* **:** marked by thoroughness or zeal

those *pl of* THAT

[1]**though** \ˈt͟hō\ *adv* **:** HOWEVER, NEVERTHELESS

[2]**though** \(ˌ)t͟hō\ *conj* **1 :** in spite of the fact that **2 :** even if

[1]**thought** *past of* THINK

[2]**thought** \ˈthȯt\ *n* **1 a :** the act or process of thinking **b :** serious consideration **:** careful attention **2 a :** power of thinking and esp. of reasoning and judging **b :** power of imagining or comprehending **3 a :** a product of thinking (as an idea, fancy, or invention) **b :** the intellectual product or the organized views and principles of a period, place, group, or individual **4 :** a slight amount **:** BIT

thought·ful \ˈthȯt-fəl\ *adj* **1 a :** absorbed in thought **:** MEDITATIVE **b :** characterized by careful reasoned thinking **2 :** MINDFUL, HEEDFUL; *esp* **:** attentive to the needs of others — **thought·ful·ly** \-fə-lē\ *adv* — **thought·ful·ness** *n*

thought·less \ˈthȯt-ləs\ *adj* **1 a :** insufficiently alert **:** CARELESS **b :** RECKLESS, RASH **2 :** devoid of thought **:** INSENSATE **3 :** lacking concern for others **:** INCONSIDERATE — **thought·less·ly** *adv* — **thought·less·ness** *n*

thou·sand \ˈthau̇z-ᵊn(d)\ *n, pl* **thousands** *or* **thousand 1** — see NUMBER table **2 :** the number in the 4th decimal place to the left of the decimal point in arabic numerals **3 :** a very large or indefinitely great number — **thousand** *adj*

thou·sandth \ˈthau̇z-ᵊn(t)th\ *n* **1 :** one of 1000 equal parts of something **2 :** the one numbered 1000 in a countable series — see NUMBER table — **thousandth** *adj*

thrall \ˈthrȯl\ *n* **1 :** SLAVE; *also* **:** SERF **2 :** the condition of a thrall **:** SLAVERY — **thrall·dom** *or* **thral·dom** \-dəm\ *n*

[1]**thrash** \ˈthrash\ *vb* **1 :** THRESH 1 **2 :** to beat soundly or strike about with or as if with a stick or whip **:** FLOG; *also* **:** DEFEAT **3 :** to swing, beat, or stir about in the manner of a rapidly moving flail **4 :** to go over again and again

[2]**thrash** *n* **:** an act of thrashing esp. of the legs in swimming

[1]**thrash·er** \ˈthrash-ər\ *n* **:** one that thrashes or threshes

[2]**thrasher** *n* **:** any of numerous long-tailed American singing birds that resemble thrushes

[1]**thread** \ˈthred\ *n* **1 :** a thin continuous filament; *esp* **:** a textile cord made by twisting together strands of spun fiber (as cotton, flax, or silk) **2 a :** something (as a streak or slender stream) suggesting a filament **b :** the ridge or groove that winds around a screw **c :** a tenuous or feeble support **3 :** a line of reasoning or train of thought — **thread·like** *adj*

[2]**thread** *vb* **1 :** to put a thread in working position in (as a needle) **2 a :** to pass through in the manner of a thread **b :** to make one's way through or between **:** wind a way **3 :** to put together on or as if on a thread **:** STRING **4 :** to interweave with or as if with threads **:** INTERSPERSE **5 :** to form a screw thread on or in **6 :** to draw out into a thread when dripped from a spoon — **thread·er** *n*

thread·bare \ˈthred-ˌba(ə)r\ *adj* **1 :** having the nap worn off so that the thread shows **:** SHABBY **2 :** HACKNEYED

thready \ˈthred-ē\ *adj* **1 :** consisting of or bearing fibers or filaments **2 :** lacking in fullness, body, or vigor **:** THIN

threat \ˈthret\ *n* **1 :** an expression of an intent to do harm or something wrong or foolish **2 :** something that threatens

threat·en \ˈthret-ᵊn\ *vb* **threat·ened; threat·en·ing** \ˈthret-niŋ, -ᵊn-iŋ\ **1 :** to utter threats **:** make threats against **2 :** to give warning of by a threat or sign **3 :** to give signs of trouble to come — **threat·en·ing·ly** *adv*

three \ˈthrē\ *n* **1** — see NUMBER table **2 :** the third in a set or series **3 :** something having three units or members — **three** *adj or pron*

3-D \ˈthrē-ˈdē\ *n* **:** three-dimensional form

three-di·men·sion·al *adj* **1 :** of, relating to, or having three dimensions **2 :** giving the illusion of depth or varying distances

three·fold \ˈthrē-ˌfōld, -ˈfōld\ *adj* **1 :** having three units or members **2 :** of or amounting to 300 percent — **threefold** *adv*

three·pence \ˈthrip-ən(t)s, ˈthrəp-, *US also* ˈthrē-ˌpen(t)s\ *n, pl* **threepence** *or* **three·penc·es 1 :** the sum of three usu. British pennies **2 :** a coin worth three pennies

three·pen·ny \ˈthrip-(ə-)nē, ˈthrəp-, *US also* ˈthrē-ˌpen-ē\ *adj*

1 : costing or worth threepence 2 : of little value : POOR

three·score \'thrē-'skō(ə)r\ *adj* : SIXTY

three·some \'thrē-səm\ *n* : a group of three persons or things

thren·o·dy \'thren-əd-ē\ *n, pl* **-dies** : a song of lamentation

thresh \'thrash, 'thresh\ *vb* 1 : to separate seed from (a harvested plant) mechanically : beat out (grain) from straw 2 : THRASH — **thresh·er** *n*

thresh·old \'thresh-,(h)ōld\ *n* 1 : the sill of a door 2 a : GATE, DOOR, ENTRANCE b : a place of beginning — **thresh·old** *adj*

threw *past of* THROW

thrice \'thrīs\ *adv* 1 : three times 2 : to a high degree

thrift \'thrift\ *n* : economical management : FRUGALITY

thrift·less \'thrift-ləs\ *adj* : wasteful of money or resources : IMPROVIDENT — **thrift·less·ness** *n*

thrifty \'thrif-tē\ *adj* 1 : inclined to save : SAVING 2 : thriving through industry and frugality — **thrift·i·ly** \-tə-lē\ *adv* — **thrift·i·ness** \-tē-nəs\ *n*

thrill \'thril\ *vb* 1 a : to experience or cause to experience a sudden sharp feeling of excitement b : to have or cause to have a shivering or tingling sensation 2 : VIBRATE, TREMBLE — **thrill** *n* — **thrill·er** *n*

thrive \'thrīv\ *vi* **throve** \'thrōv\ *or* **thrived**; **thriv·en** \'thriv-ən\; **thriv·ing** \'thrī-viŋ\ 1 : to grow vigorously : do well 2 : to gain in wealth or possessions : PROSPER, FLOURISH — **thriv·er** *n* — **thriv·ing·ly** *adv*

throat \'thrōt\ *n* 1 : the part of the neck in front of the spinal column; *also* : the passage through it to the stomach and lungs 2 : something resembling the throat esp. in being an entrance, a passageway, a constriction, or a narrowed part — **throat·ed** *adj*

throaty \'thrōt-ē\ *adj* 1 : uttered or produced from low in the throat 2 : heavy, thick, and deep as if from the throat — **throat·i·ly** \'thrōt-ᵊl-ē\ *adv* — **throat·i·ness** \'thrōt-ē-nəs\ *n*

¹throb \'thräb\ *vi* **throbbed**; **throb·bing** 1 : to pulsate or pound with abnormal force or rapidity : PALPITATE 2 : to beat or vibrate rhythmically

²throb *n* : BEAT, PULSE

throe \'thrō\ *n* 1 : PANG, SPASM 2 *pl* : a hard or painful struggle

throm·bo·sis \thräm-'bō-səs\ *n, pl* **-bo·ses** \-'bō-,sēz\ : the formation or presence of a blood clot within a blood vessel during life — **throm·bot·ic** \-'bät-ik\ *adj*

¹throne \'thrōn\ *n* 1 a : the chair of state of a high dignitary (as a king or bishop) b : the seat of a deity or devil 2 : royal power and dignity : SOVEREIGNTY

²throne *vt* : to seat on a throne : ENTHRONE

¹throng \'thrȯŋ\ *n* 1 a : a multitude of assembled persons b : CROWD 2 : a crowding together of many individuals

²throng *vb* **thronged**; **throng·ing** \'thrȯŋ-iŋ\ 1 : to crowd upon or into 2 : to crowd together in great numbers

¹throt·tle \'thrät-ᵊl\ *vb* **throt·tled**; **throt·tling** \'thrät-liŋ,-ᵊl-iŋ\ 1 a : CHOKE, STRANGLE b : to prevent or check expression or activity of : SUPPRESS 2 a : to obstruct the flow of (as fuel to an engine) by closing a valve b : to reduce the speed of (an engine) by such means

²throttle *n* 1 a : THROAT 1 b : TRACHEA 2 a : a valve controlling the volume of steam or of fuel (as gasoline) delivered to the cylinders of an engine b : a lever controlling this valve

¹through \(')thrü\ *prep* 1 a : in at one side and out at the opposite side of b : by way of c : in the midst of : AMONG 2 a : by means of b : because of 3 : over the whole surface or extent of 4 a : from the beginning to the end of b : to and including

²through \'thrü\ *adv* 1 a : from one end or side to the other b : over the whole distance 2 a : from beginning to end b : to completion, conclusion, or accomplishment 3 : to the core : COMPLETELY 4 : into the open : OUT

³through \'thrü\ *adj* 1 a : extending from one surface to another b : admitting free or continuous passage : DIRECT 2 a (1) : going from point of origin to destination without change or reshipment (2) : of or relating to such movement b : initiated at and destined for points outside a local zone 3 a : arrived at completion or accomplishment b : FINISHED

¹through·out \thrü-'au̇t\ *adv* 1 : in or to every part : EVERYWHERE 2 : from beginning to end

²throughout *prep* 1 : in or to every part of 2 : during the whole time of

throughway *var of* THRUWAY

throve *past of* THRIVE

¹throw \'thrō\ *vb* **threw** \'thrü\; **thrown** \'thrōn\; **throw·ing** 1 : to twist two or more fibers of (as silk) to form one thread 2 : to hurl or cast esp. with a quick forward motion of the arm 3 : to propel through the air in any way 4 : to cause to fall 5 : to put suddenly in a certain condition or position; *also* : to form or shape on a potter's wheel 6 : to put on or take off hastily 7 : SHED 8 : to move quickly 9 : to move (as a switch or a lever) to an open or closed position 10 : to lose (a game or contest) intentionally — **throw·er** *n*

²throw *n* 1 a : an act of throwing, hurling, or flinging b : a cast of dice 2 : the distance a missile may be thrown 3 a : a light coverlet b : a woman's scarf or light wrap

throw away \,thrō-ə-'wā\ *vt* 1 : to get rid of 2 : WASTE

throw off *vt* 1 a : to free oneself from b : to cast off often in a hurried or vigorous manner 2 : EMIT 3 : MISLEAD

throw out *vt* 1 : to reject or get rid of 2 a : to send out b : to cause to project : EXTEND 3 : DISENGAGE

throw over *vt* : FORSAKE

throw up *vb* 1 : to raise quickly 2 : to give up : QUIT 3 : to build hurriedly 4 : VOMIT

thrum \'thrəm\ *vb* **thrummed**; **thrum·ming** : to play or pluck a stringed instrument idly : STRUM — **thrum** *n*

thrush \'thrəsh\ *n* : any of numerous songbirds usu. of a plain color often with spotted underparts

¹thrust \'thrəst\ *vb* **thrust**; **thrust·ing** 1 : to push or drive with force : SHOVE 2 : STAB, PIERCE 3 : INTERJECT 4 : to press or force the acceptance of upon someone

²thrust *n* 1 a : a push or lunge with a pointed weapon b : ATTACK 2 a : a strong continued pressure b : the sideways pressure of one part of a structure against another part (as of an arch against an abutment) c (1) : the force exerted endwise through a propeller shaft to give forward motion (2) : the forwardly directed force produced (as in a rocket) by a high-speed jet of fluid discharged rearward from a nozzle

thru·way *or* **through·way** \'thrü-,wā\ *n* : EXPRESSWAY

¹thud \'thəd\ *vi* **thud·ded**; **thud·ding** : to move or strike so as to make a thud

²thud *n* 1 : BLOW 2 : a dull sound : THUMP

thug \'thəg\ *n* : a brutal ruffian or assassin

thu·li·um \'th(y)ü-lē-əm\ *n* : a rare metallic chemical element

¹thumb \'thəm\ *n* 1 : the short thick first digit of the human hand opposable to the other fingers; *also* : the corresponding digit in lower animals 2 : the part of a glove or mitten that covers the thumb

²thumb *vt* 1 a : to leaf through with the thumb : TURN b : to soil or wear by or as if by repeated thumbing 2 : to request or obtain (a ride) in a passing automobile by signaling with the thumb

thumb·nail \,thəm-,nāl\ *adj* : CONCISE, BRIEF

thumb·screw \'thəm-,skrü\ *n* 1 : a screw with a head that may be turned by the thumb and forefinger 2 : an instrument of torture for compressing the thumb by a screw

thumb·tack \-,tak\ *n* : a tack with a broad flat head for pressing into a board or wall with the thumb

¹thump \'thəmp\ *vb* 1 : to strike or beat with or as if with something thick or heavy so as to cause a dull sound 2 : POUND, KNOCK 3 : CUDGEL, THRASH 4 : to inflict or emit a thump

²thump *n* : a blow or knock with or as if with something blunt or heavy; *also* : the sound made by such a blow

[1]**thun·der** \ˈthən-dər\ *n* **1** : the loud sound that follows a flash of lightning and is caused by sudden expansion of the air in the path of the electrical discharge **2** : a loud utterance or threat **3** : BANG, RUMBLE

[2]**thunder** *vb* **thun·dered**; **thun·der·ing** \-d(ə-)riŋ\ **1 a** : to produce thunder **b** : to give forth or strike with a sound likened to thunder **2** : ROAR, SHOUT — **thun·der·er** *n*

thun·der·bolt \ˈthən-dər-ˌbōlt\ *n* : a single discharge of lightning with the accompanying thunder

thun·der·clap \-ˌklap\ *n* : a crash of thunder

thun·der·cloud \-ˌklau̇d\ *n* : a dark storm cloud that produces lightning and thunder

thun·der·head \-ˌhed\ *n* : a rounded mass of cumulus cloud often appearing before a thunderstorm

thun·der·ous \ˈthən-d(ə-)rəs\ *adj* : producing thunder; *also* : making a noise like thunder — **thun·der·ous·ly** *adv*

thun·der·show·er \ˈthən-dər-ˌshau̇(-ə)r\ *n* : a shower accompanied by lightning and thunder

thun·der·storm \-ˌstȯrm\ *n* : a storm accompanied by lightning and thunder

thun·der·struck \-ˌstrək\ *adj* : stunned as if struck by a thunderbolt : struck dumb : ASTONISHED

Thurs·day \ˈthərz-dē\ *n* : the 5th day of the week

thus \ˈt͟həs\ *adv* **1** : in this or that manner or way **2** : to this degree or extent : SO **3** : because of this or that : HENCE **4** : as an example

thwack \ˈthwak\ *vt* : to strike with or as if with something flat or heavy : WHACK — **thwack** *n*

[1]**thwart** \ˈthwȯrt, ˈthȯrt\ *adv* : ATHWART

[2]**thwart** *adj* : situated or placed across something else

[3]**thwart** *vt* **1** : OPPOSE, BAFFLE **2** : BLOCK, DEFEAT — **thwart·er** *n*

[4]**thwart** *n* : a rower's seat extending athwart a boat

thyme \ˈtīm, ˈthīm\ *n* : any of a genus of mints with small pungent aromatic leaves; *esp* : one grown for use in seasoning

thy·mus \ˈthī-məs\ *n*, *pl* **thy·mus·es** *or* **thy·mi** \-ˌmī\ : a glandular structure of uncertain function that is present in most young vertebrates typically at the base of the neck and tends to disappear or become rudimentary in the adult — **thy·mic** \-mik\ *adj*

[1]**thy·roid** \ˈthī-ˌrȯid\ *adj* : of, relating to, or being a large endocrine gland of most vertebrates that lies at the base of the neck and produces an iodine-containing hormone which affects esp. growth, development, and metabolic rate

[2]**thyroid** *n* : a thyroid gland or cartilage

ti \ˈtē\ *n* : the 7th note of the diatonic scale

ti·ara \tē-ˈar-ə, -ˈär-\ *n* **1** : a 3-tiered crown worn by the pope **2** : a decorative band or semicircular ornament for the head for formal wear by women

tib·ia \ˈtib-ē-ə\ *n*, *pl* **-i·ae** \-ē-ˌē\ : the inner and usu. larger of the two bones of the vertebrate hind limb between the knee and ankle — **tib·i·al** \-ē-əl\ *adj*

tic \ˈtik\ *n* : local and habitual twitching of particular muscles esp. of the face

[1]**tick** \ˈtik\ *n* : any of numerous small 8-legged bloodsucking animals

[2]**tick** *n* **1** : a light rhythmic audible tap or beat (as of a clock); *also* : a series of such ticks **2** : a small spot or mark used to direct attention to or check something

[3]**tick** *vb* **1 a** : to make the sound of a tick or a series of ticks **b** : to mark, count, or announce by or as if by ticking beats **2** : to operate as or in the manner of a functioning mechanism : RUN **3** : to mark with a written tick : CHECK

[4]**tick** *n* : the fabric case of a mattress, pillow, or bolster; *also* : a mattress consisting of a tick and its filling

ticked \ˈtikt\ *adj* : marked with ticks : FLECKED

tick·er \ˈtik-ər\ *n* : something that ticks or produces a ticking sound: as **a** : WATCH **b** : a telegraphic receiving instrument that prints off stock quotations or news on a paper tape

[1]**tick·et** \ˈtik-ət\ *n* **1 a** : a document that serves as a certificate, license, or permit **b** : LABEL **2** : a summons or warning issued to a traffic offender **3** : a document or token showing that a fare or admission fee has been paid **4** : a list of candidates for nomination or election

[2]**ticket** *vt* **1** : to attach a ticket to : LABEL; *also* : DESIGNATE **2** : to serve with a traffic ticket

tick·ing \ˈtik-iŋ\ *n* : a strong fabric used in upholstering and as a covering for mattresses and pillows

tick·le \ˈtik-əl\ *vb* **tick·led**; **tick·ling** \ˈtik-(ə-)liŋ\ **1** : to have a tingling or prickling sensation **2 a** : to excite or stir up agreeably : PLEASE **b** : to provoke to laughter or merriment : AMUSE **3** : to touch a body part lightly so as to excite the surface nerves and cause uneasiness, laughter, or spasmodic movements — **tickle** *n* — **tick·ler** *n*

tick·lish \ˈtik-(ə-)lish\ *adj* **1** : sensitive to tickling **2 a** : TOUCHY, OVERSENSITIVE **b** : easily overturned : UNSTABLE **3** : requiring delicate handling : CRITICAL — **tick·lish·ness** *n*

tid·al \ˈtīd-ᵊl\ *adj* **1** : of or relating to tides : periodically rising and falling or flowing and ebbing **2** : dependent (as to the time of arrival or departure) on the state of the tide

tidal wave *n* **1** : an unusually high sea wave that sometimes follows an earthquake **2** : an unusual rise of water alongshore due to strong winds

tid·bit \ˈtid-ˌbit\ *n* **1** : a choice morsel of food **2** : a choice or pleasing bit (as of news)

[1]**tide** \ˈtīd\ *n* **1** : a fit or opportune time : OPPORTUNITY **2** : the alternate rising and falling of the surface of the ocean **3** : something that fluctuates like the tides of the sea

[2]**tide** *vb* **1** : to drift or cause to drift with the tide **2** : to enable to surmount or endure a difficulty

tide·land \-ˌland\ *n* **1** : land overflowed during flood tide **2** : land underlying the ocean beyond the low-water limit of the tide but within a nation's territorial waters — often used in pl.

tide·wa·ter \-ˌwȯt-ər, -ˌwät-\ *n* **1** : water overflowing land at flood tide **2** : low-lying coastal land

tid·ing \ˈtīd-iŋ\ *n* : a piece of news — usu. used in pl.

[1]**ti·dy** \ˈtīd-ē\ *adj* **1** : ADEQUATE, SATISFACTORY; *also* : DECENT, FAIR **2 a** : neat and orderly in appearance or habits **b** : METHODICAL, PRECISE **3** : LARGE, SUBSTANTIAL — **ti·di·ly** \ˈtīd-ᵊl-ē\ *adv* — **ti·di·ness** \ˈtīd-ē-nəs\ *n*

[2]**tidy** *vb* **ti·died**; **ti·dy·ing** **1** : to put in order **2** : to make things tidy

[3]**tidy** *n*, *pl* **tidies** : a piece of fancywork used to protect the back, arms, or headrest of a chair or sofa from wear or soiling

[1]**tie** \ˈtī\ *n* **1 a** : a line, ribbon, or cord used for fastening, uniting, or drawing something closed **b** (1) : a structural element (as a beam or rod) holding two pieces together (2) : one of the transverse supports to which railroad rails are fastened **2** : something that serves as a connecting link : BOND **3 a** : an equality in number (as of votes or scores) **b** : equality in a contest; *also* : a contest that ends in a draw **4** : NECKTIE

[2]**tie** *vb* **tied**; **ty·ing** \ˈtī-iŋ\ *or* **tie·ing** **1 a** : to fasten, attach, or close by means of a tie **b** : to form a knot or bow in **c** : to make by tying constituent elements **2** : to unite in marriage **3** : to restrain or constrain the acts of **4 a** : to make or have an equal score with in a contest **b** : to come up with something equal to : EQUAL **5** : to make a tie: as **a** : to make a bond or connection **b** : to make an equal score **c** : ATTACH

[1]**tier** \ˈti(ə)r\ *n* : a row, rank, or layer of articles; *esp* : one of two or more rows arranged one above another

[2]**ti·er** \ˈtī(-ə)r\ *n* : a person or thing that ties

tiered \ˈti(ə)rd\ *adj* : having or arranged in tiers

tie–up \ˈtī-ˌəp\ *n* **1** : a suspension of traffic or business **2** : CONNECTION, ASSOCIATION

[1]**tiff** \ˈtif\ *n* : a petty quarrel

[2]**tiff** *vi* : to have a minor quarrel

tif·fin \'tif-ən\ *n* : a midday meal : LUNCHEON

ti·ger \'tī-gər\ *n* **1** : a large Asiatic carnivorous mammal of the cat family having a tawny coat transversely striped with black **2** : a fierce and bloodthirsty person or quality

ti·ger·ish \'tī-g(ə-)rish\ *adj* : of, relating to, or resembling a tiger — **ti·ger·ish·ly** *adv* — **ti·ger·ish·ness** *n*

¹tight \'tīt\ *adj* **1** : so close in structure as not to permit passage of a fluid or light **2 a** : fixed very firmly in place **b** : not slack or loose : TAUT **c** : fitting too closely for comfort or free movement **3** : neat and orderly in arrangement or design : SNUG **4** : difficult to get through or out of : TRYING, EXACTING **5 a** : firm in control **b** : STINGY, MISERLY **6** : packed or compressed to the limit : entirely full **7** : DRUNK **8** : scantily supplied : SCARCE — **tight·ly** *adv* — **tight·ness** *n*

²tight *adv* **1** : TIGHTLY, FIRMLY, HARD **2** : SOUNDLY

tight·en \'tīt-ᵊn\ *vb* **tight·ened**; **tight·en·ing** \'tīt-niŋ, -ᵊn-iŋ\ : to make or become tight — **tight·en·er** \'tīt-nər, -ᵊn-ər\ *n*

tight·fist·ed \'tīt-'fis-təd\ *adj* : MISERLY, STINGY

tight·rope \'tīt-ˌrōp\ *n* : a rope or wire stretched taut for acrobats to perform on

tights \'tīts\ *n pl* : a skintight garment covering the body from the neck down or from the waist down

tight·wad \'tīt-ˌwäd\ *n* : a stingy person

tight·wire \-ˌwī(ə)r\ *n* : a tightrope made of wire

ti·gress \'tī-grəs\ *n* : a female tiger

til·de \'til-də\ *n* : a mark ˜ placed esp. over the letter *n* (as in Spanish *señor* sir) to denote the sound \nʸ\ or over vowels (as in Portuguese *irmã* sister) to indicate nasality

¹tile \'tīl\ *n* **1** *pl* **tiles** *or* **tile a** : a flat or curved piece of fired clay, stone, or concrete used esp. for roofs, floors, or walls **b** : a hollow or a concave earthenware or concrete piece used for a drain **2** : a thin piece of resilient material (as linoleum or rubber) for covering floors or walls — **til·ing** *n*

²tile *vt* **1** : to cover with tiles **2** : to install drainage tile in

¹till \tᵊl, təl, (ˌ)til\ *prep or conj* : UNTIL

²till \'til\ *vt* : to work by plowing, sowing, and raising crops from : CULTIVATE — **till·a·ble** *adj*

³till \'til\ *n* : a receptacle (as a drawer) for money

till·age \'til-ij\ *n* **1** : the operation of tilling land **2** : cultivated land

til·ler \'til-ər\ *n* : a lever used to turn the rudder of a boat from side to side

¹tilt \'tilt\ *vb* **1** : to cause to slope : INCLINE **2** : to move or shift so as to lean or incline : SLANT **3 a** : to point or thrust in or as if in a tilt **b** : to charge against **4 a** : to engage in a combat with lances : JOUST **b** : to make an impetuous attack

²tilt *n* **1** : an exercise on horseback in which two combatants charging with lances try to unhorse each other : JOUST **2 a** : an encounter (as with words) bringing about a sharp collision : ALTERCATION, QUARREL **b** : SPEED — used in the phrase *at full tilt* **3 a** : the act of tilting : the state or position of being tilted **b** : a sloping surface

tilth \'tilth\ *n* **1** : cultivation of the soil **2** : cultivated land : TILLAGE **3** : the state of being tilled

¹tim·ber \'tim-bər\ *n* **1** : wood for use in making something **2** : a squared or dressed and usu. large piece of wood **3** : wooded land or growing trees constituting a source of timber **4** : a curving frame branching outward from the keel of a ship that is usu. composed of several pieces united : RIB — **timber** *adj*

²timber *vt* **tim·bered**; **tim·ber·ing** \-b(ə-)riŋ\ : to frame, cover, or support with timbers

tim·bered \'tim-bərd\ *adj* **1** : furnished with, made of, or covered with timber **2** : having walls framed by exposed timbers

tim·ber·ing \'tim-b(ə-)riŋ\ *n* : a set of timbers : timber construction

tim·ber·line \'tim-bər-ˌlīn\ *n* : the upper limit of tree growth in mountains or high latitudes

timber wolf *n* : a large usu. gray No. American wolf

tim·bre \'tam-bər, 'tim-\ *n* : the quality given to a sound by its overtones

tim·brel \'tim-brəl\ *n* : a small hand drum or tambourine

¹time \'tīm\ *n* **1 a** : the measured or measurable period during which an action, process, or condition exists or continues : DURATION **b** : LEISURE **2** : the point or period when something occurs : OCCASION **3** : an appointed, fixed, or customary moment or hour for something to happen, begin, or end **4 a** : an historical period : AGE **b** : conditions at present or at some specified period **5 a** : LIFETIME **b** : a period or term esp. of military service **c** : a prison sentence **6** : SEASON **7 a** : rate of speed : TEMPO **b** : the grouping of the beats of music : RHYTHM **8 a** : a moment, hour, day, or year as indicated by a clock or calendar **b** : any of various systems (as sidereal or solar) of reckoning time **9 a** : one of a series of recurring instances or repeated actions **b** *pl* : multiplied instances **c** : TURN **10** : a person's experience during a specified period or on a particular occasion **11** : TIME-OUT — **in time 1** : early enough **2** : in the course of time : EVENTUALLY **3** : in correct rhythm or tempo — **on time 1** : PUNCTUAL, PUNCTUALLY **2** : on an installment payment plan

²time *vt* **1 a** : to arrange or set the time of : SCHEDULE **b** : to regulate (a watch) to keep correct time **2** : to set the tempo, speed, or duration of **3** : to cause to keep time with something **4** : to determine or recrod the time, duration, or rate of — **tim·er** *n*

³time *adj* **1 a** : of or relating to time **b** : recording time **2** : timed to ignite or explode at a specific moment **3 a** : payable on a specified future day or a certain length of time after presentation **b** : based on installment payments

time clock *n* : a clock that mechanically records the times of arrival and departure of workers

timed \'tīmd\ *adj* **1** : made to occur at or in a set time **2** : done or taking place at a time of a specified sort

time–hon·ored \'tīm-ˌän-ərd\ *adj* : honored or respected because of age or long-established usage

time·keep·er \'tīm-ˌkē-pər\ *n* **1** : TIMEPIECE **2** : a clerk who keeps records of the time worked by employees **3** : one appointed to mark and announce the time in an athletic game or contest — **time·keep·ing** *n*

time·less \'tīm-ləs\ *adj* **1 a** : having no beginning or end : UNENDING **b** : not restricted to a particular time or date **2** : not affected by time : AGELESS — **time·less·ly** *adv*

time·ly \'tīm-lē\ *adj* **1** : coming early or at the right time : OPPORTUNE **2** : appropriate or adapted to the times or the occasion — **time·li·ness** *n*

time·piece \'tīm-ˌpēs\ *n* : a device (as a clock or watch) to measure the passage of time

times \ˌtīmz\ *prep* : multiplied by

time·ta·ble \'tīm-ˌtā-bəl\ *n* **1** : a table of departure and arrival times of trains, buses, or airplanes **2** : a schedule showing a planned order or sequence

time·worn \-ˌwōrn\ *adj* **1** : worn or impaired by time **2 a** : AGE-OLD, ANCIENT **b** : HACKNEYED, STALE

tim·id \'tim-əd\ *adj* : feeling or showing a lack of courage or self-confidence : FEARFUL, SHY — **ti·mid·i·ty** \tə-'mid-ət-ē\ *n* — **tim·id·ly** *adv*

tim·ing \'tī-miŋ\ *n* **1** : selection for maximum effect of the precise moment for beginning or doing something **2** : observation and recording (as by a stopwatch) of the elapsed time of an act, action, or process

tim·o·rous \'tim-(ə-)rəs\ *adj* **1** : of a timid disposition : AFRAID **2** : expressing or suggesting timidity — **tim·o·rous·ly** *adv* — **tim·o·rous·ness** *n*

tim·o·thy \'tim-ə-thē\ *n* : a European grass with long cylindrical spikes widely grown for hay

tim·pa·ni \'tim-pə-nē\ *n pl* : a set of two or three kettledrums played by one performer — **tim·pa·nist** \-nəst\ *n*

1tin \'tin\ *n* **1 :** a soft bluish white lustrous crystalline metallic chemical element that is malleable and ductile at ordinary temperatures and that is used as a protective coating in tinfoil and in soft solders and alloys **2 :** a box, can, pan, vessel, or a sheet made of tinplate — **tin** *adj*

2tin *vt* **tinned; tin·ning :** to cover or plate with tin

1tinc·ture \'tiŋ(k)-chər\ *n* **1 a :** a substance that colors, dyes, or stains **b :** COLOR, TINT **2 a :** a characteristic quality **:** CAST **b :** a slight admixture **:** TRACE **3 :** an alcoholic solution of a medicinal substance

2tincture *vt* **1 :** to tint or stain with a color **:** TINGE **2 :** to infuse or instill with a property or quality **:** IMPREGNATE

tin·der \'tin-dər\ *n* **:** a very flammable substance that can be used as kindling — **tin·dery** \-d(ə-)rē\ *adj*

tin·der·box \-,bäks\ *n* **:** a metal box for holding tinder and usu. a flint and steel for striking a spark

tine \'tīn\ *n* **:** a slender pointed projecting part **:** PRONG

tin·foil \'tin-,fȯil\ *n* **:** a thin metal sheeting usu. of aluminum or tin-lead alloy

1tinge \'tinj\ *vt* **tinged; tinge·ing** *or* **ting·ing** \'tin-jiŋ\ **1 a :** to color slightly **:** TINT **b :** to affect or modify with a slight odor or taste **2 :** to modify in character

2tinge *n* **1 :** a slight staining or suffusing shade or color **2 :** a modifying property or influence **:** TOUCH

1tin·gle \'tiŋ-gəl\ *vi* **tin·gled; tin·gling** \-g(ə-)liŋ\ **1 a :** to feel a ringing, stinging, prickling, or thrilling sensation **b :** to cause such a sensation **2 :** TINKLE

2tingle *n* **1 :** a tingling sensation or condition **2 :** a tinkling sound — **tin·gly** \'tiŋ-g(ə-)lē\ *adj*

1tin·ker \'tiŋ-kər\ *n* **1 :** a usu. itinerant mender of household utensils (as pots and pans) **2 :** an unskilled mender **:** BUNGLER

2tinker *vb* **tin·kered; tin·ker·ing** \-k(ə-)riŋ\ **:** to work in the manner of a tinker; *esp* **:** to repair or adjust something in an unskilled or experimental manner — **tin·ker·er** *n*

1tin·kle \'tiŋ-kəl\ *vb* **tin·kled; tin·kling** \-k(ə-)liŋ\ **1 :** to make or emit a tinkle **2 a :** to cause to make a tinkle **b :** to produce by tinkling

2tinkle *n* **:** a series of short high ringing or clinking sounds — **tin·kly** \-k(ə-)lē\ *adj*

tin·ny \'tin-ē\ *adj* **1 :** of, abounding in, or yielding tin **2 :** resembling or suggestive of tin: as **a :** LIGHT, CHEAP **b :** thin in tone **:** METALLIC — **tin·ni·ly** \'tin-ᵊl-ē\ *adv* — **tin·ni·ness** \'tin-ē-nəs\ *n*

tin·plate \'tin-'plāt\ *n* **:** thin sheet iron or steel coated with tin

1tin·sel \'tin(t)-səl\ *n* **1 :** a thread, strip, or sheet of metal, paper, or plastic used to produce a glittering and sparkling appearance (as in fabrics, yarns, or decorations) **2 :** something superficially attractive or glamorous but of little real worth — **tinsel** *adj*

2tinsel *vt* **tin·seled** *or* **tin·selled; tin·sel·ing** *or* **tin·sel·ling** \-s(ə-)liŋ\ **1 :** to interweave, overlay, or adorn with or as if with tinsel **2 :** to impart a specious brightness to

tin·smith \'tin-,smith\ *n* **:** a worker who makes or repairs things of metal (as tin)

1tint \'tint\ *n* **1 :** a slight or pale coloring **:** TINGE **2 :** a light color or shade **3 :** a usu. slight modifying quality or characteristic **4 :** dye for the hair — **tint·er** *n*

2tint *vt* **:** to impart or apply a tint to **:** COLOR

tin·tin·nab·u·la·tion \,tin-tə-,nab-yə-'lā-shən\ *n* **1 :** the ringing or sounding of bells **2 :** a jingling or tinkling sound

tin·type \'tin-,tīp\ *n* **:** a photograph made on a thin iron plate having a darkened surface

tin·ware \-,wa(ə)r\ *n* **:** articles made of tinplate

ti·ny \'tī-nē\ *adj* **:** very small or diminutive **:** MINUTE — **ti·ni·ness** *n*

1tip \'tip\ *n* **1 :** the pointed or rounded end of something **:** END **2 :** a small piece or part serving as an end, cap, or point

2tip *vt* **tipped; tip·ping 1 :** to furnish with a tip **2 :** to cover or adorn the tip of

3tip *vb* **tipped; tip·ping 1 :** OVERTURN, UPSET **2 :** LEAN, SLANT, TILT **3 :** to raise and tilt forward in salute

4tip *n* **:** the act or an instance of tipping **:** TILT

5tip *vt* **tipped; tip·ping :** to strike lightly **:** TAP

6tip *vb* **tipped; tip·ping 1 :** to give a gratuity to **2 :** to give gratuities

7tip *n* **:** a gift or small sum of money tendered for a service performed or anticipated **:** GRATUITY

8tip *n* **:** an item of authoritative or confidential information

9tip *vt* **tipped; tip·ping :** to give information or advice about or to often in a secret or confidential manner

tip–off \'tip-,ȯf\ *n* **:** WARNING, TIP

tip·per \'tip-ər\ *n* **:** one that tips

tip·pet \'tip-ət\ *n* **1 :** a long hanging part of a garment (as on a sleeve or cape) **2 :** a shoulder cape usu. with hanging ends

1tip·ple \'tip-əl\ *vb* **tip·pled; tip·pling** \'tip-(ə-)liŋ\ **:** to drink intoxicating liquor esp. continuously in small amounts — **tip·pler** \-(ə-)lər\ *n*

2tipple *n* **:** an intoxicating beverage **:** DRINK

tip·staff \'tip-,staf\ *n, pl* **tip·staves** \-,stavz, -,stāvz\ **:** an officer (as a constable or bailiff) who bears a staff

tip·ster \'tip-stər\ *n* **:** one who gives or sells tips esp. for gambling or speculation

tip·sy \'tip-sē\ *adj* **1 :** unsteady, staggering, or foolish from the effects of alcohol **:** somewhat drunk **2 :** UNSTEADY, ASKEW — **tip·si·ly** \-sə-lē\ *adv* — **tip·si·ness** \-sē-nəs\ *n*

1tip·toe \'tip-,tō, -'tō\ *n* **:** the ends of the toes

2tiptoe *adv* (*or adj*) **:** on or as if on tiptoe

3tiptoe *vi* **:** to stand, raise oneself, or walk on or as if on tiptoe

1tip–top \'tip-'täp, -,täp\ *n* **:** the highest point **:** SUMMIT

2tip–top *adj* **:** EXCELLENT, FIRST-RATE — **tip–top** *adv*

ti·rade \tī-'rād, 'tī-,\ *n* **:** a long violent usu. abusive speech

1tire \'tī(ə)r\ *vb* **1 :** to become weary **2 :** to exhaust or greatly decrease the physical strength of **:** FATIGUE **3 :** BORE

2tire *n* **1 :** a metal hoop forming the tread of a wheel **2 :** a rubber cushion usu. containing compressed air that encircles a wheel

tired \'tī(ə)rd\ *adj* **:** FATIGUED, WEARY — **tired·ness** *n*

tire·less \'tī(ə)r-ləs\ *adj* **:** UNTIRING, INDEFATIGABLE — **tire·less·ly** *adv* — **tire·less·ness** *n*

tire·some \'tī(ə)r-səm\ *adj* **:** WEARISOME, TEDIOUS — **tire·some·ly** *adv* — **tire·some·ness** *n*

tir·ing–room \'tī-riŋ-,rüm, -,rům\ *n* **:** a dressing room esp. in a theater

tis·sue \'tish-(,)ü\ *n* **1 a :** a fine lightweight often sheer fabric **b :** MESH, NETWORK, WEB **2 :** a piece of soft absorbent paper **3 :** a mass or layer of cells forming a basic structural element of a plant or an animal

1tit \'tit\ *n* **:** TEAT

2tit *n* **:** TITMOUSE

ti·tan \'tīt-ᵊn\ *n* **:** one of gigantic size, power, or achievement

ti·tan·ic \tī-'tan-ik\ *adj* **:** of great magnitude, force, or power

ti·ta·ni·um \tī-'tā-nē-əm, tə-\ *n* **:** a silvery gray light strong metallic chemical element used in alloys (as steel)

1tithe \'tīth\ *vb* **1 :** to pay or give a tithe **2 :** to levy a tithe on — **tith·er** *n*

2tithe *n* **1 :** a tenth part paid in kind or money as a voluntary contribution or as a tax esp. for the support of a religious establishment **2 a :** TENTH **b :** a small part

ti·tian \'tish-ən\ *adj, often cap* **:** of a brownish orange color

tit·il·late \'tit-ᵊl-,āt\ *vt* **1 :** TICKLE **2 :** to excite pleasurably — **tit·il·la·tion** \,tit-ᵊl-'ā-shən\ *n* — **tit·il·la·tive** \'tit-ᵊl-,āt-iv\ *adj*

tit·i·vate *or* **tit·ti·vate** \'tit-ə-,vāt\ *vb* **:** to dress up **:** spruce up **:** SMARTEN — **tit·i·va·tion** \,tit-ə-'vā-shən\ *n*

1ti·tle \'tīt-ᵊl\ *n* **1 :** RIGHT, PRIVILEGE; *esp* **:** the elements constituting legal ownership **2 :** the distinguishing name of

a written, printed, or filmed production or of a musical composition or a work of art **3 :** an appellation of dignity or honor attached to a person or family **4 :** CHAMPIONSHIP 2a
²title *vt* **ti·tled; ti·tling** \'tīt-liŋ, -ᵊl-iŋ\ **:** to designate or call by a title **:** TERM, STYLE
ti·tled \'tīt-ᵊld\ *adj* **:** having a title esp. of nobility
title page *n* **:** a page of a book bearing the title and usu. the names of the author and publisher and the place of publication
tit·mouse \'tit-,maůs\ *n, pl* **tit·mice** \-,mīs\ **:** any of numerous small long-tailed songbirds
tit·ter \'tit-ər\ *vi* **1 :** to give vent to partly suppressed laughter **2 :** to laugh in a nervous manner esp. at a high pitch — **titter** *n*
tit·tle \'tit-ᵊl\ *n* **1 :** a point or small sign used as a diacritical mark in writing or printing **2 :** a very small part
tit·tle–tat·tle \'tit-ᵊl-,tat-ᵊl\ *n* **:** GOSSIP — **tittle–tattle** *vi*
tit·u·lar \'tich-(ə-)lər\ *adj* **1 a :** existing in title only **:** NOMINAL **b :** having the title belonging to an office or dignity without its duties or responsibilities **2 :** bearing a title **3 :** of, relating to, or constituting a title — **tit·u·lar·ly** *adv*
tiz·zy \'tiz-ē\ *n, pl* **tizzies :** a highly excited and distracted state of mind
TNT \,tē-,en-'tē\ *n* **:** a high explosive used in artillery shells and bombs and in blasting
¹to \tə, (')tü\ *prep* **1 a :** in the direction of and reaching **b :** in the direction of **:** so as to approach **c :** close against **:** ON **d :** as far as **2 a :** for the purpose of **:** FOR **b :** in honor of **c :** so as to become or bring about **3 a :** BEFORE **b :** UNTIL **4 a :** being a part or accessory of **b :** with the accompaniment of **:** in harmony with **5 a :** in a relation of likeness or unlikeness with **b** (1) **:** in accordance with (2) **:** within the range of **c :** contained, occurring, or included in **6 a :** with respect to **b :** affecting as the receiver or beneficiary of an action **c :** for no one except **7** — used to indicate that the following verb is an infinitive and often used by itself at the end of a clause to stand for an infinitive
²to \'tü\ *adv* **1** — used as a function word to indicate direction toward **2 :** into contact, position, or attachment esp. with a frame (as of a door) **3 :** to the matter or business at hand esp. with vigorous concentration **4 :** to a state of consciousness or awareness **5 :** at hand **:** BY
toad \'tōd\ *n* **:** any of numerous tailless leaping amphibians that as compared with the related frogs are generally more terrestrial in habit, squatter and shorter in build and with weaker hind limbs, and rough, dry, and warty rather than smooth and moist of skin
toad·stool \-,stül\ *n* **:** a fungus having an umbrella-shaped cap **:** MUSHROOM; *esp* **:** one that is poisonous or inedible
¹toady \'tōd-ē\ *n, pl* **toad·ies :** a person who flatters or fawns upon another in the hope of receiving favors
²toady *vi* **toad·ied; toad·y·ing :** to behave as a toady
to–and–fro \,tü-ən-'frō\ *adj* **:** forward and backward
¹toast \'tōst\ *vb* **1 :** to make (as bread) crisp, hot, and brown by heat **2 :** to warm thoroughly **:** become toasted
²toast *n* **1 :** sliced toasted bread browned on both sides by heat **2 a :** a person whose health is drunk or something in honor of which persons drink **b :** a highly admired person **3 :** an act of proposing or of drinking in honor of a toast
³toast *vt* **:** to propose or drink to as a toast
toast·er \'tō-stər\ *n* **:** one that toasts; *esp* **:** an electrical appliance for toasting
toast·mas·ter \'tōs(t)-,mas-tər\ *n* **:** one that presides at a banquet and introduces the after-dinner speakers
to·bac·co \tə-'bak-ō\ *n, pl* **-cos 1 :** any of a genus of chiefly American plants of the nightshade family with sticky foliage and tubular flowers; *esp* **:** a tall erect annual So. American herb grown for its leaves **2 :** the leaves of cultivated tobacco prepared for use in smoking or chewing or as snuff **3 :** manufactured products of tobacco; *also* **:** smoking as a practice
to·bac·co·nist \tə-'bak-ə-nəst\ *n* **:** a dealer in tobacco
¹to·bog·gan \tə-'bäg-ən\ *n* **1 :** a long flat-bottomed light sled made without runners and curved up at the front **2 :** a downward course or a sharp decline

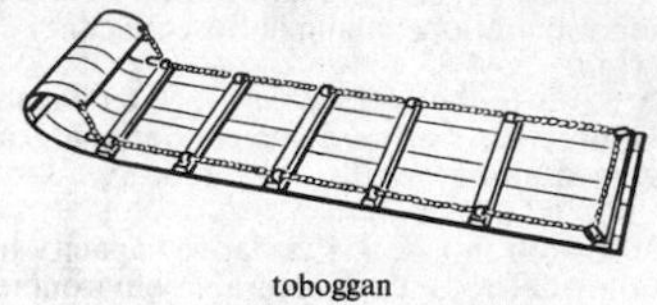
toboggan

²toboggan *vi* **1 :** to coast on a toboggan **2 :** to decline suddenly and sharply (as in value) — **to·bog·gan·er** *n*
toc·sin \'täk-sən\ *n* **1 :** an alarm bell **2 :** a warning signal
¹to·day \tə-'dā\ *adv* **1 :** on or for this day **2 :** at the present time **:** NOWADAYS
²today *n* **:** the present day, time, or age
tod·dle \'täd-ᵊl\ *vi* **tod·dled; tod·dling** \'täd-liŋ, -ᵊl-iŋ\ **:** to walk with short tottering steps in the manner of a young child — **toddle** *n* — **tod·dler** \'täd-lər, -ᵊl-ər\ *n*
tod·dy \'täd-ē\ *n, pl* **toddies :** a hot drink consisting of an alcoholic liquor, water, sugar, and spices
to–do \tə-'dü\ *n, pl* **to–dos** \-'düz\ **:** BUSTLE, STIR, COMMOTION
¹toe \'tō\ *n* **1 a :** one of the jointed members that make up the front end of a vertebrate foot **b :** the front end or part of a foot or hoof **2 :** something that is felt to resemble the toe of a foot esp. in form or position — **toe·less** \-ləs\ *adj*
²toe *vb* **toed; toe·ing :** to touch, reach, or drive with the toe
toed \'tōd\ *adj* **:** having a toe or such or so many toes — used esp. in combination
toe dance *n* **:** a dance executed on the tips of the toes — **toe–dance** \'tō-,dan(t)s\ *vi* — **toe dancer** *n*
toe·nail \'tō-,nāl, -'nāl\ *n* **:** a nail of a toe
tof·fee *or* **tof·fy** \'täf-ē\ *n, pl* **toffees** *or* **toffies :** candy of brittle but tender texture made by boiling sugar and butter together
tog \'täg\ *vt* **togged; tog·ging :** to put togs on **:** DRESS
to·ga \'tō-gə\ *n* **:** the loose outer garment worn in public by citizens of ancient Rome; *also* **:** a similar loose wrap or a professional, official, or academic gown — **to·gaed** \-gəd\ *adj*
to·geth·er \tə-'geth-ər\ *adv* **1 :** in or into one group, body, or place **2 :** in or into association, union, or contact with each other **3 a :** at one time **b :** in succession **:** without intermission **4 a :** in or by combined effort **:** JOINTLY **b :** in or into agreement **c :** so as to form an integrated or coherent whole **5 :** considered as a whole — **to·geth·er·ness** *n*
togs \'tägz\ *n pl* **:** CLOTHING; *esp* **:** a set of clothes and accessories for a specified use
¹toil \'tȯil\ *n* **:** long hard tiring labor **:** DRUDGERY
²toil *vi* **1 :** to work hard and long **:** LABOR **2 :** to proceed with laborious effort **:** PLOD — **toil·er** *n*
³toil *n* **:** SNARE, TRAP — usu. used in pl.
toi·let \'tȯi-lət\ *n* **1 :** the act or process of dressing and grooming oneself **2 a :** BATHROOM **b :** a fixture for defecation and urination; *esp* **:** WATER CLOSET
toi·let·ry \'tȯi-lə-trē\ *n, pl* **-ries :** an article or preparation used in making one's toilet — usu. used in pl.
toi·lette \twä-'let\ *n* **1 :** TOILET 1 **2 a :** formal or fashionable attire or style of dressing **b :** a particular costume or outfit
toil·some \'tȯil-səm\ *adj* **:** attended with toil or fatigue
toil·worn \-,wōrn\ *adj* **:** showing the effects of or worn out by long hard work
¹to·ken \'tō-kən\ *n* **1 :** an outward sign **2 :** SYMBOL, EMBLEM **3 a :** SOUVENIR, KEEPSAKE **b :** an indication or reminder of something **4 a :** something used or shown as a symbol of

identity, right, or authority **b** : a piece resembling a coin issued as money or for a particular use (as for a ticket on a public conveyance)

[2]**token** *adj* **1** : done or given in partial fulfillment of an obligation or undertaking **2** : SIMULATED, MINIMAL, PERFUNCTORY

to•ken•ism \'tō-kə-ˌniz-əm\ *n* : the policy or practice of accepting token integration : minimal desegregation

told *past of* TELL

tol•er•a•ble \'täl-(ə-)rə-bəl, 'täl-ər-bəl\ *adj* **1** : capable of being borne or endured **2** : moderately good or agreeable : PASSABLE — **tol•er•a•bil•i•ty** \ˌtäl-(ə-)rə-'bil-ət-ē\ *n* — **tol•er•a•bly** \'täl-(ə-)rə-blē, 'täl-ər-blē\ *adv*

tol•er•ance \'täl(-ə)-rən(t)s\ *n* **1** : relative capacity to endure or adapt physiologically to an unfavorable environmental factor **2 a** : sympathy or indulgence for beliefs or practices differing from one's own **b** : the act of allowing something : TOLERATION **3** : the allowable deviation from a standard — **tol•er•ant** \-rənt\ *adj* — **tol•er•ant•ly** *adv*

tol•er•ate \'täl-ə-ˌrāt\ *vt* **1** : to allow something to be done or to exist without making a move to stop it : put up with : ENDURE **2** : to show tolerance toward — **tol•er•a•tion** \ˌtäl-ə-'rā-shən\ *n*

[1]**toll** \'tōl\ *n* **1** : a tax paid for a privilege (as the use of a highway or bridge) **2** : a charge for a service (as placing a long-distance telephone call) **3** : the cost in loss or suffering at which something is achieved

[2]**toll** *vt* : to take as toll or take a toll from (someone)

[3]**toll** *vb* **1 a** : to announce (as a death) or summon (as defenders) by the sounding of a bell **b** : to announce (the time) by striking **2** : to sound (a bell) usu. with slow measured strokes **3** : to sound with slow measured strokes

[4]**toll** *n* : the sound of a tolling bell

toll•gate \'tōl-ˌgāt\ *n* : a point where vehicles stop to pay toll

[1]**tom•a•hawk** \'täm-i-ˌhȯk\ *n* : a light ax used as a weapon by No. American Indians

[2]**tomahawk** *vt* : to cut, strike, or kill with a tomahawk

to•ma•to \tə-'māt-ō, -'mät-\ *n, pl* **-toes** **1** : any of a genus of So. American herbs of the nightshade family; *esp* : one widely grown for its edible fruits **2** : the usu. large, rounded, and red or yellow pulpy berry of a tomato

tomb \'tüm\ *n* **1 a** : GRAVE **b** : a place of interment **2** : a house, chamber, or vault for the dead

tom•boy \'täm-ˌbȯi\ *n* : a girl of boyish behavior : HOYDEN

tomb•stone \'tüm-ˌstōn\ *n* : GRAVESTONE

tom•cat \'täm-ˌkat\ *n* : a male cat

tome \'tōm\ *n* : a usu. large or scholarly book

tom•fool \'täm-'fül\ *n* : a great fool : BLOCKHEAD, DOLT — **tomfool** *adj* — **tom•fool•ery** \täm-'fül-(ə-)rē\ *n*

[1]**to•mor•row** \tə-'mär-ō\ *adv* : on or for the day after today

[2]**tomorrow** *n* **1** : the day after the present **2** : FUTURE 1a

tom–tom \'täm-ˌtäm, 'təm-ˌtəm\ *n* : a small-headed drum commonly beaten with the hands

ton \'tən\ *n* **1** : any of various units of weight (as a metric ton) **2 a** : a unit of internal capacity for ships equal to 100 cubic feet **b** : a unit used in reckoning the displacement of ships and equal to 35 cubic feet **c** : a unit of volume for cargo freight usu. reckoned at 40 cubic feet **3** : a great quantity : LOT — used chiefly in pl.

ton•al \'tōn-ᵊl\ *adj* **1** : of, relating to, or having tonality **2** : of or relating to tone — **ton•al•ly** \-ᵊl-ē\ *adv*

to•nal•i•ty \tō-'nal-ət-ē\ *n, pl* **-ties** : tonal quality

[1]**tone** \'tōn\ *n* **1 a** : quality of vocal or musical sound **b** : a sound of definite pitch or vibration **c** : pitch, inflection, or modulation of voice esp. as an individual characteristic, a mode of emotional expression, or a linguistic device **2** : a style or manner of speaking or writing **3** : general character, quality, or trend **4 a** : color quality or value : a tint or shade of color **b** : a color that modifies another **5 a** : a healthy state of the body or any of its parts; *also* : a state of normal tension and responsiveness to stimulation **b** : RESILIENCY **6** : the general usu. harmonious effect in painting of light and shade with color

[2]**tone** *vb* **1** : to give a particular intonation or inflection to **2** : to impart tone to : STRENGTHEN **3** : to soften, blend, or harmonize in color, appearance, or sound — **ton•er** *n*

tong \'täŋ, 'tȯŋ\ *n* : a secret society of Chinese in the U.S.

tongs \'täŋz, 'tȯŋz\ *n pl* : any of numerous grasping devices consisting commonly of two pieces joined at one end by a pivot or hinged like scissors

[1]**tongue** \'təŋ\ *n* **1** : a fleshy movable process of the floor of the mouth in most vertebrates that bears sensory organs and small glands and functions esp. in taking and swallowing food and in man as a speech organ **2** : the flesh of a tongue (as of the ox or sheep) used as food **3** : the power of communication through speech **4 a** : LANGUAGE; *esp* : a spoken language **b** : manner or quality of utterance with respect to tone or sound, the sense of what is expressed, or the intention of the speaker **5** : something resembling an animal's tongue in being elongated and fastened at one end only — **tongue•less** \-ləs\ *adj* — **tongue•like** *adj*

[2]**tongue** *vb* **tongued**; **tongu•ing** \'təŋ-iŋ\ **1** : to touch or lick with or as if with the tongue **2** : to articulate notes on a wind instrument by means of the tongue

tongue in cheek *adv* (*or adj*) : with insincerity, irony, or whimsical exaggeration

tongue–tied \'təŋ-ˌtīd\ *adj* : unable to speak clearly or freely usu. from abnormal shortness of the membrane under the tongue or from shyness

[1]**ton•ic** \'tän-ik\ *adj* **1** : improving physical or mental tone : INVIGORATING **2** : relating to or based on the first tone of a scale — **ton•i•cal•ly** \'tän-i-k(ə-)lē\ *adv*

[2]**tonic** *n* **1** : a tonic agent (as a drug) **2** : the first degree of a major or minor scale **3** : a voiced sound

[1]**to•night** \tə-'nīt\ *adv* : on this present night or the night following this present day

[2]**tonight** *n* : the present or the coming night

ton•nage \'tən-ij\ *n* **1** : a duty on ships based on tons carried **2** : ships in terms of the total number of tons registered or carried **3** : the cubical content of a ship in units of 100 cubic feet **4** : total weight in tons shipped, carried, or mined

ton•neau \tə-'nō\ *n* : the rear seating compartment of an automobile

ton•sil \'tän(t)-səl\ *n* : either of a pair of oval masses of spongy tissue in the throat at the back of the mouth — **ton•sil•lar** \-sə-lər\ *adj*

ton•sil•lec•to•my \ˌtän(t)-sə-'lek-tə-mē\ *n, pl* **-mies** : the surgical removal of the tonsils

ton•sil•li•tis \-'līt-əs\ *n* : inflammation of the tonsils

ton•so•ri•al \tän-'sōr-ē-əl\ *adj* : of or relating to a barber or his work

ton•sure \'tän-chər\ *n* **1 a** : the Roman Catholic or Eastern rite of admission to the clerical state by the clipping or shaving of the head **b** : the shaven crown or patch worn by monks and many clerics **2** : a bald spot resembling a tonsure — **ton•sured** \-chərd\ *adj*

too \(')tü\ *adv* **1** : ALSO, BESIDES **2 a** : EXCESSIVELY **b** : to such a degree as to be regrettable **c** : VERY

took *past of* TAKE

[1]**tool** \'tül\ *n* **1** : an instrument (as a hammer, saw, wrench) used or worked by hand or by a machine; *also* : a machine that operates tools for shaping work **2 a** : an instrument or apparatus used in performing an operation or necessary in the practice of a vocation or profession **b** : a means to an end **3** : a person used or manipulated by another : DUPE

[2]**tool** *vb* **1** : DRIVE **2** : to shape, form, or finish with a tool; *esp* : to letter or ornament (as a book cover) by means of hand

tools 3 : to equip a plant or industry with machines and tools for production

[1]**toot** \'tüt\ *vb* 1 : to sound a short blast 2 : to blow or sound an instrument (as a horn) — **toot·er** *n*

[2]**toot** *n* : a short blast (as on a horn)

tooth \'tüth\ *n, pl* **teeth** \'tēth\ 1 : one of the hard bony structures borne esp. on the jaws of vertebrates and used for seizing and chewing food and as weapons 2 : TASTE, LIKING 3 : a projection resembling or suggesting the tooth of an animal in shape, arrangement, or action 4 : one of the projections on the rim of a cogwheel : COG 5 *pl* : effective means of enforcement — **tooth·less** \-ləs\ *adj* — **tooth·like** *adj*

tooth·ache \-ˌāk\ *n* : pain in or about a tooth

tooth and nail *adv* : with every available means

tooth·brush \'tüth-ˌbrəsh\ *n* : a brush for cleaning the teeth

toothed \'tütht\ *adj* 1 : provided with teeth or such or so many teeth 2 : NOTCHED, JAGGED

tooth·paste \'tüth-ˌpāst\ *n* : a paste dentifrice

tooth·pick \-ˌpik\ *n* : a pointed instrument (as a small flat tapering splinter) used for clearing the teeth of substances lodged between them

tooth powder *n* : a dentifrice in powder form

tooth·some \'tüth-səm\ *adj* 1 : pleasing to the taste : DELICIOUS 2 : ATTRACTIVE, LUSCIOUS

toothy \'tü-thē\ *adj* : having or showing prominent teeth — **tooth·i·ly** \-thə-lē\ *adv*

[1]**top** \'täp\ *n* 1 a : the highest point, level, or part of something b : the upper end, edge, or surface 2 : the stalk and leaves of a plant and esp. of one with edible roots 3 : an integral part serving as an upper piece, lid, or covering 4 : a platform high up on the lower mast of a ship serving to spread the topmost rigging 5 : the highest position or rank : ACME; *also* : one in such a position — **topped** \'täpt\ *adj*

[2]**top** *vt* **topped**; **top·ping** 1 : to remove or cut the top of 2 a : to cover with a top or on the top : provide, form, or serve as a top : CROWN, CAP b : to supply with a decorative or protective finish or a final touch 3 a : to be or become higher than b : to be superior to : EXCEL, SURPASS c : to gain ascendancy over : DOMINATE 4 a : to rise to, reach, or be at the top of b : to go over the top of : CLEAR, SURMOUNT 5 : to strike above the center

[3]**top** *adj* : of, relating to, or at the top : HIGHEST, UPPERMOST

[4]**top** *n* : a child's toy that has a tapering point on which it is made to spin

to·paz \'tō-ˌpaz\ *n* : a hard mineral consisting of a silicate of aluminum and occurring in crystals of various colors with the yellow variety being the one usu. cut and prized as a gem

top·coat \'täp-ˌkōt\ *n* : a lightweight overcoat

top·er \'tō-pər\ *n* : a heavy drinker; *esp* : DRUNKARD

top hat *n* : a man's tall-crowned hat usu. of beaver or silk

top–heavy \'täp-ˌhev-ē\ *adj* : having the top part too heavy for the lower part : lacking in stability

top·ic \'täp-ik\ *n* 1 : a heading in an outlined argument or exposition 2 : the subject of a discourse or a section of it

top·i·cal \'täp-i-kəl\ *adj* 1 a : of or relating to a place b : local or designed for local application 2 a : of, relating to, or arranged by topics b : referring to the topics of the day or place — **top·i·cal·i·ty** \ˌtäp-ə-'kal-ət-ē\ *n* — **top·i·cal·ly** \'täp-i-k(ə-)lē\ *adv*

top·knot \'täp-ˌnät\ *n* 1 : an ornament (as a knot of ribbons or a pompon) forming a headdress or worn as part of a coiffure 2 : a crest of feathers or hair on the top of the head

top·mast \-ˌmast, -məst\ *n* : the mast that is next above the lower mast and topmost in a fore-and-aft rig

top·most \-ˌmōst\ *adj* : highest of all : UPPERMOST

top–notch \-'näch\ *adj* : of the highest quality : FIRST-RATE — **top·notch** *n* — **top·notch·er** *n*

to·pog·ra·pher \tə-'päg-rə-fər\ *n* : one skilled in topography

top·o·graph·ic \ˌtäp-ə-'graf-ik\ *adj* : TOPOGRAPHICAL 1

top·o·graph·i·cal \-'graf-i-kəl\ *adj* 1 : of, relating to, or concerned with topography 2 : of, relating to, or concerned with the artistic representation of a particular locality — **top·o·graph·i·cal·ly** \-k(ə-)lē\ *adv*

to·pog·ra·phy \tə-'päg-rə-fē\ *n* 1 : the art or practice of detailing on maps or charts natural and man-made features of a place or region esp. so as to show elevations 2 : the configuration of a surface including its relief and the position of its natural and man-made features

top·ping \'täp-iŋ\ *n* : something that forms a top: as a : GARNISH b : a flavorful addition (as of sauce or nuts) served on top of a dessert

top·ple \'täp-əl\ *vb* **top·pled**; **top·pling** \'täp-(ə-)liŋ\ 1 : to fall or cause to fall from or as if from being top-heavy : OVERTURN 2 : to be or seem unsteady : TOTTER 3 : OVERTHROW

top·sail \'täp-ˌsāl, -səl\ *n* : the sail next above the lowermost sail on a mast in a square-rigged ship

top secret *adj* : demanding inviolate secrecy among top officials or a select few

top·soil \'täp-ˌsȯil\ *n* : a surface soil; *esp* : the organic layer in which plants have most of their roots

[1]**top·sy–tur·vy** \ˌtäp-sē-'tər-vē\ *adv* 1 : upside down 2 : in utter confusion or disorder

[2]**topsy–turvy** *adj* : turned topsy-turvy : totally disordered

toque \'tōk\ *n* : a woman's small hat usu. without a brim made in any of various soft close-fitting shapes

tor \'tȯ(ə)r\ *n* : a high craggy hill

To·rah \'tōr-ə\ *n* 1 : a scroll of the first five books of the Old Testament used in a synagogue; *also* : these five books 2 : the body of divine knowledge and law found in the Jewish scriptures and oral tradition

torch \'tȯrch\ *n* 1 : a flaming light made of something that burns brightly (as resinous wood) and usu. carried in the hand 2 : something (as wisdom or knowledge) likened to a torch as giving light or guidance — **torch·bear·er** \-ˌbar-ər\ *n* — **torch·light** \-ˌlīt\ *n*

tore *past of* TEAR

tor·e·a·dor \'tȯr-ē-ə-ˌdȯr\ *n* : BULLFIGHTER

[1]**tor·ment** \'tȯr-ˌment\ *n* 1 : the infliction of torture (as by rack or wheel) 2 : extreme pain or anguish of body or mind : AGONY 3 : a source of vexation or pain

[2]**tor·ment** \tȯr-'ment, 'tȯr-ˌ\ *vt* 1 a : to cause severe suffering of body or mind to : DISTRESS b : to cause worry or vexation to : HARASS 2 : DISTORT, TWIST — **tor·men·tor** \-ər\ *n*

torn *past part of* TEAR

tor·na·do \tȯr-'nād-ō\ *n, pl* **-does** *or* **-dos** : a violent destructive whirling wind accompanied by a funnel-shaped cloud that progresses in a narrow path over the land

[1]**tor·pe·do** \tȯr-'pēd-ō\ *n, pl* **-does** : a self-propelling cigar-shaped submarine projectile filled with an explosive charge that is released from a ship against another

[2]**torpedo** *vt* 1 : to hit with or destroy by a torpedo 2 : to destroy or nullify altogether : WRECK

tor·pid \'tȯr-pəd\ *adj* 1 a : having lost motion or the power of exertion or feeling : DORMANT b : sluggish in functioning or acting 2 : lacking in energy or vigor : APATHETIC, DULL — **tor·pid·i·ty** \tȯr-'pid-ət-ē\ *n* — **tor·pid·ly** *adv*

tor·por \'tȯr-pər\ *n* 1 : temporary loss or suspension of motion or feeling : extreme sluggishness 2 : DULLNESS, APATHY

torque \'tȯrk\ *n* : a force which produces or tends to produce rotation or torsion

tor·rent \'tȯr-ənt\ *n* 1 : a violent or rushing stream of a liquid (as water or lava) 2 : a raging flood : a tumultuous outpouring

tor·ren·tial \tȯ-'ren-chəl\ *adj* 1 a : relating to or having the character of a torrent b : caused by or resulting from action of rapid streams 2 : resembling a torrent in violence or rapidity of flow — **tor·ren·tial·ly** \-'rench-(ə-)lē\ *adv*

tor·rid \'tȯr-əd\ *adj* **1 a :** parched with heat esp. of the sun **:** HOT **b :** giving off intense heat **:** SCORCHING **2 :** ARDENT, PASSIONATE — **tor·rid·i·ty** \tȯ-'rid-ət-ē\ *n* — **tor·rid·ly** *adv* — **tor·rid·ness** *n*

torrid zone *n* **:** the belt of the earth between the tropics over which the sun is vertical at some period of the year

tor·sion \'tȯr-shən\ *n* **1 :** the act or process of turning or twisting **2 :** the state of being twisted

tor·so \'tȯr-sō\ *n, pl* **torsos** *or* **tor·si** \-ˌsē\ **:** the trunk of the human body

tort \'tȯrt\ *n* **:** a wrongful act except one involving a breach of contract for which the injured party can recover damages in a civil action

tor·til·la \tȯr-'tē-(y)ə\ *n* **:** a round flat cake of unleavened cornmeal bread with a topping or filling of ground meat or cheese

tor·toise \'tȯrt-əs\ *n* **:** TURTLE; *esp* **:** a land turtle

tor·toise·shell \'tȯrt-əs(h)-ˌshel\ *n* **:** a mottled horny substance that covers the bony shell of some sea turtles and is used in making various ornamental articles

tor·tu·ous \'tȯrch-(ə-)wəs\ *adj* **1 :** marked by repeated twists, bends, or turns **:** WINDING **2 a :** marked by devious or indirect tactics **:** CROOKED, TRICKY **b :** CIRCUITOUS, INVOLVED — **tor·tu·ous·ly** *adv* — **tor·tu·ous·ness** *n*

[1]**tor·ture** \'tȯr-chər\ *n* **1 :** the infliction of intense pain (as from burning, crushing, or wounding) esp. to punish or obtain a confession **2 a :** anguish of body or mind **:** AGONY **b :** something that causes agony or pain

[2]**torture** *vt* **tor·tured**; **tor·tur·ing** \'tȯrch-(ə-)riŋ\ **1 :** to punish or coerce by inflicting excruciating pain **2 :** to cause intense suffering to **:** TORMENT **3 :** to twist or wrench out of shape **:** DISTORT — **tor·tur·er** *n*

tor·tur·ous \'tȯrch-(ə-)rəs\ *adj* **:** causing torture **:** cruelly painful — **tor·tur·ous·ly** *adv*

To·ry \'tōr-ē\ *n, pl* **Tories** **1 :** a member of a British political group of the 18th and early 19th centuries favoring royal authority and the established church and seeking to preserve the traditional political structure **2 :** an American upholding the cause of the British Crown during the American Revolution **:** LOYALIST **3** *often not cap* **:** an extreme conservative esp. in politics and economics — **Tory** *adj*

[1]**toss** \'tȯs, 'täs\ *vb* **1 :** to keep throwing here and there or backward and forward **:** cause to pitch or roll **2 :** to throw with a quick light motion **3 :** to lift with a sudden motion **4 :** to pitch or bob about rapidly **5 :** to be restless **:** fling oneself about **6 :** to stir or mix lightly

[2]**toss** *n* **:** an act or instance of tossing

toss·pot \-ˌpät\ *n* **:** DRUNKARD

tot \'tät\ *n* **1 :** a small child **:** TODDLER **2 :** a small drink or allowance of liquor

[1]**to·tal** \'tōt-ᵊl\ *adj* **1 :** of or relating to the whole of something **2 :** making up the whole **:** ENTIRE **3 :** COMPLETE, UTTER **4 :** making use of every means to carry out a planned program

[2]**total** *n* **1 :** a product of addition **:** SUM **2 :** an entire quantity

[3]**total** *vt* **to·taled** *or* **to·talled**; **to·tal·ing** *or* **to·tal·ling** **1 :** to add up **:** COMPUTE **2 :** to amount to **:** NUMBER

to·tal·i·tar·i·an \(ˌ)tō-ˌtal-ə-'ter-ē-ən\ *adj* **:** of or relating to a political regime based on subordination of the individual to the state and strict control of all aspects of life esp. by coercive measures; *also* **:** advocating, constituting, or characteristic of such a regime — **totalitarian** *n* — **to·tal·i·tar·i·an·ism** \-ē-ə-ˌniz-əm\ *n*

to·tal·i·ty \tō-'tal-ət-ē\ *n, pl* **-ties** **:** an aggregate amount **:** SUM, WHOLE

to·tal·ize \'tōt-ᵊl-ˌīz\ *vt* **1 :** to add up **:** TOTAL **2 :** to express as a whole **:** SUMMARIZE

to·tal·ly \'tōt-ᵊl-ē\ *adv* **1 :** in a total manner **:** WHOLLY **2 :** as a whole **:** in toto

tote \'tōt\ *vt* **:** to carry by hand; *also* **:** PACK, HAUL — **tot·er** *n*

to·tem \'tōt-əm\ *n* **:** an object (as an animal or plant) serving as the emblem of a family or clan and often as a reminder of its ancestry; *also* **:** a usu. carved or painted representation of such an object — **to·tem·ic** \tō-'tem-ik\ *adj*

totem pole *n* **:** a pole carved and painted with totemic symbols

[1]**tot·ter** \'tät-ər\ *vi* **1 a :** to tremble or rock as if about to fall **:** SWAY **b :** to become unstable **:** threaten to collapse **2 :** to move unsteadily **:** STAGGER, WOBBLE — **tot·tery** \-ə-rē\ *adj*

[2]**totter** *n* **:** an unsteady gait **:** WOBBLE

tot·ter·ing \'tät-ə-riŋ\ *adj* **1 a :** unstable in condition **b :** walking unsteadily **2 :** lacking firmness or stability **:** INSECURE

tou·can \'tü-ˌkan, tü-'\ *n* **:** any of a family of fruit-eating birds of tropical America with brilliant coloring and a very large but light and thin-walled bill

[1]**touch** \'təch\ *vb* **1 :** to feel or handle (as with fingers or hands) esp. so as to perceive through the tactile sense **2 a :** to bring or come into or be in contact with something **b :** to come near to or have a common boundary with something **:** ADJOIN **c :** to come near to being something mentioned **3 a :** to hit lightly **b :** to affect physically by some contact or agent; *also* **:** to have a usu. slight injurious physical effect on **4 a :** to lay hands on (as in taking, using, or examining) **b :** to act on or tamper with so as to damage in some way or degree; *esp* **:** to commit violence upon **c :** to make use of esp. as food or drink **5 :** to speak or write of something briefly or casually **:** mention in passing **6 :** to relate or be of concern to **:** affect the interest of **7 a :** to affect the mind or spirit of **:** IMBUE; *also* **:** to be or become disordered in mind **b :** to move emotionally **8 a :** to reach as a limit **:** ATTAIN **b :** to come close **:** APPROACH **9 :** to make a usu. brief or incidental stop in port **10 :** to rival in quality or value **:** stand comparison with **11 a :** to receive (as money) for a purpose or as a recompense **b :** to induce to give or lend **12 a :** to improve or alter with or as if with slight strokes of a brush or pencil **b :** to mark or change slightly (as in color or aspect) — **touch·a·ble** *adj* — **touch·er** *n*

[2]**touch** *n* **1 :** a light stroke, tap, or blow **2 :** the act or fact of touching or being touched **3 a :** the special sense by which light pressure or traction is perceived **b :** a particular sensation conveyed by this sense **4 :** a state of contact or communication **:** close relationship **5 :** quality or kind esp. as attested by authority; *also* **:** an attesting mark (as on silver) **6 a :** manner of touching or striking esp. the keys of a keyboard; *also* **:** the character of response of such keys to being struck **b :** an individual productive act or its product (as a line or dash of color) esp. in an artistic production **c :** skillful or distinctive manner or method **7 :** a small amount **:** TRACE

touch and go *n* **:** a highly uncertain or precarious situation — **touch–and–go** \ˌtəch-ən-'gō\ *adj*

touch·down \'təch-ˌdau̇n\ *n* **:** the act of scoring six points in American football by being lawfully in possession of the ball on, above, or behind an opponent's goal line

[1]**touch·ing** \'təch-iŋ\ *prep* **:** in reference to **:** CONCERNING

[2]**touching** *adj* **:** arousing tenderness or compassion **:** PATHETIC — **touch·ing·ly** *adv*

touch·stone \'təch-ˌstōn\ *n* **:** a test or criterion for judging

touchy \'təch-ē\ *adj* **1 :** marked by readiness to take offense on slight provocation **2 :** acutely sensitive or irritable **3 :** calling for tact, care, or caution in treatment — **touch·i·ly** \'təch-ə-lē\ *adv* — **touch·i·ness** \'təch-ē-nəs\ *n*

[1]**tough** \'təf\ *adj* **1 :** able to undergo great strain **:** flexible and not brittle **2 :** not easily chewed **3 :** able to stand hard work and hardship **:** ROBUST **4 a :** hard to influence **:** STUBBORN **b :** very difficult **5 :** hardened in vice **:** ROWDY, LAWLESS **6 :** free from softness or sentimentality; *esp* **:** marked by firm uncompromising determination — **tough·ly** *adv* — **tough·ness** *n*

[2]**tough** *n* **:** a tough person; *esp* **:** ROWDY

tough·en \'təf-ən\ *vb* **tough·ened**; **tough·en·ing** \'təf-(ə-)niŋ\ : to make or become tough

tou·pee \tü-'pā\ *n* : a small wig for a bald spot

[1]tour \'tů(ə)r\ *n* **1** : a period (as of duty) under some orderly schedule **2** : a trip or excursion usu. ending at the point of beginning

[2]tour *vb* : to make a tour of : travel as a tourist

tour de force \ˌtů(ə)rd-ə-'fōrs\ *n, pl* **tours de force** *same*\ : a feat of strength, skill, or ingenuity

tour·ist \'tůr-əst\ *n* : one who travels for pleasure — **tourist** *adj*

tour·ma·line \'tůr-mə-lən, -ˌlēn\ *n* : a mineral that when transparent is valued as a gem

tour·na·ment \'tůr-nə-mənt, 'tər-\ *n* **1 a** : a contest of skill and courage between armored knights fighting with blunted lances or swords **b** : a series of knightly contests occurring at one time and place **2** : a series of athletic contests, sports events, or games for a championship

tour·ney \'tů(ə)r-nē, 'tər-\ *n, pl* **tourneys** : TOURNAMENT

tour·ni·quet \'tůr-ni-kət, 'tər-\ *n* : a device (as a bandage twisted tight with a stick) to check bleeding or blood flow

[1]tou·sle \'taů-zəl\ *vt* **tou·sled**; **tou·sling** \'taůz-(ə-)liŋ\ : DISHEVEL, RUMPLE

[2]tousle *n* : a tangled mass or condition

[1]tout \'taůt\ *vb* **1** : to solicit or canvass for patronage, trade, votes, or support **2** : to provide tips on racehorses

[2]tout *n* : one who touts

[3]tout *vt* : to praise or publicize insistently or excessively

[1]tow \'tō\ *vt* : to draw or pull along behind : HAUL

[2]tow *n* **1** : an act or instance of towing : the fact or condition of being towed **2** : a line or rope for towing **3** : something (as a tugboat or barge) that tows or is towed

[3]tow *n* : short broken fiber from flax, hemp, or jute used for yarn, twine, or stuffing

[1]to·ward \'tō(-ə)rd\ *adj* **1** : coming soon : IMMINENT **2** : happening at the moment : AFOOT

[2]to·ward *or* **to·wards** \(')tō(-ə)rd(z), tə-'wȯrd(z), (')twȯrd(z)\ *prep* **1** : in the direction of **2 a** : along a course leading to **b** : in relation to **3** : so as to face **4** : not long before **5** : to provide part of the payment for

tow–away zone \'tō-ə-ˌwā-\ *n* : a no-parking zone from which parked vehicles are towed away

[1]tow·el \'taů(-ə)l\ *n* : a cloth or piece of absorbent paper for wiping or drying

[2]towel *vb* **-eled** *or* **-elled**; **-el·ing** *or* **-el·ling** : to rub or dry with or use a towel

tow·el·ing *or* **tow·el·ling** \'taů-(ə-)liŋ\ *n* : material for towels

[1]tow·er \'taů(-ə)r\ *n* **1** : a building or structure typically higher than its diameter and high relative to its surroundings that may stand apart (as a campanile) or be attached (as a church belfry) to a larger structure **2** : a towering citadel : FORTRESS — **tow·ered** \'taů(-ə)rd\ *adj*

[2]tower *vi* : to reach or rise to a great height

tow·er·ing \'taůr-iŋ\ *adj* **1** : impressively high or great : IMPOSING **2** : reaching a high point of intensity **3** : EXCESSIVE

tow·head \'tō-ˌhed\ *n* : a person having soft whitish hair — **tow·head·ed** \-'hed-əd\ *adj*

tow·line \'tō-ˌlīn\ *n* : a line used in towing

town \'taůn\ *n* **1 a** : a compactly settled area as distinguished from surrounding rural territory; *esp* : one larger than a village but smaller than a city **b** : CITY **2** : a New England territorial and political unit usu. containing both rural and urban areas under a single town government — **town** *adj*

town clerk *n* : an official who keeps the town records

town crier *n* : a town officer who makes public proclamations

town house *n* **1** : the city residence of one having a countryseat or a chief residence elsewhere **2** : a single-family house of two or sometimes three stories connected to another house by a common sidewall

town meeting *n* : a meeting of inhabitants or taxpayers constituting the legislative authority of a town

towns·folk \'taůnz-ˌfōk\ *n pl* : TOWNSPEOPLE

town·ship \'taůn-ˌship\ *n* **1 a** : TOWN 2 **b** : a unit of local government in some northeastern and north central states **c** : a subdivision of the county esp. in the southern U.S. **2** : a division of territory in surveys of U.S. public land containing 36 square miles

towns·man \'taůnz-mən\ *n* **1** : a native or resident of a town or city **2** : a fellow citizen of a town

towns·peo·ple \-ˌpē-pəl\ *n pl* **1** : the inhabitants of a town or city : TOWNSMEN **2** : town-dwelling or town-bred persons

tow·path \'tō-ˌpath, -ˌpȧth\ *or* **tow·ing path** \'tō-iŋ-\ *n* : a path (as along a canal) traveled by men or animals towing boats

tow·rope \'tō-ˌrōp\ *n* : a line used in towing

tox·e·mia \täk-'sē-mē-ə\ *n* : an abnormal condition associated with the presence of toxic substances in the blood — **tox·e·mic** \-mik\ *adj*

tox·ic \'täk-sik\ *adj* **1** : of, relating to, or caused by a poison or toxin **2** : POISONOUS — **tox·ic·i·ty** \täk-'sis-ət-ē\ *n*

tox·i·col·o·gy \ˌtäk-sə-'käl-ə-jē\ *n* : a science that deals with poisonous materials and their effect and with the problems involved in their use and control — **tox·i·co·log·ic** \ˌtäk-si-kə-'läj-ik\ *adj* — **tox·i·col·o·gist** \ˌtäk-sə-'käl-ə-jəst\ *n*

tox·in \'täk-sən\ *n* : a complex usu. unstable substance that is a metabolic product of a living organism (as a bacterium), that is very poisonous when introduced directly into the tissues but is usu. destroyed by the digestive process when taken by mouth, and that typically induces antibody formation

[1]toy \'tȯi\ *n* **1** : something (as a trinket) of small or no real value or importance : TRIFLE **2** : something for a child to play with **3** : something tiny — **toy** *adj* — **toy·like** *adj*

[2]toy *vi* : to amuse oneself as if with a toy — **toy·er** *n*

[1]trace \'trās\ *n* **1** : a mark or line left by something that has passed : TRAIL, TRACK; *also* : FOOTPRINT **2** : a sign or evidence of some past thing **3** : a minute amount or indication

[2]trace *vb* **1 a** : DELINEATE, SKETCH **b** : to form (as letters or figures) carefully or painstakingly **c** : to copy (as a drawing) by following the lines or letters as seen through a transparent superimposed sheet **d** : to adorn with linear ornamentation (as tracery or chasing) **2 a** : to follow the footprints, track, or trail of **b** : to study out or follow the development and progress of in detail or step by step — **trac·er** *n*

[3]trace *n* : either of two straps, chains, or lines of a harness for attaching a horse to something (as a vehicle) to be drawn

trace·a·ble \'trā-sə-bəl\ *adj* **1** : capable of being traced **2** : ATTRIBUTABLE, DUE — **trace·a·bly** \-blē\ *adv*

trac·ery \'trās(-ə)-rē\ *n, pl* **-er·ies** **1** : architectural ornamental work with branching lines; *esp* : decorative openwork in the head of a Gothic window **2** : a decorative interlacing of lines suggestive of Gothic tracery — **trac·er·ied** \-rēd\ *adj*

tra·chea \'trā-kē-ə\ *n, pl* **-che·ae** \-kē-ˌē\ : the main trunk of the system of tubes by which air passes to and from the lungs — **tra·che·al** \-kē-əl\ *adj* — **tra·che·ate** \-kē-ˌāt\ *adj*

trac·ing \'trā-siŋ\ *n* **1** : the act of one that traces **2** : something that is traced

[1]track \'trak\ *n* **1 a** : detectable evidence that something has passed **b** : a path made by repeated footfalls : TRAIL **c** (1) : a course laid out esp. for racing (2) : the parallel rails of a railroad **2** : the course along which something moves **3 a** : a sequence of events : a train of ideas : SUCCESSION **b** : awareness of a fact or progression **4 a** : the width of a wheeled vehicle from wheel to wheel **b** : either of two endless metal belts on which a vehicle (as a tank) travels **5** : track-and-field sports — **in one's tracks** : on the spot : INSTANTLY

[2]track *vb* **1** : to follow the tracks or traces of : TRAIL **2** : to trace by following the signs or course of **3** : to pass over

: TRAVERSE 4 : to make tracks upon or with — **track•er** *n*
track–and–field \ˌtrak-ən-ˈfēld\ *adj* : of or relating to a sport performed on a racing track or on the adjacent field
track•less \ˈtrak-ləs\ *adj* : having no track : UNTROD — **track•less•ly** *adv* — **track•less•ness** *n*
[1]**tract** \ˈtrakt\ *n* : a pamphlet or leaflet intended to draw attention or gain support for something
[2]**tract** *n* 1 a : an indefinite stretch esp. of land b : a defined area esp. of land 2 : a system of body parts or organs that collectively serve some special purpose
trac•ta•ble \ˈtrak-tə-bəl\ *adj* 1 : easily led, taught, or controlled : DOCILE 2 : easily handled, managed, or wrought : MALLEABLE — **trac•ta•bil•i•ty** \ˌtrak-tə-ˈbil-ət-ē\ *n* — **trac•ta•ble•ness** *n* — **trac•ta•bly** \ˈtrak-tə-blē\ *adv*
trac•tion \ˈtrak-shən\ *n* 1 : the act of drawing : the state of being drawn; *also* : the force exerted in drawing 2 : the drawing of a vehicle by motive power; *also* : the motive power employed 3 : the adhesive friction of a body on a surface on which it moves — **trac•tion•al** \-shnəl, -shən-ᵊl\ *adj*
trac•tive \ˈtrak-tiv\ *adj* : serving to pull : used in pulling
trac•tor \ˈtrak-tər\ *n* 1 : an automotive vehicle that is borne on four wheels or beltlike metal tracks and used for drawing, pushing, or bearing implements or vehicles 2 : a truck with short chassis and no body used in combination with a trailer for the highway hauling of freight
[1]**trade** \ˈtrād\ *n* 1 : a customary course of action : PRACTICE 2 a : the business or work in which one engages regularly : OCCUPATION b : an occupation requiring manual or mechanical skill : CRAFT c : the persons engaged in an occupation, business, or industry 3 : the business of buying and selling or bartering commodities : COMMERCE; *also* : TRAFFIC, MARKET 4 a : an act or instance of trading : TRANSACTION; *esp* : an exchange of property without use of money b : a firm's customers c : the concerns engaged in a business or industry
[2]**trade** *vb* 1 a : to give in exchange for another commodity : BARTER; *also* : to make an exchange of b : to buy and sell (as stock) regularly 2 a : to engage in the exchange, purchase, or sale of goods b : to make one's purchases : SHOP
[3]**trade** *adj* 1 : of, relating to, or used in trade 2 : intended for persons in a business or industry 3 : of, composed of, or representing the trades or trade unions
trade in *vt* : to turn in as usu. part payment for a purchase
trade–in \ˈtrād-ˌin\ *n* : something given in trade usu. as part payment of the price of another
[1]**trade•mark** \-ˌmärk\ *n* : a device (as a word) pointing distinctly to the origin or ownership of merchandise to which it is applied and legally reserved to the exclusive use of the owner as maker or seller
[2]**trademark** *vt* : to secure trademark rights for : register the trademark of
trad•er \ˈtrād-ər\ *n* 1 : a person who trades 2 : a ship engaged in trade
trade school *n* : a secondary school teaching the skilled trades
trades•man \ˈtrādz-mən\ *n* 1 : one who runs a retail store : SHOPKEEPER 2 : a workman in a skilled trade : CRAFTSMAN
trades•peo•ple \-ˌpē-pəl\ *n pl* : TRADESMEN 1
trade union *n* : LABOR UNION
trade wind *n* : a wind blowing almost continually in the same course, from northeast to southwest in a belt north of the equator and from southeast to northwest in one south of the equator
tra•di•tion \trə-ˈdish-ən\ *n* : the handing down of information, beliefs, or customs from one generation to another; *also* : something thus handed down — **tra•di•tion•al** \-ˈdish-nəl, -ən-ᵊl\ *adj* — **tra•di•tion•al•ly** \-ē\ *adv*
tra•di•tion•al•ism \-ˈdish-nə-ˌliz-əm, -ən-ᵊl-ˌiz-\ *n* : the doctrines or practices of those who follow or accept tradition — **tra•di•tion•al•ist** \-nə-ləst, -ən-ᵊl-əst\ *n or adj*
tra•duce \trə-ˈd(y)üs\ *vt* 1 : to injure the reputation of by falsehood or misrepresentation : DEFAME 2 : to make a mock of : BETRAY — **tra•duc•er** *n*
[1]**traf•fic** \ˈtraf-ik\ *n* 1 : the business of carrying passengers or goods 2 : the business of buying and selling : TRADE, COMMERCE 3 : DEALINGS, FAMILIARITY 4 : the persons or goods carried by train, boat, or airplane or passing along a road, river, or air route; *also* : the motions or activity of such persons or carriers
[2]**traffic** *vi* **traf•ficked**; **traf•fick•ing** : to carry on traffic : TRADE, DEAL — **traf•fick•er** *n*
tra•ge•di•an \trə-ˈjēd-ē-ən\ *n* 1 : a writer of tragedies 2 : an actor of tragic roles
tra•ge•di•enne \trə-ˌjēd-ē-ˈen\ *n* : an actress who plays tragic roles
trag•e•dy \ˈtraj-əd-ē\ *n, pl* **-dies** 1 : a serious drama typically describing a conflict between the protagonist and a superior force (as destiny) and having a sorrowful or disastrous conclusion that excites pity or terror 2 a : a disastrous event : CALAMITY b : MISFORTUNE 3 : tragic quality or element
trag•ic \ˈtraj-ik\ *adj* 1 : of, marked by, or expressive of tragedy 2 a : dealing with or treated in tragedy b : appropriate to or typical of tragedy 3 a : DEPLORABLE, LAMENTABLE b : marked by a sense of tragedy — **trag•i•cal•ly** \-i-k(ə-)lē\ *adv* — **trag•i•cal•ness** \-i-kəl-nəs\ *n*
tragi•com•e•dy \ˌtraj-i-ˈkäm-əd-ē\ *n* : a drama or a situation blending tragic and comic elements
[1]**trail** \ˈtrāl\ *vb* 1 : to drag or draw along behind 2 : to lag behind 3 : to carry or bring along as a burden or bother 4 : to follow in the tracks of : PURSUE 5 : to hang or let hang so as to touch the ground 6 : to grow to such a length as to hang down or rest on or creep over the ground 7 : DWINDLE
[2]**trail** *n* 1 : something that trails or is trailed 2 a : something that follows or moves along as if being drawn along : TRAIN b : a chain of consequences : AFTERMATH 3 a : a trace or mark left by something that has passed or been drawn along b (1) : a track made by passage through a wilderness : a beaten path (2) : a marked path through a forest or mountainous region
trail•blaz•er \-ˌblā-zər\ *n* 1 : one that marks or points out a trail to guide others 2 : PIONEER — **trail•blaz•ing** *adj*
trail•er \ˈtrā-lər\ *n* 1 : a trailing plant 2 a : a vehicle designed to be hauled (as by a tractor) b : a vehicle designed to serve wherever parked as a dwelling or as a place of business
[1]**train** \ˈtrān\ *n* 1 : a part of a gown that trails behind the wearer 2 : RETINUE 3 : a moving file of persons, vehicles, or animals 4 a : regular or proper order designed to lead to some result b : a connected series c : accompanying circumstances : AFTERMATH 5 : a connected line of railroad cars with or without a locomotive
[2]**train** *vb* 1 : to direct the growth of (a plant) usu. by bending, pruning, and tying 2 : to teach in an art, profession, or trade 3 : to make ready (as by exercise) for a test of skill 4 : to aim (as a gun) at a target : bring to bear 5 : to undergo instruction, discipline, or drill — **train•a•ble** *adj* — **train•ee** \trā-ˈnē\ *n* — **train•er** *n*
train•ing \ˈtrā-niŋ\ *n* 1 : the course followed by one who trains or is being trained 2 : the condition of one who has trained for a test or contest
train•load \ˈtrān-ˈlōd\ *n* : the full freight or passenger capacity of a railroad train
train•man \ˈtrān-mən\ *n* : a member of a railroad train crew supervised by a conductor
traipse \ˈtrāps\ *vi* : to walk or trudge about — **traipse** *n*
trait \ˈtrāt\ *n* : a distinguishing quality (as of personality or physical makeup) : PECULIARITY, CHARACTERISTIC
trai•tor \ˈtrāt-ər\ *n* 1 : one who betrays another's trust or is false to an obligation or duty 2 : one who commits treason — **trai•tress** \ˈtrā-trəs\ *n*

trai·tor·ous \'trāt-ə-rəs, 'trā-trəs\ *adj* **1** : guilty or capable of treason **2** : constituting treason — **trai·tor·ous·ly** *adv*

tra·jec·to·ry \trə-'jek-t(ə-)rē\ *n, pl* **-ries** : the curve that a body (as a planet in its orbit, a projectile, or a rocket) describes in space

tram \'tram\ *n* : a cart or wagon running on rails (as in a mine)

tram·car \-ˌkär\ *n* : TRAM

¹tram·mel \'tram-əl\ *n* : something impeding activity, progress, or freedom : RESTRAINT — usu. used in pl.

²trammel *vt* **-meled** *or* **-melled**; **-mel·ing** *or* **-mel·ling** \'tram-(ə-)liŋ\ **1** : to catch or hold in or as if in a net : ENMESH **2** : to prevent or impede the free play of : CONFINE

¹tramp \'tramp, *1 & 2 are also* 'trämp\ *vb* **1** : to walk heavily **2** : to tread on forcibly and repeatedly : TRAMPLE **3 a** : to travel or wander through on foot **b** : to travel as a tramp

²tramp \'tramp, *3 is also* 'trämp\ *n* **1** : a begging or thieving vagrant **2** : a walking trip : HIKE **3** : the succession of sounds made by the beating of marching feet **4** : a ship not making regular trips but taking cargo to any port

¹tram·ple \'tram-pəl\ *vb* **tram·pled**; **tram·pling** \-p(ə-)liŋ\ **1** : to tramp or tread heavily so as to bruise, crush, or injure **2** : to tread on forcibly and repeatedly : TRAMPLE **3 a** : to travel or wander through on foot **b** : to travel as a tramp

²trample *n* : the act or sound of trampling

tram·po·line \ˌtram-pə-'lēn\ *n* : a resilient canvas sheet or web supported by springs in a metal frame used as a springboard

tram·way \'tram-ˌwā\ *n* : a road or way for trams

trance \'tran(t)s\ *n* **1** : a state of partly suspended animation or inability to function **2** : a somnolent state (as of deep hypnosis) **3** : a state of profound abstraction or absorption

tran·quil \'traŋ-kwəl, 'tran-\ *adj* **1 a** : free from agitation : SERENE **b** : free from disturbance or turmoil : QUIET **2** : STEADY, STABLE — **tran·quil·ly** \-kwə-lē\ *adv* — **tran·quil·ness** *n*

tran·quil·ize *or* **tran·quil·lize** \-kwə-ˌlīz\ *vb* : to make or become tranquil or relaxed; esp : to ease the mental tension and anxiety of usu. by means of drugs

tran·quil·iz·er \-ˌlī-zər\ *n* : one that tranquilizes; *esp* : a drug used to reduce anxiety and tension

tran·quil·li·ty *or* **tran·quil·i·ty** \tran-'kwil-ət-ē, traŋ-\ *n* : the quality or state of being tranquil

trans·act \tran(t)s-'akt, tranz-\ *vb* **1** : to carry through : bring about **2** : to carry on : CONDUCT — **trans·ac·tor** \-'ak-tər\ *n*

trans·ac·tion \-'ak-shən\ *n* **1** : an act, process, or instance of transacting **2 a** : something transacted; *esp* : a business deal **b** *pl* : the record of the meeting of a society : PROCEEDINGS — **trans·ac·tion·al** \-shnəl, -shən-ᵊl\ *adj*

trans·at·lan·tic \ˌtran(t)s-ət-'lant-ik, ˌtranz-\ *adj* : extending across or situated beyond the Atlantic ocean

tran·scend \tran-'send\ *vb* **1 a** : to rise above or go beyond the limits of : EXCEED **b** : to be prior to, beyond, and above (the universe or material existence) **2** : SURPASS

tran·scend·ence \-'sen-dən(t)s\ *n* : the quality or state of being transcendent

tran·scend·ent \-dənt\ *adj* **1** : exceeding usual limits : SURPASSING **2** : extending or lying beyond the limits of ordinary experience **3** : transcending the universe or material existence — **tran·scend·ent·ly** *adv*

tran·scen·den·tal \ˌtran-ˌsen-'dent-ᵊl, ˌtran(t)sən-\ *adj* **1** : TRANSCENDENT **2** : of or relating to transcendentalism — **tran·scen·den·tal·ly** \-ᵊl-ē\ *adv*

tran·scen·den·tal·ism \-ᵊl-ˌiz-əm\ *n* : a philosophy holding that ultimate reality is unknowable and asserting the primacy of the spiritual over the material and empirical — **tran·scen·den·tal·ist** \-ᵊl-əst\ *adj or n*

transcendental meditation *n* : a technique of meditation in which a mantra is chanted in order to foster calm, creativity, and spiritual well-being

trans·con·ti·nen·tal \ˌtran(t)s-ˌkänt-ᵊn-'ent-ᵊl\ *adj* **1** : extending or going across a continent **2** : situated on the farther side of a continent

tran·scribe \tran-'skrīb\ *vt* **1 a** : to make a written copy of **b** : to make a copy of (dictated or recorded matter) in longhand or on a typewriter **2 a** : to represent (speech sounds) by means of phonetic symbols **b** : to transfer (data) from one recording form to another **c** : to record (as on magnetic tape) for later broadcast **3** : to make a musical transcription of **4** : to broadcast recorded matter — **tran·scrib·er** *n*

tran·script \'tran-ˌskript\ *n* **1 a** : a written, printed, or typed copy **b** : an official copy (as of a student's educational record) **2** : a copy or rendering in an art form

tran·scrip·tion \tran-'skrip-shən\ *n* **1** : an act, process, or instance of transcribing **2** : COPY, TRANSCRIPT **3** : an arrangement of a musical composition for some instrument or voice other than the original — **tran·scrip·tion·al** \-shnəl, -shən-ᵊl\ *adj* — **tran·scrip·tion·al·ly** \-ē\ *adv*

tran·sept \'tran-ˌsept\ *n* : the part forming the arms of a cross-shaped church

¹trans·fer \tran(t)s-'fər, 'tran(t)s-ˌ\ *vb* **trans·ferred**; **trans·fer·ring** **1 a** : to convey from one person, place, or situation to another : TRANSPORT **b** : to cause to pass from one to another : TRANSMIT **2** : to make over the possession or ownership of : CONVEY **3** : to print or otherwise copy from one surface to another by contact **4** : to move to a different place, region, or situation; *esp* : to withdraw from one educational institution to enroll at another **5** : to change from one vehicle or transportation line to another — **trans·fer·a·bil·i·ty** \(ˌ)tran(t)s-ˌfər-ə-'bil-ət-ē\ *n* — **trans·fer·a·ble** \tran(t)s-'fər-ə-bəl\ *adj* — **trans·fer·al** \-'fər-əl\ *n* — **trans·fer·rer** *or* **trans·fer·or** \-'fər-ər\ *n*

²trans·fer \'tran(t)s-ˌfər\ *n* **1** : conveyance of right, title, or interest in real or personal property from one person to another **2** : an act, process, or instance of transferring : TRANSFERENCE **3** : one that transfers or is transferred **4** : a place where a transfer is made (as of trains to ferries) **5** : a ticket entitling a passenger on a public conveyance to continue his journey on another route

trans·fer·ence \tran(t)s-'fər-ən(t)s\ *n* : an act, process, or instance of transferring : TRANSFER

trans·fig·u·ra·tion \(ˌ)tran(t)s-ˌfig-(y)ə-'rā-shən\ *n* : a change of form or appearance; *esp* : a glorifying or exalting change

trans·fig·ure \tran(t)s-'fig-yər\ *vt* **1** : to change the form or appearance of : METAMORPHOSE **2** : EXALT, GLORIFY

trans·fix \tran(t)s-'fiks\ *vt* **1** : to pierce through with or as if with a pointed weapon : IMPALE **2** : to hold motionless by or as if by piercing — **trans·fix·ion** \-'fik-shən\ *n*

trans·form \tran(t)s-'fȯrm\ *vb* **1 a** : to change in composition, structure, or character : CONVERT **b** : to change in outward appearance **2** : to change (a current) in potential (as from high voltage to low) or in type — **trans·form·a·tive** \-'fȯr-mət-iv\ *adj* — **trans·form·er** *n*

trans·for·ma·tion \ˌtran(t)s-fər-'mā-shən\ *n* : an act, process, or instance of transforming or being transformed

trans·fuse \tran(t)s-'fyüz\ *vt* **1 a** : to cause to pass from one to another : TRANSMIT **b** : to diffuse into or through : PERMEATE **2 a** : to transfer (as blood or saline) into a vein of a man or animal **b** : to subject (a patient) to transfusion — **trans·fus·i·ble** *or* **trans·fus·a·ble** \-'fyü-zə-bəl\ *adj* — **trans·fu·sion** \-'fyü-zhən\ *n*

trans·gress \tran(t)s-'gres, tranz-\ *vb* **1** : to go beyond limits set by : VIOLATE **2** : to pass beyond or go over a limit or boundary **3** : to violate a command or law : SIN — **trans·gres·sor** \-'gres-ər\ *n*

trans·gres·sion \-'gresh-ən\ *n* : an act, process, or instance of transgressing; *esp* : violation of a law, command, or duty

tran·sience \'tran-chən(t)s\ *n* : the quality or state of being transient

[1]**tran·sient** \-chənt\ *adj* **1** : not lasting or staying long **2** : changing in form or appearance : SHIFTING — **tran·sient·ly** *adv*
[2]**transient** *n* : one that is transient
tran·sis·tor \tran-ˈzis-tər, -ˈsis-\ *n* **1** : an electronic device similar to the electron tube in use (as amplification and rectification) consisting of a small block of a semiconductor that has at least three electrodes **2** : a transistorized radio
tran·sis·tor·ize \-tə-ˌrīz\ *vt* : to equip with transistors
tran·sit \ˈtran(t)s-ət, ˈtranz-\ *n* **1 a** : an act, process, or instance of passing through or over : PASSAGE **b** (1) : conveyance of persons or things from one place to another (2) : local transportation of people by public conveyance or a system of such transportation **2** : a surveyor's instrument for measuring angles
tran·si·tion \tran(t)s-ˈish-ən, tranz-\ *n* : a passing from one state, stage, place, or subject to another : CHANGE — **tran·si·tion·al** \-ˈish-nəl, -ən-ᵊl\ *adj*
tran·si·tive \ˈtran(t)s-ət-iv, ˈtranz-\ *adj* **1** : having or containing an object required to complete its meaning **2** : TRANSITIONAL — **tran·si·tive·ly** *adv* — **tran·si·tive·ness** *n* — **tran·si·tiv·i·ty** \ˌtran(t)s-ə-ˈtiv-ət-ē, ˌtranz-\ *n*
tran·si·to·ry \ˈtran(t)s-ə-ˌtōr-ē, ˈtranz-\ *adj* : lasting only a short time : SHORT-LIVED, TEMPORARY
trans·late \tran(t)s-ˈlāt, tranz-\ *vb* **1 a** : to bear or change from one place, state, form, or appearance to another : TRANSFER, TRANSFORM **b** : to convey to heaven or to a nontemporal condition without death **2 a** : to turn from one language into another **b** : to transfer or turn from one set of symbols into another : TRANSCRIBE **c** : PARAPHRASE, EXPLAIN — **trans·lat·a·bil·i·ty** \-ˌlāt-ə-ˈbil-ət-ē\ *n* — **trans·lat·a·ble** *adj* — **trans·la·tor** \-ˈlāt-ər\ *n*
trans·la·tion \tran(t)s-ˈlā-shən, tranz-\ *n* : an act, process, or instance of translating: as **a** : a rendering from one language into another; *also* : the product of such a rendering **b** : TRANSFORMATION — **trans·la·tion·al** \-shnəl, -shən-ᵊl\ *adj*
trans·lit·er·ate \tran(t)s-ˈlit-ə-ˌrāt, tranz-\ *vt* : to represent or spell in the characters of another alphabet — **trans·lit·er·a·tion** \-ˌlit-ə-ˈrā-shən\ *n*
trans·lu·cence \tran(t)s-ˈlüs-ᵊn(t)s, tranz-\ *or* **trans·lu·cen·cy** \-ᵊn-sē\ *n* : the quality or state of being translucent
trans·lu·cent \-ᵊnt\ *adj* : admitting and diffusing light so that objects beyond cannot be clearly distinguished — **trans·lu·cent·ly** *adv*
trans·mi·gra·tion \ˌtran(t)s-ˌmī-ˈgrā-shən, ˌtranz-\ *n* **1** : the changing of one's home from one country to another : MIGRATION **2** : the passing of a soul into another body after death — **trans·mi·grate** \tran(t)s-ˈmī-ˌgrāt, tranz-\ *vi*
trans·mis·si·ble \tran(t)s-ˈmis-ə-bəl, tranz-\ *adj* : capable of being transmitted — **trans·mis·si·bil·i·ty** \-ˌmis-ə-ˈbil-ət-ē\ *n*
trans·mis·sion \-ˈmish-ən\ *n* **1** : an act, process, or instance of transmitting **2** : the passage of radio waves in the space between transmitting and receiving stations **3** : the gears by which power is transmitted from an automobile engine to the live axle **4** : something transmitted
trans·mit \tran(t)s-ˈmit, tranz-\ *vb* **trans·mit·ted**; **trans·mit·ting** **1 a** : to send or transfer from one person or place to another : FORWARD **b** : to convey by or as if by inheritance **2 a** : to cause (as light or force) to pass or be conveyed through space or a medium **b** : to send out a signal either by radio waves or over a wire — **trans·mit·ta·ble** *adj* — **trans·mit·tal** \-ˈmit-ᵊl\ *n*
trans·mit·ter \-ˈmit-ər\ *n* **1** : one that transmits **2** : the part of a telephone into which one speaks **3** : the apparatus that sends out radio or television signals or the building in which it is housed
trans·mu·ta·tion \ˌtran(t)s-myu̇-ˈtā-shən, ˌtranz-\ *n* : an act or instance of transmuting or being transmuted
trans·mute \tran(t)s-ˈmyüt, tranz-\ *vb* : to change or alter in form, appearance, or nature : CONVERT — **trans·mut·a·ble** *adj*
trans·oce·an·ic \(ˌ)tran(t)s-ˌō-shē-ˈan-ik, (ˌ)tranz-\ *adj* **1** : lying or dwelling beyond the ocean **2** : crossing or extending across the ocean
tran·som \ˈtran(t)-səm\ *n* **1** : a transverse piece in a structure : CROSSPIECE; *esp* : a horizontal crossbar in a window, over a door, or between a door and a window or fanlight above it **2** : a window above a door or other window built on and commonly hinged to a transom
tran·son·ic \tran-ˈsän-ik\ *adj* : being or relating to a speed approximating the speed of sound in air
trans·pa·cif·ic \ˌtran(t)s-pə-ˈsif-ik\ *adj* : crossing or extending across or situated beyond the Pacific ocean
trans·par·en·cy \tran(t)s-ˈpar-ən-sē\ *n*, *pl* **-cies** **1** : the quality or state of being transparent **2** : a picture or design on glass, thin cloth, paper, or film viewed by light shining through it or by projection
trans·par·ent \-ənt\ *adj* **1 a** : having the property of transmitting light so that bodies lying beyond are entirely visible **b** : fine or sheer enough to be seen through **2 a** : FRANK, GUILELESS **b** : easily detected or seen through : OBVIOUS — **trans·par·ent·ly** *adv* — **trans·par·ent·ness** *n*
tran·spi·ra·tion \ˌtran(t)s-pə-ˈrā-shən\ *n* : the act or process or an instance of transpiring; *esp* : the passage of watery vapor from a living body through a membrane or pores
tran·spire \tran(t)s-ˈpī(ə)r\ *vb* **1** : to pass off or give passage to (a fluid) through pores or interstices; *esp* : to excrete watery vapor through a membrane or pores **2** : to become known or apparent : come to light **3** : to come to pass : OCCUR
[1]**trans·plant** \tran(t)s-ˈplant\ *vb* **1** : to lift and reset (a plant) in another soil or situation **2** : to remove from one place and settle or introduce elsewhere : TRANSPORT **3** : to transfer (an organ or tissue) from one part or individual to another **4** : to admit of being transplanted — **trans·plant·a·ble** *adj* — **trans·plan·ta·tion** \ˌtran(t)s-ˌplan-ˈtā-shən\ *n* — **trans·plant·er** *n*
[2]**trans·plant** \ˈtran(t)s-ˌplant\ *n* **1** : the act or process of transplanting **2** : something transplanted
[1]**trans·port** \tran(t)s-ˈpōrt\ *vt* **1** : to convey from one place to another : CARRY **2** : ENRAPTURE **3** : to send to a penal colony overseas — **trans·port·a·ble** *adj* — **trans·port·er** *n*
[2]**trans·port** \ˈtran(t)s-ˌpōrt\ *n* **1** : the act of transporting : TRANSPORTATION **2** : strong or intensely pleasurable emotion : ECSTASY, RAPTURE **3 a** : a ship for carrying soldiers or military equipment **b** : a vehicle (as a truck or plane) used to transport persons or goods
trans·por·ta·tion \ˌtran(t)s-pər-ˈtā-shən\ *n* **1** : an act, process, or instance of transporting or being transported **2 a** : means of conveyance or travel from one place to another **b** : public conveyance of passengers or goods esp. as a commercial enterprise
trans·pose \tran(t)s-ˈpōz\ *vt* **1** : TRANSFORM, TRANSMUTE **2** : TRANSLATE **3** : to transfer from one place or period to another : SHIFT **4** : to change the relative place or normal order of : alter the sequence of **5** : to write or perform (a musical composition) in a different key — **trans·po·si·tion** \ˌtran(t)s-pə-ˈzish-ən\ *n*
trans·ship \tran-ˈship, tran(t)s-\ *vb* : to transfer for further transportation from one ship or conveyance to another — **trans·ship·ment** *n*
tran·sub·stan·ti·a·tion \ˌtran(t)-səb-ˌstan-chē-ˈā-shən\ *n* : the change in the consecrated bread and wine at Mass in substance but not in appearance to the body and blood of Christ
[1]**trans·verse** \tran(t)s-ˈvərs, tranz-ˈ, ˈtran(t)s-ˌ, ˈtranz-ˌ\ *adj* : lying or being across : set crosswise — **trans·verse·ly** *adv*
[2]**trans·verse** \ˈtran(t)s-ˌvərs, ˈtranz-\ *n* : something transverse
[1]**trap** \ˈtrap\ *n* **1** : a device (as a snare or pitfall) for catching animals; *esp* : one that holds by springing shut suddenly **2** : something by which one is caught or stopped unawares **3 a** : a device for hurling clay pigeons into the air **b** : a hazard

on a golf course consisting of a depression containing sand **4** : a light usu. one-horse carriage with springs **5** : any of various devices for preventing passage of something often while allowing other matter to proceed

²trap *vb* **trapped**; **trap·ping** **1 a** : to catch in or as if in a trap : ENSNARE **b** : to place in a restricted position : CONFINE **2** : to provide with a trap **3** : to engage in trapping animals (as for fur) — **trap·per** *n*

³trap *n* : any of various dark-colored fine-grained igneous rocks used esp. in road making

trap·door \'trap-'dō(ə)r\ *n* : a lifting or sliding door covering an opening in a roof, ceiling, or floor

tra·peze \tra-'pēz\ *n* : a gymnastic or acrobatic apparatus consisting of a short horizontal bar suspended at a height by two parallel ropes

trap·e·zoid \'trap-ə-ˌzȯid\ *n* : a quadrilateral having only two sides parallel

trap·ping \'trap-iŋ\ *n* **1** : CAPARISON 1 — usu. used in pl. **2** *pl* : outward decoration or dress : ORNAMENTS

trap·shoot·ing \'trap-ˌshüt-iŋ\ *n* : shooting at clay pigeons sprung into the air from a trap — **trap·shoot·er** *n*

trash \'trash\ *n* **1** : something worth little or nothing: as **a** : JUNK, RUBBISH **b** : NONSENSE **c** : inferior or worthless artistic matter **2** : a worthless person; *also* : RIFFRAFF

trashy \'trash-ē\ *adj* : resembling trash : WORTHLESS

trau·ma \'trau̇-mə, 'trȯ-\ *n, pl* **trau·ma·ta** \-mət-ə\ *or* **traumas** **1** : a bodily or mental injury usu. caused by an external agent **2** : a cause of trauma — **trau·mat·ic** \trə-'mat-ik, trȯ-, trau̇-\ *adj* — **trau·mat·i·cal·ly** \-'mat-i-k(ə-)lē\ *adv*

¹tra·vail \trə-'vāl, 'trav-ˌāl\ *n* **1 a** : work esp. of a painful or laborious nature : TOIL **b** : a piece of work : TASK **c** : AGONY, TORMENT **2** : LABOR, PARTURITION

²travail *vi* : to labor hard : TOIL

¹trav·el \'trav-əl\ *vb* **-eled** *or* **-elled**; **-el·ing** *or* **-el·ling** \'trav-(ə-)liŋ\ **1** : to journey from place to place or to a distant place **2** : to journey from place to place selling or taking orders **3 a** : to move or advance from one place to another **b** : to undergo transportation **4** : to journey through or over

²travel *n* **1 a** : the act of traveling : PASSAGE **b** : JOURNEY, TRIP — often used in pl. **2** *pl* : an account of one's travels **3** : the number traveling : TRAFFIC **4 a** : MOVEMENT, PROGRESSION **b** : the motion of a piece of machinery; *esp* : reciprocating motion

trav·eled *or* **trav·elled** \'trav-əld\ *adj* **1** : experienced in travel **2** : used by travelers

trav·el·er *or* **trav·el·ler** \'trav-(ə-)lər\ *n* : one that travels

trav·el·ing bag \'trav-(ə-)liŋ-\ *n* : a bag carried by hand and designed to hold a traveler's clothing and personal articles

trav·el·ogue \'trav-ə-ˌlȯg\ *n* : a usu. illustrated lecture on travel

¹trav·erse \'trav-ərs\ *n* **1** : something that crosses or lies across **2** : OBSTACLE, ADVERSITY

²tra·verse \trə-'vərs\ *vb* **1** : to go against or act in opposition to : OPPOSE, THWART **2** : to pass through, across, or over **3** : to make a study of : EXAMINE **4** : to ascend, descend, or cross (a slope or gap) at an angle **5** : to move back and forth or from side to side **6** : to move or turn laterally : SWIVEL — **tra·vers·a·ble** *adj* — **tra·vers·er** *n*

³trav·erse \'trav-(ˌ)ərs, trə-'vərs\ *adj* : TRANSVERSE

trav·er·tine \'trav-ər-ˌtēn\ *n* : a crystalline mineral formed by deposition from spring waters

¹trav·es·ty \'trav-ə-stē\ *n, pl* **-ties** : a burlesque and usu. grotesque translation or imitation

²travesty *vt* **-tied**; **-ty·ing** : to make a travesty of : PARODY

¹trawl \'trȯl\ *vb* : to fish or catch with a trawl — **trawl·er** *n*

²trawl *n* : a large conical net dragged along the sea bottom in fishing

tray \'trā\ *n* : an open receptacle with flat bottom and low rim for holding, carrying, or exhibiting articles

treach·er·ous \'trech-(ə-)rəs\ *adj* **1** : guilty of or inclined to treachery **2 a** : UNRELIABLE **b** : giving a false appearance of safety — **treach·er·ous·ly** *adv* — **treach·er·ous·ness** *n*

treach·ery \'trech-(ə-)rē\ *n, pl* **-er·ies** **1** : violation of allegiance or of faith and confidence **2** : an act of perfidy or treason

¹tread \'tred\ *vb* **trod** \'träd\; **trod·den** \'träd-ᵊn\ *or* **trod**; **tread·ing** **1 a** : to step or walk on or over **b** : to walk along : FOLLOW **2 a** : to beat or press with the feet : TRAMPLE **b** : to subdue or repress as if by trampling : CRUSH **3 a** : to form by treading : BEAT **b** : to execute by stepping or dancing **4 a** : to set foot **b** : to put one's foot : STEP — **tread·er** *n*

²tread *n* **1** : a mark made by or as if by treading **2** : the action, manner, or sound of treading or stepping **3 a** : the part of a sole that touches the ground **b** : the part of a thing on which it runs **4** : the horizontal part of a step

trea·dle \'tred-ᵊl\ *n* : a lever or other device pressed by the foot to drive a machine

tread·mill \'tred-ˌmil\ *n* **1** : a device moved by persons treading on steps set around the rim of a wide wheel or by animals walking on an endless belt **2** : a wearisome routine

trea·son \'trēz-ᵊn\ *n* : the offense of attempting by overt acts to overthrow the government of the state to which one owes allegiance or to bring about its defeat in war

trea·son·a·ble \'trēz-nə-bəl, -ᵊn-ə-bəl\ *adj* : relating to, consisting of, or involving treason — **trea·son·a·bly** \-blē\ *adv*

trea·son·ous \'trēz-nəs, -ᵊn-əs\ *adj* : TREASONABLE

¹trea·sure \'trezh-ər\ *n* **1 a** (1) : wealth (as money, jewels, or precious metals) stored up or hoarded (2) : RICHES **b** : a store of money in reserve **2** : something of great worth or value; *also* : a person esteemed as rare or precious

²treasure *vt* **trea·sured**; **trea·sur·ing** \-(ə-)riŋ\ **1** : to collect and store up (something of value) for future use : HOARD **2** : to hold or keep as precious : CHERISH

trea·sur·er \'trezh-rər, 'trezh-ər-ər\ *n* : a person trusted with charge of a treasure or a treasury; *esp* : an officer of a club, business, or government who has charge of money taken in and paid out

treasure trove \'trezh-ər-ˌtrōv\ *n* **1** : treasure found buried in the ground or hidden away and of unknown ownership **2** : a discovery or something discovered that is full of things to be treasured

trea·sury \'trezh-(ə-)rē\ *n, pl* **trea·sur·ies** **1 a** : a place in which stores of wealth are kept **b** : the place of deposit and disbursement of collected funds; *esp* : one where public revenues are deposited, kept, and disbursed **c** : funds kept in a place of deposit **2** *cap* : a governmental department in charge of finances

¹treat \'trēt\ *vb* **1** : to discuss terms of accommodation or settlement : NEGOTIATE **2 a** : to deal with a matter esp. in writing : DISCOURSE **b** : to present or represent artistically **c** : to deal with : HANDLE **3 a** : to bear the expense of another's entertainment **b** : to provide with free food, entertainment, or enjoyment **4 a** : to behave or act toward : USE **b** : to regard and deal with in a specified manner **5** : to care for or deal with medically or surgically **6** : to subject to some action (as of a chemical) — **treat·er** *n*

²treat *n* **1** : an entertainment given without expense to those invited **2** : an esp. unexpected source of pleasure or amusement

trea·tise \'trēt-əs\ *n* : a book or an article treating a subject systematically

treat·ment \'trēt-mənt\ *n* **1** : the act or manner or an instance of treating someone or something : HANDLING, USAGE **2** : a substance or technique used in treating

trea·ty \'trēt-ē\ *n, pl* **treaties** **1** : the action of treating and esp. of negotiating **2** : an agreement or arrangement made by negotiation; *esp* : a contract between two or more states

[1]tre·ble \'treb-əl\ *n* **1** : the highest of the four voice parts in vocal music : SOPRANO **2** : a high-pitched or shrill voice, tone, or sound **3** : the upper half of the musical pitch range

[2]treble *adj* **1 a** : having three parts **b** : triple in number or amount **2 a** : relating to or having the range of a musical treble **b** : high-pitched : SHRILL — **tre·bly** \'treb-(ə-)lē\ *adv*

[3]treble *vb* **tre·bled**; **tre·bling** \'treb-(ə-)liŋ\ : to make or become three times the size, amount, or number

[1]tree \'trē\ *n* **1** : a woody perennial plant having a single usu. tall main stem with few or no branches on its lower part **2** : a piece of wood usu. adapted to a particular use **3** : something in the form of or felt to resemble a tree — **tree·less** \-ləs\ *adj* — **tree·like** *adj*

[2]tree *vt* **treed**; **tree·ing** **1 a** : to drive to or up a tree **b** : to bring to bay : CORNER **2** : to furnish or fit with a tree

tre·foil \'trē-ˌfȯil\ *n* **1** : CLOVER; *also* : any of several leguminous herbs having leaves with three leaflets **2** : an ornament or symbol with three leaflike parts

[1]trek \'trek\ *n* : a slow or difficult journey or migration

[2]trek *vi* **trekked**; **trek·king** : to make one's way arduously — **trek·ker** *n*

[1]trel·lis \'trel-əs\ *n* : a frame of latticework used esp. as a screen or a support for climbing plants

[2]trellis *vt* **1** : to provide with or train on a trellis **2** : to cross or interlace on or through : INTERWEAVE

[1]trem·ble \'trem-bəl\ *vi* **trem·bled**; **trem·bling** \-b(ə-)liŋ\ **1** : to shake involuntarily (as with fear or cold) : SHIVER **2** : to move, sound, pass, or come to pass as if shaken or tremulous **3** : to be affected with fear or doubt — **trem·bler** \-b(ə-)lər\ *n*

[2]tremble *n* **1** : a fit or spell of involuntary shaking or quivering **2** : a tremor or series of tremors

trem·bly \'trem-b(ə-)lē\ *adj* : TREMBLING, TREMULOUS

tre·men·dous \tri-'men-dəs\ *adj* **1** : such as may excite trembling or arouse dread, awe, or terror : DREADFUL **2** : astonishing by reason of extreme size, power, greatness, or excellence — **tre·men·dous·ly** *adv* — **tre·men·dous·ness** *n*

trem·o·lo \'trem-ə-ˌlō\ *n, pl* **-los** : a rapid fluttering of a musical tone or alternating tones to produce a tremulous effect

trem·or \'trem-ər\ *n* **1** : a trembling or shaking usu. from weakness or disease **2** : a quivering or vibratory motion (as of the earth or a leaf) **3** : a feeling of uncertainty or insecurity

trem·u·lant \'trem-yə-lənt\ *adj* : TREMULOUS, TREMBLING

trem·u·lous \'trem-yə-ləs\ *adj* **1** : characterized by or affected with trembling or tremors **2** : affected with timidity : TIMOROUS **3** : such as is caused by a tremulous state **4** : exceedingly sensitive — **trem·u·lous·ly** *adv* — **trem·u·lous·ness** *n*

[1]trench \'trench\ *n* **1** : a long narrow cut in land : DITCH; *also* : a similar depression in an ocean floor **2** : a long ditch protected by a bank of earth thrown before it that is used to shelter soldiers

[2]trench *vb* **1** : to protect with or as if with a trench **2** : to cut a trench in **3** : to come close : VERGE

trench·ant \'tren-chənt\ *adj* **1** : having a sharp edge or point : CUTTING **2** : sharply clear : PENETRATING **3** : mentally energetic — **trench·ant·ly** *adv*

trench·er \'tren-chər\ *n* : a wooden platter for serving food

trench·er·man \-mən\ *n* : a hearty eater

[1]trend \'trend\ *vi* **1 a** : to extend in a general direction **b** : to veer in a new direction : BEND **2 a** : to show a tendency : INCLINE **b** : SHIFT

[2]trend *n* **1** : general direction taken **2 a** : a prevailing tendency or inclination : DRIFT **b** : a general movement : SWING **c** : a current style or preference **d** : a line of development

tre·pan \tri-'pan\ *vt* **tre·panned**; **tre·pan·ning** : to remove a disk from (the skull) — **trep·a·na·tion** \ˌtrep-ə-'nā-shən\ *n*

trep·i·da·tion \ˌtrep-ə-'dā-shən\ *n* : a state of alarm : FEAR

[1]tres·pass \'tres-pəs, -ˌpas\ *n* **1** : a violation of morals : TRANSGRESSION; *esp* : SIN **2** : wrongful entry on real property

[2]trespass *vi* **1** : ERR, SIN **2** : to commit a trespass; *esp* : to enter unlawfully upon the land of another — **tres·pass·er** *n*

tress \'tres\ *n* **1** : a long lock of hair **2** *pl* : the long unbound hair of a woman

tres·tle \'tres-əl\ *n* **1** : a braced frame consisting usu. of a horizontal piece with spreading legs at each end that supports something (as a tabletop or drawing board) **2** : a braced framework of timbers or steel for carrying a road or railroad over a depression

trey \'trā\ *n, pl* **treys** : a card or dice with three spots

tri·ad \'trī-ˌad, -əd\ *n* : a union or group of three usu. closely related persons or things

[1]tri·al \'trī(-ə)l\ *n* **1** : the action or process of trying or putting to the proof : TEST **2** : formal examination before a competent tribunal of the matter in issue in a civil or criminal case **3** : a test of faith, patience, or stamina **4** : a temporary use or experiment to test quality, value, or usefulness **5** : ATTEMPT, EFFORT

[2]trial *adj* **1** : of, relating to, or used in a trial **2** : made or done as a test or experiment **3** : used or tried out in a test

tri·an·gle \'trī-ˌaŋ-gəl\ *n* : a polygon having three sides

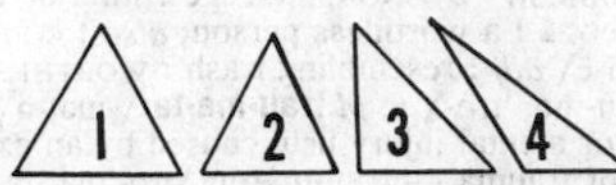

triangles: *1* equilateral, *2* isosceles, *3* right-angled, *4* obtuse

tri·an·gu·lar \trī-'aŋ-gyə-lər\ *adj* **1 a** : of, relating to, or having the form of a triangle **b** : having a triangular base or principal surface **2** : of, relating to, or involving three parts or persons — **tri·an·gu·lar·i·ty** \(ˌ)trī-ˌaŋ-gyə-'lar-ət-ē\ *n* — **tri·an·gu·lar·ly** *adv*

tri·an·gu·late \trī-'aŋ-gyə-ˌlāt\ *vt* **1** : to divide into triangles **2** : to survey, map, or determine by triangulation

tri·an·gu·la·tion \(ˌ)trī-ˌaŋ-gyə-'lā-shən\ *n* : the measurement of the elements necessary to determine the network of triangles into which any part of the earth's surface is divided in surveying

trib·al \'trī-bəl\ *adj* : of, relating to, or characteristic of a tribe — **trib·al·ly** *adv*

tribe \'trīb\ *n* **1** : a usu. primitive social group comprising numerous families, clans, or generations **2** : a group of persons having a common character, occupation, or interest **3** : a group of related plants or animals

tribes·man \'trībz-mən\ *n* : a member of a tribe

trib·u·la·tion \ˌtrib-yə-'lā-shən\ *n* : distress or suffering resulting from oppression, persecution, or affliction; *also* : a trying experience

tri·bun·al \trī-'byün-ᵊl, trib-'yün-\ *n* **1** : the seat of a judge **2** : a court of justice **3** : something that decides or determines

trib·une \'trib-ˌyün, trib-'yün\ *n* **1** : an official in ancient Rome with the function of protecting the plebeian citizen from arbitrary action by patrician magistrates **2** : a defender of the people — **trib·une·ship** \-ˌship\ *n*

[1]trib·u·tary \'trib-yə-ˌter-ē\ *adj* **1** : paying tribute to another : SUBJECT **2** : paid or owed as tribute **3** : CONTRIBUTORY **4** : flowing into a larger stream or a lake

[2]tributary *n, pl* **-tar·ies** **1** : a ruler or state that pays tribute **2** : a stream feeding a larger stream or a lake

trib·ute \'trib-ˌyüt, -yət\ *n* **1 a** : a payment made by one ruler or nation to another to show submission or to secure peace or protection **b** : a tax to raise money for this payment **2** : a gift or service showing respect, gratitude, or affection; *esp* : PRAISE, CREDIT

trice \'trīs\ *n* : a brief space of time : INSTANT — used chiefly in the phrase *in a trice*

tri·ceps \'trī-ˌseps\ *n, pl* **tri·ceps·es** : a 3-headed muscle along the back of the upper arm

tri·chi·na \trə-'kī-nə\ *n, pl* **-nae** \-(ˌ)nē\ : a small slender worm that in the larval state is parasitic in the muscles of flesh-eating mammals (as man and hog)

trich·i·no·sis \ˌtrik-ə-'nō-səs\ *n, pl* **-no·ses** \-'nō-ˌsēz\ : a disease caused by trichinae and marked esp. by muscular pain, fever, and swelling

¹trick \'trik\ *n* **1 a** : a crafty procedure or practice meant to deceive or defraud **b** : a mischievous act : PRANK **c** : an indiscreet or childish action **d** : a dexterous or ingenious feat designed to puzzle or amuse **2 a** : an habitual peculiarity of behavior or manner **b** : a characteristic and identifying feature **c** : an optical illusion **3 a** : a quick or artful way of getting a result : KNACK **b** : a technical device (as of an art or craft) **4** : the cards played in one round of a card game **5** : a tour of duty : SHIFT

²trick *adj* **1** : of or relating to or involving tricks or trickery **2** : TRIG **3** : somewhat defective and unreliable

³trick *vt* **1** : to deceive by cunning or artifice : CHEAT **2** : to dress or adorn esp. fancifully or ornately

trick·ery \'trik-(ə-)rē\ *n, pl* **-er·ies** : the use of tricks to deceive or defraud

¹trick·le \'trik-əl\ *vi* **trick·led**; **trick·ling** \'trik-(ə-)liŋ\ **1** : to issue or fall in drops **2** : to flow in a thin gentle stream

²trickle *n* : a trickling stream : DRIBBLE, DRIP

trick·ster \'trik-stər\ *n* : one who tricks or cheats

tricky \'trik-ē\ *adj* **1** : of or characteristic of a trickster : SLY **2** : requiring skill, aptitude, or caution **3** : TRICK 3 — **trick·i·ness** *n*

¹tri·col·or \'trī-ˌkəl-ər\ *n* : a flag of three colors

²tricolor *or* **tri·col·ored** \'trī-ˌkəl-ərd\ *adj* : having or using three colors

tri·cor·nered \'trī-'kȯr-nərd\ *adj* : having three corners

tri·cot \'trē-kō, 'trī-kət\ *n* **1** : a plain warp-knitted fabric (as for underwear) of nylon, wool, rayon, silk, or cotton **2** : a twilled clothing fabric of wool or wool and cotton

tri·cus·pid \(')trī-'kəs-pəd\ *n* : a tooth having three cusps

tri·cy·cle \'trī-ˌsik-əl\ *n* : a 3-wheeled vehicle propelled by pedals, hand levers, or a motor

tri·dent \'trīd-ᵊnt\ *n* : a 3-pronged spear

tried \'trīd\ *adj* : found good, faithful, or trustworthy through experience or testing

tri·en·ni·al \(')trī-'en-ē-əl\ *adj* **1** : consisting of or lasting for three years **2** : occurring or being done every three years — **triennial** *n* — **tri·en·ni·al·ly** \-ē-ə-lē\ *adv*

tri·en·ni·um \trī-'en-ē-əm\ *n, pl* **-ni·ums** *or* **-nia** \-ē-ə\ : a period of three years

tri·er \'trī(-ə)r\ *n* : someone or something that tries

¹tri·fle \'trī-fəl\ *n* : something of little value or importance; *esp* : an insignificant amount (as of money)

²trifle *vb* **tri·fled**; **tri·fling** \-f(ə-)liŋ\ **1 a** : to talk in a jesting or mocking manner with intent to delude or mislead **b** : to act heedlessly or frivolously : PLAY **2** : to waste time : DALLY **3** : to spend or waste in trifling or on trifles **4** : to handle something idly : TOY — **tri·fler** \-f(ə-)lər\ *n*

tri·fling \'trī-fliŋ\ *adj* : lacking in significance or solid worth: as **a** : FRIVOLOUS **b** : TRIVIAL

¹tri·fo·cal \(')trī-'fō-kəl\ *adj* : having three focal lengths

²trifocal *n* : a trifocal glass or lens

trig \'trig\ *adj* : stylishly trim : SMART, NEAT

¹trig·ger \'trig-ər\ *n* : the part of the lock of a firearm that releases the hammer and so fires the gun

²trigger *vb* **trig·gered**; **trig·ger·ing** \'trig-(ə-)riŋ\ **1** : to fire by pulling a mechanical trigger **2** : to initiate, actuate, or set in motion as if by pulling a trigger

trig·o·no·met·ric \ˌtrig-ə-nə-'me-trik\ *adj* : of, relating to, or in accordance with trigonometry — **trig·o·no·met·ri·cal** \-tri-kəl\ *adj* — **trig·o·no·met·ri·cal·ly** \-tri-k(ə-)lē\ *adv*

trig·o·nom·e·try \ˌtrig-ə-'näm-ə-trē\ *n* : the study of the properties of triangles and trigonometric functions and of their applications

¹trill \'tril\ *n* **1** : the alternation of two musical tones a scale degree apart **2** : a sound felt to resemble a musical trill : WARBLE **3** : the rapid vibration of one speech organ against another (as of the tip of the tongue against the ridge of the teeth); *also* : a speech sound so made

²trill *vb* **1** : to utter as or with a trill **2** : to play or sing with a trill : QUAVER — **trill·er** *n*

tril·o·gy \'tril-ə-jē\ *n, pl* **-gies** : a series of three dramas or sometimes three literary or musical compositions that although each is in one sense complete are closely related and develop a single theme

¹trim \'trim\ *vb* **trimmed**; **trim·ming** **1 a** : to embellish with ribbons, lace, or ornaments : ADORN **b** : to arrange a display of goods in (a shop window) **2 a** : to administer a beating to : THRASH; *also* : to defeat resoundingly **b** : to worst in a bargain **3 a** : to make trim and neat esp. by cutting or clipping **b** : to free of excess or extraneous matter by or as if by cutting **4 a** : to cause (a ship or boat) to assume a desirable position in the water by arrangement of ballast, cargo, or passengers; *also* : to adjust (as an airplane, blimp, or submarine) for horizontal movement or for motion upward or downward **b** : to adjust (as a sail) to a desired position **5 a** : to maintain neutrality between opposing parties **b** : to change one's views for reasons of expediency

²trim *adj* : neat, orderly, and compact in line or structure — **trim·ly** *adv* — **trim·ness** *n*

³trim *adv* : TRIMLY

⁴trim *n* **1 a** : the readiness of a ship for sailing **b** : the readiness of a person or thing for action or use : FITNESS **2 a** : material used for ornament or trimming **b** : the woodwork in the finish of a building esp. around openings **3** : the position of a ship in the water **4** : something that is trimmed off

tri·mes·ter \(')trī-'mes-tər, 'trī-ˌ\ *n* **1** : a period of three or about three months **2** : one of three terms into which an academic year is sometimes divided

trim·e·ter \'trim-ət-ər\ *n* : a line consisting of three metrical feet

trim·mer \'trim-ər\ *n* **1 a** : one that trims articles **b** : an instrument or machine with which trimming is done **2** : a beam that holds the end of a header in floor framing **3** : a person who modifies his opinions out of expediency

trim·ming \'trim-iŋ\ *n* **1** : the action of one that trims **2** : BEATING, DEFEAT **3** : something that trims, ornaments, or completes **4** *pl* : parts removed by trimming

tri·month·ly \(')trī-'mən(t)th-lē\ *adj* : occurring every three months

trine \'trīn\ *adj* : THREEFOLD, TRIPLE

trin·i·tar·i·an \ˌtrin-ə-'ter-ē-ən\ *adj* **1** *cap* : of or relating to the Trinity, the doctrine of the Trinity, or adherents to that doctrine **2** : having three parts or aspects

Trinitarian *n* : one who subscribes to the doctrine of the Trinity — **Trin·i·tar·i·an·ism** \-ē-ə-ˌniz-əm\ *n*

Trin·i·ty \'trin-ət-ē\ *n, pl* **-ties** **1** : the unity of Father, Son, and Holy Spirit as three persons in one Godhead **2** *not cap* : TRIAD

trin·ket \'triŋ-kət\ *n* **1** : a small ornament (as a jewel or ring) **2** : a thing of little value : TRIFLE

trio \'trē-ō\ *n, pl* **tri·os** **1 a** : a musical composition for three voices or three instruments **b** : a dance by three people **c** : the performers of a musical or dance trio **2** : a group or set of three

¹trip \'trip\ *vb* **tripped**; **trip·ping** **1 a** : to move (as in dancing or walking) with light quick steps **b** : to perform (as a dance) lightly or nimbly **2** : to catch one's foot while walking or

running : cause to stumble **3 a** : to make or cause to make a mistake : SLIP, BLUNDER **b** : to catch in a misstep, fault, or blunder; *also* : EXPOSE **4** : to put (as a mechanism) into operation usu. by release of a catch or detent; *also* : to become operative **5** : to get high on a psychedelic drug (as LSD)
²trip *n* **1** : VOYAGE, JOURNEY **2** : ERROR, MISSTEP **3** : a quick light step **4** : a false step : STUMBLE **5 a** : the action of tripping mechanically **b** : a device (as a catch or detent) for tripping a mechanism **6** : an intense visionary experience undergone by a person who has taken a psychedelic drug (as LSD)
tri·par·tite \(ˈ)trī-ˈpär-ˌtīt\ *adj* **1** : having three parts **2** : having three corresponding parts or copies **3** : made between or involving three parties — **tri·par·tite·ly** *adv*
tripe \ˈtrīp\ *n* **1** : stomach tissue of a ruminant and esp. of the ox for use as food **2** : something poor, worthless, or offensive
¹tri·ple \ˈtrip-əl\ *vb* **tri·pled**; **tri·pling** \ˈtrip-(ə-)liŋ\ : to make or become three times as great or as many : multiply by three
²triple *n* **1 a** : a triple sum, quantity, or number **b** : a combination, group, or series of three **2** : a hit in baseball that enables the batter to reach third base
³triple *adj* **1** : having three units or members **2** : being three times as great or as many **3** : three times repeated
tri·plet \ˈtrip-lət\ *n* **1** : a unit of three lines of verse **2** : a combination, set, or group of three **3** : one of three offspring born at one birth
¹tri·plex \ˈtrip-ˌleks, ˈtrī-ˌpleks\ *adj* : TRIPLE
²triplex *n* : something that is triplex
¹trip·li·cate \ˈtrip-li-kət\ *adj* **1** : repeated three times **2** : THIRD
²triplicate *n* **1** : one of three like things **2** : three copies all alike
³trip·li·cate \-lə-ˌkāt\ *vt* : to make triple or provide in triplicate — **trip·li·ca·tion** \ˌtrip-lə-ˈkā-shən\ *n*
tri·ply \ˈtrip-(ə-)lē\ *adv* : in a triple degree, amount, or manner
tri·pod \ˈtrī-ˌpäd\ *n* : something (as a caldron, stool, or camera stand) that rests on three legs
trip·ping·ly \ˈtrip-iŋ-lē\ *adv* : NIMBLY; *also* : FLUENTLY
trip·tych \ˈtrip-(ˌ)tik\ *n* : a picture or carving in three panels side by side
tri·reme \ˈtrī-ˌrēm\ *n* : an ancient galley having three banks of oars
tri·sect \ˈtrī-ˌsekt, trī-ˈ\ *vt* : to divide into three usu. equal parts — **tri·sec·tion** \ˈtrī-ˌsek-shən, trī-ˈ\ *n* — **tri·sec·tor** \ˈtrī-ˌsek-tər, trī-ˈ\ *n*
tri·syl·lab·ic \ˌtrī-sə-ˈlab-ik\ *adj* : having three syllables — **tri·syl·la·ble** \ˈtrī-ˌsil-ə-bəl, (ˈ)trī-ˈ\ *n*
trite \ˈtrīt\ *adj* : so common that the novelty has worn off : STALE, HACKNEYED — **trite·ly** *adv* — **trite·ness** *n*
trit·i·um \ˈtrit-ē-əm, ˈtrish-ē-\ *n* : a radioactive isotope of hydrogen with atoms of three times the mass of ordinary light hydrogen atoms
trit·u·rate \ˈtrich-ə-ˌrāt\ *vt* **1** : CRUSH, GRIND **2** : to reduce to a fine powder by rubbing or grinding — **trit·u·ra·tion** \ˌtrich-ə-ˈrā-shən\ *n* — **trit·u·ra·tor** \ˈtrich-ə-ˌrāt-ər\ *n*
¹tri·umph \ˈtrī-əm(p)f\ *n* **1** : an ancient Roman ceremonial honoring a general for a decisive victory over a foreign enemy **2** : joy or exultation of victory or success **3** : a military victory or conquest; *also* : any notable success
²triumph *vi* **1** : to celebrate victory or success often boastfully or exultingly **2** : to obtain victory : PREVAIL, WIN
tri·um·phal \trī-ˈəm(p)-fəl\ *adj* : of, relating to, or used in a triumph
tri·um·phant \trī-ˈəm(p)-fənt\ *adj* **1** : VICTORIOUS **2** : rejoicing for or celebrating victory — **tri·um·phant·ly** *adv*
tri·um·vir \trī-ˈəm-vər\ *n* : one of a commission or ruling body of three esp. in ancient Rome
tri·um·vi·rate \-və-rət\ *n* **1** : the office or term of office of a triumvir **2** : government by three persons who share authority and responsibility **3** : a group of three persons who share power or office
tri·une \ˈtrī-ˌ(y)ün\ *adj* : three in one
triv·et \ˈtriv-ət\ *n* **1** : a three-legged stand or support **2** : an ornamental metal plate on very short legs used under a hot dish to protect the table
triv·ia \ˈtriv-ē-ə\ *n sing or pl* : unimportant matters : TRIFLES
triv·i·al \ˈtriv-ē-əl\ *adj* **1** : ORDINARY, COMMONPLACE **2** : of little worth or importance — **triv·i·al·ly** \-ē-ə-lē\ *adv*
triv·i·al·i·ty \ˌtriv-ē-ˈal-ət-ē\ *n*, *pl* **-ties** **1** : the quality or state of being trivial **2** : something trivial : TRIFLE
tro·che \ˈtrō-kē\ *n* : a usu. circular medicinal tablet or lozenge used esp. as a demulcent
tro·chee \ˈtrō-(ˌ)kē\ *n* : a metrical foot consisting of one accented syllable followed by one unaccented syllable (as in *hungry*) — **tro·cha·ic** \trō-ˈkā-ik\ *adj*
trod *past of* TREAD
trodden *past part of* TREAD
troi·ka \ˈtrȯi-kə\ *n* **1** : a Russian vehicle drawn by three horses abreast; *also* : a team for such a vehicle **2** : an administrative or ruling body of three **3** : a group of three
¹troll \ˈtrōl\ *vb* **1 a** : to sing the parts of (as a round) in succession **b** : to sing loudly or in a jovial manner **2** : to speak or recite in a rolling voice **3** : to angle or angle for with a hook and line drawn through the water — **troll·er** *n*
²troll *n* **1** : a lure or a line with its lure and hook used in trolling **2** : a song sung in parts successively : ROUND
³troll *n* : a fabled dwarf or giant of Teutonic folklore inhabiting caves or hills
trol·ley *or* **trol·ly** \ˈträl-ē\ *n*, *pl* **trolleys** *or* **trollies** **1 a** : a device for carrying current from a wire to an electrically driven vehicle **b** : TROLLEY CAR **2** : a wheeled carriage running on an overhead rail or track
trolley bus *n* : a bus powered by electric power from two overhead wires
trolley car *n* : a streetcar that runs on tracks and gets its electric power through a trolley
trol·lop \ˈträl-əp\ *n* **1** : a slovenly woman : SLATTERN **2** : a loose woman : WANTON
trom·bone \träm-ˈbōn\ *n* : a brass wind instrument that has a cupped mouthpiece, that consists of a long cylindrical metal tube bent twice upon itself and ending in a bell, and that has a movable slide with which to vary the pitch — **trom·bon·ist** \-ˈbō-nəst\ *n*

trombone

¹troop \ˈtrüp\ *n* **1 a** : a group of soldiers **b** : a cavalry unit corresponding to an infantry company **c** : armed forces : SOLDIERS — usu. used in pl. **2** : a collection of beings or things **3** : a unit of boy or girl scouts under a leader
²troop *vi* **1** : to move or gather in crowds **2** : ASSOCIATE
troop·er \ˈtrü-pər\ *n* **1** : CAVALRYMAN **2 a** : a mounted policeman **b** : a state policeman
troop·ship \ˈtrüp-ˌship\ *n* : a ship for carrying troops
trope \ˈtrōp\ *n* : the use of a word or expression in a figurative sense
tro·phy \ˈtrō-fē\ *n*, *pl* **trophies** **1 a** : a memorial of an ancient Greek or Roman victory raised on the field of battle **b** : a representation of such a memorial (as on a medal) **2** : something taken in battle or conquest esp. as a memorial **3** : something (as a loving cup) given to commemorate a victory or as an award for achievement **4** : SOUVENIR, MEMENTO
¹trop·ic \ˈträp-ik\ *n* **1** : either of the two parallels of the earth's

latitude that are approximately 23½ degrees north of the equator and approximately 23½ degrees south of the equator 2 *pl, often cap* : the region lying between the two tropics

²**tropic** *adj* : of, relating to, or occurring in the tropics : TROPICAL

trop·i·cal *adj* 1 \'träp-i-kəl\ : of, located in, or used in the tropics 2 \'trō-pi-kəl, 'träp-i-\ : FIGURATIVE, METAPHORICAL — **trop·i·cal·ly** \-k(ə-)lē\ *adv*

tropic of Cancer : the parallel of latitude that is 23½ degrees north of the equator and is the northernmost latitude reached by the overhead sun

tropic of Capricorn : the parallel of latitude that is 23½ degrees south of the equator and is the southernmost latitude reached by the overhead sun

tro·po·sphere \'trō-pə-ˌsfi(ə)r, 'träp-ə-\ *n* : the portion of the atmosphere which is below the stratosphere and extends outward about 7 to 10 miles from the earth's surface — **tro·po·spher·ic** \ˌtrō-pə-'sfi(ə)r-ik, ˌträp-ə-, -'sfer-\ *adj*

¹**trot** \'trät\ *n* 1 a (1) : a moderately fast gait of a quadruped (as a horse) in which the legs move in diagonal pairs (2) : a jogging gait of man that falls between a walk and a run b : a ride on horseback 2 : PONY 3

²**trot** *vb* **trot·ted**; **trot·ting** 1 a : to ride, drive, or go at a trot b : to cause to go at a trot 2 : HURRY — **trot·ter** *n*

¹**troth** \'tròth, 'träth, 'trōth\ *n* 1 : loyal or pledged faithfulness : FIDELITY 2 : one's pledged word; *also* : BETROTHAL

²**troth** \'träth, 'tròth, 'trō*th*\ *vt* : PLEDGE, BETROTH

trou·ba·dour \'trü-bə-ˌdōr\ *n* : one of a class of lyric poets and poet-musicians often of knightly rank who flourished from the 11th to the end of the 13th century chiefly in Provence, the south of France, and the north of Italy

¹**trou·ble** \'trəb-əl\ *vb* **trou·bled**; **trou·bling** \'trəb-(ə-)liŋ\ 1 a : to agitate or become agitated mentally or spiritually : WORRY, DISTURB b : to produce physical disorder in : AFFLICT c : to put to exertion or inconvenience 2 : to put into confused motion 3 : to make an effort : take pains

²**trouble** *n* 1 a : the quality or state of being troubled : MISFORTUNE b : an instance of distress, annoyance, or perturbation 2 a : civil disorder b : EXERTION, PAINS c (1) : a condition of physical distress (2) : DISEASE, AILMENT (3) : MALFUNCTION d : a source of distress

trou·ble·shoot·er \-ˌshüt-ər\ *n* : a man expert in resolving disputes or problems — **trou·ble·shoot** \-ˌshüt\ *vi*

trou·ble·some \'trəb-əl-səm\ *adj* 1 : giving trouble or anxiety : VEXATIOUS 2 : DIFFICULT, BURDENSOME — **trou·ble·some·ly** *adv* — **trou·ble·some·ness** *n*

trou·blous \'trəb-ləs\ *adj* 1 : full of trouble : AFFLICTED; *also* : AGITATED, STORMY 2 : causing trouble : TURBULENT

trough \'tròf\ *n, pl* **troughs** \'tròfs, 'tròvz\ 1 : a long shallow often V-shaped receptacle for the drinking water or feed of domestic animals 2 a : a gutter along the eaves of a house b : a long and narrow or shallow depression (as between waves or hills)

trounce \'traůn(t)s\ *vt* : to thrash or punish severely: as a : FLOG, CUDGEL b : to defeat decisively

¹**troupe** \'trüp\ *n* : COMPANY, TROOP; *esp* : a group of performers on the stage

²**troupe** *vi* : to travel in a troupe; *also* : to perform as a member of a theatrical troupe — **troup·er** *n*

trou·ser \'traů-zər\ *adj* : of, relating to, or designed for trousers

trou·sers \'traů-zərz\ *n pl* : an outer garment extending from the waist to the ankle or sometimes only to the knee, covering each leg separately, and worn typically by men and boys

trous·seau \'trü-ˌsō\ *n, pl* **trous·seaux** \-ˌsōz\ *or* **trous·seaus** : the personal possessions of a bride usu. including clothes, accessories, and household linens and wares

trout \'traůt\ *n, pl* **trout** : any of various fishes mostly smaller than the related salmons, restricted to cool clear fresh waters, and highly regarded as table and game fish

trove \'trōv\ *n* 1 : DISCOVERY, FIND 2 : a valuable collection

¹**trow·el** \'traů(-ə)l\ *n* 1 : a small hand tool consisting of a flat blade with a handle used for spreading and smoothing mortar or plaster 2 : a small hand tool with a curved blade used by gardeners

²**trowel** *vt* **-eled** *or* **-elled**; **-el·ing** *or* **-el·ling** : to smooth, mix, or apply with a trowel

troy \'tròi\ *adj* : expressed in troy weight

troy weight *n* : a series of units of weight based on a pound of 12 ounces and the ounce of 20 pennyweights or 480 grains

tru·ant \'trü-ənt\ *n* : one who shirks duty; *esp* : one who stays out of school without permission — **tru·an·cy** \-ən-sē\ *n* — **truant** *adj*

truce \'trüs\ *n* 1 : an interruption of warfare by mutual agreement : ARMISTICE 2 : a temporary rest : RESPITE

¹**truck** \'trək\ *vb* : to exchange goods : BARTER

²**truck** *n* 1 : BARTER 2 : goods for barter or for small trade 3 : close association : DEALINGS 4 : payment of wages in goods instead of cash 5 : vegetables grown for market 6 : small articles of little value; *also* : RUBBISH

³**truck** *n* 1 : a vehicle (as a small flat-topped car on wheels, a two-wheeled barrow with long handles, or a strong heavy wagon or automobile) for carrying heavy articles 2 : a swiveling carriage with springs and one or more pairs of wheels used to carry an end of a railroad car or a locomotive

⁴**truck** *vb* 1 : to transport on or by truck 2 : to be employed as a truck driver — **truck·er** *n*

truck·le \'trək-əl\ *vi* **truck·led**; **truck·ling** \'trək-(ə-)liŋ\ : to act in a subservient manner : yield to the will of another

truckle bed *n* : TRUNDLE BED

truck–trail·er \'trək-'trā-lər\ *n* : a combination of a trailer and the truck that draws it

truc·u·lence \'trək-yə-lən(t)s, 'trük-\ *n* : the quality or state of being truculent

truc·u·lent \-lənt\ *adj* 1 : feeling or displaying ferocity : CRUEL, FIERCE, SAVAGE 2 : DEADLY, DESTRUCTIVE 3 : scathingly harsh 4 : BELLIGERENT, PUGNACIOUS — **truc·u·lent·ly** *adv*

¹**trudge** \'trəj\ *vb* 1 : to walk or march steadily and usu. laboriously 2 : to walk or march along or over — **trudg·er** *n*

²**trudge** *n* : a long tiring walk : TRAMP

¹**true** \'trü\ *adj* 1 : FAITHFUL, LOYAL 2 : that can be relied on : CERTAIN 3 a : corresponding to fact or actuality : ACCURATE, CORRECT b : logically necessary 4 : SINCERE 5 : properly so called : GENUINE; *also* : TYPICAL 6 : placed or formed accurately 7 : RIGHTFUL, LEGITIMATE — **true·ness** *n*

²**true** *n* 1 : TRUTH, REALITY — usu. used with *the* 2 : the quality or state of being accurate (as in alignment or adjustment) — used in the phrases *in true* and *out of true*

³**true** *vt* **trued**; **true·ing** : to make level, square, balanced, or concentric : bring to desired mechanical accuracy or form

⁴**true** *adv* 1 : TRUTHFULLY 2 a : ACCURATELY b : without variation from type

true–blue \'trü-'blü\ *adj* : marked by unswerving loyalty

true·love \'trü-ˌləv\ *n* : one truly beloved or loving

truf·fle \'trəf-əl, 'trüf-\ *n* : the usu. dark wrinkled edible fruit of a European underground fungus; *also* : this fungus

tru·ism \'trü-ˌiz-əm\ *n* : an obvious truth — **tru·is·tic** \trü-'is-tik\ *adj*

trull \'trəl\ *n* : TROLLOP, STRUMPET

tru·ly \'trü-lē\ *adv* 1 : SINCERELY — often used as a complementary close after *yours* 2 : TRUTHFULLY 3 : ACCURATELY 4 a : INDEED — often used as an intensive or interjectionally to express astonishment or doubt b : GENUINELY 5 : PROPERLY, RIGHTFULLY

¹**trump** \'trəmp\ *n* : TRUMPET : the sound of a trumpet

²**trump** *n* : a card of a suit any of whose cards will win over a card that is not a trump; *also* : the suit — often used in pl.

[3]**trump** *vb* **1** : to take with a trump **2** : to play a trump **3** : to get the better of : OUTDO

trum·pery \'trəm-p(ə-)rē\ *n, pl* **-per·ies** **1** : trivial or useless articles : RUBBISH **2** : worthless nonsense — **trumpery** *adj*

[1]**trum·pet** \'trəm-pət\ *n* **1** : a wind instrument consisting of a long cylindrical metal tube commonly once or twice curved and ending in a bell **2** : a trumpet player **3** : something that resembles a trumpet or its tonal quality — **trum·pet·like** *adj*

[2]**trumpet** *vb* **1** : to blow a trumpet **2** : to sound or proclaim on or as if on a trumpet

trum·pet·er \'trəm-pət-ər\ *n* : a trumpet player

trump up *vt* : to concoct esp. with intent to deceive

[1]**trun·cate** \'trəŋ-ˌkāt\ *vt* : to shorten by or as if by cutting off : LOP — **trun·ca·tion** \ˌtrəŋ-'kā-shən\ *n*

[2]**trun·cate** \'trəŋ-ˌkāt\ *adj* : having the end square or blunt

trun·cat·ed \-ˌkāt-əd\ *adj* **1 a** : cut short : CURTAILED **b** : lacking an expected or normal element (as a syllable) at beginning or end **2** : TRUNCATE

trun·cheon \'trən-chən\ *n* **1** : a shattered spear or lance **2** : a policeman's billy

[1]**trun·dle** \'trən-dᵊl\ *n* **1 a** : a small wheel or roller **b** : CIRCLET, HOOP **2** : a low-wheeled cart or truck

[2]**trundle** *vb* **trun·dled**; **trun·dling** \'trən-dliŋ, -dᵊl-iŋ\ **1 a** : to propel by causing to rotate : ROLL **b** : to progress by revolving **2** : to transport in a wheeled vehicle : HAUL, WHEEL

trundle bed *n* : a low bed usu. on casters that can be slid under a higher bed

[1]**trunk** \'trəŋk\ *n* **1 a** : the main stem of a tree apart from branches or roots **b** : the body of a person or lower animal apart from the head and limbs **c** : the main or basal part of something **d** : a trunk line **2 a** : a box or chest for holding clothes or other goods esp. for traveling **b** : the enclosed space usu. in the rear of an automobile for carrying articles (as luggage) **3** : the long versatile muscular nose of an elephant; *also* : PROBOSCIS **4** *pl* : men's shorts worn chiefly for sports

[2]**trunk** *adj* **1** : being or relating to a main line of a system (as of a railroad, pipeline, or canal) **2** : being or relating to the circuit between two telephone exchanges

[1]**truss** \'trəs\ *vt* **1 a** : to secure tightly : BIND **b** : to arrange for cooking by binding close the wings or legs of **2** : to support, strengthen, or stiffen by a truss — **truss·er** *n*

[2]**truss** *n* **1** : BUNDLE, PACK **2** : a rigid framework of beams, bars, or rods **3** : a device worn to hold a hernia in place

[1]**trust** \'trəst\ *n* **1 a** : assured reliance on the character, ability, strength, or truth of someone or something **b** : one in which confidence is placed **2 a** : dependence on something future or contingent : HOPE **b** : reliance on future payment for goods delivered : CREDIT **3 a** : property held or managed by one person or concern (as a bank) for the benefit of another **b** : a combination of firms or corporations formed by a legal agreement; *esp* : one that reduces or threatens to reduce competition **4 a** : something (as a public office) committed to one to be used or cared for in the interest of another **b** : responsible charge or office **c** : CARE, CUSTODY

[2]**trust** *vb* **1 a** : to place confidence : DEPEND **b** : to be confident : HOPE **2** : to commit or place in one's care or keeping : ENTRUST **3 a** : to rely on the truthfulness or accuracy of : BELIEVE **b** : to place confidence in : rely on **c** : to hope or expect confidently **4** : to sell to in confidence of later payment : extend credit to — **trust·er** *n*

trust·ee \ˌtrəs-'tē\ *n* : a person to whom property is legally committed in trust

trust·ful \'trəst-fəl\ *adj* : full of trust : CONFIDING — **trust·ful·ly** \-fə-lē\ *adv* — **trust·ful·ness** *n*

trust·ing \'trəs-tiŋ\ *adj* : having trust, faith, or confidence : TRUSTFUL — **trust·ing·ly** *adv*

trust·wor·thy \'trəst-ˌwər-t͟hē\ *adj* : worthy of confidence : DEPENDABLE — **trust·wor·thi·ness** *n*

[1]**trusty** \'trəs-tē\ *adj* : TRUSTWORTHY, DEPENDABLE

[2]**trusty** \'trəs-tē, ˌtrəs-'tē\ *n, pl* **trust·ies** : a trusty or trusted person; *esp* : a convict considered trustworthy and allowed special privileges

truth \'trüth\ *n, pl* **truths** \'trüt͟hz, 'trüths\ **1** : TRUTHFULNESS, HONESTY; *esp* : conformity (as in art) with what is natural, substantial, or convincing **2** : something that is real or true: as **a** (1) : a judgment, proposition, idea, or statement that is or is accepted as true (2) : the body of such truths **b** (1) : the real state of things : FACT (2) : the body of real things, events, and facts : ACTUALITY **3** : agreement with fact or among propositions : the property of being in accord with what is, has been, or must be — **in truth** : in fact : ACTUALLY

truth·ful \'trüth-fəl\ *adj* : telling or disposed to tell the truth — **truth·ful·ly** \-fə-lē\ *adv* — **truth·ful·ness** *n*

[1]**try** \'trī\ *vb* **tried**; **try·ing** **1 a** : to examine or investigate judicially **b** : to conduct the trial of **2 a** : to put to test or trial **b** : to test to the limit or breaking point : STRAIN **3** : to melt down and procure in a pure state : RENDER **4** : to make an effort to do : ENDEAVOR

[2]**try** *n, pl* **tries** : an experimental trial : ATTEMPT

try·ing \'trī-iŋ\ *adj* : causing distress or annoyance : hard to bear or endure

tryst \'trist, 'trīst\ *n* **1** : an agreement (as between lovers) to meet **2** : an appointed meeting or meeting place

T–shirt \'tē-ˌshərt\ *n* : a collarless short-sleeved cotton undershirt for men; *also* : a cotton or wool jersey outer shirt of similar design

[1]**tub** \'təb\ *n* **1** : a wide low bucketlike vessel **2** : an old or slow boat **3** : BATHTUB; *also* : BATH **4** : the amount that a tub will hold

[2]**tub** *vb* **tubbed**; **tub·bing** : to wash or bathe in a tub

tu·ba \'t(y)ü-bə\ *n* : a large low-pitched brass wind instrument; *esp* : one with a conical bore and cup-shaped mouthpiece

tub·by \'təb-ē\ *adj* : PUDGY, FAT

tube \'t(y)üb\ *n* **1 a** : a hollow elongated cylinder; *esp* : one to convey fluids **b** : a slender channel within a plant or animal body : DUCT **2** : any of various usu. cylindrical structures or devices: as **a** : a round metal container from which a paste is dispensed by squeezing **b** : TUNNEL — **tubed** \'t(y)übd\ *adj* — **tube·less** \'t(y)üb-ləs\ *adj* — **tube·like** *adj*

tu·ber \'t(y)ü-bər\ *n* : a short fleshy usu. underground stem (as of a potato plant) bearing minute scalelike leaves each with a bud at its base

tu·ber·cle \'t(y)ü-bər-kəl\ *n* **1** : a small knobby prominence or outgrowth esp. on a plant or animal : NODULE **2** : a small abnormal lump in the substance of an organ or in the skin; *esp* : one caused by tuberculosis — **tu·ber·cled** \-kəld\ *adj*

tu·ber·cu·lar \t(y)ü-'bər-kyə-lər\ *adj* **1** : relating to, resembling, or constituting a tubercle : TUBERCULATE **2** : characterized by tubercular lesions **3** : of, relating to, or affected with tuberculosis : TUBERCULOUS — **tu·ber·cu·lar·ly** *adv*

tu·ber·cu·late \t(y)ü-'bər-kyə-lət\ *or* **tu·ber·cu·lat·ed** \-ˌlāt-əd\ *adj* **1** : having or beset with tubercles **2** : TUBERCULAR

tu·ber·cu·lo·sis \t(y)ü-ˌbər-kyə-'lō-səs\ *n* : a communicable disease of some vertebrates caused by the tubercle bacillus and typically marked by wasting, fever, and formation of cheesy tubercles that in man primarily occur in the lungs

tu·ber·cu·lous \t(y)ü-'bər-kyə-ləs\ *adj* : being or affected or associated with tuberculosis — **tu·ber·cu·lous·ly** *adv*

tube·rose \'t(y)üb-ˌrōz; 't(y)ü-bə-ˌrōz, -bə-ˌrōs\ *n* : a Mexican bulbous herb of the amaryllis family grown for its spike of fragrant white flowers

tu·ber·ous \'t(y)ü-b(ə-)rəs\ *adj* **1 a** : consisting of or resembling a tuber **b** : bearing tubers **2** : of, relating to, or being a plant tuber or tuberous root — **tu·ber·ous·ly** *adv*

tub·ing \'t(y)ü-biŋ\ *n* **1** : material in the form of a tube; *also* : a length or piece of tube **2** : a series or system of tubes

tu·bu·lar \'t(y)ü-byə-lər\ *adj* **1** : having the form of or consisting of a tube **2** : made or provided with tubes

tu·bule \'t(y)ü-byül\ *n* : a small tube

¹tuck \'tək\ *vb* **1 a** : to pull up or draw together into folds **b** : to make a tuck in **2** : to put or fit into a snug position or place **3 a** : to push in the loose end of so as to hold tightly **b** : to cover by tucking in bedclothes

²tuck *n* : a stitched fold (as in a garment)

¹tuck·er \'tək-ər\ *n* **1** : one that tucks **2** : a piece of lace or cloth in the neckline of a dress

²tucker *vt* **tuck·ered**; **tuck·er·ing** \'tək-(ə-)riŋ\ : EXHAUST

Tues·day \'t(y)üz-dē\ *n* : the 3d day of the week

tu·fa \'t(y)ü-fə\ *n* : a porous rock formed as a deposit from springs or streams — **tu·fa·ceous** \t(y)ü-'fā-shəs\ *adj*

¹tuft \'təft\ *n* **1 a** : a small cluster of long flexible outgrowths (as hairs or feathers) **b** : a bunch of soft fluffy threads cut off short and used as ornament **2** : CLUMP, CLUSTER **3** : MOUND

²tuft *vt* **1** : to provide or adorn with a tuft **2** : to make (as a mattress) firm by stitching at intervals and sewing on tufts

¹tug \'təg\ *vb* **tugged**; **tug·ging** **1 a** : to pull hard **b** : to move by pulling hard : DRAG, HAUL; *also* : to carry with difficulty **2** : to struggle in opposition : CONTEND — **tug·ger** *n*

²tug *n* **1 a** : a harness trace **b** : a rope or chain used for pulling **2 a** : an act or instance of tugging : PULL **b** : a struggle between opposing individuals or forces **3** : a strong pulling force or straining effort **4** : TUGBOAT

tug·boat \'təg-ˌbōt\ *n* : a strongly built powerful boat used for towing and pushing

tug–of–war \ˌtəg-ə(v)-'wȯ(ə)r\ *n*, *pl* **tugs–of–war** **1** : a struggle for supremacy **2** : an athletic contest in which two teams pull against each other at opposite ends of a rope

tu·i·tion \t(y)u̇-'ish-ən\ *n* **1** : the act or profession of teaching : INSTRUCTION **2** : the price of or payment for instruction — **tu·i·tion·al** \-'ish-nəl, -ən-ᵊl\ *adj*

tu·lip \'t(y)ü-ləp\ *n* : any of a genus of Eurasian bulbous herbs of the lily family that are widely grown for their showy flowers; *also* : the flower or bulb of a tulip

tulip tree *n* : a tall No. American timber tree with large greenish yellow tulip-shaped flowers and soft white wood

tulle \'tül\ *n* : a sheer often stiffened silk, rayon, or nylon net

¹tum·ble \'təm-bəl\ *vb* **tum·bled**; **tum·bling** \-b(ə-)liŋ\ **1 a** : to perform gymnastic feats of rolling and turning **b** : to turn end over end in falling or flight **2 a** : to fall suddenly and helplessly **b** : to suffer a sudden decline, downfall, or defeat : COLLAPSE **3** : to move or go hurriedly and confusedly **4** : to come to understand **5 a** : to throw or push and cause to topple or tumble **b** : to toss about or together into a confused mass **c** : RUMPLE, DISORDER

²tumble *n* **1** : a disorderly state or collection **2** : an act or instance of tumbling

tum·ble·down \ˌtəm-bəl-ˌdau̇n\ *adj* : DILAPIDATED, RAMSHACKLE

tum·bler \'təm-blər\ *n* **1** : one that tumbles: as **a** : GYMNAST, ACROBAT **b** : a pigeon that habitually somersaults backward in flight **2** : a drinking glass without foot or stem and orig. with pointed or convex base **3** : a movable part in a lock that must be adjusted (as by a key) before the bolt can be thrown

tum·ble·weed \'təm-bəl-ˌwēd\ *n* : a plant that breaks away from its roots in autumn and is blown about by the wind

tum·brel *or* **tum·bril** \'təm-brəl\ *n* : a farmer's cart used during the French Revolution to carry condemned persons to the guillotine

tu·mid \'t(y)ü-məd\ *adj* **1** : marked by swelling : SWOLLEN, ENLARGED **2** : BOMBASTIC, TURGID — **tu·mid·i·ty** \t(y)ü-'mid-ət-ē\ *n*

tum·my \'təm-ē\ *n*, *pl* **tummies** : STOMACH 1c

tu·mor \'t(y)ü-mər\ *n* : an abnormal mass of tissue that is not inflammatory, arises without obvious cause from cells of preexistent tissue, and possesses no physiologic function — **tu·mor·like** *adj* — **tu·mor·ous** \'t(y)üm-(ə-)rəs\ *adj*

tu·mult \'t(y)ü-ˌməlt\ *n* **1** : violent and disorderly commotion or disturbance (as of a crowd of people) with uproar and confusion **2** : violent agitation of mind

tu·mul·tu·ous \t(y)u̇-'məl-chə-wəs, -chəs\ *adj* : marked by tumult and esp. by violent or overwhelming turbulence or upheaval — **tu·mul·tu·ous·ly** *adv* — **tu·mul·tu·ous·ness** *n*

tun \'tən\ *n* **1** : a large cask for liquids and esp. wine **2** : the capacity of a tun; *esp* : a measure of 252 gallons

tu·na \'t(y)ü-nə\ *n*, *pl* **tuna** *or* **tunas** : any of several mostly large active sea fishes (as an albacore or bonito) related to the mackerels and valued for food and sport

tun·a·ble \'t(y)ü-nə-bəl\ *adj* : capable of being tuned

tun·dra \'tən-drə\ *n* : a treeless plain of arctic and subarctic regions

¹tune \'t(y)ün\ *n* **1 a** : a succession of pleasing musical tones : MELODY **b** : the musical setting of a song **2** : correct musical pitch or consonance **3 a** : AGREEMENT, HARMONY **b** : general attitude **4** : AMOUNT, EXTENT

²tune *vb* **1** : to come or bring into harmony : ATTUNE **2** : TUNE IN **3** : to adjust in musical pitch **4** : to adjust for precise functioning — **tun·er** *n*

tune·ful \'t(y)ün-fəl\ *adj* : MELODIOUS, MUSICAL — **tune·ful·ly** *adv* — **tune·ful·ness** *n*

tune–up \'t(y)ün-ˌəp\ *n* : a general adjustment to ensure efficient functioning

tung·sten \'təŋ(k)-stən\ *n* : a gray-white heavy ductile hard metallic chemical element that is used esp. for electrical purposes and in hardening alloys (as steel)

tu·nic \'t(y)ü-nik\ *n* **1** : a simple belted knee-length or longer slip-on garment worn by ancient Greeks and Romans **2** : a long usu. plain and close-fitting jacket with high collar worn esp. as part of a uniform **3** : a blouse or jacket reaching to or just below the hips

tun·ing fork \'t(y)ü-niŋ-\ *n* : a 2-pronged metal instrument that gives a fixed tone when struck and is useful for tuning musical instruments and ascertaining standard pitch

¹tun·nel \'tən-ᵊl\ *n* : an enclosed passage (as a tube or conduit); *esp* : one underground (as under an obstruction or in a mine) — **tun·nel·like** \-ᵊl-ˌ(l)īk\ *adj*

²tunnel *vb* **-neled** *or* **-nelled**; **-nel·ing** *or* **-nel·ling** \'tən-liŋ, -ᵊl-iŋ\ : to make or use a tunnel or form a tunnel in — **tun·nel·er** \'tən-lər, -ᵊl-ər\ *n*

tun·ny \'tən-ē\ *n*, *pl* **tunnies** : TUNA

tuque \'t(y)ük\ *n* : a warm knitted usu. pointed cap

tur·ban \'tər-bən\ *n* **1** : a headdress worn chiefly in countries of the eastern Mediterranean and southern Asia esp. by Muslims and made of a cap around which is wound a long cloth **2** : a woman's close-fitting hat without a brim

tur·bid \'tər-bəd\ *adj* **1 a** : thick or opaque with roiled sediment **b** : heavy with smoke or mist : DENSE **2** : CONFUSED, MUDDLED — **tur·bid·i·ty** \ˌtər-'bid-ət-ē\ *n* — **tur·bid·ly** *adv*

tur·bine \'tər-bən, -ˌbīn\ *n* : an engine whose central driving shaft is fitted with vanes whirled around by the pressure of water or hot gases (as steam or exhaust gases)

tur·bo·jet \'tər-bō-ˌjet\ *n* : an airplane powered by turbojet engines

turbojet engine *n* : an airplane propulsion system in which the power developed by a turbine is used to drive a compressor that supplies air to a burner and hot gases from the burner pass through the turbine and thence to a rearward-directed thrust-producing exhaust nozzle

tur·bo·prop \'tər-bō-ˌpräp\ *n* **1** : TURBO-PROPELLER ENGINE **2** : an airplane powered by turbo-propeller engines

tur·bo–pro·pel·ler engine \ˌtər-bō-prə-'pel-ər-\ *n* : a jet engine having a turbine-driven propeller and designed to produce thrust principally by means of a propeller although additional thrust is usu. obtained from the hot exhaust gases which issue in a jet

tur·bot \'tər-bət\ *n, pl* **turbot** : a large brownish European flatfish highly esteemed as a food fish; *also* : any of various flatfishes resembling this

tur·bu·lence \'tər-byə-lən(t)s\ *n* : the quality or state of being turbulent: as **a** : wild commotion **b** : irregular atmospheric motion esp. when characterized by up and down currents **c** : departure in a fluid from a smooth flow

tur·bu·lent \-lənt\ *adj* **1** : causing unrest, violence, or disturbance **2** : characterized by agitation or tumult : TEMPESTUOUS — **tur·bu·lent·ly** *adv*

tu·reen \tə-'rēn, tyu̇-\ *n* : a deep bowl from which food (as soup) is served at table

turf \'tərf\ *n, pl* **turfs** \'tərfs\ *or* **turves** \'tərvz\ **1** : the upper layer of soil bound by grass and plant roots into a thick mat; *also* : a piece of this **2 a** : PEAT **b** : a piece of peat dried for fuel **3 a** : a track or course for horse racing **b** : the sport or business of horse racing — **turfy** \'tər-fē\ *adj*

tur·gid \'tər-jəd\ *adj* **1** : being in a state of distension : SWOLLEN; *esp* : exhibiting turgor **2** : excessively embellished in style or language : BOMBASTIC, POMPOUS — **tur·gid·i·ty** \ˌtər-'jid-ət-ē\ *n* — **tur·gid·ly** *adv* — **tur·gid·ness** *n*

tur·gor \'tər-gər, -ˌgȯr\ *n* : the normal state of firmness and tension typical of living cells

tur·key \'tər-kē\ *n* **1** : a large American bird which is related to the common fowl, is of wide range in No. America, and is domesticated in most parts of the world **2** : FAILURE, FLOP

turkey buzzard *n* : an American vulture common in So. and Central America and in the southern U.S.

Turk·ish bath \ˌtər-kish-\ *n* : a bath in which the bather passes through a series of rooms heated to increasingly extreme temperatures by steam and then receives a rubdown, massage, and cold shower

Turkish towel *n* : a towel made of cotton terry cloth

tur·moil \'tər-ˌmȯil\ *n* : an utterly confused or extremely agitated state or condition

¹turn \'tərn\ *vb* **1 a** : to move or cause to move around an axis or center : ROTATE, REVOLVE; *also* : to operate or cause to operate by so turning **b** : to whirl giddily : become dizzy **c** : to have as a center (as of interest) or a decisive factor **d** : to execute by revolving **e** : to revolve mentally : PONDER **2 a** : to alter or reverse in position usu. by moving through an arc: as (1) : to delve in or plow so as to turn (2) : to make over by reversing the material and refastening **b** : to disturb or upset the order or state or balance of **c** : to injure by a sudden twist : WRENCH; *also* : to fold or cause to fold back **3 a** : to take or cause to take or move in another, an opposite, or a particular direction; *also* : to pass with a change of direction **b** : to alter from a previous or anticipated course **c** (1) : to change one's attitude or reverse one's course of action to one of opposition or hostility; *also* : DEFECT (2) : to attack suddenly and usu. unexpectedly and violently **d** : to bring to bear : TRAIN; *also* : to direct or point usu. toward or away from something **e** : to influence toward a change (as in one's way of life) **f** : DEVOTE, APPLY **g** : to cause to recoil **h** : to drive or send from or to a specified place or condition **i** : to seek out as a source of something **4** : to change or cause to change: as **a** : TRANSFORM, BECOME **b** : to cause to spoil : SOUR **c** : to change in color **d** : to give a particular nature or appearance to **e** : TRANSLATE, PARAPHRASE **f** : to exchange for something else **g** : to be inconstant : VARY **5 a** : to give a rounded form to by means of a lathe and cutting tool **b** : to give a well-rounded or graceful shape or form to **c** : to become or cause to become bent **6** : to gain in the course of business

²turn *n* **1** : the action or an act of turning about a center or axis **2 a** : a change or changing of direction, course, or position **b** : a place where something turns : BEND, CURVE **c** (1) : a change or changing of condition or trend (2) : a usu. sudden and brief spell of disorder of body or spirits; *esp* : a state of nervous shock or faintness **3** : a short walk or ride **4** : an act affecting another **5 a** : a period of action or activity : SPELL **b** : place or appointed time in a succession or scheduled order **6** : special purpose or need **7 a** : distinctive quality or character **b** : the form in accord with which something is fashioned : CAST **c** : manner of arrangement esp. in being coiled or twisted; *also* : a single round (as of a rope) **d** : a special adaptive twist or interpretation **8** : particular or special aptitude or skill : BENT — **at every turn** : CONSTANTLY, CONTINUOUSLY — **to a turn** : precisely right : PERFECTLY

turn·about \'tərn-ə-ˌbau̇t\ *n* : a change or reversal of direction, trend, policy, or role

turn·buck·le \'tərn-ˌbək-əl\ *n* : a link with a screw thread at one or both ends used for tightening a rod or stay

turn·coat \-ˌkōt\ *n* : one who forsakes his party or principles

turn down \'tərn-'dau̇n, ˌtərn-\ *vt* **1** : to reduce in height or intensity by turning a control **2** : DECLINE, REJECT — **turn·down** \'tərn-ˌdau̇n\ *adj or n*

turn in *vb* **1 a** : to give up or hand over **b** : to inform on : BETRAY **c** : to acquit oneself of **2** : to go to bed

tur·nip \'tər-nəp\ *n* : either of two biennial herbs of the mustard family with thick roots eaten as a vegetable or fed to stock

turn·key \'tərn-ˌkē\ *n* : one who has charge of a prison's keys

turn off *vt* **1** : DISMISS, DISCHARGE **2** : to turn aside or aside from something **3** : to stop the functioning or flow of by or as if by turning a control

turn·off \'tərn-ˌȯf\ *n* **1** : a turning off **2** : a place where one turns off

turn on *vt* : to cause to function or flow by or as if by turning a control

turn out *vb* **1** : to put out of some shelter : EVICT **2** : to empty of contents; *also* : CLEAN **3** : to make with rapidity or regularity **4** : to equip, dress, or finish in a careful or elaborate way **5** : to turn off (as a light) **6 a** : to come out in answer to a summons **b** : to get out of bed **7** : to prove ultimately to be

turn·out \'tərn-ˌau̇t\ *n* **1** : an act of turning out **2** : a gathering of people for a special purpose **3** : a widened space (as in a highway) for vehicles to pass or park **4** : a clearing out for cleaning **5 a** : a carriage with its team and equipment **b** : an outfit of clothes : COSTUME **6** : YIELD, OUTPUT

turn over *vb* **1** : to hand over : TRANSFER **2** : to heave with nausea

¹turn·over \'tərn-ˌō-vər\ *n* **1** : UPSET, SPILL **2** : a shifting usu. in position or opinion **3** : a pie or tart with one half of the crust turned over the other **4** : the amount of business done or work accomplished; *also* : the rate at which material is processed **5** : the buying, selling, and replacing of goods considered as one complete process **6** : the number of employees hired in a given time to replace those leaving

²turn·over \ˌtərn-ˌō-vər\ *adj* : capable of being turned over

turn·pike \'tərn-ˌpīk\ *n* **1** : a toll bar : TOLLGATE **2 a** : a toll road; *esp* : a toll expressway **b** : a main road

turn·spit \-ˌspit\ *n* **1** : one that turns a spit **2** : a rotatable spit

turn·stile \-ˌstīl\ *n* : a post with arms pivoted on the top set in a passageway so that persons can pass through only on foot one by one

turn·ta·ble \-ˌtā-bəl\ *n* : a circular platform that revolves (as for turning wheeled vehicles or a phonograph record)

turn to *vi* : to apply oneself to work : act vigorously

turn up *vb* **1** : to bring or come to light usu. unexpectedly or after being lost **2** : to raise or increase by or as if by adjusting a control **3 a** : to turn out to be : become evident **b** : to put in an appearance **4** : to happen unexpectedly

turn·up \ˌtərn-ˌəp\ *adj* **1** : turned up **2** : made or fitted to be turned up

tur·pen·tine \'tər-pən-ˌtīn\ *n* **1 :** an oleoresin obtained from various conifers (as some pines and firs) **2 a :** an essential oil obtained from turpentines by distillation and used esp. as a solvent and thinner **b :** a similar oil obtained by distillation or carbonization of pinewood

tur·pi·tude \'tər-pə-ˌt(y)üd\ *n* **:** inherent baseness **:** DEPRAVITY

tur·quoise \'tər-ˌk(w)ȯiz\ *n* **1 :** a mineral that is a blue, bluish green, or greenish gray hydrous basic copper aluminum phosphate, takes a high polish, and sometimes is valued as a gem **2 :** a variable color averaging a light greenish blue

tur·ret \'tər-ət\ *n* **1 :** a little tower often at a corner of a building **2 :** a pivoted and revolvable holder in a machine tool **3 a :** a gunner's fixed or movable enclosure in an airplane **b :** a revolving structure on a warship or on a tank in which guns are mounted — **tur·ret·ed** *adj*

tur·tle \'tərt-ᵊl\ *n, pl* **turtles :** any of an order of land, freshwater, and marine reptiles with a toothless horny beak and a bony shell which encloses the trunk and into which the head, limbs, and tail usu. may be withdrawn

tur·tle·dove \-ˌdəv\ *n* **:** any of several small wild pigeons esp. of an Old World genus noted for plaintive cooing

tur·tle·neck \-ˌnek\ *n* **:** a high close-fitting turnover collar used esp. for sweaters; *also* **:** a sweater with a turtleneck

turves *pl of* TURF

tush \'təsh\ *interj* — used to express disdain or reproach

tusk \'təsk\ *n* **1 :** a long greatly enlarged tooth (as of an elephant, walrus, or boar) that projects when the mouth is closed and serves for digging food or as a weapon **2 :** a tooth-shaped part — **tusked** \'təskt\ *adj*

¹tus·sle \'təs-əl\ *vi* **tus·sled; tus·sling** \'təs-(ə-)liŋ\ **:** to struggle roughly **:** SCUFFLE

²tussle *n* **1 :** a physical contest or struggle **:** SCUFFLE **2 :** a rough argument, controversy, or struggle against difficult odds

tus·sock \'təs-ək\ *n* **:** a compact tuft esp. of grass or sedge; *also* **:** a hummock in marsh bound together by plant roots — **tus·socky** \'təs-ə-kē\ *adj*

tut *a t-sound made by suction rather than explosion; often read as* 'tət\ *or* **tut–tut** *interj* — used to express disapproval or disbelief

tu·te·lage \'t(y)üt-ᵊl-ij\ *n* **1 :** an act of guarding or protecting **:** GUARDIANSHIP **2 :** the state of being under a guardian or tutor; *also* **:** the right, power, or influence of a tutor over his pupil **3 :** INSTRUCTION

tu·te·lary \'t(y)üt-ᵊl-ˌer-ē\ *adj* **1 :** having the guardianship of a person or a thing **2 :** of or relating to a guardian

¹tu·tor \'t(y)üt-ər\ *n* **:** a person charged with the instruction and guidance of another: as **a :** a private teacher **b :** a college teacher esp. in a British university who guides the individual studies of undergraduates in his field **c :** a college or university teacher ranking below an instructor

²tutor *vb* **:** to teach usu. individually

¹tu·to·ri·al \t(y)ü-'tōr-ē-əl\ *adj* **:** of, relating to, or involving a tutor

²tutorial *n* **:** a class conducted by a tutor for one student or a small number of students

tux \'təks\ *n* **:** TUXEDO

tux·e·do \ˌtək-'sēd-ō\ *n, pl* **-dos** *or* **-does 1 :** a usu. black or blackish blue jacket **2 :** semiformal evening dress for men

TV \(')tē-'vē\ *n* **:** TELEVISION

twad·dle \'twäd-ᵊl\ *n* **:** silly idle talk **:** DRIVEL

twain \'twān\ *n* **1 :** TWO **2 :** COUPLE, PAIR

¹twang \'twaŋ\ *n* **1 :** a harsh quick ringing sound like that of a plucked bowstring **2 a :** nasal speech or resonance **b :** the characteristic speech of a region, locality, or group of people

²twang *vb* **twanged; twang·ing** \'twaŋ-iŋ\ **1 :** to sound or cause to sound with a twang **2 :** to speak with a nasal intonation

¹tweak \'twēk\ *vt* **:** to pinch and pull with a sudden jerk and twist **:** TWITCH

²tweak *n* **:** an act of tweaking **:** PINCH

tweed \'twēd\ *n* **1 :** a rough woolen fabric made usu. in twill weaves **2** *pl* **:** tweed clothing; *esp* **:** a tweed suit

tweedy \'twēd-ē\ *adj* **1 :** of or resembling tweed **2 a :** given to wearing tweeds **b :** informal or suggestive of the outdoors in taste or habits

¹tweet \'twēt\ *n* **:** a chirping note

²tweet *vb* **:** CHIRP

tweeze \'twēz\ *vt* **:** to pluck or remove with tweezers

tweez·ers \'twē-zərz\ *n pl* **:** a small metal instrument that is usu. held between the thumb and forefinger, is used for plucking, holding, or manipulating, and consists of two legs joined at one end

twelfth \'twelfth, 'twelft\ *n* — see NUMBER table — **twelfth** *adj or adv*

twelve \'twelv\ *n* **1** — see NUMBER table **2 :** the 12th in a set or series **3 :** something having 12 units or members — **twelve** *adj or pron*

twelve·month \-ˌmən(t)th\ *n* **:** YEAR

twen·ti·eth \'twent-ē-əth\ *n* — see NUMBER table — **twentieth** *adj*

twen·ty \'twent-ē\ *n, pl* **twenties** — see NUMBER table — **twenty** *adj or pron*

twen·ty–twen·ty \ˌtwent-ē-'twent-ē\ *adj* **:** of normal acuity — often written 20/20

twerp \'twərp\ *n* **:** a silly, insignificant, or contemptible person

twice \'twīs\ *adv* **:** two times

¹twid·dle \'twid-ᵊl\ *vb* **twid·dled; twid·dling** \'twid-liŋ, -ᵊl-iŋ\ **1 :** to be busy with trifles **:** FIDDLE **2 :** to rotate lightly or idly

²twiddle *n* **:** an act of twiddling **:** TURN, TWIST

twig \'twig\ *n* **:** a small shoot or branch — **twigged** \'twigd\ *adj* — **twig·gy** \'twig-ē\ *adj*

twi·light \'twī-ˌlīt\ *n* **1 :** the light from the sky between full night and sunrise or between sunset and full night **2 :** a state of indistinctness or of deepening darkness — **twilight** *adj*

twilight sleep *n* **:** a state produced by injection of drugs in which awareness and memory of pain is dulled or effaced

¹twill \'twil\ *n* **1 :** a fabric with a twill weave **2 :** a textile weave that produces a pattern of diagonal lines or ribs

²twill *vt* **:** to make (cloth) with a twill weave

¹twin \'twin\ *adj* **1 :** born with one other or as a pair at one birth **2 a :** made up of two similar, related, or connected members or parts **b :** being one of a pair

²twin *n* **1 :** either of two offspring produced at a birth **2 :** one of two persons or things closely related to or resembling each other

³twin *vb* **twinned; twin·ning 1 :** to bring together in close association **:** COUPLE **2 :** to bring forth twins

¹twine \'twīn\ *n* **1 :** a strong string of two or more strands twisted together **2 a :** an act of twining or interlacing **b :** TANGLE

²twine *vb* **1 :** to twist together **:** WEAVE **2 :** to coil or cause to coil about a support **3 :** WIND, MEANDER

¹twinge \'twinj\ *vb* **twinged; twing·ing** *or* **twinge·ing :** to affect with or feel a sudden sharp local pain

²twinge *n* **:** a sudden sharp stab (as of pain or distress)

¹twin·kle \'twiŋ-kəl\ *vb* **twin·kled; twin·kling** \'twiŋ-k(ə-)liŋ\ **1 :** to shine or cause to shine with a flickering or sparkling light **:** SCINTILLATE **2 :** to appear bright with merriment **3 a :** to move or flutter rapidly **b :** FLIT — **twin·kler** \-k(ə-)lər\ *n*

²twinkle *n* **1 :** a wink of the eyelids **2 :** the instant's duration of a wink **3 :** SPARKLE, FLICKER — **twin·kly** \-k(ə-)lē\ *adj*

twin·kling \'twiŋ-k(ə-)liŋ\ *n* **1 a :** a winking of the eye **b :** INSTANT **2 :** SCINTILLATION

¹twirl \'twərl\ *vb* **1 :** to revolve or cause to revolve rapidly **2 :** to pitch in a baseball game **3 :** CURL, TWIST — **twirl·er** *n*

²twirl *n* **1 :** an act of twirling **2 :** COIL, WHORL

¹twist \'twist\ *vb* **1 :** to unite by winding one thread, strand, or wire around another **2** : TWINE, COIL **3 a** : to turn so as to sprain or hurt **b** : to alter the meaning of : PERVERT **c** : CONTORT **d** : to pull off, rotate, or break by a turning force **e** : WARP, DEFORM **4** : to follow a winding course : SNAKE **5 a** : to turn or change shape under a turning force **b** : SQUIRM, WRITHE **6** : to turn around

²twist *n* **1** : something formed by twisting or winding **2 a** : an act of twisting : the state of being twisted **b** : a spiral turn or curve; *also* : SPIN **3 a** : a turning aside : DEFLECTION **b** : ECCENTRICITY, BIAS **c** : DISTORTION, WRENCH **4 a** : an unexpected turn or development **b** : VARIATION **c** : DEVICE, GIMMICK

twist·er \'twis-tər\ *n* **1** : one that twists; *esp* : a ball with a forward and spinning motion **2** : a tornado or waterspout in which the rotatory ascending column of air is esp. apparent

twit \'twit\ *vt* **twit·ted**; **twit·ting** : to subject to light ridicule or reproach : RALLY

¹twitch \'twich\ *vb* **1** : to move or pull with a sudden motion : JERK **2** : PLUCK, SNATCH **3** : QUIVER

²twitch *n* **1** : an act of twitching **2 a** : a short sharp contraction of muscle fibers **b** : a slight jerk of a body part

¹twit·ter \'twit-ər\ *vb* **1** : to utter successive chirping noises **2** : to talk in a chattering fashion **3** : to tremble or cause to tremble with agitation : FLUTTER

²twitter *n* **1** : a trembling agitation : QUIVER **2** : the chirping of birds **3** : a light chattering : GABBLE

twixt \(')twikst\ *prep* : BETWEEN

two \'tü\ *n* **1** — see NUMBER table **2** : the second in a set or series **3** : something having two units or members — **two** *adj or pron*

two–faced \'tü-'fāst\ *adj* **1** : having two faces **2** : DOUBLE-DEALING, FALSE

two·fold \'tü-ˌfōld, -'fōld\ *adj* **1** : having two units or members **2** : of or amounting to 200 percent — **twofold** *adv*

two·pence \'təp-ən(t)s, *US also* 'tü-ˌpen(t)s\ *n* : the sum of two pence

two·pen·ny \'təp-(ə-)nē, *US also* 'tü-ˌpen-ē\ *adj* : of the value of or costing twopence

two·some \'tü-səm\ *n* : a group of two persons or things

two–step \'tü-ˌstep\ *n* **1** : a ballroom dance executed in march or polka time **2** : a piece of music for the two-step — **two–step** *vi*

two–time \'tü-ˌtīm\ *vt* **1** : to betray (a spouse or lover) by secret lovemaking with another **2** : DOUBLE-CROSS

two–winged fly \ˌtü-ˌwiŋd-\ *n* : any of a large group of insects mostly with one pair of functional wings and another pair that if present are reduced to balancing organs

ty·coon \tī-'kün\ *n* : a businessman of exceptional wealth and power

tying *pres part of* TIE

tyke \'tīk\ *n* **1** : DOG, CUR **2** : a small child

tympani *n pl* : TIMPANI

tym·pan·ic \tim-'pan-ik\ *adj* **1** : of, relating to, or being a tympanum **2** : resembling a drum

tym·pa·num \'tim-pə-nəm\ *n, pl* **-na** \-nə\ : EARDRUM

¹type \'tīp\ *n* **1 a** : a person or thing believed to foreshadow or symbolize another **b** : one having qualities of a higher category : MODEL **2 a** : a rectangular block typically of metal or wood bearing a relief character from which an inked print is made **b** : a collection of such blocks or the letters printed from them **3 a** : general form or character common to a number of individuals that distinguishes them as an identifiable class **b** : a particular kind, class, or group

²type *vb* **1** : TYPIFY **2** : TYPEWRITE **3** : to identify as belonging to a type: as **a** : to determine the natural type of (as a blood sample) **b** : TYPECAST

type·cast \'tīp-ˌkast\ *vt* **1** : to cast (an actor) in a part calling for the same characteristics as those possessed by the actor himself **2** : to cast repeatedly in the same type of role

type·face \-ˌfās\ *n* : all type of a single design

type·script \-ˌskript\ *n* : typewritten matter

type·set·ter \-ˌset-ər\ *n* : one (as a compositor) that sets printing type — **type·set·ting** *adj or n*

type·write \'tīp-ˌrīt\ *vb* : to write with a typewriter

type·writ·er \-ˌrīt-ər\ *n* **1** : a machine for writing in characters similar to those produced by printer's type by means of keyboard-operated types striking through an inked ribbon **2** : TYPIST

type·writ·ing \-ˌrīt-iŋ\ *n* **1** : the act or study of or skill in using a typewriter **2** : the printing done with a typewriter

¹ty·phoid \'tī-ˌfȯid, (')tī-'\ *adj* : of, relating to, or being typhoid

²typhoid *n* : a communicable bacterial disease marked esp. by fever, diarrhea, prostration, headache, and intestinal inflammation

ty·phoon \tī-'fün\ *n* : a tropical cyclone occurring in the region of the Philippines or the China sea

ty·phus \'tī-fəs\ *n* : a severe disease marked by high fever, stupor alternating with delirium, intense headache, and a dark red rash and transmitted esp. by body lice

typ·i·cal \'tip-i-kəl\ *adj* **1** : being or having the nature of a type : SYMBOLIC **2** : combining or exhibiting the essential characteristics of a group — **typ·i·cal·i·ty** \ˌtip-ə-'kal-ət-ē\ *n* — **typ·i·cal·ly** \'tip-i-k(ə-)lē\ *adv*

typ·i·fy \'tip-ə-ˌfī\ *vt* **-fied**; **-fy·ing** : to have or embody the essential or main characteristics of

typ·ist \'tī-pəst\ *n* : one who typewrites

ty·po \'tī-pō\ *n, pl* **typos** : a typographical error

ty·pog·ra·pher \tī-'päg-rə-fər\ *n* **1** : COMPOSITOR **2** : PRINTER **3** : a specialist in the choice and arrangement of type matter

ty·pog·ra·phy \-fē\ *n* **1** : LETTERPRESS **2** : the art of letterpress printing **3** : the style, arrangement, or appearance of letterpress matter — **ty·po·graph·ic** \ˌtī-pə-'graf-ik\ *adj* — **ty·po·graph·i·cal** \-'graf-i-kəl\ *adj* — **ty·po·graph·i·cal·ly** \-i-k(ə-)lē\ *adv*

ty·ran·ni·cal \tə-'ran-i-kəl, tī-\ *adj* : of, relating to, or characteristic of a tyrant or tyranny : DESPOTIC — **ty·ran·ni·cal·ly** \-'ran-i-k(ə-)lē\ *adv*

tyr·an·nize \'tir-ə-ˌnīz\ *vb* **1** : to exercise arbitrary power **2** : to treat tyrannically : OPPRESS

tyr·an·nous \'tir-ə-nəs\ *adj* : marked by tyranny; *esp* : unjustly severe — **tyr·an·nous·ly** *adv*

tyr·an·ny \'tir-ə-nē\ *n, pl* **-nies** **1 a** : a government in which absolute power is vested in a single ruler **b** : the office, authority, and administration of such a ruler **2** : arbitrary and despotic government; *esp* : rigorous, cruel, and oppressive government **3** : SEVERITY, RIGOR **4** : a tyrannical act

ty·rant \'tī-rənt\ *n* **1** : an absolute ruler unrestrained by law or constitution **2 a** : a ruler who exercises absolute power oppressively or brutally **b** : one resembling such a tyrant in the harsh use of authority or power

ty·ro \'tī-rō\ *n, pl* **tyros** : a beginner in learning

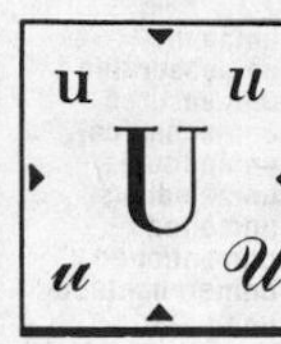

u \ˈyü\ *n, often cap* : the 21st letter of the English alphabet
ubiq·ui·tous \yu̇-ˈbik-wət-əs\ *adj* : existing or being everywhere at the same time : widely or generally present — **ubiq·ui·tous·ly** *adv* — **ubiq·ui·tous·ness** *n* — **ubiq·ui·ty** \-wət-ē\ *n*
U–boat \ˈyü-ˈbōt\ *n* : a German submarine
ud·der \ˈəd-ər\ *n* : a large pendulous organ consisting of two or more mammary glands enclosed in a common envelope and each provided with a nipple
ugh *often read as* ˈəg *or* ˈək\ *interj* — used to indicate the sound of a cough or grunt or to express disgust or horror
ug·ly \ˈəg-lē\ *adj* **1** : FRIGHTFUL, DIRE **2 a** : offensive to the sight : UNSIGHTLY, HIDEOUS **b** : offensive or unpleasing to any sense **3** : morally offensive or objectionable : REPULSIVE **4 a** : likely to cause inconvenience or discomfort : TROUBLESOME **b** : SURLY, QUARRELSOME — **ug·li·ness** *n*
ukase \yü-ˈkās\ *n* : an edict esp. of a Russian emperor or government
uku·le·le \ˌyü-kə-ˈlā-lē\ *n* : a small guitar popularized in Hawaii, strung usu. with four strings, and played with the fingers or a pick
ul·cer \ˈəl-sər\ *n* **1** : a necrotic or eroded sore that often discharges pus **2** : something that festers and corrupts like an open sore
ul·cer·ate \ˈəl-sə-ˌrāt\ *vb* : to cause or become affected with an ulcer — **ul·cer·a·tion** \ˌəl-sə-ˈrā-shən\ *n*
ul·cer·ous \ˈəls-(ə-)rəs\ *adj* **1** : being or marked by ulceration **2** : affected with an ulcer : ULCERATED
ul·ster \ˈəl-stər\ *n* : a long loose overcoat
ul·te·ri·or \ˌəl-ˈtir-ē-ər\ *adj* **1** : situated beyond or on the farther side **2** : lying farther away : more remote **3** : going beyond what is openly said or shown — **ul·te·ri·or·ly** *adv*
ul·ti·ma \ˈəl-tə-mə\ *n* : the last syllable of a word
ul·ti·mate \ˈəl-tə-mət\ *adj* **1 a** : most remote in space or time : FARTHEST **b** : last in a progression : FINAL **c** : EXTREME, UTMOST **2** : finally reckoned **3 a** : FUNDAMENTAL, ABSOLUTE, SUPREME **b** : incapable of further analysis, division, or separation : ELEMENTAL **4** : MAXIMUM — **ul·ti·mate·ly** *adv*
ul·ti·ma·tum \ˌəl-tə-ˈmāt-əm, -ˈmät-\ *n, pl* **-tums** *or* **-ta** \-ə\ : a final proposition, condition, or demand; *esp* : one whose rejection will bring about an end of negotiations and a resort to direct action (as by force)
ul·ti·mo \ˈəl-tə-ˌmō\ *adj* : of or occurring the month preceding the present
¹ul·tra \ˈəl-trə\ *adj* : going beyond others or beyond due limit
²ultra *n* : EXTREMIST
ul·tra·con·serv·a·tive \ˌəl-trə-kən-ˈsər-vət-iv\ *adj* : extremely conservative
ul·tra·high frequency \ˌəl-trə-ˌhī-\ *n* : any radio frequency in the range between 300 and 3000 megacycles — abbr. *uhf*
ul·tra·ma·rine \ˌəl-trə-mə-ˈrēn\ *n* **1** : a deep blue pigment **2** : a vivid blue
ul·tra·mod·ern \-ˈmäd-ərn\ *adj* : extreme or excessively modern in idea, style, or tendency — **ul·tra·mod·ern·ist** \-ər-nəst\ *n*
¹ul·tra·son·ic \-ˈsän-ik\ *adj* : SUPERSONIC — **ul·tra·son·i·cal·ly** \-ˈsän-i-k(ə-)lē\ *adv*
²ultrasonic *n* : a supersonic wave or frequency
ul·tra·vi·o·let \-ˈvī-ə-lət\ *adj* **1** : situated beyond the visible spectrum at its violet end and having a wavelength shorter than those of visible light but longer than those of X rays **2** : relating to, producing, or employing ultraviolet radiation — **ultraviolet** *n*
ul·u·late \ˈəl-yə-ˌlāt, ˈ(y)ül-\ *vi* : HOWL, WAIL — **ul·u·lant** \-lənt\ *adj* — **ul·u·la·tion** \ˌəl-yə-ˈlā-shən, ˌ(y)ül-yə-\ *n*
um·bel \ˈəm-bəl\ *n* : a flat or rounded flower cluster in which the individual flower stalks all arise at one point on the main stem — **um·bel·late** \ˈəm-bə-ˌlāt, ˌəm-ˈbel-ət\ *adj*
um·ber \ˈəm-bər\ *n* : a brown earth valued as a pigment — **umber** *adj*
um·bil·i·cal \ˌəm-ˈbil-i-kəl\ *adj* : of, relating to, or adjacent to the navel
umbilical cord *n* : a cord arising from the navel that connects the fetus with the placenta
um·bil·i·cus \ˌəm-ˈbil-i-kəs\ *n, pl* **-bil·i·ci** \-ˈbil-ə-ˌkī\ *or* **-bil·i·cus·es** : a depression in the abdominal wall at the point of attachment of the umbilical cord to the fetus
um·bra \ˈəm-brə\ *n, pl* **umbras** *or* **um·brae** \-(ˌ)brē\ **1** : a shaded area **2** : the conical part of the shadow of a celestial body excluding all light from the primary source
um·brage \ˈəm-brij\ *n* **1 a** : a growth (as of tangled branches) that gives shade **b** : SHADE **2** : RESENTMENT, OFFENSE — **um·bra·geous** \ˌəm-ˈbrā-jəs\ *adj*
um·brel·la \ˌəm-ˈbrel-ə\ *n* **1** : a collapsible shade for protection against weather consisting of fabric stretched over hinged ribs radiating from a center pole; *esp* : a small one for carrying in the hand **2** : the bell-shaped or saucer-shaped largely gelatinous body proper of most jellyfishes
umi·ak \ˈü-mē-ˌak\ *n* : an open Eskimo boat made of a wooden frame covered with hide
um·laut \ˈu̇m-ˌlau̇t, ˈüm-\ *n* **1 a** : the change of a vowel caused by partial assimilation to a succeeding sound **b** : a vowel resulting from such partial assimilation **2** : a diacritical mark ¨ placed esp. over a German vowel to indicate umlaut
¹um·pire \ˈəm-ˌpī(ə)r\ *n* **1** : one having authority to decide finally a controversy or question between parties **2** : an official in a sport who rules on plays
²umpire *vb* : to supervise or act as umpire
un- *prefix* **1** : not : IN-, NON- **2** : opposite of : contrary to

unabashed
unabated
unabbreviated
unabridged
unabsolved
unabsorbable
unabsorbed
unacademic
unaccented
unaccentuated
unacceptable
unaccepted
unacclimated
unacclimatized
unaccommodated
unaccommodating
unaccomplished
unaccountability
unaccredited
unacknowledged
unacquainted
unactable
unacted
unadaptable
unadapted
unadjusted
unadmirable
unadvantageous
unadventurous
unadvertised
unadvisable
unaesthetic
unaffiliated
unafraid
unaged
unaggressive
unaided
unaimed
unaired
unalarmed
unalike
unallied
unallowable
unalterability
unalterable
unalterableness
unalterably
unaltered
unambiguous
unambiguously
unambitious
unamiable
unanalyzable
unanchored
unanimated
unannounced
unanswerable
unanswered
unanticipated
unapologetic
unappalled
unapparent
unappealing
unappeased
unappetizing
unappreciated
unappreciative
unapproachable
unapproached
unappropriated
unapproved
unarmored
unarrested
unarticulated
unartistic
unashamed
unashamedly
unaspirated
unaspiring
unassailed
unassisted
unassociated
unastronomical
unattainable
unattempted
unattended
unattested
unattractive
unattractiveness
unauspicious
unauthentic
unauthenticated
unauthenticity
unauthorized
unavailable
unavenged
unavowed
unawakened
unawed
unbaked
unbandage
unbaptized
unbeautiful
unbefitting
unblamable
unblamed
unbleached
unblemished
unblenching
unblessed
unblinking
unborrowed
unbought
unbound
unbracketed
unbranded
unbreakable
unbridgeable
unbridged
unbrotherly

unbruised
unbrushed
unbudging
unburdened
unburied
unburned
unburnished
unburnt
unbusinesslike
uncalled
uncanceled
uncanonical
uncapitalized
uncared-for
uncaring
uncastrated
uncataloged
uncaught
uncensored
uncensured
unchallenged
unchangeable
unchanged
unchanging
unchaperoned
uncharacteristic
uncharged
unchary
unchastened
unchecked
unchivalrous
unchristened
uncircumcised
uncircumcision
unclaimed
unclassifiable
uncleaned
unclear
uncleared
unclosed
unclothed
unclouded
uncluttered
uncoated
uncocked
uncoiled
uncoined
uncollected
uncollectible
uncolored
uncombed
uncombined
uncomely
uncomforted
uncompanionable
uncompensated
uncomplaining
uncompleted
uncomplicated
uncomplimentary
uncompounded
uncomprehended
uncomprehending
uncomprehensible
unconcealed
unconfined
unconfirmed
unconformable
unconformably
uncongealed
uncongenial
unconnected
unconquered
unconscientious
unconsecrated
unconsidered
unconsolidated
unconstrained
unconsumed
uncontaminated
uncontested
uncontradicted
uncontrolled
unconverted
unconvinced
unconvincing
uncooked
uncooperative
uncoordinated
uncordial
uncorked
uncorrected
uncorroborated
uncorrupted
uncountable
uncourteous
uncovered
uncredited
uncrippled
uncropped
uncrossed
uncrowded
uncrowned
uncrystallized
uncultivable
uncultivated
uncultured
uncurbed
uncured
uncurious
uncurrent
uncurtained
undamaged
undamped
undated
undazzled
undecipherable
undecked
undeclared
undeclinable
undecorated
undefeated
undefended
undefiled
undefinable
undefined
undelayed
undeliverable
undemanding
undemocratic
undenominational
undependable
undeserved
undeserving
undesigning
undesired
undetachable
undetected
undeterminable
undetermined
undeterred
undeveloped
undifferentiated
undigested
undignified
undiluted
undiminished
undiminishing
undimmed
undiplomatic
undirected
undiscerning
undischarged
undisciplined
undisclosed
undiscoverable
undiscovered
undiscriminating
undisguised
undismayed
undisputed
undissolved
undistinguishable
undistinguished
undistributed
undisturbed
undiversified
undivided
undivulged
undogmatic
undomestic
undomesticated
undone
undoubled
undoubting
undrained
undramatic
undraped
undrawn
undreamed
undreamt
undrinkable
undulled
undutiful
undutifully
undutifulness
undyed
uneager
unease
uneatable
uneaten
uneconomic
uneconomical
unedifying
uneducable
uneducated
unembarrassed
unembellished
unemotional
unemphatic
unemphatically
unenclosed
unencumbered
unendorsed
unendurable
unenduring
unenforceable
unenforced
unengaged
unenjoyable
unenlarged
unenlightened
unenrolled
unenterprising
unentertaining
unenthusiastic
unenviable
unenvied
unenvious
unequipped
unessential
unethical
unexaggerated
unexamined
unexcelled
unexceptional
unexchangeable
unexcited
unexciting
unexecuted
unexhausted
unexpanded
unexpended
unexperienced
unexpired
unexplainable
unexplained
unexploded
unexplored
unexposed
unexpressed
unexpurgated
unextended
unextinguished
unfading
unfaltering
unfashionable
unfastened
unfathomable
unfathomed
unfavored
unfeasible
unfed
unfeminine
unfenced
unfermentable
unfermented
unfertilized
unfilled
unfiltered
unfinished
unfired
unfitted
unfitting
unflagging
unflattering
unflavored
unflexed
unforced
unforeseeable
unforeseen
unforested
unforgivable
unforgiving
unforked
unformulated
unfortified
unframed
unfree
unfrozen
unfulfilled
unfunded
unfurnished
ungallant
ungarnished
ungathered
ungentle
ungentlemanly
ungifted
unglazed
unglue
ungoverned
ungraded
ungrammatical
ungrudging
unguided
unhackneyed
unhallowed
unhampered
unhanged
unhardened
unharmed
unharmonious
unharnessed
unhatched
unheeded
unheeding
unheralded
unheroic
unheroical
unhesitating
unhindered
unhonored
unhoped-for
unhoused
unhurried
unhurt
unhygienic
unideal
unidentified
unidiomatic
unilluminated
unimaginable
unimaginably
unimaginative
unimpaired
unimpassioned
unimpeded
unimportant
unimposing
unimpressionable
unimpressive
unimproved
unincorporated
uninfected
uninflammable
uninflected
uninfluenced
uninformed
uninhabitable
uninhabited
uninitiated
uninjured
uninspired
uninspiring
uninstructed
uninsulated
uninsured
unintelligibility
unintended
uninteresting
unintermitted
unintermittent
uninventive
uninvested
uninvited
uninviting
unjoined
unjointed
unjustifiable
unjustified
unkept
unknowable
unknowledgeable
unlabeled
unlabored
unladylike
unlaid
unlamented
unleavened
unlicensed
unlighted
unlikable
unlined
unlisted
unlit
unlivable
unlobed
unlovable
unloved
unloving
unmagnetized
unmagnified
unmailable
unmalleable
unmanageable
unmanufactured
unmapped
unmarked
unmarketable
unmarred
unmarried
unmastered
unmatched
unmated
unmeant
unmeasurable
unmeasured
unmechanical
unmeditated
unmelodious
unmelted
unmentioned
unmerchantable
unmerited
unmethodical
unmetrical
unmilitary
unmilled
unmingled
unmitigable
unmixed
unmodified
unmodulated
unmolested
unmortgaged
unmotivated
unmounted
unmovable
unmoving
unmusical
unnameable
unnamed
unnaturalized
unnavigable
unnecessary
unneighborly
unnoted
unnoticeable
unnoticed
unobjectionable
unobliging
unobscured
unobservant
unobserved
unobserving
unobstructed
unobtainable
unoffending
unofficial
unopened
unopposed
unordained
unordered
unoriginal
unorthodox
unostentatious
unowned
unpaid
unpainted
unpaired
unpalatable
unpardonable
unpardoned
unparenthesized
unpartisan
unpartitioned
unpasteurized
unpastoral
unpatient
unpatriotic
unpaved
unpedigreed
unpeopled
unperceivable
unperceived
unperceiving
unperceptive
unperformed
unperplex
unpersuasive
unperturbed
unphilosophic
unphilosophical

unphonetic
unpitied
unpitying
unplaced
unplanned
unplanted
unplayable
unpleasing
unpledged
unplowed
unpoetic
unpoetical
unpointed
unpolarized
unpolished
unpolitical
unpolled
unpolluted
unposed
unpossessing
unpowered
unpractical
unpracticed
unprejudiced
unpremeditated
unprepared
unprepossessing
unprescribed
unpresentable
unpressed
unpretending
unpretty
unprevailing
unpreventable
unprinted
unprivileged
unprocessed
unproductive
unprofaned
unprofessed
unprofound
unprogressive
unprohibited
unpromising
unprompted
unpronounceable
unpronounced
unpropitious
unproportionate
unproportioned
unprosperous
unprotected
unprotesting
unproved
unproven
unprovided
unprovoked
unpruned
unpublished
unpunctual
unpunished
unpurchasable
unpure
unquenchable
unquenched
unquestioned
unraised
unransomed
unrated
unratified
unravished
unready
unrealistic
unrealizable
unrealized
unrecognizable
unrecognized
unrecompensed
unreconcilable
unreconciled
unrecorded
unredeemable
unredeemed
unrefined
unreflecting
unreflective
unreformable
unreformed
unregarded
unregimented
unregistered
unregulated
unrehearsed
unrelated
unrelaxed
unrelaxing
unreliability
unreliable
unrelieved
unreligious
unremarkable
unremembered
unremitted
unremunerated
unremunerative
unrenowned
unrent
unrented
unrepaid
unrepaired
unrepealed
unrepentant
unreported
unrepresentative
unrepresented
unrepressed
unreproved
unrequited
unresistant
unresisted
unresisting
unresolved
unresponsive
unrestful
unrestraint
unrestricted
unretentive
unretracted
unreturnable
unreturned
unrevealed
unrevenged
unrevoked
unrewarded
unrewarding
unrhymed
unrhythmic
unrhythmical
unrightful
unrinsed
unripened
unromantic
unroofed
unruled
unsafe
unsaid
unsaintly
unsalable
unsalaried
unsalted
unsanctified
unsanctioned
unsanitary
unsated
unsatiated
unsatisfactory
unsatisfied
unsatisfying
unsaved
unscaled
unscanned
unscarred
unscented
unscheduled
unscholarly
unscorched
unscreened
unscriptural
unsealed
unseasoned
unseaworthy
unseconded
unsecured
unseeded
unseeing
unseen
unsegmented
unselected
unselfconscious
unsensitive
unsentimental
unseparated
unserved
unserviceable
unset
unsettlement
unsexual
unshaded
unshadowed
unshakable
unshaken
unshapely
unshared
unsharp
unshaved
unshaven
unshed
unsheltered
unshielded
unshorn
unshrinkable
unshrinking
unshut
unsifted
unsigned
unsingable
unsinkable
unsized
unslacked
unslaked
unsmiling
unsnuffed
unsociability
unsociable
unsoiled
unsold
unsoldierly
unsolicited
unsolicitous
unsolid
unsolvable
unsolved
unsophistication
unsorted
unsounded
unsoured
unsown
unspecialized
unspecific
unspecified
unspent
unspiritual
unsplit
unspoiled
unspoken
unsportsmanlike
unspun
unsquared
unstained
unstatesmanlike
unsterilized
unstinted
unstinting
unstopped
unstrained
unstratified
unstriated
unstriped
unstuck
unsubdued
unsubstantiated
unsuccessful
unsuccessfully
unsuggestive
unsuited
unsullied
unsupervised
unsupportable
unsupported
unsuppressed
unsure
unsurmountable
unsurpassable
unsurpassed
unsusceptible
unsuspected
unsuspecting
unsuspicious
unsustained
unswayed
unsweetened
unswept
unswerving
unsworn
unsymmetrical
unsympathetic
unsympathizing
unsystematic
unsystematical
unsystematized
untactful
untainted
untalented
untalked-of
untamable
untamed
untanned
untapped
untarnished
untaxed
unteachable
untechnical
untempered
untenable
untenanted
untended
unterrified
untested
unthankful
unthatched
unthawed
untheatrical
unthoughtful
unthreaded
unthrifty
untidily
untidiness
untidy
untillable
untilled
untired
untiring
untouched
untraceable
untracked
untrained
untrammeled
untransferable
untranslatable
untranslated
untraveled
untraversed
untreated
untrimmed
untrod
untrodden
untroubled
untrustworthy
untufted
untunable
untwisted
untypical
unusable
unuttered
unvalued
unvaried
unvarying
unveiled
unventilated
unveracious
unverifiable
unverified
unversed
unvexed
unvisited
unvocal
unvulcanized
unwalled
unwanted
unwarlike
unwarranted
unwashed
unwatched
unwatered
unwavering
unweaned
unwearable
unwearied
unwearying
unweathered
unwedded
unweeded
unwelcome
unwelded
unwifely
unwilled
unwinking
unwished
unwitnessed
unwomanly
unwon
unwooded
unworkable
unworked
unworkmanlike
unworn
unworried
unwounded
unwoven
unwrinkled
unwrought

un·able \'ən-'ā-bəl\ *adj* : not able : INCAPABLE

un·ac·com·pa·nied \,ən-ə-'kəmp-(ə-)nēd\ *adj* : not accompanied; *esp* : being without instrumental accompaniment

un·ac·count·a·ble \,ən-ə-'kaunt-ə-bəl\ *adj* **1** : not to be accounted for : INEXPLICABLE, STRANGE, MYSTERIOUS **2** : not to be called to account : not responsible — **un·ac·count·a·bly** \-blē\ *adv*

un·ac·count·ed \-'kaunt-əd\ *adj* : not accounted : UNEXPLAINED — often used with *for*

un·ac·cus·tomed \,ən-ə-'kəs-təmd\ *adj* **1** : UNUSUAL, UNFAMILIAR **2** : not used : not habituated

un·adorned \,ən-ə-'dörnd\ *adj* : not adorned : lacking embellishment or decoration : BARE, PLAIN, SIMPLE

un·adul·ter·at·ed \,ən-ə-'dəl-tə-,rāt-əd\ *adj* : PURE, UNMIXED — **un·adul·ter·at·ed·ly** *adv*

un·ad·vised \,ən-əd-'vīzd\ *adj* **1** : done without due consideration **2** : not prudent — **un·ad·vis·ed·ly** \-'vī-zəd-lē\ *adv*

un·af·fect·ed \,ən-ə-'fek-təd\ *adj* **1** : not influenced or changed mentally, physically, or chemically **2** : free from affectation : GENUINE — **un·af·fect·ed·ly** *adv* — **un·af·fect·ed·ness** *n*

un·alien·a·ble \'ən-'āl-yə-nə-bəl, -'ā-lē-ə-nə-\ *adj* : INALIENABLE

un·aligned \,ən-ᵊl-'īnd\ *adj* : not associated with any one of competing international blocs

un·al·loyed \,ən-ᵊl-'öid\ *adj* : not alloyed : UNMIXED, PURE

un–Amer·i·can \,ən-ə-'mer-ə-kən\ *adj* : not American : not

characteristic of or consistent with American customs, principles, or traditions — **un–Amer·i·can·ism** \-kə-ˌniz-əm\ *n*
una·nim·i·ty \ˌyü-nə-ˈnim-ət-ē\ *n* : the quality or state of being unanimous
unan·i·mous \yu̇-ˈnan-ə-məs\ *adj* **1** : being of one mind **2** : assented to by all — **unan·i·mous·ly** *adv*
un·apt \ˈən-ˈapt\ *adj* **1** : UNSUITABLE, INAPPROPRIATE **2** : not accustomed and not likely **3** : INAPT, DULL, BACKWARD — **un·apt·ly** *adv* — **un·apt·ness** *n*
un·arm \ˈən-ˈärm\ *vt* : DISARM
un·armed \-ˈärmd\ *adj* : not armed or armored
un·asked \ˈən-ˈaskt\ *adj* : not asked or asked for
un·as·sail·a·ble \ˌən-ə-ˈsā-lə-bəl\ *adj* : not liable to doubt, attack, or question — **un·as·sail·a·bly** \-blē\ *adv*
un·as·sert·ive \-ˈsərt-iv\ *adj* : not assertive : MODEST, SHY
un·as·sum·ing \ˌən-ə-ˈsü-miŋ\ *adj* : not putting on airs : MODEST, RETIRING — **un·as·sum·ing·ly** *adv*
un·at·tached \ˌən-ə-ˈtacht\ *adj* **1** : not attached **2** : not married or engaged
un·avail·ing \ˌən-ə-ˈvā-liŋ\ *adj* : of no avail : not successful : VAIN — **un·avail·ing·ly** *adv*
un·avoid·a·ble \ˌən-ə-ˈvȯid-ə-bəl\ *adj* : not avoidable : INEVITABLE — **un·avoid·a·bly** \-blē\ *adv*
[1]**un·aware** \ˌən-ə-ˈwa(ə)r\ *adv* : UNAWARES
[2]**unaware** *adj* : not aware : IGNORANT — **un·aware·ness** *n*
un·awares \-ˈwarz\ *adv* **1** : without warning : by surprise **2** : without knowing : UNINTENTIONALLY
un·bal·ance \ˈən-ˈbal-ən(t)s\ *vt* : to put out of balance
un·bal·anced \-ən(t)st\ *adj* **1** : not in equilibrium **2** : mentally disordered or deranged **3** : not adjusted so as to make credits equal to debits **4** : having more players on one side of the center than on the other
un·bar \ˈən-ˈbär\ *vt* **-barred**; **-bar·ring** : to remove a bar from : UNBOLT, OPEN
un·bear·a·ble \ˈən-ˈbar-ə-bəl\ *adj* : greater than can be borne — **un·bear·a·bly** \-blē\ *adv*
un·beat·a·ble \-ˈbēt-ə-bəl\ *adj* : not capable of being defeated
un·beat·en \-ˈbēt-ᵊn\ *adj* **1** : not pounded or beaten : not whipped **2** : UNTROD **3** : UNDEFEATED
un·be·com·ing \ˌən-bi-ˈkəm-iŋ\ *adj* : not becoming : UNSUITABLE — **un·be·com·ing·ly** *adv* — **un·be·com·ing·ness** *n*
un·be·known \-bi-ˈnōn\ *or* **un·be·knownst** \-ˈnōn(t)st\ *adj* : happening without one's knowledge — usu. used with *to*
un·be·lief \ˌən-bə-ˈlēf\ *n* : the withholding or absence of belief
un·be·liev·a·ble \-ˈlē-və-bəl\ *adj* : too improbable for belief — **un·be·liev·a·bly** \-blē\ *adv*
un·be·liev·er \-ˈlē-vər\ *n* **1** : one who does not believe : DOUBTER **2** : one who does not believe in a particular religious faith : INFIDEL
un·be·liev·ing \-ˈlē-viŋ\ *adj* : marked by unbelief — **un·be·liev·ing·ly** *adv*
un·bend \ˈən-ˈbend\ *vb* **-bent** \-ˈbent\; **-bend·ing** **1** : to free from being bent : make or become straight **2** : UNTIE **3** : to make or become less stiff or more affable : RELAX
un·bend·ing \-ˈben-diŋ\ *adj* : formal and distant in manner
un·bi·ased \-ˈbī-əst\ *adj* : free from bias; *esp* : UNPREJUDICED, IMPARTIAL
un·bid·den \-ˈbid-ᵊn\ *adj* : not bidden : UNASKED, UNINVITED
un·bind \-ˈbīnd\ *vt* **-bound** \-ˈbau̇nd\; **-bind·ing** **1** : to remove a band from : free from fastenings : UNTIE, UNFASTEN, LOOSE **2** : to set free : RELEASE
un·blush·ing \-ˈbləsh-iŋ\ *adj* **1** : not blushing **2** : SHAMELESS, UNABASHED — **un·blush·ing·ly** *adv*
un·bod·ied \-ˈbäd-ēd\ *adj* **1** : having no body : INCORPOREAL; *also* : DISEMBODIED **2** : FORMLESS
un·bolt \ˈən-ˈbōlt\ *vt* : to open or unfasten by withdrawing a bolt
un·bolt·ed \-ˈbōl-təd\ *adj* : not sifted; *also* : COARSE
un·bon·net·ed \-ˈbän-ət-əd\ *adj* : BAREHEADED
un·born \-ˈbȯrn\ *adj* : not born : not brought into life; *also* : still to appear : FUTURE
un·bo·som \-ˈbu̇z-əm\ *vb* **1** : to give expression to : DISCLOSE, REVEAL **2** : to disclose the thoughts or feelings of oneself
un·bound·ed \-ˈbau̇n-dəd\ *adj* : having no bounds or limits
un·bowed \-ˈbau̇d\ *adj* **1** : not bowed down **2** : UNSUBDUED
un·braid \-ˈbrād\ *vt* : to separate the strands of : UNRAVEL
un·bri·dled \-ˈbrīd-ᵊld\ *adj* **1** : not confined by a bridle **2** : UNRESTRAINED, UNGOVERNED
un·bro·ken \-ˈbrō-kən\ *adj* **1** : not damaged : WHOLE **2** : not subdued or tamed **3** : not interrupted : CONTINUOUS
un·buck·le \ˈən-ˈbək-əl\ *vt* : to unfasten the buckle of
un·built \-ˈbilt\ *adj* **1** : not built : not yet constructed **2** : not built on
un·bur·den \-ˈbərd-ᵊn\ *vt* **1** : to free or relieve from a burden **2** : to relieve oneself of (as cares, fears, or worries) : cast off
un·but·ton \-ˈbət-ᵊn\ *vt* : to unfasten the buttons of
un·cage \-ˈkāj\ *vt* : to release from or as if from a cage
un·called–for \-ˈkȯld-ˌfȯr\ *adj* : not called for : not needed or wanted : not proper
un·can·ny \-ˈkan-ē\ *adj* **1** : seeming to have a supernatural character or origin : MYSTERIOUS **2** : being beyond what is normal or expected : suggesting superhuman or supernatural powers — **un·can·ni·ly** \-ˈkan-ᵊl-ē\ *adv*
un·cap \-ˈkap\ *vt* **-capped**; **-cap·ping** : to remove a cap or covering from
un·ceas·ing \-ˈsē-siŋ\ *adj* : never ceasing : CONTINUOUS, INCESSANT — **un·ceas·ing·ly** *adv*
un·cer·e·mo·ni·ous \ˌən-ˌser-ə-ˈmō-nē-əs\ *adj* : acting without or lacking ordinary courtesy — **un·cer·e·mo·ni·ous·ly** *adv* — **un·cer·e·mo·ni·ous·ness** *n*
un·cer·tain \ˈən-ˈsərt-ᵊn\ *adj* **1** : not determined or fixed **2** : subject to chance or change : not dependable **3** : not sure **4** : not definitely known — **un·cer·tain·ly** *adv* — **un·cer·tain·ness** *n*
un·cer·tain·ty \-ᵊn-tē\ *n* **1** : lack of certainty : DOUBT **2** : something that is uncertain
un·chain \ˈən-ˈchān\ *vt* : to free by or as if by removing a chain : set loose
un·char·i·ta·ble \-ˈchar-ət-ə-bəl\ *adj* : not charitable; *esp* : severe in judging others — **un·char·i·ta·ble·ness** *n* — **un·char·i·ta·bly** \-blē\ *adv*
un·chart·ed \-ˈchärt-əd\ *adj* : not recorded or plotted on a map, chart, or plan : UNKNOWN
un·chaste \-ˈchāst\ *adj* : not chaste : lacking in chastity — **un·chaste·ly** *adv* — **un·chaste·ness** *n* — **un·chas·ti·ty** \-ˈchas-tət-ē\ *n*
un·chris·tian \-ˈkris-chən\ *adj* **1** : contrary to the Christian spirit or character **2** : BARBAROUS, UNCIVILIZED
un·civ·il \ˈən-ˈsiv-əl\ *adj* : lacking in courtesy : ILL-MANNERED, IMPOLITE
un·civ·i·lized \-ˈsiv-ə-ˌlīzd\ *adj* **1** : not civilized : BARBAROUS **2** : remote from civilization : WILD
un·clad \-ˈklad\ *adj* : not clothed : UNDRESSED, NAKED
un·clasp \-ˈklasp\ *vt* : to release from a clasp
un·clas·si·fied \-ˈklas-ə-ˌfīd\ *adj* : not classified; *esp* : not subject to a security classification
un·cle \ˈəŋ-kəl\ *n* **1** : the brother of one's father or mother **2** : the husband of one's aunt
un·clean \ˈən-ˈklēn\ *adj* **1** : morally or spiritually impure **2** : prohibited by ritual law for use or contact **3** : DIRTY, FILTHY — **un·clean·ness** *n*
[1]**un·clean·ly** \-ˈklen-lē\ *adj* : morally or physically unclean — **un·clean·li·ness** *n*
[2]**un·clean·ly** \-ˈklēn-lē\ *adv* : in an unclean manner
un·clench \-ˈklench\ *vb* : to open from a clenched position
Un·cle Sam \ˌəŋ-kəl-ˈsam\ *n* **1** : the U. S. government per-

sonified **2 :** the American nation or people

un·cloak \ˈən-ˈklōk\ *vb* **1 :** to remove a cloak or cover from **2 :** REVEAL, UNMASK **3 :** to take off a cloak

un·close \-ˈklōz\ *vb* **:** OPEN

un·clothe \-ˈklōt͟h\ *vt* **:** to strip of clothes or a covering

un·co \ˈən-kō, -kə\ *adv* **:** EXTREMELY, REMARKABLY, UNCOMMONLY

un·coil \ˈən-ˈkȯil\ *vb* **:** to release or become released from a coiled state **:** UNWIND

un·com·fort·a·ble \-ˈkəm(p)(f)-tə-bəl, -ˈkəm(p)-fərt-ə-bəl\ *adj* **1 :** causing discomfort **2 :** feeling discomfort **:** UNEASY — **un·com·fort·a·bly** \-blē\ *adv*

un·com·mit·ted \ˌən-kə-ˈmit-əd\ *adj* **:** not committed; *esp* **:** not pledged to a particular belief, allegiance, or program

un·com·mon \ˈən-ˈkäm-ən\ *adj* **1 :** not ordinarily encountered **:** UNUSUAL **2 :** REMARKABLE, EXCEPTIONAL — **un·com·mon·ly** *adv* — **un·com·mon·ness** *n*

un·com·mu·ni·ca·tive \ˌən-kə-ˈmyü-nə-ˌkāt-iv, -ni-kət-\ *adj* **:** not inclined to talk or impart information **:** RESERVED

un·com·pro·mis·ing \ˈən-ˈkäm-prə-ˌmī-ziŋ\ *adj* **:** not making or accepting a compromise **:** making no concessions **:** INFLEXIBLE, UNYIELDING — **un·com·pro·mis·ing·ly** *adv*

un·con·cern \ˌən-kən-ˈsərn\ *n* **1 :** lack of care or interest **:** INDIFFERENCE **2 :** freedom from excessive concern

un·con·cerned \-ˈsərnd\ *adj* **1 :** not involved **:** not having any part or interest **2 :** not anxious or upset **:** free of worry — **un·con·cern·ed·ly** \-ˈsər-nəd-lē\ *adv* — **un·con·cern·ed·ness** \-nəd-nəs\ *n*

un·con·di·tion·al \ˌən-kən-ˈdish-nəl, -ˈdish-ən-ᵊl\ *adj* **:** not limited **:** ABSOLUTE — **un·con·di·tion·al·ly** \-ē\ *adv*

un·con·di·tioned \-ˈdish-ənd\ *adj* **1 :** not subject to conditions **2 :** not dependent on conditioning or learning **:** INHERENT

un·con·quer·a·ble \ˈən-ˈkäŋ-k(ə-)rə-bəl\ *adj* **:** incapable of being conquered or overcome **:** INDOMITABLE — **un·con·quer·a·bly** \-blē\ *adv*

un·con·scion·a·ble \-ˈkänch-(ə-)nə-bəl\ *adj* **1 :** not being in accordance with what is right or just **:** UNREASONABLE, EXCESSIVE **2 :** not guided or controlled by conscience — **un·con·scion·a·bly** \-blē\ *adv*

¹un·con·scious \-ˈkän-chəs\ *adj* **1 :** having lost consciousness **2 :** not aware **3 :** not realized by oneself **:** not consciously done — **un·con·scious·ly** *adv* — **un·con·scious·ness** *n*

²unconscious *n* **:** the part of one's mental life that is not ordinarily available to consciousness and is manifested in spontaneous overt behavior (as slips of the tongue) or in dreams

un·con·sti·tu·tion·al \ˌən-ˌkän(t)-stə-ˈt(y)üsh-nəl, -ən-ᵊl\ *adj* **:** not according to or consistent with the constitution of a state or society — **un·con·sti·tu·tion·al·i·ty** \-ˌt(y)ü-shə-ˈnal-ət-ē\ *n* — **un·con·sti·tu·tion·al·ly** \-ˈt(y)üsh-nə-lē, -ən-ᵊl-ē\ *adv*

un·con·trol·la·ble \ˌən-kən-ˈtrō-lə-bəl\ *adj* **:** incapable of being controlled **:** UNGOVERNABLE — **un·con·trol·la·bly** \-blē\ *adv*

un·con·ven·tion·al \ˌən-kən-ˈvench-nəl, -ən-ᵊl\ *adj* **:** not conventional **:** not bound by or in accordance with convention **:** being out of the ordinary — **un·con·ven·tion·al·i·ty** \-ˌven-chə-ˈnal-ət-ē\ *n* — **un·con·ven·tion·al·ly** \-ˈvench-nə-lē, -ən-ᵊl-ē\ *adv*

un·cork \ˈən-ˈkȯrk\ *vt* **1 :** to draw a cork from **2 a :** to release from a sealed or pent-up state **b :** to let go **:** RELEASE

un·count·ed \-ˈkau̇nt-əd\ *adj* **1 :** not counted **2 :** INNUMERABLE

un·cou·ple \-ˈkəp-əl\ *vt* **-cou·pled; -cou·pling** \-ˈkəp-(ə-)liŋ\ **:** DISCONNECT

un·couth \-ˈküth\ *adj* **1 :** strange, awkward, and clumsy in shape or appearance **2 :** vulgar in conduct or speech **:** RUDE

un·cov·er \-ˈkəv-ər\ *vb* **1 :** to make known **:** bring to light **:** DISCLOSE, REVEAL **2 :** to expose to view by removing some covering **3 a :** to take the cover from **b :** to remove the hat from; *also* **:** to take off the hat as a token of respect

un·crit·i·cal \-ˈkrit-i-kəl\ *adj* **:** showing lack or improper use of critical standards or procedures — **un·crit·i·cal·ly** \-k(ə-)lē\ *adv*

un·cross \-ˈkrȯs\ *vt* **:** to change from a crossed position

unc·tion \ˈəŋ(k)-shən\ *n* **1 :** the act of anointing as a rite of consecration or healing **2 :** exaggerated, assumed, or superficial earnestness of language or manner

unc·tu·ous \ˈəŋ(k)-ch(ə-w)əs\ *adj* **1 :** being like an ointment esp. in smooth greasy texture or appearance; *also* **:** OILY, FATTY **2 :** full of unction in speech and manner; *esp* **:** insincerely smooth — **unc·tu·ous·ly** *adv* — **unc·tu·ous·ness** *n*

un·curl \ˈən-ˈkərl\ *vb* **:** to make or become straightened out from a curled or coiled position

un·cut \-ˈkət\ *adj* **1 :** not cut down or cut into **2 :** not shaped by cutting **3 :** not having the folds of the leaves slit **4 :** not abridged or curtailed

un·daunt·ed \-ˈdȯnt-əd\ *adj* **:** not daunted **:** not discouraged or dismayed **:** FEARLESS — **un·daunt·ed·ly** *adv*

un·de·ceive \ˌən-di-ˈsēv\ *vt* **:** to free from deception, illusion, or error

un·de·cid·ed \-ˈsīd-əd\ *adj* **1 :** not yet decided **:** not settled **2 :** uncertain what to do — **un·de·cid·ed·ly** *adv*

un·de·mon·stra·tive \ˌən-di-ˈmän(t)-strət-iv\ *adj* **:** restrained or reserved in expression of feeling **:** not effusive — **un·de·mon·stra·tive·ly** *adv* — **un·de·mon·stra·tive·ness** *n*

un·de·ni·a·ble \ˌən-di-ˈnī-ə-bəl\ *adj* **1 :** plainly true **:** INCONTESTABLE **2 :** unquestionably excellent or genuine — **un·de·ni·a·ble·ness** *n* — **un·de·ni·a·bly** \-blē\ *adv*

¹un·der \ˈən-dər\ *adv* **1 :** in or into a position below or beneath something **2 :** below some quantity, level, or norm — often used in combination **3 :** in or into a condition of subjection, subordination, or unconsciousness **4 :** so as to be covered or hidden

²un·der \ˌən-dər, ˈən-\ *prep* **1 a :** lower than and overhung, surmounted, or sheltered by **b :** below the surface of **c :** in or into such a position as to be covered or concealed by **2 a (1) :** subject to the authority or guidance of **(2) :** with the guarantee of **b :** controlled, limited, or oppressed by **c :** subject to the action or effect of **3 :** within the group or designation of **4 a :** less or lower than (as in size, amount, or rank) **b :** below the standard or required degree of

³under \ˈən-dər\ *adj* **1 a :** lying or placed below, beneath, or on the ventral side **b :** facing or protruding downward — often used in combination **2 :** lower in rank or authority **:** SUBORDINATE **3 :** lower than usual, proper, or desired in amount, quality, or degree

un·der·achiev·er \ˌən-də-rə-ˈchē-vər\ *n* **:** a student who fails to achieve his scholastic potential

un·der·act \ˌən-dər-ˈakt\ *vb* **:** to perform feebly or with restraint: as **a :** to perform (a dramatic part) with less than the requisite skill or vigor **b :** to perform with restraint for greater dramatic impact or personal force

un·der·age \-ˈāj\ *adj* **:** of less than mature or legal age

un·der·arm \-ˈärm\ *adj* **:** placed under or on the underside of the arm — **underarm** *n*

un·der·bel·ly \ˈən-dər-ˌbel-ē\ *n* **:** the under surface of a body or mass; *also* **:** a vulnerable area

un·der·bid \ˌən-dər-ˈbid\ *vb* **-bid; -bid·ding 1 :** to bid less than (a competing bidder) **2 :** to bid too low (as in cards)

un·der·bred \ˌən-dər-ˈbred\ *adj* **1 :** marked by lack of good breeding **:** ILL-BRED **2 :** of inferior or mixed breed

un·der·brush \ˈən-dər-ˌbrəsh\ *n* **:** shrubs and small trees growing among large trees **:** UNDERGROWTH

un·der·car·riage \-ˌkar-ij\ *n* **1 :** a supporting framework (as of an automobile) **2 :** the landing gear of an airplane

un·der·charge \ˌən-dər-ˈchärj\ *vt* **:** to charge (as a person) too little — **un·der·charge** \ˈən-dər-ˌchärj\ *n*

un·der·class·man \ˌən-dər-ˈklas-mən\ *n* **:** a member of the freshman or sophomore class

un·der·clothes \'ən-dər-ˌklō(th)z\ *n pl* : UNDERWEAR
un·der·cloth·ing \-ˌklō-thiŋ\ *n* : UNDERWEAR
un·der·coat \-ˌkōt\ *n* **1** : a coat or jacket formerly worn under another **2** : a growth of short hair or fur partly concealed by a longer growth **3** : a coat of paint under another — **undercoat** *vb*
un·der·cov·er \ˌən-dər-'kəv-ər\ *adj* : acting or executed in secret; *esp* : employed or engaged in spying or secret investigation
un·der·cur·rent \'ən-dər-ˌkər-ənt\ *n* **1** : a current below the upper currents or surface **2** : a hidden tendency of opinion or feeling often contrary to the one publicly shown
un·der·cut \ˌən-dər-'kət\ *vb* **-cut**; **-cut·ting** **1 a** : to cut away the under part of **b** : to perform the action of cutting away beneath **2** : to cut away material from the underside of (an object) so as to leave an overhanging portion in relief **3** : to offer to sell at lower prices than or to work for lower wages than (a competitor) **4** : to strike (the ball) in golf, tennis, or field hockey with a downward glancing blow so as to give a backspin or elevation to the shot — **un·der·cut** \'ən-dər-ˌkət\ *n*
un·der·de·vel·op \ˌən-dər-di-'vel-əp\ *vt* : to develop to a point below that which is usual or required
un·der·de·vel·oped \-'vel-əpt\ *adj* **1** : not normally or adequately developed **2** : failing to reach a potential level of economic development (as from lack of capital)
un·der·dog \'ən-dər-ˌdȯg\ *n* **1** : the losing dog in a fight **2** : the loser or predicted loser in a struggle
un·der·done \ˌən-dər-'dən\ *adj* : not thoroughly done or cooked : RARE
un·der·es·ti·mate \ˌən-dər-'es-tə-ˌmāt\ *vt* **1** : to estimate as being less than the actual size, quantity, or number **2** : to place too low a value on : UNDERRATE — **un·der·es·ti·mate** \-mət\ *n* — **un·der·es·ti·ma·tion** \-ˌes-tə-'mā-shən\ *n*
un·der·ex·pose \-ik-'spōz\ *vt* : to expose (a photographic plate or film) for less time than is needed — **un·der·ex·po·sure** \-'spō-zhər\ *n*
un·der·feed \-'fēd\ *vt* **-fed** \-'fed\; **-feed·ing** **1** : to feed with too little food **2** : to feed with fuel from the underside
un·der·foot \ˌən-dər-'fu̇t\ *adv* **1** : under the feet **2** : close about one's feet : in the way
un·der·gar·ment \'ən-dər-ˌgär-mənt\ *n* : a garment to be worn under another
un·der·go \ˌən-dər-'gō\ *vt* **-went** \-'went\; **-gone** \-'gȯn\; **-go·ing** \-'gō-iŋ\ **1** : to submit or be subjected to : ENDURE **2** : to pass through : EXPERIENCE
un·der·grad·u·ate \-'graj-ə-wət, -ˌwāt\ *n* : a student at a college or university who has not taken a first degree
¹un·der·ground \ˌən-dər-'grau̇nd\ *adv* **1** : beneath the surface of the earth **2** : in or into hiding or secret operation
²un·der·ground \'ən-dər-ˌgrau̇nd\ *adj* **1** : being, growing, operating, or situated below the surface of the ground **2** : conducted by secret means
³un·der·ground \'ən-dər-ˌgrau̇nd\ *n* **1** : a space under the surface of the ground; *esp* : an underground railway **2** : a secret political movement or group; *esp* : an organized body working in secret to overthrow a government or an occupying power
un·der·growth \'ən-dər-ˌgrōth\ *n* : low growth on the floor of a forest including seedlings and saplings, shrubs, and herbs
¹un·der·hand \'ən-dər-ˌhand\ *adv* **1** : in an underhand or secret manner **2** : with an underhand motion
²underhand *adj* **1** : marked by secrecy, chicanery, and deception : not honest and aboveboard : SLY **2** : performed with the hand kept below the level of the shoulder
un·der·hand·ed \ˌən-dər-'han-dəd\ *adj* (*or adv*) : UNDERHAND — **un·der·hand·ed·ly** *adv* — **un·der·hand·ed·ness** *n*
¹un·der·lay \ˌən-dər-'lā\ *vt* **-laid** \-'lād\; **-lay·ing** **1** : to cover, line, or traverse the bottom of : give support to on the underside or below **2** : to raise or support by something laid under
²un·der·lay \'ən-dər-ˌlā\ *n* : something that is laid under
un·der·lie \ˌən-dər-'lī\ *vt* **-lay** \-'lā\; **-lain** \-'lān\; **-ly·ing** \-'lī-iŋ\ **1** : to lie or be situated under **2** : to be at the basis of : form the foundation of : SUPPORT
un·der·line \'ən-dər-ˌlīn, ˌən-dər-'\ *vt* **1** : to draw a line under : UNDERSCORE **2** : EMPHASIZE — **un·der·line** \'ən-dər-ˌlīn\ *n*
un·der·ling \'ən-dər-liŋ\ *n* : one who is under the orders of another : SUBORDINATE, INFERIOR
un·der·ly·ing \ˌən-dər-ˌlī-iŋ\ *adj* **1** : lying under or below **2** : FUNDAMENTAL, BASIC
un·der·mine \ˌən-dər-'mīn\ *vt* **1** : to dig out or wear away the supporting earth beneath **2** : to weaken or wear away secretly or gradually
un·der·most \'ən-dər-ˌmōst\ *adj* : lowest in relative position — **undermost** *adv*
¹un·der·neath \ˌən-dər-'nēth\ *prep* **1** : directly under **2** : under subjection to
²underneath *adv* **1** : under or below an object or a surface : BENEATH **2** : on the lower side
un·der·nour·ished \-'nər-isht\ *adj* : supplied with insufficient nourishment and esp. foods for sound health and growth — **un·der·nour·ish·ment** \-'nər-ish-mənt\ *n*
un·der·pants \'ən-dər-ˌpan(t)s\ *n pl* : short or long pants worn under an outer garment : DRAWERS
un·der·part \-ˌpärt\ *n* **1** : a part lying on the lower side esp. of a bird or mammal **2** : a subordinate or auxiliary part or role
un·der·pass \-ˌpas\ *n* : a passage underneath something (as for a road passing under a railroad or another road)
un·der·pay \ˌən-dər-'pā\ *vt* **-paid** \-'pād\; **-pay·ing** : to pay too little
un·der·pin \-'pin\ *vt* **1** : to form part of, strengthen, or replace the foundation of **2** : SUPPORT, SUBSTANTIATE
un·der·pin·ning \'ən-dər-ˌpin-iŋ\ *n* **1** : the material and construction (as a foundation) used for support of a structure **2** : SUPPORT, PROP
un·der·play \ˌən-dər-'plā\ *vb* : to treat or handle with restraint; *esp* : to play a role with subdued force
un·der·priv·i·leged \-'priv-(ə-)lijd\ *adj* : having fewer esp. economic and social privileges than others
un·der·rate \ˌən-də(r)-'rāt\ *vt* : to rate too low : UNDERVALUE
un·der·score \'ən-dər-ˌskōr\ *vt* **1** : to draw a line under : UNDERLINE **2** : EMPHASIZE — **underscore** *n*
un·der·sea \ˌən-dər-ˌsē\ *adj* **1** : being or carried on under the sea or under the surface of the sea **2** : designed for use under the surface of the sea
un·der·sec·re·tary \ˌən-dər-'sek-rə-ˌter-ē\ *n* : a secretary immediately subordinate to a principal secretary
un·der·sell \-'sel\ *vt* **-sold** \-'sōld\; **-sell·ing** : to sell articles cheaper than
un·der·shirt \'ən-dər-ˌshərt\ *n* : a collarless undergarment with or without sleeves
un·der·shot \ˌən-dər-ˌshät\ *adj* **1** : having the lower incisor teeth or lower jaw projecting beyond the upper when the mouth is closed **2** : moved by water passing beneath
un·der·side \'ən-dər-ˌsīd, ˌən-dər-'\ *n* : the side or surface lying underneath
un·der·signed \'ən-dər-ˌsīnd\ *n, pl* **undersigned** : one who signs his name at the end of a document
un·der·sized \ˌən-dər-'sīzd\ *adj* : smaller than is usual or standard
un·der·skirt \'ən-dər-ˌskərt\ *n* : a skirt worn under an outer skirt; *esp* : PETTICOAT
un·der·slung \ˌən-dər-'sləŋ\ *adj* : suspended so as to extend below the axles
un·der·stand \ˌən-dər-'stand\ *vb* **-stood** \-'stu̇d\; **-stand·ing** **1** : to grasp the meaning of : COMPREHEND **2** : to have thorough acquaintance with **3** : GATHER, INFER **4** : INTERPRET,

EXPLAIN 5 : to have a sympathetic attitude 6 : to accept as settled 7 : to supply in thought as though expressed — **un·der·stand·a·bil·i·ty** \-ˌstan-də-ˈbil-ət-ē\ *n* — **un·der·stand·a·ble** *adj* — **un·der·stand·a·bly** \-ˈstan-də-blē\ *adv*

¹un·der·stand·ing \ˌən-dər-ˈstan-diŋ\ *n* 1 : knowledge and ability to apply judgment : INTELLIGENCE 2 : ability to comprehend and judge 3 **a** : agreement of opinion or feeling **b** : a mutual agreement informally or tacitly entered into

²understanding *adj* : endowed with understanding : TOLERANT, SYMPATHETIC — **un·der·stand·ing·ly** *adv*

un·der·state \ˌən-dər-ˈstāt\ *vt* 1 : to represent as less than is the case 2 : to state with restraint esp. for greater effect — **un·der·state·ment** *n*

un·der·stood \ˌən-dər-ˈstu̇d\ *adj* 1 : agreed upon 2 : IMPLICIT

¹un·der·study \ˈən-dər-ˌstəd-ē\ *vb* 1 : to study another actor's part in order to be his substitute in an emergency 2 : to prepare as understudy to (as an actor)

²understudy *n* : one who stands prepared to act another's part or take over another's duties

un·der·sur·face \-ˌsər-fəs\ *n* : UNDERSIDE

un·der·take \ˌən-dər-ˈtāk\ *vt* **-took** \-ˈtu̇k\; **-tak·en** \-ˈtā-kən\ 1 : to take upon oneself as a task : enter upon 2 : to put oneself under obligation : AGREE 3 : GUARANTEE, PROMISE

un·der·tak·er \ˈən-dər-ˌtā-kər\ *n* : a person whose business is to prepare the dead for burial and to take charge of funerals

un·der·tak·ing *2 is* ˈən-dər-ˌtā-kiŋ, *other senses are also* ˌən-dər-ˈ\ *n* 1 : the act of a person who undertakes something 2 : the business of an undertaker 3 : something undertaken 4 : PROMISE, GUARANTEE

un·der·tone \ˈən-dər-ˌtōn\ *n* 1 : a low or subdued tone 2 : a subdued color (as seen through and modifying another color)

un·der·tow \-ˌtō\ *n* : a current beneath the surface of the water that moves away from or along the shore while the surface water above it moves toward the shore

un·der·trick \-ˌtrik\ *n* : a trick by which a declarer in bridge falls short of making his contract

un·der·val·ue \ˌən-dər-ˈval-yü\ *vt* 1 : to value below the real worth 2 : to set little value on — **un·der·val·u·a·tion** \-ˌval-yə-ˈwā-shən\ *n*

un·der·wa·ter \ˌən-dər-ˌwȯt-ər, -ˌwät-\ *adj* : lying, growing, worn, or operating below the surface of the water — **un·der·wa·ter** \-ˈwȯt-, -ˈwät-\ *adv*

under way *adv* 1 : in motion; *also* : into motion from a standstill 2 : in progress : AFOOT

un·der·wear \ˈən-dər-ˌwa(ə)r\ *n* : a garment worn next to the skin and under other clothing

¹un·der·weight \ˌən-dər-ˈwāt\ *n* : weight below what is normal, average, or necessary

²underweight *adj* : weighing less than the normal or requisite amount

un·der·world \ˈən-dər-ˌwərld\ *n* 1 : the place of departed souls : HADES 2 : the side of the earth opposite to one 3 : a social sphere below the level of ordinary life; *esp* : the world of organized crime

un·der·write \ˈən-də(r)-ˌrīt, ˌən-də(r)-ˈ\ *vb* **-wrote** \-ˌrōt, -ˈrōt\; **-writ·ten** \-ˌrit-ᵊn, -ˈrit-\; **-writ·ing** \-ˌrīt-iŋ, -ˈrīt-\ 1 : to write under or at the end of something else 2 : to set one's name to (an insurance policy) and thereby become answerable to the insured for a designated loss or damage : insure life or property 3 : to subscribe to : agree to 4 **a** : to undertake the sale of (a security issue) and agree to purchase on a fixed date any remaining unsold **b** : to guarantee financial support of — **un·der·writ·er** *n*

un·de·sir·a·bil·i·ty \ˌən-di-ˌzī-rə-ˈbil-ət-ē\ *n* : the quality or state of being undesirable

¹un·de·sir·a·ble \-ˈzī-rə-bəl\ *adj* : not desirable : UNWANTED — **un·de·sir·a·ble·ness** *n* — **un·de·sir·a·bly** \-blē\ *adv*

²undesirable *n* : one that is undesirable

un·de·vi·at·ing \ˈən-ˈdē-vē-ˌāt-iŋ\ *adj* : keeping a true course : UNSWERVING — **un·de·vi·at·ing·ly** *adv*

un·dies \ˈən-dēz\ *n pl* : UNDERWEAR; *esp* : women's underwear

un·do \ˌən-ˈdü\ *vb* **-did** \-ˈdid\; **-done** \-ˈdən\; **-do·ing** 1 : to make or become unfastened or loosened : OPEN, UNTIE 2 : to make of no effect or as if not done : make null : REVERSE 3 **a** : to ruin the worldly means, reputation, or hopes of **b** : to disturb the composure of : UPSET — **un·do·er** *n*

un·do·ing \-ˈdü-iŋ\ *n* 1 : LOOSING, UNFASTENING 2 : RUIN; *also* : a cause of ruin 3 : ANNULMENT, REVERSAL

un·doubt·ed \ˈən-ˈdau̇t-əd\ *adj* : not doubted or called into question : CERTAIN

un·doubt·ed·ly \-əd-lē\ *adv* : beyond doubt : CERTAINLY

un·drape \-ˈdrāp\ *vt* : to strip of drapery : UNVEIL

¹un·dress \-ˈdres\ *vb* : to remove the clothes or covering of

²undress *n* 1 : informal dress: as **a** : a loose robe or dressing gown **b** : ordinary dress 2 : NUDITY

un·dressed \-ˈdrest\ *adj* : not dressed: as **a** : partially, improperly, or informally clothed **b** : not fully processed or finished **c** : not cared for or tended

un·due \-ˈd(y)ü\ *adj* 1 : not due : not yet payable 2 **a** : INAPPROPRIATE, UNSUITABLE **b** : exceeding or violating propriety or fitness

un·du·lant \ˈən-jə-lənt, ˈən-d(y)ə-\ *adj* : UNDULATING

un·du·late \-ˌlāt\ *vb* 1 : to form or move in waves : FLUCTUATE 2 : to rise and fall in volume, pitch, or cadence 3 : to present a wavy appearance

un·du·la·tion \ˌən-jə-ˈlā-shən, ˌən-d(y)ə-\ *n* 1 **a** : the action of undulating **b** : a wavelike motion to and fro in a fluid or elastic medium : VIBRATION 2 : a wavy appearance or form

un·du·la·to·ry \ˈən-jə-lə-ˌtōr-ē, ˈən-d(y)ə-\ *adj* : of or relating to undulation : UNDULATING

un·du·ly \ˈən-ˈd(y)ü-lē\ *adv* : in an undue manner; *esp* : EXCESSIVELY

un·dy·ing \-ˈdī-iŋ\ *adj* : not dying : IMMORTAL, PERPETUAL

un·earned \-ˈərnd\ *adj* : not gained by labor, service, or skill

un·earth \ˈən-ˈərth\ *vt* 1 : to drive or draw from the earth : dig up 2 : to bring (as a secret) to light : DISCOVER

un·earth·ly \-lē\ *adj* 1 : not of or belonging to the earth 2 : SUPERNATURAL, WEIRD, TERRIFYING — **un·earth·li·ness** *n*

un·easy \-ˈē-zē\ *adj* 1 : not easy in manner : AWKWARD 2 : disturbed by pain or worry : RESTLESS — **un·eas·i·ly** \-ˈēz-(ə-)lē\ *adv* — **un·eas·i·ness** \-ˈē-zē-nəs\ *n*

un·em·ploy·a·ble \ˌən-im-ˈplȯi-ə-bəl\ *adj* : not capable of being employed; *esp* : not capable of holding a job — **unemployable** *n*

un·em·ployed \-ˈplȯid\ *adj* : not employed: **a** : not being used **b** : not engaged in a gainful occupation

un·em·ploy·ment \-ˈplȯi-mənt\ *n* : the state of being out of work : lack of employment

un·end·ing \ˈən-ˈen-diŋ\ *adj* : having no ending : ENDLESS — **un·end·ing·ly** *adv*

¹un·equal \-ˈē-kwəl\ *adj* 1 **a** : not of the same measurement, quantity, or number as another **b** : not like or not the same as another in degree, worth, or status 2 : not uniform : VARIABLE, UNEVEN 3 : badly balanced or matched 4 : INADEQUATE, INSUFFICIENT — **un·equal·ly** \-kwə-lē\ *adv*

²unequal *n* : one that is not equal to another

un·equaled \-ˈē-kwəld\ *adj* : not equaled : UNPARALLELED

un·equiv·o·cal \ˌən-i-ˈkwiv-ə-kəl\ *adj* : leaving no doubt : CLEAR, UNAMBIGUOUS — **un·equiv·o·cal·ly** \-k(ə-)lē\ *adv*

un·err·ing \ˈən-ˈe(ə)r-iŋ, -ˈər-iŋ\ *adj* : making no errors : CERTAIN, UNFAILING — **un·err·ing·ly** *adv*

un·even \-ˈē-vən\ *adj* 1 : ODD 2a 2 **a** : not even : not level or smooth : RUGGED, RAGGED **b** : varying from the straight or parallel **c** : not uniform : IRREGULAR **d** : varying in quality — **un·even·ly** *adv* — **un·even·ness** *n*

un·event·ful \ˌən-i-ˈvent-fəl\ *adj* : not eventful : lacking inter-

esting or noteworthy happenings
un·ex·am·pled \ˌən-ig-ˈzam-pəld\ *adj* : having no example or parallel : UNPRECEDENTED
un·ex·cep·tion·a·ble \ˌən-ik-ˈsep-sh(ə-)nə-bəl\ *adj* : not open to objection or criticism : beyond reproach : UNIMPEACHABLE — **un·ex·cep·tion·a·bly** \-blē\ *adv*
un·ex·pect·ed \ˌən-ik-ˈspek-təd\ *adj* : not expected : UNFORESEEN — **un·ex·pect·ed·ly** *adv* — **un·ex·pect·ed·ness** *n*
un·fail·ing \ˈən-ˈfā-liŋ\ *adj* : not failing or liable to fail: **a** : CONSTANT, UNFLAGGING **b** : EVERLASTING, INEXHAUSTIBLE **c** : INFALLIBLE — **un·fail·ing·ly** *adv* — **un·fail·ing·ness** *n*
un·fair \-ˈfa(ə)r\ *adj* **1** : marked by injustice, partiality, or deception : UNJUST, DISHONEST **2** : not equitable in business dealings — **un·fair·ly** *adv* — **un·fair·ness** *n*
un·faith·ful \-ˈfāth-fəl\ *adj* : not faithful: **a** : not adhering to vows, allegiance, or duty : DISLOYAL **b** : not faithful to marriage vows **c** : INACCURATE, UNTRUSTWORTHY — **un·faith·ful·ly** \-fə-lē\ *adv* — **un·faith·ful·ness** *n*
un·fa·mil·iar \ˌən-fə-ˈmil-yər\ *adj* : not familiar: **a** : not well known : STRANGE **b** : not well acquainted — **un·fa·mil·iar·i·ty** \-ˌmil-ˈyar-ət-ē, -ˌmil-ē-ˈar-\ *n* — **un·fa·mil·iar·ly** *adv*
un·fas·ten \ˈən-ˈfas-ᵊn\ *vb* : to make or become loose : UNDO, DETACH, UNTIE
un·fa·vor·a·ble \-ˈfāv-(ə-)rə-bəl, -ˈfā-vər-bəl\ *adj* : not favorable: as **a** : OPPOSED, NEGATIVE **b** : not propitious : DISADVANTAGEOUS — **un·fa·vor·a·ble·ness** *n* — **un·fa·vor·a·bly** \-blē\ *adv*
un·feel·ing \-ˈfē-liŋ\ *adj* **1** : lacking feeling : INSENSATE **2** : lacking kindness or sympathy : HARDHEARTED, CRUEL — **un·feel·ing·ly** *adv* — **un·feel·ing·ness** *n*
un·feigned \-ˈfānd\ *adj* : not counterfeit : not hypocritical : GENUINE — **un·feign·ed·ly** \-ˈfā-nəd-lē, -ˈfān-dlē\ *adv*
un·fet·ter \-ˈfet-ər\ *vt* **1** : to free from fetters **2** : LIBERATE
un·fil·i·al \-ˈfil-ē-əl, -ˈfil-yəl\ *adj* : not observing the obligations of a child to a parent : UNDUTIFUL
¹un·fit \-ˈfit\ *adj* : not fit: **a** : not adapted to a purpose : UNSUITABLE **b** : INCAPABLE, INCOMPETENT **c** : physically or mentally unsound — **un·fit·ly** *adv* — **un·fit·ness** *n*
²unfit *vt* : to make unfit : DISABLE, DISQUALIFY
un·fix \ˈən-ˈfiks\ *vt* **1** : to loosen from a fastening : DETACH, DISENGAGE **2** : to make unstable : UNSETTLE
un·flap·pa·ble \-ˈflap-ə-bəl\ *adj* : not easily upset or panicked
un·fledged \-ˈflejd\ *adj* **1** : not feathered or ready for flight **2** : IMMATURE, CALLOW
un·flinch·ing \-ˈflin-chiŋ\ *adj* : not flinching or shrinking : STEADFAST — **un·flinch·ing·ly** *adv*
un·fold \-ˈfōld\ *vb* **1 a** : to open the folds of : spread or cause to spread or straighten out from a folded position or arrangement **b** : UNWRAP **2 a** : BLOSSOM **b** : DEVELOP **3** : to open out or cause to open out gradually to the view or understanding
un·fold·ed \-ˈfōl-dəd\ *adj* : not folded
un·for·get·ta·ble \ˌən-fər-ˈget-ə-bəl\ *adj* : not to be forgotten : lasting in memory — **un·for·get·ta·bly** \-blē\ *adv*
un·formed \ˈən-ˈfȯrmd\ *adj* : not arranged in regular shape, order, or relations: **a** : UNDEVELOPED, IMMATURE **b** : INCHOATE, SHAPELESS
¹un·for·tu·nate \-ˈfȯrch-(ə-)nət\ *adj* **1 a** : not fortunate : UNLUCKY **b** : marked or accompanied by or resulting in misfortune **2 a** : UNSUITABLE, INFELICITOUS **b** : DEPLORABLE — **un·for·tu·nate·ly** *adv*
²unfortunate *n* : an unfortunate person
un·found·ed \-ˈfau̇n-dəd\ *adj* : lacking a sound basis
un·fre·quent·ed \ˌən-frē-ˈkwent-əd; ˌən-ˈfrē-kwənt-, ˈən-\ *adj* : not often visited or traveled over
un·friend·ly \ˈən-ˈfren-dlē\ *adj* **1** : not friendly : not kind : HOSTILE **2** : not favorable — **un·friend·li·ness** *n*
un·frock \-ˈfräk\ *vt* **1** : to divest of a frock **2** : to deprive (as a priest) of the right to exercise the functions of office
un·fruit·ful \-ˈfrüt-fəl\ *adj* **1** : not bearing fruit or offspring **2** : not producing a desired result : not resulting in gain — **un·fruit·ful·ly** \-fə-lē\ *adv* — **un·fruit·ful·ness** *n*
un·furl \-ˈfərl\ *vb* : to loose from a furled state : open or spread
un·gain·ly \-ˈgān-lē\ *adj* : CLUMSY, AWKWARD — **un·gain·li·ness** *n*
un·gen·er·ous \-ˈjen-(ə-)rəs\ *adj* : not generous: **a** : PETTY, MEAN **b** : STINGY — **un·gen·er·ous·ly** *adv*
un·gird \-ˈgərd\ *vt* : to divest of a restraining band or girdle
un·god·ly \-ˈgäd-lē, -ˈgȯd-\ *adj* **1 a** : IMPIOUS, IRRELIGIOUS **b** : SINFUL, WICKED **2** : OUTRAGEOUS — **un·god·li·ness** *n*
un·gov·ern·a·ble \-ˈgəv-ər-nə-bəl\ *adj* : not capable of being governed, guided, or restrained — **un·gov·ern·a·bly** \-blē\ *adv*
un·grace·ful \-ˈgrās-fəl\ *adj* : not graceful : AWKWARD — **un·grace·ful·ly** \-fə-lē\ *adv* — **un·grace·ful·ness** *n*
un·gra·cious \-ˈgrā-shəs\ *adj* **1** : not courteous : RUDE **2** : not pleasing : DISAGREEABLE — **un·gra·cious·ly** *adv* — **un·gra·cious·ness** *n*
un·grate·ful \ˈən-ˈgrāt-fəl\ *adj* **1** : not thankful for favors **2** : not pleasing : DISAGREEABLE — **un·grate·ful·ly** \-fə-lē\ *adv* — **un·grate·ful·ness** *n*
un·ground·ed \-ˈgrau̇n-dəd\ *adj* **1** : UNFOUNDED, BASELESS **2** : not instructed or informed
un·guard·ed \-ˈgärd-əd\ *adj* **1** : vulnerable to attack : UNPROTECTED **2** : free from guile or wariness : DIRECT, INCAUTIOUS — **un·guard·ed·ly** *adv*
un·guent \ˈəŋ-gwənt\ *n* : a soothing or healing salve
¹un·gu·late \ˈəŋ-gyə-lət\ *adj* : having hoofs
²ungulate *n* : a hoofed mammal (as a cow, horse, or rhinoceros)
un·hand \ˈən-ˈhand\ *vt* : to remove the hand from : let go
un·hand·some \-ˈhan(t)-səm\ *adj* : not handsome: as **a** : not beautiful : HOMELY **b** : UNBECOMING, UNSEEMLY **c** : DISCOURTEOUS, RUDE — **un·hand·some·ly** *adv*
un·handy \-ˈhan-dē\ *adj* **1** : hard to handle : INCONVENIENT **2** : lacking in skill or dexterity : AWKWARD — **un·hand·i·ness** *n*
un·hap·py \-ˈhap-ē\ *adj* **1** : not fortunate : UNLUCKY **2** : not cheerful : SAD, MISERABLE **3** : INAPPROPRIATE — **un·hap·pi·ly** \-ˈhap-ə-lē\ *adv* — **un·hap·pi·ness** \-ˈhap-i-nəs\ *n*
un·har·ness \-ˈhär-nəs\ *vt* : to divest of harness
un·healthy \-ˈhel-thē\ *adj* **1** : not conducive to health **2** : not in good health : SICKLY, DISEASED **3 a** : RISKY, UNSOUND **b** : BAD, INJURIOUS — **un·health·i·ly** \-thə-lē\ *adv* — **un·health·i·ness** \-thē-nəs\ *n*
un·heard \ˈən-ˈhərd\ *adj* **1** : not perceived by the ear **2** : not given a hearing
un·heard–of \-ˌəv, -ˌäv\ *adj* : previously unknown : UNPRECEDENTED
un·hinge \ˈən-ˈhinj\ *vt* **1** : to remove (as a door) from the hinges **2** : to make unstable : UNSETTLE, DISRUPT
un·hitch \-ˈhich\ *vt* : to free from being hitched
un·ho·ly \-ˈhō-lē\ *adj* : not holy : PROFANE, WICKED — **un·ho·li·ness** *n*
un·hook \-ˈhu̇k\ *vt* **1** : to remove from a hook **2** : to unfasten by disengaging a hook
un·horse \-ˈhȯrs\ *vt* : to dislodge from or as if from a horse
uni·cam·er·al \ˌyü-ni-ˈkam(-ə)-rəl\ *adj* : having or consisting of a single legislative chamber — **uni·cam·er·al·ly** \-rə-lē\ *adv*
uni·cel·lu·lar \-ˈsel-yə-lər\ *adj* : having or consisting of a single cell — **uni·cel·lu·lar·i·ty** \-ˌsel-yə-ˈlar-ət-ē\ *n*
uni·fi·a·ble \ˈyü-nə-ˌfī-ə-bəl\ *adj* : capable of being unified
uni·fi·ca·tion \ˌyü-nə-fə-ˈkā-shən\ *n* : the act, process, or result of unifying : the state of being unified
¹uni·form \ˈyü-nə-ˌfȯrm\ *adj* **1** : having always the same form, manner, or degree : not varying or variable **2** : of the same form with others : conforming to one rule — **uni·form·ly** *adv*
²uniform *vt* : to clothe with a uniform
³uniform *n* : distinctive dress worn by members of a particular group (as an army or a police force)

uni·form·i·ty \ˌyü-nə-ˈfȯr-mət-ē\ *n, pl* **-ties** : the quality or state or an instance of being uniform
uni·fy \ˈyü-nə-ˌfī\ *vt* **-fied; -fy·ing** : to make into a unit or a coherent whole : UNITE — **u·ni·fi·er** *n*
uni·lat·er·al \ˌyü-ni-ˈlat-ə-rəl, -ˈla-trəl\ *adj* : of, relating to, having, or done by one side only — **uni·lat·er·al·ly** \-ē\ *adv*
un·im·peach·a·ble \ˌən-im-ˈpē-chə-bəl\ *adj* : not impeachable : not to be called in question : not liable to accusation : IRREPROACHABLE, BLAMELESS — **un·im·peach·a·bly** \-blē\ *adv*
un·in·hib·it·ed \ˌən-in-ˈhib-ət-əd\ *adj* : free from inhibition; *esp* : boisterously informal — **un·in·hib·it·ed·ly** *adv*
un·in·tel·li·gent \ˌən-in-ˈtel-ə-jənt\ *adj* : lacking intelligence : UNWISE, IGNORANT — **un·in·tel·li·gent·ly** *adv*
un·in·tel·li·gi·ble \-ˈtel-ə-jə-bəl\ *adj* : not intelligible : OBSCURE — **un·in·tel·li·gi·ble·ness** *n* — **un·in·tel·li·gi·bly** \-blē\ *adv*
un·in·ten·tion·al \ˌən-in-ˈtench-nəl, -ˈten-chən-ᵊl\ *adj* : not intentional — **un·in·ten·tion·al·ly** \-ē\ *adv*
un·in·ter·est·ed \ˈən-ˈin-trəs-təd, -ˈint-ə-ˌres-\ *adj* **1** : having no interest and esp. no property interest in **2** : not having the mind or feelings engaged : not having the curiosity or sympathy aroused
un·in·ter·rupt·ed \ˌən-ˌint-ə-ˈrəp-təd\ *adj* : not interrupted : CONTINUOUS — **un·in·ter·rupt·ed·ly** *adv*
union \ˈyü-nyən\ *n* **1 a** : an act or instance of uniting two or more things into one: as (1) : the formation of a single political unit from two or more separate and independent units (2) : a uniting in marriage (3) : the growing together of severed parts **b** : a unified condition : COMBINATION, JUNCTION **2** : something formed by a combining of parts or members: as **a** : a confederation of independent individuals (as nations or persons) for some common purpose **b** : a political unit constituting an organic whole formed from several units that may have been previously independent **c** : LABOR UNION **d** *cap* : an organization on a college or university campus providing recreational, social, cultural, and sometimes dining facilities; *also* : the building housing it **3 a** : a device emblematic of the union of two or more sovereignties borne on a national flag **b** : the upper inner corner of a flag **4 a** : a device for connecting parts (as of a machine) **b** : a coupling for pipes
Union *adj* : of, relating to, or being the side favoring the federal union in the U.S. Civil War
union·ism \ˈyü-nyə-ˌniz-əm\ *n* : the principle or policy of forming or adhering to a union: as **a** *cap* : adherence to the policy of a firm federal union prior to or during the U.S. Civil War **b** : the principles, theory, or system of trade unions — **union·ist** \-yə-nəst\ *n, often cap*
union·ize \ˈyü-nyə-ˌnīz\ *vt* : to cause to become a member of or subject to the rules of a labor union : form into a labor union — **union·i·za·tion** \ˌyü-nyə-nə-ˈzā-shən\ *n*
union jack *n* **1** : a flag consisting of the part of a national flag that signifies union; *esp* : a U.S. flag consisting of a blue field with one white star for each state **2** *cap U & J* : the national flag of the United Kingdom
unique \yu̇-ˈnēk\ *adj* **1** : being the only one of its kind **2** : very unusual : NOTABLE — **unique·ly** *adv* — **unique·ness** *n*
uni·son \ˈyü-nə-sən, -zən\ *n* **1** : sameness or identity in pitch **2** : the condition of being tuned or sounded at the same pitch or at an octave **3** : exact agreement : ACCORD
unit \ˈyü-nət\ *n* **1** : the first and least whole number : ONE **2** : a definite quantity (as of length, time, or value) adopted as a standard of measurement **3 a** : a single thing or person or group that is a constituent of a whole **b** : a part of a military establishment that has a prescribed organization
Uni·tar·i·an \ˌyü-nə-ˈter-ē-ən\ *n* : a member of a denomination that stresses individual freedom of belief, the free use of reason in religion, a united world community, and liberal social action — **Unitarian** *adj* — **Uni·tar·i·an·ism** \-ē-ə-ˌniz-əm\ *n*
uni·tary \ˈyü-nə-ˌter-ē\ *adj* **1 a** : of or relating to a unit **b** : based on or characterized by unity or units **2** : having the character of a unit : UNDIVIDED, WHOLE
unite \yu̇-ˈnīt\ *vb* **1 a** : to put or come together to form a single unit **b** : to cause to adhere **c** : to link by a legal or moral bond **2** : to become one or as if one **3** : to join in action : act as if one — **unit·er** *n*
unit·ed \yu̇-ˈnīt-əd\ *adj* **1** : made one : COMBINED **2** : relating to or produced by joint action **3** : being in agreement : HARMONIOUS — **unit·ed·ly** *adv*
unit·ize \ˈyü-nət-ˌīz\ *vb* : to convert into a unit
uni·ty \ˈyü-nət-ē\ *n, pl* **-ties** **1** : the quality or state of being one : SINGLENESS, ONENESS **2** : CONCORD, HARMONY **3** : continuity without change **4** : a definite mathematical quantity or combination of quantities taken as one or for which 1 is made to stand in a calculation **5** : reference of all the parts of an artistic or literary composition to a single main idea : singleness of effect or style **6** : totality of related parts
uni·valve \ˈyü-ni-ˌvalv\ *n* : a mollusk having a shell with one valve
uni·ver·sal \ˌyü-nə-ˈvər-səl\ *adj* **1** : including or covering all or a whole without limit or exception **2 a** : present or occurring everywhere **b** : existent or operative everywhere or under all conditions **3 a** : embracing a major part or the greatest portion **b** : comprehensively broad and versatile **4** : affirming or denying something of all members of a class **5** : adapted or adjustable to meet varied requirements (as of use, shape, or size) — **uni·ver·sal·ly** \-s(ə-)lē\ *adv* — **uni·ver·sal·ness** *n*
uni·ver·sal·i·ty \ˌyü-nə-(ˌ)vər-ˈsal-ət-ē\ *n* : the quality or state of being universal (as in range, occurrence, or appeal)
uni·verse \ˈyü-nə-ˌvərs\ *n* **1** : the whole body of things and phenomena observed or postulated : COSMOS **2 a** : a systematic whole held to arise by and persist through the direct intervention of divine power **b** : the world of human experience
uni·ver·si·ty \ˌyü-nə-ˈvər-sət-ē, -ˈvər-stē\ *n, pl* **-ties** : an institution of higher learning authorized to grant degrees in various special fields (as law, medicine, and theology) as well as in the arts and sciences generally
un·just \ˈən-ˈjəst\ *adj* : characterized by injustice : deficient in justice and fairness — **un·just·ly** *adv* — **un·just·ness** *n*
un·kempt \-ˈkem(p)t\ *adj* **1 a** : not combed **b** : deficient in order or neatness of person **2** : ROUGH, UNPOLISHED
un·kind \-ˈkīnd\ *adj* : deficient in kindness or sympathy : HARSH, CRUEL — **un·kind·ly** *adv* — **un·kind·ness** *n*
un·kind·ly \-ˈkīn-dlē\ *adj* : UNKIND — **un·kind·li·ness** *n*
un·knit \ˈən-ˈnit\ *vb* : UNDO, UNRAVEL
un·know·ing \ˈən-ˈnō-iŋ\ *adj* : not knowing — **un·know·ing·ly** *adv*
¹un·known \-ˈnōn\ *adj* : not known; *also* : having an unknown value
²unknown *n* : one that is unknown
un·lace \ˈən-ˈlās\ *vt* : to loose by undoing a lacing
un·lade \-ˈlād\ *vb* **1** : to take the load or cargo from **2** : DISCHARGE, UNLOAD
un·lash \-ˈlash\ *vt* : to untie the lashing of : LOOSE, UNDO
un·latch \-ˈlach\ *vb* **1** : to open or loose by lifting the latch **2** : to become loosed or opened
un·law·ful \-ˈlȯ-fəl\ *adj* **1** : not lawful : contrary to law : ILLEGAL **2** : ILLEGITIMATE — **un·law·ful·ly** \-f(ə-)lē\ *adv* — **un·law·ful·ness** *n*
un·learn \-ˈlərn\ *vt* : to put out of one's knowledge or memory
un·learned *adj* **1** \-ˈlər-nəd\ : not learned : UNEDUCATED, ILLITERATE **2** \-ˈlərnd\ : not learned by study : not known **3** \-ˈlərnd\ : not learned by previous experience
un·leash \-ˈlēsh\ *vt* : to free from or as if from a leash
un·less \ən-ˌles\ *conj* : except on the condition that : if not
un·let·tered \ˈən-ˈlet-ərd\ *adj* **1** : not educated **2** : ILLITERATE
¹un·like \-ˈlīk\ *prep* **1** : different from **2** : not characteristic of

3 : in a different manner from
[2]**unlike** *adj* : not like: as **a** : marked by dissimilarity : DIFFERENT **b** : UNEQUAL — **un·like·ness** *n*
un·like·li·hood \-'lī-klē-,hu̇d\ *n* : IMPROBABILITY
un·like·ly \-'lī-klē\ *adj* **1** : not likely : IMPROBABLE **2** : likely to fail : UNPROMISING — **un·like·li·ness** *n*
un·lim·ber \'ən-'lim-bər\ *vb* : to prepare for action
un·lim·it·ed \-'lim-ət-əd\ *adj* **1** : lacking any controls **2** : BOUNDLESS, INFINITE **3** : not bounded by exceptions
un·load \-'lōd\ *vb* **1 a** : to take away or off : REMOVE; *also* : to get rid of **b** : to take a load from; *also* : to relieve or set free : UNBURDEN **2** : to get rid of or be relieved of a load or burden **3** : to sell in volume : DUMP
un·lock \-'läk\ *vb* **1** : to open or unfasten through release of a lock **2** : RELEASE **3** : DISCLOSE, REVEAL
un·looked–for \-'lu̇kt-,fȯr\ *adj* : UNEXPECTED
un·loose \'ən-'lüs\ *vt* **1** : to relax the strain of **2** : to release from or as if from restraints : set free **3** : UNTIE
un·loos·en \-'lüs-ᵊn\ *vt* : UNLOOSE
un·love·ly \-'ləv-lē\ *adj* : having no charm or appeal : not amiable : DISAGREEABLE — **un·love·li·ness** *n*
un·lucky \-'lək-ē\ *adj* **1** : marked by adversity or failure **2** : likely to bring misfortune **3** : producing dissatisfaction : REGRETTABLE — **un·luck·i·ly** \-'lək-ə-lē\ *adv*
un·man \-'man\ *vt* **1** : to deprive of manly courage **2** : to deprive of men
un·man·ly \-'man-lē\ *adj* : not manly: as **a** : being of weak character : COWARDLY **b** : EFFEMINATE — **un·man·li·ness** *n*
un·manned \-'mand\ *adj* : having no men aboard
[1]**un·man·ner·ly** \-'man-ər-lē\ *adv* : in an unmannerly fashion
[2]**unmannerly** *adj* : RUDE, IMPOLITE — **un·man·ner·li·ness** *n*
un·mask \'ən-'mask\ *vb* **1** : to strip of a mask or a disguise **2** : to take off one's own disguise (as at a masquerade)
un·mean·ing \-'mē-niŋ\ *adj* : having no meaning : SENSELESS
un·meet \-'mēt\ *adj* : not meet : UNSUITABLE, IMPROPER
un·men·tion·a·ble \-'mənch-(ə-)nə-bəl\ *adj* : not fit or proper to be talked about
un·mer·ci·ful \-'mər-si-fəl\ *adj* : not merciful : MERCILESS, CRUEL — **un·mer·ci·ful·ly** \-f(ə-)lē\ *adv*
un·mind·ful \-'mīn(d)-fəl\ *adj* : not mindful
un·mis·tak·a·ble \,ən-mə-'stā-kə-bəl\ *adj* : not capable of being mistaken or misunderstood : CLEAR, OBVIOUS — **un·mis·tak·a·bly** \-blē\ *adv*
un·mit·i·gat·ed \'ən-'mit-ə-,gāt-əd\ *adj* **1** : not softened or lessened **2** : ABSOLUTE, DOWNRIGHT — **un·mit·i·gat·ed·ly** *adv*
un·moor \-'mu̇(ə)r\ *vb* **1** : to loose from or as if from moorings **2** : to cast off moorings
un·mor·al \-'mȯr-əl\ *adj* : having no moral quality or relation : being neither moral nor immoral — **un·mor·al·ly** \-ə-lē\ *adv*
un·moved \-'müvd\ *adj* **1** : not moved : remaining in the same place **2** : FIRM, RESOLUTE **3** : not disturbed emotionally
un·muz·zle \-'məz-əl\ *vt* : to remove a muzzle from
un·nat·u·ral \'ən-'nach-(ə-)rəl\ *adj* **1** : not being in accordance with nature or consistent with a normal course of events **2 a** : not according with normal feelings or behavior : PERVERSE, ABNORMAL **b** : ARTIFICIAL, CONTRIVED **c** : STRANGE, IRREGULAR — **un·nat·u·ral·ly** \-'nach-(ə-)rə-lē, -'nach-ər-lē\ *adv* — **un·nat·u·ral·ness** *n*
un·nec·es·sar·i·ly \,ən-,nes-ə-'ser-ə-lē\ *adv* **1** : not by necessity **2** : to an unnecessary degree
un·nerve \'ən-'nərv\ *vt* : to deprive of nerve, courage, or self-control
un·num·bered \'ən-'nəm-bərd\ *adj* **1** : INNUMERABLE **2** : not having an identifying number
un·ob·tru·sive \,ən-əb-'trü-siv\ *adj* : not obtrusive : not blatant or aggressive : INCONSPICUOUS — **un·ob·tru·sive·ly** *adv*
un·oc·cu·pied \'ən-'äk-yə-,pīd\ *adj* **1** : not busy : UNEMPLOYED **2** : not occupied : EMPTY
un·of·fi·cial \,ən-ə-'fish-əl\ *adj* : not official — **un·of·fi·cial·ly** \-'fish-(ə-)lē\ *adv*
un·or·ga·nized \'ən-'ȯr-gə-,nīzd\ *adj* : not subjected to organization: as **a** : not formed or brought into an integrated or ordered whole **b** : not organized into unions
un·pack \-'pak\ *vb* **1** : to separate and remove things packed **2** : to open and remove the contents of
un·par·al·leled \-'par-ə-,leld\ *adj* : having no parallel; *esp* : having no equal or match : UNSURPASSED
un·par·lia·men·ta·ry \,ən-,pär-lə-'ment-ə-rē, -,pärl-yə-, -'men-trē\ *adj* : contrary to parliamentary practice
un·per·son \'ən-'pərs-ᵊn\ *n* : an individual who usu. for political or ideological reasons is removed completely from recognition, cognizance, consideration, or memory
un·pin \'ən-'pin\ *vt* : to remove a pin from : UNFASTEN
un·pleas·ant \-'plez-ᵊnt\ *adj* : not pleasant : not amiable or agreeable : DISPLEASING — **un·pleas·ant·ly** *adv*
un·pleas·ant·ness \-nəs\ *n* **1** : the quality or state of being unpleasant **2** : an unpleasant situation, experience, or event
un·plumbed \'ən-'pləmd\ *adj* **1** : not tested with a plumb line **2 a** : not measured with a plumb **b** : not explored in depth, intensity, or significance
un·pop·u·lar \'ən-'päp-yə-lər\ *adj* : not popular : viewed or received unfavorably : disliked by many people — **un·pop·u·lar·i·ty** \,ən-,päp-yə-'lar-ət-ē\ *n*
un·prec·e·dent·ed \'ən-'pres-ə-,dent-əd\ *adj* : having no precedent : NOVEL, UNEXAMPLED — **un·prec·e·dent·ed·ly** *adv*
un·pre·dict·a·ble \,ən-pri-'dik-tə-bəl\ *adj* : not predictable — **un·pre·dict·a·bil·i·ty** \-,dik-tə-'bil-ət-ē\ *n* — **un·pre·dict·a·bly** \-'dik-tə-blē\ *adv*
un·pre·ten·tious \,ən-pri-'ten-chəs\ *adj* : not pretentious : not showy or pompous : SIMPLE, MODEST — **un·pre·ten·tious·ly** *adv* — **un·pre·ten·tious·ness** *n*
un·prin·ci·pled \'ən-'prin(t)-sə-pəld\ *adj* : lacking moral principles : UNSCRUPULOUS
un·print·a·ble \-'print-ə-bəl\ *adj* : unfit to be printed
un·pro·fes·sion·al \,ən-prə-'fesh-nəl, -ən-ᵊl\ *adj* : not professional; *esp* : not conforming to the standards of one's profession — **un·pro·fes·sion·al·ly** \-ē\ *adv*
un·prof·it·a·ble \'ən-'präf-ət-ə-bəl, -'präf-tə-bəl\ *adj* : not profitable : USELESS — **un·prof·it·a·bly** \-blē\ *adv*
un·qual·i·fied \-'kwäl-ə-,fīd\ *adj* **1** : not fit : not having requisite qualifications **2** : not modified or restricted by reservations — **un·qual·i·fied·ly** \-,fī(-ə)d-lē\ *adv*
un·ques·tion·a·ble \-'kwes-chə-nə-bəl\ *adj* **1** : acknowledged as beyond question or doubt **2** : not questionable : INDISPUTABLE — **un·ques·tion·a·bly** \-blē\ *adv*
un·ques·tion·ing \-chə-niŋ\ *adj* : not questioning : accepting without examination or hesitation — **un·ques·tion·ing·ly** *adv*
un·qui·et \-'kwī-ət\ *adj* **1** : not quiet, AGITATED, TURBULENT **2** : physically, emotionally, or mentally restless : UNEASY — **un·qui·et·ly** *adv* — **un·qui·et·ness** *n*
un·quote \'ən-,kwōt\ *vi* : to state that the matter preceding is quoted
un·rav·el \'ən-'rav-əl\ *vb* **1** : to separate the threads of : DISENTANGLE **2** : SOLVE **3** : to become unraveled
un·read \-'red\ *adj* **1** : not read **2** : UNEDUCATED
un·read·a·ble \-'rēd-ə-bəl\ *adj* **1** : too dull or unattractive to read **2** : not legible or decipherable : ILLEGIBLE — **un·read·a·bil·i·ty** \,ən-,rēd-ə-'bil-ət-ē\ *n*
un·re·al \-'rē(-ə)l\ *adj* : lacking in reality, substance, or genuineness : ARTIFICIAL
un·re·al·i·ty \,ən-rē-'al-ət-ē\ *n* **1 a** : the quality or state of being unreal : NONEXISTENCE **b** : something unreal, insubstantial, or visionary **2** : ineptitude in dealing with reality
un·rea·son·a·ble \'ən-'rēz-nə-bəl, -ᵊn-ə-bəl\ *adj* **1 a** : not governed by or acting according to reason **b** : not conformable to

reason : ABSURD **2** : exceeding the bounds of reason or moderation — **un·rea·son·a·ble·ness** *n* — **un·rea·son·a·bly** \-blē\ *adv*
un·rea·soned \-'rēz-ᵊnd\ *adj* : not based on reason or reasoning
un·rea·son·ing \-'rēz-niŋ, -ᵊn-iŋ\ *adj* : not reasoning; *esp* : not using or showing the use of reason as a guide or control
un·reel \'ən-'rēl\ *vb* : to unwind from or as if from a reel
un·re·gen·er·ate \ˌən-ri-'jen-(ə-)rət\ *adj* : not reborn spiritually : not at peace with God : SINFUL, WICKED
un·re·lent·ing \ˌən-ri-'lent-iŋ\ *adj* **1** : not softening or yielding in determination : HARD, STERN **2** : not letting up or weakening in vigor or pace — **un·re·lent·ing·ly** *adv*
un·re·mit·ting \ˌən-ri-'mit-iŋ\ *adj* : not stopping : UNCEASING, PERSEVERING — **un·re·mit·ting·ly** *adv*
un·re·served \ˌən-ri-'zərvd\ *adj* **1** : not held in reserve : not kept back **2** : having or showing no reserve in manner or speech — **un·re·serv·ed·ly** \-'zər-vəd-lē\ *adv* — **un·re·serv·ed·ness** \-'zər-vəd-nəs\ *n*
un·rest \'ən-'rest\ *n* : want of rest : a disturbed or uneasy state
un·re·strained \ˌən-ri-'strānd\ *adj* **1** : not restrained : IMMODERATE, UNCONTROLLED **2** : free of constraint : SPONTANEOUS — **un·re·strain·ed·ly** \-'strā-nəd-lē\ *adv*
un·righ·teous \'ən-'rī-chəs\ *adj* **1** : not righteous : SINFUL, WICKED **2** : UNJUST, UNMERITED — **un·righ·teous·ly** *adv* — **un·righ·teous·ness** *n*
un·ripe \-'rīp\ *adj* **1** : not ripe : IMMATURE **2** : UNREADY, UNSEASONABLE — **un·ripe·ness** *n*
un·ri·valed *or* **un·ri·valled** \-'rī-vəld\ *adj* : having no rival
un·roll \-'rōl\ *vb* **1** : to unwind a roll of : open out **2** : DISPLAY, DISCLOSE **3** : to become unrolled or spread out
un·round \-'raůnd\ *vt* : to pronounce (a sound) without, or with decreased, rounding of the lips — **un·round·ed** *adj*
un·ruf·fled \-'rəf-əld\ *adj* **1** : not upset or agitated **2** : not ruffled : SMOOTH
un·ruly \'ən-'rü-lē\ *adj* : not yielding readily to rule or restraint : UNCONTROLLABLE — **un·rul·i·ness** *n*
un·sad·dle \-'sad-ᵊl\ *vb* **1** : to remove the saddle from a horse **2** : UNHORSE
un·sa·vory \-'sāv(-ə)-rē\ *adj* **1** : having little or no taste **2** : having a bad taste or smell **3** : morally offensive
un·say \-'sā\ *vt* **-said** \-'sed\; **-say·ing** \-'sā-iŋ\ : to take back (something said) : RETRACT, WITHDRAW
un·scathed \'ən-'skāth̲d\ *adj* : wholly unharmed : not injured
un·schooled \-'sküld\ *adj* : not schooled : UNTAUGHT, UNTRAINED
un·sci·en·tif·ic \ˌən-ˌsī-ən-'tif-ik\ *adj* **1** : not used in scientific work **2** : not according with the principles and methods of science
un·scram·ble \'ən-'skram-bəl\ *vt* **1** : to separate (as a conglomeration or tangle) into original components : RESOLVE, CLARIFY **2** : to restore (as a radio message) to intelligible form
un·screw \-'skrü\ *vb* **1** : to draw the screws from **2** : to loosen or withdraw by turning
un·scru·pu·lous \-'skrü-pyə-ləs\ *adj* : not scrupulous : UNPRINCIPLED — **un·scru·pu·lous·ly** *adv* — **un·scru·pu·lous·ness** *n*
un·seal \-'sēl\ *vt* : to break or remove the seal of : OPEN
un·search·a·ble \-'sər-chə-bəl\ *adj* : not to be searched or explored : INSCRUTABLE — **un·search·a·bly** \-blē\ *adv*
un·sea·son·a·ble \-'sēz-nə-bəl, -ᵊn-ə-bəl\ *adj* : not seasonable : happening or coming at the wrong time : UNTIMELY — **un·sea·son·a·ble·ness** *n* — **un·sea·son·a·bly** \-blē\ *adv*
un·seat \'ən-'sēt\ *vt* **1** : to dislodge from one's seat esp. on horseback **2** : to dislodge from a place or position; *esp* : to remove from political office
¹un·seem·ly \-'sēm-lē\ *adj* : not seemly : UNBECOMING
²unseemly *adv* : in an unseemly manner
un·seen \-'sēn\ *adj* : not seen or perceived : INVISIBLE
un·seg·re·gat·ed \-'seg-ri-ˌgāt-əd\ *adj* : not segregated; *esp* : free from racial segregation
un·self·ish \-'sel-fish\ *adj* : not selfish : GENEROUS — **un·self·ish·ly** *adv* — **un·self·ish·ness** *n*
un·set·tle \-'set-ᵊl\ *vb* : to move or loosen from a settled state : make or become displaced or disturbed
un·set·tled \-ᵊld\ *adj* **1** : not settled : not fixed (as in position or character) **2** : not calm : DISTURBED **3** : not decided in mind : UNDETERMINED **4** : not paid; *also* : not disposed of according to law **5** : not occupied by settlers
un·sex \'ən-'seks\ *vt* : to deprive of sex or of qualities typical of one's sex
un·shack·le \-'shak-əl\ *vt* : to loose from shackles
un·shaped \-'shāpt\ *adj* : not shaped: as **a** : not dressed or finished to final form **b** : imperfect in form or formulation
un·sheathe \-'shēth̲\ *vt* : to draw from or as if from a sheath or scabbard
un·ship \-'ship\ *vb* **1** : to remove from a ship **2** : to remove or become removed from position
un·shod \-'shäd\ *adj* : lacking shoes
un·sight·ly \-'sīt-lē\ *adj* : unpleasant to the sight : UGLY
un·skilled \-'skild\ *adj* **1** : not skilled; *esp* : not skilled in a specified branch of work : lacking technical training **2** : not requiring skill **3** : marked by lack of skill
un·skill·ful \-'skil-fəl\ *adj* : not skillful : lacking in skill or proficiency — **un·skill·ful·ly** \-fə-lē\ *adv* — **un·skill·ful·ness** *n*
un·snarl \-'snärl\ *vt* : to disentangle a snarl in
un·so·phis·ti·cat·ed \ˌən(t)-sə-'fis-tə-ˌkāt-əd\ *adj* : not sophisticated: as **a** : not changed or corrupted : GENUINE **b** (1) : not worldly-wise : lacking sophistication (2) : lacking adornment or complexity of structure : PLAIN, SIMPLE
un·sought \'ən-'sȯt\ *adj* : not sought : not searched for or asked for : not obtained by effort
un·sound \-'saůnd\ *adj* : not sound: as **a** : not healthy or whole **b** : not mentally normal : not wholly sane **c** : not firmly made, placed, or fixed **d** : not valid or true : INVALID, SPECIOUS — **un·sound·ly** *adv* — **un·sound·ness** *n*
un·spar·ing \-'spa(ə)r-iŋ\ *adj* **1** : not merciful or forbearing : RUTHLESS **2** : not frugal : LIBERAL — **un·spar·ing·ly** *adv*
un·speak·a·ble \-'spē-kə-bəl\ *adj* **1** : impossible to express in words **2** : extremely bad — **un·speak·a·bly** \-blē\ *adv*
un·spot·ted \-'spät-əd\ *adj* : not spotted : free from spot or stain; *esp* : free from moral stain
un·sta·ble \-'stā-bəl\ *adj* : not stable : not firm or fixed : not constant: as **a** : FLUCTUATING, IRREGULAR **b** : FICKLE, VACILLATING; *also* : having defective emotional control **c** : readily changing in chemical composition or physical state or properties; *esp* : tending to decompose spontaneously — **un·sta·ble·ness** *n* — **un·sta·bly** \-b(ə-)lē\ *adv*
un·steady \-'sted-ē\ *adj* : not steady : UNSTABLE — **un·stead·i·ly** \-'sted-ᵊl-ē\ *adv* — **un·stead·i·ness** \-'sted-ē-nəs\ *n*
un·stint·ing·ly \'ən-'stint-iŋ-lē\ *adv* : FREELY, GENEROUSLY
un·stop \-'stäp\ *vt* **1** : to free from an obstruction : OPEN **2** : to remove a stopper from
un·strap \-'strap\ *vt* : to remove or loose a strap from
un·stressed \-'strest\ *adj* : not stressed; *esp* : not bearing a stress or accent
un·string \-'striŋ\ *vt* **-strung** \-'strəŋ\; **-string·ing** \-'striŋ-iŋ\ **1** : to loosen or remove the strings of **2** : to remove from a string **3** : to make weak, disordered, or unstable
un·stud·ied \-'stəd-ēd\ *adj* **1** : not acquired by study **2** : not studied or planned with a certain effect in mind : NATURAL, UNFORCED
un·sub·stan·tial \ˌən(t)-səb-'stan-chəl\ *adj* : lacking substance, firmness, or strength — **un·sub·stan·ti·al·i·ty** \-ˌstan-chē-'al-ət-ē\ *n* — **un·sub·stan·tial·ly** \-'stanch-(ə-)lē\ *adv*
un·suit·a·ble \'ən-'süt-ə-bəl\ *adj* : not suitable or fitting : UNBECOMING, INAPPROPRIATE — **un·suit·a·bly** \-blē\ *adv*

un·sung \-'səŋ\ *adj* **1** : not sung **2** : not celebrated in song or verse
un·tan·gle \'ən-'taŋ-gəl\ *vt* **1** : to remove a tangle from : DISENTANGLE **2** : to straighten (as something complex or confused) out : RESOLVE
un·taught \-'tȯt\ *adj* **1** : not instructed or trained : IGNORANT **2** : NATURAL, SPONTANEOUS
un·teth·er \-'teth-ər\ *vt* : to free from a tether
un·think·a·ble \-'thiŋ-kə-bəl\ *adj* : not to be thought of or considered as possible
un·think·ing \-'thiŋ-kiŋ\ *adj* **1** : not taking thought : HEEDLESS, UNMINDFUL **2** : not indicating thought or reflection **3** : not having the power of thought — **un·think·ing·ly** *adv*
un·thought–of \-'thȯt-ˌəv, -ˌäv\ *adj* : not thought of : not considered : not imagined
un·thread \-'thred\ *vt* **1** : to draw or take out a thread from **2** : to loosen the threads or connections of **3** : to make one's way through
un·tie \-'tī\ *vb* **-tied**; **-ty·ing** *or* **-tie·ing** **1** : to free from something that ties, fastens, or restrains : UNBIND **2 a** : to disengage the knotted parts of **b** : DISENTANGLE, RESOLVE **3** : to become loosened or unbound
[1]**un·til** \ən-ˌtil, ˌən-\ *prep* : up to the time of
[2]**until** *conj* **1** : up to the time that **2** : to the point or degree that
[1]**un·time·ly** \'ən-'tīm-lē\ *adv* **1** : at an inopportune time : UNSEASONABLY **2** : PREMATURELY
[2]**untimely** *adj* **1** : occurring or done before the due, natural, or proper time : too early : PREMATURE **2** : INOPPORTUNE, UNSEASONABLE — **un·time·li·ness** *n*
un·ti·tled \-'tīt-ᵊld\ *adj* **1** : having no title esp. of nobility **2** : not named
un·to \'ən-tə, -tü\ *prep* : TO
un·told \'ən-'tōld\ *adj* **1** : not told : not revealed **2** : not counted : VAST, NUMBERLESS
[1]**un·touch·a·ble** \-'təch-ə-bəl\ *adj* : forbidden to the touch — **un·touch·a·bil·i·ty** \ˌən-ˌtəch-ə-'bil-ət-ē\ *n*
[2]**untouchable** *n* : one that is untouchable; *esp* : a member of a large formerly segregated hereditary group in India having in traditional Hindu belief the quality of defiling by contact a member of a higher caste
un·to·ward \'ən-'tō(-ə)rd\ *adj* **1** : difficult to manage : STUBBORN, WILLFUL **2** : INCONVENIENT, TROUBLESOME, AWKWARD — **un·to·ward·ly** *adv* — **un·to·ward·ness** *n*
un·tried \-'trīd\ *adj* **1** : not tested or proved by experience or trial **2** : not tried in court
un·true \-'trü\ *adj* **1** : not faithful : DISLOYAL **2** : not according with a standard of correctness : not level or exact **3** : not according with the facts : FALSE — **un·tru·ly** \-'trü-lē\ *adv*
un·truth \-'trüth\ *n* **1** : lack of truthfulness : FALSITY **2** : something that is untrue : FALSEHOOD
un·truth·ful \-'trüth-fəl\ *adj* : not containing or telling the truth : FALSE, INACCURATE — **un·truth·ful·ly** \-fə-lē\ *adv* — **un·truth·ful·ness** *n*
un·tu·tored \'ən-'t(y)üt-ərd\ *adj* : UNTAUGHT, UNLEARNED, IGNORANT
un·twine \-'twīn\ *vb* **1** : to unwind the twisted or tangled parts of : DISENTANGLE **2** : to remove by unwinding **3** : to become disentangled or unwound
un·twist \-'twist\ *vb* **1** : to separate the twisted parts of : UNTWINE **2** : to become untwined
un·used \-'yüzd, *in the phrase "unused to" usually* -'yüs(t)\ *adj* **1** : not habituated : UNACCUSTOMED **2** : not used
un·usu·al \-'yüzh-(ə-w)əl\ *adj* : not usual : UNCOMMON, RARE — **un·usu·al·ly** \-ē\ *adv* — **un·usu·al·ness** *n*
un·ut·ter·a·ble \-'ət-ə-rə-bəl\ *adj* **1** : not capable of being pronounced : UNPRONOUNCEABLE **2** : not capable of being put into words : INEXPRESSIBLE — **un·ut·ter·a·bly** \-blē\ *adv*
un·var·nished \'ən-'vär-nisht\ *adj* **1** : not varnished **2** : not heightened or exaggerated : not embellished : PLAIN
un·veil \-'vāl\ *vb* **1** : to remove a veil or covering from : DISCLOSE **2** : to remove a veil : reveal oneself
un·voiced \-'vȯist\ *adj* **1** : not verbally expressed **2** : VOICELESS 2
un·war·rant·a·ble \-'wȯr-ənt-ə-bəl\ *adj* : not justifiable : INEXCUSABLE — **un·war·rant·a·bly** \-blē\ *adv*
un·wary \-'wa(ə)r-ē\ *adj* : not alert : easily fooled or surprised
un·weave \'ən-'wēv\ *vt* **-wove** \-'wōv\; **-wo·ven** \-'wō-vən\; **-weav·ing** : DISENTANGLE, RAVEL
un·well \-'wel\ *adj* **1** : being in poor health : AILING, SICK **2** : MENSTRUATING
un·wept \-'wept\ *adj* : not mourned : UNLAMENTED
un·whole·some \-'hōl-səm\ *adj* : detrimental to physical, mental, or moral well-being : UNHEALTHY
un·wieldy \-'wēl-dē\ *adj* : not easily handled or managed because of size or weight : AWKWARD — **un·wield·i·ness** *n*
un·will·ing \'ən-'wil-iŋ\ *adj* : not willing — **un·will·ing·ly** *adv* — **un·will·ing·ness** *n*
un·wind \-'wīnd\ *vb* **-wound** \-'waùnd\; **-wind·ing** **1 a** : to cause to uncoil : wind off **b** : to become uncoiled or disentangled **c** : to free from or as if from a binding or wrapping **2** : to make or become free of tension : RELAX
un·wise \-'wīz\ *adj* : not wise : FOOLISH — **un·wise·ly** *adv*
un·wit·ting \-'wit-iŋ\ *adj* **1** : not intended : INADVERTENT **2** : not knowing : UNAWARE — **un·wit·ting·ly** *adv*
un·wont·ed \-'wȯnt-əd, -'wōnt-\ *adj* : being out of the ordinary : RARE, UNUSUAL — **un·wont·ed·ly** *adv* — **un·wont·ed·ness** *n*
un·world·ly \-'wərl-(d)lē\ *adj* **1** : not of this world; *esp* : SPIRITUAL **2 a** : not wise in the ways of the world : NAÏVE **b** : not swayed by mundane considerations — **un·world·li·ness** *n*
un·wor·thy \'ən-'wər-thē\ *adj* **1** : BASE, DISHONORABLE **2** : not meritorious : not worthy : UNDESERVING — **un·wor·thi·ly** \-thə-lē\ *adv* — **un·wor·thi·ness** \-thē-nəs\ *n*
un·wrap \-'rap\ *vt* : to remove the wrapping from : DISCLOSE
un·writ·ten \-'rit-ᵊn\ *adj* **1** : not reduced to writing : ORAL, TRADITIONAL **2** : containing no writing : BLANK
un·yield·ing \-'yēl-diŋ\ *adj* **1** : characterized by lack of softness or flexibility **2** : characterized by firmness or obduracy
un·yoke \-'yōk\ *vt* **1** : to free (as oxen) from a yoke **2** : SEPARATE, DISCONNECT
un·zip \-'zip\ *vb* : to open by means of a zipper
[1]**up** \'əp\ *adv* **1 a** : in or to a higher position or level : away from the center of the earth **b** : from beneath a surface (as ground or water) **c** : from below the horizon **d** : in or into an upright position **e** : out of bed **2** : with greater intensity **3 a** : in or into a better or more advanced state **b** : in or into a state of greater intensity or activity **4 a** : into existence, evidence, or knowledge **b** : into consideration **5** : into possession or custody **6 a** : ENTIRELY, COMPLETELY **b** — used as a function word for emphasis **7** : ASIDE, BY **8** : into a state of closure or confinement **9 a** : so as to arrive or approach **b** : in a direction conventionally opposite to down **c** : so as to be even with, overtake, or arrive at **10** : in or into parts **11** : to a stop **12 a** : in advance **b** : for each side
[2]**up** *adj* **1 a** : risen above the horizon **b** : being out of bed **c** : relatively high **d** : RAISED, LIFTED **e** : BUILT **f** : grown above a surface **g** : moving, inclining, or directed upward or in a direction regarded as up **2 a** : marked by agitation, excitement, or activity **b** : READY; *esp* : highly prepared **c** : going on : taking place **3** : EXPIRED, ENDED **4** : well informed **5** : being ahead or in advance of an opponent **6 a** : presented for or under consideration **b** : charged before a court — **up to** **1** : capable of performing or dealing with **2** : engaged in **3** : being the responsibility of
[3]**up** *vb* **upped** *or in 1* **up**; **upped**; **up·ping**; **ups** *or in 1* **up** **1** : to

act abruptly or surprisingly — usu. followed by *and* and another verb **2 :** to rise from a lying or sitting position **3 :** to move or cause to move upward : ASCEND, RAISE

[4]**up** \(ˌ)əp, ˈəp\ *prep* **1 :** to, toward, or at a higher point of **2 a** (1) **:** toward the source of (2) **:** toward the northern part of **b :** to, toward, or in the inner part of **3 :** ALONG

[5]**up** \ˈəp\ *n* **1 :** an upward course or slope **2 :** a period or state of prosperity or success

[1]**up·beat** \ˈəp-ˌbēt\ *n* **:** an unaccented beat in a musical measure; *esp* **:** the last beat of the measure

[2]**upbeat** *adj* **:** OPTIMISTIC, CHEERFUL

up·braid \ˌəp-ˈbrād\ *vt* **:** to criticize, reproach, or scold severely or vehemently — **up·braid·er** *n*

up·bring·ing \ˈəp-ˌbriŋ-iŋ\ *n* **:** the process of bringing up and training

up·com·ing \ˌəp-ˌkəm-iŋ\ *adj* **:** FORTHCOMING, APPROACHING

[1]**up–coun·try** \ˌəp-ˌkən-trē\ *adj* **:** of or relating to the interior of a country or a region — **up–coun·try** \ˈəp-\ *n*

[2]**up–coun·try** \ˌəp-ˈkən-trē\ *adv* **:** to or in the interior of a country or a region

up·date \ˌəp-ˈdāt\ *vt* **:** to bring up to date

up·draft \ˈəp-ˌdraft, -ˌdráft\ *n* **:** an upward movement of gas (as air)

up·end \ˌəp-ˈend\ *vb* **:** to set, stand, or rise on end

[1]**up·grade** \ˈəp-ˌgrād\ *n* **1 :** an upward grade or slope **2 a :** INCREASE, RISE **b :** a rise toward a better state or position

[2]**up·grade** \-ˌgrād\ *vt* **:** to raise to a higher grade or position

up·growth \ˈəp-ˌgrōth\ *n* **:** the process of growing up **:** upward growth **:** DEVELOPMENT; *also* **:** a product or result of this

up·heav·al \ˌəp-ˈhē-vəl\ *n* **1 :** the action or an instance of upheaving esp. of part of the earth's crust **2 :** an instance of violent agitation or change

up·heave \ˌəp-ˈhēv\ *vb* **-heaved; -heav·ing :** to heave or lift up from beneath — **up·heav·er** *n*

[1]**up·hill** \ˈəp-ˈhil\ *adv* **1 :** upward on a hill or incline **2 :** against difficulties

[2]**up·hill** \ˌəp-ˌhil\ *adj* **1 :** situated on elevated ground **2 :** going up **:** ASCENDING **3 :** DIFFICULT, LABORIOUS

up·hold \ˌəp-ˈhōld\ *vt* **-held** \-ˈheld\; **-hold·ing 1 a :** to give support to **b :** to support against an opponent **2 a :** to keep elevated **b :** to lift up — **up·hold·er** *n*

up·hol·ster \(ˌ)əp-ˈhōl-stər\ *vt* **-stered; -ster·ing** \-st(ə-)riŋ\ **:** to furnish with or as if with upholstery — **up·hol·ster·er** \-stər-ər, -strər\ *n*

up·hol·stery \-st(ə-)rē\ *n, pl* **-ster·ies :** materials (as fabric, padding, and springs) used to make a soft covering esp. for a seat

up·keep \ˈəp-ˌkēp\ *n* **1 :** the act or cost of maintaining in good condition **:** MAINTENANCE **2 :** the state of being maintained

up·land \ˈəp-lənd, -ˌland\ *n* **:** high land esp. at some distance from the sea — **upland** *adj*

[1]**up·lift** \(ˌ)əp-ˈlift\ *vb* **1 :** to lift up **:** ELEVATE **2 :** to improve the condition of esp. spiritually, socially, or intellectually **3 :** RISE — **up·lift·er** *n*

[2]**up·lift** \ˈəp-ˌlift\ *n* **:** an act, process, or result of uplifting: as **a :** the uplifting of a part of the earth's surface **b :** moral or social improvement; *also* **:** a movement to make such improvement **c :** influences intended to uplift

up·most \ˈəp-ˌmōst\ *adj* **:** UPPERMOST

up·on \ə-ˈpón, -ˈpän\ *prep* **:** ON

[1]**up·per** \ˈəp-ər\ *adj* **1 :** higher in physical position, rank, or order **2 :** constituting the smaller and more restricted branch of a bicameral legislature **3 :** being toward the interior **:** further inland **4 :** NORTHERN

[2]**upper** *n* **:** one that is upper: as **a :** the parts of a shoe or boot above the sole **b :** an upper tooth or denture **c :** an upper berth

up·per·case \ˌəp-ər-ˈkās\ *adj* **:** CAPITAL — **uppercase** *n*

upper class *n* **:** a social class occupying a position above the middle class and having the highest status in a society — **up·per–class** \ˌəp-ər-ˈklas\ *adj*

up·per·class·man \ˌəp-ər-ˈklas-mən\ *n* **:** a junior or senior in a college or high school

up·per·cut \ˈəp-ər-ˌkət\ *n* **:** a swinging blow (as in boxing) directed upward with a bent arm — **uppercut** *vb*

upper hand *n* **:** MASTERY, ADVANTAGE

up·per·most \ˈəp-ər-ˌmōst\ *adv* **:** in or into the highest or most prominent position — **uppermost** *adj*

up·per·part \-ˌpärt\ *n* **:** a part lying on the upper side

up·pish \ˈəp-ish\ *adj* **:** UPPITY

up·pi·ty \ˈəp-ət-ē\ *adj* **:** putting on airs of superiority

up·raise \ˌəp-ˈrāz\ *vt* **:** to raise or lift up **:** ELEVATE

up·rear \-ˈri(ə)r\ *vb* **1 :** to lift up **:** RAISE, ERECT **2 :** RISE

[1]**up·right** \ˈəp-ˌrīt\ *adj* **1 a :** PERPENDICULAR, VERTICAL **b :** erect in carriage or posture **2 :** morally correct **:** HONEST, HONORABLE — **up·right·ly** *adv* — **up·right·ness** *n*

[2]**upright** *n* **1 :** the state of being upright **:** PERPENDICULAR **2 :** something upright

upright piano *n* **:** a piano whose strings run vertically

[1]**up·rise** \ˌəp-ˈrīz\ *vi* **-rose** \-ˈrōz\; **-ris·en** \-ˈriz-ᵊn\; **-ris·ing** \-ˈrī-ziŋ\ **1 a :** to rise to a higher position **b :** to get up (as from sleep or a sitting position) **c :** to come into view esp. from below the horizon **2 :** to swell in sound **:** increase in size or volume — **up·ris·er** *n*

[2]**up·rise** \ˈəp-ˌrīz\ *n* **1 :** an act or instance of uprising **2 :** an upward slope

up·ris·ing \ˈəp-ˌrī-ziŋ\ *n* **:** an act or instance of rising up; *esp* **:** INSURRECTION, REVOLT

up·roar \ˈəp-ˌrōr\ *n* **:** a state of commotion, excitement, or violent disturbance

up·roar·i·ous \ˌəp-ˈrōr-ē-əs\ *adj* **1 :** marked by uproar **2 :** extremely funny — **up·roar·i·ous·ly** *adv*

up·root \ˌəp-ˈrüt, -ˈru̇t\ *vt* **1 :** to remove by or as if by pulling up by the roots **2 :** to displace from a country or traditional habitat — **up·root·er** *n*

[1]**up·set** \ˌəp-ˈset\ *vb* **-set; -set·ting 1 :** to force or be forced out of the usual upright, level, or proper position **:** OVERTURN, CAPSIZE **2 a :** to disturb emotionally **b :** to make somewhat ill **3 a :** to throw into disorder **:** DISARRANGE **b :** INVALIDATE **c :** to defeat unexpectedly — **up·set·ter** *n*

[2]**up·set** \ˈəp-ˌset\ *n* **1 :** an act or result of upsetting **:** a state of being upset **2 a :** a minor physical disorder **b :** an emotional disturbance

up·shot \ˈəp-ˌshät\ *n* **:** final result **:** OUTCOME

up·side \ˈəp-ˌsīd\ *n* **:** the upper side or part

up·side down \ˌəp-ˌsīd-ˈdau̇n\ *adv* **1 :** with the upper and the lower parts reversed in position **2 :** in or into great disorder — **upside–down** *adj*

[1]**up·stage** \ˈəp-ˈstāj\ *adv* **:** toward or at the rear of a stage

[2]**upstage** *adj* **:** of or relating to the rear of a stage

[3]**up·stage** \ˌəp-ˈstāj\ *vt* **1 :** to force (an actor) to face away from the audience by staying upstage **2 :** to treat snobbishly

[1]**up·stairs** \ˈəp-ˈsta(ə)rz\ *adv* **1 :** up the stairs **:** to or on a higher floor **2 :** to or at a high altitude or higher position

[2]**up·stairs** \-ˌsta(ə)rz\ *adj* **1 :** situated above the stairs **2 :** of or relating to the upper floors

[3]**up·stairs** \ˈəp-ˈ, ˈəp-ˌ\ *n* **:** the part of a building above the ground floor

up·stand·ing \ˌəp-ˈstan-diŋ, ˈəp-ˌ\ *adj* **1 :** ERECT **2 :** marked by integrity **:** STRAIGHTFORWARD — **up·stand·ing·ness** *n*

up·start \ˈəp-ˌstärt\ *n* **:** one that has risen suddenly (as from a low position to wealth or power) **:** PARVENU; *esp* **:** one that claims more personal importance than he warrants — **up·start** \ˌəp-ˌ\ *adj*

[1]**up·state** \ˈəp-ˌstāt\ *adj* **:** of, relating to, characteristic of, or being a part of a state away from a large city and esp. to the north

²upstate *n* : an upstate region — **up·stat·er** \-ˈstāt-ər\ *n*
up·stream \ˈəp-ˈstrēm\ *adv* : at or toward the source of a stream — **upstream** *adj*
up·stroke \ˈəp-ˌstrōk\ *n* : an upward stroke (as of a pen)
up·surge \ˈəp-ˌsərj\ *n* : a rapid or sudden rise
up·sweep \ˈəp-ˌswēp\ *vb* **-swept** \-ˌswept\; **-sweep·ing** : to sweep upward : curve or slope upward — **upsweep** *n*
up·swept \ˈəp-ˌswept\ *adj* : swept upward
up·swing \ˈəp-ˌswiŋ\ *n* : an upward swing; *esp* : a marked increase or rise (as in activity)
up·take \ˈəp-ˌtāk\ *n* **1** : UNDERSTANDING, COMPREHENSION **2** : a flue leading upward **3** : an act or instance of absorbing and incorporating esp. into a living organism
up to *prep* **1** : as far as a designated part or place **2** : to or in fulfillment of **3 a** : to the limit of **b** : as many or as much as **4** : UNTIL, TILL
up–to–date \ˌəp-tə-ˈdāt\ *adj* **1** : extending up to the present time **2** : abreast of the times (as in style or technique) : MODERN — **up–to–date·ness** *n*
up·town \ˈəp-ˈtaủn\ *adv* : toward, to, or in the upper part of a town — **up·town** \-ˌtaủn\ *adj*
¹up·turn \ˈəp-ˌtərn, ˌəp-ˈ\ *vb* **1** : to turn up or over **2** : to turn or direct upward
²up·turn \ˈəp-ˌtərn\ *n* : an upward turn (as toward better conditions or higher prices)
¹up·ward \ˈəp-wərd\ *or* **up·wards** \-wərdz\ *adv* **1** : in a direction from lower to higher **2** : toward a higher or better condition **3** : toward a greater amount or higher number, degree, or rate
²upward *adj* **1** : directed toward or situated in a higher place or level : ASCENDING **2** : ascending toward a head, origin, or source — **up·ward·ly** *adv* — **up·ward·ness** *n*
upwards of *adv* : more than : in excess of
up·wind \ˈəp-ˈwind\ *adv* (*or adj*) : in the direction from which the wind is blowing
ura·ni·um \yủ-ˈrā-nē-əm\ *n* : a heavy white metallic radioactive chemical element used as a source of atomic energy
ur·ban \ˈər-bən\ *adj* : of, relating to, characteristic of, or constituting a city
ur·bane \ˌər-ˈbān\ *adj* : notably polite or finished in manner : POLISHED — **ur·bane·ly** *adv*
ur·ban·i·ty \ˌər-ˈban-ət-ē\ *n, pl* **-ties** **1** : the quality or state of being urbane **2** *pl* : urbane acts or conduct
ur·ban·ize \ˈər-bə-ˌnīz\ *vt* **1** : to cause to take on urban characteristics **2** : to impart an urban way of life to — **ur·ban·i·za·tion** \ˌər-bə-nə-ˈzā-shən\ *n*
ur·chin \ˈər-chən\ *n* **1** : HEDGEHOG **2** : a pert or roguish youngster
urea \yủ-ˈrē-ə\ *n* : a soluble weakly basic nitrogenous compound that is the chief solid component of mammalian urine and an end product of protein decomposition — **ure·ic** \-ˈrē-ik\ *adj*
ure·mia \yủ-ˈrē-mē-ə\ *n* : accumulation in the blood usu. in severe kidney disease of constituents normally eliminated in the urine resulting in a severe toxic condition — **ure·mic** \-mik\ *adj*
ure·ter \ˈyủr-ət-ər\ *n* : a duct that carries urine from a kidney to the bladder or cloaca
ure·thra \yủ-ˈrē-thrə\ *n, pl* **-thras** *or* **-thrae** \-(ˌ)thrē\ : the canal that in most mammals carries off the urine from the bladder and in the male serves also as a genital duct — **ure·thral** \-thrəl\ *adj*
¹urge \ˈərj\ *vb* **1** : to present, advocate, or demand something earnestly **2 a** : to try to persuade or sway **b** : to serve as a motive or reason for **3** : to press or impel to some course or activity (as greater speed) — **urg·er** *n*
²urge *n* **1** : the act or process of urging **2** : a force or impulse that urges
ur·gent \ˈər-jənt\ *adj* **1 a** : calling for immediate attention : PRESSING **b** : conveying a sense of urgency **2** : urging insistently — **ur·gen·cy** \-jən-sē\ *n* — **ur·gent·ly** *adv*
uric \ˈyủr-ik\ *adj* : of, relating to, or found in urine
uric acid *n* : a white odorless nearly insoluble nitrogenous acid that is present in small quantity in mammalian urine and is the chief nitrogenous excretion in birds and lower forms
uri·nal \ˈyủr-ən-ᵊl\ *n* **1** : a receptacle for urine **2** : a place for urinating
uri·nal·y·sis \ˌyủr-ə-ˈnal-ə-səs\ *n, pl* **uri·nal·y·ses** \-ə-ˌsēz\ : the analysis of urine
uri·nary \ˈyủr-ə-ˌner-ē\ *adj* **1** : relating to, occurring in, or constituting the organs concerned with the formation and discharge of urine **2** : of, relating to, or used for urine **3** : excreted as or in urine
uri·nate \ˈyủr-ə-ˌnāt\ *vi* : to discharge urine — **uri·na·tion** \ˌyủr-ə-ˈnā-shən\ *n*
urine \ˈyủr-ən\ *n* : waste material that is secreted by the kidney, is rich in end products of protein metabolism together with salts and pigments, and is usu. a yellowish liquid in mammals but semisolid in birds and reptiles
urn \ˈərn\ *n* **1** : a vessel that typically has the form of a vase on a pedestal and often is used for preserving the ashes of the dead **2** : a closed vessel usu. with a spigot for serving a hot beverage
ur·ti·car·ia \ˌərt-ə-ˈkar-ē-ə\ *n* : HIVES — **ur·ti·car·i·al** \-ē-əl\ *adj*
us \(ˈ)əs\ *pron, objective case of* WE
us·a·ble \ˈyü-zə-bəl\ *adj* : suitable or fit for use — **us·a·bil·i·ty** \ˌyü-zə-ˈbil-ət-ē\ *n* — **us·a·bly** \ˈyü-zə-blē\ *adv*
us·age \ˈyü-sij, -zij\ *n* **1 a** : customary practice or procedure **b** : the way in which words and phrases are actually used in a language community **2 a** : the action or mode of using : USE **b** : manner of treating
¹use \ˈyüs\ *n* **1 a** : the act or practice of employing something : EMPLOYMENT, APPLICATION **b** : the fact or state of being used **c** : way of using **d** : USAGE, CUSTOM **2 a** : the privilege or benefit of using something **b** : the ability or power to use something (as a limb or faculty) **c** (1) : the legal enjoyment of property; *esp* : the physical occupation of real property that constitutes an element of ownership (2) : a legal arrangement resembling a trust whereby one person is invested with the legal possession or occupation of real property for the benefit of another party; *also* : the benefit or profit conferred **3 a** : a particular service or end : OBJECT, FUNCTION **b** : the quality of being suitable for employment : USEFULNESS, UTILITY **c** : the occasion or need to employ **4** : ESTEEM, LIKING
²use \ˈyüz\ *vb* **used** \ˈyüzd, *in the phrase "used to" usually* ˈyüs(t)\; **us·ing** \ˈyü-ziŋ\ **1** : ACCUSTOM, HABITUATE **2** : to put into action or service : EMPLOY **3** : to consume or take (as liquor or drugs) regularly **4** : to carry out a purpose or action by means of : UTILIZE **5** : to expend or consume by putting to use **6** : to behave toward : TREAT **7** — used in the past with *to* to indicate a former practice, fact, or state — **us·er** \ˈyü-zər\ *n*
used \ˈyüzd, *in the phrase "used to" usually* ˈyüs(t)\ *adj* **1** : employed in accomplishing something **2** : that has endured use; *esp* : SECONDHAND **3** : ACCUSTOMED, HABITUATED
use·ful \ˈyüs-fəl\ *adj* : capable of being put to use : USABLE; *also* : of a kind to be valuable or productive — **use·ful·ly** \-fə-lē\ *adv* — **use·ful·ness** *n*
use·less \ˈyüs-ləs\ *adj* : having or being of no use : UNSERVICEABLE, WORTHLESS — **use·less·ly** *adv* — **use·less·ness** *n*
¹ush·er \ˈəsh-ər\ *n* **1** : an officer who walks before a person of rank **2** : one who escorts persons to seats (as in a theater)
²usher *vt* **ush·ered**; **ush·er·ing** \ˈəsh-(ə-)riŋ\ **1** : to conduct to a place **2** : to precede as an usher, forerunner, or harbinger **3** : INAUGURATE, INTRODUCE

usu·al \'yüzh-(ə-w)əl\ *adj* **1 :** accordant with usage, custom, or habit **:** NORMAL **2 :** commonly or ordinarily used **3 :** found in ordinary practice or in the ordinary course of events **:** ORDINARY — **usu·al·ly** \-ē\ *adv* — **usu·al·ness** *n*
usu·fruct \'yü-zə-,frəkt\ *n* **:** the legal right of using and enjoying the fruits or profits of something belonging to another
usu·rer \'yü-zhər-ər\ *n* **:** one that lends money esp. at an excessively high rate of interest
usu·ri·ous \yu̇-'zhu̇r-ē-əs\ *adj* **:** practicing, involving, or constituting usury
usurp \yu̇-'sərp, -'zərp\ *vt* **:** to seize and hold by force or without right — **usur·pa·tion** \,yü-sər-'pā-shən, ,yü-zər-\ *n* — **usurp·er** *n*
usu·ry \'yüzh-(ə-)rē\ *n, pl* **usuries 1 :** the lending of money with an interest charge for its use **2 :** an excessive rate or amount of interest charged; *esp* **:** interest above an established legal rate
uten·sil \yu̇-'ten(t)-səl\ *n* **1 :** an instrument or vessel used in a household and esp. a kitchen **2 :** an article serving a useful purpose
uter·us \'yüt-ə-rəs\ *n, pl* **uteri** \-,rī\ **:** an organ of the female mammal for containing and usu. for nourishing the young during development previous to birth — **uter·ine** \-rən, -,rīn\ *adj*
¹util·i·tar·i·an \yu̇-,til-ə-'ter-ē-ən, ,yü-\ *n* **:** an advocate or adherent of utilitarianism
²utilitarian *adj* **1 :** of or relating to utilitarianism **2 a :** of or relating to utility **b :** aiming at usefulness rather than beauty **c :** serving a useful purpose
util·i·tar·i·an·ism \-ē-ə-,niz-əm\ *n* **:** a doctrine that one's conduct should be determined by the usefulness of its consequences; *esp* **:** a theory that the aim of action should be the greatest happiness of the greatest number
¹util·i·ty \yü-'til-ət-ē\ *n, pl* **-ties 1 a :** the quality or state of being useful **:** USEFULNESS **b :** capacity to satisfy human wants **2 :** something useful or designed for use **3 a :** a business organization performing a public service and subject to special governmental regulation **b** (1) **:** a public service or a commodity provided by a public utility (2) **:** equipment (as plumbing) to provide such or a similar service
²utility *adj* **1 :** capable of serving as a substitute in various roles or positions **2 :** being of a usable but inferior grade **3 :** serving primarily for usefulness rather than beauty **:** UTILITARIAN **4 :** designed for general use
uti·lize \'yüt-ᵊl-,īz\ *vt* **:** to make use of **:** convert to use — **uti·liz·a·ble** *adj* — **uti·li·za·tion** \,yüt-ᵊl-ə-'zā-shən\ *n*
ut·most \'ət-,mōst\ *adj* **1 :** situated at the farthest or most distant point **:** EXTREME **2 :** of the greatest or highest degree, quantity, number, or amount — **utmost** *n*
uto·pia \yu̇-'tō-pē-ə\ *n* **1** *often cap* **:** a place of ideal perfection esp. in laws, government, and social conditions **2 :** an impractical scheme for social improvement
¹uto·pi·an \-pē-ən\ *adj, often cap* **1 :** of, relating to, or having the characteristics of a utopia **2 :** proposing or advocating ideal social and political schemes that are impractical
²utopian *n* **1 :** a believer in the perfectibility of human society **2 :** one that proposes or advocates utopian schemes — **uto·pi·an·ism** \-pē-ə-,niz-əm\ *n*
¹ut·ter \'ət-ər\ *adj* **:** ABSOLUTE, TOTAL — **ut·ter·ly** *adv*
²utter *vt* **1 a :** to send forth usu. as a sound **b :** to express in usu. spoken words **2 :** to put (as currency) into circulation — **ut·ter·a·ble** *adj* — **ut·ter·er** *n*
ut·ter·ance \'ət-ə-rən(t)s\ *n* **1 :** something uttered; *esp* **:** an oral or written statement **2 :** the action of uttering with the voice **:** SPEECH **3 :** power, style, or manner of speaking
ut·ter·most \'ət-ər-,mōst\ *adj* **:** EXTREME, UTMOST — **uttermost** *n*
uvu·la \'yü-vyə-lə\ *n, pl* **-las** *or* **-lae** \-,lē\ **:** the pendent fleshy lobe at the back of the palate — **uvu·lar** \-lər\ *adj*
ux·o·ri·ous \,ək-'sōr-ē-əs, ,əg-'zōr-\ *adj* **:** excessively fond of or submissive to a wife — **ux·o·ri·ous·ly** *adv* — **ux·o·ri·ous·ness** *n*

v \'vē\ *n, often cap* **1 :** the 22d letter of the English alphabet **2 :** the roman numeral 5
va·can·cy \'vā-kən-sē\ *n, pl* **-cies 1 a :** a vacating of an office, post, or property **b :** the time such office or property is vacant **2 :** a vacant office, post, or tenancy **3 :** empty space **4 :** the state of being vacant **:** VACUITY
va·cant \'vā-kənt\ *adj* **1 :** being without an occupant **:** not used **2 :** free from business or care **3 :** BRAINLESS, FOOLISH — **va·cant·ly** *adv* — **va·cant·ness** *n*
va·cate \'vā-,kāt, vā-'\ *vt* **1 :** to make void **:** ANNUL **2 :** to make vacant **:** leave empty
¹va·ca·tion \vā-'kā-shən\ *n* **:** a period of rest from work **:** HOLIDAY
²vacation *vi* **-tioned; -tion·ing** \-sh(ə-)niŋ\ **:** to take or spend a vacation — **va·ca·tion·er** *n*
va·ca·tion·ist \-sh(ə-)nəst\ *n* **:** a person taking a vacation
vac·ci·nate \'vak-sə-,nāt\ *vb* **:** to inoculate (a person) with a related harmless virus in order to produce immunity to smallpox; *also* **:** to administer a vaccine to usu. by injection — **vac·ci·na·tor** \-,nāt-ər\ *n*
vac·ci·na·tion \,vak-sə-'nā-shən\ *n* **1 :** the act of vaccinating **2 :** the scar left by vaccinating
vac·cine \vak-'sēn, 'vak-,\ *n* **:** material (as a preparation of killed or modified virus or bacteria) used in vaccinating — **vaccine** *adj*
vac·il·late \'vas-ə-,lāt\ *vi* **1 :** FLUCTUATE, OSCILLATE **2 :** to incline first to one course or opinion and then to another **:** WAVER — **vac·il·la·tion** \,vas-ə-'lā-shən\ *n* — **vac·il·la·tor** \'vas-ə-,lāt-ər\ *n* — **vac·il·la·to·ry** \-lə-,tōr-ē\ *adj*
va·cu·i·ty \va-'kyü-ət-ē, və-\ *n, pl* **-ties 1 :** an empty space **2 a :** the state, fact, or quality of being vacuous **:** EMPTINESS, HOLLOWNESS **b :** vacancy of mind **3 :** a vacuous or inane thing
vac·u·ous \'vak-yə-wəs\ *adj* **1 :** EMPTY **2 :** marked by lack of ideas or intelligence **:** STUPID, INANE — **vac·u·ous·ly** *adv* — **vac·u·ous·ness** *n*
¹vac·u·um \'vak-yə(-wə)m, -yüm\ *n, pl* **-u·ums** *or* **-ua** \-yə-wə\ **1 a :** a space absolutely devoid of matter **b :** a space partially exhausted (as to the highest degree possible) by artificial means (as a special pump) **2 a :** a vacant space **:** VOID **b :** a state of isolation from outside influences
²vacuum *vt* **:** to use a vacuum device (as a cleaner) on
vacuum bottle *n* **:** a cylindrical container with a vacuum between an inner and an outer wall used to keep liquids either hot or cold
vacuum cleaner *n* **:** an electrical appliance for cleaning (as floors, carpets, tapestry, or upholstered work) by suction
vacuum tube *n* **:** an electron tube having a high degree of vacuum

va·de me·cum \ˌvād-ē-ˈmē-kəm\ *n, pl* **vade mecums** **1 :** a book for ready reference : MANUAL **2 :** something regularly carried about by a person

[1]**vag·a·bond** \ˈvag-ə-ˌbänd\ *adj* **1 :** moving from place to place without a fixed home : WANDERING **2 a :** of, relating to, or characteristic of a wanderer **b :** leading an unsettled, irresponsible, or disreputable life

[2]**vagabond** *n* **:** one who leads a vagabond life; *esp* : TRAMP — **vag·a·bond·age** \-ˌbän-dij\ *n*

va·ga·ry \ˈvā-gə-rē, və-ˈge(ə)r-ē\ *n, pl* **-ries :** an eccentric or unpredictable manifestation, action, or notion

va·gi·na \və-ˈjī-nə\ *n, pl* **-nae** \-(ˌ)nē\ *or* **-nas :** a canal that leads from the uterus to the external opening of the genital canal — **va·gi·nal** \və-ˈjīn-ᵊl, ˈvaj-ən-\ *adj*

va·gran·cy \ˈvā-grən(t)-sē\ *n, pl* **-cies** **1 :** VAGARY **2 :** the state or action of being vagrant

[1]**va·grant** \ˈvā-grənt\ *n* **:** one who wanders idly from place to place without a home or apparent means of support

[2]**vagrant** *adj* **1 :** wandering about from place to place usu. with no means of support **2 a :** having a fleeting, wayward, or inconstant quality **b :** having no fixed course : RANDOM

vague \ˈvāg\ *adj* **1 a :** not clearly expressed : stated in indefinite terms **b :** not having a precise meaning **2 :** not clearly felt, grasped, or understood : INDISTINCT **3 :** not thinking or expressing one's thoughts clearly or precisely **4 :** not sharply outlined : HAZY — **vague·ly** *adv* — **vague·ness** *n*

vain \ˈvān\ *adj* **1 :** WORTHLESS **2 :** not succeeding : FUTILE **3 :** proud of one's looks or abilities : CONCEITED — **vain·ly** *adv* — **vain·ness** *n* — **in vain 1 :** to no purpose : without success **2 :** IRREVERENTLY, BLASPHEMOUSLY

vain·glo·ri·ous \(ˈ)vān-ˈglōr-ē-əs\ *adj* **:** marked by vainglory : BOASTFUL — **vain·glo·ri·ous·ly** *adv*

vain·glo·ry \ˈvān-ˌglōr-ē\ *n* **1 :** excessive or ostentatious pride esp. in one's achievements **2 :** vain display or show : VANITY

val·ance \ˈval-ən(t)s, ˈvāl-\ *n* **1 :** a drapery hung along the edge of a bed, table, altar, canopy, or shelf **2 :** a short drapery or wood or metal frame used as a decorative heading to conceal the top of curtains and fixtures

[1]**vale** \ˈvāl\ *n* **:** VALLEY, DALE

[2]**va·le** \ˈväl-(ˌ)ā, ˈwäl-\ *n* **:** a salutation of leave-taking

val·e·dic·tion \ˌval-ə-ˈdik-shən\ *n* **:** an act or utterance of leave-taking : FAREWELL

val·e·dic·to·ri·an \ˌval-ə-ˌdik-ˈtōr-ē-ən\ *n* **:** the student usu. of the highest rank in a graduating class who delivers the valedictory oration at the commencement exercises

[1]**val·e·dic·to·ry** \-ˈdik-t(ə-)rē\ *adj* **:** of or relating to leave-taking : FAREWELL; *esp* : given at a leave-taking ceremony (as school commencement exercises)

[2]**valedictory** *n, pl* **-ries :** a valedictory oration or statement

va·lence \ˈvā-lən(t)s\ *n* **:** the degree of combining power of an element or radical as shown by the number of atomic weights of a univalent element (as hydrogen) with which the atomic weight of the element will combine or for which it can be substituted

Va·len·ci·ennes \və-ˌlen(t)-sē-ˈen(z), ˌval-ən-sē-\ *n* **:** a fine handmade lace

val·en·tine \ˈval-ən-ˌtīn\ *n* **1 :** a sweetheart chosen or complimented on St. Valentine's Day **2 :** a gift or greeting sent or given on St. Valentine's Day

val·et \ˈval-ət, va-ˈlā\ *n* **:** a male servant or hotel employee who takes care of a man's clothes and performs personal services

val·e·tu·di·nar·i·an \ˌval-ə-ˌt(y)üd-ᵊn-ˈer-ē-ən\ *n* **:** a person of a weak or sickly constitution; *esp* : one whose chief concern is his invalidism — **valetudinarian** *adj* — **val·e·tu·di·nar·i·an·ism** \-ˌiz-əm\ *n*

val·iant \ˈval-yənt\ *adj* **1 :** boldly brave : COURAGEOUS **2 :** VALOROUS, HEROIC — **val·iant·ly** *adv* — **val·iant·ness** *n*

val·id \ˈval-əd\ *adj* **1 :** founded on truth or fact : WELL-GROUNDED **2 :** binding in law : SOUND **3 :** appropriate for the end in view : EFFECTIVE — **val·id·ly** *adv* — **val·id·ness** *n*

val·i·date \ˈval-ə-ˌdāt\ *vi* **1 :** to make valid **2 :** CONFIRM, SUBSTANTIATE — **val·i·da·tion** \ˌval-ə-ˈdā-shən\ *n*

va·lid·i·ty \və-ˈlid-ət-ē\ *n* **:** the quality or state of being valid

va·lise \və-ˈlēs\ *n* **:** TRAVELING BAG

val·ley \ˈval-ē\ *n, pl* **valleys** **1 :** a long depression of the earth's surface usu. between ranges of hills or mountains **2 a :** HOLLOW, DEPRESSION **b :** the place of meeting of two slopes of a roof forming a drainage channel

val·or \ˈval-ər\ *n* **:** personal bravery in combat

val·or·ous \ˈval-ə-rəs\ *adj* **1 :** possessing or exhibiting valor : BRAVE **2 :** characterized by or performed with valor — **val·or·ous·ly** *adv*

valse \väls\ *n* **:** WALTZ; *esp* : a concert waltz

[1]**val·u·a·ble** \ˈval-yə(-wə)-bəl\ *adj* **1 a :** having monetary value **b :** worth a great deal of money **2 :** having value : of great use or service — **val·u·a·ble·ness** *n* — **val·u·a·bly** \-blē\ *adv*

[2]**valuable** *n* **:** a personal possession (as a jewel) of relatively great monetary value — usu. used in pl.

val·u·a·tion \ˌval-yə-ˈwā-shən\ *n* **1 :** the act or process of valuing; *esp* : appraisal of property **2 :** the estimated or determined value **3 :** judgment or appreciation of worth or character — **val·u·a·tion·al** \-shnəl, -shən-ᵊl\ *adj* — **val·u·a·tion·al·ly** \-ē\ *adv*

[1]**val·ue** \ˈval-yü\ *n* **1 :** a fair return or equivalent in goods, services, or money for something exchanged **2 :** the amount of another commodity for which a given thing can be exchanged; *esp* : the amount of money that something will bring : monetary worth **3 :** relative worth, utility, or importance : degree of excellence **4 a :** a numerical quantity assigned or computed **b :** the magnitude of a physical quantity **c :** precise signification **d :** the sound or sounds answering to a letter or orthographic item **5 :** the relative duration of a musical note **6 a :** relative lightness or darkness of a color : LUMINOSITY **b :** the relation of one part in a picture to another with respect to lightness and darkness **7 :** something intrinsically valuable or desirable **8 :** DENOMINATION 4

[2]**value** *vt* **1 a :** to estimate or assign the monetary worth of : APPRAISE **b :** to rate or scale in usefulness, importance, or general worth : EVALUATE **2 :** to consider or rate highly : PRIZE, ESTEEM — **val·u·er** *n*

val·ued \-yüd\ *adj* **:** highly regarded : ESTEEMED

val·ue·less \ˈval-yü-ləs\ *adj* **:** of no value : WORTHLESS

valve \ˈvalv\ *n* **1 :** a structure esp. in a bodily channel (as a vein) that closes temporarily to obstruct passage of material or permits movement of a fluid in one direction only **2 a :** a mechanical device by which the flow of liquid, gas, or loose material in bulk may be started, stopped, or regulated by a movable part; *also* : the movable part of such a device **b :** a device in a brass wind instrument for quickly varying the tube length in order to change the fundamental tone by some definite interval **3 :** one of the distinct and usu. movably jointed pieces of which the shell of some shell-bearing animals and esp. bivalve mollusks consists **4 :** one of the segments or pieces into which a ripe seed capsule or pod separates — **valved** \ˈvalvd\ *adj*

val·vu·lar \ˈval-vyə-lər\ *adj* **1 :** resembling or functioning as a valve; *also* : opening by valves **2 :** of or relating to a valve esp. of the heart

[1]**vamp** \ˈvamp\ *n* **:** the part of a shoe upper or boot upper covering esp. the front part of the foot

[2]**vamp** *vt* **1 a :** to provide (a shoe) with a new vamp **b :** to piece (something old) with a new part : PATCH **2 :** INVENT, FABRICATE

[3]**vamp** *n* **:** a woman who uses her charm or wiles to seduce and exploit men

[4]**vamp** *vt* : to practice seductive wiles on
vam·pire \'vam-,pī(ə)r\ *n* **1** : the body of a dead person believed to come from the grave at night and suck the blood of persons asleep **2 a** : one who lives by preying on others **b** : a woman who exploits and ruins her lover **3** : any of various bats believed to feed on blood; *also* : any of various So. American bats that feed on blood and are dangerous to man and domestic animals esp. as vectors of disease (as rabies)
[1]**van** \'van\ *n* : VANGUARD
[2]**van** *n* : a usu. enclosed wagon or truck used for transportation of goods or animals
va·na·di·um \və-'nād-ē-əm\ *n* : a grayish malleable metallic chemical element found combined in minerals and used esp. to form alloys (as of steel)
van·dal \'van-dᵊl\ *n* : one who willfully destroys, damages, or defaces public or private property
van·dal·ism \'van-dᵊl-,iz-əm\ *n* : willful or malicious destruction or defacement of public or private property
van·dal·ize \'van-dᵊl-,īz\ *vt* : to subject to vandalism
Van·dyke \van-'dīk\ *n* : a trim pointed beard
vane \'vān\ *n* **1** : a movable device attached to an elevated object (as a spire) for showing the direction of the wind **2** : a flat or curved extended surface attached to an axis and moved by the wind or water; *also* : a device revolving in a manner resembling this and moving in water or air — **vaned** \'vānd\ *adj*
van·guard \'van-,gärd\ *n* **1** : the troops moving at the head of an army **2** : the forefront of an action or movement or those in the forefront
va·nil·la \və-'nil-ə\ *n* **1** : any of a genus of tropical American climbing orchids **2** : the long pod of a vanilla that is an important article of commerce for the flavoring extract that it yields; *also* : this extract
van·ish \'van-ish\ *vi* **1** : to pass quickly from sight : DISAPPEAR **2** : to pass completely from existence — **van·ish·er** *n*
van·i·ty \'van-ət-ē\ *n, pl* **-ties** **1** : something that is vain **2** : the quality or fact of being vain: as **a** : WORTHLESSNESS, EMPTINESS **b** : FUTILITY **c** : inflated pride in oneself or one's appearance : CONCEIT **3** : a fashionable article or knickknack **4** : [3]COMPACT 1
van·quish \'vaŋ-kwish, 'van-\ *vt* **1** : to overcome in battle : subdue completely **2** : to gain mastery over (as an emotion or temptation or competitor) : DEFEAT — **van·quish·a·ble** *adj* — **van·quish·er** *n*
van·tage \'vant-ij\ *n* **1** : superiority in a contest **2** : a position giving a strategic advantage, commanding perspective, or comprehensive view **3** : ADVANTAGE 3
van·ward \'van-wərd\ *adj* : located in the vanguard : ADVANCED — **vanward** *adv*
vap·id \'vap-əd\ *adj* : lacking liveliness, tang, briskness, or force : FLAT, UNINTERESTING — **va·pid·i·ty** \va-'pid-ət-ē\ *n* — **vap·id·ly** \'vap-əd-lē\ *adv* — **vap·id·ness** *n*
[1]**va·por** \'vā-pər\ *n* **1** : fine particles of matter (as fog or smoke) floating in the air and clouding it **2** : a substance in a gaseous state; *esp* : such a substance that is liquid under ordinary conditions **3** : something insubstantial or fleeting
[2]**vapor** *vi* **va·pored**; **va·por·ing** \-p(ə-)riŋ\ **1 a** : to rise or pass off in vapor **b** : to emit vapor **2** : to indulge in bragging, blustering, or idle talk — **va·por·er** \-pər-ər\ *n*
va·por·ing \'vā-p(ə-)riŋ\ *n* : the act or speech of one that vapors; *esp* : an idle, extravagant, or high-flown expression or speech — usu. used in pl.
va·por·ize \'vā-pə-,rīz\ *vb* **1** : to turn from a liquid or solid into vapor **2** : to cause to become ethereal or dissipated — **va·por·iz·a·ble** *adj* — **va·por·i·za·tion** \,vā-pə-rə-'zā-shən\ *n*
va·por·iz·er \'vā-pə-,rī-zər\ *n* : a device that vaporizes something (as a fuel oil or a medicated liquid)
va·por·ous \'vā-p(ə-)rəs\ *adj* **1** : consisting or characteristic of vapor **2** : containing or obscured by vapors : MISTY **3** : UNSUBSTANTIAL, VAGUE — **va·por·ous·ly** *adv* — **va·por·ous·ness** *n*
va·pory \'vā-p(ə-)rē\ *adj* : VAPOROUS, VAGUE
va·que·ro \vä-'ke(ə)r-ō\ *n, pl* **-ros** : a ranch hand : COWBOY
[1]**var·i·a·ble** \'ver-ē-ə-bəl\ *adj* **1 a** : able or apt to vary : CHANGEABLE **b** : FICKLE, INCONSTANT **2 a** : characterized by variations **b** : not true to type : ABERRANT **3** : having the characteristics of a variable — **var·i·a·bil·i·ty** \,ver-ē-ə-'bil-ət-ē\ *n* — **var·i·a·ble·ness** *n* — **var·i·a·bly** \'ver-ē-ə-blē\ *adv*
[2]**variable** *n* **1** : something that is variable **2 a** : a quantity that may assume any one of a set of values **b** : a symbol in a mathematical formula representing a variable
var·i·ance \'ver-ē-ən(t)s\ *n* **1** : the fact, quality, or state of being variable or variant : DIFFERENCE, DEVIATION **2** : the fact or state of being in disagreement : DISSENSION, DISPUTE — **at variance** : not in harmony or agreement
[1]**var·i·ant** \'ver-ē-ənt\ *adj* : differing from others of its kind or class and esp. from others regarded as representing a norm, standard, or type
[2]**variant** *n* : one of two or more individuals exhibiting usu. slight differences: as **a** : one that exhibits variation from a type or norm **b** : one of two or more different spellings or pronunciations of the same word
var·i·a·tion \,ver-ē-'ā-shən\ *n* **1 a** : the act or process of varying : the state or fact of being varied **b** : an instance of varying **c** : the extent to which or range in which a thing varies **2** : the repetition of a musical theme with modifications in rhythm, tune, harmony, or key **3 a** : divergence in qualities from those typical or usual to a group **b** : an individual or group exhibiting variation — **var·i·a·tion·al** \-shnəl, -shən-ᵊl\ *adj* — **var·i·a·tion·al·ly** \-ē\ *adv*
vari·col·ored \'ver-i-,kəl-ərd\ *adj* : having various colors : VARIEGATED
var·i·cose \'var-ə-,kōs\ *adj* : abnormally swollen or dilated
var·ied \'ve(ə)r-ēd\ *adj* **1** : CHANGED, ALTERED **2** : having numerous forms or types : DIVERSE **3** : VARIEGATED — **var·ied·ly** *adv*
var·ie·gate \'ver-(ē-)ə-,gāt\ *vt* **1** : to diversify in external appearance esp. with different colors **2** : to enliven by variety — **var·ie·ga·tion** \,ver-(ē-)ə-'gā-shən\ *n* — **var·ie·ga·tor** \'ver-(ē-)ə-,gāt-ər\ *n*
var·ie·gat·ed \'ver-(ē-)ə-,gāt-əd\ *adj* **1** : having patches, stripes, or marks of different colors **2** : full of variety
va·ri·e·ty \və-'rī-ət-ē\ *n, pl* **-ties** **1** : the quality or state of having different forms or types **2** : a number or collection of different things : ASSORTMENT **3 a** : something differing from others of the same general kind **b** : any of various groups of plants or animals of less than specific rank **4** : entertainment consisting of successive unrelated performances (as dances, skits, or acrobatic feats) — **va·ri·e·tal** \-ət-ᵊl\ *adj* — **va·ri·e·tal·ly** \-ᵊl-ē\ *adv*
var·i·o·rum \,ver-ē-'ōr-əm\ *n* : an edition or text esp. of a classical author with notes by different persons and often with variant readings of the text
var·i·ous \'ver-ē-əs\ *adj* **1** : marked by variation or variety (as in appearance or properties) : of differing kinds : DIVERSIFIED **2 a** : differing one from another : UNLIKE **b** : VARIANT **3** : consisting of an indefinite number greater than one : SUNDRY, DIVERS — **var·i·ous·ly** *adv* — **var·i·ous·ness** *n*
var·let \'vär-lət\ *n* : a low fellow
[1]**var·nish** \'vär-nish\ *n* **1 a** : a liquid preparation that is spread like paint and dries to a hard lustrous typically transparent coating **b** : the covering or glaze given by the application of varnish **2** : outside show : GLOSS — **var·nishy** \-ni-shē\ *adj*
[2]**varnish** *vt* : to cover with or as if with varnish
var·si·ty \'vär-sət-ē, -stē\ *n, pl* **-ties** : a first team representing a university, college, school, or club — **varsity** *adj*

vary \'ve(ə)r-ē\ *vb* **var·ied**; **var·y·ing** : to differ or cause to differ: as **a** : to make a usu. minor or partial change in **b** : to give variety to : DIVERSIFY **c** : to exhibit or undergo change; *also* : to be different **d** : to take on successive values **e** : to diverge structurally or physiologically from typical members of a group — **var·y·ing·ly** *adv*

vas·cu·lar \'vas-kyə-lər\ *adj* : of, relating to, or being an anatomical vessel or a system of these; *also* : supplied with or made up of such vessels and esp. blood vessels — **vas·cu·lar·i·ty** \,vas-kyə-'lar-ət-ē\ *n*

vase \'vās, 'vāz\ *n* : a usu. round vessel of greater depth than width used chiefly for ornament or for flowers

vaso·mo·tor \,vas-ō-'mōt-ər\ *adj* : of, relating to, or being nerves or centers controlling the size of blood vessels

vas·sal \'vas-əl\ *n* **1** : a person under the protection of another who is his feudal lord and to whom he has vowed homage and fealty : a feudal tenant **2** : one in a subservient or subordinate position — **vassal** *adj*

vas·sal·age \-ij\ *n* **1** : the condition of being a vassal **2** : homage and loyalty due a lord from his vassal **3** : a politically dependent territory

¹vast \'vast\ *adj* : very great in size, amount, degree, intensity, or esp. in extent — **vast·ly** *adv* — **vast·ness** *n*

²vast *n* : a boundless space : IMMENSITY

vat \'vat\ *n* : a large vessel (as a cistern, tub, or barrel) esp. for liquids

vau·de·ville \'vòd(-ə)-vəl, 'vōd-, -,vil\ *n* : light theatrical entertainment featuring usu. unrelated variety acts (as songs, dances, and sketches)

¹vault \'vòlt\ *n* **1 a** : an arched structure of masonry usu. forming a ceiling or roof **b** : something suggesting a vault esp. in arched or domed structure **2 a** : a space covered by an arched structure; *esp* : an underground passage or room **b** : an underground storage compartment **c** : a room or compartment for the safekeeping of valuables **3 a** : a burial chamber **b** : a case usu. of metal or concrete in which a casket is enclosed at burial

²vault *vt* : to form or cover with or as if with a vault : ARCH

³vault *vb* : to execute a leap using the hands or a pole; *also* : to leap over — **vault·er** *n*

⁴vault *n* : an act of vaulting : LEAP

vault·ed \'vòl-təd\ *adj* **1** : built in the form of a vault : ARCHED **2** : covered with a vault

vault·ing \-tiŋ\ *adj* : leaping upwards; *esp* : straining unreasonably or arrogantly toward the heights

¹vaunt \'vònt\ *vb* : BRAG, BOAST — **vaunt·er** *n* — **vaunt·ing·ly** *adv*

²vaunt *n* **1** : a vainglorious display (as of worth or accomplishment) **2** : a bragging assertive speech

veal \'vēl\ *n* **1** : CALF; *esp* : VEALER **2** : the flesh of a young calf

veal·er \'vē-lər\ *n* : a calf grown for or suitable for veal

vec·tor \'vek-tər\ *n* : an organism (as an insect) that transmits disease germs — **vec·to·ri·al** \vek-'tōr-ē-əl\ *adj*

ve·dette \vi-'det\ *n* : a mounted sentinel stationed in advance of pickets

¹veer \'vi(ə)r\ *vb* : to change direction or course : TURN; *esp* : to shift in a clockwise direction — **veer·ing·ly** *adv*

²veer *n* : a change in course or direction

vee·ry \'vi(ə)r-ē\ *n, pl* **veeries** : a tawny brown thrush common in woodlands of the eastern U.S.

¹veg·e·ta·ble \'vej-tə-bəl, 'vej-ət-ə-bəl\ *adj* **1** : of, relating to, or made up of plants **2** : obtained from plants **3** : suggesting that of a plant (as in monotony) — **veg·e·ta·bly** \-blē\ *adv*

²vegetable *n* **1** : PLANT 1 **2** : a usu. herbaceous plant grown for an edible part that is usu. eaten with the principal course of a meal; *also* : such edible part

veg·e·tal \'vej-ət-ᵊl\ *adj* **1** : VEGETABLE **2** : VEGETATIVE

¹veg·e·tar·i·an \,vej-ə-'ter-ē-ən\ *n* : one who believes in or practices living solely on vegetables, fruits, grains, and nuts or excluding meat from the diet — **veg·e·tar·i·an·ism** \-ē-ə-,niz-əm\ *n*

²vegetarian *adj* **1** : of or relating to vegetarians **2** : consisting wholly of vegetables

veg·e·tate \'vej-ə-,tāt\ *vb* : to live or grow in the manner of a plant; *esp* : to lead a passive effortless existence

veg·e·ta·tion \,vej-ə-'tā-shən\ *n* **1** : the act or process of vegetating **2** : inert existence **3** : plant life or cover (as of an area) — **veg·e·ta·tion·al** \-shnəl, -shən-ᵊl\ *adj*

veg·e·ta·tive \'vej-ə-,tāt-iv\ *adj* **1** : of, relating to, or functioning in nutrition and growth as contrasted with reproduction **2** : VEGETABLE 3 — **veg·e·ta·tive·ly** *adv* — **veg·e·ta·tive·ness** *n*

ve·he·ment \'vē-ə-mənt\ *adj* : marked by forceful energy : POWERFUL: as **a** : intensely emotional : IMPASSIONED, FERVID **b** : deeply felt and usu. of a kind to compel attention — **ve·he·mence** \-mən(t)s\ *n* — **ve·he·ment·ly** *adv*

ve·hi·cle \'vē-,(h)ik-əl\ *n* **1** : a medium through which something is administered, transmitted, expressed, achieved, or displayed **2** : something used to transport persons or goods : CONVEYANCE

ve·hic·u·lar \vē-'hik-yə-lər\ *adj* : of, relating to, or designed for vehicles esp. motor vehicles

¹veil \'vāl\ *n* **1 a** : a length of cloth or net worn esp. by women over the head and shoulders or attached to a hat or headdress and sometimes (as in eastern countries) drawn also over the face **b** : something that covers or obscures like a veil **2** : the vows or life of a nun

²veil *vt* : to cover, provide, obscure, or conceal with or as if with a veil

veil·ing \'vā-liŋ\ *n* **1** : VEIL **2** : a light sheer fabric (as net or chiffon) suitable for veils

¹vein \'vān\ *n* **1** : a fissure in rock filled with mineral matter **2 a** : one of the tubular branching vessels that carry blood from the capillaries toward the heart **b** : one of the vascular bundles forming the framework of a leaf **c** : one of the thickened ribs that stiffen the wings of an insect **3** : something like a vein usu. in irregular linear form or in forming a channel; *esp* : a wavy band or streak (as of a different color or texture) **4 a** : a distinctive mode of expression : STYLE **b** : a pervasive element or quality : STRAIN **c** : MOOD — **vein·al** \-ᵊl\ *adj* — **veined** \'vānd\ *adj* — **veiny** \'vā-nē\ *adj*

²vein *vt* : to form veins in or mark with veins

ve·lar \'vē-lər\ *adj* : of, relating to, or forming a velum — **velar** *n*

veld *or* **veldt** \'felt, 'velt\ *n* : open grassland esp. of southern Africa usu. with scattered shrubs or trees

vel·lum \'vel-əm\ *n* **1** : a fine-grained lambskin, kidskin, or calfskin prepared esp. for writing on or for binding books **2** : a strong cream-colored paper resembling vellum — **vellum** *adj*

ve·loc·i·pede \və-'läs-ə-,pēd\ *n* : a lightweight wheeled vehicle propelled by the rider; *esp* : TRICYCLE

ve·loc·i·ty \və-'läs-ət-ē, -'läs-tē\ *n, pl* **-ties** : quickness of motion : SPEED

ve·lour *or* **ve·lours** \və-'lù(ə)r\ *n, pl* **velours** \-'lù(ə)rz\ : a usu. heavy fabric with a pile or napped surface resembling velvet

ve·lum \'vē-ləm\ *n* : a membrane or anatomical partition resembling a veil or curtain

¹vel·vet \'vel-vət\ *n* **1** : a usu. silk or synthetic fabric with a thick soft pile of short erect threads **2** : something suggesting velvet (as in softness); *esp* : the soft vascular skin covering the developing antler of a deer **3** : an unanticipated gain or profit

²velvet *adj* **1** : made of or covered with velvet **2** : resembling or suggesting velvet : VELVETY

vel·ve·teen \,vel-və-'tēn\ *n* : a cotton fabric made in imitation of velvet

vel·vety \'vel-vət-ē\ *adj* **1** : soft and smooth like velvet

2 : smooth to the taste : MILD

ve•nal \'vēn-ᵊl\ *adj* **1** : willing to take bribes : open to corrupt influences **2** : influenced by bribery : CORRUPT — **ve•nal•i•ty** \vi-'nal-ət-ē\ *n* — **ve•nal•ly** \'vēn-ᵊl-ē\ *adv*

ve•na•tion \vā-'nā-shən, vē-\ *n* : an arrangement or system of veins — **ve•na•tion•al** \-shnəl, -shən-ᵊl\ *adj*

venation in leaves

vend \'vend\ *vb* : to sell or offer for sale esp. as a hawker or peddler — **vend•er** \'ven-dər\ *or* **ven•dor** \'ven-dər, ven-'dȯ(ə)r\ *n* — **vend•i•ble** *or* **vend•a•ble** \'ven-də-bəl\ *adj*

ven•det•ta \ven-'det-ə\ *n* : a feud in which the relatives of a murdered man try to take vengeance by killing the murderer or his relatives

[1]**ve•neer** \və-'ni(ə)r\ *n* **1** : a thin sheet of a material; *esp* : a layer of a valuable or beautiful wood glued to an inferior wood **2** : a protective or ornamental facing (as of brick or stone) **3** : a superficial or false show : GLOSS

[2]**veneer** *vt* : to overlay with a veneer — **ve•neer•er** *n*

ven•er•a•ble \'ven-ər-(ə-)bəl, 'ven-rə-bəl\ *adj* **1** : made sacred by association (as religious or historic) **2 a** : calling forth respect through age, character, and attainments **b** : impressive by reason of age — **ven•er•a•bil•i•ty** \ˌven-(ə-)rə-'bil-ət-ē\ *n* — **ven•er•a•ble•ness** *n* — **ven•er•a•bly** \'ven-ər-(ə-)-blē, 'ven-rə-blē\ *adv*

ven•er•ate \'ven-ə-ˌrāt\ *vt* : to regard with reverential respect or with admiration and deference — **ven•er•a•tor** \-ˌrāt-ər\ *n*

ven•er•a•tion \ˌven-ə-'rā-shən\ *n* **1** : the act of venerating : the state of being venerated **2** : a feeling of reverence or deep respect : DEVOTION

ve•ne•re•al \və-'nir-ē-əl\ *adj* : of or relating to sexual intercourse or to diseases transmitted by it

[1]**ven•ery** \'ven-ə-rē\ *n* : the art, act, or practice of hunting

[2]**venery** *n* : the pursuit of sexual indulgence or pleasure; *also* : sexual intercourse

ve•ne•tian blind \və-ˌnē-shən-\ *n* : a blind having thin horizontal slats that can be set to overlap to keep out light or tipped to let light come in between them

ven•geance \'ven-jən(t)s\ *n* : punishment inflicted in retaliation for an injury or offense : RETRIBUTION — **with a vengeance 1** : VIOLENTLY **2** : EXTREMELY

venge•ful \'venj-fəl\ *adj* : filled with a desire for revenge : VINDICTIVE — **venge•ful•ly** \-fə-lē\ *adv* — **venge•ful•ness** *n*

ve•ni•al \'vē-nē-əl, -nyəl\ *adj* : FORGIVABLE, EXCUSABLE — **ve•ni•al•ly** \-ē\ *adv* — **ve•ni•al•ness** *n*

ven•i•son \'ven-ə-sən, -ə-zən\ *n* : the flesh of a deer

ven•om \'ven-əm\ *n* **1** : poisonous matter normally secreted by an animal (as a snake, scorpion, or bee) and communicated chiefly by biting or stinging **2** : something that embitters or blights the mind or spirit : MALIGNITY

ven•om•ous \'ven-ə-məs\ *adj* **1** : filled with venom: as **a** : POISONOUS **b** : SPITEFUL, MALIGNANT **2** : secreting and using venom — **ven•om•ous•ly** *adv* — **ven•om•ous•ness** *n*

ve•nous \'vē-nəs\ *adj* **1** : of, relating to, or full of veins **2** : being purplish red oxygen-deficient blood present in most veins — **ve•nous•ly** *adv*

[1]**vent** \'vent\ *vt* **1 a** : to provide with an outlet **b** : to serve as an outlet for **2** : to give expression to **3** : to relieve by venting

[2]**vent** *n* : OUTLET; *esp* : an opening (as the anus or a flue) for the escape of a gas or liquid or for the relief of pressure

ven•ti•late \'vent-ᵊl-ˌāt\ *vt* **1** : to discuss freely and openly : make public **2 a** : to expose to air and esp. to a current of fresh air **b** : to provide with ventilation — **ven•ti•la•tive** \-ˌāt-iv\ *adj*

ven•ti•la•tion \ˌvent-ᵊl-'ā-shən\ *n* **1** : the act or process of ventilating **2** : circulation of air **3** : a system or means of providing fresh air

ven•ti•la•tor \'vent-ᵊl-ˌāt-ər\ *n* : one that ventilates; *esp* : a contrivance for introducing fresh air or expelling foul or stagnant air

ven•tral \'ven-trəl\ *adj* **1** : of or relating to the belly : ABDOMINAL **2** : of or relating to or located on or near the surface of the body that in man is the front but in most other animals is the lower surface — **ven•tral•ly** \-trə-lē\ *adv*

ven•tri•cle \'ven-tri-kəl\ *n* : a cavity of a bodily part or organ: as **a** : a chamber of the heart which receives blood from a corresponding atrium and from which blood is forced into the arteries **b** : one of the communicating cavities in the brain that are continuous with the central canal of the spinal cord

ven•tril•o•quism \ven-'tril-ə-ˌkwiz-əm\ *n* : the production of the voice in such a manner that the sound appears to come from a source other than the vocal organs of the speaker — **ven•tri•lo•qui•al** \ˌven-trə-'lō-kwē-əl\ *adj* — **ven•tri•lo•qui•al•ly** \-kwē-ə-lē\ *adv* — **ven•tril•o•quist** \ven-'tril-ə-kwəst\ *n* — **ven•tril•o•quis•tic** \(ˌ)ven-ˌtril-ə-'kwis-tik\ *adj*

[1]**ven•ture** \'ven-chər\ *vb* **ven•tured**; **ven•tur•ing** \'vench-(ə-)riŋ\ **1** : to expose to hazard : RISK **2** : to face the risks and dangers of : BRAVE **3** : to offer at the risk of rebuff or censure **4** : to proceed despite danger : DARE — **ven•tur•er** \'vench-(ə-)rər\ *n*

[2]**venture** *n* **1** : an undertaking involving chance, risk, or danger; *esp* : a speculative business enterprise **2** : a venturesome act

ven•ture•some \'ven-chər-səm\ *adj* **1** : disposed to court danger or take risks : DARING **2** : involving risk : HAZARDOUS — **ven•ture•some•ly** *adv* — **ven•ture•some•ness** *n*

ven•tur•ous \'vench-(ə-)rəs\ *adj* **1** : VENTURESOME **2** : HAZARDOUS — **ven•tur•ous•ly** *adv* — **ven•tur•ous•ness** *n*

ven•ue \'ven-yü\ *n* **1** : the place in which alleged events from which a legal action arises take place **2** : the place from which the jury is drawn and in which trial is held

ve•ra•cious \və-'rā-shəs\ *adj* **1** : TRUTHFUL, HONEST **2** : ACCURATE, TRUE — **ve•ra•cious•ly** *adv* — **ve•ra•cious•ness** *n*

ve•rac•i•ty \və-'ras-ət-ē\ *n, pl* **-ties 1** : devotion to the truth : TRUTHFULNESS **2** : ACCURACY, CORRECTNESS **3** : something true

ve•ran•da *or* **ve•ran•dah** \və-'ran-də\ *n* **1** : PORCH **2** : a long roofed gallery extending along one or more sides of a building

verb \'vərb\ *n* : a word that characteristically is the grammatical center of a predicate and expresses an act, occurrence, or mode of being

[1]**ver•bal** \'vər-bəl\ *adj* **1 a** : of, relating to, or consisting of words **b** : of, relating to, or involving words only rather than meaning or substance or effective action **2** : of, relating to, or formed from a verb **3** : spoken rather than written **4** : word-for-word : VERBATIM — **ver•bal•ly** \-bə-lē\ *adv*

[2]**verbal** *n* : a word that combines characteristics of a verb with those of a noun or adjective

ver•bal•ize \'vər-bə-ˌlīz\ *vb* **1** : to speak, write, or express in wordy or empty fashion **2** : to express something in words : describe verbally **3** : to convert into a verb — **ver•bal•i•za•tion** \ˌvər-bə-lə-'zā-shən\ *n* — **ver•bal•iz•er** *n*

ver•ba•tim \(ˌ)vər-'bāt-əm\ *adv (or adj)* : word for word : in the same words : LITERAL

ver•be•na \(ˌ)vər-'bē-nə\ *n* : VERVAIN; *esp* : any of numerous garden plants of hybrid origin widely grown for their showy spikes of white, pink, red, or blue flowers which are borne in profusion over a long season

ver·bi·age \'vər-bē-ij\ *n* **1 :** superfluity of words in proportion to sense or content : WORDINESS **2 :** DICTION, WORDING

ver·bose \(,)vər-'bōs\ *adj* : excessively wordy : PROLIX — **ver·bose·ly** *adv* — **ver·bose·ness** *n* — **ver·bos·i·ty** \-'bäs-ət-ē\ *n*

ver·dant \'vərd-ᵊnt\ *adj* **1 a :** green in color **b :** green with growing plants **2 :** unripe in experience or judgment — **ver·dan·cy** \-ᵊn-sē\ *n* — **ver·dant·ly** *adv*

ver·dict \'vər-(,)dikt\ *n* **1 :** the finding or decision of a jury on the matter submitted to them in trial **2 :** OPINION, JUDGMENT

ver·di·gris \'vərd-ə-,grēs, -,gris\ *n* : a green or greenish blue poisonous pigment produced by the action of acetic acid on copper or found on brass surfaces exposed to weather

ver·dure \'vər-jər\ *n* : the greenness of growing vegetation; *also* : such vegetation itself — **ver·dured** \-jərd\ *adj* — **ver·dur·ous** \'vərj-(ə-)rəs\ *adj* — **ver·dur·ous·ness** *n*

[1]**verge** \'vərj\ *n* **1 a :** a staff carried as an emblem of authority or office **b :** an area around a place or within which jurisdiction is exercised **2 a :** something that borders, limits, or bounds : EDGE, BOUNDARY **b :** BRINK, THRESHOLD

[2]**verge** *vi* **1 :** to be contiguous **2 :** to be on the verge

[3]**verge** *vi* **1 :** to move or extend in some direction or toward some condition : INCLINE **2 :** to be in transition or change

verg·er \'vər-jər\ *n* : a church official who keeps order during services or serves as an usher or a sacristan

ver·i·fi·a·ble \'ver-ə-,fī-ə-bəl\ *adj* : capable of being verified — **ver·i·fi·a·ble·ness** *n* — **ver·i·fi·a·bly** \-blē\ *adv*

ver·i·fy \'ver-ə-,fī\ *vt* **-fied; -fy·ing 1 :** to prove to be true or correct : CONFIRM **2 :** to check or test the accuracy of — **ver·i·fi·ca·tion** \,ver-ə-fə-'kā-shən\ *n* — **ver·i·fi·er** *n*

ver·i·ly \'ver-ə-lē\ *adv* : in fact : CERTAINLY

veri·sim·i·lar \,ver-ə-'sim-ə-lər\ *adj* : having the appearance of truth : PROBABLE — **veri·sim·i·lar·ly** *adv*

veri·si·mil·i·tude \-sə-'mil-ə-,t(y)üd\ *n* **1 :** the quality or state of being verisimilar **2 :** something verisimilar

ver·i·ta·ble \'ver-ət-ə-bəl\ *adj* : ACTUAL, TRUE — **ver·i·ta·ble·ness** *n* — **ver·i·ta·bly** \-blē\ *adv*

ver·i·ty \'ver-ət-ē\ *n, pl* **-ties 1 :** the quality or state of being true or real **2 :** a true fact or statement **3 :** HONESTY, VERACITY

ver·meil *n* **1** \'vər-məl, -,māl\ : VERMILION **2** \ve(ə)r-'mā\ : gilded silver, bronze, or copper — **vermeil** *adj*

ver·mi·cel·li \,vər-mə-'chel-ē, -'sel-\ *n* : a food like spaghetti but of smaller diameter

ver·mi·form \'vər-mə-,fȯrm\ *adj* : resembling a worm in shape

vermiform appendix *n* : the intestinal appendix

ver·mi·fuge \'vər-mə-,fyüj\ *adj* : serving to destroy or expel parasitic worms — **vermifuge** *n*

ver·mil·ion *or* **ver·mil·lion** \vər-'mil-yən\ *n* : any of a number of very bright red colors not quite as bright as scarlet; *also* : a pigment yielding one of these colors

ver·min \'vər-mən\ *n, pl* **vermin 1 :** small common harmful or objectionable animals (as fleas or mice) that are difficult to control **2 :** a noxious or offensive person

ver·min·ous \'vər-mə-nəs\ *adj* : consisting of or full of vermin — **ver·min·ous·ly** *adv*

ver·mouth \vər-'müth\ *n* : a white wine flavored with aromatic herbs and used as an aperitif or in mixed drinks

[1]**ver·nac·u·lar** \və(r)-'nak-yə-lər\ *adj* **1 :** using a language or dialect native to a region or country rather than a literary, cultured, or foreign language **2 :** of, relating to, or used in the normal spoken form of a language — **ver·nac·u·lar·ly** *adv*

[2]**vernacular** *n* **1 :** a vernacular language **2 :** the mode of expression of a group or class **3 :** a common name of a plant or animal as distinguished from the latinized taxonomic name

ver·nal \'vərn-ᵊl\ *adj* **1 :** of, relating to, or occurring in the spring **2 :** fresh or new like the spring; *also* : YOUTHFUL — **ver·nal·ly** \-ᵊl-ē\ *adv*

ver·ni·er \'vər-nē-ər\ *n* **1 :** a short scale made to slide along the divisions of a graduated instrument for indicating parts of divisions **2 :** a small auxiliary device used with a main device to obtain fine adjustment

ve·ron·i·ca \və-'rän-i-kə\ *n* : SPEEDWELL

ver·sa·tile \'vər-sət-ᵊl\ *adj* **1 :** changing or fluctuating readily : VARIABLE **2 :** embracing a variety of subjects, fields, or skills; *also* : turning with ease from one thing or position to another **3 :** having many uses or applications — **ver·sa·tile·ly** \-ᵊl-(l)ē\ *adv* — **ver·sa·tile·ness** *n* — **ver·sa·til·i·ty** \,vər-sə-'til-ət-ē\ *n*

verse \'vərs\ *n* **1 :** a line of metrical writing **2 a :** metrical writing distinguished from poetry esp. by its lower level of intensity **b :** POETRY **c :** POEM **3 :** STANZA **4 :** one of the short divisions into which a chapter of the Bible is traditionally divided

versed \'vərst\ *adj* : made familiar by study or experience : SKILLED

ver·si·cle \'vər-si-kəl\ *n* : a short verse or sentence said or sung in public worship by a priest or minister and followed by a response from the people

ver·si·fi·ca·tion \,vər-sə-fə-'kā-shən\ *n* **1 :** the making of verses **2 :** metrical structure : PROSODY

ver·si·fy \'vər-sə-,fī\ *vb* **-fied; -fy·ing 1 :** to compose or turn into verse **2 :** to relate or describe in verse — **ver·si·fi·er** *n*

ver·sion \'vər-zhən\ *n* **1 :** a translation from another language; *esp* : a translation of the Bible or a part of it **2 a :** an account or description from a particular point of view esp. as contrasted with another account **b :** an adaptation of a literary or musical work **3 :** a form or variant of an original — **ver·sion·al** \'vərzh-nəl, -ən-ᵊl\ *adj*

vers li·bre \ve(ə)r-'lēbrᵊ\ *n, pl* **vers li·bres** *same*\ : FREE VERSE

ver·so \'vər-sō\ *n, pl* **versos :** a left-hand page

verst \'vərst\ *n* : a Russian unit of distance equal to 0.6629 miles

ver·sus \'vər-səs, -səz\ *prep* **1 :** AGAINST **2 :** in contrast to or as the alternative of

ver·te·bra \'vərt-ə-brə\ *n, pl* **-brae** \-(,)brē, -,brā\ *or* **-bras** : one of the bony or cartilaginous segments composing the spinal column

ver·te·bral \(')vər-'tē-brəl, 'vert-ə-\ *adj* : of, relating to, or made up of vertebrae : SPINAL — **ver·te·bral·ly** \-brə-lē\ *adv*

[1]**ver·te·brate** \'vərt-ə-brət, -,brāt\ *adj* **1 :** having a spinal column **2 :** of or relating to the vertebrates

[2]**vertebrate** *n* : any of a large group of animals (as mammals, birds, reptiles, amphibians, or fishes) with a segmented spinal column

ver·tex \'vər-,teks\ *n, pl* **ver·ti·ces** \'vərt-ə-,sēz\ **1 a :** the point opposite to and farthest from the base in a figure **b :** ZENITH 1 **2 :** a principal or highest point : SUMMIT, APEX

ver·ti·cal \'vərt-i-kəl\ *adj* **1 :** situated at the highest point : directly overhead or in the zenith **2 :** perpendicular to the plane of the horizon or to a primary axis : UPRIGHT — **vertical** *n* — **ver·ti·cal·i·ty** \,vərt-ə-'kal-ət-ē\ *n* — **ver·ti·cal·ly** \'vərt-i-k(ə-)lē\ *adv* — **ver·ti·cal·ness** *n*

ver·ti·cil \'vərt-ə-,sil\ *n* : a circle of similar parts (as leaves, flowers, or inflorescences) about the same point on an axis : WHORL — **ver·ti·cil·late** \,vərt-ə-'sil-ət\ *adj* — **ver·ti·cil·late·ly** *adv* — **ver·ti·cil·la·tion** \,vərt-ə-,sil-'ā-shən\ *n*

ver·tig·i·nous \(,)vər-'tij-ə-nəs\ *adj* **1 :** marked by, suffering from, or tending to cause dizziness **2 :** marked by turning : ROTARY — **ver·tig·i·nous·ly** *adv*

ver·ti·go \'vərt-i-,gō\ *n, pl* **ver·ti·goes** *or* **ver·tig·i·nes** \(,)vər-'tij-ə-,nēz\ : DIZZINESS, GIDDINESS

ver·vain \'vər-,vān\ *n* : any of a genus of mostly American herbs or low woody plants with often showy heads or spikes of 5-parted regular flowers

verve \ˈvərv\ *n* **1** : the spirit and enthusiasm that animate artistic composition or performance : VIVACITY **2** : ENERGY, VITALITY

[1]very \ˈver-ē\ *adj* **1 a** : properly entitled to the name or designation : TRUE **b** : ACTUAL, REAL **2 a** : EXACT, PRECISE **b** : exactly suitable or necessary **3** : ABSOLUTE, UTTER **4** : MERE, BARE **5** : SELFSAME, IDENTICAL **6** — used as an intensive

[2]very *adv* **1** : to a high degree : EXCEEDINGLY **2** : in actual fact : TRULY

very high frequency *n* : a radio frequency in the range between 30 and 300 megacycles

very low frequency *n* : a radio frequency in the range between 10 and 30 kilocycles

ves·i·cant \ˈves-i-kənt\ *n* : an agent (as a drug or a plant substance) that causes blistering — **vesicant** *adj*

ves·i·cle \ˈves-i-kəl\ *n* : a membranous and usu. fluid-filled pouch in a plant or animal; *also* : a small abnormal elevation of the outer layer of skin enclosing a watery liquid : BLISTER — **ve·sic·u·lar** \və-ˈsik-yə-lər\ *adj* — **ve·sic·u·lar·ly** *adv*

[1]ves·per \ˈves-pər\ *n* : a vesper bell

[2]vesper *adj* : of or relating to vespers or the evening

ves·pers \ˈves-pərz\ *n pl, often cap* : a late afternoon or evening worship service

ves·per·tine \ˈves-pər-ˌtīn\ *adj* **1 a** : of, relating to, or occurring in the evening **b** : resembling that of evening **2** : active or flourishing in the evening : CREPUSCULAR

ves·sel \ˈves-əl\ *n* **1** : a hollow or concave utensil (as a hogshead, bottle, kettle, cup, or bowl) for holding something **2** : a craft bigger than a rowboat for navigation of the water **3** : a tube or canal (as an artery) in which a body fluid is contained and conveyed or circulated

[1]vest \ˈvest\ *vb* **1 a** : to place or give a right, authority, or title into the possession or discretion of some person or body **b** : to become legally vested **2** : to clothe with or as if with a garment; *esp* : to garb in ecclesiastical vestments **3** : to put on garments; *esp* : to robe in ecclesiastical vestments

[2]vest *n* **1 a** : a man's sleeveless garment worn under a suit coat **b** : a similar garment for women **2** : a knitted undershirt for women **3** : a plain or decorative piece used to fill in the front neckline of a woman's outer garment (as a waist, coat, or gown)

ves·ta \ˈves-tə\ *n* : a short match with a shank of wax; *also* : a short wooden match

[1]ves·tal \ˈvest-ᵊl\ *adj* **1** : of or relating to a vestal virgin **2** : CHASTE — **ves·tal·ly** \-ᵊl-ē\ *adv*

[2]vestal *n* **1** : a virgin consecrated to the Roman goddess Vesta and to the service of watching the sacred fire perpetually kept burning on her altar **2** : a chaste woman

vest·ee \ve-ˈstē\ *n* **1** : DICKEY; *esp* : one made to resemble a vest and worn under a coat **2** : VEST 3

ves·tib·u·lar \ve-ˈstib-yə-lər\ *adj* : of, relating to, or functioning as a vestibule

ves·ti·bule \ˈves-tə-ˌbyül\ *n* **1 a** : a passage, hall, or room between the outer door and the interior of a building : LOBBY **b** : an enclosed entrance at the end of a railway passenger car **2** : any of various bodily cavities mostly serving as or resembling an entrance to some other cavity or space

ves·tige \ˈves-tij\ *n* **1** : a visible sign left by something vanished or lost **2** : a minute remaining amount — **ves·ti·gial** \ve-ˈstij-(ē-)əl\ *adj* — **ves·ti·gial·ly** \-ē\ *adv*

vest·ment \ˈves(t)-mənt\ *n* **1 a** : an outer garment; *esp* : a robe of ceremony or office **b** *pl* : CLOTHING, GARB **2** : a ceremonial garment worn by a person officiating or assisting at a religious service — **vest·ment·al** \ves(t)-ˈment-ᵊl\ *adj*

vest–pock·et \ˌvest-ˌpäk-ət\ *adj* : adapted to fit into the vest pocket : of very small size or scope

ves·try \ˈves-trē\ *n, pl* **vestries** **1 a** : a room in a church building for sacred furnishings (as vestments) **b** : a storage place for clothing **c** : a room used for church meetings and classes **2** : an elective body administering the finances, property, and ministerial relations of an Episcopal parish

ves·try·man \-mən\ *n* : a member of a vestry

ves·ture \ˈves-chər\ *n* **1** : a covering garment (as a robe or vestment) **2** : CLOTHING, APPAREL

[1]vet \ˈvet\ *n* : VETERINARIAN, VETERINARY

[2]vet *vt* **vet·ted**; **vet·ting** **1** : to provide veterinary care for (an animal) or medical care for (a person) **2** : to subject to expert appraisal or correction

[3]vet *adj or n* : VETERAN

vetch \ˈvech\ *n* : any of a genus of herbaceous twining plants related to the pea that include valuable fodder and soil-building plants

vet·er·an \ˈvet-ə-rən, ˈve-trən\ *n* **1** : a person who has had long experience in something and esp. in war **2** : a former member of the armed forces esp. in war — **veteran** *adj*

Veterans Day *n* : November 11 observed as a legal holiday in commemoration of the end of hostilities in 1918 and 1945

vet·er·i·nar·i·an \ˌvet-ə-rən-ˈer-ē-ən, ˌve-trən-, ˌvet-ᵊn-\ *n* : one qualified and authorized to treat diseases and injuries of animals

[1]vet·er·i·nary \ˈvet-ə-rən-ˌer-ē, ˈve-trən-, ˈvet-ᵊn-\ *adj* : of, relating to, or being the medical care of animals and esp. domestic animals

[2]veterinary *n, pl* **-nar·ies** : VETERINARIAN

[1]ve·to \ˈvēt-ō\ *n, pl* **vetoes** **1** : an authoritative prohibition : INTERDICTION **2 a** : a power of one branch of a government to forbid or prohibit the carrying out of projects attempted by another department; *esp* : the power of a chief executive to prevent permanently or temporarily the enactment of measures passed by a legislature **b** : the exercise of such authority

[2]veto *vt* : to refuse to admit or approve : PROHIBIT; *esp* : to refuse assent to (a legislative bill) so as to prevent enactment or cause reconsideration — **ve·to·er** *n*

vex \ˈveks\ *vt* **1 a** : to bring trouble, distress, or agitation to **b** : to irritate or annoy by petty provocations : HARASS **c** : PUZZLE, BAFFLE **2** : to debate or discuss at length **3** : to shake or toss about : BATTER

vex·a·tion \vek-ˈsā-shən\ *n* **1** : the quality or state of being vexed : IRRITATION **2** : the act of harassing or vexing : TROUBLING **3** : a cause of trouble or worry

vex·a·tious \-shəs\ *adj* **1 a** : causing vexation : DISTRESSING **b** : intended to harass **2** : full of disorder or stress : TROUBLED — **vex·a·tious·ly** *adv*

via \ˌvī-ə, ˌvē-ə\ *prep* : by way of

vi·a·ble \ˈvī-ə-bəl\ *adj* **1** : capable of living; *esp* : born alive with such form and development of organs as to be normally capable of living **2** : capable of growing or developing **3** : WORKABLE — **vi·a·bil·i·ty** \ˌvī-ə-ˈbil-ət-ē\ *n* — **vi·a·bly** \ˈvī-ə-blē\ *adv*

vi·a·duct \ˈvī-ə-ˌdəkt\ *n* : a bridge with high supporting towers or piers for carrying a road or railroad over something (as a gorge or a highway)

vi·al \ˈvī(-ə)l\ *n* : a small vessel for liquids (as medicines or chemicals)

vi·and \ˈvī-ənd\ *n* **1** : an article of food **2** *pl* : PROVISIONS, FOOD

vi·at·i·cum \vī-ˈat-i-kəm\ *n, pl* **-cums** *or* **-ca** \-kə\ **1 a** : an allowance (as of transportation or supplies and money) for traveling expenses **b** : provisions for a journey **2** : Communion given to a person in danger of death

vi·bran·cy \ˈvī-brən-sē\ *n, pl* **-cies** : the quality or state of being vibrant : VIBRATION

vi·brant \ˈvī-brənt\ *adj* **1 a** (1) : VIBRATING, PULSING (2) : pulsating with life, vigor, or activity **b** (1) : readily set in vibration (2) : RESPONSIVE, SENSITIVE **2** : sounding as a result of vibration : RESONANT — **vi·brant·ly** *adv*

vi·brate \'vī-ˌbrāt\ *vb* **1** : to swing or move back and forth **2** : to set in vibration **3** : to oscillate very rapidly so as to produce a quivering effect or sound : SHAKE, QUIVER **4** : THRILL **5** : FLUCTUATE

vi·bra·tile \'vī-brət-ᵊl, -brə-ˌtīl\ *adj* : characterized by vibration

vi·bra·tion \vī-'brā-shən\ *n* **1 a** : the action of vibrating : the state of being vibrated **b** : motion or a movement to and fro : OSCILLATION **c** : a periodic motion of the particles of an elastic body or medium rapidly to and fro (as when a stretched cord is pulled or struck and produces a musical tone or when particles of air transmit sounds to the ear) **d** : a quivering or trembling motion **2** : vacillation in opinion or action : WAVERING — **vi·bra·tion·al** \-shnəl, -shən-ᵊl\ *adj* — **vi·bra·tion·less** \-shən-ləs\ *adj*

vi·bra·tor \'vī-ˌbrāt-ər\ *n* : one that vibrates or causes vibration

vi·bra·to·ry \'vī-brə-ˌtōr-ē\ *adj* **1** : consisting in, capable of, or causing vibration **2** : VIBRANT, VIBRATING

vi·bur·num \vī-'bər-nəm\ *n* : any of a genus of widely distributed shrubs or trees of the honeysuckle family with white or rarely pink flowers in broad clusters

vic·ar \'vik-ər\ *n* **1** : SUBSTITUTE, AGENT; *esp* : an administrative deputy **2** : an Anglican parish priest who does not hold the right to the tithes **3** : an Anglican clergyman in charge of a dependent parish — **vic·ar·ship** \-ˌship\ *n*

vic·ar·age \'vik-ə-rij\ *n* **1** : the benefice or house of a vicar **2** : VICARIATE

vi·car·i·ate \vī-'kar-ē-ət\ *n* : the office, jurisdiction, or tenure of a vicar

vi·car·i·ous \vī-'kar-ē-əs\ *adj* **1** : serving instead of or for another or something else **2** : performed or suffered by one person as a substitute for another or to the benefit or advantage of another : SUBSTITUTIONARY **3** : experienced or realized through imaginative or sympathetic participation in the experience of another — **vi·car·i·ous·ly** *adv* — **vi·car·i·ous·ness** *n*

vice \'vīs\ *n* **1 a** : moral depravity or corruption : WICKEDNESS **b** : a moral fault or failing **c** : FOIBLE **2** : BLEMISH, DEFECT **3** : an abnormal behavior pattern in a domestic animal detrimental to its health or usefulness

vice admiral *n* : a commissioned officer in the navy ranking next below an admiral

vi·cen·ni·al \vī-'sen-ē-əl\ *adj* : occurring once every 20 years

vice–pres·i·dent \'vīs-'prez-əd-ənt, -'prez-dənt, -ə-ˌdent\ *n* : an official (as of a government) whose rank is next below that of the president and who takes the place of the president when necessary — **vice–pres·i·den·cy** \-'prez-əd-ən-sē, -'prez-dən-sē, -ə-ˌden-sē\ *n*

vice·re·gal \-'rē-gəl\ *adj* : of or relating to a viceroy or viceroyalty — **vice·re·gal·ly** \-gə-lē\ *adv*

vice·roy \'vīs-ˌrȯi\ *n* : the governor of a country or province who rules as the representative of his king or sovereign — **vice·roy·ship** \-ˌship\ *n*

vice·roy·al·ty \'vīs-ˌrȯi(-ə)l-tē\ *n* : the office, jurisdiction, or term of service of a viceroy

vi·ce ver·sa \ˌvī-si-'vər-sə, (ˈ)vīs-'vər-\ *adv* : with the alternation or order changed : CONVERSELY

vi·chys·soise \ˌvish-ē-'swäz, ˌvēsh-\ *n* : a soup made esp. from pureed leeks or onions and potatoes and usu. served cold

vi·chy water \'vish-ē-\ *n* : SODA WATER 1

vic·i·nage \'vis-ᵊn-ij\ *n* : a neighboring or surrounding district : VICINITY

vi·cin·i·ty \və-'sin-ət-ē\ *n, pl* **-ties** **1** : the quality or state of being near : PROXIMITY **2** : a surrounding area or district : NEIGHBORHOOD

vi·cious \'vish-əs\ *adj* **1** : given to or constituting vice or immorality : DEPRAVED, WICKED **2** : DEFECTIVE, FAULTY; *also* : INVALID **3** : IMPURE, NOXIOUS **4** : dangerously aggressive : SAVAGE **5** : MALICIOUS, SPITEFUL — **vi·cious·ly** *adv* — **vi·cious·ness** *n*

vi·cis·si·tude \və-'sis-ə-ˌt(y)üd, vī-\ *n* : a change or succession from one thing to another; *esp* : an irregular, unexpected, or surprising change — **vi·cis·si·tu·di·nous** \-ˌsis-ə-'t(y)üd-ᵊn-əs\ *adj*

vic·tim \'vik-təm\ *n* **1** : a living being offered as a sacrifice in a religious rite **2** : an individual injured or killed (as by disease or accident) **3** : a person cheated, fooled, or damaged whether by someone else or by some impersonal force

vic·tim·ize \'vik-tə-ˌmīz\ *vt* : to make a victim of esp. by deception : CHEAT — **vic·tim·i·za·tion** \ˌvik-tə-mə-'zā-shən\ *n* — **vic·tim·iz·er** *n*

vic·tor \'vik-tər\ *n* : one that defeats an enemy or opponent : WINNER — **victor** *adj*

vic·to·ria \vik-'tōr-ē-ə\ *n* : a low four-wheeled pleasure carriage for two with a folding top and a raised seat in front for the driver

vic·to·ri·ous \vik-'tōr-ē-əs\ *adj* : having won a victory : CONQUERING — **vic·to·ri·ous·ly** *adv*

vic·to·ry \'vik-t(ə-)rē\ *n, pl* **-ries** **1** : the overcoming of an enemy or opponent **2** : achievement of success in a struggle against odds or difficulties

¹vict·ual \'vit-ᵊl\ *n* **1** : food usable by man **2** *pl* : supplies of food : PROVISIONS

²victual *vb* **-ualed** *or* **-ualled**; **-ual·ing** *or* **-ual·ling** **1** : to supply with food **2** : EAT **3** : to lay in provisions

vict·ual·ler *or* **vict·ual·er** \'vit-ᵊl-ər\ *n* **1** : the keeper of a restaurant or tavern **2** : one that furnishes provisions (as to an army or a ship)

vi·cu·ña *or* **vi·cu·na** \vī-'k(y)ü-nə, vi-'kün-yə\ *n* **1** : a wild ruminant of the Andes that is related to the domesticated llama and alpaca **2 a** : the wool from the vicuña's fine lustrous undercoat **b** : a fabric made of vicuña wool; *also* : a sheep's-wool imitation of this

vi·de \'vīd-ē, 'vē-ˌdā\ *v imper* : SEE — used to direct a reader to another item

vi·de·li·cet \və-'del-ə-ˌset, vī-\ *adv* : that is to say : NAMELY

¹vid·eo \'vid-ē-ˌō\ *adj* : relating to or used in the transmission or reception of the television image

²video *n* : TELEVISION

vid·eo·tape \'vid-ē-ō-ˌtāp\ *vt* : to make a video tape recording of

vie \'vī\ *vi* **vied**; **vy·ing** \'vī-iŋ\ : to strive for superiority : CONTEND — **vi·er** \'vī(-ə)r\ *n*

¹view \'vyü\ *n* **1** : the act of seeing or examining : INSPECTION; *also* : SURVEY **2** : manner of looking at or regarding something : OPINION, JUDGMENT **3** : SCENE, PROSPECT **4** : extent or range of vision : SIGHT **5 a** : something that is looked toward or kept in sight : OBJECT **b** : something that is expected or anticipated **6** : a pictorial representation : SKETCH — **in view of** : in regard to : in consideration of

²view *vt* **1** : SEE, BEHOLD **2** : to look at attentively : SCRUTINIZE **3** : to survey or examine mentally : CONSIDER

view·er \-ər\ *n* : one that views: as **a** : an optical device used in viewing **b** : a person who watches television

view·point \'vyü-ˌpȯint\ *n* : STANDPOINT

vi·ges·i·mal \vī-'jes-ə-məl\ *adj* : based on the number 20

vig·il \'vij-əl\ *n* **1 a** : a watch formerly kept on the night before a religious feast with devotions (as prayer) **b** : the day before a religious feast observed as a day of spiritual preparation **2** : the act of keeping awake at times when sleep is customary; *also* : a period of wakefulness **3** : an act of surveillance (as for protection) : WATCH

vig·i·lance \'vij-ə-lən(t)s\ *n* : the quality or state of being vigilant : WATCHFULNESS

vig·i·lant \-lənt\ *adj* : alertly watchful esp. to avoid danger — **vig·i·lant·ly** *adv*

vig·i·lan·te \ˌvij-ə-ˈlant-ē\ *n* **:** a member of a local volunteer committee organized to suppress and punish crime esp. where the processes of law seem inadequate

vi·gnette \vin-ˈyet\ *n* **1 :** a running ornament (as of vine leaves, tendrils, and grapes) put on or just before a title page or at the beginning or end of a chapter; *also* **:** a small decorative design or picture so placed **2 :** a picture (as an engraving or photograph) that shades off gradually into the surrounding ground **3 :** a brief word picture **:** SKETCH

vig·or \ˈvig-ər\ *n* **1 :** active strength or energy of body or mind **2 :** INTENSITY, FORCE

vig·or·ous \ˈvig-(ə-)rəs\ *adj* **1 :** having vigor **:** ROBUST **2 :** done with vigor **:** carried out forcefully and energetically — **vig·or·ous·ly** *adv* — **vig·or·ous·ness** *n*

Vi·king \ˈvī-kiŋ\ *n* **:** one of the pirate Scandinavians plundering the coasts of Europe in the 8th to 10th centuries

¹vile \ˈvīl\ *adj* **1 :** of small worth or account **:** COMMON; *also* **:** MEAN **2 a :** morally base **:** WICKED **b :** physically repulsive **:** FOUL **3 :** DEGRADED, LOW **4 :** DISGUSTING, CONTEMPTIBLE — **vile·ly** \ˈvīl-lē\ *adv* — **vile·ness** *n*

²vile *adv* **:** in a vile manner **:** VILELY

vil·i·fy \ˈvil-ə-ˌfī\ *vt* **-fied; -fy·ing 1 :** to lower in estimation or importance **:** DEGRADE **2 :** to utter slanderous and abusive statements against **:** DEFAME — **vil·i·fi·ca·tion** \ˌvil-ə-fə-ˈkā-shən\ *n* — **vil·i·fi·er** *n*

vil·la \ˈvil-ə\ *n* **1 :** a country estate **2 :** the rural or suburban residence of a person of wealth

vil·lage \ˈvil-ij\ *n* **1 :** a settlement usu. larger than a hamlet and smaller than a town **2 :** the residents of a village

vil·lag·er \ˈvil-ij-ər\ *n* **:** an inhabitant of a village

vil·lain \ˈvil-ən\ *n* **1 :** VILLEIN **2 :** EVILDOER, CRIMINAL **3 :** a scoundrel in a story or play — **vil·lain·ess** \ˈvil-ə-nəs\ *n*

vil·lain·ous \ˈvil-ə-nəs\ *adj* **1 :** befitting a villain **:** DEPRAVED **2 :** highly objectionable **:** WRETCHED — **vil·lain·ous·ly** *adv* — **vil·lain·ous·ness** *n*

vil·lainy \ˈvil-ə-nē\ *n, pl* **-lain·ies 1 :** villainous conduct; *also* **:** a villainous act **2 :** villainous character or nature **:** WICKEDNESS

vil·lein \ˈvil-ən, ˈvil-ˌān\ *n* **1 :** a free peasant of any of various feudal classes **2 :** an unfree peasant standing as the slave of his feudal lord but free in his legal relations with others

vil·len·age \ˈvil-ə-nij\ *n* **1 :** tenure of land given by a feudal lord to a villein **2 :** the status of a villein

vil·lous \ˈvil-əs\ *adj* **:** covered or furnished with fine hairs or villi — **vil·los·i·ty** \vil-ˈäs-ət-ē\ *n* — **vil·lous·ly** \ˈvil-əs-lē\ *adv*

vil·lus \ˈvil-əs\ *n, pl* **vil·li** \ˈvil-ˌī\ **:** a small slender usu. vascular process; *esp* **:** one of the tiny finger-shaped processes of the mucous membrane of the small intestine that function in the absorption of nutriments

vim \ˈvim\ *n* **:** robust energy and enthusiasm **:** VITALITY

vin·ai·grette \ˌvin-i-ˈgret\ *n* **:** a small ornamental box or bottle with perforated top used for holding an aromatic preparation (as smelling salts)

vin·ci·ble \ˈvin(t)-sə-bəl\ *adj* **:** capable of being overcome or subdued **:** SURMOUNTABLE

vin·di·cate \ˈvin-də-ˌkāt\ *vt* **1 a :** EXONERATE, ABSOLVE **b** (1) **:** CONFIRM, SUBSTANTIATE (2) **:** to provide justification or defense for **:** JUSTIFY **c :** to protect from attack or encroachment **:** DEFEND **2 :** to maintain a right to **:** ASSERT — **vin·di·ca·tor** \-ˌkāt-ər\ *n* — **vin·di·ca·to·ry** \-di-kə-ˌtōr-ē\ *adj*

vin·di·ca·tion \ˌvin-də-ˈkā-shən\ *n* **:** the act of vindicating **:** the state of being vindicated; *esp* **:** justification against denial or censure **:** DEFENSE

vin·dic·tive \vin-ˈdik-tiv\ *adj* **1 a :** disposed to seek revenge **:** VENGEFUL **b :** intended for or involving revenge **2 :** VICIOUS, SPITEFUL — **vin·dic·tive·ly** *adv* — **vin·dic·tive·ness** *n*

vine \ˈvīn\ *n* **1 :** GRAPE 2 **2 :** a plant whose stem requires support and which climbs by tendrils or twining or creeps along the ground; *also* **:** the stem of such a plant

vin·e·gar \ˈvin-i-gər\ *n* **:** a sour liquid obtained by the fermentation of cider, wine, or malt and used to flavor or preserve foods

vin·e·gary \-g(ə-)rē\ *adj* **1 :** resembling vinegar **:** SOUR **2 :** disagreeable, bitter, or irascible in character or manner **:** CRABBED

vine·yard \ˈvin-yərd\ *n* **:** a planting of grapevines

vi·nous \ˈvī-nəs\ *adj* **1 :** of, relating to, or made with wine **2 :** showing the effects of the use of wine

vin·tage \ˈvint-ij\ *n* **1 a** (1) **:** the grapes or wine produced during one season (2) **:** WINE; *esp* **:** a wine of a particular type, region, and year and usu. of superior quality **b :** a collection of contemporaneous and similar persons or things **:** CROP **2 :** the act or time of gathering grapes or making wine **3 a :** a period of origin or manufacture **b :** length of existence **:** AGE — **vintage** *adj*

vint·ner \ˈvint-nər\ *n* **:** a wine merchant

viny \ˈvī-nē\ *adj* **1 :** of, relating to, or resembling vines **2 :** covered with or abounding in vines

vi·nyl \ˈvīn-ᵊl\ *n* **:** any of various tough plastics used esp. for coatings, sheeting, tile, flooring, and molded objects

vi·ol \ˈvī-əl, ˈvīl\ *n* **:** a bowed stringed instrument like the violin but weaker in tone and simpler in construction and playing technique

vi·o·la \vē-ˈō-lə\ *n* **:** a stringed musical instrument like a violin but slightly larger and lower in pitch

vi·o·la·ble \ˈvī-ə-lə-bəl\ *adj* **:** capable of being or likely to be violated — **vi·o·la·bil·i·ty** \ˌvī-ə-lə-ˈbil-ət-ē\ *n*

vi·o·late \ˈvī-ə-ˌlāt\ *vt* **1 :** to fail to keep **:** BREAK, DISREGARD **2 :** to do harm to the person or esp. the chastity of; *esp* **:** RAPE **3 :** PROFANE, DESECRATE **4 :** INTERRUPT, DISTURB — **vi·o·la·tor** \-ˌlāt-ər\ *n*

vi·o·la·tion \ˌvī-ə-ˈlā-shən\ *n* **:** the act of violating **:** the state of being violated: as **a :** INFRINGEMENT, TRANSGRESSION **b :** an act of irreverence or desecration **:** PROFANATION **c :** INTERRUPTION, DISTURBANCE **d :** RAPE

vi·o·lence \ˈvī-ə-lən(t)s\ *n* **1 a :** the use of physical force in a manner calculated to do harm to a person or his property **b :** injury esp. to something that merits respect or reverence **:** OUTRAGE; *also* **:** improper or damaging treatment or interference (as by alteration of the wording or sense of a text) **2 :** a violent act **3 a :** vigor in physical and esp. in destructive action **:** ENERGY **b :** vehemence in feeling, behavior, or emotion **:** ARDOR, PASSION

vi·o·lent \-lənt\ *adj* **1 :** marked by extreme force or sudden intense activity **2 a :** notably furious or vehement; *also* **:** excited or mentally disordered to the point of loss of self-control **b :** EXTREME, INTENSE **3 :** caused by force **:** not natural — **vi·o·lent·ly** *adv*

vi·o·let \ˈvī-ə-lət\ *n* **1 :** any of a genus of low plants with mostly heart-shaped leaves and both aerial and underground flowers; *esp* **:** one with small usu. solid-colored flowers **2 :** a variable color averaging a reddish blue

vi·o·lin \ˌvī-ə-ˈlin\ *n* **1 :** a bowed stringed instrument with four strings tuned at intervals of a fifth distinguished from the viol in having a shallower body, shoulders at right angles with the neck, and a more curved bridge **2 :** VIOLINIST

vi·o·lin·ist \-ˈlin-əst\ *n* **:** one who plays the violin

vi·o·lon·cel·lo \ˌvī-ə-lən-ˈchel-ō, ˌvē-\ *n* **:** CELLO

vi·os·ter·ol \vī-ˈäs-tə-ˌrȯl, -ˌrōl\ *n* **:** a vitamin D esp. when dissolved in an edible vegetable oil

VIP \ˌvē-ˌī-ˈpē\ *n* **:** a person of great influence or prestige; *esp* **:** a high official with special privileges

vi·per *n* \ˈvī-pər\ *n* **1 a :** any of a family of sluggish heavy-bodied broad-headed Old World venomous snakes with hollow tubular fangs **b :** PIT VIPER **c :** a venomous or reputedly venomous snake **2 :** a malignant or treacherous person — **vi·per·ine** \-pə-ˌrīn\ *adj*

vi·ra·go \və-ˈräg-ō, -ˈrāg-, ˈvir-ə-ˌgō\ *n, pl* **-goes** *or* **-gos** : a loud overbearing woman : TERMAGANT — **vi·rag·i·nous** \və-ˈraj-ə-nəs\ *adj*

vi·ral \ˈvī-rəl\ *adj* : of, relating to, or caused by a virus

vir·eo \ˈvir-ē-ˌō\ *n, pl* **-e·os** : any of a family of small insect-eating songbirds that are chiefly olive-green or grayish in color

vi·res·cent \və-ˈres-ᵊnt, vī-\ *adj* : beginning to be green : GREENISH

¹vir·gin \ˈvər-jən\ *n* : a girl or woman who has not had sexual intercourse

²virgin *adj* **1** : being a virgin : CHASTE, MODEST **2** : PURE, FRESH, UNSOILED; *esp* : not altered by human activity **3** : being used or worked for the first time or produced by a simple extractive process

¹vir·gin·al \ˈvər-jən-ᵊl\ *adj* : of, relating to, characteristic of, or suitable for a virgin or virginity; *esp* : CHASTE — **vir·gin·al·ly** \-ᵊl-ē\ *adv*

²virginal *n* : a small rectangular spinet having no legs and only one wire to a note

Vir·gin·ia creeper \vər-ˌjin-yə-\ *n* : a common No. American tendril-climbing vine of the grape family having leaves with five leaflets and bluish black berries

Virginia reel *n* : a country-dance in which all couples in turn participate in a series of figures

vir·gin·i·ty \(ˌ)vər-ˈjin-ət-ē\ *n, pl* **-ties** : the quality or state of being virgin : CHASTITY; *esp* : MAIDENHOOD

vir·gule \ˈvər-gyül\ *n* : a mark / used typically to denote "or" (as in *and/or*) or "per" (as in *feet/second*)

vir·i·des·cent \ˌvir-ə-ˈdes-ᵊnt\ *adj* : slightly green : GREENISH

vir·ile \ˈvir-əl\ *adj* **1** : having the nature, powers, or qualities of a man **2 a** : ENERGETIC, VIGOROUS **b** : MASTERFUL, FORCEFUL

vi·ril·i·ty \və-ˈril-ət-ē\ *n* : the quality or state of being virile: **a** : MANHOOD **b** : manly vigor : MASCULINITY

vir·tu \ˌvər-ˈtü, vi(ə)r-\ *n* **1** : a taste for or knowledge of curios or objets d'art **2** : productions of art esp. of a curious or antique nature

vir·tu·al \ˈvər-ch(ə-w)əl\ *adj* : being in essence or effect but not in fact or name — **vir·tu·al·i·ty** \ˌvər-chə-ˈwal-ət-ē\ *n* — **vir·tu·al·ly** \ˈvər-ch(ə-w)ə-lē, ˈvərch-lē\ *adv*

vir·tue \ˈvər-chü\ *n* **1** : moral action or excellence : MORALITY; *esp* : CHASTITY **2** : a particular moral excellence **3 a** : an active beneficial power **b** : a desirable or commendable quality or trait : MERIT — **by virtue of** *or* **in virtue of** : through the force of : by authority of

vir·tu·os·i·ty \ˌvər-chə-ˈwäs-ət-ē\ *n, pl* **-ties** : great technical skill in the practice of the fine arts

vir·tu·o·so \ˌvər-chə-ˈwō-sō, -zō\ *n, pl* **-sos** *or* **-si** \-(ˌ)sē, -(ˌ)zē\ **1** : one skilled in or having a taste for the fine arts **2** : one who excels in the technique of an art; *esp* : a musical performer (as on the violin) — **virtuoso** *adj*

vir·tu·ous \ˈvər-chə-wəs\ *adj* : having virtue and esp. moral virtue; *esp* : CHASTE — **vir·tu·ous·ly** *adv* — **vir·tu·ous·ness** *n*

vir·u·lent \ˈvir-(y)ə-lənt\ *adj* **1 a** : marked by a rapid, severe, and malignant course **b** : able to overcome bodily defensive mechanisms **2** : extremely poisonous or venomous : NOXIOUS **3** : full of malice : MALIGNANT **4** : objectionably harsh or strong — **vir·u·lence** \-lən(t)s\ *or* **vir·u·len·cy** \-lən-sē\ *n* — **vir·u·lent·ly** *adv*

vi·rus \ˈvī-rəs\ *n* **1 a** : any of a large group of infective agents that are too small to be seen with a light microscope and that remain active after passing through a filter too fine for a bacterium to pass **b** : a disease caused by a virus **2** : something (as a corrupting influence) that poisons the mind or spirit

¹vi·sa \ˈvē-zə\ *n* **1** : an endorsement made on a passport by the proper authorities denoting that it has been examined and that the bearer may proceed **2** : a signature of formal approval by a superior upon a document

²visa *vt* **vi·saed** \-zəd\; **vi·sa·ing** \-zə-iŋ\ : to give a visa to

vis·age \ˈviz-ij\ *n* **1** : the face or countenance of a person or sometimes a lower animal **2** : ASPECT, APPEARANCE — **vis·aged** \-ijd\ *adj*

¹vis–à–vis \ˌvē-zə-ˈvē\ *n, pl* **vis–à–vis** \-zə-ˈvē(z)\ **1** : one that is face to face with another **2** : TÊTE-À-TÊTE

²vis–à–vis *prep* **1** : face to face with : OPPOSITE **2** : in relation to **3** : as compared with

³vis–à–vis *adv* : in company : TOGETHER

viscera *pl of* VISCUS

vis·cer·al \ˈvis-ə-rəl\ *adj* **1** : felt in or as if in the viscera : DEEP **2** : of, relating to, or being the viscera — **vis·cer·al·ly** \-rə-lē\ *adv*

vis·cid \ˈvis-əd\ *adj* **1** : STICKY, VISCOUS **2** : covered with a sticky layer — **vis·cid·i·ty** \vis-ˈid-ət-ē\ *n* — **vis·cid·ly** *adv*

¹vis·cose \ˈvis-ˌkōs\ *adj* **1** : VISCOUS **2** : of, relating to, or made from viscose

²viscose *n* **1** : a viscous golden-brown solution made by chemically treating cellulose and used in making rayon **2** : viscose rayon

vis·cos·i·ty \vis-ˈkäs-ət-ē\ *n, pl* **-ties** : the quality of being viscous; *esp* : a tendency of a liquid to flow slowly resulting from friction of its molecules

vis·count \ˈvī-ˌkaủnt\ *n* : a member of the British peerage ranking below an earl and above a baron

vis·count·ess \-əs\ *n* **1** : the wife or widow of a viscount **2** : a woman who holds the rank of a viscount in her own right

vis·cous \ˈvis-kəs\ *adj* **1** : somewhat sticky or glutinous : ADHESIVE, VISCID **2** : having or characterized by viscosity — **vis·cous·ly** *adv* — **vis·cous·ness** *n*

vis·cus \ˈvis-kəs\ *n, pl* **vis·cera** \ˈvis-ə-rə\ : an internal organ of the body; *esp* : one (as the heart, liver, or intestine) located in the great cavity of the trunk proper

¹vise \ˈvīs\ *n* : any of various tools having two jaws for holding work that operate usu. by a screw, lever, or cam

²vi·sé \ˈvē-ˌzā, vē-ˈ\ *vt* **vi·séd**; **vi·sé·ing** : VISA

³visé *n* : VISA

vis·i·bil·i·ty \ˌviz-ə-ˈbil-ət-ē\ *n* **1** : the quality or state of being visible **2** : the degree of clearness of the atmosphere esp. as affording clear vision toward the horizon

vis·i·ble \ˈviz-ə-bəl\ *adj* **1** : capable of being seen : apparent to the eye **2** : APPARENT, DISCOVERABLE — **vis·i·ble·ness** *n* — **vis·i·bly** \-blē\ *adv*

¹vi·sion \ˈvizh-ən\ *n* **1 a** : something seen in a dream, trance, or ecstasy **b** : an object of imagination **c** : a manifestation to the senses of something immaterial **2 a** : the act or power of imagination **b** : unusual discernment or foresight **3 a** : the act or power of seeing : SIGHT **b** : the special sense by which the qualities of an object (as color, luminosity, or shape and size) constituting its appearance are perceived and which is mediated by the eye **4** : something seen; *esp* : a lovely or charming sight — **vi·sion·al** \ˈvizh-nəl, -ən-ᵊl\ *adj* — **vi·sion·al·ly** \-ē\ *adv* — **vi·sion·less** \ˈvizh-ən-ləs\ *adj*

²vision *vt* **vi·sioned**; **vi·sion·ing** \ˈvizh-(ə-)niŋ\ : IMAGINE, ENVISION

¹vi·sion·ary \ˈvizh-ə-ˌner-ē\ *adj* **1** : given to dreaming or imagining **2** : resembling a vision esp. in fanciful or impractical quality — **vi·sion·ar·i·ness** *n*

²visionary *n, pl* **-ar·ies** **1** : one who sees visions : SEER **2** : one whose ideas or projects are impractical : DREAMER

¹vis·it \ˈviz-ət\ *vb* **vis·it·ed** \ˈviz-ət-əd, ˈviz-təd\; **vis·it·ing** \ˈviz-ət-iŋ, ˈviz-tiŋ\ **1** : to go to see in order to comfort or help **2 a** : to pay a call upon as an act of friendship or courtesy **b** : to go or come to see in an official or professional capacity **c** : to dwell with temporarily as a guest **3 a** : to come to or upon as a reward, affliction, or punishment **b** : INFLICT **4** : to make a visit or frequent or regular visits **5** : CHAT, CONVERSE

[2]**visit** *n* **1 :** a brief stay : CALL **2 :** a stay as a guest or nonresident **3 :** an official or professional call

vis·i·tant \'viz-ət-ənt, 'viz-tənt\ *n* **:** VISITOR; *esp* **:** one thought to come from a spirit world

vis·i·ta·tion \,viz-ə-'tā-shən\ *n* **1 :** VISIT; *esp* **:** an official visit (as for inspection) **2 a :** a special dispensation of divine favor or wrath **b :** a severe trial : AFFLICTION — **vis·i·ta·tion·al** \-shnəl, -shən-ᵊl\ *adj*

vis·i·tor \'viz-ət-ər, 'viz-tər\ *n* **:** one that visits: as **a :** one that makes formal visits of inspection **b :** TOURIST, TRAVELER

vi·sor \'vī-zər\ *n* **1 :** the front piece of a helmet; *esp* **:** a movable upper piece **2 :** a projecting part (as on a cap or an automobile windshield) to protect or shade the eyes — **vi·sored** \-zərd\ *adj* — **vi·sor·less** \-zər-ləs\ *adj*

vis·ta \'vis-tə\ *n* **1 :** a distant view through or along an avenue or opening : PROSPECT **2 :** an extensive mental view over a stretch of time or a series of events

vi·su·al \'vizh-(ə-w)əl\ *adj* **1 :** of, relating to, or used in vision **2 :** attained or maintained by sight **3 a :** VISIBLE **b :** producing mental images : VIVID **4 :** primarily appealing to the sense of sight or employing this as a medium (as of education) — **vi·su·al·ly** \-ē\ *adv*

vi·su·al·ize \'vizh-ə-(wə-),līz\ *vb* **:** to make visible; *esp* **:** to see or form a mental image : ENVISAGE — **vi·su·al·i·za·tion** \,vizh-ə-(wə-)lə-'zā-shən\ *n*

vi·ta \'vīt-ə, 'wē-,tä\ *n, pl* **vi·tae** \'vīt-ē, 'wē-,tī\ **:** a brief autobiographical sketch

vi·tal \'vīt-ᵊl\ *adj* **1 :** of, relating to, or characteristic of life **:** showing the qualities of living things **2 :** concerned with or necessary to the maintenance of life **3 :** full of vitality : ANIMATED **4 :** FATAL, MORTAL **5 :** of first importance : BASIC — **vi·tal·ly** \-ᵊl-ē\ *adv*

vi·tal·i·ty \vī-'tal-ət-ē\ *n, pl* **-ties 1 a :** the peculiarity distinguishing the living from the nonliving **b :** capacity to live and develop; *also* **:** physical or mental vigor esp. when highly developed **2 a :** power of enduring or continuing **b :** lively and animated character : VIGOR

vi·tal·ize \'vīt-ᵊl-,īz\ *vt* **:** to endow with vitality : ANIMATE — **vi·tal·i·za·tion** \,vīt-ᵊl-ə-'zā-shən\ *n*

vi·tals \'vīt-ᵊlz\ *n pl* **1 :** vital organs **2 :** essential parts

vi·ta·min \'vīt-ə-mən\ *n* **:** any of various organic substances that are essential in tiny amounts to most animals and some plants and are mostly obtained from foods

vitamin A *n* **:** a vitamin (as from egg yolk or fish-liver oils) required for healthy epithelium and sight

vitamin B *n* **:** any of various vitamins important in metabolic reactions and as growth factors; *esp* **:** THIAMINE

vitamin C *n* **:** a vitamin esp. from fruits and leafy vegetables that functions chiefly as a cellular enzyme and is used to prevent scurvy

vitamin D *n* **:** a vitamin esp. from fish-liver oils that is essential to normal bone formation

vi·ti·ate \'vish-ē-,āt\ *vt* **1 :** to injure the quality of : SPOIL, DEBASE **2 :** to destroy the validity of — **vi·ti·a·tion** \,vish-ē-'ā-shən\ *n* — **vi·ti·a·tor** \'vish-ē-,āt-ər\ *n*

vit·re·ous \'vi-trē-əs\ *adj* **1 :** of, relating to, derived from, or resembling glass : GLASSY **2 :** of, relating to, or being the vitreous humor — **vit·re·ous·ness** *n*

vitreous humor *n* **:** the clear colorless transparent jelly that fills the eyeball posterior to the lens

vit·ri·fy \'vi-trə-,fī\ *vb* **-fied; -fy·ing :** to change into glass or a glassy substance by heat and fusion — **vit·ri·fi·a·ble** *adj* — **vit·ri·fi·ca·tion** \,vi-trə-fə-'kā-shən\ *n*

vit·ri·ol \'vi-trē-əl\ *n* **1 a :** a sulfate of any of various metals (as copper, iron, or zinc) **b :** SULFURIC ACID **2 :** something resembling vitriol in caustic quality; *esp* **:** virulence of feeling or of speech — **vit·ri·ol·ic** \,vi-trē-'äl-ik\ *adj*

vi·tu·per·ate \vī-'t(y)ü-pə-,rāt, və-\ *vt* **:** to abuse or censure severely : BERATE — **vi·tu·per·a·tive** \-'t(y)ü-p(ə-)rət-iv, -pə-,rāt-\ *adj* — **vi·tu·per·a·tive·ly** *adv* — **vi·tu·per·a·tor** \-pə-,rāt-ər\ *n*

vi·tu·per·a·tion \-,t(y)ü-pə-'rā-shən\ *n* **:** sustained and bitter railing and condemnation

vi·va \'vē-və, -,vä\ *interj* — used to express goodwill or approval

vi·va·ce \vē-'väch-ā\ *adv* (*or adj*) **:** in a brisk spirited manner — used as a direction in music

vi·va·cious \və-'vā-shəs, vī-\ *adj* **:** lively in temper or conduct **:** SPRIGHTLY — **vi·va·cious·ly** *adv* — **vi·va·cious·ness** *n*

vi·vac·i·ty \-'vas-ət-ē\ *n* **:** the quality or state of being vivacious

[1]**vi·va vo·ce** \,vī-və-'vō-sē\ *adv* **:** by word of mouth : ORALLY

[2]**viva voce** *adj* **:** expressed or conducted by word of mouth : ORAL

viv·id \'viv-əd\ *adj* **1 :** having the appearance of vigorous life or freshness : very lively **2 :** very strong or intense **3 :** producing a strong or clear impression on the senses : SHARP; *esp* **:** producing distinct mental images **4 :** acting clearly and vigorously — **viv·id·ly** *adv* — **viv·id·ness** *n*

viv·i·fy \'viv-ə-,fī\ *vt* **-fied; -fy·ing 1 :** to endue with life : QUICKEN, ANIMATE **2 :** to make vivid — **viv·i·fi·ca·tion** \,viv-ə-fə-'kā-shən\ *n* — **viv·i·fi·er** *n*

vi·vip·a·rous \vī-'vip-(ə-)rəs\ *adj* **:** producing living young from within the body rather than from eggs — **vi·vi·par·i·ty** \,vī-və-'par-ət-ē\ *n* — **vi·vip·a·rous·ly** *adv* — **vi·vip·a·rous·ness** *n*

vivi·sec·tion \,viv-ə-'sek-shən\ *n* **:** the cutting of or operation on a living animal usu. for scientific investigation; *also* **:** animal experimentation esp. if considered to cause distress to the subject — **vivi·sect** \'viv-ə-,sekt\ *vb* — **vivi·sec·tion·al** \,viv-ə-'sek-shnəl, -shən-ᵊl\ *adj* — **vivi·sec·tion·al·ly** \-ē\ *adv* — **vivi·sec·tion·ist** \-'sek-sh(ə-)nəst\ *n* — **vivi·sec·tor** \'viv-ə-,sek-tər\ *n*

vix·en \'vik-sən\ *n* **1 :** a female fox **2 :** a shrewish ill-tempered woman — **vix·en·ish** \-s(ə-)nish\ *adj*

viz·ard \'viz-ərd\ *n* **:** a mask for disguise or protection

vi·zier \və-'zi(ə)r\ *n* **:** a high executive officer of various Muslim countries and esp. of the former Turkish Empire — **vi·zier·i·al** \-'zir-ē-əl\ *adj*

vo·ca·ble \'vō-kə-bəl\ *n* **:** a word composed of various sounds or letters without regard to its meaning

vo·cab·u·lary \vō-'kab-yə-,ler-ē\ *n, pl* **-lar·ies 1 :** a list or collection of words or of words and phrases usu. alphabetically arranged and explained or defined **2 :** a sum or stock of words employed by a language, group, individual, or work or in a field of knowledge

vocabulary entry *n* **:** a word (as the noun *book*), hyphened or open compound (as the verb *baby-sit* or the noun *boric acid*), word element (as the prefix *re-*), abbreviation (as *agt*), verbalized symbol (as *Na*), or term (as *man in the street*) entered alphabetically in a dictionary for the purpose of definition or identification or expressly included as an inflectional form (as the noun *mice* or the verb *saw*) or as a derived form (as the noun *godlessness* or the adverb *globally*) or related phrase (as *in spite of*) run on at its base word and usu. set in a type (as boldface) readily distinguishable from that of the lightface running text which defines, explains, or identifies the entry

[1]**vo·cal** \'vō-kəl\ *adj* **1 :** uttered by the voice : ORAL **2 :** relating to, composed or arranged for, or sung by the human voice **3 :** VOCALIC **4 a :** having or exercising the power of producing voice, speech, or sound **b :** EXPRESSIVE **c :** full of voices : RESOUNDING **d :** given to expressing oneself freely or insistently : OUTSPOKEN **e :** expressed in words **5 :** of, relating to, or resembling the voice — **vo·cal·ly** \-kə-lē\ *adv*

[2]**vocal** *n* **1 :** a vocal sound **2 :** the vocal solo in a dance or jazz number

vo·cal·ic \vō-'kal-ik\ *adj* **1 :** marked by or consisting of vow-

els **2 :** of, relating to, or functioning as a vowel — **vo·cal·i·cal·ly** \-ˈkal-i-k(ə-)lē\ *adv*
vo·cal·ist \ˈvō-kə-ləst\ *n* **:** SINGER
vo·cal·i·za·tion \ˌvō-kə-lə-ˈzā-shən\ *n* **:** an act, process, or instance of vocalizing
vo·cal·ize \ˈvō-kə-ˌlīz\ *vb* **1 a :** to give vocal expression to **b :** SING; *esp* **:** to sing without words (as in practicing) **2 a :** VOICE **b :** to convert to a vowel — **vo·cal·iz·er** *n*
vo·ca·tion \vō-ˈkā-shən\ *n* **1 :** a summons or strong inclination to a particular state or course of action; *esp* **:** a divine call to the religious life **2 :** the work in which a person is regularly employed **:** OCCUPATION
vo·ca·tion·al \-shnəl, -shən-ᵊl\ *adj* **1 :** of, relating to, or concerned with a vocation **2 :** concerned with choice of or training in a skill or trade to be pursued as a career — **vo·ca·tion·al·ly** \-ē\ *adv*
voc·a·tive \ˈväk-ət-iv\ *adj* **:** of, relating to, or constituting a grammatical case marking the one addressed — **vocative** *n* — **voc·a·tive·ly** *adv*
vo·cif·er·ate \vō-ˈsif-ə-ˌrāt\ *vb* **:** to cry out or utter loudly **:** CLAMOR, SHOUT — **vo·cif·er·a·tion** \-ˌsif-ə-ˈrā-shən\ *n*
vo·cif·er·ous \vō-ˈsif-(ə-)rəs\ *adj* **:** making a loud outcry **:** NOISY, CLAMOROUS — **vo·cif·er·ous·ly** *adv* — **vo·cif·er·ous·ness** *n*
vod·ka \ˈväd-kə\ *n* **:** a colorless and unaged alcoholic liquor distilled from a mash (as of rye or wheat)
vogue \ˈvōg\ *n* **1 a :** popular acceptation or favor **:** POPULARITY **b :** a period of popularity **2 :** something or someone in fashion at a particular time — **vogue** *adj*
vogu·ish \ˈvō-gish\ *adj* **1 :** FASHIONABLE, SMART **2 :** suddenly or temporarily popular
¹**voice** \ˈvȯis\ *n* **1 a :** sound produced through the mouth by vertebrates and esp. by human beings in speaking or shouting **b** (1) **:** musical sound produced by the vocal cords (2) **:** the power or ability to produce musical tones (3) **:** SINGER (4) **:** one of the melodic parts in a vocal or instrumental composition (5) **:** condition of the vocal organs with respect to production of musical tones **c :** expiration of air with the vocal cords drawn close so as to vibrate audibly (as in uttering vowels and some consonants) **d :** the faculty of utterance **:** SPEECH **2 :** a sound resembling or suggesting vocal utterance **3 :** a medium of expression **4 a :** wish, choice, or opinion openly or formally expressed **b :** right of expression **:** SUFFRAGE **5 :** distinction of form of a verb to indicate the relation of the subject of the verb to the action which the verb expresses
²**voice** *vt* **1 :** UTTER **2 :** to regulate the tone of (as organ pipes) **3 :** to pronounce (as a consonant) with voice
voiced \ˈvȯist\ *adj* **1 a :** furnished with a voice **b :** expressed by the voice **2 :** uttered with voice — **voiced·ness** \ˈvȯis(t)-nəs, ˈvȯi-səd-nəs\ *n*
voice·less \ˈvȯis-ləs\ *adj* **1 :** having no voice **:** MUTE **2 :** not voiced — **voice·less·ly** *adv* — **voice·less·ness** *n*
voice·print \ˈvȯis-ˌprint\ *n* **:** a spectrographically produced individually distinctive pattern of certain voice characteristics that is an effective agent of identification
¹**void** \ˈvȯid\ *adj* **1 :** containing nothing **2 :** IDLE, LEISURE **3 a :** UNOCCUPIED, VACANT **b :** DESERTED **4 a :** WANTING, DEVOID **b :** having no members or examples **5 :** of no legal force or effect **:** NULL
²**void** *n* **1 a :** empty space **:** EMPTINESS, VACUUM **b :** OPENING, GAP **2 :** LACK, ABSENCE **3 :** a feeling of want or hollowness
³**void** *vt* **1 a :** to make empty or vacant **:** CLEAR **b :** VACATE, LEAVE **2 :** DISCHARGE, EMIT **3 :** NULLIFY, ANNUL — **void·er** *n*
void·a·ble \ˈvȯid-ə-bəl\ *adj* **:** capable of being voided
voile \ˈvȯil\ *n* **:** a soft sheer fabric of silk, cotton, rayon, or wool used esp. for curtains or women's summer clothing
vol·a·tile \ˈväl-ət-ᵊl\ *adj* **1 :** readily becoming a vapor at a relatively low temperature **2 a :** LIGHTHEARTED, LIVELY **b :** easily aroused **c :** tending to erupt into violent action **:** EXPLOSIVE **3 :** CHANGEABLE, FICKLE **4 :** TRANSITORY — **vol·a·tile·ness** *n* — **vol·a·til·i·ty** \ˌväl-ə-ˈtil-ət-ē\ *n*
vol·a·til·ize \ˈväl-ət-ᵊl-ˌīz\ *vb* **:** to pass off or make pass off in vapor — **vol·a·til·i·za·tion** \ˌväl-ət-ᵊl-ə-ˈzā-shən\ *n*
vol·can·ic \väl-ˈkan-ik\ *adj* **1 a :** of or relating to a volcano **b :** having volcanoes **2 :** explosively violent **:** VOLATILE — **vol·can·i·cal·ly** \-ˈkan-i-k(ə-)lē\ *adv*
vol·ca·no \väl-ˈkā-nō\ *n, pl* **-noes** *or* **-nos :** a vent in the earth's crust from which molten or hot rock and steam issue; *also* **:** a hill or mountain composed wholly or in part of the ejected material
vole \ˈvōl\ *n* **:** any of various small rodents closely related to the lemmings and muskrats but in general resembling stocky mice or rats
vo·li·tion \vō-ˈlish-ən\ *n* **1 :** the act or power of making one's own choices or decisions **:** WILL **2 :** the choice made or decision reached — **vo·li·tion·al** \-ˈlish-nəl, -ən-ᵊl\ *adj*
¹**vol·ley** \ˈväl-ē\ *n, pl* **volleys 1 a :** a flight of missiles (as arrows or bullets) **b :** simultaneous discharge of a number of missile weapons (as rifles) **c :** the flight of the ball in tennis or its course before striking the ground; *also* **:** a return of the ball before it touches the ground **2 :** a bursting forth of many things at once
²**volley** *vb* **vol·leyed; vol·ley·ing 1 :** to discharge in a volley **2 :** to propel an object while in the air and before touching the ground; *esp* **:** to hit a tennis ball on the volley
vol·ley·ball \ˈväl-ē-ˌbȯl\ *n* **:** a game played by volleying a large inflated ball over a net
¹**vol·plane** \ˈväl-ˌplān\ *n* **:** a glide in an airplane
²**volplane** *vi* **:** to glide in or as if in an airplane
volt \ˈvōlt\ *n* **:** the unit of electromotive force equal to a force that when steadily applied to a conductor whose resistance is one ohm will produce a current of one ampere
volt·age \ˈvōl-tij\ *n* **:** electromotive force measured in volts
vol·ta·ic \väl-ˈtā-ik, vōl-\ *adj* **:** of, relating to, or producing direct electric current by chemical action (as in a battery)
volte–face \ˌvȯlt-(ə-)ˈfäs\ *n* **:** a facing about esp. in policy **:** ABOUT-FACE
volt·me·ter \ˈvōlt-ˌmēt-ər\ *n* **:** an instrument for measuring in volts the differences of potential between different points of an electrical circuit
vol·u·ble \ˈväl-yə-bəl\ *adj* **:** characterized by ready or rapid speech **:** GLIB, FLUENT — **vol·u·bil·i·ty** \ˌväl-yə-ˈbil-ət-ē\ *n* — **vol·u·bly** \ˈväl-yə-blē\ *adv*
vol·u·ble·ness \ˈväl-yə-bəl-nəs\ *n* **:** VOLUBILITY
vol·ume \ˈväl-yəm\ *n* **1 :** BOOK **2 :** any of a series of books forming a complete work or collection **3 :** space occupied **:** bounded space as measured in cubic units **4 :** a large amount **:** MASS **5 :** intensity or quantity of tone **:** LOUDNESS
vol·u·met·ric \ˌväl-yu̇-ˈme-trik\ *adj* **:** of or relating to the measurement of volume — **vol·u·met·ri·cal·ly** \-tri-k(ə-)lē\ *adv*
vo·lu·mi·nous \və-ˈlü-mə-nəs\ *adj* **1 :** consisting of many folds, coils, or convolutions **:** WINDING **2 a :** having or marked by great volume or bulk **:** LARGE; *esp* **:** FULL **b :** NUMEROUS **3 a :** filling or capable of filling a large volume or several volumes **b :** writing or speaking much or at great length — **vo·lu·mi·nous·ly** *adv* — **vo·lu·mi·nous·ness** *n*
vol·un·tar·i·ly \ˌväl-ən-ˈter-ə-lē\ *adv* **:** of one's own free will
¹**vol·un·tary** \ˈväl-ən-ˌter-ē\ *adj* **1 :** done, given, or made in accordance with one's own free will or choice **2 :** not accidental **:** INTENTIONAL **3 :** of or relating to the will **:** controlled by the will
²**voluntary** *n, pl* **-tar·ies :** a prefatory often extemporized musical piece; *also* **:** an organ piece played before, during, or after a religious service

¹vol•un•teer \\,väl-ən-'ti(ə)r\\ *n* : one who enters into or offers himself for any service of his own free will; *esp* : one who enters into military service voluntarily

²volunteer *adj* : of, relating to, or consisting of volunteers : VOLUNTARY

³volunteer *vb* **1** : to offer or bestow voluntarily **2** : to offer oneself as a volunteer

vo•lup•tu•ary \\və-'ləp-chə-,wer-ē\\ *n, pl* **-ar•ies** : one whose chief interest is luxury and the gratification of sensual appetites — **voluptuary** *adj*

vo•lup•tu•ous \\və-'ləp-chə-wəs, -chəs\\ *adj* **1** : giving pleasure to the senses : providing sensual or sensuous gratification **2** : being a voluptuary — **vo•lup•tu•ous•ly** *adv* — **vo•lup•tu•ous•ness** *n*

vo•lute \\və-'lüt\\ *n* : a spiral or scroll-shaped form or ornament — **volute** *or* **vo•lut•ed** \\-'lüt-əd\\ *adj*

¹vom•it \\'väm-ət\\ *n* : an act or instance of disgorging the contents of the stomach through the mouth; *also* : the disgorged matter

²vomit *vb* **1** : to disgorge the contents of the stomach through the mouth **2** : to spew forth : BELCH, GUSH — **vom•it•er** *n*

voo•doo \\'vüd-ü\\ *n, pl* **voodoos 1** : VOODOOISM **2 a** : one who deals in spells and necromancy **b (1)** : a sorcerer's spell (2) : a hexed object — **voodoo** *adj*

voo•doo•ism \\'vüd-ü-,iz-əm\\ *n* **1** : a religion derived from African ancestor worship and consisting largely of magic and sorcery **2** : the practice of witchcraft — **voo•doo•ist** \\'vüd-,ü-əst\\ *n* — **voo•doo•is•tic** \\,vüd-ü-'is-tik\\ *adj*

vo•ra•cious \\vò-'rā-shəs, və-\\ *adj* **1** : greedy in eating : RAVENOUS **2** : excessively eager : INSATIABLE — **vo•ra•cious•ly** *adv* — **vo•rac•i•ty** \\-'ras-ət-ē\\ *n*

vor•tex \\'vȯr-,teks\\ *n, pl* **vor•ti•ces** \\'vȯrt-ə-,sēz\\ **1** : a mass of fluid and esp. of a liquid having a whirling motion tending to form a cavity in the center and to draw things toward this cavity **2** : a whirling mass (as a whirlwind, tornado, or waterspout); *esp* : WHIRLPOOL, EDDY

vor•ti•cal \\'vȯrt-i-kəl\\ *adj* : of, relating to, or resembling a vortex : SWIRLING

vo•ta•ry \\'vōt-ə-rē\\ *n, pl* **-ries 1 a** : ENTHUSIAST, DEVOTEE **b** : a devoted adherent or admirer **2** : a devout or zealous worshiper

¹vote \\'vōt\\ *n* **1 a** : a formal expression of opinion or will; *esp* : one given as an indication of approval or disapproval of a proposal or a candidate for office **b** : the total number of such expressions of opinion made known at a single time (as at an election) **c** : BALLOT 1 **2** : the collective opinion of a body of persons expressed by voting **3** : the right to cast a vote : SUFFRAGE **4 a** : the act or process of voting **b** : a method of voting **5 a** : VOTER **b** : a group of voters with common characteristics

²vote *vb* **1** : to express one's wish or choice by a vote : cast a vote **2** : to make into law by a vote **3** : ELECT **4** : to declare by common consent **5** : PROPOSE, SUGGEST

vot•er \\'vōt-ər\\ *n* : one that votes or has the legal right to vote

vo•tive \\'vōt-iv\\ *adj* : offered or performed in fulfillment of a vow or in gratitude or devotion — **vo•tive•ly** *adv* — **vo•tive•ness** *n*

vouch \\'vau̇ch\\ *vb* **1** : PROVE, SUBSTANTIATE **2** : to give a guarantee : become surety **3 a** : to supply supporting evidence or testimony **b** : to give personal assurance

vouch•er \\'vau̇-chər\\ *n* **1** : one who vouches for another **2** : a document that serves to establish the truth of something; *esp* : a paper (as a receipt) showing payment of a bill or debt

vouch•safe \\vau̇ch-'sāf\\ *vt* : to grant in the manner of one doing a favor : condescend to give or grant

¹vow \\'vau̇\\ *n* : a solemn promise or assertion; *esp* : one by which a person binds himself to an act, service, or condition

²vow *vb* **1** : to make a vow or as a vow **2** : to bind or consecrate by a vow

³vow *vb* : AVOW, DECLARE

vow•el \\'vau̇(-ə)l\\ *n* **1** : a speech sound in the articulation of which the oral part of the breath channel is not blocked and is not constricted enough to cause audible friction **2** : a letter representing a vowel; *esp* : any of the letters *a, e, i, o, u,* and sometimes *y* in English — **vow•el•like** *adj*

vox po•pu•li \\'väks-'päp-yə-,lī\\ *n* : popular sentiment

¹voy•age \\'vȯi-ij\\ *n* **1** : a journey by water : CRUISE **2** : a journey through air or space

²voyage *vb* **1** : to take a trip : TRAVEL **2** : SAIL, TRAVERSE — **voy•ag•er** *n*

voya•geur \\,vwä-,yä-'zhər\\ *n* : a man employed by a fur company to transport goods and men to and from remote stations in the Northwest

vul•can•ite \\'vəl-kə-,nīt\\ *n* : a hard vulcanized rubber

vul•can•ize \\'vəl-kə-,nīz\\ *vb* : to treat rubber or similar plastic material chemically in order to give it useful properties (as elasticity, strength, or stability) — **vul•can•i•za•tion** \\,vəl-kə-nə-'zā-shən\\ *n* — **vul•can•iz•er** *n*

vul•gar \\'vəl-gər\\ *adj* **1 a** : generally used, applied, or accepted **b** : having or understanding in the ordinary sense **2** : VERNACULAR **3 a** : of or relating to the common people : PLEBEIAN **b** : generally current : PUBLIC **c** : of the usual, typical, or ordinary kind **4 a** : lacking in cultivation, perception, or taste : COARSE **b** : morally crude or undeveloped : GROSS **c** : ostentatious or excessive in expenditure or display : PRETENTIOUS **5 a** : offensive in language : EARTHY **b** : OBSCENE, PROFANE — **vul•gar•ly** *adv*

vul•gar•i•an \\,vəl-'gar-ē-ən\\ *n* : a vulgar person

vul•gar•ism \\'vəl-gə-,riz-əm\\ *n* **1 a** : a word or expression originated or used chiefly by illiterate persons **b** : a coarse word or phrase **2** : VULGARITY

vul•gar•i•ty \\,vəl-'gar-ət-ē\\ *n, pl* **-ties 1** : the quality or state of being vulgar **2** : something vulgar

vul•gar•ize \\'vəl-gə-,rīz\\ *vt* : to make vulgar : COARSEN — **vul•gar•i•za•tion** \\,vəl-gə-rə-'zā-shən\\ *n*

Vul•gate \\'vəl-,gāt\\ *n* : a Latin version of the Bible authorized and used by the Roman Catholic Church

vul•ner•a•ble \\'vəln-(ə-)rə-bəl, 'vəl-nər-bəl\\ *adj* **1** : capable of being wounded **2** : open to attack or damage : ASSAILABLE **3** : liable to increased penalties but entitled to increased bonuses in a game of contract bridge — **vul•ner•a•bil•i•ty** \\,vəln-(ə-)rə-'bil-ət-ē\\ *n* — **vul•ner•a•bly** \\'vəln-(ə-)rə-blē, 'vəl-nər-blē\\ *adv*

vul•pine \\'vəl-,pīn\\ *adj* : of, relating to, or resembling a fox esp. in cunning : CRAFTY

vul•ture \\'vəl-chər\\ *n* : any of various large birds that are related to the hawks and eagles but have weaker claws and the head usu. naked and that subsist chiefly or entirely on carrion

vul•va \\'vəl-və\\ *n* : the external parts of the female genital organs; *also* : the opening between their projecting parts — **vul•val** \\'vəl-vəl\\ *or* **vul•var** \\-vər\\ *adj*

vying *pres part of* VIE

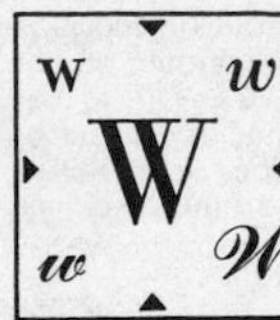

w \'dəb-əl-(,)yü, -yə\ *n, often cap* : the 23d letter of the English alphabet
wacky \'wak-ē\ *adj* : absurdly or amusingly eccentric or irrational : CRAZY — **wack·i·ly** \'wak-ə-lē\ *adv* — **wack·i·ness** \'wak-ē-nəs\ *n*
[1]**wad** \'wäd\ *n* **1** : a small mass, bundle, or tuft: as **a** : a soft mass of usu. light fibrous material **b** : a pliable pad or plug (as of felt) used to retain a powder charge in a gun or cartridge **c** : a roll of paper money **2** : a considerable amount (as of money)
[2]**wad** *vt* **wad·ded**; **wad·ding** **1** : to form into a wad **2** : to push a wad into **3** : to hold in by a wad **4** : to stuff or line with a wad or padding
wad·ding \'wäd-iŋ\ *n* **1** : wads or material for making wads **2** : a soft mass or sheet of short loose fibers used for stuffing or padding
[1]**wad·dle** \'wäd-ᵊl\ *vi* **wad·dled**; **wad·dling** \'wäd-liŋ, -ᵊl-iŋ\ : to walk with short steps swaying from side to side like a duck
[2]**waddle** *n* : an awkward clumsy swaying gait
[1]**wade** \'wād\ *vb* **1** : to step in or through a medium (as water) offering more resistance than air **2** : to move or proceed with difficulty or labor and often with determined vigor **3** : to pass or cross by wading
[2]**wade** *n* : an act of wading
wad·er \'wād-ər\ *n* **1** : one that wades **2** : WADING BIRD **3** *pl* : high waterproof boots or trousers for wading
wa·di \'wäd-ē\ *n* : a stream bed or valley esp. of southwestern Asia and northern Africa that is usu. dry except during the rainy season
wad·ing bird \'wād-iŋ-\ *n* : a long-legged bird (as a sandpiper or heron) that wades in water in search of food
wa·fer \'wā-fər\ *n* **1 a** : a thin crisp cake or cracker **b** : a round thin piece of unleavened bread in the Eucharist **2** : something (as a piece of candy or an adhesive seal) resembling a wafer esp. in thin round form
waf·fle \'wäf-əl\ *n* : a crisp cake of pancake batter baked in a waffle iron
waffle iron *n* : a cooking utensil with two hinged metal parts that shut upon each other and impress surface projections on a waffle
[1]**waft** \'wäft, 'waft\ *vb* : to cause to move or go lightly by or as if by the impulse of wind or waves
[2]**waft** *n* **1** : a slight breeze : PUFF **2** : the act of waving
[1]**wag** \'wag\ *vb* **wagged**; **wag·ging** : to swing to and fro or from side to side — **wag·ger** *n*
[2]**wag** *n* **1** : WIT, JOKER **2** : an act of wagging : a wagging movement
[1]**wage** \'wāj\ *vb* **1** : to engage in or carry on **2** : to be in process of being waged
[2]**wage** *n* **1** : payment for labor or services usu. according to contract and on an hourly, daily, or piecework basis **2** *pl* : RECOMPENSE, REWARD
[1]**wa·ger** \'wā-jər\ *n* **1** : something risked on an uncertain event : STAKE **2** : an act of betting : GAMBLE
[2]**wager** *vb* **wa·gered**; **wa·ger·ing** \'wāj-(ə-)riŋ\ : to hazard on an issue : RISK, VENTURE; *esp* : GAMBLE, BET — **wa·ger·er** *n*
wag·gery \'wag-ə-rē\ *n, pl* **-ger·ies** **1** : mischievous merriment : PLEASANTRY **2** : JEST; *esp* : PRACTICAL JOKE
wag·gish \'wag-ish\ *adj* **1** : resembling or characteristic of a wag : FROLICSOME **2** : done or made in waggery or for sport : HUMOROUS — **wag·gish·ly** *adv* — **wag·gish·ness** *n*
wag·gle \'wag-əl\ *vb* **wag·gled**; **wag·gling** \'wag-(ə-)liŋ\ : to move backward and forward or from side to side : WAG — **waggle** *n* — **wag·gly** \-(ə-)lē\ *adj*
wag·on \'wag-ən\ *n* **1** : a four-wheeled vehicle; *esp* : one drawn by animals and used for carrying goods **2** : a child's four-wheeled cart **3** : STATION WAGON **4** : PATROL WAGON — **wag·on·er** *n* — **on the wagon** : abstaining from alcoholic liquors
wag·on·ette \,wag-ə-'net\ *n* : a light wagon with two facing seats along the sides back of a transverse front seat
wag·tail \'wag-,tāl\ *n* : any of numerous slender mostly Old World birds related to the pipits and having a very long tail that is habitually jerked up and down
wa·hoo \'wä-,hü\ *n, pl* **wahoos** : any of various American trees or shrubs
waif \'wāf\ *n* **1** : something found without an owner and esp. by chance **2** : a stray person or animal; *esp* : a homeless child
[1]**wail** \'wāl\ *vb* **1** : to express sorrow audibly : LAMENT **2** : to make a sound suggestive of a mournful cry **3** : to express dissatisfaction plaintively : COMPLAIN — **wail·er** *n*
[2]**wail** *n* **1 a** : a usu. prolonged cry or sound expressing grief or pain **b** : a sound suggestive of this **2** : a querulous expression of grievance : COMPLAINT
wain \'wān\ *n* : a usu. large and heavy vehicle for farm use
[1]**wain·scot** \'wān-skət, -,skōt, -,skät\ *n* **1** : a usu. paneled and wooden lining of an interior wall **2** : the lower three or four feet of an interior wall when finished differently from the remainder of the wall
[2]**wainscot** *vt* **-scot·ed** *or* **-scot·ted**; **-scot·ing** *or* **-scot·ting** : to line with or as if with boards or paneling
wain·scot·ing \-,skōt-iŋ, -,skät-, -skət-\ *or* **wain·scot·ting** \-,skät-, -skət-\ *n* : material for wainscot : WAINSCOT
wain·wright \'wān-,rīt\ *n* : a maker and repairer of wagons
waist \'wāst\ *n* **1** : the narrowed part of the body between the chest and hips **2** : a part resembling the human waist esp. in narrowness or central position **3** : a garment or the part of a garment that covers the body from the neck to the waist
waist·band \'wās(t)-,band\ *n* : a band (as of trousers or a skirt) fitting around the waist
waist·line \'wāst-,līn\ *n* **1** : a line surrounding the waist at its narrowest part; *also* : the length of this line **2** : the line at which the waist and skirt of a dress meet
[1]**wait** \'wāt\ *vb* **1** : to remain inactive in readiness (as for action) or expectation (as of a coming event) : AWAIT **2** : POSTPONE, DELAY **3** : to attend as a waiter : SERVE **4** : to be ready — **wait on** *or* **wait upon** **1** : SERVE **2** : to make a formal call on — **wait up** : to delay going to bed
[2]**wait** *n* : an act or period of waiting
wait·er \'wāt-ər\ *n* **1** : one that waits upon another; *esp* : a man who waits on table **2** : TRAY
wait·ing room \'wāt-iŋ-\ *n* : a room (as at a railroad station) for the use of persons waiting
wait·ress \'wā-trəs\ *n* : a woman who waits on table
waive \'wāv\ *vt* **1** : to give up claim to **2** : to put off the consideration of : POSTPONE
waiv·er \'wā-vər\ *n* : the act of waiving a right, claim, or privilege or an instrument evidencing such an act
[1]**wake** \'wāk\ *vb* **waked** \'wākt\ *or* **woke** \'wōk\; **waked** *or* **wo·ken** \'wō-kən\; **wak·ing** **1 a** : to be or remain awake **b** : to remain awake on watch esp. over a corpse **2** : AWAKE — often used with *up* — **wak·er** *n*
[2]**wake** *n* : a watch held over the body of a dead person prior to burial and sometimes accompanied by festivity
[3]**wake** *n* : the track left by a moving body (as a ship) in the water; *also* : a track or path left
wake·ful \'wāk-fəl\ *adj* : not sleeping or able to sleep — **wake·ful·ly** \-fə-lē\ *adv* — **wake·ful·ness** *n*
wak·en \'wā-kən\ *vb* **wak·ened**; **wak·en·ing** \'wāk-(ə-)niŋ\ : AWAKE — often used with *up* — **wak·en·er** \-(ə-)nər\ *n*
wale \'wāl\ *n* **1** : a streak or ridge made on the skin usu. by a rod or whip : WHEAL **2** : a narrow raised surface or ridge (as on cloth)
[1]**walk** \'wȯk\ *vb* **1 a** : to move or cause to move along on foot

usu. at a natural unhurried gait **b** : to pass over, through, or along by walking **c** : to perform or affect by walking **2** : to follow a course of action or way of life **3** : to take or cause to take first base with a base on balls **4** : to move or cause to move in a manner suggestive of walking — **walk away from 1** : to outrun or get the better of without difficulty **2** : to survive (an accident) with little or no injury — **walk into 1 a** : ATTACK **b** : to reprimand or criticize severely **2** : to eat or drink greedily — **walk off with 1** : STEAL **2** : to win or gain esp. by outdoing one's competitors without difficulty — **walk over** : to disregard the wishes or feelings of

²walk *n* **1** : a going on foot **2** : a place, path, or course for walking **3** : distance to be walked **4 a** : manner of living : CONDUCT, BEHAVIOR **b** : social or economic status **5 a** : manner of walking **b** : a slow 4-beat gait of a horse **6** : BASE ON BALLS

walk·away \ˈwȯ-kə-ˌwā\ *n* : an easily won contest

walk·er \ˈwȯ-kər\ *n* : one that walks or is used in walking; *esp* : a framework with wheels designed to support one learning to walk

walk·ie–talk·ie \ˈwȯ-kē-ˈtȯ-kē\ *n* : a small portable radio set for receiving and sending messages

walk–in \ˈwȯk-ˌin\ *adj* : large enough to be walked into

walk out *vi* **1** : to go on strike **2** : to leave suddenly often as an expression of disapproval — **walk out on** : to leave in the lurch : ABANDON, DESERT

walk·out \ˈwȯk-ˌau̇t\ *n* : STRIKE 2a

walk·over \ˈwȯk-ˌō-vər\ *n* : a one-sided contest or an easy or uncontested victory

walk–up \-ˌəp\ *n* : a building or apartment house without an elevator — **walk–up** *adj*

walk·way \-ˌwā\ *n* : a passage for walking : WALK

¹wall \ˈwȯl\ *n* **1** : a structure (as of brick or stone) raised to some height and meant to enclose or shut off a space; *esp* : a side of a room or building **2** : something like a wall; *esp* : something that acts as a barrier or defense **3** : a material layer enclosing space — **walled** \ˈwȯld\ *adj* — **wall–like** *adj*

²wall *vt* **1** : to provide, separate with, or surround with or as if with a wall **2** : to close (an opening) with or as if with a wall

wal·la·by \ˈwäl-ə-bē\ *n, pl* **-bies** : any of various small or medium-sized usu. brightly colored kangaroos

wall·board \ˈwȯl-ˌbōrd\ *n* : a structural material (as of wood pulp, gypsum, or plastic) made in large rigid sheets and used esp. for sheathing interior walls and ceilings

wal·let \ˈwäl-ət\ *n* **1** : a bag or sack for carrying things on a journey **2** : a pocketbook with compartments (as for change and cards)

wall·eye \ˈwȯl-ˌī\ *n* **1 a** : an eye with a whitish iris or an opaque white cornea **b** : an eye that turns outward showing more than a normal amount of white **2** : a large vigorous American freshwater food and sport fish that has prominent eyes and is related to the perches — **wall·eyed** \-ˈīd\ *adj*

wall·flow·er \ˈwȯl-ˌflau̇(-ə)r\ *n* **1** : any of several Old World perennial plants of the mustard family; *esp* : one widely grown for its showy fragrant flowers **2** : a person who from shyness or unpopularity remains on the sidelines of a social activity (as a dance)

¹wal·lop \ˈwäl-əp\ *n* **1** : a powerful blow or impact **2** : the ability (as of a boxer) to hit hard

²wallop *vt* **1** : to beat soundly : TROUNCE **2** : to hit with force : SOCK — **wal·lop·er** *n*

wal·lop·ing \ˈwäl-ə-piŋ\ *adj* **1** : LARGE, WHOPPING **2** : exceptionally fine or impressive

¹wal·low \ˈwäl-ō\ *vi* **1** : to roll oneself about in or as if in deep mud **2** : to live or be filled with excessive pleasure in some condition **3** : to become or remain helpless — **wal·low·er** *n*

²wallow *n* **1** : an act or instance of wallowing **2** : a muddy or dust-filled area used by animals for wallowing

wall·pa·per \ˈwȯl-ˌpā-pər\ *n* : decorative paper for the walls of a room — **wallpaper** *vb*

wal·nut \ˈwȯl-(ˌ)nət\ *n* **1 a** : an edible nut with a furrowed usu. rough shell and an adherent husk; *also* : any of several trees related to the hickories that produce such nuts **b** : the usu. reddish to dark brown wood of a walnut widely used for cabinetwork and veneers **c** : a hickory nut or tree **2** : a moderate reddish brown

wal·rus \ˈwȯl-rəs, ˈwäl-\ *n, pl* **walrus** *or* **wal·rus·es** : either of two large mammals of northern seas related to the seals and hunted esp. for the hide, the ivory tusks of the males, and oil

¹waltz \ˈwȯl(t)s\ *n* **1** : a gliding dance in ¾ time with strong accent on the first beat **2** : music for or suitable for waltzing

²waltz *vb* **1** : to dance a waltz **2** : to move or advance easily or conspicuously — **waltz·er** *n*

wam·pum \ˈwäm-pəm\ *n* : beads of shells strung in strands, belts, or sashes and used by No. American Indians as money and ornaments

wan \ˈwän\ *adj* **1 a** : SICKLY, PALLID **b** : FEEBLE **2** : DIM, FAINT **3** : LANGUID — **wan·ly** *adv* — **wan·ness** *n*

wand \ˈwänd\ *n* **1** : a fairy's, diviner's, or magician's staff **2** : any of various light rods

wan·der \ˈwän-dər\ *vb* **wan·dered**; **wan·der·ing** \-d(ə-)riŋ\ **1** : to move about aimlessly or without a fixed course or goal : RAMBLE **2 a** : to deviate (as from a course) : STRAY **b** : to go astray in conduct or thought; *esp* : to become delirious or mentally disoriented — **wander** *n* — **wan·der·er** *n*

wan·der·lust \ˈwän-dər-ˌləst\ *n* : strong or unconquerable longing for or impulse toward wandering

¹wane \ˈwān\ *vi* : to be diminished : grow smaller or less: as **a** : to undergo gradual diminution after being at the full **b** : to lose power, prosperity, or influence **c** : to draw toward an end

²wane *n* **1** : the act or process of waning **2** : a period or time of waning

wan·gle \ˈwaŋ-gəl\ *vb* **wan·gled**; **wan·gling** \-g(ə-)liŋ\ **1 a** : to obtain by sly, roundabout, or underhand means **b** : to use trickery or devious or questionable means to achieve an end **2 a** : to work by skill or indirection : MANIPULATE **b** : FINAGLE — **wan·gler** \-g(ə-)lər\ *n*

¹want \ˈwȯnt\ *vb* **1** : to be without : LACK **2** : to fall short by **3** : to feel or suffer the need of **4** : NEED, REQUIRE **5** : to desire earnestly : WISH

²want *n* **1 a** : a lack of a required or usual amount **b** : dire need : DESTITUTION **2** : something wanted : NEED, DESIRE **3** : personal defect : FAULT

want·ing \ˈwȯnt-iŋ\ *adj* **1** : not present or in evidence : ABSENT **2 a** : falling below standards or expectations **b** : lacking in ability or capacity : DEFICIENT

¹wan·ton \ˈwȯnt-ᵊn\ *adj* **1** : FROLICSOME **2** : UNCHASTE, LEWD; *also* : SENSUAL **3 a** : MERCILESS, INHUMANE **b** : having no just cause : MALICIOUS **4** : UNRESTRAINED, EXTRAVAGANT, LUXURIANT — **wan·ton·ly** *adv* — **wan·ton·ness** *n*

²wanton *n* : a wanton individual; *esp* : a lascivious person

³wanton *vb* **1** : to be wanton or act wantonly **2** : to pass or waste wantonly

wap·i·ti \ˈwäp-ət-ē\ *n, pl* **-tis** *or* **-ti** : the American elk

¹war \ˈwȯ(ə)r\ *n* **1 a** : a state or period of usu. open and declared armed hostile conflict between states or nations **b** : the art or science of warfare **2 a** : a state of hostility, conflict, or antagonism **b** : a struggle between opposing forces or for a particular end

²war *vi* **warred**; **war·ring** **1** : to engage in warfare **2** : to be in conflict

¹war·ble \ˈwȯr-bəl\ *n* **1** : a melodious succession of low pleasing sounds **2** : a musical trill

²warble *vb* **war·bled**; **war·bling** \-b(ə-)liŋ\ **1** : to sing or render in a trilling manner or with many turns and variations **2** : to

express by or as if by warbling
war·bler \'wȯr-blər\ *n* **1** : one that warbles : SONGSTER **2 a** : any of numerous small Old World singing birds many of which are noted songsters and are closely related to the thrushes **b** : any of numerous small brightly colored American songbirds with a usu. weak and unmusical song
war·bon·net \'wȯr-ˌbän-ət\ *n* : an Indian ceremonial headdress with a feathered extension down the back
war club *n* : a club-shaped implement used as a weapon
war cry *n* **1** : a cry used by a body of fighters in war **2** : a slogan used esp. to rally people to a cause
[1]**ward** \'wȯrd\ *n* **1 a** : a guarding or being under guard; *esp* : CUSTODY **b** : a body of guards **2 a** : a division (as a cell or block) of a prison **b** : a division in a hospital **3** : a division of a city for electoral or administrative purposes **4 a** : a person (as a child or lunatic) under the protection of a court or a guardian **b** : a person or body of persons under the protection or tutelage of a government — **ward·ed** \-əd\ *adj*
[2]**ward** *vt* **1** : to keep watch over : GUARD **2** : to turn aside : DEFLECT — usu. used with *off*
war dance *n* : a dance performed by primitive peoples as preparation for battle or in celebration of victory
war·den \'wȯrd-ᵊn\ *n* **1** : GUARDIAN, KEEPER **2** : the governor of a town, district, or fortress **3 a** : an official charged with special supervisory duties or with the enforcement of specified laws or regulations **b** : an official in charge of the operation of a prison **c** : any of various British administrative officials **4 a** : one of two ranking lay officers of an Episcopal parish **b** : any of various British college officials
ward·er \'wȯrd-ər\ *n* : WATCHMAN, WARDEN
ward·robe \'wȯrd-ˌrōb\ *n* **1 a** : a room or closet where clothes are kept **b** : CLOTHESPRESS **2** : a collection of wearing apparel (as of one person or for one activity)
ward·room \-ˌrüm, -ˌru̇m\ *n* : the space in a warship allotted for living quarters to the commissioned officers excepting the captain; *esp* : the room assigned to these officers for meals
ward·ship \-ˌship\ *n* **1** : GUARDIANSHIP **2** : the state of being under a guardian
ware \'wa(ə)r\ *n* **1 a** : manufactured articles or products of art or craft : GOODS — often used in combination **b** : an article of merchandise **2** : items (as dishes) of fired clay : POTTERY
[1]**ware·house** \'wa(ə)r-ˌhau̇s\ *n* : a place for the storage of merchandise or commodities — **ware·house·man** \-mən\ *n*
[2]**ware·house** \-ˌhau̇z, -ˌhau̇s\ *vt* : to deposit, store, or stock in or as if in a warehouse
war·fare \'wȯr-ˌfa(ə)r\ *n* **1** : military operations between enemies : WAR; *also* : an activity undertaken by one country to weaken or destroy another **2** : STRUGGLE, CONFLICT
war–horse \-ˌhȯrs\ *n* **1** : a horse used in war : CHARGER **2** : a veteran soldier or public person (as a politician)
war·like \-ˌlīk\ *adj* **1** : fond of war **2** : of, relating to, or having to do with war **3** : threatening war : HOSTILE
war·lock \-ˌläk\ *n* : SORCERER, WIZARD
war·lord \-ˌlȯrd\ *n* **1** : a high military leader **2** : a military commander exercising local civil power by force
[1]**warm** \'wȯrm\ *adj* **1 a** : having or giving out heat to a moderate or adequate degree **b** : serving to retain heat (as of the body) **c** : feeling or inducing sensations of heat **2 a** : showing or marked by strong feeling : ARDENT **b** : marked by tense excitement or hot anger **3** : marked by or tending toward injury, distress, or pain **4 a** : newly made : FRESH **b** : near to a goal **5** : giving a pleasant impression of warmth, cheerfulness, or friendliness; *esp* : of a hue in the range yellow through orange to red — **warm·ly** *adv* — **warm·ness** *n*
[2]**warm** *vb* **1** : to make or become warm **2 a** : to give a feeling of warmth or vitality to **b** : to experience feelings of affection or pleasure **3** : to reheat (cooked food) for eating **4 a** : to make or become ready for operation or performance by preliminary exercise or operation — often used with *up* **b** : to become increasingly ardent, interested, or competent
warm–blood·ed \'wȯrm-'bləd-əd\ *adj* : able to maintain a relatively high and constant body temperature essentially independent of that of the surroundings
warm·heart·ed \-'härt-əd\ *adj* : marked by warmth of feeling — **warm·heart·ed·ness** *n*
warm·ish \'wȯr-mish\ *adj* : somewhat warm
war·mon·ger \'wȯr-ˌməŋ-gər, -ˌmäŋ-\ *n* : one who urges or attempts to stir up war : JINGO — **war·mon·ger·ing** \-g(ə-)riŋ\ *n*
warmth \'wȯrm(p)th\ *n* **1** : the quality or state of being warm **2** : emotional intensity (as of enthusiasm, anger, or love)
warn \'wȯrn\ *vb* **1 a** : to give notice to beforehand esp. of danger or evil **b** : ADMONISH, COUNSEL **c** : to notify esp. in advance : INFORM **2** : to order to go or stay away — **warn·er** *n*
[1]**warn·ing** \'wȯr-niŋ\ *n* **1** : the act of warning : the state of being warned **2** : something that warns or serves to warn
[2]**warning** *adj* : serving as an alarm, signal, summons, or admonition — **warn·ing·ly** \-niŋ-lē\ *adv*
[1]**warp** \'wȯrp\ *n* **1 a** : a series of yarns extended lengthwise in a loom and crossed by the woof **b** : FOUNDATION, BASE **2 a** : a twist or curve that has developed in something orig. flat or straight **b** : a mental twist or aberration
[2]**warp** *vb* **1 a** : to turn or twist out of shape and esp. out of a plane; *also* : to become so turned or twisted **b** : to cause to judge, choose, or act wrongly : PERVERT **c** : FALSIFY, DISTORT **2** : to move (as a ship) or become moved by hauling on a line attached to a fixed object
war paint *n* : paint put on parts of the body (as the face) by American Indians on going to war
war·path \'wȯr-ˌpath, -ˌpȧth\ *n* **1** : the route taken by a party of American Indians going on a warlike expedition **2** : a hostile course of action or frame of mind
[1]**war·rant** \'wȯr-ənt\ *n* **1 a** : AUTHORIZATION **b** : JUSTIFICATION, GROUND **2** : evidence of authorization (as a document); *esp* : a legal writ authorizing an officer to make an arrest, seizure, or search **3** : a certificate of appointment issued to an officer of lower rank than a commissioned officer
[2]**warrant** *vt* **1 a** : to declare or maintain positively **b** : to assure (a person) of the truth of what is said **2** : to guarantee (something) to be as appears or as represented **3** : to guarantee security or immunity to : SECURE **4** : SANCTION, AUTHORIZE **5 a** : to give proof of : ATTEST **b** : GUARANTEE **6** : to serve as or give ground or reason for : JUSTIFY — **war·rant·er** \-ənt-ər\ *or* **war·ran·tor** \ˌwȯr-ən-'tȯ(ə)r\ *n*
warrant officer *n* : an officer in the armed forces ranking next below a commissioned officer
war·ran·ty \'wȯr-ənt-ē\ *n, pl* **-ties** : an expressed or implied statement that some situation or thing is as it appears or is represented to be; *esp* : a usu. written guarantee of the integrity of a product and of the maker's responsibility for the repair or replacement of defective parts
war·ren \'wȯr-ən\ *n* **1** : a place for keeping small game (as hare or pheasant) **2** : an area where rabbits breed **3** : a crowded tenement or district
war·rior \'wȯr-yər, 'wȯr-ē-ər\ *n* : a man engaged or experienced in warfare
war·ship \'wȯr-ˌship\ *n* : a government ship employed for war purposes; *esp* : one armed for combat
wart \'wȯrt\ *n* **1 a** : a horny projection on the skin caused by a virus **b** : any of numerous similar skin lesions **2** : a protuberance (as on a plant) resembling a wart — **wart·ed** \'wȯrt-əd\ *adj* — **warty** \-ē\ *adj*
wart·hog \'wȯrt-ˌhȯg, -ˌhäg\ *n* : any of a genus of African wild hogs with two pairs of rough warty protuberances on the face and large protruding tusks
war·time \'wȯr-ˌtīm\ *n* : a period during which a war is in progress

wary \'wa(ə)r-ē\ *adj* : marked by keen caution; *esp* : watchfully prudent in detecting and escaping danger — **war·i·ly** \'war-ə-lē\ *adv* — **war·i·ness** \'war-ē-nəs\ *n*

was *past 1st & 3d sing of* BE

¹wash \'wȯsh, 'wäsh\ *vb* **1** : to cleanse with or as if with a liquid (as water) **2** : to wet thoroughly with liquid **3** : to flow along the border of **4** : to pour or flow in a stream or current **5** : to move or carry by the action of water **6** : to cover or daub lightly with a liquid (as whitewash or varnish) **7** : to run water over in order to separate valuable matter from refuse **8** : to bear washing without injury **9** : to stand a test or proof **10** : to be worn away by washing

²wash *n* **1 a** : the act or process or an instance of washing or being washed **b** : articles to be washed or being washed **2** : the surging action of waves or its sound **3 a** : a piece of ground washed by the sea or river **b** : BOG, MARSH **c** : a shallow body of water or creek **4** : worthless esp. liquid waste : REFUSE **5** : the liquid with which something is washed or tinted **6** : LOTION **7** : a disturbance in the air produced by the passage of an airfoil or propeller

³wash *adj* : WASHABLE

wash·a·ble \'wȯsh-ə-bəl, 'wäsh-\ *adj* : capable of being washed without damage — **wash·a·bil·i·ty** \ˌwȯsh-ə-'bil-ət-ē, ˌwäsh-\ *n*

wash and wear *adj* : of, relating to, or constituting a fabric or garment not needing to be ironed after washing

wash·ba·sin \'wȯsh-ˌbās-ᵊn, 'wäsh-\ *n* : WASHBOWL

wash·board \-ˌbōrd\ *n* : a grooved board to scrub clothes on

wash·bowl \-ˌbōl\ *n* : a large bowl for water to wash one's hands and face

wash·cloth \-ˌklȯth\ *n* : a cloth for washing one's face and body

washed–out \'wȯsht-'au̇t, 'wäsht-\ *adj* **1** : faded in color **2** : depleted in vigor or animation : EXHAUSTED

wash·er \'wȯsh-ər, 'wäsh-\ *n* **1** : one that washes **2** : a ring (as of metal or leather) used to make something fit tightly or to prevent rubbing

wash·er·wom·an \-ˌwu̇m-ən\ *n* : a woman who works at washing clothes

wash·house \'wȯsh-ˌhau̇s, 'wäsh-\ *n* : a house or building used or equipped for washing; *esp* : one for washing clothes

wash·ing \'wȯsh-iŋ, 'wäsh-\ *n* : articles washed or to be washed

washing soda *n* : SAL SODA

Wash·ing·ton pie \ˌwȯsh-iŋ-tən-, ˌwäsh-\ *n* : cake layers put together with a jam or jelly filling

Washington's Birthday *n* : February 22 observed as a legal holiday

wash out *vb* **1** : to deplete the strength or vitality of **2** : to eliminate or be eliminated as useless or unsatisfactory

wash·out \'wȯsh-ˌau̇t, 'wäsh-\ *n* **1** : the washing out or away of earth esp. in a roadbed by a freshet; *also* : a place where earth is washed away **2** : one that fails to measure up : FAILURE; *esp* : one who fails in a course of training or study (as military flight training)

wash·room \-ˌrüm, -ˌru̇m\ *n* : a room equipped with washing and toilet facilities : LAVATORY

wash·stand \-ˌstand\ *n* **1** : a stand holding articles needed for washing one's face and hands **2** : a washbowl permanently set in place and attached to water pipes and drainpipes

wash·tub \-ˌtəb\ *n* : a tub for washing clothes or for soaking them prior to washing

wash up *vt* : ELIMINATE, FINISH

wash·wom·an \'wȯsh-ˌwu̇m-ən, 'wäsh-\ *n* : WASHERWOMAN

washy \'wȯsh-ē, 'wäsh-\ *adj* **1** : WEAK, WATERY **2** : deficient in color : PALLID **3** : lacking in vigor, individuality, or definiteness

¹wasp \'wäsp, 'wȯsp\ *n* : a winged insect related to the bees and ants that has a slender body with the abdomen attached by a narrow stalk and in females and workers a powerful sting

²wasp *n, often cap* : a white Protestant esp. of English ancestry

wasp·ish \'wäs-pish, 'wȯs-\ *adj* **1** : SNAPPISH, IRRITABLE **2** : resembling a wasp in form; *esp* : slightly built — **wasp·ish·ly** *adv* — **wasp·ish·ness** *n*

¹was·sail \'wäs-əl, wä-'sāl\ *n* **1** : an early English toast to someone's health **2** : a liquor formerly drunk in England on festive occasions **3** : riotous drinking : REVELRY

²wassail *vb* : to hold a wassail : CAROUSE — **was·sail·er** *n*

Was·ser·mann test \ˌwäs-ər-mən-, ˌväs-\ *n* : a test for the detection of syphilitic infection

wast·age \'wā-stij\ *n* : loss by use, decay, erosion, or leakage or through wastefulness

¹waste \'wāst\ *n* **1 a** : a sparsely settled or barren region : DESERT **b** : uncultivated land **c** : a broad and empty expanse (as of water) **2** : the act or an instance of wasting : the state of being wasted **3** : gradual loss or decrease by use, wear, or decay **4 a** : damaged, defective, or superfluous material produced by a manufacturing process **b** (1) : refuse (as garbage, sewage, or rubbish) that accumulates about habitations (2) : material (as excrement) that is produced by a living body and is of no value to the organism that produces it

²waste *vb* **1** : DEVASTATE **2** : to wear away or diminish gradually : CONSUME **3 a** : to spend money or use property carelessly : SQUANDER **b** : to allow to be used inefficiently or become dissipated **4** : to lose or cause to lose weight, strength, or vitality — often used with *away* **5 a** : to become diminished in bulk or substance **b** : to become consumed — **wast·er** *n*

³waste *adj* **1** : being wild and uninhabited : DESOLATE, BARREN **2** : RUINED, DEVASTATED **3** : thrown away as worthless after being used **4** : of no further use to a person, animal, or plant

waste·bas·ket \'wās(t)-ˌbas-kət\ *n* : an open receptacle for wastepaper

waste·ful \'wāst-fəl\ *adj* : given to or marked by waste : LAVISH, PRODIGAL — **waste·ful·ly** \-fə-lē\ *adv* — **waste·ful·ness** *n*

waste·land \'wāst-ˌland\ *n* : barren or uncultivated land

waste·pa·per \'wās(t)-'pā-pər\ *n* : paper discarded as used, superfluous, or not fit for use

wast·rel \'wā-strəl\ *n* : WASTER, SPENDTHRIFT

¹watch \'wäch\ *vb* **1** : to stay awake intentionally (as at the bedside of a sick person or for purposes of religious devotion) **2** : to be on the alert : be on one's guard **3** : to be on the lookout **4** : to keep guard **5** : to keep one's eyes on : keep in view **6** : to keep in view so as to prevent harm or warn of danger **7** : to keep oneself informed about **8** : to be on the alert for the chance to make use of — **watch·er** *n*

²watch *n* **1 a** : the act of keeping awake to guard, protect, or attend **b** : a state of alert and continuous attention **c** : close observation : SURVEILLANCE **2** : one of the indeterminate wakeful intervals marking the passage of night — usu. used in pl. **3** : one that watches : LOOKOUT, WATCHMAN **4 a** : a portion of time during which a part of a ship's company is on duty **b** : the part of a ship's company required to be on duty during a particular watch **5** : a portable timepiece designed to be worn (as on the wrist) or carried in the pocket

watch·case \-ˌkās\ *n* : the outside metal covering of a watch

watch·dog \-ˌdȯg\ *n* **1** : a dog kept to guard property **2** : one that guards against loss, waste, theft, or undesirable practices

watch·ful \-fəl\ *adj* : steadily attentive and alert esp. to danger — **watch·ful·ly** \-fə-lē\ *adv* — **watch·ful·ness** *n*

watch·mak·er \'wäch-ˌmā-kər\ *n* : one that makes or repairs watches or clocks — **watch·mak·ing** \-kiŋ\ *n*

watch·man \-mən\ *n* : a person assigned to watch : GUARD

watch out *vi* : to be vigilant — often used with *for*

watch·tow·er \'wäch-ˌtau̇(-ə)r\ *n* : a tower for a lookout

watch·word \-ˌwərd\ *n* **1** : a secret word used as a signal or sign of recognition **2 :** a motto used as a slogan or rallying cry

¹**wa·ter** \'wȯt-ər, 'wät-\ *n* **1 a :** the liquid that descends from the clouds as rain and forms streams, lakes, and seas **b :** a natural mineral water — usu. used in pl. **2** *pl* **:** a band of water bordering on and under the control of a country **3 :** travel or transportation on water **4 :** the level of water at a particular state of the tide : TIDE **5 :** liquid containing or resembling water **6 :** a watery fluid (as tears, urine, or sap) formed or circulating in a living body **7 a :** the limpidity and luster of a precious stone and esp. a diamond **b :** a wavy lustrous pattern (as of a textile) — **in deep water :** in serious difficulties

²**water** *vb* **1 :** to supply with or get or take water **2 :** to treat with or as if with water; *esp* **:** to impart a lustrous appearance and wavy pattern to (cloth) by calendering **3 :** to dilute by or as if by the addition of water **4 :** to form or secrete water or watery matter (as tears or saliva)

water bed *n* **:** a bed whose mattress is a plastic bag filled with water

wa·ter·borne \'wȯt-ər-ˌbōrn, 'wät-\ *adj* **:** supported or carried by water

water buffalo *n* **:** an often domesticated Asiatic buffalo somewhat resembling a large ox

water closet *n* **:** a compartment or room with a bowl-shaped fixture for defecation and excretion that can be flushed : BATHROOM; *also* **:** the fixture together with its accessories

wa·ter·col·or \'wȯt-ər-ˌkəl-ər, 'wät-\ *n* **1 :** a paint whose liquid part is water **2 :** a picture painted with watercolor **3 :** the art of painting with watercolor

wa·ter·course \-ˌkōrs\ *n* **1 :** a bed over which or channel through which water flows **2 :** a stream of water (as a river, brook, or underground stream)

wa·ter·cress \-ˌkres\ *n* **:** a perennial cress found chiefly in springs or running water and used in salads or as a potherb

wa·ter·fall \-ˌfȯl\ *n* **:** a perpendicular or very steep descent of the water of a stream

wa·ter·fowl \-ˌfau̇l\ *n* **1 :** a bird that frequents water; *esp* **:** a swimming bird **2 waterfowl** *pl* **:** swimming game birds as distinguished from upland game birds and shorebirds

wa·ter·front \-ˌfrənt\ *n* **:** land or a section of a town bordering on a body of water

wat·er·ing place \'wȯt-ə-riŋ-, 'wät-\ *n* **:** a health or recreational resort featuring mineral springs or water activities

wa·ter·less \'wȯt-ər-ləs, 'wät-\ *adj* **1 :** destitute of water : DRY **2 :** not requiring water (as for cooling or cooking)

water lily *n* **:** an aquatic plant with usu. showy flowers

wa·ter·line \'wȯt-ər-ˌlīn, 'wät-\ *n* **:** any of several lines that are marked upon the outside of a ship and correspond with the surface of the water when it is afloat on an even keel

wa·ter·logged \-ˌlȯgd, -ˌlägd\ *adj* **:** so filled or soaked with water as to be heavy or hard to manage

wa·ter·loo \ˌwȯt-ər-'lü, ˌwät-\ *n* **:** a decisive defeat

wa·ter·man \'wȯt-ər-mən, 'wät-\ *n* **:** a man who lives and works on or near water; *esp* **:** a boatman who works for hire

wa·ter·mark \-ˌmärk\ *n* **1 :** a mark that indicates a line to which water has risen **2 :** a mark (as the maker's name or trademark) made in paper during manufacture and visible when the paper is held up to the light

wa·ter·mel·on \-ˌmel-ən\ *n* **1 :** a large oblong or rounded fruit with a sweet watery red pulp and many seeds **2 :** a widely grown African vine of the gourd family whose fruits are watermelons

water moccasin *n* **:** a venomous pit viper of the southern U.S. closely related to the copperhead

water polo *n* **:** a goal game played in water by teams of swimmers with a ball resembling a soccer ball

wa·ter·pow·er \'wȯt-ər-ˌpau̇(-ə)r, 'wät-\ *n* **:** the power of moving water used to run machinery (as for generating electricity)

¹**wa·ter·proof** \ˌwȯt-ər-'prüf, ˌwät-\ *adj* **:** not letting water through — **wa·ter·proof·ness** *n*

²**wa·ter·proof** \'wȯt-ər-ˌ, 'wät-\ *n* **:** a waterproof fabric

³**wa·ter·proof** \ˌwȯt-ər-', ˌwät-\ *vt* **:** to make waterproof

wa·ter·proof·ing \-'prü-fiŋ\ *n* **:** something (as a coating) capable of imparting waterproofness

wa·ter–re·pel·lent \ˌwȯt-ə(r)-ri-'pel-ənt, ˌwät-\ *adj* **:** treated with a finish that is resistant but not impervious to penetration by water

wa·ter–re·sis·tant \-ri-'zis-tənt\ *adj* **:** resistant to but not wholly proof against the action or entry of water

wa·ter·shed \'wȯt-ər-ˌshed, 'wät-\ *n* **1 :** a dividing ridge (as a mountain range) separating one drainage area from others **2 :** the whole area that drains into a particular river or lake

wa·ter·side \-ˌsīd\ *n* **:** the land bordering a body of water

water ski *n* **:** a ski used on water

wa·ter–ski \'wȯt-ər-ˌskē, 'wät-\ *vi* **:** to ski on water while towed by a speedboat

wa·ter–soak \-ˌsōk\ *vt* **:** to soak in water

wa·ter·spout \-ˌspau̇t\ *n* **1 :** a pipe for carrying off water from a roof **2 :** a slender funnel-shaped cloud that extends down to a cloud of spray torn up from water by a whirlwind

water sprite *n* **:** a sprite held to inhabit or haunt water

water table *n* **:** the upper limit of the ground wholly saturated with water

wa·ter·tight \ˌwȯt-ər-'tīt, ˌwät-\ *adj* **1 :** of such tight construction or fit as to be waterproof **2 :** leaving no possibility of misconstruction or evasion — **wa·ter·tight·ness** *n*

wa·ter·way \'wȯt-ər-ˌwā, 'wät-\ *n* **:** a channel or a body of water by which ships can travel

wa·ter·wheel \-ˌhwēl\ *n* **:** a wheel made to turn by a flow of water against it

water wings *n pl* **:** an air-filled device to give support to the body of a person swimming or learning to swim

wa·ter·works \'wȯt-ər-ˌwərks, 'wät-\ *n pl* **:** the system of reservoirs, channels, mains, and pumping and purifying equipment by which a water supply is obtained and distributed

wa·ter·worn \-ˌwōrn\ *adj* **:** worn, smoothed, or polished by the action of water

wa·tery \'wȯt-ə-rē, 'wät-\ *adj* **1 :** of or having to do with water **2 :** containing, full of, or giving out water **3 :** being like water : THIN, WEAK **4 :** being soft and soggy — **wa·ter·i·ness** *n*

watt \'wät\ *n* **:** a unit of electric power equal to the power produced in a circuit when a pressure of one volt causes a current of one ampere to flow

watt·age \-ij\ *n* **:** amount of power expressed in watts

wat·tle \'wät-ᵊl\ *n* **1 a :** a fabrication of poles interwoven with slender branches, withes, or reeds and used esp. formerly in building **b :** material for such construction **2 :** a fleshy process hanging usu. about the head or neck (as of a bird) — **wat·tled** \-ᵊld\ *adj*

¹**wave** \'wāv\ *vb* **1 :** to float, play, or shake in an air current : move or cause to move loosely to and fro : FLUTTER **2 :** to motion with the hands or with something held in them in signal or salute **3 a :** to become moved or brandished to and fro **b :** BRANDISH, FLOURISH **4 :** to move before the wind with a wavelike motion **5 :** to follow or cause to follow a curving line or take a wavy form : UNDULATE — **wav·er** *n*

²**wave** *n* **1 :** a moving swell or crest on the surface of water **2 :** a wavelike formation or shape **3 :** the action or process of making wavy or curly **4 :** a waving motion (as of the hand or a flag) **5 :** FLOW, GUSH **6 :** a surge or rapid increase **7 :** a disturbance that transfers energy progressively from point to point — **wave·like** *adj*

waved \'wāvd\ *adj* **:** having a wavelike form or outline

wave·length \'wāv-ˌleŋ(k)th\ *n* **:** the distance (as from crest to crest) in the line of advance of a wave from any one point to the next corresponding point

wave·less \-ləs\ *adj* : having no waves : CALM
wave·let \-lət\ *n* : a little wave : RIPPLE
[1]**wa·ver** \ˈwā-vər\ *vi* **wa·vered**; **wa·ver·ing** \ˈwāv-(ə-)riŋ\ 1 : to vacillate irresolutely between choices : fluctuate in opinion, allegiance, or direction 2 a : to weave or sway unsteadily to and fro : REEL, TOTTER b : QUIVER, FLICKER c : FALTER 3 : to give an unsteady sound : QUAVER — **wa·ver·er** *n* — **wa·ver·ing·ly** \ˈwāv-(ə-)riŋ-lē\ *adv*
[2]**waver** *n* : an act of wavering, quivering, or fluttering
wavy \ˈwā-vē\ *adj* : having waves : moving in waves — **wav·i·ly** \-və-lē\ *adv* — **wav·i·ness** *n*
[1]**wax** \ˈwaks\ *n* 1 : a yellowish plastic substance secreted by bees and used by them for constructing the honeycomb 2 : any of various substances resembling beeswax in physical or chemical properties; *esp* : a solid mixture of higher hydrocarbons — **wax·like** *adj*
[2]**wax** *vt* : to treat or rub with wax
[3]**wax** *vi* 1 : to grow larger or greater: as a : to grow in volume or duration b : to increase in apparent size and brightness 2 : to pass from one state to another : BECOME
wax·en \ˈwak-sən\ *adj* 1 : made of wax 2 : resembling wax
wax myrtle *n* : any of various trees or shrubs with aromatic foliage; *esp* : an American shrub having small hard berries with a thick coating of white wax used for candles
wax·wing \ˈwaks-ˌwiŋ\ *n* : any of several singing birds that are mostly brown with a showy crest and velvety plumage
wax·work \-ˌwərk\ *n* 1 : an effigy in wax usu. of a person 2 *pl* : an exhibition of wax effigies
waxy \ˈwak-sē\ *adj* 1 : made of or full of or covered with wax 2 : resembling wax : WAXEN — **wax·i·ness** *n*
[1]**way** \ˈwā\ *n* 1 a : a track for travel or passage : PATH, ROAD, STREET b : an opening for passage (as through a crowd or a gate) 2 : the course traveled from one place to another : ROUTE 3 a : a course of action b : opportunity, capability, or fact of doing as one pleases c : POSSIBILITY 4 a : manner in which something is done or happens : METHOD, MODE b : FEATURE, RESPECT c : the usual or characteristic state of affairs d : STATE, CONDITION 5 a : a particular or characteristic mode or trick of behavior b : a regular continued course (as of life or action) 6 a : the length of a course : DISTANCE b : progress along a course 7 : something (as a locality) having direction as an attribute 8 a : room or chance to progress or advance b : place for something else 9 a : a guiding track that facilitates passage or movement b *pl* : an inclined support on which a ship is built and from which it is launched 10 : CATEGORY, KIND 11 : motion or speed of a boat through the water — **by way of** 1 : for the purpose of 2 : by the route through : VIA — **out of the way** 1 : WRONG, IMPROPER 2 : SECLUDED, REMOTE — **under way** 1 : in motion through the water 2 : in progress
[2]**way** *adj* : of, connected with, or constituting an intermediate point on a route
[3]**way** *adv* : [1]AWAY 7
way·bill \ˈwā-ˌbil\ *n* : a document prepared by the carrier of a shipment of goods and containing details of the shipment, route, and charges
way·far·er \ˈwā-ˌfar-ər\ *n* : a traveler esp. on foot — **way·far·ing** *adj*
way·lay \ˈwā-ˌlā\ *vt* **-laid** \-ˌlād\; **-lay·ing** : to lie in wait for often in order to seize, rob, or kill
way–out \ˈwā-ˈau̇t\ *adj* : FAR-OUT
way·side \ˈwā-ˌsīd\ *n* : the side of or land adjacent to a road or path — **wayside** *adj*
way·ward \ˈwā-wərd\ *adj* 1 : taking one's own and usu. irregular or improper way : DISOBEDIENT 2 : CONTRARY, PERVERSE 3 : following no clear principle or law — **way·ward·ly** *adv* — **way·ward·ness** *n*
way·worn \-ˌwōrn\ *adj* : wearied by traveling
we \(ˈ)wē\ *pron* 1 : I and one or more others — used as pronoun of the 1st person plural 2 : I — used by a sovereign or an editor or writer
weak \ˈwēk\ *adj* 1 : lacking strength: as a : deficient in physical vigor : FEEBLE, DEBILITATED b : not able to sustain or resist much weight, pressure, or strain c : deficient in vigor of mind or character; *also* : resulting from or indicative of such deficiency d : DILUTE 2 : not factually grounded or logically presented 3 a : not able to function properly b : lacking skill or proficiency : indicative of a lack of skill or aptitude c : wanting in vigor of expression or effect 4 a : not having or exerting authority b : INEFFECTIVE, IMPOTENT — **weak·ly** *adv*
weak·en \ˈwē-kən\ *vb* **weak·ened**; **weak·en·ing** \ˈwēk-(ə-)niŋ\ : to make or become weak or weaker
weak·fish \ˈwēk-ˌfish\ *n* : any of several marine food fishes related to the perches; *esp* : a common sport and market fish of the eastern coast of the U.S.
weak–kneed \ˈwēk-ˈnēd\ *adj* : lacking willpower or resolution
weak·ling \ˈwēk-liŋ\ *n* : one that is weak in body, character, or mind — **weakling** *adj*
weak·ly \ˈwēk-lē\ *adj* : FEEBLE, WEAK
weak–mind·ed \ˈwēk-ˈmīn-dəd\ *adj* 1 : lacking in judgment or good sense 2 : FEEBLE-MINDED — **weak–mind·ed·ness** *n*
weak·ness \ˈwēk-nəs\ *n* 1 : the quality or state of being weak; *also* : an instance or period of being weak 2 : FAULT, DEFECT 3 : an object of special desire or fondness
[1]**weal** \ˈwēl\ *n* : WELL-BEING, PROSPERITY
[2]**weal** *n* : WELT
weald \ˈwēld\ *n* 1 : a heavily wooded area : FOREST 2 : a wild or uncultivated usu. upland region
wealth \ˈwelth\ *n* 1 : abundance of possessions or resources : AFFLUENCE 2 : abundant supply : PROFUSION 3 a : all property that has a money or an exchange value b : all material objects that have economic utility; *esp* : those in existence at any one time
wealthy \ˈwel-thē\ *adj* 1 : having wealth : AFFLUENT 2 : characterized by abundance : AMPLE — **wealth·i·ly** \-thə-lē\ *adv* — **wealth·i·ness** *n*
wean \ˈwēn\ *vt* 1 : to accustom (as a child) to take food otherwise than by nursing 2 : to turn (one) away from something long desired or followed
wean·ling \-liŋ\ *n* : one newly weaned — **weanling** *adj*
weap·on \ˈwep-ən\ *n* 1 : something (as a gun, knife, or club) that may be used to fight with 2 : a means by which one contends against another
weap·on·ry \-rē\ *n* : the science of designing and making weapons
[1]**wear** \ˈwa(ə)r\ *vb* **wore** \ˈwō(ə)r\; **worn** \ˈwōrn\; **wear·ing** 1 a : to bear on the person or use habitually for clothing or adornment b : to carry on the person 2 : to have or show an appearance of 3 a : to impair, diminish, or decay by use or attrition b : to produce gradually by friction or attrition c : to exhaust or lessen the strength of : WEARY, FATIGUE 4 : to endure use : last under use or the passage of time 5 a : to diminish or fail with the passage of time b : to grow or become by attrition or use — **wear·a·ble** *adj* — **wear·er** *n* — **wear on** : IRRITATE, FRAY
[2]**wear** *n* 1 : the act of wearing : the state of being worn : USE 2 : clothing or an article of clothing usu. of a particular kind or for a special occasion or use 3 : wearing quality : durability under use 4 : the result of wearing or use : diminution or impairment due to use
wear·ing \ˈwa(ə)r-iŋ\ *adj* : subjecting to or inflicting wear; *esp* : FATIGUING — **wear·ing·ly** *adv*
wea·ri·some \ˈwir-ē-səm\ *adj* : causing weariness
wear off *vi* : to diminish gradually (as in effect)
wear out *vb* 1 : to make or become useless by wear 2 : TIRE, WEARY; *also* : EXHAUST
[1]**wea·ry** \ˈwi(ə)r-ē\ *adj* 1 : worn out in strength, endurance,

vigor, or freshness **2 :** expressing or characteristic of weariness **3 :** having one's patience, tolerance, or pleasure exhausted — used with *of* **4 :** TIRESOME — **wea·ri·ly** \'wir-ə-lē\ *adv* — **wea·ri·ness** *n*

²weary *vb* **wea·ried**; **wea·ry·ing :** to become or make weary

wea·sand \'wēz-ᵊnd\ *n* **:** THROAT; *also* **:** WINDPIPE

¹wea·sel \'wē-zəl\ *n, pl* **weasel** *or* **weasels :** any of various small slender active carnivorous mammals related to the minks

²weasel *vi* **wea·seled**; **wea·sel·ing** \'wēz-(ə-)liŋ\ **1 :** to speak evasively **:** EQUIVOCATE **2 :** to escape from or evade a situation or obligation — often used with *out*

¹weath·er \'weth-ər\ *n* **:** state of the atmosphere with respect to heat or cold, wetness or dryness, calm or storm, clearness or cloudiness **:** meteorological condition; *also* **:** a particular and esp. a disagreeable atmospheric state — **under the weather :** somewhat ill or drunk

²weather *vb* **weath·ered**; **weath·er·ing** \'weth-(ə-)riŋ\ **1 a :** to expose to or endure the action of the elements **b :** to alter (as in color or texture) by exposure **2 :** to sail or pass to the windward of **3 :** to bear up against and come safely through

weath·er–beat·en \'weth-ər-,bēt-ᵊn\ *adj* **:** worn or altered by exposure to weather

weath·er·board \-,bōrd\ *n* **:** CLAPBOARD, SIDING

weath·er–bound \-,baund\ *adj* **:** kept in port or at anchor or from travel or sport by bad weather

weath·er·cock \-,käk\ *n* **1 :** a vane often in the figure of a cock mounted so as to turn freely with the wind and show its direction **2 :** one that changes readily or often

weath·er·ing \'weth-(ə-)riŋ\ *n* **:** alteration of exposed objects by action of the elements; *esp* **:** physical disintegration and chemical decomposition of earth materials at or near the earth's surface

weath·er·man \'weth-ər-,man\ *n* **:** one who reports and forecasts the weather **:** METEOROLOGIST

weath·er·proof \,weth-ər-'prüf\ *adj* **:** able to withstand exposure to weather without damage or loss of function — **weatherproof** *vt* — **weath·er·proof·ness** *n*

weather strip *n* **:** a strip of material used to make a seal where a door or window joins the sill or casing — **weath·er–strip** \'weth-ər-,strip\ *vt*

weather vane *n* **:** VANE 1

¹weave \'wēv\ *vb* **wove** \'wōv\; **wo·ven** \'wō-vən\; **weav·ing** **1 a :** to form by interlacing strands of material; *esp* **:** to make (cloth) on a loom by interlacing warp and filling threads **b :** to interlace (as threads) into a fabric and esp. cloth **2 :** SPIN 2b **3 a :** to produce by elaborately combining elements **:** CONTRIVE **b :** to unite in a coherent whole **c :** to introduce as an appropriate element **:** work in **4 :** to direct or move in a winding or zigzag course esp. to avoid obstacles — **weav·er** *n*

²weave *n* **:** a pattern or method of weaving

¹web \'web\ *n* **1 :** a fabric on a loom or in process of being removed from a loom **2 a :** COBWEB 1 **b :** SNARE, ENTANGLEMENT **3 :** a membrane of an animal or plant; *esp* **:** one uniting toes (as of many birds) **4 :** NETWORK **5 :** the series of barbs implanted on each side of the shaft of a feather

²web *vb* **webbed**; **web·bing 1 :** to cover or provide with webs or a network **2 :** ENTANGLE, ENSNARE **3 :** to make a web

web·bing \'web-iŋ\ *n* **:** a strong closely woven tape used esp. for straps, harness, or upholstery

web–foot·ed \'web-'fu̇t-əd\ *adj* **:** having webbed toes

wed \'wed\ *vb* **wed·ded**; **wed·ding 1 :** to take, give, or join in marriage **:** enter into matrimony **:** MARRY **2 :** to unite firmly

wed·ding \'wed-iŋ\ *n* **1 :** a marriage ceremony usu. with accompanying festivities **:** NUPTIALS **2 :** a joining in close association **3 :** a wedding anniversary or its celebration — usu. used in combination

¹wedge \'wej\ *n* **1 :** a piece of wood or metal tapered to a thin edge and used esp. to split wood or rocks and in lifting heavy weights **2 :** something (as a piece of pie or land or a flight of wild geese) shaped like a wedge **3 :** a thing that serves to make a gradual opening or cause a change in something

²wedge *vt* **1 :** to fasten or tighten by or as if by driving in a wedge **2 :** to press or force (something) into a narrow space **3 :** to separate or split with or as if with a wedge

wed·lock \'wed-,läk\ *n* **:** the state of being married **:** MARRIAGE — **out of wedlock :** with the natural parents not legally married to each other

Wednes·day \'wenz-dē\ *n* **:** the 4th day of the week

wee \'wē\ *adj* **1 :** very small **:** TINY **2 :** very early

¹weed \'wēd\ *n* **:** a plant of no value and usu. of rank growth; *esp* **:** one that tends to overgrow or choke out more desirable plants — **weed·less** \-ləs\ *adj*

²weed *vb* **1 :** to free from or remove weeds or something harmful, inferior, or superfluous **2 :** to get rid of (weeds or unwanted items) — **weed·er** *n*

³weed *n* **:** GARMENT; *esp* **:** dress worn (as by a widow) as a sign of mourning — usu. used in pl.

weedy \'wēd-ē\ *adj* **1 :** abounding with or consisting of weeds **2 :** resembling a weed esp. in rank growth or ready propagation **3 :** noticeably lean and scrawny **:** LANKY

week \'wēk\ *n* **1 a :** seven successive days **b :** a calendar period of seven days beginning with Sunday and ending with Saturday **2 :** the working or school days of the calendar week

week·day \-,dā\ *n* **:** a day of the week except Sunday or sometimes except Saturday and Sunday

week·end \-,end\ *n* **:** the end of the week; *esp* **:** the period between the close of one working or school week and the beginning of the next

¹week·ly \'wē-klē\ *adj* **1 :** occurring, done, produced, or issued every week **2 :** computed in terms of one week — **weekly** *adv*

²weekly *n, pl* **weeklies :** a weekly publication

weep \'wēp\ *vb* **wept** \'wept\; **weep·ing 1 a :** to express emotion and esp. sorrow by shedding tears **:** BEWAIL **b :** to pour forth (tears) **:** CRY **2 :** to give off (liquid) slowly or in drops **:** OOZE

weep·er \'wē-pər\ *n* **:** one that weeps

weep·ing \'wē-piŋ\ *adj* **1 :** TEARFUL; *also* **:** RAINY **2 :** having slender pendent branches

wee·vil \'wē-vəl\ *n* **:** any of numerous mostly small beetles having the head long and usu. curved downward to form a snout and including many very injurious to plants or plant products — **wee·vily** *or* **wee·vil·ly** \'wēv-(ə-)lē\ *adj*

weft \'weft\ *n* **1 a :** WOOF 1 **b :** yarn used for the woof **2 :** WEB, FABRIC; *also* **:** an article of woven fabric

¹weigh \'wā\ *vb* **1 a :** to ascertain the heaviness of by or as if by a balance **b :** to have weight or a specified weight **2 a :** to consider carefully **:** PONDER **b :** to merit consideration as important **:** COUNT **3 :** to heave up (an anchor) preparatory to sailing **4 :** to measure or apportion (a definite quantity) on or as if on a scales **5 a :** to press down with or as if with a heavy weight **b :** to have a saddening or disheartening effect — **weigh·a·ble** *adj* — **weigh·er** *n*

²weigh *n* **:** WAY — used in the phrase *under weigh*

¹weight \'wāt\ *n* **1 a :** quantity as determined by weighing **b :** the property of a body that is measurable by weighing **c :** the standard or established amount that something should weigh **d :** something with weight **:** material substance **2 a :** a quantity or portion weighing a usu. specified amount **b :** the amount that something weighs **c :** relative heaviness (as of a textile) — usu. used in combination **3 a :** a unit (as a pound or kilogram) of weight or mass **b :** an integrated system of such units **4 a :** an object (as a piece of metal) of known weight for balancing a scale in weighing other objects **b :** a heavy object used to hold or press down something else **5 a :** something

heavy : LOAD **b** : an immaterial burden or pressure **6** : relative importance or claim to consideration : NOTE
²weight *vt* **1** : to load or make heavy with or as if with a weight **2** : to oppress with a burden **3** : to assign a relative importance to (as in a statistical study)
weight·less \'wāt-ləs\ *adj* **1** : having little weight **2** : lacking apparent gravitational pull — **weight·less·ly** *adv* — **weight·less·ness** *n*
weighty \'wāt-ē\ *adj* **1** : having much weight : HEAVY **2 a** : of much importance or consequence : SERIOUS, MOMENTOUS **b** : expressing seriousness : SOLEMN **3** : exerting authority or influence — **weight·i·ly** \'wāt-ᵊl-ē\ *adv* — **weight·i·ness** *n*
weir \'wa(ə)r, 'wi(ə)r\ *n* **1** : a fence set in a stream to catch fish **2** : a dam in a stream to raise the water level or divert its flow
weird \'wi(ə)rd\ *adj* **1 a** : of, relating to, or caused by witchcraft or the supernatural : MAGICAL **b** : UNEARTHLY, MYSTERIOUS **2** : of strange or extraordinary character : ODD, FANTASTIC — **weird·ly** *adv* — **weird·ness** *n*
¹wel·come \'wel-kəm\ *interj* — used to express a greeting to a guest or newcomer upon his arrival
²welcome *vt* **1** : to greet hospitably and with courteous cordiality **2** : to meet or face with pleasure
³welcome *adj* **1** : received gladly **2** : giving pleasure : PLEASING **3** : willingly permitted to do, have, or enjoy something
⁴welcome *n* : a cordial greeting or reception
¹weld \'weld\ *vb* **1** : to join (pieces of metal or plastic) by heating and allowing the edges to flow together or by hammering or pressing together **2** : to join as if by welding — **weld·er** *n*
²weld *n* **1** : a welded joint **2** : union by welding
wel·fare \'wel-ˌfa(ə)r\ *n* **1** : the state of doing well esp. in respect to happiness, well-being, or prosperity **2** : RELIEF 1b — **welfare** *adj*
wel·kin \'wel-kən\ *n* **1** : SKY **2** : AIR
¹well \'wel\ *n* **1 a** : an issue of water from the earth : a pool fed by a spring **b** : a source of supply : WELLSPRING **2** : a hole sunk into the earth to reach a natural deposit (as of water, oil, or gas) **3** : an enclosure in the middle of a ship's hold about the pumps **4** : an open space extending vertically through floors of a structure (as for a staircase) **5** : something (as a container or space) suggesting a well for water
²well *vb* : to rise to the surface and flow forth : RUN, GUSH
³well *adv* **bet·ter** \'bet-ər\; **best** \'best\ **1 a** : in a pleasing or desirable manner : SATISFACTORILY, FORTUNATELY **b** : in a good or proper manner : EXCELLENTLY, SKILLFULLY **2** : ABUNDANTLY, FULLY **3** : with reason or courtesy : PROPERLY **4** : COMPLETELY, THOROUGHLY **5** : INTIMATELY, CLOSELY **6** : CONSIDERABLY, FAR **7** : without trouble or difficulty **8** : EXACTLY, DEFINITELY — **as well 1** : in addition : ALSO **2** : without real loss or gain : EQUALLY — **as well as** : and not only : and in addition
⁴well *interj* **1** — used to express surprise or expostulation **2** — used to indicate resumption of a thread of discourse or to introduce a remark
⁵well *adj* **1** : SATISFACTORY, PLEASING **2 a** : PROSPEROUS, WELL-OFF **b** : being in satisfactory condition or circumstances **3** : ADVISABLE, DESIRABLE **4 a** : free or recovered from infirmity or disease : HEALTHY **b** : CURED, HEALED **5** : being a cause for thankfulness : FORTUNATE
well–ad·vised \ˌwel-əd-'vīzd\ *adj* : acting wisely or properly : based on wise counsel : DISCREET, PRUDENT
well–be·ing \'wel-'bē-iŋ\ *n* : the state of being happy, healthy, or prosperous : WELFARE
well·born \'wel-'bȯrn\ *adj* : born of good stock either socially or genetically
well–bred \-'bred\ *adj* : having or displaying good breeding
well–de·fined \ˌwel-di-'fīnd\ *adj* : having clearly distinguishable limits or boundaries
well–dis·posed \-dis-'pōzd\ *adj* : disposed to be friendly, favorable, or sympathetic
well–done \'wel-'dən\ *adj* **1** : rightly or properly performed **2** : cooked thoroughly
well–fa·vored \'wel-'fā-vərd\ *adj* : HANDSOME
well–fixed \-'fikst\ *adj* : well-off financially
well–found·ed \-'fau̇n-dəd\ *adj* : based on sound reasoning, information, judgment, or grounds
well–groomed \-'grümd, -'gru̇md\ *adj* : well and neatly dressed or cared for : scrupulously neat
well–ground·ed \-'grau̇n-dəd\ *adj* : having a firm foundation
well–heeled \'wel-'hēld\ *adj* : WELL-FIXED
well–knit \-'nit\ *adj* : well and firmly formed or framed
well–known \-'nōn\ *adj* : fully or widely known
well–mean·ing \-'mē-niŋ\ *adj* : having or based on good intentions
well–nigh \-'nī\ *adv* : ALMOST, NEARLY
well–off \'wel-'ȯf\ *adj* : being in good condition or circumstances; *esp* : WELL-TO-DO
well–or·dered \-'ȯrd-ərd\ *adj* : having an orderly procedure or arrangement
well·spring \'wel-ˌspriŋ\ *n* : SPRING, FOUNTAINHEAD
well–timed \'wel-'tīmd\ *adj* : occurring opportunely : TIMELY
well–to–do \ˌwel-tə-'dü\ *adj* : having more than adequate material resources : PROSPEROUS
well–turned \'wel-'tərnd\ *adj* **1** : pleasingly rounded : SHAPELY **2** : pleasingly and appropriately expressed
well–wish·er \'wel-ˌwish-ər\ *n* : one that wishes well to another — **well–wish·ing** *adj or n*
well–worn \-'wōrn\ *adj* **1 a** : worn by much use **b** : made stale by overuse : TRITE **2** : worn well or properly
Welsh rabbit \'welsh-\ *n* : melted often seasoned cheese poured over toast or crackers
Welsh rare·bit \-'ra(ə)r-bət\ *n* : WELSH RABBIT
¹welt \'welt\ *n* **1 a** : the narrow strip of leather between a shoe upper and sole to which other parts are stitched **b** : any of various distinguishable margins, inserts, or strips **2 a** : a ridge or lump raised on the skin usu. by a blow **b** : a heavy blow
²welt *vt* **1** : to furnish with a welt **2 a** : to raise a welt on **b** : to hit hard
¹wel·ter \'wel-tər\ *vi* **1 a** : to twist or roll one's body about : WALLOW **b** : to rise and fall or toss about in or with waves; *also* : to be in a turmoil of waves **2 a** : to lie soaked or drenched **b** : to become deeply sunk or involved
²welter *n* **1** : a state of wild disorder : TURMOIL **2** : a chaotic mass or jumble
wel·ter·weight \-ˌwāt\ *n* : a boxer weighing more than 135 but not over 147 pounds
wen \'wen\ *n* : a cyst formed by obstruction of a skin gland and filled with fatty material
wench \'wench\ *n* **1** : a young woman : GIRL **2** : a female servant
wend \'wend\ *vb* : to direct one's course : proceed on (one's way)
went *past of* GO
wept *past of* WEEP
were *past 2d sing, past pl, or past subjunctive of* BE
were·wolf \'wi(ə)r-ˌwu̇lf, 'wər-, 'we(ə)r-\ *n, pl* **were·wolves** \-ˌwu̇lvz\ : a person held to be transformed or able to transform into a wolf
¹west \'west\ *adv* : to or toward the west
²west *adj* **1** : situated toward or at the west **2** : coming from the west
³west *n* **1 a** : the general direction of sunset **b** : the compass point directly opposite to east **2** *cap* : regions or countries west of a specified or implied point — **west·er·ly** \'wes-tər-lē\ *adv or adj* — **west·ward** \'wes-twərd\ *adv or adj* — **west·wards** \-twərdz\ *adv*

west·bound \'wes(t)-ˌbau̇nd\ *adj* : headed west

[1]**west·ern** \'wes-tərn\ *adj* **1** *often cap* : of, relating to, or characteristic of a region conventionally designated West **2** : lying toward or coming from the west **3** *cap* : of or relating to the Roman Catholic or Protestant segment of Christianity — **West·ern·er** \-tə(r)-nər\ *n* — **west·ern·most** \-tərn-ˌmōst\ *adj*

[2]**western** *n* **1** : one that is produced in or characteristic of a western region and esp. the western U.S. **2** *often cap* : a novel, story, motion picture, or broadcast dealing with life in the western U.S. during the latter half of the 19th century

west·ern·ize \'wes-tər-ˌnīz\ *vt* : to give western characteristics to — **west·ern·i·za·tion** \ˌwes-tər-nə-'zā-shən\ *n*

[1]**wet** \'wet\ *adj* **1 a** : consisting of, containing, covered with, or soaked with liquid (as water) **b** : RAINY **2** : still moist enough to smudge or smear **3** : permitting or advocating the manufacture and sale of alcoholic liquor **4** : involving the use or presence of liquid **5** : perversely wrong : MISGUIDED — **wet·ly** *adv* — **wet·ness** *n*

[2]**wet** *n* **1** : WATER; *also* : WETNESS, MOISTURE **2** : rainy weather : RAIN **3** : an advocate of a wet liquor policy

[3]**wet** *vb* **wet** *or* **wet·ted**; **wet·ting** : to make or become wet

wet blanket *n* : one that quenches or dampens enthusiasm or pleasure — **wet–blan·ket** \'wet-'blaŋ-kət\ *vt*

weth·er \'weth-ər\ *n* : a male sheep castrated before sexual maturity

wet·land \'wet-ˌland\ *n* : land containing much soil moisture : swampy or boggy land

wet nurse *n* : one that cares for and suckles young not her own

wet·tish \'wet-ish\ *adj* : somewhat wet : MOIST

[1]**whack** \'hwak\ *vb* **1** : to strike with a smart or resounding blow **2** : to cut with or as if with a whack : CHOP

[2]**whack** *n* **1** : a smart or resounding blow; *also* : the sound of or as if of such a blow **2** : CONDITION; *esp* : proper working order **3 a** : an opportunity or attempt to do something : CHANCE **b** : a single action or occasion : TIME

[1]**whale** \'hwāl\ *n, pl* **whale** *or* **whales** **1** : a sea mammal that superficially resembles a large fish and is valued commercially for its oil, flesh, and sometimes whalebone **2** : a person or thing impressive in size or qualities

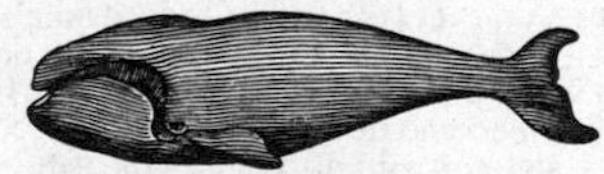

whale

[2]**whale** *vi* : to engage in whale fishing

[3]**whale** *vt* **1** : THRASH **2** : to strike or hit vigorously

whale·boat \-ˌbōt\ *n* : a long narrow rowboat made with both ends sharp and sloping and used by whalers

whale·bone \-ˌbōn\ *n* : a horny substance found in two rows of long plates attached along the upper jaw of some whales

whal·er \'hwā-lər\ *n* **1** : a person or ship engaged in whale fishing **2** : WHALEBOAT

wharf \'hwȯrf\ *n, pl* **wharves** \'hwȯrvz\ : a structure built along or at an angle from the shore of navigable waters so that ships may lie alongside to receive and discharge cargo and passengers

wharf·in·ger \'hwȯr-fən-jər\ *n* : the operator or manager of a commercial wharf

[1]**what** \(')hwät, (')hwət\ *pron* **1** — used as an interrogative in asking about the identity or nature of a thing or about the character, occupation, or position of a person **2** : that which : the one or ones that **3** : WHATEVER 1

[2]**what** *adv* **1 a** : in what respect : HOW **b** : how much **2** — used with *with* to introduce a prepositional phrase that expresses cause

[3]**what** *adj* **1 a** — used as an interrogative expressing inquiry about the identity or nature of a person, object, or matter **b** : how remarkable or surprising **2** : WHATEVER 1a

[1]**what·ev·er** \hwät-'ev-ər, (ˌ)hwət-\ *pron* **1** : anything or everything that **2** : no matter what

[2]**whatever** *adj* **1 a** : any . . . that : all . . . that **b** : no matter what **2** : of any kind at all

what·not \'hwät-ˌnät, 'hwət-\ *n* : a light open set of shelves for bric-a-brac

what·so·ev·er \ˌhwät-sə-'wev-ər, ˌhwət-\ *pron or adj* : WHATEVER

wheal \'hwēl\ *n* : a suddenly formed elevation of the skin surface: as **a** : WELT **b** : a flat burning or itching eminence on the skin

wheat \'hwēt\ *n* **1** : a cereal grain that yields a fine white flour, is the chief breadstuff of temperate climates, and is important in animal feeds **2** : any of several grasses whose white to dark red grains are wheat — **wheat·en** \-ᵊn\ *adj*

wheat germ *n* : the embryo of the wheat kernel separated in milling and used esp. as a source of vitamins

whee·dle \'hwēd-ᵊl\ *vb* **whee·dled**; **whee·dling** \'hwēd-liŋ, -ᵊl-iŋ\ **1** : to coax or entice by soft words or flattery **2** : to gain or get by wheedling

[1]**wheel** \'hwēl\ *n* **1** : a disk or circular frame capable of turning on a central axis **2** : something that is like a wheel (as in being round or in turning on an axis) **3** : a device the main part of which is a wheel **4** : BICYCLE **5** : a circular frame which when turned controls some apparatus **6 a** : a curving or circular movement **b** : a rotation or turn usu. about an axis or center; *esp* : a turning movement of troops or ships in line in which the units preserve alignment and relative positions as they change direction **7 a** : a moving power : MECHANISM **b** : a person of importance esp. in an organization — **wheeled** \'hwēld\ *adj*

[2]**wheel** *vb* **1** : to carry or move on wheels or in a vehicle with wheels **2** : to turn or cause to turn on an axis or in a circle : REVOLVE **3** : to change direction as if revolving on an axis

wheel·bar·row \'hwēl-ˌbar-ō\ *n* : a small vehicle with handles and one or more wheels for carrying small loads

wheel·base \-ˌbās\ *n* : the distance in inches between the front and rear axles of an automotive vehicle

wheel·chair \-ˌche(ə)r\ *n* : a chair mounted on wheels esp. for the use of invalids

wheel·er \'hwē-lər\ *n* **1** : one that wheels **2** : WHEELHORSE **3** : something (as a vehicle) that has wheels — used esp. in combinations

wheel·er–deal·er \-ˌdē-lər\ *n* : a shrewd operator esp. in business or politics

wheel·horse \'hwēl-ˌhȯrs\ *n* **1** : a horse in a position nearest the wheels in a tandem or similar arrangement **2** : a steady and effective worker esp. in a political body

wheel·house \-ˌhau̇s\ *n* : PILOTHOUSE

wheel·wright \-ˌrīt\ *n* : a man whose occupation is to make or repair wheels and wheeled vehicles

[1]**wheeze** \'hwēz\ *vi* **1** : to breathe with difficulty usu. with a whistling sound **2** : to make a sound resembling that of wheezing

[2]**wheeze** *n* **1** : a sound of wheezing **2 a** : GAG, JOKE **b** : a trite saying

wheezy \'hwē-zē\ *adj* **1** : inclined to wheeze **2** : having a wheezing sound — **wheez·i·ly** \-zə-lē\ *adv* — **wheez·i·ness** \-zē-nəs\ *n*

whelk \'hwelk\ *n* : any of numerous large marine snails; *esp* : one much used as food in Europe

whelm \'hwelm\ *vb* : to overcome or engulf completely : OVERWHELM

[1]**whelp** \'hwelp\ *n* : one of the young of various carnivorous mammals and esp. of the dog

²whelp *vb* **1 :** to give birth to (whelps) **2 :** to bring forth whelps
¹when \(ˈ)hwen, hwən\ *adv* **1 :** at what time **2 :** at or during which time
²when *conj* **1 a :** at or during the time that : WHILE **b :** just after the time that **c :** every time that **2 :** in the event that : IF **3 :** in spite of the fact that : THOUGH
³when \ˌhwen\ *pron* : what or which time
whence \(ˈ)hwen(t)s\ *adv* **1 :** from what place, source, or cause **2 :** from or out of which
¹when·ev·er \hwen-ˈev-ər, hwən-\ *conj* : at any or every time that
²whenever *adv* : at whatever time
when·so·ev·er \ˈhwen(t)-sə-ˌwev-ər, ˈwen(t)-\ *conj* : WHENEVER
¹where \(ˈ)hwe(ə)r\ *adv* **1 :** at, in, or to which place, circumstances, or respect **2 :** in, at, or to which **3 :** from what place or source
²where *conj* **1 a :** at or in the place at or in which **b :** to the place at, in, or to which **2 :** WHEREVER **3 :** in a case, situation, or respect in which
³where \ˈhwe(ə)r\ *n* **1 :** PLACE, LOCATION **2 :** what place, source, or cause
¹where·abouts \-ə-ˌbau̇ts\ *adv* : about where : near what place
²whereabouts *n sing or pl* : the place or general locality where a person or thing is
where·as \hwer-ˈaz\ *conj* **1 :** in view of the fact that : SINCE — used esp. to introduce a preamble **2 :** while on the contrary
where·at \-ˈat\ *conj* **1 :** at or toward which **2 :** in consequence of which : WHEREUPON
where·by \-ˈbī\ *conj* : by, through, or in accordance with which
¹where·fore \ˈhwe(ə)r-ˌfōr\ *adv* **1 :** for what reason or purpose : WHY **2 :** THEREFORE
²wherefore *n* : a statement giving an explanation : REASON
¹where·in \hwer-ˈin\ *adv* : in what : in what particular or respect
²wherein *conj* : in which : WHERE
where·of \-ˈəv, -ˈäv\ *conj* **1 :** of what **2 :** of which or whom
where·on \-ˈȯn, -ˈän\ *adv* : on which
where·to \ˈhwer-ˌtü\ *conj* : to which
where·un·to \hwer-ˈən-tü\ *conj* : WHERETO
where·up·on \ˈhwer-ə-ˌpȯn, -ˌpän\ *conj* **1 :** on which **2 :** closely following and in consequence of which
¹wher·ev·er \hwer-ˈev-ər\ *adv* : where in the world
²wherever *conj* **1 :** at, in, or to whatever place **2 :** in any circumstance in which
where·with \ˈhwer-ˌwith, -ˌwith\ *adv* : with or by means of which
where·with·al \ˈhwe(ə)r-with-ˌȯl, -with-\ *n* : MEANS, RESOURCES; *esp* : MONEY
wher·ry \ˈhwer-ē\ *n, pl* **wherries :** any of various light boats; *esp* : a long light rowboat pointed at both ends
whet \ˈhwet\ *vt* **whet·ted; whet·ting 1 :** to sharpen by rubbing on or with something (as a stone) **2 :** STIMULATE
wheth·er \ˈhweth-ər\ *conj* **1 a** (1) **:** if it is or was true that (2) **:** if it is or was better **b :** whichever is or was the case, namely, that **2 :** EITHER
whet·stone \ˈhwet-ˌstōn\ *n* : a stone for whetting sharp-edged tools
whew *often read as* ˈhwü, ˈhyü\ *n* : a sound like a half-formed whistle uttered as an exclamation — used interjectionally chiefly to express amazement, discomfort, or relief
whey \ˈhwā\ *n* : the watery part of milk that separates after the milk sours and thickens
¹which \(ˈ)hwich\ *adj* **1 :** being what one or ones out of a group — used as an interrogative **2 :** WHICHEVER
²which *pron* **1 :** what one or ones out of a group — used as an interrogative **2 :** WHICHEVER **3** — used to introduce a relative clause and to serve as a substitute within that clause for the substantive modified by that clause; used in any grammatical relation except that of a possessive; used esp. in reference to animals, inanimate objects, groups, or ideas
¹which·ev·er \hwich-ˈev-ər\ *pron* : whatever one or ones out of a group
²whichever *adj* : being whatever one or ones out of a group : no matter which
which·so·ev·er \ˌhwich-sə-ˈwev-ər\ *pron or adj* : WHICHEVER
whick·er \ˈhwik-ər\ *vi* : NEIGH, WHINNY — **whicker** *n*
¹whiff \ˈhwif\ *n* **1 :** a quick puff or slight gust esp. of air, odor, gas, smoke, or spray **2 :** an inhalation of odor, gas, or smoke
²whiff *vb* **1 :** to expel or blow away in or as if in whiffs **2 :** to inhale an odor **3 :** to strike out in baseball
whif·fle·tree \ˈhwif-əl-(ˌ)trē\ *n* : the pivoted swinging bar to which the traces of a harness are fastened and by which a vehicle or implement is drawn
Whig \ˈhwig\ *n* **1 :** a member or supporter of a British political group of the 18th and early 19th centuries seeking to limit royal authority and increase parliamentary power **2 :** an American favoring independence from Great Britain during the American Revolution **3 :** a member or supporter of an American political party formed about 1834 to oppose the Democrats — **Whig** *adj* — **Whig·gish** \-ish\ *adj*
¹while \ˈhwīl\ *n* **1 :** a period or time **2 :** the time and effort used (as in the performance of an action) : TROUBLE
²while *conj* **1 a :** during the time that **b :** as long as **2 :** in spite of the fact that : THOUGH
³while *vt* : to cause to pass esp. without boredom or in a pleasant manner — usu. used with *away*
whi·lom \ˈhwī-ləm\ *adj* : FORMER
whim \ˈhwim\ *n* : a sudden wish, desire, or change of mind : a sudden notion or fancy
¹whim·per \ˈhwim-pər\ *vi* **whim·pered; whim·per·ing**\-p(ə-)riŋ\ : to make a low whining plaintive or broken sound
²whimper *n* : a whimpering cry or sound
whim·si·cal \ˈhwim-zi-kəl\ *adj* **1 :** full of whims : CAPRICIOUS **2 :** resulting from or characterized by whim or caprice : ERRATIC — **whim·si·cal·i·ty** \ˌhwim-zə-ˈkal-ət-ē\ *n* — **whim·si·cal·ly** \ˈhwim-zi-k(ə-)lē\ *adv*
whim·sy *or* **whim·sey** \ˈhwim-zē\ *n, pl* **whimsies** *or* **whimseys 1 :** WHIM, CAPRICE **2 :** a fanciful or fantastic device, object, or creation esp. in writing or art
¹whine \ˈhwīn\ *vi* **1 :** to utter a usu. high-pitched plaintive or distressed cry; *also* : to make a sound similar to such a cry **2 :** to utter a complaint with or as if with a whine — **whin·er** *n*
²whine *n* **1 :** a prolonged usu. high-pitched cry expressive of distress or pain; *also* : a sound resembling such a cry **2 :** a complaint uttered with or as if with a whine
¹whin·ny \ˈhwin-ē\ *vi* **whin·nied; whin·ny·ing :** to neigh esp. in a low or gentle fashion
²whinny *n, pl* **whinnies :** NEIGH
¹whip \ˈhwip\ *vb* **whipped; whip·ping 1 :** to take, pull, snatch, jerk, or otherwise move very quickly and forcefully **2 a :** to strike with a slender lithe implement (as a lash or rod) esp. as a punishment; *also* : SPANK **b :** to drive or urge on by or as if by using a whip **3 a :** to bind or wrap (as a rope or fishing rod) with cord in order to protect and strengthen **b :** to wind or wrap around something **4 :** to thoroughly overcome : DEFEAT **5 :** to stir up : INCITE **6 :** to produce in a hurry **7 :** to beat (as eggs or cream) into a froth **8 :** to gather together or hold together for united action **9 a :** to move nimbly or briskly **b :** to thrash about flexibly in the manner of a whiplash
²whip *n* **1 :** an instrument consisting usu. of a handle and lash forming a flexible rod that is used for whipping **2 :** a stroke or cut with or as if with a whip **3 :** a dessert made by whipping a portion of the ingredients **4 :** one that handles a whip; *esp* : a driver of horses : COACHMAN **5 :** a member of a legislative

body appointed by his party to enforce discipline and to secure the attendance of party members at important sessions **6** : a whipping or thrashing motion — **whip·like** *adj*

whip·cord \-ˌkȯrd\ *n* **1** : a thin tough cord made of braided or twisted hemp or catgut **2** : a cloth that is made of hard-twisted yarns and has fine diagonal cords or ribs

whip·lash \-ˌlash\ *n* : the lash of a whip

whip·per·snap·per \ˈhwip-ər-ˌsnap-ər\ *n* : a diminutive, insignificant, or presumptuous person

whip·pet \ˈhwip-ət\ *n* : a small swift slender dog of greyhound type that is often used for racing

whip·ping boy \ˈhwip-iŋ-\ *n* : SCAPEGOAT

whip·poor·will \ˌhwip-ər-ˈwil, ˈhwip-ər-ˌ\ *n* : a nocturnal American bird with dull plumage

¹whip·saw \ˈhwip-ˌsȯ\ *n* **1** : a narrow saw tapering from butt to point and having hook teeth **2** : a 2-man crosscut saw

²whipsaw *vt* **whip·sawed**; **whip·saw·ing** **1** : to saw with a whipsaw **2** : to worst in two opposite ways at once, by a two-phase operation, or by the collusive action of two opponents

¹whir \ˈhwər\ *vb* **whirred**; **whir·ring** : to fly, revolve, or move rapidly with a whir

²whir *n* : a continuous fluttering or vibratory sound made by something in rapid motion

¹whirl \ˈhwərl\ *vb* **1** : to move or drive in a circle or similar curve esp. with force or speed **2 a** : to turn or cause to turn on or around an axis : SPIN **b** : to turn abruptly : WHEEL **3** : to pass, move, or go quickly **4** : to become giddy or dizzy : REEL — **whirl·er** *n*

²whirl *n* **1 a** : a rapid rotating or circling movement **b** : something undergoing a rotating movement : VORTEX **2 a** : a confused tumult : BUSTLE **b** : a confused or giddy mental state **3** : an experimental attempt : TRY

whirl·i·gig \ˈhwər-li-ˌgig\ *n* **1** : a child's toy having a whirling motion **2** : something that continuously whirls or changes; *also* : a whirling course

whirl·pool \ˈhwərl-ˌpül\ *n* : water moving rapidly in a circle so as to produce a depression in the center into which floating objects may be drawn : EDDY, VORTEX

whirl·wind \-ˌwind\ *n* **1** : a small rotating windstorm marked by an inward and upward spiral motion of the lower air **2** : a confused rush : WHIRL

¹whish \ˈhwish\ *vb* **1** : to urge on or cause to move with a rushing sound **2** : to make a sibilant sound **3** : to move with a whish esp. at high speed : WHIZ

²whish *n* : a rushing sound : SWISH

¹whisk \ˈhwisk\ *n* **1** : a quick light brushing or whipping motion **2 a** : a small usu. wire kitchen implement used for hand beating of food **b** : a flexible bunch (as of twigs, feathers, or straw) attached to a handle for use as a brush

²whisk *vb* **1** : to move nimbly and quickly **2** : to move or convey briskly **3** : to mix or fluff up by or as if by beating with a whisk **4** : to brush or wipe off lightly

whisk broom *n* : a small broom with a short handle used esp. as a clothes brush

whis·ker \ˈhwis-kər\ *n* **1 a** : a hair of the beard **b** *pl* : the part of the beard growing on the sides of the face or on the chin **2** : one of the long projecting hairs or bristles growing near the mouth of an animal (as a cat) — **whis·kered** \-kərd\ *adj*

whis·key *or* **whis·ky** \ˈhwis-kē\ *n, pl* **whiskeys** *or* **whis·kies** : a distilled alcoholic liquor made from fermented mash of grain (as rye, corn, barley, or wheat)

¹whis·per \ˈhwis-pər\ *vb* **whis·pered**; **whis·per·ing** \-p(ə-)riŋ\ **1** : to speak very low or under the breath **2** : to tell or utter by whispering **3** : to make a low rustling sound — **whis·per·er** \-pər-ər\ *n*

²whisper *n* **1 a** : an act or instance of whispering; *esp* : speech without vibration of the vocal cords **b** : a sibilant sound that resembles whispered speech **2** : something communicated by or as if by whispering : HINT, RUMOR

whist \ˈhwist\ *n* : a card game for four players in two partnerships

¹whis·tle \ˈhwis-əl\ *n* **1** : a device by which a shrill sound is produced **2 a** : a shrill clear sound produced by forcing breath out or air in through the puckered lips **b** : the sound or signal produced by a whistle or as if by whistling; *esp* : the shrill clear note of a bird or other animal

²whistle *vb* **whis·tled**; **whis·tling** \ˈhwis-(ə-)liŋ\ **1 a** : to utter a shrill clear sound by blowing or drawing air through the puckered lips **b** : to utter a shrill note or call resembling a whistle **c** : to make a shrill clear sound esp. by rapid movement **d** : to blow or sound a whistle **2** : to give a signal or issue an order or summons by or as if by whistling **3** : to send, bring, signal, or call by or as if by whistling **4** : to produce, utter, or express by whistling — **whis·tler** \-(ə-)lər\ *n*

whit \ˈhwit\ *n* : the smallest part or particle imaginable : BIT

¹white \ˈhwīt\ *adj* **1 a** : free from color **b** : of the color of new snow or milk; *esp* : of the color white **c** : light or pallid in color **d** : lustrous pale gray : SILVERY; *also* : made of silver **2** : of, relating to, or being a member of a group or race characterized by reduced pigmentation **3** : free from spot or blemish: as **a** : free from moral impurity : INNOCENT **b** : unmarked by writing or printing **c** : not intended to cause harm **d** : FAVORABLE, FORTUNATE **4 a** : wearing or habited in white **b** : marked by the presence of snow : SNOWY **5** : notably ardent : PASSIONATE **6** : conservative or reactionary in political outlook and action

²white *n* **1** : the characteristic color of fresh snow **2** : a white or light-colored part of something: as **a** : a mass of albuminous material surrounding the yolk of an egg **b** : the white part of the ball of the eye **c** : the light-colored pieces in a 2-handed board game or the player by whom these are played **3** : one that is or approaches the color white **4** : a person belonging to a light-skinned race **5** : a member of a conservative or reactionary political group

white ant *n* : TERMITE

white·bait \ˈhwīt-ˌbāt\ *n* : the young of a European herring used as food

white blood cell *n* : a blood cell that does not contain hemoglobin : LEUKOCYTE

white·cap \ˈhwīt-ˌkap\ *n* : a wave crest breaking into foam

white–col·lar \ˈhwīt-ˈkäl-ər\ *adj* : of, relating to, or constituting the class of salaried employees whose duties call for well-groomed appearance

white elephant *n* **1** : something requiring much care and expense and yielding little profit **2** : an object no longer wanted by its owner though not without value to others

white–faced \ˈhwīt-ˈfāst\ *adj* : having a wan pale face

white feather *n* : a mark or symbol of cowardice

white·fish \ˈhwīt-ˌfish\ *n* : any of various freshwater food fishes related to the salmons and trouts and mostly greenish above and silvery white below

white flag *n* : a flag of plain white used as a flag of truce or as a token of surrender

White·hall \ˈhwīt-ˌhȯl\ *n* : the British government

White House *n* **1** : the presidential mansion in Washington **2** : the executive department of the U.S. government

white lead *n* : a heavy white poisonous carbonate of lead chiefly used as a pigment

white matter *n* : the whitish part of nervous tissue consisting mostly of nerve-cell processes

whit·en \ˈhwīt-ᵊn\ *vb* **whit·ened**; **whit·en·ing** \ˈhwīt-niŋ, -ᵊn-iŋ\ : to make or become white or whiter

white·ness \ˈhwīt-nəs\ *n* : the quality or state of being white

¹white·wash \ˈhwīt-ˌwȯsh, -ˌwäsh\ *vt* **1** : to whiten with whitewash **2** : to clear of a charge of wrongdoing by offering excuses, hiding facts, or conducting a perfunctory investigation **3 :** to hold (an opponent) scoreless

²**whitewash** *n* **1 :** a composition (as of lime and water) for whitening structural surfaces **2 a :** a clearing by whitewashing **b :** a defeat in a contest in which the loser fails to score

white·wood \-ˌwu̇d\ *n* **1 :** any of various trees with pale or white wood **2 :** the wood of a whitewood and esp. of the tulip tree

whith·er \ˈhwit͟h-ər\ *adv* **1 :** to what place **2 :** to what situation, position, degree, or end **3 a :** to the place at, in, or to which **b :** to which place **4 :** to whatever place

whith·er·so·ev·er \ˌhwit͟h-ər-sə-ˈwev-ər\ *conj* **:** to whatever place

¹**whit·ing** \ˈhwīt-iŋ\ *n, pl* **whiting** *or* **whitings :** any of several edible fishes (as the hake) found mostly near seacoasts

²**whiting** *n* **:** calcium carbonate prepared as fine powder and used esp. as a pigment and in putty

whit·ish \ˈhwīt-ish\ *adj* **:** somewhat white

whit·low \ˈhwit-ˌlō\ *n* **:** ²FELON

Whit·sun·day \ˈhwit-ˈsən-dē, -ˈsən-\ *n* **:** PENTECOST

whit·tle \ˈhwit-ᵊl\ *vb* **whit·tled**; **whit·tling** \ˈhwit-liŋ, -ᵊl-iŋ\ **1 a :** to pare or cut off chips from the surface of (wood) with a knife **b :** to shape or form by so paring or cutting **2 :** to reduce, remove, or destroy gradually as if by cutting off bits with a knife **:** PARE — **whit·tler** \ˈhwit-lər, -ᵊl-ər\ *n*

¹**whiz** *or* **whizz** \ˈhwiz\ *vb* **whizzed**; **whiz·zing 1 :** to hum, whir, or hiss like a speeding object (as an arrow or ball) passing through air **2 :** to fly or move swiftly with a whiz **3 :** to rotate very rapidly — **whiz·zer** *n*

²**whiz** *or* **whizz** *n, pl* **whiz·zes 1 :** a hissing, buzzing, or whirring sound **2 :** a movement or passage of something accompanied by a whizzing sound

³**whiz** *n, pl* **whiz·zes :** WIZARD 2

whiz·bang *or* **whizz·bang** \ˈhwiz-ˌbaŋ\ *n* **:** someone or something conspicuous for noise, speed, or startling effect

whiz–bang *adj* **:** EXCELLENT, NOTABLE

who *pron* **1** \(ˈ)hü\ **:** what or which person or persons — used as an interrogative; used by speakers on all educational levels and by many reputable writers as the object of a verb or a following preposition **2** \(ˌ)hü, ü\ — used to introduce a relative clause and to serve as a substitute within that clause for the substantive modified by that clause; used esp. in reference to persons; used by speakers on all educational levels and by many reputable writers as the object of a verb

who·dun·it \hü-ˈdən-ət\ *n* **:** a detective story or mystery story presented as a novel, play, or motion picture

who·ev·er \hü-ˈev-ər\ *pron* **:** whatever person — used in any grammatical relation except that of a possessive

¹**whole** \ˈhōl\ *adj* **1 :** being in healthy or sound condition **:** free from defect or damage **:** WELL, INTACT **2 :** having all its proper parts or elements **3 a :** constituting the total sum of **:** INTEGRAL **b :** each or all of the **4 a :** constituting an undivided unit **b :** directed to one end **:** CONCENTRATED **5 :** seemingly complete or total

²**whole** *n* **1 :** a complete amount or sum **:** a number, aggregate, or totality lacking no part, member, or element **2 :** something constituting a complex unity **:** a coherent system or organization of parts fitting or working together as one — **on the whole 1 :** in view of all the circumstances or conditions **:** all things considered **2 :** in general **:** in most instances **:** TYPICALLY

whole·heart·ed \ˈhōl-ˈhärt-əd\ *adj* **:** undivided in purpose, enthusiasm, or will **:** HEARTY, ZESTFUL — **whole·heart·ed·ly** *adv* — **whole·heart·ed·ness** *n*

whole note *n* **:** a time unit of musical notation equal in value to four quarter notes or two half notes or one measure in common time

whole number *n* **:** INTEGER

¹**whole·sale** \ˈhōl-ˌsāl\ *n* **:** the sale of commodities in quantity usu. for resale by a retail merchant

²**wholesale** *adj* **1 :** of, relating to, or engaged in wholesaling **2 :** performed on a large scale esp. without discrimination — **wholesale** *adv*

³**wholesale** *vb* **:** to sell at wholesale — **whole·sal·er** *n*

whole·some \ˈhōl-səm\ *adj* **1 a :** promoting mental, spiritual, or bodily health or well-being **b :** not detrimental to health or well-being; *esp* **:** fit for food **2 :** sound in body, mind, or morals **:** HEALTHY **3 :** based on well-grounded fear **:** PRUDENT — **whole·some·ly** *adv* — **whole·some·ness** *n*

whole step *n* **:** a musical interval comprising two half steps

whole wheat *adj* **:** made of ground entire wheat kernels

whol·ly \ˈhō(l)-lē\ *adv* **1 :** to the full or entire extent **:** COMPLETELY, TOTALLY **2 :** to the exclusion of other things

whom *pron, objective case of* WHO — used as an interrogative \(ˈ)hüm\ or relative \(ˌ)hüm, üm\; used as object of a verb or a preceding preposition or less frequently as the object of a following preposition though now often considered stilted esp. as an interrogative and esp. in oral use

whom·ev·er \hü-ˈmev-ər\ *objective case of* WHOEVER

whom·so \ˈhüm-ˌsō\ *objective case of* WHOSO

whom·so·ev·er \ˌhüm-sə-ˈwev-ər\ *objective case of* WHOSOEVER

¹**whoop** \ˈh(w)üp, ˈh(w)u̇p\ *vb* **1 :** to shout or call loudly and vigorously **2 :** to make the sound that follows an attack of coughing in whooping cough **3 :** to go or pass with a loud noise **4 a :** to utter or express with a whoop **b :** to urge, drive, or cheer on with a whoop — **whoop it up 1 :** to celebrate riotously **:** CAROUSE **2 :** to stir up enthusiasm

²**whoop** *n* **1 :** a whooping sound or utterance **:** SHOUT, HOOT **2 :** a crowing sound accompanying the intake of breath after a coughing attack in whooping cough

¹**whoop·ee** \ˈ(h)wu̇p-(ˌ)ē, ˈ(h)wü-(ˌ)pē\ *interj* — used to express exuberant delight

²**whoopee** *n* **:** boisterous convivial fun

whoop·ing cough \ˈh(w)ü-piŋ-, ˈh(w)u̇p-iŋ-\ *n* **:** an infectious disease esp. of children marked by a convulsive cough sometimes followed by a whoop

whop·per \ˈhwäp-ər\ *n* **1 :** something unusually large or extreme of its kind **2 :** a monstrous lie

whop·ping \ˈhwäp-iŋ\ *adj* **:** extremely large

whore \ˈhō(ə)r\ *n* **:** PROSTITUTE

whorl \ˈhwȯrl, ˈhwərl\ *n* **1 :** a row of parts (as leaves or petals) encircling an axis and esp. a stem **2 :** something that whirls, coils, or spirals or whose form suggests such movement **:** COIL, SPIRAL **3 :** one of the turns of a snail shell — **whorled** \ˈhwȯrld, ˈhwərld\ *adj*

¹**whose** \(ˈ)hüz\ *adj* **:** of or relating to whom or which esp. as possessor, agent, or object of an action

²**whose** *pron* **:** whose one **:** whose ones — used without a following noun as a pronoun equivalent in meaning to the adjective *whose*

whose·so·ev·er \ˌhüz-sə-ˈwev-ər\ *adj* **:** of or relating to whomsoever

who·so \ˈhü-ˌsō\ *pron* **:** WHOEVER

who·so·ev·er \ˌhü-sə-ˈwev-ər\ *pron* **:** WHOEVER

¹**why** \(ˈ)hwī\ *adv* **:** for what cause, reason, or purpose

²**why** *conj* **1 :** the cause, reason, or purpose for which **2 :** for which **:** on account of which

³**why** \ˈhwī\ *n, pl* **whys :** REASON, CAUSE

⁴**why** \(ˌ)wī, (ˌ)hwī\ *interj* — used to express surprise, hesitation, approval, disapproval, or impatience

wick \ˈwik\ *n* **:** a cord, strip, or ring of loosely woven material through which a liquid (as melted tallow, wax, or oil) is drawn by capillary action to the top in a candle, lamp, or oil stove for burning

wick·ed \ˈwik-əd\ *adj* **1 :** morally bad **:** EVIL **2 a :** FIERCE, VICIOUS **b :** causing or likely to cause harm or trouble **c :** RE-

PUGNANT, VILE **d** : disposed to mischief : ROGUISH — **wick·ed·ly** *adv* — **wick·ed·ness** *n*

wick·er \'wik-ər\ *n* **1** : a small pliant twig or osier : WITHE **2 a** : WICKERWORK **b** : something made of wicker — **wicker** *adj*

wick·er·work \-,wərk\ *n* : work of osiers, twigs, or rods

wick·et \'wik-ət\ *n* **1** : a small gate or door; *esp* : one in or near a larger one **2** : a small window with a grille or grate (as at a ticket office) **3** : either of the 2 sets of 3 rods topped by 2 crosspieces at which the ball is bowled in cricket **4** : an arch or hoop in croquet

wick·ing \'wik-iŋ\ *n* : material for wicks

wick·i·up \'wik-ē-,əp\ *n* : a hut used by nomadic Indians of the western and southwestern U.S. with a usu. oval base and a rough frame covered with reed mats, grass, or brushwood

¹wide \'wīd\ *adj* **1** : covering a vast area : VAST **2** : measured across or at right angles to length **3** : having a generous measure across : BROAD **4** : opened as far as possible **5** : not limited : EXTENSIVE **6** : far from the goal, mark, or truth — **wide·ly** *adv* — **wide·ness** *n*

²wide *adv* **1 a** : over a great distance or extent : WIDELY **b** : over a specified distance, area, or extent **2 a** : so as to leave much space or distance between **b** : so as to pass at or clear by a considerable distance **3** : COMPLETELY, FULLY **4** : so as to diverge or miss : ASTRAY

wide–awake \,wīd-ə-'wāk\ *adj* : fully awake; *also* : KNOWING, ALERT — **wide–awake·ness** *n*

wide–eyed \'wīd-'īd\ *adj* **1** : having the eyes wide open **2** : struck with wonder or astonishment : AMAZED **3** : marked by unsophisticated or uncritical acceptance or admiration

wide·mouthed \-'mau̇t͟hd, -'mau̇tht\ *adj* **1** : having a wide mouth **2** : having one's mouth opened wide (as in awe)

wid·en \'wīd-ᵊn\ *vb* **wid·ened**; **wid·en·ing** \'wīd-niŋ, -ᵊn-iŋ\ : to make or become wide or wider : BROADEN

wide·spread \'wīd-'spred\ *adj* **1** : widely extended or spread out **2** : widely diffused or prevalent

wid·geon \'wij-ən\ *n, pl* **widgeon** *or* **widgeons** : any of several freshwater ducks between the teal and the mallard in size

¹wid·ow \'wid-ō\ *n* : a woman who has lost her husband by death; *esp* : one who has not remarried — **wid·ow·hood** \-,hu̇d\ *n*

²widow *vt* : to cause to become a widow

wid·ow·er \'wid-ə-wər\ *n* : a man who has lost his wife by death and has not married again

width \'width\ *n* **1** : a distance from side to side : the measurement taken at right angles to the length : BREADTH, WIDENESS **2 a** : largeness of extent or scope; *also* : FULLNESS **b** : GENEROSITY **3** : a measured and cut piece of material

wield \'wēld\ *vt* **1** : to handle (as a tool) effectively **2** : to exert one's authority by means of — **wield·er** *n*

wie·ner \'wē-nər\ *n* : FRANKFURTER

wife \'wīf\ *n, pl* **wives** \'wīvz\ **1** : a woman acting in a specified capacity — used in combination **2** : a married woman

wife·ly \'wī-flē\ *adj* : of, relating to, or befitting a wife — **wife·li·ness** *n*

wig \'wig\ *n* : a manufactured covering of hair for the head usu. made of human hair; *also* : TOUPEE

wigged \'wigd\ *adj* : wearing a wig

wig·gle \'wig-əl\ *vb* **wig·gled**; **wig·gling** \'wig-(ə-)liŋ\ **1** : to move to and fro with quick jerky or shaking motions : JIGGLE **2** : to proceed with twisting and turning movements : WRIGGLE — **wiggle** *n*

wig·gler \'wig-(ə-)lər\ *n* **1** : one that wiggles **2** : a larval or pupal mosquito

wig·gly \'wig-(ə-)lē\ *adj* **1** : tending to wiggle **2** : WAVY

wight \'wīt\ *n* : a living being : CREATURE

wig·let \'wig-lət\ *n* : a small wig used to cover the hair partially or to enhance a coiffure

¹wig·wag \'wig-,wag\ *vb* **wig·wagged**; **-wag·ging** **1** : to signal by or as if by a flag or light waved according to a code **2** : to make or cause to make a signal (as with the hand or arm)

²wigwag *n* **1** : the art or practice of wigwagging **2** : a wigwagged message

wig·wam \'wig-,wäm\ *n* : a hut of the Indians of the eastern U.S. having typically an arched framework of poles overlaid with bark, rush mats, or hides

¹wild \'wīld\ *adj* **1 a** : living in a state of nature and not ordinarily tame or domesticated **b** : growing or produced without the aid and care of man; *also* : related to or resembling a corresponding cultivated or domesticated organism **c** : of or relating to wild organisms **2** : not inhabited or cultivated : WASTE, DESOLATE **3 a** : not subjected to restraint or regulation : UNCONTROLLED, UNRULY **b** : TURBULENT, STORMY **c** : EXTRAVAGANT, FANTASTIC **d** : indicative of strong passion, desire, or emotion **4** : UNCIVILIZED, SAVAGE **5** : deviating from the natural or expected course **6** : having a denomination determined by the holder — **wild·ly** *adv* — **wild·ness** *n*

²wild *n* **1** : WILDERNESS **2** : a natural uncultivated or undomesticated state or existence

³wild *adv* **1** : WILDLY **2** : without regulation or control

¹wild·cat \'wīl(d)-,kat\ *n, pl* **wildcats** *or* **wildcat** **1** : any of various small or medium-sized cats (as the lynx or ocelot) **2** : a savage quick-tempered person

²wildcat *adj* **1** : financially irresponsible or unreliable **2** : of, relating to, or being an oil or gas well drilled in territory not known to be productive **3** : begun by a group of workers without union approval or in violation of a contract

wil·der·ness \'wil-dər-nəs\ *n* : an uncultivated and uninhabited region : wild or waste land

wild–eyed \'wīld-'īd\ *adj* **1** : appearing or being furious or raving **2** : RADICAL, EXTREME

wild·fire \'wīl(d)-,fī(ə)r\ *n* : a sweeping and destructive conflagration

wild·fowl \'wīl(d)-,fau̇l\ *n* : a game bird; *esp* : a game waterfowl (as a wild duck or goose) — **wild·fowl·er** *n* — **wild·fowl·ing** *n*

wild–goose chase *n* : the pursuit of something unattainable

wild·life \'wīl-,(d)līf\ *n* : creatures that are neither human nor domesticated; *esp* : mammals, birds, and fishes hunted by man — **wildlife** *adj*

wild rice *n* : a tall aquatic No. American perennial grass yielding an edible grain

wild·wood \'wīl-,(d)wu̇d\ *n* : a wood unaltered or unfrequented by man

¹wile \'wīl\ *n* **1** : a trick or stratagem intended to ensnare or deceive; *also* : a beguiling or playful trick **2** : TRICKERY, GUILE

²wile *vt* : LURE, ENTICE

wil·i·ness \'wī-lē-nəs\ *n* : the quality or state of being wily

¹will \wəl, (ə)l, (')wil\ *vb, past* **would** \wəd, (ə)d, (')wu̇d\; *pres sing & pl* **will** **1** : DESIRE, WISH **2** — used as an auxiliary verb (1) to express desire, willingness, or in negative constructions refusal (2) to express frequent, customary, or habitual action or natural tendency (3) to express simple futurity (4) to express capability or sufficiency (5) to express probability or recognition and often equivalent to the simple verb (6) to express determination or willfulness, and (7) to express a command

²will \'wil\ *n* **1** : wish or desire often combined with determination **2** : something desired; *esp* : a choice or determination of one having authority or power **3** : the act, process, or experience of willing : VOLITION **4 a** : the mental powers manifested as wishing, choosing, desiring, intending **b** : a disposition to act according to principles or ends **5** : SELF-CONTROL **6** : a legal declaration in which a person states how he wishes his property to be disposed of after his death

³will \'wil\ *vb* **1** : to dispose of by or as if by a will : BEQUEATH

2 a : to determine by an act of choice b : DECREE, ORDAIN c : INTEND, PURPOSE 3 : to exercise the will 4 : CHOOSE

willed \'wild\ *adj* : having a will esp. of a specified kind

wil·let \'wil-ət\ *n, pl* **willet** : a large shorebird of the eastern and Gulf coasts and the central parts of No. America

will·ful *or* **wil·ful** \'wil-fəl\ *adj* 1 : governed by will without regard to reason : OBSTINATE 2 : done deliberately : INTENTIONAL — **will·ful·ly** \-fə-lē\ *adv* — **will·ful·ness** *n*

will·ing \'wil-iŋ\ *adj* 1 : inclined or favorably disposed in mind : READY 2 : prompt to act or respond 3 : done, borne, or accepted of choice or without reluctance : VOLUNTARY 4 : of or relating to the will or power of choosing : VOLITIONAL — **will·ing·ly** *adv* — **will·ing·ness** *n*

will–o'–the–wisp \,wil-ə-t͟hə-'wisp\ *n* 1 : a light that appears at night over marshy grounds 2 : a delusive goal or hope

wil·low \'wil-ō\ *n* : any of numerous trees and shrubs bearing catkins of flowers without petals and including forms of value for wood, osiers, or tanbark — **willow** *adj* — **wil·low·like** *adj*

wil·lowy \'wil-ə-wē\ *adj* 1 : abounding with willows 2 a : resembling a willow : PLIANT b : gracefully tall and slender

will·pow·er \'wil-,paů(-ə)r\ *n* : energetic determination

wil·ly–nil·ly \,wil-ē-'nil-ē\ *adv (or adj)* : by compulsion : HELPLESSLY

[1]**wilt** \'wilt\ *vb* 1 : to lose or cause to lose freshness and become limp : DROOP 2 : to grow weak or faint : LANGUISH

[2]**wilt** *n* 1 : an act or instance of wilting : the state of being wilted 2 : a plant disorder (as a fungus disease) in which the soft tissues lose their turgor and droop and often shrivel

wily \'wī-lē\ *adj* : full of guile : TRICKY

wim·ble \'wim-bəl\ *n* : any of various instruments for boring holes

wim·ple \'wim-pəl\ *n* : a cloth covering worn outdoors over the head and around the neck and chin by women esp. in the late medieval period and by some nuns

[1]**win** \'win\ *vb* **won** \'wən\; **win·ning** 1 : to gain the victory in or as if in a contest : SUCCEED 2 : to get possession of esp. by effort : GAIN 3 a : to gain in or as if in battle or contest b : to be the victor in 4 : to obtain by work : EARN 5 : to solicit and gain the favor of; *esp* : to induce to accept oneself in marriage

[2]**win** *n* : VICTORY; *esp* : first place at the finish of a horse race

wince \'win(t)s\ *vi* : to shrink back involuntarily (as from pain) : FLINCH — **wince** *n*

winch \'winch\ *n* : a machine that has a roller on which rope is coiled for hauling or hoisting and is operated by a crank

[1]**wind** \'wind\ *n* 1 : a movement of the air of any velocity 2 : a force or agency that carries along or influences : TENDENCY, TREND 3 a : BREATH 2a b : the pit of the stomach : SOLAR PLEXUS 4 : gas generated in the stomach or the intestines 5 : something insubstantial; *esp* : idle words 6 a : air carrying a scent (as of a hunter or game) b : slight information esp. about something secret 7 a : wind instruments esp. as distinguished from strings and percussion b *pl* : players of wind instruments — **have the wind of** : to have a superior position to — **in the wind** : about to happen : ASTIR, AFOOT

[2]**wind** *vt* 1 : to get a scent of 2 : to cause to be out of breath 3 : to allow (as a horse) to rest so as to recover breath

[3]**wind** \'wīnd, 'wind\ *vt* **wound** \'waůnd\; **wind·ing** : to sound (as a horn) by blowing

[4]**wind** \'wīnd\ *vb* **wound** \'waůnd\; **wind·ing** 1 : BEND, WARP 2 : to have a curving course or shape 3 : to move or lie so as to encircle 4 a : ENTANGLE, INVOLVE b : to introduce sinuously or stealthily : INSINUATE 5 a : to encircle or cover with something pliable b : to turn completely or repeatedly about an object c : to hoist or haul by means of a rope or chain d (1) : to tighten the spring of (2) : CRANK e : to raise to a high level (as of excitement) 6 a : to cause to move in a curving line or path b : to traverse on a curving course — **wind·er** *n*

[5]**wind** \'wīnd\ *n* : COIL, TURN

wind·age \'win-dij\ *n* 1 : the influence of the wind in turning the course of a projectile 2 : the amount of deflection caused by the wind

wind·bag \'win(d)-,bag\ *n* : an idly talkative person

wind·blown \-,blōn\ *adj* : blown by the wind; *also* : having the appearance of being blown by the wind

wind·break \-,brāk\ *n* : something (as a growth of trees or shrubs) serving to break the force of wind

wind·burn \-,bərn\ *n* : skin irritation caused by wind — **wind·burned** \-,bərnd\ *adj*

wind·chill \'win(d)-,chil\ *n* : a still-air temperature that has the same cooling effect on exposed human flesh as a given combination of temperature and wind speed

wind·fall \-,fȯl\ *n* 1 : something (as a tree or fruit) blown down by the wind 2 : an unexpected or sudden gift, gain, or advantage

wind·flow·er \-,flaů(-ə)r\ *n* : ANEMONE

wind·ing \'wīn-diŋ\ *n* : material (as wire) wound or coiled about an object (as an armature); *also* : a single turn of the wound material

wind·ing–sheet \-,shēt\ *n* : SHROUD

wind instrument *n* : a musical instrument (as a flute or horn) sounded by wind and esp. by the breath

wind·jam·mer \'win(d)-,jam-ər\ *n* : a sailing ship; *also* : one of its crew

wind·lass \'win-dləs\ *n* : a winch used esp. on ships for hauling and hoisting

wind·mill \'win(d)-,mil\ *n* : a mill or a machine worked by the wind turning sails or vanes at the top of a tower

win·dow \'win-dō\ *n* 1 : an opening esp. in the wall of a building for admission of light and air usu. closed by casements or sashes containing glass 2 : WINDOWPANE 3 : something suggestive of or functioning like a window

window box *n* : a box in which to grow plants on a windowsill

win·dow·pane \-,pān\ *n* : a pane in a window

win·dow–shop \-,shäp\ *vi* : to look at the displays in store windows without going inside the stores to make purchases — **win·dow–shop·per** *n*

win·dow·sill \-,sil\ *n* : the horizontal member at the bottom of a window opening

wind·pipe \'win(d)-,pīp\ *n* : a firm tubular passage connecting the pharynx and lungs : TRACHEA

wind·proof \-'prüf\ *adj* : proof against the wind

wind·row \'win-,(d)rō\ *n* 1 : hay raked up into a row to dry 2 : a row of something (as sand or dry leaves) heaped up by or as if by the wind — **windrow** *vt*

wind·shield \'win(d)-,shēld\ *n* : a transparent screen (as of glass) in front of the occupants of a vehicle to protect them from the wind

wind·storm \-,stȯrm\ *n* : a storm marked by high wind with little or no precipitation

wind·swept \-,swept\ *adj* : swept by or as if by wind

wind up \(')wīn-'dəp\ *vb* 1 : to bring or come to a conclusion : END 2 : to put in order : SETTLE 3 : to arrive in a place, situation, or condition at the end or as a result of a course of action 4 : to go into a windup before pitching a baseball

[1]**wind·up** \'wīn-,dəp\ *n* 1 a : the act of bringing to an end b : a concluding act or part : FINISH 2 : a preliminary swing of the arm before pitching a baseball

[2]**windup** *adj* : operated by a spring wound up by hand

[1]**wind·ward** \'win-(d)wərd\ *adj* : moving or situated toward the direction from which the wind is blowing

[2]**windward** *n* : the side or direction from which the wind is blowing

windy \'win-dē\ *adj* 1 : having wind : exposed to winds 2 : indulging in or characterized by useless talk — **wind·i·ly** \-də-lē\ *adv* — **wind·i·ness** \-dē-nəs\ *n*

1wine \'wīn\ *n* **1 :** fermented grape juice containing varying percentages of alcohol **2 :** the usu. fermented juice of a plant product (as a fruit) used as a beverage

2wine *vb* **1 :** to treat to wine **2 :** to drink wine

win·ery \'wīn-(ə-)rē\ *n, pl* **-er·ies :** a wine-making establishment

wine·shop \'wīn-ˌshäp\ *n* **:** a tavern that specializes in serving wine

1wing \'wiŋ\ *n* **1 :** one of the movable feathered or membranous paired appendages by means of which a bird, bat, or insect is able to fly **2 :** an appendage or part likened to a wing in shape, appearance, or position: as **a :** a flat or broadly expanded plant or animal part; *esp* **:** either lateral petal of a pealike flower **b :** a turned-back or extended edge on an article of clothing **c :** a sidepiece at the top of an armchair **d :** one of the airfoils that develop a major part of the lift which supports a heavier-than-air aircraft **3 :** a means of flight or rapid progress **4 :** the act or manner of flying **:** FLIGHT **5 :** a side or outlying region or district **6 :** a part or feature usu. projecting from and subordinate to the main or central part **7** *pl* **:** the area at the side of the stage out of sight **8 a :** a section of an army or fleet **b :** one of the positions or players on each side of a center position (as in hockey) **9 :** either of two opposing groups in an organization **:** FACTION — **wing·less** \-ləs\ *adj* — **on the wing :** in flight **:** FLYING — **under one's wing :** under one's protection **:** in one's charge or care

2wing *vb* **1 :** to pass through in flight **:** FLY **2 :** to wound in the wing; *also* **:** to wound without killing

wing·back \-ˌbak\ *n* **:** an offensive football halfback who lines up outside the offensive end

wing·ding \'wiŋ-ˌdiŋ\ *n* **:** a wild or lively or lavish party

winged \'wiŋd *also except for "esp." sense* 'wiŋ-əd\ *adj* **1 :** having wings esp. of a specified character **2 a :** soaring with or as if with wings **:** ELEVATED **b :** SWIFT, RAPID

wing·span \'wiŋ-ˌspan\ *n* **:** WINGSPREAD; *esp* **:** the distance between the tips of an airplane's wings

wing·spread \-ˌspred\ *n* **:** the spread of the wings; *esp* **:** the distance between the tips of the fully extended wings of a winged animal

1wink \'wiŋk\ *vb* **1 :** to close and open the eyes quickly **:** BLINK **2 :** to avoid seeing **:** pretend not to look **:** pay no attention **3 :** FLICKER, TWINKLE **4 :** to close and open one eye quickly as a signal or hint

2wink *n* **1 :** a brief period of sleep **:** NAP **2 a :** a hint or sign given by winking **b :** an act of winking **3 :** INSTANT

win·kle \'wiŋ-kəl\ *n* **1 :** 2PERIWINKLE **2 :** any of various whelks that feed esp. on oysters and clams

win·na·ble \'win-ə-bəl\ *adj* **:** able to be won

win·ner \'win-ər\ *n* **:** one that wins

1win·ning \'win-iŋ\ *n* **1 :** the act of one that wins **:** VICTORY **2 :** something won; *esp* **:** money won at gambling — often used in pl.

2winning *adj* **:** ATTRACTIVE, CHARMING — **win·ning·ly** *adv*

win·now \'win-ō\ *vt* **1 a :** to remove (as chaff from grain) by a current of air **b :** to subject (as grain) to a current of air to remove waste **2 :** to get rid of (something unwanted) or to sort or separate (something) as if by winnowing

win·some \'win(t)-səm\ *adj* **1 :** causing joy or pleasure **:** WINNING, CHARMING **2 :** CHEERFUL, GAY — **win·some·ly** *adv* — **win·some·ness** *n*

1win·ter \'wint-ər\ *n* **1 a :** the season between autumn and spring comprising in the northern hemisphere usu. the months of December, January, and February **b :** the colder half of the year **2 :** YEAR **3 :** a time or season of inactivity or decay

2winter *vb* **win·tered; win·ter·ing** \'wint-ə-riŋ, 'win-triŋ\ **1 :** to pass or live through the winter **2 :** to keep, feed, or manage during the winter

3winter *adj* **:** occurring in or surviving the winter; *esp* **:** sown in autumn for harvesting in the following spring or summer

win·ter·green \'wint-ər-ˌgrēn\ *n* **1 :** any of several low-growing evergreen plants related to the heaths; *esp* **:** one with white bell-shaped flowers followed by spicy red berries **2 :** an essential oil from the common wintergreen or its flavor; *also* **:** something flavored with it

win·ter–kill \-ˌkil\ *vb* **:** to kill or die by exposure to winter conditions

win·ter·time \-ˌtīm\ *n* **:** the winter season

win·try \'win-trē\ *adj* **1 :** of or characteristic of winter **:** coming in winter **:** having to do with winter **2 :** CHILLING, COLD, CHEERLESS — **win·tri·ly** \-trə-lē\ *adv* — **win·tri·ness** \-trē-nəs\ *n*

winy \'wī-nē\ *adj* **1 :** having the taste or qualities of wine **:** VINOUS **2 :** EXHILARATING

1wipe \'wīp\ *vt* **1 :** to clean or dry by rubbing **2 :** to remove by or as if by rubbing **3 :** to erase completely **:** DESTROY **4 :** to pass or draw over a surface — **wip·er** *n*

2wipe *n* **1 :** an act or instance of wiping **2 :** something used for wiping

wir·a·ble \'wī-rə-bəl\ *adj* **:** capable of being wired

1wire \'wī(ə)r\ *n* **1 a :** metal in the form of a usu. very flexible thread or slender rod **b :** a thread or rod of metal **2 a :** a system of wires used to operate the puppets in a puppet show **b :** hidden or secret influences on a person or organization — usu. used in pl. **3 a :** a line of wire for conducting electrical current **b :** a telephone or telegraph wire or system **c :** TELEGRAM, CABLEGRAM — **wire·like** *adj* — **under the wire 1 :** at the finish line **2 :** at the last moment

2wire *vb* **1 :** to provide with wire; *also* **:** to provide with electricity **2 :** to send or send word to by telegraph **3 :** to send a telegraphic message

wired \'wī(ə)rd\ *adj* **:** reinforced or bound with wire

wire·haired \'wī(ə)r-'ha(ə)rd\ *adj* **:** having a stiff wiry outer coat of hair

1wire·less \'wī(ə)r-ləs\ *adj* **:** having no wire or wires

2wireless *n* **:** a system for communicating by code signals and radio waves and without connecting wires — **wireless** *vb*

1wire·tap \'wī(ə)r-ˌtap\ *vi* **:** to tap a telephone or telegraph wire to get information — **wire·tap·per** *n*

2wiretap *n* **:** the act or an instance of wiretapping

wire·worm \-ˌwərm\ *n* **:** the slender hard-coated larva of certain beetles often destructive to plant roots

wir·i·ness \'wī-rē-nəs\ *n* **:** the quality or state of being wiry

wir·ing \'wī(ə)r-iŋ\ *n* **1 :** the act of providing or using wire **2 :** a system of wires; *esp* **:** an arrangement of wires used for electric distribution

wiry \'wī(ə)r-ē\ *adj* **1 :** of, relating to, or resembling wire **2 :** being slender yet strong and sinewy

wis·dom \'wiz-dəm\ *n* **1 a :** accumulated learning **:** KNOWLEDGE **b :** ability to discern inner qualities and relationships **c :** good sense **:** JUDGMENT **2 :** a wise attitude or course of action **3 :** the teachings of the ancient wise men

wisdom tooth *n* **:** the last tooth of the full set on each half of each jaw in man

1wise \'wīz\ *n* **:** WAY, MANNER, FASHION — used in such phrases as *in any wise, in no wise, in this wise*

2wise *adj* **1 :** having or showing wisdom, good sense, or good judgment **:** SENSIBLE **2 :** aware of what is going on **:** INFORMED — **wise·ly** *adv*

3wise *vb* **:** to make or become informed or knowledgeable — used with *up*

wise·acre \'wī-ˌzā-kər\ *n* **:** one who pretends to knowledge or cleverness **:** SMART ALECK

1wise·crack \'wīz-ˌkrak\ *n* **:** a clever, smart, or flippant remark

2wisecrack *vi* **:** to make a wisecrack — **wise·crack·er** *n*

wise guy \'wīz-ˌgī\ *n* **:** a cocky conceited fellow

wise·ness \'wīz-nəs\ *n* **:** the quality or state of being wise

wi·sen·hei·mer \'wīz-ᵊn-ˌhī-mər\ *n* **:** one who has the air of knowing all about something or everything **:** WISEACRE

ə abut ᵊ kitten ər further a back ā bake ä cot, cart au̇ out ch chin e less ē easy g gift i trip ī life

¹wish \'wish\ *vb* **1** : to have a desire : long for : WANT **2** : to form or express a desire concerning **3** : to request by expressing a desire

²wish *n* **1 a** : an act or instance of wishing or desire : WANT **b** : an object of desire : GOAL **2 a** : an expressed will or desire : MANDATE **b** : a request or command couched as a wish **3** : an invocation of good or evil fortune on someone

wish•bone \'wish-ˌbōn\ *n* : a forked bone in front of the breastbone of a bird

wish•ful \'wish-fəl\ *adj* **1** : having a wish : DESIROUS **2** : according with wishes rather than fact — **wish•ful•ly** \-fə-lē\ *adv* — **wish•ful•ness** *n*

wishy–washy \'wish-ē-ˌwȯsh-ē, -ˌwäsh-\ *adj* : WEAK, INSIPID; *also* : morally feeble

wisp \'wisp\ *n* **1** : a small bunch of hay or straw **2 a** : a thin strip or fragment **b** : a thready streak **c** : something frail, slight, or fleeting — **wispy** \'wis-pē\ *adj*

wis•tar•ia \wis-'tir-ē-ə, -'ter-\ *n* : WISTERIA

wis•te•ria \wis-'tir-ē-ə\ *n* : any of various chiefly Asiatic mostly woody leguminous vines having compound leaves and showy blue, white, purple, or rose pealike flowers in long hanging clusters

wist•ful \'wist-fəl\ *adj* : full of unfulfilled longing or desire : YEARNING — **wist•ful•ly** \-fə-lē\ *adv* — **wist•ful•ness** *n*

wit \'wit\ *n* **1** : reasoning power : INTELLIGENCE **2 a** : mental soundness : SANITY — usu. used in pl. **b** : RESOURCEFULNESS, INGENUITY; *esp* : quickness and cleverness in handling words and ideas **3 a** : a talent for making clever remarks **b** : one noted for making witty remarks — **at one's wit's end** : at a loss for a means of solving a problem

¹witch \'wich\ *n* **1** : a person believed to have magic powers **2** : an ugly old woman : HAG **3** : a charming girl or woman

²witch *vb* **1** : BEWITCH **2** : DOWSE

witch•craft \'wich-ˌkraft\ *n* : the power or practices of a witch

witch doctor *n* : a professional worker of magic in a primitive society

witch•ery \'wich-(ə-)rē\ *n, pl* **-er•ies 1 a** : the practice of witchcraft : SORCERY **b** : an act of witchcraft **2** : an irresistible fascination : CHARM

witch ha•zel \'wich-ˌhā-zəl\ *n* **1** : a No. American shrub with slender-petaled yellow flowers borne in late fall **2** : an alcoholic solution of material from the bark of the common witch hazel used as a soothing and mildly astringent lotion

witch–hunt \-ˌhənt\ *n* **1** : a searching out and persecution of persons accused of witchcraft **2** : the searching out and deliberate harassment of those (as political opponents) with unpopular views — **witch–hunt•er** *n*

witch•ing \'wich-iŋ\ *adj* **1** : of, relating to, or suitable for sorcery or supernatural occurrences **2** : BEWITCHING, FASCINATING

with \(ˈ)wit͟h, (ˈ)with\ *prep* **1 a** : in opposition to : AGAINST **b** : so as to be separated from **2** : in mutual relation to **3** : as regards : TOWARD **4 a** : compared to : equal to **b** : on the side of : FAVORING **c** : as well as **5 a** : in the judgment or estimation of **b** : in the experience or practice of **6 a** : by means of **b** : because of **7** : having or showing as manner of action or attendant circumstance **8 a** : in possession of : HAVING **b** : characterized or distinguished by **9 a** : in the company of : in addition to **b** : inclusive of : CONTAINING **10 a** : at the time of : at the same time as **b** : in proportion to **11** : in the possession or care of **12** : in spite of **13** : in the direction of

with•al \wit͟h-'ȯl, with-\ *adv* **1** : together with this : BESIDES **2** : on the other hand : NEVERTHELESS

with•draw \wit͟h-'drȯ, with-\ *vb* **-drew** \-'drü\; **-drawn** \-'drȯn\; **-draw•ing 1** : to take back or away usu. from a holder, a place, or a condition : draw away : REMOVE **2** : to call back (as from consideration) : RECALL, RESCIND; *also* : RETRACT, RECANT **3 a** : to go away : RETREAT, LEAVE **b** : to terminate one's participation or involvement in something

with•draw•al \-'drȯ(-ə)l\ *n* : an act or instance of withdrawing

with•drawn \-'drȯn\ *adj* **1** : ISOLATED, SECLUDED **2** : socially detached and unresponsive

withe \'with\ *n* : a slender flexible branch or twig; *esp* : one used as a band or rope

with•er \'wit͟h-ər\ *vb* **with•ered**; **with•er•ing** \'wit͟h-(ə-)riŋ\ **1** : to become dry and sapless; *esp* : to shrivel from or as if from loss of bodily moisture **2** : to lose vitality, force, or freshness **3** : to cause to wither **4** : to cause to feel shriveled or blighted

with•er•ing *adj* : acting or serving to cut down or destroy

with•ers \'wit͟h-ərz\ *n pl* : the ridge between the shoulder bones of a horse

with•hold \with-'hōld, wit͟h-\ *vt* **-held** \-'held\; **-hold•ing 1** : to hold back : RESTRAIN; *also* : RETAIN **2** : to refrain from granting, giving, or allowing — **with•hold•er** *n*

with•hold•ing tax \-'hōl-diŋ-\ *n* : a tax on income withheld at the source

¹with•in \wit͟h-'in, with-\ *adv* **1** : in or into the interior : INSIDE **2** : inside oneself : INWARDLY

²within *prep* **1** : in or into the inner part of **2** : in or into the limits or compass of: as **a** : not beyond the quantity or limitations of **b** : in or into the range of

¹with•out \wit͟h-'au̇t, with-\ *prep* **1** : OUTSIDE **2 a** : not having : LACKING **b** : with absence or omission of

²without *adv* **1** : on the outside : EXTERNALLY **2** : with something lacking or absent

with•stand \with-'stand, wit͟h-\ *vt* **-stood** \-'stu̇d\; **-stand•ing** : to stand against : RESIST; *esp* : to oppose successfully

withy \'wit͟h-ē\ *n, pl* **with•ies** : WITHE

wit•less \'wit-ləs\ *adj* : lacking wit or understanding : mentally defective : FOOLISH — **wit•less•ly** *adv* — **wit•less•ness** *n*

¹wit•ness \'wit-nəs\ *n* **1 a** : attestation of a fact or event : TESTIMONY **b** : public testimony to a religious faith **2** : one that gives evidence; *esp* : one who testifies in a cause or before a court **3 a** : one present at a transaction so as to be able to testify to its having taken place **b** : one who has personal knowledge or experience of something **4** : something serving as evidence or proof : SIGN

²witness *vb* **1** : to bear witness : ATTEST, TESTIFY **2** : to act as legal witness of **3** : to furnish proof of **4** : to be a witness of

wit•ted \'wit-əd\ *adj* : having wit or understanding — usu. used in combination

wit•ti•cism \'wit-ə-ˌsiz-əm\ *n* : a witty saying

wit•ty \'wit-ē\ *adj* : marked by or full of wit : AMUSING — **wit•ti•ly** \'wit-ᵊl-ē\ *adv* — **wit•ti•ness** \'wit-ē-nəs\ *n*

wive \'wīv\ *vb* **1** : to marry a woman **2** : to take for a wife

wives *pl of* WIFE

wiz•ard \'wiz-ərd\ *n* **1** : MAGICIAN, SORCERER **2** : a very clever or skillful person

wiz•ard•ry \'wiz-ər-drē\ *n, pl* **-ries 1** : the art or practices of a wizard : SORCERY **2** : a seemingly magical transforming power or influence

wiz•en \'wiz-ᵊn\ *vb* : WITHER, SHRIVEL

woad \'wōd\ *n* : a European herb of the mustard family formerly grown for the blue dyestuff yielded by its leaves; *also* : this dyestuff

¹wob•ble \'wäb-əl\ *vb* **wob•bled**; **wob•bling** \'wäb-(ə-)liŋ\ **1 a** : to move or cause to move with an irregular rocking or side-to-side motion **b** : TREMBLE, QUAVER **2** : WAVER, VACILLATE — **wob•bler** \-(ə-)lər\ *n* — **wob•bly** \-(ə-)lē\ *adj*

²wobble *n* : a wobbling action or movement

¹woe \'wō\ *interj* — used to express grief, regret, or distress

²woe *n* **1** : a condition of deep suffering from misfortune, affliction, or grief **2** : CALAMITY, MISFORTUNE

woe•be•gone \'wō-bi-ˌgȯn\ *adj* **1** : exhibiting great woe, sorrow, or misery **2** : DISMAL, DESOLATE

woe·ful \'wō-fəl\ *adj* **1** : full of woe : AFFLICTED **2** : involving, bringing, or relating to woe **3** : PALTRY, DEPLORABLE — **woe·ful·ly** \-f(ə-)lē\ *adv* — **woe·ful·ness** *n*
woke *past of* WAKE
woken *past part of* WAKE
wold \'wōld\ *n* : an upland plain or stretch of rolling country without woods
wolf \'wu̇lf\ *n, pl* **wolves** \'wu̇lvz\ **1** : any of several large erect-eared bushy-tailed mammals that resemble the related dogs and are crafty, rapacious, and very destructive to game, sheep, and cattle **2 a** : a person resembling a wolf (as in ferocity or guile); *esp* : a man forward and zealous in attentions to women **b** : a destructive agency; *esp* : dire poverty — **wolf·ish** \'wu̇l-fish\ *adj* — **wolf·like** *adj* — **wolf in sheep's clothing** : one who cloaks a hostile intention with a friendly manner
wolf·hound \'wu̇lf-ˌhau̇nd\ *n* : any of several large dogs used in hunting large animals (as wolves)
wol·fram \'wu̇l-frəm\ *n* : TUNGSTEN
wolfs·bane \'wu̇lfs-ˌbān\ *n* : ACONITE 1; *esp* : a highly variable yellow-flowered Eurasian herb
wol·ver·ine \ˌwu̇l-və-'rēn\ *n* : a blackish shaggy-furred carnivorous mammal of northern No. America that is related to the martens and sables and is noted for its cunning and gluttony
wom·an \'wu̇m-ən\ *n, pl* **wom·en** \'wim-ən\ **1** : an adult female person **2** : WOMANKIND **3** : a female servant or attendant — **woman** *adj*
wom·an·hood \'wu̇m-ən-ˌhu̇d\ *n* **1** : the state of being a woman **2** : womanly qualities **3** : WOMEN
wom·an·ish \'wu̇m-ə-nish\ *adj* **1** : characteristic of a woman **2** : suitable to a woman rather than to a man
wom·an·kind \'wu̇m-ən-ˌkīnd\ *n* : female human beings : WOMEN
wom·an·like \-ˌlīk\ *adj* : resembling or characteristic of a woman : WOMANLY
wom·an·ly \-lē\ *adj* : marked by qualities characteristic of a woman — **wom·an·li·ness** *n* — **womanly** *adv*
woman suffrage *n* : the possession and exercise of the suffrage by women
womb \'wüm\ *n* **1** : UTERUS **2** : a place where something is generated or developed
wom·bat \'wäm-ˌbat\ *n* : any of several stocky burrowing Australian marsupials resembling small bears
wom·en·folk \'wim-ən-ˌfōk\ *or* **wom·en·folks** \-ˌfōks\ *n pl* : WOMEN
won *past of* WIN
[1]**won·der** \'wən-dər\ *n* **1 a** : a cause of astonishment or surprise : MARVEL **b** : MIRACLE **2 a** : a feeling (as of awed astonishment or of uncertainty) aroused by something extraordinary or affecting **b** : the quality of exciting wonder
[2]**wonder** *vb* **won·dered**; **won·der·ing** \-d(ə-)riŋ\ **1** : to feel surprise or amazement **2** : to feel curiosity or doubt
wonder drug *n* : a medicinal substance of outstanding effectiveness
won·der·ful \'wən-dər-fəl\ *adj* **1** : exciting wonder : MARVELOUS, ASTONISHING **2** : unusually good : ADMIRABLE — **won·der·ful·ly** \-f(ə-)lē\ *adv*
won·der·land \'wən-dər-ˌland, -lənd\ *n* **1** : a fairylike imaginary realm **2** : a place that excites admiration or wonder
won·der·ment \-mənt\ *n* **1** : ASTONISHMENT, SURPRISE **2** : curiosity about something
won·drous \'wən-drəs\ *adj* : WONDERFUL, MARVELOUS — **won·drous·ly** *adv* — **won·drous·ness** *n*
[1]**wont** \'wȯnt, 'wōnt\ *adj* : ACCUSTOMED, USED
[2]**wont** *n* : CUSTOM, USAGE
wont·ed \'wȯnt-əd, 'wōnt-\ *adj* : ACCUSTOMED, USUAL
woo \'wü\ *vb* **1** : to try to gain the love of : make love : COURT **2** : to seek usu. urgently to gain or bring about
[1]**wood** \'wu̇d\ *n* **1 a** : a dense growth of trees usu. greater in extent than a grove and smaller than a forest — often used in pl. **b** : WOODLAND **2** : a hard fibrous substance that is basically xylem and makes up the greater part of the stems and branches of trees or shrubs beneath the bark; *also* : this material suitable or prepared for some use (as burning or building) **3** : something made of wood; *esp* : a golf club having a wooden head
[2]**wood** *adj* **1** : WOODEN **2** : suitable for cutting or working wood **3** *or* **woods** \'wu̇dz\ : living or growing in woods
[3]**wood** *vb* **1** : to supply or load with wood esp. for fuel : take on wood **2** : to cover with a growth of trees or plant with trees
wood alcohol *n* : a poisonous flammable liquid used as a solvent and antifreeze
wood·bine \'wu̇d-ˌbīn\ *n* : any of several climbing vines
wood block *n* : WOODCUT
wood·chuck \'wu̇d-ˌchək\ *n* : a grizzled thickset marmot of the northeastern U.S. and Canada
wood·cock \-ˌkäk\ *n, pl* **woodcocks** *or* **woodcock** : either of two long-billed mottled and usu. brown birds related to the snipe; *esp* : an American upland game bird
wood·craft \-ˌkraft\ *n* : knowledge about the woods and how to take care of oneself in them
wood·cut \-ˌkət\ *n* **1** : a printing surface consisting of a wooden block with a usu. pictorial design cut with the grain **2** : a print from a woodcut
wood·cut·ter \-ˌkət-ər\ *n* : one that cuts wood esp. as an occupation
wood·ed \'wu̇d-əd\ *adj* : covered with trees
wood·en \'wu̇d-ᵊn\ *adj* **1** : made of wood **2 a** : lacking resilience : STIFF **b** : lacking ease, interest, or zest — **wood·en·ly** *adv* — **wood·en·ness** *n*
wood·en·ware \'wu̇d-ᵊn-ˌwa(ə)r\ *n* : articles made of wood for domestic use
[1]**wood·land** \'wu̇d-lənd, -ˌland\ *n* : land covered with woody vegetation : FOREST — **wood·land·er** *n*
[2]**woodland** *adj* **1** : of, relating to, or being woodland **2** : growing or living in woodland
wood·lot \'wu̇d-ˌlät\ *n* : a relatively small area of trees kept usu. to meet fuel and timber needs
wood louse *n* : a small flat grayish crustacean that lives esp. under stones and bark
wood nymph *n* : a nymph living in woods
wood·peck·er \'wu̇d-ˌpek-ər\ *n* : any of numerous usu. brightly marked birds with specialized feet and stiff spiny tail feathers used in climbing or resting on tree trunks and a very hard bill used to drill into trees for insects
wood·ruff \-(ˌ)rəf\ *n* : a small European sweet-scented herb used in perfumery and for flavoring wine
wood·shed \-ˌshed\ *n* : a shed for storing wood and esp. firewood
woods·man \'wu̇dz-mən\ *n* : one who frequents or works in the woods; *esp* : one skilled in woodcraft
woodsy \'wu̇d-zē\ *adj* : relating to or suggestive of woods
wood·wind \'wu̇d-ˌwind\ *n* : one of a group of wind instruments including flutes, clarinets, oboes, bassoons, and sometimes saxophones — **woodwind** *adj*
wood·work \-ˌwərk\ *n* : work made of wood; *esp* : interior fittings (as moldings or stairways) of wood
wood·work·ing \-ˌwər-kiŋ\ *n* : the act, process, or occupation of working with wood — **wood·work·er** *n* — **woodworking** *adj*
woody \'wu̇d-ē\ *adj* **1** : abounding or overgrown with trees **2** : of or containing wood or wood fibers : LIGNEOUS **3** : characteristic of or resembling wood — **wood·i·ness** *n*
wood·yard \'wu̇d-ˌyärd\ *n* : a yard for storing or sawing wood
woof \'wu̇f, 'wüf\ *n* **1** : the threads that cross the warp in a woven fabric **2** : a woven fabric or its texture
wool \'wu̇l\ *n* **1** : the heavy soft wavy or curly undercoat of

various mammals and esp. the sheep **2** : a product (as a textile) of wool **3 a** : a woollike substance **b** : short thick often crisp curly hair on a human head — **wooled** \'wu̇ld\ *adj*

¹wool·en *or* **wool·len** \'wu̇l-ən\ *adj* **1** : made of wool **2** : of or relating to the manufacture or sale of woolen products

²woolen *or* **woollen** *n* **1** : a fabric made of wool **2** : garments of woolen fabric — usu. used in pl.

wool–gath·er \'wu̇l-ˌgat͟h-ər\ *vi* : to indulge in woolgathering — **wool·gath·er·er** *n*

wool·gath·er·ing \-ˌgat͟h-(ə-)riŋ\ *n* : the act of indulging in vagrant fancies

¹wool·ly \'wu̇l-ē\ *adj* **1 a** : of, relating to, or bearing wool **b** : resembling wool **2** : CONFUSED, BLURRY **3** : marked by a lack of order or restraint — **wool·li·ness** *n*

²woolly *n, pl* **woollies** : a garment made from wool; *esp* : underclothing of knitted wool — usu. used in pl.

wool·sack \'wu̇l-ˌsak\ *n* : a sack for wool

woo·zy \'wü-zē\ *adj* **1** : BEFUDDLED **2** : affected with dizziness, mild nausea, or weakness : SICK — **woo·zi·ly** \-zə-lē\ *adv* — **woo·zi·ness** \-zē-nəs\ *n*

¹word \'wərd\ *n* **1 a** : something that is said **b** *pl* : TALK, DISCOURSE **c** : a brief remark or conversation **2 a** : a speech sound or series of speech sounds that symbolizes and communicates a meaning without being divisible into smaller units capable of independent use **b** : a written or printed character or combination of characters representing a spoken word **3** : ORDER, COMMAND **4** *often cap* **a** : the second person of the Trinity through whom all things were created **b** : GOSPEL 1a **c** : the expressed or manifested mind and will of God **5** : NEWS, INFORMATION **6** : PROMISE, DECLARATION **7** : a quarrelsome utterance or conversation — usu. used in pl. **8** : a verbal signal : PASSWORD — **word for word** : VERBATIM

²word *vt* : to express in words : PHRASE

word·book \'wərd-ˌbu̇k\ *n* : VOCABULARY, DICTIONARY

word·ing \'wərd-iŋ\ *n* : expression in words : PHRASING

word·less \'wərd-ləs\ *adj* **1** : not expressed in or accompanied by words **2** : SILENT, INARTICULATE — **word·less·ly** *adv*

word of mouth : oral communication

wordy \'wərd-ē\ *adj* : using or containing many words : VERBOSE — **word·i·ly** \'wərd-ᵊl-ē\ *adv* — **word·i·ness** \'wərd-ē-nəs\ *n*

wore *past of* WEAR

¹work \'wərk\ *n* **1** : the use of one's strength or ability in order to get something done or to achieve some desired result; *esp* : such work undertaken as one's regular employment **2** : something that needs to be done : TASK, JOB **3** : DEED, ACHIEVEMENT **4** : the material on which effort is put in the process of making something **5** : something produced by mental exertion or physical labor; *esp* : an artistic production **6** : an engineering structure **7** *pl* : a place where industrial labor is carried on **8** *pl* : the working or moving parts of a mechanical device **9** : manner of working **10** : a fortified structure **11** : the transference of energy when a force produces movement of a body **12** *pl* **a** : everything possessed, available, or belonging **b** : subjection to drastic treatment — **at work 1** : engaged in working : BUSY; *esp* : engaged in one's regular occupation **2** : having effect : OPERATING, FUNCTIONING — **out of work** : without regular employment : JOBLESS

²work *adj* **1** : suitable or styled for wear while working **2** : used for work

³work *vb* **worked** \'wərkt\ *or* **wrought** \'rȯt\; **work·ing 1** : to bring to pass : EFFECT **2** : to fashion or create a product by expending labor upon **3 a** : to prepare for use by stirring or kneading **b** : to bring into a desired form by a gradual process of cutting, hammering, scraping, pressing, or stretching **4** : to set or keep in motion or operation **5** : to solve (a problem) by reasoning or calculation **6 a** : to cause to toil or labor : get work out of **b** : to make use of : EXPLOIT **7** : to pay for with labor or service **8 a** : to get (as oneself or an object) into or out of a condition or position by stages **b** : CONTRIVE, ARRANGE **9 a** : to practice trickery or cajolery on for some end **b** : EXCITE, PROVOKE **10** : to exert oneself physically or mentally; *esp* : to perform work regularly for wages **11** : to function or operate according to plan or design **12** : to produce a desired effect : SUCCEED **13** : to make way slowly and with difficulty **14** : to permit of being worked **15 a** : to be in agitation or restless motion **b** : FERMENT 1 **c** : to move slightly in relation to another part **d** : to get into a specified condition by slow or imperceptible movements — **work on 1** : AFFECT **2** : to strive to influence or persuade

work·a·ble \'wər-kə-bəl\ *adj* **1** : capable of being worked **2** : PRACTICABLE, FEASIBLE — **work·a·bil·i·ty** \ˌwər-kə-'bil-ət-ē\ *n* — **work·a·ble·ness** *n*

work·a·day \'wər-kə-ˌdā\ *adj* **1** : relating to or suited for working days **2** : PROSAIC, ORDINARY

work·bench \'wərk-ˌbench\ *n* : a bench on which work esp. of mechanics, machinists, and carpenters is performed

work·book \-ˌbu̇k\ *n* **1** : a booklet outlining a course of study **2** : a workman's manual **3** : a record book of work done **4** : a student's individual book of problems to be solved directly on the pages

work·day \-ˌdā\ *n* **1** : a day on which work is performed as distinguished from Sunday or a holiday **2** : the period of time in a day during which work is performed — **workday** *adj*

work·er \'wər-kər\ *n* **1 a** : one that works **b** : a member of the working class **2** : one of the members of a colony of social ants, bees, wasps, or termites that are incompletely developed sexually and usu. sterile and that perform most of the labor and protective duties of the colony

work·house \'wərk-ˌhau̇s\ *n* : an institution where persons who have committed a minor offense are confined

¹work·ing \'wər-kiŋ\ *adj* **1 a** : doing work esp. for a living **b** : FUNCTIONING **2** : relating to work : taken up with work : used in or fitted for use in work **3** : good enough to allow work or further work to be done

²working *n* : an excavation or group of excavations made in mining, quarrying, or tunneling — usu. used in pl.

work·ing·man \'wər-kiŋ-ˌman\ *n* : one who works for wages usu. at manual labor or in industry

work·man \'wərk-mən\ *n* **1** : WORKINGMAN **2** : ARTISAN, CRAFTSMAN

work·man·like \-ˌlīk\ *or* **work·man·ly** \-lē\ *adj* : worthy of a good workman : SKILLFUL

work·man·ship \-ˌship\ *n* **1** : the art or skill of a workman **2** : the quality or character of a piece of work

work out *vb* **1 a** : SOLVE **b** : to bring about esp. by resolving difficulties **c** : DEVELOP, ELABORATE **2** : to exhaust (as a mine) by working

work·out \'wərk-ˌau̇t\ *n* : a practice or exercise to test or improve one's fitness esp. for athletic competition, ability, or performance

work·room \'wərk-ˌrüm, -ˌru̇m\ *n* : a room used esp. for manual work

work·shop \-ˌshäp\ *n* **1** : a small establishment where manufacturing or handicrafts are carried on **2** : a seminar emphasizing free discussion, exchange of ideas, and practical methods and given mainly for adults already employed in the field

work·ta·ble \-ˌtā-bəl\ *n* : a table for holding working materials and implements (as for needlework)

work·wom·an \-ˌwu̇m-ən\ *n* : a woman who works esp. at manual labor or in industry

world \'wərld\ *n* **1** : UNIVERSE, CREATION **2** : the earth with its inhabitants and all things upon it **3** : people in general : MANKIND **4** : a state of existence : scene of life and action **5** : a great number or quantity **6** : a part or section of the earth or its inhabitants by itself **7** : the affairs of men **8** : a heavenly body esp. if inhabited **9** : a distinctive class of persons

or their sphere of interest — **in the world** : among innumerable possibilities : EVER — used as an intensive — **out of this world** : of extraordinary excellence : SUPERB
world·ling \'wərl-(d)liŋ\ *n* : a person engrossed in the concerns of this present world
world·ly \'wərl-(d)lē\ *adj* **1** : of, relating to, or devoted to this world and its pursuits rather than to spiritual affairs **2** : WORLDLY-WISE — **world·li·ness** *n*
world·ly–wise \'wərl-(d)lē-ˌwīz\ *adj* : wise as to things and ways of this world
world·wide \'wərl-'dwīd\ *adj* : extended throughout the world
¹worm \'wərm\ *n* **1 a** : EARTHWORM; *also* : a closely related and similar animal **b** : any of various small long usu. naked and soft-bodied creeping animals (as a maggot) **2 a** : a human being who is an object of contempt, loathing, or pity : WRETCH **b** : something that inwardly torments or devours **3** *pl* : infestation with or disease caused by parasitic worms **4** : something (as a mechanical device) spiral or wormlike in form or appearance: as **a** : the thread of a screw **b** : a short revolving screw whose threads gear with the teeth of another mechanical part — **worm** *adj* — **worm·like** *adj*
²worm *vb* **1** : to move or cause to move or proceed sinuously or insidiously **2** : to insinuate or introduce (oneself) by devious or subtle means **3** : to free (as a dog) from worms **4** : to obtain or extract by artful or insidious questioning or by pleading, asking, or persuading — **worm·er** *n*
worm–eat·en \'wərm-ˌēt-ᵊn\ *adj* **1 a** : eaten or burrowed by worms **b** : PITTED **2** : WORN-OUT, ANTIQUATED
worm gear *n* **1** : WORM WHEEL **2** : a gear of a worm and a worm wheel working together
worm·hole \'wərm-ˌhōl\ *n* : a hole or passage burrowed by a worm
worm wheel *n* : a toothed wheel gearing with the thread of a worm
worm·wood \'wərm-ˌwu̇d\ *n* **1** : any of several woody herbs related to the daisies; *esp* : a European plant yielding a bitter slightly aromatic dark green oil used in absinthe **2** : something bitter or grievous : BITTERNESS
wormy \'wər-mē\ *adj* **1** : containing, infested with, or damaged by worms **2** : resembling or suggestive of a worm
worn *past part of* WEAR
worn–out \'wōrn-'au̇t\ *adj* : exhausted or used up by or as if by wear
wor·ri·ment \'wər-ē-mənt\ *n* : an act or instance of worrying; *also* : TROUBLE, WORRY
wor·ri·some \-səm\ *adj* **1** : causing distress or worry **2** : inclined to worry or fret — **wor·ri·some·ly** *adv*
¹wor·ry \'wər-ē\ *vb* **wor·ried**; **wor·ry·ing** **1** : to shake and tear or mangle with the teeth **2** : to torment with anxiety : FRET, TROUBLE **3** : to feel or express great anxiety — **wor·ri·er** *n*
²worry *n, pl* **worries** **1** : ANXIETY **2** : a cause of anxiety
¹worse \'wərs\ *adj, comparative of* BAD *or of* ILL **1** : of inferior quality, value, or condition : POORER **2 a** : more unfavorable, unpleasant, or painful; *esp* : more unwell : SICKER **b** : more faulty, unsuitable, or incorrect **c** : less skillful or efficient **3** : bad, evil, or corrupt in a greater degree
²worse *n* **1** : one that is worse **2** : a greater degree of ill or badness
³worse *adv, comparative of* BAD *or of* ILL : in a worse manner : to a worse extent or degree
wors·en \'wərs-ᵊn\ *vb* **wors·ened**; **wors·en·ing** \'wərs-niŋ, -ᵊn-iŋ\ : to make or become worse
¹wor·ship \'wər-shəp\ *n* **1** : reverence toward God, a god, or a sacred object; *also* : the expression of such reverence **2** : extravagant respect or admiration for or devotion to an object of esteem
²worship *vb* **-shiped** *or* **-shipped**; **-ship·ing** *or* **-ship·ping** **1** : to honor or reverence as a divine being or supernatural power **2** : to regard with extravagant respect, honor, or devotion : IDOLIZE **3** : to perform or take part in worship or an act of worship — **wor·ship·er** *or* **wor·ship·per** *n*
wor·ship·ful \-fəl\ *adj* : VENERATING, WORSHIPING — **wor·ship·ful·ly** \-fə-lē\ *adv* — **wor·ship·ful·ness** *n*
¹worst \'wərst\ *adj, superlative of* BAD *or of* ILL **1** : most bad, evil, ill, or corrupt **2 a** : most unfavorable, unpleasant, or painful **b** : most unsuitable, faulty, unattractive, or ill-conceived **c** : least skillful or efficient **3** : most wanting in quality, value, or condition
²worst *n* **1** : one that is worst **2** : the greatest degree of ill or badness
³worst *adv, superlative of* ILL *or of* BAD *or* BADLY : to the extreme degree of badness or inferiority : in the worst manner
⁴worst *vt* : to get the better of : DEFEAT
wor·sted \'wu̇s-təd, 'wərs-\ *n* **1** : a smooth compact yarn from long wool fibers used esp. for firm napless fabrics, carpeting, or knitting **2** : a fabric made from worsted yarns — **worsted** *adj*
¹wort \'wərt, 'wȯrt\ *n* : PLANT; *esp* : an herbaceous plant — usu. used in combination
²wort *n* : a dilute solution of sugars obtained by infusion from malt and fermented to form beer
¹worth \'wərth\ *prep* **1 a** : equal in value to **b** : having possessions or income equal to **2** : deserving of **3** : capable of
²worth *n* **1 a** : monetary value **b** : the equivalent of a specified amount or figure **2** : the value of something measured by its qualities or by the esteem in which it is held **3 a** : moral or personal value **b** : MERIT, EXCELLENCE **4** : WEALTH, RICHES
worth·less \'wərth-ləs\ *adj* **1 a** : lacking worth : VALUELESS **b** : USELESS **2** : LOW, DESPICABLE — **worth·less·ly** *adv* — **worth·less·ness** *n*
worth·while \'wərth-'hwīl\ *adj* : being worth the time or effort spent — **worth·while·ness** *n*
¹wor·thy \'wər-t͟hē\ *adj* **1 a** : having worth or value : ESTIMABLE **b** : HONORABLE, MERITORIOUS **2** : having sufficient worth — **wor·thi·ly** \-t͟hə-lē\ *adv* — **wor·thi·ness** \-t͟hē-nəs\ *n*
²worthy *n, pl* **worthies** : a worthy person
would \wəd, (ə)d, (')wu̇d\ *past of* WILL **1** : strongly desire : WISH **2** — used as an auxiliary verb (1) with *rather* or *sooner* to express preference between alternatives, (2) to express wish, desire, or intent, (3) to express willingness or preference, (4) to express plan or intention, (5) to express custom or habitual action, (6) to express consent or choice, (7) to express contingency or possibility, (8) to express completion of a statement of desire, request, or advice, and (9) to express probability or presumption in past or present time **3** : COULD **4** — used as an auxiliary verb (1) to express a request with which voluntary compliance is expected and (2) to express doubt or uncertainty **5** : SHOULD
would–be \'wu̇d-ˌbē\ *adj* : desiring or professing to be
¹wound \'wünd\ *n* **1** : an injury involving cutting or breaking of bodily tissue (as by violence, accident, or surgery) **2** : an injury or hurt to feelings or reputation
²wound *vb* **1** : to cause a wound to or in **2** : to inflict a wound
³wound \'wau̇nd\ *past of* WIND
wove *past of* WEAVE
woven *past part of* WEAVE
¹wrack \'rak\ *n* **1** : RUIN, DESTRUCTION **2** : a remnant of something destroyed
²wrack *n* **1 a** : a wrecked ship **b** : WRECKAGE **c** : WRECK **2 a** : marine vegetation; *esp* : KELP **b** : dried seaweeds
³wrack *vb* : ²RACK
⁴wrack *n* : ¹RACK 1
wraith \'rāth\ *n* **1 a** : an apparition of a living person in his exact likeness seen usu. just before his death **b** : GHOST, SPECTER **2** : an insubstantial appearance of something
¹wran·gle \'raŋ-gəl\ *vb* **wran·gled**; **wran·gling** \-g(ə-)liŋ\ **1** : to

dispute angrily or peevishly : BICKER **2** : ARGUE **3** : to obtain by persistent arguing **4** : to herd and care for (livestock and esp. horses) on the range
[2]**wrangle** *n* **1** : an angry, noisy, or prolonged dispute or quarrel **2** : CONTROVERSY
wran·gler \-g(ə-)lər\ *n* **1** : one that wrangles or bickers **2** : a ranch hand who takes care of the saddle horses
[1]**wrap** \'rap\ *vb* **wrapped**; **wrap·ping** **1 a** : to cover esp. by winding or folding **b** : to envelop and secure for transportation or storage : BUNDLE **c** : ENFOLD, EMBRACE **d** : to coil, fold, draw, or twine about something **2 a** : SURROUND, ENVELOP **b** : SUFFUSE **c** : to involve completely : ENGROSS **3** : to conceal or obscure as if by enveloping or enfolding **4** : to put on clothing : DRESS **5** : to be subject to covering, enclosing, or packaging
[2]**wrap** *n* **1** : WRAPPER, WRAPPING **2** : an article of clothing that may be wrapped round a person; *esp* : an outer garment
wrap·per \'rap-ər\ *n* **1** : that in which something is wrapped: as **a** : a tobacco leaf used for the outside covering esp. of cigars **b** (1) : a book jacket (2) : the paper cover of a book not bound in boards **c** : a paper wrapped around a newspaper or magazine in the mail **2** : one that wraps **3** : an article of clothing worn wrapped around the body
wrap·ping \'rap-iŋ\ *n* : something used to wrap an object
wrap up *vt* **1** : END, CONCLUDE **2** : to make a single comprehensive report of
wrap–up \'rap-ˌəp\ *n* : a summarizing news report
wrasse \'ras\ *n* : any of various usu. brilliantly colored spiny-finned fishes with a long deep narrow body that include important food fishes esp. of warm seas
wrath \'rath\ *n* **1** : violent anger : RAGE **2** : retributory punishment for sin or crime — **wrathy** \-ē\ *adj*
wrath·ful \'rath-fəl\ *adj* **1** : filled with wrath **2** : arising from, marked by, or indicative of wrath — **wrath·ful·ly** \-fə-lē\ *adv*
wreak \'rēk\ *vt* **1** : to exact as a punishment : INFLICT **2** : to give free scope or rein to
wreath \'rēth\ *n, pl* **wreaths** \'rēt͟hz, 'rēths\ : something intertwined into a circular shape; *esp* : GARLAND, CHAPLET
wreathe \'rēt͟h\ *vb* **1** : to twist or contort so as to show folds, coils, or creases **2 a** : to shape into a wreath **b** : to take on the shape of a wreath : move or extend in circles or spirals **c** : to cause to coil about something **3** : to encircle or adorn with or as if with a wreath
[1]**wreck** \'rek\ *n* **1** : goods cast upon the land by the sea after a shipwreck **2** : broken remains (as of a ship or vehicle after heavy damage by storm, collision, or fire) **3** : something disabled or in a state of ruin or dilapidation; *also* : an individual broken in health or strength **4** : SHIPWRECK **5** : the action of breaking up or destroying something : WRECKING
[2]**wreck** *vt* **1 a** : SHIPWRECK **b** : to damage or ruin by breaking up **c** : to involve in disaster or ruin **2** : WREAK 1
wreck·age \'rek-ij\ *n* **1** : the act of wrecking : the state of being wrecked **2** : the remains of a wreck
wreck·er \'rek-ər\ *n* **1** : one that wrecks **2** : a person who searches for or works upon wrecks of vessels **3** : a truck equipped to remove wrecked or disabled cars
wren \'ren\ *n* : any of various small mostly brown singing birds with short wings and tail
[1]**wrench** \'rench\ *vb* **1** : to move with a violent twist **2** : to pull, strain, or tighten with violent twisting or force **3** : to injure or disable by a violent twisting or straining **4** : to change (as the meaning of a word) violently **5** : to snatch forcibly : WREST **6** : to cause to suffer anguish : RACK
[2]**wrench** *n* **1 a** : a violent twisting or a pull with or as if with twisting **b** : a sharp twist or sudden jerk straining muscles or ligaments; *also* : the resultant injury (as of a joint) **c** : ALTERATION; *esp* : DISTORTION **d** : acute emotional distress : sudden violent mental change **2** : a hand or power tool for holding, twisting, or turning an object (as a bolt or nut)

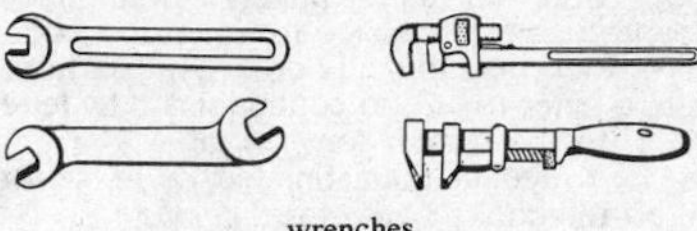

wrenches

[1]**wrest** \'rest\ *vt* **1** : to pull, force, or move by violent wringing or twisting movements **2** : to gain with difficulty by or as if by force or violence **3 a** : to divert to an unnatural or improper use **b** : DISTORT — **wrest·er** *n*
[2]**wrest** *n* : a forcible twist : WRENCH
[1]**wres·tle** \'res-əl\ *vb* **wres·tled**; **wres·tling** \'res-(ə-)liŋ\ **1** : to grapple with an opponent in an attempt to trip him or throw him down **2** : to contend against in wrestling **3** : to struggle for mastery — **wres·tler** \'res-lər\ *n*
[2]**wrestle** *n* : the action or an instance of wrestling : STRUGGLE
wres·tling \'res-liŋ\ *n* : the sport of hand-to-hand combat between two unarmed contestants who seek to throw each other
wretch \'rech\ *n* **1** : a miserable unhappy person **2** : a base, despicable, or vile person
wretch·ed \'rech-əd\ *adj* **1** : deeply afflicted, dejected, or distressed : MISERABLE **2** : WOEFUL, GRIEVOUS **3** : hatefully contemptible : DESPICABLE **4** : very poor in quality or ability : INFERIOR — **wretch·ed·ly** *adv* — **wretch·ed·ness** *n*
wrig·gle \'rig-əl\ *vb* **wrig·gled**; **wrig·gling** \'rig-(ə-)liŋ\ **1** : to move to and fro with short writhing motions like a worm : SQUIRM; *also* : to progress by such movements **2** : to extricate or insinuate oneself or reach a goal by maneuvering, equivocation, or ingratiation — **wriggle** *n* — **wrig·gly** \-(ə-)lē\ *adj*
wrig·gler \'rig-(ə-)lər\ *n* : one that wriggles; *esp* : WIGGLER 2
wright \'rīt\ *n* : a workman in wood : CARPENTER — usu. used in combination
wring \'riŋ\ *vb* **wrung** \'rəŋ\; **wring·ing** \'riŋ-iŋ\ **1** : to squeeze or twist esp. so as to make dry or to extract moisture or liquid **2** : to get by or as if by twisting or pressing **3 a** : to twist so as to strain or sprain : CONTORT **b** : to twist together (clasped hands) as a sign of anguish **4** : to place or insert by a twisting movement **5** : to affect painfully as if by wringing **6** : to shake (a hand) vigorously in greeting — **wring** *n*
wring·er \'riŋ-ər\ *n* : one that wrings; *esp* : a machine or device for pressing out liquid or moisture
[1]**wrin·kle** \'riŋ-kəl\ *n* **1** : a crease or small fold on a surface (as in the skin or in cloth) **2 a** : METHOD, TECHNIQUE; *also* : information about a method : HINT **b** : an innovation in method, technique, or equipment — **wrin·kly** \-k(ə-)lē\ *adj*
[2]**wrinkle** *vb* **wrin·kled**; **wrin·kling** \-k(ə-)liŋ\ : to develop or cause to develop wrinkles
wrist \'rist\ *n* : the joint or the region of the joint between the human hand and the arm or a corresponding part on a lower animal
wrist·band \'ris(t)-ˌband\ *n* **1** : the part of a sleeve covering the wrist **2** : a band encircling the wrist
wrist·let \'ris(t)-lət\ *n* : a band encircling the wrist; *esp* : a close-fitting knitted band worn for warmth
wrist·watch \'rist-ˌwäch\ *n* : a small watch attached to a bracelet or strap to fasten about the wrist
writ \'rit\ *n* **1** : something written : WRITING **2 a** : a legal order in writing issued under seal in the name of the sovereign or of a court or judicial officer commanding the person to whom it is directed to perform or refrain from performing a specified act **b** : a written order constituting a symbol of the power and authority of the issuer
write \'rīt\ *vb* **wrote** \'rōt\; **writ·ten** \'rit-ᵊn\; **writ·ing** \'rīt-iŋ\

1 : to form letters or words with pen or pencil 2 : to form the letters or the words of (as on paper) : INSCRIBE 3 : to put down on paper : give expression to in writing 4 : to make up and set down for others to read : COMPOSE 5 : to pen, dictate, or typewrite a letter to 6 : to communicate by letter : CORRESPOND 7 : to be fitted for writing

write off *vt* 1 : to reduce the estimated value of : DEPRECIATE 2 : to take off the books : CANCEL

writ·er \'rīt-ər\ *n* : one that writes esp. as a business or occupation : AUTHOR

write–up \'rīt-,əp\ *n* : a written account (as in a newspaper); *esp* : a flattering article

writhe \'rīth\ *vb* 1 : to twist and turn this way and that 2 : to suffer with shame or confusion : SQUIRM

writ·ing \'rīt-iŋ\ *n* 1 **a** : the act or process of one that writes : the formation of letters to express words and ideas **b** : HANDWRITING 2 **a** : something (as a letter, book, or document) that is written or printed **b** : INSCRIPTION 3 : a style or form of composition 4 : the occupation of a writer

¹wrong \'rȯŋ\ *n* 1 : an injurious, unfair, or unjust act 2 : that which is wrong : principles, practices, or conduct contrary to justice, goodness, equity, or law 3 **a** : the state, position, or fact of being or doing wrong **b** : the state of being guilty 4 : a violation of the legal rights of another; *esp* : TORT

²wrong *adj* 1 : not according to the moral standard : SINFUL, IMMORAL 2 : not right or proper according to a code, standard, or convention : IMPROPER 3 : not suitable or appropriate 4 : not according to truth or facts : INCORRECT 5 : not satisfactory (as in condition, results, health, or temper) 6 : constituting a side or part of something opposite to the principal one or one turned down, inward, or away, or least finished or polished — **wrong** *adv* — **wrong·ly** *adv* — **wrong·ness** *n*

³wrong *vt* **wronged**; **wrong·ing** \'rȯŋ-iŋ\ 1 : to do wrong to : INJURE, HARM 2 : to make unjust remarks about : DISHONOR, MALIGN — **wrong·er** *n*

wrong·do·er \'rȯŋ-'dü-ər\ *n* : a person who does wrong and esp. moral wrong — **wrong·do·ing** *n*

wrong·ful \'rȯŋ-fəl\ *adj* 1 : WRONG, UNJUST 2 : UNLAWFUL — **wrong·ful·ly** \-fə-lē\ *adv* — **wrong·ful·ness** *n*

wrong·head·ed \'rȯŋ-'hed-əd\ *adj* : stubborn in adherence to wrong opinion or principles : PERVERSE — **wrong·head·ed·ly** *adv* — **wrong·head·ed·ness** *n*

wroth \'rȯth, 'rōth\ *adj* : filled with wrath : ANGRY

wrought \'rȯt\ *adj* 1 : FASHIONED, FORMED 2 : ORNAMENTED 3 : MANUFACTURED 4 : beaten into shape by tools : HAMMERED 5 : deeply stirred : EXCITED

wrought iron *n* : a commercial form of iron that is tough, malleable, and relatively soft

wrung *past of* WRING

wry \'rī\ *adj* 1 : turned abnormally to one side : CONTORTED 2 : made by distortion of the facial muscles 3 : cleverly and often ironically or grimly humorous — **wry·ly** *adv* — **wry·ness** *n*

wry·neck \'rī-,nek\ *n* 1 : a disorder marked by a twisting of the neck and an unnatural position of the head 2 : any of several atypical woodpeckers with soft tail feathers and a peculiar way of twisting the neck

wurst \'wərst, 'wu̇rst\ *n* : SAUSAGE

¹x \'eks\ *n, often cap* 1 : the 24th letter of the English alphabet 2 : the roman numeral 10 3 : an unknown quantity

²x *vt* **x–ed** *also* **x'd** *or* **xed** \'ekst\; **x–ing** *or* **x'ing** \'ek-siŋ\ 1 : to mark with an *x* 2 : to cancel or obliterate with a series of *x's* — usu. used with *out*

xe·bec \'zē-,bek\ *n* : a usu. 3-masted Mediterranean sailing ship with long overhanging bow and stern

xe·nia \'zē-nē-ə\ *n* : the effect of genes introduced by a male nucleus on seed-plant structures (as endosperm or fruit) other than an embryo

xe·non \'zē-,nän\ *n* : a heavy gaseous chemical element occurring in air in minute quantities

xeno·pho·bia \,zen-ə-'fō-bē-ə\ *n* : fear and hatred of strangers or foreigners or of anything that is strange or foreign — **xeno·phobe** \'zen-ə-,fōb\ *n* — **xeno·pho·bic** \,zen-ə-'fō-bik\ *adj*

xe·ric \'zi(ə)r-ik\ *adj* 1 : low or deficient in available moisture for the support of life 2 : XEROPHYTIC — **xe·ri·cal·ly** \'zir-i-k(ə-)lē\ *adv*

xe·ro·phyte \'zir-ə-,fīt\ *n* : a plant adapted for growth with a limited water supply esp. by means of mechanisms that limit transpiration or that provide for the storage of water — **xe·ro·phyt·ic** \,zir-ə-'fit-ik\ *adj* — **xe·ro·phyt·i·cal·ly** \-'fit-i-k(ə-)lē\ *adv* — **xe·ro·phyt·ism** \'zir-ə-,fīt-,iz-əm\ *n*

Xmas \'kris-məs, 'eks-məs\ *n* : CHRISTMAS

X ray \'eks-,rā\ *n* 1 : any of the electromagnetic radiations of the same nature as light rays but of very short wavelength that are generated by a stream of electrons striking against a metal surface in vacuum and that are able to penetrate various thicknesses of solids 2 : photograph taken by the use of X rays — **X–ray** *adj*

x–ray *vt, often cap X* : to examine, treat, or photograph with X rays

xy·lem \'zī-ləm, -,lem\ *n* : a complex tissue of higher plants that transports water and dissolved materials upward, functions also in support and storage, lies internal to the phloem, and typically constitutes the woody element (as of a plant stem) — **xy·la·ry** \'zī-lə-rē\ *adj*

xy·lo·phone \'zī-lə-,fōn\ *n* : a musical instrument consisting of a series of wooden bars graduated in length to sound the musical scale and played by striking with two wooden hammers — **xy·lo·phon·ist** \-,fō-nəst\ *n*

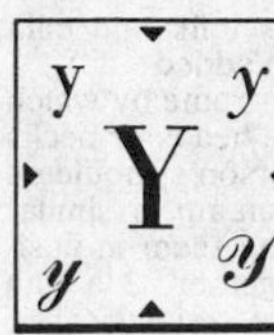

y \'wī\ *n, often cap* : the 25th letter of the English alphabet

¹yacht \'yät\ *n* : any of various relatively small sailing or mechanically driven ships that usu. have a sharp prow and graceful lines and are used esp. for pleasure cruising or racing

²yacht *vi* : to race or cruise in a yacht

yacht•ing \'yät-iŋ\ *n* : the action, fact, or pastime of racing or cruising in a yacht

yachts•man \'yäts-mən\ *n* : a person who owns or sails a yacht

ya•hoo \'yā-hü, 'yä-\ *n, pl* **yahoos** : an uncouth or rowdy person

Yah•weh \'yä-ˌwā, -ˌvā\ *n* : the God of the Hebrews

¹yak \'yak\ *n* : a large long-haired wild or domesticated ox of Tibet and adjacent elevated parts of central Asia

²yak *n* : persistent or voluble talk — **yak** *vi*

yam \'yam\ *n* **1** : an edible starchy tuberous root of a twining vine that is a staple food in tropical areas **2** : a moist-fleshed and usu. orange-fleshed sweet potato

yam•mer \'yam-ər\ *vi* **yam•mered**; **yam•mer•ing** \'yam-(ə-)riŋ\ **1** : WHIMPER **2** : CHATTER — **yammer** *n*

¹yank \'yaŋk\ *n* : a strong sudden pull : JERK

²yank *vb* : to pull or pull on or out with a quick vigorous movement

Yank \'yaŋk\ *n* : YANKEE

Yan•kee \'yaŋ-kē\ *n* **1 a** : a native or inhabitant of New England **b** : a native or inhabitant of the northern U.S. **2** : a native or inhabitant of the U.S. — **Yankee** *adj*

¹yap \'yap\ *vi* **yapped**; **yap•ping** **1** : to bark in yaps : YELP **2** : CHATTER, SCOLD

²yap *n* **1** : a quick sharp bark : YELP **2** : often complaining chatter

¹yard \'yärd\ *n* **1** : any of various units of measure; *esp* : a unit of length equal in the U.S. to 0.9144 meter **2** : a long spar tapered toward the ends that supports and spreads the head of a sail

²yard *n* **1 a** : a small usu. enclosed area open to the sky and adjacent to a building **b** : the grounds of a building or group of buildings **2 a** : an enclosure for livestock **b** : an area with its buildings and facilities set aside for a particular business or activity **c** : a system of railroad tracks for storage and maintenance of cars and making up trains

³yard *vb* : to drive into, gather, or confine in or as if in a yard

yard•age \'yärd-ij\ *n* : an aggregate number of yards; *also* : the length, extent, or volume of something as measured in yards

yard•arm \'yärd-ˌärm\ *n* : either end of the yard of a square-rigged ship

yard•mas•ter \-ˌmas-tər\ *n* : the man in charge of operations in a railroad yard

yard•stick \-ˌstik\ *n* **1** : a measuring stick a yard long **2** : a rule or standard by which something is measured or judged

¹yarn \'yärn\ *n* **1 a** : textile fiber (as spun wool, cotton, flax, or silk) for use in weaving, knitting, or the manufacture of thread **b** : a similar strand of metal, glass, asbestos, paper, or plastic **2** : an interesting or exciting story often told without regard for strict accuracy

²yarn *vi* : to tell a yarn

yar•row \'yar-ō\ *n* : a strong-scented herb related to the daisies that has finely divided leaves and white or rarely pink flowers in flat clusters

yaw \'yȯ\ *vi* : to turn abruptly from a straight course : SWERVE, VEER — **yaw** *n*

yawl \'yȯl\ *n* **1** : a ship's small boat **2** : a fore-and-aft rigged sailboat carrying a mainsail and one or more jibs

¹yawn \'yȯn\ *vb* **1** : to open wide : GAPE **2** : to open the mouth wide usu. as an involuntary reaction to fatigue or boredom **3** : to utter with a yawn — **yawn•er** *n*

²yawn *n* : a deep usu. involuntary intake of breath through the wide-open mouth

yawn•ing \'yȯ-niŋ\ *adj* **1** : wide open : CAVERNOUS **2** : showing fatigue or boredom by yawns

¹yawp *or* **yaup** \'yȯp\ *vi* **1** : to make a raucous noise : SQUAWK **2** : CLAMOR, COMPLAIN — **yawp•er** *n*

²yawp *n* : a raucous noise : SQUAWK

yaws \'yȯz\ *n sing or pl* : a tropical disease caused by a spirochete and marked by ulcerating surface lesions with later bone involvement

¹yea \'yā\ *adv* **1** : YES — used in oral voting **2** — used as a function word to introduce a more explicit or emphatic phrase

²yea *n* **1** : AFFIRMATION, ASSENT **2 a** : an affirmative vote **b** : a person casting a yea vote

yean•ling \'(y)ēn-liŋ\ *n* : LAMB, KID

year \'yi(ə)r\ *n* **1** : the period of one apparent revolution of the sun around the ecliptic or of the earth's revolution around the sun amounting to approximately 365¼ days **2 a** : a period of 365 days or in leap year 366 days beginning January 1 **b** : a period of time equal to this but beginning at a different time **3** : a continuous period of time that constitutes the period of some event (as revolution of a planet about its sun) or activity whether greater or less than the calendar year

year•book \-ˌbu̇k\ *n* **1** : a book published yearly esp. as a report : ANNUAL **2** : a school publication recording the history and activities of a graduating class

year•ling \-liŋ\ *n* : one (as a horse) that is or is rated as a year old — **yearling** *adj*

year•long \-'lȯŋ\ *adj* : lasting through a year

year•ly \-lē\ *adj* **1** : occurring, done, produced, or acted upon every year : ANNUAL **2** : computed in terms of one year — **yearly** *adv*

yearn \'yərn\ *vi* **1** : to feel a longing or craving **2** : to feel tenderness or compassion — **yearn•er** *n*

yearn•ing \'yər-niŋ\ *n* : a tender or urgent longing

yeast \'yēst\ *n* **1 a** : a surface froth or a sediment that occurs esp. in sweet liquids in which it promotes alcoholic fermentation, consists largely of cells of a tiny fungus, and is used esp. in the making of alcoholic liquors and as a leaven in baking **b** : a commercial product containing yeast plants in a moist or dry medium **c** : any of various tiny fungi that are usu. one-celled and reproduce by budding; *esp* : one present and functionally active in a yeast froth or sediment **2** : foam or spume esp. of waves **3** : something that causes ferment or activity — **yeasty** \'yē-stē\ *adj*

¹yell \'yel\ *vb* **1** : to utter a loud cry, scream, or shout **2** : to give a cheer usu. in unison **3** : to utter or declare with or as if with a yell : SHOUT — **yell•er** *n*

²yell *n* **1** : SCREAM, SHOUT **2** : a usu. rhythmic cheer used esp. in schools or colleges to encourage athletic teams

¹yel•low \'yel-ō\ *adj* **1 a** : of the color yellow **b** : yellowish from age, disease, or discoloration **c** : having a yellow complexion or skin **2 a** : featuring sensational or scandalous items or ordinary news sensationally distorted **b** : COWARDLY

²yellow *vb* : to make or turn yellow

³yellow *n* **1** : a color whose hue resembles that of ripe lemons or sunflowers or is that of the portion of the spectrum lying between green and orange **2** : something yellow or marked by a yellow color **3** *pl* **a** : JAUNDICE **b** : any of several plant virus diseases marked by yellowing of the foliage and stunting

yellow fever *n* : an acute destructive infectious disease of warm regions marked by sudden onset, prostration, fever, jaundice, and often hemorrhage and caused by a virus transmitted by a mosquito

yel•low•ish \'yel-ə-wish\ *adj* : somewhat yellow

yellow jack *n* **1** : YELLOW FEVER **2** : a flag raised on ships in quarantine

yellow jacket *n* : any of various small yellow-marked social

wasps that commonly nest in the ground
[1]**yelp** \'yelp\ *vi* : to utter a sharp quick shrill cry — **yelp·er** *n*
[2]**yelp** *n* : a sharp shrill bark or cry (as of a dog)
yen \'yen\ *n* : an intense desire : URGE, LONGING
yeo·man \'yō-mən\ *n* **1 a** : an attendant or officer in a royal or noble household **b** : a naval petty officer who performs clerical duties **2** : a small farmer who cultivates his own land; *esp* : one of a class of English freeholders below the gentry
yeo·man·ly \-lē\ *adj* : becoming to a yeoman : STURDY, SELF-RELIANT, LOYAL
yeo·man·ry \'yō-mən-rē\ *n* : the body of yeomen and esp. of small landed proprietors
[1]**yes** \'yes\ *adv* **1** — used as a function word to express assent or agreement **2** — used as a function word to introduce correction or contradiction of a negative assertion, direction, or request **3** — used as a function word to introduce a more emphatic or explicit phrase **4** — used as a function word to indicate interest or attentiveness
[2]**yes** *n* : an affirmative reply
yes–man \'yes-ˌman\ *n* : a person who agrees with everything that is said to him; *esp* : one who endorses without criticism every opinion or proposal of a superior
[1]**yes·ter·day** \'yes-tərd-ē\ *adv* **1** : on the day preceding today **2** : at a time not long past : only a short time ago
[2]**yesterday** *n* **1** : the day next before the present **2** : recent time : time not long past
yes·ter·year \'yes-tər-ˌyi(ə)r\ *n* **1** : last year **2** : the recent past
[1]**yet** \(')yet\ *adv* **1 a** : in addition : BESIDES **b** : EVEN 2b **2 a** (1) : up to now : so far (2) : at this or that time : so soon as now **b** : continuously up to the present or a specified time : STILL **c** : at a future time : EVENTUALLY **3** : NEVERTHELESS, HOWEVER
[2]**yet** *conj* : despite that fact : BUT
yew \'yü\ *n* **1** : any of a genus of evergreen trees and shrubs with stiff poisonous needles and fleshy fruits **2** : the wood of a yew; *esp* : the heavy fine-grained wood of an Old World yew that is used for bows and small articles
[1]**yield** \'yēld\ *vb* **1** : to give up possession of on claim or demand : hand over possession of **2** : to give (oneself) up to an inclination, temptation, or habit **3 a** : to bear or bring forth as a natural product esp. as a result of cultivation **b** : to furnish as return or result of expended effort **c** : to furnish as profit or interest **d** : to produce as revenue : bring in **4** : to be fruitful or productive **5** : to give up **6** : to give way to pressure or influence **7** : to give way under physical force so as to bend, stretch, or break **8** : to give place or precedence — **yield·er** *n*
[2]**yield** *n* : something yielded : PRODUCT; *esp* : the amount or quantity produced or returned
yield·ing \'yēl-diŋ\ *adj* **1** : lacking rigidity or stiffness : FLEXIBLE **2** : disposed to submit or comply
yip \'yip\ *vi* **yipped**; **yip·ping** : YELP — used chiefly of a dog — **yip** *n*
[1]**yo·del** \'yōd-ᵊl\ *vb* **-deled** *or* **-delled**; **-del·ing** *or* **-del·ling** \'yōd-liŋ, -ᵊl-iŋ\ : to sing by suddenly changing from the natural voice to falsetto and the reverse; *also* : to shout or call in this manner — **yo·del·er** \'yōd-lər, -ᵊl-ər\ *n*
[2]**yodel** *n* : a song or refrain sung by yodeling; *also* : a yodeled shout
yo·ga \'yō-gə\ *n* **1** *cap* : a Hindu theistic philosophy teaching the suppression of all activity of body, mind, and will in order that the self may realize its distinction from them and attain liberation **2** : a system of exercises for attaining bodily or mental control and well-being — **yo·gic** \-gik\ *adj, often cap*
yo·gi \'yō-gē\ *n* **1** : a person who practices yoga **2** *cap* : an adherent of Yoga philosophy
yo·gurt *or* **yo·ghurt** \'yō-gərt\ *n* : a fermented slightly acid semifluid milk food made of skimmed cow's milk and milk solids to which cultures of bacteria have been added
[1]**yoke** \'yōk\ *n, pl* **yokes 1 a** : a wooden bar or frame by which two draft animals (as oxen) are coupled at the heads or necks for working together **b** : a frame fitted to a person's shoulders to carry a load in two equal portions **c** : a clamp or similar piece that embraces two parts to hold or unite them in position **2** *pl usu* **yoke** : two animals yoked together **3 a** : an oppressive agency **b** : SERVITUDE, BONDAGE **c** : TIE, LINK **4** : a fitted or shaped piece at the top of a skirt or at the shoulder of various garments
[2]**yoke** *vb* **1 a** : to put a yoke on or couple with a yoke **b** : to attach (a draft animal) to something **2** : to join as if by a yoke **3** : to put to work
yoke·fellow \-ˌfel-ō\ *n* : a close companion : MATE
yo·kel \'yō-kəl\ *n* : RUSTIC, BUMPKIN
yolk \'yōk, 'yōlk\ *n* **1 a** : the yellow inner mass of the egg of a bird or reptile **b** : the material stored in an ovum that supplies food material to the developing embryo **2** : oily material in raw sheep wool — **yolk** *adj* — **yolked** \'yō(l)kt\ *adj* — **yolky** \'yō(l)-kē\ *adj*
Yom Kip·pur \ˌyȯm-'kip-ər, ˌyōm-, -ki-'pu̇(ə)r\ *n* : a Jewish holiday observed in September or October with fasting and prayer as a day of atonement
[1]**yon** \'yän\ *adj* : YONDER
[2]**yon** *adv* **1** : YONDER **2** : THITHER
[1]**yon·der** \'yän-dər\ *adv* : at or to that place : over there
[2]**yonder** *adj* **1** : farther removed : more distant **2** : being at a distance within view
yore \'yō(ə)r\ *n* : time long past — usu. used in the phrase *of yore*
you \(')yü, yə\ *pron* **1** : the one or ones spoken to — used as the pronoun of the 2d person singular or plural in any grammatical relation except that of a possessive; used formerly only as a plural pronoun of the 2d person in the objective case **2** : [2]ONE 1b
[1]**young** \'yəŋ\ *adj* **young·er** \'yəŋ-gər\; **young·est** \'yəŋ-gəst\ **1 a** : being in the first or an early stage of life, growth, or development **b** : JUNIOR 1a **2** : having little experience **3** : recently come into being : NEW **4** : of, relating to, or having the characteristics of youth or a young person **5** *cap* : belonging to or representing a new or revived usu. political group or movement — **young·ness** *n*
[2]**young** *n, pl* **young 1** *pl* **a** : young persons : YOUTH **b** : immature offspring esp. of lower animals **2** : a single recently born or hatched animal — **with young** : PREGNANT — used of animals
young·er \'yəŋ-gər\ *n* : an inferior in age : JUNIOR — usu. used with a possessive pronoun
young·est \'yəŋ-gəst\ *n* : one that is the least old esp. of a family
young·ish \'yəŋ-ish\ *adj* : somewhat young
young·ling \'yəŋ-liŋ\ *n* : one that is young : a young person or animal — **youngling** *adj*
young·ster \'yəŋ(k)-stər\ *n* **1** : a young person : YOUTH **2** : CHILD
youn·ker \'yəŋ-kər\ *n* **1** : a young man **2** : CHILD, YOUNGSTER
your \yər, (')yu̇(ə)r, (')yō(ə)r\ *adj* **1** : of or relating to you esp. as possessor, agent, or object of an action **2** : of or relating to one **3** — used before a title of honor in address
yours \'yu̇(ə)rz, 'yō(ə)rz\ *pron* : your one : your ones — used without a following noun as a pronoun equivalent in meaning to the adjective *your;* often used esp. with an adverbial modifier in the complimentary close of a letter
your·self \yər-'self\ *pron, pl* **your·selves** \-'selvz\ **1 a** : that identical one that is you — used reflexively, for emphasis, or in absolute constructions **b** : your normal, healthy, or sane condition or self **2** : ONESELF

youth \'yüth\ *n, pl* **youths** \'yüt͟hz, 'yüths\ **1 :** the time of life marked by growth and development; *esp* **:** the period between childhood and maturity **2 a :** a young man **b :** young persons — usu. pl. in constr. **3 :** YOUTHFULNESS
youth•ful \'yüth-fəl\ *adj* **1 :** of, relating to, or appropriate to youth **2 :** being young and not yet mature **3 :** FRESH, VIGOROUS — **youth•ful•ly** \-fə-lē\ *adv* — **youth•ful•ness** *n*
[1]**yowl** \'yau̇l\ *vi* **:** to utter a loud long often mournful cry **:** WAIL
[2]**yowl** *n* **:** a loud long mournful wail or howl (as of a cat)
yt•ter•bi•um \i-'tər-bē-əm\ *n* **:** a metallic chemical element that occurs in several minerals
yt•tri•um \'i-trē-əm\ *n* **:** a metallic chemical element usu. included among the rare-earth metals with which it occurs in minerals
yuc•ca \'yək-ə\ *n* **:** any of a genus of plants of the lily family growing in dry regions and having stiff sharp-pointed fibrous leaves mostly in a rosette at the base and whitish flowers usu. in erect clusters
yule \'yül\ *n, often cap* **:** the feast of the nativity of Jesus Christ **:** CHRISTMAS
yule log *n, often cap Y* **:** a large log formerly put on the hearth on Christmas Eve as the foundation of the fire
yule•tide \'yül-,tīd\ *n, often cap* **:** the Christmas season

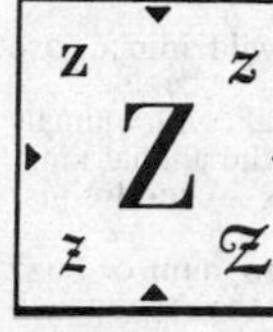

z \'zē\ *n, often cap* **:** the 26th letter of the English alphabet
[1]**za•ny** \'zā-nē\ *n, pl* **zanies :** CLOWN, BUFFOON; *also* **:** SIMPLETON
[2]**zany** *adj* **1 :** being or having the characteristics of a zany **2 :** fantastically or irrationally ludicrous **:** CRAZY — **za•ni•ly** \'zān-ᵊl-ē\ *adv* — **za•ni•ness** \'zā-nē-nəs\ *n*
zeal \'zēl\ *n* **:** eagerness and ardent interest in pursuit of something **:** FERVOR
zeal•ot \'zel-ət\ *n* **:** a zealous person; *esp* **:** a fanatical partisan — **zealot** *adj* — **zeal•ot•ry** \'zel-ə-trē\ *n*
zeal•ous \'zel-əs\ *adj* **:** filled with, characterized by, or due to zeal — **zeal•ous•ly** *adv* — **zeal•ous•ness** *n*
ze•bra \'zē-brə\ *n* **:** any of several fleet African mammals related to the horse but distinctively and conspicuously patterned in stripes of black or dark brown and white or buff — **ze•brine** \-,brīn\ *adj* — **ze•broid** \-,brȯid\ *adj*
ze•bu \'zē-b(y)ü\ *n* **:** an Asiatic ox domesticated and differentiated into many breeds and distinguished from European cattle with which it crosses freely by a large fleshy hump over the shoulders and a loose skin prolonged into dewlap and folds
zeit•geist \'tsīt-,gīst, 'zīt-\ *n* **:** the general intellectual, moral, and cultural state of an era
Zen \'zen\ *n* **:** a Japanese Buddhist sect that teaches self-discipline, meditation, and attainment of enlightenment by direct intuition and characteristically expresses its teachings by means of paradoxical and nonlogical statements
ze•na•na \zə-'nän-ə\ *n* **:** HAREM, SERAGLIO
ze•nith \'zē-nəth\ *n* **1 :** the point in the heavens directly overhead **2 :** the highest point **:** APEX, SUMMIT
zeph•yr \'zef-ər\ *n* **1 a :** a breeze from the west **b :** a gentle breeze **2 :** a fine soft wool yarn
zep•pe•lin \'zep-(ə-)lən\ *n* **:** a rigid airship consisting of a cylindrical trussed and covered frame supported by internal gas cells
[1]**ze•ro** \'zē-rō\ *n, pl* **zeros 1 a :** the numerical symbol 0 **b :** the number represented by the symbol 0 — see NUMBER table **2 a :** the point from which the graduation of a scale (as of a thermometer) commences **b :** the temperature represented by the zero mark on a thermometer **3 :** the lowest point **:** NADIR
[2]**zero** *vb* **1 :** to concentrate firepower (as of artillery) on the exact range of — usu. used with *in* **2 :** to adjust fire on a specific target — usu. used with *in*
zero hour *n* **1 :** the hour at which a previously planned military movement is scheduled to start **2 :** the moment at which an ordeal is to begin **:** the moment of crisis
zest \'zest\ *n* **1 :** a quality of enhancing enjoyment **:** PIQUANCY **2 :** keen enjoyment **:** RELISH, GUSTO — **zest•ful** \-fəl\ *adj* — **zest•ful•ly** \-fə-lē\ *adv* — **zest•ful•ness** *n* — **zesty** \'zes-tē\ *adj*
[1]**zig•zag** \'zig-,zag\ *n* **:** a line or course made up of sharp opposite angles or turns at short and rather regular intervals; *also* **:** one of the units making it up
[2]**zigzag** *adv* **:** in or by a zigzag path or course
[3]**zigzag** *adj* **:** having short sharp turns or angles
[4]**zigzag** *vi* **zig•zagged; zig•zag•ging :** to lie in, proceed along, or consist of a zigzag course
zinc \'ziŋk\ *n* **:** a bluish white metallic chemical element that tarnishes only slightly in moist air at ordinary temperatures and is used esp. as a protective coating for iron
zinc ointment *n* **:** an ointment containing about 20 percent of zinc oxide and used in treating skin diseases
zinc oxide *n* **:** an infusible white solid used esp. as a pigment, in compounding rubber, and in pharmaceutical and cosmetic preparations
zing \'ziŋ\ *n* **1 :** a shrill humming noise **2 :** VITALITY, VIM — **zing** *vi*
zin•nia \'zin-ē-ə, 'zin-yə, 'zēn-\ *n* **:** any of a small genus of tropical American herbs related to the daisies and having showy long-lasting flower heads
Zi•on \'zī-ən\ *n* **1 a :** the Jewish people **:** ISRAEL **b :** the Jewish homeland as a symbol of Judaism or of Jewish national aspiration **c :** the ideal nation or society envisaged by Judaism **2 :** HEAVEN **3 :** UTOPIA
Zi•on•ism \'zī-ə-,niz-əm\ *n* **:** a theory, plan, or movement for setting up a Jewish national or religious community in Palestine — **Zi•on•ist** \-nəst\ *adj or n* — **Zi•on•is•tic** \,zī-ə-'nis-tik\ *adj*
[1]**zip** \'zip\ *vb* **zipped; zip•ping :** to move or act with speed and vigor
[2]**zip** *n* **1 :** a sudden sharp hissing or sibilant sound **2 :** ENERGY, VIM
[3]**zip** *vb* **zipped; zip•ping :** to close or open or attach by means of a zipper
zip code \'zip-,\ *n, often cap Z & I & P* **1 :** a 5-digit code that identifies each postal delivery area in the U.S. **2 :** a 5-digit number placed after the name or abbreviation of the state in the address on postal matter
zip gun *n* **:** a gun that is made from a toy pistol or a length of pipe, is usu. powered by a rubber band, and fires a .22 caliber bullet
zip•per \'zip-ər\ *n* **:** a fastener consisting of two rows of metal or plastic teeth on strips of tape and a sliding piece that closes an opening by drawing the teeth together
zip•py \'zip-ē\ *adj* **:** full of zip **:** BRISK, SNAPPY
zir•con \'zər-,kän\ *n* **1 :** a crystalline mineral which is a silicate of zirconium and of which several transparent varieties are used as gems **2 :** a gem cut from zircon

zir·co·ni·um \ˌzər-ˈkō-nē-əm\ *n* : a steel-gray strong ductile metallic chemical element with a high melting point that is highly resistant to corrosion and is used in alloys and in refractories and ceramics

zith·er \ˈzit͟h-ər, ˈzith-\ *n* : a many-stringed musical instrument played with the tips of the fingers and a plectrum — **zith·er·ist** \-ə-rəst\ *n*

zo·di·ac \ˈzōd-ē-ˌak\ *n* **1** : an imaginary belt in the heavens that encompasses the apparent paths of all the principal planets except Pluto, that has as its central line the apparent path of the sun, and that is divided into 12 constellations or signs each taken for astrological purposes to extend 30 degrees of longitude **2** : a figure representing the signs of the zodiac and their symbols — **zo·di·a·cal** \zō-ˈdī-ə-kəl\ *adj*

zodiac

zom·bi *or* **zom·bie** \ˈzäm-bē\ *n* : a will-less and speechless human in the West Indies capable only of automatic movement who is held to have died and been reanimated but often believed to have been drugged into catalepsy for the hours of interment

zon·al \ˈzōn-ᵊl\ *adj* : of, relating to, or having the form of a zone

zon·ate \ˈzō-ˌnāt\ *adj* : marked with or arranged in zones — **zo·na·tion** \zō-ˈnā-shən\ *n*

¹zone \ˈzōn\ *n* **1** : any of five great divisions of the earth's surface with respect to latitude and temperature **2** : a distinctive belt, layer, or series of layers of earth materials (as rock) **3** : a region or area set off as distinct from surrounding or adjoining parts or created for a particular purpose

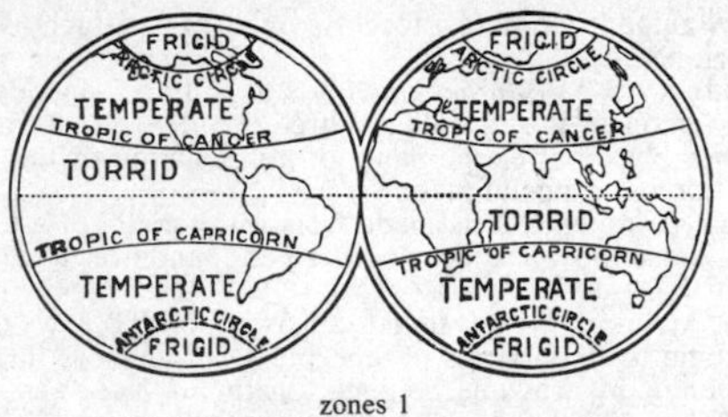

zones 1

²zone *vt* **1** : to surround with a zone : ENCIRCLE **2** : to arrange in or mark off into zones; *esp* : to divide (as a city) into sections reserved for different purposes

zoo \ˈzü\ *n, pl* **zoos** : a zoological garden or collection of living animals

zoo·ge·og·ra·phy \ˌzō-ə-jē-ˈäg-rə-fē\ *n* : a branch of biogeography concerned with the geographical distribution of animals — **zoo·ge·og·ra·pher** \-fər\ *n* — **zoo·ge·o·graph·ic** \-ˌjē-ə-ˈgraf-ik\ *or* **zoo·ge·o·graph·i·cal** \-ˈgraf-i-kəl\ *adj* — **zoo·ge·o·graph·i·cal·ly** \-i-k(ə-)lē\ *adv*

zo·oid \ˈzō-ˌȯid\ *n* : an entity (as a blood cell) that resembles (as in independent motility) but is not wholly the same as a separate individual organism; *esp* : a more or less independent animal (as a polyp of a colonial coral) produced by other than direct sexual methods — **zo·oi·dal** \zō-ˈȯid-ᵊl\ *adj*

zo·o·log·i·cal \ˌzō-ə-ˈläj-i-kəl\ *adj* **1** : of, relating to, or occupied with zoology **2** : of, relating to, or affecting lower animals often as distinguished from man — **zo·o·log·i·cal·ly** \-i-k(ə-)lē\ *adv*

zoological garden *n* : a garden or park where wild animals are kept for exhibition

zo·ol·o·gy \zō-ˈäl-ə-jē\ *n* **1** : a science that deals with animals and is the branch of biology concerned with the animal kingdom and animal life **2** : animal life : FAUNA — **zo·ol·o·gist** \-jəst\ *n*

¹zoom \ˈzüm\ *vb* **1** : to move with a loud low hum or buzz **2** : to climb for a short time at an angle greater than that which can be maintained in steady flight

²zoom *n* **1** : an act or process of zooming **2** : a zooming sound

zoo·mor·phic \ˌzō-ə-ˈmȯr-fik\ *adj* **1** : having the form of an animal **2** : of, relating to, or being a deity conceived of in animal form or with the attributes of an animal — **zoo·mor·phism** \-ˌfiz-əm\ *n*

zoo·phyte \ˈzō-ə-ˌfīt\ *n* : any of numerous invertebrate animals (as a coral or sponge) suggesting plants in appearance or mode of growth — **zoo·phyt·ic** \ˌzō-ə-ˈfit-ik\ *adj*

zoo·spore \ˈzō-ə-ˌspōr\ *n* : an independently motile spore

Zou·ave \zü-ˈäv\ *n* **1** : a member of a French infantry unit orig. composed of Algerians wearing a brilliant uniform and conducting a quick spirited drill **2** : a member of a military unit modeled on the Algerian Zouaves

zounds \ˈzau̇n(d)z\ *interj* — used as a mild oath

zuc·chet·to \zü-ˈket-ō\ *n, pl* **-tos** : a small round skullcap worn by Roman Catholic ecclesiastics

zwie·back \ˈswē-ˌbak, ˈswī-\ *n* : a usu. sweetened bread enriched with eggs that is baked and then sliced and toasted until dry and crisp

zy·gote \ˈzī-ˌgōt\ *n* : a cell formed by the union of two gametes — **zy·got·ic** \zī-ˈgät-ik\ *adj* — **zy·got·i·cal·ly** \-ˈgät-i-k(ə-)lē\ *adv*

zy·mase \ˈzī-ˌmās\ *n* : an enzyme or enzyme complex that promotes fermentation of simple sugars

ABBREVIATIONS

AND SYMBOLS FOR CHEMICAL ELEMENTS

Most of these abbreviations have been normalized to one form. Variation in use of periods, in typeface, and in capitalization is frequent and widespread (as *mph, MPH, m.p.h., Mph*)

a acre, alto, answer, are
A ace, argon
AA Alcoholics Anonymous, associate in arts
A and M agricultural and mechanical
AB able-bodied seaman, bachelor of arts
abbr abbreviation
abl ablative
abp archbishop
abs absolute
ac account
Ac actinium
AC alternating current, ante Christum (L, before Christ), area code
acad academic, academy
acc, accus accusative
accel accelerando
acct account
ack acknowledge, acknowledgment
act active, actual
AD after date, anno Domini
ADC aide-de-camp
addn addition
adj adjective, adjutant
ad loc ad locum (L, to or at the place)
ADM admiral
adv adverb, adverbial, advertisement
ad val ad valorem
advt advertisement
AEF American Expeditionary Force
AF air force, audio frequency
AFB air force base
afft affidavit
AFL–CIO American Federation of Labor and Congress of Industrial Organizations
Afr Africa, African
Ag argentum (L, silver)
AG adjutant general, attorney general
agcy agency
agric agricultural, agriculture
agt agent
AK Alaska
Al aluminum
Al, Ala Alabama
alc alcohol
ald alderman
alg algebra
alk alkaline
alt alternate, altitude
Alta Alberta
alter alteration
a.m. ante meridiem
Am America, American, americium
AM amplitude modulation, master of arts
amb ambassador
amdt amendment
Amer America, American
amp ampere
amt amount
anal analogy, analysis, analytic
anc ancient
ann annals, annual
anon anonymous
ans answer
ant antonym
a/o account of
ap apothecaries'
AP additional premium, Associated Press
APO army post office
app apparatus, appendix
appl applied
Apr April
apt apartment
aq aqua, aqueous
ar arrival, arrive
Ar argon
AR Arkansas
Aram Aramaic
arch, archit architecture
arith arithmetic
Ariz Arizona
Ark Arkansas
arr arranged, arrival, arrive
art article, artificial
As arsenic
assn association
assoc associate, association
asst assistant
At astatine
Atl Atlantic
atm atmosphere, atmospheric
att attached, attention, attorney
attn attention
attrib attributive, attributively
atty attorney
Au aurum (L, gold)
Aug August
auth authentic, author, authorized
aux auxiliary
av avenue, average, avoirdupois
AV audiovisual
avdp avoirdupois
ave avenue
avg average
avn aviation
AZ Arizona

b back, bass, book, born
B bachelor, bishop, boron
Ba barium
BA bachelor of arts
bal balance
bar barometer, barometric, barrel
Bart baronet
bbl barrel
B.C. before Christ, British Columbia
BCS bachelor of commercial science
bd board, bound
BD bachelor of divinity
bdl bundle
Be beryllium
BE bill of exchange
bet between
bf boldface
bg bag
Bi bismuth
bib Bible, biblical
BID bis in die (L, twice a day)
biog biographical, biography
biol biologic, biological, biology
bk bank, book
Bk berkelium
bkt basket
bl bale
B/L bill of lading
bldg building
blvd boulevard
BO body odor, branch office
BOQ bachelor officers' quarters
bor borough
bot botanical, botany, bottom
bp bishop, boiling point
bpl birthplace
br branch
Br British, bromine
brig brigade, brigadier
Brit Britain, British
bro brother
bros brothers
BS bachelor of science
BSc bachelor of science
bskt basket
Bt baronet
bu bushel
bull bulletin
bur bureau
bus business
BV Blessed Virgin
B.W.I. British West Indies
bx box

c cape, carat, cent, centimeter, century, chapter, circa, copyright, cup
C carbon, Celsius, centigrade
ca centare, circa
CA calcium
CA California, chartered accountant, chief accountant
cal calendar, caliber, calorie
Cal large calorie
Calif, Cal California
Can, Canad Canadian
canc canceled
cap capacity, capital, capitalize, capitalized
caps capitals, capsule
Capt captain
card cardinal
CARE Co-operative for American Remittances to Everywhere
cat catalog
Cb columbium
CB citizens band
CBD cash before delivery
cc cubic centimeter
CC carbon copy, common carrier
cd cord
Cd cadmium
CDR commander
Ce cerium
CE chemical engineer, civil engineer
Celt Celtic
cen central
cent centigrade, central, century
cert certificate, certification, certified, certify
cf confer (L, compare)
Cf californium
cg, cgm centigram
CG coast guard
ch chain, chapter, church
CH clearinghouse, courthouse, customhouse
chap chapter
chem chemical, chemist, chemistry
chg change, charge
Chin Chinese
chm, chmn chairman
chron chronicle, chronological, chronology
CIA Central Intelligence Agency
C in C commander in chief
cir, circ circular
cit citation, cited, citizen
civ civil, civilian
ck cask, check
cl centiliter, class
Cl chlorine
CL carload
clk clerk
clo clothing
cm centimeter
Cm curium
CM Congregation of the Mission
cml commercial
CNO chief of naval operations
co company, county
c/o care of
Co cobalt
CO cash order, Colorado, commanding officer, conscientious objector
COD cash on delivery, collect on delivery
C of C Chamber of Commerce
C of S chief of staff
col column
Col colonel
coll college
Colo Colorado
com commander, commerce, commissioner, committee, common
comb combination, combining
comdg commanding
comdr commander
comdt commandant
coml commercial
comm commission, commonwealth
comp comparative, compiled, compiler, composition, compound
comr commissioner
con consul, contra (L, against)
conc concentrated
conf conference
cong congress
conj conjunction
Conn Connecticut
cons conservative, consonant
consol consolidated
const constant, constitution, constitutional
constr construction
cont containing, contents, continent, continental, continued, control
contd continued
contg containing
contr contract, contraction
contrib contribution, contributor
corp corporal, corporation

corr corrected, correction, correspondence, corresponding
cos companies, counties
COS cash on shipment, chief of staff
cp compare, coupon
CP chemically pure, communist party
CPA certified public accountant
cpd compound
Cpl corporal
CPO chief petty officer
CPS cycles per second
cr credit, creditor, crown
Cr chromium
cresc crescendo
crit critical, criticism
cs case, cases
c/s cycles per second
Cs cesium
CS chief of staff, civil service
CSA Confederate States of America
CSSR Congregation of the Most Holy Redeemer (L, Congregatio Sanctissimi Redemptoris)
CST Central standard time
ct carat, cent, count, court
CT Connecticut
ctn carton
ctr center
cu cubic
Cu cuprum (L, copper)
cur currency, current
CV cardiovascular
CWO cash with order, chief warrant officer
cwt hundredweight
cyc, cycl cyclopedia
cyl cylinder
CZ Canal Zone

d date, daughter, day, degree, density, died, penny
D Democrat, Democratic, deuterium, diameter, dollar, Dutch
DA district attorney
dag dekagram
dal dekaliter
dam dekameter
DAR Daughters of the American Revolution
dat dative
db debenture, decibel
dbl double
DC da capo (It, from the beginning), direct current, District of Columbia, Doctor of Chiropractic
DD doctor of divinity
DDD direct distance dialing
DDS doctor of dental science, doctor of dental surgery
DE Delaware
deb debenture
dec decrease
Dec December
def definite, definition
deg degree
del delegate, delegation
Del Delaware
dely delivery
Dem Democrat, Democratic
dent dental, dentistry
dep depart, departure, deposit, deputy
dept department
deriv derivation, derivative
det detached, detachment, detail
DEW distant early warning
DFC distinguished flying cross
DFM distinguished flying medal
dg decigram
DG Dei gratia (LL, by the grace of God)
DH designated hitter
dia, diam diameter
diag diagonal, diagram
dial dialect
dict dictionary
diff difference
dig digest
dil dilute
dim dimension, diminished, diminuendo, diminutive
dir director
disc discount
dist distance, district
distn distillation
distr distribute, distribution
div divided, dividend, division
dk dark
dkg dekagram
dkl dekaliter
dkm dekameter
dks dekastere
dl deciliter
DLitt, DLit doctór of letters, doctor of literature
DLO dead letter office
dm decimeter
dn down
DNA deoxyribonucleic acid
do ditto
DOA dead on arrival
doc document
dol dollar
dom domestic, dominion
doz dozen
DP data processing
dpt department
dr debit, debtor, dram, drive
Dr doctor
ds decistere
DS dal segno (It, from the sign), days after sight
DSC distinguished service cross
DSM distinguished service medal
DSO distinguished service order
DST daylight saving time
Du Dutch
dup, dupl duplicate
DV Deo volente (L, God willing), Douay Version
DVM doctor of veterinary medicine
dwt pennyweight
DX distance
Dy dysprosium
dz dozen

E east, eastern, einsteinium, English, excellent
ea each
eccl ecclesiastic, ecclesiastical
ecol ecological, ecology
econ economics, economist
ed edited, edition, editor, education
EDT Eastern daylight time
educ education, educational
e.g. exempli gratia (L, for example)
ehf extremely high frequency
el, elev elevation
elec electric, electrical, electricity
elem elementary
emer emeritus
EMF electromotive force
emp emperor, empress
emu electromagnetic unit
enc, encl enclosure
ency, encyc encyclopedia
eng engine, engineer, engineering
Eng England, English
engr engineer, engraved, engraving
enl enlarged, enlisted
ENS ensign
env envelope
EOM end of month
EP extended play
eq equal, equation
equip equipment
equiv equivalent
Er erbium
Es einsteinium
esp especially
ESP extrasensory perception
esq esquire
est established, estimate, estimated
EST Eastern standard time
ETA estimated time of arrival
et al et alii (L, and others)
etc et cetera
ETD estimated time of departure
et seq et sequens (L, and the following one), et sequentes *or* et sequentia (L, and those that follow)
Eu europium
Eur Europe, European
EV electron volt
evap evaporate
ex example, express, extra
exc excellent, except
exch exchange, exchanged
ex div without dividend
exec executive
exp expense, export, exported, express
expt experiment
exptl experimental
ext extension, exterior, external, extra, extract

f female, feminine, focal length, folio, following, forte, frequency
F Fahrenheit, fluorine, French
fac facsimile, faculty
FADM fleet admiral
Fahr Fahrenheit
FAO Food and Agriculture Organization of the United Nations
FAS free alongside
fath fathom
FBI Federal Bureau of Investigation
fcy fancy
FDIC Federal Deposit Insurance Corporation
Fe ferrum (L, iron)
Feb February
fed federal, federation
fem female, feminine
fem feminine
FEPC Fair Employment Practices Commission
ff folios, following, fortissimo
FICA Federal Insurance Contributions Act
FIFO first in, first out
fig figurative, figuratively, figure
fin finance, financial, finish
fl flourished, fluid
FL, Fla Florida
fl dr fluidram
fl oz fluidounce
fm fathom
Fm fermium
FM frequency modulation
fn footnote
fo, fol folio
FOB free on board
FOC free of charge
for foreign, forestry
FOR free on rail
FOS free on steamer
FOT free on truck
fp freezing point
fpm feet per minute
FPO fleet post office
fps feet per second
fr father, friar, from
Fr francium, French
freq frequent, frequently
Fri Friday
front frontispiece
FRS Federal Reserve System
frt freight
frwy freeway
FSH follicle-stimulating hormone
ft feet, foot, fort
fur furlong
fut future
fwd forward

g acceleration of gravity, gauge, gram, gravity
G German, good
ga gauge
Ga gallium, Georgia
GA general agent, general assembly, general average, Georgia
Gael Gaelic
gal gallon
galv galvanized
gar garage
GAW guaranteed annual wage
gaz gazette, gazetteer
GB Great Britain
GCA ground-controlled approach
Gd gadolinium
gds goods
Ge germanium
gen general, genitive
genl general
geog geographic, geographical, geography
geol geologic, geological, geology
geom geometrical, geometry
ger gerund
Ger German, Germany
GHQ general headquarters
gi gill
GI general issue, government issue
Gk Greek
gm gram
GM general manager, grand master
Gmc Germanic
GNP gross national product
GOP Grand Old Party (Republican)
Goth Gothic
gov governor
govt government
gp group
GP general practitioner
GPO general post office, Government Printing Office
GQ general quarters
gr grade, grain, gram, gravity, gross
grad graduate
gram grammar
gro gross
gt great
Gt Brit Great Britain

h hard, hardness, hour, husband
H hydrogen
ha hectare
Hb hemoglobin
HC House of Commons
hd head
hdkf handkerchief
hdqrs headquarters
hdwe hardware
He helium
HE high explosive, His Eminence, His Excellency

Heb Hebrew
hf half, high frequency
Hf hafnium
Hg hydrargyrum (L, mercury)
hgt height
HH Her Highness, His Highness, His Holiness
HI Hawaii
hist historian, historical, history
HL House of Lords
HM Her Majesty, His Majesty
HMS Her Majesty's Ship, His Majesty's Ship
Ho holmium
hon honorable, honorary
hor horizontal
hort horticultural, horticulture
hosp hospital
HP high pressure, horsepower
HQ headquarters
hr hour
HR House of Representatives
HRH Her Royal Highness, His Royal Highness
HS high school
ht height
hwy highway
hy henry

I interstate, iodine, island, isle
Ia, IA Iowa
ib, ibid ibidem
ICBM intercontinental ballistic missile
id idem
ID Idaho, identification
i.e. id est (L, that is)
IF intermediate frequency
IGY International Geophysical Year
IL Illinois
ill, illus, illust illustrated, illustration
Ill Illinois
ILS instrument landing system
imit imitative
imp imperative, imperfect, imperial, import, imported, imprimatur
in inch
In indium
IN Indiana
inc incorporated, increase, incomplete
incl including, inclusive
incog incognito
ind independent, index, industrial, industry
Ind Indian, Indiana
indef indefinite
indic indicative
infl influenced
INRI Iesus Nazarenus Rex Iudaeorum (L, Jesus of Nazareth, King of the Jews)
ins inches, insurance
inst instant, institute, institution
instr instructor, instrument
int interest, interior, internal, international
interj interjection
intl international
inv invoice
IPA International Phonetic Alphabet
i.q. idem quod (L, the same as)
IQ intelligence quotient
Ir iridium, Irish
IRBM intermediate range ballistic missile
IrGael Irish Gaelic
is island
ISBN International Standard Book Number
ISV International Scientific Vocabulary
It, Ital Italian
ital italic, italicized
IU international unit
IV intravenous

J jack
Jan January
Jap Japan, Japanese
JCS joint chiefs of staff
jct junction
jg junior grade
jnt, jt joint
jour journal
JP jet propulsion, justice of the peace
jr, jun junior
junc junction
juv juvenile

k karat, knit
K kalium (L, potassium), king
Kans Kansas
kc kilocycle
KC King's Counsel
kc/s kilocycles per second
kg, kgm kilogram
KG knight of the Garter
KKK Ku Klux Klan
kl kiloliter
km kilometer
KP kitchen police
Kr krypton
KS Kansas
kt karat, knight
kw kilowatt
kwh, kwhr kilowatt-hour
Ky, KY Kentucky

l left, length, line, liter
L lake, large, Latin, libra (L, pound)
La lanthanum, Louisiana
LA Los Angeles, Louisiana
lang language
lat latitude
Lat Latin
lb libra (L, pound)
lc lowercase
LC letter of credit, Library of Congress
LCL less-than-carload lot
ld load, lord
ldg landing, loading
lect lecture
leg legal, legislative, legislature
legis legislative, legislature
lf lightface, low frequency
lg long, large
LGk Late Greek
li link
Li lithium
LI Long Island
lib liberal, librarian, library
lieut lieutenant
LIFO last in, first out
lin lineal, linear
liq liquid, liquor
lit liter, literal, literally, literary, literature
lith, litho lithography
LittD, LitD doctor of letters, doctor of literature
ll lines
LL Late Latin
LLD doctor of laws
LM lunar module
loc cit loco citato (L, in the place cited)
log logarithm
long longitude
loq loquitur (L, he speaks, she speaks)
LP low pressure
LPN licensed practical nurse
Lr lawrencium
LS letter signed, locus sigilli (L, place of seal)
lt light
Lt lieutenant
LT long ton
LTC, LT Col lieutenant colonel
ltd limited
LTL less-than-truckload lot
ltr letter
Lu lutetium
lub lubricant, lubricating
lv leave

m male, married, masculine, meridian, meridies (L, noon), meter, mile, mill, minute, month, moon
M master, medium, mille (L, thousand), monsieur
MA Massachusetts, master of arts
mach machine, machinery, machinist
mag magazine, magnetism, magneto, magnitude
Maj major
man manual
Man Manitoba
mar maritime
Mar March
masc masculine
Mass Massachusetts
math mathematical, mathematician, mathematics
MATS Military Air Transport Service
max maximum
mc megacycle
MC master of ceremonies, member of congress
Md Maryland, mendelevium
MD doctor of medicine, Maryland
mdse merchandise
Me Maine
ME Maine, mechanical engineer, Middle English
meas measure
mech mechanical, mechanics
med medical, medicine, medieval, medium
mem member, memoir, memorial
mer meridian
Messrs messieurs
met metropolitan
Mex Mexican, Mexico
mf medium frequency
mfd manufactured
mfg manufacturing
mfr manufacture, manufacturer
mg milligram
Mg magnesium
mgr manager, monseigneur, monsignor
mgt management
mi mile, mill
MI, Mich Michigan
mid middle
mil military
min minimum, mining, minor, minute
Minn Minnesota
misc miscellaneous
Miss Mississippi
mk mark
ML Medieval Latin
Mlle mademoiselle
mm millimeter
MM Maryknoll Missioners, messieurs
Mme madame
Mn manganese
MN Minnesota
mo month
Mo Missouri, molybdenum
MO mail order, medical officer, Missouri, money order
mod moderate, modern
mol molecular, molecule
MOM middle of month
Mon Monday
Mont Montana
mos months
mp melting point
MP member of parliament, metropolitan police, military police
mpg miles per gallon
mph miles per hour
Mr mister
Mrs mistress
MS manuscript, master of science, Mississippi, motor ship
msgr monseigneur, monsignor
MSgt master sergeant
MSS manuscripts
MST Mountain standard time
mt mount, mountain
MT metric ton, Montana
mtg, mtge mortgage
mtn mountain
mun, munic municipal
mus museum, music

n net, neuter, new, noon, note, noun, number
N knight, nitrogen, normal, north, northern
Na natrium (L, sodium)
NAS naval air station
NASA National Aeronautics and Space Administration
nat national, native, natural
natl national
NATO North Atlantic Treaty Organization
naut nautical
nav naval, navigable, navigation
Nb niobium
NB nota bene
NB New Brunswick
NBS National Bureau of Standards
NC no charge, North Carolina
NCO noncommissioned officer
Nd neodymium
ND no date, North Dakota
N Dak North Dakota
NE neon
NE Nebraska, New England, northeast
Nebr, Neb Nebraska
neg negative
neut neuter
Nev Nevada
NF no funds
Nfld Newfoundland
NG National Guard, no good
NH New Hampshire
Ni nickel
NJ New Jersey
NL New Latin, night letter
N Mex, NM New Mexico
no north, number
No nobelium
nol pros nolle prosequi (L, to be unwilling to prosecute)
nom nominative
non seq non sequitur

Nov November
Np neptunium
NP no protest, notary public
NS Nova Scotia
NSF not sufficient funds
NSW New South Wales
NT New Testament
NTP normal temperature and pressure
nt wt net weight
numis numismatic, numismatics
NV Nevada
NW northwest
NY New York
NYC New York City
NZ New Zealand

o ocean, ohm
O oxygen
o/a on account, on or about
OAS Organization of American States
ob obiit (L, he died, she died)
obj object, objective
obl oblique, oblong
obs obsolete
obv obverse
OCS officer candidate school
oct octavo
Oct October
o/d on demand
OD officer of the day, olive drab, overdose, overdraft, overdrawn
OE Old English
OF Old French
off office, officer, official
OFM Order of Friars Minor
OG original gum
OH Ohio
OHG Old High German
OIr Old Irish
OK, Okla Oklahoma
ON Old Norse
Ont Ontario
op opus, out of print
OP Order of Preachers
op cit opere citato (L, in the work cited)
opp opposite
opt optical, optician, optional
OR operating room, Oregon
orch orchestra
ord order, ordnance
Oreg, Ore Oregon
org organization, organized
orig original, originally
o/s out of stock
Os osmium
OS ordinary seaman
OSB Order of St. Benedict
OT Old Testament, overtime
OTS officers' training school
oz ounce

p page, participle, past, penny, per, piano, pint, purl
P pawn, phosphorus, pressure
pa per annum
Pa Pennsylvania, protactinium
PA passenger agent, Pennsylvania, power of attorney, press agent, private account, public address, purchasing agent
Pac Pacific
pam pamphlet
par paragraph, parallel, parish
part participle, particular
pass passenger, passive
pat patent
payt payment
Pb plumbum (L, lead)
pc percent, piece, postcard
pd paid
Pd palladium
PD per diem (L, by the day), police department, potential difference
PE physical education
ped pedal
PEI Prince Edward Island
penin peninsula
Penn, Penna Pennsylvania
per period
perf perfect, perforated
perh perhaps
perm permanent
perp perpendicular
pers person, personal
pert pertaining
pf, pfd preferred
PFC private first class
pg page
Pg Portuguese
PG postgraduate
pharm pharmaceutical, pharmacist, pharmacy
PhD doctor of philosophy
philos philosopher, philosophy
phon phonetics
phr phrase
phys physical, physician, physics
pk park, peak, peck
pkg package
pkt packet
pkwy parkway
pl place, plate, plural
pm premium
p.m. post meridiem
Pm promethium
PM paymaster, police magistrate, postmaster, postmortem, prime minister, provost marshal
pmk postmark
pmt payment
Po polonium
PO petty officer, post office
POC port of call
POE port of embarkation, port of entry
Pol Poland, Polish
polit political, politician
pop popular, population
Port Portugal, Portuguese
pos position, positive
poss possessive
POW prisoner of war
pp pages, pianissimo
PP parcel post, past participle, postpaid, prepaid
ppd postpaid, prepaid
PPS post postscriptum (L, an additional postscript)
ppt precipitate
pptn precipitation
PQ Province of Quebec
pr pair, price
Pr praseodymium
PR payroll, public relations, Puerto Rico
prec preceding
pred predicate
pref preface, preference, preferred, prefix
prem premium
prep preparatory, preposition
pres present, president
prev previous
prf proof
prim primary
prin principal
PRO public relations officer
prob probable, probably, problem
proc proceedings
prod production
prof professor
pron pronoun, pronounced, pronunciation
prop property, proposition, proprietor
Prot Protestant
prov province, provincial, provisional
PS postscriptum (L, postscript), public school
pseud pseudonym
psi pounds per square inch
PST Pacific standard time
psych psychology
psychol psychologist, psychology
pt part, payment, pint, point, port
Pt platinum
PTA parent-teacher association
pte private (British)
ptg printing
PTO please turn over
Pu plutonium
pub public, publication, published, publisher, publishing
publ publication, published
pvt private
PW prisoner of war
pwt pennyweight
PX post exchange

q quart, quarto, query, question, quire
Q queen
QC Queen's Counsel
QED quod erat demonstrandum (L, which was to be demonstrated)
QID quater in die (L, four times a day)
Qld, Q'land Queensland
QM quartermaster
QMC quartermaster corps
QMG quartermaster general
qq v quae vide (L pl., which see)
qr quarter, quire
qt quart
qt quiet
qto quarto
qty quantity
quad quadrant
Que Quebec
quot quotation
qv quod vide (L, which see)
qy query

r rare, right, river
R rabbi, radius, Republican, resistance, rook
Ra radium
RA regular army, royal academy
rad radical, radio, radius
RADM rear admiral
RAF Royal Air Force
Rb rubidium
RBC red blood cells, red blood count
RBI runs batted in
RC Red Cross, Roman Catholic
RCMP Royal Canadian Mounted Police
rd road, rod, round
RD rural delivery
Re rhenium
rec receipt, record, recording, recreation
recd received
recip reciprocal, reciprocity
rec sec recording secretary
rect rectangle, rectangular, receipt, rectified
ref referee, reference, referred, reformed, refunding
refl reflex, reflexive
reg region, register, registered, regular, regulation
regt regiment
rel relating, relative
relig religion
rep report, reporter, representative, republic
Rep Republican
repl replace, replacement
rept report
req require, required, requisition
res research, reserve, residence, resolution
resp respective, respectively
ret retain, retired, return
retd retained, retired, returned
rev revenue, reverend, reverse, review, reviewed, revised, revision, revolution
RF radio frequency
RFD rural free delivery
Rh rhodium
RI Rhode Island
RIP requiescat in pace (L, may he [she] rest in peace)
riv river
rm ream, room
Rn radon
RN registered nurse, Royal Navy
Rom Roman, Romania, Romanian
ROTC Reserve Officers' Training Corps
rpm revolutions per minute
RPO railway post office
rps revolutions per second
rpt repeat, report
RR railroad, rural route
RS recording secretary
RSVP répondez s'il vous plait (Fr, please reply)
RSWC right side up with care
rt right
rte route
Ru ruthenium
Rum Rumania, Rumanian
Russ Russia, Russian
ry railway

s second, section, semi, series, shilling, sine, singular, son, soprano, stere
S saint, senate, small, south, southern, sulfur
SA Salvation Army, sex appeal, sine anno (L, without date), South Africa, subject to approval
SAC Strategic Air Command
sanit sanitary, sanitation
Sask Saskatchewan
sat saturate, saturated, saturation
Sat Saturday
S Aust, SA South Australia
sb substantive
Sb stibium (L, antimony)
SB bachelor of science
sc scale, scene, science, scilicet (L, namely)
Sc scandium, Scots
SC South Carolina
Scand Scandinavian
ScD doctor of science
ScGael Scottish Gaelic
sch school
sci science, scientific

scil scilicet (L, namely)
Scot Scotland, Scottish
script scripture
SD sea-damaged, sine die (L, without day), South Dakota, special delivery
S Dak South Dakota
Se selenium
SE southeast
SEATO Southeast Asia Treaty Organization
sec second, secondary, secretary, section, secundum (L, according to)
sect section
secy secretary
sel select, selected, selection
sem seminary
sen senate, senator, senior
sep separate
Sept, Sep September
seq sequens (L, the following)
seqq sequentia (L pl., the following)
ser serial, series
serg, sergt sergeant
serv service
sf science fiction
SFC sergeant first class
sg senior grade, singular
Sgt sergeant
sh share
Shak Shakespeare
shf superhigh frequency
shpt, shipt shipment
sht sheet
shtg shortage
Si silicon
sig signal, signature
sing singular
SJ Society of Jesus
Skt Sanskrit
Slav Slavic
sm small
Sm samarium
SM master of science, sergeant major
SN stannum (LL, tin)
so south
soc social, society
sol solicitor
soln solution
sop soprano
soph sophomore
sp special, species, specimen, spelling, spirit
Sp Spain, Spanish
SPCA Society for the Prevention of Cruelty to Animals
SPCC Society for the Prevention of Cruelty to Children
spec special
specif specific, specifically
sp. gr. specific gravity
spp species (pl)
sq squadron, square
sr senior
Sr senor, sister, strontium
SR seaman recruit
Sra senora
Sres señores
SRO standing room only
Srta senorita
SS saints, steamship, Sunday school
SSG, SSgt staff sergeant
ssp subspecies
SSS Selective Service System
st saint, stanza, state, stitch, stone, strait, street
ST short ton
sta station
stat statute
stbd starboard
std standard
ste sainte (F, female saint)
stg, ster sterling
stk stock
STP standard temperature and pressure
stud student
subj subject, subjunctive
suff sufficient, suffix
Sun Sunday
sup superior, supplement, supplementary, supply, supra (L, above)
superl superlative
supp, suppl supplement, supplementary
supt superintendent
surg surgeon, surgery, surgical
surv survey, surveying, surveyor
SV sub verbo *or* sub voce (L, under the word)
Sw, Swed Sweden, Swedish
SW shipper's weight, shortwave, southwest
syll syllable
sym symbol, symmetrical
syn synonym, synonymous, synonymy
syst system

t metric ton, teaspoon, temperature, tenor, ton, troy
T tablespoon
Ta tantalum
tan tangent
Tb terbium
TB trial balance
tbs, tbsp tablespoon
Tc technetium
TD touchdown
TDN total digestible nutrients
Te tellurium
tech technical, technically, technician, technological, technology
tel telegram, telegraph, telephone
teleg telegraphy
temp temperature, temporary, tempore (L, in the time of)
Tenn Tennessee
ter terrace, territory
terr territory
Tex Texas
Th thorium, Thursday
ThD doctor of theology
theat theatrical
therm thermometer
thou thousand
Thurs, Thur, Thu Thursday
Ti titanium
TID ter in die (L, three times a day)
tinct tincture
TKO technical knockout
tkt ticket
Tl thallium
TLC tender loving care
Tm thulium
TM trademark
tn ton, town
TN Tennessee
tnpk turnpike
TO telegraph office
tot total
tp title page, township
tpk turnpike
tr translated, translation, translator, transpose
trans transaction, transitive, translated, translation, translator, transportation, transverse
treas treasurer, treasury
trib tributary
trig trigonometry
TSgt technical sergeant
tsp teaspoon
TT tuberculin tested
Tues, Tue Tuesday
TX Texas

u unit
U university, uranium
UAR United Arab Republic
uc upper case
UFO unidentified flying object
uhf ultrahigh frequency
UK United Kingdom
ult ultimate, ultimo
UMT Universal Military Training
UN United Nations
UNESCO United Nations Educational, Scientific, and Cultural Organization
UNICEF United Nations Children's Fund
univ universal, university
UNRWA United Nations Relief and Works Agency
UPI United Press International
US United States
USA United States Army, United States of America
USAF United States Air Force
USCG United States Coast Guard
USM United States mail
USMA United States Military Academy
USMC United States Marine Corps
USN United States Navy
USNA United States Naval Academy
USNR United States Naval Reserve
USP United States Pharmacopeia
USS United States Ship
USSR Union of Soviet Socialist Republics
usu usual, usually
UT Utah
UV ultraviolet
UW underwriter

v vector, velocity, verb, verse, versus, vice, vide (L, see), voice, volume, vowel
V vanadium, victory, volt, voltage
Va Virginia
VA Veterans Administration, vice admiral, Virginia
VADM vice admiral
val value
var variable, variant, variation, variety, various
vb verb
VC Victoria Cross, Vietcong
VD venereal disease
veg vegetable
vel vellum, velocity
ven venerable
vert vertical
VFW Veterans of Foreign Wars
vhf very high frequency
vi verb intransitive, vide infra (L, see below)
VI Virgin Islands
vic vicinity
Vic Victoria
vil village
vis visibility, visual
viz videlicet (L, namely)
vlf very low frequency
voc vocative
vol volume, volunteer
vou voucher
VP vice-president
vs verse, versus, vide supra (L, see above)
vss verses, versions
vt verb transitive
Vt, VT Vermont
vv verses, vice versa

w water, watt, week, weight, wide, width, wife, with
W Welsh, west, western, wolfram (G, tungsten)
WA Washington
war warrant
Wash Washington
W Aust, WA Western Australia
WBC white blood cells
WC water closet, without charge
Wed Wednesday
wf wrong font
wh which
whf wharf
WHO World Health Organization
whs, whse warehouse
whsle wholesale
WI West Indies, Wisconsin
wid widow, widower
Wis, Wisc Wisconsin
wk week, work
WL wavelength
wmk watermark
w/o without
WO warrant officer
wpm words per minute
wrnt warrant
wt weight
W Va, WV West Virginia
WW World War
WY, Wyo Wyoming

Xe xenon
XL extra large
Xn Christian
Xnty Christianity

y yard, year
Y YMCA, yttrium
Yb ytterbium
yd yard
YMCA Young Men's Christian Association
YMHA Young Men's Hebrew Association
yr year, your
yrbk yearbook
yrs years, yours
YT Yukon Territory
YWCA, YW Young Women's Christian Association
YWHA Young Women's Hebrew Association

z zero
Zn zinc
zool zoological, zoology
Zr zirconium

A PRONOUNCING VOCABULARY OF COMMON ENGLISH GIVEN NAMES

The following vocabulary presents given names that are most frequent in English use. The list is not exhaustive either of the names themselves or of the variant spellings of those names which are entered. Compound or double names and surnames used as given names are not entered except in cases where long-continued or common use gives them an independent character.

Besides the pronunciations of the names, the list usually provides at least one of the following kinds of information at each entry: (1) etymology, indicating the language source but not the original form of the name, and (2) meaning where known or ascertainable with reasonable certainty.

I NAMES OF MEN

Aar·on \'ar-ən, 'er-\ [Heb]
Abra·ham \'ā-brə-ˌham\ [Heb]
Ad·am \'ad-əm\ [Heb] man
Ad·di·son \'ad-ə-sən\ [fr. a surname]
Adolph \'ad-ˌälf, 'ā-ˌdälf\ [Gmc] noble wolf, *i.e.,* noble hero
Adri·an \'ā-drē-ən\ [L] of Hadria, ancient town in central Italy
Al \'al\ *dim of* AL-
Al·an \'al-ən\ [Celt]
Al·bert \'al-bərt\ [Gmc] illustrious through nobility
Al·bin \'al-bən\ [L] white
Al·den \'ȯl-dən\ [OE] old friend
Al·ex \'al-iks, 'el-\ *or* **Al·ec** \-ik\ *dim of* ALEXANDER
Al·ex·an·der \ˌal-ig-'zan-dər, ˌel-\ [Gk] a defender of men
Al·fred \'al-frəd, -fərd\ [OE] elf counsel, *i.e.,* good counsel
Al·len *or* **Al·lan** *or* **Al·lyn** \'al-ən\ *var of* ALAN
Al·ton \'ȯlt-ᵊn, 'alt-\ [prob. fr. a surname]
Al·va *or* **Al·vah** \'al-və\ [Heb]
Al·vin \'al-vən\ [Gmc] *prob* noble friend
Amos \'ā-məs\ [Heb]
An·dre \'än-(ˌ)drā\ [F] *var of* ANDREW
An·drew \'an-(ˌ)drü\ [Gk] manly
An·dy \'an-dē\ *dim of* ANDREW
An·ge·lo \'an-jə-ˌlō\ [It, fr. Gk] angel, messenger
An·gus \'aŋ-gəs\ [Celt]
An·tho·ny \'an(t)-thə-nē, *chiefly Brit* 'an-tə-\ [L]
An·ton \'ant-ᵊn, 'an-ˌtän\ [G & Slav] *var of* ANTHONY
An·to·nio \an-'tō-nē-ˌō\ [It] *var of* ANTHONY
Ar·chie \'är-chē\ *dim of* ARCHIBALD
Ar·den \'ärd-ᵊn\ [prob. fr. a surname]
Ar·len *or* **Ar·lin** \'är-lən\ [prob. fr. a surname]
Ar·lo \'är-(ˌ)lō\
Ar·mand \'är-ˌmänd, -mənd\ [F] *var of* HERMAN
Arne \'ärn\ [Scand] eagle
Ar·nold \'ärn-ᵊld\ [Gmc] power of an eagle
Ar·thur \'är-thər\ [prob. L]
Ar·vid \'är-vəd\ [Scand] eagle forest
Au·brey \'ȯ-brē\ [Gmc] elf ruler
Au·gust \'ȯ-gəst\ [L] August, majestic
Aus·tin \'ȯs-tən, 'äs-\ *alter of* AUGUSTINE

Bai·ley \'bā-lē\ [fr. a surname]
Bar·clay \'bär-klē\ [fr. a surname]
Bar·net *or* **Bar·nett** \bär-'net\ [fr. a surname]
Bar·ney \'bär-nē\ *dim of* BERNARD
Bar·rett \'bar-ət\ [fr. a surname]
Bar·ry *or* **Bar·rie** \'bar-ē\ [Ir]
Bart \'bärt\ *dim of* BARTHOLOMEW
Bar·ton \'bärt-ᵊn\ [fr. a surname]
Ba·sil \'baz-əl, 'bas-, 'bās-, 'bāz-\ [Gk] kingly, royal
Ben \'ben\ *or* **Ben·nie** *or* **Ben·ny** \'ben-ē\ *dim of* BENJAMIN
Ben·ja·min \'benj-(ə-)mən\ [Heb] son of the right hand
Ben·nett \'ben-ət\ [OF] *var of* BENEDICT
Ben·ton \'bent-ᵊn\ [fr. a surname]
Ber·nard \'bər-nərd, (ˌ)bər-'närd\ *or* **Bern·hard** \'bərn-ˌhärd\ [Gmc] bold as a bear
Ber·nie \'bər-nē\ *dim of* BERNARD
Bert *or* **Burt** \'bərt\ *dim of* -BERT *or* BERT-
Ber·tram \'bər-trəm\ [Gmc] bright raven
Bill \'bil\ *or* **Bil·ly** *or* **Bil·lie** \'bil-ē\ *dim of* WILLIAM
Blaine \'blān\ [fr. a surname]
Blair \'bla(ə)r, 'ble(ə)r\ [fr. a surname]
Bob·by \'bäb-ē\ *or* **Bob** \'bäb\ *dim of* ROBERT
Bo·ris \'bōr-əs, 'bȯr-, 'bär-\ [Russ]
Boyd \'bȯid\ [fr. a surname]
Brad·ford \'brad-fərd\ [fr. a surname]
Brad·ley \'brad-lē\ [fr. a surname]
Brent \'brent\ [fr. a surname]
Bri·an *or* **Bry·an** \'brī-ən\ [Celt]
Brooks \'brůks\ [fr. a surname]
Bruce \'brüs\ [fr. a surname]
Bru·no \'brü-(ˌ)nō\ [It, fr. Gmc] brown
Bryce *or* **Brice** \'brīs\ [fr. a surname]
Bud·dy \'bəd-ē\ [prob. alter. of *brother*]
Bu·ford \'byü-fərd\ [fr. a surname]
Burke \'bərk\ [fr. a surname]
Bur·ton \'bərt-ᵊn\ [fr. a surname]
By·ron \'bī-rən\ [fr. a surname]

Cal·vin \'kal-vən\ [fr. a surname]
Cam·er·on \'kam-(ə-)rən\ [fr. a surname]
Carl \'kär(-ə)l\ *var of* KARL
Car·los \'kär-ləs, -ˌlōs\ [Sp] *var of* CHARLES
Carl·ton *or* **Carle·ton** \'kär(-ə)l-tən, 'kärlt-ᵊn\ [fr. a surname]
Car·lyle \kär-'lī(ə)l, 'kär-ˌ\ [fr. a surname]
Car·men \'kär-mən\ [Sp, fr. L] song
Car·roll \'kar-əl\ [fr. a surname]
Car·son \'kärs-ᵊn\ [fr. a surname]
Car·ter \'kärt-ər\ [fr. a surname]
Cary *or* **Car·ey** \'ka(ə)r-ē, 'ke(ə)r-ē\ [fr. a surname]
Ce·cil \'sē-səl, 'ses-əl\ [L]
Charles \'chär(-ə)lz\ [Gmc] man of the common people
Ches·ter \'ches-tər\ [fr. a surname]
Chris \'kris\ *dim of* CHRISTOPHER
Chris·tian \'kris(h)-chən\ [Gk] Christian (the believer)
Chris·to·pher \'kris-tə-fər\ [Gk] Christ bearer
Clar·ence \'klar-ən(t)s\ [fr. the English dukedom]
Clark *or* **Clarke** \'klärk\ [fr. a surname]
Claude *or* **Claud** \'klȯd\ [L]
Clay \'klā\ *dim of* CLAYTON
Clay·ton \'klāt-ᵊn\ [fr. a surname]
Clem \'klem\ *dim of* CLEMENT
Clem·ent \'klem-ənt\ [L] mild, merciful
Clif·ford \'klif-ərd\ [fr. a surname]
Clif·ton \'klif-tən\ [fr. a surname]
Clint \'klint\ *dim of* CLINTON
Clin·ton \'klint-ᵊn\ [fr. a surname]
Clyde \'klīd\ [fr. a surname]
Co·lin \'käl-ən, 'kō-lən\ *or* **Col·lin** \'käl-ən\ *dim of* NICHOLAS
Con·rad \'kän-ˌrad, -rəd\ [Gmc] bold counsel
Con·stan·tine \'kän(t)-stən-ˌtēn, -ˌtīn\ [L]
Cor·ne·lius \kȯr-'nēl-yəs\ [L]
Coy \'kȯi\ [fr. a surname]
Craig \'krāg\ [fr. a surname]
Cur·tis \'kərt-əs\ [OF] courteous
Cyr·il \'sir-əl\ [Gk] lordly
Cy·rus \'sī-rəs\ [OPer]

Dale \'dā(ə)l\ [fr. a surname]
Dal·las \'dal-əs, -is\ [fr. a surname]
Dal·ton \'dȯlt-ᵊn\ [fr. a surname]
Dan \'dan\ [Heb] judge
Da·na \'dā-nə\ [fr. a surname]
Dan·iel \'dan-yəl *also* 'dan-ᵊl\ [Heb] God has judged
Dan·ny \'dan-ē\ *dim of* DANIEL
Dar·old \'dar-əld\ *perh alter of* DARRELL
Dar·rell *or* **Dar·rel** *or* **Dar·ryl** *or* **Dar·yl** \'dar-əl\ [fr. a surname]
Dar·win \'där-wən\ [fr. a surname]
Dave \'dāv\ *dim of* DAVID
Da·vid \'dā-vəd\ [Heb] beloved
Da·vis \'dā-vəs\ [fr. a surname]
Dean *or* **Deane** \'dēn\ [fr. a surname]
Del·a·no \'del-ə-ˌnō\ [fr. a surname]
Del·bert \'del-bərt\ *dim of* ADALBERT
Del·mar \'del-mər, -ˌmär\ *or* **Del·mer** \-mər\ [fr. a surname]
Den·nis *or* **Den·is** \'den-əs\ [OF, fr. Gk] belonging to Dionysus, god of wine
Den·ny \'den-ē\ *dim of* DENNIS
Den·ton \'dent-ᵊn\ [fr. a surname]
Der·ek \'der-ik\ [MD, fr. Gmc] ruler of the people
Dew·ey \'d(y)ü-ē\ [fr. a surname]
De·witt \di-'wit\ [fr. a surname]
Dex·ter \'dek-stər\ [L] on the right hand, fortunate
Dick \'dik\ *dim of* RICHARD
Die·ter \'dēt-ər\ [G] *var of* DIETRICH
Dirk \'dərk\ [D] *var of* DEREK
Dom·i·nic *or* **Dom·i·nick** \'däm-ə-(ˌ)nik\ [L] belonging to the Lord
Don *or* **Donn** \'dän\ *dim of* DONALD
Don·al \'dän-ᵊl\ *var of* DONALD
Don·ald \'dän-ᵊld\ [ScGael] world ruler
Don·nie \'dän-ē\ *dim of* DON
Don·o·van \'dän-ə-vən, 'dən-\ [fr. a surname]
Doug \'dəg\ *dim of* DOUGLAS
Doug·las *or* **Doug·lass** \'dəg-ləs\ [fr. a surname]
Doyle \'dȯi(ə)l\ [fr. a surname]
Duane \dü-'än, 'dwān\ [fr. a surname]
Dud·ley \'dəd-lē\ [fr. a surname]

Dun·can \'dəŋ-kən\ [ScGael] brown head
Dur·ward \'dər-wərd\ [fr. a surname]
Dwayne *or* **Dwaine** \'dwān\ [fr. a surname]
Dwight \'dwīt\ [fr. a surname]

Earl *or* **Earle** \'ər(-ə)l\ [OE] warrior, noble
Ed \'ed\ *dim of* ED-
Ed·die *or* **Ed·dy** \'ed-ē\ *dim of* ED
Ed·gar \'ed-gər\ [OE] spear of wealth
Ed·mund *or* **Ed·mond** \'ed-mənd\ [OE] protector of wealth
Ed·son \'ed-sən\ [fr. a surname]
Ed·ward \'ed-wərd\ [OE] guardian of wealth
Ed·win \'ed-wən\ [OE] friend of wealth
El·bert \'el-bərt\ *var of* ALBERT
El·don *or* **El·den** \'el-dən\ [prob. fr. a surname]
Eli \'ē-,lī\ [Heb] high
E·li·as \i-'lī-əs\ [Gr] *var of* ELIJAH
El·liott *or* **El·liot** *or* **El·iot** \'el-ē-ət, 'el-yət\ [fr. a surname]
El·lis \'el-əs\ *var of* ELIAS
Ells·worth \'elz-(,)wərth\ [fr. a surname]
El·mer \'el-mər\ [fr. a surname]
El·mo \'el-(,)mō\ [It, fr. Gk] lovable
El·ton \'elt-ᵊn\ [fr. a surname]
El·vin \'el-vən\ [fr. a surname]
El·wood *or* **Ell·wood** \'el-,wu̇d\ [fr. a surname]
El·wyn *or* **El·win** \'el-wən\ [fr. a surname]
Eman·u·el *or* **Em·man·u·el** \i-'man-yə(-wə)l\ [Heb] God with us
Em·er·son \'em-ər-sən\ [fr. a surname]
Emil \'ā-məl\ *or* **Emile** \ā-'mē(ə)l\ [L]
Em·mett \'em-ət\ [fr. a surname]
Em·o·ry *or* **Em·ery** \'em-(ə-)rē\ [Gmc]
Er·ic *or* **Er·ich** *or* **Er·ik** \'er-ik\ [Scand]
Er·nest *or* **Ear·nest** \'ər-nəst\ [G] earnestness
Er·nie \'ər-nē\ *dim of* ERNEST
Ernst \'ərn(t)st, 'e(ə)rn(t)st\ [G] *var of* ERNEST
Er·rol \'er-əl\ [prob. fr. a surname]
Er·vin \'ər-vən\ [fr. a surname]
Er·win \'ər-wən\ [fr. a surname]
Ethan \'ē-thən\ [Heb] strength
Eu·gene \yu̇-'jēn, 'yü-,\ [Gk] wellborn
Ev·an \'ev-ən\ [W] *var of* JOHN
Ev·er·ett \'ev-(ə-)rət\ [fr. a surname]

Fe·lix \'fē-liks\ [L] happy, prosperous
Fer·di·nand \'fərd-ᵊn-,and\ [Gmc] *prob* venture of a military expedition
Fer·nan·do \fər-'nan-(,)dō\ [Sp] *var of* FERDINAND
Fletch·er \'flech-ər\ [fr. a surname]
Floyd \'flȯid\ [fr. a surname]
For·rest *or* **For·est** \'fȯr-əst, 'fär-\ [fr. a surname]
Fos·ter \'fȯs-tər, 'fäs-\ [fr. a surname]
Fran·cis \'fran(t)-səs\ [OIt & OF] Frenchman
Fran·cis·co \fran-'sis-(,)kō\ [Sp] *var of* FRANCIS
Frank \'fraŋk\ [Gmc] freeman, Frank
Frank·lin *or* **Frank·lyn** \'fraŋ-klən\ [fr. a surname]
Fred \'fred\ *dim of* -FRED *or* FRED-
Fred·die \'fred-ē\ *dim of* FREDERICK
Fred·er·ick *or* **Fred·er·ic** *or* **Fred·rick** *or* **Fred·ric** \'fred-(ə-)rik\ [Gmc] peaceful ruler
Free·man \'frē-mən\ [fr. a surname]
Fritz \'frits\ [G] *dim of* FRIEDRICH

Ga·bri·el \'gā-brē-əl\ [Heb] man of God
Ga·len \'gā-lən\ [Gk]
Gar·land \'gär-lənd\ [fr. a surname]
Gar·rett \'gar-ət\ [fr. a surname]
Garth \'gärth\ [fr. a surname]
Gary \'ga(ə)r-ē, 'ge(ə)r-ē\ *or* **Gar·ry** \'gar-\ [prob. fr. a surname]
Gay·lord \'gā-,lȯ(ə)rd\ [fr. a surname]
Gene \'jēn\ *dim of* EUGENE
Geof·frey \'jef-rē\ [OF, fr. Gmc]
George \'jȯ(ə)rj\ [Gk] of or relating to a farmer
Ger·ald \'jer-əld\ [Gmc] spear dominion
Ge·rard \jə-'rärd, *chiefly Brit* 'jer-,ärd, -ərd\ *or* **Ger·hard** \'ge(ə)r-,härd\ [Gmc] strong with the spear
Ger·ry \'jer-ē\ *var of* JERRY
Gil·bert \'gil-bərt\ [Gmc] *prob* illustrious through hostages
Giles \'jī(ə)lz\ [OF, fr. LL]
Glenn *or* **Glen** \'glen\ [fr. a surname]
Gor·don \'gȯrd-ᵊn\ [fr. a surname]
Gra·dy \'grād-ē\ [fr. a surname]
Gra·ham \'grā-əm, 'gra(-ə)m\ [fr. a surname]
Grant \'grant\ [fr. a surname]
Gran·ville \'gran-,vil\ [fr. a surname]
Gray \'grā\ [fr. a surname]
Gregg *or* **Greg** \'greg\ *dim of* GREGORY
Greg·o·ry \'greg-(ə-)rē\ [LGk] vigilant
Gro·ver \'grō-vər\ [fr. a surname]
Gus \'gəs\ *dim of* -GUS- *or* GUS-
Gus·tav *or* **Gus·tave** \'gəs-təv\ [Gmc] *dim of* GUSTAVUS
Guy \'gī\ [OF, fr. Gmc]

Hal \'hal\ *dim of* HENRY
Hall \'hȯl\ [fr. a surname]
Ham·il·ton \'ham-əl-tən, -əlt-ᵊn\ [fr. a surname]
Hans \'hanz, 'hän(t)s\ [G] *dim of* JOHANNES
Har·lan \'här-lən\ *or* **Har·land** \-lənd\ [fr. a surname]
Har·ley \'här-lē\ [fr. a surname]
Har·low \'här-(,)lō\ [fr. a surname]
Har·mon \'här-mən\ [fr. a surname]
Har·old \'har-əld\ [OE] army dominion
Har·ris \'har-əs\ [fr. a surname]
Har·ri·son \'har-ə-sən\ [fr. a surname]
Har·ry \'har-ē\ *dim of* HENRY
Har·vey \'här-vē\ [fr. a surname]
Hayes \'hāz\ [fr. a surname]
Hec·tor \'hek-tər\ [Gk] holding fast
Hel·mut \'hel-mət, -,müt\ [G] helmet courage
Hen·ry \'hen-rē\ [Gmc] ruler of the home
Her·bert \'hər-bərt\ [Gmc] illustrious by reason of an army
Her·man *or* **Her·mann** \'hər-mən\ [Gmc] warrior
Her·schel *or* **Her·shel** \'hər-shəl\ [fr. a surname]
Hi·ram \'hī-rəm\ [Phoenician]
Ho·bart \'hō-bərt, -,bärt\ [fr. a surname]
Hol·lis \'häl-əs\ [fr. a surname]
Ho·mer \'hō-mər\ [Gk]
Hor·ace \'hȯr-əs, 'här-\ [L]
How·ard \'hau̇(-ə)rd\ [fr. a surname]
How·ell \'hau̇(-ə)l\ [W]
Hoyt \'hȯit\ [fr. a surname]
Hu·bert \'hyü-bərt\ [Gmc] bright in spirit
Hud·son \'həd-sən\ [fr. a surname]
Hugh \'hyü\ *or* **Hu·go** \'hyü-(,)gō\ [Gmc] *prob* mind, spirit

Ian \'ē-ən\ [ScGael] *var of* JOHN
Ira \'ī-rə\ [Heb] *prob* watchful
Ir·ving \'ər-viŋ\ *or* **Ir·vin** \-vən\ [fr. a surname]
Ir·win \'ər-wən\ [fr. a surname]
Isaac \'ī-zik, -zək\ [Heb] he laughs
Ivan \'ī-vən\ [Russ] *var of* JOHN

Jack \'jak\ *dim of* JOHN
Jack·son \'jak-sən\ [fr. a surname]
Ja·cob \'jā-kəb, -kəp\ [Heb] supplanter
Jacques *or* **Jacque** \'zhäk\ [F] *var of* JAMES
Jake \'jāk\ *dim of* JACOB
James \'jāmz\ [OF, fr. LL *Jacobus*] *var of* JACOB
Jan \'jan\ [D & LG] *var of* JOHN
Jar·ed \'jar-əd, 'jer-\ [Heb] descent
Ja·son \'jās-ᵊn\ [Gk] *prob* healer
Jay \'jā\ [prob. fr. a surname]
Jef·frey *or* **Jeff·ery** *or* **Jef·fry** \'jef-(ə-)rē\ *var of* GEOFFREY
Jer·ald *or* **Jer·old** *or* **Jer·rold** \'jer-əld\ *var of* GERALD
Jer·e·my \'jer-ə-mē\ *or* **Jer·e·mi·ah** \,jer-ə-'mī-ə\ [Heb] *prob* Yahweh exalts
Je·rome \jə-'rōm, *Brit also* 'jer-əm\ [Gk] bearing a holy name
Jer·ry *or* **Jere** \'jer-ē\ *dim of* GER- *or* JER-
Jes·se \'jes-ē\ [Heb]
Jim \'jim\ *or* **Jim·my** *or* **Jim·mie** \'jim-ē\ *dim of* JAMES
Joe \'jō\ *dim of* JOSEPH
Jo·el \'jō-əl\ [Heb] Yahweh is God
John \'jän\ [Heb] Yahweh is gracious
Jon \'jän\ *var of* JOHN
Jon·a·than \'jän-ə-thən\ [Heb] Yahweh has given
Jo·seph *or* **Jo·sef** \'jō-zəf *also* -səf\ [Heb] he shall add
Josh·u·a \'jäsh-(ə-)wə\ [Heb] Yahweh saves
Jud·son \'jəd-sən\ [fr. a surname]
Jules \'jülz\ [F] *var of* JULIUS
Ju·lian *or* **Ju·lien** \'jül-yən\ [L] sprung from or belonging to Julius
Ju·lius \'jül-yəs\ *or* **Ju·lio** \-(,)yō\ [L]
Jus·tin \'jəs-tən\ *or* **Jus·tus** \-təs\ [L] just

Karl \'kär(-ə)l\ [G & Scand] *var of* CHARLES
Keith \'kēth\ [fr. a surname]
Kel·ly \'kel-ē\ [fr. a surname]
Ken \'ken\ *dim of* KENNETH
Ken·dall \'ken-dᵊl\ [fr. a surname]
Ken·neth \'ken-əth\ [ScGael]
Kent \'kent\ [prob. fr. a surname]
Ken·ton \'kent-ᵊn\ [fr. a surname]
Ker·mit \'kər-mət\ [prob. fr. a surname]
Ker·ry \'ker-ē\ [prob. fr. the county of Ireland]
Kev·in \'kev-ən\ [OIr]
Kir·by \'kər-bē\ [fr. a surname]
Kirk \'kərk\ [fr. a surname]
Klaus \'klau̇s, 'klȯs\ [G] *dim of* NIKOLAUS
Kurt \'kərt, 'ku̇(ə)rt\ [G] *dim of* CONRAD

La·mar \lə-'mär\ [fr. a surname]
Lance \'lan(t)s\ *dim of* LANCELOT
Lane \'lān\ [fr. a surname]
Lan·ny \'lan-ē\ *prob dim of* LAWRENCE
Lar·ry \'lar-ē\ *dim of* LAWRENCE
Lars \'lärz\ [Sw] *var of* LAWRENCE
Lasz·lo \'laz-(,)lō\ [Hung]
Law·rence *or* **Lau·rence** \'lȯr-ən(t)s, 'lär-\ [L] of Laurentum, ancient city in central Italy
Lee *or* **Leigh** \'lē\ [fr. a surname]
Leigh·ton *or* **Lay·ton** \'lāt-ᵊn\ [fr. a surname]
Le·land \'lē-lənd\ [fr. a surname]
Leo \'lē-(,)ō\ [L] lion
Le·on \'lē-,än, -ən\ [Sp] *var of* LEO
Leon·ard \'len-ərd\ [G] strong or brave as a lion
Le·roy \li-'rȯi, 'lē-,\ [OF] royal
Les·lie \'les-lē *also* 'lez-\ [fr. a surname]
Les·ter \'les-tər\ [fr. a surname]
Lew·is \'lü-əs\ *var of* LOUIS
Lin·coln \'liŋ-kən\ [fr. a surname]
Li·o·nel \'lī-ən-ᵊl, -ə-,nel\ [OF] young lion
Lloyd *or* **Loyd** \'lȯid\ [W] gray
Lo·gan \'lō-gən\ [fr. a surname]
Lon \'län\ *dim of* ALONZO
Lon·nie *or* **Lon·ny** \'län-ē\ *dim of* LON
Lo·ren \'lōr-ən, 'lȯr-\ *dim of* LORENZO
Lou·ie \'lü-ē\ *var of* LOUIS
Lou·is *or* **Lu·is** \'lü-əs, 'lü-ē\ [Gmc] famous warrior
Low·ell \'lō-əl\ [fr. a surname]
Lu·cian \'lü-shən\ [Gk]
Lud·wig \'ləd-(,)wig, 'lüd-\ [G] *var of* LOUIS
Luke \'lük\ [Gk] *prob dim of* LUCIUS
Lu·ther \'lü-thər\ [fr. a surname]
Lyle \'lī(ə)l\ [fr. a surname]
Ly·man \'lī-mən\ [fr. a surname]
Lynn \'lin\ [fr. a surname]

Mack *or* **Mac** \'mak\ [fr. surnames beginning with *Mc* or *Mac*, fr. Gael *mac* son]
Mal·colm \'mal-kəm\ [ScGael] servant of (St.) Columba

Man·fred \'man-frəd\ [Gmc] peace among men
Man·u·el \'man-yə(-wə)l\ [Sp & Pg] *var of* EMMANUEL
Mar·cus \'mär-kəs\ [L]
Ma·rio \'mär-ē-,ō\ [It] *var of* MARIUS
Mar·i·on \'mer-ē-ən, 'mar-\ [fr. a surname]
Mark *or* **Marc** \'märk\ *var of* MARCUS
Mar·lin \'mär-lən\ [prob. fr. a surname]
Mar·shall *or* **Mar·shal** \'mär-shəl\ [fr. a surname]
Mar·tin \'märt-ᵊn\ [LL] of Mars
Mar·vin \'mär-vən\ [prob. fr. a surname]
Ma·son \'mās-ᵊn\ [fr. a surname]
Mat·thew \'math-(,)yü *also* 'math-(,)ü\ [Heb] gift of Yahweh
Mau·rice \'mȯr-əs, 'mär-; mȯ-'rēs\ [LL] *prob* Moorish
Max \'maks\ *dim of* MAXIMILIAN
Max·well \'mak-,swel, -swəl\ [fr. a surname]
May·nard \'mā-nərd\ [Gmc] bold in strength
Mel·ville \'mel-,vil\ [fr. a surname]
Mel·vin *or* **Mel·vyn** \'mel-vən\ [prob. fr. a surname]
Mer·e·dith \'mer-əd-əth\ [W]
Merle \'mər(-ə)l\ [F] blackbird
Mer·lin *or* **Mer·lyn** \'mər-lən\ [Celt]
Mer·rill \'mer-əl\ [fr. a surname]
Mer·ritt \'mer-ət\ [fr. a surname]
Mer·vin \'mər-vən\ *var of* MARVIN
Mi·chael \'mī-kəl\ [Heb] who is like God?
Mick·ey \'mik-ē\ *dim of* MICHAEL
Mike \'mīk\ *dim of* MICHAEL
Mi·lan \'mī-lən\ [prob. fr. the city in Italy]
Miles *or* **Myles** \'mī(ə)lz\ [Gmc]
Mil·ford \'mil-fərd\ [fr. a surname]
Mil·lard \'mil-ərd, mil-'ärd\ [fr. a surname]
Mi·lo \'mī-(,)lō\ [prob. L]
Mil·ton \'milt-ᵊn\ [fr. a surname]
Mitch·ell \'mich-əl\ [fr. a surname]
Mon·roe \mən-'rō, 'mən-,\ [fr. a surname]
Mon·te *or* **Mon·ty** \'mänt-ē\ *dim of* MONTAGUE
Mor·gan \'mȯr-gən\ [W] *prob* dweller on the sea
Mor·ris \'mȯr-əs, 'mär-\ *var of* MAURICE
Mor·ton \'mȯrt-ᵊn\ [fr. a surname]
Mur·ray \'mər-ē, 'mə-rē\ [fr. a surname]
My·ron \'mī-rən\ [Gk]

Na·than \'nā-thən\ [Heb] given, gift
Na·than·iel \nə-'than-yəl\ [Heb] gift of God
Ned \'ned\ *dim of* ED-
Neil *or* **Neal** \'nē(ə)l\ [Celt]
Nel·son \'nel-sən\ [fr. a surname]
Nev·ille \'nev-əl\ [fr. a surname]
Nev·in \'nev-ən\ [fr. a surname]
New·ell \'n(y)ü-əl\ [fr. a surname]
New·ton \'n(y)üt-ᵊn\ [fr. a surname]
Nich·o·las \'nik-(ə-)ləs\ [Gk] victorious among the people
Nick \'nik\ *dim of* NICHOLAS
Niles \'nī(ə)lz\ [fr. a surname]
Nils \'nils, 'nē(ə)ls\ [Scand]
No·ah \'nō-ə\ [Heb] rest
No·el \'nō-əl\ [F, fr. L] Christmas
No·lan \'nō-lən\ [fr. a surname]
Nor·bert \'nȯr-bərt\ [Gmc] shining in the north
Nor·man \'nȯr-mən\ [Gmc] Norseman, Norman
Nor·ris \'nȯr-əs, 'när-\ [fr. a surname]
Nor·ton \'nȯrt-ᵊn\ [fr. a surname]

Olin *or* **Olen** \'ō-lən\ [fr. a surname]
Ol·i·ver \'äl-ə-vər\ [OF]
Ol·lie \'äl-ē\ *dim of* OLIVER
Ora \'ōr-ə, 'ȯr-\
Or·lan·do \ȯr-'lan-(,)dō\ [It] *var of* ROLAND
Or·rin \'ȯr-ən, 'är-\ *or* **Orin** *or* **Oren** \'ȯr-, 'är-, 'ōr-\ [prob. fr. a surname]
Or·ville *or* **Or·val** \'ȯr-vəl\ [prob. fr. a surname]
Os·car \'äs-kər\ [OE] spear of a deity
Otis \'ōt-əs\ [fr. a surname]
Ot·to \'ät-(,)ō\ [Gmc] *prob* propertied
Ow·en \'ō-ən\ [OW]

Palm·er \'päm-ər, 'päl-mər\ [fr. a surname]
Par·ker \'pär-kər\ [fr. a surname]
Pat \'pat\ *dim of* PATRICK
Pat·rick \'pa-trik\ [L] patrician
Paul \'pȯl\ [L] little
Pe·dro \'pē-(,)drō, 'pā-\ [Sp] *var of* PETER
Per·cy \'pər-sē\ [fr. a surname]
Per·ry \'per-ē\ [fr. a surname]
Pete \'pēt\ *dim of* PETER
Pe·ter \'pēt-ər\ [Gk] rock
Phil \'fil\ *dim of* PHILIP
Phil·ip *or* **Phil·lip** \'fil-əp\ [Gk] lover of horses
Pierre \pē-'e(ə)r, 'pi(ə)r\ [F] *var of* PETER
Por·ter \'pōrt-ər, 'pȯrt-\ [fr. a surname]
Pres·ton \'pres-tən\ [fr. a surname]

Quen·tin \'kwent-ᵊn\ [LL] of or relating to the fifth

Ra·fa·el *or* **Ra·pha·el** \'raf-ē-əl, 'rā-fē-\ [Heb] God has healed
Ra·leigh \'rȯl-ē, 'räl-\ [fr. a surname]
Ralph \'ralf, *Brit also* 'rāf\ [Gmc] wolf in counsel
Ra·mon \rə-'mōn, 'rā-mən\ [Sp] *var of* RAYMOND
Ran·dall *or* **Ran·dal** \'ran-dᵊl\ *var of* RANDOLPH
Ran·dolph \'ran-,dälf\ [Gmc] shield wolf
Ran·dy \'ran-dē\ *dim of* RANDOLPH
Ray \'rā\ *dim of* RAYMOND
Ray·mond \'rā-mənd\ [Gmc] wise protection
Reed *or* **Reid** \'rēd\ [fr. a surname]
Reg·i·nald \'rej-ən-ᵊld\ [Gmc] wise dominion
Re·gis \'rē-jəs\ [fr. a proper name]
Re·ne \'ren-(,)ā, rə-'nā, 'rā-nē, 'rē-nē\ [F, fr. L] reborn
Reu·ben *or* **Ru·ben** \'rü-bən\ [Heb]
Rex \'reks\ [L] king
Reyn·old \'ren-ᵊld\ *var of* REGINALD
Rich·ard \'rich-ərd\ [Gmc] strong in rule
Ri·ley \'rī-lē\ [fr. a surname]
Rob·ert \'räb-ərt\ [Gmc] bright in fame
Ro·ber·to \rə-'bərt-(,)ō, rō-, -'be(ə)rt-\ [Sp & It] *var of* ROBERT
Rob·in \'räb-ən\ *dim of* ROBERT
Rod·er·ick \'räd-(ə-)rik\ [Gmc] famous ruler
Rod·ney \'räd-nē\ [fr. a surname]
Rog·er *or* **Rod·ger** \'räj-ər\ [Gmc] famous spear
Rog·ers \'räj-ərz\ [fr. a surname]
Ro·land \'rō-lənd\ *or* **Rol·land** \'räl-ənd\ *or* **Row·land** \'rō-lənd\ [Gmc] famous land
Rolf \'rälf\ *var of* RUDOLPH
Rol·lin \'räl-ən\ *var of* ROLAND
Ron \'rän\ *dim of* RONALD
Ron·al \'rän-ᵊl\ *var of* RONALD
Ron·ald \'rän-ᵊld\ [ON] *var of* REGINALD
Ron·nie *or* **Ron·ny** \'rän-ē\ *dim of* RONALD
Ros·coe \'räs-(,)kō, 'rȯs-\ [fr. a surname]
Ross \'rȯs\ [fr. a surname]
Roy \'rȯi\ [ScGael]
Roy·al \'rȯi(-ə)l\ [prob. fr. a surname]
Royce \'rȯis\ [fr. a surname]
Ru·dolph *or* **Ru·dolf** \'rü-,dälf\ [Gmc] famous wolf
Ru·dy \'rüd-ē\ *dim of* RUDOLPH
Ru·fus \'rü-fəs\ [L] red, red-haired
Ru·pert \'rü-pərt\ *var of* ROBERT
Rus·sell *or* **Rus·sel** \'rəs-əl\ [fr. a surname]
Ry·land \'rī-lənd\ [fr. a surname]

Sal·va·tore \'sal-və-,tō(ə)r, -,tȯ(ə)r; ,sal-və-'tōr-ē, -'tȯr-\ [It] savior
Sam \'sam\ *dim of* SAMUEL
Sam·my *or* **Sam·mie** \'sam-ē\ *dim of* SAM
Sam·u·el \'sam-yə(-wə)l\ [Heb] name of God
San·ford \'san-fərd\ [fr. a surname]
Saul \'sȯl\ [Heb] asked for
Scott \'skät\ [fr. a surname]
Sean \'shȯn\ [Ir] *var of* JOHN
Seth \'seth\ [Heb]
Sey·mour \'sē-,mō(ə)r, -,mȯ(ə)r\ [fr. a surname]
Shel·by \'shel-bē\ [fr. a surname]
Shel·don \'shel-dən\ [fr. a surname]
Sher·i·dan \'sher-əd-ᵊn\ [fr. a surname]
Sher·man \'shər-mən\ [fr. a surname]
Sher·win \'shər-wən\ [fr. a surname]
Sher·wood \'shər-,wu̇d, 'she(ə)r-\ [fr. a surname]
Sid·ney *or* **Syd·ney** \'sid-nē\ [fr. a surname]
Sieg·fried \'sig-,frēd, 'sēg-\ [Gmc] victorious peace
Sig·mund \'sig-mənd\ [Gmc] victorious protection
Si·mon \'sī-mən\ [Heb]
Sol·o·mon \'säl-ə-mən\ [Heb] peaceable
Spen·cer \'spen(t)-sər\ [fr. a surname]
Stan \'stan\ *dim of* STANLEY
Stan·ford \'stan-fərd\ [fr. a surname]
Stan·ley \'stan-lē\ [fr. a surname]
Stan·ton \'stant-ᵊn\ [fr. a surname]
Ste·fan \'stef-ən, -,än\ [Pol] *var of* STEPHEN
Ste·phen *or* **Ste·ven** *or* **Ste·phan** \'stē-vən\ [Gk] crown
Ster·ling \'stər-liŋ\ [fr. a surname]
Steve \'stēv\ *dim of* STEVEN
Stu·art *or* **Stew·art** \'st(y)ü-ərt, 'st(y)u̇(-ə)rt\ [fr. a surname]
Syl·ves·ter \sil-'ves-tər\ [L] woodsy, of the woods

Tay·lor \'tā-lər\ [fr. a surname]
Ted \'ted\ *or* **Ted·dy** \'ted-ē\ *dim of* EDWARD, THEODORE
Ter·ence *or* **Ter·rance** *or* **Ter·rence** \'ter-ən(t)s\ [L]
Ter·rell *or* **Ter·rill** \'ter-əl\ [fr. a surname]
Ter·ry \'ter-ē\ *dim of* TERENCE
Thad \'thad\ *dim of* THADDEUS
Thad·de·us \'thad-ē-əs\ [Gk]
The·o·dore \'thē-ə-,dō(ə)r, -,dȯ(ə)r, -əd-ər\ [Gk] gift of God
The·ron \'thir-ən\ [Gk]
Thom·as \'täm-əs\ [Aram] twin
Thur·man \'thər-mən\ [fr. a surname]
Thur·ston \'thər-stən\ [Scand] Thor's stone
Tim \'tim\ *dim of* TIMOTHY
Tim·o·thy \'tim-ə-thē\ [Gk] revering God
To·by \'tō-bē\ *dim of* TOBIAS
Todd \'täd\ [prob. fr. a surname]
Tom \'täm\ *or* **Tom·my** *or* **Tom·mie** \'täm-ē\ *dim of* THOMAS
To·ny \'tō-nē\ *dim of* ANTHONY
Tra·cy \'trā-sē\ [fr. a surname]
Trav·is \'trav-əs\ [fr. a surname]
Trent \'trent\ [fr. a surname]
Troy \'trȯi\ [prob. fr. a surname]
Tru·man \'trü-mən\ [fr. a surname]
Ty·rone \'tī-,rōn, tī-'; tir-'ōn\ [prob. fr. the county in Ireland]

Val \'val\ *dim of* VALENTINE
Van \'van\ [fr. surnames beginning with *Van,* fr. D *van* of]
Vance \'van(t)s\ [fr. a surname]
Vaughn \'vȯn, 'vän\ [fr. a surname]
Verne *or* **Vern** \'vərn\ *prob alter of* VERNON
Ver·non \'vər-nən\ [prob. fr. a surname]
Vic·tor \'vik-tər\ [L] conqueror
Vin·cent \'vin(t)-sənt\ [LL] of or relating to the conquering one
Vir·gil \'vər-jəl\ [L]

Wade \'wād\ [fr. a surname]
Wal·do \'wȯl-(,)dō, 'wäl-\ [fr. a surname]
Wal·lace *or* **Wal·lis** \'wäl-əs\ [fr. a surname]
Wal·ter \'wȯl-tər\ [Gmc] army of dominion
Wal·ton \'wȯlt-ᵊn\ [fr. a surname]
Ward \'wȯ(ə)rd\ [fr. a surname]
War·ner \'wȯr-nər\ [fr. a surname]
War·ren \'wȯr-ən, 'wär-\ [fr. a surname]
Wayne \'wān\ [fr. a surname]
Wel·don \'wel-dən\ [fr. a surname]
Wen·dell \'wen-dᵊl\ [fr. a surname]

Wer·ner \'wər-nər, 'we(ə)r-\ [Gmc] army of the Varini, a Germanic people
Wes·ley \'wes-lē *also* 'wez-\ [fr. a surname]
Wil·bert \'wil-bərt\ [fr. a surname]
Wil·bur *or* **Wil·ber** \'wil-bər\ [fr. a surname]
Wil·burn \'wil-bərn\ [fr. a surname]
Wi·ley *or* **Wy·lie** \'wī-lē\ [fr. a surname]
Wil·ford \'wil-fərd\ [fr. a surname]
Wil·fred \'wil-frəd\ [OE] desired peace
Will \'wil\ *or* **Wil·lie** \-ē\ *dim of* WILLIAM
Wil·lard \'wil-ərd\ [fr. a surname]
Wil·liam \'wil-yəm\ [Gmc] desired helmet
Wil·lis \'wil-əs\ [fr. a surname]
Wil·mer \'wil-mər\ [fr. a surname]
Wil·son \'wil-sən\ [fr. a surname]
Wil·ton \'wilt-ᵊn\ [fr. a surname]
Win·field \'win-ˌfēld\ [fr. a surname]
Win·fred \'win-frəd\ [OE] *prob* joyous peace
Win·ston \'win(t)-stən\ [fr. a surname]
Win·ton \'wint-ᵊn\ [fr. a surname]
Wolf·gang \'wu̇lf-ˌgaŋ\ [OHG] path of a wolf
Wood·row \'wu̇d-(ˌ)rō\ [fr. a surname]
Wy·att \'wī-ət\ [fr. a surname]

Yale \'yā(ə)l\ [fr. a surname]

Zane \'zān\ [fr. a surname]

II NAMES OF WOMEN

Ab·by \'ab-ē\ *dim of* ABIGAIL
Ab·i·gail \'ab-ə-ˌgāl\ [Heb] *prob* source of joy
Ada \'ād-ə\ [Heb] *prob* ornament
Ad·e·laide \'ad-ᵊl-ˌād\ [Gmc] of noble rank
Adele \ə-'del\ [Gmc] noble
Adri·enne \'ā-drē-ˌen, -ən\ [F] *fem of* ADRIEN
Ag·nes \'ag-nəs\ [LL]
Ai·leen \ī-'lēn\ [IrGael] *var of* HELEN
Al·ber·ta \al-'bərt-ə\ *fem of* ALBERT
Al·ex·an·dra \ˌal-ig-'zan-drə, ˌel-\ [Gk] *fem of* ALEXANDER
Al·ice *or* **Al·yce** \'al-əs\ [OF] *var of* ADELAIDE
Ali·cia \ə-'lish-ə\ [ML] *var of* ADELAIDE
Al·li·son *or* **Al·li·son** \'al-ə-sən\ [OF] *dim of* ALICE
Al·ma \'al-mə\ [L] nourishing, cherishing
Al·ta \'al-tə\ [L] high
Al·va \'al-və\ [Sp, fr. L] white
Aman·da \ə-'man-də\ [L] worthy to be loved
Ame·lia \ə-'mēl-yə\ [Gmc]
Amy \'ā-mē\ [L] beloved
An·as·ta·sia \ˌan-ə-'stā-zh(ē-)ə\ [LGk] of the resurrection
An·drea \'an-drē-ə, an-'drā-ə\ *fem of* ANDREW
An·ge·la \'an-jə-lə\ [It, fr. Gk] angel
An·ge·line \'an-jə-ˌlīn, -ˌlēn\ *dim of* ANGELA
Ani·ta \ə-'nēt-ə\ [Sp] *dim of* ANN
Ann *or* **Anne** \'an\ *or* **An·na** \'an-ə\ [Heb] grace
An·na·belle \'an-ə-ˌbel\ *prob var of* MABEL
An·nette \a-'net, ə-\ *or* **An·net·ta** \-'net-ə\ [F] *dim of* ANN
An·nie \'an-ē\ *dim of* ANN
An·toi·nette \ˌan-t(w)ə-'net\ [F] *dim of* ANTONIA
April \'ā-prəl\ [E] April (the month)
Ar·dell *or* **Ar·delle** \är-'del\ *var of* ADELE
Ar·dis \'ärd-əs\
Ar·lene *or* **Ar·leen** *or* **Ar·line** \är-'lēn\
As·trid \'as-trəd\ [Scand] beautiful as a deity
Au·drey \'ȯ-drē\ [OE] noble strength

Ba·bette \ba-'bet\ [F] *dim of* ELIZABETH
Bar·ba·ra \'bär-b(ə-)rə\ [Gk] foreign
Be·atrice \'bē-ə-trəs *also* bē-'a-trəs\ [It, fr. ML] she that makes happy
Becky \'bek-ē\ *dim of* REBECCA
Ber·na·dette \ˌbər-nə-'det\ [F] *fem of* BERNARD
Ber·na·dine \'bər-nə-ˌdēn\ *fem of* BERNARD
Ber·nice \(ˌ)bər-'nēs, 'bər-nəs\ [Gk] bringing victory
Ber·tha \'bər-thə\ [Gmc] bright
Ber·yl \'ber-əl\ [Gk] beryl (the mineral)
Bes·sie \'bes-ē\ *dim of* ELIZABETH
Beth \'beth\ *dim of* ELIZABETH
Bet·sy *or* **Bet·sey** \'bet-sē\ *dim of* ELIZABETH
Bet·ty *or* **Bet·te** *or* **Bet·tye** *or* **Bet·tie** \'bet-ē\ *dim of* ELIZABETH
Beu·lah \'byü-lə\ [Heb] married
Bev·er·ly *or* **Bev·er·ley** \'bev-ər-lē\ [prob. fr. a surname]
Bil·lie \'bil-ē\ *fem of* BILLY
Blanche \'blanch\ [OF, fr. Gmc] white
Bob·bie \'bäb-ē\ *dim of* ROBERTA
Bo·ni·ta \bə-'nēt-ə\ [Sp] pretty
Bon·nie \'bän-ē\ [ME] pretty
Bren·da \'bren-də\ [Scand]
Bri·gitte \'brij-ət, brə-'jit\ [G] *var of* BRIDGET

Ca·mil·la \kə-'mil-ə\ [L] freeborn girl attendant at a sacrifice
Ca·mille \kə-'mē(ə)l\ [F] *var of* CAMILLA
Can·da·ce \kan-'dā-sē, 'kan-də-(ˌ)sē, 'kan-dəs\ [Gk]
Car·la \'kär-lə\ [It] *fem of* CARLO
Car·lene \kär-'lēn\ *var of* CARLA
Car·lot·ta \kär-'lät-ə\ [It] *var of* CHARLOTTE
Car·men \'kär-mən\ *or* **Car·mine** \kär-'mēn, 'kär-mən\ [Sp, fr. L] song
Car·ol *or* **Car·ole** *or* **Car·yl** \'kar-əl\ *dim of* CAROLYN
Car·o·lyn \'kar-ə-lən\ *or* **Car·o·line** \-lən, -ˌlīn\ [It] *fem of* CHARLES
Car·rie \'kar-ē\ *dim of* CAROLINE
Cath·er·ine *or* **Cath·a·rine** \'kath-(ə-)rən\ [LGk]
Cath·leen \kath-'lēn\ [IrGael] *var of* CATHERINE
Cath·ryn \'kath-rən\ *var of* CATHERINE
Cathy *or* **Cath·ie** \'kath-ē\ *dim of* CATHERINE
Ce·cile \sə-'sē(ə)l\ *var of* CECILIA
Ce·ci·lia \sə-'sēl-yə, -'sil-\ *or* **Ce·ce·lia** \-'sēl-\ [L] *fem of* CECIL
Ce·leste \sə-'lest\ [L] heavenly
Ce·lia \'sēl-yə\ *dim of* CECILIA
Char·lene \shär-'lēn\ *fem of* CHARLES
Char·lotte \'shär-lət\ [F] *fem dim of* CHARLES
Cher·ie \'sher-ē\ [F] dear
Cher·ry \'cher-ē\ [E] cherry
Cher·yl \'cher-əl, 'sher-\ *prob var of* CHERRY
Chloe \'klō-ē\ [Gk] young verdure
Chris·tine \kris-'tēn\ *or* **Chris·ti·na** \-'tē-nə\ [Gk] Christian
Cin·dy \'sin-dē\ *dim of* LUCINDA
Claire *or* **Clare** \'kla(ə)r, 'kle(ə)r\ *var of* CLARA
Clara \'klar-ə\ [L] bright
Cla·rice \'klar-əs, klə-'rēs\ *dim of* CLARA
Clau·dette \klȯ-'det\ [F] *fem of* CLAUDE
Clau·dia \'klȯd-ē-ə\ [L] *fem of* CLAUDE
Clau·dine \klȯ-'dēn\ [F] *fem of* CLAUDE
Cleo \'klē-(ˌ)ō\ *dim of* CLEOPATRA
Co·lette \kä-'let\ [OF] *fem dim of* NICHOLAS
Col·leen \kä-'lēn\ [IrGael] girl
Con·nie \'kän-ē\ *dim of* CONSTANCE
Con·stance \'kän(t)-stən(t)s\ [L] constancy
Co·ra \'kōr-ə, 'kȯr-\ [Gk] maiden
Co·rinne *or* **Cor·rine** \kə-'rin, -'rēn\ [Gk] *dim of* CORA
Cor·ne·lia \kȯr-'nēl-yə\ [L] *fem of* CORNELIUS
Cyn·thia \'sin(t)-thē-ə\ [Gk] she of Mount Cynthus on the island of Delos (i.e. the goddess Artemis, supposed to have been born there)

Dai·sy \'dā-zē\ [E] daisy
Dale \'dā(ə)l\ [E] valley
Da·na \'dā-nə\ [fr. a surname]
Daph·ne \'daf-nē\ [Gk] laurel
Dar·la \'där-lə\ [deriv. of *darling*]
Dar·lene \där-'lēn\ [deriv. of *darling*]
Dawn \'dȯn, 'dän\ [E] dawn
De·an·na \dē-'an-ə\ *or* **De·anne** \-'an\ *var of* DIANA
Deb·o·rah *or* **Deb·o·ra** \'deb-(ə-)rə\ [Heb] bee
Deb·ra \'deb-rə\ *var of* DEBORAH
Dee \'dē\ *prob dim of* EDITH
Deir·dre \'di(ə)r-drē, 'de(ə)r-\ [IrGael]
De·lia \'dēl-yə\ [Gk] she of Delos (i.e. the goddess Artemis)
Del·la \'del-ə\ *dim of* -DEL *or* -DEL-
De·lo·res \də-'lōr-əs, -'lȯr-\ *var of* DOLORES
De·na *or* **Dee·na** \'dē-nə\ *dim of* GERALDINE
De·nise \də-'nēz, -'nēs\ [F] *fem of* DENIS
Di·ana *or* **Di·an·na** \dī-'an-ə\ [L]
Di·ane *or* **Di·anne** *or* **Di·an** *or* **Di·ann** \dī-'an\ [F] *var of* DIANA
Di·na *or* **Di·nah** \'dī-nə\ [Heb] judged
Dix·ie \'dik-sē\ [E] *prob* Dixie (nickname for the southern states of the U.S.)
Do·lo·res \də-'lōr-əs, -'lȯr-\ [Sp, fr. L] sorrows (i.e. those of the Virgin Mary)
Don·na \'dän-ə\ *or* **Do·na** \'dän-ə, 'dō-nə\ [It, fr. L] lady
Do·ra \'dōr-ə, 'dȯr-\ *dim of* -DORA
Dor·cas \'dȯr-kəs\ [Gk] gazelle
Do·reen \dȯ-'rēn, də-\ [IrGael]
Dor·is \'dȯr-əs, 'där-\ [Gk] *prob* Dorian
Dor·o·thy \'dȯr-ə-thē, 'där-\ *or* **Dor·o·thea** \ˌdȯr-ə-'thē-ə, ˌdär-\ [LGk] goddess of gifts

Edith *or* **Edythe** \'ēd-əth\ [OE]
Ed·na \'ed-nə\ [Aram] *prob var of* ANN
Ed·wi·na \e-'dwē-nə, -'dwin-ə\ *fem of* EDWIN
Ef·fie \'ef-ē\ *dim of* EUPHEMIA
Ei·leen \ī-'lēn\ [IrGael]
Elaine \i-'lān\ [OF] *var of* HELEN
El·ea·nor *or* **El·i·nor** *or* **El·ea·nore** \'el-ə-nər, -ˌnȯ(ə)r, -ˌnō(ə)r\ [OProv] *var of* HELEN
Ele·na \'el-ə-nə, ə-'lē-nə\ [It] *var of* HELEN
Elise \ə-'lēz, -'lēs\ [F] *var of* ELIZABETH
Eliz·a·beth *or* **Elis·a·beth** \i-'liz-ə-bəth\ [Heb] God has sworn
El·la \'el-ə\ [OF]
El·len *or* **El·lyn** \'el-ən\ *var of* HELEN
El·o·ise \'el-ə-ˌwēz, ˌel-ə-'\ [OF, fr. Gmc]
El·sa \'el-sə\ [G] *dim of* ELIZABETH
El·sie \'el-sē\ *dim of* ELIZABETH
El·va \'el-və\ [Gmc] elf
Em·i·ly *or* **Em·i·lie** \'em-(ə-)lē\ [L] *fem of* EMIL
Em·ma \'em-ə\ [Gmc] *var of* ERMA
Enid \'ē-nəd\ [W]
Er·i·ka \'er-i-kə\ *fem of* ERIC
Er·ma \'ər-mə\ [Gmc] *dim of* ERM-
Er·na \'ər-nə\ *dim of* ERNESTINE
Er·nes·tine \'ər-nə-ˌstēn\ *fem of* ERNEST
Es·telle \e-'stel\ *or* **Es·tel·la** \e-'stel-ə\ [OProv, fr. L] star
Es·ther \'es-tər\ [prob. fr. Per] *prob* star
Eth·el \'eth-əl\ [OE] noble

Et·ta \'et-ə\ *dim of* HENRIETTA
Eu·ge·nia \yu̇-'jēn-yə\ *or* **Eu·ge·nie** \-'jē-nē\ *fem of* EUGENE
Eu·nice \'yü-nəs\ [Gk] having (i.e. bringing) happy victory
Eva \'ē-və\ *var of* EVE
Evan·ge·line \i-'van-jə-lən, -ˌlēn, -ˌlīn\ [Gk] bringing good news
Eve \'ēv\ [Heb] life, living
Ev·e·lyn \'ev-(ə-)lən, *chiefly Brit* 'ēv-\ [OF, fr. Gmc]

Faith \'fāth\ [E] faith
Faye *or* **Fay** \'fā\ *dim of* FAITH
Fe·lice \fə-'lēs\ [L] happiness
Fern *or* **Ferne** \'fərn\ [E] fern
Flo·ra \'flōr-ə, 'flȯr-\ [L] goddess of flowers
Flor·ence \'flȯr-ən(t)s, 'flär-\ [L] bloom, prosperity
Fran·ces \'fran(t)-səs, -səz\ *fem of* FRANCIS
Fran·cine \fran-'sēn\ [F] *prob dim of* FRANCES
Fre·da *or* **Frie·da** \'frēd-ə\ *dim of* WINIFRED
Fred·er·ic·ka *or* **Fred·er·i·ca** \ˌfred-(ə-)'rē-kə, -'rik-ə\ *fem of* FREDERICK

Gail *or* **Gayle** *or* **Gale** \'gā(ə)l\ *dim of* ABIGAIL
Gay \'gā\ [E] gay
Ge·ne·va \jə-'nē-və\ *var of* GENEVIEVE
Gen·e·vieve \'jen-ə-ˌvēv\ [prob. fr. Celt]
George·ann \jȯr-'jan\ [*George* + *Ann*]
Geor·gia \'jȯr-jə\ *fem of* GEORGE
Geor·gi·na \jȯr-'jē-nə\ *fem of* GEORGE
Ger·al·dine \'jer-əl-ˌdēn\ *fem of* GERALD
Ger·trude \'gər-ˌtrüd\ [Gmc] spear strength
Gin·ger \'jin-jər\ [E] ginger
Gi·sela \jə-'sel-ə, -'zel-\ [Gmc] pledge
Glad·ys \'glad-əs\ [W]
Glen·da \'glen-də\ *prob var of* GLENNA
Glen·na \'glen-ə\ *fem of* GLENN
Glo·ria \'glōr-ē-ə, 'glȯr-\ [L] glory
Grace \'grās\ [L] favor, grace
Gre·ta \'grēt-ə, 'gret-\ *dim of* MARGARET
Gretch·en \'grech-ən\ [G] *dim of* MARGARET
Gwen \'gwen\ *dim of* GWENDOLYN
Gwen·do·lyn \'gwen-də-lən\ [W]

Han·nah \'han-ə\ [Heb] *var of* ANN
Har·ri·et *or* **Har·ri·ett** *or* **Har·ri·ette** \'har-ē-ət\ *var of* HENRIETTA
Hat·tie \'hat-ē\ *dim of* HARRIET
Ha·zel \'hā-zəl\ [E] hazel
Heath·er \'heth-ər\ [ME] heather (the shrub)
Hei·di \'hīd-ē\ [G] *dim of* ADELAIDE
He·laine \hə-'lān\ *var of* HELEN
Hel·en \'hel-ən\ *or* **He·le·na** \'hel-ə-nə, hə-'lē-nə\ [Gk]
He·lene \hə-'lēn\ [F] *var of* HELEN
Hel·ga \'hel-gə\ [Scand] holy
Hen·ri·et·ta \ˌhen-rē-'et-ə\ [MF] *fem of* HENRY
Her·mine \'hər-ˌmēn\ [G] *prob fem of* HERMAN
Hes·ter \'hes-tər\ *var of* ESTHER
Hil·da \'hil-də\ [OE] battle
Hil·de·gard *or* **Hil·de·garde** \'hil-də-ˌgärd\ [Gmc] *prob* battle enclosure
Hol·ly \'häl-ē\ [E] holly
Hope \'hōp\ [E] hope

Ida \'īd-ə\ [Gmc]
Ila \'ī-lə\
Ilene \ī-'lēn\ *var of* EILEEN
Ilo·na \ī-'lō-nə, il-'ō-\ [Hung] *var of* HELEN
Imo·gene \'im-ə-ˌjēn, 'ī-mə-\
Ina \'ī-nə\
Inez \ī-'nez, 'ī-nəz\ [Sp] *var of* AGNES
In·grid \'iŋ-grəd\ [Scand] beautiful as Ing (an ancient Germanic god)
Irene \ī-'rēn\ [Gk] peace
Iris \'ī-rəs\ [Gk] rainbow
Ir·ma \'ər-mə\ *var of* ERMA
Is·a·bel *or* **Is·a·belle** \'iz-ə-ˌbel\ [OProv] *var of* ELIZABETH
Iva \'ī-və\ *perh dim of* GODIVA

Jac·que·line *or* **Jac·que·lyn** *or* **Jac·que·lin** \'jak-(w)ə-lən, -ˌlēn\ [OF] *fem of* JACOB
Jan \'jan\ *dim of* JANET
Jane *or* **Jayne** \'jān\ [OF] *var of* JOAN
Ja·net *or* **Ja·nette** \'jan-ət, jə-'net\ *dim of* JANE
Ja·nice \'jan-əs, jə-'nēs\ *or* **Jan·is** \'jan-əs\ *prob dim of* JANE
Ja·nie \'jā-nē\ *dim of* JANE
Jean *or* **Jeanne** \'jēn\ [OF] *var of* JOAN
Jea·nette *or* **Jean·nette** \jə-'net\ [F] *dim of* JEANNE
Jean·nie *or* **Jean·ie** \'jē-nē\ *dim of* JEAN
Jean·nine *or* **Jea·nine** \jə-'nēn\ [F] *dim of* JEANNE
Jen·nie *or* **Jen·ny** \'jen-ē\ *dim of* JANE
Jen·ni·fer \'jen-ə-fər\ [Celt]
Jer·al·dine \'jer-əl-ˌdēn\ *var of* GERALDINE
Jer·i·lyn \'jer-ə-lən\ *var of* GERALDINE
Jer·ry *or* **Jeri** *or* **Jer·rie** \'jer-ē\ *dim of* GERALDINE
Jes·si·ca \'jes-i-kə\ [prob. Heb]
Jes·sie \'jes-ē\ [Sc] *dim of* JANET
Jew·el *or* **Jew·ell** \'jü(-ə)l, 'ju̇(-ə)l\ [E] jewel
Jill \'jil\ *dim of* JULIANA
Jo \'jō\ *dim of* JOSEPHINE
Joan *or* **Joann** *or* **Joanne** \'jō(-ə)n, jō-'an\ [Gk] *fem of* JOHN
Jo·an·na \jō-'an-ə\ *or* **Jo·han·na** \-'(h)an-ə\ *var of* JOAN
Joc·e·lyn \'jäs-(ə-)lən\ [OF, fr. Gmc]
Jo·lene \jō-'lēn\ *prob dim of* JO
Jo·se·phine \'jō-zə-ˌfēn *also* 'jō-sə-\ *fem of* JOSEPH
Joy \'jȯi\ [E] joy
Joyce \'jȯis\ [OF]
Jua·ni·ta \wä-'nēt-ə\ [Sp] *fem dim of* JOHN
Ju·dith \'jüd-əth\ [Heb] Jewess
Ju·dy *or* **Ju·di** *or* **Ju·die** \'jüd-ē\ *dim of* JUDITH
Ju·lia \'jül-yə\ [L] *fem of* JULIUS
Ju·li·ana \ˌjü-lē-'an-ə\ [LL] *fem of* JULIAN
Ju·li·anne *or* **Ju·li·ann** \ˌjü-lē-'an, jül-'yan\ *var of* JULIANA
Ju·lie \'jü-lē\ [MF] *var of* JULIA
Ju·liet \'jül-yət, -ē-ˌet, -ē-ət; ˌjül-ē-'et, jül-'yet, 'jül-ˌyet\ [It] *dim of* JULIA
June \'jün\ [E] June (the month)
Jus·tine \ˌjəs-'tēn\ [F] *fem of* JUSTIN

Kar·en *or* **Kar·in** *or* **Kaa·ren** \'kar-ən, 'kär-\ [Scand] *var of* CATHERINE
Kar·la \'kär-lə\ *var of* CARLA
Kar·ol \'kar-əl\ *var of* CAROL
Kar·o·lyn \'kar-ə-lən\ *var of* CAROLYN
Kate \'kāt\ *dim of* CATHERINE
Kath·er·ine *or* **Kath·a·rine** *or* **Kath·ryn** \'kath-(ə-)rən\ *var of* CATHERINE
Kath·leen \kath-'lēn\ [IrGael] *var of* CATHERINE
Kathy \'kath-ē\ *dim of* CATHERINE
Ka·tie \'kāt-ē\ *dim of* KATE
Kay *or* **Kaye** \'kā\ *dim of* CATHERINE
Kit·ty \'kit-ē\ *dim of* CATHERINE
Kris·tin \'kris-tən\ [Scand] *var of* CHRISTINE
Kris·tine \kris-'tēn\ *var of* CHRISTINE

La·na \'lan-ə, 'län-ə, 'lā-nə\
Lau·ra \'lȯr-ə, 'lär-\ [ML] *prob fem dim of* LAWRENCE
Lau·rel \'lȯr-əl, 'lär-\ [E] laurel
Lau·rie \'lȯr-ē, 'lär-\ *dim of* LAURA
La·verne *or* **La·vern** \lə-'vərn\
Le·ah \'lē-ə\ [Heb] *prob* wild cow
Le·anne \lē-'an\ [prob. fr. *Lee* + *Ann*]
Lee \'lē\ [fr. a surname]
Lei·la *or* **Le·la** \'lē-lə\ [Per] dark as night
Le·lia \'lēl-yə\ [L]
Le·na \'lē-nə\ [G] *dim of* HELENA & MAGDALENA
Le·nore \lə-'nō(ə)r, -'nȯ(ə)r\ *or* **Le·no·ra** \lə-'nōr-ə, -'nȯr-\ *var of* LEONORA
Le·o·na \lē-'ō-nə\ *fem of* LEON
Le·o·no·ra \ˌlē-ə-'nōr-ə, -'nȯr-\ *var of* ELEANOR

Les·lie *or* **Les·ley** \'les-lē *also* 'lez-\ [fr. a surname]
Le·ta \'lēt-ə\
Le·ti·tia \li-'tish-ə, -'tē-shə\ [L] gladness
Lib·by \'lib-ē\ *dim of* ELIZABETH
Li·la \'lī-lə\ *var of* LEILA
Lil·lian \'lil-yən, 'lil-ē-ən\ *prob dim of* ELIZABETH
Lil·lie \'lil-ē\ *dim of* LILLIAN
Lily \'lil-ē\ [E] lily
Lin·da *or* **Lyn·da** \'lin-də\ *dim of* -LINDA
Li·sa \'lī-zə, 'lē-\ *dim of* ELIZABETH
Lo·is \'lō-əs\ [Gk]
Lo·la \'lō-lə\ [Sp] *dim of* DOLORES
Lon·na \'län-ə\ *fem of* LON
Lo·ra \'lōr-ə, 'lȯr-\ *var of* LAURA
Lo·re·lei \'lōr-ə-ˌlī, 'lȯr-\ [G]
Lo·rene \lō-'rēn\ *dim of* LORA
Lo·ret·ta \lə-'ret-ə, lō-\ [ML] *var of* LAURETTA
Lor·na \'lȯr-nə\
Lor·raine *or* **Lo·raine** \lə-'rān, lō-\ [prob. fr. *Lorraine*, region in northeast France]
Lou \'lü\ *dim of* LOUISE
Lou·ise \lu̇-'ēz\ *or* **Lou·i·sa** \-'ē-zə\ *fem of* LOUIS
Lu·anne \lü-'an\ [*Lu-* + *Anne*]
Lu·cille *or* **Lu·cile** \lü-'sē(ə)l\ [L] *prob dim of* LUCIA
Lu·cin·da \lü-'sin-də\ [L] *var of* LUCY
Lu·cre·tia \lü-'krē-shə\ [L]
Lu·cy \'lü-sē\ *or* **Lu·cia** \'lü-shə\ [L] *fem of* LUCIUS
Lu·el·la \lu̇-'el-ə\ [prob. fr. *Lou* (dim. of *Louise*) + *Ella*]
Lyd·ia \'lid-ē-ə\ [Gk] Lydian woman
Ly·nette \lə-'net\ [W]
Lynne *or* **Lynn** \'lin\ *var of* -LYN

Ma·bel \'mā-bəl\ [L] lovable
Mad·e·line *or* **Mad·e·leine** *or* **Mad·e·lyn** \'mad-ᵊl-ən\ [Gk] woman of Magdala, ancient town in northern Palestine
Madge \'maj\ *dim of* MARGARET
Ma·mie \'mā-mē\ *dim of* MARGARET
Ma·ra \'mär-ə\ *var of* MARY
Mar·cel·la \mär-'sel-ə\ [L] *fem of* MARCELLUS
Mar·cia \'mär-shə\ [L] *fem of* MARCUS
Mar·ga·ret \'mär-g(ə-)rət\ [Gk] pearl
Mar·gery \'märj-(ə-)rē\ [OF] *var of* MARGARET
Mar·gie \'mär-jē\ *dim of* MARGARET
Mar·go \'mär-(ˌ)gō\ *var of* MARGOT
Mar·got \'mär-(ˌ)gō, -gət\ *dim of* MARGARET
Mar·gue·rite \ˌmär-g(y)ə-'rēt\ [OF] *var of* MARGARET
Ma·ria \mə-'rē-ə *also* -'rī-\ *var of* MARY
Mar·i·an \'mer-ē-ən, 'mar-\ *var of* MARIANNE
Mar·i·anne \ˌmer-ē-'an, ˌmar-\ *or* **Mar·i·an·na** \-'an-ə\ [F] *dim of* MARY
Ma·rie \mə-'rē\ [OF] *var of* MARY
Mar·i·et·ta \ˌmer-ē-'et-ə, ˌmar-\ *dim of* MARY
Mar·i·lee \'mer-ə-(ˌ)lē, 'mar-\ [prob. fr. *Mary* + *Lee*]
Mar·i·lyn *or* **Mar·i·lynn** *or* **Mar·y·lyn** \'mer-ə-lən, 'mar-\ [prob. fr. *Mary* + *-lyn*]
Ma·ri·na \mə-'rē-nə\ [LGk]
Mar·i·on \'mer-ē-ən, 'mar-\ *dim of* MARY
Mar·jo·rie *or* **Mar·jo·ry** \'märj-(ə-)rē\ *var of* MARGERY
Mar·la \'mär-lə\ *prob dim of* MARLENE
Mar·lene \mär-'lēn(-ə), -'lā-nə\ [G] *dim of* MAGDALENE
Mar·lyn \'mär-lən\ *prob var of* MARLENE
Mar·lys \'mär-ləs\
Mar·na \'mär-nə\
Mar·sha \'mär-shə\ *var of* MARCIA
Mar·ta \'märt-ə\ [It] *var of* MARTHA
Mar·tha \'mär-thə\ [Aram] lady
Mar·va \'mär-və\ *prob fem of* MARVIN
Mary \'me(ə)r-ē, 'ma(ə)r-ē, 'mā-rē\ [Gk, fr. Heb]
Mary·ann *or* **Mary·anne** \ˌmer-ē-'an, ˌmar-ē-, ˌmā-rē-\ [*Mary* + *Ann*]

Mary·el·len \ˌmer-ē-ˈel-ən, ˌmar-ē-, ˌmā-rē-\ [*Mary + Ellen*]
Mar·y·lon \ˈmer-ə-lən, ˈmar-\ *var of* MARILYN
Maude \ˈmȯd\ [OF] *var of* MATILDA
Mau·reen *or* **Mau·rine** \mȯ-ˈrēn\ *dim of* MAURA
Max·ine \mak-ˈsēn\ [F] *fem dim of* MAXIMILIAN
May *or* **Mae** \ˈmā\ *dim of* MARY
Mel·a·nie \ˈmel-ə-nē\ [Gk] blackness
Mel·ba \ˈmel-bə\ [E] woman of Melbourne, Australia
Me·lin·da \mə-ˈlin-də\ *prob alter of* BELINDA
Me·lis·sa \mə-ˈlis-ə\ [Gk] bee
Mel·va \ˈmel-və\ *prob fem of* MELVIN
Mer·e·dith \ˈmer-əd-əth\ [W]
Merle \ˈmər(-ə)l\ [F] blackbird
Mer·ri·ly \ˈmer-ə-lē\ *alter of* MARILEE
Mer·ry \ˈmer-ē\ [E] merry
Mi·chele *or* **Mi·chelle** \mi-ˈshel\ [F] *fem of* MICHAEL
Mil·dred \ˈmil-drəd\ [OE] gentle strength
Mil·li·cent \ˈmil-ə-sənt\ [Gmc]
Mil·lie \ˈmil-ē\ *dim of* MILDRED
Min·nie \ˈmin-ē\ [Sc] *dim of* MARY
Mir·i·am \ˈmir-ē-əm\ [Heb] *var of* MARY
Mit·zi \ˈmit-sē\ *prob dim of* MARGARET
Mol·ly *or* **Mol·lie** \ˈmäl-ē\ *dim of* MARY
Mo·na \ˈmō-nə\ [IrGael]
Mon·i·ca \ˈmän-i-kə\ [LL]
Mu·ri·el \ˈmyu̇r-ē-əl\ [prob. Celt]
My·ra \ˈmī-rə\
Myr·na \ˈmər-nə\
Myr·tle \ˈmərt-ᵊl\ [Gk] myrtle

Na·dine \nā-ˈdēn, nə-\ [F, fr. Russ] hope
Nan \ˈnan\ *dim of* ANN
Nan·cy \ˈnan(t)-sē\ *dim of* ANN
Nan·nette *or* **Na·nette** \na-ˈnet, nə-\ [F] *dim of* ANN
Na·o·mi \nā-ˈō-mē\ [Heb] pleasant
Nat·a·lie \ˈnat-ᵊl-ē\ [LL] of or relating to Christmas
Ne·dra \ˈned-rə, ˈnē-drə\
Nel·da \ˈnel-də\
Nel·lie \ˈnel-ē\ *or* **Nell** \ˈnel\ *dim of* -EL-
Net·tie \ˈnet-ē\ [Sc] *dim of* JANET
Ne·va \ˈnē-və\
Ni·na \ˈnī-nə, ˈnē-\ [Russ] *dim of* ANN
Ni·ta \ˈnēt-ə\ [Sp] *dim of* JUANITA
No·la \ˈnō-lə\
No·na \ˈnō-nə\ [L] ninth
No·ra \ˈnōr-ə, ˈnȯr-\ *dim of* -NOR-
No·reen \nȯ-ˈrēn\ [IrGael] *dim of* NORA
Nor·ma \ˈnȯr-mə\ [It]

Ol·ga \ˈäl-gə, ˈōl-\ [Russ] *var of* HELGA
Ol·ive \ˈäl-iv, -əv\ *or* **O·liv·ia** \ə-ˈliv-ē-ə, ō-\ [L] olive
Opal \ˈō-pəl\ [E] opal

Pa·me·la \ˈpam-ə-lə; pə-ˈmē-lə, pa-\
Pa·tri·cia \pə-ˈtrish-ə, -ˈtrē-shə\ [L] *fem of* PATRICK
Pat·sy \ˈpat-sē\ *dim of* PATRICIA
Pat·ty *or* **Pat·ti** *or* **Pat·tie** \ˈpat-ē\ *dim of* PATRICIA

Pau·la \ˈpȯ-lə\ [L] *fem of* PAUL
Pau·lette \pȯ-ˈlet\ *fem dim of* PAUL
Pau·line \pȯ-ˈlēn\ *fem dim of* PAUL
Pearl \ˈpər(-ə)l\ [E] pearl
Peg·gy \ˈpeg-ē\ *dim of* MARGARET
Pe·nel·o·pe \pə-ˈnel-ə-pē\ [Gk]
Pen·ny \ˈpen-ē\ *dim of* PENELOPE
Phoe·be \ˈfē-bē\ [Gk] shining
Phyl·lis \ˈfil-əs\ [Gk] green leaf
Pol·ly \ˈpäl-ē\ *dim of* MARY
Por·tia \ˈpōr-shə, ˈpȯr-\ [L]
Pris·cil·la \prə-ˈsil-ə\ [L]
Pru·dence \ˈprüd-ᵊn(t)s\ [E] prudence

Ra·chel \ˈrā-chəl\ [Heb] ewe
Rae \ˈrā\ *dim of* RACHEL
Ra·mo·na \rə-ˈmō-nə\ [Sp] *fem of* RAMON
Re·ba \ˈrē-bə\ *dim of* REBECCA
Re·bec·ca \ri-ˈbek-ə\ [Heb]
Re·gi·na \ri-ˈjē-nə, -ˈjī-\ [L] queen
Re·na \ˈrē-nə\
Re·nee \rə-ˈnā, ˈren-(ˌ)ā, ˈrā-nē, ˈrē-nē\ [F, fr. L] reborn
Rhea \ˈrē-ə\ [Gk]
Rho·da \ˈrōd-ə\ [Gk] rose
Ri·ta \ˈrēt-ə\ [It] *dim of* MARGARET
Ro·ber·ta \rə-ˈbərt-ə, rō-\ *fem of* ROBERT
Rob·in *or* **Rob·yn** \ˈräb-ən\ [E] robin
Ro·chelle \rō-ˈshel\ [prob. fr. a surname]
Ro·na *or* **Rho·na** \ˈrō-nə\
Ron·da \ˈrän-də\ *var of* RHONDA
Ron·nie \ˈrän-ē\ *dim of* VERONICA
Ro·sa·lie \ˈrō-zə-(ˌ)lē, ˈräz-ə-\ [L] festival of roses
Ro·sa·lind \ˈräz-(ə-)lənd, ˈrō-zə-lənd\ [Sp, prob. fr. Gmc]
Rose \ˈrōz\ *or* **Ro·sa** \ˈrō-zə\ [L] rose
Rose·anne \rō-ˈzan\ [*Rose + Anne*]
Rose·mary \ˈrōz-ˌmer-ē\ *or* **Rose·ma·rie** \ˌrōz-mə-ˈrē\ [E] rosemary
Ro·set·ta \rō-ˈzet-ə\ *dim of* ROSE
Ros·lyn \ˈräz-lən\ *or* **Ro·sa·lyn** *or* **Ro·se·lyn** \ˈräz-(ə-)lən, ˈrō-zə-lən\ *var of* ROSALIND
Ro·we·na \rə-ˈwē-nə\ [perh. fr. OE]
Rox·anne \räk-ˈsan\ [OPer]
Ru·by \ˈrü-bē\ [E] ruby
Ruth \ˈrüth\ [Heb]
Ruth·ann \rü-ˈthan\ [*Ruth + Ann*]

Sa·bra \ˈsā-brə\ *dim of* SABRINA
Sa·die \ˈsād-ē\ *dim of* SARA
Sal·ly *or* **Sal·lie** \ˈsal-ē\ *dim of* SARA
San·dra \ˈsan-drə, ˈsän-\ *dim of* ALEXANDRA
Sar·ah *or* **Sara** \ˈser-ə, ˈsar-ə, ˈsā-rə\ [Heb] princess
Sara·lee \ˈser-ə-(ˌ)lē, ˈsar-\ [prob. fr. *Sara + Lee*]
Saun·dra \ˈsȯn-drə, ˈsän-\ *var of* SANDRA
Sel·ma \ˈsel-mə\ [Sw] *fem dim of* ANSELM
Shari \ˈsha(ə)r-ē, ˈshe(ə)r-\ *dim of* SHARON
Shar·lene \shär-ˈlēn\ *var of* CHARLENE
Shar·on *or* **Shar·ron** \ˈshar-ən, ˈsher-\ [Heb] *prob* plain *n*
Shei·la \ˈshē-lə\ [IrGael] *var of* CECILIA

She·lia \ˈshēl-yə\ *var of* SHEILA
Shel·ley \ˈshel-ē\ [fr. a surname]
Sher·rill *or* **Sher·yl** \ˈsher-əl\ [prob. fr. a surname]
Sher·ry *or* **Sher·rie** *or* **Sheri** \ˈsher-ē\
Shir·ley \ˈshər-lē\ [fr. a surname]
Sig·rid \ˈsig-rəd\ [Scand] beautiful as victory
Son·dra \ˈsän-drə\ *var of* SANDRA
So·nia *or* **So·nya** *or* **So·nja** \ˈsō-nyə, ˈsȯ-\ [Russ] *dim of* SOPHIA
So·phia \sə-ˈfē-ə, -ˈfī-\ *or* **So·phie** \ˈsō-fē\ [Gk] wisdom
Stel·la \ˈstel-ə\ [L] star
Steph·a·nie \ˈstef-ə-nē\ *fem of* STEPHEN
Sue \ˈsü\ *or* **Su·sie** \ˈsü-zē\ *dim of* SUSAN
Su·el·len \sü-ˈel-ən\ [*Sue + Ellen*]
Su·san *or* **Su·zan** \ˈsüz-ᵊn\ *dim of* SUSANNA
Su·san·na *or* **Su·san·nah** \sü-ˈzan-ə\ [Heb] lily
Su·zanne *or* **Su·sanne** *or* **Su·zann** \sü-ˈzan\ [F] *var of* SUSAN
Syb·il \ˈsib-əl\ [Gk] sibyl
Syl·via \ˈsil-vē-ə\ [L] she of the forest

Ta·mara \tə-ˈmar-ə\ [prob. fr. Georgian]
Tan·ya \ˈtan-yə\ [Russ] *dim of* TATIANA
Te·re·sa \tə-ˈrē-sə\ *var of* THERESA
Ter·ry *or* **Ter·ri** \ˈter-ē\ *dim of* THERESA
Thel·ma \ˈthel-mə\
The·o·do·ra \ˌthē-ə-ˈdōr-ə, -ˈdȯr-\ [LGk] *fem of* THEODORE
The·re·sa *or* **Te·re·sa** \tə-ˈrē-sə\ [LL]
The·rese \tə-ˈrēs\ *var of* THERESA
Ti·na \ˈtē-nə\ *dim of* -TINA
To·by \ˈtō-bē\
To·ni \ˈtō-nē\ *dim of* ANTONIA
Tru·dy \ˈtrüd-ē\ *dim of* GERTRUDE

Ur·su·la \ˈər-sə-lə\ [LL] little she-bear

Val·er·ie \ˈval-ə-rē\ [L] *prob* strong
Vel·ma \ˈvel-mə\
Ve·ra \ˈvir-ə\ [Russ] faith
Ver·na \ˈvər-nə\ *prob fem of* VERNON
Ve·ron·i·ca \və-ˈrän-i-kə\ [LL]
Vicki *or* **Vicky** *or* **Vick·ie** \ˈvik-ē\ *dim of* VICTORIA
Vic·to·ria \vik-ˈtōr-ē-ə, -ˈtȯr-\ [L] victory
Vi·da \ˈvēd-ə, ˈvīd-\ *fem dim of* DAVID
Vi·o·la \vī-ˈō-lə, vē-ˈō-, ˈvī-ə-, ˈvē-ə-\ [L] violet
Vi·o·let \ˈvī-ə-lət\ [OF, fr. L] violet
Vir·gin·ia \vər-ˈjin-yə, -ˈjin-ē-ə\ [L]
Viv·i·an \ˈviv-ē-ən\ [LL]

Wan·da \ˈwän-də\ [Pol]
Wen·dy \ˈwen-dē\
Wil·da \ˈwil-də\ *var of* WILLA
Wil·la \ˈwil-ə\ *or* **Wil·lie** \ˈwil-ē\ *prob fem dim of* WILLIAM
Wil·ma \ˈwil-mə\ *prob fem dim of* WILLIAM
Win·i·fred \ˈwin-ə-frəd\ [W]

Yvette \i-ˈvet\ [F]
Yvonne \i-ˈvän\ [F]

Zel·da \ˈzel-də\ *dim of* GRISELDA

FOREIGN WORDS AND PHRASES

INCLUDING STATE AND NATIONAL MOTTOES

ab·eunt stu·dia in mo·res \'äb-e-,ủnt-'stüd-ē-,ä-,in-'mō-,rās\ [L] : practices zealously pursued pass into habits

ab in·cu·na·bu·lis \,äb-,iŋ-kə-'näb-ə-,lēs\ [L] : from the cradle : from infancy

à bon chat, bon rat \à-bō^{n}-'shà bō^{n}-'rà\ [F] : to a good cat, a good rat : a retaliation in kind

à bouche ou·verte \à-bü-shü-vert\ [F] : with open mouth : eagerly : uncritically

ab ovo us·que ad ma·la \äb-'ō-vō-,ủs-kwe-,äd-'mäl-ä\ [L] : from egg to apples : from soup to nuts : from beginning to end

à bras ou·verts \à-brà-zü-ver\ [F] : with open arms : cordially

ab·sit in·vi·dia \'äb-,sit-in-'wid-ē-,ä\ [L] : let there be no envy or ill will

ab uno dis·ce om·nes \äb-'ü-nō-,dis-ke-'ȯm-,nās\ [L] : from one learn to know all

ab ur·be con·di·ta \äb-'ủr-be-'kȯn-də-,tä\ [L] : from the founding of the city (Rome, founded 753 B.C.) — used by the Romans in reckoning dates

ab·usus non tol·lit usum \'äb-,ü-səs-,nōn-,tȯ-lət-'ü-səm\ [L] : abuse does not take away use, i.e., is not an argument against proper use

à compte \à-kō^{n}t\ [F] : on account

à coup sûr \à-kü-sue̅r\ [F] : with sure stroke : surely

ad ar·bi·tri·um \,ad-är-'bi-trē-əm\ [F] : at will : arbitrarily

ad as·tra per as·pera \ad-'as-trə-,pər-'as-pə-rə\ [L] : to the stars by hard ways — motto of Kansas

ad ex·tre·mum \,ad-ik-'strē-məm\ [L] : to the extreme : at last

ad ka·len·das Grae·cas \,äd-kə-'len-dəs-'grī-,käs\ [L] : at the Greek calends : never (since the Greeks had no calends)

ad pa·tres \äd-'pä-,trās\ [L] : (gathered) to his fathers : deceased

à droite \à-drwät\ [F] : to or on the right hand

ad un·guem \äd-'ủŋ-,gwem\ [L] : to the fingernail : to a nicety : exactly (from the use of the fingernail to test the smoothness of marble)

ad utrum·que pa·ra·tus \,äd-ủ-'trủm-kwe-pə-'rät-əs\ [L] : prepared for either (event)

ad vi·vum \äd-'wē-,wủm\ [L] : to the life

ae·gri som·nia \,ī-grē-'sȯm-nē-,ä\ [L] : a sick man's dreams

ae·quam ser·va·re men·tem \'ī-,kwäm-ser-,wä-rē-'men-,tem\ [L] : to preserve a calm mind

ae·quo ani·mo \,ī-,kwō-'än-ə-,mō\ [L] : with even mind : calmly

ae·re per·en·ni·us \'ī-re-pə-'ren-ē-ủs\ [L] : more lasting than bronze

à gauche \à-gōsh\ [F] : to or on the left hand

age quod agis \'äg-e-,kwȯd-'äg-is\ [L] : do what you are doing : to the business at hand

à grands frais \à-grä^{n}-fre\ [F] : at great expense

à huis clos \à-w^{y}ē-klō\ [F] : with closed doors

aide–toi, le ciel t'aidera \ed-twà lə-'syel-te-drà\ [F] : help yourself (and) heaven will help you

aî·né \e-nā\ [F] : elder : senior (masc.)

aî·née \e-nā\ [F] : elder : senior (fem.)

à l'aban·don \à-là-bä^{n}-dō^{n}\ [F] : carelessly : in disorder

à la belle étoile \à-là-bel-ā-twàl\ [F] : under the beautiful star : in the open air at night

à la bonne heure \à-là-bȯ-nœr\ [F] : at a good time : well and good : all right

à la fran·çaise \à-là-frä^{n}-sez\ [F] : in the French style

à l'an·glaise \à-lä^{n}-glez\ [F] : in the English style

alea jac·ta est \'äl-ē-,ä-,yäk-tə-'est\ [L] : the die is cast

à l'im·pro·viste \à-la^{n}-prȯ-vēst\ [F] : unexpectedly

ali·quan·do bo·nus dor·mi·tat Ho·me·rus \,äl-ə-,kwän-dō-'bȯ-nəs-dȯr-,mē-,tät-hō-'mer-əs\ [L] : sometimes (even) good Homer nods

alis vo·lat pro·pri·is \'äl-,ēs-'wȯ-,lät-'prō-prē-,ēs\ [L] : she flies with her own wings — motto of Oregon

al–ki \'al-,kī, -,kē\ [Chinook Jargon] : by and by — motto of Washington

alo·ha oe \ä-,lō-hä-'ȯi, ə-,lō-ə-\ [Hawaiian] : love to you : greetings : farewell

al·ter idem \,ȯl-tər-'ī-,dem, ,äl-tər-'ē-\ [L] : second self

a max·i·mis ad mi·ni·ma \ä-'mäk-sə-,mēs-,äd-'min-ə-,mä\ [L] : from the greatest to the least

ami·cus hu·ma·ni ge·ner·is \ä-'mē-kəs-hü-,män-ē-'gen-ə-rəs\ [L] : friend of the human race

ami·cus us·que ad aras \-,ủs-kwe-,äd-'är-,äs\ [L] : a friend as far as to the altars, i.e., except in what is contrary to one's religion; *also* : a friend to the last extremity

ami de cour \à-,mēd-ə-'kủr\ [F] : court friend : insincere friend

amor pa·tri·ae \,äm-,ȯr-'pä-trē-,ī\ [L] : love of one's country

amor vin·cit om·nia \'ä-,mȯr-,wiŋ-kit-'ȯm-nē-,ä\ [L] : love conquers all things

an·cienne no·blesse \ä^{n}-syen-nȯ-bles\ [F] : old-time nobility : the French nobility before the Revolution of 1789

an·guis in her·ba \,äŋ-gwəs-in-'her-,bä\ [L] : snake in the grass

ani·mal bi·pes im·plu·me \'än-i-,mäl-,bip-,äs-im-'plü-me\ [L] : two-legged animal without feathers (i.e., man)

ani·mis opi·bus·que pa·ra·ti \'än-ə-,mēs-,ȯ-pə-'bủs-kwe-pə-'rä-,tē\ [L] : prepared in spirits and resources — one of the mottoes of South Carolina

an·no ae·ta·tis su·ae \'än-ō-ī-,tät-əs-'sü-,ī\ [L] : in the (specified) year of his (or her) age

an·no mun·di \,än-ō-'mủn-dē\ [L] : in the year of the world — used in reckoning dates from the supposed period of the creation of the world, esp. as fixed by James Ussher at 4004 B.C. or by the Jews at 3761 B.C.

an·no ur·bis con·di·tae \,än-ō-,ủr-bəs-'kȯn-də-,tī\ [L] : in the year of the founded city (Rome, founded 753 B.C.)

an·nu·it coep·tis \,än-ə-,wit-'kȯip-,tēs\ [L] : He (God) has smiled on our undertakings — motto on the reverse of the great seal of the United States

à peu près \à-pœ̄-pre\ [F] : nearly : approximately

à pied \à-pyā\ [F] : on foot

après moi le dé·luge \à-pre-mwà-lə-dā-lue̅zh\ [F] : after me the deluge (attributed to Louis XV)

à pro·pos de bottes \à-prə-pōd-(ə-)bȯt\ [F] : apropos of boots — used to change the subject

à pro·pos de rien \-pō-də-rya^{n}\ [F] : apropos of nothing

aqua et ig·ni in·ter·dic·tus \,äk-wä-et-'ig-nē-,int-ər-'dik-təs\ [L] : forbidden to be furnished with water and fire : outlawed

Ar·ca·des am·bo \,är-kə-,des-'äm-bō\ [L] : both Arcadians : two persons of like occupations or tastes; *also* : two rascals

a ri·ve·der·ci \,är-ē-vā-'der-chē\ [It] : till we meet again — used as a formula of farewell

ar·rec·tis au·ri·bus \ä-'rek-,tēs-'aủ-ri-,bủs\ [L] : with ears pricked up : attentively

ars est ce·la·re ar·tem \,ärs-,est-kā-,lär-ē-'är-,tem\ [L] it is (true) art to conceal art

ars lon·ga, vi·ta bre·vis \ärs-'lȯŋ-,gä ,wē-,tä-'bre-wəs\ [L] : art is long, life is short

à tort et à tra·vers \à-tȯr-tā-à-trà-ver\ [F] : wrong and crosswise : at random : without rhyme or reason

au bout de son la·tin \ō-büd-(ə-)sō^{n}-là-ta^{n}\ [F] : at the end of one's Latin : at the end of one's mental resources

au con·traire \ō-kō^{n}-trer\ [F] : on the contrary

au·de·mus ju·ra no·stra de·fen·de·re \aủ-'dā-məs-,yủr-ə-'nȯ-strə-dā-'fen-də-re\ [L] : we dare defend our rights — motto of Alabama

au·den·tes for·tu·na ju·vat \aủ-'den-,tās-fȯr-,tü-nə-'yü-,wät\ [L] : fortune favors the bold

au fond \ō-fō^{n}\ [F] : at bottom : fundamentally

au grand sé·rieux \ō-grä^{n}-sā-ryœ̄\ [F] : in all seriousness

au pays des aveu·gles les borgnes sont rois \ō-pā-ē-dā-zà-vœ̄g-lə-lā-bȯrn^{y}-ə-sō^{n}-rwä\ [F] : in the country of the blind the one-eyed men are kings

au·rea me·di·o·cri·tas \'aủ-rē-ə-,med-ē-'ō-krə-,täs\ [L] : the golden mean

au reste \ō-rest\ [F] : for the rest : besides

au·spi·ci·um me·li·o·ris ae·vi \aủ-'spik-ē-,ủm-,mel-ē-,ōr-əs-'ī-,wē\ [L] : an omen of a better age — motto of the Order of St. Michael and St. George

aus·si·tôt dit, aus·si·tôt fait \ō-sē-tō-'dē- ō-sē-tō-'fe\ [F] : no sooner said than done

aut Cae·sar aut ni·hil \aủt-'kī-,sär-,aủt-'nē-,hil\ [L] : either a Caesar or nothing

aut Cae·sar aut nul·lus \-'nủl-əs\ [L] : either a Caesar or a nobody

au·tres temps, au·tres mœurs \ō-trə-tä^{n} ō-trə-mœrs\ [F] : other times, other customs

aut vin·ce·re aut mo·ri \aủt-'wiŋ-kə-re-,aủt-'mȯ-,rē\ [L] : either to conquer or to die

aux armes \ō-zàrm\ [F] : to arms

ave at·que va·le \'ä-,wā-,ät-kwe-'wä-,lā\ [L] : hail and farewell

à vo·tre san·té \à-vȯt-sä^{n}-tā, -vȯ-trə-\ [F] : to your health — used as a toast

beaux yeux \bō-zyœ̄\ [F] : beautiful eyes : beauty of face

bien en·ten·du \bya^{n}-nä^{n}-tä^{n}-due̅\ [F] : well understood : of course

bien·sé·ance \bya^{n}-sā-ä^{n}s\ [F] : propriety

bis dat qui ci·to dat \'bis-,dät-kwē-'ki-tō-,dät\ [L] : he gives twice who gives promptly

bon gré, mal gré \'bō^{n}-,grā-'màl-,grā\ [F] : whether with good grace or bad : willy-nilly

bo·nis avi·bus \,bȯ-,nēs-'ä-wi-,bủs\ [L] : under good auspices

bon jour \bō^{n}-zhür\ [F] : good day : good morning

bonne foi \bȯn-fwä\ [F] : good faith

bon soir \bō^{n}-swàr\ [F] : good evening

bru·tum ful·men \,brüt-əm-'fủl-mən\ [L] : insensible thunderbolt : a futile threat or display of force

ca·dit quae·stio \ˌkäd-ət-ˈkwī-stē-ˌō\ [L] : the question drops : the argument collapses
cau·sa si·ne qua non \ˈkau̇-ˌsä-ˌsin-ē-kwä-ˈnōn\ [L] : an indispensable cause or condition
ca·ve ca·nem \ˌkä-wā-ˈkän-ˌem\ [L] : beware the dog
ce·dant ar·ma to·gae \ˈkā-ˌdänt-ˌär-mə-ˈtō-ˌgī\ [L] : let arms yield to the toga : let military power give way to civil power — motto of Wyoming
c'est à dire \se-tȧ-dēr\ [F] : that is to say : namely
c'est au·tre chose \se-tōt-shōz, -tō-trə-\ [F] : that's a different thing
c'est plus qu'un crime, c'est une faute \se-plüē-kœⁿ-krēm se-tüēn-fōt\ [F] : it is worse than a crime, it is a blunder
ce·tera de·sunt \ˌkāt-ə-ˌrä-ˈdā-ˌsu̇nt\ [L] : the rest is missing
cha·cun à son gout \shȧ-kœ̄ⁿ-nȧ-sōⁿ-gü\ [F] : everyone to his taste
châ·teau en Es·pagne \shä-tō-äⁿ-nes-pȧnʸ\ [F] : castle in Spain : a visionary project
cher·chez la femme \sher-shā-lȧ-fȧm\ [F] : look for the woman
che sa·rà, sa·rà \ˌkā-sä-ˌrä-sä-ˈrä\ [It] : what will be, will be
che·val de ba·taille \shə-vȧl-də-bȧ-tī\ [F] : war-horse : argument constantly relied on : favorite subject
co·gi·to, er·go sum \ˈkō-gə-ˌtō-ˌer-gō-ˈsu̇m\ [L] : I think, therefore I exist
com·pa·gnon de voy·age \kōⁿ-pȧ-nʸōⁿ-də-vwȧ-yȧzh\ [F] : traveling companion
compte rendu \kōⁿt-räⁿ-dū̅\ [F] : report (as of proceedings in an investigation)
coup de maî·tre \küd-(ə-)metrᵊ\ [F] : master stroke
coup d'es·sai \kü-dā-se\ [F] : experiment : trial
coûte que coûte \küt-kə-küt\ [F] : cost what it may
cre·do quia ab·sur·dum est \ˌkrād-ō-ˈkwē-ä-äp-ˌsu̇rd-əm-ˈest\ [L] I believe it because it is absurd
cres·cit eun·do \ˌkres-kət-ˈeu̇n-dō\ [L] : it grows as it goes — motto of New Mexico
crux cri·ti·co·rum \ˈkru̇ks-ˌkrit-ə-ˈkōr-əm\ [L] : crux of critics
cum gra·no sa·lis \ku̇m-ˌgrän-ō-ˈsäl-əs\ [L] : with a grain of salt
cus·tos mo·rum \ˌku̇s-ˌtōs-ˈmōr-əm\ [L] : guardian of manners or morals : censor

d'ac·cord \dȧ-kȯr\ [F] : in accord : agreed
dame d'hon·neur \dȧm-dȯ-nœr\ [F] : lady-in-waiting
dam·nant quod non in·tel·li·gunt \ˈdäm-ˌnänt-ˌkwȯd-ˌnōn-in-ˈtel-ə-ˌgu̇nt\ [L] : they condemn what they do not understand
de bonne grâce \də-bȯn-gräs\ [F] : with good grace : willingly
de gus·ti·bus non est dis·pu·tan·dum \dā-ˈgu̇s-ti-ˌbu̇s-ˌnōn-ˌest-ˌdis-pu̇-ˈtän-ˌdu̇m\ [L] : there is no disputing about tastes
de in·te·gro \dā-ˈint-ə-ˌgrō\ [L] : anew : afresh
de l'au·dace, en·core de l'au·dace, et tou·jours de l'au·dace \də-lō-ˈdȧs äⁿ-ˈkȯr-də-lō-dȧs ā-tü-ˈzhür-də-lō-dȧs\ [F] : audacity, more audacity, and ever more audacity
de·len·da est Car·tha·go \dā-ˈlen-dä-ˌest-kär-ˈtäg-ō\ [L] : Carthage must be destroyed
de·li·ne·a·vit \dā-ˌlē-nā-ˈä-wit\ [L] : he (or she) drew it
de mal en pis \də-mȧ-läⁿ-pē\ [F] : from bad to worse
de mi·ni·mis non cu·rat lex \dā-ˈmin-ə-ˌmēs-ˌnōn-ˌkü-ˌrät-ˈleks\ [L] : the law takes no account of trifles
de mor·tu·is nil ni·si bo·num \dā-ˈmȯrt-ə-ˌwēs-ˌnēl-ˌnis-ē-ˈbō-ˌnu̇m\ [L] : of the dead (say) nothing but good
Deo fa·ven·te \ˌdā-ō-fä-ˈwen-te\ [L] : with God's favor
Deo gra·ti·as \ˌdā-ō-ˈgrät-ē-ˌäs\ [L] : thanks (be) to God
de pro·fun·dis \ˌdā-prō-ˈfu̇n-dēs, -ˈfən-\ [L] : out of the depths
der Geist der stets ver·neint \dər-ˈgīst-dər-ˌshtāts-fer-ˈnīnt\ [G] : the spirit that ever denies — applied originally to Mephistopheles
de·si·pe·re in lo·co \dā-ˈsip-ə-re-in-ˈlō-kō\ [L] : to indulge in trifling at the proper time
Deus vult \ˌdā-əs-ˈwu̇lt\ [L] : God wills it — rallying cry of the First Crusade
di·es fau·stus \ˌdē-ˌās-ˈfau̇-stəs\ [L] : lucky day
di·es in·fau·stus \-ˈin-ˌfau̇-stəs\ [L] : unlucky day
di·es irae \-ˈē-ˌrī, -ˌrā\ [L] : day of wrath — used of the Judgment Day
Dieu et mon droit \dyœ̄-ā-mōⁿ-drwä\ [F] : God and my right — motto on the British royal arms
Dieu vous garde \dyœ̄-vü-gȧrd\ [F] : God keep you
di·ri·go \ˈdē-ri-ˌgō\ [L] : I direct — motto of Maine
dis ali·ter vi·sum \ˌdēs-ˌäl-ə-ˌter-ˈwē-ˌsu̇m\ [L] : the gods decreed otherwise
di·tat De·us \ˌdē-ˌtät-ˈdā-ˌu̇s\ [L] : God enriches — motto of Arizona
di·vi·de et im·pe·ra \ˈdē-wi-ˌde-ˌet-ˈim-pə-ˌrä\ [L] : divide and rule
do·cen·do dis·ci·mus \dȯ-ˌken-dō-ˈdis-ki-ˌmu̇s\ [L] : we learn by teaching
Do·mi·ne, di·ri·ge nos \ˈdȯ-mi-ˌne-ˌdē-ri-ˌge-ˈnōs\ [L] : Lord, direct us — motto of the City of London
Do·mi·nus vo·bis·cum \ˌdȯ-mi-ˌnu̇s-wō-ˈbēs-ˌku̇m\ [L] : the Lord be with you
dul·ce et de·co·rum est pro pa·tria mo·ri \ˌdu̇l-ˌket-de-ˈkōr-ˌest-prō-ˌpä-trē-ˌä-ˈmȯ-ˌrē\ [L] : it is sweet and seemly to die for one's country
dum spi·ro, spe·ro \du̇m-ˈspē-rō-ˈspā-rō\ [L] : while I breathe I hope — one of the mottoes of South Carolina
dum vi·vi·mus vi·va·mus \du̇m-ˈwē-wē-ˌmu̇s-wē-ˈwäm-u̇s\ [L] : while we live, let us live
dux fe·mi·na fac·ti \ˌdu̇ks-ˌfā-mi-nä-ˈfäk-ˌtē\ [L] : a woman was leader of the exploit

ec·ce sig·num \ˌek-e-ˈsig-ˌnu̇m\ [L] : behold the sign : look at the proof
e con·tra·rio \ˌā-kȯn-ˈträr-ē-ˌō\ [L] : on the contrary
écra·sez l'in·fâme \ā-krä-zā-laⁿ-fäm\ [F] : crush the infamous thing
eheu fu·ga·ces la·bun·tur an·ni \ˌā-ˌheu̇-fü-ˈgä-ˌkās-lä-ˌbu̇n-ˌtu̇r-ˈän-ˌē\ [L] : alas! the fleeting years glide on
ein fes·te Burg ist un·ser Gott \īn-ˌfes-tə-ˈbu̇rk-ist-ˌu̇n-zər-ˈgȯt\ [G] : a mighty fortress is our God
em·bar·ras de ri·chesses \äⁿ-bȧ-räd-(ə-)rē-shes\ [F] : embarrassing surplus of riches : confusing abundance
em·bar·ras du choix \äⁿ-bȧ-rä-dūe̅-shwä\ [F] : embarrassing variety of choice
en ami \äⁿ-nȧ-mē\ [F] : as a friend
en ef·fet \äⁿ-nā-fe\ [F] : in fact : indeed
en fa·mille \äⁿ-fȧ-mēy\ [F] : in one's family : at home
en·fant gâ·té \äⁿ-fäⁿ-gä-tā\ [F] : spoiled child
en·fants per·dus \äⁿ-fäⁿ-per-dūe̅\ [F] : lost children : soldiers sent to a dangerous post
en·fin \äⁿ-faⁿ\ [F] : in conclusion : in a word
en gar·çon \äⁿ-gȧr-sōⁿ\ [F] : as or like a bachelor
en pan·tou·fles \äⁿ-päⁿ-tüflᵊ\ [F] : in slippers : at ease : informally
en plein air \äⁿ-ple-ner\ [F] : in the open air
en plein jour \äⁿ-plaⁿ-zhür\ [F] : in broad day
en rè·gle \äⁿ-reglᵊ\ [F] : in order : in due form
en re·tard \äⁿr-(ə-)tȧr\ [F] : behind time : late
en re·traite \äⁿ-rə-tret\ [F] : in retreat : in retirement
en re·vanche \äⁿr-(ə-)väⁿsh\ [F] : in return : in compensation
en·se pe·tit pla·ci·dam sub li·ber·ta·te qui·e·tem \ˌen-se-ˌpet-ət-ˈpläk-i-ˌdäm-su̇b-ˌlē-ber-ˌtä-te-kwē-ˈā-ˌtem\ [L] : with the sword she seeks calm repose under liberty — motto of Massachusetts
e plu·ri·bus unum \ˌē-ˌplu̇r-ə-bəs-ˈ(y)ü-nəm, ˌā-ˌplu̇r-ə-bəs-ˈü-\ [L] : one out of many — motto of the United States
e pur si muo·ve \ā-ˌpür-sē-ˈmwȯ-vā\ [It] : and yet it does move — attributed to Galileo after recanting his assertion of the earth's motion
er·ra·re hu·ma·num est \e-ˈrär-e-hü-ˌmän-əm-ˈest\ [L] : to err is human
es·prit de l'es·ca·lier \es-prēd-les-kȧ-lyā\ *or* **es·prit d'es·ca·lier** \-prē-des-\ [F] : spirit of the staircase : repartee thought of only too late, on the way home
es·se quam vi·de·ri \ˈes-e-ˌkwäm-wi-ˈdā-rē\ [L] : to be rather than to seem — motto of North Carolina
est mo·dus in re·bus \est-ˈmȯ-ˌdu̇s-in-ˈrā-ˌbu̇s\ [L] : there is a proper measure in things, i.e., the golden mean should always be observed
es·to per·pe·tua \ˈes-ˌtō-per-ˈpet-ə-ˌwä\ [L] : may she endure forever — motto of Idaho
et hoc ge·nus om·ne \et-ˌhōk-ˌgen-əs-ˈȯm-ne\ *or* **et id ge·nus om·ne** \et-ˌid-\ [L] : and everything of this kind
et in Ar·ca·dia ego \ˌet-in-är-ˌkäd-ē-ə-ˈeg-ō\ [L] : I too (lived) in Arcadia
et sic de si·mi·li·bus \et-ˌsēk-dā-sə-ˈmil-ə-ˌbu̇s\ [L] : and so of like things
et tu Bru·te \et-ˈtü-ˈbrü-te\ [L] : thou too, Brutus — exclamation attributed to Julius Caesar on seeing his friend Brutus among his assassins
eu·re·ka \yu̇-ˈrē-kə\ [Gk] : I have found it — motto of California
Ewig–Weib·li·che \ˌā-vik̲-ˈvīp-li-k̲ə\ [G] : eternal feminine
ex ani·mo \ek-ˈsän-ə-ˌmō\ [L] : from the heart : sincerely
ex·cel·si·or \ik-ˈsel-sē-ər, eks-ˈkel-sē-ˌȯr\ [L] : still higher — motto of New York
ex·cep·tio pro·bat re·gu·lam de re·bus non ex·cep·tis \eks-ˈkep-tē-ˌō-ˌprō-ˌbät-ˈrā-gə-ˌläm-dā-ˈrā-ˌbu̇s-ˌnōn-eks-ˈkep-ˌtēs\ [L] : an exception establishes the rule as to things not excepted
ex·cep·tis ex·ci·pi·en·dis \eks-ˈkep-ˌtēs-eks-ˌkip-ē-ˈen-ˌdēs\ [L] : with the proper or necessary exceptions
ex·i·tus ac·ta pro·bat \ˈek-sə-ˌtu̇s-ˌäk-tə-ˈprō-ˌbät\ [L] : the event justifies the deed
ex li·bris \eks-ˈlē-brəs\ [L] : from the books of — used on bookplates
ex me·ro mo·tu \ˌeks-ˌmer-ō-ˈmō-tü\ [L] : out of mere impulse : of one's own accord
ex ne·ces·si·ta·te rei \ˌeks-nə-ˌkes-ə-ˈtä-te-ˈrā(-ˌē)\ [L] : from the necessity of the case
ex ni·hi·lo ni·hil fit \eks-ˈnē-hi-ˌlō-ˌnē-ˌhil-ˈfit\ [L] : from nothing nothing is produced
ex pe·de Her·cu·lem \eks-ˌped-e-ˈher-kə-ˌlem\ [L] : from the foot (we may judge of the size of) Hercules : from a part we may judge of the whole
ex·per·to cre·di·te \eks-ˌper-ˌtō-ˈkrād-ə-ˌte\ [L] : believe one who has had experience
ex un·gue le·o·nem \eks-ˈu̇ŋ-gwe-le-ˈō-ˌnem\ [L] : from the claw (we may judge of) the lion : from a part we may judge of the whole
ex vi ter·mi·ni \eks-ˌwē-ˈter-mə-ˌnē\ [L] : from the force of the term

fa·ci·le prin·ceps \ˌfäk-i-le-ˈpriŋ-ˌkeps\ [L] : easily first

fa·ci·lis de·scen·sus Aver·no \ˈfäk-i-ˌlis-dā-ˌskān-ˌsu̇s-ä-ˈwer-nō\ *or* **facilis descensus Aver·ni** \-(ˌ)nē\ [L] : the descent to Avernus is easy : the road to evil is easy

faire sui·vre \fer-sw^{y}ēvr^{ə}\ [F] : have forwarded : please forward

fas est et ab ho·ste do·ce·ri \ˈfäs-ˈest-et-äb-ˈhȯ-ste-dȯ-ˈkā-(ˌ)rē\ [L] : it is right to learn even from an enemy

Fa·ta vi·am in·ve·ni·ent \ˌfä-tä-ˈwē-ˌäm-in-ˈwen-ē-ˌent\ [L] : the Fates will find a way

fat·ti mas·chii, pa·ro·le fe·mi·ne \ˌfät-tē-ˈmäs-ˌkē pä-ˌrȯ-lā-ˈfā-mē-ˌnā\ [It] : deeds are males, words are females : deeds are more effective than words — motto of Maryland, where it is generally interpreted as meaning "manly deeds, womanly words"

femme de cham·bre \fȧm-də-shä^{n}br^{ə}\ [F] : chambermaid : lady's maid

fe·sti·na len·te \fe-ˌstē-nə-ˈlen-ˌtā\ [L] : make haste slowly

feux d'ar·ti·fice \fœ̄-dȧr-tē-fēs\ [F] : fireworks : display of wit

fi·at ex·pe·ri·men·tum in cor·po·re vi·li \ˈfē-ˌät-ek-ˌsper-i-ˈmen-ˌtu̇m-in-ˌkȯr-pə-re-ˈwē-lē\ [L] : let experiment be made on a worthless body

fi·at ju·sti·tia, ru·at cae·lum \ˌfē-ˌät-yu̇s-ˈtit-ē-ä ˌru̇-ˌät-ˈkī-ˌlu̇m\ [L] : let justice be done though the heavens fall

fi·at lux \ˌfē-ˌät-ˈlu̇ks\ [L] : let there be light

Fi·dei De·fen·sor \ˌfid-e-ˌē-dā-ˈfān-ˌsȯr\ [L] : Defender of the Faith — a title of the sovereigns of England

fi·dus Acha·tes \ˌfēd-əs-ä-ˈkä-ˌtās\ [L] : faithful Achates : trusty friend

fille de cham·bre \fēy-də-shä^{n}br^{ə}\ [F] : lady's maid

fille d'hon·neur \fēy-dȯ-nœr\ [F] : maid of honor

fils \fēs\ [F] : son — used after French proper names to distinguish a son from his father

fi·nem re·spi·ce \ˌfē-ˌnem-ˈrā-spi-ˌke\ [L] : consider the end

fi·nis co·ro·nat opus \ˌfē-nəs-kə-ˌrō-ˌnät-ˈō-ˌpu̇s\ [L] : the end crowns the work

fluc·tu·at nec mer·gi·tur \ˈflu̇k-tə-ˌwät-ˌnek-ˈmer-gi-ˌtu̇r\ [L] : it is tossed by the waves but does not sink — motto of Paris

fors·an et haec olim me·mi·nis·se ju·va·bit \ˌfȯr-ˌsän-ˌet-ˈhīk-ˌō-lim-ˌmem-ə-ˈnis-e-yu̇-ˈwä-bit\ [L] : perhaps this too will be a pleasure to look back on one day

for·tes for·tu·na ju·vat \ˈfȯr-ˌtās-fȯr-ˌtü-nə-ˈyü-ˌwät\ [L] : fortune favors the brave

fron·ti nul·la fi·des \ˈfrȯn-ˌtē-ˌnu̇l-ə-ˈfid-ˌās\ [L] : no reliance can be placed on appearance

fu·it Il·i·um \ˈfü-ət-ˈil-ē-əm\ [L] : Troy has been (i.e., is no more)

fu·ror lo·quen·di \ˌfu̇r-ˌȯr-lȯ-ˈkwen-(ˌ)dē\ [L] : rage for speaking

fu·ror po·e·ti·cus \-pȯ-ˈāt-i-ku̇s\ [L] : poetic frenzy

fu·ror scri·ben·di \-skri-ˈben-(ˌ)dē\ [L] : rage for writing

Gal·li·ce \ˈgäl-ə-ˌke\ [L] : in French : after the French manner

gar·çon d'hon·neur \gȧr-sō^{n}-dȯ-nœr\ [F] : bridegroom's attendant

garde du corps \gȧrd-dᵫ-kȯr\ [F] : bodyguard

gar·dez la foi \gȧr-dā-lȧ-fwä\ [F] : keep faith

gau·de·a·mus igi·tur \ˌgau̇d-ē-ˈäm-əs-ˈig-ə-ˌtu̇r\ [L] : let us then be merry

gens d'é·glise \zhä^{n}-dā-glēz\ [F] : church people : clergy

gens de guerre \zhä^{n}d-(ə-)ger\ [F] : military people : soldiery

gens du monde \zhä^{n}-dᵫ-mō^{n}d\ [F] : people of the world : fashionable people

gno·thi se·au·ton \gə-ˈnō-thē-ˌse-au̇-ˈtȯn\ [Gk] : know thyself

grand monde \grä^{n}-mō^{n}d\ [F] : great world : high society

guerre à ou·trance \ger-ȧ-ü-trä^{n}s\ [F] : war to the uttermost

haut goût \ō-gü\ [F] : high flavor : slight taint of decay

hic et ubi·que \ˌhēk-et-ü-ˈbē-kwe\ [L] : here and everywhere

hic ja·cet \hik-ˈjā-sət, hēk-ˈyäk-ət\ [L] : here lies — used preceding a name on a tombstone

hinc il·lae la·cri·mae \ˌhiŋk-ˌil-ˌī-ˈläk-ri-ˌmī\ [L] : hence those tears

hoc age \hōk-ˈäg-e\ [L] : do this : apply yourself to what you are about

hoc opus, hic la·bor est \hōk-ˈō-ˌpu̇s-hēk-ˈläb-ˌȯr-ˌest\ [L] : this is the hard work, this is the toil

homme d'af·faires \ȯm-dȧ-fer\ [F] : man of business : business agent

homme d'es·prit \-des-prē\ [F] : man of wit

ho·mo sum: hu·ma·ni nil a me ali·e·num pu·to \ˈhȯ-mō-ˌsu̇m hü-ˌmän-ē-ˈnēl-ä-ˌmā-ˌäl-ē-ˈā-nəm-ˈpu̇-tō\ [L] : I am a man; I regard nothing that concerns man as foreign to my interests

ho·ni soit qui mal y pense \ȯ-nē-swȧ-kē-mȧl-ē-pä^{n}s\ [F] : shamed be he who thinks evil of it — motto of the Order of the Garter

hôtel–Dieu \ō-tel-dyœ̄\ [F] : hospital

hu·ma·num est er·ra·re \hü-ˌmän-əm-ˌest-e-ˈrär-e\ [L] : to err is human

ich dien \ik̲-ˈdēn\ [G] : I serve — motto of the Prince of Wales

ici on parle fran·çais \ē-sē-ō^{n}-pȧrl(-ə)-frä^{n}-se\ [F] : French is spoken here

id est \id-ˈest\ [L] : that is

ig·no·ran·tia ju·ris ne·mi·nem ex·cu·sat \ˌig-nə-ˌränt-ē-ä-ˈyu̇r-əs-ˈnā-mə-ˌnem-eks-ˈkü-ˌsät\ [L] : ignorance of the law excuses no one

ig·no·tum per ig·no·ti·us \ig-ˈnōt-əm-ˌper-ig-ˈnōt-ē-ˌu̇s\ [L] : (explaining) the unknown by means of the more unknown

il faut cul·ti·ver no·tre jar·din \ēl-fō-kᵫl-tē-vā-nȯt-zhȧr-da^{n}, -nȯ-trə-zhȧr-\ [F] : we must cultivate our garden : we must tend to our own affairs

in ae·ter·num \ˌin-ī-ˈter-ˌnu̇m\ [L] : forever

in du·bio \in-ˈdu̇b-ē-ˌō\ [L] : in doubt : undetermined

in fu·tu·ro \ˌin-fu̇-ˈtu̇r-ō\ [L] : in the future

in hoc sig·no vin·ces \in-hōk-ˈsig-nō-ˈviŋ-ˌkās\ [L] : by this sign (the Cross) thou shalt conquer

in li·mi·ne \in-ˈlē-mə-ˌne\ [L] : on the threshold : at the beginning

in om·nia pa·ra·tus \in-ˈȯm-nē-ə-pə-ˈrä-ˌtu̇s\ [L] : ready for all things

in par·ti·bus in·fi·de·li·um \in-ˈpärt-ə-ˌbu̇s-ˌin-fə-ˈdā-lē-ˌu̇m\ [L] : in the regions of the infidels — used of a titular bishop having no diocesan jurisdiction, usu. in non-Christian countries

in prae·sen·ti \ˌin-prī-ˈsent-ē\ [L] : at the present time

in sae·cu·la sae·cu·lo·rum \in-ˈsī-ku̇-ˌlä-ˌsī-kə-ˈlōr-əm, -ˈsā-ku̇-ˌlä-ˌsā-\ [L] : for ages of ages : forever and ever

in sta·tu quo an·te bel·lum \in-ˈstä-ˌtü-kwō-ˌänt-ē-ˈbel-əm\ [L] : in the same state as before the war

in·te·ger vi·tae sce·le·ris·que pu·rus \ˌin-tə-ˌger-ˈwē-ˌtī-ˌskel-ə-ˈris-kwe-ˈpü-rəs\ [L] : upright of life and free from wickedness

in·ter nos \ˌint-ər-ˈnōs\ [L] : between ourselves

in·tra mu·ros \ˌin-trä-ˈmü-ˌrōs\ [L] : within the walls

in usum Del·phi·ni \in-ˈü-səm-del-ˈfē-nē\ [L] : for the use of the Dauphin : expurgated

in utrum·que pa·ra·tus \ˌin-ü-ˈtru̇m-kwe-pə-ˈrä-ˌtu̇s\ [L] : prepared for either (event)

in·ve·nit \in-ˈwā-nit\ [L] : he (or she) devised it

in vi·no ve·ri·tas \in-ˌwē-nō-ˈwā-rə-ˌtäs\ [L] : there is truth in wine

in·vi·ta Mi·ner·va \in-ˈwē-ˌtä-mi-ˈner-ˌwä\ [L] : Minerva being unwilling : without natural talent or inspiration

ip·sis·si·ma ver·ba \ip-ˌsis-ə-ˌmä-ˈwer-ˌbä\ [L] : the very words

ira fu·ror bre·vis est \ˌē-rä-ˈfu̇r-ˌȯr-ˈbre-wəs-ˌest\ [L] : anger is a brief madness

jac·ta alea est \ˈyäk-ˌtä-ˌä-lē-ˌä-ˈest\ [L] : the die is cast

j'adoube \zhȧ-düb\ [F] : I adjust — used in chess when touching a piece without intending to move it

ja·nu·is clau·sis \ˌyän-ə-ˌwēs-ˈklau̇-ˌsēs\ [L] : with closed doors

je main·tien·drai \zhə-ma^{n}-tya^{n}-drā\ [F] : I will maintain — motto of the Netherlands

je ne sais quoi \zhən-(ə-)sā-kwȧ\ [F] : I don't know what : an inexpressible something

jeu de mots \zhœ̄d-(ə-)mō\ [F] : play on words : pun

Jo·an·nes est no·men eius \yō-ˈän-ās-est-ˌnō-men-ˈā-yu̇s\ [L] : John is his name — motto of Puerto Rico

jour·nal in·time \zhür-nȧl-a^{n}-tēm\ [F] : intimate journal : private diary

jus di·vi·num \ˌyüs-di-ˈwē-ˌnu̇m\ [L] : divine law

jus·ti·tia om·ni·bus \yu̇s-ˌtit-ē-ˌä-ˈȯm-ni-ˌbu̇s\ [L] : justice for all — motto of the District of Columbia

j'y suis, j'y reste \zhē-sw^{y}ē-zhē-rest\ [F] : here I am, here I remain

ktе·ma es aei \(kə-)ˈtā-ˌmä-ˌes-ä-ˈā\ [Gk] : a possession forever — applied to a work of art or literature of enduring significance

la belle dame sans mer·ci \lȧ-bel-dȧm-sä^{n}-mer-sē\ [F] : the beautiful lady without mercy

la·bo·ra·re est ora·re \ˈläb-ō-ˌrär-e-ˌest-ˈō-ˌrär-e\ [L] : to work is to pray

la·bor om·nia vin·cit \ˈlä-ˌbȯr-ˌȯm-nē-ˌä-ˈwiŋ-kit\ [L] : labor conquers all things — motto of Oklahoma

la·cri·mae re·rum \ˌläk-ri-ˌmī-ˈrā-ˌru̇m\ [L] : tears for things : pity for misfortune; *also* : tears in things : tragedy of life

lais·ser–al·ler \le-sā-ȧ-lā\ [F] : letting go : lack of restraint

lap·sus ca·la·mi \ˌläp-ˌsu̇s-ˈkäl-ə-ˌmē, ˌlap-səs-ˈkal-ə-ˌmī\ [L] : slip of the pen

lap·sus lin·guae \ˌlap-səs-ˈliŋ-ˌgwī, ˌläp-ˌsu̇s-\ [L] : slip of the tongue

la reine le veut \lȧ-ren-lə-vœ̄\ [F] : the queen wills it

la·scia·te ogni spe·ran·za, voi ch'en·tra·te \läsh-ˈshä-tā ˌō-n^{y}ē-spā-ˈrän-tsä-ˌvō-ē-kān-ˈträ-tā\ [It] : abandon all hope, ye who enter

lau·da·tor tem·po·ris ac·ti \lau̇-ˈdä-ˌtȯr-ˌtem-pə-ris-ˈäk-ˌtē\ [L] : one who praises past times

laus Deo \lau̇s-ˈdā-ō\ [L] : praise (be) to God

le roi est mort, vive le roi \lə-rwä-e-mȯr vēv-lə-rwä\ [F] : the king is dead, long live the king

le roi le veut \-lə-vœ̄\ [F] : the king wills it

le roi s'avi·se·ra \-sȧ-vēz-rȧ\ [F] : the king will consider

le style, c'est l'homme \lə-stēl-se-lȯm\ [F] : the style is the man

l'état, c'est moi \lā-tȧ-se-mwȧ\ [F] : the state, it is I

l'étoile du nord \lā-twȧl-dᵫ-nȯr\ [F] : the star of

the north — motto of Minnesota

Lie·der·kranz \'lēd-ər-ˌkräns\ [G] : wreath of songs : German singing society

lit·tera scrip·ta ma·net \ˌlit-ə-ˌrä-ˌskrip-tə-'män-et\ [L] : the written letter abides

lo·cus in quo \ˌlō-kəs-in-'kwō\ [L] : place in which

l'union fait la force \lu̅e-nyō^{n}-fe-là-fȯrs\ [F] : union makes strength — motto of Belgium

lu·sus na·tu·rae \ˌlü-səs-nə-'tu̇r-ˌī\ [L] : freak of nature

ma foi \mà-fwä\ [F] : my faith! : indeed

mag·na est ve·ri·tas et prae·va·le·bit \ˌmäg-nä-ˌest-'wā-ri-ˌtäs-et-ˌprī-wä-'lā-bit\ [L] : truth is mighty and will prevail

mag·ni no·mi·nis um·bra \ˌmäg-nē-ˌnō-mə-nis-'u̇m-brä\ [L] : the shadow of a great name

mai·son de san·té \mā-zō^{n}d-(ə-)sä^{n}-tā\ [F] : private hospital : asylum

ma·lis avi·bus \ˌmäl-ˌēs-'ä-wi-ˌbu̇s\ [L] : under evil auspices

man spricht Deutsch \män-shprikt-'dȯich\ [G] : German spoken

ma·riage de con·ve·nance \mà-ryȧzh-də-kō^{n}v-nä^{n}s\ [F] : marriage of convenience

mau·vaise honte \mō-vez-ō^{n}t\ [F] : bad shame : bashfulness

me·den agan \(ˌ)mā-ˌden-'äg-ˌän\ [Gk] : nothing in excess

me·dio tu·tis·si·mus ibis \'med-ē-ˌō-tü-ˌtis-ə-mu̇s-'ē-bis\ [L] : you will go most safely by the middle course

me ju·di·ce \mā-'yüd-ə-ke\ [L] : I being judge : in my judgment

mens sa·na in cor·po·re sa·no \māns-'sän-ä-in-ˌkȯr-pə-re-'sän-ō\ [L] : a sound mind in a sound body

me·um et tu·um \ˌmē-əm-ˌet-'tü-əm, ˌme-əm-\ [L] : mine and thine : distinction of private property

mi·ra·bi·le vi·su \mə-ˌräb-ə-lē-'wē-sü\ [L] : wonderful to behold

mi·ra·bi·lia \ˌmir-ə-'bil-ē-ə\ [L] : wonders : miracles

mo·le ru·it sua \'mō-le-ˌru̇-it-'su̇-ä\ [L] : it collapses from its own bigness

monde \mō^{n}d\ [F] : world : fashionable world : society

mon·ta·ni sem·per li·be·ri \mȯn-'tän-ē-ˌsem-pər-'lē-bə-ˌrē\ [L] : mountaineers are always free men — motto of West Virginia

mo·nu·men·tum ae·re per·en·ni·us \ˌmȯ-nə-'men-tu̇m-'ī-re-pə-'ren-ē-u̇s\ [L] : a monument more lasting than bronze — used of an immortal work of art or literature

mo·ri·tu·ri te sa·lu·ta·mus \ˌmȯr-ə-'tu̇r-ē-ˌtā-ˌsäl-ə-'täm-u̇s\ [L] : we who are about to die salute thee

mul·tum in par·vo \ˌmu̇l-təm-in-'pär-wō\ [L] : much in little

mu·ta·to no·mi·ne de te fa·bu·la nar·ra·tur \mü-ˌtät-ō-'nō-mə-ne-dā-'tā-ˌfäb-ə-lä-nä-'rä-ˌtu̇r\ [L] : with the name changed the story applies to you

na·tu·ra non fa·cit sal·tum \nä-'tü-rä-ˌnōn-ˌfäk-ət-'säl-ˌtu̇m\ [L] : nature makes no leap

ne ce·de ma·lis \nā-ˌkā-de-'mäl-ˌēs\ [L] : yield not to misfortunes

ne·mo me im·pu·ne la·ces·sit \'nā-mō-'mā-im-ˌpü-nā-lä-'kes-ət\ [L] : no one attacks me with impunity — motto of Scotland and of the Order of the Thistle

ne quid ni·mis \ˌnā-ˌkwid-'nim-əs\ [L] : not anything in excess

n'est–ce pas? \nes-pä\ [F] : isn't it so?

nil ad·mi·ra·ri \'nēl-ˌäd-mə-'rär-ē\ [L] : to be excited by nothing : equanimity

nil de·spe·ran·dum \'nēl-ˌdā-spā-'rän-du̇m\ [L] : never despair

nil si·ne nu·mi·ne \'nēl-ˌsin-e-'nü-mə-ne\ [L] : nothing without the divine will — motto of Colorado

n'im·porte \na^{n}-pȯrt\ [F] : it's no matter

no·lens vo·lens \ˌnō-ˌlenz-'vō-ˌlenz\ [L] : unwilling (or) willing : willy-nilly

non om·nia pos·su·mus om·nes \nōn-'ȯm-nē-ä-ˌpȯ-sə-mu̇s-'ȯm-ˌnās\ [L] : we can't all (do) all things

non om·nis mo·ri·ar \nōn-'ȯm-nəs-ˌmȯr-ē-ˌär\ [L] : I shall not wholly die

non sans droict \nō^{n}-sä^{n}-drwä\ [OF] : not without right — motto on Shakespeare's coat of arms

non sum qua·lis eram \ˌnōn-ˌsu̇m-ˌkwäl-əs-'er-ˌäm\ [L] : I am not what I used to be

nos·ce te ip·sum \ˌnōs-ke-ˌtā-'ip-ˌsu̇m\ [L] : know thyself

nos·tal·gie de la boue \nȯs-tàl-zhēd-(ə-)là-bü\ [F] : nostalgia for the mud : homesickness for the gutter

nous avons chan·gé tout ce·la \nü-zà-vō^{n}-shä^{n}-zhā-tü-s(ə)là\ [F] : we have changed all that

nous ver·rons ce que nous ver·rons \nü-ve-rō^{n}s-(ə-)kə-nü-ve-rō^{n}\ [F] : we shall see what we shall see

no·vus ho·mo \ˌnō-wəs-'hō-mō\ [L] : new man : man newly ennobled : upstart

no·vus or·do se·clo·rum \-'ȯr-ˌdō-sā-'klōr-əm\ [L] : a new cycle of the ages — motto on the reverse of the great seal of the United States

nu·gae \'nü-ˌgī\ [L] : trifles

nyet \'nyet\ [Russ] : no

ob·iit \'ō-bē-ˌit\ [L] : he (or she) died

ob·scu·rum per ob·scu·ri·us \əb-'skyu̇r-əm-ˌper-əb-'skyu̇r-ē-əs\ [L] : (explaining) the obscure by means of the more obscure

om·ne ig·no·tum pro mag·ni·fi·co \ˌȯm-ne-ig-'nō-ˌtu̇m-prō-mäg-'nif-i-ˌkō\ [L] : everything unknown (is taken) as grand : the unknown tends to be exaggerated in importance or difficulty

om·nia mu·tan·tur, nos et mu·ta·mur in il·lis \ˌȯm-nē-ä-mü-'tän-ˌtu̇r ˌnōs-ˌet-mü-ˌtäm-u̇r-in-'il-ˌēs\ [L] : all things are changing, and we are changing with them

om·nia vin·cit amor \'ȯm-nē-ä-ˌwiŋ-kit-'äm-ˌȯr\ [L] : love conquers all

onus pro·ban·di \ˌō-nəs-prō-'ban-ˌdī, -dē\ [L] : burden of proof

ora pro no·bis \ˌō-rä-prō-'nō-ˌbēs\ [L] : pray for us

ore ro·tun·do \ˌō-re-rō-'tu̇n-dō\ [L] : with round mouth : eloquently

oro y pla·ta \ˌōr-ō-ē-'plät-ə\ [Sp] : gold and silver — motto of Montana

o tem·po·ra! o mo·res! \ō-'tem-pə-rä-ō-'mō-ˌrās\ [L] : oh the times! oh the manners!

oti·um cum dig·ni·ta·te \'ōt-ē-ˌu̇m-ku̇m-ˌdig-nə-'tä-te\ [L] : leisure with dignity

où sont les neiges d'an·tan? \ü-sō^{n}-lā-nezh-dä^{n}-tä^{n}\ [F] : where are the snows of yesteryear?

pal·li·da Mors \ˌpal-əd-ə-'mȯrz\ [L] : pale Death

pa·nem et cir·cen·ses \'pän-ˌem-et-kir-'kān-ˌsēs\ [L] : bread and circuses : provision of the means of life and recreation by government to appease discontent

par avance \pȧr-ȧ-vä^{n}s\ [F] : in advance : by anticipation

par avion \pȧr-ȧ-vyō^{n}\ [F] : by airplane — used on airmail

par ex·em·ple \pȧr-āg-zä^{n}pl^{e}\ [F] : for example

par·tu·ri·unt mon·tes, nas·ce·tur ri·di·cu·lus mus \pär-ˌtu̇r-ē-ˌu̇nt-'mōn-ˌtās näs-'kā-ˌtu̇r-ri-ˌdik-ə-lu̇s-'mäs\ [L] : the mountains are in labor, and a ridiculous mouse will be brought forth

pa·ter pa·tri·ae \'pä-ˌter-'pä-trē-ˌī\ [L] : father of his country

pau·cis ver·bis \ˌpau̇-ˌkēs-'wer-ˌbēs\ [L] : in a few words

pax vo·bis·cum \ˌpäks-wō-'bēs-ˌku̇m\ [L] : peace (be) with you

peine forte et dure \pen-fȯr-tā-du̅er\ [F] : strong and hard punishment : torture

per an·gus·ta ad au·gus·ta \per-'än-ˌgu̇s-tə-äd-'au̇-ˌgu̇s-tə, per-'äŋ-\ [L] : through difficulties to honors

père \per\ [F] : father — used after French proper names to distinguish a father from his son

per·eant qui an·te nos nos·tra dix·e·runt \'per-e-ˌänt-kwē-ˌän-te-'nōs-'nōs-trä-dēk-'sā-ˌru̇nt\ [L] : may they perish who have expressed our bright ideas before us

per·eunt et im·pu·tan·tur \'per-e-ˌu̇nt-et-ˌim-pu̇-'tän-ˌtu̇r\ [L] : they (the hours) pass away and are reckoned on (our) account

per·fide Al·bion \per-fēd-ȧl-byō^{n}\ [F] : perfidious Albion (England)

peu à peu \pœ̄-ȧ-pœ̄\ [F] : little by little

peu de chose \pœ̄d-(ə-)shōz\ [F] : a trifle

pièce d'oc·ca·sion \pyes-dȯ-kä-zyō^{n}\ [F] : piece for a special occasion

pinx·it \'piŋk-sət\ [L] : he (or she) painted it

place aux dames \plȧs-ō-dȧm\ [F] : (make) room for the ladies

ple·no ju·re \ˌplā-nō-'yu̇r-e\ [L] : with full right

plus ça change, plus c'est la même chose \plu̅e-sȧ-shä^{n}zh plu̅e-se-lȧ-mem-shōz\ [F] : the more that changes, the more it's the same thing

po·cas pa·la·bras \ˌpō-käs-pä-'läv-räs\ [Sp] : few words

po·eta nas·ci·tur, non fit \pȯ-ˌā-tä-'näs-kə-ˌtu̇r nōn-'fit\ [L] : a poet is born, not made

pol·li·ce ver·so \ˌpȯ-li-ke-'wer-sō\ [L] : with thumb turned : with a gesture or expression of condemnation

post hoc, er·go prop·ter hoc \'pōst-ˌhōk ˌer-gō-'prōp-ter-ˌhōk\ [L] : after this, therefore on account of it (a fallacy of argument)

post ob·itum \pōst-'ō-bə-ˌtu̇m\ [L] : after death

pour ac·quit \pür-ȧ-kē\ [F] : received payment

pour le mé·rite \pür-lə-mā-rēt\ [F] : for merit

pro aris et fo·cis \prō-ˌä-ˌrēs-et-'fō-ˌkēs\ [L] : for altars and firesides

pro bo·no pu·bli·co \prō-ˌbō-nō-'pü-bli-ˌkō\ [L] : for the public good

pro hac vi·ce \prō-ˌhäk-'wik-e\ [L] : for this occasion

pro pa·tria \prō-'pä-trē-ˌä\ [L] : for one's country

pro re·ge, le·ge, et gre·ge \prō-'rā-ge-'lā-ge-et-'greg-e\ [L] : for the king, the law, and the people

pro re na·ta \ˌprō-ˌrā-'nä-tä\ [L] : for an occasion that has arisen : as needed — used in medical prescriptions

quand même \kä^{n}-mem\ [F] : even though : whatever may happen

quan·tum mu·ta·tus ab il·lo \ˌkwän-təm-mü-'tä-təs-äb-'il-ō\ [L] : how changed from what he once was

quan·tum suf·fi·cit \ˌkwän-təm-'su̇f-ə-ˌkit\ [L] : as much as suffices : a sufficient quantity — used in medical prescriptions

¿quien sa·be? \kyān-'sä-vā\ [Sp] : who knows?

qui fa·cit per ali·um fa·cit per se \kwē-ˌfäk-it-ˌper-'äl-ē-ˌu̇m-ˌfäk-it-ˌper-'sā\ [L] : he who does (anything) through another does it through himself

quis cus·to·di·et ip·sos cus·to·des? \ˌkwis-ku̇s-'tōd-ē-ˌet-ˌip-ˌsōs-ku̇s-'tō-ˌdās\ [L] : who will keep the keepers themselves?

qui s'ex·cuse s'ac·cuse \kē-'sek-ˌsku̅ez-'sȧ-ˌku̅ez\ [F] : he who excuses himself accuses himself

quis se·pa·ra·bit? \ˌkwis-ˌsā-pə-ˈräb-it\ [L] : who shall separate (us)? — motto of the Order of St. Patrick
qui trans·tu·lit sus·ti·net \kwē-ˈträns-tə-ˌlit-ˈsu̇s-tə-ˌnet\ [L] : He who transplanted sustains (us) — motto of Connecticut
qui va là? \kē-vȧ-lȧ\ [F] : who goes there?
quo·ad hoc \ˌkwō-ˌäd-ˈhōk\ [L] : as far as this : to this extent
quod erat de·mon·stran·dum \ˌkwȯd-ˈer-ˌät-ˌdem-ən-ˈstran-dəm, -ˌdā-ˌmȯn-ˈsträn-ˌdu̇m\ [L] : which was to be proved
quod erat fa·ci·en·dum \-ˌfäk-ē-ˈen-ˌdu̇m\ [L] : which was to be done
quod vi·de \kwȯd-ˈwid-ˌā\ [L] : which see
quos de·us vult per·de·re pri·us de·men·tat \kwōs-ˈde-u̇s-wu̇lt-ˈperd-ə-ˌre-ˌpri-u̇s-dā-ˈmen-ˌtät\ [L] : those whom a god wishes to destroy he first drives mad
quot ho·mi·nes, tot sen·ten·ti·ae \kwȯt-ˈhō-mə-ˌnās-ˌtȯt-sen-ˈten-tē-ˌī\ [L] : there are as many opinions as there are men
quo va·dis? \kwō-ˈwäd-əs\ [L] : whither are you going?

rai·son d'état \re-zō^{n}-dā-tȧ\ [F] : reason of state
re·cu·ler pour mieux sau·ter \rə-kue̅-lā-pür-myœ̅-sō-tā\ [F] : to draw back in order to make a better jump
reg·nat po·pu·lus \ˌreg-ˌnät-ˈpȯ-pə-ˌlu̇s\ [L] : the people rule — motto of Arkansas
re in·fec·ta \ˌrā-in-ˈfek-ˌtä\ [L] : the business being unfinished : without accomplishing one's purpose
re·li·gio lo·ci \re-ˌlig-ē-ˌō-ˈlō-ˌkē\ [L] : religious sanctity of a place
ré·pon·dez s'il vous plaît \rā-pō^{n}-dā-sēl-vü-ple\ [F] : reply, if you please
re·qui·es·cat in pa·ce \ˌrek-wē-ˈes-ˌkät-in-ˈpäk-ˌe, ˌrā-kwē-ˈes-ˌkät-in-ˈpäch-ˌā\ [L] : may he (or she) rest in peace — used on tombstones
re·spi·ce fi·nem \ˌrā-spi-ˌke-ˈfē-ˌnem\ [L] : look to the end : consider the outcome
re·sur·gam \re-ˈsu̇r-ˌgäm\ [L] : I shall rise again
re·te·nue \rət-nue̅\ [F] : self-restraint : reserve
re·ve·nons à nos mou·tons \rəv-nō^{n}-ȧ-nō-mü-tō^{n}\ [F] : let us return to our sheep : let us get back to the subject
ruse de guerre \rue̅z-də-ger\ [F] : war stratagem
rus in ur·be \ˌrüs-in-ˈu̇r-ˌbe\ [L] : country in the city

sal At·ti·cum \sal-ˈat-i-kəm\ [L] : Attic salt : wit
salle à man·ger \sȧl-ȧ-mä^{n}-zhā\ [F] : dining room
sa·lus po·pu·li su·pre·ma lex es·to \ˌsäl-ˌüs-ˈpȯ-pə-ˌlē-su̇-ˌprā-mä-ˌleks-ˈes-tō\ [L] : let the welfare of the people be the supreme law — motto of Missouri
sans doute \sä^{n}-düt\ [F] : without doubt
sans gêne \sä^{n}-zhen\ [F] : without embarrassment or constraint
sans peur et sans re·proche \sä^{n}-pœr-ā-sä^{n}-rə-prȯsh\ [Fr] : without fear and without reproach
sans sou·ci \sä^{n}-sü-sē\ [F] : without worry
sculp·sit \ˈskəlp-sət, ˈsku̇lp-\ [L] : he (or she) carved it
scu·to bo·nae vo·lun·ta·tis tu·ae co·ro·nas·ti nos \ˈskü-ˌtō-ˌbȯ-ˌnī-ˌvȯ-lün-ˈtä-tis-ˌtü-ˌī-ˌkȯr-ə-ˈnäs-tē-ˌnōs\ [L] : Thou hast crowned us with the shield of Thy good will — a motto on the Great Seal of Maryland
se·cun·dum ar·tem \se-ˌku̇n-dəm-ˈär-ˌtem\ [L] : according to the art : according to the accepted practice of a profession or trade
se·cun·dum na·tu·ram \-nä-ˈtü-ˌräm\ [L] : according to nature : naturally

se de·fen·den·do \ˈsā-ˌdā-ˌfen-ˈden-dō\ [L] : in self-defense
se ha·bla es·pa·ñol \sā-ˌäv-lä-ˌäs-pä-ˈn^{y}ȯl\ [Sp] : Spanish spoken
sem·per ea·dem \ˌsem-ˌper-ˈe-ä-ˌdem\ [L] : always the same (fem.) — motto of Queen Elizabeth I
sem·per fi·de·lis \ˌsem-pər-fə-ˈdā-ləs\ [L] : always faithful — motto of the U.S. Marine Corps
sem·per idem \ˌsem-ˌper-ˈē-ˌdem\ [L] : always the same (masc.)
sem·per pa·ra·tus \ˌsem-pər-pə-ˈrät-əs\ [L] : always prepared — motto of the U.S. Coast Guard
se non è ve·ro, è ben tro·va·to \sā-ˌnōn-e-ˈvā-rō-e-ˌben-trō-ˈvä-tō\ [It] : even if it is not true, it is well conceived
sic itur ad as·tra \sēk-ˈi-ˌtu̇r-ˌäd-ˈäs-trä\ [L] : thus one goes to the stars : such is the way to immortality
sic pas·sim \sēk-ˈpäs-im\ [L] : so everywhere
sic sem·per ty·ran·nis \ˌsik-ˌsem-pər-tə-ˈran-əs\ [L] : thus ever to tyrants — motto of Virginia
sic trans·it glo·ria mun·di \sēk-ˈträn-sət-ˌglōr-ē-ä-ˈmu̇n-dē\ [L] : so passes away the glory of the world
sic·ut pa·tri·bus sit De·us no·bis \ˌsē-ˌku̇t-ˈpä-tri-ˌbu̇s-sit-ˌde-u̇s-ˈnō-ˌbēs\ [L] : as to our fathers may God be to us — motto of Boston
si jeu·nesse sa·vait, si vieil·lesse pou·vait! \sē-ˈzhœ-nes-ˈsȧ-ve sē-ˈvye-yes-ˈpü-ve\ [F] : if youth only knew, if age only could!
si·lent le·ges in·ter ar·ma \ˌsil-ˌent-ˈlā-ˌgās-ˌint-ər-ˈär-mä\ [L] : the laws are silent in the midst of arms
s'il vous plaît \sēl-vü-ple\ [F] : if you please
si·mi·lia si·mi·li·bus cu·ran·tur \sim-ˈil-ē-ä-sim-ˈil-ə-bu̇s-kü-ˈrän-ˌtu̇r\ [L] : like is cured by like
si·mi·lis si·mi·li gau·det \ˈsim-ə-ləs-ˈsim-ə-lē-ˈgau̇-ˌdet\ [L] : like takes pleasure in like
si mo·nu·men·tum re·qui·ris, cir·cum·spi·ce \ˌsē-ˌmȯ-nə-ˌment-əm-re-ˈkwē-rəs kir-ˈku̇m-spi-ˌke\ [L] : if you seek his monument, look around — epitaph of Sir Christopher Wren in St. Paul's, London, of which he was architect
si quae·ris pen·in·su·lam amoe·nam, cir·cum·spi·ce \sē-ˌkwī-rəs-pā-ˌnin-sə-ˌläm-ə-ˈmȯi-ˌnäm kir-ˈku̇m-spi-ˌke\ [L] : if you seek a beautiful peninsula, look around — motto of Michigan
sis·te vi·a·tor \ˌsis-te-wē-ˈä-ˌtȯr\ [L] : stop, traveler — used on roadside tombs
sol·vi·tur am·bu·lan·do \ˈsȯl-wi-ˌtu̇r-ˌäm-bə-ˈlän-dō\ [L] : it is solved by walking : the problem is solved by a practical experiment
splen·di·de men·dax \ˌsplen-də-ˌdā-ˈmen-ˌdäks\ [L] : nobly untruthful
spo·lia opi·ma \ˌspȯ-lē-ə-ō-ˈpē-mə\ [L] : rich spoils : the arms taken by the victorious from the vanquished general
sta·tus in quo \ˌstät-əs-ˌin-ˈkwō\ [L] : state in which : the existing state
sta·tus quo an·te bel·lum \ˈstät-əs-kwō-ˌänt-e-ˈbel-u̇m\ [L] : the state existing before the war
sua·vi·ter in mo·do, for·ti·ter in re \ˈswä-wə-ˌter-in-ˈmȯd-ō ˈfȯrt-ə-ˌter-in-ˈrā\ [L] : gently in manner, strongly in deed
sub ver·bo \su̇b-ˈwer-bō\ *or* **sub vo·ce** \su̇b-ˈwō-ke\ [L] : under the word — introducing a cross-reference in a dictionary or index
sunt la·cri·mae re·rum \su̇nt-ˌläk-ri-ˌmī-ˈrā-ru̇m\ [L] : there are tears for things
suo ju·re \ˌsu̇-ō-ˈyu̇r-e\ [L] : in his (or her) own right
suo lo·co \-ˈlȯ-kō\ [L] : in its proper place
suo Mar·te \-ˈmär-te\ [L] : by one's own exertions
su·um cui·que \ˌsu̇-əm-ˈkwik-we\ [L] : to each his own

tant mieux \tä^{n}-myœ̅\ [F] : so much the better
tant pis \-pē\ [F] : so much the worse
tem·po·ra mu·tan·tur, nos et mu·ta·mur in il·lis \ˌtem-pə-rä-mü-ˈtän-ˌtu̇r ˌnōs-ˌet-mü-ˌtäm-ər-in-ˈil-ˌēs\ [L] : the times are changing, and we are changing with them
tem·pus edax re·rum \ˈtem-pu̇s-ˌed-ˌäks-ˈrā-ru̇m\ [L] : time, that devours all things
tem·pus fu·git \ˌtem-pəs-ˈfyü-jət, -ˈfü-git\ [L] : time flies
ti·meo Da·na·os et do·na fe·ren·tes \ˌtim-ē-ˌō-ˈdän-ä-ˌōs-ˌet-ˌdō-nä-fe-ˈren-ˌtās\ [L] : I fear the Greeks even when they bring gifts
to·ti·dem ver·bis \ˌtȯt-ə-ˌdem-ˈwer-ˌbēs\ [L] : in so many words
to·tis vi·ri·bus \ˌtō-ˌtēs-ˈwē-ri-ˌbu̇s\ [L] : with all one's might
to·to cae·lo \ˌtō-tō-ˈkī-lō\ *or* **toto coe·lo** \-ˈkȯi-lō\ [L] : by the whole extent of the heavens : diametrically
tou·jours per·drix \tü-zhür-per-drē\ [F] : always partridge : too much of a good thing
tous frais faits \tü-fre-fe\ [F] : all expenses defrayed
tout à fait \tü-tȧ-fe\ [F] : altogether : quite
tout au con·traire \tü-tō-kō^{n}-trer\ [F] : quite the contrary
tout à vous \tü-tȧ-vü\ [F] : wholly yours : at your service
tout bien ou rien \tü-ˈbya^{n}-nü-ˈrya^{n}\ [F] : everything well (done) or nothing (attempted)
tout com·pren·dre c'est tout par·don·ner \tü-kō^{n}-prä^{n}-drə se-tü-pȧr-dȯ-nā\ [F] : to understand all is to forgive all
tout court \tü-kür\ [F] : quite short : simply; *also* : brusquely
tout de même \tüt-mem\ [F] : all the same : nevertheless
tout de suite \tüt-sw^{y}ēt\ [F] : immediately; *also* : all at once : consecutively
tout en·sem·ble \tü-tä^{n}-sä^{n}bl^{ə}\ [F] : all together : general effect
tout est per·du fors l'hon·neur \tü-te-per-due̅-fȯr-lȯ-nœr\ *or* **tout est perdu hors l'honneur** \-due̅-ȯr-\ [F] : all is lost save honor
tout le monde \tül-mō^{n}d\ [F] : all the world : everybody
tria junc·ta in uno \ˌtri-ä-ˈyu̇ŋk-tä-in-ˈü-nō\ [L] : three joined in one — motto of the Order of the Bath
tru·di·tur di·es die \ˈtrüd-ə-ˌtu̇r-ˌdi-ˌās-ˈdi-ˌā\ [L] : day is pushed forth by day : one day hurries on another
tu·e·bor \tü-ˈā-ˌbȯr\ [L] : I will defend — a motto on the Great Seal of Michigan

ua mau ke ea o ka ai·na i ka po·no \ˌu̇-ä-ˈmä-u̇-ke-ˈe-ä-ō-kä-ˈä-ē-nä-ˌē-kä-ˈpō-nō\ [Hawaiian] : the life of the land is established in righteousness — motto of Hawaii
ul·ti·ma ra·tio re·gum \ˈu̇l-ti-mä-ˌrät-ē-ō-ˈrā-gu̇m\ [L] : the final argument of kings, i.e., war
und so wei·ter \u̇nt-zō-ˈvī-tər\ [G] : and so on
uno ani·mo \ˌü-nō-ˈän-ə-ˌmō\ [L] : with one mind : unanimously
ur·bi et or·bi \ˌu̇r-bē-ˌet-ˈȯr-bē\ [L] : to the city (Rome) and the world
uti·le dul·ci \ˌüt-^{ə}l-e-ˈdu̇l-ˌkē\ [L] : the useful with the agreeable
ut in·fra \u̇t-ˈin-frä\ [L] : as below
ut su·pra \u̇t-ˈsü-prä\ [L] : as above

va·de re·tro me, Sa·ta·na \ˌwä-de-ˈrā-trō-ˌmā-ˈsä-tə-ˌnä\ [L] : get thee behind me, Satan
vae vic·tis \wī-ˈwik-ˌtēs\ [L] : woe to the vanquished
va·ria lec·tio \ˌwär-ē-ä-ˈlek-tē-ˌō\ *pl* **va·ri·ae lec·ti·o·nes** \ˈwär-ē-ˌī-ˌlek-tē-ˈō-ˌnās\ [L] : variant reading

va·ri·um et mu·ta·bi·le sem·per fe·mi·na \ˌwär-ē-ˌet-ˌmü-ˈtā-bə-le-ˌsem-ˌper-ˈfā-mi-nä\ [L] : woman is ever a fickle and changeable thing
ve·di Na·po·li e poi mo·ri \ˌvā-dē-ˈnä-pō-lē-ā-ˌpȯ-ē-ˈmȯ-rē\ [It] : see Naples, and then die
ve·ni, vi·di, vi·ci \ˌwā-nē-ˌwēd-ē-ˈwē-kē\ [L] : I came, I saw, I conquered
ven·tre à terre \väⁿ-trä-ter\ [F] : belly to the ground : at very great speed
ver·ba·tim ac lit·ter·a·tim \wer-ˈbä-tim-ˌäk-ˌlit-ə-ˈrä-tim\ [L] : word for word and letter for letter
ver·bum sat sa·pi·en·ti est \ˌwer-bu̇m-ˈsät-ˌsäp-ē-ˈent-ē-ˌest\ [L] : a word to the wise is sufficient
vin·cit om·nia ve·ri·tas \ˌwiŋ-kit-ˈȯm-nē-ä-ˈwā-rə-ˌtäs\ [L] : truth conquers all things
vin·cu·lum ma·tri·mo·nii \ˌwiŋ-kə-lu̇m-ˌmä-trə-ˈmō-nē-ˌē\ [L] : bond of marriage
vir·gin·i·bus pu·er·is·que \wir-ˈgin-ə-bu̇s-ˌpu̇-ə-ˈrēs-kwe\ [L] : for girls and boys
vir·tu·te et ar·mis \wir-ˈtü-te-ˌet-ˈär-ˌmēs\ [L] : by valor and arms — motto of Mississippi
vive la reine \vēv-lä-ren\ [F] : long live the queen
vive le roi \vēv-lə-rwä\ [F] : long live the king
vix·e·re for·tes an·te Aga·mem·no·na \wik-ˌsā-re-ˈfȯr-ˌtās-ˌänt-ˌäg-ə-ˈmem-nə-ˌnä\ [L] : brave men lived before Agamemnon
vogue la ga·lère \vȯg-lä-gä-ler\ [F] : let the galley be kept rowing : keep on, whatever may happen
voi·là tout \vwä-lä-tü\ [F] : that's all
vox et prae·te·rea ni·hil \ˈwōks-et-prī-ˌter-e-ä-ˈnē-ˌhil\ [L] : voice and nothing more
vox po·pu·li vox Dei \wōks-ˈpȯ-pə-ˌlē-ˌwōks-ˈde-ē\ [L] : the voice of the people is the voice of God

Wan·der·jahr \ˈvän-dər-ˌyär\ [G] : year of wandering
wie geht's? \vē-ˈgāts\ [G] : how goes it?

CHEMICAL ELEMENTS
WITH INTERNATIONAL ATOMIC WEIGHTS

ELEMENT & SYMBOL	ATOMIC NUMBER	ATOMIC WEIGHT (C = 12)
actinium (Ac)	89	
aluminum (Al)	13	26.98154
americium (Am)	95	
antimony (Sb)	51	121.75
argon (Ar)	18	39.948
arsenic (As)	33	74.9216
astatine (At)	85	
barium (Ba)	56	137.33
berkelium (Bk)	97	
beryllium (Be)	4	9.01218
bismuth (Bi)	83	208.9808
boron (B)	5	10.81
bromine (Br)	35	79.904
cadmium (Cd)	48	112.41
calcium (Ca)	20	40.08
californium (Cf)	98	
carbon (C)	6	12.011
cerium (Ce)	58	140.12
cesium (Cs)	55	132.9054
chlorine (Cl)	17	35.453
chromium (Cr)	24	51.996
cobalt (Co)	27	58.9332
columbium (Cb)	(see niobium)	
copper (Cu)	29	63.546
curium (Cm)	96	
dysprosium (Dy)	66	162.50
einsteinium (Es)	99	
erbium (Er)	68	167.26
europium (Eu)	63	151.96
fermium (Fm)	100	
fluorine (F)	9	18.998403
francium (Fr)	87	
gadolinium (Gd)	64	157.25
gallium (Ga)	31	69.72
germanium (Ge)	32	72.59
gold (Au)	79	196.9665
hafnium (Hf)	72	178.49
helium (He)	2	4.00260
holmium (Ho)	67	164.9304
hydrogen (H)	1	1.0079
indium (In)	49	114.82
iodine (I)	53	126.9045
iridium (Ir)	77	192.22
iron (Fe)	26	55.847
krypton (Kr)	36	83.80
lanthanum (La)	57	138.9055
lawrencium (Lr)	103	
lead (Pb)	82	207.2
lithium (Li)	3	6.941
lutetium (Lu)	71	174.97
magnesium (Mg)	12	24.305
manganese (Mn)	25	54.9380
mendelevium (Md)	101	
mercury (Hg)	80	200.59
molybdenum (Mo)	42	95.94
neodymium (Nd)	60	144.24
neon (Ne)	10	20.179
neptunium (Np)	93	237.0482
nickel (Ni)	28	58.71
niobium (Nb)	41	92.9064
nitrogen (N)	7	14.0067
nobelium (No)	102	
osmium (Os)	76	190.2
oxygen (O)	8	15.9994
palladium (Pd)	46	106.4
phosphorus (P)	15	30.9738
platinum (Pt)	78	195.09
plutonium (Pu)	94	
polonium (Po)	84	
potassium (K)	19	39.0983
praseodymium (Pr)	59	140.9077
promethium (Pm)	61	
protactinium (Pa)	91	231.0359
radium (Ra)	88	226.0254
radon (Rn)	86	
rhenium (Re)	75	186.2
rhodium (Rh)	45	102.9055
rubidium (Rb)	37	85.4678
ruthenium (Ru)	44	101.07
samarium (Sm)	62	150.4
scandium (Sc)	21	44.9559
selenium (Se)	34	78.96
silicon (Si)	14	28.0855
silver (Ag)	47	107.868
sodium (Na)	11	22.9898
strontium (Sr)	38	87.62
sulfur (S)	16	32.06
tantalum (Ta)	73	180.9479
technetium (Tc)	43	98.9062
tellurium (Te)	52	127.60
terbium (Tb)	65	158.9254
thallium (Tl)	81	204.37
thorium (Th)	90	232.0381
thulium (Tm)	69	168.9342
tin (Sn)	50	118.69
titanium (Ti)	22	47.90
tungsten (W)	74	183.85
uranium (U)	92	238.029
vanadium (V)	23	50.9414
wolfram (W)	(see tungsten)	
xenon (Xe)	54	131.30
ytterbium (Yb)	70	173.04
yttrium (Y)	39	88.9059
zinc (Zn)	30	65.38
zirconium (Zr)	40	91.22

MEASURES AND WEIGHTS

linear measure

12	inches (in *or* ″)	= 1 foot (ft *or* ′)
3	feet	= 1 yard (yd)
5½	yards *or* 16½ feet	= 1 rod (rd) *or* pole (p)
40	rods	= 1 furlong (fur)
8	furlongs *or* 1760 yards *or* 5280 feet	= 1 mile (m *or* mi)

chain measure

7.92	inches	= 1 link (li)
100	links *or* 66 feet	= 1 chain (ch)
10	chains	= 1 furlong (fur)
80	chains	= 1 mile (m *or* mi)

The *engineer's chain* is 100 feet long with links one foot long (52.8 chains = 1 mile).

square measure (area)

144	square inches (sq in)	= 1 square foot (sq ft)
9	square feet	= 1 square yard (sq yd)
30¼	square yards	= 1 square rod (sq rd)
160	square rods	= 1 acre (a)

surveyor's measure (area)

625 square links (sq li)	= 1 square pole (sq p)
16 square poles	= 1 square chain (sq ch)
10 square chains	= 1 acre (a)
640 acres	= 1 square mile (sq m) *or* 1 section (sec)
36 square miles	= 1 township (tp)

miscellaneous measures of length

1 point = .013837 in	= 1/72 in (type)
1 line	= 1/12 in (type)
1 palm	= 3 in *or* 4 in
1 hand = 4 in	= 10.16 cm (height of horses)
1 span = 9 in	= 22.86 cm
1 cubit = 18 in	= 45.72 cm
1 knot = 1 nautical mile per hour	

cubic measure (volume)

1728 cubic inches (cu in)	= 1 cubic foot (cu ft)
27 cubic feet	= 1 cubic yard (cu yd)
(for measuring cordwood)	
16 cubic feet	= 1 cord foot (cd ft) *or* 4′ × 4′ × 1′
8 cord feet	= 1 cord (cd) *or* 4′ × 4′ × 8′

time measure

60 seconds (sec)	= 1 minute (min)
60 minutes	= 1 hour (hr)
24 hours	= 1 day (da)
7 days	= 1 week (wk)
30 days (commonly)	= 1 calendar month (mo)
365 days *or* 12 calendar months	= 1 common year (yr)
366 days	= 1 leap year
100 years	= 1 century

The length of the *astronomical year* is about 365¼ days, or 365 days, 5 hours, 48 minutes, 45.5 seconds. As the *common year* is 365 days, it becomes necessary once in every four years to add a day to the year making the *leap year* of 366 days.

Every year whose number is divisible by 4 without a remainder is a leap year excepting the full centuries. To be leap years, these must be divisible by 400 without a remainder; 1900, therefore, was not a leap year.

January, March, May, July, August, October, and December contain 31 days. April, June, September, and November contain 30 days. February contains 28 days except in leap years, when it contains 29 days.

circular measure

60 seconds (″)	= 1 minute (′)
60 minutes	= 1 degree (°)
90 degrees	= 1 quadrant
4 quadrants *or* 360 degrees	= 1 circle

longitude and time

1 second of longitude (″)	= 1/15 second of time
1 minute " " (′)	= 4 seconds of time
1 degree " " (°)	= 4 minutes of time
15 degrees " "	= 1 hour
360 degrees " "	= 24 hours

nautical measure

6 feet	= 1 fathom (f *or* fm)
120 fathoms	= 1 cable's length (U. S. Navy)
1 nautical mile	= 1.1516 statute miles
3 nautical miles	= 1 league
60 nautical miles	= 1 degree (of a terrestrial great circle)

dry measure (grain, fruit)

2 pints (pt)	= 1 quart (qt)
8 quarts	= 1 peck (pk)
4 pecks	= 1 bushel (bu) = 2150.42 cu in

The weight of a bushel of wheat as fixed by the United States government is 60 lb avoirdupois; of barley, 48 lb; of oats, 32 lb; of rye, 56 lb; and of Indian corn, 56 lb. In the various states a bushel of corn varies in weight from 52 to 56 lb and of barley from 32 to 50 lb. The customary legal weight of a bushel of potatoes is 60 lb but in North Carolina and West Virginia it is 56 lb.

liquid measure

4 gills (gi)	= 1 pint (pt)
2 pints	= 1 quart (qt)
4 quarts	= 1 gallon (gal) = 231 cu in
63 gallons	= 1 hogshead (hhd)

The *barrel* is usually taken to be 31½ gallons. The *imperial gallon* (of Great Britain) contains 277.420 cubic inches.

apothecaries' fluid measure (drugs)

60 minims *or* drops	= 1 fluidram
8 fluidrams	= 1 fluidounce
16 fluidounces	= 1 pint
8 pints	= 1 gallon

avoirdupois weight (ordinary commodities)

16 drams (dr)	= 1 ounce (oz)
16 ounces *or* 7000 grains	= 1 pound (lb)
14 pounds	= 1 stone (st)
100 (in England 112) pounds	= 1 hundredweight (cwt)
2000 pounds *or* 20 hundredweights	= 1 ton (tn *or* t) *or* short ton (ST)
2240 pounds *or* 20 hundredweights	= 1 long ton (LT)

troy weight (precious metals, jewels)

3.086 grains (gr)	= 1 carat (car)
24 grains	= 1 pennyweight (dwt)
20 pennyweights	= 1 ounce (oz t)
12 ounces *or* 5760 grains	= 1 pound (lb t)

apothecaries' weight (drugs)

20 grains (gr)	= 1 scruple (s ap)
3 scruples	= 1 dram (dr ap)
8 drams	= 1 ounce (oz ap)
12 ounces	= 1 pound (lb ap)

comparison of weights

	grain	ounce	pound
avoirdupois	1	437½ gr	7000 gr
troy	1	480 gr	5760 gr
apothecaries'	1	480 gr	5760 gr
175 lb troy			= 144 lb av

numbers

12 units	= 1 dozen (doz)
12 dozen	= 1 gross (gr)
12 gross	= 1 great gross
20 units	= 1 score

paper

24 sheets	= 1 quire (qr)
20 quires	= 1 ream (rm)

METRIC MEASURES AND DECIMAL EQUIVALENTS

The metric system is a decimal system of measures and weights that first came into use in France shortly after the French Revolution. It is now used for almost all scientific purposes in the United States and Great Britain, and its use is required by law in most countries. The basis of the system is the *meter* (39.37 inches), which was intended to be, and is very nearly, one ten-millionth part of the distance on a meridian from the equator to the pole. Upon the meter were based the other primary units, the *square meter,* the *cubic meter,* the *are* (100 square meters), the *liter* (the volume of a cube whose edge is one tenth of a meter), and the *gram* (the weight, nominally, of pure water at 4°C, its temperature of greatest density, contained in a cube whose edge is one hundredth of a meter).

Decimal fractions of the primary units are designated by the Latin prefixes *deci-* (10th), *centi-* (100th), *milli-* (1000th); decimal multiples are denoted by the Greek prefixes *deka-* (10 times), *hecto-* (100 times), *kilo-* (1000 times), *myria-* (10,000 times).

measures of length

10 millimeters (mm)	= 1 centimeter (cm)	= 0.3937 in
10 centimeters	= 1 decimeter (dm)	= 3.937 in
10 decimeters	= 1 meter (m)	= 39.37 in
10 meters	= 1 dekameter (dam)	= 393.7 in
10 dekameters	= 1 hectometer (hm)	= 328 ft 1 in
10 hectometers	= 1 kilometer (km)	= 0.62137 mi
10 kilometers	= 1 myriameter (mym)	= 6.2137 mi

The *micron* (μ) is one millionth of a meter or one thousandth of a millimeter.

measures of surface

100 sq millimeters (mm²)	= 1 sq centimeter (cm²)
100 sq centimeters	= 1 sq decimeter (dm²)
100 sq decimeters	= 1 sq meter (m²)
100 sq meters	= 1 sq dekameter (dam²)
100 sq dekameters	= 1 sq hectometer (hm²)
100 sq hectometers	= 1 sq kilometer (km²)

land measure

1 sq meter (m²)	= 1 centare (ca)	= 1550 sq in
100 centares *or* 100 m²	= 1 are (a)	= 119.6 sq yd
100 ares *or* 10,000 m²	= 1 hectare (ha)	= 2.471 acres
1 sq kilometer (km²)	= 1,000,000 sq meters	= .3861 sq mi

The *square kilometer* is used in surveys on a large scale or in maps or charts that show roads, plans of towns, or contour lines. The *hectare* is used for field measurements, like the *acre*. For small areas (as city lots) the *are* is generally used.

measures of capacity

The standard unit of capacity is the *liter*, equal to 1 cubic decimeter or 0.9081 dry quart or 1.0567 liquid quarts.

10 milliliters (ml)	= 1 centiliter (cl)	= 0.338 fl oz
10 centiliters	= 1 deciliter (dl)	= 6.1025 cu in
10 deciliters	= 1 liter (l)	= 0.9081 dry qt
10 liters	= 1 dekaliter (dal)	= 0.284 bu *or* 2.64 gal
10 dekaliters	= 1 hectoliter (hl)	= 2.838 bu *or* 26.418 gal
10 hectoliters	= 1 kiloliter (kl)	= 35.315 cu ft *or* 264.18 gal

weights

The standard unit of weight is the *gram,* equal to 15.432 grains.

10 milligrams (mg)	= 1 centigram (cg)	= 0.1543 gr
10 centigrams	= 1 decigram (dg)	= 1.5432 gr
10 decigrams	= 1 gram (g)	= 15.432 gr
10 grams	= 1 dekagram (dag)	= 0.3527 oz
10 dekagrams	= 1 hectogram (hg)	= 3.5274 oz
10 hectograms	= 1 kilogram *or* kilo (kg)	= 2.2046 lb
10 kilograms	= 1 myriagram (myg)	= 22.046 lb
10 myriagrams	= 1 quintal (q)	= 220.46 lb
10 quintals *or* 1000 kg	= 1 metric ton (MT *or* t)	= 2204.6 lb

measures of volume

The standard unit of volume is the *cubic meter,* equal to 1.308 cubic yards.

1000 cu millimeters (mm³)	= 1 cu centimeter (cm³)
1000 cu centimeters	= 1 cu decimeter (dm³)
1000 cu decimeters	= 1 cu meter (m³) *or* 1 stere (s)

The *stere* is used for firewood. 1 stere = 0.2759 cord; 1 decistere = 1/10 stere; 1 dekastere = 10 steres.

metric equivalents of common units

inch	= 2.54 cm	minim	= 0.062 ml
foot	= 0.3048 m	gill	= 0.118 l
yard	= 0.9144 m	liquid quart	= 0.9464 l
rod	= 5.029 m	dry quart	= 1.1012 l
mile	= 1.6093 km	gallon	= 3.7854 l
sq inch	= 6.452 cm²	peck	= 8.8098 l
sq foot	= 0.0929 m²	bushel	= 35.239 l
sq yard	= 0.8361 m²	oz av	= 28.3495 g
acre	= 0.4047 ha	lb av	= 0.4536 kg
sq mile	= 259 ha *or* 2.590 km²	ton, long	= 1.016 MT
cu inch	= 16.387 cm³	ton, short	= 0.9072 MT
cu foot	= 0.0283 m³	grain	= 0.0648 g
cu yard	= 0.7646 m³	oz troy	= 31.1035 g
fathom	= 1.829 m	lb troy	= 0.3732 kg
		cord	= 3.625 m³

DECIMAL AND FRACTIONAL EQUIVALENTS

decimal equivalents of common fractions

1/32 = .03125	1/5 = .2	4/9 = .44+	3/4 = .75
1/16 = .0625	2/9 = .22+	1/2 = .5	7/9 = .77+
1/10 = .1	1/4 = .25	5/9 = .55+	4/5 = .8
1/9 = .11+	3/10 = .3	3/5 = .6	5/6 = .833+
1/8 = .125	1/3 = .33+	5/8 = .625	7/8 = .875
1/7 = .1428+	3/8 = .375	2/3 = .66+	8/9 = .88+
1/6 = .166+	2/5 = .4	7/10 = .7	9/10 = .9

percentages and their fractional equivalents

2½% = 1/40	12½% = 1/8	25% = 1/4	50% = 1/2
5% = 1/20	16⅔% = 1/6	33⅓% = 1/3	66⅔% = 2/3
10% = 1/10	20% = 1/5	40% = 2/5	75% = 3/4

STANDARD TIME

For each zone of 15° of longitude around the world the time varies by 1 hour; however, where a country overlaps a zone or more, in order to have a uniform national time, its legal time may differ by ½ hour or less from the neighboring zone. In England, the standard time is the time when the sun crosses the meridian that passes through Greenwich (the mean solar time of Greenwich, or **Greenwich time**). In the U. S., excluding Alaska and Hawaii, there are four official standards of time, **Eastern, Central, Mountain,** and **Pacific,** based on the 75th, 90th, 105th, and 120th meridians west, 5, 6, 7, and 8 hours respectively slower than Greenwich. In addition to these standards Canada has **Newfoundland** time, 3½ hours slower than Greenwich, **Atlantic** time, 4 hours slower than Greenwich, and **Yukon** time, 9 hours slower than Greenwich. In addition to Pacific and Yukon standards, Alaska has **Alaska** time, 10 hours slower than Greenwich, and **Bering** time, 11 hours slower than Greenwich. Hawaii has **Hawaii** time, 10 hours slower than Greenwich.

STANDARD TIME AROUND THE WORLD

TIME COMPARED WITH GREENWICH TIME AND WASHINGTON, D. C., NOON

NOTE. A day, Sunday, Sept. 6, begins at the *date line* in the Pacific and moves west. Wellington, N. Z., long. 174° 50′ E, is 12 hours ahead of Greenwich. When it is 12 o'clock noon at Greenwich it is 12 o'clock midnight that evening (Sunday) at Wellington and 7 o'clock that morning at Washington. When it is 12 o'clock noon at Washington it is 5 o'clock the next morning (Monday, Sept. 7) at Wellington and 5 o'clock (17 o'clock) that afternoon (Sunday) at Greenwich.

	Difference in time from Greenwich		Local time when it is noon at Washington	
180° INTERNATIONAL DATE LINE 180°				
	hr. min.			
Wellington, N.Z.; Wake Island, 166° 35′ E	12	fast	5	A.M.[1]
New Caledonia	11	"	4	A.M.[1]
Sydney, N.S.W.; Port Moresby, Papua	10	"	3	A.M.[1]
Tokyo, Japan	9	"	2	A.M.[1]
Manila, Philippines; Shanghai, China	8	"	1	A.M.[1]
Singapore	7 30	"	12.30	A.M.[1]
Djakarta, Indonesia	7		12.00	A.M.[1]
Calcutta, India; Bombay, "	5 30	"	10.30	P.M.
Baghdad, Iraq; Moscow, U.S.S.R.	3	"	8	P.M.
Cairo, Egypt; Cape Town, South Africa	2	"	7	P.M.
Rome, Italy; Berlin, Germany; Paris, France	1	"	6	P.M.
London, England	0	"	5	P.M.
Reykjavík, Iceland	1	slow	4	P.M.
Rio de Janeiro, Brazil; Buenos Aires, Argentina	3	"	2	P.M.
Halifax, N.S. (Atlantic); Caracas, Venezuela	4	"	1	P.M.
New York, N.Y. (Eastern); Ottawa, Canada; Lima, Peru	5	"	12	noon (Sun.)
Chicago, Ill. (Central); St. Louis, Mo. "; Mexico City, Mexico	6	"	11	A.M.
Denver, Colo. (Mountain); Edmonton, Alberta	7	"	10	A.M.
San Francisco, Calif. (Pacific); Portland, Oreg. "; Juneau, Alaska "	8	"	9	A.M.
Anchorage, Alaska (Alaska); Tahiti, Society Islands; Honolulu, Hawaii (Hawaii)	10	"	7	A.M.
Nome, Alaska (Bering)	11	"	6	A.M.
Midway Island, long. 177° 20′ W[2]	12	"	5	A.M.
180° INTERNATIONAL DATE LINE 180°				

[1]The morning of the next day, Monday, Sept. 7.
[2]Actually uses the same time as Honolulu.

JEWISH YEARS 5734–5753

Jewish year		A.D.
5734	begins	Sept. 27, 1973
5735	"	Sept. 17, 1974
5736	"	Sept. 6, 1975
5737	"	Sept. 25, 1976
5738	"	Sept. 13, 1977
5739	"	Oct. 2, 1978
5740	"	Sept. 22, 1979
5741	"	Sept. 11, 1980
5742	"	Sept. 29, 1981
5743	"	Sept. 18, 1982
5744	"	Sept. 8, 1983
5745	"	Sept. 27, 1984
5746	"	Sept. 16, 1985
5747	"	Oct. 4, 1986
5748	"	Sept. 24, 1987
5749	"	Sept. 12, 1988
5750	"	Sept. 30, 1989
5751	"	Sept. 20, 1990
5752	"	Sept. 9, 1991
5753	"	Sept. 28, 1992

EASTER DATES 1973–1992

Year	Ash Wed.	Easter
1973	Mar. 7	Apr. 22
1974	Feb. 27	Apr. 14
1975	Feb. 12	Mar. 30
1976	Mar. 3	Apr. 18
1977	Feb. 23	Apr. 10
1978	Feb. 8	Mar. 26
1979	Feb. 28	Apr. 15
1980	Feb. 20	Apr. 6
1981	Mar. 4	Apr. 19
1982	Feb. 24	Apr. 11
1983	Feb. 16	Apr. 3
1984	Mar. 7	Apr. 22
1985	Feb. 20	Apr. 7
1986	Feb. 12	Mar. 30
1987	Mar. 4	Apr. 19
1988	Feb. 17	Apr. 3
1989	Feb. 8	Mar. 26
1990	Feb. 28	Apr. 15
1991	Feb. 13	Mar. 31
1992	Mar. 4	Apr. 19

THE DECLARATION OF INDEPENDENCE

IN CONGRESS, JULY 4, 1776.

The unanimous Declaration of the thirteen united States of America,

When in the Course of human events it becomes necessary for one people to dissolve the political bands which have connected them with another, and to assume among the powers of the earth, the separate and equal station to which the Laws of Nature and of Nature's God entitle them, a decent respect to the opinions of mankind requires that they should declare the causes which impel them to the separation.

We hold these truths to be self-evident, that all men are created equal, that they are endowed by their Creator with certain unalienable Rights, that among these are Life, Liberty and the pursuit of Happiness. That to secure these rights, Governments are instituted among Men, deriving their just powers from the consent of the governed, — That whenever any Form of Government becomes destructive of these ends, it is the Right of the People to alter or to abolish it, and to institute new Government, laying its foundation on such principles and organizing its powers in such form, as to them shall seem most likely to effect their Safety and Happiness. Prudence, indeed, will dictate that Governments long established should not be changed for light and transient causes; and accordingly all experience hath shewn, that mankind are more disposed to suffer, while evils are sufferable, than to right themselves by abolishing the forms to which they are accustomed. But when a long train of abuses and usurpations, pursuing invariably the same Object evinces a design to reduce them under absolute Despotism, it is their right, it is their duty, to throw off such Government, and to provide new Guards for their future security. Such has been the patient sufferance of these Colonies; and such is now the necessity which constrains them to alter their former Systems of Government. The history of the present King of Great Britain is a history of repeated injuries and usurpations, all having in direct object the establishment of an absolute Tyranny over these States. To prove this, let Facts be submitted to a candid world.

He has refused his Assent to Laws, the most wholesome and necessary for the public good.

He has forbidden his Governors to pass Laws of immediate and pressing importance, unless suspended in their operation till his Assent should be obtained; and when so suspended, he has utterly neglected to attend to them.

He has refused to pass other Laws for the accommodation of large districts of people, unless those people would relinquish the right of Representation in the Legislature, a right inestimable to them and formidable to tyrants only.

He has called together legislative bodies at places unusual, uncomfortable, and distant from the depository of their Public Records, for the sole purpose of fatiguing them into compliance with his measures.

He has dissolved Representative Houses repeatedly, for opposing with manly firmness his invasions on the rights of the people.

He has refused for a long time, after such dissolutions, to cause others to be elected; whereby the Legislative Powers, incapable of Annihilation, have returned to the People at large for their exercise; the State remaining in the mean time exposed to all the dangers of invasion from without, and convulsions within.

He has endeavoured to prevent the population of these States; for that purpose obstructing the Laws for Naturalization of Foreigners; refusing to pass others to encourage their migrations hither, and raising the conditions of new Appropriations of Lands.

He has obstructed the Administration of Justice, by refusing his Assent to Laws for establishing Judiciary Powers.

He has made Judges dependent on his Will alone, for the tenure of their offices, and the amount and payment of their salaries.

He has erected a multitude of New Offices, and sent hither swarms of Officers to harass our People, and eat out their substance.

He has kept among us, in times of peace, Standing Armies without the Consent of our legislature.

He has affected to render the Military independent of and superior to the Civil Power.

He has combined with others to subject us to a jurisdiction foreign to our constitution, and unacknowledged by our laws; giving his Assent to their Acts of pretended Legislation:

For quartering large bodies of armed troops among us:

For protecting them, by a mock Trial, from Punishment for any Murders which they should commit on the Inhabitants of these States:

For cutting off our Trade with all parts of the world:

For imposing Taxes on us without our Consent:

For depriving us in many cases, of the benefits of Trial by Jury:

For transporting us beyond Seas to be tried for pretended offences:

For abolishing the free System of English Laws in a neighbouring Province, establishing therein an Arbitrary government, and enlarging its Boundaries so as to render it at once an example and fit instrument for introducing the same absolute rule into these Colonies:

For taking away our Charters, abolishing our most valuable Laws and altering fundamentally the Forms of our Governments:

For suspending our own Legislatures, and declaring themselves invested with power to legislate for us in all cases whatsoever.

He has abdicated Government here, by declaring us out of his Protection and waging War against us.

He has plundered our seas, ravaged our Coasts, burnt our towns, and destroyed the lives of our people.

He is at this time transporting large Armies of foreign Mercenaries to compleat the works of death, desolation and tyranny, already begun with circumstances of Cruelty & Perfidy scarcely paralleled in the most barbarous ages, and totally unworthy the Head of a civilized nation.

He has constrained our fellow Citizens taken Captive on the high Seas to bear Arms against their Country, to become the executioners of their friends and Brethren, or to fall themselves by their Hands.

He has excited domestic insurrections amongst us, and has endeavoured to bring on the inhabitants of our frontiers, the merciless Indian Savages, whose known rule of warfare, is an undistinguished destruction of all ages, sexes and conditions.

In every stage of these Oppressions We have Petitioned for Redress in the most humble terms: Our repeated Petitions have been answered only by repeated injury. A Prince, whose character is thus marked by every act which may define a Tyrant, is unfit to be the ruler of a free People.

Nor have We been wanting in attentions to our Brittish brethren. We have warned them from time to time of attempts by their legislature to extend an unwarrantable jurisdiction over us. We have reminded them of the circumstances of our emigration and settlement here. We have appealed to their native justice and magnanimity, and we have conjured them by the ties of our common kindred to disavow these usurpations, which would inevitably interrupt our connections and correspondence. They too have been deaf to the voice of justice and of consanguinity. We must, therefore, acquiesce in the necessity, which denounces our Separation, and hold them, as we hold the rest of mankind, Enemies in War, in Peace Friends.

We, therefore, the Representatives of the united States of America, in General Congress, Assembled, appealing to the Supreme Judge of the world for the rectitude of our intentions, do, in the Name, and by Authority of the good People of these Colonies, solemnly publish and declare, That these United Colonies are, and of Right ought to be Free and Independent States; that they are Absolved from all Allegiance to the British Crown, and that all political connection between them and the State of Great Britain, is and ought to be totally dissolved; and that as Free and Independent States, they have full Power to levy War, conclude Peace, contract Alliances, establish Commerce, and to do all other Acts and Things which Independent States may of right do.

And for the support of this Declaration, with a firm reliance on the Protection of Divine Providence, we mutually pledge to each other our Lives, our Fortunes and our sacred Honor.

THE CONSTITUTION OF THE UNITED STATES OF AMERICA

We the People of the United States, in Order to form a more perfect Union, establish Justice, insure domestic Tranquility, provide for the common defence, promote the general Welfare, and secure the Blessings of Liberty to ourselves and our Posterity, do ordain and establish this Constitution for the United States of America.

ARTICLE I

SECTION 1. All legislative Powers herein granted shall be vested in a Congress of the United States, which shall consist of a Senate and House of Representatives.

SECTION 2. The House of Representatives shall be composed of Members chosen every second Year by the People of the several States, and the Electors in each State shall have the Qualifications requisite for Electors of the most numerous Branch of the State Legislature.

No Person shall be a Representative who shall not have attained to the age of twenty five Years, and been seven Years a Citizen of the United States, and who shall not, when elected, be an Inhabitant of that State in which he shall be chosen.

Representatives and direct Taxes shall be apportioned among the several States which may be included within this Union, according to their respective Numbers, which shall be determined by adding to the whole Number of free Persons, including those bound to Service for a Term of Years, and excluding Indians not taxed, three fifths of all other Persons.

The actual Enumeration shall be made within three Years after the first Meeting of the Congress of the United States, and within every subsequent Term of ten Years, in such Manner as they shall by Law direct. The Number of Representatives shall not exceed one for every thirty Thousand, but each State shall have at Least one Representative; and until such enumeration shall be made, the State of New Hampshire shall be entitled to chuse three, Massachusetts eight, Rhode-Island and Providence Plantations one, Connecticut five, New-York six, New Jersey four, Pennsylvania eight, Delaware one, Maryland six, Virginia ten, North Carolina five, South Carolina five, and Georgia three.

When vacancies happen in the Representation from any State, the Executive Authority thereof shall issue Writs of Election to fill such Vacancies.

The House of Representatives shall chuse their Speaker and other Officers; and shall have the sole Power of Impeachment.

SECTION 3. The Senate of the United States shall be composed of two Senators from each State, chosen by the Legislature thereof, for six Years; and each Senator shall have one Vote.

Immediately after they shall be assembled in Consequence of the first Election, they shall be divided as equally as may be into three Classes. The Seats of the Senators of the first Class shall be vacated at the Expiration of the second Year, of the second Class at the Expiration of the fourth Year, and of the third Class at the Expiration of the sixth Year, so that one third may be chosen every second Year; and if Vacancies happen by Resignation, or otherwise, during the Recess of the Legislature of any State, the Executive thereof may make temporary Appointments until the next Meeting of the Legislature, which shall then fill such Vacancies.

No Person shall be a Senator who shall not have attained to the Age of thirty Years, and been nine Years a Citizen of the United States, and who shall not, when elected, be an Inhabitant of that State for which he shall be chosen.

The Vice President of the United States shall be President of the Senate, but shall have no Vote, unless they be equally divided.

The Senate shall chuse their other Officers, and also a President pro tempore, in the Absence of the Vice President, or when he shall exercise the Office of President of the United States.

The Senate shall have the sole Power to try all Impeachments. When sitting for that Purpose, they shall be on Oath or Affirmation. When the President of the United States is tried, the Chief Justice shall preside: And no Person shall be convicted without the Concurrence of two thirds of the Members present.

Judgment in Cases of Impeachment shall not extend further than to removal from Office, and disqualification to hold and enjoy any Office of honor, Trust or Profit under the United States: but the Party convicted shall nevertheless be liable and subject to Indictment, Trial, Judgment and Punishment, according to Law.

SECTION 4. The Times, Places and Manner of holding Elections for Senators and Representatives, shall be prescribed in each State by the Legislature thereof; but the Congress may at any time by Law make or alter such Regulations, except as to the Places of chusing Senators.

The Congress shall assemble at least once in every Year, and such Meeting shall be on the first Monday in December, unless they shall by Law appoint a different Day.

SECTION 5. Each House shall be the Judge of the Elections, Returns and Qualifications of its own Members, and a Majority of each shall constitute a Quorum to do Business; but a smaller Number may adjourn from day to day, and may be authorized to compel the Attendance of absent Members, in such Manner, and under such Penalties as each House may provide.

Each House may determine the Rules of its Proceedings, punish its Members for disorderly Behaviour, and, with the Concurrence of two thirds, expel a Member.

Each House shall keep a Journal of its Proceedings, and from time to time publish the same, excepting such Parts as may in their Judgment require Secrecy; and the Yeas and Nays of the Members of either House on any question shall, at the Desire of one fifth of those Present, be entered on the Journal.

Neither House, during the Session of Congress, shall, without the Consent of the other, adjourn for more than three days, nor to any other Place than that in which the two Houses shall be sitting.

SECTION 6. The Senators and Representatives shall receive a Compensation for their Services, to be ascertained by Law, and paid out of the Treasury of the United States. They shall in all Cases, except Treason, Felony and Breach of the Peace, be privileged from Arrest during their Attendance at the Session of their respective Houses, and in going to and returning from the same; and for any Speech or Debate in either House, they shall not be questioned in any other Place.

No Senator or Representative shall, during the Time for which he was elected, be appointed to any civil Office under the Authority of the United States, which shall have been created, or the Emoluments whereof shall have been encreased during such time; and no Person holding any Office under the United States, shall be a Member of either House during his Continuance in Office.

SECTION 7. All Bills for raising Revenue shall originate in the House of Representatives; but the Senate may propose or concur with Amendments as on other Bills.

Every Bill which shall have passed the House of Representatives and the Senate, shall, before it become a Law, be presented to the President of the United States; If he approve he shall sign it, but if not he shall return it, with his Objections to that House in which it shall have originated, who shall enter the Objections at large on their Journal, and proceed to reconsider it. If after such Reconsideration two thirds of that House shall agree to pass the Bill, it shall be sent, together with the Objections, to the other House by which it shall likewise be reconsidered, and if approved by two thirds of that House, it shall become a Law. But in all such Cases the Votes of both Houses shall be determined by yeas and Nays, and the Names of the Persons voting for and against the Bill shall be entered on the Journal of each House respectively. If any Bill shall not be returned by the President within ten Days (Sundays excepted) after it shall have been presented to him, the Same shall be a Law, in like Manner as if he had signed it, unless the Congress by their Adjournment prevent its Return, in which Case it shall not be a Law.

Every Order, Resolution, or Vote to which the Concurrence of the Senate and House of Representatives may be necessary (except on a question of Adjournment) shall be presented to the President of the United States; and before the Same shall take Effect, shall be approved by him, or being disapproved by him, shall be repassed by two thirds of the Senate and House of Representatives, according to the Rules and Limitations prescribed in the Case of a Bill.

SECTION 8. The Congress shall have Power To lay and collect Taxes, Duties, Imposts and Excises, to pay the Debts and provide for the common Defence and general Welfare of the United States; but all Duties, Imposts and Excises shall be uniform throughout the United States;

To borrow Money on the credit of the United States;

To regulate Commerce with foreign Nations, and among the several States, and with the Indian Tribes;

To establish an uniform Rule of Naturalization, and uniform Laws on the subject of Bankruptcies throughout the United States;

To coin Money, regulate the Value thereof, and of foreign Coin, and fix the Standard of Weights and Measures;

To provide for the Punishment of counterfeiting the Securities and current Coin of the United States;

To establish Post Offices and post Roads;

To promote the Progress of Science and useful Arts, by securing for limited Times to Authors and Inventors the exclusive Right to their respective Writings and Discoveries;

To constitute Tribunals inferior to the supreme Court;

To define and punish Piracies and Felonies committed on the high Seas, and Offenses against the Law of Nations;

To declare War, grant Letters of Marque and Reprisal, and make Rules concerning Captures on Land and Water;

To raise and support Armies, but no Appropriation of Money to that Use shall be for a longer Term than two Years;

To provide and maintain a Navy;

To make Rules for the Government and Regulation of the land and naval Forces;

To provide for calling forth the Militia to execute the Laws of the Union, suppress Insurrections and repel Invasions;

To provide for organizing, arming, and disciplining, the Militia, and for governing such Part of them as may be employed in the Service of the United States, reserving to the States respectively, the Appointment of the Officers and the Authority of training the Militia according to the discipline prescribed by Congress;

To exercise exclusive Legislation in all Cases whatsoever, over such District (not exceeding ten Miles square) as may, by Cession of particular States, and the Acceptance of Congress, become the Seat of the Government of the United States, and to exercise like Authority over all Places purchased by the Consent of the Legislature of the State in which the Same shall be, for the Erection of Forts, Magazines, Arsenals, dock-Yards, and other needful Buildings;—And

To make all Laws which shall be necessary and proper for carrying into Execution the foregoing Powers, and all other Powers vested by this Constitution in the Government of the United States, or in any Department or Officer thereof.

SECTION 9. The Migration or Importation of such Persons as any of the States now existing shall think proper to admit, shall not be prohibited by the Congress prior to the Year one thousand eight hundred and eight, but a Tax or duty may be imposed on such Importation, not exceeding ten dollars for each Person.

The Privilege of the Writ of Habeas Corpus shall not be suspended, unless when in Cases of Rebellion or Invasion the public Safety may require it.

No Bill of Attainder or ex post facto Law shall be passed.

No Capitation, or other direct, Tax shall be laid, unless in Proportion to the Census or Enumeration herein before directed to be taken.

No Tax or Duty shall be laid on Articles exported from any State.

No Preference shall be given by any Regulation of Commerce or Revenue to the Ports of one State over those of another: nor shall Vessels bound to, or from, one State, be obliged to enter, clear or pay Duties in another.

No Money shall be drawn from the Treasury, but in Consequence of Appropriations made by Law; and a regular Statement and Account of the Receipts and Expenditures of all public Money shall be published from time to time.

No Title of Nobility shall be granted by the United States: And no Person holding any Office of Profit or Trust under them, shall, without the Consent of the Congress, accept of any present, Emolument, Office, or Title, of any kind whatever, from any King, Prince, or foreign State.

SECTION 10. No State shall enter into any Treaty, Alliance, or Confederation; grant Letters of Marque and Reprisal; coin Money; emit Bills of Credit; make any Thing but gold and silver Coin a Tender in Payment of Debts; pass any Bill of Attainder, ex post facto Law, or Law impairing the Obligation of Contracts, or grant any Title of Nobility.

No State shall, without the Consent of the Congress, lay any Imposts or Duties on Imports or Exports, except what may be absolutely necessary for executing its inspection Laws: and the net Produce of all Duties and Imposts, laid by any State on Imports or Exports, shall be for the Use of the Treasury of the United States; and all such Laws shall be subject to the Revision and Controul of the Congress.

No State shall, without the Consent of Congress, lay any Duty of Tonnage, keep Troops, or Ships of War in time of Peace, enter into any Agreement or Compact with another State, or with a foreign Power, or engage in War, unless actually invaded, or in such imminent Danger as will not admit of delay.

ARTICLE II

SECTION 1. The executive Power shall be vested in a President of the United States of America. He shall hold his Office during the Term of four Years, and, together with the Vice President, chosen for the same Term, be elected, as follows

Each State shall appoint, in such Manner as the Legislature thereof may direct, a Number of Electors, equal to the whole Number of Senators and Representatives to which the State may be entitled in the Congress: but no Senator or Representative, or Person holding an Office of Trust, or Profit under the United States, shall be appointed an Elector.

The Electors shall meet in their respective States, and vote by Ballot for two Persons, of whom one at least shall not be an Inhabitant of the same State with themselves. And they shall make a List of all the Persons voted for, and of the Number of Votes for each; which List they shall sign and certify, and transmit sealed to the Seat of the Government of the United States, directed to the President of the Senate. The President of the Senate shall, in the Presence of the Senate and House of Representatives, open all the Certificates and the Votes shall then be counted. The Person having the greatest Number of Votes shall be the President, if such Number be a Majority of the whole Number of Electors appointed; and if there be more than one who have such Majority, and have an equal Number of Votes, then the House of Representatives shall immediately chuse by Ballot one of them for President; and if no Person have a Majority, then from the five highest on the List the said House shall in like Manner chuse the President. But in chusing the President, the Votes shall be taken by States, the Representation from each State having one Vote; A quorum for this Purpose shall consist of a Member or Members from two thirds of the States, and a Majority of all the States shall be necessary to a Choice. In every Case, after the Choice of the President, the Person having the greatest Number of Votes of the Electors shall be the Vice President. But if there should remain two or more who have equal Votes, the Senate shall chuse from them by Ballot the Vice President.

The Congress may determine the Time of chusing the Electors, and the Day on which they shall give their Votes; which Day shall be the same throughout the United States.

No Person except a natural born Citizen, or a Citizen of the United States, at the time of the Adoption of this Constitution, shall be eligible to the Office of President; neither shall any Person be eligible to that Office who shall not have attained to the Age of thirty five Years, and been fourteen Years a Resident within the United States.

In Case of the Removal of the President from Office, or of his Death, Resignation, or Inability to discharge the Powers and Duties of the said Office, the Same shall devolve on the Vice President, and the Congress may by Law provide for the Case of Removal, Death, Resignation or Inability, both of the President and Vice President, declaring what Officer shall then act as President, and such Officer shall act accordingly, until the Disability be removed, or a President shall be elected.

The President shall, at stated Times, receive for his Services, a Compensation, which shall neither be encreased nor diminished during the Period for which he shall have been elected, and he shall not receive within that Period any other Emolument from the United States, or any of them.

Before he enter on the Execution of his Office, he shall take the following Oath or Affirmation:—"I do solemnly swear (or affirm) that I will faithfully execute the Office of President of the United States, and will to the best of my Ability, preserve, protect and defend the Constitution of the United States."

SECTION 2. The President shall be Commander in Chief of the Army and Navy of the United States, and of the Militia of the several States, when called into the actual Service of the United States; he may require the Opinion, in writing, of the principal Officer in each of the executive Departments, upon any Subject relating to the Duties of their respective Offices, and he shall have Power to grant Reprieves and Pardons for Offenses against the United States, except in Cases of Impeachment.

He shall have Power, by and with the Advice and Consent of the Senate, to make Treaties, provided two thirds of the Senators present concur; and he shall nominate and by and with the Advice and Consent of the Senate, shall appoint Ambassadors, other public Ministers and Consuls, Judges of the supreme Court, and all other Officers of the United States, whose Appointments are not herein otherwise provided for, and which shall be established by Law: but the Congress may by Law vest the Appointment of such inferior Officers, as they think proper, in the President alone, in the Courts of Law, or in the Heads of Departments.

The President shall have Power to fill up all Vacancies that may happen during the Recess of the Senate, by granting Commissions which shall expire at the End of their next Session.

SECTION 3. He shall from time to time give to the Congress Information of the State of the Union, and recommend to their Consideration such Measures as he shall judge necessary and expedient; he may, on extraordinary Occasions, convene both Houses, or either of them, and in Case of Disagreement between them, with Respect to the Time of Adjournment, he may adjourn them to such Time as he shall think proper; he shall receive Ambassadors and other public Ministers; he shall take Care that the Laws be faithfully executed, and shall Commission all the Officers of the United States.

SECTION 4. The President, Vice President and all civil Officers of the United States, shall be removed from Office on Impeachment for, and Conviction of, Treason, Bribery, or other high Crimes and Misdemeanors.

ARTICLE III

SECTION 1. The judicial Power of the United States, shall be vested in one supreme Court, and in such inferior Courts as the Congress may from time to time ordain and establish. The Judges, both of the supreme and inferior Courts, shall hold their offices during good Behaviour, and shall, at stated Times, receive for their Services, a Compensation, which shall not be diminished during their Continuance in Office.

SECTION 2. The judicial Power shall extend to all Cases, in Law and Equity, arising under this Constitution, the Laws of the United States, and Treaties made, or which shall be made, under their Authority: — to all Cases affecting Ambassadors, other public Ministers and Consuls; — to all Cases of admiralty and maritime Jurisdiction; — to Controversies to which the United States shall be a Party; — to Controversies between two or more States; — between a State and Citizens of another State; — between Citizens of different States; — between Citizens of the same State claiming Lands under Grants of different States, and between a State or the Citizens thereof, and foreign States, Citizens or Subjects.

In all Cases affecting Ambassadors, other public Ministers and Consuls, and those in which a State shall be Party, the supreme Court shall have original Jurisdiction. In all the other Cases before mentioned, the supreme Court shall have appellate Jurisdiction, both as to Law and Fact, with such Exceptions, and under such Regulations as the Congress shall make.

The Trial of all Crimes, except in Cases of Impeachment, shall be by Jury; and such Trial shall be held in the State where the said Crimes shall have been committed; but when not committed within any State, the Trial shall be at such Place or Places as the Congress may by Law have directed.

SECTION 3. Treason against the United States, shall consist only in levying War against them, or in adhering to their Enemies, giving them Aid and Comfort. No Person shall be convicted of Treason unless on the Testimony of two Witnesses to the same overt Act, or on Confession in open Court.

The Congress shall have Power to declare the Punishment of Treason, but no Attainder of Treason shall work Corruption of Blood, or Forfeiture except during the Life of the Person attainted.

ARTICLE IV

SECTION 1. Full Faith and Credit shall be given in each State to the public Acts, Records, and judicial Proceedings of every other State. And the Congress may by general Laws prescribe the Manner in which such Acts, Records and Proceedings shall be proved, and the Effect thereof.

SECTION 2. The Citizens of each State shall be entitled to all Privileges and Immunities of Citizens in the several States.

A Person charged in any State with Treason, Felony, or other Crime, who shall flee from Justice, and be found in another State, shall on Demand of the executive Authority of the State from which he fled, be delivered up, to be removed to the State having Jurisdiction of the Crime.

No Person held to Service or Labour in one State, under the Laws thereof, escaping into another, shall, in Consequence of any Law or Regulation therein, be discharged from such Service or Labour, but shall be delivered up on Claim of the Party to whom such Service or Labour may be due.

SECTION 3. New States may be admitted by the Congress into this Union; but no new State shall be formed or erected within the Jurisdiction of any other State; nor any State be formed by the Junction of two or more States, or Parts of States, without the Consent of the Legislatures of the States concerned as well as of the Congress.

The Congress shall have Power to dispose of and make all needful Rules and Regulations respecting the Territory or other Property belonging to the United States; and nothing in this Constitution shall be so construed as to Prejudice any Claims of the United States, or of any particular State.

SECTION 4. The United States shall guarantee to every State in this Union a Republican Form of Government, and shall protect each of them against Invasion; and on Application of the Legislature, or of the Executive (when the Legislature cannot be convened) against domestic Violence.

ARTICLE V

The Congress, whenever two thirds of both Houses shall deem it necessary, shall propose Amendments to this Constitution, or, on the Application of the Legislatures of two thirds of the several States, shall call a Convention for proposing Amendments, which, in either Case, shall be valid to all Intents and Purposes, as Part of this Constitution, when ratified by the Legislatures of three fourths of the several States, or by Conventions in three fourths thereof, as the one or the other Mode of Ratification may be proposed by the Congress; Provided that no Amendment which may be made prior to the Year One thousand eight hundred and eight shall in any Manner affect the first and fourth Clauses in the Ninth Section of the first Article; and that no State, without its Consent, shall be deprived of its equal Suffrage in the Senate.

ARTICLE VI

All Debts contracted and Engagements entered into, before the Adoption of this Constitution, shall be as valid against the United States under this Constitution, as under the Confederation.

This Constitution, and the Laws of the United States which shall be made in Pursuance thereof; and all Treaties made, or which shall be made, under the Authority of the United States, shall be the supreme Law of the Land; and the Judges in every State shall be bound thereby, any Thing in the Constitution or Laws of any State to the Contrary notwithstanding.

The Senators and Representatives before mentioned, and the Members of the several State Legislatures, and all executive and judicial Officers, both of the United States and of the several States, shall be bound by Oath or Affirmation, to support this Constitution; but no religious Test shall ever be required as a Qualification to any Office or public Trust under the United States.

ARTICLE VII

The Ratification of the Conventions of nine States, shall be sufficient for the Establishment of this Constitution between the States so ratifying the Same.

done in Convention by the Unanimous Consent of the States present the Seventeenth Day of September in the Year of our Lord one thousand seven hundred and Eighty seven and of the Independance of the United States of America the Twelfth In witness whereof We have hereunto subscribed our Names,

Go. WASHINGTON – *Presidt.*
and deputy from Virginia

In Convention Monday, September 17th 1787.
Present
The States of
New Hampshire, Massachusetts, Connecticut, Mr. Hamilton from New York, New Jersey, Pennsylvania, Delaware, Maryland, Virginia, North Carolina, South Carolina and Georgia.

Resolved,

That the preceding Constitution be laid before the United States in Congress assembled, and that it is the Opinion of this Convention, that it should afterwards be submitted to a Convention of Delegates, chosen in each State by the People thereof, under the Recommendation of its Legislature, for their Assent and Ratification; and that each Convention assenting to, and ratifying the Same, should give Notice thereof to the United States in Congress assembled. Resolved, That it is the Opinion of this Convention, that as soon as the Conventions of nine States shall have ratified this Constitution, the United States in Congress assembled should fix a Day on which Electors should be appointed by the States which shall have ratified the same, and a Day on which the Electors should assemble to vote for the President, and the Time and Place for commencing Proceedings under this Constitution. That after such Publication the Electors should be appointed, and the Senators and Representatives elected: That the Electors should meet on the Day fixed for the Election of the President, and should transmit their Votes certified, signed, sealed and directed, as the Constitution requires, to the Secretary of the United States in Congress assembled, that the Senators and Representatives should convene at the Time and Place assigned; that the Senators should appoint a President of the Senate, for the sole Purpose of receiving, opening and counting the Votes for President; and, that after he shall be chosen, the Congress, together with the President, should, without Delay, proceed to execute this Constitution.

By the Unanimous Order of the Convention

Go. WASHINGTON Presidt.

W. JACKSON Secretary.

Articles in Addition to, and Amendment of, the Constitution of the United States of America, Proposed by Congress, and Ratified by the Several States, Pursuant to the Fifth Article of the Original Constitution.

Amendment [I]

Congress shall make no law respecting an establishment of religion, or prohibiting the free exercise thereof; or abridging the freedom of speech, or of the press; or the right of the people peaceably to assemble, and to petition the Government for a redress of grievances.

Amendment [II]

A well regulated Militia, being necessary to the security of a free State, the right of the people to keep and bear Arms shall not be infringed.

Amendment [III]

No Soldier shall, in time of peace be quartered in any house, without the consent of the Owner, nor in time of war, but in a manner to be prescribed by law.

Amendment [IV]

The right of the people to be secure in their persons, houses, papers, and effects, against unreasonable searches and seizures, shall not be violated, and no Warrants shall issue, but upon probable cause, supported by Oath or affirmation, and particularly describing the place to be searched, and the persons or things to be seized.

Amendment [V]

No person shall be held to answer for a capital, or otherwise infamous crime, unless on a presentment or indictment of a Grand Jury, except in cases arising in the land or naval forces, or in the Militia, when in actual service in time of War or public danger; nor shall any person be subject for the same offence to be twice put in jeopardy of life or limb; nor shall be compelled in any criminal case to be a witness against himself, nor be deprived of life, liberty, or property, without due process of law; nor shall private property be taken for public use, without just compensation.

Amendment [VI]

In all criminal prosecutions, the accused shall enjoy the right to a speedy and public trial, by an impartial jury of the State and district wherein the crime shall have been committed, which district shall have been previously ascertained by law, and to be informed of the nature and cause of the accusation; to be confronted with the witnesses against him; to have compulsory process for obtaining witnesses in his favor, and to have the Assistance of Counsel for his defence.

Amendment [VII]

In Suits at common law, where the value in controversy shall exceed twenty dollars, the right of trial by jury shall be preserved, and no fact tried by a jury, shall be otherwise re-examined in any Court of the United States, than according to the rules of the common law.

Amendment [VIII]

Excessive bail shall not be required, nor excessive fines imposed, nor cruel and unusual punishments inflicted.

Amendment [IX]

The enumeration in the Constitution, of certain rights, shall not be construed to deny or disparage others retained by the people.

Amendment [X]

The powers not delegated to the United States by the Constitution, nor prohibited by it to the States, are reserved to the States respectively, or to the people.

Amendment [XI]

The Judicial power of the United States shall not be construed to extend to any suit in law or equity, commenced or prosecuted against one of the United States by Citizens of another State, or by Citizens or Subjects of any Foreign State.

Amendment [XII]

The Electors shall meet in their respective states, and vote by ballot for President and Vice-President, one of whom, at least, shall not be an inhabitant of the same state with themselves; they shall name in their ballots the person voted for as President, and in distinct ballots the person voted for as Vice-President, and they shall make distinct lists of all persons voted for as President, and of all persons voted for as Vice-President, and of the number of votes for each, which lists they shall sign and certify, and transmit sealed to the seat of the government of the United States, directed to the President of the Senate; — The President of the Senate shall, in the presence of the Senate and House of Representatives, open all the certificates and the votes shall then be counted; — The person having the greatest number of votes for President, shall be the President, if such number be a majority of the whole number of Electors appointed; and if no person have such majority, then from the persons having the highest numbers not exceeding three on the list of those voted for as President, the House of Representatives shall choose immediately, by ballot, the President. But in choosing the President, the votes shall be taken by States, the representation from each State having one vote; a quorum for this purpose shall consist of a member or members from two-thirds of the States, and a majority of all the States shall be necessary to a choice. And if the House of Representatives shall not choose a President whenever the right of choice shall devolve upon them, before the fourth day of March next following, then the Vice-President shall act as President, as in the case of the death or other constitutional disability of the President. — The person having the greatest number of votes as Vice-President, shall be the Vice-President, if such number be a majority of the whole number of Electors appointed, and if no person have a majority, then from the two highest numbers on the list, the Senate shall choose the Vice-President; a quorum for the purpose shall consist of two-thirds of the whole number of Senators, and a majority of the whole number shall be necessary to a choice.

But no person constitutionally ineligible to the office of President shall be eligible to that of Vice-President of the United States.

Amendment [XIII]

Section 1. Neither slavery nor involuntary servitude, except as a punishment for crime whereof the party shall have been duly convicted, shall exist within the United States, or any place subject to their jurisdiction.

Section 2. Congress shall have power to enforce this article by appropriate legislation.

Amendment [XIV]

Section 1. All persons born or naturalized in the United States, and subject to the jurisdiction thereof, are citizens of the United States and of the State wherein they reside. No State shall make or enforce any law which shall abridge the privileges or immunities of citizens of the United States; nor shall any State deprive any person of life, liberty, or property, without due process of law; nor deny to any person within its jurisdiction the equal protection of the laws.

Section 2. Representatives shall be apportioned among the several States according to their respective numbers, counting the whole number of persons in each State, excluding Indians not taxed. But when the right to vote at any election for the choice of electors for President and Vice President of the United States, Representatives in Congress, the Executive and Judicial officers of a State, or the members of the Legislature thereof, is denied to any of the male inhabitants of such State, being twenty-one years of age, and citizens of the United States, or in any way abridged, except for participation in rebellion, or other crime, the basis of representation therein shall be reduced in the proportion which the number of such male citizens shall bear to the whole number of male citizens twenty-one years of age in such State.

Section 3. No person shall be a Senator or Representative in Congress, or elector of President and Vice President, or hold any office, civil or military, under the United States, or under any State, who, having previously taken an oath, as a member of Congress, or as an officer of the United States, or as a member of any State legislature, or as an executive or judicial officer of any State, to support the Constitution of the United States, shall have engaged in insurrection or rebellion against the same, or given aid or comfort to the enemies thereof. But Congress may by a vote of two-thirds of each House, remove such disability.

Section 4. The validity of the public debt of the United States, authorized by law, including debts incurred for payment of pensions and bounties for services in suppressing insurrection or rebellion, shall not be questioned. But neither the United States, nor any State shall assume or pay any debt or obligation incurred in aid of insurrection or rebellion against the United States, or any claim for the loss or emancipation of any slave; but all such debts, obligations and claims shall be held illegal and void.

Section 5. The Congress shall have power to enforce, by appropriate legislation, the provisions of this article.

Amendment [XV]

Section 1. The right of citizens of the United States to vote shall not be denied or abridged by the United States or by any State on account of race, color, or previous condition of servitude.

Section 2. The Congress shall have power to enforce this article by appropriate legislation.

Amendment [XVI]

The Congress shall have power to lay and collect taxes on incomes, from whatever source derived, without apportionment among the several States, and without regard to any census or enumeration.

Amendment [XVII]

The Senate of the United States shall be composed of two Senators from each State, elected by the people thereof, for six years; and each Senator shall have one vote. The electors in each State shall have the qualifications requisite for electors of the most numerous branch of the State legislatures.

When vacancies happen in the representation of any State in the Senate, the executive authority of such State shall issue writs of election to fill such vacancies: *provided,* That the legislature of any State may empower the executive thereof to make temporary appointments until the people fill the vacancies by election as the legislature may direct.

This amendment shall not be so construed as to affect the election or term of any Senator chosen before it becomes valid as part of the Constitution.

Amendment [XVIII]

Section 1. After one year from the ratification of this article the manufacture, sale, or transportation of intoxicating liquors within, the importation thereof into, or the exportation thereof from the United States and all territory subject to the jurisdiction thereof for beverage purposes is hereby prohibited.

Section 2. The Congress and the several States shall have concurrent power to enforce this article by appropriate legislation.

Section 3. This article shall be inoperative unless it shall have been ratified as an amendment to the Constitution by the legislatures of the several States, as provided in the Constitution, within seven years from the date of the submission hereof to the States by the Congress.

Amendment [XIX]

The right of citizens of the United States to vote shall not be denied or abridged by the United States or by any State on account of sex.

Congress shall have power to enforce this article by appropriate legislation.

Amendment [XX]

Section 1. The terms of the President and Vice President shall end at noon on the 20th day of January, and the terms of Senators and Representatives at noon on the 3d day of January, of the years in which such terms would have ended if this article had not been ratified; and the terms of their successors shall then begin.

Section 2. The Congress shall assemble at least once in every year, and such meeting shall begin at noon on the 3d day of January, unless they shall by law appoint a different day.

Section 3. If, at the time fixed for the beginning of the term of the President, the President elect shall have died, the Vice President elect shall become President. If a President shall not have been chosen before the time fixed for the beginning of his term, or if the President elect shall have failed to qualify, then the Vice President elect shall act as President until a President shall have qualified; and the Congress may by law provide for the case wherein neither a President elect nor a Vice President elect shall have qualified, declaring who shall then act as President, or the manner in which one who is to act shall be selected, and such person shall act accordingly until a President or Vice President shall have qualified.

Section 4. The Congress may by law provide for the case of the death of any of the persons from whom the House of Representatives may choose a President whenever the right of choice shall have devolved upon them, and for the case of the death of any of the persons from whom the Senate may choose a Vice President whenever the right of choice shall have devolved upon them.

Section 5. Sections 1 and 2 shall take effect on the 15th day of October following the ratification of this article.

Section 6. This article shall be inoperative unless it shall have been ratified as an amendment to the Constitution by the legislatures of three-fourths of the several States within seven years from the date of its submission.

Amendment [XXI]

Section 1. The eighteenth article of amendment to the Constitution of the United States is hereby repealed.

Section 2. The transportation or importation into any State, Territory, or possession of the United States for delivery or use therein of intoxicating liquors, in violation of the laws thereof, is hereby prohibited.

Section 3. This article shall be inoperative unless it shall have been ratified as an amendment to the Constitution by conventions in the several States, as provided in the Constitution, within seven years from the date of the submission hereof to the States by the Congress.

Amendment [XXII]

Section 1. No person shall be elected to the office of the President more than twice, and no person who has held the office of President, or acted as President, for more than two years of a term to which some other person was elected President shall be elected to the office of the President more than once. But this Article shall not apply to any person holding the office of President when this Article was proposed by the Congress, and shall not prevent any person who may be holding the office of President, or acting as President, during the term within which this Article becomes operative from holding the office of President or acting as President during the remainder of such term.

Section 2. This article shall be inoperative unless it shall have been ratified as an amendment to the Constitution by the legislatures of three-fourths of the several States within seven years from the date of its submission to the States by the Congress.

Amendment [XXIII]

Section 1. The District constituting the seat of Government of the United States shall appoint in such manner as the Congress may direct:

A number of electors of President and Vice President equal to the whole number of Senators and Representatives in Congress to which the District would be entitled if it were a State, but in no event more than the least populous State; they shall be in addition to those appointed by the States, but they shall be considered, for the purposes of the election of President and Vice President, to be electors appointed by a State; and they shall meet in the District and perform such duties as provided by the twelfth article of amendment.

Section 2. The Congress shall have power to enforce this article by appropriate legislation.

Amendment [XXIV]

Section 1. The right of citizens of the United States to vote in any primary or other election for President or Vice President, for electors for President or Vice President, or for Senator or Representative in Congress, shall not be denied or abridged by the United States or any State by reason of failure to pay any poll tax or other tax.

Section 2. The Congress shall have power to enforce this article by appropriate legislation.

Amendment [XXV]

Section 1. In case of the removal of the President from office or of his death or resignation, the Vice President shall become President.

Section 2. Whenever there is a vacancy in the office of the Vice President, the President shall nominate a Vice President who shall take office upon confirmation by a majority vote of both Houses of Congress.

Section 3. Whenever the President transmits to the President pro tempore of the Senate and the Speaker of the House of Representatives his written declaration that he is unable to discharge the powers and duties of his office, and until he transmits to them a written declaration to the contrary, such powers and duties shall be discharged by the Vice President as Acting President.

Section 4. Whenever the Vice President and a majority of either the principal officers of the executive departments or of such other body as Congress may by law provide, transmit to the President pro tempore of the Senate and the Speaker of the House of Representatives their written declaration that the President is unable to discharge the powers and duties of his office, the Vice President shall immediately assume the powers and duties of the office as Acting President.

Thereafter, when the President transmits to the President pro tempore of the Senate and the Speaker of the House of Representatives his written declaration that no inability exists, he shall resume the powers and duties of his office unless the Vice President and a majority of either the principal officers of the executive department or of such other body as Congress may by law provide, transmit within four days to the President pro tempore of the Senate and the Speaker of the House of Representatives their written declaration that the President is unable to discharge the powers and duties of his office. Thereupon Congress shall decide the issue, assembling within forty-eight hours for that purpose if not in session. If the Congress, within twenty-one days after receipt of the latter written declaration, or, if Congress is not in session, within twenty-one days after Congress is required to assemble, determines by two-thirds vote of both Houses that the President is unable to discharge the powers and duties of his office, the Vice President shall continue to discharge the same as Acting President; otherwise, the President shall resume the powers and duties of his office.

POPULATION OF PLACES IN THE UNITED STATES

HAVING 12,000 OR MORE INHABITANTS IN 1970

A

Place	Population
Aberdeen, Md.	12,375
Aberdeen, S. Dak.	26,476
Aberdeen, Wash.	18,489
Abilene, Tex.	89,653
Abington, Mass.	12,334
Acton, Mass.	14,770
Ada, Okla.	14,859
Addison, Ill.	24,482
Adrian, Mich.	20,382
Agawam, Mass.	21,717
Aiea, Hawaii	12,560
Aiken, S.C.	13,436
Akron, Ohio	275,425
Alameda, Calif.	70,968
Alamogordo, N. Mex.	23,035
Albany, Calif.	14,674
Albany, Ga.	72,623
Albany, N.Y.	114,873
Albany, Oreg.	18,181
Albert Lea, Minn.	19,418
Albion, Mich.	12,112
Albuquerque, N. Mex.	243,751
Alexander City, Ala.	12,358
Alexandria, La.	41,557
Alexandria, Va.	110,938
Alhambra, Calif.	62,125
Alice, Tex.	20,121
Aliquippa, Pa.	22,277
Allen Park, Mich.	40,747
Allentown, Pa.	109,527
Alliance, Ohio	26,547
Alpena, Mich.	13,805
Alton, Ill.	39,700
Altoona, Pa.	62,900
Altus, Okla.	23,302
Amarillo, Tex.	127,010
Americus, Ga.	16,091
Ames, Iowa	39,505
Amherst, Mass.	26,331
Amsterdam, N.Y.	25,524
Anaheim, Calif.	166,701
Anchorage, Alaska	48,029
Anderson, Ind.	70,787
Anderson, S.C.	27,556
Andover, Mass.	23,695
Annapolis, Md.	29,592
Ann Arbor, Mich.	99,797
Anniston, Ala.	31,533
Anoka, Minn.	13,489
Ansonia, Conn.	21,160
Antioch, Calif.	28,060
Appleton, Wis.	57,143
Arcadia, Calif.	42,868
Ardmore, Okla.	20,881
Arkansas City, Kans.	13,216
Arlington, Mass.	53,524
Arlington, Tex.	90,643
Arlington Heights, Ill.	64,884
Artesia, Calif.	14,757
Arvada, Colo.	46,814
Asbury Park, N.J.	16,533
Asheville, N.C.	57,681
Ashland, Ky.	29,245
Ashland, Ohio	19,872
Ashland, Oreg.	12,342
Ashtabula, Ohio	24,313
Atchison, Kans.	12,565
Athens, Ala.	14,360
Athens, Ga.	44,342
Athens, Ohio	23,310
Atlanta, Ga.	496,973
Atlantic City, N.J.	47,859
Attleboro, Mass.	32,907
Auburn, Ala.	22,767
Auburn, Mass.	15,347
Auburn, Me.	24,151
Auburn, N.Y.	34,599
Auburn, Wash.	21,817
Augusta, Ga.	59,864
Augusta, Me.	21,945
Aurora, Colo.	74,974
Aurora, Ill.	74,182
Austin, Minn.	25,074
Austin, Tex.	251,808
Avon Lake, Ohio	12,261
Azusa, Calif.	25,217

B

Place	Population
Babylon, N.Y.	12,588
Bakersfield, Calif.	69,515
Baldwin, Pa.	26,729
Baldwin Park, Calif.	47,285
Baltimore, Md.	905,759
Bangor, Me.	33,168
Banning, Calif.	12,034
Barberton, Ohio	33,052
Barnstable, Mass.	19,842
Barrington, R.I.	17,554
Barstow, Calif.	17,442
Bartlesville, Okla.	29,683
Bartow, Fla.	12,891
Bastrop, La.	14,713
Batavia, N.Y.	17,338
Baton Rouge, La.	165,963
Battle Creek, Mich.	38,931
Bay City, Mich.	49,449
Bayonne, N.J.	72,743
Baytown, Tex.	43,980
Bay Village, Ohio	18,163
Beacon, N.Y.	13,255
Beatrice, Nebr.	12,389
Beaumont, Tex.	115,919
Beaver Dam, Wis.	14,265
Beaver Falls, Pa.	14,375
Beaverton, Oreg.	18,577
Beckley, W. Va.	19,884
Bedford, Ind.	13,087
Bedford, Mass.	13,513
Bedford, Ohio	17,552
Bedford Heights, Ohio	13,063
Beech Grove, Ind.	13,468
Beeville, Tex.	13,506
Bell, Calif.	21,836
Bellaire, Tex.	19,009
Bellefontaine Neighbors, Mo.	13,987
Belle Glade, Fla.	15,949
Belleville, Ill.	41,699
Belleville, N.J.	34,643
Bellevue, Nebr.	19,449
Bellevue, Wash.	61,102
Bellflower, Calif.	51,454
Bell Gardens, Calif.	29,308
Bellingham, Mass.	13,967
Bellingham, Wash.	39,375
Bellmawr, N.J.	15,618
Bellwood, Ill.	22,096
Belmont, Calif.	23,667
Belmont, Mass.	28,285
Beloit, Wis.	35,729
Belvidere, Ill.	14,061
Bend, Oreg.	13,710
Bennington, Vt.	14,586
Bensenville, Ill.	12,833
Benton, Ark.	16,499
Benton Harbor, Mich.	16,481
Berea, Ohio	22,396
Bergenfield, N.J.	33,131
Berkeley, Calif.	116,716
Berkeley, Mo.	19,743
Berkley, Mich.	22,618
Berlin, Conn.	14,149
Berlin, N.H.	15,256
Berwick, Pa.	12,274
Berwyn, Ill.	52,502
Bessemer, Ill.	33,428
Bethany, Okla.	21,785
Bethel Park, Pa.	34,791
Bethlehem, Pa.	72,686
Bettendorf, Iowa	22,126
Beverly, Mass.	38,348
Beverly Hills, Calif.	33,416
Beverly Hills, Mich.	13,598
Bexley, Ohio	14,888
Biddeford, Me.	19,983
Big Spring, Tex.	28,735
Billerica, Mass.	31,648
Billings, Mont.	61,581
Biloxi, Miss.	48,486
Binghamton, N.Y.	64,123
Birmingham, Ala.	300,910
Birmingham, Mich.	26,170
Bismarck, N. Dak.	34,703
Blaine, Minn.	20,640
Bloomfield, Conn.	18,301
Bloomfield, N.J.	52,029
Bloomington, Ill.	39,992
Bloomington, Ind.	42,890
Bloomington, Minn.	81,970

Bluefield, W. Va.	15,921
Blue Island, Ill	22,958
Blytheville, Ark.	24,752
Boca Raton, Fla.	28,506
Bogalusa, La.	18,412
Boise, Idaho	74,990
Boone, Iowa	12,468
Borger, Tex.	14,195
Bossier City, La.	41,595
Boston, Mass.	641,071
Boulder, Colo.	66,870
Bountiful, Utah	27,853
Bourne, Mass.	12,636
Bowie, Md.	35,028
Bowling Green, Ky.	36,253
Bowling Green, Ohio	21,760
Boynton Beach, Fla.	18,115
Bozeman, Mont.	18,670
Bradenton, Fla.	21,040
Bradford, Pa.	12,672
Braintree, Mass.	35,050
Branford, Conn.	20,444
Brattleboro, Vt.	12,239
Brawley, Calif.	13,746
Brea, Calif.	18,447
Bremerton, Wash.	35,307
Brentwood, Pa.	13,732
Bridgeport, Conn.	156,542
Bridgeton, Mo.	19,992
Bridgeton, N.J.	20,435
Bridge View, Ill.	12,522
Brigham City, Utah	14,007
Bristol, Conn.	55,487
Bristol, Pa.	12,085
Bristol, R.I.	17,860
Bristol, Tenn.	20,064
Bristol, Va.	14,857
Brockton, Mass.	89,040
Brookfield, Ill.	20,284
Brookfield, Wis.	32,140
Brookings, S. Dak.	13,717
Brookline, Mass.	58,886
Brooklyn, Ohio	13,142
Brooklyn Center, Minn.	35,173
Brooklyn Park, Minn.	26,230
Brook Park, Ohio	30,774
Brown Deer, Wis.	12,622
Brownsville, Tex.	52,522
Brownwood, Tex.	17,368
Brunswick, Ga.	19,585
Brunswick, Me.	16,195
Brunswick, Ohio	15,852
Bryan, Tex.	33,719
Bucyrus, Ohio	13,111
Buena Park, Calif.	63,646
Buffalo, N.Y.	462,768
Burbank, Calif.	88,871
Burlingame, Calif.	27,320
Burlington, Iowa	32,366
Burlington, Mass.	21,980
Burlington, N.C.	35,930
Burlington, Vt.	38,633
Burnsville, Minn.	19,940
Butler, Pa.	18,691
Butte, Mont.	23,368

C

Cahokia, Ill.	20,649
Caldwell, Idaho	14,219
Calumet City, Ill.	32,956
Camarillo, Calif.	19,219
Cambridge, Mass.	100,361
Cambridge, Ohio	13,656
Camden, Ark.	15,147
Camden, N.J.	102,551
Campbell, Calif.	24,770
Campbell, Ohio	12,577
Canton, Ill.	14,217
Canton, Mass.	17,100
Canton, Ohio	110,053
Cape Girardeau, Mo.	31,282
Carbondale, Ill.	22,816
Carbondale, Pa.	12,808
Carlisle, Pa.	18,079
Carlsbad, Calif.	14,944
Carlsbad, N. Mex.	21,297
Carpentersville, Ill.	24,059
Carrollton, Ga.	13,520
Carrollton, Tex.	13,855
Carson, Calif.	71,150
Carson City, Nev.	15,468
Carteret, N.J.	23,137
Casper, Wyo.	39,361
Cedar Falls, Iowa	29,597
Cedar Rapids, Iowa	110,642
Central Falls, R.I.	18,716
Centralia, Ill.	15,217
Cerritos, Calif.	15,856
Chambersburg, Pa.	17,315
Champaign, Ill.	56,532
Chandler, Ariz.	13,763
Chapel Hill, N.C.	25,537
Charleston, Ill.	16,421
Charleston, S.C.	66,945
Charleston, W. Va.	71,505
Charlotte, N.C.	241,178
Charlottesville, Va.	38,880
Chattanooga, Tenn.	119,082
Chelmsford, Mass.	31,432
Chelsea, Mass.	30,625
Chesapeake, Va.	89,580
Cheshire, Conn.	19,051
Chester, Pa.	56,331
Cheyenne, Wyo.	40,914
Chicago, Ill.	3,366,957
Chicago Heights, Ill.	40,900
Chickasha, Okla.	14,194
Chico, Calif.	19,580
Chicopee, Mass.	66,676
Chillicothe, Ohio	24,842
Chino, Calif.	20,411
Chippewa Falls, Wis.	12,351
Chula Vista, Calif.	67,901
Cicero, Ill.	67,058
Cincinnati, Ohio	452,524
Clairton, Pa.	15,051
Claremont, Calif.	23,464
Claremont, N.H.	14,221
Clarksburg, W. Va.	24,864
Clarksdale, Miss.	21,673
Clarksville, Ind.	13,806
Clarksville, Tenn.	31,719
Clawson, Mich.	17,617
Clayton, Mo.	16,222
Clearfield, Utah	13,316
Clearwater, Fla.	52,074
Cleburne, Tex.	16,015
Cleveland, Miss.	13,327
Cleveland, Ohio	750,903
Cleveland, Tenn.	20,651
Cleveland Heights, Ohio	60,767
Cliffside Park, N.J.	14,387
Clifton, N.J.	82,437
Clinton, Iowa	34,719
Clinton, Mass.	13,383
Clovis, Calif.	13,856
Clovis, N. Mex.	28,495
Coatesville, Pa.	12,331
Cocoa, Fla.	16,110
Coeur d'Alene, Idaho	16,228
Coffeyville, Kans.	15,116
Cohoes, N.Y.	18,613
College Park, Ga.	18,203
College Park, Md.	26,156
College Station, Tex.	17,676
Collingswood, N.J.	17,422
Collinsville, Ill.	17,773
Colonial Heights, Va.	15,097
Colorado Springs, Colo.	135,060
Colton, Calif.	19,974
Columbia, Mo.	58,804
Columbia, S.C.	113,542
Columbia, Tenn.	21,471
Columbia Heights, Minn.	23,997
Columbus, Ga.	154,168
Columbus, Ind.	27,141
Columbus, Miss.	25,795
Columbus, Nebr.	15,471
Columbus, Ohio	539,677
Commerce City, Colo.	17,407
Compton, Calif.	78,611
Concord, Calif.	85,164
Concord, Mass.	16,148
Concord, N.H.	30,022
Concord, N.C.	18,464
Conneaut, Ohio	14,522
Connersville, Ind.	17,604
Conway, Ark.	15,510
Cookeville, Tenn.	14,270
Coon Rapids, Minn.	30,505
Coos Bay, Oreg.	13,466
Coral Gables, Fla.	42,494
Corning, N.Y.	15,792
Corona, Calif.	27,519
Coronado, Calif.	20,910
Corpus Christi, Tex.	204,525
Corsicana, Tex.	19,972
Cortland, N.Y.	19,621
Corvallis, Oreg.	35,153
Coshocton, Ohio	13,747
Costa Mesa, Calif.	72,660
Cottage Grove, Minn.	13,419
Council Bluffs, Iowa	60,348
Coventry, R.I.	22,947
Covina, Calif.	30,380
Covington, Ky.	52,535
Cranston, R.I.	73,037
Crawfordsville, Ind.	13,841
Crestwood, Mo.	15,398
Crowley, La.	16,104
Crystal, Minn.	30,925
Crystal Lake, Ill.	14,541
Cudahy, Calif.	16,998
Cudahy, Wis.	22,078
Cullman, Ala.	12,601
Culver City, Calif.	31,035
Cumberland, Md.	29,724
Cumberland, R.I.	26,605
Cupertino, Calif.	18,216
Cuyahoga Falls, Ohio	49,678
Cypress, Calif.	31,026

D

Dallas, Tex.	844,401
Dalton, Ga.	18,872
Daly City, Calif.	66,922
Danbury, Conn.	50,781
Danvers, Mass.	26,151
Danville, Ill.	42,570
Danville, Va.	46,391
Darby, Pa.	13,729
Darien, Conn.	20,411
Dartmouth, Mass.	18,800
Davenport, Iowa	98,469
Davis, Calif.	23,488
Dayton, Ohio	243,601
Daytona Beach, Fla.	45,327
Dearborn, Mich.	104,199
Dearborn Heights, Mich.	80,069
Decatur, Ala.	38,044
Decatur, Ga.	21,943
Decatur, Ill.	90,397
Dedham, Mass.	26,938
Deerfield, Ill.	18,949
Deerfield Beach, Fla.	17,130
Deer Park, Tex.	12,773
Defiance, Ohio	16,281

City	Population
De Kalb, Ill.	32,949
Delano, Calif.	14,559
Delaware, Ohio	15,008
Del City, Okla.	27,133
Delray Beach, Fla.	19,366
Del Rio, Tex.	21,330
Denison, Tex.	24,923
Denton, Tex.	39,874
Denver, Colo.	514,678
De Pere, Wis.	13,309
Depew, N.Y.	22,158
Derby, Conn.	12,599
Des Moines, Iowa	200,587
Des Plaines, Ill.	57,239
Detroit, Mich.	1,511,482
Dickinson, N. Dak.	12,405
Dixon, Ill.	18,147
Dodge City, Kans.	14,127
Dolton, Ill.	25,937
Dormont, Pa.	12,856
Dothan, Ala.	36,733
Douglas, Ariz.	12,462
Dover, Del.	17,488
Dover, N.Y.	20,850
Dover, N.J.	15,039
Downers Grove, Ill.	32,751
Downey, Calif.	88,445
Dracut, Mass.	18,214
Duarte, Calif.	14,981
Dublin, Ga.	15,143
Dubuque, Iowa	62,309
Duluth, Minn.	100,578
Dumont, N.J.	17,534
Duncan, Okla.	19,718
Duncanville, Tex.	14,105
Dunedin, Fla.	17,639
Dunkirk, N.Y.	16,855
Dunmore, Pa.	17,300
Durham, N.C.	95,438
Dyersburg, Tenn.	14,523
E	
Eagle Pass, Tex.	15,364
East Chicago, Ind.	46,982
East Cleveland, Ohio	39,600
East Detroit, Mich.	45,920
East Grand Rapids, Mich.	12,565
Easthampton, Mass.	13,012
East Hartford, Conn.	57,583
East Haven, Conn.	25,120
Eastlake, Ohio	19,690
East Lansing, Mich.	47,540
East Liverpool, Ohio	20,020
East Longmeadow, Mass.	13,029
East Moline, Ill.	20,832
Easton, Mass.	12,157
Easton, Pa.	30,256
East Orange, N.J.	75,471
East Paterson, N.J.	22,749
East Peoria, Ill.	18,455
East Point, Ga.	39,315
East Providence, R.I.	48,151
East Ridge, Tenn.	21,799
East St. Louis, Ill.	69,996
Eatontown, N.J.	14,619
Eau Claire, Wis.	44,619
Ecorse, Mich.	17,515
Eden, N.C.	15,871
Edina, Minn.	44,046
Edinburg, Tex.	17,163
Edmond, Okla.	16,633
Edmonds, Wash.	23,998
El Cajon, Calif.	52,273
El Centro, Calif.	19,272
El Cerrito, Calif.	25,190
El Dorado, Ark.	25,283
El Dorado, Kans.	12,308
Elgin, Ill.	55,691
Elizabeth, N.J.	112,654
Elizabeth City, N.C.	14,069
Elizabethton, Tenn.	12,269
Elk Grove Village, Ill.	24,516
Elkhart, Ind.	43,152
Ellensburg, Wash.	13,568
Elmhurst, Ill.	50,547
Elmira, N.Y.	39,945
El Monte, Calif.	69,837
Elmwood Park, Ill.	26,160
El Paso, Tex.	322,261
El Reno, Okla.	14,510
El Segundo, Calif.	15,620
Elyria, Ohio	53,427
Emporia, Kans.	23,327
Endicott, N.Y.	16,556
Enfield, Conn.	46,189
Englewood, Colo.	33,695
Englewood, N.J.	24,985
Enid, Okla.	44,008
Enterprise, Ala.	15,591
Erie, Pa.	129,231
Erlanger, Ky.	12,676
Escanaba, Mich.	15,368
Escondido, Calif.	36,792
Euclid, Ohio	71,552
Eugene, Oreg.	76,346
Euless, Tex.	19,316
Eureka, Calif.	24,337
Evanston, Ill.	79,808
Evansville, Ind.	138,764
Everett, Mass.	42,485
Everett, Wash.	53,622
Evergreen Park, Ill.	25,487
F	
Fairbanks, Alaska	14,771
Fairborn, Ohio	32,267
Fairfax, Va.	21,970
Fairfield, Ala.	14,369
Fairfield, Calif.	44,146
Fairfield, Conn.	56,487
Fairfield, Ohio	14,680
Fairhaven, Mass.	16,332
Fair Lawn, N.J.	37,975
Fairmont, W. Va.	26,093
Fairview Park, Ohio	21,681
Fall River, Mass.	96,898
Falmouth, Mass.	15,942
Fargo, N. Dak.	53,365
Faribault, Minn.	16,595
Farmers Branch, Tex.	27,492
Farmington, Conn.	14,390
Farmington, Mich.	13,337
Farmington, N. Mex.	21,979
Fayetteville, Ark.	30,729
Fayetteville, N.C.	53,510
Fergus Falls, Minn.	12,443
Ferguson, Mo.	28,915
Ferndale, Mich.	30,850
Findlay, Ohio	35,800
Fitchburg, Mass.	43,343
Flagstaff, Ariz.	26,117
Flint, Mich.	193,317
Floral Park, N.Y.	18,422
Florence, Ala.	34,031
Florence, S.C.	25,997
Florissant, Mo.	65,908
Fond du Lac, Wis.	35,515
Fontana, Calif.	20,673
Forest Park, Ga.	19,994
Forest Park, Ill.	15,472
Forest Park, Ohio	15,139
Forrest City, Ark.	12,521
Fort Collins, Colo.	43,337
Fort Dodge, Iowa	31,263
Fort Lauderdale, Fla.	139,590
Fort Lee, N.J.	30,631
Fort Madison, Iowa	13,996
Fort Myers, Fla.	27,351
Fort Pierce, Fla.	29,721
Fort Smith, Ark.	62,802
Fort Thomas, Ky.	16,338
Fort Walton Beach, Fla.	19,994
Fort Wayne, Ind.	177,671
Fort Worth, Tex.	393,476
Fostoria, Ohio	16,037
Fountain Valley, Calif.	31,826
Foxboro, Mass.	14,218
Framingham, Mass.	64,048
Frankfort, Ind.	14,956
Frankfort, Ky.	21,356
Franklin, Mass.	17,830
Franklin, Wis.	12,247
Franklin Park, Ill.	20,497
Frederick, Md.	23,641
Fredericksburg, Va.	14,450
Freeport, Ill.	27,736
Freeport, N.Y.	40,374
Fremont, Calif.	100,869
Fremont, Nebr.	22,962
Fremont, Ohio	18,490
Fresno, Calif.	165,972
Fridley, Minn.	29,233
Fullerton, Calif.	85,826
Fulton, Mo.	12,148
Fulton, N.Y.	14,003
G	
Gadsden, Ala.	53,928
Gaffney, S.C.	13,253
Gahanna, Ohio	12,400
Gainesville, Fla.	64,510
Gainesville, Ga.	15,459
Gainesville, Tex.	13,830
Galesburg, Ill.	36,290
Galion, Ohio	13,123
Gallatin, Tenn.	13,093
Gallup, N. Mex.	14,596
Galveston, Tex.	61,809
Gardena, Calif.	41,021
Garden City, Kans.	14,708
Garden City, Mich.	41,864
Garden City, N.Y.	25,373
Garden Grove, Calif.	122,524
Gardner, Mass.	19,748
Garfield, N.J.	30,722
Garfield Heights, Ohio	41,417
Garland, Tex.	81,437
Gary, Ind.	175,415
Gastonia, N.C.	47,142
Geneva, N.Y.	16,793
Gilroy, Calif.	12,665
Girard, Ohio	14,119
Gladstone, Mo.	23,128
Glassboro, N.J.	12,938
Glastonbury, Conn.	20,651
Glen Cove, N.Y.	25,770
Glendale, Ariz.	36,228
Glendale, Calif.	132,752
Glendale, Wis.	13,436
Glendora, Calif.	31,349
Glen Ellyn, Ill.	21,909
Glen Rock, N.J.	13,011
Glens Falls, N.Y.	17,222
Glenview, Ill.	24,880
Gloucester, Mass.	27,941
Gloucester City, N.J.	14,707
Gloversville, N.Y.	19,677
Golden Valley, Minn.	24,246
Goldsboro, N.C.	26,810
Goshen, Ind.	17,171
Grand Forks, N. Dak.	39,008
Grand Island, Nebr.	31,269
Grand Junction, Colo.	20,170
Grand Prairie, Tex.	50,904
Grand Rapids, Mich.	197,649
Grandview, Mo.	17,456
Granite City, Ill.	40,440

Population of the United States

City	Population
Grants Pass, Oreg.	12,455
Great Bend, Kans.	16,133
Great Falls, Mont.	60,091
Greeley, Colo.	38,902
Green Bay, Wis.	87,809
Greenbelt, Md.	18,199
Greendale, Wis.	15,089
Greeneville, Tenn.	13,722
Greenfield, Mass.	18,116
Greenfield, Wis.	24,424
Greensboro, N.C.	144,076
Greensburg, Pa.	15,870
Greenville, Miss.	39,648
Greenville, N.C.	29,063
Greenville, Ohio	12,380
Greenville, S.C.	61,208
Greenville, Tex.	22,043
Greenwich, Conn.	59,755
Greenwood, Miss.	22,400
Greenwood, S.C.	21,069
Gretna, La.	24,875
Griffin, Ga.	22,734
Griffith, Ind.	18,168
Grosse Pointe Park, Mich.	15,585
Grosse Pointe Woods, Mich.	21,878
Groton, Conn.	38,523
Grove City, Ohio	13,911
Groves, Tex.	18,067
Guilford, Conn.	12,033
Gulfport, Miss.	40,791

H

City	Population
Hackensack, N.J.	35,911
Haddonfield, N.J.	13,118
Hagerstown, Md.	35,862
Hallandale, Fla.	23,849
Haltom City, Tex.	28,127
Hamden, Conn.	49,357
Hamilton, Ohio	67,865
Hammond, Ind.	107,790
Hammond, La.	12,487
Hampton, Va.	120,779
Hamtramck, Mich.	27,245
Hanford, Calif.	15,179
Hannibal, Mo.	18,609
Hanover, Pa.	15,623
Harahan, La.	13,037
Harlingen, Tex.	33,503
Harper Woods, Mich.	20,186
Harrisburg, Pa.	68,061
Harrisonburg, Va.	14,605
Hartford, Conn.	158,017
Harvard, Mass.	13,426
Harvey, Ill.	34,636
Hasbrouck Heights, N.J.	13,651
Hastings, Minn.	12,195
Hastings, Nebr.	23,580
Hattiesburg, Miss.	38,277
Haverhill, Mass.	46,120
Hawthorne, Calif.	53,304
Hawthorne, N.J.	19,173
Hays, Kans.	15,396
Hayward, Calif.	93,058
Hazel Park, Mich.	23,784
Hazelwood, Mo.	14,082
Hazleton, Pa.	30,426
Helena, Mont.	22,730
Hemet, Calif.	12,252
Hempstead, N.Y.	39,411
Henderson, Ky.	22,976
Henderson, Nev.	16,395
Henderson, N.C.	13,896
Hereford, Tex.	13,414
Hermosa Beach, Calif.	17,412
Hialeah, Fla.	102,297
Hibbing, Minn.	16,104
Hickory, N.C.	20,569
Hickory Hills, Ill.	13,176
Highland, Ind.	24,947
Highland Park, Ill.	32,263
Highland Park, Mich.	35,444
Highland Park, N.J.	14,385
High Point, N.C.	63,204
Hillsboro, Oreg.	14,675
Hilo, Hawaii	26,353
Hingham, Mass.	18,845
Hinsdale, Ill.	15,918
Hobart, Ind.	21,485
Hobbs, N. Mex.	26,025
Hoboken, N.J.	45,380
Hoffman Estates, Ill.	22,238
Holden, Mass.	12,564
Holland, Mich.	26,337
Holliston, Mass.	12,069
Hollywood, Fla.	106,873
Holyoke, Mass.	50,112
Homestead, Fla.	13,674
Homewood, Ala.	21,245
Homewood, Ill.	18,871
Honolulu, Hawaii	324,871
Hopewell, Va.	23,471
Hopkins, Minn.	13,428
Hopkinsville, Ky.	21,250
Hornell, N.Y.	12,144
Hot Springs, Ark.	35,631
Houma, La.	30,922
Houston, Tex.	1,232,802
Hudson, Mass.	16,084
Huntington, Ind.	16,217
Huntington, W. Va.	74,315
Huntington Beach, Calif.	115,960
Huntington Park, Calif.	33,744
Huntsville, Ala.	137,802
Huntsville, Tex.	17,610
Huron, S. Dak.	14,299
Hurst, Tex.	27,215
Hutchinson, Kans.	36,885
Hyattsville, Md.	14,998

I

City	Population
Idaho Falls, Idaho	35,776
Imperial Beach, Calif.	20,244
Independence, Mo.	111,662
Indiana, Pa.	16,100
Indianapolis, Ind.	744,624
Indio, Calif.	14,459
Inglewood, Calif.	89,985
Inkster, Mich.	38,595
Inver Grove Heights, Minn.	12,148
Iowa City, Iowa	46,850
Ironton, Ohio	15,030
Irving, Tex.	97,260
Irvington, N.J.	59,743
Ithaca, N.Y.	26,226

J

City	Population
Jackson, Mich.	45,484
Jackson, Miss.	153,968
Jackson, Tenn.	39,996
Jacksonville, Ark.	19,832
Jacksonville, Fla.	528,865
Jacksonville, Ill.	20,553
Jacksonville, N.C.	16,021
Jamestown, N.Y.	39,795
Jamestown, N. Dak.	15,385
Janesville, Wis.	46,426
Jeannette, Pa.	15,209
Jefferson City, Mo.	32,407
Jeffersonville, Ind.	20,008
Jennings, Mo.	19,379
Jersey City, N.J.	260,545
Johnson City, N.Y.	18,025
Johnson City, Tenn.	33,770
Johnston, R.I.	22,037
Johnstown, Pa.	42,476
Joliet, Ill.	80,378
Jonesboro, Ark.	27,050
Joplin, Mo.	39,256
Junction City, Kans.	19,018

K

City	Population
Kailua, Hawaii	33,783
Kalamazoo, Mich.	85,555
Kaneohe, Hawaii	29,903
Kankakee, Ill.	30,944
Kansas City, Kans.	168,213
Kansas City, Mo.	507,087
Kearney, Nebr.	19,181
Kearny, N.J.	37,585
Keene, N.H.	20,467
Kenmore, N.Y.	20,980
Kenner, La.	29,858
Kennewick, Wash.	15,212
Kenosha, Wis.	78,805
Kent, Ohio	28,183
Kent, Wash.	21,510
Kentwood, Mich.	20,310
Keokuk, Iowa	14,631
Kerrville, Tex.	12,672
Kettering, Ohio	69,599
Kewanee, Ill.	15,762
Key West, Fla.	27,563
Killeen, Tex.	35,507
Killingly, Conn.	13,573
Kingsport, Tenn.	31,938
Kingston, N.Y.	25,544
Kingston, Pa.	18,325
Kingsville, Tex.	28,711
Kinston, N.C.	22,309
Kirkland, Wash.	15,249
Kirksville, Mo.	15,560
Kirkwood, Mo.	31,890
Klamath Falls, Oreg.	15,775
Knoxville, Tenn.	174,587
Kokomo, Ind.	44,042

L

City	Population
Lackawanna, N.Y.	28,657
Laconia, N.H.	14,888
La Crosse, Wis.	51,153
Lafayette, Calif.	20,484
Lafayette, Ind.	44,955
Lafayette, La.	68,908
La Grange, Ga.	23,301
La Grange, Ill.	16,773
La Grange Park, Ill.	15,626
Laguna Beach, Calif.	14,550
La Habra, Calif.	41,350
Lake Charles, La.	77,998
Lake Forest, Ill.	15,642
Lake Jackson, Tex.	13,376
Lakeland, Fla.	41,550
Lake Oswego, Oreg.	14,573
Lakewood, Calif.	82,973
Lakewood, Colo.	92,787
Lakewood, Ohio	70,173
Lake Worth, Fla.	23,714
La Marque, Tex.	16,131
La Mesa, Calif.	39,178
La Mirada, Calif.	30,808
Lancaster, N.Y.	13,365
Lancaster, Ohio	32,911
Lancaster, Pa.	57,690
Lansdale, Pa.	18,451
Lansdowne, Pa.	14,090
Lansing, Ill.	25,805
Lansing, Mich.	131,546
La Porte, Ind.	22,140
La Puente, Calif.	31,092
Laramie, Wyo.	23,143
Laredo, Tex.	69,024
Largo, Fla.	22,031
Las Cruces, N. Mex.	37,857
Las Vegas, Nev.	125,787
Laurel, Miss.	24,145
La Verne, Calif.	12,965

City	Population
Lawndale, Calif.	24,825
Lawrence, Ind.	16,646
Lawrence, Kans.	45,698
Lawrence, Mass.	66,915
Lawton, Okla.	74,470
Layton, Utah	13,603
Leavenworth, Kans.	25,147
Lebanon, Pa.	28,572
Lebanon, Tenn.	12,492
Ledyard, Conn.	14,558
Lee's Summit, Mo.	16,230
Lenoir, N.C.	14,705
Leominster, Mass.	32,939
Lewiston, Idaho	26,068
Lewiston, Me.	41,779
Lexington, Ky.	108,137
Lexington, Mass.	31,886
Lexington, N.C.	17,205
Liberal, Kans.	13,471
Liberty, Mo.	13,679
Lima, Ohio	53,734
Lincoln, Ill.	17,582
Lincoln, Nebr.	149,518
Lincoln, R.I.	16,182
Lincoln Park, Mich.	52,984
Lincolnwood, Ill.	12,929
Linden, N.J.	41,409
Lindenhurst, N.Y.	28,338
Lindenwold, N.J.	12,199
Little Rock, Ark.	132,483
Littleton, Colo.	26,466
Livermore, Calif.	37,703
Livonia, Mich.	110,109
Lockport, N.Y.	25,399
Lodi, Calif.	28,691
Lodi, N.J.	25,213
Logan, Utah	22,333
Logansport, Ind.	19,255
Lombard, Ill.	35,977
Lomita, Calif.	19,784
Lompoc, Calif.	25,284
Long Beach, Calif.	358,633
Long Beach, N.Y.	33,127
Long Branch, N.J.	31,774
Longmeadow, Mass.	15,630
Longmont, Colo.	23,209
Longview, Tex.	45,547
Longview, Wash.	28,373
Lorain, Ohio	78,185
Los Altos, Calif.	24,956
Los Angeles, Calif.	2,816,061
Los Gatos, Calif.	23,735
Louisville, Ky.	361,472
Loveland, Colo.	16,220
Loves Park, Ill.	12,390
Lowell, Mass.	94,239
Lower Burrell, Pa.	13,654
Lubbock, Tex.	149,101
Ludlow, Mass.	17,580
Lufkin, Tex.	23,049
Lumberton, N.C.	16,961
Lynbrook, N.Y.	23,776
Lynchburg, Va.	54,083
Lyndhurst, Ohio	19,749
Lynn, Mass.	90,294
Lynnwood, Wash.	16,919
Lynwood, Calif.	43,353

M

City	Population
McAlester, Okla.	18,802
McAllen, Tex.	37,636
McKeesport, Pa.	37,977
McKinney, Tex.	15,193
Macomb, Ill.	19,643
Macon, Ga.	122,423
Madera, Calif.	16,044
Madison, Ind.	13,081
Madison, N.J.	16,710
Madison, Wis.	173,258
Madison Heights, Mich.	38,599
Madisonville, Ky.	15,332
Malden, Mass.	56,127
Mamaroneck, N.Y.	18,909
Manchester, Conn.	47,994
Manchester, N.H.	87,754
Manhattan, Kans.	27,575
Manhattan Beach, Calif.	35,352
Manitowoc, Wis.	33,430
Mankato, Minn.	30,895
Mansfield, Conn.	19,994
Mansfield, Ohio	55,047
Manteca, Calif.	13,845
Manville, N.J.	13,029
Maple Heights, Ohio	34,093
Maplewood, Minn.	25,222
Maplewood, Mo.	12,785
Marblehead, Mass.	21,295
Marietta, Ga.	27,216
Marietta, Ohio	16,861
Marinette, Wis.	12,696
Marion, Ind.	39,607
Marion, Iowa	18,028
Marion, Ohio	38,646
Markham, Ill.	15,987
Marlboro, Mass.	27,936
Marquette, Mich.	21,967
Marshall, Tex.	22,937
Marshalltown, Iowa	26,219
Marshfield, Mass.	15,223
Marshfield, Wis.	15,619
Martinez, Calif.	16,506
Martinsburg, W. Va.	14,626
Martinsville, Va.	19,653
Maryville, Tenn.	13,808
Mason City, Iowa	30,491
Massapequa Park, N.Y.	22,112
Massena, N.Y.	14,042
Massillon, Ohio	32,539
Mattoon, Ill.	19,681
Maumee, Ohio	15,937
Mayfield Heights, Ohio	22,139
Maywood, Calif.	16,996
Maywood, Ill.	30,036
Meadville, Pa.	16,573
Medford, Mass.	64,397
Medford, Oreg.	28,454
Melbourne, Fla.	40,236
Melrose, Mass.	33,180
Melrose Park, Ill.	22,706
Melvindale, Mich.	13,862
Memphis, Tenn.	623,530
Menasha, Wis.	14,905
Menlo Park, Calif.	26,734
Menomonee Falls, Wis.	31,697
Mentor, Ohio	36,912
Mequon, Wis.	12,110
Merced, Calif.	22,670
Mercer Island, Wash.	19,047
Meriden, Conn.	55,959
Meridian, Miss.	45,083
Mesa, Ariz.	62,853
Mesquite, Tex.	55,131
Methuen, Mass.	35,456
Metuchen, N.J.	16,031
Miami, Fla.	334,859
Miami, Okla.	13,880
Miami Beach, Fla.	87,072
Miamisburg, Ohio	14,797
Miami Springs, Fla.	13,279
Michigan City, Ind.	39,369
Middleboro, Mass.	13,607
Middleburg Heights, Ohio	12,367
Middlesex, N.J.	15,038
Middletown, Conn.	36,924
Middletown, N.Y.	22,607
Middletown, Ohio	48,767
Middletown, R.I.	29,621
Midland, Mich.	35,176
Midland, Tex.	59,463
Midlothian, Ill.	15,939
Midwest City, Okla.	48,114
Milford, Conn.	50,858
Milford, Mass.	19,352
Millbrae, Calif.	20,781
Millington, Tenn.	21,106
Mill Valley, Calif.	12,942
Millville, N.J.	21,366
Milpitas, Calif.	27,149
Milton, Mass.	27,190
Milwaukee, Wis.	717,099
Milwaukie, Oreg.	16,379
Minden, La.	13,996
Mineola, N.Y.	21,845
Mineral Wells, Tex.	18,411
Minneapolis, Minn.	434,400
Minnetonka, Minn.	35,776
Minot, N. Dak.	32,290
Miramar, Fla.	23,973
Mishawaka, Ind.	35,517
Mission, Tex.	13,043
Missoula, Mont.	29,497
Mitchell, S. Dak.	13,425
Moberly, Mo.	12,988
Mobile, Ala.	190,026
Modesto, Calif.	61,712
Moline, Ill.	46,237
Monessen, Pa.	15,216
Monroe, Conn.	12,047
Monroe, La.	56,374
Monroe, Mich.	23,894
Monroeville, Pa.	29,011
Monrovia, Calif.	30,015
Montclair, Calif.	22,546
Montclair, N.J.	44,043
Montebello, Calif.	42,807
Monterey, Calif.	26,302
Monterey Park, Calif.	49,166
Montgomery, Ala.	133,386
Montville, Conn.	15,662
Moore, Okla.	18,761
Moorhead, Minn.	29,687
Morgan City, La.	16,586
Morganton, N.C.	13,625
Morgantown, W. Va.	29,431
Morristown, N.J.	17,662
Morristown, Tenn.	20,318
Morton Grove, Ill.	26,369
Moscow, Idaho	14,146
Moss Point, Miss.	19,321
Moultrie, Ga.	14,302
Moundsville, W. Va.	13,560
Mountain Brook, Ala.	19,474
Mountain View, Calif.	51,092
Mount Clemens, Mich.	20,476
Mountlake Terrace, Wash.	16,600
Mount Pleasant, Mich.	20,504
Mount Prospect, Ill.	34,995
Mount Vernon, Ill.	15,980
Mount Vernon, N.Y.	72,778
Mount Vernon, Ohio	13,373
Muncie, Ind.	69,080
Mundelein, Ill.	16,128
Munhall, Pa.	16,674
Munster, Ind.	16,514
Murfreesboro, Tenn.	26,360
Murray, Ky.	13,537
Murray, Utah	21,206
Muscatine, Iowa	22,405
Muskegon, Mich.	44,631
Muskegon Heights, Mich.	17,304
Muskogee, Okla.	37,331

N

City	Population
Nacogdoches, Tex.	22,544
Nampa, Idaho	20,768
Nanticoke, Pa.	14,632
Napa, Calif.	35,978

City	Population
Naperville, Ill.	23,885
Naples, Fla.	12,042
Nashua, N.H.	55,820
Nashville, Tenn.	447,877
Natchez, Miss.	19,704
Natchitoches, La.	15,974
Natick, Mass.	31,057
National City, Calif.	43,184
Naugatuck, Conn.	23,034
Nederland, Tex.	16,810
Needham, Mass.	29,748
Neenah, Wis.	22,892
New Albany, Ind.	38,402
Newark, Calif.	27,153
Newark, Del.	20,757
Newark, N.J.	382,417
Newark, Ohio	41,836
New Bedford, Mass.	101,777
New Berlin, Wis.	26,937
New Bern, N.C.	14,660
New Braunfels, Tex.	17,859
New Brighton, Minn.	19,507
New Britain, Conn.	83,441
New Brunswick, N.J.	41,885
Newburgh, N.Y.	26,219
Newburyport, Mass.	15,807
New Canaan, Conn.	17,455
New Carrollton, Md.	13,395
New Castle, Ind.	21,215
New Castle, Pa.	38,559
New Haven, Conn.	137,707
New Hope, Minn.	23,180
New Iberia, La.	30,147
Newington, Conn.	26,037
New Kensington, Pa.	20,312
New London, Conn.	31,630
New Milford, Conn.	14,601
New Milford, N.J.	20,201
New Orleans, La.	593,471
New Philadelphia, Ohio	15,184
Newport, Ky.	25,998
Newport, R.I.	34,562
Newport Beach, Calif.	49,422
Newport News, Va.	138,177
New Providence, N.J.	13,796
New Rochelle, N.Y.	75,385
Newton, Iowa	15,619
Newton, Kans.	15,439
Newton, Mass.	91,066
Newtown, Conn.	16,942
New Ulm, Minn.	13,051
New York City, N.Y.	7,867,760
Bronx	1,472,216
Brooklyn	2,601,852
Manhattan	1,524,541
Queens	1,973,708
Richmond	295,443
Niagara Falls, N.Y.	85,615
Niles, Ill.	31,432
Niles, Mich.	12,988
Niles, Ohio	21,581
Norco, Calif.	14,511
Norfolk, Nebr.	16,607
Norfolk, Va.	307,951
Normal, Ill.	26,396
Norman, Okla.	52,117
Norridge, Ill.	16,880
Norristown, Pa.	38,169
North Adams, Mass.	19,195
Northampton, Mass.	29,664
North Andover, Mass.	16,284
North Arlington, N.J.	18,096
North Attleboro, Mass.	18,665
North Augusta, S.C.	12,883
Northbrook, Ill.	27,297
North Canton, Ohio	15,228
North Chicago, Ill.	47,275
North College Hill, Ohio	12,363
North Glenn, Colo.	27,937

City	Population
North Haven, Conn.	22,194
North Kingstown, R.I.	27,673
Northlake, Ill.	14,212
North Las Vegas, Nev.	36,216
North Little Rock, Ark.	60,040
North Miami, Fla.	34,767
North Miami Beach, Fla.	30,723
North Olmsted, Ohio	34,861
North Plainfield, N.J.	21,796
North Platte, Nebr.	19,447
North Providence, R.I.	24,337
North Richland Hills, Tex.	16,514
North Ridgeville, Ohio	13,152
North Royalton, Ohio	12,807
North Tonawanda, N.Y.	36,012
Norton, Ohio	12,308
Norton Shores, Mich.	22,271
Norwalk, Calif.	91,827
Norwalk, Conn.	79,113
Norwalk, Ohio	13,386
Norwich, Conn.	41,433
Norwood, Mass.	30,815
Norwood, Ohio	30,420
Novato, Calif.	31,006
Nutley, N.J.	32,099
O	
Oak Creek, Wis.	13,901
Oak Forest, Ill.	17,870
Oakland, Calif.	361,561
Oakland, N.J.	14,420
Oakland Park, Fla.	16,261
Oak Lawn, Ill.	60,305
Oak Park, Ill.	62,511
Oak Park, Mich.	36,762
Oak Ridge, Tenn.	28,319
Ocala, Fla.	22,583
Oceanside, Calif.	40,494
Odessa, Tex.	78,380
Ogden, Utah	69,478
Ogdensburg, N.Y.	14,554
Oil City, Pa.	15,033
Oklahoma City, Okla.	366,481
Okmulgee, Okla.	15,180
Olathe, Kans.	17,917
Olean, N.Y.	19,169
Olympia, Wash.	23,111
Omaha, Nebr.	347,328
Oneonta, N.Y.	16,030
Ontario, Calif.	64,118
Opelika, Ala.	19,027
Opelousas, La.	20,121
Orange, Calif.	77,374
Orange, Conn.	13,524
Orange, N.J.	32,566
Orange, Tex.	24,457
Orangeburg, S.C.	13,252
Oregon, Ohio	16,563
Orem, Utah	25,729
Orlando, Fla.	99,006
Ormond Beach, Fla.	14,063
Oshkosh, Wis.	53,221
Ossining, N.Y.	21,659
Oswego, N.Y.	23,844
Ottawa, Ill.	18,716
Ottumwa, Iowa	29,610
Overland, Mo.	24,949
Overland Park, Kans.	76,623
Owatonna, Minn.	15,341
Owensboro, Ky.	50,329
Owosso, Mich.	17,179
Oxford, Miss.	13,846
Oxford, Ohio	15,868
Oxnard, Calif.	71,225
Ozark, Ala.	13,555
P	
Pacifica, Calif.	36,020
Pacific Grove, Calif.	13,505

City	Population
Paducah, Ky.	31,627
Painesville, Ohio	16,536
Palatine, Ill.	25,904
Palestine, Tex.	14,525
Palisades Park, N.J.	13,351
Palm Springs, Calif.	20,936
Palo Alto, Calif.	55,966
Palos Verdes Estates, Calif.	13,641
Pampa, Tex.	21,726
Panama City, Fla.	32,096
Paramount, Calif.	34,734
Paramus, N.J.	29,495
Paris, Tex.	23,441
Parkersburg, W. Va.	44,208
Park Forest, Ill.	30,638
Park Ridge, Ill.	42,466
Parma, Ohio	100,216
Parma Heights, Ohio	27,192
Parsons, Kans.	13,015
Pasadena, Calif.	113,327
Pasadena, Tex.	89,277
Pascagoula, Miss.	27,264
Pasco, Wash.	13,920
Passaic, N.J.	55,124
Paterson, N.J.	144,824
Pawtucket, R.I.	76,984
Peabody, Mass.	48,080
Pearl City, Hawaii	19,552
Pecos, Tex.	12,682
Peekskill, N.Y.	18,881
Pekin, Ill.	31,375
Pembroke Pines, Fla.	15,520
Pendleton, Oreg.	13,197
Pensacola, Fla.	59,507
Peoria, Ill.	126,963
Perth Amboy, N.J.	38,798
Peru, Ind.	14,139
Petaluma, Calif.	24,870
Petersburg, Va.	36,103
Pharr, Tex.	15,829
Phenix City, Ala.	25,281
Philadelphia, Pa.	1,948,609
Phillipsburg, N.J.	17,849
Phoenix, Ariz.	581,562
Phoenixville, Pa.	14,823
Pico Rivera, Calif.	54,170
Pine Bluff, Ark.	57,389
Pinellas Park, Fla.	22,287
Pinole, Calif.	15,850
Piqua, Ohio	20,741
Pittsburg, Calif.	20,651
Pittsburg, Kans.	20,171
Pittsburgh, Pa.	520,117
Pittsfield, Mass.	57,020
Placentia, Calif.	21,948
Plainfield, N.J.	46,862
Plainview, Tex.	19,096
Plainville, Conn.	16,733
Plano, Tex.	17,872
Plantation, Fla.	23,523
Plant City, Fla.	15,451
Plattsburgh, N.Y.	18,715
Pleasant Hill, Calif.	24,610
Pleasanton, Calif.	18,328
Pleasantville, N.J.	13,778
Plum, Pa.	21,932
Plymouth, Mass.	18,606
Plymouth, Minn.	17,593
Pocatello, Idaho	40,036
Point Pleasant, N.J.	15,968
Pomona, Calif.	87,384
Pompano Beach, Fla.	37,724
Ponca City, Okla.	25,940
Pontiac, Mich.	85,279
Poplar Bluff, Mo.	16,653
Portage, Ind.	19,127
Portage, Mich.	33,590
Port Angeles, Wash.	16,367
Port Arthur, Tex.	57,371

City	Population
Port Chester, N.Y.	25,803
Porterville, Calif.	12,602
Port Hueneme, Calif.	14,295
Port Huron, Mich.	35,794
Portland, Me.	65,116
Portland, Oreg.	382,619
Portsmouth, N.H.	25,717
Portsmouth, Ohio	27,633
Portsmouth, R.I.	12,521
Portsmouth, Va.	110,963
Pottstown, Pa.	25,355
Pottsville, Pa.	19,715
Poughkeepsie, N.Y.	32,029
Prairie Village, Kans.	28,138
Prattville, Ala.	13,116
Prescott, Ariz.	13,030
Prichard, Ala.	41,578
Princeton, N.J.	12,311
Providence, R.I.	179,213
Provo, Utah	53,131
Pueblo, Colo.	97,453
Pullman, Wash.	20,509
Puyallup, Wash.	14,742

Q

City	Population
Quincy, Ill.	45,288
Quincy, Mass.	87,966

R

City	Population
Racine, Wis.	95,162
Rahway, N.J.	29,114
Raleigh, N.C.	121,577
Ramsey, N.J.	12,571
Randolph, Mass.	27,035
Rantoul, Ill.	25,562
Rapid City, S. Dak.	43,836
Raytown, Mo.	33,632
Reading, Mass.	22,539
Reading, Ohio	14,303
Reading, Pa.	87,643
Red Bank, N.J.	12,847
Red Bank, Tenn.	12,715
Redding, Calif.	16,659
Redlands, Calif.	36,355
Redondo Beach, Calif.	56,075
Redwood City, Calif.	55,686
Reidsville, N.C.	13,636
Reno, Nev.	72,863
Renton, Wash.	25,258
Revere, Mass.	43,159
Reynoldsburg, Ohio	13,921
Rialto, Calif.	28,370
Richardson, Tex.	48,582
Richfield, Minn.	47,231
Richland, Wash.	26,290
Richmond, Calif.	79,043
Richmond, Ind.	43,999
Richmond, Ky.	16,861
Richmond, Va.	249,621
Richmond Heights, Mo.	13,802
Ridgefield, Conn.	18,188
Ridgefield Park, N.J.	14,453
Ridgewood, N.J.	27,547
Riverdale, Ill.	15,806
River Edge, N.J.	12,850
River Forest, Ill.	13,402
River Rouge, Mich.	15,947
Riverside, Calif.	140,089
Riviera Beach, Fla.	21,401
Roanoke, Va.	92,115
Roanoke Rapids, N.C.	13,508
Robbinsdale, Minn.	16,845
Rochester, Minn.	53,766
Rochester, N.H.	17,938
Rochester, N.Y.	296,233
Rockford, Ill.	147,370
Rock Hill, S.C.	33,846
Rock Island, Ill.	50,166
Rockland, Mass.	15,674
Rockville, Md.	41,564
Rockville Centre, N.Y.	27,444
Rocky Mount, N.C.	34,284
Rocky River, Ohio	22,958
Rolla, Mo.	13,245
Rolling Meadows, Ill.	19,178
Rome, Ga.	30,759
Rome, N.Y.	50,148
Romeoville, Ill.	12,674
Roseburg, Oreg.	14,461
Roselle, N.J.	22,585
Roselle Park, N.J.	14,277
Rosemead, Calif.	40,972
Rosenberg, Tex.	12,098
Roseville, Calif.	17,895
Roseville, Mich.	60,529
Roseville, Minn.	34,518
Roswell, N. Mex.	33,908
Roy, Utah	14,356
Royal Oak, Mich.	85,499
Ruston, La.	17,365
Rutherford, N.J.	20,802
Rutland, Vt.	19,293
Rye, N.Y.	15,869

S

City	Population
Sacramento, Calif.	254,413
Saginaw, Mich.	91,849
St. Albans, W. Va.	14,356
St. Ann, Mo.	18,215
St. Augustine, Fla.	12,352
St. Charles, Ill.	12,928
St. Charles, Mo.	31,834
St. Clair Shores, Mich.	88,093
St. Cloud, Minn.	39,691
St. Joseph, Mo.	72,691
St. Louis, Mo.	622,236
St. Louis Park, Minn.	48,883
St. Matthews, Ky.	13,152
St. Paul, Minn.	309,980
St. Petersburg, Fla.	216,232
Salem Mass.	40,556
Salem, N.H.	20,142
Salem, Ohio	14,186
Salem, Oreg.	68,296
Salem, Va.	21,982
Salina, Kans.	37,714
Salinas, Calif.	58,896
Salisbury, Md.	15,252
Salisbury, N.C.	22,515
Salt Lake City, Utah	175,885
San Angelo, Tex.	63,884
San Anselmo, Calif.	13,031
San Antonio, Tex.	654,153
San Benito, Tex.	15,176
San Bernardino, Calif.	104,251
San Bruno, Calif.	36,254
San Carlos, Calif.	25,924
San Clemente, Calif.	17,063
San Diego, Calif.	696,769
San Dimas, Calif.	15,692
Sandusky, Ohio	32,674
San Fernando, Calif.	16,571
Sanford, Fla.	17,393
Sanford, Me.	15,812
San Francisco, Calif.	715,674
San Gabriel, Calif.	29,176
San Jose, Calif.	445,779
San Leandro, Calif.	68,698
San Luis Obispo, Calif.	28,036
San Marcos, Tex.	18,860
San Marino, Calif.	14,177
San Mateo, Calif.	78,991
San Pablo, Calif.	21,461
San Rafael, Calif.	38,977
Santa Ana, Calif.	156,601
Santa Barbara, Calif.	70,215
Santa Clara, Calif.	87,717
Santa Cruz, Calif.	32,076
Santa Fe, N. Mex.	41,167
Santa Fe Springs, Calif.	14,750
Santa Maria, Calif.	32,749
Santa Monica, Calif.	88,289
Santa Paula, Calif.	18,001
Santa Rosa, Calif.	50,006
Sapulpa, Okla.	15,159
Sarasota, Fla.	40,237
Saratoga, Calif.	27,110
Saratoga Springs, N.Y.	18,845
Saugus, Mass.	25,110
Sault Ste. Marie, Mich.	15,136
Savannah, Ga.	118,349
Sayreville, N.J.	32,508
Scarsdale, N.Y.	19,229
Schaumburg, Ill.	18,730
Schenectady, N.Y.	77,859
Schiller Park, Ill.	12,712
Schofield Barracks, Hawaii	13,516
Scituate, Mass.	16,973
Scottsbluff, Nebr.	14,507
Scottsdale, Ariz.	67,823
Scranton, Pa.	103,564
Seal Beach, Calif.	24,441
Seaside, Calif.	35,935
Seattle, Wash.	530,831
Secaucus, N.J.	13,228
Sedalia, Mo.	22,847
Seguin, Tex.	15,934
Selma, Ala.	27,379
Seven Hills, Ohio	12,700
Seymour, Conn.	12,776
Seymour, Ind.	13,352
Shaker Heights, Ohio	36,306
Sharon, Mass.	12,367
Sharon, Pa.	22,653
Shawnee, Kans.	20,482
Shawnee, Okla.	25,075
Sheboygan, Wis.	48,484
Sheffield, Ala.	13,115
Shelby, N.C.	16,328
Shelbyville, Ind.	15,094
Shelbyville, Tenn.	12,262
Shelton, Conn.	27,165
Sherman, Tex.	29,061
Shively, Ky.	19,223
Shorewood, Wis.	15,576
Shreveport, La.	182,064
Shrewsbury, Mass.	19,196
Sidney, Ohio	16,332
Sierra Madre, Calif.	12,140
Sikeston, Mo.	14,699
Simi Valley, Calif.	56,464
Simsbury, Conn.	17,475
Sioux City, Iowa	85,925
Sioux Falls, S. Dak.	72,488
Skokie, Ill.	68,627
Slidell, La.	16,101
Smithfield, R.I.	13,468
Smyrna, Ga.	19,157
Somerset, Mass.	18,088
Somerville, Mass.	88,779
Somerville, N.J.	13,652
South Bend, Ind.	125,580
Southbridge, Mass.	17,057
South Charleston, W. Va.	16,333
South El Monte, Calif.	13,443
South Euclid, Ohio	29,579
Southfield, Mich.	69,285
South Gate, Calif.	56,909
Southgate, Mich.	33,909
South Hadley, Mass.	17,033
South Holland, Ill.	23,931
Southington, Conn.	30,946
South Kingstown, R.I.	16,913
South Lake Tahoe, Calif.	12,921
South Miami, Fla.	19,571
South Milwaukee, Wis.	23,297
South Orange, N.J.	16,971

City	Population
South Pasadena, Calif.	22,979
South Plainfield, N.J.	21,142
South Portland, Me.	23,267
South River, N.J.	15,428
South St. Paul, Minn.	25,016
South San Francisco, Calif.	46,646
South Windsor, Conn.	15,553
Sparks, Nev.	24,187
Spartanburg, S.C.	44,546
Speedway, Ind.	15,056
Spokane, Wash.	170,516
Springdale, Ark.	16,783
Springfield, Ill.	91,753
Springfield, Mass.	163,905
Springfield, Mo.	120,096
Springfield, Ohio	81,926
Springfield, Oreg.	27,047
Spring Valley, N.Y.	18,112
Stamford, Conn.	108,798
Stanton, Calif.	17,947
State College, Pa.	33,778
Statesboro, Ga.	14,616
Statesville, N.C.	19,996
Staunton, Va.	24,504
Sterling, Ill.	16,113
Sterling Heights, Mich.	61,365
Steubenville, Ohio	30,771
Stevens Point, Wis.	23,479
Stillwater, Okla.	31,126
Stockton, Calif.	107,644
Stoneham, Mass.	20,725
Stonington, Conn.	15,940
Stoughton, Mass.	23,459
Stow, Ohio	19,847
Stratford, Conn.	49,775
Streamwood, Ill.	18,176
Streator, Ill.	15,600
Strongsville, Ohio	15,182
Struthers, Ohio	15,343
Sudbury, Mass.	13,506
Sulphur, La.	13,551
Summit, N.J.	23,620
Sumter, S.C.	24,435
Sunbury, Pa.	13,025
Sunnyvale, Calif.	95,408
Superior, Wis.	32,237
Swampscott, Mass.	13,578
Swansea, Mass.	12,640
Sweetwater, Tex.	12,020
Swissvale, Pa.	13,821
Sylacauga, Ala.	12,255
Sylvania, Ohio	12,031
Syracuse, N.Y.	197,208
T	
Tacoma, Wash.	154,581
Takoma Park, Md.	18,455
Talladega, Ala.	17,662
Tallahassee, Fla.	71,897
Tallmadge, Ohio	15,274
Tampa, Fla.	277,767
Taunton, Mass.	43,756
Taylor, Mich.	70,020
Tempe, Ariz.	62,907
Temple, Tex.	33,431
Temple City, Calif.	29,673
Tenafly, N.J.	14,827
Terre Haute, Ind.	70,286
Terrell, Tex.	14,182
Tewksbury, Mass.	22,755
Texarkana, Ark.	21,682
Texarkana, Tex.	30,497
Texas City, Tex.	38,908
The Village, Okla.	13,695
Thibodaux, La.	14,925
Thomasville, Ga.	18,155
Thomasville, N.C.	15,230
Thornton, Colo.	13,326
Thousand Oaks, Calif.	36,334
Tiffin, Ohio	21,596
Tifton, Ga.	12,179
Tinley Park, Ill.	12,382
Titusville, Fla.	30,515
Tiverton, R.I.	12,559
Toledo, Ohio	383,818
Tonawanda, N.Y.	21,898
Tooele, Utah	12,539
Topeka, Kans.	125,011
Torrance, Calif.	134,584
Torrington, Conn.	31,952
Tracy, Calif.	14,724
Traverse City, Mich.	18,048
Trenton, Mich.	24,127
Trenton, N.J.	104,638
Troy, Mich.	39,419
Troy, N.Y.	62,918
Troy, Ohio	17,186
Trumbull, Conn.	31,394
Tucson, Ariz.	262,933
Tulare, Calif.	16,235
Tullahoma, Tenn.	15,311
Tulsa, Okla.	331,638
Tupelo, Miss.	20,471
Turlock, Calif.	13,992
Tuscaloosa, Ala.	65,773
Tustin, Calif.	21,178
Twin Falls, Idaho	21,914
Two Rivers, Wis.	13,553
Tyler, Tex.	57,770
U	
Union City, Calif.	14,724
Union City, N.J.	58,537
Uniontown, Pa.	16,282
University City, Mo.	46,309
University Heights, Ohio	17,055
University Park, Tex.	23,498
Upland, Calif.	32,551
Upper Arlington, Ohio	38,630
Urbana, Ill.	32,800
Urbandale, Iowa	14,434
Utica, N.Y.	91,611
V	
Vacaville, Calif.	21,690
Valdosta, Ga.	32,303
Vallejo, Calif.	66,733
Valley Stream, N.Y.	40,413
Valparaiso, Ind.	20,020
Vancouver, Wash.	42,493
Ventura (San Buenaventura), Calif.	55,797
Vernon, Conn.	27,237
Verona, N.J.	15,067
Vicksburg, Miss.	25,478
Victoria, Tex.	41,349
Vienna, Va.	17,152
Villa Park, Ill.	25,891
Vincennes, Ind.	19,867
Vineland, N.J.	47,399
Virginia, Minn.	12,450
Virginia Beach, Va.	172,106
Visalia, Calif.	27,268
Vista, Calif.	24,688
W	
Wabash, Ind.	13,379
Waco, Tex.	95,326
Wadsworth, Ohio	13,142
Wahiawa, Hawaii	17,598
Waipahu, Hawaii	22,798
Wakefield, Mass.	25,402
Waldwick, N.J.	12,313
Walla Walla, Wash.	23,619
Wallingford, Conn.	35,714
Walnut Creek, Calif.	39,844
Walpole, Mass.	18,149
Waltham, Mass.	61,582
Warner Robins, Ga.	33,491
Warren, Mich.	179,260
Warren, Ohio	63,494
Warren, Pa.	12,998
Warrensburg, Mo.	13,125
Warrensville Heights, Ohio	18,925
Warwick, R.I.	83,694
Washington, D.C.	756,510
Washington, Ohio	12,495
Washington, Pa.	19,827
Waterbury, Conn.	108,033
Waterford, Conn.	17,227
Waterloo, Iowa	75,533
Watertown, Conn.	18,610
Watertown, Mass.	39,307
Watertown, N.Y.	30,787
Watertown, S. Dak.	13,388
Watertown, Wis.	15,683
Waterville, Me.	18,192
Watervliet, N.Y.	12,404
Watsonville, Calif.	14,569
Waukegan, Ill.	65,269
Waukesha, Wis.	40,258
Wausau, Wis.	32,806
Wauwatosa, Wis.	58,676
Waxahachie, Tex.	13,452
Waycross, Ga.	18,996
Wayland, Mass.	13,461
Wayne, Mich.	21,054
Waynesboro, Va.	16,707
Webster, Mass.	14,917
Webster Groves, Mo.	26,995
Weirton, W. Va.	27,131
Wellesley, Mass.	28,051
Wenatchee, Wash.	16,912
Weslaco, Tex.	15,313
West Allis, Wis.	71,723
West Bend, Wis.	16,555
Westboro, Mass.	12,594
Westbrook, Me.	14,444
Westbury, N.Y.	15,362
Westchester, Ill.	20,033
West Chester, Pa.	19,301
West Covina, Calif.	68,034
West Des Moines, Iowa	16,441
Westerly, R.I.	17,248
Western Springs, Ill.	12,147
Westerville, Ohio	12,530
Westfield, Mass.	31,433
Westfield, N.J.	33,720
West Hartford, Conn.	68,031
West Haven, Conn.	52,851
West Lafayette, Ind.	19,157
Westlake, Ohio	15,689
Westland, Mich.	86,749
West Memphis, Ark.	25,892
West Mifflin, Pa.	28,070
Westminster, Calif.	59,865
Westminster, Colo.	19,432
West Monroe, La.	14,868
West New York, N.J.	40,627
West Orange, N.J.	43,715
West Palm Beach, Fla.	57,375
Westport, Conn.	27,414
West St. Paul, Minn.	18,799
West Springfield, Mass.	28,461
West University Place, Tex.	13,317
West Warwick, R.I.	24,323
Westwood, Mass.	12,750
Wethersfield, Conn.	26,662
Weymouth, Mass.	54,610
Wheaton, Ill.	31,138
Wheat Ridge, Colo.	29,795
Wheeling, Ill.	14,746
Wheeling, W. Va.	48,188
White Bear Lake, Minn.	23,313
Whitefish Bay, Wis.	17,394
Whitehall, Ohio	25,263
Whitehall, Pa.	16,551
White Plains, N.Y.	50,220

White Settlement, Tex.	13,449
Whitewater, Wis.	12,038
Whitman, Mass.	13,059
Whittier, Calif.	72,863
Wichita, Kans.	276,554
Wichita Falls, Tex.	97,564
Wickliffe, Ohio	21,354
Wilkes-Barre, Pa.	58,856
Wilkinsburg, Pa.	26,780
Williamsport, Pa.	37,918
Willimantic, Conn.	14,402
Wilmar, Minn.	12,869
Willoughby, Ohio	18,634
Willowick, Ohio	21,237
Wilmette, Ill.	32,134
Wilmington, Del.	80,386
Wilmington, Mass.	17,102
Wilmington, N.C.	46,169
Wilson, N.C.	29,347
Wilton, Conn.	13,572
Winchester, Ky.	13,402
Winchester, Mass.	22,269
Winchester, Va.	14,643
Windham, Conn.	19,626
Windsor, Conn.	22,502
Windsor Locks, Conn.	15,080
Winnetka, Ill.	14,131
Winona, Minn.	26,438
Winston-Salem, N.C.	132,913
Winter Haven, Fla.	16,136
Winter Park, Fla.	21,895
Winthrop, Mass.	20,335
Wisconsin Rapids, Wis.	18,587
Woburn, Mass.	37,406
Wolcott, Conn.	12,495
Woodbury, N.J.	12,408
Woodland, Calif.	20,677
Wood River, Ill.	13,186
Woonsocket, R.I.	46,820
Wooster, Ohio	18,703
Worcester, Mass.	176,572
Worthington, Ohio	15,326
Wyandotte, Mich.	41,061
Wyoming, Mich.	56,560
Xenia, Ohio	25,373
Yakima, Wash.	45,588
Yarmouth, Mass.	12,033
Yeadon, Pa.	12,136
Yonkers, N.Y.	204,370
York, Pa.	50,335
Youngstown, Ohio	139,788
Ypsilanti, Mich.	29,538
Yuba City, Calif.	13,986
Yuma, Ariz.	29,007
Zanesville, Ohio	33,045
Zion, Ill.	17,268

POPULATION OF UNITED STATES IN 1970

SUMMARY BY STATES

(Figures in parentheses give rank of states in population)

State	Rank	Population
Alabama	(21)	3,444,165
Alaska	(50)	302,173
Arizona	(33)	1,772,482
Arkansas	(32)	1,923,295
California	(1)	19,953,134
Colorado	(30)	2,207,259
Connecticut	(24)	3,032,217
Delaware	(46)	548,104
District of Columbia		756,510
Florida	(9)	6,789,443
Georgia	(15)	4,589,575
Hawaii	(40)	768,561
Idaho	(42)	712,567
Illinois	(5)	11,113,976
Indiana	(11)	5,193,669
Iowa	(25)	2,825,041
Kansas	(28)	2,249,071
Kentucky	(23)	3,219,311
Louisiana	(20)	3,643,180
Maine	(38)	992,048
Maryland	(18)	3,922,399
Massachusetts	(10)	5,689,170
Michigan	(7)	8,875,083
Minnesota	(19)	3,805,069
Mississippi	(29)	2,216,912
Missouri	(13)	4,677,399
Montana	(43)	694,409
Nebraska	(35)	1,483,791
Nevada	(47)	488,738
New Hampshire	(41)	737,681
New Jersey	(8)	7,168,164
New Mexico	(37)	1,016,000
New York	(2)	18,190,740
North Carolina	(12)	5,082,059
North Dakota	(45)	617,761
Ohio	(6)	10,652,017
Oklahoma	(27)	2,559,253
Oregon	(31)	2,091,385
Pennsylvania	(3)	11,793,909
Rhode Island	(39)	949,723
South Carolina	(26)	2,590,516
South Dakota	(44)	665,507
Tennessee	(17)	3,924,164
Texas	(4)	11,196,730
Utah	(36)	1,059,273
Vermont	(48)	444,330
Virgina	(14)	4,648,494
Washington	(22)	3,409,169
West Virginia	(34)	1,744,237
Wisconsin	(16)	4,417,933
Wyoming	(49)	332,416
		203,184,772